Human Language Technologies: The 2010 Annual Conference of the North American Chapter of the Association for Computational Linguistics

(NAACL HLT 2010)

Los Angeles, California, USA
2-4 June 2010

ISBN: 978-1-61738-669-5

Printed from e-media with permission by:

Curran Associates, Inc.
57 Morehouse Lane
Red Hook, NY 12571

Some format issues inherent in the e-media version may also appear in this print version.

Printed by Curran Associates, Inc. (2010)

Association for Computational Linguistics
209 N. Eighth Street
Stroudsburg, Pennsylvania 18360

Phone: 1-570-476-8006
Fax: 1-570-476-0860

acl@aclweb.org

Additional copies of this publication are available from:

Curran Associates, Inc.
57 Morehouse Lane
Red Hook, NY 12571 USA
Phone: 845-758-0400
Fax: 845-758-2634
Email: curran@proceedings.com
Web: www.proceedings.com

Preface: General Chair

It is with great pleasure that I welcome you to the 2010 Human Language Technologies conference of the North American chapter of the Association for Computational Linguistics. An enormous amount of effort has gone into organizing the conference, and the result is the rich set of intellectual and social experiences that you will enjoy this week.

The NAACL HLT 2010 conference is an orchestrated production of many events. The centerpiece is the collection of carefully chosen papers, posters, and demonstrations that will be presented during the three days of the main conference. This includes the papers and posters of the Student Research Workshop, a setting that gives encouragement and opportunity for new members of our community to present their work. The main conference is preceded by a day of tutorials on topics of current interest in the field, and it is followed by a very full program of specialized workshops.

Many people have volunteered their time and energy to ensure the success of the conference. Indeed, the community as a whole has contributed by submitting papers and proposals for workshops, demos, and tutorials, by making thoughtful judgments as members of the many review committees, and for coming to participate in the events this week. These contributions are very much appreciated. The heaviest burdens have been shared by the people who agreed to lead the major subcommittees of the conference, and I want to recognize them here and explicitly thank them for their service.

To begin, I want to express my gratitude to Jill Burstein, Mary Harper, and Gerald Penn, the co-Chairs of the Program Committee. They supervised the selection of papers and scheduling for the main conference, recruiting the Area Chairs and managing the overall process. They chose the Noisy Genre theme of the conference, collaborated with the Area Chairs to select the Invited Speakers, administered the START reviewing system, and worked with the Area Chairs and the Local Arrangements Committee to assemble the final program. They also added a new feature to the program, a "one-minute madness" session to raise awareness and excitement about the poster and demo presentations.

The Program Committee co-Chairs and Area Chairs recommended a small number of papers for further consideration by the Best Papers Committee, chaired by Aravind Joshi. Tremendous thanks go to Aravind, Eugene Charniak, Michael Collins, Diane Litman, Daniel Marcu, and Drago Radev for their work in identifying the best examples of current work in the field.

The main-conference days include some other important activities. I appreciate Kristina Toutanova's effort to organize a second lunch-time Industry Panel, a follow-on to the successful panel at NAACL HLT 2009. I thank Carolyn Penstein Rosé, Chair of the Demonstration Committee, for soliciting candidates for the Demo Session and overseeing the rigorous process of review. For organizing the Student Research Workshop I thank Adriane Boyd, Mahesh Joshi, and Frank Rudzicz, the student co-Chairs, and also Julia Hockenmaier and Diane Litman for the assistance and guidance they provided as Faculty Advisors. Financial support for the student workshop came from a grant from the National Science Foundation.

I thank Richard Sproat and David Traum for serving as co-Chairs of the Workshop Committee. The workshop proposal and selection process was a joint activity of committees representing all three of this year's computational linguistics conferences, the ACL conference in Uppsala, Coling in Beijing, and NAACL HLT. Their challenge was to honor the location requests of the workshop proposers while arranging for each conference to have a broad and balanced collection of workshops. A full complement of 16 workshops were chosen for NAACL HLT, and Richard and David then became the interface with the organizers of the individual workshops as they put out their calls, reviewed submissions, and assembled final papers for the Publications Committee.

I am grateful to Jason Baldridge, Peter Clark, and Gokhan Tur for volunteering to co-Chair the Tutorial Committee and for attracting and selecting tutorials that introduce a range of novel techniques and address a number of theoretical and practical problems.

The Publications Committee is responsible for constructing the written Proceedings of the conference from the materials that come from the many sources. The Publications Committee, with Claudia Leacock and Richard Wicentowski as co-Chairs, comes in at the end of the preparation stage and must operate on a strict schedule if the Proceedings are to be available by the time the conference begins. This year Claudia and Richard have been the pioneers for two major departures from past procedure. ACL proceedings in the past have been produced by a stand-alone community-developed software package, ACLPUB; this year we are using a version of that package that has been integrated directly into the START conference-management system. This should simplify the publication process for future conferences, but Claudia and Richard endured a fair amount of first-user suffering. The second departure from past practices is that for the first time we are providing the proceedings only on a USB memory stick, unaccompanied by a hardcopy volume. I deeply appreciate the care and attention with which Claudia and Richard have carried out their responsibilities.

We are all very much indebted to David Chiang, Jason Riesa, Jonathan May, and Eduard Hovy, the co-Chairs of the Local Arrangements Committee, and to the other members of the committee from the USC Information Sciences Institute. They have been hard at work for the longest time, and the comfort and elegance of the conference setting is the result of the many decisions they have made. To highlight just a few, they selected the hotel, made sure that the session rooms are properly laid out and equipped, and planned for the reception and banquet. They also designed and maintained the very attractive and informative conference web site. Liang Huang served as Coordinator of the Student Volunteers, and Jillian Gerten and Kenji Sagae served as Exhibit Coordinators.

I am grateful to the sponsoring organizations listed above for their financial support of the conference, and to the members of the Sponsorship Committee for identifying and nurturing those important relationships. The Sponsorship Committee–Srinivas Bangalore, Christy Doran, Eduard Hovy, Stephen Pulman, and Frédérique Segond–raised money jointly for NAACL HLT and ACL this year.

The NAACL executive committee, chaired by Owen Rambow and Rebecca Hwa, provides overall supervision and maintains the continuity and traditions of the conference from year to year. They helped by identifying candidates for many of the committee positions, by resolving several significant issues of conference policy, and by overseeing the budgeting process.

Finally, my heartfelt thanks go to Priscilla Rasmussen, the Business Manager of the ACL office and for the ACL conferences, for her steady guidance through all the stages of conference preparation. Priscilla, as always, played a critical role as the voice of experience and the source of wise advice that kept everything moving in the right direction.

Ronald M. Kaplan
Powerset division of Microsoft Bing
General Chair, NAACL HLT 2010

Preface: Program Chairs

Thanks for attending NAACL HLT 2010! As can be seen in the Conference Program, the NAACL HLT program contains innovative, high-quality work spanning a large array of disciplines within computational linguistics and human language technology. This year, we have included a special Noisy Genre theme to acknowledge the significant work in that area across several disciplines. We would like to thank L.Venkata Subramaniam of IBM Research-India for this suggestion.

NAACL HLT 2010 consists of oral and poster presentations of full and short papers, tutorials, application demonstrations, and workshops. A one-minute madness session has been introduced this year to highlight the poster and demo contributions. We are excited to have two very interesting and diverse keynote speakers: David Temperley, University of Rochester, whose talk is entitled, "Music, Language, and Computational Modeling: Lessons from the Key-Finding Problem", and Steve Renals, University of Edinburgh, "Recognition and Understanding of Meetings." In addition, we have a panel session Recent and Future HLT Challenges in Industry, chaired by Kristina Toutanova, which very appropriately reflects the conference theme.

This year, 291 full papers were submitted and reviewed, of which 90 papers were accepted (a 30.9% acceptance rate); 159 short papers were submitted and reviewed, of which 56 were accepted (a 35.2% acceptance rate). One of the accepted short papers was withdrawn to appear elsewhere, leaving a total of 55 short papers in the proceedings. Eighty-six full papers and 25 short papers will be presented orally. The remaining 34 accepted full and short papers will be presented as posters. We would like to thank all of the authors for submitting such remarkable papers to the conference.

Two best papers have been selected this year, and will be presented at the conference in a special awards session. The Best Full Paper, entitled Coreference Resolution in a Modular, Entity-Centered Model, was written by Aria Haghighi and Dan Klein. The Best Short Paper, entitled "cba to check the spelling": Investigating Parser Performance on Discussion Forum Posts, was written by Jennifer Foster. Congratulations to the authors! The selection process worked as follows. The Senior Program Committee (SPC) nominated an initial set of best paper candidates for the awards; the final decisions were then made by a separate committee: Aravind Joshi (chair), Eugene Charniak, Michael Collins, Diane Litman, Daniel Marcu, and Dragomir Radev. We would like to thank the committee for reading, discussing, and contributing to the final selection process. The committee was selected to handle the breadth of expertise required to review the nominated best papers. Once the camera-ready versions of the papers were submitted by the authors, the Best Paper committee chair used the following process: (a) Committee members were asked to notify the chair about conflicts of interest. Members with conflicts of interest did not rank or discuss those papers with which they were conflicted. (b) Short papers were ranked first by committee members, and additional discussions were held to make a final decision. (c) Next, long papers were ranked by members and a smaller set of top papers were identified. Discussions were then held to make the final decision. (d) The committee chair was available to break any ties.

The review process was organized as a two-tier system with 18 SPC members and 382 reviewers. The SPC members managed the review process for both the full and short paper submissions: each paper received at least three reviews. Strict conflict-of-interest policies were in place during the review process. Specifically, authors who served on the Program Committee in any capacity were removed from any responsibility related to their paper. Any such conflict-of-interest paper was handled by another committee member. In addition, the author was prohibited from participating in any discussion or decision making related to the paper. A similar policy also applied if a Program Committee member had an institutional or personal conflict with an author. All decisions on papers with these types of conflicts were made by members without conflicts. We would not have been able to produce such an interesting conference program without the dedicated SPC members who spent many weeks handling and evaluating the submission reviews, nor without the reviewers who provided such thoughtful evaluations. The full list of the SPC members and reviewers is listed elsewhere in these Proceedings. We would also like to thank the SPC members for their best paper recommendations and suggestions for the program, and Chris Dyer for his suggestions on the Machine Translation sessions.

There were, of course, a number of additional people with whom we directly interacted, and who made significant contributions to the success of this conference. So, here are some well-deserved acknowledgements. We would like to thank Rich Gerber and the START team for their help with the system that managed paper submissions and reviews, and the Local Arrangement co-chairs, David Chiang, Eduard Hovy, Jonathan May, and Jason Riesa, for their help with organizing the program, the preparation and publication of the conference handbook, handling the NAACL HLT 2010 website, and various other tasks – a list too lengthy to name here. We would also like to thank the Publication Co-chairs, Claudia Leacock and Richard Wicentowski, for forging through a number of obstacles, and doing an excellent job of handling the preparation and printing of these proceedings. We would like to thank the Workshop Co-chairs, David Traum and Richard Sproat, the Demo Chair, Carolyn Penstein Rosé, the Tutorial Co-chairs, Jason Baldridge, Peter Clark and Gokhan Tur, and the Student Research Workshop Faculty Co-chairs, Julia Hockenmeier and Diane Litman, and Student Co-chairs, Adriane Boyd, Mahesh Joshi, and Frank Rudzicz. The hard work of all of these co-chairs contributed to the quality of the entire conference program. We would also like to thank Chris Callison-Burch for handling Student Author Support, and to Liang Huang for serving as the Student Volunteer Coordinator. We are grateful to Priscilla Rasmussen for supporting the visa application process, as well as answering a variety of our questions and concerns around general conference logistics and event planning. Finally, we would like to express our deepest thanks to the General Chair, Ron Kaplan, for his continual support and patience throughout this process.

We hope that you will have a unique and enriching conference experience!

Jill Burstein, Educational Testing Service
Mary Harper, University of Maryland; Johns Hopkins HLT COE
Gerald Penn, University of Toronto

Organizers

General Chair:

Ronald Kaplan, Powerset Division of Microsoft Bing

Program Co-Chairs:

Jill Burstein (NLP), Educational Testing Service
Mary Harper (Speech), University of Maryland and The Johns Hopkins University HLTCOE
Gerald Penn (NLP), University of Toronto

Workshop Chairs:

Richard Sproat, Oregon Health & Science University
David Traum, University of Southern California, Institute for Creative Technologies

Demo Chair:

Carolyn Penstein Rosé, Carnegie Mellon University

Tutorial Chairs:

Jason Baldridge, The University of Texas at Austin
Peter Clark, The Boeing Company
Gokhan Tur, SRI International

Publications Chairs:

Claudia Leacock, Butler Hill Group
Richard Wicentowski, Swarthmore College

Student Research Workshop Chairs:

Julia Hockenmaier (Faculty Advisor), University of Illinois at Urbana-Champaign
Diane Litman (Faculty Advisor), University of Pittsburgh
Adriane Boyd (NLP Co-Chair), University of Ohio
Mahesh Joshi (NLP Co-Chair), Carnegie Mellon University
Frank Rudzicz (Speech Co-Chair), University of Toronto

Local Arrangements Chairs:

David Chiang, University of Southern California, Information Sciences Institute
Eduard Hovy, University of Southern California, Information Sciences Institute
Jonathan May, University of Southern California, Information Sciences Institute
Jason Riesa, University of Southern California, Information Sciences Institute

Exhibits Chairs:

Jillian Gerten, University of Southern California, Institute for Creative Technologies
Kenji Sagae, University of Southern California, Information Sciences Institute

Student Volunteers Coordinator:

Liang Huang, University of Southern California, Information Sciences Institute

Sponsorship Chairs:

Srinivas Bangalore (North America), AT&T
Christy Doran (North America), MITRE
Eduard Hovy (Local), University of Southern California, Information Sciences Institute
Stephen Pulman (Europe), Oxford University
Frédérique Segond (Europe), Xerox Research Centre Europe

ACL Business Manager:

Priscilla Rasmussen

Conference Sponsors:

- AT&T Interactive (Platinum Level)
- Microsoft Research (Gold Level)
- USC Information Sciences Institute (Gold Level)
- Google (Silver Level)
- J.D. Power and Associates (Silver Level)
- Yahoo! Labs (Silver Level)
- Basis Technology (Bronze Level)
- Factual (Bronze Level)
- IBM Research (Best Student Paper Award)
- Language Weaver (Conference Bag Sponsor)

Program Committee

Senior Program Committee Members (Area Chairs):

Eugene Agichtein, Emory University
Yaser Al-Onaizan, IBM
Ciprian Chelba, Google
Mona Diab, Columbia University
Barbara Di Eugenio, University of Illinois at Chicago
Eric Fosler-Lussier, Ohio State University
Makoto Kanazawa, National Institute of Informatics, Tokyo
Damianos Karakos, Johns Hopkins University
Philip Koehn, University of Edinburgh
Mike Maxwell, University of Maryland
Diana McCarthy, Lexical Computing Ltd
Ani Nenkova, University of Pennsylvania
Stefan Oepen, University of Oslo
Dan Roth, University of Illinois at Urbana-Champaign
Noah Smith, Carnegie Mellon University
Amanda Stent, AT&T
Joel Tetreault, Educational Testing Service
Jan Wiebe, University of Pittsburgh

Paper Award Committee:

Aravind Joshi (Chair), University of Pennsylvania
Daniel Marcu, University of Southern California, Information Sciences Institute
Diane Litman, University of Pittsburgh
Drago Radev, University of Michigan
Eugene Charniak, Brown University
Michael Collins, Massachusetts Institute of Technology

Program Committee Members:

Steve Abney
Mikhail Ageev
Eneko Agirre
David Ahn
Gregory Aist
Salah Ait-Mokhtar
Cem Akkaya
Ingunn Amdal
Ron Artstein
Abhishek Arun
Necip Fazil Ayan
Jason Baldridge
Tim Baldwin
Carmen Banea
Srinivas Bangalore
Regina Barzilay
Roberto Basili
Anja Belz
Yassine Benajiba
Emily M. Bender
Shane Bergsma
Steven Bethard
Pushpak Bhattacharyya
Jiang Bian
Dan Bikel
Alexandra Birch
Steven Bird

Philippe Blache
Bernd Bohnet
Kristy Boyer
SRK Branavan
Antnio Branco
Thorsten Brants
Chris Brew
Sam Brody
Razvan Bunescu
Harry Bunt
Lukas Burget
Bill Byrne
Donna Byron
Lynne Cahill
Aoife Cahill
Chris Callison-Burch
Claire Cardie
Giuseppe Carenini
Michael Carl
Marine Carpuat
John Carroll
Francisco Casacuberta
Joyce Chai
Eugene Charniak
Ciprian Chelba
Jinying Chen
John Chen
Harr Chen
Yejin Choi
Alexander Clark
Stephen Clark
James Clarke
Martin Cmejrek
Shay Cohen
Trevor Cohn
Michael Collins
Michael Connor
John Conroy
Mark Core
Mathias Creutz
Aron Culotta
Robert Dale
Cristian Danescu-Niculescu-Mizil
Hal Daume
Anne David
Kordula De Kuthy
Eric de la Clergerie
Dina Demner Fushman
John DeNero
David DeVault
Doug Downey
Mark Dredze
Jasha Droppo
Amit Dubey
Kevin Duh
Markus Egg
Andreas Eisele
Jacob Eisenstein
Jason Eisner
Noemie Elhadad
Jonathan Elsas
Micha Elsner
Ahmad Emami
Andrea Esuli
Tanveer Faruquie
Benoit Favre
Elena Filatova
Katja Filippova
Jenny Finkel
Dan Flickinger
Kate Forbes Riley
Eric Fosler-Lussier
Davide Fossati
Jennifer Foster
George Foster
Alexander Fraser
Maria Fuentes
Pascale Fung
Ryan Gabbard
Michel Galley
Michael Gamon
Albert Gatt
Panayiotis Georgiou
Dan Gildea
Jesus Gimenez
Roxana Girju
Claudio Giuliano
Vaibhava Goel
Dan Goldwasser
Carlos Gomez Rodriguez
Jeff Good
Nancy Green
Ralph Grishman
Qi Guo
Weiwei Guo
Iryna Gurevych
Aria Haghighi
Keith Hall
Mike Hammond
Sanda Harabagiu
Mary Harper
Mark Hasegawa-Johnson
Laura Hasler
Hany Hassan
Xiaodong He
Jeff Heinz
James Henderson
Andy Hickl
Silja Hildebrand
Graeme Hirst
Hieu Hoang
Julia Hockenmaier
Kristy Hollingshead
Rebecca Hwa
Nancy Ide
Diana Inkpen
Abraham Ittycheriah
Aren Jansen
Heng Ji
Kristiina Jokinen
Doug Jones
Laura Kallmeyer
Hiroshi Kanayama
Damianos Karakos
Lauri Karttunen
Athanassios Katsamanis
Frank Keller
Cynthia Kersey
Tracy King
Brian Kingsbury
Dan Klein
Kevin Knight
Greg Kobele
Rob Koeling
Greg Kondrak
Terry Koo
Stefan Kopp

Valia Kordoni
Anna Korhonen
Sandra Kuebler
Marco Kuhlmann
Roland Kuhn
Jonas Kuhn
Seth Kulick
Mikko Kurimo
Oren Kurland
Sadao Kurohashi
Arnd Christian Knig
Philippe Langlais
Mirella Lapata
Alberto Lavelli
Matt Lease
Lin-Shan Lee
Els Lefever
James Lester
Gregor Leusch
Haizhou Li
Zhifei Li
Henry Li
Mu Li
Percy Liang
Jimmy Lin
Diane Litman
Qun Liu
Yang Liu
Zhanyi Liu
Adam Lopez
Annie Louis
Bernardo Magnini
Wolfgang Maier
Rob Malouf
Arindam Mandal
Lidia Mangu
Christopher Manning
Daniel Marcu
Lluis Marquez Villodre
David Martinez
Andre Martins
Yuval Marton
Sameer Maskey
Yuji Matsumoto
Evgeny Matusov
Arne Mauser
Mike Maxwell
James Mayfield
David McClosky
Mark McConnville
Nancy McCracken
David McDonald
Ryan McDonald
Kathy McKeown
Susan McRoy
Florian Metze
Eleni Miltsakaki
Gilad Mishne
Yusuke Miyao
Saif Mohammad
Bob Moore
Alessandro Moschitti
Dragos Munteanu
Smaranda Muresan
Gabriel Murray
Tor Andre Myrvoll
Roberto Navigli
Mark-Jan Nederhof
Sumit Negi
Hwee Tou Ng
Vincent Ng
Patrick Nguyen
Takashi Ninomiya
Joakim Nivre
Doug Oard
Franz Och
Kemal Oflazer
Alice Oh
Constantin Orasan
Miles Osborne
Lilja Ovrelid
Deepak Padmanabhan
Ulrike Pado
Alexis Palmer
Martha Palmer
Bo Pang
Marius Pasca
Becky Passonneau
Sid Patwardhan
Ted Pedersen
Slav Petrov
Christine Piatko
Daniele Pighin
Emily Pitler
Massimo Poesio
Joe Polifroni
Simone Ponzetto
Maja Popovic
Dan Povey
Sameer Pradhan
Rashmi Prasad
Chris Quirk
Stephan Raaijmakers
Bhuvana Ramabhadran
Allan Ramsay
Ari Rappoport
Ariya Rastrow
Lev Ratinov
Roi Reichart
Ehud Reiter
German Rigau
Michael Riley
Laura Rimell
Nicholas Rizzolo
Brian Roark
Horacio Rodriguez
Victoria Rosen
Antti-Veikko Rosti
Dan Roth
Shourya Roy
Marta Ruiz Costa-juss
Mark Sammons
George Saon
Murat Saraclar
Kevin Scannell
Odette Scharenborg
David Schlangen
Helmut Schmid
Hinrich Schuetze
Mike Seltzer
Hendra Setiawan
Fei Sha
Izhak Shafran
Wade Shen
Libin Shen
Nobuyuki Shimizu
Advaith Siddharthan
Khalil Simaan

Michel Simard
Kevin Small
David Smith
Mark Smucker
Swapna Somasundaran
Radu Soricut
Richard Sproat
Vivek Srikumar
Yaji Sripada
Mark Steedman
Josef Steinberger
Amanda Stent
Mark Stevenson
Carlo Strapparava
Kristina Striegnitz
Michael Strube
LV Subramaniam
Mihai Surdeanu
Hiroya Takamura
David Talbot
Simone Teufel
Joerg Tiedemann
Christoph Tillmann
Ivan Titov
Kristina Toutanova
Roy Tromble
Yoshimasa Tsuruoka
Ielka van der Sluis
Josef van Genabith
Keith Vander Linden
Balakrishnan Varadarajan
Ashish Venugopal
Yannick Versley
David Vilar
Stephan Vogel
Piek Vossen
Marilyn Walker
Stephen Wan
Wen Wang
Haifeng Wang
XingLong Wang
Qin Wang
Ye-Yi Wang
Andy Way
Bonnie Webber
David Weir
Fuiliang Weng
Michael White
Chris White
Richard Wicentowski
Theresa Wilson
Shuly Wintner
Yunfang Wu
Dekai Wu
Hua Wu
Holger Wunsch
Bing Xiang
Deyi Xiong
Puyang Xu
Jinxi Xu
Peng Xu
Wen-tau Yih
Dong Yu
Deniz Yuret
David Zajic
Richard Zens
Hao Zhang
Yue Zhang
Dongdong Zhang
Yi Zhang
Min Zhang
Ying Zhang
Tiejun Zhao
Bing Zhao
Bowen Zhou
Xiaodan Zhu
Imed Zitouni
Andreas Zollmann
Chengqing Zong
Geoff Zweig

Table of Contents

Conference Program

Wednesday, June 2, 2010

Plenary Session I

8:45–9:00 Opening Ceremony

9:00–10:10 Invited Talk: *Recognition and Understanding of Meetings*
Steve Renals

10:10–10:40 **Break**

Parsing I

10:40–11:05 *Chart Mining-based Lexical Acquisition with Precision Grammars*
Yi Zhang, Timothy Baldwin, Valia Kordoni, David Martinez and Jeremy Nicholson

11:05–11:30 *Products of Random Latent Variable Grammars*
Slav Petrov

11:30–11:55 *Automatic Domain Adaptation for Parsing*
David McClosky, Eugene Charniak and Mark Johnson

11:55–12:20 *Appropriately Handled Prosodic Breaks Help PCFG Parsing*
Zhongqiang Huang and Mary Harper

Noisy Genre I

10:40–11:05 *Using Confusion Networks for Speech Summarization*
Shasha Xie and Yang Liu

11:05–11:30 *Qme! : A Speech-based Question-Answering system on Mobile Devices*
Taniya Mishra and Srinivas Bangalore

11:30–11:55 *Dialogue-Oriented Review Summary Generation for Spoken Dialogue Recommendation Systems*
Jingjing Liu, Stephanie Seneff and Victor Zue

Wednesday, June 2, 2010 (continued)

11:55–12:20 *Minimally-Supervised Extraction of Entities from Text Advertisements*
Sameer Singh, Dustin Hillard and Chris Leggetter

Semantics I

10:40–11:05 *Taxonomy Learning Using Word Sense Induction*
Ioannis P. Klapaftis and Suresh Manandhar

11:05–11:30 *Visual Information in Semantic Representation*
Yansong Feng and Mirella Lapata

11:30–11:55 *Automatic Evaluation of Topic Coherence*
David Newman, Jey Han Lau, Karl Grieser and Timothy Baldwin

11:55–12:20 *Multi-Prototype Vector-Space Models of Word Meaning*
Joseph Reisinger and Raymond J. Mooney

Student Research Workshop I

Note: All student research workshop papers are located in a companion volume of the proceedings.

10:40–11:10 *Improving Syntactic Coordination Resolution using Language Modeling*
Philip Ogren

11:10–11:40 *On Automated Evaluation of Readability of Summaries: Capturing Grammaticality, Focus, Structure and Coherence*
Ravikiran Vadlapudi and Rahul Katragadda

11:40–12:10 *Detecting Novelty in the Context of Progressive Summarization*
Praveen Bysani

12:20–2:00 **Lunch**

Wednesday, June 2, 2010 (continued)

Machine Translation I

2:00–2:25 *Unsupervised Syntactic Alignment with Inversion Transduction Grammars*
Adam Pauls, Dan Klein, David Chiang and Kevin Knight

2:25–2:50 *Joint Parsing and Alignment with Weakly Synchronized Grammars*
David Burkett, John Blitzer and Dan Klein

2:50–3:15 *Learning Translation Boundaries for Phrase-Based Decoding*
Deyi Xiong, Min Zhang and Haizhou Li

3:15–3:40 *Hitting the Right Paraphrases in Good Time*
Stanley Kok and Chris Brockett

Noisy Genre II

2:00–2:25 *Training Paradigms for Correcting Errors in Grammar and Usage*
Alla Rozovskaya and Dan Roth

2:25–2:50 *Using Mostly Native Data to Correct Errors in Learners' Writing*
Michael Gamon

2:50–3:15 *Unsupervised Modeling of Twitter Conversations*
Alan Ritter, Colin Cherry and Bill Dolan

3:15–3:40 *Streaming First Story Detection with application to Twitter*
Saša Petrović, Miles Osborne and Victor Lavrenko

Wednesday, June 2, 2010 (continued)

Speech Processing

2:00–2:25 *Unsupervised Model Adaptation using Information-Theoretic Criterion*
Ariya Rastrow, Frederick Jelinek, Abhinav Sethy and Bhuvana Ramabhadran

2:25–2:50 *Formatting Time-Aligned ASR Transcripts for Readability*
Maria Shugrina

2:50–3:15 *Cheap, Fast and Good Enough: Automatic Speech Recognition with Non-Expert Transcription*
Scott Novotney and Chris Callison-Burch

3:15–3:40 *Contextual Information Improves OOV Detection in Speech*
Carolina Parada, Mark Dredze, Denis Filimonov and Frederick Jelinek

Student Research Workshop II

Note: All student research workshop papers are located in a companion volume of the proceedings.

2:00–2:30 *Extrinsic Parse Selection*
David Goss-Grubbs

2:30–3:00 *Towards a Matrix-based Distributional Model of Meaning*
Eugenie Giesbrecht

3:00–3:30 *Distinguishing Use and Mention in Natural Language*
Shomir Wilson

3:40–4:10 **Break**

Poster Plenary Session

4:10–5:30 One-Minute Madness: Poster and Demo Previews

5:30–6:30 **Break**

6:30–8:30 **Poster and Demo Session**

Posters

Improved Extraction Assessment through Better Language Models
Arun Ahuja and Doug Downey

Language Identification: The Long and the Short of the Matter
Timothy Baldwin and Marco Lui

Inducing Synchronous Grammars with Slice Sampling
Phil Blunsom and Trevor Cohn

Task-based Evaluation of Multiword Expressions: a Pilot Study in Statistical Machine Translation
Marine Carpuat and Mona Diab

Improving Semantic Role Labeling with Word Sense
Wanxiang Che, Ting Liu and Yongqiang Li

Extending the METEOR Machine Translation Evaluation Metric to the Phrase Level
Michael Denkowski and Alon Lavie

Testing a Grammar Customization System with Sahaptin
Scott Drellishak

Two monolingual parses are better than one (synchronous parse)
Chris Dyer

Fast Query for Large Treebanks
Sumukh Ghodke and Steven Bird

Wednesday, June 2, 2010 (continued)

Wednesday, June 2, 2010 (continued)

Information Content Measures of Semantic Similarity Perform Better Without Sense-Tagged Text
Ted Pedersen

Generating Expository Dialogue from Monologue: Motivation, Corpus and Preliminary Rules
Paul Piwek and Svetlana Stoyanchev

The Simple Truth about Dependency and Phrase Structure Representations: An Opinion Piece
Owen Rambow

Word Alignment with Stochastic Bracketing Linear Inversion Transduction Grammar
Markus Saers, Joakim Nivre and Dekai Wu

Crowdsourcing the evaluation of a domain-adapted named entity recognition system
Asad B. Sayeed, Timothy J. Meyer, Hieu C. Nguyen, Olivia Buzek and Amy Weinberg

Generalizing Hierarchical Phrase-based Translation using Rules with Adjacent Nonterminals
Hendra Setiawan and Philip Resnik

The Effect of Ambiguity on the Automated Acquisition of WSD Examples
Mark Stevenson and Yikun Guo

Word Sense Subjectivity for Cross-lingual Lexical Substitution
Fangzhong Su and Katja Markert

Query Ambiguity Revisited: Clickthrough Measures for Distinguishing Informational and Ambiguous Queries
Yu Wang and Eugene Agichtein

For the sake of simplicity: Unsupervised extraction of lexical simplifications from Wikipedia
Mark Yatskar, Bo Pang, Cristian Danescu-Niculescu-Mizil and Lillian Lee

Predicting Human-Targeted Translation Edit Rate via Untrained Human Annotators
Omar F. Zaidan and Chris Callison-Burch

Improving Semantic Role Classification with Selectional Preferences
Beñat Zapirain, Eneko Agirre, Lluís Màrquez and Mihai Surdeanu

Demonstrations

Note: Demo abstracts are located in a companion volume of the proceedings.

Wednesday, June 2, 2010 (continued)

An Overview of Microsoft Web N-gram Corpus and Applications
Kuansan Wang, Chris Thrasher, Evelyne Viegas, Xiaolong Li and Bo-june (Paul) Hsu

6:30–8:30 **Student Research Workshop Poster Session**

Note: All student research workshop papers are located in a companion volume of the proceedings.

A Learning-based Sampling Approach to Extractive Summarization
Vishal Juneja, Sebastian Germesin and Thomas Kleinbauer

Temporal Relation Identification with Endpoints
Chong Min Lee

Identifying Opinion Holders and Targets with Dependency Parser in Chinese News Texts
Bin Lu

A Data Mining Approach to Learn Reorder Rules for SMT
Avinesh PVS

Fine-Tuning in Brazilian Portuguese-English Statistical Transfer Machine Translation: Verbal Tenses
Lucia Silva

Improving Syntactic Coordination Resolution using Language Modeling
Philip Ogren

On Automated Evaluation of Readability of Summaries: Capturing Grammaticality, Focus, Structure and Coherence
Ravikiran Vadlapudi and Rahul Katragadda

Extrinsic Parse Selection
David Goss-Grubbs

Towards a Matrix-based Distributional Model of Meaning
Eugenie Giesbrecht

Distinguishing Use and Mention in Natural Language
Shomir Wilson

Thursday, June 3, 2010

	Best Paper Award Plenary Session
9:00–9:10	Best Paper Award: Introduction
9:10–9:40	*"cba to check the spelling": Investigating Parser Performance on Discussion Forum Posts* Jennifer Foster
9:40–10:15	*Coreference Resolution in a Modular, Entity-Centered Model* Aria Haghighi and Dan Klein
10:15–10:45	**Break**
	Machine Translation II
10:45–11:10	*Stream-based Translation Models for Statistical Machine Translation* Abby Levenberg, Chris Callison-Burch and Miles Osborne
11:10–11:35	*Extracting Parallel Sentences from Comparable Corpora using Document Level Alignment* Jason R. Smith, Chris Quirk and Kristina Toutanova
11:35–12:00	*Statistical Machine Translation of Texts with Misspelled Words* Nicola Bertoldi, Mauro Cettolo and Marcello Federico
12:00–12:25	*Everybody loves a rich cousin: An empirical study of transliteration through bridge languages* Mitesh M. Khapra, A Kumaran and Pushpak Bhattacharyya

Thursday, June 3, 2010 (continued)

Machine Learning I

10:45–11:10 *Discriminative Learning over Constrained Latent Representations*
Ming-Wei Chang, Dan Goldwasser, Dan Roth and Vivek Srikumar

11:10–11:35 *Some Empirical Evidence for Annotation Noise in a Benchmarked Dataset*
Beata Beigman Klebanov and Eyal Beigman

11:35–12:00 *Bayesian Inference for Finite-State Transducers*
David Chiang, Jonathan Graehl, Kevin Knight, Adam Pauls and Sujith Ravi

12:00–12:25 *Distributed Training Strategies for the Structured Perceptron*
Ryan McDonald, Keith Hall and Gideon Mann

Information Retrieval and Extraction I

10:45–11:10 *Term Weighting Schemes for Latent Dirichlet Allocation*
Andrew T. Wilson and Peter A. Chew

11:10–11:35 *Learning Dense Models of Query Similarity from User Click Logs*
Fabio De Bona, Stefan Riezler, Keith Hall, Massimiliano Ciaramita, Amaç Herdağdelen and Maria Holmqvist

11:35–12:00 *Learning to Link Entities with Knowledge Base*
Zhicheng Zheng, Fangtao Li, Minlie Huang and Xiaoyan Zhu

12:00–12:25 *Improving the Multilingual User Experience of Wikipedia Using Cross-Language Name Search*
Raghavendra Udupa and Mitesh M. Khapra

Thursday, June 3, 2010 (continued)

Morphology/Phonology

10:45–11:10 *Learning Words and Their Meanings from Unsegmented Child-directed Speech*
Bevan K. Jones, Mark Johnson and Michael C. Frank

11:10–11:35 *Subword Variation in Text Message Classification*
Robert Munro and Christopher D. Manning

11:35–12:00 *Automatic Diacritization for Low-Resource Languages Using a Hybrid Word and Consonant CMM*
Robbie Haertel, Peter McClanahan and Eric K. Ringger

12:00–12:25 *Urdu Word Segmentation*
Nadir Durrani and Sarmad Hussain

Lunch

12:40–2:00 Panel: *Recent and Future HLT Challenges in Industry*

12:25–2:15 Lunch

Machine Translation III

2:15–2:40 *Enabling Monolingual Translators: Post-Editing vs. Options*
Philipp Koehn

2:40–3:05 *Online Learning for Interactive Statistical Machine Translation*
Daniel Ortiz-Martínez, Ismael García-Varea and Francisco Casacuberta

3:05–3:30 *The Best Lexical Metric for Phrase-Based Statistical MT System Optimization*
Daniel Cer, Christopher D. Manning and Daniel Jurafsky

Thursday, June 3, 2010 (continued)

Machine Learning II

2:15–2:40 *Variational Inference for Adaptor Grammars*
Shay B. Cohen, David M. Blei and Noah A. Smith

2:40–3:05 *Type-Based MCMC*
Percy Liang, Michael I. Jordan and Dan Klein

3:05–3:30 *Painless Unsupervised Learning with Features*
Taylor Berg-Kirkpatrick, Alexandre Bouchard-Côté, John DeNero and Dan Klein

Generation

2:15–2:40 *Linguistic Steganography Using Automatically Generated Paraphrases*
Ching-Yun Chang and Stephen Clark

2:40–3:05 *Prenominal Modifier Ordering via Multiple Sequence Alignment*
Aaron Dunlop, Margaret Mitchell and Brian Roark

3:05–3:30 *Good Question! Statistical Ranking for Question Generation*
Michael Heilman and Noah A. Smith

Leixcal Semantics

2:15–2:40 *Not All Seeds Are Equal: Measuring the Quality of Text Mining Seeds*
Zornitsa Kozareva and Eduard Hovy

2:40–3:05 *Extracting Glosses to Disambiguate Word Senses*
Weisi Duan and Alexander Yates

3:05–3:30 *Can Recognising Multiword Expressions Improve Shallow Parsing?*
Ioannis Korkontzelos and Suresh Manandhar

3:30–4:00 **Break**

Thursday, June 3, 2010 (continued)

Parsing: Short Papers

4:00–4:15 *A Simple Approach for HPSG Supertagging Using Dependency Information*
Yao-zhong Zhang, Takuya Matsuzaki and Jun'ichi Tsujii

4:15–4:30 *Ensemble Models for Dependency Parsing: Cheap and Good?*
Mihai Surdeanu and Christopher D. Manning

4:30–4:45 *Enlarged Search Space for SITG Parsing*
Guillem Gascó, Joan-Andreu Sánchez and José-Miguel Benedí

4:45–5:00 *Improving Data Driven Dependency Parsing using Clausal Information*
Phani Gadde, Karan Jindal, Samar Husain, Dipti Misra Sharma and Rajeev Sangal

5:00–5:15 *A Treebank Query System Based on an Extracted Tree Grammar*
Seth Kulick and Ann Bies

5:15–5:30 *Reranking the Berkeley and Brown Parsers*
Mark Johnson and Ahmet Engin Ural

Noisy Genre: Short Papers

4:00–4:15 *An Exploration of Off Topic Conversation*
Whitney L. Cade, Blair A. Lehman and Andrew Olney

4:15–4:30 *Making Conversational Structure Explicit: Identification of Initiation-response Pairs within Online Discussions*
Yi-Chia Wang and Carolyn P. Rosé

4:30–4:45 *Engaging learning groups using Social Interaction Strategies*
Rohit Kumar and Carolyn P. Rosé

4:45–5:00 *Using Entity-Based Features to Model Coherence in Student Essays*
Jill Burstein, Joel Tetreault and Slava Andreyev

5:00–5:15 *Summarizing Microblogs Automatically*
Beaux Sharifi, Mark-Anthony Hutton and Jugal Kalita

Thursday, June 3, 2010 (continued)

Thursday, June 3, 2010 (continued)

5:00–5:15 *Softmax-Margin CRFs: Training Log-Linear Models with Cost Functions*
Kevin Gimpel and Noah A. Smith

5:15–5:30 *Bitext-Based Resolution of German Subject-Object Ambiguities*
Florian Schwarck, Alexander Fraser and Hinrich Schütze

Friday, June 4, 2010

Plenary Session II

9:00–10:10 Invited Talk: *Music, Language, and Computational Modeling: Lessons from the Key-Finding Problem*
David Temperley

10:10–10:40 **Break**

Parsing II

10:40–11:05 *An Efficient Algorithm for Easy-First Non-Directional Dependency Parsing*
Yoav Goldberg and Michael Elhadad

11:05–11:30 *From Baby Steps to Leapfrog: How "Less is More" in Unsupervised Dependency Parsing*
Valentin I. Spitkovsky, Hiyan Alshawi and Daniel Jurafsky

11:30–11:55 *Relaxed Marginal Inference and its Application to Dependency Parsing*
Sebastian Riedel and David A. Smith

11:55–12:20 *Optimal Parsing Strategies for Linear Context-Free Rewriting Systems*
Daniel Gildea

Friday, June 4, 2010 (continued)

Sentiment Analysis

Information Retrieval and Extraction II

Friday, June 4, 2010 (continued)

Lunch

12:20–2:00 Lunch

1:00–2:00 NAACL Business Meeting

Machine Translation IV

2:00–2:25 *A Direct Syntax-Driven Reordering Model for Phrase-Based Machine Translation*
Niyu Ge

2:25–2:50 *Context-free reordering, finite-state translation*
Chris Dyer and Philip Resnik

2:50–3:15 *Improved Models of Distortion Cost for Statistical Machine Translation*
Spence Green, Michel Galley and Christopher D. Manning

3:15–3:40 *Why Synchronous Tree Substitution Grammars?*
Andreas Maletti

Summarization

2:00–2:25 *An extractive supervised two-stage method for sentence compression*
Dimitrios Galanis and Ion Androutsopoulos

2:25–2:50 *Interpretation and Transformation for Abstracting Conversations*
Gabriel Murray, Giuseppe Carenini and Raymond Ng

2:50–3:15 *Quantifying the Limits and Success of Extractive Summarization Systems Across Domains*
Hakan Ceylan, Rada Mihalcea, Umut Özertem, Elena Lloret and Manuel Palomar

3:15–3:40 *Multi-document Summarization via Budgeted Maximization of Submodular Functions*
Hui Lin and Jeff Bilmes

Friday, June 4, 2010 (continued)

Discourse

4:00–4:25 *Detecting Emails Containing Requests for Action*
Andrew Lampert, Robert Dale and Cecile Paris

4:25–4:50 *Evaluating Hierarchical Discourse Segmentation*
Lucien Carroll

4:50–5:15 *Reformulating Discourse Connectives for Non-Expert Readers*
Advaith Siddharthan and Napoleon Katsos

Semantics III

4:00–4:25 *Tree Edit Models for Recognizing Textual Entailments, Paraphrases, and Answers to Questions*
Michael Heilman and Noah A. Smith

4:25–4:50 *Syntactic/Semantic Structures for Textual Entailment Recognition*
Yashar Mehdad, Alessandro Moschitti and Fabio Massimo Zanzotto

4:50–5:15 *Automatic Metaphor Interpretation as a Paraphrasing Task*
Ekaterina Shutova

5:15–5:30 **End of Main Conference**

Recognition and Understanding of Meetings

Steve Renals
Centre for Speech Technology Research, University of Edinburgh
Informatics Forum, 10 Crichton Street, Edinburgh EH8 9AB, UK
s.renals@ed.ac.uk   homepages.inf.ed.ac.uk/srenals/

Abstract

This paper is about interpreting human communication in meetings using audio, video and other signals. Automatic meeting recognition and understanding is extremely challenging, since communication in a meeting is spontaneous and conversational, and involves multiple speakers and multiple modalities. This leads to a number of significant research problems in signal processing, in speech recognition, and in discourse interpretation, taking account of both individual and group behaviours. Addressing these problems requires an interdisciplinary effort. In this paper, I discuss the capture and annotation of multimodal meeting recordings—resulting in the AMI meeting corpus—and how we have built on this to develop techniques and applications for the recognition and interpretation of meetings.

1 Introduction

On the face of it, meetings do not seem to form a compelling research area. Although many people spend a substantial fraction of their time in meetings (e.g. the 1998 3M online survey at http://www.3m.com/meetingnetwork/), for most people they are not the most enjoyable aspect of their work. However, for all the time that is spent in meetings, technological support for the meeting process is scant. Meeting records usually take the form of brief minutes, personal notes, and more recent use of collaborative web 2.0 software. Such records are labour intensive to produce—because they are manually created—and usually fail to capture much of the content of a meeting, for example the factors that led to a particular decision and the different subjective attitudes displayed by the meeting attendees. For all the time invested in meetings, very little of the wealth of information that is exchanged is explicitly preserved.

To preserve the information recorded in meetings, it is necessary to capture it. Obviously this involves recording the speech of the meeting participants. However, human communication is a multimodal activity with information being exchanged via gestures, handwritten diagrams, and numerous social signals. The creation of a rich meeting record involves the capture of data across several modalities. It is a key engineering challenge to capture such multimodal signals in a reliable, unobtrusive and flexible way, but the greater challenges arise from unlocking the multimodal recordings. If such recordings are not transcribed and indexed (at the least), then access merely corresponds to replay. And it is rare that people will have the time, or the inclination, to replay a meeting.

There is a long and interesting thread of research which is concerned to better understand the dynamics of meetings and the way that groups function (Bales, 1951; McGrath, 1991; Stasser and Taylor, 1991). The types of analyses and studies carried out by these authors is still someway beyond what we can do automatically. The first significant work on automatic processing of meetings, coupled with an exploration of how people might interact with an archive of recorded meetings, was performed in the mid 1990s (Kazman et al., 1996). This work was limited by the fact that it was not possible at

Human Language Technologies: The 2010 Annual Conference of the North American Chapter of the ACL, pages 1–9,
Los Angeles, California, June 2010.

that time to transcribe meeting speech automatically. Other early work in the area concentrated on the multimodal capture and broadcast of meetings (Roy and Luz, 1999; Cutler et al., 2002; Yong et al., 2001).

Three groups further developed approaches to automatically index the content of meetings. A team at Fuji Xerox PARC used video retrieval techniques such as keyframing to automatically generate manga-style summaries of meetings (Uchihashi et al., 1999), Waibel and colleagues at CMU used speech recognition and video tracking for meetings (Waibel et al., 2001), and Morgan and colleagues at ICSI focused on audio-only capture and speech recognition (Morgan et al., 2003). Since 2003 research in the recognition and understanding of meetings has developed substantially, stimulated by evaluation campaigns such as the NIST Rich Transcription (RT)[1] and CLEAR[2] evaluations, as well as some large multidisciplinary projects such as AMI/AMIDA[3], CHIL[4] and CALO[5].

This paper is about the work we have carried out in meeting capture, recognition and interpretation within the AMI and AMIDA projects since 2004. One of the principal outputs of these projects was a multimodal corpus of meeting recordings, annotated at a number of different levels. In section 2 we discuss collection of meeting data, and the construction of the AMI corpus. The remainder of the paper discusses the automatic recognition (section 3) and interpretation (section 4) of multimodal meeting recordings, application prototypes (section 5) and issues relating to evaluation (section 6).

2 The AMI corpus

Ideally it would not be necessary to undertake a large scale data collection and annotation exercise, every time we address a new domain. However unsupervised adaptation techniques are still rather immature, and prior to the collection of the AMI corpus, there had not been a controlled collection and multilevel annotation of multiparty interactions, recorded across multiple modalities.

[1] www.itl.nist.gov/iad/mig/tests/rt/
[2] clear-evaluation.org/
[3] www.amiproject.org/
[4] chil.server.de/
[5] caloproject.sri.com/

Figure 1: AMI instrumented meeting room: four co-located participants, one joined by video conference. In this case two microphone arrays and seven cameras were used.

One of our key motivations is the development of automatic approaches to recognise and interpret group interactions, using information spread across multiple modalities, but collected as unobtrusively as possible. This led to the design and construction of the AMI Instrumented Meeting Rooms (figure 1) at the University of Edinburgh, Idiap Research Institute, and TNO Human Factors. These rooms contained a set of standardised recording equipment including six or seven cameras (four of which would be used for close-up views in meeting of up to four people), an 8-element microphone array, a close-talking microphone for each participant (used to guarantee a clean audio signal for each speaker), as well capture of digital pens, whiteboards, shared laptop spaces, data projector and videoconferencing if used. A considerable amount of hardware was necessary for ensuring frame-level synchronisation. More recently we have used a lighter weight setup, that uses a high resolution spherical digital video camera system, and a single microphone array (7–20 elements, depending on meeting size) synchronised using software. We have also constructed a prototype system using a low-cost, flexible array of digital MEMS microphones (Zwyssig et al., 2010).

We used these instrumented meeting rooms to record the AMI Meeting Corpus (Carletta, 2007). This corpus contains over 100 hours of meeting recordings, with the different recording streams synchronised to a common timeline. The corpus contains a number of manually created and automatic annotations, synchronised to the same timeline. This includes a high-quality manual word-level transcription of the complete corpus, as well as reference automatic speech recognition output, using the speech recognition system discussed in section 3 (using 5-fold cross-validation). In addition to word-level transcriptions, the corpus includes manual annotations that describe the behaviour of meeting participants at a number of levels. These include dialogue acts, topic segmentation, extractive and abstractive summaries, named entities, limited forms of head and hand gestures, gaze direction, movement around the room, and head pose information. Some of these annotations, in particular video annotation, are expensive to perform: about 10 hours of meetings have been completely annotated at all these levels; over 70% of the corpus has been fully annotated with the linguistic annotations. NXT—the NITE XML Toolkit[6]—an XML-based open source software infrastructure for multimodal annotation was used to carry out and manage the annotations.

About 70% of the AMI corpus consists of meetings based on a design scenario, in which four participants play roles in a design team. The scenario involves four team meetings, between which the participants had tasks to accomplish. The participant roles were stimulated in real-time by email and web content. Although the use of a scenario reduces the overall realism of the meetings, we adopted this approach for several reasons, most importantly: (1) there were some preferred design outcomes, making it possible to define some objective group outcome measures; (2) the knowledge and motivation of the participants was controlled, thus removing the serious confounding factors that would arise from the long history and context found in real organisations; and (3) allowing the meeting scenario to be replicated, thus enabling system-level evaluations (as discussed in section 6). We recorded and annotated thirty replicates of the scenario: this provides an unparalleled resource for system evaluation, but also reduces the variability of the corpus (for example in terms of the language used). The remaining 30% of the corpus contains meetings that would have occurred anyway; these are meetings with a lot less control than the scenario meetings, but with greater linguistic variability.

[6] `sourceforge.net/projects/nite/`

All the meetings in the AMI corpus are spoken in English, but over half the participants are non-native speakers. This adds realism in a European context, as well as providing an additional speech recognition challenge. The corpus is publicly available[7], and is released under a licence that is based on the Creative Commons Attribution NonCommercial ShareAlike 2.5 Licence. This includes all the signals and manual annotations, plus a number of automatic annotations (e.g. speech recognition) made available to lower the startup cost of performing research on the corpus.

3 Multimodal recognition

The predominant motivation behind the collection and annotation of the AMI corpus was to enable the development of multimodal recognisers to address issues such as speech recognition, speaker diarisartion (Wooters and Huijbregts, 2007), gesture recognition (Al-Hames et al., 2007) and focus of attention (Ba and Odobez, 2008). Although speech recognition is based on the (multichannel) audio signal, the other problems can be successfully addressed by combining modalities. (There is certainly information in other modalities that has the potential to make speech recognition more accurate, but so far we have not been able to use it consistently and robustly.)

Speech recognition: The automatic transcription of what is spoken in a meeting is an essential prerequisite to interpreting a meeting. Morgan et al (2003) described the speech recognition of meetings as an "ASR-complete" problem. Developing an accurate system for meeting recognition involves the automatic segmentation of the recording into utterances from a single talker, robustness to reverberation and competing acoustic sources, handling overlapping talkers, exploitation of multiple microphone recordings, as well as the core acoustic and language modelling problems that arise when attempting to recognise spontaneous, conversational speech.

Our initial systems for meeting recognition used audio recorded with close-talking microphones, in order to develop the core acoustic modelling techniques. More recently our focus has been on recognising speech obtained using tabletop microphone

[7] `corpus.amiproject.org/`

arrays, which are less intrusive but have a lower signal-to-noise ratio. Multiple microphone systems are based on microphone array beamforming in which the individual microphone signals are filtered and summed to enhance signals coming from a particular direction, while suppressing signals from competing locations (Wölfel and McDonough, 2009).

The core acoustic and language modelling components for meeting speech recognition correspond quite closely to the state-of-the-art systems used in other domains. Acoustic modelling techniques include vocal tract length normalisation, speaker adaptation based on maximum likelihood linear transforms, and further training using a discriminative minimum Bayes risk criterion such as minimum phone error rate (Gales and Young, 2007; Renals and Hain, 2010). In addition we have employed a number of novel acoustic parameterisations including approaches based on local posterior probability estimation (Grezl et al., 2007) and pitch adaptive features (Garau and Renals, 2008), the automatic construction of domain-specific language models using documents obtained from the web by searching with n-grams obtained from meeting transcripts (Wan and Hain, 2006; Bulyko et al., 2007), and automatic approaches to acoustic segmentation optimised for meetings (Wrigley et al., 2005; Dines et al., 2006).

A feature of the systems developed for meeting recognition is the use of multiple recognition passes, cross-adaptation and model combination (Hain et al., 2007). In particular successive passes make use of more detailed—and more diverse—acoustic and language models. Different acoustic models trained on different feature representations (e.g. standard PLP features and posterior probability-based features) are cross-adapted, and different feature representations are also combined using linear transforms such as heteroscedastic linear discriminant analysis (Kumar and Andreou, 1998).

These systems have been evaluated in successive NIST RT evaluations: the core microphone array based system has a word error rate of about 40%; after adaptation and feature combination steps, this error rate can be reduced to about 30%. The equivalent close-talking microphone system has baseline word error rate of about 35%, reduced to less than 25% after further recognition passes (Hain et al., 2007). The core system runs about five times slower than real-time, and the full system is about fourteen times slower than real-time, on current commodity hardware. We have developed a low-latency real-time system (with an error rate of about 41% for microphone array input) (Garner et al., 2009), based on an open source runtime system[8].

4 Meeting interpretation

One of the interdisciplinary joys of working on meetings is that researchers with different approaches are able to build collaborations through working on common problems and common data. The automatic interpretation of meetings is a very good example: meetings form an exciting challenge for work in things such as topic identification, summarisation, dialogue act recognition and the recognition of subjective content. Although text-based approaches (using the output of a speech recognition system) form strong baselines, it is often the case that systems can be improved through the incorporation of information characteristic of spoken communication, such as prosody and speaker turn patterns, as well video information such as head or hand movements.

Segmentation: We have explored multistream statistical models to automatically segment meeting recordings. Meetings can be usefully segmented at many different levels, for example into speech and non-speech (an essential pre-processing for speech recognition), into utterances spoken by a single talker, into dialogue acts, into topics, and into "meeting phases". The latter was the subject of our first investigations in using multimodal multistream models to segment meetings.

Meetings are group events, characterised by both individual actions and group actions. To obtain structure at the group level, we and colleagues in the M4 and AMI projects investigated segmenting a meeting into a sequence of group actions such as monologue, discussion and presentation (McCowan et al., 2005). We used a number of feature streams for this segmentation and labelling task including speaker turn dynamics, prosody, lexical information,

[8] `juicer.amiproject.org/`

and participant head and hand movements (Dielmann and Renals, 2007). Our initial experiments used an HMM to model the feature streams with a single hidden state space, and resulted in an "action error rate" of over 40% (action error rate is analogous to word error rate, but defined over meeting actions, presumed not to overlap). The HMM was then substituted by a richer DBN multistream model in which each feature stream was processed independently at a lower level of the model. These partial results were then combined at a higher level, thus providing hierarchical integration of the multimodal feature streams. This multistream approach enabled a later integration of feature streams and increased flexibility in modelling the interdependences between the different streams, enabling some accommodation for asynchrony and multiple time scales. Thus use of the richer DBN multistream model resulted in a significant lowering of the action error rate to around 13%.

We extended this approach to look at a much finer grained segmentation: dialogue acts. A dialogue act can be viewed as a segment of speech labelled so as to roughly categorise the speaker's intention. In the AMI corpus each dialogue act in a meeting is given one of 15 labels, which may be categorised as information exchange, making or eliciting suggestions or offers, commenting on the discussion, social acts, backchannels, or "other". The segmentation problem is non-trivial, since a single stretch of speech (with no pauses) from a speaker may comprise several dialogue acts—and conversely a single dialogue act may contain pauses. To address the tasks of automatically segmenting the speech into dialogue acts, and assigning a label to each segment, we employed a switching dynamic Bayesian network architecture, which modelled a set of features related to lexical content and prosody and incorporates a weighted interpolated factored language model (Dielmann and Renals, 2008). The switching DBN coordinated the recognition process by integrating all the available resources. This approach was able to leverage additional corpora of conversational data by using them as training data for a factored language model which was used in conjunction with additional task specific language models. We followed this joint generative model, with a discriminative approach, based on conditional random fields, which performed a reclassification of the segmented dialogue acts.

Our experiments on dialogue act recognition used both automatic and manual transcriptions of the AMI corpus. The degradation when moving from manual transcriptions to the output of a speech recogniser was less than 10% absolute for both dialogue act classification and segmentation. Our experiments indicated that it is possible to perform automatic segmentation into dialogue acts with a relatively low error rate. However the operations of tagging and recognition into fifteen imbalanced DA categories have a relatively high error rate, even after discriminative reclassification, indicating that this remains a challenging task.

Summarisation: The automatic generation of summaries provides a natural way to succinctly describe the content of a meeting, and can be an efficient way for users to obtain information. We have focussed on extractive techniques to construct summaries, in which the most relevant parts of a meeting are located, and concatenated together to provide a 'cut-and-paste' summary, which may be textual or multimodal.

Our approach to extractive summarisation is based on automatically extracting relevant dialogue acts (or alternatively "spurts", segments spoken by a single speaker and delimited by silence) from a meeting (Murray et al., 2006). This requires (as a minimum) the automatic speech transcription and, if spurts are not used, dialogue act segmentation. Lexical information is clearly extremely important for summarisation, but we have also found speaker features (relating to activity, dominance and overlap), structural features (the length and position of dialogue acts), prosody, and discourse cues (phrases which signal likely relevance) to be important for the development of accurate methods for extractive summarisation of meetings. Furthermore we have explored reduced dimension representations of text, based on latent semantic analysis, which we found added precision to the summarisation. Using an evaluation measure referred to as weighted precision, we discovered that it is possible to reliably extract the most relevant dialogue acts, even in the presence of speech recognition errors.

5 Application prototypes

We have incorporated these meeting recognition and interpretation components in a number of applications. Our basic approach to navigating meeting archives centres on the notion of meeting browsers, in which media files, transcripts and segmentations are synchronised to a common time line. Figure 2 (a) gives an example of such a browser, which also enables a user to pan and zoom within the captured spherical video stream.

We have explored (and, as discussed below, evaluated) a number of ways of including automatically generated summaries in meeting browsers. The browser illustrated in figure 2 (b) enables navigation by the summarised transcript or via the topic segmentation. In this case the degree of summarisation is controlled by a slider, which removes those speech segments that do no contribute to the summary. We have also explored real-time (with a few utterances latency) approaches to summarisation, to facilitate meeting "catchup" scenarios, including the generation of audio only summaries, with about 60% of the speech removed (Tucker et al., 2010). Visualisations of summaries include a comic book layout (Castronovo et al., 2008), illustrated in figure 3. This is related to "VideoManga" (Uchihashi et al., 1999), but driven by transcribed speech rather than visually identified keyframes.

The availability of real-time meeting speech recognition, with phrase-level latency (Garner et al., 2009), enables a new class of applications. Within AMIDA we developed a software architecture referred to as "The Hub" to support real-time applications. The Hub is essentially a real-time annotation server, mediating between annotation producers, such as speech recognition, and annotation consumers, such as a real-time catchup browser. Of course many applications will be both producers and consumers: for instance topic segmentation consumes transcripts and speaker turn information and produces time aligned topic segments. A good example of an application made possible by real-time recognition components and the Hub is the AMIDA Content Linking Device (Popescu-Belis et al., 2008). Content linking is essentially a continual real-time search in which a repository is searched using a query constructed from the current conversational context. In this case the context is obtained from a speech recognition transcript of the past 30 seconds of the conversation, and a query is constructed using $tf{\cdot}idf$ or a similar measure, combined with predefined keywords or topic weightings. The repository to be searched may be the web, or a portion of the web, or it may be an organisational document repository, including transcribed, structured and indexed recordings of previous meetings. Figure 4 shows a basic interface to content linking. We have constructed live content-linking systems, driven by microphone array based real-time speech recognition, with the aim of presenting—without explicit query—potentially relevant documents to meeting participants.

(a) Basic web-based browser

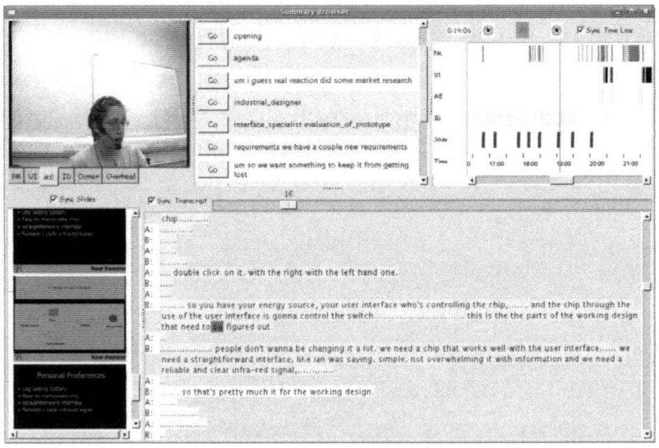

(b) Summary browser

Figure 2: Two examples of meeting browsers, both include time synchronisation with a searchable ASR transcript and speaker activities. (a) is a basic web-based browser; (b) also employs extractive summarisation and topic segmentation components.

Figure 3: Comic book display of automatically generated meeting summary.

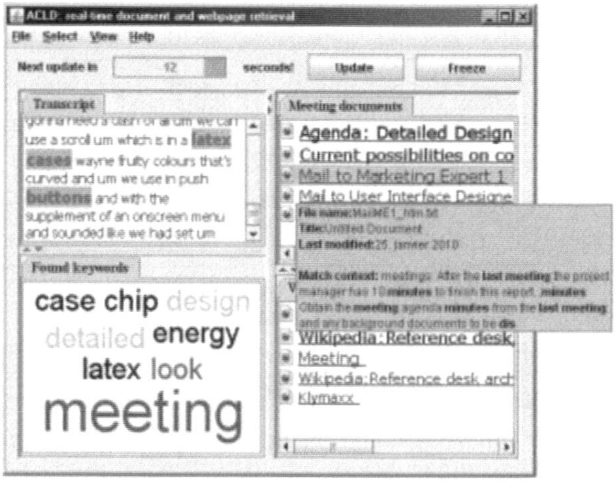

Figure 4: Demonstration screenshot of the AMI automatic content linking device. The subpanels show (clockwise from top left) the ASR transcript, relevant documents from the meeting document base, relevant web hits and a a tag cloud.

6 Evaluation

The multiple streams of data and multiple layers of annotations that make up the AMI corpus enable it to be used for evaluations of specific recognition components. The corpus has been used to evaluate many different things including voice activity detection, speaker diarisation and speech recognition (in the NIST RT evaluations), and head pose recognition (in the CLEAR evaluation). In the spoken language processing domain, the AMI corpus has been used to evaluate meeting summarisation, topic segmentation, dialogue act recognition and cross-language retrieval.

In addition to intrinsic component-level evaluations, it is valuable to evaluate complete systems, and components in a system context. In the AMI/AMIDA projects, we investigated a number of extrinsic evaluation frameworks for browsing and accessing meeting archives. The Browser Evaluation Test (BET) (Wellner et al., 2005) provides a framework for the comparison of arbitrary meeting browser setups, which may differ in terms of which content extraction or abstraction components are employed. In the BET test subjects have to answer true/false questions about a number of "observations of interest" relating to a recorded meeting, using the browser under test with a specified time limit (typically half the meeting length).

We developed of a variant of the BET to specifically evaluate different summarisation approaches. In the Decision Audit evaluation (Murray et al., 2009) the user's task is to ascertain the factors across a number of meetings that lead to a particular decision being made. A set of browsers were constructed differing in the summarisation approach employed (manual vs. ASR transcripts; extractive vs. abstractive vs. human vs. keyword-based summarisation), and the test subjects used them to perform the decision audit. Like the BET this evaluation is labour-intensive, but the results can be analysed using a battery of objective and subjective measures. Conclusions from carrying out this evaluation indicated that the task itself was quite challenging for users (even with human transcripts and summaries, most users could not find many factors involved in the decision), that automatic extractive summaries outperformed reasonably competitive baseline approaches, and that although subjects reported ASR transcripts to be unsatisfactory (due to the error rate) browsing using the ASR transcript still resulted in users' being generally able to find the relevant parts of the meeting archive.

7 Conclusions

In this paper I have given an overview of our investigations into automatic meeting recognition and interpretation. Multiparty communication is a challenging problem at many levels, from signal processing to discourse modelling. A major part of our attempt to address this problem, in an interdisciplinary way, was the collection, annotation, and distribution of the AMI meeting corpus. The AMI corpus has been at the basis of nearly all the work that we have carried out in the area, from speech recognition to summarisation. Multiparty speech recognition remains a difficult task, with a typical error rate of over 20%, however the accuracy is enough to enable various components to build on top of it. A major achievement has been the development of prototype applications that can use phrase-level latency real-time speech recognition.

Many of the automatic approaches to meeting recognition and characterisation are characterised by extensive combination at the feature stream, model and system level. In our experience, such approaches offer consistent improvements in accuracy for these complex, multimodal tasks.

Meetings serve a social function, and much of this has been ignored in our work, so far. We have focussed principally on understanding meetings in terms of their lexical content, augmented by various multimodal streams. However in many interactions, the social signals are at least as important as the propositional content of the words (Pentland, 2008); it is a major challenge to develop meeting interpretation components that can infer and take advantage of such social cues. We have made initial attempts to do this, by attempting to include aspects such as social role (Huang and Renals, 2008).

The AMI corpus involved a substantial effort from many individuals, and provides an invaluable resource. However, we do not wish to do this again, even if we are dealing with a domain that is significantly different, such as larger groups, or family "meetings". However, our recognisers rely strongly on annotated in-domain data. It is a major challenge to develop algorithms that are unsupervised and adaptive to free us from the need to collect and annotate large amount of data each time we are interested in a new domain.

Acknowledgments

This paper has arisen from a collaboration involving several laboratories. I have benefitted, in particular, from long-term collaborations with Hervé Bourlard, Jean Carletta, Thomas Hain, and Mike Lincoln, and from a number of fantastic PhD students. This work was supported by the European IST/ICT Programme Projects IST-2001-34485 (M4), FP6-506811 (AMI), FP6-033812 (AMIDA), and FP7-231287 (SSPNet). This paper only reflects the author's views and funding agencies are not liable for any use that may be made of the information contained herein.

References

M. Al-Hames, C. Lenz, S. Reiter, J. Schenk, F. Wallhoff, and G. Rigoll. 2007. Robust multi-modal group action recognition in meetings from disturbed videos with the asynchronous hidden Markov model. In *Proc IEEE ICIP*.

S. O. Ba and J. M. Odobez. 2008. Multi-party focus of attention recognition in meetings from head pose and multimodal contextual cues. In *Proc. IEEE ICASSP*.

R. F. Bales. 1951. *Interaction Process Analysis*. Addison Wesley, Cambridge MA, USA.

I. Bulyko, M. Ostendorf, M. Siu, T. Ng, A. Stolcke, and O. Cetin. 2007. Web resources for language modeling in conversational speech recognition. *ACM Transactions on Speech and Language Processing*, 5(1):1–25.

J. Carletta. 2007. Unleashing the killer corpus: experiences in creating the multi-everything AMI Meeting Corpus. *Language Resources and Evaluation*, 41:181–190.

S. Castronovo, J. Frey, and P. Poller. 2008. A generic layout-tool for summaries of meetings in a constraint-based approach. In *Machine Learning for Multimodal Interaction (Proc. MLMI '08)*. Springer.

R. Cutler, Y. Rui, A. Gupta, J. Cadiz, I. Tashev, L. He, A. Colburn, Z. Zhang, Z. Liu, and S. Silverberg. 2002. Distributed meetings: a meeting capture and broadcasting system. In *Proc. ACM Multimedia*, pages 503–512.

A. Dielmann and S. Renals. 2007. Automatic meeting segmentation using dynamic Bayesian networks. *IEEE Transactions on Multimedia*, 9(1):25–36.

A. Dielmann and S. Renals. 2008. Recognition of dialogue acts in multiparty meetings using a switching DBN. *IEEE Transactions on Audio, Speech and Language Processing*, 16(7):1303–1314.

J. Dines, J. Vepa, and T. Hain. 2006. The segmentation of multi-channel meeting recordings for automatic speech recognition. In *Proc. Interspeech*.

M. J. F. Gales and S. J. Young. 2007. The application of hidden Markov models in speech recognition. *Foundations and Trends in Signal Processing*, 1(3):195–304.

G. Garau and S. Renals. 2008. Combining spectral representations for large vocabulary continuous speech recognition. *IEEE Transactions on Audio, Speech and Language Processing*, 16(3):508–518.

P. Garner, J. Dines, T. Hain, A. El Hannani, M. Karafiat, D. Korchagin, M. Lincoln, V. Wan, and L. Zhang. 2009. Real-time ASR from meetings. In *Proc. Interspeech*.

F. Grezl, M. Karafiat, S. Kontar, and J. Cernocky. 2007. Probabilistic and bottle-neck features for lvcsr of meetings. In *Acoustics, Speech and Signal Processing, 2007. ICASSP 2007. IEEE International Conference on*, volume 4, pages IV–757–IV–760.

T. Hain, L. Burget, J. Dines, G. Garau, M. Karafiat, M. Lincoln, J. Vepa, and V. Wan. 2007. The ami system for the transcription of speech in meetings. In *Proc. IEEE ICASSP–07*.

S. Huang and S. Renals. 2008. Unsupervised language model adaptation based on topic and role information in multiparty meetings. In *Proc. Interspeech '08*.

R. Kazman, R. Al-Halimi, W. Hunt, and M. Mantei. 1996. Four paradigms for indexing video conferences. *Multimedia, IEEE*, 3(1):63–73.

N. Kumar and A. G. Andreou. 1998. Heteroscedastic discriminant analysis and reduced rank HMMs for improved recognition. *Speech Communication*, 26:283–297.

I. McCowan, D. Gatica-Perez, S. Bengio, G. Lathoud, M. Barnard, and D. Zhang. 2005. Automatic analysis of multimodal group actions in meetings. *IEEE Transactions on Pattern Analysis and Machine Intelligence*, 27(3):305–317.

J. E. McGrath. 1991. Time, interaction, and performance (TIP): A theory of groups. *Small Group Research*, 22(2):147.

N. Morgan, D. Baron, S. Bhagat, H. Carvey, R. Dhillon, J. Edwards, D. Gelbart, A. Janin, A. Krupski, B. Peskin, T. Pfau, E. Shriberg, A. Stolcke, and C. Wooters. 2003. Meetings about meetings: research at ICSI on speech in multiparty conversations. In *Proc. IEEE ICASSP*.

G. Murray, S. Renals, J. Moore, and J. Carletta. 2006. Incorporating speaker and discourse features into speech summarization. In *Proceedings of the Human Language Technology Conference of the NAACL*, pages 367–374.

G. Murray, T. Kleinbauer, P. Poller, T. Becker, S. Renals, and J. Kilgour. 2009. Extrinsic summarization evaluation: A decision audit task. *ACM Transactions on Speech and Language Processing*, 6(2):1–29.

A.S. Pentland. 2008. *Honest signals: how they shape our world*. The MIT Press.

A. Popescu-Belis, E. Boertjes, J. Kilgour, P. Poller, S. Castronovo, T. Wilson, A. Jaimes, and J. Carletta. 2008. The amida automatic content linking device: Just-in-time document retrieval in meetings. In *Machine Learning for Multimodal Interaction (Proc. MLMI '08)*.

S. Renals and T. Hain. 2010. Speech recognition. In A. Clark, C. Fox, and S. Lappin, editors, *Handbook of Computational Linguistics and Natural Language Processing*. Wiley Blackwell.

D. M. Roy and S. Luz. 1999. Audio meeting history tool: Interactive graphical user-support for virtual audio meetings. In *Proc. ESCA Workshop on Accessing Information in Spoken Audio*, pages 107–110.

G. Stasser and LA Taylor. 1991. Speaking turns in face-to-face discussions. *Journal of Personality and Social Psychology*, 60(5):675–684.

S. Tucker, O. Bergman, A. Ramamoorthy, and S. Whittaker. 2010. Catchup: a useful application of time-travel in meetings. In *Proc. ACM CSCW*, pages 99–102.

S. Uchihashi, J. Foote, A. Girgensohn, and J. Boreczky. 1999. Video manga: generating semantically meaningful video summaries. In *Proc. ACM Multimedia*, pages 383–392.

A. Waibel, M. Bett, F. Metze, K. Ries, T. Schaaf, T. Schultz, H. Soltau, H. Yu, and K. Zechner. 2001. Advances in automatic meeting record creation and access. In *Proc IEEE ICASSP*.

V. Wan and T. Hain. 2006. Strategies for language model web-data collection. In *Proc IEEE ICASSP*.

P. Wellner, M. Flynn, S. Tucker, and S. Whittaker. 2005. A meeting browser evaluation test. In *Proc. ACM CHI*, pages 2021–2024.

M. Wölfel and J. McDonough. 2009. *Distant Speech Recognition*. Wiley.

C. Wooters and M. Huijbregts. 2007. The ICSI RT07s speaker diarization system. In *Multimodal Technologies for Perception of Humans. International Evaluation Workshops CLEAR 2007 and RT 2007*, volume 4625 of *LNCS*, pages 509–519. Springer.

S. Wrigley, G. Brown, V. Wan, and S. Renals. 2005. Speech and crosstalk detection in multichannel audio. *IEEE Transactions on Speech and Audio Processing*, 13(1):84–91.

R. Yong, A. Gupta, and J. Cadiz. 2001. Viewing meetings captured by an omni-directional camera. *ACM Transactions on Computing Human Interaction*.

E. Zwyssig, M. Lincoln, and S. Renals. 2010. A digital microphone array for distant speech recognition. In *Proc. IEEE ICASSP–10*.

Chart Mining-based Lexical Acquisition with Precision Grammars

Yi Zhang,[♠] **Timothy Baldwin,**[♡◇] **Valia Kordoni,**[♠] **David Martinez**[◇] and **Jeremy Nicholson**[♡◇]
♠ DFKI GmbH and Dept of Computational Linguistics, Saarland University, Germany
♡ Dept of Computer Science and Software Engineering, University of Melbourne, Australia
◇ NICTA Victoria Research Laboratory
yzhang@coli.uni-sb.de, tb@ldwin.net, kordoni@dfki.de,
{davidm, jeremymn}@csse.unimelb.edu.au

Abstract

In this paper, we present an innovative chart mining technique for improving parse coverage based on partial parse outputs from precision grammars. The general approach of mining features from partial analyses is applicable to a range of lexical acquisition tasks, and is particularly suited to domain-specific lexical tuning and lexical acquisition using low-coverage grammars. As an illustration of the functionality of our proposed technique, we develop a lexical acquisition model for English verb particle constructions which operates over unlexicalised features mined from a partial parsing chart. The proposed technique is shown to outperform a state-of-the-art parser over the target task, despite being based on relatively simplistic features.

1 Introduction

Parsing with precision grammars is increasingly achieving broad coverage over open-domain texts for a range of constraint-based frameworks (e.g., TAG, LFG, HPSG and CCG), and is being used in real-world applications including information extraction, question answering, grammar checking and machine translation (Uszkoreit, 2002; Oepen et al., 2004; Frank et al., 2006; Zhang and Kordoni, 2008; MacKinlay et al., 2009). In this context, a "precision grammar" is a grammar which has been engineered to model grammaticality, and contrasts with a treebank-induced grammar, for example.

Inevitably, however, such applications demand complete parsing outputs, based on the assumption that the text under investigation will be completely analysable by the grammar. As precision grammars generally make strong assumptions about complete lexical coverage and grammaticality of the input, their utility is limited over noisy or domain-specific data. This lack of complete coverage can make parsing with precision grammars less attractive than parsing with shallower methods.

One technique that has been successfully applied to improve parser and grammar coverage over a given corpus is error mining (van Noord, 2004; de Kok et al., 2009), whereby n-grams with low "parsability" are gathered from the large-scale output of a parser as an indication of parser or (precision) grammar errors. However, error mining is very much oriented towards grammar engineering: its results are a mixture of different (mistreated) linguistic phenomena together with engineering errors for the grammar engineer to work through and act upon. Additionally, it generally does not provide any insight into the cause of the parser failure, and it is difficult to identify specific language phenomena from the output.

In this paper, we instead propose a **chart mining** technique that works on intermediate parsing results from a parsing chart. In essence, the method analyses the validity of different analyses for words or constructions based on the "lifetime" and probability of each within the chart, combining the constraints of the grammar with probabilities to evaluate the plausibility of each.

For purposes of exemplification of the proposed technique, we apply chart mining to a deep lexical acquisition (DLA) task, using a maximum entropy-based prediction model trained over a seed lexicon and treebank. The experimental set up is the following: given a set of sentences containing putative instances of English verb particle constructions,

Human Language Technologies: The 2010 Annual Conference of the North American Chapter of the ACL, pages 10–18,
Los Angeles, California, June 2010.

extract a list of non-compositional VPCs optionally with valence information. For comparison, we parse the same sentence set using a state-of-the-art statistical parser, and extract the VPCs from the parser output. Our results show that our chart mining method produces a model which is superior to the treebank parser.

To our knowledge, the only other work that has looked at partial parsing results of precision grammars as a means of linguistic error analysis is that of Kiefer et al. (1999) and Zhang et al. (2007a), where partial parsing models were proposed to select a set of passive edges that together cover the input sequence. Compared to these approaches, our proposed chart mining technique is more general and can be adapted to specific tasks and domains. While we experiment exclusively with an HPSG grammar in this paper, it is important to note that the proposed method can be applied to any grammar formalism which is compatible with chart parsing, and where it is possible to describe an unlexicalised lexical entry for the different categories of lexical item that are to be extracted (see Section 3.2 for details).

The remainder of the paper is organised as follows. Section 2 defines the task of VPC extraction. Section 3 presents the chart mining technique and the feature extraction process for the VPC extraction task. Section 4 evaluates the model performance with comparison to two competitor models over several different measures. Section 5 further discusses the general applicability of chart mining. Finally, Section 6 concludes the paper.

2 Verb Particle Constructions

The particular construction type we target for DLA in this paper is English Verb Particle Constructions (henceforth VPCs). VPCs consist of a head verb and one or more obligatory **particles**, in the form of intransitive prepositions (e.g., *hand in*), adjectives (e.g., *cut short*) or verbs (e.g., *let go*) (Villavicencio and Copestake, 2002; Huddleston and Pullum, 2002; Baldwin and Kim, 2009); for the purposes of our dataset, we assume that all particles are prepositional—by far the most common and productive of the three types—and further restrict our attention to single-particle VPCs (i.e., we ignore VPCs such as *get along together*).

One aspect of VPCs that makes them a particularly challenging target for lexical acquisition is that the verb and particle can be non-contiguous (for instance, *hand the paper in* and *battle right on*). This sets them apart from conventional collocations and terminology (cf., Manning and Schütze (1999), Smadja (1993) and McKeown and Radev (2000)) in that they cannot be captured effectively using n-grams, due to their variability in the number and type of words potentially interceding between the verb and the particle. Also, while conventional collocations generally take the form of compound nouns or adjective–noun combinations with relatively simple syntactic structure, VPCs occur with a range of valences. Furthermore, VPCs are highly productive in English and vary in use across domains, making them a prime target for lexical acquisition (Dehé, 2002; Baldwin, 2005; Baldwin and Kim, 2009).

In the VPC dataset we use, there is an additional distinction between compositional and non-compositional VPCs. With compositional VPCs, the semantics of the verb and particle both correspond to the semantics of the respective simplex words, including the possibility of the semantics being specific to the VPC construction in the case of particles. For example, *battle on* would be classified as compositional, as the semantics of *battle* is identical to that for the simplex verb, and the semantics of *on* corresponds to the continuative sense of the word as occurs productively in VPCs (cf., *walk/dance/drive/govern/... on*). With non-compositional VPCs, on the other hand, the semantics of the VPC is somehow removed from that of the parts. In the dataset we used for evaluation, we are interested in extracting exclusively non-compositional VPCs, as they require lexicalisation; compositional VPCs can be captured via lexical rules and are hence not the target of extraction.

English VPCs can occur with a number of valences, with the two most prevalent and productive valences being the simple transitive (e.g., *hand in the paper*) and intransitive (e.g., *back off*). For the purposes of our target task, we focus exclusively on these two valence types.

Given the above, we define the English VPC extraction task to be the production of triples of the form $\langle v, p, s \rangle$, where v is a verb lemma, p is a prepositional particle, and $s \in \{intrans, trans\}$ is the valence; additionally, each triple has to be semantically non-compositional. The triples are extracted relative to a set of putative token instances for each of the intransitive and transitive valences for a given VPC. That is, a given triple should be classified as positive if and only if it is associated with at least one non-compositional token instance in the provided token-level data.

The dataset used in this research is the one used in the LREC 2008 Multiword Expression Workshop Shared Task (Baldwin, 2008).[1] In the dataset, there is a single file for each of 4,090 candidate VPC triples, containing up to 50 sentences that have the given VPC taken from the British National Corpus. When the valence of the VPC is ignored, the dataset contains 440 unique VPCs among 2,898 VPC candidates. In order to be able to fairly compare our method with a state-of-the-art lexicalised parser trained over the WSJ training sections of the Penn Treebank, we remove any VPC types from the test set which are attested in the WSJ training sections. This removes 696 VPC types from the test set, and makes the task even more difficult, as the remaining testing VPC types are generally less frequent ones. At the same time, it unfortunately means that our results are not directly comparable to those for the original shared task.[2]

3 Chart Mining for Parsing with a Large Precision Grammar

3.1 The Technique

The chart mining technique we use in this paper is couched in a constituent-based bottom-up chart parsing paradigm. A parsing chart is a data structure that records all the (complete or incomplete) intermediate parsing results. Every passive edge on the parsing chart represents a complete local analysis covering a sub-string of the input, while each active edge predicts a potential local analysis. In this view, a full analysis is merely a passive edge that spans the whole input and satisfies certain *root conditions*. The bottom-up chart parser starts with edges instantiated from lexical entries corresponding to the input words. The grammar rules are used to incrementally create longer edges from smaller ones until no more edges can be added to the chart.

Standardly, the parser returns only outputs that correspond to passive edges in the parsing chart that span the full input string. For those inputs without a full-spanning edge, no output is generated, and the chart becomes the only source of parsing information.

A parsing chart takes the form of a hierarchy of edges. Where only passive edges are concerned, each non-lexical edge corresponds to exactly one grammar rule, and is connected with one or more daughter edge(s), and zero or more parent edge(s). Therefore, traversing the chart is relatively straightforward.

There are two potential challenges for the chart-mining technique. First, there is potentially a huge number of parsing edges in the chart. For instance, when parsing with a large precision grammar like the `HPSG` English Resource Grammar (`ERG`, Flickinger (2002)), it is not unusual for a 20-word sentence to receive over 10,000 passive edges. In order to achieve high efficiency in parsing (as well as generation), ambiguity packing is usually used to reduce the number of productive passive edges on the parsing chart (Tomita, 1985). For constraint-based grammar frameworks like `LFG` and `HPSG`, subsumption-based packing is used to achieve a higher packing ratio (Oepen and Carroll, 2000), but this might also potentially lead to an inconsistent packed parse forest that does not unpack successfully. For chart mining, this means that not all passive edges are directly accessible from the chart. Some of them are packed into others, and the derivatives of the packed edges are not generated. Because of the ambiguity packing, zero or more local analyses may exist for each passive edge on the chart, and the cross-combination of the packed daughter edges is not guaranteed to be compatible. As a result, expensive unification operations must be reapplied during the unpacking phase. Carroll and Oepen (2005) and Zhang et al. (2007b) have proposed efficient k-best unpacking algorithms that can selectively extract the most probable readings from the packed parse forest according to a discrimina-

[1] Downloadable from `http://www.csse.unimelb.edu.au/research/lt/resources/vpc/vpc.tgz`.

[2] In practice, there was only one team who participated in the original VPC task (Ramisch et al., 2008), who used a variety of web- and dictionary-based features suited more to high-frequency instances in high-density languages, so a simplistic comparison would not have been meaningful.

tive parse disambiguation model, by minimising the number of potential unifications. The algorithm can be applied to unpack any passive edges. Because of the dynamic programming used in the algorithm and the hierarchical structure of the edges, the cost of the unpacking routine is empirically linear in the number of desired readings, and $O(1)$ when invoked more than once on the same edge.

The other challenge concerns the selection of informative and representative pieces of knowledge from the massive sea of partial analyses in the parsing chart. How to effectively extract the indicative features for a specific language phenomenon is a very task-specific question, as we will show in the context of the VPC extraction task in Section 3.2. However, general strategies can be applied to generate parse ranking scores on each passive edge. The most widely used parse ranking model is the log-linear model (Abney, 1997; Johnson et al., 1999; Toutanova et al., 2002). When the model does not use non-local features, the accumulated score on a sub-tree under a certain (unpacked) passive edge can be used to approximate the probability of the partial analysis conditioned on the sub-string within that span.[3]

3.2 The Application: Acquiring Features for VPC Extraction

As stated above, the target task we use to illustrate the capabilities of our chart mining method is VPC extraction.

The grammar we apply our chart mining method to in this paper is the English Resource Grammar (ERG, Flickinger (2002)), a large-scale precision HPSG for English. Note, however, that the method is equally compatible with any grammar or grammar formalism which is compatible with chart parsing.

The lexicon of the ERG has been semi-automatically extended with VPCs extracted by Baldwin (2005). In order to show the effectiveness of chart mining in discovering "unknowns" and remove any lexical probabilities associated with pre-existing lexical entries, we block the lexical entries for the verb in the candidate VPC by substituting the input token with a DUMMY-V token, which is coupled with four candidate lexical entries of type: (1) intransitive simplex verb (*v_-_e*), (2) transitive simplex verb (*v_np_le*), (3) intransitive VPC (*v_p_le*), and (4) transitive VPC (*v_p-np_le*), respectively. These four lexical entries represent the two VPC valences we wish to distinguish between in the VPC extraction task, and the competing simplex verb candidates. Based on these lexical types, the features we extract with chart mining are summarised in Table 1. The maximal constituent (MAXCONS) of a lexical entry is defined to be the passive edge that is an ancestor of the lexical entry edge that: (i) must span over the particle, and (ii) has maximal span length. In the case of a tie, the edge with the highest disambiguation score is selected as the MAXCONS. If there is no edge found on the chart that spans over both the verb and the particle, the MAXCONS is set to be NULL, with a MAXSPAN of 0, MAXLEVEL of 0 and MAXCRANK of 4 (see Table 1). The stem of the particle is also collected as a feature.

One important characteristic of these features is that they are completely unlexicalised on the verb. This not only leads to a fair evaluation with the ERG by excluding the influence from the lexical coverage of VPCs in the grammar, but it also demonstrates that complete grammatical coverage over simplex verbs is not a prerequisite for chart mining.

To illustrate how our method works, we present the unpacked parsing chart for the candidate VPC *show off* and input sentence *The boy shows off his new toys* in Figure 1. The non-terminal edges are marked with their syntactic categories, i.e., HPSG rules (e.g., *subjh* for the subject-head-rule, *hadj* for the head-adjunct-rule, etc.), and optionally their disambiguation scores. By traversing upward through parent edges from the DUMMY-V edge, all features can be efficiently extracted (see the third column in Table 1).

It should be noted that none of these features are used to deterministically dictate the predicted VPC category. Instead, the acquired features are used as inputs to a statistical classifier for predicting the type of the VPC candidate at the token level (in the context of the given sentence). In our experiment, we used a maximum entropy-based model to do a 3-

[3]To have a consistent ranking model on any sub-analysis, one would have to retrain the disambiguation model on every passive edge. In practice, we find this to be intractable. Also, the approximation based on full-parse ranking model works reasonably well.

Feature	Description	Examples
LE:MAXCONS	A lexical entry together with the maximal constituent constructed from it	*v_-_le:subjh, v_np_le:hadj, v_p_le:subjh, v_p-np_le:subj*
LE:MAXSPAN	A lexical entry together with the length of the span of the maximal constituent constructed from the LE	*v_-_le:7, v_np_le:5, v_p_le:4, v_p-np_le:7*
LE:MAXLEVEL	A lexical entry together with the levels of projections before it reaches its maximal constituent	*v_-_le:2, v_np_le:1, v_p_le:2, v_p-np_le:3*
LE:MAXCRANK	A lexical entry together with the relative disambiguation score ranking of its maximal constituent among all MaxCons from different LEs	*v_-_le:4, v_np_le:3, v_p_le:1, v_p-np_le:2*
PARTICLE	The stem of the particle in the candidate VPC	*off*

Table 1: Chart mining features used for VPC extraction

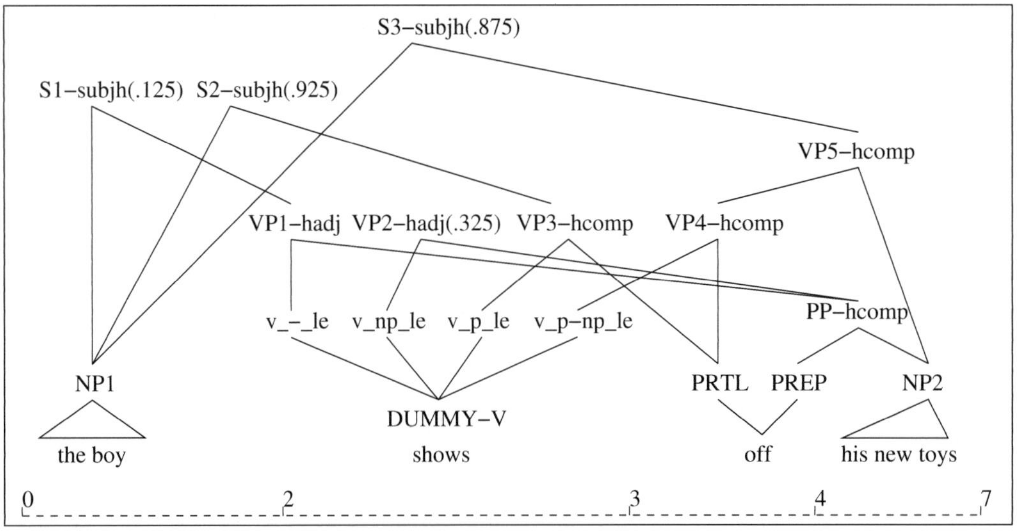

Figure 1: Example of a parsing chart in chart-mining for VPC extraction with the ERG

category classification: non-VPC, transitive VPC, or intransitive VPC. For the parameter estimation of the ME model, we use the TADM open source toolkit (Malouf, 2002). The token-level predictions are then combined with a simple majority voting to derive the type-level prediction for the VPC candidate. In the case of a tie, the method backs off to the naïve baseline model described in Section 4.2, which relies on the combined probability of the verb and particle forming a VPC.

We have also experimented with other ways of deriving type-level predictions from token-level classification results. For instance, we trained a separate classifier that takes the token-level prediction as input in order to determine the type-level VPC prediction. Our results indicate no significant difference between these methods and the basic majority voting approach, so we present results exclusively for this simplistic approach in this paper.

4 Evaluation

4.1 Experiment Setup

To evaluate the proposed chart mining-based VPC extraction model, we use the dataset from the LREC 2008 Multiword Expression Workshop shared task (see Section 2). We use this dataset to perform three distinct DLA tasks, as detailed in Table 2.

The chart mining feature extraction is implemented as an extension to the PET parser (Callmeier,

Task	Description
GOLD VPC	Determine the valence for a verb–preposition combination which is known to occur as a non-compositional VPC (i.e. known VPC, with unknown valence(s))
FULL	Determine whether each verb–preposition combination is a VPC or not, and further predict its valence(s) (i.e. unknown if VPC, and unknown valence(s))
VPC	Determine whether each verb–preposition combination is a VPC or not *ignoring valence* (i.e. unknown if VPC, and don't care about valence)

Table 2: Definitions of the three DLA tasks

2001). We use a slightly modified version of the ERG in our experiments, based on the *nov-06* release. The modifications include 4 newly-added dummy lexical entries for the verb DUMMY-V and the corresponding inflectional rules, and a lexical type prediction model (Zhang and Kordoni, 2006) trained on the LOGON Treebank (Oepen et al., 2004) for unknown word handling. The parse disambiguation model we use is also trained on the LOGON Treebank. Since the parser has no access to any of the verbs under investigation (due to the DUMMY-V substitution), those VPC types attested in the LOGON Treebank do not directly impact on the model's performance. The chart mining feature extraction process took over 10 CPU days, and collected a total of 44K events for 4,090 candidate VPC triples.[4] 5-fold cross validation is used to train/test the model. As stated above (Section 2), the VPC triples attested in the WSJ training sections of the Penn Treebank are excluded in each testing fold for comparison with the Charniak parser-based model (see Section 4.2).

4.2 Baseline and Benchmark

For comparison, we first built a naïve baseline model using the combined probabilities of the verb and particle being part of a VPC. More specifically, $P(c|v)$ and $P(c|p)$ are the probabilities of a given verb v and particle p being part of a VPC candidate of type $s \in \{intrans, trans, null\}$, for transitive VPC, intransitive VPC, and non-VPC, respectively. $\tilde{P}(s|v,p) = P(s|v) \cdot P(s|p)$ is used to approximate the joint probability of verb-particle (v,p) being of type s, and the prediction type is chosen randomly based on this probabilistic distribution. Both $P(s|v)$ and $P(s|p)$ can be estimated from a list of VPC candidate types. If v is unseen, $P(s|v)$ is set to be $\frac{1}{|V|}\sum_{v_i \in V} P(s|v_i)$ estimated over all verbs $|V|$ seen in the list of VPC candidates. The naïve baseline performed poorly, mainly because there is not enough knowledge about the context of use of VPCs. This also indicates that the task of VPC extraction is non-trivial, and that context (evidence from sentences in which the VPC putatively occurs) must be incorporated in order to make more accurate predictions.

As a benchmark VPC extraction system, we use the Charniak parser (Charniak, 2000). This statistical parser induces a context-free grammar and a generative parsing model from a training set of gold standard parse trees. Traditionally, it has been trained over the WSJ component of the Penn Treebank, and for this work we decided to take the same approach and train over sections 1 to 22, and use section 23 for parameter-tuning. After parsing, we simply search for the VPC triples in each token instance with tgrep2,[5] and decide on the classification of the candidate by majority voting over all instances, breaking ties randomly.

[4]Not all sentences in the dataset are successfully chart-mined. Due to the complexity of the precision grammar we use, the parser is unlikely to complete the parsing chart for extremely long sentences (over 50 words). Moreover, sentences which do not receive any spanning edge over the verb and the particle are not considered as an indicative event. Nevertheless, the coverage of the chart mining is much higher than the full-parse coverage of the grammar.

[5]Noting that the Penn POS tagset captures essentially the compositional vs. non-compositional VPC distinction required in the extraction task, through the use of the RP (prepositional particle, for non-compositional VPCs) and RB (adverb, for compositional VPCs) tags.

4.3 Results

The results of our experiments are summarised in Table 3. For the naïve baseline and the chart mining-based models, the results are averaged over 5-fold cross validation.

We evaluate the methods in the form of the three tasks described in Table 2. Formally, GOLD VPC equates to extracting $\langle v, p, s \rangle$ tuples from the subset of gold-standard $\langle v, p \rangle$ tuples; FULL equates to extracting $\langle v, p, s \rangle$ tuples for all VPC candidates; and VPC equates to extracting $\langle v, p \rangle$ tuples (ignoring valence) over all VPC candidates. In each case, we present the precision (P), recall (R) and F-score ($\beta = 1$: F). For multi-category classifications (i.e. the two tasks where we predict the valence s, indicated as "All" in Table 3), we micro-average the precision and recall over the two VPC categories, and calculate the F-score as their harmonic mean.

From the results, it is obvious that the chart mining-based model performs best overall, and indeed for most of the measures presented. The Charniak parser-based extraction method performs reasonably well, especially in the VPC+valence extraction task over the FULL task, where the recall was higher than the chart mining method. Although not reported here, we observe a marked improvement in the results for the Charniak parser when the VPC types attested in the WSJ are not filtered from the test set. This indicates that the statistical parser relies heavily on lexicalised VPC information, while the chart mining model is much more syntax-oriented. In error analysis of the data, we observed that the Charniak parser was noticeably more accurate at extracting VPCs where the verb was frequent (our method, of course, did not have access to the base frequency of the simplex verb), underlining again the power of lexicalisation. This points to two possibilities: (1) the potential for our method to similarly benefit from lexicalisation if we were to remove the constraint on ignoring any pre-existing lexical entries for the verb; and (2) the possibility for hybridising between lexicalised models for frequent verbs and unlexicalised models for infrequent verbs. Having said this, it is important to reinforce that lexical acquisition is usually performed in the absence of lexicalised probabilities, as if we have prior knowledge of the lexical item, there is no need to extract it. In this sense, the first set of results in Table 3 over Gold VPCs are the most informative, and illustrate the potential of the proposed approach.

From the results of all the models, it would appear that intransitive VPCs are more difficult to extract than transitive VPCs. This is partly because the dataset we use is unbalanced: the number of transitive VPC types is about twice the number of intransitive VPCs. Also, the much lower numbers over the FULL set compared to the GOLD VPC set are due to the fact that only 1/8 of the candidates are true VPCs.

5 Discussion and Future Work

The inventory of features we propose for VPC extraction is just one illustration of how partial parse results can be used in lexical acquisition tasks. The general chart mining technique can easily be adapted to learn other challenging linguistic phenomena, such as the countability of nouns (Baldwin and Bond, 2003), subcategorization properties of verbs or nouns (Korhonen, 2002), and general multiword expression (MWE) extraction (Baldwin and Kim, 2009). With MWE extraction, e.g., even though some MWEs are fixed and have no internal syntactic variability, such as *ad hoc*, there is a very large proportion of idioms that allow various degrees of internal variability, and with a variable number of elements. For example, the idiom *spill the beans* allows internal modification (*spill mountains of beans*), passivisation (*The beans were spilled in the latest edition of the report*), topicalisation (*The beans, the opposition spilled*), and so forth (Sag et al., 2002). In general, however, the exact degree of variability of an idiom is difficult to predict (Riehemann, 2001). The chart mining technique we propose here, which makes use of partial parse results, may facilitate the automatic recognition task of even more flexible idioms, based on the encouraging results for VPCs.

The main advantage, though, of chart mining is that parsing with precision grammars does not any longer have to assume complete coverage, as has traditionally been the case. As an immediate consequence, the possibility of applying our chart mining technique to evolving medium-sized grammars makes it especially interesting for lexical acquisi-

Task	VPC Type	Naïve Baseline			Charniak Parser			Chart-Mining		
		P	R	F	P	R	F	P	R	F
GOLD VPC	Intrans-VPC	0.300	0.018	0.034	0.549	0.753	0.635	0.845	0.621	0.716
	Trans-VPC	0.676	0.348	0.459	0.829	0.648	0.728	0.877	0.956	0.915
	All	0.576	0.236	0.335	0.691	0.686	0.688	0.875	0.859	**0.867**
FULL	Intrans-VPC	0.060	0.018	0.028	0.102	0.593	0.174	0.153	0.155	0.154
	Trans-VPC	0.083	0.348	0.134	0.179	0.448	0.256	0.179	0.362	0.240
	All	0.080	0.236	0.119	0.136	0.500	0.213	0.171	0.298	**0.218**
	VPC	0.123	0.348	0.182	0.173	0.782	0.284	0.259	0.332	**0.291**

Table 3: Results for the different methods over the three VPC extraction tasks detailed in Table 2

tion over low-density languages, for instance, where there is a real need for rapid-prototyping of language resources.

The chart mining approach we propose in this paper is couched in the bottom-up chart parsing paradigm, based exclusively on passive edges. As future work, we would also like to look into the top-level active edges (those active edges that are never completed), as an indication of failed assumptions. Moreover, it would be interesting to investigate the applicability of the technique in other parsing strategies, e.g., head-corner or left-corner parsing. Finally, it would also be interesting to investigate whether by using the features we acquire from chart mining enhanced with information on the prevalence of certain patterns, we could achieve performance improvements over broader-coverage treebank parsers such as the Charniak parser.

6 Conclusion

We have proposed a chart mining technique for lexical acquisition based on partial parsing with precision grammars. We applied the proposed method to the task of extracting English verb particle constructions from a prescribed set of corpus instances. Our results showed that simple unlexicalised features mined from the chart can be used to effectively extract VPCs, and that the model outperforms a probabilistic baseline and the Charniak parser at VPC extraction.

Acknowledgements

NICTA is funded by the Australian Government as represented by the Department of Broadband, Communications and the Digital Economy and the Australian Research Council through the ICT Centre of Excellence program. The first was supported by the German Excellence Cluster of Multimodal Computing and Interaction.

References

Steven Abney. 1997. Stochastic attribute-value grammars. *Computational Linguistics*, 23:597–618.

Timothy Baldwin and Francis Bond. 2003. Learning the countability of English nouns from corpus data. In *Proceedings of the 41st Annual Meeting of the Association for Computational Linguistics (ACL 2003)*, pages 463–470, Sapporo, Japan.

Timothy Baldwin and Su Nam Kim. 2009. Multiword expressions. In Nitin Indurkhya and Fred J. Damerau, editors, *Handbook of Natural Language Processing*. CRC Press, Boca Raton, USA, 2nd edition.

Timothy Baldwin. 2005. The deep lexical acquisition of English verb-particle constructions. *Computer Speech and Language, Special Issue on Multiword Expressions*, 19(4):398–414.

Timothy Baldwin. 2008. A resource for evaluating the deep lexical acquisition of English verb-particle constructions. In *Proceedings of the LREC 2008 Workshop: Towards a Shared Task for Multiword Expressions (MWE 2008)*, pages 1–2, Marrakech, Morocco.

Ulrich Callmeier. 2001. Efficient parsing with large-scale unification grammars. Master's thesis, Universität des Saarlandes, Saarbrücken, Germany.

John Carroll and Stephan Oepen. 2005. High efficiency realization for a wide-coverage unification grammar. In *Proceedings of the 2nd International Joint Conference on Natural Language Processing (IJCNLP 2005)*, pages 165–176, Jeju Island, Korea.

Eugene Charniak. 2000. A maximum entropy-based parser. In *Proceedings of the 1st Annual Meeting of the North American Chapter of Association for Computational Linguistics (NAACL2000)*, Seattle, USA.

Daniel de Kok, Jianqiang Ma, and Gertjan van Noord. 2009. A generalized method for iterative error mining in parsing results. In *Proceedings of the ACL2009 Workshop on Grammar Engineering Across Frameworks (GEAF)*, Singapore.

Nicole Dehé. 2002. *Particle Verbs in English: Syntax, Information, Structure and Intonation*. John Benjamins, Amsterdam, Netherlands/Philadelphia, USA.

Dan Flickinger. 2002. On building a more efficient grammar by exploiting types. In Stephan Oepen, Dan Flickinger, Jun'ichi Tsujii, and Hans Uszkoreit, editors, *Collaborative Language Engineering*, pages 1–17. CSLI Publications.

Anette Frank, Hans-Ulrich Krieger, Feiyu Xu, Hans Uszkoreit, Berthold Crysmann, Brigitte Jörg, and Ulrich Schäfer. 2006. Question answering from structured knowledge sources. *Journal of Applied Logic, Special Issue on Questions and Answers: Theoretical and Applied Perspectives.*, 5(1):20–48.

Rodney Huddleston and Geoffrey K. Pullum. 2002. *The Cambridge Grammar of the English Language*. Cambridge University Press, Cambridge, UK.

Mark Johnson, Stuart Geman, Stephen Canon, Zhiyi Chi, and Stefan Riezler. 1999. Estimators for stochastic unifcation-based grammars. In *Proceedings of the 37th Annual Meeting of the Association for Computational Linguistics (ACL 1999)*, pages 535–541, Maryland, USA.

Bernd Kiefer, Hans-Ulrich Krieger, John Carroll, and Rob Malouf. 1999. A Bag of Useful Techniques for Efficient and Robust Parsing. In *Proceedings of the 37th Annual Meeting of the Association for Computational Linguistics*, pages 473–480, Maryland, USA.

Anna Korhonen. 2002. *Subcategorization Acquisition*. Ph.D. thesis, University of Cambridge.

Andrew MacKinlay, David Martinez, and Timothy Baldwin. 2009. Biomedical event annotation with CRFs and precision grammars. In *Proceedings of BioNLP 2009: Shared Task*, pages 77–85, Boulder, USA.

Robert Malouf. 2002. A comparison of algorithms for maximum entropy parameter estimation. In *Proceedings of the 6th Conferencde on Natural Language Learning (CoNLL 2002)*, pages 49–55, Taipei, Taiwan.

Christopher D. Manning and Hinrich Schütze. 1999. *Foundations of Statistical Natural Language Processing*. MIT Press.

Kathleen R. McKeown and Dragomir R. Radev. 2000. Collocations. In Robert Dale, Hermann Moisl, and Harold Somers, editors, *Handbook of Natural Language Processing*.

Stephan Oepen and John Carroll. 2000. Ambiguity packing in constraint-based parsing — practical results. In *Proceedings of the 1st Annual Meeting of the North American Chapter of Association for Computational Linguistics (NAACL 2000)*, pages 162–169, Seattle, USA.

Stephan Oepen, Helge Dyvik, Jan Tore Lønning, Erik Velldal, Dorothee Beermann, John Carroll, Dan Flickinger, Lars Hellan, Janne Bondi Johannessen, Paul Meurer, Torbjørn Nordgård, and Victoria Rosén. 2004. Som å kapp-ete med trollet? Towards MRS-Based Norwegian–English Machine Translation. In *Proceedings of the 10th International Conference on Theoretical and Methodological Issues in Machine Translation*, Baltimore, USA.

Carlos Ramisch, Paulo Schreiner, Marco Idiart, and Aline Villavicencio. 2008. An evaluation of methods for the extraction of multiword expressions. In *Proceedings of the LREC 2008 Workshop: Towards a Shared Task for Multiword Expressions (MWE 2008)*, pages 50–53, Marrakech, Morocco.

Susanne Riehemann. 2001. *A Constructional Approach to Idioms and Word Formation*. Ph.D. thesis, Stanford University, CA, USA.

Ivan A. Sag, Timothy Baldwin, Francis Bond, Ann Copestake, and Dan Flickinger. 2002. Multiword expressions: A pain in the neck for NLP. In *Proceedings of the 3rd International Conference on Intelligent Text Processing and Computational Linguistics (CICLing-2002)*, pages 1–15, Mexico City, Mexico.

Frank Smadja. 1993. Retrieving collocations from text: Xtract. *Computational Linguistics*, 19(1):143–178.

Masaru Tomita. 1985. An efficient context-free parsing algorithm for natural languages. In *Proceedings of the 9th International Joint Conference on Artificial Intelligence*, pages 756–764, Los Angeles, USA.

Kristina Toutanova, Christoper D. Manning, Stuart M. Shieber, Dan Flickinger, and Stephan Oepen. 2002. Parse ranking for a rich HPSG grammar. In *Proceedings of the 1st Workshop on Treebanks and Linguistic Theories (TLT 2002)*, pages 253–263, Sozopol, Bulgaria.

Hans Uszkoreit. 2002. New chances for deep linguistic processing. In *Proceedings of the 19th international conference on computational linguistics (COLING 2002)*, Taipei, Taiwan.

Gertjan van Noord. 2004. Error mining for wide-coverage grammar engineering. In *Proceedings of the 42nd Annual Meeting of the Association for Computational Linguistics)*, pages 446–453, Barcelona, Spain.

Aline Villavicencio and Ann Copestake. 2002. Verb-particle constructions in a computational grammar of English. In *Proceedings of the 9th International Conference on Head-Driven Phrase Structure Grammar (HPSG-2002)*, Seoul, Korea.

Yi Zhang and Valia Kordoni. 2006. Automated deep lexical acquisition for robust open texts processing. In *Proceedings of the 5th International Conference on Language Resources and Evaluation (LREC 2006)*, pages 275–280, Genoa, Italy.

Yi Zhang and Valia Kordoni. 2008. Robust parsing with a large HPSG grammar. In *Proceedings of the Sixth International Language Resources and Evaluation (LREC'08)*, Marrakech, Morocco.

Yi Zhang, Valia Kordoni, and Erin Fitzgerald. 2007a. Partial parse selection for robust deep processing. In *Proceedings of ACL 2007 Workshop on Deep Linguistic Processing*, pages 128–135, Prague, Czech Republic.

Yi Zhang, Stephan Oepen, and John Carroll. 2007b. Efficiency in unification-based N-best parsing. In *Proceedings of the 10th International Conference on Parsing Technologies (IWPT 2007)*, pages 48–59, Prague, Czech.

Products of Random Latent Variable Grammars

Slav Petrov
Google Research
New York, NY, 10011
slav@google.com

Abstract

We show that the automatically induced latent variable grammars of Petrov et al. (2006) vary widely in their underlying representations, depending on their EM initialization point. We use this to our advantage, combining multiple automatically learned grammars into an unweighted product model, which gives significantly improved performance over state-of-the-art individual grammars. In our model, the probability of a constituent is estimated as a product of posteriors obtained from multiple grammars that differ only in the random seed used for initialization, without any learning or tuning of combination weights. Despite its simplicity, a product of eight automatically learned grammars improves parsing accuracy from 90.2% to 91.8% on English, and from 80.3% to 84.5% on German.

1 Introduction

Learning a context-free grammar for parsing requires the estimation of a more highly articulated model than the one embodied by the observed treebank. This is because the naive treebank grammar (Charniak, 1996) is too permissive, making unrealistic context-freedom assumptions. For example, it postulates that there is only one type of noun phrase (NP), which can appear in all positions (subject, object, etc.), regardless of case, number or gender. As a result, the grammar can generate millions of (incorrect) parse trees for a given sentence, and has a flat posterior distribution. High accuracy grammars therefore add soft constraints on the way categories can be combined, and enrich the label set with additional information. These constraints can be lexicalized (Collins, 1999; Charniak, 2000), unlexicalized (Johnson, 1998; Klein and Manning, 2003b) or automatically learned (Matsuzaki et al., 2005; Petrov et al., 2006). The constraints serve the purpose of weakening the independence assumptions, and reduce the number of possible (but incorrect) parses.

Here, we focus on the latent variable approach of Petrov et al. (2006), where an Expectation Maximization (EM) algorithm is used to induce a hierarchy of increasingly more refined grammars. Each round of refinement introduces new constraints on how constituents can be combined, which in turn leads to a higher parsing accuracy. However, EM is a local method, and there are no guarantees that it will find the same grammars when initialized from different starting points. In fact, it turns out that even though the final performance of these grammars is consistently high, there are significant variations in the learned refinements.

We use these variations to our advantage, and treat grammars learned from different random seeds as independent and equipotent experts. We use a product distribution for joint prediction, which gives more peaked posteriors than a sum, and enforces all constraints of the individual grammars, without the need to tune mixing weights. It should be noted here that our focus is on improving parsing performance using a single underlying grammar class, which is somewhat orthogonal to the issue of parser combination, that has been studied elsewhere in the literature (Sagae and Lavie, 2006; Fossum and Knight, 2009; Zhang et al., 2009). In contrast to that line of work, we also do not restrict ourselves to working with k-best output, but work directly with a packed forest representation of the posteriors, much in the spirit of Huang (2008), except that we work with several forests rather than rescoring a single one.

Human Language Technologies: The 2010 Annual Conference of the North American Chapter of the ACL, pages 19–27,
Los Angeles, California, June 2010.

In our experimental section we give empirical answers to some of the remaining theoretical questions. We address the question of averaging versus multiplying classifier predictions, we investigate different ways of introducing more diversity into the underlying grammars, and also compare combining partial (constituent-level) and complete (tree-level) predictions. Quite serendipitously, the simplest approaches work best in our experiments. A product of eight latent variable grammars, learned on the same data, and only differing in the seed used in the random number generator that initialized EM, improves parsing accuracy from 90.2% to 91.8% on English, and from 80.3% to 84.5% on German. These parsing results are even better than those obtained by discriminative systems which have access to additional non-local features (Charniak and Johnson, 2005; Huang, 2008).

2 Latent Variable Grammars

Before giving the details of our model, we briefly review the basic properties of latent variable grammars. Learning latent variable grammars consists of two tasks: (1) determining the data representation (the set of context-free productions to be used in the grammar), and (2) estimating the parameters of the model (the production probabilities). We focus on the randomness introduced by the EM algorithm and refer the reader to Matsuzaki et al. (2005) and Petrov et al. (2006) for a more general introduction.

2.1 Split & Merge Learning

Latent variable grammars split the coarse (but observed) grammar categories of a treebank into more fine-grained (but hidden) subcategories, which are better suited for modeling the syntax of natural languages (e.g. NP becomes NP_1 through NP_k). Accordingly, each grammar production $\mathrm{A}\rightarrow\mathrm{BC}$ over observed categories A,B,C is split into a set of productions $\mathrm{A}_x\rightarrow\mathrm{B}_y\mathrm{C}_z$ over hidden categories A_x,B_y,C_z. Computing the joint likelihood of the observed parse trees T and sentences w requires summing over all derivations t over split subcategories:

$$\prod_i \mathrm{P}(w_i, T_i) = \prod_i \sum_{t:T_i} \mathrm{P}(w_i, t) \quad (1)$$

Matsuzaki et al. (2005) derive an EM algorithm for maximizing the joint likelihood, and Petrov et al. (2006) extend this algorithm to use a split&merge procedure to adaptively determine the optimal number of subcategories for each observed category. Starting from a completely markovized X-Bar grammar, each category is split in two, generating eight new productions for each original binary production. To break symmetries, the production probabilities are perturbed by 1% of random noise. EM is then initialized with this starting point and used to climb the highly non-convex objective function given in Eq. 1. Each splitting step is followed by a merging step, which uses a likelihood ratio test to reverse the least useful half of the splits. Learning proceeds by iterating between those two steps for six rounds. To prevent overfitting, the production probabilities are linearly smoothed by shrinking them towards their common base category.

2.2 EM induced Randomness

While the split&merge procedure described above is shown in Petrov et al. (2006) to reduce the variance in final performance, we found after closer examination that there are substantial differences in the patterns learned by the grammars. Since the initialization is not systematically biased in any way, one can obtain different grammars by simply changing the seed of the random number generator. We trained 16 different grammars by initializing the random number generator with seed values 1 through 16, but without biasing the initialization in any other way. Figure 1 shows that the number of subcategories allocated to each observed category varies significantly between the different initialization points, especially for the phrasal categories. Figure 2 shows posteriors over the most frequent subcategories given their base category for the first four grammars. Clearly, EM is allocating the latent variables in very different ways in each case.

As a more quantitative measure of difference,[1] we evaluated all 16 grammars on sections 22 and 24 of the Penn Treebank. Figure 3 shows the performance on those two sets, and reveals that there is no single grammar that achieves the best score on both. While the parsing accuracies are consistently high,[2] there

[1] While cherry-picking similarities is fairly straight-forward, it is less obvious how to quantify differences.

[2] Note that despite their variance, the performance is always higher than the one of the lexicalized parser of Charniak (2000).

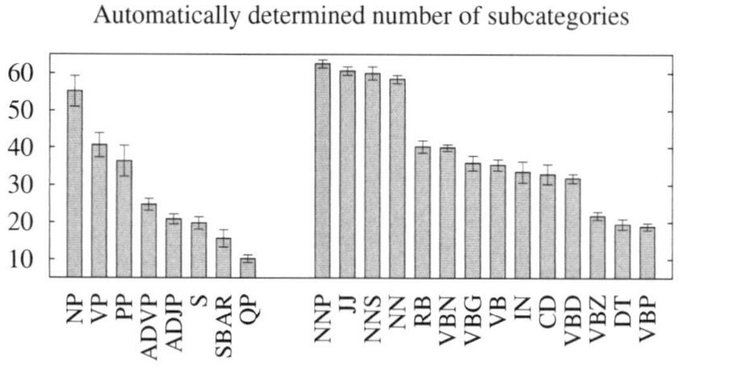

Figure 1: There is large variance in the number of subcategories (error bars correspond to one standard deviation).

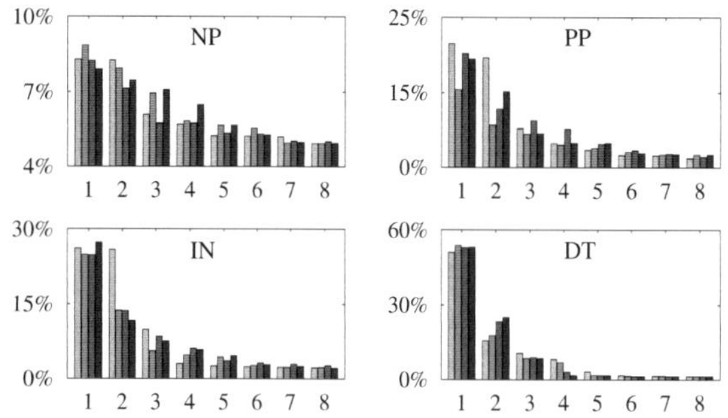

Figure 2: Posterior probabilities of the eight most frequent hidden subcategories given their observed base categories. The four grammars (indicated by shading) are populating the subcategories in very different ways.

is only a weak correlation between the accuracies on the two evaluation sets (Pearson coefficient 0.34). This suggests that no single grammar should be preferred over the others. In previous work (Petrov et al., 2006; Petrov and Klein, 2007) the final grammar was chosen based on its performance on a held-out set (section 22), and corresponds to the second best grammar in Figure 3 (because only 8 different grammars were trained).

A more detailed error analysis is given in Figure 4, where we show a breakdown of F_1 scores for selected phrasal categories in addition to the overall F_1 score and exact match (on the WSJ development set). While grammar G_2 has the highest overall F_1 score, its exact match is not particularly high, and it turns out to be the weakest at predicting quantifier phrases (QP). Similarly, the performance of the other grammars varies between the different error measures, indicating again that no single grammar dominates the others.

3 A Simple Product Model

It should be clear by now that simply varying the random seed used for initialization causes EM to discover very different latent variable grammars. While this behavior is worrisome in general, it turns out that we can use it to our advantage in this particular case. Recall that we are using EM to learn both, the data representation, as well as the parameters of the model. Our analysis showed that changing the initialization point results in learning grammars that vary quite significantly in the errors they make, but have comparable overall accuracies. This suggests that the different local maxima found by EM correspond to different data representations rather than to suboptimal parameter estimates.

To leverage the strengths of the individual grammars, we combine them in a product model. Product models have the nice property that their Kullback-Liebler divergence from the true distribution will always be smaller than the average of the KL divergences of the individual distributions (Hinton, 2001). Therefore, as long as no individual grammar G_i is significantly worse than the others, we can only benefit from combining multiple latent variable grammars and searching for the tree that maximizes

$$P(T|w) \propto \prod_i P(T|w, G_i) \qquad (2)$$

Here, we are making the assumption that the individual grammars are conditionally independent, which is of course not true in theory, but holds surprisingly well in practice. To avoid this assumption, we could use a sum model, but we will show in Section 4.1 that the product formulation performs significantly better. Intuitively speaking, products have the advantage that the final prediction has a high posterior under *all* models, giving each model veto power. This is exactly the behavior that we need in the case of parsing, where each grammar has learned different constraints for ruling out improbable parses.

3.1 Learning

Joint training of our product model would couple the parameters of the individual grammars, necessitating the computation of an intractable global partition function (Brown and Hinton, 2001). Instead, we use EM to train each grammar independently,

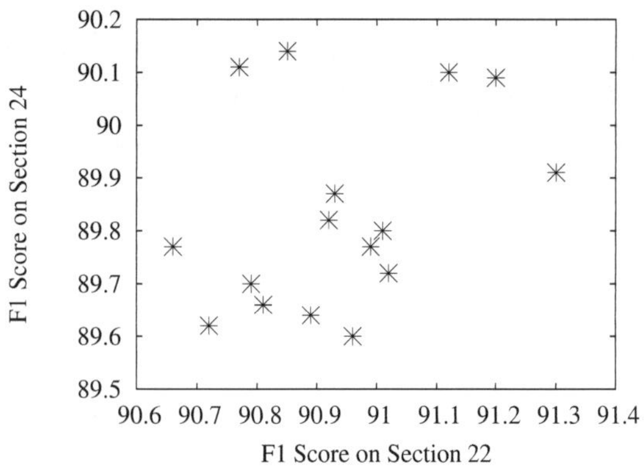

Figure 3: Parsing accuracies for grammars learned from different random seeds. The large variance and weak correlation suggest that no single grammar is to be preferred.

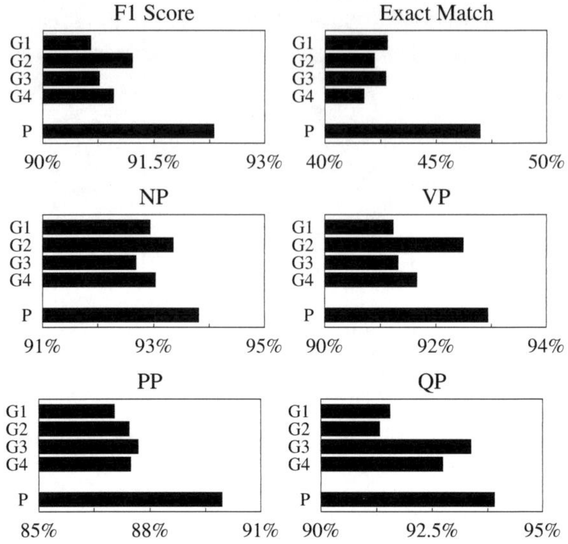

Figure 4: Breakdown of different accuracy measures for four randomly selected grammars (G_1-G_4), as well as a product model (P) that uses those four grammars. Note that no single grammar does well on all measures, while the product model does significantly better on all.

but from a different, randomly chosen starting point. To emphasize, we do not introduce any systematic bias (but see Section 4.3 for some experiments), or attempt to train the models to be maximally different (Hinton, 2002) – we simply train a random collection of grammars by varying the random seed used for initialization. We found in our experiments that the randomness provided by EM is sufficient to achieve diversity among the individual grammars, and gives results that are as good as more involved training procedures. Xu and Jelinek (2004) made a similar observation when learning random forests for language modeling.

Our model is reminiscent of Logarithmic Opinion Pools (Bordley, 1982) and Products of Experts (Hinton, 2001).[3] However, because we believe that none of the underlying grammars should be favored, we deliberately do not use any combination weights.

3.2 Inference

Computing the most likely parse tree is intractable for latent variable grammars (Sima'an, 2002), and therefore also for our product model. This is because there are exponentially many derivations over split subcategories that correspond to a single parse tree over unsplit categories, and there is no dynamic program to efficiently marginalize out the latent variables. Previous work on parse risk minimization has addressed this problem in two different ways: by changing the objective function, or by constraining the search space (Goodman, 1996; Titov and Henderson, 2006; Petrov and Klein, 2007).

The simplest approach is to stick to likelihood as the objective function, but to limit the search space to a set of high quality candidates $\mathcal{T}$:

$$T^* = \operatorname*{argmax}_{T \in \mathcal{T}} \mathrm{P}(T|w) \quad (3)$$

Because the likelihood of a given parse tree can be computed exactly for our product model (Eq. 2), the quality of this approximation is only limited by the quality of the candidate list. To generate the candidate list, we produce k-best lists of Viterbi derivations with the efficient algorithm of Huang and Chiang (2005), and erase the subcategory information to obtain parse trees over unsplit categories. We refer to this approximation as TREE-LEVEL inference, because it considers a list of complete trees from the underlying grammars, and selects the tree that has the highest likelihood under the product model. While the k-best lists are of very high quality, this is a fairly crude and unsatisfactory way of approximating the posterior distribution of the product model, as it does not allow the synthesis of new trees based on tree fragments from different grammars.

An alternative is to use a tractable objective function that allows the efficient exploration of the entire

[3]As a matter of fact, Hinton (2001) mentions syntactic parsing as one of the motivating examples for Products of Experts.

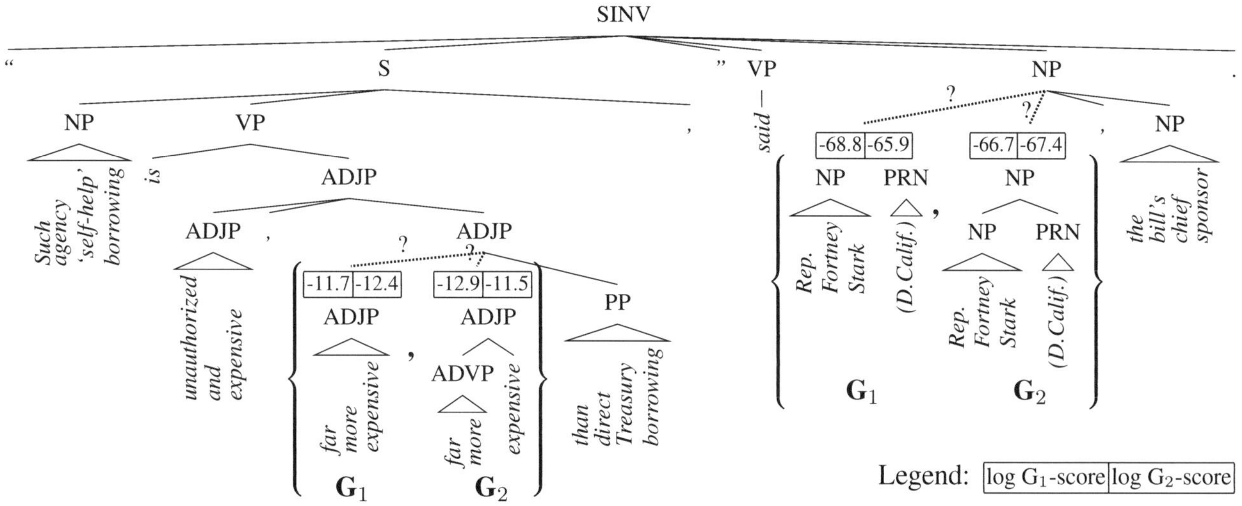

Figure 5: Grammar G_1 has a preference for flat structures, while grammar G_2 prefers deeper hierarchical structures. Both grammars therefore make one mistake each on their own. However, the correct parse tree (which uses a flat ADJP in the first slot and a hierarchical NP in the second) scores highest under the product model.

search space. Petrov and Klein (2007) present such an objective function, which maximizes the product of expected correct productions r:

$$T^* = \underset{T}{\operatorname{argmax}} \prod_{r \in T} \mathbb{E}(r|w) \tag{4}$$

These expectations can be easily computed from the inside/outside scores, similarly as in the maximum bracket recall algorithm of Goodman (1996), or in the variational approximation of Matsuzaki et al. (2005). We extend the algorithm to work over posterior distributions from multiple grammars, by aggregating their expectations into a product. In practice, we use a packed forest representation to approximate the posterior distribution, as in Huang (2008). We refer to this approximation as CONSTITUENT-LEVEL, because it allows us to form new parse trees from individual constituents.

Figure 5 illustrates a real case where the product model was able to construct a completely correct parse tree from two partially correct ones. In the example, one of the underlying grammars (G_1) had an imperfect recall score, because of its preference for flat structures (it missed an NP node in the second part of the sentence). In contrast, the other grammar (G_2) favors deeper structures, and therefore introduced a superfluous ADVP node. The product model gives each underlying grammar veto power, and picks the least controversial tree (which is the correct one in this case). Note that a sum model allows the most confident model to dominate the decision, and would chose the incorrect hierarchical ADJP construction here (as one can verify using the provided model scores).

To make inference efficient, we can use the same coarse-to-fine pruning techniques as Petrov and Klein (2007). We generate a hierarchy of projected grammars for each individual grammar and parse with each one in sequence. Because only the very last pass requires scores from the different underlying grammars, this computation can be trivially parallelized across multiple CPUs. Additionally, the first (X-Bar) pruning pass needs to be computed only once because it is shared among all grammars. Since the X-Bar pass is the bottleneck of the multipass scheme (using nearly 50% of the total processing time), the overhead of using a product model is quite manageable. It would have also been possible to use A*-search for factored models (Klein and Manning, 2003a; Sun and Tsujii, 2009), but we did not attempt this in the present work.

4 Experiments

In our experiments, we follow the standard setups described in Table 1, and use the EVALB tool for computing parsing figures. Unless noted otherwise, we use CONSTITUENT-LEVEL inference. All our experiments are based on the publicly available BerkeleyParser.[4]

[4] http://code.google.com/p/berkeleyparser

	Training Set	Dev. Set	Test Set
ENGLISH-WSJ (Marcus et al., 1993)	Sections 2-21	Section 22	Section 23
ENGLISH-BROWN (Francis et al. 1979)	see ENGLISH-WSJ	10% of the data[5]	10% of the data[5]
GERMAN (Skut et al., 1997)	Sentences 1-18,602	Sentences 18,603-19,602	Sentences 19,603-20,602

Table 1: Corpora and standard experimental setups.

4.1 (Weighted) Product vs. (Weighted) Sum

A great deal has been written on the topic of products versus sums of probability distributions for joint prediction (Genest and Zidek, 1986; Tax et al., 2000). However, those theoretical results do not apply directly here, because we are using multiple randomly permuted models from the same class, rather models from different classes. To shed some light on this issue, we addressed the question empirically, and combined two grammars into an unweighted product model, and also an unweighted sum model. The individual grammars had parsing accuracies (F_1) of 91.2 and 90.7 respectively, and their product (91.7) clearly outperformed their sum (91.3). When more grammars are added, the gap widens even further, and the trends persist independently of whether the models use TREE-LEVEL or CONSTITUENT-LEVEL inference. At least for the case of unweighted combinations, the product distribution seems to be superior.

In related work, Zhang et al. (2009) achieve excellent results with a weighted sum model. Using weights learned on a held-out set and rescoring 50-best lists from Charniak (2000) and Petrov et al. (2006), they obtain an F_1 score of 91.0 (which they further improve to 91.4 using a voting scheme). We replicated their experiment, but used an unweighted product of the two model scores. Using TREE-LEVEL inference, we obtained an F_1 score of 91.6, suggesting that weighting is not so important in the product case, as long as the classifiers are of comparable quality.[6] This is in line with previous work on product models, where weighting has been important when combining heterogenous classifiers (Heskes, 1998), and less important when the classifiers are of similar accuracy (Smith et al., 2005).

[5]See Gildea (2001) for the exact setup.

[6]The unweighted sum model, however, underperforms the individual models with an F_1 score of only 90.3.

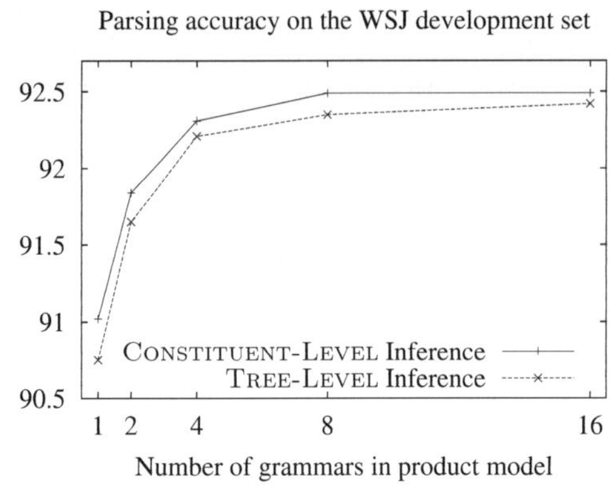

Figure 6: Adding more grammars to the product model improves parsing accuracy, while CONSTITUENT-LEVEL inference gives consistently better results.

4.2 Tree-Level vs. Constituent-Level Inference

Figure 6 shows that accuracy increases when more grammars are added to the product model, but levels off after eight grammars. The plot also compares our two inference approximations, and shows that CONSTITUENT-LEVEL inference results in a small (0.2), but consistent improvement in F_1 score.

A first thought might be that the improvement is due to the limited scope of the k-best lists. However, this is not the case, as the results hold even when the candidate set for CONSTITUENT-LEVEL inference is constrained to trees from the k-best lists. While the packed forrest representation can very efficiently encode an exponential set of parse trees, in our case the k-best lists appear to be already very diverse because they are generated by multiple grammars. Starting at 96.1 for a single latent variable grammar, merging two 50-best lists from different grammars gives an oracle score of 97.4, and adding more k-best lists further improves the oracle score to 98.6 for 16 grammars. This compares favorably to the results of Huang (2008), where the oracle score over a pruned forest is shown to be 97.8 (compared to 96.7 for a 50-best list).

The accuracy improvement can instead be explained by the change in the objective function. Recall from section Section 3.2, that CONSTITUENT-LEVEL inference maximizes the expected number of correct productions, while TREE-LEVEL inference maximizes tree-likelihood. It is therefore not too surprising that the two objective functions select the same tree only 41% of the time, even when limited to the same candidate set. Maximizing the expected number of correct productions is superior for F_1 score (see the one grammar case in Figure 6). However, as to be expected, likelihood is better for exact match, giving a score of 47.6% vs. 46.8%.

4.3 Systematic Bias

Diversity among the underlying models is what gives combined models their strength. One way of increasing diversity is by modifying the feature sets of the individual models (Baldridge and Osborne, 2008; Smith and Osborne, 2007). This approach has the disadvantage that it reduces the performance of the individual models, and is not directly applicable for latent variable grammars because the features are automatically learned. Alternatively, one can introduce diversity by changing the training distribution. Bagging (Breiman, 1996) and Boosting (Freund and Shapire, 1996) fall into this category, but have had limited success for parsing (Henderson and Brill, 2000). Furthermore boosting is impractical here, because it requires training dozens of grammars in sequence.

Since training a single grammar takes roughly one day, we opted for a different, parallelizable way of changing the training distribution. In a first experiment, we divided the training set into two disjoint sets, and trained separate grammars on each half. These truly disjoint grammars had low F_1 scores of 89.4 and 89.6 respectively (because they were trained on less data). Their combination unfortunately also achieves only an accuracy of 90.9, which is lower than what we get when training a single grammar on the entire training set. In another experiment, we used a cross-validation setup where individual sections of the treebank were held out. The resulting grammars had parsing accuracies of about 90.5, and the product model was again not able to overcome the lower starting point, despite the potentially larger diversity among the underlying grammars. It appears that any systematic bias that lowers the accuracy of the individual grammars also hurts the final performance of the product model.

4.4 Product Distribution as Smoothing

Smith et al. (2005) interpret Logarithmic Opinion Pools (LOPs) as a smoothing technique. They compare regularizing Conditional Random Fields (CRFs) with Gaussian priors (Lafferty et al., 2001), to training a set of unregularized CRFs over different feature sets and combining them in an LOP. In their experiments, both approaches work comparably well, but their combination, an LOP of regularized CRFs works best.

Not too surprisingly, we find this to be the case here as well. The parameters of each latent variable grammar are typically smoothed in a linear fashion to prevent excessive overfitting (Petrov et al., 2006). While all the experiments so far used smoothed grammars, we reran the experiments also with a set of unsmoothed grammars. The individual unsmoothed grammars have on average an 1.2% lower accuracy. Even though our product model is able to increase accuracy by combining multiple grammars, the gap to the smoothed models remains consistent. This suggests that the product model is doing more than just smoothing. In fact, because the product distribution is more peaked, it seems to be doing the opposite of smoothing.

4.5 Final Results

Our final model uses an unweighted product of eight grammars trained by initializing the random number generator with seeds 1 through 8. Table 2 shows our test set results (obtained with CONSTITUENT-LEVEL inference), and compares them to related work. There is a large body of work that has reported parsing accuracies for English, and we have grouped the different methods into categories for better overview.

Our results on the English in-domain test set are higher than those obtained by any single component parser (SINGLE). The other methods quoted in Table 2 operate over the output of one or more single component parsers and are therefore largely orthogonal to our line of work. It is nonetheless exciting to see that our product model is competitive with the discriminative rescoring methods (RE) of Charniak and Johnson (2005) and Huang (2008), achieving higher F_1 scores but lower exact match. These two methods work on top of the Charniak (2000) parser, and it would be possible to exchange that parser with our product model. We did not attempt this experiment, but we expect that those methods would stack well with our model, because they use primarily non-local features that are not available in a context-free grammar.

Techniques like self-training (SELF) and system combinations (COMBO) can further improve parsing accuracies, but are also orthogonal to our work. In particular the COMBO methods seem related to our work, but are very different in their nature. While we use multiple grammars in our work, all grammars are from the same model class for us. In contrast, those methods rely on a diverse set of individual parsers, each of which requires a significant effort to build. Furthermore, those techniques have largely relied on different voting schemes in the past (Henderson and Brill, 1999; Sagae and Lavie, 2006), and only more recently have started using actual posteriors from the underlying models (Fossum and Knight, 2009; Zhang et al., 2009). Even then, those methods operate only over k-best lists, and we are the first to work directly with parse forests from multiple grammars.

It is also interesting to note that the best results in Zhang et al. (2009) are achieved by combining k-best lists from a latent variable grammar of Petrov et al. (2006) with the self-trained reranking parser of McClosky et al. (2006). Clearly, replacing the single latent variable grammar with a product of latent variable grammars ought to improve performance.

The results on the other two corpora are similar. A product of latent variable grammars very significantly outperforms a single latent variable grammar and sets new standards for the state-of-the-art.

We also analyzed the errors of the product models. In addition to the illustrative example in Figure 5, we computed detailed error metrics for different phrasal categories. Figure 4 shows that a product of four random grammars is always better than even the best underlying grammar. The individual grammars seem to learn different sets of constraints, and the product model is able to model them all at once, giving consistent accuracy improvements across all metrics.

Type	Parser	all sentences LP	LR	EX
	ENGLISH-WSJ			
	This Paper	**92.0**	**91.7**	**41.9**
SINGLE	Charniak (2000)	89.9	89.5	37.2
SINGLE	Petrov and Klein (2007)	90.2	90.1	36.7
SINGLE	Carreras et al. (2008)	91.4	90.7	-
RE	Charniak et al. (2005)	91.8	91.2	44.8
RE	Huang (2008)	92.2	91.2	43.5
SELF	Huang and Harper (2009)	91.3[7]	91.5[7]	39.3[7]
SELF	McClosky et al. (2006)	92.5	92.1	45.3
COMBO	Sagae and Lavie (2006)	93.2	91.0	-
COMBO	Fossum and Knight (2009)	93.2	91.7	-
COMBO	Zhang et al. (2009)	93.3	92.0	-
	ENGLISH-BROWN			
	This Paper	**86.5**	**86.3**	**35.8**
SING	Charniak (2000)	82.9	82.9	31.7
SING	Petrov and Klein (2007)	83.9	83.8	29.6
RE	Charniak et al. (2005)	86.1	85.2	36.8
	GERMAN			
	This Paper	**84.5**	**84.0**	**51.2**
SING	Petrov and Klein (2007)	80.0	80.2	42.4
SING	Petrov and Klein (2008)	80.6	80.8	43.9

Table 2: Final test set accuracies for English and German.

5 Conclusions

We presented a simple product model that significantly improves parsing accuracies on different domains and languages. Our model leverages multiple automatically learned latent variable grammars, which differ only in the seed of the random number generator used to initialize the EM learning algorithm. As our analysis showed, the grammars vary widely, making very different errors. This is in part due to the fact that EM is used not only for estimating the parameters of the grammar, but also to determine the set of context-free productions that underlie it. Because the resulting data representations are largely independent, they can be easily combined in an unweighted product model. The product model does not require any additional training and is capable of significantly improving the state-of-the-art in parsing accuracy. It remains to be seen if a similar approach can be used in other cases where EM converges to widely varying local maxima.

Acknowledgements

I would like to thank Ryan McDonald for numerous discussions on this topic and his feedback on earlier versions of this paper. This work also benefited from conversations with Gideon Mann, Fernando Pereira, Dan Klein and Mehryar Mohri.

[7] Note that these results are on a modified version of the treebank where unary productions are removed.

References

J. Baldridge and M. Osborne. 2008. Active learning and logarithmic opinion pools for HPSG parse selection. *Natural Language Engineering*.

R. F. Bordley. 1982. A multiplicative formula for aggregating probability assessments. *Management Science*.

L. Breiman. 1996. Bagging predictors. *Machine Learning*.

A. Brown and G. Hinton. 2001. Products of hidden Markov models. In *AISTATS '01*.

X. Carreras, M. Collins, and T. Koo. 2008. TAG, dynamic programming, and the perceptron for efficient, feature-rich parsing. In *CoNLL '08*.

E. Charniak and M. Johnson. 2005. Coarse-to-Fine N-Best Parsing and MaxEnt Discriminative Reranking. In *ACL'05*.

E. Charniak. 1996. Tree-bank grammars. In *AAAI '96*.

E. Charniak. 2000. A maximum–entropy–inspired parser. In *NAACL '00*.

M. Collins. 1999. *Head-Driven Statistical Models for Natural Language Parsing*. Ph.D. thesis, UPenn.

V. Fossum and K. Knight. 2009. Combining constituent parsers. In *NAACL '09*.

W. N. Francis and H. Kucera. 1979. Manual of information to accompany a standard corpus of present-day edited American English. Technical report, Brown University.

Y. Freund and R. E. Shapire. 1996. Experiments with a new boosting algorithm. In *ICML '96*.

C. Genest and J. V. Zidek. 1986. Combining probability distributions: A critique and an annotated bibliography. *Statistical Science*.

D. Gildea. 2001. Corpus variation and parser performance. *EMNLP '01*.

J. Goodman. 1996. Parsing algorithms and metrics. *ACL '96*.

J. Henderson and E. Brill. 1999. Exploiting diversity in natural language processing: combining parsers. In *EMNLP '99*.

J. Henderson and E. Brill. 2000. Bagging and boosting a treebank parser. In *NAACL '00*.

T. Heskes. 1998. Selecting weighting factors in logarithmic opinion pools. In *NIPS '98*.

G. Hinton. 2001. Products of experts. In *ICANN '01*.

G. Hinton. 2002. Training products of experts by minimizing contrastive divergence. *Neural Computation*.

L. Huang and D. Chiang. 2005. Better k-best parsing. In *IWPT '05*.

Z. Huang and M. Harper. 2009. Self-training PCFG grammars with latent annotations across languages. In *EMNLP '09*.

L. Huang. 2008. Forest reranking: Discriminative parsing with non-local features. In *ACL '08*.

M. Johnson. 1998. PCFG models of linguistic tree representations. *Computational Linguistics*, 24.

D. Klein and C. Manning. 2003a. A* parsing: fast exact viterbi parse selection. In *NAACL '03*.

D. Klein and C. Manning. 2003b. Accurate unlexicalized parsing. In *ACL '03*.

J. Lafferty, A. McCallum, and F. Pereira. 2001. Conditional Random Fields: Probabilistic models for segmenting and labeling sequence data. In *ICML '01*.

M. Marcus, B. Santorini, and M. Marcinkiewicz. 1993. Building a large annotated corpus of English: The Penn Treebank. In *Computational Linguistics*.

T. Matsuzaki, Y. Miyao, and J. Tsujii. 2005. Probabilistic CFG with latent annotations. In *ACL '05*.

D. McClosky, E. Charniak, and M. Johnson. 2006. Effective self-training for parsing. In *NAACL '06*.

S. Petrov and D. Klein. 2007. Improved inference for unlexicalized parsing. In *NAACL '07*.

S. Petrov and D. Klein. 2008. Sparse multi-scale grammars for discriminative latent variable parsing. In *EMNLP '08*.

S. Petrov, L. Barrett, R. Thibaux, and D. Klein. 2006. Learning accurate, compact, and interpretable tree annotation. In *ACL '06*.

K. Sagae and A. Lavie. 2006. Parser combination by reparsing. In *NAACL '06*.

K. Sima'an. 2002. Computatoinal complexity of probabilistic disambiguation. *Grammars*.

W. Skut, B. Krenn, T. Brants, and H. Uszkoreit. 1997. An annotation scheme for free word order languages. In *ANLP '97*.

A. Smith and M. Osborne. 2007. Diversity in logarithmic opinion pools. *Lingvisticae Investigationes*.

A. Smith, T. Cohn, and M. Osborne. 2005. Logarithmic opinion pools for conditional random fields. In *ACL '05*.

X. Sun and J. Tsujii. 2009. Sequential labeling with latent variables: An exact inference algorithm and its efficient approximation. In *EACL '09*.

D. Tax, M. Van Breukelen, R. Duin, and J. Kittler. 2000. Combining multiple classifiers by averaging or by multiplying? *Pattern Recognition*.

I. Titov and J. Henderson. 2006. Loss minimization in parse reranking. In *EMNLP '06*.

P. Xu and F. Jelinek. 2004. Random forests in language modeling. In *EMNLP '04*.

H. Zhang, M. Zhang, C. L. Tan, and H. Li. 2009. K-best combination of syntactic parsers. In *EMNLP '09*.

Automatic Domain Adaptation for Parsing

David McClosky[a,b]
[a]Stanford University
Stanford, CA, USA
mcclosky@stanford.edu

Eugene Charniak[b]
[b]Brown University
Providence, RI, USA
ec@cs.brown.edu

Mark Johnson[c,b]
[c]Macquarie University
Sydney, NSW, Australia
mjohnson@science.mq.edu.au

Abstract

Current statistical parsers tend to perform well only on their training domain and nearby genres. While strong performance on a few related domains is sufficient for many situations, it is advantageous for parsers to be able to generalize to a wide variety of domains. When parsing document collections involving heterogeneous domains (e.g. the web), the optimal parsing model for each document is typically not obvious. We study this problem as a new task — *multiple source parser adaptation*. Our system trains on corpora from many different domains. It learns not only statistics of those domains but quantitative measures of domain differences and how those differences affect parsing accuracy. Given a specific target text, the resulting system proposes linear combinations of parsing models trained on the source corpora. Tested across six domains, our system outperforms all non-oracle baselines including the best domain-independent parsing model. Thus, we are able to demonstrate the value of customizing parsing models to specific domains.

1 Introduction

In statistical parsing literature, it is common to see parsers trained and tested on the same textual domain (Charniak and Johnson, 2005; McClosky et al., 2006a; Petrov and Klein, 2007; Carreras et al., 2008; Suzuki et al., 2009, among others). Unfortunately, the performance of these systems degrades on sentences drawn from a different domain. This issue can be seen across different parsing models (Sekine, 1997; Gildea, 2001; Bacchiani et al., 2006; McClosky et al., 2006b). Given that some aspects of syntax are domain dependent (typically at the lexical level), single parsing models tend to not perform well across all domains (see Table 1). Thus, statistical parsers inevitably learn some domain-specific properties in addition to the more general properties of a language's syntax. Recently, Daumé III (2007) and Finkel and Manning (2009) showed techniques for training models that attempt to separate domain-specific and general properties. However, even when given models for multiple training domains, it is not straightforward to determine which model performs best on an arbitrary piece of novel text.

This problem comes to the fore when one wants to parse document collections where each document is potentially its own domain. This shows up particularly when parsing the web. Recently, there has been much interest in applying parsers to the web for the purposes of information extraction and other forms of analysis (c.f. the CLSP 2009 summer workshop "Parsing the Web: Large-Scale Syntactic Processing"). The scale of the web demands an automatic solution to the domain detection and adaptation problems. Furthermore, it is not obvious that human annotators can determine the optimal parsing models for each web page.

Our goal is to study this exact problem. We create a new parsing task, *multiple source parser adaptation*, designed to capture cross-domain performance along with evaluation metrics and baselines. Our new task involves training parsing models on labeled and unlabeled corpora from a variety of domains (*source domains*). This is in contrast to standard domain adaptation tasks where there is a single source domain. For evaluation, one is given a text (*target text*) but not the identity of its domain. The challenge is determining how to best use the available

Human Language Technologies: The 2010 Annual Conference of the North American Chapter of the ACL, pages 28–36,
Los Angeles, California, June 2010.

	Test						
Train	BNC	GENIA	BROWN	SWBD	ETT	WSJ	Average
GENIA	66.3	**83.6**	64.6	51.6	69.0	66.6	67.0
BROWN	81.0	71.5	**86.3**	79.0	80.9	80.6	79.9
SWBD	70.8	62.9	75.5	**89.0**	75.9	69.1	73.9
ETT	72.7	65.3	75.4	75.2	81.9	73.2	73.9
WSJ	**82.5**	74.9	83.8	78.5	**83.4**	**89.0**	**82.0**

Table 1: Cross-domain *f*-score performance of the Charniak (2000) parser. Averages are macro-averages. Performance drops as training and test domains diverge. On average, the WSJ model is the most accurate.

resources from training to maximize accuracy across multiple target texts.

Broadly put, we model how domain differences influence parsing accuracy. This is done by taking several computational measures of domain differences between the target text and each source domain. We use these features in a simple linear regression model which is trained to predict the accuracy of a parsing model (or, more generally, a mixture of parsing models) on a target text. To parse the target text, one simply uses the mixture of parsing models with the highest predicted accuracy. We show that our method is able to predict these accuracies quite well and thus effectively rank parsing models formed from mixtures of labeled and automatically labeled corpora.

In Section 2, we detail recent work on similar tasks. Our regression-based approach is covered in Section 3. We describe an evaluation strategy in Section 4. Section 5 presents new baselines which are intended to give a sense of current approaches and their limitations. The results of our experiments are detailed in Section 6 where we show that our system outperforms all non-oracle baselines. We conclude with a discussion and future work (Section 7).

2 Related work

The closest work to ours is Plank and Sima'an (2008), where unlabeled text is used to group sentences from WSJ into subdomains. The authors create a model for each subdomain which weights trees from its subdomain more highly than others. Given the domain specific models, they consider different parse combination strategies. Unfortunately, these methods do not yield a statistically significant improvement.

Multiple source domain adaptation has been done for other tasks (e.g. classification in (Blitzer et al., 2007; Daumé III, 2007; Dredze and Crammer, 2008)) and is related to multitask learning. Daumé III (2007) shows that an extremely simple method delivers solid performance on a number of domain adaptation classification tasks. This is achieved by making a copy of each feature for each source domain plus the "general" pseudodomain (for capturing domain independent features). This allows the classifier to directly model which features are domain-specific. Finkel and Manning (2009) demonstrate the hierarchical Bayesian extension of this where domain-specific models draw from a general base distribution. This is applied to classification (named entity recognition) as well as dependency parsing. These works describe how to train models in many different domains but sidestep the problem of domain detection. Thus, our work is orthogonal to theirs.

Our domain detection strategy draws on work in parser accuracy prediction (Ravi et al., 2008; Kawahara and Uchimoto, 2008). These works aim to predict the parser performance on a given target sentence. Ravi et al. (2008) frame this as a regression problem. Kawahara and Uchimoto (2008) treat it as a binary classification task and predict whether a specific parse is at a certain level of accuracy or higher. Ravi et al. (2008) show that their system can be used to return a ranking over different parsing models which we extend to the multiple domain setting. They also demonstrate that training their model on WSJ allows them to accurately predict parsing accuracy on the BROWN corpus. In contrast, our models are trained over multiple domains to model which factors influence cross-domain performance.

3 Approach

We start with the assumption that all target domains are mixtures of our source domains.[1] Intuitively, these mixtures should give higher probability mass to more similar source domains. This raises the question of how to measure the similarity between domains. Our method uses multiple complementary similarity measures between the target and each source. We feed these similarity measures into a regression model which learns how domain dissimilarities hurt parse accuracy. Thus, to parse a target domain, we need only find the input that maximizes the regression function — that is, the highest scoring mixture of source domains. Our system is similar to Ravi et al. (2008) in that both use regression to predict *f*-scores and some of the features are related.

3.1 Features

Our features are designed to help the regression model determine if a particular source domain mixture is well suited for a target domain as well as the quality of a source domain mixture. While we explored a large number of features, we present here only the three that were chosen by our feature selection method (Section 6.2).

Two of our features, COSINETOP50 and UNKWORDS, are designed to approximate how similar the target domain is to a specific source domain. Only the surface form of the target text and automatic analyses are available (e.g. we can tag or parse the target text, but cannot use gold tags or trees).

Relative word frequencies are an important indicator of domain. Cosine similarity uses a spatial representation to summarize the word frequencies in a corpus as a single vector. A common method is to represent each corpus as a vector of frequencies of the k most frequent words (Schütze, 1995). This method assigns high similarity to domains with a large amount of overlap in the high-frequency vocabulary items. We experimented with several orders of magnitude for k (our feature selection method later chose $k = 50$ — see Section 6.2).

Our second feature for comparing domains, UNKWORDS, returns the percentage of words in one domain which never appear in the other domain. This can be done on the word type or token level. We opt for tokens since unknown words pose problems for parsing each time they occur. UNKWORDS provides the percentage of words in the source domain that are never seen in the target domain. Whereas COSINETOP50 examines how similar the high frequency words are from one domain, UNKWORDS tends to focus on the overlap of low frequency words.

As described, COSINETOP50 and UNKWORDS are functions only of two source domains and do not take the mixing weights of source domains into account. We experimented with several methods of incorporating mixing weights into the feature value. In practice, the one which worked best for us is to divide the mixture weight of the source domain by the raw feature value. This has the nice property that when a source is not used, the adjusted feature value is zero regardless of the raw feature value.

From pilot studies, we learned that a uniform mixture of available source domains gave strong results (further details on this in Section 5). Our last feature, ENTROPY, is intended to let the regression system leverage this and measures the entropy of the distribution over source domains. This provides a sense of uniformity.

3.2 Predicting cross-domain accuracy

For a given source domain mixture, we can create a parsing model by linearly interpolating the parsing model statistics from each source domain. The key component of our approach is a domain-aware linear regression model which predicts how well a specific parsing model will do on a given target text. The linear regressor is given values from the three features from the previous section (COSINETOP50, UNKWORDS, and ENTROPY) and returns an estimate of the *f*-score the parsing model would achieve the target text.

Training data for the regressor consists of examples of source domain mixtures and their actual *f*-scores on target texts. To produce this, we randomly sampled source domain mixtures, created parsing models for those mixtures, and then evaluated the parsing models on all of our target texts.

We used a simple technique for randomly sam-

[1]This may seem like a major limitation, but as we will show later, our method works quite well at incorporating self-trained (automatically parsed) corpora which can typically be obtained for any domain.

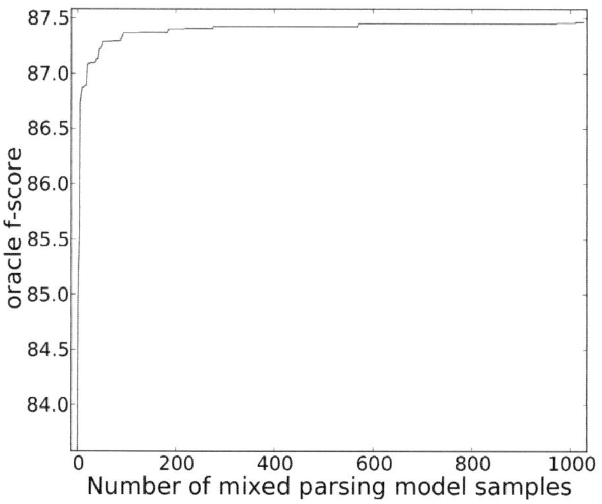

Figure 1: Cumulative oracle f-score (averaged over all target domains) as more models are randomly sampled. Most of the improvement comes the first 200 samples indicating that our samples seem to be sufficient to cover the space of good source domain mixtures.

pling source domain mixtures. First, we sample the number of source domains to use. We draw values from an exponential distribution and take their integer value until we obtain a number between two and the number of source domains. This is parametrized so that we typically only use a few corpora but still have some chance of using all of them. Once we know the number of source domains, we sample their identities uniformly at random without replacement from the list of all source domains. Finally, we sample the weights for the source domains uniformly from a simplex. The dimension of the simplex is the same as the number of source domains so we end up with a probability distribution over the sampled source domains.

In total, we sampled 1,040 source domain mixtures. We evaluated each of these source domain mixtures on the six target domains giving us 6,240 data points in total. One may be concerned that this is insufficient to cover the large space of source domain mixtures. However, we show in Figure 1 that only about 200 samples are sufficient to achieve good oracle performance[2] in practice.

Train		Test	
Source	Target	Source	Target
$\mathbf{C} \setminus \{t\}$	$\mathbf{C} \setminus \{t\}$	$\mathbf{C} \setminus \{t\}$	$\{t\}$

(a) Out-of-domain evaluation

Train		Test	
Source	Target	Source	Target
$\mathbf{C}$	$\mathbf{C} \setminus \{t\}$	$\mathbf{C}$	$\{t\}$

(b) In-domain evaluation

Table 2: List of domains allowed in single round of evaluation. In each round, the evaluation corpus is t. $\mathbf{C}$ is the set of all target domains.

4 Evaluation

Multiple-source domain adaptation is a new task for parsing and thus some thought must be given to evaluation methodology. We describe two evaluation scenarios which differ in how foreign the target text is from our source domains. Schemas for these evaluation scenarios are shown in Table 2. Note that training and testing here refer to training and testing of our regression model, **not** the parsing models.

In the first scenario, *out-of-domain evaluation*, one target domain is completely removed from consideration and only used to evaluate proposed models at test time. The regressor is trained on training points that use any of the remaining corpora, $\mathbf{C} \setminus \{t\}$, as sources or targets. For example, if $t =$ WSJ, we can train the regressor on all data points which don't use WSJ (or any self-trained corpora derived from WSJ) as a source or target domain. At test time, we are given the text of WSJ's test set. From this, our system creates a parsing model using the remaining available corpora for parsing the raw WSJ text.

This evaluation scenario is intended to evaluate how well our system can adapt to an entirely new domain with only raw text from the new domain (for example, parsing biomedical text when none is available in our list of source domains). Ideally, we would have a large number of web pages or other documents from other domains which we could use solely for evaluation. Unfortunately, at this time, only a handful of domains have been annotated with constituency structures under the same

[2]We calculate this by picking the best available model for each target domain and taking the average of their f-scores. This can pick different models for each target domain.

annotation guidelines. Instead, we hold out each hand-annotated domain, t, (including any automatically parsed corpora derived from that source domain) as a test set in a round-robin fashion.[3] For each round of the round robin we obtain an f-score and we report the mean and variance of the f-scores for each model.

The second scenario, *in-domain evaluation*, allows the target domain, t, to be used as a source domain in training but not as a target domain. This is intended to evaluate the situation where the target domain is not actually that different from our source domains. The in-domain evaluation can approximate how our system would perform when, for example, we have WSJ as a source domain and the target text is news from a source other than WSJ. Thus, our model still has to learn that WSJ and the North American News Text corpus (NANC) are good for parsing news text like WSJ without seeing any direct evaluations of the sort (WSJ and NANC can be used in models which are evaluated on all *other* corpora, though).

5 Baselines

Given that this is a new task for parsing, we needed to create baselines which demonstrate the current approaches to multiple-source domain adaptation. One approach is to take all available corpora and mix them together uniformly.[4] The UNIFORM baseline does exactly this using the available hand-built training corpora. SELF-TRAINED UNIFORM uses self-trained corpora as well. In the out-of-domain scenario, these exclude the held out domain, but in the in-domain setting, the held out domain is included. These baselines are similar to the ALL and WEIGHTED baselines in Daumé III (2007).

Another simple baseline is to use the same parsing model regardless of target domain. This is how large heterogeneous document collections are typically parsed currently. We use the WSJ corpus since it is the best single corpus for parsing all six target domains (see Table 1). We refer to this baseline as FIXED SET: WSJ. In the out-of-domain scenario, we fall back to SELF-TRAINED UNIFORM when the target domain is WSJ while the in-domain scenario uses the WSJ model throughout.

There are several interesting oracle baselines as well which serve to measure the limits of our approach. These baselines examine the resulting f-scores of models and pick the best model according to some criteria. The first oracle baseline is BEST SINGLE CORPUS which parses each corpus with the source domain that maximizes performance on the target domain. In almost all cases, this baseline selects each corpus to parse itself.

Our second oracle baseline, BEST SEEN, chooses the best parsing model from all those explored for each test set. Recall that while training the regression model in Section 3.2, we needed to explore many possible source domain mixtures to approximate the complete space of mixed parsing models. To the extent that we can fully explore the space of mixed parsing models, this baseline represents an upper bound for model mixing approaches. Since fully exploring the space of possible weightings is intractable, it is not a true upper bound. While it is theoretically possible to beat this pseudo-upper bound, (indeed, this is the mark of a good domain detection system) it is far from easy. We provide BEST SINGLE CORPUS and BEST SEEN for both in-domain and out-of-domain scenarios. The out-of-domain scenario restricts the set of possible models to those not including the target domain.

Finally, we searched for the BEST OVERALL MODEL. This is the model with the highest average f-score across all six target domains. This baseline can be thought of as an oracle version of FIXED SET: WSJ and demonstrates the limit of using a single parsing model regardless of target domain. Naturally, the very nature of this baseline places it only in the in-domain evaluation scenario. Since it was able to select the model according to f-scores on our six target domains, its performance on domains outside that set is not guaranteed.

To provide a better sense of the space of mixed parsing models, we also provide the WORST SEEN baseline which picks the worst model available for a specific target corpus.[5]

[3] Thus, the schemas in Table 2 are schemas for each round.

[4] Accounting for size so that the larger corpora don't overwhelm the smaller ones.

[5] This turns out to be GENIA for all corpora other than GENIA and SWBD when the target domain is GENIA.

6 Experiments

Our experiments use the Charniak (2000) generative parser. We describe the corpora used in our nine source and six target domains in Section 6.1. In Section 6.2, we provide a greedy strategy for picking features to include in our regression model. The results of our experiments are in Section 6.3.

6.1 Corpora

We aimed to include as many different domains as possible annotated under compatible schemes. We also tried to include human-annotated corpora and automatically labeled corpora (self-trained corpora as in McClosky et al. (2006a) which have been shown to work well across domains). Our final set includes text from news (WSJ, NANC), broadcast news (ETT), literature (BROWN, GUTENBERG), biomedical (GENIA, MEDLINE), spontaneous speech (SWBD), and the British National Corpus (BNC). In our experiments, self-trained corpora cannot be used as target domains since we lack gold annotations and BNC is not used as a source domain due to its size. An overview of our corpora is shown in Table 3.

We use news articles portion of the Wall Street Journal corpus (WSJ) from the Penn Treebank (Marcus et al., 1993) in conjunction with the self-trained North American News Text Corpus (NANC, Graff (1995)). The English Translation Treebank, ETT (Bies, 2007), is the translation[6] of broadcast news in Arabic. For literature, we use the BROWN corpus (Francis and Kučera, 1979) and the same division as (Gildea, 2001; Bacchiani et al., 2006; McClosky et al., 2006b). We also use raw sentences which we downloaded from Project Gutenberg[7] as a self-trained corpus. The Switchboard corpus (SWBD) consists of transcribed telephone conversations. While the original trees include disfluency information, we assume our speech corpora have had speech repairs excised (e.g. using a system such as Johnson et al. (2004)). Our biomedical data comes from the GENIA treebank[8] (Tateisi et al., 2005), a corpus of abstracts from the Medline database.[9] We downloaded additional sentences from Medline for our self-trained MEDLINE corpus. Unlike the other two self-trained corpora, we include two versions of MEDLINE. These differ on whether they were parsed using GENIA or WSJ as a base model to study the effect on cross-domain performance. Finally, we use a small number of sentences from the British National Corpus (BNC) (Foster and van Genabith, 2008).[10] The sentences were chosen randomly, so each one is potentially from a different domain. On the other hand, BNC can be thought of as its own domain in that it contains significant lexical differences from the American English used in our other corpora.

We preprocessed the corpora to standardize many of the annotation differences. Thus, our results on them may be slightly different than other works on these corpora. Nevertheless, these changes should not significantly impact overall the performance.

6.2 Feature selection

While our final model uses only three features, we considered many other possible features (not described due to space constraints). In order to explore these without hill climbing on our test data, we created a round-robin tuning scenario. Since the out-of-domain evaluation scenario holds out one target domain, this gives us six test evaluation rounds. For each of these six rounds, we hold out one of the remaining five target domains for tuning. This gives us 30 tuning evaluation rounds and we pick our features to optimize our aggregate performance over all of them. A model that performs well in this situation has proven that it has useful features which transfer to unknown target domains.

The next step is to determine the loss function to minimize. Our primary guide is *oracle f-score loss* which we determine as follows. We take all test data points (i.e. mixed parsing models evaluated on the target domain) and predict their f-scores with our model. In particular for this measure, we are interested in the point with the highest predicted f-score. We take its actual f-score which we call the *candidate f-score*. When tuning, we know the true f-scores of all test points. The difference between the highest f-score (the oracle f-score for

[6]The transcription and translation were done by humans.

[7]`http://gutenberg.org/`

[8]`http://www-tsujii.is.s.u-tokyo.ac.jp/GENIA/`

[9]`http://www.ncbi.nlm.nih.gov/PubMed/`

[10]`http://nclt.computing.dcu.ie/~jfoster/resources/`, downloaded January 8th, 2009.

Corpus	Source?	Target?	Average length	Train	Tune	Test
BNC		•	28.3	—	—	1,000
BROWN	•	•	20.0	19,786	2,082	2,439
ETT	•	•	25.6	2,639	1,029	1,166
GENIA	•	•	27.5	14,326	1,361	1,360
MEDLINE	•		27.2	278,192	—	—
SWBD	•	•	9.2	92,536	5,895	6,051
WSJ	•	•	25.5	39,832	1,346	2,416
NANC	•		23.2	915,794	—	—
GUTENBERG	•		26.2	689,782	—	—
MEDLINE	•		27.2	278,192	—	—

Table 3: List of source and target domains, sizes of each division in trees, and average sentence length. Indented rows indicate self-trained corpora parsed using the non-indented row as a base parser.

this dataset) and the candidate f-score is the oracle f-score loss. Ties need to be handled correctly to avoid degenerate models.[11] If there is a tie for highest predicted f-score, the candidate f-score is the one with the *lowest* actual f-score. This approach is conservative but ensures that regression models which give everything the same predicted f-score do not receive zero oracle f-score loss.

Armed with a tuning regime and a loss function, we created a procedure to pick the combination of features to use. We used a parallelized best-first search procedure. At each round, it expanded the current best set of features by adding or removing each feature where 'best' was determined by the loss function. We explored over 6,000 settings, though the best setting of (UNKWORDS, COSINETOP50, ENTROPY) was found within the first 200 settings explored. The best setting obtains an oracle f-score loss of 0.37 and a root mean squared error of 0.48 — these numbers are quite low and show the high accuracy of our regression model (similar to those in Ravi et al. (2008)). Additionally, the features are complementary in that UNKWORDS focuses on low frequency words whereas COSINETOP50 looks only at high frequency words and ENTROPY functions as a regularizer.

6.3 Results

We present an overview of our final results for out-of-domain and in-domain evaluation in Table 4. The results include the f-score macro-averaged over the six target domains and their standard deviation.

In both situations, the FIXED SET: WSJ baseline performs fairly poorly. Not surprisingly, assuming all of our target domains are close enough to WSJ works badly for our set of target domains and it does particularly poorly on SWBD and GENIA. On average, the UNIFORM baseline does slightly better for out-of-domain and over 3% better for in-domain. UNIFORM actually does fairly well on out-of-domain except on GENIA. In general, using more source domains is better which partially explains the success of UNIFORM. This seems to be the case since even if a source domain is terribly mismatched with the target domain, it may still be able to fill in some holes left by the other source domains. Of course, if it overpowers more relevant domains, performance may suffer. The SELF-TRAINED UNIFORM baseline uses even more source domains as well as the largest ones. In both scenarios, this dramatically improves performance and is the second best non-oracle system. This baseline provides more evidence as to the power of self-training for improving parser adaptation. If we excluded all self-trained corpora, our performance on this task would be substantially worse. We believe the self-trained corpora are beneficial in this task since they help reduce data sparsity of smaller corpora. The BEST SINGLE CORPUS baseline is poor in the out-of-domain scenario primarily because the actual best single corpus is excluded by the task specification in most cases. When we move to in-domain, this baseline improves

[11] For example, regression models which assign every parsing model the same f-score.

Oracle	Baseline or model	Average f-score
•	Worst seen	62.0 ± 6.1
•	Best single corpus	81.0 ± 2.9
	Fixed set: WSJ	81.0 ± 3.5
	Uniform	81.4 ± 3.6
	Self-trained uniform	83.4 ± 2.5
	Our model	84.0 ± 2.5
•	Best seen	84.3 ± 2.6

(a) Out-of-domain evaluation

Oracle	Baseline or model	Average f-score
	Fixed set: WSJ	82.0 ± 4.8
	Uniform	85.4 ± 2.4
•	Best single corpus	85.6 ± 2.9
	Self-trained uniform	86.1 ± 2.0
•	Best overall model	86.2 ± 1.9
	Our model	86.9 ± 2.4
•	Best seen	87.5 ± 2.1

(b) In-domain evaluation

Table 4: Baselines and final results for the two multiple-source domain adaptation evaluation scenarios. Results include f-scores, macro-averaged over all six target domains and their standard deviations.

but is still worse than SELF-TRAINED UNIFORM on average. It beats SELF-TRAINED UNIFORM primarily on WSJ, SWBD, and GENIA indicating that these three domains are best when not diluted by others. By definition, the WORST SEEN baseline does terribly, almost 20% worse then BEST SINGLE CORPUS.

Our model is the best non-oracle system for both evaluation scenarios. For out-of-domain evaluation, our system is only 0.3% worse than the BEST SEEN models for each target domain. For the in-domain scenario, we are within 0.6% of the BEST SEEN models. For a sense of scale, our out-of-domain and in-domain f-scores on WSJ are 83.1% and 89.8% respectively. Both numbers are quite close to the BEST SEEN baseline. Additionally, our model is 0.7% better than the BEST OVERALL MODEL. Recall that the BEST OVERALL MODEL is the single model with the best performance across all six target domains.[12] By beating this baseline, we show that there is value in customizing parsing models to the target domain. It is also interesting that the BEST OVERALL MODEL is only marginally better than SELF-TRAINED UNIFORM. Without any further information about the target corpus, an uninformed prior appears best.

7 Discussion

We have shown that for both out-of-domain and in-domain evaluations, our system is well adapted to predicting the effects of domain divergence on parsing accuracy. Using the parsing model with the highest predicted f-score leads to great performance in practice. There is a substantial benefit to doing this over existing approaches (using the same model for all domains or mixing all training data together uniformly). Creating a number of domain-specific models and mixing them together as needed is a viable approach.

One can think of our system as trying to estimate document-level context. Our representation of this context is simply a distribution over our source domains, but one can imagine more complex options such as a high-dimensional vector space. Additionally, our model separates domain and syntax estimation, but a future direction is to learn these jointly. This would combine our work with (Daumé III, 2007; Finkel and Manning, 2009).

We have focused on the Charniak (2000) parser, the first stage in the two stage Charniak and Johnson (2005) reranking parser. Applying our methods to other generative parsers (such as (Collins, 1999; Petrov and Klein, 2007)) is trivial, but it is less clear how our methods can be applied to the discriminative reranker component of the two stage parser. One avenue of approach is to incorporate the domain representation into the feature space, as in Daumé III (2007) but with more complex domain information.

Acknowledgments

This work was performed while the first author was at Brown and supported by DARPA GALE contract HR0011-06-2-0001. We would like to thank the BLLIP team and our anonymous reviewers for their comments.

[12] Somewhat surprisingly, the best overall model uses almost entirely self-trained corpora consisting of 9.5% GUTENBERG, 60.3% NANC, 26.0% MEDLINE (by GENIA), and 4.2% SWBD.

References

Michiel Bacchiani, Michael Riley, Brian Roark, and Richard Sproat. 2006. MAP adaptation of stochastic grammars. *Computer Speech and Language*, 20(1):41–68.

Ann Bies. 2007. *GALE Phase 3 Release 1 - English Translation Treebank*. Linguistic Data Consortium. LDC2007E105.

John Blitzer, Mark Dredze, and Fernando Pereira. 2007. Biographies, bollywood, boom-boxes and blenders: Domain adaptation for sentiment classification. In *Association for Computational Linguistics*, Prague, Czech Republic.

Xavier Carreras, Michael Collins, and Terry Koo. 2008. TAG, dynamic programming, and the perceptron for efficient, feature-rich parsing. In *Proceedings of CoNLL 2008*, pages 9–16, Manchester, England, August.

Eugene Charniak and Mark Johnson. 2005. Coarse-to-fine *n*-best parsing and MaxEnt discriminative reranking. In *Proceedings of the ACL 2005*, pages 173–180.

Eugene Charniak. 2000. A maximum-entropy-inspired parser. In *Proceedings of the North American Chapter of the ACL (NAACL)*, pages 132–139.

Michael Collins. 1999. *Head-driven Statistical Models for Natural Language Parsing*. Ph.D. thesis, The University of Pennsylvania.

Hal Daumé III. 2007. Frustratingly easy domain adaptation. In *Proceedings of ACL 2007*, Prague, Czech Republic.

Mark Dredze and Koby Crammer. 2008. Online methods for multi-domain learning and adaptation. In *Proceedings of the EMNLP 2008*, pages 689–697, Honolulu, Hawaii, October.

Jenny Rose Finkel and Christopher D. Manning. 2009. Hierarchical bayesian domain adaptation. In *Proceedings of HLT-NAACL 2009*, pages 602–610, Boulder, Colorado, June.

Jennifer Foster and Josef van Genabith. 2008. Parser evaluation and the bnc: Evaluating 4 constituency parsers with 3 metrics. In *Proceedings LREC 2008*, Marrakech, Morocco, May.

W. Nelson Francis and Henry Kučera. 1979. *Manual of Information to accompany a Standard Corpus of Present-day Edited American English,* for use with Digital Computers. Brown University, Providence, Rhode Island.

Daniel Gildea. 2001. Corpus variation and parser performance. In *Empirical Methods in Natural Language Processing (EMNLP)*, pages 167–202.

David Graff. 1995. *North American News Text Corpus*. Linguistic Data Consortium. LDC95T21.

Mark Johnson, Eugene Charniak, and Matthew Lease. 2004. An improved model for recognizing disfluencies in conversational speech. In *Proc. of the Rich Text 2004 Fall Workshop (RT-04F)*.

Daisuke Kawahara and Kiyotaka Uchimoto. 2008. Learning reliability of parses for domain adaptation of dependency parsing. In *Third International Joint Conference on Natural Language Processing (IJCNLP '08)*.

Mitchell P. Marcus, Beatrice Santorini, and Mary Ann Marcinkiewicz. 1993. Building a large annotated corpus of English: The Penn Treebank. *Comp. Linguistics*, 19(2):313–330.

David McClosky, Eugene Charniak, and Mark Johnson. 2006a. Effective self-training for parsing. In *Proceedings of HLT-NAACL 2006*, pages 152–159.

David McClosky, Eugene Charniak, and Mark Johnson. 2006b. Reranking and self-training for parser adaptation. In *Proceedings of COLING-ACL 2006*, pages 337–344, Sydney, Australia, July. Association for Computational Linguistics.

Slav Petrov and Dan Klein. 2007. Improved inference for unlexicalized parsing. In *Human Language Technologies 2007: The Conference of the North American Chapter of the Association for Computational Linguistics; Proceedings of the Main Conference*, pages 404–411, Rochester, New York, April. Association for Computational Linguistics.

Barbara Plank and Khalil Sima'an. 2008. Subdomain sensitive statistical parsing using raw corpora. In *Proceedings of the Sixth International Language Resources and Evaluation (LREC'08)*, Marrakech, Morocco, May.

Sujith Ravi, Kevin Knight, and Radu Soricut. 2008. Automatic prediction of parser accuracy. In *Proceedings of the 2008 Conference on Empirical Methods in Natural Language Processing*, pages 887–896, Honolulu, Hawaii, October. Association for Computational Linguistics.

Hinrich Schütze. 1995. Distributional part-of-speech tagging. In *Proceedings of the 7th conference of the EACL*, pages 141–148.

Satoshi Sekine. 1997. The domain dependence of parsing. In *Proc. Applied Natural Language Processing (ANLP)*, pages 96–102.

Jun Suzuki, Hideki Isozaki, Xavier Carreras, and Michael Collins. 2009. An empirical study of semi-supervised structured conditional models for dependency parsing. In *Proceedings EMNLP 2009*, pages 551–560, Singapore, August.

Yuka Tateisi, Akane Yakushiji, Tomoko Ohta, and Jun'ichi Tsujii. 2005. Syntax Annotation for the GENIA corpus. *Proceedings of IJCNLP 2005, Companion volume*, pages 222–227.

Appropriately Handled Prosodic Breaks Help PCFG Parsing

Zhongqiang Huang[1], **Mary Harper**[1,2]
[1]Laboratory for Computational Linguistics and Information Processing
Institute for Advanced Computer Studies
University of Maryland, College Park, MD USA
[2]Human Language Technology Center of Excellence
Johns Hopkins University, Baltimore, MD USA
{zqhuang,mharper}@umiacs.umd.edu

Abstract

This paper investigates using prosodic information in the form of ToBI break indexes for parsing spontaneous speech. We revisit two previously studied approaches, one that hurt parsing performance and one that achieved minor improvements, and propose a new method that aims to better integrate prosodic breaks into parsing. Although these approaches can improve the performance of basic probabilistic context free grammar (PCFG) parsers, they all fail to produce fine-grained PCFG models with latent annotations (PCFG-LA) (Matsuzaki et al., 2005; Petrov and Klein, 2007) that perform significantly better than the baseline PCFG-LA model that does not use break indexes, partially due to mis-alignments between automatic prosodic breaks and true phrase boundaries. We propose two alternative ways to restrict the search space of the prosodically enriched parser models to the n-best parses from the baseline PCFG-LA parser to avoid egregious parses caused by incorrect breaks. Our experiments show that all of the prosodically enriched parser models can then achieve significant improvement over the baseline PCFG-LA parser.

1 Introduction

Speech conveys more than a sequence of words to a listener. An important additional type of information that phoneticians investigate is called prosody, which includes phenomena such as pauses, pitch, energy, duration, grouping, and emphasis. For a review of the role of prosody in processing spoken language, see (Cutler et al., 1997). Prosody can help with the disambiguation of lexical meaning (via accents and tones) and sentence type (e.g., yes-no question versus statement), provide discourse-level information like focus, prominence, and discourse segment, and help a listener to discern a speaker's emotion or hesitancy, etc. Prosody often draws a listener's attention to important information through contrastive pitch or duration patterns associated words or phrases. In addition, prosodic cues can help one to segment speech into chunks that are hypothesized to have a hierarchical structure, although not necessarily identical to that of syntax. This suggests that prosodic cues may help in the parsing of speech inputs, the topic of this paper.

Prosodic information such as pause length, duration of words and phones, pitch contours, energy contours, and their normalized values have been used in speech processing tasks like sentence boundary detection (Liu et al., 2005). In contrast, other researchers use linguistic encoding schemes like ToBI (Silverman et al., 1992), which encodes tones, the degree of juncture between words, and prominence symbolically. For example, a simplified ToBI encoding scheme uses the symbol 4 for major intonational breaks, p for hesitation, and 1 for all other breaks (Dreyer and Shafran, 2007). In the literature, there have been several attempts to integrate prosodic information to improve parse accuracy of speech transcripts. These studies have used either quantized acoustic measurements of prosody or automatically detected break indexes.

Gregory et al. (2004) attempted to integrate quantized prosodic features as additional tokens in the same manner that punctuation marks are added into text. Although punctuation marks can significantly improve parse accuracy of newswire text, the quantized prosodic tokens were found harm-

Human Language Technologies: The 2010 Annual Conference of the North American Chapter of the ACL, pages 37–45,
Los Angeles, California, June 2010.

ful to parse accuracy when inserted into human-generated speech transcripts of the Switchboard corpus. The authors hypothesized that the inserted pseudo-punctuation break n-gram dependencies in the parser model, leading to lower accuracies. However, another possible cause is that the prosody has not been effectively utilized due to the fact that it is overloaded; it not only provides information about phrases, but also about the state of the speaker and his/her sentence planning process. Hence, the prosodic information may at times be more harmful than helpful to parsing performance.

In a follow-on experiment, Kahn et al. (2005), instead of using raw quantized prosodic features, used three classes of automatically detected ToBI break indexes (1, 4, or p) and their posteriors. Rather than directly incorporating the breaks into the parse trees, they used the breaks to generate additional features for re-ranking the n-best parse trees from a generative parsing model trained without prosody. They were able to obtain a significant 0.6% improvement on Switchboard over the generative parser, and a more modest 0.1% to 0.2% improvement over the reranking model that also utilizes syntactic features.

Dreyer and Shafran (2007) added prosodic breaks into a generative parsing model with latent variables. They utilized three classes of ToBI break indexes (1, 4, and p), automatically predicted by the approach described in (Dreyer and Shafran, 2007; Harper et al., 2005). Breaks were modeled as a sequence of observations parallel to the sentence and each break was generated by the preterminal of the preceding word, assuming that the observation of a break, b, was conditionally independent of its preceding word, w, given preterminal X:

$$P(w, b|X) = P(w|X)P(b|X) \quad (1)$$

Their approach has advantages over (Gregory et al., 2004) in that it does not break n-gram dependencies in parse modeling. It also has disadvantages in that the breaks are modeled by preterminals rather than higher level nonterminals, and thus cannot directly affect phrasing in a basic PCFG grammar. However, they addressed this independence drawback by splitting each nonterminal into latent tags so that the impact of prosodic breaks could be percolated into the phrasing process through the interaction of latent tags. They achieved a minor 0.2% improvement over their baseline model without prosodic cues and also found that prosodic breaks can be used to build more compact grammars.

In this paper, we re-investigate the models of (Gregory et al., 2004) and (Dreyer and Shafran, 2007), and propose a new way of modeling that can potentially address the shortcomings of the two previous approaches. We also attribute part of the failure or ineffectiveness of the previously investigated approaches to errors in the quantized prosodic tokens or automatic break indexes, which are predicted based only on acoustic cues and could misalign with phrase boundaries. We illustrate that these prosodically enriched models are in fact highly effective if we systematically eliminate bad phrase and hesitation breaks given their projection onto the reference parse trees. Inspired by this, we propose two alternative rescoring methods to restrict the search space of the prosodically enriched parser models to the n-best parses from the baseline PCFG-LA parser to avoid egregious parse trees. The effectiveness of our rescoring method suggests that the reranking approach of (Kahn et al., 2005) was successful not only because of their prosodic feature design, but also because they restrict the search space for reranking to n-best lists generated by a syntactic model alone.

2 Experimental Setup

Due to our goal of investigating the effect of prosodic information on the accuracy of state of the art parsing of conversational speech, we utilize both Penn Switchboard (Godfrey et al., 1992) and Fisher treebanks (Harper et al., 2005; Bies et al., 2006), for which we also had automatically generated break indexes from (Dreyer and Shafran, 2007; Harper et al., 2005)[1]. The Fisher treebank is a higher quality parsing resource than Switchboard due to its greater use of audio and refined specifications for sentence segmentation and disfluency markups, and so we utilize its eval set for our parser evaluation; the first 1,020 trees (7,184 words) were used for development and the remaining 3,917 trees (29,173 words) for evaluation. We utilized the Fisher dev1 and dev2 sets containing 16,519 trees (112,717 words) as the main training data source and used the Penn Switchboard

[1]A small fraction of words in the Switchboard treebank could not be aligned with the break indexes that were produced based on a later refinement of the transcription. We chose not to alter the Switchboard treebank, so in cases of missing break values, we heuristically added break *1* to words in the middle of a sentence and *4* to words that end a sentence.

treebank containing 110,504 trees (837,863 words) as an additional training source to evaluate the effect of training data size on parsing performance. The treebank trees are normalized by downcasing all terminal strings and deleting punctuation, empty nodes, and nonterminal-yield unary rules that are not related to edits.

We will compare[2] three prosodically enriched PCFG models described in the next section, with a baseline PCFG parser. We will also utilize a state of the art PCFG-LA parser (Petrov and Klein, 2007; Huang and Harper, 2009) to examine the effect of prosodic enrichment[3]. Unlike (Kahn et al., 2005), we do not remove EDITED regions prior to parsing because parsing of EDITED regions is likely to benefit from prosodic information. Also, parses from all models are compared with the gold standard parses in the Fisher evaluation set using SParseval bracket scoring (Harper et al., 2005; Roark et al., 2006) without flattening the EDITED constituents.

3 Methods of Integrating Breaks

Rather than using quantized raw acoustic features as in (Gregory et al., 2004), we use automatically generated ToBI break indexes as in (Dreyer and Shafran, 2007; Kahn et al., 2005) as the prosodic cues, and investigate three alternative methods of modeling prosodic breaks. Figure 1 shows parse trees for the four models for processing the spontaneous speech transcription *she's she would do*, where the speaker hesitated after saying *she's* and then resumed with another utterance *she would do*. Each word input into the parser has an associated break index represented by the symbol 1, 4, or p enclosed in asterisks indicating the break after the word. The automatically detected break *4* after the contraction is a strong indicator of an intonational phrase boundary that might provide helpful information for parsing if modeled appropriately. Figure 1 (a) shows the reference parse tree (thus the name REGULAR) where the break indexes are not utilized.

The first method to incorporate break indexes, BRKINSERT, shown in Figure 1 (b), treats the *p* and *4* breaks as tokens, placing them under the

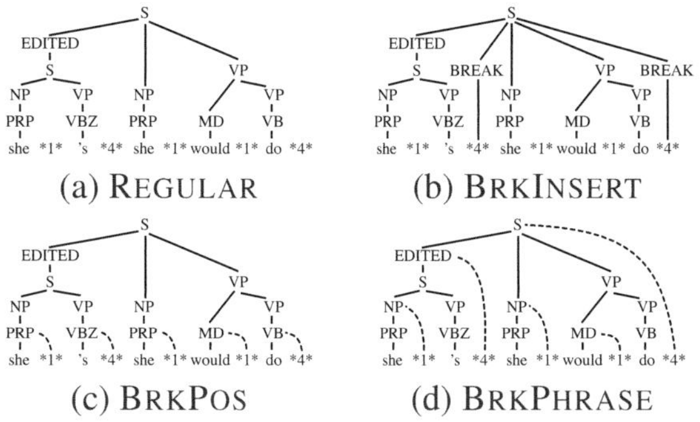

Figure 1: Modeling Methods

highest nonterminal nodes so that the order of words and breaks remain unchanged in the terminals. This is similar to (Gregory et al., 2004), except that automatically generated ToBI breaks are used rather than quantized raw prosodic tokens.

The second method, BRKPOS, shown in Figure 1 (c), treats breaks as a sequence of observations parallel to the words in the sentence as in (Dreyer and Shafran, 2007). The dotted edges in Figure 1 (c) represent the relation between preterminals and prosodic breaks, and we call them *prosodic rewrites*, with analogy to grammar rewrites and lexical rewrites. The generation of words and prosodic breaks is assumed to be conditionally independent given the preterminal, as in Equation 1.

The third new method, BRKPHRASE, shown in Figure 1 (d), also treats breaks as a sequence of observations parallel to the sentence; however, rather than associating the prosodic breaks with the preterminals, each is generated by the highest nonterminal (including preterminal) in the parse tree that covers the preceding word as the right-most terminal. The observation of break, b, is assumed to be conditionally independent of grammar or lexical rewrite, r, given the nonterminal X:

$$P(r, b|X) = P(r|X)P(b|X) \qquad (2)$$

The relation is indicated by the dotted edges in Figure 1 (d), and it is also called a *prosodic rewrite*. The potential advantage of BRKPHRASE is that it does not break or fragment n-gram dependencies of the grammar rewrites, as in the BRKINSERT method, and it directly models the dependency between breaks and phrases, which the BRKPOS method explicitly lacks.

4 Model Training

Since automatically generated prosodic breaks are incorporated into the parse trees deterministi-

[2]We use Bikel's randomized parsing evaluation comparator to determine the significance ($p < 0.005$) of the difference between two parsers' outputs.

[3]Due to the randomness of parameter initialization in the learning of PCFG-LA models with increasing numbers of latent tags, we train each latent variable grammar with 10 different seeds and report the average F score on the evaluation set.

cally for all of the three enrichment methods (BRKINSERT, BRKPOS, and BRKPHRASE), training a basic PCFG is straightforward; we simply pull the counts of grammar rules, lexical rewrites, or prosodic rewrites from the treebank and normalize them to obtain their probabilities.

As is well known in the parsing community, the basic PCFG does not provide state-of-the-art performance due to its strong independence assumptions. We can relax these assumptions by explicitly incorporating more information into the conditional history, as in Charniak's parser (Charniak, 2000); however, this would require sophisticated engineering efforts to decide what to include in the history and how to smooth probabilities appropriately due to data sparsity. In this paper, we utilize PCFG-LA models (Matsuzaki et al., 2005; Petrov and Klein, 2007) that split each nonterminal into a set of latent tags and learn complex dependencies among the latent tags automatically during training. The resulting model is still a PCFG, but it is probabilistically context free on the latent tags, and the interaction among the latent tags is able to implicitly capture higher order dependencies among the original nonterminals and observations. We follow the approach in (Huang and Harper, 2009) to train the PCFG-LA models.

5 Parsing

In a basic PCFG without latent variables, the goal of maximum probability parsing is to find the most likely parse tree given a sentence based on the grammar. Suppose our grammar is binarized (so it contains only unary and binary grammar rules). Given an input sentence $w_1^n = w_1, w_2, \cdots, w_n$, the inside probability, $P(i, j, X)$, of the most likely sub-tree that is rooted at nonterminal X and generates subsequence w_i^j can be computed recursively by:

$$P(i,j,X) = \max(\max_Y P(i,j,Y)P(X \to Y), \max_{i<k<j,Y,Z} P(i,k,Y)P(k+1,j,Z)P(X \to Y\,Z)) \quad (3)$$

Backtracing the search process then returns the most likely parse tree for the REGULAR grammar.

The same parsing algorithm can be directly applied to the BRKINSERT grammar given that the break indexes are inserted appropriately into the input sentence as additional tokens. Minor modification is needed to extend the same parsing algorithm to the BRKPOS grammar. The only difference is that the inside probability of a preterminal is set according to Equation 1. The rest of the algorithm proceeds as in Equation 3.

However, parsing with the BRKPHRASE grammar is more complicated because whether a nonterminal generates a break or not is determined by whether it is the highest nonterminal that covers the preceding word as its right-most terminal. In this case, the input observation also contains a sequence of break indexes $b_1^n = b_1, b_2, \cdots, b_n$ that is parallel to the input sentence $w_1^n = w_1, w_2, \cdots, w_n$. Let $P(i, j, X, 0)$ be the probability of the most likely sub-tree rooted at nonterminal X over span (i, j) that generates word sequence w_i^j, as well as break index sequence b_i^{j-1}, excluding b_j. According to the independence assumption in Equation 2, with the addition of prosodic edge $X \to b_j$, the same sub-tree also has the highest probability, denoted by $P(i, j, X, 1)$, of generating word sequence w_i^j together with the break index sequence b_i^j. Thus we have:

$$P(i,j,X,1) = P(i,j,X,0)P(b_j|X) \quad (4)$$

The structural constraint that a break index is only generated by the highest nonterminal that covers the preceding word as the right-most terminal enables a dynamic programming algorithm to compute $P(i, j, X, 0)$ and thus $P(i, j, X, 1)$ efficiently. If the sub-tree (without the prosodic edge that generates b_j) over span (i, j) is constructed from a unary rule rewrite $X \to Y$, then the root nonterminal Y of some best sub-tree over the same span (i, j) can not generate break b_j because it has a higher nonterminal X that also covers word w_j as its right-most terminal. If the sub-tree is constructed from a binary rule rewrite $X \to Y Z$, then the root nonterminal Y of some best sub-tree over some span (i, k) will generate break b_k because Y is the highest nonterminal that covers word w_k as the right-most terminal[4]. In contrast, the root nonterminal Z of some best sub-tree over some span $(k+1, j)$ can not generate break b_j because Z has a higher nonterminal X that also covers word w_j as its right-most terminal. Hence,

[4]Use of left-branching is required for the BRKPHRASE method to ensure that the prosodic breaks are associated with the original nonterminals, not intermediate nonterminals introduced by binarization. Binarization is needed for efficient parametrization of PCFG-LA models and left- versus right-branching binarization does not significantly affect model performance; hence, we use left-branching for all models.

$P(i,j,X,1)$ and $P(i,j,X,0)$ can be computed recursively by Equation 4 above and Equation 5 below:

$$P(i,j,X,0) = \max(\max_{Y} P(i,j,Y,0)P(X \rightarrow Y),$$
$$\max_{i<k<j,Y,Z} P(i,k,Y,1)P(k+1,j,Z,0)P(X \rightarrow Y\ Z)) \quad (5)$$

Although dynamic programming algorithms exist for maximum probability decoding of basic PCFGs without latent annotations for all four methods, it is an NP hard problem to find the most likely parse tree using PCFG-LA models. Several alternative decoding algorithms have been proposed in the literature for parsing with latent variable grammars. We use the best performing max-rule-product decoding algorithm, which searches for the best parse tree that maximizes the product of the posterior rule (either grammar, lexical, or prosodic) probabilities, as described in (Petrov and Klein, 2007) for our models with latent annotations and extend the dynamic parsing algorithm described in Equation 5 for the BRKPHRASE grammar with latent annotations.

6 Results on the Fisher Corpus

6.1 Prosodically Enriched Models

Table 1 reports the parsing accuracy of the four basic PCFGs without latent annotations when trained on the Fisher training data. All of the grammars have a low F score of around 65% due to the overly strong and incorrect independence assumptions. We observe that the BRKPHRASE grammar benefits most from breaks, significantly improving the baseline accuracy from 64.9% to 67.2%, followed by the BRKINSERT grammar, which at 66.2% achieves a smaller improvement. The BRKPOS grammar benefits the least among the three because breaks are attached to the preterminals and thus have less impact on phrasing due to the independence assumptions in the basic PCFG. In contrast, both the BRKPHRASE and BRKINSERT methods directly model the relationship between breaks and phrase boundaries through governing nonterminals; however, the BRKPHRASE method does not directly change any of the grammar rules in contrast to the BRKINSERT method that more or less breaks n-gram dependencies and fragments rule probabilities.

The bars labeled DIRECT in Figure 2 report the parsing performance of the four PCFG-LA models trained on Fisher. The introduction of latent annotations significantly boosts parsing accuracies, providing relative improvements ranging from 16.8% up to 19.0% when trained on Fisher training data due to the fact that the PCFG-LA models are able to automatically learn more complex dependencies not captured by basic PCFGs.

REGULAR	BRKINSERT	BRKPOS	BRKPHRASE
64.9	66.2	65.2	**67.2**

Table 1: Fisher evaluation parsing results for the basic PCFGs without latent annotations trained on the Fisher training set.

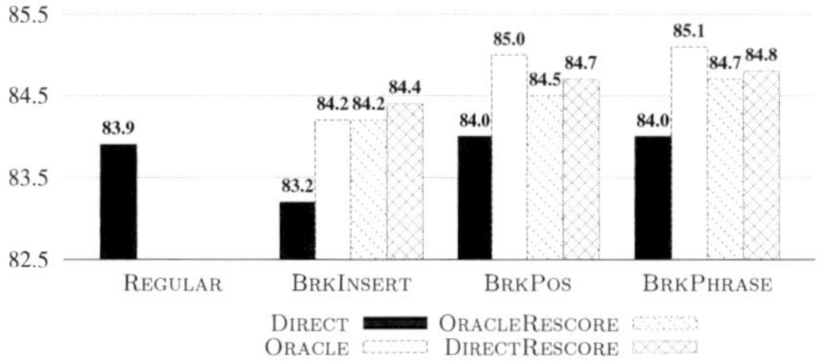

Figure 2: Parsing results on the Fisher evaluation set of the PCFG-LA models trained on the Fisher training data. The DIRECT bars represent direct parsing results for models trained and evaluated on the original data, ORACLE bars for models trained and evaluated on the modified oracle data (see Subsection 6.2), and the ORACLERESCORE and DIRECTRESCORE bars for results of the two rescoring approaches (described in Subsection 6.3) on the original evaluation data.

However, the prosodically enriched methods do not significantly improve upon the REGULAR baseline after the introduction of latent annotations. The BRKPHRASE method only achieves a minor insignificant 0.1% improvement over the REGULAR baseline; whereas, the BRKINSERT method is a significant 0.7% worse than the baseline. Similar results for BRKINSERT were reported in (Gregory et al., 2004), where they attributed the degradation to the fact that the insertion of the prosodic "punctuation" breaks the n-gram dependencies. Another possible cause is that the insertion of "bad" breaks that do not align with true phrase boundaries hurts performance more than the benefits gained from "good" breaks due to the tightly integrated relationship between phrases and breaks. For the BRKPOS method, the impact of break indexes is implicitly percolated to the nonterminals through the interaction among latent tags, as discussed in (Dreyer and Shafran, 2007), and its performance may thus be less affected by the "bad" breaks. With latent annotations (in contrast to the basic PCFG), the model is now significantly better than BRKINSERT and is on par with BRKPHRASE.

6.2 Models with Oracle Breaks

In order to determine whether "bad" breaks limit the improvements in parsing performance from prosodic enrichment, we conducted a simple oracle experiment where all *p* and *4* breaks that did not align with phrase boundaries in the treebank were systematically converted to *1* breaks[5]. When trained and evaluated on this modified oracle data, all three prosodically enriched latent variable models improve by about 1% and were then able to achieve significant improvements over the REGULAR PCFG-LA baseline, as shown by the bars labeled ORACLE in Figure 2. It should be noted, however, that the BRKINSERT method is much less effective than the other two methods in the oracle experiment, suggesting that broken n-gram dependencies affect the model in addition to the erroneous breaks.

6.3 N-Best Re-Scoring

As mentioned previously, prosody does not only provide information about phrases, but also about the state of the speaker and his/her sentence planning process. Given that our break detector utilizes only acoustic knowledge to predict breaks, the recognized *p* and *4* breaks may not correctly reflect hesitations and phrase boundaries. Incorrectly recognized breaks could hurt parsing more than the benefit brought from the correctly recognized breaks, as demonstrated by superior performance of the prosodically enhanced models in the oracle experiment. We next describe two alternative methods to make better use of automatic breaks.

In the first approach, which is called ORACLERESCORE, we train the prosodically enhanced grammars on cleaned-up break-annotated training data, where misclassified *p* and *4* breaks are converted to *1* breaks (as in the oracle experiment). If these grammars were used to directly parse the test sentences with automatically detected (unmodified) breaks, the results would be quite poor due to mismatch between the training and testing conditions. However, we can automatically bias against potentially misclassified *p* and *4* breaks if we utilize information provided by n-best parses from the baseline REGULAR PCFG-LA grammar. For each hypothesized parse tree in the n-best list, the *p* and *4* breaks that do not align with the phrase boundaries of the hypothesized parse tree are converted to *1* breaks, and then a new score is computed using the product of posterior rule probabilities[6], as in the max-rule-product criterion, for the hypothesized parse tree using the grammars trained on the cleaned-up training data. In this approach, we convert the posterior probability, $P(T|W,B)$, of parse tree T given words W and breaks B to $P(B'|W,B)P(T|W,B')$, where B' is the new break sequence constrained by T, and simplify it to $P(T|W,B')$, assuming that conversions to a new sequence of breaks as constrained by a hypothesized parse tree are equally probable given the original sequence of breaks. We consider this to be a reasonable assumption for a small n-best ($n = 50$) list with reasonably good quality.

In the second approach, called DIRECTRESCORE, we train the prosodically enhanced PCFG-LA models using unmodified, automatic breaks, and then use them to rescore the n-best lists produced by the REGULAR PCFG-LA model to avoid the poorer parse trees caused by fully trusting automatic break indexes. The size of the n-best list should not be too small or too large, or the results would be like directly parsing with REGULAR when $n = 1$ or with the prosodically enriched model when $n \to \infty$.

The ORACLERESCORE and DIRECTRESCORE bars in Figure 2 report the performance of the prosodically enriched models with the corresponding rescoring method. Both methods use the same 50-best lists produced by the baseline REGULAR PCFG-LA model using the max-rule-product criterion. Both rescoring methods produce significant improvements in the performance of all three prosodically enriched PCFG-LA models. The previously ineffective (0.7% worse than REGULAR) BRKINSERT PCFG-LA model is now 0.3% and 0.5% better than the REGULAR baseline using the ORACLERESCORE and DIRECTRESCORE approaches, respectively. The best performing BRKPOS and BRKPHRASE rescoring models are 0.6-0.9% better than the REGULAR baseline. It is interesting to note that rescoring with models trained on cleaned up prosodic breaks is somewhat poorer

[5]Other sources of errors include misclassification of *p* breaks as *1* or *4* and misclassification of *4* breaks as *1* or *p*. Although these errors are not repaired in the oracle experiment, fixing them could potentially provide greater gains.

[6]The product of posterior rule probabilities of a parse tree is more suitable for rescoring than the joint probability of the parse tree and the observables (words and breaks) because the breaks are possibly different for different trees.

than models trained using all automatic breaks.

7 Models with Augmented Training Data

Figure 3 reports the evaluation results for models that are trained on the combination of Fisher and Switchboard training data. With the additional Switchboard training data, the nonterminals can be split into more fine-grained latent tags, enabling the learning of deeper dependencies without over-fitting the limited sized Fisher training data. This improved all models by at least 2.6% absolute. Note also that the patterns observed for models trained using the larger training set are quite similar to those from using the smaller training set in Figure 2. The prosodically enriched models all benefit significantly from the oracle breaks and from the rescoring methods. The BRKPOS and BRKPHRASE methods, with the additional training data, also achieve significant improvements over the REGULAR baseline without rescoring.

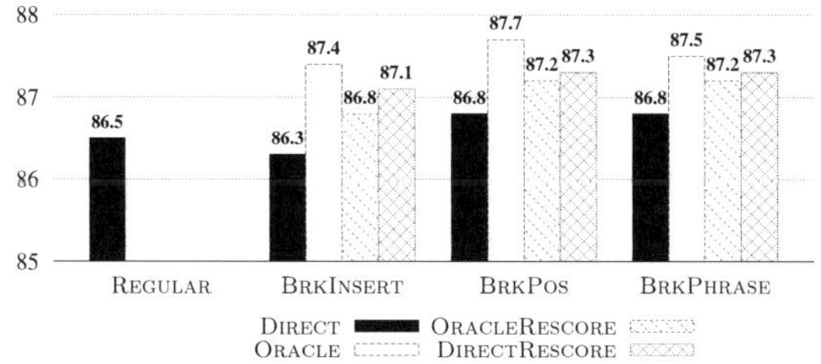

Figure 3: Parsing results on the Fisher evaluation set of the PCFG-LA models trained on the Fisher+Switchboard training data.

8 Error Analysis

In this section, we compare the errors of the BRKPHRASE PCFG-LA model and the DIRECTRESCORE approach for that model to each other and to the baseline PCFG-LA model without prosodic breaks. All models are trained and tested on Fisher as in Section 6. The results using other prosodically enhanced PCFG-LA models and their rescoring alternatives show similar patterns.

Figure 4 depicts the difference in F scores between BRKPHRASE and REGULAR and between BRKPHRASE+DIRECTRESCORE and REGULAR on a tree-by-tree basis in a 2D plot. Each quadrant also contains +/– signs roughly describing how much BRKPHRASE+DIRECTRESCORE is better (+) or worse (–) than BRKPHRASE and a pair of numbers (a, b), in which a represents the percentage of sentences in that quadrant containing *p* or *4* breaks that do not align with true phrase boundaries, and b represents the percentage of such *p* and *4* breaks among the total number of *p* and *4* breaks in that quadrant.

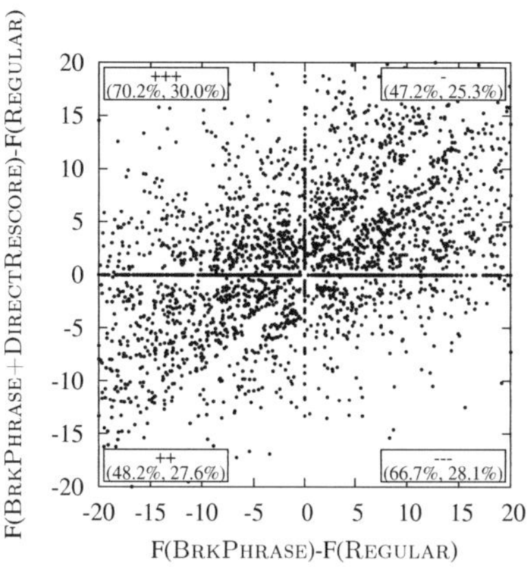

Figure 4: 2D plot of the difference in F scores between BRKPHRASE and REGULAR and between BRKPHRASE+DIRECTRESCORE and REGULAR, on a tree-by-tree basis, where each dot represents a test sentence. Each quadrant also contains +/– signs roughly describing how much BRKPHRASE+DIRECTRESCORE is better (+) or worse (–) than BRKPHRASE and a pair of numbers (a, b), in which a represents the percentage of sentences in that quadrant containing *p* or *4* breaks that do not align with true phrase boundaries, and b represents the percentage of such *p* and *4* breaks among the total number of *p* and *4* breaks in that quadrant.

Each dot in the top-right quadrant represents a test sentence for which both BRKPHRASE and BRKPHRASE+DIRECTRESCORE produce better trees than the baseline REGULAR PCFG-LA model. The BRKPHRASE+DIRECTRESCORE approach is on average slightly worse than the BRKPHRASE method (hence the single minus sign), although it also often produces better parses than BRKPHRASE alone. In contrast, the BRKPHRASE+DIRECTRESCORE approach on average makes many fewer errors than BRKPHRASE (hence + +) as can be observed in the bottom-left quadrant, where both approaches produce worse parse trees than the REGULAR baseline. The most interesting quadrant is on the top-left where the BRKPHRASE approach always produces worse parses than the REGULAR baseline while the BRKPHRASE+DIRECTRESCORE approach is able to avoid these errors while producing better parses than the baseline (hence + + +). Although the BRKPHRASE+DIRECTRESCORE approach can also produce worse parses than REGULAR, as in the bottom-right quadrant (hence – – –), altogether the quadrants suggest that, by restricting the search space to the n-best lists produced by the baseline REGULAR parser, the BRKPHRASE+DIRECTRESCORE approach is able to avoid many bad parses trees at the expense of somewhat poorer parses in cases when BRKPHRASE is able to benefit from the full search space.

The reader should note that the top-left quadrant of Figure 4 has the highest percentage (70.2%) of sentences with "bad" *p* and *4* breaks and the highest percentage (30.0%) of such "bad" breaks among all breaks. This evidence supports our argument that "bad" breaks are harmful to parsing performance and some parse errors caused by misleading breaks can be resolved by limiting the search space of the prosodically enriched models to the n-best lists produced by the baseline REGULAR parser. However, the significant presence of "bad" breaks in the top-right quadrant also suggests that the prosodically enriched models are able to produce better parses than the baseline despite the presence of "bad" breaks, probably because the models are trained on the mixture of both "good" and "bad" breaks and are able to somehow learn to use "good" breaks while avoiding being misled by "bad" breaks.

	REGULAR	BRKPHRASE	BRKPHRASE +DIRECTRESCORE
NP	90.4	90.4	**90.9**
VP	84.7	84.7	**85.6**
S	84.4	84.3	**85.2**
INTJ	93.0	**93.4**	**93.4**
PP	76.5	76.7	**77.9**
EDITED	60.4	62.2	**63.3**
SBAR	67.2	67.0	**68.8**

Table 2: F scores of the seven most frequent non-terminals of the REGULAR, BRKPHRASE, and BRKPHRASE+DIRECTRESCORE models.

Table 2 reports the F scores of the seven most frequent phrases for the REGULAR, BRKPHRASE, and BRKPHRASE+DIRECTRESCORE methods trained on Fisher. When comparing the BRKPHRASE method to REGULAR, the break indexes help to improve the score for edits most, followed by interjections and prepositional phrases; however, they do not improve the accuracy of any of the other phrases. The BRKPHRASE+DIRECTRESCORE approach obtains improvements on all of the major phrases.

Figure 5 (a) shows a reference parse tree of a test sentence. The REGULAR approach correctly parses the first half (omitted) of the sentence but it fails to correctly interpret the second half (as shown). The BRKPHRASE approach, in contrast, is misguided by the incorrectly classified interruption point *p* after word "has", and so produces an incorrect parse early in the sentence. The BRKPHRASE+DIRECTRESCORE approach is able to provide the correct tree given the n-best list produced by the REGULAR approach, despite the break index errors.

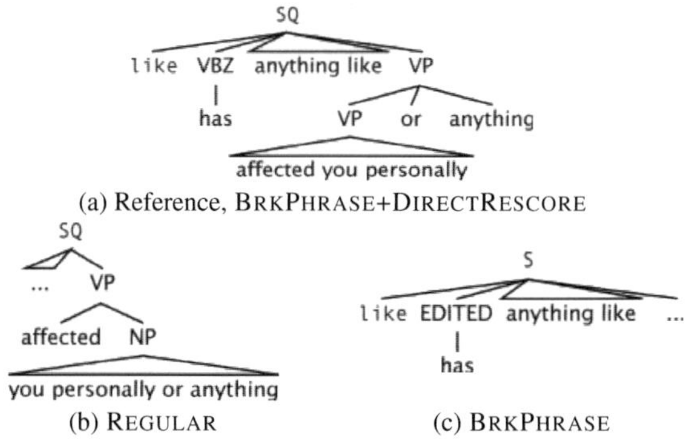

Figure 5: Parses for *like*$_{*1*}$ *has*$_{*p*}$ *anything*$_{*1*}$ *like*$_{*1*}$ *affected*$_{*1*}$ *you*$_{*4*}$ *personally*$_{*4*}$ *or*$_{*1*}$ *anything*$_{*4*}$

9 Conclusions

We have investigated using prosodic information in the form of automatically detected ToBI break indexes for parsing spontaneous speech by comparing three prosodic enrichment methods. Although prosodic enrichment improves the basic PCFGs, that performance gain disappears when latent variables are used, partly due to the impact of misclassified ("bad") breaks that are assigned to words that do not occur at phrase boundaries. However, we find that by simply restricting the search space of the three prosodically enriched latent variable parser models to the n-best parses from the baseline PCFG-LA parser, all of them attain significant improvements. Our analysis more fully explains the positive results achieved by (Kahn et al., 2005) from reranking with prosodic features and suggests that the hypothesis that inserted prosodic punctuation breaks n-gram dependencies only partially explains the negative results of (Gregory et al., 2004). Our findings from the oracle experiment suggest that integrating ToBI classification with syntactic parsing should increase the accuracy of both tasks.

Acknowledgments

We would like to thank Izhak Shafran for providing break indexes for Fisher and Switchboard and for comments on an earlier draft of this paper. This research was supported in part by NSF IIS-0703859. Opinions, findings, and recommendations expressed in this paper are those of the authors and do not necessarily reflect the views of the funding agency or the institutions where the work was completed.

References

Ann Bies, Stephanie Strassel, Haejoong Lee, Kazuaki Maeda, Seth Kulick, Yang Liu, Mary Harper, and Matthew Lease. 2006. Linguistic resources for speech parsing. In *LREC*.

Eugene Charniak. 2000. A maximum-entropy-inspired parser. In *ACL*.

Anne Cutler, Delphine Dahan, and Wilma v an Donselaar. 1997. Prosody in comprehension of spoken language: A literature review. *Language and Speech*.

Markus Dreyer and Izhak Shafran. 2007. Exploiting prosody for PCFGs with latent annotations. In *Interspeech*.

John J. Godfrey, Edward C. Holliman, and Jane McDaniel. 1992. SWITCHBOARD: Telephone speech corpus for research and development. In *ICASSP*.

Michelle L. Gregory, Mark Johnson, and Eugene Charniak. 2004. Sentence-internal prosody does not help parsing the way punctuation does. In *NAACL*.

Mary P. Harper, Bonnie J. Dorr, John Hale, Brian Roark, Izhak Shafran, Matthew Lease, Yang Liu, Matthew Snover, Lisa Yung, Anna Krasnyanskaya, and Robin Stewart. 2005. 2005 Johns Hopkins Summer Workshop Final Report on Parsing and Spoken Structural Event Detection. Technical report, Johns Hopkins University.

Zhongqiang Huang and Mary Harper. 2009. Self-training PCFG grammars with latent annotations across languages. In *EMNLP*.

Jeremy G. Kahn, Matthew Lease, Eugene Charniak, Mark Johnson, and Mari Ostendorf. 2005. Effective use of prosody in parsing conversational speech. In *EMNLP-HLT*.

Yang Liu, Andreas Stolcke, Elizabeth Shriberg, and Mary Harper. 2005. Using conditional random fields for sentence boundary detection in speech. In *ACL*.

Takuya Matsuzaki, Yusuke Miyao, and Jun'ichi Tsujii. 2005. Probabilistic CFG with latent annotations. In *ACL*.

Slav Petrov and Dan Klein. 2007. Improved inference for unlexicalized parsing. In *HLT-NAACL*.

Brian Roark, Mary Harper, Yang Liu, Robin Stewart, Matthew Lease, Matthew Snover, Izhak Shafran, Bonnie J. Dorr, John Hale, Anna Krasnyanskaya, and Lisa Yung. 2006. Sparseval: Evaluation metrics for parsing speech. In *LREC*.

Kim Silverman, Mary Beckman, John Pitrelli, Mari Ostendorf, Colin Wightman, Patti Price, Janet Pierrehumbert, and Julia Hirshberg. 1992. ToBI: A standard for labeling English prosody. In *ICSLP*.

Using Confusion Networks for Speech Summarization

Shasha Xie and Yang Liu
Department of Computer Science
The University of Texas at Dallas
{shasha,yangl}@hlt.utdallas.edu

Abstract

For extractive meeting summarization, previous studies have shown performance degradation when using speech recognition transcripts because of the relatively high speech recognition errors on meeting recordings. In this paper we investigated using confusion networks to improve the summarization performance on the ASR condition under an unsupervised framework by considering more word candidates and their confidence scores. Our experimental results showed improved summarization performance using our proposed approach, with more contribution from leveraging the confidence scores. We also observed that using these rich speech recognition results can extract similar or even better summary segments than using human transcripts.

1 Introduction

Speech summarization has received increasing interest recently. It is a very useful technique that can help users to browse a large amount of speech recordings. The problem we study in this paper is extractive meeting summarization, which selects the most representative segments from the meeting transcripts to form a summary. Compared to text summarization, speech summarization is more challenging because of not only its more spontaneous style, but also word errors in automatic speech recognition (ASR) output. Intuitively the incorrect words have a negative impact on downstream summarization performance. Previous research has evaluated summarization using either the human transcripts or ASR output with word errors. Most of the prior work showed that performance using ASR output is consistently lower (to different extent) comparing to that using human transcripts no matter whether supervised or unsupervised approaches were used.

To address the problem caused by imperfect recognition transcripts, in this paper we investigate using rich speech recognition results for summarization. N-best hypotheses, word lattices, and confusion networks have been widely used as an interface between ASR and subsequent spoken language processing tasks, such as machine translation, spoken document retrieval (Chelba et al., 2007; Chia et al., 2008), and shown outperforming using 1-best hypotheses. However, studies using these rich speech recognition results for speech summarization are very limited. In this paper, we demonstrate the feasibility of using confusion networks under an unsupervised MMR (maximum marginal relevance) framework to improve summarization performance. Our experimental results show better performance over using 1-best hypotheses with more improvement observed from using confidence measure of the words. Moreover, we find that the selected summary segments are similar to or even better than those generated using human transcripts.

2 Related Work

Many techniques have been proposed for the meeting summarization task, including both unsupervised and supervised approaches. Since we use unsupervised methods in this study, we will not describe previous work using supervised approaches because of the space limit. Unsupervised meth-

Human Language Technologies: The 2010 Annual Conference of the North American Chapter of the ACL, pages 46–54,
Los Angeles, California, June 2010.

ods are simple and robust to different corpora, and do not need any human labeled data for training. MMR was introduced in (Carbonell and Goldstein, 1998) for text summarization, and was used widely in meeting summarization (Murray et al., 2005a; Xie and Liu, 2008). Latent semantic analysis (LSA) approaches have also been used (Murray et al., 2005a), which can better measure document similarity at the semantic level rather than relying on literal word matching. In (Gillick et al., 2009), the authors introduced a concept-based global optimization framework using integer linear programming (ILP), where concepts were used as the minimum units, and the important sentences were extracted to cover as many concepts as possible. They showed better performance than MMR. In a follow-up study, (Xie et al., 2009) incorporated sentence information in this ILP framework. Graph-based methods, such as LexRank (Erkan and Radev, 2004), have been originally used for extractive text summarization, where the document is modeled as a graph and sentences as nodes, and sentences are ranked according to its similarity with other nodes. (Garg et al., 2009) proposed ClusterRank, a modified graph-based method in order to take into account the conversational speech style in meetings. Recently (Lin et al., 2009) suggested to formulate the summarization task as optimizing submodular functions defined on the document's semantic graph, and showed better performance comparing to other graph-based approaches.

Rich speech recognition results, such as N-best hypotheses and confusion networks, were first used in multi-pass ASR systems to improve speech recognition performance (Stolcke et al., 1997; Mangu et al., 2000). They have been widely used in many subsequent spoken language processing tasks, such as machine translation, spoken document understanding and retrieval. Confusion network decoding was applied to combine the outputs of multiple machine translation systems (Sim et al., 2007; Matusov et al., 2006). In the task of spoken document retrieval, (Chia et al., 2008) proposed to compute the expected word counts from document and query lattices, and estimate the statistical models from these counts, and reported better retrieval accuracy than using only 1-best transcripts. (Hakkani-Tur et al., 2006) investigated using confusion networks for name entity detection and extraction and user intent classification. They also obtained better performance than using ASR 1-best output.

There is very limited previous work using more than 1-best ASR output for speech summarization. Several studies used acoustic confidence scores in the 1-best ASR hypothesis in the summarization systems (Valenza et al., 1999; Zechner and Waibel, 2000; Hori and Furui, 2003). (Liu et al., 2010) evaluated using n-best hypotheses for meeting summarization, and showed improved performance with the gain coming mainly from the first few candidates. In (Lin and Chen, 2009), confusion networks and position specific posterior lattices were considered in a generative summarization framework for Chinese broadcast news summarization, and they showed promising results by using more ASR hypotheses. We investigate using confusion networks for meeting summarization in this study. This work differs from (Lin and Chen, 2009) in terms of the language and genre used in the summarization task, as well as the summarization approaches. We also perform more analysis on the impact of confidence scores, different pruning methods, and different ways to present system summaries.

3 Summarization Approach

In this section, we first describe the baseline summarization framework, and then how we apply it to confusion networks.

3.1 Maximum Marginal Relevance (MMR)

MMR is a widely used unsupervised approach in text and speech summarization, and has been shown perform well. We chose this method as the basic framework for summarization because of its simplicity and efficiency. We expect this is a good starting point for the study of feasibility of using confusion networks for summarization. For each sentence segment S_i in one document D, its score ($MMR(i)$) is calculated using Equation 1 according to its similarity to the entire document ($Sim_1(S_i, D)$) and the similarity to the already extracted summary ($Sim_2(S_i, Summ)$).

$$MMR(i) = \lambda \times Sim_1(S_i, D) - (1-\lambda) \times Sim_2(S_i, Summ) \quad (1)$$

where parameter λ is used to balance the two factors to ensure the selected summary sentences are relevant to the entire document (thus important), and compact enough (by removing redundancy with the currently selected summary sentences). Cosine similarity can be used to compute the similarity of two text segments. If each segment is represented as a vector, cosine similarity between two vectors (V_1, V_2) is measured using the following equation:

$$sim(V_1, V_2) = \frac{\sum_i t_{1i} t_{2i}}{\sqrt{\sum_i t_{1i}^2} \times \sqrt{\sum_i t_{2i}^2}} \quad (2)$$

where t_i is the term weight for a word w_i, for which we can use the TFIDF (term frequency, inverse document frequency) value, as widely used in the field of information retrieval.

3.2 Using Confusion Networks for Summarization

Confusion networks (CNs) have been used in many natural language processing tasks. Figure 1 shows a CN example for a sentence segment. It is a directed word graph from the starting node to the end node. Each edge represents a word with its associated posterior probability. There are several word candidates for each position. "-" in the CN represents a NULL hypothesis. Each path in the graph is a sentence hypothesis. For the example in Figure 1, *"I HAVE IT VERY FINE"* is the best hypothesis consisting of words with the highest probabilities for each position. Compared to N-best lists, confusion networks are a more compact and powerful representation for word candidates. We expect the rich information contained in the confusion networks (i.e., more word candidates and associated posterior probabilities) can help to determine words' importance for summarization.

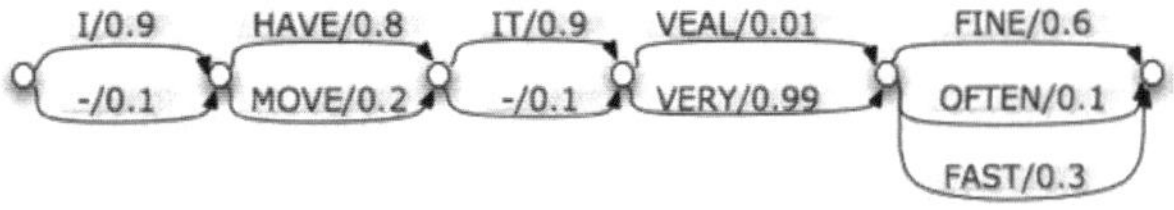

Figure 1: An example of confusion networks.

The core problems when using confusion networks under the MMR summarization framework are the definitions for S_i, D, and $Summ$, as shown in Equation 1. The extractive summary unit (for each S_i) we use is the segment provided by the recognizer. This is often different from syntactic or semantic meaningful unit (e.g., a sentence), but is a more realistic setup. Most of the previous studies for speech summarization used human labeled sentences as extraction units (for human transcripts, or map them to ASR output), which is not the real scenario when performing speech summarization on the ASR condition. In the future, we will use automatic sentence segmentation results, which we expect are better units than pause-based segmentation used in ASR. We still use a vector space model to represent each summarization unit S_i. The entire document (D) and the current selected summary ($Summ$) are formed by simply concatenating the corresponding segments S_i together. In the following, we describe different ways to represent the segments and how to present the final summary.

A. Segmentation representation

First, we construct the vector for each segment simply using all the word candidates in the CNs, without considering any confidence measure or posterior probability information. The same TFIDF computation is used as before, i.e., counting the number of times a word appears (TF) and how many documents it appears (used to calculate IDF).

Second, we leverage the confidence scores to build the vector. For the term frequency of word w_i, we calculate it by summing up its posterior probabilities $p(w_{ik})$ at each position k, that is,

$$TF(w_i) = \sum_k p(w_{ik}) \quad (3)$$

Similarly, the IDF values can also be computed using the confidence scores. The traditional method for calculating a word's IDF uses the ratio of the total number of documents (N) and the number of documents containing this word. Using the confidence scores, we calculate the IDF values as follows,

$$IDF(w_i) = log(\frac{N}{\sum_D (\max_k p(w_{ik}))}) \quad (4)$$

If a word w_i appears in the document, we find its maximum posterior probability among all the positions it occurs in the CNs, which is used to signal w_i's soft appearance in this document. We add these soft counts for all the documents as the denominator in Equation 4. Different from the traditional IDF calculation method, where the number of documents containing a word is an integer number, here the denominator can be any real number.

B. Confusion network pruning

The above vectors are constructed using the entire confusion networks. We may also use the pruned ones, in which the words with low posterior probabilities are removed beforehand. This can avoid the impact of noisy words, and increase the system speed as well. We investigate three different pruning methods, listed below.

- absolute pruning: In this method, we delete words if their posterior probabilities are lower than a predefined threshold, i.e., $p(w_i) < \theta$.
- max_diff pruning: First for each position k, we find the maximum probability among all the word candidates: $Pmax_k = \max_j p(w_{jk})$. Then we remove a word w_i in this position if the absolute difference of its probability with the maximum score is larger than a predefined threshold, i.e., $Pmax_k - p(w_{ik}) > \theta$.
- max_ratio pruning: This is similar to the above one, but instead of absolute difference, we use the ratio of their probabilities, i.e., $\frac{p(w_{ik})}{Pmax_k} < \theta$.

Again, for the last two pruning methods, the comparison is done for each position in the CNs.

C. Summary rendering

With a proper way of representing the text segments, we then extract the summary segments using the MMR method described in Section 3.1. Once the summary segments are selected using the confusion network input, another problem we need to address is how to present the final summary. When using the human transcripts or the 1-best ASR hypothesis for summarization, we can simply concatenate the corresponding transcripts of the selected sentence segments as the final summary for the users. However, when using the confusion networks as the representation of each sentence segment, we only know which segments are selected by the summarization system. To provide the final summary to the users, there are two choices. We can either use the best hypothesis from CNs of those selected segments as a text summary; or return the speech segments to the users to allow them to play it back. We will evaluate both methods in this paper. For the latter, in order to use similar word based performance measures, we will use the corresponding reference transcripts in order to focus on evaluation of the correctness of the selected summary segments.

4 Experiments

4.1 Corpus and Evaluation Measurement

We use the ICSI meeting corpus, which contains 75 recordings from natural meetings (most are research discussions) (Janin et al., 2003). Each meeting is about an hour long and has multiple speakers. These meetings have been transcribed, and annotated with extractive summaries (Murray et al., 2005b). The ASR output is obtained from a state-of-the-art SRI speech recognition system, including the confusion network for each sentence segment (Stolcke et al., 2006). The word error rate (WER) is about 38.2% on the entire corpus.

The same 6 meetings as in (Murray et al., 2005a; Xie and Liu, 2008; Gillick et al., 2009; Lin et al., 2009) are used as the test set in this study. Furthermore, 6 other meetings were randomly selected from the remaining 69 meetings in the corpus to form a development set. Each meeting in the development set has only one human-annotated summary; whereas for the test meetings, we use three summaries from different annotators as references for performance evaluation. The lengths of the reference summaries are not fixed and vary across annotators and meetings. The average word compression ratio for the test set is 14.3%, and the mean deviation is 2.9%. We generated summaries with the word compression ratio ranging from 13% to 18%, and only provide the best results in this paper.

To evaluate summarization performance, we use ROUGE (Lin, 2004), which has been widely used in previous studies of speech summarization (Zhang et al., 2007; Murray et al., 2005a; Zhu and Penn, 2006). ROUGE compares the system generated summary with reference summaries (there can be more than one reference summary), and measures different matches, such as N-gram, longest common sequence, and skip bigrams. In this paper, we present our results using both ROUGE-1 and

ROUGE-2 F-scores.

4.2 Characteristics of CNs

First we perform some analysis of the confusion networks using the development set data. We define two measurements:

- Word coverage. This is to verify that CNs contain more correct words than the 1-best hypotheses. It is defined as the percentage of the words in human transcripts (measured using word types) that appear in the CNs. We use word types in this measurement since we are using a vector space model and the multiple occurrence of a word only affects its term weights, not the dimension of the vector. Note that for this analysis, we do not perform alignment that is needed in word error rate measure — we do not care whether a word appears in the exact location; as long as a word appears in the segment, its effect on the vector space model is the same (since it is a bag-of-words model).

- Average node density. This is the average number of candidate words for each position in the confusion networks.

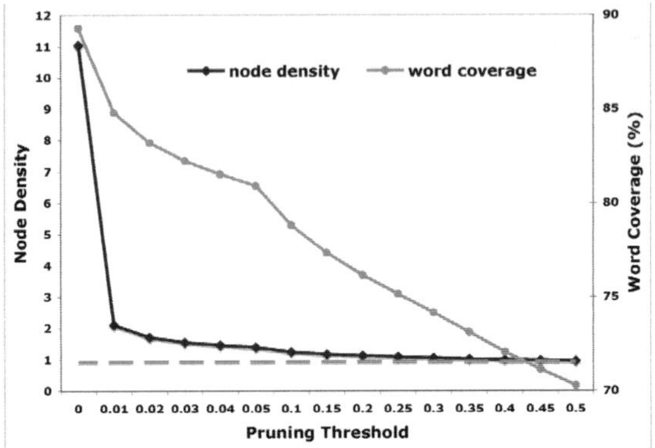

Figure 2: Average node density and word coverage of the confusion networks on the development set.

Figure 2 shows the analysis results for these two metrics, which are the average values on the development set. In this analysis we used absolute pruning method, and the results are presented for different pruning thresholds. For a comparison, we also include the results using the 1-best hypotheses (shown as the dotted line in the figure), which has an average node density of 1, and the word coverage of 71.55%. When the pruning threshold is 0, the results correspond to the original CNs without pruning.

We can see that the confusion networks include much more correct words than 1-best hypotheses (word coverage is 89.3% vs. 71.55%). When increasing the pruning thresholds, the word coverage decreases following roughly a linear pattern. When the pruning threshold is 0.45, the word coverage of the pruned CNs is 71.15%, lower than 1-best hypotheses. For node density, the non-pruned CNs have an average density of 11.04. With a very small pruning threshold of 0.01, the density decreases rapidly to 2.11. The density falls less than 2 when the threshold is 0.02, which means that for some nodes there is only one word candidate preserved after pruning (i.e., only one word has a posterior probability higher than 0.02). When the threshold increases to 0.4, the density is less than 1 (0.99), showing that on average there is less than one candidate left for each position. This is consistent with the word coverage results — when the pruning threshold is larger than 0.45, the confusion networks have less word coverage than 1-best hypotheses because even the top word hypotheses are deleted. Therefore, for our following experiments we only use the thresholds $\theta \leq 0.45$ for absolute pruning.

Note that the results in the figure are based on absolute pruning. We also performed analysis using the other two pruning methods described in Section 3.2. For those methods, because the decision is made by comparing each word's posterior probability with the maximum score for that position, we can guarantee that at least the best word candidate is included in the pruned CNs. We varied the pruning threshold from 0 to 0.95 for these pruning methods, and observed similar patterns as in absolute pruning for the word coverage and node density analysis. As expected, the fewer word candidates are pruned, the better word coverage and higher node density the pruned CNs have.

4.3 Summarization Results

4.3.1 Results on dev set using 1-best hypothesis and human transcripts

We generate the baseline summarization result using the best hypotheses from the confusion networks. The summary sentences are extracted using the MMR method introduced in Section 3.1. The term weighting is the traditional TFIDF value. The ROUGE-1 and ROUGE-2 scores for the baseline are listed in Table 1.

Because in this paper our task is to evaluate the summarization performance using ASR output, we generate an oracle result, where the summary extraction and IDF calculation are based on the human transcripts for each ASR segment. These results are also presented in Table 1. Comparing the results for the two testing conditions, ASR output and human transcripts, we can see the performance degradation due to recognition errors. The difference between them seems to be large enough to warrant investigation of using rich ASR output for improved summarization performance.

	ROUGE-1	ROUGE-2
Baseline: best hyp	65.60	26.83
Human transcript	69.98	33.21

Table 1: ROUGE results (%) using 1-best hypotheses and human transcripts on the development set.

4.3.2 Results on the dev set using CNs

A. Effect of segmentation representation

We evaluate the effect on summarization using different vector representations based on confusion networks. Table 2 shows the results on the development set using various input under the MMR framework. We also include the results using 1-best and human transcripts in the table as a comparison. The third row in the table uses the 1-best hypothesis, but the term weight for each word is calculated by considering its posterior probability in the CNs (denoted by "wp"). We calculate the TF and IDF values using Equation 3 and 4 introduced in Section 3.2. The other representations in the table are for the non-pruned and pruned CNs based on different pruning methods, and with or without using the posteriors to calculate term weights.

In general, we find that using confusion networks improves the summarization performance comparing with the baseline. Since CNs contain more candidate words and posterior probabilities, a natural question to ask is, which factor contributes more to the improved performance? We can compare the results in Table 2 across different conditions that use the same candidate words, one with standard TFIDF, and the other with posteriors for TFIDF, or that use different candidate words and the same setup for TFIDF calculation. Our results show that there is more improvement using our proposed method for TFIDF calculation based on posterior probabilities, especially ROUGE-2 scores. Even when just using 1-best hypotheses, if we consider posteriors, we can obtain very competitive results. There is also a difference in the effect of using posterior probabilities. When using the top hypotheses representation, posteriors help both ROUGE-1 and ROUGE-2 scores; when using confusion networks, non-pruned or pruned, using posterior probabilities improves ROUGE-2 results, but not ROUGE-1.

Our results show that adding more candidates in the vector representation does not necessarily help summarization. Using the pruned CNs yields better performance than the non-pruned ones. There is not much difference among different pruning methods. Overall, the best results are achieved by using pruned CNs: best ROUGE-1 result without using posterior probabilities, and best ROUGE-2 scores when using posteriors.

segment representation		ROUGE-1	ROUGE-2
Best hyp		65.60	26.83
Best hyp (wp)		66.83	29.84
Non-pruned CNs		66.58	28.22
Non-pruned CNs (wp)		66.47	29.27
Pruned CNs	Absolute	**67.44**	29.02
	Absolute (wp)	66.98	**29.99**
	Max_diff	67.29	28.97
	Max_diff (wp)	67.10	29.76
	Max_ratio	**67.43**	28.97
	Max_ratio (wp)	67.06	29.90
Human transcript		69.98	33.21

Table 2: ROUGE results (%) on the development set using different vector representations based on confusion networks: non-pruned and pruned, using posterior probabilities ("wp") and without using them.

B. Presenting summaries using human transcripts

segment representation		ROUGE-1	ROUGE-2
Best hyp		68.26	32.25
Best hyp (wp)		69.16	33.99
Non-pruned CNs		69.28	33.49
Non-pruned CNs (wp)		67.84	32.95
Pruned CNs	Absolute	69.66	34.06
	Absolute (wp)	69.37	34.25
	Max_diff	**69.88**	34.17
	Max_diff (wp)	69.38	33.94
	Max_ratio	69.76	34.06
	Max_ratio (wp)	69.44	**34.39**
Human transcript		69.98	33.21

Table 3: ROUGE results (%) on the development set using different segment representations, with the summaries constructed using the corresponding human transcripts for the selected segments.

In the above experiments, we construct the final summary using the best hypotheses from the confusion networks once the summary sentence segments are determined. Although we notice obvious improvement comparing with the baseline results, the ROUGE scores are still much lower than using the human transcripts. One reason for this is the speech recognition errors. Even if we select the correct utterance segment as in the reference summary segments, the system performance is still penalized when calculating the ROUGE scores. In order to avoid the impact of word errors and focus on evaluating whether we have selected the correct segments, next we use the corresponding human transcripts of the selected segments to obtain performance measures. The results from this experiment are shown in Table 3 for different segment representations.

We can see that the summaries formed using human transcripts are much better comparing with the results presented in Table 2. These two setups use the same utterance segments. The only difference lies in the construction of the final summary for performance measurement, using the top hypotheses or the corresponding human transcripts for the selected segments. We also notice that the difference between using 1-best hypothesis and human transcripts is greatly reduced using this new summary formulation. This suggests that the incorrect word hypotheses do not have a very negative impact in terms of selecting summary segments; however, word errors still account for a significant part of the performance degradation on ASR condition when using word-based metrics for evaluation. Using the best hypotheses with their posterior probabilities we can obtain similar ROUGE-1 score and a little higher ROUGE-2 score comparing to the results using human transcripts. The performance can be further improved using the pruned CNs.

Note that when using the non-pruned CNs and posterior probabilities for term weighting, the ROUGE scores are worse than most of other conditions. We performed some analysis and found that one reason for this is the selection of some poor segments. Most of the word candidates in the non-pruned CNs have very low confidence scores, resulting in high IDF values using our proposed methods. Since some top hypotheses are NULL words in the poorly selected summary segments, it did not affect the results when using the best hypothesis for evaluation, but when using human transcripts, it leads to lower precision and worse overall F-scores. This is not a problem for the pruned CNs since words with low probabilities have been pruned beforehand, and thus do not impact segment selection. We will investigate better methods for term weighting to address this issue in our future work.

These experimental results prove that using the confusion networks and confidence scores can help select the correct sentence segments. Even though the 1-best WER is quite high, if we can consider more word candidates and/or their confidence scores, this will not impact the process of selecting summary segments. We can achieve similar performance as using human transcripts, and sometimes even slightly better performance. This suggests using more word candidates and their confidence scores results in better term weighting and representation in the vector space model. Some previous work showed that using word confidence scores can help minimize the WER of the extracted summaries, which then lead to better summarization performance. However, we think the main reason for the improvement in our study is from selecting better utterances, as shown in Table 3. In our experiments, because different setups select different segments as the summary, we can not directly compare the WER of extracted summaries, and analyze whether lower WER is also helpful for better sum-

	output summary			
	best hypotheses		human transcripts	
	R-1	R-2	R-1	R-2
Best hyp	65.73	26.79	68.60	32.03
Best hyp (wp)	65.92	27.27	68.91	32.69
Pruned CNs	66.47	27.73	69.53	34.05
Human transcript	N/A	N/A	69.08	33.33

Table 4: ROUGE results (%) on the test set.

marization performance. In our future work, we will perform more analysis along this direction.

4.3.3 Experimental results on test set

The summarization results on the test set are presented in Table 4. We show four different evaluation conditions: baseline using the top hypotheses, best hypotheses with posterior probabilities, pruned CNs, and using human transcripts. For each condition, the final summary is evaluated using the best hypotheses or the corresponding human transcripts of the selected segments. The summarization system setups (the pruning method and threshold, λ value in MMR function, and word compression ratio) used for the test set are decided based on the results on the development set.

For the results on the test set, we observe similar trends as on the development set. Using the confidence scores and confusion networks can improve the summarization performance comparing with the baseline. The performance improvements from "Best hyp" to "Best hyp (wp)" and from "Best hyp (wp)" to "Pruned CNs" using both ROUGE-1 and ROUGE-2 measures are statistically significant according to the paired t-test ($p < 0.05$). When the final summary is presented using the human transcripts of the selected segments, we observe slightly better results using pruned CNs than using human transcripts as input for summarization, although the difference is not statistically significant. This shows that using confusion networks can compensate for the impact from recognition errors and still allow us to select correct summary segments.

5 Conclusion and Future Work

Previous research has shown performance degradation when using ASR output for meeting summarization because of word errors. To address this problem, in this paper we proposed to use confusion networks for speech summarization. Under the MMR framework, we introduced a vector representation for the segments by using more word candidates in CNs and their associated posterior probabilities. We evaluated the effectiveness of using different confusion networks, the non-pruned ones, and the ones pruned using three different methods, i.e., absolute, max_diff and max_ratio pruning. Our experimental results on the ICSI meeting corpus showed that even when we only use the top hypotheses from the CNs, considering the word posterior probabilities can improve the summarization performance on both ROUGE-1 and ROUGE-2 scores. By using the pruned CNs we can obtain further improvement. We found that more gain in ROUGE-2 results was yielded by our proposed soft term weighting method based on posterior probabilities. Our experiments also demonstrated that it is possible to use confusion networks to achieve similar or even better performance than using human transcripts if the goal is to select the right segments. This is important since one possible rendering of summarization results is to return the audio segments to the users, which does not suffer from recognition errors.

In our experiments, we observed less improvement from considering more word candidates than using the confidence scores. One possible reason is that the confusion networks we used are too confident. For example, on average 90.45% of the candidate words have a posterior probability lower than 0.01. Therefore, even though the correct words were included in the confusion networks, their contribution may not be significant enough because of low term weights. In addition, low probabilities also cause problems to our proposed soft IDF computation. In our future work, we will investigate probability normalization methods and other techniques for term weighting to cope with these problems.

6 Acknowledgment

This research is supported by NSF award IIS-0845484. Any opinions expressed in this work are those of the authors and do not necessarily reflect the views of NSF. The authors thank Shih-Hsiang Lin and Fei Liu for useful discussions.

References

Jaime Carbonell and Jade Goldstein. 1998. The use of MMR, diversity-based reranking for reordering documents and producing summaries. In *Proceedings of SIGIR*.

Ciprian Chelba, Jorge Silva, and Alex Acero. 2007. Soft indexing of speech content for search in spoken documents. In *Computer Speech and Language*, volume 21, pages 458–478.

Tee Kiah Chia, Khe Chai Sim, Haizhou Li, and Hwee Tou Ng. 2008. A lattice-based approach to query-by-example spoken document retrieval. In *Proceedings of SIGIR*.

Gunes Erkan and Dragomir R. Radev. 2004. LexRank: graph-based lexical centrality as salience in text summarization. *Artificial Intelligence Research*, 22:457–479.

Nikhil Garg, Benoit Favre, Korbinian Reidhammer, and Dilek Hakkani-Tur. 2009. ClusterRank: a graph based method for meeting summarization. In *Proceedings of Interspeech*.

Dan Gillick, Korbinian Riedhammer, Benoit Favre, and Dilek Hakkani-Tur. 2009. A global optimization framework for meeting summarization. In *Proceedings of ICASSP*.

Dilek Hakkani-Tur, Frederic Behet, Giuseppe Riccardi, and Gokhan Tur. 2006. Beyond ASR 1-best: using word confusion networks in spoken language understanding. *Computer Speech and Language*, 20(4):495 – 514.

Chiori Hori and Sadaoki Furui. 2003. A new approach to automatic speech summarization. *IEEE Transactions on Multimedia*, 5(3):368–378.

Adam Janin, Don Baron, Jane Edwards, Dan Ellis, David Gelbart, Nelson Morgan, Barbara Peskin, Thilo Pfau, Elizabeth Shriberg, Andreas Stolcke, and Chuck Wooters. 2003. The ICSI meeting corpus. In *Proceedings of ICASSP*.

Shih-Hsiang Lin and Berlin Chen. 2009. Improved speech summarization with multiple-hypothesis representations and Kullback-Leibler divergence measures. In *Proceedings of Interspeech*.

Hui Lin, Jeff Bilmes, and Shasha Xie. 2009. Graph-based submodular selection for extractive summarization. In *Proceedings of ASRU*.

Chin-Yew Lin. 2004. ROUGE: A package for automatic evaluation of summaries. In *the Workshop on Text Summarization Branches Out*.

Yang Liu, Shasha Xie, and Fei Liu. 2010. Using n-best recognition output for extractive summarization and keyword extraction in meeting speech. In *Proceedings of ICASSP*.

Lidia Mangu, Eric Brill, and Andreas Stolcke. 2000. Finding consensus in speech recognition: word error minimization and other applications of confusion networks. *Computer Speech and Language*, 14:373–400.

Evgeny Matusov, Nicola Ueffing, and Hermann Ney. 2006. Computing consensus translation from multiple machine translation systems using enhanced hypotheses alignment. In *Proceedings of EACL*.

Gabriel Murray, Steve Renals, and Jean Carletta. 2005a. Extractive summarization of meeting recordings. In *Proceedings of Interspeech*.

Gabriel Murray, Steve Renals, Jean Carletta, and Johanna Moore. 2005b. Evaluating automatic summaries of meeting recordings. In *Proceedings of the ACL Workshop on Intrinsic and Extrinsic Evaluation Measures for Machine Translation*.

Khe Chai Sim, William Byrne, Mark Gales, Hichem Sahbi, and Phil Woodland. 2007. Consensus network decoding for statistical machine translation system combination. In *Proceedings of ICASSP*.

Andreas Stolcke, Yochai Konig, and Mitchel Weintraub. 1997. Explicit word error minimization in N-best list rescoring. In *Proceedings of Eurospeech*.

Andreas Stolcke, Barry Chen, Horacio Franco, Venkata Ra mana Rao Gadde, Martin Graciarena, Mei-Yuh Hwang, Katrin Kirchhoff, Arindam Mandal, Nelson Morgan, Xin Lei, Tim Ng, and et al. 2006. Recent innovations in speech-to-text transcription at SRI-ICSI-UW. *IEEE Transactions on Audio, Speech, and Language Processing*, 14(5):1729–1744.

Robin Valenza, Tony Robinson, Marianne Hickey, and Roger Tucker. 1999. Summarization of spoken audio through information extraction. In *Proceedings of the ESCA Workshop on Accessing Information in Spoken Audio*, pages 111–116.

Shasha Xie and Yang Liu. 2008. Using corpus and knowledge-based similarity measure in maximum marginal relevance for meeting summarization. In *Proceedings of ICASSP*.

Shasha Xie, Benoit Favre, Dilek Hakkani-Tur, and Yang Liu. 2009. Leveraging sentence weights in concept-based optimization framework for extractive meeting summarization. In *Proceedings of Interspeech*.

Klaus Zechner and Alex Waibel. 2000. Minimizing word error rate in textual summaries of spoken language. In *Proceedings of NAACL*.

Jian Zhang, Ho Yin Chan, Pascale Fung, and Lu Cao. 2007. A comparative study on speech summarization of broadcast news and lecture speech. In *Proceedings of Interspeech*.

Xiaodan Zhu and Gerald Penn. 2006. Summarization of spontaneous conversations. In *Proceedings of Interspeech*.

Qme! : A Speech-based Question-Answering system on Mobile Devices

Taniya Mishra
AT&T Labs-Research
180 Park Ave
Florham Park, NJ
taniya@research.att.com

Srinivas Bangalore
AT&T Labs-Research
180 Park Ave
Florham Park, NJ
srini@research.att.com

Abstract

Mobile devices are becoming the dominant mode of information access despite being cumbersome to input text using small keyboards and browsing web pages on small screens. We present Qme!, a speech-based question-answering system that allows for spoken queries and retrieves *answers* to the questions instead of web pages. We present bootstrap methods to distinguish dynamic questions from static questions and we show the benefits of tight coupling of speech recognition and retrieval components of the system.

1 Introduction

Access to information has moved from desktop and laptop computers in office and home environments to be an any place, any time activity due to mobile devices. Although mobile devices have small keyboards that make typing text input cumbersome compared to conventional desktop and laptops, the ability to access unlimited amount of information, almost everywhere, through the Internet, using these devices have made them pervasive.

Even so, information access using text input on mobile devices with small screens and soft/small keyboards is tedious and unnatural. In addition, by the *mobile* nature of these devices, users often like to use them in hands-busy environments, ruling out the possibility of typing text. We address this issue by allowing the user to query an information repository using speech. We expect that spoken language queries to be a more natural and less cumbersome way of information access using mobile devices.

A second issue we address is related to directly and precisely answering the user's query beyond serving web pages. This is in contrast to the current approach where a user types in a query using keywords to a search engine, browses the returned results on the small screen to select a potentially relevant document, suitably magnifies the screen to view the document and searches for the answer to her question in the document. By providing a method for the user to pose her query in natural language and presenting the relevant answer(s) to her question, we expect the user's information need to be fulfilled in a shorter period of time.

We present a speech-driven question answering system, Qme!, as a solution toward addressing these two issues. The system provides a natural input modality – spoken language input – for the users to pose their information need and presents a collection of *answers* that potentially address the information need directly. For a subclass of questions that we term *static* questions, the system retrieves the answers from an archive of human generated answers to questions. This ensures higher accuracy for the answers retrieved (if found in the archive) and also allows us to retrieve related questions on the user's topic of interest. For a second subclass of questions that we term *dynamic* questions, the system retrieves the answer from information databases accessible over the Internet using web forms.

The layout of the paper is as follows. In Section 2, we review the related literature. In Section 3, we illustrate the system for speech-driven question answering. We present the retrieval methods we used to implement the system in Section 4. In Section 5, we discuss and evaluate our approach to tight coupling of speech recognition and search components. In Section 6, we present bootstrap techniques to distinguish dynamic questions from static questions, and evaluate the efficacy of these techniques on a test corpus. We conclude in Section 7.

2 Related Work

Early question-answering (QA) systems, such as Baseball (Green et al., 1961) and Lunar (Woods, 1973) were carefully hand-crafted to answer questions in a limited domain, similar to the QA components of ELIZA (Weizenbaum, 1966) and SHRDLU (Winograd, 1972). However, there has been a resurgence of QA systems following the TREC conferences with an emphasis on answering factoid questions. This work on text-based question-answering which is comprehensively summarized

Human Language Technologies: The 2010 Annual Conference of the North American Chapter of the ACL, pages 55–63,
Los Angeles, California, June 2010.

in (Maybury, 2004), range widely in terms of linguistic sophistication. At one end of the spectrum, There are linguistically motivated systems (Katz, 1997; Waldinger et al., 2004) that analyze the user's question and attempt to synthesize a coherent answer by aggregating the relevant facts. At the other end of the spectrum, there are data intensive systems (Dumais et al., 2002) that attempt to use the redundancy of the web to arrive at an answer for factoid style questions. There are also variants of such QA techniques that involve an interaction and use context to resolve ambiguity (Yang et al., 2006). In contrast to these approaches, our method matches the user's query against the *questions* in a large corpus of question-answer pairs and retrieves the associated answer.

In the information retrieval community, QA systems attempt to retrieve precise segments of a document instead of the entire document. In (Tomuro and Lytinen, 2004), the authors match the user's query against a frequently-asked-questions (FAQ) database and select the answer whose question matches most closely to the user's question. An extension of this idea is explored in (Xue et al., 2008; Jeon et al., 2005), where the authors match the user's query to a community collected QA archive such as (Yahoo!, 2009; MSN-QnA, 2009). Our approach is similar to both these lines of work in spirit, although the user's query for our system originates as a spoken query, in contrast to the text queries in previous work. We also address the issue of noisy speech recognition and assess the value of tight integration of speech recognition and search in terms of improving the overall performance of the system. A novelty in this paper is our method to address dynamic questions as a seamless extension to answering static questions.

Also related is the literature on voice-search applications (Microsoft, 2009; Google, 2009; YellowPages, 2009; vlingo.com, 2009) that provide a spoken language interface to business directories and return phone numbers, addresses and web sites of businesses. User input is typically not a free flowing natural language query and is limited to expressions with a business name and a location. In our system, users can avail of the full range of natural language expressions to express their information need.

And finally, our method of retrieving answers to dynamic questions has relevance to the database and meta search community. There is growing interest in this community to mine the "hidden" web – information repositories that are behind web forms – and provide a unified meta-interface to such information sources, for example, web sites related travel, or car dealerships. Dynamic questions can be seen as providing a natural language interface (NLI) to such web forms, similar to early work on NLI to databases (Androutsopoulos, 1995).

3 Speech-driven Question Retrieval System

We describe the speech-driven query retrieval application in this section. The user of this application provides a spoken language query to a mobile device intending to find an answer to the question. Some example users' inputs are[1] *what is the fastest animal in water, how do I fix a leaky dishwasher, why is the sky blue*. The result of the speech recognizer is used to search a large corpus of question-answer pairs to retrieve the answers pertinent to the user's static questions. For the dynamic questions, the answers are retrieved by querying a web form from the appropriate web site (e.g www.fandango.com for movie information). The result from the speech recognizer can be a single-best string or a weighted word lattice.[2] The retrieved results are ranked using different metrics discussed in the next section. In Figure 2, we illustrate the answers that `Qme`! returns for static and dynamic quesitons.

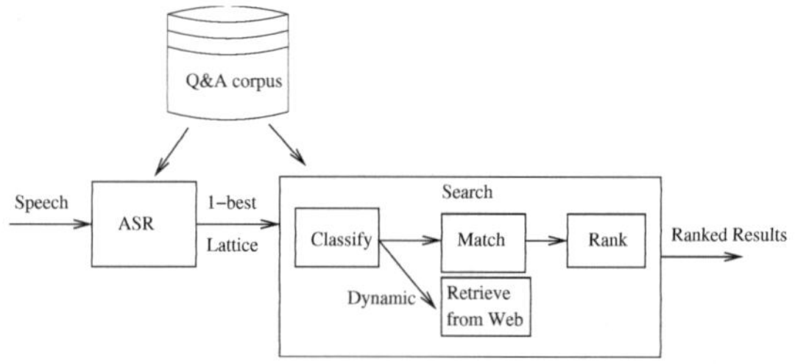

Figure 1: The architecture of the speech-driven question-answering system

4 Methods of Retrieval

We formulate the problem of answering static questions as follows. Given a question-answer archive $\mathbf{QA} = \{(q_1, a_1), (q_2, a_2), \ldots, (q_N, a_N)\}$

[1]The query is not constrained to be of any specific question type (for example, *what, where, when, how*).

[2]For this paper, the ASR used to recognize these utterances incorporates an acoustic model adapted to speech collected from mobile devices and a four-gram language model that is built from the corpus of questions.

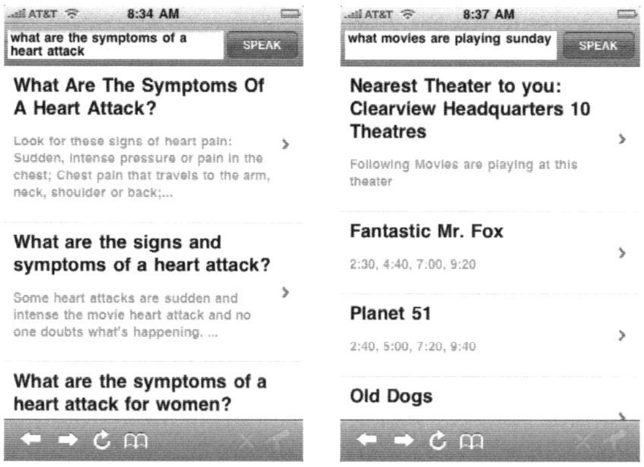

Figure 2: Retrieval results for static and dynamic questions using Qme!

of N question-answer pairs, and a user's question q_u, the task is to retrieve a subset $\mathbf{QA^r} = \{(q_1^r, a_1^r), (q_2^r, a_2^r), \ldots, (q_M^r, a_M^r)\}$ $M << N$ using a selection function $Select$ and rank the members of $\mathbf{QA^r}$ using a scoring function $Score$ such that $Score(q_u, (q_i^r, a_i^r)) > Score(q_u, (q_{i+1}^r, a_{i+1}^r))$. Here, we assume $Score(q_u, (q_i^r, a_i^r)) = Score(q_u, q_i^r)$.

The $Select$ function is intended to select the matching questions that have high "semantic" similarity to the user's question. However, given there is no objective function that measures semantic similarity, we approximate it using different metrics discussed below.

Ranking of the members of the retrieved set can be based on the scores computed during the selection step or can be independently computed based on other criteria such as popularity of the question, credibility of the source, temporal recency of the answer, geographical proximity to the answer origin.

4.1 Question Retrieval Metrics

We retrieve QA pairs from the data repository based on the similarity of match between the user's query and each of the set of questions (d) in the repository. To measure the similarity, we have experimented with the following metrics.

1. **TF-IDF metric**: The user input query and the document (in our case, questions in the repository) are represented as bag-of-n-grams (aka terms). The term weights are computed using a combination of term frequency (tf) and inverse document frequency (idf) (Robertson, 2004). If $Q = q_1, q_2, \ldots, q_n$ is a user query, then the aggregated score for a document d using a unigram model of the query and the document is given as in Equation 1. For a given query, the documents with the highest total term weight are presented as retrieved results. Terms can also be defined as n-gram sequences of a query and a document. In our experiments, we have used up to 4-grams as terms to retrieve and rank documents.
$$Score(d) = \sum_{w \in Q} tf_{w,d} \times idf_w \quad (1)$$

2. **String Comparison Metrics:** Since the length of the user query and the query to be retrieved are similar in length, we use string comparison methods such as Levenshtein edit distance (Levenshtein, 1966) and n-gram overlap (BLEU-score) (Papineni et al., 2002) as similarity metrics.

We compare the search effectiveness of these similarity metrics in Section 5.3.

5 Tightly coupling ASR and Search

Most of the speech-driven search systems use the 1-best output from the ASR as the query for the search component. Given that ASR 1-best output is likely to be erroneous, this serialization of the ASR and search components might result in sub-optimal search accuracy. A lattice representation of the ASR output, in particular, a word-confusion network (WCN) transformation of the lattice, compactly encodes the n-best hypothesis with the flexibility of pruning alternatives at each word position. An example of a WCN is shown in Figure 3. The weights on the arcs are to be interpreted as costs and the best path in the WCN is the lowest cost path from the start state (0) to the final state (4). Note that the 1-best path is *how old is mama*, while the input speech was *how old is obama* which also is in the WCN, but at a higher cost.

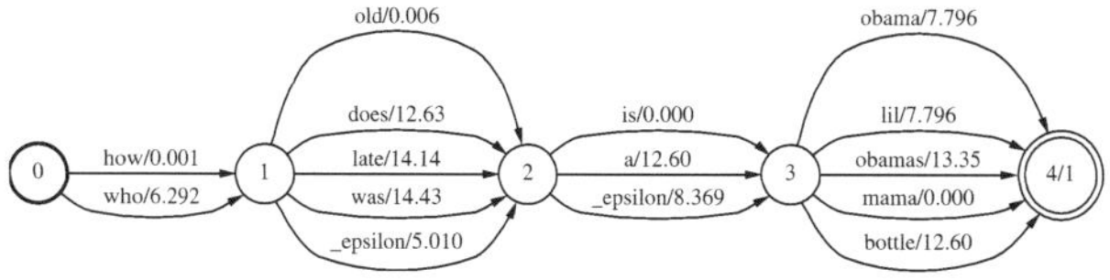

Figure 3: A sample word confusion network with arc costs as negative logarithm of the posterior probabilities.

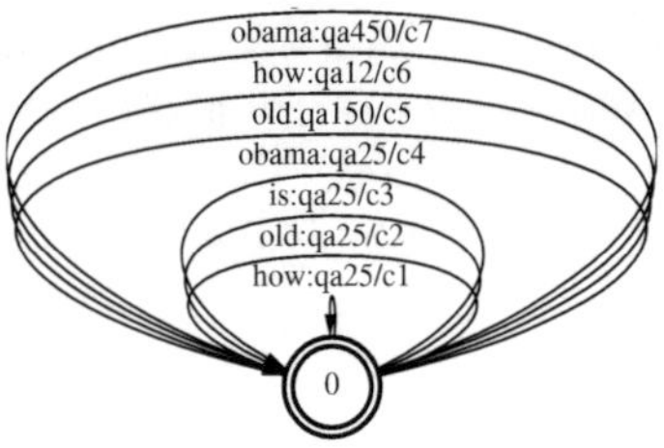

Figure 4: Example of an FST representing the search index.

5.1 Representing Search Index as an FST

Lucene (Hatcher and Gospodnetic., 2004) is an off-the-shelf search engine that implements the TF-IDF metric. But, we have implemented our own search engine using finite-state transducers (FST) for this reason. The oracle word/phrase accuracy using n-best hypotheses of an ASR is usually far greater than the 1-best output. However, using each of the n-best ($n > 1$) hypothesis as a separate query to the search component is computationally sub-optimal since the strings in the n-best hypotheses usually share large subsequences with each other. The FST representation of the search index allows us to efficiently consider lattices/WCNs as input queries.

The FST search index is built as follows. We index each question-answer (QA) pair from our repository ((q_i, a_i), qa_i for short) using the words (w_{q_i}) in question q_i. This index is represented as a weighted finite-state transducer (*SearchFST*) as shown in Figure 4. Here a word w_{q_i} (e.g *old*) is the input symbol for a set of arcs whose output symbol is the index of the QA pairs where *old* appears in the question. The weight of the arc $c_{(w_{q_i}, q_i)}$ is one of the similarity based weights discussed in Section 4.1. As can be seen from Figure 4, the words *how*, *old*, *is* and *obama* contribute a score to the question-answer pair *qa25*; while other pairs, *qa150, qa12, qa450* are scored by only one of these words.

5.2 Search Process using FSTs

A user's speech query, after speech recognition, is represented as an FSA (either 1-best or WCN), a *QueryFSA*. The *QueryFSA* (denoted as q) is then transformed into another FSA (*NgramFSA(q)*) that represents the set of n-grams of the *QueryFSA*. Due to the arc costs from WCNs, the *NgramFSA* for a WCN is a weighted FSA. The *NgramFSA* is composed with the *SearchFST* and we obtain all the arcs $(w_q, qa_{w_q}, c_{(w_q, qa_{w_q})})$ where w_q is a query term, qa_{w_q} is a QA index with the query term and, $c_{(w_q, qa_{w_q})}$ is the weight associated with that pair. Using this information, we aggregate the weight for a QA pair (qa_q) across all query words and rank the retrieved QAs in the descending order of this aggregated weight. We select the top N QA pairs from this ranked list. The query composition, QA weight aggregation and selection of top N QA pairs are computed with finite-state transducer operations as shown in Equations 2 to 5.[3]

$$D1 = \pi_2(NgramFSA(q) \circ SearchFST) \quad (2)$$

$$R1 = fsmbestpath(D1, 1) \quad (3)$$

$$D2 = \pi_2(NgramFSA(R1) \circ SearchFST) \quad (4)$$

$$TopN = fsmbestpath(fsmdeterminize(D2), N) \quad (5)$$

The process of retrieving documents using the Levenshtein-based string similarity metric can also be encoded as a composition of FSTs.

5.3 Experiments and Results

We have a fairly large data set consisting of over a million question-answer pairs collected by harvesting the web. In order to evaluate the retrieval methods discussed earlier, we use two test sets of QA pairs: a *Seen* set of 450 QA pairs and an *Unseen* set of 645 QA pairs. The queries in the *Seen* set have an exact match with some question in the database, while the queries in the *Unseen* set may not match any question in the database exactly. [4] The questions in the *Unseen* set, however, like those in the *Seen* set, also have a human generated answer that is used in our evaluations.

For each query, we retrieve the twenty most relevant QA pairs, ranked in descending order of the value of the particular metric under consideration. However, depending on whether the user query is a seen or an unseen query, the evaluation of the relevance of the retrieved question-answer pairs is different as discussed below.[5]

[3] We have dropped the need to convert the weights into the *real* semiring for aggregation, to simplify the discussion.

[4] There may however be semantically matching questions.

[5] The reason it is not a recall and precision curve is that, for the "seen" query set, the retrieval for the questions is a zero/one boolean accuracy. For the "unseen" query set there is no perfect match with the input question in the query database, and so we determine the closeness of the questions based on the closeness of the answers. Coherence attempts to capture the homogenity of the questions retrieved, with the assumption that the user might want to see similar questions as the returned results.

5.3.1 Evaluation Metrics

For the set of *Seen* queries, we evaluate the relevance of the retrieved top-20 question-answer pairs in two ways:

1. Retrieval Accuracy of Top-N results: We evaluate whether the question that matches the user query exactly is located in the top-1, top-5, top-10, top-20 or not in top-20 of the retrieved questions.

2. Coherence metric: We compute the coherence of the retrieved set as the mean of the BLEU-score between the input query and the set of top-5 retrieved questions. The intuition is that we do not want the top-5 retrieved QA pairs to distract the user by not being relevant to the user's query.

For the set of *Unseen* queries, since there are no questions in the database that exactly match the input query, we evaluate the relevance of the top-20 retrieved question-answer pairs in the following way. For each of the 645 *Unseen* queries, we know the human-generated answer. We manually annotated each unseen query with the *Best-Matched* QA pair whose answer was the closest semantic match to the human-generated answer for that unseen query. We evaluate the position of the Best-Matched QA in the list of top twenty retrieved QA pairs for each retrieval method.

5.3.2 Results

On the *Seen* set of queries, as expected the retrieval accuracy scores for the various retrieval techniques performed exceedingly well. The unigram based *tf.idf* method retrieved 93% of the user's query in the first position, 97% in one of top-5 positions and 100% in one of top-10 positions. All the other retrieval methods retrieved the user's query in the first position for all the *Seen* queries (100% accuracy).

In Table 1, we tabulate the results of the Coherence scores for the top-5 questions retrieved using the different retrieval techniques for the *Seen* set of queries. Here, the higher the n-gram the more coherent is the set of the results to the user's query. It is interesting to note that the BLEU-score and Levenshtein similarity driven retrieval methods do not differ significantly in their scores from the n-gram *tf.idf* based metrics.

Method		Coherence Metric for top-5 results
TF-IDF	unigram	61.58
	bigram	66.23
	trigram	66.23
	4-gram	69.74
BLEU-score		66.29
Levenshtein		67.36

Table 1: Coherence metric results for top-5 queries retrieved using different retrieval techniques for the *seen* set.

In Table 2, we present the retrieval results using different methods on the *Unseen* queries. For 240 of the 645 unseen queries, the human expert found that that there was no answer in the data repository that could be considered semantically equivalent to the human-generated response to that query. So, these 240 queries cannot be answered using the current database. For the remaining 405 unseen queries, over 60% have their Best-Matched question-answer pair retrieved in the top-1 position. We expect the coverage to improve considerably by increasing the size of the QA archive.

Method		Top-1	Top-20
TFIDF	Unigram	69.13	75.81
	Bigram	62.46	67.41
	Trigram	61.97	65.93
	4-gram	56.54	58.77
	WCN	70.12	78.52
Levenshtein		67.9	77.29
BLEU-score		72.0	75.31

Table 2: Retrieval results for the Unseen queries

5.3.3 Speech-driven query retrieval

In Equation 6, we show the tight integration of WCNs and *SearchFST* using the FST composition operation ($\circ$). λ is used to scale the weights[6] from the acoustic/language models on the WCNs against the weights on the *SearchFST*. As before, we use Equation 3 to retrieve the top N QA pairs. The tight integration is expected to improve both the ASR and Search accuracies by co-constraining both components.

$$D = \pi_2(Unigrams(WCN)^{\lambda} \circ SearchFST) \quad (6)$$

For this experiment, we use the speech utterances corresponding to the *Unseen* set as the test set. We use a different set of 250 *speech* queries as the

[6] fixed using the development set

development set. In Table 3, we show the Word and Sentence Accuracy measures for the best path in the WCN before and after the composition of *SearchFST* with the WCN on the development and test sets. We note that by integrating the constraints from the search index, the ASR accuracies can be improved by about 1% absolute.

Set	# of utterances	Word Accuracy	Sentence Accuracy
Dev Set	250	77.1(78.2)	54(54)
Test Set	645	70.8(72.1)	36.7(37.1)

Table 3: ASR accuracies of the best path before and after (in parenthesis) the composition of SearchFST

Since we have the speech utterances of the *Unseen* set, we were also able to compute the search results obtained by integrating the ASR WCNs with the *SearchFST*, as shown in line 5 of Table 2. These results show that the the integration of the ASR WCNs with the *SearchFST* produces higher search accuracy compared to ASR 1-best.

6 Dynamic and Static Questions

Storing previously answered questions and their answers allows `Qme!` to retrieve the answers to a subclass of questions quickly and accurately. We term this subclass as *static* questions since the answers to these questions remain the same irrespective of when and where the questions are asked. Examples of such questions are *What is the speed of light?*, *When is George Washington's birthday?*. In contrast, there is a subclass of questions, which we term *dynamic* questions, for which the answers depend on when and where they are asked. For such questions the above method results in less than satisfactory and sometimes inaccurate answers. Examples of such questions are *What is the stock price of General Motors?*, *Who won the game last night?*, *What is playing at the theaters near me?*.

We define *dynamic* questions as questions whose answers change more frequently than once a year. In dynamic questions, there may be no explicit reference to time, unlike the questions in the TERQAS corpus (Radev and Sundheim., 2002) which explicitly refer to the temporal properties of the entities being questioned or the relative ordering of past and future events. The time-dependency of a dynamic question lies in the temporal nature of its answer. For example, consider the dynamic question, "What is the address of the theater 'White Christmas' is playing at in New York?". White Christmas is a seasonal play that plays in New York every year for a few weeks in December and January, but it does not necessarily at the same theater every year. So, depending when this question is asked, the answer will be different.

Interest in temporal analysis for question-answering has been growing since the late 1990's. Early work on temporal expressions identification using a tagger led to the development of TimeML (Pustejovsky et al., 2001), a markup language for annotating temporal expressions and events in text. Other examples include QA-by-Dossier with Constraints (Prager et al., 2004), a method of improving QA accuracy by asking auxiliary questions related to the original question in order to temporally verify and restrict the original answer. (Moldovan et al., 2005) detect and represent temporally related events in natural language using logical form representation. (Saquete et al., 2009) use the temporal relations in a question to decompose it into simpler questions, the answers of which are recomposed to produce the answers to the original question.

6.1 Dynamic/Static Classification

We automatically classify questions as dynamic and static questions. Answers to static questions can be retrieved from the QA archive. To answer dynamic questions, we query the database(s) associated with the topic of the question through web forms on the Internet. We use a topic classifier to detect the topic of a question followed by a dynamic/static classifier trained on questions related to a topic, as shown in figure 5. Given the question *what movies are playing around me?*, we detect it is a movie related dynamic question and query a movie information web site (e.g. www.fandango.com) to retrieve the results based on the user's GPS information.

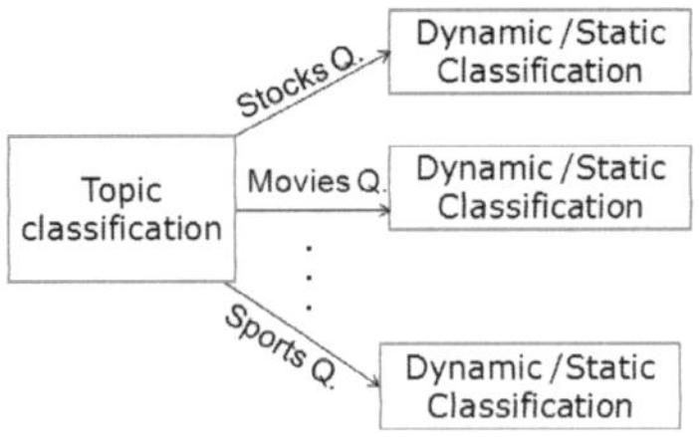

Figure 5: Chaining two classifiers

We used supervised learning to train the topic

classifier, since our entire dataset is annotated by human experts with topic labels. In contrast, to train a dynamic/static classifier, we experimented with the following three different techniques.

Baseline: We treat questions as dynamic if they contain temporal indexicals, e.g. *today*, *now*, *this week*, *two summers ago*, *currently*, *recently*, which were based on the TimeML corpus. We also included spatial indexicals such as *here*, and other substrings such as *cost of* and *how much is*. A question is considered static if it does not contain any such words/phrases.

Self-training with bagging: The general self-training with bagging algorithm (Banko and Brill, 2001) is presented in Table 6 and illustrated in Figure 7(a). The benefit of self-training is that we can build a better classifier than that built from the small seed corpus by simply adding in the large unlabeled corpus without requiring hand-labeling.

1. Create k bags of data, each of size $|L|$, by sampling with replacement from labeled set L.
2. Train k classifiers; one classifier on each of k bags.
3. Each classifier predicts labels of the unlabeled set.
4. The N labeled instances that j of k classifiers agree on with the highest average confidence is added to the labeled set L, to produce a new labeled set L'.
5. Repeat all 5 steps until stopping criteria is reached.

Figure 6: Self-training with bagging

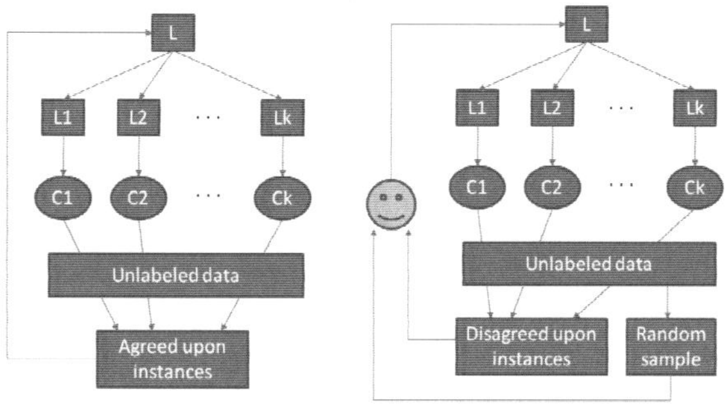

(a) (b)

Figure 7: (a) Self-training with bagging (b) Committee-based active-learning

In order to prevent a bias towards the majority class, in step 4, we ensure that the distribution of the static and dynamic questions remains the same as in the annotated seed corpus. The benefit of bagging (Breiman, 1996) is to present different views of the same training set, and thus have a way to assess the certainty with which a potential training instance can be labeled.

Active-learning: This is another popular method for training classifiers when not much annotated data is available. The key idea in active learning is to annotate only those instances of the dataset that are most difficult for the classifier to learn to classify. It is expected that training classifiers using this method shows better performance than if samples were chosen randomly for the same human annotation effort. Figure 7(b) illustrates the algorithm and Figure 8 describes the algorithm, also known as committee-based active-learning (Banko and Brill, 2001).

1. Create k bags of data, each of size $|L|$, by sampling with replacement from the labeled set L.
2. Train k classifiers, one on each bag of the k bags.
3. Each classifier predicts the labels of the unlabeled set.
4. Choose N instances from the unlabeled set for human labeling. $N/2$ of the instances are those whose labels the committee of classifiers have highest vote entropy (uncertainity). The other $N/2$ of the instances are selected randomly from the unlabeled set.
5. Repeat all 5 steps until stopping criteria is reached.

Figure 8: Active Learning algorithm

We used the maximum entropy classifier in Llama (Haffner, 2006) for all of the above classification tasks.

6.2 Experiments and Results

6.2.1 Topic Classification

The topic classifier was trained using a training set consisted of over one million questions downloaded from the web which were manually labeled by human experts as part of answering the questions. The test set consisted of 15,000 randomly selected questions. Word trigrams of the question are used as features for a MaxEnt classifier which outputs a score distribution on all of the 104 possible topic labels. The error rate results for models selecting the top topic and the top two topics according to the score distribution are shown in Table 4. As can be seen these error rates are far lower than the baseline model of selecting the most frequent topic.

Model	Error Rate
Baseline	98.79%
Top topic	23.9%
Top-two topics	12.23%

Table 4: Results of topic classification

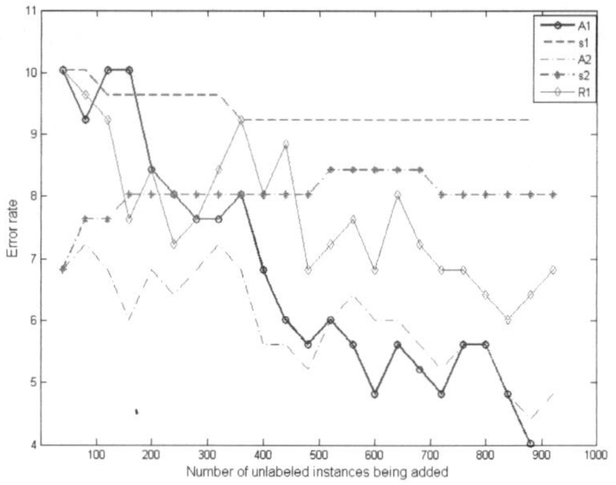

Figure 9: Change in classification results

6.2.2 Dynamic/static Classification

As mentioned before, we experimented with three different approaches to bootstrapping a dynamic/static question classifier. We evaluate these methods on a 250 question test set drawn from the broad topic of *Movies*. For the baseline model, we used the words/phrases discussed earlier based on temporal and spatial indexicals. For the "supervised" model, we use the baseline model to tag 500K examples and use the machine-annotated corpus to train a MaxEnt binary classifier with word trigrams as features. The error rate in Table 5 shows that it performs better than the baseline model mostly due to better lexical coverage contributed by the 500K examples.

Training approach	Lowest Error rate
Baseline	27.70%
"Supervised" learning	22.09%
Self-training	8.84%
Active-learning	4.02%

Table 5: Best Results of dynamic/static classification

In the *self-training* approach, we start with a small seed corpus of 250 hand-labeled examples from the *Movies* topic annotated with dynamic or static tags. We used the same set of 500K unlabeled examples as before and word trigrams from the question were used as the features for a MaxEnt classifier. We used 11 bags in the *bagging* phase of this approach and required that all 11 classifiers agree unanimously about the label of a new instance. Of all such instances, we randomly selected N instances to be added to the training set of the next iteration, while maintaining the distribution of the static and dynamic questions to be the same as that in the seed corpus. We experimented with various values of N, the number of newly labeled instances added at each iteration. The error rate at initialization is 10.4% compared to 22.1% of the "supervised" approach which can be directly attributed to the 250 hand-labeled questions. The lowest error rate of the self-training approach, obtained at N=100, is 8.84%, as shown in Table 5. In Figure 9, we show the change in error rate for N=40 (line S1 in the graph) and N=100 (line S2 in the graph).

For the *active learning* approach, we used the same set of 250 questions as the seed corpus, the same set of 500K unlabeled examples, the same test set, and the same set of word trigrams features as in the self-training approach. We used 11 bags for the bagging phase and selected top 20 new unlabeled instances on which the 11 classifiers had the greatest vote entropy to be presented to the human labeler for annotation. We also randomly selected 20 instances from the rest of the unlabeled set to be presented for annotation. The best error rate of this classifier on the test set is 4.02%, as shown in Table 5. The error rate over successive iterations is shown by line A1 in Figure 9.

In order to illustrate the benefits of selecting the examples *actively*, we repeated the experiment described above but with all 40 unlabeled instances selected randomly for annotation. The error rate over successive iterations is shown by line R1 in Figure 9. Comparing A1 to R1, we see that the error decreases faster when we select some of the unlabeled instances for annotation actively at each iteration.

7 Conclusion

In this paper, we have presented a system `Qme!`, a speech-driven question-answering system for mobile devices. We have proposed a query retrieval model for question-answering and demonstrated the mutual benefits of tightly coupling the ASR and Search components of the system. We have presented a novel concept of distinguishing questions that need dynamic information to be answered from those questions whose answers can be retrieved from an archive. We have shown results on bootstrapping such a classifier using semi-supervised learning techniques.

References

L. Androutsopoulos. 1995. Natural language interfaces to databases - an introduction. *Journal of Natural Language Engineering*, 1:29–81.

M. Banko and E. Brill. 2001. Scaling to very very large corpora for natural language disambiguation. In *Proceedings of the 39th annual meeting of the association for computational linguistics: ACL 2001*, pages 26–33.

L. Breiman. 1996. Bagging predictors. *Machine Learning*, 24(2):123–140.

S. Dumais, M. Banko, E. Brill, J. Lin, and A. Ng. 2002. Web question answering: is more always better? In *SIGIR '02: Proceedings of the 25th annual international ACM SIGIR conference on Research and development in information retrieval*, pages 291–298, New York, NY, USA. ACM.

Google, 2009. *http://www.google.com/mobile.*

B.F. Green, A.K. Wolf, C. Chomsky, and K. Laughery. 1961. Baseball, an automatic question answerer. In *Proceedings of the Western Joint Computer Conference*, pages 219–224.

P. Haffner. 2006. Scaling large margin classifiers for spoken language understanding. *Speech Communication*, 48(iv):239–261.

E. Hatcher and O. Gospodnetic. 2004. *Lucene in Action (In Action series).* Manning Publications Co., Greenwich, CT, USA.

J. Jeon, W. B. Croft, and J. H. Lee. 2005. Finding similar questions in large question and answer archives. In *CIKM '05: Proceedings of the 14th ACM international conference on Information and knowledge management*, pages 84–90, New York, NY, USA. ACM.

B. Katz. 1997. Annotating the world wide web using natural language. In *Proceedings of RIAO.*

V.I. Levenshtein. 1966. Binary codes capable of correcting deletions, insertion and reversals. *Soviet Physics Doklady*, 10:707–710.

M. T. Maybury, editor. 2004. *New Directions in Question Answering.* AAAI Press.

Microsoft, 2009. *http://www.live.com.*

D. Moldovan, C. Clark, and S. Harabagiu. 2005. Temporal context representation and reasoning. In *Proceedings of the 19th International Joint Conference on Artificial Intelligence*, pages 1009–1104.

MSN-QnA, 2009. *http://qna.live.com/.*

K. Papineni, S. Roukos, T. Ward, and W.J. Zhu. 2002. Bleu: A method for automatic evaluation of machine translation. In *Proceedings of 40th Annual Meeting of the Association of Computational Linguistics*, pages 313–318, Philadelphia, PA, July.

J. Prager, J. Chu-Carroll, and K. Czuba. 2004. Question answering using constraint satisfaction: Qa-by-dossier-with-contraints. In *Proceedings of the 42nd annual meeting of the association for computational linguistics: ACL 2004*, pages 574–581.

J. Pustejovsky, R. Ingria, R. Saurí, J. Casta no, J. Littman, and R. Gaizauskas., 2001. *The language of time: A reader*, chapter The specification languae – TimeML. Oxford University Press.

D. Radev and B. Sundheim. 2002. Using timeml in question answering. Technical report, Brandies University.

S. Robertson. 2004. Understanding inverse document frequency: On theoretical arguments for idf. *Journal of Documentation*, 60.

E. Saquete, J. L. Vicedo, P. Martínez-Barco, R. Mu noz, and H. Llorens. 2009. Enhancing qa systems with complex temporal question processing capabilities. *Journal of Artificial Intelligence Research*, 35:775–811.

N. Tomuro and S. L. Lytinen. 2004. Retrieval models and Q and A learning with FAQ files. In *New Directions in Question Answering*, pages 183–202.

vlingo.com, 2009. *http://www.vlingomobile.com/downloads.html.*

R. J. Waldinger, D. E. Appelt, J. L. Dungan, J. Fry, J. R. Hobbs, D. J. Israel, P. Jarvis, D. L. Martin, S. Riehemann, M. E. Stickel, and M. Tyson. 2004. Deductive question answering from multiple resources. In *New Directions in Question Answering*, pages 253–262.

J. Weizenbaum. 1966. ELIZA - a computer program for the study of natural language communication between man and machine. *Communications of the ACM*, 1:36–45.

T. Winograd. 1972. *Understanding Natural Language.* Academic Press.

W. A. Woods. 1973. Progress in natural language understanding - an application to lunar geology. In *Proceedings of American Federation of Information Processing Societies (AFIPS) Conference.*

X. Xue, J. Jeon, and W. B. Croft. 2008. Retrieval models for question and answer archives. In *SIGIR '08: Proceedings of the 31st annual international ACM SIGIR conference on Research and development in information retrieval*, pages 475–482, New York, NY, USA. ACM.

Yahoo!, 2009. *http://answers.yahoo.com/.*

F. Yang, J. Feng, and G. DiFabbrizio. 2006. A data driven approach to relevancy recognition for contextual question answering. In *HLT-NAACL 2006 Workshop on Interactive Question Answering*, New York, USA, June 8-9.

YellowPages, 2009. *http://www.speak4it.com.*

Dialogue-Oriented Review Summary Generation for Spoken Dialogue Recommendation Systems

Jingjing Liu, Stephanie Seneff, Victor Zue
MIT Computer Science & Artificial Intelligence Laboratory
32 Vassar Street, Cambridge, MA 02139
{jingl, seneff, zue}@csail.mit.edu

Abstract

In this paper we present an opinion summarization technique in spoken dialogue systems. Opinion mining has been well studied for years, but very few have considered its application in spoken dialogue systems. Review summarization, when applied to real dialogue systems, is much more complicated than pure text-based summarization. We conduct a systematic study on dialogue-system-oriented review analysis and propose a three-level framework for a recommendation dialogue system. In previous work we have explored a linguistic parsing approach to phrase extraction from reviews. In this paper we will describe an approach using statistical models such as decision trees and SVMs to select the most representative phrases from the extracted phrase set. We will also explain how to generate informative yet concise review summaries for dialogue purposes. Experimental results in the restaurant domain show that the proposed approach using decision tree algorithms achieves an outperformance of 13% compared to SVM models and an improvement of 36% over a heuristic rule baseline. Experiments also show that the decision-tree-based phrase selection model can achieve rather reliable predictions on the phrase label, comparable to human judgment. The proposed statistical approach is based on domain-independent learning features and can be extended to other domains effectively.

1 Introduction

Spoken dialogue systems are presently available for many purposes, such as weather inquiry (Zue et al., 2000), bus schedules and route guidance (Raux et al., 2003), customer service (Gorin et al., 1997), and train timetable inquiry (Eckert et al., 1993). These systems have been well developed for laboratory research, and some have become commercially viable.

The next generation of *intelligent* dialogue systems is expected to go beyond factoid question answering and straightforward task fulfillment, by providing active assistance and subjective recommendations, thus behaving more like human agents. For example, an intelligent dialogue system may suggest which airline is a better choice, considering cost, flight duration, take-off time, available seats, etc.; or suggest which digital camera is the most popular among teenagers or highest rated by professional photographers; or which restaurant is a perfect spot for a semi-formal business meeting or a romantic date.

Luckily, there are enormous amounts of reviews published by general users on the web every day. These are perfect resources for providing subjective recommendations and collective opinions. If there exists a systematic framework that harvests these reviews from general users, extracts the essence from the reviews and presents it appropriately in human-computer conversations, then we can enable dialogue systems to behave like a human shopping assistant, a travel agent, or a local friend who tells you where to find the best restaurant.

Summarization from online reviews, therefore, plays an important role for such dialogue systems. There have been previous studies on review analysis for text-based summarization systems (Mei et al., 2007; Titov and McDonald, 2008a; Branavan et al., 2008). Mixture models and topic models are used to predict the underlying topics of each document and generate a phrase-level summary. An aspect rating on each facet is also automatically

Human Language Technologies: The 2010 Annual Conference of the North American Chapter of the ACL, pages 64–72,
Los Angeles, California, June 2010.

learned with statistical models (Snyder and Barzilay, 2007; Titov and McDonald, 2008b; Baccianella et al., 2009). These approaches are all very effective, and the review databases generated are well presented.

So the first thought for developing a recommendation dialogue system is to use such a categorized summary in a table-lookup fashion. For example, a dialogue system for restaurant recommendations can look up a summary table as exemplified in Table 1, and generate a response utterance from each row: "Restaurant A has good service and bad food; restaurant B has good service and good food; restaurant C has great service and nice atmosphere; restaurant D has poor service and reasonable price."

Restaurant	Summary
A	Good service, bad food,
B	Good service, good food
C	Great service, nice atmosphere
D	Poor service, reasonable price

Table 1. A partial table of categorization-based review summaries.

Such a dialogue system is, however, not very informative. First of all, there is too much redundancy. Long utterances repeated in the same pattern on the same topic are quite boring, and the information density is very low. Second, such a summary is too coarse-grained to be helpful. A user querying a restaurant recommendation system expects more *fine-grained* information such as house specials, wine selections and choices on desserts rather than just general 'good food.'

In contrast to a 'text' summarization system, the textual space in a dialogue turn is often very limited. Speech is inherently serial, and it cannot be skipped and scanned easily. A dialogue system which speaks long diatribes in each single conversation turn would likely not be well received. We believe that the best unit of review summary for dialogue purposes is short succinct phrases (e.g., 'amazing sauce' and 'romantic ambiance') which are catalogued into categories to answer *high-level questions* such as "How is the *food* at this restaurant?" or "What about the *atmosphere*?" Also, domain-specific phrases are greatly needed to generate correct answers to *specific queries*, such as "Which restaurants have *fresh sushi*?" and "Show me restaurants that serve *fantastic cocktails*."

Thus, the generally used correlated topic models, although very effective in text-based systems, are not quite suitable for interactive dialogue systems. The missing piece is an *HCI-oriented (human computer interaction), fine-grained, informative* yet *concise* review summarization. A good recommendation system should be able to provide sufficient yet specific information to help users choose a restaurant, a movie or a consumer product. Figure 1 shows an example of a conversation with a good recommendation system, which 1) provides a *generalized yet high-density* review summary in *human-friendly dialogue*; 2) provides both a *coarse-grained* summary (e.g., 'authentic food') and *fine-grained* information such as house specialties.

U: Are there any French restaurants in Cambridge?
S: There are *five French restaurants* in Cambridge. *Most of them are on Backbay Street. And most of them have attentive service.*
U: Show me the ones that have nice ambiance.
S: *Two of them have nice ambiance*, Pierrot Bistrot Francais and Coriander.
U: How about the food?
S: *Pierrot Bistrot Francais has authentic food, fresh salad, and absolutely delicious spaghetti carbonara. The food at Coriander is below average. It has very greasy chicken tikka masala and dry bread.*

Figure 1. Example of a conversation with a good recommendation dialogue system ('U' denotes the user and 'S' denotes the dialogue system. The responses to the user queries are produced by our system and the actual dialogue was an illustration of system capacities).

Therefore, the task of developing recommendation dialogue systems is decomposed into three problems: 1) how to extract *context-related* phrases, both *coarse-grained* and *fine-grained*, from online reviews; 2) how to select a *representative set* from the extracted phrases to create an *informative yet concise dialogue-oriented* summary database; 3) how to generate *human-friendly dialogue responses* from the review summary database.

To tackle these problems, we propose a *three-level framework*. In previous work (Liu and Seneff, 2009), we explored the first level by proposing a linguistic parse-and-paraphrase paradigm for review phrase extraction. In this paper, we address the second problem: dialogue-oriented review summary generation. We propose an automatic approach to classifying high/low informative phrases using statistical models. Experiments conducted on a restaurant-domain dataset indicate that the proposed approach can predict phrase labels consistently with human judgment and can generate high-quality review summaries for dialogue purposes.

The rest of the paper is organized as follows: Section 2 gives an overview of the three-level framework for recommendation dialogue systems. In Section 3, we explain the proposed approach to dialogue-oriented review summary generation. Section 4 provides a systematic evaluation of the proposed approach, and Section 5 gives a further discussion on the experimental results. Section 6 summarizes the paper as well as pointing to future work.

2 System Overview

The three-level framework of a review-summary-based recommendation dialogue system is shown in Figure 2. The bottom level is linguistic phrase extraction. In previous work (Liu and Seneff, 2009), we employed a probabilistic lexicalized grammar to parse review sentences into a hierarchical representation, which we call a *linguistic frame*. From the linguistic frames, phrases are extracted by capturing a set of adjective-noun relationships. Adverbs and negations conjoined with the adjectives are also captured. We also calculated a numerical score for sentiment strength for each adjective and adverb, and further applied a cumulative offset model to assign a sentiment score to each phrase.

The approach relies on linguistic features that are independent of frequency statistics; therefore it can retrieve very rare phrases such as 'very greasy chicken tikka masala' and 'absolutely delicious spaghetti carbonara', which are very hard to derive from correlated topic models. Experimental results showed that the linguistic paradigm outperforms existing methods of phrase extraction which employ shallow parsing features (e.g., part-of-speech). The main contribution came from the linguistic frame, which preserves linguistic structure of a sentence by encoding different layers of semantic dependencies. This allows us to employ more sophisticated high-level linguistic features (e.g., long distance semantic dependencies) for phrase extraction.

However, the linguistic approach fails to distinguish highly informative and relevant phrases from uninformative ones (e.g., 'drunken husband', 'whole staff'). To apply these extracted phrases within a recommendation dialogue system, we have to filter out low quality or irrelevant phrases and maintain a concise summary database. This is the second level: dialogue-oriented review summary generation.

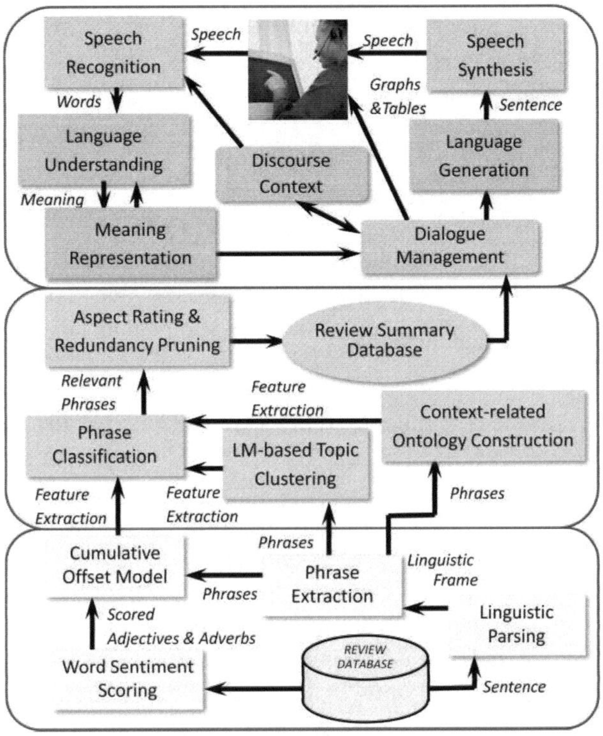

Figure 2. Three-level framework of review-based recommendation dialogue systems.

The standard of *highly informative and relevant* phrases is a very subjective problem. To gain insights on human judgment on this, the first two authors separately labeled a set of review-related phrases in a restaurant domain as 'good' and 'bad' summary phrases. We surveyed several subjects, all of whom indicated that, when querying a dialogue system for information about a restaurant, they care much more about special dishes served in this restaurant than generic descriptions such as 'good food.' This knowledge informed the annotation task: to judge whether a phrase delivered by a dialogue recommendation system would be helpful for users to make a decision. Surprisingly, although this is a difficult and subjective problem, the judgment from the two annotators is substantially consistent. By examining the annotations we observed that phrases such as 'great value' and 'good quality' are often treated as 'uninformative' as they are too common to be representative for a particular product, a restaurant or a movie. Phrases with neutral sentiment (e.g., 'green beans' and 'whole staff') are often considered as uninformative too. Phrases on specific topics such as house specialties (e.g., 'absolutely delicious spaghetti carbonara') are what the annotators care about most and are often considered as highly relevant, even though they may have only been seen once in a large database.

Driven by these criteria, from each phrase we extract a set of *statistical* features such as unigram/bigram probabilities and *sentiment* features such as sentiment orientation degree of the phrase, as well as underlying *semantic* features (e.g., whether the topic of the phrase fits in a domain-specific ontology). Classification models such as SVMs and decision tree algorithms are then trained on these features to automatically classify high/low informative phrases. Phrases identified as 'good' candidates are further pruned and catalogued to create concise summaries for dialogue purposes.

After generating the review summary database, the third level is to modify the response generation component in dialogue systems to create generalized and interactive conversations, as exemplified in Figure 1. The utterance from users is piped through speech recognition and language understanding. The meaning representation is then sent to the dialogue management component for *review-summary database lookup*. A response is then generated by the language generation component, and a speech utterance is generated by the synthesizer and sent back to the user. The dialogue system implementation is beyond the scope of this paper and will be discussed later in a separate paper.

3 Dialogue-oriented Review Summary Generation

Given an inquiry from users, the answer from a recommendation system should be helpful and relevant. So the first task is to identify a phrase as 'helpful' or not. The task of identifying a phrase as informative and relevant, therefore, is defined as a classification problem:

$$y = \bar{\theta} \cdot \bar{x} = \sum_{i=1}^{n} \theta_i x_i \qquad (1)$$

where y is the label of a phrase, assigned as '1' if the phrase is highly informative and relevant, and '-1' if the phrase is uninformative. $\bar{x}$ is the feature vector extracted from the phrase, and $\bar{\theta}$ is the coefficient vector.

We employ statistical models such as SVMs (Joachims, 1998) and decision trees (Quinlan, 1986) to train the classification model. For model learning, we employ a feature set including *statistical features*, *sentiment features* and *semantic features*.

Generally speaking, phrases with neutral sentiment are less informative than those with strong sentiment, either positive or negative. For example, 'fried seafood appetizer', 'baked halibut', 'electronic bill' and 'red drink' do not indicate whether a restaurant is worth trying, as they did not express whether the fried seafood appetizer or the baked halibut are good or bad. Therefore, we take the sentiment score of each phrase generated from a cumulative offset model (Liu and Seneff, 2009) as a *sentiment feature*. Sentiment scores of phrases are exemplified in Table 2 (on a scale of 1 to 5).

Phrase	Sc.	Phrase	Sc.
really welcoming atmosphere	4.8	truly amazing flavor	4.6
perfect portions	4.4	very tasty meat	4.3
busy place	3.1	typical Italian restaurant	3.1
a little bit high price	2.2	pretty bad soup	1.8
sloppy service	1.8	absolute worst service	1.4

Table 2. Examples of sentiment scores of phrases.

We also employ a set of *statistical features* for model training, such as the unigram probability of the adjective in a phrase, the unigram probability of the noun in a phrase, the unigram probability of the phrase and the bigram probability of the adjective-noun pair in a phrase.

Statistical features, however, fail to reveal the underlying semantic meaning of phrases. For example, phrases 'greasy chicken tikka masala' and 'drunken husband' have the same *n*-gram probabilities in our corpus (a single observation), but they should certainly not be treated as the same. To capture the semantic meanings of phrases, we first cluster the topics of phrases into generic semantic categories. The language-model based algorithm is given by:

$$P(t_c \mid t_i) = \sum_{a\in A} P(t_c|a) \cdot P(a|t_i)$$

$$= \sum_{a\in A} \frac{P(a,t_c)}{P(a)} \cdot \frac{P(a,t_i)}{P(t_i)}$$

$$= \frac{1}{P(t_i)} \sum_{a\in A} \frac{1}{P(a)} \cdot P(a,t_c) \cdot P(a,t_i) \qquad (2)$$

where A represents the set of all the adjectives in the corpus. We select a small set of initial topics with the highest frequency counts (e.g., 'food', 'service' and 'atmosphere'). For each of the other topics t_c (e.g., 'chicken', 'waitress' and 'décor'), we calculate its similarity with each initial topic t_i based on the bigram probability statistics. For those topics with conditional probability higher than a threshold for an initial topic t_i, we assign them to the cluster of t_i. We use this as a *semantic feature*, e.g., whether the topic of a phrase belongs to a generic semantic category. Table 3 gives some clustering examples.

Category	Relevant Topics
food	appetizer, beer, bread, fish, fries, ice cream, margaritas, menu, pizza, pasta, rib, roll, sauce, seafood, sandwich, steak, sushi, dessert, cocktail, brunch
service	waiter, staff, management, server, hostess, chef, bartender, waitstaff
atmosphere	décor, ambiance, music, vibe, setting, environment, crowd
price	bill, pricing, prices

Table 3. Topic to semantic category clustering.

This language-model-based method relies on bigram probability statistics and can well cluster highly frequent topics. Categories such as 'service' and 'atmosphere' contain very limited related topics, most of which have high frequencies (e.g., 'waiter', 'staff', 'ambiance' and 'vibe'). The category 'food', however, is very domain-specific and contains a very large vocabulary, from generic sub-categories such as 'sushi', 'dessert' and 'sandwich' as shown in the examples, to specific courses such as 'bosc pear bread pudding' and 'herb roasted vermont pheasant wine cap mushrooms'. These domain-specific topics have very low frequencies, yet they are very relevant and valuable. But many of them are discarded by the clustering. It would be a similar case in other domains. For example, consumer products, movies and books all have domain-independent semantic categories (e.g., 'price' and 'released date') and domain-specific categories (e.g., technical features of consumer products, casts of movies and authors of books).

To recover these context-relevant topics, we employ domain context relations such as a *context-related ontology*. A context-related ontology can be constructed from structured web resources such as online menus of restaurants, names of actors and actresses from movie databases, and specifications of products from online shops. An example of a partial online menu of a restaurant is shown in Figure 3. From these structured web resources, we can build up a hierarchical ontology, based on which a set of *semantic features* can be extracted (e.g., whether a phrase contains a course name, or an actress's name, or a dimension of technical features of a consumer product).

Entree
Roasted Pork Loin Wrapped In Bacon with watermelon and red onion salad spicy honey-mustard bbq sauce
Spicy Halibut And Clam Roast with bacon braised greens, white beans and black trumpet mushrooms
Parmesan and Caramelized Shallot Wrapper Style Ravioli turnip greens and white truffle oil
Herb Roasted Vermont Pheasant Wine Cap Mushrooms, Pearl Onions and Fava Beans
Dessert
Chocolate Tasting Plate of white chocolate bombe milk chocolate creme brulée and dark chocolate flourless cake
White Fruit Tasting Plate of warm apple strudel butterscotch, Bosc Pear bread pudding and toasted coconut panna cotta

↓

Entrée	Pork loin, bacon, watermelon, red onion salad, honey, mustard, bbq sauce
Dessert	Chocolate, milk, crème brulee, cake

Figure 3. Example of a partial online menu and an exemplary ontology derived.

After the classification, phrases identified as 'highly informative and relevant' are clustered into different aspects according to the semantic category clustering and the hierarchical ontology. An average sentiment score for each aspect is then calculated:

$$ave(s_t) = \frac{\sum_{j\in N_s} r_j}{|N_s|} \qquad (3)$$

where s_t represents the aspect s of entry t (e.g., a restaurant, a movie, or a consumer product), N_s represents the set of phrases in the cluster of aspect s, and r_j represents the sentiment score of phrase j in the cluster.

The set of phrases selected for one entry may come from several reviews on this single entry, and many of them may include the same noun (e.g., 'good fish', 'not bad fish' and 'above-average fish' for one restaurant). Thus, the next step is multi-phrase redundancy resolution. We select the phrase with a sentiment score closest to the average score of its cluster as the most representative phrase on each topic:

$$m = argmin_{j \in N_i}(|r_j - ave(s_t)|) \quad (4)$$

where $ave(s_t)$ represents the average sentiment score of aspect s, N_i represents the set of phrases on the same topic i in the cluster s, and r_j represents the sentiment score of phrase j.

This sequence of topic categorization, ontology construction, phrase pruning and redundancy elimination leads to a summary database, which can be utilized for dialogue generation in spoken recommendation systems. A review summary database entry generated by the proposed approaches is exemplified in Figure 4.

```
{ restaurant "dali restaurant and tapas bar"
   :atmosphere ( "wonderful evening", "cozy atmosphere", "fun decor", "romantic date" )
   :atmosphere_rating "4.1"
   :food ( "very fresh ingredients", "tasty fish", "creative dishes", "good sangria" )
   :food_rating "3.9"
   :service ( "fast service" )
   :service_rating "3.9"
   :general ("romantic restaurant", "small space" )
   :general_rating "3.6"            }
```

Figure 4. Example of a review summary database entry generated by the proposed approaches.

4 Experiments

In this project, we substantiate the proposed approach in a restaurant domain for our spoken dialogue system (Gruenstein and Seneff, 2007), which is a web-based multimodal dialogue system allowing users to inquire about information about restaurants, museums, subways, etc. We harvested a data collection of 137,569 reviews on 24,043 restaurants in 9 cities in the U.S. from an online restaurant evaluation website[1]. From the dataset, 857,466 sentences were subjected to parse analysis; and a total of 434,372 phrases (114,369 unique ones) were extracted from the parsable subset (78.6%) of the sentences.

Most pros/cons consist of well-formatted phrases; thus, we select 3,000 phrases extracted from pros/cons as training data. To generate a human judgment-consistent training set, we manually label the training samples with 'good' and 'bad' labels. We then randomly select a subset of 3,000 phrases extracted from review texts as the test set and label the phrases. The kappa agreement between two sets of annotations is 0.73, indicating substantial consistency. We use the two annotation sets as the ground truth.

To extract context-related semantic features, we collect a large pool of well-formatted menus from an online resource[2], which contains 16,141 restaurant menus. Based on the hierarchical structure of these collected menus, we build up a context-related ontology and extract a set of semantic features from the ontology, such as whether the topic of a phrase is on *category-level* (e.g., 'entrée', 'dessert', 'appetizers', 'salad'), whether the topic is on *course-level* (e.g., 'Roasted Pork Loin', 'Spicy Halibut and Clam Roast'), and whether the topic is on *ingredient-level* (e.g., 'beans', 'chicken', 'mushrooms', 'scallop').

We employ the three types of features as aforementioned to train the SVMs and the decision tree models. To select the most valuable features for model training, we conducted a set of leave-one-feature-out experiments for both the SVMs and the decision tree models. We found that all the features except the *adjective unigram probability* contribute positively to model learning. From further data analysis we observed that many phrases with popular adjectives have context-unrelated nouns, which makes the adjective unigram probability fail to become a dominant factor for phrase relevance. Using the adjective unigram probability as a learning feature will mislead the system into trusting an adjective that is common but has a poor bigram affinity to the noun in the phrase. Thus, we eliminate this feature for both the SVMs and the decision tree learning.

[1] http://www.citysearch.com
[2] http://www.menupages.com

To evaluate the performance of the classification models, we take a set of intuitively motivated heuristic rules as the baseline. Figure 5 gives the pseudo-code of the heuristic rule algorithm, which uses variations of all the features except the unigram probability of adjectives.

```
If(sentiment score of the phrase exists)
  if(sentiment score is within neutral range) label=-1;
  else
     if(phrase appeared in the training data)
        if((3<frequency of phrase < 100))  label = 1;
        else
           if(frequency of phrase >= 100)  label = -1;
           else  if(topic belongs to ontology) label = 1;
                    else  label = -1;
     else
        if(topic belongs to ontology)  label = 1;
        else  label = -1;
else
  if(phrase appeared in the training data)
      if((3<frequency of phrase < 100))
          if(topic belongs to ontology)  label = 1;
          else  label = -1;
      else
          if(frequency of phrase >= 100)  label = -1;
          else
             if(topic belongs to ontology)  label = 1;
             else  if(frequency of noun > 100) label = 1;
                      else  label = -1;
  else
     if(topic belongs to ontology)  label = 1;
     else   if(frequency of noun > 100)  label = 1;
              else  label = -1;
```

Figure 5. Pseudo-code of the heuristic rule algorithm.

The performance of classification by different models is shown in Table 4. Although the heuristic rule algorithm is complicated and involves human knowledge, the statistical models trained by SVMs and the decision tree algorithms both outperform the baseline significantly. The SVM model outperforms the baseline by 10.5% and 11.9% on the two annotation sets respectively. The decision tree model outperforms the baseline by 16.4% and 23.2% (average relative improvement of 36%), and it also outperforms the SVM model by 5.9% and 11.3% (average relative improvement of 13%).

The classification model using the decision tree algorithm can achieve a precision of 77.9% and 74.5% compared with the ground truth, which is quite comparable to human judgment (the precision of one annotation set based on the other is 74%). This shows that the decision tree model can predict phrase labels as reliably as human judgment.

	Baseline	**SVM**	**Decision tree**
Annotation 1	61.5%	72.0%	**77.9%**
Annotation 2	51.3%	63.2%	**74.5%**

Table 4. Precision of phrase classification using the heuristic rule baseline, the SVM model, and the decision tree algorithm.

To gain further insight on the contributions of each feature set to the decision tree learning, Table 5 gives the experimental results on leaving each feature out of model training. As shown, without semantic features, the precision is 70.6% and 65.4% on the two annotation sets, lower by 7.3% and 9.1% than the case of training the model with all the features (77.9% and 74.5%). This shows that the semantic features significantly contribute to the decision tree learning.

Feature set	**A1**	**A2**
all features	**77.9%**	**74.5%**
without bigram probability of adjective-noun pair	56.6% (-21.3%)	63.9% (-10.6%)
without unigram probability of the phrase	57.6% (-20.3%)	64.3% (-10.2%)
without unigram probability of the noun	59.8% (-18.1%)	67.8% (-6.7%)
without sentiment score of the phrase	63.4% (-14.5%)	66.6% (-7.9%)
without underlying semantic features	70.6% (-7.3%)	65.4% (-9.1%)

Table 5. Performance of the decision tree model by leaving each feature out of model training ('A1' and 'A2' represent the annotation set 1 and 2 respectively).

The experimental results also show that the feature of bigram probability of the adjective-noun pair contributes the most to the model learning. Without this feature, the precision drops by 21.3% and 10.6%, reaching the lowest precision among all the leave-one-out experiments. This confirms our observation that although a single adjective is not dominant, the pair of the adjective and the noun that co-occurs with it plays an important role in the classification.

The sentiment of phrases also plays an important role. Without sentiment features, the precision drops to 63.4% and 66.6% respectively on the two annotations, decreasing by 14.5% and 7.9%. This shows that the sentiment features contribute significantly to the classification.

5 Discussions

Experimental results show that the decision tree algorithm outperforms the SVMs on this particular classification problem, and it outperforms the heuristic rule baseline significantly. Thus, although the identification of informativeness and relevance of phrases is a rather subjective problem, which is difficult to predict using only human knowledge, it can be well defined by decision trees. Part of the reason is that the decision tree algorithm can make better use of a combination of Boolean value features (e.g., whether a topic belongs to a context-related ontology) and continuous value features. Also, as the phrase classification task is very subjective, it is very similar to a 'hierarchical *if-else* decision problem' in human cognition, where decision tree algorithms can fit well. Figure 6 shows a partial simplified decision tree learned from our model, which can give an intuitive idea of the decision tree models.

6 Related Work

Sentiment classification and opinion mining have been well studied for years. Most studies have focused on text-based systems, such as document-level sentiment classification and sentence-level opinion aggregation (Turney, 2002; Pang et al., 2002; Dave et al., 2003; Hu and Liu, 2004; Popescu and Etzioni, 2005; Wilson et al., 2005; Zhuang et al., 2006; Kim and Hovy, 2006).

There was a study conducted by Carenini et al. in 2006, which proposed a combination of a sentence extraction-based approach and a language generation-based approach for summarizing evaluative arguments. In our work, we utilize a lower-level phrase-based extraction approach, which utilizes high level linguistic features and syntactic structure to capture phrase patterns.

There was also a study on using reviews to generate a dictionary of mappings between semantic representations and realizations of concepts for dialogue systems (Higashinaka et al., 2006; Higashinaka, 2007). They also used the association between user ratings and reviews to capture semantic-syntactic structure mappings. A set of filtering rules was manually created to eliminate low-quality mappings. In our approach, we use an automatic approach to classifying high/low informative phrases. The learning features are domain-independent with no hand-crafted rules, and can be extended to other domains effortlessly.

7 Conclusions

In this paper we proposed a three-level framework for review-based recommendation dialogue systems, including linguistic phrase extraction, dialogue-oriented review summary generation, and human-friendly dialogue generation. The contributions of this paper are three-fold: 1) it identified and defined the research goal of utilizing opinion summarization for real human-computer conversation; 2) it formulated an evaluation methodology for high-density review summary for dialogue purposes; 3) it proposed an approach to automatic classification of high/low informative phrases using a decision tree model. Experimental results showed that the decision tree model significantly outperforms a heuristic rule baseline and the SVM model, and can resolve the phrase classification problem comparably to humans consistently.

Future work will focus on: 1) applying the sentiment scoring model to noun/verb sentiment assessment; 2) application of the review summary generation approach in other domains and other languages; 3) data collection on user engagement with our dialogue systems involving review-summary evaluation.

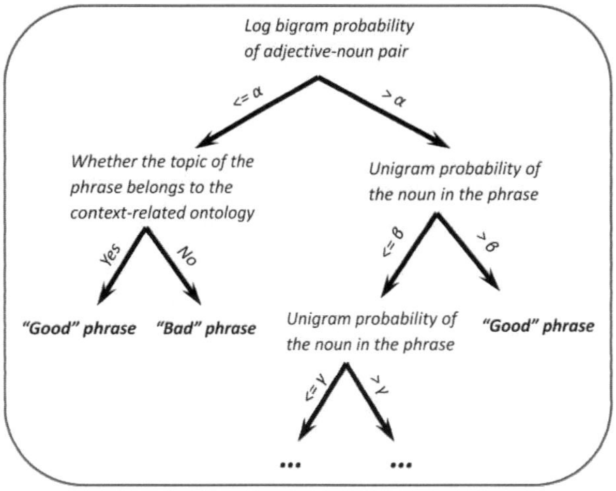

Figure 6. A partial simplified decision tree learned from our model.

References

Stefano Baccianella, Andrea Esuli, and Fabrizio Sebastiani. 2009. Multi-facet Rating of Product Reviews. In *Proceedings of European Conference on Information Retrieval.*

S.R.K. Branavan, Harr Chen, Jacob Eisenstein, and Regina Barzilay. 2008. Learning document-level semantic properties from free-text annotations. In *Proc. of ACL.*

Giuseppe Carenini, Raymond Ng, and Adam Pauls. 2006. Multi-Document Summarization of Evaluative Text. In *Proceedings of the Conference of the European Chapter of the Association for Computational Linguistics.*

Kushal Dave, Steve Lawrence, and David M. Pennock. 2003. Mining the peanut gallery: opinion extraction and semantic classification of product reviews. In *Proceedings of the International Conference on World Wide Web.*

W. Eckert, T. Kuhn, H. Niemann, S. Rieck, A. Scheuer, and E. G. Schukat-talamazzini. 1993. A Spoken Dialogue System for German Intercity Train Timetable Inquiries. In *Proc. European Conf. on Speech Technology.*

Alexander Gruenstein and Stephanie Seneff. 2007. Releasing a Multimodal Dialogue System into the Wild: User Support Mechanisms. *In Proceedings of the 8th SIGdial Workshop on Discourse and Dialogue, Antwerp, pages 111-119.*

A. L. Gorin, G. Riccardi and J. H. Wright. 1997. "How may I help you?" *Speech Communication*, vol. 23, pp. 113–127.

Ryuichiro Higashinaka, Rashmi Prasad and Marilyn Walker. 2006. Learning to Generate Naturalistic Utterances Using Reviews in Spoken Dialogue Systems. *In Proceedings of COLING-ACL.*

Ryuichiro Higashinaka, Marilyn Walker and Rashmi Prasad. 2007. An Unsupervised Method for Learning Generation Dictionaries for Spoken Dialogue Systems by Mining User Reviews. *Journal of ACM Transactions on Speech and Language Processing.*

Minqing Hu and Bing Liu. 2004. Mining and summarizing customer reviews. In *Proceedings of the 2004 ACM SIGKDD international conference on Knowledge Discovery and Data mining.*

S.M. Kim and E.H. Hovy. 2006. Identifying and Analyzing Judgment Opinions. In *Proc. of HLT/NAACL.*

Jingjing Liu and Stephanie Seneff. 2009. Review Sentiment Scoring via a Parse-and-Paraphrase Paradigm. *In proceedings of EMNLP.*

Qiaozhu Mei, Xu Ling, Matthew Wondra, Hang Su, and ChengXiang Zhai. 2007. Topic Sentiment Mixture: Modeling Facets and Opinions in Weblogs. In *Proc. of WWW.*

Bo Pang, Lillian Lee, and S. Vaithyanathan. 2002. Thumbs up? Sentiment classification using machine learning techniques. In *Proceedings of EMNLP.*

A.M. Popescu and O. Etzioni. 2005. Extracting product features and opinions from reviews. In *Proceedings of EMNLP.*

JR Quinlan, 1986. Induction of decision trees. *Machine learning*, Springer-Netherlands.

A. Raux, B. Langner, A. Black, and M. Eskenazi. 2003. LET'S GO: Improving Spoken Dialog Systems for the Elderly and Non-natives. In *Proc. Eurospeech.*

Benjamin Snyder and Regina Barzilay. 2007. Multiple Aspect Ranking using the Good Grief Algorithm. In *Proceedings of NAACL-HLT.*

Ivan Titov and Ryan McDonald. 2008a. Modeling Online Reviews with Multi-Grain Topic Models. *In Proc. of WWW.*

Ivan Titov and Ryan McDonald. 2008b. A Joint Model of Text and Aspect Ratings for Sentiment Summarization. In *Proceedings of the Annual Conference of the Association for Computational Linguistics.*

Peter D. Turney. 2002. Thumbs up or thumbs down? Sentiment orientation applied to unsupervised classification of reviews. In *Proceedings of the Annual Conference of the Association for Computational Linguistics.*

T. Joachims. 1998. Text categorization with support vector machines: Learning with many relevant features. In *Proc. of ECML*, p. 137–142.

T. Wilson, J. Wiebe, and P. Hoffmann. 2005. Recognizing Contextual Polarity in Phrase-Level Sentiment Analysis. *In Proc. of HLT/EMNLP.*

Victor Zue, Stephanie Seneff, James Glass, Joseph Polifroni, Christine Pao, Timothy J. Hazen, and Lee Hetherington. 2000. JUPITER: A Telephone-Based Conversational Interface for Weather Information. In *IEEE Transactions on Speech and Audio Processing*, Vol. 8 , No. 1.

Li Zhuang, Feng Jing, and Xiao-Yan Zhu. 2006. Movie review mining and summarization. In *Proceedings of the 15th ACM international conference on Information and knowledge management.*

Minimally-Supervised Extraction of Entities from Text Advertisements

Sameer Singh
Dept. of Computer Science
University of Massachusetts
Amherst, MA 01003
sameer@cs.umass.edu

Dustin Hillard
Advertising Sciences
Yahoo! Labs Silicon Valley
Santa Clara, CA 95054
dhillard@yahoo-inc.com

Chris Leggetter
Advertising Sciences
Yahoo! Labs Silicon Valley
Santa Clara, CA 95054
cjl@yahoo-inc.com

Abstract

Extraction of entities from ad creatives is an important problem that can benefit many computational advertising tasks. Supervised and semi-supervised solutions rely on labeled data which is expensive, time consuming, and difficult to procure for ad creatives. A small set of manually derived constraints on feature expectations over unlabeled data can be used to *partially* and *probabilistically* label large amounts of data. Utilizing recent work in constraint-based semi-supervised learning, this paper injects light weight supervision specified as these "constraints" into a semi-Markov conditional random field model of entity extraction in ad creatives. Relying solely on the constraints, the model is trained on a set of unlabeled ads using an online learning algorithm. We demonstrate significant accuracy improvements on a manually labeled test set as compared to a baseline dictionary approach. We also achieve accuracy that approaches a fully supervised classifier.

1 Introduction

Growth and competition in web search in recent years has created an increasing need for improvements in organic and sponsored search. While foundational approaches still focus on matching the exact words of a search to potential results, there is emerging need to better understand the underlying *intent* in queries and documents. The implicit intent is particularly important when little text is available, such as for user queries and advertiser creatives.

This work specifically explores the extraction of named-entities, i.e. discovering and labeling phrases in ad creatives. For example, for an ad "Move to San Francisco!", we would like to extract the entity *san francisco* and label it a CITY. Similarly, for an ad "Find DVD players at Amazon", we would extract *dvd players* as a PRODUCT and *amazon* as a ORGNAME. The named-entities provide important features to downstream tasks about what words and phrases are important, as well as information on the intent. Much recent research has focused on extracting useful information from text advertisement creatives that can be used for better retrieval and ranking of ads. Semantic annotation of queries and ad creatives allows for more powerful retrieval models. Structured representations of semantics, like the one studied in our task, can be directly framed as information extraction tasks, such as segmentation and named-entity recognition.

Information extraction methods commonly rely on labeled data for training the models. The human labeling of ad creatives would have to provide the complete segmentation and entity labels for the ads, which the information extraction algorithm would then rely on as the truth. For entity extraction from advertisements this involves familiarity with a large number of different domains, such as electronics, transportation, apparel, lodging, sports, dining, services, *etc*. This leads to an arduous and time consuming labeling process that can result in noisy and error-prone data. The problem is further compounded by the inherent ambiguity of the task, leading to the human editors often presenting conflicting and incorrect labeling.

Similar problems, to a certain degree, are also faced by a number of other machine learning tasks where completely relying on the labeled data leads to unsatisfactory results. To counter the noisy and sparse labels, *semi-supervised learning* meth-

Human Language Technologies: The 2010 Annual Conference of the North American Chapter of the ACL, pages 73–81,
Los Angeles, California, June 2010.

ods utilize unlabeled data to improve the model (see (Chapelle et al., 2006) for an overview). Furthermore, recent work on *constraint-based semi-supervised learning* allows domain experts to easily provide additional light supervision, enabling the learning algorithm to learn using the prior domain knowledge, labeled and unlabeled data (Chang et al., 2007; Mann and McCallum, 2008; Bellare et al., 2009; Singh et al., 2010).

Prior domain knowledge, if it can be easily expressed and incorporated into the learning algorithm, can often be a high-quality and cheap substitute for labeled data. For example, previous work has often used dictionaries or *lexicons* (lists of phrases of a particular label) to bootstrap the model (Agichtein and Ganti, 2004; Canisius and Sporleder, 2007), leading to a *partial* labeling of the data. Domain knowledge can also be more *probabilistic* in nature, representing the probability of certain token taking on a certain label. For most tasks, labeled data is a convenient representation of the domain knowledge, but for complex domains such as structured information extraction from ads, these alternative easily expressible representations may be as effective as labeled data.

Our approach to solving the the named entity extraction problem for ads relies completely on domain knowledge not expressed as labeled data, an approach that is termed *minimally supervised*. Each ad creative is represented as a semi-Markov conditional random field that probabilistically represents the segmentation and labeling of the creative. External domain knowledge is expressed as a set of targets for the expectations of a small subset of the features of the model. We use *alternating projections* (Bellare et al., 2009) to train our model using this knowledge, relying on the rest of the features of the model to "dissipate" the knowledge. Topic model and co-occurrence based features help this propagation by generalizing the supervision to a large number of similar ads.

This method is applied to a large dataset of text advertisements sampled from a variety of different domains. The minimally supervised model performs significantly better than a model that incorporates the domain knowledge as hard constraints. Our model also performs competitively when compared to a supervised model trained on labeled data from a similar domain (web search queries).

Background material on semi-CRFs and constraint based semi-supervised learning is summarized in Section 2. In Section 3, we describe the problem of named entity recognition in ad creatives as a semi-CRF, and describe the features in Section 4. The constraints that we use to inject supervision into our model are listed in Section 5. We demonstrate the success of our approach in Section 6. This work is compared with related literature in Section 7.

2 Background

This section covers introductory material on the probabilistic representation of our model (semi-Markov conditional random fields) and the constraint-driven semi-supervised method that we use to inject supervision into the model.

2.1 Semi-Markov Conditional Random Fields

Conditional Random Fields (CRFs) (Lafferty et al., 2001) use a Markov random field to model the conditional probability $P(\mathbf{y}|\mathbf{x})$. CRFs are commonly used to learn sequential models, where the Markov field is a linear-chain, and $\mathbf{y}$ is a linear sequence of labels and each label $y_i \in \mathcal{Y}$. Let $\mathbf{f}$ be a vector of *local feature functions* $\mathbf{f} = \langle f^1, \ldots, f^K \rangle$, each of which maps a pair $(\mathbf{x}, \mathbf{y})$ and an index i to a measurement $f^k(i, \mathbf{x}, \mathbf{y}) \in \Re$. Let $\mathbf{f}(i, \mathbf{x}, \mathbf{y})$ be the vector of these measurements, and let $\mathbf{F}(\mathbf{x}, \mathbf{y}) = \sum_i^{|\mathbf{x}|} \mathbf{f}(i, \mathbf{x}, \mathbf{y})$. CRFs use these feature functions in conjunction with the parameters θ to represent the conditional probability as follows:

$$P(\mathbf{y}|\mathbf{x}, \theta) = \frac{1}{Z(\mathbf{x})} e^{\theta \cdot \mathbf{F}(\mathbf{x}, \mathbf{y})}$$

where $Z(x) = \sum_{\mathbf{y}'} e^{\theta \cdot \mathbf{F}(\mathbf{x}, \mathbf{y}')}$.

For sequential models where the same labels appear within a sequence as contiguous blocks (*e.g.*, named entity recognition) it is more convenient to represent these blocks directly as *segments*. This representation was formulated as *semi-Markov conditional random fields (Semi-CRFs)* in (Sarawagi and Cohen, 2004). The *segmentation* of a sequence is represented by $\mathbf{s} = \langle s_1, \ldots, s_p \rangle$ where each *segment* $s_j = \langle t_j, u_j, y_j \rangle$ consists of a *start position* t_j, an *end position* u_j, and a *label* $y_j \in \mathcal{Y}$. Similar to the CRF, let $\mathbf{g}$ be the vector of *segment feature functions* $\mathbf{g} = \langle g^1, \ldots, g^K \rangle$, each of which maps the pair $(\mathbf{x}, \mathbf{s})$ and an index j to a measurement $g^k(j, \mathbf{x}, \mathbf{s}) \in \Re$, and $\mathbf{G}(\mathbf{x}, \mathbf{s}) = \sum_j^{|\mathbf{s}|} \mathbf{g}(j, \mathbf{x}, \mathbf{s})$. The conditional probability is represented as:

$$P(\mathbf{s}|\mathbf{x}, \theta) = \frac{1}{Z(\mathbf{x})} e^{\theta \cdot \mathbf{G}(\mathbf{x}, \mathbf{s})}$$

where $Z(x) = \sum_{\mathbf{s}'} e^{\theta \cdot \mathbf{G}(\mathbf{x}, \mathbf{s}')}$. To assert the Markovian assumption, each $g^k(j, \mathbf{x}, \mathbf{s})$ only computes features based on $\mathbf{x}$, s_j, and y_{j-1}[1].

An exact inference algorithm was described in (Sarawagi and Cohen, 2004), and was later improved to be more efficient (Sarawagi, 2006).

2.2 Constraint Driven Learning Using Alternating Projections

Recent work in semi-supervised learning uses constraints as external supervision (Chang et al., 2007; Mann and McCallum, 2008; Bellare et al., 2009; Singh et al., 2010). These external constraints are specified as constraints on the expectations of a set of auxiliary features $\mathbf{g}' = \{g'_1, \ldots, g'_k\}$ over the unlabeled data. In particular, given the targets $\mathbf{u} - \{u_1, \ldots, u_k\}$ corresponding to the auxiliary features $\mathbf{g}'$, the constraints can take different forms, for example $\mathbb{L}_2$ penalty ($\frac{1}{2\beta}\|u_i - \sum_j E_p[g'_i(x_j, s)]\|_2^2 = 0$), $\mathbb{L}_1$ box constraints ($|u_i - \sum_j E_p[g'_i(x_j, s)]| \leq \beta$) and Affine constraints[2] ($E_p[g'_i(x, s)] \leq u_i$). In this work, we only use the affine form of the constraints.

For an example, using domain knowledge, we may know that token "arizona" should get the label STATE in at least half of the occurrences in our data. To capture this, we introduce an auxiliary feature g' : [[Label=STATE *given* Token="arizona"]]. The affine constraint is written as $E_p[g'(x, y)] \geq 0.5$.

These constraints have been incorporated into learning using Alternating Projections (Bellare et al., 2009). Instead of directly optimizing an objective function that includes the constraints, this method considers two distributions, p_λ and $q_{\lambda,\mu}$, where $p_\lambda(\mathbf{s}|\mathbf{x}) = \frac{1}{Z(\mathbf{x})} e^{\lambda \cdot \mathbf{G}(\mathbf{x}, \mathbf{s})}$ is the usual semi-Markov model, and $q_{\lambda,\mu} = \frac{1}{Z(\mathbf{x})} e^{(\lambda \cdot \mathbf{G}(\mathbf{x}, \mathbf{s}) + \mu \cdot \mathbf{G}'(\mathbf{x}, \mathbf{s}))}$ is an auxiliary distribution that satisfies the constraints and has low divergence with the model p_λ.

In the batch setting, parameters λ and μ are learned using an EM-like algorithm, where μ is fixed while optimizing λ and vice versa. Each of the updates in these steps decomposes according to the instances, leading to a stochastic gradient based online algorithm, as follows:

1. For $t = 1, \ldots, T$, let $\eta = \frac{1}{t + t_0}$ where $t_0 = 1/\eta_0$, η_0 the initial learning rate. Let labeled and unlabeled data set sizes be m and $n - m$ respectively. Let the initial parameters be λ^0 and μ^0, and α be the weight of $\mathbb{L}_2$ regularization on λ.

2. For a new *labeled* instance x_t with segmentation s_t, set $\mu^t = \mu^{t-1}$ and $\lambda^t = \lambda^{t-1} + \eta\left[\mathbf{g}(x_t, s_t) - E_{p_{\lambda^{t-1}}}[\mathbf{g}(x_t, s)] - \frac{\alpha\lambda^{t-1}}{n}\right]$.

3. For a new *unlabeled* instance x_t, $\mu^t = \mu^{t-1} + \eta\left[\frac{u}{(n-m)} - E_{q_{\lambda^{t-1},\mu^{t-1}}}[\mathbf{g}'(x_t, s)]\right]$ and $\lambda^t = \lambda^{t-1} + \eta\left[E_{q_{\lambda^{t-1},\mu^{t-1}}}[\mathbf{g}(x_t, s)] - E_{p_{\lambda^{t-1}}}[\mathbf{g}(x_t, s)] - \frac{\alpha\lambda^{t-1}}{n}\right]$.

Online training enables scaling the approach to large data sets, as is the case with ads. In our approach we rely only on unlabeled data ($m = 0$, and step 2 of the above algorithm does not apply).

3 Model

Most text ads consist of a brief *title* and an accompanying *abstract* that provides additional information. The objective of our paper is to extract the named-entity phrases within these titles and abstracts, then label them with a *type* from a predetermined taxonomy. An example of such an extraction is shown in Fig 1.

We represent the ad creatives as a sequence of individual tokens, with a special token inserted between the title and the abstract of the ad. The distribution over possible phrases and labels of the ad is expressed as a semi-Markov conditional random field, as described earlier in Section 2.1.

3.1 Label Taxonomy

In most applications of CRFs and semi-CRFs, the domain of labels is a fixed set $\mathcal{Y}$, where each label indexes into one value. Instead, in our approach, we represent our set of labels as a taxonomy (tree). The labels higher in the taxonomy are more generic (for

[1] i.e. $g^k(j, \mathbf{x}, \mathbf{s})$ can be written as $g^k(y_{j-1}, \mathbf{x}, s_j)$

[2] where $E_p[g]$ represents the expectation of g over the unlabeled data using the model p.

Ad Title: Bradley International Airport Hotel
Ad Abstract: Marriott Hartford, CT Airport hotel - free shuttle service & parking.

Output: [Bradley International] Airport [Hotel]
[Marriott] [Hartford,] [CT] Airport [hotel] free [shuttle service & parking.]

Label	Segment
PLACE: AIRPORT	Bradley International
BUSINESS: TRAVEL	Hotel
ORGNAME: LODGING	Marriott
PLACE: CITY	Hartford
PLACE: STATE	CT
BUSINESS: TRAVEL	hotel
PRODUCT: TRAVEL	shuttle service & parking.

Figure 1: **Example Prediction:** An example of an ad creative (title and abstract), along with a set of probable extracted entities. Note that even in this relatively simple example, there is some ambiguity about what is the correct segmentation and labeling.

instance, PLACE) and the labels lower in the taxonomy are more specific (for instance, STATE may be a child of PLACE). The taxonomy of labels that we use for tagging phrases is shown in Figure 2.

When the model predicts a label for a segment, it can be from any of the levels in the tree. The benefits of this is multi-fold. First, this allows the model to be flexible in predicting labels at a lower (or higher) level based on its confidence. For example, the model may have enough evidence to label "san francisco" a CITY, however, for "georgia" it may not have enough context to discriminate between STATE or COUNTRY, but could confidently label it a PLACE. Secondly, this also allows us to design the features over multiple levels of label granularity, which leads to a more expressive model. Expectation constraints can be specified over this expanded set of features, at any level of the taxonomy.

In order to incorporate the nested labels into our model, we observe that every feature that fires for a non-leaf label should also fire for all descendants of that label, *e.g.* every feature that is active for label PLACE should also be active for a label CITY, COUNTRY, *etc* [3]. Following the observation, for every feature $g^k(\mathbf{x}, \langle t_j, u_j, y_j \rangle)$ that is active, we also fire $\forall y' \in \text{desc}(y_j), g^k(\mathbf{x}, \langle t_j, u_j, y' \rangle)$[4]. The same procedure is applied to the constraints.

4 Features

Our learning algorithm relies on constraints $\mathbf{g}'$ as supervision to extract entities, but even though constraints are designed to be generic they do not cover the whole dataset. The learning algorithm needs to propagate the supervision to instances where the constraints are not applicable, guided by the set of feature functions $\mathbf{g}$. More expressive and relevant features will provide better propagation. Even though these feature functions represent the "unsupervised" part of the model (in that they are only dependent on the unlabeled sequences), they play an important role in propagating the supervision throughout the dataset.

4.1 Sequence and Segment Features

Our first set of features are the commonly used features employed in linear-chain sequence models such as CRFs and HMMs. These consist of factors between each token and its corresponding label, and neighboring labels. They also include transition factors between the labels. These are *local feature functions* that are defined only over pairs of token-wise

[3]Note that this argument works similarly for the taxonomy represented as a DAG, where the descendants are of a node are all nodes reachable from it. We do not explore this structure of the taxonomy in this paper.

[4]This example describes when $g^k(y_{j-1}, \mathbf{x}, s_j)$ ignores y_{j-1}. For the usual case $g^k(y_{j-1}, \mathbf{x}, s_j)$, features between all pairs of descendants of y_{j-1} and y_j are enabled.

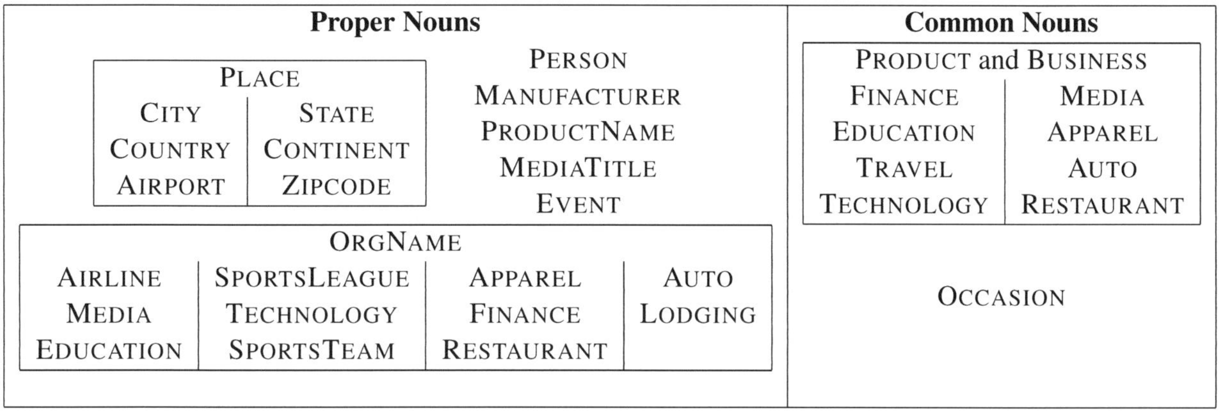

Figure 2: **Label Taxonomy:** The set of labels that are used are shown grouped by the parent label. PRODUCT and BUSINESS labels have been merged for brevity, i.e. there are two labels of each child label shown (e.g. PRODUCT: AUTO and BUSINESS: AUTO). An additional label OTHER is used for the tokens that do not belong to any entities.

labels y_j and y_{j-1}. To utilize the semi-Markov representation that allows features over the predicted segmentation, we add the segment length and prefix/suffix tokens of the segment as features.

4.2 Segment Clusters

Although the sequence and segment features capture a lot of useful information, they are not sufficient for propagation. For example, if we have a constraint about the token "london" being a CITY, but not about "boston", the model can only rely on similar contexts between 'london" and 'boston" to propagate the information. To allow more complicated propagation to occur, we use features based on a clustering of segments.

The segment cluster features are based on similarity between segments from English sentences. A large corpus of English documents were taken from web, from which 5.1 billion unique sentences were extracted. Using the co-occurrence of segments in the sentences as a distance measure, K-Means is used to identify clusters of segments as described in (Pantel et al., 2009). The cluster identity of each segment is added as a feature to the model, capturing the intuition that segments that appear in the same cluster should get the same label.

4.3 Topic Model

Most of the ads lie in separate domains with very little overlap, for example travel and electronics. Additional information about the domain can be very useful for identifying entities in the ad. For example, consider the token "amazon". It may be difficult to discern whether the token refers to the geographical region or the website from just the features in the model, however given that the domain of the ad is travel (or conversely, electronics), the choice becomes easier.

The problem of domain identification is often posed as a document classification task, which requires labeled data to train and thus is not applicable for our task. Additionally, we are not concerned with accurately specifying the exact domain of each ad, instead any information about similarity between ads according to their domains is helpful. This kind of representation can be obtained in an unsupervised fashion by using topic cluster models (Steyvers and Griffiths, 2007; Blei et al., 2003). Given a large set of unlabeled documents, topic models define a distribution of topics over each document, such that documents that are similar to each other have similar topic distributions.

The LDA (Blei et al., 2003) implementation of topic models in the Mallet toolkit (McCallum, 2002) was used to construct a model with 1000 topics for a dataset containing 3 million ads. For each ad, the discrete distribution over the topics, in conjunction with each possible label, was added as a feature. This captures a potential for each label given an approximation of the ad's domain captured as topics.

5 Constraints

Constraints are used to inject light supervision into the learning algorithm and are defined as targets u for expectations of features G' over the data. Any feature that can be included in the model can be used as a constraint. This allows us to capture a variety of different forms of domain knowledge, some of which we shall explore in this section.

Labeled data x_l, s_l can be incorporated as a special case when constraints have a target expectation of 1.0 for the features that are defined only for the sequence x_l and with segmentation s_l. This allows us to easily use labeled data in form of constraints, but in this work we do not include any labeled data. A more interesting case is that of partial labeling, where the domain expert may have prior knowledge about the probability that certain tokens and/or contexts result in a specific label. These constraints can cover more instances than labeled data, however they only provide partial and stochastic labels. All of the constraints described in this section are also included as simple features.

Many different methods have been suggested in recent work for finding the correct target values for the feature expectations. First, if ample labeled data is available, features expectations can be calculated, and assumptions can be made that the same expectations hold for the unlabeled data. This method cannot be applied to our work due to lack of labeled data. Second, for certain constraints, the prior knowledge can be used directly to specify these values. Third, if the constraints are an output of a previous machine learning model, we can use that model's confidence in the prediction as the target expectation of the constraint. Finally, a search for the ideal values of the target expectations can be performed by evaluating on small evaluation data. Our target values for feature expectations were set based on domain knowledge, then adjusted manually based on minimal manual examination of examples on a small held-out data set.

5.1 Dictionary-Based

Dictionary constraints are the form of constraints that apply to the feature between an individual token and its label. For a set of tokens in the dictionary, the constraints specify which label they are likely to be. Dictionaries can be easily constructed using various sources, for example product databases, lexicons, manual collections, or predictions from other models. These dictionary constraints are often used to bootstrap models (Agichtein and Ganti, 2004; Canisius and Sporleder, 2007) and have also been used in the ads domain (Li et al., 2009). For our application, we rely on dictionary constraints from two sources.

First, the predictions of a previous model are used to construct a dictionary. A model for entity extraction is trained on a large amount of labeled search query data. The domain and style of web queries differs from advertisements, but the set of labels is essentially the same. The supervised query entity extraction model is used to infer segments and labels for the ads domain, and each of the predicted segments are added to the dictionary of the corresponding predicted label. Even though the predictions of the model are not perfect (see Section 6.1) the predictions of some of the labels are of high precision, and thus can be used for supervision in form of noisy dictionary constraints.

The second source of prior information for dictionary constraints are external databases. Lists of various types of places can be obtained easily, for example CITY, COUNTRY, STATE, AIRPORT, etc. Additionally, product databases available internally to our research group are used for MANUFACTURERS, BRANDS, PRODUCTS, MEDIATITLE, etc. Some of these databases are noisy, and the constraints based on them are given lower target expectations.

5.2 Pattern-Based

Prior knowledge can often be easily expressed as patterns that appear for a specific domain. Pattern based matching has been used to express supervision for information extraction tasks (Califf and Mooney, 1999; Muslea, 1999). The usual use case involves a domain expert specifying a number of "prototypical" patterns, while additional patterns are discovered based on these initial patterns.

We incorporate noisy forms of patterns as constraints. Simple regular expression based patterns were used to identify and label segments for a few domains (*e.g.* "flights to {PLACE}" and "looking for {PRODUCT}?"). We do not employ a pattern-discovery algorithm for finding other contexts; the model propagates these labels, as before, using the features of the rest of the model. However if the output of a pattern-discovery algorithm is available, it can be directly incorporated into the model as additional constraints.

5.3 Domain-Based

A number of label-independent constraints are also added to avoid unrealistic segmentation predictions. For example, an expectation over segment lengths was included, which denotes that the segment length is usually 1 or 2, and almost never more than 6. A constraint is also added to avoid segments that overlap the separator token between title and abstract by ensuring that the segment that includes the separator token is always of length 1 and of label OTHER. Finally, an additional constraint ensures that the label OTHER is the most common label.

6 Results

The feature expectations of the model are calculated with modifications to an open source semi-CRF package[5]. We collect two datasets of ad creatives randomly sampled from Yahoo!'s ads database: a smaller dataset contains 14k ads and a larger dataset of 42k ads. The ads were not restricted to any particular domain (such as travel, electronics, etc.). The average length of the complete ad text was $\sim$14 tokens. Preprocessing of the text involved lower-casing, basic cleaning, and stemming.

The training time for each iteration through the data was $\sim$90 minutes for the smaller dataset and $\sim$360 minutes for the larger dataset. Inference over the dataset, using Viterbi decoding for semi-CRFs, took a total of $\sim$8 and $\sim$32 minutes. The initial learning rate η is set to 10.0.

6.1 Discussion

We compare our approach to a baseline "Dictionary" system that deterministically selects a label based on the dictionaries described in Section 5.1. A segment is given a label corresponding to the dictionary it appears in, or OTHER if it does not appear in any dictionary. In addition, we compare to an external supervised system that has been trained on tens-of-thousands of manually-annotated search queries that use the same taxonomy (the same system as used in Section 5.1 to derive dictionaries). This CRF-based model contains mostly the same features as our unsupervised system, and approximates what a fully supervised system might achieve, although it is trained on search queries. Results for our approach and these two systems are presented in Table 1. Our evaluation data consists of 2,157 randomly sampled ads that were manually labeled by professional editors. This labeled data size was too small to sufficiently train a supervised semi-CRF model that out-performed the dictionary baseline for our task (which consists of 45 potential labels).

We measure the token-wise accuracy and macro F-score over the manually labeled dataset. Typically, these metrics measure only exact matches between the true and the predicted label, but this leads to cases where the model may predict PLACE for a true CITY. To allow a "partial credit" for these cases, we introduce "weighted" version of these measures, where a predicted label is given 0.5 credit if the true label is its direct child or parent, and 0.25 credit if the true label is a sibling. Our F-score measures the recall of all true labels except OTHER and similarly the precision of all predicted labels except OTHER. We focus on these labels because the OTHER label is mostly uninformative for downstream tasks. The token-wise accuracy over all labels (including OTHER) is included as "Overall Accuracy".

Our method significantly outperforms the baseline dictionary method while approaching the results obtained with the sophisticated supervised model. Overall accuracy is 50% greater than the dictionary baseline, and comes within 10% of the supervised model[6]. Increasing unlabeled data from 14k to 42k ads provides an increase in overall accuracy and non-OTHER precision, but somewhat reduces recall for the remaining labels. We also include the F2-score which gives more weight to recall, because we are interested in extracting informative labels for downstream models (which may be able to compensate for a lower precision in label prediction). Our model trained on 14k samples out-performs the query-based supervised model in terms of F2, which is promising for future work that will incorporate predicted labels in ad retrieval and ranking systems.

[5] Available on http://crf.sourceforge.net/

[6] Comparisons and trends for normal and weighted measures are consistent throughout the results.

Table 1: **Evaluation:** Token-wise accuracy and F-score for the methods evaluated on labeled data (Normal / *Weighted*)

Metric	Dictionary	Our Method (14k)	Our Method (42k)	Query-based Sup. Model
Overall Accuracy	0.454 / *0.466*	0.596 / *0.627*	0.629 / *0.649*	0.665 / *0.685*
non-OTHER Recall	0.170 / *0.205*	0.329 / *0.412*	0.271 / *0.325*	0.286 / *0.342*
non-OTHER Precision	0.136 / *0.163*	0.265 / *0.333*	0.297 / *0.357*	0.392 / *0.469*
F1-score	0.151 / *0.182*	0.293 / *0.368*	0.283 / *0.340*	0.331 / *0.395*
F2-score	0.162 / *0.195*	0.313 / *0.393*	0.276 / *0.331*	0.303 / *0.361*

7 Related Work

Extraction of structured information from text is of interest to a large number of communities. However, in the ads domain, the task has usually been simplified to that of classification or ranking. Previous work has focused on retrieval (Raghavan and Iyer, 2008), user click prediction (Shaparenko et al., 2009; Richardson et al., 2007; Ciaramita et al., 2008), ad relevance (Hillard et al., 2010) and bounce rate prediction (Sculley et al., 2009). As far we know, our method is the only one that aims to solve a much more complex task of segmentation and entity extraction from ad creatives. Supervised methods are a poor choice to solve this task as they require large amounts of labeled ads, which is expensive, time-consuming and noisy. Most semi-supervised methods also rely on *some* labeled data, and scale badly with the size of unlabeled data, which is intractable for most ad databases.

Considerable research has been undertaken to exploit forms of domain knowledge other than labeled data to efficiently train a model while utilizing the unlabeled data. These include methods that express domain knowledge as constraints on features, which have shown to provide high accuracy on natural language datasets (Chang et al., 2007; Chang et al., 2008; Mann and McCallum, 2008; Bellare et al., 2009; Singh et al., 2010). We use the method of alternating projections for constraint-driven learning (Bellare et al., 2009) since it specifies constraints on feature expectations instead of less intuitive constraints on feature parameters (as in (Chang et al., 2008)). Additionally, the alternating projection method is computationally more efficient than Generalized Expectation (Mann and McCallum, 2008) and can be applied in an online fashion using stochastic gradient.

Our approach is most similar to (Li et al., 2009), which uses semi-supervised learning for CRFs to extract structured information from user queries. They also use a constraint-driven method that utilizes an external data source. Their method, however, relies on labeled data for part of the supervision while our method uses only unlabeled data. Also, evaluation was only shown for a small domain of user queries, while our work does not restrict itself to any specific domain of ads for evaluation.

8 Conclusions

Although important for a number of tasks in sponsored search, extraction of structured information from text advertisements is not a well-studied problem. The difficulty of the problem lies in the expensive, time-consuming and error-prone labeling process. In this work, the aim was to explore machine learning methods that do not use labeled data, relying instead on light supervision specified as constraints on feature expectations. The results clearly show this *minimally-supervised* method performs significantly better than a dictionary based baseline. Our method also approaches the performance of a supervised model trained to extract entities from web search queries. These findings strongly suggest that domain knowledge expressed in forms other than directly labeled data may be preferable in domains for which labeling data is unsuitable.

The most important limitation lies in the fact that specifying the target expectations of constraints is an ad-hoc process, and robustness of the semi-supervised learning method to noise in these target values needs to be investigated. Further research will also explore using the extracted entities from advertisements to improve downstream sponsored search tasks.

References

Eugene Agichtein and Venkatesh Ganti. 2004. Mining reference tables for automatic text segmentation. In *KDD: ACM SIGKDD International Conference on Knowledge Discovery and Data mining*, pages 20–29, New York, NY, USA.

Kedar Bellare, Gregory Druck, and Andrew McCallum. 2009. Alternating projections for learning with expectation constraints. In *UAI: Conference on Uncertainty in Artificial Intelligence*.

David M. Blei, Andrew Y. Ng, and Michael I. Jordan. 2003. Latent dirichlet allocation. *Journal on Machine Learning Research*, 3:993–1022.

Mary Elaine Califf and Raymond J. Mooney. 1999. Relational learning of pattern-match rules for information extraction. In *AAAI / IAAI '99: National conference on Artificial intelligence and the Innovative Applications of Artificial Intelligence conference*, pages 328–334.

Sander Canisius and Caroline Sporleder. 2007. Bootstrapping information extraction from field books. In *EMNLP-CoNLL: Joint Conference on Empirical Methods in Natural Language Processing and Computational Natural Language Learning*, pages 827–836.

Ming-Wei Chang, Lev Ratinov, and Dan Roth. 2007. Guiding semi-supervision with constraint-driven learning. In *ACL: Annual meeting of the Association for Computational Linguistics*, pages 280–287.

Ming-Wei Chang, Lev Ratinov, Nicholas Rizzolo, and Dan Roth. 2008. Learning and inference with constraints. In *AAAI: National Conference on Artificial Intelligence*, pages 1513–1518.

O. Chapelle, B. Schölkopf, and A. Zien, editors. 2006. *Semi-Supervised Learning (Adaptive Computation and Machine Learning)*. The MIT Press, September.

Massimiliano Ciaramita, Vanessa Murdock, and Vassilis Plachouras. 2008. Online learning from click data for sponsored search. In *WWW: International World Wide Web Conference*.

Dustin Hillard, Stefan Schroedl, Eren Manavoglu, Hema Raghavan, and Chris Leggetter. 2010. Improving ad relevance in sponsored search. In *WSDM: International conference on Web search and data mining*, pages 361–370.

John Lafferty, Andrew Mccallum, and Fernando Pereira. 2001. Conditional random fields: Probabilistic models for segmenting and labeling sequence data. In *ICML: International Conference on Machine Learning*, pages 282–289.

Xiao Li, Ye-Yi Wang, and Alex Acero. 2009. Extracting structured information from user queries with semi-supervised conditional random fields. In *SIGIR: International Conference on research and development in information retrieval*, pages 572–579. ACM.

Gideon S. Mann and Andrew McCallum. 2008. Generalized expectation criteria for semi-supervised learning of conditional random fields. In *ACL: Annual meeting of the Association for Computational Linguistics*, pages 870–878.

Andrew McCallum. 2002. Mallet: A machine learning for language toolkit. http://mallet.cs.umass.edu.

Ion Muslea. 1999. Extraction patterns for information extraction tasks: A survey. In *AAAI: Workshop on Machine Learning for Information Extraction*, pages 1–6.

Patrick Pantel, Eric Crestan, Arkady Borkovsky, Ana-Maria Popescu, and Vishnu Vyas. 2009. Web-scale distributional similarity and entity set expansion. In *EMNLP: Conference on Empirical Methods in Natural Language Processing*, pages 938–947.

Hema Raghavan and Rukmini Iyer. 2008. Evaluating vector-space and probabilistic models for query to ad matching. In *SIGIR Workshop on Information Retrieval in Advertising (IRA)*.

Matthew Richardson, Ewa Dominowska, and Robert Ragno. 2007. Predicting clicks: estimating the click-through rate for new ads. In *WWW: International World Wide Web Conference*.

Sunita Sarawagi and William W. Cohen. 2004. Semi-markov conditional random fields for information extraction. In *NIPS: Neural Information Processing Systems*.

Sunita Sarawagi. 2006. Efficient inference on sequence segmentation models. In *ICML: International Conference on Machine Learning*, pages 793–800.

D. Sculley, Robert G. Malkin, Sugato Basu, and Roberto J. Bayardo. 2009. Predicting bounce rates in sponsored search advertisements. In *KDD: ACM SIGKDD International Conference on Knowledge Discovery and Data mining*, pages 1325–1334.

Benyah Shaparenko, Ozgur Cetin, and Rukmini Iyer. 2009. Data driven text features for sponsored search click prediction. In *AdKDD: Workshop on Data mining and audience intelligence for advertising*.

Sameer Singh, Limin Yao, Sebastian Riedel, and Andrew McCallum. 2010. Constraint-driven rank-based learning for information extraction. In *North American Chapter of the Association for Computational Linguistics - Human Language Technologies (NAACL HLT)*.

Mark Steyvers and Tom Griffiths. 2007. *Probabilistic Topic Models*. Lawrence Erlbaum Associates.

Taxonomy Learning Using Word Sense Induction

Ioannis P. Klapaftis
Department of Computer Science
The University of York
York, UK, YO10 5DD
giannis@cs.york.ac.uk

Suresh Manandhar
Department of Computer Science
The University of York
York, UK, YO10 5DD
suresh@cs.york.ac.uk

Abstract

Taxonomies are an important resource for a variety of Natural Language Processing (NLP) applications. Despite this, the current state-of-the-art methods in taxonomy learning have disregarded word polysemy, in effect, developing taxonomies that conflate word senses. In this paper, we present an unsupervised method that builds a taxonomy of senses learned automatically from an unlabelled corpus. Our evaluation on two WordNet-derived taxonomies shows that the learned taxonomies capture a higher number of correct taxonomic relations compared to those produced by traditional distributional similarity approaches that merge senses by grouping the features of each word into a single vector.

1 Introduction

A concept or a sense, s, can be defined as the meaning of a word or a multiword expression. A concept s can be linguistically realised by more than one word while at the same time a word w can be the linguistic realisation of more than one concept. Given a set of concepts S, taxonomy learning is the task of hierarchically classifying the elements in S in an *automatic* manner. For example, consider a set of concepts linguistically realised by the words/multiword expressions *LAN, computer network, internet, meshwork, gauze, snood.* Taxonomy learning methods produce taxonomies, such as the ones shown in Figures 1 (a) and 1 (b).

By observing Figure 1 (a), we can express **IS-A** statements, such as *Internet* **IS-A** *Computer Network* etc. However, the same does not apply to the

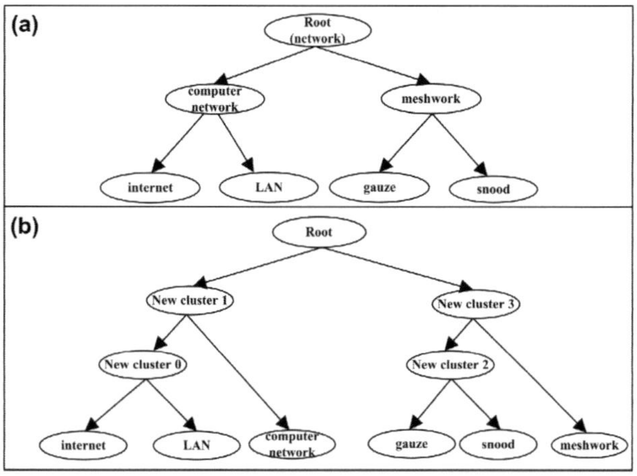

Figure 1: A labelled and an unlabelled concept taxonomy

taxonomy in Figure 1 (b), since this taxonomy is not fully labelled. Despite this, its hierarchical organisation clearly shows that the concepts are divided into groups, which are further subdivided into subgroups and so forth, until we reach a level where each concept belongs to its own group. Unlabelled taxonomies are typically produced by agglomerative hierarchical clustering algorithms (King, 1967; Sneath and Sokal, 1973).

The knowledge encoded in taxonomies can be utilised in a range of NLP applications. For instance, taxonomies can be used in information retrieval to expand a user query with semantically related words or to enhance document representation by abstracting from plain words and adding conceptual information (Cimiano, 2006). WordNet's (Fellbaum, 1998) taxonomic relations have also been used in Word Sense Disambiguation (WSD) (Navigli and Velardi, 2004b). In named entity recognition, methods relying on gazetteers could make

Human Language Technologies: The 2010 Annual Conference of the North American Chapter of the ACL, pages 82–90,
Los Angeles, California, June 2010.

use of automatically acquired taxonomies (Cimiano, 2006), while question answering systems have also benefited (Moldovan and Novischi, 2002).

Despite the wide uses of taxonomies, the majority of methods disregard or do not deal effectively with word polysemy, in effect, developing taxonomies that conflate the senses of words (see Section 2). In this work, we show that Word Sense Induction (WSI) can be effectively employed to address this limitation of existing methods.

We present a novel method that employs WSI to generate the different senses of a set of target words from an unlabelled corpus and then produces a taxonomy of senses using Hierarchical Agglomerative Clustering (HAC) (King, 1967; Sneath and Sokal, 1973). We evaluate our method on two WordNet-derived sub-taxonomies and show that our method leads to the development of concept hierarchies that capture a higher number of correct taxonomic relations in comparison to those generated by current distributional similarity approaches.

2 Related work

Initial research on taxonomy learning focused on identifying in a given text lexico-syntactic patterns that suggest hyponymy relations (Hearst, 1992). For instance, the pattern NP_0 *such as* $NP_1,\ldots,NP_n$ suggests that NP_0 is a hypernym of NP_i. For example, given the phrase *Fruits, such as oranges, apples,...*, the above pattern would suggest that *fruit* is a hypernym of *orange* and *apple*. These pattern-based approaches operate at the word level by learning lexical relations between words rather than between senses of words.

In the same spirit, other work attempted to exploit the regularities of dictionary entries to identify hyponymy relations (Amsler, 1981). For example in WordNet, *WAN* is defined as *a computer network that spans ....* Hence, one can easily induce that *WAN* is a hyponym of *computer network* by assuming that the first noun phrase in the definition is a hypernym of the target word. These approaches learn lexical relations at the sense level since dictionaries separate the senses of a word. However this would be true if and only if the glosses of the dictionaries were sense-annotated, which is not the case for the majority of electronic dictionaries (Cimiano, 2006). Another limitation is that taxonomies are built according to the sense distinctions present in dictionaries and not according to the actual use of words in the corpus.

The majority of taxonomy learning approaches are based on the *distributional hypothesis* (Harris, 1968). Typically, distributional similarity methods (Cimiano et al., 2004; Cimiano et al., 2005; Faure and Nédellec, 1998; Reinberger and Spyns, 2004; Caraballo, 1999) utilise syntactic dependencies such as subject/verb, object/verb relations, conjunctive and appositive constructions and others. These dependencies are used to extract the features that serve as the dimensions of the vector space. Each target noun is then represented as a vector of extracted features where the frequency of co-occurrence of the target noun with each feature is used to calculate the weight of that feature. The constructed vectors are the input to hierarchical clustering or *formal concept analysis* (Ganter and Wille, 1999) to produce a taxonomy. These approaches assume that a target noun is monosemous creating one vector of features for each target noun. This limitation can lead to a number of problems.

Firstly, the constructed taxonomies might be biased towards the inclusion of taxonomic relationships between the most frequent senses of target nouns, ignoring interesting taxonomic relations where less frequent senses are present. For example, consider the word *house*. Current distributional similarity methods would possibly capture the hyponyms of its Most Frequent Sense (MFS[1]), however ignoring the hyponyms of less frequent senses of *house*, e.g. *casino*, *theater*, etc. Given that word senses typically follow a Zipf distribution, these methods construct vectors dominated by the MFS of words. This bias significantly degrades the usefulness of learned taxonomies.

Secondly, given that distributional similarity approaches rely on the computation of pairwise similarities between target words, merging their senses to a single vector might lead to unreliable similarity estimates. For example, merging the features of the different senses of *house* could provide a lower similarity with its monosemous hyponym *beach house*, since only the first sense of *house* is related to *beach*

[1]WordNet: A dwelling that serves as living quarters ...

house. This problem might lead both to inclusion of incorrect or loss of correct taxonomic relations. In our work, we aim to overcome these drawbacks by identifying the different senses with which target words appear in text and then building a hierarchy of the identified senses.

Soft clustering approaches (Reinberger and Spyns, 2004; Reinberger et al., 2003) have also been applied to taxonomy learning to deal with polysemy. These methods associate each verb with a vector of features, where each feature is a noun appearing as a subject or object of that verb. That way a noun can appear in different vectors, hence in different clusters during hierarchical clustering as a result of its polysemy. However, the underlying assumption is that a verb is monosemous with respect to its associated vector of nouns. This assumption is not always valid and can cause the problems mentioned above.

Other work in taxonomy learning exploits the head/modifier relationships to create taxonomic relations (Buitelaar et al., 2004; Hwang, 1999; Sánchez and Moreno, 2005). These relations are used to create: (1) a class (concept) for each head, and (2) subclasses by adding nominal or adjectival modifiers. For example, *credit card* **IS-A** *card*. The corresponding hyponymy relations are learned at the lexical level disregarding word polysemy. Some of these approaches identified the problem of polysemy and applied sense disambiguation with respect to WordNet in order to capture the different senses of a target term (Navigli and Velardi, 2004b; Navigli and Velardi, 2004a). Specifically, the taxonomy built by exploiting head/modifiers relations was modified according to WordNet's hyponymy relations between senses of disambiguated terms. One important deficiency of using sense disambiguation is that dictionaries miss many domain-specific senses. Additionally, the fixed-list of senses paradigm prohibits learning word senses according to their use in context. The use of sense induction we propose in this paper aims to overcome these limitations.

3 Method

Given a set of words W, a WSI method is applied to each $w_i \in W$ (Section 3.1). The outcome of the first stage is a set of senses, S, where each $s_i^w \in S$ denotes the i-th sense of word $w \in W$. This set

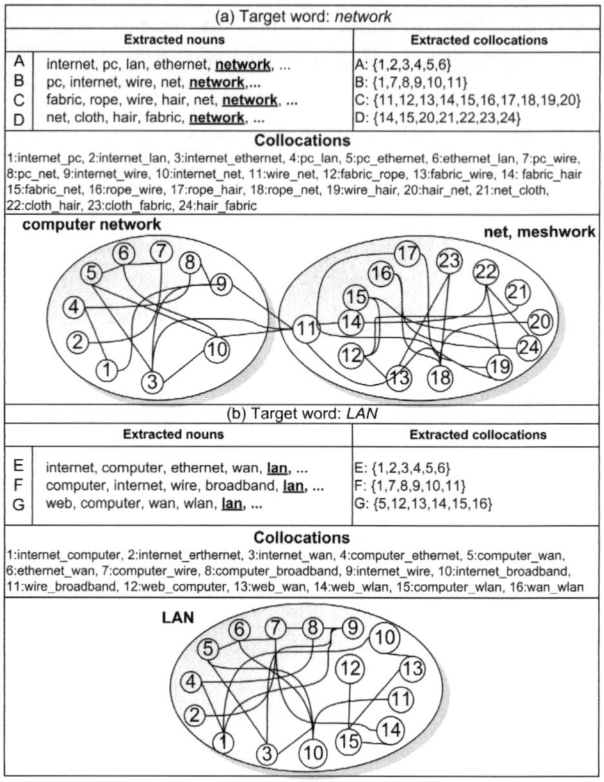

Figure 2: WSI for *network* & *LAN*

of senses is the input to hierarchical clustering that produces a hierarchy of senses (Section 3.2).

3.1 Word sense induction

WSI is the task of identifying the senses of a target word in a given text. Recent WSI methods were evaluated under the framework of SemEval-2007 WSI task (SWSI) (Agirre and Soroa, 2007). The evaluation framework defines two types of assessment, i.e. evaluation in: (1) a clustering and (2) a WSD setting. Based on this evaluation, we selected the method of Klapaftis & Manandhar (2008) (henceforth referred to as KM) that achieves high F-score in both evaluation schemes as compared to the systems participating in SWSI. We briefly describe KM mentioning its parameters used in our evaluation (Section 4). Figures 2 (a) and 2 (b) describe the different steps for inducing the senses of the target words *network* and *LAN*.

Corpus preprocessing: The input to KM is a base corpus bc, in which the target word w appears in each paragraph. In Figure 2 (a), the base corpus consists of the paragraphs *A*, *B*, *C* and *D*. The aim of this stage is to capture nouns contextually related to w. Initially, the target word is removed from bc, part-of-speech tagging is applied to each paragraph, only nouns are kept and lemmatised. In the next step, the distribution of each noun is compared to the distribution of the same noun in a reference corpus[2] using the log-likelihood ratio (G^2) (Dunning, 1993). Nouns with a G^2 below a pre-specified threshold (parameter p_1) are removed from each paragraph. Figure 2 (a) shows the remaining nouns for each paragraph of bc.

Graph creation & clustering: In the setting of KM, a collocation is a juxtaposition of two nouns within the same paragraph. Thus, each noun is combined with any other noun yielding a total of $\binom{N}{2}$ collocations for a paragraph with N nouns. Each collocation, c_{ij}, is assigned a weight that measures the relative frequency of two nouns co-occurring. This weight is the average of the conditional probabilities $p(n_i|n_j)$ and $p(n_j|n_i)$, where $p(n_i|n_j) = \frac{f(c_{ij})}{f(n_j)}$, $f(c_{ij})$ is the number of paragraphs nouns n_i, n_j co-occur and $f(n_j)$ is the number of paragraphs in which n_j appears. Collocations are filtered with respect to their frequency (parameter p_2) and weight (parameter p_3). Each retained collocation is represented as a vertex. Edges between vertices are present, if two collocations co-occur in one or more paragraphs. Figure 2 (a) shows that this process has generated 24 collocations for the target word *network*. On the top right of the figure we also observe the collocations associated with each paragraph.

In the next step, a smoothing technique is applied to discover new edges between vertices. The weight applied to each edge connecting vertices v_i and v_j (collocations c_{ab}, c_{de}) is the maximum of their conditional probabilities ($\max(p(c_{ab}|c_{de}), p(c_{de}|c_{ab}))$). Finally, the graph is clustered using Chinese whispers (Biemann, 2006). The final output is a set of senses, each one represented by a set of contextually related collocations. In Figure 2, we generated two senses for *network* and one sense for *LAN*.

3.2 Hierarchical clustering of senses

Given the set of senses S, our task at this point is to hierarchically classify the senses using HAC. Consider for example the words *network* and *LAN*, and let us assume that the WSI process has generated the senses in Figures 2 (a) and 2 (b). HAC operates by treating each sense as a singleton cluster and then successively merging the most similar clusters according to a pre-defined similarity function. This process iterates until all clusters have been merged into a single cluster taken to be the *root*.

[2]The British National Corpus, 2001, Distributed by Oxford University Computing Services.

Senses	computer network	meshwork	LAN
computer network	1	0.0	0.66
meshwork	0.0	1	0.14
LAN	0.66	0.14	1

Table 1: Similarity matrix for HAC.

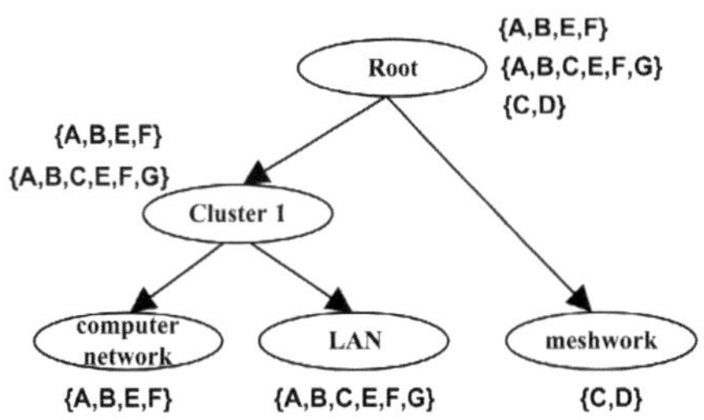

Figure 3: WSI & HAC example

To calculate the pairwise similarities between senses we exploit the attributes that represent each sense, i.e. their collocations. Let BC be the corpus resulting from the union of the base corpora of all words in W. In our example, BC would consist of the paragraphs, in which the words *network* and *LAN* appear, i.e. *A*, *B*, ..., *G*. An induced sense tags a paragraph, if one or more of its collocations appear in that paragraph. Thus, each induced sense is associated with a set of paragraph labels that denote the paragraphs tagged by that sense. Figure 3 shows the paragraph labels tagged by each sense of our example. Finally, given two senses s_i^a, s_i^b and their corresponding sets of tagged paragraphs f_i^a and f_i^b, we use the Jaccard coefficient to calculate their similarity, i.e. $\mathrm{JC}(s_i^a, s_i^b) = \frac{|f_i^a \cap f_i^b|}{|f_i^a \cup f_i^b|}$, where s_j^k denotes the j-th sense of word k. The resulting similarity matrix of our example is shown in Table 1. Given that matrix, HAC would first group *computer network* and *LAN* as they have the highest similarity (Figure 3). In the final iteration, the remaining two clusters (*Cluster 1* & *meshwork*) would be grouped to the *root*.

An important parameter of HAC is the choice of the technique for calculating cluster similarities. Note that as we move towards the higher levels of the taxonomy clusters contain more than one sets of tagged paragraphs (Figure 3 - *Cluster 1*), hence the choice of the similarity function is crucial. We experiment with three techniques, i.e. *single-linkage*, *complete-linkage* and *average-linkage*. The first one defines the similarity between two clusters as the maximum similarity among all the pairs of their corresponding feature sets. The second considers the minimum similarity among all the pairs, while the third calculates the average similarity of all the pairs.

4 Evaluation

We evaluate our method with respect to two WordNet-derived sub-taxonomies (Section 4.3). For that reason, it is necessary to map the induced senses to WordNet before applying HAC. Note that the mapping process might map more than one induced senses to the same WordNet sense. In that case, these induced senses are merged to a single one along with their corresponding collocations.

4.1 Mapping WSI clusters to WordNet senses

The process of mapping the induced senses to WordNet is straightforward. Let $w \in W$ be a word with n senses in WordNet. A WordNet sense i of w is denoted by ws_i^w, $i = [1, n]$. Let us also assume that the WSI method has produced m senses for w, where each sense j is denoted as s_j^w, $j = [1, m]$. Each induced sense s_j^w is associated with a set of features f_j^w as in the previous section. These features are the paragraphs (paragraph labels) of BC tagged by s_j^w. In the next step, each WordNet sense ws_i^w is associated with its WordNet signature g_i^w that contains the following semantic features: hypernyms/hyponyms, meronyms/holonyms and synonyms of ws_i^w. For example, the signature of the fifth WordNet sense of *network* would contain *internet*, *cyberspace* and other semantically related words. Table 2 shows partial signatures for each sense of *network*.

The signature g_i^w is used to formalise the WordNet sense ws_i^w as a set of features q_i^w. These features are the paragraphs (paragraph labels) of BC that contain one or more of the aforementioned semantically related to ws_i^w words that exist in g_i^w. Given an induced sense s_j^w, a similarity score is calculated between s_j^w and each WordNet sense of w. The maximum score determines the WordNet sense

WordNet sense	Semantically related words/phrases
1	reticulum, RF, RAS
2	communication system/equipment
3	gauze, snood, tulle
4	reseau, reticle, reticulation
5	net, internet, cyberspace

Table 2: Semantically related words/phrases to *network*

label that will be assigned to s_j^w, i.e. $label(s_j^w) = \text{argmax}_i\ JC(f_j^w, q_i^w)$, where JC is the Jaccard similarity coefficient. In the example of Figure 2 (a), the *computer network* sense would be mapped to the fifth WordNet sense of *network*, since there is a significant overlap between the paragraphs tagged by the induced and that WordNet sense.

4.2 Evaluation measures

For the purposes of this section we present one gold standard taxonomy (Figure 1 (a)) and a second derived from our method (Figure 1 (b)). The comparison of these taxonomies is based on the *semantic cotopy* of a node, which has also been used in (Maedche and Staab, 2002; Cimiano et al., 2005). In particular, the semantic cotopy of a node is defined as the set of all its super- and subnodes excluding the *root* and including that node. For example, the semantic cotopy of *computer network* in Figure 1 (a) is {*computer network, internet, LAN*}. There are two issues, which make the evaluation difficult.

The first one is that HAC produces a taxonomy in which all internal nodes are unlabelled, as opposed to the gold standard taxonomy. In Figure 1 (b), we have manually labelled internal nodes with their IDs for clarity. For example, the semantic cotopy of the node *New Cluster 1* in Figure 1 (b) is {*computer network, internet, LAN, New Cluster 1, New Cluster 0*}. By comparing the cotopies of nodes *computer network* in Figure 1 (a) and *New Cluster 1* in Figure 1 (b), we observe that the automatic method has successfully grouped all of the hypernyms and hyponyms of *computer network* under *New Cluster 1*. However, the corresponding cotopies are not identical, because the cotopy of *New Cluster 1* also includes the labels produced by HAC.

To deal with this problem, we use a version of semantic cotopy for nodes in the automatically learned taxonomy which excludes nodes that do not exist in WordNet. That way the semantic cotopies of *New Cluster 1* in Figure 1 (b) and *computer network* in

Figure 1 (a) will yield maximum similarity.

The second issue is that the nodes that exist in the gold standard taxonomy are leaf nodes in the automatically learned taxonomy. As a result, the semantic cotopy of *LAN* in Figure 1 (b) is $\{LAN\}$ since all of its supernodes do not exist in WordNet. In contrast, the semantic cotopy of *LAN* in Figure 1 (a) is $\{$*LAN, computer network*$\}$. We observe that there is an overlap between the two cotopies derived by the existence of the same concept in both taxonomies, i.e. *LAN*. In fact, all of the leaf nodes of a learned taxonomy will have a small overlap with the corresponding concept in the gold standard. For this problem, we observe that in our automatically learned taxonomies it does not make sense to calculate the semantic cotopy of leaf nodes. On the contrary, we need to evaluate the internal nodes that group the leaf nodes. Let us assume the following notation:

T_A = *automatically learned taxonomy*
η_i = *node in a taxonomy*
$C(T_A)$ = *internal nodes + leaf nodes of* T_A
$I(T_A)$ = *internal nodes of* T_A
T_G = *gold standard taxonomy*
$C(T_G)$ = *internal nodes + leaf nodes of* T_G
$I(T_G)$ = *internal nodes of* T_G
$hyper(\eta_i)$ = *supernodes of* η_i *excluding the root*
$hypo(\eta_i)$ = *subnodes of* η_i *including* η_i

For $\eta_i \in I(T_A)$, the semantic cotopy is defined as:
$SC'(\eta_i) = (hyper(\eta_i) \cup hypo(\eta_i)) \cap C(T_G)$
For $\eta_i \in C(T_G)$, the semantic cotopy is defined as:
$SC''(\eta_i) = (hyper(\eta_i) \cup hypo(\eta_i))$

$$P(\eta_i, \eta_j) = \frac{|SC'(\eta_i) \cap SC''(\eta_j)|}{|SC'(\eta_i)|} \quad (1)$$

$$R(\eta_i, \eta_j) = \frac{|SC'(\eta_i) \cap SC''(\eta_j)|}{|SC''(\eta_j)|} \quad (2)$$

$$F(\eta_i, \eta_j) = \frac{2P(\eta_i, \eta_j)R(\eta_i, \eta_j)}{P(\eta_i, \eta_j) + R(\eta_i, \eta_j)} \quad (3)$$

Precision, recall and harmonic mean of node $\eta_i \in I(T_A)$ with respect to node $\eta_j \in C(T_G)$ are defined in Equations 1, 2 and 3. The F-score, FS, of node $\eta_i \in I(T_A)$ is the maximum F attained at any $\eta_j \in C(T_G)$ ($FS(\eta_i) = \mathrm{argmax}_j F(\eta_i, \eta_j)$). Finally, the similarity TS of the entire taxonomy to the gold standard taxonomy is the average of the F-scores of each $\eta_i \in I(T_A)$ (Equation 4). The $TS(T_A, T_G)$ in Figure 1 is 0.9. All nodes of T_A have a perfect match, apart from *New Cluster 0* and *New Cluster 2*, which are matched against *computer network* and *meshwork* respectively, having a perfect precision but a lower recall since the cotopies of *computer network* and *meshwork* consist of three concepts. The automatically learned taxonomy has two redundant clusters that decrease its similarity.

$$TS(T_A, T_G) = \frac{1}{|I(T_A)|} \sum_{\eta_i \in I(T_A)} FS(\eta_i) \quad (4)$$

The similarity measure $TS(T_A, T_G)$ provides the similarity of the automatically learned taxonomy to the gold standard one, but it is not symmetric. Calculating the taxonomic similarity one way might not provide accurate results, in cases where T_A misses senses of the gold standard. This is due to the fact that we would only evaluate the internal nodes of T_A, partially ignoring the fact that T_A might have missed some parts of the gold standard taxonomy. For that reason, we also calculate $TS(T_G, T_A)$ which provides the similarity of the gold standard taxonomy to the automatically learned one. Finally, taxonomic similarities are combined to produce their harmonic mean (Equation 5).

$$TxSm(T_A, T_G) = \frac{2TS(T_G, T_A)TS(T_A, T_G)}{TS(T_G, T_A) + TS(T_A, T_G)} \quad (5)$$

4.3 Evaluation datasets & setting

The first gold standard taxonomy is derived by extracting from WordNet all the hyponyms of the senses of the word *network*. The extracted taxonomy contains 29 senses linguistically realized by 24 word sets (one sense might be expressed with more than one words), since *network* has 5 senses and *reseau* has 2 senses in the gold standard taxonomy. Note that we have disregarded senses only expressed by multiword expressions. The average polysemy of words is around 1.7. The second taxonomy is derived by extracting the concepts under the senses of the word *speaker*. The *speaker* taxonomy contains 52 senses linguistically realized by 50 word sets, since *speaker* has 3 senses included in the taxonomy. The average polysemy of words is around 1.58.

To create our datasets[3] we use the *Yahoo!* search api[4]. For each word w in each of the datasets, we is-

[3] Available in http://www.cs.york.ac.uk/aig/projects/indect/taxlearn
[4] http://developer.yahoo.com/search/ [Accessed:10/06/2009]

Parameter	Range
G^2 threshold (p_1)	5,10
Collocation frequency (p_2)	4,6,8
Collocation weight (p_3)	0.1,0.2,0.3,0.4

Table 3: Chosen parameters for the KM WSI method.

sue a query to *Yahoo!* that contains w and we download a maximum of 1000 pages. In cases where a particular sense is expressed by more than one word, the query was formulated by including all the words and putting the keyword *OR* between them. For each page we extracted fragments of text (paragraphs) that occur in <p> </p> html tags. We extracted 58956 and 78691 paragraphs for the *network* and *speaker* dataset respectively. The reason we extracted on average less content for the second dataset was that *Yahoo!* provided a small number of results for rare words such as *alliterator*, *anecdotist*, etc.

Table 3 shows the parameter ranges for the WSI method. Our method is evaluated according to these parameters. Our first baseline is *RAND*, which performs a random hierarchical clustering of senses to produce a binary tree. In each iteration two clusters are randomly chosen and form a new cluster, until we end up with one cluster taken to be the root. The performance of *RAND* is calculated by executing the random algorithm 10 times and then averaging the results. The second baseline is the taxonomy most frequent sense baseline (*TL MFS*), in which we do not perform WSI. Instead, given a parameter setting and a word w, all the collocations of w are grouped into one vector, which will possibly be dominated by collocations related to the MFS of w. WordNet mapping takes place and finally HAC with average-linkage is applied to create the taxonomy.

4.4 Results & discussion

Figures 4 (a) and 4 (b) show the performance of *HAC* with single-linkage (*HAC SNG*), average-linkage (*HAC AVG*) and complete-linkage (*HAC CMP*) against *RAND* for $p_1 = 5$ and different combinations of p_2 and p_3. It is clear that *HAC SNG* and *HAC AVG* outperform *RAND* by very large margins under all parameter combinations. In the *network* dataset, both of them achieve their highest distance from *RAND* (27.84%) at $p_2 = 8$ and $p_3 = 0.2$. In the *speaker* dataset, their highest distance from *RAND* (20.97% and 19.63% respectively) is achieved at $p_2 = 4$ and $p_3 = 0.1$. *HAC CMP* performs worse than the other HAC versions, yet it clearly outperforms *RAND* in all but one parameter combinations ($p_1 = 5$, $p_2 = 6$, $p_3 = 0.4$) in the *speaker dataset*.

Generally, for collocation weight equal to 0.4 the performance of all HAC versions drops. At this high collocation weight the WSI method produces a larger number of small clusters than in lower thresholds. This issue negatively affects both the mapping process and HAC. For example in the *speaker* dataset, for $p_1 = 5$, $p_2 = 8$ and $p_3 = 0.1$ our taxonomies contained 86.54% of the gold standard taxonomy senses. Increasing the collocation weight to 0.2 did not have any effect, but increasing the weight to 0.3 and then 0.4 led to 71.15% and 65.38% sense coverage. Overall, our conclusion is that all HAC versions exploit the WSI method and learn useful information better than chance. The picture is the same for $p_1 = 10$.

Figures 4 (c) and 4 (d) show the performance of HAC versions against the *TL MFS* baseline in the same parameter setting as above. We observe that both *HAC SNG* and *HAC AVG* perform significantly better than *TL MFS* apart from $p_3 = 0.4$, in which case all *HAC* versions perform worse. In the *network* dataset, the largest performance difference for *HAC SNG* is 10.12% and for *HAC AVG* 9.9% at $p_2 = 6$ and $p_3 = 0.2$. In the *speaker* dataset, the largest performance difference for *HAC SNG* is 10.83% and for *HAC AVG* 7.83% at $p_2 = 8$ and $p_3 = 0.2$. *HAC CMP* performs worse than *TL MFS* under most parameter settings in both datasets. The picture is the same for $p_1 = 10$.

Overall, the analysis of the WSI-based taxonomy learning approach against *TL MFS* shows that *HAC SNG* and *HAC AVG* perform better than *TL MFS* under all parameter combinations for both datasets. The main reason for their superior performance is that their learned taxonomies contain a higher number of senses than *TL MFS* as a result of the sense induction process. This greater sense coverage leads to the discovery of a higher number of correct taxonomic relations between senses than *TL MFS*, hence in a better performance. To conclude, our results verify our hypothesis and suggest that the unsupervised learning of word senses contributes to producing taxonomies with a higher similarity to the gold standard ones than traditional distributional similarity methods.

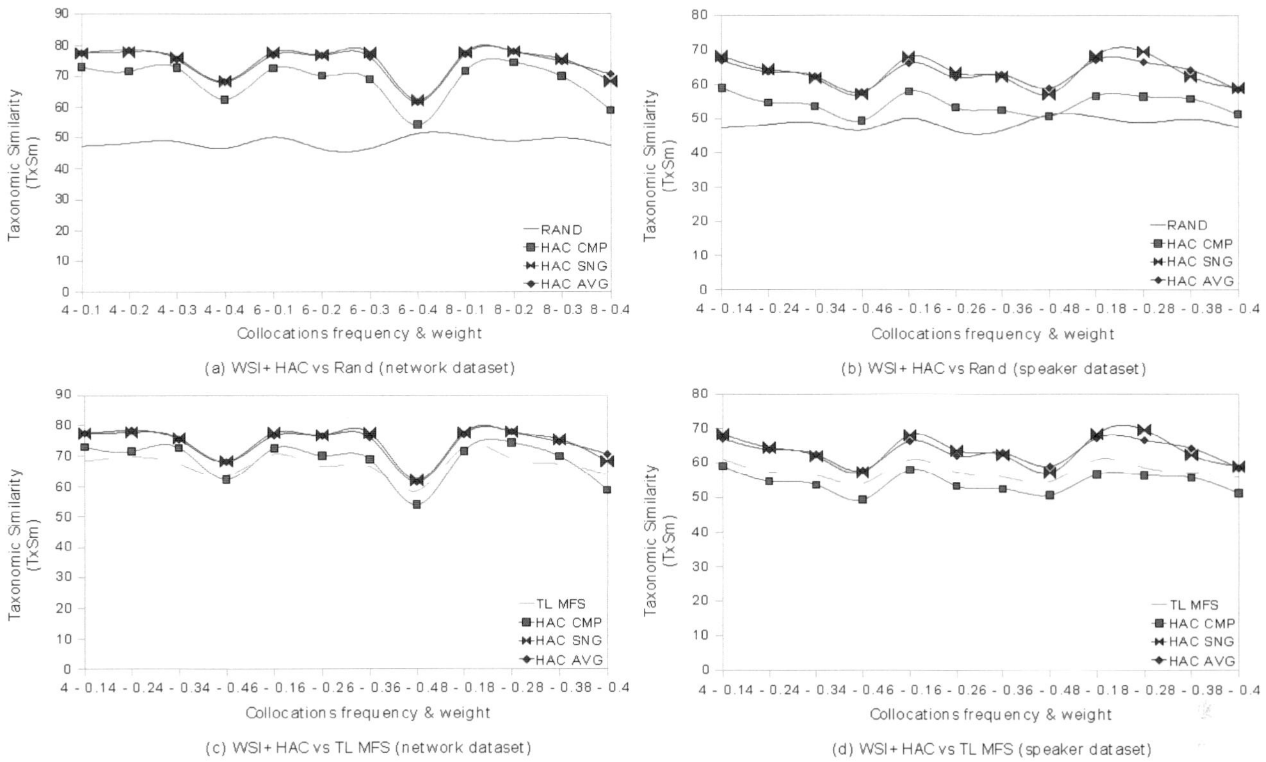

Figure 4: Performance analysis of the proposed method for $p_1 = 5$ and different combinations of p_2 and p_3.

Despite that, our evaluation also shows that in most cases *HAC CMP* is unable to exploit the induced senses and performs worse than *TL MFS*, *HAC SNG* and *HAC AVG*. This result was not expected, since *HAC SNG* employs a local criterion to merge two clusters and does not consider the global structure of the clusters, in effect, being biased towards elongated clusters. The observation of the gold standard taxonomies shows that they consist both of cohyponym concepts which are expected to be contextually related, but also of cohyponyms which are not expected to appear in similar contexts. For example, someone would expect a high similarity between *WAN*, *LAN*, or between *snood* and *tulle*. However, the same does not apply for *snood* and *cheesecloth* or *tulle* and *grillwork*, because *cheesecloth* and *grillwork* appear in significantly different contexts than *snood* and *tulle*. Despite that, all of them are cohyponyms. This issue is more prevalent in the *speaker* dataset, where concepts such as *loudspeaker*, *tannoy*, *woofer* are expected to be contextually related, while cohyponyms such as *whisperer*, *lecturer* and *interviewer* are not. This means that the gold standard taxonomies include elongated clusters and explains the superior performance of *HAC SNG*. This issue is not affecting *HAC AVG*, but it has a significant effect on *HAC CMP*. Generally, *HAC CMP* employs a non-local criterion by considering the diameter of a candidate cluster. This results in compact clusters with small diameters, as opposed to elongated ones.

5 Conclusion

We presented an unsupervised method for taxonomy learning that employs WSI to identify the senses of target words and then builds a taxonomy of these senses using HAC. We have shown that dealing with polysemy by means of sense induction helps to develop taxonomies that capture a higher number of correct taxonomic relations than traditional distributional similarity methods, which associate each target word with one vector of features, in effect, merging its senses.

Acknowledgements

This work is supported by the European Commission via the EU FP7 INDECT project, Grant No. 218086, Research area: SEC-2007-1.2-01 Intelligent Urban Environment Observation System.

References

E. Agirre and A. Soroa. 2007. SemEval-2007 Task 02: Evaluating Word Sense Induction and Discrimination Systems. In *Proceedings of the Fourth International Workshop on Semantic Evaluations*, pages 7–12, Prague, Czech Republic.

R. A. Amsler. 1981. A Taxonomy for English Nouns and Verbs. In *Proceedings of the 19th ACL Conference*, pages 133–138, Stanford, California.

C. Biemann. 2006. Chinese Whispers - An Efficient Graph Clustering Algorithm and its Application to Natural Language Processing Problems. In *Proceedings of TextGraphs*, pages 73–80, New York,USA.

P. Buitelaar, D. Olejnik, and M. Sintek. 2004. A Ptotégé Plug-in for Ontology Extraction from Text Based on Linguistic Analysis. In *Proceedings of the 1st European Semantic Web Symposium*, pages 31–44, Crete, Greece. CEUR-WS.org.

S. A. Caraballo. 1999. Automatic Construction of a Hypernym-labeled Noun Hierarchy from Text. In *Proceedings of the 37th ACL Conference*, pages 120–126, College Park, Maryland.

P. Cimiano, A. Hotho, and S. Staab. 2004. Comparing Conceptual, Divisive and Agglomerative Clustering for Learning Taxonomies from Text. In *Proceedings of the 16th ECAI Conference*, pages 435–439, Valencia, Spain.

P. Cimiano, A. Hotho, and S. Staab. 2005. Learning Concept Hieararchies from Text Corpora Using Formal Concept Analysis. *Journal of Artificial Intelligence Research*, 24:305–339.

P. Cimiano. 2006. *Ontology Learning and Population from Text: Algorithms, Evaluation and Applications*. Springer-Verlag New York, Inc., Secaucus, NJ, USA.

T. Dunning. 1993. Accurate Methods for the Statistics of Surprise and Coincidence. *Computational Linguistics*, 19(1):61–74.

D. Faure and C. Nédellec. 1998. A Corpus-based Conceptual Clustering Method for Verb Frames and Ontology Acquisition. In *LREC workshop on Adapting lexical and corpus resources to sublanguages and applications*, pages 5–12, Granada, Spain.

C. Fellbaum. 1998. *Wordnet: An Electronic Lexical Database*. MIT Press, Cambridge, Massachusetts, USA.

B. Ganter and R. Wille. 1999. *Formal Concept Analysis: Mathematical Foundations*. Springer-Verlag New York, Inc., Secaucus, NJ, USA. Translator-C. Franzke.

Z. Harris. 1968. *Mathematical Structures of Language*. Wiley, New York, USA.

M. A. Hearst. 1992. Automatic Acquisition of Hyponyms from Large Text Corpora. In *Proceedings of the 14th Coling Conference*, pages 539–545, Nantes, France.

C. H. Hwang. 1999. Incompletely and Imprecisely Speaking: Using Dynamic Ontologies for Representing and Retrieving Information. In *Proceedings of the 6th International Workshop on Knowledge Representation Meets Databases*, pages 14–20, Linkoping, Sweden. CEUR-WS.org.

B. King. 1967. Step-wise Clustering Procedures. *Journal of the American Statistical Association*, 69:86–101.

I. P. Klapaftis and S. Manandhar. 2008. Word Sense Induction Using Graphs of Collocations. In *Proceedings of the 18th ECAI Conference*, pages 298–302, Patras, Greece. IOS Press.

A. Maedche and S. Staab. 2002. Measuring Similarity between Ontologies. In *Proceedings of the European Conference on Knowledge Acquisition and Management (EKAW)*, pages 251–263, London,UK. Springer-Verlag.

D. Moldovan and A. Novischi. 2002. Lexical Chains for Question Answering. In *Proceedings of the 19th Coling Conference*, pages 1–7, Taipei, Taiwan.

R. Navigli and P. Velardi. 2004a. Learning Domain Ontologies from Document Warehouses and Dedicated web Sites. *Computational Linguistics*, 30(2):151–179.

R. Navigli and P. Velardi. 2004b. Structural Semantic Interconnection: a Knowledge-based Approach to Word Sense Disambiguation. In *Proceedings of Senseval-3: Third International Workshop on the Evaluation of Systems for the Semantic Analysis of Text*, pages 179–182, Barcelona, Spain.

M.L. Reinberger and P. Spyns. 2004. Discovering Knowledge in Texts for the Learning of Dogma-inspired Ontologies. In *Proceedings of the ECAI Workshop on Ontology Learning and Population*, pages 19–24, Valencia, Spain.

M. L. Reinberger, P. Spyns, W. Daelemans, and R. Meersman. 2003. Mining for Lexons: Applying Unsupervised Learning Methods to create ontology bases. In *CoopIS/DOA/ODBASE*, pages 803–819.

D. Sánchez and A. Moreno. 2005. Web-scale Taxonomy Learning. In *Proceedings of the Workshop on Learning and Extending Ontologies by using Machine Learning methods*, pages 53–60, Bonn, Germany.

P. H. A. Sneath and R. R. Sokal. 1973. *Numerical Taxonomy, The Principles and Practice of Numerical Classification*. W. H. Freeman, San Francisco, USA.

Visual Information in Semantic Representation

Yansong Feng and **Mirella Lapata**
School of Informatics, University of Edinburgh
10 Crichton Street, Edinburgh, EH8 9AB, UK
Y.Feng-4@sms.ed.ac.uk, mlap@inf.ed.ac.uk

Abstract

The question of how meaning might be acquired by young children and represented by adult speakers of a language is one of the most debated topics in cognitive science. Existing semantic representation models are primarily *amodal* based on information provided by the linguistic input despite ample evidence indicating that the cognitive system is also sensitive to perceptual information. In this work we exploit the vast resource of images and associated documents available on the web and develop a model of multimodal meaning representation which is based on the linguistic and visual context. Experimental results show that a closer correspondence to human data can be obtained by taking the visual modality into account.

1 Introduction

The representation and modeling of word meaning has been a central problem in cognitive science and natural language processing. Both disciplines are concerned with how semantic knowledge is acquired, organized, and ultimately used in language processing and understanding. A popular tradition of studying semantic representation has been driven by the assumption that word meaning can be learned from the linguistic environment. Words that are similar in meaning tend to behave similarly in terms of their distributions across different contexts. *Semantic space* models, among which Latent Semantic Analysis (LSA, Landauer and Dumais 1997) is perhaps known best, operationalize this idea by capturing word meaning *quantitatively* in terms of simple co-occurrence statistics. Each word w is represented by a k element vector reflecting the local distributional context of w relative to k context words. More recently, *topic models* have been gaining ground as a more structured representation of word meaning. In contrast to more standard semantic space models where word senses are conflated into a single representation, topic models assume that words observed in a corpus manifest some latent structure — word meaning is a probability distribution over a set of topics (corresponding to coarse-grained senses). Each topic is a probability distribution over words, and the content of the topic is reflected in the words to which it assigns high probability.

Semantic space (and topic) models are extracted from real language corpora, and thus provide a direct means of investigating the influence of the statistics of language on semantic representation. They have been successful in explaining a wide range of behavioral data — examples include lexical priming, deep dyslexia, text comprehension, synonym selection, and human similarity judgments (see Landauer and Dumais 1997 and the references therein). They also underlie a large number of natural language processing (NLP) tasks including lexicon acquisition, word sense discrimination, text segmentation and notably information retrieval. Despite their popularity, these models offer a somewhat impoverished representation of word meaning based solely on information provided by the linguistic input.

Many experimental studies in language acquisition suggest that word meaning arises not only from exposure to the linguistic environment but also from our interaction with the physical world. For example, infants are from an early age able to form perceptually-based category representations (Quinn et al., 1993). Perhaps unsurprisingly, words that refer to concrete entities and actions are among the first words being learned as these are directly observable in the environment (Bornstein et al., 2004). Experimental evidence also shows that children respond to categories on the basis of visual features, e.g., they generalize object names to new objects often on the basis of similarity in shape (Landau et al., 1998) and texture (Jones et al., 1991).

In this paper we aim to develop a unified mod-

Human Language Technologies: The 2010 Annual Conference of the North American Chapter of the ACL, pages 91–99,
Los Angeles, California, June 2010.

eling framework of word meaning that captures the mutual dependence between the linguistic and visual context. This is a challenging task for at least two reasons. First, in order to emulate the environment within which word meanings are acquired, we must have recourse to a corpus of verbal descriptions and their associated images. Such corpora are in short supply compared to the large volumes of solely textual data. Secondly, our model should integrate linguistic and visual information in a single representation. It is unlikely that we have separate representations for different aspects of word meaning (Rogers et al., 2004).

We meet the first challenge by exploiting multimodal corpora, namely collections of documents that contain pictures. Although large scale corpora with a one-to-one correspondence between words and images are difficult to come by, datasets that contain images and text are ubiquitous. For example, online news documents are often accompanied by pictures. Using this data, we develop a model that combines textual and visual information to learn semantic representations. We assume that images and their surrounding text have been generated by a shared set of latent variables or topics. Our model follows the general rationale of topic models — it is based upon the idea that documents are mixtures of topics. Importantly, our topics are inferred from the *joint* distribution of textual and visual words. Our experimental results show that a closer correspondence to human word similarity and association can be obtained by taking the visual modality into account.

2 Related Work

The bulk of previous work has focused on models of semantic representation that are based solely on textual data. Many of these models represent words as vectors in a high-dimensional space (e.g., Landauer and Dumais 1997), whereas probabilistic alternatives view documents as mixtures of topics, where words are represented according to their likelihood in each topic (e.g., Steyvers and Griffiths 2007). Both approaches allow for the estimation of similarity between words. Spatial models compare words using distance metrics (e.g., cosine), while probabilistic models measure similarity between terms according to the degree to which they share the same topic distributions.

Within cognitive science, the problem of how words are grounded in perceptual representations has attracted some attention. Previous modeling efforts have been relatively small-scale, using either artificial images, or data gathered from a few subjects in the lab. Furthermore, the proposed models work well for the tasks at hand (e.g., either word learning or object categorization) but are not designed as a general-purpose meaning representation. For example, Yu (2005) integrates visual information in a computational model of lexical acquisition and object categorization. The model learns a mapping between words and visual features from data provided by (four) subjects reading a children's story. In a similar vein, Roy (2002) considers the problem of learning which words or word sequences refer to objects in a synthetic image consisting of ten rectangles. Andrews et al. (2009) present a probabilistic model that incorporates perceptual information (indirectly) by combining distributional information gathered from corpus data with speaker generated feature norms[1] (which are also word-based).

Much work in computer vision attempts to learn the underlying connections between visual features and words from examples of images annotated with description keywords. The aim here is to enhance image-based applications (e.g., search or retrieval) by developing models that can label images with keywords *automatically*. Most methods discover the correlations between visual features and words by introducing latent variables. Standard latent semantic analysis (LSA) and its probabilistic variant (PLSA) have been applied to this task (Pan et al., 2004; Hofmann, 2001; Monay and Gatica-Perez, 2007). More sophisticated approaches estimate the joint distribution of words and regional image features, whilst treating annotation as a problem of statistical inference in a graphical model (Blei and Jordan, 2003; Barnard et al., 2002).

Our own work aims to develop a model of semantic representation that takes visual context into account. We do not model explicitly the correspondence of words and visual features, or learn a mapping between words and visual features. Rather, we develop a multimodal representation of meaning which is based on visual information and distributional statistics. We hypothesize that visual features are crucial in acquiring and representing meaning

[1]Participants are given a series of object names and for each object they are asked to name all the properties they can think of that are characteristic of the object.

Michelle Obama fever hits the UK

In the UK on her first visit as first lady, Michelle Obama seems to be making just as big an impact. She has attracted as much interest and column inches as her husband on this London trip; creating a buzz with her dazzling outfits, her own schedule of events and her own fanbase. Outside Buckingham Palace, as crowds gathered in anticipation of the Obamas' arrival, Mrs Obama's star appeal was apparent.

Table 1: Each article in the document collection contains a document (the title is shown in boldface), and image with related content.

and conversely, that linguistic information can be useful in isolating salient visual features. Our model extracts a semantic representation from large document collections and their associated images without any human involvement. Contrary to Andrews et al. (2009) we use visual features directly without relying on speaker generated norms. Furthermore, unlike most work in image annotation, we do not employ any goldstandard data where images have been manually labeled with their description keywords.

3 Semantic Representation Model

Much like LSA and the related topic models our model creates semantic representations from large document collections. Importantly, we assume that the documents are paired with images which in turn describe some of the document's content. Our experiments make use of news articles which are often accompanied with images illustrating events, objects or people mentioned in the text. Other datasets with similar properties include Wikipedia entries and their accompanying pictures, illustrated stories, and consumer photo collections. An example news article and its associated image is shown in Table 1 (we provide more detail on the database we used in our experiments in Section 4).

Our model exploits the redundancy inherent in this multimodal collection. Specifically, we assume that the images and their surrounding text have been generated by a shared set of topics. A potential stumbling block here is the fact that images and documents represent distinct modalities: images are commonly described by a continuous feature space (e.g., color, shape, texture; Barnard et al. 2002; Blei and Jordan 2003), whereas words are discrete. Fortunately, we can convert the visual features from a continuous onto a discrete space, thereby rendering image features more like word units. In the following we describe how we do this and then move on to present an extension of Latent Dirichlet Allocation (LDA, Blei and Jordan 2003), a topic model that can be used to represent meaning as a probability distribution over a set of multimodal topics. Finally, we discuss how word similarity can be measured under this model.

3.1 Image Processing

A large number of image processing techniques have been developed in computer vision for extracting meaningful features which are subsequently used in a modeling task. For example, a common first step to all automatic image annotation methods is partitioning the image into regions, using either an image segmentation algorithm (such as normalized cuts; Shi and Malik 2000) or a fixed-grid layout (Feng et al., 2004). In the first case the image is represented by irregular regions (see Figure 1(a)), whereas in the second case the image is partitioned into smaller scale regions which are uniformly extracted from a fixed grid (see Figure 1(b)). The obtained regions are further represented by a standard set of features including color, shape, and texture. These can be treated as continuous vectors (Blei and Jordan, 2003) or in quantized form (Barnard et al., 2002).

Despite much progress in image segmentation, there is currently no automatic algorithm that can reliably divide an image into meaningful parts. Extracting features from small local regions is thus preferable, especially for image collections that are diverse and have low resolution (this is often the case for news images). In our work we identify local regions using a difference-of-Gaussians point detector (see Figure 1(c)). This representation is based on descriptors computed over automatically detected image regions. It provides a much richer (and hopefully more informative) feature space compared to the alternative image representations discussed above. For example, an image segmentation algorithm, would extract at most 20 regions from the image in Figure 1; uniform grid segmentation yields 143

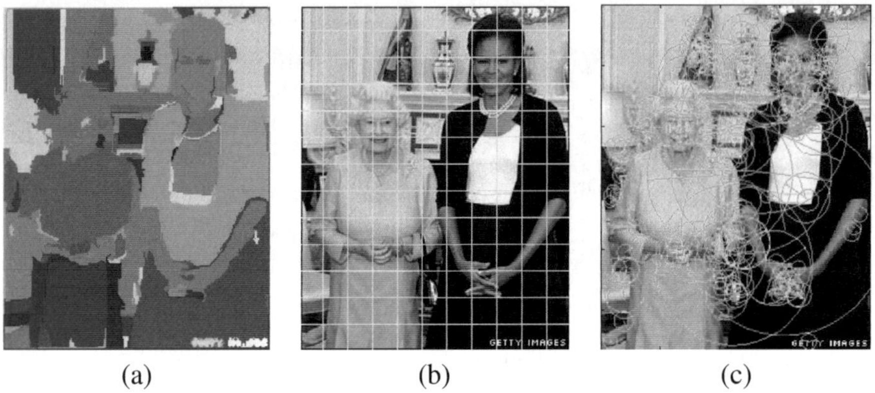

Figure 1: Image partitioned into regions of varying granularity using (a) the normalized cut image segmentation algorithm, (b) uniform grid segmentation, and (c) the SIFT point detector.

(11×13) regions, whereas an average of 240 points (depending on the image content) are detected. A non-sparse feature representation is critical in our case, since we usually do not have more than one image per document.

We compute local image descriptors using the the Scale Invariant Feature Transform (SIFT) algorithm (Lowe, 1999). Importantly, SIFT descriptors are designed to be invariant to small shifts in position, changes in illumination, noise, and viewpoint and can be used to perform reliable matching between different views of an object or scene (Mikolajczyk and Schmid, 2003; Lowe, 1999). We further quantize the SIFT descriptors using the K-means clustering algorithm to obtain a discrete set of visual terms (visiterms) which form our visual vocabulary Voc_V. Each entry in this vocabulary stands for a group of image regions which are similar in content or appearance and assumed to originate from similar objects. More formally, each image I is expressed in a bag-of-words format vector, $[v_1, v_2, ..., v_L]$, where $v_i = n$ only if I has n regions labeled with v_i. Since both images and documents in our corpus are now represented as bags-of-words, and since we assume that the visual and textual modalities express the same content, we can go a step further and represent the document and its associated image as a mixture of verbal and visual words d_{Mix}. We will then learn a topic model on this concatenated representation of visual and textual information.

3.2 Topic Model

Latent Dirichlet Allocation (Blei et al., 2003; Griffiths et al., 2007) is a probabilistic model of text generation. LDA models each document using a mixture over K topics, which are in turn characterized as distributions over words. The words in the document are generated by repeatedly sampling a topic according to the topic distribution, and selecting a word given the chosen topic. Under this framework, the problem of meaning representation is expressed as one of statistical inference: given some data — textual and visual words — infer the latent structure from which it was generated. Word meaning is thus modeled as a probability distribution over a set of latent multimodal topics.

LDA can be represented as a three level hierarchical Bayesian model. Given a corpus consisting of M documents, the generative process for a document d is as follows. We first draw the mixing proportion over topics θ_d from a Dirichlet prior with parameters α. Next, for each of the N_d words w_{dn} in document d, a topic z_{dn} is first drawn from a multinomial distribution with parameters θ_{dn}. The probability of a word token w taking on value i given that topic $z = j$ is parametrized using a matrix β with $b_{ij} = p(w = i|z = j)$. Integrating out θ_d's and z_{dn}'s, gives $P(D|\alpha, \beta)$, the probability of a corpus (or document collection):

$$\prod_{d=1}^{M} \int P(\theta_d|\alpha) \left(\prod_{n=1}^{N_d} \sum_{z_{dn}} P(z_{dn}|\theta_d) P(w_{dn}|z_{dn}, \beta) \right) d\theta_d$$

The central computational problem in topic modeling is to compute the posterior distribution $P(\theta, \mathbf{z}|\mathbf{w}, \alpha, \beta)$ of the hidden variables given a document $\mathbf{w} = (w_1, w_2, \ldots, w_N)$. Although this distribution is intractable in general, a variety of approximate inference algorithms have been proposed in the literature including variational inference which our model adopts. Blei et al. (2003) introduce a set of variational parameters, γ and ϕ, and show that a tight lower bound on the log likelihood of the probability can be found using the following optimization procedure:

$$(\gamma^*, \phi^*) = \underset{\gamma,\phi}{\operatorname{argmin}} D(q(\theta, \mathbf{z}|\gamma, \phi)||p(\theta, \mathbf{z}|\mathbf{w}, \alpha, \beta))$$

Here, D denotes the Kullback-Leibler (KL) divergence between the true posterior and the variational distribution $q(\theta, \mathbf{z}|\gamma, \phi)$ defined as: $q(\theta, \mathbf{z}|\gamma, \phi) = q(\theta|\gamma)\prod_{n=1}^{N} q(z_n|\phi_n)$, where the Dirichlet parameter γ and the multinomial parameters $(\phi_1, \dots, \phi_N)$ are the free variational parameters. Notice that the optimization of parameters $(\gamma^*(\mathbf{w}), \phi^*(\mathbf{w}))$ is document-specific (whereas α is corpus specific).

Previous applications of LDA (e.g., to document classification or information retrieval) typically make use of the posterior Dirichlet parameters $\gamma^*(\mathbf{w})$ associated with a given document. We are not so much interested in γ as we wish to obtain a semantic representation for a given word across documents. We therefore train the LDA model sketched above on a corpus of multimodal documents $\{d_{Mix}\}$ consisting of both textual and visual words. We select the number of topics, K, and apply the LDA algorithm to obtain the β parameters, where β represents the probability of a word w_i given a topic z_j, $p(w_i|z_j) = \beta_{ij}$. The meaning of w_i is thus extracted from β and is a K-element vector, whose components correspond to the probability of w_i given each latent topic assumed to have generated the document collection.

3.3 Similarity Measures

The ability to accurately measure the similarity or association between two words is often used as a diagnostic for the psychological validity of semantic representation models. In the topic model described above, the similarity between two words w_1 and w_2 can be intuitively measured by the extent to which they share the same topics (Griffiths et al., 2007). For example, we may use the KL divergence to measure the difference between the distributions p and q:

$$D(p,q) = \sum_{j=1}^{K} p_j \log_2 \frac{p_j}{q_j}$$

where p and q are shorthand for $P(w_1|z_j)$ and $P(w_2|z_j)$, respectively.

The KL divergence is asymmetric and in many applications, it is preferable to apply a symmetric measure such as the Jensen Shannon (JS) divergence. The latter measures the "distance" between p and q through $\frac{(p+q)}{2}$, the average of p and q:

$$JS(p,q) = \frac{1}{2}\left[D(p, \frac{(p+q)}{2}) + D(q, \frac{(p+q)}{2})\right]$$

An alternative approach to expressing the similarity between two words is proposed in Griffiths et al. (2007). The underlying idea is that word association can be expressed as a conditional distribution. If we have seen word w_1, then we can determine the probability that w_2 will be also generated by computing $P(w_2|w_1)$. Although the LDA generative model allows documents to contain multiple topics, here it is assumed that both w_1 and w_2 came from a single topic:

$$P(w_2|w_1) = \sum_{z=1}^{K} P(w_2|z)P(z|w_1)$$

$$P(z|w_1) \propto P(w_1|z)P(z)$$

where $p(z)$ is uniform, a single topic is sampled from the distribution $P(z|w_1)$, and an overall estimate is obtained by averaging over all topics K.

Griffiths et al. (2007) report results on modeling human association norms using exclusively $P(w_2|w_1)$. We are not aware of any previous work that empirically assesses which measure is best at capturing semantic similarity. We undertake such an empirical comparison as it is not a priory obvious how similarity is best modeled under a multimodal representation.

4 Experimental Setup

In this section we discuss our experimental design for assessing the performance of the model presented above. We give details on our training procedure and parameter estimation and present the baseline method used for comparison with our model.

Data We trained the multimodal topic model on the corpus created in Feng and Lapata (2008). It contains 3,361 documents that have been downloaded from the BBC News website.[2] Each document comes with an image that depicts some of its content. The images are usually 203 pixels wide

[2] http://news.bbc.co.uk/

and 152 pixels high. The average document length is 133.85 words. The corpus has 542,414 words in total. Our experiments used a vocabulary of 6,253 textual words. These were words that occurred at least five times in the whole corpus, excluding stopwords. The accompanying images were preprocessed as follows. We first extracted SIFT features from each image (150 on average) which we subsequently quantized into a discrete set of visual terms using K-means. As we explain below, we determined an optimal value for K experimentally.

Evaluation Our evaluation experiments compared the multimodal topic model against a standard text-based topic model trained on the same corpus whilst ignoring the images. Both models were assessed on two related tasks, that have been previously used to evaluate semantic representation models, namely word association and word similarity.

In order to simulate word association, we used the human norms collected by Nelson et al. (1999).[3] These were established by presenting a large number of participants with a cue word (e.g., *rice*) and asking them to name an associate word in response (e.g., *Chinese, wedding, food, white*). For each word, the norms provide a set of associates and the frequencies with which they were named. We can thus compute the probability distribution over associates for each cue. Analogously, we can estimate the degree of similarity between a cue and its associates using our model (and any of the measures in Section 3.3). And consequently examine (using correlation analysis) the degree of linear relationship between the human cue-associate probabilities and the automatically derived similarity values. We also report how many times the word with the highest probability under the model was the first associate in the norms. The norms contain 10,127 unique words in total. Of these, we created semantic representations for the 3,895 words that appeared in our corpus.

Our word similarity experiment used the WordSim353 test collection (Finkelstein et al., 2002) which consists of relatedness judgments for word pairs. For each pair, a similarity judgment (on a scale of 0 to 10) was elicited from human subjects (e.g., *tiger-cat* are very similar, whereas *delay–racism* are not). The average rating for each pair represents an estimate of the perceived similarity of the two words. The task varies slightly from word association. Here, participants are asked

[3] http://www.usf.edu/Freeassociation.

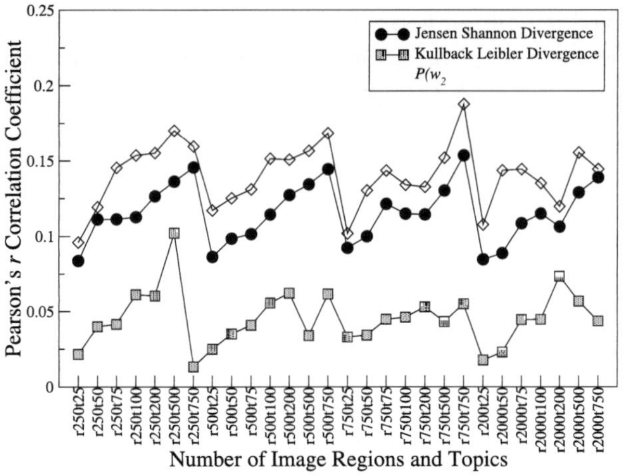

Figure 2: Performance of multimodal topic model on predicting word association under varying topics and visual terms (development set).

to rate perceived similarity rather than generate the first word that came into their head in response to a cue word. The collection contains similarity ratings for 353 word pairs. Of these, we constructed semantic representations for the 254 that appeared in our corpus. We also evaluated how well model produced similarities correlate with human ratings. Throughout this paper we report correlation coefficients using Pearson's r.

5 Experimental Results

Model Selection The multimodal topic model has several parameters that must be instantiated. These include the quantization of the image features, the number of topics, the choice of similarity function, and the values for α and β. We explored the parameter space on held-out data. Specifically, we fit the parameters for the word association and similarity models separately using a third of the association norms and WordSim353 similarity judgments, respectively. As mentioned in Section 3.1 we used K-means to quantize the image features into a discrete set of visual terms. We varied K from 250 to 2000. We also varied the number of topics from 25 to 750 for both the multimodal and text-based topic models. The parameter α was set to 0.1 and β was initialized randomly. The model was trained using variational Bayes until convergence of its bound on the likelihood objective. This took 1,000 iterations.

Figure 2 shows how word association performance varies on the development set with different numbers of topics (t) and visual terms (r) according

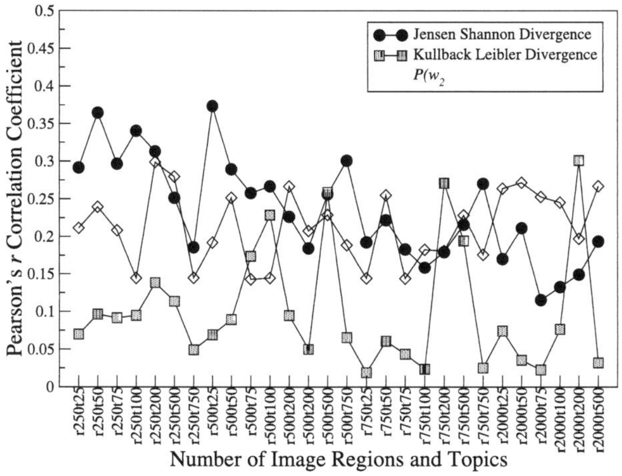

Figure 3: Performance of multimodal topic model on predicting word similarity under varying topics and visual terms (development set).

to three similarity measures: KL divergence, JS divergence, and $P(w_2|w_1)$, the probability of word w_2 given w_1 (see Section 3.3). Figure 3 shows results on the development set for the word similarity task. As far as word association is concerned, we obtain best results with $P(w_2|w_1)$, 750 visual terms and 750 topics ($r = 0.188$). On word similarity, JS performs best with 500 visual terms and 25 topics ($r = 0.374$). It is not surprising that $P(w_2|w_1)$ works best for word association. The measure expresses the associative relations between words as a conditional distribution over potential response words w_2 for cue word w_1. A symmetric function is more appropriate for word similarity as the task involves measuring the degree to which to words share some meaning (expressed as topics in our model) rather than whether a word is likely to be generated as a response to another word. These differences also lead to different parametrizations of the semantic space. A rich visual term vocabulary (750 terms) is needed for modeling association as broader aspects of word meaning are taken into account, whereas a sparser more focused representation (with 500 visual terms and 25 overall topics) is better at isolating the common semantic content between two words. We explored the parameter space for the text-based topic model in a similar fashion. On the word association task the best correlation coefficient was achieved with 750 topics and $P(w_2|w_1)$ ($r = 0.139$). On word similarity, the best results were obtained with 75 topics and the JS divergence ($r = 0.309$).

Model	Word Association	Word Similarity
UpperBnd	0.400	0.545
MixLDA	0.123	0.318
TxtLDA	0.077	0.247

Table 2: Model performance on word association and similarity (test set).

Model Comparison Table 2 summarizes our results on the test set using the optimal set of parameters as established on the development set. The first row shows how well humans agree with each other on the two tasks (UpperBnd). We estimated the intersubject correlation using leave-one-out resampling[4] (Weiss and Kulikowski, 1991). As can be seen, in all cases the topic model based on textual and visual modalities (MixLDA) outperforms the model relying solely on textual information (TxtLDA). The differences in performance are statistically significant ($p < 0.05$) using a t-test (Cohen and Cohen, 1983).

Steyvers and Griffiths (2007) also predict word association using Nelson's norms and a state-of-the-art LDA model. Although they do not report correlations, they compute how many times the word with the highest probability $P(w_2|w_1)$ under the model was the first associate in the human norms. Using a considerably larger corpus (37,651 documents), they reach an accuracy of 16.15%. Our corpus contains 3,361 documents, the MixLDA model performs at 14.15% and the LDA model at 13.16%. Using a vector-based model trained on the BNC corpus (100M words), Washtell and Markert (2009) report a correlation of 0.167 on the same association data set, whereas our model achieves a correlation of 0.123. With respect to word similarity, Marton et al. (2009) report correlations within the range of 0.31–0.54 using different instantiations of a vector-based model trained on the BNC with a vocabulary of 33,000 words. Our MixLDA model obtains a correlation of 0.318 with a vocabulary five times smaller (6,253 words). Although these results are not strictly comparable due to the different nature and size of the training data, they give some indication of the quality of our model in the context of other approaches that exploit only the textual modality. Besides, our intent is not to report the best performance possible,

[4]We correlated the data obtained from each participant with the ratings obtained from all other participants and report the average.

GAME, CONSOLE, XBOX, SECOND, SONY, WORLD, TIME, JAPAN, JAPANESE, SCHUMACHER, LAP, MICROSOFT, ALONSO, RACE, TITLE, WIN, GAMERS, LAUNCH, RENAULT, MARKET
PARTY, MINISTER, BLAIR, LABOUR, PRIME, LEADER, GOVERNMENT, TELL, BROW, MP, TONY, SIR, SECRETARY, ELECTION, CONFERENCE, POLICY, NEW, WANT, PUBLIC, SPEECH
SCHOOL, CHILD, EDUCATION, STUDENT, WORK, PUPIL, PARENT, TEACHER, GOVERNMENT, YOUNG, SKILL, AGE, NEED, UNIVERSITY, REPORT, LEVEL, GOOD, HELL, NEW, SURVEY

Table 3: Most frequent words in three topics learnt from a corpus of image-document pairs.

but to show that a model of meaning representation is more accurate when taking visual information into account.

Table 3 shows some examples of the topics found by our model, which largely form coherent blocks of semantically related words. In general, we observe that the model using image features tends to prefer words that visualize easily (e.g., CONSOLE, XBOX). Furthermore, the visual modality helps obtain crisper meaning distinctions. Here, SCHUMACHER is a very probable world for the "game" cluster. This is because the Formula One driver appears as a character in several video games discussed and depicted in our corpus. For comparison the "game" cluster for the text-based LDA model contains the words: GAME, USE, INTERNET, SITE, USE, SET, ONLINE, WEB, NETWORK, MURRAY, PLAY, MATCH, GOOD, WAY, BREAK, TECHNOLOGY, WORK, NEW, TIME, SECOND.

We believe the model presented here works better than a vanilla text-based topic model for at least three reasons: (1) the visual information helps create better clusters (i.e., conceptual representations) which in turn are used to measure similarity or association; these clusters themselves are amodal but express commonalities across the visual and textual modalities; (2) the model is also able to capture perceptual correlations between words. For example, RED is the most frequent associate for APPLE in Nelson's norms. This association is captured in our visual features (pictures with apples cluster with pictures showing red objects) even though RED does not co-occur with APPLE in our data; (3) finally, even in cases where two words are visually very different in terms of shape or color (e.g., BANANA and APPLE), they tend to appear in images with similar structure (e.g., on tables, in bowls, as being held or eaten by someone) and thus often share some common element of meaning.

6 Conclusion

In this paper we developed a computational model that unifies visual and linguistic representations of word meaning. The model learns from natural language corpora paired with images under the assumption that visual terms and words are generated by mixtures of latent topics. We have shown that a closer correspondence to human data can be obtained by explicitly taking the visual modality into account in comparison to a model that estimates the topic structure solely from the textual modality. Beyond word similarity and association, the approach is promising for modeling word learning and categorization as well as a wide range of priming studies. Outwith cognitive science, we hope that some of the work described here might be of relevance to more applied tasks such as thesaurus acquisition, word sense disambiguation, multimodal search, image retrieval, and summarization.

Future improvements include developing a non-parametric version that jointly *learns* how many visual terms and topics are optimal. Currently, the size of the visual vocabulary and the number of topics are parameters in the model, that must be tuned separately for different tasks and corpora. Another extension concerns the creation of visual terms. Our model assumes that an image is a bag of words. The assumption is convenient for modeling purposes, but clearly false in the context of visual processing. Image descriptors found closely to each other are likely to represent the same object and should form one term rather than several distinct ones (Wang and Grimson, 2007). Taking the spatial structure among visual words into account would yield better topics and overall better semantic representations. Analogously, we could represent documents by their syntactic structure (Boyd-Graber and Blei, 2009).

References

Andrews, M., G. Vigliocco, and D. Vinson. 2009. Integrating experiential and distributional data to learn semantic representations. *Psychological Review* 116(3):463–498.

Barnard, K., P. Duygulu, D. Forsyth, N. de Freitas, D. Blei, and M. Jordan. 2002. Matching words and pictures. *Journal of Machine Learning Research* 3:1107–1135.

Blei, D. and M. Jordan. 2003. Modeling annotated data. In *Proceedings of the 26th Annual International ACM SIGIR Conference*. Toronto, ON, pages 127–134.

Blei, D. M., A. Y. Ng, and M. I. Jordan. 2003. Latent Dirichlet allocation. *Journal of Machine Learning Research* 3:993–1022.

Bornstein, M. H., L. R. Cote, S. Maital, K. Painter, S.-Y. Park, and L. Pascual. 2004. Cross-linguistic analysis of vocabulary in young children: Spanish, Dutch, French, Hebrew, Italian, Korean, and American English. *Child Development* 75(4):1115–1139.

Boyd-Graber, J. and D. Blei. 2009. Syntactic topic models. In *Proceedings of the 22nd Conference on Advances in Neural Information Processing Systems*. MIT, Press, Cambridge, MA, pages 185–192.

Cohen, J. and P. Cohen. 1983. *Applied Multiple Regression/Correlation Analysis for the Behavioral Sciences*. Hillsdale, NJ: Erlbaum.

Feng, S., V. Lavrenko, and R. Manmatha. 2004. Multiple Bernoulli relevance models for image and video annotation. In *Proceedings of the International Conference on Computer Vision and Pattern Recognition*. Washington, DC, pages 1002–1009.

Feng, Y. and M. Lapata. 2008. Automatic image annotation using auxiliary text information. In *Proceedings of the ACL-08: HLT*. Columbus, pages 272–280.

Finkelstein, L., E. Gabrilovich, Y. Matias, E. Rivlin, Z. Solan, G. Wolfman, and E. Ruppin. 2002. Placing search in context: The concept revisited. *ACM Transactions on Information Systems* 20(1):116–131.

Griffiths, T. L., M. Steyvers, and J. B. Tenenbaum. 2007. Topics in semantic representation. *Psychological Review* 114(2):211–244.

Hofmann, T. 2001. Unsupervised learning by probabilistic latent semantic analysis. *Machine Learning* 41(2):177–196.

Jones, S. S., L. B. Smith, and B. Landau. 1991. Object properties and knowledge in early lexical learning. *Child Development* (62):499–516.

Landau, B., L. Smith, and S. Jones. 1998. Object perception and object naming in early development. *Trends in Cognitive Science* 27:19–24.

Landauer, T. and S. T. Dumais. 1997. A solution to Plato's problem: the latent semantic analysis theory of acquisition, induction, and representation of knowledge. *Psychological Review* 104(2):211–240.

Lowe, D. 1999. Object recognition from local scale-invariant features. In *Proceedings of International Conference on Computer Vision*. IEEE Computer Society, pages 1150–1157.

Marton, Y., S. Mohammad, and P. Resnik. 2009. Estimating semantic distance using soft semantic constraints in knowledge-source – corpus hybrid models. In *Proceedings of the 2009 Conference on Empirical Methods in Natural Language Processing*. Singapore, pages 775–783.

Mikolajczyk, K. and C. Schmid. 2003. A performance evaluation of local descriptors. In *Proceedings of the 9th International Conference on Computer Vision and Pattern Recognition*. Nice, France, volume 2, pages 257–263.

Monay, F. and D. Gatica-Perez. 2007. Modeling semantic aspects for cross-media image indexing. *IEEE Transactions on Pattern Analysis and Machine Intelligence* 29(10):1802–1817.

Nelson, D. L., C. L. McEvoy, and T.A. Schreiber. 1999. The university of South Florida word association norms.

Pan, J., H. Yang, P. Duygulu, and C. Faloutsos. 2004. Automatic image captioning. In *Proceedings of the 2004 International Conference on Multimedia and Expo*. Taipei, pages 1987–1990.

Quinn, P., P. Eimas, and S. Rosenkrantz. 1993. Evidence for representations of perceptually similar natural categories by 3-month and 4-month old infants. *Perception* 22:463–375.

Rogers, T. T., M. A. Lambon Ralph, P. Garrard, S. Bozeat, J. L. McClelland, J. R. Hodges, and K. Patterson. 2004. Structure and deterioration of semantic memory: A neuropsychological and computational investigation. *Psychological Review* 111(1):205–235.

Roy, D. 2002. Learning words and syntax for a visual description task. *Computer Speech and Language* 16(3).

Shi, J. and J. Malik. 2000. Normalized cuts and image segmentation. *IEEE Transactions on Pattern Analysis and Machine Intelligence* 22(8):888–905.

Steyvers, M. and T. Griffiths. 2007. Probabilistic topic models. In T. Landauer, D. McNamara, S Dennis, and W Kintsch, editors, *A Handbook of Latent Semantic Analysis*, Psychology Press.

Wang, X. and E. Grimson. 2007. Spatial latent Dirichlet allocation. In *Proceedings of the 20th Conference on Advances in Neural Information Processing Systems*. MI Press, Cambridge, MA, pages 1577–1584.

Washtell, J. and K. Markert. 2009. A comparison of windowless and window-based computational association measures as predictors of syntagmatic human associations. In *Proceedings of the 2009 Conference on Empirical Methods in Natural Language Processing*. Singapore, pages 628–637.

Weiss, S. M. and C. A. Kulikowski. 1991. *Computer Systems that Learn: Classification and Prediction Methods from Statistics, Neural Nets, Machine Learning, and Expert Systems*. Morgan Kaufmann, San Mateo, CA.

Yu, C. 2005. The emergence of links between lexical acquisition and object categorization: A computational study. *Connection Science* 17(3):381–397.

Automatic Evaluation of Topic Coherence

David Newman,[♠♣] **Jey Han Lau,**[♡] **Karl Grieser**[◇], and **Timothy Baldwin,**[♠♡]
♠ NICTA Victoria Research Laboratory, Australia
♣ Dept of Computer Science, University of California, Irvine
♡ Dept of Computer Science and Software Engineering, University of Melbourne, Australia
◇ Dept of Information Systems, University of Melbourne, Australia
newman@uci.edu, depthchargex@gmail.com,
kgrieser@csse.unimelb.edu.au, tb@ldwin.net

Abstract

This paper introduces the novel task of topic coherence evaluation, whereby a set of words, as generated by a topic model, is rated for coherence or interpretability. We apply a range of topic scoring models to the evaluation task, drawing on WordNet, Wikipedia and the Google search engine, and existing research on lexical similarity/relatedness. In comparison with human scores for a set of learned topics over two distinct datasets, we show a simple co-occurrence measure based on pointwise mutual information over Wikipedia data is able to achieve results for the task at or nearing the level of inter-annotator correlation, and that other Wikipedia-based lexical relatedness methods also achieve strong results. Google produces strong, if less consistent, results, while our results over WordNet are patchy at best.

1 Introduction

There has traditionally been strong interest within computational linguistics in techniques for learning sets of words (aka topics) which capture the latent semantics of a document or document collection, in the form of methods such as latent semantic analysis (Deerwester et al., 1990), probabilistic latent semantic analysis (Hofmann, 2001), random projection (Widdows and Ferraro, 2008), and more recently, latent Dirichlet allocation (Blei et al., 2003; Griffiths and Steyvers, 2004). Such methods have been successfully applied to a myriad of tasks including word sense discrimination (Brody and Lapata, 2009), document summarisation (Haghighi and Vanderwende, 2009), areal linguistic analysis (Daume III, 2009) and text segmentation (Sun et al., 2008). In each case, *extrinsic* evaluation has been used to demonstrate the effectiveness of the learned topics in the application domain, but standardly, no attempt has been made to perform *intrinsic* evaluation of the topics themselves, either qualitatively or quantitatively. In machine learning, on the other hand, researchers have modified and extended topic models in a variety of ways, and evaluated *intrinsically* in terms of model perplexity (Wallach et al., 2009), but there has been less effort on *qualitative* understanding of the semantic nature of the learned topics.

This research seeks to fill the gap between topic evaluation in computational linguistics and machine learning, in developing techniques to perform intrinsic qualitative evaluation of learned topics. That is, we develop methods for evaluating the quality of a given topic, in terms of its coherence to a human. After learning topics from a collection of news articles and a collection of books, we ask humans to decide whether individual learned topics are coherent, in terms of their interpretability and association with a single over-arching semantic concept. We then propose models to predict topic coherence, based on resources such as WordNet, Wikipedia and the Google search engine, and methods ranging from ontological similarity to link overlap and term co-occurrence. Over topics learned from two distinct datasets, we demonstrate that there is remarkable inter-annotator agreement on what is a coherent topic, and additionally that our methods based on Wikipedia are able to achieve nearly perfect agreement with humans over the evaluation of topic coherence.

This research forms part of a larger research agenda on the utility of topic modelling in gisting and visualising document collections, and ultimately enhancing search/discovery interfaces over

Human Language Technologies: The 2010 Annual Conference of the North American Chapter of the ACL, pages 100–108,
Los Angeles, California, June 2010.

document collections (Newman et al., to appeara). Evaluating topic coherence is a component of the larger question of what are good topics, what characteristics of a document collection make it more amenable to topic modelling, and how can the potential of topic modelling be harnessed for human consumption (Newman et al., to appearb).

2 Related Work

Most earlier work on intrinsically evaluating learned topics has been on the basis of perplexity results, where a model is learned on a collection of training documents, then the log probability of the unseen test documents is computed using that learned model. Usually perplexity is reported, which is the inverse of the geometric mean per-word likelihood. Perplexity is useful for model selection and adjusting parameters (e.g. number of topics T), and is the standard way of demonstrating the advantage of one model over another. Wallach et al. (2009) presented efficient and unbiased methods for computing perplexity and evaluating almost any type of topic model.

While statistical evaluation of topic models is reasonably well understood, there has been much less work on evaluating the intrinsic *semantic* quality of topics learned by topic models, which could have a far greater impact on the overall value of topic modeling for end-user applications. Some researchers have started to address this problem, including Mei et al. (2007) who presented approaches for automatic labeling of topics (which is core to the question of coherence and semantic interpretability), and Griffiths and Steyvers (2006) who applied topic models to word sense discrimination tasks. Misra et al. (2008) used topic modelling to identify semantically incoherent documents within a document collection (vs. coherent *topics*, as targeted in this research). Chang et al. (2009) presented the first human-evaluation of topic models by creating a task where humans were asked to identify which word in a list of five topic words had been randomly switched with a word from another topic. This work showed some possibly counter-intuitive results, where in some cases humans preferred models with higher perplexity. This type of result shows the need for further exploring measures other than perplexity for evaluating topic models. In earlier work, we carried out preliminary experimentation using pointwise mutual information and Google results to evaluate topic coherence over the same set of topics as used in this research (Newman et al., 2009).

Part of this research takes inspiration from the work on automatic evaluation in machine translation (Papineni et al., 2002) and automatic summarisation (Lin, 2004). Here, the development of automated methods with high correlation with human subjects has opened the door to large-scale automated evaluation of system outputs, revolutionising the respective fields. While our aspirations are more modest, the basic aim is the same: to develop a fully-automated method for evaluating a well-grounded task, which achieves near-human correlation.

3 Topic Modelling

In order to evaluate topic modelling, we require a topic model and set of topics for a given document collection. While the evaluation methodology we describe generalises to any method which generates sets of words, all of our experiments are based on *Latent Dirichlet Allocation* (LDA, aka *Discrete Principal Component Analysis*), on the grounds that it is a state-of-the-art method for generating topics.

LDA is a Bayesian graphical model for text document collections represented by bags-of-words (see Blei et al. (2003), Griffiths and Steyvers (2004), Buntine and Jakulin (2004)). In a topic model, each document in the collection of D documents is modelled as a multinomial distribution over T topics, where each topic is a multinomial distribution over W words. Typically, only a small number of words are important (have high likelihood) in each topic, and only a small number of topics are present in each document.

The collapsed Gibbs sampled topic model simultaneously learns the topics and the mixture of topics in documents by iteratively sampling the topic assignment z to every word in every document, using the Gibbs sampling update:

$$p(z_{id} = t | x_{id} = w, \mathbf{z}^{\neg id}) \propto \frac{N_{wt}^{\neg id} + \beta}{\sum_w N_{wt}^{\neg id} + W\beta} \frac{N_{td}^{\neg id} + \alpha}{\sum_t N_{td}^{\neg id} + T\alpha}$$

where $z_{id} = t$ is the assignment of the ith word in document d to topic t, $x_{id} = w$ indicates that the current observed word is w, and $\mathbf{z}^{\neg id}$ is the vector of all topic assignments not including the current word. N_{wt} represents integer count arrays (with the subscripts denoting what is counted), and α and β are Dirichlet priors.

The maximum a posterior (MAP) estimates of the topics $p(w|t)$, $t = 1 \ldots T$ are given by:

$$p(w|t) = \frac{N_{wt} + \beta}{\sum_w N_{wt} + W\beta}$$

We will follow the convention of representing a topic via its top-n words, ordered by $p(w|t)$. Here, we use the top-ten words, as they usually provide sufficient detail to convey the subject of a topic, and distinguish one topic from another. For the remainder of this paper, we will refer to individual topics by its list of top-ten words, denoted by $\mathbf{w} = (w_1, \ldots, w_{10})$.

4 Topic Evaluation Methods

We experiment with scoring methods based on WordNet (Section 4.1), Wikipedia (Section 4.2) and the Google search engine (Section 4.3). In the case of Google, we query for the entire topic, but with WordNet and Wikipedia, this takes the form of scoring each word-pair in a given topic $\mathbf{w}$ based on the component words $(w_1, \ldots, w_{10})$. Given some (symmetric) word-similarity measure $D(w_i, w_j)$, two straightforward ways of producing a combined score from the 45 (i.e. $\binom{10}{2}$) word-pair scores are: (1) the arithmetic mean, and (2) the median, as follows:

$$\text{Mean-D-Score}(\mathbf{w}) = \text{mean}\{\text{D}(w_i, w_j), ij \in 1 \ldots 10, i < j\}$$

$$\text{Median-D-Score}(\mathbf{w}) = \text{median}\{\text{D}(w_i, w_j), ij \in 1 \ldots 10, i < j\}$$

Intuitively, the median seems the more natural representation, as it is less affected by outlier scores, but we experiment with both, and fall back to empirical verification of which is the better combination method.

4.1 WordNet similarity

WordNet (Fellbaum, 1998) is a lexical ontology that represents word sense via "synsets", which are structured in a hypernym/hyponym hierarchy (nouns) or hypernym/troponym hierarchy (verbs). WordNet additionally links both synsets and words via lexical relations including antonymy, morphological derivation and holonymy/meronym.

In parallel with the development of WordNet, a number of computational methods for calculating the semantic relatedness/similarity between synset pairs (i.e. sense-specified word pairs) have been developed, as we outline below. These methods apply to *synset* rather than word pairs, so to generate a single score for a given word pair, we look up each word in WordNet and exhaustively generate scores for each sense pairing defined by them, and calculate their arithmetic mean.[1]

The majority of the methods (all methods other than HSO, VECTOR and LESK) are restricted to operating strictly over hierarchical links within a single hierarchy. As the verb and noun hierarchies are not connected (other than via derivational links), this means that it is generally not possible to calculate the similarity between noun and verb senses, for example. In such cases, we simply drop the synset pairing in question from our calculation of the mean.

The least common subsumer (LCS) is a common feature to a number of the measures, and is defined as the deepest node in the hierarchy that subsumes both of the synsets under question.

For all our experiments over WordNet, we use the `WordNet::Similarity` package.

Path distance (PATH)

The simplest of the WordNet-based measures is to count the number of nodes visited while going from one word to another via the hypernym hierarchy. The path distance between two nodes is defined as the number of nodes that lie on the shortest path between two words in the hierarchy. This

[1] We also experimented with the median, and trialled filtering the set of senses in a variety of ways, e.g. using only the first sense (the sense with the highest prior) for a given word, or using only the word senses associated with the POS with the highest prior. In all cases, the overall trend was for the correlation with the human scores to drop relative to the mean, so we only present the numbers for the mean in this paper.

count of nodes includes the beginning and ending word nodes.

Leacock-Chodorow (LCH)

The measure of semantic similarity devised by Leacock et al. (1998) finds the shortest path between two WordNet synsets ($sp(c_1, c_2)$) using hypernym and synonym relationships. This path length is then scaled by the maximum depth of WordNet (D), and the log likelihood taken:

$$sim_{lch}(c_1, c_2) = -\log \frac{sp(c_1, c_2)}{2 \cdot D}$$

Wu-Palmer (WUP)

Wu and Palmer (1994) proposed to scale the depth of the two synset nodes ($depth_{c_1}$ and $depth_{c_2}$) by the depth of their LCS ($depth(lcs_{c_1,c_2})$):

$$sim_{wup}(c_1, c_2) = \frac{2 \cdot depth(lcs_{c_1,c_2})}{depth_{c_1} + depth_{c_2} + 2 \cdot depth(lcs_{c_1,c_2})}$$

The scaling means that specific terms (deeper in the hierarchy) that are close together are more semantically similar than more general terms, which have a short path distance between them. Only hypernym relationships are used in this measure, as the LCS is defined by the common member in the concepts' hypernym path.

Hirst-St Onge (HSO)

Hirst and St-Onge (1998) define a measure of semantic similarity based on length and tortuosity of the path between nodes. Hirst and St-Onge attribute directions (up, down and horizontal) to the larger set of WordNet relationships, and identify the path from one word to another utilising all of these relationships. The relatedness score is then computed by the weighted sum of the path length between the two words ($len(c_1, c_2)$) and the number of turns the path makes ($turns(c_1, c_2)$) to take this route:

$$rel_{hso}(c_1, c_2) = C - len(c_1, c_2) - k \times turns(c_1, c_2)$$

where C and k are constants. Additionally, a set of restrictions is placed on the path so that it may not be more than a certain length, may not contain more than a set number of turns, and may only take turns in certain directions.

Resnik Information Content (RES)

Resnik (1995) presents a method for weighting edges in WordNet (avoiding the assumption that all edges between nodes have equal importance), by weighting edges between nodes by their frequency of use in textual corpora.

Resnik found that the most effective measure of comparison using this methodology was to measure the Information Content ($IC(c) = -\log p(c)$) of the subsumer with the greatest Information Content from the set of all concepts that subsumed the two initial concepts ($S(c_1, c_2)$) being compared:

$$sim_{res}(c_1, c_2) = \max_{c \in S(c_1,c_2)} [-\log p(c)]$$

Lin (LIN)

Lin (1998) expanded on the Information Theoretic approach presented by Resnik by scaling the Information Content of each node by the information content of their LCS:

$$sim_{lin}(c_1, c_2) = \frac{2 \times \log p(lcs_{c_1,c_2})}{\log p(c_1) + \log p(c_2)}$$

This measure contrasts the joint content of the two concepts with the difference between them.

Jiang-Conrath (JCN)

Jiang and Conrath (1997) define a measure that utilises the components of the information content of the LCS in a different manner:

$$sim_{jcn}(c_1, c_2) = \frac{1}{IC(a) + IC(b) - 2 \times IC(lcs_{a,b})}$$

Instead of defining commonality and difference as with Lin's measure, the key determinant is the specificity of the two nodes compared with their LCS.

Lesk (LESK)

Lesk (1986) proposed a significantly different approach to lexical similarity to that proposed in the methods presented above, using the lexical overlap in dictionary definitions (or *glosses*) to disambiguate word sense. The sense definitions that contain the most words in common indicate the most likely sense of the word given its co-occurrence with similar word senses. Banerjee and Pedersen (2002) adapted this method to utilise WordNet sense glosses rather than dictionary definitions, and expand the dictionary definitions via ontological links, and it is this method we experiment with in this paper.

Vector (VECTOR)

Schütze (1998) uses the words surrounding a term in a piece of text to form a context vector that describes the context in which the word sense appears. For a set of words associated with a target sense, a context vector is computed as the centroid vector of these words. The centroid context vectors each represent a word sense. To compare word senses, the cosine similarity of the context vectors is used.

4.2 Wikipedia

In the last few years, there has been a surge of interest in using Wikipedia to calculate semantic similarity, using the Wikipedia article content, in-article links and document categories (Strübe and Ponzetto, 2006; Gabrilovich and Markovitch, 2007; Milne and Witten, 2008). We present a selection of such methods below. There are a number of Wikipedia-based scoring methods which we do not present results for here (notably Strübe and Ponzetto (2006) and Gabrilovich and Markovitch (2007)), due to their computational complexity and uncertainty about the full implementation details of the methods.

As with WordNet, a given word will often have multiple entries in Wikipedia, grouped in a disambiguation page. For MIW, RACO and DOCSIM, we apply the same strategy as we did with WordNet, in exhaustively calculating the pairwise scores between the sets of documents associated with each term, and averaging across them.

Milne-Witten (MIW)

Milne and Witten (2008) adapted the Resnik (1995) methodology to utilise the count of links pointing to an article. As Wikipedia is self-referential (articles link to related articles), no external data is needed to find the "referred-to-edness" of a concept. Milne and Witten use an adapted Information Content measure that weights the number of links from one article to another ($c_1 \rightarrow c_2$) by the total number of links to the second article:

$$w(c_1 \rightarrow c_2) = |c_1 \rightarrow c_2| \times \log \sum_{x \in W} \frac{|W|}{|c_1, x)|}$$

where x is an article in W, Wikipedia. This measure provides the similarity of one article to another, however this is asymmetrical. The above metric is used to find the weights of all outlinks from the two articles being compared:

$$\vec{c_1} = (w(c_1 \rightarrow l_1), w(c_1 \rightarrow l_2), \cdots, w(c_1 \rightarrow l_n))$$
$$\vec{c_2} = (w(c_2 \rightarrow l_1), w(c_2 \rightarrow l_2), \cdots, w(c_2 \rightarrow l_n))$$

for the set of links l that is the union of the sets of outlinks from both articles. The overall similarity of the two articles is then calculated by taking the cosine similarity of the two vectors.

Related Article Concept Overlap (RACO)

We also determine the category overlap of two articles by examining the outlinks of both articles, in the form of the Related Article Concept Overlap (RACO) measure. The concept overlap of the sets of respective outlinks is given by the union of the two sets of categories from the outlinks from each article:

$$overlap(c_1, c_1) = \Big|\Big(\bigcup_{l \in ol(c_1)} cat(l)\Big) \bigcap \Big(\bigcup_{l \in ol(c_2)} cat(l)\Big)\Big|$$

where $ol(c_1)$ is the set of outlinks from article c_1, and $cat(l)$ is the set of categories of which the article at outlink l is a member. To account for article size (and differing number of outlinks), the Jaccard coefficient is used:

$$rel_{raco}(c_1, c_2) = \frac{\big|(\bigcup_{l \in ol(c_1)} cat(l)) \bigcap (\bigcup_{l \in ol(c_2)} cat(l))\big|}{\big|\bigcup_{l \in ol(c_1)} cat(l)\big| + \big|\bigcup_{l \in ol(c_2)} cat(l)\big|}$$

Document Similarity (DOCSIM)

In addition to these two measures of semantic relatedness, we experiment with simple cosine similarity of the text of Wikipedia articles as a measure of semantic relatedness.

Term Co-occurrence (PMI)

Another variant is to treat Wikipedia as a single meta-document and score word pairs using term co-occurrence. Here, we calculate the pointwise mutual information (PMI) of each word pair, estimated

Selected high-scoring topics (unanimous score=3):
[NEWS] *space earth moon science scientist light nasa mission planet mars ...*
[NEWS] *health disease aids virus vaccine infection hiv cases infected asthma ...*
[BOOKS] *steam engine valve cylinder pressure piston boiler air pump pipe ...*
[BOOKS] *furniture chair table cabinet wood leg mahogany piece oak louis ...*

Selected low-scoring topics (unanimous score=1):
[NEWS] *king bond berry bill ray rate james treas byrd key ...*
[NEWS] *dog moment hand face love self eye turn young character ...*
[BOOKS] *soon short longer carried rest turned raised filled turn allowed ...*
[BOOKS] *act sense adv person ppr plant sax genus applied dis ...*

Table 1: A selection of high-scoring and low-scoring topics

from the entire corpus of over two million English Wikipedia articles (~1 billion words). PMI has been studied variously in the context of collocation extraction (Pecina, 2008), and is one measure of the statistical independence of observing two words in close proximity. Using a sliding window of 10-words to identify co-occurrence, we computed the PMI of all a given word pair (w_i, w_j) as, following Newman et al. (2009):

$$\text{PMI}(w_i, w_j) = \log \frac{p(w_i, w_j)}{p(w_i)p(w_j)}$$

4.3 Search engine-based similarity

Finally, we present two search engine-based scoring methods, based on Newman et al. (2009). In this case the external data source is the entire World Wide Web, via the Google search engine. Unlike the methods presented above, here we query for the topic in its entirety,[2] meaning that we return a topic-level score rather than scores for individual word or word sense pairs. In each case, we mark each search term with the advanced search option + to search for the terms exactly as is and prevent Google from using synonyms or lexical variants of the term. An example query is: *+space +earth +moon +science +scientist +light +nasa +mission +planet +mars*.

Google title matches (TITLES)

Firstly, we score topics by the relative occurrence of their component words in the titles of documents returned by Google:

$$\text{Google-titles-match}(\mathbf{w}) = \mathbf{1}\left[w_i = v_j\right]$$

[2]All queries were run on 15/09/2009.

where $i = 1, \ldots, 10$ and $j = 1, \ldots, |V|$, v_j are all the unique terms mentioned in the titles from the top-100 search results, and **1** is the indicator function to count matches. For example, in the top-100 results for our query above, there are 194 matches with the ten topic words, so Google-titles-match$(\mathbf{w}) =$ 194.

Google log hits matches (LOGHITS)

Second, we issue queries as above, but return the log number of hits for our query:

$$\text{Google-log-hits}(\mathbf{w}) = \log_{10}(\text{\# results from search for } \mathbf{w})$$

where $\mathbf{w}$ is the search string $+w_1$ $+w_2$ $+w_3$ $\ldots$ $+w_{10}$. For example, our query above returns 171,000 results, so Google-log-hits$(\mathbf{w}) = 5.2$. and the URL titles from the top-100 results include a total of 194 matches with the ten topic words, so for this topic Google-titles-match($\mathbf{w}$)=194.

5 Experimental Setup

We learned topics for two document collections: a collection of news articles, and a collection of books. These collections were chosen to produce sets of topics that have more variable quality than one typically observes when topic modeling highly uniform content. The collection of $D = 55,000$ news articles was selected from English Gigaword, and the collection of $D = 12,000$ books was downloaded from the Internet Archive. We refer to these collections as NEWS and BOOKS, respectively.

Standard procedures were used to tokenize each collection and create the bags-of-words. We learned

Resource	Method	Median	Mean
WordNet	HSO	−0.29	0.34
	JCN	0.08	0.22
	LCH	−0.18	−0.07
	LESK	0.38	0.37
	LIN	0.18	0.25
	PATH	0.19	0.11
	RES	−0.10	0.13
	VECTOR	0.07	0.20
	WUP	0.03	0.10
Wikipedia	RACO	0.61	0.63
	MIW	0.69	0.60
	DOCSIM	0.45	0.50
	PMI	0.78	0.77
Google	TITLES	**0.80**	
	LOGHITS	0.46	
Gold-standard	IAA	0.79	0.73

Table 2: Spearman rank correlation ρ values for the different scoring methods over the NEWS dataset (best-performing method for each resource underlined; best-performing method overall in **boldface**)

Resource	Method	Median	Mean
WordNet	HSO	0.15	0.59
	JCN	−0.20	0.19
	LCH	−0.31	−0.15
	LESK	0.53	0.53
	LIN	0.09	0.28
	PATH	0.29	0.12
	RES	0.57	0.66
	VECTOR	−0.08	0.27
	WUP	0.41	0.26
Wikipedia	RACO	0.62	0.69
	MIW	0.68	0.70
	DOCSIM	0.59	0.60
	PMI	**0.74**	**0.77**
Google	TITLES	0.51	
	LOGHITS	−0.19	
Gold-standard	IAA	0.82	0.78

Table 3: Spearman rank correlation ρ values for the different scoring methods over the BOOKS dataset (best-performing method for each resource underlined; best-performing method overall in **boldface**)

topic models of NEWS and BOOKS using $T = 200$ and $T = 400$ topics respectively. We randomly selected a total of 237 topics from the two collections for user scoring. We asked $N = 9$ users to score each of the 237 topics on a 3-point scale where 3="useful" (coherent) and 1="useless" (less coherent).

We provided annotators with a rubric and guidelines on how to judge whether a topic was useful or useless. In addition to showing several examples of useful and useless topics, we instructed users to decide whether the topic was to some extent coherent, meaningful, interpretable, subject-heading-like, and something-you-could-easily-label. For our purposes, the usefulness of a topic can be thought of as whether one could imagine using the topic in a search interface to retrieve documents about a particular subject. One indicator of usefulness is the ease by which one could think of a short label to describe a topic.

Table 1 shows a selection of high- and low-scoring topics, as scored by the $N = 9$ users. The first topic illustrates the notion of labelling coherence, as *space exploration*, e.g., would be an obvious label for the topic. The low-scoring topics display little coherence, and one would not expect them to be useful as categories or facets in a search interface. Note that the useless topics from both collections are not chance artifacts produced by the models, but are in fact stable and robust statistical features in the data sets.

6 Results

The results for the different topic scoring methods over the NEWS and BOOKS collections are presented in Tables 2 and 3, respectively. In each table, we separate out the scoring methods into those based on WordNet (from Section 4.1), those based on Wikipedia (from Section 4.2), and those based on Google (from Section 4.3).

As stated in Section 4, we experiment with two methods for combining the word-pair scores (for all methods other than the two Google methods, which operate natively over a word set), namely the arithmetic mean and median. We present the numbers for these two methods in each table. In each case, we evaluate via Spearman rank correlation, reversing the sign of the calculated ρ value for PATH (as it is the only instance of a distance metric, where the gold-standard is made up of similarity values).

We include the inter-annotator agreement (IAA) in the final row of each table, which we consider to be the upper bound for the task. This is calculated as the average Spearman rank correlation between each annotator and the mean/median of the remaining annotators for that topic. Encouragingly, there is relatively little difference in the IAA between the two datasets; the median-based calculation produces slightly higher ρ values and is empirically the method of choice.[3]

Of all the topic scoring methods tested, PMI (term co-occurrence via simple pointwise mutual information) is the most consistent performer, achieving the best or near-best results over both datasets, and approaching or surpassing the inter-annotator agreement. This indicates both that the task of topic evaluation as defined in this paper is computationally tractable, and that word-pair based co-occurrence is highly successful at modelling topic coherence.

Comparing the different resources, Wikipedia is far and away the most consistent performing, with PMI producing the best results, followed by MIW and RACO, and finally DOCSIM. There is relatively little difference in results between NEWS and BOOKS for the Wikipedia methods. Google achieves the best results over NEWS, for TITLES (actually slightly above the IAA), but the results fall away sharply over BOOKS. The reason for this can be seen in the sample topics in Table 1: the topics for BOOKS tend to be more varied in word class than for NEWS, and contain less proper names; also, the genre of BOOKS is less well represented on the web. We hypothesise that Wikipedia's encyclopedic nature means that it has good coverage over both domains, and thus more robust.

Turning to WordNet, the overall results are markedly better over BOOKS, again largely because of the relative sparsity of proper names in the resource. The results for individual methods are somewhat surprising. Whereas JCN and LCH have been shown to be two of the best-performing methods over lexical similarity tasks (Budanitsky and Hirst, 2005; Agirre et al., 2009), they perform abysmally at the topic scoring task. Indeed, the spread of results across the WordNet similarity methods (notably HSO, JCN, LCH, LIN, RES and WUP) is much greater than we had expected. The single most consistent method is LESK, which is based on lexical overlap in definition sentences and makes relatively modest use of the WordNet hierarchy. Supplementary evaluation where we filtered out all proper nouns from the topics (based on simple POS priors for each word learned from an automatically-tagged version of the British National Corpus) led to a slight increase in results for the WordNet methods; the full results are omitted for reasons of space. In future work, we intend to carry out error analysis to determine why some of the methods performed so badly, or inconsistently across the two datasets.

There is no clear answer to the question of whether the mean or median is the best method for combining the pair-wise scores.

7 Conclusions

We have proposed the novel task of topic coherence evaluation as a form of intrinsic topic evaluation with relevance in document search/discovery and visualisation applications. We constructed a gold-standard dataset of topic coherence scores over the output of a topic model for two distinct datasets, and evaluated a wide range of topic scoring methods over this dataset, drawing on WordNet, Wikipedia and the Google search engine. The single best-performing method was term co-occurrence within Wikipedia based on pointwise mutual information, which achieve results very close to the inter-annotator agreement for the task. Google was also found to perform well over one of the two datasets, while the results for the WordNet-based methods were overall surprisingly low.

Acknowledgements

NICTA is funded by the Australian government as represented by Department of Broadband, Communication and Digital Economy, and the Australian Research Council through the ICT centre of Excellence programme. DN has also been supported by a grant from the Institute of Museum and Library Services, and a Google Research Award.

References

E Agirre, E Alfonseca, K Hall, J Kravalova, M Paşca, and A Soroa. 2009. A study on similarity and re-

[3]Note that the choice of mean or median for IAA is independent of that for the scoring methods, as they are combining different things: annotator scores in the one hand, and word/concept pair scores on the other.

latedness using distributional and WordNet-based approaches. In *Proc. of HLT: NAACL 2009*, pages 19–27, Boulder, Colorado.

S Banerjee and T Pedersen. 2002. An adapted Lesk algorithm for word sense disambiguation using WordNet. *Proc. of CICLing'02*, pages 136–145.

DM Blei, AY Ng, and MI Jordan. 2003. Latent Dirichlet allocation. *Journal of Machine Learning Research*, 3:993–1022.

S Brody and M Lapata. 2009. Bayesian word sense induction. In *Proc. of EACL 2009*, pages 103–111, Athens, Greece.

A Budanitsky and G Hirst. 2005. Evaluating WordNet-based Measures of Lexical Sematic Relatedness. *Computational Linguistics*, 32(1):13–47.

WL Buntine and A Jakulin. 2004. Applying discrete PCA in data analysis. In *Proc. of UAI 2004*, pages 59–66.

J Chang, J Boyd-Graber, S Gerris, C Wang, and D Blei. 2009. Reading tea leaves: How humans interpret topic models. In *Proc. of NIPS 2009*.

H Daume III. 2009. Non-parametric bayesian areal linguistics. In *Proc. of HLT: NAACL 2009*, pages 593–601, Boulder, USA.

Scott Deerwester, Susan T. Dumais, George W. Furnas, Thomas K. Landauer, and Richard Harshman. 1990. Indexing by latent semantic analysis. *Journal of the American Society of Information Science*, 41(6).

C Fellbaum, editor. 1998. *WordNet: An Electronic Lexical Database*. MIT Press, Cambridge, USA.

E Gabrilovich and S Markovitch. 2007. Computing semantic relatedness using Wikipedia-based explicit semantic analysis. In *Proc. of IJCAI'07*, pages 1606–1611, Hyderabad, India.

T Griffiths and M Steyvers. 2004. Finding scientific topics. In *Proc. of the National Academy of Sciences*, volume 101, pages 5228–5235.

T Griffiths and M Steyvers. 2006. Probabilistic topic models. In *Latent Semantic Analysis: A Road to Meaning*.

A Haghighi and L Vanderwende. 2009. Exploring content models for multi-document summarization. In *Proc. of HLT: NAACL 2009*, pages 362–370, Boulder, USA.

G Hirst and D St-Onge. 1998. Lexical chains as representations of context for the detection and correction of malapropism. In Fellbaum (Fellbaum, 1998), pages 305–332.

T Hofmann. 2001. Unsupervised learning by probabilistic latent semantic analysis. *Machine Learning*, 42(1):177–196.

JJ Jiang and DW Conrath. 1997. Semantic similarity based on corpus statistics and lexical taxonomy. In *Proc. of COLING'97*, pages 19–33, Taipei, Taiwan.

C Leacock, G A Miller, and M Chodorow. 1998. Using corpus statistics and WordNet relations for sense identification. *Computational Linguistics*, 24(1):147–65.

M Lesk. 1986. Automatic sense disambiguation using machine readable dictionaries: how to tell a pine cone from an ice cream cone. In *Proc. of SIGDOC'86*, pages 24–26, Toronto, Canada.

D Lin. 1998. Automatic retrieval and clustering of similar words. In *Proc. of COLING/ACL'98*, pages 768–774, Montreal, Canada.

C-Y Lin. 2004. ROUGE: a package for automatic evaluation of summaries. In *Proc. of the ACL 2004 Workshop on Text Summarization Branches Out (WAS 2004)*, pages 74–81, Barcelona, Spain.

Q Mei, X Shen, and CX Zhai. 2007. Automatic labeling of multinomial topic models. In *Proc. of KDD 2007*, pages 490–499.

D Milne and IH Witten. 2008. An effective, low-cost measure of semantic relatedness obtained from Wikipedia links. In *Proc. of AAAI Workshop on Wikipedia and Artificial Intelligence*, pages 25–30, Chicago, USA.

H Misra, O Cappe, and F Yvon. 2008. Using LDA to detect semantically incoherent documents. In *Proc. of CoNLL 2008*, pages 41–48, Manchester, England.

D Newman, S Karimi, and L Cavedon. 2009. External evaluation of topic models. In *Proc. of ADCS 2009*, pages 11–18, Sydney, Australia.

D Newman, T Baldwin, L Cavedon, S Karimi, D Martinez, and J Zobel. to appeara. Visualizing document collections and search results using topic mapping. *Journal of Web Semantics*.

D Newman, Y Noh, E Talley, S Karimi, and T Baldwin. to appearb. Evaluating topic models for digital libraries. In *Proc. of JCDL/ICADL 2010*, Gold Coast, Australia.

K Papineni, S Roukos, T Ward, and W-J Zhu. 2002. BLEU: a method for automatic evaluation of machine translation. In *Proc. of ACL 2002*, pages 311–318, Philadelphia, USA.

P Pecina. 2008. *Lexical Association Measures: Collocation Extraction*. Ph.D. thesis, Charles University.

P Resnik. 1995. Using information content to evaluate semantic similarity in a taxonomy. In *Proc. of IJCAI'95*, pages 448–453, Montreal, Canada.

H Schütze. 1998. Automatic word sense discrimination. *Computational Linguistics*, 24(1):97–123.

M Strübe and SP Ponzetto. 2006. WikiRelate! computing semantic relateness using Wikipedia. In *Proc. of AAAI'06*, pages 1419–1424, Boston, USA.

Q Sun, R Li, D Luo, and X Wu. 2008. Text segmentation with LDA-based Fisher kernel. In *Proc. of ACL-08: HLT*, pages 269–272.

HM Wallach, I Murray, R Salakhutdinov, and DM Mimno. 2009. Evaluation methods for topic models. In *Proc. of ICML 2009*, page 139.

D Widdows and K Ferraro. 2008. Semantic Vectors: A scalable open source package and online technology management application. In *Proc. of LREC 2008*, Marrakech, Morocco.

Z Wu and M Palmer. 1994. Verb selection and lexical selection. In *Proc. of ACL'94*, pages 133–138, Las Cruces, USA.

Multi-Prototype Vector-Space Models of Word Meaning

Joseph Reisinger
Department of Computer Science
The University of Texas at Austin
1 University Station C0500
Austin, TX 78712-0233
joeraii@cs.utexas.edu

Raymond J. Mooney
Department of Computer Science
The University of Texas at Austin
1 University Station C0500
Austin, TX 78712-0233
mooney@cs.utexas.edu

Abstract

Current vector-space models of lexical semantics create a single "prototype" vector to represent the meaning of a word. However, due to lexical ambiguity, encoding word meaning with a single vector is problematic. This paper presents a method that uses clustering to produce multiple "sense-specific" vectors for each word. This approach provides a context-dependent vector representation of word meaning that naturally accommodates homonymy and polysemy. Experimental comparisons to human judgements of semantic similarity for both isolated words as well as words in sentential contexts demonstrate the superiority of this approach over both prototype and exemplar based vector-space models.

1 Introduction

Automatically judging the degree of semantic similarity between words is an important task useful in text classification (Baker and McCallum, 1998), information retrieval (Sanderson, 1994), textual entailment, and other language processing tasks. The standard empirical approach to this task exploits the *distributional hypothesis*, i.e. that similar words appear in similar contexts (Curran and Moens, 2002; Lin and Pantel, 2002; Pereira et al., 1993). Traditionally, word types are represented by a single vector of contextual features derived from co-occurrence information, and semantic similarity is computed using some measure of vector distance (Lee, 1999; Lowe, 2001).

However, due to homonymy and polysemy, capturing the semantics of a word with a single vector is problematic. For example, the word *club* is similar to both *bat* and *association,* which are not at all similar to each other. Word meaning violates the triangle inequality when viewed at the level of word types, posing a problem for vector-space models (Tversky and Gati, 1982). A single "prototype" vector is simply incapable of capturing phenomena such as homonymy and polysemy. Also, most vector-space models are context independent, while the meaning of a word clearly depends on context. The word *club* in "The caveman picked up the *club*" is similar to *bat* in "John hit the robber with a *bat*," but not in "The *bat* flew out of the cave."

We present a new resource-lean vector-space model that represents a word's meaning by a *set* of distinct "sense specific" vectors. The similarity of two isolated words A and B is defined as the *minimum* distance between one of A's vectors and one of B's vectors. In addition, a context-dependent meaning for a word is determined by choosing one of the vectors in its set based on minimizing the distance to the vector representing the current context. Consequently, the model supports judging the similarity of both words in isolation and words in context.

The set of vectors for a word is determined by unsupervised *word sense discovery* (WSD) (Schütze, 1998), which clusters the contexts in which a word appears. In previous work, vector-space lexical similarity and word sense discovery have been treated as two separate tasks. This paper shows how they can be combined to create an improved vector-space model of lexical semantics. First, a word's contexts are clustered to produce groups of similar context vectors. An average "prototype" vector is then computed separately for each cluster, producing a set of vectors for each word. Finally, as described above, these cluster vectors can be used to determine the se-

Human Language Technologies: The 2010 Annual Conference of the North American Chapter of the ACL, pages 109–117,
Los Angeles, California, June 2010.

mantic similarity of both isolated words and words in context. The approach is completely modular, and can integrate any clustering method with any traditional vector-space model.

We present experimental comparisons to human judgements of semantic similarity for both isolated words and words in sentential context. The results demonstrate the superiority of a clustered approach over both traditional prototype and exemplar-based vector-space models. For example, given the isolated target word *singer* our method produces the most similar word *vocalist*, while using a single prototype gives *musician*. Given the word *cell* in the context: "The book was published while Piasecki was still in prison, and a copy was delivered to his *cell*." the standard approach produces *protein* while our method yields *incarcerated*.

The remainder of the paper is organized as follows: Section 2 gives relevant background on prototype and exemplar methods for lexical semantics, Section 3 presents our multi-prototype method, Section 4 presents our experimental evaluations, Section 5 discusses future work, and Section 6 concludes.

2 Background

Psychological concept models can be roughly divided into two classes:

1. *Prototype* models represented concepts by an abstract prototypical instance, similar to a cluster centroid in parametric density estimation.

2. *Exemplar* models represent concepts by a concrete set of observed instances, similar to nonparametric approaches to density estimation in statistics (Ashby and Alfonso-Reese, 1995).

Tversky and Gati (1982) famously showed that conceptual similarity violates the triangle inequality, lending evidence for exemplar-based models in psychology. Exemplar models have been previously used for lexical semantics problems such as selectional preference (Erk, 2007) and thematic fit (Vandekerckhove et al., 2009). Individual exemplars can be quite noisy and the model can incur high computational overhead at prediction time since naively computing the similarity between two words using each occurrence in a textual corpus as an exemplar requires $O(n^2)$ comparisons. Instead, the standard

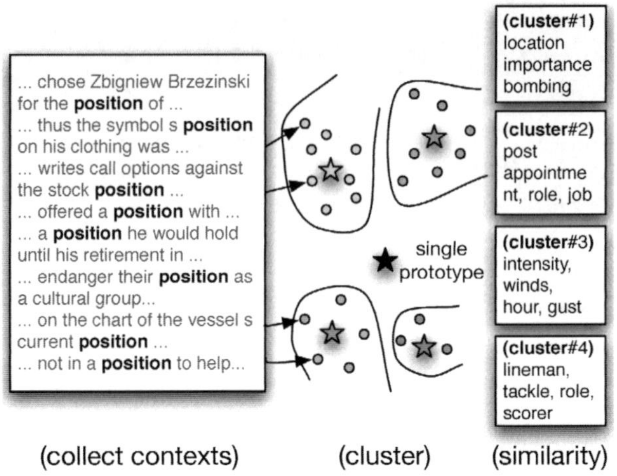

Figure 1: Overview of the multi-prototype approach to near-synonym discovery for a single target word independent of context. Occurrences are clustered and cluster centroids are used as prototype vectors. Note the "hurricane" sense of *position* (cluster 3) is not typically considered appropriate in WSD.

approach is to compute a single prototype vector for each word from its occurrences.

This paper presents a *multi-prototype* vector space model for lexical semantics with a single parameter K (the number of clusters) that generalizes both prototype ($K = 1$) and exemplar ($K = N$, the total number of instances) methods. Such models have been widely studied in the Psychology literature (Griffiths et al., 2007; Love et al., 2004; Rosseel, 2002). By employing multiple prototypes per word, vector space models can account for homonymy, polysemy and thematic variation in word usage. Furthermore, such approaches require only $O(K^2)$ comparisons for computing similarity, yielding potential computational savings over the exemplar approach when $K \ll N$, while reaping many of the same benefits.

Previous work on lexical semantic relatedness has focused on two approaches: (1) mining monolingual or bilingual dictionaries or other pre-existing resources to construct networks of related words (Agirre and Edmond, 2006; Ramage et al., 2009), and (2) using the distributional hypothesis to automatically infer a vector-space prototype of word meaning from large corpora (Agirre et al., 2009; Curran, 2004; Harris, 1954). The former approach tends to have greater precision, but depends on hand-crafted dictionaries and cannot, in general, model sense frequency (Budanitsky and Hirst, 2006). The latter approach is fundamentally more scalable as it does not rely on specific resources and can model corpus-specific sense distributions. However, the distributional approach can suffer from poor precision, as thematically similar words (e.g., *singer* and *actor*) and antonyms often occur in similar contexts (Lin et al., 2003).

Unsupervised word-sense discovery has been studied by number of researchers (Agirre and Edmond, 2006; Schütze, 1998). Most work has also focused on corpus-based distributional approaches, varying the vector-space representation, e.g. by incorporating syntactic and co-occurrence information from the words surrounding the target term (Pereira et al., 1993; Pantel and Lin, 2002).

3 Multi-Prototype Vector-Space Models

Our approach is similar to standard vector-space models of word meaning, with the addition of a per-word-type clustering step: Occurrences for a specific word type are collected from the corpus and clustered using any appropriate method (§3.1). Similarity between two word types is then computed as a function of their cluster centroids (§3.2), instead of the centroid of all the word's occurrences. Figure 1 gives an overview of this process.

3.1 Clustering Occurrences

Multiple prototypes for each word w are generated by clustering feature vectors $v(c)$ derived from each occurrence $c \in \mathcal{C}(w)$ in a large textual corpus and collecting the resulting cluster centroids $\pi_k(w), k \in [1, K]$. This approach is commonly employed in unsupervised word sense discovery; however, we do not assume that clusters correspond to traditional word senses. Rather, we only rely on clusters to capture meaningful variation in word usage.

Our experiments employ a *mixture of von Mises-Fisher distributions* (movMF) clustering method with first-order unigram contexts (Banerjee et al., 2005). Feature vectors $v(c)$ are composed of individual features $I(c, f)$, taken as all unigrams occurring $f \in \mathcal{F}$ in a 10-word window around w.

Like spherical k-means (Dhillon and Modha, 2001), movMF models semantic relatedness using cosine similarity, a standard measure of textual similarity. However, movMF introduces an additional per-cluster *concentration* parameter controlling its semantic breadth, allowing it to more accurately model non-uniformities in the distribution of cluster sizes. Based on preliminary experiments comparing various clustering methods, we found movMF gave the best results.

3.2 Measuring Semantic Similarity

The similarity between two words in a multi-prototype model can be computed straightforwardly, requiring only simple modifications to standard distributional similarity methods such as those presented by Curran (2004). Given words w and w', we define two *noncontextual clustered similarity metrics* to measure similarity of isolated words:

$$\text{AvgSim}(w, w') \stackrel{\text{def}}{=} \frac{1}{K^2} \sum_{j=1}^{K} \sum_{k=1}^{K} d(\pi_k(w), \pi_j(w'))$$

$$\text{MaxSim}(w, w') \stackrel{\text{def}}{=} \max_{1 \le j \le K, 1 \le k \le K} d(\pi_k(w), \pi_j(w'))$$

where $d(\cdot, \cdot)$ is a standard distributional similarity measure. In AvgSim, word similarity is computed as the average similarity of all pairs of prototype vectors; In MaxSim the similarity is the maximum over all pairwise prototype similarities. All results reported in this paper use *cosine* similarity, [1]

$$\text{Cos}(w, w') = \frac{\sum_{f \in \mathcal{F}} I(w, f) \cdot I(w', f)}{\sqrt{\sum_{f \in \mathcal{F}} I(w, f)^2} \sqrt{\sum_{f \in \mathcal{F}} I(w', f)^2}}$$

We compare across two different feature functions *tf-idf* weighting and χ^2 weighting, chosen due to their ubiquity in the literature (Agirre et al., 2009; Curran, 2004).

In AvgSim, all prototype pairs contribute equally to the similarity computation, thus two words are judged as similar if many of their senses are similar. MaxSim, on the other hand, only requires a single pair of prototypes to be close for the words to be judged similar. Thus, MaxSim models the similarity of words that share only a single sense (e.g. *bat* and *club*) at the cost of lower robustness to noisy clusters that might be introduced when K is large.

When contextual information is available, AvgSim and MaxSim can be modified to produce

[1]The main results also hold for *weighted Jaccard* similarity.

more precise similarity computations:

$$\text{AvgSimC}(w, w') \stackrel{\text{def}}{=} \frac{1}{K^2} \sum_{j=1}^{K} \sum_{k=1}^{K} d_{c,w,k} d_{c',w',j} d(\pi_k(w), \pi_j(w'))$$

$$\text{MaxSimC}(w, w') \stackrel{\text{def}}{=} d(\hat{\pi}(w), \hat{\pi}(w'))$$

where $d_{c,w,k} \stackrel{\text{def}}{=} d(v(c), \pi_k(w))$ is the likelihood of context c belonging to cluster $\pi_k(w)$, and $\hat{\pi}(w) \stackrel{\text{def}}{=} \pi_{\arg\max_{1 \le k \le K} d_{c,w,k}}(w)$, the maximum likelihood cluster for w in context c. Thus, AvgSimC corresponds to *soft cluster assignment*, weighting each similarity term in AvgSim by the likelihood of the word contexts appearing in their respective clusters. MaxSimC corresponds to *hard assignment*, using only the most probable cluster assignment. Note that AvgSim and MaxSim can be thought of as special cases of AvgSimC and MaxSimC with uniform weight to each cluster; hence AvgSimC and MaxSimC can be used to compare words in context to isolated words as well.

4 Experimental Evaluation

4.1 Corpora

We employed two corpora to train our models:

1. A snapshot of English Wikipedia taken on Sept. 29th, 2009. Wikitext markup is removed, as are articles with fewer than 100 words, leaving 2.8M articles with a total of 2.05B words.

2. The third edition English Gigaword corpus, with articles containing fewer than 100 words removed, leaving 6.6M articles and 3.9B words (Graff, 2003).

Wikipedia covers a wider range of sense distributions, whereas Gigaword contains only newswire text and tends to employ fewer senses of most ambiguous words. Our method outperforms baseline methods even on Gigaword, indicating its advantages even when the corpus covers few senses.

4.2 Judging Semantic Similarity

To evaluate the quality of various models, we first compared their lexical similarity measurements to human similarity judgements from the WordSim-353 data set (Finkelstein et al., 2001). This test corpus contains multiple human judgements on 353 word pairs, covering both monosemous and polysemous words, each rated on a 1–10 integer scale. Spearman's rank correlation (ρ) with average human judgements (Agirre et al., 2009) was used to measure the quality of various models.

Figure 2 plots Spearman's ρ on WordSim-353 against the number of clusters (K) for Wikipedia and Gigaword corpora, using pruned *tf-idf* and χ^2 features.[2] In general pruned *tf-idf* features yield higher correlation than χ^2 features. Using AvgSim, the multi-prototype approach ($K > 1$) yields higher correlation than the single-prototype approach ($K = 1$) across all corpora and feature types, achieving state-of-the-art results with pruned *tf-idf* features. This result is statistically significant in all cases for *tf-idf* and for $K \in [2, 10]$ on Wikipedia and $K > 4$ on Gigaword for χ^2 features.[3] MaxSim yields similar performance when $K < 10$ but performance degrades as K increases.

It is possible to circumvent the model-selection problem (choosing the best value of K) by simply combining the prototypes from clusterings of different sizes. This approach represents words using both semantically broad and semantically tight prototypes, similar to hierarchical clustering. Table 1 and Figure 2 (squares) show the result of such a *combined* approach, where the prototypes for clusterings of size 2-5, 10, 20, 50, and 100 are unioned to form a single large prototype set. In general, this approach works about as well as picking the optimal value of K, even outperforming the single best cluster size for Wikipedia.

Finally, we also compared our method to a pure exemplar approach, averaging similarity across all occurrence pairs.[4] Table 1 summarizes the results. The exemplar approach yields significantly higher correlation than the single prototype approach in all cases except Gigaword with *tf-idf* features ($p < 0.05$). Furthermore, it performs significantly *worse*

[2](**Feature pruning**) We find that results using *tf-idf* features are extremely sensitive to feature pruning while χ^2 features are more robust. In all experiments we prune *tf-idf* features by their overall weight, taking the top 5000. This setting was found to optimize the performance of the single-prototype approach.

[3]Significance is calculated using the large-sample approximation of the Spearman rank *test*; ($p < 0.05$).

[4]Averaging across all pairs was found to yield higher correlation than averaging over the most similar pairs.

Spearman's ρ	prototype	exemplar	multi-prototype (AvgSim) $K=5$	$K=20$	$K=50$	combined
Wikipedia *tf-idf*	0.53±0.02	0.60±0.06	0.69±0.02	0.76±0.01	0.76±0.01	0.77±0.01
Wikipedia χ^2	0.54±0.03	0.65±0.07	0.58±0.02	0.56±0.02	0.52±0.03	0.59±0.04
Gigaword *tf-idf*	0.49±0.02	0.48±0.10	0.64±0.02	0.61±0.02	0.61±0.02	0.62±0.02
Gigaword χ^2	0.25±0.03	0.41±0.14	0.32±0.03	0.35±0.03	0.33±0.03	0.34±0.03

Table 1: Spearman correlation on the WordSim-353 dataset broken down by corpus and feature type.

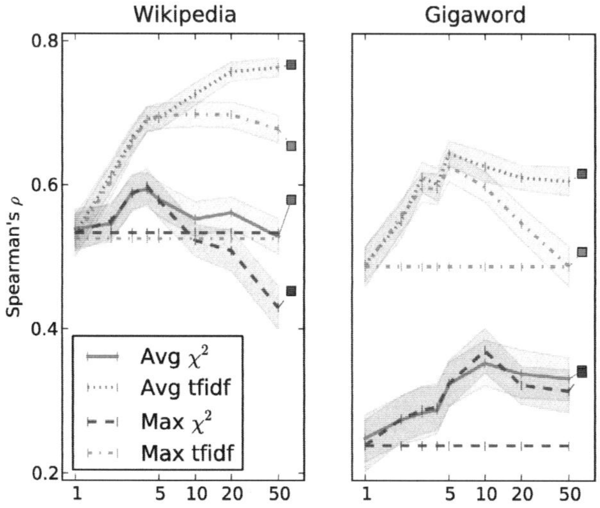

Figure 2: WordSim-353 rank correlation vs. number of clusters (log scale) for both the Wikipedia (left) and Gigaword (right) corpora. Horizontal bars show the performance of single-prototype. Squares indicate performance when combining across clusterings. Error bars depict 95% confidence intervals using the Spearman test. Squares indicate performance when combining across clusterings.

than combined multi-prototype for *tf-idf* features, and does not differ significantly for χ^2 features. Overall this result indicates that multi-prototype performs at least as well as exemplar in the worst case, and significantly outperforms when using the best feature representation / corpus pair.

4.3 Predicting Near-Synonyms

We next evaluated the multi-prototype approach on its ability to determine the most closely related words for a given target word (using the Wikipedia corpus with *tf-idf* features). The top k most similar words were computed for each prototype of each target word. Using a forced-choice setup, human subjects were asked to evaluate the quality of these *near synonyms* relative to those produced by a single prototype. Participants on Amazon's Mechanical Turk[5] (Snow et al., 2008) were asked to choose between two possible alternatives (one from a prototype model and one from a multi-prototype model) as being most similar to a given target word. The target words were presented either in isolation or in a sentential context randomly selected from the corpus. Table 2 lists the ambiguous words used for this task. They are grouped into homonyms (words with very distinct senses) and polysemes (words with related senses). All words were chosen such that their usages occur within the same part of speech.

homonymous
carrier, crane, cell, company, issue, interest, match, media, nature, party, practice, plant, racket, recess, reservation, rock, space, value
polysemous
cause, chance, journal, market, network, policy, power, production, series, trading, train

Table 2: Words used in predicting near synonyms.

In the non-contextual task, 79 unique raters completed 7,620 comparisons of which 72 were discarded due to poor performance on a known test set.[6] In the contextual task, 127 raters completed 9,930 comparisons of which 87 were discarded.

For the non-contextual case, Figure 3 left plots the fraction of raters preferring the multi-prototype prediction (using AvgSim) over that of a single prototype as the number of clusters is varied. When asked to choose between the single best word for

[5] http://mturk.com

[6] (**Rater reliability**) The reliability of Mechanical Turk raters is quite variable, so we computed an accuracy score for each rater by including a control question with a known correct answer in each HIT. Control questions were generated by selecting a random word from WordNet 3.0 and including as possible choices a word in the same synset (correct answer) and a word in a synset with a high path distance (incorrect answer). Raters who got less than 50% of these control questions correct, or spent too little time on the HIT were discarded.

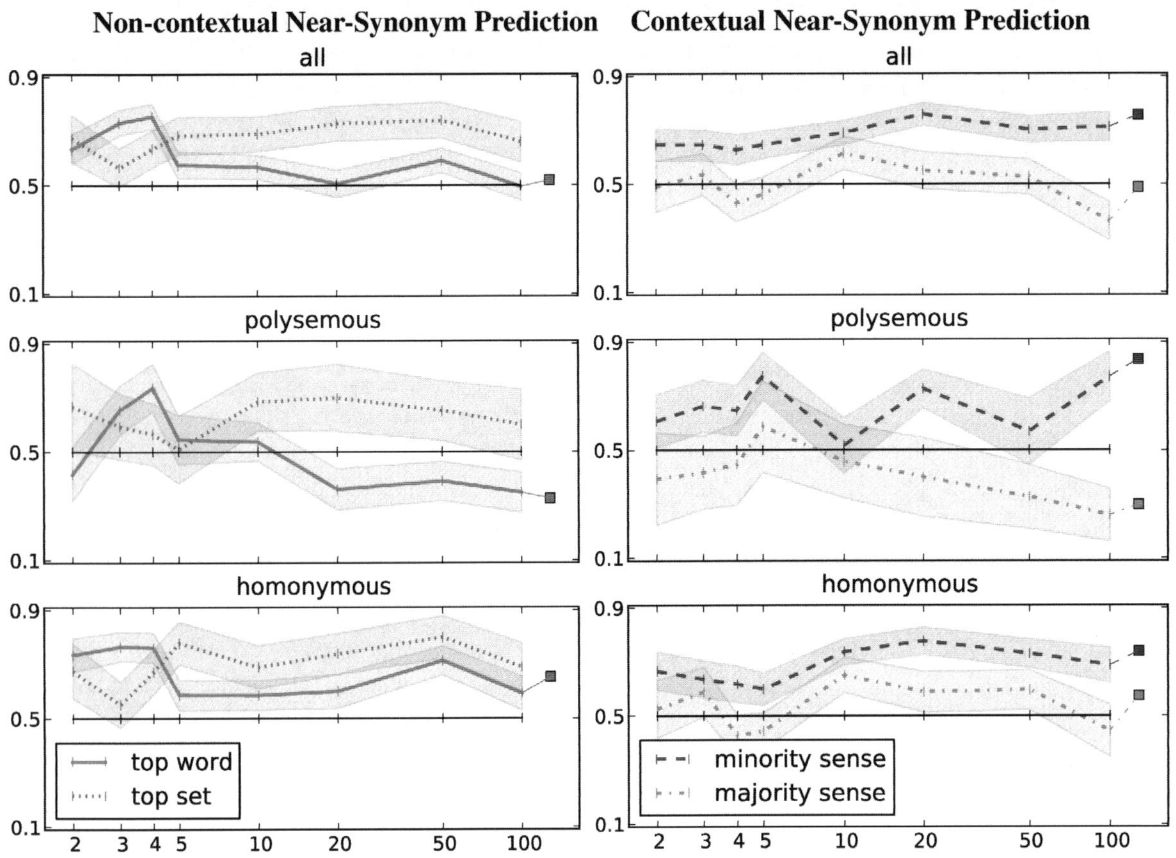

Figure 3: (**left**) Near-synonym evaluation for isolated words showing fraction of raters preferring multi-prototype results vs. number of clusters. Colored squares indicate performance when combining across clusterings. 95% confidence intervals computed using the Wald test. (**right**) Near-synonym evaluation for words in a sentential context chosen either from the minority sense or the majority sense.

each method (**top word**), the multi-prototype prediction is chosen significantly more frequently (i.e. the result is above 0.5) when the number of clusters is small, but the two methods perform similarly for larger numbers of clusters (Wald test, $\alpha = 0.05$.) Clustering more accurately identifies homonyms' clearly distinct senses and produces prototypes that better capture the different uses of these words. As a result, compared to using a single prototype, our approach produces better near-synonyms for homonyms compared to polysemes. However, given the right number of clusters, it also produces better results for polysemous words.

The near-synonym prediction task highlights one of the weaknesses of the multi-prototype approach: as the number of clusters increases, the number of occurrences assigned to each cluster decreases, increasing noise and resulting in some poor prototypes that mainly cover outliers. The word similarity task is somewhat robust to this phenomenon, but synonym prediction is more affected since only the top predicted choice is used. When raters are forced to chose between the top *three* predictions for each method (presented as **top set** in Figure 3 left), the effect of this noise is reduced and the multi-prototype approach remains dominant even for a large number of clusters. This indicates that although more clusters can capture finer-grained sense distinctions, they also can introduce noise.

When presented with words in context (Figure 3 right),[7] raters found no significant difference in the two methods for words used in their majority sense.[8] However, when a minority sense is pre-

[7]Results for the multi-prototype method are generated using AvgSimC (soft assignment) as this was found to significantly outperform MaxSimC.

[8]Sense frequency determined using Google; senses labeled manually by trained human evaluators.

sented (e.g. the "prison" sense of *cell*), raters prefer the choice predicted by the multi-prototype approach. This result is to be expected since the single prototype mainly reflects the majority sense, preventing it from predicting appropriate synonyms for a minority sense. Also, once again, the performance of the multi-prototype approach is better for homonyms than polysemes.

4.4 Predicting Variation in Human Ratings

Variance in pairwise prototype distances can help explain the variance in human similarity judgements for a given word pair. We evaluate this hypothesis empirically on WordSim-353 by computing the Spearman correlation between the *variance* of the per-cluster similarity computations, $\mathbb{V}[D]$, $D \stackrel{\text{def}}{=} \{d(\pi_k(w), \pi_j(w')) : 1 \leq k, j \leq K\}$, and the variance of the human annotations for that pair. Correlations for each dataset are shown in Figure 4 left. In general, we find a statistically significant *negative* correlation between these values using χ^2 features, indicating that as the entropy of the pairwise cluster similarities increases (i.e., prototypes become more similar, and similarities become uniform), rater disagreement increases. This result is intuitive: if the occurrences of a particular word cannot be easily separated into coherent clusters (perhaps indicating high polysemy instead of homonymy), then human judgement will be naturally more difficult.

Rater variance depends more directly on the actual word similarity: word pairs at the extreme ranges of similarity have significantly lower variance as raters are more certain. By removing word pairs with similarity judgements in the middle two quartile ranges (4.4 to 7.5) we find significantly higher variance correlation (Figure 4 right). This result indicates that multi-prototype similarity variance accounts for a secondary effect separate from the primary effect that variance is naturally lower for ratings in extreme ranges.

Although the *entropy* of the prototypes correlates with the variance of the human ratings, we find that the individual senses captured by each prototype do not correspond to human intuition for a given word, e.g. the "hurricane" sense of *position* in Figure 1. This notion is evaluated empirically by computing the correlation between the predicted similarity us-

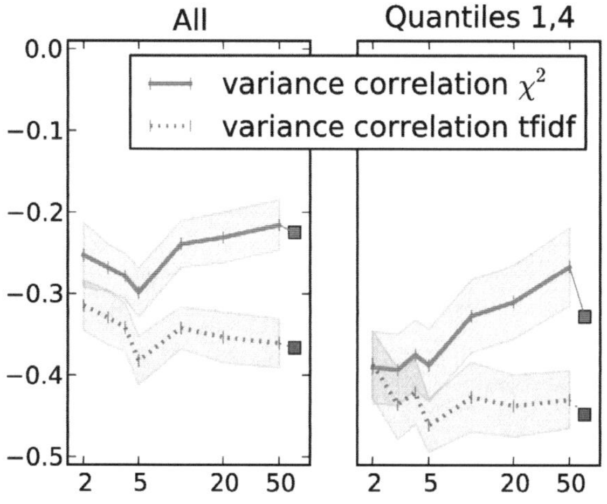

Figure 4: Plots of variance correlation; lower numbers indicate higher negative correlation, i.e. that prototype entropy predicts rater disagreement.

ing the contextual multi-prototype method and human similarity judgements for different usages of the *same* word. The Usage Similarity (USim) data set collected in Erk et al. (2009) provides such similarity scores from human raters. However, we find no evidence for correlation between USim scores and their corresponding prototype similarity scores ($\rho = 0.04$), indicating that prototype vectors may not correspond well to human senses.

5 Discussion and Future Work

Table 3 compares the inferred synonyms for several target words, generally demonstrating the ability of the multi-prototype model to improve the precision of inferred near-synonyms (e.g. in the case of *singer* or *need*) as well as its ability to include synonyms from less frequent senses (e.g., the *experiment* sense of *research* or the *verify* sense of *prove*). However, there are a number of ways it could be improved:

Feature representations: Multiple prototypes improve Spearman correlation on WordSim-353 compared to previous methods using the same underlying representation (Agirre et al., 2009). However we have not yet evaluated its performance when using more powerful feature representations such those based on Latent or Explicit Semantic Analysis (Deerwester et al., 1990; Gabrilovich and Markovitch, 2007). Due to its modularity, the multi-prototype approach can easily incorporate such advances in order to further improve its effectiveness.

Inferred Thesaurus	
bass	
single	guitar, drums, rhythm, piano, acoustic
multi	basses, contrabass, rhythm, guitar, drums
claim	
single	argue, say, believe, assert, contend
multi	assert, contend, allege, argue, insist
hold	
single	carry, take, receive, reach, maintain
multi	carry, maintain, receive, accept, reach
maintain	
single	ensure, establish, achieve, improve, promote
multi	preserve, ensure, establish, retain, restore
prove	
single	demonstrate, reveal, ensure, confirm, say
multi	demonstrate, verify, confirm, reveal, admit
research	
single	studies, work, study, training, development
multi	studies, experiments, study, investigations, training
singer	
single	musician, actress, actor, guitarist, composer
multi	vocalist, guitarist, musician, singer-songwriter, singers

Table 3: Examples of the top 5 inferred near-synonyms using the single- and multi-prototype approaches (with results merged). In general such clustering improves the precision and coverage of the inferred near-synonyms.

Nonparametric clustering: The success of the combined approach indicates that the optimal number of clusters may vary per word. A more principled approach to selecting the number of prototypes per word is to employ a clustering model with infinite capacity, e.g. the Dirichlet Process Mixture Model (Rasmussen, 2000). Such a model would allow naturally more polysemous words to adopt more flexible representations.

Cluster similarity metrics: Besides AvgSim and MaxSim, there are many similarity metrics over mixture models, e.g. KL-divergence, which may correlate better with human similarity judgements.

Comparing to traditional senses: Compared to WordNet, our best-performing clusterings are significantly more fine-grained. Furthermore, they often do not correspond to agreed upon semantic distinctions (e.g., the "hurricane" sense of *position* in Fig. 1). We posit that the finer-grained senses actually capture useful aspects of word meaning, leading to better correlation with WordSim-353. However, it would be good to compare prototypes learned from supervised sense inventories to prototypes produced by automatic clustering.

Joint model: The current method independently clusters the contexts of each word, so the senses discovered for w cannot influence the senses discovered for $w' \neq w$. Sharing statistical strength across similar words could yield better results for rarer words.

6 Conclusions

We presented a resource-light model for vector-space word meaning that represents words as collections of prototype vectors, naturally accounting for lexical ambiguity. The multi-prototype approach uses word sense discovery to partition a word's contexts and construct "sense specific" prototypes for each cluster. Doing so significantly increases the accuracy of lexical-similarity computation as demonstrated by improved correlation with human similarity judgements and generation of better near synonyms according to human evaluators. Furthermore, we show that, although performance is sensitive to the number of prototypes, combining prototypes across a large range of clusterings performs nearly as well as the ex-post best clustering. Finally, variance in the prototype similarities is found to correlate with inter-annotator disagreement, suggesting psychological plausibility.

Acknowledgements

We would like to thank Katrin Erk for helpful discussions and making the USim data set available. This work was supported by an NSF Graduate Research Fellowship and a Google Research Award. Experiments were run on the Mastodon Cluster, provided by NSF Grant EIA-0303609.

References

Eneko Agirre and Phillip Edmond. 2006. *Word Sense Disambiguation: Algorithms and Applications (Text, Speech and Language Technology)*. Springer-Verlag New York, Inc., Secaucus, NJ, USA.

Eneko Agirre, Enrique Alfonseca, Keith Hall, Jana Kravalova, Marius Paşca, and Aitor Soroa. 2009. A study on similarity and relatedness using distributional and WordNet-based approaches. In *Proc. of NAACL-HLT-09*, pages 19–27.

F. Gregory Ashby and Leola A. Alfonso-Reese. 1995. Categorization as probability density estimation. *J. Math. Psychol.*, 39(2):216–233.

L. Douglas Baker and Andrew K. McCallum. 1998. Distributional clustering of words for text classification. In *Proceedings of 21st International ACM SIGIR Conference on Research and Development in Information Retrieval*, pages 96–103.

Arindam Banerjee, Inderjit Dhillon, Joydeep Ghosh, and Suvrit Sra. 2005. Clustering on the unit hypersphere using von Mises-Fisher distributions. *Journal of Machine Learning Research*, 6:1345–1382.

Alexander Budanitsky and Graeme Hirst. 2006. Evaluating wordnet-based measures of lexical semantic relatedness. *Computational Linguistics*, 32(1):13–47.

James R. Curran and Marc Moens. 2002. Improvements in automatic thesaurus extraction. In *Proceedings of the ACL-02 workshop on Unsupervised lexical acquisition*, pages 59–66.

James R. Curran. 2004. *From Distributional to Semantic Similarity*. Ph.D. thesis, University of Edinburgh. College of Science.

Scott C. Deerwester, Susan T. Dumais, George W. Furnas, Thomas K. Landauer, and Richard A. Harshman. 1990. Indexing by latent semantic analysis. *Journal of the American Society for Information Science*, 41:391–407.

Inderjit S. Dhillon and Dharmendra S. Modha. 2001. Concept decompositions for large sparse text data using clustering. *Machine Learning*, 42:143–175.

Katrin Erk, Diana McCarthy, Nicholas Gaylord Investigations on Word Senses, and Word Usages. 2009. Investigations on word senses and word usages. In *Proc. of ACL-09*.

Katrin Erk. 2007. A simple, similarity-based model for selectional preferences. In *Proceedings of the 45th Annual Meeting of the Association for Computational Linguistics*. Association for Computer Linguistics.

Lev Finkelstein, Evgeniy Gabrilovich, Yossi Matias, Ehud Rivlin, Zach Solan, Gadi Wolfman, and Eytan Ruppin. 2001. Placing search in context: the concept revisited. In *Proc. of WWW-01*, pages 406–414, New York, NY, USA. ACM.

Evgeniy Gabrilovich and Shaul Markovitch. 2007. Computing semantic relatedness using Wikipedia-based explicit semantic analysis. In *Proc. of IJCAI-07*, pages 1606–1611.

David Graff. 2003. *English Gigaword*. Linguistic Data Consortium, Philadephia.

Tom L. Griffiths, Kevin. R. Canini, Adam N. Sanborn, and Daniel. J. Navarro. 2007. Unifying rational models of categorization via the hierarchical Dirichlet process. In *Proc. of CogSci-07*.

Zellig Harris. 1954. Distributional structure. *Word*, 10(23):146–162.

Lillian Lee. 1999. Measures of distributional similarity. In *37th Annual Meeting of the Association for Computational Linguistics*, pages 25–32.

Dekang Lin and Patrick Pantel. 2002. Concept discovery from text. In *Proc. of COLING-02*, pages 1–7.

Dekang Lin, Shaojun Zhao, Lijuan Qin, and Ming Zhou. 2003. Identifying synonyms among distributionally similar words. In *Proceedings of the Interational Joint Conference on Artificial Intelligence*, pages 1492–1493. Morgan Kaufmann.

Bradley C. Love, Douglas L. Medin, and Todd M. Gureckis. 2004. SUSTAIN: A network model of category learning. *Psych. Review*, 111(2):309–332.

Will Lowe. 2001. Towards a theory of semantic space. In *Proceedings of the 23rd Annual Meeting of the Cognitive Science Society*, pages 576–581.

Patrick Pantel and Dekang Lin. 2002. Discovering word senses from text. In *Proc. of SIGKDD-02*, pages 613–619, New York, NY, USA. ACM.

Fernando C. N. Pereira, Naftali Tishby, and Lillian Lee. 1993. Distributional clustering of English words. In *Proceedings of the 31st Annual Meeting of the Association for Computational Linguistics (ACL-93)*, pages 183–190, Columbus, Ohio.

Daniel Ramage, Anna N. Rafferty, and Christopher D. Manning. 2009. Random walks for text semantic similarity. In *Proc. of the 2009 Workshop on Graph-based Methods for Natural Language Processing (TextGraphs-4)*, pages 23–31.

Carl E. Rasmussen. 2000. The infinite Gaussian mixture model. In *Advances in Neural Information Processing Systems*, pages 554–560. MIT Press.

Yves Rosseel. 2002. Mixture models of categorization. *J. Math. Psychol.*, 46(2):178–210.

Mark Sanderson. 1994. Word sense disambiguation and information retrieval. In *Proc. of SIGIR-94*, pages 142–151.

Hinrich Schütze. 1998. Automatic word sense discrimination. *Computational Linguistics*, 24(1):97–123.

Rion Snow, Brendan O'Connor, Daniel Jurafsky, and Andrew Ng. 2008. Cheap and fast—but is it good? Evaluating non-expert annotations for natural language tasks. In *Proc. of EMNLP-08*.

Amos Tversky and Itamar Gati. 1982. Similarity, separability, and the triangle inequality. *Psychological Review*, 89(2):123–154.

Bram Vandekerckhove, Dominiek Sandra, and Walter Daelemans. 2009. A robust and extensible exemplar-based model of thematic fit. In *Proc. of EACL 2009*, pages 826–834. Association for Computational Linguistics.

Unsupervised Syntactic Alignment with Inversion Transduction Grammars

Adam Pauls Dan Klein
Computer Science Division
University of California at Berkeley
{adpauls,klein}@cs.berkeley.edu

David Chiang Kevin Knight
Information Sciences Institute
University of Southern California
{chiang,knight}@isi.edu

Abstract

Syntactic machine translation systems currently use word alignments to infer syntactic correspondences between the source and target languages. Instead, we propose an unsupervised ITG alignment model that directly aligns syntactic structures. Our model aligns spans in a source sentence to nodes in a target parse tree. We show that our model produces syntactically consistent analyses where possible, while being robust in the face of syntactic divergence. Alignment quality and end-to-end translation experiments demonstrate that this consistency yields higher quality alignments than our baseline.

1 Introduction

Syntactic machine translation has advanced significantly in recent years, and multiple variants currently achieve state-of-the-art translation quality. Many of these systems exploit linguistically-derived syntactic information either on the target side (Galley et al., 2006), the source side (Huang et al., 2006), or both (Liu et al., 2009). Still others induce their syntax from the data (Chiang, 2005). Despite differences in detail, the vast majority of syntactic methods share a critical dependence on word alignments. In particular, they infer syntactic correspondences between the source and target languages through word alignment patterns, sometimes in combination with constraints from parser outputs.

However, word alignments are not perfect indicators of syntactic alignment, and syntactic systems are very sensitive to word alignment behavior. Even a single spurious word alignment can invalidate a large number of otherwise extractable rules, while unaligned words can result in an exponentially large set of extractable rules to choose from. Researchers have worked to incorporate syntactic information into word alignments, resulting in improvements to both alignment quality (Cherry and Lin, 2006; DeNero and Klein, 2007), and translation quality (May and Knight, 2007; Fossum et al., 2008).

In this paper, we remove the dependence on word alignments and instead directly model the syntactic correspondences in the data, in a manner broadly similar to Yamada and Knight (2001). In particular, we propose an unsupervised model that aligns nodes of a parse tree (or forest) in one language to spans of a sentence in another. Our model is an instance of the inversion transduction grammar (ITG) formalism (Wu, 1997), constrained in such a way that one side of the synchronous derivation respects a syntactic parse. Our model is best suited to systems which use source- or target-side trees only.

The design of our model is such that, for divergent structures, a structurally integrated backoff to flatter word-level (or null) analyses is available. Therefore, our model is empirically robust to the case where syntactic divergence between languages prevents syntactically accurate ITG derivations.

We show that, with appropriate pruning, our model can be efficiently trained on large parallel corpora. When compared to standard word-alignment-backed baselines, our model produces more consistent analyses of parallel sentences, leading to high-count, high-quality transfer rules. End-to-end translation experiments demonstrate that these higher quality rules improve translation quality by 1.0 BLEU over a word-alignment-backed baseline.

2 Syntactic Rule Extraction

Our model is intended for use in syntactic translation models which make use of syntactic parses on either the target (Galley et al., 2006) or source side (Huang et al., 2006; Liu et al., 2006). Our model's

Human Language Technologies: The 2010 Annual Conference of the North American Chapter of the ACL, pages 118–126,
Los Angeles, California, June 2010.

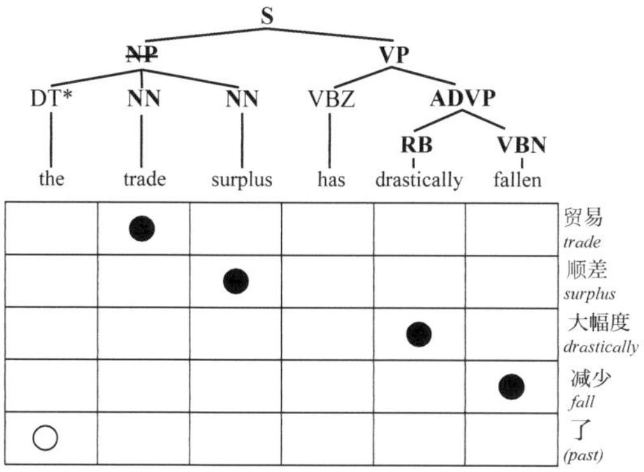

Figure 1: A single incorrect alignment removes an extractable node, and hence several desirable rules. We represent correct extractable nodes in bold, spurious extractable nodes with a *, and incorrectly blocked extractable nodes in bold strikethrough.

chief purpose is to align nodes in the syntactic parse in one language to spans in the other – an alignment we will refer to as a "syntactic" alignment. These alignments are employed by standard syntactic rule extraction algorithms, for example, the GHKM algorithm of Galley et al. (2004). Following that work, we will assume parses are present in the target language, though our model applies in either direction.

Currently, although syntactic systems make use of syntactic alignments, these alignments must be induced indirectly from word-level alignments. Previous work has discussed at length the poor interaction of word-alignments with syntactic rule extraction (DeNero and Klein, 2007; Fossum et al., 2008). For completeness, we provide a brief example of this interaction, but for a more detailed discussion we refer the reader to these presentations.

2.1 Interaction with Word Alignments

Syntactic systems begin rule extraction by first identifying, for each node in the target parse tree, a span of the foreign sentence which (1) contains every source word that aligns to a target word in the yield of the node and (2) contains no source words that align outside that yield. Only nodes for which a non-empty span satisfying (1) and (2) exists may form the root or leaf of a translation rule; for that reason, we will refer to these nodes as *extractable* nodes.

Since extractable nodes are inferred based on word alignments, spurious word alignments can rule out otherwise desirable extraction points. For example, consider the alignment in Figure 1. This alignment, produced by GIZA++ (Och and Ney, 2003), contains 4 correct alignments (the filled circles), but incorrectly aligns *the* to the Chinese past tense marker 了 (the hollow circle). This mistaken alignment produces the incorrect rule (DT $\rightarrow$ *the* ; 了), and also blocks the extraction of (VBN $\rightarrow$ *fallen* ; 减少 了).

More high-level syntactic transfer rules are also ruled out, for example, the "*the* insertion rule" (NP $\rightarrow$ *the* NN_1 NN_2 ; NN_1 NN_2) and the high-level (S $\rightarrow$ NP_1 VP_2 ; NP_1 VP_2).

3 A Syntactic Alignment Model

The most common approach to avoiding these problems is to inject knowledge about syntactic constraints into a word alignment model (Cherry and Lin, 2006; DeNero and Klein, 2007; Fossum et al., 2008).[1] While syntactically aware, these models remain limited by the word alignment models that underly them.

Here, we describe a model which directly infers alignments of nodes in the target-language parse tree to spans of the source sentence. Formally, our model is an instance of a Synchronous Context-Free Grammar (see Chiang (2004) for a review), or SCFG, which generates an English (target) parse tree T and foreign (source) sentence $\mathbf{f}$ given a target sentence $\mathbf{e}$. The generative process underlying this model produces a derivation d of SCFG rules, from which T and $\mathbf{f}$ can be read off; because we condition on $\mathbf{e}$, the derivations produce $\mathbf{e}$ with probability 1. This model places a distribution over T and $\mathbf{f}$ given by

$$p(T, \mathbf{f} \mid \mathbf{e}) = \sum_{d} p(d \mid \mathbf{e}) = \sum_{d} \prod_{r \in d} p(r \mid \mathbf{e})$$

where the sum is over derivations d which yield T and $\mathbf{f}$. The SCFG rules r come from one of 4 types, pictured in Table 1. In general, because our model can generate English trees, it permits inference over forests. Although we will restrict ourselves to a single parse tree for our experiments, in this section, we discuss the more general case.

[1]One notable exception is May and Knight (2007), who produces syntactic alignments using syntactic rules derived from word-aligned data.

Rule Type	Root	English	Foreign	Example Instantiation									
TERMINAL	E	e	$\mathbf{f}_t$	FOUR	$\rightarrow$	*four*		; 四					
UNARY	A	B	$\mathbf{f}_l\ B\ \mathbf{f}_r$	CD	$\rightarrow$	FOUR		; ϵ	FOUR	个			
BINARYMONO	A	$B\ C$	$\mathbf{f}_l\ B\ \mathbf{f}_m\ C\ \mathbf{f}_r$	NP	$\rightarrow$	NN	NN	; ϵ	NN	的	NN	ϵ	
BINARYINV	A	$B\ C$	$\mathbf{f}_l\ C\ \mathbf{f}_m\ B\ \mathbf{f}_r$	PP	$\rightarrow$	IN	NP	; 在	NP	ϵ	IN	ϵ	

Table 1: Types of rules present in the SCFG describing our model, along with some sample instantiations of each type. Empty word sequences $\mathbf{f}$ have been explicitly marked with an ϵ.

The first rule type is the TERMINAL production, which rewrites a terminal symbol[2] E as its English word e and a (possibly empty) sequence of foreign words $\mathbf{f}_t$. Generally speaking, the majority of foreign words are generated using this rule. It is only when a straightforward word-to-word correspondence cannot be found that our model resorts to generating foreign words elsewhere.

We can also rewrite a non-terminal symbol A using a UNARY production, which on the English side produces a single symbol B, and on the foreign side produces the symbol B, with sequences of words $\mathbf{f}_l$ to its left and $\mathbf{f}_r$ to its right.

Finally, there are two binary productions: BINARYMONO rewrites A with two non-terminals B and C on the English side, and the same non-terminals B and C in monotonic order on the foreign side, with sequences of words $\mathbf{f}_l$, $\mathbf{f}_r$, and $\mathbf{f}_m$ to the left, right, and the middle. BINARYINV inverts the order in which the non-terminals B and C are written on the source side, allowing our model to capture a large subset of possible reorderings (Wu, 1997).

Derivations from this model have two key properties: first, the English side of a derivation is constrained to form a valid constituency parse, as is required in a syntax system with target-side syntax; and second, for each parse node in the English projection, there is exactly one (possibly empty) contiguous span of the foreign side which was generated from that non-terminal or one of its descendants. Identifying extractable nodes from a derivation is thus trivial: any node aligned to a non-empty foreign span is extractable.

In Figure 2, we show a sample sentence pair fragment as generated by our model. Our model correctly identifies that the English *the* aligns to nothing on the foreign side. Our model also effectively captures the one-to-many alignment[3] of *elections* to 议

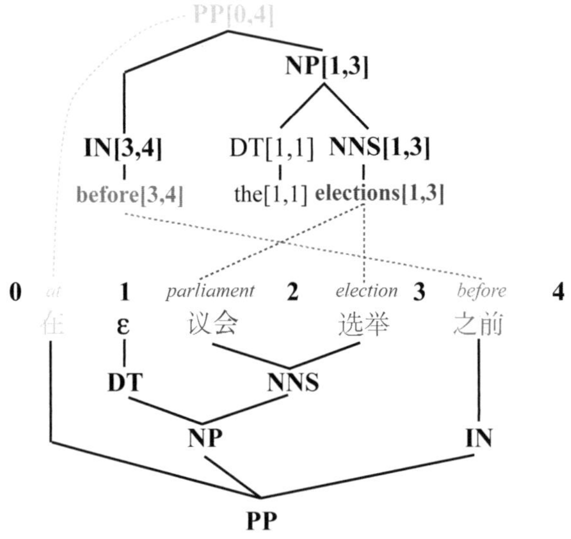

PP	$\rightarrow$	IN	NP	; 在	NP	IN
NP	$\rightarrow$	DT	NNS	; DT	NNS	
IN	$\rightarrow$	BEFORE		; BEFORE		
BEFORE	$\rightarrow$	before		; 之前		
DT	$\rightarrow$	THE		; THE		
THE	$\rightarrow$	the		; ϵ		
NNS	$\rightarrow$	ELECTIONS		; ELECTIONS		
ELECTIONS	$\rightarrow$	elections		; 议会 选举		

Figure 2: *Top:* A synchronous derivation of a small sentence pair fragment under our model. The English projection of the derivation represents a valid constituency parse, while the foreign projection is less constrained. We connect each foreign terminal with a dashed line to the node in the English side of the synchronous derivation at which it is generated. The foreign span assigned to each English node is indicated with indices. All nodes with non-empty spans, shown in boldface, are extractable nodes. *Bottom:* The SCFG rules used in the derivation.

[2]For notational convenience, we imagine that for each particular English word e, there is a special preterminal symbol E which produces it. These symbols E act like any other non-terminal in the grammar with respect to the parameterization in Section 3.1. To denote standard non-terminals, we will use A, B, and C.

[3]While our model does not explicitly produce many-to-one alignments, many-to-one rules can be discovered via rule composition (Galley et al., 2006).

会 选举. Finally, our model correctly analyzes the Chinese circumposition 在 ... 之前 (*before* ...). In this construction, 之前 carries the meaning of "before", and thus correctly aligns to *before*, while 在 functions as a generic preposition, which our model handles by attaching it to the PP. This analysis permits the extraction of the general rule (PP $\rightarrow$ IN_1 NP_2 ; 在 NP_2 IN_1), and the more lexicalized (PP $\rightarrow$ *before* NP ; 在 NP 之前).

3.1 Parameterization

In principle, our model could have one parameter for each instantiation r of a rule type. This model would have an unmanageable number of parameters, producing both computational and modeling issues – it is well known that unsupervised models with large numbers of parameters are prone to degenerate analyses of the data (DeNero et al., 2006). One solution might be to apply an informed prior with a computationally tractable inference procedure (e.g. Cohn and Blunsom (2009) or Liu and Gildea (2009)). We opt here for the simpler, statistically more robust solution of making independence assumptions to keep the number of parameters at a reasonable level.

Concretely, we define the probability of the BINARYMONO rule,[4]

$$p(r = A \rightarrow B\,C; \mathbf{f}_l\; B\; \mathbf{f}_m\; C\; \mathbf{f}_r | A, \mathbf{e}_A)$$

which conditions on the root of the rule A and the English yield $\mathbf{e}_A$, as

$$p_g(A \rightarrow B\,C \mid A, \mathbf{e}_A) \cdot p_{inv}(I \mid B, C) \cdot$$
$$p_{left}(\mathbf{f}_l \mid A, \mathbf{e}_A) \cdot p_{mid}(\mathbf{f}_m \mid A, \mathbf{e}_A) \cdot p_{right}(\mathbf{f}_r \mid A, \mathbf{e}_A)$$

In words, we assume that the rule probability decomposes into a monolingual PCFG grammar probability p_g, an inversion probability p_{inv}, and a probability of left, middle, and right word sequences p_{left}, p_{mid}, and p_{right}.[5] Because we condition on $\mathbf{e}$, the monolingual grammar probability p_g must form a distribution which produces $\mathbf{e}$ with probability 1.[6]

[4]In the text, we only describe the factorization for the BINARYMONO rule. For a parameterization of all rules, we refer the reader to Table 2.

[5]All parameters in our model are multinomial distributions.

[6]A simple case of such a distribution is one which places all of its mass on a single tree. More complex distributions can be obtained by conditioning an arbitrary PCFG on $\mathbf{e}$ (Goodman, 1998).

We further assume that the probability of producing a foreign word sequence $\mathbf{f}_l$ decomposes as:

$$p_{left}(\mathbf{f}_l \mid A, \mathbf{e}_A) = p_l(|\mathbf{f}_l| = m \mid A) \prod_{j=1}^{m} p(f_j \mid A, \mathbf{e}_A)$$

where m is the length of the sequence $\mathbf{f}_l$. The parameter p_l is a left length distribution. The probabilities p_{mid}, p_{right}, decompose in the same way, except substituting a separate length distribution p_m and p_r for p_l. For the TERMINAL rule, we emit $\mathbf{f}_t$ with a similarly decomposed distribution p_{term} using length distribution p_w.

We define the probability of generating a foreign word f_j as

$$p(f_j \mid A, \mathbf{e}_A) = \sum_{i \in \mathbf{e}_A} \frac{1}{|\,\mathbf{e}_A\,|} p_t(f_j \mid e_i)$$

with $i \in \mathbf{e}_A$ denoting an index ranging over the indices of the English words contained in $\mathbf{e}_A$. The reader may recognize the above expressions as the probability assigned by IBM Model 1 (Brown et al., 1993) of generating the words $\mathbf{f}_l$ given the words $\mathbf{e}_A$, with one important difference – the length m of the foreign sentence is often not modeled, so the term $p_l(|\mathbf{f}_l| = m \mid A)$ is set to a constant and ignored. Parameterizing this length allows our model to effectively control the number of words produced at different levels of the derivation.

It is worth noting how each parameter affects the model's behavior. The p_t distribution is a standard "translation" table, familiar from the IBM Models. The p_{inv} distribution is a "distortion" parameter, and models the likelihood of inverting non-terminals B and C. This parameter can capture, for example, the high likelihood that prepositions IN and noun phrases NP often invert in Chinese due to its use of postpositions. The non-terminal length distributions p_l, p_m, and p_r model the probability of "backing off" and emitting foreign words at non-terminals when a more refined analysis cannot be found. If these parameters place high mass on 0 length word sequences, this heavily penalizes this backoff behaviour. For the TERMINAL rule, the length distribution p_w parameterizes the number of words produced for a particular English word e, functioning similarly to the "fertilities" employed by IBM Models 3 and 4 (Brown et al., 1993). This allows us to model, for example, the tendency of English determiners *the* and *a* translate to nothing in the Chinese, and of English names to align to multiple Chinese words. In general, we expect an English word to usually align to one Chinese word, and so we place a weak Dirichlet prior on on the p_e distribution which puts extra mass on 1-length word sequences. This is helpful for avoiding the "garbage collection" (Moore, 2004) problem for rare words.

3.2 Exploiting Non-Terminal Labels

There are often foreign words that do not correspond well to any English word, which our model must also handle. We elected for a simple augmentation to our model to account for these words. When generating foreign word sequences $\mathbf{f}$ at a non-terminal (i.e. via the UNARY or BINARY productions), we also allow for the production of foreign words from the non-terminal symbol A. We modify $p(f_j \mid \mathbf{e}_A)$ from the previous section to allow production of f_j directly from the non-terminal[7] A:

$$p(f_j \mid \mathbf{e}_A) = p_{nt} \cdot p(f_j \mid A) + (1 - p_{nt}) \cdot \sum_{i \in \mathbf{e}_A} \frac{1}{|\mathbf{e}_A|} p_t(f_j \mid e_i)$$

where p_{nt} is a global binomial parameter which controls how often such alignments are made.

This necessitates the inclusion of parameters like $p_t($的 $\mid$ NP$)$ into our translation table. Generally, these parameters do not contain much information, but rather function like a traditional NULL rooted at some position in the tree. However, in some cases, the particular annotation used by the Penn Treebank (Marcus et al., 1993) (and hence most parsers) allows for some interesting parameters to be learned. For example, we found that our aligner often matched the Chinese word 了, which marks the past tense (among other things), to the preterminals VBD and VBN, which denote the English simple past and perfect tense. Additionally, Chinese measure words like 个 and 名 often align to the CD (numeral) preterminal. These generalizations can be quite useful – where a particular number might predict a measure word quite poorly, the generalization that measure words co-occur with the CD tag is very robust.

[7]For terminal symbols E, this production is not possible.

3.3 Membership in ITG

The generative process which describes our model contains a class of grammars larger than the computationally efficient class of ITG grammars. Fortunately, the parameterization described above not only reduces the number of parameters to a manageable level, but also introduces independence assumptions which permit synchronous binarization (Zhang et al., 2006) of our grammar. Any SCFG that can be synchronously binarized is an ITG, meaning that our parameterization permits efficient inference algorithms which we will make use of in the next section. Although several binarizations are possible, we give one such binarization and its associated probabilities in Table 2.

3.4 Robustness to Syntactic Divergence

Generally speaking, ITG grammars have proven more useful without the monolingual syntactic constraints imposed by a target parse tree. When derivations are restricted to respect a target-side parse tree, many desirable alignments are ruled out when the syntax of the two languages diverges, and alignment quality drops precipitously (Zhang and Gildea, 2004), though attempts have been made to address this issue (Gildea, 2003).

Our model is designed to degrade gracefully in the case of syntactic divergence. Because it can produce foreign words at any level of the derivation, our model can effectively back off to a variant of Model 1 in the case where an ITG derivation that both respects the target parse tree and the desired word-level alignments cannot be found.

For example, consider the sentence pair fragment in Figure 3. It is not possible to produce an ITG derivation of this fragment that both respects the English tree and also aligns all foreign words to their obvious English counterparts. Our model handles this case by attaching the troublesome 明天 at the uppermost VP. This analysis captures 3 of the 4 word-level correspondences, and also permits extraction of abstract rules like (S $\rightarrow$ NP VP ; NP VP) and (NP $\rightarrow$ *the* NN ; NN).

Unfortunately, this analysis leaves the English word *tomorrow* with an empty foreign span, permitting extraction of the incorrect translation (VP $\rightarrow$ *announced tomorrow* ; 公布), among others. Our

Rule Type	Root	English side	Foreign side	Probability
TERMINAL	E	e	$\mathbf{w}_t$	$p_{term}(\mathbf{w}_t \mid E)$
UNARY	A	B^u	$\mathbf{w}_l\ B^u$	$p_g(A \to B \mid A) p_{left}(\mathbf{w}_l \mid A, \mathbf{e}_A)$
	B^u	B	$B\ \mathbf{w}_r$	$p_{right}(\mathbf{w}_r \mid A, \mathbf{e}_A)$
BINARY	A	A^1	$\mathbf{w}_l\ A^1$	$p_{left}(\mathbf{w}_l \mid A, \mathbf{e}_A)$
	A^1	$B\ C^1$	$B\ C^1$	$p_g(A \to B\ C \mid A) p_{inv}(I\text{=false} \mid B, C)$
	A^1	$B\ C^1$	$C^1\ B$	$p_g(A \to B\ C \mid A) p_{inv}(I\text{=true} \mid B, C)$
	C^1	C^2	$\mathbf{f}_m\ C^2$	$p_{mid}(\mathbf{f}_m \mid A, \mathbf{e}_A)$
	C^2	C	$C\ \mathbf{f}_r$	$p_{right}(\mathbf{f}_r \mid A, \mathbf{e}_A)$

Table 2: A synchronous binarization of the SCFG describing our model.

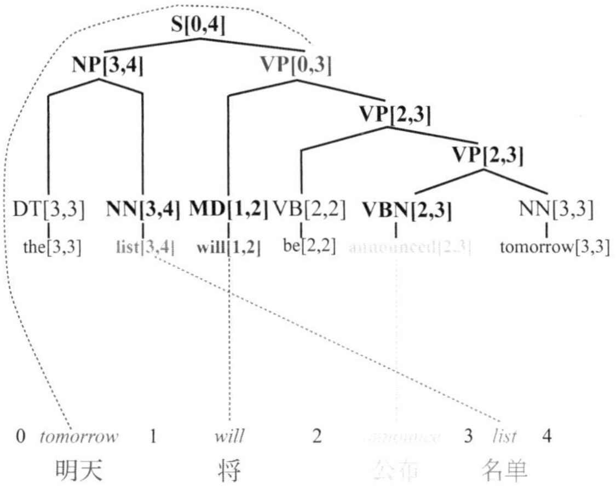

Figure 3: The graceful degradation of our model in the face of syntactic divergence. It is not possible to align all foreign words with their obvious English counterparts with an ITG derivation. Instead, our model analyzes as much as possible, but must resort to emitting 明天 high in the tree.

point here is not that our model's analysis is "correct", but "good enough" without resorting to more computationally complicated models. In general, our model follows an "extract as much as possible" approach. We hypothesize that this approach will capture important syntactic generalizations, but it also risks including low-quality rules. It is an empirical question whether this approach is effective, and we investigate this issue further in Section 5.3.

There are possibilities for improving our model's treatment of syntactic divergence. One option is to allow the model to select trees which are more consistent with the alignment (Burkett et al., 2010), which our model can do since it permits efficient inference over forests. The second is to modify the generative process slightly, perhaps by including the "clone" operator of Gildea (2003).

4 Learning and Inference

4.1 Parameter Estimation

The parameters of our model can be efficiently estimated in an unsupervised fashion using the Expectation-Maximization (EM) algorithm. The E-step requires the computation of expected counts under our model for each multinomial parameter. We omit the details of obtaining expected counts for each distribution, since they can be obtained using simple arithmetic from a single quantity, namely, the expected count of a particular instantiation of a synchronous rule r. This expectation is a standard quantity that can be computed in $O(n^6)$ time using the bitext Inside-Outside dynamic program (Wu, 1997).

4.2 Dynamic Program Pruning

While our model permits $O(n^6)$ inference over a forest of English trees, inference over a full forest would be very slow, and so we fix a single n-ary English tree obtained from a monolingual parser. However, it is worth noting that the English side of the ITG derivation is *not* completely fixed. Where our English trees are more than binary branching, we permit any binarization in our dynamic program.

For efficiency, we also ruled out span alignments that are extremely lopsided, for example, a 1-word English span aligned to a 20-word foreign span. Specifically, we pruned any span alignment in which one side is more than 5 times larger than the other.

Finally, we employ pruning based on high-precision alignments from simpler models (Cherry and Lin, 2007; Haghighi et al., 2009). We compute word-to-word alignments by finding all word pairs which have a posterior of at least 0.7 according to both forward and reverse IBM Model 1 parameters, and prune any span pairs which invalidate more than 3 of these alignments. In total, this pruning re-

Span	P	R	F1
Syntactic Alignment	50.9	**83.0**	**63.1**
GIZA++	**56.1**	67.3	61.2
Rule	P	R	F1
Syntactic Alignment	39.6	**40.3**	**39.9**
GIZA++	**46.2**	34.7	39.6

Table 3: Alignment quality results for our syntactic aligner and our GIZA++ baseline.

duced computation from approximately 1.5 seconds per sentence to about 0.3 seconds per sentence, a speed-up of a factor of 5.

4.3 Decoding

Given a trained model, we extract a tree-to-string alignment as follows: we compute, for each node in the English tree, the posterior probability of a particular foreign span assignment using the same dynamic program needed for EM. We then compute the set of span assignments which maximizes the sum of these posteriors, constrained such that the foreign span assignments nest in the obvious way. This algorithm is a natural synchronous generalization of the monolingual Maximum Constituents Parse algorithm of Goodman (1996).

5 Experiments

5.1 Alignment Quality

We first evaluated our alignments against gold standard annotations. Our training data consisted of the 2261 manually aligned and translated sentences of the Chinese Treebank (Bies et al., 2007) and approximately half a million unlabeled sentences of parallel Chinese-English newswire. The unlabeled data was subsampled (Li et al., 2009) from a larger corpus by selecting sentences which have good tune and test set coverage, and limited to sentences of length at most 40. We parsed the English side of the training data with the Berkeley parser.[8] For our baseline alignments, we used GIZA++, trained in the standard way.[9] We used the *grow-diag-final* alignment heuristic, as we found it outperformed *union* in early experiments.

We trained our unsupervised syntactic aligner on the concatenation of the labelled and unlabelled data. As is standard in unsupervised alignment models, we initialized the translation parameters p_t by first training 5 iterations of IBM Model 1 using the joint training algorithm of Liang et al. (2006), and then trained our model for 5 EM iterations. We extracted syntactic rules using a re-implementation of the Galley et al. (2006) algorithm from both our syntactic alignments and the GIZA++ alignments. We handle null-aligned words by extracting every consistent derivation, and extracted composed rules consisting of at most 3 minimal rules.

We evaluate our alignments against the gold standard in two ways. We calculated Span F-score, which compares the set of extractable nodes paired with a foreign span, and Rule F-score (Fossum et al., 2008) over minimal rules. The results are shown in Table 3. By both measures, our syntactic aligner effectively trades recall for precision when compared to our baseline, slightly increasing overall F-score.

5.2 Translation Quality

For our translation system, we used a re-implementation of the syntactic system of Galley et al. (2006). For the translation rules extracted from our data, we computed standard features based on relative frequency counts, and tuned their weights using MERT (Och, 2003). We also included a language model feature, using a 5-gram language model trained on 220 million words of English text using the SRILM Toolkit (Stolcke, 2002).

For tuning and test data, we used a subset of the NIST MT04 and MT05 with sentences of length at most 40. We used the first 1000 sentences of this set for tuning and the remaining 642 sentences as test data. We used the decoder described in DeNero et al. (2009) during both tuning and testing.

We provide final tune and test set results in Table 4. Our alignments produce a 1.0 BLEU improvement over the baseline. Our reported syntactic results were obtained when rules were thresholded by count; we discuss this in the next section.

5.3 Analysis

As discussed in Section 3.4, our aligner is designed to extract many rules, which risks inadvertently extracting low-quality rules. To quantify this, we first examined the number of rules extracted by our aligner as compared with GIZA++. After relativiz-

[8] `http://code.google.com/p/berkeleyparser/`

[9] 5 iterations of model 1, 5 iterations of HMM, 3 iterations of Model 3, and 3 iterations of Model 4.

	Tune	Test
Syntactic Alignment	**29.78**	**29.83**
GIZA++	28.76	28.84
GIZA++ high count	25.51	25.38

Table 4: Final tune and test set results for our grammars extracted using the baseline GIZA++ alignments and our syntactic aligner. When we filter the GIZA++ grammars with the same count thresholds used for our aligner ("high count"), BLEU score drops substantially.

ing to the tune and test set, we extracted approximately 32 million unique rules using our aligner, but only 3 million with GIZA++. To check that we were not just extracting extra low-count, low-quality rules, we plotted the number of rules with a particular count in Figure 4. We found that while our aligner certainly extracts many more low-count rules, it also extracts many more high-count rules.

Of course, high-count rules are not guaranteed to be high quality. To verify that frequent rules were better for translation, we experimented with various methods of thresholding to remove rules with low count extracted from using aligner. We found in early development found that removing low-count rules improved translation performance substantially. In particular, we settled on the following scheme: we kept all rules with a single foreign terminal on the right-hand side. For entirely lexical (gapless) rules, we kept all rules occurring at least 3 times. For unlexicalized rules, we kept all rules occurring at least 20 times per gap. For rules which mixed gaps and lexical items, we kept all rules occurring at least 10 times per gap. This left us with a grammar about 600 000 rules, the same grammar which gave us our final results reported in Table 4.

In contrast to our syntactic aligner, rules extracted using GIZA++ could not be so aggressively pruned. When pruned using the same count thresholds, accuracy dropped by more than 3.0 BLEU on the tune set, and similarly on the test set (see Table 4). To obtain the accuracy shown in our final results (our best results with GIZA++), we had to adjust the count threshold to include all lexicalized rules, all unlexicalized rules, and mixed rules occurring at least twice per gap. With these count thresholds, the GIZA++ grammar contained about 580 000 rules, roughly the same number as our syntactic grammar.

We also manually searched the grammars for rules that had high count in the syntactically-

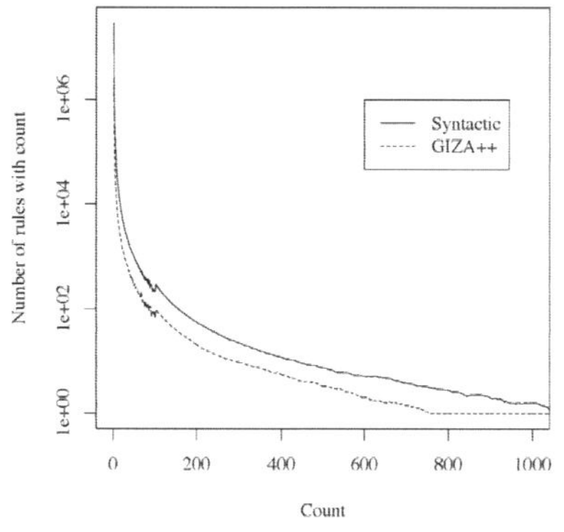

Figure 4: Number of extracted translation rules with a particular count. Grammars extracted from our syntactic aligner produce not only more low-count rules, but also more high-count rules than GIZA++.

extracted grammar and low (or 0) count in the GIZA++ grammar. Of course, we can always cherry-pick such examples, but a few rules were illuminating. For example, for the 在 ...之前 construction discussed earlier, our aligner permits extraction of the general rule (PP $\rightarrow$ IN_1 NP_2 ; 在 NP_2 IN_1) 3087 times, and the lexicalized rule (PP $\rightarrow$ *before* NP ; 在 NP 之前) 118 times. In constrast, the GIZA++ grammar extracts the latter only 23 times and the former not at all. The more complex rule (NP $\rightarrow$ NP_2 , who S_1 , ; S_1 的 NP_2), which captures a common appositive construction, was absent from the GIZA++ grammar but occurred 63 in ours.

6 Conclusion

We have described a syntactic alignment model which explicitly aligns nodes of a syntactic parse in one language to spans in another, making it suitable for use in many syntactic translation systems. Our model is unsupervised and can be efficiently trained with a straightforward application of EM. We have demonstrated that our model can accurately capture many syntactic correspondences, and is robust in the face of syntactic divergence between language pairs. Our aligner permits the extraction of more reliable, high-count rules when compared to a standard word-alignment baseline. These high-count rules also produce improvements in BLEU score.

Acknowledgements

This project is funded in part by the NSF under grant 0643742; by BBN under DARPA contract HR0011-06-C-0022; and an NSERC Postgraduate Fellowship. The authors would like to thank Michael Auli for his input.

References

Ann Bies, Martha Palmer, Justin Mott, and Colin Warner. 2007. English chinese translation treebank v 1.0. web download. In *LDC2007T02*.

Peter F. Brown, Stephen A. Della Pietra, Vincent J. Della Pietra, and Robert L. Mercer. 1993. The mathematics of statistical machine translation: Parameter estimation. *Computational Linguistics*, 19:263–311.

David Burkett, John Blitzer, and Dan Klein. 2010. Joint parsing and alignment with weakly synchronized grammar. In *Proceedings of the North American Association for Computational Linguistics*.

Colin Cherry and Dekang Lin. 2006. Soft syntactic constraints for word alignment through discriminative training. In *Proceedings of the Association of Computational Linguistics*.

Colin Cherry and Dekang Lin. 2007. Inversion transduction grammar for joint phrasal translation modeling. In *Workshop on Syntax and Structure in Statistical Translation*.

David Chiang. 2004. *Evaluating grammar formalisms for applications to natural language processing and biological sequence analysis*. Ph.D. thesis, University of Pennsylvania.

David Chiang. 2005. A hierarchical phrase-based model for statistical machine translation. In *The Annual Conference of the Association for Computational Linguistics*.

Trevor Cohn and Phil Blunsom. 2009. A Bayesian model of syntax-directed tree to string grammar induction. In *Proceedings of the Conference on Emprical Methods for Natural Language Processing*.

John DeNero and Dan Klein. 2007. Tailoring word alignments to syntactic machine translation. In *The Annual Conference of the Association for Computational Linguistics*.

John DeNero, Dan Gillick, James Zhang, and Dan Klein. 2006. Why generative phrase models underperform surface heuristics. In *Workshop on Statistical Machine Translation at NAACL*.

John DeNero, Mohit Bansal, Adam Pauls, and Dan Klein. 2009. Efficient parsing for transducer grammars. In *Proceedings of NAACL*.

Victoria Fossum, Kevin Knight, and Steven Abney. 2008. Using syntax to improve word alignment precision for syntax-based machine translation. In *Proceedings of the Third Workshop on Statistical Machine Translation*.

Michel Galley, Mark Hopkins, Kevin Knight, and Daniel Marcu. 2004. What's in a translation rule? In *Proceedings of the North American Chapter of the Association for Computational Linguistics*.

Michel Galley, Jonathan Graehl, Kevin Knight, Daniel Marcu, Steve DeNeefe, Wei Wang, and Ignacio Thayer. 2006. Scalable inference and training of context-rich syntactic translation models. In *Proceedings of the Association for Computational Linguistics*.

Daniel Gildea. 2003. Loosely tree-based alignment for machine translation. In *Proceedings of the Association for Computational Linguistics*.

Joshua Goodman. 1996. Parsing algorithms and metrics. In *Proceedings of the Association for Computational Linguistics*.

Joshua Goodman. 1998. *Parsing Inside-Out*. Ph.D. thesis, Harvard University.

Aria Haghighi, John Blitzer, John Denero, and Dan Klein. 2009. Better word alignments with supervised itg models. In *Proceedings of the Association for Computational Linguistics*.

Liang Huang, Kevin Knight, and Aravind Joshi. 2006. A syntax-directed translator with extended domain of locality. In *Proceedings of CHSLP*.

Zhifei Li, Chris Callison-Burch, Chris Dyer, Juri Ganitkevitch, Sanjeev Khudanpur, Lane Schwartz, Wren N. G. Thornton, Jonathan Weese, and Omar F. Zaidan. 2009. Joshua: an open source toolkit for parsing-based machine translation. In *Proceedings of the Fourth Workshop on Statistical Machine Translation*.

Percy Liang, Ben Taskar, and Dan Klein. 2006. Alignment by agreement. In *Proceedings of the North American Chapter of the Association for Computational Linguistics*.

Ding Liu and Daniel Gildea. 2009. Bayesian learning of phrasal tree-to-string templates. In *Proceedings of EMNLP*.

Yang Liu, Qun Liu, and Shouxun Lin. 2006. Tree-to-string alignment template for statistical machine translation. In *Proceedings of the Association for Computational Linguistics*.

Yang Liu, Yajuan Lü, and Qun Liu. 2009. Improving tree-to-tree translation with packed forests. In *Proceedings of ACL*.

M. Marcus, B. Santorini, and M. Marcinkiewicz. 1993. Building a large annotated corpus of English: The Penn Treebank. In *Computational Linguistics*.

Jonathan May and Kevin Knight. 2007. Syntactic re-alignment models for machine translation. In *Proceedings of the Conference on Emprical Methods for Natural Language Processing*.

Robert C. Moore. 2004. Improving ibm word alignment model 1. In *The Annual Conference of the Association for Computational Linguistics*.

Franz Josef Och and Hermann Ney. 2003. A systematic comparison of various statistical alignment models. *Computational Linguistics*, 29:19–51.

Franz Josef Och. 2003. Minimum error rate training in statistical machine translation. In *Proceedings of the Association for Computational Linguistics*.

Andreas Stolcke. 2002. SRILM: An extensible language modeling toolkit. In *ICSLP 2002*.

Dekai Wu. 1997. Stochastic inversion transduction grammars and bilingual parsing of parallel corpora. *Computational Linguistics*, 23:377–404.

Kenji Yamada and Kevin Knight. 2001. A syntax-based statistical translation model. In *Proceedings of the Association of Computational Linguistics*.

Hao Zhang and Daniel Gildea. 2004. Syntax-based alignment: supervised or unsupervised? In *Proceedings of the Conference on Computational Linguistics*.

Hao Zhang, Liang Huang, Daniel Gildea, and Kevin Knight. 2006. Synchronous binarization for machine translation. In *Proceedings of the North American Chapter of the Association for Computational Linguistics*.

Joint Parsing and Alignment with Weakly Synchronized Grammars

David Burkett **John Blitzer** **Dan Klein**
Computer Science Division
University of California, Berkeley
{dburkett,blitzer,klein}@cs.berkeley.edu

Abstract

Syntactic machine translation systems extract rules from bilingual, word-aligned, syntactically parsed text, but current systems for parsing and word alignment are at best cascaded and at worst totally independent of one another. This work presents a unified joint model for simultaneous parsing and word alignment. To flexibly model syntactic divergence, we develop a discriminative log-linear model over two parse trees and an ITG derivation which is encouraged but not forced to synchronize with the parses. Our model gives absolute improvements of 3.3 F_1 for English parsing, 2.1 F_1 for Chinese parsing, and 5.5 F_1 for word alignment over each task's independent baseline, giving the best reported results for both Chinese-English word alignment and joint parsing on the parallel portion of the Chinese treebank. We also show an improvement of 1.2 BLEU in downstream MT evaluation over basic HMM alignments.

1 Introduction

Current syntactic machine translation (MT) systems build synchronous context free grammars from aligned syntactic fragments (Galley et al., 2004; Zollmann et al., 2006). Extracting such grammars requires that bilingual word alignments and monolingual syntactic parses be compatible. Because of this, much recent work in both word alignment and parsing has focused on changing aligners to make use of syntactic information (DeNero and Klein, 2007; May and Knight, 2007; Fossum et al., 2008) or changing parsers to make use of word alignments (Smith and Smith, 2004; Burkett and Klein, 2008; Snyder et al., 2009). In the first case, however, parsers do not exploit bilingual information. In the second, word alignment is performed with a model that does not exploit syntactic information. This work presents a single, joint model for parsing and word alignment that allows both pieces to influence one another simultaneously.

While building a joint model seems intuitive, there is no easy way to characterize how word alignments and syntactic parses should relate to each other in general. In the ideal situation, each pair of sentences in a bilingual corpus could be syntactically parsed using a synchronous context-free grammar. Of course, real translations are almost always at least partially syntactically divergent. Therefore, it is unreasonable to expect perfect matches of any kind between the two sides' syntactic trees, much less expect that those matches be well explained at a word level. Indeed, it is sometimes the case that large pieces of a sentence pair are completely asynchronous and can only be explained monolingually.

Our model exploits synchronization where possible to perform more accurately on both word alignment and parsing, but also allows independent models to dictate pieces of parse trees and word alignments when synchronization is impossible. This notion of "weak synchronization" is parameterized and estimated from data to maximize the likelihood of the correct parses and word alignments. Weak synchronization is closely related to the quasi-synchronous models of Smith and Eisner (2006; 2009) and the bilingual parse reranking model of Burkett and Klein (2008), but those models assume that the word alignment of a sentence pair is known and fixed.

To simultaneously model both parses and align-

Human Language Technologies: The 2010 Annual Conference of the North American Chapter of the ACL, pages 127–135,
Los Angeles, California, June 2010.

ments, our model loosely couples three separate combinatorial structures: monolingual trees in the source and target languages, and a synchronous ITG alignment that links the two languages (but is not constrained to match linguistic syntax). The model has no hard constraints on how these three structures must align, but instead contains a set of "synchronization" features that are used to propagate influence between the three component grammars. The presence of synchronization features couples the parses and alignments, but makes exact inference in the model intractable; we show how to use a variational mean field approximation, both for computing approximate feature expectations during training, and for performing approximate joint inference at test time.

We train our joint model on the parallel, gold word-aligned portion of the Chinese treebank. When evaluated on parsing and word alignment, this model significantly improves over independently-trained baselines: the monolingual parser of Petrov and Klein (2007) and the discriminative word aligner of Haghighi et al. (2009). It also improves over the discriminative, bilingual parsing model of Burkett and Klein (2008), yielding the highest joint parsing F_1 numbers on this data set. Finally, our model improves word alignment in the context of translation, leading to a 1.2 BLEU increase over using HMM word alignments.

2 Joint Parsing and Alignment

Given a source-language sentence, s, and a target-language sentence, s', we wish to predict a source tree t, a target tree t', and some kind of alignment a between them. These structures are illustrated in Figure 1.

To facilitate these predictions, we define a conditional distribution $\mathrm{P}(t, a, t'|s, s')$. We begin with a generic conditional exponential form:

$$\mathrm{P}(t, a, t'|s, s') \propto \exp \theta^\top \phi(t, a, t', s, s') \quad (1)$$

Unfortunately, a generic model of this form is intractable, because we cannot efficiently sum over all triples (t, a, t') without some assumptions about how the features $\phi(t, a, t', s, s')$ decompose.

One natural solution is to restrict our candidate triples to those given by a synchronous context free grammar (SCFG) (Shieber and Schabes, 1990). Figure 1(a) gives a simple example of generation from a log-linearly parameterized synchronous grammar, together with its features. With the SCFG restriction, we can sum over the necessary structures using the $O(n^6)$ bitext inside-outside algorithm, making $\mathrm{P}(t, a, t'|s, s')$ relatively efficient to compute expectations under.

Unfortunately, an SCFG requires that *all* the constituents of each tree, from the root down to the words, are generated perfectly in tandem. The resulting inability to model any level of syntactic divergence prevents accurate modeling of the individual monolingual trees. We will consider the running example from Figure 2 throughout the paper. Here, for instance, the verb phrase *established in such places as Quanzhou, Zhangzhou, etc.* in English does not correspond to any single node in the Chinese tree. A synchronous grammar has no choice but to analyze this sentence incorrectly, either by ignoring this verb phrase in English or postulating an incorrect Chinese constituent that corresponds to it.

Therefore, instead of requiring strict synchronization, our model treats the two monolingual trees and the alignment as separate objects that can vary arbitrarily. However, the model rewards synchronization appropriately when the alignment brings the trees into correspondence.

3 Weakly Synchronized Grammars

We propose a joint model which still gives probabilities on triples (t, a, t'). However, instead of using SCFG rules to synchronously enforce the tree constraints on t and t', we only require that each of t and t' be well-formed under separate monolingual CFGs.

In order to permit efficient enumeration of all possible alignments a, we also restrict a to the set of unlabeled ITG bitrees (Wu, 1997), though again we do not require that a relate to t or t' in any particular way. Although this assumption does limit the space of possible word-level alignments, for the domain we consider (Chinese-English word alignment), the reduced space still contains almost all empirically observed alignments (Haghighi et al., 2009).[1] For

[1]See Section 8.1 for some new terminal productions required to make this true for the parallel Chinese treebank.

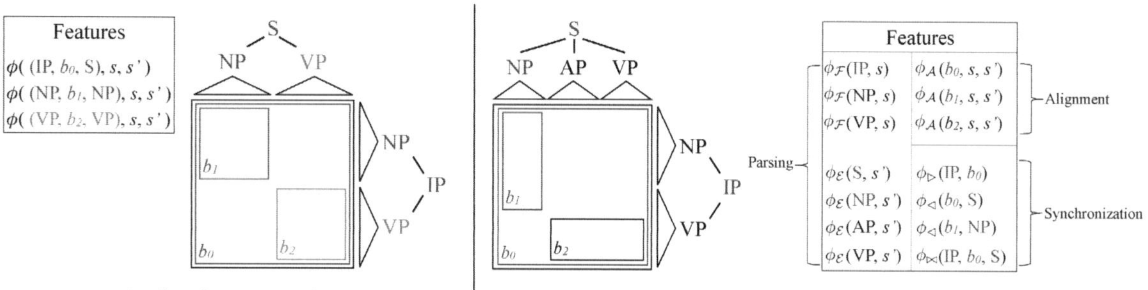

(a) Synchronous Rule

(b) Asynchronous Rule

Figure 1: Source trees, t (right), alignments, a (grid), and target trees, t' (top), and feature decompositions for synchronous (a) and weakly synchronous (b) grammars. Features always condition on bispans and/or anchored syntactic productions, but weakly synchronous grammars permit more general decompositions.

example, in Figure 2, the word alignment is ITG-derivable, and each of the colored rectangles is a bispan in that derivation.

There are no additional constraints beyond the independent, internal structural constraints on t, a, and t'. This decoupling permits derivations like that in Figure 1(b), where the top-level syntactic nodes align, but their children are allowed to diverge. With the three structures separated, our first model is a completely factored decomposition of (1).

Formally, we represent a source tree t as a set of nodes $\{n\}$, each node representing a labeled span. Likewise, a target tree t' is a set of nodes $\{n'\}$.[2] We represent alignments a as sets of *bispans* $\{b\}$, indicated by rectangles in Figure 1.[3] Using this notation, the initial model has the following form:

$$\mathrm{P}(t, a, t'|s, s') \propto \exp\left[\sum_{n\in t}\theta^\top\phi_{\mathcal{F}}(n, s)+\sum_{b\in a}\theta^\top\phi_{\mathcal{A}}(b, s, s')+\sum_{n'\in t'}\theta^\top\phi_{\mathcal{E}}(n', s')\right] \quad (2)$$

Here $\phi_{\mathcal{F}}(n, s)$ indicates a vector of source node features, $\phi_{\mathcal{E}}(n', s')$ is a vector of target node features, and $\phi_{\mathcal{A}}(b, s, s')$ is a vector of alignment bispan features. Of course, this model is completely asynchronous so far, and fails to couple the trees and alignments at all. To permit soft constraints between the three structures we are modeling, we add a set of *synchronization* features.

For $n \in t$ and $b \in a$, we say that $n \rhd b$ if n and b both map onto the same span of s. We define $b \lhd n'$ analogously for $n' \in t'$. We now consider three different types of synchronization features. Source-alignment synchronization features $\phi_{\rhd}(n, b)$ are extracted whenever $n \rhd b$. Similarly, target-alignment features $\phi_{\lhd}(b, n')$ are extracted if $b \lhd n'$. These features capture phenomena like that of bispan b_7 in Figure 2. Here the Chinese noun 地 synchronizes with the ITG derivation, but the English projection of b_7 is a distituent. Finally, we extract source-target features $\phi_{\bowtie}(n, b, n')$ whenever $n \rhd b \lhd n'$. These features capture complete bispan synchrony (as in bispan b_8) and can be expressed over triples (n, b, n') which happen to align, allowing us to reward synchrony, but not requiring it. All of these licensing conditions are illustrated in Figure 1(b).

With these features added, the final form of the model is:

$$\mathrm{P}(t, a, t'|s, s') \propto \exp\left[\sum_{n\in t}\theta^\top\phi_{\mathcal{F}}(n, s)+\sum_{b\in a}\theta^\top\phi_{\mathcal{A}}(b, s, s')+\sum_{n'\in t'}\theta^\top\phi_{\mathcal{E}}(n', s')+\sum_{n\rhd b}\theta^\top\phi_{\rhd}(n, b)+\sum_{b\lhd n'}\theta^\top\phi_{\lhd}(b, n')+\sum_{n\rhd b\lhd n'}\theta^\top\phi_{\bowtie}(n, b, n')\right] \quad (3)$$

[2]For expositional clarity, we describe n and n' as labeled spans only. However, in general, features that depend on n or n' are permitted to depend on the entire rule, and do in our final system.

[3]Alignments a link arbitrary spans of s and s' (including non-constituents and individual words). We discuss the relation to word-level alignments in Section 4.

We emphasize that because of the synchronization features, this final form does *not* admit any known efficient dynamic programming for the exact computation of expectations. We will therefore turn to a variational inference method in Section 6.

4 Features

With the model's locality structure defined, we just need to specify the actual feature function, ϕ. We divide the features into three types: parsing features ($\phi_{\mathcal{F}}(n, s)$ and $\phi_{\mathcal{E}}(n', s')$), alignment features ($\phi_{\mathcal{A}}(b, s, s')$) and synchronization features ($\phi_{\triangleright}(n, b)$, $\phi_{\triangleleft}(b, n')$, and $\phi_{\bowtie}(n, b, n')$). We detail each of these in turn here.

4.1 Parsing

The monolingual parsing features we use are simply parsing model scores under the parser of Petrov and Klein (2007). While that parser uses heavily refined PCFGs with rule probabilities defined at the refined symbol level, we interact with its posterior distribution via posterior marginal probabilities over unrefined symbols. In particular, to each unrefined anchored production ${}_i\mathrm{A}_j \rightarrow {}_i\mathrm{B}_k\mathrm{C}_j$, we associate a single feature whose value is the marginal quantity $\log \mathrm{P}({}_i\mathrm{B}_k\mathrm{C}_j|{}_i\mathrm{A}_j, s)$ under the monolingual parser. These scores are the same as the variational rule scores of Matsuzaki et al. (2005).[4]

4.2 Alignment

We begin with the same set of alignment features as Haghighi et al. (2009), which are defined only for terminal bispans. In addition, we include features on nonterminal bispans, including a bias feature, features that measure the difference in size between the source and target spans, features that measure the difference in relative sentence position between the source and target spans, and features that measure the density of word-to-word alignment posteriors under a separate unsupervised word alignment model.

[4]Of course the structure of our model permits any of the additional rule-factored monolingual parsing features that have been described in the parsing literature, but in the present work we focus on the contributions of joint modeling.

4.3 Synchronization

Our synchronization features are indicators for the syntactic types of the participating nodes. We determine types at both a coarse (more collapsed than Treebank symbols) and fine (Treebank symbol) level. At the coarse level, we distinguish between phrasal nodes (e.g. S, NP), synthetic nodes introduced in the process of binarizing the grammar (e.g. S′, NP′), and part-of-speech nodes (e.g. NN, VBZ). At the fine level, we distinguish all nodes by their exact label. We use coarse and fine types for both partially synchronized (source-alignment or target-alignment) features and completely synchronized (source-alignment-target) features. The inset of Figure 2 shows some sample features. Of course, we could devise even more sophisticated features by using the input text itself. As we shall see, however, our model gives significant improvements with these simple features alone.

5 Learning

We learn the parameters of our model on the parallel portion of the Chinese treebank. Although our model assigns probabilities to entire synchronous derivations of sentences, the parallel Chinese treebank gives alignments only at the word level (1 by 1 bispans in Figure 2). This means that our alignment variable a is not fully observed. Because of this, given a particular word alignment w, we maximize the marginal probability of the set of derivations $\mathcal{A}(w)$ that are consistent with w (Haghighi et al., 2009).[5]

$$\mathcal{L}(\theta) = \log \sum_{a \in \mathcal{A}(w_i)} \mathrm{P}(t_i, a, t_i' | s_i, s_i')$$

We maximize this objective using standard gradient methods (Nocedal and Wright, 1999). As with fully visible log-linear models, the gradient for the ith sentence pair with respect to θ is a difference of feature expectations:

$$\begin{aligned}\nabla\mathcal{L}(\theta) = &\mathrm{E}_{\mathrm{P}(a|t_i, w_i, t_i', s_i, s_i')}\left[\phi(t_i, a, t_i', s_i, s_i')\right] \\ &- \mathrm{E}_{\mathrm{P}(t, a, t'|s_i, s_i')}\left[\phi(t, a, t', s_i, s_i')\right]\end{aligned} \qquad (4)$$

[5]We also learn from non-ITG alignments by maximizing the marginal probability of the set of minimum-recall error alignments in the same way as Haghighi et al. (2009)

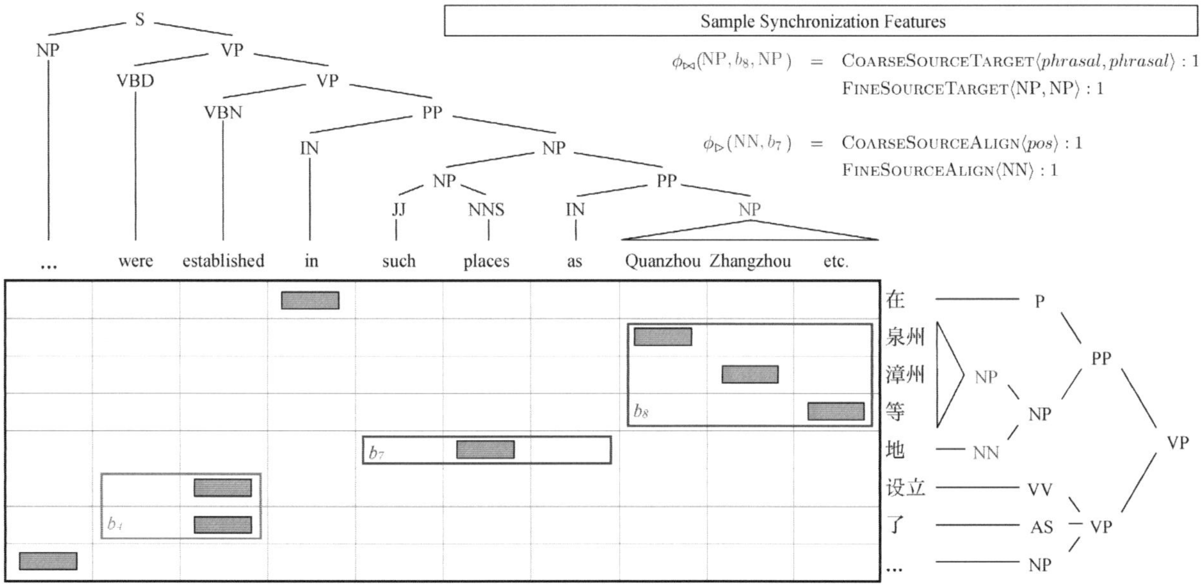

Figure 2: An example of a Chinese-English sentence pair with parses, word alignments, and a subset of the full optimal ITG derivation, including one totally unsynchronized bispan (b_4), one partially synchronized bispan (b_7), and and fully synchronized bispan (b_8). The inset provides some examples of active synchronization features (see Section 4.3) on these bispans. On this example, the monolingual English parser erroneously attached the lower PP to the VP headed by *established*, and the non-syntactic ITG word aligner misaligned 等 to *such* instead of to *etc.* Our joint model corrected both of these mistakes because it was rewarded for the synchronization of the two NPs joined by b_8.

We cannot efficiently compute the model expectations in this equation exactly. Therefore we turn next to an approximate inference method.

6 Mean Field Inference

Instead of computing the model expectations from (4), we compute the expectations for each sentence pair with respect to a simpler, fully factored distribution $Q(t, a, t') = q(t)q(a)q(t')$. Rewriting Q in log-linear form, we have:

$$Q(t, a, t') \propto \exp\left[\sum_{n \in t} \psi_n + \sum_{b \in a} \psi_b + \sum_{n' \in t'} \psi_{n'}\right]$$

Here, the ψ_n, ψ_b and $\psi_{n'}$ are variational parameters which we set to best approximate our weakly synchronized model from (3):

$$\psi^* = \underset{\psi}{\operatorname{argmin}}\ \text{KL}\left(Q_\psi || P_\theta(t, a, t'|s, s')\right)$$

Once we have found Q, we compute an approximate gradient by replacing the model expectations with expectations under Q:

$$\mathrm{E}_{Q(a|w_i)}\left[\phi(t_i, a, t'_i, s_i, s'_i)\right] - \mathrm{E}_{Q(t,a,t'|s_i,s'_i)}\left[\phi(t, a, t', s_i, s'_i)\right]$$

Now, we will briefly describe how we compute Q. First, note that the parameters ψ of Q factor along individual source nodes, target nodes, and bispans. The combination of the KL objective and our particular factored form of Q make our inference procedure a structured mean field algorithm (Saul and Jordan, 1996). Structured mean field techniques are well-studied in graphical models, and our adaptation in this section to multiple grammars follows standard techniques (see e.g. Wainwright and Jordan, 2008).

Rather than derive the mean field updates for ψ, we describe the algorithm (shown in Figure 3) procedurally. Similar to block Gibbs sampling, we iteratively optimize each component (source parse, target parse, and alignment) of the model in turn, conditioned on the others. Where block Gibbs sampling conditions on fixed trees or ITG derivations, our mean field algorithm maintains uncertainty in

Input: sentence pair (s, s')
parameter vector θ

Output: variational parameters ψ

1. Initialize

$\psi_n^0 \leftarrow \theta^\top \phi_{\mathcal{F}}(n, s)$

$\psi_b^0 \leftarrow \theta^\top \phi_{\mathcal{A}}(b, s, s')$

$\psi_{n'}^0 \leftarrow \theta^\top \phi_{\mathcal{E}}(n', s')$

$\mu_n^0 \leftarrow \sum_t q_{\psi^0}(t) I(n \in t)$, etc for μ_b^0, $\mu_{n'}^0$

2. While not converged, for each n, n', b in the monolingual and ITG charts

$$\psi_n^i \leftarrow \theta^\top \Big(\phi_{\mathcal{F}}(n, s) + \textstyle\sum_{b, n \triangleright b} \mu_b^{i-1} \phi_{\triangleright}(n, b) + \sum_{b, n \triangleright b} \sum_{n', b \triangleleft n'} \mu_b^{i-1} \mu_{n'}^{i-1} \phi_{\bowtie}(n, b, n')\Big)$$

$\mu_n^i \leftarrow \sum_t q_\psi(t) I(n \in t)$ (inside-outside)

$$\psi_b^i \leftarrow \theta^\top \Big(\phi_{\mathcal{A}}(b, s, s') + \textstyle\sum_{n, n \triangleright b} \mu_n^{i-1} \phi_{\triangleright}(n, b) + \sum_{n', b \triangleleft n'} \mu_{n'}^{i-1} \phi_{\triangleleft}(b, n') + \sum_{n, n \triangleright b} \sum_{n', b \triangleleft n'} \mu_n^{i-1} \mu_{n'}^{i-1} \phi_{\bowtie}(n, b, n')\Big)$$

$\mu_b \leftarrow \sum_a q_\psi(a) I(b \in a)$ (bitext inside-outside)

updates for $\psi_{n'}^i$, $\mu_{n'}^i$ analogous to ψ_n^i, μ_n^i

3. Return variational parameters ψ

Figure 3: Structured mean field inference for the weakly synchronized model. $I(n \in t)$ is an indicator value for the presence of node n in source tree t.

the form of monolingual parse forests or ITG forests. The key components to this uncertainty are the expected counts of particular source nodes, target nodes, and bispans under the mean field distribution:

$$\mu_n = \sum_t q_\psi(t) I(n \in t)$$
$$\mu_{n'} = \sum_{t'} q_\psi(t') I(n' \in t')$$
$$\mu_b = \sum_a q_\psi(a) I(b \in a)$$

Since dynamic programs exist for summing over each of the individual factors, these expectations can be computed in polynomial time.

6.1 Pruning

Although we can approximate the expectations from (4) in polynomial time using our mean field distribution, in practice we must still prune the ITG forests and monolingual parse forests to allow tractable inference. We prune our ITG forests using the same basic idea as Haghighi et al. (2009), but we employ a technique that allows us to be more aggressive. Where Haghighi et al. (2009) pruned bispans based on how many unsupervised HMM alignments were violated, we first train a maximum-matching word aligner (Taskar et al., 2005) using our supervised data set, which has only half the precision errors of the unsupervised HMM. We then prune every bispan which violates at least three alignments from the maximum-matching aligner. When compared to pruning the bitext forest of our model with Haghighi et al. (2009)'s HMM technique, this new technique allows us to maintain the same level of accuracy while cutting the number of bispans in half.

In addition to pruning the bitext forests, we also prune the syntactic parse forests using the monolingual parsing model scores. For each unrefined anchored production ${}_i\mathrm{A}_j \rightarrow {}_i\mathrm{B}_k\mathrm{C}_j$, we compute the marginal probability $\mathrm{P}({}_i\mathrm{A}_j, {}_i\mathrm{B}_k, {}_k\mathrm{C}_j|s)$ under the monolingual parser (these are equivalent to the maxrule scores from Petrov and Klein 2007). We only include productions where this probability is greater than 10^{-20}. Note that at training time, we are not guaranteed that the gold trees will be included in the pruned forest. Because of this, we replace the gold trees t_i, t_i' with oracle trees from the pruned forest, which can be found efficiently using a variant of the inside algorithm (Huang, 2008).

7 Testing

Once the model has been trained, we still need to determine how to use it to predict parses and word alignments for our test sentence pairs. Ideally, given the sentence pair (s, s'), we would find:

$$(t^*, w^*, t'^*) = \operatorname*{argmax}_{t,w,t'} \mathrm{P}(t, w, t'|s, s')$$
$$= \operatorname*{argmax}_{t,w,t'} \sum_{a \in \mathcal{A}(w)} \mathrm{P}(t, a, t'|s, s')$$

Of course, this is also intractable, so we once again resort to our mean field approximation. This yields the approximate solution:

$$(t^*, w^*, t'^*) = \operatorname*{argmax}_{t,w,t'} \sum_{a \in \mathcal{A}(w)} \mathrm{Q}(t, a, t')$$

However, recall that Q incorporates the model's mutual constraint into the variational parameters, which factor into $q(t)$, $q(a)$, and $q(t')$. This allows us to simplify further, and find the maximum a posteriori assignments under the variational distribution. The trees can be found quickly using the Viterbi inside algorithm on their respective qs. However, the sum for computing w^* under q is still intractable.

As we cannot find the maximum probability word alignment, we provide two alternative approaches for finding w^*. The first is to just find the Viterbi ITG derivation $a^* = \text{argmax}_a\, q(a)$ and then set w^* to contain exactly the 1x1 bispans in a^*. The second method, posterior thresholding, is to compute posterior marginal probabilities under q for each 1x1 cell beginning at position i, j in the word alignment grid:

$$m(i,j) = \sum_a q(a) I((i, i+1, j, j+1) \in a)$$

We then include $w(i,j)$ in w^* if $m(w(i,j)) > \tau$, where τ is a threshold chosen to trade off precision and recall. For our experiments, we found that the Viterbi alignment was uniformly worse than posterior thresholding. All the results from the next section use the threshold $\tau = 0.25$.

8 Experiments

We trained and tested our model on the translated portion of the Chinese treebank (Bies et al., 2007), which includes hand annotated Chinese and English parses and word alignments. We separated the data into three sets: *train*, *dev*, and *test*, according to the standard Chinese treebank split. To speed up training, we only used training sentences of length ≤ 50 words, which left us with 1974 of 2261 sentences. We measured the results in two ways. First, we directly measured F_1 for English parsing, Chinese parsing, and word alignment on a held out section of the hand annotated corpus used to train the model. Next, we further evaluated the quality of the word alignments produced by our model by using them as input for a machine translation system.

8.1 Dataset-specific ITG Terminals

The Chinese treebank gold word alignments include significantly more many-to-many word alignments than those used by Haghighi et al. (2009). We are able to produce some of these many-to-many alignments by including new many-to-many terminals in

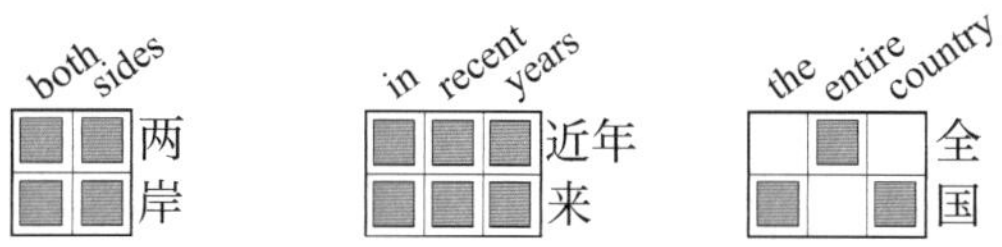

(a) 2x2 (b) 2x3 (c) Gapped 2x3

Figure 4: Examples of phrasal alignments that can be represented by our new ITG terminal bispans.

our ITG word aligner, as shown in Figure 4. Our terminal productions sometimes capture non-literal translation like *both sides* or *in recent years*. They also can allow us to capture particular, systematic changes in the annotation standard. For example, the gapped pattern from Figure 4 captures the standard that English word *the* is always aligned to the Chinese head noun in a noun phrase. We featurize these non-terminals with features similar to those of Haghighi et al. (2009), and all of the alignment results we report in Section 8.2 (both joint and ITG) employ these features.

8.2 Parsing and Word Alignment

To compute features that depend on external models, we needed to train an unsupervised word aligner and monolingual English and Chinese parsers. The unsupervised word aligner was a pair of jointly trained HMMs (Liang et al., 2006), trained on the FBIS corpus. We used the Berkeley Parser (Petrov and Klein, 2007) for both monolingual parsers, with the Chinese parser trained on the full Chinese treebank, and the English parser trained on a concatenation of the Penn WSJ corpus (Marcus et al., 1993) and the English side of *train*.[6]

We compare our parsing results to the monolingual parsing models and to the English-Chinese bilingual reranker of Burkett and Klein (2008), trained on the same dataset. The results are in Table 1. For word alignment, we compare to

[6] To avoid overlap in the data used to train the monolingual parsers and the joint model, at training time, we used a separate version of the Chinese parser, trained only on articles 400-1151 (omitting articles in *train*). For English parsing, we deemed it insufficient to entirely omit the Chinese treebank data from the monolingual parser's training set, as otherwise the monolingual parser would be trained entirely on out-of-domain data. Therefore, at training time we used two separate English parsers: to compute model scores for the *first* half of *train*, we used a parser trained on a concatenation of the WSJ corpus and the *second* half of *train*, and vice versa for the remaining sentences.

	Test Results		
	Ch F_1	Eng F_1	Tot F_1
Monolingual	83.6	81.2	82.5
Reranker	**86.0**	83.8	84.9
Joint	85.7	**84.5**	**85.1**

Table 1: Parsing results. Our joint model has the highest reported F_1 for English-Chinese bilingual parsing.

	Test Results			
	Precision	Recall	AER	F_1
HMM	86.0	58.4	30.0	69.5
ITG	**86.8**	73.4	20.2	79.5
Joint	85.5	**84.6**	**14.9**	**85.0**

Table 2: Word alignment results. Our joint model has the highest reported F_1 for English-Chinese word alignment.

the baseline unsupervised HMM word aligner and to the English-Chinese ITG-based word aligner of Haghighi et al. (2009). The results are in Table 2.

As can be seen, our model makes substantial improvements over the independent models. For parsing, we improve absolute F_1 over the monolingual parsers by 2.1 in Chinese, and by 3.3 in English. For word alignment, we improve absolute F_1 by 5.5 over the non-syntactic ITG word aligner. In addition, our English parsing results are better than those of the Burkett and Klein (2008) bilingual reranker, the current top-performing English-Chinese bilingual parser, despite ours using a much simpler set of synchronization features.

8.3 Machine Translation

We further tested our alignments by using them to train the Joshua machine translation system (Li and Khudanpur, 2008). Table 3 describes the results of our experiments. For all of the systems, we tuned on 1000 sentences of the NIST 2004 and 2005 machine translation evaluations, and tested on 400 sentences of the NIST 2006 MT evaluation. Our training set consisted of 250k sentences of newswire distributed with the GALE project, all of which were sub-sampled to have high Ngram overlap with the tune and test sets. All of our sentences were of length at most 40 words. When building the translation grammars, we used Joshua's default "tight" phrase extraction option. We ran MERT for 4 iterations, optimizing 20 weight vectors per iteration on a 200-best list.

	Rules	Tune	Test
HMM	1.1M	29.0	29.4
ITG	1.5M	**29.9**	30.4†
Joint	1.5M	29.6	**30.6**

Table 3: Tune and test BLEU results for machine translation systems built with different alignment tools. † indicates a statistically significant difference between a system's test performance and the one above it.

Table 3 gives the results. On the test set, we also ran the approximate randomization test suggested by Riezler and Maxwell (2005). We found that our joint parsing and alignment system significantly outperformed the HMM aligner, but the improvement over the ITG aligner was not statistically significant.

9 Conclusion

The quality of statistical machine translation models depends crucially on the quality of word alignments and syntactic parses for the bilingual training corpus. Our work presented the first joint model for parsing and alignment, demonstrating that we can improve results on both of these tasks, as well as on downstream machine translation, by allowing parsers and word aligners to simultaneously inform one another. Crucial to this improved performance is a notion of weak synchronization, which allows our model to learn when pieces of a grammar are synchronized and when they are not. Although exact inference in the weakly synchronized model is intractable, we developed a mean field approximate inference scheme based on monolingual and bitext parsing, allowing for efficient inference.

Acknowledgements

We thank Adam Pauls and John DeNero for their help in running machine translation experiments. We also thank the three anonymous reviewers for their helpful comments on an earlier draft of this paper. This project is funded in part by NSF grants 0915265 and 0643742, an NSF graduate research fellowship, the CIA under grant HM1582-09-1-0021, and BBN under DARPA contract HR0011-06-C-0022.

References

Ann Bies, Martha Palmer, Justin Mott, and Colin Warner. 2007. English Chinese translation treebank v 1.0. Web download. LDC2007T02.

David Burkett and Dan Klein. 2008. Two languages are better than one (for syntactic parsing). In *EMNLP*.

John DeNero and Dan Klein. 2007. Tailoring word alignments to syntactic machine translation. In *ACL*.

Victoria Fossum, Kevin Knight, and Steven Abney. 2008. Using syntax to improve word alignment for syntax-based statistical machine translation. In *ACL MT Workshop*.

Michel Galley, Mark Hopkins, Kevin Knight, and Daniel Marcu. 2004. What's in a translation rule? In *HLT-NAACL*.

Aria Haghighi, John Blitzer, John DeNero, and Dan Klein. 2009. Better word alignments with supervised ITG models. In *ACL*.

Liang Huang. 2008. Forest reranking: Discriminative parsing with non-local features. In *ACL*.

Zhifei Li and Sanjeev Khudanpur. 2008. A scalable decoder for parsing-based machine translation with equivalent language model state maintenance. In *ACL SSST*.

Percy Liang, Ben Taskar, and Dan Klein. 2006. Alignment by agreement. In *HLT-NAACL*.

Mitchell P. Marcus, Mary Ann Marcinkiewicz, and Beatrice Santorini. 1993. Building a large annotated corpus of English: The Penn Treebank. *Computational Linguistics*, 19(2):313–330.

Takuya Matsuzaki, Yusuki Miyao, and Jun'ichi Tsujii. 2005. Probabilistic CFG with latent annotations. In *ACL*.

Jon May and Kevin Knight. 2007. Syntactic re-alignment models for machine translation. In *EMNLP*.

Jorge Nocedal and Stephen J. Wright. 1999. *Numerical Optimization*. Springer.

Slav Petrov and Dan Klein. 2007. Improved inference for unlexicalized parsing. In *HLT-NAACL*.

Stefan Riezler and John Maxwell. 2005. On some pitfalls in automatic evaluation and significance testing for MT. In *Workshop on Intrinsic and Extrinsic Evaluation Methods for MT and Summarization, ACL*.

Lawrence Saul and Michael Jordan. 1996. Exploiting tractable substructures in intractable networks. In *NIPS*.

Stuart M. Shieber and Yves Schabes. 1990. Synchronous tree-adjoining grammars. In *ACL*.

David A. Smith and Jason Eisner. 2006. Quasi-synchronous grammars: Alignment by soft projection of syntactic dependencies. In *HLT-NAACL*.

David A. Smith and Jason Eisner. 2009. Parser adaptation and projection with quasi-synchronous grammar features. In *EMNLP*.

David A. Smith and Noah A. Smith. 2004. Bilingual parsing with factored estimation: using English to parse Korean. In *EMNLP*.

Benjamin Snyder, Tahira Naseem, and Regina Barzilay. 2009. Unsupervised multilingual grammar induction. In *ACL*.

Ben Taskar, Simon Lacoste-Julien, and Dan Klein. 2005. A discriminative matching approach to word alignment. In *EMNLP*.

Martin J Wainwright and Michael I Jordan. 2008. *Graphical Models, Exponential Families, and Variational Inference*. Now Publishers Inc., Hanover, MA, USA.

Dekai Wu. 1997. Stochastic inversion transduction grammars and bilingual parsing of parallel corpora. *Computational Linguistics*, 23(3):377–404.

Andreas Zollmann, Ashish Venugopal, Stephan Vogel, and Alex Waibel. 2006. The CMU-AKA syntax augmented machine translation system for IWSLT-06. In *IWSLT*.

Learning Translation Boundaries for Phrase-Based Decoding

Deyi Xiong, Min Zhang, Haizhou Li
Human Language Technology
Institute for Infocomm Research
1 Fusionopolis Way, #21-01 Connexis, Singapore 138632.
{dyxiong, mzhang, hli}@i2r.a-star.edu.sg

Abstract

Constrained decoding is of great importance not only for speed but also for translation quality. Previous efforts explore soft syntactic constraints which are based on constituent boundaries deduced from parse trees of the source language. We present a new framework to establish soft constraints based on a more natural alternative: translation boundary rather than constituent boundary. We propose simple classifiers to learn translation boundaries for any source sentences. The classifiers are trained directly on word-aligned corpus without using any additional resources. We report the accuracy of our translation boundary classifiers. We show that using constraints based on translation boundaries predicted by our classifiers achieves significant improvements over the baseline on large-scale Chinese-to-English translation experiments. The new constraints also significantly outperform constituent boundary based syntactic constrains.

1 Introduction

It has been known that phrase-based decoding (phrase segmentation/translation/reordering (Chiang, 2005)) should be constrained to some extent not only for transferring the NP-hard problem (Knight, 1999) into a tractable one in practice but also for improving translation quality. For example, Xiong et al. (2008) find that translation quality can be significantly improved by either prohibiting reorderings around punctuation or restricting reorderings within a 15-word window.

Recently, more linguistically motivated constraints are introduced to improve phrase-based decoding. (Cherry, 2008) and (Marton and Resnik, 2008) introduce syntactic constraints into the standard phrase-based decoding (Koehn et al., 2003) and hierarchical phrase-based decoding (Chiang, 2005) respectively by using a counting feature which accumulates whenever hypotheses violate syntactic boundaries of source-side parse trees. (Xiong et al., 2009) further presents a bracketing model to include thousands of context-sensitive syntactic constraints. All of these approaches achieve their improvements by guiding the phrase-based decoder to prefer translations which respect source-side parse trees.

One major problem with such constituent boundary based constraints is that syntactic structures of the source language do not necessarily reflect translation structures where the source and target language correspond to each other. In this paper, we investigate building classifiers that directly address the problem of *translation boundary*, rather than extracting constituent boundary from source-side parsers built for a different purpose. A translation boundary is a position in the source sequence which begins or ends a *translation zone* [1] spanning multiple source words. In a translation zone, the source phrase is translated as a unit. Reorderings which cross translation zones are not desirable.

Inspired by (Roark and Hollingshead, 2008) which introduces classifiers to decide if a word can begin/end a multi-word constituent, we build two discriminative classifiers to tag each word in the source sequence with a binary class label. The first classifier decides if a word can begin a multi-source-word translation zone; the second classifier decides if a word can end a multi-source-word translation

[1] We will give a formal definition of translation zone in Section 2.

Human Language Technologies: The 2010 Annual Conference of the North American Chapter of the ACL, pages 136–144,
Los Angeles, California, June 2010.

zone. Given a partial translation covering source sequence (i, j) with start word c_i and end word c_j [2], this translation can be penalized if the first classifier decides that the start word c_i can not be a beginning translation boundary or the second classifier decides that the end word c_j can not be an ending translation boundary. In such a way, we can guide the decoder to boost hypotheses that respect translation boundaries and therefore the common translation structure shared by the source and target language, rather than the syntactic structure of the source language.

We report the accuracy of such classifiers by comparing their outputs with "gold" translation boundaries obtained from reference translations on the development set. We integrate translation boundary based constraints into phrase-based decoding and display that they improve translation quality significantly in large-scale experiments. Furthermore, we confirm that they also significantly outperform constituent boundary based syntactic constraints.

2 Beginning and Ending Translation Zones

To better understand the particular task that we address in this paper, we study the distribution of classes of translation boundaries in real-world data. First, we introduce some notations. Given a source sentence $c_1...c_n$, we will say that a word c_i $(1 < i < n)$ is in the class B_y if there is a translation zone τ spanning $c_i...c_j$ for some $j > i$; and $c_i \in B_n$ otherwise. Similarly, we will say that a word c_j is in the class E_y if there is a translation zone spanning $c_i...c_j$ for some $j > i$; and $c_j \in E_n$ otherwise.

Here, a translation zone τ is a pair of aligned source phrase and target phrase

$$\tau = (c_i^j, e_p^q)$$

where τ must be consistent with the word alignment M

$$\forall (u, v) \in M, i \leq u \leq j \leftrightarrow p \leq v \leq q$$

By this, we require that no words inside the source phrase c_i^j are aligned to words outside the target phrase e_p^q and that no words outside the source phrase are aligned to words inside the target phrase.

[2]In this paper, we use c to denote the source language and e the target language.

Item	Count (M)	P (%)
Sentences	3.8	–
Words	96.9	–
Words $\in B_y$	22.7	23.4
Words $\in E_y$	41.0	42.3
Words $\notin B_y$ and $\notin E_y$	33.2	34.3

Table 1: Statistics on word classes from our bilingual training data. All numbers are calculated on the source side. P means the percentage.

This means, in other words, that the source phrase c_i^j is mapped as a unit onto the target phrase e_p^q.

When defining the B_y and E_y class, we also require that the source phrase c_i^j in the translation zone must contain multiple words $(j > i)$. Our interest is the question of whether a sequence of consecutive source words can be translated as a unit (i.e. whether there is a translation zone covering these source words). For a single-word source phrase, if it can be translated separately, it is always translated as a unit in the context of phrase-based decoding. Therefore this question does not exist.

Note that the first word c_1 and the last word c_n are unambiguous in terms of whether they begin or end a translation zone. The first word c_1 must begin a translation zone spanning the whole source sentence. The last word c_n must end a translation zone spanning the whole source sentence. Therefore, our classifiers only need to predict the other $n - 2$ words for a source sentence of length n.

Table 1 shows statistics of word classes from our training data which contain nearly 100M words in approximately 4M sentences. Among these words, only 22.7M words can begin a translation zone which covers multiple source words. 41M words can end a translation zone spanning multiple source words, which accounts for more than 42% in all words. We still have more than 33M words, accounting for 34.3%, which neither begin nor end a multi-source-word translation zone. Apparently, translations that begin/end on words $\in B_y / \in E_y$ are preferable to those which begin/end on other words.

Yet another interesting study is to compare translation boundaries with constituent boundaries deduced from source-side parse trees. In doing so, we can know further how well constituent boundary

Classification Task	Avg. Accuracy (%)
B_y/B_n	46.9
E_y/E_n	52.2

Table 2: Average classification accuracy on the development set when we treat constituent boundary deducer (according to source-side parse trees) as a translation boundary classifier.

based syntactic constraints can improve translation quality. We pair the source sentences of our development set with each of the reference translations and include the created sentence pairs in our bilingual training corpus. Then we obtain word alignments on the new corpus (see Section 5.1 for the details of learning word alignments). From the word alignments we obtain translation boundaries (see details in the next section). We parse the source sentences of our development set and obtain constituent boundaries from parse trees.

To make a clear comparison with our translation boundary classifiers (see Section 3.3), we treat constituent boundaries deduced from source-side parse trees as output from beginning/ending boundary classifiers: the constituent beginning boundary corresponds to B_y; the constituent ending boundary corresponds to E_y. We have four reference translations for each source sentence. Therefore we have four translation boundary sets, each of which is produced from word alignments between source sentences and one reference translation set. Each of the four translation boundary sets will be used as a gold standard. We calculate classification accuracy for our constituent boundary deducer on each gold standard and average them finally.

Table 2 shows the accuracy results. The average accuracies on the four gold standard sets are very low, especially for the B_y/B_n classification task. In section 3.3, we will show that our translation boundary classifiers achieve higher accuracy than that of constituent boundary deducer. This suggests that pure constituent boundary based constraints are not the best choice to constrain phrase-based decoding.

3 Learning Translation Boundaries

In this section, we investigate building classifiers to predict translation boundaries. First, we elaborate the acquisition of training instances from word alignments. Second, we build two classifiers with simple features on the obtained training instances. Finally, we evaluate our classifiers on the development set using the "gold" translation boundaries obtained from reference translations.

3.1 Obtaining Translation Boundaries from Word Alignments

We can easily obtain constituent boundaries from parse trees. Similarly, if we have a tree covering both source and target sentence, we can easily get translation boundaries from this tree. Fortunately, we can build such a tree directly from word alignments. We use (Zhang et al., 2008)'s shift-reduce algorithm (SRA) to decompose word alignments into hierarchical trees.

Given an arbitrary word-level alignment as an input, SRA is able to output a tree representation of the word alignment (a.k.a **decomposition tree**). Each node of the tree is a translation zone as we defined in the Section 2. Therefore the first word on the source side of each multi-source-word node is a beginning translation boundary ($\in B_y$); the last word on the source side of each multi-source-word node is an ending translation boundary ($\in E_y$).

Figure 1a shows an example of many-to-many alignment, where the source language is Chinese and the target language is English. Each word is indexed with their occurring position from left to right. Figure 1b is the tree representation of the word alignment after hierarchical analysis using SRA. We use $([i, j], [p, q])$ to denote a tree node, where i, j and p, q are the beginning and ending index in the source and target language, respectively. By checking nodes which cover multiple source words, we can easily decide that the source words {过去, 五, 因故} are in the class B_y and any other words are in the class B_n if we want to train a B_y/B_n classifier with class labels $\{B_y, B_n\}$. Similarly, the source words {次, 飞行, 都, 失败} are in the class E_y and any other words are in the class E_n when we train a E_y/E_n classifier with class labels $\{E_y, E_n\}$.

By using SRA on each word-aligned bilingual sentence, as described above, we can tag each source word with two sets of class labels: $\{B_y, B_n\}$ and $\{E_y, E_n\}$. The tagged source sentences will be used to train our two translation boundary classifiers.

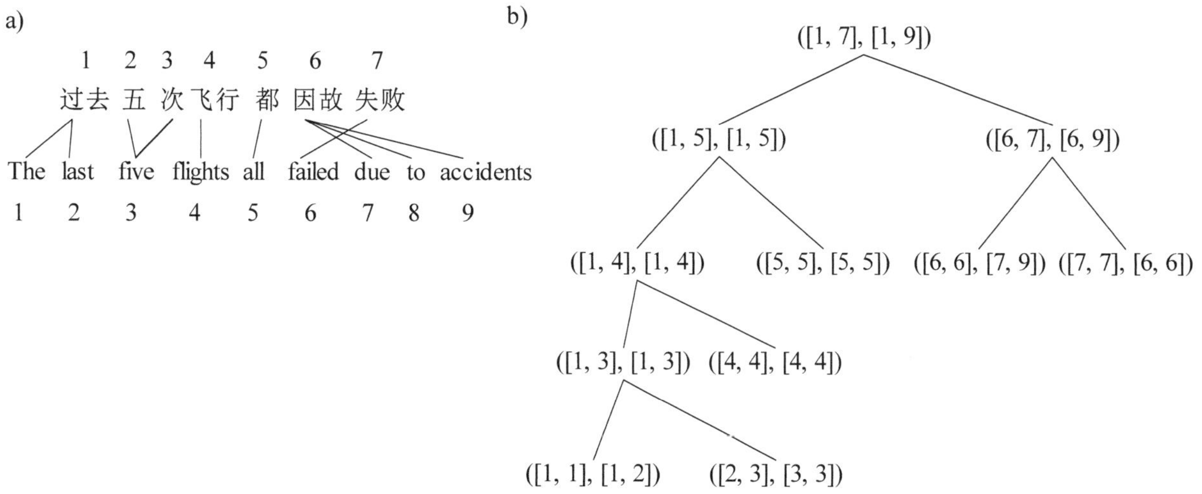

Figure 1: An example of many-to-many word alignment and its tree representation produced by (Zhang et al., 2008)'s shift-reduce algorithm.

3.2 Building Translation Boundary Classifiers

We build two discriminative classifiers based on Maximum Entropy Markov Models (MEMM) (McCallum et al., 2000). One classifier is to predict the word class $\zeta \in \{B_y, B_n\}$ for each source word. The other is to predict the word class $\zeta \in \{E_y, E_n\}$. These two classifiers are separately trained using training instances obtained from our word-aligned training data as demonstrated in the last section.

We use features from surrounding words, including 2 before and 2 after the current word position $(c_{-2}, c_{-1}, c_{+1}, c_{+2})$. We also use class features to train models with Markov order 1 (including class feature $\zeta_{c_{-1}}$), and Markov order 2 (including class features $\zeta_{c_{-1}}, \zeta_{c_{-2}}$).

3.3 Evaluating Translation Boundary Classifiers

How well can we perform these binary classification tasks using the classifiers described above? Can we obtain better translation boundary predictions than extracting constituent boundary from source-side parse trees? To investigate these questions, we evaluate our MEMM based classifiers. We trained them on our 100M-word word-aligned corpus. We ran the two trained classifiers on the development set separately to obtain the B_y/B_n words and E_y/E_n words. Then we built our four gold standards using four reference translation sets as described in Section 2. The average classification accuracy results are shown in Table 3.

	Avg. Accuracy (%)	
Classification Task	MEMM 1	MEMM 2
B_y/B_n	71.7	70.2
E_y/E_n	59.2	58.8

Table 3: Average classification accuracy on the development set for our MEMM based translation boundary classifiers with various Markov orders.

Comparing Table 3 with Table 2, we find that our MEMM based classifiers significantly outperform constituent boundary deducer in predicting translation boundaries, especially in the B_y/B_n classification task, where our MEMM based B_y/B_n classifier (Markov order 1) achieves a relative increase of 52.9% in accuracy over the constituent boundary deducer. In the E_y/E_n classification task, our classifiers also perform much better than constituent boundary deducer.

Then are our MEMM based translation boundary classifiers good enough? The accuracies are still low although they are higher than those of constituent boundary deducer. One reason why we have low accuracies is that our gold standard based evaluation is not established on real gold standards. In other words, we don't have gold standards in terms of translation boundary since different translations

Classification Task	Avg. Accuracy (%)
B_y/B_n	80.6
E_y/E_n	75.7

Table 4: Average classification accuracy on the development set when treating each reference translation set as a boundary classifier.

generate very different translation boundaries. We can measure these differences in reference translations using the same evaluation metric (classification accuracy). We treat each reference translation set as a translation boundary classifier while the other three reference translation sets as gold standards. We calculate the classification accuracy for the current reference translation set and finally average all four accuracies. Table 4 presents the results.

Comparing Table 4 with Table 3, we can see that the accuracy of our translation boundary classification approach is not that low when considering vast divergences of reference translations. The question now becomes, how can classifier output be used to constrain phrase-based decoding, and what is the impact on the system performance of using such constraints.

4 Integrating Translation Boundaries into Decoding

By running the two trained classifiers on the source sentence separately, we obtain two classified word sets: B_y/B_n words, and E_y/E_n words. We can prohibit any translations or reorderings spanning $c_i...c_j$ ($j > i$) where $c_i \notin B_y$ according to the first classifier or $c_j \notin E_y$ according to the second classifier. In such a way, we integrate translation boundaries into phrase-based decoding as hard constraints, which, however, is at the risk of producing no translation covering the whole source sentence.

Alternatively, we introduce soft constraints based on translation boundary that our classifiers predict, similar to constituent boundary based soft constraints in (Cherry, 2008) and (Marton and Resnik, 2008). We add a new feature to the decoder's log-linear model: translation boundary violation counting feature. This counting feature accumulates whenever hypotheses have a partial translation spanning $c_i...c_j$ ($j > i$) where $c_i \notin B_y$ or $c_j \notin E_y$. The

LDC ID	Description
LDC2004E12	United Nations
LDC2004T08	Hong Kong News
LDC2005T10	Sinorama Magazine
LDC2003E14	FBIS
LDC2002E18	Xinhua News V1 beta
LDC2005T06	Chinese News Translation
LDC2003E07	Chinese Treebank
LDC2004T07	Multiple Translation Chinese

Table 5: Training corpora.

weight λ_v of this feature is tuned via minimal error rate training (MERT) (Och, 2003) with other feature weights.

Unlike hard constraints, which simply prevent any hypotheses from violating translation boundaries, soft constraints allow violations of translation boundaries but with a penalty of $\exp(-\lambda_v C_v)$ where C_v is the violation count. By using soft constraints, we can enable the model to prefer hypotheses which are consistent with translation boundaries.

5 Experiment

Our baseline system is a phrase-based system using BTGs (Wu, 1997), which includes a content-dependent reordering model discriminatively trained using reordering examples (Xiong et al., 2006). We carried out various experiments to evaluate the impact of integrating translation boundary based soft constraints into decoding on the system performance on the Chinese-to-English translation task of the NIST MT-05 using large scale training data.

5.1 Experimental Setup

Our training corpora are listed in Table 5. The whole corpora consist of 96.9M Chinese words and 109.5M English words in 3.8M sentence pairs. We ran GIZA++ (Och and Ney, 2000) on the parallel corpora in both directions and then applied the "grow-diag-final" refinement rule (Koehn et al., 2005) to obtain many-to-many word alignments. From the word-aligned corpora, we extracted bilingual phrases and trained our translation model.

We used all corpora in Table 5 except for the United Nations corpus to train our MaxEnt based reordering model (Xiong et al., 2006), which consist of 33.3M Chinese words and 35.8M English words. We built a four-gram language model using the SRILM toolkit (Stolcke, 2002), which was trained on Xinhua section of the English Gigaword corpus (181.1M words).

To train our translation boundary classifiers, we extract training instances from the whole word-aligned corpora, from which we obtain 96.9M training instances for the B_y/B_n and E_y/E_n classifier. We ran the off-the-shelf MaxEnt toolkit (Zhang, 2004) to tune classifier feature weights with Gaussian prior set to 1 to avoid overfitting.

We used the NIST MT-03 evaluation test data as our development set (919 sentences in total, 27.1 words per sentence). The NIST MT-05 test set includes 1082 sentences with an average of 27.4 words per sentence. Both the reference corpus for the NIST MT-03 set and the reference corpus for the NIST MT-05 set contain 4 translations per source sentence. To compare with constituent boundary based constraints, we parsed source sentences of both the development and test sets using a Chinese parser (Xiong et al., 2005) which was trained on the Penn Chinese Treebank with an F_1-score of 79.4%.

Our evaluation metric is case-insensitive BLEU-4 (Papineni et al., 2002) using the shortest reference sentence length for the brevity penalty. Statistical significance in BLEU score differences was tested by paired bootstrap re-sampling (Koehn, 2004).

5.2 Using Translation Boundaries from Reference Translations

The most direct way to investigate the impact on the system performance of using translation boundaries is to integrate "right" translation boundaries into decoding which are directly obtained from reference translations. For both the development set and test set, we have four reference translation sets, which are named ref1, ref2, ref3 and ref4, respectively. For the development set, we used translation boundaries obtained from ref1. Based on these boundaries, we built our translation boundary violation counting feature and tuned its feature weight with other features using MERT. When we obtained the best feature weights λs, we evaluated on the test set using translation boundaries produced from ref1, ref2, ref3 and ref4 of the test set respectively.

Table 6 shows the results. We clearly see that using "right" translation boundaries to build soft constraints significantly improve the performance measured by BLEU score. The best result comes from ref4, which achieves an absolute increase of 1.16 BLEU points over the baseline. We believe that the best result here only indicates the lower bound of potential improvement when using right translation boundaries. If we have consistent translation boundaries on the development and test set (for example, we have the same 4 translators build reference translations for both the development and test set), the performance improvement will be higher.

System	BLEU-4 (%)
Base	33.05
Ref1	33.99*
Ref2	34.17*
Ref3	33.93*
Ref4	34.21*

Table 6: Results of using translation boundaries obtained from reference translations. *: significantly better than baseline ($p < 0.01$).

5.3 Using Automatically Learned Translation Boundaries

The success of using translation boundaries from reference translations inspires us to pursue translation boundaries predicted by our MEMM based classifiers. We ran our MEMM1 (Markov order 1) and MEMM2 (Markov order 2) B_y/B_n and E_y/E_n classifiers on both the development and test set. Based on translation boundaries output by MEMM1 and MEMM2 classifiers, we built our translation boundary violation feature and tuned it on the development set. The evaluation results on the test set are shown in Table 7.

From Table 7 we observe that using soft constraints based on translation boundaries from both our MEMM 1 and MEMM 2 significantly outperform the baseline. Impressively, when using outputs from MEMM 2, we achieve an absolute improvement of almost 1 BLEU point over the baseline. This result is also very close to the best result of using translation boundaries from reference translations.

To compare with constituent boundary based syntactic constraints, we also carried out experiments using two kinds of such constraints. One is the

System	BLEU-4 (%)
Base	33.05
Condeducer	33.18
XP+	33.58*
BestRef	34.21*+
MEMM 1	33.70*
MEMM 2	34.04*+

Table 7: Results of using automatically learned translation boundaries. Condeducer means using pure constituent boundary based soft constraint. XP+ is another constituent boundary based soft constraint but with distinction among special constituent types (Marton and Resnik, 2008). BestRef is the best result using reference translation boundaries in Table 6. MEMM 1 and MEMM 2 are our MEMM based translation boundary classifiers with Markov order 1 and 2. *: significantly better than baseline ($p < 0.01$). +: significantly better than XP+ ($p < 0.01$).

Condeducer which uses pure constituent boundary based syntactic constraint: any partial translations which cross any constituent boundaries will be penalized. The other is the XP+ from (Marton and Resnik, 2008) which only penalizes hypotheses which violate the boundaries of a constituent with a label from {NP, VP, CP, IP, PP, ADVP, QP, LCP, DNP}. The XP+ is the best syntactic constraint among all constraints that Marton and Resnik (2008) use for Chinese-to-English translation.

Still in Table 7, we find that both syntactic constraint Condeducer and XP+ are better than the baseline. But only XP+ is able to obtain significant improvement. Both our MEMM 1 and MEMM 2 outperform Condeducer. MEMM 2 achieves significant improvement over XP+ by approximately 0.5 BLEU points. This comparison suggests that translation boundary is a better option than constituent boundary when we build constraints to restrict phrase-based decoding.

5.4 One Classifier vs. Two Classifiers

Revisiting the classification task in this paper, we can also consider it as a sequence labeling task where the first source word of a translation zone is labeled "B", the last source word of the translation zone is labeled "E", and other words are labeled "O". To complete such a sequence labeling task, we built only one classifier which is still based on MEMM (with Markov order 2) with the same features as described in Section 3.2. We built soft constraints based on the outputs of this classifier and evaluated them on the test set. The case-insensitive BLEU score is 33.62, which is lower than the performance of using two separate classifiers (34.04).

We calculated the accuracy for class "B" by mapping "B" to B_y and "E" and "O" to B_n. The result is 67.9%. Similarly, we obtained the accuracy of class "E", which is as low as 48.6%. These two accuracies are much lower than those of using two separate classifiers, especially the accuracy of "E". This suggests that the B_y and E_y are not interrelated tightly. It is better to learn them separately with two classifiers.

Another advantage of using two separate classifiers is that we can explore more constraints. A word c_k can be possibly labeled as B_y by the first classifier and E_y by the second classifier. Therefore we can build soft constraints on span (c_i, c_k) $(c_i \in B_y, c_k \in E_y)$ and span (c_k, c_j) $(c_k \in B_y, c_j \in E_y)$. This is impossible if we use only one classifier since each word can have only one class label. We can build only one constraint on span (c_i, c_k) or span (c_k, c_j).

6 Related Work

Various approaches incorporate constraints into phrase-based decoding in a soft or hard manner. Our introduction has already briefly mentioned (Cherry, 2008) and (Marton and Resnik, 2008), which utilize source-side parse tree boundary violation counting feature to build soft constraints for phrase-based decoding, and (Xiong et al., 2009), which calculates a score to indicate to what extent a source phrase can be translated as a unit using a bracketing model with richer syntactic features. More previously, (Chiang, 2005) rewards hypotheses whenever they exactly match constituent boundaries of parse trees on the source side.

In addition, hard linguistic constraints are also explored. (Wu and Ng, 1995) employs syntactic bracketing information to constrain search in order to improve speed and accuracy. (Collins et al., 2005) and (Wang et al., 2007) use hard syntactic constraints to perform reorderings according to source-side parse trees. (Xiong et al., 2008) prohibit any swappings which violate punctuation based constraints.

Non-linguistic constraints are also widely used in phrase-based decoding. The IBM and ITG constraints (Zens et al., 2004) are used to restrict reorderings in practical phrase-based systems.

(Berger et al., 1996) introduces the concept of *rift* into a machine translation system, which is similar to our definition of translation boundary. They also use a maximum entropy model to predict whether a source position is a rift based on features only from source sentences. Our work differs from (Berger et al., 1996) in three major respects.

1) We distinguish a segment boundary into two categories: beginning and ending boundary due to their different distributions (see Table 1). However, Berger et al. ignore this difference.

2) We train two classifiers to predict beginning and ending boundary respectively while Berger et al. build only one classifier. Our experiments show that two separate classifiers outperform one classifier.

3) The last difference is how segment boundaries are integrated into a machine translation system. Berger et al. use predicted rifts to divide a long source sentence into a series of smaller segments, which are then translated sequentially in order to increase decoding speed (Brown et al., 1992; Berger et al., 1996). This can be considered as a hard integration, which may undermine translation accuracy given wrongly predicted rifts. We integrate predicted translation boundaries into phrase-based decoding in a soft manner, which improves translation accuracy in terms of BLEU score.

7 Conclusion and Future Work

In this paper, we have presented a simple approach to learn translation boundaries on source sentences. The learned translation boundaries are used to constrain phrase-based decoding in a soft manner. The whole approach has several properties.

- First, it is based on a simple classification task that can achieve considerably high accuracy when taking translation divergences into account using simple models and features.
- Second, the classifier output can be straightforwardly used to constrain phrase-based decoder.
- Finally, we have empirically shown that, to build soft constraints for phrase-based decoding, translation boundary predicted by our classifier is a better choice than constituent boundary deduced from source-side parse tree.

Future work in this direction will involve trying different methods to define more informative translation boundaries, such as a boundary to begin/end a swapping. We would also like to investigate new methods to incorporate automatically learned translation boundaries more efficiently into decoding in an attempt to further improve search in both speed and accuracy.

References

Adam L. Berger, Stephen A. Della Pietra and Vincent J. Della Pietra. 1996. A Maximum Entropy Approach to Natural Language Processing. *Computational Linguistics*, 22(1):39-71.

Peter F. Brown, Stephen A. Della Pietra, Vincent J. Della Pietra, Robert L. Mercer, and Surya Mohanty. 1992. Dividing and Conquering Long Sentences in a Translation System. In *Proceedings of the workshop on Speech and Natural Language, Human Language Technology*.

Colin Cherry. 2008. Cohesive Phrase-based Decoding for Statistical Machine Translation. In *Proceedings of ACL*.

David Chiang. 2005. A Hierarchical Phrase-based Model for Statistical Machine Translation. In *Proceedings of ACL*, pages 263–270.

Michael Collins, Philipp Koehn and Ivona Kucerova. 2005. Clause Restructuring for Statistical Machine Translation. In *Proceedings of ACL*.

Kevin Knight. 1999. Decoding Complexity in Word Replacement Translation Models. In *Computational Linguistics*, 25(4):607 – 615.

Philipp Koehn, Franz Joseph Och, and Daniel Marcu. 2003. Statistical Phrase-based Translation. In *Proceedings of HLT-NAACL*.

Philipp Koehn. 2004. Statistical Significance Tests for Machine Translation Evaluation. In *Proceedings of EMNLP*.

Philipp Koehn, Amittai Axelrod, Alexandra Birch Mayne, Chris Callison-Burch, Miles Osborne and David Talbot. 2005. Edinburgh System Description for the 2005 IWSLT Speech Translation Evaluation. In *Proceedings of IWSLT*.

Yuval Marton and Philip Resnik. 2008. Soft Syntactic Constraints for Hierarchical Phrase-Based Translation. In *Proceedings of ACL.*

Andrew McCallum, Dayne Freitag and Fernando Pereira 2000. Maximum Entropy Markov Models for Information Extraction and Segmentation. In *Proceedings of the Seventeenth International Conference on Machine Learning 2000.*

Franz Josef Och and Hermann Ney. 2000. Improved Statistical Alignment Models. In *Proceedings of ACL 2000.*

Franz Josef Och. 2003. Minimum Error Rate Training in Statistical Machine Translation. In *Proceedings of ACL 2003.*

Kishore Papineni, Salim Roukos, Todd Ward and Wei-Jing Zhu. 2002. BLEU: a Method for Automatically Evaluation of Machine Translation. In *Proceedings of ACL 2002.*

Brian Roark and Kristy Hollingshead. 2008. Classifying Chart Cells for Quadratic Complexity Context-Free Inference. In *Proceedings of COLING 2008.*

Andreas Stolcke. 2002. SRILM - an Extensible Language Modeling Toolkit. In *Proceedings of International Conference on Spoken Language Processing*, volume 2, pages 901-904.

Chao Wang, Michael Collins and Philipp Koehn 2007. Chinese Syntactic Reordering for Statistical Machine Translation. In *Proceedings of EMNLP.*

Dekai Wu and Cindy Ng. 1995. Using Brackets to Improve Search for Statistical Machine Translation In *Proceedings of PACLIC-IO, Pacific Asia Conference on Language, Information and Computation.*

Dekai Wu. 1997. Stochastic Inversion Transduction Grammars and Bilingual Parsing of Parallel Corpora. *Computational Linguistics*, 23(3):377-403.

Deyi Xiong, Shuanglong Li, Qun Liu, Shouxun Lin, Yueliang Qian. 2005. Parsing the Penn Chinese Treebank with Semantic Knowledge. In *Proceedings of IJCNLP*, Jeju Island, Korea.

Deyi Xiong, Qun Liu and Shouxun Lin. 2006. Maximum Entropy Based Phrase Reordering Model for Statistical Machine Translation. In *Proceedings of ACL-COLING 2006.*

Deyi Xiong, Min Zhang, Ai Ti Aw, Haitao Mi, Qun Liu and Shouxun Lin. 2008. Refinements in BTG-based Statistical Machine Translation. In *Proceedings of IJCNLP 2008.*

Deyi Xiong, Min Zhang, Ai Ti Aw, and Haizhou Li. 2009. A Syntax-Driven Bracketing Model for Phrase-Based Translation. In *Proceedings of ACL-IJCNLP 2009.*

Richard Zens, Hermann Ney, Taro Watanabe and Eiichiro Sumita 2004. Reordering Constraints for Phrase-Based Statistical Machine Translation. In *Proceedings of COLING.*

Hao Zhang, Daniel Gildea, and David Chiang. 2008. Extracting Synchronous Grammars Rules from Word-Level Alignments in Linear Time. In *Proceeding of COLING 2008.*

Le Zhang. 2004. Maximum Entropy Modeling Tooklkit for Python and C++. Available at http://homepages.inf.ed.ac.uk/s0450736 /maxent_toolkit.html.

Hitting the Right Paraphrases in Good Time

Stanley Kok
Department of Computer Science & Engineering
University of Washington
Seattle, WA 98195, USA
koks@cs.washington.edu

Chris Brockett
Microsoft Research
One Microsoft Way
Redmond, WA 98052, USA
chrisbkt@microsoft.com

Abstract

We present a random-walk-based approach to learning paraphrases from bilingual parallel corpora. The corpora are represented as a graph in which a node corresponds to a phrase, and an edge exists between two nodes if their corresponding phrases are aligned in a phrase table. We sample random walks to compute the average number of steps it takes to reach a ranking of paraphrases with better ones being "closer" to a phrase of interest. This approach allows "feature" nodes that represent domain knowledge to be built into the graph, and incorporates truncation techniques to prevent the graph from growing too large for efficiency. Current approaches, by contrast, implicitly presuppose the graph to be bipartite, are limited to finding paraphrases that are of length two away from a phrase, and do not generally permit easy incorporation of domain knowledge. Manual evaluation of generated output shows that our approach outperforms the state-of-the-art system of Callison-Burch (2008).

1 Introduction

Automatically learning paraphrases, or alternative ways of expressing the same meaning, is an active area of NLP research because of its usefulness in a variety of applications, e.g., question answering (Lin and Pantel, 2001; Ravichandran and Hovy, 2002; Reizler et al., 2007), document summarization (Barzilay et al., 1999; McKeown et al., 2002), natural language generation (Iordanskaja et al., 1991; Lenke, 1994; Stede, 1999), machine translation (Kauchak and Barzilay, 2006; Callison-Burch et al., 2006; Madnani et al., 2007).

Early work on paraphrase acquisition has focused on using monolingual parallel corpora (Barzilay and McKeown, 2001; Barzilay and Lee, 2003; Pang et al., 2003; Quirk et al., 2004). While effective, such methods are hampered by the scarcity of monolingual parallel corpora, an obstacle that limits both the quantity and quality of the paraphrases learned. To address this limitation, Bannard and Callison-Burch (2005) focused their attention on the abundance of bilingual parallel corpora. The crux of this system (referred to below as "BCB") is to align phrases in a bilingual parallel corpus and hypothesize English phrases as potential paraphrases if they are aligned to the same phrase in another language (the "pivot"). Callison-Burch (2008) further refines BCB with a system that constrains paraphrases to have the same syntactic structure (Syntactic Bilingual Phrases: SBP).

We take a graphical view of the state-of-the-art BCB and SBP approaches by representing the bilingual parallel corpora as a graph. A node corresponds to a phrase, and an edge exists between two nodes if their corresponding phrases are aligned. This graphical form makes the limitations of the BCB/SBP approaches more evident. The BCB/SBP graph is limited to be bipartite with English nodes on one side and foreign language nodes on the other, and an edge can only exist between nodes on different sides. This neglects information between foreign language nodes that may aid in learning paraphrases. Further, by only considering English nodes that are linked via a foreign language node as potential paraphrases,

Human Language Technologies: The 2010 Annual Conference of the North American Chapter of the ACL, pages 145–153,
Los Angeles, California, June 2010.

these approaches will fail to find paraphrases separated by distances greater than length two.

In this paper, we present HTP (Hitting Time Paraphraser), a paraphrase learning approach that is based on random walks (Lovász, 1996) and hitting times (Aldous and Fill, 2001). Hitting time measures the average number of steps one needs to take in a random traversal of a graph before reaching a destination node from a source node. Intuitively, the smaller the hitting time from a phrase E to E' (i.e., the closer E' is to E), the more likely it is that E' is a good paraphrase of E. The advantages of HTP are as follows:

- By traversing paths of lengths greater than two, our approach is able to find more paraphrases of a given phrase.
- We do not require the graph to be bipartite. Edges can exist between nodes of different foreign languages if their corresponding phrases are aligned. This allows information from foreign phrase alignments to be used in finding English paraphrases.
- We permit domain knowledge to be easily incorporated as nodes in the graph. This allows domain knowledge to favor good paraphrases over bad ones, thereby improving performance.

In this paper, we focus on learning English paraphrases. However, our system can be applied to learning paraphrases in any language.

We begin by reviewing random walks and hitting times in the next section. Then we describe our paraphrase learning algorithm (Section 3), and report our experiments (Section 4). We discuss related work in Section 5. Finally, we conclude with future work (Section 6).

2 Background

A directed graph consists of a set of nodes V, and a set of edges E. A directed edge is a pair (i, j) where $i, j \in V$. Associated with the graph is a $|V| \times |V|$ adjacency matrix W. Each entry W_{ij} in the matrix is the weight of edge (i, j), or zero if the edge does not exist.

In a *random walk* (Lovász, 1996), we traverse from node to node via the edges. Suppose at time step t, we are at node i. In the next step, we move to its neighbor j with probability proportional to the weight of the edge (i, j), i.e., with probability $W_{ij}/\sum_j W_{ij}$. This probability is known as the *transition probability* from i to j. Note that the transition probabilities from a node to its neighbors sum to 1.

The *hitting time* h_{ij} (Aldous and Fill, 2001) from node i to j is defined as the average number of steps one takes in a random walk starting from i to visit j for the first time. Hitting time has the property of being robust to noise. This is a desirable property for our system which works on bilingual parallel corpora containing numerous spurious alignments between phrases (i.e., edges between nodes). However, as observed by Liben-Nowell and Kleinberg (2003), *hitting time* has the drawback of being sensitive to portions of the graph that are far from the start node because it considers paths of length up to ∞.

To circumvent this problem, Sarkar and Moore (2007) introduced the notion of *truncated* hitting time where random walks are limited to have at most T steps. The truncated hitting time h^T_{ij} from node i to j is defined as the average number of steps one takes to reach j for the first time starting from i in a random walk that is limited to at most T steps. h^T_{ij} is defined to be 0 if $i = j$ or $T = 0$, and to be T if j is not reach in T steps. As $T \to \infty$, $h^T_{ij} \to h_{ij}$.

In a recent work, Sarkar et al. (2008) showed that truncated hitting time can be approximated accurately with high probability by sampling. They run M independent length-T random walks from node i. In m of these runs, node j is visited for the first time at time steps $t^1_j, \ldots, t^m_j$. The *estimated* truncated hitting time is given by

$$\hat{h}^T_{ij} = \frac{\sum_{k=1}^{m} t^k_j}{M} + (1 - \frac{m}{M})T \tag{1}$$

They also showed that the number of samples of random walks M has to be at least $\frac{1}{2\epsilon^2} \log \frac{2n}{d}$ in order for the estimated truncated hitting time to be a good estimate of the actual truncated hitting time with high probability, i.e., for $P(|\hat{h}^T_{ij} - h^T_{ij}| \leq \epsilon T) \geq 1 - \delta$, where n is the number of nodes in the graph, ϵ and δ are user-specified parameters, and $0 \leq \epsilon, \delta \leq 1$.

3 Hitting Time Paraphraser (HTP)

HTP takes a *query* phrase as input, and outputs a list of paraphrases, with better paraphrases at the top of

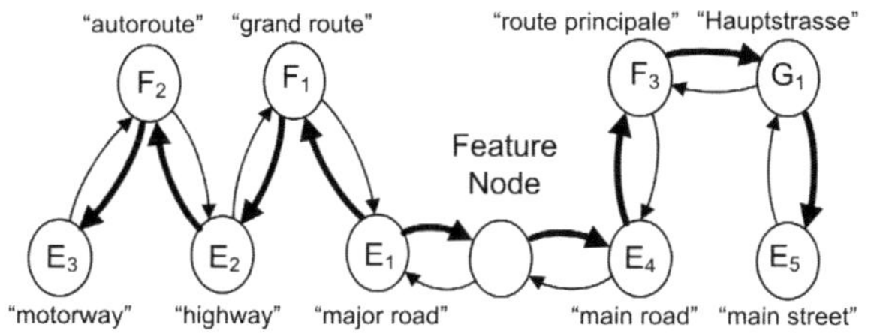

Figure 1: Graph created from English-French (E-F), English-German (E-G), and French-German (F-G) bilingual parallel corpora. Bold edges have large positive weights (high transition probabilities).

the list. HTP also requires as input a set of bilingual parallel corpora that have been processed into phrase tables of the kind used in statistical machine translation.

A bilingual parallel corpus is made up of sentences in two languages. Two sentences that are translations of one another are paired together, and a phrase in one sentence is aligned with a phrase in the other with the same meaning. From such alignments, we can count for a phrase E both the number of times it occurs ($Count_E$), and the number of times it is aligned with a phrase F in the other language ($Count_{E,F}$). With these counts we can estimate the probability of F given E as $P(F|E) = \frac{Count_{E,F}}{Count_E}$.

HTP represents the aligned phrases as a graph. A node corresponds to a phrase, and a directed edge exists from node i to j if their corresponding phrases are aligned. The weight of edge (i, j) is given by $P(j|i)$ which is computed as described in the previous paragraph.

Figure 1 gives an example of a graph created from English-French, English-German, and French-German parallel corpora. We use this figure to illustrate the strengths of HTP. First, by using moderately long random walks, HTP is able to find paraphrases that are separated by long paths. For example, there is a high probability path of length 4 $(E_1, F_1, E_2, F_2, E_3)$ from E_1 to E_3. Because of the path's high probability, it will appear in many of the random walks starting from E_1 that are sampled on the graph, and thus E_3 will be visited in many of the samples. This causes the truncated hitting time $h^T_{E_1 E_3}$ to be small, allowing HTP to find E_3 as a plausible paraphrase of E_1. Second, by allowing edges between nodes of different foreign languages

Table 1: The HTP algorithm.

---

function $HTP(E, C, d, n, m, T, \delta, l)$
  input: E, query phrase
    C, tables of aligned phrases
    d, maximum distance of nodes from E
    n, maximum number of nodes in graph
    m, number of samples of random walks
    T, maximum number of steps taken by a random walk
    δ, probability that estimated truncated hitting time deviates from actual value by a large margin (see Equation 1)
    l, number of top outgoing edges to select at each node in a random walk
  output: $(E'_1, \ldots, E'_k)$, paraphrases of E ranked in order of increasing hitting times
  calls: $CreateGraph(E, C, d, n)$ creates graph G from C containing at most n nodes that are at most d steps from E
    $EstimateHitTimes(E, G, m, T, \delta)$, estimates the truncated hitting times of each node in G by running m random walks
    $PruneNodes((E_1, \ldots, E_k), G)$, removes nodes from G if their hitting times is equal to T.
    $AddFeatureNodes(G)$, adds nodes representing domain knowledge to G

$G \leftarrow CreateGraph(E, C, d, n)$
$(E_1, \ldots, E_k) \leftarrow EstimateHitTimes(E, G, m, T, \delta)$
$G' \leftarrow PruneNodes((E_1, \ldots, E_k), G)$
$G'' \leftarrow AddFeatureNodes(G')$
$(E'_1, \ldots, E'_k) \leftarrow EstimateHitTimes(E, G'', m, T, \delta)$
return $(E'_1, \ldots, E'_k)$

(i.e., by not requiring the graph to be bipartite), HTP allows strong correlation between foreign language nodes to aid in finding paraphrases. In the figure, even though E_4 and E_5 are not linked via a common foreign language node, there is a high probability path linking them (E_4, F_3, G_1, E_5). This allows HTP to find E_5 as a reasonable paraphrase of E_4. Third, HTP enables domain knowledge to be incorporated as nodes in the graph. For example, we could incorporate the domain knowledge that phrases with lots of unigrams in common are likely to be paraphrases. In Figure 1, the "feature" node represents such knowledge, linking E_4 and E_1 as possible paraphrases even though they have no foreign language nodes in common. Note that such domain knowledge nodes can be linked to arbitrary nodes, not just English ones.

The HTP algorithm is shown in Table 1. It takes as input a query phrase and a set of bilingual phrase tables. The algorithm begins by creating a graph from the phrase tables. Then it estimates the truncated hitting times of each node from the query node by sampling random walks of length T. Next it prunes nodes (and their associated edges) if their truncated hitting times are equal to T. To the resulting graph, it then adds nodes representing domain knowledge and estimates the truncated hitting times of the nodes by sampling random walks as before. Finally, it returns the nodes in the same language as the query phrase in order of increasing hitting times.

3.1 Graph Creation

An obvious approach to creating a graph from bilingual parallel corpora is to create a node for every phrase in the corpora, and two directed edges (i, j) and (j, i) for every aligned phrase pair i and j. Let H refer to the graph that is created in this manner. Such an approach is only tractable for small bilingual parallel corpora that would result in a small H, but not for large corpora containing millions of sentences, such as those described in Section 4.1. Therefore we approximate H with a graph H' that only contains nodes "near" to the node representing the query phrase. Specifically, we perform breadth-first search starting from the query node up to a depth d, or until the number of nodes visited in the search has reached a maximum of n nodes. Some nodes at the periphery of H' have edges to nodes that are not in H' but are in H. For a periphery node j that has edges to nodes $j_1, \ldots, j_k$ outside H', we create a "dummy" node a, and replace edges $(j, j_1), \ldots, (j, j_k)$ with a single edge (j, a) with weight $\sum_{x=1}^{k} W_{j,j_x}$. We also add edges (a, j) and (a, a) (each with a heuristic weight of 0.5). The dummy nodes and their edges approximate the transition probabilities at H''s periphery. Our empirical results show that this approximation works well in practice.

3.2 Graph Pruning

After H' is created, we run M independent length-T random walks on it starting from the query node to estimate the truncated hitting times of all nodes.

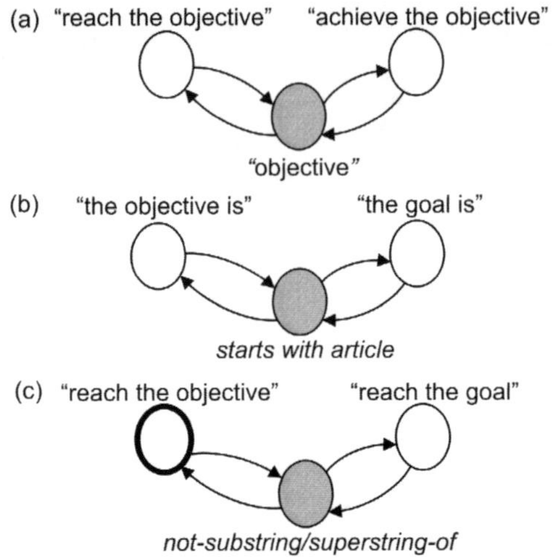

Figure 2: Feature nodes representing domain knowledge. Feature nodes are shaded. The bold node represents a query phrase. (a) n-gram nodes (b) "syntax" nodes (c) "not-substring/superstring-of" nodes.

A node in H' may have many outgoing edges, most of which may be due to spurious phrase alignments. For efficiency, and to reduce the noise due to spurious edges, we select among a node's top l outgoing edges with the highest transition probabilities, when deciding which node to visit next at each step of a random walk

For each random walk k, we record the first time that a node j is visited t_j^k. Using Equation 1, we estimate the truncated hitting time of each node. Then we remove nodes (and their associated edges) that are far from the query node, i.e., with times equal to T. Such nodes either are not visited in any of the random walks, or are always visited for the first time at step T.

3.3 Adding Domain Knowledge

Next we add nodes representing domain knowledge to the pruned graph. In this version of HTP, we implemented three types of *feature nodes*.

First, we have *n-gram nodes*. These nodes capture the domain knowledge that phrases containing many words in common are likely to be paraphrases. For each 1 to 4-gram that appears in English phrases, we create an n-gram node a. We add directed edges (a, j) and (j, a) if node j represents an English phrase containing n-gram a. For example, in Figure 2(a), "reach the objective" is connected to "objective" because it contains that unigram. Note that such nodes create short paths between nodes with many n-grams in common, thereby reducing the hitting times between them.

Second, we have *"syntax" nodes*, which represent syntactic classes of the start and end words of English phrases. We created classes such as *interrogatives* ("whose", "what", "where", etc.), *articles* ("the", "a", "an"), etc. For each class c, we create syntax nodes a_c and a'_c to respectively represent the conditions that a phrase begins and ends with a word in class c. Directed edges (a_c, j) and (j, a_c) are added if node j starts with a word in class c (similarly we add (a'_c, j) and (j, a'_c) if it ends with a word in class c). For example, in Figure 2(b), "the objective is" is linked to "starts with *article*" because it begins with "the". These syntax nodes allow HTP to capture broad commonalities about structural distribution, without requiring syntactic equivalence as in Callison-Burch 2008 (or the use of a parser).

Third, we have *"not-substring/superstring-of" nodes*. We observed that many English phrases (e.g., "reach the objective" and "reach the") that are superstrings or substrings of each other tend to be aligned to several shared non-English phrases in the bilingual parallel corpora used in our experiments. Most such English phrase pairs are not paraphrases, but they are linked by many short paths via their common aligned foreign phrase, and thus have small hitting times. To counteract this, we create a "not-substring/superstring-of" node a. The query node i is always connected to a via edges (i, a) and (a, i). We add edges (a, j) and (j, a) if English phrase j is not a substring or superstring of the query phrase (see Figure 2(c)).

With the addition of the above, each node representing an English phrase can have four kinds of outgoing edges: edges to foreign phrase nodes, and edges to the three kinds of feature nodes. Let $f_{phrase}, f_{ngram}, f_{syntax}, f_{substring}$ denote the distribution of transition probabilities among the four kinds of outgoing edges. Note that $f_{phrase} + f_{ngram} + f_{syntax} + f_{substring} = 1.0$. These values are user-specified or can be set with tuning data. An outgoing edge from English phrase node i that originally had weight (transition probability) W_{ij} will now have weight $W_{ij} \times f_{phrase}$. All k edges from i to n-gram nodes will have weight $\frac{f_{ngram}}{k}$. Likewise for edges to the other two kinds of feature nodes. Each of the k outgoing edges from a feature node is simply set to have a weight of $\frac{1}{k}$.

After adding the feature nodes, we again run M independent length-T random walks to estimate the truncated hitting times of the nodes, and return the English phrase nodes in order of increasing hitting times.

4 Experiments

We conducted experiments to investigate how HTP compares with the state of the art, and to evaluate the contributions of its components.

4.1 Dataset

We used the Europarl dataset (Koehn, 2005) for our experiments. This dataset contains English transcripts of the proceedings of the European Parliament, and their translations into 10 other European languages. In the dataset, there are about a million sentences per language, and English sentences are aligned with sentences in the other languages. Callison-Burch (2008) aligned English phrases with phrases in each of the other languages using Giza++ (Och and Ney, 2004). We used his English-foreign phrasal alignments which are publicly available on the web at http://ironman.jhu.edu/emnlp08.tar. In addition, we paired sentences of different non-English languages that correspond to the same English sentence, and aligned the phrases using 5 iterations of IBM model 1 in each direction, followed by 5 iterations of HMM alignment with paired training using the algorithm described in Liang et al. (2006). We further used the technique of Chen et al. (2009) to remove a phrase alignment F-G (where F and G are phrases in different foreign languages) if it was always aligned to different phrases in a third "bridge" foreign language. As observed by Chen et al., this helped to remove spurious alignments. We used Finnish as the bridge language; when either F or G is Finnish, we used Spanish as the bridge language; when F and G were Finnish and Spanish, we used English as the bridge language. In our experiments, we used phrases of length 1 to 4 of the following six languages: English, Danish, German, Spanish, Finnish, and Dutch. All the phrasal alignments between each pair of languages (15 in total) were used as input to HTP and its comparison systems. A small subset of the remaining phrase alignments were used for tuning parameters.

4.2 Systems

We compared HTP to the state-of-the-art SBP system (Callison-Burch, 2008). We also investigated the contribution of the feature nodes by running HTP without them. In addition, we ran HTP on a bipartite graph, i.e., one created from English-foreign phrase alignments only without any phrase alignments between foreign languages.

We used Callison-Burch (2008)'s implementation of SBP that is publicly available at http://ironman.jhu.edu/emnlp08.tar. SBP is based on BCB (Bannard and Callison- Burch, 2005) which computes the probability that English phrase E' is a paraphrase of E using the following formula:

$$P(E'|E) \approx \sum_{C \in \mathcal{C}} \sum_{F \in C} P(E'|F)P(F|E) \quad (2)$$

where $\mathcal{C}$ is set of bilingual parallel corpora, and F is a foreign language phrase. Representing phrases as nodes, and viewing $P(E'|F)$ and $P(F|E)$ as transition probabilities of edges (F, E') and (E, F), we see that BCB is summing over the transition probabilities of all length-two paths between E and E'. All E' paraphrases of E can then be ranked in order of decreasing probability as given by Equation 2. The SBP system modifies Equation 2 to incorporate syntactic information, thus:

$$P(E'|E) \approx \frac{1}{|\mathcal{C}|} \sum_{C \in \mathcal{C}} \sum_{F \in C} P(E'|F, syn_E))P(F|E, syn_E) \quad (3)$$

where syn_E is the syntax of phrase E, and $P(E'|F, syn_E)) = 0$ if E' is not of the same syntactic category. From Equation 3, we can see that SBP constrains E' to have the same syntactic structure as E. To obtain the syntactic structure of each English phrase, each English sentence in every parallel corpus has to be parsed to obtain its parse tree. An English phrase can have several syntactic structures because different parse trees can have the phrase as their leaves, and in each of these, SBP associates the phrase with all subtrees that have the phrase as their leaves. SBP thus offers several ways of choosing which syntactic structure a phrase should be associated with. In our experiments, we used the best performing method of averaging Equation 3 over all syntactic structures that E is associated with.

Table 2: Scoring Standards.

0	Clearly wrong; grammatically incorrect, or does not preserve meaning
1	Minor grammatical errors (e.g., subject-verb disagreement or wrong tense), or meaning is largely preserved but not completely
2	Totally correct; grammatically correct and meaning is preserved

4.3 Methodology

To evaluate performance, we used 33,216 English translations from the Linguistic Data Consortium's Multiple Translation Chinese (MTC) corpora (Huang et al., 2002). We randomly selected 100 1- to 4-grams that appeared in both Europarl and MTC sentences (excluding stop words, numbers, and phrases containing periods and commas). For each of those 100 phrases, we randomly selected a MTC sentence containing that phrase. We then replaced the phrase in the sentence with each paraphrase output by the systems, and evaluated the correctness of the paraphrase in the context of the sentence. We had two volunteers manually score the paraphrases on a 3-point scale (Table 2), using a simplified version of the scoring system used by Callison-Burch (2008). We deemed a paraphrase to be correct if it was scored 1 or 2, and wrong if it was scored 0. Evaluation was blind, and the paraphrases were presented randomly to the volunteers. The Kappa measure of inter-annotator agreement was 0.62, which indicates substantial agreement between the evaluators. We took the average score for each paraphrase.

The parameters used for HTP were as follows (see Table 1 for parameter descriptions): $d = 6, n = 50,000, m = 1,000,000, T = 10, \delta = 0.05, l = 20$, $f_{phrase} = 0.1$, $f_{ngram} = 0.1$, $f_{syntax} = 0.4$, $f_{substring} = 0.4$. ($\epsilon \leq 0.03$ with these values of n, m, T, and δ.)

Table 3: HTP vs. SBP.

	HTP	SBP
Correct top-1 paraphrases	71%	53%
Correct top-k paraphrases	54%	39%
Count of correct paraphrases	420	145
Correct paraphrases	43%	39%

Table 4: HTP vs. HTP without feature nodes.

	HTP	HTP-NoFeatNodes
Correct top-1 paraphrases	61%	41%
Correct top-k paraphrases	43%	29%
Count of correct paraphrases	420	283
Correct paraphrases	43%	29%

4.4 Results

HTP versus SBP. Comparison between HTP and SBP is complicated by the fact that the two systems did not output the same number of paraphrases for the 100 query phrases. HTP output paraphrases for all the query phrases, but SBP only did so for 49 query phrases. Of those 49 query phrases, HTP returned at least as many paraphrases as SBP, and for many it returned more.

To provide a fair comparison, we present results both for these 49 query phrases, and for all paraphrases returned by each of the systems. The upper half of Table 3 shows results for the 49 query phrases. The first row of Table 3 reports the percentage of top-1 paraphrases from this set that are correct, while the second row reports the percentage of correct top-k paraphrases from this set, where k is the number of queries returned by SBP, and is limited to at most 10. The value of k may differ for each query: if SBP and HTP return 3 and 20 paraphrases respectively, we only consider the top 3. On the third and fourth rows, we present the number of correct paraphrases and the percentage of correct paraphrases among the top 10 paraphrases returned by HTP for all 100 queries and the corresponding figures for the 49 queries for SBP. (When a system returned fewer than 10 paraphrases for a query, we consider all the paraphrases for that query.) It is evident from Table 3 that HTP consistently outperforms SBP: not only does it return more correct paraphrases overall (420 versus 145), it also has higher precision (43% versus 39%)

HTP and SBP respectively took 48 and 468 seconds per query on a 3 GHz machine. The times are not directly comparable because the systems are implemented in different languages (HTP in C# and SBP in Java), and use different data structures.

HTP without Feature Nodes. Both HTP and HTP minus feature nodes output paraphrases for each of the 100 query phrases. Table 4 compares performance in the same manner as in Table 3, except that the "top-1" and "top-k" results are over all 100 query phrases. We see that feature nodes boost HTP's performance, allowing HTP to return more correct paraphrases (420 versus 283), and at higher precision (43% versus 29%).

HTP with Bipartite Graph. Lastly, we investigate the contribution of alignments between foreign phrases to HTP's performance. HTP-Bipartite refers to HTP that is given a set consisting only of English-foreign phrase alignment as input. HTP-Bipartite does not return paraphrases for 5 query phrases. Thus, in Table 5, the "top-1" and "top-k" results are for the 95 query phrases for which both systems return paraphrases. From the better performance of HTP, we see that the foreign phrase alignments help in finding English paraphrases.

Table 5: HTP vs. HTP with bipartite graph.

	HTP	HTP-Bipartite
Correct top-1 paraphrases	62%	58%
Correct top-k paraphrases	46%	41%
Count of correct paraphrases	420	361
Correct paraphrases	43%	41%

5 Related Work

Random walks and hitting times have been successfully applied to a variety of applications. Brand (2005) has used hitting times for collaborative filtering, in which product recommendations to users are made based on purchase history. In computer vision, hitting times have been used to determine object shape from silhouettes (Gorelick et al., 2004), and for image segmentation (Grady and Schwartz, 2006). In social network analysis, Liben-Nowell and Kleinberg (2003) have investigated the use of hitting times for predicting relationships between entities. Recently, Mei et al. (2008) have used the hitting times of nodes in a bipartite graph created from search engine query logs to find related queries. They used an iterative algorithm to compute the hitting time, which converges slowly on large graphs. In HTP, we have sought to obviate this issue by using *truncated* hitting time that can be computed efficiently by sampling random walks.

Several approaches have been proposed to learn paraphrases. Barzilay and Mckeown (2001) acquire paraphrases from a monolingual parallel corpus using a co-training algorithm. Their co-trained classifier determines whether two phrases are paraphrases of one another using their surrounding contexts. Lin and Pantel (2001) learn paraphrases using the distributional similarity of paths in dependency trees. Ibrahim et al. (2003) generalize syntactic paths in aligned monolingual sentence pairs in order to generate paraphrases. Pang et al. (2003) merge parse trees of monolingual sentence pairs, and then compress the merged tree into a word lattice that can subsequently be used to generate paraphrases. Recently, Zhao et al. (2008) used dependency parses to learn paraphrase patterns that include part-of-speech slots. In other recent work, Das and Smith (2009) use a generative model for paraphrase detection. Rather than outputing paraphrases of an input phrase, their system detects whether two input sentences are paraphrases of one another.

6 Conclusion and Future Work

We have introduced HTP, a novel approach based on random walks and hitting times for the learning of paraphrases from bilingual parallel corpora. HTP works by converting aligned phrases into a graph, and finding paraphrases that are "close" to a phrase of interest. Compared to previous approaches, HTP is able to find more paraphrases by traversing paths of lengths longer than 2; utilizes information in the edges between foreign phrase nodes; and allows domain knowledge to be easily incorporated. Empirical results show its effectiveness in learning new paraphrases.

As future work, we plan to learn the distribution of weights on edges to phrase nodes and feature nodes automatically from data, rather than tuning them manually, and to develop a probabilistic model supporting HTP. We intend also to apply HTP to learning paraphrases in languages other than English and investigate the impact of the learned paraphrases on resource-sparse machine translation systems.

Acknowledgments

This work was done while the first author was an intern at Microsoft Research. We would like to thank Xiaodong He, Jianfeng Gao, Chris Quirk, Kristina Toutanova, Bob Moore, and other members of the MSR NLP group, along with Dengyong Zhou (TMSN) for their insightful comments and assistance in the course of this project.

References

David Aldous and Jim Fill. 2001. *Reversible Markov Chains and Random Walks on Graphs.* http://www.stat.berkeley.edu/~aldous/RWG/book.html.

Colin Bannard and Chris Callison-Burch. 2005. Paraphrasing with bilingual parallel corpora. In *Proceedings of the 43rd Annual Meeting of the ACL*, pages 597–604.

Regina Barzilay and Lillian Lee. 2003. Learning to paraphrase: an unsupervised approach using multiple-sequence alignment. In *Proceedings of HLT/NAACL*, pages 16–23.

Regina Barzilay and Kathleen McKeown. 2001. Extracting paraphrases from a parallel corpus. In *Proceedings of the 39th Annual Meeting of the ACL*, pages 50–57.

Regina Barzilay, Kathleen McKeown, and Michael Elhadad. 1999. Information fusion in the context of multi-document summarization. In *Proceedings of the 37th Annual Meeting of the ACL*, pages 550–557.

Matthew Brand. 2005. A random walks perspective on maximizing satisfaction and profit. In *Proceedings of the 8th SIAM Conference on Optimization.*

Chris Callison-Burch, Philipp Koehn, and Miles Osborne. 2006. Improved statistical machine translation using paraphrases. In *Proceedings of HLT/NAACL*, pages 17–24.

Chris Callison-Burch. 2008. Syntactic constraints on paraphrases extracted from parallel corpora. In *Proceedings of EMNLP*, pages 196–205.

Yu Chen, Martin Kay, and Andreas Eisele. 2009. Intersecting multilingual data for faster and better statistical translations. In *Proceedings of HLT/NAACL.*

Dipanjan Das and Noah A. Smith. 2009. Paraphrase identification as probabilistic quasi-synchronous recognition. In *Proceedings of the Joint Conference of the Annual Meeting of the Association for Computational Linguistics and the International Joint Conference on Natural Language Processing.*

Lena Gorelick, Meirav Galun, Eitan Sharon, Ronen Basri, and Achi Brandt. 2004. Shape representation and classification using the Poisson equation. In *Proceedings of the Conference on Computer Vision and Pattern Recognition.*

Leo Grady and Eric L. Schwartz. 2006. Isoperimetric graph partitioning for image segmentation. *IEEE Transactions on Pattern Analysis and Machine Intelligence*, 28:469–475.

Shudong Huang, David Graff, and George Doddington. 2002. Multiple-translation Chinese corpus. Linguistic Data Consortium, Philadelphia.

Ali Ibrahim, Boris Katz, and Jimmy Lin. 2003. Extracting structural paraphrases from aligned monolingual corpora. In *Proceedings of the 2nd International Workshop on Paraphrasing*, pages 57–64.

Lidija Iordanskaja, Richard Kittredge, and Alain Polguère. 1991. Lexical selection and paraphrase in a meaning-text generation model. In Cécile L. Paris, William R. Swartout, and William C. Mann, editors, *Natural Language Generation in Artificial Intelligence and Computational Linguistics*. Kluwer Academic.

David Kauchak and Regina Barzilay. 2006. Paraphrasing for automatic evaluation. In *Proceedings of HLT/NAACL*, pages 455–462.

Philipp Koehn. 2005. Europarl: A parallel corpus for statistical machine translation. In *Proceedings of the 10th Machine Translation Summit.*

Nils Lenke. 1994. Anticipating the reader's problems and the automatic generation of paraphrases. In *Proceedings of the 15th Conference on Computational Linguistics*, pages 319–323.

Percy Liang, Ben Taskar, and Dan Klein. 2006. Alignment by agreement. In *Proceedings of HLT/NAACL*, pages 104–111.

David Liben-Nowell and Jon Kleinberg. 2003. The link prediction problem for social networks. In *Proceedings of the 12th International Conference on Information and Knowledge*, pages 556–559.

Dekang Lin and Patrick Pantel. 2001. Discovery of inference rules for question answering. In *Proceedings of ACM SIGKDD Conference on Knowledge Discovery and Data Mining*, pages 323–328.

László Lovász. 1996. Random walks on graphs: A survey. In D. Miklós, V. T. Sós, and T. Szőnyi, editors, *Combinatorics, Paul Erdős is Eighty, Vol. 2*, pages 353–398.

Nitin Madnani, Necip Fazil Ayan, Philip Resnik, and Bonnie J. Dorr. 2007. Using paraphrases for parameter tuning in statistical machine translation. In *Proceedings of the 2nd Workshop on Statistical Machine Translation*, pages 120–127.

Kathleen R. McKeown, Regina Barzilay, David Evans, Vasileios Hatzivassiloglou, Judith L. Klavans, Ani Nenkova, Carl Sable, Barry Schiffman, and Sergey Sigelman. 2002. Tracking and summarizing news on a daily basis with Columbia's Newsblaster. In *Proceedings of the 2nd International Conference on HLT Research*, pages 280–285.

Qiaozhu Mei, Dengyong Zhou, and Kenneth Church. 2008. Query suggestion using hitting time. In *Proceeding of the 17th ACM Conference on Information and Knowledge Management*, pages 469–478.

Franz J. Och and Hermann Ney. 2004. The alignment template approach to statistical machine translation. *Computational Linguistics*, 30:417–449.

Bo Pang, Kevin Knight, and Daniel Marcu. 2003. Syntax-based alignment of multiple translations: Extracting paraphrases and generating new sentences. In *Proceedings of HLT/NAACL*, pages 102–109.

Chris Quirk, Chris Brockett, and William B. Dolan. 2004. Monolingual machine translation for paraphrase generation. In *Proceedings of EMNLP*, pages 142–149.

Deepak Ravichandran and Eduard Hovy. 2002. Learning surface text patterns for a question answering system. In *Proceedings of the 40th Annual Meeting of the ACL*, pages 41–47.

Stefan Reizler, Alexander Vasserman, Ioannis Tsochantaridis, Vibhu Mittal, and Yi Liu. 2007. Statistical machine translation for query expansion in answer retrieval. In *Proceedings of the 45th Annual Meeting of the ACL.*

Purnamrita Sarkar and Andrew W. Moore. 2007. A tractable approach to finding closest truncated-commute-time neighbors in large graphs. In *Proceedings of the 23th Conference on Uncertainty in Artificial Intelligence.*

Purnamrita Sarkar, Andrew W. Moore, and Amit Prakash. 2008. Fast incremental proximity search in large graphs. In *Proceedings of the 25th International Conference on Machine Learning.*

Manfred Stede. 1999. *Lexical Semantics and Knowledge Representation in Multilingual Text Generation.* Kluwer Academic Publishers.

Shiqi Zhao, Haifeng Wang, Ting Liu, and Sheng Li. 2008. Pivot approach for extracting paraphrase patterns from bilingual corpora. In *Proceedings of ACL.*

Training Paradigms for Correcting Errors in Grammar and Usage

Alla Rozovskaya and Dan Roth
University of Illinois at Urbana-Champaign
Urbana, IL 61801
{rozovska,danr}@illinois.edu

Abstract

This paper proposes a novel approach to the problem of training classifiers to detect and correct grammar and usage errors in text by selectively introducing mistakes into the training data. When training a classifier, we would like the distribution of examples seen in training to be as similar as possible to the one seen in testing. In error correction problems, such as correcting mistakes made by second language learners, a system is generally trained on correct data, since annotating data for training is expensive. Error generation methods avoid expensive data annotation and create training data that resemble non-native data with errors.

We apply error generation methods and train classifiers for detecting and correcting article errors in essays written by non-native English speakers; we show that training on data that contain errors produces higher accuracy when compared to a system that is trained on clean native data. We propose several training paradigms with error generation and show that each such paradigm is superior to training a classifier on native data. We also show that the most successful error generation methods are those that use knowledge about the article distribution and error patterns observed in non-native text.

1 Introduction

This paper considers the problem of training classifiers to detect and correct errors in grammar and word usage in text. Both native and non-native speakers make a variety of errors that are not always easy to detect. Consider, for example, the problem of context-sensitive spelling correction (e.g., (Golding and Roth, 1996; Golding and Roth, 1999; Carlson et al., 2001)). Unlike spelling errors that result in non-words and are easy to detect, context-sensitive spelling correction task involves correcting spelling errors that result in legitimate words, such as confusing *peace* and *piece* or *your* and *you're*. The typical training paradigm for these context-sensitive ambiguities is to use text assumed to be error free, replacing each target word occurrence (e.g. *peace*) with a *confusion set* consisting of, say {*peace, piece*}, thus generating both positive and negative examples, respectively, from the same context.

This paper proposes a novel error generation approach to the problem of training classifiers for the purpose of detecting and correcting grammar and usage errors in text. Unlike previous work (e.g., (Sjöbergh and Knutsson, 2005; Brockett et al., 2006; Foster and Andersen, 2009)), we selectively introduce mistakes in an appropriate proportion. In particular, to create training data that closely resemble text with naturally occurring errors, we use error frequency information and error distribution statistics obtained from corrected non-native text. We apply the method to the problem of detecting and correcting article mistakes made by learners of English as a Second Language (ESL).

The problem of correcting article errors is generally viewed as that of article *selection*, cast as a classification problem and is trained as described above: a machine learning algorithm is used to train a classifier on native English data, where the possible selections are used to generate positive and negative

Human Language Technologies: The 2010 Annual Conference of the North American Chapter of the ACL, pages 154–162,
Los Angeles, California, June 2010.

examples (e.g., (Izumi et al., 2003; Han et al., 2006; De Felice and Pulman, 2008; Gamon et al., 2008)). The classifier is then applied to non-native text to predict the correct article in context. But the article *correction* problem differs from the problem of article selection in that we know the original (*source*) article that the writer used. When proposing a correction, we would like to use information about the original article. One reason for this is that about 90% of articles are used correctly by ESL learners; this is higher than the performance of state-of-the-art classifiers for article selection. Consequently, not using the writer's article, when making a prediction, may result in making more mistakes than there are in the data. Another reason is that statistics on article errors (e.g., (Han et al., 2006; Lee and Seneff, 2008)) and in the annotation performed for the present study reveal that non-native English speakers make article mistakes in a consistent manner.

The system can consider the article used by the writer at evaluation time, by proposing a correction only when the confidence of the classifier is high enough, but the article cannot be used in training if the classifier is trained on clean native data that do not have errors. Learning Theory says that the distribution of examples seen in testing should be as similar as possible to the one seen in training, so one would like to train on errors similar to those observed in testing. Ideally, we would like to train using corrected non-native text. In that case, the original article of the writer can be used as a feature for the classifier and the correct article, as judged by a native English speaker, will be viewed as the label. However, obtaining annotated data for training is expensive and, since the native training data do not contain errors, we cannot use the writer's article as a feature for the classifier.

This paper compares the traditional training paradigm that uses native data to training paradigms that use data with artificial mistakes. We propose several methods of generating mistakes in native training data and demonstrate that they outperform the traditional training paradigm. We also show that the most successful error generation methods use knowledge about the article distribution and error patterns observed in the ESL data.

The rest of the paper is organized as follows. First, we discuss the baseline on the error correction task and show why the baselines used in selection tasks are not relevant for the error correction task. Next, we describe prior work in error generation and show the key difference of our approach. Section 4 presents the ESL data that we use and statistics on article errors. Section 5 describes training paradigms that employ error generation. In Sections 6 and 7 we present the results and discuss the results. The key findings are summarized in Table 7 in Section 6. We conclude with a brief discussion of directions for future work.

2 Measuring Success in Error Correction Tasks

The distinction between the selection and the error correction tasks alluded to earlier is important not only for training but also in determining an appropriate evaluation method.

The standard baseline used in selection tasks is the relative frequency of the most common class. For example, in word sense disambiguation, the baseline is the most frequent sense. In the task of article selection, the standard baseline used is to predict the article that occurs most frequently in the data (usually, it is the *zero* article, whose frequency is 60-70%). In this context, the performance of a state-of-the-art classifier (Knight and Chander, 1994; Minnen et al., 2000; Turner and Charniak, 2007; Gamon et al., 2008) whose accuracy is 85-87% is a significant improvement over the baseline. The majority has been used as the baseline also in the context-sensitive spelling task (e.g., (Golding and Roth, 1999)).

However, in article correction, spelling correction, and other text correction applications the split of the classes is not an appropriate baseline since the majority of the words in the confusion set are used correctly in the text. Han et al. (2006) report an average error rate of 13% on article data from TOEFL essays, which gives a baseline of 87%, versus the baseline of 60-70% used in the article selection task. Statistics on article mistakes in our data suggest a baseline of about 90%, depending on the source language of the writer. So the real baseline on the task is "do nothing". Therefore, to determine the baseline for a correction task, one needs to consider the error rate in the data.

Using the definitions of precision and recall and the "real" baseline, we can also relate the resulting accuracy of the classifier to the precision and recall on an error correction task as follows: Let P and R denote the precision and recall, respectively, of the system on an error correction task, and $Base$ denote the error rate in the data. Then the task baseline (i.e., accuracy of the data before running the system) is:

$$Baseline = 1 - Base$$

It can be shown that the error rate after running the classifier is:

$$Error = \frac{Base * (P + R - 2RP)}{P}$$

It follows that the accuracy of the system on the task is $1 - Error$.

For example, we can obtain a rough estimate on the accuracy of the system in Han et al. (2006), using precision and recall numbers by error type. Excluding the error type of category *other*, we can estimate that $Base = 0.1$, so the baseline is 0.9, average precision and recall are 0.85 and 0.25, respectively, and the resulting overall accuracy of the system is 92.2%.

3 Related Work

3.1 Generating Errors in Text

In text correction, adding mistakes in training has been explored before. Although the general approach has been to produce errors similar to those observed in the data to be corrected, mistakes were added in an ad-hoc way, without respecting the error frequencies and error patterns observed in non-native text. Izumi et al. (2003) train a maximum entropy model on error-tagged data from the Japanese Learners of English corpus (JLE, (Izumi et al., 2004)) to detect 8 error types in the same corpus. They show improvement when the training set is enhanced with sentences from the same corpus to which artificial article mistakes have been added. Though it is not clear in what proportion mistakes were added, it is also possible that the improvement was due to a larger training set. Foster and Andersen (2009) attempt to replicate naturally occurring learner mistakes in the Cambridge Learner Corpus (CLC)[1], but show a drop in accuracy when the original error-tagged data in training are replaced with corrected CLC sentences containing artificial errors.

Brockett et al. (2006) generate mass noun errors in native English data using relevant examples found in the Chinese Learners English Corpus (CLEC, (Gui and Yang, 2003)). Training data consist of an equal number of correct and incorrect sentences. Sjöbergh and Knutsson (2005) introduce split compound and agreement errors into native Swedish text: agreement errors are added in every sentence and for compound errors, the training set consists of an equal number of negative and positive examples. Their method gives higher recall at the expense of lower precision compared to rule-based grammar checkers.

To sum up, although the idea of using data with artificial mistakes is not new, the advantage of training on such data has not been investigated. Moreover, training on error-tagged data is currently unrealistic in the majority of error correction scenarios, which suggests that using text with artificial mistakes is the only alternative to using clean data. However, it has not been shown whether training on data with artificial errors is beneficial when compared to utilizing clean data. More importantly, error statistics have not been considered for error correction tasks. Lee and Seneff (2008) examine statistics on article and preposition mistakes in the JLE corpus. While they do not suggest a specific approach, they hypothesize that it might be helpful to incorporate this knowledge into a correction system that targets these two language phenomena.

3.2 Approaches to Detecting Article Mistakes

Automated methods for detecting article mistakes generally use a machine learning algorithm. Gamon et al. (2008) use a decision tree model and a 5-gram language model trained on the English Gigaword corpus (LDC2005T12) to correct errors in English article and preposition usage. Han et al. (2006) and De Felice and Pulman (2008) train a maximum entropy classifier. Yi et al. (2008) propose a web count-based system to correct determiner errors. In the above approaches, the classifiers are trained on native data. Therefore the classifiers cannot use the

[1] http://www.cambridge.org/elt

original article that the writer used as a feature. Han et al. (2006) use the *source* article at evaluation time and propose a correction only when the score of the classifier is high enough, but the *source* article is not used in training.

4 Article Errors in ESL Data

Article errors are one of the most common mistakes that non-native speakers make, especially those whose native language does not have an article system. For example, Han et al. (2006) report that in the annotated TOEFL data by Russian, Chinese, and Japanese speakers 13% of all noun phrases have an incorrect article. It is interesting to note that article errors are present even with very advanced speakers. While the TOEFL data include essays by students of different proficiency levels, we use data from very advanced learners and find that error rates on articles are similar to those reported by Han et al. (2006).

We use data from speakers of three first language backgrounds: Chinese, Czech, and Russian. None of these languages has an article system. The Czech and the Russian data come from the ICLE corpus (Granger et al., 2002), which is a collection of essays written by advanced learners of English. The Chinese data is a part of the CLEC corpus that contains essays by students of all levels of proficiency.

4.1 Data Annotation

A portion of data for each source language was corrected and error-tagged by native speakers. The annotation was performed at the sentence level: a sentence was presented to the annotator in the context of the entire essay. Essay context can become necessary, when an article is acceptable in the context of a sentence, but is incorrect in the context of the essay. Our goal was to correct all article errors, including those that, while acceptable in the context of the sentence, were not correct in the context of the essay. The annotators were also encouraged to propose more than one correction, as long as all of their suggestions were consistent with the essay context.

The annotators were asked to correct all mistakes in the sentence. The annotation schema included the following error types: mistakes in article and preposition usage, errors in *noun number*, *spelling*, *verb form*, and *word form*[2]. All other corrections were marked as *word replacement*, *word deletion*, and *word insertion*. For details about annotation and data selection, please refer to the companion paper (Rozovskaya and Roth, 2010).

4.2 Statistics on Article Errors

Traditionally, three article classes are distinguished: *the*, *a(an)*[3] and *None* (no article). The training and the test data are thus composed of two types of events:

1. All articles in the data

2. Spaces in front of a noun phrase if that noun phrase does not start with an article. To identify the beginning of a noun phrase, we ran a part-of-speech tagger and a phrase chunker[4] and excluded all noun phrases not headed[5] by a personal or demonstrative pronoun.

Table 1 shows the size of the test data by source language, proportion of errors and distribution of article classes before and after annotation and compares these distributions to the distribution of articles in English Wikipedia. The distribution before annotation shows statistics on article usage by the writers and the distribution after annotation shows statistics after the corrections made by the annotators were applied. As the table shows, the distribution of articles is quite different for native data (Wikipedia) and non-native text. In particular, non-native data have a lower proportion of *the*.

The annotation statistics also reveal that learners do not confuse articles randomly. From Table 2, which shows the distribution of article errors by type, we observe that the majority of mistakes are omissions and extraneous articles. Table 3 shows statistics on corrections by *source* and *label*, where *source* refers to the article used by the writer, and *label* refers to the article chosen by the annotator. Each entry in the table indicates $Prob(source =$

[2]Our classification, was inspired by the classification presented in Tetreault and Chodorow (2008)

[3]Henceforth, we will use *a* to refer to both *a* and *an*

[4]The tagger and the chunker are available at `http://L2R.cs.uiuc.edu/~cogcomp/software.php`

[5]We assume that the last word of the noun phrase is its head.

Source language	Number of test examples	Proportion of errors	Errors total	Article distribution	Classes		
					a	*the*	*None*
Chinese	1713	9.2%	158	Before annotation	8.5	28.2	63.3
				After annotation	9.9	24.9	65.2
Czech	1061	9.6%	102	Before annotation	9.1	22.9	68.0
				After annotation	9.9	22.3	67.8
Russian	2146	10.4%	224	Before annotation	10.5	21.7	67.9
				After annotation	12.5	20.1	67.4
English Wikipedia					9.6	29.1	61.4

Table 1: Statistics on articles in the annotated data before and after annotation.

Source language	Proportion of errors in the data	Errors total	Errors by Type			
			Extraneous	Missing a	Missing the	Confusion
Chinese	9.2%	158	57.0%	13.3%	22.8%	7.0%
Czech	9.6%	102	45.1%	14.7%	33.3%	6.9%
Russian	10.4%	224	41.5%	20.1%	25.5%	12.3%

Table 2: Distribution of article errors in the annotated data by error type. *Extraneous* refers to using *a* or *the* where *None* (no article) is correct. *Confusion* is using *a* instead of *the* or vice versa.

Label	Source language	Source		
		a	*the*	*None*
a	Chinese	81.7%	5.9%	12.4%
	Czech	81.0%	4.8%	14.3%
	Russian	75.3%	7.9%	16.9%
the	Chinese	0.2%	91.3%	8.5%
	Czech	0.9%	84.7%	14.4%
	Russian	1.9%	84.9%	13.2%
None	Chinese	0.6%	7.4%%	92.0%
	Czech	1.3%	5.2%	93.6%
	Russian	1.0%	5.4%%	93.6%

Table 3: Statistics on article corrections by the original article (*source*) and the annotator's choice (*label*). Each entry in the table indicates $Prob(source = s|label = l)$ for each article pair.

$s|label = l)$ for each article pair. We can also observe specific error patterns. For example, *the* is more likely than *a* to be used superfluously.

5 Introducing Article Errors into Training Data

This section describes experiments with error generation methods. We conduct four sets of experiments. Each set differs in how article errors are generated in the training data. We now give a description of error generation paradigms in each experimental set.

5.1 Methods of error generation

We refer to the article that the writer used in the ESL data as *source*, and *label* refers to the article that the annotator chose. Similarly, when we introduce errors into the training data, we refer to the original article as *label* and to the replacement as *source*. This is because the original article is the correct article choice, and the replacement that the classifier will see as a feature can be an error. We call this feature *source* feature. In other words, both for training (native data) and test (ESL data), *source* denotes the form that the classifier sees as a feature (which could be an error) and *label* denotes the correct article. Below we describe how errors are generated in each set of experiments.

Method 1: General With probability x each article in the training data is replaced with a different article uniformly at random, and with probability $(1 - x)$ it remains unchanged. We build six classifiers, where $x \in \{5\%, 10\%, 12\%, 14\%, 16\%, 18\%\}$. We call this method *general* since it uses no information about article distribution in the ESL data.

Method 2: ArticleDistrBeforeAnnot We use the distribution of articles in the ESL data before the annotation to change the distribution of articles in the training. Specifically, we change the articles so that their distribution approximates the distribution of articles in the ESL data. For example, the relative frequency of *the* in English Wikipedia data is 29.1%, while in the writing by Czech speakers it is 22.3%. It should be noted that this method changes the distribution only of source articles, but the distribution of labels is not affected. An additional constraint that we impose is the minimum error rate r for each article class, so that $Prob(s|l) \geq r \; \forall l \in labels$. In this fashion, for each source language we train four classifiers, where we use article distribution from Chinese, Czech, and Russian, and where we set the minimum error rate r to be $\in \{2\%, 3\%, 4\%, 5\%\}$.

Method 3: ArticleDistrAfterAnnot This method is similar to the one above but we use the distribution of articles in the ESL data after the corrections have been made by the annotators.

Method 4: ErrorDistr This method uses information about error patterns in the annotated ESL data. For example, in the Czech annotated subcorpus, label *the* corresponds to source *the* in 85% of the cases and corresponds to source *None* in 14% of the cases. In other words, in 14% of the cases where the article *the* should have been used, the writer used no article at all. Thus, with probability 14% we change *the* in the training data to *None*.

6 Experimental Results

In this section, we compare the quality of the system trained on clean native English data to the quality of the systems trained on data with errors. The errors were introduced into the training data using error generation methods presented in Section 5.

In each training paradigm, we follow a discriminative approach, using an online learning paradigm and making use of the Averaged Perceptron Algorithm (Freund and Schapire, 1999) implemented within the Sparse Network of Winnow framework (Carlson et al., 1999) – we use the regularized version in Learning Based Java[6] (LBJ, (Rizzolo and Roth, 2007)). While classical Perceptron comes with generalization bound related to the margin of the data, Averaged Perceptron also comes with a PAC-like generalization bound (Freund and Schapire, 1999). This linear learning algorithm is known, both theoretically and experimentally, to be among the best linear learning approaches and is competitive with SVM and Logistic Regression, while being more efficient in training. It also has been shown to produce state-of-the-art results on many natural language applications (Punyakanok et al., 2008).

Since the methods of error generation described in Section 5 rely on the distribution of articles and article mistakes and these statistics are specific to the first language of the writer, we conduct evaluation separately for each source language. Thus, for each language group, we train five system types: one system is trained on clean English data without errors (the same classifier for the three language groups) and four systems are trained on data with errors, where errors are produced using the four methods described in Section 5. Training data are extracted from English Wikipedia.

All of the five systems employ the same set of features based on three tokens to the right and to the left of the target article. For each context word, we use its relative position, its part-of-speech tag and the word token itself. We also use the head of the noun phrase and the conjunctions of the pairs and triples of the six tokens and their part-of-speech tags[7]. In addition to these features, the classifiers trained on data with errors also use the *source* article as a feature. The classifier that is trained on clean English data cannot use the *source* feature, since in training the *source* always corresponds to the *label*. By contrast, when the training data contain mistakes, the *source* is not always the same as the *label*, the situation that we also have with the test (ESL) data.

We refer to the classifier trained on clean data as $TrainClean$. We refer to the classifiers trained on data with mistakes as TWE (TrainWithErrors). There are four types of TWE systems for each language group, one for each of the methods of error generation described in Section 5. All results are the averaged results of training on three random samples from Wikipedia with two million training examples on each round. All five classifiers are trained on exactly the same set of Wikipedia examples, except that we add article mistakes to the data used by the TWE systems. The $TrainClean$ system achieves an accuracy of 87.10% on data from English Wikipedia. This performance is state-of-the-

[6]LBJ code is available at `http://L2R.cs.uiuc.edu/~cogcomp/asoftware.php?skey=LBJ`

[7]Details about the features are given in the paper's web page, accessible from `http://L2R.cs.uiuc.edu/~cogcomp/`

art compared to other systems reported in the literature (Knight and Chander, 1994; Minnen et al., 2000; Turner and Charniak, 2007; Han et al., 2006; De Felice and Pulman, 2008). The best results of 92.15% are reported by De Felice and Pulman (2008). But their system uses sophisticated syntactic features and they observe that the parser does not perform well on non-native data.

As mentioned in Section 4, the annotation of the ESL data consisted of correcting all errors in the sentence. We exclude from evaluation examples that have spelling errors in the 3-word window around the target article and errors on words that immediately precede or immediately follow the article, as such examples would obscure the evaluation of the training paradigms.

Tables 4, 5 and 6 show performance by language group. The tables show the accuracy and the error reduction on the test set. The results of systems TWE (methods 2 and 3) that use the distribution of articles before and after annotation are merged and appear as $ArtDistr$ in the tables, since, as shown in Table 1, these distributions are very similar and thus produce similar results. Each table compares the performance of the $TrainClean$ system to the performance of the four systems trained on data with errors.

For all language groups, all classifiers of type TWE outperform the $TrainClean$ system. The reduction in error rate is consistent when the TWE classifiers are compared to the $TrainClean$ system.

Table 7 shows results for all three languages, comparing for each language group the $TrainClean$ classifier to the best performing system of type TWE.

Training paradigm	Errors in training	Accuracy	Error reduction
$TrainClean$	0.0%	91.85%	-2.26%
$TWE(General)$	10.0%	92.57%	6.78%
$TWE(ArtDistr)$	13.2%	92.67%	**8.33%**
$TWE(ErrorDistr)$	9.2%	92.31%	3.51%
Baseline		92.03%	

Table 4: **Chinese speakers**: Performance of the $TrainClean$ system (without errors in training) and of the best classifiers of type TWE. Rows 2-4 show the performance of the systems trained with error generation methods described in 5. *Error reduction* denotes the percentage reduction in the number of errors when compared to the number of errors in the ESL data.

Training paradigm	Errors in training	Accuracy	Error reduction
$TrainClean$	0.0%	91.82%	10.31%
$TWE(General)$	18.0%	92.22%	**14.69%**
$TWE(ArtDistr)$	21.6%	92.00%	12.28%
$TWE(ErrorDistr)$	10.2%	92.15%	13.93%
Baseline		90.88%	

Table 5: **Czech speakers**: Performance of the $TrainClean$ system (without errors in training) and of the best classifiers of type TWE. Rows 2-4 show the performance of the systems trained with error generation methods described in 5. *Error reduction* denotes the percentage reduction in the number of errors when compared to the number of errors in the ESL data.

Training paradigm	Errors in training	Accuracy	Error reduction
$TrainClean$	0.0%	90.62%	5.92%
$TWE(General)$	14.0%	91.25%	12.24%
$TWE(ArtDistr)$	18.8%	91.52%	14.94%
$TWE(ErrorDistr)$	10.7%	91.63%	**16.05%**
Baseline		90.03%	

Table 6: **Russian speakers**: Performance of the $TrainClean$ system (without errors in training) and of the best classifiers of type TWE. Rows 2-4 show the performance of the systems trained with error generation methods described in 5. *Error reduction* denotes the percentage reduction in the number of errors when compared to the number of errors in the ESL data.

7 Discussion

As shown in Section 6, training a classifier on data that contain errors produces better results when compared to the $TrainClean$ classifier trained on clean native data. The key results for all language groups are summarized in Table 7. It should be noted that the $TrainClean$ system also makes use of the article chosen by the author through a confidence threshold[8]; it prefers to keep the article chosen by the user. The difference is that the $TrainClean$ system does not consider the author's article in training. The results of training with error generation are better, which shows that training on automatically corrupted data indeed helps. While the performance is different by language group, there is an observable reduction in error rate for each language group when TWE systems are used compared to $TrainClean$ approach. The reduction in error rate

[8]The decision threshold is found empirically on a subset of the ESL data set aside for development.

achieved by the best performing TWE system when compared to the error rate of the $TrainClean$ system is 10.06% for Chinese, 4.89% for Czech and 10.77% for Russian, as shown in Table 7. We also note that the best performing TWE systems for Chinese and Russian speakers are those that rely on the distribution of articles (Chinese) and the distribution of errors (Russian), but for Czech it is the $General$ TWE system that performs the best, maybe because we had less data for Czech speakers, so their statistics are less reliable.

There are several additional observations to be made. First, training paradigms that use error generation methods work better than the training approach of using clean data. Every system of type TWE outperforms the $TrainClean$ system, as evidenced by Tables 4, 5, and 6. Second, the proportion of errors in the training data should be similar to the error rate in the test data. The proportion of errors in training is shown in Tables 4, 5 and 6 in column 2. Furthermore, TWE systems $ArtDistr$ and $ErrorDistr$ that use specific knowledge about article and error distributions, respectively, work better for Russian and Chinese groups than the $General$ method that adds errors to the data uniformly at random. Since $ArtDistr$ and $ErrorDistr$ depend on the statistics of learner mistakes, the success of the systems that use these methods for error generation depends on the accuracy of these statistics, and we only have between 100 and 250 errors for each language group. It would be interesting to see whether better results can be achieved with these methods if more annotated data are available. Finally, for the same reason, there is no significant difference in the performance of methods $ArtDistrBeforeAnnot$ and $ArtDistrAfterAnnot$: With small sizes of annotated data there is no difference in article distributions before and after annotation.

8 Conclusion and Future Work

We have shown that error correction training paradigms that introduce artificial errors are superior to training classifiers on clean data. We proposed several methods of error generation that account for error frequency information and error distribution statistics from non-native text and demonstrated that the methods that work best are those that result in a training corpus that statistically resembles the non-native text. Adding information about article distribution in non-native data and statistics on specific error types is even more helpful.

We have also argued that the baselines used earlier in the relevant literature – all based on the majority of the most commonly used class – suit selection tasks, but are inappropriate for error correction. Instead, the error rate in the data should be taken into account when determining the baseline.

The focus of the present study was on training paradigms. While it is quite possible that the article correction system presented here can be improved – we would like to explore improving the system by using a more sophisticated feature set – we believe that the performance gap due to the error driven training paradigms shown here will remain. The reason is that even with better features, some of the features that hold in the native data will not be active in in the ESL writing.

Finally, while this study focused on the problem of correcting article mistakes, we plan to apply the proposed training paradigms to similar text correction problems.

Source language	Accuracy		Error reduction
	$Train$ $Clean$	TWE	
Chinese	91.85%	92.67%	**10.06%**
Czech	91.82%	92.22%	**4.89%**
Russian	90.62%	91.63%	**10.77%**

Table 7: **Improvement due to training with errors**. For each source language, the last column of the table shows the reduction in error rate achieved by the best performing TWE system when compared to the error rate of the $TrainClean$ system. The error rate for each system is computed by subtracting the accuracy achieved by the system, as shown in columns 2 and 3.

Acknowledgments

We thank Nick Rizzolo for helpful discussions on LBJ. We also thank Peter Chew and the anonymous reviewers for their insightful comments. This research is partly supported by a grant from the U.S. Department of Education.

References

C. Brockett, W. B. Dolan, and M. Gamon. 2006. Correcting ESL errors using phrasal SMT techniques. In *Proceedings of the 21st COLING and the 44th ACL*, Sydney.

A. Carlson, C. Cumby, J. Rosen, and D. Roth. The SNoW learning architecture. *Technical report.*

A. J. Carlson and J. Rosen and D. Roth. 2001. Scaling Up Context Sensitive Text Correction. *IAAI*, 45–50.

R. De Felice and S. Pulman. 2008. A Classifier-Based Approach to Preposition and Determiner Error Correction in L2 English. In *Proceedings of COLING-08.*

J. Foster and Ø. Andersen. 2009. GenERRate: Generating Errors for Use in Grammatical Error Detection. In *Proceedings of the NAACL Workshop on Innovative Use of NLP for Building Educational Applications.*

Y. Freund and R. E. Schapire. 1999. Large margin classification using the perceptron algorithm. *Machine Learning*, 37(3):277-296.

M. Gamon, J. Gao, C. Brockett, A. Klementiev, W. Dolan, D. Belenko and L. Vanderwende. 2008. Using Contextual Speller Techniques and Language Modeling for ESL Error Correction. *Proceedings of IJCNLP.*

A. R. Golding and D. Roth. 1996. Applying Winnow to Context-Sensitive Spelling Correction. *ICML*, 182–190.

A. R. Golding and D. Roth. 1999. A Winnow based approach to Context-Sensitive Spelling Correction. *Machine Learning*, 34(1-3):107–130.

S. Granger, E. Dagneaux and F. Meunier 2002. *International Corpus of Learner English.*

S. Gui and H. Yang. 2003. *Zhongguo Xuexizhe Yingyu Yuliaohu. (Chinese Learner English Corpus).* Shanghai Waiyu Jiaoyu Chubanshe. (In Chinese).

N. Han, M. Chodorow and C. Leacock. 2006. Detecting Errors in English Article Usage by Non-native Speakers. *Journal of Natural Language Engineering*, 12(2):115–129.

E. Izumi, K. Uchimoto, T. Saiga and H. Isahara. 2003. Automatic Error Detection in the Japanese Leaners English Spoken Data. *ACL.*

E. Izumi, K. Uchimoto and H. Isahara. 2004. The NICT JLE Corpus: Exploiting the Language Learner's Speech Database for Research and Education. *International Journal of the Computer, the Internet and Management*, 12(2):119–125.

K. Knight and I. Chander. 1994. Automatic Postediting of Documents. In *Proceedings of the American Association of Artificial Intelligence*, pp 779–784.

J. Lee and S. Seneff. 2008. An analysis of grammatical errors in non-native speech in English. In *Proceedings of the 2008 Spoken Language Technology Workshop*, Goa.

G. Minnen, F. Bond and A. Copestake 2000. Memory-Based Learning for Article Generation. In *Proceedings of the Fourth Conference on Computational Natural Language Learning and of the Second Learning Language in Logic Workshop*, pp 43–48.

V. Punyakanok, D. Roth, and W. Yih. The importance of syntactic parsing and inference in semantic role labeling. *Computational Linguistics*, 34(2).

N. Rizzolo and D. Roth 2007. Modeling Discriminative Global Inference. In *Proceedings of the First International Conference on Semantic Computing (ICSC)*, pp 597–604.

A. Rozovskaya and D. Roth 2010. Annotating ESL Errors: Challenges and Rewards. In *Proceedings of the NAACL Workshop on Innovative Use of NLP for Building Educational Applications.*

J. Sjöbergh and O. Knutsson. 2005. Faking errors to avoid making errors. In *Proceedings of RANLP 2005*, Borovets.

J. Tetreault and M. Chodorow. 2008. Native Judgments of Non-Native Usage: Experiments in Preposition Error Detection. *COLING Workshop on Human Judgments in Computational Linguistics*, Manchester, UK.

J. Turner and E. Charniak. 2007. Language Modeling for Determiner Selection. In *Human Language Technologies 2007: The Conference of the North American Chapter of the Association for Computational Linguistics; Companion Volume, Short Papers*, pp 177–180.

J. Wagner, J. Foster, and J. van Genabith. 2009. Judging grammaticality: Experiments in sentence classification. *CALICO Journal.* Special Issue on the 2008 Automatic Analysis of Learner Language CALICO Workshop.

Y. Xing, J. Gao, and W. Dolan. 2009. A web-based English proofing system for ESL users. In *Proceedings of IJCNLP.*

Using Mostly Native Data to Correct Errors in Learners' Writing: A Meta-Classifier Approach

Michael Gamon
Microsoft Research
One Microsoft Way
Redmond, WA 98052
mgamon@microsoft.com

Abstract

We present results from a range of experiments on article and preposition error correction for non-native speakers of English. We first compare a language model and error-specific classifiers (all trained on large English corpora) with respect to their performance in error detection and correction. We then combine the language model and the classifiers in a meta-classification approach by combining evidence from the classifiers and the language model as input features to the meta-classifier. The meta-classifier in turn is trained on error-annotated learner data, optimizing the error detection and correction performance on this domain. The meta-classification approach results in substantial gains over the classifier-only and language-model-only scenario. Since the meta-classifier requires error-annotated data for training, we investigate how much training data is needed to improve results over the baseline of not using a meta-classifier. All evaluations are conducted on a large error-annotated corpus of learner English.

1 Introduction

Research on the automatic correction of grammatical errors has undergone a renaissance in the past decade. This is, at least in part, based on the recognition that non-native speakers of English now outnumber native speakers by 2:1 in some estimates, so any tool in this domain could be of tremendous value. While earlier work in both native and non-native error correction was focused on the construction of grammars and analysis systems to detect and correct specific errors (see Heift and Schulze, 2005 for a detailed overview), more recent approaches have been based on data-driven methods.

The majority of the data-driven methods use a classification technique to determine whether a word is used appropriately in its context, continuing the tradition established for contextual spelling correction by Golding (1995) and Golding and Roth (1996). The words investigated are typically articles and prepositions. They have two distinct advantages as the subject matter for investigation: They are a closed class and they comprise a substantial proportion of learners' errors. The investigation of preposition corrections can even be narrowed further: amongst the more than 150 English prepositions, the usage of the ten most frequent prepositions accounts for 82% of preposition errors in the 20 million word *Cambridge University Press Learners' Corpus*. Learning correct article use is most difficult for native speakers of an L1 that does not overtly mark definiteness and indefiniteness as English does. Prepositions, on the other hand, pose difficulties for language learners from all L1 backgrounds (Dalgish, 1995; Bitchener et al., 2005).

Contextual classification methods represent the context of a preposition or article as a feature vector gleaned from a window of a few words around the preposition/article. Different systems typically vary along three dimensions: choice of features, choice of classifier, and choice of training data. Features range from words and morphological information (Knight and Chander, 1994) to the inclusion of part-of-speech tags (Minnen et al., 2000; Han et al., 2004, 2006; Chodorow et al., 2007; Gamon et al., 2008, 2009; Izumi et al., 2003, 2004; Tetrault and Chodorow, 2008) to features based on linguistic analysis and on WordNet (Lee, 2004; DeFelice and Pulman, 2007, 2008). Knight and Chander (1994) and Gamon et al. (2008) used decision tree classifiers but, in general, maximum entropy classifiers have become the classification

Human Language Technologies: The 2010 Annual Conference of the North American Chapter of the ACL, pages 163–171,
Los Angeles, California, June 2010.

algorithm of choice. Training data are normally drawn from sizeable corpora of native English text (*British National Corpus* for DeFelice and Pulman (2007, 2008), *Wall Street Journal* in Knight and Chander (1994), a mix of *Reuters* and *Encarta* in Gamon et al. (2008, 2009). In order to partially address the problem of domain mismatch between learners' writing and the news-heavy data sets often used in data-driven NLP applications, Han et al. (2004, 2006) use 31.5 million words from the MetaMetrics corpus, a diverse corpus of fiction, non-fiction and textbooks categorized by reading level.

In addition to the classification approach to error detection, there is a line of research - going back to at least Atwell (1987) - that uses language models. The idea here is to detect errors in areas where the language model score is suspiciously low. Atwell (1987) uses a part-of-speech tag language model to detect errors, Chodorow and Leacock (2000) use mutual information and chi square statistics to identify unlikely function word and part-of-speech tag sequences, Turner and Charniak (2007) employ a language model based on a generative statistical parser, and Stehouwer and van Zaanen (2009) investigate a diverse set of language models with different backoff strategies to determine which choice, from a set of confusable words, is most likely in a given context. Gamon et al. (2008, 2009) use a combination of error-specific classifiers and a large generic language model with hand-tuned heuristics for combining their scores to maximize precision. Finally, Yi et al. (2008) and Hermet et al. (2008) use n-gram counts from the web as a language model approximation to identify likely errors and correction candidates.

2 Our Approach

We combine evidence from the two kinds of data-driven models that have been used for error detection and correction (error-specific classifiers and a language model) through a meta-classifier. We use the term *primary models* for both the initial error-specific classifiers and a large generic language model. The *meta-classifier* takes the output of the primary models (language model scores and class probabilities) as input. Using a meta-classifier for ensemble learning has been proven effective for many machine learning problems (see e.g. Dietterich 1997), especially when the combined models are sufficiently different to make distinct kinds of errors. The meta-classification approach also has an advantage in terms of data requirements: Our primary models are trained on large sets of widely available well-formed English text. The meta-classifier, in contrast, is trained on a smaller set of error-annotated learner data. This allows us to address the problem of domain mismatch: We can leverage large well-formed data sets that are substantially different from real-life learner language for the primary models, and then fine-tune the output to learner English using a much smaller set of expensive and hard-to-come-by annotated learner writing.

For the purpose of this paper, we restrict ourselves to article and preposition errors. The questions we address are:

1. How effective is the meta-classification approach compared to either a classifier or a language model alone?
2. How much error-annotated data are sufficient to produce positive results above the baseline of using either a language model or a classifier alone?

Our evaluation is conducted on a large data set of error-annotated learner data.

3 Experimental Design

3.1 Primary Models

Our error-specific primary models are maximum entropy classifiers (Rathnaparki 1997) for articles and for prepositions. Features include contextual features from a window of six tokens to the right and left, such as lexical features (word), part-of-speech tags, and a handful of "custom features", for example lexical head of governing VP or governed NP (as determined by part-of-speech-tag based heuristics). For both articles and prepositions, we employ two classifiers: the first determines the probability that a preposition/article is present in a given context (*presence classifier*), the second classifier determines the probability that a specific article or preposition is chosen (*choice classifier*). A training event for the presence classifier is any noun phrase boundary that is a potential location for a preposition or article. Whether a location is an NP boundary and a potential site for an article/preposition is determined by a simple heuristic based on part-of-speech tags.

The candidates for article choice are *the* and *a/an*, and the choice for prepositions is limited to twelve very frequent prepositions (*in, at, on, for, since, with, to, by, about, from, of, as*) which account for 86.2 % of preposition errors in our learner data. At prediction time, the presence and choice classifiers produce a list of potential changes in preposition/article usage for the given context. Since the application of our system consists of suggesting corrections to a user, we do not consider identity operations where the suggested word choice equals the actual word choice. For a potential preposition/article location where there is no preposition/article, each of the candidates is considered for an insertion operation. For a potential location that contains a preposition/article, the possible operations include deletion of the existing token or substitution with another preposition/article from the candidate set. Training data for the classifiers is a mix of primarily well-formed data sources: There are about 2.5 million sentences, distributed roughly equally across *Reuters* newswire, *Encarta* encyclopedia, UN proceedings, *Europarl* and web-scraped general domain data[1]. From the total set of candidate operations (substitutions, insertions, and deletions) that each combination of presence and choice classifier produces for prepositions, we consider only the top three highest-scoring operations[2].

Our language model is trained on the *Gigaword* corpus (Linguistic Data Consortium, 2003) and utilizes 7-grams with absolute discount smoothing (Gao, Goodman, and Miao, 2001; Nguyen, Gao, and Mahajan, 2007). Each suggested revision from the preposition/article classifiers (top three for prepositions, all revisions from the article classifiers) are scored by the language model: for each revision, the language model score of the original and the suggested rewrite is recorded, as is the language model entropy (defined as the language model probability of the sentence, normalized by sentence length).

[1] We are not able to train the error-specific classifiers on a larger data set like the one we use for the language model. Note that the 2.5 million sentences used in the classifier training already produce 16.5 million training vectors.

[2] This increases runtime performance because fewer calls need to be made to the language model which resides on a server. In addition, we noticed that overall precision is increased by not considering the less likely suggestions by the classifier.

3.2 Meta-Classifier

For the meta-classifier we chose to use a decision tree, trained with the WinMine toolkit (Chickering 2002). The motivation for this choice is that decision trees are well-suited for continuously valued features and for non-linear decision surfaces. An obvious alternative would be to use a support vector machine with non-linear kernels, a route that we have not explored yet. The feature set for the meta-classifier consists of the following scores from the primary models, including some arithmetic combinations of scores:

- Ratio and delta of Log LM score of the original word choice and the suggested revision (2 features)
- Ratio and delta of the LM entropy for original and suggested revision (2 features).
- Products of the above ratios/deltas and classifier choice/presence probabilities
- Type of operation: deletion, insertion, substitution (3 features)
- P(presence) (1 feature)
- For each preposition/article choice: P(choice): 13 features for prepositions (12 prepositions and *other* for a preposition not in that set), 2 for articles
- Original token: *none* (for insertion) or the original preposition/article (13 features for prepositions, 2 for articles)
- Suggested token: *none* (for deletion) or the suggested preposition/article (13 features for prepositions, 2 for articles)

The total number of features is 63 for prepositions and 36 for articles.

The meta-classifier is trained by collecting suggested corrections from the primary models on the error annotated data. The error-annotation provides the binary class label, i.e. whether the suggested revision is correct or incorrect. If the suggested revision matches an annotated correction, it counts as correct, if it does not match it counts as incorrect. To give an example, the top three preposition operations for the position before *this test* in the sentence *I rely to this test* are:

Change_to_on
Delete_to
Change_to_of

The class label in this example is "suggestion correct", assuming that the change of preposition is annotated in the data. The operation *Change_to_on* in this example has the following feature values for the basic classifier and LM scores:

classifier P(choice): 0.755
classifier P(presence): 0.826
LM logP(original): -17.373
LM logP(rewrite): -14.184

An example of a path through the decision tree meta-classifier for prepositions is:

LMLogDelta is Not < -8.59 and
LMLogDelta is Not < -3.7 and
ProductRewriteLogRatioConf is Not < -0.00115 and
LMLogDelta is Not < -1.58 and
ProductOrigEntropyRatioChoiceConf is Not < -0.00443 and
choice_prob is Not < 0.206 and
Original_of is 0 and
choice_prob is Not < 0.329 and
to_prob is < 0.108 and
Suggested_on is 1 and
Original_in is 0 and
choice_prob is Not < 0.497 and
choice_prob is Not < 0.647 and
presence_prob is Not < 0.553

The leaf node at the end of this path has a 0.21 probability of changing "*to*" to "*on*" being a correct rewrite suggestion.

The features selected by the decision trees range across all of the features discussed above. For both the article and preposition meta-classifiers, the ranking of features by importance (as measured by how close to the root the decision tree uses the feature) follows the order in which features are listed.

3.3 Data

In contrast to the training data for the primary models, the meta-classifier is trained on error-annotated data from the *Cambridge University Press Learners' Corpus* (CLC). The version of CLC that we have licensed currently contains a total of 20 million words from learner English essays written as part of one of *Cambridge's English Language Proficiency Tests* (ESOL) – at all proficiency levels. The essays are annotated for error type, erroneous span and suggested correction.

We first perform a random split of the essays into 70% training, 20% test and 10% for parameter tuning. Next, we create error-specific training, tuning and test sets by performing a number of clean-up steps on the data. First, we correct all errors that were flagged as being spelling errors, since we presume that the user will perform a spelling check on the data before proceeding to grammatical proofing. Spelling errors that were flagged as morphology errors were left alone. By the same token, we corrected confused words that are covered by MS Word. We then revised British English spelling to American English spelling conventions. In addition, we eliminated all annotations for non-pertinent errors (i.e., non-preposition/article errors, or errors that do not involve any of the targeted prepositions), but we maintained the original (erroneous) text for these. This makes our task harder since we will have to learn how to make predictions in text containing multiple errors, but it also is a more realistic scenario given real learner writing. Finally, we eliminated sentences containing nested errors and immediately adjacent errors when they involve pertinent (preposition/article) errors. For example, an annotated error "*take a picture*" with the correction "*take pictures*" is annotated as two consecutive errors: "delete *a*" and "rewrite *picture* as *pictures*". Since the error involves operations on both the article and the noun, which our article correction module is not designed to cover, we eliminated the sentence from the data. (This last step eliminated 31% of the sentences annotated with preposition errors and 29% or the sentences annotated with article errors.) Sentences that were flagged for a replacement error but contained no replacement were also eliminated from the data.

The final training, tuning and test set sizes are as follows (note that for prepositions we had to reduce the size of the training set by an additional 20% in order to avoid memory limitations of our decision tree tools).

Prepositions:

train: 584,485 sentences, 68,806 prep errors
tuning: 105,166 sentences, 9918 prep errors
test: 208,724 sentences, 19,706 prep errors

Articles:

train: 737,091 sentences, 58,356 article errors
tuning: 106,052 sentences, 8341 article errors
test: 210,577 sentences, 16,742 article errors

This mix is strongly biased towards "correct" usage. After all, there are many more correct uses of articles and prepositions in the CLC data than incorrect ones. Again, this is likely to make our task harder, but more realistic, since both at training and test time we are working with the error distribution that is observed in learner data.

3.4 Evaluation

To evaluate, we run our meta-classifier system on the preposition and article test sets described in above and calculate precision and recall. Precision and recall for the overall system are controlled by thresholding the meta-classifier class probability. As a point of comparison, we also evaluate the performance of the primary models (the error-specific classifier and the language model) in isolation. Precision and recall for the error-specific classifier is controlled by thresholding class probability. To control the precision-recall tradeoff for the language model, we calculate the difference between the log probabilities of the original user input and the suggested correction. We then vary that difference across all observed values in small increments, which affects precision and recall: the higher the difference, the fewer instances we find, but the higher the reliability of these instances is.

This evaluation differs from many of the evaluations reported in the error detection/correction literature in several respects. First, the test set is a broad random sample across all proficiency levels in the CLC data. Second, it is far larger than any sets that have been so far to report results of preposition/article correction on learner data. Finally, we are only considering cases in which the system suggests a correction. In other words, we do not count as correct instances where the system's prediction matches a correct preposition/article.

This evaluation scheme, however, ignores one aspect of a real user scenario. Of all the suggested changes that are counted as wrong in our evaluation because they do not match an annotated error, some may in fact be innocuous or even helpful for a real user. Such a situation can arise for a variety of reasons: In some cases, there are legitimate alternative ways to correct an error. In other cases, the classifier has identified the location of an error although that error is of a different kind (which can be beneficial because it causes the user to make a correction - see Leacock et al., 2009). Gamon et al. (2009), for example manually evaluate preposition suggestions as belonging to one of three categories: (a) properly correcting an existing error, (b) offering a suggestion that neither improves nor degrades the user sentence, (c) offering a suggestion that would degrade the user input. Obviously, (c) is a more serious error than (b). Similarly, Tetrault and Chodorow (2008) annotate their test set with preposition choices that are valid alternatives. We do not have similar information in the CLC data, but we can perform a manual analysis of a random subset of test data to estimate an "upper bound" for our precision/recall curve. Our annotator manually categorized each suggested correction into one of seven categories.

Details of the distribution of suggested corrections into the seven categories are shown in Table 1.

Category	preps.	articles
Corrects a CLC error	32.87%	33.34%
Corrects an error that was not annotated as being that error type in CLC	11.67%	12.16%
Corrects a CLC error, but uses an alternative correction	3.62%	2.26%
Original and suggested correction are equally good	9.60%	11.30%
Error correctly detected, but the correction is wrong	8.73%	5.03%
Identifies an error site, but the actual error is not a preposition error	19.17%	12.64%
Introduces an error	14.65%	23.26%

Table 1: Manual analysis of suggested corrections on CLC data.

This analysis involves costly manual evaluation, so we only performed it at one point of the precision/recall curve (our current runtime system setting). The sample size was 6,000 sentences for prepositions and 5981 sentences for articles (half of the sentences were flagged as containing at least one article/preposition error while the other half were not). On this manual evaluation, we achieve 32.87% precision if we count all flags that do not perfectly match a CLC annotation as a false positive. Only counting the last category (introduction of an error) as a false positive, precision is at 85.34%. Similarly, for articles, the manual estimation arrives at 76.74% precision, where pure CLC annotation matching gives us 33.34%.

4 Results

Figure 1 and Figure 2 show the evaluation results of the meta-classifier for prepositions and articles, compared to the performance of the error-specific classifier and language model alone. For both prepositions and articles, the first notable observation is that the language model outperforms the classifier by a large margin. This came as a surprise to us, given the recent prevalence of classification approaches in this area of research and the fact that our classifiers produce state-of-the art performance when compared to other systems, on well-formed data. Second, the combination of scores from the classifier and language model through a meta-classifier clearly outperforms either one of them in isolation. This result, again, is consistent across prepositions and articles.

We had previously used a hand-tuned score combination instead of a meta-classifier. We also established that this heuristic performs worse than the language model for prepositions, and just about at the same level as the language model for articles. Note, though, that the manual tuning was performed to optimize performance against a different data set (the *Chinese Learners of English Corpus*: CLEC), so the latter point is not really comparable and hence is not included in the charts.

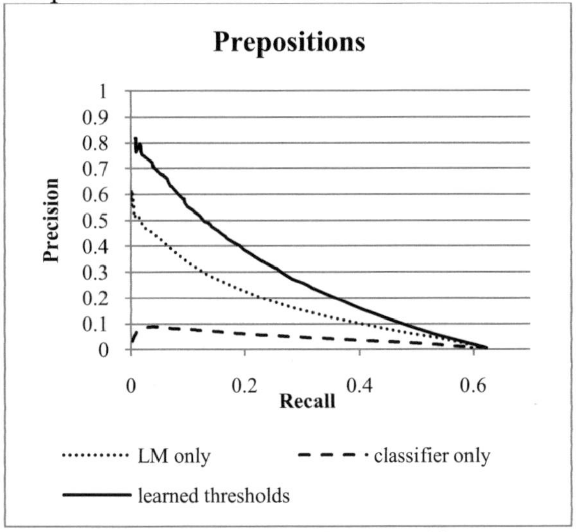

Figure 1: Precision and recall for prepositions.

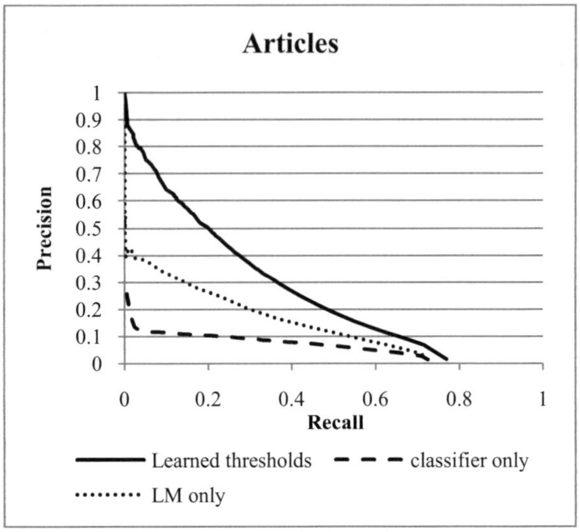

Figure 2: Precision and recall for articles.

We now turn to the question of the required amount of annotated training data for the meta-classifier. CLC is commercially available, but it is obvious that for many researchers such a corpus will be too expensive and they will have to create or license their own error-annotated corpus. Thus the question of whether one could use less annotated data to train a meta-classifier and still achieve reasonable results becomes important. Figure 3 and Figure 4 show results obtained by using decreasing amounts of training data. The dotted line shows the language model baseline. Any result below the language model performance shows that the training data is insufficient to warrant the use of a meta-classifier. In these experiments there is a clear difference between prepositions and articles. We can reduce the amount of training data for prepositions to 10% of the original data and still outperform the language model baseline. 10% of the data corresponds to 6,800 annotated preposition errors and 58,400 sentences. When we reduce the training data to 1% of the original amount (680 annotated errors, 5,800 sentences) we clearly see degraded results compared to the language model. With articles, the system is much less data-hungry. Reducing the training data to 1% (580 annotated errors, 7,400 sentences) still outperforms the language model alone. This result can most likely be explained by the different complexity of the preposition and article tasks. Article operations include only six distinct operations: deletion of *the*, deletion of *a/an*, insertion of *the*, insertion of *a/an*, change of *the* to *a/an*, and change of *a/an* to *the*. For the twelve prepositions that we work with, the total number of insertions, deletions and substitutions that require sufficient training events and might need different score combinations is 168, making the problem much harder.

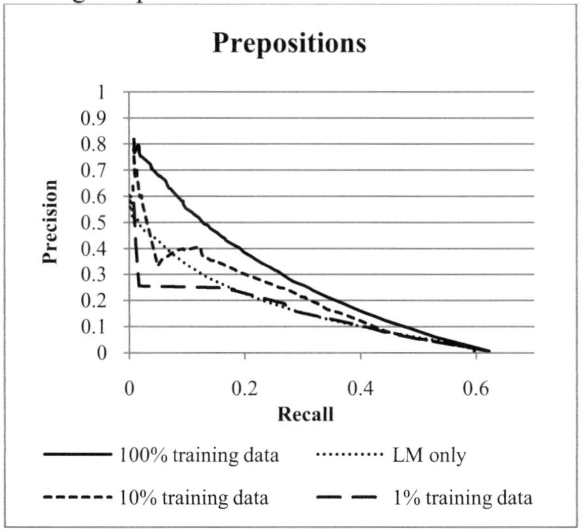

Figure 3: Using different amounts of annotated training data for the preposition meta-classifier.

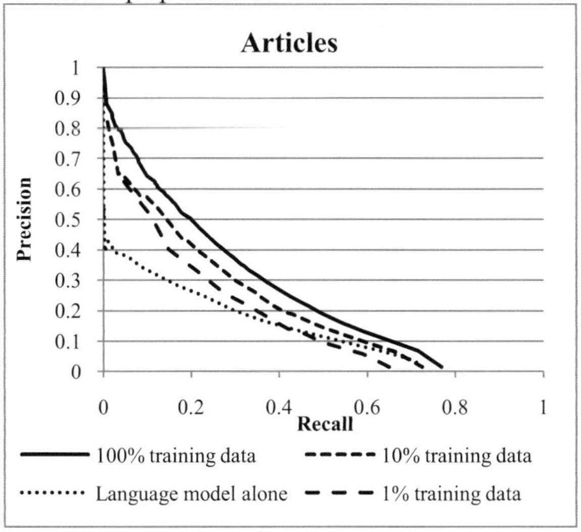

Figure 4: Using different amounts of annotated training data for the article meta-classifier.

To find out if it is possible to reduce the required amount of annotated preposition errors for a system that still covers more than one third of the preposition errors, we ran the same learning curve experiments but now only taking the four most frequent prepositions into account: *to*, *of*, *in*, *for*. In the CLC, these four prepositions account for 39.8% of preposition error flags. As in the previous experiments, however, we found that we are not able to outperform the baseline by using just 1% of annotated data.

5 Error Analysis

We have conducted a failure analysis on examples where the system produces a blatantly bad suggestion in order to see whether this decision could be attributed to the error-specific classifier or to the language model, or both, and what the underlying cause is. This preliminary analysis highlights two common causes for bad flags. One is that of frequent lower order n-grams that dominate the language model score. Consider the CLEC sentence *I get to know the world outside the campus* ***by*** *newspaper and television*. The system suggests deleting *by*. The cause of this bad decision is that the bigram *campus newspaper* is extremely likely, trumping all other n-grams, and leading to a high probability for the suggested string compared to the original: Log (P(original)) = -26.2 and Log (P(suggestion)) = -22.4. This strong imbalance of the language model score causes the meta-classifier to assign a relatively high probability to this being a correct revision, even though the error-specific classifier is on the right track and gives a relatively high probability for the presence of a preposition and the choice of *by*. A similar example, but for substitution, occurs in *They give discounts to their workers* ***on*** *books.* Here the bigram *in books* has a very high probability and the system incorrectly suggests replacing *on* with *in*. An example for insertion is seen in *Please send me the letter* ***back*** *writing what happened.* Here, the bigram *back to* causes the bad suggestion of inserting *to* after *back*. Since the language model is generally more accurate than the error-specific classifier, the meta-classifier tends to trust its score more than that of the classifier. As a result we see this kind of error quite frequently.

Another common error class is the opposite situation: the language model is on the right track, but the classifier makes a wrong assessment. Consider *Whatever direction my leg fought to stretch*, with the suggested insertion of *on* before *my leg*. Here Log (P(original)) = -31.5 and Log (P(suggestion)) = -32.1, a slight preference for the original string. The error-specific classifier, however, assigns a probability of 0.65 for a preposition to be present, and 0.80 for that preposition to be *on*. The contextual features that are important in that decision are: the insertion site is between a pronoun and a noun, it is relatively close to the beginning of the sentence, and the head of the NP *my leg* has a possible mass noun sense. An example involving deletion is in *Someone came to sort **of** it.* While the language model assigns a high probability for deleting *of,* the error-specific classifier does not. Similarly, for substitution, in *Your experience is very interesting **for** our company,* the language model suggests substituting *for* with *to* while the classifier gives the substitution a very low probability.

As can be seen from the learner sentences cited above, often, even though the sentences are grammatical, they are not idiomatic, which can confuse all of the classifiers.

6 Conclusion and Future Work

We have addressed two questions in this paper:

1. How effective is a meta-classification approach that combines language modeling and error-specific classification to the detection and correction of preposition and article errors by non-native speakers?
2. How much error-annotated data is sufficient to produce positive results using that approach?

We have shown that a meta-classifier approach outperforms using a language model or a classifier alone. An interesting side result is that the language model solidly outperforms the contextual classifier for both article and preposition correction, contrary to current practice in the field. Training data requirements for the meta-classifier vary significantly between article and preposition error detection. The article meta-classifier can be trained with as few as 600 annotated errors, but the preposition meta-classifier requires more annotated data by an order of magnitude. Still, the overall amount of expensive error-annotated data is relatively small, and the meta-classification approach makes it possible to leverage large amounts of well-formed text in the primary models, tuning to the non-native domain in the meta-classifier.

We believe that the logical next step is to combine more primary models in the meta-classifier. Candidates for additional primary models include (1) more classifiers trained either on different data sets or with a different classification algorithm, and (2) more language models, such as skip models or part-of-speech n-gram language models.

Acknowledgments

We thank Claudia Leacock from the Butler Hill Group for detailed error analysis and the anonymous reviewers for helpful and constructive feedback.

References

Eric Steven Atwell. 1987. How to detect grammatical errors in a text without parsing it. In *Proceedings of the 3rd EACL* (pp 38 – 45). Copenhagen.

John Bitchener, Stuart Young, and Denise Cameron. 2005. The effect of different types of corrective feedback on ESL student writing. *Journal of Second Language Writing*, *14*(3), 191-205.

David Maxwell Chickering. 2002. The WinMine Toolkit. *Microsoft Technical Report* 2002-103. Redmond.

Martin Chodorow, Joel Tetreault, and Na-Rae Han. 2007. Detection of grammatical errors involving prepositions. In *Proceedings of the Fourth ACL-SIGSEM Workshop on Prepositions* (pp. 25-30). Prague.

Gerard M. Dalgish. 1985. Computer-assisted ESL research and courseware development. *Computers and Composition*, *2*(4), 45-62.

Rachele De Felice and Stephen G. Pulman. 2007. Automatically acquiring models of preposition use. In *Proceedings of the Fourth ACL-SIGSEM Workshop on Prepositions* (pp. 45-50). Prague.

Rachele De Felice and Stephen Pulman. 2008. A classifier-based approach to preposition and determiner error correction in L2 English. In *Proceedings of COLING*. Manchester, UK.

Thomas G. Dietterich. 1997. Machine learning research: Four current directions. *AI Magazine*, *18*(4), 97-136.

Ted Dunning. 1993. Accurate Methods for the Statistics of Surprise and Coincidence. *Computational Linguistics*, *19*, 61-74.

Michael Gamon, Claudia Leacock, Chris Brockett, William B. Dolan, Jianfeng Gao, Dmitriy Belenko, and Alexandre Klementiev,. 2009. Using statistical techniques and web search to correct ESL errors. *CALICO Journal*, *26*(3).

Michael Gamon, Jianfeng Gao, Chris Brockett, Alexander Klementiev, William Dolan, Dmitriy Belenko, and Lucy Vanderwende. 2008. Using contextual speller techniques and language modeling for ESL error correction. In *Proceedings of IJCNLP*, Hyderabad, India.

Jianfeng Gao, Joshua Goodman, and Jiangbo Miao. 2001. The use of clustering techniques for language modeling—Application to Asian languages. *Compu-*

tational Linguistics and Chinese Language Processing, *6*(1), 27-60.

Andrew Golding. 1995. A Bayesian Hybrid for Context Sensitive Spelling Correction. In *Proceedings of the 3rd Workshop on Very Large Corpora* (pp. 39–53). Cambridge, USA.

Andrew R. Golding and Dan Roth. 1996. Applying Winnow to context-sensitive spelling correction. In *Proceedings of the Int. Conference on Machine Learning* (pp 182 –190).

Na-Rae Han, Martin Chodorow, and Claudia Leacock. 2004. Detecting errors in English article usage with a maximum entropy classifier trained on a large, diverse corpus. In *Proceedings of the 4th International Conference on Language Resources and Evaluation.* Lisbon.

Na-Rae Han, Martin Chodorow, and Claudia Leacock. 2006. Detecting errors in English article usage by non-native speakers. *Natural Language Engineering*, *12*(2), 115-129.

Trude Heift and Mathias Schulze. 2007. *Errors and Intelligence in Computer-Assisted Language Learning: Parsers and Pedagogues*. New York & London: Routledge.

Matthieu Hermet, Alain Désilets, and Stan Szpakowicz. 2008. Using the web as a linguistic resource to automatically correct lexico-yyntactic errors. In *Proceedings of the 6th Conference on Language Resources and Evaluation (LREC)*, (pp. 874 - 878).

Emi Izumi, Kiyotaka Uchimoto, Toyomi Saiga, Thepchai Supnithi and Hitoshi Isahara. 2003. Automatic error detection in the Japanese learners' English spoken data. In *Proceedings of the 41st Annual Meeting of the Association for Computational Linguistics* (pp. 145-148).

Emi Izumi, Kiyotaka Uchimoto and Hitoshi Isahara. 2004. SST speech corpus of Japanese learners' English and automatic detection of learners' errors. In *Proceedings of the 4th International Conference on Language Resources and Evaluation (LREC)*, (Vol 4, pp. 31-48).

Kevin Knight and Ishwar Chander,. 1994. Automatic postediting of documents. In *Proceedings of the 12th National Conference on Artificial Intelligence* (pp. 779-784). Seattle: Morgan Kaufmann.

Claudia Leacock, Michael Gamon, and Chris Brockett. 2009. User Input and Interactions on Microsoft ESL Assistant. In *Proceedings of the Fourth Workshop on Innovative Use of NLP for Building Educational Applications* (pp. 73-81).

John Lee. 2004. Automatic article restoration. In *Proceedings of the Human Language Technology Conference of the North American Chapter of the Association for Computational Linguistics,* (pp. 31-36). Boston.

Guido Minnen, Francis Bond, and Anne Copestake. 2000. Memory-based learning for article generation. In *Proceedings of the Fourth Conference on Computational Natural Language Learning and of the Second Learning Language in Logic Workshop* (pp. 43-48). Lisbon.

Patrick Nguyen, Jianfeng Gao, and Milind Mahajan. 2007. MSRLM: A scalable language modeling toolkit. *Microsoft Technical Report* 2007-144. Redmond.

Adwait Ratnaparkhi. 1997. A simple introduction to maximum entropy models for natural language processing. *Technical Report IRCS Report 97-98*, Institute for Research in Cognitive Science, University of Pennsylvania.

Herman Stehouwer and Menno van Zaanen. 2009. Language models for contextual error detection and correction. In *Proceedings of the EACL 2009 Workshop on Computational Linguistic Aspects of Grammatical Inference* (pp. 41-48). Athens.

Joel Tetreault and Martin Chodorow. 2008a. The ups and downs of preposition error detection in ESL. In *Proceedings of COLING*. Manchester, UK.

Joel Tetreault and Martin Chodorow. 2008b. Native judgments of non-native usage: Experiments in preposition error detection. In *Proceedings of the Workshop on Human Judgments in Computational Linguistics, 22nd International Conference on Computational Linguistics* (pp 43-48). Manchester, UK.

Jenine Turner and Eugene Charniak. 2007. Language modeling for determiner selection. In *Human Language Technologies 2007: NAACL*; Companion Volume, Short Papers (pp. 177-180). Rochester, NY.

Wikipedia. English Language. http://en.wikipedia.org/wiki/English_language

Xing Yi, Jianfeng Gao, and Bill Dolan. 2008. A web-based English proofing system for English as a second language users. In *Proceedings of the Third International Joint Conference on Natural Language Processing (IJCNLP)*. Hyderabad, India.

Unsupervised Modeling of Twitter Conversations

Alan Ritter*
Computer Sci. & Eng.
University of Washington
Seattle, WA 98195
aritter@cs.washington.edu

Colin Cherry*
National Research Council Canada
Ottawa, Ontario, K1A 0R6
Colin.Cherry@nrc-cnrc.gc.ca

Bill Dolan
Microsoft Research
Redmond, WA 98052
billdol@microsoft.com

Abstract

We propose the first unsupervised approach to the problem of modeling dialogue acts in an open domain. Trained on a corpus of noisy Twitter conversations, our method discovers dialogue acts by clustering raw utterances. Because it accounts for the sequential behaviour of these acts, the learned model can provide insight into the shape of communication in a new medium. We address the challenge of evaluating the emergent model with a qualitative visualization and an intrinsic conversation ordering task. This work is inspired by a corpus of 1.3 million Twitter conversations, which will be made publicly available. This huge amount of data, available only because Twitter blurs the line between chatting and publishing, highlights the need to be able to adapt quickly to a new medium.

1 Introduction

Automatic detection of dialogue structure is an important first step toward deep understanding of human conversations. **Dialogue acts**[1] provide an initial level of structure by annotating utterances with shallow discourse roles such as "statement", "question" and "answer". These acts are useful in many applications, including conversational agents (Wilks, 2006), dialogue systems (Allen et al., 2007), dialogue summarization (Murray et al., 2006), and flirtation detection (Ranganath et al., 2009).

Dialogue act tagging has traditionally followed an annotate-train-test paradigm, which begins with the design of annotation guidelines, followed by the collection and labeling of corpora (Jurafsky et al., 1997; Dhillon et al., 2004). Only then can one train a tagger to automatically recognize dialogue acts (Stolcke et al., 2000). This paradigm has been quite successful, but the labeling process is both slow and expensive, limiting the amount of data available for training. The expense is compounded as we consider new methods of communication, which may require not only new annotations, but new annotation guidelines and new dialogue acts. This issue becomes more pressing as the Internet continues to expand the number of ways in which we communicate, bringing us e-mail, newsgroups, IRC, forums, blogs, Facebook, Twitter, and whatever is on the horizon.

Previous work has taken a variety of approaches to dialogue act tagging in new media. Cohen et al. (2004) develop an inventory of dialogue acts specific to e-mail in an office domain. They design their inventory by inspecting a large corpus of e-mail, and refine it during the manual tagging process. Jeong et al. (2009) use semi-supervised learning to transfer dialogue acts from labeled speech corpora to the Internet media of forums and e-mail. They manually restructure the source act inventories in an attempt to create coarse, domain-independent acts. Each approach relies on a human designer to inject knowledge into the system through the inventory of available acts.

As an alternative solution for new media, we propose a series of **unsupervised** conversation models, where the discovery of acts amounts to clustering utterances with similar conversational roles. This avoids manual construction of an act inventory, and allows the learning algorithm to tell us something about how people converse in a new medium.

*This work was conducted at Microsoft Research.
[1]Also called "speech acts"

Human Language Technologies: The 2010 Annual Conference of the North American Chapter of the ACL, pages 172–180,
Los Angeles, California, June 2010.

There is surprisingly little work in unsupervised dialogue act tagging. Woszczyna and Waibel (1994) propose an unsupervised Hidden Markov Model (HMM) for dialogue structure in a meeting scheduling domain, but model dialogue state at the word level. Crook et al. (2009) use Dirichlet process mixture models to cluster utterances into a flexible number of acts in a travel-planning domain, but do not examine the sequential structure of dialogue.[2]

In contrast to previous work, we address the problem of discovering dialogue acts in an informal, open-topic domain, where an unsupervised learner may be distracted by strong topic clusters. We also train and test our models in a new medium: Twitter. Rather than test against existing dialogue inventories, we evaluate using qualitative visualizations and a novel conversation ordering task, to ensure our models have the opportunity to discover dialogue phenomena unique to this medium.

2 Data

To enable the study of large-data solutions to dialogue modeling, we have collected a corpus of 1.3 million conversations drawn from the microblogging service, Twitter. [3] To our knowledge, this is the largest corpus of naturally occurring chat data that has been available for study thus far. Similar datasets include the NUS SMS corpus (How and Kan, 2005), several IRC chat corpora (Elsner and Charniak, 2008; Forsyth and Martell, 2007), and blog datasets (Yano et al., 2009; Gamon et al., 2008), which can display conversational structure in the blog comments.

As it characterizes itself as a micro-blog, it should not be surprising that structurally, Twitter conversations lie somewhere between chat and blogs. Like blogs, conversations on Twitter occur in a public environment, where they can be collected for research purposes. However, Twitter posts are restricted to be no longer than 140 characters, which keeps interactions chat-like. Like e-mail and unlike IRC, Twitter conversations are carried out by replying to specific posts. The Twitter API provides a link from each reply to the post it is responding to, allowing

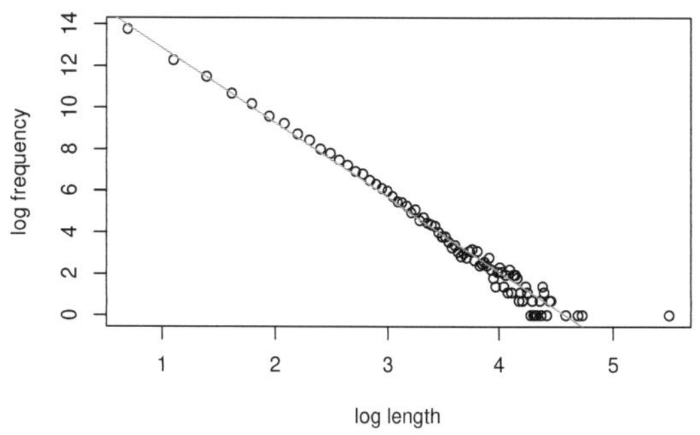

Figure 1: Conversation length versus frequency

accurate thread reconstruction without requiring a conversation disentanglement step (Elsner and Charniak, 2008). The proportion of posts on Twitter that are conversational in nature are somewhere around 37% (Kelly, 2009).

To collect this corpus, we crawled Twitter using its publicly available API. We monitored the *public timeline*[4] to obtain a sample of active Twitter users. To expand our user list, we also crawled up to 10 users who had engaged in dialogue with each seed user. For each user, we retrieved all posts, retaining only those that were in reply to some other post. We recursively followed the chain of replies to recover the entire conversation. A simple function-word-driven filter was used to remove non-English conversations.

We crawled Twitter for a 2 month period during the summer of 2009. The resulting corpus consists of about 1.3 million conversations, with each conversation containing between 2 and 243 posts. The majority of conversations on Twitter are very short; those of length 2 (one status post and a reply) account for 69% of the data. As shown in Figure 1, the frequencies of conversation lengths follow a power-law relationship.

While the style of writing used on Twitter is widely varied, much of the text is very similar to SMS text messages. This is likely because many users access Twitter through mobile devices. Posts are often highly ungrammatical, and filled with spelling errors. In order to illustrate the spelling variation found on Twitter, we ran the Jcluster word clustering algorithm (Goodman, 2001) on our cor-

[2]The Crook et al. model should be able to be combined with the models we present here.

[3]Will be available at http://www.cs.washington.edu/homes/aritter/twitter_chat/

[4]http://twitter.com/public_timeline provides the 20 most recent posts on Twitter

coming comming
enough enought enuff enuf
be4 b4 befor before
yuhr yur your yor ur youur yhur
msgs messages
couldnt culdnt cldnt cannae cudnt couldent
about bou abt abour abut bowt

Table 1: A sample of Twitter spelling variation.

pus, and manually picked out clusters of spelling variants; a sample is displayed in Table 1.

Twitter's noisy style makes processing Twitter text more difficult than other domains. While moving to a new domain (e.g. biomedical text) is a challenging task, at least the new words found in the vocabulary are limited mostly to verbs and nouns, while function words remain constant. On Twitter, even closed-class words such as prepositions and pronouns are spelled in many different ways.

3 Dialogue Analysis

We propose two models to discover dialogue acts in an unsupervised manner. An ideal model will give insight into the sorts of conversations that happen on Twitter, while providing a useful tool for later processing. We first introduce the summarization technology we apply to this task, followed by two Bayesian extensions.

3.1 Conversation model

Our base model structure is inspired by the content model proposed by Barzilay and Lee (2004) for multi-document summarization. Their sentence-level HMM discovers the sequence of topics used to describe a particular type of news event, such as earthquakes. A news story is modeled by first generating a sequence of hidden topics according to a Markov model, with each topic generating an observed sentence according to a topic-specific language model. These models capture the sequential structure of news stories, and can be used for summarization tasks such as sentence extraction and ordering.

Our goals are not so different: we wish to discover the sequential dialogue structure of conversation. Rather than learning a disaster's location is followed by its death toll, we instead wish to learn that a question is followed by an answer. An initial

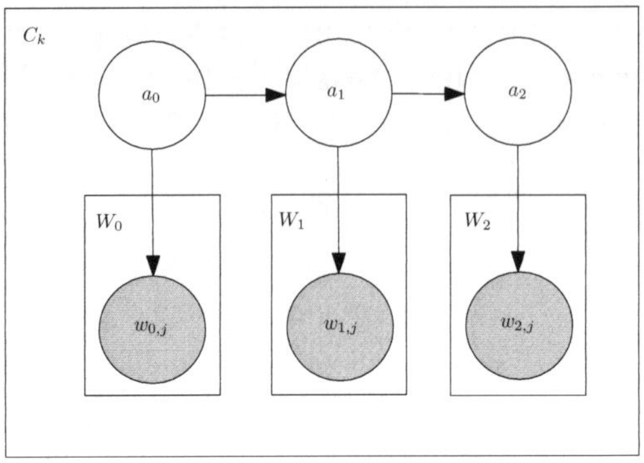

Figure 2: Conversation Model

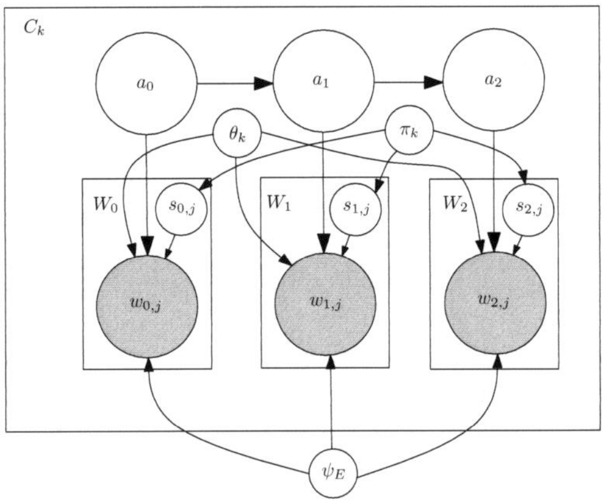

Figure 3: Conversation + Topic Model

conversation model can be created by simply applying the content modeling framework to conversation data. We rename the hidden states *acts*, and assume each post in a Twitter conversation is generated by a single act.[5] During development, we found that a unigram language model performed best as the act emission distribution.

The resulting conversation model is shown as a plate diagram in Figure 2. Each conversation C is a sequence of acts a, and each act produces a post, represented by a bag of words shown using the W plates. The number of acts available to the model is fixed; we experimented with between 5 and 40. Starting with a random assignment of acts, we train our conversation model using EM, with forward-backward providing act distributions during the expectation step. The model structure in Figure 2 is

[5]The short length of Twitter posts makes this assumption reasonable.

sadly no. some **pasta bake**, but **coffee** and **pasta bake** is not a contender for **tea** and **toast**... .	
yum! **Ground beef tacos**? We 're **grilling** out. **Turkey dogs** for me, a **Bubba Burger** for my dh, and **combo** for the kids.	
ha! They gotcha! You had to think about **Arby's** to write that tweet. **Arby's** is conducting a psychlogical study. Of **roast beef**.	
Rumbly tummy soon to be tamed by **Dominos** for **lunch**! **Nom nom nom**!	

Table 2: Example of a topical cluster discovered by the EM Conversation Model.

similar to previous HMMs for supervised dialogue act recognition (Stolcke et al., 2000), but our model is trained unsupervised.

3.2 Conversation + Topic model

Our conversations are not restricted to any particular topic: Twitter users can and will talk about anything. Therefore, there is no guarantee that our model, charged with discovering clusters of posts that aid in the prediction of the next cluster, will necessarily discover dialogue acts. The sequence model could instead partition entire conversations into topics, such as *food*, *computers* and *music*, and then predict that each topic self-transitions with high probability: if we begin talking about food, we are likely to continue to do so. Since we began with a content model, it is perhaps not surprising that our Conversation Model tends to discover a mixture of dialogue and topic structure. Several high probability posts from a topic-focused cluster discovered by EM are shown in Table 2. These clusters are undesirable, as they have little to do with dialogue structure.

In general, unsupervised sentence clustering techniques need some degree of direction when a particular level of granularity is desired. Barzilay and Lee (2004) mask named entities in their content models, forcing their model to cluster topics about earthquakes in general, and not instances of specific earthquakes. This solution is not a good fit for Twitter. As explained in Section 2, Twitter's noisiness resists off-the-shelf tools, such as named-entity recognizers and noun-phrase chunkers. Furthermore, we would require a more drastic form of preprocessing in order to mask all topic words, and not just alter the topic granularity. During development, we explored coarse methods to abstract away content while maintaining syntax, such as replacing tokens with either parts-of-speech or automatically-generated word clusters, but we found that these approaches degrade model performance.

Another approach to filtering out topic information leaves the data intact, but modifies the model to account for topic. To that end, we adopt a Latent Dirichlet Allocation, or LDA, framework (Blei et al., 2003) similar to approaches used recently in summarization (Daumé III and Marcu, 2006; Haghighi and Vanderwende, 2009). The goal of this extended model is to separate content words from dialogue indicators. Each word in a conversation is generated from one of three **sources**:

- The current post's dialogue act
- The conversation's topic
- General English

The extended model is shown in Figure 3.[6] In addition to act emission and transition parameters, the model now includes a conversation-specific word multinomial θ_k that represents the topic, as well as a universal general English multinomial ψ_E. A new hidden variable, s determines the source of each word, and is drawn from a conversation-specific distribution over sources π_k. Following LDA conventions, we place a symmetric Dirichlet prior over each of the multinomials. Dirichlet concentration parameters for act emission, act transition, conversation topic, general English, and source become the hyper-parameters of our model.

The multinomials θ_k, π_k and ψ_E create non-local dependencies in our model, breaking our HMM dynamic programing. Therefore we adopt Gibbs sampling as our inference engine. Each hidden variable is sampled in turn, conditioned on a complete assignment of all other hidden variables throughout the data set. Again following LDA convention, we carry out collapsed sampling, where the various multinomials are integrated out, and are never explicitly estimated. This results in a sampling sequence where for each post we first sample its act, and then sample a source for each word in the post. The hidden act and source variables are sampled according to the following transition distributions:

[6] This figure omits hyperparameters as well as act transition and emission multinomials to reduce clutter. Dirichlet priors are placed over all multinomials.

$$P_{trans}(a_i|\mathbf{a}_{-i}, \mathbf{s}, \mathbf{w}) \propto P(a_i|\mathbf{a}_{-i}) \prod_{j=1}^{W_i} P(w_{i,j}|\mathbf{a}, \mathbf{s}, \mathbf{w}_{-(i,j)})$$

$$P_{trans}(s_{i,j}|\mathbf{a}, \mathbf{s}_{-(i,j)}, \mathbf{w}) \propto P(s_{i,j}|\mathbf{s}_{-(i,j)}) P(w_{i,j}|\mathbf{a}, \mathbf{s}, \mathbf{w}_{-(i,j)})$$

These probabilities can be computed analogously to the calculations used in the collapsed sampler for a bigram HMM (Goldwater and Griffiths, 2007), and those used for LDA (Griffiths and Steyvers, 2004).

Note that our model contains five hyperparameters. Rather than attempt to set them using an expensive grid search, we treat the concentration parameters as additional hidden variables and sample each in turn, conditioned on the current assignment to all other variables. Because these variables are continuous, we apply slice sampling (Neal, 2003). Slice sampling is a general technique for drawing samples from a distribution by sampling uniformly from the area under its density function.

3.3 Estimating Likelihood on Held-Out Data

In Section 4.2 we evaluate our models by comparing their probability on held-out test conversations. As computing this probability exactly is intractable in our model, we employ a recently proposed Chibb-style estimator (Murray and Salakhutdinov, 2008; Wallach et al., 2009). Chibb estimators estimate the probability of unseen data, $P(\mathbf{w})$ by selecting a high probability assignment to hidden variables $\mathbf{h}^*$, and taking advantage of the following equality which can be easily derived from the definition of conditional probability:

$$P(\mathbf{w}) = \frac{P(\mathbf{w}, \mathbf{h}^*)}{P(\mathbf{h}^*|\mathbf{w})}$$

As the numerator can be computed exactly, this reduces the problem of estimating $P(\mathbf{w})$ to the easier problem of estimating $P(\mathbf{h}^*|\mathbf{w})$. Murray and Salakhutdinov (2008) provide an unbiased estimator for $P(\mathbf{h}^*|\mathbf{w})$, which is calculated using the stationary distribution of the Gibbs sampler.

3.4 Bayesian Conversation model

Given the infrastructure necessary for the Conversation+Topic model described above, it is straightforward to also implement a Bayesian version of the conversation model described in Section 3.1. This amounts to replacing the add-x smoothing of dialogue act emission and transition probabilities with (potentially sparse) Dirichlet priors, and replacing EM with Gibbs sampling. There is reason to believe that integrating out multinomials and using sparse priors will improve the performance of the conversation model, as improvements have been observed when using a Bayesian HMM for unsupervised part-of-speech tagging (Goldwater and Griffiths, 2007).

4 Experiments

Evaluating automatically discovered dialogue acts is a difficult problem. Unlike previous work, our model automatically discovers an appropriate set of dialogue acts for a new medium; these acts will not necessarily have a close correspondence to dialogue act inventories manually designed for other corpora. Instead of comparing against human annotations, we present a visualization of the automatically discovered dialogue acts, in addition to measuring the ability of our models to predict post order in unseen conversations. Ideally we would evaluate performance using an end-use application such as a conversational agent; however as this is outside the scope of this paper, we leave such an evaluation to future work.

For all experiments we train our models on a set of 10,000 randomly sampled conversations with conversation length in posts ranging from 3 to 6. Note that our implementations can likely scale to larger data by using techniques such as SparseLDA (Yao et al., 2009). We limit our vocabulary to the 5,000 most frequent words in the corpus.

When using EM, we train for 100 iterations, evaluating performance on the test set at each iteration, and reporting the maximum. Smoothing parameters are set using grid search on a development set.

When performing inference with Gibbs Sampling, we use 1,000 samples for burn-in and take 10 samples at a lag of 100. Although using multiple samples introduces the possibility of poor results due to "act drift", we found this not to be a problem in practice; in fact, taking multiple samples substantially improved performance during development.

Recall that we infer hyperparameters using slice

sampling. The concentration parameters chosen in this manner were always sparse (< 1), which produced a moderate improvement over an uninformed prior.

4.1 Qualitative Evaluation

We are quite interested in what our models can tell us about how people converse on Twitter. To visualize and interpret our competing models, we examined act-emission distributions, posts with high-confidence acts, and act-transition diagrams. Of the three competing systems, we found the Conversation+Topic model by far the easiest to interpret: the 10-act model has 8 acts that we found intuitive, while the other 2 are used only with low probability. Conversely, the Conversation model, whether trained by EM or Gibbs sampling, suffered from the inclusion of general terms and from the conflation of topic and dialogue. For example, the EM-trained conversation model discovered an "act" that was clearly a collection of posts about food, with no underlying dialogue theme (see Table 2).

In the remainder of this section, we reproduce our visualization for the 10-act Conversation+Topic model. Word lists summarizing the discovered dialogue acts are shown in Table 3. For each act, the top 40 words are listed in order of decreasing emission probability. An example post, drawn from the set of highest-confidence posts for that act, is also included. Figure 4 provides a visualization of the matrix of transition probabilities between dialogue acts. An arrow is drawn from one act to the next if the probability of transition is above 0.15.[7] Note that a uniform model would transition to each act with probability 0.10. In both Table 3 and Figure 4, we use intuitive names in place of cluster numbers. These are based on our interpretations of the clusters, and are provided only to benefit the reader when interpreting the transition diagram.[8]

From inspecting the transition diagram (Figure 4), one can see that the model employs three distinct acts to initiate Twitter conversations. These initial acts are quite different from one another, and lead to

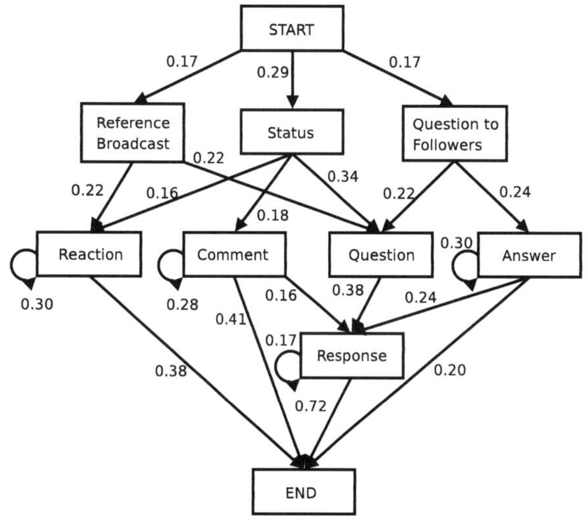

Figure 4: Transitions between dialogue acts. See table 3 for word lists and example posts for each act

different sets of possible responses. We discuss each of these in turn.

The *Status* act appears to represent a post in which the user is broadcasting information about what they are currently doing. This can be seen by the high amount of probability mass given to words like *I* and *my*, in addition to verbs such as *go* and *get*, as well as temporal nouns such as *today*, *tomorrow* and *tonight*.

The *Reference Broadcast* act consists mostly of usernames and urls.[9] Also prominent is the word *rt*, which has special significance on Twitter, indicating that the user is re-posting another user's post. This act represents a user broadcasting an interesting link or quote to their followers. Also note that this node transitions to the *Reaction* act with high probability. *Reaction* appears to cover excited or appreciative responses to new information, assigning high probability to *!*, *!!*, *!!!*, *lol*, *thanks*, and *haha*.

Finally *Question to Followers* represents a user asking a question to their followers. The presence of the question mark and WH question words indicate a question, while words like *anyone* and *know* indicate that the user is asking for information or an opinion. Note that this is distinct from the *Question* act, which is in response to an initial post.

Another interesting point is the alternation be-

[7] After setting this threshold, two Acts were cut off from the rest of the graph (had no incoming edges), and were therefore removed

[8] In some cases, the choice in name is somewhat arbitrary, ie: answer versus response, reaction versus comment.

[9] As part of the preprocessing of our corpus we replaced all usernames and urls with the special tokens *-usr-* and *-url-*.

Status	I . to ! my , is for up in ... and going was today so at go get back day got this am but Im now tomorrow night work tonight off morning home had gon need !! be just getting
	I just changed my twitter page bkgornd and now I can't stop looking at it, lol!!
Question to Followers	? you is do I to -url- what -usr- me , know if anyone why who can " this or of that how does - : on your are need any rt u should people want get did have would tell
	anyone using google voice? just got my invite, should i?? don't know what it is? -url- for the video and break down
Reference Broadcast	-usr- ! -url- rt : -usr-: - " my the , is (you new – ? !!) this for at in follow of on ¡ lol u are twitter your thanks via !!! by :) here 2 please check
	rt -usr-: -usr- word that mac lip gloss give u lock jaw! lol
Question	? you what ! are is how u do the did your that , lol where why or ?? hey about was have who it in so haha on doing going know good up get like were for there :) can
	DWL!! what song is that??
Reaction	! you I :) !! , thanks lol it haha that love so good too your thank is are u !!! was for :d me -usr- ¡ hope ? my 3 omg ... oh great hey awesome - happy now aww
	sweet! im so stoked now!
Comment	you I . to , ! do ? it be if me your know have we can get will :) but u that see lol would are so want go let up well need - come ca make or think them
	why are you in tx and why am I just now finding out about it?! i'm in dfw, till I get a job. i'll have to come to Htown soon!
Answer	. I , you it " that ? is but do was he the of a they if not would know be did or does think) like (as have what in are - no them said who say '
	my fave was "keeping on top of other week"
Response	. I , it was that lol but is yeah ! haha he my know yes you :) like too did well she so its ... though do had no - one as im thanks they think would not good oh
	nah im out in maryland, leaving for tour in a few days.

Table 3: Word lists and example posts for each Dialogue Act. Words are listed in decreasing order of probability given the act. Example posts are in *italics*.

tween the personal pronouns *you* and *I* in the acts due to the focus of conversation and speaker. The *Status* act generates the word *I* with high probability, whereas the likely response state *Question* generates *you*, followed by *Response* which again generates *I*.

4.2 Quantitative Evaluation

Qualitative evaluations are both time-consuming and subjective. The above visualization is useful for understanding the Twitter domain, but it is of little use when comparing model variants or selecting parameters. Therefore, we also propose a novel quantitative evaluation that measures the intrinsic quality of a conversation model by its ability to predict the ordering of posts in a conversation. This measures the model's predictive power, while requiring no tagged data, and no commitment to an existing tag inventory.

Our test set consists of 1,000 randomly selected conversations not found in the training data. For each conversation in the test set, we generate all $n!$ permutations of the posts. The probability of each permutation is then evaluated as if it were an unseen conversation, using either the forward algorithm (EM) or the Chibb-style estimator (Gibbs). Following work from the summarization community (Barzilay and Lee, 2004), we employ Kendall's τ to measure the similarity of the max-probability permutation to the original order.

The Kendall τ rank correlation coefficient measures the similarity between two permutations based on their agreement in pairwise orderings:

$$\tau = \frac{n_+ - n_-}{\binom{n}{2}}$$

where n_+ is the number of pairs that share the same order in both permutations, and n_- is the number that do not. This statistic ranges between -1 and +1, where -1 indicates inverse order, and +1 indicates identical order. A value greater than 0 indicates a positive correlation.

Predicting post order on open-domain Twitter conversations is a much more difficult task than on topic-focused news data (Barzilay and Lee, 2004). We found that a simple bigram model baseline does very poorly at predicting order on Twitter, achieving only a weak positive correlation of $\tau = 0.0358$ on our test data as compared with 0.19-0.74 reported by Barzilay and Lee on news data.

Note that τ is not a perfect measure of model quality for conversations; in some cases, multiple order-

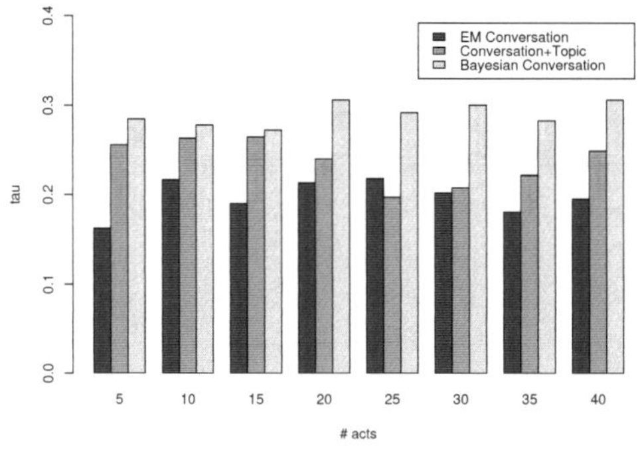

Figure 5: Performance at conversation ordering task.

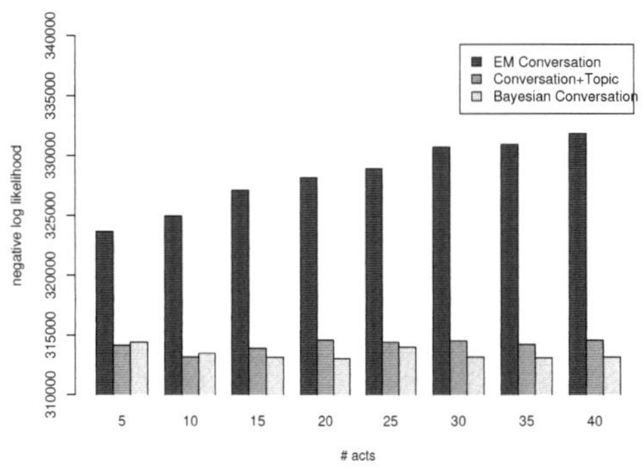

Figure 6: Negative log likelihood on held out test data (smaller values indicate higher likelihood).

ings of the same set of posts may form a perfectly acceptable conversation. On the other hand, there are often strong constraints on the type of response we might expect to follow a particular dialogue act; for example, answers follow questions. We would expect an effective model to use these constraints to predict order.

Performance at the conversation ordering task while varying the number of acts for each model is displayed in Figure 5. In general, we found that using Bayesian inference outperforms EM. Also note that the Bayesian Conversation model outperforms the Conversation+Topic model at predicting conversation order. This is likely because modeling conversation content as a sequence can in some cases help to predict post ordering; for example, adjacent posts are more likely to contain similar content words. Recall though that we found the Conversation+Topic model to be far more interpretable.

Additionally we compare the likelihood of these models on held out test data in Figure 6. Note that the Bayesian methods produce models with much higher likelihood.[10] For the EM models, likelihood tends to decrease on held out test data as we increase the number of hidden states, due to overfitting.

5 Conclusion

We have presented an approach that allows the unsupervised induction of dialogue structure from naturally-occurring open-topic conversational data. By visualizing the learned models, coherent patterns emerge from a stew of data that human readers find difficult to follow. We have extended a conversation sequence model to separate topic and dialogue words, resulting in an interpretable set of automatically generated dialogue acts. These discovered acts have interesting differences from those found in other domains, and reflect Twitter's nature as a micro-blog.

We have introduced the task of conversation ordering as an intrinsic measure of conversation model quality. We found this measure quite useful in the development of our models and algorithms, although our experiments show that it does not necessarily correlate with interpretability. We have directly compared Bayesian inference to EM on our conversation ordering task, showing a clear advantage for Bayesian methods.

Finally, we have collected a corpus of 1.3 million Twitter conversations, which we will make available to the research community, and which we hope will be useful beyond the study of dialogue. In the future, we wish to scale our models to the full corpus, and extend them with more complex notions of discourse, topic and community. Ultimately, we hope to put the learned conversation structure to use in the construction of a data-driven, conversational agent.

Acknowledgements

We are grateful to everyone in the NLP and TMSN groups at Microsoft Research for helpful discussions and feedback. We thank Oren Etzioni, Michael Gamon, Mausam and Fei Wu, and the anonymous reviewers for helpful comments on a previous draft.

[10]Likelihood of the test data is estimated using the Chibb Style estimator described in (Murray and Salakhutdinov, 2008; Wallach et al., 2009). This method under-estimates likelihood in expectation. The maximum likelihood (EM) likelihoods are exact.

References

James Allen, Nathanael Chambers, George Ferguson, Lucian Galescu, Hyuckchul Jung, Mary Swift, and William Taysom. 2007. Plow: a collaborative task learning agent. In *Proceedings of AAAI*.

Regina Barzilay and Lillian Lee. 2004. Catching the drift: Probabilistic content models, with applications to generation and summarization. In *Proceedings of HLT-NAACL*, pages 113–120.

David M. Blei, Andrew Y. Ng, and Michael I. Jordan. 2003. Latent dirichlet allocation. *J. Mach. Learn. Res.*, 3:993–1022.

William W. Cohen, Vitor R. Carvalho, and Tom M. Mitchell. 2004. Learning to classify email into "speech acts". In *Proceedings of EMNLP*.

Nigel Crook, Ramon Granell, and Stephen Pulman. 2009. Unsupervised classification of dialogue acts using a Dirichlet process mixture model. In *Proceedings of SIGDIAL*, pages 341–348.

Hal Daumé III and Daniel Marcu. 2006. Bayesian query-focused summarization. In *Proceedings of ACL*.

Rajdip Dhillon, Sonali Bhagat, Hannah Carvey, and Elizabeth Shriberg. 2004. Meeting recorder project: Dialog act labeling guide. Technical report, International Computer Science Institute.

Micha Elsner and Eugene Charniak. 2008. You talking to me? A corpus and algorithm for conversation disentanglement. In *Proceedings of ACL-HLT*.

Eric N. Forsyth and Craig H. Martell. 2007. Lexical and discourse analysis of online chat dialog. In *Proceedings of ICSC*.

Michael Gamon, Sumit Basu, Dmitriy Belenko, Danyel Fisher, Matthew Hurst, and Arnd Christian Knig. 2008. Blews: Using blogs to provide context for news articles. In *Proceedings of ICWSM*.

Sharon Goldwater and Tom Griffiths. 2007. A fully bayesian approach to unsupervised part-of-speech tagging. In *Proceedings of ACL*, pages 744–751.

Joshua T. Goodman. 2001. A bit of progress in language modeling. Technical report.

T. L. Griffiths and M. Steyvers. 2004. Finding scientific topics. *Proc Natl Acad Sci*, 101 Suppl 1:5228–5235.

Aria Haghighi and Lucy Vanderwende. 2009. Exploring content models for multi-document summarization. In *Proceedings of HLT-NAACL*, pages 362–370.

Yijue How and Min-Yen Kan. 2005. Optimizing predictive text entry for short message service on mobile phones. In *Proceedings of HCII*.

Minwoo Jeong, Chin-Yew Lin, and Gary Geunbae Lee. 2009. Semi-supervised speech act recognition in emails and forums. In *Proceedings of EMNLP*, pages 1250–1259.

Dan Jurafsky, Liz Shriberg, and Debra Biasca. 1997. Switchboard swbd-damsl shallow-discourse-function annotation coders manual, draft 13. Technical report, University of Colorado Institute of Cognitive Science.

Ryan Kelly. 2009. Pear analytics twitter study. Whitepaper, August.

Iain Murray and Ruslan Salakhutdinov. 2008. Evaluating probabilities under high-dimensional latent variable models. In *Proceedings of NIPS*, pages 1137–1144.

Gabriel Murray, Steve Renals, Jean Carletta, and Johanna Moore. 2006. Incorporating speaker and discourse features into speech summarization. In *Proceedings of HLT-NAACL*, pages 367–374.

Radford M. Neal. 2003. Slice sampling. *Annals of Statistics*, 31:705–767.

Rajesh Ranganath, Dan Jurafsky, and Dan Mcfarland. 2009. It's not you, it's me: Detecting flirting and its misperception in speed-dates. In *Proceedings of EMNLP*, pages 334–342.

Andreas Stolcke, Noah Coccaro, Rebecca Bates, Paul Taylor, Carol Van Ess-Dykema, Klaus Ries, Elizabeth Shriberg, Daniel Jurafsky, Rachel Martin, and Marie Meteer. 2000. Dialogue act modeling for automatic tagging and recognition of conversational speech. *Computational Linguistics*, 26(3):339–373.

Hanna M. Wallach, Iain Murray, Ruslan Salakhutdinov, and David M. Mimno. 2009. Evaluation methods for topic models. In *Proceedings of ICML*, page 139.

Yorick Wilks. 2006. Artificial companions as a new kind of interface to the future internet. In *OII Research Report No. 13*.

M. Woszczyna and A. Waibel. 1994. Inferring linguistic structure in spoken language. In *Proceedings of ICSLP*.

Tae Yano, William W. Cohen, and Noah A. Smith. 2009. Predicting response to political blog posts with topic models. In *Proceedings of NAACL*, pages 477–485.

Limin Yao, David Mimno, and Andrew McCallum. 2009. Efficient methods for topic model inference on streaming document collections. In *Proceedings of KDD*, pages 937–946.

Streaming First Story Detection with application to Twitter

Saša Petrović
School of Informatics
University of Edinburgh
sasa.petrovic@ed.ac.uk

Miles Osborne
School of Informatics
University of Edinburgh
miles@inf.ed.ac.uk

Victor Lavrenko
School of Informatics
University of Edinburgh
vlavrenk@inf.ed.ac.uk

Abstract

With the recent rise in popularity and size of social media, there is a growing need for systems that can extract useful information from this amount of data. We address the problem of detecting new events from a stream of Twitter posts. To make event detection feasible on web-scale corpora, we present an algorithm based on locality-sensitive hashing which is able overcome the limitations of traditional approaches, while maintaining competitive results. In particular, a comparison with a state-of-the-art system on the first story detection task shows that we achieve over an order of magnitude speedup in processing time, while retaining comparable performance. Event detection experiments on a collection of 160 million Twitter posts show that celebrity deaths are the fastest spreading news on Twitter.

1 Introduction

In the recent years, the microblogging service Twitter has become a very popular tool for expressing opinions, broadcasting news, and simply communicating with friends. People often comment on events in real time, with several hundred micro-blogs (*tweets*) posted each second for significant events. Twitter is not only interesting because of this real-time response, but also because it is sometimes ahead of newswire. For example, during the protests following Iranian presidential elections in 2009, Iranian people first posted news on Twitter, where they were later picked up by major broadcasting corporations. Another example was the swine flu outbreak when the US Centre for disease control (CDC) used Twitter to post latest updates on the pandemic. In addition to this, subjective opinion expressed in posts is also an important feature that sets Twitter apart from traditional newswire.

New event detection, also known as first story detection (FSD)[1] is defined within the topic detection and tracking as one of the subtasks (Allan, 2002). Given a sequence of stories, the goal of FSD is to identify the first story to discuss a particular *event*. In this context, an event is taken to be something that happens at some specific time and place, e.g., an earthquake striking the town of L'Aquila in Italy on April 6th 2009. Detecting new events from tweets carries additional problems and benefits compared to traditional new event detection from newswire. Problems include a much higher volume of data to deal with and also a higher level of noise. A major benefit of doing new event detection from tweets is the added social component – we can understand the impact an event had and how people reacted to it.

The speed and volume at which data is coming from Twitter warrants the use of *streaming* algorithms to make first story detection feasible. In the streaming model of computation (Muthukrishnan, 2005), items (tweets in our case) arrive continuously in a chronological order, and we have to process each new one in bounded space and time. Recent examples of problems set in the streaming model include stream-based machine translation (Levenberg and Osborne, 2009), approximating kernel matrices of data streams (Shi et al., 2009), and topic modelling on streaming document collections (Yao et al., 2009). The traditional approach to FSD, where each new story is compared to all, or a constantly growing subset, of previously seen stories, does not scale to the Twitter streaming setting. We present a FSD system that works in the streaming model and takes constant time to process each new document, while also using constant space. Constant processing time is achieved by employing *locality sensitive hashing (LSH)* (Indyk and Motwani, 1998), a randomized technique that dramatically reduces the time needed

[1] We will be using the terms first story detection and new event detection interchangeably.

Human Language Technologies: The 2010 Annual Conference of the North American Chapter of the ACL, pages 181–189,
Los Angeles, California, June 2010.

to find a nearest neighbor in vector space, and the space saving is achieved by keeping the amount of stories in memory constant.

We find that simply applying pure LSH in a FSD task yields poor performance and a high variance in results, and so introduce a modification which virtually eliminates variance and significantly improves performance. We show that our FSD system gives comparable results as a state-of-the-art system on the standard TDT5 dataset, while achieving an order of magnitude speedup. Using our system for event detection on 160 million Twitter posts shows that i) the number of users that write about an event is more indicative than the volume of tweets written about it, ii) spam tweets can be detected with reasonable precision, and iii) news about deaths of famous people spreads the fastest on Twitter.

2 First Story Detection

2.1 Traditional Approach

The traditional approach to first story detection is to represent documents as vectors in term space, where coordinates represent the (possibly IDF-weighted) frequency of a particular term in a document. Each new document is then compared to the previous ones, and if its similarity to the closest document (or centroid) is below a certain threshold, the new document is declared to be a first story. For example, this approach is used in the UMass (Allan et al., 2000) and the CMU system (Yang et al., 1998). Algorithm 1 shows the exact pseudocode used by the UMass system. Note that $dis_{min}(d)$ is the novelty score assigned to document d. Often, in order to decrease the running time, documents are represented using only n features with the highest weights.

Algorithm 1: Traditional FSD system based on nearest-neighbor search.

foreach *document d in corpus* **do**
  foreach *term t in d* **do**
    foreach *document d' that contains t* **do**
      update distance(d, d')
    end
  end
  $dis_{min}(d) = \min_{d'}\{distance(d, d')\}$
  add d to inverted index
end

2.2 Locality Sensitive Hashing

The problem of finding the nearest neighbor to a given query has been intensively studied, but as the dimensionality of the data increases none of the current solutions provide much improvement over a simple linear search (Datar et al., 2004). More recently, research has focused on solving a relaxed version of the nearest neighbor problem, the *approximate nearest neighbor*, where the goal is to report any point that lies within $(1+\epsilon)r$ distance of the query point, where r is the distance to the nearest neighbor. One of the first approaches to solving the approximate-NN problem in sublinear time was described in Indyk and Motwani (1998), where the authors introduced a new method called *locality sensitive hashing (LSH).* This method relied on hashing each query point into buckets in such a way that the probability of collision was much higher for points that are near by. When a new point arrived, it would be hashed into a bucket and the points that were in the same bucket were inspected and the nearest one returned.

Because we are dealing with textual documents, a particularly interesting measure of distance is the cosine between two documents. Allan et al. (2000) report that this distance outperforms the KL divergence, weighted sum, and language models as distance functions on the first story detection task. This is why in our work we use the hashing scheme proposed by Charikar (2002) in which the probability of two points colliding is proportional to the cosine of the angle between them. This scheme was used, e.g., for creating similarity lists of nouns collected from a web corpus in Ravichandran et al. (2005). It works by intersecting the space with random hyperplanes, and the buckets are defined by the subspaces formed this way. More precisely, the probability of two points x and y colliding under such a hashing scheme is

$$P_{coll} = 1 - \frac{\theta(x,y)}{\pi}, \quad (1)$$

where $\theta(x,y)$ is the angle between x and y. By using more than one hyperplane, we can decrease the probability of collision with a non-similar point. The number of hyperplanes k can be considered as a number of bits per key in this hashing scheme. In particular, if $x \cdot u_i < 0, i \in [1 \dots k]$ for document x and hyperplane vector u_i, we set the i-th bit to 0, and 1 otherwise. The higher k is, the fewer collisions we will have in our buckets but we will spend more time computing the hash values.[2] However, increasing k also decreases the probability of collision with the nearest neighbor, so we need multiple hash tables (each with k independently chosen random hyperplanes) to increase the chance that the nearest neighbor will collide with our point in at least one of

[2]Probability of collision under k random hyperplanes will be P^k_{coll}.

them. Given the desired number of bits k, and the desired probability of missing a nearest neighbor δ, one can compute the number of hash tables L as

$$L = \log_{1-P_{coll}^{k}} \delta. \quad (2)$$

2.3 Variance Reduction Strategy

Unfortunately, simply applying LSH for nearest neighbor search in a FSD task yields poor results with a lot of variance (the exact numbers are given in Section 6). This is because LSH only returns the true near neighbor if it is reasonably close to the query point. If, however, the query point lies far away from all other points (i.e., its nearest neighbor is far away), LSH fails to find the true near neighbor. To overcome this problem, we introduce a strategy by which, if the LSH scheme declares a document new (i.e., sufficiently different from all others), we start a search through the inverted index, but only compare the query with a fixed number of most recent documents. We set this number to 2000; preliminary experiments showed that values between 1000 and 3000 all yield very similar results. The pseudocode shown in algorithm 2 summarizes the approach based on LSH, with the lines 11 and 12 being the variance reduction strategy.

Algorithm 2: Our LSH-based approach.

```
   input: threshold t
1  foreach document d in corpus do
2      add d to LSH
3      S <- set of points that collide with d in LSH
4      dis_min(d) <- 1
5      foreach document d' in S do
6          c = distance(d, d')
7          if c < dis_min(d) then
8              dis_min(d) <- c
9          end
10     end
11     if dis_min(d) >= t then
12         compare d to a fixed number of most
           recent documents as in Algorithm 1 and
           update dis_min if necessary
13     end
14     assign score dis_min(d) to d
15     add d to inverted index
16 end
```

3 Streaming First Story Detection

Although using LSH in the way we just described greatly reduces the running time, it is still too expensive when we want to deal with *text streams.* Text streams naturally arise on the Web, where millions of new documents are published each hour. Social media sites like Facebook, MySpace, Twitter, and various blogging sites are a particularly interesting source of textual data because each new document is timestamped and usually carries additional metadata like topic tags or links to author's friends. Because this stream of documents is unbounded and coming down at a very fast rate, there is usually a limit on the amount of space/time we can spend per document. In the context of first story detection, this means we are not allowed to store all of the previous data in main memory nor compare the new document to all the documents returned by LSH.

Following the previous reasoning, we present the following desiderata for a streaming first story detection system: we first assume that each day we are presented with a large volume of documents in chronological order. A streaming FSD system should, for each document, say whether it discusses a previously unseen event and give confidence in its decision. The decision should be made in bounded time (preferably constant time per document), and using bounded space (also constant per document). Only one pass over the data is allowed and the decision has to be made immediately after a new document arrives. A system that has all of these properties can be employed for finding first stories in real time from a stream of stories coming down from the Web.

3.1 A constant space and time approach

In this section, we describe our streaming FSD system in more depth. As was already mentioned in Section 2.2, we use locality sensitive hashing to limit our search to a small number of documents. However, because there is only a finite number of buckets, in a true streaming setting the number of documents in any bucket will grow without a bound. This means that i) we would use an unbounded amount of space, and ii) the number of comparisons we need to make would also grow without a bound. To alleviate the first problem, we limit the number of documents inside a single bucket to a constant. If the bucket is full, the oldest document in the bucket is removed. Note that the document is removed only from that single bucket in one of the L hash tables – it may still be present in other hash tables. Note that this way of limiting the number of documents kept is in a way topic-specific. Luo et al. (2007) use a global constraint on the documents they keep and show that around 30 days of data needs to be kept in order to achieve reasonable performance. While using this approach also ensures that the number of comparisons made is constant, this constant can be rather large. Theoretically, a new document can collide with all of the documents that are left, and this can be quite a large number (we have to keep a sufficient portion of the data in memory to make sure we have a representative sample of the stream to compare with). That is why, in addition to limiting the number of documents in a bucket, we also limit ourselves to making a constant number of comparisons. We do this by comparing each new document with at most 3L documents it collided with. Unlike Datar et al. (2004), where any 3L documents were used, we compare to the 3L documents that collide most frequently with the new document. That is, if S is the set of all documents that collided with a new document in all L hash tables, we order the elements of S according to the number of hash tables where the collision occurred. We take the top 3L elements of that ordered set and compare the new document only to them.

4 Detecting Events in Twitter Posts

While doing first story detection on a newspaper stream makes sense because all of the incoming documents are actual stories, this is not the case with Twitter posts (tweets). The majority of tweets are not real stories, but rather updates on one's personal life, conversations, or spam. Thus, simply running a first story detection system on this data would yield an incredible amount of new stories each day, most of which would be of no interest to anyone but a few people. However, when something significant happens (e.g., a celebrity dies), a lot of users write about this either to share their opinion or just to inform others of the event. Our goal here is to automatically detect these significant events, preferably with a minimal number of non-important events.

Threading. We first run our streaming FSD system and assign a novelty score to each tweet. In addition, since the score is based on a cosine distance to the nearest tweet, for each tweet we also output which other tweet it is most similar to. This way, we can analyze *threads* of tweets, i.e., a subset of tweets which all discuss the same topic (Nallapati et al., 2004). To explain how we form threads of tweets, we first introduce the *links* relation. We say that tweet a *links* to tweet b if b is the nearest neighbor of a and $1 - \cos(a, b) < t$, where t is a user-specified threshold. Then, for each tweet a we either assign it to an existing thread if its nearest neighbor is within distance t, or say that a is the first tweet in a new thread. If we assign a to an existing thread, we assign it to the same thread to which its nearest neighbor belongs. By changing t we can control the granularity of threads. If t is set very high, we will have few very big and broad threads, whereas setting t very low will result in many very specific and very small threads. In our experiments, we set $t = 0.5$. We experimented with different values of t and found that for $t \in [0.5, 0.6]$ results are very much the same, whereas setting t outside this interval starts to impact the results in the way we just explained.

Once we have threads of tweets, we are interested in which threads grow fastest, as this will be an indication that news of a new event is spreading. Therefore, for each time interval we only output the fastest growing threads. This growth rate also gives us a way to measure a thread's impact.

5 Related Work

In the recent years, analysis of social media has attracted a lot of attention from the research community. However, most of the work that uses social media focuses on blogs (Glance et al., 2004; Bansal and Koudas, 2007; Gruhl et al., 2005). On the other hand, research that uses Twitter has so far only focused on describing the properties of Twitter itself (Java et al., 2007; Krishnamurthy et al., 2008).

The problem of online new event detection in a large-scale streaming setting was previously addressed in Luo et al. (2007). Their system used the traditional approach to FSD and then employed various heuristics to make computation feasible. These included keeping only the first stories in memory, limiting the number of terms per document, limiting the number of total terms kept, and employing parallel processing. Our randomized framework gives us a principled way to work out the errors introduced and is more general than the previously mentioned approach because we could still use all the heuristics used by Luo et al. (2007) in our system. Finally, while Luo et al. (2007) achieved considerable speedup over an existing system on a TDT corpus, they never showed the utility of their system on a truly large-scale task.

The only work we are aware of that analyzes social media in a streaming setting is Saha and Getoor (2009). There, the focus was on solving the *maximum coverage* problem for a stream of blog posts. The maximum coverage problem in their setting, dubbed *blog watch*, was selecting k blogs that maximize the cover of interests specified by a user. This work differs from Saha and Getoor (2009) in many ways. Most notably, we deal with the problem of detecting new events, and determining who was the first to report them. Also, there is a difference in the type and volume of data – while Saha and Getoor (2009) use 20 days of blog data totalling two million posts, we use Twitter data from a timespan of six months, totalling over 160 million posts.

6 Experiments

6.1 TDT5 Experimental Setup

Baseline. Before applying our FSD system on Twitter data, we first compared it to a state-of-the-art FSD system on the standard TDT5 dataset. This way, we can test if our system is on par with the best existing systems, and also accurately measure the speedup that we get over a traditional approach. In particular, we compare our system with the UMass FSD system (Allan et al., 2000). The UMass system has participated in the TDT2 and TDT3 competitions and is known to perform at least as well as other existing systems who also took part in the competition (Fiscus, 2001). Note that the UMass system uses an inverted index (as shown in Algorithm 1) which optimizes the system for speed and makes sure a minimal number of comparisons is made. We compare the systems on the English part of the TDT5 dataset, consisting of 221,306 documents from a time period spanning April 2003 to September 2003. To make sure that any difference in results is due to approximations we make, we use the same settings as the UMass system: 1-NN clustering, cosine as a similarity measure, and TFIDF weighted document representation, where the IDF weights are incrementally updated. These particular settings were found by Allan et al. (2000) to perform the best for the FSD task. We limit both systems to keeping only top 300 features in each document. Using more than 300 features barely improves performance while taking significantly more time for the UMass system.[3]

LSH parameters. In addition, our system has two LSH parameters that need to be set. The number of hyperplanes k gives a tradeoff between time spent computing the hash functions and the time spent computing the distances. A lower k means more documents per bucket and thus more distance computations, whereas a higher k means less documents per bucket, but more hash tables and thus more time spent computing hash functions. Given k, we can use equation (2) to compute L. In our case, we chose k to be 13, and L such that the probability of missing a neighbor within the distance of 0.2 is less than 2.5%. The distance of 0.2 was chosen as a reasonable estimate of the threshold when two documents are very similar. In general, this distance will depend on the application, and Datar et al. (2004) suggest guessing the value and then doing a binary search to set it more accurately. We set k to 13 because it achieved a reasonable balance between time spent computing the distances and the time spent computing the hash functions.

Evaluation metric. The official TDT evaluation requires each system to assign a confidence score for its decision, and this assignment can be made either immediately after the story arrives, or after a fixed number of new stories have been observed. Because we assume that we are working in a true streaming setting, systems are required to assign a confidence score as soon as the new story arrives. The actual performance of a system is measured in terms of *detection error tradeoff (DET)* curves and the *minimal normalized cost.* Evaluation is carried out by first sorting all stories according to their scores and then performing a threshold sweep. For each value of the threshold, stories with a score above the threshold are considered new, and all others are considered old. Therefore, for each threshold value, one can compute the probability of a *false alarm*, i.e., probability of declaring a story new when it is actually not, and the *miss probability*, i.e., probability of declaring a new story old (missing a new story). Having computed all the miss and false alarm probabilities, we can plot them on a graph showing the tradeoff between these two quantities – such graphs are called detection error tradeoff curves. The normalized cost C_{det} is computed as

$$C_{det} = C_{miss} * P_{miss} * P_{target} + C_{FA} * P_{FA} * P_{non-target},$$

where C_{miss} and C_{FA} are costs of miss and false alarm, P_{miss} and P_{FA} are probabilities of a miss and false alarm, and P_{target} and $P_{non-target}$ are the prior target and non-target probabilities. Minimal normalized cost C_{min} is the minimal value of C_{det} over all threshold values (a lower value of C_{min} indicates better performance).

6.2 TDT5 Results

All the results on the TDT5 dataset are shown in Table 1. In this section, we go into detail in explaining them. As was mentioned in Section 2.2, simply using LSH to find a nearest neighbor resulted in poor performance and a high variance of results. In particular, the mean normalized cost of ten runs of our system without the variance reduction strategy was 0.88, with a standard deviation of 0.046. When using the strategy explained in Section 2.2, the mean result dropped to 0.70, with a standard deviation of 0.004. Therefore, the results were significantly improved, while also reducing standard deviation by an order of magnitude. This shows that there is a clear advantage in using our variance reduction strategy,

[3] In other words, using more features only increases the advantage of our system over the UMass system.

Table 1: Summary of TDT5 results. Numbers next to LSH'_{ts} indicate the maximal number of documents in a bucket, measured in terms of percentage of the expected number of collisions.

	Baseline	Unbounded		Bounded			
		Pure	Variance Red.	Time	Space and Time		
System	UMass	LSH	LSH′	LSH'_t	LSH'_{ts} 0.5	LSH'_{ts} 0.3	LSH'_{ts} 0.1
C_{min}	0.69	0.88	0.70	0.71	0.76	0.75	0.73

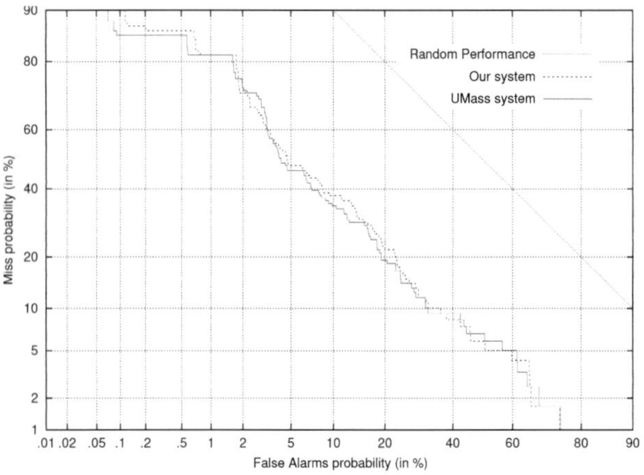

Figure 1: Comparison of our system with the UMass FSD system.

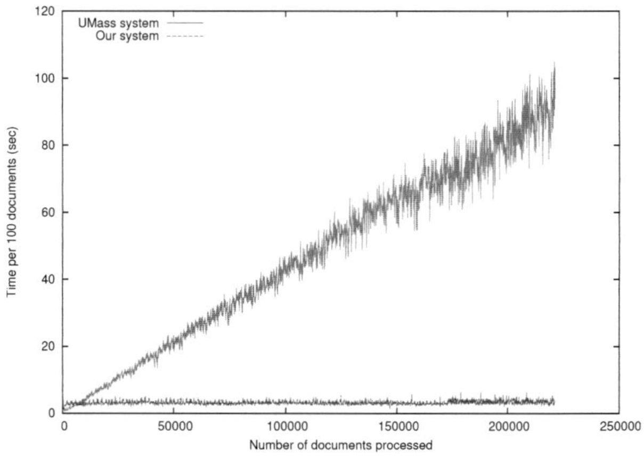

Figure 2: Comparison of processing time per 100 documents for our and the UMass system.

and all the following results we report were obtained from a system that makes use of it.

Figure 1 shows DET curves for the UMass and for our system. For this evaluation, our system was not limited in space, i.e., buckets sizes were unlimited, but the processing time per item was made constant. It is clear that UMass outperforms our system, but the difference is negligible. In particular, the minimal normalized cost C_{min} was 0.69 for the UMass system, and 0.71 for our system. On the other hand, the UMass system took 28 hours to complete the run, compared to two hours for our system. Figure 2 shows the time required to process 100 documents as a function of number of documents seen so far. We can see that our system maintains constant time, whereas the UMass system processing time grows without a bound (roughly linear with the number of previously seen documents).

The last three columns in Table 1 show the effect that limiting the bucket size has on performance. Bucket size was limited in terms of the percent of expected number of collisions, i.e., a bucket size of 0.5 means that the number of documents in a bucket cannot be more than 50% of the expected number of collisions. The expected number of collisions can be computed as $n/2^k$, where n is the total number of documents, and k is the LSH parameter explained earlier. Not surprisingly, limiting the bucket size reduced performance compared to the space-unlimited version, but even when the size is reduced to 10% of the expected number of collisions, performance remains reasonably close to the UMass system. Figure 3 shows the memory usage of our system on a month of Twitter data (more detail about the data can be found in Section 6.3). We can see that most of the memory is allocated right away, after which the memory consumption levels out. If we ran the system indefinitely, we would see the memory usage grow slower and slower until it reached a certain level at which it would remain constant.

6.3 Twitter Experimental Setup

Corpus. We used our streaming FSD system to detect new events from a collection of Twitter data gathered over a period of six months (April 1st 2009 to October 14th 2009). Data was collected through Twitter's streaming API.[4] Our corpus consists of 163.5 million timestamped tweets, totalling over 2 billion tokens. All the tweets in our corpus contain

[4]`http://stream.twitter.com/`

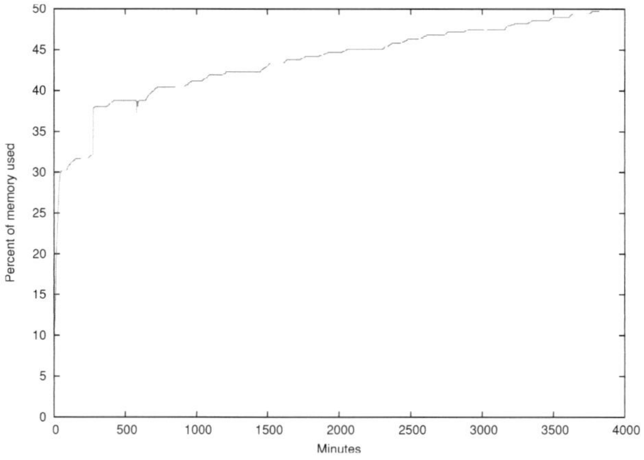

Figure 3: Memory usage on a month of Twitter data. X-axis shows how long the system has been running for.

only ASCII characters and we additionally stripped the tweets of words beginning with the @ or # symbol. This is because on Twitter words beginning with @ indicate a reply to someone, and words beginning with # are topic tags. Although these features would probably be helpful for our task, we decided not to use them as they are specific to Twitter and our approach should be independent of the stream type.

Gold standard. In order to measure how well our system performs on the Twitter data, we employed two human experts to manually label all the tweets returned by our system as either *Event*, *Neutral*, or *Spam*. Note that each tweet that is returned by our system is actually the first tweet in a thread, and thus serves as the representative of what the thread is about. Spam tweets include various advertisements, automatic weather updates, automatic radio station updates, etc. For a tweet to be labeled as an event, it had to be clear from the tweet alone what exactly happened without having any prior knowledge about the event, and the event referenced in the tweet had to be sufficiently important. Important events include celebrity deaths, natural disasters, major sports, political, entertainment, and business events, shootings, plane crashes and other disasters. Neutral tweets include everything not labeled as spam or event. Because the process of manual labeling is tedious and time-consuming, we only labeled the 1000 fastest growing threads from June 2009. Rate of growth of a thread is measured by the number of tweets that belong to that thread in a window of 100,000 tweets, starting from the beginning of the thread. Agreement between our two annotators, measured using Cohen's kappa coefficient, was substantial (kappa = 0.65). We use 820 tweets on which both annotators agreed as the gold standard.

Evaluation. Evaluation is performed by computing *average precision* (AP) on the gold standard sorted according to different criteria, where event tweets are taken to be relevant, and neutral and spam tweets are treated as non-relevant documents. Average precision is a common evaluation metric in tasks like ad-hoc retrieval where only the set of returned documents and their relevance judgements are available, as is the case here (Croft et al., 2009). Note that we are not evaluating our FSD system here. There are two main reasons for this: i) we already have a very good idea about the first story detection performance from the experiments on TDT5 data, and ii) evaluating a FSD system on this scale would be prohibitively expensive as it would involve human experts going through 30 million tweets looking for first stories. Rather, we are evaluating different methods of ranking threads which are output from a FSD system for the purpose of detecting important events in a very noisy and unstructured stream such as Twitter.

6.4 Twitter Results

Results for the average precisions are given in Table 2. Note that we were not able to compare our system with the UMass FSD system on the Twitter data, as the UMass system would not finish in any reasonable amount of time. Different rows of Table 2 correspond to the following ways of ranking the threads:

- Baseline – random ordering of threads
- Size of thread – threads are ranked according to number of tweets
- Number of users – threads are ranked according to number of unique users posting in a thread
- Entropy + users – if the entropy of a thread is < 3.5, move to the back of the list, otherwise sort according to number of unique users

Results show that ranking according to size of thread performs better than the baseline, and ranking according to the number of users is slightly better. However, a sign test showed that neither of the two ranking strategies is significantly better than the baseline. We perform the sign test by splitting the labeled data into 50 stratified samples and ranking each sample with different strategies. We then measure the number of times each strategy performed better (in terms of AP) and compute the significance levels based on these numbers. Adding the information about the entropy of the thread showed to be

Table 2: Average precision for *Events* vs. *Rest* and for *Events* and *Neutral* vs. *Spam*.

Ranking method	events vs. rest	spam vs. rest
Baseline	16.5	84.6
Size of thread	24.1	83.5
Number of users	24.5	83.9
Entropy + users	34.0	96.3

Table 3: Average precision as a function of the entropy threshold on the *Events* vs. *Rest* task.

Entropy	2	2.5	3	3.5	4	4.5
AP	24.8	27.6	30.0	34.0	33.2	29.4

very beneficial. Entropy of a thread is computed as

$$H_{thread} = -\sum_i \frac{n_i}{N} \log \frac{n_i}{N},$$

where n_i is the number of times word i appears in a thread, and $N = \sum_i n_i$ is the total number of words in a thread. We move the threads with low entropy (< 3.5) to the back of the list, while we order other threads by the number of unique users. A sign test showed this approach to be significantly better ($p \leq 0.01$) than all of the previous ranking methods. Table 3 shows the effect of varying the entropy threshold at which threads are moved to the back of the list. We can see that adding information about entropy improves results regardless of the threshold we choose. This approach works well because most spam threads have very low entropy, i.e., contain very little information.

We conducted another experiment where events and neutral tweets are considered relevant, and spam tweets non-relevant documents. Results for this experiment are given in the third column of Table 2. Results for this experiment are much better, mostly due to the large proportion of neutral tweets in the data. The baseline in this case is very strong and neither sorting according to the size of the thread nor according to the number of users outperforms the baseline. However, adding the information about entropy significantly ($p \leq 0.01$) improves the performance over all other ranking methods.

Finally, in Table 4 we show the top ten fastest growing threads in our data (ranked by the number of users posting in the thread). Each thread is represented by the first tweet. We can see from the table that events which spread the fastest on Twitter are

Table 4: Top ten fastest growing threads in our data.

# users	First tweet
7814	TMZ reporting michael jackson has had a heart attack. We r checking it out. And pulliing video to use if confirmed
7579	RIP Patrick Swayze...
3277	Walter Cronkite is dead.
2526	we lost Ted Kennedy :(
1879	RT BULLETIN – STEVE MCNAIR HAS DIED.
1511	David Carradine (Bill in "Kill Bill") found hung in Bangkok hotel.
1458	Just heard Sir Bobby Robson has died. RIP.
1426	I just upgraded to 2.0 - The professional Twitter client. Please RT!
1220	LA Times reporting Manny Ramirez tested positive for performance enhancing drugs. To be suspended 50 games.
1057	A representative says guitar legend Les Paul has died at 94

mostly deaths of famous people. One spam thread that appears in the list has an entropy of 2.5 and doesn't appear in the top ten list when using the entropy + users ranking.

7 Conclusion

We presented an approach to first story detection in a streaming setting. Our approach is based on locality sensitive hashing adapted to the first story detection task by introducing a backoff towards exact search. This adaptation greatly improved performance of the system and virtually eliminated variance in the results. We showed that, using our approach, it is possible to achieve constant space and processing time while maintaining very good results. A comparison with the UMass FSD system showed that we gain more than an order of magnitude speedup with only a minor loss in performance. We used our FSD system on a truly large-scale task of detecting new events from over 160 million Twitter posts. To the best of our knowledge, this is the first work that does event detection on this scale. We showed that our system is able to detect major events with reasonable precision, and that the amount of spam in the output can be reduced by taking entropy into account.

Acknowledgments

The authors would like to thank Donnla Osborne for her work on annotating tweets.

References

James Allan, Victor Lavrenko, Daniella Malin, and Russell Swan. 2000. Detections, bounds, and timelines: Umass and tdt-3. In *Proceedings of Topic Detection and Tracking Workshop*, pages 167–174.

James Allan. 2002. *Topic detection and tracking: event-based information organization*. Kluwer Academic Publishers.

Nilesh Bansal and Nick Koudas. 2007. Blogscope: a system for online analysis of high volume text streams. In *VLDB '07: Proceedings of the 33rd international conference on Very large data bases*, pages 1410–1413. VLDB Endowment.

Moses S. Charikar. 2002. Similarity estimation techniques from rounding algorithms. In *STOC '02: Proceedings of the thiry-fourth annual ACM symposium on Theory of computing*, pages 380–388, New York, NY, USA. ACM.

W.B. Croft, D. Metzler, and T. Strohman. 2009. *Search Engines: Information Retrieval in Practice*. Addison-Wesley Publishing.

Mayur Datar, Nicole Immorlica, Piotr Indyk, and Vahab Mirrokni. 2004. Locality-sensitive hashing scheme based on p-stable distributions. In *SCG '04: Proceedings of the twentieth annual symposium on Computational geometry*, pages 253–262, New York, NY, USA. ACM.

J. Fiscus. 2001. Overview of results (nist). In *Proceedings of the TDT 2001 Workshop*.

N. Glance, M. Hurst, and T. Tomokiyo. 2004. BlogPulse: Automated Trend Discovery for Weblogs. *WWW 2004 Workshop on the Weblogging Ecosystem: Aggregation, Analysis and Dynamics*, 2004.

Daniel Gruhl, R. Guha, Ravi Kumar, Jasmine Novak, and Andrew Tomkins. 2005. The predictive power of online chatter. In *KDD '05: Proceedings of the eleventh ACM SIGKDD international conference on Knowledge discovery in data mining*, pages 78–87, New York, NY, USA. ACM.

Piotr Indyk and Rajeev Motwani. 1998. Approximate nearest neighbors: towards removing the curse of dimensionality. In *STOC '98: Proceedings of the thirtieth annual ACM symposium on Theory of computing*, pages 604–613, New York, NY, USA. ACM.

Akshay Java, Xiaodan Song, Tim Finin, and Belle Tseng. 2007. Why we twitter: understanding microblogging usage and communities. In *WebKDD/SNA-KDD '07: Proceedings of the 9th WebKDD and 1st SNA-KDD 2007 workshop on Web mining and social network analysis*, pages 56–65, New York, NY, USA. ACM.

Balachander Krishnamurthy, Phillipa Gill, and Martin Arlitt. 2008. A few chirps about twitter. In *WOSP '08: Proceedings of the first workshop on Online social networks*, pages 19–24, New York, NY, USA. ACM.

Abby Levenberg and Miles Osborne. 2009. Stream-based randomised language models for smt. In *Proceedings of the 2009 Conference on Empirical Methods in Natural Language Processing*, pages 756–764.

Gang Luo, Chunqiang Tang, and Philip S. Yu. 2007. Resource-adaptive real-time new event detection. In *SIGMOD '07: Proceedings of the 2007 ACM SIGMOD international conference on Management of data*, pages 497–508, New York, NY, USA. ACM.

S. Muthukrishnan. 2005. *Data streams: Algorithms and applications*. Now Publishers Inc.

Ramesh Nallapati, Ao Feng, Fuchun Peng, and James Allan. 2004. Event threading within news topics. In *CIKM '04: Proceedings of the thirteenth ACM international conference on Information and knowledge management*, pages 446–453, New York, NY, USA. ACM.

Deepak Ravichandran, Patrick Pantel, and Eduard Hovy. 2005. Randomized algorithms and nlp: using locality sensitive hash function for high speed noun clustering. In *ACL '05: Proceedings of the 43rd Annual Meeting on Association for Computational Linguistics*, pages 622–629, Morristown, NJ, USA. Association for Computational Linguistics.

Barna Saha and Lise Getoor. 2009. On maximum coverage in the streaming model & application to multi-topic blog-watch. In *2009 SIAM International Conference on Data Mining (SDM09)*, April.

Qinfeng Shi, James Petterson, Gideon Dror, John Langford, Alex Smola, Alex Strehl, and Vishy Vishwanathan. 2009. Hash kernels. In *Proceedings of the 12th International Conference on Artificial Intelligence and Statistics (AISTATS)*, pages 496–503.

Yiming Yang, Tom Pierce, and Jaime Carbonell. 1998. A study of retrospective and on-line event detection. In *SIGIR '98: Proceedings of the 21st annual international ACM SIGIR conference on Research and development in information retrieval*, pages 28–36, New York, NY, USA. ACM.

Limin Yao, David Mimno, and Andrew McCallum. 2009. Efficient methods for topic model inference on streaming document collections. In *KDD '09: Proceedings of the 15th ACM SIGKDD international conference on Knowledge discovery and data mining*, pages 937–946, New York, NY, USA. ACM.

Unsupervised Model Adaptation using Information-Theoretic Criterion

Ariya Rastrow[1], Frederick Jelinek[1], Abhinav Sethy[2] and Bhuvana Ramabhadran[2]
[1]Human Language Technology Center of Excellence, and
Center for Language and Speech Processing, Johns Hopkins University
{ariya, jelinek}@jhu.edu
[2]IBM T.J. Watson Research Center, Yorktown Heights, NY, USA
{asethy, bhuvana}@us.ibm.com

Abstract

In this paper we propose a novel general framework for unsupervised model adaptation. Our method is based on entropy which has been used previously as a regularizer in semi-supervised learning. This technique includes another term which measures the stability of posteriors w.r.t model parameters, in addition to conditional entropy. The idea is to use parameters which result in both low conditional entropy and also stable decision rules. As an application, we demonstrate how this framework can be used for adjusting language model interpolation weight for speech recognition task to adapt from Broadcast news data to MIT lecture data. We show how the new technique can obtain comparable performance to completely supervised estimation of interpolation parameters.

1 Introduction

All statistical and machine learning techniques for classification, in principle, work under the assumption that

1. A reasonable amount of training data is available.

2. Training data and test data are drawn from the same underlying distribution.

In fact, the success of statistical models is crucially dependent on training data. Unfortunately, the latter assumption is not fulfilled in many applications. Therefore, model adaptation is necessary when training data is not matched (not drawn from same distribution) with test data. It is often the case where we have plenty of labeled data for one specific domain/genre (source domain) and little amount of labeled data (or no labeled data at all) for the desired domain/genre (target domain). Model adaptation techniques are commonly used to address this problem. Model adaptation starts with trained models (trained on source domain with rich amount of labeled data) and then modify them using the available labeled data from target domain (or instead unlabeled data). A survey on different methods of model adaptation can be found in (Jiang, 2008).

Information regularization framework has been previously proposed in literature to control the label conditional probabilities via input distribution (Szummer and Jaakkola, 2003). The idea is that labels should not change too much in dense regions of the input distribution. The authors use the mutual information between input features and labels as a measure of label complexity. Another framework previously suggested is to use label entropy (conditional entropy) on unlabeled data as a regularizer to Maximum Likelihood (ML) training on labeled data (Grandvalet and Bengio, 2004).

Availability of resources for the target domain categorizes these techniques into either *supervised* or *unsupervised*. In this paper we propose a general framework for unsupervised adaptation using Shannon entropy and stability of entropy. The assumption is that in-domain and out-of-domain distributions are not too different such that one can improve the performance of initial models on in-domain data by little adjustment of initial decision boundaries (learned on out-of-domain data).

Human Language Technologies: The 2010 Annual Conference of the North American Chapter of the ACL, pages 190–197,
Los Angeles, California, June 2010.

2 Conditional Entropy based Adaptation

In this section, conditional entropy and its relation to classifier performance are first described. Next, we introduce our proposed objective function for domain adaptation.

2.1 Conditional Entropy

Considering the classification problem where $\mathbf{X}$ and $\mathbf{Y}$ are the input features and the corresponding class labels respectively, the conditional entropy is a measure of the class overlap and is calculated as follows

$$H(\mathbf{Y}|\mathbf{X}) = E_{\mathbf{X}}[H(\mathbf{Y}|\mathbf{X}=x)] = \\ -\int p(x)\left(\sum_y p(y|x)\log p(y|x)\right)dx \quad (1)$$

Through *Fano's Inequality* theorem, one can see how conditional entropy is related to classification performance.

Theorem 1 (Fano's Inequality) *Suppose $P_e = P\{\hat{\mathbf{Y}} \neq \mathbf{Y}\}$ where $\hat{\mathbf{Y}} = g(X)$ are the assigned labels for the data points, based on the classification rule. Then*

$$P_e \geq \frac{H(\mathbf{Y}|\mathbf{X}) - 1}{\log(|\mathcal{Y}| - 1)}$$

where $\mathcal{Y}$ is the number of possible classes and $H(Y|X)$ is the conditional entropy with respect to true distibution.

The proof to this theorem can be found in (Cover and Thomas, 2006). This inequality indicates that $\mathbf{Y}$ can be estimated with low probability of error only if the conditional entropy $H(\mathbf{Y}|\mathbf{X})$ is small.

Although the above theorem is useful in a sense that it connects the classification problem to Shannon entropy, the true distributions are almost never known to us[1]. In most classification methods, a specific model structure for the distributions is assumed and the task is to estimate the model parameters within the assumed model space. Given the model structure and parameters, one can modify *Fano's Inequality* as follows,

Corollary 1

$$P_e(\theta) = P\{\hat{\mathbf{Y}} \neq \mathbf{Y}\ |\theta\} \geq \frac{H_\theta(\mathbf{Y}|\mathbf{X}) - 1}{\log(|\mathcal{Y}| - 1)} \quad (2)$$

where $P_e(\theta)$ is the classifier probability of error given model parameters, θ and

$$H_\theta(\mathbf{Y}|\mathbf{X}) = \\ -\int p(x)\left(\sum_y p_\theta(y|x)\log p_\theta(y|x)\right)dx$$

Here, $H_\theta(\mathbf{Y}|\mathbf{X})$ is the conditional entropy imposed by model parameters.

Eqn. 2 indicates the fact that models with low conditional entropy are preferable. However, a low entropy model does not necessarily have good performance (this will be reviewed later on) [2]

2.2 Objective Function

Minimization of conditional entropy as a framework in the classification task is not a new concept and has been tried by researchers. In fact, (Grandvalet and Bengio, 2004) use this along with the maximum likelihood criterion in a semi-supervised set up such that parameters with both maximum likelihood on labeled data and minimum conditional entropy on unlabeled data are chosen. By minimizing the entropy, the method assumes a prior which prefers minimal class overlap. Entropy minimization is used in (Li et al., 2004) as an unsupervised non-parametric clustering method and is shown to result in significant improvement over k-mean, hierarchical clustering and etc.

These methods are all based on the fact that models with low conditional entropy have their decision boundaries passing through low-density regions of the input distribution, $P(X)$. This is consistent with the assumption that classes are well separated so that one can expect to take advantage of unlabeled examples (Grandvalet and Bengio, 2004).

In many cases shifting from one domain to another domain, initial trained decision boundaries (on

[1]In fact, Theorem 1 shows how relevant the input features are for the classification task by putting a lower bound on the best possible classifier performance. As the overlap between features from different classes increases, conditional entropy increases as well, thus lowering the performance of the best possible classifier.

[2]Imagine a model which classifies any input as class 1. Clearly for this model $H_\theta(\mathbf{Y}|\mathbf{X}) = 0$.

out-of-domain data) result in high conditional entropy for the new domain, due to mismatch between distributions. Therefore, there is a need to adjust model parameters such that decision boundaries goes through low-density regions of the distribution. This motivates the idea of using minimum conditional entropy criterion for adapting to a new domain. At the same time, two domains are often close enough that one would expect that the optimal parameters for the new domain should not deviate too much from initial parameters. In order to formulate the technique mentioned in the above paragraph, let us define Θ_{init} to be the initial model parameters estimated on out-of-domain data (using labeled data). Assuming the availability of enough amount of unlabeled data for in-domain task, we try to minimize the following objective function w.r.t the parameters,

$$\theta_{\mathbf{new}} = \underset{\theta}{\operatorname{argmin}}\, H_\theta(\mathbf{Y}|\mathbf{X}) + \lambda\, ||\theta - \theta_{\mathbf{init}}||_p \tag{3}$$

where $||\theta - \theta_{\mathbf{init}}||_p$ is an L_p regularizer and tries to prevent parameters from deviating too much from their initial values[3].

Once again the idea here is to adjust the parameters (using unlabeled data) such that low-density separation between the classes is achieved. In the following section we will discuss the drawback of this objective function for adaptation in realistic scenarios.

3 Issues with Minimum Entropy Criterion

It is discussed in Section 2.2 that the model parameters are adapted such that a minimum conditional entropy is achieved. It was also discussed how this is related to finding decision boundaries through low-density regions of input distribution. However, the obvious assumption here is that the classes are well separated and there in fact exists low-density regions between classes which can be treated as boundaries. Although this is a suitable/ideal assumption for classification, in most practical problems this assumption is not satisfied and often classes overlap. Therefore, we can not expect the conditional entropy to be convex in this situation and to achieve minimization w.r.t parameters (other than the trivial solutions).

Let us clarify this through an example. Consider X to be generated by mixture of two 2-D Gaussians (each with a particular mean and covariance matrix) where each Gaussian corresponds to a particular class (binary class situation) . Also in order to have linear decision boundaries, let the Gaussians have same covariance matrix and let the parameter being estimated be the prior for class 1, $P(Y = 1)$. Fig. 1 shows two different situations with overlapping classes and non-overlapping classes. The left panel shows a distribution in which classes are well separated whereas the right panel corresponds to the situation where there is considerable overlap between classes. Clearly, in the later case there is no low-density region separating the classes. Therefore, as we change the parameter (here, the prior on the class $Y = 1$), there will not be any well defined point with minimum entropy. This can be seen from Fig. 2 where model conditional entropy is plotted vs. class prior parameter for both cases. In the case of no-overlap between classes, entropy is a convex function w.r.t the parameter (excluding trivial solutions which happens at $P(Y = 1) = 0, 1$) and is minimum at $P(Y = 1) = 0.7$ which is the true prior with which the data was generated.

We summarize issues with minimum entropy criterion and our proposed solutions as follows:

- Trivial solution: this happens when we put decision boundaries such that both classes are considered as one class (this can be avoided using the regularizer in Eqn. 3 and the assumption that initial models have a reasonable solution, e.g. close to the optimal solution for new domain)

- Overlapped Classes: As it was discussed in this section, if the overlap is considerable then the entropy will not be convex w.r.t to model parameters. We will address this issue in the next section by introducing the entropy-stability concept.

4 Entropy-Stability

It was discussed in the previous section that a minimum entropy criterion can not be used (by itself) in

[3]The other reason for using a regularizer is to prevent trivial solutions of minimum entropy criterion

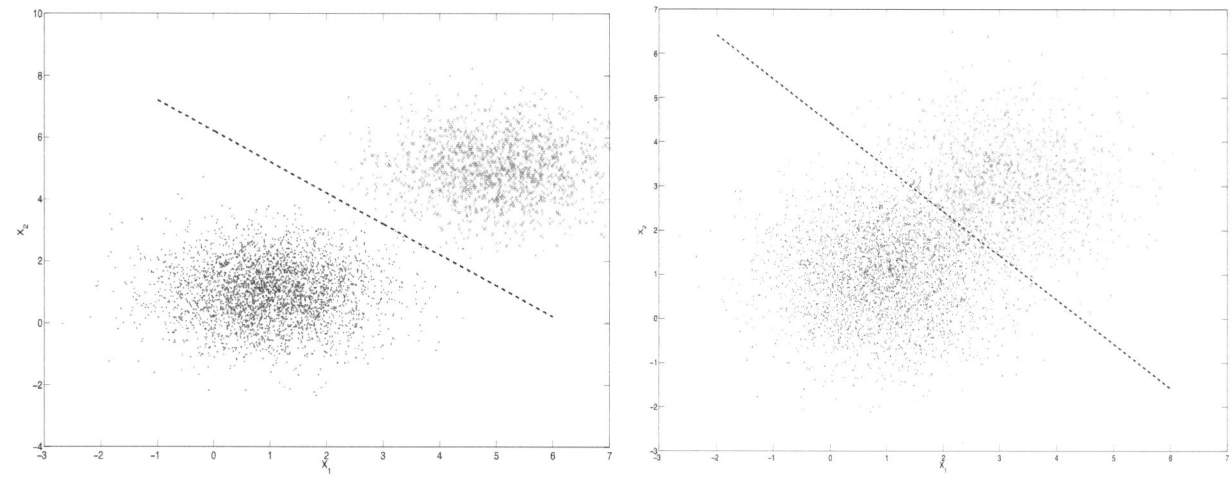

Figure 1: Mixture of two Gaussians and the corresponding Bayes decision boundary: (left) with no class overlap (right) with class overlap

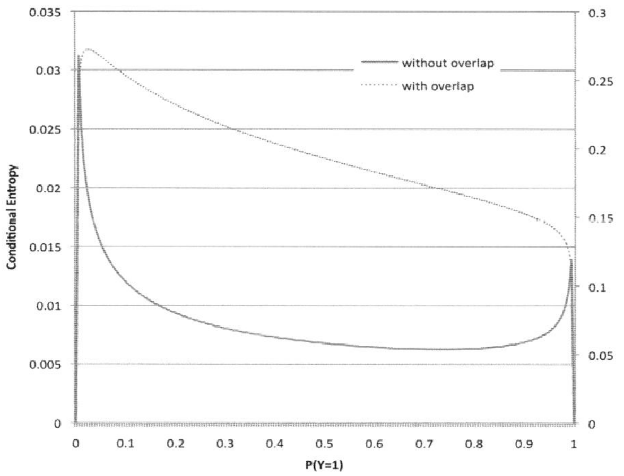

Figure 2: Condtional entropy vs. prior parameter, $P(Y = 1)$

situations where there is a considerable amount of overlap among classes. Assuming that class boundaries happen in the regions close to the tail of class distributions, we introduce the concept of *Entropy-Stability* and show how it can be used to detect boundary regions. Define *Entropy-Stability* to be the reciprocal of the following

$$\left\|\frac{\partial H_\theta(\mathbf{Y}|\mathbf{X})}{\partial \theta}\right\|_p = \left\|\int p(x) \frac{\partial \left(\sum_y p_\theta(y|x) \log p_\theta(y|x)\right)}{\partial \theta} dx\right\|_p \tag{4}$$

Recall: since θ is a vector of parameters, $\frac{\partial H_\theta(\mathbf{Y}|\mathbf{X})}{\partial \theta}$ will be a vector and by using L_p norm Entropy-stability will be a scalar.

The introduced concept basically measures the stability of label entropies w.r.t the model parameters. The idea is that we prefer models which not only have low-conditional entropy but also have stable decision rules imposed by the model. Next, we show through the following theorem how Entropy-Stability measures the stability over posterior probabilities (decision rules) of the model.

Theorem 2

$$\left\|\frac{\partial H_\theta(\mathbf{Y}|\mathbf{X})}{\partial \theta}\right\|_p = \left\|\int p(x) \left(\sum_y \frac{\partial p_\theta(y|x)}{\partial \theta} \log p_\theta(y|x)\right) dx\right\|_p$$

where the term inside the parenthesis is the weighted sum (by log-likelihood) over the gradient of posterior probabilities of labels for a given sample x

Proof The proof is straight forward and uses the fact that $\sum \frac{\partial p_\theta(y|x)}{\partial \theta} = \frac{\partial(\sum p_\theta(y|x))}{\partial \theta} = 0$.

Using Theorem 2 and Eqn. 4, it should be clear how Entropy-Stability measures the expected stability over the posterior probabilities of the model. A high value of $\left\|\frac{\partial H_\theta(\mathbf{Y}|\mathbf{X})}{\partial \theta}\right\|_p$ implies models with less stable decision rules. In order to explain how this is used for detecting boundaries (overlapped regions) we once again refer back to our mixture of Gaussians' example. As the decision boundary moves from class specific regions to overlapped regions (by changing the parameter which is here class prior probability) we expect the entropy to continuously decrease (due to the assumption that the overlaps occur at the tail of class distributions). However, as we get close to the overlapping regions the added data points from other class(es) will resist changes in the entropy. resulting in stability over the entropy until we enter the regions specific to other class(es).

In the following subsection we use this idea to propose a new objective function which can be used as an unsupervised adaptation method even for the case of input distribution with overlapping classes.

4.1 Better Objective Function

The idea here is to use the Entropy-Stability concept to accept only regions which are close to the overlapped parts of the distribution (based on our assumption, these are valid regions for decision boundaries) and then using the minimum entropy criterion we find optimum solutions for our parameters inside these regions. Therefore, we modify Eqn. 3 such that it also includes the Entropy-Stability term

$$\theta_{\mathbf{new}} = \underset{\theta}{\operatorname{argmin}} \left(H_\theta(\mathbf{Y}|\mathbf{X}) + \gamma \left\| \frac{\partial H_\theta(\mathbf{Y}|\mathbf{X})}{\partial \theta} \right\|_{p'} + \lambda \left\| \theta - \theta_{\mathbf{init}} \right\|_p \right) \quad (5)$$

The parameter γ and λ can be tuned using small amount of labeled data (Dev set).

5 Speech Recognition Task

In this section we will discuss how the proposed framework can be used in a speech recognition task. In the speech recognition task, Y is the sequence of words and X is the input speech signal. For a given speech signal, almost every word sequence is a possible output and therefore there is a need for a compact representation of output labels (words). For this, word graphs (Lattices) are generated during the recognition process. In fact, each lattice is an *acyclic directed graph* whose nodes correspond to particular instants of time, and arcs (edges connecting nodes) represent possible word hypotheses. Associated with each arc is an acoustic likelihood and language model likelihood scores. Fig. 3 shows an example of recognition lattice [4] (for the purpose of demonstration likelihood scores are not shown).

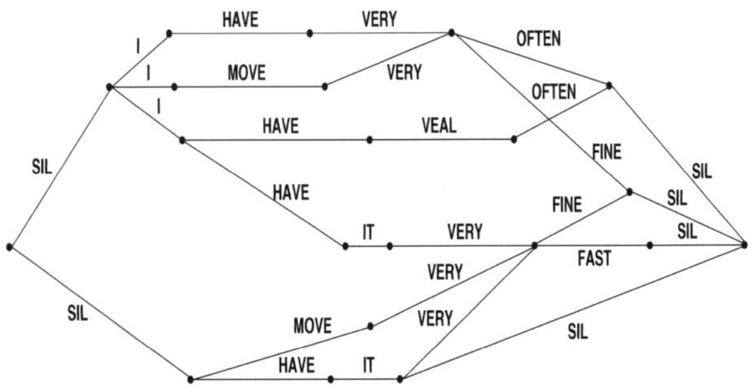

Figure 3: Lattice Example

Since lattices contain all the likely hypotheses (unlikely hypotheses are pruned during recognition and will not be included in the lattice), conditional entropy for any given input speech signal, x, can be approximated by the conditional entropy of the lattice. That is,

$$H_\theta(\mathbf{Y}|\mathbf{X} = x_i) = H_\theta(\mathbf{Y}|\mathcal{L}_i)$$

where $\mathcal{L}_i$ is the corresponding decoded lattice (given speech recognizer parameters) of utterance x_i.

For the calculation of entropy we need to know the distribution of X because $H_\theta(\mathbf{Y}|\mathbf{X}) = E_X[H_\theta(\mathbf{Y}|\mathbf{X} = x)]$ and since this distribution is not known to us, we use *Law of Large Numbers* to approximate it by the empirical average

$$H_\theta(\mathbf{Y}|\mathbf{X}) \approx -\frac{1}{N} \sum_{i=1}^{N} \sum_{y \in \mathcal{L}_i} p_\theta(y|\mathcal{L}_i) \log p_\theta(y|\mathcal{L}_i) \quad (6)$$

Here N indicates the number of unlabeled utterances for which we calculate the empirical value of conditional entropy. Similarly, expectation w.r.t input distribution in entropy-stability term is also approximated by the empirical average of samples.

Since the number of paths (hypotheses) in the lattice is very large, it would be computationally infeasible to compute the conditional entropy by enumerating all possible paths in the lattice and calculating

[4]The figure is adopted from (Mangu et al., 1999)

Element	$\langle p, r \rangle$
$\langle p_1, r_1 \rangle \otimes \langle p_2, r_2 \rangle$	$\langle p_1 p_2,\ p_1 r_2 + p_2 r_1 \rangle$
$\langle p_1, r_1 \rangle \oplus \langle p_2, r_2 \rangle$	$\langle p_1 + p_2,\ r_1 + r_2 \rangle$
0	$\langle 0, 0 \rangle$
1	$\langle 1, 0 \rangle$

Table 1: **First-Order (Expectation) semiring**: Defining *multiplication* and *sum* operations for first-order semirings.

their corresponding posterior probabilities. Instead we use Finite-State Transducers (FST) to represent the hypothesis space (lattice). To calculate entropy and the gradient of entropy, the weights for the FST are defined to be First- and Second-Order *semirings* (Li and Eisner, 2009). The idea is to use *semirings* and their corresponding operations along with the forward-backward algorithm to calculate first- and second-order statistics to compute entropy and the gradient of entropy respectively. Assume we are interested in calculating the entropy of the lattice,

$$\begin{aligned} H(p) &= -\sum_{d \in \mathcal{L}_i} \frac{p(d)}{Z} \log(\frac{p(d)}{Z}) \\ &= \log Z - \frac{1}{Z} \sum_{d \in \mathcal{L}_i} p(d) \log p(d) \\ &= \log Z - \frac{\bar{r}}{Z} \end{aligned} \quad (7)$$

where Z is the total probability of all the paths in the lattice (normalization factor). In order to do so, we need to compute $\langle Z, \bar{r} \rangle$ on the lattice. It can be proved that if we define the first-order semiring $\langle p_e, p_e \log p_e \rangle$ (p_e is the non-normalized score of each arc in the lattice) as our FST weights and define semiring operations as in Table. 1, then applying the forward algorithm will result in the calculation of $\langle Z, \bar{r} \rangle$ as the weight (semiring weight) for the final node.

The details for using Second-Order *semirings* for calculating the gradient of entropy can be found in (Li and Eisner, 2009). The same paper describes how to use the forward-backward algorithm to speed-up the this procedure.

6 Language Model Adaptation

Language Model Adaptation is crucial when the training data does not match the test data being decoded. This is a frequent scenario for all Automatic Speech Recognition (ASR) systems. The application domain very often contains named entities and N-gram sequences that are unique to the domain of interest. For example, conversational speech has a very different structure than class-room lectures. Linear Interpolation based methods are most commonly used to adapt LMs to a new domain. As explained in (Bacchiani et al., 2003), linear interpolation is a special case of Maximum A Posterior (MAP) estimation, where an N-gram LM is built on the adaptation data from the new domain and the two LMs are combined using:

$$p(w_i|h) = \lambda p_B(w_i|h) + (1 - \lambda) p_A(w_i|h)$$
$$0 \leq \lambda \leq 1$$

where p_B refers to out-of-domain (background) models and p_A is the adaptation (in-domain) models. Here λ is the interpolation weight.

Conventionally, λ is calculated by optimizing perplexity (PPL) or Word Error Rate (WER) on some held-out data from target domain. Instead using our proposed framework, we estimate λ on enough amount of unlabeled data from target domain. The idea is that resources on the new domain have already been used to build domain specific models and it does not make sense to again use in-domain resources for estimating the interpolation weight. Since we are trying to just estimate one parameter and the performance of the interpolated model is bound by in-domain/out-of-domain models, there is no need to include a regularization term in Eqn. 5. Also $\left|\left|\frac{\partial H_\theta(\mathbf{Y}|\mathbf{X})}{\partial \theta}\right|\right|_p = |\frac{\partial H_\lambda(\mathbf{Y}|\mathbf{X})}{\partial \lambda}|$ because we only have one parameter. Therefore, interpolation weight will be chosen by the following criterion

$$\hat{\lambda} = \underset{0 \leq \lambda \leq 1}{\operatorname{argmin}} H_\lambda(\mathbf{Y}|\mathbf{X}) + \gamma |\frac{\partial H_\lambda(\mathbf{Y}|\mathbf{X})}{\partial \lambda}| \quad (8)$$

For the purpose of estimating one parameter λ, we use $\gamma = 1$ in the above equation

7 Experimental Setup

The large vocabulary continuous speech recognition (LVCSR) system used throughout this paper is based on the 2007 IBM Speech transcription system for GALE Distillation Go/No-go Evaluation (Chen et al., 2006). The acoustic models used in this system are state-of-the-art discriminatively trained models and are the same ones used for all experiments presented in this paper.

For LM adaptation experiments, the out-of-domain LM (p_B, Broadcast News LM) training text consists of 335M words from the following *broadcast news* (BN) data sources (Chen et al., 2006): 1996 CSR Hub4 Language Model data, EARS BN03 closed captions, GALE Phase 2 Distillation GNG Evaluation Supplemental Multilingual data, Hub4 acoustic model training transcripts, TDT4 closed captions, TDT4 newswire, and GALE Broadcast Conversations and GALE Broadcast News. This language model is of order 4-gram with Kneser-Ney smoothing and contains $4.6M$ n-grams based on a lexicon size of $84K$.

The second source of data is the MIT lectures data set (J. Glass, T. Hazen, S. Cyphers, I. Malioutov, D. Huynh, and R. Barzilay, 2007) . This serves as the target domain (in-domain) set for language model adaptation experiments. This set is split into 8 hours for in-domain LM building, another 8 hours served as unlabeled data for interpolation weight estimation using criterion in Eqn. 8 (we refer to this as unsupervised training data) and finally 2.5 hours Dev set for estimating the interpolation weight w.r.t WER (supervised tuning) . The lattice entropy and gradient of entropy w.r.t λ are calculated on the unsupervised training data set. The results are discussed in the next section.

8 Results

In order to optimize the interpolation weight λ based on criterion in Eqn. 8, we devide $[0, 1]$ to 20 different points and evaluate the objective function (Eqn. 8) on those points. For this, we need to calculate entropy and gradient of the entropy on the decoded lattices of the ASR system on 8 hours of MIT lecture set which is used as an unlabeled training data. Fig. 4 shows the value of the objective function against different values of model parameters (interpolation weight λ). As it can be seen from this figure just considering the conditional entropy will result in a non-convex objective function whereas adding the entropy-stability term will make the objective function convex. For the purpose of the evaluation, we show the results for estimating λ directly on the transcription of the 8 hour MIT lecture data and compare it to estimated value using our framework. The results are shown in Fig. 5. Using $\lambda = 0$ and $\lambda = 1$ the WERs are 24.7% and 21.1% respectively. Using the new proposed objective function, the optimal λ is estimated to be 0.6 with WER of 20.1% (Red circle on the figure). Estimating λ w.r.t 8 hour training data transcription (supervised adaptation) will result in $\lambda = 0.7$ (green circle) and WER of 20.0%. Instead $\lambda = 0.8$ will be chosen by tuning the interpolation weight on 2.5 hour Dev set with comparable WER of 20.1%. Also it is clear from the figure that the new objective function can be used to predict the WER trend w.r.t the interpolation weight parameter.

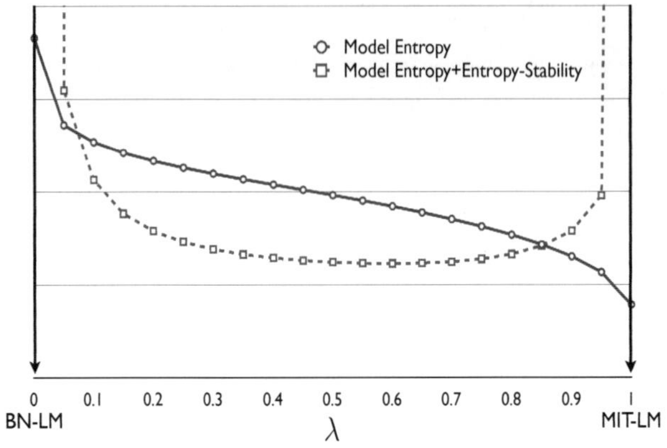

Figure 4: Objective function with and without including Entropy-Stability term vs. interpolation weight λ on 8 hours MIT lecture unlabeled data

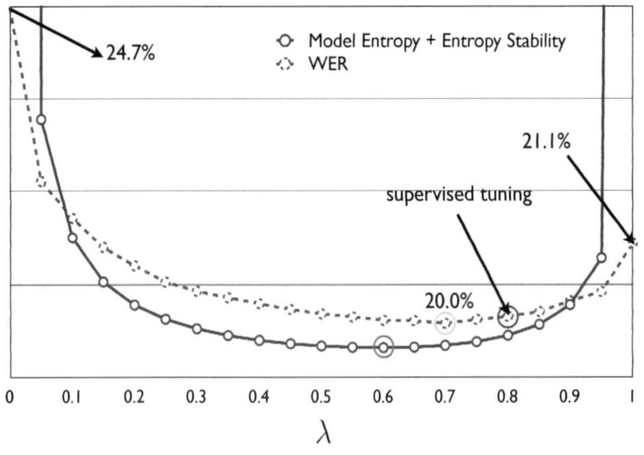

Figure 5: Estimating λ based on WER vs. the information-theoretic criterion

Therefore, it can be seen that the new unsupervised method results in the same performance as supervised adaptation in speech recognition task.

9 Conclusion and Future Work

In this paper we introduced the notion of entropy stability and presented a new criterion for unsupervised adaptation which combines conditional entropy minimization with entropy stability. The entropy stability criterion helps in selecting parameter settings which correspond to stable decision boundaries. Entropy minimization on the other hand tends to push decision boundaries into sparse regions of the input distributions. We show that combining the two criterion helps to improve unsupervised parameter adaptation in real world scenario where class conditional distributions show significant overlap. Although conditional entropy has been previously proposed as a regularizer, to our knowledge, the gradient of entropy (entropy-stability) has not been used previously in the literature. We presented experimental results where the proposed criterion clearly outperforms entropy minimization. For the speech recognition task presented in this paper, the proposed unsupervised scheme results in the same performance as the supervised technique.

As a future work, we plan to use the proposed criterion for adapting log-linear models used in Machine Translation, Conditional Random Fields (CRF) and other applications. We also plan to expand linear interpolation Language Model scheme to include history specific (context dependent) weights.

Acknowledgments

The Authors want to thank Markus Dreyer and Zhifei Li for their insightful discussions and suggestions.

References

M. Bacchiani, B. Roark, and M. Saraclar. 2003. Unsupervised language model adaptation. In *Proc. ICASSP*, pages 224–227.

S. Chen, B. Kingsbury, L. Mangu, D. Povey, G. Saon, H. Soltau, and G. Zweig. 2006. Advances in speech transcription at IBM under the DARPA EARS program. *IEEE Transactions on Audio, Speech and Language Processing*, pages 1596–1608.

Thomas M. Cover and Joy A. Thomas. 2006. *Elements of information theory*. Wiley-Interscience, 3rd edition.

Yves Grandvalet and Yoshua Bengio. 2004. Semi-supervised learning by entropy minimization. In *Advances in neural information processing systems (NIPS)*, volume 17, pages 529–536.

J. Glass, T. Hazen, S. Cyphers, I. Malioutov, D. Huynh, and R. Barzilay. 2007. Recent progress in MIT spoken lecture processing project. In *Proc. Interspeech*.

Jing Jiang. 2008. A literature survey on domain adaptation of statistical classifiers, March.

Zhifei Li and Jason Eisner. 2009. First- and second-order expectation semirings with applications to minimum-risk training on translation forests. In *EMNLP*.

Haifeng Li, Keshu Zhang, and Tao Jiang. 2004. Minimum entropy clustering and applications to gene expression analysis. In *Proceedings of IEEE Computational Systems Bioinformatics Conference*, pages 142–151.

Lidia Mangu, Eric Brill, and Andreas Stolcke. 1999. Finding consensus among words: Lattice-based word error minimization. In *Sixth European Conference on Speech Communication and Technology*.

M. Szummer and T. Jaakkola. 2003. Information regularization with partially labeled data. In *Advances in Neural Information Processing Systems*, pages 1049–1056.

Formatting Time-Aligned ASR Transcripts for Readability

Maria Shugrina*
Google Inc.
New York, NY 10011
shumash@google.com

Abstract

We address the problem of formatting the output of an automatic speech recognition (ASR) system for readability, while preserving word-level timing information of the transcript. Our system enriches the ASR transcript with punctuation, capitalization and properly written dates, times and other numeric entities, and our approach can be applied to other formatting tasks. The method we describe combines hand-crafted grammars with a class-based language model trained on written text and relies on Weighted Finite State Transducers (WFSTs) for the preservation of start and end time of each word.

1 Introduction and Prior Work

The output of a typical ASR system lacks punctuation, capitalization and proper formatting of entities such as phone numbers, time expressions and dates. Even if such automatic transcript is free of recognition errors, it is difficult for a human to parse. The proper formatting of the transcript gains particular importance in applications where the user relies on ASR output for information and where information-rich numeric entities (e.g. time expressions, monetary amounts) are common. A good example of such application is a voicemail transcription system. The goal of our work is to transform the raw transcript into its proper written form in order to optimize it for the visual scanning task by the end user. We present quantitative and qualitative evaluation of our system with a focus on numeric entity formatting, punctuation and capitalization (See Fig. 1).

Apart from text, the ASR output usually contains word-level metadata such as time-alignment and confidence. Such quantities may be useful for a variety of applications. Although simple to recover via word alignment after some types of formatting, word-level quantities may be difficult to preserve if the original text has undergone a significant transformation. We present a formal and general augmentation of our WFST-based technique that preserves word-level timing and confidence information during arbitrary formatting.

Raw Transcript:
hi bill it's tracy at around three thirty P M just got an apartment for one thousand three thirty one thousand four hundred a month my number is five five five eight eight eight eight extension is three thirty bye
Our Result:
Hi Bill, it's Tracy at around 3:30 PM, just got an apartment for 1,330 1,400 a month. My number is 555-8888 extension is 330. Bye.

Figure 1: An example of a raw transcript with ambiguous written forms and the output of our formatting system.

The problems of sentence boundary detection and punctuation of transcripts have received a substantial amount of attention, e.g. (Beeferman et al., 1998; Shriberg et al., 2000; Christensen et al., 2001; Liu et al., 2006; Gravano et al., 2009). Capitalization of ASR transcripts received less attention (Brown and Coden, 2002; Gravano et al., 2009), but there has also been work on case restoration in the context of machine translation (Chelba and Acero, 2006; Wang et al., 2006). Our work does not propose competing methods for transcript punctuation and capitalization. Instead, we aim to provide a common framework for a wide range of formatting tasks. Our method extends the approach of Gravano et al. (2009) with a general WFST formulation suitable for formatting monetary amounts, time expressions, dates, phone numbers, honorifics and more, in addition to punctuation and capitalization.

To our knowledge, this scope of the problem has not been addressed in literature. Yet such formatting can have a high impact on transcript readability. In this paper we focus on numeric entity format-

*Thank you to Michiel Bacchiani, Martin Jansche, Michael Riley and Cyril Allauzen for discussion and support.

Human Language Technologies: The 2010 Annual Conference of the North American Chapter of the ACL, pages 198–206,
Los Angeles, California, June 2010. ©2010 Association for Computational Linguistics

ting. In general, context independent rules fail to adequately perform this task due to its inherent ambiguity (See Fig. 1). For example, the spoken words "three thirty" should be written differently in these three contexts:

- meet me at **3:30**
- you owe me **330**
- dinner for **three 30** minutes later

The proper written form of a numeric entity depends on its class (time, monetary amount, etc). In this sense, formatting is related to the problem of named entity (NE) detection and value extraction, as defined by MUC-7 (Chinchor, 1997). Several authors have considered the problem of NE value extraction from raw transcripts (Huang et al., 2001; Jansche and Abney, 2002; Béchet et al., 2004; Levit et al., 2004). This is an information extraction task that involves identifying transcript words corresponding to a particular NE class and extracting an unambiguous value of that NE (e.g. the value of the date NE "december first oh nine" is "12/01/2009"). Although relevant, this information extraction does not directly address the problem of proper formatting and ordinarily requires a tagged corpus for training.

A parallel corpus containing raw transcriptions and the corresponding formatted strings would facilitate the solution to the transcript formatting problem. However, there is no such corpus available. Therefore, we follow the approach of Gravano et al. and provide an approximation that exploits readily available written text instead. In section 2 we detail our method, provide a probabilistic interpretation and present a practical formulation of the solution in terms of WFSTs. Section 3 shows how to augment the WFST formulation to preserve word-level timing and confidence. Section 4 presents both qualitative and quantitative evaluation of our system.

2 Method

First, handwritten grammars are used to generate all plausible written forms. These variants are then scored with a language model (LM) approximating probability over written strings. To overcome data sparsity associated with written numeric strings, we introduce numeric classes into the LM. In section 2.1 we give a probabilistic formulation of this approach. In section 2.2 we comment on the handwritten grammars, and in section 2.3 we discuss the class-based language model used for scoring. Section 2.4 provides the WFST formulation of the solution.

2.1 Probabilistic Formulation

The problem of estimating the best written form $\hat{w}$ of a spoken sequence of words s can be formulated as a Machine Translation (MT) problem of translating a string s from the language of spoken strings into a language of written strings. From a statistical standpoint, $\hat{w}$ can be estimated as follows:

$$\hat{w} = \underset{w}{\operatorname{argmax}}\{P(w|s)\} \approx \underset{w}{\operatorname{argmax}}\{P'(s|w)P'(w)\},$$

where $P(\cdot)$ denotes probability, and $P'(\cdot)$ a probability approximation. The probability over written strings $P(w)$ can be estimated by training an n-gram language model on amply available written text. The absence of a parallel corpus containing sequences of spoken words and their written renditions makes the conditional distribution $P(s|w)$ impossible to estimate. An approximation $P'(s|w)$ can be obtained by defining handwritten grammars that generate multiple unweighted written variants for any spoken sequence. For a given s, a collection of grammars encodes a uniform probability distribution across the set of all written variants generated for s and assigns a zero probability to any string not in this set. Such grammar-based modeling of $P(s|w)$ combined with statistical estimation of $P(w)$ takes advantage of prior knowledge, but does not share the disadvantages of rigid, fully rule-based systems.

2.2 Handwritten Grammars

Handwritten grammars $G_1 ... G_m$ are used to generate unweighted written variants for a raw string s. In Gravano's work (Gravano et al., 2009) the generated variants include optional punctuation between every two words and an optional capitalization for every word. Our system supports a wider range of variants, including but not limited to multiple variants of number formatting.

The handwritten grammars can be very restrictive or very liberal, depending on the application requirements. For example, a grammar we use to generate punctuation and capitalization only generates sentences with the first word capitalized. This enforces conventions and consistency, which the best scoring variant could occasionally violate. On the other

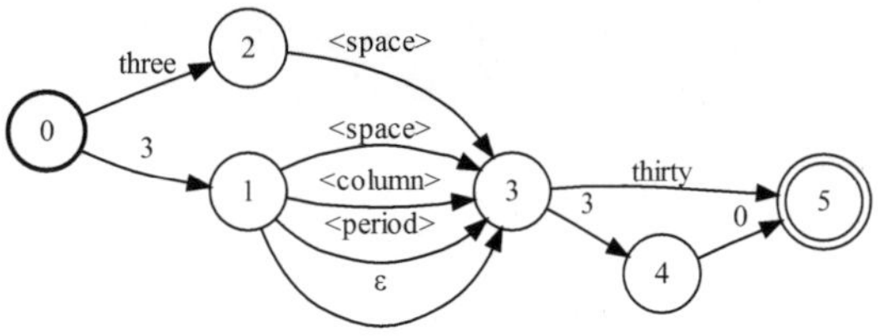

Figure 2: An FSA encoding all variants generated by the number grammar for a spoken string "three thirty".

hand, the grammar for number formatting could be very liberal in producing written variants (See Fig. 2). Jansche and Abney (2002) observe that handwritten rules deterministically tagging numeric strings of certain length as phone numbers perform surprisingly well on phone number NE identification in voicemail. If appropriate to the task, deterministic grammars can be incorporated into the grammar stack. The unweighted written variants generated by applying $G_1 ... G_m$ to s are then scored with the language model.

2.3 Language Model

The probability distribution over written text $P(w)$ can be approximated by a Katz back-off n-gram language model trained on written text in a domain semantically similar to the domain for which the ASR engine is deployed. Unlike some of the approaches used for NE identification (Jansche and Abney, 2002; Levit et al., 2004) and sentence boundary detection (Christensen et al., 2001; Shriberg et al., 2000; Liu et al., 2006), LM-based scoring cannot exploit a larger context than n tokens or prosodic features. The advantage of the LM approach is the ease of applying it to new formatting tasks: no new tagged corpus, and only trivial changes to the preprocessing of the training text would be required.

If the LM is to score written numeric strings, care must be taken in modeling numbers. Representing each written number as a token (e.g. tokens "1,235", "15") during training results in a very large model and suffers from data sparsity even with very large training corpora. An alternative approach of modeling every digit as a token (e.g. "15" is comprised of tokens "1" and "2") fails to model sufficient context for longer digit strings. A partially class-based LM remedies the drawbacks of both approaches, and has been used for tasks such as NE tagging (Béchet et al., 2004). The generalization provided by classes eliminates data sparsity, and is able to model sufficient context.

Class Set A	
Numeric range	*Interpretation*
2-9	single digits
10-12	up to hour in a 12-hour system
13-31	up to the largest day of the month
32-59	up to the largest minute in a time expression
other 2-digit	all other 2-digit numbers
other 3-digit	all 3-digit numbers
1900 - 2099	common year numbers
other 4-digit	all other 4-digit numbers
10000-99999	all 5-digit numbers; e.g. US zip-codes
$\geq$ 100000	all large numbers

Class Set B	
Numeric range	*Interpretation*
0-9	one digit string
10-99	two digit string
...	...
$10^9 - (10^{10} - 1)$	ten-digit string
$\geq 10^{10}$	longer digit string

Table 1: Two sets of number classes used in our system. Each sequence of consecutive digit characters is mapped to the appropriate class. For example, "$1,235.12" would become "⟨dollar⟩ 1 ⟨comma⟩ ⟨num_100_999⟩ ⟨period⟩ ⟨num_10_12⟩" in Class Set A and "⟨dollar⟩ ⟨num_1D⟩ ⟨comma⟩ ⟨num_3D⟩ ⟨period⟩ ⟨num_2D⟩ in Class Set B.

We experiment with two sets of classes (See Table 1). Class Set B, based on (Béchet et al., 2004), marks strings of n consecutive digits as belonging to an n-digit class, assuming nothing about the number distribution. Class Set A is based on intuition about number distribution in text (See Table 1, *Interpretation*). In section 4.4 we show that Class Set A achieves better performance on number formatting. Now that it is established that the choice of classes affects performance, future research could focus on finding an optimal set of number classes automatically. Clustering techniques, often used to derive class definitions from training text, could be applied.

Although more punctuation marks could be considered, we focus on periods and commas. Similarly to Gravano et al. (2009), we map all other punctuation marks in the training text to these two. In many formatting scenarios (e.g. spelled out acronyms, numeric ranges), spaces are ambiguous and significant, and it is therefore important to consider whitespace when scoring the written variants. Because of this, we model space as a token in the LM.

2.4 WFST Formulation

The one-best[1] ASR output s can be represented by a Finite State Acceptor (FSA) S. We describe a series of standard WFST operations on S resulting in the FSA W_{best} encoding the best estimated formatted variant $\hat{w}$. Current section assumes familiarity with WFSTs; for background see (Mohri, 2009).

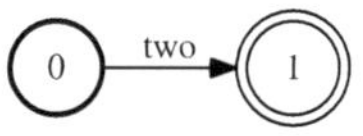

(a) S FSA

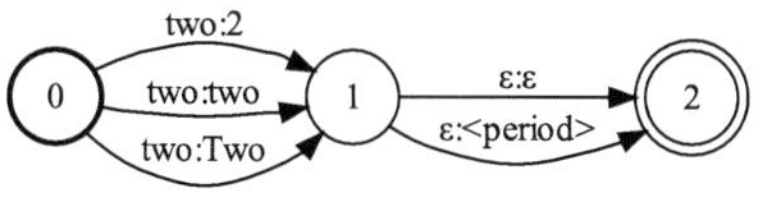

(b) W variants FST

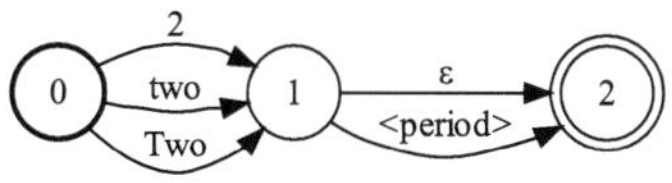

(c) W_{out} FSA

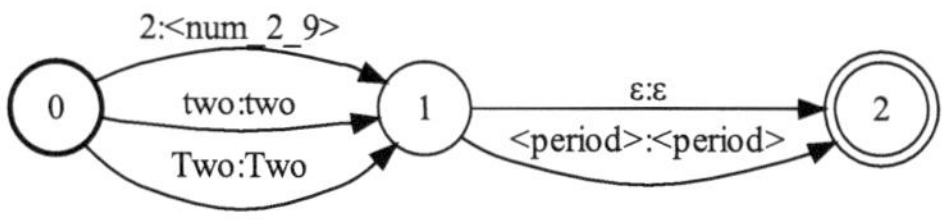

(d) W_{class} FST

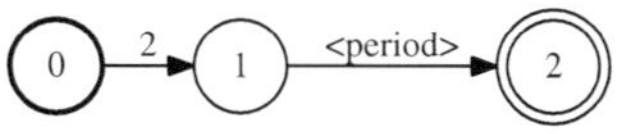

(e) W_{best} FSA

Figure 3: An example showing transducers produced during formatting.

We encode each grammar G_i as an unweighted FST T_i that transduces the raw transcript to its formatted versions. The necessity to encode them as FSTs restricts the set of grammars to regular grammars (Hopcroft and Ullman, 1979), sufficiently powerful for most formatting tasks. The back-off n-gram LM is naturally represented as a weighted deterministic FSA G with negative log probability weights (Mohri et al., 2008). The deterministic mapping of digit strings to number class tokens can also be accomplished by an unweighted transducer K, which passes all non-numeric strings unchanged.

Composing the input acceptor S with the grammar transducers T_i results in a transducer W with all written variants on the output. Projected onto its output labels, W becomes an acceptor W_{out}. W_{class}, the result of the composition of W_{out} with K, has all formatted written variants on the input side and the formatted variants with digit strings replaced by class tokens on the output. The output side of W_{class} can then be scored via composition with G to produce a weighted transducer W_{scored}. The shortest path in the Tropical Semiring on W_{scored} contains the estimate of the best written variant on the input side. This algorithm can be summarized as follows (See Fig. 3):

1. $W = S \circ T_1 \circ T_2 ... \circ T_m$
2. $W_{\text{out}} = \text{Proj}_{\text{out}}(W)$
3. $W_{\text{class}} = W_{\text{out}} \circ K$
4. $W_{\text{scored}} = W_{\text{class}} \circ G$
5. $W_{\text{best}} = \text{Proj}_{\text{in}}(\text{BestPath}(W_{\text{scored}}))$

where $\circ$ denotes FST composition, Proj_{in} and Proj_{out} denote projection on input and output labels respectively, and $\text{BestPath}(X)$ as a function returning an FST encoding the shortest path of X. The key Step 2 ensures that the target written variants are not consumed in the consequent composition operations. For efficiency reasons it is advisable to apply optimizations such as epsilon removal and determinization to the intermediate results. [2]

3 Preserving Word-Level Metadata

We extend the WFST formulation to preserve word-level timing and confidence information.

3.1 Background

A WFST is a finite set of states and transitions connecting them. Each transition has an input label, an output label and a weight in some semiring $\mathbb{K}$. A semiring is informally defined as a touple $(\mathbb{K}, \oplus, \otimes, \overline{0}, \overline{1})$, where $\mathbb{K}$ is the set of elements, $\oplus$ and $\otimes$ are the addition and multiplication operations, $\overline{0}$ is the additive identity and multiplicative annihilator, $\overline{1}$ is the multiplicative identity (See (Mohri,

[1] This WFST formulation can also be applied to the ASR lattice or n-best list with some modification to the scoring phase.

[2] Our system implements proper failure transitions available in the OpenFST Library (Allauzen et al., 2007).

2009)). By defining new semirings we can use standard FST operations to accomplish a wide range of goals.

3.2 Timing Semiring

In order to formulate time preservation within the FST formalism, we define the *timing semiring* $\mathbb{K}_t$ where each element is a pair (s, e) that can be interpreted as the start and end time of a word:

$$W_t = \{(s, e) : s, e \in \mathbb{R}^+ \cup \{0, \infty\}\}$$

$$(s_1, e_1) \oplus (s_2, e_2) = (max(s_1, s_2),\ min(e_1, e_2))$$

$$(s_1, e_1) \otimes (s_2, e_2) = (min(s_1, s_2),\ max(e_1, e_2))$$

$$\overline{0} = (0, \infty) \qquad \overline{1} = (\infty, 0)$$

Intuitively, the addition operation takes the largest interval contained by both operand intervals, while multiplication returns the smallest interval fully containing both operand intervals. [3] This definition fulfills all the semiring properties as defined in (Mohri, 2009). Note that encoding only the duration of each word is not sufficient, as there may be time gaps between the words due to the segmentation of the source audio. Let $\tilde{S}$ denote the Weighted Finite State Acceptor (WFSA) encoding the raw ASR output with the start and end time stored in the weight of each arc.

In order to preserve word-level confidence in addition to timing information, a Cartesian product of $\mathbb{K}_t$ and the Log semiring can be used to store both time and confidence in an arc weight.

3.3 Weight Synchronization

The goal is to associate the timing/confidence weights of $\tilde{S}$ with the word labels of W_{best}, the best formatted string (See Sec. 2.4). Because the weight of each transition in $\tilde{S}$ already expresses the timing/confidence corresponding to its word label, it is sufficient to associate the labels of $\tilde{S}$ with the labels of W_{best}. This is equivalent to identifying the output labels to which each input label is transduced during Step 1 in section 2.4. However, in general WFST operations may desynchronize input and output labels and weights, as the FST structure itself does not indicate a semantic correspondence between them. To alleviate this, we guarantee such a correspondence in our grammars by enforcing that for all paths in any grammar FST T_i:

- an input label appears before any of the corresponding output labels, and
- output labels corresponding to a given input label appear before the next input label.

In practice, these assumptions are usually met by handwritten grammars. Even if these assumptions are violated for a small number of paths, only small word-level timing discrepancies will be incurred. Each path in W can be thought of as a sequence of subpaths with only the first transition containing a non-ϵ input label. We say that the input label of each such subpath corresponds to that subpath's output labels.

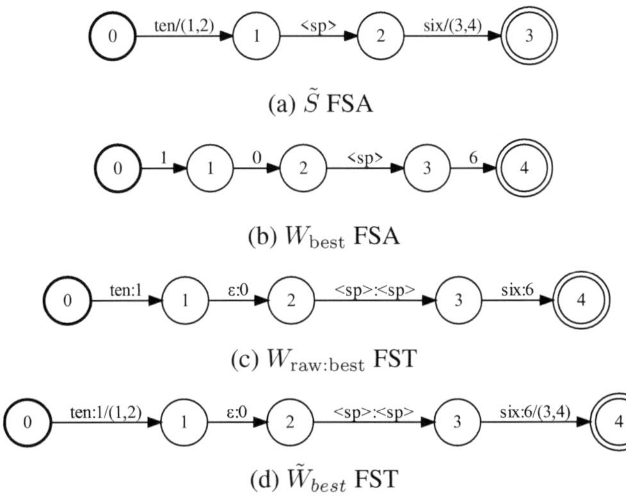

Figure 4: A small example of time preservation section of the algorithm. Arcs with non-unity timing weights show parenthesized pair of start and end time.

The best path that has input labels corresponding to the raw ASR output can be obtained by composing the variants FST W with the best formatted FSA W_{best} and picking any path. The timing weights are restored to by composing the weighted $\tilde{S}$ with this result. To preserve timing we add two more steps to Steps 1–5 in section 2.4:

6. $W_{\text{raw:best}} = \text{RmEps}(\text{AnyPath}(W \circ W_{\text{best}}))$
7. $\tilde{W}_{\text{best}} = \tilde{S} \circ \text{Map}_{\text{t}}(W_{\text{raw:best}})$

where $\text{RmEps}(X)$ applies the epsilon-removal algorithm to X (Mohri, 2009), and $\text{Map}_{\text{t}}(X)$ maps

[3] Note that this is just a Cartesian product of min-max and max-min semirings. The elements of $\mathbb{K}_t$ are not proper intervals, as it is possible for s to exceed e.

all non-zero weights of X to the unity weight in the *timing semiring*. Because $\tilde{S}$ is an epsilon-free acceptor, the result $\widetilde{W}_{\text{best}}$ will contain the original weights of $\tilde{S}$ on the arcs with the corresponding input labels (See Fig. 4 for an example). The space-delimited words and the corresponding weights can then be read off by walking $\widetilde{W}_{\text{best}}$.

4 Evaluation

Section 4.1 presents our datasets and an evaluation metric specific to number formatting, and section 4.2 describes our experimental system. We present quantitative evaluation of capitalization/punctuation performance and number formatting performance separately in sections 4.3 and 4.4. Because the ultimate goal of our work is to improve the readability of ASR transcripts, we also present the result of a user study of transcript readability in section 4.5.

4.1 Data and Metrics

The training corpus contains 185M tokens of written text normalized to contain only comma and period punctuation marks. A set of 176M tokens (TRS) is used for training and a set of 7M tokens (PTS) is held back for testing punctuation and capitalization (See Table 3). To obtain a test input (NPTS) for our system, PTS is lowercased and all punctuation is removed.

	words	commas	periods	capitals
TRS	176M	10.6M	11.8M	24.3M
PTS	7M	420K	440K	880K

Table 3: Training set TRS and test set PTS.

Number formatting is evaluated on a manually formatted test set. We manually processed the set of raw manual transcripts (NNTS) from the LDC Voicemail Part I training set (Padmanabhan et al., 1998) to obtain a reference number formatting set (NTS). All numeric entities in NTS were formatted according to the following conventions:

- all quantities under 10 are spelled out
- time is written in a 12-hour system as “xx:xx” or “xx”
- dollar amounts are written as “$x,xxx.xx” with cents included if spoken
- US phone numbers are written as “(xxx) xxx-xxxx” or “xxx-xxxx”
- other phone numbers are written as digit strings
- decimals are written as “x.x”
- large amounts include commas: “x,xxx,xxx”

All contiguous sequences of words in NTS that could be a target for number formatting were marked as *numeric entities*, whether or not these words were formatted by the labeler (for example “six” is a *numeric entity*). To evaluate number formatting performance, we process NNTS with our full experimental system, then remove all capitalization and inter-word punctuation. This result is aligned with NTS, and each entity is scored separately as totally correct or totally incorrect (See Table 2), yielding:

$$\text{Numeric Entity Error Rate} = 100 \cdot \frac{I}{N}$$

where I is the count of entities that did not match the reference entity string exactly and N is the total entity count. This error rate is independent of the numeric entity density in the test set. The errors are broken down into three types:

- incorrect formatting - when the system incorrectly formats an entity that is formatted in the reference
- overformatting - when the system formats an entity that stays unformatted in the reference
- underformatting - when the system does not format an entity formatted in the reference

Out of 1801 voicemail transcripts in NTS, 1347 contain at least one entity for a total of 3563 entities, signifying a frequent occurrence of numeric entities in voicemail. There is an average of 7 raw transcript words per entity, suggesting that in many cases entity formatting is non-trivial.

4.2 Experimental System

The experimental system includes a 5-gram LM trained on TRS with spaces treated as tokens. Number evaluation is performed with two sets of number classes, listed in Table 1. System A contains LM with classes from set A, and System B contains LM with classes from set B. The experimental setup also includes the following grammars:

- G_{phone} - deterministically formats as a phone number any string spoken like a US 7 or 10 digit phone number
- G_{number} - expands all spoken numbers to a full range of variants, with support for time expressions, ordinals, decimals, dollar amounts
- $G_{\text{cap\_punct}}$ - generates all possible combinations of commas, periods and capitals; always capitalizes the first word of a sentence

Raw:	for	**six**	people at	**five five thirty**	cost is	**eleven hundred dollars**
Ref:	for	**six**	people at	**5 5:30**	cost is	**$1,100**
Hyp:	for	**6**	people at	**5 5:30**	cost is	**11 $100**
Score:	-	incorrect	-	correct	-	incorrect

Table 2: A example of a raw transcript, reference transcript with number formatting and the hypothesis produced by the system. The entities (bold) in reference and hypothesis are aligned and scored.

4.3 Evaluation of Punctuation

To evaluate the performance of capitalization and punctuation we run System A on NPTS with only the $G_{\text{cap\_punct}}$ (in order not to introduce errors due to numeric formatting). The precision, recall and F-measure rates for periods, commas and capitals are computed using PTS as reference (See Fig. 5).

	Precision	Recall	F-Measure
Capitals	0.7902	0.5356	0.6385
Comma	0.5527	0.3129	0.3996
Period	0.6672	0.6783	0.6727

Figure 5: Punctuation and capitalization results.

It should be noted that a 5-gram language model that treats spaces as words models the same history as a 3-gram model that omits the spaces from training data. When this is taken into account, our results with a much smaller training set are comparable to Gravano et al. (2009). The F-measure scores for commas and periods are also comparable to the prosody-based work of (Christensen et al., 2001), with the precision of the period slightly lower, but compensated by recall. Thus, our system can perform additional formatting, while retaining a reasonable capitalization and punctuation performance.

4.4 Evaluation of Number Formatting

We evaluate number formatting performance of Systems A and B, which use different sets of classes for the language modeling (See Table 1). We process NNTS with both systems and score against the reference formatted set NTS to obtain Numeric Entity Error Rate (NEER). Class Set B naively breaks numbers into classes by digit count. System B using this class set performs worse than System A by 1.7% absolute (See Table 4). In particular, the overformatting rate (OFR) is higher by 1.2% absolute in System B than in System A. An example of overformatting is the mis-formatting of the English impersonal pronoun "one" as the digit "1". Such overformatting errors are much more noticeable than the underformatting errors, which are higher by 0.4% absolute in System A. This result shows that the choice of classes for the class-based LM significantly impacts number formatting performance. Superior overall performance of System A suggests that prior knowledge in the choice of classes favorably impacts performance.

	NEER	IFR	OFR	UFR
System A				
exact	16.1%	9.7%	5.4%	1.0%
ignore space	11.2%	4.9%	5.4%	1.0%
System B				
exact	17.8%	10.6%	6.6%	0.6%
ignore space	13.2%	6.0%	6.6%	0.6%

Table 4: The total NEER score, NEER due to incorrect formatting (IFR), NEER due to overformatting (OFR) and NEER due to underformatting (UFR); NEER rates with whitespace errors ignored are also listed.

In order to estimate the error rate not caused by whitespace errors, we also compute the NEER with whitespace errors ignored. It turns out that between 4 and 5% absolute of the errors are whitespace errors. Even if all whitespace errors are significant, the 83.9% of perfectly formatted entities suggests that the proposed formatting approach can achieve good performance on the number formatting task.

	entities	:	.	$	,
Reference totals	3563	310	50	39	17
System A correct	3161	232	36	33	10
System B correct	2923	204	35	31	5

Table 5: The count of formatted entities in NTS containing various formatting characters; the counts of these entities correctly formatted by the systems A and B.

To estimate how well the systems perform on specific number formatting tasks we count the number of reference entities containing certain formatting characters and compute the number of these entities correctly formatted by Systems A and B (See Table 5). The count of different formatting characters in NTS is small, but still provides an estimate of the number formatting performance for a real application like voicemail transcription. System A performs significantly better on the formatting of time expressions containing a colon, getting 74.8% correct. The NEER of System A for entities containing special formatting characters is under 28% for all formatting characters except comma, which is used inconsistently in training text.

4.5 Qualitative Evaluation

In addition to quantitative evaluation we have conducted a small-scale study of transcript readability. The study aims to compare raw ASR transcripts, ASR transcripts formatted by our system and raw manual transcripts. We have processed LDC Voicemail Part 1 with our ASR engine achieving an error rate of 30%, and have selected 50 voicemails with error rate under 30% and high informational content. Messages containing names, addresses and numbers were preferred. The word error rate on the selected voicemails is 20%. For each voicemail we have constructed three semantic multiple-choice questions, aimed at information extraction. We have asked each of 15 volunteers to answer all 3 questions about half of the voicemails. The questions were shown in sequence, while the transcript remained on the screen. The transcript for each voicemail was randomly selected to be ASR raw, ASR formatted or manual raw. The response time was measured individually for each question.

The analysis of the responses reveals a statistically significant difference in response time between formatted and raw ASR transcripts ($p = 0.02$, even allowing for per-item and per-subject effects; see also Fig. 6) and comparable accuracy. The response times for formatted ASR were comparable to the response times for manual unformatted transcripts. This suggests that for transcripts with low error rates the formatting of the ASR output significantly impacts readability. This disagrees with a similar study (Jones et al., 2003), which found no significant difference in the comprehension rates between raw ASR transcripts and capitalized, punctuated ASR output with disfluencies removed. This could be due to a number of factors, including a different type of transformation performed on the ASR transcript, a different corpus, and a lower word error rate of transcripts in our user study.

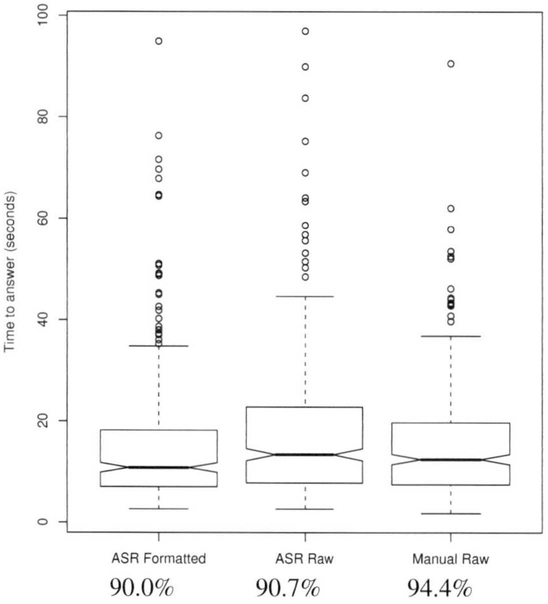

Figure 6: The standard R box plot of the response time for different transcript types and the corresponding accuracy.

5 Conclusion

We present a statistical approach suitable for a wide range of formatting tasks, including but not limited to punctuation, capitalization and numeric entity formatting. The average of 2 numeric entities per voicemail in the manually processed LDC Voicemail corpus shows that number formatting is important for applications such as voicemail transcription. Our best system achieves a Numeric Entity Error Rate of 16.1% on the ambiguous task of numeric entity formatting, while retaining capitalization and punctuation performance comparable to other published work. Our algorithm is concisely formulated in terms of WFSTs and is easily extended to new formatting tasks without the need for additional training data. In addition, the WFST formulation allows word-level timing and confidence to be retained during formatting. In order to overcome data sparsity associated with written numbers, we use a class-based language model and show that the choice of number classes significantly impacts number formatting performance. Finally, a statistically significant difference in question answering time for raw and formatted ASR transcripts in our user study demonstrates the positive impact of the transcript formatting on the readability of errorful ASR transcripts.

References

C. Allauzen, M. Riley, J. Schalkwyk, W. Skut, and M. Mohri. 2007. Openfst: A general and efficient weighted finite-state transducer library. In *Proceedings of CIAA*, pages 11–23.

F. Béchet, A. Gorin, J. Wright, and D. Hakkani-Tür. 2004. Detecting and extracting named entities from spontaneous speech in a mixed-initiative spoken dialogue context: How may i help you? *Speech Communication*, 42(2):207–225.

D. Beeferman, A. Berger, and J. Lafferty. 1998. Cyberpunc: A lightweight punctuation annotation system for speech. In *Proceedings of ICASSP*, pages 689–692.

E. Brown and A. Coden. 2002. Capitalization recovery for text. In *Information Retrieval Techniques for Speech Applications*, pages 11–22, London, UK. Springer-Verlag.

C. Chelba and A. Acero. 2006. Adaptation of maximum entropy capitalizer: Little data can help a lot. *Computer Speech and Language*, 20(4):382–399.

N. Chinchor. 1997. Muc-7 named entity task definition. In *Proceedings of MUC-7*.

H. Christensen, Y. Gotoh, and S. Renals. 2001. Punctuation annotation using statistical prosody models. In *ISCA Workshop on Prosody in Speech Recognition and Understanding*.

A. Gravano, M. Jansche, and M. Bacchiani. 2009. Restoring punctuation and capitalization in transcribed speech. In *Proceedings of ICASSP*, pages 4741–4744. IEEE Computer Society.

J. Hopcroft and J. Ullman, 1979. *Introduction to automata theory, languages, and computation*, pages 218–219. Addison-Wesley.

J. Huang, G. Zweig, and M. Padmanabhan. 2001. Information extraction from voicemail. In *Proceedings of the Conference of the ACL*, pages 290–297.

M. Jansche and S. P. Abney. 2002. Information extraction from voicemail transcripts. In *In EMNLP*.

D. Jones, F. Wolf, E. Gibson, E. Williams, E. Fedorenko, D. Reynolds, and M. Zissman. 2003. Measuring the readability of automatic speech-to-text transcripts. In *Proceedings of EUROSPEECH*, pages 1585–1588.

M. Levit, P. Haffner, A. Gorin, H. Alshawi, and E. Nöth. 2004. Aspects of named entity processing. In *Proceedings of INTERSPEECH*.

Y. Liu, E. Shriberg, A. Stolcke, D. Hillard, M. Ostendorf, and M. Harper. 2006. Enriching speech recognition with automatic detection of sentence boundaries and disfluencies. *IEEE Transactions on Audio, Speech, and Language Processing*, 14(5):1526–1540.

M. Mohri, F. Pereira, and M. Riley. 2008. Speech recognition with weighted finite-state transducers. In *Handbook on Speech Processing and Speech Communication*. Springer.

M. Mohri. 2009. Weighted automata algorithms. In *Handbook of Weighted Automata. Monographs in Theoretical Computer Science.*, pages 213–254. Springer.

M. Padmanabhan, G. Ramaswamy, B. Ramabhadran, P. Gopalakrishnan, and C. Dunn. 1998. Voicemail corpus part i. Linguistic Data Consortium, Philadelphia.

E. Shriberg, A. Stolcke, D. Hakkani-Tür, and G. Tür. 2000. Prosody-based automatic segmentation of speech into sentences and topics. *Speech Communications*, 32(1-2):127–154.

W. Wang, K. Knight, and D. Marcu. 2006. Capitalizing machine translation. In *Proceedings of HLT/ACL*, pages 1–8. Association for Computational Linguistics.

Cheap, Fast and Good Enough: Automatic Speech Recognition with Non-Expert Transcription

Scott Novotney and **Chris Callison-Burch**
Center for Language and Speech Processing
Johns Hopkins University
snovotne@bbn.com ccb@jhu.edu

Abstract

Deploying an automatic speech recognition system with reasonable performance requires expensive and time-consuming in-domain transcription. Previous work demonstrated that non-professional annotation through Amazon's Mechanical Turk can match professional quality. We use Mechanical Turk to transcribe conversational speech for as little as one thirtieth the cost of professional transcription. The higher disagreement of non-professional transcribers does not have a significant effect on system performance. While previous work demonstrated that redundant transcription can improve data quality, we found that resources are better spent collecting more data. Finally, we describe a quality control method without needing professional transcription.

1 Introduction

Successful speech recognition depends on huge investments in data collection. Even after training on 2000+ hours of transcribed conversational speech, over a billion words of language modeling text, and hand-crafted pronunciation dictionaries, state of the art systems still have an error rate of around 15% for English (Prasad et al., 2005) Transcribing the large volumes of data required for Large Vocabulary Continuous Speech Recognition (LVCSR) of new languages appears prohibitively expensive. Recent work has shown that Amazon's Mechanical Turk[1] can be used to cheaply create data for other natural language processing applications (Snow et al., 2008; Zaidan and Callison-Burch, 2009; McGraw et al., 2009). In this paper we focus on reducing the cost of transcribing conversational telephone speech (CTS) data. Previous measurements of Mechanical Turk stopped at agreement/disagreement with professional annotation. We take the next logical step and measure performance on systems trained with non-professional transcription.

Mechanical Turk is an online labor market where workers (or Turkers) perform simple tasks called Human Intelligence Tasks (HITs) for small amounts of money – frequently as little as $0.01 per HIT. Since HITs can be tasks that are difficult for computers, but easy for humans, they are ideal for natural language processing tasks (Snow et al., 2008). Mechanical Turk has even spawned a business that specializes in manual speech transcription.[2]

Automatic speech recognition (ASR) of conversational speech is an extremely difficult problem. Characteristics like rapid speech, phonetic reductions and speaking style limit the value of non-CTS data, necessitating in-domain transcription. Even a few hours of transcription is sufficient to bootstrap with unsupervised methods like self-training (Lamel et al., 2002). The speech community has built effective downstream solutions for the past twenty years despite imperfect recognition. In topic classification, 90% accuracy is possible on conversational data even with 80%+ word error rate

[1] http://www.mturk.com

[2] http://castingwords.com/

Human Language Technologies: The 2010 Annual Conference of the North American Chapter of the ACL, pages 207–215,
Los Angeles, California, June 2010.

(WER) (Gillick et al., 1993). Other successful tasks include information retrieval from speech (Miller et al., 2007) and spoken dialogue processing (Young et al., 2007). Inexpensive transcription would quickly open new languages or domains (like meeting or lecture data) for automatic speech recognition.

In this paper, we make the following points:

- Quality control isn't necessary as a system built with non-professional transcription is only 6% worse for $\frac{1}{30}$ the cost of professional transcription.
- Resources are better spent collecting more data than improving data quality.
- Transcriber skill can be accurately estimated without gold standard data.

2 Related Work

Research into Mechanical Turk by the NLP community has largely focused on comparing the quality of annotations produced by non-expert Turkers against annotations created by experts. Snow et al. (2008) conducted a comprehensive study across a variety of NLP tasks. They showed that high agreement could be reached with gold-standard expert annotation for these tasks through a weighted combination of ten redundant annotations produced by Turkers.

Callison-Burch (2009) showed similar results for machine translation evaluation, and further showed that Turkers could accomplish complex tasks like translating Urdu or creating reading comprehension tests.

McGraw et al. (2009) used Mechanical Turk to improve an English isolated word speech recognizer by having Turkers listen to a word and select from a list of probable words at a cost of $20 per hour of transcription.

Marge et al. (2010) collected transcriptions of verbal instructions to robots with clean speech. By using five duplicate transcriptions, the average transcription disagreement with experts was reduced from 4% to 2%.

Previous efforts at reducing the cost of transcription include the EARS Fisher project (Cieri et al., 2004), which collected 2000+ hours of English CTS data – an order of magnitude more than had previously been transcribed. To speed transcription and lower costs, Kimball et al. (2004) created new transcription guidelines and used automatic segmentation. These improved the speed of transcription from fifty times real time to six times real time, and made it cost effective to transcribe 2000 hours at an average of $150 per hour. Models trained on the faster transcripts exhibited almost no degradation in performance, although discrimanitve training was sensitive to transcription errrors.

3 Experiment Description

3.1 Corpora

We conducted most experiments on a twenty hour subset of the English Switchboard corpus (Godfrey et al., 1992) where two strangers converse about an assigned topic. We used two sets of transcription as our gold standard: high quality transcription from the LDC and those following the Fisher quick transcription guidelines (Kimball et al., 2004) provided by a professional transcription company. All English ASR models were tested with the carefully transcribed three hour Dev04 test set from the NIST HUB5 evaluation.[3] A 75k word lexicon taken from the EARS Fisher training corpus covers the LDC training data and has a test OOV rate of 0.18%.

We also conducted experiments in Korean and collected Hindi and Tamil data from the Callfriend corpora [4]. Participants were given a free long distance phone call to talk with friends or family in their native language, although English frequently appears. Since Callfriend was originally intended for language identification, only the 27 hour Korean portion has been transcribed by the LDC.

3.2 LVCSR System

We used Byblos, a state-of-the-art multi-pass LVCSR system with state-clustered Gaussian tied-mixture acoustic models and modified Kneser-Ney smoothed language models (Prasad et al., 2005). While understanding the system

[3] `http://www.itl.nist.gov/iad/mig/tests/ctr/1998/current-plan.html`

[4] `http://www.ldc.upenn.edu/CallFriend2/`

details is not essential for this work, we provide a brief description for completeness.

Recognition begins with cepstral feature extraction using concatenated frames with cepstral mean subtraction and HLDA to reduce the feature dimension space. Vocal track length normalization follows. Decoding then requires three passes: a fast forward pass with coarse one-gaussian-per-phone models and bigram LM followed by a backward pass with triphone models and a trigram LM to generate word confusion lattices. The lattices are rescored with a more powerful quinphone cross-word acoustic model and trigram LM to extract the one best output. These three steps are repeated after unsupervised speaker adaptation with constrained MLLR. Decoding is around ten times real time.

3.3 Transcription Task

Using language-independent speaker activity detection models, we segmented each ten minute conversation into five second utterances, greatly simplifying the transcription task (Roy and Roy, 2009). Utterances were assigned in batches of ten per HIT and played with a simple flash player with a text box for entry. All non-empty HITs were approved and we did not award bonuses except as described in Section 5.1.

3.4 Measuring Annotation Quality

The usefullness of the transcribed data is ultimately measured by how much it benefits a speech recognition system. Factors that inflate disagreement (word error rate) between Turkers and professionals do not necessarily impact system performance. These include typographical mistakes, transcription inconsistencies (like improperly marking hesitations or the many variations of `um`) and spelling variations (`geez` or `jeez` are both valid spellings). Additionally, the gold standard is itself imperfect, with typical estimates of professional disagreement around five percent. Therefore, we judge the quality of Mechanical Turk data by comparing the performance of one LVCSR system trained on Turker annotation and another trained on professional transcriptions of the same dataset.

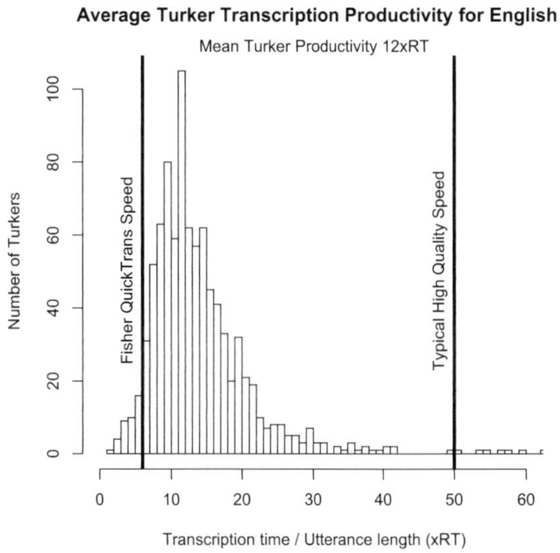

Figure 1: Histogram of per-turker transcription rate for twenty hours of English CTS data. Historical estimates for high quality transcription are 50xRT. The 2004 Fisher transcription effort achieved 6xRT and the average here is 11xRT.

4 Establishing Best Practices with English Switchboard

As an initial test to see how cheaply conversational data could be transcribed, we uploaded one hour of test data from Hub5 Dev04. We first paid \$0.20 per HIT (\$0.02 per utterance). This test finished quickly, and we measured the average disagreement with professionals at 17%. Next, we reduced payment to \$0.10 per HIT and disagreement was again 17%. Finally, we pushed the price down to \$0.05 per HIT or \$5 per hour of transcription and again disagreement was nearly identical at 18%, although a few Turkers complained about the low pay.

Using this price, we then paid for the full twenty hours to be redundantly transcribed three times. 1089 Turkers participated in the task at an incoming rate of 10 hours of transcription per day. On average, each Turker transcribed 30 utterance (earning 15 cents) at an average professional disagreement of 23%. Transcribing one minute of audio required an average eleven minutes of effort (denoted 11xRT). 63 workers transcribed more than one hundred utterances and one prolific worker transcribed 1223 utterances.

4.1 Comparing Non-Professional to Professional Transcription

Table 1 details the results of different selection methods for redundant transcription. For each method of selection, we build an acoustic and language model and report WER on the heldout test set (transcribed at very high accuracy).

We first randomly selected one of the three transcriptions per utterance (as if the data were only tanscribed once) and repeated this three times with little variance. Selecting utterances randomly by *Turker* performed similarly. Performance of an LVCSR system trained on the non-professional transcription degrades by only 2.5% absolute (6% relative) despite a disagreement of 23%. This is without any quality control besides throwing out empty utterances. The degradation held constant as we swept the amount of training data frome one to twenty hours. Bot the acoustic and language models exhibited the log-linear relationship between WER and the amount of training data. Independent of the amount of training data, the acoustic model degraded by a nearly constant 1.7% and the language model by 0.8%.

To evaluate the benefit of multiple transcriptions, we built two oracle systems. The *Turker oracle* ranks Turkers by the average error rate of their transcribed utterances against the professionals and selects utterances by Turker until the twenty hours is covered (Section 4.3 discusses a fair way to rank Turkers). The *utterance oracle* selects the best of the three different transcriptions per utterance. The best of the three Turkers per utterance wrote the best transcription two thirds of the time.

The utterance oracle only recovered half of the degradation for using non-professional transcription. Cutting the disagreement in half (from 23% to 13%) reduced the WER gap by about half (from 2.5% to 1%). Using the standard system combination algorithm ROVER (Fiscus, 1997) to combine the three transcriptions per utterance only reduced disagreement from 23% to 21%. While previous work benefited from combining multiple annotations, this task shows little benefit.

Transcription	Disagreement with LDC	ASR WER
Random Utterance	23%	42.0%
Random Turker	20%	41.4%
Oracle Utterance	13%	40.9%
Oracle Turker	18%	41.1%
Contractor	< 5%	39.6%
LDC	-	39.5%

Table 1: Quality of Non-Professional Transcription on 20 hours of English Switchboard. Even though disagreement for random selection without quality control has 23% disagreement with professional transcription, an ASR system trained on the data is only 2.5% worse than using LDC transcriptions. The upper bound for quality control (row 3) recovers only 50% of the total loss.

4.2 Combining with External Sources

While in-domain speech transcription is typically the only effective way to improve the acoustic model, out-of-domain transcripts tend to be useful for language models of conversational speech. Broadcast News (BN) transcription is particularly well suited for English Switchboard data as the topics tend to cover news items like terrorism or politics. We built a small one million word language model (to simulate a resource-poor language) and interpolated it with varying amounts of LDC or Mechanical Turk transcriptions. Figure 2 details the results.

4.3 The Value of Quality Control

With a fixed transcription budget, should one even bother with redundant transcription to improve an ASR system? To find out, we transcribed 40 additional hours of Switchboard using Mechanical Turk. Disagreement to the LDC transcriptions was 24%, similar to the initial 20 hours. The two percent degradation of test WER when using Mechanical Turk compared to LDC held up with 40 and 60 hours of training.

Given a fixed budget of 60 hours of transcription, we compared the quality of 20 hours transcribed three times to 60 hours transcribed once. The best we could hope to recover from the three redundant transcriptions is the utterance oracle. Oracle and singly transcribed data had 13% and 24% disagreement with LDC respectively. System performance was 40.9% with 20 hours of

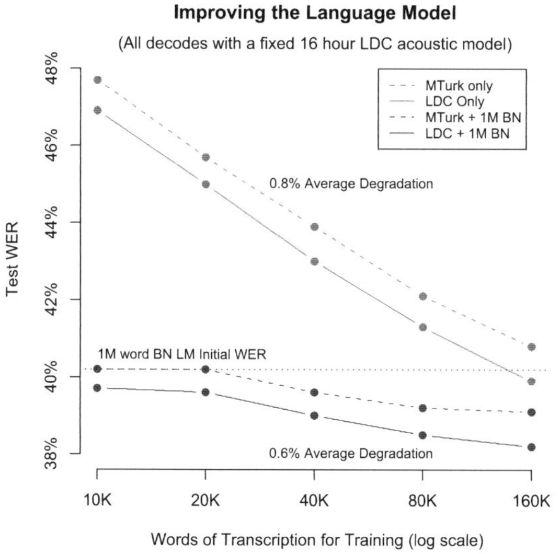

Figure 2: WER with a varied amount of LM training data and a fixed 16hr acoustic model. MTurk transcription degrades WER by 0.8% absolute across LM size. When interpolated with 1M words of broadcast news, this degradation shrinks to 0.6%.

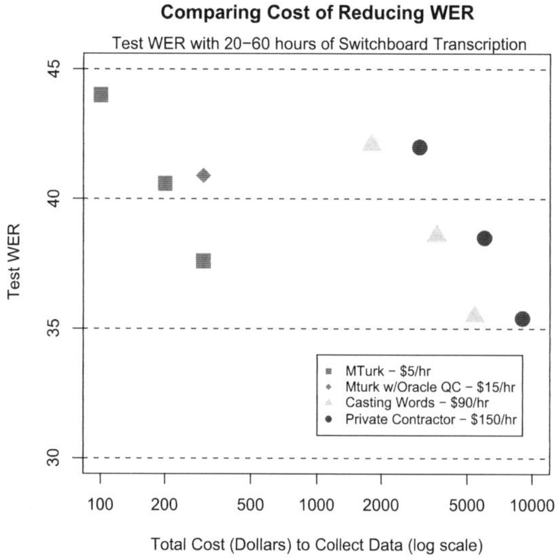

Figure 3: Historical cost estimates are $150 per hour of transcription (blue cirlces). The company Casting Words uses Turkers to transcribe English at $90 per hour which we estimated to be high quality (green triangles). Transcription without quality control on Mechanical Turk (red squares) is drastically cheaper at $5 per hour. With a fixed budget, it is better to transcribe more data at lower quality than to improve quality. Contrast the oracle WER for 20 hours transcribed three times (red diamond) with 60 hours transcribed once (bottom red square).

the former and 37.6% with 60 hours of the latter. Even though perfect selection cuts disagreement in half, three times as much data helps more.

The 2004 Fisher effort averaged a price of $150 per hour of English CTS transcription. The company CastingWords produces high quality (Passy, 2008) English transcription for $90 an hour using Mechanical Turk by a multi-pass process to collect and clean Turker-provided transcripts. While we did not use their service, we assume it is of comparable quality to the private contractor used earlier. The price for LDC transcription is not comparable here since it was intended for more precise linguistic tasks. Extrapolating from Figure 3, the entire 2000 Fisher corpus could be transcribed using Mechanical Turk at the same cost of collecting 60 hours of professional transcription.

5 Collection in Other Languages

To test the feasability of improving low-resource languages, we attempted to collect transcriptions for Korean, Hindi, Tamil CTS data. We built an LVCSR system in Korean since it is the only one with reference LDC transcriptions to use as a test set.

5.1 Korean

Korean is spoken by roughly 78 million speakers world wide and is written in Hangul, a phonetic orthography, although Chinese characters frequently appear in written text. Since Korean has essentially arbitrary spacing (Chong-Woo et al., 2001), we report Phoneme Error Rate (PER) instead of WER, which would be unfairly penalized. Both behave similarly as system performance improves. For comparison, an English WER of 39.5% has a PER of 34.8%.

We uploaded ten hours of audio to be transcribed once, again segmented into short snippets. Transcription was very slow at first and we had to pay $0.20 per HIT to attract workers. We posted a separate HIT to refer Korean transcribers, paying a 25% bonus of the income earned by referrals. This was quite successful as two referred Turkers contributed over 80% of the total transcription (at a cost of $25 per hour instead of $20). We collected three hours of transcriptions after five weeks, paying eight Turkers $113 at a transcription rate of 10xRT.

Average Turker disagreement to the LDC reference was 17% (computed at the character level). Using these transcripts to train an LVCSR system instead of those provided by LDC degraded PER by 0.8% from 51.3% to 52.1%. For comparison, a system trained on the entire 27 hours of LDC data had 41.2% PER.

Although performance seems poor, it is sufficiently good to bootstrap with acoustic model self-training (Lamel et al., 2002). The language model can be improved by finding 'conversational' web text found with n-gram queries extracted from the three hours of transcripts (Bulyko et al., 2003).

5.2 Hindi and Tamil

As a feasability experiment, we collected one hour of transcription in Hindi and Tamil, paying $20 per hour of transcription. Hindi and Tamil transcription finished in eight days, perhaps due to the high prevalence of Turkers in India (Ipeirotis, 2008). While we did not have any professional reference, Hindi speaking colleagues viewed some of the data and pointed out errors in English transliteration, but overall quality appeared fine. The true test will be to build an LVCSR system and report WER.

6 Quality Control sans Quality Data

Although we have shown that redundantly transcribing an entire corpus gives little gain, there is value in *some* amount of quality control. We could improve system performance by only rejecting Turkers with high disagreement, similar to confidence selection for active learning or unsupervised training (Ma and Schwartz,). But if we are transcribing a truly new domain, there is no gold-standard data to use as reference, so we must estimate disagreement against errorful reference. In this section we provide a practical use for quality control without gold standard reference data.

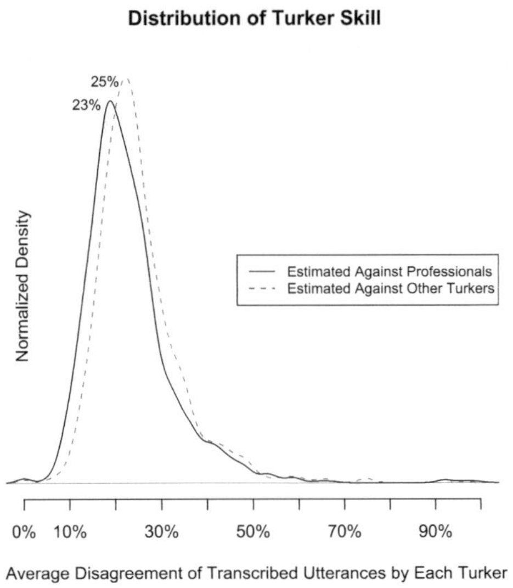

Figure 4: Each Turker was judged against professional and non-professional reference and assigned an overall disagreement. The distribution of Turker disagreement follows a gamma distribution, with a tight cluster of average Turkers and a long-tail of bad Turkers. Estimating with non-professionals (even though the reference is 23% wrong on average) is surprisingly well matched to professional estimate. Turker estimation over-estimated disagreement by only 2%.

6.1 Estimating Turker Skill

Using the twenty hour English transcriptions from Section 4, we computed disagreement for each Turker against the professional transcription for all utterances longer than four words. Note that each utterance was transcribed by three random turkers, so there is not one set of utterances which were transcribed by all turkers. Each Turker transcribed a different, partially overlapping, subset of the data.

For a particular Turker, we estimated the disagreement with other Turkers by using the two other transcripts as reference and taking the average. Figure 4 shows the density estimate of Turker disagreement when calculated against professional and non-professional transcription. On average, the non-professional estimate was 3% off from the professional disagreement.

Given that non-professional disagreement is a good estimate of professional disagreement

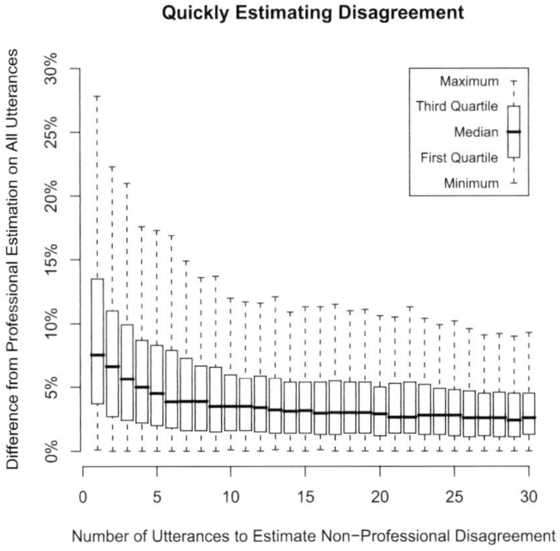

Figure 5: Boxplot of the difference of non-professional disagreement with a fixed number of utterances to professional disagreement over all utterances. While error is expectedly high with one utterance, 50% of the estimates are within 3% of the truth after ten utterances and 75% of the estimates are within 6% after fifteen utterances.

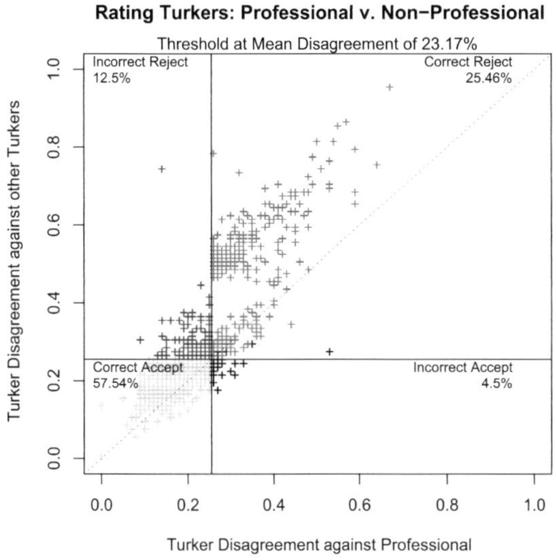

Figure 6: Each Turker is a point with professional (X axis) plotted against non-professional (Y axis) disagreement. The non-professional disagreement correlates surprisingly well with professional disagreement even though the transcripts used as reference are 23% wrong on average. By setting a selection threshold, the space is divided into four quadrants. The bottom left are correctly accepted: both non-professional and professional disagreement are below the threshold. The top left are incorrectly rejected: using their transcripts would have helped, but they don't hurt system performance, just waste money. The top right are correctly rejected for having high disagreement. The bottom right are the troublesome false positives that are included in training but actually may hurt performance. Luckily, the ratio of false negatives to false positives is usually much larger.

over all of a Turker's utterances, we wondered how few needed to be redundantly transcribed by other non-professionals. For each Turker, we started by randomly selecting one utterance and computed the non-professional disagreement. We compared the estimate to the true professional disagreement over all of the utterances and repeatedly sample 20 times. Then we increased the number of utterances used to estimate non-professional disagreement until all utterances by that Turker are selected.

Figure 5 shows a boxplot of the differences of non-professional to professional disagreement on *all* utterances. As few as fifteen utterances need to be redundantly transcribed to accurately estimate three out of four Turkers within 5% of the professional disagreement.

6.2 Finding the Right Turkers

Since we can accurately predict a Turker's skill with as few as fifteen utterances on average, we can rank Turkers by their professional and non-professional disagreemeents. By thresholding on disagreement, we can either select good turkers or equivalently reject bad turkers. We can view the ranking as a precision/recall problem to select only the 'good' Turkers below the threshold. Figure 6 plots each Turker where the X axis is the professional disagreement and the Y axis is the non-professional disagreement. Sweeping the disagreement threshold from zero to one generates Figure 7, which reports F-score (the harmonic mean of precision and recall). This section suggests a concrete qualification test by first transcribing 15-30 utterance multiple times to create a gold standard. Using the transcription from the best Turker as reference, approve new Turkers with a WER less than the average WER from the initial set.

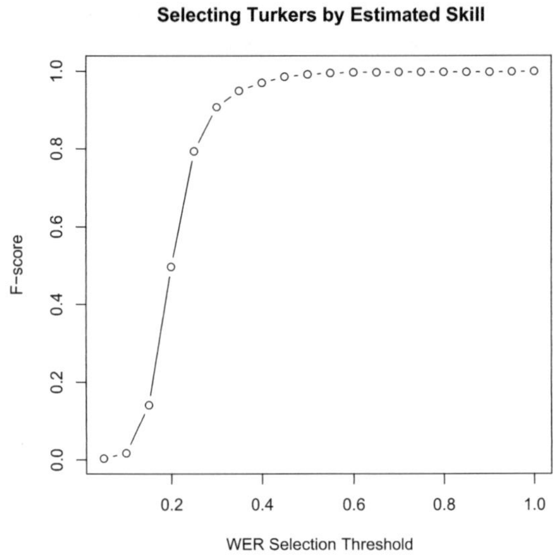

Figure 7: It is difficult to find only good Turkers since the false positives outnumber the few good workers. However, rejecting bad Turkers becomes very easy once past the mean error rate of 23%. It is better to use disagreement estimation to reject poor workers instead of finding good workers.

7 Experience with Mechanical Turk

We initially expected to invest most of our effort in managing Turker transcription. But the vast majority of Turkers completed the effort in good faith with few complaints about pay. Many left positive comments[5] despite the very difficult task. Indeed, the author's own disagreement on a few dozen English utterances were 17.7% and 26.8% despite an honest effort.

Instead, we spent most of our time normalizing the transcriptions for English acoustic model training. Every single misspelling or new word had to be mapped to a pronunciation in order to be used in training. We initially discarded any utterance with an out of vocabulary word, but after losing half of the data, we used a set of simple heuristics to produce pronunciations. Even though there were a few thousand of these errors, they were all singletons and had little effect on performance. Turkers sometimes left comments in the transcription box such as "no audio" or "man1: man2:". These errant transcriptions could be detected by force aligning the transcript with the audio and rejecting any with low scores (Lamel et al., 2000). Extending transcription to thousands of hours will require robust methods to automatically deal with errant transcripts and additionally run the risk of exhausting the available pool of workers.

Finding Korean transcribers required the most creativity. We found success in interacting with the transcribers, providing feedback, encouragement and paying bonuses for referring other workers. Cultivating workers for a new language is definitely a 'hands on' process.

For Hindi and Tamil, Turkers sometimes misinterpreted or ignored instructions and translated into English or transliterated into Roman characters. Additionally, *some* linguistic knowledge is required to classify phonemic categories (like fricative or sonorant) required for acoustic model training.

8 Conclusion

Unlike previous work which studied the quality of Mechanical Turk annotations alone, we judge its value in terms of the real task: improving system performance. Despite relatively high disagreement with professional transcription, data collected with Mechanical Turk was nearly as effective for training speech models. Since this degradation is so small, redundant annotation to improve quality is not worth the cost. Resources are better spent collecting more transcription. In addition to English, we demonstrated similar trends in Korean and also collected transcripts for Hindi and Tamil. Finally, we proposed an effective procedure to reduce costs by maintaining the quality of the annotator pool without needing high quality annotation.

Acknowledgments

This research was supported by the EuroMatrixPlus project funded by the European Commission by the DARPA GALE program under Contract No. HR0011-06-2-0001, and NSF under grant IIS-0713448 and by BBN Technologies. The views and findings are the authors' alone.

[5] One Turker left a comment "You don't grow pickles!!" in regards to the misinformed speakers she was transcribing.

References

Ivan Bulyko, Mari Ostendorf, and A. Stolcke. 2003. Getting more mileage from web text sources for conversational speech language modeling using class-dependent mixtures. In *HLT-NAACL*.

Chris Callison-Burch. 2009. Fast, Cheap, and Creative: Evaluating Translation Quality Using Amazons Mechanical Turk. *EMNLP*.

Seung-Shik Kang Chong-Woo, Chong woo Woo, and Kookmin Univerity. 2001. Automatic segmentation of words using syllable bigram statistics. In *6th Natural Language Processing Pacific Rim Symposium*.

Christopher Cieri, David Miller, and Kevin Walker. 2004. The fisher corpus: a resource for the next generations of speech-to-text. In *LREC*.

Jonathan G. Fiscus. 1997. A post-processing system to yield reduced word error rates: Recognizer output voting error reduction (rover).

L. Gillick, J. Baker, J. Bridle, M. Hunt, Y. Ito, S. Lowe, J. Orloff, B. Peskin, R. Roth, and F. Scattone. 1993. Application of large vocabulary continuous speech recognition to topic and speaker identification using telephone speech. In *ICASSP*.

Jack Godfrey, Edward Holliman, and Jane McDaniel. 1992. Switchboard: Telephone speech corpus for research and development. In *ICASSP*.

Panos Ipeirotis. 2008. Mechanical turk: The demographics. `http://behind-the-enemy-lines.blogspot.com/2010/03/new-demographics-of-mechanical-turk.html`.

Owen Kimball, Chai-Lin Kao, Teodoro Arvizo, John Makhoul, and Rukmini Iyer. 2004. Quick transcription and automatic segmentation of the fisher conversational telephone speech corpus. In *RT04 Workshop*.

Lori Lamel, Jean luc Gauvain, and Gilles Adda. 2000. Lightly supervised acoustic model training. In *ISCA ITRW ASR2000*.

Lori Lamel, Jean luc Gauvain, and Gilles Adda. 2002. Lightly supervised and unsupervised acoustic model training. *Computer Speech and Language*, 16(1).

Jeff Ma and Rich Schwartz. Unsupervised versus supervised training of acoustic models. In *INTERSPEECH*.

Matthew Marge, Satanjeev Banerjee, and Alexander Rudnicky. 2010. Using the amazon mechanical turk for transcription of spoken language. *ICASSP*, March.

Ian McGraw, Alexander Gruenstein, and Andrew Sutherland. 2009. A self-labeling speech corpus: Collecting spoken words with an online educational game. In *INTERSPEECH*.

D. Miller, M. Kleber, C. Kao, O. Kimball, T. Colthurst, S.A. Lowe, R.M. Schwartz, and H. Gish. 2007. Rapid and Accurate Spoken Term Detection. In *INTERSPEECH*.

Charles Passy. 2008. Turning audio into words on the screen. `http://online.wsj.com/article/SB122351860225518093.html`.

R. Prasad, S. Matsoukas, CL Kao, J.Z. Ma, DX Xu, T. Colthurst, O. Kimball, R. Schwartz, J.L. Gauvain, L. Lamel, et al. 2005. The 2004 BBN/LIMSI 20xRT English conversational telephone speech recognition system. In *INTERSPEECH*.

Brandon Roy and Deb Roy. 2009. Fast transcription of unstructured audio recordings. In *INTERSPEECH*.

Rion Snow, Brendan O'Connor, Daniel Jurafsky, and Andrew Y. Ng. 2008. Cheap and fast—but is it good?: evaluating non-expert annotations for natural language tasks. In *EMNLP*.

Steve. Young, Jost. Schatzmann, Karl. Weilhammer, and Hui. Ye. 2007. The hidden information state approach to dialog management. In *ICASSP*.

Omar F. Zaidan and Chris Callison-Burch. 2009. Feasibility of human-in-the-loop minimum error rate training. In *EMNLP*.

Contextual Information Improves OOV Detection in Speech

Carolina Parada, Mark Dredze
HLTCOE
Johns Hopkins University
3400 North Charles Street,
Baltimore MD 21210, USA
carolinap@jhu.edu
mdredze@cs.jhu.edu

Denis Filimonov
HLTCOE
University of Maryland,
College Park, MD 20742 USA
den@cs.umd.edu

Frederick Jelinek
HLTCOE
Johns Hopkins University
3400 North Charles Street,
Baltimore MD 21210, USA
jelinek@jhu.edu

Abstract

Out-of-vocabulary (OOV) words represent an important source of error in large vocabulary continuous speech recognition (LVCSR) systems. These words cause recognition failures, which propagate through pipeline systems impacting the performance of downstream applications. The detection of OOV regions in the output of a LVCSR system is typically addressed as a binary classification task, where each region is independently classified using local information. In this paper, we show that jointly predicting OOV regions, and including contextual information from each region, leads to substantial improvement in OOV detection. Compared to the state-of-the-art, we reduce the missed OOV rate from 42.6% to 28.4% at 10% false alarm rate.

1 Introduction

Even with a vocabulary of one hundred thousand words, a large vocabulary continuous speech recognition (LVCSR) system encounters out-of-vocabulary (OOV) words, especially in new domains or genres. New words often include named entities, foreign words, rare and invented words. Since these words were not seen during training, the LVCSR system has no way to recognize them.

OOV words are an important source of error in LVCSR systems for three reasons. First, OOVs can never be recognized by the LVCSR system, even if repeated. Second, OOV words contribute to recognition errors in surrounding words, which propagate into to later processing stages (translation, understanding, document retrieval, etc.). Third, OOVs are often information-rich nouns – mis-recognized OOVs can have a greater impact on the understanding of the transcript than other words.

One solution is to simply increase the LVCSR system's vocabulary, but there are always new words. Additionally, increasing the vocabulary size without limit can sometimes produce higher word error rates (WER), leading to a tradeoff between recognition accuracy of frequent and rare words.

A more effective solution is to detect the presence of OOVs directly. Once identified, OOVs can be flagged for annotation and addition to the system's vocabulary, or OOV segments can be transcribed with a phone recognizer, creating an open vocabulary LVCSR system. Identified OOVs prevent error propagation in the application pipeline.

In the literature, there are two basic approaches to OOV detection: 1) *filler* models, which explicitly represent OOVs using a filler, sub-word, or generic word model (Bazzi, 2002; Schaaf, 2001; Bisani and Ney, 2005; Klakow et al., 1999; Wang, 2009); and 2) confidence estimation models, which use different confidence scores to find unreliable regions and label them as OOV (Lin et al., 2007; Burget et al., 2008; Sun et al., 2001; Wessel et al., 2001).

Recently, Rastrow et al. (2009a) presented an approach that combined confidence estimation models and filler models to improve state-of-the-art results for OOV detection. This approach and other confidence based systems (Hazen and Bazzi, 2001; Lin et al., 2007), treat OOV detection as a binary classification task; each region is independently classified using local information as IV or OOV. This work moves beyond this independence assumption

Human Language Technologies: The 2010 Annual Conference of the North American Chapter of the ACL, pages 216–224,
Los Angeles, California, June 2010.

that considers regions independently for OOV detection. We treat OOV detection as a sequence labeling problem and add features based on the local lexical context of each region as well as global features from a language model using the entire utterance. Our results show that such information improves OOV detection and we obtain large reductions in error compared to the best previously reported results. Furthermore, our approach can be combined with any confidence based system.

We begin by reviewing the current state-of-the-art results for OOV detection. After describing our experimental setup, we generalize the framework to a sequence labeling problem, which includes features from the local context, lexical context, and entire utterance. Each stage yields additional improvements over the baseline system. We conclude with a review of related work.

2 Maximum Entropy OOV Detection

Our baseline system is the Maximum Entropy model with features from filler and confidence estimation models proposed by Rastrow et al. (2009a). Based on filler models, this approach models OOVs by constructing a hybrid system which combines words and sub-word units. Sub-word units, or fragments, are variable length phone sequences selected using statistical methods (Siohan and Bacchiani, 2005). The vocabulary contains a word and a fragment lexicon; fragments are used to represent OOVs in the language model text. Language model training text is obtained by replacing low frequency words (assumed OOVs) by their fragment representation. Pronunciations for OOVs are obtained using grapheme to phoneme models (Chen, 2003).

This approach also includes properties from confidence estimation systems. Using a hybrid LVCSR system, they obtain *confusion networks* (Mangu et al., 1999), compact representations of the recognizer's most likely hypotheses. For an utterance, the confusion network is composed of a sequence of *confused regions*, indicating the set of most likely word/sub-word hypotheses uttered and their posterior probabilities[1] in a specific time interval.

Figure 1 depicts a confusion network decoded by the hybrid system for a section of an utterance in our test-set. Below the network we present the reference transcription. In this example, two OOVs were uttered: "slobodan" and "milosevic" and decoded as four and three in-vocabulary words, respectively. A *confused region* (also called "bin") corresponds to a set of competing hypothesis between two nodes. The goal is to correctly label each of the "bins" as OOV or IV. Note the presence of both fragments (e.g. `s_l_ow`, `l_aa_s`) and words in some of the hypothesis bins.

For any bin of the confusion network, Rastrow et al. combine features from that region using a binary Maximum Entropy classifier (White et al., 2007). Their most effective features were:

$$\text{Fragment-Posterior} = \sum_{f \in t_j} p(f|t_j)$$

$$\text{Word-Entropy} = -\sum_{w \in t_j} p(w|t_j) \log p(w|t_j)$$

t_j is the current bin in the confusion network and f is a fragment in the hybrid dictionary.

We obtained confusion networks for a standard word based system and the hybrid system described above. We re-implemented the above features, obtaining nearly identical results to Rastrow et al. using Mallet's MaxEnt classifier (McCallum, 2002).[2] All real-valued features were normalized and quantized using the uniform-occupancy partitioning described in White et al. (2007).[3] The MaxEnt model is regularized using a Gaussian prior ($\sigma^2 = 100$), but we found results generally insensitive to σ.

3 Experimental Setup

Before we introduce and evaluate our context approach, we establish an experimental setup. We used the dataset constructed by Can et al. (2009) to evaluate Spoken Term Detection (STD) of OOVs; we refer to this corpus as OOVCORP. The corpus contains 100 hours of transcribed Broadcast News English speech emphasizing OOVs. There are 1290 unique OOVs in the corpus, which were selected with a minimum of 5 acoustic instances per word.

[1] $P(w_i|A)$: posterior probability of word i given the acoustics, which includes the language model and acoustic model scores, as described in (Mangu et al., 1999).

[2] Small differences are due to a change in MaxEnt library.

[3] All experiments use 50 partitions with a minimum of 100 training values per partition.

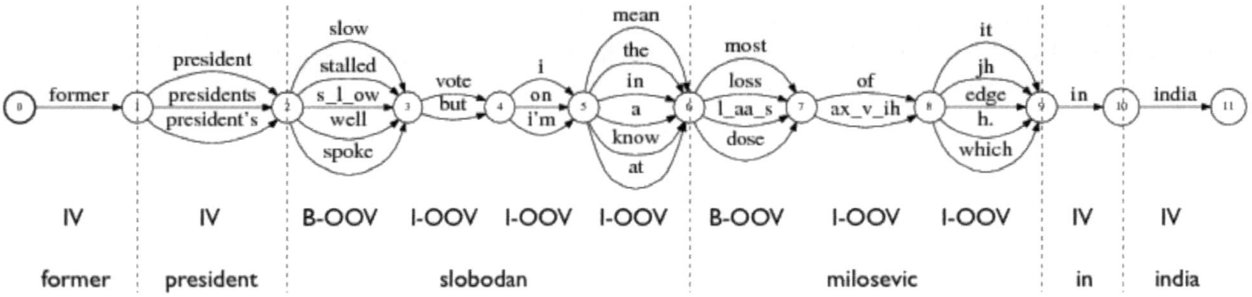

Figure 1: Example confusion network from the hybrid system with OOV regions and BIO encoding. Hypothesis are ordered by decreasing value of posterior probability. Best hypothesis is the concatenation of the top word/fragments in each bin. We omit posterior probabilities due to spacing.

Common English words were filtered out to obtain meaningful OOVs: e.g. `NATALIE`, `PUTIN`, `QAEDA`, `HOLLOWAY`. Since the corpus was designed for STD, short OOVs (less than 4 phones) were explicitly excluded. This resulted in roughly 24K (2%) OOV tokens.

For a LVCSR system we used the IBM Speech Recognition Toolkit (Soltau et al., 2005)[4] with acoustic models trained on 300 hours of HUB4 data (Fiscus et al., 1998) and excluded utterances containing OOV words as marked in OOVCORP. The language model was trained on 400M words from various text sources with a 83K word vocabulary. The LVCSR system's WER on the standard RT04 BN test set was 19.4%. Excluded utterances were divided into 5 hours of training and 95 hours of test data for the OOV detector. Both train and test sets have a 2% OOV rate. We used this split for all experiments. Note that the OOV training set is different from the LVCSR training set.

In addition to a word-based LVCSR system, we use a hybrid LVCSR system, combining word and sub-word (fragments) units. Combined word/sub-word systems have improved OOV Spoken Term Detection performance (Mamou et al., 2007; Parada et al., 2009), better phone error rates, especially in OOV regions (Rastrow et al., 2009b), and state-of-the-art performance for OOV detection. Our hybrid system's lexicon has 83K words and 20K fragments derived using Rastrow et al. (2009a). The 1290 excluded words are OOVs to both the word and hybrid systems.

Note that our experiments use a different dataset than Rastrow et. al., but we have a larger vocabulary (83K vs 20K), which is closer to most modern LVCSR system vocabularies; the resulting OOVs are more challenging but more realistic.

3.1 Evaluation

Confusion networks are obtained from both the word and hybrid LVCSR systems. In order to evaluate the performance of the OOV detector, we align the reference transcript to the audio. The LVCSR transcript is compared to the reference transcript at the confused region level, so each confused region is tagged as either OOV or IV. The OOV detector assigns a score/probability for IV/OOV to each of these regions.

Previous research reported OOV detection accuracy on all test data. However, once an OOV word has been observed in the training data for the OOV detector, even if it never appeared in the LVCSR training data, it is no longer truly OOV. The features used in previous approaches did not necessarily provide an advantage on observed versus unobserved OOVs, but our features do yield an advantage. Therefore, in the sections that follow we report unobserved OOV accuracy: OOV words that do not appear in either the OOV detector's or the LVCSR's training data. While this penalizes our results, it is a more informative metric of true system performance.

We present results using standard detection error tradeoff (DET) curves (Martin et al., 1997). DET

[4]We use the IBM system with speaker adaptive training based on maximum likelihood with no discriminative training.

curves measure tradeoffs between misses and false alarms and can be used to determine the optimal operating point of a system. The x-axis varies the false alarm rate (false positive) and the y-axis varies the miss (false negative) rate; lower curves are better.

4 From MaxEnt to CRFs

As a classification algorithm, Maximum Entropy assigns a label to each region independently. However, OOV words tend to be recognized as two or more IV words, hence OOV regions tend to co-occur. In the example of Figure 1, the OOV word "slobodan" was recognized as four IV words: "slow vote i mean". This suggests that sequence models, which jointly assign all labels in a sequence, may be more appropriate. Therefore, we begin incorporating context by moving from classification to sequence models.

MaxEnt classification models the target label as $p(y_i|\mathbf{x}_i)$, where y_i is a discrete variable representing the ith label ("IV" or "OOV") and $\mathbf{x}_i$ is a feature vector representing information for position i. The conditional distribution for y_i takes the form

$$p(y_i|\mathbf{x}_i) = \frac{1}{Z(\mathbf{x}_i)} \exp(\sum_{k=1}^{K} \lambda_k f_k(y_i, \mathbf{x}_i)) ,$$

$Z(\mathbf{x}_i)$ is a normalization term and $f(y_i, \mathbf{x}_i)$ is a vector of K features, such as those defined in Section 2. The model is trained discriminatively: parameters λ are chosen to maximize conditional data likelihood.

Conditional Random Fields (CRF) (Lafferty et al., 2001) generalize MaxEnt models to sequence tasks. While having the same model structure as Hidden Markov Models (HMMs), CRFs are trained discriminatively and can use large numbers of correlated features. Their primary advantage over MaxEnt models is their ability to find an optimal labeling for the entire sequence rather than greedy local decisions. CRFs have been used successfully used in numerous text processing tasks and while less popular in speech, still applied successfully, such as sentence boundary detection (Liu et al., 2005).

A CRF models the entire label sequence $\mathbf{y}$ as:

$$p(\mathbf{y}|\mathbf{x}) = \frac{1}{Z(\mathbf{x})} \exp(\lambda F(\mathbf{y}, \mathbf{x})) ,$$

where $F(\mathbf{y}, \mathbf{x})$ is a global feature vector for input sequence $\mathbf{x}$ and label sequence $\mathbf{y}$ and $Z(\mathbf{x})$ is a normalization term.[5]

5 Context for OOV Detection

We begin by including a minimal amount of local context in making OOV decisions: the predicted labels for adjacent confused regions (bins). This information helps when OOV bins occur in close proximity, such as successive OOV bins. This is indeed the case: in the OOV detector training data only 48% of OOV sequences contained a single bin; sequences were of length 2 (40%), 3 (9%) and 4 (2%). We found similar results in the test data. Therefore, we expect that even a minimal amount of context based on the labels of adjacent bins will help.

A natural way of incorporating contextual information is through a CRF, which introduces dependencies between each label and its neighbors. If a neighboring bin is likely an OOV, it increases the chance that the current bin is OOV.

In sequence models, another technique for capturing contextual dependence is the label encoding scheme. In information extraction, where sequences of adjacent tokens are likely to receive the same tag, the beginning of each sequence receives a different tag from words that continue the sequence. For example, the first token in a person name is labeled `B-PER` and all subsequent tokens are labeled `I-PER`. This is commonly referred to as BIO encoding (beginning, inside, outside). We applied this encoding technique to our task, labeling bins as either `IV` (in vocabulary), `B-OOV` (begin OOV) and `I-OOV` (inside OOV), as illustrated in Figure 1. This encoding allows the algorithm to identify features which might be more indicative of the beginning of an OOV sequence. We found that this encoding achieved a superior performance to a simple `IV/OOV` encoding. We therefore utilize the BIO encoding in all CRF experiments.

Another means of introducing context is through the order of the CRF model. A first order model ($n = 1$) adds dependencies only between neighboring labels, whereas an n order model creates dependencies between labels up to a distance of n positions. Higher order models capture length of label

[5] CRF experiments used the CRF++ package http://crfpp.sourceforge.net/

regions (up to length n). We experiment with both a first order and a second order CRF. Higher order models did not provide any improvements.

In order to establish a comparative baseline, we first present results using the same features from the system described in Section 2 (Word-Entropy and Fragment-Posterior). All real-valued features were normalized and quantized using the uniform-occupancy partitioning described in White et al. (2007).[6] Quantization of real valued features is standard for log-linear models as it allows the model to take advantage of non-linear characteristics of feature values and is better handled by the regularization term. As in White et. al. we found it improved performance.

Figure 2 depicts DET curves for OOV detection for the MaxEnt baseline and first and second order CRFs with BIO encoding on unobserved OOVs in the test data. We generated predictions at different false alarm rates by varying a probability threshold. For MaxEnt we used the predicted label probability and for CRFs the marginal probability of each bin's label. While the first order CRF achieves nearly identical performance to the MaxEnt baseline, the second order CRF shows a clear improvement. The second order model has a 5% absolute improvement at 10% false alarm rate, despite using the identical features as the MaxEnt baseline. Even a small amount of context as expressed through local labeling decisions improves OOV detection.

The quantization of the features yields quantized prediction scores, resulting in the non-smooth curves for the MaxEnt and 1st order CRF results. However, when using a second order CRF the OOV score varies more smoothly since more features (context labels) are considered in the prediction of the current label.

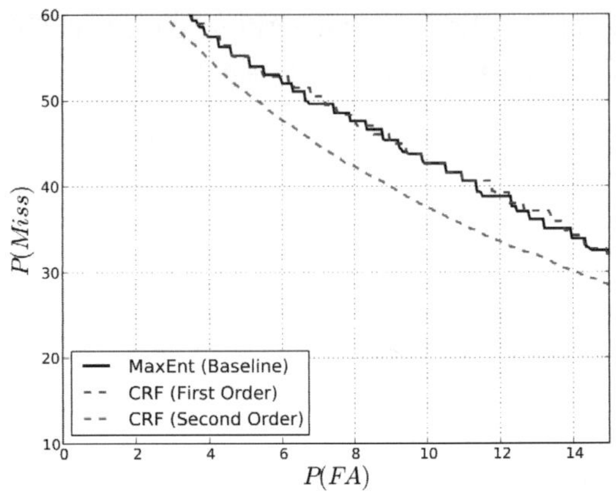

Figure 2: DET curves for OOV detection using a Maximum Entropy (MaxEnt) classifier and contextual information using a 1st order and 2nd order CRF. All models use the same baseline features (Section 2).

6 Local Lexical Context

A popular approach in sequence tagging, such as information extraction or part of speech tagging, is to include features based on local lexical content and context. In detecting a name, both the lexical form "John" and the preceding lexical context "Mr." provide clues that "John" is a name. While we do not know the actual lexical items in the speech sequence, the speech recognizer output can be used as a best guess. In the example of Figure 1, the words "former president" are good indicators that the following word is either the word "of" or a name, and hence a potential OOV. Combining this lexical context with hypothesized words can help label the subsequent regions as OOVs (note that none of the hypothesized words in the third bin are "of", names, or nouns).

Words from the LVCSR decoding of the sentence are used in the CRF OOV detector. For each bin in the confusion network, we select the word with the highest probability (best hypothesis). We then add the best hypothesis word as a feature of the form: `current_word=X`. These features capture how the LVCSR system incorrectly recognizes OOV words. However, since detection is measured on unobserved OOVs, these features alone may not help.

Instead, we turn to lexical context, which includes correctly recognized IV words. We evaluate the following sets of features derived from lexical context:

- Current bin's best hypothesis. (Current-Word)
- Unigrams and bigrams from the best hypothesis in a window of 5 words around current bin. This feature ignores the best hypothesis in the current bin, i.e., `word[-2],word[-1]` is included, but `word[-1],word[0]` is not. (Context-Bigrams)

[6]All experiments use 50 partitions with a minimum of 100 training values per partition.

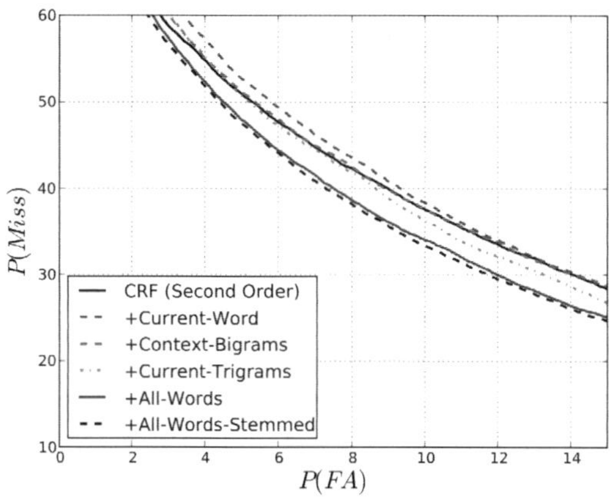

Figure 3: A second order CRF (Section 5) and additional features including including word identities from current and neighboring bins (Section 6).

- Unigrams, bigrams, and trigrams in a window of 5 words around and including current bin. (Current-Trigrams)
- All of the above features. (All-Words)
- All above features and their stems.[7] (All-Words-Stemmed)

We added these features to the second order CRF with BIO encoding and baseline features (Figure 3). As expected, the current words did not improve performance on unobserved OOVs. When the current words are combined with the lexical context and their lemmas, they give a significant boost in performance: a 4.2% absolute improvement at 10% false alarm rate over the previous CRF system, and 9.3% over the MaxEnt baseline. Interestingly, only combining context and current word gives a substantial gain. This indicates that OOVs tend to occur with certain distributional characteristics that are independent of the OOV word uttered (since we consider only unobserved OOVs), perhaps because OOVs tend to be named entities, foreign words, or rare nouns. The importance of distributional features is well known for named entity recognition and part of speech tagging (Pereira et al., 1993). Other features such as sub-strings or baseline features (Word-Entropy, Fragment-Posterior) from neighboring bins did not provide further improvement.

7 Global Utterance Context

We now include features that incorporate information from the entire utterance. The probability of an utterance as computed by a language model is often used as a measure of fluency of the utterance. We also observe that OOV words tend to take very specific syntactic roles (more than half of them are proper nouns), which means the surrounding context will have predictive lexical and *syntactic* properties. Therefore, we use a syntactic language model.

7.1 Language Models

We evaluated both a standard trigram language model and a syntactic language model (Filimonov and Harper, 2009a). The syntactic model estimates the joint probability of the word and its syntactic tag based on the preceding words and tags. The probability of an utterance w_1^n of length n is computed by summing over all latent syntactic tag assignments:

$$p(utt) = p(w_1^n) = \sum_{t_1 \dots t_n} \prod_{i-1}^{n} p(w_i, t_i | w_1^{i-1}, t_1^{i-1}) \quad (1)$$

where w_i and t_i are the word and tag at position i, and w_1^{i-1} and t_1^{i-1} are sequences of words and tags of length $i-1$ starting a position 1. The model is restricted to a trigram context, i.e., $p(w_i, t_i | w_{i-2}^{i-1}, t_{i-2}^{i-1})$; experiments that increased the order yielded no improvement.

We trained the language model on 130 million words from Hub4 CSR 1996 (Garofolo et al., 1996). The corpus was parsed using a modified Berkeley parser (Huang and Harper, 2009) and tags extracted from parse trees incorporated the word's POS, the label of its immediate parent, and the relative position of the word among its siblings.[8] The parser required separated contractions and possessives, but we recombined those words after parsing to match the LVCSR tokenization, merging their tags. Since we are considering OOV detection, the language model was restricted to LVCSR system's vocabulary.

[7] To obtain stemmed words, we use the CPAN package: http://search.cpan.org/~snowhare/Lingua-Stem-0.83.

[8] The *parent* tagset of Filimonov and Harper (2009a).

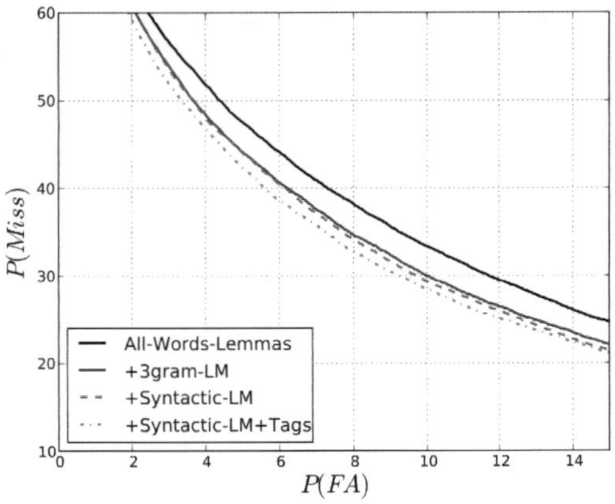

Figure 4: Features from a language model added to the best CRF from Section 6 (All-Words-Stemmed).

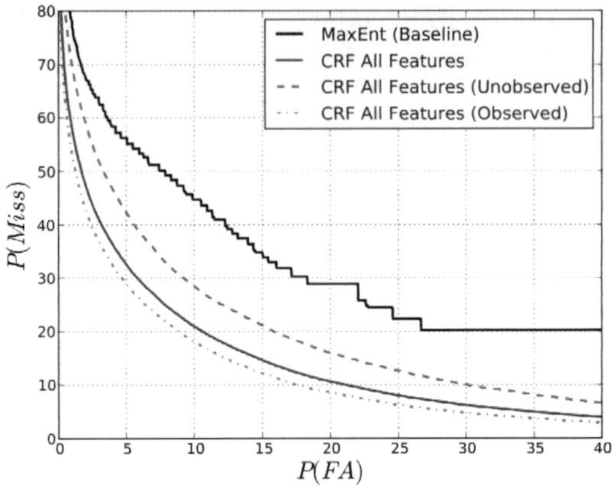

Figure 5: A CRF with all context features compared to the state-of-the-art MaxEnt baseline. Results for the CRF are shown for unobserved, observed and both OOVs.

We also used the standard trigram LM for reference. It was trained on the same data and with the same vocabulary using the SRILM toolkit. We used interpolated modified KN discounting.

7.2 Language Model Features

We designed features based on the entire utterance using the language model to measure how the utterance is effected by the current token: whether the utterance is more likely given the recognized word or some OOV word.

$$\text{Likelihood-ratio} = \log \frac{p(utt)}{p(utt|w_i = \text{unknown})}$$

$$\text{Norm-LM-score} = \frac{\log p(utt)}{length(utt)}$$

where $p(utt)$ represents the probability of the utterance using the best path hypothesis word of the LVCSR system, and $p(utt|w_i = \text{unknown})$ is the probability of the entire utterance with the current word in the LVCSR output replaced by the token <unk>, used to represent OOVs. Intuitively, when an OOV word is recognized as an IV word, the fluency of the utterance is disrupted, especially if the IV is a function word. The Likelihood-ratio is designed to show whether the utterance is more fluent (more likely) if the current word is a misrecognized OOV. [9] The second feature (Norm-LM-score) is the normalized likelihood of the utterance. An unlikely utterance biases the system to predicting OOVs.

We evaluated a CRF with these features and all lexical context features (Section 6) using both the trigram model and the joint syntactic language model (Figure 4). Each model improved performance, but the syntactic model provided the largest improvement. At 10% false alarm rate it yields a 4% absolute improvement with respect to the previous best result (All-Words-Stemmed) and 13.3% over the MaxEnt baseline. Higher order language models did not improve.

7.3 Additional Syntactic Features

We explored other syntactic features; the most effective was the 5-tag window of POS tags of the best hypothesis.[10] The additive improvement of this feature is depicted in Figure 4 labeled "+Syntactic-LM+Tags." With this feature, we achieve a small additional gain. We tried other syntactic features without added benefit, such as the most likely POS tag for <unk>in the utterance.

[9] Note that in the standard n-gram LM the feature reduces to $\log \frac{\prod_{k=i}^{i+n-1} p(w_k|w_{k-n+1}^{k-1})}{\prod_{k=i}^{i+n-1} p(w_k|w_{k-n+1}^{k-1}, w_i=\text{unknown})}$, i.e., only n n-grams actually contribute. However, in the syntactic LM, the entire utterance is affected by the change of one word through the latent states (tags) (Eq. 1), thus making it a truly global feature.

[10] The POS tags were generated by the same syntactic LM (see Section 7.1) as described in (Filimonov and Harper, 2009b). In this case, POS tags include merged tags, i.e., the vocabulary word *fred's* may be tagged as NNP-POS or NNP-VBZ.

8 Final System

Figure 5 summarizes all of the context features in a single second order BIO encoded CRF. Results are shown for state-of-the-art MaxEnt (Rastrow et al., 2009a) as well as for the CRF on unobserved, observed and combined OOVs. For unobserved OOVs our final system achieves a 14.2% absolute improvement at 10% FA rate. The absolute improvement on all OOVs was 23.7%. This result includes *observed* OOVs: words that are OOV for the LVCSR but are encountered in the OOV detector's training data. MaxEnt achieved similar performance for observed and unobserved OOVs so we only include a single combined result.

Note that the MaxEnt curve flattens at 26% false alarms, while the CRF continues to decrease. The elbow in the MaxEnt curve corresponds to the probability threshold at which no other labeled OOV region has a non-zero OOV score (regions with zero entropy and no fragments). In this case, the CRF model can still rely on the context to predict a non-zero OOV score. This helps applications where misses are more heavily penalized than false alarms.

9 Related Work

Most approaches to OOV detection in speech can be categorized as filler models or confidence estimation models. Filler models vary in three dimensions: 1) The type of filler units used: variable-length phoneme units (as the baseline system) vs joint letter sound sub-words; 2) Method used to derive units: data-driven (Bazzi and Glass, 2001) or linguistically motivated (Choueiter, 2009); 3) The method for incorporating the LVCSR system: hierarchical (Bazzi, 2002) or flat models (Bisani and Ney, 2005). Our approach can be integrated with any of these systems.

We have shown that combining the presence of sub-word units with other measures of confidence can provided significant improvements, and other proposed local confidence measures could be included in our system as well. Lin et al. (2007) uses joint word/phone lattice alignments and classifies high local miss-alignment regions as OOVs. Hazen and Bazzi (2001) combines filler models with word confidence scores, such as the minimum normalized log-likelihood acoustic model score for a word and, the fraction of the N-best utterance hypotheses in which a hypothesized word appears.

Limited contextual information has been previously exploited (although maintaining independence assumptions on the labels). Burget et al. (2008) used a neural-network (NN) phone-posterior estimator as a feature for OOV detection. The network is fed with posterior probabilities from weakly-constrained (phonetic-based) and strongly-constrained (word-based) recognizers. Their system estimates frame-based scores, and interestingly, they report large improvements when using temporal context in the NN input. This context is quite limited; it refers to posterior scores from one frame on each side. Other features are considered and combined using a MaxEnt model. They attribute this gain to sampling from neighboring phonemes. Sun et al. (2001) combines a filler-based model with a confidence approach by using several acoustic features along with context based features, such as whether the next word is a filler, acoustic confidence features for next word, number of fillers, etc.

None of these approaches consider OOV detection as a sequence labeling problem. The work of Liu et al. (2005) is most similar to the approach presented here, but applies a CRF to sentence boundary detection.

10 Conclusion and Future Work

We have presented a novel and effective approach to improve OOV detection in the output confusion networks of a LVCSR system. Local and global contextual information is integrated with sub-word posterior probabilities obtained from a hybrid LVCSR system in a CRF to detect OOV regions effectively. At a 10% FA rate, we reduce the missed OOV rate from 42.6% to 28.4%, a 33.3% relative error reduction. Our future work will focus on additional features from the recognizer aside from the single best-hypothesis, as well as other applications of contextual sequence prediction to speech tasks.

Acknowledgments

The authors thank Ariya Rastrow for providing the baseline system code, Abhinav Sethy and Bhuvana Ramabhadran for providing the data used in the experiments and for many insightful discussions.

References

Issam Bazzi and James Glass. 2001. Learning units for domain-independent out-of-vocabulary word modelling. In *Eurospeech*.

Issam Bazzi. 2002. *Modelling out-of-vocabulary words for robust speech recognition*. Ph.D. thesis, Massachusetts Institute of Technology.

M. Bisani and H. Ney. 2005. Open vocabulary speech recognition with flag hybrid models. In *INTERSPEECH*.

L. Burget, P. Schwarz, P. Matejka, M. Hannemann, A. Rastrow, C. White, S. Khudanpur, H. Hermansky, and J. Cernocky. 2008. Combination of strongly and weakly constrained recognizers for reliable detection of OOVS. In *ICASSP*.

Dogan Can, Erica Cooper, Abhinav Sethy, Chris White, Bhuvana Ramabhadran, and Murat Saraclar. 2009. Effect of pronounciations on OOV queries in spoken term detection. *ICASSP*.

Stanley F. Chen. 2003. Conditional and joint models for grapheme-to-phoneme conversion. In *Eurospeech*.

G. Choueiter. 2009. *Linguistically-motivated subword modeling with applications to speech recognition*. Ph.D. thesis, Massachusetts Institute of Technology.

Denis Filimonov and Mary Harper. 2009a. A joint language model with fine-grain syntactic tags. In *EMNLP*.

Denis Filimonov and Mary Harper. 2009b. Measuring tagging performance of a joint language model. In *Proceedings of the Interspeech 2009*.

Jonathan Fiscus, John Garofolo, Mark Przybocki, William Fisher, and David Pallett, 1998. *1997 English Broadcast News Speech (HUB4)*. Linguistic Data Consortium, Philadelphia.

John Garofolo, Jonathan Fiscus, William Fisher, and David Pallett, 1996. *CSR-IV HUB4*. Linguistic Data Consortium, Philadelphia.

Timothy J. Hazen and Issam Bazzi. 2001. A comparison and combination of methods for OOV word detection and word confidence scoring. In *Proceedings of the International Conference on Acoustics*.

Zhongqiang Huang and Mary Harper. 2009. Self-Training PCFG grammars with latent annotations across languages. In *EMNLP*.

Dietrich Klakow, Georg Rose, and Xavier Aubert. 1999. OOV-detection in large vocabulary system using automatically defined word-fragments as fillers. In *Eurospeech*.

John Lafferty, Andrew McCallum, and Fernando Pereira. 2001. Conditional random fields: Probabilistic models for segmenting and labeling sequence data. In *International Conference on Machine Learning (ICML)*.

Hui Lin, J. Bilmes, D. Vergyri, and K. Kirchhoff. 2007. OOV detection by joint word/phone lattice alignment. In *ASRU*, pages 478–483, Dec.

Yang Liu, Andreas Stolcke, Elizabeth Shriberg, and Mary Harper. 2005. Using conditional random fields for sentence boundary detection in speech. In *ACL*.

Jonathan Mamou, Bhuvana Ramabhadran, and Olivier Siohan. 2007. Vocabulary independent spoken term detection. In *SIGIR*.

L. Mangu, E. Brill, and A. Stolcke. 1999. Finding consensus among words. In *Eurospeech*.

A. Martin, G. Doddington, T. Kamm, M. Ordowski, and M. Przybocky. 1997. The DET curve in assessment of detection task performance. In *Eurospeech*.

Andrew McCallum. 2002. MALLET: A machine learning for language toolkit. `http://mallet.cs.umass.edu`.

Carolina Parada, Abhinav Sethy, and Bhuvana Ramabhadran. 2009. Query-by-example spoken term detection for OOV terms. In *ASRU*.

Fernando Pereira, Naftali Tishby, and Lillian Lee. 1993. Distributional clustering of english words. In *ACL*.

Ariya Rastrow, Abhinav Sethy, and Bhuvana Ramabhadran. 2009a. A new method for OOV detection using hybrid word/fragment system. *ICASSP*.

Ariya Rastrow, Abhinav Sethy, Bhuvana Ramabhadran, and Fred Jelinek. 2009b. Towards using hybrid, word, and fragment units for vocabulary independent LVCSR systems. *INTERSPEECH*.

T. Schaaf. 2001. Detection of OOV words using generalized word models and a semantic class language model. In *Eurospeech*.

O. Siohan and M. Bacchiani. 2005. Fast vocabulary-independent audio search using path-based graph indexing. In *INTERSPEECH*.

H. Soltau, B. Kingsbury, L. Mangu, D. Povey, G. Saon, and G. Zweig. 2005. The IBM 2004 conversational telephony system for rich transcription. In *ICASSP*.

H. Sun, G. Zhang, f. Zheng, and M. Xu. 2001. Using word confidence measure for OOV words detection in a spontaneous spoken dialog system. In *Eurospeech*.

Stanley Wang. 2009. Using graphone models in automatic speech recognition. Master's thesis, Massachusetts Institute of Technology.

F. Wessel, R. Schluter, K. Macherey, and H. Ney. 2001. Confidence measures for large vocabulary continuous speech recognition. *IEEE Transactions on Speech and Audio Processing*, 9(3).

Christopher White, Jasha Droppo, Alex Acero, and Julian Odell. 2007. Maximum entropy confidence estimation for speech recognition. In *ICASSP*.

Improved Extraction Assessment through Better Language Models

Arun Ahuja, Doug Downey
EECS Dept., Northwestern University
Evanston, IL 60208
{arun.ahuja, ddowney}@eecs.northwestern.edu

Abstract

A variety of information extraction techniques rely on the fact that instances of the same relation are "distributionally similar," in that they tend to appear in similar textual contexts. We demonstrate that extraction accuracy depends heavily on the accuracy of the language model utilized to estimate distributional similarity. An unsupervised model selection technique based on this observation is shown to reduce extraction and type-checking error by 26% over previous results, in experiments with Hidden Markov Models. The results suggest that optimizing statistical language models over unlabeled data is a promising direction for improving weakly supervised and unsupervised information extraction.

1 Introduction

Many weakly supervised and unsupervised information extraction techniques assess the correctness of extractions using the *distributional hypothesis*—the notion that words with similar meanings tend to occur in similar contexts (Harris, 1985). A candidate extraction of a relation is deemed more likely to be correct when it appears in contexts similar to those of "seed" instances of the relation, where the seeds may be specified by hand (Paşca et al., 2006), taken from an existing, incomplete knowledge base (Snow et al., 2006; Pantel et al., 2009), or obtained in an unsupervised manner using a generic extractor (Banko et al., 2007). We refer to this technique as *Assessment by Distributional Similarity* (ADS).

Typically, distributional similarity is computed by comparing co-occurrence counts of extractions and seeds with various contexts found in the corpus. *Statistical Language Models* (SLMs) include methods for more accurately estimating co-occurrence probabilities via back-off, smoothing, and clustering techniques (e.g. (Chen and Goodman, 1996; Rabiner, 1989; Bell et al., 1990)). Because SLMs can be trained from only unlabeled text, they can be applied for ADS even when the relations of interest are not specified in advance (Downey et al., 2007). Unlabeled text is abundant in large corpora like the Web, making nearly-ceaseless automated optimization of SLMs possible. But how fruitful is such an effort likely to be—to what extent does optimizing a language model over a fixed corpus lead to improvements in assessment accuracy?

In this paper, we show that an ADS technique based on SLMs is improved substantially when the language model it employs becomes more accurate. In a large-scale set of experiments, we quantify how language model perplexity correlates with ADS performance over multiple data sets and SLM techniques. The experiments show that accuracy over unlabeled data can be used for selecting among SLMs—for an ADS approach utilizing Hidden Markov Models, this results in an average error reduction of 26% over previous results in extraction and type-checking tasks.

2 Extraction Assessment with Language Models

We begin by formally defining the extraction and typechecking tasks we consider, then discuss statistical language models and their utilization for extraction assessment.

Human Language Technologies: The 2010 Annual Conference of the North American Chapter of the ACL, pages 225–228,
Los Angeles, California, June 2010.

The extraction task we consider is formalized as follows: given a corpus, a target relation R, a list of seed instances S_R, and a list of candidate extractions U_R, the task is to order elements of U_R such that correct instances for R are ranked above extraction errors. Let U_{Ri} denote the set of the ith arguments of the extractions in U_R, and let S_{Ri} be defined similarly for the seed set S_R. For relations of arity greater than one, we consider the *typechecking* task, an important sub-task of extraction (Downey et al., 2007). The typechecking task is to rank extractions with arguments that are of the proper type for a relation above type errors. As an example, the extraction `Founded(Bill Gates, Oracle)` is type correct, but is not correct for the extraction task.

2.1 Statistical Language Models

A *Statistical Language Model* (SLM) is a probability distribution $P(\mathbf{w})$ over word sequences $\mathbf{w} = (w_1, ..., w_r)$. The most common SLM techniques are *n-gram models*, which are Markov models in which the probability of a given word is dependent on only the previous $n-1$ words. The accuracy of an n-gram model of a corpus depends on two key factors: the choice of n, and the *smoothing* technique employed to assign probabilities to word sequences seen infrequently in training. We experiment with choices of n from 2 to 4, and two popular smoothing approaches, Modified Kneser-Ney (Chen and Goodman, 1996) and Witten-Bell (Bell et al., 1990).

Unsupervised *Hidden Markov Models* (HMMs) are an alternative SLM approach previously shown to offer accuracy and scalability advantages over n-gram models in ADS (Downey et al., 2007). An HMM models a sentence $\mathbf{w}$ as a sequence of observations w_i each generated by a hidden state variable t_i. Here, hidden states take values from $\{1, \ldots, T\}$, and each hidden state variable is itself generated by some number k of previous hidden states. Formally, the joint distribution of a word sequence $\mathbf{w}$ given a corresponding state sequence $\mathbf{t}$ is:

$$P(\mathbf{w}|\mathbf{t}) = \prod_i P(w_i|t_i)P(t_i|t_{i-1}, \ldots, t_{i-k}) \quad (1)$$

The distributions on the right side of Equation 1 are learned from the corpus in an unsupervised manner using Expectation-Maximization, such that words distributed similarly in the corpus tend to be generated by similar hidden states (Rabiner, 1989).

2.2 Performing ADS with SLMs

The *Assessment by Distributional Similarity* (ADS) technique is to rank extractions in U_R in decreasing order of distributional similarity to the seeds, as estimated from the corpus. In our experiments, we utilize an ADS approach previously proposed for HMMs (Downey et al., 2007) and adapt it to also apply to n-gram models, as detailed below.

Define a *context* of an extraction argument e_i to be a string containing the m words preceding and m words following an occurrence of e_i in the corpus. Let $C_i = \{c_1, c_2, ..., c_{|C_i|}\}$ be the union of all contexts of extraction arguments e_i and seed arguments s_i for a given relation R. We create a *probabilistic context vector* for each extraction e_i where the j-th dimension of the vector is the probability of the context surrounding given the extraction, $P(c_j|e_i)$, computed from the language model. [1]

We rank the extractions in U_R according to how similar their arguments' contextual distributions, $P(c|e_i)$, are to those of the seed arguments. Specifically, extractions are ranked according to:

$$f(e) = \sum_{e_i \in e} KL(\frac{\sum_{w' \in S_{Ri}} P(c|w')}{|S_{Ri}|}, P(c|e_i)) \quad (2)$$

where KL represents KL Divergence, and the outer sum is taken over arguments e_i of the extraction e.

For HMMs, we alternatively rank extractions using the HMM *state distributions* $P(t|e_i)$ in place of the probabilistic context vectors $P(c|e_i)$. Our experiments show that state distributions are much more accurate for ADS than are HMM context vectors.

3 Experiments

In this section, we present experiments showing that SLM accuracy correlates strongly with ADS performance. We also show that SLM performance can be used for model selection, leading to an ADS technique that outperforms previous results.

3.1 Experimental Methodology

We experiment with a wide range of n-gram and HMM models. The n-gram models are trained using the SRILM toolkit (Stolcke, 2002). Evaluating a

[1] For example, for context c_j = "I visited ___ in July" and extraction e_i = "Boston," $P(c_j|e_i)$ is P("I visited Boston in July") / P("Boston"), where each string probability is computed using the language model.

LM	Unary	Binary	Wikipedia
HMM 1-5	-.911	-.361	-.994
HMM 2-5	-.856	.120	-.930
HMM 3-5	-.823	-.683	.922
HMM 1-10	-.916	-.967	-.905
HMM 2-10	-.877	-.797	-.963
HMM 3-10	-.957	-.669	-.924
HMM 1-25	-.933	-.850	-.959
HMM 1-50	-.942	-.942	-.947
HMM 1-100	-.896	-.877	-.942
N-Gram	-.512	-.999	.024

Table 1: Pearson Correlation value for extraction performance (in AUC) and SLM performance (in perplexity). Extraction accuracy increases as perplexity decreases, with an average correlation coefficient of -0.742. "HMM k-T" denotes an HMM model of order k, with T states.

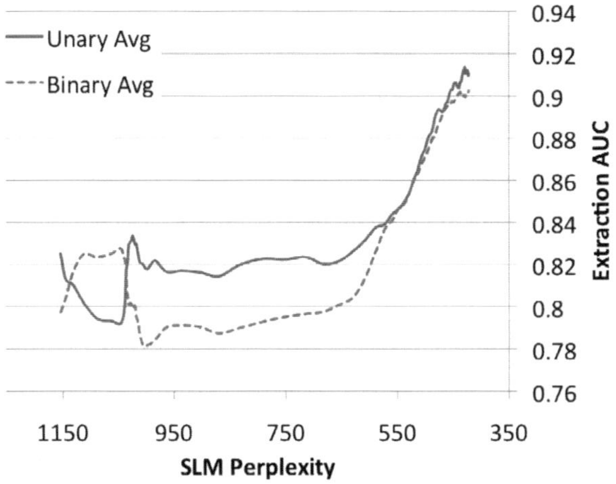

Figure 1: HMM 1-100 Performance. Information Extraction performance (in AUC) increases as SLM accuracy improves (perplexity decreases).

variety of HMM configurations over a large corpus requires a scalable training architecture. We constructed a parallel HMM codebase using the Message Passing Interface (MPI), and trained the models on a supercomputing cluster. All language models were trained on a corpus of 2.8M sentences of Web text (about 60 million tokens). SLM performance is measured using the standard perplexity metric, and assessment accuracy is measured using area under the precision-recall curve (AUC), a standard metric for ranked lists of extractions. We evaluated performance on three distinct data sets. The first two data sets evaluate ADS for unsupervised information extraction, and were taken from (Downey et al., 2007). The first, Unary, was an extraction task for unary relations (Company, Country, Language, Film) and the second, Binary, was a type-checking task for binary relations (Conquered, Founded, Headquartered, Merged). The 10 most frequent extractions served as bootstrapped seeds. The two test sets contained 361 and 265 extractions, respectively. The third data set, Wikipedia, evaluates ADS on weakly-supervised extraction, using seeds and extractions taken from Wikipedia 'List of' pages (Pantel et al., 2009). Seed sets of various sizes (5, 10, 15 and 20) were randomly selected from each list, and we present results averaged over 10 random samplings. Other members of the seed list were added to a test set as correct extractions, and elements from other lists were added as errors. The data set included 2264 extractions across 36 unary relations, including Composers and US Internet Companies.

3.2 Optimizing Language Models for IE

The first question we investigate is whether optimizing individual language models leads to better performance in ADS. We measured the correlation between SLM perplexity and ADS performance as training proceeds in HMMs, and as n and the smoothing technique vary in the n-gram models. Table 1 shows that as the SLM becomes more accurate (i.e. as perplexity decreases), ADS performance increases. The correlation is strong (averaging -0.742) and is consistent across model configurations and data sets. The low positive correlation for the n-gram models on Wikipedia is likely due to a "floor effect"; the models have low performance overall on the difficult Wikipedia data set. The lowest-perplexity n-gram model (Mod Kneser-Ney smoothing with n=3, KN3) does exhibit the best IE performance, at 0.039 (the *average* performance of the HMM models is more than twice this, at 0.084). Figure 1 shows the relationship between SLM and ADS performance in detail for the best-performing HMM configuration.

3.3 Model Selection

Different language models can be configured in different ways: for example, HMMs require choices for the hyperparameters k and T. Here, we show that

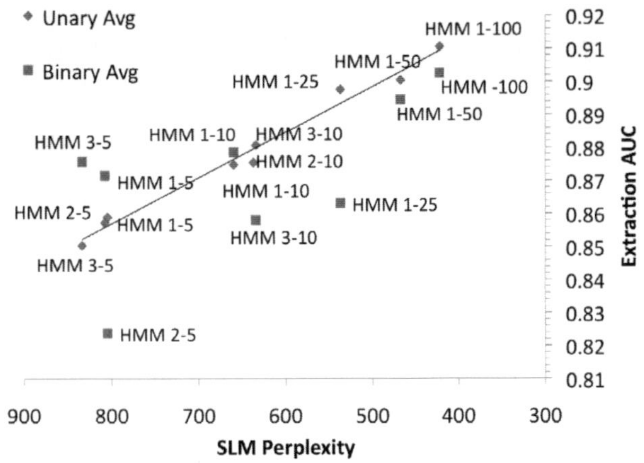

Figure 2: Model Selection for HMMs. SLM performance is a good predictor of extraction performance across model configurations.

Relation	HMM-T	Best HMM
Company	.966	**.985**
Country	.886	**.942**
Languages	**.936**	.914
Film	**.803**	.801
Unary Avg	.898	**.911**
Conquered	.917	**.923**
Founded	**.827**	.799
Merged	.920	**.925**
Headquartered	.734	**.964**
Binary Average	.849	**.903**

Table 2: Extraction Performance Results in AUC for Individual Relations. The lowest-perplexity HMM, 1-100, outperforms the HMM-T model from previous work.

SLM perplexity can be used to select a high-quality model configuration for ADS using only unlabeled data. We evaluate on the Unary and Binary data sets, since they have been employed in previous work on our corpora. Figure 2 shows that for HMMs, ADS performance increases as perplexity decreases across various model configurations (a similar relationship holds for n-gram models). A model selection technique that picks the HMM model with lowest perplexity (HMM 1-100) results in better ADS performance than previous results. As shown in Table 2, HMM 1-100 reduces error over the HMM-T model in (Downey et al., 2007) by 26%, on average. The experiments also reveal an important difference between the HMM and n-gram approaches. While KN3 is more accurate in SLM than our HMM models, it performs *worse* in ADS on average. For example, HMM 1-25 underperforms KN3 in perpexity, at 537.2 versus 227.1, but wins in ADS, 0.880 to 0.853. We hypothesize that this is because the latent state distributions in the HMMs provide a more informative distributional similarity measure. Indeed, when we compute distributional similarity for HMMs using probabilistic context vectors as opposed to state distributions, ADS performance for HMM 1-25 decreases to 5.8% *below* that of KN3.

4 Conclusions

We presented experiments showing that estimating distributional similarity with more accurate statistical language models results in more accurate extraction assessment. We note that significantly larger, more powerful language models are possible beyond those evaluated here, which (based on the trajectory observed in Figure 2) may offer significant improvements in assessment accuracy.

References

M. Banko, M. Cafarella, S. Soderland, M. Broadhead, and O. Etzioni. 2007. Open information extraction from the Web. In *Procs. of IJCAI.*

T. C. Bell, J. G. Cleary, and I. H. Witten. 1990. *Text Compression.* Prentice Hall, January.

Stanley F. Chen and Joshua Goodman. 1996. An empirical study of smoothing techniques for language modeling. In *Proc. of ACL.*

D. Downey, S. Schoenmackers, and O. Etzioni. 2007. Sparse information extraction: Unsupervised language models to the rescue. In *Proc. of ACL.*

Z. Harris. 1985. Distributional structure. In J. J. Katz, editor, *The Philosophy of Linguistics.*

M. Paşca, D. Lin, J. Bigham, A. Lifchits, and A. Jain. 2006. Names and similarities on the web: Fact extraction in the fast lane. In *Procs. of ACL/COLING 2006.*

P. Pantel, E. Crestan, A. Borkovsky, A. M. Popescu, and V. Vyas. 2009. Web-scale distributional similarity and entity set expansion. In *Proc. of EMNLP.*

L. R. Rabiner. 1989. A tutorial on Hidden Markov Models and selected applications in speech recognition. *Proceedings of the IEEE*, 77(2):257–286.

R. Snow, D. Jurafsky, and A. Y. Ng. 2006. Semantic taxonomy induction from heterogenous evidence. In *COLING/ACL 2006.*

Andreas Stolcke. 2002. SRILM – an extensible language modeling toolkit. In *Proceedings of ICSLP*, volume 2.

Language Identification: The Long and the Short of the Matter

Timothy Baldwin and **Marco Lui**
Dept of Computer Science and Software Engineering
University of Melbourne, VIC 3010 Australia
tb@ldwin.net, saffsd@gmail.com

Abstract

Language identification is the task of identifying the language a given document is written in. This paper describes a detailed examination of what models perform best under different conditions, based on experiments across three separate datasets and a range of tokenisation strategies. We demonstrate that the task becomes increasingly difficult as we increase the number of languages, reduce the amount of training data and reduce the length of documents. We also show that it is possible to perform language identification without having to perform explicit character encoding detection.

1 Introduction

With the growth of the worldwide web, ever-increasing numbers of documents have become available, in more and more languages. This growth has been a double-edged sword, however, in that content in a given language has become more prevalent but increasingly hard to find, due to the web's sheer size and diversity of content. While the majority of (X)HTML documents declare their character encoding, only a tiny minority specify what language they are written in, despite support for language declaration existing in the various (X)HTML standards.[1] Additionally, a single encoding can generally be used to render a large number of languages such that the document encoding at best filters out a subset of languages which are incompatible with the given encoding, rather than disambiguates the source language. Given this, the need for automatic means to determine the source language of web documents is crucial for web aggregators of various types.

There is widespread misconception of language identification being a "solved task", generally as a result of isolated experiments over homogeneous datasets with small numbers of languages (Hughes et al., 2006; Xia et al., 2009). Part of the motivation for this paper is to draw attention to the fact that, as a field, we are still a long way off perfect language identification of web documents, as evaluated under realistic conditions.

In this paper we describe experiments on language identification of web documents, focusing on the broad question of what combination of tokenisation strategy and classification model achieves the best overall performance. We additionally evaluate the impact of the volume of training data and the test document length on the accuracy of language identification, and investigate the interaction between character encoding detection and language identification.

One assumption we make in this research, following standard assumptions made in the field, is that all documents are monolingual. This is clearly an unrealistic assumption when dealing with general web documents (Hughes et al., 2006), and we plan to return to investigate language identification over multilingual documents in future work.

Our contributions in this paper are: the demonstration that language identification is: (a) trivial over datasets with smaller numbers of languages and approximately even amounts of training data per language, but (b) considerably harder over datasets with larger numbers of languages with more skew in the amount of training data per language; byte-based tokenisation without character encoding detection is superior to codepoint-based tokenisation

[1] http://dev.opera.com/articles/view/mama-head-structure/

Human Language Technologies: The 2010 Annual Conference of the North American Chapter of the ACL, pages 229–237,
Los Angeles, California, June 2010.

with character encoding detection; and simple cosine similarity-based nearest neighbour classification is equal to or better than models including support vector machines and naive Bayes over the language identification task. We also develop datasets to facilitate standardised evaluation of language identification.

2 Background Research

Language identification was arguably established as a task by Gold (1967), who construed it as a closed class problem: given data in each of a predefined set of possible languages, human subjects were asked to classify the language of a given test document. It wasn't until the 1990s, however, that the task was popularised as a text categorisation task.

The text categorisation approach to language identification applies a standard supervised classification framework to the task. Perhaps the best-known such model is that of Cavnar and Trenkle (1994), as popularised in the `textcat` tool.[2] The method uses a per-language character frequency model, and classifies documents via their relative "out of place" distance from each language (see Section 5.1). Variants on this basic method include Bayesian models for character sequence prediction (Dunning, 1994), dot products of word frequency vectors (Darnashek, 1995) and information-theoretic measures of document similarity (Aslam and Frost, 2003; Martins and Silva, 2005). More recently, support vector machines (SVMs) and kernel methods have been applied to the task of language identification task with success (Teytaud and Jalam, 2001; Lodhi et al., 2002; Kruengkrai et al., 2005), and Markov logic has been used for joint inferencing in contexts where there are multiple evidence sources (Xia et al., 2009).

Language identification has also been carried out via linguistically motivated models. Johnson (1993) used a list of stop words from different languages to identify the language of a given document, choosing the language with the highest stop word overlap with the document. Grefenstette (1995) used word and part of speech (POS) correlation to determine if two text samples were from the same or different languages. Giguet (1995) developed a cross-language tokenisation model and used it to identify the language of a given document based on its tokenisation similarity with training data. Dueire Lins and Gonçalves (2004) considered the use of syntactically-derived closed grammatical-class models, matching syntactic structure rather than words or character sequences.

The observant reader will have noticed that some of the above approaches make use of notions such as "word", typically based on the naive assumption that the language uses white space to delimit words. These approaches are appropriate in contexts where there is a guarantee of a document being in one of a select set of languages where words are space-delimited, or where manual segmentation has been performed (e.g. interlinear glossed text). However, we are interested in language identification of web documents, which can be in any language, including languages that do not overtly mark word boundaries, such as Japanese, Chinese and Thai; while relatively few languages fall into this categories, they are among the most populous web languages and therefore an important consideration. Therefore, approaches that assume a language is space-delimited are clearly not suitable for our purposes. Equally, approaches which make assumptions about the availability of particular resources for each language to be identified (e.g. POS taggers, or the existence of precompiled stop word lists) cannot be used.

Language identification has been applied in a number of contexts, the most immediate application being in multilingual text retrieval, where retrieval results are generally superior if the language of the query is known, and the search is restricted to only those documents predicted to be in that language (McNamee and Mayfield, 2004). It can also be used to "word spot" foreign language terms in multilingual documents, e.g. to improve parsing performance (Alex et al., 2007), or for linguistic corpus creation purposes (Baldwin et al., 2006; Xia et al., 2009; Xia and Lewis, 2009).

3 Datasets

In the experiments reported in this paper, we employ three novel datasets, with differing properties relevant to language identification research:

[2] `http://www.let.rug.nl/vannoord/TextCat/`

Corpus	Documents	Languages	Encodings	Document Length (bytes)
EUROGOV	1500	10	1	17460.5±39353.4
TCL	3174	60	12	2623.2±3751.9
WIKIPEDIA	4963	67	1	1480.8±4063.9

Table 1: Summary of the three language identification datasets

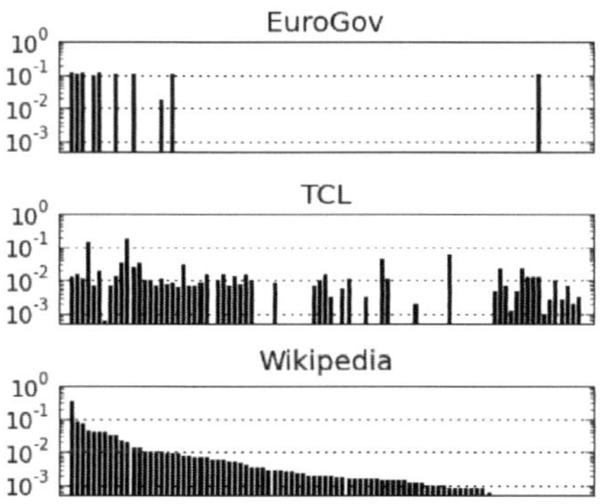

Figure 1: Distribution of languages in the three datasets (vector of languages vs. the proportion of documents in that language)

EUROGOV: longer documents, all in a single encoding, spread evenly across a relatively small number (10) of Western European languages; this dataset is comparable to the datasets conventionally used in language identification research. As the name would suggest, the documents were sourced from the EuroGOV document collection, as used in the 2005 WebCLEF task.

TCL: a larger number of languages (60) across a wider range of language families, with shorter documents and a range of character encodings (12). The collection was manually sourced by the Thai Computational Linguistics Laboratory (TCL) in 2005 from online news sources.

WIKIPEDIA: a slightly larger number of languages again (67), a single encoding, and shorter documents; the distribution of languages is intended to approximate that of the actual web. This collection was automatically constructed by taking the dumps of all versions of Wikipedia with 1000 or more documents in non-constructed languages, and randomly selecting documents from them in a bias-preserving manner (i.e. preserving the document distribution in the full collection); this is intended to represent the document language bias observed on the web. All three corpora are available on request.

We outline the characteristics of the three datasets in Table 1. We further detail the language distribution in Figure 1, using a constant vector of languages for all three datasets, based on the order of languages in the WIKIPEDIA dataset (in descending order of documents per language). Of note are the contrasting language distributions between the three datasets, in terms of both the languages represented and the relative skew of documents per language. In the following sections, we provide details of the corpus compilation and document sampling method for each dataset.

4 Document Representation

As we are interested in performing language identification over arbitrary web documents, we require a language-neutral document representation which does not make artificial assumptions about the source language of the document. Separately, there is the question of whether it is necessary to determine the character encoding of the document in order to extract out character sequences, or whether the raw byte stream is sufficient. To explore this question, we experiment with two document representations: (1) byte n-grams, and (2) codepoint n-grams. In both cases, a document is represented as a feature vector of token counts.

Byte n-grams can be extracted directly without explicit encoding detection. Codepoint n-grams, on the other hand, require that we know the character encoding of the document in order to perform tokenisation. Additionally, they should be based on a common encoding to prevent: (a) over-fragmenting the feature space (e.g. ending up with discrete feature spaces for `euc-jp`, `s-jis` and `utf-8` in the case of Japanese); and (b) spurious matches between encodings (e.g. Japanese hiragana and Korean hangul mapping onto the same codepoint in `euc-jp` and `euc-kr`, respectively). We use unicode as the common encoding for all documents.

In practice, character encoding detection is an issue only for TCL, as the other two datasets are in a single encoding. Where a character encoding was provided for a document in TCL and it was possible to transcode the document to unicode based on that encoding, we used the encoding information. In cases where a unique encoding was not provided, we used an encoding detection library based on the Mozilla browser.[3] Having disambiguated the encoding for each document, we transcoded it into unicode.

5 Models

In our experiments we use a number of different language identification models, as outlined below. We first describe the nearest-neighbour and nearest-prototype models, and a selection of distance and similarity metrics combined with each. We then present three standalone text categorisation models.

5.1 Nearest-Neighbour and Nearest-Prototype Models

The 1-nearest-neighbour (1NN) model is a common classification technique, whereby a test document D is classified based on the language of the closest training document D_i (with language $l(D_i)$), as determined by a given distance or similarity metric.

In nearest-neighbour models, each training document is represented as a single instance, meaning that the computational cost of classifying a test document is proportional to the number of training documents. A related model which aims to reduce this cost is nearest-prototype (AM), where each language is represented as a single instance, by merging all of the training instances for that language into a single centroid via the arithmetic mean.

For both nearest-neighbour and nearest-prototype methods, we experimented with three similarity and distance measures in this research:

Cosine similarity (COS): the cosine of the angle between two feature vectors, as measured by the dot product of the two vectors, normalised to unit length.

Skew divergence (SKEW): a variant of Kullback-Leibler divergence, whereby the second distribution (y) is smoothed by linear interpolation with the first (x) using a smoothing factor α (Lee, 2001):

$$s_\alpha(x, y) = D(x \mid\mid \alpha y + (1 - \alpha)x)$$

where:

$$D(x \mid\mid y) = \sum_i x_i(\log_2 x_i - \log_2 y_i)$$

In all our experiments, we set α to 0.99.

Out-of-place (OOP): a ranklist-based distance metric, where the distance between two documents is calculated as (Cavnar and Trenkle, 1994):

$$oop(D_x, D_y) = \sum_{t \in D_x \vee D_y} abs(R_{D_x}(t) - R_{D_y}(t))$$

$R_D(t)$ is the rank of term t in document D, based on the descending order of frequency in document D; terms not occurring in document D are conventionally given the rank $1 + \max_i R_D(t_i)$.

5.2 Naive Bayes (NB)

Naive Bayes is a popular text classification model, due to it being lightweight, robust and easy to update. The language of test document D is predicted by:

$$\hat{l}(D) = \arg\max_{l_i \in L} P(l_i) \prod_{j=1}^{|\mathscr{V}|} \frac{P(t_j|l_i)^{N_{D,t_j}}}{N_{D,t_j}!}$$

where L is the set of languages in the training data, N_{D,t_j} is the frequency of the jth term in D, $\mathscr{V}$ is the set of all terms, and:

$$P(t|l_i) = \frac{1 + \sum_{k=1}^{|\mathscr{D}|} N_{k,t} P(l_i|D_k)}{|\mathscr{V}| + \sum_{j=1}^{|\mathscr{V}|} \sum_{k=1}^{|\mathscr{D}|} N_{k,t_j} P(l_i|D_k)}$$

In this research, we use the `rainbow` implementation of multinominal naive Bayes (McCallum, 1996).

5.3 Support Vector Machines (SVM)

Support vector machines (SVMs) are one of the most popular methods for text classification, largely because they can automatically weight large numbers of features, capturing feature interactions in the process (Joachims, 1998; Manning et al., 2008). The basic principle underlying SVMs is to maximize the

[3] http://chardet.feedparser.org/

margin between training instances and the calculated decision boundary based on structural risk minimisation (Vapnik, 1995).

In this work, we have made use of `bsvm`,[4] an implementation of SVMs with multiclass classification support (Hsu et al., 2008). We only report results for multi-class bound-constrained support vector machines with linear kernels, as they were found to perform best over our data.

6 Experimental Methodology

We carry out experiments over the cross-product of the following options, as described above:

model ($\times 7$)**:** nearest-neighbour ($\text{COS}_{1\text{NN}}$, $\text{SKEW}_{1\text{NN}}$, $\text{OOP}_{1\text{NN}}$), nearest-prototype (COS_{AM}, SKEW_{AM}),[5] NB, SVM

tokenisation ($\times 2$)**:** byte, codepoint

n**-gram** ($\times 3$)**:** 1-gram, 2-gram, 3-gram

for a total of 42 distinct classifiers. Each classifier is run across the 3 datasets (EUROGOV, TCL and WIKIPEDIA) based on 10-fold stratified cross-validation.

We evaluate the models using micro-averaged precision ($\mathcal{P}_\mu$), recall ($\mathcal{R}_\mu$) and F-score ($\mathcal{F}_\mu$), as well as macro-averaged precision ($\mathcal{P}_M$), recall ($\mathcal{R}_M$) and F-score ($\mathcal{F}_M$). The micro-averaged scores indicate the average performance *per document*; as we always make a unique prediction per document, the micro-averaged precision, recall and F-score are always identical (as is the classification accuracy). The macro-averaged scores, on the other hand, indicate the average performance *per language*. In each case, we average the precision, recall and F-score across the 10 folds of cross validation.[6]

As a baseline, we use a majority class, or ZeroR, classifier (ZEROR), which assigns the language with highest prior in the training data to each of the test documents.

[4] `http://www.csie.ntu.edu.tw/~cjlin/bsvm/`

[5] We do not include the results for nearest-prototype classifiers with the OOP distance metric as the results were considerably lower than the other methods.

[6] Note that this means that the averaged $\mathcal{F}_M$ is not necessarily the harmonic mean of the averaged $\mathcal{P}_M$ and $\mathcal{R}_M$.

Model	Token	$\mathcal{P}_M$	$\mathcal{R}_M$	$\mathcal{F}_M$	$\mathcal{P}_\mu/\mathcal{R}_\mu/\mathcal{F}_\mu$
ZEROR	—	.020	.084	.032	.100
$\text{COS}_{1\text{NN}}$	byte	.975	.978	.976	.975
$\text{COS}_{1\text{NN}}$	codepoint	.968	.973	.970	.971
COS_{AM}	byte	.922	.938	.926	.937
COS_{AM}	codepoint	.908	.930	.913	.931
$\text{SKEW}_{1\text{NN}}$	byte	.979	.979	.979	.977
$\text{SKEW}_{1\text{NN}}$	codepoint	.978	.978	.978	.976
SKEW_{AM}	byte	.974	.972	.972	.969
SKEW_{AM}	codepoint	.974	.972	.973	.970
$\text{OOP}_{1\text{NN}}$	byte	.953	.952	.953	.949
$\text{OOP}_{1\text{NN}}$	codepoint	.961	.960	.960	.957
NB	byte	.975	.973	.974	.971
NB	codepoint	.975	.973	.974	.971
SVM	byte	**.989**	**.985**	**.987**	**.987**
SVM	codepoint	.988	.985	.986	.987

Table 2: Results for byte vs. codepoint (bigram) tokenisation over EUROGOV

7 Results

In our experiments, we first compare the different models for fixed n-gram order, then come back to vary the n-gram order. Subsequently, we examine the relative performance of the different models on test documents of differing lengths, and finally look into the impact of the amount of training data for a given language on the performance for that language.

7.1 Results for the Different Models and Tokenisation Strategies

First, we present the results for each of the classifiers in Tables 2–4, based on byte or codepoint tokenisation and bigrams. In each case, we present the best result in each column in **bold**.

The relative performance over EUROGOV and TCL is roughly comparable for all methods barring $\text{SKEW}_{1\text{NN}}$, with near-perfect scores over all 6 evaluation metrics. $\text{SKEW}_{1\text{NN}}$ is near-perfect over EUROGOV and TCL, but drops to baseline levels over WIKIPEDIA; we return to discuss this effect in Section 7.2.

In the case of EUROGOV, the near-perfect results are in line with our expectations for the dataset, based on its characteristics and results reported for comparable datasets. The results for WIKIPEDIA, however, fall off considerably, with the best model achieving an $\mathcal{F}_M$ of .671 and $\mathcal{F}_\mu$ of .869, due to

Model	Token	$\mathcal{P}_M$	$\mathcal{R}_M$	$\mathcal{F}_M$	$\mathcal{P}_\mu/\mathcal{R}_\mu/\mathcal{F}_\mu$
ZEROR	—	.003	.017	.005	.173
COS_{1NN}	byte	.981	.975	.975	.982
COS_{1NN}	codepoint	.931	.930	.925	.961
COS_{AM}	byte	.967	.975	.965	.965
COS_{AM}	codepoint	.979	**.977**	.974	.964
SKEW_{1NN}	byte	**.984**	.974	.976	**.987**
SKEW_{1NN}	codepoint	.910	.210	.320	.337
SKEW_{AM}	byte	.962	.959	.950	.972
SKEW_{AM}	codepoint	.968	.961	.957	.967
OOP_{1NN}	byte	.964	.945	.951	.974
OOP_{1NN}	codepoint	.901	.892	.893	.933
NB	byte	.905	.905	.896	.969
NB	codepoint	.722	.711	.696	.845
SVM	byte	.981	.973	**.977**	.984
SVM	codepoint	.979	.970	.974	.980

Table 3: Results for byte vs. codepoint (bigram) tokenisation over TCL

Model	Token	$\mathcal{P}_M$	$\mathcal{R}_M$	$\mathcal{F}_M$	$\mathcal{P}_\mu/\mathcal{R}_\mu/\mathcal{F}_\mu$
ZEROR	—	.004	.013	.007	.328
COS_{1NN}	byte	**.740**	**.646**	**.671**	**.869**
COS_{1NN}	codepoint	.685	.604	.625	.835
COS_{AM}	byte	.587	.634	.573	.776
COS_{AM}	codepoint	.486	.556	.483	.725
SKEW_{1NN}	byte	.005	.013	.008	.304
SKEW_{1NN}	codepoint	.006	.013	.007	.241
SKEW_{AM}	byte	.605	.617	.588	.844
SKEW_{AM}	codepoint	.552	.575	.532	.807
OOP_{1NN}	byte	.619	.518	.548	.831
OOP_{1NN}	codepoint	.598	.486	.520	.807
NB	byte	.496	.454	.442	.851
NB	codepoint	.426	.349	.360	.798
SVM	byte	.667	.545	.577	.845
SVM	codepoint	.634	.494	.536	.818

Table 4: Results for byte vs. codepoint (bigram) tokenisation over WIKIPEDIA

the larger number of languages, smaller documents, and skew in the amounts of training data per language. All models are roughly balanced in the relative scores they attain for $\mathcal{P}_M$, $\mathcal{R}_M$ and $\mathcal{F}_M$ (i.e. there are no models that have notably higher $\mathcal{P}_M$ relative to $\mathcal{R}_M$, for example).

The nearest-neighbour models outperform the corresponding nearest-prototype models to varying degrees, with the one exception of SKEW_{1NN} over WIKIPEDIA. The nearest-prototype classifiers were certainly faster than the nearest-neighbour classifiers, by roughly an order of 10, but this is more than outweighed by the drop in classification performance. With the exception of SKEW_{1NN} over WIKIPEDIA, all methods were well above the baselines for all three datasets.

The two methods which perform consistently well at this point are COS_{1NN} and SVM, with COS_{1NN} holding up particularly well under micro-averaged F-score while NB drops away over WIKIPEDIA, the most skewed dataset; this is due to the biasing effect of the prior in NB.

Looking to the impact of byte- vs. codepoint-tokenisation on classifier performance over the three datasets, we find that overall, bytes outperform codepoints. This is most notable for TCL and WIKIPEDIA, and the SKEW_{1NN} and NB models. Given this result, we present only results for byte-based tokenisation in the remainder of this paper.

The results for byte tokenisation of TCL are particularly noteworthy. The transcoding into unicode and use of codepoints, if anything, hurts performance, suggesting that implicit character encoding detection based on byte tokenisation is the best approach: it is both more accurate and simplifies the system, in removing the need to perform encoding detection prior to language identification.

7.2 Results for Differing n-gram Sizes

We present results with byte unigrams, bigrams and trigrams in Table 5 for WIKIPEDIA.[7] We omit results for the other two datasets, as the overall trend is the same as for WIKIPEDIA, with lessened relative differences between n-gram orders due to the relative simplicity of the respective classification tasks.

SKEW_{1NN} is markedly different to the other methods in achieving the best performance with unigrams, moving from the worst-performing method by far to one of the best-performing methods. This is the result of the interaction between data sparseness and heavy-handed smoothing with the α constant. Rather than using a constant α value for all n-gram orders, it may be better to parameterise it using an exponential scale such as $\alpha = 1 - \beta^n$ (with

[7]The results for OOP_{1NN} over byte trigrams are missing due to the computational cost associated with the method, and our experiment hence not having run to completion at the time of writing. Extrapolating from the results for the other two datasets, we predict similar results to bigrams.

Model	n-gram	$\mathcal{P}_M$	$\mathcal{R}_M$	$\mathcal{F}_M$	$\mathcal{P}_\mu/\mathcal{R}_\mu/\mathcal{F}_\mu$
ZEROR	—	.004	.013	.007	.328
COS_{1NN}	1	.644	.579	.599	.816
COS_{1NN}	2	.740	.646	.671	**.869**
COS_{1NN}	3	**.744**	**.656**	**.680**	.862
COS_{AM}	1	.526	.543	.487	.654
COS_{AM}	2	.587	.634	.573	.776
COS_{AM}	3	.553	.632	.545	.761
SKEW_{1NN}	1	.691	.598	.625	.848
SKEW_{1NN}	2	.005	.013	.008	.304
SKEW_{1NN}	3	.005	.013	.004	.100
SKEW_{AM}	1	.552	.569	.532	.740
SKEW_{AM}	2	.605	.617	.588	.844
SKEW_{AM}	3	.551	.631	.554	.825
OOP_{1NN}	1	.519	.446	.468	.747
OOP_{1NN}	2	.619	.518	.548	.831
NB	1	.576	.578	.555	.778
NB	2	.496	.454	.442	.851
NB	3	.493	.435	.432	.863
SVM	1	.585	.505	.523	.812
SVM	2	.667	.545	.577	.845
SVM	3	.717	.547	.594	.840

Table 5: Results for different n-gram orders over WIKIPEDIA

$\beta = 0.01$, e.g.), based on the n-gram order. We leave this for future research.

For most methods, bigrams and trigrams are better than unigrams, with the one notable exception of SKEW_{1NN}. In general, there is little separating bigrams and trigrams, although the best result for is achieved slightly more often for bigrams than for trigrams.

For direct comparability with Cavnar and Trenkle (1994), we additionally carried out a preliminary experiment with hybrid byte n-grams (all of 1- to 5-grams), combined with simple frequency-based feature selection of the top-1000 features for each n-gram order. The significance of this setting is that it is the strategy adopted by `textcat`, based on the original paper of Cavnar and Trenkle (1994) (with the one exception that we use 1000 features rather than 300, as all methods other than OOP_{1NN} benefitted from more features). The results are shown in Table 6.

Compared to the results in Table 5, SKEW_{1NN} and SKEW_{AM} both increase markedly to achieve the best overall results. OOP_{1NN}, on the other hand, rises slightly, while the remaining three methods actually

Model	$\mathcal{P}_M$	$\mathcal{R}_M$	$\mathcal{F}_M$	$\mathcal{P}_\mu/\mathcal{R}_\mu/\mathcal{F}_\mu$
ZEROR	.004	.013	.007	.328
COS_{1NN}	.735	.664	.682	.865
COS_{AM}	.592	.626	.580	.766
SKEW_{1NN}	**.789**	.708	**.729**	**.902**
SKEW_{AM}	.681	**.718**	.680	.870
OOP_{1NN}	.697	.595	.626	.864
SVM	.669	.500	.544	.832

Table 6: Results for mixed n-grams (1–5) and feature selection over WIKIPEDIA (a lá Cavnar and Trenkle (1994))

drop back slightly. Clearly, there is considerably more experimentation to be done here with mixed n-gram models and different feature selection methods, but the results indicate that some methods certainly benefit from n-gram hybridisation and feature selection, and also that we have been able to surpass the results of Cavnar and Trenkle (1994) with SKEW_{1NN} in an otherwise identical framework.

7.3 Breakdown Across Test Document Length

To better understand the impact of test document size on classification accuracy, we divided the test documents into 5 equal-size bins according to their length, measured by the number of tokens. We then computed $\mathcal{F}_\mu$ individually for each bin across the 10 folds of cross validation. We present the breakdown of results for WIKIPEDIA in Figure 2.

WIKIPEDIA shows a pseudo-logarithmic growth in $\mathcal{F}_\mu$ (= $\mathcal{P}_\mu$ = $\mathcal{R}_\mu$) as the test document size increases. This fits with our intuition, as the model has progressively more evidence to base the classification on. It also suggests that performance over shorter documents appears to be the dominating factor in the overall ranking of the different methods. In particular, COS_{1NN} and SVM appear to be able to classify shorter documents most reliably, leading to the overall result of them being the best-performing methods.

While we do not show the graph for reasons of space, the equivalent graph for EUROGOV displays a curious effect: $\mathcal{F}_\mu$ drops off as the test documents get longer. Error analysis of the data indicates that this is due to longer documents being more likely to be "contaminated" with either data from a second language or extra-linguistic data, such as large tables of numbers or chemical names. This suggests that all the models are brittle when the assump-

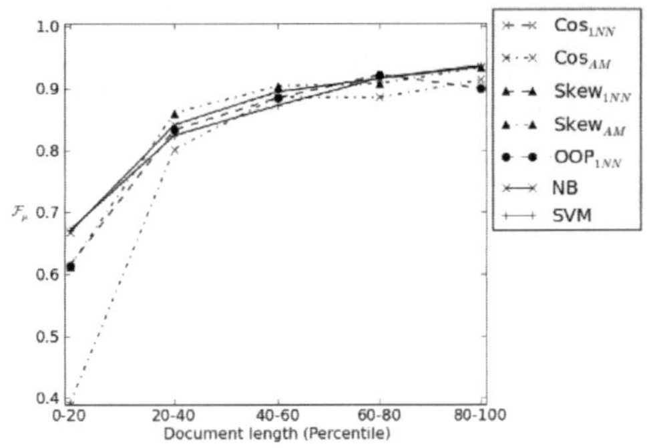

Figure 2: Breakdown of $\mathcal{F}_\mu$ over WIKIPEDIA for test documents of increasing length

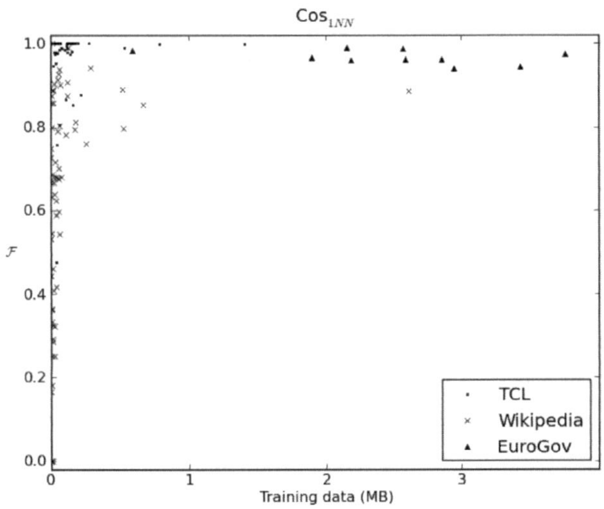

Figure 3: Per-language $\mathcal{F}_M$ for $\text{COS}_{1\text{NN}}$, relative to the training data size (in MB) for that language

tion of strict monolingualism is broken, or when the document is dominated by extra-linguistic data. Clearly, this underlines our assumption of monolingual documents, and suggests multilingual language identification is a fertile research area even in terms of optimising performance over our "monolingual" datasets.

7.4 Performance Relative to Training Data Size

As a final data point in our analysis, we calculated the $\mathcal{F}_M$ for each language relative to the amount of training data available for that language, and present the results in the form of a combined scatter plot for the three datasets in Figure 3. The differing distributions of the three datasets are self-evident, with most languages in EUROGOV (the squares) both having reasonably large amounts of training data and achieving high $\mathcal{F}_M$ values, but the majority of languages in WIKIPEDIA (the crosses) having very little data (including a number of languages with no training data, as there is a singleton document in that language in the dataset). As an overall trend, we can observe that the greater the volume of training data, the higher the $\mathcal{F}_M$ across all three datasets, but there is considerable variation between the languages in terms of their $\mathcal{F}_M$ for a given training data size (the column of crosses for WIKIPEDIA to the left of the graph is particularly striking).

8 Conclusions

We have carried out a thorough (re)examination of the task of language identification, that is predicting the language that a given document is written in, focusing on monolingual documents at present. We experimented with a total of 7 models, and tested each over two tokenisation strategies (bigrams vs. codepoints) and three token n-gram orders (unigrams, bigrams and trigrams). At the same time as reproducing results from earlier research on how easy the task can be over small numbers of languages with longer documents, we demonstrated that the task becomes much harder for larger numbers of languages, shorter documents and greater class skew. We also found that explicit character encoding detection is not necessary in language detection, and that the most consistent model overall is either a simple 1-NN model with cosine similarity, or an SVM with a linear kernel, using a byte bigram or trigram document representation. We also confirmed that longer documents tend to be easier to classify, but also that multilingual documents cause problems for the standard model of language identification.

Acknowledgements

This research was supported by a Google Research Award.

References

Beatrice Alex, Amit Dubey, and Frank Keller. 2007. Using foreign inclusion detection to improve parsing performance. In *Proceedings of the Joint Conference on Empirical Methods in Natural Language Processing and Computational Natural Language Learning 2007 (EMNLP-CoNLL 2007)*, pages 151–160, Prague, Czech Republic.

Javed A. Aslam and Meredith Frost. 2003. An information-theoretic measure for document similarity. In *Proceedings of 26th International ACM-SIGIR Conference on Research and Development in Information Retrieval (SIGIR 2003)*, pages 449–450, Toronto, Canada.

Timothy Baldwin, Steven Bird, and Baden Hughes. 2006. Collecting low-density language materials on the web. In *Proceedings of the 12th Australasian Web Conference (AusWeb06)*. `http://www.ausweb.scu.edu.au/ausweb06/edited/hughes/`.

William B. Cavnar and John M. Trenkle. 1994. N-gram-based text categorization. In *Proceedings of the Third Symposium on Document Analysis and Information Retrieval*, Las Vegas, USA.

Marc Darnashek. 1995. Gauging similarity with n-grams: Language-independent categorization of text. *Science*, 267:843–848.

Rafael Dueire Lins and Paulo Gonçalves. 2004. Automatic language identification of written texts. In *Proceedings of the 2004 ACM Symposium on Applied Computing (SAC 2004)*, pages 1128–1133, Nicosia, Cyprus.

Ted Dunning. 1994. Statistical identification of language. Technical Report MCCS 940-273, Computing Research Laboratory, New Mexico State University.

Emmanuel Giguet. 1995. Categorization according to language: A step toward combining linguistic knowledge and statistic learning. In *Proceedings of the 4th International Workshop on Parsing Technologies (IWPT-1995)*, Prague, Czech Republic.

E. Mark Gold. 1967. Language identification in the limit. *Information and Control*, 5:447–474.

Gregory Grefenstette. 1995. Comparing two language identification schemes. In *Proceedings of Analisi Statistica dei Dati Testuali (JADT)*, pages 263–268.

Chih-Wei Hsu, Chih-Chung Chang, and Chih-Jen Lin. 2008. A practical guide to support vector classification. Technical report, Department of Computer Science National Taiwan University.

Baden Hughes, Timothy Baldwin, Steven Bird, Jeremy Nicholson, and Andrew MacKinlay. 2006. Reconsidering language identification for written language resources. In *Proceedings of the 5th International Conference on Language Resources and Evaluation (LREC 2006)*, pages 485–488, Genoa, Italy.

Thorsten Joachims. 1998. Text categorization with support vector machines: learning with many relevant features. In *Proceedings of the 10th European Conference on Machine Learning*, pages 137–142, Chemnitz, Germany.

Stephen Johnson. 1993. Solving the problem of language recognition. Technical report, School of Computer Studies, University of Leeds.

Canasai Kruengkrai, Prapass Srichaivattana, Virach Sornlertlamvanich, and Hitoshi Isahara. 2005. Language identification based on string kernels. In *Proceedings of the 5th International Symposium on Communications and Information Technologies (ISCIT-2005)*, pages 896–899, Beijing, China.

Lillian Lee. 2001. On the effectiveness of the skew divergence for statistical language analysis. In *Proceedings of Artificial Intelligence and Statistics 2001 (AISTATS 2001)*, pages 65–72, Key West, USA.

Huma Lodhi, Craig Saunders, John Shawe-Taylor, Nello Cristianini, and Chris Watkins. 2002. Text classification using string kernels. *Journal of Machine Learning Research*, 2:419–444.

Christopher D. Manning, Prabhakar Raghavan, and Hinrich Schütze. 2008. *Introduction to Information Retrieval*. Cambridge University Press, Cambridge, UK.

Bruno Martins and Mário J. Silva. 2005. Language identification in web pages. In *Proceedings of the 2005 ACM symposium on Applied computing*, pages 764–768, Santa Fe, USA.

Andrew Kachites McCallum. 1996. Bow: A toolkit for statistical language modeling, text retrieval, classification and clustering. `http://www.cs.cmu.edu/~mccallum/bow`.

Paul McNamee and James Mayfield. 2004. Character N-gram Tokenization for European Language Text Retrieval. *Information Retrieval*, 7(1–2):73–97.

Olivier Teytaud and Radwan Jalam. 2001. Kernel-based text categorization. In *Proceedings of the International Joint Conference on Neural Networks (IJCNN'2001)*, Washington DC, USA.

Vladimir N. Vapnik. 1995. *The Nature of Statistical Learning Theory*. Springer-Verlag, Berlin, Germany.

Fei Xia and William Lewis. 2009. Applying NLP technologies to the collection and enrichment of language data on the web to aid linguistic research. In *Proceedings of the EACL 2009 Workshop on Language Technology and Resources for Cultural Heritage, Social Sciences, Humanities, and Education (LaTeCH – SHELT&R 2009)*, pages 51–59, Athens, Greece.

Fei Xia, William Lewis, and Hoifung Poon. 2009. Language ID in the context of harvesting language data off the web. In *Proceedings of the 12th Conference of the EACL (EACL 2009)*, pages 870–878, Athens, Greece.

Inducing Synchronous Grammars with Slice Sampling

Phil Blunsom
Computing Laboratory
Oxford University
Phil.Blunsom@comlab.ox.ac.uk

Trevor Cohn
Department of Computer Science
University of Sheffield
T.Cohn@dcs.shef.ac.uk

Abstract

This paper describes an efficient sampler for synchronous grammar induction under a non-parametric Bayesian prior. Inspired by ideas from *slice sampling*, our sampler is able to draw samples from the posterior distributions of models for which the standard dynamic programing based sampler proves intractable on non-trivial corpora. We compare our sampler to a previously proposed Gibbs sampler and demonstrate strong improvements in terms of both training log-likelihood and performance on an end-to-end translation evaluation.

1 Introduction

Intractable optimisation algorithms abound in much of the recent work in Natural Language Processing. In fact, there is an increasing acceptance that solutions to many of the great challenges of NLP (e.g. machine translation, summarisation, question answering) will rest on the quality of approximate inference. In this work we tackle this problem in the context of inducing synchronous grammars for a machine translation system. We concern ourselves with the lack of a principled, and scalable, algorithm for learning a synchronous context free grammar (SCFG) from sentence-aligned parallel corpora.

The predominant approach for learning phrase-based translation models (both finite state or synchronous grammar based) uses a cascade of heuristics beginning with predicted word alignments and producing a weighted set of translation rules (Koehn et al., 2003). Alternative approaches avoid such heuristics, instead learning structured alignment models directly from sentence aligned data (e.g., (Marcu and Wong, 2002; Cherry and Lin, 2007; DeNero et al., 2008; Blunsom et al., 2009)). Although these models are theoretically attractive, inference is intractable (at least $\mathcal{O}(|\mathbf{f}|^3|\mathbf{e}|^3)$). The efficacy of direct estimation of structured alignment models therefore rests on the approximations used to make inference practicable – typically heuristic constraints or Gibbs sampling. In this work we show that naive Gibbs sampling (specifically, Blunsom et al. (2009)) is ineffectual for inference and reliant on a high quality initialisation, mixing very slowly and being easily caught in modes. Instead, blocked sampling over sentence pairs allows much faster mixing, but done in the obvious way (following Johnson et al. (2007)) would incur a $\mathcal{O}(|\mathbf{f}|^3|\mathbf{e}|^3)$ time complexity.

Here we draw inspiration from the work of Van Gael et al. (2008) on inference in infinite hidden Markov models to develop a novel algorithm for efficient sampling from a SCFG. We develop an auxiliary variable 'slice' sampler which can dramatically reduce inference complexity, and thereby make blocked sampling practicable on real translation corpora. Our evaluation demonstrates that our algorithm mixes more quickly than the local Gibbs sampler, and produces translation models which achieve state-of-the-art BLEU scores without using GIZA++ or symmetrisation heuristics for initialisation.

We adopt the generative model of Blunsom et al. (2009) which creates a parallel sentence pair by a sequence (derivation) of SCFG productions $\mathbf{d} = (r_1, r_2, ..., r_n)$. The tokens in each language can be read off the leaves of the derivation tree while their order is defined hierarchically by the productions in use. The probability of a derivation is defined as $p(\mathbf{d}|\theta) = \prod_{r \in \mathbf{d}} \theta_r$ where θ are the model parameters which are drawn from a Bayesian prior. We deviate from that models definition of the prior over phrasal translations, instead adopting the hierarchical Dirichlet process prior from DeNero et al. (2008), which incorporates IBM Model 1. Blunsom et al. (2009) describe a blocked sampler following Johnson et al. (2007) which uses the Metropolis-Hastings algorithm to correct proposal samples drawn from an approximating SCFG, however this is discounted as impractical due to the $\mathcal{O}(|\mathbf{f}|^3|\mathbf{e}|^3)$ complexity. Instead a Gibbs sampler is used which samples local updates to the derivation structure of each training instance. This avoids the dynamic program of the

Human Language Technologies: The 2010 Annual Conference of the North American Chapter of the ACL, pages 238–241,
Los Angeles, California, June 2010. ©2010 Association for Computational Linguistics

blocked sampler but at the expense of considerably slower mixing.

Recently Bouchard-Côté et al. (2009) proposed an auxialliary variable sampler, possibly complementary to ours, which was also evaluated on synchronous parsing. Rather than slice sampling derivations in a collapsed Bayesian model, this model employed a secondary proposal model (IBM Models) and sampled expectations over rule parameters.

2 Slice Sampling a SCFG

It would be advantageous to explore a middle ground where the scope of the dynamic program is limited to high probability regions, reducing the running time to an acceptable level. By employing the technique of *slice sampling* (Neal, 2003) we describe an algorithm which stochastically samples from a reduced space of possible derivations, while ensuring that these samples are drawn from the correct distribution. We apply the slice sampler to the approximating SCFG parameterised by θ, which requires samples from an *inside* chart $p(\mathbf{d}|\theta)$ (for brevity, we omit the dependency on θ in the following).

Slice sampling is an example of *auxiliary variable sampling* in which we make use of the fact that if we can draw samples from a joint distribution, then we can trivially obtain samples from the marginal distributions: $p(\mathbf{d}) = \sum_{\mathbf{u}} p(\mathbf{d}, \mathbf{u})$, where $\mathbf{d}$ is the variable of interest and $\mathbf{u}$ is an auxiliary variable. Using a Gibbs sampler we can draw samples from this joint distribution by alternately sampling from $p(\mathbf{d}|\mathbf{u})$ and $p(\mathbf{u}|\mathbf{d})$. The trick is to ensure that $\mathbf{u}$ is defined such that drawing samples from $p(\mathbf{d}|\mathbf{u})$ is more efficient than from $p(\mathbf{d})$.

We define the variable $\mathbf{u}$ to contain a slice variable u_s for every cell of a synchronous parse chart for every training instance:[1]

$$\mathcal{S} = \{(i, j, x, y) \mid 0 \leq i < j \leq |\mathbf{f}|, 0 \leq x < y \leq |\mathbf{e}|\}$$
$$\mathbf{u} = \{u_s \in \mathbb{R} \mid 0 < u_s < 1, s \in \mathcal{S}\}$$

These slice variables act as cutoffs on the probabilities of the rules considered in each cell s: rule applications r_s with $\theta_{r_s} \leq u_s$ will be pruned from the dynamic program.[2]

Sampling $p(\mathbf{u}|\mathbf{d})$ Unlike Van Gael et al. (2008), there is not a one-to-one correspondence between the spans of the rules in $\mathbf{d}$ and the set $\mathcal{S}$, rather the derivation's rule spans form a subset of $\mathcal{S}$. This complicates our definition of $p(\mathbf{u}|\mathbf{d})$; we must provide separate accounts of how each u_s is generated depending on whether there is a corresponding rule for s, i.e., $r_s \in \mathbf{d}$. We define $p(\mathbf{u}|\mathbf{d}) = \prod_s p(u_s|\mathbf{d})$, where:

$$p(u_s|\mathbf{d}) = \begin{cases} \frac{\mathbb{I}(u_s < \theta_{r_s})}{\theta_{r_s}} & \text{, if } r_s \in \mathbf{d} \\ \beta(u_s; a, b) & \text{, else} \end{cases} \quad (1)$$

which mixes a uniform distribution and a Beta distribution[3] depending on the existence of a rule r_s in the derivation $\mathbf{d}$.[4] Eq. 1 is constructed such that only rules with probability greater than the relevant threshold, $\{r_s \mid \theta_{r_s} > u_s\}$, could have feasibly been part of a derivation resulting in auxiliary variable $\mathbf{u}$. This is critical in reasoning over the reverse conditional $p(\mathbf{d}|\mathbf{u})$ which only has to consider the reduced space of rules (formulation below in (4)). Trivially, the conditioning derivation is recoverable, $\forall r_s \in \mathbf{d}, \theta_{r_s} \geq u_s$. We parameterise the β distribution in (1) with a heavy skew towards zero in order to limit the amount of pruning and thereby include many competing derivations.[5]

Sampling $p(\mathbf{d}|\mathbf{u})$ Recall the probability of a derivation, $p(\mathbf{d}) = \prod_{r_s \in \mathbf{d}} \theta_{r_s}$. We draw samples from the joint distribution, $p(\mathbf{d}, \mathbf{u})$, holding $\mathbf{u}$ fixed:

$$\begin{aligned} p(\mathbf{d}|\mathbf{u}) &\propto p(\mathbf{d}, \mathbf{u}) = p(\mathbf{d}) \times p(\mathbf{u}|\mathbf{d}) \\ &= \left(\prod_{r_s \in \mathbf{d}} \theta_{r_s}\right) \times \left(\begin{array}{r} \prod_{u_s : r_s \in \mathbf{d}} \frac{\mathbb{I}(u_s < \theta_{r_s})}{\theta_{r_s}} \\ \times \prod_{u_s : r_s \notin \mathbf{d}} \beta(u_s; a, b) \end{array}\right) \\ &= \prod_{u_s : r_s \in \mathbf{d}} \mathbb{I}(u_s < \theta_{r_s}) \prod_{u_s : r_s \notin \mathbf{d}} \beta(u_s; a, b) \quad (2) \\ &= \prod_{u_s : r_s \in \mathbf{d}} \frac{\mathbb{I}(u_s < \theta_{r_s})}{\beta(u_s; a, b)} \prod_{u_s} \beta(u_s; a, b) \quad (3) \\ &\propto \prod_{u_s : r_s \in \mathbf{d}} \frac{\mathbb{I}(u_s < \theta_{r_s})}{\beta(u_s; a, b)} \quad (4) \end{aligned}$$

In step (2) we cancel the θ_{r_s} terms while in step (3) we introduce $\beta(u_s; a, b)$ terms to the numerator and denominator for $u_s : r_s \in \mathbf{d}$ to simplify the range

[1] The dependence on training instances is omitted here and subsequently for simplicity. Each instance is independent, and therefore this formulation can be trivially applied to a set.

[2] Alternatively, we could naively sample from a pruned chart using a fixed beam threshold. However, this would not produce samples from $p(\mathbf{d})$, but some other unknown distribution.

[3] Any distribution defined over $\{x \in \mathbb{R} \mid 0 \leq x \leq 1\}$ may be used in place of β, however this may affect the efficiency of the sampler.

[4] $\mathbb{I}(\cdot)$ returns 1 if the condition is true and 0 otherwise.

[5] We experiment with a range of $a < 1$ while fixing $b = 1$.

System	BLEU	time(s)	LLH
Moses (default settings)	47.3	–	–
LB init.	36.5	–	-257.1
M1 init.	48.8	–	-153.4
M4 init.	49.1	–	-151.4
Gibbs LB init.	45.3	44	-135.4
Gibbs M1 init.	48.2	40	-120.5
Gibbs M4 init. (Blunsom et al., 2009)	49.6	44	-110.3
Slice (a=0.15, b=1) LB init.	47.3	180	-98.9
Slice (a=0.10, b=1) M1 init.	50.4	908	-89.4
Slice (a=0.15, b=1) M1 init.	49.9	144	-90.2
Slice (a=0.25, b=1) M1 init.	49.2	80	-95.6

Table 1: IWSLT Chinese to English translation.

of the second product. The last step (4) discards the term $\prod_{u_s} \beta(u_s; a, b)$ which is constant wrt $\mathbf{d}$. The net result is a formulation which factors with the derivation structure, thereby eliminating the need to consider all $\mathcal{O}(|\mathbf{e}|^2|\mathbf{f}|^2)$ spans in $\mathcal{S}$. Critically $p(\mathbf{d}|\mathbf{u})$ is zero for all spans failing the $\mathbb{I}\,(u_s < \theta_{r_s})$ condition.

To exploit the decomposition of Equation 4 we require a parsing algorithm that only explores chart cells whose child cells have not already been pruned by the slice variables. The standard approach of using synchronous CYK (Wu, 1997) doesn't posses this property: all chart cells would be visited even if they are to be pruned. Instead we use an agenda based parsing algorithm, in particular we extend the algorithm of Klein and Manning (2004) to synchronous parsing.[6] Finally, we need a Metropolis-Hastings acceptance step to account for intra-instance dependencies (the 'rich-get-richer' effect). We omit the details, save to state that the calculation cancels to the same test as presented in Johnson et al. (2007).[7]

3 Evaluation

In the following experiments we compare the slice sampler and the Gibbs sampler (Blunsom et al., 2009), in terms of mixing and translation quality. We measure mixing in terms of training log-likelihood (LLH) after a fixed number of sampling iterations. Translations are produced using Moses (Koehn et al., 2007), initialised with the word alignments from the final sample, and are evaluated using BLEU(Papineni et al., 2001). The slice sampled models are restricted to learning binary branching one-to-one (or null) alignments,[8] while no restriction is placed on the Gibbs sampler (both use the same model, so have comparable LLH). Of particular interest is how the different samplers perform given initialisations of varying quality. We evaluate three initialisers: **M4**: the symmetrised output of GIZA++ factorised into ITG form (as used in Blunsom et al. (2009)); **M1**: the output of a heavily pruned ITG parser using the IBM Model 1 prior for the rule probabilities;[9] and **LB**: left-branching monotone derivations.[10]

We experiment with the Chinese→English translation task from IWSLT, as used in Blunsom et al. (2009).[11] Figure 1 shows LLH curves for the samplers initialised with the M1 and LB derivations, plus the curve for Gibbs sampler with the M4 initialiser.[12] Table 1 gives BLEU scores on Test-05 for phrase-based translation models built from the 1500th sample for the various models along with the average time per sample and their final log-likelihood.

4 Discussion

The results are particularly encouraging. The slice sampler uniformly finds much better solutions than the Gibbs sampler regardless of initialisation. In particular, the slice sampled model initialised with the naive LB structure achieves a higher likelihood than the M4 initialised model, although this is not reflected in their relative BLEU scores. In contrast the Gibbs sampler is more significantly affected by its initialisation, only deviating slightly before becoming trapped in a mode, as seen in Fig. 1. With sufficient (infinite) time both sampling strategies will converge on the true posterior regardless of initialisation, however the slice sampler appears to be converging much faster than the Gibbs sampler.

Interestingly, the initialisation heuristics (M1 and M4) outperform the default heuristics (Koehn et al., 2007) by a considerable margin. This is most likely because the initialisation heuristics force the alignments to factorise with an ITG, resulting in more aggressive pruning of spurious alignments which in turn allows for more and larger phrase pairs.

[6]Moreover, we only sample values for u_s as they are visited by the parser, thus avoiding the quartic complexity.

[7]Acceptance rates averaged above 99%.

[8]This restriction is not strictly necessary, however it greatly simplifies the implementation and increases efficiency.

[9]The following beam heuristics are employed: alignments to null are only permitted on the longer sentence side; words are only allowed to align to those whose relative sentence position is within ± 3 words.

[10]Words of the longer sentence are randomly assigned to null.

[11]We limit the maximum training sentence length to 40, resulting in $\sim 40k$ training sentences.

[12]The GIZA++ M4 alignments don't readily factorise to word-based ITG derivations, as such we haven't produced results for this initialiser using the slice sampler.

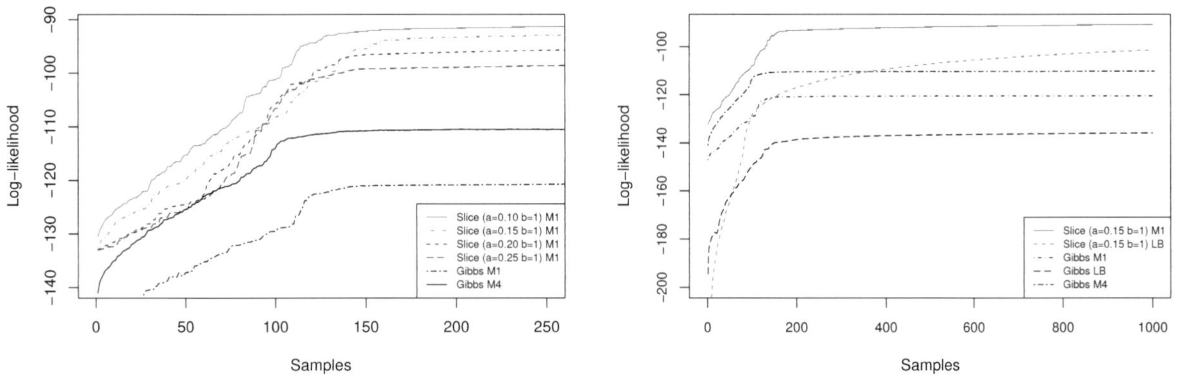

Figure 1: Training log-likelihood as a function of sampling iteration for Gibbs and slice sampling.

While the LLHs for the slice sampled models and their BLEU scores appear correlated, this doesn't extend to comparisons with the Gibbs sampled models. We believe that this is because the GIZA++ initialisation alignments also explain the data well, while not necessarily obtaining a high LLH under the ITG model. Solutions which score highly in one model score poorly in the other, despite both producing good translations.

The slice sampler is slower than the local Gibbs sampler, its speed depending on the parameterisation of the Beta distribution (affecting the width of the beam). In the extreme, exhaustive search using the full dynamic program is intractable on current hardware,[13] and therefore we have achieved our aim of mediating between local and blocked inference.

This investigation has established the promise of the SCFG slice sampling technique to provide a scalable inference algorithm for non-parametric Bayesian models. With further development, this work could provide the basis for a family of principled inference algorithms for parsing models, both monolingual and synchronous, and other models that prove intractable for exact dynamic programming.

References

P. Blunsom, T. Cohn, C. Dyer, M. Osborne. 2009. A Gibbs sampler for phrasal synchronous grammar induction. In *Proc. ACL/IJCNLP*, 782–790, Suntec, Singapore. Association for Computational Linguistics.

A. Bouchard-Côté, S. Petrov, D. Klein. 2009. Randomized pruning: Efficiently calculating expectations in large dynamic programs. In *Advances in Neural Information Processing Systems 22*, 144–152.

C. Cherry, D. Lin. 2007. Inversion transduction grammar for joint phrasal translation modeling. In *Proc. SSST*, Rochester, USA.

J. DeNero, A. Bouchard-Côté, D. Klein. 2008. Sampling alignment structure under a Bayesian translation model. In *Proc. EMNLP*, 314–323, Honolulu, Hawaii.

M. Johnson, T. Griffiths, S. Goldwater. 2007. Bayesian inference for PCFGs via Markov chain Monte Carlo. In *Proc. HLT-NAACL*, 139–146, Rochester, New York.

D. Klein, C. D. Manning, 2004. *Parsing and hypergraphs*, 351–372. Kluwer Academic Publishers, Norwell, MA, USA, 2004.

P. Koehn, F. J. Och, D. Marcu. 2003. Statistical phrase-based translation. In *Proc. HLT-NAACL*, 81–88, Edmonton, Canada.

P. Koehn, H. Hoang, A. Birch, C. Callison-Burch, M. Federico, N. Bertoldi, B. Cowan, W. Shen, C. Moran, R. Zens, C. Dyer, O. Bojar, A. Constantin, E. Herbst. 2007. Moses: Open source toolkit for statistical machine translation. In *Proc. ACL*, Prague.

D. Marcu, W. Wong. 2002. A phrase-based, joint probability model for statistical machine translation. In *Proc. EMNLP*, 133–139, Philadelphia.

R. Neal. 2003. Slice sampling. *Annals of Statistics*, 31:705–767.

K. Papineni, S. Roukos, T. Ward, W. Zhu. 2001. Bleu: a method for automatic evaluation of machine translation. Technical Report RC22176 (W0109-022), IBM Research Division, Thomas J. Watson Research Center, 2001.

J. Van Gael, Y. Saatci, Y. W. Teh, Z. Ghahramani. 2008. Beam sampling for the infinite hidden markov model. In *ICML*, 1088–1095, New York, NY, USA.

D. Wu. 1997. Stochastic inversion transduction grammars and bilingual parsing of parallel corpora. *Computational Linguistics*, 23(3):377–403.

[13] Our implementation had not completed a single sample after a week.

Task-based Evaluation of Multiword Expressions: a Pilot Study in Statistical Machine Translation

Marine Carpuat **Mona Diab**
Columbia University
Center for Computational Learning Systems
475 Riverside Drive, New York, NY 10115
{marine,mdiab}@ccls.columbia.edu

Abstract

We conduct a pilot study for task-oriented evaluation of Multiword Expression (MWE) in Statistical Machine Translation (SMT). We propose two different integration strategies for MWE in SMT, which take advantage of different degrees of MWE semantic compositionality and yield complementary improvements in SMT quality on a large-scale translation task.[1]

1 Introduction

A multiword expression (MWE) generally refers to a multiword unit or a collocation of words that cooccur together statistically more than chance. A MWE is a cover term for different types of collocations which vary in their transparency and fixedness. Identifying MWEs and understanding their meaning is considered essential to language understanding, and of crucial importance for any Natural Language Processing (NLP) applications that aim at handling robust language meaning and use. In fact, the seminal paper (Sag et al., 2002) refers to this problem as a key issue for the development of high-quality NLP applications. (Villavicencio et al., 2005) identify Machine Translation as an application of particular interest since " recognition of MWEs is necessary for systems to preserve the meaning and produce appropriate translations and avoid the generation of unnatural or nonsensical sentences in the target language."

However, statistical machine translation (SMT) typically does not model MWEs explicitly. SMT units are typically phrasal translations, defined without any direct syntactic or lexical semantic motivation: they are simply n-grams that are consistently translated in parallel corpora. Phrasal translations might indirectly capture MWEs, but they are not distinguished from any other n-gram.

As a result, the usefulness of explicitly modeling MWEs in the SMT framework has not yet been studied systematically. Previous work has focused on automatically learning and integrating translations of very specific MWE categories, such as, for instance, idiomatic Chinese four character expressions (Bai et al., 2009) or domain specific MWEs (Ren et al., 2009). MWEs have also been defined not from a lexical semantics perspective but from a SMT error reduction perspective, as phrases that are hard to align during SMT training (Lambert and Banchs, 2005). For each of these particular cases, translation quality improved by augmenting the SMT translation lexicon with the learned bilingual MWEs either directly or through improved word alignments.

In this paper, we consider a more general problem: we view SMT as an extrinsic evaluation of the usefulness of monolingual MWEs as used pervasively in natural language regardless of domain, idiomaticity and compositionality. A MWE is compositional if its meaning as a unit can be predicted from the meaning of its component words such as in *make a decision* meaning *to decide*. Some MWEs are more predictable than others, for instance, *kick the bucket*, when used idiomatically to mean *to die*, has nothing in common with the literal meaning of either *kick* or *bucket*, while *make a decision* is very clearly related to *to decide*. These expressions are

[1]The research was partially funded by IBM under the DARPA GALE project.

Human Language Technologies: The 2010 Annual Conference of the North American Chapter of the ACL, pages 242–245,
Los Angeles, California, June 2010.

both considered MWEs but have varying degrees of compositionality and predictability.

We explore strategies for integrating all MWEs along this continuum in SMT. Given a monolingual MWE lexicon, we propose (1) a **static integration** strategy that segments training and test sentences according to the MWE vocabulary, and (2) a **dynamic integration** strategy that adds a new MWE-based feature in SMT translation lexicons.

In a pilot study of the impact of WordNet MWEs on a large-scale English to Arabic SMT system, we show that static and dynamic strategies both improve translation quality and that their impact is not the same for different types of MWEs. This suggests that the proposed framework would be an interesting testbed for a task-driven evaluation of automatic MWE extraction.

2 Static integration of MWE in SMT

The first strategy for integration can be seen as a generalization of word segmentation for MWEs. Given a MWE lexicon, we identify MWEs in running text and turn them into a single unit by underscoring. We call this integration method **static**, since, once segmented, all MWEs are considered frozen from the perspective of the SMT system. During training and decoding, MWEs are handled as distinct words regardless of their compositionality, and all knowledge of the MWE components is lost.

3 Dynamic integration of MWE in SMT

The second strategy attempts to encourage cohesive translations of MWEs without ignoring their components. Word alignment and phrasal translation extraction are conducted without any MWE knowledge, so that the SMT system can learn word-for-word translations from consistently translated compositional MWEs. MWE knowledge is integrated as a feature in the translation lexicon. For each entry, in addition to the standard phrasal translation probabilities, we define a count feature that represents the number of MWEs in the input language phrase.

We refer to this integration strategy as **dynamic**, because the SMT system decides at decoding time how to segment the input sentence. The MWE feature biases the system towards using phrases that do not break MWEs. This can be seen as a generalization of the binary MWE feature in (Ren et al., 2009), repurposed for monolingual MWEs.

4 Empirical Evaluation

We evaluate the impact of MWEs in SMT on a large-scale English-Arabic translation task.

Using two languages from different families is a challenging testbed for MWEs in SMT. In contrast, very closely related languages such as English and French might present less divergence in lexicalization.

In addition, Arabic-English is a well-studied language pair in SMT, with large amounts of data available. However, we tackle the less common English to Arabic direction in order to take advantage of the rich lexical resources available for English on the input side.

Our test set consists of the 813 newswire sentences of the 2008 NIST Open Machine Translation Evaluation, which is standard evaluation data for Arabic-English translation. The first English reference translation is used as the input to our SMT system, and the single Arabic translation is used as the unique reference[2]. Translation quality is evaluated using two automatic evaluation metrics: (1) BLEUr1n4 (Papineni et al., 2002), which is based on n-gram precisions for $n = 1..4$, and (2) Translation Edit Rate (TER) (Snover et al., 2006), which generalizes edit distance beyond single-word edits.

4.1 SMT system

We use the open-source Moses toolkit (Koehn et al., 2007) to build a standard phrase-based SMT system.

Our training data consists of 2.5M sentence pairs from mostly newswire parallel corpora distributed by the Linguistic Data Consortium. The English side is tokenized using simple punctuation-based rules. The Arabic side is segmented according to the Arabic Treebank v3 tokenization scheme using the MADA+TOKAN morphological analyzer and tokenizer (Habash et al., 2009).

The parallel corpus is word-aligned using GIZA++ in both translation directions, which are

[2]We exclude weblog text since it consists of an informal mix of Modern Standard Arabic and Dialectal Arabic which is suboptimal as a reference translation.

combined by intersection and the grow-diag-final-and heuristic (Koehn et al., 2007). Phrase translations of up to 10 words are extracted in the Moses phrase-table. We use a 5-gram language model with modified Kneser-Ney smoothing. Feature weights are tuned on NIST-MT06.

4.2 English MWE

Our main source of English MWE is the WordNet 3.0 lexical database (Fellbaum, 1998). We use simple rules to augment WordNet entries with morphological variations (e.g., *keep one's eyes peeled* is expanded into *keep her eyes peeled*, etc.). In addition when marking MWEs in text, we allow matches not only with surface forms, but also with lemmatized forms (Schmid, 1994) to account for inflections. This results in a total of about 900 MWE tokens and 500 types in our evaluation test set. MWE identification in running text is performed using a straightforward maximum forward match algorithm.

Second, in order to contrast the impact of MWEs with that of frequent collocations in our dynamic integration strategy, we consider the top 500 most frequent n-grams from the SMT test set, so that the same number of n-gram types and WordNet MWEs are marked in the test set. Unlike WordNet MWEs, these n-gram represent cohesive units, but are not necessarily frozen or even a single concept. We consider n-grams up to length 10 from the phrase-table, and compute their frequency in the English side of the parallel corpus. The top 500 most frequent n-grams and the WordNet MWEs yield two very different lexicons. Only the following 10 entries appear in both: *at the same time, deputy prime minister, for the first time, in the south, in the wake of, international atomic energy agency, islamic resistance movement, on the other hand, osama bin laden, secretary of state*.

5 Static MWE Integration Improves SMT

As seen in Table 1, the static integration of the WordNet MWE lexicon by segmentation of English training and test sentences improves BLEU and TER compared to the SMT baseline. This suggests that WordNet MWEs represent useful units of meaning for alignment and translation into Arabic despite the fact that they are monolingually defined.

MWE	integration	TER	BLEU
Baseline	—	59.43	30.49
Top 500 n-grams	dynamic	59.07	30.98
WordNet MWE	dynamic	58.89	31.07
WordNet MWE	static	58.98	31.27

Table 1: Impact of MWE integration measured on NIST MT08

Consider, for instance, the following input sentence: *the special envoy of the secretary-general will submit an oral report to the international security council rather than a written report*. With static integration, the MWE *written report* is correctly translated as *tqryrA mktwbA*, while the baseline produces the incorrect translation *ktb Altqryr* (*writing the report* or *book of report*).

6 Dynamic MWE Integration Improves SMT

Dynamic integration of the WordNet MWE lexicon and the top 500 n-grams both improve BLEU and TER (Table 1), but WordNet MWEs yield slightly better scores. This confirms the ability of the dynamic integration method to handle compositional MWEs, since the most frequent n-grams are highly compositional by definition.

7 Discussion

At the corpus-level, static integration yields a slightly better BLEU score than dynamic with WordNet MWEs, while the opposite effect is observed on TER. This suggests that the two integration strategies impact translation in different ways. Sentence-level scores indeed reveal that dynamic and static integration strategies have an opposite impact on 27% of the test set (Table 2).

For instance, the dynamic approach fails for phrasal verbs such as *take out*. In *who were then allowed to take out as many unsecured loans as they wanted*, *take out* is realized as *b+ AlHSwl* (*acquire*) with the static approach, while it is entirely dropped from the dynamic translation.

In the static approach, translation quality is often degraded when our simple dictionary matching approach incorrectly detects MWE. For instance, in the sentence *the perpetration of this heinous act on our*

Dynamic integration	helps	hurts
Static integration		
helps	45%	**16%**
hurts	**11%**	28%

Table 2: Percentage of sentences where each integration strategy helps or hurts both BLEU and TER compared to the baseline SMT system.

soil, *act on* is incorrectly identified as a MWE which degrades translation fluency. This suggests that further gains in translation quality could be obtained with a more sophisticated MWE detection method.

8 Conclusion

We have proposed a framework of two complementary integration strategies for MWEs in SMT, which allows extrinsic evaluation of the usefulness of MWEs of varying degree of compositionality. We conducted a pilot study using manually defined WordNet MWE and a dictionary matching approach to MWE detection. This simple model improves English-Arabic translation quality, even on a large SMT system trained on more than 2 Million sentence pairs.

This result suggests that standard SMT phrases do not implicitly capture all useful MWE information. It would therefore be interesting to conduct this study on a larger scale, using more general MWE definitions such as automatically learned collocations (Smadja, 1993) or verb-noun constructions (Diab and Bhutada, 2009).

References

Ming-Hong Bai, Jia-Ming You, Keh-Jiann Chen, and Jason S. Chang. 2009. Acquiring translation equivalences of multiword expressions by normalized correlation frequencies. In *Proceedings of the 2009 Conference on Empirical Methods in Natural Language Processing*, pages 478–486, Singapore, August.

Mona Diab and Pravin Bhutada. 2009. Verb noun construction MWE token classification. In *Proceedings of the Workshop on Multiword Expressions: Identification, Interpretation, Disambiguation and Applications*, pages 17–22, Singapore, August.

Christiane Fellbaum, editor. 1998. *WordNet: An Electronic Lexical Database*. MIT Press.

Nizar Habash, Owen Rambow, and Ryan Roth. 2009. MADA+TOKAN: A toolkit for Arabic tokenization, diacritization, morphological disambiguation, POS tagging, stemming and lemmatization. In *Proceedings of the 2nd International Conference on Arabic Language Resources and Tools (MEDAR)*, Cairo, Egypt.

Philipp Koehn, Hieu Hoang, Alexandra Birch, Chris Callison-Burch, Marcello Federico, Nicola Bertoldi, Brooke Cowan, Wade Shen, Christine Moran, Richard Zens, Chris Dyer, Ondrej Bojar, Alexandra Constantin, and Evan Herbst. 2007. Moses: Open source toolkit for statistical machine translation. In *Annual Meeting of the Association for Computational Linguistics (ACL), demonstration session*, Prague, Czech Republic, June.

Patrik Lambert and Rafael Banchs. 2005. Data inferred multi-word expressions for statistical machine translation. In *Machine Translation Summit X*, pages 396–403, Phuket, Thailand.

Kishore Papineni, Salim Roukos, Todd Ward, and Wei-Jing Zhu. 2002. BLEU: a method for automatic evaluation of machine translation. In *Proceedings of the 40th Annual Meeting of the Association for Computational Linguistics*.

Zhixiang Ren, Yajuan Lü, Jie Cao, Qun Liu, and Yun Huang. 2009. Improving statistical machine translation using domain bilingual multiword expressions. In *Proceedings of the Workshop on Multiword Expressions: Identification, Interpretation, Disambiguation and Applications*, pages 47–54, Singapore, August.

Ivan A. Sag, Timothy Baldwin, Francis Bond, Ann A. Copestake, and Dan Flickinger. 2002. Multiword expressions: A pain in the neck for NLP. In *Proceedings of the Third International Conference on Computational Linguistics and Intelligent Text Processing*, pages 1–15, London, UK. Springer-Verlag.

Helmut Schmid. 1994. Probabilistic part–of–speech tagging using decision trees. In *Proceedings of the Conference on New Methods in Language Processing*, pages 44–49, Manchester, UK.

Frank A. Smadja. 1993. Retrieving collocations from text: Xtract. *Computational Linguistics*, 19(1):143–177.

Matthew Snover, Bonnie Dorr, Richard Schwartz, Linnea Micciulla, and John Makhoul. 2006. A study of translation edit rate with targeted human annotation. In *Proceedings of AMTA*, pages 223–231, Boston, MA. Association for Machine Translation in the Americas.

Aline Villavicencio, Francis Bond, Anna Korhonen, and Diana McCarthy. 2005. Introduction to the special issue on multiword expressions: Having a crack at a hard nut. *Computer Speech & Language*, 19(4):365 – 377. Special issue on Multiword Expression.

Improving Semantic Role Labeling with Word Sense

Wanxiang Che, Ting Liu and Yongqiang Li
Research Center for Information Retrieval
MOE-Microsoft Key Laboratory of Natural Language Processing and Speech
School of Computer Science and Technology
Harbin Institute of Technology, China, 150001
{car, tliu, yqli}@ir.hit.edu.cn

Abstract

Semantic role labeling (SRL) not only needs lexical and syntactic information, but also needs word sense information. However, because of the lack of corpus annotated with both word senses and semantic roles, there is few research on using word sense for SRL. The release of OntoNotes provides an opportunity for us to study how to use word sense for SRL. In this paper, we present some novel word sense features for SRL and find that they can improve the performance significantly.

1 Introduction

Semantic role labeling (SRL) is a kind of shallow sentence-level semantic analysis and is becoming a hot task in natural language processing. SRL aims at identifying the relations between the predicates in a sentence and their associated arguments. At present, the main stream researches are focusing on feature engineering or combination of multiple results.

Word senses are important information for recognizing semantic roles. For example, if we know "cat" is an "agent" of the predicate "eat" in a sentence, we can guess that "dog" can also be an "agent" of "eat". Word sense has been successfully used in many natural language processing tasks, such as machine translation (Chan et al., 2007; Carpuat and Wu, 2007). CoNLL 2008 shared task (Surdeanu et al., 2008) first introduced the predicate classification task, which can be regarded as the predicate sense disambiguation. Meza-Ruiz and Riedel (2009) has shown that the predicate sense can improve the final SRL performance. However, there is few discussion about the concrete influence of all word senses, i.e. the words besides predicates. The major reason is lacking the corpus, which is both annotated with all word senses and semantic roles.

The release of OntoNotes corpus provides an opportunity for us to verify whether all word senses can help SRL. OntoNotes is a large corpus annotated with constituency trees (based on Penn Treebank), predicate argument structures (based on Penn PropBank) and word senses. It has been used in some natural language processing tasks, such as joint parsing and named entity recognition (Finkel and Manning, 2009) and word sense disambiguation (Zhong et al., 2008).

In this paper, we regard the word sense information as additional SRL features. We compare three categories of word sense features (subtree-word related sense, predicate sense, and sense path) and find that the subtree-word related sense feature is ineffective, however, the predicate sense and the sense path features can improve the SRL performance significantly.

2 Data Preparation

In our experiments, we use the OntoNotes Release 2.0[1] corpus (Hovy et al., 2006). The OntoNotes project leaders describe it as "a large, multilingual richly-annotated corpus constructed at 90% internanotator agreement." The corpus has been annotated with multiple levels of annotation, including constituency trees, predicate argument structure, word senses, co-reference, and named entities. For this work, we focus on the constituency trees, word senses, and predicate argument structures. The corpus has English and Chinese portions, and we just use the English portion, which has been split into seven sections: ABC, CNN, MNB, NBC, PRI, VOA, and WSJ. These sections represent a mix of speech and newswire data.

Because we used SRL system based on dependence syntactic trees, we convert the constituency

[1] http://www.ldc.upenn.edu/Catalog/CatalogEntry.jsp?catalogId=LDC2008T04

Human Language Technologies: The 2010 Annual Conference of the North American Chapter of the ACL, pages 246–249,

trees into dependence trees with an Constituent-to-Dependency Conversion Tool[2]. In addition, we also convert the OntoNotes sense of each polysemant into WordNet sense using sense inventory file provided by OntoNotes 2.0. For an OntoNotes sense with more than one WordNet sense, we simply use the foremost (more popular) one.

3 Semantic Role Labeling System

Our baseline is a state-of-the-art SRL system based on dependency syntactic tree (Che et al., 2009). A maximum entropy (Berger et al., 1996) classifier is used to predict the probabilities of a word in the sentence to be each semantic role. A virtual role "NULL" (presenting none of roles is assigned) is added to the roles set, so it does not need semantic role identification stage anymore. For a predicate, two classifiers (one for noun predicates, and the other for verb predicates) predict probabilities of each word in a sentence to be each semantic role (including virtual role "NULL"). The features used in this stage are listed in Table 1.

Feature	Description
FirstwordLemma	The lemma of the first word in a subtree
HeadwordLemma	The lemma of the head word in a subtree
HeadwordPOS	The POS of the head word in a subtree
LastwordLemma	The lemma of the last word in a subtree
POSPath	The POS path from a word to a predicate
PathLength	The length of a path
Position	The relative position of a word with a predicate
PredicateLemma	The lemma of a predicate
RelationPath	The dependency relation path from a word to a predicate

Table 1: Features that are used in SRL.

4 Word Sense for Semantic Role Labeling

From Table 1, we can see that there are lots of lemma or POS related features. However, the lemma feature is very sparse and may result in data sparseness problem. As for the POS, it represents the syntactic information, but is not enough to distinguish different semantic roles. Therefore, we need a kind of new feature, which is general than the lemma and special than the POS.

The word sense just satisfies the requirement. Thus, we will add some new features related with word sense for SRL. Generally, the original features can be classified into three categories:

1. Subtree-word related: FirstwordLemma, LastwordLemma, HeadwordLemma, and HeadwordPOS
2. Predicate related: PredicateLemma
3. Word and predicate related: POSPath, RelationPath, PathLenght, and Position

Correspondingly, we add three categories of word sense features by replacing Lemma or POS into Sense, i.e.

1. Subtree-word related sense: FirstwordSense, LastwordSense, and HeadwordSense
2. Predicate related sense: PredicateSense
3. Word and predicate related sense: SensePath

Three strategies are designed to adopt these senses:

1. Lemma+Sense: It is the original word sense representation in OntoNotes, such as "dog.n.1". In fact, This is a specialization of the lemma.
2. Hypernym(n): It is the hypernym of a word sense, e.g. the hypernym of "dog.n.1" is "canine.n.1". The n means the level of the hypernym. With the increasing of n, the sense becomes more and more general. In theory, however, this strategy may result in inconsistent sense, e.g. word "dog" and "canine" have different hypernyms. The same problem occurs with Basic Concepts method (Izquierdo et al., 2007).
3. Root_Hyper(n): In order to extract more consistent sense, we use the hypernym of a word sense counting from the root of a sense tree, e.g. the root hypernym of "dog.n.1" is "entity.n.1". The n means the level of the root hypernym. With the increasing of n, the sense

[2]http://nlp.cs.lth.se/software/treebank_converter/

becomes more and more special. Thus, word "dog" and "canine" have the same Root_Hyper: "entity", "physical_entity", and "object" with n = 1, 2, and 3 respectively.

5 Experiments

We will do our experiments on seven of the OntoNotes English datasets described in Section 2. For each dataset, we aimed for roughly a 60% train / 20% development / 20% test split. See Table 2 for the detailed statistics. In order to examine the influence of word senses in isolation, we use the human annotated POS, parse trees, and word senses provided by OntoNotes. The lemma of each word is extracted using WordNet tool.

	Training	Developing	Testing
ABC	669 (0001-0040)	163 (0041-0054)	138 (0057-0069)
CNN	1,691 (0001-0234)	964 (0235-0331)	1,146 (0333-0437)
MNB	381 (0001-0015)	130 (0016-0020)	125 (0021-0025)
NBC	351 (0001-0025)	129 (0026-0032)	86 (0033-0039)
PRI	1,205 (0001-0067)	384 (0068-0090)	387 (0091-0112)
VOA	1,238 (0001-0159)	325 (0160-0212)	331 (0213-0264)
WSJ	8,592 (0020-1446)	2,552 (1447-1705)	3,432 (1730-2454)
All	14,127	4,647	5,645

Table 2: Training, developing and testing set sizes for the seven datasets in sentences. The file ranges (in parenthesis) refer to the numbers within the names of the original OntoNotes files.

The baseline SRL system without sense information is trained with all the training corpus as described in Section 3. Its performance on the development data is F1 = 85.48%.

Table 3 shows the performance (F1) comparison on the development data among different sense extracting strategies with different feature categories. The numbers are the parameter n used in Hypernym and Root_Hyper strategies.

From Table 3, we can find that:

1. Both of the predicate sense feature and the sense path feature can improve the performance. For the predicate sense feature, we arrive at the same conclusion with Meza-Ruiz and Riedel (2009). As for the sense path feature, it is more special than the POS, therefore, it can enhance the precision.

		Subtree-word related sense	Predicate sense	Sense path
Lemma+Sense		85.34%	86.16%	85.69%
Hypernym(n)	1	85.41%	86.12%	85.74%
	2	85.48%	86.10%	85.74%
	3	85.38%	86.10%	85.69%
Root_Hyper(n)	1	85.35%	86.07%	85.96%
	2	85.45%	86.13%	85.86%
	3	85.46%	86.05%	85.91%

Table 3: The performance comparison on the development data among different sense extracting strategies with different feature categories.

2. The subtree-word related sense is almost useless. The reason is that the original lemma and POS features have been able to describe the subtree-word related information. This kind of sense features is just reduplicate.

3. For different sense feature categories (columns), the performance is not very seriously affected by different sense extracting strategies (rows). That is to say, once the sense of a word is disambiguated, the sense expressing form is not important for SRL.

In order to further improve the performance, we add the predicate sense and the sense path features simultaneously. Here, we select the Lemma+Sense strategy for the predicate sense and the Root_Hyper(1) strategy for the sense path. The final performance achieves F1 = 86.44%, which is about 1% higher than the baseline (F1 = 85.48%).

Finally, we compare the baseline (without sense) result with the word sense result on the test data. In order to see the contribution of correct word senses, we introduce a simple sense determining strategy, which use the first (the most popular) WordNet sense for each word. The final detailed comparison results are listed in Table 4.

Averagely, both of the methods with the first sense and the correct sense can perform better than the baseline. However, the improvement of the method with the first sense is not significant (χ^2-test[3] with

[3]http://graphpad.com/quickcalcs/chisquared1.cfm

		Precision	Recall	F1
ABC	w/o sense	86.25	83.01	84.60
	first sense	84.91	81.71	83.28
	word sense	87.13	83.40	85.22
CNN	w/o sense	86.67	79.97	83.19
	first sense	86.94	80.73	83.72
	word sense	87.75	80.64	84.05
MNB	w/o sense	85.29	81.69	83.45
	first sense	85.04	81.85	83.41
	word sense	86.96	82.47	84.66
NBC	w/o sense	84.49	76.42	80.26
	first sense	84.53	76.63	80.38
	word sense	86.20	77.44	81.58
PRI	w/o sense	86.48	82.29	84.34
	first sense	86.82	83.10	84.92
	word sense	87.45	83.14	85.24
VOA	w/o sense	89.87	86.65	88.23
	first sense	90.01	86.60	88.27
	word sense	91.35	87.10	89.18
WSJ	w/o sense	88.38	82.93	85.57
	first sense	88.72	83.29	85.92
	word sense	89.25	84.00	86.54
Avg	w/o sense	87.85	82.46	85.07
	first sense	88.11	82.85	85.40
	word sense	88.84	83.37	86.02

Table 4: The testing performance comparison among the baseline without (w/o) sense information, the method with the first sense, and the method with the correct word sense.

$\rho < 0.01$). Especially, for some sections, such as ABC and MNB, it is harmful to the performance. In contrast, the correct word sense can improve the performance significantly (χ^2-test with $\rho < 0.01$)and consistently. These can further prove that the word sense can enhance the semantic role labeling.

6 Conclusion

This is the first effort to adopt the word sense features into semantic role labeling. Experiments show that the subtree-word related sense features are ineffective, but the predicate sense and the sense path features can improve the performance significantly. In the future, we will use an automatic word sense disambiguation (WSD) system to obtain word senses and study the function of WSD for SRL.

Acknowledgments

This work was supported by National Natural Science Foundation of China (NSFC) via grant 60803093, 60975055, the "863" National High-Tech Research and Development of China via grant 2008AA01Z144, and Natural Scientific Research Innovation Foundation in Harbin Institute of Technology (HIT.NSRIF.2009069).

References

Adam L. Berger, Stephen A. Della Pietra, and Vincent J. Della Pietra. 1996. A maximum entropy approach to natural language processing. *Computational Linguistics*, 22.

Marine Carpuat and Dekai Wu. 2007. Improving statistical machine translation using word sense disambiguation. In *Proceedings of EMNLP/CoNLL-2007*, pages 61–72, Prague, Czech Republic, June.

Yee Seng Chan, Hwee Tou Ng, and David Chiang. 2007. Word sense disambiguation improves statistical machine translation. In *Proceedings of ACL-2007*, pages 33–40, Prague, Czech Republic, June.

Wanxiang Che, Zhenghua Li, Yongqiang Li, Yuhang Guo, Bing Qin, and Ting Liu. 2009. Multilingual dependency-based syntactic and semantic parsing. In *Proceedings of CoNLL-2009*, pages 49–54, Boulder, Colorado, June.

Jenny Rose Finkel and Christopher D. Manning. 2009. Joint parsing and named entity recognition. In *Proceedings of NAACL/HLT-2009*, pages 326–334, Boulder, Colorado, June.

Eduard Hovy, Mitchell Marcus, Martha Palmer, Lance Ramshaw, and Ralph Weischedel. 2006. Ontonotes: The 90% solution. In *Proceedings of NAACL/HLT-2006*, pages 57–60, New York City, USA, June.

Rubén Izquierdo, Armando Suárez, and German Rigau. 2007. Exploring the automatic selection of basic level concepts. In *Proceedings of RANLP-2007*.

Ivan Meza-Ruiz and Sebastian Riedel. 2009. Jointly identifying predicates, arguments and senses using markov logic. In *Proceedings of NAACL/HLT-2009*, pages 155–163, Boulder, Colorado, June.

Mihai Surdeanu, Richard Johansson, Adam Meyers, Lluís Màrquez, and Joakim Nivre. 2008. The conll 2008 shared task on joint parsing of syntactic and semantic dependencies. In *Proceedings of CoNLL-2008*, pages 159–177, Manchester, England, August.

Zhi Zhong, Hwee Tou Ng, and Yee Seng Chan. 2008. Word sense disambiguation using OntoNotes: An empirical study. In *Proceedings of EMNLP-2008*, pages 1002–1010, Honolulu, Hawaii, October.

Extending the METEOR Machine Translation Evaluation Metric to the Phrase Level

Michael Denkowski and **Alon Lavie**
Language Technologies Institute
School of Computer Science
Carnegie Mellon University
Pittsburgh, PA 15232, USA
{mdenkows,alavie}@cs.cmu.edu

Abstract

This paper presents METEOR-NEXT, an extended version of the METEOR metric designed to have high correlation with post-editing measures of machine translation quality. We describe changes made to the metric's sentence aligner and scoring scheme as well as a method for tuning the metric's parameters to optimize correlation with human-targeted Translation Edit Rate (HTER). We then show that METEOR-NEXT improves correlation with HTER over baseline metrics, including earlier versions of METEOR, and approaches the correlation level of a state-of-the-art metric, TER-plus (TERp).

1 Introduction

Recent focus on the need for accurate automatic metrics for evaluating the quality of machine translation output has spurred much development in the field of MT. Workshops such as WMT09 (Callison-Burch et al., 2009) and the MetricsMATR08 challenge (Przybocki et al., 2008) encourage the development of new MT metrics and reliable human judgment tasks.

This paper describes our work extending the METEOR metric to improve correlation with human-targeted Translation Edit Rate (HTER) (Snover et al., 2006), a semi-automatic post-editing based metric which measures the distance between MT output and a targeted reference. We identify several limitations of the original METEOR metric and describe our modifications to improve performance on this task. Our extended metric, METEOR-NEXT, is then tuned to maximize segment-level correlation with HTER scores and tested against several baseline metrics. We show that METEOR-NEXT outperforms earlier versions of METEOR when tuned to the same HTER data and approaches the performance of a state-of-the-art TER-based metric, TER-plus.

2 The METEOR-NEXT Metric

2.1 Traditional METEOR Scoring

Given a machine translation hypothesis and a reference translation, the traditional METEOR metric calculates a lexical similarity score based on a word-to-word alignment between the two strings (Banerjee and Lavie, 2005). When multiple references are available, the hypothesis is scored against each and the reference producing the highest score is used. Alignments are built incrementally in a series of stages using the following METEOR matchers:

Exact: Words are matched if and only if their surface forms are identical.

Stem: Words are stemmed using a language-appropriate Snowball Stemmer (Porter, 2001) and matched if the stems are identical.

Synonym: Words are matched if they are both members of a synonym set according to the WordNet (Miller and Fellbaum, 2007) database. This matcher is limited to translations into English.

At each stage, one of the above matchers identifies all possible word matches between the two translations using words not aligned in previous stages. An alignment is then identified as the largest subset of these matches in which every word in each sentence aligns to zero or one words in the other sen-

Human Language Technologies: The 2010 Annual Conference of the North American Chapter of the ACL, pages 250–253,
Los Angeles, California, June 2010.

tence. If multiple such alignments exist, the alignment is chosen that best preserves word order by having the fewest crossing alignment links. At the end of each stage, matched words are fixed so that they are not considered in future stages. The final alignment is defined as the union of all stage alignments.

Once an alignment has been constructed, the total number of unigram matches (m), the number of words in the hypothesis (t), and the number of words in the reference (r) are used to calculate precision ($P = m/t$) and recall ($R = m/r$). The parameterized harmonic mean of P and R (van Rijsbergen, 1979) is then calculated:

$$F_{mean} = \frac{P \cdot R}{\alpha \cdot P + (1 - \alpha) \cdot R}$$

To account for differences in word order, the minimum number of "chunks" (ch) is calculated where a chunk is defined as a series of matched unigrams that is contiguous and identically ordered in both sentences. The fragmentation ($frag = ch/m$) is then used to calculate a fragmentation penalty:

$$Pen = \gamma \cdot frag^{\beta}$$

The final METEOR score is then calculated:

$$Score = (1 - Pen) \cdot F_{mean}$$

The free parameters α, β, and γ can be tuned to maximize correlation with various types of human judgments (Lavie and Agarwal, 2007).

2.2 Extending the METEOR Aligner

Traditional METEOR is limited to unigram matches, making it strictly a word-level metric. By focusing on only one match type per stage, the aligner misses a significant part of the possible alignment space. Further, selecting partial alignments based only on the fewest number of per-stage crossing alignment links can in practice lead to missing full alignments with the same number of matches in fewer chunks. Our extended aligner addresses these limitations by introducing support for multiple-word phrase matches and considering all possible matches in a single alignment stage.

We introduce an additional **paraphrase** matcher which matches *phrases* (one or more successive words) if one phrase is considered a paraphrase of the other by a paraphrase database. For English, we use the paraphrase database developed by Snover et al. (2009), using techniques presented by Bannard and Callison-Burch (2005).

The extended aligner first constructs a search space by applying all matchers in sequence to identify all possible matches between the hypothesis and reference. To reduce redundant matches, stem and synonym matches between pairs of words which have already been identified as exact matches are not considered. Matches have start positions and *lengths* in both sentences; a word occurring less than *length* positions after a match start is said to be *covered* by the match. As exact, stem, and synonym matches will always have length one in both sentences, they can be considered phrase matches of length one. Since other matches can cover phrases of different lengths in the two sentences, matches are now said to be one-to-one at the *phrase* level rather than the *word* level.

Once all possible matches have been identified, the aligner identifies the final alignment as the largest subset of these matches meeting the following criteria in order of importance:

1. Each word in each sentence is covered by zero or one matches
2. Largest number of covered words across both sentences
3. Smallest number of chunks, where a chunk is now defined as a series of matched phrases that is contiguous and identically ordered in both sentences
4. Smallest sum of absolute distances between match start positions in the two sentences (prefer to align words and phrases that occur at similar positions in both sentences)

The resulting alignment is selected from the full space of possible alignments and directly optimizes the statistics on which the the final score will be calculated.

2.3 Extended METEOR Scoring

Once an alignment has been chosen, the METEOR-NEXT score is calculated using extended versions of the traditional METEOR statistics. We also introduce a tunable weight vector used to dictate the relative contribution of each match type. The extended METEOR score is calculated as follows.

The number of words in the hypothesis (t) and reference (r) are counted. For each of the matchers (m_i), count the number of words covered by matches of this type in the hypothesis ($m_i(t)$) and reference ($m_i(r)$) and apply the appropriate module weight (w_i). The weighted Precision and Recall are then calculated:

$$P = \frac{\sum_i w_i \cdot m_i(t)}{t} \qquad R = \frac{\sum_i w_i \cdot m_i(r)}{r}$$

The minimum number of chunks (ch) is then calculated using the new chunk definition. Once P, R, and ch are calculated, the remaining statistics and final score can be calculated as in Section 2.1.

3 Tuning for Post-Editing Measures of Quality

Human-targeted Translation Edit Rate (HTER) (Snover et al., 2006), is a semi-automatic assessment of machine translation quality based on the number of edits required to correct translation hypotheses. A human annotator edits each MT hypothesis so that it is meaning-equivalent with a reference translation, with an emphasis on making the minimum possible number of edits. The Translation Edit Rate (TER) is then calculated using the human-edited translation as a targeted reference for the MT hypothesis. The resulting scores are shown to correlate well with other types of human judgments (Snover et al., 2006).

3.1 Tuning Toward HTER

The GALE (Olive, 2005) Phase 2 unsequestered data includes HTER scores for multiple Arabic-to-English and Chinese-to-English MT systems. We used HTER scores for 10838 segments from 1045 documents from this data set to tune both the original METEOR and METEOR-NEXT. Both were exhaustively tuned to maximize the length-weighted segment-level Pearson's correlation with the HTER scores. This produced globally optimal α, β, and γ values for METEOR and optimal α, β, γ values plus stem, synonym, and paraphrase match weights for

Task	α	β	γ
Adequacy & Fluency	0.81	0.83	0.28
Ranking	0.95	0.50	0.50
HTER	0.70	1.95	0.50
HTER (extended)	0.65	1.95	0.45
	Stem	Syn	Par
	0	0.4	0.9

Table 1: Parameter values for various METEOR tasks for translations into English.

METEOR-NEXT (with the weight of exact matches fixed at 1). Table 1 compares the new HTER parameters to those tuned for other tasks including adequacy and fluency (Lavie and Agarwal, 2007) and ranking (Agarwal and Lavie, 2008).

As observed by Snover et al. (2009), HTER prefers metrics which are more balanced between precision and recall: this results in the lowest values of α for any task. Additionally, non-exact matches receive lower weights, with stem matches receiving zero weight. This reflects a weakness in HTER scoring where words with matching stems are treated as completely dissimilar, requiring full word substitutions (Snover et al., 2006).

4 Experiments

The GALE (Olive, 2005) Phase 3 unsequestered data includes HTER scores for Arabic-to-English MT output. We created a test set from HTER scores of 2245 segments from 195 documents in this data set. Our evaluation metric (METEOR-NEXT-hter) was tested against the following established metrics: BLEU (Papineni et al., 2002) with a maximum N-gram length of 4, TER (Snover et al., 2006), versions of METEOR based on release 0.7 tuned for adequacy and fluency (METEOR-0.7-af) (Lavie and Agarwal, 2007), ranking (METEOR-0.7-rank) (Agarwal and Lavie, 2008), and HTER (METEOR-0.7-hter). Also included is the HTER-tuned version of TER-plus (TERp-hter), a metric with state-of-the-art performance in recent evaluations (Snover et al., 2009). Length-weighted Pearson's and Spearman's correlation are shown for all metrics at both the segment (Table 2) and document level (Table 3). System level correlations are not shown as the Phase 3 data only contained the output of 2 systems.

Metric	Pearson's r	Spearman's ρ
BLEU-4	-0.496	-0.510
TER	0.539	0.510
METEOR-0.7-af	-0.573	-0.561
METEOR-0.7-rank	-0.561	-0.556
METEOR-0.7-hter	-0.574	-0.562
METEOR-NEXT-hter	-0.600	-0.581
TERp-hter	0.627	0.610

Table 2: Segment level correlation with HTER.

Metric	Pearson's r	Spearman's ρ
BLEU-4	-0.689	-0.686
TER	0.675	0.679
METEOR-0.7-af	-0.696	-0.699
METEOR-0.7-rank	-0.691	-0.693
METEOR-0.7-hter	-0.704	-0.705
METEOR-NEXT-hter	-0.719	-0.713
TERp-hter	0.738	0.747

Table 3: Document level correlation with HTER.

METEOR-NEXT-hter outperforms all baseline metrics at both the segment and document level. Bootstrap sampling indicates that the segment-level correlation improvements of 0.026 in Pearson's r and 0.019 in Spearman's ρ over METEOR-0.7-hter are statistically significant at the 95% level. TERp's correlation with HTER is still significantly higher across all categories. Our metric does run significantly faster than TERp, scoring approximately 120 segments per second to TERp's 3.8.

5 Conclusions

We have presented an extended METEOR metric which shows higher correlation with HTER than baseline metrics, including traditional METEOR tuned on the same data. Our extensions are not specific to HTER tasks; improved alignments and additional features should improve performance on any task having sufficient tuning data. Although our metric does not outperform TERp, it should be noted that HTER incorporates TER alignments, providing TER-based metrics a natural advantage. Our metric also scores segments relatively quickly, making it a viable choice for tuning MT systems.

Acknowledgements

This work was funded in part by NSF grants IIS-0534932 and IIS-0915327.

References

Abhaya Agarwal and Alon Lavie. 2008. Meteor, m-bleu and m-ter: Evaluation Metrics for High-Correlation with Human Rankings of Machine Translation Output. In *Proc. of WMT08*, pages 115–118.

Satanjeev Banerjee and Alon Lavie. 2005. METEOR: An Automatic Metric for MT Evaluation with Improved Correlation with Human Judgments. In *Proc. of the ACL Workshop on Intrinsic and Extrinsic Evaluation Measures for Machine Translation and/or Summarization*, pages 65–72.

Colin Bannard and Chris Callison-Burch. 2005. Paraphrasing with bilingual parallel corpora. In *Proc. of ACL05*, pages 597–604.

Chris Callison-Burch, Philipp Koehn, Christof Monz, and Josh Schroeder. 2009. Findings of the 2009 Workshop on Statistical Machine Translation. In *Proc. of WMT09*, pages 1–28.

Alon Lavie and Abhaya Agarwal. 2007. METEOR: An Automatic Metric for MT Evaluation with High Levels of Correlation with Human Judgments. In *Proc. of WMT07*, pages 228–231.

George Miller and Christiane Fellbaum. 2007. WordNet. http://wordnet.princeton.edu/.

Joseph Olive. 2005. *Global Autonomous Language Exploitation (GALE)*. DARPA/IPTO Proposer Information Pamphlet.

Kishore Papineni, Salim Roukos, Todd Ward, and Wei-Jing Zhu. 2002. BLEU: a Method for Automatic Evaluation of Machine Translation. In *Proc. of ACL02*, pages 311–318.

Martin Porter. 2001. Snowball: A language for stemming algorithms. http://snowball.tartarus.org/texts/.

M. Przybocki, K. Peterson, and S Bronsart. 2008. Official results of the NIST 2008 "Metrics for MAchine TRanslation" Challenge (MetricsMATR08). http://nist.gov/speech/tests/metricsmatr/2008/results/.

Matthew Snover, Bonnie Dorr, Richard Schwartz, Linnea Micciulla, and John Makhoul. 2006. A Study of Translation Edit Rate with Targeted Human Annotation. In *Proc. of AMTA-2006*, pages 223–231.

Matthew Snover, Nitin Madnani, Bonnie Dorr, and Richard Schwartz. 2009. Fluency, Adequacy, or HTER? Exploring Different Human Judgments with a Tunable MT Metric. In *Proc. of WMT09*, pages 259–268.

C. van Rijsbergen, 1979. *Information Retrieval*, chapter 7. 2nd edition.

Testing a Grammar Customization System with Sahaptin

Scott Drellishak
University of Washington
Seattle, WA, USA
sfd@u.washington.edu

Abstract

I briefly describe a system for automatically creating an implemented grammar of a natural language based on answers to a web-based questionnaire, then present a grammar of Sahaptin, a language of the Pacific Northwest with complex argument-marking and agreement patterns, that was developed to test the system. The development of this grammar has proved useful in three ways: (1) verifying the correct functioning of the grammar customization system, (2) motivating the addition of a new pattern of agreement to the system, and (3) making detailed predictions that uncovered gaps in the linguistic descriptions of Sahaptin.

1 Introduction

The **LinGO Grammar Matrix** (Bender et al., 2002) is a resource for building implemented precision HPSG (Pollard and Sag, 1994) grammars of natural languages. Grammars based on the Matrix are expressed in the Type Description Language (TDL) (Krieger and Schäfer, 1994), are interpretable by the Linguistic Knowledge Building system (LKB) (Copestake, 2002) (a software tool for developing constraint-based grammars), and have semantic representations that are compatible with Minimal Recursion Semantics (MRS) (Copestake et al., 2005). The Grammar Matrix project, in particular the customization system described below, has drawn on the linguistics and linguistic typology literature during its development; the system is now complex enough that it is capable making contributions back to linguistics.

1.1 Matrix Customization System

In its earliest form, the Matrix provided a set of predefined types intended to give grammar engineers a head start, allowing them to avoid duplicating the effort required to develop analyses of linguistic structures thought to occur in all languages. However, there exist many linguistic phenomena that are widespread, but not universal. If the Matrix were restricted to supporting only what is truly universal, it would be a much less useful resource for grammar-writers working on languages containing such non-universal phenomena. Our solution has been to provide the **Matrix customization system**, which presents a linguist with a web-based typological questionnaire designed to elicit a description of a target language and, based on it, automatically produce a grammar that parses and generates the target language.[1] The grammars produced are not encumbered by phenomena that do not occur in the target language; rather, they contain just enough complexity to model it as described. Although the grammars produced by the customization system are intended as a starting point for further grammar engineering, that starting point is now far enough along that even without enhancement the grammars can be used for interesting linguistic work.

The customization system is conceived of as consisting of a set of **libraries**, each of which supports a particular linguistic phenomenon, and includes a section of the questionnaire and a syntactic analysis of the target phenomenon that can be

[1] A frozen version of the customization system as described here can be found on the Web at depts.washington.edu/uwcl/matrix/sfddiss/.

Human Language Technologies: The 2010 Annual Conference of the North American Chapter of the ACL, pages 254–262,
Los Angeles, California, June 2010.

customized and included in output grammars. Recently, I have added three new libraries to the system (Drellishak, 2009). A library for case-marking supports a variety of patterns for the marking of up to two mandatory verbal arguments, including the nominative-accusative, ergative-absolutive, and tripartite patterns, as well as various split-ergative systems and Austronesian alignment (see Blake (2001) for definitions of these terms). A library for agreement supports agreement in syntactic and semantic features between verbs and their arguments. Finally, a library for so-called direct-inverse argument marking supports languages in which the marking of verbs and verbal arguments is conditioned on a grammatical scale—for example, languages in which clauses with a first person subject and a second person object are marked differently than clauses with a second person subject and a first person object. Languages can contain none, some, or all of these phenomena, and the customization system must produce consistent grammars for every combination.

1.2 Tcsting thc Customization System

Work to add new libraries to the customization system is ongoing. Since the grammatical analyses of different phenomena can interact in unexpected ways, we utilize a system of regression testing to verify that the implementation new libraries does not break older libraries.

A customization system regression test consists of three parts. First, each test includes a stored set of answers to the questionnaire describing a language that illustrates one or more linguistic phenomena; this can be fed into the customization system to create a grammar. Second, each test has a list of strings, some grammatical and some ungrammatical in the test's language, that probe the behavior of the grammar with respect to the phenomena in question. Third, each test has the expected results, including semantic representations in the format of Oepen (2001), that are produced by the grammar when it parses the test sentences.

At the time of this writing, the regression test suite includes 112 tests that fall roughly into two categories. The first category contains small artificial languages that illustrate a single phenomenon (e.g. nominative-accusative case marking or a particular word order). The second category contains larger grammars based on natural languages that illustrate a wider range of phenomena, and therefore test the interaction of the associated libraries. The largest and most complex test in the latter category is the regression test for Sahaptin.

2 Sahaptin

Sahaptin [uma] (Penutian) is a family of closely related dialects spoken in Washington, Idaho, and Oregon. The details of Sahaptin grammar are drawn primarily from a description of the language by Rigsby and Rude (1996) (henceforth R&R). It happens that Sahaptin contains extremely complex argument marking and agreement patterns that illustrate, in a single grammar, a number of phenomena covered by my recently-implemented Matrix libraries, including:

- Case marking on verbal arguments.
- Argument marking sensitive to a grammatical scale, including patterns analyzed here as proximate and obviative marking on third-person nominals.
- Two loci of agreement (a verbal prefix and a second-position enclitic) with both the subject and the object.
- A distinction in number between singular, dual, and plural on nominals, but only between singular and plural on agreement morphology.
- An inclusive/exclusive distinction in person reflected only in the second-position enclitic.

2.1 Sahaptin Grammar

This section contains a brief sketch of the structure of Sahaptin sentences. Consider the following simple sentence:

(1) *ín=aš á-tux̣nana yáamaš-na*
I=1SG 3ABS-shot mule.deer-OBJ
'I shot the mule deer.' [uma]
(Rigsby and Rude, 1996, 676)

In (1) the first word consists of the first person singular pronoun in its unmarked form, the nominative, followed by a second-position enclitic that agrees with the pronoun. The second word is the verb, consisting of a verbal prefix appropriate to the person and number of the subject and object (glossed by

R&R as 3ABS, but see §3.6 below for a different analysis) and the verb stem. The third word consists of the noun stem meaning 'mule deer' and a suffix marking the objective case.

R&R describe several cases in Sahaptin, including an unmarked "nominative" case, a marked "objective" case, an "inverse ergative" case, and an "obviative ergative" case. In spite of their use of the term "ergative", R&R make it clear that the subject generally appears in the nominative case in both transitive and intransitive clauses, and that the object consistently appears in the objective case in transitive clauses. The "inverse ergative" and "obviative ergative" forms only occur with third person singular nominals, both nouns and pronouns, in addition to the subject and object forms, and they are used to distinguish the subject from the object in transitive clauses.

In addition to case marking on nominals, Sahaptin has two ways to cross-reference the arguments of verbs: a verbal prefix and a second-position enclitic that attaches to whichever word comes first in the sentence. R&R characterize the prefixes and enclitics in two ways: first, they provide a general description of the distribution of each; second, they provide detailed paradigms of intransitive and transitive sentence patterns that cover most, but not all, of the logical combinations.

Enclitic	**Description**
=naš ~ *=aš* ~ *=š*	"first-person singular"
=na	"first-person plural inclusive"
=nataš ~ *=ataš* ~ *=taš*	"first-person plural exclusive"
=nam ~ *=am* ~ *=m*	"second-person singular"
=pam	"second-person plural"
=maš	"second-person object with first-person subject (both singular)"
=mataš	"second-person object with first-person subject (one or both plural)"

Table 1: Sahaptin enclitics (Rigsby and Rude, 1996, 675)

R&R describe Sahaptin's second-position enclitics as shown in Table 1. Notice in particular that several of the enclitics are associated with a person and number, but R&R do not mention whether those values are associated with the subject or the object. The reason for this becomes clear when we examine the full paradigm of clauses. The enclitic *=nataš*, for example, occurs with first person plural exclusive subjects in intransitive clauses; in transitive clauses, however, it occurs when one argument is first person plural exclusive and the other is third person, regardless of which is the subject and which is the object. A similar pattern can be observed for *=na* and *=naš*. This variant of scale-sensitive argument marking motivated an enhancement to the customization system described in §5 below.

Prefix	**Description**
i-	"third-person nominative"
pa-	"third-person plural nominative"
á- ~ *áw-*	"third-person absolutive"
pá-	"inverse"
patá- ~ *patáw-*	"third-person plural subject with third-person object"

Table 2: Sahaptin prefixes (Rigsby and Rude, 1996, 675)

As for Sahaptin's verbal prefixes, R&R describe them as shown in Table 2.[2] These descriptions are less straightforward than those for the enclitics. In particular, the description of *á-* ~ *áw-* as "absolutive" is misleading. Regarding that prefix, R&R write, "...this pronominal marks subjects in intransitive clauses when they are possessors, and objects in transitive clauses when the subject is first or second person." (675) In other words, it does not occur in all transitive clauses, and only in those intransitive clauses where the subject is possessive. Furthermore, all the prefixes above appear on the verb, not the nominal arguments, as one might expect for an "absolutive" affix. In spite of the use of the term "absolutive", the distribution of the prefix *á-* ~ *áw-* does not give evidence of ergative alignment in Sahaptin. Similarly, although there is evidence of argument marking sensitive to a grammatical scale, the description of *pá-* as "inverse" is misleading, since that prefix does not appear if and only if the object outranks the subject.

[2]There are three further verbal prefixes in Sahaptin that mark reflexives and reciprocals, but there is currently no support for these phenomena in the customization system.

3 Sahaptin Test Case

The phenomena described above make Sahaptin an excellent test case for demonstrating the flexibility and expressive power of the customization system. In this section, I will show how a significant fragment of Sahaptin can be described in the customization system questionnaire, producing a grammar that correctly models some of the complexity of Sahaptin morphosyntax.

It should be noted that some aspects of Sahaptin are beyond the current capabilities of the customization system, so some simplifying assumptions were necessary. For instance, the customization system models complex morphosyntax but not complex morphophonology. In effect, the grammars it outputs expect a morpheme-by-morpheme gloss as input rather than orthography, leaving the problem of morphological analysis to other systems.[3] The Sahaptin test grammar therefore uses only a single spelling for each stem and morpheme, and the morphemes are separated by '-' or '=' characters. The facts of Sahaptin word order are also too complex for the customization system; in particular, it cannot model truly free word order (i.e., discontinuous noun phrases), and the attachment behavior of the second-position enclitic is similarly beyond its capability. However, given these simplifying assumptions, the customization system is capable of modeling all the agreement and marking patterns of Sahaptin intransitive and transitive clauses shown in Tables 7 and 8 in R&R (1996, 676).

After the design and implementation of the libraries for case, direct-inverse languages, and agreement were completed, the construction of the Sahaptin test case took only about 80 hours of work, including the creation of test sentences (described in more detail in §4 below), a linguistic analysis of Sahaptin, filling out the questionnaire to reflect that analysis, and debugging the answers to the questionnaire.

3.1 Word Order

In the test grammar, I treat Sahaptin as a VSO language, and the enclitic as a suffix on verbs. This means that the sentences recognized and generated by the grammar are in a legal word order—VSO sentences with the verb followed by the second-position enclitic are grammatical in Sahaptin—but there are other legal word orders that the test grammar will not accept. The analysis of the enclitic is therefore limited by the current capabilities of the customization system's word order library; however, if that library is enhanced in the future to support second-position clitics, the analysis presented below should transfer straightforwardly.

3.2 Number

I analyze Sahaptin as having three values of number: singular (sg), dual (du), and plural (pl). All three values are distinguished on pronouns, as shown in Table 3; however, agreement with enclitics and verbal prefixes only shows a singular/plural distinction (with dual pronouns agreeing with the plural morpheme). It will be necessary in several places for the grammar to refer to a non-singular category covering *du* and *pl*. The questionnaire allows the explicit description of such a category; however, it also allows the user to select multiple values for a feature, and from those values infers the existence of categories like *non-singular*. I have made use of the latter mechanism in this grammar.

Table 3 shows the Sahaptin pronoun forms that distinguish singular, dual, and plural; in the questionnaire, therefore, I specified a number value on each. So-called plural agreement morphemes, on the other hand, do not distinguish between the dual and plural so are simply specified as covering both values.

3.3 Person

Sahaptin distinguishes three values of person: first, second, and third. The enclitics (but, interestingly, not the pronouns) further distinguish a first person inclusive and first person exclusive. I filled out the person section of the questionnaire with answers reflecting the presence of an inclusive/exclusive distinction.

3.4 Case

As described above, Sahaptin has a nominative case that marks intransitive and transitive subjects and an objective case that marks transitive objects. This

[3]The construction of such systems is well-understood (Beesley and Karttunen, 2003), as is the method for hooking up such a system to the LKB.

	Singular		Dual		Plural	
	Subject	Object	Subject	Object	Subject	Object
1	*ín*	*ináy*	*napiiní*	*napiinamanáy*	*náma*	*naamanáy*
2	*ím*	*imanáy*	*imiiní*	*imiinamanáy*	*imáy*	*imaamanáy*
3	*pɨ́n*	*paanáy*	*piiní*	*piinamanáy*	*pmáy*	*paamanáy*
3 obv erg	*piiní*					
3 inv erg	*pnɨ́m*					

Table 3: Umatilla Sahaptin Pronouns (Rigsby and Rude, 1996, 682–683)

is the common nominative-accusative pattern, so in the case section of the questionnaire I describe it as such. Note that I do *not* analyze the inverse ergative and obviative ergative as case; see §3.6 for details.

3.5 Direct-Inverse

I analyze Sahaptin as a direct-inverse language—that is, a language whose argument marking is sensitive to a grammatical scale—though one that lacks clear direct or inverse forms of the verb, with the exception of the *pá-* prefix. The scale I propose for Sahaptin is:

(2) 1P > 2P > 3P topic > 3P non-topic

The customization system interprets this scale, creating a series of rules that constrain the value of a feature DIRECTION on verbs. This feature takes the values *direct* and *inverse* and can be used to constrain the form either of verbs themselves or of their arguments.

3.6 Other Features

I use two additional features in my analysis of Sahaptin: a semantic TOPICALITY feature and a syntactic PROXIMITY feature, both on nominals.

Marking of Sahaptin transitive clauses distinguishes between topical and non-topical third person arguments. There is no overt marking of topicality on nominals, but clausal marking is conditioned on pragmatic distinctions that influence the felicity of the sentence in different discourse contexts. In order to systematically test this aspect of Sahaptin grammar in terms of string grammaticality, I introduced an artificial mark on topical noun phrases, the suffix *-TOP*. This suffix constrains the value of the TOPICALITY feature on nominal indices.

I use the syntactic PROXIMITY feature to model the "inverse ergative" and "obviative ergative" forms of nominals. In Sahaptin transitive clauses, the inverse ergative occurs precisely when the subject is third person singular and the clause is inverse (that is, the object is higher on the scale). The obviative ergative occurs in exactly one case: when the subject is third person singular and the object is a topical third person singular. These "ergative" forms function very much like the so-called proximate and obviative forms in Algonquian languages. However, in contrast to those languages, I analyze Sahaptin as having three values of the PROXIMITY feature rather than two: *proximate*, corresponding to the inverse ergative *-nɨ́m*, which promotes the marked nominal up the scale; *obviative*, corresponding to the obviative ergative *-in*, which demotes the marked nominal down the scale; and *neutral*, the unmarked form, which does not affect the nominal's position on the scale.[4]

3.7 Lexicon

Having defined the necessary features and values, we can now describe the lexicon of the Sahaptin grammar, which includes lexical types and inflectional morphemes. In the questionnaire, inflectional morphology is described as a series of slots, each attaching to one or more lexical types or other slots, and each containing one or more morphemes, each of which in turn specifies features. In order to prevent spurious ambiguity, the features on each set of morphemes are specified in such a way that no morpheme overlaps another, but also so that no legal combination of features goes unexpressed.

The simplest grammars are those that do not resort to homophony—that is, they do not have multiple lexical items or morphemes with the same

[4]Note that, for consistency with R&R's description, I nonetheless continue to refer to the marked forms as the "inverse ergative" and "obviative ergative".

spelling but different semantics or features. It is often possible to avoid homophony by adding complexity to feature hierarchies, but overly complex hierarchies can be as difficult to manage as extensive homophony. In the Sahaptin grammar, I have attempted to strike a balance between homophony and hierarchy complexity. For example, to make the grammar easier for users to understand, I segregated verbal prefixes and enclitics each into two classes: those attaching to intransitive stems and those attaching to transitive stems. This produced two homophonous variants of the prefixes *i-* and *pa-*, and of the enclitics *=naš*, *=na*, *=nataš*, *=nam*, and *=pam*. Furthermore, the distributions of two transitive prefixes (*pá-* and the null variant) and of three transitive enclitics (*=nam*, *=pam*, and *=mataš*) were easier to model using homophonous variants. Finally, the third person singular obviative pronoun and the third person dual subject pronoun are both *piiní* (as shown in Table 3) and it seemed simplest to represent these using two separate lexical entries. The grammar, then, contains 22 lexical items, of which only two are homophonous, and 24 non-null inflectional morphemes representing 12 distinctly spelled prefixes and enclitics.

A full description of the morphosyntactic details of the Sahaptin test grammar would be too long for this paper; instead, I will provide a summary.[5] The lexicon of the test grammar contains six inflectional slots: a slot for the topic morpheme described above that attaches to nominals; a slot for verbal prefixes that attach to intransitive verbs; a slot for verbal prefixes that attach to transitive verbs; a slot for enclitics that attach to intransitive verbs; a slot for enclitics that attach to transitive verbs; and a slot that contains no overt morphemes, but is used to produce lexical rules that constrain the appearance of topic, proximate, and obviative on a verb's nominal arguments. Each of these slots contains morphemes, on which are specified values for one or more features. To give an idea of what this looks like, Table 4 shows the features that are defined for the most complex of these slots, the one that contains transitive prefixes.

4 Testing the Sahaptin Grammar

In order to test the correctness of the Sahaptin grammar, it was necessary to create a suite of test sentences, some grammatical and some not, that probe its expected lexical and grammatical coverage. I started with the sentence patterns in R&R's Tables 7 and 8 (Rigsby and Rude, 1996, 676); from each, I created a sentence with the appropriate prefix, verb, enclitic, subject, and object. In every case where a plural argument was called for, I actually created two sentences, one with a dual argument—and in cases with two plural arguments, I created four: *du/du*, *du/pl*, *pl/du*, and *pl/pl*.

All these sentences were expected to be grammatical based on the descriptions in R&R. To generate ungrammatical sentences, I initially permuted the grammatical sentences in the following ways:

1. For each grammatical sentence with a prefix, I created an ungrammatical variant with the prefix missing.
2. For each grammatical sentence with an enclitic, I created an ungrammatical variant with the enclitic missing.
3. For each grammatical sentence, I created variants that contained every incorrect prefix and variants that contained every incorrect enclitic.

After duplicates were removed, this produced a list of 89 grammatical and 220 ungrammatical sentences, for a total of 309.

The permutation of the grammatical sentences as described above was sufficient to test the phenomena of interest for intransitive sentences, producing ungrammatical sentences consisting of correctly-formed words in the correct basic word order but with an ungrammatical agreement pattern, and this permutation was a small enough job to perform by hand. For transitive sentences, though, there is a much larger space of sentences with the right word order but wrong agreement, so in order to test the grammar thoroughly, I decided to supplement the ungrammatical sentences I created by hand by writing a small program to generate every sentence containing the verb *q̓ínun* 'see' that followed the pattern:

[5] The full details of the Sahaptin grammar can be found in my dissertation (Drellishak, 2009). How the questionnaire can be filled out to model Sahaptin can be seen by visiting the customization system web site at `depts.washington.edu/uwcl/matrix/sfddiss/` and clicking the Umatilla Sahaptin link at the bottom of the main page, which fills out the questionnaire automatically.

Transitive prefix	Subject PERNUM	Subject TOPICALITY	Object PERNUM	Object TOPICALITY
i-	*3sg*			*non-topic*
pa-	*3du, 3pl*			*non-topic*
á-	*1st, 2nd*		*3rd*	
pá-	*2sg*		*1sg*	
pá-	*3sg*	*non-topic*	*3sg*	*topic*
patá-	*3du, 3pl*	*non-topic*	*3sg*	*topic*
∅	*1st*		*2nd*	
∅	*2du, 2pl*		*1st*	
∅	*2sg*		*1du, 1pl*	

Table 4: Morphemes appearing in the transitive prefix slot

(3) **prefix-*q̓ínun*=enclitic subject object**

The possible fillers for each position in (3) are shown in Table 5:

prefix	*i-, pa-, á-, pá-, patá-,* and ∅
enclitic	*=naš, =na, =nataš, =nam, =pam, =maš, =mataš,* and ∅
subject	subject forms in Table 3
object	object forms in Table 3

Table 5: Fillers for positions in (3)

As mentioned above, the lexicon of the Sahaptin grammar, and consequently the test sentences, uses the various forms of the personal pronoun to represent the possible person, number, case, and proximity values of subject and object noun phrases. In addition to plain case-marked pronouns, the subject and object positions may also contain third person pronouns marked as the topic with *-TOP*.

Generating every sentence that followed the pattern in (3) produced 6048 sentences, but some additional filtering was required. First, since it appears that topic marking is only relevant when disambiguating third person arguments, I removed all sentences where the *-TOP* suffix appeared with a first or second person pronoun. Second, 192 of the permutations of (3) are actually duplicates of the ungrammatical transitive test sentences created by hand above, so I removed those as well. After filtering, a total of 5856 programmatically-generated sentences remained. Added to the aforementioned 309 examples, this made 6165 unique test sentences.

After using the customization system to generate a grammar of Sahaptin, I used that grammar to attempt to parse every test sentence. All 89 sentences corresponding to R&R's grammatical transitive and intransitive patterns parsed and were assigned exactly one analysis.[6] Among the ungrammatical sentences, 5848 out of 5856 failed to parse, as expected. To my surprise, however, eight of the sentences did parse. These sentences were:

(4) a. *i-q̓ínun pɨ́n-TOP piinamanáy*
3SG-see 3SG.NOM-TOP 3DU.OBJ
'He saw them (DU).'

b. *i-q̓ínun pɨ́n-TOP paamanáy*
3SG-see 3SG.NOM-TOP 3PL.OBJ
'He saw them.'

c. *pa-q̓ínun piiní paanáy*
3NONSG-see 3DU.NOM 3SG.OBJ
'They (DU) saw him.'

d. *pa-q̓ínun pmáy paanáy*
3NONSG-see 3PL.NOM 3SG.OBJ
'They saw him.'

e. *pa-q̓ínun piiní-TOP piinamanáy*
3NONSG-see 3DU.NOM-TOP 3DU.OBJ
'They (DU) saw them (DU).'

f. *pa-q̓ínun piiní-TOP paamanáy*
3NONSG-see 3DU.NOM-TOP 3PL.OBJ
'They (DU) saw them.'

g. *pa-q̓ínun pmáy-TOP piinamanáy*
3NONSG-see 3PL.NOM-TOP 3DU.OBJ
'They saw them (DU).'

h. *pa-q̓ínun pmáy-TOP paamanáy*
3NONSG-see 3PL-TOP.NOM 3PL.OBJ
'They saw them.'

[6]Multiple analyses would not necessarily have been wrong—some sentences in some languages are structurally ambiguous—but the grammatical Sahaptin sentences in the test suite are marked explicitly enough for agreement that none was ambiguous.

Notice that the eight sentences fall into three patterns. The first two sentences have a third person singular topical subject and a third person non-singular non-topical object, the next two have a third person non-singular non-topical subject and a third person singular non-topical object, and the last four have a third person non-singular topical subject and a third person non-topical object. These are precisely the patterns that are absent from R&R's Table 8; corresponding sentences were therefore not included in the list of 89 grammatical sentences. In developing the Sahaptin grammar, I had, without considering these eight patterns, defined the prefixes in such a way that the grammar expected *i-* to appear in the first two sentences and *pa-* in the last six.

In order to determine whether this analysis was correct, Sharon Hargus presented the Yakima Sahaptin equivalents of the sentences in (4) by telephone to Virginia Beavert, a native speaker of that dialect, who accepted all eight of them with the readings shown in (4). Note that, in order for these sentences to be acceptable, they had to be cast in the past tense, a feature not modeled in my Sahaptin grammar fragment. Note also that Dr. Beavert considered sentence (4c) somewhat less acceptable, saying that it is "[a] little awkward, but has meaning."

The Sahaptin grammar, then, which was created using the customization system and based on its support for case, direct-inverse languages, and agreement, correctly analysed all 6165 of the test sentences, including eight that fell outside of the patterns described in the linguistic literature.

5 Summary and Discussion

Based on these results, I conclude that even Sahaptin, a language with extremely complex argument marking morphology, can be modeled using the customization system. Note that the system was not designed with the facts of Sahaptin in mind, and with two exceptions, the system did not need to be modified to enable it to handle Sahaptin.

One of the exceptions was trivial: formerly, grammars produced by the system treated '=' as punctuation, stripping it out and breaking words containing it. The other exception concerns an unusual agreement pattern I first encountered in Sahaptin: morphemes that agree, not with the subject or the object of a verb, but with the nominal argument that is more highly ranked on the direct-inverse scale. Supporting this agreement pattern proved worthwhile later, when it was used again in a test grammar for Plains Cree [crk] (Algonquian), another direct-inverse language. Although this latter change was a substantive one that allows grammars to be described more compactly, it did not increase the descriptive power of the system—languages showing that pattern of agreement could still be modeled using duplicated, homophonous morphemes. Such an enhancement to the system is an example of the feedback loop between grammar engineering and customization system development, where new languages with new phenomena (or new variations of old phenomena) inform the design and, in some cases, the descriptive power of the system.

After constructing the Sahaptin grammar and test suite described here, it was natural to include it in two places in the customization system. First, it is now one of the regression tests that is regularly run to ensure that future enhancement of the system does not break earlier features. Second, Sahaptin has been added to the list of sample grammars accessible from the main page of the questionnaire—by clicking on links in this list, users can see detailed examples of how the questionnaire can be filled out to model a target language.

The Sahaptin grammar, developed using the customization system, has proved itself useful—not only to the Grammar Matrix project, where it inspired the addition of support for scale-sensitive agreement and serves as a regression test of the correct functioning of the system, but also to the field of linguistics. By analyzing Sahaptin in the precise detail required by the customization system, I found unnoticed gaps in linguistic descriptions of the language, and in collaboration with linguists studying the language was able to help resolve those gaps.

Acknowledgments

My thanks go to Emily Bender and the Matrix team, Sharon Hargus, and Virginia Beavert. This work was supported by a gift to the Turing Center from the Utilika Foundation, by the Max Planck Institute for Evolutionary Anthropology, and by the National Science Foundation under Grant No. 0644097.

References

[Beesley and Karttunen2003] Kenneth R. Beesley and Lauri Karttunen. 2003. *Finite State Morphology*. CSLI, Stanford.

[Bender et al.2002] Emily M. Bender, Dan Flickinger, and Stephan Oepen. 2002. The grammar matrix. In *Proceedings of COLING 2002 Workshop on Grammar Engineering and Evaluation*, Taipei, Taiwan.

[Blake2001] Barry J. Blake. 2001. *Case, Second Edition*. Cambridge University Press, Cambridge.

[Copestake et al.2005] Ann Copestake, Dan Flickinger, Carl Pollard, and Ivan A. Sag. 2005. Minimal recursion semantics: An introduction. *Research on Language & Computation*, 3(2–3):281–332.

[Copestake2002] Ann Copestake. 2002. *Implementing Typed Feature Structure Grammars*. CSLI, Stanford.

[Drellishak2009] Scott Drellishak. 2009. *Widespread, but Not Universal: Improving the Typological Coverage of the Grammar Matrix*. Ph.D. thesis, University of Washington.

[Krieger and Schäfer1994] Hans-Ulrich Krieger and Ulrich Schäfer. 1994. Tdl – a type description language for constraint-based grammars. In *Proceedings of the 15th International Conference on Computational Linguistics*, pages 893–899, Kyoto, Japan.

[Oepen2001] Stephan Oepen. 2001. [incr tsdb()] — Competence and performance laboratory. User manual. Technical report, Saarbrücken, Germany.

[Pollard and Sag1994] Carl Pollard and Ivan A. Sag. 1994. *Head-Driven Phrase Structure Grammar*. CSLI, Stanford.

[Rigsby and Rude1996] Bruce Rigsby and Noel Rude. 1996. Sketch of sahaptin, a sahaptian language. In Ives Goddard, editor, *Languages*, pages 666–92. Smithsonian Institution, Washington DC.

Two monolingual parses are better than one (synchronous parse)*

Chris Dyer
UMIACS Laboratory for Computational Linguistics and Information Processing
Department of Linguistics
University of Maryland, College Park, MD 20742, USA
redpony AT umd.edu

Abstract

We describe a synchronous parsing algorithm that is based on two successive *monolingual* parses of an input sentence pair. Although the worst-case complexity of this algorithm is and must be $O(n^6)$ for binary SCFGs, its average-case run-time is far better. We demonstrate that for a number of common synchronous parsing problems, the two-parse algorithm substantially outperforms alternative synchronous parsing strategies, making it efficient enough to be utilized without resorting to a pruned search.

1 Introduction

Synchronous context free grammars (SCFGs) generalize monolingual context-free grammars to generate strings concurrently in pairs of languages (Lewis and Stearns, 1968) in much the same way that finite state transducers (FSTs) generalize finite state automata (FSAs).[1] *Synchronous parsing* is the problem of finding the best derivation, or forest of derivations, of a source and target sentence pair $\langle \mathbf{f}, \mathbf{e} \rangle$ under an SCFG, $\mathcal{G}$.[2] Solving this problem is necessary for several applications, for example, optimizing how well an SCFG translation model fits parallel training data. Wu (1997) describes a bottom-up $O(n^6)$ synchronous parsing algorithm for ITGs, a binary SCFG with a restricted form. For general grammars, the situation is even worse: the problem has been shown to be NP-hard (Satta and Peserico, 2005). Even if we restrict ourselves to binary ITGs, the $O(n^6)$ run-time makes large-scale learning applications infeasible. The usual solution is to use a heuristic search that avoids exploring edges that are likely (but not guaranteed) to be low probability (Zhang et al., 2008; Haghighi et al., 2009). In this paper, we derive an alternative synchronous parsing algorithm starting from a conception of parsing with SCFGs as a composition of binary relations. This enables us to factor the synchronous parsing problem into two successive *monolingual* parses. Our algorithm runs more efficiently than $O(n^6)$ with many grammars (including those that required using heuristic search with other parsers), making it possible to take advantage of synchronous parsing without developing search heuristics; and the SCFGs are not required to be in a normal form, making it possible to easily parse with more complex SCFG types.

2 Synchronous parsing

Before presenting our algorithm, we review the $O(n^6)$ synchronous parser for binary ITGs.[3]

2.1 ITG synchronous parsing algorithm

Wu (1997) describes a bottom-up synchronous parsing algorithm that can be understood as a generalization of the CKY algorithm. CKY defines a table consisting of n^2 cells, with each cell corresponding to a span $[i, j]$ in the input sentence; and the synchronous variant defines a table in 4 dimensions, with cells corresponding to a source span $[s, t]$ *and* a target span $[u, v]$. The bottom of the chart is initialized first, and pairs of items are combined from bottom to top. Since combining items from the n^4 cells involves considering two split points (one source, one target), it is not hard to see that this algorithm runs in time $O(n^6)$.

*This work was supported in part by the GALE program of DARPA, Contract No. HR0011-06-2-001. The author wishes to thank Philip Rensik, Adam Lopez, Phil Blunsom, and Jason Eisner for helpful discussions.

[1] SCFGs have enjoyed a resurgence in popularity as the formal basis for a number of statistical translation systems, e.g. Chiang (2007). However, translation requires only the manipulation of SCFGs using monolingual parsing algorithms.

[2] It is assumed that $n = |\mathbf{f}| \approx |\mathbf{e}|$.

[3] Generalizing the algorithm to higher rank grammars is possible (Wu, 1997), as is converting a grammar to a weakly equivalent binary form in some cases (Huang et al., 2009).

Human Language Technologies: The 2010 Annual Conference of the North American Chapter of the ACL, pages 263–266, Los Angeles, California, June 2010.

2.2 Parsing, intersection, and composition

We motivate an alternative conception of the synchronous parsing problem as follows. It has long been appreciated that monolingual parsing computes the intersection of an FSA and a CFG (Bar-Hillel et al., 1961; van Noord, 1995). That is, if S is an FSA encoding some sentence $\mathbf{s}$, intersection of S with a CFG, $\mathcal{G}$, results in a parse forest which contains all and only derivations of $\mathbf{s}$, that is $L(S) \cap L(\mathcal{G}) \in \{\{\mathbf{s}\}, \emptyset\}$.[4] Crucially for our purposes, the resulting parse forest *is also itself a CFG*.[5] Figure 1 illustrates, giving two equivalent representations of the forest $S \cap \mathcal{G}$, once as a directed hypergraph and once as a CFG. While $S \cap \mathcal{G}$ appears similar to $\mathcal{G}$, the non-terminals (NTs) of the resulting CFG are a cross product of pairs of states from S and NTs from $\mathcal{G}$.[6]

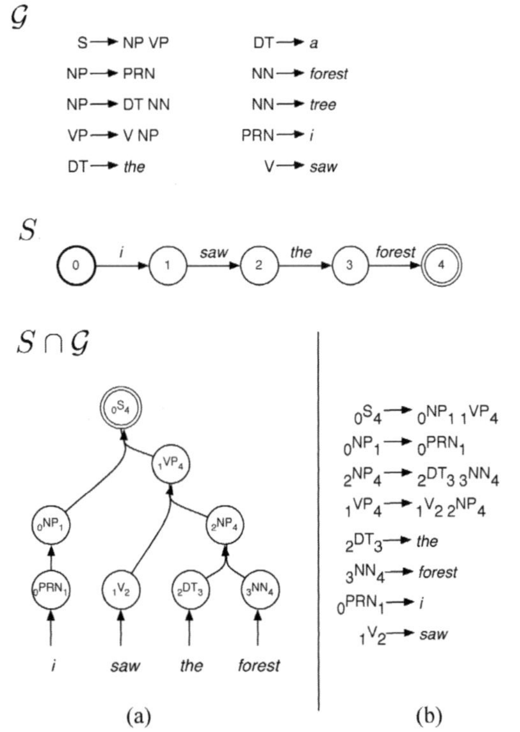

Figure 1: A CFG, $\mathcal{G}$, an FSA, S, encoding a sentence, and two equivalent representations of the parse forest $S \cap \mathcal{G}$, (a) as a directed hypergraph and (b) as a CFG.

When dealing with SCFGs, rather than intersection, parsing computes a related operation, *composition*.[7] The standard MT decoding-by-parsing task can be understood as computing the composition of an FST,[8] F, which encodes the source sentence $\mathbf{f}$ with the SCFG, $\mathcal{G}$, representing the translation model. The result is the translation forest, $F \circ \mathcal{G}$, which encodes all translations of $\mathbf{f}$ licensed by the translation model. While $\mathcal{G}$ can generate a potentially infinite set of strings in the source and target languages, $F \circ \mathcal{G}$ generates *only* $\mathbf{f}$ in the source language (albeit with possibly infinitely many derivations), but any number of different strings in the target language. It is not hard to see that a second composition operation of an FST, E, encoding the target string $\mathbf{e}$ with the e-side of $F \circ \mathcal{G}$ (again using a monolingual parsing algorithm), will result in a parse forest that exactly derives $\langle \mathbf{f}, \mathbf{e} \rangle$, which is the goal of synchronous composition. Figure 2 shows an example. In $F \circ \mathcal{G} \circ E$ the NTs (nodes) are the cross product of pairs of states from E, the NTs from $\mathcal{G}$, and pairs of states in F.

Thus, synchronous parsing is the task of computing $F \circ \mathcal{G} \circ E$. Since composition is associative, we can compute this quantity either as $(F \circ \mathcal{G}) \circ E$ or $F \circ (\mathcal{G} \circ E)$. Alternatively, we can use an algorithm that performs 3-way composition directly.

2.3 The two-parse algorithm[9]

The *two-parse algorithm* refers to performing a synchronous parse by computing either $(F \circ \mathcal{G}) \circ E$ or $F \circ (\mathcal{G} \circ E)$. Each composition operation is carried out using a standard monolingual parsing algorithm, such as Earley's or CKY. In the experiments below, since we use ϵ-free grammars, we use a variant of CKY for unrestricted CFGs (Chiang, 2007).

Once the first composition is done, the resulting parse forest must be converted into a CFG representation that the second parser can utilize. This is straightforward to do: each node becomes a unique non-terminal symbol, with its incoming edges corresponding to different ways of rewriting it. Tails of edges are non-terminal variables in the RHS of these rewrites. A single bottom-up traversal of the forest is sufficient to perform the conversion. Since

[4] $L(x)$ denotes the set of strings generated by the grammar/automaton x. In future mentions of intersection and composition operations, this will be implicit.

[5] The forest grammar derives only $\mathbf{s}$, but using possibly many derivations.

[6] Each pair of states from the FSA corresponds to a span $[i, j]$ in a CKY table.

[7] Intersection is a special case of composition where the input and output labels on the transducers are identical (Mohri, 2009).

[8] FSTs used to represent the source and target sentences have identical input and output labels on every transition.

[9] Satta (submitted) has independently derived this algorithm.

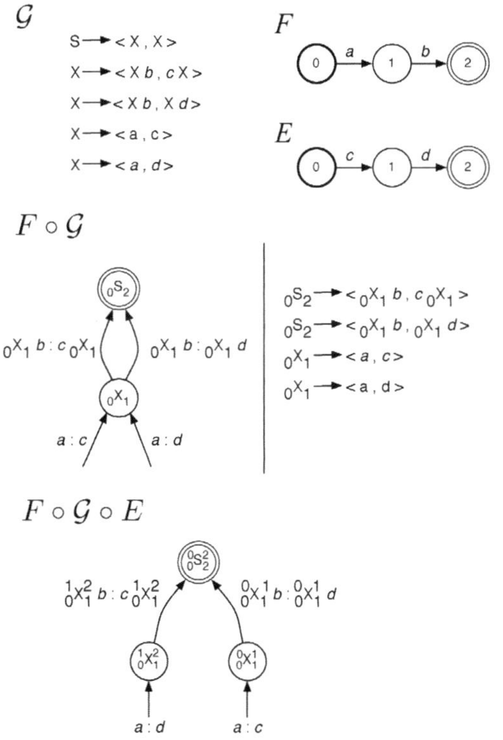

Figure 2: An SCFG, $\mathcal{G}$, two FSAs, E and F, and two equivalent representations of $F \circ \mathcal{G}$. The synchronous parse forest of the pair $\langle ab, cd \rangle$ with $\mathcal{G}$ is given under $F \circ \mathcal{G} \circ E$.

our parser operates more efficiently with a determinized grammar, we left-factor the grammar during this traversal as well.

Analysis. Monolingual parsing runs in worst case $O(|\mathcal{G}| \cdot n^3)$ time, where n is the length of the input being parsed and $|\mathcal{G}|$ is a measure of the size of the grammar (Graham et al., 1980). Since the grammar term is constant for most typical parsing applications, it is generally not considered carefully; however, in the two-parse algorithm, the size of the grammar term for the second parse is not $|\mathcal{G}|$ but $|F \circ \mathcal{G}|$, which clearly depends on the size of the input F; and so understanding the impact of this term is key to understanding the algorithm's run-time.

If $\mathcal{G}$ is an ϵ-free SCFG with non-terminals N and maximally two NTs in a rule's right hand side, and n is the number of states in F (corresponding to the number of words in the $\mathbf{f}$ in a sentence pair $\langle \mathbf{f}, \mathbf{e} \rangle$), then the number of nodes in the parse forest $F \circ \mathcal{G}$ will be $O(|N| \cdot n^2)$. This can be shown easily since by stipulation, we are able to use CKY+ to perform the parse, and there will be maximally as many nodes in the forest as there are cells in the CKY chart times the number of NTs. The number of edges will be $O(|N| \cdot n^3)$, which occurs when every node can be derived from all possible splits. This bound on the number of edges implies that $|F \circ \mathcal{G}| \in O(n^3)$.[10] Therefore, the worst case run-time of the two-parse algorithm is $O(|N| \cdot n^3 \cdot n^3 + |\mathcal{G}| \cdot n^3) = O(|N| \cdot n^6)$, the same as the bound on the ITG algorithm. We note that while the ITG algorithm requires that the SCFGs be rank-2 and in a normal form, the two-parse algorithm analysis holds as long as the grammars are rank-2 and ϵ-free.[11]

3 Experiments

We now describe two different synchronous parsing applications, with different classes of SCFGs, and compare the performance of the two-parse algorithm with that of previously used algorithms.

Phrasal ITGs. Here we compare performance of the two-parse algorithm and the $O(n^6)$ ITG parsing algorithm on an Arabic-English phrasal ITG alignment task. We used a variant of the phrasal ITG described by Zhang et al. (2008).[12] Figure 3 plots the average run-time of the two algorithms as a function of the Arabic sentence length. The two-parse approach is far more efficient. In total, aligning the 80k sentence pairs in the corpus completed in less than 4 hours with the two-parse algorithm but required more than 1 week with the baseline algorithm.[13]

"Hiero" grammars. An alternative approach to computing a synchronous parse forest is based on *cube pruning* (Huang and Chiang, 2007). While more commonly used to integrate a target m-gram LM during decoding, Blunsom et al. (2008), who required synchronous parses to discriminatively train

[10] How tight these bounds are depends on the ambiguity in the grammar w.r.t. the input: to generate n^3 edges, every item in every cell must be derivable by every combination of its subspans. Most grammars are substantially less ambiguous.

[11] Since many widely used SCFGs meet these criteria, including hierarchical phrase-based translation grammars (Chiang, 2007), SAMT grammars (Zollmann and Venugopal, 2006), and phrasal ITGs (Zhang et al., 2008), a detailed analysis of ϵ-containing and higher rank grammars is left to future work.

[12] The restriction that phrases contain exactly a single alignment point was relaxed, resulting in much larger and more ambiguous grammars than those used in the original work.

[13] A note on implementation: our ITG aligner was minimal; it only computed the probability of the sentence pair using the inside algorithm. With the two-parse aligner, we stored the complete forest during both the first and second parses.

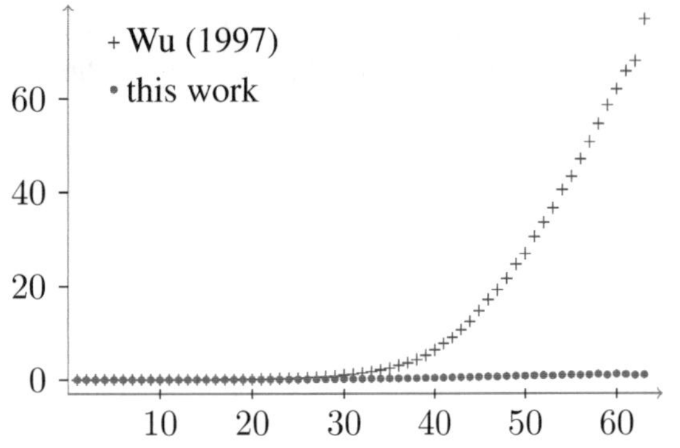

Figure 3: Average synchronous parser run-time (in seconds) as a function of Arabic sentence length (in words).

an SCFG translation model, repurposed this algorithm to discard partial derivations during translation of **f** if the derivation yielded a target m-gram not found in **e** (p.c.). We replicated their BTEC Chinese-English baseline system and compared the speed of their 'cube-parsing' technique and our two-parse algorithm.[14] The SCFG used here was extracted from a word-aligned corpus, as described in Chiang (2007).[15] The following table compares the average per sentence synchronous parse time.

Algorithm	avg. run-time (sec)
Blunsom et al. (2008)	7.31
this work	0.20

4 Discussion

Thinking of synchronous parsing as two composition operations has both conceptual and practical benefits. The two-parse strategy can outperform both the ITG parsing algorithm (Wu, 1997), as well as the 'cube-parsing' technique (Blunsom et al., 2008). The latter result points to a connection with recent work showing that determinization of edges before LM integration leads to fewer search errors during decoding (Iglesias et al., 2009).

Our results are somewhat surprising in light of work showing that 3-way composition algorithms for FSTs operate far more efficiently than performing successive pairwise compositions (Allauzen and Mohri, 2009). This is certainly because the 3-way algorithm used here (the ITG algorithm) does an exhaustive search over all n^4 span pairs without awareness of any top-down constraints. This suggests that faster composition algorithms that incorporate top-down filtering may still be discovered.

[14] To the extent possible, the two experiments were carried out using the exact same code base, which was a C++ implementation of an SCFG-based decoder.

[15] Because of the mix of terminal and non-terminal symbols, such grammars cannot be used by the ITG synchronous parsing algorithm.

References

C. Allauzen and M. Mohri. 2009. N-way composition of weighted finite-state transducers. *International Journal of Foundations of Comp. Sci.*, 20(4):613–627.

Y. Bar-Hillel, M. Perles, and E. Shamir. 1961. On formal properties of simple phrase structure grammars. *Zeitschrift für Phonetik, Sprachwissenschaft und Kommunikationsforschung*, 14:143–172.

P. Blunsom, T. Cohn, and M. Osborne. 2008. Probalistic inference for machine translation. In *EMNLP*.

D. Chiang. 2007. Hierarchical phrase-based translation. *Computational Linguistics*, 33(2):201–228.

S. L. Graham, W. L. Ruzzo, and M. Harrison. 1980. An improved context-free recognizer. *ACM Trans. Program. Lang. Syst.*, 2(3):415–462.

A. Haghighi, J. Blitzer, J. DeNero, and D. Klein. 2009. Better word alignments with supervised ITG models. In *Proc. of ACL/IJCNLP*, pages 923–931.

L. Huang and D. Chiang. 2007. Forest rescoring: Faster decoding with integrated language models. In *ACL*.

L. Huang, H. Zhang, D. Gildea, and K. Knight. 2009. Binarization of synchronous context-free grammars. *Computational Linguistics*, 35(4).

G. Iglesias, A. de Gispert, E. R. Banga, and W. Byrne. 2009. Hierarchical phrase-based translation with weighted finite state transducers. In *Proc. NAACL*.

P. M. Lewis, II and R. E. Stearns. 1968. Syntax-directed transduction. *J. ACM*, 15(3):465–488.

M. Mohri. 2009. Weighted automata algorithms. In M. Droste, W. Kuich, and H. Vogler, editors, *Handbook of Weighted Automata*, Monographs in Theoretical Computer Science, pages 213–254. Springer.

G. Satta and E. Peserico. 2005. Some computational complexity results for synchronous context-free grammars. In *Proceedings of NAACL*.

G. Satta. submitted. Translation algorithms by means of language intersection.

G. van Noord. 1995. The intersection of finite state automata and definite clause grammars. In *Proc. of ACL*.

D. Wu. 1997. Stochastic inversion transduction grammars and bilingual parsing of parallel corpora. *Computational Linguistics*, 23(3):377–404.

H. Zhang, C. Quirk, R. C. Moore, and D. Gildea. 2008. Bayesian learning of non-compositional phrases with synchronous parsing. In *Proceedings of ACL*.

A. Zollmann and A. Venugopal. 2006. Syntax augmented machine translation via chart parsing. In *Proc. of the Workshop on SMT*.

Fast Query for Large Treebanks

Sumukh Ghodke[*]
[*]Department of Computer Science
and Software Engineering,
University of Melbourne
Victoria 3010, Australia

Steven Bird[*†]
[†]Linguistic Data Consortium,
University of Pennsylvania
3600 Market Street, Suite 810
Philadelphia PA 19104, USA

Abstract

A variety of query systems have been developed for interrogating parsed corpora, or treebanks. With the arrival of efficient, wide-coverage parsers, it is feasible to create very large databases of trees. However, existing approaches that use in-memory search, or relational or XML database technologies, do not scale up. We describe a method for storage, indexing, and query of treebanks that uses an information retrieval engine. Several experiments with a large treebank demonstrate excellent scaling characteristics for a wide range of query types. This work facilitates the curation of much larger treebanks, and enables them to be used effectively in a variety of scientific and engineering tasks.

1 Introduction

The problem of representing and querying linguistic annotations has been an active area of research for several years. Much of the work has grown from efforts to curate large databases of annotated text such as *treebanks*, for use in developing and testing language technologies (Marcus et al., 1993; Abeillé, 2003; Hockenmaier and Steedman, 2007). At least a dozen linguistic tree query languages have been developed for interrogating treebanks (see §2).

While high quality syntactic parsers are able to efficiently annotate large quantities of English text (Clark and Curran, 2007), existing approaches to query do not work on the same scale. Many existing systems load the entire corpus into memory and check a user-supplied query against every tree. Others avoid the memory limitation, and use relational or XML database systems. Although these have built-in support for indexes, they do not scale up either (Ghodke and Bird, 2008; Zhang et al., 2001)).

The ability to interrogate large collections of parsed text has important practical applications. First, it opens the way to a new kind of information retrieval (IR) that is sensitive to syntactic information, permitting users to do more focussed search. At the simplest level, an ambiguous query term like *wind* or *park* could be disambiguated with the help of a POS tag (e.g. `wind/N`, `park/V`). (Existing IR engines already support query with part-of-speech tags (Chowdhury and McCabe, 1998)). More complex queries could stipulate the syntactic category of *apple* is in subject position.

A second benefit of large scale tree query is for natural language processing. For example, we might compute the likelihood that a given noun appears as the agent or patient of a verb, as a measure of animacy. We can use features derived from syntactic trees in order to support semantic role labeling, language modeling, and information extraction (Chen and Rambow, 2003; Collins et al., 2005; Hakenberg et al., 2009). A further benefit for natural language processing, though not yet realized, is for a treebank and query engine to provide the underlying storage and retrieval for a variety of linguistic applications. Just as a relational database is present in most business applications, providing reliable and efficient access to relational data, such a system would act as a repository of annotated texts, and expose an expressive API to client applications.

A third benefit of large scale tree query is to support syntactic investigations, e.g. for develop-

Human Language Technologies: The 2010 Annual Conference of the North American Chapter of the ACL, pages 267–275,
Los Angeles, California, June 2010.

ing syntactic theories or preparing materials for language learners. Published treebanks will usually not attest particular words in the context of some infrequent construction, to the detriment of syntactic studies that make predictions about such combinations, and language learners wanting to see instances of some construction involving words from some specialized topic. A much larger treebank alleviates these problems. To improve recall performance, multiple parses for a given sentence could be stored (possibly derived from different parsers).

A fourth benefit for large scale tree query is to support the curation of treebanks, a major enterprise in its own right (Abeillé, 2003). Manual selection and correction of automatically generated parse trees is a substantial part of the task of preparing a treebank. At the point of making such decisions, it is often helpful for an annotator to view existing annotations of a given construction which have already been manually validated (Hiroshi et al., 2005). Occasionally, an earlier annotation decision may need to be reconsidered in the light of new examples, leading to further queries and to corrections that are spread across the whole corpus (Wallis, 2003; Xue et al., 2005).

This paper explores a new methods for scaling up tree query using an IR engine. In §2 we describe existing tree query systems, elaborating on the design decisions, and on key aspects of their implementation and performance. In §3 we describe a method for indexing trees using an IR engine, and discuss the details of our open source implementation. In §4 we report results from a variety of experiments involving two data collections. The first collection contains of 5.5 million parsed trees, two orders of magnitude larger than those used by existing tree query systems, while the second collection contains 26.5 million trees.

2 Treebank Query

A tree query system needs to be able to identify trees having particular properties. On the face of it, this should be possible to achieve by writing simple programs over treebank files on disk. The programs would match tree structures using regular expression patterns, possibly augmented with syntax for matching tree structure. However, tree query is a more complex and interesting task, due to several factors which we list below.

Structure of the data: There are many varieties of treebank. Some extend the nested bracketing syntax to store morphological information. Others store complex attribute-value matrices in tree nodes or have tree-valued attributes (Oepen et al., 2002), or store dependency structures (Čmejrek et al., 2004), or categorial grammar derivations (Hockenmaier and Steedman, 2007). Others store multiple overlapping trees (Cassidy and Harrington, 2001; Heid et al., 2004; Volk et al., 2007).

Form of results: Do we want entire trees, or matching subtrees, or just a count of the number of results? Do we need some indication of why the query matched a particular tree, perhaps by showing how query terms relate to a hit, cf. document snippets and highlighted words in web search results? Do we want to see multiple hits when a query matches a particular tree in more than one place? Do we want to see tree diagrams, or some machine-readable tree representation that can be used in external analysis? Can a query serve to update the treebank, cf. SQL update queries?

Number of results: Do we want all results, or the first n results in document order, or the "best" n results, where our notion of best might be based on representativeness or distinctiveness.

Description language: Do we prefer to describe trees by giving examples of tree fragments, replacing some nodes replaced with wildcards (Hiroshi et al., 2005; Ichikawa et al., 2006; Mírovský, 2006)? Or do we prefer a path language (Rohde, 2005; Lai and Bird, 2010)? Or perhaps we prefer a language involving variables, quantifiers, boolean operators, and negation (König and Lezius, 2001; Kepser, 2003; Pajas and Štěpánek, 2009)? What built-in tree relations are required, beyond the typical parent/child, ancestor/descendent, sibling and temporal relations? (E.g. last child, leftmost descendent, parent's following sibling, pronoun's antecedent.) Do we need to describe tree nodes using regular expressions, or attributes and values? Do we need a type system, a pattern language, or boolean logic for talking about attribute values? The expressive requirements of the query language have been discussed at length elsewhere (Lai and Bird, 2004; Mírovský, 2008), and we will not consider them further here.

Performance: What performance is acceptable, especially as the data size grows? Do we want to optimize multiple reformulations of a query, for users who iteratively refine a query based on query results? Do we want to optimize certain query types? Are queries performed interactively or in batch mode? Is the treebank stable, or being actively revised, in which case indexes need to be easily updatable? Do we expect logically identical queries to have the same performance, so that users do not have to rewrite their queries for efficiency? Key performance measures are index size and search times.

Architecture: Is the query system standalone, or does it exist in a client-server architecture? Is there a separate user-interface layer that interacts with a data server using a well-defined API, or is it a monolithic system? Should it translate queries into another language, such as SQL (Bird et al., 2006; Nakov et al., 2005), or XQuery (Cassidy, 2002; Mayo et al., 2006), or to automata (Maryns and Kepser, 2009), in order to benefit from the performance optimizations they provide

Indexing. The indexing methods used in individual systems are usually not reported. Many systems display nearly constant time for querying a database, regardless of the selectivity of a query, a strong indicator that no indexes are being used. For example, Emu performs all queries in memory with no indexes, and several others are likely to be the same (Cassidy and Harrington, 2001; König and Lezius, 2001; Heid et al., 2004). TGrep2 (Rohde, 2005) uses a custom corpus file and processes it sentence by sentence at query execution time. Other tree query systems use hashed indexes or other types of in-memory indexes. However, a common drawback of these systems is that they are designed for treebanks that are at most a few million words in size, and do not scale well to much larger treebanks.

There are many positions to be taken on the above questions. Our goal is not to argue for a particular data format or query style, but rather to demonstrate a powerful technique for indexing and querying treebanks which should be applicable to most of the above scenarios.

3 Indexing Trees

In this section we discuss two methods of storing and indexing trees. The first uses a relational database and linguistic queries are translated into SQL, while the second uses an inverted index approach based on an open source IR engine, Lucene.[1] Relational databases are a mature technology and are known to be efficient at performing joins and accessing data using indexes. Information retrieval engines using term vectors, on the other hand, efficiently retrieve documents relevant to a query. IR engines are known to scale well, but they do not support complex queries. A common feature of both the IR and database approaches is the adoption of so-called "tree labeling" schemes.

3.1 Tree labeling schemes

Tree queries specify node labels ("value constraints") and structural relationships between nodes of interest ("structural constraints"). A simple value constraint could look for a *wh noun phrase* by specifying the `WHNP`; such queries are efficiently implemented using indexes. Structural relationships cannot be indexed like node labels. A term in a sentence will have multiple relationships with other terms in the same sentence. Indexing all pairs of terms that exist in a given structural relationship results in an explosion in the index size. Instead, the standard approach is to store position information with each occurrence of a term, using a table or a term vector, and then use the position information to find structural matches. Many systems use this approach, from early object databases such as Lore (McHugh et al., 1997), to relational representation of tree data (Bird et al., 2006) and XISS/R (Harding et al., 2003), and native XML databases such as eXist (Meier, 2003). Here, the position is encoded via node labeling schemes, and is designed so it can support efficient testing of a variety of structural relations.

A labeling scheme based on pre-order and post-order labeling of nodes is the foundation for several extended schemes. It can be used for efficiently detecting that two nodes are in a hierarchical (or inclusion) relationship. Other labeling schemes are based on the Dewey scheme, in which each node contains

[1] http://lucene.apache.org/

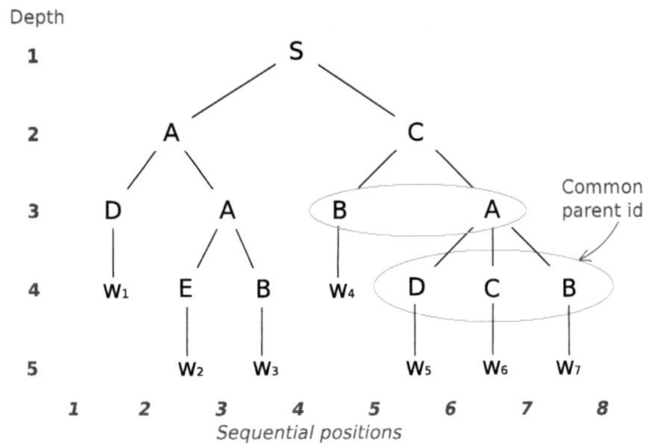

Figure 1: Generating node labels

a hierarchical label in which numbers are separated by periods (Tatarinov et al., 2002). A child node gets its label by appending its position relative to its siblings to its parent's label. This scheme can be used for efficiently detecting that two nodes are in a hierarchical or sequential (temporal) relationship.

The LPath numbering scheme assigns four integer labels to each node (Bird et al., 2006). The generation of these labels is explained with the help of an example. Figure 1 is the graphical representation of a parse tree for a sentence with 7 words, $w_1 \cdots w_7$. Let *A*, *B*, *C*, *D*, *E*, and *S* represent the annotation tags. Some nodes at different positions in the tree share a common name.

The first step in labeling is to identify the sequential positions between words, as shown beneath the parse tree in Figure 1. The left id of a terminal node is the sequence position immediately to the left of a node, while its right id is the one to its immediate right. The left id of a non-terminal node is the left id of its leftmost descendant, and the right id is the right id of its rightmost descendant. In most cases the ancestor-descendant and preceding-following relationships between two elements can be evaluated using the left and right ids alone. The sequential ids do not differentiate between two nodes where one is the lone child of the other. The depth id is therefore required in such cases and to identify the child node (depth values are shown on the left side of Figure 1). In order to check if two given nodes are siblings, the above three ids will not suffice. We therefore assign a common parent id label to siblings. These four identifiers together enable us to identify relationships between elements without traversing trees.

Node	Left	Right	Depth	Parent
A	2	4	3	2
A	1	4	2	6
A	5	8	3	8
B	3	4	4	4
B	4	5	3	8
B	7	8	4	10

Table 1: Node labels

Table 1 illustrates the node labels assigned to *A* and *B* nodes in Figure 1. We can see that the parent id of the third *A* and second *B* are equal because they are siblings.

Once these numbers are assigned to each node, the nodes can be stored independently without loss of any structural information (in either a relational database or an inverted index). At query execution time, the set of elements on either side of an operator are extracted and only those node numbers that satisfy the operator's specification are selected as the result. For example, if the operator is the child relation, and the operands are *A* and *B*, then there are two matches: $B\{3,4,4,4\}$, child of $A\{2,4,3,2\}$ and, $B\{7,8,4,10\}$, child of $A\{5,8,3,8\}$.[2] This process of finding the elements of a document that match operators is nothing other than the standard join operation (and it is implemented differently in relational databases and IR engines).

3.2 Relational database approach

Tree nodes can be stored in a relational database using a table structure (Bird et al., 2006). Each treebank would have a single table for all nodes where each node's information is stored in a tuple. The node name is stored along with other position information and the sentence id. Every node tuple also has a unique primary key. The parent id column is a foreign key, referencing the parent node's id, speeding up parent/child join operations. In practice, queries are translated from higher level linguistic query languages such as LPath into SQL automatically, allowing users to use a convenient syntax, rather than query using SQL.

Previous research on a similar database structure for containment queries in XML databases showed

[2]The node labels are represented as an ordered set here for brevity. Their positions match the headings in Table 1.

that databases are generally slower than specialised IR indexes (Zhang et al., 2001). In that work, the authors provide results comparing their IR join algorithm, the multi-predicate merge join (MPMGJN), with two standard relational join algorithms. They consider the number of comparisons performed in the standard merge join and the index nested loop join, and contrast these with their IR join algorithm. They show that the IR algorithm performs fewer comparisons than a standard merge join but greater than the index nested loop join.

The multi-predicate merge join exploits the fact that nodes are encountered in document order (i.e. a node appears before its descendents). Search within a document can be aborted as soon as it is clear that further searching will not yield further results. Importantly, this IR join algorithm is faster than both relational join algorithms in practice, since it makes much better use of the hardware disk cache. Our own experiments with a large treebank stored in an Oracle database have demonstrated that this shortcoming of relational query relative to IR query exists in the linguistic domain (Ghodke and Bird, 2008).

3.3 IR engine approach

We transform the task of searching treebanks into a conventional document retrieval task in which each sentence is treated as a document. Tree node labels are stored in inverted indexes just like words in a text index. We require two types of indexes, for frequency and position. The frequency index for a node label contains a list of sentence ids and, for each one, a count indicating the frequency of the node label in the sentence. (Labels with a frequency of zero do not appear in this index.) The position index is used to store node numbers for each occurrence of the node label. The numbers at each position are read into memory as objects only when required (at other times, the byte numbers are skipped over for efficiency). During query processing, the frequency indexes are first traversed sequentially to find a document that contains all the required elements in the query. Once a document is found, the structural constraints are checked using the data stored in the position index for that document. The document itself does not need to be loaded.

Using an inverted index for searching structured data is not new, and several XML databases already use this method to index XML elements (Meier, 2003). However, linguistic query systems are special purpose applications where the unit of retrieval is usually a sentence. A given tree may satisfy a query in multiple places, but we only identify which sentences are relevant. Finding all matches within a sentence requires further processing. [3]

Our approach has been to process each sentence as a document. By fixing the unit of retrieval to be the sentence, we are able to greatly reduce the size of intermediate results when performing a series of joins. The task is then to simply check whether a sentence satisfies a query or not. This can be done using substantially less resources than is needed for finding sets of nodes, the unit of retrieval for relational and XML databases. When processing a series of joins, we use a single buffer to store the node positions required to perform the next join in the series. After computing that join and processing another operator in the query, the buffer contents is replaced with a new set of nodes, discarding the intermediate information.

4 Experiments with IR Engine

4.1 Data

We used two data collections in our experiments. The first collection is a portion of the English Gigaword Corpus, parsed in the Penn Treebank format. We used the TnT tagger and the DBParser trained on the Wall Street Journal section of the Penn Treebank to parse sentences in the corpus. The total size of the corpus is about 5.5 million sentences. The TGrep2 corpus file for this corpus is about 1.8 GB and the Lucene index is 4 GB on disk. The second data collection is a portion of English Wikipedia, again tagged and parsed using TnT tagger and DBParser, respectively. This collection contains 26.5 million parsed sentences. The TGrep2 corpus file corresponding to this collection is about 6.6 GB and the Lucene index is 14 GB on disk.

[3] Several alternate path joins and improvements to the MPMGJN algorithm have been proposed over the years to overcome the problem of large number of intermediate nodes and to reduce unnecessary joins (Al-Khalifa et al., 2002; Li and Moon, 2001). Bruno *et al.*'s work on twig joins further improved on those efforts by processing an entire query twig in a holistic fashion (Bruno et al., 2002), and has since been further optimized.

Query	Selectivity	Data Collection 1 (5.5M sentences)					Data Collection 2 (26.5M sentences)				
		Full search			First 10		Full search			First 10	
(//N1 op N2)	N1-op-N2	cold	warm	hits	cold	warm	cold	warm	hits	cold	warm
NP/NN	L-L-L	7.326	5.533	4,814,540	0.059	0.0003	24.680	20.256	21,906,349	0.260	0.0003
VP/DT	L-H-L	4.576	3.593	17,328	0.140	0.004	13.865	11.363	91,070	0.301	0.003
NP/LST	L-L-H	4.454	0.043	6,808	0.083	0.001	16.864	0.077	2.974	0.270	0.003
VP/WHPP	L-H-H	2.445	0.034	32	1.012	0.014	8.834	0.066	29	3.653	0.015
LST\NP	H-L-L	4.444	0.043	6,808	0.080	0.001	16.814	0.077	2,974	0.271	0.003
WHPP\VP	H-H-L	2.461	0.034	32	0.990	0.013	8.726	0.065	29	3.611	0.015
LST/LS	H-L-H	0.181	0.005	10,432	0.071	0.0001	0.294	0.008	8,977	0.238	0.0002
LST/FW	H-H-H	0.123	0.009	4	0.103	0.011	0.348	0.012	9	0.408	0.012

Table 2: Execution times (in seconds) for queries of varying selectivity

4.2 Types of queries

Query performance depends largely on the nature of the individual queries, therefore we present a detailed analysis of the query types and their corresponding results in this section.

Selectivity: A query term that has few corresponding hits in the corpus will be considered to have high selectivity. The selectivity of whole queries depends not only on the selectivity of their individual elements, but also on how frequently these terms satisfy the structural constraints specified by the query.

Table 2 gives execution times for queries with varying selectivity, using our system. We assign a selectivity measure for the operator based on how often the two operands satisfy the structural condition. It is clear that when elements are very common and they frequently satisfy the structural constraints of the operator, there are bound to be more run-time structural checks and the performance deteriorates. This is demonstrated by the time taken by the first query. Note the relatively small difference in the execution time between the second and third queries. The third query contains a high selectivity element and even returns fewer matches compared to the second, but takes almost as long. This may be due to the relative frequency of the tags within each sentence, which we have not controled in this experiment. If there are several LST tags in the sentences where it appears, there are likely to be greater number of searches within each sentence. A better join algorithm would improve the performance in such cases.

A multiple regression analysis of the full search (cold start) times for collection 2 shows that low-selectivity labels contribute 9.5 seconds, and a low-selectivity operator contributes 6.7 seconds, and that this accounts for most of the variability in the timing data ($t = -1.53 + 9.51 * N_1 + 6.72 * op + 9.44 * N_2, R^2 = 0.8976$). This demonstrates that the distribution of full search (cold start) times is mostly accounted for by the index load time, with the time for computing a large join being a secondary cost. The full search (warm start) times in Table 2 pay a lesser index loading cost.

Query length: It is evident that the system must retrieve and process more term vectors as we increase the number of elements in a query. To find out exactly how the query length affects processing, we ran tests with three sets of queries. In each set we varied the number of elements in a dominance relationship with another node of the same name. The number of terms in the dominance relationship was varied from 1 to 6, where the first case is equivalent to just finding all terms with that name. In the first set, queries search for nested noun phrases (`NP`), while the second and third look for adjective phrases (`ADJP`) and list elements (`LST`) respectively.

These terms have been chosen to simultaneously study the effects of selectivity and query length, with `NP` being the least selective (or most common), followed by `ADJP`, then with `LST` being the most selective (or least common). `NP` is also more frequently self-nested than the others. Figure 2 plots query length (x-axis) against query execution time (y-axis, log scale) for the three sets, using our system. With

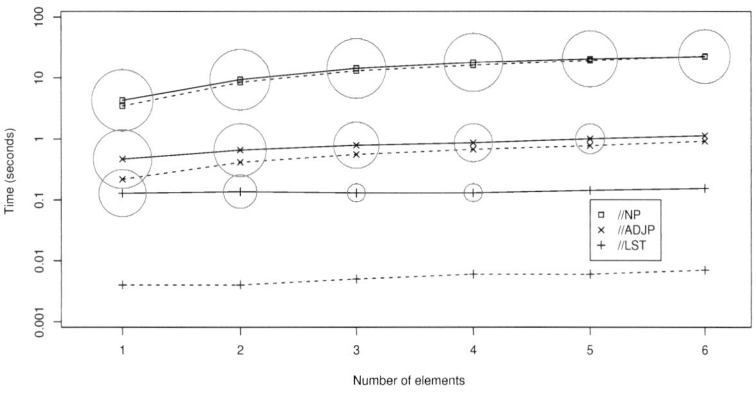

Figure 2: Variation of query execution time with query length in data collection 1

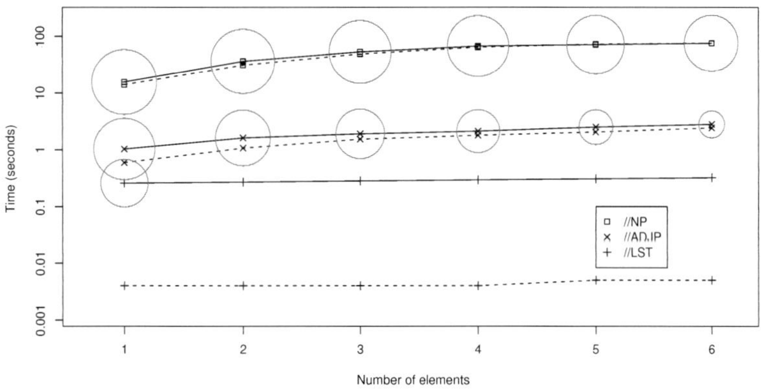

Figure 3: Variation of query execution time with query length in data collection 2

each step on the x-axis, a query will have an extra descendant node. For example, at position 3 for element `A`, the query would be `//A//A//A`.

The circles on the plot are proportional to the log of the result set size. The biggest circle is for `//NP` which is of the order of 5.4 million, while there are only 4 trees in which `LST` is nested 4 times. `LST` is not nested 5 or more times. Similarly, `ADJP` returns 0 results for the 6th test query and hence there are no circles at these locations. The thick lines on the plot indicate the average cold start run time over three runs, while the dashed line shows the minimum average run time of 4 sets, with the query executed 5 times in each set. Together, the pairs of unbroken and dashed lines indicate the variation in run time depending on the state of the system. [4]

4.3 Measurement techniques

The measurement techniques vary for TGrep and the IR based approach. In TGrep the corpus file is loaded each time during query processing, but in the IR approach an index once loaded can operate faster than a cold start.

In order to understand the variations in the operating speed we plot the variation in times from a cold start to a repeat query, as shown in Table 3.

[4]We can observe from the results that the variation between cold start and warm start correlates with query length. The length experiment here use a single term repeated multiple times. However, there is a possibility that the results may vary when the terms are different, because it would involve additional time to load the term vectors of distinct elements into memory.

Query	Data collection 1		Data collection 2	
	TGrep2	IR	TGrep2	IR
//NP	25.28	8.15	89.35	15.53
//NP//NP	25.44	10.42	88.36	35.95
//NP//NP//NP	25.45	14.96	87.48	52.81
//NP. . . //NP (4 times)	25.34	18.38	88.28	66.80
//NP. . . //NP (5 times)	25.46	20.94	87.38	70.80
//NP. . . //NP (6 times)	25.41	23.23	86.92	75.05
//ADJP	25.48	0.69	86.83	1.03
//ADJP//ADJP	25.36	0.73	86.42	1.61
//ADJP//ADJP//ADJP	25.29	0.84	86.89	1.89
//ADJP. . . //ADJP (4 times)	25.45	0.90	87.39	2.11
//ADJP. . . //ADJP (5 times)	25.23	1.03	86.50	2.49
//ADJP. . . //ADJP (6 times)	25.74	1.11	89.24	2.79
//LST	25.29	0.17	87.73	0.26
//LST//LST	25.49	0.20	87.09	0.27
//LST//LST//LST	25.38	0.20	87.66	0.28
//LST. . . //LST (4 times)	25.43	0.19	87.17	0.29
//LST. . . //LST (5 times)	25.40	0.19	88.02	0.31
//LST. . . //LST (6 times)	25.32	0.19	89.01	0.32
//NP/NN	25.66	7.33	87.63	24.68
//VP/DT	25.53	4.58	89.85	13.86
//NP/LST	25.62	4.45	86.39	16.86
//VP/WHPP	25.09	2.97	87.43	8.83
//WHPP/IN	25.75	4.44	88.48	16.81
//LST/JJ	25.46	2.46	86.57	8.73
//LST/LS	25.38	0.18	87.40	0.29
//LST/FW	25.51	0.12	87.27	0.35

Table 3: Comparison of TGrep2 and IR Engine cold start query times (seconds)

5 Conclusions

We have shown how an IR engine can be used to build a high performance tree query system. It outperforms existing approaches using indexless in-memory search, or custom indexes, or relational database systems, or XML database systems. We reported the results of a variety of experiments to demonstrate the efficiency of query for a variety of query types on two treebanks consisting of around 5 and 26 million sentences, more than two orders of magnitude larger than what existing systems support. The approach is quite general, and not limited to particular treebank formats or query languages. This work suggests that web-scale tree query may soon be feasible. This opens the door to some interesting possibilities: augmenting web search with syntactic constraints, the ability discover rare examples of particular syntactic constructions, and as a technique for garnering better statistics and more sensitive features for the purpose of constructing language models.

Acknowledgments

We gratefully acknowledge support from Microsoft Research India and the University of Melbourne.

References

Anne Abeillé, editor. 2003. *Treebanks: Building and Using Parsed Corpora*. Text, Speech and Language Technology. Kluwer.

Shurug Al-Khalifa, H.V. Jagadish, Nick Koudas, Jignesh M. Patel, Divesh Srivastava, and Yuqing Wu. 2002. Structural joins: A primitive for efficient XML query pattern matching. In *ICDE '02: Proc. 18th Intl Conf on Data Engineering*, page 141. IEEE Computer Society.

Steven Bird, Yi Chen, Susan B. Davidson, Haejoong Lee, and Yifeng Zheng. 2006. Designing and evaluating an XPath dialect for linguistic queries. In *ICDE '06: Proc. 22nd Intl Conf on Data Engineering*, page 52. IEEE Computer Society.

Nicolas Bruno, Nick Koudas, and Divesh Srivastava. 2002. Holistic twig joins: optimal XML pattern matching. In *SIGMOD '02: Proc. 2002 ACM SIGMOD Intl Conf on Management of Data*, pages 310–321. ACM.

Steve Cassidy and Jonathan Harrington. 2001. Multi-level annotation of speech: an overview of the Emu Speech Database Management System. *Speech Communication*, 33:61–77.

Steve Cassidy. 2002. Xquery as an annotation query language: a use case analysis. In *Proc. 3rd LREC*.

John Chen and Owen Rambow. 2003. Use of deep linguistic features for the recognition and labeling of semantic arguments. In *Empirical Methods in Natural Language Processing*, pages 41–48.

Abdur Chowdhury and M. Catherine McCabe. 1998. Performance improvements to vector space information retrieval systems with POS. U Maryland.

Stephen Clark and James R. Curran. 2007. Wide-coverage efficient statistical parsing with CCG and log-linear models. *Computational Linguistics*, 33(4):493–552.

Michael Collins, Brian Roark, and Murat Saraclar. 2005. Discriminative syntactic language modeling for speech recognition. In *Proc. 43rd ACL*, pages 507–514. ACL.

Sumukh Ghodke and Steven Bird. 2008. Querying linguistic annotations. In *Proc. 13th Australasian Document Computing Symposium*, pages 69–72.

Jörg Hakenberg, Illes Solt, Domonkos Tikk, Luis Tari, Astrid Rheinländer, Nguyen Quang Long, Graciela Gonzalez, and Ulf Leser. 2009. Molecular event extraction from Link Grammar parse trees. In *Proc. BioNLP 2009 Workshop*, pages 86–94. ACL.

Philip J Harding, Quanzhong Li, and Bongki Moon. 2003. XISS/R: XML indexing and storage system using RDBMS. In *Proc. 29th Intl Conf on Very Large Data Bases*, pages 1073–1076. Morgan Kaufmann.

Ulrich Heid, Holger Voormann, Jan-Torsten Milde, Ulrike Gut, Katrin Erk, and Sebastian Pado. 2004. Querying both time-aligned and hierarchical corpora with NXT search. In *Proc. 4th LREC*.

Ichikawa Hiroshi, Noguchi Masaki, Hashimoto Taiichi, Tokunaga Takenobu, and Tanaka Hozumi. 2005. eBonsai: An integrated environment for annotating treebanks. In *Proc. 2nd IJCNLP*, pages 108–113.

Julia Hockenmaier and Mark Steedman. 2007. CCGbank: A corpus of CCG derivations and dependency structures extracted from the Penn Treebank. *Computational Linguistics*, 33:355–396.

Hiroshi Ichikawa, Keita Hakoda, Taiichi Hashimoto, and Takenobu Tokunaga. 2006. Efficient sentence retrieval based on syntactic structure. In *COLING/ACL*, pages 399–406.

Stephan Kepser. 2003. Finite Structure Query: A tool for querying syntactically annotated corpora. In *Proc. 10th EACL*, pages 179–186.

Esther König and Wolfgang Lezius. 2001. The TIGER language: a description language for syntax graphs. part 1: User's guidelines. Technical report, University of Stuttgart.

Catherine Lai and Steven Bird. 2004. Querying and updating treebanks: A critical survey and requirements analysis. In *Proc. Australasian Language Technology Workshop*, pages 139–146.

Catherine Lai and Steven Bird. 2010. Querying linguistic trees. *Journal of Logic, Language and Information*, 19:53–73.

Quanzhong Li and Bongki Moon. 2001. Indexing and querying XML data for regular path expressions. In *VLDB '01: Proc. 27th Intl Conf on Very Large Data Bases*, pages 361–370. Morgan Kaufmann.

Mitchell P. Marcus, Beatrice Santorini, and Mary Ann Marcinkiewicz. 1993. Building a large annotated corpus of English: The Penn Treebank. *Computational Linguistics*, 19(2):313–30.

Hendrik Maryns and Stephan Kepser. 2009. Monasearch: Querying linguistic treebanks with monadic second-order logic. In *The 7th International Workshop on Treebanks and Linguistic Theories*.

Neil Mayo, Jonathan Kilgour, and Jean Carletta. 2006. Towards an alternative implementation of nxts query language via xquery. In *Proc. 5th Workshop on NLP and XML: Multi-Dimensional Markup in Natural Language Processing*, pages 27–34. ACL.

J. McHugh, S. Abiteboul, R. Goldman, D. Quass, and J. Widom. 1997. Lore: A database management system for semistructured data. *SIGMOD Rec.*, 26:54–66.

Wolfgang Meier. 2003. eXist: An open source native XML database. In *Revised Papers from the NODe 2002 Web and Database-Related Workshops on Web, Web-Services, and Database Systems*, pages 169–183. Springer-Verlag.

Jiří Mírovský. 2006. Netgraph: a tool for searching in Prague Dependency Treebank 2.0. In *Proc. 5th Intl Conf on Treebanks and Linguistic Theories*, pages 211–222.

Jiří Mírovský. 2008. PDT 2.0 requirements on a query language. In *Proc. 46th ACL*, pages 37–45. ACL.

Preslav Nakov, Ariel Schwartz, Brian Wolf, and Marti Hearst. 2005. Supporting annotation layers for natural language processing. In *Proc. 43rd ACL*, pages 65–68.

Stephan Oepen, Kristina Toutanova, Stuart Shieber, Christopher Manning, Dan Flickinger, and Thorsten Brants. 2002. The LinGO Redwoods Treebank: Motivation and preliminary applications. In *Proc. 19th COLING*, pages 1253–57.

Petr Pajas and Jan Štěpánek. 2009. System for querying syntactically annotated corpora. In *Proc. 47th ACL*, pages 33–36. ACL.

Douglas L. T. Rohde, 2005. *TGrep2 User Manual Version 1.15.* http://tedlab.mit.edu/ dr/TGrep2/tgrep2.pdf.

Igor Tatarinov, Stratis D. Viglas, Kevin Beyer, Jayavel Shanmugasundaram, Eugene Shekita, and Chun Zhang. 2002. Storing and querying ordered XML using a relational database system. In *SIGMOD '02: Proc. 2002 ACM SIGMOD Intl Conf on Management of Data*, pages 204–215. ACM.

M. Čmejrek, J. Cuřín, and J. Havelka. 2004. Prague czech-english dependency treebank: Any hopes for a common annotation scheme? In A. Meyers, editor, *HLT-NAACL 2004 Workshop: Frontiers in Corpus Annotation*, pages 47–54. ACL.

Martin Volk, Joakim Lundborg, and Maël Mettler. 2007. A search tool for parallel treebanks. In *Proc. Linguistic Annotation Workshop*, pages 85–92. ACL.

Sean Wallis. 2003. Completing parsed corpora. In Anne Abeillé, editor, *Treebanks: Building and Using Parsed Corpora*, Text, Speech and Language Technology, pages 61–71. Kluwer.

Naiwen Xue, Fei Xia, Fu-Dong Chiou, and Martha Palmer. 2005. The Penn Chinese TreeBank: Phrase structure annotation of a large corpus. *Natural Language Engineering*, 11:207–238.

Chun Zhang, Jeffrey Naughton, David DeWitt, Qiong Luo, and Guy Lohman. 2001. On supporting containment queries in relational database management systems. In *SIGMOD '01: Proc. ACM SIGMOD international Conference on Management of Data*, pages 425–436, New York. ACM.

Efficient Parsing of Well-Nested Linear Context-Free Rewriting Systems

Carlos Gómez-Rodríguez[1], Marco Kuhlmann[2], and Giorgio Satta[3]

[1]Departamento de Computación, Universidade da Coruña, Spain, cgomezr@udc.es
[2]Department of Linguistics and Philology, Uppsala University, Sweden, marco.kuhlmann@lingfil.uu.se
[3]Department of Information Engineering, University of Padua, Italy, satta@dei.unipd.it

Abstract

The use of well-nested linear context-free rewriting systems has been empirically motivated for modeling of the syntax of languages with discontinuous constituents or relatively free word order. We present a chart-based parsing algorithm that asymptotically improves the known running time upper bound for this class of rewriting systems. Our result is obtained through a linear space construction of a binary normal form for the grammar at hand.

1 Introduction

Since its earliest years, one of the main goals of computational linguistics has been the modeling of natural language syntax by means of formal grammars. Following results by Huybregts (1984) and Shieber (1985), special attention has been given to formalisms that enlarge the generative power of context-free grammars, but still remain below the full generative power of context-sensitive grammars. On this line of investigation, *mildly context-sensitive grammar formalisms* have been introduced (Joshi, 1985), including, among several others, the tree adjoining grammars (TAGs) of Joshi et al. (1975).

Linear context-free rewriting system (LCFRS), introduced by Vijay-Shanker et al. (1987), is a mildly context-sensitive formalism that allows the derivation of tuples of strings, i.e., discontinuous phrases. This feature has been used to model phrase structure treebanks with discontinuous constituents (Maier and Søgaard, 2008), as well as to map non-projective dependency trees into discontinuous phrase structures (Kuhlmann and Satta, 2009).

Informally, in an LCFRS G, each nonterminal can generate string tuples with a fixed number of components. The *fan-out* of G is defined as the maximum number of tuple components generated by G. During a derivation of an LCFRS, tuple components generated by the nonterminals in the right-hand side of a production are concatenated to form new tuples, possibly adding some terminal symbols. The only restriction applying to these generalized concatenation operations is linearity, that is, components cannot be duplicated or deleted.

The freedom in the rearrangement of components has specific consequences in terms of the computational and descriptional complexity of LCFRS. Even for grammars with bounded fan-out, the universal recognition problem is NP-hard (Satta, 1992), and these systems lack Chomsky-like normal forms for fixed fan-out (Rambow and Satta, 1999) that are especially convenient in tabular parsing. This is in contrast with other mildly context-sensitive formalisms, and TAG in particular: TAGs can be parsed in polynomial time both with respect to grammar size and string size, and they can be cast in normal forms having binary derivation trees only.

It has recently been argued that LCFRS might be too powerful for modeling languages with discontinuous constituents or with relatively free word order, and that additional restrictions on the rearrangement of components might be needed. More specifically, analyses of both dependency and constituency treebanks (Kuhlmann and Nivre, 2006; Havelka, 2007; Maier and Lichte, 2009) have shown that rearrangements of argument tuples almost always satisfy the so-called *well-nestedness condition*, a generalization

Human Language Technologies: The 2010 Annual Conference of the North American Chapter of the ACL, pages 276–284,
Los Angeles, California, June 2010.

of the standard condition on balanced brackets. This condition states that any two components x_1, x_2 of some tuple will never be composed with any two components y_1, y_2 of some other tuple in such a way that a 'crossing' configuration is realized.

In this paper, we contribute to a better understanding of the formal properties of well-nested LCFRS. We show that, when fan-out is bounded by any integer $\varphi \geq 1$, these systems can always be transformed, in an efficient way, into a specific normal form with no more than two nonterminals in their productions' right-hand sides. On the basis of this result, we then develop an efficient parsing algorithm for well-nested LCFRS, running in time $\mathcal{O}(\varphi \cdot |G| \cdot |w|^{2\varphi+2})$, where G and w are the input grammar and string, respectively. Well-nested LCFRS with fan-out $\varphi = 2$ are weakly equivalent to TAG, and our complexity result reduces to the well-known upper bound $\mathcal{O}(|G| \cdot |w|^6)$ for this class. For $\varphi > 2$, our upper bound is asymptotically better than the one obtained from existing parsing algorithms for general LCFRS or equivalent formalisms (Seki et al., 1991).

Well-nested LCFRS are generatively equivalent to (among others) coupled context-free grammars (CCFG), introduced by Hotz and Pitsch (1996). These authors also provide a normal form and develop a parsing algorithm for CCFGs. One difference with respect to our result is that the normal form for CCFGs allows more than two nonterminals to appear in the right-hand side of a production, even though no nonterminal may contribute more than two tuple components. Also, the construction in (Hotz and Pitsch, 1996) results in a blow-up of the grammar that is exponential in its fan-out, and the parsing algorithm that is derived runs in time $\mathcal{O}(4^{\varphi} \cdot |G| \cdot |w|^{2\varphi+2})$. Our result is therefore a considerable asymptotic improvement over the CCFG result, both with respect to the normal form construction and the parsing efficiency. Finally, under a practical perspective, our parser is a simple chart-based algorithm, while the algorithm in (Hotz and Pitsch, 1996) involves two passes and is considerably more complex to analyze and to implement than ours.

Kanazawa and Salvati (2010) mention a normal form for well-nested multiple context-free grammars.

Structure In Section 2, we introduce LCFRS and the class of well-nested LCFRS that is the focus of this paper. In Section 3, we discuss the parsing complexity of LCFRS, and show why grammars using our normal form can be parsed efficiently. Section 4 presents the transformation of a well-nested LCFRS into the normal form. Section 5 concludes the paper.

2 Linear Context-Free Rewriting Systems

We write $[n]$ to denote the set of positive integers up to and including n: $[n] = \{1, \dots, n\}$.

2.1 Linear, non-erasing functions

Let Σ be an alphabet. For integers $m \geq 0$ and $k_1, \dots, k_m, k \geq 1$, a total function

$$f : (\Sigma^*)^{k_1} \times \cdots \times (\Sigma^*)^{k_m} \to (\Sigma^*)^k$$

is called a *linear, non-erasing function* over Σ with type $k_1 \times \cdots \times k_m \to k$, if it can be defined by an equation of the form

$$f(\langle x_{1,1}, \dots, x_{1,k_1}\rangle, \dots, \langle x_{m,1}, \dots, x_{m,k_m}\rangle) = \vec{\alpha},$$

where $\vec{\alpha}$ is a k-tuple of strings over the variables on the left-hand side of the equation and Σ with the property that each variable occurs in $\vec{\alpha}$ exactly once. The values m and k are called the *rank* and the *fan-out* of f, and denoted by $\rho(f)$ and $\varphi(f)$.

2.2 Linear Context-Free Rewriting Systems

For the purposes of this paper, a *linear context-free rewriting system*, henceforth LCFRS, is a construct $G = (N, T, P, S)$, where N is an alphabet of nonterminal symbols in which each symbol A is associated with a positive integer $\varphi(A)$ called its *fan-out*, T is an alphabet of terminal symbols, $S \in N$ is a distinguished start symbol with $\varphi(S) = 1$; and P is a finite set of productions of the form

$$p = A \to f(A_1, \dots, A_m),$$

where $m \geq 0$, $A, A_1, \dots, A_m \in N$, and f is a linear, non-erasing function over the terminal alphabet T with type $\varphi(A_1) \times \cdots \times \varphi(A_m) \to \varphi(A)$, called the *composition operation* associated with p. The *rank* of G and the *fan-out* of G are defined as the maximal rank and fan-out of the composition operations of G, and are denoted by $\rho(G)$ and $\varphi(G)$.

The sets of *derivation trees* of G are the smallest indexed family of sets D_A, $A \in N$, such that, if

$$p = A \to f(A_1, \dots, A_m)$$

$$N = \{S, R\},\ T = \{a, b, c, d\},\ P = \{\, p_1 = S \to f_1(R),\ p_2 = R \to f_2(R),\ p_3 = R \to f_3 \,\},$$
$$\text{where: } f_1(\langle x_{1,1}, x_{1,2}\rangle) = \langle x_{1,1}\, x_{1,2}\rangle,\ f_2(\langle x_{1,1}, x_{1,2}\rangle) = \langle a\, x_{1,1}\, b, c\, x_{1,2}\, d\rangle,\ f_3 = \langle \varepsilon, \varepsilon\rangle.$$

Figure 1: An LCFRS that generates the string language $\{\, a^n b^n c^n d^n \mid n \geq 0 \,\}$.

is a production of G and $t_i \in D_{A_i}$ for all $i \in [m]$, then $t = p(t_1, \ldots, t_m) \in D_A$. By interpreting productions as their associated composition operations in the obvious way, a derivation tree $t \in D_A$ evaluates to a $\varphi(A)$-tuple of strings over T; we denote this tuple by $val(t)$. The *string language* generated by G, denoted by $L(G)$, is then defined as

$$L(G) = \{\, w \in T^* \mid t \in D_S,\ \langle w \rangle = val(t) \,\}.$$

Two LCFRS are called *weakly equivalent*, if they generate the same string language.

Example Figure 1 shows a sample LCFRS G with $\rho(G) = 1$ and $\varphi(G) = 2$. The sets of its derivation trees are $D_R = \{\, p_2^n(p_3) \mid n \geq 0 \,\}$ and $D_S = \{\, p_1(t) \mid t \in D_R \,\}$. The string language generated by G is $\{\, a^n b^n c^n d^n \mid n \geq 0 \,\}$.

2.3 Characteristic strings

In the remainder of this paper, we use the following convenient syntax for tuples of strings. Instead of

$$\langle v_1, \ldots, v_k \rangle, \quad \text{we write} \quad v_1 \,\$\, \cdots \,\$\, v_k,$$

using the \$-symbol to mark the component boundaries. We call this the *characteristic string* of the tuple, and an occurrence of the symbol \$ a *gap marker*. We also use this notation for composition operations. For example, the characteristic string of the operation

$$f(\langle x_{1,1}, x_{1,2}\rangle, \langle x_{2,1}\rangle) = \langle a\, x_{1,1}\, x_{2,1}, x_{1,2}\, b\rangle$$

is $a\, x_{1,1}\, x_{2,1} \,\$\, x_{1,2}\, b$. If we assume the variables on the left-hand side of an equation to be named according to the schema used in Section 2.1, then the characteristic string of a composition operation determines that operation completely. We will therefore freely identify the two, and write productions as

$$p = A \to [v_1 \,\$\, \cdots \,\$\, v_k](A_1, \ldots, A_m),$$

where the string inside the brackets is the characteristic string of some composition operation. The substrings $v_1, \ldots, v_k$ are called the *components* of the characteristic string. Note that the characteristic string of a composition operation with type $k_1 \times \cdots \times k_m \to k$ is a sequence of terminal symbols, gap markers, and variables from the set $\{\, x_{i,j} \mid i \in [m],\ j \in [k_i] \,\}$ in which the number of gap markers is $k-1$, and each variable occurs exactly once. When in the context of such a composition operation we refer to 'a variable of the form $x_{i,j}$', then it will always be the case that $i \in [m]$ and $j \in [k_i]$.

The identification of composition operations and their characteristic strings allows us to construct new operations by string manipulations: if, for example, we delete some variables from a characteristic string, then the resulting string still defines a composition operation (after a suitable renaming of the remaining variables, which we leave implicit).

2.4 Canonical LCFRS

To simplify our presentation, we will assume that LCFRS are given in a certain canonical form. Intuitively, this canonical form requires the variables in the characteristic string of a composition operation to be ordered in a certain way.

Formally, the defining equation of a composition operation f with type $k_1 \times \cdots \times k_m \to k$ is called *canonical*, if (i) the sequence obtained from f by reading variables of the form $x_{i,1}$ from left to right has the form $x_{1,1} \cdots x_{m,1}$; and (ii) for each $i \in [m]$, the sequence obtained from f by reading variables of the form $x_{i,j}$ from left to right has the form $x_{i,1} \cdots x_{i,k_i}$. An LCFRS is called *canonical*, if each of its composition operations is canonical.

We omit the proof that every LCFRS can be transformed into a weakly equivalent canonical LCFRS. However, we point out that both the normal form and the parsing algorithm that we present in this paper can be applied also to general LCFRS. This is in contrast to some left-to-right parsers in the literature on LCFRS and equivalent formalisms (de la Clergerie, 2002; Kallmeyer and Maier, 2009), which actually depend on productions in canonical form.

2.5 Well-nested LCFRS

We now characterize the class of *well-nested LCFRS* that are the focus of this paper. Well-nestedness was first studied in the context of dependency grammars (Kuhlmann and Möhl, 2007). Kanazawa (2009) defines well-nested multiple context-free grammars, which are weakly equivalent to well-nested LCFRS.

A composition operation is called *well-nested*, if it does not contain a substring of the form

$$x_{i,i_1} \cdots x_{j,j_1} \cdots x_{i,i_2} \cdots x_{j,j_2}\,, \quad \text{where } i \neq j\,.$$

For example, the operation $x_{1,1}\,x_{2,1}\$x_{2,2}\,x_{1,2}$ is well-nested, while $x_{1,1}\,x_{2,1}\,\$\,x_{1,2}\,x_{2,2}$ is not. An LCFRS is called well-nested, if it contains only well-nested composition operations.

The class of languages generated by well-nested LCFRS is properly included in the class of languages generated by general LCFRS; see Kanazawa and Salvati (2010) for further discussion.

3 Parsing LCFRS

We now discuss the parsing complexity of LCFRS, and motivate our interest in a normal form for well-nested LCFRS.

3.1 General parsing schema

A bottom-up, chart-based parsing algorithm for the class of (not necessarily well-nested) LCFRS can be defined by using the formalism of parsing schemata (Sikkel, 1997). The parsing schemata approach considers parsing as a deduction process (as in Shieber et al. (1995)), generating intermediate results called *items*. Starting with an initial set of items obtained from each input sentence, a parsing schema defines a set of *deduction steps* that can be used to infer new items from existing ones. Each item contains information about the sentence's structure, and a successful parsing process will produce at least one *final item* containing a full parse for the input.

The item set used by our bottom-up algorithm to parse an input string $w = a_1 \cdots a_n$ with an LCFRS $G = (N, T, P, S)$ will be

$$\begin{aligned}\mathcal{I} = \{[A, (l_1, r_1), \ldots, (l_k, r_k)] \mid A \in N \quad \wedge \\ 0 \leq l_i \leq r_i \leq n \quad \forall i \in [k]\},\end{aligned}$$

where an item $[A, (l_1, r_1), \ldots, (l_k, r_k)]$ can be interpreted as the set of those derivation trees $t \in D_A$ of G for which

$$\mathit{val}(t) \;=\; a_{l_1+1} \cdots a_{r_1}\ \$ \cdots \$\ a_{l_k+1} \cdots a_{r_k}\,.$$

The set of final items is thus $\mathcal{F} = \{[S, (0, n)]\}$, containing full derivation trees that evaluate to w.

For simplicity of definition of the sets of initial items and deduction steps, let us assume that productions of rank > 0 in our grammar do not contain terminal symbols in their right-hand sides. This can be easily achieved from a starting grammar by creating a nonterminal A_a for each terminal $a \in T$, a corresponding rank-0 production $p_a = A_a \to [a]()$, and then changing each occurrence of a in the characteristic string of a production to the single variable associated with the fan-out 1 nonterminal A_a. With this, our initial item set for a string $a_1 \cdots a_n$ will be

$$\mathcal{H} = \{[A_{a_i}, (i-1, i)] \mid i \in [n]\}\,,$$

and each production $p = A_0 \to f(A_1, \ldots, A_m)$ of G (excluding the ones we created for the terminals) will produce a deduction step of the form given in Figure 2a, where the indexes are subject to the following constraints, imposed by the semantics of f.

1. If the kth component of the characteristic string of f starts with $x_{i,j}$, then $l_{0,k} = l_{i,j}$.
2. If the kth component of the characteristic string of f ends with $x_{i,j}$, then $r_{0,k} = r_{i,j}$.
3. If $x_{i,j}x_{i',j'}$ is an infix of the characteristic string of f, then $r_{i,j} = l_{i',j'}$.
4. If the kth component of the characteristic string of f is the empty string, then $l_{0,k} = r_{0,k}$.

3.2 General complexity

The time complexity of parsing LCFRS with respect to the length of the input can be analyzed by counting the maximum number of indexes that can appear in an instance of the inference rule above. Although the total number of indexes is $\sum_{i=0}^{m} 2 \cdot \varphi(A_i)$, some of these indexes are equated by the constraints.

To count the number of independent indexes, consider all the indexes of the form $l_{0,i}$ (corresponding to the left endpoints of each component of the characteristic string of f) and those of the form $r_{j,k}$ for $j > 0$ (corresponding to the right endpoints of each variable in the characteristic string). By the constraints above, these indexes are mutually independent, and it is easy to check that any other index is equated to one of these: indexes $r_{0,i}$ are equated to the index $r_{j,k}$ corresponding to the last variable $x_{j,k}$ of the ith component of the characteristic string, or to $l_{0,i}$ if there is no such variable; while indexes $l_{j,k}$ with $j > 0$ are equated to an index $l_{0,i}$ if the variable $x_{j,k}$ is at the beginning of a component of the characteristic string, or to an index $r_{j',k'} (j' > 1)$ if the variable $x_{j,k}$ follows another variable $x_{j',k'}$.

$$\frac{[A_1,(l_{1,1},r_{1,1}),\ldots,(l_{1,\varphi(A_1)},r_{1,\varphi(A_1)})] \quad \cdots \quad [A_m,(l_{m,1},r_{m,1}),\ldots,(l_{m,\varphi(A_m)},r_{m,\varphi(A_m)})]}{[A_0,(l_{0,1},r_{0,1}),\ldots,(l_{0,\varphi(A_0)},r_{0,\varphi(A_0)})]}$$

(a) The general rule for a parsing schema for LCFRS

$$\frac{[B,(l_1,r_1),\ldots,(l_m,r_m)] \quad [C,(l'_1,r'_1),\ldots(l'_n,r'_n)]}{[A,(l_1,r_1),\ldots,(l_m,r'_1),\ldots(l'_n,r'_n)]}\; r_m = l'_1$$

(b) Deduction step for concatenation

$$\frac{[B,(l_1,r_1),\ldots,(l_m,r_m)] \quad [C,(l'_1,r'_1),\ldots(l'_n,r'_n)]}{[A,(l_1,r_1),\ldots,(l_i,r'_1),\ldots(l'_n,r_{i+1}),\ldots,(l_m,r_m)]}\; r_i = l'_1, r'_n = l_{i+1}$$

(c) Deduction step for wrapping

Figure 2: Deduction steps for parsing LCFRS.

Thus, the *parsing complexity* (Gildea, 2010) of a production $p = A_0 \to f(A_1,\ldots,A_m)$ is determined by $\varphi(A_0)$ l-indexes and $\sum_{i\in[m]}\varphi(A_i)$ r-indexes, for a total complexity of

$$\mathcal{O}(|w|^{\varphi(A_0)+\sum_{i\in[m]}\varphi(A_i)})$$

where $|w|$ is the length of the input string. The parsing complexity of an LCFRS will correspond to the maximum parsing complexity among its productions. Note that this general complexity matches the result given by Seki et al. (1991).

In an LCFRS of rank ρ and fan-out φ, the maximum possible parsing complexity is $\mathcal{O}(|w|^{\varphi(\rho+1)})$, obtained by applying the above expression to a production of rank ρ and where each nonterminal has fan-out φ. The asymptotic time complexity of LCFRS parsing is therefore exponential both in its rank and its fan-out. This means that it is interesting to transform LCFRS into equivalent forms that reduce their rank while preserving the fan-out. For sets of LCFRS that can be transformed into a *binary* form (i.e., such that all its rules have rank at most 2), the ρ factor in the complexity is reduced to a constant, and complexity is improved to $\mathcal{O}(|w|^{3\varphi})$ (see Gómez-Rodríguez et al. (2009) for further discussion). Unfortunately, it is known by previous results (Rambow and Satta, 1999) that it is not always possible to convert an LCFRS into such a binary form without increasing the fan-out. However, we will show that it is always possible to build such a binarization for *well-nested* LCFRS. Combining this result with the inference rule and complexity analysis given above, we would obtain a parser for well-nested LCFRS running in $\mathcal{O}(|w|^{3\varphi})$ time. But the construction of our binary normal form additionally restricts binary composition operations in the binarized LCFRS to be of two specific forms, *concatenation* and *wrapping*, which further improves the parsing complexity to $\mathcal{O}(|w|^{2\varphi+2})$, as we will see below.

3.3 Concatenation and wrapping

A composition operation is called a *concatenation operation*, if its characteristic string has the form

$$x_{1,1}\,\$\cdots\$\,x_{1,m}\,x_{2,1}\,\$\cdots\$\,x_{2,n}\,,$$

where $m, n \geq 1$. Intuitively, such an operation corresponds to the bottom-up combination of two adjacent discontinuous constituents into one. An example of a concatenation operation is the binary parsing rule used by the standard CKY parser for context-free grammars, which combines continuous constituents (represented as 1-tuples of strings in the LCFRS notation). In the general case, a concatenation operation will take an m-tuple and an n-tuple and return an $(m+n-1)$-tuple, as the joined constituents may have gaps that will also appear in the resulting tuple.

If we apply the general parsing rule given in Figure 2a to a production $A \to conc(B,C)$, where $conc$ is a concatenation operation, then we obtain the deduction step given in Figure 2b. This step uses $2m$ different l- and r-indexes, and $2n-1$ different l'- and r'-indexes (excluding l'_1 which must equal r_m), for a total of $2m+2n-1 = 2(m+n-1)+1$ indexes. Since $m+n-1$ is the fan-out of the nonterminal A, we conclude that the maximum number of indexes in the step associated with a concatenation operation in an LCFRS of fan-out φ is $2\varphi+1$.

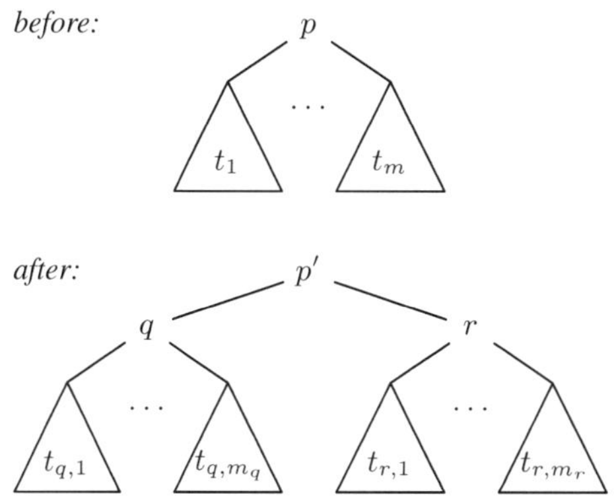

Figure 3: Transformation of derivation trees

A linear, non-erasing function is called a *wrapping operation*, if its characteristic string has the form

$$x_{1,1}\,\$\cdots\$\,x_{1,i}\,x_{2,1}\,\$\cdots\$\,x_{2,n}\,x_{1,i+1}\,\$\cdots\$\,x_{1,m}\,,$$

where $m, n \geq 1$ and $i \in [m-1]$. Intuitively, such an operation wraps the tuple derived from a nonterminal B around the tuple derived from a nonterminal C, filling the ith gap in the former. An example of a wrapping operation is the adjunction of an auxiliary tree in tree-adjoining grammar. In the general case, a wrapping operation will take an m-tuple and an n-tuple and return an $(m+n-2)$-tuple of strings: the gaps of the argument tuples appear in the obtained tuple, except for one gap in the tuple derived from B which is filled by the tuple derived from C.

By applying the general parsing rule in Figure 2a to a production $A \rightarrow \mathit{wrap}_i(B, C)$, where wrap_i is a wrapping operation, then we obtain the deduction step given in Figure 2c. This step uses $2m$ different l- and r-indexes, and $2n-2$ different l'- and r'-indexes (discounting l'_1 and r'_n which are equal to other indexes), for a total of $2m+2n-2 = 2(m+n-2)+2$ indexes. Since the fan-out of A is $m+n-2$, this means that a wrapping operation needs at most $2\varphi+2$ indexes for an LCFRS of fan-out φ.

From this, we conclude that an LCFRS of fan-out φ in which all composition operations are either concatenation operations, wrapping operations, or operations of rank 0 or 1, can be parsed in time $\mathcal{O}(|w|^{2\varphi+2})$. In particular, nullary and unary composition operations do not affect this worst-case complexity, since their associated deduction steps can never have more than 2φ indexes.

4 Transformation

We now show how to transform a well-nested LCFRS into the normal form that we have just described.

4.1 Informal overview

Consider a production $p = A \rightarrow f(A_1, \dots, A_m)$, where $m \geq 2$ and f is neither a concatenation nor a wrapping operation. We will construct new productions p', q, r such that every derivation that uses p can be rewritten into a derivation that uses the new productions, and the new productions do not license any other derivations. Formally, this can be understood as implementing a *tree transformation*, where the input trees are derivations of the original grammar, and the output trees are derivations of the new grammar. The situation is illustrated in Figure 3. The tree on top represents a derivation in the original grammar; this derivation starts with the rewriting of the nonterminal A using the production p, and continues with the subderivations $t_1, \dots, t_m$. The tree at the bottom represents a derivation in the transformed grammar. This derivation starts with the rewriting of A using the new production p', and continues with two independent subderivations that start with the new productions q and r, respectively. The sub-derivations $t_1, \dots, t_m$ have been partitioned into two sequences

$$t_{1,1}, \dots, t_{1,m_1} \quad \text{and} \quad t_{2,1}, \dots, t_{2,m_2}\,.$$

The new production p' will be either a concatenation or a wrapping operation, and the rank of both q and r will be strictly smaller than the rank of p. The transformation will continue with q and r, unless these have rank one. By applying this strategy exhaustively, we will thus eventually end up with a grammar that only has productions with rank at most 2, and in which all productions with rank 2 are either concatenation or wrapping operations.

4.2 Constructing the composition operations

To transform the production p, we first factorize the composition operation f associated with p into three new composition operations f', g, h as follows. Recall that we represent composition operations by their characteristic strings.

In the following, we will assume that no characteristic string starts or ends with a gap marker, or contains immediate repetitions of gap markers. This property can be ensured, without affecting the asymptotic complexity, by adding intermediate steps to the transformation that we report here; we omit the details due to space reasons. When this property holds, we are left with the following two cases. Let us call a sequence of variables *joint*, if it contains all and only variables associated with a given nonterminal.

Case 1 $f = x_1 \, f_1 \, x_2 \cdots x_{k-1} \, f_{k-1} \, x_k \, f^*$, where $k \geq 1$, $x_1, \ldots, x_k$ are joint variables, and the suffix f^* contains at least one variable. Let

$$g = x_1 \, f_1 \, x_2 \cdots x_{k-1} \, f_{k-1} \, x_k \,,$$

let $h = f^*$, and let $f' = \mathit{conc}$. As f is well-nested, both g and h define well-nested composition operations. By the specific segmentation of f, the ranks of these operations are strictly smaller than the rank of f. Furthermore, we have $\varphi(f) = \varphi(g) + \varphi(h) - 1$.

Case 2 $f = x_1 \, f_1 \, x_2 \cdots x_{k-1} \, f_{k-1} \, x_k$, where $k \geq 2$, $x_1, \ldots, x_k$ are joint variables, and there exist at least one i such that the sequence f_i contains at least one variable. Choose an index j as follows: if there is at least one i such that f_i contains at least one variable and one gap marker, let j be the minimal such i; otherwise, let j be the minimal i such that f_i contains at least one variable. Now, let

$$g = x_1 \, f_1 \, x_2 \cdots x_j \, \$ \, x_{j+1} \cdots x_{k-1} \, f_{k-1} \, x_k \,,$$

let $h = f_j$, and let $f' = \mathit{wrap}_j$. As in Case 1, both g and h define well-nested composition operations whose ranks are strictly smaller than the rank of f. Furthermore, we have $\varphi(f) = \varphi(g) + \varphi(h) - 2$.

Note that at most one of the two cases can apply to f. Furthermore, since f is well-nested, it is also true that at least one of the two cases applies. This is so because for two distinct nonterminals $A_i, A_{i'}$, either all variables associated with $A_{i'}$ precede the leftmost variable associated with A_i, succeed the rightmost variable associated with A_i, or are placed between two variables associated with A_i without another variable associated with A_i intervening. (Here, we have left out the symmetric cases.)

4.3 Constructing the new productions

Based on the composition operations, we now construct three new productions p', q, r as follows. Let B and C be two fresh nonterminals with $\varphi(B) = \varphi(g)$ and $\varphi(C) = \varphi(h)$, and let $p' = A \to f'(B, C)$. The production p' rewrites A into B and C and combines the two subderivations that originate at these nonterminals using either a concatenation or a wrapping operation. Now, let $A_{q,1}, \ldots, A_{q,m_q}$ and $A_{r,1}, \ldots, A_{r,m_r}$ be the sequences of nonterminals that are obtained from the sequence $A_1, \ldots, A_m$ by deleting those nonterminals that are not associated with any variable in g or h, respectively. Then, let

$$q = B \to g(A_{q,1}, \ldots, A_{q,m_q}) \quad \text{and}$$
$$r = C \to h('A_{r,1}, \ldots, A_{r,m_r}) \,.$$

4.4 Example

We now illustrate the transformation using the concrete production $p = A \to f(A_1, A_2, A_3)$, where

$$f = x_{1,1} \, x_{2,1} \, \$ \, x_{1,2} \, \$ \, x_{3,1} \,.$$

Note that this operation has rank 3 and fan-out 3.

The composition operations are constructed as follows. The operation f matches the pattern of Case 1, and hence induces the operations

$$g_1 = x_{1,1} \, x_{2,1} \, \$ \, x_{1,2} \,, \quad h_1 = \$ \, x_{3,1} \,, \quad f'_1 = \mathit{conc} \,.$$

The productions constructed from these are

$$p'_1 = A \to \mathit{conc}(B_1, C_1) \,,$$
$$q_1 = B_1 \to g_1(A_1, A_2) \,, \quad r_1 = C_1 \to h_1(A_3) \,.$$

where B_1 and C_1 are fresh nonterminals with fan-out 2. The production r_1 has rank one, so it does not require any further transformations. The transformation thus continues with q_1. The operation g_1 matches the pattern of Case 2, and induces the operations

$$g_2 = x_{1,1} \, \$ \, x_{1,2} \,, \quad h_2 = x_{2,1} \$ \,, \quad f'_2 = \mathit{wrap}_1 \,.$$

The productions constructed from these are

$$p'_2 = B_1 \to \mathit{wrap}_1(B_2, C_2) \,,$$
$$q_2 = B_2 \to g_2(A_1) \,, \quad r_2 = C_2 \to h_2(A_2) \,,$$

where B_2 and C_2 are fresh nonterminals with fan-out 2. At this point, the transformation terminates. We can now delete p from the original grammar, and replace it with the productions $\{p'_1, r_1, p'_2, q_2, r_2\}$.

4.5 Correctness

To see that the transformation is correct, we need to verify that each production of the original grammar is transformed into a set of equivalent normal-form productions, and that the fan-out of the new grammar does not exceed the fan-out of the old grammar.

For the first point, we note that the transformation preserves well-nestedness, decreases the rank of a production, and is always applicable as long as the rank of a production is at most 2 and the production does not use a concatenation or wrapping operation. That the new productions are equivalent to the old ones in the sense of Figure 3 can be proved by induction on the length of a derivation in the original and the new grammar, respectively.

Let us now convince ourselves that the fan-out of the new grammar does not exceed the fan-out of the old grammar. This is clear in Case 1, where

$$\varphi(f) = \varphi(g) + \varphi(h) - 1$$

implies that both $\varphi(g) \leq \varphi(f)$ and $\varphi(h) \leq \varphi(f)$. For Case 2, we reason as follows. The fan-out of the operation h, being constructed from an infix of the characteristic string of the original operation f, is clearly bounded by the fan-out of f. For g, we have

$$\varphi(g) = \varphi(f) - \varphi(h) + 2,$$

Now suppose that the index j was chosen according to the first alternative. In this case, $\varphi(h) \geq 2$, and

$$\varphi(g) \leq \varphi(f) - 2 + 2 = \varphi(f).$$

For the case where j was chosen according to the second alternative, $\varphi(f) < k$ (since there are no immediate repetitions of gap markers), $\varphi(h) = 1$, and $\varphi(g) \leq k$. If we assume that each nonterminal is productive, then this means that the underlying LCFRS has at least one production with fan-out k or more; therefore, the fan-out of g does not increase the fan-out of the original grammar.

4.6 Complexity

To conclude, we now briefly discuss the space complexity of the normal-form transformation. We measure it in terms of the *length* of a production, defined as the length of its string representation, that is, the string $A \to [v_1 \$ \cdots \$ v_k](A_1, \dots, A_m)$.

Looking at Figure 3, we note that the normal-form transformation of a production p can be understood as the construction of a (not necessarily complete) binary-branching tree whose leaves correspond to the productions obtained by splitting the characteristic string of p and whose non-leaf nodes are labeled with concatenation and wrapping operations. By construction, the sum of the lengths of leaf-node productions is $\mathcal{O}(|p|)$. Since the number of inner nodes of a binary tree with n leaves is bounded by $n - 1$, we know that the tree has $\mathcal{O}(\rho(p))$ inner nodes. As these nodes correspond to concatenation and wrapping operations, each inner-node production has length $\mathcal{O}(\varphi(p))$. Thus, the sum of the lengths of the productions created from $|p|$ is $\mathcal{O}(|p| + \rho(p)\varphi(p))$. Since the rank of a production is always smaller than its length, this is reduced to $\mathcal{O}(|p|\varphi(p))$.

Therefore, the size of the normal-form transformation of an LCFRS G of fan-out φ is $\mathcal{O}(\varphi|G|)$ in the worst case, and linear space in practice, since the fan-out is typically bounded by a small integer. Taking the normal-form transformation into account, our parser therefore runs in time $\mathcal{O}(\varphi \cdot |G| \cdot |w|^{2\varphi+2})$ where $|G|$ is the original grammar size.

5 Conclusion

In this paper, we have presented an efficient parsing algorithm for well-nested linear context-free rewriting systems, based on a new normal form for this formalism. The normal form takes up linear space with respect to grammar size, and the algorithm is based on a bottom-up process that can be applied to any LCFRS, achieving $\mathcal{O}(\varphi \cdot |G| \cdot |w|^{2\varphi+2})$ time complexity when applied to LCFRS of fan-out φ in our normal form. This complexity is an asymptotic improvement over existing results for this class, both from parsers specifically geared to well-nested LCFRS or equivalent formalisms (Hotz and Pitsch, 1996) and from applying general LCFRS parsing techniques to the well-nested case (Seki et al., 1991).

The class of well-nested LCFRS is an interesting syntactic formalism for languages with discontinuous constituents, providing a good balance between coverage of linguistic phenomena in natural language treebanks (Kuhlmann and Nivre, 2006; Maier and Lichte, 2009) and desirable formal properties (Kanazawa, 2009). Our results offer a further argument in support of well-nested LCFRS: while the complexity of parsing general LCFRS depends on two dimensions (rank and fan-out), this bidimensional hierarchy collapses into a single dimension in the well-nested case, where complexity is only conditioned by the fan-out.

Acknowledgments Gómez-Rodríguez has been supported by MEC/FEDER (HUM2007-66607-C04) and Xunta de Galicia (PGIDIT07SIN005206PR, Redes Galegas de PL e RI e de Ling. de Corpus, Bolsas Estadías INCITE/FSE cofinanced). Kuhlmann has been supported by the Swedish Research Council.

References

Éric Villemonte de la Clergerie. 2002. Parsing mildly context-sensitive languages with thread automata. In *19th International Conference on Computational Linguistics (COLING)*, pages 1–7, Taipei, Taiwan.

Daniel Gildea. 2010. Optimal parsing strategies for linear context-free rewriting systems. In *Human Language Technologies: The Eleventh Annual Conference of the North American Chapter of the Association for Computational Linguistics*, Los Angeles, USA.

Carlos Gómez-Rodríguez, Marco Kuhlmann, Giorgio Satta, and David J. Weir. 2009. Optimal reduction of rule length in linear context-free rewriting systems. In *Human Language Technologies: The 2009 Annual Conference of the North American Chapter of the Association for Computational Linguistics*, pages 539–547, Boulder, CO, USA.

Jiří Havelka. 2007. Beyond projectivity: Multilingual evaluation of constraints and measures on non-projective structures. In *45th Annual Meeting of the Association for Computational Linguistics (ACL)*, pages 608–615.

Günter Hotz and Gisela Pitsch. 1996. On parsing coupled-context-free languages. *Theoretical Computer Science*, 161(1–2):205–233.

Riny Huybregts. 1984. The weak inadequacy of context-free phrase structure grammars. In Ger de Haan, Mieke Trommelen, and Wim Zonneveld, editors, *Van periferie naar kern*, pages 81–99. Foris, Dordrecht, The Netherlands.

Aravind K. Joshi, Leon S. Levy, and Masako Takahashi. 1975. Tree Adjunct Grammars. *Journal of Computer and System Sciences*, 10(2):136–163.

Aravind K. Joshi. 1985. Tree Adjoining Grammars: How much context-sensitivity is required to provide reasonable structural descriptions? In *Natural Language Parsing*, pages 206–250. Cambridge University Press.

Laura Kallmeyer and Wolfgang Maier. 2009. An incremental Earley parser for simple range concatenation grammar. In *Proceedings of the 11th International Conference on Parsing Technologies (IWPT 2009)*, pages 61–64. Association for Computational Linguistics.

Makoto Kanazawa and Sylvain Salvati. 2010. The copying power of well-nested multiple context-free grammars. In *Fourth International Conference on Language and Automata Theory and Applications*, Trier, Germany.

Makoto Kanazawa. 2009. The pumping lemma for well-nested multiple context-free languages. In *Developments in Language Theory. 13th International Conference, DLT 2009, Stuttgart, Germany, June 30–July 3, 2009. Proceedings*, volume 5583 of *Lecture Notes in Computer Science*, pages 312–325.

Marco Kuhlmann and Mathias Möhl. 2007. Mildly context-sensitive dependency languages. In *45th Annual Meeting of the Association for Computational Linguistics (ACL)*, pages 160–167.

Marco Kuhlmann and Joakim Nivre. 2006. Mildly non-projective dependency structures. In *21st International Conference on Computational Linguistics and 44th Annual Meeting of the Association for Computational Linguistics (COLING-ACL), Main Conference Poster Sessions*, pages 507–514, Sydney, Australia.

Marco Kuhlmann and Giorgio Satta. 2009. Treebank grammar techniques for non-projective dependency parsing. In *Twelfth Conference of the European Chapter of the Association for Computational Linguistics (EACL)*, pages 478–486, Athens, Greece.

Wolfgang Maier and Timm Lichte. 2009. Characterizing discontinuity in constituent treebanks. In *14th Conference on Formal Grammar*, Bordeaux, France.

Wolfgang Maier and Anders Søgaard. 2008. Treebanks and mild context-sensitivity. In *13th Conference on Formal Grammar*, pages 61–76, Hamburg, Germany.

Owen Rambow and Giorgio Satta. 1999. Independent parallelism in finite copying parallel rewriting systems. *Theoretical Computer Science*, 223(1–2):87–120.

Giorgio Satta. 1992. Recognition of Linear Context-Free Rewriting Systems. In *30th Annual Meeting of the Association for Computational Linguistics (ACL)*, pages 89–95, Newark, DE, USA.

Hiroyuki Seki, Takashi Matsumura, Mamoru Fujii, and Tadao Kasami. 1991. On Multiple Context-Free Grammars. *Theoretical Computer Science*, 88(2):191–229.

Stuart M. Shieber, Yves Schabes, and Fernando Pereira. 1995. Principles and implementation of deductive parsing. *Journal of Logic Programming*, 24(1–2):3–36.

Stuart M. Shieber. 1985. Evidence against the context-freeness of natural language. *Linguistics and Philosophy*, 8(3):333–343.

Klaas Sikkel. 1997. *Parsing Schemata: A Framework for Specification and Analysis of Parsing Algorithms*. Springer.

K. Vijay-Shanker, David J. Weir, and Aravind K. Joshi. 1987. Characterizing structural descriptions produced by various grammatical formalisms. In *25th Annual Meeting of the Association for Computational Linguistics (ACL)*, pages 104–111, Stanford, CA, USA.

Utility Evaluation of Cross-document Information Extraction

Heng Ji[a], Zheng Chen[a], Jonathan Feldman[a], Antonio Gonzalez[a], Ralph Grishman[b], Vivek Upadhyay[a]
[a]Computer Science Department, Queens College and the Graduate Center, City University of New York
New York, NY 11367, USA
[b]Computer Science Department, New York University, New York, NY 10003, USA
hengji@cs.qc.cuny.edu, zchen1@gc.cuny.edu, agonzalez117@qc.cuny.edu, grishman@cs.nyu.edu, vivekqc@gmail.com

Abstract

We describe a utility evaluation to determine whether cross-document information extraction (IE) techniques measurably improve user performance in news summary writing. Two groups of subjects were asked to perform the same time-restricted summary writing tasks, reading news under different conditions: with no IE results at all, with traditional single-document IE results, and with cross-document IE results. Our results show that, in comparison to using source documents only, the quality of summary reports assembled using IE results, especially from cross-document IE, was significantly better and user satisfaction was higher. We also compare the impact of different user groups on the results.

1 Introduction

Information Extraction (IE) is a task of identifying 'facts' (entities, relations and events) within unstructured documents, and converting them into structured representations (e.g., databases). IE techniques have been effectively applied to different domains (e.g. daily news, Wikipedia, biomedical reports, financial analysis and legal documentations) and different languages. Recently we described a new cross-document IE task (Ji et al., 2009) to extract events across-documents and track them on a time line. Compared to traditional single-document IE, this new task can extract more salient, accurate and concise event information.

However, a significant question remains: will the events extracted by IE, especially this new cross-document IE task, actually help end-users to make better use of the large volumes of news? In order to investigate whether we have reached this goal, we performed an extrinsic utility (i.e., usefulness) and usability evaluation on IE results. Two groups of subjects were asked to perform the same time-restricted summary writing tasks, reading news under different conditions: with no IE results at all, with traditional single-document IE results, and with cross-document IE results. Our results show that, in comparison to using source documents only, the quality of summary reports assembled using IE techniques, especially from cross-document IE, was significantly better. Also, as extraction quality increases from no IE at all to single-document IE and then to cross-document IE, user satisfaction increases. We also compare the impact of different user groups on the results. To the best of our knowledge, this is the first systematic evaluation of cross-document IE from a usability perspective.

2 Overview of IE Systems

We applied the English single-document IE system (Ji and Grishman, 2008) and cross-document IE system presented in (Ji et al., 2009). Both systems were developed for the ACE program[1].

The single-document IE system can extract events from individual documents. The core stages include entity extraction, time expression extraction and normalization, relation extraction and event extraction. Events include the 33 distinct types defined in ACE05. The extraction results are presented in tabular form.

The cross-document IE system can identify important person entities which are frequently in-

[1] http://www.itl.nist.gov/iad/mig/tests/ace/2005/

Human Language Technologies: The 2010 Annual Conference of the North American Chapter of the ACL, pages 285–288,
Los Angeles, California, June 2010.

volved in events as 'centroid entities'; and then for each centroid entity, link and order the events centered around it on a time line and associate them to a geographical map. The event chains are presented in a user-friendly graphical interface (Ji and Chen, 2009). Both systems link the events back to their context documents.

3 Evaluation Methods

3.1 Study Execution

Our measurement challenge is to assess how IE techniques affect users' abilities to perform real-world tasks. We followed the summary writing task described in the Integrated Feasibility Experiment of the DARPA TIDES program (Colbath and Kubala, 2003) and the daily task conducted by intelligence analysts (Bodnar, 2003). Each task in our evaluation is based on writing a summary of ACE-type events involving a specific centroid entity, using one of three levels of support:

- Level (I): Read the news articles, with assistance of keyword based sentence search;
- Level (II): (I) + with assistance from single-document IE results;
- Level (III): (I) + with assistance from cross-document IE results.

The summary writing task for each entity using any level should be finished in 10 minutes. The users can choose to trust the IE results to create new sentences or select relevant sentences from the source documents. The IE systems were applied to a corpus of 106 articles from ACE 2005 training data.

3.2 Summary Scoring

We measure user responses in three aspects:

- *Observer-based Quantity* -- How many sentences are extracted in each summary? How many of them are uniquely correct?
- *Observer-based Quality*-- How fluent and coherent are the sentences in each summary?
- *User-based Usability* -- How does the user feel about the system?

3.3 User Group Selection

We selected user groups based on the principles that we should run as many tests as we can afford (Nielsen, 1994), and at least 5 to insure that we detect any major usability problems (Faulkner, 2003). Two different groups of users were asked to conduct the evaluation:

(1) Hallway Evaluation

We chose the first group of users with a "Hallway Testing" user-study method described in (Nielsen, 1994). We randomly asked 11 PhD students in the field of natural language processing to conduct the evaluation. In order to evaluate these three levels independently, each student was asked to write at most one summary, using one of the three levels, for any single centroid entity. To avoid the impact of diverse text comprehension abilities, each student was involved in all of these three levels for different centroid entities.

(2) Remote Evaluation

An effective utility evaluation will require users with a diversity of prior knowledge and computer experience. Therefore we asked the second group of 11 users in a remote usability testing mode (Hammontree et al., 1994). We sent out the request to university-wide undergraduate student mailing lists and found 11 users to work on the evaluation. The evaluation procedure follows the Hallway Testing method, except that the tests are carried out in the user's own environment (rather than labs) helping further simulate real-life scenario testing. Also the users didn't meet with the observers and thus they were not aware of any expectations for results.

4 Evaluation Results

In this section we will focus on reporting the results from Hallway Evaluation, while providing comparisons with Remote Evaluation.

4.1 Observer-based Quantity

The summaries were judged by two annotators and the judgements reconciled. A summary sentence is judged as uniquely correct if it: (1) includes relevant events involving the centroid entity; and (2) the same information was not included in previous sentences in the current summary. This metric can be considered as an approximate com bination of the "content responsiveness", "non-redundancy"and "focus" criteria in the NIST TAC summarization track[2]. Table 1 presents the

[2]http://www.nist.gov/tac/2009/Summarization/update.summ.09.guidelines.html

Cen-troid	(I)	(II)	(III)	Cen-troid	(I)	(II)	(III)	Cen-troid	(I)	(II)	(III)
Bush	3/1/0	5/1/2	6/0/0	Al-douri	4/3/3	4/2/0	6/0/1	Ba'asyir	3/1/0	3/0/0	5/0/0
Ibrahim	4/0/1	5/0/0	8/0/0	Giuliani	2/0/0	3/2/0	5/0/0	Erdogan	1/0/1	4/0/0	4/0/0
Toefting	0/0/0	7/1/0	4/0/0	Blair	2/0/1	3/0/0	5/0/0	Diller	3/0/0	4/1/0	3/0/0
Putin	2/1/0	4/3/2	7/1/1	Pasko	3/0/0	3/0/0	2/0/0	**Overall**	**27/6/6**	**45/10/5**	**55/1/2**

Table 1. # (uniquely correct sentences)/ #(redundant correct sentences)/ #(spurious sentences) in a summary in Hallway Evaluation

quantified Hallway Testing results for each centroid separately and the overall score. It shows that overall Level (II) contained 18 more correct sentences than the baseline (I), while (III) achieved 11 further correct sentences. (I) obtained significantly fewer sentences without assistance from IE tools. We conducted the Wilcoxon Matched-Pairs Signed-Ranks Test on a query entity basis for accuracy - number of (uniquely correct sentences)/number of (total extracted sentences in a summary). The results show that (III) is significantly better than (I) at a 99.2% confidence level, and better than (II) at a 96.9% confidence level. (II) is not significantly better than (I).

We can also see that for some centroid entities such as "Putin", "Al-douri" and "Giuliani", (II) generated more sentences but also introduced more redundant information. The user feedback has indicated that they did not have enough time to remove redundancy. In contrast, (III) yielded much less redundant information. In fact, the average time the users spent using (III) was only about 7.2 minutes. Therefore we can conclude that cross-document IE can produce more informative summaries in a more efficient way.

Error analysis showed that the major error types propagated from IE to summaries are as follows.

1. Event time errors. For example, the summary sentence "Toefting was convicted in September 2001 of assaulting a pair of restaurant workers in the capital" was judged as incorrect because the time argument should be "October 2002".

2. Pronoun resolution errors. When a pronoun is mistakenly linked to an entity, incorrect event arguments will be included in the summaries.

3. Event type errors. When an event is misclassified, the users tend to use incorrect templates and thus generate wrong summaries.

4. Negative events. Sometimes the event attribute classifier makes mistakes and the users include negative events in the summaries.

4.2 Impact of User Groups

In the Remote Testing, the accuracy results from the three levels are as follows: 21/37, 28/37 and 31/36. Thus both user groups benefited from using IE techniques, but the enhancements vary a lot. In the Hallway Testing, the users were better trained and more familiar with IE tools (including the graphical interface of cross-document IE); and thus they can benefit more from the IE techniques. In contrast, in the Remote Evaluation, the users had quite diverse knowledge backgrounds. For example, one remote user was only able to find 1-2 sentences using any of the three levels; while another, more skilled remote user found more than 5 sentences with any level. However the Remote Evaluation is important to gather the feedback of the more subjective usability evaluation in section 4.4. Because the users in Hallway Testing may be aware of the observations that the observer is hoping to achieve, they may provide potentially biased feedback.

4.3 Observer-based Quality

The evaluation also showed that (III) produced summaries with better quality. We asked the observers to give a score between [1, 10] to each summary according to the following TAC summarization quality criteria: Readability/Fluency, Referential Clarity and Structure/Coherence. Table 2 shows the evaluation results for the three different methods.

Criteria	(I)	(II)	(III)
Readability/Fluency	9.4	8.5	8.2
Referential Clarity	6.1	8.3	8.7
Structure/Coherence	7.1	7.6	8.5

Table 2. Observer-based Average Quality

In their detailed feedback, the users indicated that (III) has the following advantages: (1) Better pronoun resolution; (2) More complete and accurate temporal order because (III) Can recover unknown time arguments using cross-document inference. (3) Can generate abstractive summaries. For the biographical events (e.g. employment), some users were able to use specific templates such as "PER was hired by ORG at TIME" to write summaries. For example, a sentence "Bush and Blair met at Camp David and the UK three times in March 2003" was derived from three different "Contact-Meeting" events in the event chains. (4) Can connect related events into more concise summaries. For example, several events were connected to generate the following sentences "Pasko was appealed for treason crime on April 16, 2003 *and then* released on June 15, 2003". The readability scores in Table 2 also indicate that a more effective template generation method should be developed to produce more fluent summaries based on IE results.

4.4 User-based Usability

The user feedback from both evaluations also showed that (II) and (III) results were trusted almost equally, and (III) was claimed to provide the most useful functions. The positive comments about (III) include "Temporal Linking allows logical reasoning and generalization", "Centroid search helps to focus immediately", "Spatial Linking allows to browse all the places which a person has visited", "Name disambiguation helps to filter irrelevant information", "Can find key information from event chains", "Timeline helps correlate events"; and the negative comments include "Sometimes IE errors mislead locating the sentences", "No support of name pair search for meeting events", "No color emphasis of events on the original documents" and "No suggestions of templates to compose summary sentences".

5 Conclusion and Future Work

Through a utility evaluation on summary writing we have proved that IE techniques, especially cross-document IE, can aid news browsing, search and analysis. In particular, temporal event tracking across documents helps users perform better at fact-gathering than they do without IE. Users also produced more informative summaries with cross-document IE than with traditional single-document IE. We also compared and analyzed the differences between two user groups. Such measures of the benefits to the eventual end users also provided feedback on what works well and identified additional research problems, such as to expand the centroid to a pair of entities and to provide confidence metrics in the interface. In the future we aim to set up an online news article analysis system and perform larger and regular utility evaluations.

Acknowledgement

This work was supported by the U.S. NSF CAREER Award under Grant IIS-0953149, the U.S. Army Research Laboratory under Cooperative Agreement Number W911NF-09-2-0053, Google, Inc., CUNY Research Enhancement Program, Faculty Publication Program and GRTI Program. The views and conclusions contained in this document are those of the authors and should not be interpreted as representing the official policies, either expressed or implied, of the Army Research Laboratory or the U.S. Government. The U.S. Government is authorized to reproduce and distribute reprints for Government purposes notwithstanding any copyright notation here on.

References

John W. Bodnar. 2003. Warning Analysis for the Information Age: Rethinking the Intelligence Process. *Center for Strategic Intelligence Research, Joint Military Intelligence College*, Washington, D.C.

Sean Colbath and Francis Kubala. 2003. TAP-XL: An Automated Analyst's Assistant. *Proc. HLT-NAACL 2003 (demonstrations)*.

Laura Faulkner. 2003. Beyond the five-user assumption: Benefits of increased sample sizes in usability testing. *Behavior Research Methods Instruments and Computers* 35(3), 379-383.

Monty Hammontree, Paul Weiler and Nandini Nayak. 1994. Remote Usability Testing. *Interactions*. Volume 1, Issue 3. Pages: 21-25.

Heng Ji and Zheng Chen. 2009. Cross-document Temporal and Spatial Person Tracking System Demonstration. *Proc. HLT-NAACL 2009*.

Heng Ji, Ralph Grishman, Zheng Chen and Prashant Gupta. 2009. Cross-document Event Extraction, Ranking and Tracking. *Proc. Recent Advances in Natural Language Processing 2009*.

Jakob Nielsen. 1994. Usability Engineering. Morgan Kaufmann Publishers.

Evaluation Metrics for the Lexical Substitution Task

Sanaz Jabbari **Mark Hepple** **Louise Guthrie**
Department of Computer Science, University of Sheffield
211 Portobello Street, Sheffield, S1 4DP, UK
{S.Jabbari,M.Hepple,L.Guthrie}@dcs.shef.ac.uk

Abstract

We identify some problems of the evaluation metrics used for the English Lexical Substitution Task of SemEval-2007, and propose alternative metrics that avoid these problems, which we hope will better guide the future development of lexical substitution systems.

1 Introduction

The English Lexical Substitution task at SemEval-2007 (here called ELS07) requires systems to find substitutes for target words in a given sentence (McCarthy & Navigli, 2007: M&N). For example, we might replace the target word *match* with *game* in the sentence *they lost the match*. System outputs are evaluated against a set of candidate substitutes proposed by human subjects for test items. Targets are typically *sense ambiguous* (e.g. *match* in the above example), and so task performance requires a combination of *word sense disambiguation* (by exploiting the given sentential context) and (near) *synonym generation*. In this paper, we discuss some problems of the evaluation metrics used in ELS07, and then propose some alternative measures that avoid these problems, and which we believe will better serve to guide the development of lexical substitution systems in future work.[1] The subtasks within ELS07 divide into two groups, in terms of whether they focus on a system's 'best' answer for a test item, or address the broader set of answer candidates a system can produce. In what follows, we address these two cases in separate sections, and then present some results for applying our new metrics for the second case. We begin by briefly introducing the test materials that were created for the ELS07 evaluation.

2 Evaluation Materials

Briefly stated, the ELS07 dataset comprises around 2000 sentences, providing 10 test sentences each for some 201 preselected target words, which were required to be sense ambiguous and have at least one synonym, and which include nouns, verbs, adjectives and adverbs. Five human annotators were asked to suggest up to three substitutes for the target word of each test sentence, and their collected suggestions serve as the gold standard against which system outputs are compared. Around 300 sentences were distributed as development data, and the remainder retained for the final evaluation.

To assist defining our metrics, we formally describe this data as follows.[2] For each sentence t_i in the test data ($1 \leq i \leq N$, N the number of test items), let H_i denote the set of human proposed substitutes. A key aspect of the data is the *count* of human annotators that proposed each candidate (since a term appears a stronger candidate if proposed by annotators). For each t_i, there is a function $freq_i$ which returns this count for each term within H_i (and 0 for any other term), and a value $maxfreq_i$ corresponding to the maximal count for any term in H_i. The pairing of H_i and $freq_i$ in effect provides a *multiset* representation of the human answer set. We

[1] We consider here only the case of substituting for single word targets. Subtasks of ELS07 involving multi-word substitutions are not addressed.

[2] For consistency, we also restate the original ELS07 metrics in these terms, whilst preserving their essential content.

Human Language Technologies: The 2010 Annual Conference of the North American Chapter of the ACL, pages 289–292,
Los Angeles, California, June 2010.

use $|S|^i$ in what follows to denote the *multiset cardinality* of S according to $freq_i$, i.e. $\Sigma_{a \in S} freq_i(a)$. Some of the ELS07 metrics use a notion of *mode* answer m_i, which exists only for test items that have a single most-frequent human response, i.e. a *unique* $a \in H_i$ such that $freq_i(a) = maxfreq_i$. To adapt an example from M&N, an item with target word *happy* (adj) might have human answers $\{glad, merry, sunny, jovial, cheerful\}$ with counts (3,3,2,1,1) respectively. We will abbreviate this answer set as $H_i = \{G{:}3, M{:}3, S{:}2, J{:}1, Ch{:}1\}$ where it is used later in the paper.

3 Best Answer Measures

Two of the ELS07 tasks address how well systems are able to find a 'best' substitute for a test item, for which individual test items are scored as follows:

$$best(i) = \frac{\sum_{a \in A_i} freq_i(a)}{|H_i|^i \times |A_i|}$$

$$mode(i) = \begin{cases} 1 & \text{if } bg_i = m_i \\ 0 & \text{otherwise} \end{cases}$$

For the first task, a system can return a *set* of answers A_i (the answer set for item i), but since the score achieved is divided by $|A_i|$, returning multiple answers only serves to allow a system to 'hedge its bets' if it is uncertain which candidate is really the best. The optimal score on a test item is achieved by returning a single answer whose count is $maxfreq_i$, with proportionately lesser credit being received for any answer in H_i with a lesser count. For the second task, which uses the *mode* metric, only a single system answer – its 'best guess' bg_i – is allowed, and the score is simply 0 or 1 depending on whether the best guess is the mode. Overall performance is computed by averaging across a broader set of test items (which for the second task includes only items having a mode value). M&N distinguish two overall performance measures: *Recall*, which averages over all relevant items, and *Precision*, which averages only over those items *for which the system gave a non-empty response*.

We next discuss these measures and make an alternative proposal. The task for the first measure seems a reasonable one, i.e. assessing the ability of systems to provide a 'best' answer for a test item, but allowing them to offer multiple candidates (to 'hedge their bets'). However, the metric is unsatisfactory in that a system that performs optimally in terms of this task (i.e. which, for every test item, returns a single correct 'most frequent' response) will get a score that is well below 1, because the score is also divided by $|H_i|^i$, the multiset cardinality of H_i, whose size varies between test items (being a consequence of the number of alternatives suggested by the human annotators), but which is typically larger than the numerator value $maxfreq_i$ of an optimal answer (unless H_i is singleton). This problem is fixed in the following modified metric definition, by dividing instead by $maxfreq_i$, as then a response containing a single optimal answer will score 1.

$$best(i) = \frac{\sum_{a \in A_i} freq_i(a)}{maxfreq_i \times |A_i|} \qquad best_1(i) = \frac{freq_i(bg_i)}{maxfreq_i}$$

With $H_i = \{G{:}3, M{:}3, S{:}2, J{:}1, Ch{:}1\}$, for example, an optimal response $A_i = \{M\}$ receives score 1, where the original metric gives score 0.3. Singleton responses containing a correct but non-optimal answer receive proportionately lower credit, e.g. for $A_i = \{S\}$ we score 0.66 (vs. 0.2 for the original metric). For a non-singleton answer set including, say, a correct answer and an incorrect one, the credit for the correct answer will be halved, e.g. for $A_i = \{S, X\}$ we score 0.33.

Regarding the second task, we think it reasonable to have a task where systems may offer only a single 'best guess' response, but argue that the *mode* metric used has two key failings: it is too *brittle* in being applicable only to items that have a mode answer, and it *loses information* valuable to system ranking, in assigning no credit to a response that might be good but not optimal. We propose instead the $best_1$ metric above, which assigns score 1 to a best guess answer with count $maxfreq_i$, but applies to *all* test items irrespective of whether or not they have a unique mode. For answers having lesser counts, proportionately less credit is assigned. This metric is equivalent to the new *best* metric shown beside it for the case where $|A_i| = 1$.

For assessing overall performance, we suggest just taking the average of scores across *all* test items, c.f. M&N's Recall measure. Their Precision metric is presumably intended to favour a system that can tell whether it does or does not have any good answers to return. However, the ability to draw a boundary between good vs. poor candidates will be reflected widely in a system's performance and captured elsewhere (not least by the coverage metrics discussed later) and so, we argue, does not need to be separately assessed in this way. Furthermore, the fact that a system does not return any answers may have other causes, e.g. that its lexical resources have failed to yield *any* substitution candidates for a term.

4 Measures of Coverage

A third task of ELS07 assesses the ability of systems to field a wider set of good substitution candidates for a target, rather than just a 'best' candidate. This 'out of ten' (*oot*) task allows systems to offer a set A_i of *upto 10* guesses per item i, and is scored as:

$$oot(i) = \frac{\sum_{a \in A_i} freq_i(a)}{|H_i|^i}$$

Since the score is *not* divided by the answer set size $|A_i|$, no benefit derives from offering less than 10 candidates.[3] When systems are asked to field a broader set of candidates, we suggest that evaluation should assess if the response set is *good* in containing as many correct answers as possible, whilst containing as few incorrect answers as possible. In general, systems will tackle this problem by combining a means of ranking candidates (drawn from lexical resources) with a means of drawing a boundary between good and bad candidates, e.g. threshold setting.[4] Since the *oot* metric does not penalise incorrect answers, it does not encourage systems to develop such boundary methods, even though this is important to their ultimate practical utility.

The view of a 'good' answer set described above suggests a comparison of A_i to H_i using versions of 'recall' and 'precision' metrics, that incorporate the 'weighting' of human answers via $freq_i$. Let us begin by noting the obvious definitions for recall and precision metrics *without* count-weighting:

$$R(i) = \frac{|H_i \cap A_i|}{|H_i|} \qquad P(i) = \frac{|H_i \cap A_i|}{|A_i|}$$

Our definitions of these metrics, given below, *do* include count-weighting, and require some explanation. The numerator of our recall definition is $|A_i|^i$ not $|H_i \cap A_i|^i$ as $|A_i|^i = |H_i \cap A_i|^i$ (as $freq_i$ assigns 0 to any term not in H_i), an observation which also affects the numerator of our P definition. Regarding the latter's denominator, merely dividing by $|A_i|^i$ would not penalise incorrect terms (as, again, $freq_i(a) = 0$ for any $a \notin H_i$), so this is done directly by adding $k|A_i - H_i|$, where $|A_i - H_i|$ is the number of incorrect answers, and k some *penalty factor*, which might be $k = 1$ in the simplest case. (Note that our weighted R metric is in fact equivalent to the *oot* definition above.) As usual, an F-score can be computed as the harmonic mean of these values (i.e. $F = 2PR/(P + R)$). For assessing overall performance, we might average P, R and F scores across all test items.

$$R(i) = \frac{|A_i|^i}{|H_i|^i} \qquad P(i) = \frac{|A_i|^i}{|A_i|^i + k|A_i - H_i|}$$

With $H_i = \{G{:}3, M{:}3, S{:}2, J{:}1, Ch{:}1\}$, for example, the perfect response set $A_i = \{G, M, S, J, Ch\}$ gives P and R scores of 1. The response $A_i = \{G, M, S, J, Ch, X, Y, Z, V, W\}$, containing all correct answers plus 5 incorrect ones, gets $R = 1$, but only $P = 0.66$ (assuming $k = 1$, giving $10/(10 + 5)$). The response $A_i = \{G, S, J, X, Y\}$, with 3 out of 5 correct answers, plus 2 incorrect ones, gets $R = 0.6$ $(6/10)$ and $P = 0.75$ $(6/6 + 2)$)

5 Applying the Coverage measure

Although the 'best guess' task is a valuable indicator of the likely utility of a lexical substitution system within various broader applications, we would argue that the *core* task for lexical substitution is *coverage*, i.e. the ability to field a broad set of correct substitution candidates. This task requires systems both to field and rank promising candidates, and to have a means of drawing a boundary between the good and bad candidates, i.e. a *boundary strategy*.

In this section, we apply the coverage metrics to the outputs of some lexical substitution systems, and

[3]We do not consider here a related task which assesses whether the *mode* answer m_i is found within an answer set of up to 10 guesses. We do not favour the use of this metric for reasons parallel to those discussed for the *mode* metric of the previous section, i.e. *brittleness* and *information loss*.

[4]In Jabbari *et al.* (2010), we define a metric that directly addresses the ability of systems to achieve good ranking of substitution candidates. This is not itself a measure of lexical substitution task performance, but addresses a component ability that is key to the achievement of lexical substitution tasks.

Model	1	2	3	4	5	6	7	8	9	10
bow	.067	.114	.151	.173	.191	.201	.212	.219	.222	.225
lm	.119	.192	.228	.246	.256	.267	.271	.272	.271	.271
cmlc	.139	.205	.251	.271	.284	.288	.291	.290	.289	.286
KU	.173	.244	.287	.307	.318	.321	.320	.318	.314	.311

Table 3: Coverage F-scores (macro-avgd), for simple boundary strategies (with *penalty factor* $k = 1$).

	All	*By part-of-speech*			
Model	*words*	nouns	adj	verb	adv
bow	.326	.343	.334	.205	.461
lm	.393	.372	.442	.252	.562
cmlc	.414	.404	.447	.311	.534
KU	.462	.408	.511	.398	.567

Table 1: Out-of-ten recall scores for all the systems (with a subdivision by *pos* of target item).

	All	*By part-of-speech*			
Model	*words*	nouns	adj	verb	adv
bow	.298	.315	.302	.189	.422
lm	.371	.35	.408	.24	.539
cmlc	.395	.383	.419	.31	.506
KU	.435	.379	.477	.385	.536

Table 2: *Optimal* F-scores (macro-avgd) for coverage, computed over the (oot) ranked outputs of the systems (with *penalty factor* $k = 1$).

compare the indication it provides of relative system performance to that of the *oot* metric. We consider three systems described in Jabbari (2010), developed as part of an investigation into the means and benefits of combining models of lexical context: (i) *bow*: a system using a bag-of-words model to rank candidates, (ii) *lm*: using a (simple) n-gram language model, and (iii) *cmlc*: using a model that combines *bow* and *lm* models into one. We also consider the system KU, which uses a very large language model and an advanced treatment of smoothing, and which performed well at ELS07 (Yuret, 2007).[5] Table 1 shows the *oot* scores for these systems, including a breakdown by part-of-speech, which indicate a performance ranking: *bow* < *lm* < *cmlc* < KU

Our first problem is that these systems are developed for the *oot* task, not coverage, so after ranking their candidates, they do not attempt to draw a boundary between the candidates worth returning and those not. Instead, we here use the *oot* outputs to compute an *optimal* performance for each system, i.e. we find, for the ranked candidates of each question, the cut-off position giving the highest F-score, and then average these scores across questions, which tells us the F-score the system could achieve if it had an *optimal boundary strategy*. These scores, shown in Table 2, indicate a ranking of systems in line with that in Table 1, which is not surprising as both will ultimately reflect the quality of candidate ranking achieved by the systems.

Table 3 shows the coverage results achieved by applying a naive boundary strategy to the system outputs. The strategy is just to always return the top n candidates for each question, for a fixed value n. Again, performance correlates straightforwardly with the underlying quality of ranking. Comparing tables, we see, for example, that by always returning 6 candidates, the system KU could achieve a coverage of .32 as compared to the .435 optimal score.

References

D. McCarthy and R. Navigli. 2007. SemEval-2007 Task 10: English Lexical Substitution Task. *Proc. of the 4th Int. Workshop on Semantic Evaluations* (SemEval-2007), Prague.

S. Jabbari. 2010. *A Statistical Model of Lexical Context*, PhD Thesis, University of Sheffield.

S. Jabbari, M. Hepple and L.Guthrie. 2010. Evaluating Lexical Substitution: Analysis and New Measures. *Proc. of the 7th Int. Conf. on Language Resources and Evaluation* (LREC-2010). Malta.

D. Yuret. 2007. KU: Word Sense Disambiguation by Substitution. In *Proc. of the 4th Int. Workshop on Semantic Evaluations* (SemEval-2007), Prague.

[5]We thank Deniz Yuret for allowing us to use his system's outputs in this analysis.

Movie Reviews and Revenues: An Experiment in Text Regression*

Mahesh Joshi Dipanjan Das Kevin Gimpel Noah A. Smith
Language Technologies Institute
Carnegie Mellon University
Pittsburgh, PA 15213, USA
{maheshj,dipanjan,kgimpel,nasmith}@cs.cmu.edu

Abstract

We consider the problem of predicting a movie's opening weekend revenue. Previous work on this problem has used metadata about a movie—e.g., its genre, MPAA rating, and cast—with very limited work making use of text *about* the movie. In this paper, we use the text of film critics' reviews from several sources to predict opening weekend revenue. We describe a new dataset pairing movie reviews with metadata and revenue data, and show that review text can substitute for metadata, and even improve over it, for prediction.

1 Introduction

Predicting gross revenue for movies is a problem that has been studied in economics, marketing, statistics, and forecasting. Apart from the economic value of such predictions, we view the forecasting problem as an application of NLP. In this paper, we use the text of critics' reviews to predict opening weekend revenue. We also consider metadata for each movie that has been shown to be successful for similar prediction tasks in previous work.

There is a large body of prior work aimed at predicting gross revenue of movies (Simonoff and Sparrow, 2000; Sharda and Delen, 2006; *inter alia*). Certain information is used in nearly all prior work on these tasks, such as the movie's genre, MPAA rating, running time, release date, the number of screens on which the movie debuted, and the presence of particular actors or actresses in the cast. Most prior text-based work has used automatic text analysis tools, deriving a small number of aggregate statistics. For example, Mishne and Glance (2006) applied sentiment analysis techniques to pre-release and post-release blog posts about movies and showed higher correlation between actual revenue and sentiment-based metrics, as compared to mention counts of the movie. (They did not frame the task as a revenue prediction problem.) Zhang and Skiena (2009) used a news aggregation system to identify entities and obtain domain-specific sentiment for each entity in several domains. They used the aggregate sentiment scores and mention counts of each movie in news articles as predictors.

While there has been substantial prior work on using critics' reviews, to our knowledge all of this work has used polarity of the review or the number of stars given to it by a critic, rather than the review text directly (Terry et al., 2005).

Our task is related to sentiment analysis (Pang et al., 2002) on movie reviews. The key difference is that our goal is to predict a *future* real-valued quantity, restricting us from using any post-release text data such as user reviews. Further, the most important clues about revenue may have little to do with whether the reviewer *liked* the movie, but rather what the reviewer found worth mentioning. This paper is more in the tradition of Ghose et al. (2007) and Kogan et al. (2009), who used text regression to directly quantify review "value" and make predictions about future financial variables, respectively.

Our aim in using the full text is to identify particular words and phrases that predict the movie-going tendencies of the public. We can also perform syntactic and semantic analysis on the text to identify richer constructions that are good predictors. Furthermore, since we consider multiple reviews for each movie, we can compare these features across reviews to observe how they differ both in frequency and predictive performance across different media outlets and individual critics.

In this paper, we use linear regression from text and non-text (meta) features to directly predict gross revenue aggregated over the opening weekend, and the same averaged per screen.

*We appreciate reviewer feedback and technical advice from Brendan O'Connor. This work was supported by NSF IIS-0803482, NSF IIS-0844507, and DARPA NBCH-1080004.

Human Language Technologies: The 2010 Annual Conference of the North American Chapter of the ACL, pages 293–296,
Los Angeles, California, June 2010.

Domain	train	dev	test	total
Austin Chronicle	306	94	62	462
Boston Globe	461	154	116	731
LA Times	610	2	13	625
Entertainment Weekly	644	208	187	1039
New York Times	878	273	224	1375
Variety	927	297	230	1454
Village Voice	953	245	198	1396
# movies	1147	317	254	1718

Table 1: Total number of reviews from each domain for the training, development and test sets.

2 Data

We gathered data for movies released in 2005–2009. For these movies, we obtained metadata and a list of hyperlinks to movie reviews by crawling MetaCritic (`www.metacritic.com`). The metadata include the name of the movie, its production house, the set of genres it belongs to, the scriptwriter(s), the director(s), the country of origin, the primary actors and actresses starring in the movie, the release date, its MPAA rating, and its running time. From The Numbers (`www.the-numbers.com`), we retrieved each movie's production budget, opening weekend gross revenue, and the number of screens on which it played during its opening weekend. Only movies found on both MetaCritic and The Numbers were included.

Next we chose seven review websites that most frequently appeared in the review lists for movies at Metacritic, and obtained the text of the reviews by scraping the raw HTML. The sites chosen were the *Austin Chronicle*, the *Boston Globe*, the *LA Times*, *Entertainment Weekly*, the *New York Times*, *Variety*, and the *Village Voice*. We only chose those reviews that appeared on or before the release date of the movie (to ensure that revenue information is not present in the review), arriving at a set of 1718 movies with at least one review. We partitioned this set of movies temporally into training (2005–2007), development (2008) and test (2009) sets. Not all movies had reviews at all sites (see Table 1).

3 Predictive Task

We consider two response variables, both in U.S. dollars: the total revenue generated by a movie during its release weekend, and the *per screen* revenue during the release weekend. We evaluate these predictions using (1) mean absolute error (MAE) in U.S. dollars and (2) Pearson's correlation between the actual and predicted revenue.

We use linear regression to directly predict the opening weekend gross earnings, denoted y, based on features $\boldsymbol{x}$ extracted from the movie metadata and/or the text of the reviews. That is, given an input feature vector $\boldsymbol{x} \in \mathbb{R}^p$, we predict an output $\hat{y} \in \mathbb{R}$ using a linear model: $\hat{y} = \beta_0 + \boldsymbol{x}^\top \boldsymbol{\beta}$. To learn values for the parameters $\boldsymbol{\theta} = \langle \beta_0, \boldsymbol{\beta} \rangle$, the standard approach is to minimize the sum of squared errors for a training set containing n pairs $\langle \boldsymbol{x}_i, y_i \rangle$ where $\boldsymbol{x}_i \in \mathbb{R}^p$ and $y_i \in \mathbb{R}$ for $1 \leq i \leq n$:

$$\hat{\boldsymbol{\theta}} = \operatorname*{argmin}_{\boldsymbol{\theta}=(\beta_0,\boldsymbol{\beta})} \frac{1}{2n} \sum_{i=1}^{n} \left(y_i - (\beta_0 + \boldsymbol{x}_i^\top \boldsymbol{\beta}) \right)^2 + \lambda P(\boldsymbol{\beta})$$

A penalty term $P(\boldsymbol{\beta})$ is included in the objective for regularization. Classical solutions use an ℓ_2 or ℓ_1 norm, known respectively as ridge and lasso regression. Introduced recently is a mixture of the two, called the elastic net (Zou and Hastie, 2005):

$$P(\boldsymbol{\beta}) = \sum_{j=1}^{p} \left(\tfrac{1}{2}(1-\alpha)\beta_j^2 + \alpha|\beta_j| \right)$$

where $\alpha \in (0, 1)$ determines the trade-off between ℓ_1 and ℓ_2 regularization. For our experiments we used the elastic net and specifically the `glmnet` package which contains an implementation of an efficient coordinate ascent procedure for training (Friedman et al., 2008).

We tune the α and λ parameters on our development set and select the model with the $\langle \alpha, \lambda \rangle$ combination that yields minimum MAE on the development set.

4 Experiments

We compare predictors based on metadata, predictors based on text, and predictors that use both kinds of information. Results for two simple baselines of predicting the training set mean and median are reported in Table 2 (Pearson's correlation is undefined since the standard deviation is zero).

4.1 Metadata Features

We considered seven types of metadata features, and evaluated their performance by adding them to our pool of features in the following order: whether the film is of U.S. origin, running time (in minutes), the logarithm of its budget, # opening screens, genre (e.g., Action, Comedy) and MPAA rating (e.g., G, PG, PG-13), whether the movie opened on a holiday weekend or in summer months, total count as well as of presence of individual Oscar-winning actors and directors and high-grossing actors. For the first task of predicting the total opening weekend revenue of a movie, the best-performing feature set in terms of MAE turned out to be all the features. However, for the second task of predicting the *per screen* revenue, addition of the last feature subset consisting of information related to the actors and directors hurt performance (MAE increased). Therefore, for the second task, the best performing set contained only the first six types of metadata features.

4.2 Text Features

We extract three types of text features (described below). We only included feature instances that occurred in at least five different movies' reviews. We stem and downcase individual word components in all our features.

I. n-grams. We considered unigrams, bigrams, and trigrams. A 25-word stoplist was used; bigrams and trigrams were only filtered if all words were stopwords.

II. Part-of-speech n-grams. As with words, we added unigrams, bigrams, and trigrams. Tags were obtained from the Stanford part-of-speech tagger (Toutanova and Manning, 2000).

III. Dependency relations. We used the Stanford parser (Klein and Manning, 2003) to parse the critic reviews and extract syntactic dependencies. The dependency relation features consist of just the relation part of a dependency triple $\langle$relation, head word, modifier word$\rangle$.

We consider three ways to combine the collection of reviews for a given movie. The first ("$-$") simply concatenates all of a movie's reviews into a single document before extracting features. The second ("$+$") conjoins each feature with the source site (e.g., *New York Times*) from whose review it was extracted. A third version (denoted "B") combines both the site-agnostic and site-specific features.

	Features	Site	Total MAE ($M)	Total r	Per Screen MAE ($K)	Per Screen r
	Predict mean		11.672	–	6.862	–
	Predict median		10.521	–	6.642	–
meta	Best		5.983	0.722	6.540	0.272
text	I	–	8.013	0.743	6.509	0.222
		+	7.722	0.781	6.071	0.466
	see Tab. 3	B	7.627	0.793	6.060	0.411
	I ∪ II	–	8.060	0.743	6.542	0.233
		+	**7.420**	0.761	6.240	0.398
		B	7.447	0.778	6.299	0.363
	I ∪ III	–	8.005	0.744	6.505	0.223
		+	7.721	0.785	6.013	**0.473**
		B	7.595	**0.796**	†**6.010**	0.421
meta ∪ text	I	–	5.921	**0.819**	6.509	0.222
		+	5.757	0.810	6.063	0.470
		B	5.750	**0.819**	6.052	0.414
	I ∪ II	–	5.952	0.818	6.542	0.233
		+	5.752	0.800	6.230	0.400
		B	5.740	**0.819**	6.276	0.358
	I ∪ III	–	5.921	**0.819**	6.505	0.223
		+	**5.738**	0.812	6.003	**0.477**
		B	5.750	**0.819**	†**5.998**	0.423

Table 2: Test-set performance for various models, measured using mean absolute error (MAE) and Pearson's correlation (r), for two prediction tasks. Within a column, **boldface** shows the best result among "text" and "meta ∪ text" settings. †Significantly better than the meta baseline with $p < 0.01$, using the Wilcoxon signed rank test.

4.3 Results

Table 2 shows our results for both prediction tasks. For the total first-weekend revenue prediction task, metadata features baseline result ($r^2 = 0.521$) is comparable to that reported by Simonoff and Sparrow (2000) on a similar task of movie gross prediction ($r^2 = 0.446$). Features from critics' reviews by themselves improve correlation on both prediction tasks, however improvement in MAE is only observed for the *per screen* revenue prediction task.

A combination of the meta and text features achieves the best performance both in terms of MAE and r. While the text-only models have some high negative weight features, the combined models do not have any negatively weighted features and only a very few metadata features. That is, the text is able to substitute for the other metadata features.

Among the different types of text-based features that we tried, lexical n-grams proved to be a strong baseline to beat. None of the "I ∪ $*$" feature sets are significantly better than n-grams alone, but adding the dependency relation features (set III) to the n-grams does improve the performance enough to make it significantly better than the metadata-only baseline for per screen revenue prediction.

Salient Text Features: Table 3 lists some of the highly weighted features, which we have categorized manually. The features are from the text-only model annotated in Table 2 (total, not per screen). The feature weights can be directly interpreted as U.S. dollars contributed to the predicted value $\hat{y}$ by each occurrence of the feature. Sentiment-related features are not as prominent as might be expected, and their overall proportion in the set of features with non-zero weights is quite small (estimated in preliminary trials at less than 15%). Phrases that refer to metadata are the more highly weighted and frequent ones. Consistent with previous research, we found some positively-oriented sentiment features to be predictive. Some other prominent features not listed in the table correspond to special effects ("*Boston Globe*: of_the_art", "and_cgi"), particular movie franchises ("shrek_movies", "*Variety*: chronicle_of", "voldemort"), hype/expectations ("blockbuster", "anticipation"), film festival ("*Variety*: canne" with negative weight) and time of release ("summer_movie").

5 Conclusion

We conclude that text features from pre-release reviews can substitute for and improve over a strong metadata-based first-weekend movie revenue prediction. The dataset used in this paper has been made available for research at `http://www.ark.cs.cmu.edu/movie$-data`.

	Feature	Weight ($M)
rating	pg	+0.085
	New York Times: adult	-0.236
	New York Times: rate_r	-0.364
sequels	this_series	+13.925
	LA Times: the_franchise	+5.112
	Variety: the_sequel	+4.224
people	*Boston Globe*: will_smith	+2.560
	Variety: brittany	+1.128
	^_producer_brian	+0.486
genre	*Variety*: testosterone	+1.945
	Ent. Weekly: comedy_for	+1.143
	Variety: a_horror	+0.595
	documentary	-0.037
	independent	-0.127
sentiment	*Boston Globe*: best_parts_of	+1.462
	Boston Globe: smart_enough	+1.449
	LA Times: a_good_thing	+1.117
	shame_$	-0.098
	bogeyman	-0.689
plot	*Variety*: torso	+9.054
	vehicle_in	+5.827
	superhero_$	+2.020

Table 3: Highly weighted features categorized manually. ^ and $ denote sentence boundaries. "brittany" frequently refers to Brittany Snow and Brittany Murphy. "^_producer_brian" refers to producer Brian Grazer (*The Da Vinci Code*, among others).

References

J. Friedman, T. Hastie, and R. Tibshirani. 2008. Regularized paths for generalized linear models via coordinate descent. Technical report, Stanford University.

A. Ghose, P. G. Ipeirotis, and A. Sundararajan. 2007. Opinion mining using econometrics: A case study on reputation systems. In *Proc. of ACL*.

D. Klein and C. D. Manning. 2003. Fast exact inference with a factored model for natural language parsing. In *Advances in NIPS 15*.

S. Kogan, D. Levin, B. R. Routledge, J. Sagi, and N. A. Smith. 2009. Predicting risk from financial reports with regression. In *Proc. of NAACL*, pages 272–280.

G. Mishne and N. Glance. 2006. Predicting movie sales from blogger sentiment. In *AAAI Spring Symposium on Computational Approaches to Analysing Weblogs*.

B. Pang, L. Lee, and S. Vaithyanathan. 2002. Thumbs up? Sentiment classification using machine learning techniques. In *Proc. of EMNLP*, pages 79–86.

R. Sharda and D. Delen. 2006. Predicting box office success of motion pictures with neural networks. *Expert Systems with Applications*, 30(2):243–254.

J. S. Simonoff and I. R. Sparrow. 2000. Predicting movie grosses: Winners and losers, blockbusters and sleepers. *Chance*, 13(3):15–24.

N. Terry, M. Butler, and D. De'Armond. 2005. The determinants of domestic box office performance in the motion picture industry. *Southwestern Economic Review*, 32:137–148.

K. Toutanova and C. D. Manning. 2000. Enriching the knowledge sources used in a maximum entropy part-of-speech tagger. In *Proc. of EMNLP*, pages 63–70.

W. Zhang and S. Skiena. 2009. Improving movie gross prediction through news analysis. In *Web Intelligence*, pages 301–304.

H. Zou and T. Hastie. 2005. Regularization and variable selection via the elastic net. *Journal Of The Royal Statistical Society Series B*, 67(5):768–768.

Using Gaussian Mixture Models to Detect Figurative Language in Context

Linlin Li and Caroline Sporleder
Saarland University, Postfach 15 11 50
66041 Saarbrücken, Germany
{linlin, csporled}@coli.uni-saarland.de

Abstract

We present a Gaussian Mixture model for detecting different types of figurative language in context. We show that this model performs well when the parameters are estimated in an unsupervised fashion using EM. Performance can be improved further by estimating the parameters from a small annotated data set.

1 Introduction

Figurative language employs words in a way that deviates from their normal meaning. It includes idiomatic usage, metaphor, metonymy or other types of creative language. Being able to detect figurative language is important for a number of NLP applications, e.g., machine translation.

Simply checking the input against an idiom dictionary does not solve the problem. While some expressions (e.g., *trip the light fantastic*) are always used idiomatically, many expressions (e.g., *spill the beans*), can take on a literal meaning as well. Whether such expression is used idiomatically or not has to be inferred from the discourse context. Likewise, simple dictionary look-up would not work for truly creative, one-off usages; these can neither be found in a dictionary nor can they be detected by standard idiom extraction methods, which apply statistical measures to accumulated corpus evidence for an expression to assess its 'idiomaticity'. An example of a fairly creative usage can be found in (1), which is a variation of the idiom *put a sock in*.

(1) **Take the sock out of your mouth** and create a brand-new relationship with your mom.

We propose a method for detecting figurative language in context. Because we use context information rather than corpus statistics, our approach works also for truly creative usages.

2 Related Work

Most studies on the detection of idioms and other types of figurative language focus on one of three aspects: type-based extraction (detect idioms on the type level), token-based classification (given a potentially idiomatic phrase in context, decide whether it is used idiomatically), token-based detection (detect figurative expressions in running text).

Type-based extractions exploit the fact that idioms have many properties which differentiate them from other expressions, e.g., they often exhibit a degree of syntactic and lexical fixedness. These properties can be used to identify potential idioms, for instance, by employing measures of association strength between the elements of an expression (Lin, 1999).

Type-based approaches are unsuitable for expressions which can be used both figuratively and literally. These have to be disambiguated in context. *Token-based classification* aims to do this. A number of token-based approaches have been proposed: supervised (Katz and Giesbrecht, 2006), weakly supervised (Birke and Sarkar, 2006), and unsupervised (Fazly et al., 2009; Sporleder and Li, 2009).

Finally, *token-based detection* can be viewed as a two stage task which is the combination of type-based extraction and token-based classification. There has been relatively little work on this so far. One exception are Fazly et al. (2009) who detect idiom types by using statistical methods that model the general idiomaticity of an expression and then combine this with a simple second-stage process that detects whether the target expression is used figuratively in a given context, based on whether the expression occurs in canonical form or not.

However, modeling token-based detection as a

Human Language Technologies: The 2010 Annual Conference of the North American Chapter of the ACL, pages 297–300,
Los Angeles, California, June 2010.

combination of type-based extraction and token-based classification has some drawbacks. First, type-based approaches typically compute statistics from multiple occurrences of a target expression, hence they cannot be applied to novel usages. Second, these methods were developed to detect figuratively used multi-word expressions (MWEs) and do not work for figuratively used individual words, like *sparrow* in example (2). Ideally, one would like to have a generic model that can detect any type of figurative usage in a given context. The model we propose in this paper is one step in this direction.

(2) During the Iraq war, he was a **sparrow**; he didn't condone the bloodshed but wasn't bothered enough to go out and protest.

3 Using Gaussian Mixture Model to Detect Figurative Language

We address the problem by using Gaussian Mixture Models (GMMs). We assume that the literal (l) and non-literal (n) data are generated by two different Gaussians (*literal* and *nonliteral* Gaussian). The token-based detection task is done by comparing which Gaussian has the higher probability of generating a specific instance.

The Gaussian mixture model is defined as:

$$p(x) = \sum_{c \in \{l,n\}} w_c \times N(x|\mu_c, \Sigma_c)$$

Where, c is the category of the Gaussian, μ_c is the mean, Σ_c is the covariance matrix, and w_c is the Gaussian weight.

Our method is based on the insight that figurative language exhibits less semantic cohesive ties with the context than literal language (Sporleder and Li, 2009). We use Normalized Google Distance to model semantic relatedness (Cilibrasi and Vitanyi, 2007) and represent the data by five types of semantic relatedness features $x = (x1, x2, x3, x4, x5)$:

$x1$ is the average relatedness between the target expression and context words,

$$x1 = \frac{2}{|T| \times |C|} \sum_{(w_i, c_j) \in T \times C} relatedness(w_i, c_j)$$

where w_i is a component word of the target expression (T); c_j is one of the context words (C); $|T|$ is the total number of words in the target expression, and $|C|$ is the total number of words in the context. The term $\frac{2}{|T| \times |C|}$ is the normalization factor, which is the total number of relatedness pairs between target component words and context words.

$x2$ is the average semantic relatedness in the context of the target expression,

$$x2 = \frac{1}{\binom{|C|}{2}} \sum_{(c_i, c_j) \in C \times C, i \neq j} relatedness(c_i, c_j)$$

$x3$ is the difference between the average semantic relatedness between the target expression and the context words and the average semantic relatedness of the context (i.e., $x3 = x1 - x2$). It is an indicator of how strongly the target expression is semantically related to the discourse context.

$x4$ is the feature used by Sporleder and Li (2009) for predicting literal or idiomatic use in the cohesion graph based method,

$$x4 = \begin{cases} 1 & \text{if } x3 < 0 \\ 0 & \text{else} \end{cases}$$

$x5$ is a high dimensional vector which represents the top relatedness scores between the component words of the target expression and the context,

$$x5(k) = \max_{(w_i, c_j) \in T \times C} (k, \{relatedness(w_i, c_j)\})$$

where the function $max(k, A)$ is defined to choose the kth highest element from the set A.[1]

The detection task is done by a Bayes decision rule, which chooses the category by maximizing the probability of fitting the data into the different Gaussian components:

$$c(x) = \arg\max_{i \in \{l,n\}} \{w_i \times N(x|\mu_i, \Sigma_i)\}$$

4 Evaluating the GMM Approach

4.1 Data

We evaluate our method on two data sets. The first set (*idiom set*) is taken from Sporleder and Li (2009) and consists of 3964 idiom occurrences (17 idiom types) which were manually labeled as 'literal' or 'figurative'. The second data set (*V+NP set*), consists of a randomly selected sample of 500 V+NP constructions from the Gigaword corpus, which were manually labeled.

To determine how well our model deals with different types of figurative usage, we distinguish four phenomena: *Phrase-level figurative* means that the

[1]We set k to be 100 in our experiment.

whole phrase is used figuratively. We further divide this class into expressions which are potentially ambiguous between literal and figurative usage (**nsa**), e.g., *spill the beans*, and those that are unambiguously figurative irrespective of the context (**nsu**), e.g., *trip the light fantastic*. The latter can, theoretically, be detected by dictionary look-up, the former cannot. The label *token-level figurative* (**nw**) is used when part of the phrase is used figuratively (e.g., *sparrow* in (2)). Often it is difficult to determine whether a word is still used in a 'literal' sense or whether it is already used figuratively. Since we are interested in improving the performance of NLP applications such as MT, we take a pragmatic approach and classify usages as 'figurative' if they are not lexicalized, i.e., if the specific sense is not listed in a dictionary.[2] For example, we would classify *summit* in the 'meeting' sense as 'literal' (**l**). In our data set, 7.3% of the instances were annotated as 'nsa', 1.9% as 'nsu', 9.2% as 'nw' and 81.5% as 'l'. A randomly selected sample (100 instances) was annotated independently by a second annotator. The kappa score (Cohen, 1960) is 0.84, which suggest that the annotations are reliable.

4.2 GMM Estimated by EM

We used the MatLab package provided by Calinon (2009) for estimating the GMM model. The GMM is trained by the EM algorithm. The priors of Gaussian components, means and covariance of each components, are initialized by the k-means clustering algorithm (Hartigan, 1975).

To determine whether the GMM is able to perform token-based idiom classification, we applied it to the idiom data set. The results (see Table 1) show that the GMM can distinguish usages quite well and gains equally good results as Sporleder and Li's cohesion graph method (*Co-Graph*). In addition, this method can deal with unobserved occurrences of non-literal language.

Table 2 shows the results on the second data set. The baseline predicts 'idiomatic' and 'literal' according to a biased probability which is based on the true distribution in the annotated set. *GMM* shows the performance on the whole V+NP set. We also split the test set into three different subsets to determine how the GMM performs on distinguishing literal usage from the different types of figurative usage: *GMM{nsu, l}*, *GMM{nsa, l}*, *GMM{nw, l}*.

Model	C	Pre.	Rec.	F-S.	Acc.
Co-Graph	n	90.55	80.66	85.32	78.38
	l	50.04	69.72	58.26	
GMM	n	90.69	80.66	85.38	78.39
	l	50.17	70.15	58.50	

Table 1: Results on the idiom data set, n(on-literal) is the union of the predefined three sub-classes (nsu, nsa, nw), l(iteral), Acc(uracy), Pre(cision), Rec(all), F-S(core)

Model	C	Pre.	Rec.	F-S.	Acc.
Baseline	n	21.79	22.67	22.22	71.87
	l	83.19	82.47	82.83	
Co-Graph	n	37.29	84.62	51.76	70.92
	l	95.12	67.83	79.19	
GMM	n	40.71	73.08	52.29	75.41
	l	92.58	75.94	83.44	
GMM{nsu,l}	n	8.79	1.00	16.16	76.49
	l	1.00	75.94	86.33	
GMM{nsa,l}	n	22.43	77.42	34.78	76.06
	l	97.40	75.94	85.34	
GMM{nw,l}	n	23.15	64.10	34.01	74.74
	l	94.93	75.94	84.38	

Table 2: Results on the V+NP data set, Gaussian component parameters estimated by EM

The unsupervised GMM model beats the baseline and achieves good results on the V+NP data set. It also outperforms the Co-Graph approach, which suggests that the statistical model, GMM, is more likely to boost the performance by capturing statistical properties of the data for more difficult cases (*idioms* vs. *general figurative usages*), compared with the Co-Graph approach.

In conclusion, the model is not only able to classify idiomatic expressions but also to detect new figurative expressions. However, the performance on the second data set is worse compared with running the same model on the idiom data set. This is because the V+NP data set contains more difficult examples, e.g., expressions which are only partially figurative (e.g., (2)). One would expect the literal part of the expression to exhibit cohesive ties with the context, hence the cohesion based features may fail to detect this type of figurative usage. Consequently the performance of the GMM is lower for figuratively used words ('nw') than for idioms ('nsa', 'nsu'). However, even for 'nw' cases the model still obtains a relatively high accuracy.

[2]We used `http://www.askoxford.com`.

4.3 GMM estimated from Annotated Data

In a second experiment, we tested how well the GMM performs when utilizing the annotated idiom data set to estimate the two Gaussian components instead of using EM. We give equal weights to the two Gaussian components and predict the label on the V+NP data set by fixing the mixture model which is estimated from the training set (GMM+f). This method further improves the performance compared to the unsupervised approach (Table 3).

We also experimented with setting a threshold and abstaining from making a prediction when the probability of an instance belonging to the Gaussian is below the threshold (GMM+f+s). Table 3 shows the performance when only evaluating on the subset for which a classification was made. It can be seen that the accuracy and the overall performance on the literal class improve, but the precision for the nonliteral class remains relatively low, i.e., many literal instances are still misclassified as 'non-literal'. One reason for this may be that there are a few instances containing named entities, which exhibit weak cohesive ties with the context even if though they are used literally. Using a named-entity tagger before applying the GMM might solve the problem.

Model	C	Pre.	Rec.	F-S.	Acc.
GMM+f	n	42.22	73.08	53.52	76.60
	l	92.71	77.39	84.36	
GMM+f+s	n	41.38	54.55	47.06	83.44
	l	92.54	87.94	90.18	

Table 3: Results on the V+NP data set, Gaussian component parameters estimated by annotated data

Finally, Table 4 shows the result when using different idioms to generate the nonliteral Gaussian. The literal Gaussian can be generated from the automatically obtained nonliteral examples by Li and Sporleder (2009). We found the estimation of the GMM is not sensitive to idioms; our model is robust and can use any existing idiom data to discover new figurative expressions. Furthermore, Table 4 also shows that the GMM does not need a large amount of annotated data for parameter estimation. A few hundred instances are sufficient.

5 Conclusion

We described a GMM based approach for detecting figurative expressions. This method not only works for distinguishing literal and non-literal usages of a potential idiomatic expression in a discourse context, but also discovers new figurative expressions.

The components of the GMM can be effectively estimated using the EM algorithm. The performance can be further improved when employing an annotated data set for parameter estimation. Our results show that the estimation of Gaussian components are not idiom-dependent. Furthermore, a small annotated data set is enough to obtain good results.

Train (size)	C	Pre.	Rec.	F-S.	Acc.
bite one's tongue (166)	n	40.79	79.49	53.91	74.94
	l	94.10	73.91	82.79	
break the ice (541)	n	39.05	52.56	44.81	76.12
	l	88.36	81.45	84.77	

Table 4: Results on the V+NP dataset, Gaussian component parameters estimated on different idioms

Acknowledgments

This work was funded by the DFG within the Cluster of Excellence "Multimodal Computing and Interaction". Thanks to Benjamin Roth for discussions and comments.

References

J. Birke, A. Sarkar. 2006. A clustering approach for the nearly unsupervised recognition of nonliteral language. In *Proceedings of EACL-06*.

S. Calinon. 2009. *Robot Programming by Demonstration: A Probabilistic Approach*. EPFL/CRC Press.

R. L. Cilibrasi, P. M. B. Vitanyi. 2007. The Google similarity distance. *IEEE Trans. on Knowl. and Data Eng.*, 19(3):370–383.

J. Cohen. 1960. A coefficient of agreement for nominal scales. *Educational and Psychological Measurements*, 20:37–46.

A. Fazly, P. Cook, S. Stevenson. 2009. Unsupervised type and token identification of idiomatic expressions. *Computational Linguistics*, 35(1):61–103.

J. A. Hartigan. 1975. *Clustering Algorithm*. Wiley.

G. Katz, E. Giesbrecht. 2006. Automatic identification of non-compositional multi-word expressions using latent semantic analysis. In *Proceedings of the ACL06 Workshop on Multiword Expressions: Identifying and Exploiting Underlying Properties*.

L. Li, C. Sporleder. 2009. Contextual idiom detection without labelled data. In *Proceedings of EMNLP-09*.

D. Lin. 1999. Automatic identification of noncompositional phrases. In *Proceedings of ACL-99*.

C. Sporleder, L. Li. 2009. Unsupervised recognition of literal and non-literal use of idiomatic expressions. In *Proceedings of EACL-09*.

Improving Phrase-Based Translation with Prototypes of Short Phrases

Frank Liberato[†], **Behrang Mohit**[‡], **Rebecca Hwa**[†‡]
[†]Department of Computer Science [‡]Intelligent Systems Program
University of Pittsburgh
{frank,behrang,hwa@cs.pitt.edu}

Abstract

We investigate methods of generating additional bilingual phrase pairs for a phrase-based decoder by translating short sequences of source text. Because our translation task is more constrained, we can use a model that employs more linguistically rich features than a traditional decoder. We have implemented an example of this approach. Experimental results suggest that the phrase pairs produced by our method are useful to the decoder, and lead to improved sentence translations.

1 Introduction

Recently, there have been a number of successful attempts at improving phrase-based statistical machine translation by exploiting linguistic knowledge such as morphology, part-of-speech tags, and syntax. Many translation models use such knowledge before decoding (Xia and McCord, 2004) and during decoding (Birch et al., 2007; Gimpel and Smith, 2009; Koehn and Hoang, 2007; Chiang et al., 2009), but they are limited to simpler features for practical reasons, often restricted to conditioning left-to-right on the target sentence. Traditionally, n-best rerankers (Shen et al., 2004) have applied expensive analysis after the translation process, on both the source and target side, though they suffer from being limited to whatever is on the n-best list (Hasan et al., 2007).

We argue that it can be desirable to pre-translate parts of the source text before sentence-level decoding begins, using a richer model that would typically be out of reach during sentence-level decoding. In this paper, we describe a particular method of generating additional bilingual phrase pairs for a new source text, using what we call *phrase prototypes*, which are are learned from bilingual training data. Our goal is to generate improved translations of relatively short phrase pairs to provide the SMT decoder with better phrasal choices. We validate the idea through experiments on Arabic-English translation. Our method produces a 1.3 BLEU score increase (3.3% relative) on a test set.

2 Approach

Re-ranking tends to use expensive features of the entire source and target sentences, s and t, and alignments, a, to produce a score for the translation. We will call this scoring function $\phi(s,t,a)$. While $\phi(\cdot)$ might capture quite a bit of linguistic information, it can be problematic to use this function for decoding directly. This is due to both the expense of computing it, and the difficulty in using it to guide the decoder's search. For example, a choice of $\phi(\cdot)$ that relies on a top-down parser is difficult to integrate into a left-to-right decoder (Charniak et al., 2003).

Our idea is to use an expensive scoring function to guide the search for potential translations for *part* of a source sentence, S, even if translating all of it isn't feasible. We can then provide these translations to the decoder, along with their scores, to incorporate them as it builds the complete translation of S. This differs from approaches such as (Och and Ney, 2004) because we generate new phrase pairs in isolation, rather than incorporating everything into the sentence-level decoder. The baseline system is the Moses phrase-based translation system (Koehn

Human Language Technologies: The 2010 Annual Conference of the North American Chapter of the ACL, pages 301–304,
Los Angeles, California, June 2010.

et al., 2007).

2.1 Description of Our Scoring Function

For this work, we consider a scoring function based on part-of-speech (POS) tags, $\phi_{POS}(\cdot)$. It operates in two steps: it converts the source and target phrases, plus alignments, into what we call a *phrase prototype*, then assigns a score to it based on how common that prototype was during training.

Each phrase pair prototype is a tuple containing the source prototype, target prototype, and alignment prototype, respectively. The source and target prototypes are a mix of surface word forms and POS tags, such as the Arabic string $\langle$`NN Al JJ`$\rangle$, or the English string $\langle$`NN NN`$\rangle$. For example, the source and target prototypes above might be used in the phrase prototype $\langle \texttt{NN}_0\ \texttt{Al}\ \texttt{JJ}_1\ ,\ \texttt{NN}_1\ \texttt{NN}_0 \rangle$, with the alignment prototype specified implicitly via subscripts for brevity. For simplicity, the alignment prototype is restricted to allow a source or target word/tag to be unaligned, plus 1:1 alignments between them. We do not consider 1:many, many:1, or many:many alignments in this work.

For any input $\langle s, t, a \rangle$, it is possible to construct potentially many phrase prototypes from it by choosing different subsets of the source and target words to represent as POS tags. In the above example, the Arabic determiner `Al` could be converted into an unaligned POS tag, making the source prototype $\langle$`NN DT JJ`$\rangle$. For this work, we convert all aligned words into POS tags. As a practical concern, we insist that unaligned words are always kept as their surface form.

$\phi_{POS}(s, t, a)$ assign a score based on the probability of the resulting prototypes; more likely prototypes should yield higher scores. We choose:

$$\phi_{POS}(s, t, a) = p(SP, AP|TP) \cdot p(TP, AP|SP)$$

where SP is the source prototype constructed from s, t, a. Similarly, TP and AP are the target and alignment prototypes, respectively.

To compute $\phi_{POS}(\cdot)$, we must build a model for each of $p(SP, AP|TP)$ and $p(TP, AP|SP)$. To do this, we start with a corpus of aligned, POS-tagged bilingual text. We then find phrases that are consistent with (Koehn et al., 2003). As we extract these phrase pairs, we convert each into a phrase prototype by replacing surface forms with POS tags for all aligned words in the prototype.

After we have processed the bilingual training text, we have collected a set of phrase prototypes and a count of how often each was observed.

2.2 Generating New Phrases

To generate phrases, we scan through the source text to be translated, finding any span of source words that matches the source prototype of at least one phrase prototype. For each such phrase, and for each phrase prototype which it matches, we generate all target phrases which also match the target and alignment prototypes.

To do this, we use a word-to-word dictionary to generate all target phrases which honor the alignments required by the alignment prototype. For each source word which is aligned to a POS tag in the target prototype, we substitute all single-word translations in our dictionary[1].

For each target phrase that we generate, we must ensure that it matches the target prototype. We give each phrase to a POS tagger, and check the resulting tags against any tags in the target prototype. If there are no mismatches, then the phrase pair is retained for the phrase table, else it is discarded. In the latter case, $\phi_{POS}(\cdot)$ would assign this pair a score of zero.

2.3 Computing Phrase Weights

In the Moses phrase table, each entry has four parameters: two lexical weights, and the two conditional phrase probabilities $p(s|t)$ and $p(t|s)$. While the lexical weights can be computed using the standard method (Koehn et al., 2003), estimating the conditional phrase probabilities is not straightforward for our approach because they are not observed in bilingual training data. Instead, we estimate the *maximum* conditional phrase probabilities that would be assigned by the sentence-level decoder for this phrase pair, as if it had generated the target string from the source string using the baseline phrase table[2]. To do this efficiently, we use some

[1] Since we required that all unaligned target words are kept as surface forms in the target prototype, this is sufficient. If we did not insist this, then we might be faced with the unenviable task of choosing a target languange noun, without further guidance from the source text.

[2] If we use these probabilities for our generated phrase pair's probability estimates, then the sentence-level decoder would see

simplifying assumptions: we do not restrict how often a source word is used during the translation, and we ignore distortion / reordering costs. These admit a simple dynamic programming solution.

We must also include the score from $\phi_{POS}(\cdot)$, to give the decoder some idea of our confidence in the generated phrase pair. We include the phrase pair's score as an additional weight in the phrase table.

3 Experimental Setup

The Linguistic Data Consortium Arabic-English corpus2[3] is used to train the baseline MT system (34K sentences, about one million words), and to learn phrase prototypes. The LDC multi-translation Arabic-English corpus (NIST2003)[4] is used for tuning and testing; the tuning set consists of the first 500 sentences, and the test set consists of the next 500 sentences. The language model is a 4-gram model built from the English side of the parallel corpus, plus the English side of the wmt07 German-English and French-English news commentary data. The baseline translation system is Moses (Koehn et al., 2007), with the `msd-bidirectional-fe` reordering model. Evaluation is done using the BLEU (Papineni et al., 2001) metric with four references. All text is lowercased before evaluation; recasing is not used. We use the Stanford Arabic POS Tagging system, based on (Toutanova et al., 2003)[5]. The word-to-word dictionary that is used in the phrase generation step of our method is extracted from the highest-scoring translations for each source word in the baseline phrase table. For some closed-class words, we use a small, manually constructed dictionary to reduce the noise in the phrase table that exists for very common words. We use this in place of a stand-alone dictionary to reduce the need for additional resources.

4 Experiments

To see the effect on the BLEU score of the resulting sentence-level translation, we vary the amount of bilingual data used to build the phrase prototypes.

(approximately) no difference between building the generated phrase using the baseline phrase table, or using our generated phrase pair directly.

[3]Catalogue numbers LDC2004T17 and LDC2004T18

[4]Catalogue number: LDC2003T18

[5]It is available at http://nlp.stanford.edu/software/tagger.shtml

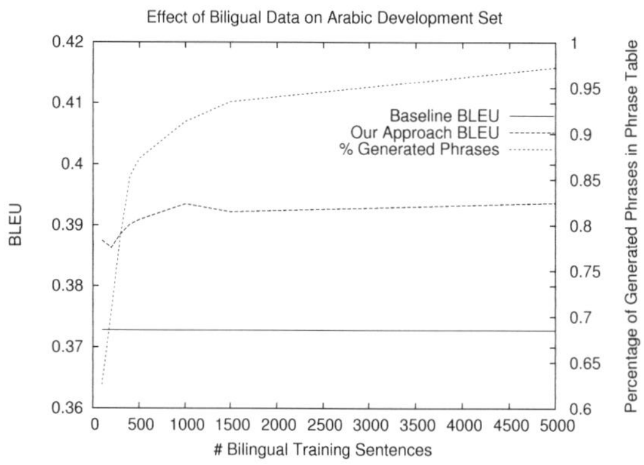

Figure 1: Bilingual training size vs. BLEU score (middle line, left axis) and phrase table composition (top line, right axis) on Arabic Development Set. The baseline BLEU score (bottom line) is included for comparison.

As we increase the amount of training data, we expect that the phrase prototype extraction algorithm will observe more phrase prototypes. This will cause it to generate more phrase pairs, introducing both more noise and more good phrases into the phrase table. Because quite a few phrase prototypes are built in any case, we require that each is seen at least three times before we use it to generate phrases. Phrase prototypes seen fewer times than this are discarded before phrase generation begins. Varying this minimum support parameter does not affect the results noticeably.

The results on the tuning set are seen in Figure 1. The BLEU score on the tuning set generally improves as the amount of bilingual training data is increased, even as the percentage of generated phrases approaches 100%. Manual inspection of the phrase pairs reveals that many are badly formed; this suggests that the language model is doing its job in filtering out disfluent phrases.

Using the first 5,000 bilingual training sentences to train our model, we compare our method to the baseline moses system. Each system was tuned via MERT (Och, 2003) before running it on the test set. The tuned baseline system scores 38.45. Including our generated phrases improves this by 1.3 points to 39.75. This is a slightly smaller gain than exists in the tuning set experiment, due in part that we did not run MERT for experiment shown in Figure 1.

5 Discussion

As one might expect, generated phrases both help and hurt individual translations. A sentence that can be translated starting with the phrase "`korea added that the syrian prime minister`" is translated by the baseline system as "`korean | foreign minister | added | that | the syrian`". While "`the syrian foreign minister`" is an unambiguous source phrase, the baseline phrase table does not include it; the language and reordering models must stitch the translation together. Ours method generates "`the syrian foreign minister`" directly.

Generated phrases are not always correct. For example, a generated phrase causes our system to choose "`europe role`", while the baseline system picks "`the role of | europe`". While the same prototype is used (correctly) for reordering Arabic "$\mathtt{NN}_0$ $\mathtt{JJ}_1$" constructs into English as "$\mathtt{NN}_1$ $\mathtt{NN}_0$" in many instances, it fails in this case. The language model shares the blame, since it does not prefer the correct phrase over the shorter one. In contrast, a 5-gram language model based on the LDC Web IT 5-gram counts[6] prefers the correct phrase.

6 Conclusion

We have shown that translating short spans of source text, and providing the results to a phrase-based SMT decoder can improve sentence-level machine translation. Further, it permits us to use linguistically informed features to guide the generation of new phrase pairs.

Acknowledgements

This work is supported by U.S. National Science Foundation Grant IIS-0745914. We thank the anonymous reviewers for their suggestions.

References

A. Birch, M. Osborne, and P. Koehn. 2007. CCG supertags in factored statistical machine translation. In *Proc. of the Second Workshop on SMT.*

E. Charniak, K. Knight, and K. Yamada. 2003. Syntax-based language models for statistical machine translation. In *Proceedings of MT Summit IX.*

D. Chiang, K. Knight, and W. Wang. 2009. 11,001 new features for statistical machine translation. In *NAACL '09: Proceedings of Human Language Technologies: The 2009 Annual Conference of the North American Chapter of the Assoc. for Computational Linguistics.*

K. Gimpel and N.A. Smith. 2009. Feature-rich translation by quasi-synchronous lattice parsing. In *Proc. of EMNLP.*

S. Hasan, R. Zens, and H. Ney. 2007. Are very large n-best lists useful for SMT? *Proc. NAACL, Short paper,* pages 57–60.

P. Koehn and H. Hoang. 2007. Factored translation models. In *Proceedings of the 2007 Joint Conference on Empirical Methods in Natural Language Processing and Computational Natural Language Learning (EMNLP-CoNLL),* pages 868–876.

P. Koehn, F.J. Och, and D. Marcu. 2003. Statistical phrase-based translation. In *Proceedings of the 2003 Conference of the North American Chapter of the Association for Computational Linguistics on Human Language Technology-Volume 1,* page 54.

P. Koehn, H. Hoang, A. Birch, C. Callison-Burch, M. Federico, N. Bertoldi, B. Cowan, W. Shen, C. Moran, R. Zens, et al. 2007. Moses: Open source toolkit for statistical machine translation. In *Annual meeting-Association for Computational Linguistics,* volume 45, page 2.

F. J. Och and H. Ney. 2004. The alignment template approach to statistical machine translation. *Computational Linguistics,* 30(4):417–449.

F.J. Och. 2003. Minimum error rate training in statistical machine translation. In *Proc. of the 41st Annual Meeting on Assoc. for Computational Linguistics.*

K. Papineni, S. Roukos, T. Ward, and W.J. Zhu. 2001. Bleu: a method for automatic evaluation of machine translation. In *Proc. of the 40th Annual Meeting of Association for Computational Linguistics.*

L. Shen, A. Sarkar, and F.J. Och. 2004. Discriminative reranking for machine translation. In *Proceedings of the Joint HLT and NAACL Conference (HLT 04),* pages 177–184.

K. Toutanova, D. Klein, C. D. Manning, and Y. Singer. 2003. Feature-rich part-of-speech tagging with a cyclic dependency network. In *NAACL '03: Proceedings of the 2003 Conference of the North American Chapter of the Association for Computational Linguistics on Human Language Technology.*

F. Xia and M. McCord. 2004. Improving a statistical mt system with automatically learned rewrite patterns. In *COLING '04: Proceedings of the 20th international conference on Computational Linguistics.*

[6]Catalogue number LDC2006T13.

Putting the User in the Loop: Interactive Maximal Marginal Relevance for Query-Focused Summarization

Jimmy Lin, Nitin Madnani, and **Bonnie J. Dorr**
University of Maryland
College Park, MD 20742, USA
jimmylin@umd.edu, {nmadnani,bonnie}@umiacs.umd.edu

Abstract

This work represents an initial attempt to move beyond "single-shot" summarization to *interactive* summarization. We present an extension to the classic Maximal Marginal Relevance (MMR) algorithm that places a user "in the loop" to assist in candidate selection. Experiments in the complex interactive Question Answering (ciQA) task at TREC 2007 show that interactively-constructed responses are significantly higher in quality than automatically-generated ones. This novel algorithm provides a starting point for future work on interactive summarization.

1 Introduction

Document summarization, as captured in modern comparative evaluations such as TAC and DUC, is mostly conceived as a "one-shot" task. However, researchers have long known that information seeking is an iterative activity, which suggests that an interactive approach might be worth exploring.

This paper present a simple extension of a well-known algorithm, Maximal Marginal Relevance (MMR) (Goldstein et al., 2000), that places the user in the loop. MMR is an iterative algorithm, where at each step a candidate extract c (e.g., a sentence) is assigned the following score:

$$\lambda \text{Rel}(q, c) - (1 - \lambda) \max_{s \in S} \text{Sim}(s, c)$$

The score consists of two components: the relevance of the candidate c with respect to the query q (Rel) and the similarity of the candidate c to each extract s in the current summary S (Sim). The maximum score from these similarity comparisons is subtracted from the relevance score, subjected to a tuning parameter that controls the emphasis on relevance and anti-redundancy. Scores are recomputed after each step and the algorithm iterates until a stopping criterion has been met (e.g., length quota).

We propose a simple extension to MMR: at each step, we interactively ask the user to select the best sentence for inclusion in the summary. That is, instead of the system automatically selecting the candidate with the highest score, it presents the user with a ranked list of candidates for selection.

2 Complex, Interactive QA

One obstacle to assessing the effectiveness of interactive summarization algorithms is the lack of a suitable evaluation vehicle. Given the convergence of complex QA and summarization (particularly the query-focused variant) in recent years, we found an appropriate evaluation vehicle in the ciQA (complex, interactive Question Answering) task at TREC 2007 (Dang et al., 2007).

Information needs in the ciQA task, called topics, consist of two parts: the question template and the narrative. The question template is a stylized information need that has a fixed structure and free slots whose instantiation varies across different topics. The narrative is unstructured prose that elaborates on the information need. For the evaluation, NIST assessors developed 30 topics, grouped into five templates. See Figure 1 for an example.

Participants in the task were able to deploy fully-functional web-based QA systems, with which the

Human Language Technologies: The 2010 Annual Conference of the North American Chapter of the ACL, pages 305–308,
Los Angeles, California, June 2010.

Template: What evidence is there for transport of [drugs] from [Mexico] to [the U.S.]?
Narrative: The analyst would like to know of efforts to curtail the transport of drugs from Mexico to the U.S. Specifically, the analyst would like to know of the success of the efforts by local or international authorities.

Figure 1: Example topic from the TREC 2007 ciQA task.

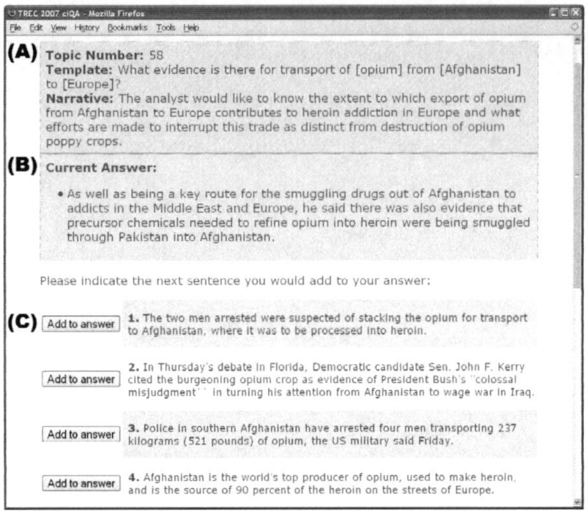

Figure 2: Screenshot of the interface for interactive MMR, which shows the current topic (A), the current answer (B), and a ranked list of document extracts (C).

NIST assessors interacted (serving as surrogates for users). Upon receiving the topics, participants first submitted an initial run. During a pre-arranged period of time shortly thereafter, each assessor was given five minutes to interact with the participant's system, live over the web. After this interaction period, participants submitted a final run, which had presumably gained the benefit of user interaction. By comparing initial and final runs, it was possible to quantify the effect of the interaction.

The target corpus was AQUAINT-2, which consists of around 970k documents totaling 2.5 GB. System responses consisted of multi-line answers and were evaluated using the "nugget" methodology with the "nugget pyramid" extension (Lin and Demner-Fushman, 2006).

3 Experiment Design

This section describes our experiments for the TREC 2007 ciQA task. In summary: the initial run was generated automatically using standard MMR. The web-based interactions consisted of iterations of interactive MMR, where the user selected the best candidate extract at each step. The final run consisted of the output of interactive MMR padded with automatically-generated output.

Sentence extracts were used as the basic response unit. For each topic, the top 100 documents were retrieved from the AQUAINT-2 collection with Lucene, using the topic template verbatim as the query. Neither the template structure nor the narrative text were exploited. All documents were then broken into individual sentences, which served as the pool of candidates. The relevance of each sentence was computed as the sum of the inverse document frequencies of matching terms from the topic template. Redundancy was computed as the cosine similarity between the current answer (consisting of all previously-selected sentences) and the current candidate. The relevance and redundancy scores were then normalized and combined ($\lambda = 0.8$). For the initial run, the MMR algorithm iterated until 25 candidates had been selected.

For interactive MMR, a screenshot of the web-based system is shown in Figure 2. The interface consists of three elements: at the top (label A) is the current topic; in the middle (label B) is the current answer, containing user selections from previous iterations; the bottom area (label C) shows a ranked list of candidate sentences ordered by MMR score. At each iteration, the user is asked to select one candidate by clicking the "Add to answer" button next to that candidate. The selected candidate is then added to the current answer. Ten answer candidates are shown per page. Clicking on a button labeled "Show more candidates" at the bottom of the page (not shown in the screenshot) displays the next ten candidates. In the ciQA 2007 evaluation, NIST assessors engaged with this interface for the entire allotted five minute interaction period. Note that this simple interface was designed only to assess the effectiveness of interactive MMR, and not intended to represent an actual interactive system.

To prevent users from seeing the same sentences repeatedly once a candidate selection has been recorded, we divide the scores of all candidates ranked higher than the selected candidate by two (an

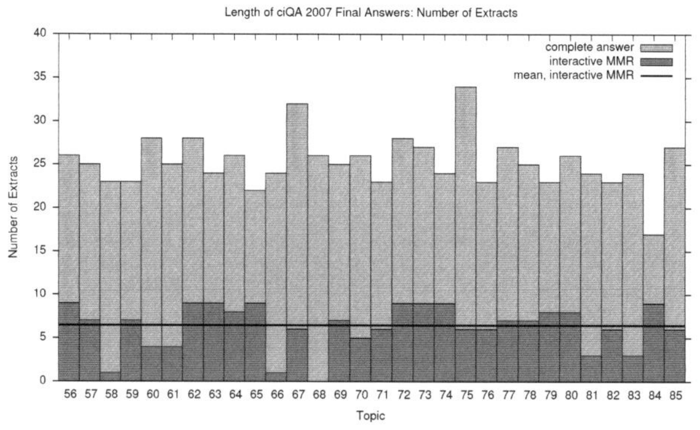

Figure 3: Per-topic lengths of final run in terms of number of extracts. Bars show contribution from interactive MMR (darker) and "padding" (lighter).

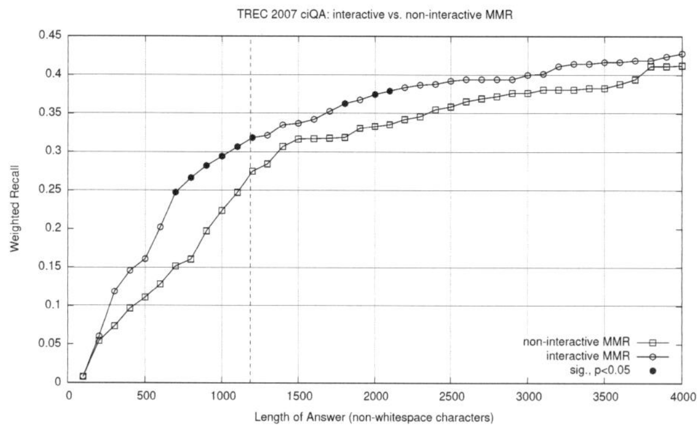

Figure 4: Weighted recall at different length increments, comparing interactive and non-interactive MMR.

arbitrary constant). For example, if the user clicked on candidate five, scores for candidates one through four are cut in half. Previous studies have shown that users generally examine ranked lists in order, so the lack of a selection can be interpreted as negative feedback (Joachims et al., 2007).

The answers constructed interactively were submitted to NIST as the final (post-interaction) run. However, since these answers were significantly shorter than the initial run (given the short interaction period), the responses were "padded" by running additional iterations of automatic MMR until a length quota of 4000 characters had been achieved.

4 Results and Discussion

First, we present descriptive statistics of the final run submitted to NIST. Lengths of the answers on a per-topic basis are shown in Figure 3 in terms of number of extracts: darker bars show the number of manually-selected extracts for each topic during the five-minute interaction period (i.e., the number of interactive MMR iterations). The average across all topics was 6.5 iterations, shown by the horizontal line; the average length of answers (all user selections) was 1186 characters. The average rank of the user selection was 4.9, and the user selected the top ranking sentence 28% of the time. Note that the interaction period included system processing as well as delays caused by network traffic. The number of extracts contained in the padding is shown by the lighter gray portions of the bars. For topic 68, the system did not record any user interactions (possibly resulting from a network glitch).

The official metric for the ciQA task was F-measure, but a disadvantage of this single-point metric is that it doesn't account for answers of varying lengths. An alternative proposed by Lin (2007) and used as the secondary metric in the evaluation is recall-by-length plots, which characterize weighted nugget recall at varying length increments. Weighted recall captures how much relevant information is contained in the system response (weighted by each nugget's importance, with an upper bound of one). Responses that achieve higher nugget recall at shorter length increments are desirable in providing concise, informative answers.

Recall-by-length plots for both the initial run (non-interactive MMR) and final run (interactive MMR with padding) are shown in Figure 4, in length increments of 1000 characters. The vertical dotted line denotes the average length of interactive MMR answers (without padding). Taking length as a proxy for time, one natural interpretation of this plot is how quickly users are able to "learn" about the topic of interest under the two conditions.

We see that interactive MMR yields higher weighted recall at all length increments. The Wilcoxon signed-rank test was applied to assess the statistical significance of the differences in weighted recall at each length increment. Solid circles in the graph represent improvements that are statistically significant ($p < 0.05$). Furthermore, in the 700–1000 character range, weighted recall is significantly higher for interactive MMR at the 99% level.

Viewing weighted recall as a proxy for answer quality, interactive MMR yields responses that are significantly better than non-interactive MMR at a range of length increments. This is an important finding, since effective interaction techniques that require little training and work well in limited-duration settings are quite elusive. Often, user input actually makes answers worse. Results from both ciQA 2006 and ciQA 2007 show that, overall, F-measure improved little between initial and final runs. Although it is widely accepted that user feedback can enhance interactive IR, effective interaction techniques to exploit this feedback are by no means obvious.

To better understand the characteristics of interactive MMR, it is helpful to compare our experiments with the ciQA task-wide baseline. As a reference for all participants, the organizers of the task submitted a pair of runs to help calibrate effectiveness. According to Dang et al. (2007), the first run was prepared by submitting the question template verbatim as a query to Lucene to retrieve the top 20 documents. These documents were then tokenized into individual sentences. Sentences that contained at least one non-stopword from the question were retained and returned as the initial run (up to a quota of 5,000 characters). Sentence order within each document and across the ranked list was preserved. The interaction associated with this run asked the assessor for relevance judgments on each of the sentences. Three options were given: "relevant", "not relevant", and "no opinion". The final run was prepared by removing sentences judged not relevant.

Other evidence suggests that the task-wide sentence retrieval algorithm represents a strong baseline. Similar algorithms performed well in other complex QA tasks—in TREC 2003, a sentence retrieval variant beat all but one run on definition questions (Voorhees, 2003). The sentence retrieval baseline also performed well in ciQA 2006.

The MMR runs are compared to the task-wide reference runs in Figure 5: diamonds denote the sentence retrieval baseline and triangles mark the manual sentence selection final run. The manual sentence selection run outperforms the sentence retrieval baseline (as expected), but its weighted recall is still below that of interactive MMR across almost all length increments. The weighted recall of interactive MMR is significantly better at 1000 characters (at the 95% level), but nowhere else. So, the bottom line is: for limited-duration interactions, interactive

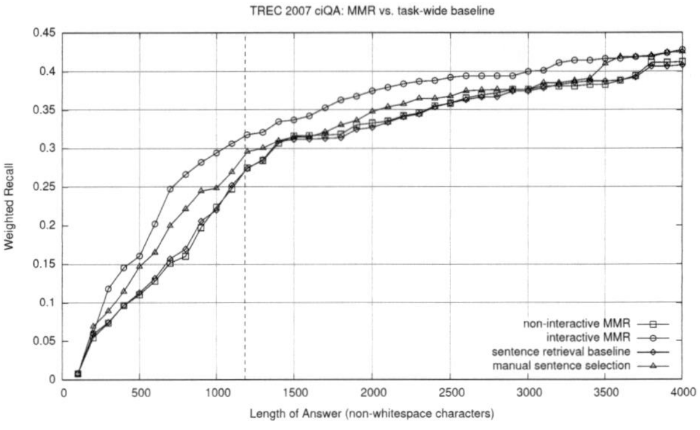

Figure 5: Weighted recall at different length increments, comparing MMR with the task-wide baseline.

MMR is more effective than simply asking for relevance judgments, but not significantly so.

5 Conclusion

We present an interactive extension of the Maximal Marginal Relevance algorithm for query-focused summarization. Results from the TREC 2007 ciQA task demonstrate it is a simple yet effective technique for involving users in interactively constructing responses to complex information needs. These results provide a starting point for future work in interactive summarization.

Acknowledgments

This work was supported in part by NLM/NIH. The first author would like to thank Esther and Kiri for their loving support.

References

H. Dang, J. Lin, and D. Kelly. 2007. Overview of the TREC 2007 question answering track. *TREC 2007*.

J. Goldstein, V. Mittal, J. Carbonell, and J. Callan. 2000. Creating and evaluating multi-document sentence extract summaries. *CIKM 2000*.

T. Joachims, L. Granka, B. Pan, H. Hembrooke, F. Radlinski, and G. Gay. 2007. Evaluating the accuracy of implicit feedback from clicks and query reformulations in Web search. *TOIS*, 25(2):1–27.

J. Lin and D. Demner-Fushman. 2006. Will pyramids built of nuggets topple over? *HLT/NAACL 2006*.

J. Lin. 2007. Is question answering better than information retrieval? Towards a task-based evaluation framework for question series. *HLT/NAACL 2007*.

E. Voorhees. 2003. Overview of the TREC 2003 question answering track. *TREC 2003*.

Improving Blog Polarity Classification via Topic Analysis and Adaptive Methods

Feifan Liu
University of Wisconsin, Milwaukee
liuf@uwm.edu

Dong Wang, Bin Li, Yang Liu
The University of Texas at Dallas
dongwang,yangl@hlt.utdallas.edu

Abstract

In this paper we examine different linguistic features for sentimental polarity classification, and perform a comparative study on this task between blog and review data. We found that results on blog are much worse than reviews and investigated two methods to improve the performance on blogs. First we explored information retrieval based topic analysis to extract relevant sentences to the given topics for polarity classification. Second, we adopted an adaptive method where we train classifiers from review data and incorporate their hypothesis as features. Both methods yielded performance gain for polarity classification on blog data.

1 Introduction

Sentimental analysis is a task of text categorization that focuses on recognizing and classifying opinionated text towards a given subject. Different levels of sentimental analysis has been performed in prior work, from binary classes to more fine grained categories. Pang et al. (2002) defined this task as a binary classification task and applied it to movie reviews. More sentiment classes, such as document objectivity and subjectivity as well as different rating scales on the subjectivity, have also been taken into consideration (Pang and Lee, 2005; Boiy et al., 2007). In terms of granularity, this task has been investigated from building word level sentiment lexicon (Turney, 2002; Moilanen and Pulman, 2008) to detecting phrase-level (Wilson et al., 2005; Agarwal et al., 2009) and sentence-level (Riloff and Wiebe, 2003; Hu and Liu, 2004) sentiment orientation. However, most previous work has mainly focused on reviews (Pang et al., 2002; Hu and Liu, 2004), news resources (Wilson et al., 2005), and multi-domain adaptation (Blitzer et al., 2007; Mansour et al., 2008). Sentiment analysis on blogs (Chesley et al., 2005; Kim et al., 2009) is still at its early stage.

In this paper we investigate binary polarity classification (positive vs. negative). We evaluate the genre effect between blogs and review data and show the difference of feature effectiveness. We demonstrate improved polarity classification performance in blogs using two methods: (a) integrating topic relevance analysis to perform topic specific polarity classification; (b) adopting an adaptive method by incorporating multiple classifiers' hypotheses from different review domains as features. Our manual analysis also points out some challenges and directions for further study in blog domain.

2 Features for Polarity Classification

For the binary polarity classification task, we use a supervised learning framework to determine whether a document is positive or negative. We used a subjective lexicon, containing 2304 positive words and 4145 negative words respectively, based on (Wilson et al., 2005). The features we explored are listed below.

(i) Lexical features (LF)

We use the bag of words for the lexical features as they have been shown very useful in previous work.

(ii) Polarized lexical features (PL)

We tagged each sentiment word in our data set with its polarity tag based on the sentiment lexicon ("POS" for positive, and "NEG" for negative), along with its part-of-speech tag. For example, in the sentence "It is good, and I like it", "good" is tagged as "POS/ADJ", "like" is tagged as "POS/VRB". Then we encode the number of the polarized tags in a document as features.

(iii) Polarized bigram features (PB)

Contextual information around the polarized words can be useful for sentimental analysis. A word may flip the polarity of its neighboring sentiment words even though this word itself is not necessarily a negative word. For example, in "Given her sudden celebrity with those on the left..." (a sentence in a political blog), "sudden" preceding "celebrity" implies the author's negative attitude towards "her". We combine the sentiment word's polarized tag and its following and preceding word or its part-of-speech to comprise different bigram features to represent this kind of contextual information. For ex-

Human Language Technologies: The 2010 Annual Conference of the North American Chapter of the ACL, pages 309–312,
Los Angeles, California, June 2010.

ample, in "I recommend this.", "recommend" is a positive verb, denoted as "POS/VRB", and the bigram features including this tag and its previous word "I" are "I_POS/VRB" and "pron_POS/VRB".

(iv) Transition word features (T)

Transition words, such as "although", "even though", serve as function words that may change the literal opinion polarity in the current sentence. This information has not been widely explored for sentiment analysis. In this study, we compiled a transition word list containing 31 words. We use the co-occurring feature between a transition word and its nearby content words (noun, verb, adjective and adverb) or polarized tags of sentiment words within the same sentence, but not spanning over other transition words. For example, in "Although it is good", we use features like "although_is","although_good" and "although_POS/ADJ", where "POS/ADJ" is the PL feature for word "good".

3 Feature Effectiveness on Blogs and Reviews

The blog data we used is from the TREC Blog Track evaluation in 2006 and 2007. The annotation was conducted for the 100 topics used in the evaluation (blogs are relevant to a given topic and also opinionated). We use 6,896 positive and 5,300 negative blogs. For the review data, we combined multiple review data sets from (Pang et al., 2002; Blitzer et al., 2007) together. It contains reviews from movies and four product domains (kitchen, electronics, books, and dvd), each of which has 1000 negative and 1000 positive samples. For the data without sentence information (e.g., blog data, some review data), we generated sentences using the maximum entropy sentence boundary detection tool[1]. We used TnT tagger to obtain the part-of-speech tags for these data sets.

For classification, we use the maximum entropy classifier[2] with a Gaussian prior of 1 and 100 iterations in model training. For all the experiments below, we use a 10-fold cross validation setup and report the average classification accuracy. Table 1 shows classification results using various feature sets on blogs and review data. We keep the lexical feature (LF) as a base feature, and investigate the effectiveness of adding more different features. We used Wilcox signed test for statistical significance test. Symbols "†" and "§" in the table indicate the significant level of 0.05 and 0.1 respectively, compared to the baseline performance using LF feature setup.

For the review domain, most of the feature sets can significantly improve the classification performance over the baseline of using "LF" features. "PB" features yielded more significant improvement than "PL" or "T" feature categories. Combining "PL" and "T" features resulted in some slight further improvement, achieving the best accuracy of 83.94%. We notice that incorporating our proposed transition feature (T) always achieves some gain on different feature settings, suggesting that those transition features are useful for sentimental analysis on reviews.

Feature Set	Blogs	Reviews
LF	72.07	81.67
LF+PL	70.93	81.93
LF+PB	72.44	83.62†
LF+T	72.17	81.76
LF+PL+PB	70.81	83.61†
LF+PL+T	72.74	82.13§
LF+PB+T	72.29	83.73†
LF+PL+PB+T	71.85	83.94†

Table 1: Polarity classification results (accuracy in %) using different features for blogs and reviews.

From Table 1, we can see that overall the performance on blogs is worse than on the review data. We hypothesize this may be due to the large variation in terms of contents and styles in blogs. Regarding the feature effectiveness, we also observe some differences between blogs and reviews. Adding the polarized bigram feature and transition feature (PB and T) individually can yield some improvement; however, adding both of them did not result in any further improvement – performance degrades compared to LF+PB. Interestingly, although "PL" feature alone does not seem to help, by adding "PL" and "T" together, the performance achieved the best accuracy of 72.74%. We also found that adding all the features together hurts the performance, suggesting that different features interact with each other and some do not combine well (e.g., PB and T features). In addition, all the improvements here are not statistically significant.

Note that for the blog data, we randomly split them for the cross validation experiments regardless of the queries. In order to better understand whether the poor results on blog data is due to the effect of different queries, we performed another experiment where for each query, we randomly divided the corresponding blogs into training and test splits. Only 66 queries were kept for this experiments – we did not include those queries that have fewer than 10 relevant blogs. The results for the query balanced split on blogs are shown in Figure 1. We also include results for the five individual review data sets in order to see the topic effect. We present results using four representative feature sets chosen according to Table 1. For the review data, we notice some difference across different data sets, suggesting their inherent difference in terms of task difficulty. We observe slight performance increase for some feature sets using the query balanced setup for blog data, but overall it is still much worse than the review data. This shows that the query unbalanced training/test split does not explain the performance gap between blogs and reviews. This is consistent with (Zhang et al., 2007) that found that a query-independent classifier performs even better than query-dependent one. We expect that the

[1]http://stp.ling.uu.se/~gustav/java/classes/MXTERMINATOR.html
[2]http://homepages.inf.ed.ac.uk/s0450736/maxent_toolkit.html

query unbalanced setup is more realistic, therefore, in the following experiments, we continue with this setup.

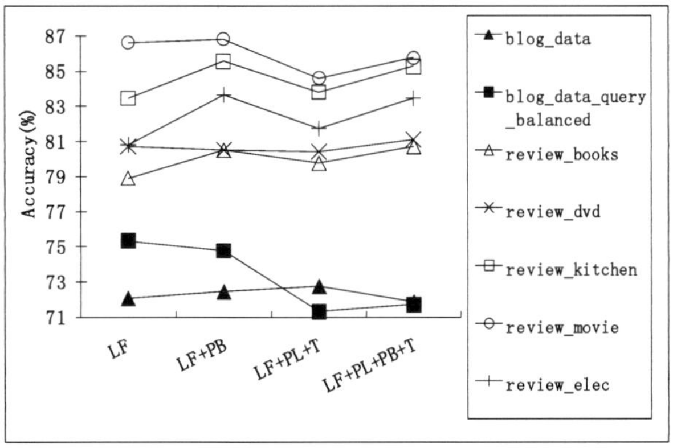

Figure 1: Polarity classification results on query balanced blog data and five individual review data sets.

4 Improving Blog Polarity Classification

To improve the performance of polarity classification on blogs, we propose two methods: (a) extract only topic-relevant segments from blogs for sentiment analysis; (b) apply adaptive methods to leverage review data.

4.1 Using topic-relevant blog context

Generally a review is written towards one product or one kind of service, but a blog may cover several topics with possibly different opinions towards each topic. The blog data we used is annotated based on some specific topics in the TREC Blog Track evaluation. Take topic 870 in the data as an example, "Find opinions on alleged use of steroids by baseball player Barry". There is one blog that talks about 5 different baseball players in issues of using steroids. Since the reference opinion tag of a blog is determined by polarity towards the given query topic, it might be confusing for the classifier if we use the whole blog to derive features. Recently topic analysis has been used for polarity classification (Zhang et al., 2007; Titov and McDonald, 2008; Wiegand and Klakow, 2009). We take a different approach in this study.

In order to obtain a topic-relevant context, we retrieved the top 10 relevant sentences corresponding to the given topic using the Lemur toolkit[3]. Then we used these sentences and their immediate previous and following sentences for feature extraction in the same way as what we did on the whole blog. In addition to using all the words in the relevant context, we also investigated using only content words since those are more topic indicative than function words. We extracted content words (nouns, verbs, adjectives and adverbs) from each blog in their original order and apply the same feature extraction process as for using all the words.

[3]http://www.lemurproject.org/lemur/

Table 2 shows the blog polarity classification results using the whole blog vs. relevant context composed of all the words or only content words. For the significance test, the comparison was done for using relevant context with all the words vs. using the whole blog; and using content words only vs. using all the words in relevant context. Each comparison was with respect to the same feature setup. We observe improved polarity classification performance when using sentence retrieval based topic analysis to extract relevant context. Using all the words in the topic relevant context, all the improvements compared to using the original entire blog are statistically significant at the level of 0.01. We also notice that unlike on the entire blog document, the "PL" features contribute positively when combined with "LF". All the feature settings with "PL" perform very well. The best accuracy of 75.32% is achieved using feature combination of "LF+PL" or "LF+PL+T". This suggests that polarized lexical features suffered from the off-topic content when using the entire blog and are more useful within contexts of certain topics.

When using content words only, we observe consistent gain across all the feature sets. Three feature settings, "LF+PB","LF+T" and "LF+PL+PB+T", achieve statistically significant further improvement (compared to using all the words of relevant contexts). The best accuracy (75.6%) is achieved by using the "LF+PB" features.

Feature Set	Whole Blog	Relevant Context	
		All Words	Content Words
LF	72.07	74.92†	75.14
LF+PL	70.93	75.32†	75.34
LF+PB	72.44	75.03†	75.6†
LF+T	72.17	75.01†	75.35§
LF+PL+PB	70.81	75.27†	75.35
LF+PL+T	72.74	75.32†	75.41
LF+PB+T	72.29	75.17†	75.42
LF+PL+PB+T	71.85	75.21†	75.45§

Table 2: Blog polarity classification results (accuracy in %) using topic relevant context composed of all the words or only content words.

4.2 Adaptive methods using review data

Domain adaptation has been studied in some previous work (e.g., (Blitzer et al., 2007; Mansour et al., 2008)). In this paper, we evaluate two adaptive approaches in order to leverage review data to improve blog polarity classification. In the first approach, in each of the 10-fold cross-validation training, we pool the blog training data (90% of the entire blog data) together with all the review data from 5 different domains. In the second method, we augment features with hypotheses obtained from classifiers trained using other domain data. Specifically, we first trained 5 classifiers from 5 review domain data sets respectively, and encoded the hypotheses from different classifiers as features for blog training (together with the original features of the blog data). Results of these two approaches are shown in Table 3. We use the topic relevant context with content words only in this experiment, and present results for different feature combinations (except the baseline "LF" setting). The significance test is conducted in comparison to the results using only blog data for training, for the same feature setting.

We find that the first approach does not yield any gain, even though the added data is about the same size as the blog data. It indicates that due to the large difference between the two genres, simply combining blogs and reviews in training is not effective. However, we can see that using augmented features in training significantly improved the performance across different feature sets. The best result is achieved using "LF+T" features, 76.84% compared with the best accuracy of 75.6% when using the blog data only ("LF+PB" features).

Feature Set	Only Blog	Pool Data	Augment Features
LF+PL	75.34	75.05	76.12†
LF+PB	75.6	74.35	76.28†
LF+T	75.35	74.47	76.84†
LF+PL+PB	75.35	74.94	76.7†
LF+PL+T	75.41	74.85	76.32†
LF+PB+T	75.42	74.46	76.3†
LF+PL+PB+T	75.45	74.96	76.53†

Table 3: Results (accuracy in %) of blog polarity classification using two methods leveraging review data.

4.3 Error analysis

Notice that after achieving some improvements the performance on blogs is still much worse than on review data. Thus we performed a manual error analysis for a better understanding of the difficulties of sentiment analysis on blog data, and identified the following challenges.

(a) Idiomatic expressions. Compared to reviews, bloggers seem to use more idioms. For example, "Of course he has me over the barrel..." expresses negative opinion, however, there are no superficially indicative features.

(b) Ironic writing style. Some bloggers prefer ironic style especially when speaking against something or somebody, whereas opinions are often expressed using plain writing style in reviews. Simply using the surface word level features is not able to model these properly.

(c) Background knowledge. In some political blogs, the polarized expressions are implicit. Correctly recognizing them requires background knowledge and deeper language analysis techniques.

5 Conclusions and Future Work

In this paper, we have evaluated various features and the domain effect on sentimental polarity classification. Our experiments on blog and review data demonstrated different feature effectiveness and the overall poorer performance on blogs than reviews. We found that the polarized features and the transition word features we introduced are useful for polarity classification. We also show that by extracting topic-relevant context and considering only content words, the system can achieve significantly better performance on blogs. Furthermore, an adaptive method using augmented features can effectively leverage data from other domains, and yield improvement compared to using in-domain training or training on combined data from different domains. For our future work, we plan to investigate other adaption methods, and try to address some of the problems identified in our error analysis.

6 Acknowledgment

The authors thank the three anonymous reviewers for their suggestions.

References

Apoorv Agarwal, Fadi Biadsy, and Kathleen McKeown. 2009. Contextual phrase-level polarity analysis using lexical affect scoring and syntactic n-grams. In *Proc. of EACL*.

John Blitzer, Mark Dredze, and Fernando Pereira. 2007. Biographies, bollywood, boom-boxes and blenders: Domain adaptation for sentiment classification. In *Proc. of ACL*.

Erik Boiy, Pieter Hens, Koen Deschacht, and Marie-Francine Moens. 2007. Automatic sentiment analysis in on-line text. In *Proc. of ELPUB*.

Paula Chesley, Bruce Vincent, Li Xu, and Rohini K. Srihari. 2005. Using verbs and adjectives to automatically classify blog sentiment. In *Proc. of AAAI*.

Minqing Hu and Bing Liu. 2004. Mining and summarizing customer reviews. In *Proc. of ACM SIGKDD*.

Jungi Kim, Jin-Ji Li, and Jong-Hyeok Lee. 2009. Discovering the discriminative views: Measuring term weights for sentiment analysis. In *Proc. of ACL-IJCNLP*.

Yishay Mansour, Mehryar Mohri, and Afshin Rostamizadeh. 2008. Domain adaptation with multiple sources. In *Proc. of NIPS*.

Karo Moilanen and Stephen Pulman. 2008. The good, the bad, and the unknown: Morphosyllabic sentiment tagging of unseen words. In *Proc. of ACL*.

Bo Pang and Lillian Lee. 2005. Seeing stars: Exploiting class relationships for sentiment categorization with respect to rating scales. In *Proc. of ACL*.

Bo Pang, Lilian Lee, and Shrivakumar Vaithyanathan. 2002. Thumbs up? sentiment classification using machine learning techniques. In *Proc. of EMNLP*.

Ellen Riloff and Janyce Wiebe. 2003. Learning extraction patterns for subjective expressions. In *Proc. of EMNLP*.

Ivan Titov and Ryan McDonald. 2008. Modeling online reviews with multi-grain topic models. In *Proc. of WWW*.

Peter D. Turney. 2002. Thumbs up or thumbs down? semantic orientation applied to unsupervised classification of reviews. In *Proc. of ACL*.

Michael Wiegand and Dietrich Klakow. 2009. Topic-Related polarity classification of blog sentences. In *Proc. of the 14th Portuguese Conference on Artificial Intelligence: Progress in Artificial Intelligence*, pages 658–669.

Theresa Wilson, Janyce Wiebe, and Paul Hoffmann. 2005. Recognizing contextual polarity in phrase-level sentiment analysis. In *Proc. of HLT-EMNLP*.

Wei Zhang, Clement Yu, and Weiyi Meng. 2007. Opinion retrieval from blogs. In *Proc. of CIKM*, pages 831–840.

Creating Local Coherence: An Empirical Assessment

Annie Louis
University of Pennsylvania
Philadelphia, PA 19104, USA
lannie@seas.upenn.edu

Ani Nenkova
University of Pennsylvania
Philadelphia, PA 19104, USA
nenkova@seas.upenn.edu

Abstract

Two of the mechanisms for creating natural transitions between adjacent sentences in a text, resulting in local coherence, involve discourse relations and switches of focus of attention between discourse entities. These two aspects of local coherence have been traditionally discussed and studied separately. But some empirical studies have given strong evidence for the necessity of understanding how the two types of coherence-creating devices interact. Here we present a joint corpus study of discourse relations and entity coherence exhibited in news texts from the Wall Street Journal and test several hypotheses expressed in earlier work about their interaction.

1 Introduction

Coherent discourse is characterized by local properties that are crucial for comprehension. In fact, a long line of linguistics and computational linguistics tradition has proposed that several levels of structure contribute to the creation of coherent discourse. Among these, the attentional structure (Grosz et al., 1995) and the relational structure (Mann and Thompson, 1988) of text, are the most widely discussed in the literature.

Centering theory (Grosz et al., 1995) is the dominant approach for describing and analyzing attentional structure. It assumes that readers of the text focus (center) their attention on a small number of salient discourse entities at a time and that there are preferred patterns for switching attention between entities mentioned in adjacent sentences. Relational structure theories, on the other hand, describe how certain discourse (also called rhetorical or coherence) relations such as CONTRAST and CAUSE are inferred by the reader between adjacent units of text. The existence of richly annotated corpora and the development of automatic applications based on the theories have allowed empirical assessments of the validity and generality of these theories individually.

Such work has also provided increasingly strong evidence that attentional and relational structures need to be taken into account simultaneously. The motivation behind such proposals have been the empirical findings that "weak" discourse relations such as ELABORATION are the most common type of relations, and that a large percentage of adjacent sentences in fact do not have *any* entities in common.

In particular, a corpus based evaluation of Centering theory found that only 42% of pairs of adjacent sentences have at least one entity in common and hypothesized that discourse relations are responsible for creating local coherence in the remaining cases (Poesio et al., 2004). At the same time, the work of Knott et al. (2001) has discussed several theoretical complications arising from the existence of the very common and semantically weak ELABORATION relation. These researchers propose that replacing ELABORATION by an account of entity coherence such as Centering will be most beneficial. But work in information ordering (Karamanis, 2007) has not been able to confirm such claims that better results can be obtained by combining entity coherence with discourse relations.

Till recently, the absence of large corpora annotated for both discourse relations and coreference information has prohibited a detailed joint analysis of attentional and relational structure. We combine two

This work was partially supported by NSF Grant IIS -07-05671.

Human Language Technologies: The 2010 Annual Conference of the North American Chapter of the ACL, pages 313–316,
Los Angeles, California, June 2010.

recently released corpora: discourse relations from the Penn Discourse Treebank and coreference annotations from the OntoNotes corpus, to assess the prevalence and interplay between factors that create local coherence in newspaper text.

Specifically, in our study we examine how three hypotheses formulated in prior work play out in the Wall Street Journal texts in our corpus:

Hypothesis 1 Adjacent sentences that do not share entities are related by non-elaboration discourse relations [Poesio et al. (2004) Sec. 5.2.2 Pg. 354].

Hypothesis 2 Adjacent sentences joined by non-elaboration discourse relation have lower entity coherence: such pairs are less likely to mention the same entities [Knott et al. (2001) Sec. 7 Pg. 10].

Hypothesis 3 Almost all pairs of sentences in a coherent text either share entities or participate in non-elaboration discourse relation (Knott et al., 2001; Poesio et al., 2004).

None of these hypotheses are validated. We find that only 38.65% of pairs that do not share entities participate in "core" relations such as temporal, contingency or comparison; the rate of coreference in these "core" relations is similar to that in weaker elaboration relations; about 30% of all sentence pairs neither share entities nor participate in a "core" discourse relation.

2 Data

In order to jointly analyze both discourse relations and noun phrase coreference between adjacent sentences, we combine annotations from two corpora, OntoNotes and the Penn Discourse Treebank. The two individual corpora are larger, but a smaller subset of 590 Wall Street Journal articles appear in both. All our analysis is for *adjacent sentences within paragraphs* in this subset of texts.

Penn Discourse Treebank The Penn Discourse Treebank (PDTB) (Prasad et al., 2008) is the largest available corpus of annotations for discourse relations, covering one million words of the Wall Street Journal (WSJ). In the PDTB, two kinds of discourse relations are annotated. In *explicit relations*, a discourse connective such as "because", "but" or "so" is present, as in the example below.

[Ex. 1] There is an incredible pressure on school systems and teachers to raise test scores. *So* efforts to beat the tests are also on the rise.

On the other hand, relations can also exist without an explicit signal. In *Ex. 2*, it is clear that the second sentence is the *result* of the event mentioned in the first.

[Ex. 2] In July, the Environmental Protection Agency imposed a gradual ban on virtually all uses of asbestos. By 1997, almost all remaining uses of cancer-causing asbestos will be outlawed.

Such relations are called *implicit relations*. In the PDTB, they are annotated between all adjacent sentences within a paragraph which do not already participate in an explicit discourse relation.

For both implicit and explicit relations, the semantic sense of the discourse relation is assigned from a hierarchy of senses. There are four classes of discourse relations at the topmost general level. The second level senses are shown within parantheses: Comparison (*Concession, Contrast, Pragmatic Concession/Contrast*), Contingency (*Cause, Condition, Pragmatic Cause/Condition*), Temporal (*Asynchronous, Synchronous*) and Expansion (*Alternative, Conjunction, Exception, Instantiation, List, Restatement*).

Some of the adjacent sentences in the texts, however, were found not to have a discourse relation between the events or propositions mentioned in them. Instead, they were related because both sentences mention the same entity, directly or indirectly, and the second sentence provides some further description of that entity. An *Entity Relation (EntRel)* was annotated for such sentence pairs as below.

[Ex. 3] Pierre Vinken, 61 years old, will join the board as a nonexecutive director Nov. 29. Mr. Vinken is chairman of Elsevier N.V., the Dutch publishing group.

OntoNotes For coreference information, we use the WSJ portion of the OntoNotes corpus version 2.9 (Hovy et al., 2006) which contains 590 documents. For these documents, we also have the PDTB annotations available. In OntoNotes, all noun phrases–pronouns, names and nominals are marked for coreference without any limitation to specific semantic categories.

3 Corpus study findings

For ease of presentation in the following analysis, we will call the Expansion and Entity relations "weak" and Temporal, Contingency and Compari-

0 to 100	0.41		500 to 1000	0.50
100 to 200	0.37		above 1000	0.51
200 to 500	0.48			

Table 1: Proportion of sentence pairs that *don't share* any entities for different document lengths (in words)

Type	Relation	No shared entities
	Temporal	122 (2.98)
Core	Contingency	752 (18.40)
	Comparison	706 (17.27)
Weak	Expansion	1870 (45.74)
	EntRel	638 (15.61)

Table 2: Distribution of the 4088 *non-entity sharing* sentence pairs. The proportions are shown in brackets.

Type	Relation	Total	Share entities
	Temporal	365	243 (66.57)
Core	Contingency	1570	818 (52.10)
	Comparison	1477	771 (52.20)
Weak	Expansion	3569	1699 (47.60)
	EntRel	1424	786 (55.20)

Table 3: Rate of *entity sharing*

	Share entities	No sharing
core relations	1832 (21.80)	1580 (18.80)
weak relations	2485 (29.56)	2508 (29.84)

Table 4: Total number (proportion) of sentence pairs in the corpus in the given categories

son relations "core", following the intuition that the semantics of the latter class is much more clearly defined. Implicit and explicit relations were not distinguished in the analysis.[1]

Hypothesis 1 The first hypothesis is that adjacent sentences that do not share entities participate in core relations and so remain locally coherent.

Pairs of adjacent sentences that do not share any entities are common. In prior work, Poesio et al. (2004) found that 58% of adjacent sentence pairs in their corpus of museum object descriptions did not have overlapping mentions of any entity. The distribution in the WSJ texts is similar, as seen in Table 1. Depending on the length of the article, 37% to 51% of sentence pairs do not have any entity in common.[2]

Table 2 shows the distribution of discourse relations for the 4088 sentence pairs in the corpus that do not share any entities. Contrary to expectation, the majority of such pairs, 61%, are related by a weak discourse relation. Especially unexpected is the high percentage of *entity relations (EntRel)* that don't have actual entity overlap:

[Ex. 4] All four demonstrators were arrested. The law, which Bush allowed to take effect without his signature, went into force Friday.

[Ex. 5] Authorities in Hawaii said the wreckage of a missing commuter plane with 20 people aboard was spotted in a remote valley on the island of Molokai. There wasn't any evidence of survivors.

Hypothesis 2 The second hypothesis states that adjacent sentences joined by a core discourse relation are less likely to mention the same entities in comparison to weak relations. But as Table 3 reveals, this is generally not the case.

Adjacent sentences in Temporal relation are very likely to share entities—almost 70% of them do. Over half of all Contingency and Comparison relations also share entities. But, the rates of sharing in Comparison and Contingency relations are significantly lower compared to Entity relations (under a two-sided binomial test). *Ex. 6* shows a Contingency relation without entity sharing.

[Ex. 6] Without machines, good farms can't get bigger. So the potato crop, once 47 million tons, is down to 35.

However, adjacent sentences with Expansion relation turn out least likely to share entities. The entity sharing rates of all the other relations were found to be significantly higher than Expansion.

Hypothesis 3 Finally, we test the hypothesis that the majority of adjacent sentences exhibit coherence because they either share entities or form the arguments of a core discourse relation.

This hypothesis is not supported in the WSJ data (see Table 4): 30% of all sentence pairs are in a weak discourse relation—Expansion or EntRel—and do not have any entities in common. In a sense, neither of the theories of entity or relational coherence can explain what mechanisms create the local coherence for these pairs. In order to glean some insights of how coherence is created there, we examine the behavior of different types of Elaboration relations (Table 5). There is a wide variation between the dif-

[1]For brevity we present combined results for both implicit and explicit relations. However, most of our conclusions remain the same when the two types are distinguished.

[2]There are around 100 documents in each length range.

Alternative	67 (0.63)	Instantiation	490 (0.34)
Restatement	960 (0.56)	List	165 (0.28)
Conjunction	1021 (0.48)	EntRel	1424 (0.55)

Table 5: Total number of different Expansion relations and their coreference probability (in brackets)

ferent types of Expansions.

When the function of an expansion sentence is to provide an *alternative explanation* or *restate* an utterance, the probability of entity overlap is very high and patterns similarily with entity relations (around 60%). Below is an example restatement sentence.

[Ex. 7] $\{$Researchers in Belgium$\}_r$ said $\{$they$\}_r$ have developed a genetic engineering technique for creating hybrid plants for a number of crops, such as cotton, soybeans and rice. $\{$The scientists at Plant Genetic Systems N.V.$\}_r$ isolated a gene that could lead to a generation of plants possessing a high-production trait.

However, the two classes–Instantiation and List largely appear with very little entity overlap, 37% and 29% respectively. An Instantiation relation is used to provide an example and hence has little overlap with the previous sentence (Ex. 8 and 9).

[Ex. 8] There may be a few cases where the law breaking is well pinpointed and so completely non-invasive of the rights of others that it is difficult to criticize it. The case of Rosa Parks, the black woman who refused to sit at the back of the bus, comes to mind as an illustration.

[Ex. 9] The economy is showing signs of weakness, particularly among manufacturers. Exports, which played a key role in fueling growth over the last two years, seem to have stalled.

List relations, on the other hand, connect sentences where each of them elaborates on a common proposition mentioned earlier in the discourse. Here is an example five sentence paragraph with list relations but no entity repetition at all.

> **[Ex. 10]** Designs call for a L-shaped structure with a playground in the center. *[Implicit List]* There will be recreation and movie rooms. *[Implicit List]* Teens will be able to listen to music with headsets. *[Implicit List]* Study halls, complete with reference materials will be available. *[Explicit List]* And there will be a nurse's station and rooms for children to meet with the social workers.

In *Ex. 10*, as well as some others, a broad notion of entity coherence–bridging anaphora can be applied. Poesio et al. (2004) also note this fact, but also say that such instances are very difficult to annotate reliably. Our work is based on coreference annotations which can be marked with considerably high inter-annotator agreement.

4 Conclusions

The recent release of corpora annotated for coreference and discourse relations for the same texts have made possible to empirically assess claims about the interaction between two types of local coherence: relational and entity. We find that about half of the pairs of adjacent sentences do not share any entities at all, and about 60% are related by weak discourse relations. We test the hypothesis from prior work that these two types of coherence are complementary to each other and taken together explain most local coherence. We find that the two types of coherence mechanisms are neither mutually exclusive nor do they explain all the data. Future work in discourse analysis will need to develop better understanding of how the two types of coherence interact.

References

B. Grosz, A. Joshi, and S. Weinstein. 1995. Centering: a framework for modelling the local coherence of discourse. *Computational Linguistics*, 21(2):203–226.

E. Hovy, M. Marcus, M. Palmer, L. Ramshaw, and R. Weischedel. 2006. Ontonotes: the 90% solution. In *Proceedings of NAACL-HLT*, pages 57–60.

N. Karamanis. 2007. Supplementing entity coherence with local rhetorical relations for information ordering. *Journal of Logic, Language and Information*, 16(4):445–464.

A. Knott, J. Oberlander, M. O'Donnell, and C. Mellish. 2001. Beyond elaboration: the interaction of relations and focus in coherent text. In *Text Representation: Linguistic and Psycholinguistic Aspects, chapter 7*, pages 181–196.

W.C. Mann and S.A. Thompson. 1988. Rhetorical structure theory: Towards a functional theory of text organization. *Text*, 8.

M. Poesio, R. Stevenson, B. Di Eugenio, and J. Hitzeman. 2004. Centering: A parametric theory and its instantiations. *Computational Linguistics*, pages 309–363.

R. Prasad, N. Dinesh, A. Lee, E. Miltsakaki, L. Robaldo, A. Joshi, and B. Webber. 2008. The penn discourse treebank 2.0. In *Proceedings of LREC'08*.

Time-Efficient Creation of an Accurate Sentence Fusion Corpus

Kathleen McKeown, Sara Rosenthal, Kapil Thadani and **Coleman Moore**
Columbia University
New York, NY 10027, USA
{kathy,sara,kapil}@cs.columbia.edu, cjm2140@columbia.edu

Abstract

Sentence fusion enables summarization and question-answering systems to produce output by combining fully formed phrases from different sentences. Yet there is little data that can be used to develop and evaluate fusion techniques. In this paper, we present a methodology for collecting fusions of similar sentence pairs using Amazon's Mechanical Turk, selecting the input pairs in a semi-automated fashion. We evaluate the results using a novel technique for automatically selecting a representative sentence from multiple responses. Our approach allows for rapid construction of a high accuracy fusion corpus.

1 Introduction

Summarization and question-answering systems must transform input text to produce useful output text, condensing an input document or document set in the case of summarization and selecting text that meets the question constraints in the case of question answering. While many systems use sentence extraction to facilitate the task, this approach risks including additional, irrelevant or non-salient information in the output, and the original sentence wording may be inappropriate for the new context in which it appears. Instead, recent research has investigated methods for generating new sentences using a technique called *sentence fusion* (Barzilay and McKeown, 2005; Marsi and Krahmer, 2005; Filippova and Strube, 2008) where output sentences are generated by fusing together portions of related sentences.

While algorithms for automated fusion have been developed, there is no corpus of human-generated fused sentences available to train and evaluate such systems. The creation of such a dataset could provide insight into the kinds of fusions that people produce. Furthermore, since research in the related task of sentence compression has benefited from the availability of training data (Jing, 2000; Knight and Marcu, 2002; McDonald, 2006; Cohn and Lapata, 2008), we expect that the creation of this corpus might encourage the development of supervised learning techniques for automated sentence fusion.

In this work, we present a methodology for creating such a corpus using Amazon's Mechanical Turk[1], a widely used online marketplace for crowdsourced task completion. Our goal is the generation of accurate fusions between pairs of sentences that have some information in common. To ensure that the task is performed consistently, we abide by the distinction proposed by Marsi and Krahmer (2005) between *intersection* fusion and *union* fusion. Intersection fusion results in a sentence that contains only the information that the sentences had in common and is usually shorter than either of the original sentences. Union fusion, on the other hand, results in a sentence that contains all information content from the original two sentences. An example of intersection and union fusion is shown in Figure 1.

We solicit multiple annotations for both union and intersection tasks separately and leverage the different responses to automatically choose a representative response. Analysis of the responses shows that our approach yields 95% accuracy on the task of union fusion. This is a promising first step and indicates that our methodology can be applied towards efficiently building a highly accurate corpus for sentence fusion.

[1] https://www.mturk.com

Human Language Technologies: The 2010 Annual Conference of the North American Chapter of the ACL, pages 317–320,
Los Angeles, California, June 2010.

1. Palin actually turned against the bridge project only after it became a national symbol of wasteful spending.
2. Ms. Palin supported the bridge project while running for governor, and abandoned it after it became a national scandal.
Intersection: Palin turned against the bridge project after it became a national scandal.
Union: Ms. Palin supported the bridge project while running for governor, but turned against it when it became a national scandal and a symbol of wasteful spending.

Figure 1: Examples of intersection and union

2 Related Work

The combination of fragments of sentences on a common topic has been studied in the domain of single document summarization (Jing, 2000; Daumé III and Marcu, 2002; Xie et al., 2008). In contrast to these approaches, sentence fusion was introduced to combine fragments of sentences with common information for multi-document summarization (Barzilay and McKeown, 2005). Automated fusion of sentence pairs has since received attention as an independent task (Marsi and Krahmer, 2005; Filippova and Strube, 2008). Although generic fusion of sentence pairs based on importance does not yield high agreement when performed by humans (Daumé III and Marcu, 2004), fusion in the context of a query has been shown to produce better agreement (Krahmer et al., 2008). We examine similar fusion annotation tasks in this paper, but we asked workers to provide two specific types of fusion, intersection and union, thus avoiding the less specific definition based on importance. Furthermore, as our goal is the generation of corpora, our target for evaluation is *accuracy* rather than agreement.

This work studies an approach to the automatic construction of large fusion corpora using workers through Amazon's Mechanical Turk service. Previous studies using this online task marketplace have shown that the collective judgments of many workers are comparable to those of trained annotators on labeling tasks (Snow et al., 2008) although these judgments can be obtained at a fraction of the cost and effort. However, our task presents an additional challenge: building a corpus for sentence fusion requires workers to enter free text rather than simply choose between predefined options; the results are prone to variation and this makes comparing and aggregating multiple responses problematic.

A. After a decade on the job, Gordon had become an experienced cop.
B. Gordon has a lot of experience in the police force.

Figure 2: An example of sentences that were judged to be too similar for inclusion in the dataset

3 Collection Methodology

Data collection involved the identification of the types of sentence pairs that would make suitable candidates for fusion, the development of a system to automatically identify good pairs and manual filtering of the sentence pairs to remove erroneous choices. The selected sentence pairs were then presented to workers on Mechanical Turk in an interface that required them to manually type in a fused sentence (intersection or union) for each case.

Not all pairs of related sentences are useful for the fusion task. When sentences are too similar, the result of fusion is simply one of the input sentences. For example (Fig. 2), if sentence A contains all the information in sentence B but not vice versa, then B is also their intersection while A is their union and no sentence generation is required. On the other hand, if the two sentences are too dissimilar, then no intersection is possible and the union is just the conjunction of the sentences.

We experimented with different similarity metrics aimed at identifying pairs of sentences that were inappropriate for fusion. The sentences in this study were drawn from clusters of news articles on the same event from the Newsblaster summarization system (McKeown et al., 2002). While these clusters are likely to contain similar sentences, they will contain many more dissimilar than similar pairs and thus a metric that emphasizes precision over recall is important. We computed pairwise similarity between sentences within each cluster using three standard metrics: word overlap, n-gram overlap and cosine similarity. Bigram overlap yielded the best precision in our experiments. We empirically arrived at a lower threshold of .35 to remove dissimilar sentences and an upper threshold of .65 to avoid near-identical sentences, yielding a false-positive rate of 44.4%. The remaining inappropriate pairs were then manually filtered. This semi-automated procedure enabled fast selection of suitable sentence pairs: one person was able to select 30 pairs an hour yielding the 300 pairs for the full experiment in ten hours.

Responses	Intersection	Union
All (1500)	0.49	0.88
Representatives (300)	0.54	0.95

Table 1: Union and intersection accuracy

3.1 Using Amazon's Mechanical Turk

Based on a pilot study with 20 sentence pairs, we designed an interface for the full study. For intersection tasks, the interface posed the question "*How would you combine the following two sentences into a single sentence conveying only the information they have in common?*". For union tasks, the question was "*How would you combine the following two sentences into a single sentence that contains ALL of the information in each?*".

We used all 300 pairs of similar sentences for both union and intersection and chose to collect five worker responses per pair, given the diversity of responses that we found in the pilot study. This yielded a total of 3000 fused sentences with 1500 intersections and 1500 unions.

3.2 Representative Responses

Using multiple workers provides little benefit unless we are able to harness the collective judgments of their responses. To this end, we experiment with a simple technique to select one representative response from all responses for a case, hypothesizing that such a response would have a lower error rate. We test the hypothesis by comparing the accuracy of representative responses with the average accuracy over all responses.

Our strategy for selecting representatives draws on the common assumption used in human computation that human agreement in independently-generated labels implies accuracy (von Ahn and Dabbish, 2004). We approximate agreement between responses using a simple and transparent measure for overlap: cosine similarity over stems weighted by *tf-idf* where *idf* values are learned over the Gigawords corpus[2]. After comparing all responses in a pairwise fashion, we need to choose a representative response. As using the centroid directly might not be robust to the presence of erroneous responses, we first select the pair of responses with the greatest overlap as *candidates* and then choose the candidate which has the greatest total overlap with all other responses.

[2]LDC Catalog No. LDC2003T05

Errors	Intersection	Union
Missing clause	2	7
Union/Intersection	46	6
S1/S2	21	8
Additional clause	10	1
Lexical	3	1

Table 2: Errors seen in 30 random cases (150 responses)

4 Results and Error Analysis

For evaluating accuracy, fused sentences were manually compared to the original sentence pairs. Due to the time-consuming nature of the evaluation, 50% of the 300 cases were randomly selected for analysis. 10% were initially analyzed by two of the authors; if a disagreement occurred, the authors discussed their differences and came to a unified decision. The remaining 40% were then analyzed by one author. In addition to this high-level analysis, we further analyzed 10% of the cases to identify the the types of errors made in fusion as well as the techniques used and the effect of task difficulty on performance.

The accuracy for intersection and union tasks is shown in Table 1. For both tasks, accuracy of the selected representatives significantly exceeded the average response accuracy. In our error analysis, we found that workers often answered the intersection task by providing a union, possibly due to a misinterpretation of the question. This caused intersection accuracy to be significantly worse than union. We analyzed the impact of this error by computing accuracy on the first 30 cases (10%) without this error and the accuracy for intersection increased 22%.

Error types were categorized as "missing clause", "using union for intersection and vice versa", "choosing an input sentence (S1/S2)", "additional clause" and "lexical error". Table 2 shows the number of occurrences of each in 10% of the cases.

We binned the sentence pairs according to the difficulty of the fusion task for each pair (easy/medium/hard) and found that performance was not dependent on difficulty level; accuracy was relatively similar across bins. We also observed that workers typically performed fusion by selecting one sentence as a base and removing clauses or merging in additional clauses from the other sentence.

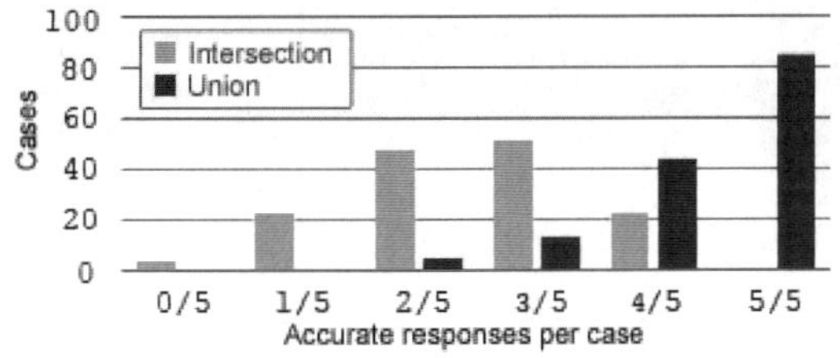

Figure 3: Number of cases in which $x/5$ workers provided accurate responses for fusion

In order to determine the benefit of using many workers, we studied the number of workers who answered correctly for each case. Figure 3 reveals that 2/5 or more workers (summing across columns) responded accurately in 99% of union cases and 82% of intersection cases. The intersection results are skewed due to the question misinterpretation issue which, though it was the most common error, was made by 3/5 workers only 17% of the time. Thus, in the majority of the cases, accurate fusions can still be found using the representative method.

5 Conclusion

We presented a methodology to build a fusion corpus which uses semi-automated techniques to select similar sentence pairs for annotation on Mechanical Turk[3]. Additionally, we showed how multiple responses for each fusion task can be leveraged by automatically selecting a representative response. Our approach yielded 95% accuracy for union tasks, and while intersection fusion accuracy was much lower, our analysis showed that workers sometimes provided unions instead of intersections and we suspect that an improved formulation of the question could lead to better results. Construction of the fusion dataset was relatively fast; it required only ten hours of labor on the part of a trained undergraduate and seven days of active time on Mechanical Turk.

Acknowledgements

This material is based on research supported in part by the U.S. National Science Foundation (NSF) under IIS-05-34871 Any opinions, findings and conclusions or recommendations expressed in this material are those of the authors and do not necessarily reflect the views of the NSF.

[3]The corpus described in this work is available at http://www.cs.columbia.edu/~kathy/fusioncorpus

References

Regina Barzilay and Kathleen R. McKeown. 2005. Sentence fusion for multidocument news summarization. *Computational Linguistics*, 31(3):297–328.

Trevor Cohn and Mirella Lapata. 2008. Sentence compression beyond word deletion. In *Proceedings of COLING*, pages 137–144.

Hal Daumé III and Daniel Marcu. 2002. A noisy-channel model for document compression. In *Proceedings of ACL*, pages 449–456.

Hal Daumé III and Daniel Marcu. 2004. Generic sentence fusion is an ill-defined summarization task. In *Proceedings of the ACL Text Summarization Branches Out Workshop*, pages 96–103.

Katja Filippova and Michael Strube. 2008. Sentence fusion via dependency graph compression. In *Proceedings of EMNLP*, pages 177–185.

Hongyan Jing. 2000. Sentence reduction for automatic text summarization. In *Proceedings of Applied Natural Language Processing*, pages 310–315.

Kevin Knight and Daniel Marcu. 2002. Summarization beyond sentence extraction: a probabilistic approach to sentence compression. *Artificial Intelligence*, 139(1):91–107.

Emiel Krahmer, Erwin Marsi, and Paul van Pelt. 2008. Query-based sentence fusion is better defined and leads to more preferred results than generic sentence fusion. In *Proceedings of ACL*, pages 193–196.

Erwin Marsi and Emiel Krahmer. 2005. Explorations in sentence fusion. In *Proceedings of the European Workshop on Natural Language Generation*, pages 109–117.

Ryan McDonald. 2006. Discriminative sentence compression with soft syntactic evidence. In *Proceedings of EACL*, pages 297–304.

Kathleen R. McKeown, Regina Barzilay, David Evans, Vasileios Hatzivassiloglou, Judith L. Klavans, Ani Nenkova, Carl Sable, Barry Schiffman, and Sergey Sigelman. 2002. Tracking and summarizing news on a daily basis with Columbia's Newsblaster. In *Proceedings of HLT*, pages 280–285.

Rion Snow, Brendan O'Connor, Daniel Jurafsky, and Andrew Y. Ng. 2008. Cheap and fast—but is it good?: Evaluating non-expert annotations for natural language tasks. In *Proceedings of EMNLP*, pages 254–263.

Luis von Ahn and Laura Dabbish. 2004. Labeling images with a computer game. In *Proceedings of the SIGCHI conference on Human Factors in Computing Systems*, pages 319–326.

Zhuli Xie, Barbara Di Eugenio, and Peter C. Nelson. 2008. From extracting to abstracting: Generating quasi-abstractive summaries. In *Proceedings of LREC*, May.

Towards Cross-Lingual Textual Entailment

Yashar Mehdad[1,2], **Matteo Negri**[1], **Marcello Federico**[1]
FBK-Irst[1], University of Trento[2]
Trento, Italy
{mehdad,negri,federico}@fbk.eu

Abstract

This paper investigates *cross-lingual textual entailment* as a semantic relation between two text portions in different languages, and proposes a prospective research direction. We argue that cross-lingual textual entailment (CLTE) can be a core technology for several cross-lingual NLP applications and tasks. Through preliminary experiments, we aim at proving the feasibility of the task, and providing a reliable baseline. We also introduce new applications for CLTE that will be explored in future work.

1 Introduction

Textual Entailment (TE) (Dagan and Glickman, 2004) has been proposed as a generic framework for modeling language variability. Given two texts T and H, the task consists in deciding if the meaning of H can be inferred from the meaning of T. So far, TE has been only applied in a *monolingual* setting, where both texts are assumed to be written in the same language. In this work, we propose and investigate a *cross-lingual* extension of TE, where we assume that T and H are written in different languages.

The great potential of integrating (monolingual) TE recognition components into NLP architectures has been reported in several works, such as question answering (Harabagiu and Hickl, 2006), information retrieval (Clinchant et al., 2006), information extraction (Romano et al., 2006), and document summarization (Lloret et al., 2008).

To the best of our knowledge, mainly due to the absence of cross-lingual TE (CLTE) recognition components, similar improvements have not been achieved yet in any cross-lingual application. As a matter of fact, despite the great deal of attention that TE has received in recent years (also witnessed by five editions of the Recognizing Textual Entailment Challenge[1]), interest for cross-lingual extensions has not been in the mainstream of TE research, which until now has been mainly focused on the English language.

Nevertheless, the strong interest towards cross-lingual NLP applications (both from the market and research perspectives, as demonstrated by successful evaluation campaigns such as CLEF[2]) is, to our view, a good reason to start investigating CLTE, as well. Along such direction, research can now benefit from recent advances in other fields, especially machine translation (MT), and the availability of: *i)* large amounts of parallel and comparable corpora in many languages, *ii)* open source software to compute word-alignments from parallel corpora, and *iii)* open source software to set-up strong MT baseline systems. We strongly believe that all these resources can potentially help in developing inference mechanisms on multilingual data.

Building on these considerations, this paper aims to put the basis for future research on the cross-lingual Textual Entailment task, in order to allow for semantic inference across languages in different NLP tasks. Among these, as a long-term goal, we plan to adopt CLTE to support the alignment of text portions that express the same meaning in different languages. As a possible application scenario, CLTE

[1] http://pascallin.ecs.soton.ac.uk/Challenges/RTE/
[2] www.clef-campaign.org/

Human Language Technologies: The 2010 Annual Conference of the North American Chapter of the ACL, pages 321–324,
Los Angeles, California, June 2010.

can be used to address *content merging* tasks in tidy multilingual environments, such as commercial Web sites, digital libraries, or user generated content collections. Within such framework, as it will be discussed in the last section of this paper, CLTE components can be used for automatic content synchronization in a concurrent, collaborative, and multilingual editing setting, *e.g.* Wikipedia.

2 Cross Lingual Textual Entailment

Adapting the definition of TE we define CLTE as a relation between two natural language portions in different languages, namely a text T (*e.g.* in English), and a hypothesis H (*e.g.* in French), that holds if a human after reading T would infer that H is most likely true, or otherwise stated, the meaning of H can be entailed (inferred) from T.

We can see two main orthogonal directions for approaching CLTE: *i)* simply bring CLTE back to the monolingual case by translating H into the language of T, or vice-versa; *ii)* try to embed cross-lingual processing techniques inside the TE recognition process. In the following, we briefly overview and motivate each approach.

Basic approaches. The simplest approach is to add a MT component to the front-end of an existing TE engine. For instance, let the French hypothesis H be translated into English and then run the TE engine on T and the translation of H. There are several good reasons to follow this divide-and-conquer approach, as well as some drawbacks. Decoupling the cross-lingual and the entailment components results in a simple and modular architecture that, according to well known software engineering principles, results easier to develop, debug, and maintain. Moreover, a decoupled CLTE architecture would allow for easy extensions to other languages as it just requires extra MT systems. Along the same idea of pivoting through English, in fact, the same TE system can be employed to perform CLTE between any language pair, once MT is available from each language into English. A drawback of the decoupled approach is that as MT is still far from being perfect, translation errors are propagated to the TE engine and might likely affect performance. To cope with this issue, we explored the alternative approach of applying TE on a list of n-best translations provided by the MT engine, and take a final decision based on some system combination criterion. This latter approach potentially reduces the impact of translation errors, but might significantly increase the computational requirements of CLTE.

Advanced approaches. The idea is to move towards a cross-lingual TE approach that takes advantage of a tighter integration of MT and TE algorithms and techniques. This could result in methods for recognizing TE across languages without translating the texts and, in principle, with a lower complexity. When dealing with phrase-based statistical MT (Koehn et al., 2007), a possible approach is to extract information from the phrase-table to enrich the inference and entailment rules which could be used in a distance based entailment system. As an example the entailment relations between the French phrase "*ordinateur portable*" and the English phrase "*laptop*", or between the German phrase "*europaeischen union*" and the English word "*Europe*" could be captured from parallel corpora through statistical phrase-based MT approaches.

There are several implications that make this approach interesting. First of all, we believe that research on CLTE can employ inference mechanisms and semantic knowledge sources to augment existing MT methods, leading to improvements in the translation quality (*e.g.* (Padó et al., 2009)). In addition, the acquired rules could as well enrich the available multilingual resources and dictionaries such as MultiWordNet[3].

3 Feasibility studies

The main purpose of our preliminary experiments is to verify the feasibility of CLTE, as well as setting baseline results to be further improved over time. To this aim, we started by adopting the basic approach previously discussed. In particular, starting from an English/French corpus of T-H pairs, we automatically translated each H fragment from French into English.

Our decisions build on several motivations. First of all, the reason for setting English and French as a first language pair for experiments is to rely on higher quality translation models, and larger amounts of parallel data for future improvements.

[3]http://multiwordnet.fbk.eu/

Second, the reason for translating the hypotheses is that, according to the notion of TE, they are usually shorter, less detailed, and barely complex in terms of syntax and concepts with respect to the texts. This makes them easier to translate preserving the original meaning. Finally, from an application-oriented perspective, working with English Ts seems more promising due the richness of English data available (*e.g.* in terms of language variability, and more detailed elaboration of concepts). This increases the probability to discover entailment relations with Hs in other languages.

In order to create a realistic and standard setting, we took advantage of the available RTE data, selecting the RTE3 development set and manually translating the hypotheses into French. Since the manual translation requires trained translators, and due to time and logistics constraints, we obtained 520 translated hypotheses (randomly selected from the entire RTE3 development set) which built our bilingual entailment corpus for evaluation.

In the initial step, following our basic approach, we translated the French hypotheses to English using Google[4] and Moses[5]. We trained a phrase-base translation model using Europarl[6] and News Commentary parallel corpora in Moses, applying a 6-gram language model trained on the New York Times portion of the English Gigaword corpus[7].

As a TE engine , we used the EDITS[8] package (Edit Distance Textual Entailment Suite). This system is an open source software package based on edit distance algorithms, which computes the T-H distance as the cost of the edit operations (*i.e.* insertion, deletion and substitution) that are necessary to transform T into H. By defining the edit distance algorithm and a cost scheme (*i.e.* which defines the costs of each edit operation), this package is able to learn a distance model over a set of training pairs, which is used to decide if an entailment relation holds over each test pair.

In order to obtain a monolingual TE model, we trained and tuned (Mehdad, 2009) our model on the RTE3 test set, to reduce the overfitting bias, since our original data was created over the RTE3 development set. Moreover, we used a set of lexical entailment rules extracted from Wikipedia and WordNet, as described in (Mehdad et al., 2009). To begin with, we used this model to classify the created cross-lingual entailment corpus in three different settings: 1) hypotheses translated by Google, 2) hypotheses translated by Moses (1st best), and 3) the original RTE3 monolingual English pairs.

Results reported in Table 1 show that using Google as a translator, in comparison with the original manually-created data, does not cause any drop in performance. This confirms that merely translating the hypothesis using a very good translation model (Google) is a feasible and promising direction for CLTE. Knowing that Google has one of the best French-English translation models, the downtrend of results using Moses translator, in contrast with Google, is not out of our expectation. Trying to bridge this gap brings us to the next round of experiments, where we extracted the n-best translations produced by Moses, to have a richer lexical variability, beneficial for improving the TE recognition. The graph in Figure 1 shows an incremental improvement when the n-best translated hypotheses are used. Besides that, trying to reach a more monotonic distribution of the results, we normalized the ranking score (from 0 to 1) given by Moses, and in each step we chose the first n results over a normalized score. In this way, having the hypotheses with the score of above 0.4, we achieved the highest accuracy of 62.9%. This is exactly equal to adopting the 30-best hypotheses translated by Moses. Using this method, we could improve the performance up to 1.5% above the 1st best results, achieving almost the same level of performance obtained with Google.

	Orig.	**Google**	**Moses** 1st best	**Moses** 30 best	**Moses** > 0.4
Acc.	63.48	63.48	61.37	62.90	62.90

Table 1: Results comparison over 520 test pairs.

4 A possible application scenario

Among the many possible applications, the task of managing textual information in multiple languages represents an ideal application scenario for CLTE. Along such direction, our long-term goal is to use

[4]http://translate.google.com

[5]http://www.statmt.org/moses/

[6]http://www.statmt.org/europarl/

[7]http://www.ldc.upenn.edu

[8]http://edits.fbk.eu/

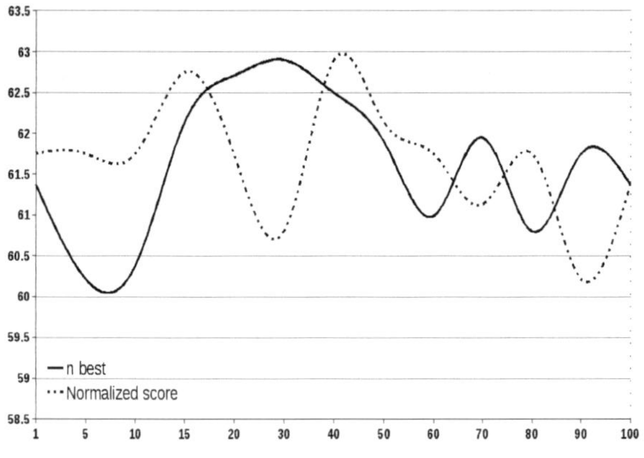

Figure 1: Accuracy gained by n-best Moses translations.

CLTE components in the task of *synchronizing* the content of documents about the same topic (*e.g.* Wikipedia articles), written in different languages. Currently, multilingual Wikis rely on users to manually translate different Wiki pages on the same subject. This is not only a time-consuming procedure but also the source of many inconsistencies, as users update the different language versions separately, and every update would require translators to compare the different language versions and synchronize the updates. Our goal is to automate this process by integrating MT and CLTE in a two-step process where: *i)* CLTE is used to identify text portions that should "migrate" from one page to the other, and *ii)* MT is used to actually translate these portions in the appropriate target language.

The adoption of entailment-based techniques to address the multilingual content synchronization task looks promising, as several issues inherent to such task can be formalized as TE-related problems. Given two pages (P1 and P2), these issues include identifying (and then properly managing):

1. Text portions in P1 and P2 that express exactly the same meaning (bi-directional entailment, or semantic equivalence) and which should not migrate across pages;

2. Text portions in P1 that are more specific than portions of P2 (unidirectional entailment between P2 and P1 or vice-versa) and should replace them;

3. Text portions in P1 describing facts that are not present in P2, and which should be added in P2 or vice-versa (the "unknown" cases in RTE parlance);

4. Meaning discrepancies between text portions in P1 and text portions in P2 ("contradictions" in RTE parlance).

5 Conclusion

This paper presented a preliminary investigation towards cross-lingual Textual Entailment, focusing on possible research directions and alternative methodologies. Baseline results have been provided to demonstrate the potentialities of a simple approach that integrates MT and monolingual TE components. Overall, our work sets a novel framework for further studies and experiments to improve cross-lingual NLP tasks. In particular, CLTE can be scaled to more complex problems, such as cross-lingual content merging and synchronization.

Acknowledgments

This work has been partially supported by the EC-funded project CoSyne (FP7-ICT-4-24853)

References

S. Clinchant, C. Goutte, and E. Gaussier. 2006. Lexical entailment for information retrieval. In *Proc. ECIR'06.*

I. Dagan and O. Glickman. 2004. Probabilistic textual entailment: Generic applied modeling of language variability. *Proc. of the PASCAL Workshop of Learning Methods for Text Understanding and Mining.*

S. Harabagiu and A. Hickl. 2006. Methods for using textual entailment in open-domain question answering. In *Proc. COLING/ACL 2006.*

P. Koehn et al. 2007. Moses: Open source toolkit for statistical machine translation. In *Proc. ACL07 Demo and Poster Sessions.*

E. Lloret, Ó. Ferrández, R. Muñoz, and M. Palomar. 2008. A text summarization approach under the influence of textual entailment. In *Proc. NLPCS 2008.*

Y. Mehdad, M. Negri, E. Cabrio, M. Kouylekov, and B. Magnini. 2009. Edits: An open source framework for recognizing textual entailment. In *Proc. TAC 2009. To appear.*

Yashar Mehdad. 2009. Automatic cost estimation for tree edit distance using particle swarm optimization. In *Proc. ACL '09.*

S. Padó, M. Galley, D. Jurafsky, and C. D. Manning. 2009. Textual entailment features for machine translation evaluation. In *Proc. StatMT '09.*

L. Romano, M. Kouylekov, I. Szpektor, I. Dagan, and A. Lavelli. 2006. Investigating a generic paraphrase-based approach for relation extraction. In *Proc. EACL 2006.*

A Comparative Study of Word Co-occurrence for Term Clustering in Language Model-based Sentence Retrieval

Saeedeh Momtazi
Spoken Language Systems
Saarland University
saeedeh.momtazi
@lsv.uni-saarland.de

Sanjeev Khudanpur
Center for Language
and Speech Processing
Johns Hopkins University
khudanpur@jhu.edu

Dietrich Klakow
Spoken Language Systems
Saarland University
dietrich.klakow
@lsv.uni-saarland.de

Abstract

Sentence retrieval is a very important part of question answering systems. Term clustering, in turn, is an effective approach for improving sentence retrieval performance: the more similar the terms in each cluster, the better the performance of the retrieval system. A key step in obtaining appropriate word clusters is accurate estimation of *pairwise* word similarities, based on their tendency to co-occur in similar contexts. In this paper, we compare four different methods for estimating word co-occurrence frequencies from two different corpora. The results show that different, commonly-used contexts for defining word co-occurrence differ significantly in retrieval performance. Using an appropriate co-occurrence criterion and corpus is shown to improve the mean average precision of sentence retrieval form 36.8% to 42.1%.

1 Corpus-Driven Clustering of Terms

Since the search in Question Answering (QA) is conducted over smaller segments of text than in document retrieval, the problems of data sparsity and exact matching become more critical. The idea of using class-based language model by applying term clustering, proposed by Momtazi and Klakow (2009), is found to be effective in overcoming these problems.

Term clustering has a very long history in natural language processing. The idea was introduced by Brown et al. (1992) and used in different applications, including speech recognition, named entity tagging, machine translation, query expansion, text categorization, and word sense disambiguation. In most of the studies in term clustering, one of several well-know *notions of co-occurrence*—appearing in the same document, in the same sentence or following the same word—has been used to estimate term similarity. However, to the best of our knowledge, none of them explored the relationship between different notions of co-occurrence and the effectiveness of their resulting clusters in an end task.

In this research, we present a comprehensive study of how different notions of co-occurrence impact retrieval performance. To this end, the Brown algorithm (Brown et al., 1992) is applied to pairwise word co-occurrence statistics based on different *definitions* of word co-occurrence. Then, the word clusters are used in a class-based language model for sentence retrieval. Additionally, impact of corpus size and domain on co-occurrence estimation is studied.

The paper is organized as follows. In Section 2, we give a brief description of class-based language model for sentence retrieval and the Brown word clustering algorithm. Section 3 presents different methods for estimating the word co-occurrence. In Section 4, experimental results are presented. Finally, Section 5 summarizes the paper.

2 Term Clustering Method and Application

In language model-based sentence retrieval, the probability $P(Q|S)$ of generating query Q conditioned on a candidate sentence S is first calculated. Thereafter sentences in the search collection are ranked in descending order of this probability. For word-based unigram, $P(Q|S)$ is estimated as

$$P(Q|S) = \prod_{i=1...M} P(q_i|S), \qquad (1)$$

where M is the number of query terms, q_i denotes the ith query term in Q, and S is the sentence model.

Human Language Technologies: The 2010 Annual Conference of the North American Chapter of the ACL, pages 325–328,
Los Angeles, California, June 2010.

For class-based unigrams, $P(Q|S)$ is computed using only the *cluster labels* of the query terms as

$$P(Q|S) = \prod_{i=1...M} P(q_i|C_{q_i}, S)P(C_{q_i}|S), \quad (2)$$

where C_{q_i} is the cluster that contains q_i and $P(q_i|C_{q_i}, S)$ is the emission probability of the ith query term given its cluster and the sentence. $P(C_{q_i}|S)$ is analogous to the sentence model $P(q_i|S)$ in (1), but is based on clusters instead of terms. To calculate $P(C_{q_i}|S)$, each cluster is considered an atomic entity, with Q and S interpreted as sequences of such entities.

In order to cluster lexical items, we use the algorithm proposed by Brown et al (1992), as implemented in the SRILM toolkit (Stolcke, 2002). The algorithm requires an input corpus statistics in the form $\langle w, w', f_{ww'} \rangle$, where $f_{ww'}$ is the number of times the word w' is seen in the context w. Both w and w' are assumed to come from a common vocabulary. Beginning with each vocabulary item in a separate cluster, a bottom-up approach is used to merge the pair of clusters that minimizes the loss in *Average Mutual Information* (AMI) between the word cluster $C_{w'}$ and its context cluster C_w. Different words seen in the same contexts are good candidates for merger, as are different contexts in which the same words are seen.

While originally proposed with bigram statistics, the algorithm is *agnostic* to the definition of co-occurrence. E.g. if $\langle w, w' \rangle$ are verb-object pairs, the algorithm clusters verbs based on their selectional preferences, if $f_{ww'}$ is the number of times w and w' appear in the same document, it will produce semantically (or topically) related word-clusters, etc.

Several notions of co-occurrence have been used in the literature to cluster words, as described next.

3 Notions of Word Co-occurrence

Co-occurrence in a Document

If two content words w and w' are seen in the same document, they are usually topically related. In this notion of co-occurrence, how near or far away from each other they are in the document is irrelevant, as is their order of appearance in the document. *Document-wise* co-occurrence has been successfully used in many NLP applications such as automatic thesaurus generation (Manning et al., 2008)

Statistics of document-wise co-occurrence may be collected in two different ways. In the first case, $f_{ww'} = f_{w'w}$ is simply the number of documents that contain both w and w'. This is usually the notion used in ad hoc retrieval. Alternatively, we may want to treat each *instance* of w' in a document that contains an instance of w to be a co-occurrence event. Therefore if w' appears three times in a document that contains two instances of w, the former method counts it as one co-occurrence, while the latter as six co-occurrences. We use the latter statistic, since we are concerned with retrieving sentence sized "documents," wherein a repeated word is more significant.

Co-occurrence in a Sentence

Since topic changes sometimes happen within a single document, and our end task is sentence retrieval, we also investigate the notion of word co-occurrence in a smaller segment of text such as a sentence. In contrast to the document-wise model, *sentence-wise* co-occurrence does not consider whole documents, and only concerns itself with the number of times that two words occur in the same sentence.

Co-occurrence in a Window of Text

The *window-wise* co-occurrence statistic is an even narrower notion of context, considering only terms in a window surrounding w'. Specifically, a window of a fixed size is moved along the text, and $f_{ww'}$ is set as the number of times both w and w' appear in the window. Since the window size is a free parameter, different sizes may be applied. In our experiments we use two window sizes, 2 and 5, that have been studied in related research (Church and Hanks, 1990).

Co-occurrence in a Syntactic Relationship

Another notion of word similarity derives from having the same syntactic relationship with the context w. This *syntax-wise* co-occurrence statistic is similar to the sentence-wise co-occurrence, in that co-occurrence is defined at the sentence level. However, in contrast to the sentence-wise model, w and w' are said to co-occur only if there is a syntactic relation between them in that sentence. E.g., this type of co-occurrence can help cluster nouns that are used as objects of same verb, such as 'tea', 'water', and 'cola,' which all are used with the verb 'drink'.

To gather such statistics, all sentences in the corpus must be syntactically parsed. We found that a dependency parser is an appropriate tool for our goal: it directly captures dependencies between words without the mediation of any virtual (nonterminal) nodes. Having all sentences in the parsed format, $f_{ww'}$ is defined as the number of times that the words w and w' have a parent-child relationship of *any syntactic type* in the dependency parse tree. For our experiments we use MINIPAR (Lin, 1998) to parse the whole corpus due to its robustness and speed.

4 Sentence Retrieval Experiments

4.1 Derivatives of the TREC QA Data Sets

The set of questions from the TREC 2006 QA track[1] was used as the test data to evaluate our models, while the TREC 2005 set was used for development.

The TREC 2006 QA task contains 75 question-series, each on one topic, for a total of 403 factoid questions which is used as queries for sentence retrieval. For sentence-level relevance judgments, the *Question Answer Sentence Pair* corpus of Kaisser and Lowe (2008) was used. All the documents that contain relevant sentences are from the NIST AQUAINT1 corpus.

QA systems typically employ sentence retrieval after initial, high quality document retrieval. To simulate this, we created a separate *search collection* for each question using all sentences from all documents relevant to the topic (question-series) from which the question was derived. On average, there are 17 relevant documents per topic, many *not* relevant to the question itself: they may be relevant to another question. So the sentence search collection is realistic, even if somewhat optimistic.

4.2 Corpora for Term Clustering

We investigated two different corpora[2], *AQUAINT1* and *Google n-grams*, to obtain word co-occurrence statistics for term clustering. Based on this we can also evaluate the impact of corpus size and corpus domain on the result of term clustering.

AQUAINT1 consists of English newswire text extracted from the Xinhua, the New York Times and the Associated Press Worldstream News Services.

The Google *n*-gram counts were generated from publicly accessible English web pages. Since there is no possibility of extracting document-wise, sentence-wise or syntax-wise co-occurrence statistics from the Google *n*-gram corpus, we only collect window-wise statistics to the extent available in the corpus.

Corpus	Co-occurrence	# Word Pairs
AQUAINT1	document	368,109,133
AQUAINT1	sentence	104,084,473
AQUAINT1	syntax	12,343,947
AQUAINT1	window-5	46,307,650
AQUAINT1	window-2	14,093,661
Google *n*-grams	window-5	12,005,479
Google *n*-grams	window-2	328,431,792

Table 1: Statistics for different notions of co-occurrence.

Table 1 shows the number of word pairs extracted from the two corpora with different definitions of co-occurrence. The statistics only include word pairs for which both constituent words are present in the 35,000 word vocabulary of our search collection.

4.3 Sentence Retrieval Results and Discussion

Sentence retrieval performance for term clustering using different definitions of word co-occurrence is shown in Figure 1. Since the Brown algorithm requires specifying the number of clusters, tests were conducted for 50, 100, 200, 500, and 1000 clusters of the term vocabulary. The baseline system is the word-based sentence retrieval model of Equation (1).

Figure 1(a) shows the *Mean Average Precision* (MAP) for class-based sentence retrieval of Equation (2) using clusters based on different co-occurrence statistics from AQUAINT1. Note that

(i) the best result achieved by sentence-wise co-occurence is better the best result of document-wise, perhaps due to more local and relevant information that it captures;

(ii) all the results achieved by syntax-wise co-occurrence are better than sentence-wise, indicating that merely co-occurring in a sentence is not very indicative of word similarity, while relations extracted from syntactic structure improve system performance significantly;

(iii) window-2 significantly outperforms all other notions of co-occurrence; i.e., the bigram statistics achieve the best clustering results. In comparison, window-5 has the worst results, with performance very close to baseline.

Although window-5 co-occurrence has been reported

[1]See `http://trec.nist.gov`.

[2]See catalog numbers LDC2002T31 and LDC2006T13 respectively at `http://www.ldc.upenn.edu/Catalog`.

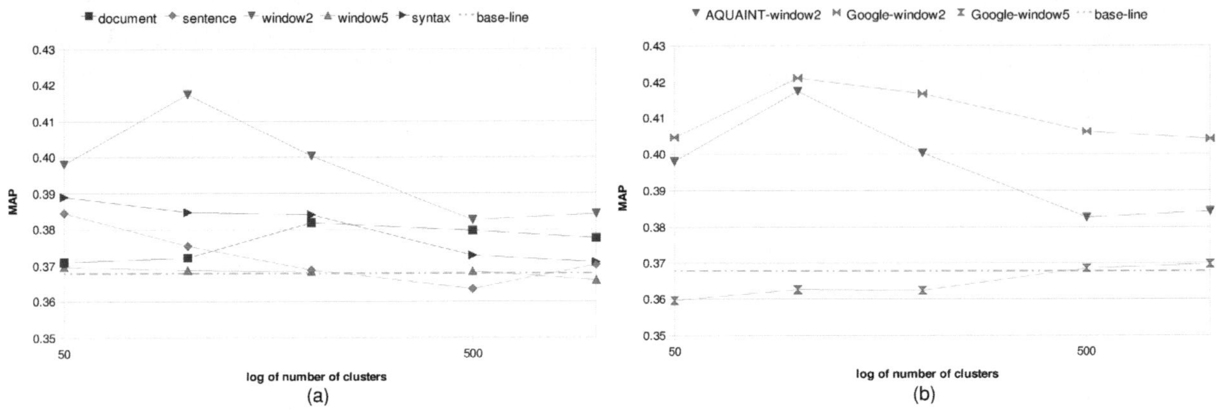

Figure 1: MAP of sentence retrieval for different word co-occurrence statistics from AQUAINT1 and Google *n*-grams.

to be effective in other applications, it is not helpful in sentence retrieval.

Figure 1(b) shows the MAP for class-based sentence retrieval of Equation (2) when window-wise co-occurrence statistics from the Google *n*-grams are used. For better visualization, we repeated the MAP results using AQUAINT1 window-2 co-occurrence statistics from Figure 1(a) in 1(b). Note that

(iv) window-2 co-occurrence statistics significantly outperform window-5 for the Google *n*-grams, consistent with results from AQUAINT1;

(v) Google *n*-gram window-2 co-occurrence statistics consistently result in better MAP than AQUAINT window-2.

The last result indicates that even though the Google *n*-grams are from a different (and much broader) domain than the test data, they significantly improve the system performance due to sheer size. Finally

(vi) Google *n*-gram window-2 MAP curve is flatter than AQUAINT window-2; i.e., performance is not very sensitive to the number of clusters.

The best overall result is from Google window-2 co-occurrence statistics with 100 clusters, achieving 42.1% MAP while the best result derived from AQUAINT1 is 41.7% MAP for window-2 co-occurrence with 100 clusters, and the MAP of the word-based model (baseline) is 36.8%.

5 Concluding Remarks

We compared different notions of word co-occurrence for clustering terms, using document-wise, sentence-wise, window-wise, and syntax-wise co-occurrence statistics derived from AQUAINT1. We found that different notions of co-occurrence significantly change the behavior of a sentence retrieval system, in which window-wise model with size 2 achieves the best result. In addition, Google *n*-grams were used for window-wise model to study the impact of corpus size and domain on the clustering result. The result showed that although the domain of the Google *n*-grams is dissimilar to the test set, it outperforms models derived from AQUAINT1 due to sheer size.

Acknowledgments

Saeedeh Momtazi is funded by the German research foundation DFG through the International Research Training Group (IRTG 715).

References

P.F. Brown, V.J.D. Pietra, P.V. Souza, J.C. Lai, and R.L. Mercer. 1992. Class-based n-gram models of natural language. *Computational Linguistics*, 18(4):467–479.

K.W. Church and P. Hanks. 1990. Word association norms, mutual information, and lexicography. *Computational Linguistics*, 16(1):22–29.

M. Kaisser and J.B. Lowe. 2008. Creating a research collection of question answer sentence pairs with Amazon's mechanical turk. In *Proc. of LREC*.

D. Lin. 1998. Dependency-based evaluation of MINIPAR. In *Proc. of the Evaluation of Parsing Systems Workshop*.

C.D. Manning, P. Raghavan, and H. Schütze. 2008. *Introduction to Information Retrieval*. Cambridge University Press.

S. Momtazi and D. Klakow. 2009. A word clustering approach for language model-based sentence retrieval in question answering systems. In *Proc. of ACM CIKM*.

A. Stolcke. 2002. SRILM - an extensible language modeling toolkit. In *Proc. of ICSLP*.

Information Content Measures of Semantic Similarity Perform Better Without Sense-Tagged Text

Ted Pedersen
Department of Computer Science
University of Minnesota, Duluth
Duluth, MN 55812
tpederse@d.umn.edu
http://wn-similarity.sourceforge.net

Abstract

This paper presents an empirical comparison of similarity measures for pairs of concepts based on Information Content. It shows that using modest amounts of untagged text to derive Information Content results in higher correlation with human similarity judgments than using the largest available corpus of manually annotated sense–tagged text.

1 Introduction

Measures of semantic similarity based on WordNet have been widely used in Natural Language Processing. These measures rely on the structure of WordNet to produce a numeric score that quantifies the degree to which two concepts (represented by a sense or synset) are similar (or not). In their simplest form these measures use path length to identify concepts that are physically close to each other and therefore considered to be more similar than concepts that are further apart.

While this is a reasonable first approximation to semantic similarity, there are some well known limitations. Most significant is that path lengths between very specific concepts imply much smaller distinctions in semantic similarity than do comparable path lengths between very general concepts. One proposed improvement is to augment concepts in WordNet with *Information Content* values derived from sense–tagged corpora or from raw unannotated corpora (Resnik, 1995).

This paper shows that Information Content measures based on modest amounts of unannotated corpora have greater correlation with human similarity judgements than do those based on the largest corpus of sense-tagged text currently available.[1] The key to this success is not in the specific type of corpora used, but rather in increasing the number of concepts in WordNet that have counts associated with them. These results show that Information Content measures of semantic similarity can be significantly improved without requiring the creation of sense–tagged corpora (which is very expensive).

1.1 Information Content

Information Content (IC) is a measure of specificity for a concept. Higher values are associated with more specific concepts (e.g., *pitch_fork*), while those with lower values are more general (e.g., *idea*). Information Content is computed based on frequency counts of concepts as found in a corpus of text. The frequency associated with a concept is incremented in WordNet each time that concept is observed, as are the counts of the ancestor concepts in the WordNet hierarchy (for nouns and verbs). This is necessary because each occurrence of a more specific concept also implies the occurrence of the more general ancestor concepts.

When a corpus is sense–tagged, mapping occurrences of a word to a concept is straightforward (since each sense of a word corresponds with a concept or synset in WordNet). However, if the text has not been sense–tagged then all of the possible senses of a given word are incremented (as are their ancestors). For example, if *tree* (as a plant) occurs in a sense–tagged text, then only the concept associated

[1]These experiments were done with version 2.05 of WordNet::Similarity (Pedersen et al., 2004).

Human Language Technologies: The 2010 Annual Conference of the North American Chapter of the ACL, pages 329–332,

with tree as a kind of plant would be incremented. If the text is untagged, then all of the possible senses of *tree* would be incremented (such as the mathematical sense of tree, a shoe tree, a plant, etc.) In this case the frequency of all the occurrences of a word are divided equally among the different possible senses. Thus, if a word occurs 42 times in a corpus and there are six possible senses (concepts), each sense and all of their ancestors would have their frequency incremented by seven.[2]

For each concept (synset) c in WordNet, Information Content is defined as the negative log of the probability of that concept (based on the observed frequency counts):

$$IC(c) = -logP(c)$$

Information Content can only be computed for nouns and verbs in WordNet, since these are the only parts of speech where concepts are organized in hierarchies. Since these hierarchies are separate, Information Content measures of similarity can only be applied to pairs of nouns or pairs of verbs.

2 Semantic Similarity Measures

There are three Information Content measures implemented in WordNet::Similarity: (res) (Resnik, 1995), (jcn) (Jiang and Conrath, 1997), and (lin) (Lin, 1998).

These measures take as input two concepts c_1 and c_2 (i.e., senses or synsets in WordNet) and output a numeric measure of similarity. These measures all rely to varying degrees on the idea of a least common subsumer (LCS); this is the most specific concept that is a shared ancestor of the two concepts. For example, the LCS of *automobile* and *scooter* is *vehicle*.

The Resnik (res) measure simply uses the Information Content of the LCS as the similarity value:

$$res(c_1, c_2) = IC(LCS(c_1, c_2))$$

The Resnik measure is considered somewhat coarse, since many different pairs of concepts may share the same LCS. However, it is less likely to suffer from zero counts (and resulting undefined values) since in general the LCS of two concepts will not be a very specific concept (i.e., a leaf node in WordNet), but will instead be a somewhat more general concept that is more likely to have observed counts associated with it.

Both the Lin and Jiang & Conrath measures attempt to refine the Resnik measure by augmenting it with the Information Content of the individual concepts being measured in two different ways:

$$lin(c_1, c_2) = \frac{2*res(c_1,c_2)}{IC(c_1)+IC(c_2)}$$

$$jcn(c_1, c_2) = \frac{1}{IC(c_1)+IC(c_2)-2*res(c_1,c_2)}$$

All three of these measures have been widely used in the NLP literature, and have tended to perform well in a wide range of applications such as word sense disambiguation, paraphrase detection, and Question Answering (c.f., (Resnik, 1999)).

3 Experimental Data

Information Content in WordNet::Similarity is (by default) derived from SemCor (Miller et al., 1993), a manually sense–tagged subset of the Brown Corpus. It is made up of approximately 676,000 words, of which 226,000 are sense–tagged. SemCor was originally created using sense–tags from version 1.6 of WordNet, and has been mapped to subsequent versions to stay current.[3] This paper uses version 3.0 of WordNet and SemCor.

WordNet::Similarity also includes a utility (rawtextFreq.pl) that allows a user to derive Information Content values from any corpus of plain text. This utility is used with the untagged version of SemCor and with various portions of the English GigaWord corpus (1st edition) to derive alternative Information Content values.

English GigaWord contains more than 1.7 billion words of newspaper text from the 1990's and early 21st century, divided among four different sources: Agence France Press English Service (afe), Associated Press Worldstream English Service (apw), The New York Times Newswire Service (nyt), and The Xinhua News Agency English Service (xie).

This paper compares the ranking of pairs of concepts according to Information Content measures in WordNet::Similarity with a number of manually created gold standards. These include the (RG) (Rubenstein and Goodenough, 1965) collection of 65 noun

[2]This is the –resnik counting option in WordNet::Similarity.

[3]http://www.cse.unt.edu/~rada/downloads.html

Table 1: Rank Correlation of Existing Measures

measure	WS	MC	RG
vector	**.46**	**.89**	**.73**
lesk	.42	.83	.68
wup	.34	.74	.69
lch	.28	.71	.70
path	.26	.68	.69
random	-.20	-.16	.15

pairs, the (MC) (Miller and Charles, 1991) collection of 30 noun pairs (a subset of RG), and the (WS) WordSimilarity-353 collection of 353 pairs (Finkelstein et al., 2002). RG and MC have been scored for similarity, while WS is scored for relatedness, which is a more general and less well–defined notion than similarity. For example *aspirin* and *headache* are clearly related, but they aren't really similar.

4 Experimental Results

Table 1 shows the Spearman's rank correlation of several other measures of similarity and relatedness in WordNet::Similarity with the gold standards discussed above. The WordNet::Similarity vector relatedness measure achieves the highest correlation, followed closely by the adapted lesk measure. These results are consistent with previous findings (Patwardhan and Pedersen, 2006). This table also shows results for several path–based measures.[4]

Table 2 shows the correlation of jcn, res, and lin when Information Content is derived from 1) the sense-tagged version of SemCor (semcor), 2) SemCor without sense tags (semcor-raw), and 3) steadily increasing subsets of the 133 million word xie portion of the English GigaWord corpus. These subsets start with the entire first month of xie (199501, from January 1995) and then two months (199501-02), three months (199501-03), up through all of 1995 (199501-12). Thereafter the increments are annual, with two years of data (1995-1996), then three (1995-1997), and so on until the entire xie corpus is used (1995-2001). The afe, apw, and nyt portions of GigaWord are also used individually and then combined all together along with xie *(all)*.

[4] *wup* is the Wu & Palmer measure, *lch* is the Leacock & Chodorow measure, *path* relies on edge counting, and *random* provides a simple sanity check.

The size (in tokens) of each corpus is shown in the second column of Table 2 *(size)*, which is expressed in thousands (k), millions (m), and billions (b).

The third column (*cover*) shows what percentage of the 96,000 noun and verb synsets in WordNet receive a non-zero frequency count when Information Content is derived from the specified corpus. These values show that the 226,000 sense–tagged instances in SemCor cover about 24%, and the untagged version of SemCor covers 37%. As it happens the correlation results for semcor-raw are somewhat better than semcor, suggesting that coverage is at least as important (if not more so) to the performance of Information Content measures than accurate mapping of words to concepts.

A similar pattern can be seen with the xie results in Table 2. This again shows that an increase in WordNet coverage is associated with increased performance of the Information Content measures. As coverage increases the correlation improves, and in fact the results are better than the path–based measures and approach those of lesk and vector (see Table 1). The one exception is with respect to the WS gold standard, where vector and lesk perform much better than the Information Content measures. However, this seems reasonable since they are relatedness measures, and the WS corpus is annotated for relatedness rather than similarity.

As a final test of the hypothesis that coverage matters as much or more than accurate mapping of words to concepts, a simple baseline method was created that assigns each synset a count of 1, and then propagates that count up to the ancestor concepts. This is equivalent to doing add-1 smoothing without any text (add1only). This results in correlation nearly as high as the best results with xie and semcor-raw, and is significantly better than semcor.

5 Conclusions

This paper shows that semantic similarity measures based on Information Content can be significantly improved by increasing the coverage of the frequency counts used to derive Information Content. Increased coverage can come from unannotated text or simply assigning counts to every concept in WordNet and does not require sense–tagged text.

Table 2: Rank Correlation of Information Content Measures From Different Corpora

			jcn			lin			res		
corpus	size	cover	WS	MC	RG	WS	MC	RG	WS	MC	RG
semcor	226 k	.24	.21	.72	.51	.30	.73	.58	.38	.74	.69
semcor-raw	670 k	.37	.26	.82	.58	.32	.79	.65	.38	.76	.70
xie:											
199501	1.2 m	.35	.35	.78	.57	.37	.75	.63	.37	.73	.68
199501-02	2.3 m	.39	.31	.79	.65	.32	.75	.67	.36	.73	.68
199501-03	3.8 m	.42	.34	.88	.69	.34	.81	.70	.37	.75	.69
199501-06	7.9 m	.46	.36	.88	.69	.36	.81	.70	.37	.75	.69
199501-09	12 m	.49	.36	.88	.69	.36	.81	.70	.37	.75	.69
199501-12	16 m	.51	.37	.87	.73	.36	.81	.71	.37	.75	.69
1995-1996	34 m	.56	.37	.88	.73	.36	.81	.72	.37	.75	.69
1995-1997	53 m	.58	.37	.88	.73	.36	.81	.71	.37	.75	.69
1995-1998	73 m	.60	.37	.89	.73	.36	.81	.72	.37	.75	.69
1995-1999	94 m	.62	.36	.88	.73	.36	.81	.72	.37	.76	.69
1995-2000	115 m	.63	.36	.89	.73	.36	.81	.71	.37	.76	.70
1995-2001	133 m	.64	.36	.88	.73	.36	.81	.71	.37	.76	.70
afe	174 m	.66	**.36**	**.88**	**.81**	.36	.80	.78	.37	.77	.79
apw	560 m	.75	.36	.84	.78	.36	.79	.78	.37	.76	.79
nyt	963 m	.83	.36	.84	.78	.36	.79	.77	.37	.77	.80
all	1.8 b	.85	.34	.85	.79	.35	.80	.78	.37	.77	.79
add1only	96 k	1.00	.36	.85	.73	.37	.77	.73	.39	.76	.70

Acknowledgements

Many thanks to Siddharth Patwardhan and Jason Michelizzi for their exceptional work on WordNet::Similarity over the years, which has made this and a great deal of other research possible.

References

L. Finkelstein, E. Gabrilovich, Y. Matias, E. Rivlin, Z. Solan, G. Wolfman, and E. Ruppin. 2002. Placing search in context: The concept revisited. *ACM Transactions on Information Systems*, 20(1):116–131.

J. Jiang and D. Conrath. 1997. Semantic similarity based on corpus statistics and lexical taxonomy. In *Proceedings on International Conference on Research in Computational Linguistics*, pages 19–33, Taiwan.

D. Lin. 1998. An information-theoretic definition of similarity. In *Proceedings of the International Conference on Machine Learning*, Madison, August.

G.A. Miller and W.G. Charles. 1991. Contextual correlates of semantic similarity. *Language and Cognitive Processes*, 6(1):1–28.

G.A. Miller, C. Leacock, R. Tengi, and R. Bunker. 1993. A semantic concordance. In *Proceedings of the Workshop on Human Language Technology*, pages 303–308.

S. Patwardhan and T. Pedersen. 2006. Using WordNet-based Context Vectors to Estimate the Semantic Relatedness of Concepts. In *Proceedings of the EACL 2006 Workshop on Making Sense of Sense: Bringing Computational Linguistics and Psycholinguistics Together*, pages 1–8, Trento, Italy, April.

T. Pedersen, S. Patwardhan, and J. Michelizzi. 2004. Wordnet::Similarity - Measuring the relatedness of concepts. In *Proceedings of Fifth Annual Meeting of the North American Chapter of the Association for Computational Linguistics*, pages 38–41, Boston, MA.

P. Resnik. 1995. Using information content to evaluate semantic similarity in a taxonomy. In *Proceedings of the 14th International Joint Conference on Artificial Intelligence*, pages 448–453, Montreal, August.

P. Resnik. 1999. Semantic similarity in a taxonomy: An information-based measure and its application to problems of ambiguity in natural language. *Journal of Artificial Intelligence Research*, 11:95–130.

H. Rubenstein and J.B. Goodenough. 1965. Contextual correlates of synonymy. *Computational Linguistics*, 8:627–633.

Generating Expository Dialogue from Monologue: Motivation, Corpus and Preliminary Rules

Paul Piwek
Centre for Research in Computing
The Open University
Walton Hall, Milton Keynes, UK
p.piwek@open.ac.uk

Svetlana Stoyanchev
Centre for Research in Computing
The Open University
Walton Hall, Milton Keynes, UK
s.stoyanchev@open.ac.uk

Abstract

Generating expository dialogue from monologue is a task that poses an interesting and rewarding challenge for Natural Language Processing. This short paper has three aims: firstly, to motivate the importance of this task, both in terms of the benefits of expository dialogue as a way to present information and in terms of potential applications; secondly, to introduce a parallel corpus of monologues and dialogues which enables a data-driven approach to this challenge; and, finally, to describe work-in-progress on semi-automatic construction of Monologue-to-Dialogue (M2D) generation rules.

1 Introduction

The tasks of text generation – e.g., Reiter et al. (2005) and Demir et al. (2008) – and generation in dialogue – e.g., Stent (2002) and DeVault et al. (2008) – are central topics in Natural Language Generation (NLG). What sets the two tasks apart is the interactive nature of dialogue, where participants need to adapt their contributions to each other.

This paper introduces an NLG task, the generation of expository dialogue, to the Computational Linguistics community which occupies the middle ground between these two tasks. An expository dialogue is an authored conversation between two fictive characters. It can be presented as text, audio or film. Although there is no real-time interactivity, in expository dialogue the contributions of the characters do need to mesh with each other. The main purpose of expository dialogue is to present information (a description, explanation or definition) to the reader, hearer or viewer, in contrast with dramatic dialogue, which tells a story.

The use of expository dialogue goes back as far as Plato (c. 470-399 BC), who expressed his ideas as dialogues between Socrates and his contemporaries. Recently, a number of empirical studies show that for some purposes expository dialogue has advantages over monologue: for learners, dialogue can be more memorable, stimulate them to formulate their own questions (Craig et al., 2000), and get them to talk with each other (Lee et al., 1998). Expository dialogue has also been found to be more effective for persuasion (Suzuki and Yamada, 2004).

Additionally, dialogue lends itself very well for multimedia presentations by computer-animated agents (André et al., 2000; van Deemter et al., 2008). Potential application domains include education, (serious) games and E-Health. In education, information from textbooks could be presented in dialogue form, possibly using virtual reality platforms such as Second Life. Automatically generating dialogue from text for non-player characters could have a tremendous impact on the gaming industry; e.g., (IGDA Game Writers SIG, 2003) state that the amount of dialogue script for a character-driven computer game is usually many times that for the average film. In connection with E-health, consider patient information leaflets, which are often left unread; presenting them as movies between a virtual pharmacist and client may help address this. Thus instead of being presented with

(1) a. You can take aspirin,
    b. if you have a headache.

Human Language Technologies: The 2010 Annual Conference of the North American Chapter of the ACL, pages 333–336,
Los Angeles, California, June 2010.

c. Though aspirin does have side effects:

d. it can harm circulation.

the patient could watch a movie on their mobile device of an exchange between a virtual client (*layman*, L) and pharmacist (*expert*, E):

(2) *L*: What if I have a headache?
E: You can take aspirin
L: But does it have side effects?
E: Yes, it can harm circulation.

So far, research on generating expository dialogue has been firmly rooted in classical AI approaches. Work in this area starts from knowledge representations or databases (André et al., 2000), and even research that does take text as input – e.g., Piwek et al. (2007) describe a system for generating dialogues such as Example 2 – relies on handcrafted rules. Two challenges present themselves for NLP research: 1) generation of expository dialogue from text, and 2) use of data-driven, rather than manually authored, generation rules.

Apart from the cost of manually authoring generation rules, previous research has found that human-authored rules can result in 'too much information [being] given too quickly' (Williams et al., 2007), which can be addressed by conversational padding. We argue that rather than trying to invent padding rules, the best strategy is to learn rules automatically from professionally authored dialogues.

2 The CODA Corpus

To make inroads into data-driven dialogue generation, we first need to have the necessary resources. We propose to view Monologue-to-Dialogue (M2D) generation as analogous to machine translation; consequently we need a parallel corpus for learning mappings from the source (monologue) to the target (dialogue) texts. In the ongoing CODA[1] project we have created such a corpus. It consists of professionally authored dialogues[2] that have been aligned with monologues (written by ourselves) expressing the same information. Since our ultimate aim is to generate dialogues that resemble those written by

[1]COherent Dialogue Automatically generated from text

[2]Most dialogues are from the Gutenberg library to facilitate our planned release of the corpus to the research community.

Sp	Dialog act	Dialogue Turn	Monologue
E:	Complex Question	When you have a pain in your foot, how do you know it?	When you have a pain in your foot (i) you know it because you
L:	Explain	I feel it.	can feel it. (ii)
E:	Explain-Contradict	But you do not feel it until a nerve reports the hurt to the brain.	But you do not feel it until a nerve reports the hurt to the brain. (iii)
E:	YN-Question	Yet the brain is the seat of the mind , is it not?	Yet the brain is the seat of the mind. (iv)

Table 1: Parallel Monologue and Dialogue Example from Mark Twain's "What is Man?"

acclaimed authors, we started with professionally authored dialogues and created the corresponding monologues. From a practical point of view, it was more feasible to use existing dialogue by acclaimed authors than to hire professional authors to write dialogue based on monologues.

We have annotated both dialogues and monologues: dialogue with dialogue acts and monologue with discourse relations.[3] We achieved 91% agreement on segmentation and *kappa*=.82 for dialogue act annotation on 11 dialogue act tags. We developed a *D2MTranslation* tool for monologue authoring, segmentation and dialogue annotation.

In January 2010, the corpus included 500 turns from "What is man?", a dialogue by Mark Twain, and 88 turns from "Evolving Algebras", an academic paper in the form of dialogue by Yuri Gurevich.[4] Both of these expository dialogues present conversation between an *expert* (Old Man in Twain and Author in Gurevich) and a *layman* (Young Man in Twain and Quisani in Gurevich). Table 1 shows an example of a dialogue fragment, aligned monologue and dialogue act annotations. The discourse structure of the monologue is depicted in Figure 1.

Table 2 shows the distribution of the dialogue acts between expert and layman. In both dialogues, the

[3]See (Stoyanchev and Piwek, 2010) for details.

[4]In addition to these dialogues we are working on a dialogue by Berkeley (Three Dialogues between Hylas and Philonous) and a selection of shorter fragments (for copyrights reasons) by authors such as Douglas Hofstadter and Paul Feyerabend.

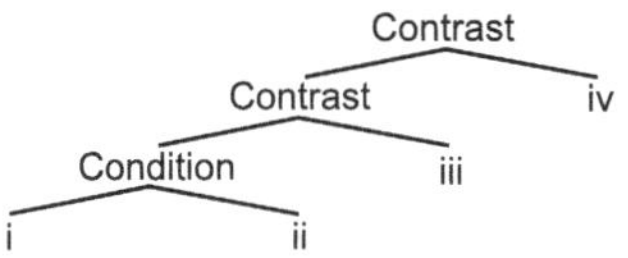

Figure 1: Discourse structure of the monologue in Table 1

most frequent dialogue act is *Explain*, where a character presents information (as a new idea or as a response to another utterance). Also, in both dialogues the *layman* asks more often for clarification than the *expert*. The distribution over information requests (yes/no, factoid, and complex questions) and responses (yes, no, factoid) differs between the two dialogues: in Twain's dialogue, the expert mostly requests information and the layman responds to requests, whereas in Gurevich's dialogue it is the other way around.

The differences in style suggests that the M2D mapping rules will be author or style-specific. By applying M2D rules obtained from two different authors (e.g., Twain and Gurevich) to the same text (e.g., the aspirin example) we can generate two different dialogues. This will enable us to vary the presentation style of automatically generated dialogues.

	Twain		Gurevich	
Tag	Expert	Layman	Expert	Layman
Explain	69	55	49	24
Clarify	1	15	0	6
Request	60	26	2	29
Response	14	43	9	0

Table 2: Dialogue act tag frequencies for *expert* and *layman* in a sample of 250 turns from Twain and 88 turns from Gurevich dialogues.

3 Rules

We automatically derive M2D rules from the aligned discourse relations and dialogue acts in our parallel corpus of monologues and dialogues. Table 3 shows three rules generated from the parallel dialogue–monologue fragment in Table 1. The first rule, R1, is based on the complete discourse structure of the monologue (i–iv), whereas R2 and R3 are based on only a part of it: R2 is based on i–iii, whereas R3 is based on i and ii. By generating rules from subtrees of a discourse structure, we obtain several rules from a single dialogue fragment in the corpus.

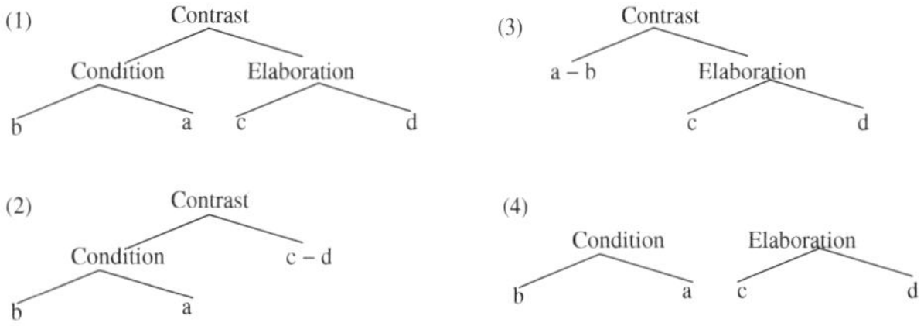

Figure 2: Discourse structures of the monologue in Example 1. a-b and c-d indicate a concatenation of two clauses.

Let us illustrate the use of such rules by applying them to Example 1 about aspirin. The relations between the clauses of the example are depicted in Figure 2 (1). To generate a dialogue, we apply a matching M2D rule. Alternatively, we can first simplify the discourse structure of the monologue by removing relation nodes as illustrated in Figure 2 (2–4).

The simplified structure in Figure 2 (2) matches rule R2 from Table 3. By applying R2 we generate the dialogue in Table 4: the expert asks a complex question composed of clauses a and b, which the layman answers with an explanation generated from the same set of clauses. Then the expert offers a contradicting explanation generated from c and d. To generate dialogue sentences for a corresponding discourse structure we are adapting the approach to paraphrasing of Barzilay and McKeown (2001).

4 Conclusion

This short paper presented three angles on the Monologue-to-Dialogue (M2D) task. First, as an opinion piece, it motivates the task of generating expository dialogue from monologue. We described empirical research that provides evidence for the effectiveness of expository dialogue and discussed applications from education, gaming and E-health. Second, we introduced the CODA corpus for addressing the task. Finally, we reported on work-in-progress on semi-automatic construction of M2D rules. Our implemented algorithm extracts several M2D rules from the corpus that are applicable even to a relatively simple input. Additionally, frequency analysis of dialogue tags suggests that there is scope for generating different dialogue styles.

The timeliness of this research is evidenced by the emergence of a Question Generation (QG) commu-

ID	Dialogue Structure	Monologue Structure
R1	E: Complex Question (i-ii) L: Explain (i-ii) E: Explain-Contradict (iii) E: YNQuestion (iv)	Contrast (Contrast (Condition(i,ii), iii, iv))
R2	E: Complex Question (i-ii) L: Explain(i-ii) E: Explain-Contradict (iii)	Contrast (Condition(i,ii), iii)
R3	E: Complex Question (i-ii) L: Explain (i-ii)	Condition (i,ii)

Table 3: Monologue-to-Dialogue rules extracted from the parallel example in Table 1

Sp	Dialogue act	Dialogue Turn
E:	Complex Question a-b	If you have a headache, what do you do?
L:	Explain a-b	Take aspirin.
E:	Explain-Contradict c-d	But aspirin does have side effects: it can harm circulation

Table 4: A dialogue generated from the monologue about aspirin by applying the rule R2 (see Table 3)

nity. QG is a subtask of M2D. The first QG workshop was held at the end of 2008, resulting in proposals for a Shared Task and Evaluation Campaign (Rus and Graesser, 2009) for 2010. The CODA corpus should prove to be a useful resource not only for M2D researchers, but also for the QG community.

Acknowledgments

The research reported in this paper was funded by the UK Engineering and Physical Sciences Research Council under grant EP/G/020981/1.

References

E. André, T. Rist, S. van Mulken, M. Klesen, and S. Baldes. 2000. The automated design of believable dialogues for animated presentation teams. In *Embodied Conversational Agents*, pages 220–255. MIT Press, Cambridge, Mass.

R. Barzilay and K. McKeown. 2001. Extracting paraphrases from a parallel corpus. In *Proc. of ACL/EACL*, Toulouse.

S. Craig, B. Gholson, M. Ventura, A. Graesser, and the Tutoring Research Group. 2000. Overhearing dialogues and monologues in virtual tutoring sessions. *International Journal of Artificial Intelligence in Education*, 11:242–253.

S. Demir, S. Carberry, and K. McCoy. 2008. Generating Textual Summaries of Bar Charts . In *Procs of INLG 2008*, Ohio, June.

D. DeVault, D. Traum, and R. Artstein. 2008. Making Grammar-Based Generation Easier to Deploy in Dialogue Systems. In *Procs SIGdial 2008*, Ohio, June.

J. Lee, F. Dinneen, and J. McKendree. 1998. Supporting student discussions: it isn't just talk. *Education and Information Technologies*, 3:217–229.

P. Piwek, H. Hernault, H. Prendinger, and M. Ishizuka. 2007. T2D: Generating Dialogues between Virtual Agents Automatically from Text. In *Intelligent Virtual Agents*, LNAI 4722, pages 161–174. Springer Verlag.

E. Reiter, S. Sripada, J. Hunter, J. Yu, and I. Davy. 2005. Choosing Words in Computer-Generated Weather Forecasts. *Artificial Intelligence*, 167:137–169.

V. Rus and A. Graesser, editors. 2009. *The Question Generation Shared Task and Evaluation Challenge*. The University of Memphis. Available at: http://www.questiongeneration.org/.

IGDA Game Writers SIG. 2003. International game developers association's (IGDA) guide to writing for games. IGDA White Paper.

A. Stent. 2002. A conversation acts model for generating spoken dialogue contributions. *Computer Speech and Language*, 16(3-4):313–352.

S. Stoyanchev and P. Piwek. 2010. Constructing the CODA corpus. In *Procs of LREC 2010*, Malta, May.

S. V. Suzuki and S. Yamada. 2004. Persuasion through overheard communication by life-like agents. In *Procs of the 2004 IEEE/WIC/ACM International Conference on Intelligent Agent Technology*, Beijing, September.

K. van Deemter, B. Krenn, P. Piwek, M. Klesen, M. Schröder, and S. Baumann. 2008. Fully generated scripted dialogue for embodied agents. *Artificial Intelligence Journal*, 172(10):1219–1244.

S. Williams, P. Piwek, and R. Power. 2007. Generating Monologue and Dialogue to Present Personalised Medical Information to Patients. In *Procs ENLG 2007*, pages 167–170, Schloss Dagstuhl, Germany.

The Simple Truth about Dependency and Phrase Structure Representations

An Opinion Piece

Owen Rambow
CCLS, Columbia University
New York, NY, USA
rambow@ccls.columbia.edu

Abstract

There are many misconceptions about dependency representations and phrase structure representations for syntax. They are partly due to terminological confusion, partly due to a lack of meta-scientific clarity about the roles of representations and linguistic theories. This opinion piece argues for a simple but clear view of syntactic representation.

1 Introduction

To the machine learning community, treebanks are just collections of data, like pixels with captions, structural and behavioral facts about genes, or observations about wild boar populations. In contrast, to us computational linguists, treebanks are not naturally occurring data at all: they are the result of a very complex annotation process. While the text that is annotated (usually) is naturally occurring, the annotation itself is already the result of a scientific activity. This opinion piece argues that the level of discourse about treebanks often found in our community does not reflect this fact (presumably due to the influence of the brute machine learning perspective). We, as a community of computational linguists, need to be very precise when talking about treebanks and syntactic representations in general.

So let's start with three very important concepts which we must always distinguish. The **representation type**: what type of mathematical object is used to represent syntactic facts? In this opinion piece, I only consider dependency trees (DTs) and phrase structure trees (PSTs) (Section 2). The represented **syntactic content**: the morphological and syntactic facts of the analyzed sentence (Section 3). The **syntactic theory**: it explains how syntactic content is represented in the chosen representation type (Section 4).

A crucial confusing factor is the fact that the terms *dependency* and *phrase structure* both have both a mathematical and a linguistic meaning. The mathematical meaning refers **representation types**. The linguistic meaning refers to **syntactic content**. I discuss this issue in Section 3. I discuss the issue of converting between DTs and PSTs in Section 5, as an example of how my proposed conceptualization of syntactic representation throws light on a computational problem.

This opinion piece will be a success if after reading it, the reader concludes that actually he or she knew this all along. In fact, this opinion piece does not advocate for a controversial position; its mission is to make its readers be more precise when talking about syntactic representations. This opinion piece is intentionally polemical for rhetorical reasons.

2 DTs and PSTs as Representation Types

Assume we have two disjoint symbol sets: a set of terminal symbols which contains the words of the language we are describing; and a set of nonterminal symbols. A **Dependency Tree** (DT) is a tree in which all nodes are labeled with words (elements of the set of terminal symbols) or empty strings. A **Phrase Structure Tree** (PST) is a tree in which all and only the leaf nodes are labeled with words or empty strings, and internal nodes are labeled with nonterminal symbols. There is nothing more to the

Human Language Technologies: The 2010 Annual Conference of the North American Chapter of the ACL, pages 337–340,
Los Angeles, California, June 2010.

definitions. Trees of both types can have many other properties which are not part of the two definitions, and which do not follow from the definitions. I mention some such properties.

Unordered trees. DTs and PSTs can be ordered or unordered. For example, the Prague Theory (Sgall et al., 1986) uses unordered DTs at the deeper level of representation and ordered DTs at a more surfacy level. GPSG (Gazdar et al., 1985) uses unordered trees (or at any rate context-free rules whose right-hand side is ordered by a separate component of the grammar), as does current Chomskyan theory (the PST at spell-out may be unordered).

Empty categories. Empty categories can be empty pronouns, or traces, which are co-indexed with a word elsewhere in the tree. Empty pronouns are widely used in both DT- and PST-based representations. While most DT-based approaches do not use traces, Lombardo and Lesmo (1998) do; and while traces are commonly found in PST-based approaches, there are many that do not use them, such as the c-structure of LFG.

Discontinuous Constituents or **Non-Projectivity**. Both types of trees can be used with or without discontinuous constituents; PSTs are more likely to use traces to avoid discontinuous constituents, but linguistic proposals for PSTs with discontinuous constituents have been made (work by McCawley, or (Becker et al., 1991)).

Labeled Arcs. In DTs, arcs often have labels; arcs in PSTs usually do not, but we can of course label PST arcs as well, as is done in the German TIGER corpus.I note that in both DTs and PSTs we can represent the arc label as a feature on the daughter node, or as a separate node.

3 Syntactic Content

While there is lots of disagreement about the proper **representation type** for syntax, there is actually a broad consensus among theoretical and descriptive syntacticians of all persuasions about the range of syntactic phenomena that *exist*. What exactly is this content, then? It is not a theory-neutral representation of syntax (Section 4). Rather, it is the *empirical matter* which linguistic theory attempts to represent or explain. We cannot represent it without a theory, but we can refer to it without a theory, using names such as *control constructions* or *transitive verb*. In the same manner, we use the word *light* and physicists will agree on what the phenomenon is, but we cannot represent light within a theory without choosing a representation as either particles or wave.

Note that in linguistics, the terms *dependency* and *phrase structure* refer to **syntactic content**, i.e., syntactic facts we can represent. **Syntactic dependency** is direct relation between words. Usually, this relation is labeled (or typed), and is identical to (or subsumes) the notion of **grammatical function**, which covers relations such as SUBJECT, OBJECT, TEMPORAL-ADJUNCT and so forth. **Syntactic phrase structure**, also known as **syntactic constituency structure** is recursive representation using sets of one or more linguistic units (words and empty strings), such that at each level, each set (constituent) acts as a unit syntactically. Linguistic phrase structure is most conveniently expressed in a phrase structure tree, while linguistic dependency is most conveniently expressed in a dependency tree. However, we can express the same content in either type of tree! For example, the English Penn Treebank (PTB) encodes the predicate-argument structure of English using structural conventions and special nonterminal labels ("dashtags"), such as NP-SBJ. And a dependency tree represents constituency: each node can be interpreted both as a preterminal node (X^0) and as a node heading a constituent containing all terminals included in the subtree it heads (the XP). Of course, what is more complex to encode in a DT are intermediate projections, such as VP. I leave a fuller discussion aside for lack of space, but I claim that the syntactic content which is expressed in intermediate projections can also be expressed in a DT, through the use of features and arc labels.

4 Syntactic Theory

The choice of representation type does not determine the representation for a given sentence. This is obvious, but it needs to be repeated; I have heard "What is the DT for this sentence?" one too many times. There are many possible DTs and PSTs, proposed by serious syntacticians, for even simple sentences, even when the syntacticians agree on what the syntactic content (a transitive verb with SVO order, for example) of the analysis should be! What is going on?

In order to make sense of this, we need a third player in addition to the **representation type** and the **content**. This is the **syntactic theory**. A linguistic theory chooses a representation type and then defines a coherent mapping for a well-defined set of content to the chosen representation type. Here, "coherent representation" means that the different choices made for conceptually independent content are also representationally independent, so that we can compose representational choices. Note that a theory can decide to omit some content; for example, we can have a theory which does not distinguish raising from control (the English PTB does not).

There are different types of syntactic theories. A **descriptive theory** is an account of the syntax of one language. Examples of descriptive grammars include works such as Quirk for English, or the annotation manuals of monolingual treebanks, such as (Marcus et al., 1994; Maamouri et al., 2003). The annotation manual serves two purposes: it tells the annotators how to represent a syntactic phenomenon, and it tells the users of the treebank (us!) how to interpret the annotation. A treebank without manual is meaningless. And an arborescent structure does not mean the same thing in all treebanks (for example, a "flat NP" indicates an unannotated constituent in the English ATB but a fully annotated construction in the Arabic Treebank is).

An **explanatory theory** is a theory which attempts to account for the syntax of all languages, for example by reducing their diversity to a set of principles and finite-valued parameters. Linguistic theories (and explanatory theories in particular) often take the form of a one-to-many mapping from a simple representation of syntactic dependency (predicate-argument structure) to a structural representation that determines surface word order. The linguistic theory itself is formulated as a (computational) device that relates the deeper level to the more surfacy level. LFG has a very pure expression of this approach, with the deeper level expressed using a DT (actually, dependency directed acyclic graphs, but the distinction is not relevant here), and the surface level expressed using a PST. But the Chomskyan approaches fit the same paradigm, as do many other theories of syntax.

Therefore, there is no theory-neutral representation of a sentence or a set of sentences, because *every* representation needs a theory for us to extract its meaning! Often what is meant by "theory-neutral tree" is a tree which is interpreted using some notion of consensus theory, perhaps a stripped-down representation which omits much content for which there is no consensus on how to represent it.

5 Converting Between DTs and PSTs

Converting a set of DS annotations to PS or *vice versa* means that we want to obtain a representation which expresses exactly the same **content**. This is frequently done these days as interest in dependency parsing grows but many languages only have PS treebanks. However, this process is often not understood.

To start, I observe that uninterpreted structures (i.e., structures without a syntactic theory, or trees from a treebank without a manual) cannot be converted from or into, as we do not know what they mean and we cannot know if we are preserving the same content or not.

Now, my central claim about the possibility of automatically converting between PSTs and DTs is the following. If we have an interpretation for the source representation and the goal representation (as we must in order for this task to be meaningful), then we can convert any facts that are represented in the source structure, and we cannot convert any facts that are not represented in the source structure. It is that simple. If we are converting from a source which contains less information than the target, then we cannot succeed. For example, if we are converting from a PS treebank that does not distinguish particles from prepositions to a DS treebank that does, then we will fail. General claims about the possibility of conversion ("it is easier to convert PS to DS than DS to PS") are therefore *meaningless*. It only matters **what** is represented, not **how** it is represented.

There is, however, no guarantee that there is a *simple* algorithm for conversion, such as a parametrized head percolation algorithm passed down from researcher to researcher like a sorcerer's incantation. In general, if the two representations are independently devised and both are linguistically motivated, then we have no reason to believe that the conversion can be done using a specific simple approach, or using conversion rules which have some fixed property (say, the depth of the trees in the rules templates). In the general case, the only way to write an automatic converter between two representations is to study the two annotation manuals and to create a case-by-case converter, covering all linguistic phenomena represented in the target representation.

Machine learning-based conversion (for example, (Xia and Palmer, 2001)) is an interesting exercise, but it does not give us any general insights into dependency or phrase structure. Suppose the source contains all the information that the target should contain. Then if machine learning-based conversion fails or does not perform completely correctly, the exercise merely shows that the machine learning is not adequate. Now suppose that the source does not contain all the information that the target should contain. Then no fancy machine learning can ever provide a completely correct conversion. Also, note that unlike, for example, parsers which are based on machine learning and which learn about a natural phenomenon (language use), machine learning of conversion merely learns an artificial phenomenon: the relation between the two syntactic theories in question, which are created by researchers. (Of course, in practice, machine learning of automatic conversion between DT to PSTs is useful.)

6 Conclusion

I have argued that when talking about dependency and phrase structure representations, one should always distinguish the type of representation (dependency or phrase structure) from the content of the representation, and one needs to understand (and make explicit if it is implicit) the linguistic theory that relates content to representation. Machine learning researchers have the luxury of treating syntactic representations as mere fodder for their mills; we as computational linguists do not, since this is our area of expertise.

Acknowledgments

I would like to thank my colleagues on the Hindi-Urdu treebank project (Bhatt et al., 2009) (NSF grant CNS-0751089) for spirited discussions about the issues discussed here. I would like to thank Sylvain Kahane, Yoav Goldberg, and Joakim Nivre for comments that have helped me improve this paper. The expressed opinions have been influenced by far too many people to thank individually here.

References

Tilman Becker, Aravind Joshi, and Owen Rambow. 1991. Long distance scrambling and tree adjoining grammars. In *Fifth Conference of the European Chapter of the Association for Computational Linguistics (EACL'91)*, pages 21–26. ACL.

Rajesh Bhatt, Bhuvana Narasimhan, Martha Palmer, Owen Rambow, Dipti Sharma, and Fei Xia. 2009. A multi-representational and multi-layered treebank for hindi/urdu. In *Proceedings of the Third Linguistic Annotation Workshop*, pages 186–189, Suntec, Singapore.

Gerald Gazdar, Ewan Klein, Geoffrey Pullum, and Ivan Sag. 1985. *Generalized Phrase Structure Grammar*. Harvard University Press, Cambridge, Mass.

Vincenzo Lombardo and Leonardo Lesmo. 1998. Formal aspects and parsing issue of dependency theory. In *36th Meeting of the Association for Computational Linguistics and 17th International Conference on Computational Linguistics (COLING-ACL'98)*, pages 787–793, Montréal, Canada.

Mohamed Maamouri, Ann Bies, Hubert Jin, and Tim Buckwalter. 2003. Arabic treebank: Part 1 v 2.0. Distributed by the Linguistic Data Consortium. LDC Catalog No.: LDC2003T06.

Mohamed Maamouri, Ann Bies, and Tim Buckwalter. 2004. The Penn Arabic Treebank: Building a large-scale annotated arabic corpus. In *NEMLAR Conference on Arabic Language Resources and Tools*, Cairo, Egypt.

M. Marcus, G. Kim, M. Marcinkiewicz, R. MacIntyre, A. Bies, M. Ferguson, K. Katz, and B. Schasberger. 1994. The Penn Treebank: Annotating predicate argument structure. In *Proceedings of the ARPA Human Language Technology Workshop*.

Igor A. Mel'čuk. 1988. *Dependency Syntax: Theory and Practice*. State University of New York Press, New York.

P. Sgall, E. Hajičová, and J. Panevová. 1986. *The meaning of the sentence and its semantic and pragmatic aspects*. Reidel, Dordrecht.

Fei Xia and Martha Palmer. 2001. Converting dependency structure to phrase structures. In *hlt2001*, pages 61–65.

Word Alignment with Stochastic Bracketing Linear Inversion Transduction Grammar

Markus SAERS and **Joakim NIVRE**
Computational Linguistics Group
Dept. of Linguistics and Philology
Uppsala University
Sweden
first.last@lingfil.uu.se

Dekai WU
Human Language Technology Center
Dept. of Computer Science and Engineering
HKUST
Hong Kong
dekai@cs.ust.hk

Abstract

The class of Linear Inversion Transduction Grammars (LITGs) is introduced, and used to induce a word alignment over a parallel corpus. We show that alignment via Stochastic Bracketing LITGs is considerably faster than Stochastic Bracketing ITGs, while still yielding alignments superior to the widely-used heuristic of intersecting bidirectional IBM alignments. Performance is measured as the translation quality of a phrase-based machine translation system built upon the word alignments, and an improvement of 2.85 BLEU points over baseline is noted for French–English.

1 Introduction

Machine translation relies heavily on word alignments, which are usually produced by training IBM-models (Brown et al., 1993) in both directions and combining the resulting alignments via some heuristic. Automatically training an Inversion Transduction Grammar (ITG) has been suggested as a viable way of producing superior alignments (Saers and Wu, 2009). The main problem of using Bracketing ITGs for alignment is that exhaustive biparsing runs in $\mathcal{O}(n^6)$ time. Several ways to lower the complexity of ITGs has been suggested, but in this paper, a different approach is taken. Instead of using full ITGs, we explore the possibility of subjecting the grammar to a linear constraint, making exhaustive biparsing of a sentence pair in $\mathcal{O}(n^4)$ time possible. This can be further improved by applying pruning.

2 Background

A transduction is the bilingual version of a language. A language (L_l) can be formally viewed as a set of sentences, sequences of tokens taken from a specified vocabulary (V_l). A transduction ($T_{e,f}$) between two languages (L_e and L_f) is then a set of sentence pairs, sequences of bitokens from the cross production of the vocabularies of the two languages being transduced ($V_{e,f} = V_e \times V_f$). This adds an extra layer of complexity to finding transductions from raw bitexts, as an alignment has to be imposed.

Simple (STG) and Syntax Directed (SDTG) Transduction Grammars (Aho and Ullman, 1972) can be used to parse transductions between context-free languages. Both work fine as long as a grammar is given and parsing is done as transduction, that is: a sentence in one language is rewritten into the other language. In NLP, interest has shifted away from hand-crafted grammars, towards stochastic grammars induced from corpora. To induce a stochastic grammar from a parallel corpus, expectations of all possible parses over a sentence pair are typically needed. STGs can biparse sentence pairs in polynomial time, but are unable to account for the complexities typically found in natural languages. SDTGs do account for the complexities in natural languages, but are intractable for biparsing.

Inversion transductions (Wu, 1995; Wu, 1997) are a special case of transductions that are not monotone, but where permutations are severely limited. By limiting the possible permutations, biparsing becomes tractable. This in turn means that ITGs can be induced from parallel corpora in polynomial time,

Human Language Technologies: The 2010 Annual Conference of the North American Chapter of the ACL, pages 341–344,
Los Angeles, California, June 2010.

as well as account for most of the reorderings found between natural languages.

An Inversion transduction is limited so that it must be expressible as non-overlapping groups, internally permuted either by the identity permutation or the inversion permutation (hence the name). This requirement also means that the grammar is binarizable, yielding a two-normal form. A production with the identity permutation is written inside square brackets, while productions with the inversion permutation is written inside angled brackets. This gives us a two-normal form that looks like this (where e/f is a biterminal):

$$A \rightarrow [B\ C]$$
$$A \rightarrow \langle B\ C \rangle$$
$$A \rightarrow e/f$$

The time complexity for exhaustive ITG biparsing is $\mathcal{O}(Gn^6)$, which is typically too large to be applicable to large grammars and long sentence. The grammar constant G can be eliminated by limiting the grammar to a bracketing ITG (BITG), which only has one nonterminal symbol. Saers & Wu (2009) show that it is possible to apply exhaustive biparsing to a large parallel corpus ($\sim 100,000$ sentence pairs) of short sentences ($\leq$10 tokens in both language). The word alignments read off the Viterbi parse also increased translation quality when used instead of the alignments from bidirectional IBM alignments.

The $\mathcal{O}(n^6)$ time complexity is somewhat prohibitive for large corpora, so pruning in some form is needed. Saers, Nivre & Wu (2009) introduce a beam pruning scheme, which reduces time complexity to $\mathcal{O}(bn^3)$. They also show that severe pruning is possible without significant deterioration in alignment quality. Haghighi et. al (2009) use a simpler aligner as guidance for pruning, which reduce the time complexity by two orders of magnitude, and also introduce block ITG, which gives many-to-one instead of one-to-one alignments. Zhang et. al (2008) present a method for evaluating spans in the sentence pair to determine whether they should be excluded or not. The algorithm has a best case time complexity of $\mathcal{O}(n^3)$.

In this paper we introduce Linear ITG (LITG), and apply it to a word-alignment task which is evaluated by the phrase-based statistical machine translation (PBSMT) system that can be built from that.

3 Stochastic Bracketing Linear Inversion Transduction Grammar

A Bracketing Linear Inversion Transduction Grammar (BLITG) is a BITG where rules may have at most one nonterminal symbol in their production. This gives us a normal form that is somewhat different from the usual ITG:

$$X \rightarrow [Xe/f]$$
$$X \rightarrow [e/fX]$$
$$X \rightarrow \langle Xe/f \rangle$$
$$X \rightarrow \langle e/fX \rangle$$
$$X \rightarrow \epsilon/\epsilon$$

where one but not both of the tokens in the biterminal may be the empty string ϵ, if a nonterminal is produced. By associating each rule with a probability, we get a Stochastic BLITG (SBLITG).

3.1 Biparsing Algorithm

The sentence pair to be biparsed consists of two vectors of tokens ($\mathbf{e}$ and $\mathbf{f}$). An item is represented as a nonterminal (X), and one span in each of the languages ($e_{s..t}$ and $f_{u..v}$). For notational convenience, an item will be written as the nonterminal with the spans as subscripts ($X_{s,t,u,v}$). The length of an item is defined as the sum of the length of the two spans: $|X_{s,t,u,v}| = t - s + v - u$. Items are gathered in buckets, B_n, according to their length so that $X_{s,t,u,v} \in B_{|X_{s,t,u,v}|}$. The algorithm is initialized with the item spanning the entire sentence pair:

$$X_{0,|\mathbf{e}|,0,|\mathbf{f}|} \in B_{|X_{0,|\mathbf{e}|,0,|\mathbf{f}|}|}$$

Starting from this top bucket, buckets are processed in larger to smaller order: $B_n, B_{n-1}, \ldots, B_1$. While processing a bucket, only smaller items are added, meaning that B_0 is fully constructed by the time B_1 has been processed. Each item in B_0 can have the rule $X \rightarrow \epsilon/\epsilon$ applied to it, eliminating the nonterminal and halting processing. If there are no items in B_0, parsing has failed.

To process a bucket, each item is extended by all applicable rules, and the nonterminals in the productions are added to their respective buckets.

System	BLEU	NIST	Phrases
GIZA++ (`intersect`)	0.2629	6.7968	146,581,109
GIZA++ (`grow-diag-final`)	0.2632	6.7410	1,298,566
GIZA++ (`grow-diag-final-and`)	0.2742	6.9228	7,340,369
SBLITG ($b = 25$)	**0.3027**	**7.3664**	13,551,915
SBLITG ($b = \infty$)	0.3008	7.3303	12,673,361

Table 1: Results for French–English.

$$\begin{aligned} X_{s,t,u,v} \rightarrow & \\ & [e_{s,s+1}/f_{u,u+1}\ X_{s+1,t,u+1,v}] \\ \mid\ & [X_{s,t-1,u,v-1}\ e_{t-1,t}/f_{v-1,v}] \\ \mid\ & \langle e_{s,s+1}/f_{v-1,v}\ X_{s+1,t,u,v-1}\rangle \\ \mid\ & \langle X_{s,t-1,u+1,v}\ e_{t-1,t}/f_{u,u+1}\rangle \\ \mid\ & [e_{s,s+1}/\epsilon\ X_{s+1,t,u,v}] \mid \langle e_{s,s+1}/\epsilon\ X_{s+1,t,u,v}\rangle \\ \mid\ & [\epsilon/f_{u,u+1}\ X_{s,t,u+1,v}] \mid \langle X_{s,t,u+1,v}\ \epsilon/f_{u,u+1}\rangle \\ \mid\ & [X_{s,t-1,u,v}\ e_{t-1,t}/\epsilon] \mid \langle X_{s,t-1,u,v}\ e_{t-1,t}/\epsilon\rangle \\ \mid\ & [X_{s,t,u,v-1}\ \epsilon/f_{v-1,v}] \mid \langle \epsilon/f_{v-1,v}\ X_{s,t,u,v-1}\rangle \end{aligned}$$

Note that there are two productions on each of the four last rows. These are distinct rules, but the symbols in the productions are identical. This phenomenon is due to the fact that the empty symbols can be "read" off either end of the span. In our experiments, such rules were merged into their non-inverting form, effectively eliminating the last four inverted rules (productions enclosed in angled brackets) above.

3.2 Analysis

Let n be the length of the longer sentence in the pair. The number of buckets will be $\mathcal{O}(n)$, since the longest item will be at most $2n$ long. Within a bucket, there can be $\mathcal{O}(n^2)$ starting points for items, but once the length of one of the spans is fixed, the length of the other follows, adding a factor $\mathcal{O}(n)$, making the total number of items in a bucket $\mathcal{O}(n^3)$. Each item in a bucket can be analyzed in 8 possible ways, requiring $\mathcal{O}(1)$ time. In summary, we have: $\mathcal{O}(n) \times \mathcal{O}(n^3) \times \mathcal{O}(1) = \mathcal{O}(n^4)$

The pruning scheme works by limiting the number of items that are processed from each bucket, reducing the cost of processing a bucket from $\mathcal{O}(n^3)$ to $\mathcal{O}(b)$, where b is the beam width. This gives time complexity $\mathcal{O}(n) \times \mathcal{O}(b) \times \mathcal{O}(1) = \mathcal{O}(bn)$.

4 Experiments

We used the guidelines of the shared task of WMT'08[1] to train our baseline system as well as our experimental system. This includes induction of word alignments with GIZA++ (Och and Ney, 2003), induction of a Phrase-based SMT system (Koehn et al., 2007), and tuning with minimum error rate training (Och, 2003), as well as applying some utility scripts provided for the workshop. The translation model is combined with a 5-gram language model (Stolcke, 2002).

Our experimental system uses alignments from the Viterbi parses, extracted during EM training of an SBLITG on the training corpus, instead of GIZA++. Since EM will converge fairly slowly, it was limited to 10 iterations, after which it was halted.

We used the French–English part of the WMT'08 shared task, but limited the training set to sentence pairs where both sentences were of length 20 or less. This was necessary in order to carry out exhaustive search in the SBLITG algorithm. In total, we had 381,780 sentence pairs for training, and 2,000 sentence pairs each for tuning and testing. The language model was trained with the entire training set.

To evaluate the systems we used BLEU (Papineni et al., 2002) and NIST (Doddington, 2002)

Results are presented in Table 1. It is interesting to note that there is no correlation between the number of phrases extracted and translation quality. The only explanation for the results we are seeing is that the SBLITGs find *better* phrases. Since the only difference is the word alignment strategy, this suggests that the word alignments from SBLITGs are better suited for phrase extraction than those from bidirectional IBM-models. The fact that SBLITGs extract more phrases than bidirectional IBM-models under

[1]`http://www.statmt.org/wmt08/`

the grow-diag-x heuristics is significant, since more phrases means that more translation possibilities are extracted. The fact that SBLITGs extract fewer phrases than bidirectional IBM-models under the intersect heuristic is also significant, since it implies that simply adding more phrases is a bad strategy. Combined, the two observations leads us to believe that there are some alignments missed by the bidirectional IBM-models that are found by the SBLITG-models. It is also interesting to see that the pruned version outperforms the exhaustive version. We believe this to be because the pruned version approaches the correct grammar faster than the exhaustive. That would mean that the exhaustive SBLITG would be better in the limit, but the experiment was limited to 10 iterations.

5 Conclusion

In this paper we have focused on the benefits of applying SBLITGs to the task of inducing word alignments, which leads to a 2.85 BLEU points improvement compared to the standard model (heuristically combined bidirectional IBM-models). In the future, we hope that LITGs will be a spring board towards full ITGs, with more interesting nonterminals than the BITGs seen in the literature so far. With the possibility of inducing full ITG from parallel corpora it becomes viable to use ITG decoders directly as machine translation systems.

Acknowledgments

This work was funded by the Swedish National Graduate School of Language Technology (GSLT), the Defense Advanced Research Projects Agency (DARPA) under GALE Contract No. HR0011-06-C-0023, and the Hong Kong Research Grants Council (RGC) under research grants GRF621008, DAG03/04.EG09, RGC6256/00E, and RGC6083/99E. Any opinions, findings and conclusions or recommendations expressed in this material are those of the authors and do not necessarily reflect the views of DARPA.The computations were performed on UPPMAX resources under project p2007020.

References

A. V. Aho and J. D. Ullman. 1972. *The Theory of Parsing, Translation, and Compiling*. Prentice-Halll, Englewood Cliffs, New Jersey.

P. F. Brown, S. A. Della Pietra, V. J. Della Pietra, and R. L. Mercer. 1993. The mathematics of statistical machine translation: Parameter estimation. *Computational Linguistics*, 19(2):263–311.

G. Doddington. 2002. Automatic evaluation of machine translation quality using n-gram co-occurrence statistics. In *Proceedings of Human Language Technology conference (HLT-2002)*, San Diego, California.

A. Haghighi, J. Blitzer, J. DeNero, and D. Klein. 2009. Better word alignments with supervised itg models. In *Proceedings of ACL/IJCNLP 2009*, pages 923–931, Singapore.

P. Koehn, H. Hoang, A. Birch, C. Callison-Burch, M. Federico, N. Bertoldi, B. Cowan, W. Shen, C. Moran, R. Zens, C. Dyer, O. Bojar, A. Constantin, and E. Herbst. 2007. Moses: Open source toolkit for statistical machine translation. In *Proceedings of the ACL 2007 Demo and Poster Session*, pages 177–180, Prague, Czech Republic.

F. J. Och and H. Ney. 2003. A systematic comparison of various statistical alignment models. *Computational Linguistics*, 29(1):19–51.

F. J. Och. 2003. Minimum error rate training in statistical machine translation. In *Proceedings of ACL 2003*, pages 160–167, Sapporo, Japan.

K. Papineni, S. Roukos, T. Ward, and W. Zhu. 2002. Bleu: a method for automatic evaluation of machine translation. In *Proceedings of ACL 2002*, pages 311–318, Philadelphia, Pennsylvania.

M. Saers and D. Wu. 2009. Improving phrase-based translation via word alignments from Stochastic Inversion Transduction Grammars. In *Proceedings of SSST-3 at NAACL HLT 2009*, pages 28–36, Boulder, Colorado.

M. Saers, J. Nivre, and D. Wu. 2009. Learning stochastic bracketing inversion transduction grammars with a cubic time biparsing algorithm. In *Proceedings of IWPT'09*, pages 29–32, Paris, France.

A. Stolcke. 2002. SRILM – an extensible language modeling toolkit. In *International Conference on Spoken Language Processing*, Denver, Colorado.

D. Wu. 1995. An algorithm for simultaneously bracketing parallel texts by aligning words. In *Proceedings of WVLC-3*, pages 69–82, Cambridge, Massachusetts.

D. Wu. 1997. Stochastic inversion transduction grammars and bilingual parsing of parallel corpora. *Computational Linguistics*, 23(3):377–403.

H. Zhang, C. Quirk, R. C. Moore, and D. Gildea. 2008. Bayesian learning of non-compositional phrases with synchronous parsing. In *Proceedings of ACL/HLT 2008*, pages 97–105, Columbus, Ohio.

Crowdsourcing the evaluation of a domain-adapted named entity recognition system

Asad B. Sayeed, Timothy J. Meyer, Hieu C. Nguyen, Olivia Buzek
Department of Computer Science
University of Maryland
College Park, MD 20742
asayeed@cs.umd.edu, tmeyer1@umd.edu, {hcnguyen88,olivia.buzek}@gmail.com

Amy Weinberg
Department of Linguistics
University of Maryland
College Park, MD 20742
weinberg@umiacs.umd.edu

Abstract

Named entity recognition systems sometimes have difficulty when applied to data from domains that do not closely match the training data. We first use a simple rule-based technique for domain adaptation. Data for robust validation of the technique is then generated, and we use crowdsourcing techniques to show that this strategy produces reliable results even on data not seen by the rule designers. We show that it is possible to extract large improvements on the target data rapidly at low cost using these techniques.

1 Introduction

1.1 Named entities and errors

In this work, we use crowdsourcing to generate evaluation data to validate simple techniques designed to adapt a widely-used high-performing named entity recognition system to new domains. Specifically, we achieve a roughly 10% improvement in precision on text from the information technology (IT) business press via *post hoc* rule-based error reduction. We first tested the system on a small set of data that we annotated ourselves. Then we collected data from Amazon Mechanical Turk in order to demonstrate that the gain is stable. To our knowledge, there is no previous work on crowdsourcing as a rapid means of evaluating error mitigation in named entity recognizer development.

Named entity recognition (NER) is a well-known problem in NLP which feeds into many other related tasks such as information retrieval (IR) and machine translation (MT) and more recently social network discovery and opinion mining. Generally, errors in the underlying NER technology correlate with a steep price in performance in the NLP systems further along a processing pipeline, as incorrect entities propagate into incorrect translations or erroneous graphs of social networks.

Not all errors carry the same price. In some applications, omitting a named entity has the consequence of reducing the availability of training data, but including an incorrectly identified piece of text *as* as a named entity has the consequence of producing misleading results. Our application would be opinion mining; an omitted entity may prevent the system from attributing an opinion to a source, but an incorrect entity reveals non-existent opinion sources.

Machine learning is currently used extensively in building NER systems. One such system is BBN's Identifinder (Bikel et al., 1999). The IdentiFinder algorithm, based on Hidden Markov Models, has been shown to achieve F-measure scores above 90% when the training and testing data happen to be derived from Wall Street Journal text produced in the 1990s. We use IdentiFinder 3.3 as a starting point for performance improvement in this paper.

The use of machine learning in existing systems requires us to produce new and costly training data if we want to adapt these systems directly to other domains. Our *post hoc* error reduction strategy is therefore profoundly different: it relieves us of the burden of generating complete training examples. The data we generate are strictly corrections of the existing system's output. Our thus cheaper evaluation is therefore primarily on improvements to pre-

Human Language Technologies: The 2010 Annual Conference of the North American Chapter of the ACL, pages 345–348,
Los Angeles, California, June 2010.

cision, while minimizing damage to recall, unlike an evaluation based on retraining with new, fully-annotated text.

1.2 Crowdsourcing

Crowdsourcing is the use of the mass collaboration of Internet passers-by for large enterprises on the World Wide Web such as Wikipedia and survey companies. However, a generalized way to monetize the many small tasks that make up a larger task is relatively new. Crowdsourcing platforms like Amazon Mechanical Turk have allowed some NLP researchers to acquire data for small amounts of money from large, unspecified groups of Internet users (Snow et al., 2008; Callison-Burch, 2009).

The use of crowdsourcing for an NLP annotation task required careful definition of the specifics of the task. The individuals who perform these tasks have no specific training, and they are trying to get through as many tasks as they can, so each task must be specified very simply and clearly.

Part of our work was to define a named entity error detection task simply enough that the results would be consistent across anonymous annotators.

2 Methodology

2.1 Process overview

The overall process for running this experiment was as follows (figure 1).

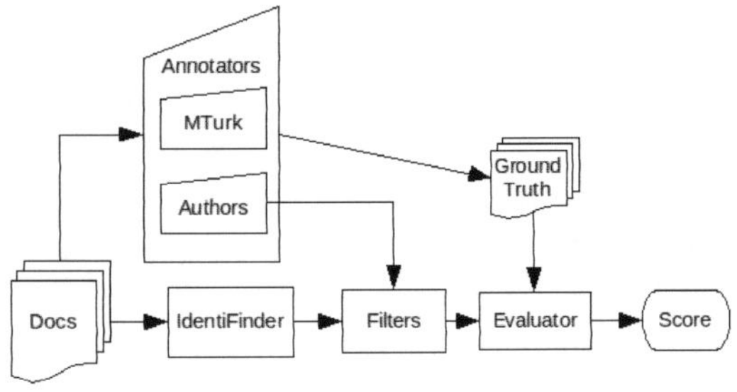

Figure 1: Diagram of data pipeline.

First, we performed an initial performance assessment of IdentiFinder on our domain. We selected 200 articles from an IT trade journal. IdentiFinder was used to tag persons and organizations in these documents. Domain experts (in this case, the authors of this paper) analyzed the entity tags produced by the NER system and annotated the erroneous tags. We built an error reduction system based on our error analysis. We then ran the IdentiFinder output through the error reduction system and evaluated its performance against our annotations.

Next, we constructed an Amazon Mechanical Turk-based interface for naïve web users or "Turkers" to annotate the IdentiFinder entities for errors. We measured the interannotator agreement between the Turkers and the domain experts, and we evaluated the IdentiFinder output and the repaired output against the expert-generated and Turker gold standards.

We selected a new batch of 800 articles and ran IdentiFinder and the filters on them, and we again ran our Mechanical Turk application on the IdentiFinder output. We measured the performance of IdentiFinder and filtered output against the Turker annotations.

2.2 Performance evaluation

Performance is evaluated in terms of standard precision and recall of entities. If the system output contains a person or organization labelled correctly as such, it considers this to be a hit. If it contains a person or organization that is mislabelled or otherwise incorrect in the gold standard annotation, it is a miss. We compute the F-measure as the harmonic mean of precision and recall.

As the IdentiFinder output is the baseline, and we ignore missed entities, by definition the baseline recall is 100%.

3 Experiments and results

Here we delve into further detail about the techniques we used and the results that they yielded. The results are summarized in table 1.

3.1 Baseline performance assessment

We randomly selected 200 documents from InformationWeek, a major weekly magazine in the IT business press. Running them through IdentiFinder produces NIST ACE-standard XML entity markup. We focused on the ENAMEX tags of person and organization type that IdentiFinder produces.

After we annotated the ENAMEX tags for errors, we found that closer inspection of the errors in the IdentiFinder output allowed us to classify the majority of them into three major categories:

Annotator	Collection	System	Precision	Recall	F-measure
Authors	200 document	IdentiFinder only	0.74	1	0.85
Authors	200 document	Filtered	0.86	0.98	0.92
MTurk	200 document	IdentiFinder only	0.69	1	0.82
MTurk	200 document	Filtered	0.79	0.97	0.87
MTurk	800 document	IdentiFinder only	0.67	1	0.80
MTurk	800 document	Filtered	0.77	0.95	0.85

Table 1: Results of evaluation of different document sets against ground truth source by annotation technique.

- IdentiFinder tags words that are simply not named entities.
- IdentiFinder assigns the wrong category (person or organization) to an entity.
- IdentiFinder includes extraneous words in an otherwise correct entity.

The second and third types of error are particularly challenging. An example of the second type is the following:

> **Yahoo** is a reasonably strong competitor to *Google*. It gets about half as much online revenue and search traffic as *Google*, ...

Google is marked twice incorrectly as being a person rather than an organization.

Finally, here is an example of the third error type:

> A San Diego bartender reported that *Bill Gates danced* the night away in his bar on Nov. 11.

IdentiFinder incorrectly marks "danced" as part of a person tag.

We were able to find the precision of IdentiFinder against our annotations: 0.74. This is poorer than the reported performance of IdentiFinder on Wall Street Journal text (Bikel et al., 1999).

3.2 Domain-specific error reduction

We wrote a series of rule-based filters to remove instances of the error types—of which there were many subtypes—described in the previous section. For instance, the third example above was eliminated via the use of a part-of-speech tagger; "danced" was labelled as a verb, and entities with tagged verbs were removed. In the second case, the mislabelling of Google as a person rather than an organization is identified by looking at IdentiFinder's majority labelling of Google throughout the corpus—as an organization. Simple rules about capitalization allow instances like the first example to be identified as errors.

This step increases the precision of the system output to 86%, while only sacrificing a tiny amount of recall. We see that this 10% increase is maintained even on the Mechanical Turk-generated annotations.

3.3 Mechanical Turk tasks

The basic unit of Mechanical Turk is the Human Intelligence Task (HIT). Turkers select HITs presented as web pages and perform the described task. Data-collectors create HITs and pay Amazon to disburse small amounts of money to Turkers who complete them.

We designed our Mechanical Turk process so that every HIT we create corresponds to an IdentiFinder-marked document. Within its corresponding HIT, each document is broken up into paragraphs. Following every paragraph is a table whose rows consist of every person/organization ENAMEX discovered by IdentiFinder and whose columns consist of one of the four categories: "Person," "Organization," "Neither," and "Don't Know." Then for each entity, the user selects exactly one of the four options.

Each HIT is assigned to three different Turkers. Every entity in that HIT is assigned a person or organization ENAMEX tag if two of the three Turkers agreed it was one of those (majority vote); otherwise, it is marked as an invalid entity.

We calculated the agreement between our annotations and those developed from the Turker majority vote scheme. This yields a Cohen's κ of 0.68. We considered this to be substantial agreement.

After processing the same 200 document set from our own annotation, we found that the precision of IdentiFinder was 69%, but after error reduction, it increased to 79% with only a miniscule loss of known valid entities (recall).

We then took another 800 documents from InformationWeek and ran them through IdentiFinder. We did not annotate these documents ourselves, but instead turned them over to Turkers. IdentiFinder output alone has a 67% precision, but after error reduction, it rises to 77%, and recall is still minimally affected.

4 Discussion

4.1 Benefits

It appears that high-performing NER systems exhibit rather severe domain adaption problems. The performance of IdentiFinder is quite low on the IT business press. However, a simple rule-based system was able to gain 10% improvement in precision with little recall sacrificed. This is a particularly important improvement in applications with low tolerance for erroneous entities.

However, rule-based systems built by experts are known to be vulnerable to new data unseen by the experts. In order to apply this domain-specific error reduction reliably, it has to be tested on data gathered elsewhere. We used crowdsourced data to show that the rule-based system was robust when confronted with data that the designers did not see.

One danger in crowdsourcing is a potential lack of commitment on the part of the annotators, as they attempt to get through tasks as quickly as possible. It turns out that in an NER context, we can design a crowdsourced task that yields relatively reliable results across data sets by ensuring that for every data point, there were multiple annotators making only simple decisions about entity classification.

This method also provides us with a source of easily acquired supervised training data for testing more advanced techniques, if required.

4.2 Costs

It took not more than an estimated two person weeks to complete this work. This includes doing the expert annotations, designing the Mechanical Turk tasks, and building the domain-specific error reduction rules.

For each HIT, each annotator was paid 0.05 USD. For three annotators for 1000 documents, that is 150.00 USD (plus additional small Amazon surcharges and any taxes that apply).

5 Conclusions and Future Work

This work was done on a single publication in a single domain. One future experiment would be to see whether these results are reliable across other publications in the domain. Another set of experiments would be to determine the optimum number of annotators; we assumed three, but cross-domain results may be more stable with more annotators.

Retraining an NER system for a particular domain can be expensive if new annotations must be generated from scratch. While there is work on using advanced machine learning techniques for domain transfer (Guo et al., 2009), simply repairing the the errors *post hoc* via a rule-based system can have a low cost for high gains. This work shows a case where the results are reliable and the verification simple, in a context where reducing false positives is a high priority.

Acknowledgements

This paper is based upon work supported by the National Science Foundation under Grant IIS-0729459. This research was also supported in part by NSF award IIS-0838801.

References

Daniel M. Bikel, Richard Schwartz, and Ralph M. Weischedel. 1999. An algorithm that learns what's in a name. *Mach. Learn.*, 34(1-3).

Chris Callison-Burch. 2009. Fast, cheap, and creative: Evaluating translation quality using Amazon's Mechanical Turk. In *EMNLP 2009*, Singapore, August.

Honglei Guo, Huijia Zhu, Zhili Guo, Xiaoxun Zhang, Xian Wu, and Zhong Su. 2009. Domain adaptation with latent semantic association for named entity recognition. In *NAACL 2009*, Morristown, NJ, USA.

Rion Snow, Brendan O'Connor, Daniel Jurafsky, and Andrew Y. Ng. 2008. Cheap and fast—but is it good?: evaluating non-expert annotations for natural language tasks. In *EMNLP 2008*, Morristown, NJ, USA.

Generalizing Hierarchical Phrase-based Translation using Rules with Adjacent Nonterminals

Hendra Setiawan and Philip Resnik
UMIACS Laboratory for Computational Linguistics and Information Processing
University of Maryland, College Park, MD 20742, USA
hendra, resnik @umd.edu

Abstract

Hierarchical phrase-based translation (Hiero, (Chiang, 2005)) provides an attractive framework within which both short- and long-distance reorderings can be addressed consistently and efficiently. However, Hiero is generally implemented with a constraint preventing the creation of rules with adjacent nonterminals, because such rules introduce computational and modeling challenges. We introduce methods to address these challenges, and demonstrate that rules with adjacent nonterminals can improve Hiero's generalization power and lead to significant performance gains in Chinese-English translation.

1 Introduction

Hierarchical phrase-based translation (Hiero, (Chiang, 2005)) has proven to be a very useful compromise between syntactically informed and purely corpus-driven translation. By automatically learning synchronous grammar rules from parallel text, Hiero captures short- and long-distance reorderings consistently and efficiently. However, implementations of Hiero generally forbid adjacent nonterminal symbols on the source side of hierarchical rules, a practice we will refer to as the *non-adjacent nonterminals constraint*. The main argument against such rules is that they cause the system to produce multiple derivations that all lead to the same translation – a form of redundancy known as *spurious ambiguity*. Spurious ambiguity can lead to drastic reductions in decoding efficiency, and the obvious solutions, such as reducing beam width, erode translation quality.

In Section 2, we argue that the non-adjacent nonterminals constraints severely limits Hiero's generalization power, limiting its coverage of important reordering phenomena. In Section 3, we discuss the challenges that arise in relaxing this constraint. In Section 4 we introduce new methods to address those challenges, and Section 5 validates the approach empirically.

Improving Hiero via variations on rule pruning and filtering is well explored, e.g., (Chiang, 2005; Chiang et al., 2008; Zollmann and Venugopal, 2006), to name just a few. These proposals differ from each other mainly in the specific linguistic knowledge being used, and on which side the constraints are applied. In contrast, we complement previous work by showing that *adding* rules to Hiero can provide benefits if done judiciously.

2 Judicious Use of Adjacent Nonterminals

Our motivations largely follow Menezes and Quirk's (2007) discussion of reorderings and generalization. As a specific example, we will use a Chinese to English verb phrase (VP) translation (Fig. 1), which represents one of the most prominent phrase constructions in Chinese. Here the construction of the Chinese VP involves joining a prepositional phrase (PP) and a smaller verbal phrase (VP-A), with the preposition at the beginning as a PP marker. In the translation, the VP-A precedes the PP, a shift from pre-verbal PP in Chinese to post-verbal in English.

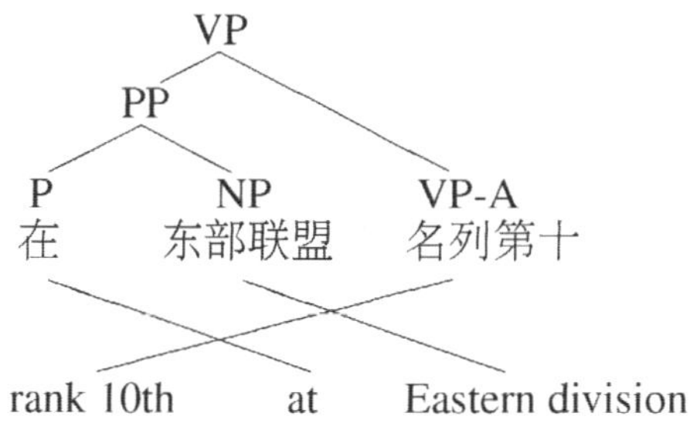

Figure 1: A Chinese-English verb phrase translation

Human Language Technologies: The 2010 Annual Conference of the North American Chapter of the ACL, pages 349–352,
Los Angeles, California, June 2010.

Hiero can correctly translate the example if it learns any of the following rules from training data:

$$X \rightarrow \langle \text{在 } X_1 \text{ 名列第十, rank 10th at } X_1 \rangle \quad (1)$$

$$X \rightarrow \langle \text{在东部联盟 } X_1, X_1 \text{ at Eastern div.} \rangle \quad (2)$$

$$X \rightarrow \langle X_1 \text{ 东部联盟 } X_2, X_2\ X_1 \text{ Eastern div.} \rangle \quad (3)$$

However, in practice, data sparsity makes the chance of learning these rules rather slim. For instance, learning Rule 1 depends on training data containing instances of the shift with identical wording for the VP-A, which belongs to an open word class.

If Hiero fails to learn any of the above rules, it will apply the "glue rules" $S \rightarrow \langle S\ X_1,\ S\ X_1 \rangle$ and $S \rightarrow \langle X,\ X \rangle$. But these glue rules clearly cannot model the VP-A's movement. In failing to learn Rules 1-3, Hiero has no choice but to translate VP-A in a monotone order.

On the other hand, consider the following rules with adjacent nonterminals on the source side (or *XX rules*, for brevity):

$$X \rightarrow \langle \text{在 } X_1 X_2, X_2 \text{ at } X_1 \rangle \quad (4)$$

$$X \rightarrow \langle X_1 X_2 \text{ 名列第十, rank 10th } X_1 X_2 \rangle \quad (5)$$

$$X \rightarrow \langle X_1 X_2, X_2 X_1 \rangle \quad (6)$$

Note that although XX rules 4-6 can potentially increase the chance of modeling the pre-verbal to post-verbal shift, not all of them are beneficial to learn. For instance, Rule 5 models the word order shift but introduces spurious ambiguity, since the nonterminals are translated in monotone order. Rule 6, which resembles the inverted rule of the Inversion Transduction Grammar (Wu, 1997), is highly ambiguous because its application has no lexical grounding. Rule 4 avoids both problems, and is also easier to learn, since it is lexically anchored by a preposition, 在(at), which we can expect to appear frequently in training. These observations will motivate us to focus on rules that model non-monotone reordering of phrases surrounding a lexical item on the target side.

3 Addressing XX Rule Challenges

The first challenge created by introducing XX rules is computational: relaxing the constraint significantly increases the grammar size. Motivated by our earlier discussion, we address this by permitting only rules that model non-monotone reordering, i.e. those rules whose nonterminals are projected into the target language in a different word order, leaving monotone mappings to be handled by the glue rules as previously. This choice helps keep the search space more manageable, and also avoids spurious ambiguity. In addition, we disallow rules in which nonterminals are adjacent on both the source and target sides, by imposing the non adjacent nonterminal constraint on the target side whenever the constraint is relaxed on the source side. This forces any non-monotone reorderings to always be grounded in lexical evidence. We refer to the permitted subset of XX rules as *XX-nonmono* rules.

The second challenge involves modeling: introducing XX rules places them in competition with the existing glue rules. In particular, these two kinds of rules try to model the same phenomena, namely the translations of phrases that appear next to each other. However, they differ in terms of the features associated with the rules. XX rules will be associated with the same features as any other hierarchical rules, since they are all learned via an identical training method. In contrast, glue rules are introduced into the grammar in an *ad hoc* manner, and the only feature associated with them is a "glue penalty". These distinct feature sets makes direct comparison of scores unreliable. As a result the decoder may simply prefer to always select glue rules because they are associated with fewer features resulting in adjacent phrases always being translated in a monotone order. To address this issue, we introduce a new model, which we call the *target-side function words orientation-based model*, or simply P_{ori_t}, which evaluates the application of the two kinds of rules on the same context, i.e. for our example, it is the function word 在(at).

4 Target-side Function Words Orientation-based Model

The P_{ori_t} model is motivated by the *function words reordering hypothesis* (Setiawan et al., 2007), which suggests that function words encode essential information about the (re)ordering of their neighboring phrases. In contrast to Setiawan et al. (2007), who looked at neighboring contexts for function words on the source side, we focus here on modeling the influence of function words on neighboring phrases on the *target* side. We argue that this focus better fits our purpose, since the phrases that we want to model are the function words' neighbors on the target side, as illustrated in Fig. 1.

To develop this idea, we first define an ori_t function that takes a source function word as a reference point, along with its neighboring phrase on the target side. The ori_t function outputs one of the following orientation values (Nagata et al., 2006): Monotone-Adjacent (MA); Reverse-Adjacent (RA); Monotone-Gap (MG); and Reverse-Gap (RG). The Monotone/Reverse distinction indicates whether the source order follows the target order. The Adjacent/Gap distinction indicates whether the two phrases are adjacent or separated by an intervening phrase on the source side. For example, in Fig. 1, the value of ori_t for right neighbor *Eastern division* with respect to function word 在 (at) is MA, since its corresponding source phrase 东部联盟 is adjacent to 在 (at) and their order is preserved on the English side. The value for left neighbor *rank 10th* with respect to 在 (at) is RG, since 名列第十 is separated from 在 (at) and their order is reversed on the English side.

More formally, we define $P_{ori_t}(ori_t(Y, X)|Y)$, where $ori_t(Y, X) \in \{\mathrm{MA}, \mathrm{RA}, \mathrm{MG}, \mathrm{RG}\}$ is the orientation of a target phrase X with a source function word Y as the reference point.[1]

We estimate the orientation model using maximum likelihood, which involves counting and normalizing events of interest: $(Y, o = ori_t(Y, X))$. Specifically, we estimate $P_{ori_t}(o|Y) = C(Y, o)/C(Y, \cdot)$. Collecting training counts $C(Y, o)$ involves several steps. First, we run GIZA++ on the training bitext and apply the "grow-diag-final" heuristic over the training data to produce a bi-directional word alignment. Then, we enumerate all occurrences of Y and determine $ori_t(Y, X)$. To ensure uniqueness, we enforce that neighbor X be the longest possible phrase that satisfies the consistency constraint (Och and Ney, 2004). Determining $ori_t(Y, X)$ can then be done in a straightforward manner by looking at the monotonicity (monotone or reverse) and adjacency (adjacent or gap) between Y's and X.

[1] In fact, separate models are developed for left and right neighbors, although for clarity we suppress this distinction throughout.

	MT06	MT08
baseline	30.58	23.59
+itg	29.82	23.21
+XX	30.10	22.86
+XX-nonmono	*30.96*	*24.07*
$+ori_t$	30.19	*23.69*
+XX-nonmono+ori_t	***31.49***	***24.73***

Table 1: Experimental results where better than baseline results are *italicized*, and statistically significant better ($p < 0.01$) are in **bold**.

5 Experiments

We evaluated the generalization of Hiero to include XX rules on a Chinese-to-English translation task. We treat the $N = 128$ most frequent words in the corpus as function words, an approximation that has worked well in the past and minimized dependence on language-specific resources (Setiawan et al., 2007). We report BLEU r4n4 and assess significance using the standard bootstrapping approach.

We trained on the NIST MT06 Eval corpus excluding the UN data (approximately 900K sentence pairs), segmenting Chinese using the Harbin segmenter (Zhao et al., 2001). Our 5-gram language model with modified Kneser-Ney smoothing was trained on the English side of our training data plus portions of the Gigaword v2 English corpus. We optimized the feature weights using minimum error rate training, using the NIST MT03 test set as the development set. We report the results on the NIST 2006 evaluation test (MT06) and the NIST 2008 evaluation test (MT08).

Table 1 reports experiments in an incremental fashion, starting from the baseline model (the original Hiero), then adding different sets of rules, and finally adding the orientation-based model. In our first experiments, we investigated the introduction of three different sets of XX rules. First (+itg), we simply add the ITG's inverted rule (Rule 6) to the baseline system in an ad-hoc manner, similar to the glue rules. This hurts performance consistently across MT06 and MT08 sets, which we suspect is a result of ITG rule applications often aggravating search error. Second (+XX), we permitted general XX rules. This results in a grammar size increase of 25-26%, filtering out rules irrelevant for the test set, and leads to a significant performance drop, again perhaps attributable to search error. When we inspected the rules, we observe that the majority of these rules involve spurious word insertions. Third (+XX-nonmono), we introduced only XX-nonmono rules; this produced only a 5% additional rules, and yielded a marginal but consistent gain.

In a second experiment ($+ori_t$), we introduced the target-side function words orientation-based model. Note that this experiment is orthogonal to the first set, since we introduce no additional rules. Results are mixed, worse for MT06 but better (with significance) for MT08. Here, we suspect the model's potential has not been fully realized, since Hiero only considers monotone reordering in unseen cases.

Finally, we combine both the XX-nonmono rules and the P_{ori_t} model (+XX-nonmono+ori_t). The combination produces a significant, consistent gain across all test sets. This result suggests that the orientation model contributes more strongly in unseen cases when Hiero also considers non-monotone reordering. We interpret this result as a validation of our hypothesis that carefully relaxing the non-adjacent constraint improves translation.

6 Discussion and Future Work

To our knowledge, the work reported here is the first to relax the non-adjacent nonterminals constraint in hierarchical phrase-based models. The results confirm that judiciously *adding* rules to a Hiero grammar, adjusting the modeling accordingly, can achieve significant gains.

Although we found that XX-nonmono rules performed better than general XX rules, we believe the latter may nonetheless prove useful. Manually inspecting our system's output, we find that the output is often shorter than the references, and the missing words often correspond to function words that are modeled by those rules. Using XX rules to model legitimate word insertions is a topic for future work.

Acknowledgments

The authors gratefully acknowledge partial support from the GALE program of the Defense Advanced Research Projects Agency, Contract No. HR0011-06-2-001. Any opinions, findings, conclusions or recommendations expressed in this paper are those of the authors and do not necessarily reflect the views of the sponsors.

References

David Chiang, Yuval Marton, and Philip Resnik. 2008. Online large-margin training of syntactic and structural translation features. In *Proceedings of the 2008 Conference on Empirical Methods in Natural Language Processing*, pages 224–233, Honolulu, Hawaii, October.

David Chiang. 2005. A hierarchical phrase-based model for statistical machine translation. In *Proceedings of the 43rd Annual Meeting of the Association for Computational Linguistics (ACL'05)*, pages 263–270, Ann Arbor, Michigan, June. Association for Computational Linguistics.

Arul Menezes and Chris Quirk. 2007. Using dependency order templates to improve generality in translation. In *Proceedings of the Second Workshop on Statistical Machine Translation*, pages 1–8, Prague, Czech Republic, June. Association for Computational Linguistics.

Masaaki Nagata, Kuniko Saito, Kazuhide Yamamoto, and Kazuteru Ohashi. 2006. A clustered global phrase reordering model for statistical machine translation. In *Proceedings of the 21st International Conference on Computational Linguistics and 44th Annual Meeting of the Association for Computational Linguistics*, pages 713–720, Sydney, Australia, July. Association for Computational Linguistics.

Franz Josef Och and Hermann Ney. 2004. The alignment template approach to statistical machine translation. *Computational Linguistics*, 30(4):417–449.

Hendra Setiawan, Min-Yen Kan, and Haizhou Li. 2007. Ordering phrases with function words. In *Proceedings of the 45th Annual Meeting of the Association of Computational Linguistics*, pages 712–719, Prague, Czech Republic, June. Association for Computational Linguistics.

Dekai Wu. 1997. Stochastic inversion transduction grammars and bilingual parsing of parallel corpora. *Computational Linguistics*, 23(3):377–404, Sep.

Tiejun Zhao, Yajuan Lv, Jianmin Yao, Hao Yu, Muyun Yang, and Fang Liu. 2001. Increasing accuracy of chinese segmentation with strategy of multi-step processing. *Journal of Chinese Information Processing (Chinese Version)*, 1:13–18.

Andreas Zollmann and Ashish Venugopal. 2006. Syntax augmented machine translation via chart parsing. In *Proceedings on the Workshop on Statistical Machine Translation*, pages 138–141, New York City, June. Association for Computational Linguistics.

The Effect of Ambiguity on the Automated Acquisition of WSD Examples

Mark Stevenson and Yikun Guo
Department of Computer Science,
University of Sheffield,
Regent Court, 211 Portobello,
Sheffield, S1 4DP
United Kingdom
m.stevenson@dcs.shef.ac.uk and g.yikun@dcs.shef.ac.uk

Abstract

Several methods for automatically generating labeled examples that can be used as training data for WSD systems have been proposed, including a semi-supervised approach based on relevance feedback (Stevenson et al., 2008a). This approach was shown to generate examples that improved the performance of a WSD system for a set of ambiguous terms from the biomedical domain. However, we find that this approach does not perform as well on other data sets. The levels of ambigu ity in these data sets are analysed and we suggest this is the reason for this negative result.

1 Introduction

Several studies, for example (Mihalcea et al., 2004; Pradhan et al., 2007), have shown that supervised approaches to Word Sense Disambiguation (WSD) outperform unsupervised ones. But these rely on labeled training data which is difficult to create and not always available (e.g. (Weeber et al., 2001)). Various techniques for creating labeled training data automatically have been suggested in the literature. Stevenson et al. (2008a) describe a semi-supervised approach that used relevance feedback (Rocchio, 1971) to analyse existing labeled examples and use the information produced to generate further ones. The approach was tested on the biomedical domain and the additional examples found to improve performance of a WSD system. However, biomedical documents represent a restricted domain. In this paper the same approach is tested against two data sets that are not limited to a single domain.

2 Application to a Range of Data Sets

In this paper the relevance feedback approach described by Stevenson et al. (2008a) is evaluated using three data sets: the **NLM-WSD** corpus (Weeber et al., 2001) which Stevenson et al. (2008a) used for their experiments, the **Senseval-3** lexical sample task (Mihalcea et al., 2004) and the coarse-grained version of the **SemEval** English lexical sample task (Pradhan et al., 2007).

2.1 Generating Examples

To generate examples for a particular sense of an ambiguous term all of the examples where the term is used in that sense are considered to be "relevant documents" while the examples in which any other sense of the term is used are considered to be "irrelevant documents". Relevance feedback (Rocchio, 1971) is used to generate a set of query terms designed to identify relevant documents, and therefore instances of the sense. The top five query terms are used to retrieve documents and these are used as labeled examples of the sense. Further details of this process are described by Stevenson et al. (2008a).

This process requires a collection of documents that can be queried to generate the additional examples. For the NLM-WSD data set we used PubMed, a database of biomedical journal abstracts queried using the Entrez retrieval system (http://www.ncbi.nlm.nih.gov/sites/gquery). The British National Corpus (BNC) was used for Senseval-3 and SemEval.[1] Lucene (http://lucene.apache.org) was used to index the BNC and retrieve examples.

[1] We also experimented with the English WaCky corpus (Baroni et al., 2009) which contains nearly 2 billion words automatically retrieved from the web. However, results were not as good as when the BNC was used.

Human Language Technologies: The 2010 Annual Conference of the North American Chapter of the ACL, pages 353–356,
Los Angeles, California, June 2010.

2.2 WSD System

We use a WSD system that has been shown to perform well when evaluated against ambiguities found in both general text and the biomedical domain (Stevenson et al., 2008b). Medical Subject Headings (MeSH), a controlled vocabulary used for document indexing, are obtained from PubMed and used as additional features for the NLM-WSD data set since they have been shown to improve performance. The features are combined using the Vector Space Model, a simple memory-based learning algorithm.

2.3 Experiment

Experiments were carried out comparing performance when the WSD system was trained using either the examples in the original data set (**original**), the examples generated from these using the relevance feedback approach (**additional**) or a combination of these (**combined**). The Senseval-3 and SemEval corpora are split into training and test portions so the training portion is used as the original data set and the WSD system evaluated against the held-back data. As there is no such recognised standard split for the NLM-WSD corpus, 10-fold cross-validation was used. For each fold the training portion is used as the original data set and automatically generated examples created by examining just that part of the data. Evaluation is carried out against the fold's test data and the average result across the 10 folds reported.

Table 1 shows the results of this experiment.[2] Examples generated using the relevance feedback approach only improve results for one data set, the NLM-WSD corpus. In this case there is a significant improvement (Mann-Whitney, $p < 0.01$) when the original and automatically generated examples are combined. There is no such improvement for the other two data sets: WSD results using the additional data are noticeably worse than when the original data is used alone and, although performance improves when these examples are combined with the original data, results are still lower than using the original data. When examples are combined there is a drop in performance of 1.2% and 2.9% for SemEval and Senseval-3 respectively.

[2]Results reported here for the NLM-WSD corpus are slightly different from those reported by (Stevenson et al., 2008a). We used an additional feature (MeSH headings), which improved the baseline performance, and more query terms which improved the quality of the additional examples for all three data sets.

Corpus	Original	Additional	Combined
NLM-WSD	87.9	87.6	89.2
SemEval	83.7	74.6	82.5
Senseval-3	68.8	56.3	65.9

Table 1: Results of relevance feedback approach applied to three data sets

These results indicate that the relevance feedback approach described by Stevenson et al. (2008a) is not able to generate useful examples for the Senseval-3 and SemEval data sets, although it can for the NLM-WSD data set. We hypothesise that these corpora contain different levels of ambiguity which effect suitability of the approach.

3 Analysis of Ambiguities

The three data sets are compared using measures designed to determine the level of ambiguity they contain. Section 3.1 reports results using various widely used measures based on the distribution of senses. Section 3.2 introduces a measure based on the semantic similarity between the possible senses of ambiguous terms.

3.1 Sense Distributions

Three measures for characterising the difficulty of WSD data sets based on their sense distribution were used. The first is the widely applied most frequent sense (MFS) baseline (McCarthy et al., 2004), i.e. the proportion of examples for an ambiguous term that are labeled with the commonest sense. The second is number of senses per ambiguous term. The final measure, the entropy of the sense distribution, has been shown to be a good indication of disambiguation difficulty (Kilgarriff and Rosenzweig, 2000). For two of these measures (number of senses and entropy) a higher figure indicates greater ambiguity while for the MFS measure a lower figure indicates a more difficult data set.

Table 2 shows the results of computing these measures averaged across all terms in the corpus. For two measures (number of senses and entropy) the NLM-WSD corpus is least ambiguous, Senseval-3 the most ambiguous with SemEval between them. The MFS scores are very similar for two data sets (NLM-WSD and SemEval), both of which are much higher than for Senseval-3.

These measures suggest that the NLM-WSD corpus is less ambiguous than the other two and also that the Senseval-3 corpus is the most ambiguous of the three.

Corpus	MFS	Senses	Entropy
NLM-WSD	78.0	2.63	0.73
SemEval	78.4	3.60	0.91
Senseval-3	53.8	6.43	1.75

Table 2: Properties of Data Sets using sense distribution measures

3.2 Semantic Similarity

We also developed a measure that takes into account the similarity in meaning between the possible senses for an ambiguous term. This measure is similar to the one used by Passoneau et al. (2009) to analyse levels of inter-annotator agreement in word sense annotation. Our measure is shown in equation 1 where $Senses$ is the set of possible senses for an ambiguous term, $|Senses| = n$ and $\binom{Senses}{2}$ is the set of all subsets of $Senses$ containing two of its members (i.e the set of unordered pairs). The similarity between a pair of senses, $sim(x, y)$, can be computed using any lexical similarity measure, see Pedersen et al. (2004). Essentially this measure computes the mean of the similarities between each pair of senses for the term.

$$sim\_measure = \frac{\sum_{\{x,y\} \epsilon \binom{Senses}{2}} sim(x, y)}{\binom{n}{2}} \quad (1)$$

One problem with comparing the data sets used here is that they use a range of sense inventories. Although lexical similarity measures have been applied to WordNet (Pedersen et al., 2004) and UMLS (Pedersen et al., 2007), it is not clear that the scores they produce can be meaningfully compared. To avoid this problem we mapped the sense inventories onto a single resource: WordNet version 3.0.

The mapping was most straightforward for Senseval-3 which uses WordNet 1.7.1 and could be automatically mapped onto WordNet 3.0 senses using publicly available mappings (Daudé et al., 2000). The SemEval data contains a mapping from the OntoNotes senses to groups of WordNet 2.1 senses. The first sense from this group was mapped to WordNet 3.0 using the same mappings.

Mapping the NLM-WSD corpus was more problematic and had to be carried out manually by comparing sense definitions in UMLS and WordNet 3.0. We had expected this process to be difficult but found clear mappings for the majority of senses. There were even found cases in which the sense definitions were identical in both resources. (The most likely reason for this is that some of the resources that are included in the UMLS were used to compile WordNet.) Another, more serious, problem is related to the annotation scheme used in the NLM-WSD corpus. If none of the possible senses in UMLS were judged to be appropriate the annotators could label the sense as "None". We did not map these senses since it would require examining each instance to determine the most appropriate sense or senses in WordNet and we expected this to be error prone. In addition, there is no guarantee that all of the instances of a particular term labeled with "None" refer to the same meaning. All of the "None" senses were removed from the NLM-WSD data set and any terms where there were more than ten instances marked as "None" were also rejected from the similarity analysis. This allowed us to compute the similarity score for just 20 examples (40% of the total) although we felt that this was a large enough sample to provide insight into the data set.

The `WordNet::Similarity` package (Pedersen et al., 2004) was used to compute similarity scores. Results are reported for three of the measures in this package. (Other measures produced similar results.) The simple **path** measure computes the similarity between a pair of nodes in WordNet as the reciprocal of the number of edges in the shortest path between them, the **LCh** measure (Leacock et al., 1998) also uses information about the length of the shortest path between a pair of nodes and combines this with information about the maximum depth in WordNet and the **JCn** measure (Jaing and Conrath, 1997) makes use of information theory to assign probabilities to each of the nodes in the WordNet hierarchy and computes similarity based on these scores.

Table 3 shows the values of equation 1 for the three similarity measures with scores averaged across terms. These results indicate that for all measures the Senseval-3 data set contains the most ambiguity and NLM-WSD the least. This analysis is consistent with the one carried out using measures based on sense distributions (Section 3.1)

Corpus	Measure		
	Path	JCn	LCh
NLM-WSD	0.074	0.032	1.027
SemEval	0.136	0.061	1.292
Senseval-3	0.159	0.063	1.500

Table 3: Semantic similarity for each data set using a variety of measures

and suggest that the senses in the NLM-WSD data set are more clearly distinguished than the other two.

4 Conclusion

This paper has explored a semi-supervised approach to the generation of labeled training data for WSD that is based on relevance feedback (Stevenson et al., 2008a). It was tested on three data sets but was only found to generate examples that were accurate enough to improve WSD performance for one of these. The data set in which a performance improvement was observed represented a limited domain (biomedicine) while the other two were not restricted in this way. Measures designed to quantify the level of ambiguity were applied to these data sets including ones based on the distribution of senses and another designed to quantify similarities between senses. These measures provided evidence that the corpus for which the relevance feedback approach was successful contained less ambiguity than the other two and this suggests that the relevance feedback approach is most appropriate when the level of ambiguity is low.

The experiments described in this paper highlight the importance of the level of ambiguity on the relevance feedback approach's ability to generate useful labeled examples. Since it is semi-supervised the ambiguity level can be checked using the measures used in this paper (Section 3) and the performance of any automatically generated examples can be compared with the manually labeled ones (see Section 2.3) before deciding whether or not they should be applied.

References

M. Baroni, S. Bernardini, A. Ferraresi, and E. Zanchetta. 2009. The wacky wide web: a collection of very large linguistically processed web-crawled corpora. *Language Resources and Evaluation*, 43(3):209–226.

J. Daudé, L. Padró, and G. Rigau. 2000. Mapping wordnets using structural information. In *Proceedings of ACL '00*, pages 504–511, Hong Kong.

J. Jaing and D. Conrath. 1997. Semantic similarity based on corpus statistics and lexical taxonomy. In *Proceedings of International Conference on Research in Computational Linguistics*, Taiwan.

A. Kilgarriff and J. Rosenzweig. 2000. Framework and results for English SENSEVAL. *Computers and the Humanities*, 34(1-2):15–48.

C. Leacock, M. Chodorow, and G. Miller. 1998. Using corpus statistics and WordNet relations for sense identification. *Computational Linguistics*, 24(1):147–165.

D. McCarthy, R. Koeling, J. Weeds, and J. Carroll. 2004. Finding predominant word senses in untagged text. In *Proceedings of ACL'04*, pages 279–286, Barcelona, Spain.

R. Mihalcea, T. Chklovski, and A. Kilgarriff. 2004. The Senseval-3 English lexical sample task. In *Proceedings of Senseval-3*, pages 25–28, Barcelona, Spain.

R. Passoneau, A. Salleb-Aouissi, and N. Ide. 2009. Making sense of word sense variation. In *Proceedings of SEW-2009*, pages 2–9, Boulder, Colorado.

T. Pedersen, S. Patwardhan, and Michelizzi. 2004. Wordnet::similarity - measuring the relatedness of concepts. In *Proceedings of AAAI-04*, pages 1024–1025, San Jose, CA.

T. Pedersen, S. Pakhomov, S. Patwardhan, and C. Chute. 2007. Measures of semantic similarity and relateness in the biomedical domain. *Journal of Biomedical Informatics*, 40(3):288–299.

S. Pradhan, E. Loper, D. Dligach, and M. Palmer. 2007. SemEval-2007 Task-17: English Lexical Sample, SRL and All Words. In *Proceedings of SemEval-2007*, pages 87–92, Prague, Czech Republic.

J. Rocchio. 1971. Relevance feedback in Information Retrieval. In G. Salton, editor, *The SMART Retrieval System – Experiments in Automatic Document Processing*. Prentice Hall, Englewood Cliffs, NJ.

M. Stevenson, Y. Guo, and R. Gaizauskas. 2008a. Acquiring Sense Tagged Examples using Relevance Feedback. In *Proceedings of the Coling 2008*, pages 809–816, Manchester, UK, August.

M. Stevenson, Y. Guo, R. Gaizauskas, and D. Martinez. 2008b. Disambiguation of biomedical text using diverse sources of information. *BMC Bioinformatics*, 9(Suppl 11):S7.

M. Weeber, J. Mork, and A. Aronson. 2001. Developing a Test Collection for Biomedical Word Sense Disambiguation. In *Proceedings of AMIA Symposium*, pages 746–50, Washington, DC.

Word Sense Subjectivity for Cross-lingual Lexical Substitution

Fangzhong Su
School of Computing
University of Leeds, UK
scsfs@leeds.ac.uk

Katja Markert
School of Computing
University of Leeds, UK
scskm@leeds.ac.uk

Abstract

We explore the relation between word sense subjectivity and cross-lingual lexical substitution, following the intuition that good substitutions will transfer a word's (contextual) sentiment from the source language into the target language. Experiments on English-Chinese lexical substitution show that taking a word's subjectivity into account can indeed improve performance. We also show that just using word sense subjectivity can perform as well as integrating fully-fledged fine-grained word sense disambiguation for words which have both subjective and objective senses.

1 Introduction

Cross-lingual lexical substitution has been proposed as a Task at SemEval-2010.[1] Given a target word and its context in a source language (like English), the goal is to provide correct translations for that word in a target language (like Chinese). The translations must fit the given context.

In this paper, we explore the relation between the sentiment of the used word in the source language and translation choice in the target language, focusing on English as the source and Chinese as the target language. Our work is motivated by the intuition that most good word translations will be *sentiment-invariant*, i.e. if a source word is used in a subjective (opinion-carrying) sense it will be often translated with a subjective sense in the target language whereas if it used in an objective sense, it will be translated with an objective sense. As an example, consider the two words *positive* and *collaborate* with example senses from WordNet 2.0 below.

(1) positive—greater than zero; "positive numbers" (*objective*)

(2) plus, positive—involving advantage or good; "a plus (or positive) factor" (*subjective*)

(3) collaborate, join forces, cooperate—work together on a common enterprise of project; "We joined forces with another research group"(*objective*)

(4) collaborate—cooperate as a traitor; (*subjective*)

In most cases, if the word *positive* is used in the sense *"greater than zero"* (**objective**) in an English context, the corresponding Chinese translation is "正的"; if *"involving advantage or good"*(**subjective**) is used, its Chinese translations are "积极的, 好的". Similarly, for the word *collaborate*, the sense *"work together on a common enterprise of project"* (**objective**) corresponds to "合作, 协作" in Chinese translation, and *"cooperate as a traitor"* (**subjective**) corresponds to "勾结, 狼狈为奸". Therefore, subjectivity information should be effective for improving lexical translation for what we previously (Su and Markert, 2008) termed *subjectivity-ambiguous* words, i.e. words with both subjective and objective senses such as *positive* and *collaborate* above.

We therefore incorporate subjectivity word sense disambiguation (SWSD) as defined in Akkaya et al. (2009) into lexical substitution. SWSD is a binary classification task that decides in context whether a word occurs with one of its subjective or one of its objective senses. In contrast to standard

[1] http://lit.csci.unt.edu/index.php/Semeval_2010

Human Language Technologies: The 2010 Annual Conference of the North American Chapter of the ACL, pages 357–360,
Los Angeles, California, June 2010. ©2010 Association for Computational Linguistics

multi-class Word Sense Disambiguation (WSD), it uses a coarse-grained sense inventory that allows to achieve higher accuracy than WSD and therefore introduces less noise when embedded in another task such as word translation. For example, the accuracy reported in Akkaya et al. (2009) for SWSD is over 20% higher than for standard WSD. Coarse-grained senses are also easier to annotate, so getting training data for learning is less arduous. On the minus side, SWSD can only be useful for subjectivity-ambiguous words. However, we showed (Su and Markert, 2008) that subjectivity-ambiguity is frequent (around 30% of common words).

2 Related Work

McCarthy and Navigli (2007) organized a monolingual English lexical substitution task in Semeval-2007, i.e finding English substitutions for an English target word. Mihalcea et al. organize an English-Spanish lexical substitution task in SemEval-2010. Approaches to lexical substitution in the past competitions did not use sentiment features.

Independent of these lexical substitution tasks, the connection between word senses and word translation has been explored in Chan et al. (2007) and Carpuat and Wu (2007), who predict the probabilities of a target word being translated as an item in a "sense inventory", where the sense inventory is a list of possible translations. They then incorporate these probabilities into machine translation. However, they do not consider sentiment explicitly.

Subjectivity at the word sense level has been discussed by (Wiebe and Mihalcea, 2006; Su and Markert, 2008; Akkaya et al., 2009). Wiebe and Mihalcea (2006) and Su and Markert (2008) both show that this is a well-defined concept via human annotation as well as automatic recognition. Akkaya et al. (2009) show that subjectivity word sense disambiguation (SWSD) can boost the performance of a sentiment analysis system. None of these paper considers the impact of word sense subjectivity on cross-lingual lexical substitution.

3 Methodology

3.1 Task and Dataset

We constructed an English-Chinese lexical substitution gold standard by translating the English target words in the SENSEVAL 2 and SENSEVAL 3 lexical sample training and test sets into Chinese. We choose the SENSEVAL datasets as they are relatively domain-independent and also because we can use them for our SWSD/WSD subtasks as well. The translation is carried out by two native Chinese speakers with a good command of English. First, candidate Chinese translations (denoted by **T**) of the English target words are provided from the on-line English-Chinese dictionary *iciba*[2], which is composed of more than 150 different English-Chinese dictionaries. To reduce annotation bias, the order of the Senseval sentences is randomized. The annotators then independently assign the most fitting Chinese translation(s) (from **T**) for the English target words in the given Senseval sentences. For the agreement study, different Chinese translations (for example, "权威" and "泰斗" of the word *authority*) that are actually synonyms are merged. The observed agreement between the two annotators is 86.7%. Finally, the two annotators discuss the disagreed examples together, leading to a gold standard.

Since we evaluate how word sense subjectivity affects cross-lingual lexical substitution, we limited our study to the SENSEVAL words that are subjectivity-ambiguous. Therefore, following the annotation schemes in (Su and Markert, 2008; Wiebe and Mihalcea, 2006), all senses of all target words in SENSEVAL 2&3 are annotated by a near-native English speaker as *subjective* or*objective*. This annotator was not involved in the English to Chinese translation. We also discard subjectivity-ambiguous words if its *subjective* or *objective* senses do not appear in both training and test set. In total we collect 28 subjectivity-ambiguous words. Their English example sentences and translations yield 2890 training sentence pairs and 1444 test sentence pairs.

3.2 Algorithms

For the English-Chinese lexical substitution task, we first develop a basic system (called **B**) to assign Chinese translations to the target English words in context. This system uses only standard contextual features from the English sentences (see Section 3.3). We then add word sense subjectivity information to

[2]http://www.iciba.com

the basic system (see Section 3.4). We also compare including word sense subjectivity to the inclusion of full fine-grained sense information (Section 3.5).

All systems are supervised classifiers trained on the SENSEVAL training data and evaluated on the SENSEVAL test data for each of the 28 words. We employ an SVM classifier from the `libsvm` package[3] with a linear kernel.

3.3 Common Features

In the basic system **B**, we adopt features which are commonly used in WSD or lexical translation.

Surrounding Words: Lemmatized bag of words with stop word filtering.

Part-of-Speech (POS): The POS of the neighbouring words of the target word. We extract POS tag of the 3 words to the right and left together with position information.

Collocation: The neighbouring words of the target word. We extract 4 lemmatized words to the right and left, together with position information.

Syntactic Relations: We employ the MaltParser[4] for dependency parsing and extract 4 features: the head word of the target word, POS of the head word, the dependency relation between head word and target word, and the relative position (left or right) of the head word to the target word.

3.4 Subjectivity Features

We add a feature that incorporates whether the original English word is used subjectively or objectively. For an upper bound, we use the SENSEVAL gold standard sense annotation (**gold-subj**), mapped onto binary subjective/objective labels. For a more realistic assessment, we use SWSD to derive the subjectivity sense label automatically (**auto-subj**) using standard supervised binary SVMs and the features in Section 3.3 on the SENSEVAL data.

3.5 Sense Features

We compare using subjectivity information to using full fine-grained word sense information, incorporating a feature that specifies the exact word sense of the target word to be translated. This setting also compares the SENSEVAL gold standard (**gold-senses**) and automatically predicted sense information (**auto-senses**), the latter via supervised multiclass learning on the SENSEVAL dataset.

4 Experiments and Evaluation

For the English-Chinese lexical substitution task, we evaluate 6 different methods: **Baseline** (assign the most frequent translation to all examples), **B** (use common features), **B+gold subj** (incorporate gold standard word sense subjectivity), **B+gold sense** (incorporate gold standard sense), **B+auto subj** (incorporate automatically predicted word sense subjectivity), and **B+auto sense** (incorporate automatically predicted fine-grained senses). We measure lexical substitution accuracy on the SENSEVAL test data by comparing to the human gold standard annotation (see Section 3.1). Results are listed in Table 1.

Results. Table 1 shows that our standard lexical substitution system **B** improves strongly (near 11% average accuracy gain) over the most frequent translation baseline. Incorporating sense subjectivity as in **B+gold subj** leads to a further strong improvement, confirming our hypothesis that word sense subjectivity can improve lexical substitution. Incorporating fine-grained senses **B+gold senses** yields only a slightly higher gain, showing that a coarse-grained subjective/objective classification might be sufficient for subjectivity-ambiguous words for aiding translation. In addition, the small gain using fine-grained senses might disappear in practice as automatic WSD is a more challenging task than SWSD: in our experiment, **B+auto sense** performs worse than **B+auto subj**. The current improvement of **B+auto subj** over **B** is significant (McNemar test at the 5% level). The difference between the actual performance of word sense subjectivity and its potential as exemplified in **B+gold subj** is, obviously, caused by imperfect performance of the SWSD component, mostly due to a distributional bias in the SENSEVAL training data, with few examples for rarer senses of the target words.

For some words (such as *authority* and *stress*), the additional sense subjectivity feature does not improve lexical substitution, even when gold standard labels are used. There are two main reasons for this. First, one candidate Chinese translation might cover

[3] `http://www.csie.ntu.edu.tw/~cjlin/libsvm`

[4] `http://w3.msi.vxu.se/~nivre/research/MaltParser.html`

Table 1: Accuracy of lexical substitution with different different feature settings

Word	Subjectivity of Senses	Baseline	Basic (B)	B+gold subj	B+gold senses	B+auto subj	B+auto senses
authority	3-S 4-O	50.5%	70.3%	70.3%	84.6%	70.3%	79.1%
blind	2-S 1-O	87.0%	88.9%	94.4%	94.4%	88.9%	88.9%
cool	3-S 3-O	46.0%	46.0%	68.0%	68.0%	58.0%	48.0%
dyke	1-S 1-O	89.3%	89.3%	92.9%	92.9%	89.3%	89.3%
fatigue	1-S 2-O 1-B	80.0%	80.0%	82.5%	85.0%	82.5%	82.5%
fine	5-S 4-O	78.5%	78.5%	90.8%	80.0%	80.0%	78.5%
nature	1-S 3-O 1-B	53.3%	62.2%	73.3%	71.1%	64.4%	62.2%
oblique	1-S 1-O	65.5%	75.9%	86.2%	89.7%	79.3%	79.3%
sense	3-S 2-O	47.5%	67.5%	77.5%	77.5%	75.0%	72.5%
simple	2-S 2-O 1-B	71.2%	71.2%	75.8%	74.2%	72.7%	71.2%
stress	3-S 2-O	92.1%	92.1%	92.1%	92.1%	92.1%	92.1%
collaborate	1-S 1-O	90.0%	90.0%	93.3%	93.3%	93.3%	90.0%
drive	3-S 5-O 1-B	51.4%	78.4%	89.2%	86.5%	83.8%	78.4%
play	4-S 13-O 1-B	23.3%	40.0%	48.3%	56.7%	41.7%	43.3%
see	7-S 11-O	30.9%	36.8%	58.8%	61.8%	42.6%	38.2%
strike	3-S 10-O 1-B	20.5%	27.3%	43.2%	45.5%	29.5%	38.6%
treat	2-S 4-O	36.4%	61.4%	65.9%	81.8%	56.8%	65.9%
wander	1-S 2-O 1-B	79.2%	81.3%	83.3%	83.3%	81.3%	81.3%
work	2-S 9-O 2-B	56.8%	56.8%	75.0%	75.0%	63.6%	61.4%
appear	1-S 2-O	42.7%	63.4%	80.2%	90.8%	65.6%	66.4%
express	2-S 2-O	81.5%	81.5%	90.7%	88.9%	83.3%	81.5%
hot	3-S 4-O 1-B	85.0%	85.0%	85.0%	85.0%	85.0%	85.0%
image	3-S 4-O	56.7%	83.6%	94.0%	92.5%	85.1%	79.1%
interest	2-S 4-O 1-B	38.7%	73.1%	84.9%	88.2%	74.2%	71.0%
judgment	4-S 3-O	46.9%	65.6%	78.1%	75.0%	68.8%	62.5%
miss	3-S 5-O	50.0%	63.3%	70.0%	66.7%	63.3%	60.0%
solid	4-S 10-O	40.0%	40.0%	44.0%	48.0%	44.0%	44.0%
watch	3-S 4-O	86.3%	86.3%	90.2%	88.2%	86.3%	86.3%
AVERAGE		**57.4%**	**68.5%**	**77.9%**	**80.2%**	**70.7%**	**70.1%**

both subjective and objective uses of the word. For example, both the objective sense (*"physics force that produces strain on a physical body"*) and subjective senses (*"difficulty that causes worry or emotional emotional tension"* and *" a state of mental or emotional strain or suspense"*) of *stress* are often translated as "压力" in Chinese. Second, in some cases, subjectivity word sense disambiguation is too coarse-grained and finer-grained WSD is actually necessary. For example, the subjective usages of *authority* in SENSEVAL examples are often translated as "专家, 权威", "自信" or "可信" (called **List-S**), and objective usages are often translated as "局, 部","当局","权力, 职权" or "授权, 批准" (called **List-O**). In this case, word sense subjectivity might help to distinguish **List-S** from **List-O**, but not among the candidate translations within a single list.

5 Discussion

We tackle cross-lingual lexical substitution as a supervised task, using sets of manual translations for a target word as training data even for baseline system **B**. However, we do not necessarily need dedicated human translated data as we could also use existing parallel texts in which the target word occurs. Therefore, we think that a supervised approach to lexical substitution is feasible. However, we do need additional monolingual sense-tagged data in the source language for incorporating our word sense subjectivity features.[5] Although a disadvantage, more and more sense-tagged data does become available (such as OntoNotes). We also only need tagging at a coarse-grained sense level, which is much easier to create than fine-grained data.

6 Conclusion and Future Work

We investigate the relation between word sense subjectivity and cross-lingual lexical substitution. The experimental results show that incorporating word sense subjectivity into a standard supervised classification model yields a significantly better performance for an English-Chinese lexical substitution task. We also compare the effect of sense subjectivity to the effect of fine-grained sense information on lexical substitution. The differences between the two methods turn out to be small, making a case for the "easier", coarse-grained SWSD over WSD for subjectivity-ambiguous words. Future work will widen the study by (i) looking at a wider range of words and languages, (ii) improving automatic SWSD results for better application and (iii) integrating unsupervised subjectivity features into cross-lingual lexical substitution.

References

Cem Akkaya, Janyce Wiebe, and Rada Mihalcea. 2009. Subjectivity Word Sense Disambiguation. *Proceedings of EMNLP'09.*

Marine Carpuat and Dekai Wu. 2007. Improving Statistical Machine Translation Using Word Sense Disambiguation. *Proceedings of EMNLP'07.*

Yee Seng Chan, Hwee Tou Ng, and David Chiang. 2007. Word Sense Disambiguation Improves Statistical Machine Translation. *Proceedings of ACL'07.*

Diana McCarthy and Roberto Navigli. 2007. SemEval-2007 Task 10: English Lexical Substitution Task. *Proceedings of SemEval-2007.*

Fangzhong Su and Katja Markert. 2008. From Words to Senses: A Case Study in Subjectivity Recognition. *Proceedings of COLING'08.*

Janyce Wiebe and Rada Micalcea. 2006. Word Sense and Subjectivity. *Proceedings of ACL'06.*

[5] In our case, this is the same data as the data the lexical substitution algorithms are trained on, but this is not mandatory.

Query Ambiguity Revisited: Clickthrough Measures for Distinguishing Informational and Ambiguous Queries

Yu Wang
Math & Computer Science Department
Emory University
yu.wang@emory.edu

Eugene Agichtein
Math & Computer Science Department
Emory University
eugene@mathcs.emory.edu

Abstract

Understanding query ambiguity in web search remains an important open problem. In this paper we reexamine query ambiguity by analyzing the result clickthrough data. Previously proposed clickthrough-based metrics of query ambiguity tend to conflate informational and ambiguous queries. To distinguish between these query classes, we introduce novel metrics based on the entropy of the click distributions of individual searchers. Our experiments over a clickthrough log of commercial search engine demonstrate the benefits of our approach for distinguishing informational from truly ambiguous queries.

1 Introduction

Since query interpretation is the first crucial step in the operation of the web search engines, more reliable query intent classification, such as detecting whether a query is ambiguous, could allow a search engine to provide more diverse results, better query suggestions, or otherwise improve user experience.

In this paper we re-examine query ambiguity in connection with searcher clickthrough behavior. That is, we posit that clickthrough information could provide important evidence for classifying query ambiguity. However, we find that previously proposed clickthrough-based measures tend to conflate informational and ambiguous queries. We propose a novel clickthrough measure for query classification, *user click entropy*, and show that it helps distinguish between informational and truly ambiguous queries.

Previous research on this topic focused on binary classification of query ambiguity. Notably, (Teevan et al., 2008) used click entropy as a proxy for query ambiguity to estimate the potential for search personalization. (Mei and Church, 2008) considered click entropy as measure of search difficulty. More broadly, clickthrough information has been used for many other tasks such as improving search ranking (Zhu and Mishne, 2009), learning semantic categories (Komachi et al., 2009), and for topical query classification (Li et al., 2008). However, our work sheds new light on distinguishing between informational and ambiguous queries, by using clickthrough data. Our contributions include:

- More precise definition of query ambiguity in terms of clickthrough behavior (Section 2).
- Entropy-based formalization of resulting click behaviors (Section 3).
- Empirical validation of our methods on a large real query and clickthrough log (Section 4).

2 Defining Query Ambiguity

In this study we focus on two orthogonal query intent dimensions, adapted from the top level of user goal taxonomies such as (Rose and Levinson, 2004). Specifically, a query could be *ambiguous* or *unambiguous*; as well as *informational* or *navigational*. Consider the example queries of each type below:

	Ambiguous	Unambiguous
Informational	"al pacino"	"lyrics"
Navigational	"people"	"google"

The query "al pacino", the name of a famous actor, is a typical ambiguous and informational query. In the clickthrough logs that we examined, the most popular searcher destinations include sites with pictures of Al Pacino, movie sites, and biography sites – corresponding to different informational intents. In contrast, the query "lyrics" has an unambiguous informational intent, which is to explore websites with song lyrics. For the ambiguous navigational query "people", popular destinations include people.com, Yahoo People or People's United Bank. Finally, the

Human Language Technologies: The 2010 Annual Conference of the North American Chapter of the ACL, pages 361–364,
Los Angeles, California, June 2010.

query "google" is unambiguous and navigational, with over 94% of the clicks on the Google's homepage.

Definitions of query classes: we now more formally define the query classes we consider:

- **Clear**: Unambiguous navigational query, such as "google".
- **Informational**: Unambiguous informational query, such as "lyrics"
- **Ambiguous**: Ambiguous informational or navigational query, such as "people" or "al pacino".

The key challenge in distinguishing the last two classes, Informational and Ambiguous, is that the overall clickthrough patterns for these classes are similar: in both cases, there are clicks on many results, without a single dominant result for the query.

3 Clickthrough Measures for Distinguishing Ambiguous and Informational Queries

In this section we describe the features used to represent a query for intent classification, listed in Table 1. In addition to popular features such as clickthrough frequency and query length, we introduce novel features related to user click entropy, to capture the distinction between informational and ambiguous queries.

Overall Entropy: Previous methods for query classification utilize entropy of all result clicks for a query, or overall entropy (the uncertainty associated with obtaining a click on any specific result), defined as:

$$H(R_q) = -\sum_{r \in R_q} p(r) \log p(r)$$

R_q is the set of results r, clicked by all users after submitting the query q. For example, a clear query "target" has the overall entropy of 0.36, and most results corresponding to this query point to Target's company website. The click log data shows that 85% of the users click the Target website for this query. In contrast, an unclear query "lyrics" has the overall entropy of 2.26. However, overall entropy is insufficient for distinguishing between informational and ambiguous queries. To fill this gap, we introduce new clickthrough metrics to detect such ambiguous queries.

User Entropy: Recall, that both informational queries and ambiguous queries could have high overall entropy, making it difficult to distinguish them. Thus, we introduce a new metric, *user entropy of a query q* $H(U_q)$, as the average entropy of a distribution of clicks for each *searcher*:

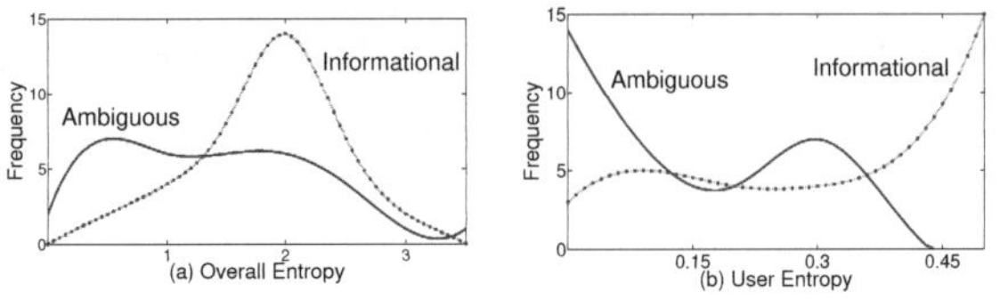

Figure 1: Frequency of ambiguous and informational queries by Overall Entropy (a) and User Entropy (b).

$$H(U_q) = \frac{-\sum_{u \in U_q} \sum_{r \in R_u} p(r) \log p(r)}{|U_q|}$$

where U_q is the set of users who have submitted the query q, and R_u is the set of results r, clicked by the user u. For the example informational query "lyrics", a single user may click many different URLs, thereby increasing user entropy of this query to 0.317. While for an ambiguous query, which has multiple meanings, a user typically searches for only one meaning of this query at a time, so the results clicked by each user will concentrate on one topic. For example, the query "people" is ambiguous, and has the overall entropy of 1.73 due to the variety of URLs clicked. However, a particular user usually clicks only one of the websites, resulting in low *user entropy* of 0.007. Figure 1 illustrates the difference in the distributions of informational and ambiguous queries according to their overall and user entropy values: more informational queries tend to have medium to high User Entropy values, compared to the truly ambiguous queries.

Domain Entropy: One problem with the above measures is that clickthrough data for individual URLs is sparse. A common approach is to *backoff* to the URLs domain, with the assumption that URLs within the same domain usually relate to the same topic or concept. Therefore, domain entropy $H(D_q)$ of a query may be more robust, and is defined as:

$$H(D_q) = -\sum_{d \in D_q} p(d) \log p(d)$$

where D_q are the domains of all URL clicked for q. For example, the query "excite" is a navigational and clear query, as all the different clicked URLs for this query are within the same domain, *excite.com*.

Query Feature	Description
QueryLength	Number of tokens (words) in the query
ClickFrequency	Number of total clicks for this query
OverallEntropy	Entropy of all URLs for this query
UserEntropy*	Average entropy of the URLs clicked by one user for this query
OverallDomainEntropy	Entropy of all URL domains for this query
UserDomainEntropy*	Average entropy of URL domains clicked by one user for this query
RelativeUserEntropy*	Fraction of UserEntropy divided by OverallEntropy
RelativeOverallEntropy*	Fraction of OverallEntropy divided by UserEntropy
RelativeUserDomainEntropy*	Fraction of UserDomainEntropy divided by OverallDomainEntropy
RelativeOverallDomainEntropy*	Fraction of OverallDomainEntropy divided by UserDomainEntropy

Table 1: Features used to represent a query (* indicates features derived from User Entropy).

While this query has high Overall and User Entropy values, the Domain Entropy is low, as all the clicked URLs for this query are within the same domain.

The features described here can then be used as input to many available classifiers. In particular, we use the Weka toolkit[1], as described below.

4 Experimental Results

We describe the dataset and annotation process, and then present and analyze the experimental results.

Dataset: We use an MSN Search query log (from 2006 Microsoft data release) with 15 million queries, from US users, sampled over one month. Queries with click frequency under 10 are discarded. As a result, 84,703 unique queries remained, which form our universe of queries. To separately analyze queries with different frequencies, we divide the queries into three groups: low frequency group (10-100 clicks), medium frequency group (100-1000 clicks) and high frequency group (over 1000 clicks). From each group, we draw a random sample of 50 queries for manual labeling, for the total of 150 queries. Each query was labeled by three members of our lab. The inter-annotator agreeement was 85%, and Cohen's Kappa value was 0.77.

Table 2 reports the distribution of query classes in our dataset. Note that low frequency queries dominate, but are equally represented in the data samples used for classification training and prediction (we will separately analyze performance on different query frequency groups).

Results: Table 3 shows that best classification required User Entropy features. The Weka classifiers were Naive Bayes (NB), Logistic Regression (Logistic), and Support Vector Machines (SVM).

[1]http://www.cs.waikato.ac.nz/ml/weka/

	Clear	Informational	Ambiguous	Frequency (%)
High	76%	8%	16%	255 (0.3%)
Medium	52%	20%	28%	3802 (4.5%)
Low	32%	46%	22%	80646 (95.2%)

Table 2: Frequency distribution of different query types

	All	Clear		Informational		Ambiguous	
	Ac.	Pre.	Rec.	Pre.	Rec.	Pre.	Rec.
All features							
NB	0.72	**0.90**	0.85	**0.77**	0.54	0.42	**0.61**
Logistic	**0.77**	0.84	0.98	0.68	0.73	0.59	0.30
SVM	0.76	0.79	1.00	0.69	0.78	**0.71**	0.15
Without user entropy							
NB	0.73	0.85	0.95	0.63	0.73	0.39	0.21
Logistic	0.73	0.84	0.95	0.63	0.68	0.47	0.27
SVM	0.74	0.79	1.00	0.65	0.76	0.50	0.09

Table 3: Classification performance by query type

	High	Mid	Low		
	Ac.	Ac.	Ac.	Pre.	Rec.
All features					
NB	0.76	0.76	0.74	**0.80**	**0.74**
Logistic	0.78	0.76	0.70	0.68	0.7
SVM	0.78	0.72	**0.79**	0.69	0.72
Without user entropy					
NB	0.80	0.76	0.70	0.66	0.70
Logistic	0.80	**0.82**	0.66	0.63	0.66
SVM	0.80	0.78	0.68	0.62	0.68

Table 4: Classification performance by query frequency

Recall, that low frequency queries dominate our dataset, so we focus on performance of low frequency queries, as reported in Table 4. The respective χ^2 values are reported in (Table 5). The features *UserDomainEntropy* and *UserEntropy* correlate the most with manual query intent labels.

As an alternative to direct multiclass classification described above, we first classify clear vs. unclear queries, and only then attempt to distinguish ambiguous and informational queries (within the un-

Feature	χ^2 *(multiclass)*	χ^2 *(binary)*
UserDomainEntropy	132.9618	23.3629
UserEntropy	128.0111	21.6112
RelativeOverallEntropy	96.6842	20.0255
RelativeUserEntropy	98.6842	20.0255
OverallEntropy	96.1205	0

Table 5: χ^2 values of top five features for *multiclass* classification (*clear* vs. *informational* vs. *ambiguous*) and for and for *binary* classification (*informational* vs. *ambiguous*), given the manual *unclear* label.

	Overall	*Informational*		*Ambiguous*	
	Ac.	Pre.	Rec.	Pre.	Rec.
With User Entropy features					
NB	**0.72**	**0.82**	0.60	0.65	**0.85**
Logistic	0.71	0.74	0.70	0.69	0.73
SVM	0.65	0.64	0.73	0.64	0.55
Without User Entropy features					
NB	0.66	0.65	0.76	0.67	0.55
Logistic	0.68	0.69	0.73	0.68	0.64
SVM	0.68	0.67	**0.81**	**0.72**	0.55

Table 6: Binary classification performance for queries manually labeled as unclear.

clear category). For classification between clear and unclear queries, the accuracy was 90%, precision was 91%, and recall was 90%. The results for subsequently classifying ambiguous vs. information queries are reported in Table 6. For this task, User Entropy features are beneficial, while the χ^2 value or Overall Entropy is 0, supporting our claim that User Entropy is more useful for distinguishing informational from ambiguous queries.

Discussion: Interestingly, User Entropy does not show a large effect on classification of High and Medium frequency queries. However, as Table 2 indicates, High and Medium frequency queries are largely *clear* (76% and 52%, respectively). As discussed above, User Entropy helps classify unclear queries, but there are fewer such queries among the High frequency group, which also tend to have larger click entropy in general.

An *ambiguous* query is difficult to detect when most users interpret it only one way. For instance, query "ako" was annotated as *ambiguous*, as it could refer to different popular websites, such as the site for Army Knowledge Online and the company site for A.K.O., Inc. However, most users select the result for the Army Knowledge Online site, making the overall entropy low, resulting in prediction as a *clear* query. On the positive side, we find that User Entropy helps detect ambiguous queries, such as "laguna beach", which was labeled *ambiguous* as it could refer to both a geographical location and a popular MTV show. As a result, while the Overall Entropy value of the clickthrough is high, the low User Entropy value identifies the query as truly ambiguous and not informational.

In summary, our techniques are of most help for Low frequency queries and moderately helpful for Medium frequency queries. These results are promising, as Low frequency queries make up the majority of queries processed by search engines, and also contain the highest proportion of informational queries, which our techniques can identify.

5 Conclusions

We explored clickthrough-based metrics for distinguishing between ambiguous and informational queries - which, while exhibiting similar *overall* clickthrough distributions, can be more accurately identified by using our User Entropy-based features. We demonstrated substantial improvements for *low-frequency* queries, which are the most frequent in query logs. Hence, our results are likely to have noticeable impact in a real search setting.

Acknowledgments: This work was partially supported by grants from Yahoo! and Microsoft.

References

M. Komachi, S. Makimoto, K. Uchiumi, and M. Sassano. 2009. Learning semantic categories from clickthrough logs. In *Proc. of ACL-IJCNLP*.

X. Li, Y.Y. Wang, and A.Acero. 2008. Learning query intent from regularized click graphs. In *SIGIR*, pages 339–346.

Q. Mei and K. Church. 2008. Entropy of search logs: how hard is search? with personalization? with backoff? In *Proc. of WSDM*, pages 45–54.

D. E. Rose and D. Levinson. 2004. Understanding user goals in web search. In *Proc. of WWW*, pages 13–19.

J. Teevan, S. T. Dumais, and D. J. Liebling. 2008. To personalize or not to personalize: modeling queries with variation in user intent. In *Proc. of SIGIR*, pages 163–170.

G. Zhu and G. Mishne. 2009. Mining rich session context to improve web search. In *Proc. of KDD*, pages 1037–1046.

For the sake of simplicity: Unsupervised extraction of lexical simplifications from Wikipedia

Mark Yatskar, Bo Pang, Cristian Danescu-Niculescu-Mizil and Lillian Lee
my89@cornell.edu, bopang@yahoo-inc.com, cristian@cs.cornell.edu, llee@cs.cornell.edu

Abstract

We report on work in progress on extracting lexical simplifications (e.g., "*collaborate*" → "*work together*"), focusing on utilizing edit histories in Simple English Wikipedia for this task. We consider two main approaches: (1) deriving simplification probabilities via an edit model that accounts for a mixture of different operations, and (2) using metadata to focus on edits that are more likely to be simplification operations. We find our methods to outperform a reasonable baseline and yield many high-quality lexical simplifications not included in an independently-created manually prepared list.

1 Introduction

Nothing is more simple than greatness; indeed, to be simple is to be great. —Emerson, *Literary Ethics*

Style is an important aspect of information presentation; indeed, different contexts call for different styles. Here, we consider an important dimension of style, namely, *simplicity*. Systems that can rewrite text into simpler versions promise to make information available to a broader audience, such as non-native speakers, children, laypeople, and so on.

One major effort to produce such text is the Simple English Wikipedia (henceforth SimpleEW)[1], a sort of spin-off of the well-known English Wikipedia (henceforth ComplexEW) where human editors enforce simplicity of language through rewriting. The crux of our proposal is to learn lexical simplifications from SimpleEW edit histories, thus leveraging the efforts of the 18K pseudonymous individuals who work on SimpleEW. Importantly, not all the changes on SimpleEW are simplifications; we thus also make use of ComplexEW edits to filter out non-simplifications.

Related work and related problems Previous work usually involves general syntactic-level transformation rules [1, 9, 10].[2] In contrast, we explore data-driven methods to learn *lexical simplifications* (e.g., "*collaborate*" → "*work together*"), which are highly specific to the lexical items involved and thus cannot be captured by a few general rules.

Simplification is strongly related to but distinct from paraphrasing and machine translation (MT). While it can be considered a directional form of the former, it differs in spirit because simplification must trade off meaning preservation (central to paraphrasing) against complexity reduction (not a consideration in paraphrasing). Simplification can also be considered to be a form of MT in which the two "languages" in question are highly related. However, note that ComplexEW and SimpleEW do not together constitute a clean parallel corpus, but rather an extremely noisy comparable corpus. For example, Complex/Simple same-topic document pairs are often written completely independently of each other, and even when it is possible to get good sentence alignments between them, the sentence pairs may reflect operations other than simplification, such as corrections, additions, or edit spam.

Our work joins others in using Wikipedia revisions to learn interesting types of directional lexical relations, e.g, "eggcorns"[3] [7] and entailments [8].

2 Method

As mentioned above, a key idea in our work is to utilize SimpleEW edits. The primary difficulty in working with these modifications is that they include not only simplifications but also edits that serve other functions, such as spam removal or correction of grammar or factual content ("fixes"). We describe two main approaches to this problem: a probabilistic model that captures this mixture of different edit operations (§2.1), and the use of *metadata* to filter out undesirable revisions (§2.2).

[1] `http://simple.wikipedia.org`

[2] One exception [5] changes verb tense and replaces pronouns. Other lexical-level work focuses on medical text [4, 2], or uses frequency-filtered WordNet synonyms [3].

[3] A type of lexical corruption, e.g., "acorn"→"eggcorn".

Human Language Technologies: The 2010 Annual Conference of the North American Chapter of the ACL, pages 365–368,
Los Angeles, California, June 2010.

2.1 Edit model

We say that the kth article in a Wikipedia corresponds to (among other things) a title or *topic* (e.g., "Cat") and a sequence $\vec{d_k}$ of article versions caused by successive edits. For a given lexical item or phrase A, we write $A \in \vec{d_k}$ if there is any version in $\vec{d_k}$ that contains A. From each $\vec{d_k}$ we extract a collection $e_k = (e_{k,1}, e_{k,2}, \ldots, e_{k,n_k})$ of *lexical edit instances, repeats allowed*, where $e_{k,i} = A \to a$ means that phrase A in one version was changed to a in the next, $A \neq a$; e.g., "*stands for*" $\to$ "*is the same as*". (We defer detailed description of how we extract lexical edit instances from data to §3.1.) We denote the collection of $\vec{d_k}$ in ComplexEW and SimpleEW as C and S, respectively.

There are at least four possible edit operations: *fix* (o_1), *simplify* (o_2), *no-op* (o_3), or *spam* (o_4). However, for this initial work we assume $P(o_4) = 0$.[4]

Let $P(o_i \mid A)$ be the probability that o_i is applied to A, and $P(a \mid A, o_i)$ be the probability of $A \to a$ given that the operation is o_i. The key quantities of interest are $P(o_2 \mid A)$ in S, which is the probability that A should be simplified, and $P(a \mid A, o_2)$, which yields proper simplifications of A. We start with an equation that models the probability that a phrase A is edited into a:

$$P(a \mid A) = \sum_{o_i \in \Omega} P(o_i \mid A) P(a \mid A, o_i), \quad (1)$$

where Ω is the set of edit operations. This involves the desired parameters, which we solve for by estimating the others from data, as described next.

Estimation Note that $P(a \mid A, o_3) = 0$ if $A \neq a$. Thus, if we have estimates for o_1-related probabilities, we can derive o_2-related probabilities via Equation 1. To begin with, we make the working assumption that occurrences of simplification in ComplexEW are negligible in comparison to fixes. Since we are also currently ignoring edit spam, we thus assume that only o_1 edits occur in ComplexEW.[5]

Let $f_C(A)$ be the fraction of $\vec{d_k}$ in C containing A in which A is modified: $f_C(A) = \frac{|\{\vec{d_k} \in C \mid \exists a, i \text{ such that } e_{k,i} = A \to a\}|}{|\{\vec{d_k} \in C \mid A \in \vec{d_k}\}|}$.

We similarly define $f_S(A)$ on $\vec{d_k}$ in S. Note that we count topics (version sequences), not individual versions: if A appears at some point and is not edited until 50 revisions later, we should *not* conclude that A is unlikely to be rewritten; for example, the intervening revisions could all be minor additions, or part of an edit war.

If we assume that the probability of any particular fix operation being applied in SimpleEW is proportional to that in ComplexEW— e.g., the SimpleEW fix rate might be dampened because already-edited ComplexEW articles are copied over — we have[6]

$$\widehat{P}(o_1 \mid A) = \alpha f_C(A)$$

where $0 \leq \alpha \leq 1$. Note that in SimpleEW,

$$P(o_1 \vee o_2 \mid A) = P(o_1 \mid A) + P(o_2 \mid A),$$

where $P(o_1 \vee o_2 \mid A)$ is the probability that A is changed to a different word in SimpleEW, which we estimate as $\widehat{P}(o_1 \vee o_2 \mid A) = f_S(A)$. We then set

$$\boxed{\widehat{\mathbf{P}}(\mathbf{o_2} \mid \mathbf{A}) = \max(\mathbf{0}, \mathbf{f_S}(\mathbf{A}) - \alpha \mathbf{f_C}(\mathbf{A})).}$$

Next, under our working assumption, we estimate the probability of A being changed to a as a fix by the proportion of ComplexEW edit instances that rewrite A to a:

$$\widehat{P}(a \mid A, o_1) = \frac{|\{(k,i) \text{ pairs} \mid e_{k,i} = A \to a \wedge \vec{d_k} \in C\}|}{\sum_{a'} |\{(k,i) \text{ pairs} \mid e_{k,i} = A \to a' \wedge \vec{d_k} \in C\}|}.$$

A natural estimate for the conditional probability of A being rewritten to a under any operation type is based on observations of $A \to a$ in SimpleEW, since that is the corpus wherein both operations are assumed to occur:

$$\widehat{P}(a \mid A) = \frac{|\{(k,i) \text{ pairs} \mid e_{k,i} = A \to a \wedge \vec{d_k} \in S\}|}{\sum_{a'} |\{(k,i) \text{ pairs} \mid e_{k,i} = A \to a' \wedge \vec{d_k} \in S\}|}.$$

Thus, from (1) we get that for $A \neq a$:

$$\boxed{\widehat{\mathbf{P}}(\mathbf{a} \mid \mathbf{A}, \mathbf{o_2}) = \frac{\widehat{\mathbf{P}}(\mathbf{a} \mid \mathbf{A}) - \widehat{\mathbf{P}}(\mathbf{o_1} \mid \mathbf{A}) \widehat{\mathbf{P}}(\mathbf{a} \mid \mathbf{A}, \mathbf{o_1})}{\widehat{\mathbf{P}}(\mathbf{o_2} \mid \mathbf{A})}.}$$

2.2 Metadata-based methods

Wiki editors have the option of associating a comment with each revision, and such comments sometimes indicate the intent of the revision. We therefore sought to use comments to identify "trusted"

[4]Spam/vandalism detection is a direction for future work.

[5]This assumption also provides useful constraints to EM, which we plan to apply in the future, by reducing the number of parameter settings yielding the same likelihood.

[6]Throughout, "hats" denote estimates.

revisions wherein the extracted lexical edit instances (see §3.1) would be likely to be simplifications.

Let $\vec{r}_k = (r_k^1, \ldots, r_k^i, \ldots)$ be the sequence of revisions for the kth article in SimpleEW, where r_k^i is the set of lexical edit instances ($A \rightarrow a$) extracted from the ith modification of the document. Let c_k^i be the comment that accompanies r_k^i, and conversely, let $R(Set) = \{r_k^i | c_k^i \in Set\}$.

We start with a seed set of trusted comments, $Seed$. To initialize it, we manually inspected a small sample of the 700K+ SimpleEW revisions that bear comments, and found that comments containing a word matching the regular expression *simpl* (e.g, "simplify") seem promising. We thus set $Seed := \{ * \mathsf{simpl} * \}$ (abusing notation).

The SIMPL **method** Given a set of trusted revisions $TRev$ (in our case $TRev = R(Seed)$), we score each $A \rightarrow a \in TRev$ by the point-wise mutual information (PMI) between A and a.[7] We write RANK($TRev$) to denote the PMI-based ranking of $A \rightarrow a \in TRev$, and use SIMPL to denote our most basic ranking method, RANK($R(Seed)$).

Two ideas for bootstrapping We also considered bootstrapping as a way to be able to utilize revisions whose comments are not in the initial $Seed$ set.

Our first idea was to iteratively expand the set of trusted comments to include those that most often accompany already highly ranked simplifications. Unfortunately, our initial implementations involved many parameters (upper and lower comment-frequency thresholds, number of highly ranked simplifications to consider, number of comments to add per iteration), making it relatively difficult to tune; we thus omit its results.

Our second idea was to iteratively expand the set of trusted revisions, adding those that contain already highly ranked simplifications. While our initial implementation had fewer parameters than the method sketched above, it tended to terminate quickly, so that not many new simplifications were found; so, again, we do not report results here.

An important direction for future work is to differentially weight the edit instances within a revision, as opposed to placing equal trust in all of them; this could prevent our bootstrapping methods from giving common fixes (e.g., "*a*" → "*the*") high scores.

3 Evaluation[8]

3.1 Data

We obtained the revision histories of both SimpleEW (November 2009 snapshot) and ComplexEW (January 2008 snapshot). In total, ~1.5M revisions for 81733 SimpleEW articles were processed (only 30% involved textual changes). For ComplexEW, we processed ~16M revisions for 19407 articles.

Extracting lexical edit instances. For each article, we aligned sentences in each pair of adjacent versions using tf-idf scores in a way similar to Nelken and Shieber [6] (this produced satisfying results because revisions tended to represent small changes). From the aligned sentence pairs, we obtained the aforementioned lexical edit instances $A \rightarrow a$. Since the focus of our study was not word alignment, we used a simple method that identified the longest differing segments (based on word boundaries) between each sentence, except that to prevent the extraction of entire (highly non-matching) sentences, we filtered out $A \rightarrow a$ pairs if either A or a contained more than five words.

3.2 Comparison points

Baselines RANDOM returns lexical edit instances drawn uniformly at random from among those extracted from SimpleEW. FREQUENT returns the most frequent lexical edit instances extracted from SimpleEW.

Dictionary of simplifications The SimpleEW editor "Spencerk" (Spencer Kelly) has assembled a list of simple words and simplifications using a combination of dictionaries and manual effort[9]. He provides a list of 17,900 simple words — words that do not need further simplification — and a list of 2000 transformation pairs. We did not use Spencerk's set as the gold standard because many transformations we found to be reasonable were not on his list. Instead, we measured our agreement with the list of transformations he assembled (SPLIST).

[7]PMI seemed to outperform raw frequency and conditional probability.

[8]Results at http://www.cs.cornell.edu/home/llee/data/simple

[9]http://www.spencerwaterbed.com/soft/simple/about.html

3.3 Preliminary results

The top 100 pairs from each system (edit model[10] and SIMPL and the two baselines) plus 100 randomly selected pairs from SPLIST were mixed and all presented in random order to three native English speakers and three non-native English speakers (all non-authors). Each pair was presented in random orientation (i.e., either as $A \rightarrow a$ or as $a \rightarrow A$), and the labels included "simpler", "more complex", "equal", "unrelated", and "?" ("hard to judge"). The first two labels correspond to simplifications for the orientations $A \rightarrow a$ and $a \rightarrow A$, respectively. Collapsing the 5 labels into "simplification", "not a simplification", and "?" yields reasonable agreement among the 3 native speakers ($\kappa = 0.69$; 75.3% of the time all three agreed on the same label). While we postulated that non-native speakers[11] might be more sensitive to what was simpler, we note that they disagreed more than the native speakers ($\kappa = 0.49$) and reported having to consult a dictionary. The native-speaker majority label was used in our evaluations.

Here are the results; "-x-y" means that x and y are the number of instances discarded from the precision calculation for having no majority label or majority label "?", respectively:

Method	Prec@100	# of pairs
SPLIST	86% (-0-0)	2000
Edit model	77% (-0-1)	1079
SIMPL	66% (-0-0)	2970
FREQUENT	17% (-1-7)	-
RANDOM	17% (-1-4)	-

Both baselines yielded very low precisions — clearly not all (frequent) edits in SimpleEW were simplifications. Furthermore, the edit model yielded higher precision than SIMPL for the top 100 pairs. (Note that we only examined one simplification per A for those A where $\widehat{P}(o_2 \mid A)$ was well-defined; thus "# of pairs" does not directly reflect the full potential recall that either method can achieve.) Both, however, produced many high-quality pairs (62% and 71% of the *correct* pairs) *not* included in SPLIST. We also found the pairs produced by these two systems to be complementary to each other. We believe that these two approaches provide a good starting point for further explorations.

Finally, some examples of simplifications found by our methods: "*stands for*" $\rightarrow$ "*is the same as*", "*indigenous*" $\rightarrow$ "*native*", "*permitted*" $\rightarrow$ "*allowed*", "*concealed*" $\rightarrow$ "*hidden*", "*collapsed*" $\rightarrow$ "*fell down*", "*annually*" $\rightarrow$ "*every year*".

3.4 Future work

Further evaluation could include comparison with machine-translation and paraphrasing algorithms. It would be interesting to use our proposed estimates as initialization for EM-style iterative re-estimation. Another idea would be to estimate *simplification priors* based on a model of inherent lexical complexity; some possible starting points are number of syllables (which is used in various readability formulae) or word length.

Acknowledgments We first wish to thank Ainur Yessenalina for initial investigations and helpful comments. We are also thankful to R. Barzilay, T. Bruce, C. Callison-Burch, J. Cantwell, M. Dredze, C. Napoles, E. Gabrilovich, & the reviewers for helpful comments; W. Arms and L. Walle for access to the Cornell Hadoop cluster; J. Cantwell for access to computational resources; R. Hwa & A. Owens for annotation software; M. Ulinski for preliminary explorations; J. Cantwell, M. Ott, J. Silverstein, J. Yatskar, Y. Yatskar, & A. Yessenalina for annotations. Supported by NSF grant IIS-0910664.

References

[1] R. Chandrasekar, B. Srinivas. Automatic induction of rules for text simplification. *Knowledge-Based Systems*, 1997.

[2] L. Deléger, P. Zweigenbaum. Extracting lay paraphrases of specialized expressions from monolingual comparable medical corpora. *Workshop on Building and Using Comparable Corpora*, 2009.

[3] S. Devlin, J. Tait. The use of a psycholinguistic database in the simplification of text for aphasic readers. In *Linguistic Databases*, 1998.

[4] N. Elhadad, K. Sutaria. Mining a lexicon of technical terms and lay equivalents. *Workshop on BioNLP*, 2007.

[5] B. Beigman Klebanov, K. Knight, D. Marcu. Text simplification for information-seeking applications. *OTM Conferences*, 2004.

[6] R. Nelken, S. M. Shieber. Towards robust context-sensitive sentence alignment for monolingual corpora. *EACL*, 2006.

[7] R. Nelken, E. Yamangil. Mining Wikipedia's article revision history for training computational linguistics algorithms. *WikiAI*, 2008.

[8] E. Shnarch, L. Barak, I. Dagan. Extracting lexical reference rules from Wikipedia. *ACL*, 2009.

[9] A. Siddharthan, A. Nenkova, K. McKeown. Syntactic simplification for improving content selection in multi-document summarization. *COLING*, 2004.

[10] D. Vickrey, D. Koller. Sentence simplification for semantic role labeling/ *ACL*, 2008.

[10] We only considered those A such that $freq(A \rightarrow *) > 1 \wedge freq(A) > 100$ on both SimpleEW and ComplexEW. The final top 100 $A \rightarrow a$ pairs were those with As with the highest $P(o_2 \mid A)$. We set $\alpha = 1$.

[11] Native languages: Russian; Russian; Russian and Kazakh.

Predicting Human-Targeted Translation Edit Rate via Untrained Human Annotators

Omar F. Zaidan and **Chris Callison-Burch**
Dept. of Computer Science, Johns Hopkins University
Baltimore, MD 21218, USA
{ozaidan,ccb}@cs.jhu.edu

Abstract

In the field of machine translation, automatic metrics have proven quite valuable in system development for tracking progress and measuring the impact of incremental changes. However, human judgment still plays a large role in the context of *evaluating* MT systems. For example, the GALE project uses human-targeted translation edit rate (HTER), wherein the MT output is scored against a post-edited version of itself (as opposed to being scored against an existing human reference). This poses a problem for MT researchers, since HTER is not an easy metric to calculate, and would require hiring and training human annotators to perform the editing task. In this work, we explore soliciting those edits from *untrained* human annotators, via the online service Amazon Mechanical Turk. We show that the collected data allows us to predict HTER-ranking of documents at a significantly higher level than the ranking obtained using automatic metrics.

1 Introduction

In the early days of machine translation (MT), it was typical to evaluate MT output by soliciting judgments from human subjects, such as evaluating the fluency and adequacy of MT output (LDC, 2005). While this approach was appropriate (indeed desired) for evaluating a system, it was not a practical means of tracking the progress of a system during its development, since collecting human judgments is both costly and time-consuming. The introduction of automatic metrics like BLEU contributed greatly to MT research, for instance allowing researchers to measure and evaluate the impact of small modifications to an MT system.

However, manual evaluation remains a core component of system evaluation. Teams on the GALE project, a DARPA-sponsored MT research program, are evaluated using the HTER metric, which is a version of TER whereby the output is scored against a post-edited version of itself, instead of a preexisting reference. Moreover, emphasis is placed on performing well across all documents and across all genres. Therefore, it is important for a research team to be able to evaluate their system using HTER, or at least determine the ranking of the documents according to HTER, for purposes of error analysis. Instead of hiring a human translator and training them, we propose moving the task to the virtual world of Amazon's Mechanical Turk (AMT), hiring workers to edit the MT output and predict HTER from those edits. We show that edits collected this way are better at predicting document ranking than automatic metrics, and furthermore that it can be done at a low cost, both in terms of time and money.

The paper is organized as follows. We first discuss options available to predict HTER, such as automatic metrics. We then discuss the possibility of relying on human annotators, and the inherent difficulty in training them, before discussing the concept of soliciting edits over AMT. We detail the task given to the workers and summarize the data that we collected, then show how we can combine their data to obtain significanly better rank predictions of documents.

2 Human-Targeted TER

Translation edit rate (TER) measures the number of edits required to transform a hypothesis into an appropriate sentence in terms of grammaticality and meaning (Snover et al., 2006). While TER usually scores a hypothesis against an existing reference sentence, *human-targeted* TER scores a hypothesis against a post-edited version of itself.

Human Language Technologies: The 2010 Annual Conference of the North American Chapter of the ACL, pages 369–372,
Los Angeles, California, June 2010.

While HTER has been shown to correlate quite well with human judgment of MT quality, it is quite challenging to obtain HTER scores for MT output, since this would require hiring and training human subjects to perform the editing task. Therefore, other metrics such as BLEU or TER are used as proxies for HTER.

2.1 Amazon's Mechanical Turk

The high cost associated with hiring and training a human editor makes it difficult to imagine an alternative to automatic metrics. However, we propose soliciting edits from workers on Amazon's Mechanical Turk (AMT). AMT is a virtual marketplace where "requesters" can post tasks to be completed by "workers" (aka *Turkers*) around the world. Two main advantages of AMT are the pre-existing infrastructure, and the low cost of completing tasks, both in terms of time and money. Data collected over AMT has already been used in several papers such as Snow et al. (2008) and Callison-Burch (2009).

When a requester creates a task to be completed over AMT, it is typical to have completed by more than one worker. The reason is that the use of AMT for data collection has an inherent problem with data quality. A requester has fewer tools at their disposal to ensure workers are doing the task properly (via training, feedback, etc) when compared to hiring annotators in the 'real' world. Those redundant annotations are therefore collected to increase the likelihood of at least one submission from a faithful (and competent) worker.

2.2 AMT for HTER

The main idea it to mimic the real-world HTER setup by supplying workers with the original MT output that needs to be edited. The worker is also given a human reference, produced independently from the MT output. The instructions ask the worker to modify the MT output, using as few edits as possible, to match the human reference in meaning and grammaticality.

The submitted edited hypothesis can then be used as the reference for calculating HTER. The idea is that, with this setup, a competent worker would be able to closely match the editing behavior of the professionally trained editor.

3 The Datasets

We solicited edits of the output from one of GALE's teams on the Arabic-to-English task. This MT output was submitted by this team and HTER-scored by LDC-hired human translators. Therefore, we already had the edits produced by a professional translator. These edits were used as the "gold-standard" to evaluate the edits solicited from AMT and to evaluate our methods of combining Turkers' submissions.

The MT output is a translation of more than 2,153 Arabic segments spread across 195 documents in 4 different genres: broadcast conversations (BC), broadcast news (BN), newswire (NW), and blogs (WB). Table 1 gives a summary of each genre's dataset.

Genre	# docs	Segs/doc	Words/seg
BC	40	15.8	28.3
BN	48	9.6	36.1
NW	54	8.7	39.5
WB	53	11.1	31.6

Table 1: The 4 genres of the dataset.

For each of the 2,153 MT output segments, we collected edits from 5 distinct workers on AMT, for a total of 10,765 post-edited segments by a total of about 500 distinct workers.[1] The segments were presented in 1,210 groups of up to 15 segments each, with a reward of \$0.25 per group. Hence the total rewards to workers was around \$300, at a rate of 36 post-edited segments per dollar (or 2.8 pennies per segment).

4 What are we measuring?

We are interested in predicting the ranking the documents according to HTER, not necessarily predicting the HTER itself (though of course attempting to predict the latter accurately is the cornerstone of our approach to predict the former). To measure the quality of a predicted ranking, we use Spearman's rank correlation coefficient, ρ, where we first convert the raw scores into ranks and then use the following formula to measure correlation:

$$\rho(X,Y) = 1 - \frac{6\sum_{i=1}^{n}(rank(x_i) - rank(y_i))^2}{n(n^2-1)}$$

[1] Data available at `http://cs.jhu.edu/~ozaidan/hter`.

where n is the number of documents, and each of X and Y is a vector of n HTER scores.

Notice that values for ρ range from −1 to 1, with +1 indicating perfect rank correlation, −1 perfect inverse correlation, and 0 no correlation. That is, for a fixed X, the best-correlated Y is that for which $\rho(X,Y)$ is highest.

5 Combining Tukers' Edits

Once we have collected edits from the human workers, how should we attempt to predict HTER from them? If we could assume that all Turkers are doing the task faithfully (and doing it adequately), we should use the annotations of the worker performing the least amount of editing, since that would mirror the real-life scenario.

However, data collected from AMT should be treated with caution, since a non-trivial portion of the collected data is of poor quality. Note that this does not necessarily indicate a 'cheating' worker, for even if a worker is acting in good faith, they might not be able to perform the task adequately, due to misunderstanding the task, or neglecting to attempt to use a small number of edits.

And so we need to combine the redundant edits in an intelligent manner. Recall that, given a segment, we collected edits from multiple workers. Some baseline methods include taking the minimum over the edits, taking the median, and taking the average.

Once we start thinking of averages, we should consider taking a *weighted* average of the edits for a segment. The weight associated with a worker should reflect our confidence in the quality of that worker's edits. But how can we evaluate a worker in the first place?

5.1 Self Verification of Turkers

We have available "gold-standard" editing behavior for the segments, and we treat a small portion of the segments edited by a Turker as a verification dataset. On that portion, we evaluate how closely the Turker matches the LDC editor, and weight them accordingly when predicting the number of edits of the rest of that group's segments. Specifically, the Turker's weight is the absolute difference between the Turker's edit count and the professional editor's edit count.

Notice that we are not simply interested in a worker whose edited submission closely matches the edited submission of the professional translator. Rather, we are interested in mirroring the professional translator's edit *rate*. That is, the closer a Turker's edit *rate* is to the LDC editor's, the more we should prefer the worker. This is a subtle point, but it is indeed possible for a Turker to have similar edit rate as the LDC editor but still require a large number of edits to get the LDC editor's submission itself.

6 Experiments

We examine the effectiveness of any of the above methods by comparing the resulting document ranking versus the desired ranking by HTER. In addition to the above methods, we use a baseline a ranking predicted by TER to a human reference. (For clarity, we omit discussion with other metrics such as BLEU and (TER–BLEU)/2, since those baselines are not as strong as the TER baseline.

6.1 Experimental Setup

We examine each genre individually, since genres vary quite a bit in difficulty, and, more importantly, we care about the internal ranking within each genre, to mirror the GALE evaluation procedure.

We examine the effect of varying the amount of data by which we judge a Turker's data quality. The amount of this "verification" data is varied as a percentage of the total available segments. Those segments are chosen at random, and we perform 100 trials for each point.

6.2 Experimental Results

Figure 1 shows the rank correlations for various methods across different sizes of verification subsets. Notice that some methods, such as the TER baseline, have horizontal lines, since these do not rate a Turker based on a verification subset.

It is worth noting that the oracle performs very well. This is an indication that predicting HTER accurately is mostly a matter of identifying the best worker. While oracle scenarios usually represent unachievable upper bounds, keep in mind that there are only a very small number of editors per segment (five, as opposed to oracle scenarios dealing with 100-best lists, etc).

Other than that, in general, it is possible to achieve very high rank correlation using Turkers' data, significantly outperforming the TER ranking, even with a small verification subset. The genres do vary quite a bit in difficulty for Turkers, with BC and especially NW being quite difficult, though in the case of NW for instance, this is due to the human reference doing quite well to begin with, rather than Turkers performing poorly.

7 Conclusions and Future Work

We proposed soliciting edits of MT output via Amazon's Mechanical Turk and showed we can predict ranking significantly better than an automatic metric. The next step is to explicitly identify undesired worker behavior, such as not editing the MT output at all, or using the human reference as is instead of editing the MT output. This can be detected by not limiting our verification to comparing behavior to the professional editor's, but also by comparing submitted edits to the MT output itself and to the human reference. In other words, a worker's submission could be characterized in terms of its distance to the MT output and to the human reference, thus building a complete 'profile' of the worker, and adding another component to guard against poor data quality and to reward the desired behavior.

Acknowledgments

This work was supported by the EuroMatrixPlus Project (funded by the European Commission), and by the DARPA GALE program under Contract No. HR0011-06-2-0001. The views and findings are the authors' alone.

References

Chris Callison-Burch. 2009. *Fast, Cheap, and Creative: Evaluating Translation Quality Using Amazon's Mechanical Turk.* In Proceedings of EMNLP.

LDC. 2005. *Linguistic data annotation specification: Assessment of fluency and adequacy in translations.* Revision 1.5.

Matthew Snover, Bonnie J. Dorr, Richard Schwartz. 2006. *A Study of Translation Edit Rate with Targeted Human Annotation.* Proceedings of AMTA.

Rion Snow, Brendan O'Connor, Daniel Jurafsky, and Andrew Y. Ng. 2008. *Cheap and fast – but is it good? Evaluating non-expert annotations for natural language tasks.* In Proceedings of EMNLP.

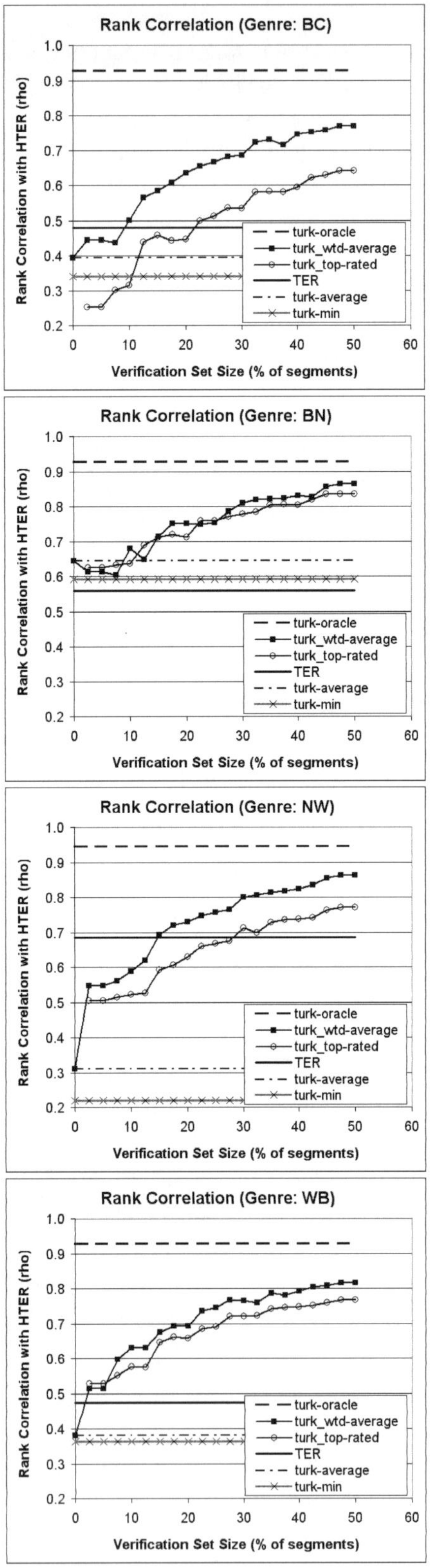

Figure 1: Rank correlation between predicted ranking and HTER ranking for different prediction schemes, across the four genres, and across various sizes of the worker verification set.

Improving Semantic Role Classification with Selectional Preferences

Beñat Zapirain, Eneko Agirre
IXA NLP Group
Basque Country Univ.
{benat.zapirain,e.agirre}@ehu.es

Lluís Màrquez
TALP Research Center
Technical Univ. of Catalonia
lluism@lsi.upc.edu

Mihai Surdeanu
Stanford NLP Group
Stanford Univ.
mihais@stanford.edu

Abstract

This work incorporates Selectional Preferences (SP) into a Semantic Role (SR) Classification system. We learn separate selectional preferences for noun phrases and prepositional phrases and we integrate them in a state-of-the-art SR classification system both in the form of features and individual class predictors. We show that the inclusion of the refined SPs yields statistically significant improvements on both in domain and out of domain data (14.07% and 11.67% error reduction, respectively). The key factor for success is the combination of several SP methods with the original classification model using meta-classification.

1 Introduction

Semantic Role Labeling (SRL) is the process of extracting simple event structures, i.e., "who" did "what" to "whom", "when" and "where". Current systems usually perform SRL in two pipelined steps: argument *identification* and argument *classification*. While identification is mostly syntactic, classification requires semantic knowledge to be taken into account. Semantic information is usually captured through lexicalized features on the predicate and the head–word of the argument to be classified. Since lexical features tend to be sparse, SRL systems are prone to overfit the training data and generalize poorly to new corpora.

Indeed, the SRL evaluation exercises at CoNLL-2004 and 2005 (Carreras and Màrquez, 2005) observed that all systems showed a significant performance degradation ($\sim$10 F_1 points) when applied to test data from a different genre of that of the training set. Pradhan et al. (2008) showed that this performance degradation is essentially caused by the argument classification subtask, and suggested the lexical data sparseness as one of the main reasons. The same authors studied the contribution of the different feature types in SRL and concluded that the lexical features were the most salient features in argument classification (Pradhan et al., 2007).

In recent work, we showed (Zapirain et al., 2009) how automatically generated selectional preferences (SP) for verbs were able to perform better than pure lexical features in a role classification experiment, disconnected from a full-fledged SRL system. SPs introduce semantic generalizations on the type of arguments preferred by the predicates and, thus, they are expected to improve results on infrequent and unknown words. The positive effect was especially relevant for out-of-domain data. In this paper we advance (Zapirain et al., 2009) in two directions:
(1) We learn separate SPs for prepositions and verbs, showing improvement over using SPs for verbs alone.
(2) We integrate the information of several SP models in a state-of-the-art SRL system (SwiRL[1]) and show significant improvements in SR classification. The key for the improvement lies in a meta-classifier, trained to select among the predictions provided by several role classification models.

2 SPs for SR Classification

SPs have been widely believed to be an important knowledge source when parsing and performing SRL, especially role classification. Still, present parsers and SRL systems use just lexical features, which can be seen as the most simple form of SP,

[1] http://www.surdeanu.name/mihai/swirl/

Human Language Technologies: The 2010 Annual Conference of the North American Chapter of the ACL, pages 373–376,
Los Angeles, California, June 2010.

where the headword needs to be seen in the training data, and otherwise the SP is not satisfied. Gildea and Jurafsky (2002) showed barely significant improvements in semantic role classification of NPs for FrameNet roles using distributional clusters. In (Erk, 2007) a number of SP models are tested in a pseudo-task related to SRL. More recently, we showed (Zapirain et al., 2009) that several methods to automatically generate SPs generalize well and outperform lexical match in a large dataset for semantic role classification, but the impact on a full system was not explored.

In this work we apply a subset of the SP methods proposed in (Zapirain et al., 2009). These methods can be split in two main families, depending on the resource used to compute similarity: WordNet-based methods and distributional methods. Both families define a similarity score between a word (the headword of the argument to be classified) and a set of words (the headwords of arguments of a given role).

WordNet-based similarity: One of the models that we used is based on Resnik's similarity measure (1993), referring to it as res. The other model is an in-house method (Zapirain et al., 2009), referred as wn, which only takes into account the depth of the most common ancestor, and returns SPs that are as specific as possible.

Distributional similarity: Following (Zapirain et al., 2009) we considered both first order and second order similarity. In first order similarity, the similarity of two words was computed using the cosine (or Jaccard measure) of the co-occurrence vectors of the two words. Co-occurrence vectors where constructed using freely available software (Padó and Lapata, 2007) run over the British National Corpus. We used the optimal parameters (Padó and Lapata, 2007, p. 179). We will refer to these similarities as sim_{cos} and sim_{Jac}, respectively. In contrast, second order similarity uses vectors of similar words, i.e., the similarity of two words was computed using the cosine (or Jaccard measure) between the thesaurus entries of those words in Lin's thesaurus (Lin, 1998). We refer to these as sim^2_{cos} and sim^2_{Jac}.

Given a target sentence with a verb and its arguments, the task of SR classification is to assign the correct role to each of the arguments. When using SPs alone, we only use the headwords of the arguments, and each argument is classified independently of the rest. For each headword, we select the role (r) of the verb (c) which fits best the head word (w), where the goodness of fit ($SP_{sim}(v, r, w)$) is modeled using one of the similarity models above, between the headword w and the headwords seen in training data for role r of verb v. This selection rule is formalized as follows:

$$R_{sim}(v, w) = \arg \max_{r \in Roles(v)} SP_{sim}(v, r, w) \quad (1)$$

In our previous work (Zapirain et al., 2009), we modelled SPs for pairs of predicates (verbs) and arguments, independently of the fact that the argument is a core argument (typically a noun) or an adjunct argument (typically a prepositional phrase). In contrast, (Litkowski and Hargraves, 2005) show that prepositions have SPs of their own, especially when functioning as adjuncts. We therefore decided to split SPs according to whether the potential argument is a Prepositional Phrase (PP) or a Noun Phrase (NP). For NPs, which tend to be core arguments[2], we use the SPs of the verb (as formalized above). For PPs, which have an even distribution between core and adjunct arguments, we use the SPs of the prepositions alone, ignoring the verbs. Implementation wise, this means that in Eq. (1), we change v for p, where p is the preposition heading the PP.

3 Experiments with SPs in isolation

In this section we evaluate the use of SPs for classification in isolation, i.e., we use formula 1, and no other information. In addition we contrast the use of both verb-role and preposition-role SPs, as compared to the use of verb-role SPs alone.

The dataset used in these experiments (and in Section 4) is the same as provided by the CoNLL-2005 shared task on SRL (Carreras and Màrquez, 2005). This dataset comprises several sections of the PropBank corpus (news from the WSJ) as well as an extract of the Brown Corpus. Sections 02-21 are used for generating the SPs and training, Section 00 for development, and Section 23 for testing, as customary. The Brown Corpus is used for out-of-domain testing, but due to the limited size of the provided section, we extended it with instances from SemLink[3]. Since the focus of this work is on argument

[2]In our training data, NPs are adjuncts only 5% of the times
[3]`http://verbs.colorado.edu/semlink/`

	Verb-Role SPs						Preposition-Role and Verb-Role SPs					
	WSJ-test			Brown			WSJ-test			Brown		
	prec.	rec.	F_1	prec.	rec.	F_1	prec.	rec.	F_1	prec.	rec.	F_1
lexical	**70.75**	26.66	39.43	**59.39**	05.51	10.08	**82.98**	43.77	57.31	**68.47**	13.60	22.69
SP_{res}	45.07	37.11	40.71	36.34	27.58	31.33	63.47	53.24	57.91	55.12	44.15	49.03
SP_{wn}	55.44	45.58	50.03	41.76	31.58	35.96	65.70	63.88	64.78	60.08	48.10	53.43
$SP_{sim_{Jac}}$	48.85	46.38	47.58	42.10	34.34	37.82	61.83	61.40	61.61	55.42	53.45	54.42
$SP_{sim_{cos}}$	53.13	50.44	51.75	43.24	35.27	38.85	64.67	64.22	64.44	56.56	54.54	55.53
$SP_{sim^2_{Jac}}$	61.76	**58.63**	**60.16**	51.97	**42.39**	**46.69**	70.82	**70.33**	**70.57**	62.37	**60.15**	**61.24**
$SP_{sim^2_{cos}}$	61.12	58.12	59.63	51.92	42.35	46.65	70.28	69.80	70.04	62.36	60.14	61.23

Table 1: Results for SPs in isolation, left for verb SPs, and right both preposition and verb SPs.

Labels proposed by the base models
Number of base models that proposed this datum's label
List of actual base models that proposed this datum's label

Table 2: Features of the binary meta-classifier.

classification, we use the gold PropBank data to identify argument boundaries. Considering that SPs can handle only nominal arguments, in these experiments we used only arguments mapped to NPs and PPs containing a nominal head. From the training sections, we extracted over 140K such arguments for the supervised generation of SPs. The development and test sections contain over 5K and 8K examples, respectively, and the portion of the Brown Corpus comprises an amount of 8.1K examples.

Table 1 lists the results of the different SPs in isolation. The results reported in the left part of Table 1 are comparable to those we reported in (Zapirain et al., 2009). The differences are due to the fact that we do not discard roles like MOD, DIS, NEG and that our previous work used only the subset of the data that could be mapped to VerbNet (around 50%). All in all, the table shows that splitting SPs into verb and preposition SPs yields better results, both in precision and recall, improving F_1 up to 10 points in some cases.

4 Integrating SPs in a SRL system

For these experiments we modified SwiRL (Surdeanu et al., 2007): (a) we matched the gold boundaries against syntactic constituents predicted internally using the Charniak parser (Charniak, 2000); and (b) we classified these constituents with their semantic role using a modified version of SwiRL's feature set.

We explored two different strategies for integrating SPs in SwiRL. The first, obvious method is to extend SwiRL's feature set with features that model the preferences of the SPs, i.e., for each SP model SP_i we add a feature whose value is R_i. The second method combines SwiRL's classification model and our SP models using meta-classification. We opted for a binary classification approach: first, for each constituent we generate n datums, one for each distinct role label proposed by the pool of base models; then we use a binary meta-classifier to label each candidate role as correct or incorrect. Table 2 lists the features of the meta-classifier. We trained the meta-classifier on the usual PropBank training partition, using cross-validation to generate outputs for the base models that require the same training material. At prediction time, for each candidate constituent we selected the role label that was classified as correct with the highest confidence.

Table 3 compares the performance of both combination approaches against the standalone SwiRL classifier. We show results for both core arguments (Core), adjunct arguments (Arg) and all arguments combined (All). In the table, the SwiRL+SP_* models stand for SwiRL classifiers enhanced with one feature from the corresponding SP. Adding more than one SP-based feature to SwiRL did not improve results. Our conjecture is that the SwiRL classifier enhanced with SP-based features does not learn relevant weights for these features because their signal is "drowned" by SwiRL's large initial feature set and the correlation between the different SPs. This observation motivated the development of the meta-classifier. The meta-classifier shown in the table combines the output of the SwiRL+SP_* models with the predictions of SP models used in isolation. We implemented the meta-classifier using Support Vector Machines (SVM)[4] with a quadratic polynomial kernel, and

[4] http://svmlight.joachims.org

	WSJ-test			Brown		
	Core	Adj	All	Core	Adj	All
SwiRL	93.25	81.31	90.83	84.42	57.76	79.52
$+SP_{Res}$	93.17	81.08	90.76	84.52	59.24	79.86
$+SP_{wn}$	92.88	81.11	90.56	84.26	59.69	79.73
$+SP_{sim_{Jac}}$	93.37	80.30	90.86	84.43	59.54	79.83
$+SP_{sim_{cos}}$	93.33	80.92	90.87	85.14	60.16	80.50
$+SP_{sim^2_{Jac}}$	93.03	82.75	90.95	85.62	59.63	80.75
$+SP_{sim^2_{cos}}$	93.78	80.56	91.23	84.95	61.01	80.48
Meta	**94.37**	**83.40**	**92.12**	**86.20**	**63.40**	**81.91**

Table 3: Classification accuracy for the combination approaches. $+SP_x$ stands for SwiRL plus each SP model.

$C = 0.01$ (tuned in development).

Table 3 indicates that four out of the six SwiRL+SP_* models perform better than SwiRL in domain (WSJ-test), and all of them outperform SwiRL out of domain (Brown). However, the improvements are small and, generally, not statistically significant. On the other hand, the meta-classifier outperforms SwiRL both in domain (14.07% error reduction) and out of domain (11.67% error reduction), and the differences are statistically significant (measured using two-tailed paired t-test at 99% confidence interval on 100 samples generated using bootstrap resampling). We also implemented two unsupervised voting baselines, one unweighted (each base model has the same weight) and one weighted (each base model is weighted by its accuracy in development). However, none of these baselines outperformed the standalone SwiRL classifier. This is further proof that, for SR classification, meta-classification is crucial because it can learn the distinct specializations of the various base models.

Finally, Table 3 shows that our approach yields consistent improvements for both core and adjunct arguments. Out of domain, we see a bigger accuracy improvement for adjunct arguments (5.64 absolute points) vs. core arguments (1.78 points). This is to be expected, as most core arguments fall under the Arg0 and Arg1 classes, which can typically be disambiguated based on syntactic information, i.e., subject vs. object. On the other hand, there are no syntactic hints for adjunct arguments, so the system learns to rely more on SP information in this case.

5 Conclusions

This paper is the first work to show that SPs improve a state-of-the-art SR classification system. Several decisions were crucial for success: (a) we deployed separate SP models for verbs and prepositions, which in conjunction outperform SP models for verbs alone; (b) we incorporated SPs into SR classification using a meta-classification approach that combines eight base models, developed from variants of a state-of-the-art SRL system and the above SP models. We show that the resulting system outperforms the original SR classification system for arguments mapped to nominal or prepositional constituents. The improvements are statistically significant both on in-domain and out-of-domain data sets.

Acknowledgments

This work was partially supported by projects KNOW-2 (TIN2009-14715-C04-01 / 04), KYOTO (ICT-2007-211423) and OpenMT-2 (TIN2009-14675C03)

References

X. Carreras and L. Màrquez. 2005. Introduction to the CoNLL-2005 Shared Task: Semantic role labeling. In *Proc. of CoNLL*.

E. Charniak. 2000. A maximum-entropy-inspired parser. In *Proc. of NAACL*.

K. Erk. 2007. A simple, similarity-based model for selectional preferences. In *Proc. of ACL*.

D. Gildea and D. Jurafsky. 2002. Automatic labeling of semantic roles. *Computational Linguistics*, 28(3).

D. Lin. 1998. Automatic retrieval and clustering of similar words. In *Proc. of COLING-ACL*.

K. Litkowski and O. Hargraves. 2005. The preposition project. In *Proceedings of the Workshop on The Linguistic Dimensions of Prepositions and their Use in Computational Linguistic Formalisms and Applications*.

S. Padó and M. Lapata. 2007. Dependency-based construction of semantic space models. *Computational Linguistics*, 33(2).

S. Pradhan, W. Ward, and J. Martin. 2007. Towards robust semantic role labeling. In *Proc. of NAACL-HLT*.

S. Pradhan, W. Ward, and J. Martin. 2008. Towards robust semantic role labeling. *Computational Linguistics*, 34(2).

P. Resnik. 1993. Semantic classes and syntactic ambiguity. In *Proc. of HLT*.

M. Surdeanu, L. Màrquez, X. Carreras, and P.R. Comas. 2007. Combination strategies for semantic role labeling. *Journal of Artificial Intelligence Research*, 29.

B. Zapirain, E. Agirre, and L. Màrquez. 2009. Generalizing over lexical features: Selectional preferences for semantic role classification. In *Proc. of ACL-IJCNLP*.

Generalizing Syntactic Structures for Product Attribute Candidate Extraction

Yanyan Zhao, Bing Qin, Shen Hu, Ting Liu
Harbin Institute of Technology, Harbin, China
{yyzhao,bqin,shu,tliu}@ir.hit.edu.cn

Abstract

Noun phrases (NP) in a product review are always considered as the product attribute candidates in previous work. However, this method limits the recall of the product attribute extraction. We therefore propose a novel approach by generalizing syntactic structures of the product attributes with two strategies: intuitive heuristics and syntactic structure similarity. Experiments show that the proposed approach is effective.

1 Introduction

Product attribute extraction is a fundamental task of sentiment analysis. It aims to extract the product attributes from a product review, such as "picture quality" in the sentence "The picture quality of Canon is perfect." This task is usually performed in two steps: product attribute candidate extraction and candidate classification.

Almost all the previous work pays more attention to the second step, fewer researchers make in-depth research on the first step. They simply choose the NPs in a product review as the product attribute candidates (Hu and Liu, 2004; Popescu and Etzioni, 2005; Yi et al., 2003). However, this method limits the recall of the product attribute extraction for two reasons. First, there exist other structures of the product attributes except NPs. Second, the syntactic parsing is not perfect, especially for the Non-English languages, such as Chinese. Experiments on three Chinese datasets[1] show that nearly 15% product attributes are lost, when only using NPs as the candidates. Obviously, if using the candidate classification techniques on these NP candidates, it would lead to poor performance (especially for recall) for the final product attribute extraction.

Based on the above discussion, it can be observed that product attribute candidate extraction is well worth studying. In this paper, we propose an approach by generalizing the *syntactic structures* of the product attributes to solve this problem. Figure 1 lists some syntactic structure samples from an annotated corpus, including the special forms of NPs in Figure 1(a) and other syntactic structures, such as VP or IP in Figure 1(b). We can find that the syntactic structures can not only cover more phrase types besides NP, but also describe the detailed forms of the product attributes.

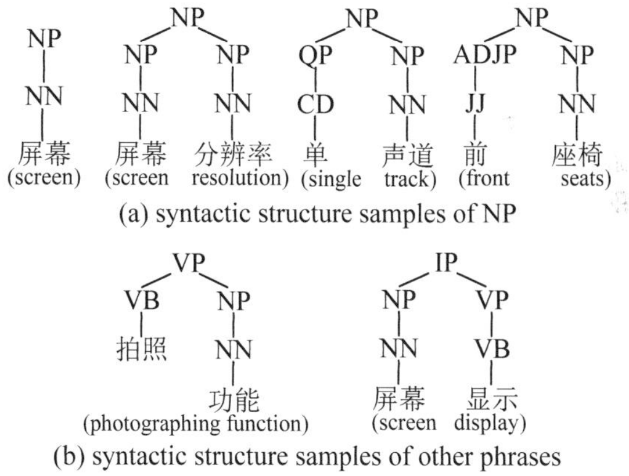

Figure 1: Syntactic structure samples of the product attributes (acquired by an automatic phrase parser).

In order to exploit more and useful syntactic structures, two generalization strategies: intuitive heuristics and syntactic structure similarity are used. Experiments on three Chinese domain-specific datasets show that our approach can significantly improve the recall of the product attribute candidate extraction, and furthermore, improve the performance of the final product attribute extraction.

[1] It refers to the training data in Section 3.1.

Human Language Technologies: The 2010 Annual Conference of the North American Chapter of the ACL, pages 377–380,
Los Angeles, California, June 2010.

2 Approach

The standard syntactic structures of the product attributes can be collected from a training set[2]. Then a simple method of *exact matching* can be used to select the product attribute candidates from the test set. In particular, for a syntactic structure[3] T in the test set, if T exactly matches with one of the standard syntactic structures, then its corresponding string can be treated as a product attribute candidate.

However, this method fails to handle similar syntactic structures, such as the two structures in Figure 2. Besides, this method treats the syntactic structure as a whole during exact matching, without considering any structural information. Therefore, it is difficult to describe the syntactic structure information explicitly. All of these prevent this method from generalizing unseen data well.

To overcome the above problems, two generalization strategies are proposed in this paper. One is to generalize the syntactic structures with two intuitive heuristics. The other is to deeply mine the syntactic structure by decomposing it into several substructures. Both strategies will be introduced in the following subsections.

2.1 Intuitive Heuristics

Two intuitive heuristics are adopted to generalize the syntactic structures.

Heu1: For the near-synonymic grammar tags in syntactic structures, we can generalize them by a normalized one. Such as the red boxes in Figure 2, the POSs "NNS" and "NN" show the same syntactic meaning, we can generalize "NNS" with "NN". The near-synonymic grammar tags are listed in Table 1.

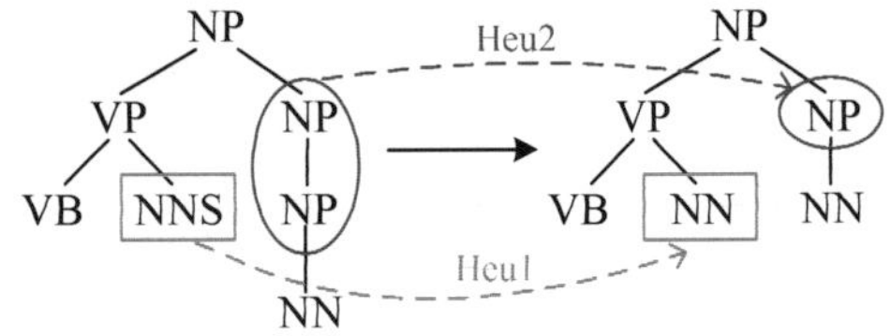

Figure 2: Generalizing a syntactic structure with two intuitive heuristics.

Heu2: For the sequence of identical grammar tags in syntactic structures, we can replace them with one. The reason is that the sequential grammar tags always describe the same syntactic function as one grammar tag. Such as the blue circles in Figure 2.

Replaced by	Near-synonymic grammar tags
JJ	JJR, JJS
NN	NNS, NNP, NNPS, CD, NR
RB	RBR, RBS
VB	VBD, VBG, VBN, VBP, VBZ, VV
S	SBAR, SBARQ, SINU, SQ

Table 1: The near-synonymic grammar tags.

2.2 Syntactic Structure Similarity

The heuristic generalization strategy is too restrictive to give a good coverage. Moreover, after this kind of generalization, the syntactic structure is used as a whole in exact matching all the same. Thus, as an alternative to the exact matching, tree kernel based methods can be used to implicitly explore the substructures of the syntactic structure in a high-dimensional space. This kind of methods can directly calculate the similarity between two substructure vectors using a kernel function. Tree kernel based methods are effective in modeling structured features, which are widely used in many natural language processing tasks, such as syntactic parsing (Collins and Duffy, 2001) and semantic role labeling (Che et al., 2008) and so on.

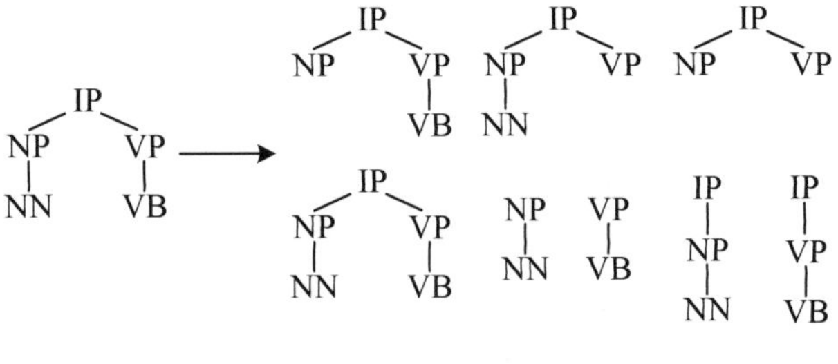

Figure 3: Substructures from a syntactic structure.

In this paper, the syntactic structure for a product attribute can be decomposed into several substructures, such as in Figure 3. Correspondingly, the syntactic structure T can be represented by a vector of integer counts of each substructure type:

$$\begin{aligned}\Phi(T) &= (\phi_1(T), \phi_2(T), ..., \phi_n(T)) \\ &= (\text{\# of substructures of type } 1, \\ &= \text{\# of substructures of type } 2, \\ &\quad ..., \\ &= \text{\# of substructures of type } n)\end{aligned}$$

[2]We use Dan Bikel's phrase parser for syntactic parsing.

[3]We simply select the syntactic structures of the strings under three words or four words with "的"("of" in English).

After syntactic structure decomposition, we can count the number of the common substructures as the similarity between two syntactic structures. The commonly used convolution tree kernel is applied in this paper. Its kernel function is defined as follows:

$$K(T_1, T_2) = \langle \Phi(T_1), \Phi(T_2) \rangle = \sum_i (\phi_i(T_1) \cdot \phi_i(T_2))$$

Based on these, for a syntactic structure T in the test set, we can compute the similarity between T and all the standard syntactic structures by the above kernel function. A similarity threshold th_{sim}[4] is set to determine whether the string from T is a correct product attribute candidate.

3 Experiments

3.1 Datasets and Evaluation Metrics

Three domain-specific datasets are used in the experiments, which is from an official Chinese Opinion Analysis Evaluation 2008 (COAE2008) (Zhao et al., 2008). Table 2 shows the statistics of the three datasets, each of which is divided into training, development and test data in a proportion of 2:1:1.

Domain	# of sentences	# of standard product attributes
Camera	1,780	1,894
Car	2,166	2,504
Phone	2,196	2,293

Table 2: The datasets for three product domains.

Two evaluation metrics, recall and noise ratio, are designed to evaluate the performance of the product attribute candidate extraction. Recall refers to the proportion of correctly identified attribute candidates in all standard product attributes. Noise ratio refers to the proportion of incorrectly identified attribute candidates in all candidates.

3.2 Comparative methods

We choose the method, which considers NPs as the product attribute candidates, as the baseline (shown as **NPs_based**).

Besides, in order to assess the two generalization strategies' effectiveness, four experiments are designed as follows:

[4]In the experiments, th_{sim} is set to 0.7, which is tuned on the development set.

SynStru_based: It refers to the syntactic structure exact matching method, which is implemented without the two proposed generation strategies.

SynStru_*h*: It refers to the strategy only using the first generalization.

SynStru_*kernel*: It refers to the strategy only using the second generalization.

SynStru_*h+kernel*: It refers to the strategy using both two generalizations, i.e., it refers to our approach in this paper.

3.3 Results

Table 3 lists the comparative performances on the test data between our approach and the comparative methods for product attribute candidate extraction.

Domain	Method	Recall	Noise ratio
Camera	NPs_based	81.20%	63.64%
	SynStru_based	84.80%	67.67%
	SynStru_*h*	92.08%	74.74%
	SynStru_*kernel*	92.51%	75.92%
	SynStru_*h+kernel*	92.72%	76.25%
Car	NPs_based	85.25%	69.35%
	SynStru_based	86.31%	72.66%
	SynStru_*h*	93.78%	78.01%
	SynStru_*kernel*	94.56%	79.50%
	SynStru_*h+kernel*	94.71%	80.44%
Phone	NPs_based	84.11%	63.76%
	SynStru_based	86.26%	67.09%
	SynStru_*h*	93.13%	73.62%
	SynStru_*kernel*	93.47%	75.11%
	SynStru_*h+kernel*	93.63%	75.35%

Table 3: Comparisons between our approach and the comparative methods for product attribute candidate extraction.

Analyzing the recalls in Table 3, we can find that:

1. The performance of SynStru_based method is better than NPs_based method for each domain. This can illustrate that syntactic structures can cover more forms of the product attributes. However, the recall of SynStru_based method is not high, either.

2. The two generalization strategies, SynStru_*h* and SynStru_*kernel* can both significantly improve the performance for each domain, comparing to the SynStru_based method. This can illustrate that our two generalization strategies are helpful.

3. Our approach SynStru_*h+kernel* achieves the best performance. This can illustrate that the two generalization strategies are complementary to each

other. And further, mining and generalizing the syntactic structures is effective for candidate extraction.

However, the noise ratio for each domain is increasing when employing our approach. That's because, more kinds of syntactic structures are considered, more noise is added. However, we can easily remove the noise in the candidate classification step. Thus in the next section, we will assess our candidate extraction approach by applying it to the product attribute extraction task.

4 Application in Product Attribute Extraction

For the extracted product attribute candidates, we train a maximum entropy (ME) based binary classifier to find the correct product attributes. Several commonly used features are listed in Table 4.

Feature	Description
lexical	the words of the product attribute(PA)
	the POS for each word of the PA
	three words before the PA
	three words after the PA
	the words' number of the PA
syntactic	the syntactic structure of the PA
binary (Y/N)	Is there a stop word in the PA?
	Is there a polarity word in the PA?
	Is there an English word or number in the PA?

Table 4: The feature set for product attribute extraction.

Table 5 shows the product attribute extraction performances on the test data. We can find that the performance (F1) of our approach is better than NPs_based method for each domain. We discuss the results as follows:

1. Comparing to the NPs_based method, the recall of our approach increases a lot for each domain. This demonstrates that generalized syntactic structures can cover more forms of product attributes.

2. Comparing to the NPs_based method, the precision of our approach also increases for each domain. That's because syntactic structures are more specialized than the phrase forms (such as NP, VP) in the previous work, which can filter some noises from the phrase(NP) candidates.

5 Conclusion

This paper describes a simple but effective way to extract the product attribute candidates from product reviews. The proposed approach is based on deep analysis into syntactic structures of the product attributes, via intuitive heuristics and syntactic structure decomposition. Experimental results indicate that our approach is promising. In future, we will try more syntactic structure generalization strategies.

Domain	Method	R (%)	P (%)	F1 (%)
Camera	NPs_based	59.62	68.38	63.70
	Our approach	62.96	73.32	67.74
Car	NPs_based	59.94	64.87	62.31
	Our approach	67.34	65.90	66.61
Phone	NPs_based	58.53	71.14	64.22
	Our approach	67.84	76.13	71.74

Table 5: Comparisons between our approach and the NPs_based method for product attribute extraction.

Acknowledgments

This work was supported by National Natural Science Foundation of China (NSFC) via grant 60803093, 60975055, and the "863" National High- Tech Research and Development of China via grant 2008AA01Z144.

References

Wanxiang Che, Min Zhang, AiTi Aw, Chew Lim Tan, Ting Liu, and Sheng Li. 2008. Using a hybrid convolution tree kernel for semantic role labeling. *ACM Trans. Asian Lang. Inf. Process.*, 7(4).

Michael Collins and Nigel Duffy. 2001. Convolution kernels for natural language. In *NIPS*, pages 625–632.

Minqing Hu and Bing Liu. 2004. Mining opinion features in customer reviews. In *Proceedings of AAAI-2004*, pages 755–760.

Ana-Maria Popescu and Oren Etzioni. 2005. Extracting product features and opinions from reviews. In *hltemnlp2005*, pages 339–346.

Jeonghee Yi, Tetsuya Nasukawa, Razvan Bunescu, and Wayne Niblack. 2003. Sentiment analyzer: Extracting sentiments about a given topic using natural language processing techniques. In *Proceedings of the IEEE International Conference on Data Mining*.

Jun Zhao, Hongbo Xu, Xuanjing Huang, Songbo Tan, Kang Liu, and Qi Zhang. 2008. Overview of chinese opinion analysis evaluation 2008.

"cba to check the spelling"
Investigating Parser Performance on Discussion Forum Posts

Jennifer Foster
National Centre for Language Technology
School of Computing
Dublin City University
jfoster@computing.dcu.ie

Abstract

We evaluate the Berkeley parser on text from an online discussion forum. We evaluate the parser output with and without gold tokens and spellings (using Sparseval and Parseval), and we compile a list of problematic phenomena for this domain. The Parseval f-score for a small development set is 77.56. This increases to 80.27 when we apply a set of simple transformations to the input sentences and to the Wall Street Journal (WSJ) training sections.

1 Introduction

Parsing techniques have recently become efficient enough for parsers to be used as part of a pipeline in a variety of tasks. Another recent development is the rise of user-generated content in the form of blogs, wikis and discussion forums. Thus, it is both interesting and necessary to investigate the performance of NLP tools trained on edited text when applied to unedited Web 2.0 text. McClosky et al. (2006) report a Parseval f-score decrease of 5% when a WSJ-trained parser is applied to Brown corpus sentences. In this paper, we move even further from the WSJ by investigating the performance of the Berkeley parser (Petrov et al., 2006) on user-generated content.

We create gold standard phrase structure trees for the posts on two threads of the same online discussion forum. We then parse the sentences in one thread, our development set, with the Berkeley parser under three conditions: 1) when it performs its own tokenisation, 2) when it is provided with gold tokens and 3) when misspellings in the input have been corrected. A qualitative evaluation is then carried out on parser output under the third condition. Based on this evaluation, we identify some "low-hanging fruit" which we attempt to handle either by transforming the input sentence or by transforming the WSJ training material. The success of these transformations is evaluated on our development and test sets, with encouraging results.

2 Parser Evaluation Experiments

Data Our data consists of sentences that occur on the BBC Sport 606 Football discussion forum. The posts on this forum are quite varied, ranging from throwaway comments to more considered essay-like contributions. The development set consists of 42 posts (185 sentences) on a thread discussing a controversial refereeing decision in a soccer match.[1] The test set is made up of 40 posts (170 sentences) on a thread discussing a player's behaviour in the same match.[2] The average sentence length in the development set is 18 words and the test set 15 words. Tokenisation and spelling correction were carried out by hand on the sentences in both sets.[3] They were then parsed using Bikel's parser (Bikel, 2004) and corrected by hand using the Penn Treebank Bracketing Guidelines (Bies et al., 1995).

Parser The Berkeley parser is an unlexicalised phrase structure parser which learns a latent variable PCFG by iteratively splitting the treebank non-

[1] http://www.bbc.co.uk/dna/606/F15264075?thread=7065503&show=50

[2] http://www.bbc.co.uk/dna/606/F15265997?thread=7066196&show=50

[3] Note that abbreviated forms such as *cos* which are typical of computer-mediated communication are not corrected.

Human Language Technologies: The 2010 Annual Conference of the North American Chapter of the ACL, pages 381–384,
Los Angeles, California, June 2010.

terminals, estimating rule probabilities for the new grammar using EM and merging the less useful splits. We train a PCFG from WSJ2-21 by carrying out five cycles of the split-merge process (SM5).

Tokenisation and Spelling Effects In the first experiment, the parser is given the original development set sentences which contain spelling mistakes and which have not been tokenised. We ask the parser to perform its own tokenisation. In the second experiment, the parser is given the hand-tokenised sentences which still contain spelling mistakes. These are corrected for the third experiment.

Since the yields of the parser output and gold trees are not guaranteed to match exactly, we cannot use the `evalb` implementation of the Parseval evaluation metrics. Instead we use Sparseval (Roark et al., 2006), which was designed to be used to evaluate the parsing of *spoken* data and can handle this situation. An unaligned dependency evaluation is carried out: head-finding rules are used to convert a phrase structure tree into a dependency graph. Precision and recall are calculated over the dependencies

The Sparseval results are shown in Table 1. For the purposes of comparison, the WSJ23 performance is displayed in the top row. We can see that performance suffers when the parser performs its own tokenisation. A reason for this is the under-use of apostrophes in the forum data, with the result that words such as *didnt* and *im* remain untokenised and are tagged by the parser as common nouns:

(NP (NP (DT the) (NNS refs)) (SBAR (S (NP (NN ***didnt****))*
(VP want to make it to obvious))))

To properly see the effect of the 39 spelling errors on parsing accuracy, we factor out the mismatches between the correctly spelled words in the reference set and their incorrectly spelled equivalents. We do this by evaluating against a version of the gold standard which contains the original misspellings (third row). We can see that the effect of spelling errors is quite small. The Berkeley parser's mechanism for handling unknown words makes use of suffix information and it is able to ignore many of the content word spelling errors. It is the errors in function words that appear to cause a greater problem:

(NP (DT the) (JJ zealous) (NNS fans) ***(NN whpo)*** *(NN care) (JJR more))*

Test Set	R	P	F
WSJ 23	88.66	88.66	88.66
Football	68.49	70.74	69.60
Football Gold Tokens	71.54	73.25	72.39
Ft Gold Tok (misspelled gold)	73.49	75.25	74.36
Football Gold Tokens+Spell	73.94	75.59	74.76

Table 1: **Sparseval** scores for Berkeley SM5

Test Set	R	P	F
WSJ 23	88.88	89.46	89.17
Football Gold Tokens+Spell	78.15	76.97	77.56

Table 2: **Parseval** scores for Berkeley SM5

Gold Tokens and Spelling Leaving aside the problems of automatic tokenisation and spelling correction, we focus on the results of the third experiment. The Parseval results are given in Table 2. Note that the performance degradation is quite large, more than has been reported for the Charniak parser on the Brown corpus. We examine the parser output for each sentence in the development set. The phenomena which lead the parser astray are listed in Table 3. One problem is coordination which is difficult for parsers on in-domain data but which is exacerbated here by the omission of conjunctions, the use of a comma as a conjunction and the tendency towards unlike constituent coordination.

Parser Comparison We test the lexicalised Charniak parser plus reranker (Charniak and Johnson, 2005) on the development set sentences. We also test the Berkeley parser with an SM6 grammar. The f-scores are shown in Table 4. The parser achieving the highest score on WSJ23, namely, the C&J reranking parser, also achieves the highest score on our development set. The difference between the two Berkeley grammars supports the claim that an SM6 grammar overfits to the WSJ (Petrov and Klein, 2007). However, the differences between the four parser/grammar configurations are small.

Parser	WSJ23	Football
Berkeley SM5	89.17	77.56
Berkeley SM6	89.56	77.01
Charniak First-Stage	89.13	77.13
C & J Reranking	91.33	78.33

Table 4: Cross-parser and cross-grammar comparison

Problematic Phenomena	Examples
Idioms/Fixed Expressions	*Spot on* `(S (VP (VB Spot) (PP (IN on))) (. .))`

Acronyms	*lmao*
	`(S (NP (PRP you))`
	`(VP (VBZ have) (RB n't) (VP (VBN done)`
	`(NP (ADVP (RB that) (RB once)) (DT this) (NN season))`
	`(NP (NN lmao)))))`

Missing subject	*Does n't change the result though*
	`(SQ (VBZ Does) (RB n't) (NP (NN change))`
	`(NP (DT the) (NN result)) (ADVP (RB though)) (. !))`

Lowercase proper nouns	*paul scholes* `(NP (JJ paul) (NNS scholes))`

Coordination	*Very even game and it's sad that...*
	`(S (ADVP (RB Very))`
	`(NP (NP (JJ even) (NN game)) (CC and) (NP (PRP it)))`
	`(VP (VBZ 's) (ADJP (JJ sad)) (SBAR (IN that)...`

Adverb/Adjective Confusion	*when playing bad*
	`(SBAR (WHADVP (WRB when))`
	`(S (VP (VBG playing) (ADJP (JJ bad)))))`

CAPS LOCK IS ON	*YOU GOT BEATEN BY THE BETTER TEAM*
	`(S (NP (PRP YOU)) (VP (VBP GOT) (NP (NNP BEATEN)`
	`(NNP BY) (NNP THE) (NNP BETTER) (NNP TEAM))))`

cos instead of *because*	*or it was cos you lost*
	`(VP (VBD was) (ADJP (NN cos)`
	`(SBAR (S (NP (PRP you)) (VP (VBD lost))))))`

Table 3: Phenomena which lead the parser astray. The output of the parser is given for each example.

3 Initial Improvements

Parsing performance on noisy data can be improved by transforming the input data so that it resembles the parser's training data (Aw et al., 2006), transforming the training data so that it resembles the input data (van der Plas et al., 2009), applying semi-supervised techniques such as the self-training protocol used by McClosky et al. (2006), and changing the parser internals, e.g. adapting the parser's unknown word model to take into account variation in capitalisation and function word misspelling.[4]

We focus on the first two approaches and attempt to transform both the input data and the WSJ training material. The transformations that we experiment with are shown in Table 5. The treebank transformations are performed in such a way that their frequency distribution mirrors their distribution in the development data. We remove discourse-marking acronyms such as *lol*[5] from the input sentence, but do not attempt to handle acronyms which are integrated into the sentence.[6]

We examine the effect of each transformation on development set parsing performance and discard those which do not improve performance. We keep all the input sentence transformations and those treebank transformations which affect lexical rules, i.e. changing the endings on adverbs and changing the first character of proper nouns. The treebank transformations which delete subject pronouns and coordinating conjunctions are not as effective. They work in individual cases, e.g. the original analysis of the sentence *Will be here all day* is
(S (NP (NNP Will)) (VP be here all day) (. .))
After applying the treebank transformation, it is
(S (VP (MD Will) (VP be here all day)) (. .))
Their overall effect is, however, negative. It is likely that, for complex phenomena such as coordination and subject ellipsis, the development set is still too small to inform how much of and in what way the original treebank should be transformed. The results of applying the effective transformations to the development set and the test set are shown in Table 6.

[4]Even when spelling errors have been corrected, unknown words are still an issue: 8.5% of the words in the football development set do not occur in WSJ2-21, compared to 3.6% of the words in WSJ23.

[5]In a study of teenage instant messaging, Tagliamonte and Dennis (2008) found that forms such as *lol* are not as ubiquitous as is commonly perceived. Although only occurring a couple of times in our data, they are problematic for the parser.

[6]An example is: *your loss to Wigan would be more scrutunized (**cba** to check spelling) than it has been this year*

Input Sentence
cos $\rightarrow$ *because*
Sentences consisting of all uppercase characters converted to standard capitalisation *DEAL WITH IT* $\rightarrow$ *Deal with it*
Remove certain acronyms *lol* $\rightarrow \epsilon$
Treebank
Delete subject noun phrases when the subject is a pronoun *(S (NP (PRP It)) (VP (VBD arrived)...* $\longrightarrow$ *(S (VP (VBD arrived)...*
Delete or replace conjunctions with a comma (for sentence coordination) *(S ...) (CC and) (S ...)* $\longrightarrow$ *(S ...) (, ,) (S ...)* OR *(S ...) (CC and) (S ...)* $\longrightarrow$ *(S ...) (S ...)*
Delete *ly* from adverbs *(VP (VBD arrived) (ADVP (RB quickly)))* $\longrightarrow$ *(VP (VBD arrived) (ADVP (RB quick)))*
Replace uppercase first character in proper nouns *(NP (NP (NNP Warner) (POS 's)) (NN price))* $\longrightarrow$ *(NP (NP (NNP warner) (POS 's)) (NN price))*

Table 5: Input Sentence and Treebank Transformations

Configuration	Recall	Precision	F-Score
Baseline Dev	78.15	76.97	77.56
Transformed Dev	80.83	79.73	80.27
Baseline Test	77.61	79.14	78.37
Transformed Test	80.10	79.77	79.93

Table 6: Effect of transformations on dev and test set

The recall and precision improvements on the development set are statistically significant ($p < 0.02$), as is the recall improvement on the test set ($p < 0.05$).

4 Conclusion

Ongoing research on the problem of parsing unedited informal text has been presented. At the moment, because of the small size of the data sets and the variety of writing styles in the development set, only tentative conclusions can be drawn. However, even this small data set reveals clear problems for WSJ-trained parsers: the handling of long coordinated sentences (particularly in the presence of erratic punctuation usage), domain-specific fixed expressions and unknown words. We have presented some preliminary experimental results using simple transformations to both the input sentence and the parser's training material. Treebank transformations need to be more thoroughly explored with use made of the Switchboard corpus as well as the WSJ.

Acknowledgments

Thanks to the reviewers and to Emmet Ó Briain, Deirdre Hogan, Adam Bermingham, Joel Tetreault.

References

AiTi Aw, Min Zhang, Juan Xiao, and Jian Su. 2006. A phrase-based statistical model for SMS text normalisation. In *Proceedings of the 21st COLING/44th ACL.*

Ann Bies, Mark Ferguson, Karen Katz, and Robert MacIntyre. 1995. Bracketing guidelines for Treebank II style, Penn Treebank Project. Technical Report Tech Report MS-CIS-95-06, University of Pennsylvania.

Daniel Bikel. 2004. Intricacies of Collins Parsing Model. *Computational Linguistics*, 30(4):479–511.

Eugene Charniak and Mark Johnson. 2005. Course-to-fine n-best-parsing and maxent discriminative reranking. In *Proceedings of the 43rd ACL.*

David McClosky, Eugene Charniak, and Mark Johnson. 2006. Reranking and self-training for parser adaptation. In *Proceedings of the 21st COLING/44th ACL.*

Slav Petrov and Dan Klein. 2007. Improved inference for unlexicalized parsing. In *Proceedings of HLT NAACL 2007.*

Slav Petrov, Leon Barrett, Romain Thibaux, and Dan Klein. 2006. Learning accurate, compact and interpretable tree annotation. In *Proceedings of the 21st COLING and the 44th ACL.*

Brian Roark, Mary Harper, Eugene Charniak, Bonnie Dorr, Mark Johnson, Jeremy G. Kahn, Yang Liu, Mari Ostendorf, John Hale, Anna Krasnyanskaya, Matthew Lease, Izhak Shafran, Matthew Snover, Robin Stewart, and Lisa Yung. 2006. SParseval: Evaluation metrics for parsing speech. In *Proceedings of LREC.*

Sali A. Tagliamonte and Derek Dennis. 2008. Linguistic ruin? LOL! Instant messaging and teen language. *American Speech*, 83(1).

Lonneke van der Plas, James Henderson, and Paola Merlo. 2009. Domain adaptation with artificial data for semantic parsing of speech. In *Proceedings of HLT NAACL 2009, Companion Volume: Short Papers.*

Coreference Resolution in a Modular, Entity-Centered Model

Aria Haghighi
Computer Science Division
University of California, Berkeley
aria42@cs.berkeley.edu

Dan Klein
Computer Science Division
University of California, Berkeley
klein@cs.berkeley.edu

Abstract

Coreference resolution is governed by syntactic, semantic, and discourse constraints. We present a generative, model-based approach in which each of these factors is modularly encapsulated and learned in a primarily unsupervised manner. Our semantic representation first hypothesizes an underlying set of latent *entity types*, which generate specific entities that in turn render individual mentions. By sharing lexical statistics at the level of abstract entity types, our model is able to substantially reduce semantic compatibility errors, resulting in the best results to date on the complete end-to-end coreference task.

1 Introduction

Coreference systems exploit a variety of information sources, ranging from syntactic and discourse constraints, which are highly configurational, to semantic constraints, which are highly contingent on lexical meaning and world knowledge. Perhaps because configurational features are inherently easier to learn from small data sets, past work has often emphasized them over semantic knowledge.

Of course, all state-of-the-art coreference systems have needed to capture semantic compatibility to some degree. As an example of nominal headword compatibility, a "president" can be a "leader" but cannot be not an "increase." Past systems have often computed the compatibility of specific headword pairs, extracted either from lexical resources (Ng, 2007; Bengston and Roth, 2008; Rahman and Ng, 2009), web statistics (Yang et al., 2005), or surface syntactic patterns (Haghighi and Klein, 2009). While the pairwise approach has high precision, it is neither realistic nor scalable to explicitly enumerate all pairs of compatible word pairs. A more compact approach has been to rely on named-entity recognition (NER) systems to give coarse-grained entity types for each mention (Soon et al., 1999; Ng and Cardie, 2002). Unfortunately, current systems use small inventories of types and so provide little constraint. In general, coreference errors in state-of-the-art systems are frequently due to poor models of semantic compatibility (Haghighi and Klein, 2009).

In this work, we take a primarily unsupervised approach to coreference resolution, broadly similar to Haghighi and Klein (2007), which addresses this issue. Our generative model exploits a large inventory of distributional entity types, including standard NER types like PERSON and ORG, as well as more refined types like WEAPON and VEHICLE. For each type, distributions over typical heads, modifiers, and governors are learned from large amounts of unlabeled data, capturing type-level semantic information (e.g. "spokesman" is a likely head for a PERSON). Each entity inherits from a type but captures entity-level semantic information (e.g. "giant" may be a likely head for the Microsoft entity but not all ORGs). Separately from the type-entity semantic module, a log-linear discourse model captures configurational effects. Finally, a mention model assembles each textual mention by selecting semantically appropriate words from the entities and types.

Despite being almost entirely unsupervised, our model yields the best reported end-to-end results on a range of standard coreference data sets.

2 Key Abstractions

The key abstractions of our model are illustrated in Figure 1 and described here.

Mentions: A mention is an observed textual reference to a latent real-world entity. Mentions are as-

Human Language Technologies: The 2010 Annual Conference of the North American Chapter of the ACL, pages 385–393,
Los Angeles, California, June 2010.

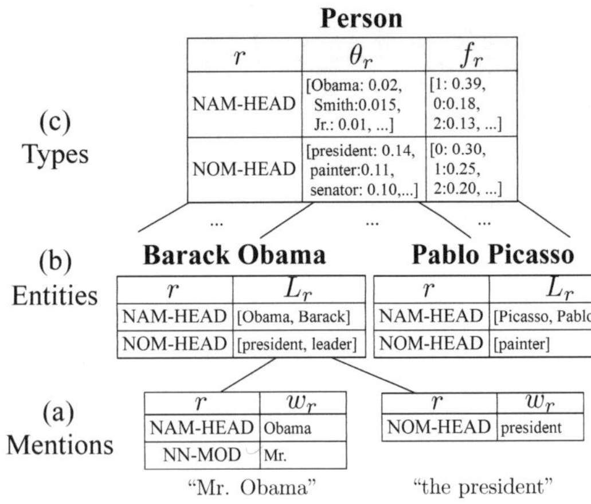

Figure 1: The key abstractions of our model (Section 2). (a) Mentions map properties (r) to words (w_r). (b) Entities map properties (r) to word lists (L_r). (c) Types map properties (r) to distributions over property words (θ_r) and the fertilities of those distributions (f_r). For (b) and (c), we only illustrate a subset of the properties.

sociated with nodes in a parse tree and are typically realized as NPs. There are three basic forms of mentions: proper (denoted NAM), nominal (NOM), and pronominal (PRO). We will often describe proper and nominal mentions together as *referring* mentions.

We represent each mention M as a collection of key-value pairs. The keys are called *properties* and the values are words. For example, the left mention in Figure 1(a) has a proper head property, denoted NAM-HEAD, with value "Obama." The set of properties we consider, denoted $\mathcal{R}$, includes several varieties of heads, modifiers, and governors (see Section 5.2 for details). Not every mention has a value for every property.

Entities: An entity is a specific individual or object in the world. Entities are always latent in text. Where a mention has a single word for each property, an entity has a *list* of signature words. Formally, entities are mappings from properties $r \in \mathcal{R}$ to lists L_r of "canonical" words which that entity uses for that property. For instance in Figure 1(b), the list of nominal heads for the Barack Obama entity includes "president."

Types: Coreference systems often make a mention / entity distinction. We extend this hierarchy to include *types*, which represent classes of entities (PERSON, ORGANIZATION, and so on). Types allow the sharing of properties across entities and mediate the generation of entities in our model (Section 3.1). See Figure 1(c) for a concrete example.

We represent each type τ as a mapping between properties r and pairs of multinomials (θ_r, f_r). Together, these distributions control the lists L_r for entities of that type. θ_r is a unigram distribution of words that are semantically licensed for property r. f_r is a "fertility" distribution over the integers that characterizes entity list lengths. For example, for the type PERSON, θ_r for proper heads is quite flat (there are many last names) but f_r is peaked at 1 (people have a single last name).

3 Generative Model

We now describe our generative model. At the parameter level, we have one parameter group for the types $\boldsymbol{\tau} = (\phi, \tau_1, \ldots, \tau_t)$, where ϕ is a multinomial prior over a fixed number t of types and the $\{\tau_i\}$ are the parameters for each individual type, described in greater detail below. A second group comprises log-linear parameters $\boldsymbol{\pi}$ over discourse choices, also described below. Together, these two groups are drawn according to $P(\boldsymbol{\tau}|\boldsymbol{\lambda})P(\boldsymbol{\pi}|\sigma^2)$, where $\boldsymbol{\lambda}$ and σ^2 are a small number of scalar hyper-parameters described in Section 4.

Conditioned on the parameters $(\boldsymbol{\tau}, \boldsymbol{\pi})$, a document is generated as follows: A *semantic module* generates a sequence $\mathbf{E}$ of entities. $\mathbf{E}$ is in principle infinite, though during inference only a finite number are ever instantiated. A *discourse module* generates a vector $\mathbf{Z}$ which assigns an entity index Z_i to each mention position i. Finally, a *mention generation module* independently renders the sequence of mentions ($\mathbf{M}$) from their underlying entities. The syntactic position and structure of mentions are treated as observed, including the mention forms (pronominal, etc.). We use $\mathbf{X}$ to refer to this ungenenerated information. Our model decomposes as follows:

$$
\begin{aligned}
&P(\mathbf{E}, \mathbf{Z}, \mathbf{M}|\boldsymbol{\tau}, \boldsymbol{\pi}, \mathbf{X}) = \\
&\quad P(\mathbf{E}|\boldsymbol{\tau}) \text{ [Semantic, Section 3.1]} \\
&\quad P(\mathbf{Z}|\boldsymbol{\pi}, \mathbf{X}) \text{ [Discourse, Section 3.2]} \\
&\quad P(\mathbf{M}|\mathbf{Z}, \mathbf{E}, \boldsymbol{\tau}) \text{ [Mention, Section 3.3]}
\end{aligned}
$$

We detail each of these components in subsequent sections.

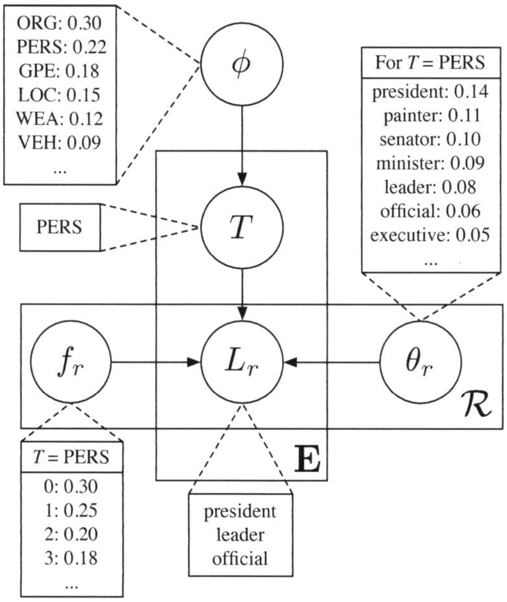

Figure 2: Depiction of the entity generation process (Section 3.1). Each entity draws a type (T) from ϕ, and, for each property $r \in \mathcal{R}$, forms a word list (L_r) by choosing a length from T's f_r distribution and then independently drawing that many words from T's θ_r distribution. Example values are shown for the person type and the nominal head property (NOM-HEAD).

3.1 Semantic Module

The semantic module is responsible for generating a sequence of entities. Each entity E is generated independently and consists of a type indicator T, as well as a collection $\{L_r\}_{r \in \mathcal{R}}$ of word lists for each property. These elements are generated as follows:

Entity Generation

Draw entity type $T \sim \phi$

For each mention property $r \in \mathcal{R}$,

Fetch $\{(f_r, \theta_r)\}$ for τ_T

Draw word list length $|L_r| \sim f_r$

Draw $|L_r|$ words from $w \sim \theta_r$

See Figure 2 for an illustration of this process. Each word list L_r is generated by first drawing a list length from f_r and then independently populating that list from the property's word distribution θ_r.[1] Past work has employed broadly similar distributional models for unsupervised NER of proper mentions (Collins and Singer, 1999; Elsner et al., 2009). However, to our knowledge, this is the first work to incorporate such a model into an entity reference process.

[1]There is one exception: the sizes of the proper and nominal head property lists are jointly generated, but their word lists are still independently populated.

3.2 Discourse Module

The discourse module is responsible for choosing an entity to evoke at each of the n mention positions. Formally, this module generates an entity assignment vector $\mathbf{Z} = (Z_1, \ldots, Z_n)$, where Z_i indicates the entity index for the ith mention position. Most linguistic inquiry characterizes NP anaphora by the pairwise relations that hold between a mention and its antecedent (Hobbs, 1979; Kehler et al., 2008). Our discourse module utilizes this pairwise perspective to define each Z_i in terms of an intermediate "antecedent" variable A_i. A_i either points to a previous antecedent mention position ($A_i < i$) and "steals" its entity assignment or begins a new entity ($A_i = i$). The choice of A_i is parametrized by affinities $s_{\boldsymbol{\pi}}(i, j; \mathbf{X})$ between mention positions i and j. Formally, this process is described as:

Entity Assignment

For each mention position, $i = 1, \ldots, n$,

Draw antecedent position $A_i \in \{1, \ldots, i\}$:

$$P(A_i = j|X) \propto s_{\boldsymbol{\pi}}(i, j; X)$$

$$Z_i = \begin{cases} Z_{A_i}, \text{ if } A_i < i \\ K + 1, \text{ otherwise} \end{cases}$$

Here, K denotes the number of entities allocated in the first i-1 mention positions. This process is an instance of the sequential distance-dependent Chinese Restaurant Process (DD-CRP) of Blei and Frazier (2009). During inference, we variously exploit both the A and Z representations (Section 4).

For nominal and pronoun mentions, there are several well-studied anaphora cues, including centering (Grosz et al., 1995), nearness (Hobbs, 1978), and deterministic constraints, which have all been utilized in prior coreference work (Soon et al., 1999; Ng and Cardie, 2002). In order to combine these cues, we take a log-linear, feature-based approach and parametrize $s_{\boldsymbol{\pi}}(i, j; X) = \exp\{\boldsymbol{\pi}^\top \mathbf{f_X}(i, j)\}$, where $\mathbf{f_X}(i, j)$ is a feature vector over mention positions i and j, and $\boldsymbol{\pi}$ is a parameter vector; the features may freely condition on $\mathbf{X}$. We utilize the following features between a mention and an antecedent: tree distance, sentence distance, and the syntactic positions (subject, object, and oblique) of the mention and antecedent. Features for starting a new entity include: a definiteness feature (extracted from the mention's determiner), the top CFG rule of the mention parse node, its syntactic role, and a bias feature. These features are conjoined with the mention form (nominal or pronoun). Additionally, we restrict pronoun antecedents to the current and last two sentences, and the current and last three sentences for nominals. Additionally, we disallow nominals from having direct pronoun antecedents.

In addition to the above, if a mention is in a deterministic coreference configuration, as defined in Haghighi and Klein (2009), we force it to take the required antecedent. In general, antecedent affinities learn to prefer close antecedents in prominent syntactic positions. We also learn that new entity nominals are typically indefinite or have SBAR complements (captured by the CFG feature).

In contrast to nominals and pronouns, the choice of entity for a proper mention is governed more by entity frequency than antecedent distance. We capture this by setting $s_{\boldsymbol{\pi}}(i, j; \mathbf{X})$ in the proper case to 1 for past positions and to a fixed α otherwise. [2]

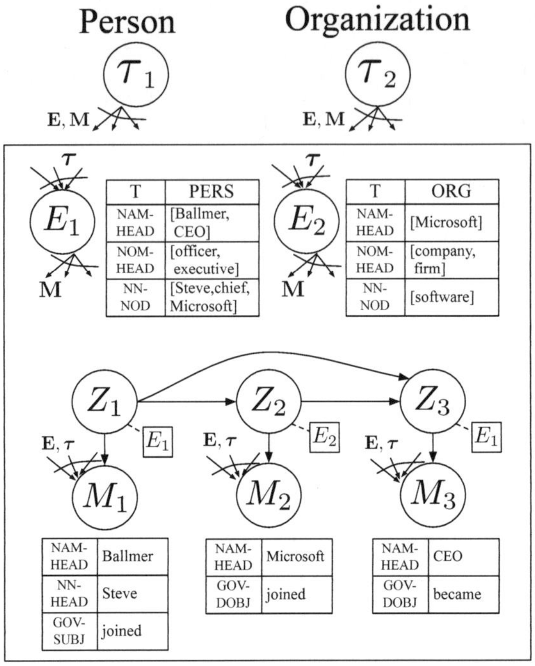

Figure 3: Depiction of the discourse module (Section 3.2); each random variable is annotated with an example value. For each mention position, an entity assignment (Z_i) is made. Conditioned on entities (E_{Z_i}), mentions (M_i) are rendered (Section 3.3). The $\overset{\mathbf{Y}}{\nearrow\!\!\!\!\nwarrow}$ symbol denotes that a random variable is the parent of all $\mathbf{Y}$ random variables.

3.3 Mention Module

Once the semantic module has generated entities and the discourse model selects entity assignments, each mention M_i generates word values for a set of observed properties R_i:

Mention Generation

For each mention M_i, $i = 1, \ldots, n$

Fetch $(T, \{L_r\}_{r \in \mathcal{R}})$ from E_{Z_i}

Fetch $\{(f_r, \theta_r)\}_{r \in \mathcal{R}}$ from $\mathcal{T}_T$

For $r \in R_i$:

$$w \sim (1 - \alpha_r)\textsc{Uniform}(L_r) + (\alpha_r)\theta_r$$

For each property r, there is a hyper-parameter α_r which interpolates between selecting a word from the entity list L_r and drawing from the underlying type property distribution θ_r. Intuitively, a small value of α_r indicates that an entity prefers to re-use a small number of words for property r. This is typically the case for proper and nominal heads as well as modifiers. At the other extreme, setting α_r to 1 indicates the property isn't particular to the entity itself, but rather only on its type. We set α_r to 1 for pronoun heads as well as for the governor of the head properties.

4 Learning and Inference

Our learning procedure involves finding parameters and assignments which are likely under our model's posterior distribution $P(\mathbf{E}, \mathbf{Z}, \boldsymbol{\tau}, \boldsymbol{\pi} | \mathbf{M}, \mathbf{X})$. The model is modularized in such a way that running EM on all variables simultaneously would be very difficult. Therefore, we adopt a variational approach which optimizes various subgroups of the variables in a round-robin fashion, holding approximations to the others fixed. We first describe the variable groups, then the updates which optimize them in turn.

Decomposition: We decompose the entity vari-

[2] As Blei and Frazier (2009) notes, when marginalizing out the A_i in this trivial case, the DD-CRP reduces to the traditional CRP (Pitman, 2002), so our discourse model roughly matches Haghighi and Klein (2007) for proper mentions.

ables $\mathbf{E}$ into types, $\mathbf{T}$, one for each entity, and word lists, $\mathbf{L}$, one for each entity and property. We decompose the mentions $\mathbf{M}$ into *referring* mentions (propers and nominals), $\mathbf{M}^r$, and pronominal mentions, $\mathbf{M}^p$ (with sizes n_r and n_p respectively). The entity assignments $\mathbf{Z}$ are similarly divided into $\mathbf{Z}^r$ and $\mathbf{Z}^p$ components. For pronouns, rather than use $\mathbf{Z}^p$, we instead work with the corresponding antecedent variables, denoted $\mathbf{A}^p$, and marginalize over antecedents to obtain $\mathbf{Z}^p$.

With these variable groups, we would like to approximation our model posterior $P(\mathbf{T}, \mathbf{L}, \mathbf{Z}^r, \mathbf{A}^p, \boldsymbol{\tau}, \boldsymbol{\pi} | \mathbf{M}, \mathbf{X})$ using a simple factored representation. Our variational approximation takes the following form:

$$Q(\mathbf{T}, \mathbf{L}, \mathbf{Z}^r, \mathbf{A}^p, \boldsymbol{\tau}, \boldsymbol{\pi}) = \delta_r(\mathbf{Z}^r, \mathbf{L}) \left(\prod_{k=1}^{n} q_k(T_k)\right) \left(\prod_{i=1}^{n_p} r_i(A_i^p)\right) \delta_s(\boldsymbol{\tau})\delta_d(\boldsymbol{\pi})$$

We use a mean field approach to update each of the RHS factors in turn to minimize the KL-divergence between the current variational posterior and the true model posterior. The δ_r, δ_s, and δ_d factors place point estimates on a single value, just as in hard EM. Updating these factors involves finding the value which maximizes the model (expected) log-likelihood under the other factors. For instance, the δ_s factor is a point estimate of the type parameters, and is updated with:[3]

$$\delta_s(\boldsymbol{\tau}) \leftarrow \operatorname*{argmax}_{\boldsymbol{\tau}} \mathbb{E}_{Q_{-\delta_s}} \ln P(\mathbf{E}, \mathbf{Z}, \mathbf{M}, \boldsymbol{\tau}, \boldsymbol{\pi}) \quad (1)$$

where $Q_{-\delta_s}$ denotes all factors of the variational approximation except for the factor being updated. The r_i (pronoun antecedents) and q_k (type indicator) factors maintain a soft approximation and so are slightly more complex. For example, the r_i factor update takes the standard mean field form:

$$r_i(A_i^p) \propto \exp\{\mathbb{E}_{Q_{-r_i}} \ln P(\mathbf{E}, \mathbf{Z}, \mathbf{M}, \boldsymbol{\tau}, \boldsymbol{\pi})\} \quad (2)$$

We briefly describe the update for each additional factor, omitting details for space.

Updating type parameters $\delta_s(\boldsymbol{\tau})$: The type parameters $\boldsymbol{\tau}$ consist of several multinomial distributions which can be updated by normalizing expected counts as in the EM algorithm. The prior $P(\boldsymbol{\tau}|\boldsymbol{\lambda})$ consists of several finite Dirichlet draws for each multinomial, which are incorporated as pseudocounts.[4] Given the entity type variational posteriors $\{q_k(\cdot)\}$, as well as the point estimates of the $\mathbf{L}$ and $\mathbf{Z}^r$ elements, we obtain expected counts from each entity's attribute word lists and referring mention usages.

Updating discourse parameters $\delta_d(\boldsymbol{\pi})$: The learned parameters for the discourse module rely on pairwise antecedent counts for assignments to nominal and pronominal mentions.[5] Given these expected counts, which can be easily obtained from other factors, the update reduces to a weighted maximum entropy problem, which we optimize using LBFGS. The prior $P(\boldsymbol{\pi}|\sigma^2)$ is a zero-centered normal distribution with shared diagonal variance σ^2, which is incorporated via L2 regularization during optimization.

Updating referring assignments and word lists $\delta_r(\mathbf{Z}^r, \mathbf{L})$: The word lists are usually concatenations of the words used in nominal and proper mentions and so are updated together with the assignments for those mentions. Updating the $\delta_r(\mathbf{Z}^r, \mathbf{L})$ factor involves finding the referring mention entity assignments, $\mathbf{Z}^r$, and property word lists $\mathbf{L}$ for instantiated entities which maximize $\mathbb{E}_{Q_{-\delta_r}} \ln P(\mathbf{T}, \mathbf{L}, \mathbf{Z}^r, \mathbf{A}^p, \mathbf{M}, \boldsymbol{\tau}, \boldsymbol{\pi})$. We actually only need to optimize over $\mathbf{Z}^r$, since for any $\mathbf{Z}^r$, we can compute the optimal set of property word lists $\mathbf{L}$. Essentially, for each entity we can compute the L_r which optimizes the probability of the referring mentions assigned to the entity (indicated by $\mathbf{Z}^r$). In practice, the optimal L_r is just the set of property words in the assigned mentions. Of course enumerating and scoring all $\mathbf{Z}^r$ hypotheses is intractable, so we instead utilize a left-to-right sequential beam search. Each partial hypothesis is an assignment to a prefix of mention positions and is scored as though it were a complete hypothesis. Hypotheses are extended via adding a new mention to an existing entity or creating a new one. For our experiments, we limited the number of hypotheses on the beam to the top fifty and did not notice an improvement in model score from increasing beam size.

[3]Of course during learning, the argmax is performed over the entire document collection, rather than a single document.

[4]See software release for full hyper-parameter details.

[5]Propers have no learned discourse parameters.

Updating pronominal antecedents $r_i(A_i^p)$ and entity types $q_k(T_k)$: These updates are straightforward instantiations of the mean-field update (2).

To produce our final coreference partitions, we assign each referring mention to the entity given by the δ_r factor and each pronoun to the most likely entity given by the r_i.

4.1 Factor Staging

In order to facilitate learning, some factors are initially set to fixed heuristic values and only learned in later iterations. Initially, the assignment factors δ_r and $\{r_i\}$ are fixed. For δ_r, we use a deterministic entity assignment $\mathbf{Z}^r$, similar to the Haghighi and Klein (2009)'s SYN-CONSTR setting: each referring mention is coreferent with any past mention with the same head or in a deterministic syntactic configuration (appositives or predicative nominatives constructions).[6] The $\{r_i\}$ factors are heuristically set to place most of their mass on the closest antecedent by tree distance. During training, we proceed in stages, each consisting of 5 iterations:

Stage	Learned	Fixed	$B^3 All$
1	$\delta_s, \delta_d, \{q_k\}$	$\{r_i\}$,δ_r	74.6
2	$\delta_s, \delta_d, \{q_k\}, \delta_r$	$\{r_i\}$	76.3
3	$\delta_s, \delta_d, \{q_k\}, \delta_r, \{r_i\}$	–	78.0

We evaluate our system at the end of stage using the $B^3 All$ metric on the A05CU development set (see Section 5 for details).

5 Experiments

We considered the challenging end-to-end system mention setting, where in addition to predicting mention partitions, a system must identify the mentions themselves and their boundaries automatically. Our system deterministically extracts mention boundaries from parse trees (Section 5.2). We utilized no coreference annotation during training, but did use minimal prototype information to prime the learning of entity types (Section 5.3).

5.1 Datasets

For evaluation, we used standard coreference data sets derived from the ACE corpora:

- **A04CU**: Train/dev/test split of the newswire portion of the ACE 2004 training set[7] utilized in Culotta et al. (2007), Bengston and Roth (2008) and Stoyanov et al. (2009). Consists of 90/68/38 documents respectively.
- **A05ST**: Train/test split of the newswire portion of the ACE 2005 training set utilized in Stoyanov et al. (2009). Consists of 57/24 documents respectively.
- **A05RA**: Train/test split of the ACE 2005 training set utilized in Rahman and Ng (2009). Consists of 482/117 documents respectively.

For all experiments, we evaluated on the dev and test sets above. To train, we included the text of all documents above, though of course not looking at either their mention boundaries or reference annotations in any way. We also trained on the following much larger unlabeled datasets utilized in Haghighi and Klein (2009):

- **BLLIP**: 5k articles of newswire parsed with the Charniak (2000) parser.
- **WIKI**: 8k abstracts of English Wikipedia articles parsed by the Berkeley parser (Petrov et al., 2006). Articles were selected to have subjects amongst the frequent proper nouns in the evaluation datasets.

5.2 Mention Detection and Properties

Mention boundaries were automatically detected as follows: For each noun or pronoun (determined by parser POS tag), we associated a mention with the maximal NP projection of that head or that word itself if no NP can be found. This procedure recovers over 90% of annotated mentions on the A05CU dev set, but also extracts many unannotated "spurious" mentions (for instance events, times, dates, or abstract nouns) which are not deemed to be of interest by the ACE annotation conventions.

Mention properties were obtained from parse trees using the the Stanford typed dependency extractor (de Marneffe et al., 2006). The mention properties we considered are the mention head (annotated with mention type), the typed modifiers of the head, and the governor of the head (conjoined with

[6] Forcing appositive coreference is essential for tying proper and nominal entity type vocabulary.

[7] Due to licensing restriction, the formal ACE test sets are not available to non-participants.

	MUC			$B^3 All$			$B^3 None$			Pairwise F_1		
System	P	R	F1	P	R	F1	P	R	F1	P	R	F1
ACE2004-STOYANOV-TEST												
Stoyanov et al. (2009)	-	-	62.0	-	-	76.5	-	-	75.4	-	-	-
Haghighi and Klein (2009)	**67.5**	61.6	64.4	77.4	69.4	73.2	77.4	67.1	71.3	58.3	44.5	50.5
THIS WORK	67.4	**66.6**	**67.0**	**81.2**	**73.3**	**77.0**	**80.6**	**75.2**	**77.3**	59.2	50.3	54.4
ACE2005-STOYANOV-TEST												
Stoyanov et al. (2009)	-	-	67.4	-	-	73.7	-	-	72.5	-	-	-
Haghighi and Klein (2009)	73.1	58.8	65.2	82.1	63.9	71.8	81.2	61.6	70.1	66.1	37.9	48.1
THIS WORK	**74.6**	**62.7**	**68.1**	**83.2**	**68.4**	**75.1**	**82.7**	**66.3**	**73.6**	**64.3**	**41.4**	**50.4**
ACE2005-RAHMAN-TEST												
Rahman and Ng (2009)	75.4	64.1	69.3	-	-	-	**54.4**	70.5	61.4	-	-	-
Haghighi and Klein (2009)	72.9	60.2	67.0	53.2	73.1	61.6	52.0	72.6	60.6	57.0	44.6	50.0
THIS WORK	**77.0**	**66.9**	**71.6**	**55.4**	**74.8**	**63.8**	54.0	**74.7**	**62.7**	**60.1**	**47.7**	**53.0**

Table 1: Experimental results with system mentions. All systems except Haghighi and Klein (2009) and current work are fully supervised. The current work outperforms all other systems, supervised or unsupervised. For comparison purposes, the $B^3 None$ variant used on A05RA is calculated slightly differently than other $B^3 None$ results; see Rahman and Ng (2009).

the mention's syntactic position). We discard determiners, but make use of them in the discourse component (Section 3.2) for NP definiteness.

5.3 Prototyping Entity Types

While it is possible to learn type distributions in a completely unsupervised fashion, we found it useful to prime the system with a handful of important types. Rather than relying on fully supervised data, we took the approach of Haghighi and Klein (2006). For each type of interest, we provided a (possibly-empty) prototype list of proper and nominal head words, as well as a list of allowed pronouns. For instance, for the PERSON type we might provide:

NAM	Bush, Gore, Hussein
NOM	president, minister, official
PRO	he, his, she, him, her, you, ...

The prototypes were used as follows: Any entity with a prototype on any proper or nominal head word attribute list (Section 3.1) was constrained to have the specified type; i.e. the q_k factor (Section 4) places probability one on that single type. Similarly to Haghighi and Klein (2007) and Elsner et al. (2009), we biased these types' pronoun distributions to the allowed set of pronouns.

In general, the choice of entity types to prime with prototypes is a domain-specific question. For experiments here, we utilized the types which are annotated in the ACE coreference data: person (PERS), organization (ORG), geo-political entity (GPE), weapon (WEA), vehicle (VEH), location (LOC), and facility (FAC). Since the person type in ACE conflates individual persons with groups of people (e.g., *soldier* vs. *soldiers*), we added the group (GROUP) type and generated a prototype specification.

We obtained our prototype list by extracting at most four common proper and nominal head words from the newswire portions of the 2004 and 2005 ACE training sets (A04CU and A05ST); we chose prototype words to be minimally ambiguous with respect to type.[8] When there are not at least three proper heads for a type (WEA for instance), we did not provide any proper prototypes and instead strongly biased the type fertility parameters to generate empty NAM-HEAD lists.

Because only certain semantic types were annotated under the arbitrary ACE guidelines, there are many mentions which do not fall into those limited categories. We therefore prototype (refinements of) the ACE types and then add an equal number of unconstrained "other" types which are automatically induced. A nice consequence of this approach is that we can simply run our model on *all* mentions, discarding at evaluation time any which are of non-prototyped types.

5.4 Evaluation

We evaluated on multiple coreference resolution metrics, as no single one is clearly superior, partic-

[8]Meaning those headwords were assigned to the target type for more than 75% of their usages.

ularly in dealing with the system mention setting. We utilized MUC (Vilain et al., 1995), $B^3 All$ (Stoyanov et al., 2009), $B^3 None$ (Stoyanov et al., 2009), and Pairwise F1. The $B^3 All$ and $B^3 None$ are B^3 variants (Bagga and Baldwin, 1998) that differ in their treatment of spurious mentions. For Pairwise F1, precision measures how often pairs of predicted coreferent mentions are in the same annotated entity. We eliminated any mention pair from this calculation where both mentions were spurious.[9]

5.5 Results

Table 1 shows our results. We compared to two state-of-the-art supervised coreference systems. The Stoyanov et al. (2009) numbers represent their THRESHOLD_ESTIMATION setting and the Rahman and Ng (2009) numbers represent their highest-performing cluster ranking model. We also compared to the strong deterministic system of Haghighi and Klein (2009).[10] Across all data sets, our model, despite being largely unsupervised, consistently outperforms these systems, which are the best previously reported results on end-to-end coreference resolution (i.e. including mention detection). Performance on the A05RA dataset is generally lower because it includes articles from blogs and web forums where parser quality is significantly degraded.

While Bengston and Roth (2008) do not report on the full system mention task, they do report on the more optimistic setting where mention detection is performed but non-gold mentions are removed for evaluation using an oracle. On this more lenient setting, they report 78.4 B^3 on the A04CU test set. Our model yields 80.3.

6 Analysis

We now discuss errors and improvements made by our system. One frequent source of error is the merging of mentions with explicitly contrasting modifiers, such as *new president* and *old president*. While it is not unusual for a single entity to admit multiple modifiers, the particular modifiers *new* and *old* are incompatible in a way that *new* and *popular* are not. Our model does not represent the negative covariance between these modifiers.

We compared our output to the deterministic system of Haghighi and Klein (2009). Many improvements arise from correctly identifying mentions which are semantically compatible but which do not explicitly appear in an appositive or predicate-nominative configuration in the data. For example, *analyst* and *it* cannot corefer in our system because *it* is not a likely pronoun for the type PERSON.

While the focus of our model is coreference resolution, we can also isolate and evaluate the type component of our model as an NER system. We test this component by presenting our learned model with boundary-annotated non-pronominal entities from the A05ST dev set and querying their predicted type variable T. Doing so yields 83.2 entity classification accuracy under the mapping between our prototyped types and the coarse ACE types. Note that this task is substantially more difficult than the unsupervised NER in Elsner et al. (2009) because the inventory of named entities is larger (7 vs. 3) and because we predict types over nominal mentions that are more difficult to judge from surface forms. In this task, the plurality of errors are confusions between the GPE (geo-political entity) and ORG entity types, which have very similar distributions.

7 Conclusion

Our model is able to acquire and exploit knowledge at either the level of individual entities ("Obama" is a "president") and entity types ("company" can refer to a corporation). As a result, it leverages semantic constraints more effectively than systems operating at either level alone. In conjunction with reasonable, but simple, factors capturing discourse and syntactic configurational preferences, our entity-centric semantic model lowers coreference error rate substantially, particularly on semantically disambiguated references, giving a sizable improvement over the state-of-the-art.[11]

Acknowledgements: This project is funded in part by the Office of Naval Research under MURI Grant No. N000140911081.

[9] Note that we are still penalized for marking a spurious mention coreferent with an annotated one.

[10] Haghighi and Klein (2009) reports on true mentions; here, we report performance on automatically detected mentions.

[11] See *nlp.cs.berkeley.edu* and *aria42.com/software.html* for software release.

References

A Bagga and B Baldwin. 1998. Algorithms for scoring coreference chains. In *Linguistic Coreference Workshop (LREC)*.

Eric Bengston and Dan Roth. 2008. Understanding the Value of Features for Corefernce Resolution. In *Empirical Methods in Natural Language Processing (EMNLP)*.

David Blei and Peter I. Frazier. 2009. Distance Dependent Chinese Restaurant Processes. http://arxiv.org/abs/0910.1022/.

Eugene Charniak. 2000. Maximum Entropy Inspired Parser. In *North American Chapter of the Association of Computational Linguistics (NAACL)*.

Michael Collins and Yoram Singer. 1999. Unsupervised Models for Named Entity Classification. In *Empirical Methods in Natural Language Processing (EMNLP)*.

Mike Collins. 1999. *Head-Driven Statistical Models for Natural Language Parsing*. Ph.D. thesis, University of Pennsylvania.

A Culotta, M Wick, R Hall, and A McCallum. 2007. First-order Probabilistic Models for Coreference Resolution. In *Proceedings of the conference on Human Language Technology and Empirical Methods in Natural Language Processing (NAACL-HLT)*.

M. C. de Marneffe, B. Maccartney, and C. D. Manning. 2006. Generating Typed Dependency Parses from Phrase Structure Parses. In *LREC*.

M Elsner, E Charniak, and M Johnson. 2009. Structured generative models for unsupervised named-entity clustering. In *Proceedings of Human Language Technologies: The 2009 Annual Conference of the North American Chapter of the Association for Computational Linguistics*, pages 164–172.

Barbara J. Grosz, Aravind K. Joshi, and Scott Weinstein. 1995. Centering: A Framework for Modeling the Local Coherence of Discourse. *Computational Linguistics*, 21(2):203–225.

Aria Haghighi and Dan Klein. 2006. Prototype-Driven Learning for Sequence Models. In *HLT-NAACL*. Association for Computational Linguistics.

Aria Haghighi and Dan Klein. 2007. Unsupervised Coreference Resolution in a Nonparametric Bayesian Model. In *Proceedings of the 45th Annual Meeting of the Association of Computational Linguistics*. Association for Computational Linguistics.

Aria Haghighi and Dan Klein. 2009. Simple Coreference Resolution with Rich Syntactic and Semantic Features. In *Proceedings of the 2009 Conference on Empirical Conference in Natural Language Processing*.

J. R. Hobbs. 1978. Resolving Pronoun References. *Lingua*, 44.

J. R. Hobbs. 1979. Coherence and Coreference. *Cognitive Science*, 3:67–90.

Andrew Kehler, Laura Kertz, Hannah Rohde, and Jeffrey Elman. 2008. Coherence and Coreference Revisited.

Vincent Ng and Claire Cardie. 2002. Improving Machine Learning Approaches to Coreference Resolution. In *Association of Computational Linguists (ACL)*.

Vincent Ng. 2005. Machine Learning for Coreference Resolution: From Local Classification to Global Ranking. In *Association of Computational Linguists (ACL)*.

Vincent Ng. 2007. Shallow semantics for coreference resolution. In *IJCAI'07: Proceedings of the 20th international joint conference on Artifical intelligence*, pages 1689–1694.

Slav Petrov, Leon Barrett, Romain Thibaux, and Dan Klein. 2006. Learning Accurate, Compact, and Interpretable Tree Annotation. In *Proceedings of the 21st International Conference on Computational Linguistics and 44th Annual Meeting of the Association for Computational Linguistics*, pages 433–440, Sydney, Australia, July. Association for Computational Linguistics.

J. Pitman. 2002. Combinatorial Stochastic Processes. In *Lecture Notes for St. Flour Summer School*.

A Rahman and V Ng. 2009. Supervised models for coreference resolution. In *Proceedings of the 2009 Conference on Empirical Conference in Natural Language Processing*.

W.H. Soon, H. T. Ng, and D. C. Y. Lim. 1999. A Machine Learning Approach to Coreference Resolution of Noun Phrases.

V Stoyanov, N Gilbert, C Cardie, and E Riloff. 2009. Conundrums in Noun Phrase Coreference Resolution: Making Sense of the State-of-the-art. In *Associate of Computational Linguistics (ACL)*.

Marc Vilain, John Burger, John Aberdeen, Dennis Connolly, and Lynette Hirschman. 1995. A model-theoretic coreference scoring scheme. In *MUC-6*.

X Yang, J Su, and CL Tan. 2005. Improving pronoun resolution using statistics-based semantic compatibility information. In *Association of Computational Linguists (ACL)*.

Stream-based Translation Models for Statistical Machine Translation

Abby Levenberg
School of Informatics
University of Edinburgh
a.levenberg@ed.ac.uk

Chris Callison-Burch
Computer Science Department
Johns Hopkins University
ccb@cs.jhu.edu

Miles Osborne
School of Informatics
University of Edinburgh
miles@inf.ed.ac.uk

Abstract

Typical statistical machine translation systems are trained with static parallel corpora. Here we account for scenarios with a continuous incoming stream of parallel training data. Such scenarios include daily governmental proceedings, sustained output from translation agencies, or crowd-sourced translations. We show incorporating recent sentence pairs from the stream improves performance compared with a static baseline. Since frequent batch retraining is computationally demanding we introduce a fast incremental alternative using an online version of the EM algorithm. To bound our memory requirements we use a novel data-structure and associated training regime. When compared to frequent batch retraining, our online time and space-bounded model achieves the same performance with significantly less computational overhead.

1 Introduction

There is more parallel training data available today than there has ever been and it keeps increasing. For example, the European Parliament[1] releases new parallel data in 22 languages on a regular basis. Project Syndicate[2] translates editorials into seven languages (including Arabic, Chinese and Russian) every day. Existing translation systems often get 'crowd-sourced' improvements such as the option to contribute a better translation to GoogleTranslate[3]. In these and many other instances, the data can be viewed as an incoming *unbounded stream* since the corpus grows continually with time. Dealing with such unbounded streams of parallel sentences presents two challenges: making retraining efficient and operating within a bounded amount of space.

Statistical Machine Translation (SMT) systems are typically batch trained, often taking many CPU-days of computation when using large volumes of training material. Incorporating new data into these models forces us to retrain from scratch. Clearly, this makes rapidly adding newly translated sentences into our models a daunting engineering challenge. We introduce an adaptive training regime using an online variant of EM that is capable of incrementally adding new parallel sentences without incurring the burdens of full retraining.

For situations with large volumes of incoming parallel sentences we are also forced to consider placing space-bounds on our SMT system. We introduce a dynamic suffix array which allows us to add and delete parallel sentences, thereby maintaining bounded space despite processing a potentially high-rate input stream of unbounded length.

Taken as a whole we show that online translation models operating within bounded space can perform as well as systems which are batch-based and have no space constraints thereby making our approach suitable for stream-based translation.

2 Stepwise Online EM

The EM algorithm is a common way of inducing latent structure from unlabeled data in an unsupervised manner (Dempster et al., 1977). Given a set of unlabeled examples and an initial, often uniform guess at a probability distribution over the latent variables, the EM algorithm maximizes the marginal

[1] http://www.europarl.europa.eu

[2] http://www.project-syndicate.org

[3] http://www.translate.google.com

Human Language Technologies: The 2010 Annual Conference of the North American Chapter of the ACL, pages 394–402,
Los Angeles, California, June 2010.

log-likelihood of the examples by repeatedly computing the expectation of the conditional probability of the latent data with respect to the current distribution, and then maximizing the expectations over the observations into a new distribution used in the next iteration. EM (and related variants such as variational or sampling approaches) form the basis of how SMT systems learn their translation models.

2.1 Batch vs. Online EM

Computing an expectation for the conditional probabilities requires collecting the *sufficient statistics* **S** over the set of n unlabeled examples. In the case of a multinomial distribution, **S** is comprised of the counts over each conditional observation occurring in the n examples. In traditional *batch* EM, we collect the counts over the entire dataset of n unlabeled training examples via the current 'best-guess' probability model $\hat{\theta}_t$ at iteration t (E-step) before normalizing the counts into probabilities $\bar{\theta}(\mathbf{S})$ (M-step)[4]. After each iteration all the counts in the sufficient statistics vector **S** are cleared and the count collection begins anew using the new distribution $\hat{\theta}_{t+1}$.

When we move to processing an incoming data stream, however, the batch EM algorithm's requirement that all data be available for each iteration becomes impractical since we do not have access to all n examples at once. Instead we receive examples from the input stream incrementally. For this reason online EM algorithms have been developed to update the probability model $\hat{\theta}$ incrementally without needing to store and iterate through all the unlabeled training data repeatedly.

Various online EM algorithms have been investigated (see Liang and Klein (2009) for an overview) but our focus is on the *stepwise online* EM (sOEM) algorithm (Cappe and Moulines, 2009). Instead of iterating over the full set of training examples, sOEM stochastically approximates the batch E-step and incorporates the information from the newly available streaming observations in steps. Each step is called a *mini-batch* and is comprised of one or more new examples encountered in the stream.

Unlike in batch EM, in sOEM the expected counts are retained between EM iterations and not cleared.

[4]As the M-step can be computed in closed form we designate it in this work as $\bar{\theta}(\mathbf{S})$.

Algorithm 1: Batch EM for Word Alignments

Input: $\{F$(source)$,E$ (target)$\}$ sentence-pairs
Output: MLE $\hat{\theta}_T$ over alignments $\mathbf{a}$
$\hat{\theta}_0 \leftarrow$MLE initialization;
for *iteration* $k = 0, \ldots, T$ **do**
  $S \leftarrow 0$;   `// reset counts`
  foreach $(f, e) \in \{F, E\}$ **do**   `// E-step`
    $S \leftarrow S + \sum_{a' \in \mathbf{a}} \Pr(f, a'|e; \hat{\theta}_t)$;
  end
  $\hat{\theta}_{t+1} \leftarrow \bar{\theta}_t(S)$;   `// M-step`
end

That is, for each new example we interpolate its expected count with the existing set of sufficient statistics. For each step we use a *stepsize* parameter γ which mixes the information from the current example with information gathered from all previous examples. Over time the sOEM model probabilities begin to stabilize and are guaranteed to converge to a local maximum (Cappe and Moulines, 2009).

Note that the stepsize γ has a dependence on the current mini-batch. As we observe more incoming data the model's current probability distribution is closer to the true distribution so the new observations receive less weight. From Liang and Klein (2009), if we set the stepsize as $\gamma_t = (t+2)^{-\alpha}$, with $0.5 < \alpha \leq 1$, we can guarantee convergence in the limit as $n \rightarrow \infty$. If we set α low, γ weighs the newly observed statistics heavily whereas if γ is low new observations are down-weighted.

2.2 Batch EM for Word Alignments

Batch EM is used in statistical machine translation to estimate word alignment probabilities between parallel sentences. From these alignments, bilingual rules or phrase pairs can be extracted. Given a set of parallel sentence examples, $\{\mathbf{F}, \mathbf{E}\}$, with $\mathbf{F}$ the set of source sentences and $\mathbf{E}$ the corresponding target sentences, we want to find the latent alignments $\mathbf{a}$ for a sentence pair $(\mathbf{f}, \mathbf{e}) \in \{\mathbf{F}, \mathbf{E}\}$ that defines the most probable correspondence between words f_j and e_i such that $a_j = i$. We can induce these alignments using an *HMM-based* alignment model where the probability of alignment a_j is dependent only on the previous alignment at a_{j-1} (Vogel et al., 1996).

We can write

$$\Pr(\mathbf{f}, \mathbf{a} \mid \mathbf{e}) = \sum_{a' \in \mathbf{a}} \prod_{j=1}^{|\mathbf{f}|} p(a_j \mid a_{j-1}, |\mathbf{e}|) \cdot p(f_j \mid e_{a_j})$$

where we assume a first-order dependence on previously aligned positions.

To find the most likely parameter weights for the translation and alignment probabilities for the HMM-based alignments, we employ the EM algorithm via dynamic programming. Since HMMs have multiple local minima, we seed the HMM-based model probabilities with a better than random guess using IBM Model 1 (Brown et al., 1993) as is standard. IBM Model 1 is of the same form as the HMM-based model except it uses a uniform distribution instead of a first-order dependency. Although a series of more complex models are defined, IBM Models 2 to Model 6 (Brown et al., 1993; Och and Ney, 2003), researchers typically find that extracting phrase pairs or translation grammar rules using Model 1 and the HMM-based alignments results in equivalently high translation quality. Nevertheless, there is nothing in our approach which limits us to using just Model 1 and the HMM model.

A high-level overview of the standard, batch EM algorithm applied to HMM-based word alignment model is shown in Algorithm 1.

2.3 Stepwise EM for Word Alignments

Application of sOEM to HMM and Model 1 based word aligning is straightforward. The process of collecting the counts over the expected conditional probabilities inside each iteration loop remains the same as in the batch case. However, instead of clearing the sufficient statistics between the iterations we retain them and interpolate them with the batch of counts gathered in the next iteration.

Algorithm 2 shows high level pseudocode of our sOEM framework as applied to HMM-based word alignments. Here we have an unbounded input stream of source and target sentences $\{\mathbf{F}, \mathbf{E}\}$ which we do not have access to in its entirety at once. Instead we observe mini-batches $\{\mathbf{M}\}$ comprised of chronologically ordered strict subsets of the full stream. To word align the sentences for each mini-batch $\mathbf{m} \in \mathbf{M}$, we use the probability assigned by the current model parameters and then interpolate

Algorithm 2: sOEM Algorithm for Word Alignments

Input: mini-batches of sentence pairs $\{M : M \subset \{F(source), E(target)\}\}$
Input: stepsize weight α
Output: MLE $\hat{\theta}_T$ over alignments $\mathbf{a}$
$\hat{\theta}_0$ ←MLE initialization;
$S \leftarrow 0$; $k = 0$;
foreach *mini-batch* $\{m : m \in M\}$ **do**
  for *iteration* $t = 0, \ldots, T$ **do**
    foreach $(f, e) \in \{m\}$ **do** // E-step
      $\bar{s} \leftarrow \sum_{a' \in \mathbf{a}} \Pr(f, a' | e; \hat{\theta}_t)$;
    end
    $\gamma = (k+2)^{-\alpha}; k = k + 1$; // stepsize
    $S \leftarrow \gamma \bar{s} + (1 - \gamma) S$; // interpolate
    $\hat{\theta}_{t+1} \leftarrow \bar{\theta}_t(S)$; // M-step
  end
end

the newest sufficient statistics $\bar{s}$ with our full count vector $\mathbf{S}$ using an interpolation parameter γ. The interpolation parameter γ has a dependency on how far along the input stream we are processing.

3 Dynamic Suffix Arrays

So far we have shown how to incrementally retrain translation models. We now consider how we might bound the space we use for them when processing (potentially) unbounded streams of parallel data.

Suffix arrays are space-efficient data structures for fast searching over large text strings (Manber and Myers, 1990). Treating the entire corpus as a single string, a suffix array holds in lexicographical order (only) the starting index of each suffix of the string. After construction, since the corpus is now ordered, we can query the suffix array quickly using binary search to efficiently find all occurrences of a particular token or sequence of tokens. Then we can easily compute, on-the-fly, the statistics required such as translation probabilities for a given source phrase. Suffix arrays can also be compressed, which make them highly attractive structures for representing massive translation models (Callison-Burch et al., 2005; Lopez, 2008).

We need to delete items if we wish to maintain

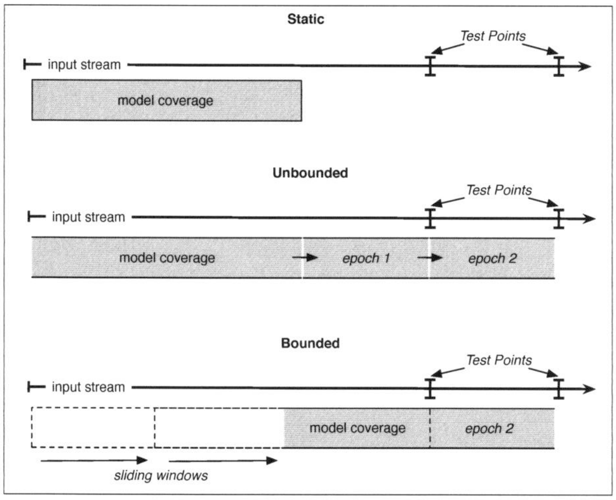

Figure 1: Streaming coverage conditions. In traditional batch based modeling the coverage of a trained model never changes. Unbounded coverage operates without any memory constraints so the model is able to continually add data from the input stream. Bounded coverage uses just a fixed window.

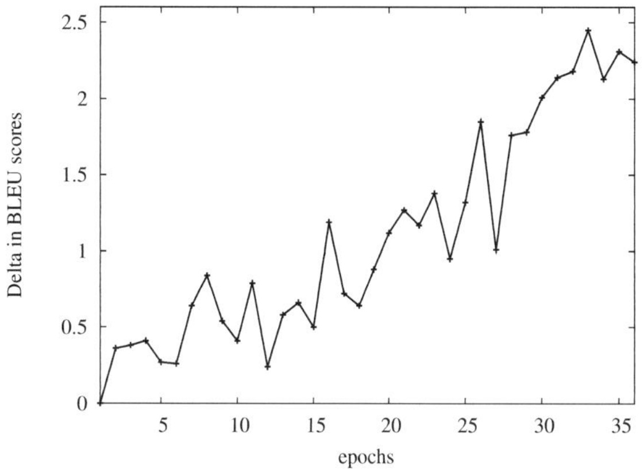

Figure 2: Recency effects to SMT performance. Depicted are the differences in BLEU scores for multiple test points decoded by a static baseline system and a system batched retrained on a fixed sized window prior to the test point in question. The results are accentuated at the end of the timeline when more time has passed confirming that recent data impacts translation performance.

constant space when processing unbounded streams. Standard suffix arrays are static, store a fixed corpus and do not support deletions. Nevertheless, a dynamic variant of the suffix array does support deletions as well as insertions and therefore can be used in our stream-based approach (Salson et al., 2009). Using a dynamic suffix array, we can compactly represent the set of parallel sentences from which we eventually extract grammar rules. Furthermore, when incorporating new parallel sentences, we simply insert them into the array and, to maintain constant space usage, we delete an equivalent number.

4 Experiments

In this section we describe the experiments conducted comparing various batch trained translation models (TMs) versus online incrementally retrained TMs in a full SMT setting with different conditions set on model coverage. We used publicly available resources for all our tests. We start by showing that recency motivates incremental retraining.

4.1 Effects of Recency on SMT

For language modeling, it is known that performance can be improved using the criterion of *recency* where training data is drawn from times chronologically closer to the test data (Rosenfeld, 1995). Given an incoming stream of parallel text, we gauged the extent to which incorporating recent data into a TM affects translation quality.

We used the Europarl corpus[5] with the Fr-En language pair using French as source and English as target. Europarl is released in the format of a daily parliamentary session per time-stamped file. The actual dates of the full corpus are interspersed unevenly (they do not convene daily) over a continuous timeline corresponding to the parliament sessions from April,1996 through October, 2006, but for conceptual simplicity we treated the corpus as a continual input stream over consecutive days.

As a baseline we aligned the first 500k sentence pairs from the beginning of the corpus timeline. We extracted a grammar for and translated 36 held out test documents that were evenly spaced along the remainder of the Europarl timeline. These test documents effectively divided the remaining training data into *epochs* and we used a *sliding window* over the timeline to build 36 distinct, overlapping training sets of 500k sentences each.

We then translated all 36 test points again using a new grammar for each document extracted from only the sentences contained in the epoch that was before it. To explicitly test the effect of recency

[5]Available at `http://www.statmt.org/europarl`

on the TM all other factors of the SMT pipeline remained constant including the language model and the feature weights. Hence, the only change from the static baseline to the epochs performance was the TM data which was based on recency. Note that at this stage we did not use any incremental retraining.

Results are shown in Figure 2 as the differences in BLEU score (Papineni et al., 2001) between the baseline TM versus the translation models trained on material chronologically closer to the given test point. The consistently positive deltas in BLEU scores between the model that is never retrained and the models that are retrained show that we achieve a higher translation performance when using more up-to-date TMs that incorporate recent sentence pairs. As the chronological distance between the initial, static model and the retrained models increases, we see ever-increasing differences in translation performance. This underlines the need to retrain translation models with timely material.

4.2 Unbounded and Bounded Translation Model Retraining

Here we consider how to process a stream along two main axes: by bounding time (batch versus incremental retraining) and by bounding space (either using all the stream seen so far, or only using a fixed sized sample of it).

To ensure the recency results reported above were not limited to French-English, this time our parallel input stream was generated from the German-English language pair of Europarl with German as source and English again as target. For testing we held out a total of 22k sentences from 10 evenly spaced intervals in the input stream which divided the input stream into 10 epochs. Stream statistics for three example epochs are shown in Table 1. We held out 4.5k sentence pairs as development data to optimize the feature function weights using minimum error rate training (Och, 2003) and these weights were used by all models. We used *Joshua* (Li et al., 2009), a syntax-based decoder with a suffix array implementation, and rule induction via the standard *Hiero* grammar extraction heuristics (Chiang, 2007) for the TMs. Note that nothing hinges on whether we used a syntax or a phrase-based system.

We used a 5-gram, Kneser-Ney smoothed language model (LM) trained on the initial segment of the target side parallel data used in the first baseline as described further in the next subsection. As our initial experiments aim to isolate the effect of changes to the TM on overall translation system performance, our in-domain LM remains static for every decoding run reported below until indicated.

Ep	From–To	Sent Pairs	Source/Target
00	04/1996–12/2000	600k	15.0M/16.0M
03	02/2002–09/2002	70k	1.9M/2.0M
06	10/2003–03/2004	60k	1.6M/1.7M
10	03/2006–09/2006	73k	1.9M/2.0M

Table 1: Date ranges, total sentence pairs, and source and target word counts encountered in the input stream for example epochs. Epoch 00 is baseline data that is also used as a seed corpus for the online models.

We used the open-source toolkit GIZA++ (Och and Ney, 2003) for all word alignments. For the online adaptation experiments we modified Model 1 and the HMM model in GIZA++ to use the sOEM algorithm. Batch baselines were aligned using the standard version of GIZA++. We ran the batch and incremental versions of Model 1 and HMM for the same number of iterations each in both directions.

4.3 Time and Space Bounds

For both batch and sOEM we ran a number of experiments listed below corresponding to the different training scenarios diagrammed in Figure 1.

1. **Static**: We used the first half of the input stream, approximately 600k sentences and 15/16 million source/target words, as parallel training data. We then translated each of the 10 test sets using the static model. This is the traditional approach and the coverage of the model never changes.

2. **Unbounded Space**: Batch or incremental retraining with no memory constraint. For each epoch in the stream, we retrained the TM using *all* the data from the beginning of the input stream until just before the present with respect to a given test point. As more time passes our training data set grows so each *batch* run of GIZA++ takes more time. Overall this is the most computationally expensive approach.

			Baseline		Unbounded		Bounded	
Epoch	Test Date	Test Sent.	Train Sent.	Rules	Train Sent.	Rules	Train Sent.	Rules
03	09/23/2002	1.0k	580k	4.0M	800k	5.0M	580k	4.2M
06	03/29/2004	1.5k	580k	5.0M	1.0M	7.0M	580k	5.5M
10	09/26/2006	3.5k	580k	8.5M	1.3M	14.0M	580k	10.0M

Table 2: Translation model statistics for example epochs and the next test dates grouped by experimental condition. *Test* and *Train Sent.* is the number of sentence pairs in test and training data respectively. *Rules* is the count of unique Hiero grammar rules extracted for the corresponding test set.

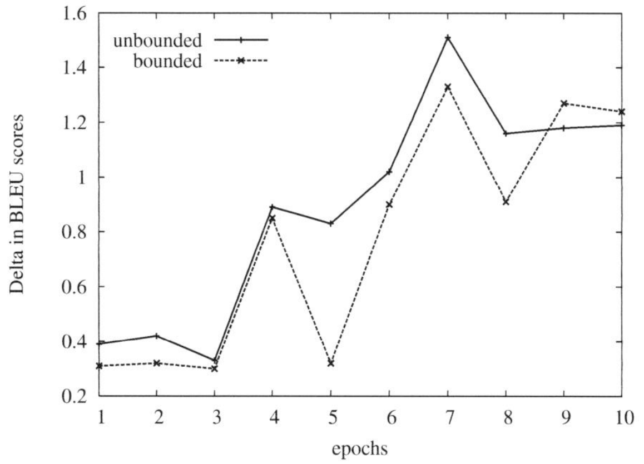

Figure 3: Static vs. online TM performance. Gains in translation performance measured by BLEU are achieved when recent German-English sentence pairs are automatically incorporated into the TM. Shown are relative BLEU improvements for the online models against the static baseline.

3. **Bounded Space**: Batch and incremental retraining with an enforced memory constraint. Here we batch or incrementally retrain using a *sliding window* approach where the training set size (the number of sentence pairs) remains constant. In particular, we ensured that we used the same number of sentences as the baseline. Each batch run of GIZA++ takes approximately the same time.

The *time* for aligning in the sOEM model is unaffected by the bounded/unbounded conditions since we always only align the mini-batch of sentences encountered in the last epoch. In contrast, for batch EM we must realign all the sentences in our training set from scratch to incorporate the new training data.

Similarly *space* usage for the batch training grows with the training set size. For sOEM, in theory memory used is with respect to vocabulary size (which grows slowly with the stream size) since we retain count history for the entire stream. To make space usage truly constant, we filter for just the needed word pairs in the current epoch being aligned. This effectively means that online EM is more memory efficient than the batch version. As our experiments will show, the sufficient statistics kept between epochs by sOEM benefits performance compared to the batch models which can only use information present within the batch itself.

4.4 Incremental Retraining Procedure

Our incremental adaptation procedure was as follows: after the latest mini-batch of sentences had been aligned using sOEM we added all newly aligned sentence pairs to the dynamic suffix arrays. For the experiments where our memory was bounded, we also *deleted* an equal number of sentences from the suffix arrays before extracting the Hiero grammar for the next test point. For the unbounded coverage experiments we deleted nothing prior to grammar extraction. Table 2 presents statistics for the number of training sentence pairs and grammar rules extracted for each coverage condition for various test points.

4.5 Results

Figure 3 shows the results of the static baseline against both the unbounded and bounded online EM models. We can see that both the online models outperform the static baseline. On average the unconstrained model that contains more sentence pairs for rule extraction slightly outperforms the bounded condition which uses less data per epoch. However, the static baseline and the bounded models both use the same number of sentence-pairs for TM training. We see there is a clear gain by incorporating recent sentence-pairs made available by the stream.

	Static Baseline	Retrained (Unbounded)		Retrained (Bounded)	
Test Date	Batch	Batch	Online	Batch	Online
09/23/2002	26.10	**26.60**	26.43	26.19	*26.40*
03/29/2004	27.40	28.33	**28.42**	28.06	*28.38*
09/26/2006	28.56	29.74	**29.75**	29.73	*29.80*

Table 3: Sample BLEU results for all baseline and online EM model conditions. The *static baseline* is a traditional model that is never retrained. The *batch unbounded* and *batch bounded* models incorporate new data from the stream but retraining is slow and computationally expensive (best results are bolded). In contrast both unbounded and bounded online models incrementally retrain only the mini-batch of new sentences collected from the incoming stream so quickly adopt the new data (best results are italicized).

Table 3 gives results of the online models compared to the batch retrained models. For presentation clarity we show only a sample of the full set of ten test points though all results follow the pattern that using more aligned sentences to derive our grammar set resulted in slightly better performance versus a restricted training set. However, for the same coverage constraints not only do we achieve comparable performance to batch retrained models using the sOEM method of incremental adaptation, we are able to align and adopt new data from the input stream orders of magnitude quicker since we only align the mini-batch of sentences collected from the last epoch. In the bounded condition, not only do we benefit from quicker adaptation, we also see that sOEM models slightly outperform the batch based models due to the online algorithm employing a longer history of count-based evidence to draw on when aligning new sentence pairs.

Figure 4 shows two example test sentences that benefited from the online TM adaptation. Translations from the online model produce more and longer matching phrases for both sentences (e.g., "creation of such a", "of the occupying forces") leading to more fluent output as well as the improvements achieved in BLEU scores.

We experimented with a variety of interpolation parameters (see Algorithm 2) but found no significant difference between them (the biggest improvement gained over all test points for all parameter settings was less than 0.1% BLEU).

4.6 Increasing LM Coverage

A natural and interesting extension to the experiments above is to use the target side of the incoming stream to extend the LM coverage alongside the TM.

Test Date	Static	Unbounded	Bounded
09/23/2002	26.46	27.11	26.96
03/29/2004	28.11	29.53	29.20
09/26/2006	29.53	30.94	30.88

Table 4: Unbounded LM coverage improvements. Shown are the BLEU scores for each experimental conditional when we allow the LM coverage to increase.

It is well known that more LM coverage (via larger training data sets) is beneficial to SMT performance (Brants et al., 2007) so we investigated whether recency gains for the TM were additive with recency gains afforded by a LM.

To test this we added all the target side data from the beginning of the stream to the most recent epoch into the LM training set before each test point. We then batch retrained[6] and used the new LM with greater coverage for the next decoding run. Experiments were for the static baseline and online models.

Results are reported in Table 4. We can see that increasing LM coverage is complimentary to adapting the TM with recent data. Comparing Tables 3 and 4, for the bounded condition, adapting only the TM achieved an absolute improvement of +1.24 BLEU over the static baseline for the final test point. We get another absolute gain of +1.08 BLEU by allowing the LM coverage to adapt as well. Using an online, adaptive model gives a total gain of +2.32 BLEU over a static baseline that does not adapt.

[6] Although we batch retrain the LMs we could use an online LM that incorporates new vocabulary from the input stream as in Levenberg and Osborne (2009).

Source: Die Kommission ist bereit, an der Schaffung eines solchen Rechtsrahmens unter Zugrundelegung von vier wesentlichen Prinzipien mitzuwirken.

Reference: The commission is willing to cooperate in the creation of such a legal framework on the basis of four essential principles.

Static: The commission is prepared, in the creation of a legal framework, taking account of four fundamental principles them.

Online: The commission is prepared to participate in the creation of such a legal framework, based on four fundamental principles.

Source: Unser Standpunkt ist klar und allseits bekannt: Wir sind gegen den Krieg und die Besetzung des Irak durch die USA und das Vereinigte Königreich, und wir verlangen den unverzüglichen Abzug der Besatzungsmächte aus diesem Land.

Reference: Our position is clear and well known: we are against the war and the US-British occupation in Iraq and we demand the immediate withdrawal of the occupying forces from that country.

Static: Our position is clear and we all know: we are against the war and the occupation of Iraq by the United States and the United Kingdom, and we are calling for the immediate withdrawal of the besatzungsmächte from this country.

Online: Our position is clear and well known: we are against the war and the occupation of Iraq by the United States and the United Kingdom, and we demand the immediate withdrawal of the occupying forces from this country .

Figure 4: Example sentences and improvements to their translation fluency by the adaptation of the TM with recent sentences. In both examples we get longer matching phrases in the online translation compared to the static one.

5 Related Work

5.1 Translation Model Domain Adaptation

Our work is related to domain adaptation for translation models. See, for example, Koehn and Schroeder (2007) or Bertoldi and Federico (2009). Most techniques center around using mixtures of translation models. Once trained, these models generally never change. They therefore fall under the *batch* training regime. The focus of this work instead is on incremental retraining and also on supporting bounded memory consumption. Our experiments examine updating model parameters in a single domain over different periods in time. Naturally, we could also use domain adaptation techniques to further improve how we incorporate new samples.

5.2 Online EM for SMT

For stepwise online EM for SMT models, the only prior work we are aware of is Liang and Klein (2009), where variations of online EM were experimented with on various NLP tasks including word alignments. They showed application of sOEM can produce quicker convergence compared to the batch EM algorithm. However, the model presented does not incorporate any unseen data, instead iterating over a static data set multiple times using sOEM. For Liang and Klein (2009) incremental retraining is simply an alternative way to use a fixed training set.

5.3 Streaming Language Models

Recent work in Levenberg and Osborne (2009) presented a streaming LM that was capable of adapting to an unbounded monolingual input stream in constant space and time. The LM has the ability to add or delete n-grams (and their counts) based on feedback from the decoder after translation points. The model was tested in an SMT setting and results showed recent data benefited performance. However, adaptation was only to the LM and no tests were conducted on the TM.

6 Conclusion and Future Work

We have presented an online EM approach for word alignments. We have shown that, for a SMT system, incorporating recent parallel data into a TM from an input stream is beneficial to translation performance compared to a traditional, static baseline.

Our strategy for populating the suffix array was simply to use a first-in, first-out stack. For future work we will investigate whether information provided by the incoming stream coupled with the feedback from the decoder allows for more sophisticated adaptation strategies that reinforce useful word alignments and delete bad or unused ones.

In the near future we also hope to test the online EM setup in an application setting such as a computer aided translation or crowdsourced generated streams via Amazon's Mechanical Turk.

Acknowledgements

Research supported by EuroMatrixPlus funded by the European Commission, by the DARPA GALE program under Contract Nos. HR0011-06-2-0001 and HR0011-06-C-0022, and the NSF under grant IIS-0713448.

References

Nicola Bertoldi and Marcello Federico. 2009. Domain adaptation for statistical machine translation with monolingual resources. In *WMT09: Proceedings of the Fourth Workshop on Statistical Machine Translation*, pages 182–189, Morristown, NJ, USA. Association for Computational Linguistics.

Thorsten Brants, Ashok C. Popat, Peng Xu, Franz J. Och, and Jeffrey Dean. 2007. Large language models in machine translation. In *Proceedings of the 2007 Joint Conference on Empirical Methods in Natural Language Processing and Computational Natural Language Learning (EMNLP-CoNLL)*, pages 858–867.

Peter F. Brown, Vincent J. Della Pietra, Stephen A. Della Pietra, and Robert L. Mercer. 1993. The mathematics of statistical machine translation: parameter estimation. *Computational Linguistics*, 19(2):263–311.

Chris Callison-Burch, Colin Bannard, and Josh Schroeder. 2005. Scaling phrase-based statistical machine translation to larger corpora and longer phrases. In *Proceedings of the 43rd Annual Meeting of the Association for Computational Linguistics (ACL'05)*, pages 255–262, Ann Arbor, Michigan, June. Association for Computational Linguistics.

Olivier Cappe and Eric Moulines. 2009. Online EM algorithm for latent data models. *Journal Of The Royal Statistical Society Series B*, 71:593.

David Chiang. 2007. Hierarchical phrase-based translation. *Computational Linguistics*, 33(2):201–228.

A. P. Dempster, N. M. Laird, and D. B. Rubin. 1977. Maximum likelihood from incomplete data via the EM algorithm. *Journal of the Royal Statistical Society. Series B (Methodological)*, 39:1–38.

Philipp Koehn and Josh Schroeder. 2007. Experiments in domain adaptation for statistical machine translation. In *Proceedings of the Second Workshop on Statistical Machine Translation*, pages 224–227, Prague, Czech Republic, June. Association for Computational Linguistics.

Abby Levenberg and Miles Osborne. 2009. Stream-based randomised language models for SMT. In *Proceedings of the Conference on Empirical Methods in Natural Language Processing (EMNLP)*.

Zhifei Li, Chris Callison-Burch, Chris Dyer, Juri Ganitkevitch, Sanjeev Khudanpur, Lane Schwartz, Wren N. G. Thornton, Jonathan Weese, and Omar F. Zaidan. 2009. Joshua: an open source toolkit for parsing-based machine translation. In *WMT09: Proceedings of the Fourth Workshop on Statistical Machine Translation*, pages 135–139, Morristown, NJ, USA. Association for Computational Linguistics.

Percy Liang and Dan Klein. 2009. Online EM for unsupervised models. In *North American Association for Computational Linguistics (NAACL)*.

Adam Lopez. 2008. Tera-scale translation models via pattern matching. In *Proceedings of the 22nd International Conference on Computational Linguistics (Coling 2008)*, pages 505–512, Manchester, UK, August. Coling 2008 Organizing Committee.

Udi Manber and Gene Myers. 1990. Suffix arrays: A new method for on-line string searches. In *The First Annual ACM-SIAM Symposium on Dicrete Algorithms*, pages 319–327.

Franz Josef Och and Hermann Ney. 2003. A systematic comparison of various statistical alignment models. *Computational Linguistics*, 29(1):19–51, March.

Franz Josef Och. 2003. Minimum error rate training in statistical machine translation. In *ACL '03: Proceedings of the 41st Annual Meeting on Association for Computational Linguistics*, pages 160–167, Morristown, NJ, USA. Association for Computational Linguistics.

Kishore Papineni, Salim Roukos, Todd Ward, and Wei-Jing Zhu. 2001. Bleu: a method for automatic evaluation of machine translation. In *ACL '02: Proceedings of the 40th Annual Meeting on Association for Computational Linguistics*, pages 311–318, Morristown, NJ, USA. Association for Computational Linguistics.

Ronald Rosenfeld. 1995. Optimizing lexical and n-gram coverage via judicious use of linguistic data. In *In Proc. European Conf. on Speech Technology*, pages 1763–1766.

Mikaël Salson, Thierry Lecroq, Martine Léonard, and Laurent Mouchard. 2009. Dynamic extended suffix arrays. *Journal of Discrete Algorithms*, March.

Stephan Vogel, Hermann Ney, and Christoph Tillmann. 1996. HMM-based word alignment in statistical translation. In *Proceedings of the 16th conference on Computational linguistics*, pages 836–841, Morristown, NJ, USA. Association for Computational Linguistics.

Extracting Parallel Sentences from Comparable Corpora using Document Level Alignment

Jason R. Smith[*]
Center for Lang. and Speech Processing
Johns Hopkins University
Baltimore, MD 21218
jsmith@cs.jhu.edu

Chris Quirk and Kristina Toutanova
Microsoft Research
One Microsoft Way
Redmond, WA 98052
{chrisq,kristout}@microsoft.com

Abstract

The quality of a statistical machine translation (SMT) system is heavily dependent upon the amount of parallel sentences used in training. In recent years, there have been several approaches developed for obtaining parallel sentences from non-parallel, or comparable data, such as news articles published within the same time period (Munteanu and Marcu, 2005), or web pages with a similar structure (Resnik and Smith, 2003). One resource not yet thoroughly explored is Wikipedia, an online encyclopedia containing linked articles in many languages. We advance the state of the art in parallel sentence extraction by modeling the document level alignment, motivated by the observation that parallel sentence pairs are often found in close proximity. We also include features which make use of the additional annotation given by Wikipedia, and features using an automatically induced lexicon model. Results for both accuracy in sentence extraction and downstream improvement in an SMT system are presented.

1 Introduction

For any statistical machine translation system, the size of the parallel corpus used for training is a major factor in its performance. For some language pairs, such as Chinese-English and Arabic-English, large amounts of parallel data are readily available, but for most language pairs this is not the case. The domain of the parallel corpus also strongly influences the quality of translations produced. Many parallel corpora are taken from the news domain, or from parliamentary proceedings. Translation quality suffers when a system is not trained on any data from the domain it is tested on.

While parallel corpora may be scarce, comparable, or semi-parallel corpora are readily available in several domains and language pairs. These corpora consist of a set of documents in two languages containing similar information. (See Section 2.1 for a more detailed description of the types of non-parallel corpora.) In most previous work on extraction of parallel sentences from comparable corpora, some coarse document-level similarity is used to determine which document pairs contain parallel sentences. For identifying similar web pages, Resnik and Smith (2003) compare the HTML structure. Munteanu and Marcu (2005) use publication date and vector-based similarity (after projecting words through a bilingual dictionary) to identify similar news articles.

Once promising document pairs are identified, the next step is to extract parallel sentences. Usually, some seed parallel data is assumed to be available. This data is used to train a word alignment model, such as IBM Model 1 (Brown et al., 1993) or HMM-based word alignment (Vogel et al., 1996). Statistics from this word alignment model are used to train a classifier which identifies bilingual sentence pairs as parallel or not parallel. This classifier is applied to all sentence pairs in documents which were found to be similar. Typically, some pruning is done to reduce the number of sen-

[*]This research was conducted during the author's internship at Microsoft Research.

Human Language Technologies: The 2010 Annual Conference of the North American Chapter of the ACL, pages 403–411,
Los Angeles, California, June 2010.

tence pairs that need to be classified.

While these methods have been applied to news corpora and web pages, very little attention has been given to Wikipedia as a source of parallel sentences. This is surprising, given that Wikipedia contains annotated article alignments, and much work has been done on extracting bilingual lexicons on this dataset. Adafre and de Rijke (2006) extracted similar sentences from Wikipedia article pairs, but only evaluated precision on a small number of extracted sentences.

In this paper, we more thoroughly investigate Wikipedia's viability as a comparable corpus, and describe novel methods for parallel sentence extraction. Section 2 describes the multilingual resources available in Wikipedia. Section 3 gives further background on previous methods for parallel sentence extraction on comparable corpora, and describes our approach, which finds a global sentence alignment between two documents. In Section 4, we compare our approach with previous methods on datasets derived from Wikipedia for three language pairs (Spanish-English, German-English, and Bulgarian-English), and show improvements in downstream SMT performance by adding the parallel data we extracted.

2 Wikipedia as a Comparable Corpus

Wikipedia (Wikipedia, 2004) is an online collaborative encyclopedia available in a wide variety of languages. While the English Wikipedia is the largest, with over 3 million articles, there are 24 language editions with at least 100,000 articles.

Articles on the same topic in different languages are also connected via "interwiki" links, which are annotated by users. This is an extremely valuable resource when extracting parallel sentences, as the document alignment is already provided. Table 1 shows how many of these "interwiki" links are present between the English Wikipedia and the 16 largest non-English Wikipedias.

Wikipedia's markup contains other useful indicators for parallel sentence extraction. The many hyperlinks found in articles have previously been used as a valuable source of information. (Adafre and de Rijke, 2006) use matching hyperlinks to identify similar sentences. Two links match if the articles they refer to are connected by an "interwiki" link. Also, images in Wikipedia are often stored in a central source across different languages; this allows identification of captions which may be parallel (see Figure 1). Finally, there are other minor forms of markup which may be useful for finding similar content across languages, such as lists and section headings. In Section 3.3, we will explain how features are derived from this markup.

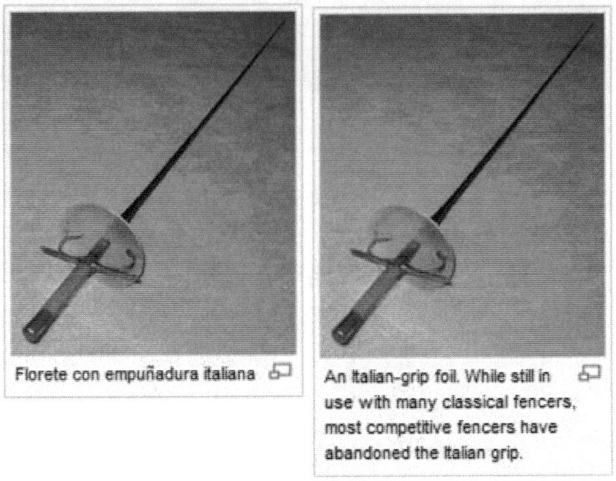

Figure 1: Captions for an image of a foil in English and Spanish

2.1 Types of Non-Parallel Corpora

Fung and Cheung (2004) give a more fine-grained description of the types of non-parallel corpora, which we will briefly summarize. A *noisy parallel corpus* has documents which contain many parallel sentences in roughly the same order. *Comparable corpora* contain topic aligned documents which are not translations of each other. The corpora Fung and Cheung (2004) examine are *quasi-comparable*: they contain bilingual documents which are not necessarily on the same topic.

Wikipedia is a special case, since the aligned article pairs may range from being almost completely parallel (e.g., the Spanish and English entries for "Antiparticle") to containing almost no parallel sentences (the Spanish and English entries for "John Calvin"), despite being topic-aligned. It is best characterized as a mix of noisy parallel and comparable article pairs. Some Wikipedia authors will translate articles from another language; others

French 496K	German 488K	Polish 384K	Italian 380K	Dutch 357K	Portuguese 323K	Spanish 311K	Japanese 252K
Russian 232K	Swedish 197K	Finnish 146K	Chinese 142K	Norwegian 141K	Volapük 106K	Catalan 103K	Czech 87K

Table 1: Number of aligned bilingual articles in Wikipedia by language (paired with English).

write the content themselves. Furthermore, even articles created through translations may later diverge due to independent edits in either language.

3 Models for Parallel Sentence Extraction

In this section, we will focus on methods for extracting parallel sentences from aligned, comparable documents. The related problem of automatic document alignment in news and web corpora has been explored by a number of researchers, including Resnik and Smith (2003), Munteanu and Marcu (2005), Tillmann and Xu (2009), and Tillmann (2009). Since our corpus already contains document alignments, we sidestep this problem, and will not discuss further details of this issue. That said, we believe that our methods will be effective in corpora without document alignments when combined with one of the aforementioned algorithms.

3.1 Binary Classifiers and Rankers

Much of the previous work involves building a binary classifier for sentence pairs to determine whether or not they are parallel (Munteanu and Marcu, 2005; Tillmann, 2009). The training data usually comes from a standard parallel corpus. There is a substantial class imbalance ($O(n)$ positive examples, and $O(n^2)$ negative examples), and various heuristics are used to mitigate this problem. Munteanu and Marcu (2005) filter out negative examples with high length difference or low word overlap (based on a bilingual dictionary).

We propose an alternative approach: we learn a ranking model, which, for each sentence in the *source* document, selects either a sentence in the *target* document that it is parallel to, or "null". This formulation of the problem avoids the class imbalance issue of the binary classifier.

In both the binary classifier approach and the ranking approach, we use a Maximum Entropy classifier, following Munteanu and Marcu (2005).

3.2 Sequence Models

In Wikipedia article pairs, it is common for parallel sentences to occur in clusters. A global sentence alignment model is able to capture this phenomenon. For both parallel and comparable corpora, global sentence alignments have been used, though the alignments were monotonic (Gale and Church, 1991; Moore, 2002; Zhao and Vogel, 2002). Our model is a first order linear chain Conditional Random Field (CRF) (Lafferty et al., 2001). The set of source and target sentences are observed. For each *source* sentence, we have a hidden variable indicating the corresponding *target* sentence to which it is aligned (or null). The model is similar to the discriminative CRF-based word alignment model of (Blunsom and Cohn, 2006).

3.3 Features

Our features can be grouped into four categories.

Features derived from word alignments

We use a feature set inspired by (Munteanu and Marcu, 2005), who defined features primarily based on IBM Model 1 alignments (Brown et al., 1993). We also use HMM word alignments (Vogel et al., 1996) in both directions (*source* to *target* and *target* to *source*), and extract the following features based on these four alignments:[1]

1. Log probability of the alignment
2. Number of aligned/unaligned words
3. Longest aligned/unaligned sequence of words
4. Number of words with fertility 1, 2, and 3+

We also define two more features which are independent of word alignment models. One is a sentence length feature taken from (Moore, 2002),

[1]These are all derived from the one best alignment, and normalized by sentence length.

which models the length ratio between the *source* and *target* sentences with a Poisson distribution. The other feature is the difference in relative document position of the two sentences, capturing the idea that the aligned articles have a similar topic progression.

The above features are all defined on sentence pairs, and are included in the binary classifier and ranking model.

Distortion features

In the sequence model, we use additional distortion features, which only look at the difference between the position of the previous and current aligned sentences. One set of features bins these distances; another looks at the absolute difference between the expected position (one after the previous aligned sentence) and the actual position.

Features derived from Wikipedia markup

Three features are derived from Wikipedia's markup. The first is the number of matching links in the sentence pair. The links are weighted by their inverse frequency in the document, so a link that appears often does not contribute much to this feature's value. The image feature fires whenever two sentences are captions of the same image, and the list feature fires when two sentences are both items in a list. These last two indicator features fire with a negative value when the feature matches on one sentence and not the other.

None of the above features fire on a null alignment, in either the ranker or CRF. There is also a bias feature for these two models, which fires on all non-null alignments.

Word-level induced lexicon features

A common problem with approaches for parallel sentence classification, which rely heavily on alignment models trained from unrelated corpora, is low recall due to unknown words in the candidate sentence-pairs. One approach that begins to address this problem is the use of self-training, as in (Munteanu and Marcu, 2005). However, a self-trained sentence pair extraction system is only able to acquire new lexical items that occur in parallel sentences. Within Wikipedia, many linked article pairs do not contain any parallel sentences, yet contain many words and phrases that are good translations of each other.

In this paper we explore an alternative approach to lexicon acquisition for use in parallel sentence extraction. We build a lexicon model using an approach similar to ones developed for unsupervised lexicon induction from monolingual or comparable corpora (Rapp, 1999; Koehn and Knight, 2002; Haghighi et al., 2008). We briefly describe the lexicon model and its use in sentence-extraction.

The lexicon model is based on a probabilistic model $P(w_t|w_s, T, S)$ where w_t is a word in the target language, w_s is a word in the source language, and T and S are linked articles in the target and source languages, respectively.

We train this model similarly to the sentence-extraction ranking model, with the difference that we are aligning word pairs and not sentence pairs. The model is trained from a small set of annotated Wikipedia article pairs, where for some words in the source language we have marked one or more words as corresponding to the source word (in the context of the article pair), or have indicated that the source word does not have a corresponding translation in the target article. The word-level annotated articles are disjoint from the sentence-aligned articles described in Section 4. The following features are used in the lexicon model:

Translation probability. This is the translation probability $p(w_t|w_s)$ from the HMM word alignment model trained on the seed parallel data. We also use the probability in the other direction, as well as the log-probabilities in the two directions.

Position difference. This is the absolute value of the difference in relative position of words w_s and w_t in the articles S and T.

Orthographic similarity. This is a function of the edit distance between source and target words. The edit distance between words written in different alphabets is computed by first performing a deterministic phonetic translation of the words to a common alphabet. The translation is inexact and this is a promising area for improvement. A similar source of information has been used to create seed lexicons in (Koehn and Knight, 2002) and as part of the feature space in (Haghighi et al., 2008).

Context translation probability. This feature looks at all words occurring next to word w_s in the article S and next to w_t in the article T in a local context window (we used one word to the left and one word to the right), and computes several scoring functions measuring the translation correspondence between the contexts (using the IBM Model 1 trained from seed parallel data). This feature is similar to distributional similarity measures used in previous work, with the difference that it is limited to contexts of words within a linked article pair.

Distributional similarity. This feature corresponds more closely to context similarity measures used in previous work on lexicon induction. For each source headword w_s, we collect a distribution over context positions $o \in \{-2, -1, +1, +2\}$ and context words v_s in those positions based on a count of times a context word occurred at that offset from a headword: $P(o, v_s|w_s) \propto weight(o) \cdot C(w_s, o, v_s)$. Adjacent positions -1 and $+1$ have a weight of 2; other positions have a weight of 1. Likewise we gather a distribution over target words and contexts for each target headword $P(o, v_t|w_t)$. Using an IBM Model 1 word translation table $P(v_t|v_s)$ estimated on the seed parallel corpus, we estimate a cross-lingual context distribution as $P(o, v_t|w_s) = \sum_{v_s} P(v_t|v_s) \cdot P(o, v_s|w_s)$. We define the similarity of a words w_s and w_t as one minus the Jensen-Shannon divergence of the distributions over positions and target words.[2]

Given this small set of feature functions, we train the weights of a log-linear ranking model for $P(w_t|w_s, T, S)$, based on the word-level annotated Wikipedia article pairs. After a model is trained, we generate a new translation table $P_{lex}(t|s)$ which is defined as $P_{lex}(t|s) \propto \sum_{t \in T, s \in S} P(t|s, T, S)$. The summation is over occurrences of the source and target word in linked Wikipedia articles. This new translation table is used to define another HMM word-alignment model (together with distortion probabilities trained from parallel data) for use in the sentence extraction models. Two copies of each feature using the HMM word alignment model are generated: one using the seed data HMM model, and another using this new HMM model.

The training data for Bulgarian consisted of two partially annotated Wikipedia article pairs. For German and Spanish we used the feature weights of the model trained on Bulgarian, because we did not have word-level annotated Wikipedia articles.

4 Experiments

4.1 Data

We annotated twenty Wikipedia article pairs for three language pairs: Spanish-English, Bulgarian-English, and German-English. Each sentence in the *source* language was annotated with possible parallel sentences in the *target* language (the target language was English in all experiments). The pairs were annotated with a quality level: **1** if the sentences contained some parallel fragments, **2** if the sentences were mostly parallel with some missing words, and **3** if the sentences appeared to be direct translations. In all experiments, sentence pairs with quality **2** or **3** were taken as positive examples. The resulting datasets are available at http://research.microsoft.com/en-us/people/chrisq/wikidownload.aspx.

For our seed parallel data, we used the Europarl corpus (Koehn, 2005) for Spanish and German and the JRC-Aquis corpus for Bulgarian, plus the article titles for parallel Wikipedia documents, and translations available from Wiktionary entries.[3]

4.2 Intrinsic Evaluation

Using 5-fold cross-validation on the 20 document pairs for each language condition, we compared the binary classifier, ranker, and CRF models for parallel sentence extraction. To tune for precision/recall, we used minimum Bayes risk decoding. We define the loss $L(\tau, \mu)$ of picking target sentence τ when the correct target sentence is μ as 0 if $\tau = \mu$, λ if $\tau =$ NULL and $\mu \neq$ NULL, and 1 otherwise. By modifying the null loss λ, the precision/recall trade-off can be adjusted. For the CRF model, we used posterior decoding to make the minimum risk decision rule tractable. As a summary measure of the performance of the models at different levels of recall we use average precision as defined in (Ido

[2]We restrict our attention to words with ten or more occurrences, since rare words have poorly estimated distributions. Also we discard the contribution from any context position and word pair that relates to more than 1,000 distinct source or target words, since it explodes the computational overhead and has little impact on the final similarity score.

[3]Wiktionary is an online collaborative dictionary, similar to Wikipedia.

Language Pair	Binary Classifier			Ranker			CRF		
	Avg Prec	R@90	R@80	Avg Prec	R@90	R@80	Avg Prec	R@90	R@80
English-Bulgarian	75.7	33.9	56.2	76.3	38.8	57.0	**80.6**	**52.9**	**59.5**
English-Spanish	90.4	81.3	87.6	93.4	81.0	84.5	**94.7**	**87.6**	**90.2**
English-German	61.8	9.4	27.5	66.4	25.7	42.4	**78.9**	**52.2**	**54.7**

Table 2: Average precision, recall at 90% precision, and recall at 80% precision for each model in all three language pairs. In these experiments, the Wikipedia features and lexicon features are omitted.

Setting	Ranker			CRF		
	Avg Prec	R@90	R@80	Avg Prec	R@90	R@80
English-Bulgarian						
One Direction	76.3	38.8	57.0	80.6	52.9	59.5
Intersected	78.2	47.9	60.3	79.9	38.8	57.0
Intersected +Wiki	80.8	39.7	68.6	82.1	53.7	62.8
Intersected +Wiki +Lex	89.3	64.4	79.3	**90.9**	**72.0**	**81.8**
English-Spanish						
One Direction	93.4	81.0	84.5	94.7	87.6	90.2
Intersected	94.3	82.4	89.0	95.4	88.5	91.8
Intersected +Wiki	94.5	82.4	89.0	95.6	89.2	92.7
Intersected +Wiki +Lex	95.8	87.4	91.1	**96.4**	**90.4**	**93.7**
English-German						
One Direction	66.4	25.7	42.4	78.9	52.2	54.7
Intersected	71.9	36.2	43.8	80.9	54.0	67.0
Intersected +Wiki	74.0	38.8	45.3	82.4	56.9	**71.0**
Intersected +Wiki +Lex	78.7	46.4	59.1	**83.9**	**58.7**	68.8

Table 3: Average precision, recall at 90% precision, and recall at 80% precision for the Ranker and CRF in all three language pairs. "+Wiki" indicates that Wikipedia features were used, and "+Lex" means the lexicon features were used.

et al., 2006). We also report recall at precision of 90 and 80 percent. Table 2 compares the different models in all three language pairs.

In our next set of experiments, we looked at the effects of the Wikipedia specific features. Since the ranker and CRF are asymmetric models, we also experimented with running the models in both directions and combining their outputs by intersection. These results are shown in Table 3.

Identifying the agreement between two asymmetric models is a commonly exploited trick elsewhere in machine translation. It is mostly effective here as well, improving all cases except for the Bulgarian-English CRF where the regression is slight. More successful are the Wikipedia features, which provide an auxiliary signal of potential parallelism.

The gains from adding the lexicon-based features can be dramatic as in the case of Bulgarian (the CRF model average precision increased by nearly 9 points). The lower gains on Spanish and German may be due in part to the lack of language-specific training data. These results are very promising and motivate further exploration. We also note that this is perhaps the first successful practical application of an automatically induced word translation lexicon.

4.3 SMT Evaluation

We also present results in the context of a full machine translation system to evaluate the potential utility of this data. A standard phrasal SMT system (Koehn et al., 2003) serves as our testbed, using a conventional set of models: phrasal models of source given target and target given source; lexical weighting models in both directions, language model, word count, phrase count, distortion penalty, and a lexicalized reordering model. Given that the extracted Wikipedia data takes the standard form of parallel sentences, it would be easy to exploit this same data in a number of systems.

For each language pair we explored two training conditions. The "Medium" data condition used easily downloadable corpora: Europarl for German-English and Spanish-English, and JRC/Acquis for Bulgarian-English. Additionally we included titles of all linked Wikipedia articles as parallel sentences in the medium data condition. The "Large" data condition includes all the medium data, and also includes using a broad range of available sources such as data scraped from the web (Resnik and Smith, 2003), data from the United Nations, phrase books, software documentation, and more.

In each condition, we explored the impact of including additional parallel sentences automatically extracted from Wikipedia in the system training data. For German-English and Spanish-English, we extracted data with the null loss adjusted to achieve an estimated precision of 95 percent, and for English-Bulgarian a precision of 90 percent. Table 4 summarizes the characteristics of these data sets. We were pleasantly surprised at the amount of parallel sentences extracted from such a varied comparable corpus. Apparently the average Wikipedia article contains at least a handful of parallel sentences, suggesting this is a very fertile ground for training MT systems.

The extracted Wikipedia data is likely to make the greatest impact on broad domain test sets – indeed, initial experimentation showed little BLEU gain on in-domain test sets such as Europarl, where out-of-domain training data is unlikely to provide appropriate phrasal translations. Therefore, we experimented with two broad domain test sets.

First, Bing Translator provided a sample of translation requests along with translations in German-English and Spanish-English, which acted our standard development and test set. Unfortunately no such tagged set was available in Bulgarian-English, so we held out a portion of the large system's training data to use for development and test. In each language pair, the test set was split into a development portion ("Dev A") used for minimum error rate training (Och, 2003) and a test set ("Test A") used for final evaluation.

Second, we created new test sets in each of the three language pairs by sampling parallel sentences from held out Wikipedia articles. To ensure that this test data was clean, we manually filtered the sentence pairs that were not truly parallel and edited them as necessary to improve adequacy. We called this "Wikitest". This test set is available at http://research.microsoft.com/en-us/people/chrisq/wikidownload.aspx. Characteristics of these test sets are summarized in Table 5.

We evaluated the resulting systems using BLEU-4 (Papineni et al., 2002); the results are presented in Table 6. First we note that the extracted Wikipedia data are very helpful in medium data conditions, significantly improving translation performance in all conditions. Furthermore we found that the extracted Wikipedia sentences substantially improved translation quality on held-out Wikipedia articles. In every case, training on medium data plus Wikipedia extracts led to equal or better translation quality than the large system alone. Furthermore, adding the Wikipedia data to the large data condition still made substantial improvements.

5 Conclusions

Our first substantial contribution is to demonstrate that Wikipedia is a useful resource for mining parallel data. The sheer volume of extracted parallel sentences within Wikipedia is a somewhat surprising result in the light of Wikipedia's construction. We are also releasing several valuable resources to the community to facilitate further research: manually aligned document pairs, and an edited test set. Hopefully this will encourage research into Wikipedia as a resource for machine translation.

Secondly, we improve on prior pairwise models by introducing a ranking approach for sentence pair extraction. This ranking approach sidesteps the problematic class imbalance issue, resulting in improved average precision while retaining simplicity and clarity in the models.

Also by modeling the sentence alignment of the articles globally, we were able to show a substantial improvement in task accuracy. Furthermore a

		German	English	Spanish	English	Bulgarian	English
Medium	sentences	924,416	924,416	957,884	957,884	413,514	413,514
	types	351,411	320,597	272,139	247,465	115,756	69,002
	tokens	11,556,988	11,751,138	18,229,085	17,184,070	10,207,565	10,422,415
Large	sentences	6,693,568	6,693,568	7,727,256	7,727,256	1,459,900	1,459,900
	types	1,050,832	875,041	1,024,793	952,161	239,076	137,227
	tokens	100,456,622	96,035,475	155,626,085	137,559,844	29,741,936	29,889,020
Wiki	sentences	1,694,595	1,694,595	1,914,978	1,914,978	146,465	146,465
	types	578,371	525,617	569,518	498,765	107,690	74,389
	tokens	21,991,377	23,290,765	29,859,332	28,270,223	1,455,458	1,516,231

Table 4: Statistics of the training data size in all three language pairs.

		German	English	Spanish	English	Bulgarian	English
Dev A	sentences	2,000	2,000	2,000	2,000	2,000	2,000
	tokens	16,367	16,903	24,571	21,493	39,796	40,503
Test A	sentences	5,000	5,000	5,000	5,000	2,473	2,473
	tokens	42,766	43,929	68,036	60,380	52,370	52,343
Wikitest	sentences	500	500	500	500	516	516
	tokens	8,235	9,176	10,446	9,701	7,300	7,701

Table 5: Statistics of the test data sets.

Language pair	Training data	Dev A	Test A	Wikitest
Spanish-English	Medium	32.6	30.5	33.0
	Medium+Wiki	36.7 (+4.1)	33.8 (+3.3)	39.1 (+6.1)
	Large	39.2	**37.4**	38.9
	Large+Wiki	**39.5** (+0.3)	37.3 (-0.1)	**41.1** (+2.2)
German-English	Medium	28.7	26.6	13.0
	Medium+Wiki	31.5 (+2.8)	29.6 (+3.0)	18.2 (+5.2)
	Large	**35.0**	33.7	17.1
	Large+Wiki	34.8 (-0.2)	**33.9** (+0.2)	**20.2** (+3.1)
Bulgarian-English	Medium	36.9	26.0	27.8
	Medium+Wiki	37.9 (+1.0)	27.6 (+1.6)	37.9 (+10.1)
	Large	**51.7**	**49.6**	36.0
	Large+Wiki	**51.7**(+0.0)	49.4 (-0.2)	**39.5**(+3.5)

Table 6: BLEU scores under various training and test conditions. The first column is from minimum error rate training; the next two columns are on held-out test sets. For training data conditions including extracted Wikipedia sentences, parenthesized values indicate absolute BLEU difference against the corresponding system without Wikipedia extracts.

small sample of annotated articles is sufficient to train these global level features, and the learned classifiers appear very portable across languages. It is difficult to say whether such improvement will carry over to other comparable corpora with less document structure and meta-data. We plan to address this question in future work.

Finally, initial investigations have shown that substantial gains can be achieved by using an induced word-level lexicon in combination with sentence extraction. This helps address modeling word pairs that are out-of-vocabulary with respect to the seed parallel lexicon, while avoiding some of the issues in bootstrapping.

References

S. F Adafre and M. de Rijke. 2006. Finding similar sentences across multiple languages in wikipedia. In *Proceedings of EACL*, pages 62–69.

Phil Blunsom and Trevor Cohn. 2006. Discriminative word alignment with conditional random fields. In *Proceedings of ACL*.

P. F Brown, V. J Della Pietra, S. A Della Pietra, and R. L Mercer. 1993. The mathematics of statistical machine translation: Parameter estimation. *Computational linguistics*, 19(2):263–311.

P. Fung and P. Cheung. 2004. Multi-level bootstrapping for extracting parallel sentences from a quasi-comparable corpus. In *Proceedings of the 20th international conference on Computational Linguistics*, page 1051.

W. A Gale and K. W Church. 1991. Identifying word correspondences in parallel texts. In *Proceedings of the workshop on Speech and Natural Language*, pages 152–157.

Aria Haghighi, Percy Liang, Taylor Berg-Kirkpatrick, and Dan Klein. 2008. Learning bilingual lexicons from monolingual corpora. In *Proceedings of ACL*, pages 771–779.

Roy Bar-Haim Ido, Ido Dagan, Bill Dolan, Lisa Ferro, Danilo Giampiccolo, Bernardo Magnini, and Idan Szpektor. 2006. The second pascal recognising textual entailment challenge.

P. Koehn and K. Knight. 2002. Learning a translation lexicon from monolingual corpora. In *Proceedings of the ACL Workshop on Unsupervised Lexical Acquisition*.

Philipp Koehn, Franz Josef Och, and Daniel Marcu. 2003. Statistical phrase-based translation. In *Proceedings of HLT/NAACL*, pages 127–133, Edmonton, Canada, May.

P. Koehn. 2005. Europarl: A parallel corpus for statistical machine translation. In *MT summit*, volume 5.

J. Lafferty, A. McCallum, and F. Pereira. 2001. Conditional random fields: Probabilistic models for segmenting and labeling sequence data. In *Proceedings of the 18th International Conference on Machine Learning*, pages 282–289.

R. C Moore. 2002. Fast and accurate sentence alignment of bilingual corpora. *Lecture Notes in Computer Science*, 2499:135–144.

D. S Munteanu and D. Marcu. 2005. Improving machine translation performance by exploiting non-parallel corpora. *Computational Linguistics*, 31(4):477–504.

Franz Josef Och. 2003. Minimum error rate training in statistical machine translation. In *Proceedings of the Annual Meeting of the Association for Computational Linguistics*, pages 160–167, Sapporo, Japan.

Kishore Papineni, Salim Roukos, Todd Ward, and Wei-Jing Zhu. 2002. BLEU: a method for automatic evaluation of machine translation. In *Proceedings of the Annual Meeting of the Association for Computational Linguistics*, pages 311–318, Philadelpha, Pennsylvania, USA.

R. Rapp. 1999. Automatic identification of word translations from unrelated English and German corpora. In *Proceedings of ACL*.

P. Resnik and N. A Smith. 2003. The web as a parallel corpus. *Computational Linguistics*, 29(3):349–380.

C. Tillmann and J. Xu. 2009. A simple sentence-level extraction algorithm for comparable data. In *Proceedings of HLT/NAACL*, pages 93–96.

C. Tillmann. 2009. A Beam-Search extraction algorithm for comparable data. In *Proceedings of ACL*, pages 225–228.

S. Vogel, H. Ney, and C. Tillmann. 1996. HMM-based word alignment in statistical translation. In *Proceedings of the 16th conference on Computational linguistics-Volume 2*, pages 836–841.

Wikipedia. 2004. Wikipedia, the free encyclopedia. [Online; accessed 20-November-2009].

B. Zhao and S. Vogel. 2002. Adaptive parallel sentences mining from web bilingual news collection. In *Proceedings of the 2002 IEEE International Conference on Data Mining*, page 745. IEEE Computer Society.

Statistical Machine Translation of Texts with Misspelled Words

Nicola Bertoldi **Mauro Cettolo** **Marcello Federico**
FBK - Fondazione Bruno Kessler
via Sommarive 18 - 38123 Povo, Trento, Italy
{bertoldi,cettolo,federico}@fbk.eu

Abstract

This paper investigates the impact of misspelled words in statistical machine translation and proposes an extension of the translation engine for handling misspellings. The enhanced system decodes a word-based confusion network representing spelling variations of the input text.

We present extensive experimental results on two translation tasks of increasing complexity which show how misspellings of different types do affect performance of a statistical machine translation decoder and to what extent our enhanced system is able to recover from such errors.

1 Introduction

With the widespread adoption of the Internet, of modern communication, multimedia and mobile device technologies, the amount of multilingual information distributed and available to anyone, anywhere, has exploded. So called social media have rapidly reshaped information exchange among Internet users, providing new means of communication (blogs, tweets, etc.), collaboration (e.g. wikis), and sharing of multimedia content, and entertainment. In particular, social media have today become also an important market for advertisement as well as a global forum for consumer opinions (Kushal et al., 2003).

The growing spread of user-generated content is scaling-up the potential demand for on-line machine translation (MT) but also setting new challenges to the field of natural language processing (NLP) in general. The language written and spoken in the social media presents an impressive variety of content and styles (Schler et al., 2006), and writing conventions that rapidly evolve over time. Moreover, much of the content is expressed in informal style, that more or less violates the standard grammar, contains many abbreviations and acronyms, and finally many misspelled words. From the point of view of MT, language of social media is hence very different from the one represented in the text corpora nowadays available to train statistical MT systems.

Facing all these challenges, we pragmatically scaled down our ambition and decided to investigate a basic, somehow preliminary, well defined problem: the impact of misspelled words in statistical MT. Unintentional typing errors are indeed remarkably frequent in online chats, blogs, wikis, reviews, and hence constitute a major source of noise (Subramaniam et al., 2009).

In this paper we aim at studying performance degradation of statistical MT under different levels and kinds of noise, and at analyzing to what extent statistical MT is able to recover from errors by enriching its input with spelling variations.

After a brief overview of NLP literature related to noisy texts, in Section 3 we consider different types of misspellings and derive simple but realistic models that are able to reproduce them. Such models are then used to generate errors in texts passed to a phrase-based statistical MT system. Next, in Section 4 we introduce an extension of a statistical MT system able to handle misspellings by exploiting confusion network decoding (Bertoldi et al., 2008).

Experiments are reported in Section 5 that in-

Human Language Technologies: The 2010 Annual Conference of the North American Chapter of the ACL, pages 412–419,
Los Angeles, California, June 2010.

vestigate the trade-off between complexity of the extended MT decoder versus translation accuracy. Moreover, as the proposed model for handling misspellings embeds specific assumptions on how errors are generated, we also measure the robustness of the enhanced MT decoder with respect to different noise sources. Experiments are reported on two tasks of different complexity, the translation of Europarl texts and weather bulletins, involving English and Italian languages.

2 Previous Work

Most contributions addressing NLP of noisy user-generated content are from the text mining community. A survey about the different types of noise that might affect text mining is in (Subramaniam et al., 2009), while an analysis of how noise phenomena, commonly occurring in blogs, affect an opinion mining application is in (Dey and Haque, 2009).

Concerning spelling correction literature, many works apply the noisy channel model which consists of two components: a source model (prior of word probabilities) and a channel (error) model, that accounts for spelling transformations on letter sequences. Several approaches have been proposed under this framework, that mainly differ in the employed error model; see for example: (Church and Gale, 1991), (Brill and Moore, 2000) and (Toutanova and Moore, 2002).

Comprehensive surveys on methods to model and recover spelling errors can be found in (Kukich, 1992) and (Pedler, 2007); in particular, the latter work is specifically centered on methods for correcting so-called real-word errors (cf. Section 3). The detection of errors and the suggestion of corrections typically rely on the availability of text corpora or human-made lexical resources. Search for correct alternatives can be based on word similarity measures, such as the edit distance (Mitton, 1995), anagram hashing (Reynaert, 2006), and semantic distance based on WordNet (Hirst and Budanitsky, 2005). More sophisticated approaches have been proposed by (Fossati and Di Eugenio, 2008), that mixes surface and Part-Of-Speech Information, and (Schaback and Li, 2007), which combines similarity measures at the character, phonetic, word, syntax, and semantic levels into one global feature-based framework.

*a) *W *w had just come in from Australia [Australia]*
*b) good service we *staid one week. [Tahiti]*
*c) The room was *exellent but the hallway was *filty . [NJ]*
*d) is a good place to stay, if you are looking for a hotel *arround LAX airport. [Tahiti]*
*e) The staff was *freindly ... I was *conerned about the noise [CT]*

Table 1: Examples of misspellings found in on-line reviews of an hotel close to Los Angeles Int'l Airport. Corresponding corrections are: a) *We*, ϵ, b) *stayed*, c) *excellent*, *filthy*, d) *around*, e) *friendly*, *concerned*.

Concerning the literature of statistical MT, interest in noisy data has been so far considering issues different from misspelled words. For instance, (Davis et al., 1995) and (Vogel, 2003) address training methods coping with noisy parallel data, in the sense that translations do not perfectly match. Work on speech translation (Casacuberta et al., 2008) focused instead on efficient methods to couple speech recognition and MT in order to avoid error propagation. Very recently, (Carrera et al., 2009) conducted a qualitative study on the impact of noisy social media content on statistical and rule-based MT. Unfortunately, this work does not report any quantitative result, it is only based on a small selection of examples that are manually evaluated, and finally it does not address the problem of integrating error correction with MT.

3 Types of Misspellings

In general, a misspelled word is a sequence of letters that corresponds to no correctly spelled word of the same language (*non-word error*), or to a correct spelling of another word (*real-word error*). In the examples shown in Table 1, all marked errors are non-word errors, but the one in sentence b), which indeed is likely a misspelling of the word *stayed*.

Causes of a misspelling may be an unintentional typing error (e.g. **freindly* for *friendly*), or lack of knowledge about the proper spelling. Typing errors can originate from six different typing operations (Kukich, 1992): substitution, insertion, deletion, transposition, run-on, and split.[1] Lack of knowledge could be the cause of the misspelled **exellent* in sentence c).

[1] Run-on and split are the special cases of deleting and inserting blank spaces, respectively.

1.	*your - you're*
2.	*then - than*
3.	*its - it's*
4.	*to - too - two*
5.	*were - where - we're*
6.	*there - their - they're*
7.	*a - an - and*
8.	*off - of*
9.	*here - hear*
10.	*lose - loose*

Table 2: List of frequent real-word errors found in blogs. Source: http://www.theprobabilist.com.

An interesting combination of cause and effect is when lack of linguistic competence results in confusing the spelling of a word with the spelling of another word that sounds similarly (Hirst and Budanitsky, 2005). This could be likely the case of the Polynesian tourist that authored sentence b).

A short list of words frequently confused in blogs is reported in Table 2 while a longer list can be found in the Wikipedia.[2] Real-word errors typically fool spell checkers because their identification requires analyzing the context in which they occur.

In this paper, we automatically corrupt clean text with three types of noise described below. This procedure permits us to analyze the MT performance against different sources and levels of noise and to systematically evaluate our error-recovering strategy.

Non-word Noise We randomly replace words in the text according to a list of 4,100 frequently non-word errors provided in the Wikipedia. A qualitative analysis of these errors reveals that all of them originate by one or two keyboard typing errors of the kind described beforehand. Practically, non-word noise is introduced by defining a desired level of corruption of the source text.

Real-word Noise Similarly to the previous case, real-word errors are automatically introduced by another list of frequently misused words in the Wikipedia. This list contains about 300 pairs of confusable words to which we also added the 10 frequent real-word errors occurring in blogs reported in Table 2.

[2]See Wikipedia's "list of frequently misused English words".

Random Noise Finally, we may corrupt the original text by randomly replacing, inserting, and deleting characters in it up to a desired percentage.

4 Error-recovering Statistical MT

An enhancement of a statistical MT system is proposed with the goal of improving robustness to misspellings in the input. Rrror recovery is realized by performing a sequence of actions before the actual translation, which create reliable spelling alternatives of the input and store them into a compact word-based Confusion Network (CN).

Starting from the possibly noisy input text, spelling variations are generated by assuming that each character is a potential typing error, independent from other characters.

The variants are represented as a character-based CN that models possible substitutions, insertion, deletions of each character, with an empirically determined weight assigned to each alternative. The network is then searched by a non-monotonic search process that scores possible character sequences through a character n-gram language model, and outputs a set of multiple spelling variants that is finally converted into a word-based CN. The resulting word-based network is finally passed to the MT engine. In the following, more details are provided on the augmented MT system with the help of Figure 1, which shows how the system acts on the corrupted example "all off ame", supposed to be "hall of fame".

Step 1 The input text (**a**) is split into a sequence of characters (**b**) including punctuation marks and blank spaces (␣), which are here considered as standard characters. Moreover, single characters interleaved with the conventional empty character ϵ.

Step 2 A CN (**c**) is built by adding all alternative characters of the keyboard to each input character, including the space character ␣ and the empty character. When the string character is ␣, the only admitted alternative is ϵ. Possible alternative spellings of the original string correspond to paths in the CN. Notice that each CN column beginning with a standard character permits to manage insertion, substitution and split errors, while each column beginning with the empty character permits to handle deletion and run-on errors.

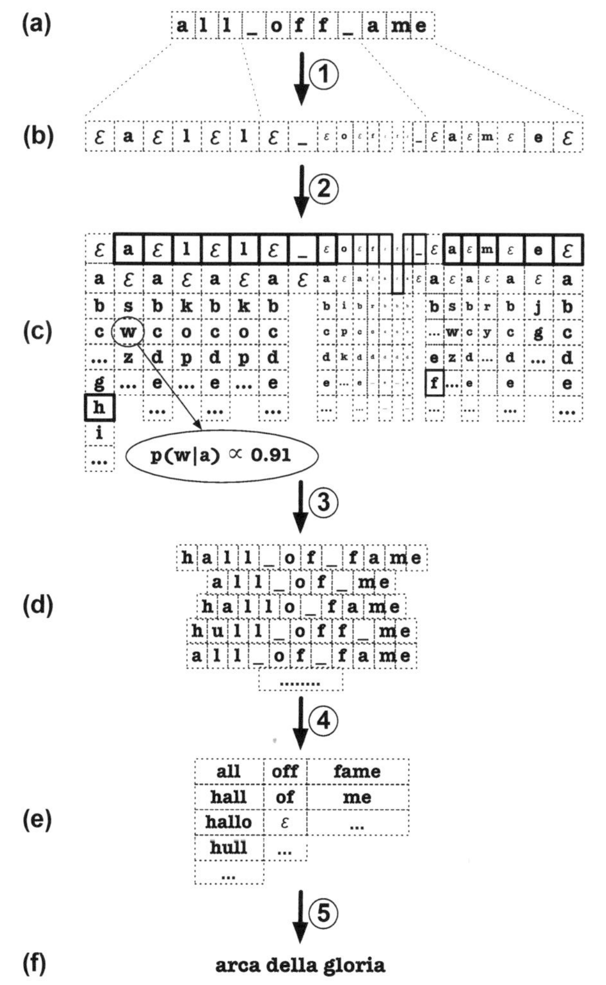

Figure 1: The whole process to translate the mistaken input *"all off ame [hall of fame]"* into *"arca della gloria"*.

A probability distribution of confusable keystrokes is generated based on the distance between the keys on a standard QWERTY keyboard. This distribution is intended to model how a spelling error is actually produced. Hence, character alternatives in the CN are associated to a probability given by:

$$p(x|y) \propto \cdot \frac{1}{k \cdot d(x, y) + 1} \qquad (1)$$

where $d(x, y)$ is the physical distance between the key of x and the key of y on the keyboard layout; for example, the character *a* has a distance of 3 from the character c on the considered keyboard layout. The free parameter k tunes the discriminative power of the model between correct and wrong typing. In this paper, k was empirically set to 0.1. The ϵ and ␣ characters are assigned a default distance of 9 and 999 from any other character, respectively.

For the sake of clarity, the probability $p(w|a)$ of just one entry is reported in Figure 1.

Step 3 The generation of spelling variations (**d**) is operated by means of the same decoder employed for translation (see below), but in a much simplified configuration which does not exploit any translation model. It is designed to search the input character-based CN for the n-best character sequences which better "correct" the mistaken input. In Figure 1 the best sequence is marked by bold boxes (**c**), and the empty character ϵ is removed for the sake of clarity (**d**). This process relies only on the character-based 6-gram language model trained on monolingual data in the source language. It is worth noticing that the generated spelling alternatives may in principle still contain non-words, just because they are selected by a character-based language model, which does not explicitly embed the notion of word.

Transposition errors are modeled both (i) indirectly through consecutive substitutions with appropriate characters and (ii) directly by permitting some rc-ordcrings of adjacent characters. Moreover, preliminary experiments revealed that the explicit handling of deletion and run-on errors by interleaving input characters with the empty character ϵ (Step 1) is crucial to achieve good performance. Although the size of the character-based CN doubles, its decoding time increases only by a small factor.

Step 4 The n-best character sequences (**d**) are transformed into a word-based CN (**e**) (Mangu et al., 2000). First, each character-based sequence is transformed into a unifilar word-based lattice, whose edges correspond to words and timestamps to the character positions. Then, the unifilar lattices are put in parallel to create one lattice with all spelling variations of the input text (**a**). Finally, a word-based CN is generated by means of the *lattice-tool* available in the SRILM Toolkit (Stolcke, 2002).

Step 5 Translation of the CN (**e**) is performed with the Moses decoder (Koehn et al., 2007), that has been successfully applied mainly to text translation, but also to process multiple input hypotheses (Bertoldi et al., 2008), representing, for example, speech transcriptions, word segmentations, texts with possible punctuation marks, etc. In general,

set	#sent.	English		Italian	
		#wrd	dict.	#wrd	dict.
EP train	1.2M	36M	106K	35M	146K
test	2K	60K	6.5K	60K	8.3K
WF train	42K	996K	2641	994K	2843
test	328	8789	606	8704	697

Table 3: Statistics of train/test data of the Europarl (EP) and the Weather Forecast (WF) tasks.

Moses looks for the best translation exploring the search space defined by a set of feature functions (models), which are log-linearly interpolated with weights estimated during a tuning stage.

The rationale of storing the spelling alternatives into a word-based CN instead of n-best list is two-fold: (i) the CN contains a significantly larger number of variations, and (ii) the translation system is much more efficient to translate CNs instead of n-best lists.

5 Experiments

Extensive experiments have been conducted on the Europarl shared task, from English to Italian, as specified by the Workshop on Statistical Machine Translation of the ACL 2008.[3] Additional experiments were conducted on a smaller task, namely the translation of weather forecast bulletins between the same language pair. Statistics on texts employed in experiments are reported in Table 3.

For both tasks, we created evaluation data by artificially corrupting input text with the noise sources described in Section 3. The module for generating spelling variations (Step 3) was trained on additional 4M and 16M running words in English and Italian, respectively.

We empirically investigated the following issues: (a) performance of the standard MT engine versus nature and level of the input noise; (b) performance of the error-recovering MT engine versus number of provided spelling variations; (c) portability of the approach to another task and translation direction; (d) computational requirements of the approach.

5.1 Impact of Noise

The first set of experiments involved the translation of corrupted versions of the Europarl test set. Figure 2 plots three curves of BLEU(%) scores, corresponding to different noise sources and noise ratios, given in terms of percentage of word error rate. It also shows the BLEU score on the original clean text. Notice that this baseline performance (25.16) represents the state-of-the-art[4] for this task.

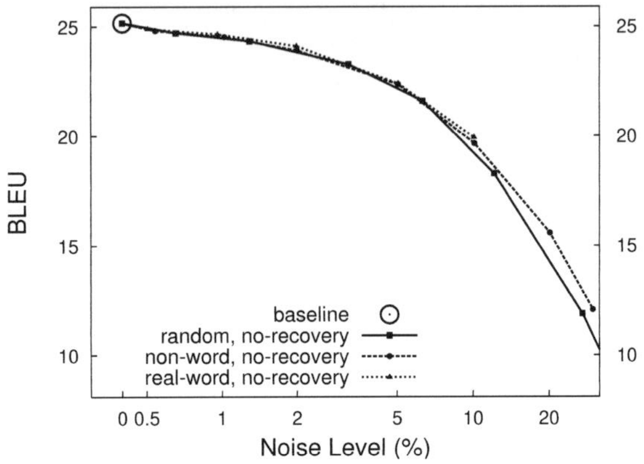

Figure 2: Translation performance as function of the noise level (in log-scale) for different types of noise.

The major outcome of these experiments is that the different types of errors seem to affect MT performance in a very similar manner. Quantitatively, performance degradation begins even for low noise levels – about 0.5 absolute BLEU loss at 1% of noise level – and reaches 50% when text corruption reaches the level of 30%. The similar impact of non-word and random errors is somehow expected. The plain reason is that both types of errors very likely[5] generate Out-Of-Vocabulary (OOV) words.

We find instead less predictable that the impact of real-word errors is indistinguishable from that of the other two noise sources. Notice also that most of the real-word errors produce indeed words known to the MT system. Hence, the question regards the behavior of the MT system when the sentence includes on OOV word or an out-of-context known word. Empirically it seems that in both cases the decoder produces translations with the same amount of errors. In some sense, the good news is that real-word errors do not induce more translation errors than OOV words do.

[3] http://www.statmt.org/wmt08/

[4] http://matrix.statmt.org/matrix

[5] Modulo noise in the parallel data and the chance that a random error generates a true word.

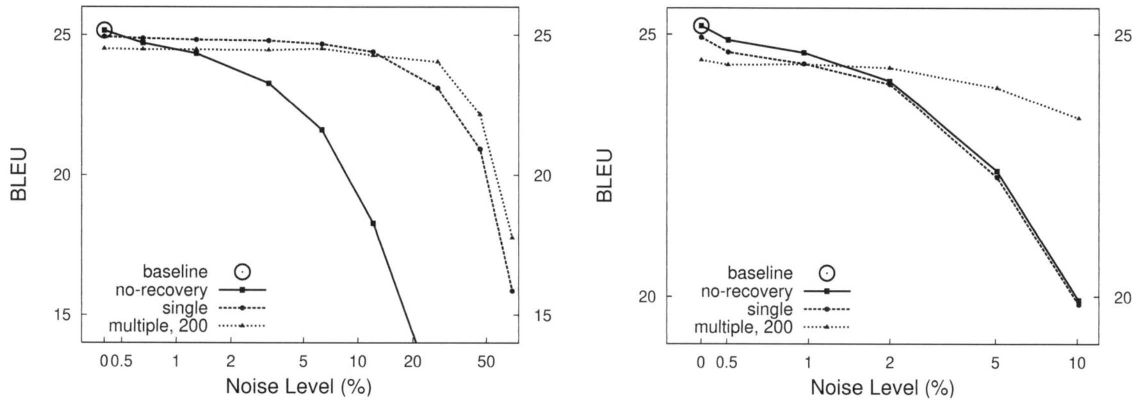

Figure 3: Performance of error-recovering method with random (left) and real-word (right) noise.

5.2 Impact of Multiple Corrections

Experiments presented here address evaluation of our enhanced MT system. In addition to nature and level of noise, translation performance is also analyzed with respect to the number (1 and 200) of spelling alternatives generated at Step 3. Figure 3 plots BLEU scores for random (left plot) and real-word (right plot) noises. For comparison purposes, the curves with no error recovery are also shown. Results with non-word noise are not provided since they are pretty similar to those with random noise. It is worth noticing that real-word errors are recovered in a different way than random errors; in fact, for the latter a single spelling alternative seems sufficient to guarantee a substantial error recovery, whereas for real-word errors this is not the case.

Concerning the use of spelling variations, it is worth remarking that our system is able to fully recover from both random and non-word errors up to noise levels of 10%, which remains high even for noise levels up to 20%, where the BLEU degradation is limited to around 5% relative.

Real-word errors are optimally recovered in the case of multiple spelling variations until they do not exceed 2% of the words in the input text; after that, the decrement of the MT quality becomes significant but still limited to about 5% BLEU relative for a noise level of 10%. So the question arises about what could be a realistic real-word noise level. Clearly this question is not easy to address. However, to get a rough idea we can look at the examples reported in Table 1. These five sentences were extracted from a text of about 100 words (of which Table 1 only shows the sentences containing errors) that contain in total 8 errors: 7 of which are non-words and 1 is a real-word. Although from these figures reliable statistics cannot be estimated, a reasonable assumption could be that a global noise level of 10%[6] might contain a 1/10 ratio for real-word vs. non-word errors. Thus, looking at the real-word error curve of Figure 3, the inability to recover errors for noise levels greater than 2-5% should actually be acceptable given this empirical observation.

Another relevant remark from Figure 3 is that for low noise levels (less than 1%) the use of the error-recovering module is counterproductive, since it introduces more errors than those actually affecting the original input text, causing a slight degradation of the translation performance. If the computational cost to generate variants, which will be analyzed in the next paragraph, is also taken into account, it results evident the importance of designing a good strategy for enabling or disabling on demand the error-recovering stage. A starting point for defining an effective activation strategy is the estimation of the noise rate. For doing this, non-words can be counted by exploiting proper dictionaries or spell checkers; concerning real-word noise, its rate can be inferred either from the non-word rate, or by means of the perplexity, which is expected to become higher as the real-word error rate increases (Subramaniam et al., 2009). Once the noise level of the input text is known, the decision of activating the correction module can be easily taken on a

[6] By the way, at this noise rate, an error-recovering strategy would be highly recommended.

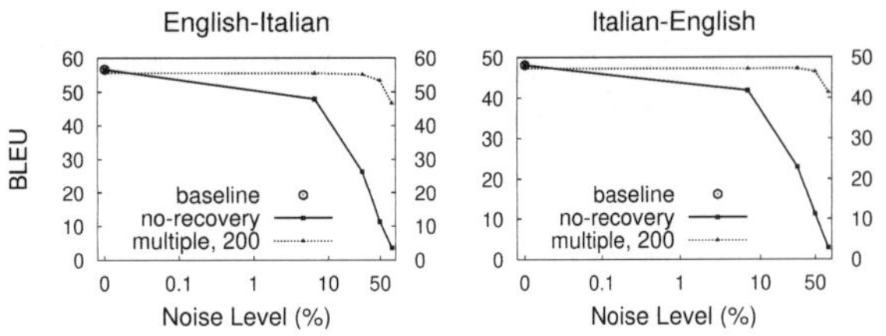

Figure 4: Effects of random noise and noise correction on translation performance for the WF task.

threshold basis. Alternatively, the proper working point, in terms of precision and recall, of the correction model could be dynamically chosen as a function of the actual noise level.

5.3 Computational Costs

Although our investigation does not address explicitly computational aspects of translating noisy input, nevertheless some general considerations can be drawn.

The effectiveness of our recovering approach relies on the compact representation of many spelling alternatives in a word-based CN. The CN decoding has been shown to be efficient, just minimally larger than the single string decoding (Bertoldi et al., 2008). On the contrary, in the current enhanced MT setting, the sequence of Steps 1 to 4 for building the CN from the noisy input text is quite costly. Rather than to an intrinsic complexity, this is due to our choice of creating a rich character-based CN in Step 3 for the sake of flexibility and to a naive implementation of Step 4.

5.4 Portability

So far we have analyzed in detail our approach on the medium-large sized Europarl task, for the English-to-Italian translation direction. For assessing portability, we also considered a simpler task –the translation of weather forecast bulletins– where the translation quality is definitely higher, for the same language pair but in both translation directions. The choice of the weather forecast task is not by chance. In fact, as the automatically translated bulletins are published on the Web, a very high translation quality is required, and then the presence of any typing error in the original text could be a concern. (By the way, for this task the presence of real-word errors is very marginal.)

Figure 4 plots curves of MT performance under random noise conditions against multiple spelling variations, for two translation directions. It can be noticed that the error-recovering system behaves qualitatively as for the Europarl task but even better from a quantitative viewpoint. Again, the recovering model introduces spurious errors which affect translation quality for low levels of noisy input, but in this case the break-even point is less than 0.1% noise level. On the other side, errors corrupting the input text are fully recovered up to 30-40% of noise levels, for which the BLEU score would be more than halved for non-corrected texts.

6 Future Work

There are a number of important issues that this work has still left open. First of all, we focused on a specific way of generating spelling variations, based on single characters, but other possible choices should be investigated and compared to our approach, like the use of n-grams of words.

An important open question regards efficiency of the proposed recovering strategy, since the problem has been only sketched in Section 5.3. It is our intention to analyze the intrinsic complexity of our model, possibly discover its bottlenecks and implement a more efficient solution.

Another topic, mentioned in Section 5.2, is the activation strategy of the misspelling recovery. Some further investigation is required on how its working point can be effectively selected; in fact, since the enhanced system necessarily introduces spurious errors, it would be desirable to increase its precision for low-corrupted input texts.

7 Conclusions

This paper addressed the issue of automatically translating written texts that are corrupted by misspelling errors. An enhancement of a state-of-the-art statistical MT system is proposed which efficiently performs the translation of multiple spelling variants of noisy input. These alternatives are generated by a character-based error recovery system under the assumption that misspellings are due to typing errors.

The enhanced MT system has been tested on texts corrupted with increasing noise levels of three different sources: random, non-word, and real-word errors.

Analysis of experimental results has led us to draw the following conclusions:

- The impact of misspelling errors on MT performance depends on the noise rate, but not on the noise source.
- The capability of the enhanced MT system to recover from errors differs according to the noise source: real-word noise is significantly harder to remove than random and non-word noise, which behave substantially the same.
- The exploitation of several spelling alternatives permits to almost fully recover from errors if the noise rate does not exceed 10% for non-word noise and 2% for real-word noise, which are likely above the corruption level observed in many social media.
- Finally, performance slightly decreases when input text is correct or just mistaken at a negligible level, because the error recovery module rewards recall rather than precision and hence tends to overgenerate correction alternatives, even if not needed.

Acknowledgments

This work was supported by the EuroMatrixPlus project (IST-231720), which is funded by the EC under the 7th Framework Programme for Research and Technological Development.

References

N. Bertoldi, et al. 2008. Efficient speech translation through confusion network decoding. *IEEE Transactions on Audio, Speech, and Language Processing*, 16(8):1696–1705.

E. Brill and R. C. Moore. 2000. An improved error model for noisy channel spelling correction. In *Proceedings of ACL*. Hong Kong.

J. Carrera, et al. 2009. Machine translation for cross-language social media. http://www.promt.com/company/technology/pdf/machine_translation_for_cross_language_social_media.pdf.

F. Casacuberta, et al. 2008. Recent efforts in spoken language processing. *IEEE Signal Processing Magazine*, 25(3):80–88.

K. W. Church and W. A. Gale. 1991. Probability scoring for spelling correction. *Statistics and Computing*, 1(2):93–103.

M. W. Davis, et al. 1995. Text alignment in the real world: Improving alignments of noisy translations using common lexical features, string matching strategies and n-gram comparisons. In *Proceedings of EACL*, Dublin, Ireland.

L. Dey and S. M. Haque. 2009. Studying the effects of noisy text on text mining applications. In *Proceedings of AND*, pages 107–114, Barcelona, Spain.

D. Fossati and B. Di Eugenio. 2008. I saw tree trees in the park: How to correct real-word spelling mistakes. In *Proceedings of LREC*, Marrakech, Morocco.

G. Hirst and A. Budanitsky. 2005. Correcting real-word spelling errors by restoring lexical cohesion. *Natural Language Engineering*, 11(01):87–111.

P. Koehn, et al. 2007. Moses: Open source toolkit for statistical machine translation. In *Proceedings of ACL - Demo and Poster Sessions*, pages 177–180, Prague, Czech Republic.

K. Kukich. 1992. Spelling correction for the telecommunications network for the deaf. *Communications of the ACM*, 35(5):80–90.

D. Kushal, et al. 2003. Mining the peanut gallery: opinion extraction and semantic classification of product reviews. In *Proceedings of the WWW conference*, pages 519–528, Budapest, Hungary.

L. Mangu, et al. 2000. Finding consensus in speech recognition: Word error minimization and other applications of confusion networks. *Computer, Speech and Language*, 14(4):373–400.

R. Mitton. 1995. *English Spelling and the Computer (Studies in Language and Linguistics)*. Addison Wesley Publishing Company.

J. Pedler. 2007. *Computer correction of real-word spelling errors in dyslexic text*. Ph.D. thesis, University of London.

M. Reynaert. 2006. Corpus-induced corpus cleanup. In *Proceedings of LREC*, Genoa, Italy.

J. Schaback and F. Li. 2007. Multi-level feature extraction for spelling correction. In *IJCAI - Workshop on Analytics for Noisy Unstructured Text Data*, pages 79–86, Hyderabad, India.

J. Schler, et al. 2006. Effects of age and gender on blogging. In *Proceedings of AAAI-CAAW*, Palo Alto, CA.

A. Stolcke. 2002. Srilm - an extensible language modeling toolkit. In *Proceedings of ICSLP*, Denver, CO.

L. V. Subramaniam, et al. 2009. A survey of types of text noise and techniques to handle noisy text. In *Proceedings of AND*, pages 115–122, Barcelona, Spain.

K. Toutanova and R. C. Moore. 2002. Pronunciation modeling for improved spelling correction. In *Proceedings of ACL*, pages 144–151, Philadelphia, PA

S. Vogel. 2003. Using noisy biligual data for statistical machine translation. In *Proceedings of EACL*, Budapest, Hungary.

Everybody loves a rich cousin: An empirical study of transliteration through bridge languages

Mitesh M. Khapra
Indian Institute of Technology
Bombay,
Powai, Mumbai 400076,
India
miteshk@cse.iitb.ac.in

A Kumaran
Microsoft Research India,
Bangalore,
India
a.kumaran@microsoft.com

Pushpak Bhattacharyya
Indian Institute of Technology
Bombay,
Powai, Mumbai 400076,
India
pb@cse.iitb.ac.in

Abstract

Most state of the art approaches for machine transliteration are data driven and require significant parallel names corpora between languages. As a result, developing transliteration functionality among n languages could be a resource intensive task requiring parallel names corpora in the order of ${}^{n}C_2$. In this paper, we explore ways of reducing this high resource requirement by leveraging the available parallel data between subsets of the n languages, transitively. We propose, and show empirically, that reasonable quality transliteration engines may be developed between two languages, X and Y, even when no direct parallel names data exists between them, but only transitively through language Z. Such systems alleviate the need for $O({}^{n}C_2)$ corpora, significantly. In addition we show that the performance of such transitive transliteration systems is in par with direct transliteration systems, in practical applications, such as CLIR systems.

1 Introduction

Names and Out Of Vocabulary (OOV) terms appear very frequently in written and spoken text and hence play a very important role in several Natural Language Processing applications. Several studies have shown that handling names correctly across languages can significantly improve the performance of CLIR Systems (Mandl and Womser-Hacker, 2004) and the utility of machine translation systems. The fact that translation lexicons or even statistical dictionaries derived from parallel data do not provide a good coverage of name and OOV translations, underscores the need for good transliteration engines to transform them between the language.

The importance of machine transliteration, in the above context, is well realized by the research community and several approaches have been proposed to solve the problem. However, most state of the art approaches are data driven and require significant parallel names corpora between languages. Such data may not always be available between every pair of languages, thereby limiting our ability to support transliteration functionality between many language pairs, and subsequently information access between languages. For example, let us consider a practical scenario where we have six languages from four different language families as shown in Figure 1. The nodes in the graph represent languages and the edges indicate the availability of data between that language pair and thus the availability of a Machine Transliteration system for that pair. It is easy to see the underlying characteristics of the graph. Data is available between a language pair due to one of the following three reasons:

Politically related languages: Due to the political dominance of English it is easy to obtain parallel names data between English and most languages.

Genealogically related languages: Arabic and Hebrew share a common origin and there is a significant overlap between their phoneme and grapheme inventory. It is easy to obtain parallel names data between these two languages.

Demographically related languages: Hindi and Kannada are languages spoken in the Indian subcontinent, though they are from different language families. However, due to the shared culture and demographics, it is easy to create parallel names data between these two languages.

Human Language Technologies: The 2010 Annual Conference of the North American Chapter of the ACL, pages 420–428,
Los Angeles, California, June 2010.

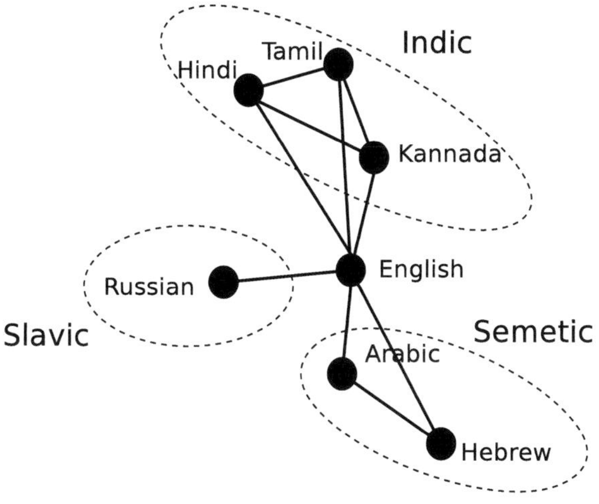

Figure 1: A connected graph of languages

On the other hand, for politically, demographically and genealogically unrelated languages such as, say, Hindi and Hebrew, parallel data is not readily available, either due to the unavailability of skilled bilingual speakers. Even the argument of using Wikipedia resources for such creation of such parallel data does not hold good, as the amount of interlinking may be very small to yield data. For example, only 800 name pairs between Hindi and Hebrew were mined using a state of the art mining algorithm (Udupa et al., 2009), from Wikipedia interwiki links.

We propose a methodology to develop a practical Machine Transliteration system between any two nodes of the above graph, provided a two-step path exists between them. That is, even when no parallel data exists between X & Y but sufficient data exists between X & Z and Z & Y it is still possible to develop transliteration functionality between X & Y by combining a $X \rightarrow Z$ system with a $Z \rightarrow Y$ system. For example, given the graph of Figure 1, we explore the possibility of developing transliteration functionality between Hindi and Russian even though no direct data is available between these two languages. Further, we show that in many cases the bridge language can be suitably selected to ensure optimal MT accuracy.

To establish the practicality and utility of our approach we integrated such a bridge transliteration system with a standard CLIR system and compared its performance with that of a direct transliteration system. We observed that such a bridge system performs well in practice and in specific instances results in improvement in CLIR performance over a baseline system further strengthening our claims that such bridge systems are good practical solutions for alleviating the resource scarcity problem.

To summarize, our main contributions in this paper are:

1. Constructing bridge transliteration systems and establishing empirically their quality.

2. Demonstrating their utility in providing practical transliteration functionality between two languages X & Y with no direct parallel data between them.

3. Demonstrating that in specific cases it is possible to select the bridge language so that optimal Machine Transliteration accuracy is ensured while stepping through the bridge language.

1.1 Organization of the Paper

This paper is organized in the following manner. In section 2 we present the related work and highlight the lack of work on transliteration in resource scarce scenarios. In section 3 we discuss the methodology of bridge transliteration. Section 4 discusses the experiments and datasets used. Section 4.3 discusses the results and error analysis. Section 5 discusses orthographic characteristics to be considered while selecting the bridge language. Section 6 demonstrates the effectiveness of such bridge systems in a practical scenario, *viz.*, Cross Language Information Retrieval. Section 7 concludes the paper, highlighting future research issues.

2 Related Work

Current models for transliteration can be classified as grapheme-based, phoneme-based and hybrid models. Grapheme-based models, such as, Source Channel Model (Lee and Choi, 1998), Maximum Entropy Model (Goto et al., 2003), Conditional Random Fields (Veeravalli et al., 2008) and Decision Trees (Kang and Choi, 2000) treat transliteration as an orthographic process and try to map the source language graphemes directly to the target language graphemes. Phoneme based models, such as, the ones based on Weighted Finite State

Transducers (WFST) (Knight and Graehl, 1997) and extended Markov window (Jung et al., 2000) treat transliteration as a phonetic process rather than an orthographic process. Under such frameworks, transliteration is treated as a conversion from source grapheme to source phoneme followed by a conversion from source phoneme to target grapheme. Hybrid models either use a combination of a grapheme based model and a phoneme based model (Stalls and Knight, 1998) or capture the correspondence between source graphemes and source phonemes to produce target language graphemes (Oh and Choi, 2002).

A significant shortcoming of all the previous works was that none of them addressed the issue of performing transliteration in a resource scarce scenario, as there was always an implicit assumption of availability of data between a pair of languages. In particular, none of the above approaches address the problem of developing transliteration functionality between a pair of languages when no direct data exists between them but sufficient data is available between each of these languages and an intermediate language. Some work on similar lines has been done in Machine Translation (Wu and Wang, 2007) wherein an intermediate bridge language (say, Z) is used to fill the data void that exists between a given language pair (say, X and Y). In fact, recently it has been shown that the accuracy of a $X \rightarrow Z$ Machine Translation system can be improved by using additional $X \rightarrow Y$ data provided Z and Y share some common vocabulary and cognates (Nakov and Ng, 2009). However, no such effort has been made in the area of Machine Transliteration. To the best of our knowledge, this work is the first attempt at providing a practical solution to the problem of transliteration in the face of resource scarcity.

3 Bridge Transliteration Systems

In this section, we explore the salient question *"Is it possible to develop a practical machine transliteration system between X and Y, by composing two intermediate $X \rightarrow Z$ and $Z \rightarrow Y$ transliteration systems?"* We use a standard transliteration methodology based on orthography for all experiments (as outlined in section 3.1), to ensure the applicability of the methodology to a variety of languages.

3.1 CRF based transliteration engine

Conditional Random Fields ((Lafferty et al., 2001)) are undirected graphical models used for labeling sequential data. Under this model, the conditional probability distribution of the target word given the source word is given by,

$$P(Y|X;\lambda) = \frac{1}{N(X)} \cdot e^{\sum_{t=1}^{T}\sum_{k=1}^{K} \lambda_k f_k(Y_{t-1},Y_t,X,t)} \quad (1)$$

where,

$$\begin{aligned} X &= source\ word \\ Y &= target\ word \\ T &= length\ of\ source\ word \\ K &= number\ of\ features \\ \lambda_k &= feature\ weight \\ N(X) &= normalization\ constant \end{aligned}$$

CRF++ [1], an open source implementation of CRF was used for training and decoding (*i.e.* transliterating the names). GIZA++ (Och and Ney, 2003), a freely available implementation of the IBM alignment models (Brown et al., 1993) was used to get character level alignments for the name pairs in the parallel names training corpora. Under this alignment, each character in the source word is aligned to zero or more characters in the corresponding target word. The following features are then generated using this character-aligned data (here e_i and h_i form the *i*-th pair of aligned characters in the source word and target word respectively):

- h_i and e_j such that $i-2 \leq j \leq i+2$
- h_i and source character bigrams ($\{e_{i-1}, e_i\}$ or $\{e_i, e_{i+1}\}$)
- h_i and source character trigrams ($\{e_{i-2}, e_{i-1}, e_i\}$ or $\{e_{i-1}, e_i, e_{i+1}\}$ or $\{e_i, e_{i+1}, e_{i+2}\}$)
- h_i, h_{i-1} and e_j such that $i-2 \leq j \leq i+2$
- h_i, h_{i-1} and source character bigrams
- h_i, h_{i-1} and source character trigrams

[1] http://crfpp.sourceforge.net/

3.2 Bridge Transliteration Methodology

In this section, we outline our methodology for composing transitive transliteration systems between X and Y, using a bridge language Z, by chaining individual direct transliteration systems. Our approach of using bridge transliteration for finding the best target string (Y^*), given the input string X can be represented by the following probabilistic expression:

$$\begin{aligned} Y^* &= \arg\max_Y P(Y|X) \\ &= \sum_Z P(Y, Z|X) \\ &= \sum_Z P(Y|Z, X) * P(Z|X) \end{aligned} \quad (2)$$

We simplify the above expression, by assuming that Y is independent of X given Z; the linguistic intuition behind this assumption is that the *top-k* outputs of the $X \rightarrow Z$ system corresponding to a string in X, capture all the transliteration information necessary for transliterating to Y. Subsequently, in section 5 we discuss the characteristics of the effective bridge languages to maximize the capture of necessary information for the second stage of the transliteration, namely for generating correct strings of Z. Thus,

$$Y^* = \sum_Z P(Y|Z) * P(Z|X) \quad (3)$$

The probabilities $P(Y|Z)$ and $P(Z|X)$ in Equation (3) are derived from the two stages of the bridge system. Specifically, we assume that the parallel names corpora are available between the language pair, X and Z, and the language pair, Z and Y. We train two baseline CRF based transliteration systems (as outlined in Section 3.1), between the language X and Z, and Z and Y. Each name in language X was provided as an input into $X \rightarrow Z$ transliteration system, and the top-10 candidate strings in language Z produced by this first stage system were given as an input into the second stage system $Z \rightarrow Y$. The results were merged using Equation (2). Finally, the top-10 outputs of this system were selected as the output of the bridge system.

4 Experiments

It is a well known fact that transliteration is lossy, and hence the transitive systems may be expected to suffer from the accumulation of errors in each stage, resulting in a system that is of much poorer quality than a direct transliteration system. In this section, we set out to quantify this expected loss in accuracy, by a series of experiments in a set of languages using bridge transliteration systems and a baseline direct systems. We conducted a comprehensive set of experiments in a diverse set of languages, as shown in Figure 1, that include English, Indic (Hindi and Kannada), Slavic (Russian) and Semitic (Arabic and Hebrew) languages. The datasets and results are described in the following subsections.

4.1 Datasets

To be consistent, for training each of these systems, we used approximately 15K name pairs corpora (as this was the maximum data available for some language pairs). While we used the NEWS 2009 training corpus (Li et al., 2009) as a part of our training data, we enhanced the data set to about 15K by adding more data of similar characteristics (such as, name origin, domain, length of the name strings, *etc.*), taken from the same source as the original NEWS 2009 data. For languages such as Arabic and Hebrew which were not part of the NEWS 2009 shared task, the data was created along the same lines. All results are reported on the standard NEWS 2009 test set, wherever applicable. The test set consists of about 1,000 name pairs in languages X and Y; to avoid any bias, it was made sure that there is no overlap between the test set with the training sets of both the $X \rightarrow Z$ and $Z \rightarrow Y$ systems. To establish a baseline, the same CRF based transliteration system (outlined in Section 3.1) was trained with a 15K name pairs corpora between the languages $X \rightarrow Y$. The same test set used for testing the transitive systems was used for testing the direct system as well. As before, to avoid any bias, we made sure that there is no overlap between the test set and the training set for the direct system as well.

4.2 Results

We produce top-10 outputs from the bridge system as well from the direct system and compare their performance. The performance is measured using the following standard measures, *viz.*, top-1 accuracy (ACC-1) and Mean F-score. These measures are described in detail in (Li et al., 2009). Table 1

Language Pair	ACC-1	Relative change in ACC-1	Mean F-score	Relative change in Mean F-score
Hin-Rus	0.507		0.903	
Hin-Eng-Rus	0.466	-8.08%	0.886	-1.88%
Hin-Ara	0.458		0.897	
Hin-Eng-Ara	0.420	-8.29%	0.876	-2.34%
Eng-Heb	0.544		0.917	
Eng-Ara-Heb	0.544	0%	0.917	0%
Hin-Eng	0.422		0.884	
Hin-Kan-Eng	0.382	-9.51%	0.871	-1.47%

Table 1: Stepping through an intermediate language

presents the performance measures, both for a direct system (say, Hin-Rus), and a transitional system (say, Hin-Eng-Rus), in 4 different transitional systems, between English, Indic, Semitic and Slavic languages. In each case, we observe that the transitional systems have a slightly lower quality, with an absolute drop in accuracy (ACC-1) of less than 0.05 (relative drop under 10%), and an absolute drop in Mean F-Score of 0.02 (relative drop under 3%).

4.3 Analysis of Results

Intuitively, one would expect that the errors of the two stages of the transitive transliteration system (i.e., $X \rightarrow Z$, and $Z \rightarrow Y$) to compound, leading to a considerable loss in the overall performance of the system. Given that the accuracies of the direct transliteration systems are as given in Table 2, the transitive systems are expected to have accuracies close to the product of the accuracies of the individual stages, for independent systems.

Language Pair	ACC-1	Mean F-Score
Hin-Eng	0.422	0.884
Eng-Rus	0.672	0.935
Eng-Ara	0.514	0.905
Ara-Heb	1.000	1.000
Hin-Kan	0.433	0.879
Kan-Eng	0.434	0.886

Table 2: Performance of Direct Transliteration Systems

However, as we observe in Table 1, the relative drop in the accuracy (ACC-1) is less than 10% from that of the direct system, which goes against our intuition. To identify the reasons for the better than expected performance, we performed a detailed error analysis of each stage of the bridge transliteration systems, and the results are reported in Tables 3 – 5. We draw attention to two interesting facts which account for the better than expected performance of the bridge system:

Improved 2nd stage performance on correct inputs: In each one of the cases, as expected, the ACC-1 of the first stage is same as the ACC-1 of the $X \rightarrow Z$ system. However, we notice that the ACC-1 of the second stage *on the correct strings output in the first stage*, is significantly better than the the ACC-1 of the $Z \rightarrow Y$ system! For example, the ACC-1 of the Eng-Rus system is 67.2% (see Table 2), but, that of the 2nd stage Eng-Rus system is 77.8%, namely, on the strings that are transliterated correctly by the first stage. Our analysis indicate that there are two reasons for such improvement: First, the strings that get transliterated correctly in the first stage are typically shorter or less ambiguous and hence have a better probability of correct transliterations in the both stages. This phenomenon could be verified empirically: Names like गोपाल {Gopal}, रमेश {Ramesh}, राम {Ram} are shorter and in general have less ambiguity on target orthography. Second, also significantly, the use of top-10 outputs from the first stage as input to the second stage provides a better opportunity for the second stage to produce correct string in Z. Again, this phenomenon is verified by providing increasing number of *top-n* results to the 2nd stage.

Hi→En→Ru		En → Ru (Stage-2)		Stage-2 Acc.
		Correct	Error	
Hi→En (Stage-1)	Correct	263	75	**77.81%**
	Error	**119**	362	**24.74%**

Table 3: Error Analysis for Hi→En→Ru

Hi→En→Ar		En → Ar (Stage-2)		Stage-2 Acc.
		Correct	Error	
Hi→En (Stage-1)	Correct	221	127	**63.50%**
	Error	**119**	340	**25.70%**

Table 4: Error Analysis for Hi→En→Ar

2nd stage error correction on incorrect inputs: The last rows in each of the above tables 3 – 5 report the performance of the second stage system on strings that were transliterated incorrectly by the first stage. While we expected the second row to produce incorrect transliterations nearly for all inputs (as the input themselves were incorrect in Z), we find to our surprise that upto 25% of the erroneous strings in Z were getting transliterated correctly in Y! This provides credence to our hypothesis that sufficient transliteration information is captured in the 1st stage output (*even when incorrect*) that may be exploited in the 2nd stage. Empirically, we verified that in most cases (nearly 60%) the errors were due to the incorrectly transliterated vowels, and in many cases, they get corrected in the second stage, and re-ranked higher in the output. Figure 2 shows a few examples of such error corrections in the second stage.

Hindi input	Erroneous English by Hi-En system	Correct English (reference)	Correct Russian by En-Ru system
बेरीलियम	berillium	beryllium	бериллий
दंबार्टन	dambarton	dumbarton	дамбартон
हब	hab	hub	хаб
कोच	coch	coach	кох

Figure 2: Examples of error corrections

Hi→Ka→En		Ka → En (Stage-2)		Stage-2 Acc.
		Correct	Error	
Hi→Ka (Stage-1)	Correct	225	196	**53.44%**
	Error	**151**	400	**27.40%**

Table 5: Error Analysis for Hi→Ka→En

5 Characteristics of the bridge language

An interesting question that we explore in this section is *"how the choice of bridge language influence the performance of the bridge system?"*. The underlying assumption in transitive transliteration systems (as expressed in Equation 3), is that *"Y is independent of X given Z"*. In other words, we assume that the representations in the language will Z *"capture sufficient transliteration information from X to produce correct strings in Y"*. We hypothesize that two parameters of the bridge language, namely, the orthography inventory and the phoneme-to-grapheme entropy, that has most influence on the quality of the transitional systems, and provide empirical evidence for this hypothesis.

5.1 Richer Orthographic Inventory

In each of the successful bridge systems (that is, those with a relative performance drop of less than 10%), presented in Table 1, namely, *Hin-Eng-Ara*, *Eng-Ara-Heb* and *Hin-Kan-Eng*, the bridge language has, in general, richer orthographic inventory than the target language. Arabic has a reduced set of vowels, and hence poorer orthographic inventory compared with English. Similarly, between the closely related Semitic languages Arabic-Hebrew, there is a many-to-one mapping from Arabic to Hebrew, and between Kannada-English, Kannada has nearly a superset of vowels and consonants as compared to English or Hindi.

As an example for a poor choice of Z, we present a transitional system, *Hindi → Arabic → English*, in Table 6, in which the transitional language z (Arabic) has smaller orthographic inventory than Y (English).

Arabic has a reduced set of vowels and, unlike English, in most contexts short vowels are optional. As a result, when Arabic is used as the bridge language the loss of information (in terms of vowels) is large

Language Pair	ACC-1	Relative change in ACC-1
Hin-Eng	0.422	
Hin-Ara-Eng	0.155	-64.28%

Table 6: Incorrect choice of bridge language

and the second stage system has no possibility of recovering from such a loss. The performance of the bridge system confirms such a drastic drop in ACC-1 of nearly 64% compared with the direct system.

5.2 Higher Phoneme-Grapheme Entropy

We also find that the entropy in phoneme - grapheme mapping of a language indicate a good correlation with a good choice for a transition language. In a good transitional system (say, *Hin-Eng-Rus*), English has a more ambiguous phoneme-to-grapheme mapping than Russian; for example, in English the phoneme 's' as in *Sam* or *Cecilia* can be represented by the graphemes 'c' and 's', whereas Russian uses only a single character to represent this phoneme. In such cases, the ambiguity introduced by the bridge language helps in recovering from errors in the $X \rightarrow Z$ system. The relative loss of ACC-1 for this transitional system is only about 8%. The Table 7 shows another transitional system, in which a poor choice was for the transitional language was made.

Language Pair	ACC-1	Relative change in ACC-1
Hin-Eng	0.422	
Hin-Tam-Eng	0.231	-45.26%

Table 7: Incorrect choice of bridge language

Tamil has a reduced set of consonants compared with Hindi or English. For example, the Hindi consonants (k, kh, g, gh) are represented by a single character in Tamil. As a result, when Tamil is used as the bridge language it looses information (in terms of consonants) and results in a significant drop in performance (nearly a 45% drop in ACC-1) for the bridge system.

6 Effectiveness of Bridge Transliteration on CLIR System

In this section, we demonstrate the effectiveness of our bridge transliteration system on a downstream application, namely, a Crosslingual Information Retrieval system. We used the standard document collections from CLEF 2006 (Nardi and Peters, 2006), CLEF 2007 (Nardi and Peters, 2007) and FIRE 2008 (FIRE, 2008). We used Hindi as the query language. All the three fields (title, description and narration) of the topics were used for the retrieval. Since the collection and topics are from the previous years, their relevance judgments were also available as a reference for automatic evaluation.

6.1 Experimental Setup

We used primarily the statistical dictionaries generated by training statistical word alignment models on an existing Hindi-English parallel corpora. As with any CLIR system that uses translation lexicon, we faced the problem of out-of-vocabulary (OOV) query terms that need to be transliterated, as they are typically proper names in the target language. First, for comparison, we used the above mentioned CLIR system with no transliteration engine (*Basic*), and measured the crosslingual retrieval performance. Clearly, the OOV terms would not be converted into target language, and hence contribute nothing to the retrieval performance. Second, we integrated a direct machine transliteration system between Hindi and English (*D-HiEn*), and calibrated the improvement in performance. Third, we integrate, instead of a direct system, a bridge transliteration system between Hindi and English, transitioning through Kannada (*B-HiKaEn*). For both, direct as well as bridge transliteration, we retained the top-5 transliterations generated by the appropriate system, for retrieval.

6.2 Results and Discussion

The results of the above experiments are given in Table 7. The current focus of these experiments is to answer the question of *whether the bridge machine transliteration systems used to transliterate the OOV words in Hindi queries to English* (by stepping through Kannada) *performs at par with a direct transliteration system.* As expected, enhancing the CLIR system with a machine transliteration sys-

Collection	CLIR System	MAP	Relative MAP change from *Basic*	Recall	Relative Recall change from *Basic*
CLEF 2006	Basic	0.1463	-	0.4952	-
	D-HiEn	0.1536	+4.98%	0.5151	+4.01%
	B-HiKaEn	0.1529	+4.51%	0.5302	+7.06%
CLEF 2007	Basic	0.2521	-	0.7156	-
	D-HiEn	0.2556	+1.38%	0.7170	+ 0.19%
	B-HiKaEn	0.2748	+9.00%	0.7174	+ 0.25%
FIRE 2008	Basic	0.4361	-	0.8457	-
	D-HiEn	0.4505	+3.30%	0.8506	+0.57%
	B-HiKaEn	0.4573	+4.86%	0.8621	+1.93%

Table 8: CLIR Experiments with bridge transliteration systems

tem (*D-HiEn*) gives better results over a CLIR system with no transliteration functionality (*Basic*). On the standard test collections, the bridge transliteration system performs in par or better than the direct transliteration system in terms of MAP as well as recall. Even though, the bridged system is of slightly lesser quality in ACC-1 in Hi-Ka-En, compared to Hi-En (see Table 1), the top-5 results had captured the correct transliteration, as shown in our analysis. A detailed analysis of the query translations produced by the above systems showed that in some cases the bridge systems does produce a better transliteration thereby leading to a better MAP. As an illustration, consider the OOV terms वेटिकन {`Vatican`} and नेस्ले {`Nestle`} and the corresponding transliterations generated by the different systems. The Direct-HiEn system was unable to

OOV term	D-HiEn	B-HiKaEn
वेटिकन (`vatican`)	vetican	vetican
	veticon	vettican
	vettican	**vatican**
	vetticon	watican
	wetican	wetican
नेस्ले (`nestle`)	nesle	**nestle**
	nesly	nesle
	nesley	nesley
	nessle	nestley
	nesey	nesly

Table 9: Sample output in direct and bridge systems

generate the correct transliteration in the top-5 results whereas the B-HiKaEn was able to produce the correct transliteration in the top-5 results thereby resulting in an improvement in MAP for these queries.

7 Conclusions

In this paper, we introduced the idea of bridge transliteration systems that were developed employing well-studied orthographic approaches between constituent languages. We empirically established the quality of such bridge transliteration systems and showed that quite contrary to our expectations, the quality of such systems does not degrade drastically as compared to the direct systems. Our error analysis showed that these better-than-expected results can be attributed to (i) Better performance (∼10-12%) of the second stage system on the strings transliterated correctly by the first stage system and (ii) Significant (∼25%) error correction in the second stage. Next, we highlighted that the performance of such bridge systems will be satisfactory as long as the orthographic inventory of the bridge language is either richer or more ambiguous as compared to the target language. We showed that our results are consistent with this hypothesis and provided two examples where there is a significant drop in the accuracy when the bridge language violates the above constraints. Finally, we showed that a state of the art CLIR system integrated with a bridge transliteration system performs in par with the same CLIR system integrated with a direct transliteration system, vindicating our claim that such bridge transliteration systems can be use in real-world applications to alleviate the resource requirement of ${}^nC_2$ parallel names corpora.

References

Peter E Brown, Vincent J. Della Pietra, Stephen A. Della Pietra, and Robert L. Mercer. 1993. The mathematics of statistical machine translation: parameter estimation. *Computational Linguistics*, 19:263–311.

FIRE. 2008. Forum for information retrieval evaluation.

Isao Goto, Naoto Kato, Noriyoshi Uratani, and Terumasa Ehara. 2003. Transliteration considering context information based on the maximum entropy method. In *Proceedings of MT-Summit IX*, pages 125–132.

Sung Young Jung, SungLim Hong, and Eunok Paek. 2000. An english to korean transliteration model of extended markov window. In *Proceedings of the 18th conference on Computational linguistics*, pages 383–389.

Byung-Ju Kang and Key-Sun Choi. 2000. Automatic transliteration and back-transliteration by decision tree learning. In *Proceedings of the 2nd International Conference on Language Resources and Evaluation*, pages 1135–1411.

Kevin Knight and Jonathan Graehl. 1997. Machine transliteration. In *Computational Linguistics*, pages 128–135.

John D. Lafferty, Andrew Mccallum, and Fernando C. N. Pereira. 2001. Conditional random fields: Probabilistic models for segmenting and labeling sequence data. In *ICML '01: Proceedings of the Eighteenth International Conference on Machine Learning*, pages 282–289, San Francisco, CA, USA.

Jae Sung Lee and Key-Sun Choi. 1998. English to korean statistical transliteration for information retrieval. In *Computer Processing of Oriental Languages*, pages 17–37.

Haizhou Li, A Kumaran, , Min Zhang, and Vladimir Pervouvhine. 2009. Whitepaper of news 2009 machine transliteration shared task. In *Proceedings of the 2009 Named Entities Workshop: Shared Task on Transliteration (NEWS 2009)*, pages 19–26, Suntec, Singapore, August. Association for Computational Linguistics.

Thomas Mandl and Christa Womser-Hacker. 2004. How do named entities contribute to retrieval effectiveness? In *CLEF*, pages 833–842.

Preslav Nakov and Hwee Tou Ng. 2009. Improved statistical machine translation for resource-poor languages using related resource-rich languages. In *Proceedings of the 2009 Conference on Empirical Methods in Natural Language Processing*, pages 1358–1367, Singapore, August. Association for Computational Linguistics.

A Nardi and C Peters. 2006. Working notes for the clef 2006 workshop.

A Nardi and C Peters. 2007. Working notes for the clef 2007 workshop.

Franz Josef Och and Hermann Ney. 2003. A systematic comparison of various statistical alignment models. *Computational Linguistics*, 29(1):19–51.

Jong-hoon Oh and Key-Sun Choi. 2002. An english-korean transliteration model using pronunciation and contextual rules. In *Proceedings of the 19th International Conference on Computational Linguistics (COLING)*, pages 758–764.

Bonnie Glover Stalls and Kevin Knight. 1998. Translating names and technical terms in arabic text. In *Proceedings of COLING/ACL Workshop on Computational Approaches to Semitic Languages*, pages 34–41.

Raghavendra Udupa, K Saravanan, Anton Bakalov, and Abhijit Bhole. 2009. "they are out there, if you know where to look: Mining transliterations of oov query terms for cross language information retrieval". In *ECIR'09: Proceedings of the 31st European Conference on IR research on Advances in Information Retrieval*, pages 437–448, Toulouse, France.

Suryaganesh Veeravalli, Sreeharsha Yella, Prasad Pingali, and Vasudeva Varma. 2008. Statistical transliteration for cross language information retrieval using hmm alignment model and crf. In *Proceedings of the 2nd workshop on Cross Lingual Information Access (CLIA) Addressing the Information Need of Multilingual Societies*.

Hua Wu and Haifeng Wang. 2007. Pivot language approach for phrase-based statistical machine translation. *Machine Translation*, 21(3):165–181.

Discriminative Learning over Constrained Latent Representations

Ming-Wei Chang and **Dan Goldwasser** and **Dan Roth** and **Vivek Srikumar**
University of Illinois at Urbana Champaign
Urbana, IL 61801
{mchang,goldwas1,danr,vsrikum2}@uiuc.edu

Abstract

This paper proposes a general learning framework for a class of problems that require learning over latent intermediate representations. Many natural language processing (NLP) decision problems are defined over an expressive intermediate representation that is not explicit in the input, leaving the algorithm with both the task of recovering a good intermediate representation and learning to classify correctly. Most current systems separate the learning problem into two stages by solving the first step of recovering the intermediate representation heuristically and using it to learn the final classifier. This paper develops a novel joint learning algorithm for both tasks, that uses the final prediction to guide the selection of the best intermediate representation. We evaluate our algorithm on three different NLP tasks – transliteration, paraphrase identification and textual entailment – and show that our joint method significantly improves performance.

1 Introduction

Many NLP tasks can be phrased as decision problems over complex linguistic structures. Successful learning depends on correctly encoding these (often latent) structures as features for the learning system. Tasks such as transliteration discovery (Klementiev and Roth, 2008), recognizing textual entailment (RTE) (Dagan et al., 2006) and paraphrase identification (Dolan et al., 2004) are a few prototypical examples. However, the input to such problems does not specify the latent structures and the problem is defined in terms of surface forms only. Most current solutions transform the raw input into a meaningful intermediate representation[1], and then encode its structural properties as features for the learning algorithm.

Consider the RTE task of identifying whether the meaning of a short text snippet (called the *hypothesis*) can be inferred from that of another snippet (called the *text*). A common solution (MacCartney et al., 2008; Roth et al., 2009) is to begin by defining an alignment over the corresponding entities, predicates and their arguments as an intermediate representation. A classifier is then trained using features extracted from the intermediate representation. The idea of using a intermediate representation also occurs frequently in other NLP tasks (Bergsma and Kondrak, 2007; Qiu et al., 2006).

While the importance of finding a good intermediate representation is clear, emphasis is typically placed on the later stage of extracting features over this intermediate representation, thus separating learning into **two stages** – specifying the latent representation, and then extracting features for learning. The latent representation is obtained by an inference process using predefined models or well-designed heuristics. While these approaches often perform well, they ignore a useful resource when generating the latent structure – the labeled data for the final learning task. As we will show in this paper, this results in degraded performance for the actual classification task at hand. Several works have considered this issue (McCallum et al., 2005; Goldwasser and Roth, 2008b; Chang et al., 2009; Das and Smith, 2009); however, they provide solutions

[1] In this paper, the phrases "intermediate representation" and "latent representation" are used interchangeably.

Human Language Technologies: The 2010 Annual Conference of the North American Chapter of the ACL, pages 429–437,
Los Angeles, California, June 2010.

that do not easily generalize to new tasks.

In this paper, we propose a unified solution to the problem of learning to make the classification decision **jointly** with determining the intermediate representation. Our *Learning Constrained Latent Representations (***LCLR***) framework* is guided by the intuition that there is *no* intrinsically good intermediate representation, but rather that a representation is good only to the extent to which it improves performance on the final classification task. In the rest of this section we discuss the properties of our framework and highlight its contributions.

Learning over Latent Representations This paper formulates the problem of *learning over latent representations* and presents a novel and general solution applicable to a wide range of NLP applications. We analyze the properties of our learning solution, thus allowing new research to take advantage of a well understood learning and optimization framework rather than an ad-hoc solution. We show the generality of our framework by successfully applying it to three domains: transliteration, RTE and paraphrase identification.

Joint Learning Algorithm In contrast to most existing approaches that employ domain specific heuristics to construct intermediate representations to learn the final classifier, our algorithm learns to construct the optimal intermediate representation to support the learning problem. Learning to represent is a difficult structured learning problem however, unlike other works that use labeled data at the intermediate level, our algorithm only uses the binary supervision supplied for the final learning problem.

Flexible Inference Successful learning depends on constraining the intermediate representation with task-specific knowledge. Our framework uses the declarative Integer Linear Programming (ILP) inference formulation, which makes it easy to define the intermediate representation and to inject knowledge in the form of *constraints*. While ILP has been applied to structured output learning, to the best of our knowledge, this is the first work that makes use of ILP in formalizing the general problem of learning intermediate representations.

2 Preliminaries

We introduce notation using the Paraphrase Identification task as a running example. This is the binary classification task of identifying whether one sentence is a paraphrase of another. A paraphrase pair from the MSR Paraphrase corpus (Quirk et al., 2004) is shown in Figure 1. In order to identify that the sentences paraphrase each other , we need to align constituents of these sentences. One possible alignment is shown in the figure, in which the dotted edges correspond to the aligned constituents. An alignment can be specified using binary variables corresponding to every edge between constituents, indicating whether the edge is included in the alignment. Different activations of these variables induce the space of *intermediate representations*.

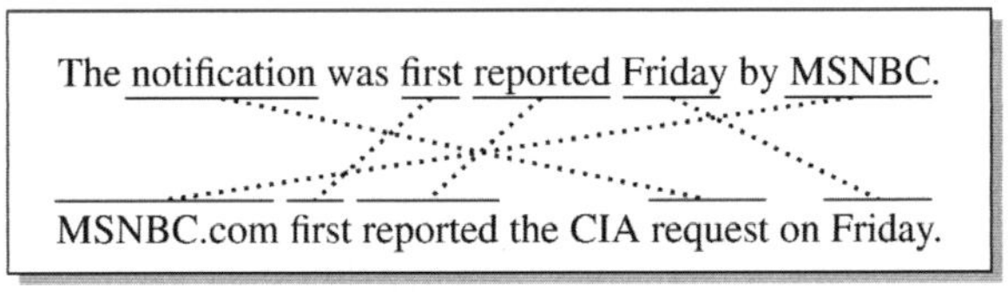

Figure 1: The dotted lines represent a possible intermediate representation for the paraphrase identification task. Since different representation choices will impact the binary identification decision directly, our approach chooses the representation that facilitates the binary learning task.

To formalize this setting, let $\mathbf{x}$ denote the input to a decision function, which maps $\mathbf{x}$ to $\{-1, 1\}$. We consider problems where this decision depends on an intermediate representation (for example, the collection of all dotted edges in Figure 1), which can be represented by a binary vector $\mathbf{h}$.

In the literature, a common approach is to separate the problem into two stages. First, a generation stage predicts $\mathbf{h}$ for each $\mathbf{x}$ using a pre-defined model or a heuristic. This is followed by a learning stage, in which the classifier is trained using $\mathbf{h}$. In our example, if the generation stage predicts the alignment shown, then the learning stage would use the features computed based on the alignments. Formally, the two-stage approach uses a pre-defined inference procedure that finds an intermediate representation $\mathbf{h}'$. Using features $\Phi(\mathbf{x}, \mathbf{h}')$ and a learned weight vector θ, the example is classified as positive if $\theta^T \Phi(\mathbf{x}, \mathbf{h}') \geq 0$.

However, in the two stage approach, the latent representation, which is provided to the learning algorithm, is determined before learning starts, and without any feedback from the final task. It is dictated by the intuition of the developer. This approach makes two implicit assumptions: first, it assumes the existence of a "correct" latent representation and, second, that the model or heuristic used to generate it is the correct one for the learning problem at hand.

3 Joint Learning with an Intermediate Representation

In contrast to two-stage approaches, we use the annotated data for the final classification task to learn a suitable intermediate representation which, in turn, helps the final classification.

Choosing a good representation is an optimization problem that selects which of the elements (features) of the representation best contribute to successful classification given some legitimacy constraints; therefore, we (1) set up the optimization framework that finds legitimate representations (Section 3.1), and (2) learn an objective function for this optimization problem, such that it makes the best final decision (Section 3.2.)

3.1 Inference

Our goal is to correctly predict the final label rather than matching a "gold" intermediate representation. In our framework, attempting to learn the final decision drives both the selection of the intermediate representation and the final predictions.

For each $\mathbf{x}$, let $\Gamma(\mathbf{x})$ be the set of all substructures of all possible intermediate representations. In Figure 1, this could be the set of all alignment edges connecting the constituents of the sentences. Given a vocabulary of such structures of size N, we denote intermediate representations by $\mathbf{h} \in \{0,1\}^N$, which "select" the components of the vocabulary that constitute the intermediate representation. We define $\phi_s(\mathbf{x})$ to be a feature vector over the substructure s, which is used to describe the characteristics of s, and define a weight vector $\mathbf{u}$ over these features.

Let $\mathcal{C}$ denote the set of feasible intermediate representations $\mathbf{h}$, specified by means of linear constraints over $\mathbf{h}$. While $\Gamma(\mathbf{x})$ might be large, the set of those elements in $\mathbf{h}$ that are active can be constrained by controlling $\mathcal{C}$. After we have learned a weight vector $\mathbf{u}$ that scores intermediate representations for the final classification task, we define our decision function as

$$f_{\mathbf{u}}(\mathbf{x}) = \max_{\mathbf{h}\in\mathcal{C}} \mathbf{u}^T \sum_{s\in\Gamma(\mathbf{x})} h_s \phi_s(\mathbf{x}), \qquad (1)$$

and classify the input as positive if $f_{\mathbf{u}}(\mathbf{x}) \geq 0$.

In Eq. (1), $\mathbf{u}^T\phi_s(\mathbf{x})$ is the score associated with the substructure s, and $f_{\mathbf{u}}(\mathbf{x})$ is the score for the entire intermediate representation. Therefore, our decision function $f_{\mathbf{u}}(\mathbf{x}) \geq 0$ makes use of the intermediate representation and its score to classify the input. An input is labeled as positive if its underlying intermediate structure allows it to cross the decision threshold. The intermediate representation is chosen to maximize the overall score of the input. This design is especially beneficial for many phenomena in NLP, where only positive examples have a meaningful underlying structure. In our paraphrase identification example, good alignments generally exist only for positive examples.

One unique feature of our framework is that we treat Eq. (1) as an Integer Linear Programming (ILP) instance. A concrete instantiation of this setting to the paraphrase identification problem, along with the actual ILP formulation is shown in Section 4.

3.2 Learning

We now present an algorithm that learns the weight vector $\mathbf{u}$. For a loss function $\ell : \mathbb{R} \to \mathbb{R}$, the goal of learning is to solve the following optimization problem:

$$\min_{\mathbf{u}} \frac{\lambda}{2}\|\mathbf{u}\|^2 + \sum_i \ell\left(-y_i f_{\mathbf{u}}(\mathbf{x}_i)\right) \qquad (2)$$

Here, λ is the regularization parameter. Substituting Eq. (1) into Eq. (2), we get

$$\min_{\mathbf{u}} \frac{\lambda}{2}\|\mathbf{u}\|^2 + \sum_i \ell\left(-y_i \max_{\mathbf{h}\in\mathcal{C}} \mathbf{u}^T \sum_{s\in\Gamma(\mathbf{x})} h_s\phi_s(\mathbf{x}_i)\right) \qquad (3)$$

Note that there is a maximization term inside the global minimization problem, making Eq. (3) a nonconvex problem. The minimization drives $\mathbf{u}$ towards smaller empirical loss while the maximization uses $\mathbf{u}$ to find the best representation for each example.

The algorithm for Learning over Constrained Latent Representations (LCLR) is listed in Algorithm 1. In each iteration, first, we find the best feature representations for all positive examples (lines 3-5). This step can be solved with an off-the-shelf ILP solver. Having fixed the representations for the positive examples, we update the $\mathbf{u}$ by solving Eq. (4) at line 6 in the algorithm. It is important to observe

Algorithm 1 *LCLR* :The algorithm that optimizes (3)

1: initialize: $\mathbf{u} \leftarrow \mathbf{u}_0$
2: **repeat**
3: **for all** positive examples $(\mathbf{x}_i, y_i = 1)$ **do**
4: Find $\mathbf{h}_i^* \leftarrow \arg\max_{\mathbf{h} \in \mathcal{C}} \sum_s h_s \mathbf{u}^T \phi_s(\mathbf{x}_i)$
5: **end for**
6: Update $\mathbf{u}$ by solving

$$\min_{\mathbf{u}} \frac{\lambda}{2}\|\mathbf{u}\|^2 + \sum_{i:y_i=1} \ell(-\mathbf{u}^T \sum_s h_{i,s}^* \phi_s(\mathbf{x}_i)) + \sum_{i:y_i=-1} \ell(\max_{\mathbf{h} \in \mathcal{C}} \mathbf{u}^T \sum_s h_s \phi_s(\mathbf{x}_i)) \quad (4)$$

7: **until** convergence
8: return $\mathbf{u}$

Algorithm 2 Cutting plane algorithm to optimize Eq. (4)

1: for each negative example x_j, $H_j \leftarrow \emptyset$
2: **repeat**
3: **for** each negative example x_j **do**
4: Find $\mathbf{h}_j^* \leftarrow \arg\max_{\mathbf{h} \in \mathcal{C}} \sum_s h_s \mathbf{u}^T \phi_s(\mathbf{x}_j)$
5: $H_j \leftarrow H_j \cup \{\mathbf{h}_j^*\}$
6: **end for**
7: Solve

$$\min_{\mathbf{u}} \frac{\lambda}{2}\|\mathbf{u}\|^2 + \sum_{i:y_i=1} \ell(-\mathbf{u}^T \sum_s h_{i,s}^* \phi_s(\mathbf{x}_i)) + \sum_{i:y_i=-1} \ell(\max_{\mathbf{h} \in H_j} \mathbf{u}^T \sum_s h_s \phi_s(\mathbf{x}_i)) \quad (5)$$

8: **until** no new element is added to any H_j
9: return $\mathbf{u}$

that for positive examples in Eq. (4), we use the intermediate representations $\mathbf{h}^*$ from line 4.

Algorithm 1 satisfies the following property:

Theorem 1 *If the loss function ℓ is a non-decreasing function, then the objective function value of Eq.* (3) *is guaranteed to decrease in every iteration of Algorithm 1. Moreover, if the loss function is also convex, then Eq.* (4) *in Algorithm 1 is convex.*

Due to the space limitation, we omit the proof.

Theoretically, we can use any loss function that satisfies the conditions of the theorem. In the experiments in this paper, we use the squared-hinge loss function: $\ell(-yf_{\mathbf{u}}(\mathbf{x})) = \max(0, 1 - yf_{\mathbf{u}}(\mathbf{x}))^2$.

Recall that Eq. (4) is not the traditional SVM or logistic regression formulation. This is because inside the inner loop, the best representation for each negative example must be found. Therefore, we need to perform inference for every negative example when updating the weight vector solution. Instead of solving a difficult non-convex optimization problem (Eq. (3)), LCLR iteratively solves a series of easier problems (Eq. (4)). This is especially true for our loss function because Eq. (4) is convex and can be solved efficiently.

We use a cutting plane algorithm to solve Eq. (4). A similar idea has been proposed in (Joachims et al., 2009). The algorithm for solving Eq. (4) is presented as Algorithm 2. This algorithm uses a "cache" H_j to store all intermediate representations for negative examples that have been seen in previous iterations (lines 3-6) [2]. The difference between Eq. (5) in line 7 of Algorithm 2 and Eq. (4) is that in Eq. (5), we do not search over the entire space of intermediate representations. The search space for the minimization problem Eq. (5) is restricted to the cache H_j. Therefore, instead of solving the minimization problem Eq. (4), we can now solve several simpler problems shown in Eq. (5). The algorithm is guaranteed to stop (line 8) because the space of intermediate representations is finite. Furthermore, in practice, the algorithm needs to consider only a small subset of "hard" examples before it converges.

Inspired by (Hsieh et al., 2008), we apply an efficient coordinate descent algorithm for the *dual* formulation of (5) which is guaranteed to find its global minimum. Due to space considerations, we do not present the derivation of dual formulation and the details of the optimization algorithm.

4 Encoding with ILP: A Paraphrase Identification Example

In this section, we define the latent representation for the paraphrase identification task. Unlike the earlier example, where we considered the alignment of lexical items, we describe a more complex intermediate representation by aligning graphs created using semantic resources.

An input example is represented as two acyclic

[2]In our implementation, we keep a global cache H_j for each negative example x_j. Therefore, in Algorithm 2, we start with a non-empty cache improving the speed significantly.

graphs, G_1 and G_2, corresponding to the first and second input sentences. Each vertex in the graph contains word information (lemma and part-of-speech) and the edges denote dependency relations, generated by the Stanford parser (Klein and Manning, 2003). The intermediate representation for this task can now be defined as an alignment between the graphs, which captures lexical and syntactic correlations between the sentences.

We use $V(G)$ and $E(G)$ to denote the set of vertices and edges in G respectively, and define four hidden variable types to encode vertex and edge mappings between G_1 and G_2.

- The **word-mapping** variables, denoted by h_{v_1,v_2}, define possible pairings of vertices, where $v_1 \in V(G_1)$ and $v_2 \in V(G_2)$.
- The **edge-mapping** variables, denoted by h_{e_1,e_2}, define possible pairings of the graphs edges, where $e_1 \in E(G_1)$ and $e_2 \in E(G_2)$.
- The **word-deletion** variables $h_{v_1,*}$ (or h_{*,v_2}) allow for vertices $v_1 \in V(G_1)$ (or $v_2 \in V(G_2)$) to be deleted. This accounts for omission of words (like function words).
- The **edge-deletion** variables, $h_{e_1,*}$ (or h_{*,e_2}) allow for deletion of edges from G_1 (or G_2).

Our inference problem is to find the optimal set of hidden variable activations, restricted according to the following set of linear constraints

- Each vertex in G_1 (or G_2) can either be mapped to a single vertex in G_2 (or G_1) or marked as deleted. In terms of the **word-mapping** and **word-deletion** variables, we have

$$\forall v_1 \in V(G_1); h_{v_1,*} + \sum_{v_2 \in V(G_2)} h_{v_1,v_2} = 1 \quad (6)$$

$$\forall v_2 \in V(G_2); h_{*,v_2} + \sum_{v_1 \in V(G_1)} h_{v_1,v_2} = 1 \quad (7)$$

- Each edge in G_1 (or G_2) can either be mapped to a single edge in G_2 (or G_1) or marked as deleted. In terms of the **edge-mapping** and **edge-deletion** variables, we have

$$\forall e_1 \in E(G_1); h_{e_1,*} + \sum_{e_2 \in E(G_2)} h_{e_1,e_2} = 1 \quad (8)$$

$$\forall e_2 \in E(G_2); h_{*,e_2} + \sum_{e_1 \in E(G_1)} h_{e_1,e_2} = 1 \quad (9)$$

- The edge mappings can be active if, and only if, the corresponding node mappings are active. Suppose $e_1 = (v_1, v'_1) \in E(G_1)$ and $e_2 = (v_2, v'_2) \in E(G_2)$, where $v_1, v'_1 \in V(G_1)$ and $v_2, v'_2 \in V(G_2)$. Then, we have

$$h_{v_1,v_2} + h_{v'_1,v'_2} - h_{e_1,e_2} \leq 1 \quad (10)$$

$$h_{v_1,v_2} \geq h_{e_1,e_2}; h_{v'_1,v'_2} \geq h_{e_1,e_2} \quad (11)$$

These constraints define the feasible set for the inference problem specified in Equation (1). This inference problem can be formulated as an ILP problem with the objective function from Equation (1):

$$\max_{\mathbf{h}} \quad \sum_s h_s \mathbf{u}^T \phi_s(\mathbf{x})$$
$$\text{subject to} \quad (6)\text{-}(11); \ \forall s; h_s \in \{0,1\} \quad (12)$$

This example demonstrates the use of integer linear programming to define intermediate representations incorporating domain intuition.

5 Experiments

We applied our framework to three different NLP tasks: transliteration discovery (Klementiev and Roth, 2008), RTE (Dagan et al., 2006), and paraphrase identification (Dolan et al., 2004).

Our experiments are designed to answer the following research question: "Given a binary classification problem defined over latent representations, will the joint LCLR algorithm perform better than a two-stage approach?" To ensure a fair comparison, both systems use the same feature functions and definition of intermediate representation. We use the same ILP formulation in both configurations, with a single exception – the objective function parameters: the two stage approach uses a task-specific heuristic, while LCLR learns it iteratively.

The ILP formulation results in very strong two stage systems. For example, in the paraphrase identification task, even our two stage system is the current state-of-the-art performance. In these settings, the improvement obtained by our joint approach is non-trivial and can be clearly attributed to the superiority of the joint learning algorithm. Interestingly, we find that our more general approach is better than specially designed joint approaches (Goldwasser and Roth, 2008b; Das and Smith, 2009).

Since the objective function (3) of the joint approach is not convex, a good initialization is required. We use the weight vector learned by the two stage approach as the starting point for the joint approach. The algorithm terminates when the relative improvement of the objective is smaller than 10^{-5}.

5.1 Transliteration Discovery

Transliteration discovery is the problem of identifying if a word pair, possibly written using two different character sets, refers to the same underlying entity. The intermediate representation consists of all possible character mappings between the two character sets. Identifying this mapping is not easy, as most writing systems do not perfectly align phonetically and orthographically; rather, this mapping can be context-dependent and ambiguous.

For an input pair of words (w_1, w_2), the intermediate structure $\mathbf{h}$ is a mapping between their characters, with the latent variable h_{ij} indicating if the ith character in w_1 is aligned to the jth character in w_2. The feature vector associated with the variable h_{ij} contains unigram character mapping, bigram character mapping (by considering surrounding characters). We adopt the *one-to-one mapping* and *non-crossing* constraint used in (Chang et al., 2009).

We evaluated our system using the English-Hebrew corpus (Goldwasser and Roth, 2008a), which consists of 250 positive transliteration pairs for training, and 300 pairs for testing. As negative examples for training, we sample 10% from random pairings of words from the positive data. We report two evaluation measurements – (1) the Mean Reciprocal Rank (MRR), which is the average of the multiplicative inverse of the rank of the correct answer, and (2) the accuracy (Acc), which is the percentage of the top rank candidates being correct.

We initialized the two stage inference process as detailed in (Chang et al., 2009) using a Romanization table to assign uniform weights to prominent character mappings. This initialization procedure resembles the approach used in (Bergsma and Kondrak, 2007). An alignment is first built by solving the constrained optimization problem. Then, a support vector machine with squared-hinge loss function is used to train a classifier using features extracted from the alignment. We refer to this two stage approach as *Alignment+Learning*.

The results summarized in Table 1 show the significant improvement obtained by the joint approach (95.4% MRR) compared to the two stage approach

Transliteration System	Acc	MRR
(Goldwasser and Roth, 2008b)	N/A	89.4
Alignment + Learning	80.0	85.7
LCLR	**92.3**	**95.4**

Table 1: Experimental results for transliteration. We compare a *two-stage* system: "Alignment+Learning" with LCLR, our *joint* algorithm. Both "Alignment+Learning" and LCLR use the same features and the same intermediate representation definition.

(85.7%). Moreover, LCLR outperforms the joint system introduced in (Goldwasser and Roth, 2008b).

5.2 Textual Entailment

Recognizing Textual Entailment (RTE) is an important textual inference task of predicting if a given *text* snippet, entails the meaning of another (the *hypothesis*). In many current RTE systems, the entailment decision depends on successfully aligning the constituents of the text and hypothesis, accounting for the internal linguistic structure of the input.

The raw input – the text and hypothesis – are represented as directed acyclic graphs, where vertices correspond to words. Directed edges link verbs to the head words of semantic role labeling arguments produced by (Punyakanok et al., 2008). All other words are connected by dependency edges. The intermediate representation is an alignment between the nodes and edges of the graphs. We used three hidden variable types from Section 4 – **word-mapping**, **word-deletion** and **edge-mapping**, along with the associated constraints as defined earlier. Since the text is typically much longer than the hypothesis, we create **word-deletion** latent variables (and features) only for the hypothesis.

The second column of Table 2 lists the resources used to generate features corresponding to each hidden variable type. For word-mapping variables, the features include a WordNet based metric (WNSim), indicators for the POS tags and negation identifiers. We used the state-of-the-art coreference resolution system of (Bengtson and Roth, 2008) to identify the canonical entities for pronouns and extract features accordingly. For word deletion, we use only the POS tags of the corresponding tokens (generated by the LBJ POS tagger[3]) to generate features. For edge

[3] http://L2R.cs.uiuc.edu/~cogcomp/software.php

Hidden Variable	RTE features	Paraphrase features
word-mapping	WordNet, POS, Coref, Neg	WordNet, POS, NE, ED
word-deletion	POS	POS, NE
edge-mapping	NODE-INFO	NODE-INFO, DEP
edge-deletion	N/A	DEP

Table 2: Summary of latent variables and feature resources for the entailment and paraphrase identification tasks. See Section 4 for an explanation of the hidden variable types. The linguistic resources used to generate features are abbreviated as follows – POS: Part of speech, Coref: Canonical coreferent entities; NE: Named Entity, ED: Edit distance, Neg: Negation markers, DEP: Dependency labels, NODE-INFO: corresponding node alignment resources, N/A: Hidden variable not used.

Entailment System	**Acc**
Median of TAC 2009 systems	61.5
Alignment + Learning	65.0
LCLR	**66.8**

Table 3: Experimental results for recognizing textual entailment. The first row is the median of best performing systems of all teams that participated in the RTE5 challenge (Bentivogli et al., 2009). *Alignment + Learning* is our two-stage system implementation, and LCLR is our joint learning algorithm. Details about these systems are provided in the text.

mapping variables, we include the features of the corresponding word mapping variables, scaled by the word similarity of the words forming the edge.

We evaluated our system using the RTE-5 data (Bentivogli et al., 2009), consisting of 600 sentence pairs for training and testing respectively, in which positive and negative examples are equally distributed. In these experiments the joint LCLR algorithm converged after 5 iterations.

For the two stage system, we used WN-Sim to score alignments during inference. The word-based scores influence the edge variables via the constraints. This two-stage system (the Alignment+Learning system) is significantly better than the median performance of the RTE-5 submissions. Using LCLR further improves the result by almost 2%, a substantial improvement in this domain.

5.3 Paraphrase Identification

Our final task is Paraphrase Identification, discussed in detail at Section 4. We use all the four hidden variable types described in that section. The features used are similar to those described earlier

Paraphrase System	**Acc**
Experiments using (Dolan et al., 2004)	
(Qiu et al., 2006)	72.00
(Das and Smith, 2009)	73.86
(Wan et al., 2006)	75.60
Alignment + Learning	76.23
LCLR	**76.41**
Experiments using **Extended data set**	
Alignment + Learning	72.00
LCLR	**72.75**

Table 4: Experimental Result For Paraphrasing Identification. Our joint LCLR approach achieves the best results compared to several previously published systems, and our own two stage system implementation (*Alignment + Learning*). We evaluated the systems performance across two datasets: (Dolan et al., 2004) dataset and the Extended dataset, see the text for details. Note that LCLR outperforms (Das and Smith, 2009), which is a specifically designed joint approach for this task.

for the RTE system and are summarized in Table 2.

We used the MSR paraphrase dataset of (Dolan et al., 2004) for empirical evaluation. Additionally, we generated a second corpus (called the *Extended dataset*) by sampling 500 sentence pairs from the MSR dataset for training and using the entire test collection of the original dataset. In the Extended dataset, for every sentence pair, we extended the longer sentence by concatenating it with itself. This results in a more difficult inference problem because it allows more mappings between words. Note that the performance on the original dataset sets the ceiling on the second one.

The results are summarized in Table 4. The first part of the table compares the LCLR system with a two stage system (*Alignment + Learning*) and three published results that use the MSR dataset. (We only list single systems in the table[4]) Interestingly, although still outperformed by our joint LCLR algorithm, the two stage system is able perform significantly better than existing systems for that dataset (Qiu et al., 2006; Das and Smith, 2009; Wan et al., 2006). We attribute this improvement, consistent across both the ILP based systems, to the intermediate representation we defined.

We hypothesize that the similarity in performance between the joint LCLR algorithm and the two stage

[4]Previous work (Das and Smith, 2009) has shown that combining the results of several systems improves performance.

(*Alignment* + *Learning*) systems is due to the limited intermediate representation space for input pairs in this dataset. We evaluated these systems on the more difficult *Extended* dataset. Results indeed show that the margin between the two systems increases as the inference problem becomes harder.

6 Related Work

Recent NLP research has largely focused on two-stage approaches. Examples include RTE (Zanzotto and Moschitti, 2006; MacCartney et al., 2008; Roth et al., 2009); string matching (Bergsma and Kondrak, 2007); transliteration (Klementiev and Roth, 2008); and paraphrase identification (Qiu et al., 2006; Wan et al., 2006).

(MacCartney et al., 2008) considered constructing a latent representation to be an independent task and used manually labeled *alignment* data (Brockett, 2007) to tune the inference procedure parameters. While this method identifies alignments well, it does not improve entailment decisions. This strengthens our intuition that the latent representation should be guided by the final task.

There are several exceptions to the two-stage approach in the NLP community (Haghighi et al., 2005; McCallum et al., 2005; Goldwasser and Roth, 2008b; Das and Smith, 2009); however, the intermediate representation and the inference for constructing it are closely coupled with the application task. In contrast, LCLR provides a general formulation that allows the use of expressive constraints, making it applicable to many NLP tasks.

Unlike other latent variable SVM frameworks (Felzenszwalb et al., 2009; Yu and Joachims, 2009) which often use task-specific inference procedure, LCLR utilizes the declarative inference framework that allows using *constraints* over intermediate representation and provides a general platform for a wide range of NLP tasks.

The optimization procedure in this work and (Felzenszwalb et al., 2009) are quite different. We use the coordinate descent and cutting-plane methods ensuring we have fewer parameters and the inference procedure can be easily parallelized. Our procedure also allows different loss functions. (Cherry and Quirk, 2008) adopts the Latent SVM algorithm to define a language model. Unfortunately, their implementation is not guaranteed to converge.

In CRF-like models with latent variables (McCallum et al., 2005), the decision function marginalizes over the all hidden states when presented with an input example. Unfortunately, the computational cost of applying their framework is prohibitive with constrained latent representations. In contrast, our framework requires only the *best* hidden representation instead of marginalizing over all possible representations, thus reducing the computational effort.

7 Conclusion

We consider the problem of learning over an intermediate representation. We assume the existence of a latent structure in the input, relevant to the learning problem, but not accessible to the learning algorithm. Many NLP tasks fall into these settings and each can consider a different hidden input structure. We propose a unifying thread for the different problems and present a novel framework for Learning over Constrained Latent Representations (LCLR). Our framework can be applied to many different latent representations such as parse trees, orthographic mapping and tree alignments. Our approach contrasts with existing work in which learning is done over a *fixed* representation, as we advocate *jointly* learning it with the final task.

We successfully apply the proposed framework to three learning tasks – Transliteration, Textual Entailment and Paraphrase Identification. Our joint LCLR algorithm achieves superior performance in all three tasks. We attribute the performance improvement to our novel training algorithm and flexible inference procedure, allowing us to encode domain knowledge. This presents an interesting line of future work in which more linguistic intuitions can be encoded into the learning problem. For these reasons, we believe that our framework provides an important step forward in understanding the problem of learning over hidden structured inputs.

Acknowledgment We thank James Clarke and Mark Sammons for their insightful comments. This research was partly sponsored by the Army Research Laboratory (ARL) (accomplished under Cooperative Agreement Number W911NF-09-2-0053) and by Air Force Research Laboratory (AFRL) under prime contract no. FA8750-09-C-0181. Any opinions, findings, and conclusion or recommendations expressed in this material are those of the author(s) and do not necessarily reflect the view of the ARL or of AFRL.

References

E. Bengtson and D. Roth. 2008. Understanding the value of features for coreference resolution. In *EMNLP*.

L. Bentivogli, I. Dagan, H. T. Dang, D. Giampiccolo, and B. Magnini. 2009. The fifth PASCAL recognizing textual entailment challenge. In *Proc. of TAC Workshop*.

S. Bergsma and G. Kondrak. 2007. Alignment-based discriminative string similarity. In *ACL*.

C. Brockett. 2007. Aligning the RTE 2006 corpus. In *Technical Report MSR-TR-2007-77, Microsoft Research*.

M. Chang, D. Goldwasser, D. Roth, and Y. Tu. 2009. Unsupervised constraint driven learning for transliteration discovery. In *NAACL*.

C. Cherry and C. Quirk. 2008. Discriminative, syntactic language modeling through latent svms. In *Proc. of the Eighth Conference of AMTA*.

I. Dagan, O. Glickman, and B. Magnini, editors. 2006. *The PASCAL Recognising Textual Entailment Challenge*.

D. Das and N. A. Smith. 2009. Paraphrase identification as probabilistic quasi-synchronous recognition. In *ACL*.

W. Dolan, C. Quirk, and C. Brockett. 2004. Unsupervised construction of large paraphrase corpora: Exploiting massively parallel news sources. In *COLING*.

P. F. Felzenszwalb, R. B. Girshick, D. McAllester, and D. Ramanan. 2009. Object detection with discriminatively trained part based models. *IEEE Transactions on Pattern Analysis and Machine Intelligence*.

D. Goldwasser and D. Roth. 2008a. Active sample selection for named entity transliteration. In *ACL*. Short Paper.

D. Goldwasser and D. Roth. 2008b. Transliteration as constrained optimization. In *EMNLP*.

A. Haghighi, A. Ng, and C. Manning. 2005. Robust textual inference via graph matching. In *HLT-EMNLP*.

C.-J. Hsieh, K.-W. Chang, C.-J. Lin, S. S. Keerthi, and S. Sundararajan. 2008. A dual coordinate descent method for large-scale linear svm. In *ICML*.

T. Joachims, T. Finley, and Chun-Nam Yu. 2009. Cutting-plane training of structural svms. *Machine Learning*.

D. Klein and C. D. Manning. 2003. Fast exact inference with a factored model for natural language parsing. In *NIPS*.

A. Klementiev and D. Roth. 2008. Named entity transliteration and discovery in multilingual corpora. In Cyril Goutte, Nicola Cancedda, Marc Dymetman, and George Foster, editors, *Learning Machine Translation*.

B. MacCartney, M. Galley, and C. D. Manning. 2008. A phrase-based alignment model for natural language inference. In *EMNLP*.

A. McCallum, K. Bellare, and F. Pereira. 2005. A conditional random field for discriminatively-trained finite-state string edit distance. In *UAI*.

V. Punyakanok, D. Roth, and W. Yih. 2008. The importance of syntactic parsing and inference in semantic role labeling. *Computational Linguistics*.

L. Qiu, M.-Y. Kan, and T.-S. Chua. 2006. Paraphrase recognition via dissimilarity significance classification. In *EMNLP*.

C. Quirk, C. Brockett, and W. Dolan. 2004. Monolingual machine translation for paraphrase generation. In *EMNLP*.

D. Roth, M. Sammons, and V.G. Vydiswaran. 2009. A framework for entailed relation recognition. In *ACL*.

S. Wan, M. Dras, R. Dale, and C. Paris. 2006. Using dependency-based features to take the p̈ara-farceöut of paraphrase. In *Proc. of the Australasian Language Technology Workshop (ALTW)*.

C. Yu and T. Joachims. 2009. Learning structural svms with latent variables. In *ICML*.

F. M. Zanzotto and A. Moschitti. 2006. Automatic learning of textual entailments with cross-pair similarities. In *ACL*.

Some Empirical Evidence for Annotation Noise in a Benchmarked Dataset

Beata Beigman Klebanov
Kellogg School of Management
Northwestern University
beata@northwestern.edu

Eyal Beigman
Washington University in St. Louis
beigman@wustl.edu

Abstract

A number of recent articles in computational linguistics venues called for a closer examination of the type of noise present in annotated datasets used for benchmarking (Reidsma and Carletta, 2008; Beigman Klebanov and Beigman, 2009). In particular, Beigman Klebanov and Beigman articulated a type of noise they call *annotation noise* and showed that in worst case such noise can severely degrade the generalization ability of a linear classifier (Beigman and Beigman Klebanov, 2009). In this paper, we provide quantitative empirical evidence for the existence of this type of noise in a recently benchmarked dataset. The proposed methodology can be used to zero in on unreliable instances, facilitating generation of cleaner gold standards for benchmarking.

1 Introduction

Traditionally, studies in computational linguistics use few trained annotators. Lately this might be changing, as inexpensive annotators are available in large numbers through projects like Amazon Mechanical Turk or through online games where annotations are produced as a by-product (Poesio et al., 2008; von Ahn, 2006), and, at least for certain tasks, the quality of multiple non-expert annotations is close to that of a small number of experts (Snow et al., 2008; Callison-Burch, 2009).

Apart from the reduced costs, mass annotation is a promising way to get detailed information about the dataset, such as the level of difficulty of the difference instances. Such information is important both from the linguistic and from the machine learning perspective, as the existence of a group of instances difficult enough to look like they have been labeled by random guesses can in the worst case induce the machine learner training on the dataset to misclassify a constant proportion of easy, non-controversial instances, as well as produce incorrect comparative results in a benchmarking setting (Beigman Klebanov and Beigman, 2009; Beigman and Beigman Klebanov, 2009) .

In this article, we employ annotation generation models to estimate the types of instances in a multiply annotated dataset for a binary classification task. We provide the first quantitative empirical demonstration, to our knowledge, of the existence of what Beigman Klebanov and Beigman (2009) call "annotation noise" in a benchmarked dataset, that is, for a case where instances cannot be plausibly assigned to just two classes, and where instances in the third class can be plausibly described as having been annotated by flips of a nearly fair coin. The ability to identify such instances helps improve the gold standard by eliminating them, and allows further empirical investigation of their impact on machine learning for the task in question.

2 Generative models of annotation

We present a graphical model for the generation of annotations. The basic idea is that there are different types of instances that induce different responses from annotators. Each instance may have a true label of "0" or "1", however, the researcher's access to it is mediated by annotators who are guessing the true label by flipping a coin, where the bias of the coin depends on the type of the instance. The bias of the coin essentially models the difficulty of label-

Human Language Technologies: The 2010 Annual Conference of the North American Chapter of the ACL, pages 438–446,
Los Angeles, California, June 2010.

ing the instance; coins biased close to 0 and 1 correspond to instances that are easy to classify; a fair coin represents instances that are very difficult if not impossible to classify correctly with the given pool of annotators. The model presented in Beigman Klebanov and Beigman (2009) is a special case with 3 types (A,B,C) where p_A=0, p_C=1 (easy cases), and $0<p_B<1$ represents the hard cases, the harder the closer p_B is to 0.5. Models used here are a type of latent class models (McCutcheon, 1987) widely used in the *Biometrics* community (Espeland and Handelman, 1989; Yang and Becker, 1997; Albert et al., 2001; Albert and Dodd, 2004).

The goal of modeling is to determine whether more than two types of instances need to be postulated, to estimate how difficult each type is, and to identify the troublemaking instances.

The graphical model is presented in figure 1. We assume the dataset of size N is a mixture of k different types of instances. The proportion of types is given by $\theta = (\theta_1, \ldots, \theta_k)$, and coin biases for each type are given by $p = (p_1, \ldots, p_k)$. Each instance is annotated by n i.i.d coinflips, and random variable $x \in \{0, \ldots, n\}$ counts the number of "1"s in the n annotations given to an instance. Each instance belongs to a type $t \in \{1, ..., k\}$, characterized by a coin with the probability p_t of annotating with the label "1". Conditioned on t, the number of "1"s in n annotations has a binomial distribution with parameter p_t: $\Pr(x = j|t) = \binom{n}{j} p_t^j (1 - p_t)^{n-j}$.

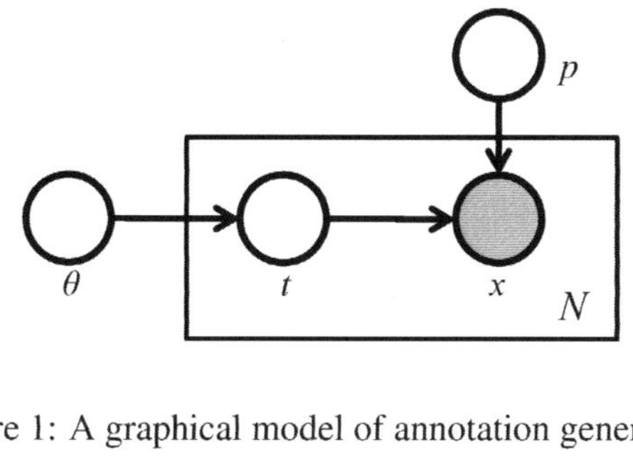

Figure 1: A graphical model of annotation generation.

The probability of observing j "1"s out of n annotations for an instance given θ and p is therefore $\Pr(x = j|\theta, p) = \sum_{t=1}^{k} \Pr(t|\theta) \cdot \Pr(x = j|t) = = \binom{n}{j} \sum_{t=1}^{k} \theta_t p_t^j (1 - p_t)^{n-j}$. The annotations are thus generated by a superposition of k binomials.

3 Data

3.1 Recognizing Textual Entailment -1

For the experiments reported here we use the 800 item test data of the first Recognizing Textual Entailment benchmark (RTE-1) from Dagan et al. (2006). This task drew a lot of attention in the community, with a series of benchmarks in 2005-2007.

The task is defined as follows: "... *textual entailment* is defined as a directional relationship between pairs of text expressions, denoted by *T* - the entailing "Text", and *H* - the entailed "Hypothesis". We say that *T* entails *H* if the meaning of *H* can be inferred from the meaning of T, as would typically be interpreted by people. This somewhat informal definition is based on (and assumes) common human understanding of language as well as common background knowledge" (Dagan et al., 2006). Further guidelines included an instruction to disregard tense differences, to accept cases where the inference is "very probable (but not completely certain)" and to avoid cases where the inference "has some positive probability that is not clearly very high." An example of a true entailment is the pair *T-H*: (T) Cavern Club sessions paid the Beatles £15 evenings and £5 lunchtime. (H) The Beatles perform at Cavern.

Although annotated by a small number of experts for the benchmark, the RTE-1 dataset has been later transferred to a mass annotation framework by Snow et al. (2008), who submitted simplified guidelines to the Amazon Mechanical Turk workplace (henceforth, AMT), collected 10 annotations per item from the total of 164 annotators, and showed that majority vote by Turkers agreed with expert annotation in 89.7% of the cases. We call the Snow et al. (2008) Turker annotations SRTE dataset, and use it in section 6. The instructions, followed by two examples, read: "Please state whether the second sentence (the Hypothesis) is implied by the information in the first sentence (the Text), i.e., please state whether the Hypothesis can be determined to be true given that the Text is true. Assume that you do not know anything about the situation except what the Text itself says. Also, note that every part of the Hypothesis must be implied by the Text in order for it to be true." The guidelines for Turkers are somewhat different from the original, not mentioning the issue of highly probable though not certain inference or a special treatment of tense mismatch between *H* and *T*, as well as discouraging reliance on background knowledge.

Using Snow et al. (2008) instructions, we collected 20 annotations for each of the 800 items through AMT from the total of 441 annotators. Each annotator did the minimum of 2 items, and was paid \$0.01 for 2 items, for the total annotator cost of \$80. We used only annotators with prior AMT approval rate of at least 95%, that is, only people whose performance in previous tasks on AMT was almost always approved by the requester of the task. Our design is thus somewhat different from Snow et al. (2008), as we paid more and selected annotators with a stake in their AMT reputation.

3.2 Preparing the data for model fitting

We collected the annotations in two separate batches of 10 annotations per item, using the same set of instructions, incentives, and examples. We hypothesized that controlling for these elements, we would get two random samples from the same distribution of Turkers, and hence will have two samples to make sure a model fitted on one sample generalized to the other. It turned out, however, that a 3-Binomial model with a good fit on one of the samples was rejected with high probability for the other.[1] Thus, on the one hand, the variations between annotators in each sample were not as high as to preclude a model that captures only instance variability from fitting well; on the other hand, evidently, the two samples did not come from the same annotator distribution, but differed systematically due to factors we did not control for.[2] In order for our models not to inherit a systematic bias of any of the two samples, we mixed the two samples, and constructed two sets, BRTEa and BRTEb, each with 10 annotations per item, by randomly splitting the 20 answers per item into two groups, allowing the same annotator to contribute to different groups on different instances. Indeed, after the randomization, a model fitted for BRTEa produced excellent generalization on BRTEb, as we will see in section 4.2.

[1]For details of the model fitting procedure, see section 4.

[2]Such factors could be the hour and day of assignment, as the composition of AMT's global 24/7 workforce could differ systematically by day and hour.

4 Fitting a model to BRTE data

Using the model template presented in section 2, we successively attempt to fit a model with $k = 2, 3, \ldots$ until a model with a good fit is found or no degrees of freedom are left. For a given k, we fit the parameters θ and p using non-linear least squares trust-region method as implemented in the default version of MATLAB's *lsqnonlin* function. We then use χ^2 to measure goodness of fit; a model that cannot be rejected with 95% confidence (p>0.05) would be considered a good fit. In all cases N=800, n=10, as we use 10 annotations for each instance.

4.1 Mixture of 2 Binomials

Suppose k=2, with types t_0 and t_1. The best fit yields p_0=0.237, p_1=0.867, $\theta_0=\frac{431}{800}$, θ_1=1-θ_0. The model (shown in figure 2) is a poor fit, with χ^2=73.66 well above the critical value of 14.07 for df=7, p=0.05.[3]

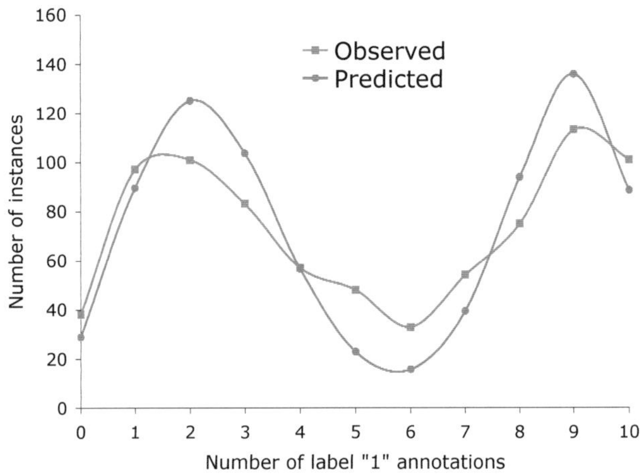

Figure 2: Fitting the model B1+B2 to BRTEa data. B1$\sim \mathcal{B}(10,0.237)$ on 431 instances, B2$\sim \mathcal{B}(10,0.867)$ on 369 instances. The point (x,y) means that there are y instances given label "1" in exactly x out of 10 annotations.

4.2 Model M: Mixture of 3 Binomials

Suppose now k=3. The best fitting model M=B1+B2+B3 is specified in figure 3; M fits the data very well. Assuming B1 and B3 reflect items

[3]For degrees of freedom, we take the number of datapoints being fitted (11), take one degree of freedom off for knowing in advance the total number of instances, and take off additional 3 degrees of freedom for estimating p_0, p_1, and θ_0 from the data. We are therefore left with 7 degrees of freedom in this case.

with uncontroversial labels "0" and "1", respectively, the model suggests that detecting "0" (no textual entailment) is somewhat more difficult for non-experts than detecting "1" (there is textual entailment) in this dataset, with the rate of incorrect predictions of about 20% and 10%, respectively.[4] The model also predicts that $\frac{159}{800} \approx 20\%$ of the data are difficult cases, with annotators flipping a close-to-a-fair coin (p=0.5487).

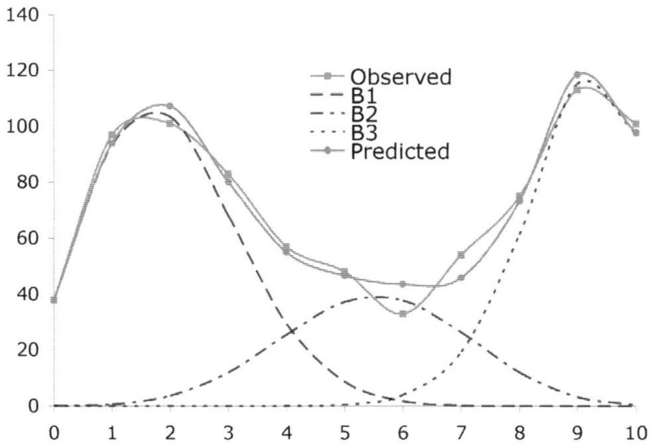

Figure 3: Fitting the model M=B1+B2+B3 to BRTEa data. B1$\sim$ $\mathcal{B}$(10,0.1978) on 343 instances, B2$\sim$ $\mathcal{B}$(10,0.5487) on 159 instances, B3$\sim$ $\mathcal{B}$(10,0.8942) on 298 instances. The binomials are shown in grey lines. The model M fits with χ^2=5.091; for df=5, this corresponds to p=0.4.

We use the dataset BRTEb to test the model developed on BRTEa. The model fits with χ^2=13.13, which, for df=10,[5] corresponds to p=0.2154.

We therefore conclude that, after eliminating systematic differences between annotators, we were unable to fit a model with two types of instances, whereas a model with three types of instances provides a good fit both for the dataset on which it is estimated and for a new dataset. This constitutes empirical evidence for the existence of a group of instances with near-random labels in this recently benchmarked dataset, at least for our pool of more than 400 non-expert annotators.

5 Could annotator heterogeneity provide an alternative explanation?

In the previous section, we established that instance heterogeneity can explain the observations. We might however ask whether a different model could provide a similarly fitting explanation. Specifically, heterogeneity among annotators has been seen as a major source of noise in the aggregate data and there are several works attempting to separate high quality annotators from low quality ones (Raykar et al., 2009; Donmez et al., 2009; Sheng et al., 2008; Carpenter, 2008). Could we explain the observed behavior with a model with only two types of instances that allows for annotator heterogeneity?

In this section we construct such a model. We show that this model entails an instance distribution that is a superposition of two normal distributions. We subsequently show that the best fitting two-Gaussian model does not provide a good fit.

We use a generation model similar to those in (Raykar et al., 2009; Carpenter, 2008) but with weaker parametric assumptions. The graphical model is given in figure 4.

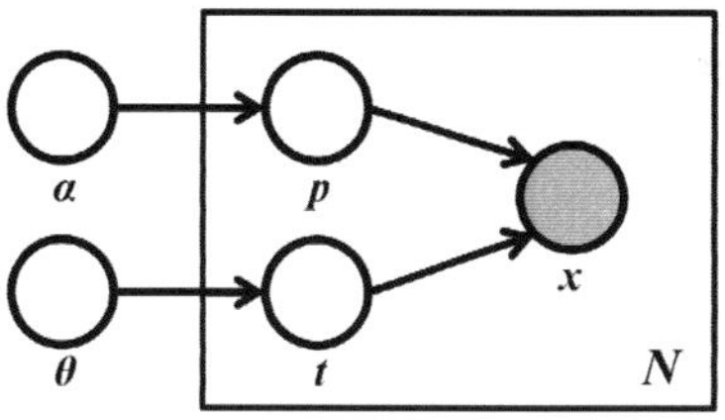

Figure 4: Annotation generation model with annotator heterogeneity.

We assume there are two types of instances $t \in \{0,1\}$ with the proportions $\theta = (\theta_0, \theta_1)$. The $2n$ probabilities $p = (p_{t1}, \ldots, p_{tn})$ for $t = 0, 1$ correspond to coins drawn independently from some distribution with parameter $\alpha = (\alpha_1, \ldots, \alpha_n)$. We make no assumption on the functional form apart from a positive probability to draw a value between 0 and 1, this in particular is true for the beta distribution used in (Raykar et al., 2009; Carpenter, 2008). As before, the number of "1"s attributed to an instance of type t is a random variable x, determined

[4] We note that any conclusions from the model hold for the particular 800 item dataset in question, and not for the task of recognizing textual entailment in general, as the dataset is not necessarily a representative sample. In fact, we know from Dagan et al. (2006) that these 800 items are not a random sample, but rather what remained after some 400 instances were removed due to disagreements between expert annotators or due to the judgment of one of organizers of the RTE-1 challenge.

[5] No parameters are fitted using the BRTEb data.

by independent flips of the n coins that correspond to the value of t. The marginal distribution of x is:

$$Pr(x = j|\theta, \alpha) =$$

$$= \sum_{t=0,1} \Pr(t|\theta) \int_{[0,1]^n} \Pr(p_t|\alpha)\cdot\Pr(x = j|p_t, t, \alpha)dp_t$$

$$= \sum_{t=0,1} \theta_t \int_{[0,1]^n} \Pr(p_t|\alpha) \left(\sum_{|S|=j} \prod_{i\in S} p_{ti} \prod_{i\notin S}(1 - p_{ti}) \right) dp_t$$

Let $x_1, \ldots, x_N$ be the random variables corresponding to the number of "1"s attributed to instances $1, \ldots, N$. W.l.g we assume instances $1, \ldots, N'$ are all of type t_0 ($N' = \theta_0 \cdot N$) and the rest of type t_1. Since $0 \leq x_j \leq n$ it follows that $\mathbb{E}(x_j)$, $Var(x_j) < \infty$ for $j = 1, \ldots, N$. If for each instance the coin-flips are independent, we can think of this as a two step process where we first draw the coins and then flip them. Thus, $x_1, \ldots, x_{N'}$ are i.i.d and the central limit theorem implies that the average number of "1"s on t_0 instances, namely the random variable $y_0 = \frac{1}{N'} \sum_{j=1}^{N'} x_j$ has an approximately normal distribution.[6] Making the same argument for the distribution of y_1 for instances of type t_1, it follows that the number of "1"s attributed to an instance of any type $y = y_0 + y_1$ would have a distribution that is a superposition of two Gaussians.

The best least-squares fit of all two-Gaussian models to BRTEa data is produced by G=N1+N2, N1$\sim$ $\mathcal{N}$(2.22, 1.73) on 418 instances, N2$\sim$ $\mathcal{N}$(9.07,1.41) on 382 instances; G is shown in figure 5. G fits with χ^2=36.77, much above the critical value χ^2=11.07 for df=5, p=0.05. We can thus rule out annotator heterogeneity as the only explanation of the observed pattern of responses.

6 Testing M on SRTE data

We further test M on the annotations collected by Snow et al. (2008) for the same 800 item dataset. While the instructions and the task were identical in BRTEa, BRTEb, and BRTE datasets, and in all cases each item was given 10 annotations, the incentive design was different (see section 3).

[6]It can be shown that $y_0 \sim \mathcal{N}(\mu, \sigma)$ for $\mu = n \cdot \mathbb{E}_{Dist(\alpha)}(p)$ and $\sigma = \sqrt{Var_{Dist(\alpha)}(p) \cdot n}$, using the expectation and variance of the coin parameter for type t_0 instances. For example, for a beta distribution with parameters α and β these would be $\mu = \frac{\alpha}{\alpha+\beta} n$ and $\sigma = \sqrt{\frac{\alpha\beta}{\alpha+\beta} n}$.

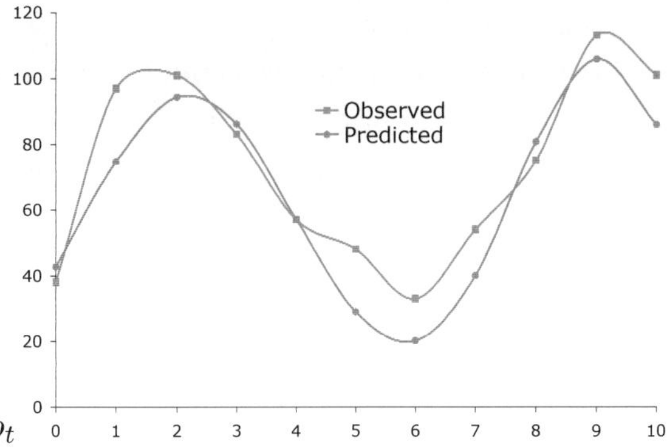

Figure 5: Model G's fit to BRTEa data, G= N1+N2, a mixture of two Gaussians.

Figure 6 shows that model M=B1+B2+B3 does not fit well, as SRTE dataset exhibits a rather different distribution from both BRTE datasets. In particular, it is clear that had a model been fitted on SRTE data, the coin flipping probabilities for the clear types, B1 and B3, would have to be moved towards 0.5; that is, an average annotator in SRTE dataset had worse ability to detect clear 0s and clear 1s than an average BRTE annotator. We note that BRTEa and BRTEb agreed with expert annotation in 92.5% and 90.8% of the instances, respectively, both better than 89.7% in SRTE.[7] Since we offered somewhat better incentives in BRTE, it is tempting to attribute the observed better quality of BRTE annotations to the improved incentives, although it is possible that some other uncontrolled AMT-related factor is responsible for the difference between the datasets, just as we found for our original two collected samples (see section 3.2).

Supposing the main source of misfit is difference in incentives, we conjecture that the difference between the 441 BRTE annotators and the 164 SRTE ones is due to the existence in SRTE of unmotivated, or "lazy" annotators, that is, people who flipped the same coin on every instance, no matter what type. Our hypothesis is that once an annotator is diligent (and motivated) enough to pay attention to the data, her annotations can be described by model M, but some annotators are not sufficiently diligent.

[7]Turker annotations were aggregated using majority vote, as in Snow et al. (2008) section 4.3.

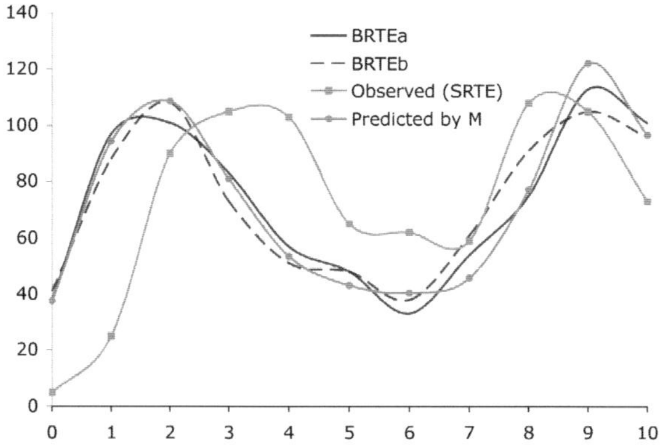

Figure 6: Model M's fit to SRTE data. BRTEa and BRTEb are shown in grey lines.

In this model we assume there are three types of instances as before, and two types of annotators $a \in \{D, L\}$, for Diligent and Lazy, with their proportions in the population $\xi = (\xi_D, \xi_L)$. The corresponding graphical model is shown in figure 7.

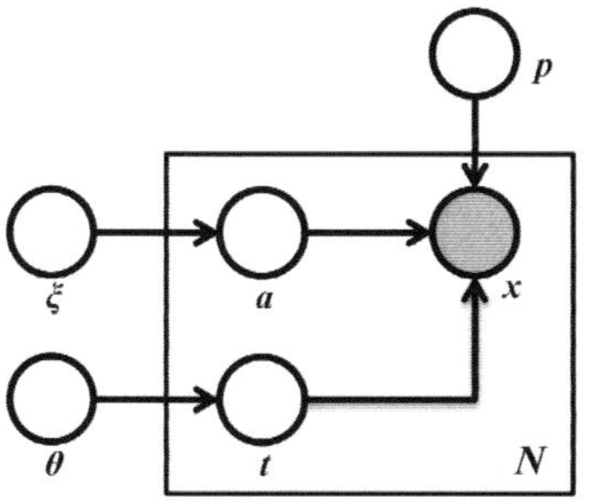

Figure 7: Annotation generation with diligent and lazy annotators.

We assume that diligent annotators flip coins corresponding to the types of instances, whereas lazy annotators always flip the same coin p_L.

Let n_D and n_L=$n - n_D$ be the number of diligent and lazy annotations given to a certain instance, thus $\Pr(n_D{=}r|\xi){=}\binom{n}{r}\xi_D^r\xi_L^{n-r}$, and the probability of observing j label "1" annotations for an instance of type t is given by:

$$\Pr(x = j|t, \xi, p) = \sum_{r=1}^{n}\left[\binom{n}{r}\xi_D^r\xi_L^{n-r} \times \right.$$

$$\times \left[\sum_{(j_1,j_2)\in S}\binom{r}{j_1}p_t^{j_1}(1-p_t)^{r-j_1} \times \right.$$

$$\left.\left.\times \binom{n-r}{j_2}p_L^{j_2}(1-p_L)^{n-r-j_2}\right]\right]$$

where S=$\{(j_1, j_2)$:j_1+j_2=j; j_1≤r;j_2≤n-r$\}$. Finally, $\Pr(x{=}j|\theta, \xi, p){=}\sum_{t=1}^{k}\theta_t \Pr(x{=}j|t, \xi, p)$.

We assume that model M provides the values for θ and p for all diligent annotators, and estimate ξ and p_L, the proportion of the lazy annotators and the coin they flip. The best fitting model yields ξ=(0.79,0.21), and p_L=0.74, predicting that about one-fifth of SRTE annotators are lazy.[8] This model fits with χ^2=14.63, which is below the critical level of χ^2=15.51 for df=8,p=0.05, hence a hypothesis that model M behavior for the diligent annotators and flipping a coin with bias 0.74 for the lazy ones generated the SRTE data cannot be rejected with high confidence. We note that Carpenter (2008) arrived at a similar conclusion – that there are quite a few annotators making random guesses in SRTE dataset – by means of jointly estimating annotator accuracies.

7 Discussion

To summarize our findings: With systematic differences between annotators smoothed out, there is evidence that non-expert annotators performing RTE task on RTE-1 test data tend to flip a close-to-fair coin on about 20% of instances, according to the best fitting model.[9] This constitutes, to our knowledge, the first empirical evidence for the existence of the kind of noise termed annotation noise in Beigman Klebanov and Beigman (2009). Given Beigman Klebanov and Beigman (2009) warning against annotation noise in test data and their finding in Beigman and Beigman Klebanov (2009) that annotation noise in training data can potentially devastate a linear classifier learning from the data, the immediate usefulness of our result is that instances of this difficult type can be identified, removed from the dataset before further benchmarking, and pos-

[8]A more precise statement is that there are about one-fifth lazy potential annotators in the SRTE pool for any given item. It is possible that the length of stay of an annotator in the pool is not independent of her diligence; for example, Callison-Burch (2009) found in his AMT experiments with tasks related to machine translation that lazy annotators tended to stay longer and do more annotations.

[9]Beigman Klebanov and Beigman (2009) discuss the connection between noise models and inter-annotator agreement.

sibly used in a controlled fashion for subsequent studies of the impact of annotation noise on specific learning algorithms and feature spaces for this task.

The current literature on generating benchmarking data from AMT annotations overwhelmingly considers annotator heterogeneity as the source of observed discrepancies, with instances falling into two classes only. Our results suggest that, at least in RTE data, instance heterogeneity cannot be ignored.

It also transpired that small variations in incentives (as between SRTE and BRTE), and even unknown factors possibly related to differences in the composition of AMT's workforce can lead to systematic differences in the resulting annotator pools, which results in annotations that are described by models with somewhat different parameter values. This can potentially limit the usefulness of our main finding, because it is not clear how reliable the identification of hard cases is using any particular group of Turkers. While this is a valid concern in general, we show in section 7.1 that many items consistently found to be hard by different groups of Turkers warrant at least an additional examination, as they often represent borderline cases of highly or not-so-highly probable inferences, corruption of meaning by ungrammaticality, or difficulties related to the treatment of time references and background knowledge.

Finally, our findings seem to be at odds with the fact that the 800 items analyzed here were left after all items on which two experts disagreed and all items that looked controversial to the arbiter were removed (see section 3). One potential explanation is that things that are hard for Turkers are not necessarily hard for experts. Yet it is possible that two or three annotators, graduate students or faculty in computational linguistics, are an especially homogenous and small pool of people to base gold standard annotations of the way things are "typically interpreted by people" upon. Furthermore, there is some evidence from additional expert re-annotations of this dataset that some controversies remain; we discuss relation to expert annotations in section 7.2.

7.1 Hard cases

We examine some of the instances that in all likelihood belong to the difficult type, according to Turkers. We focus on items that received between 4 and 7 class "1" annotations in SRTE and in each of our two datasets (before randomization).

(1) **T**: Saudi Arabia, the biggest oil producer in the world, was once a supporter of Osama bin Laden and his associates who led attacks against the United States. **H**: Saudi Arabia is the world's biggest oil exporter.

(2) **T**: Seiler was reported missing March 27 and was found four days later in a marsh near her campus apartment. **H**: Abducted Audrey Seiler found four days after missing.

(3) **T**: The spokesman for the rescue authorities, Linart Ohlin, said that the accident took place between 01:00 and dawn today, Friday (00:00 GMT) in a disco behind the theatre, where "hundreds" of young people were present. **H**: The fire happened in the early hours of Friday morning, and hundreds of young people were present.

(4) **T**: William Leonard Jennings sobbed loudly as was charged with killing his 3-year-old son, Stephen, who was last seen alive on Dec.12, 1962. **H**: William Leonard Jennings killed his 3-year-old son, Stephen.

Labeling of examples 1-4 seems to hinge on the assessment of the likelihood of an alternative explanation. Thus, it is possible that the biggest producer of oil is not the biggest exporter, because, for example, its internal consumption is much higher than in the second-biggest producer. In 2, abduction is a possible cause for being missing, but how relatively probable is it? Similarly, fire is a kind of accident, but can we infer that there was fire from a report about an accident? In 4, could the man have sobbed because on top of loosing his son he was also being falsely accused of having killed him? Experts marked all five as true entailments, while many Turkers had reservations.

(5) **T**: Bush returned to the White House late Saturday while his running mate was off campaigning in the West. **H**: Bush left the White House.

(6) **T**: De la Cruz's family said he had gone to Saudi Arabia a year ago to work as a driver after a long period of unemployment. **H**: De la Cruz was unemployed.

(7) **T**: Measurements by ground-based instruments around the world have shown a decrease of up to 10 percent in sunlight from the late 1950s to the early 1990s. **H**: The world is about 10 per cent darker than half a century ago.

In examples 5-7 time seems to be an issue. If Bush returned to White House, he must have left it beforehand, but does this count as entailment, or is the hypothesis referencing a time concurrent with the text, in which case *T* and *H* are in contradiction? In 6, can *H* be seen as referring to some time more than a year ago? In 7, if the hypothesis is taken to be stated in mid- or late-2000s, the time of annotation, half a century ago would reach to late 1950s, but it is possible that further substantial reduction occurred between early 1990s mentioned in the text and mid 2000s, amounting to much more than 10%. Experts labeled example 5 as false, 6 and 7 as true.

(8) **T**: On 2 February 1990, at the opening of Parliament, he declared that apartheid had failed and that the bans on political parties, including the ANC, were to be lifted. **H**: Apartheid in South Africa was abolished in 1990.

(9) **T**: Kennedy had just won California's Democratic presidential primary when Sirhan shot him in Los Angeles on June 5, 1968. **H**: Sirhan killed Kennedy.

Labeling examples 8 and 9 (both true according to the experts) requires knowledge about South African and American politics, respectively. Was the ban on ANC the only or the most important manifestation of apartheid? Was abolishing apartheid merely an issue of declaring that it failed? In 9, killing is a potential but not necessary outcome of shooting, so details of Robert Kennedy's case need to be known to the annotator to render the case-specific judgment.

(10) **T**: The version for the PC has essentially the same packaging as those for the big game consoles, but players have been complaining that it offers significantly less versatility when it comes to swinging through New York. **H**: Players have been complaining that it sells significantly less versatility when it comes to swinging through New York.

(11) **T**: During his trip to the Middle East that took three days, Clinton made the first visit by an American president to the Palestinian Territories and participated in a three-way meeting with Israeli Prime Minister Benjamin Netanyahu and Palestinian President Yasser Arafat. **H**: During his trip to the east of the Middle which lasted three days, the Clinton to first visit to American President to the occupied Palestinian territories and participated in meeting tripartite co-operation with Israeli Prime Minister Benjamin Netanyahu and Palestinian President, Yasser Arafat.

(12) **T**: The ISM non-manufacturing index rose to 64.8 in July from 59.9 in June. **H**: The non-manufacturing index of the ISM raised 64.8 in July from 59.9 in June.

(13) **T**: Henryk Wieniawski, a Polish-born musician, was known for his special preference for resurrecting neglected or lost works for the violin. **H**: Henryk Wieniawski was born in Polish.

Examples 10-13 were labeled as false by experts, possibly betraying over-sensitivity to the failings of language technology. *Sells* is not an ideal substitution for *offers*, but in a certain sense versatility is sold as part of a product. In 11-13, some Turkers felt the hypothesis is not too bad a rendition of the text or of its part, while experts seemed to hold MT to a higher standard.

7.2 Turkers vs experts

Model M puts 159 items in the difficult type B2. While M is the best fitting model, it is possible to find a model that still fits with $p>0.05$ but places a smaller number of items in B2, in order to obtain a conservative estimate on the number of difficult cases. The model with B1$\sim \mathcal{B}(10, 0.21)$ on 373 items, B2$\sim \mathcal{B}(10,0.563)$ on 110 items, B3$\sim \mathcal{B}(10,0.89)$ on 327 items still produces a fit with $p>0.05$, but going down to 100 instances in B2 makes it impossible to find a good fit with a 3 type model. There are therefore about 110 difficult cases by a conservative estimate. Assuming there remain 110 hard cases in the 800 item dataset for which even experts flip a fair coin, we expect about 55 disagreements between the 800 item gold standard from RTE-1 and a replication by a new expert, or an agreement of $\frac{745}{800}$=93% on average. This estimate is consistent with reports of 91% to 96% replication accuracy for the expert annotations on various subsets of the data by different groups of experts (see section 2.3 in Dagan et al. (2006)).

Acknowledgments

We would like to thank the anonymous reviewers of this and the previous draft for helping us improve the paper significantly. We also thank Amar Cheema for his advice on AMT.

References

Paul Albert and Lori Dodd. 2004. A Cautionary Note on the Robustness of Latent Class Models for Estimating Diagnostic Error without a Gold Standard. *Biometrics*, 60(2):427–435.

Paul Albert, Lisa McShane, Joanna Shih, and The U.S. National Cancer Institute Bladder Tumor Marker Network. 2001. Latent Class Modeling Approaches for Assessing Diagnostic Error without a Gold Standard: With Applications to p53 Immunohistochemical Assays in Bladder Tumors. *Biometrics*, 57(2):610–619.

Eyal Beigman and Beata Beigman Klebanov. 2009. Learning with Annotation Noise. In *Proceedings of the 47th Annual Meeting of the Association for Computational Linguistics*, pages 280–287, Singapore.

Beata Beigman Klebanov and Eyal Beigman. 2009. From Annotator Agreement to Noise Models. *Accepted to Computational Linguistics*.

Chris Callison-Burch. 2009. Fast, Cheap, and Creative: Evaluating Translation Quality Using Amazon's Mechanical Turk. In *Proceedings of the Empirical Methods in Natural Language Processing Conference*, pages 286–295, Singapore.

Bob Carpenter. 2008. Multilevel Bayesian Models of Categorical Data Annotation. *Unpublished manuscript*, last accessed 28 July 2009 at lingpipe.files.wordpress.com/2009/01/anno-bayes-entities-09.pdf.

Ido Dagan, Oren Glickman, and Bernardo Magnini. 2006. The PASCAL Recognising Textual Entailment Challenge. In J. Quiñonero Candela, I. Dagan, B. Magnini, and F. d'Alché-Buc, editors, *Machine Learning Challenges*, pages 177–190. Springer.

Pinar Donmez, Jaime Carbonell, and Jeff Schneider. 2009. Efficiently Learning and Accuracy of Labeling Sources for Selective Sampling. In *Proceedings of the 15th International Conference on Knowledge Discovery and Data Mining*, pages 259–268, Paris, France.

Mark Espeland and Stanley Handelman. 1989. Using Class Models to Characterize and Assess Relative Error in Discrete Measurements. *Biometrics*, 45(2):587–599.

Allan McCutcheon. 1987. *Latent Class Analysis*. Newbury Park, CA, USA: Sage.

Massimo Poesio, Udo Kruschwitz, and Jon Chamberlain. 2008. ANAWIKI: Creating Anaphorically Annotated Resources through Web Cooperation. In *Proceedings of the 6th International Conference on Language Resources and Evaluation*, Marrakech, Morocco.

Vikas Raykar, Shipeng Yu, Linda Zhao, Anna Jerebko, Charles Florin, Gerardo Hermosillo Valadez, Luca Bogoni, and Linda Moy. 2009. Supervised Learning from Multiple Experts: Whom to Trust when Everyone Lies a Bit. In *Proceedings of the 26th Annual International Conference on Machine Learning*, pages 889–896, Montreal, Canada.

Dennis Reidsma and Jean Carletta. 2008. Reliability Measurement without Limits. *Computational Linguistics*, 34(3):319–326.

Victor Sheng, Foster Provost, and Panagiotis Ipeirotis. 2008. Get Another Label? Improving Data Quality and Data Mining Using Multiple, Noisy Labelers. In *Proceedings of the 14th International Conference on Knowledge Discovery and Data Mining*, pages 614–622, Las Vegas, Nevada, USA.

Rion Snow, Brendan O'Connor, Daniel Jurafsky, and Andrew Ng. 2008. Cheap and Fast - But is it Good? Evaluating Non-Expert Annotations for Natural Language Tasks. In *Proceedings of the Empirical Methods in Natural Language Processing Conference*, pages 254–263, Honolulu, Hawaii.

Luis von Ahn. 2006. Games with a Purpose. *Computer*, 39(6):92–94.

Ilsoon Yang and Mark Becker. 1997. Latent Variable Modeling of Diagnostic Accuracy. *Biometrics*, 53(3):948–958.

Bayesian Inference for Finite-State Transducers*

David Chiang[1] **Jonathan Graehl**[1] **Kevin Knight**[1] **Adam Pauls**[2] **Sujith Ravi**[1]

[1]Information Sciences Institute
University of Southern California
4676 Admiralty Way, Suite 1001
Marina del Rey, CA 90292

[2]Computer Science Division
University of California at Berkeley
Soda Hall
Berkeley, CA 94720

Abstract

We describe a Bayesian inference algorithm that can be used to train any cascade of weighted finite-state transducers on end-to-end data. We also investigate the problem of automatically selecting from among multiple training runs. Our experiments on four different tasks demonstrate the genericity of this framework, and, where applicable, large improvements in performance over EM. We also show, for unsupervised part-of-speech tagging, that automatic run selection gives a large improvement over previous Bayesian approaches.

1 Introduction

In this paper, we investigate Bayesian inference for weighted finite-state transducers (WFSTs). Many natural language models can be captured by weighted finite-state transducers (Pereira et al., 1994; Sproat et al., 1996; Knight and Al-Onaizan, 1998; Clark, 2002; Kolak et al., 2003; Mathias and Byrne, 2006), which offer several benefits:

- WFSTs provide a uniform knowledge representation.
- Complex problems can be broken down into a cascade of simple WFSTs.
- Input- and output-epsilon transitions allow compact designs.
- Generic algorithms exist for doing inferences with WFSTs. These include best-path decoding, k-best path extraction, composition, intersection, minimization, determinization, forward-backward training, forward-backward pruning, stochastic generation, and projection.
- Software toolkits implement these generic algorithms, allowing designers to concentrate on novel models rather than problem-specific inference code. This leads to faster scientific experimentation with fewer bugs.

Weighted tree transducers play the same role for problems that involve the creation and transformation of tree structures (Knight and Graehl, 2005). Of course, many problems do not fit either the finite-state string or tree transducer framework, but in this paper, we concentrate on those that do.

Bayesian inference schemes have become popular recently in natural language processing for their ability to manage uncertainty about model parameters and to allow designers to incorporate prior knowledge flexibly. Task-accuracy results have generally been favorable. However, it can be time-consuming to apply Bayesian inference methods to each new problem. Designers typically build custom, problem-specific sampling operators for exploring the derivation space. They may factor their programs to get some code re-use from one problem to the next, but highly generic tools for string and tree processing are not available.

In this paper, we marry the world of finite-state machines with the world of Bayesian inference, and we test our methods across a range of natural language problems. Our contributions are:

- We describe a Bayesian inference algorithm that can be used to train any cascade of WFSTs on end-to-end data.
- We propose a method for automatic *run selec-*

*The authors are listed in alphabetical order. Please direct correspondence to Sujith Ravi (sravi@isi.edu). This work was supported by NSF grant IIS-0904684 and DARPA contract HR0011-06-C0022.

Human Language Technologies: The 2010 Annual Conference of the North American Chapter of the ACL, pages 447–455,
Los Angeles, California, June 2010.

tion, i.e., how to automatically select among multiple training runs in order to achieve the best possible task accuracy.

The natural language applications we consider in this paper are: (1) unsupervised part-of-speech (POS) tagging (Merialdo, 1994; Goldwater and Griffiths, 2007), (2) letter substitution decipherment (Peleg and Rosenfeld, 1979; Knight et al., 2006; Ravi and Knight, 2008), (3) segmentation of space-free English (Goldwater et al., 2009), and (4) Japanese/English phoneme alignment (Knight and Graehl, 1998; Ravi and Knight, 2009a). Figure 1 shows how each of these problems can be represented as a cascade of finite-state acceptors (FSAs) and finite-state transducers (FSTs).

2 Generic EM Training

We first describe forward-backward EM training for a single FST M. Given a string pair (v, w) from our training data, we transform v into an FST M_v that just maps v to itself, and likewise transform w into an FST M_w. Then we compose M_v with M, and compose the result with M_w. This composition follows Pereira and Riley (1996), treating epsilon input and output transitions correctly, especially with regards to their weighted interleaving. This yields a derivation lattice D, each of whose paths transforms v into w.[1] Each transition in D corresponds to some transition in the FST M. We run the forward-backward algorithm over D to collect fractional counts for the transitions in M. After we sum fractional counts for all examples, we normalize with respect to competing transitions in M, assign new probabilities to M, and iterate. Transitions in M compete with each other if they leave the same state with the same input symbol, which may be empty (ϵ).

In order to train an FSA on observed string data, we convert the FSA into an FST by adding an input-epsilon to every transition. We then convert each training string v into the string pair (ϵ, v). After running the above FST training algorithm, we can remove all input-ϵ from the trained machine.

It is straightforward to modify generic training to support the following controls:

[1]Throughout this paper, we do not assume that lattices are acyclic; the algorithms described work on general graphs.

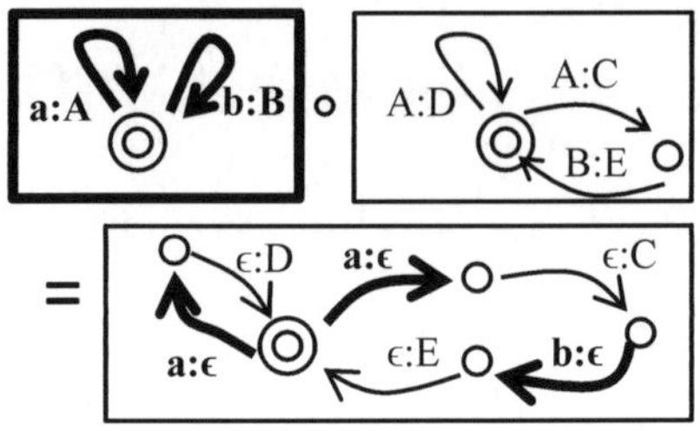

Figure 2: Composition of two FSTs maintaining separate transitions.

Maximum iterations and early stopping. We specify a maximum number of iterations, and we halt early if the ratio of $\log P(\text{data})$ from one iteration to the next exceeds a threshold (such as 0.99999).

Initial point. Any probabilities supplied on the pre-trained FST are interpreted as a starting point for EM's search. If no probabilities are supplied, EM begins with uniform probabilities.

Random restarts. We can request n random restarts, each from a different, randomly-selected initial point.

Locking and tying. Transitions on the pre-trained FST can be marked as locked, in which case EM will not modify their supplied probabilities. Groups of transitions can be tied together so that their fractional counts are pooled, and when normalization occurs, they all receive the same probability.

Derivation lattice caching. If memory is available, training can cache the derivation lattices computed in the first EM iteration for all training pairs. Subsequent iterations then run much faster. In our experiments, we observe an average 10-fold speedup with caching.

Next we turn to training a *cascade* of FSTs on end-to-end data. The algorithm takes as input: (1) a sequence of FSTs, and (2) pairs of training strings (v, w), such that v is accepted by the first FST in the cascade, and w is produced by the last FST. The algorithm outputs the same sequence of FSTs, but with trained probabilities.

To accomplish this, we first compose the supplied FSTs, taking care to keep the transitions from different machines separate. Figure 2 illustrates this with a small example. It may thus happen that a single transition in an input FST is represented multiple times in the composed device, in which case their prob-

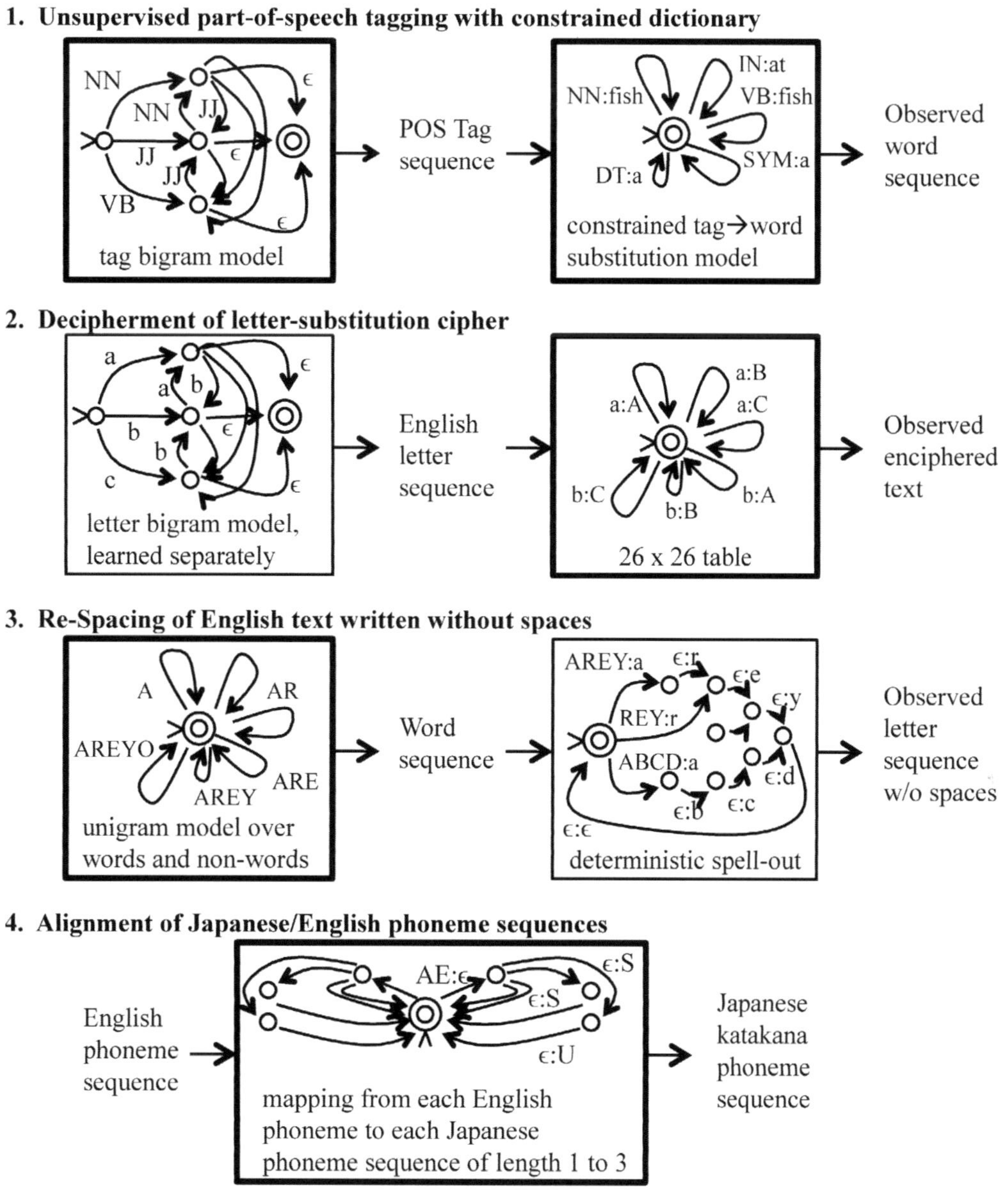

Figure 1: Finite-state cascades for five natural language problems.

abilities are tied together. Next, we run FST training on the end-to-end data. This involves creating derivation lattices and running forward-backward on them. After FST training, we de-compose the trained device back into a cascade of trained machines.

When the cascade's first machine is an FSA, rather than an FST, then the entire cascade is viewed as a generator of strings rather than a transformer of strings. Such a cascade is trained on observed strings rather than string pairs. By again treating the first FSA as an FST with empty input, we can train using the FST-cascade training algorithm described in the previous paragraph.

Once we have our trained cascade, we can apply it to new data, obtaining (for example) the k-best output strings for an input string.

3 Generic Bayesian Training

Bayesian learning is a wide-ranging field. We focus on training using Gibbs sampling (Geman and Geman, 1984), because it has been popularly applied in the natural language literature, e.g., (Finkel et al., 2005; DeNero et al., 2008; Blunsom et al., 2009).

Our overall plan is to give a generic algorithm for Bayesian training that is a "drop-in replacement" for EM training. That is, we input an FST cascade and data and output the same FST cascade with trained weights. This is an approximation to a purely Bayesian setup (where one would always integrate over all possible weightings), but one which makes it easy to deploy FSTs to efficiently decode new data. Likewise, we do not yet support non-parametric approaches—to create a drop-in replacement for EM, we require that all parameters be specified in the initial FST cascade. We return to this issue in Section 5.

3.1 Particular Case

We start with a well-known application of Bayesian inference, unsupervised POS tagging (Goldwater and Griffiths, 2007). Raw training text is provided, and each potential corpus tagging corresponds to a hidden derivation of that data. Derivations are created and probabilistically scored as follows:

1. $i \leftarrow 1$
2. Choose tag t_1 according to $P_0(t_1)$
3. Choose word w_1 according to $P_0(w_1 \mid t_1)$
4. $i \leftarrow i + 1$
5. Choose tag t_i according to

$$\frac{\alpha P_0(t_i \mid t_{i-1}) + c_1^{i-1}(t_{i-1}, t_i)}{\alpha + c_1^{i-1}(t_{i-1})} \quad (1)$$

6. Choose word w_i according to

$$\frac{\beta P_0(w_i \mid t_i) + c_1^{i-1}(t_i, w_i)}{\beta + c_1^{i-1}(t_i)} \quad (2)$$

7. With probability P_{quit}, quit; else go to 4.

This defines the probability of any given derivation. The base distribution P_0 represents prior knowledge about the distribution of tags and words, given the relevant conditioning context. The c_1^{i-1} are the counts of events occurring before word i in the derivation (the "cache").

When α and β are large, tags and words are essentially generated according to P_0. When α and β are small, tags and words are generated with reference to previous decisions inside the cache.

We use Gibbs sampling to estimate the distribution of tags given words. The key to efficient sampling is to define a sampling operator that makes some small change to the overall corpus derivation. With such an operator, we derive an incremental formula for re-scoring the probability of an entire new derivation based on the probability of the old derivation. Exchangeability makes this efficient—we pretend like the area around the small change occurs at the end of the corpus, so that both old and new derivations share the same cache. Goldwater and Griffiths (2007) choose the re-sampling operator "change the tag of a single word," and they derive the corresponding incremental scoring formula for unsupervised tagging. For other problems, designers develop different sampling operators and derive different incremental scoring formulas.

3.2 Generic Case

In order to develop a generic algorithm, we need to abstract away from these problem-specific design choices. In general, hidden derivations correspond to paths through derivation lattices, so we first

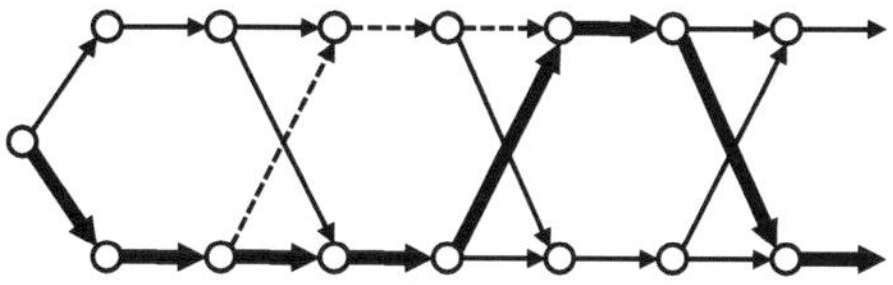

Figure 3: Changing a decision in the derivation lattice. All paths generate the observed data. The bold path represents the current sample, and the dotted path represents a sidetrack in which one decision is changed.

compute derivation lattices for our observed training data through our cascade of FSTs. A random path through these lattices constitutes the initial sample, and we calculate its derivation probability directly.

One way to think about a generic small change operator is to consider a single transition in the current sample. This transition will generally compete with other transitions. One possible small change is to "sidetrack" the derivation to a competing derivation. Figure 3 shows how this works. If the sidetrack path quickly re-joins the old derivation path, then an incremental score can be computed. However, sidetracking raises knotty questions. First, what is the proper path continuation after the sidetracking transition is selected? Should the path attempt to re-join the old derivation as soon as possible, and if so, how is this efficiently done? Then, how can we compute new derivation scores for all possible sidetracks, so that we can choose a new sample by an appropriate weighted coin flip? Finally, would such a sampler be reversible? In order to satisfy theoretical conditions for Gibbs sampling, if we move from sample A to sample B, we must be able to immediately get back to sample A.

We take a different tack here, moving from pointwise sampling to blocked sampling. Gao and Johnson (2008) employed blocked sampling for POS tagging, and the approach works nicely for arbitrary derivation lattices. We again start with a random derivation for each example in the corpus. We then choose a training example and exchange its entire derivation lattice to the end of the corpus. We create a weighted version of this lattice, called the *proposal lattice*, such that we can approximately sample whole paths by stochastic generation. The probabilities are based on the event counts from the rest of the sample (the cache), and on the base distribution, and are computed in this way:

$$P(r \mid q) = \frac{\alpha P_0(r \mid q) + c(q, r)}{\alpha + c(q)} \tag{3}$$

where q and r are states of the derivation lattice, and the $c(\cdot)$ are counts collected from the corpus minus the entire training example being resampled. This is an approximation because we are ignoring the fact that $P(r \mid q)$ in general depends on choices made earlier in the lattice. The approximation can be corrected using the Metropolis-Hastings algorithm, in which the sample drawn from the proposal lattice is accepted only with a certain probability α; but Gao and Johnson (2008) report that $\alpha > 0.99$, so we skip this step.

3.3 Choosing the best derivations

After the sampling run has finished, we can choose the best derivations using two different methods. First, if we want to find the MAP derivations of the training strings, then following Goldwater and Griffiths (2007), we can use *annealing*: raise the probabilities in the sampling distribution to the $\frac{1}{T}$ power, where T is a temperature parameter, decrease T towards zero, and take a single sample.

But in practice one often wants to predict the MAP derivation for a new string w' not contained in the training data. To approximate the distribution of derivations of w' given the training data, we average the transition counts from all the samples (after burn-in) and plug the averaged counts into (3) to obtain a single proposal lattice.[2] The predicted derivation is the Viterbi path through this lattice. Call this method *averaging*. An advantage of this approach is that the trainer, taking a cascade of FSAs as input, outputs a weighted version of the same cascade, and this trained cascade can be used on unseen examples without having to rerun training.

3.4 Implementation

That concludes the generic Bayesian training algorithm, to which we add the following controls:

[2] A better approximation might have been to build a proposal lattice for each sample (after burn-in), and then construct a single FSA that computes the average of the probability distributions computed by all the proposal lattices. But this FSA would be rather large.

Number of Gibbs sampling iterations. We execute the full number specified.

Base distribution. Any probabilities supplied on the pre-trained FST are interpreted as base distribution probabilities. If no probabilities are supplied, then the base distribution is taken to be uniform.

Hyperparameters. We supply a distinct α for each machine in the FST cascade. We do not yet support different α values for different states within a single FST.

Random restarts. We can request multiple runs from different, randomly-selected initial samples.

EM-based initial point. If random initial samples are undesirable, we can request that the Gibbs sampler be initialized with the Viterbi path using parameter values obtained by n iterations of EM.

Annealing schedule. If annealing is used, it follows a linear annealing schedule with starting and stopping temperature specified by the user.

EM and Bayesian training for arbitrary FST cascades are both implemented in the finite-state toolkit Carmel, which is distributed with source code.[3] All controls are implemented as command-line switches. We use Carmel to carry out the experiments in the next section.

4 Run Selection

For both EM and Bayesian methods, different training runs yield different results. EM's objective function (probability of observed data) is very bumpy for the unsupervised problems we work on—different initial points yield different trained WFST cascades, with different task accuracies. Averaging task accuracies across runs is undesirable, because we want to deploy a particular trained cascade in the real world, and we want an estimate of its performance. Selecting the run with the best task accuracy is illegal in an unsupervised setting. With EM, we have a good alternative: select the run that maximizes the objective function, i.e., the likelihood of the observed training data. We find a decent correlation between this value and task accuracy, and we are generally able to improve accuracy using this run selection method. Figure 4 shows a scatterplot of 1000 runs for POS tagging. A single run with a uniform start yields 81.8%

[3]http://www.isi.edu/licensed-sw/carmel

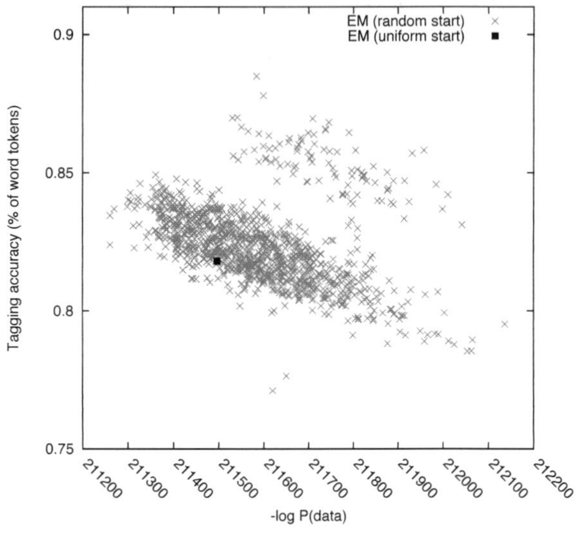

Figure 4: Multiple EM restarts for POS tagging. Each point represents one random restart; the y-axis is tagging accuracy and the x-axis is EM's objective function, $-\log P(\text{data})$.

accuracy, while automatic selection from 1000 runs yields 82.4% accuracy.

Gibbs sampling runs also yield WFST cascades with varying task accuracies, due to random initial samples and sampling decisions. In fact, the variation is even larger than what we find with EM. It is natural to ask whether we can do automatic run selection for Gibbs sampling. If we are using annealing, it makes sense to use the probability of the final sample, which is supposed to approximate the MAP derivation. When using averaging, however, choosing the final sample would be quite arbitrary. Instead, we propose choosing the run that has the highest average log-probability (that is, the lowest entropy) after burn-in. The rationale is that the runs that have found their way to high-probability peaks are probably more representative of the true distribution, or at least capture a part of the distribution that is of greater interest to us.

We find that this method works quite well in practice. Figure 5 illustrates 1000 POS tagging runs for annealing with automatic run selection, yielding 84.7% accuracy. When using averaging, however, automatic selection from 1000 runs (Figure 6) produces a much higher accuracy of 90.7%. This is better than accuracies reported previously using

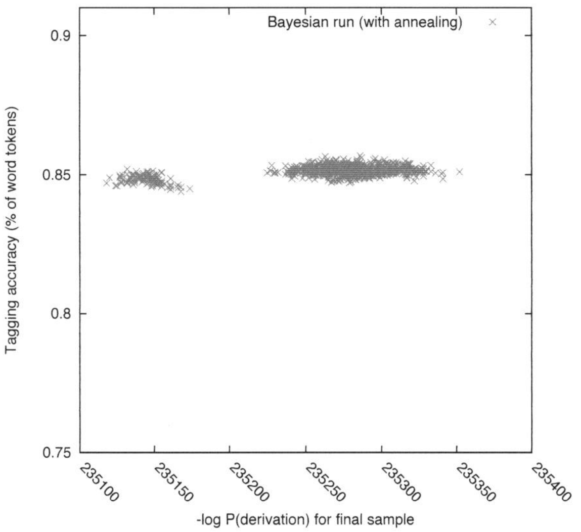

Figure 5: Multiple Bayesian learning runs (using *annealing* with temperature decreasing from 2 to 0.08) for POS tagging. Each point represents one run; the y-axis is tagging accuracy and the x-axis is the $-\log P$(derivation) of the final sample.

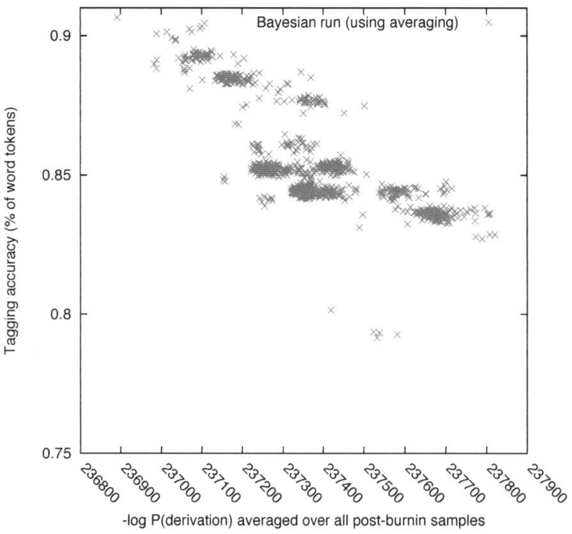

Figure 6: Multiple Bayesian learning runs (using *averaging*) for POS tagging. Each point represents one run; the y-axis is tagging accuracy and the x-axis is the average $-\log P$(derivation) over all samples after burn-in.

Bayesian methods (85.2% from Goldwater and Griffiths (2007), who use a trigram model) and close to the best accuracy reported on this task (91.8% from Ravi and Knight (2009b), who use an integer linear program to minimize the model directly).

5 Experiments and Results

We run experiments for various natural language applications and compare the task accuracies achieved by the EM and Bayesian learning methods. The tasks we consider are:

Unsupervised POS tagging. We adopt the common problem formulation for this task described by Merialdo (1994), in which we are given a raw 24,115-word sequence and a dictionary of legal tags for each word type. The tagset consists of 45 distinct grammatical tags. We use the same modeling approach as as Goldwater and Griffiths (2007), using a probabilistic tag bigram model in conjunction with a tag-to-word model.

Letter substitution decipherment. Here, the task is to decipher a 414-letter substitution cipher and uncover the original English letter sequence. The task accuracy is defined as the percent of ciphertext tokens that are deciphered correctly. We work on the same standard cipher described in previous literature (Ravi and Knight, 2008). The model consists of an English letter bigram model, whose probabilities are fixed and an English-to-ciphertext channel model, which is learnt during training.

Segmentation of space-free English. Given a space-free English text corpus (e.g., `iwalkedtothe...`), the task is to segment the text into words (e.g., `i walked to the ...`). Our input text corpus consists of 11,378 words, with spaces removed. As illustrated in Figure 1, our method uses a unigram FSA that models every letter sequence seen in the data, which includes both words and non-words (at most 10 letters long) composed with a deterministic spell-out model. In order to evaluate the quality of our segmented output, we compare it against the gold segmentation and compute the word token f-measure.

Japanese/English phoneme alignment. We use the problem formulation of Knight and Graehl (1998). Given an input English/Japanese katakana phoneme sequence pair, the task is to produce an alignment that connects each English

	MLE	Bayesian		
	EM	prior	VB-EM	Gibbs
POS tagging	82.4	$\alpha = 10^{-2}, \beta = 10^{-1}$	84.1	90.7
Letter decipherment	83.6	$\alpha = 10^{6}, \beta = 10^{-2}$	83.6	88.9
Re-spacing English	0.9	$\alpha = 10^{-8}, \beta = 10^{4}$	0.8	42.8
Aligning phoneme strings*	100	$\alpha = 10^{-2}$	99.9	99.1

Table 1: Gibbs sampling for Bayesian inference outperforms both EM and Variational Bayesian EM. *The output of EM alignment was used as the gold standard.

phoneme to its corresponding Japanese sounds (a sequence of one or more Japanese phonemes). For example, given a phoneme sequence pair ((`AH B AW T`) → (`a b a u t o`)), we have to produce the alignments ((`AH` → `a`), (`B` → `b`), (`AW` → `a u`), (`T` → `t o`)). The input data consists of 2,684 English/Japanese phoneme sequence pairs. We use a model that consists of mappings from each English phoneme to Japanese phoneme sequences (of length up to 3), and the mapping probabilities are learnt during training. We manually analyzed the alignments produced by the EM method for this task and found them to be nearly perfect. Hence, for the purpose of this task we treat the EM alignments as our gold standard, since there are no gold alignments available for this data.

In all the experiments reported here, we run EM for 200 iterations and Bayesian for 5000 iterations (the first 2000 for burn-in). We apply automatic run selection using the objective function value for EM and the averaging method for Bayesian.

Table 1 shows accuracy results for our four tasks, using run selection for both EM and Bayesian learning. For the Bayesian runs, we compared two inference methods: Gibbs sampling, as described above, and Variational Bayesian EM (Beal and Ghahramani, 2003), both of which are implemented in Carmel. We used the hyperparameters (α, β) as shown in the table. Setting a high value yields a final distribution that is close to the original one (P_0). For example, in letter decipherment we want to keep the language model probabilities fixed during training, and hence we set the prior on that model to be very strong ($\alpha = 10^6$). Table 1 shows that the Bayesian methods consistently outperform EM for all the tasks (except phoneme alignment, where EM was taken as the gold standard). Each iteration of Gibbs sampling was 2.3 times slower than EM for POS tagging, and in general about twice as slow.

6 Discussion

We have described general training algorithms for FST cascades and their implementation, and examined the problem of run selection for both EM and Bayesian training. This work raises several interesting points for future study.

First, is there an efficient method for performing pointwise sampling on general FSTs, and would pointwise sampling deliver better empirical results than blocked sampling across a range of tasks?

Second, can generic methods similar to the ones described here be developed for cascades of tree transducers? It is straightforward to adapt our methods to train a single tree transducer (Graehl et al., 2008), but as most types of tree transducers are not closed under composition (Gécseg and Steinby, 1984), the compose/de-compose method cannot be directly applied to train cascades.

Third, what is the best way to extend the FST formalism to represent non-parametric Bayesian models? Consider the English re-spacing application. We currently take observed (un-spaced) data and build a giant unigram FSA that models every letter sequence seen in the data of up to 10 letters, both words and non-words. This FSA has 207,253 transitions. We also define P_0 for each individual transition, which allows a preference for short words. This set-up works fine, but in a nonparametric approach, P_0 is defined more compactly and without a word-length limit. An extension of FSTs along the lines of recursive transition networks may be appropriate, but we leave details for future work.

References

Matthew J. Beal and Zoubin Ghahramani. 2003. The Variational Bayesian EM algorithm for incomplete data: with application to scoring graphical model structures. *Bayesian Statistics*, 7:453–464.

Phil Blunsom, Trevor Cohn, Chris Dyer, and Miles Osborne. 2009. A Gibbs sampler for phrasal synchronous grammar induction. In *Proceedings of ACL-IJCNLP 2009*.

Alexander Clark. 2002. Memory-based learning of morphology with stochastic transducers. In *Proceedings of ACL 2002*.

John DeNero, Alexandre Bouchard-Côté, and Dan Klein. 2008. Sampling alignment structure under a Bayesian translation model. In *Proceedings of EMNLP 2008*.

Jenny Rose Finkel, Trond Grenager, and Christopher Manning. 2005. Incorporating non-local information into information extraction systems by Gibbs sampling. In *Proceedings of ACL 2005*.

Jianfeng Gao and Mark Johnson. 2008. A comparison of Bayesian estimators for unsupervised Hidden Markov Model POS taggers. In *Proceedings of EMNLP 2008*.

Ferenc Gécseg and Magnus Steinby. 1984. *Tree Automata*. Akadémiai Kiadó, Budapest.

Stuart Geman and Donald Geman. 1984. Stochastic relaxation, Gibbs distributions and the Bayesian restoration of images. *IEEE Transactions on Pattern Analysis and Machine Intelligence*, 6(6):721–741.

Sharon Goldwater and Thomas L. Griffiths. 2007. A fully Bayesian approach to unsupervised part-of-speech tagging. In *Proceedings of ACL 2007*.

Sharon Goldwater, Thomas L. Griffiths, and Mark Johnson. 2009. A Bayesian framework for word segmentation: Exploring the effects of context. *Cognition*, 112(1):21 – 54.

Jonathan Graehl, Kevin Knight, and Jonathan May. 2008. Training tree transducers. *Computational Linguistics*, 34(3):391–427.

Kevin Knight and Yaser Al-Onaizan. 1998. Translation with finite-state devices. In *Proceedings of AMTA 1998*.

Kevin Knight and Jonathan Graehl. 1998. Machine transliteration. *Computational Linguistics*, 24(4):599–612.

Knight Knight and Jonathan Graehl. 2005. An overview of probabilistic tree transducers for natural language processing. In *Proceedings of CICLing-2005*.

Kevin Knight, Anish Nair, Nishit Rathod, and Kenji Yamada. 2006. Unsupervised analysis for decipherment problems. In *Proceedings of COLING-ACL 2006*.

Okan Kolak, Willian Byrne, and Philip Resnik. 2003. A generative probabilistic OCR model for NLP applications. In *Proceedings of HLT-NAACL 2003*.

Lambert Mathias and William Byrne. 2006. Statistical phrase-based speech translation. In *Proceedings of ICASSP 2006*.

Bernard Merialdo. 1994. Tagging English text with a probabilistic model. *Computational Linguistics*, 20(2):155–171.

Shmuel Peleg and Azriel Rosenfeld. 1979. Breaking substitution ciphers using a relaxation algorithm. *Communications of the ACM*, 22(11):598–605.

Fernando C. N. Pereira and Michael D. Riley. 1996. Speech recognition by composition of weighted finite automata. *Finite-State Language Processing*, pages 431–453.

Fernando Pereira, Michael Riley, and Richard Sproat. 1994. Weighted rational transductions and their applications to human language processing. In *ARPA Human Language Technology Workshop*.

Sujith Ravi and Kevin Knight. 2008. Attacking decipherment problems optimally with low-order n-gram models. In *Proceedings of EMNLP 2008*.

Sujith Ravi and Kevin Knight. 2009a. Learning phoneme mappings for transliteration without parallel data. In *Proceedings of NAACL HLT 2009*.

Sujith Ravi and Kevin Knight. 2009b. Minimized models for unsupervised part-of-speech tagging. In *Proceedings of ACL-IJCNLP 2009*.

Richard Sproat, Chilin Shih, William Gale, and Nancy Chang. 1996. A stochastic finite-state word-segmentation algorithm for Chinese. *Computational Linguistics*, 22(3):377–404.

Distributed Training Strategies for the Structured Perceptron

Ryan McDonald **Keith Hall** **Gideon Mann**
Google, Inc., New York / Zurich
{ryanmcd|kbhall|gmann}@google.com

Abstract

Perceptron training is widely applied in the natural language processing community for learning complex structured models. Like all structured prediction learning frameworks, the structured perceptron can be costly to train as training complexity is proportional to inference, which is frequently non-linear in example sequence length. In this paper we investigate distributed training strategies for the structured perceptron as a means to reduce training times when computing clusters are available. We look at two strategies and provide convergence bounds for a particular mode of distributed structured perceptron training based on iterative parameter mixing (or averaging). We present experiments on two structured prediction problems – named-entity recognition and dependency parsing – to highlight the efficiency of this method.

1 Introduction

One of the most popular training algorithms for structured prediction problems in natural language processing is the perceptron (Rosenblatt, 1958; Collins, 2002). The structured perceptron has many desirable properties, most notably that there is no need to calculate a partition function, which is necessary for other structured prediction paradigms such as CRFs (Lafferty et al., 2001). Furthermore, it is robust to approximate inference, which is often required for problems where the search space is too large and where strong structural independence assumptions are insufficient, such as parsing (Collins and Roark, 2004; McDonald and Pereira, 2006; Zhang and Clark, 2008) and machine translation (Liang et al., 2006). However, like all structured prediction learning frameworks, the structure perceptron can still be cumbersome to train. This is both due to the increasing size of available training sets as well as the fact that training complexity is proportional to inference, which is frequently non-linear in sequence length, even with strong structural independence assumptions.

In this paper we investigate distributed training strategies for the structured perceptron as a means of reducing training times when large computing clusters are available. Traditional machine learning algorithms are typically designed for a single machine, and designing an efficient training mechanism for analogous algorithms on a computing cluster – often via a map-reduce framework (Dean and Ghemawat, 2004) – is an active area of research (Chu et al., 2007). However, unlike many batch learning algorithms that can easily be distributed through the gradient calculation, a distributed training analog for the perceptron is less clear cut. It employs online updates and its loss function is technically non-convex.

A recent study by Mann et al. (2009) has shown that distributed training through parameter mixing (or averaging) for maximum entropy models can be empirically powerful and has strong theoretical guarantees. A parameter mixing strategy, which can be applied to any parameterized learning algorithm, trains separate models in parallel, each on a disjoint subset of the training data, and then takes an average of all the parameters as the final model. In this paper, we provide results which suggest that the perceptron is ill-suited for straight-forward parameter mixing, even though it is commonly used for large-scale structured learning, e.g., Whitelaw et al. (2008) for named-entity recognition. However, a slight mod-

Human Language Technologies: The 2010 Annual Conference of the North American Chapter of the ACL, pages 456–464,
Los Angeles, California, June 2010.

ification we call *iterative parameter mixing* can be shown to: 1) have similar convergence properties to the standard perceptron algorithm, 2) find a separating hyperplane if the training set is separable, 3) reduce training times significantly, and 4) produce models with comparable (or superior) accuracies to those trained serially on all the data.

2 Related Work

Distributed cluster computation for many batch training algorithms has previously been examined by Chu et al. (2007), among others. Much of the relevant prior work on online (or sub-gradient) distributed training has been focused on asynchronous optimization via gradient descent. In this scenario, multiple machines run stochastic gradient descent simultaneously as they update and read from a shared parameter vector asynchronously. Early work by Tsitsiklis et al. (1986) demonstrated that if the delay between model updates and reads is bounded, then asynchronous optimization is guaranteed to converge. Recently, Zinkevich et al. (2009) performed a similar type of analysis for online learners with asynchronous updates via stochastic gradient descent. The asynchronous algorithms in these studies require shared memory between the distributed computations and are less suitable to the more common cluster computing environment, which is what we study here.

While we focus on the perceptron algorithm, there is a large body of work on training structured prediction classifiers. For batch training the most common is conditional random fields (CRFs) (Lafferty et al., 2001), which is the structured analog of maximum entropy. As such, its training can easily be distributed through the gradient or sub-gradient computations (Finkel et al., 2008). However, unlike perceptron, CRFs require the computation of a partition function, which is often expensive and sometimes intractable. Other batch learning algorithms include M^3Ns (Taskar et al., 2004) and Structured SVMs (Tsochantaridis et al., 2004). Due to their efficiency, online learning algorithms have gained attention, especially for structured prediction tasks in NLP. In addition to the perceptron (Collins, 2002), others have looked at stochastic gradient descent (Zhang, 2004), passive aggressive algorithms (McDonald et al., 2005; Crammer et al., 2006), the recently introduced confidence weighted learning (Dredze et al., 2008) and coordinate descent algorithms (Duchi and Singer, 2009).

Perceptron($\mathcal{T} = \{(\mathbf{x}_t, \mathbf{y}_t)\}_{t=1}^{|\mathcal{T}|}$)
1. $\mathbf{w}^{(0)} = \mathbf{0}$; $k = 0$
2. for $n : 1..N$
3. for $t : 1..T$
4. Let $\mathbf{y}' = \arg\max_{\mathbf{y}'} \mathbf{w}^{(k)} \cdot \mathbf{f}(\mathbf{x}_t, \mathbf{y}')$
5. if $\mathbf{y}' \neq \mathbf{y}_t$
6. $\mathbf{w}^{(k+1)} = \mathbf{w}^{(k)} + \mathbf{f}(\mathbf{x}_t, \mathbf{y}_t) - \mathbf{f}(\mathbf{x}_t, \mathbf{y}')$
7. $k = k + 1$
8. return $\mathbf{w}^{(k)}$

Figure 1: The perceptron algorithm.

3 Structured Perceptron

The structured perceptron was introduced by Collins (2002) and we adopt much of the notation and presentation of that study. The structured percetron algorithm – which is identical to the multi-class perceptron – is shown in Figure 1. The perceptron is an online learning algorithm and processes training instances one at a time during each epoch of training. Lines 4-6 are the core of the algorithm. For a input-output training instance pair $(\mathbf{x}_t, \mathbf{y}_t) \in \mathcal{T}$, the algorithm predicts a structured output $\mathbf{y}' \in \mathcal{Y}_t$, where $\mathcal{Y}_t$ is the space of permissible structured outputs for input $\mathbf{x}_t$, e.g., parse trees for an input sentence. This prediction is determined by a linear classifier based on the dot product between a high-dimensional feature representation of a candidate input-output pair $\mathbf{f}(\mathbf{x}, \mathbf{y}) \in \mathbb{R}^M$ and a corresponding weight vector $\mathbf{w} \in \mathbb{R}^M$, which are the parameters of the model[1]. If this prediction is incorrect, then the parameters are updated to add weight to features for the corresponding correct output $\mathbf{y}_t$ and take weight away from features for the incorrect output $\mathbf{y}'$. For structured prediction, the inference step in line 4 is problem dependent, e.g., CKY for context-free parsing.

A training set $\mathcal{T}$ is separable with margin $\gamma > 0$ if there exists a vector $\mathbf{u} \in \mathbb{R}^M$ with $||\mathbf{u}|| = 1$ such that $\mathbf{u} \cdot \mathbf{f}(\mathbf{x}_t, \mathbf{y}_t) - \mathbf{u} \cdot \mathbf{f}(\mathbf{x}_t, \mathbf{y}') \geq \gamma$, for all $(\mathbf{x}_t, \mathbf{y}_t) \in \mathcal{T}$, and for all $\mathbf{y}' \in \mathcal{Y}_t$ such that $\mathbf{y}' \neq \mathbf{y}_t$. Furthermore, let $R \geq ||\mathbf{f}(\mathbf{x}_t, \mathbf{y}_t) - \mathbf{f}(\mathbf{x}_t, \mathbf{y}')||$, for all $(\mathbf{x}_t, \mathbf{y}_t) \in \mathcal{T}$ and $\mathbf{y}' \in \mathcal{Y}_t$. A fundamental theorem

[1]The perceptron can be kernalized for non-linearity.

of the perceptron is as follows:

Theorem 1 (Novikoff (1962)). *Assume training set $\mathcal{T}$ is separable by margin γ. Let k be the number of mistakes made training the perceptron (Figure 1) on $\mathcal{T}$. If training is run indefinitely, then $k \leq \frac{R^2}{\gamma^2}$.*

Proof. See Collins (2002) Theorem 1. □

Theorem 1 implies that if $\mathcal{T}$ is separable then 1) the perceptron will converge in a finite amount of time, and 2) will produce a $\mathbf{w}$ that separates $\mathcal{T}$. Collins also proposed a variant of the structured perceptron where the final weight vector is a weighted average of all parameters that occur during training, which he called the *averaged perceptron* and can be viewed as an approximation to the voted perceptron algorithm (Freund and Schapire, 1999).

4 Distributed Structured Perceptron

In this section we examine two distributed training strategies for the perceptron algorithm based on parameter mixing.

4.1 Parameter Mixing

Distributed training through parameter mixing is a straight-forward way of training classifiers in parallel. The algorithm is given in Figure 2. The idea is simple: divide the training data $\mathcal{T}$ into S disjoint *shards* such that $\mathcal{T} = \{\mathcal{T}_1, \ldots, \mathcal{T}_S\}$. Next, train perceptron models (or any learning algorithm) on each shard in parallel. After training, set the final parameters to a weighted mixture of the parameters of each model using mixture coefficients $\boldsymbol{\mu}$. Note that we call this strategy *parameter mixing* as opposed to *parameter averaging* to distinguish it from the averaged perceptron (see previous section). It is easy to see how this can be implemented on a cluster through a map-reduce framework, i.e., the map step trains the individual models in parallel and the reduce step mixes their parameters. The advantages of parameter mixing are: 1) that it is parallel, making it possibly to scale to extremely large data sets, and 2) it is resource efficient, in particular with respect to network usage as parameters are not repeatedly passed across the network as is often the case for exact distributed training strategies.

For maximum entropy models, Mann et al. (2009) show it is possible to bound the norm of the difference between parameters trained on all the data serially versus parameters trained with parameter mixing. However, their analysis requires a stability bound on the parameters of a regularized maximum entropy model, which is not known to hold for the perceptron. In Section 5, we present empirical results showing that parameter mixing for distributed perceptron can be sub-optimal. Additionally, Dredze et al. (2008) present negative parameter mixing results for confidence weighted learning, which is another online learning algorithm. The following theorem may help explain this behavior.

PerceptronParamMix($\mathcal{T} = \{(\mathbf{x}_t, \mathbf{y}_t)\}_{t=1}^{|\mathcal{T}|}$)
1. Shard $\mathcal{T}$ into S pieces $\mathcal{T} = \{\mathcal{T}_1, \ldots, \mathcal{T}_S\}$
2. $\mathbf{w}^{(i)} = \text{Perceptron}(\mathcal{T}_i)$ †
3. $\mathbf{w} = \sum_i \mu_i \mathbf{w}^{(i)}$ ‡
4. return $\mathbf{w}$

Figure 2: Distributed perceptron using a parameter mixing strategy. † Each $\mathbf{w}^{(i)}$ is computed in parallel. ‡ $\boldsymbol{\mu} = \{\mu_1, \ldots, \mu_S\}$, $\forall \mu_i \in \boldsymbol{\mu} : \mu_i \geq 0$ and $\sum_i \mu_i = 1$.

Theorem 2. *For a any training set $\mathcal{T}$ separable by margin γ, the perceptron algorithm trained through a parameter mixing strategy (Figure 2) does not necessarily return a separating weight vector* $\mathbf{w}$.

Proof. Consider a binary classification setting where $\mathcal{Y} = \{0, 1\}$ and $\mathcal{T}$ has 4 instances. We distribute the training set into two shards, $\mathcal{T}_1 = \{(\mathbf{x}_{1,1}, \mathbf{y}_{1,1}), (\mathbf{x}_{1,2}, \mathbf{y}_{1,2})\}$ and $\mathcal{T}_2 = \{(\mathbf{x}_{2,1}, \mathbf{y}_{2,1}), (\mathbf{x}_{2,2}, \mathbf{y}_{2,2})\}$. Let $\mathbf{y}_{1,1} = \mathbf{y}_{2,1} = 0$ and $\mathbf{y}_{1,2} = \mathbf{y}_{2,2} = 1$. Now, let $\mathbf{w}, \mathbf{f} \in \mathbb{R}^6$ and using block features, define the feature space as,

$$\begin{array}{ll} \mathbf{f}(\mathbf{x}_{1,1}, 0) = [1\,1\,0\,0\,0\,0] & \mathbf{f}(\mathbf{x}_{1,1}, 1) = [0\,0\,0\,1\,1\,0] \\ \mathbf{f}(\mathbf{x}_{1,2}, 0) = [0\,0\,1\,0\,0\,0] & \mathbf{f}(\mathbf{x}_{1,2}, 1) = [0\,0\,0\,0\,0\,1] \\ \mathbf{f}(\mathbf{x}_{2,1}, 0) = [0\,1\,1\,0\,0\,0] & \mathbf{f}(\mathbf{x}_{2,1}, 1) = [0\,0\,0\,0\,1\,1] \\ \mathbf{f}(\mathbf{x}_{2,2}, 0) = [1\,0\,0\,0\,0\,0] & \mathbf{f}(\mathbf{x}_{2,2}, 1) = [0\,0\,0\,1\,0\,0] \end{array}$$

Assuming label 1 tie-breaking, parameter mixing returns $\mathbf{w}^1$=[1 1 0 -1 -1 0] and $\mathbf{w}^2$=[0 1 1 0 -1 -1]. For any $\boldsymbol{\mu}$, the mixed weight vector $\mathbf{w}$ will not separate all the points. If both μ_1/μ_2 are non-zero, then all examples will be classified 0. If μ_1=1 and μ_2=0, then $(\mathbf{x}_{2,2}, \mathbf{y}_{2,2})$ will be incorrectly classified as 0 and $(\mathbf{x}_{1,2}, \mathbf{y}_{1,2})$ when μ_1=0 and μ_2=1. But there is a separating weight vector $\mathbf{w}$ = [-1 2 -1 1 -2 1]. □

This counter example does not say that a parameter mixing strategy will not converge. On the contrary, if $\mathcal{T}$ is separable, then each of its subsets is separable and converge via Theorem 1. What it does say is that, independent of $\boldsymbol{\mu}$, the mixed weight vector produced after convergence will not necessarily separate the entire data, even when $\mathcal{T}$ is separable.

4.2 Iterative Parameter Mixing

Consider a slight augmentation to the parameter mixing strategy. Previously, each parallel perceptron was trained to convergence before the parameter mixing step. Instead, shard the data as before, but train a single epoch of the perceptron algorithm for each shard (in parallel) and mix the model weights. This mixed weight vector is then re-sent to each shard and the perceptrons on those shards reset their weights to the new mixed weights. Another single epoch of training is then run (again in parallel over the shards) and the process repeats. This *iterative parameter mixing* algorithm is given in Figure 3.

Again, it is easy to see how this can be implemented as map-reduce, where the map computes the parameters for each shard for one epoch and the reduce mixes and re-sends them. This is analogous to batch distributed gradient descent methods where the gradient for each shard is computed in parallel in the map step and the reduce step sums the gradients and updates the weight vector. The disadvantage of iterative parameter mixing, relative to simple parameter mixing, is that the amount of information sent across the network will increase. Thus, if network latency is a bottleneck, this can become problematic. However, for many parallel computing frameworks, including both multi-core computing as well as cluster computing with high rates of connectivity, this is less of an issue.

Theorem 3. *Assume a training set $\mathcal{T}$ is separable by margin γ. Let $k_{i,n}$ be the number of mistakes that occurred on shard i during the nth epoch of training. For any N, when training the perceptron with iterative parameter mixing (Figure 3),*

$$\sum_{n=1}^{N}\sum_{i=1}^{S}\mu_{i,n}k_{i,n} \leq \frac{R^2}{\gamma^2}$$

Proof. Let $\mathbf{w}^{(i,n)}$ to be the weight vector for the ith shard after the nth epoch of the main loop and let $\mathbf{w}^{([i,n]-k)}$ be the weight vector that existed on shard i in the nth epoch k errors before $\mathbf{w}^{(i,n)}$. Let

PerceptronIterParamMix($\mathcal{T} = \{(\mathbf{x}_t, \mathbf{y}_t)\}_{t=1}^{|\mathcal{T}|}$)
Shard $\mathcal{T}$ into S pieces $\mathcal{T} = \{\mathcal{T}_1, \ldots, \mathcal{T}_S\}$
$\mathbf{w} = \mathbf{0}$
for $n : 1..N$
  $\mathbf{w}^{(i,n)} =$ OneEpochPerceptron($\mathcal{T}_i, \mathbf{w}$) †
  $\mathbf{w} = \sum_i \mu_{i,n}\mathbf{w}^{(i,n)}$ ‡
return $\mathbf{w}$

OneEpochPerceptron($\mathcal{T}, \mathbf{w}^*$)
1. $\mathbf{w}^{(0)} = \mathbf{w}^*$; $k = 0$
2. for $t : 1..T$
3.   Let $\mathbf{y}' = \arg\max_{\mathbf{y}'} \mathbf{w}^{(k)} \cdot \mathbf{f}(\mathbf{x}_t, \mathbf{y}')$
4.   if $\mathbf{y}' \neq \mathbf{y}_t$
5. $\mathbf{w}^{(k+1)} = \mathbf{w}^{(k)} + \mathbf{f}(\mathbf{x}_t, \mathbf{y}_t) - \mathbf{f}(\mathbf{x}_t, \mathbf{y}')$
6. $k = k + 1$
7. return $\mathbf{w}^{(k)}$

Figure 3: Distributed perceptron using an iterative parameter mixing strategy. † Each $\mathbf{w}^{(i,n)}$ is computed in parallel. ‡ $\boldsymbol{\mu}_n = \{\mu_{1,n}, \ldots, \mu_{S,n}\}$, $\forall \mu_{i,n} \in \boldsymbol{\mu}_n$: $\mu_{i,n} \geq 0$ and $\forall n$: $\sum_i \mu_{i,n} = 1$.

$\mathbf{w}^{(\text{avg},n)}$ be the mixed vector from the weight vectors returned after the nth epoch, i.e.,

$$\mathbf{w}^{(\text{avg},n)} = \sum_{i=1}^{S}\mu_{i,n}\mathbf{w}^{(i,n)}$$

Following the analysis from Collins (2002) Theorem 1, by examining line 5 of OneEpochPerceptron in Figure 3 and the fact that $\mathbf{u}$ separates the data by γ:

$$\begin{aligned}
\mathbf{u}\cdot\mathbf{w}^{(i,n)} &= \mathbf{u}\cdot\mathbf{w}^{([i,n]-1)} \\
&\quad + \mathbf{u}\cdot(\mathbf{f}(\mathbf{x}_t,\mathbf{y}_t) - \mathbf{f}(\mathbf{x}_t,\mathbf{y}')) \\
&\geq \mathbf{u}\cdot\mathbf{w}^{([i,n]-1)} + \gamma \\
&\geq \mathbf{u}\cdot\mathbf{w}^{([i,n]-2)} + 2\gamma \\
\ldots &\geq \mathbf{u}\cdot\mathbf{w}^{(\text{avg},n-1)} + k_{i,n}\gamma \quad \text{(A1)}
\end{aligned}$$

That is, $\mathbf{u}\cdot\mathbf{w}^{(i,n)}$ is bounded below by the average weight vector for the n-1st epoch plus the number of mistakes made on shard i during the nth epoch times the margin γ. Next, by OneEpochPerceptron line 5, the definition of R, and $\mathbf{w}^{([i,n]-1)}(\mathbf{f}(\mathbf{x}_t,\mathbf{y}_t) - \mathbf{f}(\mathbf{x}_t,\mathbf{y}')) \leq 0$ when line 5 is called:

$$\begin{aligned}
\|\mathbf{w}^{(i,n)}\|^2 &= \|\mathbf{w}^{([i,n]-1)}\|^2 \\
&\quad + \|\mathbf{f}(\mathbf{x}_t,\mathbf{y}_t) - \mathbf{f}(\mathbf{x}_t,\mathbf{y}')\|^2 \\
&\quad + 2\mathbf{w}^{([i,n]-1)}(\mathbf{f}(\mathbf{x}_t,\mathbf{y}_t) - \mathbf{f}(\mathbf{x}_t,\mathbf{y}')) \\
&\leq \|\mathbf{w}^{([i,n]-1)}\|^2 + R^2 \\
&\leq \|\mathbf{w}^{([i,n]-2)}\|^2 + 2R^2 \\
\ldots &\leq \|\mathbf{w}^{(\text{avg},n-1)}\|^2 + k_{i,n}R^2 \quad \text{(A2)}
\end{aligned}$$

That is, the squared L2-norm of a shards weight vector is bounded above by the same value for the average weight vector of the n-1st epoch and the number of mistakes made on that shard during the nth epoch times R^2.

Using A1/A2 we prove two inductive hypotheses:

$$\mathbf{u} \cdot \mathbf{w}^{(\text{avg},N)} \geq \sum_{n=1}^{N} \sum_{i=1}^{S} \mu_{i,n} k_{i,n} \gamma \qquad \text{(IH1)}$$

$$\|\mathbf{w}^{(\text{avg},N)}\|^2 \leq \sum_{n=1}^{N} \sum_{i=1}^{S} \mu_{i,n} k_{i,n} R^2 \qquad \text{(IH2)}$$

IH1 implies $\|\mathbf{w}^{(\text{avg},N)}\| \geq \sum_{n=1}^{N} \sum_{i=1}^{S} \mu_{i,n} k_{i,n} \gamma$ since $\mathbf{u} \cdot \mathbf{w} \leq \|\mathbf{u}\|\|\mathbf{w}\|$ and $\|\mathbf{u}\| = 1$.

The base case is $\mathbf{w}^{(\text{avg},1)}$, where we can observe:

$$\mathbf{u} \cdot \mathbf{w}^{\text{avg},1} = \sum_{i=1}^{S} \mu_{i,1} \mathbf{u} \cdot \mathbf{w}^{(i,1)} \geq \sum_{i=1}^{S} \mu_{i,1} k_{i,1} \gamma$$

using A1 and the fact that $\mathbf{w}^{(\text{avg},0)} = \mathbf{0}$ for the second step. For the IH2 base case we can write:

$$\begin{aligned} \|\mathbf{w}^{(\text{avg},1)}\|^2 &= \left\| \sum_{i=1}^{S} \mu_{i,1} \mathbf{w}^{(i,1)} \right\|^2 \\ &\leq \sum_{i=1}^{S} \mu_{i,1} \|\mathbf{w}^{(i,1)}\|^2 \leq \sum_{i=1}^{S} \mu_{i,1} k_{i,1} R^2 \end{aligned}$$

The first inequality is Jensen's inequality, and the second is true by A2 and $\|\mathbf{w}^{(\text{avg},0)}\|^2 = 0$.

Proceeding to the general case, $\mathbf{w}^{(\text{avg},N)}$:

$$\begin{aligned} \mathbf{u} \cdot \mathbf{w}^{(\text{avg},N)} &= \sum_{i=1}^{S} \mu_{i,N} (\mathbf{u} \cdot \mathbf{w}^{(i,N)}) \\ &\geq \sum_{i=1}^{S} \mu_{i,N} (\mathbf{u} \cdot \mathbf{w}^{(\text{avg},N-1)} + k_{i,N}\gamma) \\ &= \mathbf{u} \cdot \mathbf{w}^{(\text{avg},N-1)} + \sum_{i=1}^{S} \mu_{i,N} k_{i,N} \gamma \\ &\geq \left[\sum_{n=1}^{N-1} \sum_{i=1}^{S} \mu_{i,n} k_{i,n} \gamma \right] + \sum_{i=1}^{S} \mu_{i,N} k_{i,N} \\ &= \sum_{n=1}^{N} \sum_{i=1}^{S} \mu_{i,n} k_{i,n} \gamma \end{aligned}$$

The first inequality uses A1, the second step $\sum_i \mu_{i,N} = 1$ and the second inequality the inductive hypothesis IH1. For IH2, in the general case, we can write:

$$\begin{aligned} \|\mathbf{w}^{(\text{avg},N)}\|^2 &\leq \sum_{i=1}^{S} \mu_{i,N} \|\mathbf{w}^{(i,N)}\|^2 \\ &\leq \sum_{i=1}^{S} \mu_{i,N} (\|\mathbf{w}^{(\text{avg},N-1)}\|^2 + k_{i,N} R^2) \\ &= \|\mathbf{w}^{(\text{avg},N-1)}\|^2 + \sum_{i=1}^{S} \mu_{i,N} k_{i,N} R^2 \\ &\leq \left[\sum_{n=1}^{N-1} \sum_{i=1}^{S} \mu_{i,n} k_{i,n} R^2 \right] + \sum_{i=1}^{S} \mu_{i,N} k_{i,N} R^2 \\ &= \sum_{n=1}^{N} \sum_{i=1}^{S} \mu_{i,n} k_{i,n} R^2 \end{aligned}$$

The first inequality is Jensen's, the second A2, and the third the inductive hypothesis IH2. Putting together IH1, IH2 and $\|\mathbf{w}^{(\text{avg},N)}\| \geq \mathbf{u} \cdot \mathbf{w}^{(\text{avg},N)}$:

$$\left[\sum_{n=1}^{N} \sum_{i=1}^{S} \mu_{i,n} k_{i,n} \right]^2 \gamma^2 \leq \left[\sum_{n=1}^{N} \sum_{i=1}^{S} \mu_{i,n} k_{i,n} \right] R^2$$

which yields: $\sum_{n=1}^{N} \sum_{i=1}^{S} \mu_{i,n} k_{i,n} \leq \frac{R^2}{\gamma^2}$ □

4.3 Analysis

If we set each $\boldsymbol{\mu}_n$ to be the uniform mixture, $\mu_{i,n} = 1/S$, then *Theorem 3 guarantees convergence to a separating hyperplane.* If $\sum_{i=1}^{S} \mu_{i,n} k_{i,n} = 0$, then the previous weight vector already separated the data. Otherwise, $\sum_{n=1}^{N} \sum_{i=1}^{S} \mu_{i,n} k_{i,n}$ is still increasing, but is bounded and cannot increase indefinitely. Also note that if $S = 1$, then $\mu_{1,n}$ must equal 1 for all n and this bound is identical to Theorem 1.

However, we are mainly concerned with how fast convergence occurs, which is directly related to the number of training epochs each algorithm must run, i.e., N in Figure 1 and Figure 3. For the non-distributed variant of the perceptron we can say that $N_{\text{non\_dist}} \leq R^2/\gamma^2$ since in the worst case a single mistake happens on each epoch.[2] For the distributed case, consider setting $\mu_{i,n} = k_{i,n}/k_n$, where $k_n = \sum_i k_{i,n}$. That is, we mix parameters proportional to the number of errors each made during the previous epoch. Theorem 3 still implies convergence to a separating hyperplane with this choice. Further, we can

[2] It is not hard to derive such degenerate cases.

bound the required number of epochs N_{dist}:

$$N_{\text{dist}} \leq \sum_{n=1}^{N_{\text{dist}}} \prod_{i=1}^{S} [k_{i,n}]^{\frac{k_{i,n}}{k_n}} \leq \sum_{n=1}^{N_{\text{dist}}} \sum_{i=1}^{S} \frac{k_{i,n}}{k_n} k_{i,n} \leq \frac{R^2}{\gamma^2}$$

Ignoring when all $k_{i,n}$ are zero (since the algorithm will have converged), the first inequality is true since either $k_{i,n} \geq 1$, implying that $[k_{i,n}]^{k_{i,n}/k_n} \geq 1$, or $k_{i,n} = 0$ and $[k_{i,n}]^{k_{i,n}/k_n} = 1$. The second inequality is true by the generalized arithmetic-geometric mean inequality and the final inequality is Theorem 3. Thus, the worst-case number of epochs is identical for both the regular and distributed perceptron – but the distributed perceptron can theoretically process each epoch S times faster. This observation holds only for cases where $\mu_{i,n} > 0$ when $k_{i,n} \geq 1$ and $\mu_{i,n} = 0$ when $k_{i,n} = 0$, which does not include uniform mixing.

5 Experiments

To investigate the distributed perceptron strategies discussed in Section 4 we look at two structured prediction tasks – named entity recognition and dependency parsing. We compare up to four systems:

1. **Serial (All Data)**: This is the classifier returned if trained serially on all the available data.
2. **Serial (Sub Sampling)**: Shard the data, select one shard randomly and train serially.
3. **Parallel (Parameter Mix)**: Parallel strategy discussed in Section 4.1 with uniform mixing.
4. **Parallel (Iterative Parameter Mix)**: Parallel strategy discussed in Section 4.2 with uniform mixing (Section 5.1 looks at mixing strategies).

For all four systems we compare results for both the standard perceptron algorithm as well as the averaged perceptron algorithm (Collins, 2002).

We report the final test set metrics of the converged classifiers to determine whether any loss in accuracy is observed as a consequence of distributed training strategies. We define convergence as either: 1) the training set is separated, or 2) the training set performance measure (accuracy, f-measure, etc.) does not change by more than some pre-defined threshold on three consecutive epochs. As with most real world data sets, convergence by training set separation was rarely observed, though in both cases training set accuracies approached 100%. For both tasks we also plot test set metrics relative to the user wall-clock taken to obtain the classifier. The results were computed by collecting the metrics at the end of each epoch for every classifier. All experiments used 10 shards (Section 5.1 looks at convergence relative to different shard size).

Our first experiment is a named-entity recognition task using the English data from the CoNLL 2003 shared-task (Tjong Kim Sang and De Meulder, 2003). The task is to detect entities in sentences and label them as one of four types: people, organizations, locations or miscellaneous. For our experiments we used the entire training set (14041 sentences) and evaluated on the official development set (3250 sentences). We used a straight-forward IOB label encoding with a 1st order Markov factorization. Our feature set consisted of predicates extracted over word identities, word affixes, orthography, part-of-speech tags and corresponding concatenations. The evaluation metric used was micro f-measure over the four entity class types.

Results are given in Figure 4. There are a number of things to observe here: 1) training on a single shard clearly provides inferior performance to training on all data, 2) the simple parameter mixing strategy improves upon a single shard, but does not meet the performance of training on all data, 3) iterative parameter mixing achieves performance as good as or better than training serially on all the data, and 4) the distributed algorithms return better classifiers much quicker than training serially on all the data. This is true regardless of whether the underlying algorithm is the regular or the averaged perceptron. Point 3 deserves more discussion. In particular, the iterative parameter mixing strategy has a higher final f-measure than training on all the data serially than the standard perceptron (f-measure of 87.9 vs. 85.8). We suspect this happens for two reasons. First, the parameter mixing has a bagging like effect which helps to reduce the variance of the per-shard classifiers (Breiman, 1996). Second, the fact that parameter mixing is just a form of parameter averaging perhaps has the same effect as the averaged perceptron.

Our second set of experiments looked at the much more computationally intensive task of dependency parsing. We used the Prague Dependency Treebank (PDT) (Hajič et al., 2001), which is a Czech

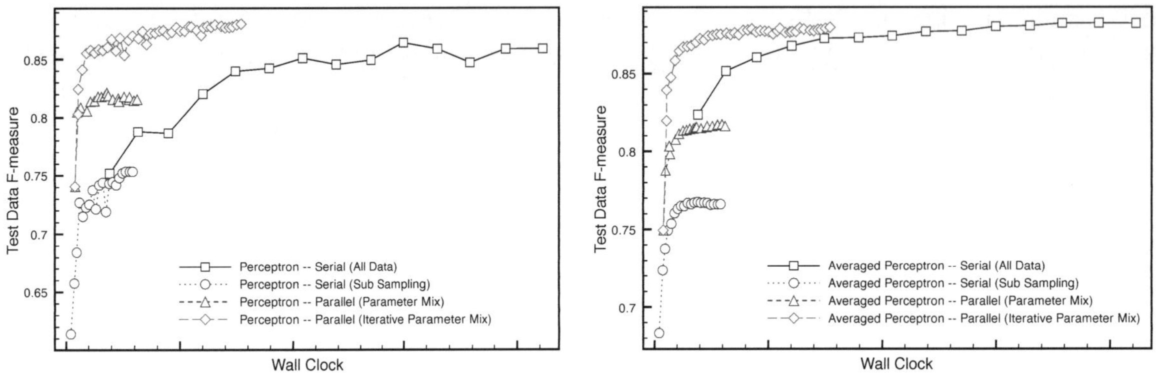

	Reg. Perceptron F-measure	Avg. Perceptron F-measure
Serial (All Data)	85.8	88.2
Serial (Sub Sampling)	75.3	76.6
Parallel (Parameter Mix)	81.5	81.6
Parallel (Iterative Parameter Mix)	87.9	88.1

Figure 4: NER experiments. Upper figures plot test data f-measure versus wall clock for both regular perceptron (left) and averaged perceptron (right). Lower table is f-measure for converged models.

language treebank and currently one of the largest dependency treebanks in existence. We used the CoNLL-X training (72703 sentences) and testing splits (365 sentences) of this data (Buchholz and Marsi, 2006) and dependency parsing models based on McDonald and Pereira (2006) which factors features over pairs of dependency arcs in a tree. To parse all the sentences in the PDT, one must use a non-projective parsing algorithm, which is a known NP-complete inference problem when not assuming strong independence assumptions. Thus, the use of approximate inference techniques is common in order to find the highest weighted tree for a sentence. We use the approximate parsing algorithm given in McDonald and Pereira (2006), which runs in time roughly cubic in sentence length. To train such a model is computationally expensive and can take on the order of days to train on a single machine.

Unlabeled attachment scores (Buchholz and Marsi, 2006) are given in Figure 5. The same trends are seen for dependency parsing that are seen for named-entity recognition. That is, iterative parameter mixing learns classifiers faster and has a final accuracy as good as or better than training serially on all data. Again we see that the iterative parameter mixing model returns a more accurate classifier than the regular perceptron, but at about the same level as the averaged perceptron.

5.1 Convergence Properties

Section 4.3 suggests that different weighting strategies can lead to different convergence properties, in particular with respect to the number of epochs. For the named-entity recognition task we ran four experiments comparing two different mixing strategies – uniform mixing ($\mu_{i,n}{=}1/S$) and error mixing ($\mu_{i,n}{=}k_{i,n}/k_n$) – each with two shard sizes – $S = 10$ and $S = 100$. Figure 6 plots the number of training errors per epoch for each strategy.

We can make a couple observations. First, the mixing strategy makes little difference. The reason being that the number of observed errors per epoch is roughly uniform across shards, making both strategies ultimately equivalent. The other observation is that increasing the number of shards can slow down convergence when viewed relative to epochs[3]. Again, this appears in contradiction to the analysis in Section 4.3, which, at least for the case of error weighted mixtures, implied that the number of epochs to convergence was independent of the number of shards. But that analysis was based on worst-case scenarios where a single error occurs on a single shard at each epoch, which is unlikely to occur in real world data. Instead, consider the uni-

[3]As opposed to raw wall-clock/CPU time, which benefits from faster epochs the more shards there are.

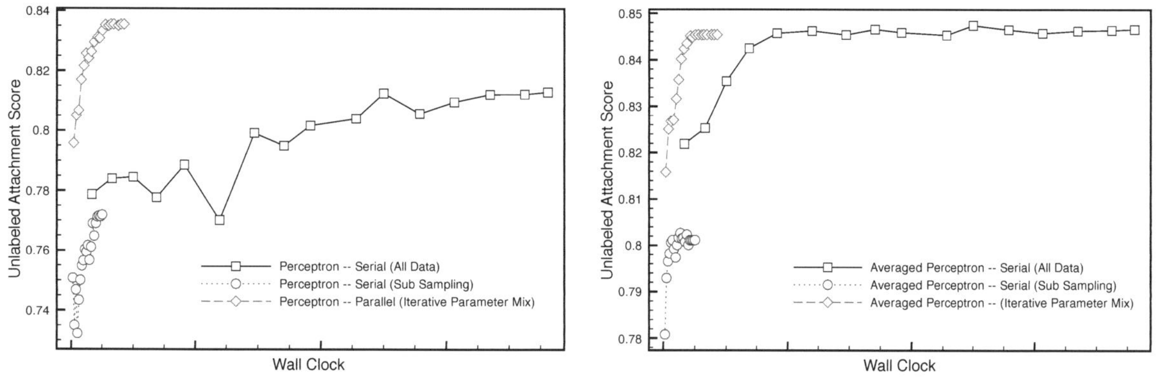

	Reg. Perceptron Unlabeled Attachment Score	Avg. Perceptron Unlabeled Attachment Score
Serial (All Data)	81.3	84.7
Serial (Sub Sampling)	77.2	80.1
Parallel (Iterative Parameter Mix)	83.5	84.5

Figure 5: Dependency Parsing experiments. Upper figures plot test data unlabeled attachment score versus wall clock for both regular perceptron (left) and averaged perceptron (right). Lower table is unlabeled attachment score for converged models.

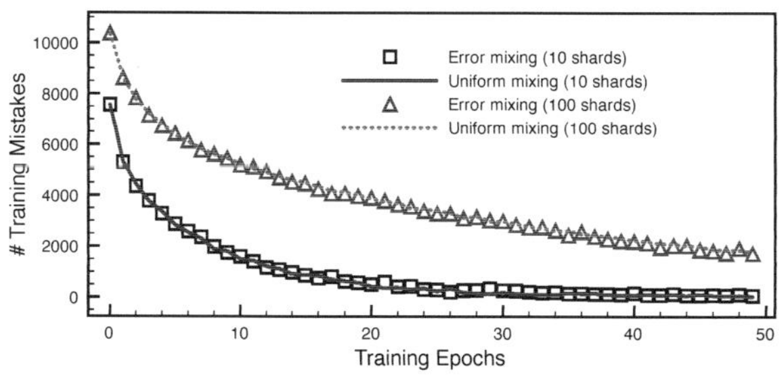

Figure 6: Training errors per epoch for different shard size and parameter mixing strategies.

form mixture case. Theorem 3 implies:

$$\sum_{n=1}^{N}\sum_{i=1}^{S}\frac{k_{i,n}}{S} \leq \frac{R^2}{\gamma^2} \quad \Longrightarrow \quad \sum_{n=1}^{N}\sum_{i=1}^{S} k_{i,n} \leq S \times \frac{R^2}{\gamma^2}$$

Thus, for cases where training errors are uniformly distributed across shards, it is possible that, in the worst-case, convergence may slow proportional the the number of shards. This implies a trade-off between slower convergence and quicker epochs when selecting a large number of shards. In fact, we observed a tipping point for our experiments in which increasing the number of shards began to have an adverse effect on training times, which for the named-entity experiments occurred around 25-50 shards. This is both due to reasons described in this section as well as the added overhead of maintaining and summing multiple high-dimensional weight vectors after each distributed epoch.

It is worth pointing out that a linear term S in the convergence bound above is similar to convergence/regret bounds for asynchronous distributed online learning, which typically have bounds linear in the asynchronous delay (Mesterharm, 2005; Zinkevich et al., 2009). This delay will be on average roughly equal to the number of shards S.

6 Conclusions

In this paper we have investigated distributing the structured perceptron via simple parameter mixing strategies. Our analysis shows that an iterative parameter mixing strategy is both guaranteed to separate the data (if possible) and significantly reduces the time required to train high accuracy classifiers. However, there is a trade-off between increasing training times through distributed computation and slower convergence relative to the number of shards. Finally, we note that using similar proofs to those given in this paper, it is possible to provide theoretical guarantees for distributed online passive aggressive learning (Crammer et al., 2006), which is a form of large-margin perceptron learning. Unfortunately space limitations prevent exploration here.

Acknowledgements: We thank Mehryar Mohri, Fernando Periera, Mark Dredze and the three anonymous reviews for their helpful comments on this work.

References

L. Breiman. 1996. Bagging predictors. *Machine Learning*, 24(2):123–140.

S. Buchholz and E. Marsi. 2006. CoNLL-X shared task on multilingual dependency parsing. In *Proceedings of the Conference on Computational Natural Language Learning*.

C.T. Chu, S.K. Kim, Y.A. Lin, Y.Y. Yu, G. Bradski, A.Y. Ng, and K. Olukotun. 2007. Map-Reduce for machine learning on multicore. In *Advances in Neural Information Processing Systems*.

M. Collins and B. Roark. 2004. Incremental parsing with the perceptron algorithm. In *Proceedings of the Conference of the Association for Computational Linguistics*.

M. Collins. 2002. Discriminative training methods for hidden Markov models: Theory and experiments with perceptron algorithm. In *Proceedings of the Conference on Empirical Methods in Natural Language Processing*.

K. Crammer, O. Dekel, J. Keshet, S. Shalev-Shwartz, and Y. Singer. 2006. Online passive-aggressive algorithms. *The Journal of Machine Learning Research*, 7:551–585.

J. Dean and S. Ghemawat. 2004. MapReduce: Simplified data processing on large clusters. In *Sixth Symposium on Operating System Design and Implementation*.

M. Dredze, K. Crammer, and F. Pereira. 2008. Confidence-weighted linear classification. In *Proceedings of the International Conference on Machine learning*.

J. Duchi and Y. Singer. 2009. Efficient learning using forward-backward splitting. In *Advances in Neural Information Processing Systems*.

J.R. Finkel, A. Kleeman, and C.D. Manning. 2008. Efficient, feature-based, conditional random field parsing. In *Proceedings of the Conference of the Association for Computational Linguistics*.

Y. Freund and R.E. Schapire. 1999. Large margin classification using the perceptron algorithm. *Machine Learning*, 37(3):277–296.

J. Hajič, B. Vidova Hladka, J. Panevová, E. Hajičová, P. Sgall, and P. Pajas. 2001. Prague Dependency Treebank 1.0. LDC, 2001T10.

J. Lafferty, A. McCallum, and F. Pereira. 2001. Conditional random fields: Probabilistic models for segmenting and labeling sequence data. In *Proceedings of the International Conference on Machine Learning*.

P. Liang, A. Bouchard-Côté, D. Klein, and B. Taskar. 2006. An end-to-end discriminative approach to machine translation. In *Proceedings of the Conference of the Association for Computational Linguistics*.

G. Mann, R. McDonald, M. Mohri, N. Silberman, and D. Walker. 2009. Efficient large-scale distributed training of conditional maximum entropy models. In *Advances in Neural Information Processing Systems*.

R. McDonald and F. Pereira. 2006. Online learning of approximate dependency parsing algorithms. In *Proceedings of the Conference of the European Chapter of the Association for Computational Linguistics*.

R. McDonald, K. Crammer, and F. Pereira. 2005. Online large-margin training of dependency parsers. In *Proceedings of the Conference of the Association for Computational Linguistics*.

C. Mesterharm. 2005. Online learning with delayed label feedback. In *Proceedings of Algorithmic Learning Theory*.

A.B. Novikoff. 1962. On convergence proofs on perceptrons. In *Symposium on the Mathematical Theory of Automata*.

F. Rosenblatt. 1958. The perceptron: A probabilistic model for information storage and organization in the brain. *Psychological Review*, 65(6):386–408.

B. Taskar, C. Guestrin, and D. Koller. 2004. Max-margin Markov networks. In *Advances in Neural Information Processing Systems*.

E. F. Tjong Kim Sang and F. De Meulder. 2003. Introduction to the CoNLL-2003 Shared Task: Language-Independent Named Entity Recognition. In *Proceedings of the Conference on Computational Natural Language Learning*.

J. N. Tsitsiklis, D. P. Bertsekas, and M. Athans. 1986. Distributed asynchronous deterministic and stochastic gradient optimization algorithms. *IEEE Transactions on Automatic Control*, 31(9):803–812.

I. Tsochantaridis, T. Hofmann, T. Joachims, and Y. Altun. 2004. Support vector machine learning for interdependent and structured output spaces. In *Proceedings of the International Conference on Machine learning*.

C. Whitelaw, A. Kehlenbeck, N. Petrovic, and L. Ungar. 2008. Web-scale named entity recognition. In *Proceedings of the International Conference on Information and Knowledge Management*.

Y. Zhang and S. Clark. 2008. A tale of two parsers: Investigating and combining graph-based and transition-based dependency parsing using beam-search. In *Proceedings of the Conference on Empirical Methods in Natural Language Processing*.

T. Zhang. 2004. Solving large scale linear prediction problems using stochastic gradient descent algorithms. In *Proceedings of the International Conference on Machine Learning*.

M. Zinkevich, A. Smola, and J. Langford. 2009. Slow learners are fast. In *Advances in Neural Information Processing Systems*.

Term Weighting Schemes for Latent Dirichlet Allocation

Andrew T. Wilson
Sandia National Laboratories
PO Box 5800, MS 1323
Albuquerque, NM 87185-1323, USA
atwilso@sandia.gov

Peter A. Chew
Moss Adams LLP
6100 Uptown Blvd. NE, Suite 400
Albuquerque, NM 87110-4489, USA
Peter.Chew@MossAdams.com

Abstract

Many implementations of Latent Dirichlet Allocation (LDA), including those described in Blei et al. (2003), rely at some point on the removal of stopwords, words which are assumed to contribute little to the meaning of the text. This step is considered necessary because otherwise high-frequency words tend to end up scattered across many of the latent topics without much rhyme or reason. We show, however, that the 'problem' of high-frequency words can be dealt with more elegantly, and in a way that to our knowledge has not been considered in LDA, through the use of appropriate weighting schemes comparable to those sometimes used in Latent Semantic Indexing (LSI). Our proposed weighting methods not only make theoretical sense, but can also be shown to improve precision significantly on a non-trivial cross-language retrieval task.

1 Introduction

Latent Dirichlet Allocation (LDA) (Blei et al., 2003), like its more established competitors Latent Semantic Indexing (LSI) (Deerwester et al., 1990) and Probabilistic Latent Semantic Indexing (PLSI) (Hofmann, 1999), is a model which is applicable to the analysis of text corpora. It is claimed to differ from LSI in that LDA is a generative Bayesian model (Blei et al., 2003), although this may depend upon the manner in which one approaches LSI (see for example Chew et al. (2010)). In LDA as applied to text analysis, each document in the corpus is modeled as a mixture over an underlying set of topics, and each topic is modeled as a probability distribution over the terms in the vocabulary.

As the newest among the above-mentioned techniques, LDA is still in a relatively early stage of development. It is also sufficiently different from LSI, probably the most popular and well-known compression technique for information retrieval (IR), that many practitioners of LSI may perceive a 'barrier to entry' to LDA. This in turn perhaps explains why notions such as term weighting, which have been commonplace in LSI for some time (Dumais, 1991), have not yet found a place in LDA. In fact, it is often assumed that weighting is unnecessary in LDA. For example, Blei et al. (2003) contrast the use of tf-idf weighting in both non-reduced space (Salton and McGill, 1983) and LSI on the one hand with PLSI and LDA on the other, where no mention is made of weighting. Ramage et al. (2008) propose a simple term-frequency weighting scheme for tagged documents within the framework of LDA, although term weighting is not their focus and their scheme is intended to incorporate document tags into the same model that represents the documents themselves.

In this paper, we produce evidence that term weighting should be given consideration within LDA. First and foremost, this is shown empirically through a non-trivial multilingual retrieval task which has previously been used as the basis for tests of variants of LSI. We also show that term weighting allows one to avoid maintenance of stoplists, which can be awkward especially for multilingual data. With appropriate term weighting, high-frequency words (which might otherwise be eliminated as stopwords) are assigned naturally to topics

Human Language Technologies: The 2010 Annual Conference of the North American Chapter of the ACL, pages 465–473,
Los Angeles, California, June 2010.

by LDA, rather than dominating and being scattered across many topics as happens with the standard uniform weighting. Our approach belies the usually unstated, but widespread, assumption in papers on LDA that the removal of stopwords is a necessary pre-processing step (see e.g. Blei et al. (2003); Griffiths and Steyvers (2004)).

It might seem that to demonstrate this it would be necessary to perform a test that directly compares the results when stoplists are used to those when weighting are used. However, we believe that stopwords are highly ad-hoc to begin with. Assuming a vocabulary of n words and a stoplist of x items, there are (at least in theory) $\binom{n}{x}$ possible stoplists. To be sure that *no* stoplist improves on a particular term weighting scheme we would have to test every one of these. In addition, our tests are with a multilingual dataset, which raises the issue that a domain-appropriate stoplist for a particular corpus and language may not be available. This is even more true if we pre-process the dataset morphologically (for example, with stemming). Therefore, rather than attempting a direct comparison of this type, we take the position that it is possible to sidestep the need for stoplists and to do so in a non-ad-hoc way.

The paper is organized as follows. Section 2 describes the general framework of LDA, which has only very recently been applied to cross-language IR. In Section 3, we look at alternatives to the 'standard' uniform weighting scheme (i.e., lack of weighting scheme) commonly used in LDA. Section 4 discusses the framework we use for empirical testing of our hypothesis that a weighting scheme would be beneficial. We present the results of this comparison in Section 5 along with an impressionistic comparison of the output of the different alternatives. We conclude in Section 6.

2 Latent Dirichlet Allocation

Our IR framework is multilingual Latent Dirichlet Allocation (LDA), first proposed by Blei et al. (2003) as a general Bayesian framework with initial application to topic modeling. It is only very recently that variants of LDA have been applied to cross-language IR: examples are Cimiano et al. (2009) and Ni et al. (2009).

As an approach to topic modeling, LDA relies on the idea that the tokens in a document are drawn independently from a set of topics where each topic is a distribution over types (words) in the vocabulary. The mixing coefficients for topics within each document and weights for types in each topic can be specified *a priori* or learned from a training corpus. Blei et al. initially proposed a variational model (2003) for learning topics from data. Griffiths and Steyvers (2004) later developed a Markov chain Monte Carlo approach based on collapsed Gibbs sampling.

In this model, the mixing weights for topics within each document and the multinomial coefficients for terms within each topic are hidden (latent) and must be learned from a training corpus. Blei et al. (2003) proposed LDA as a general Bayesian framework and gave a variational model for learning topics from data. Griffiths and Steyvers (2004) subsequently developed a stochastic learning algorithm based on collapsed Gibbs sampling. In this paper we will focus on the Gibbs sampling approach.

2.1 Generative Document Model

The LDA algorithm models the D documents in a corpus as mixtures of K topics where each topic is in turn a distribution over W terms. Given $\boldsymbol{\theta}$, the matrix of mixing weights for topics within each document, and ϕ, the matrix of multinomial coefficients for each topic, we can use this formulation to describe a generative model for documents (Alg. 1).

Restating the LDA model in linear-algebraic terms, we can say that the product of ϕ (the $K \times W$ column-stochastic topic-by-type matrix) and $\boldsymbol{\theta}$ (the $D \times K$ column-stochastic topic-by-document matrix) is the original $D \times W$ term-by-document matrix. In this sense, LDA computes a matrix factorization of the term-by-document matrix in the same way that LSI or non-negative matrix factorization (NMF) do. In fact, LDA is a special case of NMF, but unlike in NMF, there is a unique factorization in LDA. We see this as a feature recommending LDA above NMF.

Our objective is to reverse the generative model to learn the contents of $\boldsymbol{\theta}$ and ϕ given a training corpus D, a number of topics K, and symmetric Dirichlet prior distributions over both $\boldsymbol{\theta}$ and ϕ with hyperparameters α and β, respectively.

for $k = 1$ to K **do**
  Draw $\phi^k \sim$ Dirichlet(β)
end for
for $d = 1$ to D **do**
  Draw $\theta \sim$ Dirichlet(α)
  Draw $N \sim$ Poisson(ξ)
  for $i = 1$ to N **do**
    Draw $z \sim$ Multinomial(θ)
    Draw $w \sim$ Multinomial($\phi^{(z)}$)
  end for
end for

Algorithm 1: Generative algorithm for LDA. This will generate D documents with N tokens each. Each token is drawn from one of K topics. The distributions over topics and terms have Dirichlet hyperparameters α and β respectively. The Poisson distribution over the token count may be replaced with any other convenient distribution.

2.2 Learning Topics via Collapsed Gibbs Sampling

Rather than learn $\boldsymbol{\theta}$ and ϕ directly, we use collapsed Gibbs sampling (Geman et al. (1993), Chatterji and Pachter (2004)) to learn the latent assignment of tokens to topics $\mathbf{z}$ given the observed tokens $\mathbf{x}$.

The algorithm operates by repeatedly sampling each z_{ij} from a distribution conditioned on the values of all other elements of $\mathbf{z}$. This requires maintaining counts of tokens assigned to topics globally and within each document. We use the following notation for these sums:

N_{ijk}: Number of tokens of type w_i in document d_j assigned to topic k

N_{ijk}^{-st}: The sum N_{ijk} with the contribution of token x_{st} excluded

We indicate summation over all values of an index with $(\cdot)$.

Given the current state of $\mathbf{z}$ the conditional probability of z_{ij} is:

$$p(z_{ij} = k|\mathbf{z}^{-ij}, \mathbf{x}, d, \alpha, \beta) = p(x_{ij}|\phi^k) \quad p(k|d_j) \quad \propto \frac{N_{i(\cdot)k}^{-ij} + \beta}{N_{(\cdot)(\cdot)k}^{-ij} + W\beta} \frac{N_{(\cdot)jk}^{-ij} + \alpha}{N_{(\cdot)j(\cdot)} + T\alpha} \tag{1}$$

As Griffiths and Steyvers (2004) point out, this is an intuitive result. The first term, $p(x_{ij}|\phi^k)$, indicates the importance of term x_{ij} in topic k. The second term, $p(k|d_j)$, indicates the importance of topic k in document j. The sum of the terms is normalized implicitly to 1 when we draw each new z_{ij}.

We sample a new value for z_{ij} for every token x_{ij} during each iteration of Gibbs sampling. We run the sampler for a burn-in period of a few hundred iterations to allow it to reach its converged state and then estimate $\boldsymbol{\theta}$ and ϕ from $\mathbf{z}$ as follows:

$$\theta_{jk} = \frac{N_{(\cdot)jk} + \alpha}{N_{(\cdot)j(\cdot)} + T\alpha} \tag{2}$$

$$\phi_{ki} = \frac{N_{i(\cdot)k} + \beta}{N_{(\cdot)(\cdot)k} + W\beta} \tag{3}$$

2.3 Classifying New Documents

In LSI, new documents not in the original training set can be 'projected' into the semantic space of the training set. The equivalent process in LDA is one of *classification*: given a corpus D' of one or more new documents we use the existing topics ϕ to compute a maximum a posteriori estimate of the mixing coefficients $\boldsymbol{\theta}'$. This follows the same Monte Carlo process of repeatedly resampling a set of token-to-topic assignments $\mathbf{z}'$ for the tokens $\mathbf{x}'$ in the new documents. These new tokens are used to compute the first term $p(k|d_j)$ in Eq. 1. We re-use the topic assignments $\mathbf{z}$ from the training corpus to compute the second term $p(x_{ij}|\phi_k)$. Tokens with new types that were not present in the vocabulary of the training corpus do not participate in classification.

The resulting distribution $\boldsymbol{\theta}'$ essentially encodes how likely each new document is to relate to each of the K topics. We can use this matrix to compute pairwise similarities between any two documents from either corpus (training or newly-classified). Whereas in LSI it may make sense to compute similarity between documents using the cosine metric (since the 'dimensions' defining the space are orthogonal), we compute similarities in LDA using either the symmetrized Kullback-Leibler (KL) or Jensen-Shannon (JS) divergences (Kullback and Leibler (1951), Lin (2002)) since these are methods of measuring the similarity between probability distributions.

3 Term Weighting Schemes and LDA

The standard approach presented above assumes, effectively, that each token is equally important in calculating the conditional probabilities. From both an information-theoretic and a linguistic point of view, however, it is clear that this is not the case. In English, a term such as 'the' which occurs with high frequency in many documents does not contribute as much to the meaning of each document as a lower-frequency term such as 'corpus'. It is an axiom of information theory that an event a's information content (in bits) is equal to $\log_2 \frac{1}{p(a)} = -\log_2 p(a)$.

Treating tokens as events, we can say that the information content of a particular token of type t is $-\log_2 p(t)$. Furthermore, as is well-known, we can estimate $p(t)$ from observed frequencies in a corpus: it is simply the number of tokens of type t in the corpus, divided by the total number of tokens in the corpus. For high-probability terms such as 'the', therefore, $-\log_2 p(t)$ is low. Our basic hypothesis is that recalculating $p(z_{ij}|\mathbf{z}, \mathbf{x}, \alpha, \beta)$ to take the information content of each token into account will improve the results of LDA. Specifically, we have incorporated a weighting term into Eq. 1 by replacing the counts denoted N with weights denoted M.

$$p(z_{ij} = k|\mathbf{z}^{-ij}, \mathbf{x}, d, \alpha, \beta) \propto \frac{M_{i(\cdot)k}^{-ij} + \beta}{M_{(\cdot)(\cdot)k}^{-ij} + W\beta} \frac{M_{(\cdot)jk}^{-ij} + \alpha}{M_{(\cdot)j(\cdot)} + T\alpha} \tag{4}$$

Here M_{ijk} is the total *weight* of tokens of type i in document j assigned to topic k instead of the total *number* of tokens. All of the machinery for Gibbs sampling and the estimation of $\boldsymbol{\theta}$ and $\boldsymbol{\phi}$ from $\mathbf{z}$ remains unchanged.

We appeal to an urn model to explain the intuition behind this approach. In the original LDA formulation, each topic ϕ can be modeled as an urn containing a large number of balls of uniform size. Each ball assumes one of W different colors (one color for each term in the vocabulary). The frequency of occurrence of each color in the urn is proportional to the corresponding term's weight in topic ϕ. We incorporate a term weighting scheme by making the size of each ball proportional to the weight of its corresponding term. This makes the probability of drawing the ball for a term w proportional to both the term weight $m(w)$ and its multinomial weight ϕ^w:

$$p(w|\phi, \beta, m) = \frac{\phi^w \, m(w)}{\sum_{w \in W} m(w)} \tag{5}$$

We can now expand Eq. 4 to obtain a new sampling equation for use with the Gibbs sampler.

$$p(z_{ij} = k|\mathbf{z}^{-ij}, \mathbf{x}, \mathbf{d}, m, \alpha, \beta) = \frac{m(x_i) N_{i(\cdot)k}^{-ij} + \beta}{\sum_w m(w) N_{w(\cdot)k}^{-ij} + W\beta} \frac{\sum_w m(w) N_{wjk}^{-ij} + \alpha}{\sum_w m(w) N_{wj(\cdot)} + T\alpha} \tag{6}$$

If all weights $m(w) = 1$ this reduces immediately to the standard LDA formulation in Eq. 1.

The information measure we describe above is constant for a particular term across the entire corpus, but it is possible to conceive of other, more sophisticated weighting schemes as well, for example those where term weights vary by document. Pointwise mutual information (PMI) is one such weighting scheme which has a solid basis in information theory and has been shown to work well in the context of LSI (Chew et al., 2010). According to PMI, the weight of a given term w in a given document d is the pointwise mutual information of the term and document, or $-\log_2 \frac{p(w|d)}{p(w)}$. Extending the LDA model to accommodate PMI is straightforward. We replace $m(x_i)$ and $m(w)$ in Eq. 4 with $m(x_i, d)$ as follows.

$$\begin{aligned} m(x_i, d) &= -\log_2 \frac{p(x_i|d)}{p(x_i)} \\ &= -\log_2 \frac{\#[\text{tokens of type } x_i \text{ in } d]}{\#[\text{tokens of type } x_i]} \end{aligned} \tag{7}$$

It is possible for PMI of a term within a document to be negative. When this happens, we clamp the weight of the offending term to zero in that document. In practice, we observe this only with common words (e.g. 'and', 'in', 'of', 'that', 'the' and 'to' in English) that are assigned very low weight everywhere else in the corpus. This clamping does not noticeably affect the results.

In the next sections, we describe tests which have enabled us to evaluate empirically which of these formulations works best in practice.

4 Testing Framework

In this paper, we chose to test our hypotheses with the same cross-language retrieval task used in a number of previous studies of LSI (e.g. Chew and Abdelali (2007)). Briefly, the task is to train an IR model on one particular multilingual corpus, then deploy it on a separate multilingual corpus, using a document in one language to retrieve related documents in other languages. This task is difficult because of the size of the datasets involved. Its usefulness becomes apparent when we consider the following two use cases: a human wishing (1) to use a search engine to retrieve relevant documents in many languages regardless of the language in which the query is posed; or (2) to produce a clustering or visualization of documents according to their topics even when the documents are in different languages.

The training corpus consists of the text of the Bible in 31,226 parallel chunks, corresponding generally to verses, in Arabic, English, French, Russian and Spanish. These data were obtained from the Unbound Bible project (Biola University (2006)). The test data, obtained from `http://www.kuran.gen.tr/`, is the text of the Quran in the same 5 languages, in 114 parallel chunks corresponding to suras (chapters). The task, in short, is to use the training data to inform whatever linguistic, semantic, or statistical model is being tested, and then to infer characteristics of the test data in such a way that the test documents can automatically be matched with their translations in other languages. Though the documents come from a specific domain (scriptural texts), what is of interest is comparative results using different weighting schemes, holding the datasets and other settings constant. The training and test datasets are large enough to allow statistically significant observations to be made, and if a significant difference is observed between experiments using two settings, it is to be expected that similar basic differences would be observed with any other set of training and test data. In any case, it should be noted that the Bible and Quran were written centuries apart, and in different original languages; we believe this contributes to a clean separation of training and test data, and makes for a non-trivial retrieval task.

In our framework, a term-by-document matrix is formed from the Bible as a parallel verse-aligned corpus. We employed two different approaches to tokenization, one (word-based tokenization) in which text was tokenized at every non-word character, and the other (unsupervised morpheme-based tokenization) in which after word-based tokenization, a further pre-processing step (based on Goldsmith (2001)) was performed to add extra breaks at every morpheme. It is shown elsewhere (Chew et al., 2010) that this step leads to improved performance with LSI. In each verse, all languages are concatenated together, allowing terms (either morphemes or words) from all languages to be represented in every verse. Cross-language homographs such as 'mien' in English and French are treated as distinct terms in our framework. Thus, if there are L languages, D documents (each of which is translated into each of the L languages), and W distinct linguistic terms across all languages, then the term-by-document matrix is of dimensions W by D (not W by $D \times L$); with the Bible as a training corpus, the actual numbers in our case are 160,345 $\times$ 31,226. As described in Sec. 2.2, we use this matrix as the input to a collapsed Gibbs sampling algorithm to learn the latent assignment of tokens in all five languages to language-independent topics, as well as the latent assignment of language-independent topics to the multilingual (parallel) documents. In general, we specified, arbitrarily but consistently across all tests, that the number of topics to be learned should be 200. Other parameters for the Gibbs sampler held constant were the number of iterations for burn-in (200) and the number of iterations for sampling (1).

To evaluate our different approaches to weighting, we use classification as described in Sec. 2.3 to obtain, for each document from the Quran test corpus, a probability distribution across the topics learned from the Bible. While in training we have D multilingual documents, in testing we have $D' \times L$ documents, each in a specific language, for which a distribution is computed. For the Quran data, this amounts to $114 \times 5 = 570$ documents. This is because our goal is to match documents with their translations in other languages using just the probability distributions. For each source-language/target-language pair L_1 and L_2, we obtain the similarity of each of the 114 documents in L_1 to each of the 114 documents in L_2. We found that similarity here is best computed using the Jensen-Shannon divergence

	Tokenization	
Weighting Scheme	Word	Morpheme
Unweighted	0.505	0.544
$\log p(w\|L)$	0.616	0.641
PMI	0.612	**0.686**

Table 1: Summary of comparison results. This table shows the average precision at one document (P1) for each of the tokenization and weighting schemes we evaluated. Detailed results are presented in Table 2.

(Lin, 2002) and so this measure was used in all tests. Ultimately, the measure of how well a particular method performs is average precision at 1 document (P1). Among the various measurements for evaluating the performance of IR systems (Salton and McGill (1983), van Rijsbergen (1979)), this is a fairly standard measure. For a particular source-target pair, this is the percentage (out of 114 cases) where a document in L_1 is most similar to its mate in L_2. With 5 languages, there are 25 source-target pairs, and we can also calculate average P1 across all language pairs. Here, we average across 114 $\times$ 25 (or 2,850) cases. This is why even small differences in P1 can be statistically significant.

5 Results

First, we present a summary of our results in Table 1 which clearly demonstrates that it is better in LDA to use some kind of weighting scheme rather than the uniform weights in the standard LDA formulation from Eq. 1. This is true whether tokenization is by word or by morpheme. All increases from the baseline precision at 1 document (0.505 and 0.544 respectively), whether under log or PMI weighting, are highly significant ($p < 10^{-11}$). Furthermore, all increases in precision when moving from word-based to morphology-based tokenization are also highly significant ($p < 5 \times 10^{-5}$ without weighting, $p < 5 \times 10^{-3}$ with log-weighting, and $p < 2 \times 10^{-15}$ with PMI weighting). The best result overall, where P1 is 0.686, is obtained with morphological tokenization and PMI weighting (parallel to the results in (Chew et al., 2010) with LSI), and again the difference between this result and its nearest competitor of 0.641 is highly significant ($p < 3 \times 10^{-6}$). We return to comment below on lack of an increase in P1 when moving from log-weighting to PMI-weighting under word-based tokenization.

These results can also be broken out by language pair, as shown in Table 2. Here, it is apparent that Arabic, and to a lesser extent Russian, are harder languages in the IR problem at hand. Our intuition is that this is connected with the fact that these two languages have a more complex morphological structure: words are formed by a process of agglutination. A consequence of this is that single Arabic and Russian tokens can less frequently be mapped to single tokens in other languages, which appears to "confuse" LDA (and also, as we have found, LSI). The complex morphology of Russian and Arabic is also reflected in the type-token ratios for each language: in our English Bible, there are 12,335 types (unique words) and 789,744 tokens, a type-token ratio of 0.0156. The ratios for French, Spanish, Russian and Arabic are 0.0251, 0.0404, 0.0843 and 0.1256 respectively. Though the differences may not be explicable in purely statistical terms (there may be linguistic factors at play which cannot be reduced to statistics), it seems plausible that choosing a suboptimal term-weighting scheme could exacerbate any intrinsic problems of statistical imbalance. Considering this, it is interesting to note that the greatest gains, when moving from unweighted LDA to either form of weighted LDA, are often to be found where Russian and/or Arabic are involved. This, to us, shows the value of using a multilingual dataset as a testbed for our different formulations of LDA: it allows problems which may not be apparent when working with a monolingual dataset to come more easily to light.

We have mentioned that the best results are with PMI and morphological tokenization, and also that there is an increase in precision for many language of the pairs when morphological (as opposed to word-based) tokenization is employed. To us, the results leave little doubt that both weighting and morphological tokenization are independently beneficial. It appears, though, that morphology and weighting are also complementary and synergistic strategies for improving the results of LDA: for example, a suboptimal approach in tokenization may at best place an upper bound on the overall precision achievable, and perhaps at worst undo the benefits of a good weighting scheme. This may explain the one apparently anomalous result, which is the lack of an increase in

		Original Words					Morphological Tokenization					
		EN	ES	RU	AR	FR	EN	ES	RU	AR	FR	
	EN	1.000	0.500	0.447	0.132	0.816	1.000	0.500	0.658	0.211	0.640	EN
	ES	0.649	1.000	0.307	0.175	0.781	0.605	1.000	0.482	0.175	0.737	ES
LDA	RU	0.430	0.316	1.000	0.149	0.430	0.553	0.421	1.000	0.272	0.553	RU
	AR	0.070	0.149	0.114	1.000	0.096	0.123	0.105	0.228	1.000	0.114	AR
	FR	0.781	0.693	0.421	0.175	1.000	0.693	0.640	0.667	0.211	1.000	FR
	EN	1.000	0.518	0.518	0.228	0.658	1.000	0.675	0.561	0.219	0.754	EN
	ES	0.558	1.000	0.605	0.254	0.763	0.711	1.000	0.570	0.289	0.860	ES
Log-WLDA	RU	0.605	0.615	1.000	0.298	0.702	0.684	0.667	1.000	0.289	0.728	RU
	AR	0.404	0.430	0.526	1.000	0.439	0.430	0.439	0.535	1.000	0.404	AR
	FR	0.667	0.667	0.658	0.281	1.000	0.711	0.667	0.561	0.289	1.000	FR
	EN	1.000	0.579	0.658	0.272	0.702	1.000	0.719	0.658	0.342	0.851	EN
	ES	0.596	1.000	0.623	0.246	0.693	0.816	1.000	0.675	0.272	0.798	ES
PMI-WLDA	RU	0.649	0.579	1.000	0.307	0.693	0.702	0.693	1.000	0.360	0.772	RU
	AR	0.351	0.368	0.421	1.000	0.351	0.456	0.474	0.509	1.000	0.377	AR
	FR	0.693	0.667	0.605	0.254	1.000	0.825	0.772	0.719	0.333	1.000	FR

Table 2: Full results for precision at one document for all combinations of LDA, Log-WLDA, PMI-WLDA, word tokenization and morphological tokenization.

precision moving from log-WLDA to PMI-WLDA under word-based tokenization: if word-based tokenization is suboptimal, PMI weighting cannot compensate for that. Effectively, for best results, the right strategies have to be pursued with respect *both* to morphology *and* to weighting.

Finally, we can illustrate the differences between weighted and unweighted LDA in another way. As discussed earlier, each topic in LDA is a probability distribution over terms. For each topic, we can list the most probable terms in decreasing order of probability; this gives a sense of what each topic is 'about' and whether the groupings of terms appear reasonable. Since we use 200 topics, an exhaustive listing is impractical here, but in Table 3 we present some representative examples from unweighted LDA and PMI-WLDA that we judged to be of interest. It appears to us that the groupings are not perfect under either LDA or PMI-WLDA; under both methods, we find examples of rather heterogeneous topics, whereas we would like each topic to be semantically focused. Still, a comparison of the output with LDA and PMI-WLDA sheds some light on why PMI-WLDA makes it less necessary to remove stopwords. Note that all words listed for the top two topics under LDA would commonly be considered stopwords. This might also be true of the words in topic 1 for PMI-WLDA, but in the latter case, the topic is actually one of the most semantically focused in that the top words have a clear semantic connection to one another. This cannot be said of topics 1 and 2 in LDA. For one thing, many of the same terms that appear in topic 1 reappear in topic 2, making the two topics hard to distinguish from one another. Secondly, the terms have only a loose semantic connection to one another: 'the', 'and', and 'of' are all high-frequency and likely to co-occur, but they are different parts of speech and have very different functions in English. One might say that topics 1 and 2 in LDA are a rag-bag of high-frequency words, and it is unsurprising that these topics do little to help characterize documents in our cross-language IR task. The same cannot be said of any of the top 5 topics in PMI-WLDA. We believe this illustrates well, and at a fundamental level, why weighted forms of LDA work better in practice than unweighted LDA.

6 Conclusion

We have conducted a series of experiments to evaluate the effect of different weighting schemes on Latent Dirichlet Allocation. Our results demonstrate, perhaps contrary to the conventional wisdom that weighting is unnecessary in LDA, that weighting schemes (and other pre-processing strategies) simi-

Topic	Weighting Scheme: LDA (no weighting) 1	2	3	4	5	PMI-WLDA 1	2	3	4	5
Terms	the	the	vanité	as	cárcel	under	city	coeur	sat	colère
	et	de	vanidad	comme	prison	sous	ville	heart	assis	ira
	and	et	vanity	como	السجن	под	ciudad	corazón	vent	wrath
	los	of	باطل	как	prison	تحت	لمدينة	сердце	wind	anger
	и	and	суета	un	темницу	debajo	город	сердца	viento	furor
	y	y	aflicción	a	prisonniers	ombre	twelve	قلبه	sentado	гнев
	les	de	poursuite	one	темницы	bases	douze	قلب	ветер	fureur
	á	и	الباطل	كما	bound	basas	doce	قلبي	الريح	غضب
	de	la	prédicateur	une	prisión	sombra	دينة	قلبك	sitting	гнева
	of	la	وقبض	واحد	prisoners	dessous	города	сердцем	сел	contre

Table 3: Top 10 terms within top 5 topics for each of LDA and PMI-WLDA. Terms that appear twice within the same topic (e.g. 'la' in LDA topic 2) are words from different languages with the same spelling (here Spanish and French).

lar to those commonly employed in other approaches to IR (such as LSI) can significantly improve the performance of a system. Our approach also runs counter to the standard position in LDA that it is necessary or desirable to remove stopwords as a preprocessing step, and we have presented an alternative approach of applying an appropriate weighting scheme within LDA. This approach is preferable because it is considerably less ad-hoc than the construction of stoplists. We have shown mathematically how alternative weighting schemes can be incorporated into the Gibbs sampling model. We have also demonstrated that, far from being arbitrary, the introduction of weighting into the LDA model has a solid and rational basis in information and probability theory, just as the basic LDA model itself has.

In future work, we would like to explore further enhancements to weighting in LDA. There are many variants which can be considered: one example is the incorporation of word order and context through an n-gram model based on conditional probabilities. We also aim to evaluate LDA against LSI with a view to establishing whether one can be said to outperform the other consistently in terms of precision, with appropriate settings held constant. Finally, we would like to determine whether other techniques which have been shown to benefit LSI can also be usefully brought to bear in LDA, just as we have shown here in the case of term weighting.

References

David M. Blei, Andrew Y. Ng, and Michael I. Jordan. 2003. Latent Dirichlet Allocation. *Journal of Machine Learning Research 3*, pages 993–1022.

Sourav Chatterji and Lior Pachter. 2004. Multiple Organism Gene Finding by Collapsed Gibbs Sampling. In *RECOMB '04: Proceedings of the eighth annual international conference on Research in computational molecular biology*, pages 187–193, New York, NY, USA. ACM.

Peter A. Chew and Ahmed Abdelali. 2007. Benefits of the 'Massively Parallel Rosetta Stone': Cross-Language Information Retrieval with Over 30 Languages. In Association for Computational Linguistics, editor, *Proceedings of the 45th meeting of the Association of Computational Linguistics*, pages 872–879.

Peter A. Chew, Brett W. Bader, Stephen Helmreich, Ahmed Abdelali, and Stephen J. Verzi. 2010. An Information-Theoretic, Vector-Space-Model Approach to Cross-Language Information Retrieval. *Journal of Natural Language Engineering*. Forthcoming.

Philipp Cimiano, Antje Schultz, Sergej Sizov, Philipp Sorg, and Steffen Staab. 2009. Explicit Versus Latent Concept Models for Cross-Language Information Retrieval. In *Proceedings of the 21st International Joint Conference on Artificial Intelligence*, pages 1513–1518.

Scott Deerwester, Susan T. Dumais, George W. Furnas, Thomas K. Landauer, and Richard Harshman. 1990. Indexing by Latent Semantic Analysis. *Journal of the American Society of Information Science*, 41(6):391–407.

Susan T. Dumais. 1991. Improving the Retrieval of Information from External Sources. *Behavior Research Methods, Instruments and Computers*, 23(2):229–236.

Stuart Geman, Donald Geman, K. Abend, T. J. Harley, and L. N. Kanal. 1993. Stochastic Relaxation, Gibbs Distributions and the Bayesian Restoration of Images*. *Journal of Applied Statistics*, 20(5):25–62.

J. Goldsmith. 2001. Unsupervised Learning of the Morphology of a Natural Language. *Computational Linguistics*, 27(2):153–198.

Thomas L. Griffiths and Mark Steyvers. 2004. Finding Scientific Topics. In *Proceedings of the National Academy of Sciences USA*, volume 101, pages 5228–5235.

Thomas Hofmann. 1999. Probablistic Latent Semantic Indexing. In *Proceedings of the 22nd Annual International SIGIR Conference*, pages 53–57.

Solomon Kullback and Richard A. Leibler. 1951. On Information and Sufficiency. *Annals of Mathematical Statistics*, 22:49–86.

J. Lin. 2002. Divergence Measures based on the Shannon Entropy. *IEEE Transactions on Information Theory*, 37(1):145–151, August.

Xiaochuan Ni, Jian-Tao Sun, Jian Hu, and Zheng Chen. 2009. Mining Multilingual Topics from Wikipedia. In *18th International World Wide Web Conference*, pages 1155–1155, April.

Daniel Ramage, Paul Heymann, Christopher D. Manning, and Hector Garcia-Molina. 2008. Clustering the Tagged Web. In *Second ACM International Conference on Web Search and Data Mining (WSDM 2009)*, November.

G. Salton and M. McGill, editors. 1983. *Introduction to Modern Information Retrieval*. McGraw-Hill.

Biola University. 2006. The Unbound Bible. http://www.unboundbible.com.

C.J. van Rijsbergen. 1979. *Information Retrieval*. Butterworth-Heinemann.

Learning Dense Models of Query Similarity from User Click Logs

Fabio De Bona*
Friedrich Miescher Laboratory
of the Max Planck Society
Tübingen, Germany
fabio@tuebingen.mpg.de

Stefan Riezler
Google Research
Zürich, Switzerland
riezler@google.com

Keith Hall
Google Research
Zürich, Switzerland
kbhall@google.com

Massimiliano Ciaramita
Google Research
Zürich, Switzerland
massi@google.com

Amaç Herdağdelen*
University of Trento
Rovereto, Italy
amac@herdagdelen.com

Maria Holmqvist*
Linkopings University
Linkopings, Sweden
marho@ida.liu.se

Abstract

The goal of this work is to integrate query similarity metrics as features into a dense model that can be trained on large amounts of query log data, in order to rank query rewrites. We propose features that incorporate various notions of syntactic and semantic similarity in a generalized edit distance framework. We use the implicit feedback of user clicks on search results as weak labels in training linear ranking models on large data sets. We optimize different ranking objectives in a stochastic gradient descent framework. Our experiments show that a pairwise SVM ranker trained on multipartite rank levels outperforms other pairwise and listwise ranking methods under a variety of evaluation metrics.

1 Introduction

Measures of query similarity are used for a wide range of web search applications, including query expansion, query suggestions, or listings of related queries. Several recent approaches deploy user query logs to learn query similarities. One set of approaches focuses on user reformulations of queries that differ only in one phrase, e.g., Jones et al. (2006). Such phrases are then identified as candidate expansion terms, and filtered by various signals such as co-occurrence in similar sessions, or log-likelihood ratio of original and expansion phrase. Other approaches focus on the relation of queries and search results, either by clustering queries based on their search results, e.g., Beeferman and Berger (2000), or by deploying the graph of queries and results to find related queries, e.g., Sahami and Heilman (2006).

The approach closest to ours is that of Jones et al. (2006). Similar to their approach, we create a training set of candidate query rewrites from user query logs, and use it to train learners. While the dataset used in Jones et al. (2006) is in the order of a few thousand query-rewrite pairs, our dataset comprises around 1 billion query-rewrite pairs. Clearly, manual labeling of rewrite quality is not feasible for our dataset, and perhaps not even desirable. Instead, our intent is to learn from large amounts of user query log data. Such data permit to learn smooth models because of the effectiveness of large data sets to capture even rare aspects of language, and they also are available as *in the wild*, i.e., they reflect the actual input-output behaviour that we seek to automate (Halevy et al., 2009). We propose a technique to automatically create weak labels from co-click information in user query logs of search engines. The central idea is that two queries are related if they lead to user clicks on the same documents for a large amount of documents. A manual evaluation of a small subset showed that a determination of positive versus negative rewrites by thresholding the number of co-clicks correlates well with human judgements of similarity, thus justifying our method of eliciting labels from co-clicks.

Similar to Jones et al. (2006), the features of our models are not based on word identities, but instead on general string similarity metrics. This leads to dense rather than sparse feature spaces. The dif-

*The work presented in this paper was done while the authors were visiting Google Research, Zürich.

Human Language Technologies: The 2010 Annual Conference of the North American Chapter of the ACL, pages 474–482,
Los Angeles, California, June 2010.

ference of our approach to Jones et al. (2006) lies in our particular choice of string similarity metrics. While Jones et al. (2006) deploy "syntactic" features such as Levenshtein distance, and "semantic" features such as log-likelihood ratio or mutual information, we combine syntactic and semantic aspects into generalized edit-distance features where the cost of each edit operation is weighted by various term probability models.

Lastly, the learners used in our approach are applicable to very large datasets by an integration of linear ranking models into a stochastic gradient descent framework for optimization. We compare several linear ranking models, including a log-linear probability model for bipartite ranking, and pairwise and listwise SVM rankers. We show in an experimental evaluation that a pairwise SVM ranker trained on multipartite rank levels outperforms state-of-the-art pairwise and listwise ranking methods under a variety of evaluation metrics.

2 Query Similarity Measures

2.1 Semantic measures

In several of the similarity measures we describe below, we employ *pointwise mutual information* (PMI) as a measure of the association between two terms or queries. Let w_i and w_j be two strings that we want to measure the amount of association between. Let $\mathrm{p}(w_i)$ and $\mathrm{p}(w_j)$ be the probability of observing w_i and w_j in a given model; e.g., relative frequencies estimated from occurrence counts in a corpus. We also define $\mathrm{p}(w_i, w_j)$ as the joint probability of w_i and w_j; i.e., the probability of the two strings occurring together. We define PMI as follows:

$$\mathrm{PMI}(w_i, w_j) = \log \frac{\mathrm{p}(w_i, w_j)}{\mathrm{p}(w_i)\mathrm{p}(w_j)}. \quad (1)$$

PMI has been introduced by Church and Hanks (1990) as word assosiatio ratio, and since then been used extensively to model semantic similarity. Among several desirable properties, it correlates well with human judgments (Recchia and Jones, 2009).

2.2 Taxonomic normalizations

As pointed out in earlier work, query transitions tend to correlate with taxonomic relations such as generalization and specialization (Lau and Horvitz, 1999; Rieh and Xie, 2006). Boldi et al. (2009) show how knowledge of transition types can positively impact query reformulation. We would like to exploit this information as well. However, rather than building a dedicated supervised classifier for this task we try to capture it directly at the source. First, we notice how string features; e.g., length, and edit distance already model this phenomenon to some extent, and in fact are part of the features used in Boldi et al. (2009). However, these measures are not always accurate and it is easy to find counterexamples both at the term level (e.g., "camping" to "outdoor activities" is a generalization) and character level ("animal pictures" to "cat pictures" is a specialization). Secondly, we propose that by manipulating PMI we can directly model taxonomic relations to some extent.

Rather than using raw PMI values we renormalize them. Notice that it is not obvious in our context how to interpret the relation between strings co-occurring less frequently than random. Such noisy events will yield negative PMI values since $p(w_i, w_j) < p(w_i)p(w_j)$. We enforce zero PMI values for such cases. If PMI is thus constrained to non-negative values, normalization will bound PMI to the range between 0 and 1.

The first type of normalization, called *joint normalization*, uses the negative log joint probability and is defined as

$$\mathrm{PMI(J)}(w_i, w_j) = \mathrm{PMI}(w_i, w_j)/{-\log}(\mathrm{p}(w_i, w_j)).$$

The jointly normalized PMI(J) is a symmetric measure between w_i and w_j in the sense that $\mathrm{PMI(J)}(w_i, w_j) = \mathrm{PMI(J)}(w_j, w_i)$. Intuitively it is a measure of the amount of shared information between the two strings relative to the sum of individual strings information. The advantages of the joint normalization of PMI have been noticed before (Bouma, 2009).

To capture asymmetries in the relation between two strings, we introduce two non-symmetric normalizations which also bound the measure between 0 and 1. The second normalization is called *specialization normalization* and is defined as

$$\mathrm{PMI(S)}(w_i, w_j) = \mathrm{PMI}(w_i, w_j)/ - \log(\mathrm{p}(w_i)).$$

The reason we call it specialization is that PMI(S) favors pairs where the second string is a specialization of the first one. For instance, PMI(S) is at its maximum when $\mathrm{p}(w_i, w_j) = \mathrm{p}(w_j)$ and that means the conditional probability $\mathrm{p}(w_i|w_j)$ is 1 which is an indication of a specialization relation.

The last normalization is called the *generalization normalization* and is defined in the reverse direction as

$$\mathrm{PMI(G)}(w_i, w_j) = \mathrm{PMI}(w_i, w_j) / -\log(\mathrm{p}(w_j)).$$

Again, PMI(G) is a measure between 0 and 1 and is at its maximum value when $\mathrm{p}(w_j|w_i)$ is 1.

The three normalizations provide a richer representation of the association between two strings. Furthermore, jointly, they model in an information-theoretic sense the generalization-specialization dimension directly. As an example, for the query transition "apple" to "mac os" PMI(G)=0.2917 and PMI(S)=0.3686; i.e., there is more evidence for a specialization. Conversely for the query transition "ferrari models" to "ferrari" we get PMI(G)=1 and PMI(S)=0.5558; i.e., the target is a "perfect" generalization of the source[1].

2.3 Syntactic measures

Let V be a finite vocabulary and ξ be the null symbol. An edit operation: insertion, deletion or substitution, is a pair $(a, b) \in \{V \cup \{\xi\} \times V \cup \{\xi\}\} \setminus \{(\xi, \xi)\}$. An alignment between two sequences w_i and w_j is a sequence of edit operations $\omega = (a_1, b_1), ..., (a_n, b_n)$. Given a non-negative cost function c, the cost of an alignment is $c(\omega) = \sum_{i=1}^{n} c(\omega_i)$. The Levenshtein distance, or edit distance, defined over V, $d_V(w_i, w_j)$ between two sequences is the cost of the least expensive sequence of edit operations which transforms w_i into w_j (Levenshtein, 1966). The distance computation can be performed via dynamic programming in time $O(|w_i||w_j|)$. Similarity at the string, i.e., character or term, level is an indicator of semantic similarity. Edit distance captures the amount of overlap between the queries as sequences of symbols and has been previously used in information retrieval (Boldi et al., 2009; Jones et al., 2006).

We use two basic Levenshtein distance models. The first, called Edit1 (E1), employs a unit cost function for each of the three operations. That is, given a finite vocabulary T containing all terms occurring in queries:

$$\forall a, b \in T, c_{\mathrm{E1}}(a, b) = 1 \text{ if}(a \neq b), 0 \text{ else}.$$

The second, called Edit2 (E2), uses unit costs for insertion and deletion, but computes the character-based edit distance between two terms to decide on the substitution cost. If two terms are very similar at the character level, then the cost of substitution is lower. Given a finite vocabulary T of terms and a finite vocabulary A of characters, the cost function is defined as:

$$\forall a, b \in T, c_{E2}(a, b) = d_A(a, b) \text{ if} a \wedge b \neq \xi, 1 \text{ else}.$$

where $d_A(a, b)$ is linearly scaled between 0 and 1 dividing by $\max(|a|, |b|)$.

We also investigate a variant of the edit distance algorithm in which the terms in the input sequences are sorted, alphabetically, before the distance computation. The motivation behind this variant is the observation that linear order in queries is not always meaningful. For example, it seems reasonable to assume that "brooklyn pizza" and "pizza brooklyn" denote roughly the same user intent. However, the pair has an edit distance of two (delete-insert), while the distance between "brooklyn pizza" and the less relevant "brooklyn college" is only one (substitute). The sorted variant relaxes the ordering constraint.

2.4 Generalized measures

In this section we extend the edit distance framework introduced in Section 2.3 with the semantic similarity measures described in Section 2.1, using the taxonomic normalizations defined in Section 2.2.

Extending the Levenshtein distance framework to take into account semantic similarities between terms is conceptually simple. As in the Edit2 model above we use a modified cost function. We introduce a *cost matrix* encoding individual costs for term substitution operations; the cost is defined in terms of the normalized PMI measures of Section 2.2, recall that these measures range between 0 and 1. Given a normalized similarity measure f, an entry in a cost matrix S for a term pair (w_i, w_j) is defined as:

$$s(w_i, w_j) = 2 - 2f(w_i, w_j) + \epsilon$$

[1]The values are computed from Web counts.

We call these models SEdit (SE), where S specifies the cost matrix used. Given a finite term vocabulary T and cost matrix S, the cost function is defined as:

$$\forall a, b \in T, c_{SE}(a, b) = s(a, b) \text{ if} a \wedge b \neq \xi, 1 \text{ else.}$$

The cost function has the following properties. Since insertion and deletion have unit cost, a term is substituted only if a substitution is "cheaper" than deleting and inserting another term, namely, if the similarity between the terms is not zero. The ϵ correction, coupled with unit insertion and deletion cost, guarantees that for an unrelated term pair a combination of insertion and deletion will always be less costly then a substitution. Thus in the computation of the optimal alignment, each operation cost ranges between 0 and 2.

As a remark on efficiency, we notice that here the semantic similarities are computed between terms, rather than full queries. At the term level, caching techniques can be applied more effectively to speed up feature computation. The cost function is implemented as a pre-calculated matrix, in the next section we describe how the matrix is estimated.

2.5 Cost matrix estimation

In our experiments we evaluated two different sources to obtain the PMI-based cost matrices. In both cases, we assumed that the cost of the substitution of a term with itself (i.e. identity substitution) is always 0. The first technique uses a probabilistic clustering model trained on queries and clicked documents from user query logs. The second model estimates cost matrices directly from user session logs, consisting of approximately 1.3 billion U.S. English queries. A session is defined as a sequence of queries from the same user within a controlled time interval. Let q_s and q_t be a query pair observed in the session data where q_t is issued immediately after q_s in the same session. Let $q'_s = q_s \setminus q_t$ and $q'_t = q_t \setminus q_s$, where $\setminus$ is the set difference operator. The co-occurrence count of two terms w_i and w_j from a query pair q_s, q_t is denoted by $n_{i,j}(q_s, q_t)$ and is defined as:

$$n_{i,j}(q_s, q_t) = \begin{cases} 1 \text{ if } w_i = w_j \wedge w_i \in q_s \wedge w_j \in q_t \\ 1/(|q'_s|\,|q'_t|) \text{ if } w_i \in q'_s \wedge w_j \in q'_t \\ 0 \text{ else.} \end{cases}$$

In other words, if a term occurs in both queries, it has a co-occurrence count of 1. For all other term pairs, a normalized co-occurrence count is computed in order to make sure the sum of co-occurrence counts for a term $w_i \in q_s$ sums to 1 for a given query pair. The normalization is an attempt to avoid the under representation of terms occurring in both queries.

The final co-occurrence count of two arbitrary terms w_i and w_j is denoted by $N_{i,j}$ and it is defined as the sum over all query pairs in the session logs, $N_{i,j} = \sum_{q_s, q_t} n_{i,j}(q_s, q_t)$. Let $N = \sum_{w_i, w_j} N_{i,j}$ be the sum of co-occurrence counts over all term pairs. Then we define a joint probability for a term pair as $\mathrm{p}(w_i, w_j) = \frac{N_{i,j}}{N}$. Similarly, we define the single-occurrence counts and probabilities of the terms by computing the marginalized sums over all term pairs. Namely, the probability of a term w_i occurring in the source query is $\mathrm{p}(i, \cdot) = \sum_{w_j} N_{i,j}/N$ and similarly the probability of a term w_j occurring in the target query is $\mathrm{p}(\cdot, j) = \sum_{w_i} N_{i,j}/N$. Plugging in these values in Eq. (1), we get the $\mathrm{PMI}(w_i, w_j)$ for term pair w_i and w_j, which are further normalized as described in Section 2.2.

More explanation and evaluation of the features described in this section can be found in Ciaramita et al. (2010).

3 Learning to Rank from Co-Click Data

3.1 Extracting Weak Labels from Co-Clicks

Several studies have shown that implicit feedback from clickstream data is a weaker signal than human relevance judgements. Joachims (2002) or Agrawal et al. (2009) presented techniques to convert clicks into labels that can be used for machine learning. Our goal is not to elicit relevance judgments from user clicks, but rather to relate queries by pivoting on commonly clicked search results. The hypothesis is that two queries are related if they lead to user clicks on the same documents for a large amount of documents. This approach is similar to the method proposed by Fitzpatrick and Dent (1997) who attempt to measure the relatedness between two queries by using the normalized intersection of the top 200 retrieval results. We add click information to this setup, thus strengthening the preference for precision over recall in the extraction of related queries.

Table 1: Statistics of co-click data sets.

	train	dev	test
number of queries	250,000	2,500	100
average number of rewrites per query	4,500	4,500	30
percentage of rewrites with ≥ 10 coclicks	0.2	0.2	43

In our experiments we created two ground-truth ranking scenarios from the co-click signals. In a first scenario, called *bipartite ranking*, we extract a set of positive and a set of negative query-rewrite pairs from the user logs data. We define positive pairs as queries that have been co-clicked with at least 10 different results, and negative pairs as query pairs with fewer than 10 co-clicks. In a second scenario, called *multipartite ranking*, we define a hierarchy of levels of "goodness", by combining rewrites with the same number of co-clicks at the same level, with increasing ranks for higher number of co-clicks. Statistics on the co-click data prepared for our experiments are given in Table 1.

For training and development, we collected query-rewrite pairs from user query logs that contained at least one positive rewrite. The training set consists of about 1 billion of query-rewrite pairs; the development set contains 10 million query-rewrite pairs. The average number of rewrites per query is around 4,500 for the training and development set, with a very small amount of 0.2% positive rewrites per query. In order to confirm the validity of our co-click hypothesis, and for final evaluation, we held out another sample of query-rewrite pairs for manual evaluation. This dataset contains 100 queries for each of which we sampled 30 rewrites in descending order of co-clicks, resulting in a high percentage of 43% positive rewrites per query. The query-rewrite pairs were annotated by 3 raters as follows: First the raters were asked to rank the rewrites in descending order of relevance using a graphical user interface. Second the raters assigned rank labels and binary relevance scores to the ranked list of rewrites. This labeling strategy is similar to the labeling strategy for synonymy judgements proposed by Rubenstein and Goodenough (1965). Inter-rater agreements on binary relevance judgements, and agreement between rounded averaged human relevance scores and assignments of positive/negative labels by the co-click threshold of 10 produced a Kappa value of 0.65 (Siegel and Castellan, 1988).

3.2 Learning-to-Rank Query Rewrites

3.2.1 Notation

Let $S = \{(x_q, y_q)\}_{q=1}^{n}$ be a training sample of queries, each represented by a set of rewrites $x_q = \{x_{q1}, \ldots, x_{q,n(q)}\}$, and set of rank labels $y_q = \{y_{q1}, \ldots, y_{q,n(q)}\}$, where $n(q)$ is the number of rewrites for query q. For full rankings of all rewrites for a query, a total order on rewrites is assumed, with rank labels taking on values $y_{qi} \in \{1, \ldots, n(q)\}$. Rewrites of equivalent rank can be specified by assuming a partial order on rewrites, where a multipartite ranking involves $r < n(q)$ relevance levels such that $y_{qi} \in \{1, \ldots, r\}$, and a bipartite ranking involves two rank values $y_{qi} \in \{1, 2\}$ with relevant rewrites at rank 1 and non-relevant rewrites at rank 2.

Let the rewrites in x_q be identified by the integers $\{1, 2, \ldots, n(q)\}$, and let a permutation π_q on x_q be defined as a bijection from $\{1, 2, \ldots, n(q)\}$ onto itself. Let Π_q denote the set of all possible permutations on x_q, and let π_{qi} denote the rank position of x_{qi}. Furthermore, let (i, j) denote a pair of rewrites in x_q and let $\mathcal{P}_q$ be the set of all pairs in x_q.

We associate a feature function $\phi(x_{qi})$ with each rewrite $i = 1, \ldots, n(q)$ for each query q. Furthermore, a partial-order feature map as used in Yue et al. (2007) is created for each rewrite set as follows:

$$\phi(x_q, \pi_q) = \frac{1}{|\mathcal{P}_q|} \sum_{(i,j)\in\mathcal{P}_q} \phi(x_{qi}) - \phi(x_{qj}) \mathrm{sgn}(\frac{1}{\pi_{qi}} - \frac{1}{\pi_{qj}}).$$

The goal of learning a ranking over the rewrites x_q for a query q can be achieved either by sorting the rewrites according to the rewrite-level ranking function $f(x_{qi}) = \langle w, \phi(x_{qi})\rangle$, or by finding the permutation that scores highest according to a query-level ranking function $f(x_q, \pi_q) = \langle w, \phi(x_q, \pi_q)\rangle$.

In the following, we will describe a variety of well-known ranking objectives, and extensions thereof, that are used in our experiments. Optimization is done in a stochastic gradient descent (SGD) framework. We minimize an empirical loss objective

$$\min_w \sum_{x_q, y_q} \ell(w)$$

by stochastic updating

$$w_{t+1} = w_t - \eta_t g_t$$

where η_t is a learning rate, and g_t is the gradient

$$g_t = \nabla \ell(w)$$

where

$$\nabla \ell(w) = \left\langle \frac{\partial}{\partial w_1}\ell(w), \frac{\partial}{\partial w_2}\ell(w), \ldots, \frac{\partial}{\partial w_n}\ell(w) \right\rangle.$$

3.2.2 Listwise Hinge Loss

Standard ranking evaluation metrics such as (Mean) Average Precision (Manning et al., 2008) are defined on permutations of whole lists and are not decomposable over instances. Joachims (2005), Yue et al. (2007), or Chakrabarti et al. (2008) have proposed multivariate SVM models to optimize such listwise evaluation metrics. The central idea is to formalize the evaluation metric as a prediction loss function L, and incorporate L via margin rescaling into the hinge loss function, such that an upper bound on the prediction loss is achieved (see Tsochantaridis et al. (2004), Proposition 2).

The loss function is given by the following listwise hinge loss:

$$\ell_{lh}(w) = (L(y_q, \pi_q^*) - \langle w, \phi(x_q, y_q) - \phi(x_q, \pi_q^*)\rangle)_+$$

where π_q^* is the maximizer of the $\max_{\pi_q \in \Pi_q \setminus y_q} L(y_q, \pi_q^*) + \langle w, \phi(x_q, \pi_q^*)\rangle$ expression, $(z)_+ = \max\{0, z\}$ and $L(y_q, \pi_q) \in [0, 1]$ denotes a prediction loss of a predicted ranking π_q compared to the ground-truth ranking y_q.[2]

In this paper, we use Average Precision (AP) as prediction loss function s.t.

$$L_{AP}(y_q, \pi_q) = 1 - AP(y_q, \pi_q)$$

where AP is defined as follows:

$$AP(y_q, \pi_q) = \frac{\sum_{j=1}^{n(q)} Prec(j) \cdot (|y_{qj} - 2|)}{\sum_{j=1}^{n(q)} (|y_{qj} - 2|)},$$

$$Prec(j) = \frac{\sum_{k:\pi_{qk} \leq \pi_{qj}} (|y_{qk} - 2|)}{\pi_{qj}}.$$

[2]We slightly abuse the notation y_q to denote the permutation on x_q that is induced by the rank labels. In case of full rankings, the permutation π_q corresponding to ranking y_q is unique. For multipartite and bipartite rankings, there is more than one possible permutation for a given ranking, so that we let π_q denote a permutation that is consistent with ranking y_q.

Note that the ranking scenario is in this case bipartite with $y_{qi} \in \{1, 2\}$.

The derivatives for ℓ_{lh} are as follows:

$$\frac{\partial}{\partial w_k}\ell_{lh} = \begin{cases} 0 \text{ if } \left(\langle w, \phi(x_q, y_q) - \phi(x_q, \pi_q^*)\rangle\right) \\ \qquad > L(y_q, \pi_q^*), \\ -(\phi_k(x_q, y_q) - \phi_k(x_q, \pi_q^*)) \text{ else.} \end{cases}$$

SGD optimization involves computing π_q^* for each feature and each query, which can be done efficiently using the greedy algorithm proposed by Yue et al. (2007). We will refer to this method as the *SVM-MAP* model.

3.2.3 Pairwise Hinge Loss for Bipartite and Multipartite Ranking

Joachims (2002) proposed an SVM method that defines the ranking problem as a pairwise classification problem. Cortes et al. (2007) extended this method to a magnitude-preserving version by penalizing a pairwise misranking by the magnitude of the difference in preference labels. A position-sensitive penalty for pairwise ranking SVMs was proposed by Riezler and De Bona (2009) and Chapelle and Keerthi (2010), and earlier for perceptrons by Shen and Joshi (2005). In the latter approaches, the magnitude of the difference in inverted ranks is accrued for each misranked pair. The idea is to impose an increased penalty for misrankings at the top of the list, and for misrankings that involve a difference of several rank levels.

Similar to the listwise case, we can view the penalty as a prediction loss function, and incorporate it into the hinge loss function by rescaling the margin by a pairwise prediction loss function $L(y_{qi}, y_{qj})$. In our experiments we used a position-sensitive prediction loss function

$$L(y_{qi}, y_{qj}) = \left|\frac{1}{y_{qi}} - \frac{1}{y_{qj}}\right|$$

defined on the difference of inverted ranks. The margin-rescaled pairwise hinge loss is then defined as follows:

$$\ell_{ph}(w) = \sum_{(i,j) \in \mathcal{P}_q} (L(y_{qi}, y_{qj}) - \langle w, \phi(x_{qi}) - \phi(x_{qj})\rangle \operatorname{sgn}(\frac{1}{y_{qi}} - \frac{1}{y_{qj}}))_+$$

Table 2: Experimental evaluation of *random* and *best feature* baselines, and *log-linear*, *SVM-MAP*, *SVM-bipartite*, *SVM-multipartite*, and *SVM-multipartite-margin-rescaled* learning-to-rank models on manually labeled test set.

	MAP	NDCG@10	AUC	Prec@1	Prec@3	Prec@5
Random	51.8	48.7	50.4	45.6	45.6	46.6
Best-feature	71.9	70.2	74.5	70.2	68.1	68.7
SVM-bipart.	73.7	73.7	74.7	79.4	70.1	70.1
SVM-MAP	74.3	75.2	75.3	76.3	71.8	72.0
Log-linear	74.7	75.1	75.7	75.3	72.2	71.3
SVM-pos.-sens.	75.7	76.0	76.6	82.5	72.9	73.0
SVM-multipart.	**76.5**	**77.3**	**77.2**	**83.5**	**74.2**	**73.6**

The derivative of ℓ_{ph} is calculated as follows:

$$\frac{\partial}{\partial w_k}\ell_{lp} = \begin{cases} 0 \text{ if } (\langle w, \phi(x_{qi}) - \phi(x_{qj})\rangle \\ \quad \text{sgn}(\frac{1}{y_{qi}} - \frac{1}{y_{qj}})) > L(y_{qi}, y_{qj}), \\ -(\phi_k(x_{qi}) - \phi_k(x_{qj}))\text{sgn}(\frac{1}{y_{qi}} - \frac{1}{y_{qj}}) \\ \quad \text{else.} \end{cases}$$

Note that the effect of inducing a position-sensitive penalty on pairwise misrankings applies only in case of full rankings on $n(q)$ rank levels, or in case of multipartite rankings involving $2 < r < n(q)$ rank levels. Henceforth we will refer to margin-rescaled pairwise hinge loss for multipartite rankings as the *SVM-pos.-sens.* method.

Bipartite ranking is a special case where $L(y_{qi}, y_{qj})$ is constant so that margin rescaling does not have the effect of inducing position-sensitivity. This method will be referred to as the *SVM-bipartite* model.

Also note that for full ranking or multipartite ranking, predicting a low ranking for an instance that is ranked high in the ground truth has a domino effect of accruing an additional penalty at each rank level. This effect is independent of margin-rescaling. The method of pairwise hinge loss for multipartite ranking with constant margin will henceforth be referred to as the *SVM-multipartite* model.

Computation in SGD optimization is dominated by the number of pairwise comparisons $|\mathcal{P}_q|$ for each query. For full ranking, a comparison of $|\mathcal{P}_q| = \binom{n(q)}{2}$ pairs has to be done. In the case of multipartite ranking at r rank levels, each including $|l_i|$ rewrites, pairwise comparisons between rewrites at the same rank level can be ignored. This reduces the number of comparisons to $|\mathcal{P}_q| = \sum_{i=1}^{r-1}\sum_{j=i+1}^{r}|l_i||l_j|$. For bipartite ranking of p positive and n negative instances, $|\mathcal{P}_q| = p \cdot n$ comparisons are necessary.

3.2.4 Log-linear Models for Bipartite Ranking

A probabilistic model for bipartite ranking can be defined as the conditional probability of the set of relevant rewrites, i.e., rewrites at rank level 1, given all rewrites at rank levels 1 and 2. A formalization in the family of log-linear models yields the following logistic loss function ℓ_{llm} that was used for discriminative estimation from sets of partially labeled data in Riezler et al. (2002):

$$\ell_{llm}(w) = -\log \frac{\sum_{x_{qi}\in x_q | y_{qi}=1} e^{\langle w, \phi(x_{qi})\rangle}}{\sum_{x_{qi}\in x_q} e^{\langle w, \phi(x_{qi})\rangle}}.$$

The gradient of ℓ_{llm} is calculated as a difference between two expectations:

$$\frac{\partial}{\partial w_k}\ell_{llm} = -p_w\left[\phi_k | x_q; y_{qi} = 1\right] + p_w\left[\phi_k | x_q\right].$$

The SGD computation for the log-linear model is dominated by the computation of expectations for each query. The logistic loss for bipartite ranking is henceforth referred to as the *log-linear* model.

4 Experimental Results

In the experiments reported in this paper, we trained linear ranking models on 1 billion query-rewrite pairs using 60 dense features, combined of the building blocks of syntactic and semantic similarity metrics under different estimations of cost matrices. Development testing was done on a data set that was held-out from the training set. Final testing was carried out on the manually labeled dataset. Data statistics for all sets are given in Table 1.

Table 3: P-values computed by approximate randomization test for 15 pairwise comparisons of result differences.

	Best-feature	SVM-bipart.	SVM-MAP	Log-linear	SVM-pos.-sens.	SVM-multipart.
Best-feature	-	< 0.005	< 0.005	< 0.005	< 0.005	< 0.005
SVM-bipart.	-	-	**0.324**	< 0.005	< 0.005	< 0.005
SVM-MAP	-	-	-	**0.374**	< 0.005	< 0.005
Log-linear	-	-	-	-	**0.053**	< 0.005
SVM-pos.-sens.	-	-	-	-	-	< 0.005
SVM-multipart.	-	-	-	-	-	-

Model selection was performed by adjusting meta-parameters on the development set. We trained each model at constant learning rates $\eta \in \{1, 0.5, 0.1, 0.01, 0.001\}$, and evaluated each variant after every fifth out of 100 passes over the training set. The variant with the highest MAP score on the development set was chosen and evaluated on the test set. This early stopping routine also served for regularization.

Evaluation results for the systems are reported in Table 2. We evaluate all models according to the following evaluation metrics: Mean Average Precision (MAP), Normalized Discounted Cumulative Gain with a cutoff at rank 10 (NDCG@10), Area-under-the-ROC-curve (AUC), Precision@n[3]. As baselines we report a random permutation of rewrites (*random*), and the single dense feature that performed best on the development set (*best-feature*). The latter is the log-probability assigned to the query-rewrite pair by the probabilistic clustering model used for cost matrix estimation (see Section 2.5). P-values are reported in Table 3 for all pairwise comparisons of systems (except the random baseline) using an Approximate Randomization test where stratified shuffling is applied to results on the query level (see Noreen (1989)). The rows in Tables 2 and 3 are ranked according to MAP values of the systems. *SVM-multipartite* outperforms all other ranking systems under all evaluation metrics at a significance level ≥ 0.995. For all other pairwise comparisons of result differences, we find result differences of systems ranked next to each other to be not statistically significant. All systems outperform the *random* and *best-feature* baselines with statistically significant result differences. The distinctive advantage of the *SVM-multipartite* models lies in the possibility to rank rewrites with very high co-click numbers even higher than rewrites with reasonable numbers of co-clicks. This preference for ranking the top co-clicked rewrites high seems the best avenue for transferring co-click information to the human judgements encoded in the manually labeled test set. Position-sensitive margin rescaling does not seem to help, but rather seems to hurt.

[3]For a definition of these metrics see Manning et al. (2008)

5 Discussion

We presented an approach to learn rankings of query rewrites from large amounts of user query log data. We showed how to use the implicit co-click feedback about rewrite quality in user log data to train ranking models that perform well on ranking query rewrites according to human quality standards. We presented large-scale experiments using SGD optimization for linear ranking models. Our experimental results show that an SVM model for multipartite ranking outperforms other linear ranking models under several evaluation metrics. In future work, we would like to extend our approach to other models, e.g., sparse combinations of lexicalized features.

References

R. Agrawal, A. Halverson, K. Kenthapadi, N. Mishra, and P. Tsaparas. 2009. Generating labels from clicks. In *Proceedings of the 2nd ACM International Conference on Web Search and Data Mining*, Barcelona, Spain.

Doug Beeferman and Adam Berger. 2000. Agglomerative clustering of a search engine query log. In *Proceedings of the 6th ACM SIGKDD International Conference on Knowledge Discovery and Data Mining (KDD'00)*, Boston, MA.

P. Boldi, F. Bonchi, C. Castillo, and S. Vigna. 2009. From 'Dango' to 'Japanese cakes': Query reformulation models and patterns. In *Proceedings of Web Intelligence*. IEEE Cs Press.

G. Bouma. 2009. Normalized (pointwise) mutual information in collocation extraction. In *Proceedings of GSCL*.

Soumen Chakrabarti, Rajiv Khanna, Uma Sawant, and Chiru Bhattacharayya. 2008. Structured learning for non-smooth ranking losses. In *Proceedings of the 14th ACM SIGKDD Conference on Knowledge Discovery and Data Mining (KDD'08)*, Las Vegas, NV.

Olivier Chapelle and S. Sathiya Keerthi. 2010. Efficient algorithms for ranking with SVMs. *Information Retrieval Journal*.

Kenneth Church and Patrick Hanks. 1990. Word association norms, mutual information and lexicography. *Computational Linguistics*, 16(1):22–29.

Massimiliano Ciaramita, Amaç Herdağdelen, Daniel Mahler, Maria Holmqvist, Keith Hall, Stefan Riezler, and Enrique Alfonseca. 2010. Generalized syntactic and semantic models of query reformulation. In *Proceedings of the 33rd ACM SIGIR Conference*, Geneva, Switzerland.

Corinna Cortes, Mehryar Mohri, and Asish Rastogi. 2007. Magnitude-preserving ranking algorithms. In *Proceedings of the 24th International Conference on Machine Learning (ICML'07)*, Corvallis, OR.

Larry Fitzpatrick and Mei Dent. 1997. Automatic feedback using past queries: Social searching? In *Proceedings of the 20th Annual International ACM SIGIR Conference*, Philadelphia, PA.

Alon Halevy, Peter Norvig, and Fernando Pereira. 2009. The unreasonable effectiveness of data. *IEEE Intelligent Systems*, 24:8–12.

Thorsten Joachims. 2002. Optimizing search engines using clickthrough data. In *Proceedings of the 8th ACM SIGKDD Conference on Knowledge Discovery and Data Mining (KDD'08)*, New York, NY.

Thorsten Joachims. 2005. A support vector method for multivariate performance measures. In *Proceedings of the 22nd International Conference on Machine Learning (ICML'05)*, Bonn, Germany.

Rosie Jones, Benjamin Rey, Omid Madani, and Wiley Greiner. 2006. Generating query substitutions. In *Proceedings of the 15th International World Wide Web conference (WWW'06)*, Edinburgh, Scotland.

T. Lau and E. Horvitz. 1999. Patterns of search: analyzing and modeling web query refinement. In *Proceedings of the seventh international conference on User modeling*, pages 119–128. Springer-Verlag New York, Inc.

V.I. Levenshtein. 1966. Binary codes capable of correcting deletions, insertions, and reversals. *Soviet Physics Doklady*, 10(8):707–710.

Christopher D. Manning, Prabhakar Raghavan, and Hinrich Schütze. 2008. *Introduction to Information Retrieval*. Cambridge University Press.

Eric W. Noreen. 1989. *Computer Intensive Methods for Testing Hypotheses. An Introduction*. Wiley, New York.

G. Recchia and M.N. Jones. 2009. More data trumps smarter algorithms: comparing pointwise mutual information with latent semantic analysis. *Behavioral Research Methods*, 41(3):647–656.

S.Y. Rieh and H. Xie. 2006. Analysis of multiple query reformulations on the web: the interactive information retrieval context. *Inf. Process. Manage.*, 42(3):751–768.

Stefan Riezler and Fabio De Bona. 2009. Simple risk bounds for position-sensitive max-margin ranking algorithms. In *Proceedings of the Workshop on Advances in Ranking at the 23rd Annual Conference on Neural Information Processing Systems (NIPS'09)*, Whistler, Canada.

Stefan Riezler, Tracy H. King, Ronald M. Kaplan, Richard Crouch, John T. Maxwell, and Mark Johnson. 2002. Parsing the Wall Street Journal using a Lexical-Functional Grammar and discriminative estimation techniques. In *Proceedings of the 40th Annual Meeting of the Association for Computational Linguistics (ACL'02)*, Philadelphia, PA.

Herbert Rubenstein and John B. Goodenough. 1965. Contextual correlates of synonymy. *Communications of the ACM*, 10(3):627–633.

Mehran Sahami and Timothy D. Heilman. 2006. A web-based kernel function for measuring the similarity of short text snippets. In *Proceedings of the 15th International World Wide Web conference (WWW'06)*, Edinburgh, Scotland.

Libin Shen and Aravind K. Joshi. 2005. Ranking and reranking with perceptron. *Journal of Machine Learning Research*, 60(1-3):73–96.

Sidney Siegel and John Castellan. 1988. *Nonparametric Statistics for the Behavioral Sciences. Second Edition*. MacGraw-Hill, Boston, MA.

Ioannis Tsochantaridis, Thomas Hofmann, Thorsten Joachims, and Yasemin Altun. 2004. Support vector machine learning for interdependent and structured output spaces. In *Proceedings of the 21st International Conference on Machine Learning (ICML'04)*, Banff, Canada.

Yisong Yue, Thomas Finley, Filip Radlinski, and Thorsten Joachims. 2007. A support vector method for optimizing average precision. In *Proceedings of the 30th Annual International ACM SIGIR Conference*, Amsterdam, The Netherlands.

Learning to Link Entities with Knowledge Base

Zhicheng Zheng, Fangtao Li, Minlie Huang, Xiaoyan Zhu
State Key Laboratory of Intelligent Technology and Systems
Tsinghua National Laboratory for Information Science and Technology
Department of Computer Science and Technology, Tsinghua University, Beijing 100084, China
{zhengzc04,fangtao06}@gmail.com, {aihuang,zxy-dcs}@tsinghua.edu.cn

Abstract

This paper address the problem of entity linking. Specifically, given an entity mentioned in unstructured texts, the task is to link this entity with an entry stored in the existing knowledge base. This is an important task for information extraction. It can serve as a convenient gateway to encyclopedic information, and can greatly improve the web users' experience. Previous learning based solutions mainly focus on classification framework. However, it's more suitable to consider it as a ranking problem. In this paper, we propose a learning to rank algorithm for entity linking. It effectively utilizes the relationship information among the candidates when ranking. The experiment results on the TAC 2009[1] dataset demonstrate the effectiveness of our proposed framework. The proposed method achieves 18.5% improvement in terms of accuracy over the classification models for those entities which have corresponding entries in the Knowledge Base. The overall performance of the system is also better than that of the state-of-the-art methods.

1 Introduction

The entity linking task is to map a named-entity mentioned in a text to a corresponding entry stored in the existing Knowledge Base. The Knowledge Base can be considered as an encyclopedia for entities. It contains definitional, descriptive or relevant information for each entity. We can acquire the knowledge of entities by looking up the Knowledge Base. Wikipedia is an online encyclopedia, and now it becomes one of the largest repositories of encyclopedic knowledge. In this paper, we use Wikipedia as our Knowledge Base.

Entity linking can be used to automatically augment text with links, which serve as a convenient gateway to encyclopedic information, and can greatly improve user experience. For example, Figure 1 shows news from BBC.com. When a user is interested in "Thierry Henry", he can acquire more detailed information by linking *"Thierry Henry"* to the corresponding entry in the Knowledge Base.

Figure 1: Entity linking example

Entity linking is also useful for some information extraction (IE) applications. We can make use of information stored in the Knowledge Base to assist the IE problems. For example, to answer the question *"When was the famous basketball player Jordan born?"*, if the Knowledge Base contains the en-

[1] http://www.nist.gov/tac/

Human Language Technologies: The 2010 Annual Conference of the North American Chapter of the ACL, pages 483–491,
Los Angeles, California, June 2010.

tity of basketball player Michael Jordan and his information (such as infobox[2] in Wikipedia), the correct answer *"February 17, 1963"* can be easily retrieved.

Entity linking encounters the problem of entity ambiguity. One entity may refer to several entries in the Knowledge Base. For example, the entity "Michael Jordan" can be linked to the basketball player or the professor in UC Berkeley.

Previous solutions find that classification based methods are effective for this task (Milne and Witten, 2008). These methods consider each candidate entity independently, and estimate a probability that the candidate entry corresponds to the target entity. The candidate with the highest probability was chosen as the target entity. In this way, it's more like a ranking problem rather than a classification problem. Learning to rank methods take into account the relations between candidates, which is better than considering them independently. Learning to rank methods are popular in document information retrieval, but there are few studies on information extraction. In this paper, we investigate the application of learning to rank methods to the entity linking task. And we compare several machine learning methods for this task. We investigate the pairwise learning to rank method, Ranking Perceptron (Shen and Joshi, 2005), and the listwise method, ListNet (Cao et al., 2007). Two classification methods, SVM and Perceptron, are developed as our baselines. In comparison, learning to rank methods show significant improvements over classification methods, and ListNet achieves the best result. The best overall performance is also achieved with our proposed framework.

This paper is organized as follows. In the next section we will briefly review the related work. We present our framework for entity linking in section 3. We then describe in section 4 learning to rank methods and features for entity linking. A top1 candidate validation module will be explained in section 5. Experiment results will be discussed in section 6. Finally, we conclude the paper and discusses the future work in section 7.

[2]Infoboxes are tables with semi-structured information in some pages of Wikipedia

2 Related Work

There are a number of studies on named entity disambiguation, which is quite relevant to entity linking. Bagga and Baldwin (1998) used a Bag of Words (BOW) model to resolve ambiguities among people. Mann and Yarowsky (2003) improved the performance of personal names disambiguation by adding biographic features. Fleischman (2004) trained a Maximum Entropy model with Web Features, Overlap Features, and some other features to judge whether two names refer to the same individual. Pedersen (2005) developed features to represent the context of an ambiguous name with the statistically significant bigrams.

These methods determined to which entity a specific name refer by measuring the similarity between the context of the specific name and the context of the entities. They measured similarity with a BOW model. Since the BOW model describes the context as a term vector, the similarity is based on co-occurrences. Although a term can be one word or one phrase, it can't capture various semantic relations. For example, "Michael Jordan now is the boss of Charlotte Bobcats" and "Michael Jordan retired from NBA". The BOW model can't describe the relationship between *Charlotte Bobcats* and *NBA*. Malin and Airoldi (2005) proposed an alternative similarity metric based on the probability of walking from one ambiguous name to another in a random walk within the social network constructed from all documents. Minkov (2006) considered extended similarity metrics for documents and other objects embedded in graphs, facilitated via a lazy graph walk, and used it to disambiguate names in email documents. Bekkerman and McCallum (2005) disambiguated web appearances of people based on the link structure of Web pages. These methods tried to add background knowledge via social networks. Social networks can capture the relatedness between terms, so the problem of a BOW model can be solved to some extent. Xianpei and Jun (2009) proposed to use Wikipedia as the background knowledge for disambiguation. By leveraging Wikipedia's semantic knowledge like social relatedness between named entities and associative relatedness between concepts, they can measure the similarity between entities more accurately. Cucerzan (2007) and

Bunescu (2006) used Wikipedia's category information in the disambiguation process. Using different background knowledge, researcher may find different efficient features for disambiguation.

Hence researchers have proposed so many efficient features for disambiguation. It is important to integrate these features to improve the system performance. Some researchers combine features by manual rules or weights. However, it is not convenient to directly use these rules or weights in another data set. Some researchers also try to use machine learning methods to combine the features. Milne and Witten (2008) used typical classifiers such as Naive Bayes, C4.5 and SVM to combine features. They trained a two-class classifier to judge whether a candidate is a correct target. And then when they try to do disambiguation for one query, each candidate will be classified into the two classes: correct target or incorrect target. Finally the candidate answer with the highest probability will be selected as the target if there are more than one candidates classified as answers. They achieve great performance in this way with three efficient features. The classifier based methods can be easily used even the feature set changed. However, as we proposed in Introduction, it's not the best way for such work. We'll detail the learning to rank methods in the next section.

3 Framework for Entity Linking

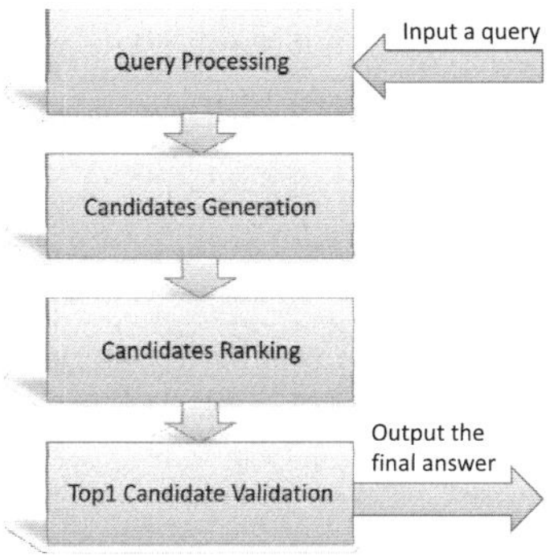

Figure 2: The framework for entity linking

Entity linking is to align a named-entity mentioned in a text to a corresponding entry stored in the existing Knowledge Base. We proposed a framework to solve the "entity linking" task. As illustrated in Figure 2, when inputting a query which is an entity mentioned in a text, the system will return the target entry in Knowledge Base with four modules:

1. Query Processing. First, we try to correct the spelling errors in the queries by using query spelling correction supplied by Google. Second, we expand the query in three ways: expanding acronym queries from the text where the entity is located, expanding queries with the corresponding redirect pages of Wikipedia and expanding queries by using the anchor text in the pages from Wikipedia.

2. Candidates Generation. With the queries generated in the first step, the candidate generation module retrieves the candidates from the Knowledge Base. The candidate generation module also makes use of the disambiguation pages in Wikipedia. If there is a disambiguation page corresponding to the query, the linked entities listed in the disambiguation page are added to the candidate set.

3. Candidates Ranking. In the module, we rank all the candidates with learning to rank methods.

4. Top1 Candidate Validation. To deal with those queries without appropriate matching, we finally add a validation module to judge whether the top one candidate is the target entry.

The detail information of ranking module and validation module will be introduced in next two sections.

4 Learning to Rank Candidates

In this section we first introduce the learning to rank methods, and then describe the features for ranking methods.

4.1 Learning to rank methods

Learning to rank methods are popular in the area of document retrieval. There are mainly two types of learning to rank methods: pairwise and listwise. The pairwise approach takes as instances object pairs in a ranking list for a query in learning. In this way, it transforms the ranking problem to the classification problem. Each pair from ranking list is labeled based on the relative position or with the score of ranking objects. Then a classification model can be trained on the labeled data and then be used for ranking. The pairwise approach has advantages in that the existing methodologies on classification can be applied directly. The listwise approach takes candidate lists for a query as instances to train ranking models. Then it trains a ranking function by minimizing a listwise loss function defined on the predicted list and the ground truth list.

To describe the learning to rank methods, we first introduce some notations:

- Query set Q = $\{ \; ^{(\,)} \; = 1 : \; \}$.
- Each query $^{(\,)}$ is associated with a list of objects(in document retrieval, the objects should be documents), $^{(\,)} = \{ \; ^{(\,)} \; = 1 : \; ^{(\,)}\}$.
- Each object list has a labeled score list $^{(\,)} = \{ \; ^{(\,)} \; = 1 : \; ^{(\,)}\}$ represents the relevance degree between the objects and the query.
- Features vectors $^{(\,)}$ from each query-object pair, $= 1 : \; ^{(\,)}$.
- Ranking function f, for each $^{(\,)}$ it outputs a score $(\; ^{(\,)})$. After the training phase, to rank the objects, just use the ranking function f to output the score list of the objects, and rank them with the score list.

In the paper we will compare two different learning to rank approaches: Ranking Perceptron for pairwise and ListNet for listwise. A detailed introduction on Ranking Perceptron (Shen and Joshi, 2005) and ListNet (Cao et al., 2007) is given.

4.1.1 Ranking Perceptron

Ranking Perceptron is a pairwise learning to rank method. The score function $(\; ^{(\,)})$ is defined as $< \; , \; ^{(\,)} >$.

For each pair $(\; ^{(\,)}_1, \; ^{(\,)}_2)$, $(\; ^{(\,)}_1 - \; ^{(\,)}_2)$ is computed. With a given margin function $(\; ^{(\,)}_1, \; ^{(\,)}_2)$ and a positive rate , if $(\; ^{(\,)}_1 - \; ^{(\,)}_2) \leq (\; ^{(\,)}_1, \; ^{(\,)}_2)$, an update is performed:

$$^{+1} = \; + (\; ^{(\,)}_1 - \; ^{(\,)}_2) \; (\; ^{(\,)}_1, \; ^{(\,)}_2)$$

After iterating enough times, we can use the function to rank candidates.

SOME FORMULAS/TEXT MAY BE MISSING DUE TO FORMATTING ISSUES IN THE ORIGINAL E-MEDIA VERSION

4.1.2 ListNet

ListNet takes lists of objects as instances in learning. It uses a probabilistic method to calculate the listwise loss function.

ListNet transforms into probability distributions both the scores of the objects assigned by the oracle ranking function and the real score of the objects given by human.

Let denote a permutation on the objects. In ListNet algorithm, the probability of with given scores is defined as: $(\;) = \; _{=1} \; \frac{(\; (\;)) (\;)}{(\quad)}$

Then the top k probability of $\mathcal{G} \; (\; _1, \; _2, \ldots, \;)$ can be calculated as:

$$(\mathcal{G} \; (\; _1, \; _2, \ldots, \;)) = \; _{=1} \; \frac{(\;)}{(\;)}$$

The ListNet uses a listwise loss function with Cross Entropy as metric:

$$(\; ^{(\,)}, \; ^{(\,)}) = - \sum_{\forall \; \in \mathcal{G}} \; _{(\,)}(\;) \; (\; _{(\,)}(\;))$$

Denote as the ranking function based on Neural Network model . The gradient of $(\; ^{(\,)}, \; ^{(\,)}(\;))$ with respect to parameter can be calculated as:

$$= \frac{\partial \; (\; ^{(\,)}, \; ^{(\,)}(\;))}{\partial}$$

$$= - \sum_{\forall \; \in \mathcal{G}} \frac{\partial \; _{(\,)(\;)}(\;)}{\partial} \; \frac{_{(\,)}(\;)}{_{(\,)(\;)}(\;)}$$

In each iteration, the is updated with $- \; \times$ in a gradient descent way. Here is the learning rate.

To train a learning to rank model, the manually evaluated score list for each query's candidate list is required. We assign 1 to the real target entity and 0 to the others.

4.2 Features for Ranking

In the section, we will introduce the features used in the ranking module. For convenience, we define some symbols first:

Q represents a query, which contains a named entity mentioned in a text. CSet represents the candidate entries in Knowledge Base for the query Q. C represents a candidate in CSet.

Q's nameString represents the name string of Q. Q's sourceText represents the source text of Q. Q's querySet represents the queries which are expansions of Q's nameString.

C's title represents the title of corresponding Wikipedia article of C. C's titleExpand represents the union set of the redirect set of C and the anchor text set of C. C's article represents the Wikipedia article of C.

C's nameEntitySet represents the set of all named entities in C's article labeled by Stanford NER (Finkel et al., 2005). Q's nameEntitySet represents the set of all named entities in Q's sourceText.

C's countrySet represents the set of all countries in C's article, and we detect the countries from text via a manual edited country list. Q's countrySet represents the set of all countries in Q's sourceText. C's countrySetInTitle represents the set of countries exist in one of the string s from C's titleExpand.

C's citySetInTitle represents the set of all cities exist in one of the string s from C's titleExpand, and we detect the cities from text via a manual edited list of famous cities. Q's citySet represents the set of all cities in Q's sourceText.

Q's type represents the type of query Q. It's labeled by Stanford NER. C's type is manually labeled already in the Knowledge Base.

The features that used in the ranking module can be divided into 3 groups: Surface, Context and Special. Each of these feature groups will be detailed next.

4.2.1 Surface Features

The features in Surface group are used to measure the similarity between the query string and candidate entity's name string.

StrSimSurface. The feature value is the maximum similarity between the Q's nameString and each string s in the set C's titleExpand. The string similarity is measured with edit distance.

ExactEqualSurface. The feature value is 1 if there is a string s in set C's titleExpand same as the Q's nameString, or the Candidate C is extracted from the disambiguation page. In other case, the feature value is set to 0.

StartWithQuery. The feature value is 1 if there is a string s in set C's titleExpand starting with the Q's nameString, and C's ExactEqualSurface is not 1. In other case, the feature value is set to 0.

EndWithQuery. The feature value is 1 if there is a string s in set C's titleExpand ending with the Q's nameString, and C's ExactEqualSurface is not 1. In other case, the feature value is set to 0.

StartInQuery. The feature value is 1 if there is a string s in set C's titleExpand that s is the prefix of the Q's nameString, and C's ExactEqualSurface is not 1. In other case, the feature value is set to 0.

EndInQuery. The feature value is 1 if there is a string s in set C's titleExpand that s is the postfix of the Q's nameString, and C's ExactEqualSurface is not 1. In other case, the feature value is set to 0.

EqualWordNumSurface. The feature value is the maximum number of same words between the Q's nameString and each string s in the set C's titleExpand.

MissWordNumSurface. The feature value is the minimum number of different words between the Q's nameString and each string s in the set C's titleExpand.

4.2.2 Context Features

The features in Context group are used to measure the context relevance between query and the candidate entity. We mainly consider the TF-IDF similarity and named entity co-occurrence.

TFSimContext. The feature value is the TF-IDF similarity between the C's article and Q's sourceText.

TFSimRankContext. The feature value is the inverted rank of C's TFSimContext in the CSet.

AllWordsInSource. The feature value is 1 if all words in C's title exist in Q's sourceText, and in other case, the feature value is set to 0.

NENumMatch. The feature value is the number of of same named entities between C's nameEntitySet and Q's nameEntitySet. Two named entities are judged to be the same if and only if the two named entities' strings are identical.

4.2.3 Special Features

Besides the features above, we also find that the following features are quite significant in the entity linking task: country names, city names and types of queries and candidates.

CountryInTextMatch. The feature value is the number of same countries between C's countrySet and Q's countrySet.

CountryInTextMiss. The feature value is the number of countries that exist in Q's countrySet but do not exist in C's countrySet.

CountryInTitleMatch. The feature value is the number of same countries between C's countrySetInTitle and Q's countrySet.

CountryInTitleMiss. The feature value is the number of countries that exist in C's countrySetInTitle but do not exist in Q's countrySet.

CityInTitleMatch. The feature value is the number of same cities between C's citySetInTitle and Q's citySet.

TypeMatch. The feature value is 0 if C's type is not consistent with Q's type, in other case, the feature value is set to 1.

When ranking the candidates in CSet, the features' value was normalized into [0, 1] to avoid noise caused by large Integer value or small double value.

5 Top 1 Candidate Validation

To deal with those queries without target entities in the Knowledge Base, we supply a Top 1 candidate validation module. In the module, a two-class classifier is used to judge whether the top one candidate is the true target entity. The top one candidate selected from the ranking module can be divided into two classes: target and non-target, depending on whether it's the correct target link of the query. According to the performance of classification, SVM is chosen as the classifier (In practice, the libsvm package is used) and the SVM classifier is trained on the entire training set.

Most of the features used in the validation module are the same as those in ranking module, such as StrSimSurface, EqualWordNumSurface, MissWordNumSurface, TFSimContext, AllWordsInSource, NENumMatch and TypeMatch. We also design some other features, as follows:

AllQueryWordsInWikiText. The feature value is one if Q's textRetrievalSet contains C, and in other case the feature value is set to zero. The case that Q's textRetrievalSet contains C means the candidate C's article contains the Q's nameString.

CountryInTextPer. The feature is the percentage of countries from Q's countrySet exist in C's countrySet too. The feature can be seen as a normalization of CountryInTextMatch/Miss features in ranking module.

ScoreOfRank. The feature value is the score of the candidate given by the ranking module. The ScoreOfRank takes many features in ranking module into consideration, so only fewer features of ranking module are used in the classifier.

6 Experiment and Analysis

6.1 Experiment Setting

Algorithm	Accuracy	Improvement over SVM
ListNet	**0.9045**	+18.5%
Ranking Perceptron	0.8842	+15.8%
SVM	0.7636	-
Perceptron	0.7546	-1.2%

Table 1: Evaluation of different ranking algorithm

Set	Features in Set
Set1	Surface Features
Set2	Set1+TF-IDF Features
Set3	Set2+AllWordsInSource
Set4	Set3+NENumMatch
Set5	Set4+CountryInTitle Features
Set6	Set5+CountryInText Features
Set7	Set6+CityInTitleMatch
Set8	Set7+MatchType

Table 2: Feature Sets

Entity linking is initiated as a task in this year's TAC-KBP[3] track, so we use the data from this track. The entity linking task in the KBP track is to map an entity mentioned in a news text to the Knowledge Base, which consist of articles from Wikipedia. The KBP track gives a sample query set which consists of 416 queries for developing. The test set consists of 3904 queries. 2229 of these queries can't be mapped to Knowledge Base, for which the systems should return NIL links. The remaining 1675 queries all can be aligned to Knowledge Base. We will firstly analyze the ranking methods with those non-NIL queries, and then with an additional validation module, we train and test with all queries including NIL queries.

As in the entity linking task of KBP track, the accuracy is taken as

$$\text{accuracy} = \frac{\#(\text{correct answered queries})}{\#(\text{total queries})}$$

6.2 Evaluation of Machine Learning Methods in ranking

As mentioned in the section of related work, learning to rank methods in entity linking performs better than the classification methods. To justify this, some experiments are designed to evaluate the performance of our ranking module when adopting different algorithms.

To evaluate the performance of the ranking module, we use all the queries which can be aligned to a target entry in the Knowledge Base. The training set contains 285 valid queries and the test set contains 1675.

[3]http://apl.jhu.edu/ paulmac/kbp.html

Three algorithms are taken into comparison: ListNet, Ranking Perceptron, and classifier based methods. The classifier based methods are trained by dividing the candidates into two classes: target and non-target. Then, the candidates are ranked according to their probability of being classified as target. two different classifiers are tested here, SVM and Perceptron.

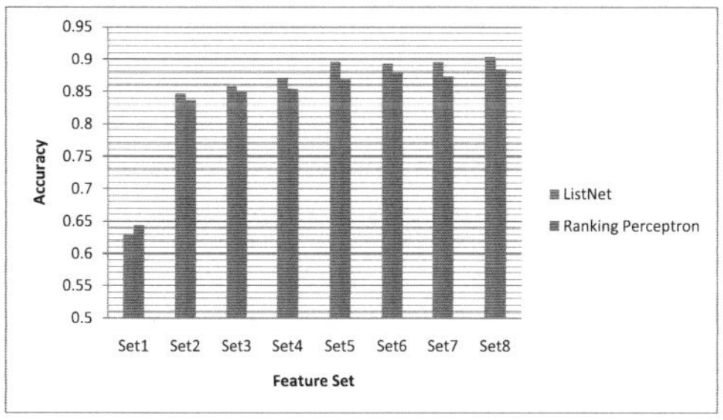

Figure 3: Comparison of ListNet and Ranking Perceptron

As shown in Table 1, the two learning to rank methods perform much better than the classification based methods. The experiment results prove our point that the learning to rank algorithms are more suitable in this work. And the ListNet shows slight improvement over Ranking Perceptron, but since the improvement is not so significant, maybe it depends on the feature set. To confirm this, we compare the two algorithms with different features, as showed in Table 2. In Figure 3, The ListNet outperforms Ranking Perceptron with all feature sets except Set1, which indicates that the listwise approach is more suitable than the pairwise approach. The pairwise approach suffers from two problems: first, the objective of learning is to minimize classification er-

Systems	Accuracy of all queries	Accuracy of non-NIL queries	Accuracy of NIL queries
System1	0.8217	0.7654	0.8641
System2	0.8033	0.7725	0.8241
System3	0.7984	0.7063	0.8677
ListNet+SVM	**0.8494**	**0.79**	**0.8941**

Table 3: Evaluation of the overall performance, compared with KBP results (System 1-3 demonstrate the top three ranked systems)

rors but not to minimize the errors in ranking; second, the number of pairs generated from list varies largely from list to list, which will result in a model biased toward lists with more objects. The issues are also discussed in (Y.B. Cao et al., 2006; Cao et al., 2007). And the listwise approach can fix the problems well.

As the feature sets are added incrementally, it can be used for analyzing the importance of the features to the ranking task. Although Surface Group only takes into consideration the candidate's title and the query's name string, its accuracy is still higher than 60%. This is because many queries have quite small number of candidates, the target entry can be picked out with the surface features only. The result shows that after adding the TF-IDF similarity related features, the accuracy increases significantly to 84.5%. Although TF-IDF similarity is a simple way to measure the contextual similarity, it performs well in practice. Another improvement is achieved when adding the CountryInTitleMatch and CountryInTitleMiss features. Since a number of queries in test set need to disambiguate candidates with different countries in their titles, the features about country in the candidates' title are quite useful to deal with these queries. But it doesn't mean that the features mentioned above are the most important. Because many features correlated with each other quite closely, adding these features doesn't lead to remarkable improvement. The conclusion from the results is that the Context Features significantly improve the ranking performance and the Special Features are also useful in the entity linking task.

6.3 Overall Performance Evaluation

We are also interested in overall performance with the additional validation module. We use all the 3904 queries as the test set, including both NIL and non-NIL queries. The top three results from the KBP track (McNamee and Dang, 2009) are selected as comparison. The evaluation result in Table 3 shows that our proposed framework outperforms the best result in the KBP track, which demonstrates the effectiveness of our methods.

7 Conclusions and Future Work

This paper demonstrates a framework of learning to rank for linking entities with the Knowledge Base. Experimenting with different ranking algorithms, it shows that the learning to rank methods perform much better than the classification methods in this problem. ListNet achieves 18.5% improvement over SVM, and Ranking Perceptron gets 15.8% improvement over SVM. We also observe that the listwise learning to rank methods are more suitable for this problem than pairwise methods. We also add a validation module to deal with those entities which have no corresponding entry in the Knowledge Base. We also evaluate the proposed method on the whole data set given by the KBP track, for which we add a binary SVM classification module to validate the top one candidate. The result of experiment shows the proposed strategy performs better than all the systems participated in the entity linking task.

In the future, we will try to develop more sophisticated features in entity linking and design a typical learning to rank method for the entity linking task.

Acknowledgments

This work was partly supported by the Chinese Natural Science Foundation under grant No.60973104 and No. 60803075, partly carried out with the aid of a grant from the International Development Research Center, Ottawa, Canada IRCI project from the International Development.

References

Bagga and Baldwin. 1998. *Entity-Based Cross-Document Coreferencing Using the Vector Spcae Model. in Proceedings of HLT/ACL.*

Gideon S. Mann and David Yarowsky. 2003. *Unsupervised Personal Name Disambiguation. in Proceedings of CONIL.*

Michael Ben Fleishman. 2004. *Multi-Document Person Name Resolution. in Proceedings of ACL.*

Ted Pedersen, Amruta Purandare and Anagha Kulkarni. 2005. *Name Discrimination by Clustering Similar Contexts. in Proceedings of CICLing.*

B.Malin and E. Airoldi. 2005. *A Network Analysis Model for Disambiguation of Names in Lists. in Proceedings of CMOT.*

Einat Minkov, William W. Cohen and Andrew Y. Ng. 2006. *Contextual Search and Name Disambiguation in Email Using Graph. in Proceedings of SIGIR.*

Ron Bekkerman and Andrew McCallum. 2005. *Disambiguating Web Appearances of People in a Social Network. in Proceedings of WWW.*

Xianpei Han and Jun Zhao. 2009. *Named Entity Disambiguation by Leveraging Wikipedia Semantic Knowledge. in Proceedings of CIKM.*

David Milne and Ian H. Witten. 2008. *Learning to Link with Wikipedia. in Proceedings of CIKM.*

Herbrich, R., Graepel, T. and Obermayer K. 1999. *Support vector learning for ordinal regression. in Proceedings of ICANN.*

Freund, Y., Iyer, R., Schapire, R. E. and Singer, Y. 1998. *An efficient boosting algorithm for combining preferences. in Proceedings of ICML.*

Burges, C., Shaked, T., Renshaw, E., Lazier, A., Deeds, M., Hamilton, N. and Hullender, G. 2005. *Learning to rank using gradient descent. in Proceedings of ICML.*

Cao, Y. B., Xu, J., Liu, T. Y., Li, H., Huang, Y. L. and Hon, H. W. 2006. *Adapting ranking SVM to document retrieval. in Proceedings of SIGIR.*

Cao, Z., Qin, T., Liu, T. Y., Tsai, M. F. and Li, H. 2007. *Learning to rank: From pairwise approach to listwise approach. in Proceedings of ICML.*

Qin, T., Zhang, X.-D., Tsai, M.-F., Wang, D.-S., Liu, T.Y., and Li, H. 2007. *Query-level loss functions for information retrieval. in Proceedings of Information processing and management.*

L. Shen and A. Joshi. 2005. *Ranking and Reranking with Perceptron. Machine Learning,*60(1-3),pp. 73-96.

Silviu Cucerzan. 2007. *Large-Scale Named Entity Disambiguation Based on Wikipedia Data. in Proceedings of EMNLP-CoNLL.*

Razvan Bunescu and Marius Pasca. 2006. *Using Encyclopedic Knowledge for Named Entity Disambiguation. in Proceedings of EACL.*

Paul McNamee and Hoa Dang. 2009. *Overview of the TAC 2009 Knowledge Base Population Track (DRAFT). in Proceedings of TAC.*

Jenny Rose Finkel, Trond Grenager, and Christopher Manning. 2005. *Incorporating Non-local Information into Information Extraction Systems by Gibbs Sampling. Proceedings of the 43nd Annual Meeting of the Association for Computational Linguistics (ACL 2005)*, pp. 363-370.

Improving the Multilingual User Experience of Wikipedia Using Cross-Language Name Search

Raghavendra Udupa
Microsoft Research India
Bangalore, India.

Mitesh Khapra *
Indian Institute of Technology Bombay
Powai, India.

Abstract

Although Wikipedia has emerged as a powerful collaborative Encyclopedia on the Web, it is only partially multilingual as most of the content is in English and a small number of other languages. In real-life scenarios, non-English users in general and ESL/EFL [1] users in particular, have a need to search for relevant English Wikipedia articles as no relevant articles are available in their language. The multilingual experience of such users can be significantly improved if they could express their information need in their native language while searching for English Wikipedia articles. In this paper, we propose a novel cross-language name search algorithm and employ it for searching English Wikipedia articles in a diverse set of languages including Hebrew, Hindi, Russian, Kannada, Bangla and Tamil. Our empirical study shows that the multilingual experience of users is significantly improved by our approach.

1 Introduction

Since its inception in 2001, Wikipedia has emerged as the most famous free, web-based, collaborative, and multilingual encyclopedia with over 13 million articles in over 270 languages. However, Wikipedia exhibits severe asymmetry in the distribution of its content in the languages of the world with only a small number of languages dominating (see Table 1). As a consequence, most users of the under-represented languages of the world have no choice but to consult foreign language Wikipedia articles for satisfying their information needs.

Table 1: Linguistic asymmetry of Wikipedia

Language	Speakers	Contributors	Articles
English	1500M	47.1%	3,072,373
Russian	278M	5.2%	441,860
Hebrew	10M	0.7%	97,987
Hindi	550M	0.06%	50,926
Bangla	230M	0.02%	20,342
Tamil	66M	0.04%	19,472
Kannada	47M	0.02%	7,185

Although consulting foreign language Wikipedia is not a solution for the problem of linguistic asymmetry, in the specific case of ESL/EFL users who form a sizable fraction of Internet users of the world [2], it is arguably the most practical option today. Typically, ESL/EFL users are reasonably good at reading and extracting relevant information from English content but not so good at expressing their information needs in English. In particular, getting the spellings of foreign names in English correctly is very difficult for most ESL/EFL users due to the differences in the way a foreign name is pronounced in the native languages. For instance, Japanese EFL speakers often break consonant clusters in foreign names using vowels (see Table 2) and Hindi ESL speakers find it difficult to differentiate between 'an', 'en', and 'on' in English names (such as 'Clin-

*This work was done when the author was a summer intern at Microsoft Research India.

[1] *English as Second Language* and *English as Foreign Language*.

[2] As per some estimates, there are about 1 Billion ESL and EFL speakers in the world today and their number is growing.

Human Language Technologies: The 2010 Annual Conference of the North American Chapter of the ACL, pages 492–500,
Los Angeles, California, June 2010.

ton') and will most likely use 'an' ('Clintan').

Table 2: Influence of native language on the English spelling of names.

Wikipedia Entity	Hindi	Japanese	Kannada
Stephen Hawking	Stefan Hoking	Suchifun Houkingu	Steephan Haakimg
Paul Krugman	Pol Crugmun	Pooru Kuruguman	Paal Kragaman
Haroun al-Rashid	Haroon al-Rashid	Haruun aru-Rasheedo	Haroon al-Rasheed
Subrahmaniya Bharati	Subramaniya Bharati	Suburaamaniya Bahaarachi	Subrahmanya Bharathi

In principle, English spell-checkers (Ahmad and Kondrak, 2005) can handle the problem of incorrect spellings in the queries formed by ESL/EFL users. But in practice, there are two difficulties. Firstly, most English spell-checkers do not have a good coverage of names which form the bulk of user queries. Secondly, spelling correction of names is difficult because spelling mistakes are markedly influenced by the native language of the user. Not surprisingly, Wikipedia's inbuilt spell-checker suggests *"Suchin Housing"* as the only alternative to the query *"Suchifun Houkingu"* instead of the correct entity *"Stephen Hawking"* (See Table 3 for more examples).

The inability of ESL/EFL speakers to express their information needs correctly in English and the poor performance of spell-checkers highlight the need for a practical solution for the linguistic asymmetry problem of Wikipedia. In this work, we argue the multilingual user experience of ESL/EFL users can be significantly improved by allowing them to express their information need in their native language. While it might seem that we would need a fully functional cross-language retrieval system that supports translation of non-English queries to English, we note that a good number of the pages in Wikipedia are on people. This empirical fact allows us to improve the multilingual experience of ESL/EFL Wikipedia users by means of cross-language name search which is less resource demanding than a fully functional cross-language retrieval system.

There are several challenges that need to be addressed in order to enable cross-language name search in Wikipedia.

Table 3: Spelling suggestions by Wikipedia.

User Input	Wikipedia's Suggestion	Correct Spelling
Suchifun Houkingu	Suchin Housing	Stephen Hawking
Stefan Hoking	Stefan Ho king	Stephen Hawking
Pol Crugman	Poll Krugman	Paul Krugman
Paal Kragaman	Paul Krugman	Paul Krugman
Suburaamaniya Bahaarachi	Subramaniya Baracchi	Subrahmaniya Bharati

- Firstly, name queries are expressed by ESL/EFL users in the native languages using the orthography of those languages. Transliterating the name into Latin script using a Machine Transliteration system is an option but state-of-the-art Machine Transliteration technologies are still far away from producing the correct transliteration. Further, as pointed out by (Udupa et al., 2009a), it is not enough if a Machine Transliteration system generates a correct transliteration; it must produce the transliteration that is present in the Wikipedia title.

- Secondly, there are about 6 million titles (including redirects) in English Wikipedia which rules out the naive approach of comparing the query with every one of the English Wikipedia titles for transliteration equivalence as is done typically in transliteration mining tasks. A practical cross-language name search system for Wikipedia must be able to search millions of Wikipedia titles in a fraction of a second and return the most relevant titles.

- Thirdly, names are typically multi-word and as a consequence there might not be an exact match between the query and English Wikipedia titles. Any cross-language name search system for Wikipedia must be able to deal with multi-word names and partial matches effectively.

- Fourthly, the cross-language name search system must be tolerant to spelling variations in the query as well as the Wikipedia titles.

In this work, we propose a novel approach to cross-language name search in Wikipedia that addresses all the challenges described above. Further, our approach does not depend on either spell-checkers or Machine Transliteration. Rather we transform the problem into a geometric search problem and employ a state-of-the-art geometric algorithm for searching a very large database of names. This enables us to accurately search the relevant Wikipedia titles for a given user query in a fraction of a second even on a single processor.

1.1 Our Contributions

Our contributions can be summarized as follows:

1. We introduce a language and orthography independent geometric representation for single-word names (Section 3.1).

2. We model the problem of learning the geometric representation of names as a multi-view learning problem and employ the machinery of Canonical Correlation Analysis (CCA) to compute a low-dimensional Euclidean feature space. We map both foreign single-word names and English single-word names to points in the common feature space and the similarity between two single-word names is an exponentially decaying function of the squared geometric distance between the corresponding points (Section 3).

3. We model the problem of searching a database of names as a geometric nearest neighbor problem in low-dimensional Euclidean space and employ the well-known ANN algorithm for approximate nearest neighbors to search for the equivalent of a query name in the English Wikipedia titles (Arya et al., 1998) (Section 3.3).

4. We introduce a simple and efficient algorithm for computing the similarity scores of multi-word names from the single-word similarity scores (Section 3.4).

5. We show experimentally that our approach significantly improves the multilingual experience of ESL/EFL users (Section 4).

2 Related Work

Although approximate similarity search is well-studied, we are not aware of any non-trivial cross-language name search algorithm in the literature. However, several techniques for mining name transliterations from monolingual and comparable corpora have been studied (Pasternack and Roth, 2009), (Goldwasser and Roth, 2008), (Klementiev and Roth, 2006), (Sproat et al., 2006), (Udupa et al., 2009b). These techniques employ various transliteration similarity models. Character unigrams and bigrams were used as features to learn a discriminative transliteration model and time series similarity was combined with the transliteration similarity model (Klementiev and Roth, 2006). A generative transliteration model was proposed and used along with cross-language information retrieval to mine named entity transliterations from large comparable corpora (Udupa et al., 2009b). However, none of these transliteration similarity models are applicable for searching very large name databases as they rely on brute-force search. Not surprisingly, (Pasternack and Roth, 2009) report that *".. testing [727 single word English names] with fifty thousand [Russian] candidates is a large computational hurdle (it takes our model about seven hours)"*.

Several algorithms for string similarity search have been proposed and applied to various problems (Jin et al., 2005). None of them are directly applicable to cross-language name search as they are based on the assumption that the query string shares the same alphabet as the database strings.

Machine Transliteration has been studied extensively in the context of Machine Translation and Cross-Language Information Retrieval (Knight and Graehl, 1998), (Virga and Khudanpur, 2003), (Kuo et al., 2006), (Sherif and Kondrak, 2007), (Ravi and Knight, 2009), (Li et al., 2009), (Khapra and Bhattacharyya, 2009). However, Machine Transliteration followed by string similarity search gives less-than-satisfactory solution for the cross-language name search problem as we will see later in Section 4.

CCA was introduced by Hotelling in 1936 and has

been applied to various problems including CLIR, Text Clustering, and Image Retrieval (Hardoon et al., 2004). Recently, CCA has gained importance in the Machine Learning community as a technique for multi-view learning. CCA computes a common semantic feature space for two-view data and allows users to query a database using either of the two views. CCA has been used in bilingual lexicon extraction from comparable corpora (Gaussier et al., 2004) and monolingual corpora (Haghighi et al., 2008).

Nearest neighbor search is a fundamental problem where challenge is to preprocess a set of points in some metric space into a geometric data structure so that given a query point, its k-nearest neighbors in the set can be reported as fast as possible. It has applications in many areas including pattern recognition and classification, machine learning, data compression, data mining, document retrieval and statistics. The brute-force search algorithm can find the nearest neighbors in running time proportional to the product of the number of points and the dimension of the metric space. When the dimension of the metric space is small, there exist algorithms which give better running time than brute-force search. However, the search time grows exponentially with the dimension and none of the algorithms do significantly better than brute-force search for high-dimensional data. Fortunately, efficient algorithms exist if instead of exact nearest neighbors, we ask for approximate nearest neighbors (Arya et al., 1998).

3 Cross-Language Name Search as a Geometric Search Problem

The key idea behind our approach is the following: if we can embed names as points (or equivalently as vectors) in a suitable geometric space, then the problem of searching a very large database of names can be casted as a geometric search problem, i.e. one of finding the nearest neighbors of the query point in the database.

As illustrative examples, consider the names *Stephen* and *Steven*. A simple geometric representation for these names is the one induced by their corresponding features: $\{St, te, ep, ph, he, en\}$ and $\{St, te, ev, ve, en\}$ [3]. In this representation, each character bigram constitutes a dimension of the geometric feature space whose coordinate value is the number of times the bigram appears in the name. It is possible to find a low-dimensional representation for the names by using Principal Components Analysis or any other dimensionality reduction technique on the bigram feature vectors. However, the key point to note is that once we have an appropriate geometric representation for names, the similarity between two names can be computed as

$$K_{mono}\left(name1, name2\right) = e^{-||\phi_1 - \phi_2||^2/2\epsilon^2} \quad (1)$$

where ϕ_1 and ϕ_2 are the feature vectors of the two names and ϵ is a constant. Armed with the geometric similarity measure, we can leverage geometric search techniques for finding names similar to the query.

In the case of cross-language name search, we need a feature representation of names that is language/script independent. Once we map names in different languages/scripts to the same feature space, we can essentially treat similarity search as a geometric search problem.

3.1 Language/Script Independent Geometric Representation of Names

To obtain language/script independent geometric representation of names, we start by forming the language/script specific feature vectors as described in Section 3. Given two names, *Stephen* in Latin script and स्टीफन in Devanagari script, we form the corresponding character bigram feature vectors ϕ (using features $\{St, te, ep, ph, en\}$) and ψ (using features {स्ट, टी, ीफ, फन}) respectively. We then map these vectors to a common geometric feature space using two linear transformations A and B:

$$\phi \rightarrow A^T\phi = \phi_s \in R^d \quad (2)$$

$$\psi \rightarrow B^T\psi = \psi_s \in R^d \quad (3)$$

The vectors ϕ_s and ψ_s can be viewed as language/script independent representation of the names *Stephen* and स्टीफन.

[3]Here, we have employed character bigrams as features. In principle, we can use any suitable set of features including phonetic features extracted from the strings.

3.1.1 Cross-Language Similarity of Names

In order to search a database of names in English when the query is in a native language, say Hindi, we need to be able to measure the similarity of a name in Devangari script with names in Latin script. The language/script independent representation gives a natural way to measure the similarity of names across languages. By embedding the language/script specific feature vectors ϕ and ψ in a common feature space via the projections A and B, we can compute the similarity of the corresponding names as follows:

$$K_{cross}\left(name1, name2\right) = e^{-||\phi_s - \psi_s||^2/2\epsilon^2} \quad (4)$$

It is easy to see from Equation 4 that the similarity score of two names is small when the projections of the names are negatively correlated.

3.2 Learning Common Feature Space using CCA

Ideally, the transformations A and B should be such that similar names in the two languages are mapped to close-by points in the common geometric feature space. It is possible to learn such transformations from a training set of name transliterations in the two languages using the well-known multi-view learning framework of Canonical Correlation Analysis (Hardoon et al., 2004). By viewing the language/script specific feature vectors as two representations/views of the same semantic object, the entity whose name is written as $Stephen$ in English and as स्टीफन in Hindi, we can employ the machinery of CCA to find the transformations A and B.

Given a sample of multivariate data with two views, CCA finds a linear transformation for each view such that the correlation between the projections of the two views is maximized. Consider a sample $Z = \{(x_i, y_i)\}_{i=1}^N$ of multivariate data where $x_i \in R^m$ and $y_i \in R^n$ are two views of the object. Let $X = \{x_i\}_{i=1}^N$ and $Y = \{y_i\}_{i=1}^N$. Assume that X and Y are centered[4], i.e., they have zero mean. Let a and b be two directions. We can project X onto the direction a to get $U = \{u_i\}_{i=1}^N$ where $u_i = a^T x_i$. Similarly, we can project Y onto the direction b to get the projections $V = \{v_i\}_{i=1}^n$ where $v_i = b^T y_i$. The aim of CCA is to find a pair of directions (a, b) such that the projections U and V are maximally correlated. This is achieved by solving the following optimization problem:

$$\begin{aligned}\rho &= max_{(a,b)} \frac{< Xa, Xb >}{||Xa||||Xb||} \\ &= max_{(a,b)} \frac{a^T XY^T b}{\sqrt{a^T XX^T a}\sqrt{b^T YY^T b}}\end{aligned}$$

The objective function of Equation 5 can be maximized by solving the following generalized eigen value problem (Hardoon et al., 2004):

$$\begin{aligned}XY^T \left(YY^T\right)^{-1} YX^T a &= \lambda^2 XX^T a \\ \left(YY^T\right)^{-1} YX^T a &= \lambda b\end{aligned}$$

The subsequent basis vectors can be found by adding the orthogonality of bases constraint to the objective function. Although the number of basis vectors can be as high as $\min\{Rank(X), Rank(Y)\}$, in practice, only the first few basis vectors are used since the correlation of the projections is high for these vectors and small for the remaining vectors.

Let A and B be the first $d > 0$ basis vectors computed by CCA.

Figure 1: Projected names (English-Hindi).

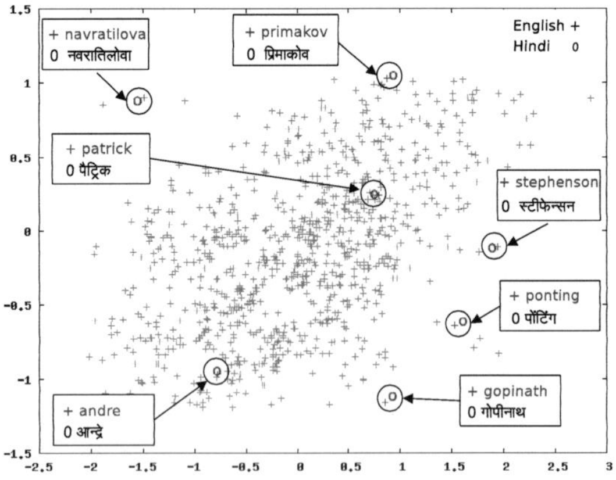

3.2.1 Common Geometric Feature Space

As described in Section 3.1, we represent names as points in the common geometric feature space defined by the projection matrices A and B. Figure 1

[4] If X and Y are not centered, they can be centered by subtracting the respective means.

shows a 2-dimensional common feature space computed by CCA for English (Latin script) and Hindi (Devanagari script) names. As can be seen from the figure, names that are transliterations of each other are mapped to near-by points in the common feature space.

Figure 2 shows a 2-dimensional common feature space for English (Latin script) and Russian (Cyrillic script) names. As can be seen from the figure, names that are transliterations of each other are mapped to near-by points in the common feature space.

Figure 2: Projected names (English-Russian).

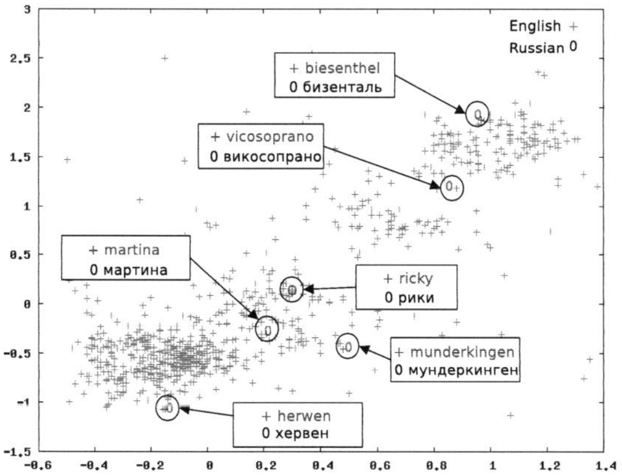

3.3 Querying the Name Database

Given a database $D = \{e_i\}_{i=1}^{M}$ of single-word names in English, we first compute their language/script specific feature vectors $\phi^{(i)}$, $i = 1, \ldots, M$. We then compute the projections $\phi_s^{(i)} = A^T\phi^{(i)}$. Thus, we transform the name database D into a set of vectors $\{\phi_s^{(1)}, \ldots, \phi_s^{(M)}\}$ in R^d.

Given a query name h in Hindi, we compute its language/script specific feature vector ψ and project it on to the common feature space to get $\psi_s = B^T\psi \in R^d$. Names similar to h in the database D can be found as solutions of the k-nearest neighbor problem:

$$\begin{aligned} e_{i_k} &= argmax_{e_i \in D - \{e_{i_j}\}_{j=1}^{k-1}} K_{cross}(e_i, h) \\ &= argmax_{e_i \in D - \{e_{i_j}\}_{j=1}^{k-1}} e^{-\|\phi_s^{(i)} - \psi_s\|^2/2\epsilon^2} \\ &= argmin_{e_i \in D - \{e_{i_j}\}_{j=1}^{k-1}} \|\phi_s^{(i)} - \psi_s\| \end{aligned}$$

Unfortunately, computing exact k-nearest neighbors in dimensions much higher than 8 is difficult and the best-known methods are only marginally better than brute-force search (Arya et al., 1998). Fortunately, there exist very efficient algorithms for computing approximate nearest neighbors and in practice they do nearly as well as the exact nearest neighbors algorithms (Arya et al., 1998). It is also possible to control the tradeoff between accuracy and running time by specifiying a maximum approximation error bound. We employ the well-known Approximate Nearest Neighbors (aka ANN) algorithm by Arya and Mount which is known to do well in practice when $d \leq 100$ (Arya et al., 1998).

3.4 Combining Single-Word Similarities

The approach described in the previous sections works only for single-word names. We need to combine the similarities at the level of individual words into a similarity function for multi-word names. Towards this end, we form a weighted bipartite graph from the two multi-word names as follows:

We first tokenize the Hindi query name into single word tokens and find the nearest English neighbors for each of these Hindi tokens using the method outlined section 3.3. We then find out all the English Words which contain one or more of the English neighbors thus fetched. Let $E = e_1e_2 \ldots e_I$ be one such multi-word English name and $H = h_1h_2 \ldots h_J$ be the multi-word Hindi query. We form a weighted bipartite graph $G = (S \cup T, W)$ with a node s_i for the ith word e_i in E and node t_j for the jth word h_j in H. The weight of the edge (s_i, t_j) is set as $w_{ij} = K_{cross}(e_i, h_j)$.

Let w be the weight of the maximum weighted bipartite matching in the graph G. We define the similarity between E and H as follows:

$$K_{cross}(E, H) = \frac{w}{|I - J| + 1}. \quad (5)$$

The numerator of the right hand side of Equation 5 favors name pairs which have a good number of high quality matches at the individual word level whereas the denominator penalizes pairs that have disproportionate lengths.

Note that, in practice, both I and J are small and hence we can find the maximum weighted bipartite matching very easily. Further, most edge weights in

Figure 3: Combining Single-Word Similarities.

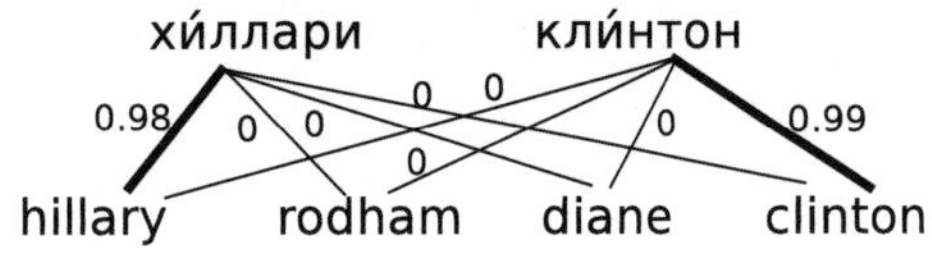

the bipartite graph are negligibly small. Therefore, even a greedy matching algorithm suffices in practice.

4 Experiments and Results

In the remainder of this section, we refer to our system by GEOM-SEARCH.

4.1 Experimental Setup

We tested our cross language name search system using six native languages, *viz.*, Russian, Hebrew, Hindi, Kannada, Tamil and Bangla. For each of these languages, we created a test set consisting of 1000 multi-word name queries and found manually the most relevant Wikipedia article for each query in the test set. The Wikipedia articles thus found and all the redirect titles that linked to them formed the gold standard for evaluating the performance of our system.

In order to compare the performance of GEOM-SEARCH with a reasonable baseline, we implemented the following baseline: We used a state-of-the art Machine Transliteration system to generate the best transliteration of each of the queries. We used the edit distance between the transliteration and the single-word English name as the similarity score. We combined single word similarities using the approach described in Section 3.4. We refer to this baseline by TRANS-SEARCH.

Note that several English Wikipedia names sometimes get the same score for a query. Therefore, we used a tie-aware mean-reciprocal rank measure to evaluate the performance (McSherry and Najork, 2008).

4.2 GEOM-SEARCH

The training and search procedure employed by GEOM-SEARCH are described below.

4.2.1 CCA Training

We learnt the linear transformations A and B that project the language/script specific feature vectors to the common feature space using the approach discussed in Section 3.2. The learning algorithm requires a training set consisting of pairs of single-word names in English and the respective native language. We used approximately $15,000$ name pairs for each native language.

A key parameter in CCA training is the number of dimensions of the common feature space. We found the optimal number of dimensions using a tuning set consisting of $1,000$ correct name pairs and $1,000$ incorrect name pairs for each native language. We found that $d = 50$ is a very good choice for each native language.

Another key aspect of training is the choice of language/script specific features. For the six languages we experimented with and also for English, we found that character bigrams formed a good set of features. We note that for languages such as Chinese, Japanese, and Korean, unigrams are the best choice. Also, for these languages, it may help to syllabify the English name.

4.2.2 Search

As a pre-processing step, we extracted a list of 1.3 million unique words from the Wikipedia titles. We computed the language/script specific feature vector for each word in this list and projected the vector to the common feature space as described in Section 3.1. The low-dimensional embeddings thus computed formed the input to the ANN algorithm.

We tokenized each query in the native language into constituent words. For each constituent, we first computed the language/script specific feature vector, projected it to the common feature space, and found the k-nearest neighbors using the ANN algorithm. We used k=100 for all our experiments.

After finding the nearest neighbors and the corresponding similarity scores, we combined the scores using the approach described in Section 3.4.

4.3 TRANS-SEARCH

The training and search procedure employed by TRANS-SEARCH are described below.

Figure 4: Top scoring English Wikipedia page retrieved by GEOM-SEARCH

Hebrew		Russian	
אלכסנדר ריבאק	Alexander Rybak	мёзер юстус	Justus Moser
אילת מזר	Eilat Mazar	спалланцани ладзаро	Lazzaro Spallanzani
לריאה קינגסטון	Laryea Kingston	бахтияр теймур	Teymur Bakhtiar
אליאס פיגרואה	Elias Figueroa	исраэлс йозеф	Jozef Israels
פדורה ברביירי	Fedora Barbieri	бэкон фрэнсис	Francis Bacon
Hindi		**Kannada**	
आन्द्रे अगासी	Andre Agassi	ಬೆಂಜಮಿನ್ ನೆತನ್ಯಾಹು	Benjamin Netanyahu
ऐल्बर्ट आइनस्टाइन	Albert Einstein	ವಿನ್ಸೆಂಟ್ ವಾನ್ ಗೋ	Vincent Van Gogh
अकिरा कुरोसावा	Kurosawa Akira	ಬರ್ನಾರ್ಡ್ ಕುರ್ಟೋಯಿಸ್	Bernard Courtois
अर्नेस्ट हेमिंगवे	Ernest Hemingway	ಪೆರ್ ತಿಯೊಡೊರ್ ಕ್ಲೀವ್	Per Teodor Cleve
जेम्स वाट	James Watt	ಸ್ಪೆನ್ಸರ್ ಟ್ರೇಸಿ	Spencer Tracy

4.3.1 Transliteration Training

We used a state-of-the-art CRF-based transliteration technique for transliterating the native language names (Khapra and Bhattacharyya, 2009). We used CRF++, an open-source CRF training tool, to train the transliteration system. We used exactly the same features and parameter settings as described in (Khapra and Bhattacharyya, 2009). As in the case of CCA, we use around $15,000$ single word name pairs in the training.

4.3.2 Search

The preprocessing step for TRANS-SEARCH is the same as that for GEOM-SEARCH. We transliterated each constituent of the query into English and find all single-word English names that are at an edit distance of at most 3. We computed the similarity score as described in Section 3.4.

4.4 Evaluation

We evaluated the performance of GEOM-SEARCH and TRANS-SEARCH using a tie-aware mean reciprocal rank (MRR). Table 4 compares the average time per query and the MRR of the two systems.

GEOM-SEARCH performed significantly better than the transliteration based baseline system for all the six languages. On an average, the relevant English Wikipedia page was found in the top 2 results produced by GEOM-SEARCH for all the six native languages. Clearly, this shows that GEOM-SEARCH is highly effective as a cross-langauge name search system. The good results also validate our claim that cross-language name search can improve the multi-lingual user experience of ESL/EFL users.

Table 4: MRR and average time per query (in seconds) for the two systems.

Language	GEOM		TRANS	
	Time	MRR	Time	MRR
Hin	0.51	0.686	2.39	0.485
Tam	0.23	0.494	2.16	0.291
Kan	1.08	0.689	2.17	0.522
Ben	1.30	0.495	–	–
Rus	0.15	0.563	1.65	0.476
Heb	0.65	0.723	–	–

5 Conclusions

GEOM-SEARCH, a geometry-based cross-language name search system for Wikipedia, improves the multilingual experience of ESL/EFL users of Wikipedia by allowing them to formulate queries in their native languages. Further, it is easy to integrate a Machine Translation system with GEOM-SEARCH. Such a system would find the relevant English Wikipedia page for a query using GEOM-SEARCH and then translate the relevant Wikipedia pages to the native language using the Machine Translation system.

6 Acknowledgement

We thank Jagadeesh Jagarlamudi and Shaishav Kumar for their help.

References

Farooq Ahmad and Grzegorz Kondrak. 2005. Learning a spelling error model from search query logs. In *HLT '05: Proceedings of the conference on Human Language Technology and Empirical Methods in Natural Language Processing*, pages 955–962, Morristown, NJ, USA. Association for Computational Linguistics.

Sunil Arya, David M. Mount, Nathan S. Netanyahu, Ruth Silverman, and Angela Y. Wu. 1998. An optimal algorithm for approximate nearest neighbor searching fixed dimensions. *J. ACM*, 45(6):891–923.

Éric Gaussier, Jean-Michel Renders, Irina Matveeva, Cyril Goutte, and Hervé Déjean. 2004. A geometric view on bilingual lexicon extraction from comparable corpora. In *ACL*, pages 526–533.

Dan Goldwasser and Dan Roth. 2008. Transliteration as constrained optimization. In *EMNLP*, pages 353–362.

Aria Haghighi, Percy Liang, Taylor Berg-Kirkpatrick, and Dan Klein. 2008. Learning bilingual lexicons from monolingual corpora. In *Proceedings of ACL-08: HLT*, pages 771–779, Columbus, Ohio, June. Association for Computational Linguistics.

David R. Hardoon, Sándor Szedmák, and John Shawe-Taylor. 2004. Canonical correlation analysis: An overview with application to learning methods. *Neural Computation*, 16(12):2639–2664.

Liang Jin, Nick Koudas, Chen Li, and Anthony K. H. Tung. 2005. Indexing mixed types for approximate retrieval. In *VLDB*, pages 793–804.

Mitesh Khapra and Pushpak Bhattacharyya. 2009. Improving transliteration accuracy using word-origin detection and lexicon lookup. In *Proceedings of the 2009 Named Entities Workshop: Shared Task on Transliteration (NEWS 2009)*. Association for Computational Linguistics.

Alexandre Klementiev and Dan Roth. 2006. Named entity transliteration and discovery from multilingual comparable corpora. In *HLT-NAACL*.

Kevin Knight and Jonathan Graehl. 1998. Machine transliteration. *Computational Linguistics*, 24(4):599–612.

Jin-Shea Kuo, Haizhou Li, and Ying-Kuei Yang. 2006. Learning transliteration lexicons from the web. In *ACL*.

John D. Lafferty, Andrew McCallum, and Fernando C. N. Pereira. 2001. Conditional random fields: Probabilistic models for segmenting and labeling sequence data. In *ICML*, pages 282–289.

Haizhou Li, A Kumaran, Vladimir Pervouchine, and Min Zhang. 2009. Report of news 2009 machine transliteration shared task. In *Proceedings of the 2009 Named Entities Workshop: Shared Task on Transliteration (NEWS 2009)*. Association for Computational Linguistics.

Frank McSherry and Marc Najork. 2008. Computing information retrieval performance measures efficiently in the presence of tied scores. In *ECIR*, pages 414–421.

Jeff Pasternack and Dan Roth. 2009. Learning better transliterations. In *CIKM*, pages 177–186.

Sujith Ravi and Kevin Knight. 2009. Learning phoneme mappings for transliteration without parallel data. In *NAACL-HLT*.

Hanan Samet. 2006. *Foundations of Multidimensional and Metric Data Structures (The Morgan Kaufmann Series in Computer Graphics)*. Morgan Kaufmann, August.

Tarek Sherif and Grzegorz Kondrak. 2007. Substring-based transliteration. In *ACL*.

Richard Sproat, Tao Tao, and ChengXiang Zhai. 2006. Named entity transliteration with comparable corpora. In *ACL*.

Raghavendra Udupa, K. Saravanan, Anton Bakalov, and Abhijit Bhole. 2009a. "they are out there, if you know where to look": Mining transliterations of oov query terms for cross-language information retrieval. In *ECIR*, pages 437–448.

Raghavendra Udupa, K. Saravanan, A. Kumaran, and Jagadeesh Jagarlamudi. 2009b. Mint: A method for effective and scalable mining of named entity transliterations from large comparable corpora. In *EACL*, pages 799–807.

Paola Virga and Sanjeev Khudanpur. 2003. Transliteration of proper names in cross-language applications. In *SIGIR*, pages 365–366.

Learning Words and Their Meanings from Unsegmented Child-directed Speech

Bevan K. Jones & Mark Johnson
Dept of Cognitive and Linguistic Sciences
Brown University
Providence, RI 02912, USA
{Bevan_Jones,Mark_Johnson}@Brown.edu

Michael C. Frank
Dept of Brain and Cognitive Science
Massachusetts Institute of Technology
Cambridge, MA 02139, USA
mcfrank@mit.edu

Abstract

Most work on language acquisition treats word segmentation—the identification of linguistic segments from continuous speech—and word learning—the mapping of those segments to meanings—as separate problems. These two abilities develop in parallel, however, raising the question of whether they might interact. To explore the question, we present a new Bayesian segmentation model that incorporates aspects of word learning and compare it to a model that ignores word meanings. The model that learns word meanings proposes more adult-like segmentations for the meaning-bearing words. This result suggests that the non-linguistic context may supply important information for learning word segmentations as well as word meanings.

1 Introduction

Acquiring a language entails mastering many learning tasks simultaneously, including identifying where words begin and end in continuous speech and learning meanings for those words. It is common to treat these tasks as separate, sequential processes, where segmentation is a prerequisite to word learning but otherwise there are few if any dependencies. The earliest evidence of segmentation, however, is for words bordering a child's own name (Bortfeld et al., 2005). In addition, infants begin learning their first words before they achieve adult-level competence in segmentation. These two pieces of evidence raise the question of whether the tasks of meaning learning and segmentation might mutually inform one another.

To explore this question we present a joint model that simultaneously identifies word boundaries and attempts to associate meanings with words. In doing so we make two contributions. First, by modeling the two levels of structure in parallel we simulate a more realistic situation. Second, a joint model allows us to explore possible synergies and interactions. We find evidence that our joint model performs better on a segmentation task than an alternative model that does not learn word meanings.

The picture in Figure 1 depicts a language learning situation from our corpus (originally from Fernald and Morikawa, 1993; recoded in Frank et al., 2009) where a mother talks while playing with various toys. Setting down the dog and picking up the hand puppet of a pig, she asks, "Is that the pig?" Starting out, a young learner not only does not know that the word "pig" refers to the puppet but does not even know that "pig" is a word at all. Our model simulates the learning task, taking as input the unsegmented phonemic representation of the speech along with the set of objects in the non-linguistic context as shown in Figure 1 (a), and infers both a segmentation and a word-object mapping as in Figure 1 (b).

One can formulate the word learning task as that of finding a reasonably small set of reusable word-meaning pairs consistent with the underlying communicative intent. Infant directed speech often refers to objects in the immediate environment, and early word learning seems to involve associating frequently co-occurring word-object pairs (Akhtar and Montague, 1999; Markman, 1990). Several computational models are based on this idea that a word

Human Language Technologies: The 2010 Annual Conference of the North American Chapter of the ACL, pages 501–509,
Los Angeles, California, June 2010.

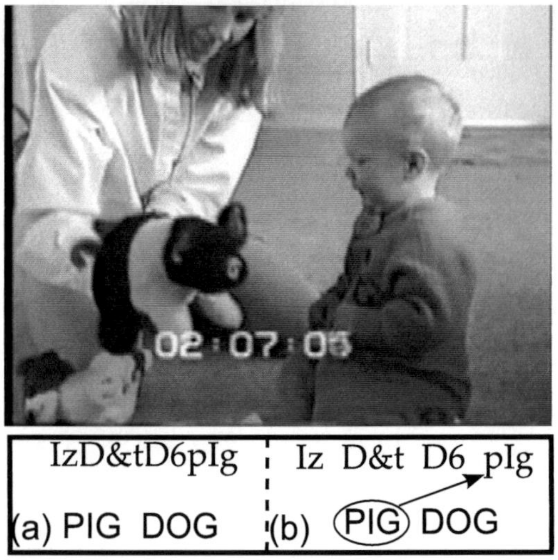

Figure 1: (a) The input to our system for the utterance "Is that the pig?" consists of an unsegmented sequence of phonemes and the set of objects representing the non-linguistic context. These objects were manually identified by inspecting the associated video, a frame from which is shown above. (b) The gold-standard segmentation and word-object assignments of the same utterance, against which the output of our system is evaluated (all words except "pIg" are mapped to a special "null" object, as explained in the text).

that frequently occurs in the presence of an object and not so frequently in its absence is likely to refer to that object (Frank et al., 2009a; Siskind, 1996; Yu and Ballard, 2007). Importantly, all these models assume words are pre-segmented in the input.

While the word segmentation task relates less clearly to the communicative content, it can be formulated according to a similar objective, that of attempting to explain the sound sequences in the input in terms of some reasonably small set of reusable units, or words. Computational models have successfully addressed the problem in much this way (Johnson and Goldwater, 2009; Goldwater et al., 2009; Brent, 1999), and the general approach is consistent with experimental observations that humans are sensitive to statistics of sound sequences (Saffran et al., 1996; Frank et al., 2007).

The two tasks can be integrated in a relatively seamless way, since, as we have just formulated them, they have a common objective, that of finding a minimal, consistent set of reusable units. However, the two deal with different types of information with different dependencies. The basic idea is that learning a vocabulary that both meets the constraints of the word-learning task and is consistent with the objective of the segmentation task can yield a better segmentation. That is, we hope to find a synergy in the joint inference of meaning and segmentation.

Note that to the best of our knowledge there is very little computational work that combines word form and word meaning learning (Frank et al. 2006 takes a first step but their model is applicable only to small artificial languages). Frank et al. (2009a) and Regier (2003) review pure word learning models and, in addition to the papers we have already cited, Brent (1999) presents a fairly comprehensive review of previous pure segmentation models. However, none of the models reviewed make any attempt to jointly address the two problems. Similarly, in the behavioral literature on development, we are aware of only one segmentation study (Graf-Estes et al., 2007) that involves non-linguistic context, though this study treats the two tasks sequentially rather than jointly.

We now describe our model and inference procedure and follow with evaluation and discussion.

2 Model Definition

Cross-situational meaning learning in our joint word learning and segmenting model is inspired by the model of Frank et al. (2009a). Our model can be viewed as a variant of the Latent Dirichlet Allocation (LDA) topic model of Blei et al. (2003), where topics are drawn from the objects in the non-linguistic context. The model associates each utterance with a single referent object, the topic, and every word in the utterance is either generated from a distribution over words associated with that object or else from a distribution associated with a special "null" object shared by all utterances. Note that in this paper we use "topic" to denote the referent object of an utterance, otherwise we depart from topic modeling convention and use the term "object" instead.

Segmentation is based on the unigram model proposed by Brent (1999) and reformulated by Goldwater et al. (2009) in terms of a Dirichlet process. Since both LDA and the unigram segmenter are based on unigram distributions it is relatively straightforward

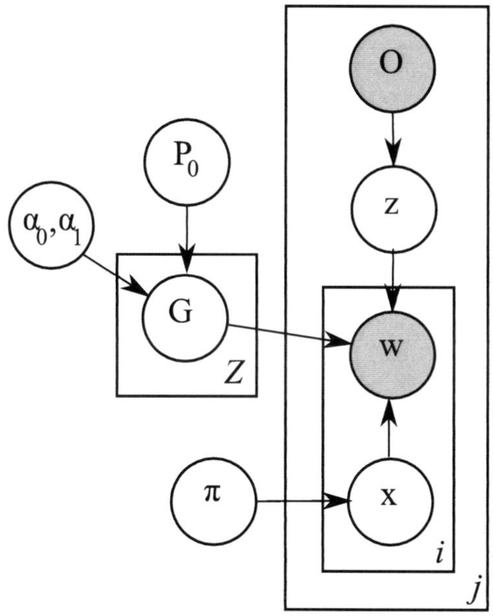

Figure 2: Topical Unigram Model: O_j is the set of objects in the non-linguistic context of the jth utterance, z_j is the utterance topic, w_{ji} is the ith word of the utterance, x_{ji} is the category of the word (referring or non-referring), and the other variables are distribution parameters.

to integrate the two to simultaneously infer word boundaries and word-object associations.

Figure 2 illustrates a slightly simplified form of the model, and the the relevant distributions are as follows:

$$\begin{aligned} z|O &\sim Uniform(O) \\ G_z|z,\alpha_0,\alpha_1,P_0 &\sim \begin{cases} DP(\alpha_1,P_0) & \text{if } z \neq 0 \\ DP(\alpha_0,P_0) & \text{otherwise} \end{cases} \\ \pi &\sim Beta(1,1) \\ x|\pi &\sim Bernoulli(\pi) \\ w|G,z,x &\sim \begin{cases} G_z & \text{if } x = 1 \\ G_0 & \text{if } x = 0 \end{cases} \end{aligned}$$

Note that $Uniform(O)$ denotes a discrete uniform distribution over the elements of the set O. P_0 is described later.

Briefly, each utterance has a single topic z_j, drawn from the objects in the non-linguistic context O_j, and then for each word w_{ji} we first flip a coin x_{ji} to determine if it refers to the topic or not. Then, depending on x_{ji} the word is either drawn from a distribution specific to the topic ($x_{ji} = 1$) or from a distribution associated with the "null" object ($x_j i = 0$). In slightly greater detail but still glossing over the details of how the multinomial parameters are generated, the generative story proceeds as follows:

1. For each utterance, indexed by j
2. (a) Pick a single topic z_j uniformly from the set of objects in the environment O_j
   (b) For each word w_{ji} of the utterance
   (c) i. Determine if it refers to z_j or not by setting x_{ji} to 1 (referring) with probability π, and to 0 (non-referring) otherwise.
       ii. if x_{ji} is 1, draw w_{ji} from the topic specific distribution over words G_{z_j}.
       iii. otherwise, draw w_{ji} from G_0, the distribution over words associated with the "null" object.

This generative story is a simplification since it does not describe how we model utterance boundaries. It is important for segmentation purposes to explicitly model utterance boundaries since, unlike utterance-internal word boundaries, we assume utterance boundaries are observed. Thus, the story is complicated by the fact that there is a chance each time we generate a word that we also generate an utterance boundary. The choice of whether to terminate the utterance or not is captured by a $Bernoulli(\gamma)$ random variable $\$_{ji}$ indicating whether the ith word was the last word of the jth utterance.

$$\begin{aligned} \gamma &\sim Beta(1,1) \\ \$|\gamma &\sim Bernoulli(\gamma) \end{aligned}$$

The G_z multinomial parameters are generated from a Dirichlet process with base distribution over words, P_0, which describes how new word types are generated from their constituent phonemes. Phonemes are generated sequentially, i.i.d. uniformly from m phonemic types. In addition, there is a probability $p_\#$ of generating a word boundary.

$$P_0(w) = (1 - p_\#)^{|w|-1} p_\# \frac{1}{m^{|w|}}$$

The concentration parameters α_0 and α_1 also play a critical role in the generation of words and word types. Any given word has a certain probability of either being produced from the set of previously seen word types, or from an entirely new one. The greater the concentration parameter, the more likely the model is to appeal to the base distribution P_0 to introduce a new word type.

Like Frank et al. (2009a), we distinguish between two coarse grammatical categories, referring and non-referring. Referring words are generated by the topic, while non-referring words are drawn from G_0, a distribution associated with the "null" object. The distinction ensures sparse word-object maps that obey the principle of mutual exclusion. Otherwise all words in the utterance would be associated with the topic object, resulting in a very large set of words for each object that is very likely to overlap with the words for other objects. As a further bias toward a small lexicon, we employ different concentration parameters (α_0 and α_1) for the non-referring and referring words, using a much smaller value for the referring words. Intuitively, there should be a relatively small prior probability of introducing a new word-object pair, corresponding to a small α_1 value. On the other hand, most other words don't refer to the topic object (or any other object for that matter), corresponding to a much larger α_0 value.

Note that this topical unigram model is a straightforward generalization of the unigram segmentation model (Goldwater et al., 2009) to the case of multiple topics. In fact, if all words were assumed to refer to the same object (or to no object at all) the models would be identical.

Unlike LDA, each "document" has only one topic, which is necessitated by the fact that in our model documents correspond single utterances. The utterances in our corpus of child directed speech are often only four or five words long, whereas the general LDA model assumes documents are much larger. Thus, there may not be enough words to infer a useful utterance specific distribution over topics. Consequently, rather than inferring a separate topic distribution for each utterance, we simply assume a uniform distribution over objects in the non-linguistic context. In effect, we rely entirely on the non-linguistic context and word-object associations to infer topics. Though necessitated by data sparsity issues, we also note that it is very rare in our corpus for utterances to refer to more than one object in the non-linguistic context, so the choice of a single topic may also be a more accurate model. In fact, even with multi-sentence documents, LDA may perform better if only one topic is assumed per sentence (Gruber et al., 2007).

3 Inference

We use a collapsed Gibbs sampling procedure, integrating over all possible G_z, π, and γ values and then iteratively sample values for each variable conditioned on the current state of all other variables. We visit each utterance once per iteration, sample a topic, and then visit each possible word boundary location to sample the boundary and word categories simultaneously according to their joint probability.

A single topic is sampled for each utterance, conditioned on the words and their current determinations as referring or non-referring. Since z_j is drawn from a uniform distribution, this probability is simply proportionate to the conditional probability of the words given z_j and the x_{ji} variables.

$$P(z_j|\mathbf{w_j}, \mathbf{x_j}, \mathbf{h}^{-j}) \propto \frac{\Gamma(\sum_w^{W_j} n_{w,z_j}^{(\mathbf{h}^-)} + \alpha_1 P_0(w))}{\Gamma(\sum_w^{W_j} n_{w,z_j}^{(\mathbf{h})} + \alpha_1 P_0(w))} \cdot \prod_w^{W_j} \frac{\Gamma(n_{w,z_j}^{(\mathbf{h})} + \alpha_1 P_0(w))}{\Gamma(n_{w,z_j}^{(\mathbf{h}^-)} + \alpha_1 P_0(w))}$$

Here, $P(z_j|\mathbf{w_j}, \mathbf{x_j}, \mathbf{h}^{-\mathbf{j}})$ is the probability of topic z_j given the current hypothesis $\mathbf{h}$ for all variables excluding those for the current utterance. Also, $n_{w,z_j}^{(\mathbf{h}^{-j})}$ is the count of occurrences of word type w that refer to topic z_j among the current variable assignments, and W_j is the set of word types appearing in utterance j. The vectors of word and category variables in utterance j are represented as $\mathbf{w_j}$ and $\mathbf{x_j}$, respectively. Note that only referring words have any bearing on the appropriate selection of z_j and so all factors involving only non-referring words are absorbed by the constant of proportionality.

The word categories can be sampled conditioned on the current word boundary states according to the following conditional probability, where $n_{x_{ji}}^{(\mathbf{h}^{-ji})}$ is the number of words categorized according to label

x_{ji} over the entire corpus excluding word w_{ji}.

$$\begin{aligned} P(x_{ji}|w_{ji}, z_j, \mathbf{h}^{-ji}) &\propto P(w_{ji}|z_j, x_{ji}, \mathbf{h}^{-ji}) \\ &\cdot P(x_{ji}|\mathbf{h}^{-ji}) \\ &= \frac{n^{(\mathbf{h}^{-ji})}_{w_{ji},x_{ji}z_j} + \alpha_{x_{ji}} P_0(w_{ji})}{n^{(\mathbf{h}^{-ji})}_{\bullet,x_{ji}z_j} + \alpha_{x_{ji}}} \cdot \frac{n^{(\mathbf{h}^{-ji})}_{x_{ji}} + 1}{n^{(\mathbf{h}^{-ji})}_{\bullet} + 2} \end{aligned} \quad (1)$$

In practice, however, we actually sample the word category variables jointly with the boundary states, using a scheme similar to that outlined in Goldwater et al. (2009). We visit each possible word boundary location (any point between two consecutive phonemes) and compute probabilities for the hypotheses for which the phonemic environment makes up either one word or two. As illustrated below there are two sets of cases: those where we treat the segment as a single word, and those where we treat it as two words.

$$\begin{array}{ccc} x_1 & & x_2 \quad x_3 \\ \ldots\#w_1\#\ldots & \text{vs.} & \ldots\#w_2\#w_3\#\ldots \\ \uparrow & & \uparrow \end{array}$$

The probabilities of the hypotheses can be derived by application of equation 1. Since the $\mathbf{x}$ variables can each describe two possible events, there are a total of six different cases to consider for each boundary assignment: two cases without and four with a word boundary.

The probability of each of the two cases without a word boundary can be computed as follows:

$$\begin{aligned} P(w_1, x_1|z, \mathbf{h}^-) = &\frac{n^{(\mathbf{h}^-)}_{w_1,x_1z} + \alpha_{x_1} P_0(w_1)}{n^{(\mathbf{h}^-)}_{\bullet,x_1z} + \alpha_{x_1}} \\ &\cdot \frac{n^{(\mathbf{h}^-)}_{x_1} + 1}{n^{(\mathbf{h}^-)}_{\bullet} + 2} \cdot \frac{n^{(\mathbf{h}^-)}_{\$_1} + 1}{n^{(\mathbf{h}^-)}_{\bullet} + 2} \end{aligned}$$

Here $\mathbf{h}^-$ signifies the current hypothesis for all variables excluding those for the current segment and $n^{(\mathbf{h}^-)}_{\$_1}$ is the count for $\mathbf{h}^-$ of either utterance final words if w_1 is utterance final or non-utterance final words if w_1 is also not utterance final.

In the four cases with a word boundary, we have two words and two categories to sample.

$$\begin{aligned} P(w_2, x_2, w_3, x_3|z, \mathbf{h}^-) = &\frac{n^{(\mathbf{h}^-)}_{w_2,x_2z} + \alpha_{x_2} P_0(w_2)}{n^{(\mathbf{h}^-)}_{\bullet,x_2z} + \alpha_{x_2}} \\ &\cdot \frac{n^{(\mathbf{h}^-)}_{x_2} + 1}{n^{(\mathbf{h}^-)}_{\bullet} + 2} \cdot \frac{n^{(\mathbf{h}^-)}_{\$_2=0} + 1}{n^{(\mathbf{h}^-)}_{\bullet} + 2} \\ &\cdot \frac{n^{(\mathbf{h}^-)}_{w_3,x_3z} + \delta_{x_2}(x_3)\delta_{w_2}(w_3) + \alpha_{x_3} P_0(w_3)}{n^{(\mathbf{h}^-)}_{\bullet,x_3z} + \delta_{x_2}(x_3) + \alpha_{x_3}} \\ &\cdot \frac{n^{(\mathbf{h}^-)}_{x_3} + \delta_{x_2}(x_3) + 1}{n^{(\mathbf{h}^-)}_{\bullet} + 3} \cdot \frac{n^{(\mathbf{h}^-)}_{\$_3} + \delta_{\$_2}(\$_3) + 1}{n^{(\mathbf{h}^-)}_{\bullet} + 3} \end{aligned}$$

Here $\delta_x(y)$ is 1 if $x = y$ and 0 otherwise.

4 Results & Model Comparisons

4.1 Corpus

Our training corpus (Fernald and Morikawa, 1993; Frank et al., 2009b) consists of about 22,000 words and 5,600 utterances. Video recordings consisting of mother-child play over pairs of toys were orthographically transcribed, and each utterance was annotated with the set of objects present in the non-linguistic context. The object referred to by the utterance, if any, was noted, as described in Frank et al. (2009b). We used the VoxForge dictionary to map orthographic words to phoneme sequences in a process similar to that described in Brent (1999).

Figure 1 (a) presents an example of the coding of phonemic transcription and non-linguistic context for a single utterance. The input to the system consists solely of the phonemic transcription and the objects in the non-linguistic context.

4.2 Evaluation

We ran the sampler ten times for 100,000 iterations with parameter settings of $\alpha_1 = 0.01$, $\alpha_0 = 20$, and $p_{\#} = 0.5$, keeping only the final sample for evaluation. We defined the word-object pairs for a sample as the words in the referring category that were paired at least once with a particular topic. These pairs were then compared against a gold standard set of word-object pairs, while segmentation performance was evaluated by comparing the final boundary assignments against the gold standard segmentation.

4.2.1 Word Learning

To explore the contribution of word boundaries to the joint word learning and segmenting task, we compare our full joint model against a variant that only infers topics, using the gold standard segmentation as input. In this way we also reproduce the usual assumption of a sequential relationship between segmentation and word learning and test the necessity of the simplifying assumption. The results are shown in Table 2. We compare them with three different metric types: topic accuracy; precision, recall, and F-score of the word-object pairs; and Kullback-Liebler (KL) divergence.

First, treating utterances with no referring words as though they have no topic, we compute the accuracy of the inferred topics. Note that we don't report accuracy for the the variant with no non-linguistic context, since in this case the objects are interchangeable, and we have a problem identifying which cluster corresponds to which topic. Table 2 shows that the joint segmentation and word learning model gets the topic right for 81% of the utterances. The variant that assumes pre-segmented input does comparably well with an accuracy of 79%. Surprisingly, it seems that knowing the gold segmentation doesn't add very much, at least for the topic inference task.

To evaluate how well we discovered the word-object map, we manually compiled a list of all the nouns in the corpus that named one of the 30 objects. We used this set of nouns, cross-referenced with their topic objects, as a gold standard set of word-object pairs. By counting the co-occurrences, we also compute a gold standard probability distribution for the words given the topic, $P(w|z, x = 1)$.

Precision, recall and F-score are computed as per Frank et al. (2009a). In particular, precision is the fraction of gold pairs among the sampled set and recall is the fraction of sampled pairs among the gold standard pairs.

$$\text{p} = \frac{|\text{Sampled} \cap \text{Gold}|}{|\text{Sampled}|}, \qquad \text{r} = \frac{|\text{Sampled} \cap \text{Gold}|}{|\text{Gold}|}$$

KL divergence is a way of measuring the difference between distributions. Small numbers generally indicate a close match and is zero only when the two are equal. Using the empirical distribution over gold topics $P(z)$, we use the standard formula for KL divergence to compare the gold standard distribution P against the inferred distribution Q. I.e., we compute $D_{KL}(P(w,z)||Q(w,z))$.

The model learns fairly meaningful word-object associations; results are shown in Table 2. As in the case of topic accuracy, the joint and word learning only variants perform similarly, this time with somewhat better performance for the easier task with an F-score and KL divergence of 0.31 and 1.82 vs. 0.28 and 2.78 for the joint task.

Table 1 illustrates the sort of word-object pairs the model discovers. As can be seen, many of the errors are due to the segmentation, usually under-segmentation errors where it segments two words as one. This is a general problem with the unigram segmenter on which our model is based (Goldwater et al., 2009). Yet, even though these segmentation errors are also counted as word learning errors, they are often still meaningful in the sense that the true referring word is a subsequence.

So, word segmentation has an impact on word learning. Yet, the joint model still tends to uncover reasonable meanings. The next question is whether these meanings have an impact on the segmentation.

Object	Words			
BOX	thebox	box		
BRUSH	brush			
BUNNY	rabbit	Rosie		
BUS	bus			
CAR	car	thecar		
CHEESE	cheese			
DOG	thedoggy	doggy		
DOLL	doll	thedoll	yeah	benice
DOUGH	dough			
ERNIE	Ernie			

Table 1: Subset of an inferred word-object mapping. For clarity, the proposed words have been converted to standard English orthography.

	p	r	f	KL	acc
Joint	**0.21**	0.45	0.28	2.78	**0.81**
Gold Seg	**0.21**	**0.60**	**0.31**	**1.82**	0.79

Table 2: Word Learning Performance. Comparing precision, recall, and F-score of word-object pairs, $D_{KL}(P(w,z)||Q(w,z))$, and accuracy of utterance topics for the full joint model and a variant that only infers meanings given a gold standard segmentation.

	NoCon	Random	Joint
Referring Nouns	0.36	0.35	**0.50**
Neighbors	0.33	0.33	**0.37**
Utt Final Nouns	0.36	0.36	**0.52**
Entire Corpus	0.53	0.53	**0.54**

Table 3: Segmentation performance. F-score for three subsets and the full corpus for three variants: the model without non-linguistic context, the model with random topics, and the full joint model.

4.2.2 Word Segmentation

To measure the impact of word learning on segmentation, we again compare the model on the full joint task against two other variants: one where topics are randomly selected, and one that ignores the non-linguistic context. For the random topics variant, we choose each topic during initialization according to the empirical distribution over gold topics and treat these topic assignments as observed variables for subsequent iterations. The variant that ignores non-linguistic context draws topics uniformly from the entire set of objects ever discussed in the corpus, another test of the contribution of the non-linguistic context to segmentation. We report token F-score, computed as per Goldwater et al. (2009), where any segment proposed by the model is a true positive only if it matches the gold segmentation and is a false positive otherwise. Any segment in the gold data not found by the model is a false negative.

Table 3 shows the segmentation performance for various subsets as well as for the entire corpus. Because we are primarily interested in synergies between word learning and segmentation, we focus on the words most directly impacted by the meanings: gold standard referring nouns and their neighboring words.

The model behaves the same with randomized topics as without context; it learns none of the gold standard pairs (no matter how we identify clusters with topics for the contextless case). On all subsets, the full joint model outperforms the other two variants. In particular, the greatest gain is for the referring nouns, with a 21% reduction in error. Also, similar to the findings of Bortfeld et al. (2005) regarding 6 month olds' abilities to segment words adjoining a familiar name, we also find that neighboring words benefit from sharing a word boundary with a learned word.

The model performs exceptionally well on utterance final referring nouns, with a 24% reduction in error. This may explain certain psycholinguistic observations. Frank et al. (2006) performed an artificial language experiment with humans subjects demonstrating that adults were able to learn words at the same time as they learned to segment the language. However, subjects did much better on a word learning task when the meaning bearing words were consistently placed at the end of utterances. There are several possible reasons why this might have been the case. For instance, it is common in English for the object noun to occur at the end of the sentence, and since the subjects were all English speakers, they may have found it easier to learn an artificial language with a similar pattern. However, our model predicts another simple possibility: the segmentation task is easier at the end because one of the two word boundaries is already known (the utterance boundary itself).

4.3 Discussion

The word learning model generally prefers a very sparse word-to-object map. This is enforced by using a concentration parameter α_1 that is quite small relative to the α_0 parameter, and it biases the model so that the distributions over referring words are very different from that over non-referring words. A small concentration parameter biases the estimator to prefer a small set of word types. In contrast, the relatively large concentration parameter for the non-referring words tends to result in most of the words receiving highest probability as non-referring words. The model thus categorizes words accordingly. It is in part due to this tendency towards sparse word-object maps that the model enforces mutual exclusivity, a phenomenon well documented among natural word learners (Markman, 1990).

Aside from contributing to mutual exclusivity and specialization among the topical word distributions, the small concentration parameter also has important implications for the segmentation task. A very small value for α_1 discourages the learner from acquiring more word types for each meaning than absolutely necessary, thereby forcing the segmenter to use fewer types to explain the sequence of phonemes. A model without any notion of meaning cannot maintain separate distributions for different topics, and must in some sense treat all words as non-referring. A segmenting model without meanings cannot share the word learner's reluctance to propose new meaning-bearing word types and might propose three separate types for "your book", "a book", and "the book". However, with a small enough prior on new referring word types, the word learner that discovers a common referent for all three sequences and, preferring fewer referring word types, is more likely to discover the common subsequence "book". With a single word-object pair ("book", BOOK), the word learner could explain reference for all three sequences instead of using the three separate pairs ("yourbook", BOOK), ("abook", BOOK), and ("thebook", BOOK).

While relying on non-linguistic context helps segment the meaning-bearing words, the overall improvement is small in our current corpus. One reason for this small improvement was that only 9% of the tokens in the corpus were referring words. In corpora containing a larger variety of objects – and in cases where sub- and super-ordinate labels like "eyes" and "ears" are coded – this percentage is likely to be much higher, leading to a greater boost in overall segmentation performance.

We should acknowledge that the decisions entailed in enriching the annotations are neither trivial nor without theoretic implication, however. It is not immediately obvious how to represent the non-linguistic correlates of verbs, for instance. Developmentally, verbs are typically acquired much later than nouns, and it has been argued that this may be due to the difficulty of producing a cognitive representation of the associated meaning (Gentner and Boroditsky, 2001). Even among concrete nouns, not all are equal. Children tend to have a bias toward whole objects when mapping novel words to their non-linguistic counterparts (Markman, 1990). Decisions about more sophisticated encoding of non-linguistic information may thus require more knowledge about children's representations of the world around them

5 Conclusion and Future Work

We find (1) that it is possible to jointly infer both meanings and a segmentation in a fully unsupervised way and (2) that doing so improves the segmentation performance of our model. In particular, we found that although the word learning side suffered from segmentation errors, and performed worse than a model that learned from a gold standard segmentation, the loss was only slight. On the other hand, segmentation performance for the meaning bearing words improved a great deal. The first result suggests that is not necessary to assume fully segmented input in order to learn word meanings, and that the segmentation and word learning tasks can be effectively modeled in parallel, allowing us to explore potential developmental interactions. The second result suggests that synergies do actually exist and argue not only that we can model the two as parallel processes, but that doing so could prove fruitful.

Our model is relatively simple both in terms of word learning and in terms of word segmentation. For instance, social cues and shared attention, or discourse effects, might all play a role (Frank et al., 2009b). Shared features or other relationships can also potentially impact how quickly one might generalize a label to multiple instances (Tenenbaum and Xu, 2000). There are many ways to elaborate on the word learning task, with additional potential synergistic implications.

We might also elaborate the linguistic structures we incorporate into the word learning model. For instance, Johnson (2008) explores synergies in syllable and morphological structures in word segmentation. Aspects of linguistic structure, such as morphology, may contribute to word meaning learning beyond its contribution to word segmentation performance.

Acknowledgments

This research was funded by NSF awards 0544127 and 0631667 to Mark Johnson and by NSF DDRIG 0746251 to Michael C. Frank. We would also like to thank Anne Fernald for providing the corpus and Maeve Cullinane for help in coding it.

References

Nameera Akhtar and Lisa Montague. 1999. Early lexical acquisition: The role of cross-situational learning. *First Language*, 19(57 Pt 3):347–358.

David Blei, Andrew Ng, and Michael Jordan. 2003. Latent dirichlet allocation. *Journal of Machine Learning Research*, 3:993–1022.

Heather Bortfeld, James L. Morgan, Roberta Michnick Golinkoff, and Karen Rathbun. 2005. Mommy and me: Familiar names help launch babies into speechstream segmentation. *Psychological Science*, 16(4):298–304.

Michael R. Brent. 1999. An efficient, probabilistically sound algorithm for segmentation and word discovery. *Machine Learning*, 34:71–105.

Anne Fernald and Hiromi Morikawa. 1993. Common themes and cultural variations in japanese and american mothers' speech to infants. In *Child Development*, number 3, pages 637–656, June.

Michael C. Frank, Vikash Mansinghka, Edward Gibson, and Joshua B. Tenenbaum. 2006. Word segmentation as word learning: Integrating stress and meaning with distributional cues. In *Proceedings of the 31st Annual Boston University Conference on Language Development*.

Michael C. Frank, Sharon Goldwater, Vikash Mansinghka, Tom Griffiths, and Joshua Tenenbaum. 2007. Modeling human performance in statistical word segmentation. *Proceedings of the 29th Annual Meeting of the Cognitive Science Society*, pages 281–286.

Michael C. Frank, Noah D. Goodman, and Joshua B. Tenenbaum. 2009a. Using speakers' referential intentions to model early cross-situational word learning. *Psychological Science*, 5:578–585.

Michael C. Frank, Noah D. Goodman, Joshua B. Tenenbaum, and Anne Fernald. 2009b. Continuity of discourse provides information for word learning.

Dedre Gentner and Lera Boroditsky. 2001. Individuation, relativity, and early word learning. *Language, culture, & cognition*, 3:215–56.

Sharon Goldwater, Thomas L. Griffiths, and Mark Johnson. 2009. A bayesian framework for word segmentation: Exploring the effects of context. *Cognition*, 112(1):21–54.

Katharine Graf-Estes, Julia L. Evans, Martha W. Alibali, and Jenny R. Saffran. 2007. Can infants map meaning to newly segmented words? statistical segmentation and word learning. *Psychological Science*, 18(3):254–260.

Amit Gruber, Michal Rosen-Zvi, and Yair Weiss. 2007. Hidden topic markov models. In *Artificial Intelligence and Statistics (AISTATS)*, March.

Mark Johnson and Sharon Goldwater. 2009. Improving nonparameteric bayesian inference: experiments on unsupervised word segmentation with adaptor grammars. In *Proceedings of Human Language Technologies: The 2009 Annual Conference of the North American Chapter of the Association for Computational Linguistics*, pages 317–325, Boulder, Colorado, June. Association for Computational Linguistics.

Mark Johnson. 2008. Using adaptor grammars to identifying synergies in the unsupervised acquisition of linguistic structure. In *Proceedings of the 46th Annual Meeting of the Association of Computational Linguistics*, Columbus, Ohio. Association for Computational Linguistics.

Ellen M. Markman. 1990. Constraints children place on word learning. *Cognitive Science*, 14:57–77.

Terry Regier. 2003. Emergent constraints on word-learning: A computational review. *Trends in Cognitive Sciences*, 7:263–268.

Jenny R. Saffran, Elissa L. Newport, and Richard N. Aslin. 1996. Word segmentation: The role of distributional cues. *Journal of memory and Language*, 35:606–621.

Jeffrey M. Siskind. 1996. A computational study of cross-situational techniques for learning word-to-meaning mappings. *Cognition*, 61(1-2):39–91.

Joshua B. Tenenbaum and Fei Xu. 2000. Word learning as bayesian inference. In *Proceedings of the 22nd Annual Conference of the Cognitive Science Society*, pages 517–522.

Chen Yu and Dana H. Ballard. 2007. A unified model of early word learning: Integrating statistical and social cues. *Neurocomputing*, 70(13-15):2149–2165.

Subword Variation in Text Message Classification

Robert Munro
Department of Linguistics
Stanford University
Stanford, CA 94305
rmunro@stanford.edu

Christopher D. Manning
Department of Computer Science
Stanford University
Stanford, CA 94305
manning@stanford.edu

Abstract

For millions of people in less resourced regions of the world, text messages (SMS) provide the only regular contact with their doctor. Classifying messages by medical labels supports rapid responses to emergencies, the early identification of epidemics and everyday administration, but challenges include text-brevity, rich morphology, phonological variation, and limited training data. We present a novel system that addresses these, working with a clinic in rural Malawi and texts in the Chichewa language. We show that modeling morphological and phonological variation leads to a substantial average gain of F=0.206 and an error reduction of up to 63.8% for specific labels, relative to a baseline system optimized over word-sequences. By comparison, there is no significant gain when applying the same system to the English translations of the same texts/labels, emphasizing the need for subword modeling in many languages. Language independent morphological models perform as accurately as language specific models, indicating a broad deployment potential.

1 Introduction

The whole world is texting, but rarely in English. Africa has seen the greatest recent uptake of cellphones, with an 8-fold increase over the last 5 years and saturation possible in another 5 (Buys et al., 2009). This is a leapfrog technology – for the majority of new users cellphones are the *only* form of remote communication, surpassing landlines, (non-mobile) internet access and even grid electricity, with costs making texts the dominant communication method. This has led social development organizations to leverage mobile technologies to support health (Leach-Lemens, 2009), banking (Peevers et al., 2008), access to market information (Jagun et al., 2008), literacy (Isbrandt, 2009) and emergency response (Munro, 2010). The possibility to automate many of these services through text-classification is huge, as are the potential benefits – those with the least resources have the most to gain.

However, the data presents many challenges, as text messages are brief, most languages have rich morphology, spellings may be overly-phonetic, and there is often limited training data. We partnered with a medical clinic in rural Malawi and FrontlineSMS:Medic, whose text message management systems serve a patient population of over 2 million in less developed regions of the world. The system allows remote community health workers (CHWs) to communicate directly with more qualified medical staff at centralized clinics, many for the first time.

We present a short-message classification system that incorporates morphological and phonological/orthographic variation, with substantial improvements over a system optimized on word-sequences alone. The average gain is F=0.206 with an error reduction of up to 63.8% for specific labels. For 6 of the 9 labels this more than *doubles* the accuracy. By comparison, there is *not* a significant gain in accuracy when applying the same system to the English translations of the same texts/labels, emphasizing the need for modeling subword structures, but also highlighting why morphology has been peripheral in text classification until now.

Human Language Technologies: The 2010 Annual Conference of the North American Chapter of the ACL, pages 510–518,
Los Angeles, California, June 2010.

2 Language and data

Chichewa is a Bantu language with about 13 million speakers in Southern Africa including 65% of Malawians. We limit examples to the nouns: *odwala* 'patient', *mankhwala* 'medicine'; verb: *fun* 'want'; and the 1st person pronoun/marker: *ndi-* 'I'. Chichewa is closely related to many neighboring languages – more than 100 million people could recognize *ndifuna* as 'I want'.

The morphological complexity is average with about 2-3 morpheme boundaries per word, but this is rich and complex compared to estimates for English, Spanish and Chinese with average of 0.33, 0.85 and 0.01 morpheme boundaries per word. A typical verb is *ndimakafunabe*, 'I am still wanting', consisting of six morphemes, *ndi-ma-ka-fun-a-be*, expressing: 1st person Subject; present tense; noun-class (gender) agreement with the Object; 'want'; verb part-of-speech; and incompletive aspect.

2.1 Labels

The text messages are coded for 0-9 labels in 3 groupings (with counts):

Administrative: related to the clinic:

1. Patient-related (394)
2. Clinic-admin: meetings, supplies etc (169)
3. Technological: phone-credit, batteries etc (21)

Requests: from Community Health Workers:

4. Response: any action requested by CHW (124)
5. Request for doctor (62)
6. Medical advice: CHW asking for advice (23)

Illness: changes of interest to monitoring bodies:

7. TB: tuberculosis (44)
8. HIV: HIV, AIDS and/or treatments (45)
9. Death: reported death of a patient (30)

The groupings correspond to the three main stakeholders of the messages: the clinic itself, interested in classifying messages according to internal work-practices; the Community Health Workers and their patients, acting as the direct care-givers outside the clinic; and broader bodies like the World Health Organization who are interested in monitoring diseases and early identification of epidemics (biosurveillance). The labels are the three most frequent labels required by each of these user groups.

We analyzed 4 months of texts messages with approximately 1,500 labels from 600 messages, consisting of 8,000 words and 30,000 morphemes. While this is small, the final system is being piloted at a clinic in rural Malawi, where users can define new labels at any time according to changing work-practices, new diseases etc. If more than 4 months of manually labeling were required it could limit the utility and user acceptance.

All the messages were translated into English by a medical practitioner, allowing us to make cross-linguistic comparisons of our system.

2.2 Variation

The variation in the data is large. There are >40 forms for 'patient' and only 32% are *odwala*. Of the rest, >50% occur only once. The variation results from morphology: *ndi-odwala*; phonology: *odwa<u>r</u>a*, *ndi<u>w</u>odwala*, and compounding: *ndatindidziwewodwala*. There are also >10 spellings for the English borrowing: *patient*, *pachenti* etc, and 3 for the synonym *matenda*.

Similarly, there are >20 forms for 'medicine'. For *fun* 'want', there are >30 forms with >80% occuring only once. There are >200 forms containing *ndi* and no one form accounts for more than 5% of the instances.

The co-occurrence of *ndi* and *fun* within a word is a strong non-redundant predictor for several labels, but >75% of forms occur only once and >85% of the forms are non-contiguous, as above and in the most frequent *ndi-ma-funa* 'I currently want'.

By contrast, in the English translations 'needing' occurs just once but all other forms of 'patient', 'medicine' and '(I) want/need' are frequent.

This brief introduction to the language and data should make it clear that specialized methods are required for modeling variation in text messages, especially in many languages where text messaging is the dominant form of digital communication.

3 Morphological models

We compared language specific and language independent morphological models, comparing 3 methods (with *ndimafuna* as an example):

Stemmed: {*ndi, fun*}
Segmented: {*ndi, ma, fun, a*}
Morph-config: {*ndi-ma, ndi-fun, ndi-a, ma-fun...*}

We also looked at character ngrams, as used by Hidalgo et al. (2006) for morphological variation in English and Spanish. The results converged with those of the segmented model, which is not surprising as the most frequent features would be similar and increasing data items would overcome the sparcity. We leave more sophisticated character ngram modeling for future work.

3.1 Language specific

For the language specific morphological models we implemented a morphological parser as a set of context-free grammars for all possible prefixes and suffixes according to the formal definitions of Chichewa morphology in Mchombo (2004).

We identified stems by parsing potential prefixes and suffixes, segmenting a word w into n morphemes $w_{m,0}, \ldots, w_{m,n-1}$ leaving a stem w_s with length $len(w_s)$ and corpus frequency of $f(w_s)$, such that $len(w_s) > 0$ (ie, there must be a stem). Where multiple parses could be applied, we minimized $len(w_s)$, then maximized n.

3.2 Language independent

For the language independent morphological models we adapted the word-segmenter of Goldwater, Griffiths and Johnson (2009), to morphological parsing (see Related Work for other algorithms we tested/considered). It was suited to our task because a) it is largely nonparametric, meaning that it can be deployed as a black-box before language-specific properties are known b) it favored recall over precision (see the Results for discussion) and c) using a segmentation algorithm, rather than explicitly modeling morphology, also addresses compounds.

This model uses a *Hierarchical Dirichlet Process* (HDP) (Teh et al., 2005). Every morpheme in the corpus m_i is drawn from a distribution G which consists of possible morphemes (the affixes and stems) and probabilities associated with each morpheme. G is generated from a Dirichlet Process (DP) distribution $DP(\alpha_0, P_0)$, with morphemes sampled from P_0 and their probabilities determined by a concentration parameter α_0. The context-sensitive model where H_m is the DP for a specific morpheme is:

$$\begin{aligned} m_i | m_{i-1} = m, H_m &\sim H_m & \forall m \\ H_m | \alpha_1, G &\sim DP(\alpha_1, G) & \forall m \\ G | \alpha_0, P &\sim DP(\alpha_0, P_0) & \end{aligned}$$

Note that this part of our model is identical to the bigram HDP in Goldwater et al. (2009), except that we possess a set of morphemes, not words. Because word boundaries are already marked in the majority of the messages, we constrain the model to treat all existing word boundaries in the corpus as morpheme boundaries, thus constraining the model to morpheme and compound segmentation.

Unlike word-segmentation, not all tokens in the morpheme lexicon are equal, as we want to model stems separately from affixes in the stemmed models. We assume a) the free morphemes (stems and through compounding) are the least frequent and therefore have the lowest final probability, $P(m)$, in the HDP model; and b) each word w must have at least one free morpheme, the stem w_s ($w_s \neq \emptyset$).[1]

The token-optimal process for identifying stems is straightforward and efficient. The words are sorted by the $argmin$ probabilities of $P(w_{m,0}), \ldots, P(w_{m,n-1})$. For each word w, unless w_s can be identified by a previously observed free morpheme, w_s is identified as $argmin(P(w_{m,0}), \ldots, P(w_{m,n-1}))$ and w_s is added to our lexicon of free morphemes. This algorithm iterates over the words with one extra pass to mark all free morphemes in each word (assuming that there might be compounds we missed on the first pass). The cost, where M is the total number of morphemes and W the total number of words, is $O(log(W) + M)$.

This process has the potential to miss free morphemes that only happened to occur in compounds with less-probable stems, but this did not occur in our data.

4 Phonological/Orthographic Models

We compared three models of phonological/orthographic variation:

Chichewa: Chichewa specific
Script: Roman script specific
Indep: language independent

We refer to these using the term 'phonology' very broadly. The majority of the variation stems from

[1]Note that identifying stems must be a separate step – if we allowed multiple free morphemes for each word to enter the lexicon without penalty in the HDP model it would converge on a zero-penalty distribution where *all* morphemes were free.

the phonology, but also from phonetic variation as expressed in a given writing system, and variation in the writing system itself arising from fluent speakers with varying literacy.

4.1 Chichewa specific

For the language specific normalization, we applied a set of heuristics to the data, based on the variation given in (Paas, 2005) and our own knowledge of how Bantu languages are expressed in Roman scripts. The heuristics were used to normalize all alternates, eg: $\{iwo \rightarrow i\emptyset o\}$ and $\{r \rightarrow l\}$, resulting in *ndiwodwara* $\rightarrow$ *ndiodwala*.

The heuristics represented forms for phonemes with the same potential place of articulation ('c/k'), forms with an adjacent place-of-articulation that are common phonological alternates ('l/r', 'e,i'), voicing alternations ('s/z'), or language-internal phonological processes like the insertion of a glide between vowels that the morphology has made adjacent (like we pronounce but don't spell in 'go(w)ing' in English).

We also implemented hard-coded acronym-recovery methods for acronyms associated with the 'Illness' labels: 'HIV', 'TB', 'AIDS', 'ARV'.

4.2 Script specific

The script specific techniques used the same sets of alternates in the language specific model, but normalized such that the heuristic H was applied to a word w in the corpus C resulting in an alternate w', iff $w' \in C$. This method limits the alternates to those whose existence is supported by the data. It is therefore more conservative than the previous method.

For more general acronym identification, we adapted the method of Schwartz & Hearst (2003). We created a set of candidate acronyms by identifying capitalized sequences in non-capitalized contexts and period-delimited single character sequences. All case-insensitive sequences that were segmented by consistent non-alphabetic characters were then identified as acronyms, provided that they ended in a non-alphabetic character. We could not define a similar acronym-start boundary, as prefixes were often added to acronyms, even when the acronyms themselves contained spaces, eg: '*aT. B.*'.

4.3 Language independent

For complete language independence we applied a noise-reduction algorithm to the stream of characters in order to learn the heuristics that represented potential phonological alternates by identifying all minimal pairs of characters sequences (sequences that alternated by one character, include the absence of a character).

Given all sequences of characters, we identified all pairs of sequences of length $> l$ that differed by one character c_1, where c_1 could be null. We then ranked the pairs of alternating sequences by descending length and applied a threshold t, selecting the t longest sequences, creating alternating patterns from all pairs. Regardless of l or t, the resulting heuristics did not resemble those in 4.1 or 4.2.

We did not implement any acronym identification methods, for obvious reasons.

5 Results

The results are compared to a baseline system optimized over word sequences (words and ngrams but no subword modeling). All results presented here are from a MaxEnt model using a leave-one-out cross-validation.

For the English translations of the texts there was no phonological/orthographic variation beyond that resulting from morphology, so we only applied the language independent morphological models.

5.1 Morphology

With the exception of the unsupervised stemming, all the morphological models led to substantial gains in accuracy. As Table 1 shows, the most accurate system used the language specific segmentation, with an average accuracy of F=0.476, a macro-average gain of 22.4%.

The greatest increase in accuracy occured where verbs were the best predictors – the words with the most complex morphology. The 'Response' label showed the greatest relative gain in accuracy for those with a non-zero baseline, where the accuracy increased 4-fold from F=0.113 to F=0.442. It is expected that a label predicated on requests for action should rely on the isolation of verb stems, but this is still a very substantial gain. In contrast to this 391.2% gain in accuracy for Chichewa, the gain for

Label	Baseline	Stemmed		Segmented		Morph-Config		Gain	
		Chich	Indep	Chich	Indep	Chich	Indep	Best	Final
Patient-related	0.830	0.842	0.735	0.857	0.832	0.851	0.867	+3.7	+3.7
Clinic-admin	0.358	0.490	0.295	0.612	0.561	0.577	0.580	+25.5	+22.2
Technological	0	0	0	0.320	0.174	0.320	0.091	+32.0	+09.1
Response	0.113	0.397	0.115	0.440	0.477	0.459	0.442	+36.4	+32.9
Request for doctor	0.121	0.312	0.090	0.505	0.395	0.477	0.375	+38.4	+25.4
Medical advice	0	0	0	0.083	0.160	0.083	0.083	+16.0	+08.3
HIV	0.379	0.597	0	0.554	0.357	0.484	0.351	+21.8	(-2.8)
TB	0.235	0.357	0	0.414	0.200	0.386	0.327	+17.8	+09.2
Death	0.235	0.333	0.229	0.500	0.667	0.462	0.723	+48.8	+48.8
Average.	0.252	0.370	0.163	0.476	0.425	0.455	0.427	+22.4	+17.4

Table 1: Morphology results: F-values for leave-one-out cross-validation comparing different morphological models. *Indep* = language independent, *Chich* = specific to Chichewa, ( ) = not significant ($\rho > 0.05, \chi^2$), *Final* = Gain of the 'Morph-Config, Indep' model over the Baseline.

English, while still relying on the isolation of verb stems, only increased the accuracy by 5.4%.

The unsupervised stemming underperformed the baseline model by 8.9%, due to over-segmentation. Compared to the Chichewa stemmer, we estimate that the unsupervised stemmer had 90-95% recall and 40-50% precision, resulting in over-stemmed tokens. However, this seemed to be favor the *segmented* and *morph-config* models, as unnecessary segmentation can be recovered when the tokens are sequenced or re-configured, with the supervised model arriving at the optimal weights for each candidate token or sequence. This can be seen by comparing the stemmed and morph-config results for the Chichewa-specific and language independent results. The difference in stemming is 20.7% but for the morph-config models it is only 2.8%. A loss in segmentation recall could not be recovered in the same way, as adjacent non-segmented morphemes will remain one token. This leads us to conclude that recall should be weighted more highly than precision in unsupervised morphological models applied to supervised classification tasks.

5.2 Phonology

For the phonological models the results in Table 2 show that the script-specific model was the most accurate with an average of F=0.443, a gain of 19.1% over the baseline.

There are correlations between morphological variation and phonological variation, with the gains similar for each label in Table 1 and Table 2. This is because much phonological variation often arises from the morphology, as in *ndiwodwala* where the glide *w* is pronounced and variably written between the vowels made adjacent through morphology. It is also because more morphologically complex words are longer and simply have more potential for phonological and written variation. The were greater gains in identifying the 'TB' and 'HIV' labels here than in the morphological models as the result of acronym identification.

The language independent model did not perform well. Despite changing the data considerably, there was little change in the accuracy, indicating that the changes it made were largely random with respect to the target concepts. The most frequent alternations in large contexts were noun-class prefixes differing by a single character, which has the potential to change the meaning, and this seemed to negate any gains from normalization.

While language independent results would have been ideal, a system with script-specific assumptions is realistic. It is likely that text messages are regularly sent in 1000s of languages but less than 10 scripts, and our definition of 'script specific' would be considered 'language independent' elsewhere. For example, in the Morpho Challenge (see

	Baseline	Model			Gain	
Label		Chichewa	Script	Indep	Best	Final
Patient-related	0.830	0.842	0.848	0.838	(+1.8)	(+1.8)
Clinic-admin	0.358	0.511	0.594	0.358	+23.6	+23.6
Technological	0	0.091	0.091	0	+9.1	+9.1
Response	0.113	0.420	0.473	0.207	+36.0	+36.0
Request for doctor	0.121	0.154	0.354	0	+23.3	+23.3
Medical advice	0	0.375	0.222	0.121	+37.5	+22.2
HIV	0.379	0.508	0.492	0.379	+12.9	+11.3
TB	0.235	0.327	0.492	0.235	+25.7	+25.7
Death	0.235	0.333	0.421	0.235	+18.6	+18.6
Average	0.252	0.396	0.443	0.264	+19.1	+19.1

Table 2: Phonological results: F-values for leave-one-out cross-validation comparing different phonological models. *Chichewa* = Chichewa specific heuristics, *Script* = specific to Roman scripts, *Indep* = language independent, ( ) = not significant ($\rho > 0.05, \chi^2$), *Final* = Gain of the 'Script' model over the Baseline.

Related Work) Arabic data was converted to Roman script, and it is likely that the methods could be adapted with some success to any alphabetic script.

5.3 Combined results

Table 3 gives the final results, comparing the systems over the original text messages and the English translations of the same messages. The most accurate results were achieved by applying the phonological normalization before the morphological segmentation, giving a (macro) average of 0.459 which is an increase of 20.6% over the baseline. The increase in accuracy was not cumulative – the combined system outperforms both the standalone phonological and morphological systems, but with a comparatively modest gain.

The final English system is 9.2% more accurate than the final Chichewa system, but the Chichewa system has closed the gap considerably as the English baseline system was 25.7% more accurate than the baseline Chichewa system. Assuming that the potential accuracy is approximately equal (given both languages are encoding exactly the same information) we conclude that we have made substantial gains in accuracy but there are further large gains to be made. Therefore, while we have not solved the problem of text message classification in morphologically rich languages, we have been able to make promising gains in an exciting new area of research.

5.4 Practical effectiveness

The FrontlineSMS system currently allows users to filter messages by keywords, similar to many email clients. Because of the large number of variants per word this is sub optimal in many languages. We defined a second baseline to model an idealized version of the current system that assumes oracle knowledge of the keyword/label and the optimal order in which to apply rules created from this knowledge. The only constraint was that we excluded words that occurred only once. In essence, it is a MaxEnt model that includes seen test items and assigns a label according to the single strongest feature for each test item.

Here, we evaluated the systems according to Micro-F, recall and precision, as these give a better gauge of the frequency of error per incoming text, and therefore the usability for someone needing to correct mislabeled texts. We also calculated the Micro-F for each label/non-label decision to give exact figures per classification decision. The results are in Table 4. The Micro-F is 0.684 as compared to 0.403 for the keyword system. The higher precision is also promising, indicating that when we assign a label we are more often correct. By adjusting the precision and recall through label confidence thresholds, 90% precision can be achieved with 35.3% recall.[2] In terms of usability, the Label/no-Label re-

[2]We confirmed significance relative to confidence by ROC analysis – results omitted for space.

	Chichewa			English		
Label	**Baseline**	**Final Sys**	**Gain**	**Baseline**	**Final Sys**	**Gain**
Patient-related	0.830	**0.847**	(+1.7)	0.878	**0.878**	0
Clinic-admin	0.358	**0.624**	+26.6	0.682	**0.717**	(+3.4)
Technological	0	**0.174**	+17.4	0.174	**0.320**	+14.6
Response	0.113	**0.476**	+36.3	0.573	**0.555**	(-1.8)
Request for doctor	0	**0.160**	+16.0	0.160	**0.357**	+19.7
Medical advice	0.121	**0.500**	+37.9	0.560	**0.580**	(+2.0)
HIV	0.379	**0.357**	(-2.2)	0.414	**0.576**	+16.2
TB	0.235	**0.351**	+11.6	0.557	**0.533**	(-2.4)
Death	0.235	**0.638**	+40.3	0.591	**0.439**	-15.2
Average	0.252	**0.459**	+20.6	0.510	**0.551**	+4.1
Micro F	**0.593**	**0.684**	**+9.1**	**0.728**	**0.737**	**(+0.9)**

Table 3: Final Results, comparing the systems in Chichewa and the English translations.

sults are very promising, reducing errors from 1 in 4 to 1 in 20.

The learning rates in Figure 1 show that the learners are converging on accurate models after only seeing a handful of text messages. This figure also makes it clear that subword processing gives relatively little gain to the English translations. The disparity between the final model and the baseline widens as more items are seen, indicating that the failure of the word-optimal baseline model is not just due to a lack of training items.

5.5 Other models investigated

Much recent work in text classification has been in machine-learning, comparing models over constant features. We tested SVMs and joint learning strategies. The gains were significant but small and did not closed the gap between systems with and without subword modeling. We therefore omit these for space and scope.

However, one interesting result came from extending the feature space with topics derived from *Latent Dirichlet Allocation* (LDA) using similar methods to Ramage et al. (2009). This produced significant gains (micro-F=0.029), halving the remaining gap with the English system, but only when the topics were derived from modeling non-contiguous morpheme sequences, not words-alone or segmented morphemes. We found that the different surface forms of each word cooccurred *less* often than chance (0.46 as often as chance for the different forms of *odwala*) forming disjunctive distributions. We suspect that this acts as a bias against robust unsupervised clustering of the different forms.

6 Related Work

To our best knowledge, no prior researchers have worked on subword models for text message categorization, or any NLP task with the Chichewa, but we build on many recent developments in computational morphology and NLP for Bantu languages.

Badenhorst et al. (2009) found substantial variation in a speech recognition corpus for 9 Southern Bantu languages, where accurate models could also be built with limited data. Morphological segmentation improved Swahili-English machine translation in De Pauw et al. (2009), even in the absense of gold standard reference segmentations, as was the case here. The complexity and necessity of modeling non-contiguous morphemes in Bantu languages is discussed by Pretorius et al. (2009).

Computational morphology (Goldsmith, 2001; Creutz, 2006; Kurimo et al., 2008; Johnson and Goldwater, 2009; Goldwater et al., 2009) has begun to play a prominent role in machine translation and speech recognition for morphologically rich languages (Goldwater and McClosky, 2005; Tachbelie et al., 2009). In the current-state-of-the-art, a combination of the *ParaMor* (Monson et al., 2008) and *Morfessor* (Creutz, 2006) algorithms achieved

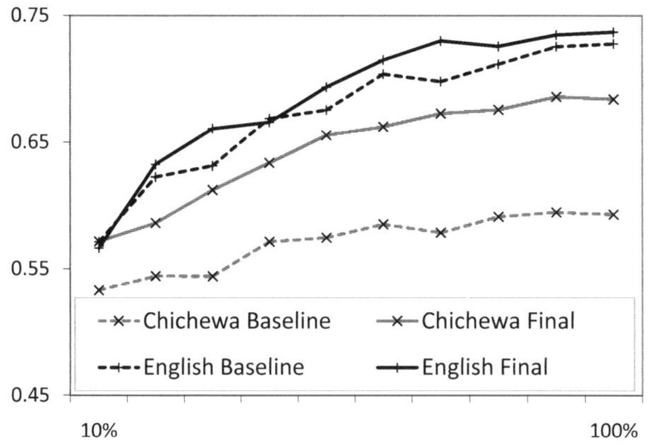

Figure 1: The learning rate, comparing micro-F for the Chichewa and English systems on different training set sizes. A random stratified sample was used for subsets.

the most accurate results in 2008 Morpho Challenge Workshop (Kurimo et al., 2008). *ParaMor* assumes a single affix and is not easily adapted to more complex morphologies, but we were able to test and evaluate *Morfessor* and the earlier *Linguistica* (Goldsmith, 2001). Both were more accurate for segmentation than our adaptation of Goldwater et al. (2009), but with lower recall. For the reasons discussed in Section 5.3 this meant less accuracy in classification. Goldwater et al. have also used the Pitman-Yor algorithm for morphological modeling (Goldwater et al., 2006). In results too recent to test here, Pitman-Yor has been used for segmentation with accuracy comparable to the HDP model but with greater efficiency (Mochihashi et al., 2009). Biosurveillance systems currently use simple rule-based pre-processing for subword models. Dara et al. (2008) found only modest gains, although the data was limited to English.

For text message classification, prior work is limited to identifying SPAM (Healy et al., 2005; Hidalgo et al., 2006; Cormack et al., 2007), where specialized algorithms and feature representations were also found to improve accuracy. For written variation, Kobus et al. (2008) focussed on SMS-specific abbreviations in French. Unlike their data, SMS-specific abbreviations were not present in our data. This is consistent with the reports on SMS practices in the related isiXhosa language (Deumert and Masinyana, 2008), but it may also be because the data we used contained professional communications not personal messages.

	Label class		**Label/No-Label**	
	KWF	Final	KWF	Final
F-val	0.403	0.684	0.713	0.950
Prec.	0.265	0.796	0.570	0.972
Rec.	0.842	0.599	0.953	0.929

Table 4: Micro-F, precision and recall, compared with the oracle keyword system. *KWF* = Oracle Keyword Filter.

7 Conclusions

We have demonstrated that subword modeling in Chichewa leads to significant gains in classifying text messages according to medical labels, reducing the error from 1 in 4 to 1 in 20 in a system that should generalize to other languages with similar morphological complexity.

The rapid expansion of cellphone technologies has meant that digital data is now being generated in 100s, if not 1000s, of languages that have not previously been the focus of language technologies. The results here therefore represent just one of a large number of potential new applications for short-message classification systems.

Acknowledgements

Thank you to FrontlineSMS:Medic and the health care workers they partner with. The first author was supported by a Stanford Graduate Fellowship.

References

Jaco Badenhorst, Charl van Heerden, Marelie Davel, and Etienne Barnard. 2009. Collecting and evaluating speech recognition corpora for nine Southern Bantu languages. In *The EACL Workshop on Language Technologies for African Languages.*

Piet Buys, Susmita Dasgupta, Timothy S. Thomas, and David Wheeler. 2009. Determinants of a digital divide in Sub-Saharan Africa: A spatial econometric analysis of cell phone coverage. *World Development*, 37(9).

Gordon V. Cormack, José Mara Gómez Hidalgo, and Enrique Puertas Sánz. 2007. Feature engineering for mobile (SMS) spam filtering. In *The 30th annual international ACM SIGIR conference on research and development in information retrieval.*

Mathias Creutz. 2006. *Induction of the Morphology of Natural Language: Unsupervised Morpheme Segmentation with Application to Automatic Speech Recognition.* Ph.D. thesis, University of Technology, Helsinki.

Jagan Dara, John N. Dowling, Debbie Travers, Gregory F. Cooper, and Wendy W. Chapman. 2008. Evaluation of preprocessing techniques for chief complaint classification. *Journal of Biomedical Informatics*, 41(4):613–23.

Ana Deumert and Sibabalwe Oscar Masinyana. 2008. Mobile language choices: the use of English and isiXhosa in text messages (SMS) evidence from a bilingual South African sample. *English World-Wide*, 29(2):117–147.

John Goldsmith. 2001. Unsupervised learning of the morphology of a natural language. *Computational Linguistics*, 27(2):153–198.

Sharon Goldwater and David McClosky. 2005. Improving statistical MT through morphological analysis. In *Human Language Technology Conference and Conference on Empirical Methods in Natural Language Processing*.

Sharon Goldwater, Thomas L. Griffiths, and Mark Johnson. 2006. Interpolating between types and tokens by estimating power-law generators. *Advances in Neural Information Processing Systems*, 18.

Sharon Goldwater, Thomas L. Griffiths, and Mark Johnson. 2009. A bayesian framework for word segmentation: Exploring the effects of context. *Cognition*, 112(1):21–54.

Matt Healy, Sarah Jane Delany, and Anton Zamolotskikh. 2005. An assessment of case-based reasoning for Short Text Message Classification. In *The 16th Irish Conference on Artificial Intelligence & Cognitive Science*.

José Mara Gómez Hidalgo, Guillermo Cajigas Bringas, Enrique Puertas Sánz, and Francisco Carrero Garca. 2006. Content based SMS spam filtering. In *ACM symposium on Document engineering*.

Scott Isbrandt. 2009. Cell Phones in West Africa: improving literacy and agricultural market information systems in Niger. White paper: Projet Alphabétisation de Base par Cellulaire.

Abi Jagun, Richard Heeks, and Jason Whalley. 2008. The impact of mobile telephony on developing country micro-enterprise: A Nigerian case study. *Information Technologies and International Development*, 4.

Mark Johnson and Sharon Goldwater. 2009. Improving nonparameteric Bayesian inference: experiments on unsupervised word segmentation with adaptor grammars. In *Human Language Technologies*.

Catherine Kobus, François Yvon, and Geéraldine Damnati. 2008. Normalizing SMS: are two metaphors better than one? In *The 22nd International Conference on Computational Linguistics*.

Mikko Kurimo, Matti Varjokallio, and Ville Turunen. 2008. Unsupervised morpheme analysis. In *Morpho Challenge Workshop*, Finland. Helsinki University of Technology.

Carole Leach-Lemens. 2009. Using mobile phones in HIV care and prevention. *HIV and AIDS Treatment in Practice*, 137.

Sam Mchombo. 2004. *The Syntax of Chichewa*. Cambridge University Press, New York, NY.

Daichi Mochihashi, Takeshi Yamada, and Naonori Ueda. 2009. Bayesian unsupervised word segmentation with nested Pitman-Yor language modeling. In *The 47th Annual Meeting of the Association for Computational Linguistics*.

Christian Monson, Jaime Carbonell, Alon Lavie, and Lori Levin. 2008. ParaMor: finding paradigms across morphology. *Lecture Notes in Computer Science*, 5152.

Robert Munro. 2010. Haiti Emergency Response: the power of crowdsourcing and SMS. In *Haiti Crisis Relief 2.0*, Stanford, CA.

Steven Paas. 2005. *English Chichewa-Chinyanja Dictionary*. Mvunguti Books, Zomba, Malawi.

Guy De Pauw, Peter Waiganjo Wagacha, and Gilles-Maurice de Schryver. 2009. The SAWA Corpus: a parallel corpus of English - Swahili. In *The EACL Workshop on Language Technologies for African Languages*.

Gareth Peevers, Gary Douglas, and Mervyn A. Jack. 2008. A usability comparison of three alternative message formats for an SMS banking service. *International Journal of Human-Computer Studies*, 66.

Rigardt Pretorius, Ansu Berg, Laurette Pretorius, and Biffie Viljoen. 2009. Setswana tokenisation and computational verb morphology: Facing the challenge of a disjunctive orthography. In *The EACL Workshop on Language Technologies for African Languages*.

Daniel Ramage, David Hall, Ramesh Nallapati, and Christopher D. Manning. 2009. Labeled LDA: A supervised topic model for credit attribution in multi-labeled corpora. In *Proceedings of the 2009 Conference on Empirical Methods in Natural Language Processing*, Singapore.

Ariel S. Schwartz and Marti A. Hearst. 2003. A simple algorithm for identifying abbreviation definitions in biomedical texts. In *The Pacific Symposium on Biocomputing*, University of California, Berkeley.

Martha Yifiru Tachbelie, Solomon Teferra Abate, and Wolfgang Menzel. 2009. Morpheme-based language modeling for amharic speech recognition. In *The 4th Language and Technology Conference*.

Yee Whye Teh, Michael I. Jordan, Matthew J. Beal, and David M. Blei. 2005. Hierarchical Dirichlet processes. *In Advances in Neural Information Processing Systems*, 17.

Automatic Diacritization for Low-Resource Languages Using a Hybrid Word and Consonant CMM

Robbie A. Haertel, Peter McClanahan, and Eric K. Ringger
Department of Computer Science
Brigham Young University
Provo, Utah 84602, USA
rah67@cs.byu.edu, petermcclanahan@gmail.com, ringger@cs.byu.edu

Abstract

We are interested in diacritizing Semitic languages, especially Syriac, using only diacritized texts. Previous methods have required the use of tools such as part-of-speech taggers, segmenters, morphological analyzers, and linguistic rules to produce state-of-the-art results. We present a low-resource, data-driven, and language-independent approach that uses a hybrid word- and consonant-level conditional Markov model. Our approach rivals the best previously published results in Arabic (15% WER with case endings), without the use of a morphological analyzer. In Syriac, we reduce the WER over a strong baseline by 30% to achieve a WER of 10.5%. We also report results for Hebrew and English.

1 Introduction

Abjad writing systems omit vowels and other diacritics. The ability to restore these diacritics is useful for personal, industrial, and governmental purposes—especially for Semitic languages. In its own right, the ability to diacritize can aid language learning and is necessary for speech-based assistive technologies, including speech recognition and text-to-speech. Diacritics are also useful for tasks such as segmentation, morphological disambiguation, and machine translation, making diacritization important to Natural Language Processing (NLP) systems and intelligence gathering. In alphabetic writing systems, similar techniques have been used to restore accents from plain text (Yarowsky, 1999) and could be used to recover missing letters in the compressed writing styles found in email, text, and instant messages.

We are particularly interested in diacritizing Syriac, a low-resource dialect of Aramaic, which possesses properties similar to Arabic and Hebrew. This work employs conditional Markov models (CMMs) (Klein and Manning, 2002) to diacritize Semitic (and other) languages and requires only diacritized texts for training. Such an approach is useful for languages (like Syriac) in which annotated data and linguistic tools such as part-of-speech (POS) taggers, segmenters, and morphological analyzers are not available. Our main contributions are as follows: (1) we introduce a hybrid word and consonant CMM that allows access to the diacritized form of the previous words; (2) we introduce new features available in the proposed model; and (3) we describe an efficient, approximate decoder. Our models significantly outperform existing low-resource approaches across multiple related and unrelated languages and even achieve near state-of-the-art results when compared to resource-rich systems.

In the next section, we review previous work relevant to our approach. Section 3 then motivates and describes the models and features used in our framework, including a description of the decoder. We describe our data in Section 4 and detail our experimental setup in Section 5. Section 6 presents our results. Finally, Section 7 briefly discusses our conclusions and offers ideas for future work.

2 Previous Work

Diacritization has been receiving increased attention due to the rising interest in Semitic languages, cou-

Human Language Technologies: The 2010 Annual Conference of the North American Chapter of the ACL, pages 519–527,
Los Angeles, California, June 2010.

pled with the importance of diacritization to other NLP-related tasks. The existing approaches can be categorized based on the amount of resources they require, their basic unit of analysis, and of course the language they are targeting. Probabilistic systems can be further divided into generative and conditional approaches.

Existing methodologies can be placed along a continuum based on the quantity of resources they require—a reflection of their cost. Examples of resources used include morphological analyzers (Habash and Rambow, 2007; Ananthakrishnan et al., 2005; Vergyri and Kirchhoff, 2004; El-Sadany and Hashish, 1989), rules for grapheme-to-sound conversion (El-Imam, 2008), transcribed speech (Vergyri and Kirchhoff, 2004), POS tags (Zitouni et al., 2006; Ananthakrishnan et al., 2005), and a list of prefixes and suffixes (Nelken and Shieber, 2005). When such resources exist for a particular language, they typically improve performance. For instance, Habash and Rambow's (2007) approach reduces the error rate of Zitouni et al.'s (2006) by as much as 30% through its use of a morphological analyzer. In fact, such resources are not always available. Several data-driven approaches exist that require only diacritized texts (e.g., Kübler and Mohamed, 2008; Zitouni et al., 2006; Gal, 2002) which are relatively inexpensive to obtain: most literate speakers of the target language could readily provide them.

Apart from the quantity of resources required, diacritization systems also differ in their basic unit of analysis. A consonant-based approach treats each consonant[1] in a word as a potential host for one or more (possibly null) diacritics; the goal is to predict the correct diacritic(s) for each consonant (e.g., Kübler and Mohamed, 2008). Zitouni et al. (2006) extend the problem to a sequence labeling task wherein they seek the best *sequence* of diacritics for the consonants. Consequently, their approach has access to previously chosen diacritics.

Alternatively, the basic unit of analysis can be the full, undiacritized word. Since morphological analyzers produce analyses of undiacritized words, diacritization approaches that employ them typically fall into this category (e.g., Habash and Rambow, 2007; Vergyri and Kirchoff, 2004). Word-based, low-resource solutions tend to treat the problem as word-level sequence labeling (e.g., Gal, 2002).

Unfortunately, word-based techniques face problems due to data sparsity: not all words in the test set are seen during training. In contrast, consonant-based approaches rarely face the analogous problem of previously unseen consonants. Thus, one low-resource solution to data sparsity is to use consonant-based techniques for unknown words (Ananthakrishnan et al., 2005; Nelken and Shieber, 2005).

Many of the existing systems, especially recent ones, are probabilistic or contain probabilistic components. Zitouni et al. (2006) show the superiority of their conditional-based approaches over the best-performing generative approaches. However, the instance-based learning approach of Kübler and Mohamed (2008) slightly outperforms Zitouni et al. (2006). In the published literature for Arabic, the latter two have the best low-resource solutions. Habash and Rambow (2007) is the state-of-the-art, high-resource solution for Arabic. To our knowledge, no work has been done in this area for Syriac.

3 Models

In this work, we are concerned with diacritization for Syriac for which a POS tagger, segmenter, and other tools are not readily available, but for which diacritized text is obtainable.[2] Use of a system dependent on a morphological analyzer such as Habash and Rambow's (2007) is therefore not cost-effective. Furthermore, we seek a system that is applicable to a wide variety of languages. Although Kübler and Mohamed's (2008) approach is competitive to Zitouni et al.'s (2006), instance-based approaches tend to suffer with the addition of new features (their own experiments demonstrate this). We desire to add linguistically relevant features to improve performance and thus choose to use a conditional model. However, unlike Zitouni et al. (2006), we use a hybrid word- and consonant-level approach based on the following observations (statistics taken from the Syriac training and development sets explained in Section 4):

[1]We refer to all graphemes present in undiacritized texts as consonants.

[2]Kiraz (2000) describes a morphological analyzer for Syriac that is not publicly available and is costly to reproduce.

1. Many undiacritized words are unambiguous: 90.8% of the word types and 63.5% of the tokens have a single diacritized form.

2. Most undiacritized word types have only a few possible diacritizations: the average number of possible diacritizations is 1.11.

3. Low-frequency words have low ambiguity: Undiacritized types occurring fewer than 5 times have an average of 1.05 possible diacritizations.

4. Diacritized words not seen in the training data occur infrequently at test time: 10.5% of the diacritized test tokens were not seen in training.

5. The diacritics of previous words can provide useful morphological information such as person, number, and gender.

Contrary to observations 1 and 2, consonant-level approaches dedicate modeling capacity to an exponential (in the number of consonants) number of possible diacritizations of a word. In contrast, a word-level approach directly models the (few) diacritized forms seen in training. Furthermore, word-based approaches naturally have access to the diacritics of previous words if used in a sequence labeler, as per observation 5. However, without a "backoff" strategy, word-level models cannot predict a diacritized form not seen in the training data. Also, low-frequency words by definition have less information from which to estimate parameters. In contrast, abundant information exists for each diacritic in a consonant-level system. To the degree to which they hold, observations 3 and 4 mitigate these latter two problems. Clearly a hybrid approach would be advantageous.

To this end we employ a CMM in which we treat the problem as an instance of sequence labeling at the word level with less common words being handled by a consonant-level CMM. Let $\mathbf{u}$ be the undiacriatized words in a sentence. Applying an order o Markov assumption, the distribution over sequences of diacritized words $\mathbf{d}$ is:

$$P(\mathbf{d}|\mathbf{u}) = \prod_{i=1}^{\|\mathbf{d}\|} P(d_i|\mathbf{d}_{i-o\ldots i-1}, \mathbf{u}; \boldsymbol{\omega}, \boldsymbol{\gamma}, \alpha) \quad (1)$$

in which the local conditional distribution of a diacritized word is an interpolation of a word-level model ($\boldsymbol{\omega}_{u_i}$) and a consonant-level model ($\boldsymbol{\gamma}$):

$$\begin{aligned} P(d_i|\mathbf{d}_{i-o\ldots i-1}, \mathbf{u}; \boldsymbol{\omega}, \boldsymbol{\gamma}, \alpha) = \\ \alpha P(d_i|\mathbf{d}_{i-o\ldots i-1}, \mathbf{u}; \boldsymbol{\omega}_{u_i}) + \\ (1-\alpha) P(d_i|\mathbf{d}_{i-o\ldots i-1}, \mathbf{u}; \boldsymbol{\gamma}) \end{aligned}$$

We let the consonant-level model be a standard CMM, similar to Zitouni et al. (2006), but with access to previously diacritized words. Note that the order of this "inner" CMM need not be the same as that of the outer CMM.

The parameter α reflects the degree to which we trust the word-level model. In the most general case, α can be a function of the undiacritized words and the previous o diacritized words. Based on our earlier enumerated observations, we use a simple delta function for α: we let α be 0 when $\mathbf{u}_i$ is rare and 1 otherwise. We leave discussion for what constitutes a "rare" undiacritized type for Section 5.2.

Figure 1b presents a graphical model of a simple example sentence in Syriac. The diacritization for non-rare words is predicted for a whole word, hence the random variable D for each such word. These diacritized words D_i depend on previous D_{i-1} as per equation (1) for an order-1 CMM (note that the capitalized A, I, and O are in fact consonants in this transliteration). Because "NKTA" and "RGT" are rare, their diacritization is represented by a consonant-level CMM: one variable for each possible diacritic in the word. Importantly, these consonant-level models have access to the previously diacritized word (D_4 and D_6, respectively).

We use log-linear models for all local distributions in our CMMs, i.e., we use maximum entropy (maxent) Markov models (McCallum et al., 2000; Berger et al., 1996). Due to the phenomenon known as *d*-separation (Pearl and Shafer, 1988), it is possible to independently learn parameters for each word model $\boldsymbol{\omega}_{u_i}$ by training only on those instances for the corresponding word. Similarly, the consonant model can be learned independent of the word models. We place a spherical normal prior centered at zero with a standard deviation of 1 over the weights of all models and use an L-BFGS minimizer to find the MAP estimate of the weights for all the models (words and consonant).

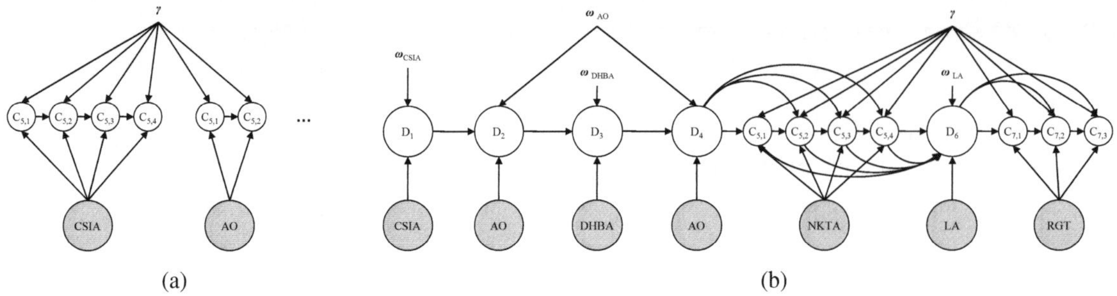

Figure 1: Graphical models of Acts 20:33 in Syriac, *CSIA AO DHBA AO NKTA LA RGT* 'silver or gold or garment I have not coveted,' using Kiraz's (1994) transliteration for (a) the initial portion of a consonant-level-only model and (b) a combined word- and consonant-level model. For clarity, both models assume a consonant-level Markov order of 1; (b) shows a word-level Markov order of 1. For simplicity, the figure further assumes that additional features come only from the current (undiacritized) word.

Note that Zitouni et al.'s (2006) model is a special case of equation (1) where all words are rare, the word-level Markov order (o) is 0, and the consonant-level Markov order is 2. A simplified version of Zitouni's model is presented in Figure 1a.

3.1 Features

Our features are based on those found in Zitouni et al. (2006), although we have added a few of our own which we consider to be one of the contributions of this paper. Unlike their work, our consonant-level model has access to previously diacritized words, allowing us to exploit information noted in observation 5.

Each of the word-level models shares the same set of features, defined by the following templates:

- The prefixes and suffixes (up to 4 characters) of the previously *diacritized* words.
- The string of the actual diacritics, including the null diacritic, from each of the previous o diacritized words and n-grams of these strings; a similar set of features is extracted but without the null diacritics.
- Every possible (overlapping) n-gram of all sizes from $n = 1$ to $n = 5$ of undiacritized words contained within the window defined by 2 words to the right and 2 to the left. These templates yield 15 features for each token.
- The count of how far away the current token is from the beginning/end of the sentence up to the Markov order; also, their binary equivalents.

The first two templates rely on diacritizations of previous words, in keeping with observation 5.

The consonant-level model has the following feature templates:

- The current consonant.
- Previous diacritics (individually, and n-grams of diacritics ending in the diacritic prior to the current consonant, where n is the consonant-level Markov order).
- Conjunctions of the first two templates.
- Indicators as to whether this is the first or last consonant.
- The first three templates independently conjoined with the current consonant.
- Every possible (overlapping) n-gram of all sizes from $n = 1$ to $n = 11$ consisting of consonants contained within the window defined by 5 words to the right and 5 to the left.
- Same as previous, but available diacritics are included in the window.
- Prefixes and suffixes (of up to length 4) of previously diacritized words conjoined with previous diacritics in the current token, both individually and n-grams of such.

This last template is only possible because of our model's dependency on previous diacritized words.

3.2 Decoder

Given a sentence consisting of undiacritized words, we seek the most probable sequence of diacritized words, i.e., $\arg\max_{\mathbf{d}} P(\mathbf{d}|\mathbf{u}...)$. In sentences containing no rare words, the well-known Viterbi algorithm can be used to find the optimum.

However, as can be seen in Figure 1b, predictions in the consonant-level model (e.g., $C_{5,1...4}$) depend on previously diacritized words (D_4), and some diacritized words (e.g., D_6) depend on diacritics in the previous rare word ($C_{5,1...4}$). These dependencies introduce an exponential number of states (in the length of the word) for rare words, making exact decoding intractable. Instead, we apply a non-standard beam during decoding to limit the number of states for rare words to the n-best (locally). This is accomplished by using an independent "inner" n-best decoder for the consonant-level CMM to produce the n-best diacritizations for the rare word given the previous diacritized words and other features. These become the only states to and from which transitions in the "outer" word-level decoder can be made. We note this is the same type of decoding that is done in pipeline models that use n-best decoders (Finkel et al., 2006). Additionally, we use a traditional beam-search of width 5 to further reduce the search space both in the outer and inner CMMs.

4 Data

Although our primary interest is in the Syriac language, we also experimented with the Penn Arabic Treebank (Maamouri et al., 2004) for the sake of comparison with other approaches. We include Hebrew to provide results for yet another Semitic language. We also apply the models to English to show that our method and features work well outside of the Semitic languages. A summary of the datasets, including the number of diacritics, is found in Figure 2. The number of diacritics shown in the table is less than the number of possible predictions since we treat contiguous diacritics between consonants as a single prediction.

For our experiments in Syriac, we use the New Testament portion of the Peshitta (Kiraz, 1994) and treat each verse as if it were a sentence. The diacritics we predict are the five short vowels, as well as *Sěyāmē*, *Rukkākhā*, *Quššāyā*, and *linea ocultans*.

lang	diacs	train	dev	test
Syriac	9	87,874	10,747	11,021
Arabic	8	246,512	42,105	51,664
Hebrew	17	239,615	42,133	49,455
English	5	1,004,073	80,156	89,537

Figure 2: Number of diacritics and size (in tokens) of each dataset

For Arabic, we use the training/test split defined by Zitouni et al. (2006). We group all words having the same P index value into a sentence. We build our own development set by removing the last 15% of the sentences of the training set. Like Zitouni, when no solution exists in the treebank, we take the first solution as the gold tag. Zitouni et al. (2006) report results on several different conditions, but we focus on the most challenging of the conditions: we predict the standard three short vowels, three *tanween*, *sukuun*, *shadda*, and all case endings. (Preliminary experiments show that our models perform equally favorably in the other scenarios as well.)

For Hebrew, we use the Hebrew Bible (Old Testament) in the Westminster Leningrad Codex (Zefania XML Project, 2009). As with Syriac, we treat each verse as a sentence and remove the paragraph markers (*pe* and *samekh*). There is a large number of diacritics that could be predicted in Hebrew and no apparent standardization in the literature. For these reasons, we attempt to predict as many diacritics as possible. Specifically, we predict the diacritics whose unicode values are 05B0-B9, 05BB-BD, 05BF, 05C1-C2, and 05C4. We treat the following list of punctuation as consonants: *maqaf*, *paseq*, *sof pasuq*, *geresh*, and *gershayim*. The cantillation marks are removed entirely from the data.

Our English data comes from the Penn Treebank (Marcus et al., 1994). We used sections 0–20 as training data, 21–22 as development data, and 23–24 as our test set. Unlike words in the Semitic languages, English words can begin with a vowel, requiring us to prepend a prosthetic consonant to every word; we also convert all English text to lowercase.

5 Experiments

For all feature engineering and tuning, we trained and tested on training and development test sets, respectively (as specified above). Final results are reported by folding the development test set into the training data and evaluating on the blind test set. We retain only those features that occur more than once.

For each approach, we report the Word Error Rate (WER) (i.e., the percentage of words that were incorrectly diacritized), along with the Diacritic Error Rate (DER) (i.e., the percentage of diacritics, including the null diacritic, that were incorrectly predicted). We also report both WER and DER for only those words that were not seen during training (UWER and UDER, respectively). We found that precision, recall, and f-score were nearly perfectly correlated with DER; hence, we omit this information for brevity.

5.1 Models for Evaluation

In previous work, Kübler et al. (2008) report the lowest error rates of the low-resource models. Although their results are not directly comparable to Zitouni et al. (2006), we have independently confirmed that the former slightly outperforms the latter using the same diacritics and on the same dataset (see Figure 4), thereby providing the strongest published baseline for Arabic on a common dataset. We denote this model as **`kübler`** and use it as a strong baseline for all datasets.

For the Arabic results, we additionally include Zitouni et al.'s (2006) lexical model (**`zitouni-lex`**) and their model that uses a segmenter and POS tagger (**`zitouni-all`**), which are not immediately available to us for Syriac. For yet another point of reference for Arabic, we provide the results from the state-of-the-art (resource-rich) approach of Habash and Rambow (2007) (**`habash`**). This model is at an extreme advantage, having access to a full morphological analyzer. Note that for these three models we simply report their published results and do not attempt to reproduce them.

Since **`kübler`** is of a different model class than ours, we consider an additional baseline that is a consonant-level CMM with access to the same information, namely, only those consonants within a window of 5 to either side (**`ccmm`**). This is equivalent to a special case of our hybrid model wherein both the word-level and the consonant-level Markov order are 0. The features that we extract from this window are the windowed n-gram features.

In order to assess the utility of previous diacritics and how effectively our features leverage them, we build a model based on the methodology from Section 3 but specify that all words are rare, effectively creating a consonant-only model that has access to the diacritics of previous words. We call this model **`cons-only`**. We note that the main difference between this model and **`zitouni-lex`** are features that depend on previous diacritized words.

Finally, we present results using our full hybrid model (**`hybrid`**). We use a Markov order of 2 at the word and consonant level for both **`hybrid`** and **`cons-only`**.

5.2 Consonant-Level Model and Rare Words

The hybrid nature of **`hybrid`** naturally raises the question of whether or not the inner consonant model should be trained only on rare words or on all of the data. In other words, is the distribution of diacritics different in rare words? If so, the consonant model should be trained only on rare words. To answer this question, we trained our consonant-level model (**`cons-only`**) on words occurring fewer than n times. We swept the value of the threshold n and compared the results to the same model trained on a random selection of words. As can be seen in Figure 3, the performance on unknown words (both UWER and UDER) using a model trained on rare words can be much lower than using a model trained on the same amount of randomly selected data. In fact, training on rare words can lead to a lower error rate on unknown words than training on all tokens in the corpus. This suggests that the distribution of diacritics in rare words is different from the distribution of diacritics in general. This difference may come from foreign words, especially in the Arabic news corpus.

While this phenomenon is more pronounced in some languages and with some models more than others, it appears to hold in the cases we tried. We found the WER for unknown words to be lowest for a threshold of 8, 16, 32, and 32 for Syriac, Arabic, Hebrew, and English, respectively.

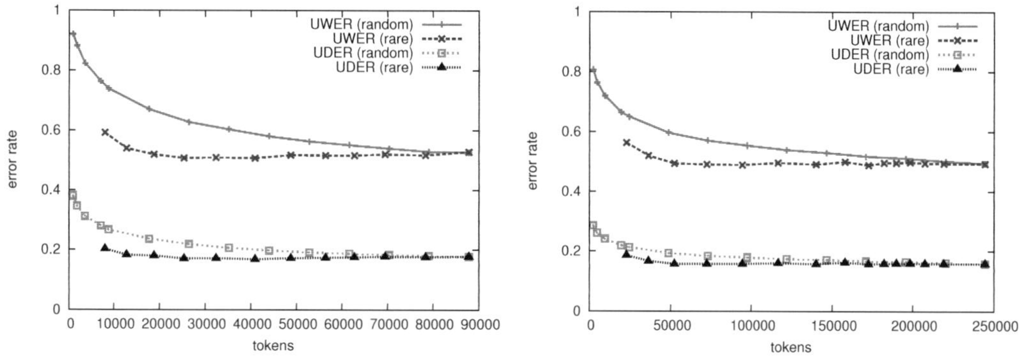

(a) Syriac (b) Arabic

Figure 3: Learning curves showing impact on consonant-level models when training on rare tokens for Syriac and Arabic. Series marked "rare" were trained with the least common tokens in the dataset.

	Approach	WER	DER	UWER	UDER
Syriac	kübler	15.04	5.23	64.65	18.21
	ccmm	13.99	4.82	**54.54**	**15.18**
	cons-only	12.31	5.03	55.68	19.09
	hybrid	**10.54**	**4.29**	55.16	18.86
Arabic	zitouni-lex	25.1	8.2	NA	NA
	kübler	23.61	7.25	66.69	20.51
	ccmm	22.63	6.61	57.71	16.10
	cons-only	**15.02**	**5.15**	48.10	15.76
	hybrid	17.87	5.67	**47.85**	**15.63**
	zitouni-all	18.0	5.5	NA	NA
	habash	14.9	4.8	NA	NA
Hebrew	kübler	30.60	12.96	89.52	36.86
	ccmm	29.67	12.05	80.02	**29.39**
	cons-only	23.39	10.92	75.70	33.34
	hybrid	**22.18**	**10.71**	**74.38**	32.40
English	kübler	10.54	4.38	**54.96**	**16.31**
	ccmm	11.60	4.71	58.55	16.34
	cons-only	8.71	3.87	58.93	17.85
	hybrid	**5.39**	**2.38**	57.24	16.51

Figure 4: Results for all languages and approaches

6 Discussion of Results

Since Syriac is of primary interest to us, we begin by examining the results from this dataset. Syriac appears to be easier to diacritize than Arabic, considering it has a similar number of diacritics and only one-third the amount of data. On this dataset, `hybrid` has the lowest WER and DER, achieving nearly 30% and 18% reduction in WER and DER, respectively, over `kübler`; it reduces both error rates over `cons-only` by more than 14%. These results attest to the effectiveness of our model in accounting for the observations made in Section 3.

A similar pattern holds for the Hebrew and English datasets, namely that `hybrid` reduces the WER over `kübler` by 28% to upwards of 50%; `cons-only` also consistently and significantly outperforms `kübler` and `ccmm`. However, the reduction in error rate for our `cons-only` and `hybrid` models tends to be lower for DER than WER in all languages except for English. In the case of `hybrid`, this is probably because it is inherently word-based. Having access to entire previous diacritized words may be a contributing factor as well, especially in `cons-only`.

When comparing model classes (`kübler` and `ccmm`), it appears that performance is comparable across all languages, with the maxent approach enjoying a slight advantage except in English. Interestingly, the maxent solution usually handles unknown words better, although it does not specifically target this case. Both models outperform `zitouni-lex` in Arabic, despite the fact that they use a much simpler feature set, most notably, the lack of previous diacritics. In the case of `ccmm` this may be attributable in part to our use of an L-BFGS optimizer, convergence criteria, feature selection, or other potential differences not noted in Zitouni et al. (2006). We note that the maxent-based approaches are much more time and memory intensive.

Using the Arabic data, we are able to compare our methods to several other published results.

The **cons-only** model significantly outperforms **zitouni-all** despite the additional resources to which the latter has access. This is evidence supporting our hypothesis that the diacritics from previous words in fact contain useful information for prediction. This empirically suggests that the independence assumptions in consonant-only models are too strict.

Perhaps even more importantly, our low-resource method approaches the performance of **habash**. We note that the differences may not be statistically significant, and also that Habash and Rambow (2007) omit instances in the data that lack solutions. In fact, **cons-only** has a lower WER than all but two of the seven techniques used by Habash and Rambow (2007), which use a morphological analyzer.

Interestingly, **hybrid** does worse than **cons-only** on this dataset, although it is still competitive with **zitouni-all**. We hypothesize that the observations from Section 3 do not hold as strongly for this dataset. For this reason, using a smooth interpolation function (rather than the abrupt one we employ) may be advantageous and is an interesting avenue for future research.

One last observation is that the approaches that use diacritics from previous words (i.e., **cons-only** and **hybrid**) usually have lower sentence error rates (not shown in Figure 4). This highlights an advantage of observation 5: that dependencies on previously diacritized words can help ensure a consistent tagging within a sentence.

7 Conclusions and Future Work

In this paper, we have presented a low-resource solution for automatic diacritization. Our approach is motivated by empirical observations of the ambiguity and frequency of undiacritized and diacritized words as well as by the hypothesis that diacritics from previous words provide useful information. The main contributions of our work, based on these observations, are (1) a hybrid word-level CMM combined with a consonant-level model for rare words, (2) a consonant-level model with dependencies on previous diacritized words, (3) new features that leverage these dependencies, and (4) an efficient, approximate decoder for these models. As expected, the efficacy of our approach varies across languages, due to differences in the actual ambiguity and frequency of words in these languages. Nevertheless, our models consistently reduce WER by 15% to nearly 50% over the best performing low-resource models in the literature. In Arabic, our models approach state-of-the-art despite not using a morphological analyzer. Arguably, our results have brought diacritization very close to being useful for practical application, especially when considering that we evaluated our method on the most difficult task in Arabic, which has been reported to have double the WER (Zitouni et al., 2006).

The success of this low-resource solution naturally suggests that where more resources are available (e.g., in Arabic), they could be used to further reduce error rates. For instance, it may be fruitful to incorporate a morphological analyzer or segmentation and part-of-speech tags.

In future work, we would like to consider using CRFs in place of MEMMs. Also, other approximate decoders used in pipeline approaches could be explored as alternatives to the one we used (e.g., Finkel et al., 2006). Additionally, we wish to include our model as a stage in a pipeline that segments, diacritizes, and labels morphemes. Since obtaining data for these tasks is substantially more expensive, we hope to use active learning to obtain more data.

Our framework is applicable for any sequence labeling task that can be done at either a word or a sub-word (e.g., character) level. Segmentation and lemmatization are particularly promising tasks to which our approach could be applied.

Finally, for the sake of completeness, we note that more recent work has been done based on our baseline models that has emerged since the preparation of the current work, particularly Zitouni et al. (2009) and Mohamed et al. (2009). We wish to address any improvements captured by this more recent work such as the use of different data sets and addressing problems with the *hamza* to decrease error rates.

Acknowledgments

We thank Imed Zitouni, Nizar Habash, Sandra Kübler, and Emad Mohamed for their assistance in reconstructing datasets, models, and features.

References

S. Ananthakrishnan, S. Narayanan, and S. Bangalore. 2005. Automatic diacritization of Arabic transcripts for automatic speech recognition. In *Proceedings of the International Conference on Natural Language Processing*.

A. L. Berger, S. Della Pietra, and V. J. Della Pietra. 1996. A maximum entropy approach to natural language processing. *Computational Linguistics*, 22:39–71.

Y. A. El-Imam. 2008. Synthesis of the intonation of neutrally spoken Modern Standard Arabic speech. *Signal Processing*, 88(9):2206–2221.

T. A. El-Sadany and M. A. Hashish. 1989. An Arabic morphological system. *IBM Systems Journal*, 28(4):600–612.

J. R. Finkel, C. D. Manning, and A. Y. Ng. 2006. Solving the problem of cascading errors: Approximate Bayesian inference for linguistic annotation pipelines. In *Proceedings of the 2006 Conference on Empirical Methods in Natural Language Processing*, pages 618–626.

Y. Gal. 2002. An HMM approach to vowel restoration in Arabic and Hebrew. In *Proceedings of the ACL-02 Workshop on Computational Approaches to Semitic Languages*, pages 1–7.

N. Habash and O. Rambow. 2007. Arabic diacritization through full morphological tagging. In *Human Language Technologies 2007: The Conference of the North American Chapter of the Association for Computational Linguistics; Companion Volume, Short Papers*, pages 53–56.

G. Kiraz. 1994. Automatic concordance generation of Syriac texts. In R. Lavenant, editor, *VI Symposium Syriacum 1992*, pages 461–471, Rome, Italy.

G. A. Kiraz. 2000. Multitiered nonlinear morphology using multitape finite automata: a case study on Syriac and Arabic. *Computational Linguistics*, 26(1):77–105.

D. Klein and C. D. Manning. 2002. Conditional structure versus conditional estimation in NLP models. In *Proceedings of the 2002 Conference on Empirical Methods in Natural Language Processing*, pages 9–16.

S. Kübler and E. Mohamed. 2008. Memory-based vocalization of Arabic. In *Proceedings of the LREC Workshop on HLT and NLP within the Arabic World*.

M. Maamouri, A. Bies, T. Buckwalter, and W. Mekki. 2004. The Penn Arabic Treebank: Building a large-scale annotated Arabic corpus. In *Proceedings of the NEMLAR Conference on Arabic Language Resources and Tools*, pages 102–109.

M. P. Marcus, B. Santorini, and M. A. Marcinkiewicz. 1994. Building a large annotated corpus of English: The Penn Treebank. *Computational Linguistics*, 19:313–330.

A. McCallum, D. Freitag, and F. Pereira. 2000. Maximum entropy Markov models for information extraction and segmentation. In *Proceedings of the 17th International Conference on Machine Learning*, pages 591–598.

E. Mohamed and S. Kübler. 2009. Diacritization for real-world Arabic texts. In *Proceedings of Recent Advances in Natural Language Processing 2009*.

R. Nelken and S. M. Shieber. 2005. Arabic diacritization using weighted finite-state transducers. In *Proceedings of the ACL Workshop on Computational Approaches to Semitic Languages*, pages 79–86.

J. Pearl and G. Shafer. 1988. *Probabilistic reasoning in intelligent systems: networks of plausible inference*. Morgan Kaufman, San Mateo, CA.

D. Vergyri and K. Kirchhoff. 2004. Automatic diacritization of Arabic for acoustic modeling in speech recognition. In *Proceedings of the COLING 2004 Workshop on Computational Approaches to Arabic Script-based Languages*, pages 66–73.

D. Yarowsky. 1999. A comparison of corpus-based techniques for restoring accents in Spanish and French text. *Natural language processing using very large corpora*, pages 99–120.

Zefania XML Project. 2009. Zefania XML bible: Leningrad codex. `http://sourceforge.net/projects/zefania-sharp/files/Zefania\%20XML\%20Bibles\%204\%20hebraica/Leningrad\%20Codex/sf_wcl.zip/download`.

I. Zitouni and R. Sarikaya. 2009. Arabic diacritic restoration approach based on maximum entropy models. *Computer Speech & Language*, 23(3):257–276.

I. Zitouni, J. S. Sorensen, and R. Sarikaya. 2006. Maximum entropy based restoration of Arabic diacritics. In *Proceedings of the 21st International Conference on Computational Linguistics and 44th Annual Meeting of the Association for Computational Linguistics*, pages 577–584.

Urdu Word Segmentation

Nadir Durrani
Institute for NLP
Universität Stuttgart
durrani@ims.uni-stuttgart.de

Sarmad Hussain
Center for Research in Urdu Language Processing
National University of Computer and Emerging Sciences
sarmad.hussain@nu.edu.pk

Abstract

Word Segmentation is the foremost obligatory task in almost all the NLP applications where the initial phase requires tokenization of input into words. Urdu is amongst the Asian languages that face word segmentation challenge. However, unlike other Asian languages, word segmentation in Urdu not only has space omission errors but also space insertion errors. This paper discusses how orthographic and linguistic features in Urdu trigger these two problems. It also discusses the work that has been done to tokenize input text. We employ a hybrid solution that performs an n-gram ranking on top of rule based maximum matching heuristic. Our best technique gives an error detection of 85.8% and overall accuracy of 95.8%. Further issues and possible future directions are also discussed.

1 Introduction

All language processing applications require input text to be tokenized into words for further processing. Languages like English normally use white spaces or punctuation marks to identify word boundaries, though with some complications, e.g. the word "e.g." uses a period in between and thus the period does not indicate a word boundary. However, many Asian languages like Thai, Khmer, Lao and Dzongkha do not have word boundaries and thus do not use white space to consistently mark word endings. This makes the process of tokenization of input into words for such languages very challenging.

Urdu is spoken by more than 100 million people, mostly in Pakistan and India[1]. It is an Indo-Aryan language, written using Arabic script from right to left, and Nastalique writing style (Hussain, 2003). Nastalique is a cursive writing system, which also does not have a concept of space. Thus, though space is used in typing the language, it serves other purposes, as discussed later in this paper. This entails that space cannot be used as a reliable delimiter for words. Therefore, Urdu shares the word segmentation challenge for language processing, like other Asian languages.

This paper explains the problem of word segmentation in Urdu. It gives details of work done to investigate linguistic typology of words and motivation of using space in Urdu. The paper then presents an algorithm developed to automatically process the input to produce consistent word segmentation, and finally discusses the results and future directions.

2 Urdu Writing System

Urdu is written in cursive Arabic script. Characters in general join with the neighbors within a word and in doing so acquire different shapes. Logically, a character can acquire up to four shapes, i.e. initial, medial, final position in a connected sequence or an isolated form. The characters having this four-way shaping are known as *joiners*. However, another set of characters only join with characters before them but do not join with character after them, and are termed as *non-joiners*. The non-joiners only have final and isolated forms. For example Arabic Letter Farsi Yeh ی is a joiner and has four shapes ﯾ, ﯿ, ﯽ and ﯼ respectively and Arabic letter Dal د is a non-joiner and has two forms د and ﺪ only. The shape that these characters acquire depends upon the context.

Table 1 lists the orthographic rules that Urdu characters follow. For example, the table shows that in the middle of a word, if the character is a non-joiner, it acquires final shape when following a

[1] Ethnologue.com
http://www.ethnologue.com/14/show_language.asp?code=URD

Human Language Technologies: The 2010 Annual Conference of the North American Chapter of the ACL, pages 528–536,
Los Angeles, California, June 2010.

joiner and isolated shape when following a non-joiner. This joining behavior results in formation of multiple connected portions within a word, each called a *ligature*.

Word	J-Shape	Example	NJ-Shape	Example
Start	I	مسجد	I_s	دجال
Middle	M after J	نمرہ	F after J	بندر
	I after NJ	دمبا	I_s after J	نادر
End	F after J	عجم	F after J	بند
	I_s after NJ	کام	I_s after NJ	رد
J = Joiners, NJ = Non-Joiners I = Initial, I_s = Isolated, M = Medial, F = Final Underlined = Shape in Consideration				

Table 1: Orthographic Rules for Urdu

The concept of space as a word boundary marker is not present in Urdu writing. As an Urdu learner, a person is not taught to leave a space between words, but only to generate correct shaping while writing. Thus, the concept of space is only learnt later on when the person learns how to use a computer. However, space is introduced as a tool to control the correct letter shaping and not to consistently separate words. For example, the native speaker learns to insert a space within the word ضرورت مند ("needy") to generate the correct shape of ت. Without space it appears as ضرورتمند which is visually incorrect. On contrary, the user finds it unnecessary to insert a space between the two words اردومرکز ("Urdu Center"), because the correct shaping is produced automatically as the first word ends with a non-joiner. Therefore اردومرکز and اردو مرکز look identical.

Though space character is not present in Urdu, with increasing usage of computer it is now being used, both to generate correct shaping (as discussed above) and also to separate words (a habit being carried over to Urdu from English literate computer users). This makes space an unreliable cue for word boundary. The problem is further obfuscated by the lack of a clear definition of a work in Urdu in some contexts. The next section discusses these issues.

3 Segmentation Issues in Urdu Text

The segmentation challenges can be divided into two categories, challenges caused due to joiner and non-joiner characters.

3.1 Space Omission

As discussed, for words ending with non-joiners correct shaping is generated even when space is not typed and thus, many times a user omits the space. Though there is no visible implication, from the perspective of computational processing not typing a space merges current word with the next word. Figure 1 below illustrates an example, where the phrase has eight words (or tokens) each ending with a non-joiner and thus the whole phrase can be written without a space and is still visibly same and equally readable.

قافلے کے صدر احمد شیر ڈوگر نے کہا

(a)

قافلےکےصدراحمدشیرڈوگرنےکہا

(b)

Figure 1: All Words Ending with Non-Joiners (a) with Spaces, (b) without Spaces between Words ("Troop Leader Ahmed Sher Dogar Said")

Another frequent set of space omissions are caused due to variation in the definition of a word in Urdu. There are certain function words in Urdu which may be combined with other function words and content words by some writers but may be written separately by others. Shape variation may also occur in some of these cases, but is overlooked by the writers. Table 2 gives some examples of such cases. Though the merged form is not considered correct diction, it is still frequently used and thus has to be handled. It is not considered spelling error but a writing variation.

POS	Combined	Separated	Translation
P_n+CM	آپکا	آپ کا	Yours
D+ NN	اسوقت	اس وقت	at that time
CM+ NN	کیطرف	کی طرف	Towards
V+TA	کریگی	کرے گی	will do
CM + P	کیلیے	کے لیے	For
P_n = Pronoun, D = Demonstrative, NN = Noun, CM = Case Marker, V=Verb, P = Particle			

Table 2: Multiple Words Written in Connected Form Causing Shaping Changes

Due to reasonable frequency of such cases, these may be considered as acceptable alternatives, and thus Urdu word segmentation system would need to deal with both forms and consider them equivalent. This process is productively applicable and not limited to a few pre-determined cases. Additional complication in the process arises from the fact that in some cases (last two cases in Table 2) the spellings also change when two words are written in combined form, due to the way these characters are encoded. Urdu considers ی and ے both logically same characters at a certain level, though with different shapes to indicated different vowels (Hussain, 2004). In combined form they render the same shape. However, Unicode terms ے as a non-joiner with no medial shape. Thus, the Urdu writers use ی to generate the medial position of ے in combined form.

3.2 Space Insertion

When multiple morphemes are juxtaposed within a word, many of them tend to retain their shaping as separate ligatures. If ending characters are joiners, space is usually inserted by writers to prevent them from joining and thus to retain the separate ligature identity. This causes an extra space within a word. Though this creates the visually acceptable form, it creates two tokens from a single word in the context of its processing. If the writers do not type a space between these two morphemes within a word they would join and create a visually incorrect shape. Such examples are common in Urdu[2]. Few of these cases are given in Table 3.

Class	A	B	Translation
i	شادی شدہ	شادیشدہ	Married
ii	موم بتی	مومبتی	Candle
iii	خواہ مخواہ	خواہمخواہ	Unnecessarily
iv	ٹیلی فون	ٹیلیفون	Telephone
v	پی ایچ ڈی	پیایچڈی	PhD
i= Affixation, ii = Compounding , iii = Reduplication, iv = Foreign Word, v = Abbreviations			

Table 3: (A) Separated Form (Correct Shaping, but Two Tokens), (B) Combined Form (Erroneous Shaping, with one Token)

As categorized in Table 3, the space insertion problem is caused due to multiple reasons. Data analyzed shows that space is inserted (i) to keep affixes separate from the stem, (ii) in some cases, to keep two words compounded together from visually merging, (iii) to keep reduplicated words from combining, (iv) to enhance readability of some foreign words written in Urdu, and (v) to keep English letters separate and readable when English abbreviations are transliterated.

3.3 Extent of Segmentation Issues in Urdu

In an earlier work on Urdu spell checking (Naseem and Hussain, 2007) report that a significant number of spelling errors[3] are due to irregular use of space, as discussed above. The study does a spelling check of an Urdu corpus. The errors reported by the spelling checker are manually analyzed. A total of 975 errors are found and of which 736 errors were due to irregular use of space (75.5%) and 239 errors are non-space-related errors (24.5%). Of the space related errors, majority of errors (672 or 70% of total errors) are due to space omission and 53 errors (5%) were due to space insertion. Thus irregular use of space causes an extremely high percentage of all errors and has to be addressed for all language processing applications for Urdu.

A study of Urdu words was also conducted as part of the current work. Text was used from popular Urdu online news sites (www.bbc.co.uk/urdu and http://search.jang.com.pk/). A data of 5,000 words from both corpora was observed and space insertion and omission cases were counted. These counts are given in Table 4. Counts for Space Insertion are sub-divided into the four categories identified earlier.

Problem	BBC	Jang	Total
Space Omission	373	563	936
Space Insertion			
Affixation	298	467	765
Reduplication	52	76	128
Compounding	133	218	351
Abbreviation	263	199	462
Total	1119	1523	2642

Table 4: Space Omission and Insertion Counts from Online BBC and Jang Urdu News Websites

The data shows that a significantly high percentage of errors related to space, with significant errors

[2] Though Unicode recommends using Zero Width Non-Joiner character in these context, this is not generally known by Urdu typists and thus not practiced; Further, this character is not available on most Urdu keyboards.

[3] Errors based on tokenization on space and punctuation markers

related to both omission and insertion. Within insertion errors, affixation, compounding and abbreviation related errors are more significant (because reduplication is a less frequent phenomenon).

In summary, the space related errors are significant and must be addressed as a precursor to any significant language and speech processing of the language

3.4 Ambiguity in Defining Urdu Word

Another confounding factor in this context it that there is no clear agreement on word boundaries of Urdu in some cases.

Compound words are hard to categorize as single or multiple words. Urdu forms compounds in three ways: (i) by placing two words together, e.g. ماں باپ ("parents", literally "father mother"), (ii) by putting a combining mark between them[4], e.g. وزیر اعظم ("prime minister"), and (iii) by putting the conjunction و between two words, e.g. نظم و ضبط ("Discipline").

Similarly certain cases of reduplication are also considered a single word by a native speaker, e.g. فرفر ("fluently") and برابر ("equal"), while others are not, e.g. آہستہ آہستہ ("slowly"). There are also cases which are ambiguous, as there is no agreement even within native speakers.

Moreover, certain function words, normally case markers, postpositions and auxiliaries, may be written joined with other words in context or separately. The words like کے لیے may also be written in joined form کیلیے, and the different forms may be perceived as multiple or single words respectively.

This is demonstrated by the results of a study done with 30 native speakers of Urdu (including university students, language researchers and language teachers). The subjects were asked to mark whether they considered some text a single word or a sequence of two words. Some relevant results are given in Table 5. The table indicates that for the types of phenomena in Table 4, the native speakers do not always agree on the word boundary, that certain cases are very ambiguous, and that writing with or without space also changes the perception of where the word boundary should lie.

Word(s)	# of Words		Category
	1	2	
وزیرمملکت	24	6	Compounding with conjunctive diacritic
حکومتِ پاکستان	17	13	-do-
صورتِ حال	28	2	-do-
صورتحال	28	2	-do-
امن وامان	25	5	Compounding with conjunctive character و
نشو ونما	29	1	-do-
عقیدت مندی	30	0	Suffixation
جرائم پیشہ	22	8	-do-
جگہ جگہ	3	27	Reduplication
ساتھ ساتھ	3	27	-do-
ہوگی	15	15	Space omission between two auxiliaries
جائیگا	18	12	Space omission between verb and auxiliary
جائے گا	5	25	Same as above but without space omission

Table 5: Survey on Word Definition

As the word boundary is ambiguously perceived, it is not always clear when to mark it. To develop a more consistent solution, the current work tags the different levels of boundaries, and it is left up to the application provider using the output to decide which tags to translate to word level boundaries. Free morphemes are placed and identified at first level. At second level we identify strings that are clearly lexicalized as a single word. Compounds, reduplication and abbreviations are dealt at third level.

4 Summary of Existing Techniques

Rule based techniques have been extensively used for word segmentation. Techniques including longest matching (Poowarawan, 1986; Rarunrom, 1991) try to match longest possible dictionary look-up. If a match is found at n^{th} letter next look-up is performed starting from $n+1$ index. Longest matching with word binding force is used for Chinese word segmentation (Wong and Chang, 1997). However, the problem with this technique is that it consistently segments a letter sequence the same way, and does not take the context into account.

[4] The diacritics (called *zer-e-izafat* or *hamza-e-izafat*) are optional, and are not written in the example given.

Thus, shorter word sequences are never generated, even where they are intended.

Maximum matching is another rule based technique that was proposed to solve the shortcomings of longest matching. It generates all possible segmentations out of a given sequence of characters using dynamic programming. It then selects the best segmentation based on some heuristics. Most popularly used heuristic selects the segmentation with minimum number of words. This heuristic fails when alternatives have same number of words. Some additional heuristics are then often applied, including longest match (Sornlertlamvanich, 1995). Many variants of maximum matching have been applied (Liang, 1986; Li et al., 1991; Gu and Mao, 1994; Nie et al., 1994).

There is a third category of rule based techniques, which also use additional linguistic information for generating intermediate solutions which are then eventually mapped onto words. For example, rule based techniques have also been applied to languages like Thai and Lao to determine syllables, before syllables are eventually mapped onto words, e.g. see (Phissamy et al., 2007).

There has been an increasing application of statistical methods, including n-grams, to solve word segmentation. These techniques are based at letters, syllables and words, and use contextual information to resolve segmentation ambiguities, e.g. (Aroonmanakul, 2002; Krawtrakul et al., 1997). The limitation of statistical methods is that they only use immediate context and long distance dependencies cannot be directly handled. Also the performance is based on training corpus. Nevertheless, statistical methods are considered to be very effective to solve segmentation ambiguities.

Finally, another class of segmentation techniques applies several types of features, e.g. Winnow and RIPPER algorithms (Meknavin et al., 1997; Blum 1997). The idea is to learn several sources of features that characterize the context in which each word tends to occur. Then these features are combined to remove the segmentation ambiguities (Charoenpornsawat and Kijsirikul 1998).

5 Segmentation Model for Urdu

Although many other languages share the same problem of word boundary identification for language processing, Urdu problem is unique due to its cursive script and its irregular use of space to create proper shaping. Though other languages only have space omission challenge, Urdu has both omission and insertion problems further confounding the issue.

We employ a combination of techniques to investigate an effective algorithm to achieve Urdu segmentation. These techniques are incorporated based on knowledge of Urdu linguistic and writing system specific information for effective segmentation. For space omission problem a rule based maximum matching technique is used to generate all the possible segmentations. The resulting possibilities are ranked using three different heuristics, namely min-word, unigram and bigram techniques.

For space insertion, we first sub-classify the problem based on linguistic information, and then use different techniques for the different cases. Space insertion between affixes is done by extracting all possible affixes from Urdu corpus. Some affixes in Urdu are also free morphemes so it is important to identify in segmentation process whether or not they are part of preceding or following word. For example ناک is also a free morpheme ("nose") and a suffix that makes adjective from noun, e.g. in word خطر ناک ("dangerous"). This is done based on the part of speech information of the words in the context.

Reduplication is handled using edit distance algorithm. In Urdu the reduplicated morpheme is either the same or a single edit-distance from the base morpheme, e.g. فرفر has same string repeated, برابر has one insertion, and ٹھیک ٹھاک has one substitution. Thus, if a string is less than two edits from its neighbor it is an instance of reduplication[5]. As the examples suggest, the reduplication may not only be limited to word initial position and may also occur word medially. However, if the length of base word is less than four, it is further to avoid function words (case markers, postpositions, aux-

[5] Insertion, deletion and substitution are all considered contributing a single edit distance here.

iliaries, etc.) from being mistakenly identified as a case of reduplication, e.g. کیا گیا ("was done") has two words with a single edit distance but is not a reduplicated sequence.

Urdu does not abbreviate strings, but abbreviations from English are frequently transliterated into Urdu. This sequence can be effectively recognized by developing a simple finite automaton. The automaton treats marks all such co-occurring morphemes because they are likely to be an English abbreviation transliterated into Urdu, e.g. پی ایچ ڈی ("PhD"). If such morphemes are preceding proper names then these are not combined as they are more likely to be the initials of an abbreviated name, e.g. این ڈی شاکر ("N. D. Shakir"). This approach confuses the morpheme کے (genitive case marker) of Urdu with the transliteration of English letter "k". If we write پی ایچ ڈی کے بعد ("after PhD"), it is interpreted as "P H D K after". This has to be explicitly handled.

As classification of compounds into one or two word sequences is unclear, unambiguous cases are explicitly handled via lexical look-up. An initial lexicon of 1850 compound words has been developed for the system based on a corpus of Urdu. Common foreign words are also included in this list.

5.1 Algorithm

The segmentation process starts with preprocessing, which involves removing diacritics (as they are optionally used in Urdu and not considered in the current algorithm because they are frequently incorrectly marked by users[6]) and normalizing the input text to remove encoding ambiguities[7]. Input is then tokenized based on space and punctuation characters in the input stream. As has been discussed, space does not necessarily indicate word boundary. However presence of space does imply word or morpheme boundary in many cases, which can still be useful. The tokenization process gives what we call an Orthographic Word (OW). OW is used instead of "word" because one OW may eventually give multiple words and multiple OWs may combine to give a single word. Keeping space related information also keeps the extent of problem to be solved within a reasonable computational complexity. For example input string نادر خان درانی (the name of the first author) with spaces giving three OWs, creates 2 x 1 x 7 = 14 possible segmentations when sent separately to the maximum matching module (space omission error removal - see Figure 2). However, if we remove the spaces from the input and send input as a single OW نادرخاندرانی to maximum matching process, we get 77 possible segmentations. This number grows exponentially with the length of input sentence. Throwing away space character means we are losing important information so we keep that intact to our use.

After pre-processing a series of modules further process the input string and convert the OWs into a sequence of words. This is summarized in Figure 2 and explained below.

Each OW is sent to a module which deals with space omission errors. This module extracts all possible morpheme segmentations out of an OW. Ten best segmentations of these are selected based on minimum-word heuristic. This heuristic prefers segmentations with minimum number of morphemes. Such a heuristic is important to prevent the search space to explode. We observed that using 10-best segmentations proved to be sufficient in most cases as OW normally encapsulates two or three Urdu words but as a heuristic we also added a feature which increases this number of 10-best segmentations to 15, 20, 25-best and so on depending upon number of characters in an OW. Ten best segmentations for each OW are merged with the extracted segmentations of other OWs. Up till here we have successfully resolved all space omission errors and the input sentence has been segmented into morphemes. The 10^n (where 'n' is No. of OWs) segmentations are then passed on to space insertion error removal module. This module has several sub-modules that handle different linguistic phenomena like reduplication, affixation, abbreviations and compounding.

[6] The word اعلیٰ is written with the super-script Alef placed on Lam and Yay characters. The latter variation is correct but the former incorrect variation is also common in the corpus.

[7] Unicode provides multiple codes for a few letters, and both composed and decomposed forms for others. These have to be mapped onto same underlying encoding sequence for further processing. See http://www.crulp.org/software/langproc/urdunormalization.htm for details.

The reduplication identification module employs single edit distance algorithm to see if adjacent morphemes are at single edit-distance of each other. If the edit distance is less than two, then the reduplication is identified and marked.

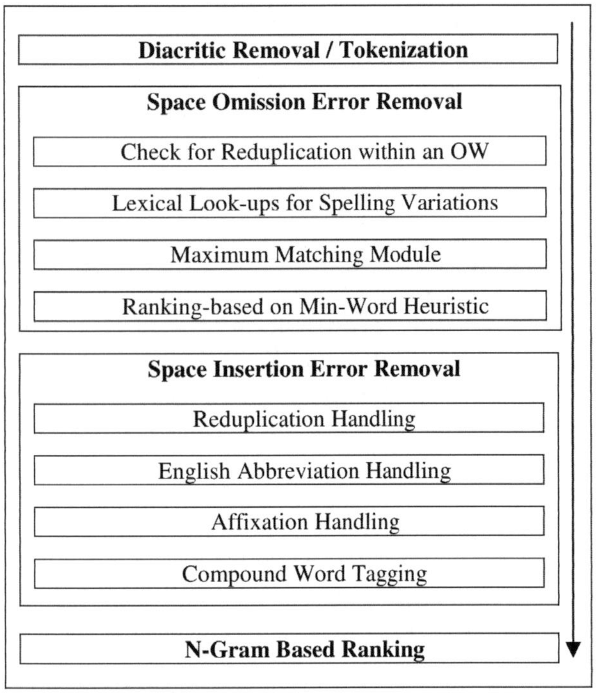

Figure 2: Urdu Word Segmentation Process

For example the module will correctly recognize consecutively occurring OWs بھولا and بھالا as a case of reduplication. Reduplication is also applied earlier in space omission error module as there may also be a case of reduplication within a single OW. This module handles such cases, by dividing words in halves and identifying possible reduplications. Thus, if the words are written without space, e.g. بھولابھالا (innocent) they are still identified and tagged as reduplicated words بھولا and بھالا.

This list of words is then fed into an automaton which recognizes the sequence of abbreviations generated by transliterating English letters.

A complete affix list is compiled, and in the next stage the short listed word sequences are processed through a process which looks through this list to determine if any of the OWs may be combined. Part of speech information of stem is also used to confirm if OWs can be merged.

Urdu compounds are finally identified. This is done by using a compound list generated through the corpus. As compounding is arbitrary, where speakers are not certain in many cases that a sequence of morphemes form a single compound or not, the segmentation process leaves this level to the discretion of the user. Whichever compounds are listed in a compound lexicon are treated as a single compound word. Those not listed are not tagged as compounds. User may enhance this list arbitrarily. The lexicon is initialized with a list of non-controversial compound, as verified from published dictionaries.

Eventually, all the segmentations are re-ranked. We used three different re-ranking methods namely minimum-word heuristic, unigram and bi-gram based sequence probabilities, comparative analysis.

Based on the segmentation process, the output sequence contains the following tagging. As discussed earlier, the word segmentation may be defined based on this tagging by the individual application using this process.

Phenomenon	Tags	Examples
Word	<W></W>	<W>اعلان</W>
Root	<R></R>	<W><R>ضرورت</R> <S>مند</S></W>
Suffix	<S></S>	<W><R>حیرت</R> <S>انگیز</S></W>
Prefix	<P></P>	<W><P>بد</P> <R>تہذیبی</R></W>
XY Compounds	<C1></C1>	<C1><W>انشاء</W> <W>اللّٰہ</W></C1>
X-e-Y Compounds	<C2></C2>	<C2><W>وزیر</W> <W>اعلی</W></C2>
X-o-Y Compounds	<C3></C3>	<C3><W>گرد</W> <W>و</W> <W>نواح</W></C3>
Reduplication	<Rd></Rd>	<Rd><W>ٹھیک</W> <W>ٹھاک</W></Rd>
Abbreviations	<A></A>	<A><W>پی</W> <W>سی</W> </A>

Figure 3: Urdu Word Segmentation Tag Set

A regular word is tagged using <w> …</w> pair. Roots, suffixes and prefixes are also tagged within a word. Reduplication, compounding and abbreviations are all considered to be multi-word tags and relevant words are grouped within these tags. Three different kind of compounding is separately tagged.

6 Results

The algorithm was tested on a very small, manually segmented corpus of 2367 words. The corpus we selected contained 404 segmentation errors with 221 cases of space omissions and 183 cases of space insertions. In space insertion category there were 66 cases of affixation, 63 cases of compounding, 32 cases of reduplication and 22 cases of abbreviations. The results for all three techniques are shown below:

Categories	Errors	%ages
Affixation	59/66	89.39
Reduplication	27/32	84.37
Abbreviations	19/22	86.36
Compounds	28/63	44.44
Total	133/183	72.67

Table 6: Percentages of Number of Errors Detected in Different Categories of Space Insertion Error

There were 221 cases of space omission errors where multiple words were written in a continuum. Given below is a table that shows how many of these were correctly identified by each of the used techniques. Clearly, statistical techniques outperform a simple minimum number of words heuristic. Bigrams are likely to produce better results if the training corpus is improved. Our training corpus contained manually segmented 70K words. The bigram probabilities are obtained using SRILM-Toolkit (Stolcke, 2002).

Categories	Errors	%ages
Maximum Matching	186/221	84.16
Unigram	214/221	96.83
Bigram	209/221	94.5

Table 7: %age of No. of Errors Detected in Space Omission with Different Ranking Techniques

Following table gives cumulative results for correctly identified space omission and insertion errors.

Categories	Errors	%ages
Maximum Matching	323/404	79.95
Unigram	347/404	85.8
Bigram	339/404	83.9

Table 8: %age of No. of Errors Detected Cumulatively

Final table counts total number of words (reduplication, compounds and abbreviations cases are inclusive) in test corpus and total number of correctly identified words after running the entire segmentation process.

Categories	Detected	%ages
Maximum Matching	2209/2367	93.3
Unigram	2269/2367	95.8
Bigram	2266/2367	95.7

Table 9: Percentage of Correctly Detected Words

7 Future Work

This work presents a preliminary effort on word segmentation problem in Urdu. It is a multi-dimensional problem. Each dimension requires a deeper study and analysis. Each sub-problem has been touched in this work and a basic solution for all has been devised. However to improve on results each of these modules require a separate analysis and study. Statistics is only used in ranking of segmentations. In future work bi-gram statistics can be used to merge morphemes. More data can be tagged to find out joining probabilities for the affixes that occur as free morpheme. Such analysis will reveal whether an affix is more inclined towards joining or occurs freely more frequently. Similarly a corpus can be tagged on compounds. For each morpheme its probability to occur in compound can be calculated. If two or more morphemes with higher compounding probabilities co-occur they can be joined together. Similarly corpus can be tagged for abbreviations.

Ranking of segmentations and affix merging can be improved if POS tags are also involved with bigram probabilities. Use of POS tags with n-gram technique is proven to be very helpful in solving unknown word problems. Our model does not explicitly handle unknown words. Currently the maximum matching module splits an unknown OW into smaller Urdu morphemes. For example کولیسینکوف(Kolesnikov) is erroneously split into کولی،سین،کو،ف. More serious problems occur in cases when OW is a mixture of known and unknown words. For example in case فریزرکوجاناہے ("Fraser must go"). All these are to be addressed in future work.

References

Andreas, S. 2002. SRILM - an extensible language modeling toolkit. In Intl. Conf. Spoken Language Processing, Denver, Colorado.

Aroonmanakul, W. 2002. Collocation and Thai Word Segmentation. In *proceeding of SNLPOriental* COCOSDA.

Blum, A. 1997. Empirical Support for Winnow and Weighted-Majority Algorithm: Results on a Calendar Scheduling Domain, Machine Learning, 26:5-23.

Charoenpornsawat, P., Kijsirikul, B. 1998. Feature-Based Thai Unknown Word Boundary Identification Using Winnow. In *Proceedings of the 1998 IEEE Asia-Pacific Conference on Circuits and Systems (APCCAS'98).*

Gu, P. and Mao, Y. 1994. The adjacent matching algorithm of Chinese automatic word segmentation and its implementation in the QHFY Chinese-English system. In *International Conference on Chinese Computing*, Singapore.

Hussain, S. 2003. www. LICT4D . asia / Fonts / Nafees_Nastalique. In the *Proceedings of 12th AMIC Annual Conference on E-Worlds: Governments, Business and Civil Society, Asian Media Information Center,* Singapore. Also available at http://www.crulp.org/Publication/papers/2003/www.LICT4D.asia.pdf.

Hussain, S. 2004. Letter to Sound Rules for Urdu Text to Speech System. In the *Proceedings of Workshop on Computational Approaches to Arabic Script-based Languages,* COLING 2004, Geneva, Switzerland, 2004.

Krawtrakul, A., Thumkanon. C., Poovorawan. Y. and Suktarachan. M. 1997. Automatic Thai Unknown Word Recognition. In *Proceedings of the natural language Processing* Pacific Rim Symposium.

Li, B.Y., S. Lin, C.F. Sun, and M.S. Sun. 1991. A maximum-matching word segmentation algorithm using corpus tags for disambiguation. In *ROCLING IV*, pages: 135-146, Taipei. ROCLING

Liang, N. 1986. A written Chinese automatic segmentation system-CDWS. In *Journal of Chinese Information Processing*, 1(1):44-52.

Meknavin. S., Charenpornsawat. P. and Kijsirikul. B. 1997. Feature-based Thai Words Segmentation. NLPRS, Incorporating SNLP.

Naseem, T., Hussain, S. 2007. Spelling Error Trends in Urdu. In the *Proceedings of Conference on Language Technology (CLT07),* University of Peshawar, Pakistan.

Nie, J., Jin W., and Hannan, M. 1994. A hybrid approach to unknown word detection and segmentation of Chinese. In *International Conference on Chinese Computing,* Singapore.

Phissamay, P., Dalolay,V., Chanhsililath, C., Silimasak, O. Hussain, S., and Durrani, N. 2007. Syllabification of Lao Script for Line Breaking. In *PAN Localization Working Papers 2004-2007.* .

Poowarawan, Y., 1986. Dictionary-based Thai Syllable Separation. In *Proceedings of the Ninth Electronics Engineering Conference*

Rarunrom, S., 1991. Dictionary-based Thai Word Separation. Senior Project Report.

Sornlertlamvanich, V. 1995. Word Segmentation for Thai in a Machine Translation System (in Thai), *Papers on Natural Language Processing, NECTEC, Thailand*

Wong, P., Chan, C. 1996. Chinese Word Segmentation based on Maximum Matching and Word Binding Force. In *Proceedings of COLING 96*, pp. 200-203.

Enabling Monolingual Translators: Post-Editing vs. Options

Philipp Koehn
University of Edinburgh
10 Crichton Street
Edinburgh, EH8 9AB
Scotland, United Kingdom
pkoehn@inf.ed.ac.uk

Abstract

We carried out a study on monolingual translators with no knowledge of the source language, but aided by post-editing and the display of translation options. On Arabic-English and Chinese-English, using standard test data and current statistical machine translation systems, 10 monolingual translators were able to translate 35% of Arabic and 28% of Chinese sentences correctly on average, with some of the participants coming close to professional bilingual performance on some of the documents.

While machine translation systems have advanced greatly over the last decade, nobody seriously expects human-level performance any time soon, except for very constraint settings. But are todays systems good enough to enable monolingual speakers of the target language without knowledge of the source language to generate correct translations? And what type of assistance from machine translation is most helpful for such translators?

We carried out a study that involved monolingual translators who had no knowledge of Chinese and Arabic to translate documents from the NIST 2008[1] test sets, being assisted by statistical machine translation systems trained on data created under the GALE[2] research program.

Our study shows that monolingual translators were able to translate 35% of Arabic and 28% of Chinese sentences, under a strict standard of correctness that scored professional bilingual translations as 61% and 66% correct for Arabic and Chinese, respectively. We found also large variability among the participants and between the documents in the study, indicating the importance of general language skills and domain knowledge. The results suggest that a skilled monolingual translator can compete with a bilingual translator, when using todays machine translation systems.

1 Related Work

The use of human translators in combination with machine translation is as old as the emergence of the first effective machine translation systems. Typically, this takes the form of a human translator post-editing machine translation output, and rarely of a human translator guiding the decisions of a machine translation system. Recent examples of using post-editing of machine translation in tools for translation tools are the Google Translator Toolkit (Galvez and Bhansali, 2009) and the WikiBabel project (Kumaran et al., 2008).

A recent seminal effort on building interactive machine translation systems (Langlais et al., 2000; Barrachina et al., 2009) looked at a tighter integration of machine translation and human translation by developing a prediction model that interactively suggests translations to the human translator, taking her prior translation decisions into account. This approach was recently re-implemented and extended by Koehn (2009).

Our study uses both post-editing and the extended interactive machine translation approach as types of assistance for translations. In our case, however, we look at monolingual translators, while prior work has focused on bilingual translators.

Another effort to enable monolingual translators looked at a more linguistically motivated tool using syntactic analysis to inform their translation decisions (Albrecht et al., 2009).

The quality of the translations produced by

[1]http://www.itl.nist.gov/iad/mig/tests/mt/
[2]http://www.darpa.mil/ipto/programs/gale/gale.asp

Human Language Technologies: The 2010 Annual Conference of the North American Chapter of the ACL, pages 537–545,
Los Angeles, California, June 2010.

monolingual translators was previously explored by Callison-Burch (2005) in a submission to the NIST 2005 evaluation campaign, but not properly evaluated. The idea of using post-editing by monolingual speakers without access to the source as a metric to evaluate machine translation quality of different systems was explored by Callison-Burch et al. (2009) in the WMT 2009 shared task.

2 Human Translation

Except for constraint settings with a very limited domain, translation quality by trained humans is much higher than automatic translation methods. Especially for the commercially most relevant field of publication-quality translation of official reports, product manuals, promotion material, web sites, and so on, machine translation currently plays at most a supportive role.

2.1 Translation Tools

The main draw-back of relying on professional human translators is their high cost. A number of technological advances in the industry have increased the productivity of translators, and thus lowered their cost, over the last two decades. The pervasive use of computers and the Internet has reduced the cost of management, and helped a industry where translation is outsources many times over: from the original customer to a translation agency, from a translation agency to freelance translators, and maybe some additional levels in between.

The use of computers has also led to the adoption of tools such as translation memories[3] (databases of translated material that are queried for fuzzy matches, i.e. translated sentences similar to the one to be processed), monolingual and bilingual concordances (showing words used in context, and their translations), terminology databases, online dictionaries and thesauri, and basic editing tools such as word processors and spell checkers (Desilets, 2009).

The use of machine translation has not yet made great inroads into the toolbox of professional translators. Being reduced to mere post-editors of badly machine translated texts is not an appealing prospect, and machine translation is generally considered (rightly or wrongly) not yet good enough to increase productivity. More innovative use of machine translations such as interactive machine translation (Langlais et al., 2000) has not advanced much beyond the research stage. There is rich potential for improvements and entirely new tools.

2.2 Translation Skills

A fully qualified professional translator has to have two sets of skills when translating a text. On the one hand the language skills to generally understand the source language and to write well in the target language, and on the other hand the domain knowledge to understand the content of a possibly very specialized technical document. Both skill sets may be hard to find, especially in combination.

In fact, it is common practice in the translation industry to differentiate translators according to their qualifications. For instance, junior translators may produce the first draft, and senior translators edit it — which they will be able to do much faster than a translation from scratch by themselves.

Human translation is also performed in a non-professional environment by generally less qualified volunteer translators. To give just a few example: there are vibrant communities that concern themselves with the translation of Wikipedia articles[4] (Kumaran et al., 2008), open source software documentation,[5] movie subtitles,[6] and even material such as the TED conference talks.[7]

Research has shown that less qualified translators are able to increase their productivity and quality disproportionally when given automatic assistance (Koehn and Haddow, 2009). Assistance may be as limited as offering machine translation in a post-editing environment, as for instance provided by Google Translator Toolkit[8] (Galvez and Bhansali, 2009) which provides a special function to translate Wikipedia articles.

In this context, our work looks at one extreme of the skill range: translators that have no knowledge of the source language. While we would not expect them to compete with professional translators that have this knowledge, their inferior performance may

[3] for instance: Trados, http://www.trados.com/

[4] http://en.wikipedia.org/wiki/Wikipedia:Translation

[5] http://l10n.kde.org/

[6] http://www.opensubtitles.org/

[7] http://www.ted.com/translate/

[8] http://translate.google.com/toolkit/

Figure 1: Translation Options shown to the monolingual translator. The machine translation of the Arabic input sentence is: *The us house of representatives adopted thursday a law calls for the withdrawal of us combat troops from iraq by the first of april 2008, defying once again president george bush who opposed to setting any date.*

be remedied as suggested above: their texts may be edited by a more qualified translator, or their domain knowledge may augment the language skills of a collaborating translator.

From the view of human translation, the main question that this paper is trying to answer is: how well can monolingual translators perform, given the current quality of machine translation, and what types of assistance offered by a machine translation system is most helpful?

3 Machine Translation

Statistical machine translation has made great progress over the last two decades, with changing models, learning methods, decoding algorithms, decision rules, etc. While there is increasing effort to build grammar-based translation models that take into account the recursive nature of language, currently the most popular models are still phrase-based.

3.1 Phrase-Based Models

In phrase based models, the input is segmented into text chunks (that do not have to correspond to linguistic phrases), each is translated and may be reordered, and the output is assembled with the help of a language model. The translations for individual phrases are called translation options. Typically, up to 20 translation options for each input phrase are considered during decoding.

The large number of translation options and their even larger combinatorial arrangement creates a search space that is too large to exhaustively explore, creating the need for a heuristic search algorithm. During the heuristic search a search graph is constructed. This search graph can be converted into a word lattice, which is useful for n-best list generation, or in our case interactive machine translation.

3.2 Interactive Machine Translation

The by-products of phrase-based models have been used in a type of computer aided translation tool called interactive machine translation. In these setups, the human translator is creating the translation, but receives suggestions how to complete the sentence or is offered alternative translation options for the input words and phrases.

The translation options that the decoder is using are ranked based on their probability and presented to the human translator, as done by Koehn (2009). Sentence completion prediction is based on the search graph (Barrachina et al., 2009). If the human translator starts a translation that diverges from the suggestion, the interactive translation tool quickly computes a approximate match in the search graph and uses this as a starting point for further predictions.

In our experiments, we offer both translation options and interactive sentence completion predictions to the user. See Figure 1 for an example.

3.3 Arabic and Chinese

This paper is using machine translation systems for Arabic–English and Chinese–English that were developed in the context of the recent GALE research program funded by DARPA.

The choice of these two languages pairs has two motivations: first, a lot of resources have gone into improving translation quality for these language pairs. An important question is how the improvements in translation quality can be utilized.

The second motivation for choosing Arabic–English and Chinese–English is that they are undecipherably foreign for a typical European or American speaker of English. The fact that both languages are written in a different script already makes it impossible to spot cognates, except for the occasional number. In our study, the test subjects had to practically exclusively rely on the given sentence translations or phrase translations options.

3.4 Evaluation of Machine Translation

Chinese–English is considered significantly harder than Arabic–English, as measured by automatic metrics (which measure similarity to a human reference translation), human evaluation metrics such as HTER (which measures the number of editing steps necessary to correct the output into an acceptable translation), or human judgment on the correctness of the translation, its fluency or adequacy (which is typically measured on a scale from 1 to 5).

All these metrics have been criticized in the past as too simple, biased towards statistical systems, non-repeatable, having low intra and inter-annotator agreement, or plainly too expensive to use. How to properly evaluate machine translation quality is still an open problem.

From the view of machine translation evaluation, this paper explores the question if current machine translation systems have reached the goal to bring across the meaning of a foreign text. The ability of a monolingual target language speaker to produce correct translations (based on her understanding of the machine translation output) is a test for this goal. It sets aside the problems of clumsy wordings and grammatical errors. To relate this to traditional error metrics in machine translation: we focus on the adequacy opposed to the fluency of translation.

Language	Sentences	Words
Arabic	9,320,356	228,712,189
Chinese	2,039,399	49,564,193

Table 1: Training data: number of sentences and English words in the parallel training data

4 Experiment

We trained translation models using Moses (Koehn et al., 2007) on the bilingual data provided by the LDC, with additional monolingual data from the English Gigaword corpus for an interpolated 5-gram language model. Basic statistics about the corpus are given in Table 1. The systems are close to the state of the art.

We used four news stories for each of the two languages for the monolingual translators. The news stories were selected from the evaluation sets of the 2008 machine translation evaluation campaign organized by NIST. See Table 2 for details. The news stories are rather short (around 10 sentences each), since we opted for a variety of stories rather than long stories.

The evaluation set comes with four reference translations. This allowed us to use one of the reference translation as gold standard for the evaluation, and the other three reference translations as competitors for the monolingual translations.

We recruited 10 monolingual translators, students at the University of Edinburgh for the study. None of the students had knowledge of either Chinese or Arabic. Each translator was given all eight stories to translate, half of the stories with only the machine translation output (Post-editing task) and half of the stories with interactive assistance as described in Section 3.2: prediction of sentence completion and translation options (Options).

In both cases, we also displayed the Arabic or Chinese source sentence to the translator, which may show some clues regarding punctuation, numbers, or the length of source words. The translators had no knowledge of the source script.

After all the translations were completed, we assessed the translation quality. Since we did not have access to bilingual speakers for this, we resorted to the standard manual setup, where human judges are asked to assess the quality of each sentence transla-

Story	Headline	Sent.	Words
1: Chinese	White House Pushes for Nuclear Inspectors to Be Sent as Soon as Possible to Monitor North Korea's Closure of Its Nuclear Reactors	6	207
2: Chinese	Torrential Rains Hit Western India, 43 People Dead	10	204
3: Chinese	Research Shows a Link between Arrhythmia and Two Forms of Genetic Variation	7	247
4: Chinese	Veteran US Goalkeeper Keller May Retire after America's Cup	10	367
5: Arabic	Britain: Arrests in Several Cities and Explosion of Suspicious Car	7	224
6: Arabic	Ban Ki-Moon Withdraws His Report on the Sahara after Controversy Surrounding Its Content	8	310
7: Arabic	Pakistani Opposition Leaders Call on Musharraf to Resign.	11	312
8: Arabic	Al-Maliki: Iraqi Forces Are Capable of Taking Over the Security Dossier Any Time They Want	8	255

Table 2: News stories used in the experiment with headlines from the reference translation

Assistance	Arabic	Chinese
Bilingual	61±6%	66±6%
Postediting	35±4%	26±4%
Options	34±4%	30±4%

Table 3: Correctness of translations (with 95% confidence interval) under the two types of assistance, compared against professional reference translations

tion compared to a reference translation in context — the first reference translation in the NIST evaluation set which was produced by a professional translation agency.

We used a strict evaluation metric: a binary judgment, if the translation is correct. Correct was defined as *a fluent translation that contains the same meaning in the document context.* The reference translation was shown with its document context (two sentences before and after). We used a variant of the web-based evaluation tool of the 2009 Workshop on Statistical Machine Translation.

5 Results

The headline results are displayed in Table 3. The bilingual translations which were taken from the other three reference sets score surprisingly low: only about two thirds of the sentences were deemed to be correct by our judges. This is a better result than the monolingual translators performance, who translate around one third of the sentences correctly, except for a statistically significant worse showing for post-editing Chinese–English.

Translator	Arabic	Chinese
bi1	67±10%	65±11%
bi2	49±10%	67±10%
bi3	67±10%	67±9%
mono1	48±11%	31±11%
mono2	29±10%	21±8%
mono3	26±10%	12±7%
mono4	50±11%	26±11%
mono5	25±10%	25±10%
mono6	26±9%	18±9%
mono7	23±10%	29±10%
mono8	50±11%	50±10%
mono9	42±10%	37±11%
mono10	25±9%	32±10%

Table 4: Correctness by translator (note: different bilingual translators for Arabic and Chinese)

Translation speed of the monolingual translators varied, but it was mostly around 500 words per hour (7 seconds per word), which is roughly comparable to the lower end of professional translation speed.

Table 4 shows the performance of the individual translators. The 95% confidence intervals are very wide, due to the few sentences that were translated by each translator, but some monolingual translators are significantly better than others. Some of the monolingual translators seem to compete head-to-head with the professional bilingual translators: three monolingual translators perform as well as one of the bilingual translators for Arabic–English, albeit one has to be cautioned by the wide confidence intervals. See also Figure 2 for a graphical display.

Story	BLEU	Bilingual	Post-ed.	Options
1: Chinese	42.8	76±16%	32±13%	40±13%
2: Chinese	24.8	70±10%	39±8%	33±9%
3: Chinese	35.1	61±12%	19±8%	17±7%
4: Chinese	26.7	64±11%	12±6%	36±9%
5: Arabic	43.6	60±14%	10±6%	13±7%
6: Arabic	48.5	57±13%	34±9%	43±9%
7: Arabic	60.5	72±10%	45±8%	36±9%
8: Arabic	55.7	50±13%	45±10%	39±10%

Table 5: Correctness by story and BLEU score of MT

	Length	Bilingual	Post-ed.	Options
Arabic	≤15 words	81±16%	56±15%	48±16%
Arabic	16–30 words	54±10%	41±8%	37±7%
Arabic	>30 words	62±8%	27±6%	29±6%
Chinese	≤15 words	60±12%	48±10%	21±9%
Chinese	16–30 words	73±13%	25±9%	32±10%
Chinese	>30 words	68±8%	17±5%	33±6%

Table 6: Correctness by sentence length

Similarly, performance on the different stories varies (Table 5, Figure 3): For instance, the monolingual translators struggled with the Chinese medical and sports stories (no. 3 and 4) and the Arabic car explosion story (no. 5), while even on average, they are close to bilingual translation quality on the Arabic stories 6 and 8. Note that correctness correlates mildly with BLEU.

Surprisingly, we did not find a consistent effect of sentence length on the quality of the translations (see Table 6). We expected to find worse translations among the longer sentences, but this is not the case for the all conditions.

6 Analysis

Our results have shown that monolingual translators are often able to produce correct translation when post-editing output from current Arabic–English and Chinese–English machine translation systems. For Chinese–English, they are better when given additional assistance in form of translation options and interactive machine translation.

We give in Figure 4 examples for translations by machine translation, as well as monolingual and bilingual translators.

One puzzle is the low score for the professional human translators, as only two thirds of their trans-

(a) Critical judges

REF: *Torrential Rains Hit Western India, 43 People Dead*

BI: *Heavy Rains Plague Western India Leaving 43 Dead*

(b) Mistakes by the professional translators

REF: *Over just two days on the 29th and 30th, rainfall in Mumbai reached 243 mm.*

BI: *The rainfall in Mumbai had reached 243 cm over the two days of the 29th and 30th alone.*

(c) Bad English by monolingual translators

MONO: *The western region of india heavy rain killed 43 people.*

(d) Mistranslated / untranslated name

REF: *Johndroe said that the two leaders ...*

MT: *Strong zhuo, pointing out that the two presidents ...*

MONO: *Qiang Zhuo pointed out that the two presidents ...*

(e) Wrong relationship between entities

REF: *The next match against Colombia will probably be the US team's and Keller's last performance in this America's Cup competition.*

MT: *The colombian team for the match, and it is very likely that the united states and kai in the americas cup final performance.*

MONO6: *The Colombian team and the United States are very likely to end up in the Americas Cup as the final performance.*

MONO8: *The next match against Colombia is likely to be the United States' and Keller's final performance in the current Copa America.*

(f) Badly muddled machine translation

REF: *In the current America's cup, he has, just as before, been given an important job to do by head coach Bradley, but he clearly cannot win the match singlehanded. The US team, made up of "young guards,"...*

MT: *He is still being head coach bradley appointed to important, it's even a fist ", four young guards at the beginning of the ", the united states is...*

MONO: *He is still being considered important by head coach Bradley who appointed him. It is a fight with "four young guards at the beginning of their careers", but the United States...*

Figure 4: Examples of translations

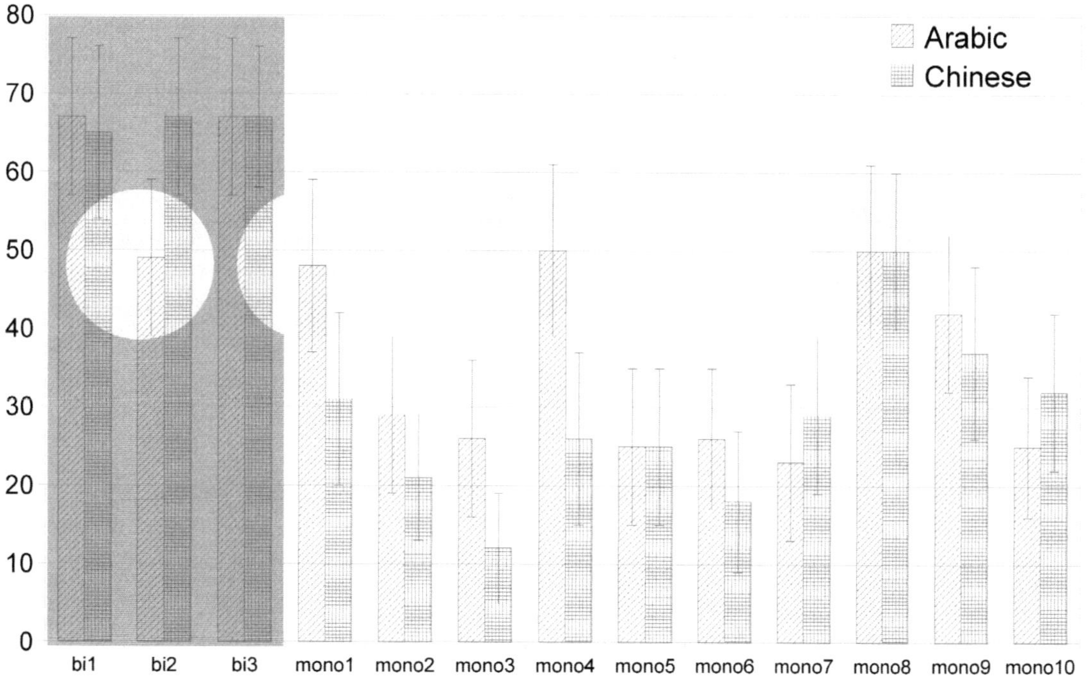

Figure 2: Quality of different bilingual and monolingual translators: For Arabic, three monolingual translators are as good as the worst bilingual translator (around 50% of sentences judged as correct). For detailed numbers, see Table 4.

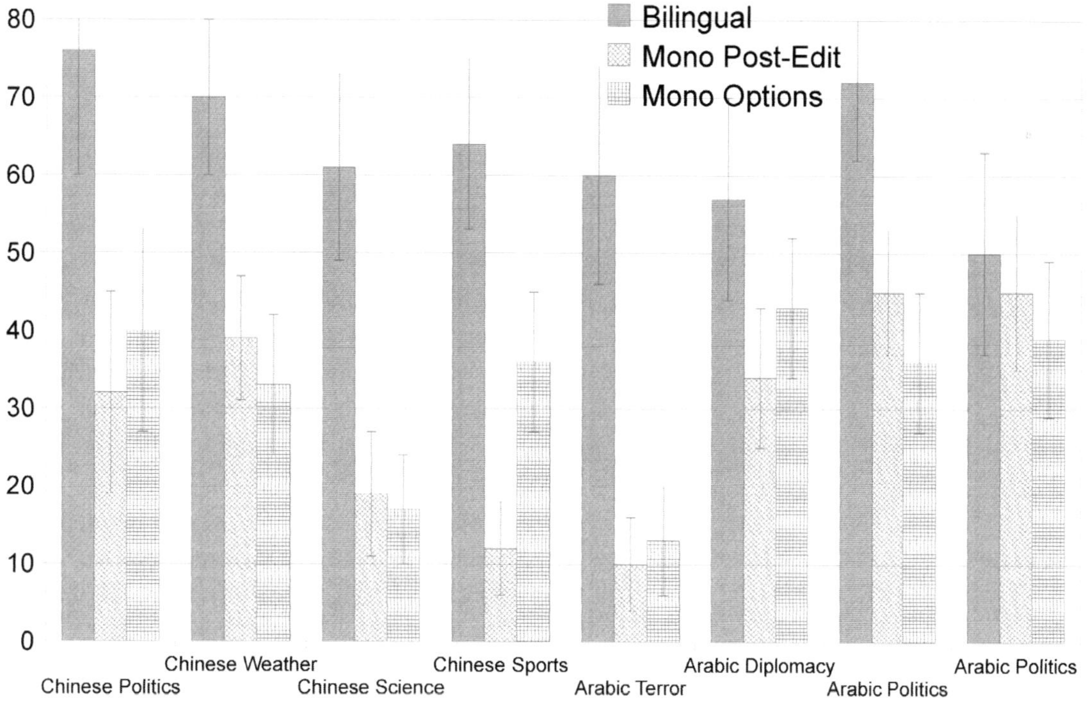

Figure 3: Translation quality of monolingual translators differs significantly between stories: For the last Ararbic politics stories average performance is close to bilingual quality, while it is bad for the Chinese science and sports as well as the Arabic terror story. For detailed numbers, please see Table 5.

lations were deemed to be correct. The example (a) shows such a translation, and it is hard to tell why it was deemed wrong by all three judges who looked at it. There are real mistakes in the professional translations, as example (b) shows, which mistakes the rain fall amount as *243cm* instead of *243mm*.

Some monolingual translators, by the way, also had problems with that number. The machine translation system is not very well in translating numbers, which could be relatively easily addressed.

Sometimes monolingual translators are just not thorough enough in their efforts, as example (c) shows, where the output does have the correct meaning elements, but it is just not correct English. These type of examples explain the big difference between the different monolingual translators.

A severe problem for monolingual translators are untranslated or mistranslated names. In example (d) *Johndroe* was referred to by monolingual translators as *Qiang Zhuo* or *Strong Zhuo*. The statistical machine translation system we used has no special name transliteration component, so often a name remains untranslated. Without given the right translation as a choice, the monolingual is in no position of completing a correct translation.

The monolingual translators' world and domain knowledge helps them a great deal to piece together translations, but sometimes it is not enough, as example (e) shows. There is some connection between *final performance*, *United States* and *Columbia*, but it is not the final performance for both teams as MONO6 renders it. Translator MONO8 got it right, but other translators made different mistakes.

Finally, there are some cases, as example (f) shows, where the machine translation is just so bad, that monolingual translators have no chance to render a proper translation of the sentence, especially when only post-editing.

7 Conclusion

We approached this study from two directions: the motivation to enable monolingual translators and the need for a way to assess the quality of todays machine translation systems.

Coming from a human translator's perspective, we asked what type of assistance machine translation can provide for a human translator. We compared the use of interactive machine translation against post-editing, and found no significant difference for Arabic (34% vs. 35%), but better performance with richer assistance for Chinese (30% vs. 26%). We believe that there is ample opportunity to provide additional assistance and we will explore this in future work.

Coming from a machine translation perspective, we asked if current systems are good enough to bring across the meaning of documents, even if generating output language with grammatical and idiomatic mistakes. Given the harsh metric we use to assess translation quality (complete correctness of a sentence), we showed that monolingual translators were able to produce translations that were on average 35% (Arabic) and 28% (Chinese) correct, compared to 61% (Arabic) and 66% (Chinese) correctness for professional bilingual translations.

Arguable, the method we use to assess the preservation of meaning in machine translation is superior to subjective adequacy judgments: it separates the task of defining the meaning of a machine translation from the assessment of its correctness.

We identified name and number translation as important aspects to improve performance on this task.

We also learned that there are significant difference between human translators, which indicates that general language skills and effort are very important. We also learned that the performance varies significantly for different documents in a way that hints at the importance of domain knowledge. In conclusion, a good monolingual translator has good language skills in the target language and understands the domain. In this case, this study suggests, she may be as good as a professional bilingual translator.

Acknowledgement

This work was supported in part by the GALE program of the Defense Advanced Research Projects Agency, Contract No. HR0011-06-C-0022, and in part by the EuroMatrixPlus project funded by the European Commission (7th Framework Programme). This study was made possible by the work of the monolingual translators.

References

Albrecht, J., Hwa, R., and Marai, G. E. (2009). Correcting automatic translations through collaborations between MT and monolingual target-language users. In *Proceedings of the 12th Conference of the European Chapter of the ACL (EACL 2009)*, pages 60–68, Athens, Greece. Association for Computational Linguistics.

Barrachina, S., Bender, O., Casacuberta, F., Civera, J., Cubel, E., Khadivi, S., Lagarda, A., Ney, H., Tomás, J., Vidal, E., and Vilar, J.-M. (2009). Statistical approaches to computer-assisted translation. *Computational Linguistics*, 35(1):3–28.

Callison-Burch, C. (2005). Linear B system description for the 2005 NIST MT evaluation exercise. In *Proceedings of Machine Translation Evaluation Workshop*.

Callison-Burch, C., Koehn, P., Monz, C., and Schroeder, J. (2009). Findings of the 2009 Workshop on Statistical Machine Translation. In *Proceedings of the Fourth Workshop on Statistical Machine Translation*, pages 1–28, Athens, Greece. Association for Computational Linguistics.

Desilets, A. (2009). Up close and personal with a translator - how translators really work. In *Machine Translation Summit XII*. Tutorial.

Galvez, M. and Bhansali, S. (2009). Translating the world's information with google translator toolkit.

Koehn, P. (2009). A web-based interactive computer aided translation tool. In *Proceedings of the ACL Interactive Poster and Demonstration Sessions*.

Koehn, P. and Haddow, B. (2009). Interactive assistance to human translators using statistical machine translation methods. In *Machine Translation Summit XII*.

Koehn, P., Hoang, H., Birch, A., Callison-Burch, C., Federico, M., Bertoldi, N., Cowan, B., Shen, W., Moran, C., Zens, R., Dyer, C. J., Bojar, O., Constantin, A., and Herbst, E. (2007). Moses: Open source toolkit for statistical machine translation. In *Proceedings of the 45th Annual Meeting of the Association for Computational Linguistics Companion Volume Proceedings of the Demo and Poster Sessions*, pages 177–180, Prague, Czech Republic. Association for Computational Linguistics.

Kumaran, A., Saravanan, K., and Maurice, S. (2008). wikiBABEL; community creation of multilingual data. In *Babel Wiki Workshop 2008: Cross-Language Communication*.

Langlais, P., Foster, G., and Lapalme, G. (2000). Transtype: a computer-aided translation typing system. In *Proceedings of the ANLP-NAACL 2000 Workshop on Embedded Machine Translation Systems*.

Online Learning for Interactive Statistical Machine Translation

Daniel Ortiz-Martínez
Dpto. de Sist. Inf. y Comp.
Univ. Politéc. de Valencia
46071 Valencia, Spain
dortiz@dsic.upv.es

Ismael García-Varea
Dpto. de Informática
Univ. de Castilla-La Mancha
02071 Albacete, Spain
ivarea@info-ab.uclm.es

Francisco Casacuberta
Dpto. de Sist. Inf. y Comp.
Univ. Politéc. de Valencia
46071 Valencia, Spain
fcn@dsic.upv.es

Abstract

State-of-the-art Machine Translation (MT) systems are still far from being perfect. An alternative is the so-called Interactive Machine Translation (IMT) framework. In this framework, the knowledge of a human translator is combined with a MT system. The vast majority of the existing work on IMT makes use of the well-known *batch learning* paradigm. In the batch learning paradigm, the training of the IMT system and the interactive translation process are carried out in separate stages. This paradigm is not able to take advantage of the new knowledge produced by the user of the IMT system. In this paper, we present an application of the *online learning* paradigm to the IMT framework. In the online learning paradigm, the training and prediction stages are no longer separated. This feature is particularly useful in IMT since it allows the user feedback to be taken into account. The online learning techniques proposed here incrementally update the statistical models involved in the translation process. Empirical results show the great potential of online learning in the IMT framework.

1 Introduction

Information technology advances have led to the need for more efficient translation methods. Current MT systems are not able to produce ready-to-use texts. Indeed, MT systems usually require human post-editing to achieve high-quality translations.

One way of taking advantage of MT systems is to combine them with the knowledge of a human translator in the IMT paradigm, which is a special type of the computer-assisted translation paradigm (Isabelle and Church, 1997). An important contribution to IMT technology was pioneered by the *TransType* project (Foster et al., 1997; Langlais et al., 2002) where data driven MT techniques were adapted for their use in an interactive translation environment.

Following the TransType ideas, Barrachina et al. (2009) proposed a new approach to IMT, in which fully-fledged statistical MT (SMT) systems are used to produce full target sentence hypotheses, or portions thereof, which can be partially or completely accepted and amended by a human translator. Each partial, correct text segment is then used by the SMT system as additional information to achieve improved suggestions. Figure 1 illustrates a typical IMT session.

source($\mathbf{f}$): Para ver la lista de recursos
reference($\hat{\mathbf{e}}$): To view a listing of resources

inter.-0	$\mathbf{e}_p$						
	$\mathbf{e}_s$	*To*	*view*	*the*	*resources*	*list*	
inter.-1	$\mathbf{e}_p$	To	view				
	k			**a**			
	$\mathbf{e}_s$				*list*	*of*	*resources*
inter.-2	$\mathbf{e}_p$	To	view	a	list		
	k				**i**		
	$\mathbf{e}_s$				*ng*	*resources*	
inter.-3	$\mathbf{e}_p$	To	view	a	listing		
	k					**o**	
	$\mathbf{e}_s$					*f*	*resources*
accept	$\mathbf{e}_p$	To	view	a	listing	of	resources

Figure 1: IMT session to translate a Spanish sentence into English. In interaction-0, the system suggests a translation ($\mathbf{e}_s$). In interaction-1, the user moves the mouse to accept the first eight characters "To view " and presses the **a** key (k), then the system suggests completing the sentence with "*list of resources*" (a new $\mathbf{e}_s$). Interactions 2 and 3 are similar. In the final interaction, the user accepts the current suggestion.

In this paper, we also focus on the IMT framework. Specifically, we present an IMT system that is able to learn from user feedback. For this purpose, we apply the *online learning* paradigm to the IMT framework. The online learning techniques that we propose here allow the statistical models involved in the translation process to be incrementally updated.

Human Language Technologies: The 2010 Annual Conference of the North American Chapter of the ACL, pages 546–554,
Los Angeles, California, June 2010.

Figure 2 (inspired from (Vidal et al., 2007)) shows a schematic view of these ideas. Here, $\mathbf{f}$ is the input sentence and $\mathbf{e}$ is the output derived by the IMT system from $\mathbf{f}$. By observing $\mathbf{f}$ and $\mathbf{e}$, the user interacts with the IMT system until the desired output $\hat{\mathbf{e}}$ is produced. The input sentence $\mathbf{f}$ and its desired translation $\hat{\mathbf{e}}$ can be used to refine the models used by the system. In general, the model is initially obtained through a classical batch training process from a previously given training sequence of pairs ($\mathbf{f}_i$,$\mathbf{e}_i$) from the task being considered. Now, the models can be extended with the use of valuable user feedback.

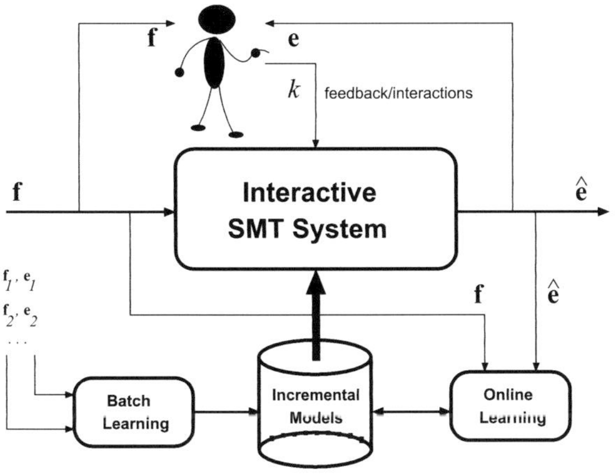

Figure 2: An Online Interactive SMT system

2 Interactive machine translation

IMT can be seen as an evolution of the SMT framework. Given a sentence $\mathbf{f}$ from a source language $\mathcal{F}$ to be translated into a target sentence $\mathbf{e}$ of a target language $\mathcal{E}$, the fundamental equation of SMT (Brown et al., 1993) is the following:

$$\hat{\mathbf{e}} = \underset{\mathbf{e}}{\operatorname{argmax}} \{Pr(\mathbf{e} \mid \mathbf{f})\} \quad (1)$$

$$= \underset{\mathbf{e}}{\operatorname{argmax}} \{Pr(\mathbf{f} \mid \mathbf{e})\, Pr(\mathbf{e})\} \quad (2)$$

where $Pr(\mathbf{f} \mid \mathbf{e})$ is approximated by a *translation model* that represents the correlation between the source and the target sentence and where $Pr(\mathbf{e})$ is approximated by a *language model* representing the well-formedness of the candidate translation $\mathbf{e}$.

State-of-the-art statistical machine translation systems follow a loglinear approach (Och and Ney, 2002), where direct modelling of the posterior probability $Pr(\mathbf{e} \mid \mathbf{f})$ of Equation (1) is used. In this case, the decision rule is given by the expression:

$$\hat{\mathbf{e}} = \underset{\mathbf{e}}{\operatorname{argmax}} \left\{ \sum_{m=1}^{M} \lambda_m h_m(\mathbf{e}, \mathbf{f}) \right\} \quad (3)$$

where each $h_m(\mathbf{e}, \mathbf{f})$ is a feature function representing a statistical model and λ_m its weight.

Current MT systems are based on the use of phrase-based models (Koehn et al., 2003) as translation models. The basic idea of Phrase-based Translation (PBT) is to segment the source sentence into phrases, then to translate each source phrase into a target phrase, and finally to reorder the translated target phrases in order to compose the target sentence. If we summarize all the decisions made during the phrase-based translation process by means of the hidden variable $\tilde{a}_1^K$, we obtain the expression:

$$Pr(\mathbf{f}|\mathbf{e}) = \sum_{K, \tilde{a}_1^K} Pr(\tilde{f}_1^K, \tilde{a}_1^K \mid \tilde{e}^K) \quad (4)$$

where each $\tilde{a}_k \in \{1 \ldots K\}$ denotes the index of the target phrase $\tilde{e}$ that is aligned with the k-th source phrase $\tilde{f}_k$, assuming a segmentation of length K.

According to Equation (4), and following a maximum approximation, the problem stated in Equation (2) can be reframed as:

$$\hat{\mathbf{e}} \approx \arg\max_{\mathbf{e},\mathbf{a}} \{p(\mathbf{e}) \cdot p(\mathbf{f}, \mathbf{a} \mid \mathbf{e})\} \quad (5)$$

In the IMT scenario, we have to find an extension $\mathbf{e}_s$ for a given prefix $\mathbf{e}_p$. To do this we reformulate Equation (5) as follows:

$$\hat{\mathbf{e}}_s \approx \arg\max_{\mathbf{e}_s,\mathbf{a}} \{p(\mathbf{e}_s \mid \mathbf{e}_p) \cdot p(\mathbf{f}, \mathbf{a} \mid \mathbf{e}_p, \mathbf{e}_s)\} \quad (6)$$

where the term $p(\mathbf{e}_p)$ has been dropped since it does depend neither on $\mathbf{e}_s$ nor on $\mathbf{a}$.

Thus, the search is restricted to those sentences $\mathbf{e}$ which contain $\mathbf{e}_p$ as prefix. It is also worth mentioning that the similarities between Equation (6) and Equation (5) (note that $\mathbf{e}_p\mathbf{e}_s \equiv \mathbf{e}$) allow us to use the same models whenever the search procedures are adequately modified (Barrachina et al., 2009).

Following the loglinear approach stated in Equation (3), Equation (6) can be rewriten as:

$$\hat{\mathbf{e}}_s = \underset{\mathbf{e}_s,\mathbf{a}}{\operatorname{argmax}} \left\{ \sum_{m=1}^{M} \lambda_m h_m(\mathbf{e}, \mathbf{a}, \mathbf{f}) \right\} \quad (7)$$

which is the approach that we follow in this work.

A common problem in IMT arises when the user sets a prefix ($\mathbf{e}_p$) which cannot be found in the phrase-based statistical translation model. Different solutions have been proposed to deal with this problem. The use of word translation graphs, as a compact representation of all possible translations of a source sentence, is proposed in (Barrachina et al., 2009). In (Ortiz-Martínez et al., 2009), a technique based on the generation of partial phrase-based alignments is described. This last proposal has also been adopted in this work.

3 Related work

In this paper we present an application of the online learning paradigm to the IMT framework. In the online learning setting, models are trained sample by sample. Our work is also related to model adaptation, although model adaptation and online learning are not exactly the same thing.

The online learning paradigm has been previously applied to train discriminative models in SMT (Liang et al., 2006; Arun and Koehn, 2007; Watanabe et al., 2007; Chiang et al., 2008). These works differ from the one presented here in that we apply online learning techniques to train generative models instead of discriminative models.

In (Nepveu et al., 2004), dynamic adaptation of an IMT system via cache-based model extensions to language and translation models is proposed. The work by Nepveu et al. (2004) constitutes a domain adaptation technique and not an online learning technique, since the proposed cache components require pre-existent models estimated in batch mode. In addition to this, their IMT system does not use state-of-the-art models.

To our knowledge, the only previous work on online learning for IMT is (Cesa-Bianchi et al., 2008), where a very constrained version of online learning is presented. This constrained version of online learning is not able to extend the translation models due to technical problems with the efficiency of the learning process. In this paper, we present a purely statistical IMT system which is able to incrementally update the parameters of all of the different models that are used in the system, including the translation model, breaking with the above mentioned constraints. What is more, our system is able to learn from scratch, that is, without any preexisting model stored in the system. This is demonstrated empirically in section 5.

4 Online IMT

In this section we propose an online IMT system. First, we describe the basic IMT system involved in the interactive translation process. Then we introduce the required techniques to incrementally update the statistical models used by the system.

4.1 Basic IMT system

The basic IMT system that we propose uses a log-linear model to generate its translations. According to Equation (7), we introduce a set of seven feature functions (from h_1 to h_7):

- **n-gram language model (h_1)**
  $h_1(\mathbf{e}) = \log(\prod_{i=1}^{|\mathbf{e}|+1} p(e_i|e_{i-n+1}^{i-1}))$, [1] where $p(e_i|e_{i-n+1}^{i-1})$ is defined as follows:

$$p(e_i|e_{i-n+1}^{i-1}) = \frac{\max\{c_X(e_{i-n+1}^{i}) - D_n, 0\}}{c_X(e_{i-n+1}^{i-1})} + \frac{D_n}{c_X(e_{i-n+1}^{i-1})} N_{1+}(e_{i-n+1}^{i-1}\bullet) \cdot p(e_i|e_{i-n+2}^{i-1}) \quad (8)$$

where $D_n = \frac{c_{n,1}}{c_{n,1}+2c_{n,2}}$ is a fixed discount ($c_{n,1}$ and $c_{n,2}$ are the number of n-grams with one and two counts respectively), $N_{1+}(e_{i-n+1}^{i-1}\bullet)$ is the number of unique words that follows the history e_{i-n+1}^{i-1} and $c_X(e_{i-n+1}^{i})$ is the count of the n-gram e_{i-n+1}^{i}, where $c_X(\cdot)$ can represent true counts $c_T(\cdot)$ or modified counts $c_M(\cdot)$. True counts are used for the higher order n-grams and modified counts for the lower order n-grams. Given a certain n-gram, its modified count consists in the number of different words that precede this n-gram in the training corpus.

Equation (8) corresponds to the probability given by an n-gram language model with an interpolated version of the Kneser-Ney smoothing (Chen and Goodman, 1996).

[1] $|\mathbf{e}|$ is the length of $\mathbf{e}$, e_0 denotes the *begin-of-sentence* symbol, $e_{|\mathbf{e}|+1}$ denotes the *end-of-sentence* symbol, $e_i^j \equiv e_i...e_j$

- **target sentence-length model** (h_2)
$h_2(\mathbf{e}, \mathbf{f}) = \log(p(|\mathbf{f}| \mid |\mathbf{e}|)) = \log(\phi_{|\mathbf{e}|}(|\mathbf{f}|+0.5) - \phi_{|\mathbf{e}|}(|\mathbf{f}| - 0.5))$, where $\phi_{|\mathbf{e}|}(\cdot)$ denotes the cumulative distribution function (cdf) for the normal distribution (the cdf is used here to integrate the normal density function over an interval of length 1). We use a specific normal distribution with mean $\mu_{|\mathbf{e}|}$ and standard deviation $\sigma_{|\mathbf{e}|}$ for each possible target sentence length $|\mathbf{e}|$.

- **inverse and direct phrase-based models** (h_3, h_4)
$h_3(\mathbf{e}, \mathbf{a}, \mathbf{f}) = \log(\prod_{k=1}^{K} p(\tilde{f}_k|\tilde{e}_{\tilde{a}_k}))$, where $p(\tilde{f}_k|\tilde{e}_{\tilde{a}_k})$ is defined as follows:

$$p(\tilde{f}_k|\tilde{e}_{\tilde{a}_k}) = \beta \cdot p_{phr}(\tilde{f}_k|\tilde{e}_{\tilde{a}_k}) + (1-\beta).p_{hmm}(\tilde{f}_k|\tilde{e}_{\tilde{a}_k}) \quad (9)$$

In Equation (9), $p_{phr}(\tilde{f}_k|\tilde{e}_{\tilde{a}_k})$ denotes the probability given by a statistical phrase-based dictionary used in regular phrase-based models (see (Koehn et al., 2003) for more details). $p_{hmm}(\tilde{f}_k|\tilde{e}_{\tilde{a}_k})$ is the probability given by an HMM-based (intra-phrase) alignment model (see (Vogel et al., 1996)):

$$p_{hmm}(\tilde{f}|\tilde{e}) = \epsilon \sum_{a_1^{|\tilde{f}|}} \prod_{j=1}^{|\tilde{f}|} p(\tilde{f}_j|\tilde{e}_{a_j}) \cdot p(a_j|a_{j-1}, |\tilde{e}|) \quad (10)$$

The HMM-based alignment model probability is used here for smoothing purposes as described in (Ortiz-Martínez et al., 2009).

Analogously h_4 is defined as:
$h_4(\mathbf{e}, \mathbf{a}, \mathbf{f}) = \log(\prod_{k=1}^{K} p(\tilde{e}_{\tilde{a}_k}|\tilde{f}_k))$

- **target phrase-length model** (h_5)
$h_5(\mathbf{e}, \mathbf{a}, \mathbf{f}) = \log(\prod_{k=1}^{K} p(|\tilde{e}_k|))$, where $p(|\tilde{e}_k|) = \delta(1-\delta)^{|\tilde{e}_k|}$. h_5 implements a target phrase-length model by means of a geometric distribution with probability of success on each trial δ. The use of a geometric distribution penalizes the length of target phrases.

- **source phrase-length model** (h_6)
$h_6(\mathbf{e}, \mathbf{a}, \mathbf{f}) = \log(\prod_{k=1}^{K} p(|\tilde{f}_k| \mid |\tilde{e}_{\tilde{a}_k}|))$, where $p(|\tilde{f}_k| \mid |\tilde{e}_{\tilde{a}_k}|) = \delta(1-\delta)^{abs(|\tilde{f}_k|-|\tilde{e}_{\tilde{a}_k}|)}$ and $abs(\cdot)$ is the absolute value function. A geometric distribution is used to model this feature (it penalizes the difference between the source and target phrase lengths).

- **distortion model** (h_7)
$h_7(\mathbf{a}) = \log(\prod_{k=1}^{K} p(\tilde{a}_k|\tilde{a}_{k-1}))$, where $p(\tilde{a}_k|\tilde{a}_{k-1}) = \delta(1-\delta)^{abs(b_{\tilde{a}_k} - l_{\tilde{a}_{k-1}})}$, $b_{\tilde{a}_k}$ denotes the beginning position of the source phrase covered by $\tilde{a}_k$ and $l_{\tilde{a}_{k-1}}$ denotes the last position of the source phrase covered by $\tilde{a}_{k-1}$. A geometric distribution is used to model this feature (it penalizes the reorderings).

The log-linear model, which includes the above described feature functions, is used to generate the suffix $\mathbf{e}_s$ given the user-validated prefix $\mathbf{e}_p$. Specifically, the IMT system generates a partial phrase-based alignment between the user prefix $\mathbf{e}_p$ and a portion of the source sentence $\mathbf{f}$, and returns the suffix $\mathbf{e}_s$ as the translation of the remaining portion of $\mathbf{f}$ (see (Ortiz-Martínez et al., 2009)).

4.2 Extending the IMT system from user feedback

After translating a source sentence $\mathbf{f}$, a new sentence pair $(\mathbf{f}, \mathbf{e})$ is available to feed the IMT system (see Figure 1). In this section we describe how the log-linear model described in section 4.1 is updated given the new sentence pair. To do this, a set of *sufficient statistics* that can be incrementally updated is maintained for each feature function $h_i(\cdot)$. A sufficient statistic for a statistical model is a statistic that captures all the information that is relevant to estimate this model.

Regarding feature function h_1 and according to equation (8), we need to maintain the following data: $c_{k,1}$ and $c_{k,2}$ given any order k, $N_{1+}(\cdot)$, and $c_X(\cdot)$ (see section 4.1 for the meaning of each symbol). Given a new sentence $\mathbf{e}$, and for each k-gram e_{i-k+1}^{i} of $\mathbf{e}$ where $1 \leq k \leq n$ and $1 \leq i \leq |\mathbf{e}|+1$, we modify the set of sufficient statistics as it is shown in Algorithm 1. The algorithm checks the changes in the counts of the k-grams to update the set of sufficient statistics. Sufficient statistics for D_k are updated following the auxiliar procedure shown in Algorithm 2.

Feature function h_2 requires the incremental calculation of the mean $\mu_{|\mathbf{e}|}$ and the standard deviation $\sigma_{|\mathbf{e}|}$ of the normal distribution associated to a target sentence length $|\mathbf{e}|$. For this purpose the procedure described in (Knuth, 1981) can be used. In this procedure, two quantities are maintained for each normal distribution: $\mu_{|\mathbf{e}|}$ and $S_{|\mathbf{e}|}$. Given a new sentence

input : n (higher order), e^i_{i-k+1} (k-gram),
$\mathcal{S} = \{\forall j(c_{j,1}, c_{j,2}), N_{1+}(\cdot), c_X(\cdot)\}$
(current set of sufficient statistics)
output : $\mathcal{S}$ (updated set of sufficient statistics)
begin
  if $c_T(e^i_{i-k+1}) = 0$ **then**
    if $k - 1 \geq 1$ **then**
      updD ($\mathcal{S}$,k-1,$c_M(e^{i-1}_{i-k+2})$,$c_M(e^{i-1}_{i-k+2})$+1)
      if $c_M(e^{i-1}_{i-k+2}) = 0$ **then**
        $N_{1+}(e^{i-1}_{i-k+2}) = N_{1+}(e^{i-1}_{i-k+2}) + 1$
      $c_M(e^{i-1}_{i-k+2}) = c_M(e^{i-1}_{i-k+2}) + 1$
      $c_M(e^i_{i-k+2}) = c_M(e^{i}$
    if $k = n$ **then**
      $N_{1+}(e^{i-1}_{i-k+1}) = N_{1+}(e^{i-1}_{i-k+1}) + 1$
  if $k = n$ **then**
    updD ($\mathcal{S}$,k,$c_T(e^i_{i-k+1})$,$c_T(e^{i}$$_{i-k+1}) + 1)$
  $c_T(e^{i-1}_{i-k+1})$=$c_T(e^{i-1}_{i-k+1}) + 1$
  $c_T(e^i_{i-k+1})$=$c_T(e^i$
end

Algorithm 1: Pseudocode for updating the sufficient statistics of a given k-gram

input : $\mathcal{S}$ (current set of sufficient statistics),k
(order), c (current count), c' (new count)
output : $(c_{k,1}, c_{k,2})$ (updated sufficient statistics)
begin
  if $c = 0$ **then**
    if $c' = 1$ **then** $c_{k,1} = c_{k,1} + 1$
    if $c' = 2$ **then** $c_{k,2} = c_{k,2} + 1$
  if $c = 1$ **then**
    $c_{k,1} = c_{k,1} - 1$
    if $c' = 2$ **then** $c_{k,2} = c_{k,2} + 1$
  if $c = 2$ **then** $c_{k,2} = c_{k,2} - 1$
end

Algorithm 2: Pseudocode for the updD procedure

pair $(\mathbf{f}, \mathbf{e})$, the two quantities are updated using a recurrence relation:

$$\mu_{|\mathbf{e}|} = \mu'_{|\mathbf{e}|} + (|\mathbf{f}| - \mu'_{|\mathbf{e}|})/c(|\mathbf{e}|) \tag{11}$$

$$S_{|\mathbf{e}|} = S'_{|\mathbf{e}|} + (|\mathbf{f}| - \mu'_{|\mathbf{e}|})(|\mathbf{f}| - \mu_{|\mathbf{e}|}) \tag{12}$$

where $c(|\mathbf{e}|)$ is the count of the number of sentences of length $|\mathbf{e}|$ that have been seen so far, and $\mu'_{|\mathbf{e}|}$ and $S'_{|\mathbf{e}|}$ are the quantities previously stored ($\mu_{|\mathbf{e}|}$ is initialized to the source sentence length of the first sample and $S_{|\mathbf{e}|}$ is initialized to zero). Finally, the standard deviation can be obtained from S as follows: $\sigma_{|\mathbf{e}|} = \sqrt{S_{|\mathbf{e}|}/(c(|\mathbf{e}|) - 1)}$.

Feature functions h_3 and h_4 implement inverse and direct smoothed phrase-based models respectively. Since phrase-based models are symmetric models, only an inverse phrase-based model is maintained (direct probabilities can be efficiently obtained using appropriate data structures, see (Ortiz-Martínez et al., 2008)). The inverse phrase model probabilities are estimated from the phrase counts:

$$p(\tilde{f}|\tilde{e}) = \frac{c(\tilde{f}, \tilde{e})}{\sum_{\tilde{f}'} c(\tilde{f}', \tilde{e})} \tag{13}$$

According to Equation (13), the set of sufficient statistics to be stored for the inverse phrase model consists of a set of phrase counts ($c(\tilde{f}, \tilde{e})$ and $\sum_{\tilde{f}'} c(\tilde{f}', \tilde{e})$ must be stored separately). Given a new sentence pair $(\mathbf{f}, \mathbf{e})$, the standard phrase-based model estimation method uses a word alignment matrix between $\mathbf{f}$ and $\mathbf{e}$ to extract the set of phrase pairs that are *consistent* with the word alignment matrix (see (Koehn et al., 2003) for more details). Once the consistent phrase pairs have been extracted, the phrase counts are updated. The word alignment matrices required for the extraction of phrase pairs are generated by means of the HMM-based models used in the feature functions h_3 and h_4.

Inverse and direct HMM-based models are used here for two purposes: to smooth the phrase-based models via linear interpolation and to generate word alignment matrices. The weights of the interpolation can be estimated from a development corpus. Equation (10) shows the expression of the probability given by an inverse HMM-based model. The probability includes lexical probabilities $p(f_j|e_i)$ and alignment probabilities $p(a_j|a_{j-1}, l)$. Since the alignment in the HMM-based model is determined by a hidden variable, the EM algorithm is required to estimate the parameters of the model (see (Och and Ney, 2003)). However, the standard EM algorithm is not appropriate to incrementally extend our HMM-based models because it is designed to work in batch training scenarios. To solve this problem, we apply the incremental view of the EM algorithm described in (Neal and Hinton, 1998). According to (Och and Ney, 2003), the lexical probability for a pair of words is given by the expression:

$$p(f|e) = \frac{c(f|e)}{\sum_{f'} c(f'|e)} \quad (14)$$

where $c(f|e)$ is the *expected* number of times that the word e is aligned to the word f. The alignment probability is defined in a similar way:

$$p(a_j|a_{j-1}, l) = \frac{c(a_j|a_{j-1}, l)}{\sum_{a'_j} c(a'_j|a_{j-1}, l)} \quad (15)$$

where $c(a_j|a_{j-1}, l)$ denotes the expected number of times that the alignment a_j has been seen after the previous alignment a_{j-1} given a source sentence composed of l words.

Given the equations (14) and (15), the set of sufficient statistics for the inverse HMM-based model consists of a set of expected counts (numerator and denominator values are stored separately). Given a new sentence pair $(\mathbf{f}, \mathbf{e})$, we execute a new iteration of the incremental EM algorithm on the new sample and collect the contributions to the expected counts.

The parameters of the direct HMM-based model are estimated analogously to those of the inverse HMM-based model. Once the direct and the inverse HMM-based model parameters have been modified due to the presentation of a new sentence pair to the IMT system, both models are used to obtain word alignments for the new sentence pair. The resulting direct and inverse word alignment matrices are combined by means of the *symmetrization* alignment operation (Och and Ney, 2003) before extracting the set of consistent phrase pairs.

HMM-based alignment models are used here because, according to (Och and Ney, 2003) and (Toutanova et al., 2002), they outperform IBM 1 to IBM 4 alignment models while still allowing the exact calculation of the likelihood for a given sentence pair.

The δ parameters of the geometric distributions associated to the feature functions h_5, h_6 and h_7 are left fixed. Because of this, there are no sufficient statistics to store for these feature functions.

Finally, the weights of the log-linear combination are not modified due to the presentation of a new sentence pair to the system. These weights can be adjusted off-line by means of a development corpus and well-known optimization techniques.

5 Experiments

This section describes the experiments that we carried out to test our online IMT system.

5.1 Experimental setup

The experiments were performed using the XEROX XRCE corpus (SchlumbergerSema S.A. et al., 2001), which consists of translations of Xerox printer manuals involving three different pairs of languages: French-English, Spanish-English, and German-English. The main features of these corpora are shown in Table 1. Partitions into training, development and test were performed. This corpus is used here because it has been extensively used in the literature on IMT to report results.

IMT experiments were carried out from English to the other three languages.

5.2 Assessment criteria

The evaluation of the techniques presented in this paper were carried out using the *Key-stroke and mouse-action ratio* (KSMR) measure (Barrachina et al., 2009). This is calculated as the number of keystrokes plus the number of *mouse movements* plus one more count per sentence (aimed at simulating the user action needed to accept the final translation), the sum of which is divided by the total number of reference characters. In addition to this, we also used the well-known BLEU score (Papineni et al., 2001) to measure the translation quality of the first translation hypothesis produced by the IMT system for each source sentence (which is automatically generated without user intervention).

5.3 Online IMT results

To test the techniques proposed in this work, we carried out experiments in two different scenarios. In the first one, the first 10 000 sentences extracted from the training corpora were interactively translated by means of an IMT system without any preexistent model stored in memory. Each time a new sentence pair was validated, it was used to incrementally train the system. Figures 3a, 3b and 3c show the evolution of the KSMR with respect to the number of sentence pairs processed by the IMT system; the results correspond to the translation from English to Spanish, French and German, respectively. In addi-

		En	Sp	En	Fr	En	Ge
Train	Sent. pairs	55761		52844		49376	
	Running words	571960	657172	542762	573170	506877	440682
	Vocabulary	25627	29565	24958	27399	24899	37338
Dev.	Sent. pairs	1012		994		964	
	Running words	12111	13808	9480	9801	9162	8283
	Perplexity (3-grams)	46.2	34.0	96.2	74.1	68.4	124.3
Test	Sent. pairs	1125		984		996	
	Running words	7634	9358	9572	9805	10792	9823
	Perplexity (3-grams)	107.0	59.6	192.6	135.4	92.8	169.2

Table 1: XEROX corpus statistics for three different language pairs (from English (En) to Spanish (Sp), French (Fr) and German (Ge))

tion, for each language pair we interactively translated the original portion of the training corpus and the same portion of the original corpus after being randomly shuffled.

As these figures show, the results clearly demonstrate that the IMT system is able to learn from scratch. The results were similar for the three languages. It is also worthy of note that the obtained results were better in all cases for the original corpora than for the shuffled ones. This is because, in the original corpora, similar sentences appear more or less contiguosly (due to the organization of the contents of the printer manuals). This circumstance increases the accuracy of the online learning, since with the original corpora the number of *lateral effects* ocurred between the translation of similar sentences is decreased. The online learning of a new sentence pair produces a lateral effect when the changes in the probability given by the models not only affect the newly trained sentence pair but also other sentence pairs. A lateral effect can cause that the system generates a wrong translation for a given source sentence due to undesired changes in the statistical models.

The accuracy were worse for shuffled corpora, since shuffling increases the number of lateral effects that may occur between the translation of similar sentences (because they no longer appear contiguously). A good way to compare the quality of different online IMT systems is to determine their robustness in relation to sentence ordering. However, it can generally be expected that the sentences to be translated in an interactive translation session will be in a non-random order.

Alternatively, we carried out experiments in a different learning scenario. Specifically, the XEROX test corpora were interactively translated from the English language to the other three languages, comparing the performance of a batch IMT system with

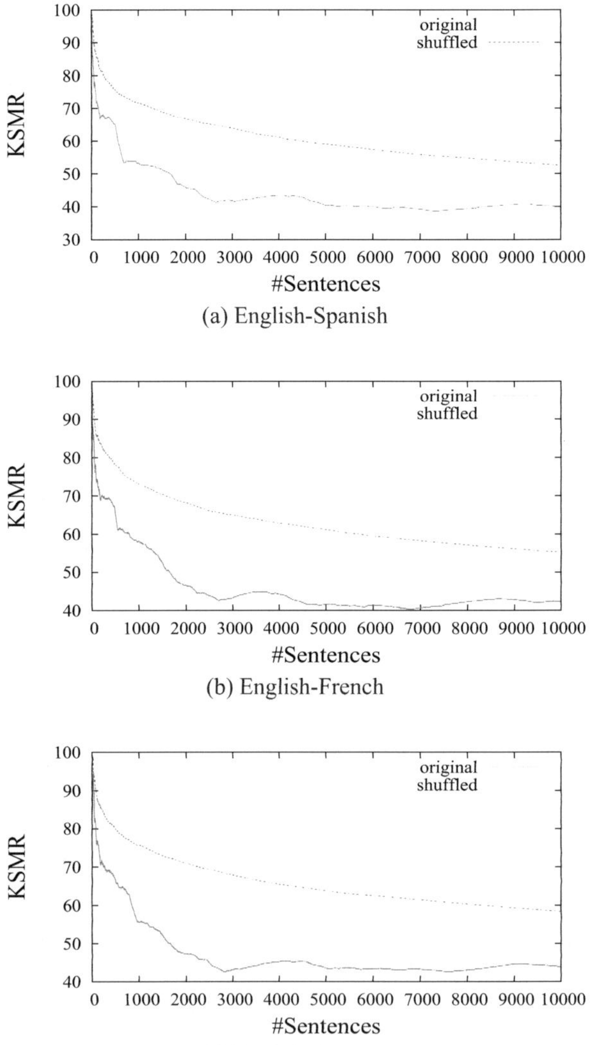

(a) English-Spanish
(b) English-French
(c) English-German

Figure 3: KSMR evolution translating a portion of the training corpora that of an online IMT system. The batch IMT system is a conventional IMT system which is not able to take advantage of user feedback after each translation while the online IMT system uses the new sentence pairs provided by the user to revise the statistical models. Both systems were initialized with a log-linear model trained in batch mode by means of the XEROX training corpora. The weights of the log-linear combination were adjusted for the development corpora by means of the downhill-simplex algorithm. Table 2 shows the obtained results. The table shows the BLEU score and the KSMR for the batch and the online IMT systems (95% confidence intervals are shown). The BLEU score was calculated from the first translation hypothesis produced by the IMT system for each source sentence. The table also shows the average online learning time (LT) for each new sample presented to the system[2]. All the improvements obtained with the online IMT system were statistically significant. Also, the average learning times clearly allow the system to be used in a real-time scenario.

	IMT system	BLEU	KSMR	LT (s)
En-Sp	batch	55.1± 2.3	18.2± 1.1	-
	online	60.6± 2.3	15.8± 1.0	0.04
En-Fr	batch	33.7± 2.0	33.9± 1.3	-
	online	42.2± 2.2	27.9± 1.3	0.09
En-Ge	batch	20.4± 1.8	40.3± 1.2	-
	online	28.0± 2.0	35.0± 1.3	0.07

Table 2: BLEU and KSMR results for the XEROX test corpora using the batch and the online IMT systems. The average online learning time (LT) in seconds is shown for the online system

Finally, in Table 3 a comparison of the KSMR results obtained by the online IMT system with state-of-the-art IMT systems is reported (95% confidence intervals are shown). We compared our system with those presented in (Barrachina et al., 2009): the alignment templates (AT), the stochastic finite-state transducer (SFST), and the phrase-based (PB) approaches to IMT. The results were obtained using the same Xerox training and test sets (see Table 1) for the four different IMT systems. Our system outperformed the results obtained by these systems.

[2]All the experiments were executed on a PC with a 2.40 Ghz Intel Xeon processor with 1GB of memory.

	AT	PB	SFST	Online
En-Sp	23.2±1.3	16.7±1.2	21.8±1.4	15.8± 1.0
En-Fr	40.4±1.4	35.8±1.3	43.8±1.6	27.9± 1.3
En-Ge	44.7±1.2	40.1±1.2	45.7±1.4	35.0± 1.3

Table 3: KSMR results comparison of our system and three different state-of-the-art batch systems

6 Conclusions

We have presented an online IMT system. The proposed system is able to incrementally extend the statistical models involved in the translation process, breaking technical limitations encountered in other works. Empirical results show that our techniques allow the IMT system to learn from scratch or from previously estimated models.

One key aspect of the proposed system is the use of HMM-based alignment models trained by means of the incremental EM algorithm.

The incremental adjustment of the weights of the log-linear models and other parameters have not been tackled here. For the future we plan to incorporate this functionality into our IMT system.

The incremental techniques proposed here can also be exploited to extend SMT systems (in fact, our proposed IMT system is based on an incrementally updateable SMT system). For the near future we plan to study possible aplications of our techniques in a fully automatic translation scenario.

Finally, it is worthy of note that the main ideas presented here can be used in other interactive applications such as Computer Assisted Speech Transcription, Interactive Image Retrieval, etc (see (Vidal et al., 2007) for more information). In conclusion, we think that the online learning techniques proposed here can be the starting point for a new generation of interactive pattern recognition systems that are able to take advantage of user feedback.

Acknowledgments

Work supported by the EC (FEDER/FSE), the Spanish Government (MEC, MICINN, MITyC, MAEC, "Plan E", under grants MIPRCV "Consolider Ingenio 2010" CSD2007-00018, iTrans2 TIN2009-14511, erudito.com TSI-020110-2009-439), the Generalitat Valenciana (grant Prometeo/2009/014), the Univ. Politécnica de Valencia (grant 20091027) and the Spanish JCCM (grant PBI08-0210-7127).

References

A. Arun and P. Koehn. 2007. Online learning methods for discriminative training of phrase based statistical machine translation. In *Proc. of the MT Summit XI*, pages 15–20, Copenhagen, Denmark, September.

S. Barrachina, O. Bender, F. Casacuberta, J. Civera, E. Cubel, S. Khadivi, A. Lagarda, H. Ney, J. Tomás, and E. Vidal. 2009. Statistical approaches to computer-assisted translation. *Computational Linguistics*, 35(1):3–28.

Peter F. Brown, Stephen A. Della Pietra, Vincent J. Della Pietra, and R. L. Mercer. 1993. The mathematics of statistical machine translation: Parameter estimation. *Computational Linguistics*, 19(2):263–311.

N. Cesa-Bianchi, G. Reverberi, and S. Szedmak. 2008. Online learning algorithms for computer-assisted translation. Deliverable D4.2, SMART: Stat. Multilingual Analysis for Retrieval and Translation, Mar.

S.F. Chen and J. Goodman. 1996. An empirical study of smoothing techniques for language modeling. In *Proc. of the ACL*, pages 310–318, San Francisco.

D. Chiang, Y. Marton, and P. Resnik. 2008. Online large-margin training of syntactic and structural translation features. In *Proc. of EMNLP*.

George Foster, Pierre Isabelle, and Pierre Plamondon. 1997. Target-text mediated interactive machine translation. *Machine Translation*, 12(1):175–194.

P. Isabelle and K. Church. 1997. Special issue on new tools for human translators. *Machine Translation*, 12(1–2).

D.E. Knuth. 1981. *Seminumerical Algorithms*, volume 2 of *The Art of Computer Programming*. Addison-Wesley, Massachusetts, 2nd edition.

P. Koehn, F. J. Och, and D. Marcu. 2003. Statistical phrase-based translation. In *Proc. of the HLT/NAACL*, pages 48–54, Edmonton, Canada, May.

P. Langlais, G. Lapalme, and M. Loranger. 2002. Transtype: Development-evaluation cycles to boost translator's productivity. *Machine Translation*, 15(4):77–98.

P. Liang, A. Bouchard-Côté, D. Klein, and B. Taskar. 2006. An end-to-end discriminative approach to machine translation. In *Proc. of the 44th ACL*, pages 761–768, Morristown, NJ, USA.

R.M. Neal and G.E. Hinton. 1998. A view of the EM algorithm that justifies incremental, sparse, and other variants. In *Proceedings of the NATO-ASI on Learning in graphical models*, pages 355–368, Norwell, MA, USA.

L. Nepveu, G. Lapalme, P. Langlais, and G. Foster. 2004. Adaptive language and translation models for interactive machine translation. In *Proc. of EMNLP*, pages 190–197, Barcelona, Spain, July.

Franz Josef Och and Hermann Ney. 2002. Discriminative Training and Maximum Entropy Models for Statistical Machine Translation. In *Proc. of the 40th ACL*, pages 295–302, Philadelphia, PA, July.

Franz Josef Och and Hermann Ney. 2003. A systematic comparison of various statistical alignment models. *Computational Linguistics*, 29(1):19–51, March.

D. Ortiz-Martínez, I. García-Varea, and Casacuberta F. 2008. The scaling problem in the pattern recognition approach to machine translation. *Pattern Recognition Letters*, 29:1145–1153.

Daniel Ortiz-Martínez, Ismael García-Varea, and Francisco Casacuberta. 2009. Interactive machine translation based on partial statistical phrase-based alignments. In *Proc. of RANLP*, Borovets, Bulgaria, sep.

Kishore A. Papineni, Salim Roukos, Todd Ward, and Wei-Jing Zhu. 2001. Bleu: a method for automatic evaluation of machine translation. Technical Report RC22176 (W0109-022), IBM Research Division, Thomas J. Watson Research Center, Yorktown Heights, NY, September.

SchlumbergerSema S.A., ITI Valencia, RWTH Aachen, RALI Montreal, Celer Soluciones, Société Gamma, and XRCE. 2001. TT2. TransType2 - computer assisted translation. Project Tech. Rep.

Kristina Toutanova, H. Tolga Ilhan, and Christopher Manning. 2002. Extensions to hmm-based statistical word alignment models. In *Proc. of EMNLP*.

E. Vidal, L. Rodríguez, F. Casacuberta, and I. García-Varea. 2007. Interactive pattern recognition. In *Proc. of the 4th MLMI*, pages 60–71. Brno, Czech Republic, 28-30 June.

Stephan Vogel, Hermann Ney, and Christoph Tillmann. 1996. HMM-based word alignment in statistical translation. In *Proc. of COLING*, pages 836–841, Copenhagen, Denmark, August.

T. Watanabe, J. Suzuki, H. Tsukada, and H. Isozaki. 2007. Online large-margin training for statistical machine translation. In *Proc. of EMNLP and CoNLL*, pages 764–733, Prage, Czeck Republic.

The Best Lexical Metric for Phrase-Based Statistical MT System Optimization

Daniel Cer, Christopher D. Manning and Daniel Jurafsky
Stanford University
Stanford, CA 94305, USA

Abstract

Translation systems are generally trained to optimize BLEU, but many alternative metrics are available. We explore how optimizing toward various automatic evaluation metrics (BLEU, METEOR, NIST, TER) affects the resulting model. We train a state-of-the-art MT system using MERT on many parameterizations of each metric and evaluate the resulting models on the other metrics and also using human judges. In accordance with popular wisdom, we find that it's important to train on the same metric used in testing. However, we also find that training to a newer metric is only useful to the extent that the MT model's structure and features allow it to take advantage of the metric. Contrasting with TER's good correlation with human judgments, we show that people tend to prefer BLEU and NIST trained models to those trained on edit distance based metrics like TER or WER. Human preferences for METEOR trained models varies depending on the source language. Since using BLEU or NIST produces models that are more robust to evaluation by other metrics and perform well in human judgments, we conclude they are still the best choice for training.

1 Introduction

Since their introduction, automated measures of machine translation quality have played a critical role in the development and evolution of SMT systems. While such metrics were initially intended for evaluation, popular training methods such as minimum error rate training (MERT) (Och, 2003) and margin infused relaxed algorithm (MIRA) (Crammer and Singer, 2003; Watanabe et al., 2007; Chiang et al., 2008) train translation models toward a specific evaluation metric. This makes the quality of the resulting model dependent on how accurately the automatic metric actually reflects human preferences.

The most popular metric for both comparing systems and tuning MT models has been BLEU. While BLEU (Papineni et al., 2002) is relatively simple, scoring translations according to their n-gram overlap with reference translations, it still achieves a reasonable correlation with human judgments of translation quality. It is also robust enough to use for automatic optimization. However, BLEU does have a number of shortcomings. It doesn't penalize n-gram scrambling (Callison-Burch et al., 2006), and since it isn't aware of synonymous words or phrases, it can inappropriately penalize translations that use them.

Recently, there have been efforts to develop better evaluation metrics. Metrics such as *Translation Edit Rate* (TER) (Snover et al., 2006; Snover et al., 2009) and METEOR[1] (Lavie and Denkowski, 2009) perform a more sophisticated analysis of the translations being evaluated and the scores they produce tend to achieve a better correlation with human judgments than those produced by BLEU (Snover et al., 2009; Lavie and Denkowski, 2009; Przybocki et al., 2008; Snover et al., 2006).

Their better correlations suggest that we might obtain higher quality translations by making use of these new metrics when training our models. We expect that training on a specific metric will produce the best performing model according to that met-

[1]METEOR: Metric for Evaluation of Translation with Explicit ORdering.

Human Language Technologies: The 2010 Annual Conference of the North American Chapter of the ACL, pages 555–563,
Los Angeles, California, June 2010.

ric. Doing better on metrics that better reflect human judgments seems to imply the translations produced by the model would be preferred by human judges.

However, there are four potential problems. First, some metrics could be susceptible to systematic exploitation by the training algorithm and result in model translations that have a high score according to the evaluation metric but that are of low quality.[2] Second, other metrics may result in objective functions that are harder to optimize. Third, some may result in better generalization performance at test time by not encouraging overfitting of the training data. Finally, as a practical concern, metrics used for training cannot be too slow.

In this paper, we systematically explore these four issues for the most popular metrics available to the MT community. We examine how well models perform both on the metrics on which they were trained and on the other alternative metrics. Multiple models are trained using each metric in order to determine the stability of the resulting models. Select models are scored by human judges in order to determine how performance differences obtained by tuning to different automated metrics relates to actual human preferences.

The next sections introduce the metrics and our training procedure. We follow with two sets of core results, machine evaluation in section 5, and human evaluation in section 6.

2 Evaluation Metrics

Designing good automated metrics for evaluating machine translations is challenging due to the variety of acceptable translations for each foreign sentence. Popular metrics produce scores primarily based on matching sequences of words in the system translation to those in one or more reference translations. The metrics primarily differ in how they account for reorderings and synonyms.

2.1 BLEU

BLEU (Papineni et al., 2002) uses the percentage of n-grams found in machine translations that also occur in the reference translations. These n-gram precisions are calculated separately for different n-gram lengths and then combined using a geometric mean. The score is then scaled by a brevity penalty if the candidate translations are shorter than the references, $BP = \min(1.0, e^{1-len(R)/len(T)})$. Equation 1 gives BLEU using n-grams up to length N for a corpus of candidate translations T and reference translations R. A variant of BLEU called the NIST metric (Doddington, 2002) weights n-gram matches by how informative they are.

$$\text{BLEU:}N = \left(\prod_{n=1}^{N} \frac{n\text{-grams}(T \bigcap R)}{n\text{-grams}(T)} \right)^{\frac{1}{N}} BP \quad (1)$$

While easy to compute, BLEU has a number of shortcomings. Since the order of matching n-grams is ignored, n-grams in a translation can be randomly rearranged around non-matching material or other n-gram breaks without harming the score. BLEU also does not explicitly check whether information is missing from the candidate translations, as it only examines what fraction of candidate translation n-grams are in the references and not what fraction of references n-grams are in the candidates (i.e., BLEU ignores n-gram recall). Finally, the metric does not account for words and phrases that have similar meanings.

2.2 METEOR

METEOR (Lavie and Denkowski, 2009) computes a one-to-one alignment between matching words in a candidate translation and a reference. If a word matches multiple other words, preference is given to the alignment that reorders the words the least, with the amount of reordering measured by the number of crossing alignments. Alignments are first generated for exact matches between words. Additional alignments are created by repeatedly running the alignment procedure over unaligned words, first allowing for matches between word stems, and then allowing matches between words listed as synonyms in WordNet. From the final alignment, the candidate translation's unigram precision and recall is calculated, $P = \frac{\text{matches}}{\text{length trans}}$ and $R = \frac{\text{matches}}{\text{length ref}}$. These two are then combined into a weighted harmonic mean (2). To penalize reorderings, this value is then scaled by a fragmentation penalty based on the number of chunks the two sentences would need to be broken

[2]For example, BLEU computed without the brevity penalty would likely result in models that have a strong preference for generating pathologically short translations.

into to allow them to be rearranged with no crossing alignments, $P_{\beta,\gamma} = 1 - \gamma\left(\frac{\text{chunks}}{\text{matches}}\right)^{\beta}$.

$$F_{\alpha} = \frac{PR}{\alpha P + (1-\alpha)R} \quad (2)$$

$$\text{METEOR}_{\alpha,\beta,\gamma} = F_{\alpha} \cdot P_{\beta,\gamma} \quad (3)$$

Equation 3 gives the final METEOR score as the product of the unigram harmonic mean, F_{α}, and the fragmentation penalty, $P_{\beta,\gamma}$. The free parameters α, β, and γ can be used to tune the metric to human judgments on a specific language and variation of the evaluation task (e.g., ranking candidate translations vs. reproducing judgments of translations adequacy and fluency).

2.3 Translation Edit Rate

TER (Snover et al., 2006) searches for the shortest sequence of edit operations needed to turn a candidate translation into one of the reference translations. The allowable edits are the insertion, deletion, and substitution of individual words and swaps of adjacent sequences of words. The swap operation differentiates TER from the simpler word error rate (WER) metric (Nießen et al., 2000), which only makes use of insertions, deletions, and substitutions. Swaps prevent phrase reorderings from being excessively penalized. Once the shortest sequence of operations is found,[3] TER is calculated simply as the number of required edits divided by the reference translation length, or average reference translation length when multiple are available (4).

$$\text{TER} = \frac{\text{min edits}}{\text{avg ref length}} \quad (4)$$

TER-Plus (TERp) (Snover et al., 2009) extends TER by allowing the cost of edit operations to be tuned in order to maximize the metric's agreement with human judgments. TERp also introduces three new edit opertions: word stem matches, WordNet synonym matches, and multiword matches using a table of scored paraphrases.

[3]Since swaps prevent TER from being calculated exactly using dynamic programming, a beam search is used and this can overestimate the number of required edits.

3 MERT

MERT is the standard technique for obtaining a machine translation model fit to a specific evaluation metric (Och, 2003). Learning such a model cannot be done using gradient methods since the value of the objective function only depends on the translation model's $\arg\max$ for each sentence in the tuning set. Typically, this optimization is performed as a series of line searches that examines the value of the evaluation metric at critical points where a new translation $\arg\max$ becomes preferred by the model. Since the model score assigned to each candidate translation varies linearly with changes to the model parameters, it is possible to efficiently find the global minimum along any given search direction with only $O(n^2)$ operations when n-best lists are used.

Using our implementation of MERT that allows for pluggable optimization metrics, we tune models to BLEU:N for $N = 1 \ldots 5$, TER, two configurations of TERp, WER, several configurations of METEOR, as well as additive combinations of these metrics. The TERp configurations include the default configuration of TERp and TERpA: the configuration of TERp that was trained to match human judgments for NIST Metrics MATR (Matthew Snover and Schwartz, 2008; Przybocki et al., 2008). For METEOR, we used the standard METEOR English parameters ($\alpha = 0.8, \beta = 2.5, \gamma = 0.4$), and the English parameters for the ranking METEOR ($\alpha = 0.95, \beta = 0.5, \gamma = 0.5$),[4] which was tuned to maximize the metric's correlation with WMT-07 human ranking judgements (Agarwal and Lavie, 2008). The default METEOR parameters favor longer translations than the other metrics, since high α values place much more weight on unigram recall than precision. Since this may put models tuned to METEOR at a disadvantage when being evaluated by the other metrics, we also use a variant of the standard English model and of ranking METEOR with α set to 0.5, as this weights both recall and precision equally.

For each iteration of MERT, 20 random restarts were used in addition to the best performing point discovered during earlier iterations of training.[5]

[4]Agarwal and Lavie (2008) report $\gamma = 0.45$, however the 0.8.2 release of METEOR uses $\gamma = 0.5$ for ranking English.

[5]This is not necessarily identical with the point returned by the most recent MERT iteration, but rather can be any point

Since MERT is known to be sensitive to what restart points are provided, we use the same series of random restart points for each model. During each iteration of MERT, the random seed is based on the MERT iteration number. Thus, while a different set of random points is selected during each MERT iteration, on any given iteration all models use the same set of points. This prevents models from doing better or worse just because they received different starting points. However, it is still possible that certain random starting points are better for some evaluation metrics than others.

4 Experiments

Experiments were run using Phrasal (Cer et al., 2010), a left-to-right beam search decoder that achieves a matching BLEU score to Moses (Koehn et al., 2007) on a variety of data sets. During decoding we made use of a stack size of 100, set the distortion limit to 6, and retrieved 20 translation options for each unique source phrase.

Using the selected metrics, we train both Chinese to English and Arabic to English models.[6] The Chinese to English models are trained using NIST MT02 and evaluated on NIST MT03. The Arabic to English experiments use NIST MT06 for training and GALE dev07 for evaluation. The resulting models are scored using all of the standalone metrics used during training.

4.1 Arabic to English

Our Arabic to English system was based on a well ranking 2009 NIST submission (Galley et al., 2009). The phrase table was extracted using all of the allowed resources for the constrained Arabic to English track. Word alignment was performed using the Berkeley cross-EM aligner (Liang et al., 2006). Phrases were extracted using the grow heuristic (Koehn et al., 2003). However, we threw away all phrases that have a $P(e|f) < 0.0001$ in order to reduce the size of the phrase table. From the aligned data, we also extracted a hierarchical reordering model that is similar to popular lexical reordering models (Koehn et al., 2007) but that models swaps containing more than just one phrase (Galley and Manning, 2008). A 5-gram language model was created with the SRI language modeling toolkit (Stolcke, 2002) using all of the English material from the parallel data employed to train the phrase table as well as Xinhua Chinese English Parallel News (LDC2002E18).[7] The resulting decoding model has 16 features that are optimized during MERT.

4.2 Chinese to English

For our Chinese to English system, our phrase table was built using 1,140,693 sentence pairs sampled from the GALE Y2 training data. The Chinese sentences were word segmented using the 2008 version of Stanford Chinese Word Segmenter (Chang et al., 2008; Tseng et al., 2005). Phrases were extracted by running GIZA++ (Och and Ney, 2003) in both directions and then merging the alignments using the grow-diag-final heuristic (Koehn et al., 2003). From the merged alignments we also extracted a bidirectional lexical reordering model conditioned on the source and the target phrases (Koehn et al., 2007). A 5-gram language model was created with the SRI language modeling toolkit (Stolcke, 2002) and trained using the Gigaword corpus and English sentences from the parallel data. The resulting decoding model has 14 features to be trained.

5 Results

As seen in tables 1 and 2, the evaluation metric we use during training has a substantial impact on performance as measured by the various other metrics. There is a clear block structure where the best class of metrics to train on is the same class that is used during evaluation. Within this block structure, we make three primary observations. First, the best performing model according to any specific metric *configuration* is usually not the model we trained to that configuration. In the Chinese results, the model trained on BLEU:3 scores 0.74 points higher on BLEU:4 than the model actually trained to BLEU:4. In fact, the BLEU:3 trained model outperforms all other models on BLEU:N metrics. For the Arabic results, training on NIST scores 0.27 points higher

returned during an earlier iteration of MERT.

[6]Given the amount of time required to train a TERpA model, we only present TERpA results for Chinese to English.

[7]In order to run multiple experiments in parallel on the computers available to us, the system we use for this work differs from our NIST submission in that we remove the Google n-gram language model. This results in a performance drop of less than 1.0 BLEU point on our dev data.

Train\Eval	BLEU:1	BLEU:2	BLEU:3	BLEU:4	BLEU:5	NIST	TER	TERp	WER	TERpA	METR	METR-r	METR $\alpha = 0.5$	METR-r $\alpha = 0.5$
BLEU:1	75.98	55.39	40.41	29.64	21.60	11.94	78.07	78.71	68.28	73.63	41.98	59.63	42.46	60.02
BLEU:2	76.58	57.24	42.84	32.21	24.09	12.20	77.09	77.63	67.16	72.54	43.20	60.91	43.59	61.56
BLEU:3	**76.74**	**57.46**	**43.13**	**32.52**	**24.44**	12.22	76.53	77.07	66.81	72.01	42.94	60.57	43.40	60.88
BLEU:4	76.24	56.86	42.43	31.80	23.77	12.14	76.75	77.25	66.78	72.01	43.29	60.94	43.10	61.27
BLEU:5	76.39	57.14	42.93	32.38	24.33	12.40	75.42	75.77	65.86	70.29	43.02	61.22	43.57	61.43
NIST	76.41	56.86	42.34	31.67	23.57	12.38	75.20	75.72	65.78	70.11	43.11	61.04	43.78	**61.84**
TER	73.23	53.39	39.09	28.81	21.18	**12.73**	**71.33**	**71.70**	63.92	**66.58**	38.65	55.49	41.76	59.07
TERp	72.78	52.90	38.57	28.32	20.76	12.68	71.76	72.16	64.26	66.96	38.51	56.13	41.48	58.73
TERpA	71.79	51.58	37.36	27.23	19.80	12.54	72.26	72.56	64.58	67.30	37.86	55.10	41.16	58.04
WER	74.49	54.59	40.30	29.88	22.14	12.64	71.85	72.34	**63.82**	67.11	39.76	57.29	42.37	59.97
METR	73.33	54.35	40.28	30.04	22.39	11.53	84.74	85.30	71.49	79.47	**44.68**	62.14	42.99	60.73
METR-r	74.20	54.99	40.91	30.66	22.98	11.74	82.69	83.23	70.49	77.77	44.64	**62.25**	43.44	61.32
METR:0.5	76.36	56.75	42.48	31.98	24.00	12.44	74.94	75.32	66.09	70.14	42.75	60.98	**43.86**	61.38
METR-r:0.5	76.49	56.93	42.36	31.70	23.68	12.21	77.04	77.58	67.12	72.23	43.26	61.03	43.63	61.67
Combined Models														
BLEU:4-TER	75.32	55.98	41.87	31.42	23.50	12.62	72.97	73.38	64.46	67.95	41.50	59.11	43.50	60.82
BLEU:4-2TERp	75.22	55.76	41.57	31.11	23.25	12.64	72.48	72.89	64.17	67.43	41.12	58.82	42.73	60.86
BLEU:4+2MTR	75.77	56.45	42.04	31.47	23.48	11.98	79.96	80.65	68.85	74.84	44.06	61.78	43.70	61.48

Table 1: Chinese to English test set performance on MT03 using models trained using MERT on MT02. In each column, cells shaded blue are better than average and those shaded red are below average. The intensity of the shading indicates the degree of deviation from average. For BLEU, NIST, and METEOR, higher is better. For edit distance metrics like TER and WER, lower is better.

Train\Eval	BLEU:1	BLEU:2	BLEU:3	BLEU:4	BLEU:5	NIST	TER	TERp	WER	METR	METR-r	METR $\alpha = 0.5$	METR-r $\alpha = 0.5$
BLEU:1	79.90	65.35	54.08	45.14	37.81	10.68	46.19	61.04	49.98	49.74	67.79	49.19	68.12
BLEU:2	80.03	65.84	54.70	45.80	38.47	10.75	45.74	60.63	49.24	50.02	68.00	49.71	68.27
BLEU:3	79.87	65.71	54.59	45.67	38.34	10.72	45.86	60.80	49.18	49.87	68.32	49.61	67.67
BLEU:4	80.39	66.14	54.99	46.05	38.70	10.82	45.25	59.83	48.69	49.65	68.13	49.66	67.92
BLEU:5	79.97	65.77	54.64	45.76	38.44	10.75	45.66	60.55	49.11	49.89	68.33	49.64	68.19
NIST	80.41	66.27	55.22	46.32	38.98	**10.96**	44.11	57.92	47.74	48.88	67.85	**49.88**	**68.52**
TER	79.69	65.52	54.44	45.55	38.23	10.75	43.36	56.12	**47.11**	47.90	66.49	49.55	68.12
TERp	79.27	65.11	54.13	45.35	38.12	10.75	**43.36**	**55.92**	47.14	47.83	66.34	49.43	67.94
WER	79.42	65.28	54.30	45.51	38.27	10.78	43.44	56.13	47.13	47.82	66.33	49.38	67.88
METR	75.52	60.94	49.84	41.17	34.12	9.93	52.81	70.08	55.72	50.92	68.55	48.47	66.89
METR-r	77.42	62.91	51.67	42.81	35.61	10.24	49.87	66.26	53.17	**50.95**	**69.29**	49.29	67.89
METR:0.5	79.69	65.14	53.94	45.03	37.72	10.72	45.80	60.44	49.34	49.78	68.31	49.23	67.72
METR-r:0.5	79.76	65.12	53.82	44.88	37.57	10.67	46.53	61.35	50.17	49.66	68.57	49.58	68.25
Combined Models													
BLEU:4-TER	80.37	66.31	55.27	46.36	39.00	10.96	43.94	57.46	47.46	49.00	67.10	49.85	68.41
BLEU:4-2TERp	79.65	65.53	54.54	45.75	38.48	10.80	43.42	56.16	47.15	47.90	65.93	49.09	67.90
BLEU:4+2METR	79.43	64.97	53.75	44.87	37.58	10.63	46.74	62.03	50.35	50.42	68.92	49.70	68.37

Table 2: Arabic to English test set performance on dev07 using models trained using MERT on MT06. As above, in each column, cells shaded blue are better than average and those shaded red are below average. The intensity of the shading indicates the degree of deviation from average.

on BLEU:4 than training on BLEU:4, and outperforms all other models on BLEU:N metrics.

Second, the edit distance based metrics (WER, TER, TERp, TERpA)[8] seem to be nearly interchangeable. While the introduction of swaps allows the scores produced by the TER metrics to achieve better correlation with human judgments, our models are apparently unable to exploit this during training. This maybe due to the monotone nature of the reference translations and the fact that having multiple references reduces the need for reorderings. However, it is possible that differences between training to WER and TER would become more apparent using models that allow for longer distance reorderings or that do a better job of capturing what reorderings are acceptable.

Third, with the exception of BLEU:1, the performance of the BLEU, NIST, and the METEOR α=.5 models appears to be more robust across the other evaluation metrics than the standard METEOR, METEOR ranking, and edit distance based models (WER, TER, TERp, an TERpA). The latter models tend to do quite well on metrics similar to what they were trained on, while performing particularly poorly on the other metrics. For example, on Chinese, the TER and WER models perform very well

[8] In our implementation of multi-reference WER, we use the length of the references that result in the lowest sentence level WER to divide the edit costs. In contrast, TER divides by the average reference length. This difference can sometimes result in WER being lower than the corresponding TER. Also, as can be seen in the Arabic to English results, TERp scores sometimes differ dramatically from TER scores due to normalization and tokenization differences (e.g., TERp removes punctuation prior to scoring, while TER does not).

on other edit distance based metrics, while performing poorly on all the other metrics except NIST. While less pronounced, the same trend is also seen in the Arabic data. Interestingly enough, while the TER, TERp and standard METEOR metrics achieve good correlations with human judgments, models trained to them are particularly mismatched in our results. The edit distance models do terribly on METEOR and METEOR ranking, while METEOR and METEOR ranking models do poorly on TER, TERp, and TERpA.

Training Metric	Itr	MERT Time	Training Metric	Itr	MERT Time
BLEU:1	13	21:57	NIST	15	78:15
BLEU:2	15	32:40	TER	7	21:00
BLEU:3	19	45:08	TERp	9	19:19
BLEU:4	10	24:13	TERpA	8	393:16
BLEU:5	16	46:12	WER	13	33:53
BL:4-TR	9	21:07	BL:4-2TRp	8	22:03
METR	12	39:16	METR 0.5	18	42:04
METR R	12	47:19	METR R:0.5	13	25:44

Table 3: Chinese to English MERT iterations and training times, given in hours:mins and excluding decoder time.

5.1 Other Results

On the training data, we see a similar block structure within the results, but there is a different pattern among the top performers. The tables are omitted, but we observe that, for Chinese, the BLEU:5 model performs best on the training data according to all higher order BLEU metrics (4-7). On Arabic, the BLEU:6 model does best on the same higher order BLEU metrics (4-7). By rewarding higher order n-gram matches, these objectives actually find minima that result in more 4-gram matches than the models optimized directly to BLEU:4. However, the fact that this performance advantage disappears on the evaluation data suggests these higher order models also promote overfitting.

Models trained on additive metric blends tend to smooth out performance differences between the classes of metrics they contain. As expected, weighting the metrics used in the additive blends results in models that perform slightly better on the type of metric with the highest weight.

Table 3 reports training times for select Chinese to English models. Training to TERpA is very computationally expensive due to the implementation of the paraphrase table. The TER family of metrics tends to converge in fewer MERT iterations than those trained on other metrics such as BLEU, METEOR or even WER. This suggests that the learning objective provided by these metrics is either easier to optimize or they more easily trap the search in local minima.

5.2 Model Variance

One potential problem with interpreting the results above is that learning with MERT is generally assumed to be noisy, with different runs of the algorithm possibly producing very different models. We explore to what extent the results just presented were affected by noise in the training procedure. We perform multiple training runs using select evaluation metrics and examining how consistent the resulting models are. This also allows us to determine whether the metric used as a learning criteria influences the stability of learning. For these experiments, Chinese to English models are trained 5 times using a different series of random starting points. As before, 20 random restarts were used during each MERT iteration.

In table 4, models trained to BLEU and METEOR are relatively stable, with the METEOR:0.5 trained models being the most stable. The edit distance models, WER and TERp, vary more across training runs, but still do not exceed the interesting cross metric differences seen in table 1. The instability of WER and TERp, with TERp models having a standard deviation of 1.3 in TERp and 2.5 in BLEU:4, make them risky metrics to use for training.

6 Human Evaluation

The best evaluation metric to use during training is the one that ultimately leads to the best translations according to human judges. We perform a human evaluation of select models using Amazon Mechanical Turk, an online service for cheaply performing simple tasks that require human intelligence. To use the service, tasks are broken down into individual units of work known as human intelligence tasks (HITs). HITs are assigned a small amount of money that is paid out to the workers that complete them. For many natural language annotation tasks, including machine translation evaluation, it is possible to obtain annotations that are as good as those pro-

Train\Eval σ	BLEU:1	BLEU:3	BLEU:4	BLEU:5	TERp	WER	METEOR	METEOR:0.5
BLEU:1	**0.17**	0.56	0.59	0.59	0.36	0.58	0.42	0.24
BLEU:3	0.38	0.41	0.38	0.32	0.70	0.49	0.44	0.33
BLEU:4	0.27	0.29	0.29	0.27	0.67	0.50	0.41	0.29
BLEU:5	**0.17**	0.14	0.19	0.21	0.67	0.75	0.34	0.17
TERp	1.38	2.66	2.53	2.20	1.31	1.39	1.95	1.82
WER	0.62	1.37	1.37	1.25	1.31	1.21	1.10	1.01
METEOR	0.80	0.56	0.48	0.44	3.71	2.69	0.69	1.10
METEOR:0.5	0.32	**0.11**	**0.09**	**0.11**	**0.23**	**0.12**	**0.07**	**0.11**

Table 4: MERT model variation for Chinese to English. We train five models to each metric listed above. The collection of models trained to a given metric is then evaluated using the other metrics. We report the resulting standard devation for the collection on each of the metrics. The collection with the lowest varience is bolded.

Model Pair	% Preferred	p-value
Chinese		
METR R vs. TERp	60.0	0.0028
BLEU:4 vs. TERp	57.5	0.02
NIST vs. TERp	55.0	0.089
NIST vs. TERpA	55.0	0.089
BLEU:4 vs. TERpA	54.5	0.11
BLEU:4 vs. METR R	54.5	0.11
METR:0.5 vs. METR	54.5	0.11
METR:0.5 vs. METR R	53.0	0.22
METR vs. BLEU:4	52.5	0.26
BLEU:4 vs. METR:0.5	52.5	0.26
METR vs. TERp	52.0	0.31
NIST vs. BLEU:4	52.0	0.31
BLEU:4 vs. METR R:0.5	51.5	0.36
WER vs. TERp	51.5	0.36
TERpA vs. TERp	50.5	0.47
Arabic		
BLEU:4 vs. METR R	62.0	< 0.001
NIST vs. TERp	56.0	0.052
BLEU:4 vs. METR:0.5	55.5	0.069
BLEU:4 vs. METR	54.5	0.11
METR R:0.5 vs METR R	54.0	0.14
NIST vs. BLEU:4	51.5	0.36
WER vs. TERp	51.5	0.36
METR:0.5 vs METR	51.5	0.36
TERp vs. BLEU:4	51.0	0.42
BLEU:4 vs. METR R:0.5	50.5	0.47

Table 5: Select pairwise preference for models trained to different evaluation metrics. For A vs. B, *preferred* indicates how often A was preferred to B. We bold the better training metric for statistically significant differences.

duced by experts by having multiple workers complete each HIT and then combining their answers (Snow et al., 2008; Callison-Burch, 2009).

We perform a pairwise comparison of the translations produced for the first 200 sentences of our Chinese to English test data (MT03) and our Arabic to English test data (dev07). The HITs consist of a pair of machine translated sentences and a single human generated reference translation. The reference is chosen at random from those available for each sentence. Capitalization of the translated sentences is restored using an HMM based truecaser (Lita et al., 2003). Turkers are instructed to "...select the machine translation generated sentence that is easiest to read and best conveys what is stated in the reference". Differences between the two machine translations are emphasized by being underlined and bold faced.[9] The resulting HITs are made available only to workers in the United States, as pilot experiments indicated this results in more consistent preference judgments. Three preference judgments are obtained for each pair of translations and are combined using weighted majority vote.

As shown in table 5, in many cases the quality of the translations produced by models trained to different metrics is remarkably similar. Training to the simpler edit distance metric WER produces translations that are as good as those from models tuned to the similar but more advanced TERp metric that allows for swaps. Similarly, training to TERpA, which makes use of both a paraphrase table and edit costs

[9]We emphasize relative differences between the two translations rather than the difference between each translation and the reference in order to avoid biasing evaluations toward edit distance metrics.

tuned to human judgments, is no better than TERp.

For the Chinese to English results, there is a statistically significant human preference for translations that are produced by training to BLEU:4 and a marginally significant preferences for training to NIST over the default configuration of TERp. This contrasts sharply with earlier work showing that TER and TERp correlate better with human judgements than BLEU (Snover et al., 2009; Przybocki et al., 2008; Snover et al., 2006). While it is assumed that, by using MERT, "improved evaluation measures lead directly to improved machine translation quality" (Och, 2003), these results show improved correlations with human judgments are **not always** sufficient to establish that tuning to a metric will result in higher quality translations. In the Arabic results, we see a similar pattern where NIST is preferred to TERp, again with marginal signficance. Strangely, however, there is no real difference between TERp vs. BLEU:4.

For Arabic, training to ranking METEOR is worse than BLEU:4, with the differences being very significant. The Arabic results also trend toward suggesting that BLEU:4 is better than either standard METEOR and METEOR α 0.5. However, for the Chinese models, training to standard METEOR and METEOR α 0.5 is about as good as training to BLEU:4. In both the Chinese and Arabic results, the METEOR α 0.5 models are at least as good as those trained to standard METEOR and METEOR ranking. In contrast to the cross evaluation metric results, where the differences between the α 0.5 models and the standard METEOR models were always fairly dramatic, the human preferences suggest there is often not much of a difference in the true quality of the translations produced by these models.

7 Conclusion

Training to different evaluation metrics follows the expected pattern whereby models perform best on the same type of metric used to train them. However, models trained using the n-gram based metrics, BLEU and NIST, are more robust to being evaluated using the other metrics.

Edit distance models tend to do poorly when evaluated on other metrics, as do models trained using METEOR. However, training models to METEOR can be made more robust by setting α to 0.5, which balances the importance the metric assigns to precision and recall.

The fact that the WER, TER and TERp models perform very similarly suggests that current phrase-based translation systems lack either the features or the model structure to take advantage of swap edit operations. The situation might be improved by using a model that does a better job of both capturing the structure of the source and target sentences and their allowable reorderings, such as a syntactic tree-to-string system that uses contextually rich rewrite rules (Galley et al., 2006), or by making use of larger more fine grained feature sets (Chiang et al., 2009) that allow for better discrimination between hypotheses.

Human results indicate that edit distance trained models such as WER and TERp tend to produce lower quality translations than BLEU or NIST trained models. Tuning to METEOR works reasonably well for Chinese, but is not a good choice for Arabic. We suspect that the newer RYPT metric (Zaidan and Callison-Burch, 2009), which directly makes use of human adequacy judgements of substrings, would obtain better human results than the automated metrics presented here. However, like other metrics, we expect performance gains still will be sensitive to how the mechanics of the metric interact with the structure and feature set of the decoding model being used.

BLEU and NIST's strong showing in both the machine and human evaluation results indicates that they are still the best general choice for training model parameters. We emphasize that improved metric correlations with human judgments do not imply that models trained to a metric will result in higher quality translations. We hope future work on developing new evaluation metrics will explicitly explore the translation quality of models trained to them.

Acknowledgements

The authors thank Alon Lavie for suggesting setting α to 0.5 when training to METEOR. This work was supported by the Defense Advanced Research Projects Agency through IBM. The content does not necessarily reflect the views of the U.S. Government, and no official endorsement should be inferred.

References

Abhaya Agarwal and Alon Lavie. 2008. METEOR, M-BLEU and M-TER: Evaluation metrics for high-correlation with human rankings of machine translation output. In *StatMT workshop at ACL*.

Chris Callison-Burch, Miles Osborne, and Philipp Koehn. 2006. Re-evaluating the role of BLEU in machine translation research. In *EACL*.

Chris Callison-Burch. 2009. Fast, cheap, and creative: Evaluating translation quality using Amazon's Mechanical Turk. In *EMNLP*.

Daniel Cer, Michel Galley, Christopher D. Manning, and Dan Jurafsky. 2010. Phrasal: A statistical machine translation toolkit for exploring new model features. In *NAACL*.

Pi-Chuan Chang, Michel Galley, and Christopher D. Manning. 2008. Optimizing chinese word segmentation for machine translation performance. In *StatMT workshop at ACL*.

David Chiang, Yuval Marton, and Philip Resnik. 2008. Online large-margin training of syntactic and structural translation features. In *EMNLP*.

David Chiang, Kevin Knight, and Wei Wang. 2009. 11,001 new features for statistical machine translation. In *NAACL*.

Koby Crammer and Yoram Singer. 2003. Ultraconservative online algorithms for multiclass problems. *JMLR*, 3:951–991.

George Doddington. 2002. Automatic evaluation of machine translation quality using n-gram co-occurrence statistics. In *HLT*.

Michel Galley and Christopher D. Manning. 2008. A simple and effective hierarchical phrase reordering model. In *EMNLP*.

Michel Galley, Jonathan Graehl, Kevin Knight, Daniel Marcu, Steve DeNeefe, Wei Wang, and Ignacio Thayer. 2006. Scalable inference and training of context-rich syntactic translation models. In *ACL*.

Michel Galley, Spence Green, Daniel Cer, Pi-Chuan Chang, and Christopher D. Manning. 2009. Stanford university's arabic-to-english statistical machine translation system for the 2009 NIST evaluation. In *NIST Open Machine Translation Evaluation Meeting*.

Philipp Koehn, Franz Josef Och, and Daniel Marcu. 2003. Statistical phrase-based translation. In *NAACL*.

Philipp Koehn, Hieu Hoang, Alexandra Birch, Chris Callison-Burch, Marcello Federico, Nicola Bertoldi, Brooke Cowan, Wade Shen, Christine Moran, Richard Zens, Chris Dyer, Ondrej Bojar, Alexandra Constantin, and Evan Herbst. 2007. Moses: Open source toolkit for statistical machine translation. In *ACL*.

Alon Lavie and Michael J. Denkowski. 2009. The METEOR metric for automatic evaluation of machine translation. *Machine Translation*, 23.

Percy Liang, Ben Taskar, and Dan Klein. 2006. Alignment by agreement. In *NAACL*.

Lucian Vlad Lita, Abe Ittycheriah, Salim Roukos, and Nanda Kambhatla. 2003. tRuEcasIng. In *ACL*.

Bonnie Dorr Matthew Snover, Nitin Madnani and Richard Schwartz. 2008. TERp system description. In *MetricsMATR workshop at AMTA*.

Sonja Nießen, Franz Josef Och, and Hermann Ney. 2000. An evaluation tool for machine translation: Fast evaluation for MT research. In *LREC*.

Franz Josef Och and Hermann Ney. 2003. A systematic comparison of various statistical alignment models. *Computational Linguistics*, 29(1):19–51.

Franz Josef Och. 2003. Minimum error rate training in statistical machine translation. In *ACL*.

Kishore Papineni, Salim Roukos, Todd Ward, and Wei-Jing Zhu. 2002. BLEU: a method for automatic evaluation of machine translation. In *ACL*.

M. Przybocki, K. Peterson, and S. Bronsart. 2008. Official results of the "Metrics for MAchine TRanslation" Challenge (MetricsMATR08). Technical report, NIST, `http://nist.gov/speech/tests/metricsmatr/2008/results/`.

Matthew Snover, Bonnie Dorr, Richard Schwartz, Linnea Micciulla, and John Makhoul. 2006. A study of translation edit rate with targeted human annotation. In *AMTA*.

Matthew Snover, Nitin Madnani, Bonnie J. Dorr, and Richard Schwartz. 2009. Fluency, adequacy, or HTER?: exploring different human judgments with a tunable MT metric. In *StatMT workshop at EACL)*.

Rion Snow, Brendan O'Connor, Daniel Jurafsky, and Andrew Ng. 2008. Cheap and fast – but is it good? Evaluating non-expert annotations for natural language tasks. In *EMNLP*.

Andreas Stolcke. 2002. SRILM – an extensible language modeling toolkit. In *ICSLP*.

Huihsin Tseng, Pichuan Chang, Galen Andrew, Daniel Jurafsky, and Christopher D. Manning. 2005. A conditional random field word segmenter. In *SIGHAN*.

Taro Watanabe, Jun Suzuki, Hajime Tsukada, and Hideki Isozaki. 2007. Online large-margin training for statistical machine translation. In *EMNLP-CoNLL*.

Omar F. Zaidan and Chris Callison-Burch. 2009. Feasibility of human-in-the-loop minimum error rate training. In *EMNLP*, pages 52–61, August.

Variational Inference for Adaptor Grammars

Shay B. Cohen
School of Computer Science
Carnegie Mellon University
Pittsburgh, PA 15213, USA
scohen@cs.cmu.edu

David M. Blei
Computer Science Department
Princeton University
Princeton, NJ 08540, USA
blei@cs.princeton.edu

Noah A. Smith
School of Computer Science
Carnegie Mellon University
Pittsburgh, PA 15213, USA
nasmith@cs.cmu.edu

Abstract

Adaptor grammars extend probabilistic context-free grammars to define prior distributions over trees with "rich get richer" dynamics. Inference for adaptor grammars seeks to find parse trees for raw text. This paper describes a variational inference algorithm for adaptor grammars, providing an alternative to Markov chain Monte Carlo methods. To derive this method, we develop a stick-breaking representation of adaptor grammars, a representation that enables us to define adaptor grammars with recursion. We report experimental results on a word segmentation task, showing that variational inference performs comparably to MCMC. Further, we show a significant speed-up when parallelizing the algorithm. Finally, we report promising results for a new application for adaptor grammars, dependency grammar induction.

1 Introduction

Recent research in unsupervised learning for NLP focuses on Bayesian methods for probabilistic grammars (Goldwater and Griffiths, 2007; Toutanova and Johnson, 2007; Johnson et al., 2007). Such methods have been made more flexible with nonparametric Bayesian (NP Bayes) methods, such as Dirichlet process mixture models (Antoniak, 1974; Pitman, 2002). One line of research uses NP Bayes methods on whole tree structures, in the form of **adaptor grammars** (Johnson et al., 2006; Johnson, 2008b; Johnson, 2008a; Johnson and Goldwater, 2009), in order to identify recurrent subtree patterns.

Adaptor grammars provide a flexible distribution over parse trees that has more structure than a traditional context-free grammar. Adaptor grammars are used via posterior inference, the computational problem of determining the posterior distribution of parse trees given a set of observed sentences. Current posterior inference algorithms for adaptor grammars are based on MCMC sampling methods (Robert and Casella, 2005). MCMC methods are theoretically guaranteed to converge to the true posterior, but come at great expense: they are notoriously slow to converge, especially with complex hidden structures such as syntactic trees. Johnson (2008b) comments on this, and suggests the use of **variational inference** as a possible remedy.

Variational inference provides a deterministic alternative to sampling. It was introduced for Dirichlet process mixtures by Blei and Jordan (2005) and applied to infinite grammars by Liang et al. (2007). With NP Bayes models, variational methods are based on the stick-breaking representation (Sethuraman, 1994). Devising a stick-breaking representation is a central challenge to using variational inference in this setting.

The rest of this paper is organized as follows. In §2 we describe a stick-breaking representation of adaptor grammars, which enables variational inference (§3) and a well-defined incorporation of recursion into adaptor grammars. In §4 we give an empirical comparison of the algorithm to MCMC inference and describe a novel application of adaptor grammars to unsupervised dependency parsing.

2 Adaptor Grammars

We review adaptor grammars and develop a stick-breaking representation of the tree distribution.

2.1 Definition of Adaptor Grammars

Adaptor grammars capture syntactic regularities in sentences by placing a nonparametric prior over the distribution of syntactic trees that underlie them. The model exhibits "rich get richer" dynamics: once a tree is generated, it is more likely to reappear.

Adaptor grammars were developed by Johnson et al. (2006). An adaptor grammar is a tuple $\boldsymbol{A} = \langle \boldsymbol{G}, \mathcal{M}, \boldsymbol{a}, \boldsymbol{b}, \boldsymbol{\alpha} \rangle$, which contains: (i) a context-free grammar $\boldsymbol{G} = \langle \mathcal{W}, \mathcal{N}, \boldsymbol{R}, S \rangle$ where $\mathcal{W}$ is the set of

Human Language Technologies: The 2010 Annual Conference of the North American Chapter of the ACL, pages 564–572,
Los Angeles, California, June 2010.

terminals, $\mathcal{N}$ is the set of nonterminals, $\boldsymbol{R}$ is a set of production rules, and $S \in \mathcal{N}$ is the start symbol—we denote by $\boldsymbol{R}_A$ the subset of $\boldsymbol{R}$ with left-hand side A; (ii) a set of adapted nonterminals, $\mathcal{M} \subseteq \mathcal{N}$; and (iii) parameters $\boldsymbol{a}$, $\boldsymbol{b}$ and $\boldsymbol{\alpha}$, which are described below.

An adaptor grammar assumes the following generative process of trees. First, the multinomial distributions $\boldsymbol{\theta}$ for a PCFG based on $\boldsymbol{G}$ are drawn from Dirichlet distributions. Specifically, multinomial $\boldsymbol{\theta}_A \sim \mathrm{Dir}(\alpha_A)$ where $\boldsymbol{\alpha}$ is collection of Dirichlet parameters, indexed by $A \in \mathcal{N}$.

Trees are then generated top-down starting with S. Any non-adapted nonterminal $A \in \mathcal{N} \setminus \mathcal{M}$ is expanded by drawing a rule from $\boldsymbol{R}_A$. There are two ways to expand $A \in \mathcal{M}$:

1. With probability $(n_z - b_A)/(n_A + a_A)$ we expand A to subtree z (a tree rooted at A with a yield in $\mathcal{W}^*$), where n_z is the number of times the tree z was previously generated and n_A is the total number of subtrees (tokens) previously generated root being A. We denote by $\boldsymbol{a}$ the *concentration parameters* and $\boldsymbol{b}$ the *discount parameters*, both indexed by $A \in \mathcal{M}$. We have $a_A \geq 0$ and $b_A \in [0, 1]$.
2. With probability $(a_A + k_A b_A)/(n_A + a_A)$, A is expanded as in a PCFG by a draw from $\boldsymbol{\theta}_A$ over $\boldsymbol{R}_A$, where k_A is the number of subtrees (types) previously generated with root A.

For the expansion of adapted nonterminals, this process can be explained using the Chinese restaurant process (CRP) metaphor: a "customer" (corresponding to a partially generated tree) enters a "restaurant" (corresponding to a nonterminal) and selects a "table" (corresponding to a subtree) to attach to the partially generated tree. If she is the first customer at the table, the PCFG $\langle \boldsymbol{G}, \boldsymbol{\theta} \rangle$ produces the new table's associated "dish" (a subtree).[1]

When adaptor grammars are defined using the CRP, the PCFG $\boldsymbol{G}$ has to be non-recursive with respect to the adapted nonterminals. More precisely, for $A \in \mathcal{N}$, denote by $\mathrm{Reachable}(\boldsymbol{G}, A)$ all the nonterminals that can be reached from A using a partial derivation from $\boldsymbol{G}$. Then we restrict $\boldsymbol{G}$ such that for all $A \in \mathcal{M}$, we have $A \notin \mathrm{Reachable}(\boldsymbol{G}, A)$. Without this restriction, we might end up in a situation where the generative process is ill-defined: in the CRP terminology, a customer could enter a restaurant and select a table whose dish is still in the process of being selected.[2] In the more general form of adaptor grammars with arbitrary adaptors, the problem amounts to mutually dependent definitions of distributions which rely on the others to be defined. We return to this problem in §3.1.

Inference The inference problem is to compute the posterior distribution of parse trees given observed sentences $\boldsymbol{x} = \langle x_1, \ldots, x_n \rangle$. Typically, inference with adaptor grammars is done with Gibbs sampling. Johnson et al. (2006) use an embedded Metropolis-Hastings sampler (Robert and Casella, 2005) inside a Gibbs sampler. The proposal distribution is a PCFG, resembling a tree substitution grammar (TSG; Joshi, 2003). The sampler of Johnson et al. is based on the representation of the PY process as a distribution over partitions of integers. This representation is not amenable to variational inference.

2.2 Stick-Breaking Representation

To develop a variational inference algorithm for adaptor grammars, we require an alternative representation of the model in §2.1. The CRP-based definition implicitly marginalizes out a random distribution over trees. For variational inference, we construct that distribution.

We first review the Dirichlet process and its stick-breaking representation. The Dirichlet process defines a distribution over distributions. Samples from the Dirichlet process tend to deviate from a *base distribution* depending on a *concentration parameter*. Let $G \sim \mathrm{DP}(G_0, a)$ be a distribution sampled from the Dirichlet process with base distribution G_0

[1] We note that our construction deviates from the strict definition of adaptor grammars (Johnson et al., 2006): (i) in our construction, we assume (as prior work does in practice) that the adaptors in $\boldsymbol{A} = \langle \boldsymbol{G}, \mathcal{M}, \boldsymbol{a}, \boldsymbol{b}, \boldsymbol{\alpha} \rangle$ follow the Pitman-Yor (PY) process (Pitman and Yor, 1997), though in general other stochastic processes might be used; and (ii) we place a symmetric Dirichlet over the parameters of the PCFG, $\boldsymbol{\theta}$, whereas Johnson et al. used a fixed PCFG for the definition (though they experimented with a Dirichlet prior).

[2] Consider the simple grammar with rules { S → S S, S → a }. Assume that a customer enters the restaurant for S. She sits at a table, and selects a dish, a subtree, which starts with the rule S → S S. Perhaps the first child S is expanded by S → a. For the second child S, it is possible to re-enter the "S restaurant" and choose the first table, where the "dish" subtree is still being generated.

and concentration parameter a. The distribution G is discrete, which means it puts positive mass on a countable number of atoms drawn from G_0. Repeated draws from G exhibit the "clustering property," which means that they will be assigned to the same value with positive probability. Thus, they exhibit a partition structure. Marginalizing out G, the distribution of that partition structure is given by a CRP with parameter a (Pitman, 2002).

The stick-breaking process gives a constructive definition of G (Sethuraman, 1994). With the stick-breaking process (for the PY process), we first sample "stick lengths" $\boldsymbol{\pi} \sim \text{GEM}(a, b)$ (in the case of Dirichlet process, we have $b = 0$). The GEM partitions the interval $[0, 1]$ into countably many segments. First, draw $v_i \sim \text{Beta}(1 - b, a + ib)$ for $i \in \{1, \ldots\}$. Then, define $\pi_i \triangleq v_i \prod_{j=1}^{i-1}(1 - v_j)$. In addition, we also sample infinitely many "atoms" independently $z_i \sim G_0$. Define G as:

$$G(z) = \sum_{i=1}^{\infty} \pi_i \delta(z_i, z) \tag{1}$$

where $\delta(z_i, z)$ is 1 if $z_i = z$ and 0 otherwise. This random variable is drawn from a Pitman-Yor process. Notice the discreteness of G is laid bare in the stick-breaking construction.

With the stick-breaking representation in hand, we turn to a constructive definition of the distribution over trees given by an adaptor grammar. Let $A_1, \ldots, A_K$ be an enumeration of the nonterminals in $\mathcal{M}$ which satisfies: $i \leq j \Rightarrow A_j \notin \text{Reachable}(\boldsymbol{G}, A_i)$. (That this exists follows from the assumption about the lack of recursiveness of adapted nonterminals.) Let $\text{Yield}(z)$ be the yield of a tree derivation z. The process that generates observed sentences $\boldsymbol{x} = \langle x_1, \ldots, x_n \rangle$ from the adaptor grammar $\boldsymbol{A} = \langle \boldsymbol{G}, \mathcal{M}, \boldsymbol{a}, \boldsymbol{b}, \boldsymbol{\alpha} \rangle$ is as follows:

1. For each $A \in \mathcal{N}$, draw $\boldsymbol{\theta}_A \sim \text{Dir}(\alpha_A)$.
2. For A from A_1 to A_K, define G_A as follows:
   (a) Draw $\boldsymbol{\pi}_A \mid a_A, b_A \sim \text{GEM}(a_A, b_A)$.
   (b) For $i \in \{1, \ldots\}$, grow a tree $z_{A,i}$ as follows:
      i. Draw $A \rightarrow B_1 \ldots B_n$ from $\boldsymbol{R}_A$.
      ii. $z_{A,i} =$

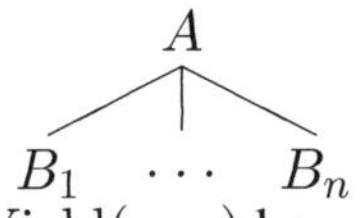

      iii. While $\text{Yield}(z_{A,i})$ has nonterminals:
         A. Choose an unexpanded nonterminal B from yield of $z_{A,i}$.
         B. If $B \in \mathcal{M}$, expand B according to G_B (defined on previous iterations of step 2).
         C. If $B \in \mathcal{N} \setminus \mathcal{M}$, expand B with a rule from $\boldsymbol{R}_B$ according to $\text{Mult}(\boldsymbol{\theta}_B)$.
   (c) For $i \in \{1, \ldots\}$, define $G_A(z_{A,i}) = \pi_{A,i}$
3. For $i \in \{1, \ldots, n\}$ draw z_i as follows:
   (a) If $S \in \mathcal{M}$, draw $z_i \mid G_S \sim G_S$.
   (b) If $S \notin \mathcal{M}$, draw z_i as in 2(b) (omitted for space).
4. Set $x_i = \text{Yield}(z_i)$ for $i \in \{1, \ldots, n\}$.

Here, there are four collections of hidden variables: the PCFG multinomials $\boldsymbol{\theta} = \{\boldsymbol{\theta}_A \mid A \in \mathcal{N}\}$, the stick length proportions $\boldsymbol{v} = \{\boldsymbol{v}_A \mid A \in \mathcal{M}\}$ where $\boldsymbol{v}_A = \langle v_{A,1}, v_{A,2}, \ldots \rangle$, the adapted nonterminals' subtrees $\boldsymbol{z}_A = \{z_{A,i} \mid A \in \mathcal{M}; i \in \{1, \ldots\}\}$ and the derivations $\boldsymbol{z}_{1:n} = z_1, \ldots, z_n$. The symbol $\boldsymbol{z}$ refers to the collection of $\{\boldsymbol{z}_A \mid A \in \mathcal{M}\}$, and $\boldsymbol{z}_{1:n}$ refers to the derivations of the data $\boldsymbol{x}$.

Note that the distribution in 2(c) is defined with the GEM distribution, as mentioned earlier. It is a sample from the Pitman-Yor process (or the Dirichlet process), which is later used in 3(a) to sample trees for an adapted non-terminal.

3 Variational Inference

Variational inference is a deterministic alternative to MCMC, which casts posterior inference as an optimization problem (Jordan et al., 1999; Wainwright and Jordan, 2008). The optimized function is a bound on the marginal likelihood of the observations, which is expressed in terms of a so-called "variational distribution" over the hidden variables. When the bound is tightened, that distribution is close to the posterior of interest. Variational methods tend to converge faster than MCMC, and can be more easily parallelized over multiple processors in a framework such as MapReduce (Dean and Ghemawat, 2004).

The variational bound on the likelihood of the data is:

$$\log p(\boldsymbol{x} \mid \boldsymbol{a}, \boldsymbol{\alpha}) \geq H(q) + \sum_{A \in \mathcal{M}} \mathbb{E}_q[\log p(\boldsymbol{v}_A \mid a_A)]$$
$$+ \sum_{A \in \mathcal{M}} \mathbb{E}_q[\log p(\boldsymbol{\theta}_A \mid \boldsymbol{\alpha}_A)]$$
$$+ \sum_{A \in \mathcal{M}} \mathbb{E}_q[\log p(\boldsymbol{z}_A \mid \boldsymbol{v}, \boldsymbol{\theta})] + \mathbb{E}_q[\log p(\boldsymbol{z} \mid \boldsymbol{v}_A)]$$

Expectations are taken with respect to the variational distribution $q(\boldsymbol{v}, \boldsymbol{\theta}, \boldsymbol{z})$ and $H(q)$ is its entropy.

Before tightening the bound, we define the functional form of the variational distribution. We use the mean-field distribution in which all of the hidden variables are independent and governed by individual variational parameters. (Note that in the true posterior, the hidden variables are highly coupled.) To account for the infinite collection of random variables, for which we cannot define a variational distribution, we use the truncated stick distribution (Blei and Jordan, 2005). Hence, we assume that, for all $A \in \mathcal{M}$, there is some value N_A such that $q(v_{A,N_A} = 1) = 1$. The assigned probability to parse trees in the stick will be 0 for $i > N_A$, so we can ignore $z_{A,i}$ for $i > N_A$. This leads to a factorized variational distribution:

$$q(\boldsymbol{v}, \boldsymbol{\theta}, \boldsymbol{z}) = \prod_{A \in \mathcal{M}} \left(q(\boldsymbol{\theta}_A) \prod_{i=1}^{N_A} q(v_{A,i}) \times q(z_{A,i}) \right) \times \prod_{i=1}^{n} q(z_i) \quad (2)$$

It is natural to define the variational distributions over $\boldsymbol{\theta}$ and $\boldsymbol{v}$ to be Dirichlet distributions with parameters $\boldsymbol{\tau}_A$ and Beta distributions with parameters $\gamma_{A,i}$, respectively. The two distributions over trees, $q(z_{A,i})$ and $q(z_i)$, are more problematic. For example, with $q(z_i \mid \boldsymbol{\phi})$, we need to take into account different subtrees that could be generated by the model and use them with the proper probabilities in the variational distribution $q(z_i \mid \boldsymbol{\phi})$. We follow and extend the idea from Johnson et al. (2006) and use *grammatons* for these distributions. Grammatons are "mini-grammars," inspired by the grammar $\boldsymbol{G}$.

For two strings in $s, t \in \mathcal{W}^*$, we use "$t \subseteq s$" to mean that t is a substring of s. In that case, a grammaton is defined as follows:

Definition 1. *Let $\boldsymbol{A} = \langle \boldsymbol{G}, \mathcal{M}, \boldsymbol{a}, \boldsymbol{b}, \boldsymbol{\alpha} \rangle$ be an adaptor grammar with $\boldsymbol{G} = \langle \mathcal{W}, \mathcal{N}, \boldsymbol{R}, S \rangle$. Let s be a finite string over the alphabet of $\boldsymbol{G}$ and $A \in \mathcal{N}$. Let $\mathcal{U}$ be the set of nonterminals $\mathcal{U} \triangleq \mathrm{Reachable}(\boldsymbol{G}, A) \cap (\mathcal{N} \setminus \mathcal{M})$. The grammaton $\boldsymbol{G}(A, s)$ is the context-free grammar with the start symbol A and the rules*

$$R_A \cup \left(\bigcup_{B \in \mathcal{U}} R_B \right) \cup \bigcup_{A \to B_1 \ldots B_n \in R_A} \; \bigcup_{i \in \{i \mid B_i \in \mathcal{M}\}} \{B_i \to t \mid t \subseteq s\}.$$

Using a grammaton, we define the distributions $q(z_{A,i} \mid \boldsymbol{\phi}_A)$ and $q(z_i \mid \boldsymbol{\phi})$. This requires a preprocessing step (described in detail in §3.3) that defines, for each $A \in \mathcal{M}$, a list of strings $\boldsymbol{s}_A = \langle s_{A,1}, \ldots, s_{A,N_A} \rangle$. Then, for $q(z_{A,i} \mid \boldsymbol{\phi}_A)$ we use the grammaton $\boldsymbol{G}(A, s_{A,i})$ and for $q(z_i \mid \boldsymbol{\phi})$ we use the grammaton $\boldsymbol{G}(A, x_i)$ where x_i is the ith observed sentence. We parametrize the grammaton with weights $\boldsymbol{\phi}_A$ (or $\boldsymbol{\phi}$) for each rule in the grammaton. This makes the variational distributions over the trees for strings $\boldsymbol{s}$ (and trees for $\boldsymbol{x}$) globally normalized weighted grammars. Choosing such distributions is motivated by their ability to make the variational bound tight (similar to Cohen et al., 2008, and Cohen and Smith, 2009). In practice we do not have to use rewrite rules for all strings $t \subseteq s$ in the grammaton. It suffices to add rewrite rules only for the strings $t = s_{A,i}$ that have some grammaton attached to them, $\boldsymbol{G}(A, s_{A,i})$.

The variational distribution above yields a variational inference algorithm for approximating the posterior by estimating $\gamma_{A,i}$, $\boldsymbol{\tau}_A$, $\boldsymbol{\phi}_A$ and $\boldsymbol{\phi}$ iteratively, given a fixed set of hyperparameters $\boldsymbol{a}$, $\boldsymbol{b}$ and $\boldsymbol{\alpha}$. Let r be a PCFG rule. Let $\tilde{f}(r, s_{B,k}) = \mathbb{E}_{q(z_k \mid \boldsymbol{\phi}_{B,k})}[f(r; z_k)]$, where $f(r; z_k)$ counts the number of times that rule r is applied in the derivation z_k. Let $A \to \beta$ denote a rule from $\boldsymbol{G}$. The quantity $\tilde{f}(r, s_{B,k})$ is computed using the inside-outside (IO) algorithm. Fig. 1 gives the variational inference updates.

Variational EM We use variational EM to fit the hyperparameters. Variational EM is an EM algorithm where the E step is replaced by variational inference (Fig. 1). The M-step optimizes the hyperparameters ($\boldsymbol{a}$, $\boldsymbol{b}$ and $\boldsymbol{\alpha}$) with respect to expected sufficient statistics under the variational distribution. We use Newton-Raphson for each (Boyd and Vandenberghe, 2004); Fig. 2 gives the objectives.

3.1 Note about Recursive Grammars

With recursive grammars, the stick-breaking process representation gives probability mass to events which are ill-defined. In step 2(iii)(c) of the stick-breaking representation, we assign nonzero probability to an event in which we choose to expand the current tree using a subtree with the same index that we are currently still expanding (see footnote 2). In short, with recursive grammars, we can get "loops" inside the trees.

We would still like to use recursion in the cases which are not ill-defined. In the case of recursive grammars, there is no problem with the stick-breaking representation and the order by which we enumerate the nonterminals. This is true because the stick-breaking process separates allocating the probabilities for each index in the stick and allocating the atoms for each index in the stick.

Our variational distributions give probability 0 to any event which is ill-defined in the sense mentioned above. Optimizing the variational bound in this case is equivalent to optimizing the same variational bound with a model p' that (i) starts with p, (ii) assigns probability 0 to ill-defined events, and (iii) renormalizes:

Proposition 2. *Let $p(\boldsymbol{x}, \boldsymbol{z})$ be a probability distribution, where $z \in \mathcal{Z}$, and let $\mathcal{S} \subset \mathcal{Z}$. Let $Q = \{q \mid q(z) = 0, \forall z \in \mathcal{S}\}$, a set of distributions. Then:*

$$\operatorname*{argmax}_{q \in Q} \mathbb{E}_q[\log p(\boldsymbol{x}, \boldsymbol{z})] = \operatorname*{argmax}_{q} \mathbb{E}_q[\log p'(\boldsymbol{x}, \boldsymbol{z})]$$

where $p'(\boldsymbol{x}, \boldsymbol{z})$ is a probability distribution defined as $p'(\boldsymbol{x}, \boldsymbol{z}) = p(\boldsymbol{x}, \boldsymbol{z}) / \sum_{\boldsymbol{z} \in \mathcal{S}} p(\boldsymbol{x}, \boldsymbol{z})$ for $\boldsymbol{z} \in \mathcal{S}$ and 0 otherwise.

For this reason, our variational approximation allows the use of recursive grammars. The use of recursive grammars with MCMC methods is problematic, since it has no corresponding probabilistic interpretation, enabled by zeroing events that are ill-defined in the variational distribution. There is no underlying model such as p', and thus the inference algorithm is invalid.

3.2 Time Complexity

The algorithm in Johnson et al. (2006) works by sampling from a PCFG containing rewrite rules that rewrite to a whole tree fragment. This requires a procedure that uses the inside-outside algorithm. Despite the grammar being bigger (because of the rewrite rules to a string), the asymptotic complexity of the IO algorithm stays $O(|\mathcal{N}|^2|x_i|^3 + |\mathcal{N}|^3|x_i|^2)$ where $|x_i|$ is the length of the ith sentence.[3]

[3] This analysis is true for CNF grammars augmented with rules rewriting to a whole string, like those used in our study.

$$\begin{aligned}
\gamma^1_{A,i} &= 1 - b_A + \textstyle\sum_{B \in \mathcal{M}} \sum_{k=1}^{N_B} \tilde{f}(A \to s_{A,i}, s_{B,k}) \\
\gamma^2_{A,i} &= a_A + i b_A \\
&\quad + \textstyle\sum_{j=1}^{i-1} \sum_{B \in \mathcal{M}} \sum_{k=1}^{N_B} \tilde{f}(A \to s_{A,j}, s_{B,k}) \\
\tau_{A,A\to\beta} &= \textstyle\sum_{B \in \mathcal{M}} \sum_{k=1}^{N_B} \tilde{f}(A \to \beta, s_{B,k}) \\
\phi_{A,A\to s_{A,i}} &= \Psi(\gamma^1_{A,i}) - \Psi(\gamma^1_{A,i} + \gamma^2_{A,i}) \\
&\quad + \textstyle\sum_{j=1}^{i-1} \left(\Psi(\gamma^2_{A,i}) - \Psi(\gamma^1_{A,i} + \gamma^2_{A,i})\right) \\
\phi_{A,A\to\beta} &= \Psi(\tau_{A,A\to\beta}) - \Psi\left(\textstyle\sum_\beta \tau_{A,A\to\beta}\right)
\end{aligned}$$

Figure 1: Updates for variational inference with adaptor grammars. Ψ is the digamma function.

Our algorithm requires running the IO algorithm for each yield in the variational distribution, for each nonterminal, and for each sentence. However, IO runs with much smaller grammars coming from the grammatons. The cost of running the IO algorithm on the yields in the sticks for $A \in \mathcal{M}$ can be taken into account parsing a string that appears in the corpus with the full grammars. This leads to an asymptotic complexity of $O(|\mathcal{N}|^2|x_i|^3 + |\mathcal{N}|^3|x_i|^2)$ for the ith sentence in the corpus each iteration.

Asymptotically, both sampling and variational EM behave the same. However, there are different constants that hide in these asymptotic runtimes: the number of iterations that the algorithm takes to converge (for which variational EM generally has an advantage over sampling) and the number of additional rewrite rules that rewrite to a string representing a tree (for which MCMC has a relative advantage, because it does not use a fixed set of strings; instead, the size of the grammars it uses grow as sampling proceeds). In §4, we see that variational EM and sampling methods are similar in the time it takes to complete because of a trade-off between these two constants. Simple parallelization, however, which is possible only with variational inference, provides significant speed-ups.[4]

3.3 Heuristics for Variational Inference

For the variational approximation from §3, we need to decide on a set of strings, $s_{A,i}$ (for $A \in \mathcal{M}$ and $i \in \{1, \ldots, N_A\}$) to define the grammatons in the

[4] Newman et al. (2009) show how to parallelize sampling algorithms, but in general, parallelizing these algorithms is more complicated than parallelizing variational algorithms and requires further approximation.

$$\max_{\alpha_A} \quad \log\Gamma(|R_A|\alpha_A) - |R_A|\log\Gamma(\alpha_A) + (\alpha_A - 1)\left(\sum_{A\to\beta\in R_A}\Psi(\tau_{A\to\beta}) - \Psi\left(\sum_{A\to\beta\in R_A}\tau_{A\to\beta}\right)\right)$$
$$\max_{a_A} \quad \sum_{i=1}^{N_A} a_A\left(\Psi(\gamma^2_{A,i}) - \Psi(\gamma^1_{A,i} + \gamma^2_{A,i})\right) + \log\Gamma(a_A + 1 + ib_A) - \log\Gamma(ib_A + a_A)$$
$$\max_{b_A} \quad \sum_{i=1}^{N_A} ib_A\left(\Psi(\gamma^2_{A,i}) - \Psi(\gamma^1_{A,i} + \gamma^2_{A,i})\right) + \log\Gamma(a_A + 1 + ib_A) - \log\Gamma(1 - b_A) - \log\Gamma(ib_A + a_A)$$

Figure 2: Variational M-step updates. Γ is the gamma function.

nonparametric stick. Any set of strings will give a valid approximation, but to make the variational approximation as accurate as possible, we require that: (i) the strings in the set must be likely to be generated using the adaptor grammar as constituents headed by the relevant nonterminal, and (ii) strings that are more likely to be generated should be associated with a lower index in the stick. The reason for the second requirement is the exponential decay of coefficients as the index increases.

We show that a simple heuristic leads to an order over the strings generated by the adaptor grammars that yields an accurate variational estimation. We begin with a weighted context-free grammar $\boldsymbol{G}_{\text{heur}}$ that has the same rules as in $\boldsymbol{G}$, only the weight for all of its rules is 1. We then compute the quantity:

$$c(A, s) = \frac{1}{n}\left(\sum_{i=1}^{n} \mathbb{E}_{\boldsymbol{G}_{\text{heur}}}[f_i(z; A, s)]\right) - \rho \log |s| \qquad (3)$$

where $f_i(z; A, s)$ is a function computing the count of constituents headed by A with yield s in the tree z for the sentence x_i. This quantity can be computed by using the IO algorithm on $\boldsymbol{G}_{\text{heur}}$. The term $\rho \log |s|$ is subtracted to avoid preference for shorter constituents, similar to Mochihashi et al. (2009).

While computing $c(A, s)$ using the IO algorithm, we sort the set of all substrings of s according to their expected counts (aggregated over all strings s). Then, we use the top N_A strings in the sorted list for the grammatons of A.[5]

3.4 Decoding

The variational inference algorithm gives a distributions over parameters and hidden structures (through the grammatons). We experiment with two commonly used decoding methods: Viterbi decoding and minimum Bayes risk decoding (MBR; Goodman, 1996).

To parse a string with Viterbi (or MBR) decoding, we find the tree with highest score for the grammaton which is attached to that string. For all rules which rewrite to strings in the resulting tree, we again perform Viterbi (or MBR) decoding recursively using other grammatons.

4 Experiments

We describe experiments with variational inference for adaptor grammars for word segmentation and dependency grammar induction.

4.1 Word Segmentation

We follow the experimental setting of Johnson and Goldwater (2009), who present state-of-the-art results for inference with adaptor grammars using Gibbs sampling on a segmentation problem. We use the standard Brent corpus (Brent and Cartwright, 1996), which includes 9,790 unsegmented phonemic representations of utterances of child-directed speech from the Bernstein-Ratner (1987) corpus.

Johnson and Goldwater (2009) test three grammars for this segmentation task. The first grammar is a character unigram grammar ($\boldsymbol{G}_{\text{Unigram}}$). The second grammar is a grammar that takes into consideration collocations ($\boldsymbol{G}_{\text{Colloc}}$) which includes the rules { Sentence → Colloc, Sentence → Colloc Sentence, Colloc → Word$^+$, Word → Char$^+$ }. The third grammar incorporates more prior knowledge about the syllabic structure of English ($\boldsymbol{G}_{\text{Syllable}}$). $\boldsymbol{G}_{\text{Unigram}}$ and $\boldsymbol{G}_{\text{Syllable}}$ can be found in Johnson and Goldwater (2009). Once an utterance is parsed, Word constituents denote segments.

The value of ρ (penalty term for string length) had little effect on our results and was fixed at $\rho = -0.2$. When N_A (number of strings used in the variational distributions) is fixed, we use N_A = 15,000. We report results using Viterbi and MBR decoding. Johnson and Goldwater (2009) experimented with two

[5] The requirement to select N_A in advance is strict. We experimented with dynamic expansions of the stick, in the spirit of Kurihara et al. (2006) and Wang and Blei (2009), but we did not achieve better performance and it had an adverse effect on runtime. For completeness, we give these results in §4.

grammar	model	this paper Vit.	this paper MBR	J&G 2009 SA	J&G 2009 MM
G_{Unigram}	Dir	0.49	**0.84**	0.57	0.54
	PY	0.49	**0.84**	0.81	0.75
	PY+inc	0.42	0.59	-	-
G_{Colloc}	Dir	0.40	**0.86**	0.75	0.72
	PY	0.40	**0.86**	0.83	**0.86**
	PY+inc	0.43	0.60	-	-
G_{Syllable}	Dir	0.77	0.83	0.84	0.84
	PY	0.77	0.83	**0.89**	0.88
	PY+inc	0.75	0.76	-	-

Table 1: F_1 performance for word segmentation on the Brent corpus. Dir. stands for Dirichlet Process adaptor ($\boldsymbol{b} = 0$), PY stands for Pitman-Yor adaptor ($\boldsymbol{b}$ optimized), and PY+inc. stands for Pitman-Yor with iteratively increasing N_A for $A \in \mathcal{M}$ (see footnote 5). J&G 2009 are the results adapted from Johnson and Goldwater (2009); SA is sample average decoding, and MM is maximum marginal decoding.

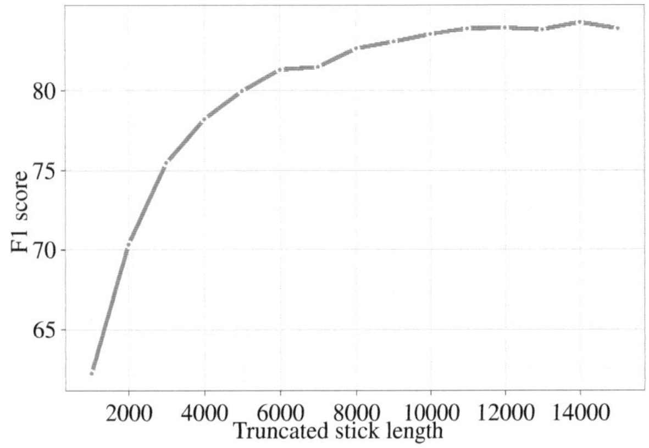

Figure 3: F_1 performance of $\boldsymbol{G}_{\text{Unigram}}$ as influenced by the length of the stick, N_{Word}.

decoding methods, sample average (SA) and maximal marginal decoding (MM), which are closely related to Viterbi and MBR, respectively. With MM, we marginalize the tree structure, rather than the word segmentation induced, similar to MBR decoding. With SA, we compute the probability of a whole tree, by averaging its count in the samples, an approximation to finding the tree with highest probability, like Viterbi.

Table 1 gives the results for our experiments. Notice that the results for the Pitman-Yor process and the Dirichlet process are similar. When inspecting the learned parameters, we noticed that the discount parameters ($\boldsymbol{b}$) learned by the variational inference algorithm for the Pitman-Yor process are very close to 0. In this case, the Pitman-Yor process is reduced to the Dirichlet process.

Similar to Johnson and Goldwater's comparisons, we see superior performance when using minimum Bayes risk over Viterbi decoding. Further notice that the variational inference algorithm obtains significantly superior performance for simpler grammars than Johnson et al., while performance using the syllable grammar is lower. The results also suggest that it is better to decide ahead on the set of strings available in the sticks, instead of working gradually and increase the size of the sticks as described in footnote 5. We believe that the reason is that the variational inference algorithm settles in a trajectory that uses fewer strings, then fails to exploit the strings that are added to the stick later. Given that selecting N_A in advance is advantageous, we may inquire if choosing N_A to be too large can lead to degraded performance, because of fragmention of the grammar. Fig. 3 suggests it is not the case, and performance stays steady after N_A reaches a certain value.

One of the advantages of variational approximation over sampling methods is the ability to run for fewer iterations. For example, with $\boldsymbol{G}_{\text{Unigram}}$ convergence typically takes 40 iterations with variational inference, while Johnson and Goldwater (2009) ran their sampler for 2,000 iterations, for which 1,000 were for burning in. The inside-outside algorithm dominates the iteration's runtime, both for sampling and variational EM. Each iteration with sampling, however, takes less time, despite the asymptotic analysis in §3.2, because of different implementations and the different number of rules that rewrite to a string. We now give a comparison of clock time for $\boldsymbol{G}_{\text{Unigram}}$ for variational inference and sampling as described in Johnson and Goldwater (2009).[6] Replicating the experiment in Johnson and Goldwater (first row in Table 1) took 2 hours and 11 minutes. With the variational approximation, we had the following: (i) the preprocessing (§3.3) step took 114 seconds; (ii) each iteration took approximately 204 seconds, with convergence after 40 iterations, leading to 8,160 seconds of pure varia-

[6]We used the code and data available at `http://www.cog.brown.edu/~mj/Software.htm`. The machine used for this comparison is a 64-bit machine with 2.6GHz CPU, 4MB of cache memory and 8GB of RAM.

tional EM processing; (iii) parsing took another 952 seconds. The total time is 2 hours and 34 minutes.

At first glance it seems that variational inference is slower than MCMC sampling. However, note that the cost of the grammar preprocessing step is amortized over all experiments with the specific grammar, and the E-step with variational inference can be parallelized, while sampling requires an update of a global set of parameters after each tree update. We ran our algorithm on a cluster of 20 1.86GHz CPUs and achieved a significant speed-up: preprocessing took 34 seconds, each variational EM iteration took 43 seconds and parsing took 208 seconds. The total time was 47 minutes, which is 2.8 times faster than sampling.

4.2 Dependency Grammar Induction

We conclude our experiments with preliminary results for unsupervised syntax learning. This is a new application of adaptor grammars, which have so far been used in segmentation (Johnson and Goldwater, 2009) and named entity recognition (Elsner et al., 2009).

The grammar we use is the dependency model with valence (DMV Klein and Manning, 2004) represented as a probabilistic context-free grammar, $\boldsymbol{G}_{\text{DMV}}$ (Smith, 2006). We note that $\boldsymbol{G}_{\text{DMV}}$ is recursive; this is not a problem (§3.1).

We used part-of-speech sequences from the *Wall Street Journal* Penn Treebank (Marcus et al., 1993), stripped of words and punctuation. We follow standard parsing conventions and train on sections 2–21 and test on section 23 (while using sentences of length 10 or less). Because of the unsupervised nature of the problem, we report results on the training set, in addition to the test set.

The nonterminals that we adapted correspond to nonterminals that define noun constituents. We then use the preprocessing step defined in §3.3 with a uniform grammar and take the top 3,000 strings for each nonterminal of a noun constituent.

The results are in Table 4.2. We report attachment accuracy, the fraction of parent-child relationships that the algorithm classified correctly. Notice that the results are not very different for Viterbi and MBR decoding, unlike the case with word segmentation. It seems like the DMV grammar, applied to this task, is more robust to changes in decoding mechanism. Adaptor grammars improve performance over classic EM and variational EM with a Dirichlet prior significantly.

	model	Vit.	MBR
train	non-Bayesian	48.2	48.3
train	Dirichlet prior	48.3	48.6
train	Adaptor grammar	**54.0**	†53.7
test	non-Bayesian	45.8	46.1
test	Dirichlet prior	45.9	46.1
test	Adaptor grammar	48.3	**50.2**

Table 2: Attachment accuracy for different models for dependency grammar induction. Bold marks best overall accuracy per evaluation set, and † marks figures that are not significantly worse (binomial sign test, $p < 0.05$).

We note that adaptor grammars are not limited to a selection of a Dirichlet distribution as a prior for the grammar rules. Our variational inference algorithm, for example, can be extended to use the logistic normal prior instead of the Dirichlet, shown successful by Cohen and Smith (2009).[7]

5 Conclusion

We described a variational inference algorithm for adaptor grammars based on a stick-breaking process representation, which solves a problem with adaptor grammars and recursive PCFGs. We tested it for a segmentation task, and showed results which are either comparable or an imporvement of state of the art. We showed that significant speed-ups can be obtained using parallelization of the algorithm. We also tested the algorithm on a novel task for adaptor grammars, dependency grammar induction. We showed that an improvement can be obtained using adaptor grammars over non-Bayesian and parametric baselines.

Acknowledgments

The authors would like to thank the anonymous reviewers, Jordan Boyd-Graber, Reza Haffari, Mark Johnson, and Chong Wang for their useful feedback and comments. This work was supported by the following grants: ONR 175-6343 and NSF CAREER 0745520 to Blei; NSF IIS-0836431 and IIS-0915187 to Smith.

[7] The performance of Cohen and Smith (2009), like the performance of Headden et al. (2009), is greater than what we report, but those developments are orthogonal to the contributions of this paper.

References

C. Antoniak. 1974. Mixtures of Dirichlet processes with applications to Bayesian nonparametric problems. *The Annals of Statistics*, 2(6):1152–1174.

N. Bernstein-Ratner. 1987. The phonology of parent child speech. *Children's Language*, 6.

D. Blei and M. Jordan. 2005. Variational inference for Dirichlet process mixtures. *Journal of Bayesian Analysis*, 1(1):121–144.

S. Boyd and L. Vandenberghe. 2004. *Convex Optimization*. Cambridge Press.

M. Brent and T. Cartwright. 1996. Distributional regularity and phonotactic constraints are useful for segmentation. *Cognition*, 6:93–125.

S. B. Cohen and N. A. Smith. 2009. Shared logistic normal distributions for soft parameter tying in unsupervised grammar induction. In *Proc. of NAACL-HLT*.

S. B. Cohen, K. Gimpel, and N. A. Smith. 2008. Logistic normal priors for unsupervised probabilistic grammar induction. In *NIPS*.

J. Dean and S. Ghemawat. 2004. MapReduce: Simplified data processing on large clusters. In *Proc. of OSDI*.

M. Elsner, E. Charniak, and M. Johnson. 2009. Structured generative models for unsupervised named-entity clustering. In *Proc. of NAACL-HLT*.

S. Goldwater and T. L. Griffiths. 2007. A fully Bayesian approach to unsupervised part-of-speech tagging. In *Proc. of ACL*.

J. Goodman. 1996. Parsing algorithms and metrics. In *Proc. of ACL*.

W. P. Headden, M. Johnson, and D. McClosky. 2009. Improving unsupervised dependency parsing with richer contexts and smoothing. In *Proc. of NAACL-HLT*.

M. Johnson and S. Goldwater. 2009. Improving nonparameteric Bayesian inference experiments on unsupervised word segmentation with adaptor grammars. In *Proc. of NAACL-HLT*.

M. Johnson, T. L. Griffiths, and S. Goldwater. 2006. Adaptor grammars: A framework for specifying compositional nonparameteric Bayesian models. In *NIPS*.

M. Johnson, T. L. Griffiths, and S. Goldwater. 2007. Bayesian inference for PCFGs via Markov chain Monte Carlo. In *Proc. of NAACL*.

M. Johnson. 2008a. Unsupervised word segmentation for Sesotho using adaptor grammars. In *Proceedings of the Tenth Meeting of ACL Special Interest Group on Computational Morphology and Phonology*.

M. Johnson. 2008b. Using adaptor grammars to identify synergies in the unsupervised acquisition of linguistic structure. In *Proc. of ACL*.

M. I. Jordan, Z. Ghahramani, T. S. Jaakola, and L. K. Saul. 1999. An introduction to variational methods for graphical models. *Machine Learning*, 37(2):183–233.

A. Joshi. 2003. Tree adjoining grammars. In R. Mitkov, editor, *The Oxford Handbook of Computational Linguistics*, pages 483–501. Oxford University Press.

D. Klein and C. D. Manning. 2004. Corpus-based induction of syntactic structure: Models of dependency and constituency. In *Proc. of ACL*.

K. Kurihara, M. Welling, and N. A. Vlassis. 2006. Accelerated variational Dirichlet process mixtures. In *NIPS*.

P. Liang, S. Petrov, M. Jordan, and D. Klein. 2007. The infinite PCFG using hierarchical Dirichlet processes. In *Proc. of EMNLP*.

M. P. Marcus, B. Santorini, and M. A. Marcinkiewicz. 1993. Building a large annotated corpus of English: The Penn treebank. *Computational Linguistics*, 19:313–330.

D. Mochihashi, T. Yamada, and N. Ueda. 2009. Bayesian unsupervised word segmentation with nested Pitman-Yor language modeling. In *Proc. of ACL*.

D. Newman, A. Asuncion, P. Smyth, and M. Welling. 2009. Distributed algorithms for topic models. *Journal of Machine Learning Research*, 10:1801–1828.

J. Pitman and M. Yor. 1997. The two-parameter Poisson-Dirichlet distribution derived from a stable subordinator. *Annals of Probability*, 25(2):855–900.

J. Pitman. 2002. *Combinatorial Stochastic Processes*. Lecture Notes for St. Flour Summer School. Springer-Verlag, New York, NY.

C. P. Robert and G. Casella. 2005. *Monte Carlo Statistical Methods*. Springer.

J. Sethuraman. 1994. A constructive definition of Dirichlet priors. *Statistica Sinica*, 4:639–650.

N. A. Smith. 2006. *Novel Estimation Methods for Unsupervised Discovery of Latent Structure in Natural Language Text*. Ph.D. thesis, Johns Hopkins University.

K. Toutanova and M. Johnson. 2007. A Bayesian LDA-based model for semi-supervised part-of-speech tagging. In *Proc. of NIPS*.

M. J. Wainwright and M. I. Jordan. 2008. Graphical models, exponential families, and variational inference. *Foundations and Trends in Machine Learning*, 1:1–305.

C. Wang and D. M. Blei. 2009. Variational inference for the nested Chinese restaurant process. In *NIPS*.

Type-Based MCMC

Percy Liang
UC Berkeley
pliang@cs.berkeley.edu

Michael I. Jordan
UC Berkeley
jordan@cs.berkeley.edu

Dan Klein
UC Berkeley
klein@cs.berkeley.edu

Abstract

Most existing algorithms for learning latent-variable models—such as EM and existing Gibbs samplers—are *token-based*, meaning that they update the variables associated with one sentence at a time. The incremental nature of these methods makes them susceptible to local optima/slow mixing. In this paper, we introduce a *type-based sampler*, which updates a block of variables, identified by a *type*, which spans multiple sentences. We show improvements on part-of-speech induction, word segmentation, and learning tree-substitution grammars.

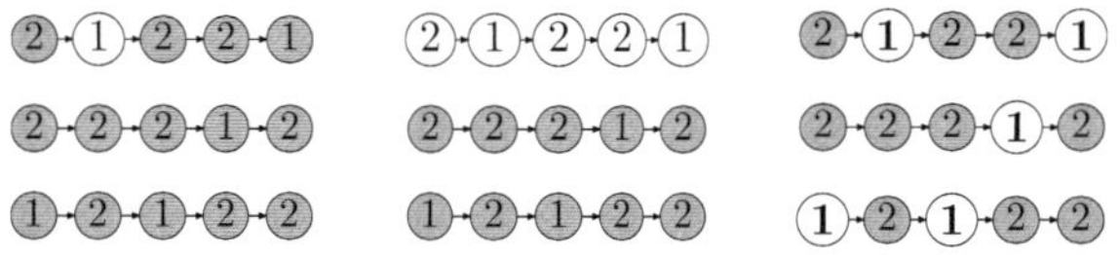

(a) token-based (b) sentence-based (c) type-based

Figure 1: Consider a dataset of 3 sentences, each of length 5. Each variable is labeled with a *type* (1 or 2). The unshaded variables are the ones that are updated jointly by a sampler. The token-based sampler updates the variable for one token at a time (a). The sentence-based sampler updates all variables in a sentence, thus dealing with intra-sentential dependencies (b). The type-based sampler updates all variables of a particular type (1 in this example), thus dealing with dependencies due to common parameters (c).

1 Introduction

A long-standing challenge in NLP is the unsupervised induction of linguistic structures, for example, grammars from raw sentences or lexicons from phoneme sequences. A fundamental property of these unsupervised learning problems is multimodality. In grammar induction, for example, we could analyze subject-verb-object sequences as either *((subject verb) object)* (mode 1) or *(subject (verb object))* (mode 2).

Multimodality causes problems for token-based procedures that update variables for one example at a time. In EM, for example, if the parameters already assign high probability to the *((subject verb) object)* analysis, re-analyzing the sentences in E-step only reinforces the analysis, resulting in EM getting stuck in a local optimum. In (collapsed) Gibbs sampling, if all sentences are already analyzed as *((subject verb) object)*, sampling a sentence *conditioned* on all others will most likely not change its analysis, resulting in slow mixing.

To combat the problems associated with token-based algorithms, we propose a new sampling algorithm that operates on *types*. Our sampler would, for example, be able to change all occurrences of *((subject verb) object)* to *(subject (verb object))* in one step. These type-based operations are reminiscent of the type-based grammar operations of early chunk-merge systems (Wolff, 1988; Stolcke and Omohundro, 1994), but we work within a sampling framework for increased robustness.

In NLP, perhaps the the most simple and popular sampler is the *token-based Gibbs sampler*,[1] used in Goldwater et al. (2006), Goldwater and Griffiths (2007), and many others. By sampling only one

[1] In NLP, this is sometimes referred to as simply the collapsed Gibbs sampler.

Human Language Technologies: The 2010 Annual Conference of the North American Chapter of the ACL, pages 573–581,
Los Angeles, California, June 2010.

variable at a time, this sampler is prone to slow mixing due to the strong coupling between variables. A general remedy is to sample blocks of coupled variables. For example, the *sentence-based sampler* samples all the variables associated with a sentence at once (e.g., the entire tag sequence). However, this blocking does not deal with the strong type-based coupling (e.g., all instances of a word should be tagged similarly). The type-based sampler we will present is designed exactly to tackle this coupling, which we argue is stronger and more important to deal with in unsupervised learning. Figure 1 depicts the updates made by each of the three samplers.

We tested our sampler on three models: a Bayesian HMM for part-of-speech induction (Goldwater and Griffiths, 2007), a nonparametric Bayesian model for word segmentation (Goldwater et al., 2006), and a nonparametric Bayesian model of tree substitution grammars (Cohn et al., 2009; Post and Gildea, 2009). Empirically, we find that type-based sampling improves performance and is less sensitive to initialization (Section 5).

2 Basic Idea via a Motivating Example

The key technical problem we solve in this paper is finding a block of variables which are both *highly coupled* and yet *tractable to sample jointly*. This section illustrates the main idea behind type-based sampling on a small word segmentation example.

Suppose our dataset $\mathbf{x}$ consists of n occurrences of the sequence a b. Our goal is infer $\mathbf{z} = (z_1, \dots, z_n)$, where $z_i = 0$ if the sequence is one word *ab*, and $z_i = 1$ if the sequence is two, *a* and *b*. We can model this situation with a simple generative model: for each $i = 1, \dots, n$, generate one or two words with equal probability. Each word is drawn independently based on probabilities $\theta = (\theta_a, \theta_b, \theta_{ab})$ which we endow with a uniform prior $\theta \sim \text{Dirichlet}(1, 1, 1)$.

We marginalize out θ to get the following standard expression (Goldwater et al., 2009):

$$p(\mathbf{z} \mid \mathbf{x}) \propto \frac{1^{(m)} 1^{(m)} 1^{(n-m)}}{3^{(n+m)}} \stackrel{\text{def}}{=} g(m), \quad (1)$$

where $m = \sum_{i=1}^{n} z_i$ is the number of two-word sequences and $a^{(k)} = a(a+1)\cdots(a+k-1)$ is the *ascending factorial*.[2] Figure 2(a) depicts the resulting bimodal posterior.

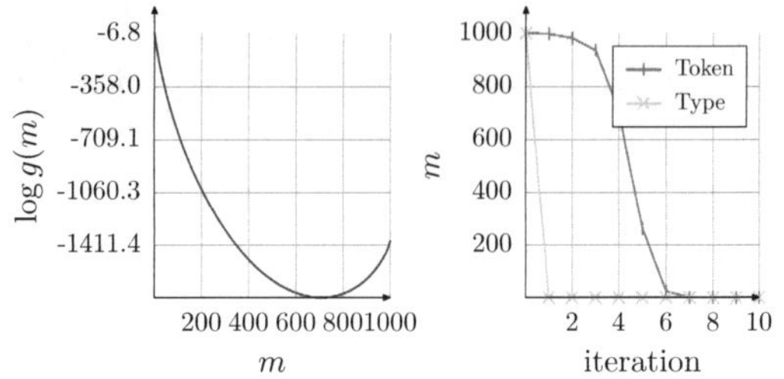

(a) bimodal posterior (b) sampling run

Figure 2: (a) The posterior (1) is sharply bimodal (note the log-scale). (b) A run of the token-based and type-based samplers. We initialize both samplers with $m = n$ ($n = 1000$). The type-based sampler mixes instantly (in fact, it makes independent draws from the posterior) whereas the token-based sampler requires five passes through the data before finding the high probability region $m \approxeq 0$.

A token-based sampler chooses one z_i to update according to the posterior $p(z_i \mid \mathbf{z}_{-i}, \mathbf{x})$. To illustrate the mixing problem, consider the case where $m = n$, i.e., all sequences are analyzed as two words. From (1), we can verify that $p(z_i = 0 \mid \mathbf{z}_{-i}, \mathbf{x}) = O(\frac{1}{n})$. When $n = 1000$, this means that there is only a 0.002 probability of setting $z_i = 0$, a very unlikely but necessary first step to take to escape this local optimum. Indeed, Figure 2(b) shows how the token-based sampler requires five passes over the data to finally escape.

Type-based sampling completely eradicates the local optimum problem in this example. Let us take a closer look at (1). Note that $p(\mathbf{z} \mid \mathbf{x})$ only depends on a single integer m, which only takes one of $n+1$ values, not on the particular $\mathbf{z}$. This shows that the z_is are *exchangeable*. There are $\binom{n}{m}$ possible values of $\mathbf{z}$ satisfying $m = \sum_i z_i$, each with *the same* probability $g(m)$. Summing, we get:

$$p(m \mid \mathbf{x}) \propto \sum_{\mathbf{z}:m=\sum_i z_i} p(\mathbf{x}, \mathbf{z}) = \binom{n}{m} g(m). \quad (2)$$

A sampling strategy falls out naturally: First, sample the number m via (2). Conditioned on m, choose

[2]The ascending factorial function arises from marginalizing Dirichlet distributions and is responsible the rich-gets-richer phenomenon: the larger n is, more we gain by increasing it.

the particular $\mathbf{z}$ uniformly out of the $\binom{n}{m}$ possibilities. Figure 2(b) shows the effectiveness of this type-based sampler.

This simple example exposes the fundamental challenge of multimodality in unsupervised learning. Both $m = 0$ and $m = n$ are modes due to the rich-gets-richer property which arises by virtue of all n examples sharing the same parameters $\boldsymbol{\theta}$. This sharing is a double-edged sword: It provides us with clustering structure but also makes inference hard. Even though $m = n$ is much worse (by a factor exponential in n) than $m = 0$, a naïve algorithm can easily have trouble escaping $m = n$.

3 Setup

We will now present the type-based sampler in full generality. Our sampler is applicable to any model which is built out of local multinomial choices, where each multinomial has a Dirichlet process prior (a Dirichlet prior if the number of choices is finite). This includes most probabilistic models in NLP (excluding ones built from log-linear features).

As we develop the sampler, we will provide concrete examples for the Bayesian hidden Markov model (HMM), the Dirichlet process unigram segmentation model (USM) (Goldwater et al., 2006), and the probabilistic tree-substitution grammar (PTSG) (Cohn et al., 2009; Post and Gildea, 2009).

3.1 Model parameters

A model is specified by a collection of multinomial parameters $\boldsymbol{\theta} = \{\theta_r\}_{r \in \mathcal{R}}$, where $\mathcal{R}$ is an index set. Each vector θ_r specifies a distribution over outcomes: outcome o has probability θ_{ro}.

- HMM: Let K is the number of states. The set $\mathcal{R} = \{(q,k) : q \in \{\text{T},\text{E}\}, k = 1,\dots,K\}$ indexes the K transition distributions $\{\theta_{(\text{T},k)}\}$ (each over outcomes $\{1,\dots,K\}$) and K emission distributions $\{\theta_{(\text{E},k)}\}$ (each over the set of words).
- USM: $\mathcal{R} = \{0\}$, and θ_0 is a distribution over (an infinite number of) words.
- PTSG: $\mathcal{R}$ is the set of grammar symbols, and each θ_r is a distribution over labeled tree fragments with root label r.

$\mathcal{R}$	index set for parameters
$\boldsymbol{\theta} = \{\theta_r\}_{r \in \mathcal{R}}$	multinomial parameters
$\boldsymbol{\mu} = \{\mu_r\}_{r \in \mathcal{R}}$	base distributions (fixed)
$\mathcal{S}$	set of sites
$\mathbf{b} = \{b_s\}_{s \in \mathcal{S}}$	binary variables (to be sampled)
$\mathbf{z}$	latent structure (set of choices)
$\mathbf{z}^{-s}$	choices not depending on site s
$\mathbf{z}^{s:b}$	choices after setting $b_s = b$
$\Delta\mathbf{z}^{s:b}$	$\mathbf{z}^{s:b} \backslash \mathbf{z}^{-s}$: new choices from $b_s = b$
$S \subset \mathcal{S}$	sites selected for sampling
m	# sites in S assigned $b_s = 1$
$\mathbf{n} = \{n_{ro}\}$	counts (sufficient statistics of $\mathbf{z}$)

Table 1: Notation used in this paper. Note that there is a one-to-one mapping between $\mathbf{z}$ and $(\mathbf{b}, \mathbf{x})$. The information relevant for evaluating the likelihood is $\mathbf{n}$. We use the following parallel notation: $\mathbf{n}^{-s} = \mathbf{n}(\mathbf{z}^{-s}), \mathbf{n}^{s:b} = \mathbf{n}(\mathbf{z}^{s:b}), \Delta\mathbf{n}^{s} = \mathbf{n}(\Delta\mathbf{z}^{s})$.

3.2 Choice representation of latent structure z

We represent the latent structure $\mathbf{z}$ as a set of local *choices*:[3]

- HMM: $\mathbf{z}$ contains elements of the form (T, i, a, b), denoting a transition from state a at position i to state b at position $i+1$; and (E, i, a, w), denoting an emission of word w from state a at position i.
- USM: $\mathbf{z}$ contains elements of the form (i, w), denoting the generation of word w at character position i extending to position $i + |w| - 1$.
- PTSG: $\mathbf{z}$ contains elements of the form (x, t), denoting the generation of tree fragment t rooted at node x.

The choices $\mathbf{z}$ are connected to the parameters $\boldsymbol{\theta}$ as follows: $p(\mathbf{z} \mid \boldsymbol{\theta}) = \prod_{z \in \mathbf{z}} \theta_{z.r, z.o}$. Each choice $z \in \mathbf{z}$ is identified with some $z.r \in \mathcal{R}$ and outcome $z.o$. Intuitively, choice z was made by drawing drawing $z.o$ from the multinomial distribution $\theta_{z.r}$.

3.3 Prior

We place a Dirichlet process prior on θ_r (Dirichlet prior for finite outcome spaces): $\theta_r \sim \text{DP}(\alpha_r, \mu_r)$, where α_r is a concentration parameter and μ_r is a fixed base distribution.

[3]We assume that $\mathbf{z}$ contains both a latent part and the observed input $\mathbf{x}$, i.e., $\mathbf{x}$ is a deterministic function of $\mathbf{z}$.

Let $n_{ro}(\mathbf{z}) = |\{z \in \mathbf{z} : z.r = r, z.o = o\}|$ be the number of draws from θ_r resulting in outcome o, and $n_{r\cdot} = \sum_o n_{ro}$ be the number of times θ_r was drawn from. Let $\mathbf{n}(\mathbf{z}) = \{n_{ro}(\mathbf{z})\}$ denote the vector of sufficient statistics associated with choices $\mathbf{z}$. When it is clear from context, we simply write $\mathbf{n}$ for $\mathbf{n}(\mathbf{z})$. Using these sufficient statistics, we can write $p(\mathbf{z} \mid \boldsymbol{\theta}) = \prod_{r,o} \theta_{ro}^{n_{ro}(\mathbf{z})}$.

We now marginalize out $\boldsymbol{\theta}$ using Dirichlet-multinomial conjugacy, producing the following expression for the likelihood:

$$p(\mathbf{z}) = \prod_{r \in \mathcal{R}} \frac{\prod_o (\alpha_{ro}\mu_{ro})^{(n_{ro}(\mathbf{z}))}}{\alpha_r^{(n_{r\cdot}(\mathbf{z}))}}, \tag{3}$$

where $a^{(k)} = a(a+1)\cdots(a+k-1)$ is the ascending factorial. (3) is the distribution that we will use for sampling.

4 Type-Based Sampling

Having described the setup of the model, we now turn to posterior inference of $p(\mathbf{z} \mid \mathbf{x})$.

4.1 Binary Representation

We first define a new representation of the latent structure based on binary variables $\mathbf{b}$ so that there is a bijection between $\mathbf{z}$ and $(\mathbf{b}, \mathbf{x})$; $\mathbf{z}$ was used to define the model, $\mathbf{b}$ will be used for inference. We will use $\mathbf{b}$ to exploit the ideas from Section 2. Specifically, let $\mathbf{b} = \{b_s\}_{s \in \mathcal{S}}$ be a collection of binary variables indexed by a set of *sites* $\mathcal{S}$.

- HMM: If the HMM has $K = 2$ states, $\mathcal{S}$ is the set of positions in the sequence. For each $s \in \mathcal{S}$, b_s is the hidden state at s. The extension to general K is considered at the end of Section 4.4.
- USM: $\mathcal{S}$ is the set of non-final positions in the sequence. For each $s \in \mathcal{S}$, b_s denotes whether a word boundary exists between positions s and $s+1$.
- PTSG: $\mathcal{S}$ is the set of internal nodes in the parse tree. For $s \in \mathcal{S}$, b_s denotes whether a tree fragment is rooted at node s.

For each site $s \in \mathcal{S}$, let $\mathbf{z}^{s:0}$ and $\mathbf{z}^{s:1}$ denote the choices associated with the structures obtained by setting the binary variable $b_s = 0$ and $b_s = 1$, respectively. Define $\mathbf{z}^{-s} \stackrel{\text{def}}{=} \mathbf{z}^{s:0} \cap \mathbf{z}^{s:1}$ to be the set of choices that do not *depend* on the value of b_s, and $\mathbf{n}^{-s} \stackrel{\text{def}}{=} \mathbf{n}(\mathbf{z}^{-s})$ be the corresponding counts.

- HMM: $\mathbf{z}^{-s}$ includes all *but* the transitions into and out of the state at s plus the emission at s.
- USM: $\mathbf{z}^{-s}$ includes all except the word ending at s and the one starting at $s+1$ if there is a boundary ($b_s = 1$); except the word covering s if no boundary exists ($b_s = 0$).
- PTSG: $\mathbf{z}^{-s}$ includes all except the tree fragment rooted at node s and the one with leaf s if $b_s = 1$; except the single fragment containing s if $b_s = 0$.

4.2 Sampling One Site

A token-based sampler considers one site s at a time. Specifically, we evaluate the likelihoods of $\mathbf{z}^{s:0}$ and $\mathbf{z}^{s:1}$ according to (3) and sample b_s with probability proportional to the likelihoods. Intuitively, this can be accomplished by removing choices that depend on b_s (resulting in $\mathbf{z}^{-s}$), evaluating the likelihood resulting from setting b_s to 0 or 1, and then adding the appropriate choices back in.

More formally, let $\Delta\mathbf{z}^{s:b} \stackrel{\text{def}}{=} \mathbf{z}^{s:b} \backslash \mathbf{z}^{-s}$ be the new choices that would be added if we set $b_s = b \in \{0, 1\}$, and let $\Delta\mathbf{n}^{s:b} \stackrel{\text{def}}{=} \mathbf{n}(\Delta\mathbf{z}^{s:b})$ be the corresponding counts. With this notation, we can write the posterior as follows:

$$p(b_s = b \mid \mathbf{b} \backslash \mathbf{b}_s) \propto \tag{4}$$
$$\prod_{r \in \mathcal{R}} \frac{\prod_o (\alpha_{ro}\mu_{ro} + n_{ro}^{-s})^{(\Delta n_{ro}^{s:b})}}{(\alpha_r + n_{r\cdot}^{-s})^{(\Delta n_{r\cdot}^{s:b})}}.$$

The form of the conditional (4) follows from the joint (3) via two properties: additivity of counts ($\mathbf{n}^{s:b} = \mathbf{n}^{-s} + \Delta\mathbf{n}^{s:b}$) and a simple property of ascending factorials ($a^{(k+\delta)} = a^{(k)}(a+k)^{(\delta)}$).

In practice, most of the entries of $\Delta\mathbf{n}^{s:b}$ are zero. For the HMM, $n_{ro}^{s:b}$ would be nonzero only for the transitions into the new state (b) at position s ($z_{s-1} \to b$), transitions out of that state ($b \to z_{s+1}$), and emissions from that state ($b \to x_s$).

4.3 Sampling Multiple Sites

We would like to sample multiple sites jointly as in Section 2, but we cannot choose any arbitrary subset $S \subset \mathcal{S}$, as the likelihood will in general depend on the exact assignment of $\mathbf{b}_S \stackrel{\text{def}}{=} \{b_s\}_{s \in S}$, of which

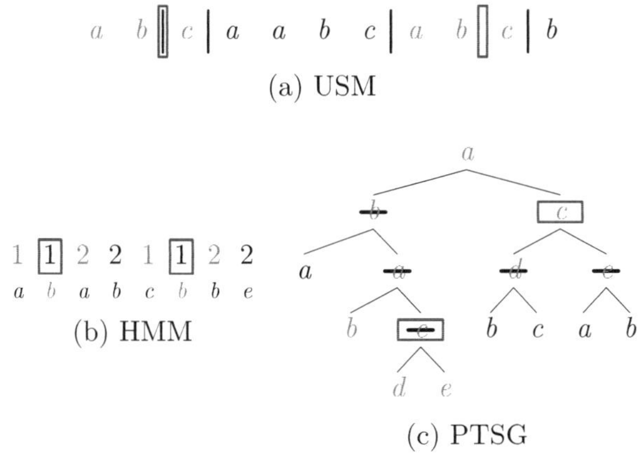

Figure 3: The type-based sampler jointly samples all variables at a set of sites S (in green boxes). Sites in S are chosen based on types (denoted in red). (a) HMM: two sites have the same type if they have the same previous and next states and emit the same word; they conflict unless separated by at least one position. (b) USM: two sites have the same type if they are both of the form $ab|c$ or abc; note that occurrences of the same letters with other segmentations do not match the type. (c) PTSG: analogous to the USM, only for tree rather than sequences.

there are an exponential number. To exploit the exchangeability property in Section 2, we need to find sites which look "the same" from the model's point of view, that is, the likelihood only depends on $\mathbf{b}_S$ via $m \stackrel{\text{def}}{=} \sum_{s \in S} b_s$.

To do this, we need to define two notions, *type* and *conflict*. We say sites s and s' have the same *type* if the counts added by setting either b_s or $b_{s'}$ are the same, that is, $\Delta \mathbf{n}^{s:b} = \Delta \mathbf{n}^{s':b}$ for $b \in \{0, 1\}$. This motivates the following definition of the *type* of site s with respect to $\mathbf{z}$:

$$t(\mathbf{z}, s) \stackrel{\text{def}}{=} (\Delta \mathbf{n}^{s:0}, \Delta \mathbf{n}^{s:1}), \qquad (5)$$

We say that s and s' have the same type if $t(\mathbf{z}, s) = t(\mathbf{z}, s')$. Note that the actual choices added ($\Delta \mathbf{z}^{s:b}$ and $\Delta \mathbf{z}^{s':b}$) are in general different as s and s' correspond to different parts of the latent structure, but the model only depends on counts and is indifferent to this. Figure 3 shows examples of same-type sites for our three models.

However, even if all sites in S have the same type, we still cannot sample $\mathbf{b}_S$ jointly, since changing one b_s might change the type of another site s'; indeed, this dependence is reflected in (5), which shows that types depend on $\mathbf{z}$. For example, $s, s' \in S$ conflict when $s' = s + 1$ in the HMM or when s and s' are boundaries of one segment (USM) or one tree fragment (PTSG). Therefore, one additional concept is necessary: We say two sites s and s' *conflict* if there is some choice that depends on both b_s and $b_{s'}$; formally, $(\mathbf{z} \backslash \mathbf{z}^{-s}) \cap (\mathbf{z} \backslash \mathbf{z}^{-s'}) \neq \emptyset$.

Our key mathematical result is as follows:

Proposition 1 *For any set $S \subset \mathcal{S}$ of non-conflicting sites with the same type,*

$$p(\mathbf{b}_S \mid \mathbf{b} \backslash \mathbf{b}_S) \propto g(m) \qquad (6)$$

$$p(m \mid \mathbf{b} \backslash \mathbf{b}_S) \propto \binom{|S|}{m} g(m), \qquad (7)$$

for some easily computable $g(m)$, where $m = \sum_{s \in S} b_s$.

We will derive $g(m)$ shortly, but first note from (6) that the likelihood for a particular setting of $\mathbf{b}_S$ depends on $\mathbf{b}_S$ only via m as desired. (7) sums over all $\binom{|S|}{m}$ settings of $\mathbf{b}_S$ with $m = \sum_{s \in S} b_s$. The algorithmic consequences of this result is that to sample $\mathbf{b}_S$, we can first compute (7) for each $m \in \{0, \ldots, |S|\}$, sample m according to the normalized distribution, and then choose the actual $\mathbf{b}_S$ uniformly subject to m.

Let us now derive $g(m)$ by generalizing (4). Imagine removing all sites S and their dependent choices and adding in choices corresponding to some assignment $\mathbf{b}_S$. Since all sites in S are non-conflicting and of the same type, the count contribution $\Delta \mathbf{n}^{s:b}$ is the same for every $s \in S$ (i.e., sites in S are exchangeable). Therefore, the likelihood of the new assignment $\mathbf{b}_S$ depends only on the new counts:

$$\Delta \mathbf{n}^{S:m} \stackrel{\text{def}}{=} m \Delta \mathbf{n}^{s:1} + (|S| - m) \Delta \mathbf{n}^{s:0}. \qquad (8)$$

Using these new counts in place of the ones in (4), we get the following expression:

$$g(m) = \prod_{r \in \mathcal{R}} \frac{\prod_o (\alpha_{ro}\mu_{ro} + n_{ro}(\mathbf{z}^{-S}))^{(\Delta n_{ro}^{S:m})}}{\alpha_r + n_{r\cdot}(\mathbf{z}^{-S})^{(\Delta n_{r\cdot}^{S:m})}}. \qquad (9)$$

4.4 Full Algorithm

Thus far, we have shown how to sample $\mathbf{b}_S$ given a set $S \subset \mathcal{S}$ of non-conflicting sites with the same type. To complete the description of the type-based

Type-Based Sampler

for each iteration $t = 1, \ldots, T$:
  for each pivot site $s_0 \in \mathcal{S}$:
    $S \leftarrow \text{TB}(\mathbf{z}, s_0)$ (S is the type block centered at s_0)
    decrement $\mathbf{n}$ and remove from $\mathbf{z}$ based on $\mathbf{b}_S$
    sample m according to (7)
    sample $M \subset S$ with $|M| = m$ uniformly at random
    set $b_s = \mathbb{I}[s \in M]$ for each $s \in S$
    increment $\mathbf{n}$ and add to $\mathbf{z}$ accordingly

Figure 4: Pseudocode for the general type-based sampler. We operate in the binary variable representation $\mathbf{b}$ of $\mathbf{z}$. Each step, we jointly sample $|S|$ variables (of the same type).

sampler, we need to specify how to choose S. Our general strategy is to first choose a *pivot site* $s_0 \in \mathcal{S}$ uniformly at random and then set $S = \text{TB}(\mathbf{z}, s_0)$ for some function TB. Call S the *type block* centered at s_0. The following two criteria on TB are sufficient for a valid sampler: (A) $s_0 \in S$, and (B) the type blocks are *stable*, which means that if we change $\mathbf{b}_S$ to any $\mathbf{b}'_S$ (resulting in a new $\mathbf{z}'$), the type block centered at s_0 with respect to $\mathbf{z}'$ does not change (that is, $\text{TB}(\mathbf{z}', s_0) = S$). (A) ensures ergodicity; (B), reversibility.

Now we define TB as follows: First set $S = \{s_0\}$. Next, loop through all sites $s \in \mathcal{S}$ with the same type as s_0 in some fixed order, adding s to S if it does not conflict with any sites already in S. Figure 4 provides the pseudocode for the full algorithm.

Formally, this sampler cycles over $|\mathcal{S}|$ transition kernels, one for each pivot site. Each kernel (indexed by $s_0 \in \mathcal{S}$) defines a blocked Gibbs move, i.e. sampling from $p(\mathbf{b}_{\text{TB}(\mathbf{z},s_0)} \mid \cdots)$.

Efficient Implementation There are two operations we must perform efficiently: (A) looping through sites with the same type as the pivot site s_0, and (B) checking whether such a site s conflicts with any site in S. We can perform (B) in $O(1)$ time by checking if any element of $\Delta\mathbf{z}^{s:b_s}$ has already been removed; if so, there is a conflict and we skip s. To do (A) efficiently, we maintain a hash table mapping type t to a doubly-linked list of sites with type t. There is an $O(1)$ cost for maintaining this data structure: When we add or remove a site s, we just need to add or remove neighboring sites s' from their respective linked lists, since their types depend on b_s. For example, in the HMM, when we remove site s, we also remove sites $s-1$ and $s+1$.

For the USM, we use a simpler solution: maintain a hash table mapping each word w to a list of positions where w occurs. Suppose site (position) s straddles words a and b. Then, to perform (A), we retrieve the list of positions where *a*, *b*, and *ab* occur, intersecting the a and b lists to obtain a list of positions where a b occurs. While this intersection is often much smaller than the pre-intersected lists, we found in practice that the smaller amount of bookkeeping balanced out the extra time spent intersecting. We used a similar strategy for the PTSG, which significantly reduces the amount of bookkeeping.

Skip Approximation Large type blocks mean larger moves. However, such a block S is also sampled more frequently—once for every choice of a pivot site $s_0 \in S$. However, we found that empirically, $\mathbf{b}_S$ changes very infrequently. To eliminate this apparent waste, we use the following approximation of our sampler: do not consider $s_0 \in \mathcal{S}$ as a pivot site if s_0 belongs to some block which was already sampled in the current iteration. This way, each site is considered roughly once per iteration.[4]

Sampling Non-Binary Representations We can sample in models without a natural binary representation (e.g., HMMs with with more than two states) by considering random binary slices. Specifically, suppose $b_s \in \{1, \ldots, K\}$ for each site $s \in \mathcal{S}$. We modify Figure 4 as follows: After choosing a pivot site $s_0 \in \mathcal{S}$, let $k = b_{s_0}$ and choose k' uniformly from $\{1, \ldots, K\}$. Only include sites in one of these two states by re-defining the type block to be $S = \{s \in \text{TB}(\mathbf{z}, s_0) : b_s \in \{k, k'\}\}$, and sample $\mathbf{b}_S$ restricted to these two states by drawing from $p(\mathbf{b}_S \mid \mathbf{b}_S \in \{k, k'\}^{|S|}, \cdots)$. By choosing a random k' each time, we allow $\mathbf{b}$ to reach any point in the space, thus achieving ergodicity just by using these binary restrictions.

5 Experiments

We now compare our proposed type-based sampler to various alternatives, evaluating on marginal like-

[4]A site could be sampled more than once if it belonged to more than one type block during the iteration (recall that types depend on $\mathbf{z}$ and thus could change during sampling).

lihood (3) and accuracy for our three models:

- HMM: We learned a $K = 45$ state HMM on the Wall Street Journal (WSJ) portion of the Penn Treebank (49208 sentences, 45 tags) for part-of-speech induction. We fixed α_r to 0.1 and μ_r to uniform for all r.

  For accuracy, we used the standard metric based on greedy mapping, where each state is mapped to the POS tag that maximizes the number of correct matches (Haghighi and Klein, 2006). We did not use a tagging dictionary.

- USM: We learned a USM model on the Bernstein-Ratner corpus from the CHILDES database used in Goldwater et al. (2006) (9790 sentences) for word segmentation. We fixed α_0 to 0.1. The base distribution μ_0 penalizes the length of words (see Goldwater et al. (2009) for details). For accuracy, we used word token F_1.

- PTSG: We learned a PTSG model on sections 2–21 of the WSJ treebank.[5] For accuracy, we used EVALB parsing F_1 on section 22.[6] Note this is a supervised task with latent-variables, whereas the other two are purely unsupervised.

5.1 Basic Comparison

Figure 5(a)–(c) compares the likelihood and accuracy (we use the term *accuracy* loosely to also include F_1). The initial observation is that the type-based sampler (TYPE) outperforms the token-based sampler (TOKEN) across all three models on both metrics.

We further evaluated the PTSG on parsing. Our standard treebank PCFG estimated using maximum likelihood obtained 79% F_1. TOKEN obtained an F_1 of 82.2%, and TYPE obtained a comparable F_1 of 83.2%. Running the PTSG for longer continued to improve the likelihood but actually hurt parsing accuracy, suggesting that the PTSG model is overfitting.

To better understand the gains from TYPE over TOKEN, we consider three other alternative samplers. First, annealing ($\text{TOKEN}_{\text{anneal}}$) is a commonly-used technique to improve mixing, where (3) is raised to some inverse temperature.[7] In Figure 5(a)–(c), we see that unlike TYPE, $\text{TOKEN}_{\text{anneal}}$ does not improve over TOKEN uniformly: it hurts for the HMM, improves slightly for the USM, and makes no difference for the PTSG. Although annealing does increase mobility of the sampler, this mobility is undirected, whereas type-based sampling increases mobility in purely model-driven directions.

Unlike past work that operated on types (Wolff, 1988; Brown et al., 1992; Stolcke and Omohundro, 1994), type-based sampling makes stochastic choices, and moreover, these choices are reversible. Is this stochasticity important? To answer this, we consider a variant of TYPE, $\text{TYPE}_{\text{greedy}}$: instead of sampling from (7), $\text{TYPE}_{\text{greedy}}$ considers a type block S and sets b_s to 0 for all $s \in S$ if $p(\mathbf{b}_S = (0, \dots, 0) \mid \cdots) > p(\mathbf{b}_S = (1, \dots, 1) \mid \cdots)$; else it sets b_s to 1 for all $s \in S$. From Figure 5(a)–(c), we see that greediness is disastrous for the HMM, hurts a little for USM, and makes no difference on the PTSG. These results show that stochasticity can indeed be important.

We consider another block sampler, SENTENCE, which uses dynamic programming to sample all variables in a sentence (using Metropolis-Hastings to correct for intra-sentential type-level coupling). For USM, we see that SENTENCE performs worse than TYPE and is comparable to TOKEN, suggesting that type-based dependencies are stronger and more important to deal with than intra-sentential dependencies.

5.2 Initialization

We initialized all samplers as follows: For the USM and PTSG, for each site s, we place a boundary (set $b_s = 1$) with probability η. For the HMM, we set b_s to state 1 with probability η and a random state with

[5] Following Petrov et al. (2006), we performed an initial preprocessing step on the trees involving Markovization, binarization, and collapsing of unary chains; words occurring once are replaced with one of 50 "unknown word" tokens, using base distributions $\{\mu_r\}$ that penalize the size of trees, and sampling the hyperparameters (see Cohn et al. (2009) for details).

[6] To evaluate, we created a grammar where the rule probabilities are the mean values under the PTSG distribution: this involves taking a weighted combination (based on the concentration parameters) of the rule counts from the PTSG samples and the PCFG-derived base distribution. We used the decoder of DeNero et al. (2009) to parse.

[7] We started with a temperature of 10 and gradually decreased it to 1 during the first half of the run, and kept it at 1 thereafter.

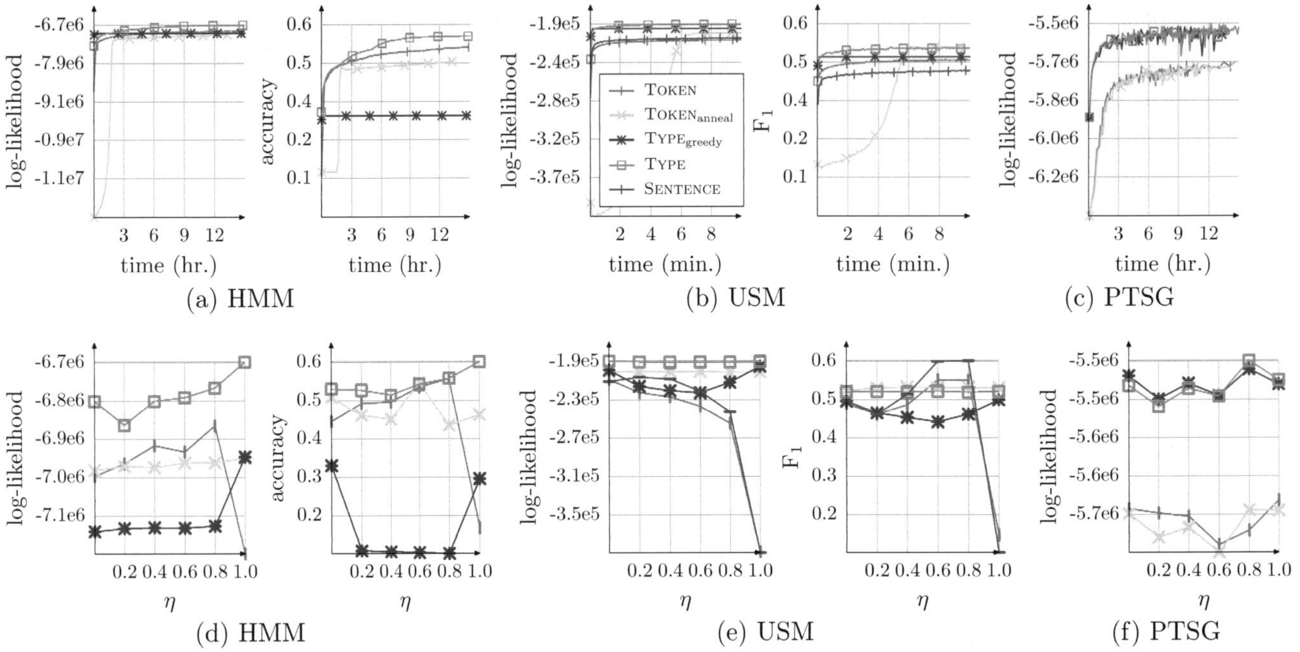

Figure 5: (a)–(c): Log-likelihood and accuracy over time. TYPE performs the best. Relative to TYPE, $\text{TYPE}_{\text{greedy}}$ tends to hurt performance. TOKEN generally works worse. Relative to TOKEN, $\text{TOKEN}_{\text{anneal}}$ produces mixed results. SENTENCE behaves like TOKEN. (d)–(f): Effect of initialization. The metrics were applied to the current sample after 15 hours for the HMM and PTSG and 10 minutes for the USM. TYPE generally prefers larger η and outperform the other samplers.

probability $1 - \eta$. Results in Figure 5(a)–(c) were obtained by setting η to maximize likelihood.

Since samplers tend to be sensitive to initialization, it is important to explore the effect of initialization (parametrized by $\eta \in [0, 1]$). Figure 5(d)–(f) shows that TYPE is consistently the best, whereas other samplers can underperform TYPE by a large margin. Note that TYPE favors $\eta = 1$ in general. This setting maximizes the number of initial types, and thus creates larger type blocks and thus enables larger moves. Larger type blocks also mean more dependencies that TOKEN is unable to deal with.

6 Related Work and Discussion

Block sampling, on which our work is built, is a classical idea, but is used restrictively since sampling large blocks is computationally expensive. Past work for clustering models maintained tractability by using Metropolis-Hastings proposals (Dahl, 2003) or introducing auxiliary variables (Swendsen and Wang, 1987; Liang et al., 2007). In contrast, our type-based sampler simply identifies tractable blocks based on exchangeability.

Other methods for learning latent-variable models include EM, variational approximations, and uncollapsed samplers. All of these methods maintain distributions over (or settings of) the latent variables of the model and update the representation iteratively (see Gao and Johnson (2008) for an overview in the context of POS induction). However, these methods are at the core all token-based, since they only update variables in a single example at a time.[8]

Blocking variables by type—the key idea of this paper—is a fundamental departure from token-based methods. Though type-based changes have also been proposed (Brown et al., 1992; Stolcke and Omohundro, 1994), these methods operated greedily, and in Section 5.1, we saw that being greedy led to more brittle results. By working in a sampling framework, we were able bring type-based changes to fruition.

[8]While EM technically updates all distributions over latent variables in the E-step, this update is performed *conditioned on* model parameters; it is this coupling (made more explicit in collapsed samplers) that makes EM susceptible to local optima.

References

P. F. Brown, V. J. D. Pietra, P. V. deSouza, J. C. Lai, and R. L. Mercer. 1992. Class-based n-gram models of natural language. *Computational Linguistics*, 18:467–479.

T. Cohn, S. Goldwater, and P. Blunsom. 2009. Inducing compact but accurate tree-substitution grammars. In *North American Association for Computational Linguistics (NAACL)*, pages 548–556.

D. B. Dahl. 2003. An improved merge-split sampler for conjugate Dirichlet process mixture models. Technical report, Department of Statistics, University of Wisconsin.

J. DeNero, M. Bansal, A. Pauls, and D. Klein. 2009. Efficient parsing for transducer grammars. In *North American Association for Computational Linguistics (NAACL)*, pages 227–235.

J. Gao and M. Johnson. 2008. A comparison of Bayesian estimators for unsupervised hidden Markov model POS taggers. In *Empirical Methods in Natural Language Processing (EMNLP)*, pages 344–352.

S. Goldwater and T. Griffiths. 2007. A fully Bayesian approach to unsupervised part-of-speech tagging. In *Association for Computational Linguistics (ACL)*.

S. Goldwater, T. Griffiths, and M. Johnson. 2006. Contextual dependencies in unsupervised word segmentation. In *International Conference on Computational Linguistics and Association for Computational Linguistics (COLING/ACL)*.

S. Goldwater, T. Griffiths, and M. Johnson. 2009. A Bayesian framework for word segmentation: Exploring the effects of context. *Cognition*, 112:21–54.

A. Haghighi and D. Klein. 2006. Prototype-driven learning for sequence models. In *North American Association for Computational Linguistics (NAACL)*, pages 320–327.

P. Liang, M. I. Jordan, and B. Taskar. 2007. A permutation-augmented sampler for Dirichlet process mixture models. In *International Conference on Machine Learning (ICML)*.

S. Petrov, L. Barrett, R. Thibaux, and D. Klein. 2006. Learning accurate, compact, and interpretable tree annotation. In *International Conference on Computational Linguistics and Association for Computational Linguistics (COLING/ACL)*, pages 433–440.

M. Post and D. Gildea. 2009. Bayesian learning of a tree substitution grammar. In *Association for Computational Linguistics and International Joint Conference on Natural Language Processing (ACL-IJCNLP)*.

A. Stolcke and S. Omohundro. 1994. Inducing probabilistic grammars by Bayesian model merging. In *International Colloquium on Grammatical Inference and Applications*, pages 106–118.

R. H. Swendsen and J. S. Wang. 1987. Nonuniversal critical dynamics in MC simulations. *Physics Review Letters*, 58:86–88.

J. G. Wolff. 1988. Learning syntax and meanings through optimization and distributional analysis. In *Categories and processes in language acquisition*, pages 179–215.

Painless Unsupervised Learning with Features

Taylor Berg-Kirkpatrick   Alexandre Bouchard-Côté   John DeNero   Dan Klein
Computer Science Division
University of California at Berkeley
{tberg, bouchard, denero, klein}@cs.berkeley.edu

Abstract

We show how features can easily be added to standard generative models for unsupervised learning, without requiring complex new training methods. In particular, each component multinomial of a generative model can be turned into a miniature logistic regression model if feature locality permits. The intuitive EM algorithm still applies, but with a gradient-based M-step familiar from discriminative training of logistic regression models. We apply this technique to part-of-speech induction, grammar induction, word alignment, and word segmentation, incorporating a few linguistically-motivated features into the standard generative model for each task. These feature-enhanced models each outperform their basic counterparts by a substantial margin, and even compete with and surpass more complex state-of-the-art models.

1 Introduction

Unsupervised learning methods have been increasingly successful in recent NLP research. The reasons are varied: increased supplies of unlabeled data, improved understanding of modeling methods, additional choices of optimization algorithms, and, perhaps most importantly for the present work, incorporation of richer domain knowledge into structured models. Unfortunately, that knowledge has generally been encoded in the form of conditional independence structure, which means that injecting it is both tricky (because the connection between independence and knowledge is subtle) and time-consuming (because new structure often necessitates new inference algorithms).

In this paper, we present a range of experiments wherein we improve existing unsupervised models by declaratively adding richer features. In particular, we parameterize the local multinomials of existing generative models using features, in a way which does not require complex new machinery but which still provides substantial flexibility. In the feature-engineering paradigm, one can worry less about the backbone structure and instead use hand-designed features to declaratively inject domain knowledge into a model. While feature engineering has historically been associated with discriminative, supervised learning settings, we argue that it can and should be applied more broadly to the unsupervised setting.

The idea of using features in unsupervised learning is neither new nor even controversial. Many top unsupervised results use feature-based models (Smith and Eisner, 2005; Haghighi and Klein, 2006). However, such approaches have presented their own barriers, from challenging normalization problems, to neighborhood design, to the need for complex optimization procedures. As a result, most work still focuses on the stable and intuitive approach of using the EM algorithm to optimize data likelihood in locally normalized, generative models.

The primary contribution of this paper is to demonstrate the clear empirical success of a simple and accessible approach to unsupervised learning with features, which can be optimized by using standard NLP building blocks. We consider the same generative, locally-normalized models that dominate past work on a range of tasks. However, we follow Chen (2003), Bisani and Ney (2008), and Bouchard-Côté et al. (2008), and allow each component multinomial of the model to be a miniature multi-class logistic regression model. In this case, the EM algorithm still applies with the E-step unchanged. The M-step involves gradient-based training familiar from standard supervised logistic regression (i.e., maximum entropy models). By integrating these two familiar learning techniques, we add features to unsupervised models without any

Human Language Technologies: The 2010 Annual Conference of the North American Chapter of the ACL, pages 582–590,
Los Angeles, California, June 2010.

specialized learning or inference.

A second contribution of this work is to show that further gains can be achieved by directly optimizing data likelihood with LBFGS (Liu et al., 1989). This alternative optimization procedure requires no additional machinery beyond what EM uses. This approach is still very simple to implement, and we found that it empirically outperforms EM.

This paper is largely empirical; the underlying optimization techniques are known, even if the overall approach will be novel to many readers. As an empirical demonstration, our results span an array of unsupervised learning tasks: part-of-speech induction, grammar induction, word alignment, and word segmentation. In each task, we show that declaring a few linguistically motivated feature templates yields state-of-the-art results.

2 Models

We start by explaining our feature-enhanced model for part-of-speech (POS) induction. This particular example illustrates our approach to adding features to unsupervised models in a well-known NLP task. We then explain how the technique applies more generally.

2.1 Example: Part-of-Speech Induction

POS induction consists of labeling words in text with POS tags. A hidden Markov model (HMM) is a standard model for this task, used in both a frequentist setting (Merialdo, 1994; Elworthy, 1994) and in a Bayesian setting (Goldwater and Griffiths, 2007; Johnson, 2007).

A POS HMM generates a sequence of words in order. In each generation step, an observed word emission y_i and a hidden successor POS tag z_{i+1} are generated independently, conditioned on the current POS tag z_i . This process continues until an absorbing stop state is generated by the transition model.

There are two types of conditional distributions in the model—emission and transition probabilities—that are both multinomial probability distributions. The joint likelihood factors into these distributions:

$$P_{\boldsymbol{\theta}}(\mathbf{Y}=\mathbf{y},\mathbf{Z}=\mathbf{z}) = P_{\boldsymbol{\theta}}(Z_1=z_1)\cdot \prod_{i=1}^{|\mathbf{z}|} P_{\boldsymbol{\theta}}(Y_i=y_i|Z_i=z_i)\cdot P_{\boldsymbol{\theta}}(Z_{i+1}=z_{i+1}|Z_i=z_i)$$

The emission distribution $P_{\boldsymbol{\theta}}(Y_i = y_i|Z_i = z_i)$ is parameterized by conditional probabilities $\theta_{y,z,\text{EMIT}}$ for each word y given tag z. Alternatively, we can express this emission distribution as the output of a logistic regression model, replacing the explicit conditional probability table by a logistic function parameterized by weights and features:

$$\theta_{y,z,\text{EMIT}}(\mathbf{w}) = \frac{\exp\langle \mathbf{w}, \mathbf{f}(y,z,\text{EMIT})\rangle}{\sum_{y'}\exp\langle \mathbf{w}, \mathbf{f}(y',z,\text{EMIT})\rangle}$$

This feature-based logistic expression is equivalent to the flat multinomial in the case that the feature function $\mathbf{f}(y, z, \text{EMIT})$ consists of all indicator features on tuples (y, z, EMIT), which we call BASIC features. The equivalence follows by setting weight $w_{y,z,\text{EMIT}} = \log(\theta_{y,z,\text{EMIT}})$.[1] This formulation is known as the natural parameterization of the multinomial distribution.

In order to enhance this emission distribution, we include coarse features in $\mathbf{f}(y, z, \text{EMIT})$, in addition to the BASIC features. Crucially, these features can be active across multiple (y, z) values. In this way, the model can abstract general patterns, such as a POS tag co-occurring with an inflectional morpheme. We discuss specific POS features in Section 4.

2.2 General Directed Models

Like the HMM, all of the models we propose are based on locally normalized generative decisions that condition on some context. In general, let $\mathbf{X} = (\mathbf{Z}, \mathbf{Y})$ denote the sequence of generation steps (random variables) where $\mathbf{Z}$ contains all hidden random variables and $\mathbf{Y}$ contains all observed random variables. The joint probability of this directed model factors as:

$$P_{\mathbf{w}}(\mathbf{X}=\mathbf{x}) = \prod_{i\in I} P_{\mathbf{w}}\left(X_i = x_i \middle| X_{\pi(i)} = x_{\pi(i)}\right),$$

where $X_{\pi(i)}$ denotes the parents of X_i and I is the index set of the variables in $\mathbf{X}$.

In the models that we use, each factor in the above expression is the output of a local logistic regression

[1]As long as no transition or emission probabilities are equal to zero. When zeros are present, for instance to model that an absorbing stop state can only transition to itself, it is often possible to absorb these zeros into a *base measure*. All the arguments in this paper carry with a structured base measure; we drop it for simplicity.

model parameterized by $\mathbf{w}$:

$$P_{\mathbf{w}}(X_i = d | X_{\pi(i)} = c) = \frac{\exp\langle \mathbf{w}, \mathbf{f}(d, c, t)\rangle}{\sum_{d'} \exp\langle \mathbf{w}, \mathbf{f}(d', c, t)\rangle}$$

Above, d is the generative decision value for X_i picked by the model, c is the conditioning context tuple of values for the parents of X_i, and t is the type of decision being made. For instance, the POS HMM has two types of decisions: transitions and emissions. In the emission model, the type t is EMIT, the decision d is a word and the context c is a tag. The denominator normalizes the factor to be a probability distribution over decisions.

The objective function we derive from this model is the marginal likelihood of the observations $\mathbf{y}$, along with a regularization term:

$$L(\mathbf{w}) = \log P_{\mathbf{w}}(\mathbf{Y} = \mathbf{y}) - \kappa ||\mathbf{w}||_2^2 \quad (1)$$

This model has two advantages over the more prevalent form of a feature-rich unsupervised model, the globally normalized Markov random field.[2] First, as we explain in Section 3, optimizing our objective does not require computing expectations over the joint distribution. In the case of the POS HMM, for example, we do not need to enumerate an infinite sum of products of potentials when optimizing, in contrast to Haghighi and Klein (2006). Second, we found that locally normalized models empirically outperform their globally normalized counterparts, despite their efficiency and simplicity.

3 Optimization

3.1 Optimizing with Expectation Maximization

In this section, we describe the EM algorithm applied to our feature-rich, locally normalized models. For models parameterized by standard multinomials, EM optimizes $L(\boldsymbol{\theta}) = \log P_{\boldsymbol{\theta}}(\mathbf{Y} = \mathbf{y})$ (Dempster et al., 1977). The E-step computes expected counts for each tuple of decision d, context c, and multinomial type t:

$$e_{d,c,t} \leftarrow \mathbb{E}_{\boldsymbol{\theta}}\left[\sum_{i \in I} \mathbb{1}(X_i = d, X_{\pi(i)} = c, t) \middle| \mathbf{Y} = \mathbf{y}\right] \quad (2)$$

[2]The locally normalized model class is actually equivalent to its globally normalized counterpart when the former meets the following three conditions: (1) The graphical model is a directed tree. (2) The BASIC features are included in $\mathbf{f}$. (3) We do not include regularization in the model ($\kappa = 0$). This follows from Smith and Johnson (2007).

These expected counts are then normalized in the M-step to re-estimate $\boldsymbol{\theta}$:

$$\theta_{d,c,t} \leftarrow \frac{e_{d,c,t}}{\sum_{d'} e_{d',c,t}}$$

Normalizing expected counts in this way maximizes the expected complete log likelihood with respect to the current model parameters.

EM can likewise optimize $L(\mathbf{w})$ for our locally normalized models with logistic parameterizations. The E-step first precomputes multinomial parameters from $\mathbf{w}$ for each decision, context, and type:

$$\theta_{d,c,t}(\mathbf{w}) \leftarrow \frac{\exp\langle \mathbf{w}, \mathbf{f}(d, c, t)\rangle}{\sum_{d'} \exp\langle \mathbf{w}, \mathbf{f}(d', c, t)\rangle}$$

Then, expected counts $\mathbf{e}$ are computed according to Equation 2. In the case of POS induction, expected counts are computed with the forward-backward algorithm in both the standard and logistic parameterizations. The only change is that the conditional probabilities $\boldsymbol{\theta}$ are now functions of $\mathbf{w}$.

The M-step changes more substantially, but still relies on canonical NLP learning methods. We wish to choose $\mathbf{w}$ to optimize the regularized expected complete log likelihood:

$$\ell(\mathbf{w}, \mathbf{e}) = \sum_{d,c,t} e_{d,c,t} \log \theta_{d,c,t}(\mathbf{w}) - \kappa ||\mathbf{w}||_2^2 \quad (3)$$

We optimize this objective via a gradient-based search algorithm like LBFGS. The gradient with respect to $\mathbf{w}$ takes the form

$$\nabla \ell(\mathbf{w}, \mathbf{e}) = \sum_{d,c,t} e_{d,c,t} \cdot \Delta_{d,c,t}(\mathbf{w}) - 2\kappa \cdot \mathbf{w} \quad (4)$$

$$\Delta_{d,c,t}(\mathbf{w}) = \mathbf{f}(d, c, t) - \sum_{d'} \theta_{d',c,t}(\mathbf{w}) \mathbf{f}(d', c, t)$$

This gradient matches that of regularized logistic regression in a supervised model: the difference Δ between the observed and expected features, summed over every decision and context. In the supervised case, we would observe the count of occurrences of (d, c, t), but in the unsupervised M-step, we instead substitute expected counts $e_{d,c,t}$.

This gradient-based M-step is an iterative procedure. For each different value of $\mathbf{w}$ considered during the search, we must recompute $\boldsymbol{\theta}(\mathbf{w})$, which requires computation in proportion to the size of the parameter space. However, $\mathbf{e}$ stays fixed throughout the M-step. Algorithm 1 outlines EM in its entirety. The subroutine climb$(\cdot, \cdot, \cdot)$ represents a generic optimization step such as an LBFGS iteration.

Algorithm 1 Feature-enhanced EM

```
repeat
    Compute expected counts e                 ▷ Eq. 2
    repeat
        Compute ℓ(w, e)                       ▷ Eq. 3
        Compute ∇ℓ(w, e)                      ▷ Eq. 4
        w ← climb(w, ℓ(w, e), ∇ℓ(w, e))
    until convergence
until convergence
```

3.2 Direct Marginal Likelihood Optimization

Another approach to optimizing Equation 1 is to compute the gradient of the log marginal likelihood directly (Salakhutdinov et al., 2003). The gradient turns out to have the same form as Equation 4, with the key difference that $e_{d,c,t}$ is recomputed for every different value of $\mathbf{w}$. Algorithm 2 outlines the procedure. Justification for this algorithm appears in the Appendix.

Algorithm 2 Feature-enhanced direct gradient

```
repeat
    Compute expected counts e                 ▷ Eq. 2
    Compute L(w)                              ▷ Eq. 1
    Compute ∇ℓ(w, e)                          ▷ Eq. 4
    w ← climb(w, L(w), ∇ℓ(w, e))
until convergence
```

In practice, we find that this optimization approach leads to higher task accuracy for several models. However, in cases where computing $e_{d,c,t}$ is expensive, EM can be a more efficient alternative.

4 Part-of-Speech Induction

We now describe experiments that demonstrate the effectiveness of locally normalized logistic models. We first use the bigram HMM described in Section 2.1 for POS induction, which has two types of multinomials. For type EMIT, the decisions d are words and contexts c are tags. For type TRANS, the decisions and contexts are both tags.

4.1 POS Induction Features

We use the same set of features used by Haghighi and Klein (2006) in their baseline globally normalized Markov random field (MRF) model. These are all coarse features on emission contexts that activate for words with certain orthographic properties. We use only the BASIC features for transitions. For an emission with word y and tag z, we use the following feature templates:

BASIC:	$\mathbb{1}(y = \cdot, z = \cdot)$
CONTAINS-DIGIT:	Check if y contains digit and conjoin with z: $\mathbb{1}(\text{containsDigit}(y) = \cdot, z = \cdot)$
CONTAINS-HYPHEN:	$\mathbb{1}(\text{containsHyphen}(x) = \cdot, z = \cdot)$
INITIAL-CAP:	Check if the first letter of y is capitalized: $\mathbb{1}(\text{isCap}(y) = \cdot, z = \cdot)$
N-GRAM:	Indicator functions for character n-grams of up to length 3 present in y.

4.2 POS Induction Data and Evaluation

We train and test on the entire WSJ tag corpus (Marcus et al., 1993). We attempt the most difficult version of this task where the only information our system can make use of is the unlabeled text itself. In particular, we do not make use of a tagging dictionary. We use 45 tag clusters, the number of POS tags that appear in the WSJ corpus. There is an identifiability issue when evaluating inferred tags. In order to measure accuracy on the hand-labeled corpus, we map each cluster to the tag that gives the highest accuracy, the many-1 evaluation approach (Johnson, 2007). We run all POS induction models for 1000 iterations, with 10 random initializations. The mean and standard deviation of many-1 accuracy appears in Table 1.

4.3 POS Induction Results

We compare our model to the basic HMM and a bigram version of the feature-enhanced MRF model of Haghighi and Klein (2006). Using EM, we achieve a many-1 accuracy of 68.1. This outperforms the basic HMM baseline by a 5.0 margin. The same model, trained using the direct gradient approach, achieves a many-1 accuracy of 75.5, outperforming the basic HMM baseline by a margin of 12.4. These results show that the direct gradient approach can offer additional boosts in performance when used with a feature-enhanced model. We also outperform the globally normalized MRF, which uses the same set of features and which we train using a direct gradient approach.

To the best of our knowledge, our system achieves the best performance to date on the WSJ corpus for totally unsupervised POS tagging.[3]

5 Grammar Induction

We next apply our technique to a grammar induction task: the unsupervised learning of dependency parse trees via the dependency model with valence (DMV) (Klein and Manning, 2004). A dependency parse is a directed tree over tokens in a sentence. Each edge of the tree specifies a directed dependency from a head token to a dependent, or argument token. Thus, the number of dependencies in a parse is exactly the number of tokens in the sentence, not counting the artificial root token.

5.1 Dependency Model with Valence

The DMV defines a probability distribution over dependency parse trees. In this head-outward attachment model, a parse and the word tokens are derived together through a recursive generative process. For each token generated so far, starting with the root, a set of left dependents is generated, followed by a set of right dependents.

There are two types of multinomial distributions in this model. The Bernoulli STOP probabilities $\theta_{d,c,\text{STOP}}$ capture the valence of a particular head. For this type, the decision d is whether or not to stop generating arguments, and the context c contains the current head h, direction δ and adjacency adj. If a head's stop probability is high, it will be encouraged to accept few arguments. The ATTACH multinomial probability distributions $\theta_{d,c,\text{ATTACH}}$ capture attachment preferences of heads. For this type, a decision d is an argument token a, and the context c consists of a head h and a direction δ.

We take the same approach as previous work (Klein and Manning, 2004; Cohen and Smith, 2009) and use gold POS tags in place of words.

[3] Haghighi and Klein (2006) achieve higher accuracies by making use of labeled prototypes. We do not use any external information.

5.2 Grammar Induction Features

One way to inject knowledge into a dependency model is to encode the similarity between the various morphological variants of nouns and verbs. We encode this similarity by incorporating features into both the STOP and the ATTACH probabilities. The attachment features appear below; the stop feature templates are similar and are therefore omitted.

BASIC:	$\mathbb{1}(a = \cdot, h = \cdot, \delta = \cdot)$
NOUN:	Generalize the morphological variants of nouns by using isNoun($\cdot$): $\mathbb{1}(a = \cdot, \text{isNoun}(h) = \cdot, \delta = \cdot)$ $\mathbb{1}(\text{isNoun}(a) = \cdot, h = \cdot, \delta = \cdot)$ $\mathbb{1}(\text{isNoun}(a) = \cdot, \text{isNoun}(h) = \cdot, \delta = \cdot)$
VERB:	Same as above, generalizing verbs instead of nouns by using isVerb($\cdot$)
NOUN-VERB:	Same as above, generalizing with $\text{isVerbOrNoun}(\cdot) = \text{isVerb}(\cdot) \vee \text{isNoun}(\cdot)$
BACK-OFF:	We add versions of all other features that ignore direction or adjacency.

While the model has the expressive power to allow specific morphological variants to have their own behaviors, the existence of coarse features encourages uniform analyses, which in turn gives better accuracies.

Cohen and Smith's (2009) method has similar characteristics. They add a shared logistic-normal prior (SLN) to the DMV in order to tie multinomial parameters across related derivation events. They achieve their best results by only tying parameters between different multinomials when the corresponding contexts are headed by nouns and verbs. This observation motivates the features we choose to incorporate into the DMV.

5.3 Grammar Induction Data and Evaluation

For our English experiments we train and report directed attachment accuracy on portions of the WSJ corpus. We work with a standard, reduced version of WSJ, WSJ10, that contains only sentences of length 10 or less after punctuation has been removed. We train on sections 2-21, and use section 22 as a development set. We report accuracy on section 23. These are the same training, development, and test sets used by Cohen and Smith (2009). The regularization parameter (κ) is tuned on the development set to maximize accuracy.

For our Chinese experiments, we use the same corpus and training/test split as Cohen and Smith

(2009). We train on sections 1-270 of the Penn Chinese Treebank (Xue et al., 2002), similarly reduced (CTB10). We test on sections 271-300 of CTB10, and use sections 400-454 as a development set.

The DMV is known to be sensitive to initialization. We use the deterministic harmonic initializer from Klein and Manning (2004). We ran each optimization procedure for 100 iterations. The results are reported in Table 1.

5.4 Grammar Induction Results

We are able to outperform Cohen and Smith's (2009) best system, which requires a more complicated variational inference method, on both English and Chinese data sets. Their system achieves an accuracy of 61.3 for English and an accuracy of 51.9 for Chinese.[4] Our feature-enhanced model, trained using the direct gradient approach, achieves an accuracy of 63.0 for English, and an accuracy of 53.6 for Chinese. To our knowledge, our method for feature-based dependency parse induction outperforms all existing methods that make the same set of conditional independence assumptions as the DMV.

6 Word Alignment

Word alignment is a core machine learning component of statistical machine translation systems, and one of the few NLP tasks that is dominantly solved using unsupervised techniques. The purpose of word alignment models is to induce a correspondence between the words of a sentence and the words of its translation.

6.1 Word Alignment Models

We consider two classic generative alignment models that are both used heavily today, IBM Model 1 (Brown et al., 1994) and the HMM alignment model (Ney and Vogel, 1996). These models generate a hidden alignment vector $\mathbf{z}$ and an observed foreign sentence $\mathbf{y}$, all conditioned on an observed English sentence $\mathbf{e}$. The likelihood of both models takes the form:

$$P(\mathbf{y}, \mathbf{z}|\mathbf{e}) = \prod_j p(z_j = i|z_{j-1}) \cdot \theta_{y_j, e_i, \text{ALIGN}}$$

[4]Using additional bilingual data, Cohen and Smith (2009) achieve an accuracy of 62.0 for English, and an accuracy of 52.0 for Chinese, still below our results.

	Model	Inference	Reg	Eval
POS Induction			κ	Many-1
WSJ	Basic-HMM	EM	–	63.1 (1.3)
WSJ	Feature-MRF	LBFGS	0.1	59.6 (6.9)
WSJ	Feature-HMM	EM	1.0	68.1 (1.7)
WSJ		LBFGS	1.0	**75.5** (1.1)
Grammar Induction			κ	Dir
WSJ10	Basic-DMV	EM	–	47.8
WSJ10	Feature-DMV	EM	0.05	48.3
WSJ10		LBFGS	10.0	**63.0**
WSJ10	(Cohen and Smith, 2009)			61.3
CTB10	Basic-DMV	EM	–	42.5
CTB10	Feature-DMV	EM	1.0	49.9
CTB10		LBFGS	5.0	**53.6**
CTB10	(Cohen and Smith, 2009)			51.9
Word Alignment			κ	AER
NIST ChEn	Basic-Model 1	EM	–	38.0
NIST ChEn	Feature-Model 1	EM	–	**35.6**
NIST ChEn	Basic-HMM	EM	–	33.8
NIST ChEn	Feature-HMM	EM	–	**30.0**
Word Segmentation			κ	F1
BR	Basic-Unigram	EM	–	76.9 (0.1)
BR	Feature-Unigram	EM	0.2	84.5 (0.5)
BR		LBFGS	0.2	**88.0** (0.1)
BR	(Johnson and Goldwater, 2009)			87

Table 1: Locally normalized feature-based models outperform all proposed baselines for all four tasks. LBFGS outperformed EM in all cases where the algorithm was sufficiently fast to run. Details of each experiment appear in the main text.

The distortion term $p(z_j = i|z_{j-1})$ is uniform in Model 1, and Markovian in the HMM. See Liang et al. (2006) for details on the specific variant of the distortion model of the HMM that we used. We use these standard distortion models in both the baseline and feature-enhanced word alignment systems.

The bilexical emission model $\theta_{y,e,\text{ALIGN}}$ differentiates our feature-enhanced system from the baseline system. In the former, the emission model is a standard conditional multinomial that represents the probability that decision word y is generated from context word e, while in our system, the emission model is re-parameterized as a logistic regression model and feature-enhanced.

Many supervised feature-based alignment models have been developed. In fact, this logistic parameterization of the HMM has been proposed before and yielded alignment improvements, but was trained using supervised estimation techniques (Varea et al., 2002).[5] However, most full translation systems to-

[5]Varea et al. (2002) describes unsupervised EM optimization with logistic regression models at a high level—their *dynamic training* approach—but provides no experiments.

day rely on unsupervised learning so that the models may be applied easily to many language pairs. Our approach provides efficient and consistent unsupervised estimation for feature-rich alignment models.

6.2 Word Alignment Features

The BASIC features on pairs of lexical items provide strong baseline performance. We add coarse features to the model in order to inject prior knowledge and tie together lexical items with similar characteristics.

BASIC:	$\mathbb{1}(e = \cdot, y = \cdot)$
EDIT-DISTANCE:	$\mathbb{1}(\text{dist}(y, e) = \cdot)$
DICTIONARY:	$\mathbb{1}((y, e) \in D)$ for dictionary D.
STEM:	$\mathbb{1}(\text{stem}(e) = \cdot, y = \cdot)$ for Porter stemmer.
PREFIX:	$\mathbb{1}(\text{prefix}(e) = \cdot, y = \cdot)$ for prefixes of length 4.
CHARACTER:	$\mathbb{1}(e = \cdot, \text{charAt}(y, i) = \cdot)$ for index i in the Chinese word.

These features correspond to several common augmentations of word alignment models, such as adding dictionary priors and truncating long words, but here we integrate them all coherently into a single model.

6.3 Word Alignment Data and Evaluation

We evaluate on the standard hand-aligned portion of the NIST 2002 Chinese-English development set (Ayan et al., 2005). The set is annotated with sure S and possible P alignments. We measure alignment quality using alignment error rate (AER) (Och and Ney, 2000).

We train the models on 10,000 sentences of FBIS Chinese-English newswire. This is not a large-scale experiment, but large enough to be relevant for low-resource languages. LBFGS experiments are not provided because computing expectations in these models is too computationally intensive to run for many iterations. Hence, EM training is a more appropriate optimization approach: computing the M-step gradient requires only summing over word type pairs, while the marginal likelihood gradient needed for LBFGS requires summing over training sentence alignments. The final alignments, in both the baseline and the feature-enhanced models, are computed by training the generative models in both directions, combining the result with hard union competitive thresholding (DeNero and Klein, 2007), and using agreement training for the HMM (Liang et al., 2006). The combination of these techniques yields a state-of-the-art unsupervised baseline for Chinese-English.

6.4 Word Alignment Results

For both IBM Model 1 and the HMM alignment model, EM training with feature-enhanced models outperforms the standard multinomial models, by 2.4 and 3.8 AER respectively.[6] As expected, large positive weights are assigned to both the dictionary and edit distance features. Stem and character features also contribute to the performance gain.

7 Word Segmentation

Finally, we show that it is possible to improve upon the simple and effective word segmentation model presented in Liang and Klein (2009) by adding phonological features. Unsupervised word segmentation is the task of identifying word boundaries in sentences where spaces have been removed. For a sequence of characters $\mathbf{y} = (y_1, ..., y_n)$, a segmentation is a sequence of segments $\mathbf{z} = (z_1, ..., z_{|\mathbf{z}|})$ such that $\mathbf{z}$ is a partition of $\mathbf{y}$ and each z_i is a contiguous subsequence of $\mathbf{y}$. Unsupervised models for this task infer word boundaries from corpora of sentences of characters without ever seeing examples of well-formed words.

7.1 Unigram Double-Exponential Model

Liang and Klein's (2009) unigram double-exponential model corresponds to a simple derivational process where sentences of characters $\mathbf{x}$ are generated a word at a time, drawn from a multinomial over all possible strings $\theta_{z,\text{SEGMENT}}$. For this type, there is no context and the decision is the particular string generated. In order to avoid the degenerate MLE that assigns mass only to single segment sentences it is helpful to independently generate a length for each segment from a fixed distribution. Liang and Klein (2009) constrain individual segments to have maximum length 10 and generate lengths from the following distribution: $\theta_{l,\text{LENGTH}} = \exp(-l^{1.6})$ when $1 \le l \le 10$. Their model is deficient since it is possible to generate

[6]The best published results for this dataset are supervised, and trained on 17 times more data (Haghighi et al., 2009).

lengths that are inconsistent with the actual lengths of the generated segments. The likelihood equation is given by:

$$P(\mathbf{Y} = \mathbf{y}, \mathbf{Z} = \mathbf{z}) =$$
$$\theta_{\text{STOP}} \prod_{i=1}^{|\mathbf{z}|} \left[(1 - \theta_{\text{STOP}})\, \theta_{z_i,\text{SEGMENT}} \exp(-|z_i|^{1.6})\right]$$

7.2 Segmentation Data and Evaluation

We train and test on the phonetic version of the Bernstein-Ratner corpus (1987). This is the same set-up used by Liang and Klein (2009), Goldwater et al. (2006), and Johnson and Goldwater (2009). This corpus consists of 9790 child-directed utterances transcribed using a phonetic representation. We measure segment F1 score on the entire corpus.

We run all word segmentation models for 300 iterations with 10 random initializations and report the mean and standard deviation of F1 in Table 1.

7.3 Segmentation Features

The SEGMENT multinomial is the important distribution in this model. We use the following features:

BASIC:	$\mathbb{1}(z = \cdot)$
LENGTH:	$\mathbb{1}(\text{length}(z) = \cdot)$
NUMBER-VOWELS:	$\mathbb{1}(\text{numVowels}(z) = \cdot)$
PHONO-CLASS-PREF:	$\mathbb{1}(\text{prefix}(\text{coarsePhonemes}(z)) = \cdot)$
PHONO-CLASS-PREF:	$\mathbb{1}(\text{suffix}(\text{coarsePhonemes}(z)) = \cdot)$

The phonological class prefix and suffix features project each phoneme of a string to a coarser class and then take prefix and suffix indicators on the string of projected characters. We include two versions of these features that use projections with different levels of coarseness. The goal of these features is to help the model learn general phonetic shapes that correspond to well-formed word boundaries.

As is the case in general for our method, the feature-enhanced unigram model still respects the conditional independence assumptions that the standard unigram model makes, and inference is still performed using a simple dynamic program to compute expected sufficient statistics, which are just segment counts.

7.4 Segmentation Results

To our knowledge our system achieves the best performance to date on the Bernstein-Ratner corpus, with an F1 of 88.0. It is substantially simpler than the non-parametric Bayesian models proposed by Johnson et al. (2007), which require sampling procedures to perform inference and achieve an F1 of 87 (Johnson and Goldwater, 2009). Similar to our other results, the direct gradient approach outperforms EM for feature-enhanced models, and both approaches outperform the baseline, which achieves an F1 of 76.9.

8 Conclusion

We have shown that simple, locally normalized models can effectively incorporate features into unsupervised models. These enriched models can be easily optimized using standard NLP building blocks. Beyond the four tasks explored in this paper—POS tagging, DMV grammar induction, word alignment, and word segmentation—the method can be applied to many other tasks, for example grounded semantics, unsupervised PCFG induction, document clustering, and anaphora resolution.

Acknowledgements

We thank Percy Liang for making his word segmentation code available to us, and the anonymous reviewers for their comments.

Appendix: Optimization

In this section, we derive the gradient of the log marginal likelihood needed for the direct gradient approach. Let $\mathbf{w}_0$ be the current weights in Algorithm 2 and $\mathbf{e} = \mathbf{e}(\mathbf{w}_0)$ be the expectations under these weights as computed in Equation 2. In order to justify Algorithm 2, we need to prove that $\nabla L(\mathbf{w}_0) = \nabla \ell(\mathbf{w}_0, \mathbf{e})$.

We use the following simple lemma: if ϕ, ψ are real-valued functions such that: (1) $\phi(\mathbf{w}_0) = \psi(\mathbf{w}_0)$ for some $\mathbf{w}_0$; (2) $\phi(\mathbf{w}) \leq \psi(\mathbf{w})$ on an open set containing $\mathbf{w}_0$; and (3), ϕ and ψ are differentiable at $\mathbf{w}_0$; then $\nabla\psi(\mathbf{w}_0) = \nabla\phi(\mathbf{w}_0)$.

We set $\psi(\mathbf{w}) = L(\mathbf{w})$ and $\phi(\mathbf{w}) = \ell(\mathbf{w}, \mathbf{e}) - \sum_{\mathbf{z}} P_{\mathbf{w}_0}(\mathbf{Z} = \mathbf{z}|\mathbf{Y} = \mathbf{y}) \log P_{\mathbf{w}_0}(\mathbf{Z} = \mathbf{z}|\mathbf{Y} = \mathbf{y})$. If we can show that ψ, ϕ satisfy the conditions of the lemma we are done since the second term of ϕ depends on $\mathbf{w}_0$, but not on $\mathbf{w}$.

Property (3) can be easily checked, and property (2) follows from Jensen's inequality. Finally, property (1) follows from Lemma 2 of Neal and Hinton (1998).

References

N. F. Ayan, B. Dorr, and C. Monz. 2005. Combining word alignments using neural networks. In *Empirical Methods in Natural Language Processing*.

N. Bernstein-Ratner. 1987. *The phonology of parent-child speech*. K. Nelson and A. van Kleeck.

M. Bisani and H. Ney. 2008. Joint-sequence models for grapheme-to-phoneme conversion.

A. Bouchard-Côté, P. Liang, D. Klein, and T. L. Griffiths. 2008. A probabilistic approach to language change. In *Neural Information Processing Systems*.

P. F. Brown, S. A. Della Pietra, V. J. Della Pietra, and R. L. Mercer. 1994. The mathematics of statistical machine translation: Parameter estimation. *Computational Linguistics*.

S. F. Chen. 2003. Conditional and joint models for grapheme-to-phoneme conversion. In *Eurospeech*.

S. B. Cohen and N. A. Smith. 2009. Shared logistic normal distributions for soft parameter tying in unsupervised grammar induction. In *North American Chapter of the Association for Computational Linguistics*.

A. P. Dempster, N. M. Laird, and D. B. Rubin. 1977. Maximum likelihood from incomplete data via the EM algorithm. *Journal of the Royal Statistical Society. Series B (Methodological)*.

J. DeNero and D. Klein. 2007. Tailoring word alignments to syntactic machine translation. In *Association for Computational Linguistics*.

D. Elworthy. 1994. Does Baum-Welch re-estimation help taggers? In *Association for Computational Linguistics*.

S. Goldwater and T. L. Griffiths. 2007. A fully Bayesian approach to unsupervised part-of-speech tagging. In *Association for Computational Linguistics*.

S. Goldwater, T. L. Griffiths, and M. Johnson. 2006. Contextual dependencies in unsupervised word segmentation. In *International Conference on Computational Linguistics/Association for Computational Linguistics*.

A. Haghighi and D. Klein. 2006. Prototype-driven learning for sequence models. In *Association for Computational Linguistics*.

A. Haghighi, J. Blitzer, J. DeNero, and D. Klein. 2009. Better word alignments with supervised ITG models. In *Association for Computational Linguistics*.

M. Johnson and S. Goldwater. 2009. Improving non-parametric Bayesian inference: Experiments on unsupervised word segmentation with adaptor grammars. In *North American Chapter of the Association for Computational Linguistics*.

M. Johnson, T. L. Griffiths, and S. Goldwater. 2007. Adaptor grammars: a framework for specifying compositional nonparametric Bayesian models. In *Neural Information Processing Systems*.

M. Johnson. 2007. Why doesnt EM find good HMM POS-taggers? In *Empirical Methods in Natural Language Processing/Computational Natural Language Learning*.

D. Klein and C. D. Manning. 2004. Corpus-based induction of syntactic structure: Models of dependency and constituency. In *Association for Computational Linguistics*.

P. Liang and D. Klein. 2009. Online EM for unsupervised models. In *North American Chapter of the Association for Computational Linguistics*.

P. Liang, B. Taskar, and D. Klein. 2006. Alignment by agreement. In *North American Chapter of the Association for Computational Linguistics*.

D. C. Liu, J. Nocedal, and C. Dong. 1989. On the limited memory BFGS method for large scale optimization. *Mathematical Programming*.

M. P. Marcus, M. A. Marcinkiewicz, and B. Santorini. 1993. Building a large annotated corpus of English: the penn treebank. *Computational Linguistics*.

B. Merialdo. 1994. Tagging English text with a probabilistic model. *Computational Linguistics*.

R. Neal and G. E. Hinton. 1998. A view of the EM algorithm that justifies incremental, sparse, and other variants. In *Learning in Graphical Models*. Kluwer Academic Publishers.

H. Ney and S. Vogel. 1996. HMM-based word alignment in statistical translation. In *International Conference on Computational Linguistics*.

F. J. Och and H. Ney. 2000. Improved statistical alignment models. In *Association for Computational Linguistics*.

R. Salakhutdinov, S. Roweis, and Z. Ghahramani. 2003. Optimization with EM and expectation-conjugate-gradient. In *International Conference on Machine Learning*.

N. A. Smith and J. Eisner. 2005. Contrastive estimation: Training log-linear models on unlabeled data. In *Association for Computational Linguistics*.

N. A. Smith and M. Johnson. 2007. Weighted and probabilistic context-free grammars are equally expressive. *Computational Linguistics*.

I. G. Varea, F. J. Och, H. Ney, and F. Casacuberta. 2002. Refined lexicon models for statistical machine translation using a maximum entropy approach. In *Association for Computational Linguistics*.

N. Xue, F-D Chiou, and M. Palmer. 2002. Building a large-scale annotated Chinese corpus. In *International Conference on Computational Linguistics*.

Linguistic Steganography Using Automatically Generated Paraphrases

Ching-Yun Chang
University of Cambridge
Computer Laboratory
Ching-Yun.Chang@cl.cam.ac.uk

Stephen Clark
University of Cambridge
Computer Laboratory
Stephen.Clark@cl.cam.ac.uk

Abstract

This paper describes a method for checking the acceptability of paraphrases in context. We use the Google n-gram data and a CCG parser to certify the paraphrasing grammaticality and fluency. We collect a corpus of human judgements to evaluate our system. The ultimate goal of our work is to integrate text paraphrasing into a Linguistic Steganography system, by using paraphrases to hide information in a cover text. We propose automatically generated paraphrases as a new and useful source of transformations for Linguistic Steganography, and show that our method for checking paraphrases is effective at maintaining a high level of imperceptibility, which is crucial for effective steganography.

1 Introduction

Steganography is concerned with hiding information in some cover medium, by manipulating properties of the medium in such a way that the hidden information is not easily detectable by an observer (Fridrich, 2009). The covert communication is such that the very act of communication is to be kept secret from outside observers. A related area is Watermarking, in which modifications are made to a cover medium in order to identify it, for example for the purposes of copyright. Here the changes may be known to an observer, and the task is to make the changes in such a way that the watermark cannot easily be removed.

There is a large literature on image steganography and watermarking, in which images are modified to encode a hidden message or watermark. Image stegosystems exploit the redundancy in an image representation together with limitations of the human visual system. For example, a standard image stegosystem uses the least-significant-bit (LSB) substitution technique. Since the difference between 11111111 and 11111110 in the value for red/green/blue intensity is likely to be undetectable by the human eye, the LSB can be used to hide information other than colour, without being perceptable by a human observer.[1]

A key question for any steganography system is the choice of cover medium. Given the ubiquitous nature of natural languages and electronic text, text is an obvious medium to consider. However, the literature on Linguistic Steganography, in which linguistic properties of a text are modified to hide information, is small compared with other media (Bergmair, 2007). The likely reason is that it is easier to make changes to images and other non-linguistic media which are undetectable by an observer. Language has the property that even small local changes to a text, e.g. replacing a word by a word with similar meaning, may result in text which is anomalous at the document level, or anomalous with respect to the state of the world. Hence finding linguistic transformations which can be applied reliably and often is a challenging problem for Linguistic Steganography.

In this paper we focus on steganography rather than watermarking, since we are interested in the requirement that any changes to a text be imperceptible to an observer. Figure 1 shows the Linguistic Steganography framework. First, some secret message, represented as a sequence of bits, is hidden in a

[1]The observer may also be a computer program, designed to detect statistical anomalies in the image representation which may indicate the presence of hidden information.

Human Language Technologies: The 2010 Annual Conference of the North American Chapter of the ACL, pages 591–599,
Los Angeles, California, June 2010.

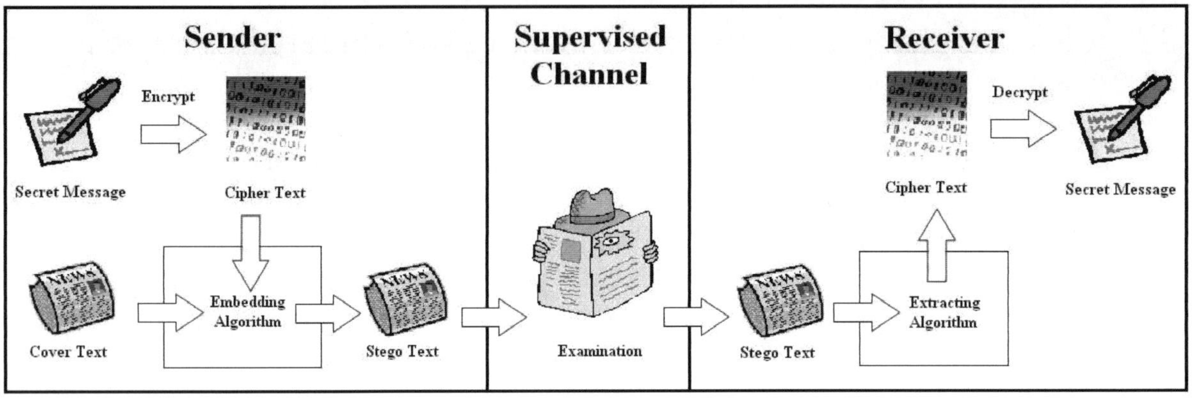

Figure 1: The Linguistic Steganography framework

cover text using the embedding algorithm, resulting in the *stego text*.[2] Next, the stego text passes the human observer, who is happy for innocuous messages to pass between the sender and receiver, but will examine the text for any suspicious looking content. Once the stego text reaches the receiver, the hidden message is recovered using the extracting algorithm.

There is a fundamental tradeoff in all steganography systems, and one that is especially apparent in the Linguistic Steganography framework: the tradeoff between *imperceptibility* and *payload*. Payload is the number of bits that can be encoded per unit of cover medium, for example per sentence in the linguistic case. The tradeoff arises because any attempt to hide additional information in the cover text, through the application of more linguistic transformations, is likely to increase the chances of raising the suspicions of the observer, by introducing anomalies into the text.

The key elements of a Linguistic Steganography system are the linguistic transformation and the embedding method. In this paper we focus on the linguistic transformation. Section 5 describes a possible embedding method for our framework, and for readers unfamiliar with linguistic steganography shows how linguistic transformations can be used to embed hidden bits in text.

Section 2 describes some of the previous transformations used in Linguistic Steganography. Note that we are concerned with transformations which are linguistic in nature, rather than dealing with superficial properties of the text, e.g. the amount of white space between words (Por et al., 2008). Our proposed method is based on the automatically acquired paraphrase dictionary described in Callison-Burch (2008), in which the application of paraphrases from the dictionary encodes secret bits. One advantage of the dictionary is that it has wide coverage, being automatically extracted; however, a disadvantage is that it contains many paraphrases which are either inappropriate, or only appropriate in certain contexts. Since we require any changes to be imperceptible to a human observer, it is crucial to our system that any uses of paraphrasing are grammatical and retain the meaning of the original cover text.

In order to test the grammaticality and meaning preserving nature of a paraphrase, we employ a simple technique based on checking whether the contexts containing the paraphrase are in the Google n-gram corpus. This technique is based on the simple hypothesis that, if the paraphrase in context has been used many times before on the web, then it is an appropriate use. We test our n-gram-based system against some human judgements of the grammaticality of paraphrases in context. We find that using larger contexts leads to a high precision system (100% when using 5-grams), but at the cost of a reduced recall. This precision-recall tradeoff reflects the inherent tradeoff between imperceptibility and payload in a Linguistic Steganography system. We also experiment with a CCG parser (Clark and Curran, 2007), requiring that the contexts surrounding the original phrase and paraphrase are assigned

[2]The message may have been encrypted initially also, as in the figure, but this is not important in this paper; the key point is that the hidden message is a sequence of bits.

the same CCG lexical categories by the parser. This method increases the precision of the Google n-gram check with a slight loss in recall.

A contribution of this paper is to advertise the Linguistic Steganography problem to the ACL community. The requirement that any linguistic transformation maintain the grammaticality and meaning of the cover text makes the problem a strong test for existing NLP technology.

2 Previous Work

2.1 Synonym Substitution

The simplest and most straightforward subliminal modification of text is to substitute selected words with their synonyms. The first lexical substitution method was proposed by Chapman and Davida (1997). Later works, such as Atallah et al. (2001a), Bolshakov (2004), Taskiran et al. (2006) and Topkara et al. (2006b), further made use of part-of-speech taggers and electronic dictionaries, such as WordNet and VerbNet, to increase the robustness of the method. Taskiran et al. (2006) attempt to use context by prioritizing the alternatives using an n-gram language model; that is, rather than randomly choose an option from the synonym set, the system relies on the language model to select the synonym. Topkara et al. (2005) and Topkara et al. (2006b) report an average embedding capacity of 0.67 bits per sentence for the synonym substitution method.

2.2 Syntactic Transformations

The second and the most widely used manipulations for linguistic steganography are syntactic transformations. This method is based on the fact that a sentence can be transformed into more than one semantically equivalent syntactic structure, using transformations such as passivization, topicalization and clefting. The first syntactic transformation method is presented by Atallah et al. (2001a). Later, Atallah et al. (2001b) embedded information in the tree structure of the text by adjusting the structural properties of intermediate representations of sentences. In other words, instead of performing lexical substitution directly to the text, the secret message is embedded into syntactic parse trees of the sentences. Liu et al. (2005), Meral et al. (2007), Murphy (2001), Murphy and Vogel (2007) and Topkara et al. (2006a) all belong to the syntactic transformation category. After embedding the secret message, modified deep structure forms are converted into the surface structure format via language generation tools. Atallah et al. (2001b) and Topkara et al. (2006a) attained the embedding capacity of 0.5 bits per sentence with the syntactic transformation method.

2.3 Semantic Transformations

The semantic transformation method is the most sophisticated approach for linguistic steganography, and perhaps impractical given the current state-of-the-art for NLP technology. It requires some sophisticated tools and knowledge to model natural language semantics. Atallah et al. (2002) used semantic transformations and embed information in text-meaning representation (TMR) trees of the text by either pruning, grafting or substituting the tree structure with information available from ontological semantic resources. Vybornova and Macq (2007) aimed to embed information by exploiting the linguistic phenomenon of presupposition, with the idea that some presuppositional information can be removed without changing the meaning of a sentence.

3 Data Resources

3.1 Paraphrase Dictionary

The cover text used for our experiments consists of newspaper sentences from Section 00 of the Penn Treebank (Marcus et al., 1993). Hence we require possible paraphrases for phrases that occur in Section 00. The paraphrase dictionary that we use was generated for us by Chris Callison-Burch, using the technique described in Callison-Burch (2008), which exploits a parallel corpus and methods developed for statistical machine translation.

Table 1 gives summary statistics of the paraphrase dictionary and its coverage on Section 00 of the Penn Treebank. The length of the extracted n-gram phrases ranges from unigrams to five-grams. The coverage figure gives the percentage of sentences which have at least one phrase in the dictionary. The coverage is important for us because it determines the payload capacity of the embedding method described in Section 5.

Table 2 lists some examples 5-gram phrases and paraphrases from the dictionary. The format of the

N-gram	Number of phrases	Coverage on section 00 (%)
Unigrams	5,856	99
Bigrams	13,473	96
Trigrams	6,574	65
Four-grams	1,604	40
Five-grams	295	10

Table 1: Statistics for the paraphrase dictionary

Original phrase	Paraphrases
the end of this year	later this year
	the end of the year
	year end
a number of people	some of my colleagues
	differences
	the European peoples party
	the PPE group

Table 2: Example phrases and paraphrases from the dictionary

dictionary is a mapping from phrases to sets of possible paraphrases. Each paraphrase also has a probability, based on a statistical machine translation model, but we do not use that feature here. The examples show that, while some of the paraphrases are of a high quality, some are not. For example, *differences* is unlikely to be a suitable paraphrase for *a number of people* in any context. Moreover, there are some ⟨phrase, paraphrase⟩ pairs which are only suitable in particular contexts. For example, *year end* is an unsuitable paraphrase for *the end of this year* in the sentence *The chart compares the gold price at the end of last year with the end of this year*. Barzilay and McKeown (2001) also note that the applicability of paraphrases is strongly influenced by context. Section 4 describes our method for determining if a paraphrase is suitable in a given context.

3.2 Google N-gram Data

The Google n-gram data was collected by Google Research for statistical language modelling, and has been used for many tasks such as lexical disambiguation (Bergsma et al., 2009), and contains English n-grams and their observed frequency counts, for counts of at least 40. The striking feature of the n-gram corpus is the large number of n-grams and the size of the counts, since the counts were extracted from over 1 trillion word tokens of English text on publicly accessible Web pages collected in January 2006. For example, the 5-gram phrase *the part that you were* has a count of 103. The compressed data is around 24 GB on disk.

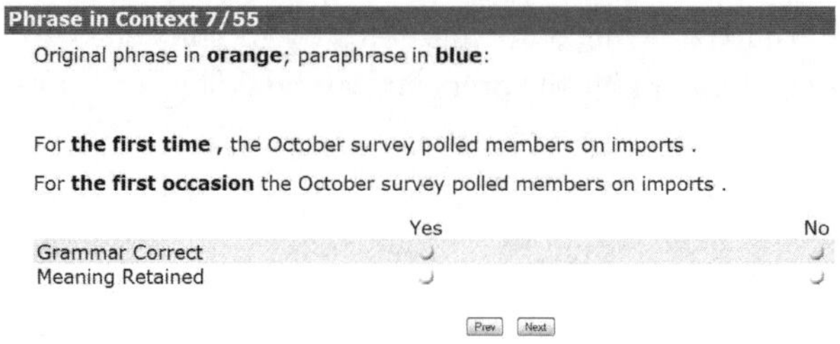

Figure 2: The web-based annotation system

3.3 Paraphrase Judgement Corpus

The focus of the paper is to develop an automatic system for checking the grammaticality and fluency of paraphrases in context. In order to evaluate the system, we collected some human judgements, based on 70 sentences from Section 00 of the Penn Treebank. For each sentence, we took every phrase in the sentence which is in the dictionary, and for each paraphrase of that phrase, replaced the phrase with the paraphrase to create an instance. This procedure resulted in 500 cases of paraphrases in context.

Each case was then evaluated by a human judge, using a web-based annotation system that we developed. The judges were asked to judge each case on two dimensions: a) whether the paraphrase is *grammatical* in context; and b) whether the paraphrase *retains the meaning* of the original phrase given the context. Figure 2 gives a screen shot of the annotation system.

50 of the 500 cases were judged by two judges, in order to obtain some indication of whether the grammaticality and meaning retention judgements are viable; the rest were judged by one annotator. (The 500 instances were randomly distributed among 10 native speakers, each being given 55 instances to judge.) For the meaning retention check, only 34 out of the 50 cases received the same judgement. One reason for the low agreement may be that, for 11 of the 16 disagreement cases, we were asking annota-

tors to judge the meaning retention of paraphrases which had been judged to be ungrammatical in context, which may not be a meaningful task. For the grammatical check, 42 out of the 50 cases received the same judgement, a much higher level of agreement.

Since the meaning retention judgements were unreliable, we used only the grammatical judgements to evaluate our system. Hence we are interested in evaluating whether our n-gram and parser-based systems can determine if a paraphrase is *grammatical* in context. Meaning retention is important for the imperceptibility requirement, but grammaticality is even more so, since ungrammatical sentences will be easy for an observer to spot. However, we recognise that only testing for grammaticality does not fully test the imperceptibility properties of the system, only part of it.

For the 8 cases which received different judgements on grammaticality, the second author of this paper made the definitive judgement, which resulted in a test set of 308 paraphrases judged as grammatical in context, and 192 paraphrases judged as ungrammatical in context.

4 Proposed Method and Experiments

4.1 Google N-gram Method

The main idea for testing the use of paraphrases is to check if the various contextual n-grams appear in the Google n-gram data, or were already in the original sentence (before paraphrasing). Let us first define some notation to be used in describing the method. The leftmost and rightmost $<m>$ words in the phrase/paraphrase are represented as $<m>IN_{Left}$ and $<m>IN_{Right}$, respectively. Words at the left and right side of the substituted phrase are defined as $<c>OUT_{Left}$ and $<c>OUT_{Right}$, where $<c>$ is an integer which indicates the number of words represented. Also, we define a context window pair $W^{<c>}_{<n>} = (W_L{}^{<c>}_{<n>}, W_R{}^{<c>}_{<n>})$, where $W_L{}^{<c>}_{<n>}$ is composed by $<c>OUT_{Left}$ concatenated with $<n-c>IN_{Left}$, and $W_R{}^{<c>}_{<n>}$ is composed by $<n-c>IN_{Right}$ concatenated with $<c>OUT_{Right}$. Figure 3 gives an example of the context window pairs W_3^1 and W_3^2 in the sentence *Soviets said that it is* ***too early to*** *say whether that will happen* where the phrase *too early to* is being considered in context.

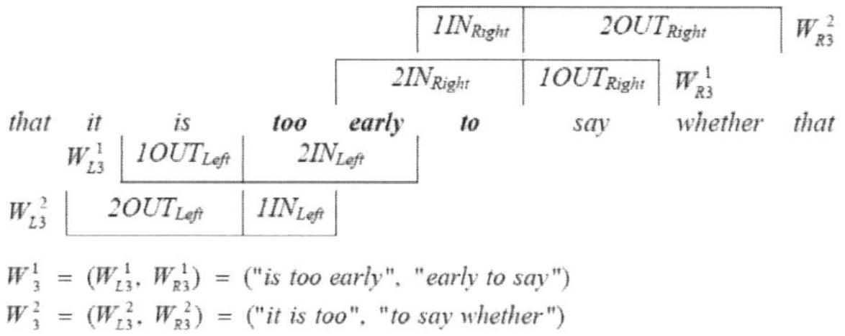

Figure 3: An example of the context window pair

INPUT: $S, P, P', n, maxC$
OUTPUT: the acceptability of paraphrase P' checked by $(n,\ maxC)$

FOR each context size C from 1 to $maxC$
  GET a context window pair W_n^C
  IF $O(W_n^C)$ is zero **THEN**
    OUTPUT paraphrase P' fails
END FOR
OUTPUT paraphrase P' passes

Figure 4: Procedure for checking acceptability

We define a *google-count function G()*. This function takes a context window pair $W^{<c>}_{<n>}$ as input and outputs a frequency count pair of $W^{<c>}_{<n>}$ recorded in the Google n-gram data. If a context window cannot be found in the Google n-gram data, the frequency count of that window is zero. Also, we define a binary *occurrence function O()*. It is used to determine whether a context window pair can be passed as acceptable. The input of this function is $W^{<c>}_{<n>}$. The function outputs one if either both $W_L{}^{<c>}_{<n>}$ and $W_R{}^{<c>}_{<n>}$ already occurred in the original sentence (before paraphrasing) or if the frequency counts output by *G*($W^{<c>}_{<n>}$) are both greater than zero.

The two major components in our method are the paraphrase dictionary and the Google n-gram data. Once a phrase P in the cover sentence S is matched with that in the paraphrase dictionary, we test the use of its paraphrase P' by the following method. This method takes into account maximum C contextual words at both sides of the target phrase, and uses Google n-gram data as a check, where n = 2, 3, 4 or 5, and $maxC$ = 1 to $n - 1$. Each pair of $(n,\ maxC)$ provides a separate check, by considering both left and right contexts for these values.

Figure 4 describes the procedure for checking the

acceptability of paraphrasing phrase P with P' in a given sentence S, given the n-gram size and the maximum considered context size $maxC$. For example, we want to check the acceptability of the paraphrase in context shown in Figure 3 by using google tri-gram data (n = 3) and taking maximum context size equal to two into consideration ($maxC$ = 2). The procedure starts from taking context size C equal to one into account, namely checking the occurrence of W_3^1. If the paraphrase P' passes the current test, in the next iteration it will be tested by taking one more context word into account, namely W_3^2. However, If the paraphrase P' fails the current (n, C) check the checking procedure will terminate and report that the paraphrase fails. In contrast, if the paraphrase passes all the (n, C) checks where C = 1 to $maxC$, the procedure determines the paraphrase as acceptable. What is happening is that an n-gram window is effectively being shifted across the paraphrase boundary to include different amounts of context and paraphrase.

4.2 Syntactic Filter

In order to improve the grammaticality checking, we use a parser as an addition to the basic Google n-gram method. We use the Clark and Curran (2007) CCG parser to analyse the sentence before and after paraphrasing. Combinatory Categorial Grammar (CCG) is a lexicalised grammar formalism, in which CCG lexical categories — typically expressing subcategorisation information — are assigned to each word in a sentence. The grammatical check works by checking if the words in the sentence outside of the phrase and paraphrase receive the same lexical categories before and after paraphrasing. If there is any change in lexical category assignment to these words then the paraphrase is judged ungrammatical. Hence the grammar check is at the word, rather than derivation, level; however, CCG lexical categories contain a large amount of syntactic information which this method is able to exploit.

4.3 Results

The test corpus described in Section 3.3 was split into development and test data: 100 instances for development and 400 for testing. The development data was used for preliminary experiments. For the test data, 246 of the examples (61.5%) had been judged as grammatical, and 154 (38.5%) had been judged as ungrammatical by the annotators.

	Acc%	P%	R%	F%
baseline	61.5	61.5	100.0	76.2
parser	68.3	67.4	93.9	78.4

Table 3: Grammar check using CCG parser

The performance of the system is evaluated using accuracy, precision, recall and balanced F-measure. Accuracy is the percentage of correct judgements over all grammatical and ungrammatical paraphrases. Precision is the percentage of paraphrases judged grammatical by the system which are judged grammatical by the human judges, and recall is the percentage of paraphrases judged grammatical by human judges which are also judged grammatical by the system. Precision and recall are relevant in our setting because high precision implies high imperceptibility, since grammatical phrases in context are less likely to be viewed as suspicious by the observer; whereas high recall maximises the payload (given the dictionary), since high recall implies that phrases are being paraphrased where possible (and hence embedding as much information as possible).

An accuracy baseline is obtained by always returning the majority class, in this case always judging the paraphrase grammatical, which gives an accuracy of 61.5%. Table 3 gives the performance when only the CCG parser is used for checking grammaticality. As far as steganography is concerned, the precision is low, since over 30% of the paraphrases used are ungrammatical, which is likely to raise the suspicions of the observer.

Table 4 gives the results for the Google n-gram method, for various n-gram and context sizes. As the n-gram size increases — meaning that a larger part of the context is used — the accuracy falls below that of the baseline. However, from a steganography aspect, accuracy is not useful, since the trade-off between precision and recall is more relevant. As expected, with larger n-grams checking the left and right contexts, the precision increases, reaching 100% for the 5-grams. Hence, as far as grammaticality judgements are concerned, the imperceptibility requirement is completely satisified. However, the large drop in recall means that the imperceptibil-

N-gram	Context Size	Accuracy (%)	Precision (%)	Recall (%)	F-measure (%)
2-gram	1	62.0	62.1	98.0	76.0
3-gram	1	62.5	65.1	84.2	73.4
	2	67.3	72.9	74.4	73.6
4-gram	1	58.5	71.3	54.5	61.8
	2	53.2	84.7	29.3	43.5
	3	51.8	89.6	24.4	38.3
5-gram	1	54.8	85.0	32.1	46.6
	2	43.5	95.5	8.5	15.7
	3	41.0	100.0	4.1	7.8
	4	41.0	100.0	4.1	7.8

Table 4: Performance of google n-gram method

N-gram	Context Size	Accuracy (%)	Precision (%)	Recall (%)	F-measure (%)
2-gram	1	68.0	67.7	91.9	78.0
3-gram	1	67.3	70.9	79.3	74.9
	2	69.5	77.7	70.7	74.0
4-gram	1	59.5	75.6	50.4	60.5
	2	53.8	88.6	28.5	43.1
	3	52.0	92.2	24.0	38.1
5-gram	1	53.8	86.8	29.3	43.8
	2	43.3	95.2	8.1	15.0
	3	41.0	100.0	4.1	7.8
	4	41.0	100.0	4.1	7.8

Table 5: Performance of google n-gram method with the CCG parser filter

ity is achieved at the cost of a reduced payload, since many of the grammatical paraphrases that could be used to embed information are being discarded.

Table 5 shows the results for the Google n-gram method followed by the parser check; that is, if the Google n-gram method judges the paraphrase to be grammatical, then it is passed to the CCG parser for an additional check. Adding the parser generally increases the precision with a slight loss in recall. Which settings are best to use in practice would depend on how the steganography user wished to trade off imperceptibility for payload.

5 Possible embedding method

In this section, we propose a linguistic hiding method which can be integrated with an automatic paraphrasing system. It needs a large paraphrase dictionary to determine modifiable phrases and provide available paraphrases. The embedding capacity of the proposed linguistic stegosystem relies on the number of paraphrasable sentences in the cover text. If every sentence in the cover text is paraphrasable, the system can have the maximum embedding capacity equal to 1 bit per sentence which is comparable to other linguistic steganography methods using syntactic transformations and synonym substitution.

5.1 Data Embedding Procedure

First the sentences in a cover text T are identified using a sentence segmentation algorithm, giving N sentences s_1, s_2,..., s_N. The paraphrasability of each sentence is then checked using our automatic method. If a sentence contains at least one paraphrasable phrase, we call the sentence a *paraphrasable sentence* or a *non-paraphrasable sentence* otherwise. Let D be the maximum number of sentence boundaries between two subsequent paraphrasable sentences in T. Thus, for every D sentences within a cover text T, there will be at least one paraphrasable sentence. Let every unit of D sentences serve as one embedding unit in which a single secret bit can be embedded. If we want to embed 0 in an embedding unit, we transform all the paraphrasable sentences in this embedding unit to non-paraphrasable sentences (assuming certain properties of the dictionary; see end of this section for discussion). If we want to embed 1, we leave the embedding unit without any modifications.

Figure 5 demonstrates the embedding of the secret bitstring 101 in a cover text containing nine sentences t_1, t_2,..., t_9 defined by a sentence segmentation algorithm. First, t_1, t_3, t_4, t_7 and t_9 are determined as paraphrasable sentences and thus D, the

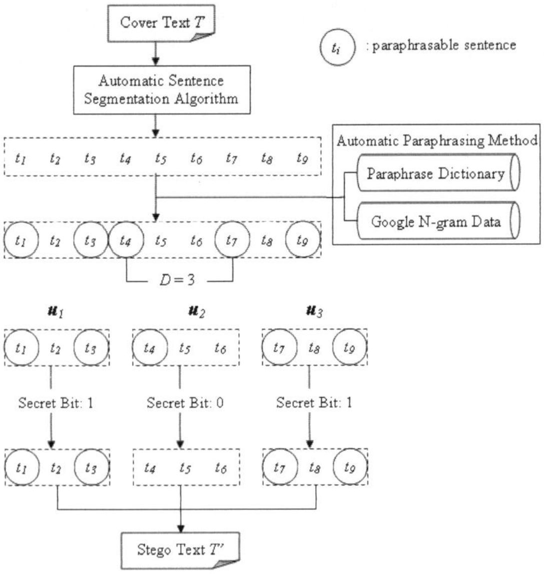

Figure 5: Embedding secret bits in a cover text using sentence segmentation method

size of an embedding unit, is 3. Next, we segment the cover text into three embedding units u_1, u_2 and u_3, each of which contains three sentences. Since we want to embed secret bits 101 in u_1, u_2 and u_3 respectively, the embedding unit u_2 should contain no paraphrasable sentence. That is, the paraphrasable phrase in t_4 should be replaced by its paraphrase. Finally, the stego text is output and sent along with the private key *D* to the other party. A private key is known only to the parties that exchange messages.

In order for this method to work, we require certain properties of the paraphrase dictionary. For example, it is crucial that, once a phrase has been paraphrased, it does not produce another phrase that can be paraphrased. This can be achieved by simply requiring that any paraphrase 'on the RHS' of the dictionary does not also appear as a phrase on the LHS. In fact, this is not so unnatural for the Callison-Burch dictionary, which consists of phrases mapped to sets of paraphrases, many of which only appear on one side.

5.2 Data Extracting Procedure

For extracting the secret data, first, the stego text T' undergoes sentence segmentation, and *N* defined sentences s'_1, s'_2,..., s'_N are obtained. According to the private key *D*, every *D* sentences are treated as an information unit, and in each unit we check the occurrence of paraphrasable sentences making use of our paraphrasing method. If an information unit contains at least one paraphrasable sentence, this information unit implies the embedding of 1. In contrast, if none of the sentences in the information unit are paraphrasable, it implies the embedding of 0. Hence, in order to recover the hidden message, the receiver requires the sentence segmentation algorithm, the paraphrase dictionary, the automatic program determining grammaticality of paraphrases in context, and the secret key D. The extraction process essentially reverses the embedding method.

6 Conclusions

The contributions of this paper are to develop an automatic system for checking the grammaticality and fluency of paraphrases in context, and the proposal of using paraphrases as a suitable transformation for Linguistic Steganography. An advantage of our proposed method is that it is somewhat language and domain independent, requiring only a paraphrase dictionary and a Google n-gram corpus, both of which are likely to be available for a range of languages in the future.

There are various practical issues in the application of Linguistic Steganography systems that we have chosen to ignore. For example, we have not discussed the choice of cover text. If a newspaper article were chosen as the cover text, then any changes could be easily found in practice by comparing the stego text with the original article, which is likely to be readily available. Another interesting question that we have not addressed is whether some languages are better suited to Linguistic Steganography than others, or whether some languages are better suited to particular linguistic transformations than others. Finally, we have only evaluated our grammatical checker and not the steganography system itself (other than giving an indication of the likely payload). How best to evaluate the imperceptibility of such a system we leave to future work.

Acknowledgements

We would like to thank Chris Callison-Burch for providing the paraphrase dictionary, Katja Markert, Stephen Pulman, Laura Rimell, and the anonymous reviewers for useful comments. Ching-Yun Chang was funded by an Oxford University Clarendon scholarship.

References

Mikhail J. Atallah, Craig J. McDonough, Victor Raskin, and Sergei Nirenburg. 2001a. Natural language processing for information assurance and security: an overview and implementations. In *Proceedings of the 2000 workshop on New security paradigms*, pages 51–65, Ballycotton, County Cork, Ireland.

Mikhail J. Atallah, Victor Raskin, Michael C. Crogan, Christian Hempelmann, Florian Kerschbaum, Dina Mohamed, and Sanket Naik. 2001b. Natural language watermarking: design, analysis, and a proof-of-concept implementation. In *Proceedings of the 4th International Information Hiding Workshop*, volume 2137, pages 185–199, Pittsburgh, Pennsylvania.

Mikhail J. Atallah, Victor Raskin, Christian F. Hempelmann, Mercan Karahan, Umut Topkara, Katrina E. Triezenberg, and Radu Sion. 2002. Natural language watermarking and tamperproofing. In *Proceedings of the 5th International Information Hiding Workshop*, pages 196–212, Noordwijkerhout, The Netherlands.

Regina Barzilay and Kathleen R. McKeown. 2001. Extracting paraphrases from a parallel corpus. In *Proceedings of the 39th ACL*, pages 50–57, Toulouse.

Richard Bergmair. 2007. A comprehensive bibliography of linguistic steganography. In *Proceedings of the SPIE Conference on Security, Steganography, and Watermarking of Multimedia Contents*, volume 6505.

Shane Bergsma, Dekang Lin, and Randy Goebel. 2009. Web-scale n-gram models for lexical disambiguation. In *Proceedings of the 21st International Joint Conference on Artifical Intelligence*, pages 1507–1512, Pasadena, CA.

Igor A. Bolshakov. 2004. A method of linguistic steganography based on coladdressally-verified synonym. In *Information Hiding: 6th International Workshop*, volume 3200, pages 180–191, Toronto, Canada.

Chris Callison-Burch. 2008. Syntactic constraints on paraphrases extracted from parallel corpora. In *Proceedings of the EMNLP Conference*, pages 196–205, Honolulu, Hawaii.

Mark Chapman and George I. Davida. 1997. Hiding the hidden: A software system for concealing ciphertext as innocuous text. In *Proceedings of the First International Conference on Information and Communication Security*, volume 1334, pages 335–345, Beijing.

Stephen Clark and James R. Curran. 2007. Wide-coverage efficient statistical parsing with CCG and log-linear models. *Comp. Ling.*, 33(4):493–552.

Jessica Fridrich. 2009. *Steganography in Digital Media: Principles, Algorithms, and Applications*. Cambridge University Press, first edition.

Yuling Liu, Xingming Sun, and Yong Wu. 2005. A natural language watermarking based on Chinese syntax. In *Advances in Natural Computation*, volume 3612, pages 958–961, Changsha, China.

Mitchell P. Marcus, Beatrice Santorini, and Mary A. Marcinkiewicz. 1993. Building a large annotated corpus of English: the Penn Treebank. *Computational Linguistics*, 19:313–330.

Hasan M. Meral, Emre Sevinc, Ersin Unkar, Bulent Sankur, A. Sumru Ozsoy, and Tunga Gungor. 2007. Syntactic tools for text watermarking. In *Proceedings of the SPIE Conference on Security, Steganography, and Watermarking of Multimedia Contents*, volume 6505, San Jose, CA.

Brian Murphy and Carl Vogel. 2007. The syntax of concealment: reliable methods for plain text information hiding. In *Proceedings of the SPIE Conference on Security, Steganography, and Watermarking of Multimedia Contents*, volume 6505, San Jose, CA.

Brian Murphy. 2001. Syntactic information hiding in plain text. Masters Thesis. Trinity College Dublin.

Lip Y. Por, Ang T. Fong, and B. Delina. 2008. Whitesteg: a new scheme in information hiding using text steganography. *WSEAS Transactions on Computers*, 7:735–745.

Cuneyt M. Taskiran, Mercan Topkara, and Edward J. Delp. 2006. Attacks on linguistic steganography systems using text analysis. In *Proceedings of the SPIE Conference on Security, Steganography, and Watermarking of Multimedia Contents*, volume 6072, pages 97–105, San Jose, CA.

Mercan Topkara, Cuneyt M. Taskiran, and Edward J. Delp. 2005. Natural language watermarking. In *Proceedings of the SPIE Conference on Security, Steganography, and Watermarking of Multimedia Contents*, volume 5681, pages 441–452, San Jose, CA.

Mercan Topkara, Umut Topkara, and Mikhail J. Atallah. 2006a. Words are not enough: sentence level natural language watermarking. In *Proceedings of the ACM Workshop on Content Protection and Security*, pages 37–46, Santa Barbara, CA.

Umut Topkara, Mercan Topkara, and Mikhail J. Atallah. 2006b. The hiding virtues of ambiguity: quantifiably resilient watermarking of natural language text through synonym substitutions. In *Proceedings of the 8th Workshop on Multimedia and Security*, pages 164–174, Geneva, Switzerland.

M. Olga Vybornova and Benoit Macq. 2007. A method of text watermarking using presuppositions. In *Proceedings of the SPIE Conference on Security, Steganography, and Watermarking of Multimedia Contents*, volume 6505, San Jose, CA.

Prenominal Modifier Ordering via Multiple Sequence Alignment

Aaron Dunlop
Oregon Health & Science University
Portland, OR
dunlopa@cslu.ogi.edu

Margaret Mitchell
University of Aberdeen
Aberdeen, Scotland, U.K.
m.mitchell@abdn.ac.uk

Brian Roark
Oregon Health & Science University
Portland, OR
roark@cslu.ogi.edu

Abstract

Producing a fluent ordering for a set of prenominal modifiers in a noun phrase (NP) is a problematic task for natural language generation and machine translation systems. We present a novel approach to this issue, adapting multiple sequence alignment techniques used in computational biology to the alignment of modifiers. We describe two training techniques to create such alignments based on raw text, and demonstrate ordering accuracies superior to earlier reported approaches.

1 Introduction

Natural language generation and machine translation systems must produce text which not only conforms to a reasonable grammatical model, but which also sounds smooth and natural to a human consumer. Ordering prenominal modifiers in noun phrases is particularly difficult in these applications, as the rules underlying these orderings are subtle and not well understood. For example, the phrase "big red ball" seems natural, while "red big ball" seems more marked, suitable only in specific contexts. There is some consensus that the order of prenominal modifiers in noun phrases is governed in part by semantic constraints, but there is no agreement on the exact constraints necessary to specify consistent orderings for any given set of modifiers. General principles of modifier ordering based on semantic constraints also fall short on larger domains, where it is not always clear how to map prenominal modifiers to proposed semantic groups.

With the recent advantages of large corpora and powerful computational resources, work on automatically ordering prenominal modifiers has moved away from approaches based on general principles, and towards learning ordering preferences empirically from existing corpora. Such approaches have several advantages: (1) The predicted orderings are based on prior evidence from 'real-world' texts, ensuring that they are therefore reasonably natural. (2) Many (if not all) prenominal modifiers can be ordered. (3) Expanding the training data with more and larger corpora often improves the system without requiring significant manual labor.

In this paper, we introduce a novel approach to prenominal modifier ordering adapted from multiple sequence alignment (MSA) techniques used in computational biology. MSA is generally applied to DNA, RNA, and protein sequences, aligning three or more biological sequences in order to determine, for example, common ancestry (Durbin et al., 1999; Gusfield, 1997; Carrillo and Lipman, 1988). MSA techniques have not been widely applied in NLP, but have produced some promising results for building a generation mapping dictionary (Barzilay and Lee, 2002), paraphrasing (Barzilay and Lee, 2003), and phone recognition (White et al., 2006).

We believe that multiple sequence alignment is well-suited for aligning linguistic sequences, and that these alignments can be used to predict prenominal modifier ordering for any given set of modifiers. Our technique utilizes simple features within the raw text, and does not require any semantic information. We achieve good performance using this approach, with results competitive with earlier work (Shaw and Hatzivassiloglou, 1999; Malouf, 2000; Mitchell, 2009) and higher recall and F-measure than that reported in Mitchell (2009) when tested on the same corpus.

Human Language Technologies: The 2010 Annual Conference of the North American Chapter of the ACL, pages 600–608,
Los Angeles, California, June 2010. ©2010 Association for Computational Linguistics

2 Related work

In one of the first attempts at automatically ordering prenominal modifiers, Shaw and Hatzivassiloglou (1999) present three empirical methods to order a variety of prenominal modifier types. Their approach provides ordering decisions for adjectives, gerunds (such as "running" in "running man"), and past participles (such as "heated" in "heated debate"), as well as for modifying nouns (such as "baseball" in "baseball field"). A morphology module transforms plural nouns and comparative/superlative forms into their base forms, increasing the frequency counts for each modifier. We will briefly recap their three methods, which are categorized as the *direct evidence* method, the *transitivity* method, and the *clustering* method.

Given prenominal modifiers a and b in a training corpus, the *direct evidence* method compares frequency counts of the ordered sequences $<a,b>$ and $<b,a>$. This approach works well, but is limited by data sparsity; groups of two or more modifiers before a noun are relatively infrequent in traditional corpora, and finding the same pair of modifiers together more than once is particularly rare.

To overcome this issue, Shaw and Hatzivassiloglou's *transitivity* and *clustering* methods make inferences about unseen orderings among prenominal modifiers. In the transitivity method, given three modifiers a,b,c, where a precedes b and b precedes c, the model concludes that a precedes c. The clustering method calculates a similarity score between modifiers based on where the modifiers occur in relation to the other modifiers in the corpus. Those modifiers that are most similar are clustered together, and ordering decisions can be made between modifiers in separate clusters. All three approaches are designed to order pairs of modifiers; it is unclear how to extend these approaches to order groups larger than a pair.

Shaw and Hatzivassiloglou find that NPs with only adjectives as modifiers (including gerunds and past participles) are considerably easier to order than those which contain both adjectives and nouns. They also find large differences in accuracy across domains; their systems achieve much lower overall accuracy on financial text (the Wall Street Journal (WSJ) corpus (Marcus et al., 1999)) than on medical discharge summaries.

Looking at all modifier pairs, the authors achieve their highest prediction accuracy of 90.7% using the transitivity technique on a medical corpus. We do not have access to this corpus, but we do have access to the WSJ corpus, which provides a way to compare our methods. On this corpus, their model produces predictions for 62.5% of all modifier pairs and achieves 83.6% accuracy when it is able to make a prediction. Random guessing on the remainder yields an overall accuracy of 71.0%.

Malouf (2000) also examines the problem of prenominal modifier ordering. He too proposes several statistical techniques, achieving results ranging from 78.3% to 91.9% accuracy. He achieves his best results by combining memory-based learning and positional probability to modifiers from the first 100 million tokens of the BNC. However, this evaluation is limited to the ordering of prenominal adjectives, which is a considerably simpler task than ordering all types of prenominal modifiers. Malouf's approaches are also limited to ordering pairs of modifiers.

Mitchell (2009) proposes another approach, grouping modifiers into classes and ordering based on those classes. A modifier's class is assigned based on its placement before a noun, relative to the other modifiers it appears with. Classes are composed of those modifiers that tend to be placed closer to the head noun, those modifiers that tend to be placed farther from the head noun, etc., with each class corresponding to a general positional preference. Unlike earlier work, these classes allow more than one ordering to be proposed for some pairs of modifiers.

Combining corpora of various genres, Mitchell's system achieves a *token precision* of 89.6% (see Section 4 for discussion and comparison of various evaluation metrics). However, the model only makes predictions for 74.1% of all modifier pairs in the test data, so recall is quite low (see Tables 4 and 6).

Overall, previous work in noun-phrase ordering has produced impressive accuracies in some domains, but currently available systems tend to adapt poorly to unseen modifiers and do not generalize well to unseen domains.

3 Methods

3.1 Multiple Sequence Alignment

Multiple sequence alignment algorithms align sequences of discrete tokens into a series of columns. They attempt to align identical or easily-substitutable tokens within a column, inserting gaps when such gaps will result in a better alignment (more homogeneous token assignments within each column). For example, consider the simple alignment shown in Table 1. The two sequences 'GAACTGAT' and 'AAGTGTAT' are aligned to maximize the number of identical items that appear in the same column, substituting tokens (column 3), and inserting gaps (columns 1 and 6)[1].

A full MSA is generally constructed by iteratively aligning each new sequence with an identical or similar sequence already in the MSA (so-called "progressive alignment"). The costs of token substitution are often taken from a hand-tuned substitution matrix. A cost may also be associated with inserting a gap into the existing MSA (a "gap penalty"). Once the full MSA has been constructed, a Position Specific Score Matrix (PSSM) can be induced, in which each token (including a special gap token) is assigned a separate alignment cost for each column. An unseen sequence can then be aligned with the full MSA by Viterbi search.

Predicting sequence ordering within a noun phrase is a natural application for MSA techniques, and it seems reasonable to propose that aligning an unseen set of modifiers with such an MSA model will yield acceptable orderings. Table 2 illustrates how MSA may be applied to modifiers before a noun. Given an NP preceded by modifiers *hungry*, *big*, and *Grizzly*, alignment of the modifiers with NPs seen in the training corpus determines the prenominal ordering *big hungry Grizzly*. We then align every permutation of the NP and choose the best-scoring alignment.

[1]See Durbin et al. (1999) for details on standard alignment techniques.

G	A	C	T	G	-	A	T
-	A	G	T	G	T	A	T
1	2	3	4	5	6	7	8

Table 1: Alignment of the two DNA sequences 'GAACTGAT' and 'AAGTGTAT'.

small	clumsy	black	bear
big	-	black	cow
two-story	-	brown	house
big	clumsy	-	bull
small	fuzzy	brown	duck
large	-	green	house
big	hungry	Grizzly	bear

Table 2: Example noun-phrase alignment.

The vocabulary for a linguistic alignment is large enough to render a hand-tuned substitution matrix impractical, so we instead construct a cost function based on features of the token under consideration and those of the other tokens already aligned in a column.

We know of no prior work on methods for training such an alignment. We present and compare two training methods, each of which produces competitive ordering accuracies. Both training methods share the feature-set described in Table 3. In each case, we train an MSA by aligning each instance in the training data.

3.2 Maximum Likelihood Training

In our alignment approach, the features listed in Table 3 are grouped into several classes. All observed words are a class, all observed stems are a class (Porter, 1980), and so on. We treat each indicator feature as a separate class, and make the assumption that classes are independent of one another. This assumption is clearly false, but serves as a reasonable first approximation, similar to the independence assumption in Naïve Bayesian analysis. After aligning each instance, we estimate the probability of a feature appearing in a column as the simple maximum likelihood estimate given the observed occurrences

Identity Features	
Word	Token
Stem	Word stem, derived by the Porter Stemmer
Length	'Binned' length indicators: 1, 2, 3, 4, 5-6, 7-8, 9-12, 13-18, >18 characters
Indicator Features	
Capitalized	Token begins with a capital
All-caps	Entire token is capitalized
Hyphenated	Token contains a hyphen
Numeric	Entire token is numeric (e.g. 234)
Initial Numeric	Token begins with a numeral (e.g. 123, 2-sided)
Endings	Token ends with *-al*, *-ble*, *-ed*, *-er*, *-est*, *-ic*, *-ing*, *-ive*, *-ly*

Table 3: Description of the feature-set.

within its class.[2] This produces a new PSSM with which to align the next instance.

Our problem differs from alignment of biological sequences in that we have little prior knowledge of the similarity between sequences. 'Similarity' can be defined in many ways; for biological sequences, a simple Levenshtein distance is effective, using a matrix of substitution costs or simple token identity (equivalent to a matrix with cost 0 on the diagonal and 1 everywhere else). These matrices are constructed and tuned by domain experts, and are used both in choosing alignment order (i.e., which sequence to align next) and during the actual alignment. When aligning biological sequences, it is customary to first calculate the pairwise distance between each two sequences and then introduce new sequences into the MSA in order of similarity. In this way, identical sequences may be aligned first, followed by less similar sequences (Durbin et al., 1999).

However, we have no principled method of determining the 'similarity' of two words in an NP. We have no a priori notion of what the cost of substituting 'two-story' for 'red' should be. Lacking this prior knowledge, we have no optimal alignment order and we must in effect learn the substitution costs as we construct the MSA. Therefore, we choose to add instances in the order they occur in the corpus, and to iterate over the entire MSA, re-introducing each sequence.

[2]We treat two special symbols for gaps and unknown words as members of the word class.

This allows a word to 'move' from its original column to a column which became more likely as more sequences were aligned. Each iteration is similar to a step in the EM algorithm: create a model (build up an MSA and PSSM), apply the model to the data (re-align all sequences), and repeat. Randomly permuting the training corpus did not change our results significantly, so we believe our results are not greatly dependent on the initial sequence order.

Instead of assigning substitution costs, we compute the cost of aligning a word into a particular column, as follows:

$$\mathbb{C} = \text{The set of } i \text{ feature classes, } C_i \in \mathbb{C}$$

$$j = \text{Features } 1 \ldots |C_i| \text{ from class } C_i$$

$$cnt(i,j,k) = \text{The count of instances of feature } j \text{ from class } i \text{ in column } k$$

$$\lambda_i = \text{Laplace smoothing count for feature class } C_i$$

$$A = \text{The number of aligned instances}$$

$$f(w,i,j) = \begin{cases} 1 & \text{if word } w \text{ has feature } j \text{ from } C_i, \\ 0 & \text{otherwise} \end{cases}$$

These help define feature positional probabilities for column k:

$$p(i,j,k) = \frac{cnt(i,j,k) + \lambda_i}{A + \lambda_i \cdot |C_i|} \quad (1)$$

That is, the probability of feature j from class i occurring in column k is a simple maximum-likelihood estimate — count the number of times we have already aligned that feature in the column and divide by the number of sequences aligned. We smooth that probability with simple Laplace smoothing.

We can now calculate the probability of aligning a word w into column k by multiplying the product of the probabilities of aligning each of the word's features. Taking the negative log to convert that probability into a cost function:

$$c(w,k) = -\sum_{i=1}^{|\mathbb{C}|}\sum_{j=1}^{|C_i|} \log\left(p(i,j,k)\cdot f(w,i,j)\right) \quad (2)$$

Finally, we define the cost of inserting a new column into the alignment to be equal to the number of columns in the existing alignment, thereby increasingly penalizing each inserted column until additional columns become prohibitively expensive.

$$i(j) = I \cdot \text{Length of existing alignment} \quad (3)$$

The longest NPs aligned were 7 words, and most ML MSAs ended with 12-14 columns. We experimented with various column insertion costs and values for the smoothing λ and found no significant differences in overall performance.

3.3 Discriminative Training

We also trained a discriminative model, using the same feature-set. Discriminative training does not require division of the features into classes or the independence assumption discussed in Section 3.2. We again produced a cost vector for each column. We fixed the alignment length at 8 columns, allowing alignment of the longest instances in our test corpus.

Our training data consists of ordered sequences, but the model we are attempting to learn is a set of column probabilities. Since we have no gold-standard MSAs, we instead align the ordered NPs with the current model and treat the least cost alignment of the correct ordering as the reference for training.

We trained this model using the averaged perceptron algorithm (Collins, 2002). A perceptron learns from classifier errors, i.e., when it misorders an NP. At each training instance, we align all possible permutations of the modifiers with the MSA. If the least cost alignment does not correspond to the correct ordering of the modifiers, we update the perceptron to penalize features occurring in that alignment and to reward features occurring in the least cost alignment corresponding to the correct ordering, using standard perceptron updates.

Examining every permutation of the NP involves a non-polynomial cost, but the sequences under consideration are quite short (less than 1% of the NPs in our corpus have more than 3 modifiers, and the longest has 6; see Table 7). So exhaustive search is practical for our problem; if we were to apply MSA to longer sequences, we would need to prune heavily.[3]

4 Evaluation

We trained and tested on the same corpus used by Mitchell (2009), including identical 10-fold cross-validation splits. The corpus consists of all NPs extracted from the Penn Treebank, the Brown corpus, and the Switchboard corpus (Marcus et al., 1999; Kucera and Francis, 1967; Godfrey et al., 1992). The corpus is heavily biased toward WSJ text (74%), with approximately 13% of the NPs from each of the other corpora.

We evaluated our system using several related but distinct metrics, and on both modifier pairs and full NPs.

We define:

$\mathbb{T}$ = The set of unique orderings found in the test corpus

$\mathbb{P}$ = The set of unique orderings predicted by the system

Type Precision ($|\mathbb{P} \cap \mathbb{T}|/|\mathbb{P}|$) measures the probability that a predicted ordering is 'reasonable' (where 'reasonable' is defined as orderings which are found in the test corpus).

[3]The same issue arises when evaluating candidate orderings; see Section 4.

	Token Accuracy	Type Precision	Type Recall	Type F-measure
Mitchell	N/A	**90.3%** (2.2)	67.2% (3.4)	77.1%
ML MSA	85.5% (1.0)	84.6% (1.1)	84.7% (1.1)	84.7%
Perceptron MSA	**88.9%** (0.7)	88.2% (0.8)	**88.1%** (0.8)	**88.2%**

Table 4: Results on the combined WSJ, Switchboard, and Brown corpus; averages and standard deviations over a 10-fold cross validation. Winning scores are in bold.

Type Recall ($|\mathbb{P} \cap \mathbb{T}|/|\mathbb{T}|$) measures the percentage of 'reasonable' orderings which the system recreates.

Note that these two metrics differ only in notation from those used by Mitchell (2009).

We also define a third metric, **Token Accuracy**, which measures accuracy on each individual ordering in the test corpus, rather than on *unique* orderings. This penalizes producing orderings which are legal, but uncommon. For example, if $\{a,b\}$ occurs eight times in the test corpus as $<a,b>$ and two times as $<b,a>$, we will be limited to a maximum accuracy of 80% (presuming our system correctly predicts the more common ordering). However, even though suggesting $<b,a>$ is not strictly incorrect, we generally prefer to reward a system that produces more common orderings, an attribute not emphasized by type-based metrics. Our test corpus does not contain many ambiguous pairings, so our theoretical maximum token accuracy is 99.8%.

We define:

$$o_{1..N} = \text{All modifier orderings in the test data}$$

$$pred(o_i) = \text{The predicted ordering for modifiers in } o_i$$

$$a_i = \begin{cases} 1 & \text{if } pred(o_i) = o_i, \\ 0 & \text{otherwise} \end{cases}$$

$$\textbf{Token Accuracy} = \sum_{i=0}^{N} \frac{a_i}{N}$$

4.1 Pairwise Ordering

Most earlier work has focused on ordering pairs of modifiers. The results in Table 4 are directly comparable to those found in Mitchell (2009). Mitchell's earlier approach does not generate a prediction when the system has insufficient evidence, and allows generation of multiple predictions given conflicting evidence. In theory, generating multiple predictions could improve recall, but in practice her system appears biased toward under-predicting, favoring precision. Our approach, in contrast, forces prediction of a single ordering for each test instance, occasionally costing some precision (in particular in cross-domain trials; see Table 5), but consistently balancing recall and precision.

Our measurement of Token Accuracy is comparable to the accuracy measure reported in Shaw and Hatzivassiloglou (1999) and Malouf (2000) (although we evaluate on a different corpus). Their approaches produce a single ordering for each test instance evaluated, so for each incorrectly ordered modifier pair, there is a corresponding modifier pair in the test data that was not predicted.

Shaw and Hatzivassiloglou found financial text particularly difficult to order, and reported that their performance dropped by 19% when they included nouns as well as adjectives. Malouf's system surpasses theirs, achieving an accuracy of 91.9%. However, his corpus was derived from the BNC — he did not attempt to order financial text — and he ordered only adjectives as modifiers. In contrast, our test corpus consists mainly of WSJ text, and we test on all forms of prenominal modifiers. We believe this to be a considerably more difficult task, so our peak performance of 88.9% would appear to be — at worst — quite competitive.

Table 5 presents an evaluation of cross-domain generalization, splitting the same corpus by genre — Brown, Switchboard, and WSJ. In each trial, we train on two genres and test on

	Training Corpora	Testing Corpus	Token Accuracy	Type Precision	Type Recall	Type F-measure
Mitchell	Brown+WSJ	Swbd	N/A	**94.2%**	58.2%	72.0%
	Swbd+WSJ	Brown	N/A	**87.0%**	51.2%	64.5%
	Swbd+Brown	WSJ	N/A	**82.4%**	27.2%	40.9%
ML MSA	Brown+WSJ	Swbd	74.6%	74.7%	75.3%	75.0%
	Swbd+WSJ	Brown	75.3%	74.7%	74.9%	74.8%
	Swbd+Brown	WSJ	70.2%	71.6%	71.8%	71.7%
Perceptron MSA	Brown+WSJ	Swbd	**77.2%**	78.2%	**77.6%**	**77.9%**
	Swbd+WSJ	Brown	**76.4%**	76.7%	**76.4%**	**76.5%**
	Swbd+Brown	WSJ	**77.9%**	77.5%	**77.3%**	**77.4%**

Table 5: Cross-domain generalization.

	Token Accuracy	Token Precision	Token Recall	Token F-measure
Mitchell	N/A	**94.4%**	78.6% (1.2)	85.7%
ML MSA	76.9% (1.6)	76.5% (1.4)	76.5% (1.4)	76.50%
Perceptron MSA	**86.7%** (0.9)	86.7% (0.9)	**86.7%** (0.9)	**86.7%**

Table 6: Full NP ordering accuracies; averages and standard deviations over a 10-fold cross validation. To compare directly with Mitchell (2009), we report *token* precision and recall instead of type. Our system always proposes one and only one ordering, so token accuracy, precision, and recall are identical.

the third.[4] Our results mirror those in the previous trials — forcing a prediction costs some precision (vis-a-vis Mitchell's 2009 system), but our recall is dramatically higher, resulting in more balanced performance overall.

4.2 Full NP Ordering

We now extend our analysis to ordering entire NPs, a task we feel the MSA approach should be particularly suited to, since (unlike pairwise models) it can model positional probabilities over an entire NP. To our knowledge, the only previously reported work on this task is Mitchell's (2009). We train this model on the full NP instead of on modifier pairs; this makes little difference in pairwise accuracy, but improves full-NP ordering considerably.

As seen in Table 6, both MSA models perform quite well, the perceptron-trained MSA again outperforming the maximum likelihood model. However, we were somewhat disappointed in the performance on longer sequences. We expected the MSA to encode enough global information to perform accurate full sequence ordering, but found the accuracy drops off dramatically on NPs with more modifiers. In fact, the accuracy on longer sequences is worse than we would expect by simply extending a pairwise model. For instance, ordering three modifiers requires three pairwise decisions. We predict pairwise orderings with 88% accuracy, so we would expect no worse than $(.88)^3$, or 68% accuracy on such sequences. However, the pairwise accuracy declines on longer NPs, so it underperforms even that theoretical minimum. Sparse training data for longer NPs biases the model strongly toward short sequences and transitivity (which our model does not encode) may become important when ordering several modifiers.

[4]Note that the WSJ corpus is much larger than the other two, comprising approximately 84% of the total.

Modifiers	Frequency	Token Accuracy	Pairwise Accuracy
2	89.1%	89.7%	89.7%
3	10.0%	64.5%	84.4%
4	0.9%	37.2%	80.7%

Table 7: Descriminative model performance on NPs of various lengths, including pairwise measures.

5 Ablation Tests

We performed limited ablation testing on the discriminative model, removing features individually and comparing token accuracy (see Table 8). We found that few of the features provided great benefit individually; the overall system performance remains dominated by the word. The word and stem features appear to capture essentially the same information; note that performance does not decline when the word or stem features are ablated, but drops drastically when both are omitted. Performance declines slightly more when ending features are ablated as well as words and stems, so it appears that — as expected — the information captured by ending features overlaps somewhat with lexical identity. The effects of individual features are all small and none are statistically significant.

Feature(s)	Gain/Loss
Word	0.0
Stem	0.0
Capitalization	-0.1
All-Caps	0.0
Numeric	-0.2
Initial-numeral	0.0
Length	-0.1
Hyphen	0.0
-al	0.0
-ble	-0.4
-ed	-0.4
-er	0.0
-est	-0.1
-ic	+0.1
-ing	0.0
-ive	-0.1
-ly	0.0
Word and stem	-22.9
Word, stem, and endings	-24.2

Table 8: Ablation test results on the discriminative model.

6 Summary and Future Directions

We adapted MSA approaches commonly used in computational biology to linguistic problems and presented two novel methods for training such alignments. We applied these techniques to the problem of ordering prenominal modifiers in noun phrases, and achieved performance competitive with — and in many cases, superior to — the best results previously reported.

In our current work, we have focused on relatively simple features, which should be adaptable to other languages without expensive resources or much linguistic insight. We are interested in exploring richer sources of features for ordering information. We found simple morphological features provided discriminative clues for otherwise ambiguous instances, and believe that richer morphological features might be helpful even in a language as morphologically impoverished as English. Boleda et al. (2005) achieved promising preliminary results using morphology for classifying adjectives in Catalan.

Further, we might be able to capture some of the semantic relationships noted by psychological analyses (Ziff, 1960; Martin, 1969) by labeling words which belong to known semantic classes (e.g., colors, size denominators, etc.). We intend to explore deriving such labels from resources such as WordNet or OntoNotes.

We also plan to continue exploration of MSA training methods. We see considerable room for refinement in generative MSA models; our maximum likelihood training provides a strong starting point for EM optimization, conditional likelihood, or gradient descent methods. We are also considering applying maximum entropy approaches to improving the discriminative model.

Finally (and perhaps most importantly), we expect that our model would benefit from additional training data, and plan to train on a larger, automatically-parsed corpus.

Even in its current form, our approach improves the state-of-the-art, and we believe MSA techniques can be a useful tool for ordering prenominal modifiers in NLP tasks.

7 Acknowledgements

This research was supported in part by NSF Grant #IIS-0811745. Any opinions, findings, conclusions or recommendations expressed in this publication are those of the authors and do not necessarily reflect the views of the NSF.

References

Regina Barzilay and Lillian Lee. 2002. Bootstrapping lexical choice via multiple-sequence alignment. In *Proceedings of the ACL-02 conference on Empirical methods in natural language processing - Volume 10*, pages 164–171, Philadelphia. Association for Computational Linguistics.

Regina Barzilay and Lillian Lee. 2003. Learning to paraphrase: An unsupervised approach using multiple-sequence alignment. In *Proceedings of the Human Language Technology Conference of the North American Chapter of the Association for Computational Linguistics (HLT-NAACL)*, volume 15, pages 201–31, Edmonton, Canada. Association for Computational Linguistics.

Gemma Boleda, Toni Badia, and Sabine Schulte im Walde. 2005. Morphology vs. syntax in adjective class acquisition. In *Proceedings of the ACL-SIGLEX Workshop on Deep Lexical Acquisition*, pages 77–86, Ann Arbor, Michigan, June. Association for Computational Linguistics.

Humberto Carrillo and David Lipman. 1988. The multiple sequence alignment problem in biology. *SIAM Journal on Applied Mathematics*, 48(5):1073–1082, October.

Michael Collins. 2002. Discriminative training methods for hidden markov models: theory and experiments with perceptron algorithms. In *Proceedings of the ACL-02 conference on Empirical methods in natural language processing*, volume 10, pages 1–8, Philadelphia, July. Association for Computational Linguistics.

Richard Durbin, Sean R. Eddy, Anders Krogh, and Graeme Mitchison. 1999. *Biological Sequence Analysis: Probabilistic Models of Proteins and Nucleic Acids.* Cambridge University Press, West Nyack, NY, July.

John J. Godfrey, Edward C. Holliman, and Jane McDaniel. 1992. SWITCHBOARD: telephone speech corpus for research and development. In *Acoustics, Speech, and Signal Processing, IEEE International Conference on*, volume 1, pages 517–520, Los Alamitos, CA, USA. IEEE Computer Society.

Dan Gusfield. 1997. *Algorithms on Strings, Trees and Sequences: Computer Science and Computational Biology.* Cambridge University Press, West Nyack, NY, May.

H. Kucera and W. N Francis. 1967. *Computational analysis of present-day American English.* Brown University Press, Providence, RI.

Robert Malouf. 2000. The order of prenominal adjectives in natural language generation. In *Proceedings of the 38th Annual Meeting of the Association for Computational Linguistics*, pages 85–92, Hong Kong, October. Association for Computational Linguistics.

Mitchell P Marcus, Beatrice Santorini, Mary Ann Marcinkiewicz, and Ann Taylor. 1999. *Treebank-3.* Linguistic Data Consortium, Philadelphia.

J. E. Martin. 1969. Semantic determinants of preferred adjective order. *Journal of Verbal Learning & Verbal Behavior. Vol*, 8(6):697–704.

Margaret Mitchell. 2009. Class-Based ordering of prenominal modifiers. In *Proceedings of the 12th European Workshop on Natural Language Generation (ENLG 2009)*, pages 50–57, Athens, Greece, March. Association for Computational Linguistics.

M.F. Porter. 1980. An algorithm for suffix stripping. *Program*, 14(3):130—137.

James Shaw and Vasileios Hatzivassiloglou. 1999. Ordering among premodifiers. In *Proceedings of the 37th Annual Meeting of the Association for Computational Linguistics*, pages 135–143, College Park, Maryland, USA, June. Association for Computational Linguistics.

Christopher White, Izhak Shafran, and Jean luc Gauvain. 2006. Discriminative classifiers for language recognition. In *Proceedings of the 2006 IEEE International Conference on Acoustics, Speech, and Signal Processing (ICASSP)*, pages 213–216, Toulouse, France. IEEE.

Paul Ziff. 1960. *Semantic Analysis.* Cornell University Press, Ithaca, New York.

Good Question! Statistical Ranking for Question Generation

Michael Heilman   Noah A. Smith
Language Technologies Institute
Carnegie Mellon University
Pittsburgh, PA 15213, USA
{mheilman,nasmith}@cs.cmu.edu

Abstract

We address the challenge of automatically generating questions from reading materials for educational practice and assessment. Our approach is to overgenerate questions, then rank them. We use manually written rules to perform a sequence of general purpose syntactic transformations (e.g., subject-auxiliary inversion) to turn declarative sentences into questions. These questions are then ranked by a logistic regression model trained on a small, tailored dataset consisting of labeled output from our system. Experimental results show that ranking nearly doubles the percentage of questions rated as acceptable by annotators, from 27% of all questions to 52% of the top ranked 20% of questions.

1 Introduction

In this paper, we focus on question generation (QG) for the creation of educational materials for reading practice and assessment. Our goal is to generate fact-based questions about the content of a given article. The top-ranked questions could be filtered and revised by educators, or given directly to students for practice. Here we restrict our investigation to questions about factual information in texts.

We begin with a motivating example. Consider the following sentence from the Wikipedia article on the history of Los Angeles:[1] *During the Gold Rush years in northern California, Los Angeles became known as the "Queen of the Cow Counties" for its role in supplying beef and other foodstuffs to hungry miners in the north.*

Consider generating the following question from that sentence: *What did Los Angeles become known as the "Queen of the Cow Counties" for?*

We observe that the QG process can be viewed as a two-step process that essentially "factors" the problem into simpler components.[2] Rather than simultaneously trying to remove extraneous information and transform a declarative sentence into an interrogative one, we first transform the input sentence into a simpler sentence such as *Los Angeles become known as the "Queen of the Cow Counties" for its role in supplying beef and other foodstuffs to hungry miners in the north*, which we then can then transform into a more succinct question.

Question transformation involves complex long distance dependencies. For example, in the question about Los Angeles, the word *what* at the beginning of the sentence is a semantic argument of the verb phrase *known as …* at the end of the question. The characteristics of such phenomena are (arguably) difficult to learn from corpora, but they have been studied extensively in linguistics (Ross, 1967; Chomsky, 1973). We take a rule-based approach in order to leverage this linguistic knowledge.

However, since many phenomena pertaining to question generation are not so easily encoded with rules, we include statistical ranking as an integral component. Thus, we employ an overgenerate-and-rank approach, which has been applied successfully in areas such as generation (Walker et al., 2001; Langkilde and Knight, 1998) and syntactic parsing (Collins, 2000). Since large datasets of the appropriate domain, style, and form of questions are not available to train our ranking model, we learn to rank from a relatively small, tailored dataset of human-labeled output from our rule-based system.

The remainder of the paper is organized as fol-

[1] "History of Los Angeles." *Wikipedia*. 2009. Wikimedia Foundation, Inc. Retrieved Nov. 17, 2009 from: http://en.wikipedia.org/wiki/History_of_Los_Angeles.

[2] The motivating example does not exhibit lexical semantic variations such as synonymy. In this work, we do not model complex paraphrasing, but believe that paraphrase generation techniques could be incorporated into our approach.

Human Language Technologies: The 2010 Annual Conference of the North American Chapter of the ACL, pages 609–617,
Los Angeles, California, June 2010.

lows. §2 clarifies connections to prior work and enumerates our contributions. §3 discusses particular terms and conventions we will employ. §4 discusses rule-based question transformation. §5 describes the data used to learn and to evaluate our question ranking model, and §6 then follows with details on the ranking approach itself. We then present and discuss results from an evaluation of ranked question output in §7 and conclude in §8.

2 Connections with Prior Work

The generation of questions by humans has long motivated theoretical work in linguistics (e.g., Ross, 1967), particularly work that portrays questions as transformations of canonical declarative sentences (Chomsky, 1973).

Questions have also been a major topic of study in computational linguistics, but primarily with the goal of *answering* questions (Dang et al., 2008). While much of the question answering research has focused on retrieval or extraction (e.g., Ravichandran and Hovy, 2001; Hovy et al., 2001), models of the transformation from answers to questions have also been developed (Echihabi and Marcu, 2003) with the goal of finding correct answers *given* a question (e.g., in a source-channel framework). Also, Harabagiu et al. (2005) present a system that automatically generates questions from texts to predict which user-generated questions the text might answer. In such work on question answering, question generation models are typically not evaluated for their intrinsic quality, but rather with respect to their utility as an intermediate step in the question answering process.

QG is very different from many natural language generation problems because the input is natural language rather than a formal representation (cf. Reiter and Dale, 1997). It is also different from some other tasks related to generation: unlike machine translation (e.g., Brown et al., 1990), the input and output for QG are in the same language, and their length ratio is often far from one to one; and unlike sentence compression (e.g., Knight and Marcu, 2000), QG may involve substantial changes to words and their ordering, beyond simple removal of words.

Some previous research has directly approached the topic of generating questions for educational purposes (Mitkov and Ha, 2003; Kunichika et al., 2004; Gates, 2008; Rus and Graessar, 2009; Rus and Lester, 2009), but to our knowledge, none has involved statistical models for choosing among output candidates. Mitkov et al. (2006) demonstrated that automatic generation and manual correction of questions can be more time-efficient than manual authoring alone. Much of the prior QG research has evaluated systems in specific domains (e.g., introductory linguistics, English as a Second Language), and thus we do not attempt empirical comparisons. Existing QG systems model their transformations from source text to questions with many complex rules for specific question types (e.g., a rule for creating a question *Who did the* `Subject Verb`*?* from a sentence with SVO word order and an object referring to a person), rather than with sets of general rules.

This paper's contributions are as follows:

- We apply statistical ranking to the task of *generating* natural language questions. In doing so, we show that question rankings are improved by considering features beyond surface characteristics such as sentence lengths.
- We model QG as a two-step process of first simplifying declarative input sentences and then transforming them into questions, the latter step being achieved by a sequence of general rules.
- We incorporate linguistic knowledge to explicitly model well-studied phenomena related to long distance dependencies in WH questions, such as noun phrase island constraints.
- We develop a QG evaluation methodology, including the use of broad-domain corpora.

3 Definitions and Conventions

The term "source sentence" refers to a sentence taken directly from the input document, from which a question will be generated (e.g., *Kenya is located in Africa.*). The term "answer phrase" refers to phrases in declarative sentences which may serve as targets for WH-movement, and therefore as possible answers to generated questions (e.g., *in Africa*). The term "question phrase" refers to the phrase containing the WH word that replaces an answer phrase (e.g., *Where* in *Where is Kenya located?*).

To represent the syntactic structure of sentences, we use simplified Penn Treebank-style phrase structure trees, including POS and category labels, as produced by the Stanford Parser (Klein and Manning, 2003). Noun phrase heads are selected using Collins' rules (Collins, 1999).

To implement the rules for transforming source sentences into questions, we use `Tregex`, a tree query language, and `Tsurgeon`, a tree manipulation language built on top of `Tregex` (Levy and Andrew, 2006). The `Tregex` language includes various relational operators based on the primitive relations of immediate dominance (denoted "<") and immediate precedence (denoted "."). `Tsurgeon` adds the ability to *modify* trees by relabeling, deleting, moving, and inserting nodes.

4 Rule-based Overgeneration

Many useful questions can be viewed as lexical, syntactic, or semantic transformations of the declarative sentences in a text. We describe how to model this process in two steps, as proposed in §1.[3]

4.1 Sentence Simplification

In the first step for transforming sentences into questions, each of the sentences from the source text is expanded into a set of derived declarative sentences (which also includes the original sentence) by altering lexical items, syntactic structure, and semantics. Many existing NLP transformations could potentially be exploited in this step, including sentence compression, paraphrase generation, or lexical semantics for word substitution.

In our implementation, a set of transformations derive a simpler form of the source sentence by removing phrase types such as leading conjunctions, sentence-level modifying phrases, and appositives. `Tregex` expressions identify the constituents to move, alter, or delete. Similar transformations have been utilized in previous work on headline generation (Dorr and Zajic, 2003) and summarization (Toutanova et al., 2007).

To enable questions about syntactically embedded content, our implementation also extracts a set of declarative sentences from any finite clauses, relative clauses, appositives, and participial phrases that appear in the source sentence. For example, it transforms the sentence *Selling snowballed because of waves of automatic stop-loss orders, which are triggered by computer when prices fall to certain levels* into *Automatic stop-loss orders are triggered by computer when prices fall to certain levels*, from which the next step will produce *What are triggered by computer when prices fall to certain levels?*.

4.2 Question Transformation

In the second step, the declarative sentences derived in step 1 are transformed into sets of questions by a sequence of well-defined syntactic and lexical transformations (subject-auxiliary inversion, WH-movement, etc.). It identifies the answer phrases which may be targets for WH-movement and converts them into question phrases.[4]

In the current implementation, answer phrases can be noun phrases or prepositional phrases, which enables *who*, *what*, *where*, *when*, and *how much* questions. The system could be extended to transform other types of phrases into other types of questions (e.g., *how*, *why*, and *what kind of*). It should be noted that the transformation from answer to question is achieved by applying a series of general-purpose rules. This would allow, for example, the addition of a rule to generate *why* questions that builds off of the existing rules for subject-auxiliary inversion, verb decomposition, etc. In contrast, previous QG approaches have employed separate rules for specific sentence types (e.g., Mitkov and Ha, 2003; Gates, 2008).

For each sentence, many questions may be produced: there are often multiple possible answer phrases, and multiple question phrases for each answer phrase. Hence many candidates may result from the transformations.

These rules encode a substantial amount of linguistic knowledge about the long distance dependencies prevalent in questions, which would be challenging to learn from existing corpora of questions and answers consisting typically of only thousands of examples (e.g., Voorhees, 2003).

Specifically, the following sequence of transfor-

[3] See Heilman and Smith (2009) for details on the rule-based component.

[4] We leave the generation of correct answers and distractors to future work.

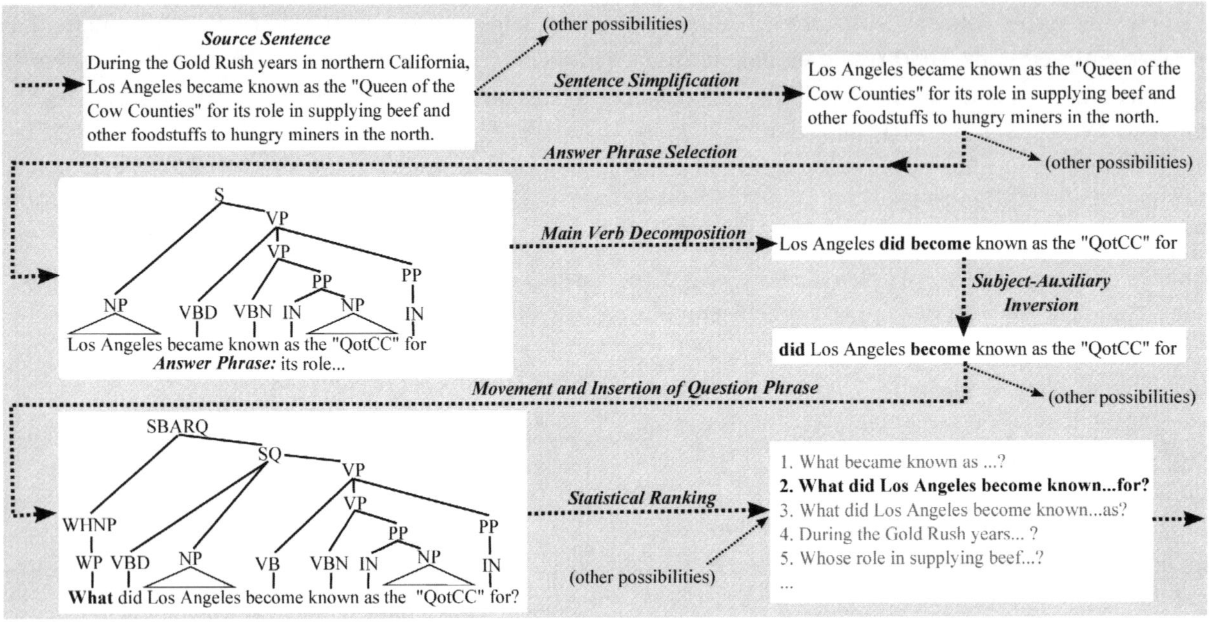

Figure 1: An illustration of the sequence of steps for generating questions. For clarity, trees are not shown for all steps. Also, while many questions may be generated from a single source sentence, only one path is shown.

mations is performed, as illustrated in Figure 1: mark phrases that cannot be answer phrases due to constraints on WH movement (§4.2.1, not in figure); select an answer phrase, remove it, and generate possible question phrases for it (§4.2.2); decompose the main verb; invert the subject and auxiliary verb; and insert one of the possible question phrases.

Some of these steps do not apply in all cases. For example, no answer phrases are removed when generating yes-no questions.

4.2.1 Marking Unmovable Phrases

In English, various constraints determine whether phrases can be involved in WH-movement and other phenomena involving long distance dependencies. In a seminal dissertation, Ross (1967) described many of these phenomena. Goldberg (2006) provides a concise summary of them.

For example, noun phrases are "islands" to movement, meaning that constituents dominated by a noun phrase typically cannot undergo WH-movement. Thus, from *John liked the book that I gave him*, we generate *What did John like?* but not **Who did John like the book that gave him?*.

We operationalize this linguistic knowledge to appropriately restrict the set of questions produced. Eight `Tregex` expressions mark phrases that cannot be answer phrases due to WH-movement constraints. For example, the following expression encodes the noun phrase island constraint described above, where `unmv` indicates unmovable noun phrases: `NP << NP=unmv`.

4.2.2 Generating Possible Question Phrases

After marking unmovable phrases, we iteratively remove each possible answer phrase and generate possible question phrases from it. The system annotates the source sentence with a set of entity types taken from the BBN Identifinder Text Suite (Bikel et al., 1999) and then uses these entity labels along with the syntactic structure of a given answer phrase to generate zero or more question phrases, each of which is used to generate a final question. (This step is skipped for yes-no questions.)

5 Rating Questions for Evaluation and Learning to Rank

Since different sentences from the input text, as well as different transformations of those sentences, may be more or less likely to lead to high-quality questions, each question is scored according to features of the source sentence, the input sentence, the question, and the transformations used in its generation. The scores are used to rank the questions. This is an example of an "overgenerate-and-rank" strategy (Walker et al., 2001; Langkilde and Knight, 1998).

This section describes the acquisition of a set of rated questions produced by the steps described above. Separate portions of these labeled data will be used to develop a discriminative question ranker (§6), and to evaluate ranked lists of questions (§7).

Fifteen native English-speaking university students rated a set of questions produced from steps 1 and 2, indicating whether each question exhibited any of the deficiencies listed in Table 1.[5] If a question exhibited no deficiencies, raters were asked to label it "acceptable." Annotators were asked to read the text of a newswire or encyclopedia article (§5.1 describes the corpora used), and then rate approximately 100 questions generated from that text. They were asked to consider each question independently, such that similar questions about the same information would receive similar ratings.

For a predefined training set, each question was rated by a single annotator (not the same for each question), leading to a large number of diverse examples. For the test set, each question was rated by three people (again, not the same for each question) to provide a more reliable gold standard. To assign final labels to the test data, a question was labeled as acceptable only if a majority of the three raters rated it as acceptable (i.e., without deficiencies).[6]

An inter-rater agreement of Fleiss's $\kappa = 0.42$ was computed from the test set's acceptability ratings. This value corresponds to "moderate agreement" (Landis and Koch, 1977) and is somewhat lower than for other rating schemes.[7]

5.1 Corpora

The training and test datasets consisted of 2,807 and 428 questions, respectively. The questions were generated from three corpora.

The first corpus was a random sample from the featured articles in the English Wikipedia[8] with between 250 and 2,000 word tokens. This English Wikipedia corpus provides expository texts written at an adult reading level from a variety of domains, which roughly approximates the prose that a secondary or post-secondary student would encounter. By choosing from the featured articles, we intended to select well-edited articles on topics of general interest. The training set included 1,328 questions about 12 articles, and the test set included 120 questions about 2 articles from this corpus.

The second corpus was a random sample from the articles in the Simple English Wikipedia of similar length. This corpus provides similar text but at a reading level corresponding to elementary education or intermediate second language learning.[9] The training set included 1,195 questions about 16 articles, and the test set included 118 questions about 2 articles from this corpus.

The third corpus was Section 23 of the *Wall Street Journal* data in the Penn Treebank (Marcus et al., 1993).[10] The training set included 284 questions about 8 articles, and the test set included 190 questions about 2 articles from this corpus.

6 Ranking

We use a discriminative ranker to rank questions, similar to the approach described by Collins (2000) for ranking syntactic parses. Questions are ranked by the predictions of a logistic regression model of question acceptability. Given the question q and source text t, the model defines a binomial distribution $p(R \mid q, t)$, with binary random variable R ranging over a ("acceptable") and u ("unacceptable").

We estimate the parameters by optimizing the regularized log-likelihood of the training data (cf. §5.1) with a variant of Newton's method (le Cessie and

[5]The ratings from one person were excluded due to an extremely high rate of accepting questions as error-free and other irregularities.

[6]The percentages in Table 1 do not add up to 100% for two reasons: first, questions are labeled acceptable in the test set only if the majority of raters labeled them as having no deficiencies, rather than the less strict criterion of requiring no deficiencies to be identified by a majority of raters; second, the categories are not mutually exclusive.

[7]E.g., Dolan and Brockett (2005) and Glickman et al. (2005) report κ values around 0.6 for paraphrase identification and textual entailment, respectively.

[8]The English and Simple English Wikipedia data were downloaded on December 16, 2008 from `http://en.wikipedia.org` and `http://simple.wikipedia.org`, respectively.

[9]The subject matter of the articles in the two Wikipedia corpora was not matched.

[10]In separate experiments with the Penn Treebank, gold-standard parses led to an absolute increase of 15% in the percentage of acceptable questions (Heilman and Smith, 2009).

Question Deficiency	Description	%
Ungrammatical	The question is not a valid English sentence. (e.g., *In what were nests excavated exposed to the sun?* from ... *eggs are usually laid* ..., *in nests excavated in pockets of earth exposed to the sun.*. This error results from the incorrect attachment by the parser of *exposed to the sun* to the verb phrase headed by *excavated*)	14.0
Does not make sense	The question is grammatical but indecipherable. (e.g., *Who was the investment?*)	20.6
Vague	The question is too vague to know exactly what it is asking about, even after reading the article (e.g., *What do modern cities also have?* from ..., *but modern cities also have many problems*).	19.6
Obvious answer	The correct answer would be obvious even to someone who has not read the article (e.g., a question where the answer is obviously the subject of the article).	0.9
Missing answer	The answer to the question is not in the article.	1.4
Wrong WH word	The question would be acceptable if the WH phrase were different (e.g., a *what* question with a person's name as the answer).	4.9
Formatting	There are minor formatting errors (e.g., with respect to capitalization, punctuation).	8.9
Other	The question was unacceptable for other reasons.	1.2
None	The question exhibits none of the above deficiencies and is thus acceptable.	27.3

Table 1: Deficiencies a question may exhibit, and the percentages of test set questions labeled with them.

van Houwelingen, 1997). In our experiments, the regularization constant was selected through cross-validation on the training data.

The features used by the ranker can be organized into several groups described in this section. This feature set was developed by an analysis of questions generated from the training set. The numbers of distinct features for each type are denoted in parentheses, with the second number, after the addition symbol, indicating the number of histogram features (explained below) for that type.

Length Features (3 + 24) The set includes integer features for the numbers of tokens in the question, the source sentence, and the answer phrase from which the WH phrase was generated. These numbers of tokens will also be used for computing the histogram features discussed below.

WH Words (9 + 0) The set includes boolean features for the presence of each possible WH word in the question.

Negation (1 + 0) This is a boolean feature for the presence of *not*, *never*, or *no* in the question.

N-Gram Language Model Features (6 + 0) The set includes real valued features for the log likelihoods and length-normalized log likelihoods of the question, the source sentence, and the answer phrase. Separate likelihood features are included for unigram and trigram language models. These language models were estimated from the written portion of the American National Corpus Second Release (Ide and Suderman, 2004), which consists of approximately 20 million tokens, using Kneser and Ney (1995) smoothing.

Grammatical Features (23 + 95) The set includes integer features for the numbers of proper nouns, pronouns, adjectives, adverbs, conjunctions, numbers, noun phrases, prepositional phrases, and subordinate clauses in the phrase structure parse trees for the question and answer phrase. It also includes one integer feature for the number of modifying phrases at the start of the question (e.g., as in *At the end of the Civil War, who led the Union Army?*); three boolean features for whether the main verb is in past, present, or future tense; and one boolean feature for whether the main verb is a form of *be*.

Transformations (8 + 0) The set includes binary features for the possible syntactic transformations (e.g., removal of appositives and parentheticals, choosing the subject of source sentence as the answer phrase).

Vagueness (3 + 15) The set includes integer features for the numbers of noun phrases in the question, source sentence, and answer phrase that are potentially vague. We define this set to include pronouns as well as common nouns that are not specified by a subordinate clause, prepositional phrase, or possessive. In the training data, we observed many vague questions resulting from such noun phrases (e.g., *What is the bridge named for?*).

Histograms In addition to the integer features for lengths, counts of grammatical types, and counts of vague noun phrases, the set includes binary "histogram" features for each length or count. These features indicate whether a count or length exceeds various thresholds: 0, 1, 2, 3, and 4 for counts; 0, 4, 8, 12, 16, 20, 24, and 28 for lengths. We aim to account for potentially non-linear relationships between question quality and these values (e.g., most good questions are neither very long nor very short).

7 Evaluation and Discussion

This section describes the results of experiments to evaluate the quality of generated questions before and after ranking. Results are aggregated across the 3 corpora (§5.1). The evaluation metric we employ is the percentage of test set questions labeled as acceptable. For rankings, our metric is the percentage of the top $N\%$ labeled as acceptable, for various N.

7.1 Results for Unranked Questions

First, we present results for the *unranked* questions produced by the rule-based overgenerator. As shown in Table 1, 27.3% of test set questions were labeled acceptable (i.e., having no deficiencies) by a majority of raters.[11]

The most frequent deficiencies were ungrammaticality (14.0%), vagueness (19.6%), and semantic errors labeled with the "Does not make sense" category (20.6%). Formatting errors (8.9%) were due to both straightforward issues with pre-processing and more challenging issues such as failing to identifying named entities (e.g., *Who was nixon's second vice president?*).

While Table 1 provides data on how often bad questions were generated, a measure of how often good questions were not generated would require knowing the number of *possible* valid questions. Instead, we provide a measure of *productivity*: the system produced an average of 6.0 acceptable questions per 250 words (i.e., the approximate average number of words on a single page in a printed book).

7.2 Configurations and Baselines

For ranking experiments, we present results for the following configurations of features:

[11] 12.1% of test set questions were unanimously acceptable.

All This configuration includes the entire set of features described in §6.

Surface Features This configuration includes only features that can be computed from the surface form of the question, source sentence, and answer phrase—that is, without hidden linguistic structures such as parts of speech or syntactic structures. Specifically, it includes features for lengths, length histograms, WH words, negation, and language model likelihoods.

Question Only This configuration includes all features of questions, but no features involving the source sentence or answer phrase (e.g., it does not include source sentence part of speech counts). It does not include transformation features.

We also present two baselines for comparison:

Random The expectation of the performance if questions were ranked randomly.

Oracle The expected performance if all questions that were labeled acceptable were ranked higher than all questions that were labeled unacceptable.

7.3 Ranking Results

Figure 2 shows that the percentage of questions rated as acceptable generally increases as the set of questions is restricted from the full 428 questions in the test set to only the top ranked questions. While 27.3% of all test set questions were acceptable, 52.3% of the top 20% of ranked questions were acceptable. Thus, the quality of the top fifth was nearly doubled by ranking with all the features.

Ranking with surface features also improved question quality, but to a lesser extent. Thus, unobserved linguistic features such as parts of speech and syntax appear to add value for ranking questions.[12]

The ranker seems to have focused on the "Does not make sense" and "Vague" categories. The percentage of nonsensical questions dropped from 20.6% to 4.7%, and vagueness dropped from 19.6%

[12] Ranking with all features was statistically significantly better ($p < .05$) in terms of the percentage of acceptable questions in the top ranked 20% than ranking with the "question only" or "surface" configurations, or the random baseline, as verified by computing 95% confidence intervals with the BC_a Bootstrap (Efron and Tibshirani, 1993).

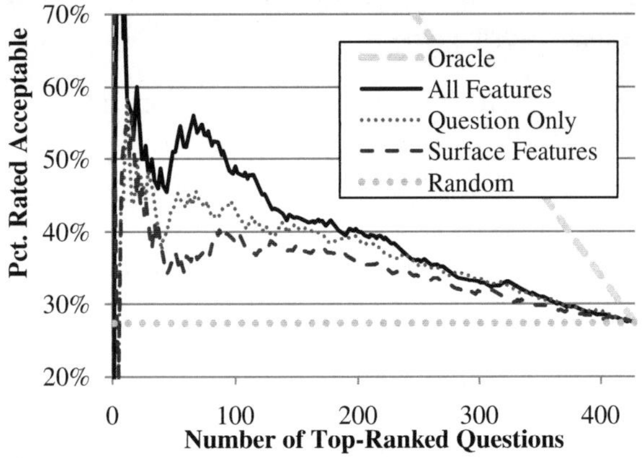

Figure 2: A graph of the percentage of acceptable questions in the top-N questions in the test set, using various rankings, for N varying from 0 to the size of the test set. The percentages become increasingly unstable when restricted to very few questions (e.g., < 50).

Features	#	Top 20%	Top 40%
All	187	52.3	40.8
All – Length	160	52.3	42.1
All – WH	178	50.6	39.8
All – Negation	186	51.7	39.3
All – Lang. Model	181	51.2	39.9
All – Grammatical	69	43.2	38.7
All – Transforms	179	46.5	39.0
All – Vagueness	169	48.3	41.5
All – Histograms	53	49.4	39.8
Surface	43	39.5	37.6
Question Only	91	41.9	39.5
Random	-	27.3	27.3
Oracle	-	100.0	87.3

Table 2: The total numbers of features (#) and the percentages of the top 20% and 40% of ranked test set questions labeled acceptable, for rankers built from variations of the complete set of features ("All"). E.g., "All – WH" is the set of all features *except* WH word features.

to 7.0%, while ungrammaticality dropped from 14.0% to 10.5%, and the other, less prevalent, categories changed very little.[13]

7.4 Ablation Study

Ablation experiments were also conducted to study the effects of removing each of the different types of features. Table 2 presents the percentages of acceptable test set questions in the top 20% and top 40% when they are scored by rankers trained with various feature sets that are defined by removing various feature types from the set of all possible features.

Grammatical features appear to be the most important: removing them from the feature set resulted in a 9.0% absolute drop in acceptability in the top 20% of questions, from 52.3% to 43.3%.

Some of the features did not appear to be particularly helpful, notably the N-gram language model features. We speculate that they might improve results when used with a larger, less noisy training set.

Performance did not drop precipitously upon the removal of any particular feature type, indicating a high amount of shared variance among the features. However, removing several types of features at once led to somewhat larger drops in performance. For example, using only surface features led to a 12.8% drop in acceptability in the top 20%, and using only features of questions led to a 10.4% drop.

8 Conclusion

By ranking the output of rule-based natural language generation system, existing knowledge about WH-movement from linguistics can be leveraged to model the complex transformations and long distance dependencies present in questions. Also, in this overgenerate-and-rank framework, a statistical ranker trained from a small set of annotated questions can capture trends related to question quality that are not easily encoded with rules. In our experiments, we found that ranking approximately doubled the acceptability of the top-ranked questions generated by our approach.

Acknowledgments

We acknowledge partial support from the Institute of Education Sciences, U.S. Department of Education, through Grant R305B040063 to Carnegie Mellon University; and from the National Science Foundation through a Graduate Research Fellowship for the first author and grant IIS-0915187 to the second author. We thank the anonymous reviewers for their comments.

[13]We speculate that improvements in syntactic parsing and entity recognition would reduce the proportion of ungrammatical questions and incorrect WH words, respectively.

References

D. M. Bikel, R. Schwartz, and R. M. Weischedel. 1999. An algorithm that learns what's in a name. *Machine Learning*, 34(1-3).

P. F. Brown, J. Cocke, S. A. Della Pietra, V. J. Della Pietra, F. Jelinek, J. D. Lafferty, R. L. Mercer, and P. S. Roossin. 1990. A statistical approach to machine translation. *Computational Linguistics*, 16(2).

N. Chomsky. 1973. Conditions on transformations. *A Festschrift for Morris Halle*.

M. Collins. 1999. *Head-Driven Statistical Models for Natural Language Parsing*. Ph.D. thesis, University of Pennsylvania.

M. Collins. 2000. Discriminative reranking for natural language parsing. In *Proc. of ICML*.

H. T. Dang, D. Kelly, and J. Lin. 2008. Overview of the TREC 2007 question answering track. In *Proc. of TREC*.

W. B. Dolan and C. Brockett. 2005. Automatically constructing a corpus of sentential paraphrases. In *Proc. of IWP*.

B. Dorr and D. Zajic. 2003. Hedge Trimmer: A parse-and-trim approach to headline generation. In *Proc. of Workshop on Automatic Summarization*.

A. Echihabi and D. Marcu. 2003. A noisy-channel approach to question answering. In *Proc. of ACL*.

B. Efron and R. Tibshirani. 1993. *An Introduction to the Bootstrap*. Chapman & Hall/CRC.

D. M. Gates. 2008. Generating reading comprehension look-back strategy questions from expository texts. Master's thesis, Carnegie Mellon University.

O. Glickman, I. Dagan, and M. Koppel. 2005. A probabilistic classification approach for lexical textual entailment. In *Proc. of AAAI*.

A. Goldberg. 2006. *Constructions at Work: The Nature of Generalization in Language*. Oxford University Press, New York.

S. Harabagiu, A. Hickl, J. Lehmann, and D. Moldovan. 2005. Experiments with interactive question-answering. In *Proc. of ACL*.

Michael Heilman and Noah A. Smith. 2009. Question generation via overgenerating transformations and ranking. Technical Report CMU-LTI-09-013, Language Technologies Institute, Carnegie Mellon University.

E. Hovy, U. Hermjakob, and C. Lin. 2001. The use of external knowledge in factoid QA. In *Proc. of TREC*.

N. Ide and K. Suderman. 2004. The american national corpus first release. In *Proc. of LREC*.

D. Klein and C. D. Manning. 2003. Fast exact inference with a factored model for natural language parsing. In *Advances in NIPS 15*.

R. Kneser and H. Ney. 1995. Improved backing-off for m-gram language modeling. In *Proc. of IEEE Int. Conf. Acoustics, Speech and Signal Processing*.

K. Knight and D. Marcu. 2000. Statistics-based summarization - step one: Sentence compression. In *Proc. of the Seventeenth National Conference on Artificial Intelligence and Twelfth Conference on Innovative Applications of Artificial Intelligence*.

H. Kunichika, T. Katayama, T. Hirashima, and A. Takeuchi. 2004. Automated question generation methods for intelligent English learning systems and its evaluation. In *Proc. of ICCE*.

J. R. Landis and G. G. Koch. 1977. The measurement of observer agreement for categorical data. *Biometrics*, 33.

I. Langkilde and Kevin Knight. 1998. Generation that exploits corpus-based statistical knowledge. In *Proc. of ACL*.

S. le Cessie and J. C. van Houwelingen. 1997. Ridge estimators in logistic regression. *Applied Statistics*, 41.

R. Levy and G. Andrew. 2006. Tregex and Tsurgeon: tools for querying and manipulating tree data structures. In *Proc. of LREC*.

M. P. Marcus, B. Santorini, and M. A. Marcinkiewicz. 1993. Building a large annotated corpus of English: The Penn Treebank. *Computational Linguistics*, 19.

R. Mitkov and L. A. Ha. 2003. Computer-aided generation of multiple-choice tests. In *Proc. of the HLT-NAACL 03 workshop on Building educational applications using natural language processing*.

R. Mitkov, L. A. Ha, and N. Karamanis. 2006. A computer-aided environment for generating multiple-choice test items. *Natural Language Engineering*, 12(2).

D. Ravichandran and E. Hovy. 2001. Learning surface text patterns for a question answering system. In *Proc. of ACL*.

E. Reiter and R. Dale. 1997. Building applied natural language generation systems. *Nat. Lang. Eng.*, 3(1).

J. R. Ross. 1967. *Constraints on Variables in Syntax*. Phd dissertation, MIT, Cambridge, MA.

V. Rus and A. Graessar, editors. 2009. *The Question Generation Shared Task and Evaluation Challenge*. `http://www.questiongeneration.org`.

V. Rus and J. Lester, editors. 2009. *Proc. of the 2nd Workshop on Question Generation*. IOS Press.

K. Toutanova, C. Brockett, M. Gamon, J. Jagarlamudi, H. Suzuki, and L. Vanderwende. 2007. The PYTHY summarization system: Microsoft research at duc 2007. In *Proc. of DUC*.

E. M. Voorhees. 2004. Overview of the TREC 2003 question answering track. In *Proc. of TREC 2003*.

M. A. Walker, O. Rambow, and M. Rogati. 2001. Spot: a trainable sentence planner. In *Proc. of NAACL*.

Not All Seeds Are Equal: Measuring the Quality of Text Mining Seeds

Zornitsa Kozareva and Eduard Hovy
USC Information Sciences Institute
4676 Admiralty Way
Marina del Rey, CA 90292-6695
{kozareva,hovy}@isi.edu

Abstract

Open-class semantic lexicon induction is of great interest for current knowledge harvesting algorithms. We propose a general framework that uses patterns in bootstrapping fashion to learn open-class semantic lexicons for different kinds of relations. These patterns require seeds. To estimate the *goodness* (the potential yield) of new seeds, we introduce a regression model that considers the connectivity behavior of the seed during bootstrapping. The generalized regression model is evaluated on six different kinds of relations with over 10000 different seeds for English and Spanish patterns. Our approach reaches robust performance of 90% correlation coefficient with 15% error rate for any of the patterns when predicting the *goodness* of seeds.

1 Introduction: What is a Good Seed?

The automated construction of semantically typed lexicons (terms classified into their appropriate semantic class) from unstructured text is of great importance for various kinds of information extraction (Grishman and Sundheim, 1996), question answering (Moldovan et al., 1999), and ontology population (Suchanek et al., 2007). Maintaining large semantic lexicons is a time-consuming and tedious task, because open classes (such as: all singers, all types of insects) are hard to cover completely, and even closed classes (such as: all countries, all large software companies) change over time. Since it is practically impossible for a human to collect such knowledge adequately, many supervised, unsupervised, and semi-supervised techniques have been developed.

All these techniques employ some sort of context to specify the appearance in text of the desired information. This approach is based on the general intuition, dating back at least to the distributional similarity idea of (Harris, 1954), that certain contexts are specific enough to constrain terms or expressions within them to be specific classes or types. Often, the context is a string of words with an empty slot for the desired term(s); sometimes, it is a regular expression-like pattern that includes word classes (syntactic or semantic); sometimes, it is a more abstract set of features, including orthographic features like capitalization, words, syntactic relations, semantic types, and other characteristics, which is the more complete version of the distributional similarity approach.

In early information extraction work, these contexts were constructed manually, and resembled regular expressions (Appelt et al., 1995). More recently, researchers have focused on learning them automatically. Since unsupervised algorithms require large training data and may or may not produce the types and granularities of the semantic class desired by the user, and supervised algorithms may require a lot of manual oversight, semi-supervised algorithms have become more popular. They require only a couple of seeds (examples filling the desired semantic context) to enable the learning mechanism to learn patterns that extract from unlabeled texts additional instances of the same class (Riloff and Jones, 1999; Etzioni et al., 2005; Pasca, 2004).

Sometimes, the pattern(s) learned are satisfactory

Human Language Technologies: The 2010 Annual Conference of the North American Chapter of the ACL, pages 618–626,
Los Angeles, California, June 2010.

enough to need no further elaboration. They are applied to harvest as many additional terms of the desired type as possible (for example, the instance-learning pattern '*<type> such as ?*' introduced in (Hearst, 1992)). More often, the method is applied recursively: once some pattern(s) have been learned, they are used to find additional terms, which are then used as new seeds in the patterns to search for additional new patterns, etc., until no further patterns are found. At that point, the satisfactory patterns are selected and large-scale harvesting proceeds as usual. In an interesting variation of this method, (Kozareva et al., 2008) describe the 'doubly-anchored pattern' (DAP) that includes a seed term in conjunction with the open slot for the desired terms to be learned, making the pattern itself recursive by allowing learned terms to replace the initial seed terms directly: '*<type> such as <seed> and ?*'.

Context-based information harvesting is well understood and has been the focus of extensive research. The core unsolved problem is the selection of seeds. In current knowledge harvesting algorithms, seeds are chosen either at random (Davidov et al., 2007; Kozareva et al., 2008), by picking the top N most frequent terms of the desired class (Riloff and Jones, 1999; Igo and Riloff, 2009), or by asking experts (Pantel et al., 2009). None of these methods is quite satisfactory. (Etzioni et al., 2005) report on the impact of seed set noise on the final performance of semantic class learning, and Pantel et al. observe a tremendous variation in the entity set expansion depending on the initial seed set composition. These studies show that the selection of 'good' seeds is very important. Recently, (Vyas et al., 2009) proposed an automatic system for improving the seeds generated by editors (Pantel et al., 2009). The results show 34% improvement in final performance using the appropriate seed set. However, using editors to select seeds or to guide their seed selection process is expensive and therefore not always possible. Because of this, we address in this paper two questions: "*What is a good seed?*" and "*How can the goodness of seeds be automatically measured without human intervention?*".

The contributions of this paper are as follows:

- First, we use recursive patterns to automatically learn seeds for open-class semantic lexicons.
- Second, we define what the 'goodness' of a seed term is. Then we introduce a regression model of seed quality measurement that, after a certain amount of training, automatically estimates the goodness of new seeds with above 90% accuracy for bootstrapping with the given relation.
- Next, importantly, we discover that training a regression model on certain relations enables one to predict the goodness of a seed even for other relations that have never been seen before, with an accuracy rate of over 80%.
- We conduct experiments with six kinds of relations and more than 10000 automatically harvested seed examples in both English and Spanish.

The rest of the paper is organized as follows. In the next section, we review related work. Section 3 describes the recursive pattern bootstrapping (Kozareva et al., 2008). Section 4 presents our seed quality measurement regression model. Section 5 discusses experiments and results. Finally, we conclude in Section 6.

2 Related Work

Seeds are used in automatic pattern extraction from text corpora (Riloff and Jones, 1999) and from the Web (Banko, 2009). Seeds are used to harvest instances (Pasca, 2004; Etzioni et al., 2005; Kozareva et al., 2008) or attributes of a given class (Paşca and Van Durme, 2008), or to learn concept-specific relations (Davidov et al., 2007), or to expand already existing entity sets (Pantel et al., 2009). As mentioned above, (Etzioni et al., 2005) report that seed set composition affects the correctness of the harvested instances, and (Pantel et al., 2009) observe an increment of 42% precision and 39% recall between the best and worst performing seed sets for the task of entity set expansion.

Because of the large diversity of the usage of seeds, there has been no general agreement regarding exactly how many seeds are necessary for a given task. According to (Pantel et al., 2009) 10 to 20 seeds are a sufficient starting set in a distributional similarity model to discover as many new correct instances as may ever be found. This observation differs from the claim of (Paşca and Van Durme, 2008) that 1 or 2 instances are sufficient to discover thousands of instance attributes. For some pattern-based algorithms one to two seeds are sufficient (Davidov et al., 2007; Kozareva et al., 2008), some require ten seeds (Riloff and Jones, 1999; Igo and Riloff, 2009), and others use a variation of 1, 5, 10 to 25 seeds (Talukdar et al., 2008).

As mentioned, seed selection is not yet well understood. Seeds may be chosen at random (Davidov et al., 2007; Kozareva et al., 2008), by picking the most frequent terms of the desired class (Riloff and Jones, 1999; Igo and Riloff, 2009), or by asking humans (Pantel et al., 2009). The intuitions for seed selection that experts develop over time seem to prefer instances that are neither ambiguous nor too frequent, but that at the same time are prolific and quickly lead to the discovery of a diverse set of instances. These criteria are vague and do not always lead to the discovery of good seeds. For some approaches, infrequent and ambiguous seeds are acceptable while for others they lead to deterioration in performance. For instance, the DAP (Kozareva et al., 2008) performance is not affected by the ambiguity of the seed, because the class and the seed in the pattern mutually disambiguate each other, while for the distributional similarity model of (Pantel et al., 2009), starting with an ambiguous seed leads to 'leakage' and the harvesting of non-true class instances. (Kozareva et al., 2008) show that for the closed class *country*, both high-frequency seeds like *USA* and low-frequency seeds like *Burkina Faso* can equally well yield all remaining instances. An open question to which no-one provides an answer is whether and which high/low frequency seeds can yield all instances of large, open classes like people or singers.

3 Bootstrapping Recursive Patterns

There are many algorithms for harvesting information from the Web. The main objective of our work is not the creation of a new algorithm, but rather determining the effect of seed selection on the general class of recursive bootstrapping harvesting algorithms for the acquisition of semantic lexicons for open class relations. For our experiments, since it is time-consuming and difficult for humans to provide large sets of seeds to start the bootstrapping process, we employ the recursive DAP mechanism introduced by (Kozareva et al., 2008) that produces seeds on its own.

The algorithm starts with a *seed* of type *class* which is fed into the doubly-anchored pattern '*<class> such as <seed> and* *' and learns in the * position new instances of type *class*. The newly learned instances are then systematically placed into the position of the *seed* in the DAP pattern, and the harvesting process is repeated until no new instances are found. The general framework is as follows:

1. Given:
   a language L={English, Spanish}
   a pattern P_i={e.g., [verb prep, noun, verb]}
   a seed $seed$ for P_i
2. Build a query in DAP-like fashion for P_i using template T_i of the type 'class such as $seed$ and *', '* and $seed$ verb prep', '* and $seed$ noun', '* and $seed$ verb'
3. submit T_i to Yahoo! or another search engine
4. extract instances occupying the * position
5. take instances from 4. and go to 2.
6. repeat steps 2–5 until no new instances are found

At the end of bootstrapping, the harvested instances can be considered to be seeds with which the bootstrapping procedure could have been initiated. We can now compare any of them to study their relative 'goodness' as bootstrapping seeds.

4 Seed Quality Measurement

4.1 Problem Formulation

We define our task as:

Task Definition: Given a seed and a pattern in a language (say English or Spanish), (1) use the bootstrapping procedure to learn instances from the Web; (2) build a predictive model to estimate the 'goodness' of seeds (whether generated by a human or learned) .

Given a desired semantic class, a recursive harvesting pattern expressing its context, and a seed term for use in this pattern, we define the 'goodness' of the seed as consisting of two measures:

- the *yield*: the total number of instances learned, not counting duplicates, until the bootstrapping procedure has run to exhaustion;
- the *distance*: the number of iterations required by the process to reach exhaustion.

Our approach is to build a model of the behavior of many seeds for the given pattern. Any new seed can then be compared against this model, once its basic characteristics have been determined, and its yield and distance estimates produced. In order to determine the characteristics of the new seed, it first has to be employed in the pattern for a small number of iterations. The next subsection describes the regression model we employ in our approach.

4.2 Regression Model

Given a seed s, we seek to predict the yield g of s as defined above. We do this via a parametrized function f:$\hat{g} = f(s; w)$, where $w \in R^d$ are the weights. Our approach is to learn w from a collection of N training examples $\{< s_i, g_i >\}_{i=1}^{N}$, where each s_i is a seed and each $g_i \in R$.

Support vector regression (Drucker et al., 1996) is a well-known method for training a regression model by solving the following optimization problem:

$$\min_{w \in R^s} \frac{1}{2}||w||^2 + \frac{C}{N} \sum_{i=1}^{N} \underbrace{\max(0, |g_i - f(s_i; w)| - \epsilon)}_{\epsilon\text{-insensitive loss function}}$$

where C is a regularization constant and ϵ controls the training error. The training algorithm finds weights w that define a function f minimizing the empirical risk.

Let h be a function from seeds into some vector-space representation $\subseteq R^d$, then the function f takes the form: $f(s; w) = h(s)^T w = \sum_{i=1}^{N} \alpha_i K(s, s_i)$, where f is re-parameterized in terms of a polynomial kernel function K with dual weights α_i. K measures the similarity between two seeds. Full details of the regression model and its implementation are beyond the scope of this paper; for more details see (Schölkopf and Smola, 2001; Smola et al., 2003). In our experimental study, we use the freely available implementation of SVM in Weka (Witten and Frank, 2005).

To evaluate the quality of our prediction model, we compare the actual yield of a seed with the predicted value obtained, and compute the correlation coefficient and the relative absolute error.

5 Experiments and Results

5.1 Data Collection

We conducted an exhaustive evaluation study with the open semantic classes *people* and *city*, initiated with the seeds *John* and *London*. For each class, we submitted the DAP patterns as web queries to Yahoo!Boss and retrieved the top 1000 web snippets for each query, keeping only unique instances. In total, we collected 1.5GB of snippets for people and 1.9GB of snippets for cities. The algorithm ran until complete exhaustion, requiring 19 iterations for people and 12 for cities. The total number of unique harvested instances was 3798 for people and 5090 for cities. We used all instances as seeds and instantiated for each seed the bootstrapping process from the very beginning. This resulted in 3798 and 5090 separate bootstrapping runs for people and cities respectively. For each seed, we recorded the total number of instances learned at the end of bootstrapping, the number of iterations, and the number of unique instances extracted on each iteration. After the harvesting part terminated, we analyzed the connectivity / bootstrapping behavior of the seeds, and produced the regression model.

5.2 Seed Characteristics

For many knowledge harvesting algorithms, the selection of a non-ambiguous seeds is of great importance. In the DAP bootstrapping framework, the ambiguity of the seed is eliminated as the *class* and the *seed* mutually disambiguate each other. Of great importance to the bootstrapping algorithm is the selection of a seed that can yield a large number of instances and can keep the bootstrapping process energized.

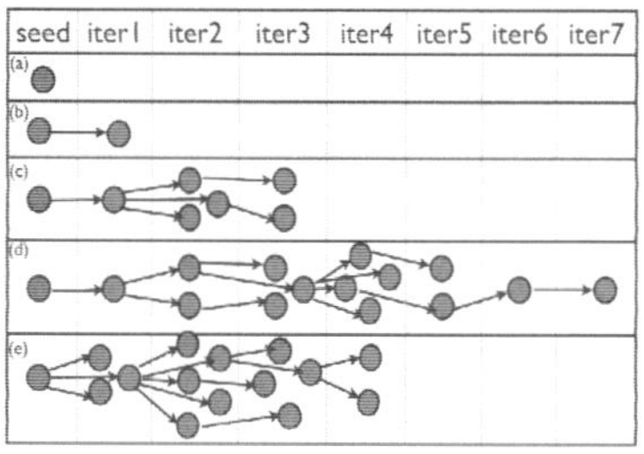

Figure 1: Seed Connectivity

Figure 1 shows the different kinds of seeds we found on analyzing the results of the bootstrapping process. Based on the yield learned on each iteration, we identify four major kinds of seeds: **hermit**, **one-step**, **mid**, and **high** connectors. In the figure, seed (a) is a hermit because it does not discover other instances. Seed (b) is a one-step connector as it discovers instances on the first iteration but then becomes inactive. Seeds (d) and (e) are high connectors because they find a rich population of instances. Seed (c) is a mid connector because it has lower yield than (d) and (e), but higher than (a) and (b).

Table 1 shows the results of classifying the 3798 people and 5090 city seeds into the four kinds of seed. The majority of the seeds for both patterns are hermits, from 23 to 41% are high connectors, and the rest are one-step and mid connectors. For each kind of seed, we also show three examples.

people such as X and *		examples
#hermit	2271 (60%)	Leila, Anne Boleyn, Sophocles
#one-step	329 (9%)	Helene, Frida Kahlo, Cornelius
#mid	315 (8%)	Brent, Ferdinand, Olivia
#high	883 (23%)	Diana, Donald Trump, Christopher
cities such as X and *		examples
#hermit	2393 (47%)	Belfast, Najafabad, El Mirador
#one-step	406 (8%)	Durnstein, Wexford, Al-Qaim
#mid	207 (4%)	Bialystok, Gori, New Albany
#high	2084 (41%)	Vienna, Chicago, Marrakesh

Table 1: Connectivity-based Seed Classification.

This study shows that humans are very likely to choose non-productive seeds for bootstrapping: it is difficult for a human to know a priori that a name like Diana will be more productive than Leila, Helene, or Olivia.

Another interesting characteristic of a seed is the speed of learning. Some seeds, such as (e), extract large quantity of instances from the very beginning, resulting in fewer bootstrapping iterations, while others, such as (d), spike much later, resulting in more. In our analysis, we found that some high connector seeds of the people pattern can learn the whole population in 12 iterations, while others require from 15 to 20 iterations. Figure 2 shows the speed of learning of ten high connector seeds for the *people* pattern. The y axis shows the number of unique instances harvested on each iteration. Intuitively, a good seed is the one that produces a large *yield* of instances in short *distance*. Thus the 'goodness' of seed (e) is better than that of seed (d).

As shown in Figure 2, for each seed, we observe a single hump that corresponds to the point in which a seed generates the maximum number of instances. The peak occurs on different iterations because it is dependent both on the yield learned with each iteration and the total distance, for each seed. The occurrence of a single hump reveals regularity in the connectivity behavior of seeds, and is discussed in the Conclusion. We model this behavior as features in our regression model and use it to measure the quality of new seeds. The next subsection explains the features of the regression model and the experimental results obtained.

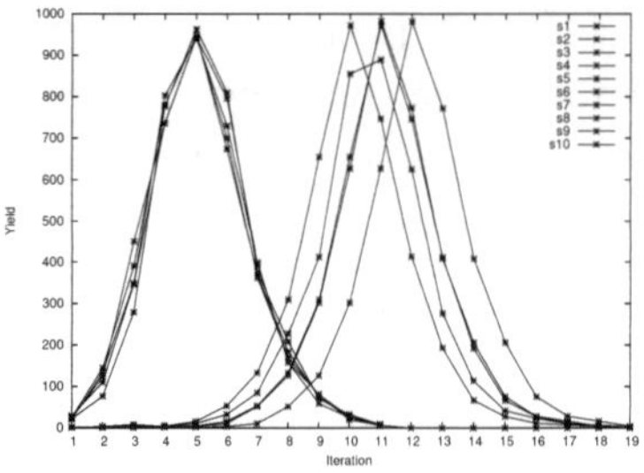

Figure 2: Seed Learning Speed

5.3 Predicting the Goodness of Seeds

Building a pattern specific model: For each pattern, we build N different regression models, where N corresponds to the total number of bootstrapping iterations of the pattern. For regression model R_i, we use the yield of a seed from iterations 1 to i as features. This information is used to model the activity of the seed in the bootstrapping process and later on to predict the extraction power of new seeds. For example, in Figure 1 on the first iteration seeds (b), (c), and (d) have the same low connectivity compared to seed (e). As bootstrapping progresses, seed (d) reaches productive neighbors that discover more instances, while seeds (b) and (c) become inactive. This example shows that the yield in the initial stage of bootstrapping is not sufficient to accurately predict the quality of the seeds. Since we do not know exactly how many iterations are necessary to accurately determine the 'goodness' of seeds, we model the yield learned on each iteration by each seed and subsequently include this information in the regression models.

The yield of a seed s_k at iteration i is computed as $yield(s_k)_i = \sum_{m=1}^{n}(s_m)$, where n is the total number of unique instances s_m harvested on iteration i. $Yield(s_k)_i$ is high when s_k discovers a large number of instances (new seeds), and small otherwise. For hermit seeds, $yield$=0 at any iteration, because the seeds are totally isolated and do not discover other instances (seeds). For example, when building the second regression model R_2 using seeds (d) and (e) from Figure 1, the feature values corresponding to each seed in R_2 are: $yield(s_d)_1$=1 and $yield(s_d)_2$=2 for seed (d), and $yield(s_e)_1$=3 and $yield(s_e)_2$=5 for seed (e).

Results: Figure 3 shows the correlation coefficients (cc) and the relative absolute errors of each regression model R_i for the *people* and *city* patterns. The results are computed over ten-fold cross validation of the 3798 people and 5090 city seeds. The x axis shows the regression model R_i,. The y axis in the two upper graphs shows the correlation coefficient of the predicted and the actual total yield of the seeds using R_i, and in the two lower graphs, the y axis shows the error rate of each R_i.

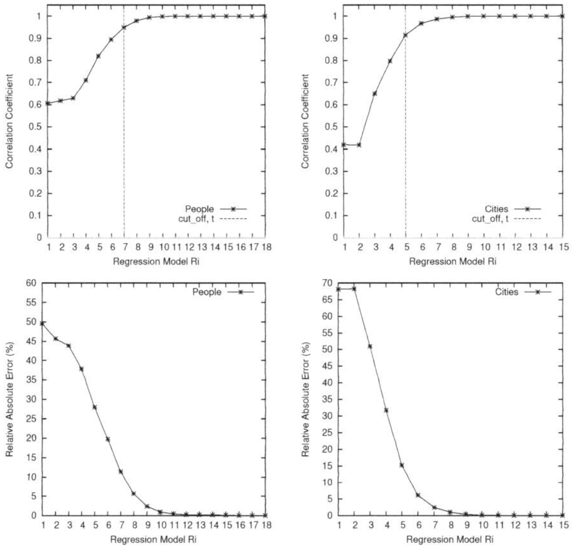

Figure 3: Regression for People and City.

We consider as a baseline model the regression R_1 which uses only the yield of the seeds on first iteration. The prediction of R_1 has cc=0.6 with 50% error for people and cc=0.4 with 70% error for cities. These results confirm our previous observation that the quality of the seeds cannot be accurately measured in the very beginning of bootstrapping. However, by the ninth iteration, the regression models for people and cities reach cc=1.0 with 5% error rate. To make such an accurate prediction, the model uses around one half of all bootstrapping iterations—generally, just past the hump in Figure 2, once the yield starts dropping.

Often in real applications or when under limited resources (e.g., a fixed amount of Web queries per day), running half the bootstrapping iterations is not feasible. This problem can be resolved by employing different stopping criteria, at the cost of lower cc and greater error. For example, one cut-off point can be the (averaged) iteration number of the hump for the given pattern. For people, the average hump occurs at the seventh iteration, and for the city at the fifth iteration. At this point, both patterns have a cc=0.9 with 15% error rate. An alternative stopping point can be the fourth iteration, where cc=0.7–0.8 with 35% error.

Overall, our study shows that it is possible to model the behavior of seeds and use it to accurately predict the 'goodness' of previously unseen seeds. The results obtained for both *people* and *city* patterns are very promising. However, a disadvantage of this regression is that it requires training over the whole extent of the given pattern. Also, each regression model is specific to the particular pattern it is trained over. Next, we propose a generalized regression model which surmounts the problem of training pattern-specific regression models.

5.4 Generalized Model for Goodness of Seeds

We built a generalized regression model (RG) combining evidence from the people and city patterns. We generated the features of each model as previously described in Section 5.3. From each pattern, we randomly picked 1000 examples which resulted in 30% of the people and 20% of the city seeds. We used these seed examples to train the RG_i models. In total, we built 15 RG_i, which is the maximum number of overlapping iterations between the two patterns. We tested our RG model with the remaining 2798 people and 4090 city seeds.

Figure 4 shows the results of the RG_i models for the people and city patterns. In the first two iterations, the predictions of the RG model are poorer compared to the pattern-specific regression. On the fourth iteration, both models have cc=0.7 and 0.8 for the people and city patterns respectively. The error rates of the generalized model are 41% and 35% for people and city, while for the pattern-specific model the errors are 37% and 32%. The early iterations show a difference of around 4% in the error rate of the two models, but around the ninth iteration both models have comparable results.

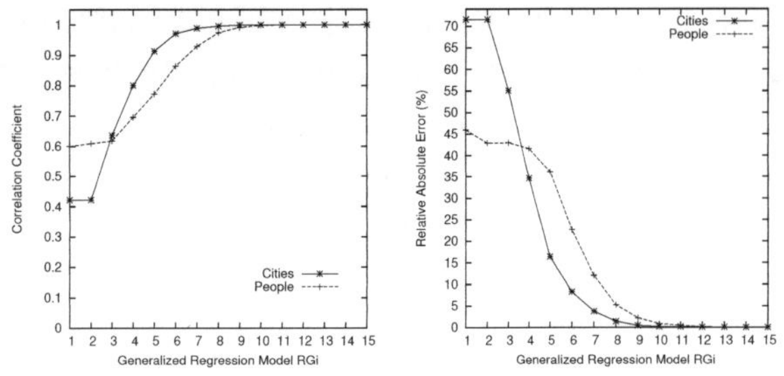

Figure 4: Generalized Regression for People and City.

This study shows that it is possible to combine evidence from two patterns harvesting different semantic information to predict accurately the behavior of unseen seed examples for either of the two patterns.

5.5 Evaluating the Generalized Model on Different Languages and Kinds of Patterns

So far, we have studied the performance of the generalized seed quality prediction method for specific patterns in English. However, the connectivity behavior of the seeds might change for other languages and kinds of patterns, making the generalized model impractical to use in such cases. To verify this, we evaluated the generalized model (RG) from Section 5.4 with the people and city patterns in Spanish (‘ *gente como X y ** ’ and ‘ *ciudades como X y ** ’), as well as with two new kinds of patterns (‘ ** and X fly to*’ and ‘ ** and X work for*’[1]). For each pattern, we ran the bootstrapping process from Section 3 until exhaustion and collected all seeds.

First, for each pattern we studied the connectivity behavior of the seeds. Table 2 shows the obtained results. The distribution is similar to the seed distribution for the English people and cities patterns. Although the total number of harvested instances (i.e., seeds) is different for each pattern, the proportion of hermits to other seeds remains larger. From 20% to 37% of the seeds are high connectors, and the rest are one-step and mid connectors. This analysis shows that the connectivity behavior of seeds across different languages and patterns is similar, at least for the examples studied. In addition to the seed analysis, we show in the table the total number of bootstrapping iterations for each pattern. The ‘*work for*’ and ‘*fly to*’ patterns run for a longer distance compared to the other patterns. While for the majority of the patterns the hump is observed on the fifth or seventh iteration, for these two patterns the average peak is observed on the fifteenth.

[1]The X indicates the position of the seed and (*) corresponds to the instances learned during bootstrapping.

	gente como X y	ciudades como X y
#hermit	318 (56%)	1061 (51%)
#one-step	58 (10%)	150 (8%)
#mid	79 (14%)	79 (4%)
#high	117 (20%)	795 (38%)
tot#iter	20	16
	and X fly to	and X work for
#hermit	389 (45%)	1262 (48%)
#one-step	87 (9%)	238 (9%)
#mid	75 (8%)	214 (8%)
#high	322 (37%)	922 (35%)
tot#iter	26	33

Table 2: Seed Classification for Spanish and Verb-Prep Patterns.

Second, we test the RG_i models from Section 5.4, which were trained on people and cities, to predict the total yield of the seeds in the new patterns. Figure 5 shows the correlation coefficient and the relative absolute error results of each pattern for RG_i.

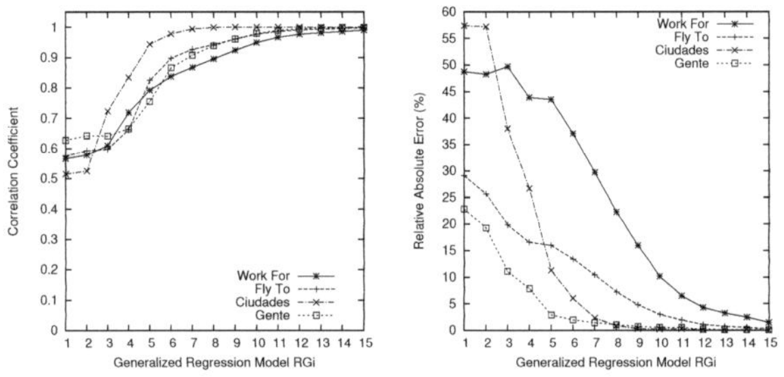

Figure 5: Generalized Regression for Different Languages and Patterns.

Interestingly, we found that our generalized method has consistent performance across the different languages and patterns. On the twelfth iteration, the model is able to predict the ‘goodness’ of seeds with cc=1.0 and from 0.4% to 8.0% error rate. Around the fifth and sixth iterations, all patterns reach cc=0.8 with error of 5% to 15%. The higher error bound is for patterns like ‘work for’ and ‘fly to’ which run for a longer distance. This experimental study confirms the robustness of our generalized model which is trained on the behavior of seeds from one kind of pattern and tested with seeds in different languages and on completely different kinds of patterns.

6 Conclusions and Future Work

It would, a fortiori, seem impossible to estimate the goodness of a seed term used in a recursive bootstrapping pattern for harvesting information from the web. After all, its eventual total yield and distance depend on the cumulation of the terms produced in each iteration of the bootstrapping, and there are no external constraints or known web language structure to be exploited.

We have shown that it is possible to create, using regression, a model of the grown behavior of seeds for a given pattern, and fitting it with an indication of a new seed's growth (considering its grown behavior in a limited number of bootstrapping iterations) in order to obtain a quite reliable estimate of the new seed's eventual yield and distance.

Going further, we are delighted to observe that the regularity of the single-hump harvesting behavior makes it possible to learn a regression model that enables one to predict, with some accuracy, both the yield and the distance of a new seed, even when the pattern being considered is not yet seen. All that is required is the indication of the seed's growth behavior, obtained through a number of iterations using the pattern of interest.

Our ongoing analysis takes the following approach. Let T_i be the set of all new terms (terms not yet found) harvested during iteration i. Then $T_0 = \{t_{0,1}\}$, just the initial seed term. Let $NY(t_{i,j})$ be the novel yield of term $t_{i,j}$, that is, the number of as yet undiscovered terms produced by a single application of the pattern using the term $t_{i,j}$. Notice that bootstrapping ceases when for some $i = d$ (the distance), $\sum_j NY(t_{d,j}) = 0$. Since the total number of terms that can be learned, $\sum_{i=0}^{d} \sum_j NY(t_{i,j}) = N$, is finite and fixed, there are exactly three alternatives for the growth of the NY curve when it is shown summed over each iteration: (i) either $\sum_j NY(t_{i,j}) = \sum_j NY(t_{i+1,j})$ and there is no larger NY sum for any iteration; or (ii) $\sum_j NY(t_{i,j})$ grows to a maximal value for some iteration $i = m$ and then decreases again; or (iii) $\sum_j NY(t_{i,j})$ reaches more than one locally maximal value at different iterations. The first case, in which exactly the same number of new terms is harvested every iteration for several or all iterations, would require that each new term once learned yields precisely and only one subsequent new term, or that the number of hermits is exactly balanced by the NY of one or more of the other terms in that iteration. This situation is so unlikely as to be dismissed outright. Case (ii), in which there is a single hump, appears to be how text is written on the web, as shown in Figure 2. Case (iii), the multi-hump case, would require that the terms be linked in semi-disconnected 'islands', with a relatively much smaller inter-island connectivity than intra-island one. Given our studies, it appears that language on the web is not organized this way, at least not for the patterns we studied. However, it is not impossible: this two-hump case would have to have occurred in (Kozareva et al., 2008) when the ambiguous seed term *Georgia* was used in the DAP '*states such as Georgia and **', where initially the US states were harvested but, at some point, the learned term Georgia also initiated harvesting of the ex-USSR states. Such 'leakage' into a new semantic domain requires not only ambiguity of the seed but also parallel ambiguity of the class term, which is highly unlikely as well.

Accepting case (ii), therefore, we postulate that for any (or all regular) patterns there is some iteration m in which $\sum_j NY(t_{m,j})$ is maximal. The question is how rapidly the summed NY curve approaches it and then abates again. This depends on the out-degree connectivity of terms overall. In the population of N terms for a given semantic pattern, is the distribution of out-degrees Poisson (or Zipfian), or is it normal (Gaussian)? In the former case, there will be a few high-degree connector terms and a large number (the long tail) of one-step and hermit terms; in the latter, there will be a small but equal number of low-end and high-end connector terms, with the bulk of terms falling in the mid-connector range. One direction of our ongoing work is to determine this distribution, and to empirically derive its parameters. It might be possible to discover some interesting regularities about the (preferential) uses of terms within semantic domains, as reflected in term network connectivity.

Although not all seeds are equal, it appears to be possible to treat them with a single regression model, regardless of pattern, to predict their 'goodness'.

Acknowledgments: This research was supported by NSF grant IIS-0705091.

References

Douglas E. Appelt, Jerry R. Hobbs, John Bear, David Israel, Megumi Kameyama, Andy Kehler, David Martin, Karen Myers, and Mabry Tyson. 1995. SRI International FASTUS system MUC-6 test results and analysis. In *Proceedings of the Sixth Message Understanding Conference (MUC-6)*, pages 237–248.

Michele Banko. 2009. Open information extraction from the web. In *Ph.D. Dissertation from University of Washington*.

Dmitry Davidov, Ari Rappoport, and Moshel Koppel. 2007. Fully unsupervised discovery of concept-specific relationships by web mining. In *Proc. of the 45th Annual Meeting of the Association of Computational Linguistics*, pages 232–239, June.

Harris Drucker, Chris J.C. Burges, Linda Kaufman, Alex Smola, and Vladimir Vapnik. 1996. Support vector regression machines. In *Advances in NIPS*, pages 155–161.

Oren Etzioni, Michael Cafarella, Doug Downey, Ana-Maria Popescu, Tal Shaked, Stephen Soderland, Daniel S. Weld, and Alexander Yates. 2005. Unsupervised named-entity extraction from the web: an experimental study. *Artificial Intelligence*, 165(1):91–134, June.

Ralph Grishman and Beth Sundheim. 1996. Message understanding conference-6: a brief history. In *Proceedings of the 16th conference on Computational linguistics*, pages 466–471.

Zellig S. Harris. 1954. Distributional structure. *Word*, 10:140–162.

Marti Hearst. 1992. Automatic acquisition of hyponyms from large text corpora. In *Proc. of the 14th conference on Computational linguistics*, pages 539–545.

Sean Igo and Ellen Riloff. 2009. Corpus-based semantic lexicon induction with web-based corroboration. In *Proceedings of the Workshop on Unsupervised and Minimally Supervised Learning of Lexical Semantics*.

Zornitsa Kozareva, Ellen Riloff, and Eduard Hovy. 2008. Semantic class learning from the web with hyponym pattern linkage graphs. In *Proceedings of ACL-08: HLT*, pages 1048–1056.

Dan I. Moldovan, Sanda M. Harabagiu, Marius Pasca, Rada Mihalcea, Richard Goodrum, Roxana Girju, and Vasile Rus. 1999. Lasso: A tool for surfing the answer net. In *TREC*.

Marius Paşca and Benjamin Van Durme. 2008. Weakly-supervised acquisition of open-domain classes and class attributes from web documents and query logs. In *Proceedings of ACL-08: HLT*.

Patrick Pantel, Eric Crestan, Arkady Borkovsky, Ana-Maria Popescu, and Vishnu Vyas. 2009. Web-scale distributional similarity and entity set expansion. In *Proceedings of the 2009 Conference on Empirical Methods in Natural Language Processing*, pages 938–947, August.

Marius Pasca. 2004. Acquisition of categorized named entities for web search. In *Proc. of the thirteenth ACM international conference on Information and knowledge management*, pages 137–145.

Ellen Riloff and Rosie Jones. 1999. Learning dictionaries for information extraction by multi-level bootstrapping. In *AAAI '99/IAAI '99: Proceedings of the sixteenth national conference on Artificial intelligence and the eleventh Innovative applications of artificial intelligence conference innovative applications of artificial intelligence*.

Bernhard Schölkopf and Alexander J. Smola. 2001. *Learning with Kernels: Support Vector Machines, Regularization, Optimization, and Beyond (Adaptive Computation and Machine Learning)*. The MIT Press.

Alex J. Smola, Bernhard Schlkopf, and Bernhard Sch Olkopf. 2003. A tutorial on support vector regression. Technical report, Statistics and Computing.

Fabian M. Suchanek, Gjergji Kasneci, and Gerhard Weikum. 2007. Yago: a core of semantic knowledge. In *WWW '07: Proceedings of the 16th international conference on World Wide Web*, pages 697–706.

Partha Pratim Talukdar, Joseph Reisinger, Marius Pasca, Deepak Ravichandran, Rahul Bhagat, and Fernando Pereira. 2008. Weakly-supervised acquisition of labeled class instances using graph random walks. In *Proceedings of the Conference on Empirical Methods in Natural Language Processing, EMNLP 2008*, pages 582–590.

Vishnu Vyas, Patrick Pantel, and Eric Crestan. 2009. Helping editors choose better seed sets for entity set expansion. In *Proceedings of the 18th ACM Conference on Information and Knowledge Management, CIKM*, pages 225–234.

Ian H. Witten and Eibe Frank. 2005. *Data Mining: Practical Machine Learning Tools and Techniques*. Morgan Kaufmann, second edition.

Extracting Glosses to Disambiguate Word Senses

Weisi Duan
Carnegie Mellon University
Language Technologies Institute
5000 Forbes Ave.
Gates Hillman Complex 5407
Pittsburgh, PA 15213
wduan@cs.cmu.edu

Alexander Yates
Temple University
Computer and Information Sciences
1805 N. Broad St.
Wachman Hall 303A
Philadelphia, PA 19122
yates@temple.edu

Abstract

Like most natural language disambiguation tasks, word sense disambiguation (WSD) requires world knowledge for accurate predictions. Several proxies for this knowledge have been investigated, including labeled corpora, user-contributed knowledge, and machine readable dictionaries, but each of these proxies requires significant manual effort to create, and they do not cover all of the ambiguous terms in a language. We investigate the task of automatically extracting world knowledge, in the form of glosses, from an unlabeled corpus. We demonstrate how to use these glosses to automatically label a training corpus to build a statistical WSD system that uses no manually-labeled data, with experimental results approaching that of a supervised SVM-based classifier.

1 Introduction

For many semantic natural language processing tasks, systems require world knowledge to disambiguate language utterances. Word sense disambiguation (WSD) is no exception — systems for WSD require world knowledge to figure out which aspects of a word's context indicate one sense over another. A fundamental problem for WSD is that the required knowledge is open-ended. That is, for every ambiguous term, new kinds of information about the world become important, and the knowledge that a system may have acquired for previously-studied ambiguous terms may have little or no impact on the next ambiguous term. Thus open-ended knowledge acquisition is a fundamental obstacle to strong performance for this disambiguation task.

Researchers have investigated a variety of techniques that address this knowledge acquisition bottleneck in different ways. Supervised WSD techniques, for instance, can learn to associate features in the context of a word with a particular sense of that word. Knowledge-based techniques rely on machine-readable dictionaries or lexical resources like WordNet (Fellbaum, 1998) to provide the necessary knowledge. And most recently, systems have used resources like Wikipedia, which contain user-contributed knowledge in the form of sense-disambiguated links, to acquire world knowledge for WSD. Yet each of these approaches is limited by the amount of manual effort that is needed to build the necessary resources, and as a result the techniques are limited to a subset of English words for which the manually-constructed resources are available.

In this work we investigate an alternative approach that attacks the problem of knowledge acquisition head-on. We use information extraction (IE) techniques to extract *glosses*, or short textual characterizations of the meaning of one sense of a word. In the ideal case, we would extract full logical forms to define word senses, but here we instead focus on a more feasible, but still very useful, sub-task: for a given word sense, extract a collection of terms that are highly correlated with that sense and no other sense of the ambiguous word. Our system requires as input only an unlabeled corpus of documents that each contain the ambiguous term of interest.

In experiments, we demonstrate that our gloss extraction system can often determine key aspects of a word's senses. In one experiment our system was able to extract glosses with 60% precision for 20 ambiguous biomedical terms, while discovering 7 senses of those terms that never appeared in a widely-used dictionary of biomedical terminology. In addition, we demonstrate that our extracted glosses are useful for real WSD problems: our sys-

Human Language Technologies: The 2010 Annual Conference of the North American Chapter of the ACL, pages 627–635,
Los Angeles, California, June 2010. ©2010 Association for Computational Linguistics

tem outperforms a state-of-the-art unsupervised system, and it comes close to the performance of a supervised WSD system on a challenging dataset.

In the next section, we describe previous work. In Section 3, we formally define the gloss extraction task and refine it into a sub-task that is feasible for an IE approach, and Section 5 presents our technique for using extracted glosses in a WSD task. Section 6 discusses our experiments and results.

2 Previous Work

Many previous systems (Cui et al., 2007; Androutsopoulos and Galanis, 2005) have studied the related task of answering definitional questions on the Web, such as "What does cold mean?". Such systems are focused on information retrieval for human consumption, and especially on recall of definitional information (Velardi et al., 2008). They generally do not consider the problem of how to merge the large number of similar extracted definitions into a single item (Fujii and Ishikawa, 2000), so that the overall result contains one definition per sense of the word. A separate approach (Pasca, 2005) relies on the WordNet lexical database to supply the set of senses, and extracts alternate glosses for the senses that have already been defined. When glosses are to be used by computational methods, as in a WSD system in our case, it becomes critical that the system extract one coherent gloss per sense. As far as we are aware, no previous system has extracted glosses for word sense disambiguation.

Gloss extraction is related to the task of ontology extraction, in which systems extract hierarchies of word classes (Snow et al., 2006; Popescu et al., 2004). Gloss extraction differs from ontology extraction in that it extracts definitional information characterizing senses of a single word, rather than trying to place a word in a hierarchy of other words.

Most WSD systems have relied on hand-labeled training examples (Leroy and Rindflesch, 2004; Joshi et al., 2005; Mohammad and Pedersen, 2004) or on dictionary glosses (Lesk, 1986; Stevenson and Wilks, 2001) or the WordNet hierarchy (Boyd-Graber et al., 2007) to help make disambiguation choices. In recent coarse-grained evaluations, such systems have achieved accuracies of close to 90% (Pradhan et al., 2007; Agirre and Soroa, 2007; Schijvenaars et al., 2005). However, by some estimates, English contains over a million word types, and new words and new senses are added to the language every day. It is unreasonable to expect that any system will have access to hand-labeled training examples or useful dictionary glosses for each of them.

More recent techniques based on user-contributed knowledge (Mihalcea, 2007; Chklovski and Mihalcea, 2002; Milne and Witten, 2008), such as that found in Wikipedia, suffer from similar problems – Wikipedia contains many articles on well known entities, categories, and events, but very few articles that disambiguate verbs, adjectives, adverbs, and certain kinds of nouns which are poorly represented in an encyclopedia.

On the other hand, word usages in large corpora like the Web reflect nearly all of the word senses in use in English today, albeit without manually-supplied labels. Unsupervised approaches to WSD use clustering techniques to group instances of words into clusters that correspond to different senses (Pantel and Lin, 2002). While such systems are more general than supervised and dictionary-based approaches in that they can handle any word type and word sense, they have lagged behind other approaches in terms of accuracy thus far – for example, the best system in the recent word sense induction task of Semeval 2007 (Agirre and Soroa, 2007) achieved an F1 score of 78.7, slightly below the baseline (78.9) in which all instances of a word are part of a single cluster. Part of the problem is that the clustering techniques operate in a bag-of-words-like representation. This is an extremely high-dimensional space, and it is difficult in such a space to determine which dimensions are noise and which ones correlate with different senses. Our gloss extraction technique helps to address this curse of dimensionality by reducing the large vocabulary of a corpus to a much smaller set of terms that are highly relevant for WSD. Others (Kulkarni and Pedersen, 2005) have used feature selection techniques like mutual information to reduce dimensionality, but so far these techniques have only been able to find features that correlate with an ambiguous term. With gloss extraction, we are able to find features that correlate with individual senses of a term.

3 Overview: The Gloss Extraction Task

Given an input corpus C of documents where each document contains at least one instance of a *keyword* k, a Gloss Extraction system should produce a set of *glosses* $G = \{g_i\}$, where each g_i is a logical expression defining the meaning of a particular sense s_i of

Glosses:
1. cold(a) $\equiv$ isA(a, b) $\wedge$ disease(b) $\wedge$ symptom(a, c) $\wedge$ possibly-includes(c, d) $\wedge$ fever(d)
2. cold(a) $\equiv$ isA(a, b) $\wedge$ physical-entity(b) $\wedge$ temperature(a, c) $\wedge$ less-than(c, 25C)

Sense Indicators:
1. common cold, virus, symptom, fever
2. hot, ice cold, lukewarm, cold room, room temperature

Figure 1: **Example glosses and sense indicators for two senses of the word *cold*.**

k, to the exclusion of all other senses of k. Note that the system must discover the appropriate number of senses in addition to the gloss for each sense.

While extraction technology has made impressive advancements, it is not yet at a stage where it can produce full logical forms for sense glosses. As a first step towards this goal, we introduce the task of Sense Indicator Extraction, in which each gloss g_i consists of a set of features that, when present in the context of an instance of k, strongly indicate that the instance has sense s_i, and no other sense. Examples of both tasks are given in Figure 1. The Sense Indicator Extraction task represents a nontrivial extraction challenge, but it is much more feasible than full Gloss Extraction. And the task preserves key properties of Gloss Extraction: the results are quite useful for word sense disambiguation. The results are also readily interpreted upon inspection, making it easy to monitor a system's accuracy.

4 Extracting Word Sense Glosses

We present the GLOSSY system, an unsupervised information extraction system for Sense Indicator Extraction. GLOSSY proceeds in two phases: a *collocation detection* phase, in which the system detects components of the glosses, and an *arrangement* phase, in which the system decides how many distinct senses there are, and puts together the components of the glosses.

4.1 Collocation Detection

The first major challenge to a Gloss Extraction system is that the space of possible features is enormous, and almost all of them are irrelevant to the task at hand. Supervised techniques can use labeled examples to provide clues, but in an unsupervised setting the curse of dimensionality can be overwhelming. Indeed, unsupervised WSD techniques suffer from exactly this problem.

GLOSSY's answer to this problem is based on the following observation: pairs of potential features which rarely or never co-occur in the same document in a large corpus are likely to represent features for two distinct senses. The well-known observation that words rarely exhibit more than one sense per discourse (Yarowsky, 1995) implies that features closely associated with a particular sense have a low probability of appearing in the same document as features associated with another sense. Features that are independent of any particular sense of the keyword, on the other hand, have no such restriction, and are just as likely to appear in the context of one sense as any other. As a consequence, a low count for the co-occurrence of two potential features over a large corpus of documents for keyword k is a reliable indicator that the two features are part of the glosses of two distinct senses of k.

GLOSSY's collocation detector begins by indexing the corpus and counting the frequency of each vocabulary word. Using the index, the collocation detector determines all pairs of potential features such that each feature appears at least T times, and the pair of features never co-occurs in the same document. We call the pairs that this step finds the "non-overlapping" features. Finally, we rank the feature pairs according to the total number of documents they appear in, and choose the most frequent N pairs. This excludes non-overlapping pairs that have not been seen often enough to provide reliable evidence that they are features of different senses, and it cuts down on processing time for the next phase of the algorithm. The collocation detector outputs the set of features $F = \{f | \exists_{f'}(f, f')$ or (f', f) is one of the top N non-overlapping pairs$\}$. The GLOSSY system uses stems, words, and bigrams as potential features. We use $N = 100$ and $T = 50$ in our experiments. Figure 2 shows an example corpus and the set of features that the collocation detector would output.

Corpus of documents for term `cold`**:**
DOCUMENT 1: "Symptoms of the common cold may include fever, headache, sore throat, and coughing."
DOCUMENT 2: "Hibernation is a common response to the cold winter weather of temperate climates."

Non-overlapping feature pairs:
(symptoms,temperate) (headache, climate) (cold winter, common cold) (*response*, headache)

Detected collocations:
symptoms, temperate, headache, climate, cold winter, common cold, *response*

Arranged glosses:
`cold 1`: symptoms, common cold, headache
`cold 2`: temperate, climate, cold winter

Figure 2: **Example operation of the GLOSSY extraction system.** The collocation detector finds potential features using its non-overlapping pair heuristic. The arranger selects a subset of the potential features (in this example, it drops the feature *response*) and clusters them to produces glosses containing sense indicators.

4.2 Arranging Glosses

Given the corpus $\mathcal{C}$ for keyword k and the features F that GLOSSY's collocation detector has discovered, the arrangement phase groups these features into coherent sense glosses. Figure 2 shows an example of how the features found during collocation detection may be arranged to form coherent glosses for two senses of the word "cold."

GLOSSY's Arranger component uses a combination of a small set of statistics to determine whether a particular arrangement of the features into glosses is warranted, based on the given corpus. Let $\mathcal{A} \subset 2^F$ be an arrangement of the features into clusters representing glosses. We require that clusters in $\mathcal{A}$ be disjoint, but we do not require every feature in F to be included in a cluster in $\mathcal{A}$ — in other words, $\mathcal{A}$ is a partition of a subset of F. We define a scoring function S that is a linear interpolation of several statistics of the arrangement $\mathcal{A}$ and the corpus $\mathcal{C}$:

$$S(\mathcal{A}|\mathcal{C}, \mathbf{w}) = \sum_i w_i f_i(\mathcal{A}, \mathcal{C}) \qquad (1)$$

After experimenting with a number of options, we settled on the following for our statistics f_i:

NUMCLUSTERS: the number of clusters in $\mathcal{A}$. We use a negative weight for this statistic to favor fewer senses and encourage clustering.

DOCSCOVERED: the total number of documents in $\mathcal{C}$ in which at least one feature from $\mathcal{A}$ appears. We use this statistic to encourage the Arranger to find an arrangement that explains the sense of as many examples of the keyword as possible.

BADOVERLAPS: the number of pairs of features that co-occur in at least one document in $\mathcal{C}$, and that belong to different clusters of $\mathcal{A}$. A negative weight for this statistic encourages overlapping feature pairs to be placed in the same cluster.

BADNONOVERLAPS: the number of pairs of features that never co-occur in $\mathcal{C}$, and that belong to the same cluster in $\mathcal{A}$. A negative weight for this statistic encourages non-overlapping feature pairs to be placed in different clusters.

Given such an optimization function, the Arranger attempts to maximize its value by searching for an optimal $\mathcal{A}$. Note that this is a structured prediction task in which the choice for some sub-component of $\mathcal{A}$ can greatly affect the choice of other clusters and features. GLOSSY addresses this optimization problem with a greedy hill-climbing search with random restarts. Each round of hill-climbing is initialized with a randomly chosen subset of features, which are then all assigned to a single cluster. Using a randomly chosen search operator from a pre-defined set, the search procedure attempts to move to a new arrangement $\mathcal{A}'$. It accepts the move to $\mathcal{A}'$ if the optimization function gives a higher value than at the previous state; otherwise, it continues from the previous state. Our set of search operators include a move that splits a cluster; a move that joins two clusters; a move that swaps a feature from one cluster to another; a move that removes a feature from the arrangement altogether; and a move that adds a feature from the pool of unused features. We used 100 rounds of hill-climbing, and found that each round converged in fewer than 1000 moves.

To estimate the weights w_i for each of the four features of the Arranger, we use a development corpus consisting of 185 documents each containing the same ambiguous term, and each labeled with sense information. Because of the small number of parameters, we performed a grid search on the development data for the optimal values of the weights.

5 A Bootstrapping WSD System

Yarowsky (1995) first recognized that it is possible to use a small number of features for different senses to bootstrap an unsupervised word sense disambiguation system. In Yarowsky's work, his system requires an initial, manually-supplied collocation as a feature for each sense of a keyword. In contrast, we can use GLOSSY's extracted glosses to supply starter features fully automatically, using only an unlabeled corpus. Thus GLOSSY complements the efforts of Yarowsky and other bootstrapping techniques for WSD (Diab, 2004; Mihalcea, 2002).

Building on their efforts, we design a bootstrapping WSD system using GLOSSY's extracted glosses as follows. Let $\mathcal{A}$ be the arranged features representing glosses for a keyword. We first retrieve all the documents from our unlabeled corpus which contain features in $\mathcal{A}$. We then label appearances of the target word according to the cluster of the features that appear in that document. If features for more than one cluster appear in the same document, we discard it. The result is an automatically labeled corpus containing examples of all the extracted senses.

We use this automatically labeled "bootstrap corpus" to perform supervised WSD. This allows our system a great deal of flexibility once the bootstrap corpus is created: we can use any features of the corpus, plus the labels, in our classifier. Importantly, this means we do not need to rely on just the features in the extracted glosses. We use a multi-class SVM classifier with a linear kernel and default parameter settings. We use LibSVM (Chang and Lin, 2001) for all of our experiments. We use standard features for supervised WSD (Liu et al., 2004): all stems, words, bigrams, and trigrams within a context window of 20 words surrounding the ambiguous term.

6 Experiments

We ran two types of experiments, one to measure the accuracy of our sense gloss extractor, and one to measure the usefulness of the extracted knowledge for word sense disambiguation.

6.1 Data

We use a dataset of biomedical literature abstracts from Duan *et al.*(2009). The data contains a set of documents for 21 ambiguous terms. We reserved one of these terms ("MCP") for setting parameters, and ran our algorithms on the remaining keywords. The ambiguous terms vary from acronyms (7 terms), which are common and important in biomedical literature, to ambiguous biomedical terminology (3 terms), to terms like "culture" and "mole" that have some biomedical senses and some senses that are part of the general lexicon (11 terms). There were on average 271 labeled documents per term; the smallest number of documents for a term is 125, and the largest is 503. For every ambiguous term, we added on average 9625 (minimum of 1544, maximum of 15711) unlabeled documents to our collection by searching for the term on PubMed Central and downloading additional PubMed abstracts.

6.2 Extracting Glosses

We measured the performance of GLOSSY's gloss extraction by comparing the extracted glosses with definitions contained in the Unified Medical Language System (UMLS) Metathesaurus. First, for each ambiguous term, we looked up the set of exact matches for that term in the Metathesaurus, and downloaded definitions for all of the different senses listed under that term. Wherever possible, we used the MeSH definition of a sense; when that was unavailable, we used the definition from the NCI Thesaurus; and when both were unavailable, we used the definition from the resource listed first. 34 senses (40%) had no available definitions at all, but in all cases, the Metathesaurus lists a short (usually 1-3 word) gloss of the sense, which we used instead.

We manually aligned extracted glosses with UMLS senses in a way that maximizes the number of matched senses for every ambiguous term. We consider an extracted gloss to match a UMLS sense when the extracted gloss unambiguously refers to a single sense of the ambiguous term, and that sense matches the definition in UMLS. Typically, this means that the extracted features in the gloss overlap content words in the UMLS definition (*e.g.*, the extracted feature "symptoms" for the "common cold" sense of the term "cold"). In some cases, however, there was no strict overlap in content words between the extracted gloss and the UMLS definition, but the sense of the extracted gloss still unambiguously matched a unique UMLS sense: *e.g.*, for the term "transport," the extracted gloss "intracellular transport" was matched with the UMLS sense of "Molecular Transport," which the NCI Thesaurus defines as, "Any subcellular or molecular process involved in translocation of a biological entity, such as a macromolecule, from one site or compartment to another." In the end, such matchings were determined by hand. Table 1 shows extracted glosses and UMLS definitions for the term "mole."

For each ambiguous term, we measure the number of extracted glosses, the number of UMLS senses, and the number of matches between the two. We report on the precision (number of matches / number of extracted glosses), recall (number of matches / number of UMLS senses), and F1 score (harmonic mean of precision and recall). Table 2 shows the average of the precision and recall numbers over all terms. Since these terms have different numbers of senses, we can compute this average in two different ways: a Macro average, in which each term has equal weight in the average; and a Micro average, in which each term's weight in the average is proportional to the number of senses (extracted senses for the precision, and UMLS senses for the recall). We report on both.

A strict matching between GLOSSY's glosses and UMLS senses is potentially unfair to GLOSSY in several ways: GLOSSY may discover valid senses that happen not to appear in UMLS; UMLS senses may overlap one another, and so multiple UMLS senses may match a single GLOSSY gloss; and the two sets of senses may differ in granularity. For the sake of repeatable experiments, in this evaluation we make no attempt to change existing UMLS senses.

However, to highlight one particular strength of the Gloss Extraction paradigm, we do consider a separate evaluation that allows for new senses that GLOSSY discovers, but do not appear in UMLS. For instance, "biliopancreatic diversion" and "bipolar disorder" are both valid senses for the acronym "BPD." GLOSSY discovers both, but UMLS does not contain entries for either, so in our original evaluation both senses would count against GLOSSY's precision. To correct for this, our second evaluation adds senses to the list of UMLS senses whenever GLOSSY discovers valid entries missing from the Metathesaurus. The last five columns of Table 2 show our results under these conditions.

Despite the difficulty of the task, GLOSSY is able to find glosses with 53% precision and 47% recall (Macro average, no discovered senses) using only unlabeled corpora as input, and it is extracting roughly the right number of senses for each ambiguous term. In addition, GLOSSY is able to identify 7 valid senses missing from UMLS for the 20 terms in our evaluation. Including these senses in the evaluation increases GLOSSY's F1 by 6.2 points Micro (4.7 Macro). We are quite encouraged by the results, especially because they hold promise for WSD. Note that in order to improve upon a WSD baseline which tags all instances of a word as the same sense, GLOSSY only needs to be able to separate one sense from the rest. GLOSSY is finding between 1.85 and 2.2 correct glosses per term, more than enough to help with WSD.

6.3 WSD with Extracted Glosses

While extracting glosses is an important application in its own right, we also aim to show that this extracted knowledge is useful for an established application: namely, word sense disambiguation. Our next experiment compares the performance of our WSD system with an established unsupervised algorithm, and with a supervised technique — support vector machines (SVMs).

Using the same dataset as above, we trained GLOSSY on the ambiguous term "MCP", and tested it on the remaining ones. For comparison, we also report the state-of-the-art results of Duan *et al.*'s (2009) SENSATIONAL system, and the results of a BASELINE system that lumps all documents into a single cluster. SENSATIONAL is a fast clustering system based on minimum spanning trees and a pruning mechanism that eliminates noisy points from consideration during clustering. Since SENSATIONAL uses both "MCP" and "white" to train a small set of parameters, we leave "white" out of our comparison as well. We measure accuracy by aligning each system's clusters with the gold standard clusters in such a way as to maximize the number of elements that belong to aligned clusters. We use an implementation of the MaxFlow algorithm to determine this alignment. We then compute accuracy

	GLOSSY		UMLS
1.	choriocarcinoma, invasive, complete, hydatidiform mole, hydatidiform	1.	Hydatidiform Mole – Trophoblastic hyperplasia associated with normal gestation, or molar pregnancy. ...Hydatidiform moles or molar pregnancy may be categorized as complete or partial based on their gross morphology, histopathology, and karyotype.
2.	grams per mole	2.	Mole, unit of measurement – A unit of amount of substance, one of the seven base units of the International System of Units. It is the amount of substance that contains as many elementary units as there are atoms in 0.012 kg of carbon-12.
3.	mole fractions	-	
-		3.	Nevus – A circumscribed stable malformation of the skin ....
-		4.	Talpidae – Any of numerous burrowing mammals found in temperate regions ...

Table 1: GLOSSY**'s extracted glosses and UMLS dictionary entries for the example term "mole".**

	GLOSSY	Without Discovered Senses					With Discovered Senses				
		UMLS					UMLS				
	Senses	Senses	Matches	P	R	F1	Senses	Matches	P	R	F1
Macro Avg	4.35	4.25	1.85	53.1	47.1	49.9	4.6	2.2	60.6	49.7	54.6
Micro Avg	N/A	N/A	N/A	42.5	43.5	43.0	N/A	N/A	50.6	47.8	49.2

Table 2: GLOSSY **can automatically discover glosses that match definitions in an online dictionary.** "Without Discovered Senses" counts only the senses that are listed in the UMLS Metathesaurus; "With Discovered Senses" enhances the Metathesaurus with 7 new senses that GLOSSY has automatically discovered.

as the percentage of elements that belong to aligned clusters. This metric is very similar to the so-called "supervised" evaluation of Agirre *et al.* (2006).

The first four columns of Table 3 show our results. Clearly, both SENSATIONAL and GLOSSY outperform the BASELINE significantly, and traditionally this is a difficult baseline for unsupervised WSD systems to beat. SENSATIONAL outperforms GLOSSY by approximately 6%. There appear to be two reasons for this. In other experiments, SENSATIONAL has been shown to be competitive with supervised systems, but only when the corpus consists mostly of two, fairly well-balanced senses, as is true for this particular dataset, where the two most common senses always covered at least 70% of the examples for every ambiguous term.

A more serious problem for GLOSSY is that the unlabeled corpus that it extracts glosses from may not match well with the labeled test data. If the relative frequency of senses in the unlabeled documents does not match the relative frequency of senses in the labeled test set, GLOSSY may not extract the right set of glosses. Manual inspection of the extracted glosses shows that this is indeed a problem: for example, the labeled data contains two senses of the word "mole": a discolored area of skin (78%), and a burrowing mammal (22%); our unlabeled data contains both of these senses, but the additional sense of "mole" as a unit of measurement is by far predominant. GLOSSY manages to extract glosses for "skin" and "unit of measurement," but misses out on "mammal" as a result of the skew in the data.

Note that this problem, though serious for our experiments, is largely artificial from the point of view of applications. In a typical usage of a WSD system, there is a supply of data that the system needs to disambiguate, and accuracy is measured on a labeled sample of this data. Here, we started from a sample of labeled data, constructed a larger corpus that does not necessarily match it, and then ran our algorithm.

To correct for the artificial bias in our experiment, we ran a second test in which we manually labeled a random sample of 100 documents for each ambiguous term from the larger unlabeled corpus. We used a subset of 14 of the 21 keywords in the original dataset. As before, we compared our system against SENSATIONAL and the most-frequent-sense BASELINE. We also compare against an SVM system using 3-fold cross-validation. We use a linear kernel SVM, with the same set of features that are available

Keyword	Duan *et al.*(2009) Data Num. senses	BASE-LINE	GLOSSY	SENSE-ATIONAL	Sampled Data Num. senses	BASE-LINE	SENSE-ATIONAL	GLOSSY	SVM
ANA	2	63.1	87.9	100	13	75	79	74	75.8
BPD	3	39.8	71.6	52.9	7	33	48	85	66.7
BSA	2	50.1	77.9	94.7	5	97	53	89	87.9
CML	2	55.0	99.2	89.5	4	81	75	84	75.8
MAS	2	50.0	100	100	35	46	90	67	66.7
VCR	2	79.2	79.2	64.0	8	72	32	72	75.8
cold	3	37.1	73.3	66.8	3	87	81	44	90.9
culture	2	52.0	67.1	81.7	3	74	39	62	66.7
discharge	2	66.3	82.4	95.1	5	57	41	84	54.5
fat	2	50.6	50.1	53.2	2	97	60	97	97.0
mole	2	78.3	71.3	95.8	7	78	47	57	84.8
pressure	2	52.1	69.8	86.4	5	47	60	65	75.8
single	2	50.0	59.7	99.5	4	53	63	37	45.4
white	-	-	-	-	7	32	33	58	51.5
fluid	2	64.3	83.5	99.6	-	-	-	-	-
glucose	2	50.5	64.5	50.5	-	-	-	-	-
inflammation	3	35.5	52.8	50.4	-	-	-	-	-
inhibition	2	50.4	50.4	54.2	-	-	-	-	-
nutrition	3	38.8	53.8	54.9	-	-	-	-	-
transport	2	50.6	41.1	56.8	-	-	-	-	-
AVERAGE	2.16	53.4	70.3	76.1	7.71	66.3	57.2	69.6	72.5
Diff from BL	-	0.0	+16.9	+22.7	-	0.0	-9.1	+3.3	+6.2

Table 3: GLOSSY**'s extracted glosses can be used to create an unsupervised WSD system that achieves an accuracy within 3% of a supervised system.** Our WSD system outperforms our BASELINE system, widely recognized as a difficult baseline for unsupervised WSD, by 16.9% and 3.3% on two different datasets.

to the SVM in the GLOSSY system. We run our unsupervised systems on all of the unlabeled data, and then intersect the resulting clusters with the document set that we randomly sampled.

The last four columns of Table 3 show our results. The sampled data set appears to be a significantly harder test, since even the supervised SVM achieves only a 6% gain over the BASELINE. The SENSATIONAL system does significantly worse on this data, where there is a wider variation in the distribution of senses. The GLOSSY system outperforms both the SENSATIONAL system and the BASELINE.

7 Conclusion and Future Work

Gloss Extraction is an important, and difficult task of extracting definitions of words from unlabeled text. The GLOSSY system succeeds at a more feasible refinement of this task, the Sense Indicator Extraction task. GLOSSY's extractions have proven useful as seed definitions in an unsupervised WSD task. There is a great deal of room for future work in expanding the ability of Gloss Extraction systems to extract sense glosses that more closely match the meanings of a word. An important first step in this direction is to extract relations, rather than ngrams, that make up the definition a word's senses.

Acknowledgments

Presentation of this work was supported by the Institute of Education Sciences, U.S. Department of Education, through Grant R305A080157 to Carnegie Mellon University. The opinions expressed are those of the authors and do not necessarily represent the views of the Institute or the U.S. Department of Education. The authors thank the anonymous reviewers for their helpful suggestions and comments.

References

Eneko Agirre and Aitor Soroa. 2007. Semeval 2007 task 02: Evaluating word sense induction and discrimination systems. In *Proceedings of the Fourth International Workshop on Semantic Evaluations (SemEval)*, pages 7–12.

E. Agirre, O. Lopez de Lacalle, D. Martinez, and A. Soroa. 2006. Evaluating and optimizing the parameters of an unsupervised graph-based WSD algorithm. In *Proceedings of the NAACL Textgraphs Workshop*.

I. Androutsopoulos and D. Galanis. 2005. A practically unsupervised learning method to identify single-snippet answers to definition questions on the web. In *Proceedings of HLT-EMNLP*, pages 323–330.

Jordan Boyd-Graber, David M. Blei, and Xiaojin Zhu. 2007. A topic model for word sense disambiguation. In *Empirical Methods in Natural Language Processing*.

Chih-Chung Chang and Chih-Jen Lin, 2001. *LIBSVM: a library for support vector machines*.

T. Chklovski and R. Mihalcea. 2002. Building a sense tagged corpus with Open Mind Word Expert. In *Proceedings of the Workshop on Word Sense Disambiguation: Recent Successes and Future Directions*.

H. Cui, M.K. Kan, and T.S. Chua. 2007. Soft pattern matching models for definitional question answering. *ACM Trans. Information Systems*, 25(2):1–30.

Mona Diab. 2004. Relieving the data acquisition bottleneck in word sense disambiguation. In *Proceedings of the ACL*.

Weisi Duan, Min Song, and Alexander Yates. 2009. Fast max-margin clustering for unsupervised word sense disambiguation in biomedical texts. *BMC Bioinformatics*, 10(S3)(S4).

Christiane Fellbaum, editor. 1998. *WordNet: An Electronic Lexical Database*. Bradford Books.

A. Fujii and T. Ishikawa. 2000. Utilizing the world wide web as an encyclopedia: Extracting term descriptions from semi-structured texts. In *Proceedings of ACL*, pages 488–495.

M. Joshi, T. Pedersen, and R. Maclin. 2005. A comparative study of support vector machines applied to the supervised word sense disambiguation problem in the medical domain. In *Proceedings of the Second Indian International Conference on Artificial Intelligence*.

Anagha Kulkarni and Ted Pedersen. 2005. Name discrimination and email clustering using unsupervised clustering and labeling of similar contexts. In *Proceedings of the Second Indian International Conference on Artificial Intelligence*, pages 703–722.

Gondy Leroy and Thomas C. Rindflesch. 2004. Using symbolic knowledge in the umls to disambiguate words in small datasets with a naive bayes classifier. In *MEDINFO*.

M.E. Lesk. 1986. Automatic sense disambiguation using machine readable dictionaries: How to tell a pine cone from an ice cream cone. In *Proceedings of the SIGDOC Conference*.

Hongfang Liu, Virginia Teller, and Carol Friedman. 2004. A multi-aspect comparison study of supervised word sense disambiguation. *Journal of the American Medical Informatics Association*, 11:320–331.

Rada Mihalcea. 2002. Bootstrapping large sense-tagged corpora. In *International Conference on Languages Resources and Evaluations (LREC)*.

Rada Mihalcea. 2007. Using wikipedia for automatic word sense disambiguation. In *Proceedings of the NAACL*.

David Milne and Ian H. Witten. 2008. Learning to link with wikipedia. In *Proceedings of the 17th Conference on Information and Knowledge Management (CIKM)*.

S. Mohammad and Ted Pedersen. 2004. Combining lexical and syntactic features for supervised word sense disambiguation. In *Proceedings of CoNLL*.

P. Pantel and D. Lin. 2002. Discovering word senses from text. In *Procs. of ACM Conference on Knowledge Discovery and Data Mining (KDD-02)*.

Marius Pasca. 2005. Finding instance names and alternative glosses on the web: WordNet reloaded. In *Computational Linguistics and Intelligent Text Processing*, pages 280–292. Springer Berlin / Heidelberg.

Ana-Maria Popescu, Alexander Yates, and Oren Etzioni. 2004. Class extraction from the world wide web. In *AAAI-04 ATEM Workshop*, pages 65–70.

Sameer Pradhan, Edward Loper, Dmitriy Dligach, and Martha Palmer. 2007. Semeval-2007 task-17: English lexical sample, srl and all words. In *Proceedings of the Fourth International Workshop on Semantic Evaluations (SemEval)*.

B.J. Schijvenaars, B. Mons, M. Weeber, M.J. Schuemie, E.M. van Mulligen, H.M. Wain, and J.A. Kors. 2005. Thesaurus-based disambiguation of gene symbols. *BMC Bioinformatics*, 6.

R. Snow, D. Jurafsky, and A. Y. Ng. 2006. Semantic taxonomy induction from heterogenous evidence. In *COLING/ACL*.

M. Stevenson and Yorick Wilks. 2001. The interaction of knowledge sources in word sense disambiguation. *Computational Linguistics*, 27(3):321–349.

Paola Velardi, Roberto Navigli, and Pierluigi D'Amadio. 2008. Mining the web to create specialized glossaries. *IEEE Intelligent Systems*, 23(5):18–25.

David Yarowsky. 1995. Unsupervised word sense disambiguation rivaling supervised methods. In *Proceedings of the ACL*.

Can Recognising Multiword Expressions Improve Shallow Parsing?

Ioannis Korkontzelos, Suresh Manandhar
Department of Computer Science
The University of York
Heslington, York, YO10 5NG, UK
{johnkork, suresh}@cs.york.ac.uk

Abstract

There is significant evidence in the literature that integrating knowledge about multiword expressions can improve shallow parsing accuracy. We present an experimental study to quantify this improvement, focusing on *compound nominals*, *proper names* and *adjective-noun constructions*. The evaluation set of multiword expressions is derived from *WordNet* and the textual data are downloaded from the web. We use a classification method to aid human annotation of output parses. This method allows us to conduct experiments on a large dataset of unannotated data. Experiments show that knowledge about multiword expressions leads to an increase of between 7.5% and 9.5% in accuracy of shallow parsing in sentences containing these multiword expressions.

1 Introduction

Multiword expressions are sequences of words that tend to co-occur more frequently than chance and are characterised by various levels of idiosyncracy (Baldwin et al., 2003; Baldwin, 2006). There is extended literature on various issues relevant to multiword expression; recognition, classification, lexicography, etc. (see Section 6). The vast majority of these publications identifies as motivation for multiword expression research its potential contribution to deep or shallow parsing. On the other side of this issue, the state-of-the-art parsing systems seem to ignore the fact that treating multiword expressions as syntactic units would potentially increase parser's accuracy.

In this paper, we present an experimental study attempting to estimate the contribution of integrating multiword expressions into shallow parsing. We focus on multiword expressions that consist of two successive tokens; in particular, *compound nominals proper names* and *adjective-noun constructions*. We also present a detailed classification method to aid human annotation during the procedure of deciding if a parse is correct or wrong. We present experimental results about the different classes of changes that occur in the parser output while unifying multiword expression components.

We conclude that treating known multiwords expressions as singletons leads to an increase of between 7.5% and 9.5% in accuracy of shallow parsing of sentences containing these multiword expressions. Increase percentages are higher for multiword expressions that consist of an adjective followed by a noun (12% to 15%); and even higher for non-compositional multiword expressions[1] that consist of an adjective and a noun (15.5% to 19.5%).

The rest of the paper is structured as follows: In Section 2 we present how multiword expressions can be annotated in text and used by a shallow parser. In Section 3 we present an overview of our experimental process. Section 4 explains how the set of target multiword expressions and textual corpora were created. In Section 5 we present and discuss the results of the experimental process. In Section 6 we present parts of the related literature. Section 7 concludes the paper and proposes some future work.

[1]Compositionality is defined as the degree to which the meaning of a multiword expression can be predicted by combining the meanings of its components (Nunberg et al., 1994).

Human Language Technologies: The 2010 Annual Conference of the North American Chapter of the ACL, pages 636–644,
Los Angeles, California, June 2010.

2 Annotating Multiword expressions

In this paper, we present a study to inspect the extent to which knowledge of multiword expressions improves shallow parsing. Our approach focuses on English multiword expressions that appear as sequences in text. In particular, we focus on *compound nominals* (e.g. lemon tree), *proper names* (e.g. prince Albert) and *adjective-noun constructions* (e.g. red carpet).

Shallow or deep parsing should treat multiword expression as units that cannot be divided in any way. We replace the multiword expression tokens with a special made up token, i.e. the multiword expression constituents joined with an underscore. For example, we replace all occurrences of "lemon tree" with "lemon_tree".

We choose to replace the multiword expression words with a token that does not exist in the dictionary of the part of speech tagger. This is quite an important decision. Usually, a part of sheech tagger assigns to an unknown words the part of speech that best fits to it with respect to the parts of speech of the words around it and the training data. This is a desirable behaviour for our purposes.

The experimental results of our study quantify the difference between the shallow parser output of a big number of sentences after the replacement and the shallow parser output of the same sentences before the replacement. The comparison is done ignoring changes of parts of speech, assigned by the part of speech tagger.

3 Evaluation

The target of our experiment is to evaluate whether replacing the multiword expression tokens with a single token, unknown to the part of speech tagger, improves shallow parsing accuracy. The ideal way to perform this evaluation would be to use a corpus with manual annotation about parsing and multiword expressions. Given this corpus we would be able to measure the accuracy of a shallow (or deep) parser before and after replacing multiword expressions. However, to the best of our knowledge there is no corpus available to include this type of annotations in English.

Instead, there are two options: Firstly, we can use treebank data, where manual parsing annotation

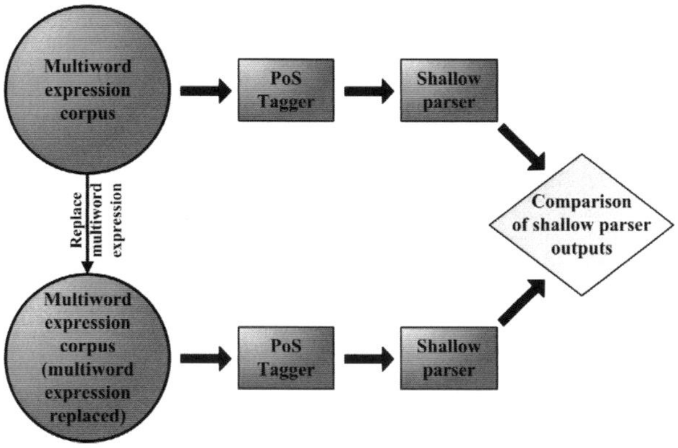

Figure 1: Evaluation process

is readily available, and manually annotate multiword expressions. The advantage of this approach is that results are directly comparable with other results of the literature, due to the use of benchmark data. Manual annotation of multiword expressions is a very time- and effort-consuming process due to the large size of most treebanks. Alternatively, multiword expression annotation could be done using a method of recognition. Annotating the multiword expressions that appear in *WordNet* could be a safe decision, in terms of correctness, however, *WordNet* is reported to have limited coverage of multiword expressions (Baldwin, 2006; Laporte and Voyatzi, 2008). *WordNet* covers only 9.1 % and 16.1 % of the datasets of Nicholson and Baldwin (2008) (484 noun compounds) and Kim and Baldwin (2008) (2169 noun compounds), respectively.

Secondly, we can use a set of multiword expressions as a starting point and then create corpora that contain instances of these multiword expressions. In succession, these sentences need to be manually annotated in terms of parsing, and this requires huge human effort. Alternatively, we can parse the corpora before and after replacing the multiword expression and then compare the parser output. This is the evaluation procedure that we chose to follow, and is shown in Figure 1.

The above procedure is only able to retrieve instances where the replacement of the multiword expression leads to a different parsing, a different allocation of tokens to phrases. It is not able to spot instances where the parser output remains unchanged after the replacement, no matter if they are correct. Since we are interested in measuring if replacing

Example A - Replacement causes no change	
Before:	*[NP they] [VP jumped] [PP over] [NP a bonfire] and [VP rolled] [NP a fire wheel] .*
After:	*[NP they] [VP jumped] [PP over] [NP a bonfire] and [VP rolled] [NP a fire_wheel] .*

Example B - Replacement corrects an error	
Before:	*[NP the blades] [VP ignited] and [NP he] [VP threw]* ***[NP the fire] wheel up*** *[PP into] [NP the air] .*
After:	*[NP the blades] [VP ignited] and [NP he] [VP threw]* ***[NP the fire_wheel] [PRT up]*** *[PP into] [NP the air] .*

Table 1: 2 shallow parsing examples. Multiword expression: *"fire wheel"*

multiword expressions with a single token improves parsing accuracy, we are not interested in instances that remain unchanged. We focus on instances that changed; either they were corrected or they were made wrong or they remain erroneous. For example, the shallow parser output for example A in Table 1 did not change after the replacement. Example B in Table 1 shows a sentence which was corrected after the replacement.

Instead of manually annotating the sentences whose parser output changed after the replacement as corrected or not, we identify a number of change classes under which we classify all these sentences. In the following section, we present the change classes. For each we thoroughly discuss whether its form guarantees that its sentences are wrongly parsed before the change and correctly parsed after the change. In this case, the sentences of the corresponding class should be counted as false positives. We also discuss the opposite; if the form of each change class guarantees that its sentences are correctly parsed before the change and wrongly parsed after the change. In this case, the sentences of the corresponding class should be counted as true negatives. For this discussion we hypothesize that among the possible output shallow parses for a given sentence the correct one has (a) the smallest number phrases, and (b) the smallest number of tokens not assigned to any phrase.

3.1 Shallow parsing change classes

In this section, we present a classification of cases where the shallow parser output of the sentence is different from the parser output of the same sentence after replacing the multiword expression with a single token. The secondary focus of this discussion is to estimate whether the specific form of each change class can lead to a safe conclusion about if the parser output of the sentence under discussion: (a) was wrong before the replacement and was then corrected, (b) was correct before the replacement and was then made wrong, or (c) was wrong before the replacement and remained wrong. For this discussion, we refer to words that are not assigned to any phase in the shallow parser output as "leaves".

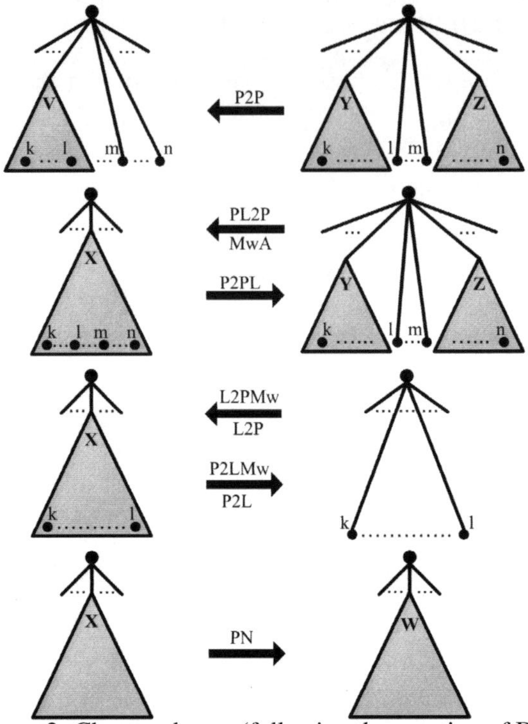

Figure 2: Change classes (following the notation of Bille (2005)). Triangles denote phrases and uppercase bold letters $V...Z$ denote phrase labels. Lowercase letters $k...n$ denote parsing leaves. For change classes *P2LMw* and *L2PMw*, X includes the multiword expression tokens. For change classes *P2L* and *L2P* it does not. For change class *MwA*, the multiword expression tokens are not assigned to the same phrase Y or Z.

Hypothesis: We base our analysis on the hypothesis that among the possible output shallow parses for a given sentence the correct one has (a) the smallest number phrases, and (b) the smallest number of leaves. The theoretical intuitions behind the hypothesis are: (a) parse trees with just leaves are partial parse trees and hence should not be preferred over complete parse trees. (b) when mistaken parse trees are generally larger (with more phrases). We checked the hypothesis by manually annotating 80 randomly chosen instances; 10 for each change class that is counted as correct or wrong (see Table 2). 74 instances validated the hypothesis (92.5%).

Table 2 shows one example for each change class. Figure 2 presents the classes as transformations between trees, following the notation of Bille (2005).

Change class *P2LMw* (***P***hrase to ***L***eaves including the ***M***ulti***w***ord expression) Before replacing the multiword expression sequence with a single token, the multiword expression is assigned to some phrase, possibly together with other words. After the replacement, the components of that phrase are not assigned to any phrase, but instead as leaves.

Change class *P2L* (***P***hrase to ***L***eaves excluding the multiword expression) Similarly to change class *P2LMw*, before the replacement, some successive tokens excluding the multiword expression itself are assigned to some phrase. After the replacement, the components of that phrase appear as leaves.

Change class *L2PMw* (***L***eaves to ***P***hrase including the ***M***ulti***w***ord expression) The changes covered by this class are the opposite changes of change class *P2LMw*. Before the replacing the multiword expression sequence with a single token, the multiword expression sequence is not assign to any phrase possibly among other words. After the replacement, the multiword expression is assigned to a phrase.

Change class *L2P* (***L***eaves to ***P***hrase excluding the multiword expression) Similarly to change class *L2PMw*, before the replacement, one or more successive tokens excluding the multiword expression itself appear as leaves. After the replacement, these tokens are assigned to a phrase.

Change class *PL2P* (***P***hrases or ***L***eaves to ***P***hrase) After the replacement, the tokens of more than one phrases or leaves are assigned to a single phrase.

Change class *P2PL* (***P***hrase to ***P***hrases or ***L***eaves) In contrast to change class *PL2P*, after the replacement, the tokens of one phrase either are assigned to more than one phrases or appear as leaves.

Change class *PN* (***P***hrase label ***N***ame) After replacing the multiword expression sequence with a single token, one phrase appears with a different phrase label, although it retains exactly the same component tokens.

Change class *PoS* (***P***art ***o***f ***S***peech) After replacing the multiword expression sequence with a single token, one or more tokens appears with a different part of speech. This class of changes comes from the part of speech tagger, and are out of the scope of this study. Thus, in the results section we show a size estimate of this class, and then we present results about change classes, ignoring change class *PoS*.

Change class P2P (***P***hrases to less ***P***hrases) After replacing the multiword expression sequence with a single token, the component tokens of more than one successive phrases α are assigned to a different set of successive phrases β. However, it is always the case that phrases α are less than phrases β ($|\alpha| < |\beta|$).

Change class MwA (***M***ulti***w***ord expression ***A***llocation) Before replacing the multiword expression sequence, the multiword expression constituents are assigned to different phrases.

The instances of change classes where the parser output after the replacement has more parsing leaves or phrases than before are counted towards sentences that were parsed wrongly after the replacement. For these classes, change classes *P2LMw*, *P2L* and *P2PL*, most probably the parser output after the replacement is wrong.

In contrast, the instances of change classes where a sequence of tokens is assigned to a phrase, or many phrases are merged are counted towards sentences that were parsed wrongly before the replacement and correctly after the replacement. These changes, that are described by classes *L2PMw*, *L2P*, *PL2P* and *P2P*, most probably describe improvements in shallow parsing. The instances of change class *MwA* are counted as correct after the replacement because by definition all tokens of a multiword expression are expected to be assigned to the same phrase.

The instances of change class *PN* can be either correct or wrong after the replacement. For this reason, we present our results as ranges (see Table 4). The minimum value is computed when the instances of class *PN* are counted as wrong after the replacement. In contrast, the maximum value is computed when the instances of this class are counted as correct after the replacement.

3.2 Shallow parsing complex change classes

During the inspection of instances where the shallow parser output before the replacement is dif-

P2LMw	B	**[NP the(DT) action(NN) officer(NN)]** [NP logistic(JJ) course(NN)] [VP is(VBZ) designed(VBN)] [VP to(TO) educate(VB)] and(CC) [VP train(VB)] [NP military(JJ) personnel(NNS)] ...	✗
	A	**the(DT) action_officer(NN)** [NP logistic(JJ) course(NN)] [VP is(VBZ) designed(VBN)] [VP to(TO) educate(VB)] and(CC) [VP train(VB)] [NP military(JJ) personnel(NNS)] ...	
P2L	B	... [NP the(DT) action(NN) officer(NN)] **[PP in(IN)]** [NP armenia(NN)] [VP signed(VBN)] ...	✗
	A	... [NP the(DT) action_officer(NN)] **in(IN)** [NP armenia(NN)] [VP signed(VBN)] ...	
L2PMw	B	“(“) **affirmative(JJ) action(NN) officer(NN)** “(“) [NP aao(NN)] [VP refers(VBZ)] [PP to(TO)] [NP the(DT) regional(JJ) affirmative(JJ) action(NN) officer(NN)] or(CC) [NP director(NN)] ...	✓
	A	“(“) **[NP affirmative(JJ) action_officer(NN)]** “(“) [NP aao(NN)] [VP refers(VBZ)] [PP to(TO)] [NP the(DT) regional(JJ) affirmative(JJ) action_officer(NN)] or(CC) [NP director(NN)] ...	
L2P	B	[NP the(DT) action(NN) officer(NN)] **usually(RB)** [VP delivers(VBZ)] ...	✓
	A	[NP the(DT) action_officer(NN)] **[ADVP usually(RB)]** [VP delivers(VBZ)] ...	
PL2P	B	... [VP to(TO) immediately(RB) report(VB)] [NP the(DT) incident(NN)] [PP to(TO)] **[NP the(DT) equal(JJ) opportunity(NN)] and(CC) [NP affirmative(JJ) action(NN) officer(NN)]** .(.)	✓
	A	... [VP to(TO) immediately(RB) report(VB)] [NP the(DT) incident(NN)] [PP to(TO)] **[NP the(DT) equal(JJ) opportunity(NN) and(CC) affirmative(JJ) action_officer(NN)]** .(.)	
P2PL	B	... [NP action(NN) officer(NN)] **[VP shall(MD) prepare(VB) and(CC) transmit(VB)]** ...	✗
	A	... [NP action_officer(NN)] **[VP shall(MD) prepare(VB)] and(CC) [VP transmit(VB)]** ...	
PN	B	... [NP an(DT) action(NN) officer(NN)] **[SBAR for(IN)]** [NP communications(NNS)] ...	?
	A	... [NP an(DT) action_officer(NN)] **[PP for(IN)]** [NP communications(NNS)] ...	
PoS	B	... [NP security(NN) officer(NN)] or(CC) “(“) [NP **youth(JJ)** action(NN) officer(NN)] .(.) “(“)	?
	A	... [NP security(NN) officer(NN)] or(CC) “(“) [NP **youth(NN)** action_officer(NN)] .(.) “(“)	
P2P	B	... ,(,) [PP as(IN)] **[NP a(DT) past(JJ) action(NN) officer(NN)] and(CC) command(NN) and(CC) control(NN) and(CC)** [NP intelligence(NN) communications(NNS) inspector(NN)] ...	✓
	A	... ,(,) [PP as(IN)] **[NP a(DT) past(JJ) action_officer(NN) and(CC) command(NN) and(CC) (control(NN)] and(CC)** [NP intelligence(NN) communications(NNS) inspector(NN)] ...	
MwA	B	**the(DT) campus(NN) affirmative(JJ) action(NN) [NP officer(NN)]** [VP serves(VBZ)] ...	✓
	A	**[NP the(DT) campus(NN) affirmative(JJ) action_officer(NN)]** [VP serves(VBZ)]...	

Table 2: Examples for change classes. Multiword expression: *"action officer"*. Parts of speech appear within parentheses. "B" stands for "before" and "A" for "after" (multiword expression replacement). ✓or ✗ denote change classes that count positively or negatively towards improving shallow parsing. *?* denotes classes that are treated specially.

ferent from the shallow parser output after the replacement, we came across a number of instances that were classified in more than one class of the previous subsection. In other words, two or more classes of change happened. For example, in a number of instances, before the replacement, the multiword expression constituents are assigned to different phrases (change class *MwA*). After the replacement, the tokens of more than one phrases are assigned to a single phrase (change class *PL2P*). These instances consist new complex change classes and are named as the sum of names of the participating classes. The instances of the example above consist the complex change class *PL2P+MwA*.

4 Target multiword expressions and corpora collection

We created our set of target multiword expressions using *WordNet 3.0* (Miller, 1995). Out of its $52,217$ multiword expressions we randomly chose 120. Keeping the ones that consist of two tokens resulted in the 118 expressions of Table 3. Manually inspecting these multiword expressions proved that they are all *compound nominals*, *proper names* or *adjective-noun constructions*. Each multiword expression was manually tagged as compositional or non-compositional, following the procedure described in Korkontzelos and Manandhar (2009). Table 3 shows the chosen multiword expressions together with information about their compositionality and the parts of speech of their components.

Compositional Multiword expressions (Noun - Noun sequences)				
action officer (3119)	bile duct (21649)	cartridge brass (479)	field mushroom (789)	fire wheel (480)
key word (3131)	king snake (2002)	labor camp (3275)	life form (5301)	oyster bed (1728)
pack rat (3443)	palm reading (4428)	paper chase (1115)	paper gold (1297)	paper tiger (1694)
picture palace (2231)	pill pusher (924)	pine knot (1026)	potato bean (265)	powder monkey (1438)
prison guard (4801)	rat race (2556)	road agent (1281)	sea lion (9113)	spin doctor (1267)
tea table (62)	telephone service (9771)	upland cotton (3235)	vegetable sponge (806)	winter sweet (460)
Non-Compositional Multiword expressions (Noun - Noun sequences)				
agony aunt (751)	air conditioner (24202)	band aid (773)	beach towel (1937)	car battery (3726)
checker board (1280)	corn whiskey (1862)	corner kick (2882)	cream sauce (1569)	fire brigade (5005)
fish finger (1423)	flight simulator (5955)	honey cake (843)	jazz band (6845)	jet plane (1466)
laser beam (16716)	lemon tree (3805)	lip service (3388)	love letter (3265)	luggage van (964)
memory device (4230)	monkey puzzle (1780)	motor pool (3184)	power cord (5553)	prince Albert (2019)
sausage pizza (598)	savoy cabbage (1320)	surface fire (2607)	torrey tree (10)	touch screen (9654)
water snake (2649)	water tank (5158)	wood aster (456)		
Compositional Multiword expressions (Adjective - Noun sequences)				
basic color (2453)	cardiac muscle (6472)	closed chain (1422)	common iguana (668)	cubic meter (4746)
eastern pipistrel (128)	graphic designer (8228)	hard candy (2357)	ill health (2055)	kinetic theory (2934)
male parent (1729)	medical report (3178)	musical harmony (1109)	mythical monster (770)	red fox (10587)
relational adjective (279)	parking brake (7199)	petit juror (991)	taxonomic category (1277)	thick skin (1338)
toxic waste (7220)	universal donor (1454)	parenthesis-free notation (113)		
Non-Compositional Multiword expressions (Adjective - Noun sequences)				
black maria (930)	dead end (5256)	dutch oven (4582)	golden trumpet (607)	green light (5960)
high jump (4455)	holding pattern (3622)	joint chiefs (2865)	living rock (985)	magnetic head (2457)
missing link (5314)	personal equation (873)	personal magnetism (2869)	petit four (1506)	pink lady (1707)
pink shower (351)	poor devil (1594)	public eye (3231)	quick time (2323)	red devil (2043)
red dwarf (6526)	red tape (2024)	round window (1380)	silent butler (332)	small beer (2302)
small voice (4313)	stocking stuffer (7486)	sweet bay (1367)	teddy boy (2413)	think tank (4586)

Table 3: 118 multiword expressions randomly chosen from *WordNet*. The size of the respective corpus in sentences appears within parentheses.

For each multiword expression we created a different corpus. Each consists of webtext snippets of length 15 to 200 tokens in which the multiword expression appears. Snippets were collected following Korkontzelos and Manandhar (2009). Given a multiword expression, a set of queries is created: All synonyms of the multiword expression extracted from WordNet are collected[2]. The multiword expression is paired with each synonym to create a set of queries. For each query, snippets are collected by parsing the web-pages returned by *Yahoo!*. The union of all snippets produces the multiword expression corpus.

In Table 3, the number of collected corpus sentences for each multiword expression are shown within parentheses. *GENIA* tagger (Tsuruoka et al., 2005) was used as part of speech tagger. *SNoW-based Shallow Parser* (Munoz et al., 1999) was used for shallow parsing.

[2] e.g. for "red carpet", corpora are collected for "red carpet" and "carpet". The synonyms of "red carpet" are "rug", "carpet" and "carpeting".

5 Experimental results and discussion

The corpora collecting procedure of Section 4 resulted in a corpus of $376,007$ sentences, each one containing one or more multiword expressions. In $85,527$ sentences (22.75%), the shallow parser output before the replacement is different than the shallow parser output after the replacement. 7.20% of these change instances are due to one or more parts of speech changes, and are classified to change class *PoS*. In other words, in 7.20% of cases where there is a difference between the shallow parses before and after replacing the multiword expression tokens there is one or more tokens that were assigned a different part of speech. However, excluding parts of speech from the comparison, there is no other difference between the two parses.

The focus of this study is to quantify the effect of unifying multiword expressions in shallow parsing. Part of speech tagging is a component of our approach and parts of speech are not necessarily parts of the parser output. For this reason, we chose to ignore part of speech changes, the changes of class *PoS*. Below, we discuss results for all other classes.

Multiword expressions			Shallow Parsing improvement	
class	*PS*	sentences	min.	max.
On average	-	376,007	7.47%	9.49%
Comp.	N N	93,166	5.54%	7.19%
Non-Comp.	N N	127,875	3.66%	4.44%
Comp.	J N	68,707	7.34%	9.21%
Non-Comp.	J N	86,259	15.32%	19.67%
-	N N	221,041	4.45%	5.60%
	J N	154,966	11.78%	15.03%
Comp.	-	161,873	6.30%	8.05%
Non-Comp.	-	214,134	8.36%	10.57%

Table 4: Summary of results. *PS*: parts of speech, Comp: compositional, N: noun, J: adjective, min.: minimum, max.: maximum.

Table 4 shows a summary of our results. The first two columns describe classes of multiword expression with respect to compositionality and the parts of speech of the component words. The first line accounts for the average of all multiword expressions, the second one for compositional multiword expressions made of nouns, etc. The third column shows the number of corpus sentences of each class.

For each one of the classes of Table 4, the fourth and fifth columns show the minimum and maximum improvement in shallow parsing, respectively, caused by unifying multiword expression tokens. Let $\|X\|$ be the function that returns the number of instances assigned to change class X. With respect to the discussion of Subsection 3.1 about how the instances of each class should be counted towards the final results, the minimum and maximum improvements in shallow parsing are:

$$
\begin{aligned}
min &= -\|P2LMw\| - \|P2L\| + \|L2PMw\| + \|L2P\| + \\
&\quad + \|PL2P\| - \|P2PL\| + \|PL2P{+}MwA\| + \\
&\quad + \|P2P\| + \|P2P{+}MwA\| - \|PN\| \qquad (1) \\
max &= -\|P2LMw\| - \|P2L\| + \|L2PMw\| + \|L2P\| + \\
&\quad + \|PL2P\| - \|P2PL\| + \|PL2P{+}MwA\| + \\
&\quad + \|P2P\| + \|P2P{+}MwA\| + \|PN\| \qquad (2)
\end{aligned}
$$

On average of all multiword expressions, unifying multiword expression tokens contributes from 7.47% to 9.49% in shallow parsing accuracy. It should be noted that this improvement is reported on sentences which contain at least one known multiword expression. To project this improvement on any general text, one needs to know the percentage of sentences that contain known multiword expressions. Then the projected improvement can be computed by multiplying these two percentages.

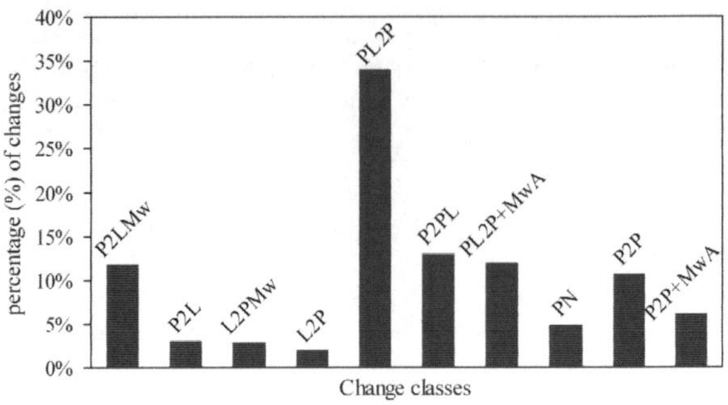

Figure 3: Average change percentages per change class.

Table 4 shows that the increase in shallow parsing accuracy is lower for expressions that consist of nouns than for those that consist of an adjective and a noun. Moreover, the improvement is higher for non-compositional expressions than compositional ones. This is expected, due to the idiosyncratic nature of non-compositional multiword expressions. The highest improvement, 15.32% to 19.67%, occurs for non-compositional multiword expressions that consist of an adjective followed by a noun.

Figure 3 shows the percentage of each class over the sum of sentences whose parse before unifying multiword expression tokens is different for the parse after the replacement. The most common change class is *PL2P*. It contains sentences in the shallow parser output of which many phrases or leaves were all assigned to a single phrase. 34.03% of the changes are classified in this class. The least common classes are change classes *P2L*, *L2PMw* and *L2P*. Each of these accounts for less than 3% of the overall changes.

6 Related Work

There have been proposed several ways to classify multiword expressions according to various properties such as compositionality and institutionalisation[3] (Moon, 1998; Sag et al., 2002; Baldwin, 2006). There is a large variety of methods in the literature that address recognising multiword expressions or some subcategory. McCarthy (2006) divides multiword expression detect-

[3]Institutionalisation is the degree that a multiword expression is accepted as lexical item through consistent use over time.

ing methods into statistical (e.g. pointwise mutual information (*PMI*)), translation-based, dictionary-based, substitution-based, and distributional. Statistical methods score multiword expression candidates based on co-occurrence counts (Manning and Schutze, 1999; Dunning, 1993; Lin, 1999; Frantzi et al., 2000). Translation-based methods usually take advantage of alignment to discover potential multiword expressions (Venkatapathy and Joshi, 2005).

Other methods use dictionaries to reveal semantic relationships between the components of potential multiword expressions and their context (Baldwin et al., 2003; Hashimoto et al., 2006). Substitution-based methods decide for multiword expressions by substituting their components with other similar words and measuring their frequency of occurrence (Lin, 1999; Fazly and Stevenson, 2006). These techniques can be enriched with selectional preference information (Van de Cruys and Moirón, 2007; Katz and Giesbrecht, 2006). Fazly and Stevenson (2007) propose measures for *institutionalisation*, *syntactic fixedness* and *compositionality* based on the selectional preferences of verbs. There are several studies relevant to detecting compositionality of noun-noun, verb-particle and light verb constructions and verb-noun pairs (e.g. Katz and Giesbrecht (2006)).

To the best of our knowledge there are no approaches integrating multiword expression knowledge in deep or shallow parsing. However, there are several attempts to integrate other forms of lexical semantics into parsing. Bikel (2000) merged the Brown portion of the Penn Treebank with SemCor, and used it to evaluate a generative bilexical model for joint word sense disambiguation and parsing. Similarly, Agirre et al. (Agirre et al., 2008) integrated semantic information in the form of semantic classes and observed significant improvement in parsing and PP attachment tasks. Xiong et al. (2005) integrated first-sense and hypernym features in a generative parse model applied to the Chinese Penn Treebank and achieved significant improvement over their baseline model. Fujita et al. (2007) extended this work by implementing a discriminative parse selection model, incorporating word sense information and achieved great improvements as well. Examples of integrating selectional preference information into parsing are Dowding et al. (1994) and Hektoen (1997).

7 Conlusion and future work

In this paper, we presented an experimental study attempting to estimate the contribution of unifying multiword expression components into shallow parsing. The evaluation is done based on 118 multiword expressions extracted from *WordNet 3.0*. They consist of two successive components and are in particular, *compound nominals*, *proper names* or *adjective-noun constructions*.

Instead of using pre-annotated text, we collected sentences that contain the above multiword expressions from the web. We applied shallow parsing before and after unifying multiword expression tokens and compared the outputs. We presented a detailed classification of changes in the shallow parser output to aid human annotation during the procedure of deciding if a parser output is correct or wrong.

We presented experimental results about change classes and about the overall improvement of unifying multiword expression tokens with respect to compositionality and the parts of speech of their components. We conclude that unifying the tokens of known multiwords expressions leads to an increase of between 7.5% and 9.5% in accuracy of shallow parsing of sentences that contain these multiword expressions. Increase percentages are higher on *adjective-noun constructions* (12% to 15%); and even higher on non-compositional *adjective-noun constructions* (15.5% to 19.5%).

Future work will focus in conducting similar experiments for multiword expressions longer than two words. One would expect that due to their size, a wrong interpretation of their structure would affect the shallow parser output more than it does for multiword expressions consisting of two words. Thus, unifying multiword expressions longer than two words would potentially contribute more to shallow parsing accuracy.

Furthermore, the evaluation results presented in this paper could be strengthened by adding manual multiword expression annotation to some treebank. This would provide a way to avoid the change class analysis presented in Subsection 3.1 and compute statistics more accurately. Finally, the results of this paper suggest that implementing a parser able to recognise multiword expressions would be very helpful towards high accuracy parsing.

References

E. Agirre, T. Baldwin, and D. Martinez. 2008. Improving parsing and PP attachment performance with sense information. In *Proceedings of ACL*, pages 317–325, USA. ACL.

T. Baldwin, C. Bannard, T. Tanaka, and D. Widdows. 2003. An empirical model of multiword expression decomposability. In *proceedings of the ACL workshop on MWEs*, pages 89–96, USA. ACL.

T. Baldwin. 2006. Compositionality and multiword expressions: Six of one, half a dozen of the other? In *proceedings of the ACL workshop on MWEs*, Australia. ACL.

D. Bikel. 2000. A statistical model for parsing and word-sense disambiguation. In *proceedings of the 2000 Joint SIGDAT conference: EMNLP/VLC*, pages 155–163, USA. ACL.

P. Bille. 2005. A survey on tree edit distance and related problems. *Theoretical Computer Science*, 337(1-3):217–239.

J. Dowding, R. Moore, F. Andryt, and D. Moran. 1994. Interleaving syntax and semantics in an efficient bottom-up parser. In *proceedings of ACL*, pages 110–116, USA. ACL.

T. Dunning. 1993. Accurate methods for the statistics of surprise and coincidence. *Computational Linguistics*, 19(1):61–74.

A. Fazly and S. Stevenson. 2006. Automatically constructing a lexicon of verb phrase idiomatic combinations. In *Proceedings of EACL*, pages 337–344, Italy.

A. Fazly and S. Stevenson. 2007. Distinguishing subtypes of multiword expressions using linguistically-motivated statistical measures. In *proceedings of the ACL workshop on MWEs*, pages 9–16, Czech Republic. ACL.

K. Frantzi, S. Ananiadou, and H. Mima. 2000. Automatic recognition of multi-word terms: the c-value/nc-value method. *International Journal on Digital Libraries*, 3(2):115–130.

S. Fujita, F. Bond, S. Oepen, and T. Tanaka. 2007. Exploiting semantic information for hpsg parse selection. In *proceedings of DeepLP*, pages 25–32, USA. ACL.

C. Hashimoto, S. Sato, and T. Utsuro. 2006. Detecting japanese idioms with a linguistically rich dictionary. *Language Resources and Evaluation*, 40(3):243–252.

E. Hektoen. 1997. Probabilistic parse selection based on semantic cooccurrences. In *proceedings of IWPT*, pages 113–122, USA.

G. Katz and E. Giesbrecht. 2006. Automatic identification of non-compositional multi-word expressions using latent semantic analysis. In *proceedings of the ACL workshop on MWEs*, pages 12–19, Australia. ACL.

S. Kim and T. Baldwin. 2008. Standardised evaluation of english noun compound interpretation. In *proceedings of the LREC workshop on MWEs*, pages 39–42, Morocco.

I. Korkontzelos and S. Manandhar. 2009. Detecting compositionality in multi-word expressions. In *proceedings of ACL-IJCNLP*, Singapore.

E. Laporte and S. Voyatzi. 2008. An Electronic Dictionary of French Multiword Adverbs. In *proceedings of the LREC workshop on MWEs*, pages 31–34, Marocco.

D. Lin. 1999. Automatic identification of non-compositional phrases. In *proceedings of ACL*, pages 317–324, USA. ACL.

C. Manning and H. Schutze, 1999. *Foundations of Statistical NLP, Collocations*, chapter 5. MIT Press.

D. McCarthy. 2006. Automatic methods to detect the compositionality of MWEs. presentation slides. url: www.sunum.org/myfiles/B2/McCarthyCollocIdioms06.ppt last accessed: 28/11/2009.

G. Miller. 1995. Wordnet: a lexical database for english. *Communications of the ACM*, 38(11):39–41.

R. Moon. 1998. *Fixed Expressions and Idioms in English. A Corpus-based Approach.* Oxford: Clarendon Press.

M. Munoz, V. Punyakanok, D. Roth, and D. Zimak. 1999. A learning approach to shallow parsing. In *proceedings of EMNLP/VLC*, pages 168–178, USA.

J. Nicholson and T. Baldwin. 2008. Interpreting compound nominalisations. In *proceedings of the LREC workshop on MWEs*, pages 43–45, Morocco.

G. Nunberg, T. Wasow, and I. Sag. 1994. Idioms. *Language*, 70(3):491–539.

I. Sag, T. Baldwin, F. Bond, A. Copestake, and D. Flickinger. 2002. Multiword expressions: A pain in the neck for nlp. In *proceedings of CICLing*, pages 1–15, Mexico.

Y. Tsuruoka, Y. Tateishi, J. Kim, T. Ohta, J. McNaught, S. Ananiadou, and J. Tsujii. 2005. Developing a robust part-of-speech tagger for biomedical text. *Advances in Informatics*, pages 382–392.

T. Van de Cruys and B. Moirón. 2007. Semantics-based multiword expression extraction. In *proceedings of the ACL workshop on MWEs*, pages 25–32, Czech Republic. ACL.

S. Venkatapathy and A. Joshi. 2005. Measuring the relative compositionality of verb-noun (V-N) collocations by integrating features. In *proceedings of HLT*, pages 899–906, USA. ACL.

D. Xiong, S. Li, Q. Liu, S. Lin, and Y. Qian. 2005. Parsing the penn chinese treebank with semantic knowledge. In *proceedings of IJCNLP*, pages 70–81, Korea.

A Simple Approach for HPSG Supertagging Using Dependency Information

Yao-zhong Zhang † **Takuya Matsuzaki** † **Jun'ichi Tsujii**†‡§

† Department of Computer Science, University of Tokyo
‡ School of Computer Science, University of Manchester
§National Centre for Text Mining, UK
{yaozhong.zhang, matuzaki, tsujii}@is.s.u-tokyo.ac.jp

Abstract

In a supertagging task, sequence labeling models are commonly used. But their limited ability to model long-distance information presents a bottleneck to make further improvements. In this paper, we modeled this long-distance information in dependency formalism and integrated it into the process of HPSG supertagging. The experiments showed that the dependency information is very informative for supertag disambiguation. We also evaluated the improved supertagger in the HPSG parser.

1 Introduction

Supertagging is a widely used speed-up technique for lexicalized grammar parsing. It was first proposed for lexicalized tree adjoining grammar (LTAG) (Bangalore and Joshi, 1999), then extended to combinatory categorial grammar (CCG) (Clark, 2002) and head-driven phrase structure grammar (HPSG) (Ninomiya et al., 2006). For deep parsing, supertagging is an important preprocessor: an accurate supertagger greatly reduces search space of a parser. Not limited to parsing, supertags can be used for NP chunking (Shen and Joshi, 2003), semantic role labeling (Chen and Rambow, 2003) and machine translation (Birch et al., 2007; Hassan et al., 2007) to explore rich syntactic information contained in them.

Generally speaking, supertags are lexical templates extracted from a grammar. These templates encode possible syntactic behavior of a word. Although the number of supertags is far larger than the 45 POS tags defined in Penn Treebank, sequence labeling techniques are still effective for supertagging. Previous research (Clark, 2002) showed that a POS sequence is very informative for supertagging, and some extent of local syntactic information can be captured by the context of surrounding words and POS tags. However, since the context window length is limited for the computational cost reasons, there are still long-range dependencies which are not easily captured in sequential models (Zhang et al., 2009). In practice, the multi-tagging technique proposed by Clark (2002) assigned more than one supertag to each word and let the ambiguous supertags be selected by the parser. As for other NLP applications which use supertags, resolving more supertag ambiguities in supertagging stage is preferred. With this consideration, we focus on supertagging and aim to make it as accurate as possible.

In this paper, we incorporated long-distance information into supertagging. First, we used dependency parser formalism to model long-distance relationships between the input words, which is hard to model in sequence labeling models. Then, we combined the dependency information with local context in a simple point-wise model. The experiments showed that dependency information is very informative for supertagging and we got a competitive 93.70% on supertagging accuracy (fed golden POS). In addition, we also evaluated the improved supertagger in the HPSG parser.

2 HPSG Supertagging and Dependency

2.1 HPSG Supertags

HPSG (Pollard and Sag, 1994) is a lexicalist grammar framework. In HPSG, a large number of lexical entries is used to describe word-specific syntactic characteristics, while only a small number of schemas is used to explain general construction rules. These lexical entries are called "HPSG supertags". For example, one possible supertag for the word "like" is written like "[NP.nom<V.bse>NP.acc]_lxm", which indicates

Human Language Technologies: The 2010 Annual Conference of the North American Chapter of the ACL, pages 645–648,
Los Angeles, California, June 2010.

the head syntactic category of "like" is verb in base form. It has a NP subject and a NP complement. With such fine-grained grammatical type distinctions, the number of supertags is much larger than the number of tags used in other sequence labeling tasks. The HPSG grammar used in our experiment includes 2,308 supertags. This increases computational cost of sequence labeling models.

2.2 Why Use Dependency in Supertagging

By analyzing the internal structure of the supertags, we found that subject and complements are two important syntactic properties for each supertag. If we could predict subject and complements of the word well, supertagging would be an easier job to do. However, current widely used sequence labeling models have the limited ability to catch these long-distance syntactic relations. In supertagging stage, tree structures are still not constructed. Dependency formalism is an alternative way to describe these two syntactic properties. Based on this observation, we think dependency information could assist supertag prediction.

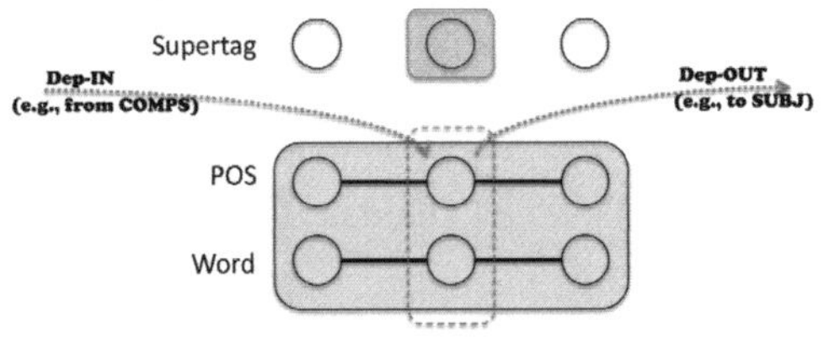

Figure 1: Model structure of incorporating dependency information into the supertagging stage. Dotted arrows describe the augmented long distance dependency information provided for supertag prediction.

3 Our Method

3.1 Modeling Dependency for Supertags

First of all, we need to characterize the dependency between words for supertagging. Since exact dependency locations are not encoded in supertags, to make use of state-of-the-art dependency parser, we recover HPSG supertag dependencies with the aid of HPSG treebanks. The dependencies are extracted from each branch in the HPSG trees by regarding the non-head daughter as the modifier of the head-daughter. HPSG schemas are expressed in dependency arcs.

To model the dependency, we follow mainstream dependency parsing formalism. Two representative methods for dependency parsing are transition-based model like MaltParser (Nivre, 2003) and graph-based model like MSTParser[1] (McDonald et al., 2005). Previous research (Nivre and McDonald, 2008) showed that MSTParser is more accurate than MaltParser for long dependencies. Since our motivation is to capture long-distance dependency as a complement for local supertagging models, we use the projective MSTParser formalism to model dependencies.

MOD-IN	$\{(p_i \Leftarrow p_j)\&s_j \mid (j,i) \in E\}$ $\{(p_i \Leftarrow w_j)\&s_j \mid (j,i) \in E\}$ $\{(w_i \Leftarrow p_j)\&s_j \mid (j,i) \in E\}$ $\{(w_i \Leftarrow w_j)\&s_j \mid (j,i) \in E\}$
MOD-OUT	$\{(p_i \Rightarrow p_j)\&s_i \mid (i,j) \in E\}$ $\{(p_i \Rightarrow w_j)\&s_i \mid (i,j) \in E\}$ $\{(w_i \Rightarrow p_j)\&s_i \mid (i,j) \in E\}$ $\{(w_i \Rightarrow w_j)\&s_i \mid (i,j) \in E\}$

Table 1: Non-local feature templates used for supertagging. Here, p, w and s represent POS, word and schema respectively. Direction (Left/Right) from MODIN/MODOUT word to the current word is also considered in the feature templates.

3.2 Integrating Dependency into Supertagging

There are several ways to combine long-distance dependency into supertagging. Integrating dependency information into training process would be more intuitive. Here, we use feature-based integration. The base model is a point-wise averaged perceptron (PW-AP) which has been shown very effective (Zhang et al., 2009). The improved model structure is described in Figure 1. The long-distance information is formalized as first-order dependency. For the word being predicted, we extract its modifiers (MODIN) and its head (MODOUT) (Table 1) based on first-order dependency arcs. Then MODIN and MODOUT relations are combined as features with local context for supertag prediction. To compare with previous work, the basic local context features are the same as in Matsuzaki et al. (2007).

[1]http://sourceforge.net/projects/mstparser/

4 Experiments

We evaluated dependency-informed supertagger (PW-DEP) both by supertag accuracy [2] and by a HPSG parser. The experiments were conducted on WSJ-HPSG treebank (Miyao, 2006). Sections 02-21 were used to train the dependency parser, the dependency-informed supertagger and the HPSG parser. Section 23 was used as the testing set. The evaluation metric for HPSG parser is the accuracy of predicate-argument relations in the parser's output, as in previous work (Sagae et al., 2007).

Model	**Dep Acc%**†	**Acc%**
PW-AP	/	91.14
PW-DEP	90.98	**92.18**
PW-AP (gold POS)	/	92.48
PW-DEP (gold POS)	92.05	**93.70**
	100	**97.43**

Table 2: Supertagging accuracy on section 23. (†) Dependencies are given by MSTParser evaluated with labeled accuracy. PW-AP is the baseline point-wise averaged perceptron model. PW-DEP is point-wise dependency-informed model. The automatically tagged POS tags were given by a maximum entropy tagger with 97.39% accuracy.

4.1 Results on Supertagging

We first evaluated the upper-bound of dependency-informed supertagging model, given gold standard first-order dependencies. As shown in Table 2, with such long-distance information supertagging accuracy can reach 97.43%. Comparing to point-wise model (PW-AP) which only used local context (92.48%), this absolute 4.95% gain indicated that dependency information is really informative for supertagging. When automatically predicted dependency relations were given, there still were absolute 1.04% (auto POS) and 1.22% (gold POS) improvements from baseline PW-AP model.

We also compared supertagging results with previous works (reported on section 22). Here we mainly compared the dependency-informed point-wise models with perceptron-based Bayes point machine (BPM) plus CFG-filter (Zhang et al., 2009). To the best of our knowledge, these are the state-of-the-art results on the same dataset with gold POS

[2]"UNK" supertags are ignored in evaluation as previous.

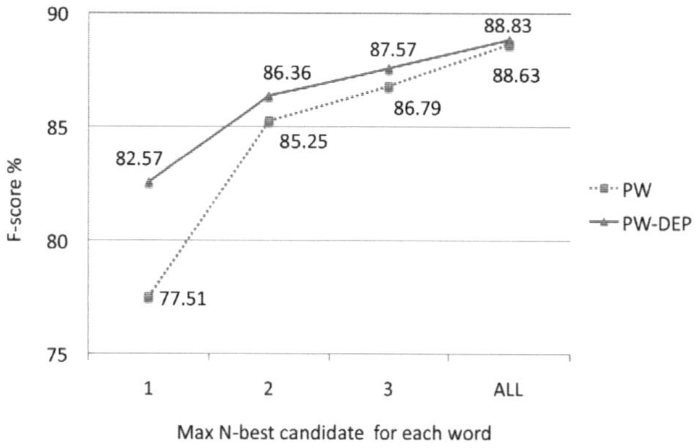

Figure 2: HPSG Parser F-score on section 23, given automatically tagged POS.

tags. CFG-filtering can be considered as an alternative way of incorporating long-distance constraints on supertagging results. Although our baseline system was slightly behind (PW-AP: 92.16% vs. BPM:92.53%), the final accuracies of grammatically constrained models were very close (PW-DEP: 93.53% vs. BPM-CFG: 93.60%); They were not statistically significantly different (P-value is 0.26). As the result of oracle PW-DEP indicated, supertagging accuracy can be further improved with better dependency modeling (e.g., with a semi-supervised dependency parser), which makes it more extensible and attractive than using CFG-filter after the supertagging process.

4.2 HPSG parsing results

We also evaluated the dependency-informed supertagger in a HPSG parser. Considering the efficiency, we use the HPSG parser[3] described by Matsuzaki et al. (2007).

In practice, several supertag candidates are reserved for each word to avoid parsing failure. To evaluate the quality of the two supertaggers, we restricted the number of each word's supertag candidates fed to the HPSG parser. As shown in Figure 2, for the case when only one supertag was predicted for each word, F-score of the HPSG parser using dependency-informed supertagger is 5.06% higher than the parser using the baseline supertagger module. As the candidate number increased, the gap narrowed: when all candidates were given, the gains gradually came down to 0.2%. This indicated that

[3]Enju v2.3.1, http://www-tsujii.is.s.u-tokyo.ac.jp/enju.

improved supertagger can optimize the search space of the deep parser, which may contribute to more accurate and fast deep parsing. From another aspect, supertagging can be viewed as an interface to combine different types of parsers.

As for the overall parsing time, we didn't optimize for speed in current setting. The parsing time[4] saved by using the improved supertagger (around 6.0 ms/sen, 21.5% time reduction) can not compensate for the extra cost of MSTParser (around 73.8 ms/sen) now. But there is much room to improve the final speed (e.g., optimizing the dependency parser for speed or reusing acquired dependencies for effective pruning). In addition, small beam-size can be "safely" used with improved supertagger for speed.

Using shallow dependencies in deep HPSG parsing has been previously explored by Sagae et al. (2007), who used dependency constraints in schema application stage to guide HPSG tree construction (F-score was improved from 87.2% to 87.9% with a single shift-reduce dependency parser). Since the baseline parser is different, we didn't make a direct comparison here. However, it would be interesting to compare these two different ways of incorporating the dependency parser into HPSG parsing. We left it as further work.

5 Conclusions

In this paper, focusing on improving the accuracy of supertagging, we proposed a simple but effective way to incorporate long-distance dependency relations into supertagging. The experiments mainly showed that these long-distance dependencies, which are not easy to model in traditional sequence labeling models, are very informative for supertag predictions. Although these were preliminary results, the method shows its potential strength for related applications. Not limited to HPSG, it can be extended to other lexicalized grammar supertaggers.

Acknowledgments

Thanks to the anonymous reviewers for valuable comments. We also thank Goran Topic for his selfless help. The first author was supported by The University of Tokyo Fellowship (UT-Fellowship). This work was partially supported by Grant-in-Aid for Specially Promoted Research (MEXT, Japan).

[4]Tested on section 23 (2291 sentences) using an AMD Opteron 2.4GHz server, given all supertag candidates.

References

Srinivas Bangalore and Aravind K. Joshi. 1999. Supertagging: An approach to almost parsing. *Computational Linguistics*, 25:237–265.

Alexandra Birch, Miles Osborne, and Philipp Koehn. 2007. CCG supertags in factored statistical machine translation. In *Proceedings of the Second Workshop on Statistical Machine Translation*.

John Chen and Owen Rambow. 2003. Use of deep linguistic features for the recognition and labeling of semantic arguments. In *Proceedings of EMNLP-2003*.

Stephen Clark. 2002. Supertagging for combinatory categorial grammar. In *Proceedings of the 6th International Workshop on Tree Adjoining Grammars and Related Frameworks (TAG+ 6)*, pages 19–24.

Hany Hassan, Mary Hearne, and Andy Way. 2007. Supertagged phrase-based statistical machine translation. In *Proceedings of ACL 2007*, pages 288–295.

Takuya Matsuzaki, Yusuke Miyao, and Jun'ichi Tsujii. 2007. Efficient hpsg parsing with supertagging and cfg-filtering. In *Proceedings of IJCAI-07*.

Ryan McDonald, Koby Crammer, and Fernando Pereira. 2005. Online large-margin training of dependency parsers. In *Proceedings of ACL-05*.

Yusuke Miyao. 2006. *From Linguistic Theory to Syntactic Analysis: Corpus-Oriented Grammar Development and Feature Forest Model*. Ph.D. Dissertation, The University of Tokyo.

Takashi Ninomiya, Yoshimasa Tsuruoka, Takuya Matsuzaki, and Yusuke Miyao. 2006. Extremely lexicalized models for accurate and fast hpsg parsing. In *Proceedings of EMNLP-2006*, pages 155–163.

Joakim Nivre and Ryan McDonald. 2008. Integrating graph-based and transition-based dependency parsers. In *Proceedings of ACL-08: HLT*.

J. Nivre. 2003. An efficient algorithm for projective dependency parsing. In *Proceedings of IWPT-03*, pages 149–160. Citeseer.

Carl Pollard and Ivan A. Sag. 1994. *Head-driven Phrase Structure Grammar*. University of Chicago / CSLI.

Kenji Sagae, Yusuke Miyao, and Jun'ichi Tsujii. 2007. Hpsg parsing with shallow dependency constraints. In *Proceedings of ACL-07*.

Libin Shen and Aravind K. Joshi. 2003. A snow based supertagger with application to np chunking. In *Proceedings of ACL 2003*, pages 505–512.

Yao-zhong Zhang, Takuya Matsuzaki, and Jun'ichi Tsujii. 2009. Hpsg supertagging: A sequence labeling view. In *Proceedings of IWPT-09*, Paris, France.

Ensemble Models for Dependency Parsing: Cheap and Good?

Mihai Surdeanu and Christopher D. Manning
Computer Science Department
Stanford University, Stanford, CA 94305
{mihais,manning}@stanford.edu

Abstract

Previous work on dependency parsing used various kinds of combination models but a systematic analysis and comparison of these approaches is lacking. In this paper we implemented such a study for English dependency parsing and find several non-obvious facts: (a) the diversity of base parsers is more important than complex models for learning (e.g., stacking, supervised meta-classification), (b) approximate, linear-time re-parsing algorithms guarantee well-formed dependency trees without significant performance loss, and (c) the simplest scoring model for re-parsing (unweighted voting) performs essentially as well as other more complex models. This study proves that fast and accurate ensemble parsers can be built with minimal effort.

1 Introduction

Several ensemble models have been proposed for the parsing of syntactic dependencies. These approaches can generally be classified in two categories: models that integrate base parsers at learning time, e.g., using stacking (Nivre and McDonald, 2008; Attardi and Dell'Orletta, 2009), and approaches that combine independently-trained models only at parsing time (Sagae and Lavie, 2006; Hall et al., 2007; Attardi and Dell'Orletta, 2009). In the latter case, the correctness of the final dependency tree is ensured by: (a) selecting entire trees proposed by the base parsers (Henderson and Brill, 1999); or (b) re-parsing the pool of dependencies proposed by the base models (Sagae and Lavie, 2006). The latter approach was shown to perform better for constituent parsing (Henderson and Brill, 1999).

While all these models achieved good performance, the previous work has left several questions unanswered. Here we answer the following questions, in the context of English dependency parsing:

	Devel	In domain		Out of domain	
	LAS	LAS	UAS	LAS	UAS
MST	85.36	87.07	89.95	80.48	86.08
$\text{Malt}_{\overrightarrow{AE}}$	84.24	85.96	88.64	78.74	84.18
$\text{Malt}_{\overrightarrow{CN}}$	83.75	85.61	88.14	78.55	83.68
$\text{Malt}_{\overrightarrow{AS}}$	83.74	85.36	88.06	77.23	82.39
$\text{Malt}_{\overleftarrow{AS}}$	82.43	83.90	86.70	76.69	82.57
$\text{Malt}_{\overleftarrow{CN}}$	81.75	83.53	86.17	77.29	83.02
$\text{Malt}_{\overleftarrow{AE}}$	80.76	82.51	85.35	76.18	82.02

Table 1: Labeled attachment scores (LAS) and unlabeled attachment scores (UAS) for the base models. The parsers are listed in descending order of LAS in the development partition.

1. When combining models at parsing time, what is the best scoring model for candidate dependencies during re-parsing? Can a meta classifier improve over unsupervised voting?
2. Are (potentially-expensive) re-parsing strategies justified for English? What percentage of trees are not well-formed if one switches to a light word-by-word voting scheme?
3. How important is the integration of base parsers at learning time?
4. How do ensemble models compare against state-of-the-art supervised parsers?

2 Setup

In our experiments we used the syntactic dependencies from the CoNLL 2008 shared task corpus (Surdeanu et al., 2008).

We used seven base parsing models in this paper: six are variants of the Malt parser[1] and the seventh is the projective version of MSTParser that uses only first-order features[2] (or MST for short). The six Malt

[1] http://maltparser.org/

[2] http://sourceforge.net/projects/mstparser/

Human Language Technologies: The 2010 Annual Conference of the North American Chapter of the ACL, pages 649–652,
Los Angeles, California, June 2010.

# of parsers	Unweighted		Weighted by POS of modifier		Weighted by label of dependency		Weighted by dependency length		Weighted by sentence length	
	LAS	UAS	LAS	UAS	LAS	UAS	LAS	UAS	LAS	UAS
3	86.03	89.44	86.02	89.43	85.53	88.97	85.85	89.23	86.03	89.45
4	86.79	90.14	86.68	90.07	86.38	89.78	86.46	89.79	86.84	90.18
5	86.98	90.33	86.95	90.30	86.60	90.06	86.87	90.22	86.86	90.22
6	87.14	**90.51**	**87.17**	90.50	86.74	90.22	86.91	90.23	87.04	90.37
7	86.81	90.21	86.82	90.21	86.50	90.01	86.71	90.08	86.80	90.19

Table 2: Scores of unsupervised combination models using different voting strategies. The combined trees are assembled using a word-by-word voting scheme.

parser variants are built by varying the parsing algorithm (we used three parsing models: Nivre's arc-eager (AE), Nivre's arc-standard (AS), and Covington's non-projective model (CN)), and the parsing direction (left to right (→) or right to left (←)), similar to (Hall et al., 2007). The parameters of the Malt models were set to the values reported in (Hall et al., 2007). The MST parser was used with the default configuration. Table 1 shows the performance of these models in the development and test partitions.

3 Experiments

3.1 On scoring models for parser combination

The most common approach for combining independently-trained models at parsing time is to assign each candidate dependency a score based on the number of votes it received from the base parsers. Considering that parsers specialize in different phenomena, these votes can be weighted by different criteria. To understand the importance of such weighting strategies we compare several voting approaches in Table 2: in the "unweighted" strategy all votes have the same weight; in all other strategies each vote is assigned a value equal to the accuracy of the given parser in the particular instance of the context considered, e.g., in the "weighted by POS of modifier" model we use the accuracies of the base models for each possible part-of-speech (POS) tag of a modifier token. In the table we show results as more base parsers are added to the ensemble (we add parsers in the order given by Table 1). The results in Table 2 indicate that weighting strategies do not have an important contribution to overall performance. The only approach that outperforms the LAS score of the unweighted voting model is the model that weighs parsers by their accuracy for a given modifier POS tag, but the improvement is marginal. On the other hand, the number of base parsers in the ensemble pool is crucial: performance generally continues to improve as more base parsers are considered. The best ensemble uses 6 out of the 7 base parsers.[3]

	POS(m)	POS(m) × POS(h)	length(s)
MST	38	56	26
$\text{Malt}_{AE}^{\rightarrow}$	0	6	6
$\text{Malt}_{CN}^{\rightarrow}$	0	14	7
$\text{Malt}_{AS}^{\rightarrow}$	0	61	0
$\text{Malt}_{AS}^{\leftarrow}$	0	0	3
$\text{Malt}_{CN}^{\leftarrow}$	0	9	0
$\text{Malt}_{AE}^{\leftarrow}$	0	0	0

Table 3: Total number of minority dependencies with precision larger than 50%, for different base parsers and most representative features (m - modifier, h - head, s - sentence). These are counts of tokens, computed in the development corpus of 33,368 dependencies.

It is often argued that the best way to re-score candidate dependencies is not through voting but rather through a meta-classifier that selects candidate dependencies based on their likelihood of belonging to the correct tree. Unlike voting, a meta-classifier can combine evidence from multiple contexts (such as the ones listed in Table 2). However, in our experiments such a meta-classifier[4] did not offer any gains over the much simpler unweighted voting strategy. We explain these results as follows: the meta-classifier can potentially help only when it proposes dependencies that disagree with the majority vote. We call such dependencies *minority dependencies*.[5] For a given parser and context instance (e.g., a modifier POS), we define precision of minority dependencies as the ratio of minority dependencies in this group that are correct. Obviously, a

[3]We drew similar conclusions when we replaced voting with the re-parsing algorithms from the next sub-section.

[4]We implemented a L2-regularized logistic regression classifier using as features: identifiers of the base models, POS tags of head and modifier, labels of dependencies, length of dependencies, length of sentence, and combinations of the above.

[5](Henderson and Brill, 1999) used a similar framework in the context of constituent parsing and only three base parsers.

group of minority dependencies provides beneficial signal only if its precision is larger than 50%. Table 3 lists the total number of minority dependencies in groups with precision larger than 50% for all our base parsers and the most representative features. The table shows that the number of minority dependencies with useful signal is extremely low. All in all, it accounts for less than 0.7% of all dependencies in the development corpus.

3.2 On re-parsing algorithms

To guarantee that the resulting dependency tree is well-formed, most previous work used the dynamic programming algorithm of Eisner (1996) for re-parsing (Sagae and Lavie, 2006; Hall et al., 2007).[6] However, it is not clear that this step is necessary. In other words, how many sentences are not well-formed if one uses a simple word-by-word voting scheme? To answer this, we analyzed the output of our best word-by-word voting scheme (six base parsers weighted by the POS of the modifier). The results for both in-domain and out-of-domain testing corpora are listed in Table 4. The table shows that the percentage of badly-formed trees is relatively large: almost 10% out of domain. This indicates that the focus on algorithms that guarantee well-formed trees is justified.

However, it is not clear how the Eisner algorithm, which has runtime complexity of $O(n^3)$ (n – number of tokens per sentence), compares against approximate re-parsing algorithms that have lower runtime complexity. One such algorithm was proposed by Attardi and Dell'Orletta (2009). The algorithm, which has a runtime complexity of $O(n)$, builds dependency trees using a greedy top-down strategy, i.e., it starts by selecting the highest-scoring root node, then the highest-scoring children, etc. We compare these algorithms against the word-by-word voting scheme in Table 5.[7] The results show that both algorithms pay a small penalty for guaranteeing well-formed trees. This performance drop is statistically significant out of domain. On the other hand, the difference between the Eisner and Attardi algorithms is not statistically significant out of domain.

	In domain	Out of domain
Zero roots	0.83%	0.70%
Multiple roots	3.37%	6.11%
Cycles	4.29%	4.23%
Total	7.46%	9.64%

Table 4: Percentage of badly-formed dependency trees when base parsers are combined using a word-by-word voting scheme. The different error classes do not sum up to the listed total because the errors are not mutually exclusive.

	In domain		Out of domain	
	LAS	UAS	LAS	UAS
Word by word	88.89	91.52	82.13*	87.51*
Eisner	88.83*	91.47*	81.99	87.32
Attardi	88.70	91.34	81.82	87.29

Table 5: Scores of different combination schemes. * indicates that a model is significantly different than the next lower ranked model.

This experiment proves that approximate re-parsing algorithms are a better choice for practical purposes, i.e., ensemble parsing in domains different from the training material of the base models.

3.3 On parser integration at learning time

Recent work has shown that the combination of base parsers at learning time, e.g., through stacking, yields considerable benefits (Nivre and McDonald, 2008; Attardi and Dell'Orletta, 2009). However, it is unclear how these approaches compare against the simpler ensemble models, which combine parsers only at runtime. To enable such a comparison, we reimplemented the best stacking model from (Nivre and McDonald, 2008) – MST_{Malt} – which trains a variant of the MSTParser that uses additional features extracted from the output of a Malt parser.

In Table 6, we compare this stacking approach against four variants of our ensemble models. The superscript in the ensemble name indicates the runtime complexity of the model ($O(n^3)$ or $O(n)$). The cubic-time models use all base parsers from Table 1 and the Eisner algorithm for re-parsing. The linear-time models use only Malt-based parsers and the Attardi algorithm for re-parsing. The subscript in the model names indicates the percentage of available base parsers used, e.g., $\text{ensemble}^3_{50\%}$ uses only the first three parsers from Table 1. These results show that MST_{Malt} is statistically equivalent to an ensemble that uses MST and two Malt variants, and both our $\text{ensemble}_{100\%}$ models are significantly better than MST_{Malt}. While this comparison is somewhat unfair (MST_{Malt} uses two base models, whereas our ensemble models use at least three) it

[6]We focus on projective parsing algorithms because 99.6% of dependencies in our data are projective (Surdeanu et al., 2008).

[7]Statistical significance was performed using Dan Bikel randomized parsing evaluation comparator at 95% confidence.

	In domain		Out of domain	
	LAS	UAS	LAS	UAS
$\text{ensemble}^3_{100\%}$	88.83*	91.47*	81.99*	87.32*
$\text{ensemble}^1_{100\%}$	88.01*	90.76*	80.78	86.55
$\text{ensemble}^3_{50\%}$	87.45	90.17	81.12	86.62
MST_{Malt}	87.45*	90.22*	80.25*	85.90*
$\text{ensemble}^1_{50\%}$	86.74	89.62	79.44	85.54

Table 6: Comparison of different combination strategies.

	In domain		Out of domain	
	LAS	UAS	LAS	UAS
CoNLL 2008, #1	90.13*	92.45*	82.81*	88.19*
$\text{ensemble}^3_{100\%}$	88.83*	91.47*	81.99*	87.32*
CoNLL 2008, #2	88.14	90.78	80.80	86.12
$\text{ensemble}^1_{100\%}$	88.01	90.76	80.78	86.55

Table 7: Comparison with state of the art parsers.

does illustrate that the advantages gained from combining parsers at learning time can be easily surpassed by runtime combination models that have access to more base parsers. Considering that variants of shift-reduce parsers can be generated with minimal effort (e.g., by varying the parsing direction, learning algorithms, etc.) and combining models at runtime is simpler than combining them at learning time, we argue that runtime parser combination is a more attractive approach.

3.4 Comparison with the state of the art

In Table 7 we compare our best ensemble models against the top two systems of the CoNLL-2008 shared task evaluation. The table indicates that our best ensemble model ranks second, outperforming significantly 19 other systems. The only model performing better than our ensemble is a parser that uses higher-order features and has a higher runtime complexity ($O(n^4)$) (Johansson and Nugues, 2008). While this is certainly proof of the importance of higher-order features, it also highlights a pragmatic conclusion: in out-of-domain corpora, an ensemble of models that use only first-order features achieves performance that is within 1% LAS of much more complex models.

4 Conclusions

This study unearthed several non-intuitive yet important observations about ensemble models for dependency parsing. First, we showed that the diversity of base parsers is more important than complex learning models for parser combination, i.e., (a) ensemble models that combine several base parsers at runtime performs significantly better than a state-of-the-art model that combines two parsers at learning time, and (b) meta-classification does not outperform unsupervised voting schemes for the re-parsing of candidate dependencies when six base models are available. Second, we showed that well-formed dependency trees can be guaranteed without significant performance loss by linear-time approximate re-parsing algorithms. And lastly, our analysis indicates that unweighted voting performs as well as weighted voting for the re-parsing of candidate dependencies. Considering that different base models are easy to generate, this work proves that ensemble parsers that are both accurate and fast can be rapidly developed with minimal effort.

Acknowledgments

This material is based upon work supported by the Air Force Research Laboratory (AFRL) under prime contract no. FA8750-09-C-0181. Any opinions, findings, and conclusion or recommendations expressed in this material are those of the authors and do not necessarily reflect the view of the Air Force Research Laboratory (AFRL).

We thank Johan Hall, Joakim Nivre, Ryan McDonald, and Giuseppe Attardi for their help in understanding details of their models.

References

G. Attardi and F. Dell'Orletta. 2009. Reverse revision and linear tree combination for dependency parsing. In *Proc. of NAACL-HLT*.

J. Eisner. 1996. Three new probabilistic models for dependency parsing: An exploration. In *Proc. of COLING*.

J. Hall, J. Nilsson, J. Nivre, G. Eryigit, B. Megyesi, M. Nilsson, and M. Saers. 2007. Single malt or blended? A study in multilingual parser optimization. In *Proc. of CoNLL Shared Task*.

J. C. Henderson and E. Brill. 1999. Exploiting diversity in natural language processing: Combining parsers. In *Proc. of EMNLP*.

R. Johansson and P. Nugues. 2008. Dependency-based syntactic semantic analysis with PropBank and NomBank. In *Proc. of CoNLL Shared Task*.

J. Nivre and R. McDonald. 2008. Integrating graph-based and transition-based dependency parsers. In *Proc. of ACL*.

K. Sagae and A. Lavie. 2006. Parser combination by reparsing. In *Proc. of NAACL-HLT*.

M. Surdeanu, R. Johansson, A. Meyers, L. Marquez, and J. Nivre. 2008. The CoNLL-2008 shared task on joint parsing of syntactic and semantic dependencies. In *Proc. of CoNLL*.

Enlarged Search Space for SITG Parsing

Guillem Gascó, Joan-Andreu Sánchez, José-Miguel Benedí
Institut Tecnològic d'Informàtica, Universitat Politècnica de València
Camí de Vera s/n, València, 46022, Spain
ggasco@iti.upv.es,{jandreu,jbenedi}@dsic.upv.es

Abstract

Stochastic Inversion Transduction Grammars constitute a powerful formalism in Machine Translation for which an efficient Dynamic Programming parsing algorithm exists. In this work, we review this parsing algorithm and propose important modifications that enlarge the search space. These modifications allow the parsing algorithm to search for more and better solutions.

1 Introduction

Syntax Machine Translation has received great attention in the last few years, especially for pairs of languages that are sufficiently non-monotonic. Several works have explored the use of syntax for Machine Translation (Wu, 1997; Chiang, 2007). In (Wu, 1997), Stochastic Inverse Transduction Grammars (SITGs) were introduced for describing structurally correlated pairs of languages. SITGs can be used to simultaneously analyze two strings from different languages and to correlate them. An efficient Dynamic Programming parsing algorithm for SITGs was presented in (Wu, 1997). This algorithm is similar to the CKY algorithm for Probabilistic Context Free Grammars. The parsing algorithm does not allow the association of two items that have the empty string in one of their sides. This limitation restricts the search space and prevents the algorithm from exploring some valid parse trees.

In this paper, we review Wu's parsing algorithm for SITGs (referred to as the original algorithm) and propose some modifications to increase the search space in order to make it possible to find these valid parse trees.

2 SITG Parsing

SITGs (Wu, 1997) can be viewed as a restricted subset of Stochastic Syntax-Directed Transduction Grammars (Maryanski and Thomason, 1979). Formally, a SITG in Chomsky Normal Form can be defined as a set of lexical rules that are noted as $A \rightarrow x/\epsilon$, $A \rightarrow \epsilon/y$, $A \rightarrow x/y$; direct syntactic rules that are noted as $A \rightarrow [BC]$; and inverse syntactic rules that are noted as $A \rightarrow \langle BC \rangle$, where A, B, C are non-terminal symbols, x, y are terminal symbols, ϵ is the empty string, and each rule has a probability value p attached. The sum of the probabilities of the rules with the same non-terminal in the left side must be equal to 1. When a direct syntactic rule is used in parsing, both strings are parsed with the syntactic rule $A \rightarrow BC$. When an inverse rule is used in parsing, one string is parsed with the syntactic rule $A \rightarrow BC$, and the other string is parsed with the syntactic rule $A \rightarrow CB$.

An efficient Viterbi-like parsing algorithm that is based on a Dynamic Programming Scheme was proposed in (Wu, 1997). It allows us to obtain the most probable parse tree that simultaneously analyzes two strings, $X = x_1 ... x_{|X|}$ and $Y = y_1 ... x_{|Y|}$, i.e. the bilingual string X/Y. It has a time complexity of $O(|X|^3|Y|^3|R|)$, where $|R|$ is the number of rules of the grammar.

The parsing algorithm is based on the definition of:

$$\delta_{ijkl}(A) = \widehat{\Pr}(A \stackrel{*}{\Rightarrow} x_{i+1} \cdots x_j / y_{k+1} \cdots y_l)$$

as the maximum probability of any parsing tree that simultaneously generates the substrings $x_{i+1} \cdots x_j$ and $y_{k+1} \cdots y_l$ from the non-terminal symbol A.

In (Wu, 1997), the parsing algorithm was defined as follows:

Human Language Technologies: The 2010 Annual Conference of the North American Chapter of the ACL, pages 653–656,
Los Angeles, California, June 2010. ©2010 Association for Computational Linguistics

1. Initialization

$$\delta_{i-1,i,k-1,k}(A) = p(A \to x_i/y_k) \quad 1 \le i \le |X|, 1 \le k \le |Y|,$$
$$\delta_{i-1,i,k,k}(A) = p(A \to x_i/\epsilon) \quad 1 \le i \le |X|, 0 \le k \le |Y|,$$
$$\delta_{i,i,k-1,k}(A) = p(A \to \epsilon/y_k) \quad 0 \le i \le |X|, 1 \le k \le |Y|,$$

2. Recursion

For all $A \in N$ and i, j, k, l such that
$$\begin{cases} 0 \le i < j \le |X|, \\ 0 \le k < l \le |Y|, \\ j - i + l - k > 2, \end{cases} \quad (1)$$

$$\delta_{ijkl}(A) = \max(\delta^{[]}_{ijkl}(A), \delta^{\langle\rangle}_{ijkl}(A))$$

where

$$\delta^{[]}_{ijkl}(A) = \max_{\substack{B,C \in N \\ i \le I \le j, k \le K \le l \\ (I-i)(j-I)+(K-k)(l-K)>0}} p(A \to [BC])\delta_{iIkK}(B)\delta_{IjKl}(C) \quad (2)$$

$$\delta^{\langle\rangle}_{ijkl}(A) = \max_{\substack{B,C \in N \\ i \le I \le j, k \le K \le l \\ (I-i)(j-I)+(K-k)(l-K)>0}} p(A \to \langle BC\rangle)\delta_{iIKl}(B)\delta_{IjkK}(C) \quad (3)$$

This algorithm cannot provide the correct parsing tree in some situations. For example, consider the SITG shown in Fig. 1. If the input pair is a/b,

p	S	$\to [SS]$	p	S	$\to \langle SS\rangle$
q	S	$\to \epsilon/b$	q	S	$\to a/\epsilon$
$1-2p-2q$	S	$\to a/b$			

Figure 1: Example SITG.

this SITG provides the parse tree (a) that is shown in Fig. 2 with probability $1 - 2p - 2q$. However, the parse tree (b) is more likely if $1 - 2p - 2q < 2pq$. The above parsing algorithm is not able to obtain this parse tree due to the restriction $j - i + l - k > 2$ in (1). This restriction does not allow the algorithm to consider two subproblems in which each substring has length 1 which have not been previously considered in the initialization step. Changing this restriction to $j - i + l - k \ge 2$ is not enough to tackle this situation since the restriction

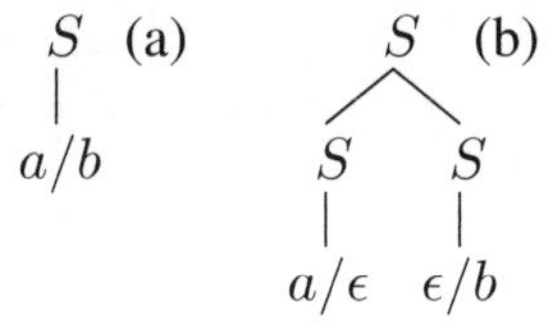

Figure 2: Parse tree (a) can be obtained with Wu's algorithm for a/b, but parse tree (b) cannot be obtained.

$(I-i)(j-I)+(K-k)(l-K) \neq 0$ in expression (2) is not accomplished given that $I = i$ or $I = j$, and $K = k$ or $l = K$ (similarly in expression (3)).

From now on, we will use the term *non-explored trees* to denote the set of trees that are possible when rules of the grammar are applied but cannot be explored with Wu's algorithm. In fact, this situation appears for other paired strings (see Fig. 3) in which a string in one side is associated with the empty string in the other side through rules that are not lexical rules. For example, in Fig. 3b, substring aa could be associated with ϵ. However,this parse tree cannot be obtained with the algorithm due to the search restrictions described above.

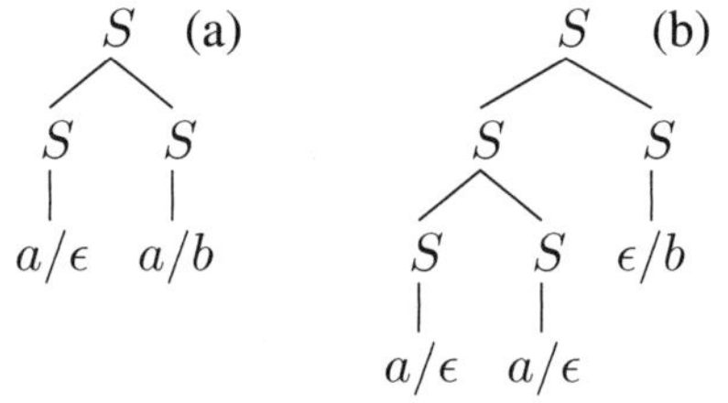

Figure 3: Parse tree (a) can be obtained with Wu's algorithm for aa/b, but parse tree (b) would be more probable if $pq^2 > 1 - 2p - 2q$.

The changes needed in the algorithm to be able to find the sort of parsing trees described above are the following:

- Changing restriction $j - i + l - k > 2$ in (1) to $j-i+l-k \ge 2$. Note that this new restriction is redundant and could be removed.
- Changing restriction $(I-i)(j-I)+(K-k)(l-K) \neq 0$ to $((j-I)+(l-K))*((I-i)+(K-k)) \neq 0$ in (2) and to $((j-I)+(K-k))*((I-i)+(l-K)) \neq 0$ in (3) in order to guarantee the algorithm's termination.

3 Search under SITG Constraints

The modifications that have been introduced in Section 2 enlarge the search space and allow the parsing algorithm to explore a greater number of possible solutions. We illustrate this situation with an example. Consider the SITG introduced in Figure 1. Fig. 4 shows the possible complete matched trees for the input pair a/b that are considered in the search process with the modifications introduced.

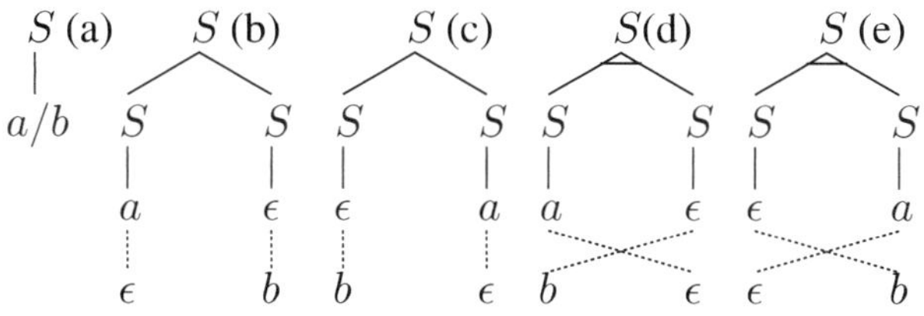

Figure 4: Parse trees for input pair a/b that are taken into account in the search process with the modifications.

Without these modifications, the parsing algorithm only takes into account tree (a) of Fig. 4. For this grammar, we have computed the growth in number of complete matched trees. Table 1 shows how the search space grows notably with the modifications introduced.

n	Wu's alg.	Modified alg.	ratio
1	1	5	0.200
2	34	290	0.117
3	1,928	34,088	0.057
4	131,880	5,152,040	0.026
5	10,071,264	890,510,432	0.011
6	827,969,856	167,399,588,160	0.005

Table 1: Growth in number of explored trees for the original and modified parsing algorithms (n is the length of the input pair strings and the last column represents the ratio between columns two and three).

As a preliminary experiment and in order to evaluate empirically the Wu's parsing algorithm versus the modified algorithm, we parsed first 100K sentence of German-English Europarl corpus. The lexical rules in the Bracketing SITG used for parsing were obtained from a probabilistic dictionary by aligning with IBM3 model (NULL aligments were also included). In this experiment, the modified algorithm obtained a more probable parse tree for 6% of the sentences. If we added brackets to the sentences separately with monolingual parsers, we could use a parsing algorithm similar to the algorithm that is described in (Sánchez and Benedí, 2006). The monolingual brackets restricted the parse tree to those that were compatible with the brackets. In that case the modified algorithm obtained a more probable parse tree for 14% of the sentences.

4 Inside Probability

The parsing algorithm described above computes the most likely parse tree for a given paired string X/Y. However, in some cases (Wu, 1995; Huang and Zhou, 2009), we need the inside probability ($\beta_{0,|X|,0,|Y|}(S)$), i.e., the probability that the grammar assigns to the whole set of parse trees that yield X/Y. If the maximizations are replaced by sums, the algorithm can be used to compute the inside probability. However, as stated above, the original algorithm cannot find the whole set of trees for a given paired string in some cases. These non-explored trees have a probability greater than 0.

As an example, we computed the amount of probability lost in the inside computation using the original algorithm with the grammar shown in Fig. 1. Let Γ be the amount of probability of the non-explored trees (the lost probability). It must be noted that since height 1 trees are all reachable, we must accumulate lost probability for trees of height 2 or more. Hence, let γ be the amount of lost probability for trees of height 2 or more. Note that all such trees must have initially used the production $S \to SS$ inversely or directly. Thus, $\Gamma = 2p \cdot \gamma$. Fig. 5 shows the kinds of non-explored trees. Then γ is:

$$\gamma = 4 \cdot q^2 + 2 \cdot 2p \cdot (1-2p) \cdot \gamma + (2p)^2 \cdot (2\gamma(1-\gamma) + \gamma^2)$$

The first addend is the probability of the non-explored trees of height 2 (Fig. 5a). The second addend is the probability that one of the subtrees uses a syntactic production, this new subtree produces a non-explored tree ($2p \cdot \gamma$) and the other subtree

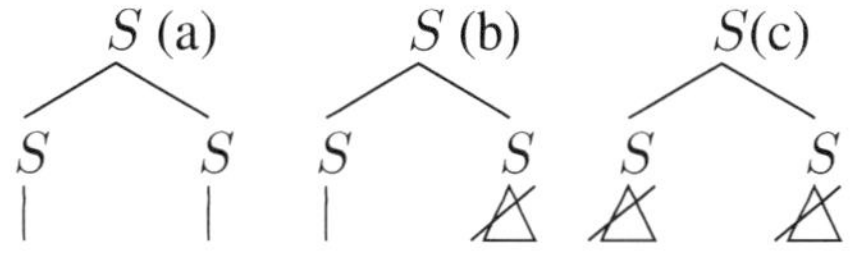

Figure 5: Partial representation of non-explored parse trees from the non-terminal string SS introduced after the first derivation step: (a) both non-terminals yield a terminal in one side and the empty string in the other; (b) one of the non-terminals uses a lexical production and the other non-terminal yields a non-explored tree; (c) both non-terminals use a syntactic production and one (or both) yields a non-explored tree.

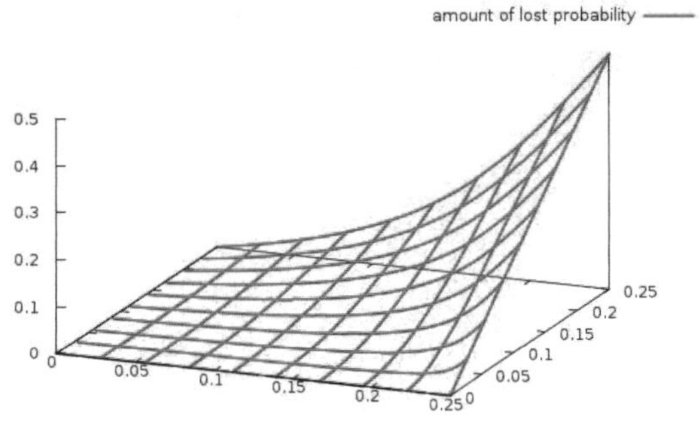

Figure 6: Amount of lost probability for values of p and q.

rewrites itself using a lexical production $(1-2p)$. Note that the non-explored tree can be yielded from either the left or the right non-terminal, (Fig. 5b). The third addend is the probability that both non-terminals use a syntactic production $(2p)^2$ and either one $(2(\gamma)(1-\gamma))$ or both (γ^2) subtrees are non-explored trees (Fig. 5c). If we isolate Γ, we get

$$\Gamma = 2p \cdot \frac{1 - 4p \pm \sqrt{16p^2 - 8p + 1 + 64p^2q^2}}{4p^2}$$

Since the solution with the positive square root takes values greater than 1, we can discard it.

Fig. 6 shows the probability accumulated in the non-explored trees for values of p and q between 0 and 0.25 (higher values of p produce inconsistent SITGs). That is the amount of probability lost in the inside parsing for the whole language generated by the grammar shown in Fig. 1.

In order to prove the loss of probability produced by the original algorithm, we use the grammar in Fig. 1 with $p = q = 0.2$. We parse all the paired strings X/Y such that $|X| + |Y| \leq l$, where l is a fixed maximum length. We repeat the same experiment using the modified algorithm. Fig. 7 shows the accumulated inside probabilities for both original and modified algorithms and the theoretical maximums ($1-\Gamma$ for the original algorithm and 1 for the modified algorithm). Note that the computed results approach the theoretical maximums and the modified algorithm covers the whole search space.

5 Conclusions

SITGs have proven to be a powerful tool in Syntax Machine Translation. However, the algorithms have been proposed do not explore all the possible parse trees. This work proposes modifications of the algorithms to be able to explore the whole search space.

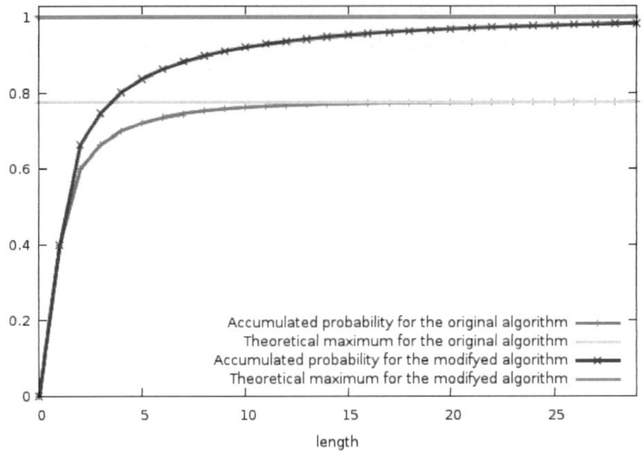

Figure 7: Accumulated inside probability for the original and modified algorithms.

Using an example, we have shown that the modifications allow a complete search. As future work, we plan to proove the correctness of the modified algorithm and to study the impact of these modifications on the use of SITGs for Machine Translation, and the estimation of SITGs.

Acknowledgments

Work supported by the EC (FSE), the Spanish Government (MICINN, "Plan E") under grants MIPRCV "Consolider Ingenio 2010" CSD2007-00018, iTrans2 TIN2009-14511 and the Generalitat Valenciana grant Prometeo/2009/014 and BFPI/2007/117.

References

D. Chiang. 2007. Hierarchical phrase-based translation. *Computational Linguistics*, 33(2):201–228.

S. Huang and B. Zhou. 2009. An em algorithm for scfg in formal syntax-based translation. In *ICASSP*, pages 4813–4816, Taiwan, China, April.

F.J. Maryanski and M.T. Thomason. 1979. Properties of stochastic syntax-directed tranlation schemata. *Journal of Computer and Information Sciences*, 8(2):89–110.

J.A. Sánchez and J.M. Benedí. 2006. Stochastic inversion transduction grammars for obtaining word phrases for phrase-based statistical machine translation. In *Proc. of Workshop on Statistical Machine Translation. HLT-NAACL 06*, pages 130–133.

D. Wu. 1995. Trainable coarse bilingual grammars for parallel text bracketing. In *Proceedings of the Third Annual Workshop on Very Large Corpora*, pages 69–81.

D. Wu. 1997. Stochastic inversion transduction grammars and bilingual parsing of parallel corpora. *Computational Linguistics*, 23(3):377–404.

Improving Data Driven Dependency Parsing using Clausal Information

Phani Gadde, Karan Jindal, Samar Husain, Dipti Misra Sharma, Rajeev Sangal
Language Technologies Research Centre, IIIT-Hyderabad, India.
phani.gadde@research.iiit.ac.in, karan_jindal@students.iiit.ac.in,
{samar,dipti,sangal}@mail.iiit.ac.in

Abstract

The paper describes a data driven dependency parsing approach which uses clausal information of a sentence to improve the parser performance. The clausal information is added automatically during the parsing process. We demonstrate the experiments on Hindi, a language with relatively rich case marking system and free-word-order. All the experiments are done using a modified version of MSTParser. We did all the experiments on the ICON 2009 parsing contest data. We achieved an improvement of 0.87% and 0.77% in unlabeled attachment and labeled attachment accuracies respectively over the baseline parsing accuracies.

1 Introduction

Linguistic analysis of morphologically rich free-word-order languages (MoRFWO) using dependency framework have been argued to be more effective (Shieber, 1985; Mel'čuk, 1988, Bharati et al., 1993). Not surprisingly, most parsers for such languages are dependency based (Nivre et al., 2007a; Bharati et al., 2008a; Hall et al., 2007). In spite of availability of annotated treebanks, state-of-the-art parsers for MoRFWO have not reached the performance obtained for English. Some of the reasons stated for the low performance are small treebank size, complex linguistic phenomenon, long-distance dependencies, and non-projective structures (Nivre et al., 2007a, 2007b; Bharati et al., 2008a).

Several approaches have been tried to handle these difficulties in such languages. For Hindi, Bharati et al. (2008a) and Ambati et al. (2009) used semantic features in parsing to reduce the negative impact of unavailable syntactic features and showed that use of minimal semantics can help in identifying certain core dependency labels. Various attempts have proved to simplify the structure by dividing the sentence into suitable linguistic units (Attardi and Dell'Orletta 2008; Bharati et al., 1993, 2008b, 2009; Husain et al., 2009). These approaches handle complex structures by breaking the parsing process into several steps. Attardi and Dell'Orletta (2008) used chunk information as a feature to MaltParser (Nivre et al., 2007a) for parsing English. Bharati et al., 1993 used the notion of local word groups, while Bharati et al., 2009 and Husain et al., 2009 used clauses.

In this paper, we describe a data driven dependency parsing approach which uses clausal information of a sentence to improve the parser performance. Previous attempts at data driven parsing for Hindi have failed to exploit this feature explicitly. The clausal information is added automatically during the parsing process. We demonstrate the experiments on Hindi[1]. All the experiments are done using a modified version of MSTParser (McDonald et al., 2005a and the references therein) (henceforth MST) on the ICON 2009 parsing contest[2] (Husain, 2009) data. We achieved an improvement of 0.87% and 0.77% in unlabeled attachment and labeled attachment accuracies respectively over the baseline parsing accuracies.

---

[1] Hindi is a verb final language with free word order and a rich case marking system. It is an official language of India and is spoken by ~800 million people.
[2] http://www.icon2009.in/contests.html

Human Language Technologies: The 2010 Annual Conference of the North American Chapter of the ACL, pages 657–660,
Los Angeles, California, June 2010.

2 Why Clausal Information?

Traditionally, a clause is defined as a group of words having a subject and a predicate. Clause boundary identification is the process of dividing the given sentence into a set of clauses. It can be seen as a partial parsing step after chunking, in which one tries to divide the sentence into meaningful units. It is evident that most of the dependents of words in a clause appear inside the same clause; in other words the dependencies of the words in a clause are mostly localized within the clause boundary.

In the dependency parsing task, a parser has to disambiguate between several words in the sentence to find the parent/child of a particular word. This work is to see whether the clause boundary information can help the parser to reduce the search space when it is trying to find the correct parent/child for a word. The search space of the parser can be reduced by a large extent if we solve a relatively small problem of identifying the clauses. Interestingly, it has been shown recently that most of the non-projective cases in Hindi are inter-clausal (Mannem et al., 2009). Identifying clausal boundaries, therefore, should prove to be helpful in parsing non-projective structures. The same holds true for many long-distance dependencies.

3 Experimental Setup

3.1 Dataset

The experiments reported in this paper have been done on Hindi; the data was released as part of the ICON 2009 parsing contest (Husain, 2009). The sentences used for this contest are subset of the Hyderabad Dependency Treebank (HyDT) developed for Hindi (Begum et al., 2008). The dependency relations in the treebank are syntactico-semantic. The dependency tagset in the annotation scheme has around 28 relations. The dependency trees in the treebank show relations between chunk heads. Note, therefore, that the experiments and results described in this paper are based on parse trees that have chunk head as nodes.

The data provided in the task contained morphological features along with the lemma, POS tag, and coarse POS tag, for each word. These are six morphological features namely category, gender, number, person, vibhakti[3] or TAM[4] markers of the node

3.2 Clause Boundary Identifier

We used the Stage1[5] parser of Husain et al. (2009), to provide the clause boundary information that is then incorporated as features during the actual parsing process. The Stage1 parser uses MST to identify just the intra-clausal relations. To achieve this, Husain et al., introduce a special dummy node named _ROOT_ which becomes the head of the sentence. All the clauses are connected to this dummy node with a dummy relation. In effect the Stage1 parser gives only intra-clausal relations. In the current work, we used MaltParser[6] (Nivre et al., 2007b) (henceforth Malt) to do this task. This is because Malt performs better than MST in case of intra-clausal relations, which are mostly short distance dependencies. We use the same algorithm and feature setting of Bharati et al., (2008a) to train the Stage1 parser.

Since the above tool parses clauses, therefore along with the clause boundary information we also know the root of the clausal sub-tree. Several experiments were done to identify the most optimal set of clausal features available from the partial parse. The best results are obtained when the clause boundary information, along with the head information i.e. head node of a clause, is given as a feature to each node.

We trained the Stage1 parser by converting the treebank data into the stage1 format, following the steps that were given in Husain et al. (2009). This conversion depends on the definition of the clause. We experimented with different definitions of clause in order to tune the tool to give the optimal clause boundary and head information required for parsing. For the results reported in this paper, a clause is a sequence of words, with a single verb, unless the verb is a child of another verb.

---

[3] Vibhakti is a generic term for preposition, post-position and suffix.

[4] TAM: Tense, Aspect and Modality.

[5] Stage1 handles intra-clausal dependency relations. These relations generally correspond to the argument structure of the verb, noun-noun genitive relation, infinitive-noun relation, adjective-noun, adverb-verb relations, etc.

[6] Malt version 1.2

	Precision	Recall
Clause Boundary	84.83%	91.23%
Head Information	92.42%	99.40%

Table 1. Accuracies of the features being used

Table 1 gives the accuracy of the clausal information being used as features in parsing. It is clear from Table1 that the tool being used doesn't have very high clause boundary identification performance; nevertheless, the performance is sufficient enough to make an improvement in parsing experiments. On the other hand, the head of the clause (or, the root head in the clausal sub-tree) is identified efficiently. All the above experiments for parameter tuning were done on the development data of the ICON 2009 parsing contest.

3.3 Parser

We used MSTParser[7] for the actual parsing step. MST uses Chu-Liu-Edmonds Maximum Spanning Tree Algorithm for non-projective parsing and Eisner's algorithm for projective parsing (Eisner, 1996). It uses online large margin learning as the learning algorithm (McDonald et al., 2005b).

We modified MST so that it uses the clause boundary. Unlike the normal features that MST uses, the clause boundary features span across many words.

.

4 Experiments and Results

We experimented with different combinations of the information provided in the data (as mentioned in 3.1). Vibhakti and TAM fields gave better results than others. This is consistent with the best previous settings for Hindi parsing (Bharati et al., 2008a, Ambati et al., 2009). We used the results obtained using this setting as our baseline (F1).

We first experimented by giving only the clause inclusion (boundary) information to each node (F2). This feature should help the parser reduce its search space during parsing decisions. Then, we provided only the head and non-head information (whether that node is the head of the clause or not) (F3). The head or non-head information helps in handling complex sentences that have more than one clause and each verb in the sentence has its own argument structure. We achieved the best performance by using both as features (F4) during the parsing process.

	LA (%)	UA (%)	L (%)
F1	73.62	91.00	76.04
F2	72.66	91.00	74.74
F3	73.88	91.35	75.78
F4	74.39	91.87	76.21

Table 2. Parsing accuracies with different features

Table 2 gives the results for all the settings. It is interesting to note that the boundary information (F1) alone does not cross the baseline; however this feature is reliable enough to give the best performance when combined with F3.

5 Observations

We see from the above results (F4 in Table 2) that there is a rise of 0.87% in UA (unlabeled attachment) and 0.77% in LA (labeled attachment) over previous best (F1). This shows the positive effect of using the clausal information during the parsing process.

We analyzed the performance of both the parsers in handling the long distance dependencies and non-projective dependencies. We found that the non-projective arcs handled by F4 have a precision and recall of 41.1% and 50% respectively for UA, compared to 30.5% and 39.2% for the same arcs during F1.

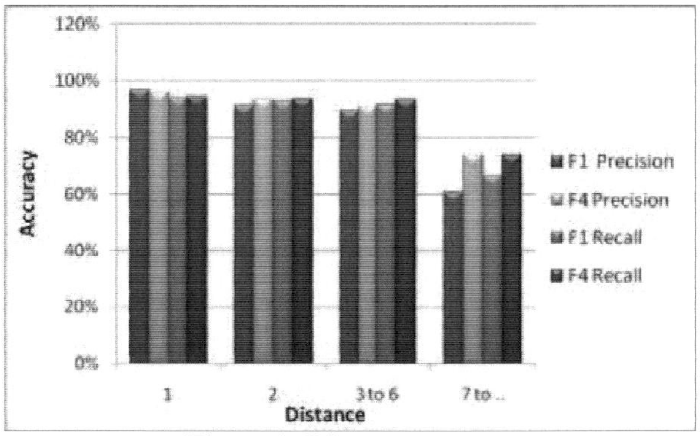

Figure 1. Distance stats

Figure 1 compares the accuracies of the dependencies at various distances. It is clear that the effect of clausal information become more

[7] MST version 0.4b

pronounced as the distance increases. This means F4 does help the parser in effectively handling long distance dependencies as well.

6 Conclusion and Future Work

The results show that there is a significant improvement in the parsing accuracy when the clausal information is being used.

The clausal information is presently being used only as attachment features in MST. Experiments can be done in future, to find out if there is a label bias to the clause boundary, which also helps in reducing the search space for specific labels. Improving the feature set for the labeled parse also improves the unlabeled attachment accuracy, as MST does attachments and labels in a single step, and the labels of processed nodes will also be taken in features.

We can see from Table1 that the precision of the clause boundary is 84.83%. Using a tool, targeted at getting just the clausal information, instead of using a parser can improve the accuracy of the clausal information, which helps improving parsing.

References

B. R. Ambati, P. Gadde, and K. Jindal. 2009. Experiments in Indian Language Dependency Parsing. In *Proceedings of the ICON09 NLP Tools Contest: Indian Language Dependency Parsing,* pp 32-37.

B. R. Ambati, P. Gade and C. GSK. 2009. Effect ofMinimal Semantics on Dependency Parsing. In the *Proceedings of RANLP 2009 Student Research Workshop*.

G. Attardi and F. Dell'Orletta. Chunking and Dependency Parsing. *LREC Workshop on Partial Parsing: Between Chunking and Deep Parsing*. Marrakech, Morocco. 2008.

R. Begum, S. Husain, A. Dhwaj, D. Sharma, L. Bai, and R. Sangal. 2008. Dependency annotation scheme for Indian languages. *In Proceedings of IJCNLP-2008.*

A. Bharati and R. Sangal. 1993. Parsing Free Word Order Languages in the Paninian Framework. *Proceedings of ACL:93.*

A. Bharati, S. Husain, B. Ambati, S. Jain, D. Sharma and R. Sangal. 2008a. Two Semantic features make all the difference in Parsing accuracy. In *Proceedings. of International Conference on Natural Language Processing-2008.*

A. Bharati, S. Husain, D. Sharma, and R. Sangal. 2008b. A two stage constraint based dependency parser for free word order languages. *In Proceedings. of COLIPS International Conference on Asian Language Processing. Thailand. 2008.*

A. Bharati, S. Husain, D. M. Sharma and R. Sangal. Two stage constraint based hybrid approach to free word order language dependency parsing. In the *Proceedings of the 11th International Conference on Parsing Technologies (IWPT09). Paris. 2009.*

J. Hall, J. Nilsson, J. Nivre, G. Eryigit, B. Megyesi, M. Nilsson,M. Saers.2007. Single Malt or Blended? A Study in Multilingual Parser Optimization. In *Proceedings of the CoNLL Shared Task Session of EMNLP-CoNLL 2007.*

S. Husain. 2009. Dependency Parsers for Indian Languages. In *Proceedings of ICON09 NLP Tools Contest:Indian Language Dependency Parsing. Hyderabad, India. 2009.*

S. Husain, P. Gadde, B. Ambati, D. M. Sharma and Rajeev Sangal. 2009. A modular cascaded approach to complete parsing. In the *Proceedings of COLIPS International Conference on Asian Language Processing. Singapore. 2009.*

P. Mannem and H. Chaudhry.2009. Insights into Non-projectivity in Hindi. In *ACL-IJCNLP Student paper workshop. 2009.*

R. McDonald, F. Pereira, K. Ribarov, and J. Hajic. 2005a. Non-projective dependency parsing using spanning tree algorithms. In the *Proceedings of HLT/EMNLP*, pp. 523–530.

R. McDonald, K. Crammer, and F. Pereira. 2005b. Online large-margin training of dependency parsers. In the *Proceedings of ACL 2005.* pp. 91–98.

I. A. Mel'Cuk. 1988. Dependency *Syntax: Theory and Practice*, State University Press of New York.

J. Nivre, J. Hall, S. Kubler, R. McDonald, J. Nilsson, S. Riedel and D. Yuret. 2007a. The CoNLL 2007 Shared Task on Dependency Parsing. In *Proceedings of the CoNLL Shared Task Session of EMNLP-CoNLL 2007.*

J. Nivre, J. Hall, J. Nilsson, A. Chanev, G. Eryigit, S. Kübler, S. Marinov and E Marsi. 2007b. MaltParser: A language-independent system for data-driven dependency parsing. *Natural Language Engineering*, 13(2), 95-135.

S. M. Shieber. 1985. Evidence against the context-freeness of natural language. In *Linguistics and Philosophy*, p. 8, 334–343.

A Treebank Query System Based on an Extracted Tree Grammar

Seth Kulick and **Ann Bies**
Linguistic Data Consortium
University of Pennsylvania
3600 Market St., Suite 810
Philadelphia, PA 19104
{skulick,bies}@ldc.upenn.edu

Abstract

Recent work has proposed the use of an extracted tree grammar as the basis for treebank analysis and search queries, in which queries are stated over the elementary trees, which are small chunks of syntactic structure. However, this work was lacking in two crucial ways. First, it did not allow for including lexical properties of tokens in the search. Second, it did not allow for using the derivation tree in the search, describing how the elementary trees are connected together. In this work we describe an implementation that overcomes these problems.

1 Introduction

(Kulick and Bies, 2009) describe the need for treebank search that compares two sets of trees over the same tokens. Their motivation is the problem of comparing different annotations of the same data, such as with inter-annotator agreement evaluation during corpus construction. The typical need is to recognize which annotation decisions the annotators are disagreeing on. This is similar to the problem of determining where the gold trees and parser output differ, which can also be viewed as two annotations of the same data.

As they point out, for this purpose it would be useful to be able to state queries in a way that relates to the decisions that annotators actually make, or that a parser mimics. They provide examples suggesting that (parent, head, sister) relations as in e.g. (Collins, 2003) are not sufficient, and that what is needed is the ability to state queries in terms of small chunks of syntactic structure.

Their solution is to use an extracted tree grammar, inspired by Tree Adjoining Grammar (Joshi and Schabes, 1997). The "elementary trees" of the TAG-like grammar become the objects on which queries can be stated. They demonstrate how the "lexicalization" property of the grammar, in which each elementary tree is associated with one or more token, allows for the the queries to be carried out in parallel across the two sets of trees.

However, the work was lacking in two crucial ways. First, it did not allow for including lexical properties of a token, such as its Part-of-Speech tag, together with the elementary tree search. This made it impossible to formulate such queries as "find all ADVP elementary trees for which the head of the tree is a `NOUN_NUM`". Even more seriously, there was no way to search over the "derivation tree", which encodes how the extracted elementary trees combine together to create the original tree. This made it impossible to carry out searches such as "find all verb frames with a `PP-LOC` modifying it", and in general to search for the crucial question of where annotators disagree on attachment decisions.

In this paper we describe how we have solved these two problems.

2 Tree Extraction

Following (Kulick and Bies, 2009), we draw our examples from the Arabic Treebank[1] For our gram-

[1]Part 3, v3.1 - Linguistic Data Consortium LDC2008E22. Also, we use the Buckwalter Arabic transliteration scheme `http://www.qamus.org/transliteration.htm`.

Human Language Technologies: The 2010 Annual Conference of the North American Chapter of the ACL, pages 661–664,
Los Angeles, California, June 2010.

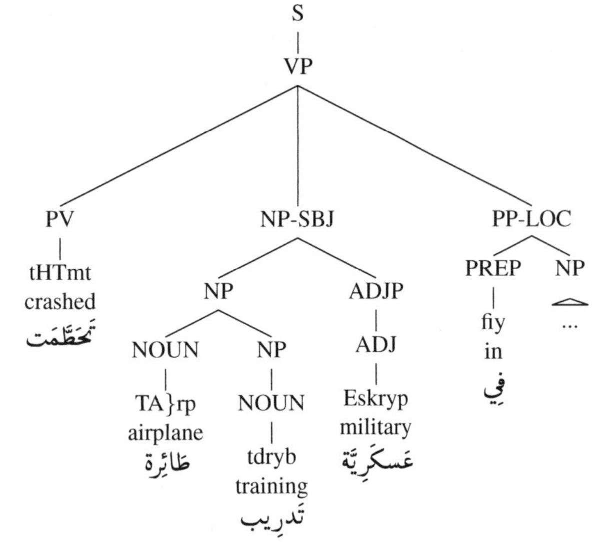

Figure 1: Sample tree

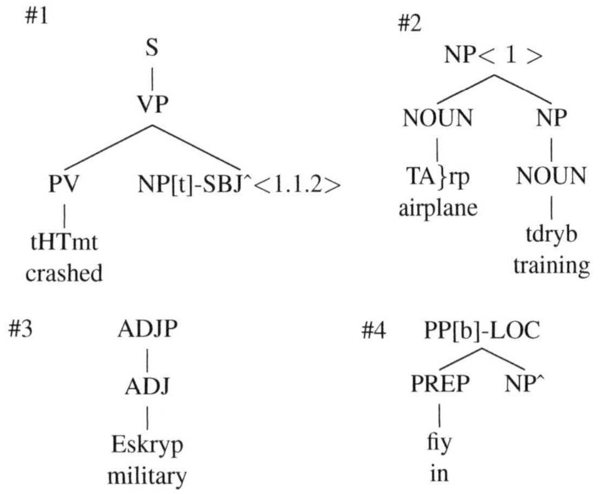

Figure 2: Extracted trees from Figure 1

mar we use a TAG variant with tree-substitution, sister-adjunction, and Chomsky-adjunction (Chiang, 2003), using head rules to decompose the full trees and extract the elementary trees. Sister adjunction attaches a tree (or single node) as a sister to another node, and Chomsky-adjunction forms a recursive structure as well, duplicating a node. As one example, the full tree is shown in Figure 1, and the extracted elementary trees[2] are shown in Figure 2. We briefly mention two unusual features of this extraction, and refer the reader to (Kulick and Bies, 2009) for detail and justification.

(1)The function tags are included in the tree extraction, with the syntactic tags such as `SBJ` treated

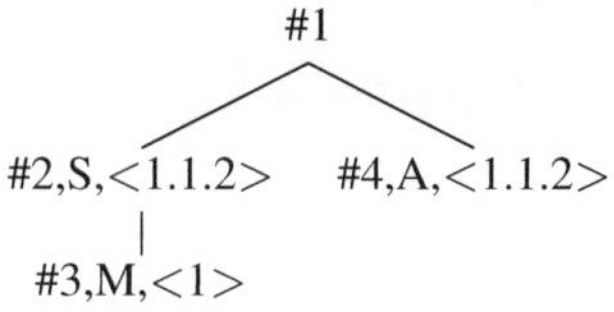

Figure 3: Derivation Tree for Figures 1 and 2

as a top feature value, and semantic tags such as `LOC` treated as a bottom feature value, extending the traditional TAG feature system to handle function tags.

(2) Etree #2 consists of two anchors, rather than splitting up the tree decomposition further. This is because this is an instance of the "construct state" construction in Arabic, in which two or more words are grouped tightly together.

The nodes in the elementary trees are numbered with their Gorn address, and we make two such addresses explicit, in trees #1 and #2. These addresses appear in the derivation tree in Figure 3. Each node in the derivation tree refers to one etree in Figure 2, and each node (except the root) is labelled with the address in the parent etree to which it attaches, and the attachment type (`M` for Chomsky-adjunction, `A` for sister-adjunction, and `S` for substitution).[3] The ^ symbol at the node `NP[t]-SBJ` in tree #1 indicates that it is a substitution node. Etree #3 Chomsky-adjoins at the root of etree #2, thus forming a a new NP node. Etree #4 sister-adjoins at the `NP[t]-SBJ` node in etree #1, thus becoming a sister to that node.

It is often the case that the same elementary tree structure will be repeated in different elementary trees extracted from a corpus. We call each such structure an "etree template", and a particular instance of that template, together with the "anchors" (tokens) used in that instance of the template, is called an "etree instance".

The extracted tokens, etree templates, etree instances, and derivation trees are stored in a MySQL database for later search. The derivation tree is implemented with a simple "adjacency list" representation as is often done in database representations of hierarchical structure. The database schema is organized with appropriate indexing so that a full tree is represented by a derivation tree, with integers point-

[2]We will use "etree" as shorthand for "elementary tree".

[3]This derivation tree is slightly simplified, since with sister-adjunction it includes more information to indicate the direction and order of attachment.

```
LEX   : (L1) text="fiy"
ETREE: (E1) (S (VP A$
                   NP[t]-SBJ^{dta:1}))
       (E2) (PP A${lex:L1} NP^)
DTREE: (D1) E2
       (D2) (E1 E2{dta:1})
```

Figure 4: Examples of one lexical restriction, two etree queries, and two dtree queries

ing to the etree instances, which in turn use integers to represent the etree template in that etree instance and also point to the anchors of that etree instance.

The section of ATB we are working with has 402,246 tokens, resulting in 319,981 etree instances and only 2804 etree templates, which gives an indication of the huge amount of duplication of structure in a typical treebank representation. From the perspective of database organization, the representation of the etree templates can be perhaps be viewed as a type of database "normalization", in which duplicate information is placed in a separate table.

3 Query Processing

We now describe the algorithm used for searching on the database with the extracted tree grammar, focusing on how the algorithm now allows searching based on the derivation tree and lexical information.

Queries are specified as "etree queries" and "dtree queries". Sample queries are shown in Figure 4. The query processing is as follows:

Step 1:
The etree templates are searched to determine which match a given etree query.[4] This is a simple tree matching between each template and query, all of which are small small trees. It is within this tree matching that several of the typical relations can be specified, such as precedence and dominance. A table stores the information on which templates match which queries.

In addition, the Etree queries can now include two new properties. First, they can include a specification for a lexical restriction, such as `lex:L1` in `E2` in Figure 4. However, step 1 of the query processing does not actually check this, since it is simply going through each template, without examining any anchors, to determine which have the appropriate structure to match a query. Therefore, we store in another table the information that for a (template, query) to match it must be the case that an anchor at a particular address in that template satisfies a particular lexical restriction. It in effect produces specialized information for the given template as to what additional restrictions apply for that (template, query) pair to succeed as a match, in each etree instance that uses that etree template. For example, in this case the stored information specifies that an etree instance with template `(PP A NP^)` matches the query `E2` if the instance has an anchor with the text `fiy` at address 1.1 (the anchor `A`).

Similarly, the etree query can include a specification `dta` (as in `E1`), for "derivation tree address", indicating that the corresponding address in each matching template needs to be stored for later reference in derivation tree searching. In this case, the template for etree instance #1 will match etree query `E1`, with the additional information stored that the address `1.1.2` will be used for later processing.

An important point here is that this additional information is not necessarily the same for the different templates that otherwise match a query. For example, the two templates

```
(1)       (S (VP A NP[t]-SBJ<1.1.2>)
(2) (SBAR (S (VP A NP[t]-SBJ<1.1.1.2>))
```

both match query `E1`, but for (1) the stored address `dta:1` is `1.1.2`, while for (2) the stored address is is `1.1.1.2`. The same point holds for the address of the anchor with a lexical restriction.

Step 2:
For a given query, the matching etree instances are found. First it finds all etree instances such that the (template, query) is a match for the instance's etree template. It then filters this list by checking the lexical restriction, if any, for the anchor at the appropriate address in the etree instance, using the information stored from step 1. In the above example, this will select etree instance #4 as satisfying query `E2`, since the template for instance #4 was determined in step 1 to match E2, and the particular instance #4

[4]Each etree query has a "distinguished" anchor marked `A$` that indicates the anchor (word) of an etree template that is associated with that query. The reason for that is that if an etree template has more than one anchor, we only want one to trigger that query, so that the etree is not counted twice.

also satisfies the lexical restriction in query `E2`.

Step 3:

The final results are reported using the dtree queries. Some dtree queries are singletons naming an etree query, such as `D1`, indicating that the dtree query is simply that etree query. In this example, any etree instance that satisfies the etree query `E2` is reported as satisfying the dtree query `D1`.

The dtree query can also specify nodes in a derivation tree that must satisfy specified etree queries and also be in a certain relationship in the derivation tree. For example, dtree query `D2` in Figure 4 specifies that the query is for two nodes in a parent-child relationship in the derivation tree, such that the parent node is for an etree instance that satisfies etree query `E1`, and the child is an instance that satisfies etree query `E2`. Furthermore, the address in the derivation tree is the same as the address `dta:1` that was identified during Step 1. Note that the address is located on the parent tree during Step 1, but appears in the derivation tree on the child node.

Steps 1 and 2 identify etree instance #1 as satisfying etree query `E1`, with `dta:1` stored as address `<1.1.2>` for the template used by instance #1. These steps also identifed etree instance #4 as satisfying etree query `E2`. Step 3 now determines that etree instances #1 and #4 are in a derivation tree relationship that satisfies dtree query `D2`, by checking for a parent-child relationship between them with the address `<1.1.2>`.[5] So dtree query D1 is finding all PP etrees headed by "fiy", and dtree query D2 is finding all clauses with a subject after the verb, with a PP attaching next to the subject, where the PP is headed by "fiy".

We consider the distinguished anchor (see footnote 4) for a dtree query to be the distinguished anchor of the parent node. The earlier work on comparing two sets of trees (Kulick and Bies, 2009) can then use this to report such searches as "the annotators agree on the same verbal structure, but one has a PP modification and the other does not".

4 Conclusion and Future Work

Our immediate concern for future work is to work closely with the ATB team to ensure that the desired queries are possible and are integrated into the work on comparing two sets of trees. We expect that this will involve further specification of how queries select etree templates (Step 1), in interesting ways that can take advantage of the localized search space, such as searching for valency of verbs.

We are also working on an evaluation of the speed of this system, in comparison to systems such as (Ghodke and Bird, 2008) and Corpus Search[6]. The search algorithm described above for derivation tree searches can be made more efficient by only looking for relevant etree instances in the context of walking down the derivation tree. In general, while searching for etree instances is very efficient, even with lexical restrictions, complex searches over the derivation tree will be less so. However, our hope, and expectation, is that the vast majority of real-life dtree queries will be local (parent,child,sister) searches on the derivation tree, since each node of the derivation tree already encodes small chunks of structure.

Acknowledgements

We thank Aravind Joshi, Anthony Kroch, Mitch Marcus, and Mohamed Maamouri for useful discussions. This work was supported in part by the Defense Advanced Research Projects Agency, GALE Program Grant No. HR0011-06-1-0003 (both authors) and by the GALE program, DARPA/CMO Contract No. HR0011-06-C-0022 (first author). The content of this paper does not necessarily reflect the position or the policy of the Government, and no official endorsement should be inferred.

References

David Chiang. 2003. Statistical parsing with an automatically extracted tree adjoining gramar. In *Data Oriented Parsing*. CSLI.

Michael Collins. 2003. Head-driven statistical models for natural language parsing. *Computational Linguistics*, 29:589–637.

Sumukh Ghodke and Steven Bird. 2008. Querying linguistic annotations. In *Proceedings of the Thirteenth Australasian Document Computing Symposium.*

A.K. Joshi and Y. Schabes. 1997. Tree-adjoining grammars. In G. Rozenberg and A. Salomaa, editors, *Handbook of Formal Languages, Volume 3.*

Seth Kulick and Ann Bies. 2009. Treebank analysis and search using an extracted tree grammar. In *Proceedings of The Eigth International Workshiop on Treebanks and Linguistic Theories.*

[5] It is also possible to specify the nature of that relationship by the attachment type, substitution or modification.

[6] `http://corpussearch.sourceforge.net.`

Reranking the Berkeley and Brown Parsers*

Mark Johnson
Department of Computing
Macquarie University
Sydney, Australia
mjohnson@science.mq.edu.au

Ahmet Engin Ural
Cognitive and Linguistic Sciences
Brown University
Providence, RI, USA
aeural@gmail.com

Abstract

The Brown and the Berkeley parsers are two state-of-the-art generative parsers. Since both parsers produce n-best lists, it is possible to apply reranking techniques to the output of both of these parsers, and to their union. We note that the standard reranker feature set distributed with the Brown parser does not do well with the Berkeley parser, and propose an extended set that does better. An ablation experiment shows that different parsers benefit from different reranker features.

1 Introduction

Syntactic parsing is the task of identifying the phrases and clauses in natural language sentences. It has been intensively studied primarily because it is generally believed that identifying syntactic structure is a first step towards semantic interpretation. This paper focuses on parsing the Wall Street Journal (WSJ) section of the University of Pennsylvania treebank corpus (Marcus et al., 1993). There are a large number of different approaches to this task. For simplicity we focus on two popular generative statistical parsing models: Charniak's "Maximum Entropy Inspired" parser (Charniak and Johnson, 2005) and Petrov's "split-merge" parser (Petrov et al., 2006). We follow conventional informal usage and refer to these as the "Brown" and the "Berkeley" parsers respectively.

* We would like to thank Eugene Charniak and the other members of BLLIP for their helpful advice on this work. Naturally all errors remain our own.

Briefly, the Berkeley parser is a smoothed PCFG whose non-terminals are refinements of the original treebank grammar obtained by an automatic split-merge procedure, while the Brown parser is effectively a smoothed PCFG whose non-terminals encode a wide variety of manually chosen conditioning information, such as heads, governors, etc. The Berkeley parser is usually viewed as unlexicalized (although the preterminals may be split so finely that they may be viewed as identifying lexical clusters), while essentially every distribution used in the Brown parser conditions on lexical information. Even from this cursory description it is clear that these parsers parsers extract generalizations from the training data in different ways.

This paper applies reranking (Collins and Koo, 2005) to the n-best output of both parsers individually, as well as to an n-best list consisting of the union of the outputs of both parsers. We are interested to see whether the same kinds of features improve the performance of both the Berkeley and the Brown parsers, or whether successful reranking requires features that are specially tuned to the parser it is applied to. Finally, we are interested in the performance of the reranker trained on the union n-best lists. Combining the output of multiple parsers in other more complex ways has been previously demonstrated to improve overall accuracy, so it is interesting to see if the relatively simple method used here improves parsing accuracy as well.

The approach of Zhang et al. (2009) is closest to the work described here. They combine n-best lists produced by the same parsers as we do, but use only a relatively small set of features (the log probabil-

Human Language Technologies: The 2010 Annual Conference of the North American Chapter of the ACL, pages 665–668,
Los Angeles, California, June 2010. ©2010 Association for Computational Linguistics

Trees	Reranker features	
	standard	extended
Berkeley	91.6	91.7
Brown	**91.8**	91.6
Combined	**91.8**	**91.9**

Table 1: The f-scores on section 22 of rerankers trained on folds 1–18 by minimizing a regularized "MaxEnt" objective (negative log likelihood with a Gaussian regularizer) using L-BFGS. The weight of the regularizer was tuned to optimize f-score on folds 19–20.

ity of the parses plus a constituent overlap feature), while we investigate models with millions of features here. They report a higher f-score than we do when they replace the generative Brown parser with the the self-trained discriminatively-reranked parser of McClosky et al. (2006), but with inputs provided by the generative Berkeley and Brown n-best parsers they report an f-score of 91.43 on section 23, which is consistent with the results reported here.

2 Experimental setup

We ran both parsers in 50-best mode, and constructed 20-fold cross-validated training data as described in Collins and Koo (2005) and Charniak and Johnson (2005), i.e., the trees in sections 2–21 of the WSJ treebank were divided into 20 equal-sized folds, and the parses for each fold were generated by a parser trained on the trees in the other folds. Then sections 22, 23 and 24 were parsed using the standard "out-of-the-box" parser. Following the suggestion in Collins and Koo (2005), in order to avoid over-training on section 23 all reranking experiments reported here (except the final one) used folds 1–18 as training data, used folds 19–20 as development data and used section 22 as test data. (The averaged perceptron algorithm does not require development data, so the experiments using that algorithm report averages over folds 19–20 and section 22).

The Berkeley parser can be run in many modes; in order to produce the 20-fold training data we ran the Berkeley trainer with 6 splits, and ran the resulting parsers in "accurate" mode. It failed to produce any parses for 12 sentences in sections 2–21 and one sentence in section 24. The Brown parser was trained using the "out-of-the-box" settings, and produced parses for all sentences.

Using the reranker features distributed with the Brown reranker (Charniak and Johnson, 2005), which we call the "standard" set below, we obtained no overall improvement in f-score when either reranking the Berkeley parser n-best lists alone, or when the Berkeley parses were combined with the Brown parses.

However, it is possible that these results reflect the fact that the features used by the reranker were chosen because they improve the Brown parser, i.e., they are the result of feature selection based on reranking the Brown parser's n-best lists. In order to determine if this is the case, we developed an "extended" feature set that incorporates a wider set of features, specifically including features that capture global properties of the tree that might be harder for the Berkeley parser to learn.

Our extended feature set consists of 4,256,553 features, which are instances of 162 feature classes, which in turn are grouped into 20 feature "super-classes". By contrast, the standard feature set contains 1,333,950 features in 90 feature classes, grouped into 14 super-classes. A brief description of the extended feature set super-classes follows:

Parser: an indicator feature indicating which parsers generated this parse,

RelLogP: the log probability of this parse according to each parser,

InterpLogCondP: an indicator feature based on the binned log conditional probability according to each parser,

RightBranch: an indicator function of each node that lies on the right-most branch of the parse tree,

Heavy: an indicator function based on the size and location of each nonterminal (designed to identify the locations of "heavy" phrases),

LeftBranchLength: an indicator function of the binned length of each left-branching chain,

RightBranchLength: an indicator function of the binned length of each right-branching chain,

Rule: an indicator function of parent and children categories, optionally with head POS annotations,

NNGram: and indicator function of parent and n-gram sequences of children categories, optionally head

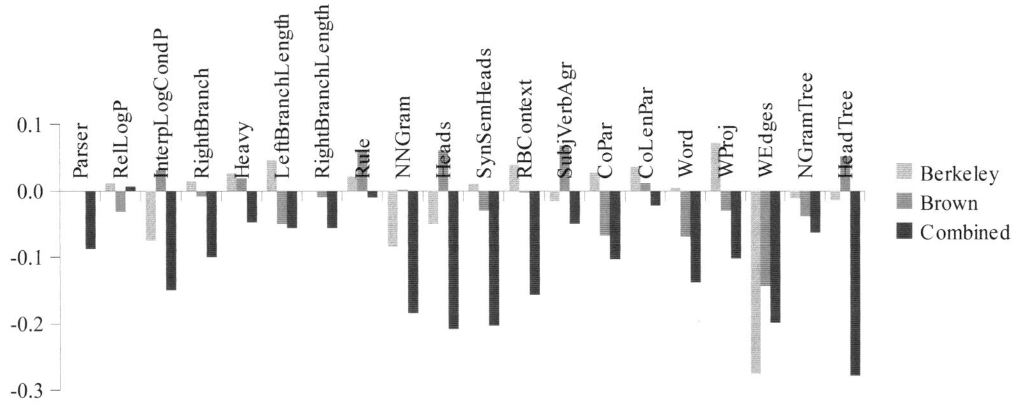

Figure 1: The average change in f-score on folds 19–20 and section 22 caused by removing a feature superclass from the extended feature set and retraining. Difference in scores less that 0.1% are probably not significant. In this experiment all rerankers were trained using the averaged perceptron algorithm. With the full extended feature set, rerankers trained with the averaged perceptron algorithm achieve f-scores of 91.2% on both the Berkeley and Brown parses, and 91.6% on the combined parses.

annotated, inspired by the n-gram rule features described in Collins and Koo (2005),

Heads: an indicator function of "head-to-head" dependencies,

SynSemHeads: an indicator function of the pair of syntactic (i.e., functional) and semantic (i.e., lexical) heads of each non-terminal,

RBContext: an indicator function of how much each subtree deviates from from right-branching,

SubjVerbAgr: an indicator function of whether subject-verb agreement is violated,

CoPar: an indicator function that fires when conjoined phrases in a coordinate structure have approximately parallel syntactic structure,

CoLenPar: an indicator function that fires when conjoined phrases in a coordinate structure have approximately the same length,

Word: an indicator function that identifies words and their preterminals,

WProj: an indicator function that identifies words and their phrasal projections up to their maximal projection,

WEdges: an indicator function that identifies the words and POS tags appearing at the edges of each nonterminal,

NGramTree: an indicator function of the subtree consisting of nodes connecting each pair of adjacent words in the parse tree, and

HeadTree: a tree fragment consisting of a head word and its projection up to its maximal projection, plus all of the siblings of each node in this sequence (this is like an auxiliary tree in a TAG).

The InterpLogCondP features were designed to capture non-linearities in the way that the Berkeley and Brown parsers assign probabilities to trees. We deliberately added features that incorporated linguistic notions such as head, governor and maximal projection, as the Berkeley parser does not explicitly condition on such information (in contrast to the Brown parser, which does).

In fact, as the reader can verify the differences in f-scores between rerankers containing the extended features and the standard features is minimal. In order to better study the importance of the various features we conducted an ablation study, in which we trained rerankers which were missing one feature superclass from the 20 superclasses of the extended feature set. In order to speed training time we used the averaged perceptron algorithm (Collins, 2002) (it converges an order of magnitude faster than the L-BFGS algorithm we used in the other experiments, but the f-score of the model estimated with the averaged perceptron is approximately 0.1% lower than when using L-BFGS). The results from this experiment are shown in Figure 1. The averaged perceptron algorithm does not rely on the development data (folds 19–20), so the results we report are average f-scores on the development data and on section 22 (we did this because the differences are small, so a larger evaluation set may be able to detect differences more reliably).

It is interesting that linguistically-informed features (such as Heads, SynSemHeads and HeadTree) seem to be much more important when reranking the combined n-best lists than when reranking the output of either parser alone. This suggests that the log probability scores from both parsers are internally consistent, but need to be recalibrated when the parses are combined. The log probability scores from the parsers themselves (in the form of the InterpLogCondP feature) are also supplying useful information that the reranker features on their own are not providing. Finally, the WEdges feature, which identifies the words and POS at the left and right boundaries of each nonterminal, also provides extremely useful information, especially for reranking the Berkeley parser.

3 Conclusion

Reranking is a straight-forward method for improving the accuracy of n-best parsers. While one might have hoped that reranking the n-best output of the Berkeley parser, or the union of the outputs of the Berkeley and Brown parsers, would dramatically improve overall f-score, this seems not to be the case. It's possible that the features of current rerankers have been implicitly designed to work well with parsers like the Brown parser, but a reranker with a dramatically enlarged feature set performs only marginally better. This result was confirmed by training a reranker with the extended features on the union of the output of the Berkeley and Brown parsers on sections 2–21 and testing on section 23 (i.e., the standard WSJ parsing evaluation), which achieved an f-score of 91.49%; approximately 0.1% higher than a reranker with the standard feature set trained on the output of the Brown parser alone.

Acknowledgments

This research was funded by NSF awards 0530118, 0544127 and 0631667.

References

Eugene Charniak and Mark Johnson. 2005. Coarse-to-fine n-best parsing and MaxEnt discriminative reranking. In *Proceedings of the 43rd Annual Meeting of the Association for Computational Linguistics*, pages 173–180, Ann Arbor, Michigan, June. Association for Computational Linguistics.

Michael Collins and Terry Koo. 2005. Discriminative reranking for natural language parsing. *Computational Linguistics*, 31(1):25–70.

Michael Collins. 2002. Discriminative training methods for hidden Markov models: Theory and experiments with perceptron algorithms. In *Proceedings of the 2002 Conference on Empirical Methods in Natural Language Processing*, pages 1–8. Association for Computational Linguistics.

Michell P. Marcus, Beatrice Santorini, and Mary Ann Marcinkiewicz. 1993. Building a large annotated corpus of English: The Penn Treebank. *Computational Linguistics*, 19(2):313–330.

David McClosky, Eugene Charniak, and Mark Johnson. 2006. Effective self-training for parsing. In *Proceedings of the Human Language Technology Conference of the NAACL, Main Conference*, pages 152–159, New York City, USA, June. Association for Computational Linguistics.

Slav Petrov, Leon Barrett, Romain Thibaux, and Dan Klein. 2006. Learning accurate, compact, and interpretable tree annotation. In *Proceedings of the 21st International Conference on Computational Linguistics and 44th Annual Meeting of the Association for Computational Linguistics*, pages 433–440, Sydney, Australia. Association for Computational Linguistics.

Hui Zhang, Min Zhang, Chew Lim Tan, and Haizhou Li. 2009. K-best combination of syntactic parsers. In *Proceedings of the 2009 Conference on Empirical Methods in Natural Language Processing*, pages 1552–1560, Singapore. Association for Computational Linguistics.

An Exploration of Off Topic Conversation

Whitney L. Cade
University of Memphis
365 Innovation Drive
Memphis, TN 38152-3115
wlcade@memphis.edu

Blair A. Lehman
University of Memphis
365 Innovation Drive
Memphis, TN 38152-3115
baleh-man@memphis.edu

Andrew Olney
University of Memphis
365 Innovation Drive
Memphis, TN 38152-3115
aolney@memphis.edu

Abstract

In a corpus of expert tutoring dialogue, conversation that is considered to be "off topic" (non-pedagogical) according to a previous coding scheme is explored for its value in tutoring dynamics. Using the Linguistic Inquiry and Word Count (LIWC) tool, phases of tutoring categorized as "off topic" were compared with interactive problem solving phases to explore how the two differ on the emotional, psychological, and topical dimensions analyzed by LIWC. The results suggest that conversation classified as "off topic" serves as motivation and broad pedagogy in tutoring. These findings can be used to orient future research on "off topic" conversation, and help to make sense of both previous coding schemes and noisy data sets.

1 Introduction

Methods of investigating a large and noisy data set are of paramount importance in computational linguistics. Quite often, qualitative coding schemes are used to capture snapshots of the data set, but these may gloss over finer details or miss the larger picture. Add to that the messy and unpredictable nature of naturalistic data, and analysis becomes even more complicated. Therefore, a multi-method approach to understanding pre-existing coding schemes and orienting future in-depth analyses of those schemes proves to be a useful means of exploring one's data.

Dialogue, particularly tutorial dialogue, is one area where large, noisy data sets are common. Computer and human tutoring data have been parsed, coded, and tested by a number of researchers, and much effort has been put into making sense of the variability in the task-oriented dialogue (e.g. Chi, Roy, and Hausmann, 2008; Graesser, Person, and Magliano, 1995; Person, Lehman, and Ozbun, 2007). This work has all been in pursuit of a deep understanding of the complex interaction between the human tutor and student, which, if understood, could be used to boost the efficacy of artificially intelligent computer tutors. Expert human tutoring has been found to increase learning gains by as much as 2 sigmas (Bloom, 1984), which makes understanding their methods and motives the goal of any tutor research.

The corpus under examination here was collected with the express purpose of understanding how truly expert tutors manage a tutoring session, with an emphasis on creating a corpus of naturalistic dialogue data. The corpus has been investigated at two different grain sizes, a dialogue move level and a sustained phases level. Our study investigates in detail an "other" category that these coding schemes, which emphasize the pedagogy of the tutors and the students reactions, classify as "off topic" conversation. Off topic conversation, by virtue of its name, does not address the tutoring task in which the tutor and student are engaged. However, given the prevalence of off topic conversation in the corpus, it is perhaps more likely that the function or utility of off topic conversation in expert tutoring is indirect rather than non-existent, suggesting that the noisiest part of the tutoring dialogue corpus, off topic conversation, should be further explored.

Because any topic not pertaining to the topic at hand may be broached in off topic conversation and because the dialogue itself is full of false

Human Language Technologies: The 2010 Annual Conference of the North American Chapter of the ACL, pages 669–672,
Los Angeles, California, June 2010.

starts, interruptions, and fragmented sentences, it is reasonable to explore off topic conversation using a bag of words method that is applicable to a variety of formal and informal texts. One such method is the Linguistic Inquiry and Word Count (LIWC) tool developed by Pennebaker et al., (2001), which looks for words that fall into specific, predetermined categories such as COGNITIVE MECHANISMS and POSITIVE EMOTIONS, then reports the percent of words in the document that fall into that category. LIWC provides over 70 possible categories, and can help sketch a rough picture of the verbal dynamics of a text (Mairesse and Walker, 2006; Mihalcea and Strapparava, 2009). Using a readily available tool like LIWC allows an examination of the variability within off topic conversation based on predetermined LIWC features. We can also compare these results to a prominent pedagogical category, such as scaffolding, that a current coding scheme particularly emphasizes, and examine the differences between the two.

In this analysis, the task-orientation and utility of "off topic" conversation are investigated by comparing its outcome scores in certain dimensions of LIWC to a classic pedagogical and interactive phase of tutoring: scaffolding (Rogoff and Gardner, 1984). Scaffolding, previously identified in a tutorial dialogue coding scheme (Cade, Copeland, Person, and D'Mello, 2008), involves much of the conversational give-and-take expected in casual off topic conversation, but is considered to be a very focused, on task phase of tutoring. Knowing how off topic conversation differs from scaffolding may help further exploration of this forgotten phase of tutoring. Likewise, it would give us direction in how to structure future coding schemes that would help bring clarity to the data set.

2 Methods

In this study, pedagogical and non-pedagogical phases of expert tutoring sessions were compared on linguistic dimensions to get at the diverse nature of off topic conversation within a naturalistic expert tutoring session.

The corpus under examination was collected in a previous study on expert human tutors. Therefore, what follows is a brief synopsis of how this corpus was collected.

Ten expert math and science tutors (4 male and 6 female) were recruited through local tutoring agencies and schools. Tutors were considered "expert" when they met the following criteria: they had to be licensed to teach at the secondary level, have five or more years of tutoring experience, be employed by a professional tutoring agency, and come highly recommended by school personnel who specialize in providing support to students who are struggling academically. Student participants were in grades 7 to 12, except for one who was obtaining a GED. All of the students were in academic trouble and actively sought out tutoring.

All sessions were unobtrusively videotaped at the location decided upon by the tutor and student. The researcher turned on the camera and left the room when the session began. Each student participated in a maximum of two tutorial sessions, while each tutor participated in between two and eight tutoring sessions. These 50 1-hour tutoring sessions were then transcribed.

Two previously identified phases of tutoring (or "modes"), Off Topic and Scaffolding, were compared to investigate their psychological, emotional, and topical differences. To do this, instances of each mode were extracted from 30 sessions (all sessions that contained at least one Off Topic and one Scaffolding mode). If a session had multiple occurrences of a single mode, those modes were compiled into a single document. Documents were capped at 1000 words each to prevent differences in word count between the modes from affecting the outcomes. These documents were also separated by speaker (tutor or student); speakers may be differentially motivated to broach certain topics, and so separating out these effects leads to more specific identification of conversational dynamics. Each session's Scaffolding and Off Topic document was then analyzed using LIWClite 7, which calculates the percentage of each document's words that fall into specific, predefined categories. Though this version of LIWC offers over 70 linguistic categories, only 15 were of interest in determining the nature of off topic conversation: SOCIAL PROCESSES (ex: *mate*, *talk*, *they*), FAMILY (*daughter*, *husband*, *aunt*), FRIENDS (*buddy*, *neighbor*), AFFECTIVE PROCESSES (*happy*, *cried*), POSITIVE EMOTION (*nice*, *sweet*), NEGATIVE EMOTIONN (*hurt*, *ugly*, *nasty*) ANXIETY (*worried*, *nervous*), TENTATIVENESS (*maybe*, *perhaps*), CERTAINTY (*always*, *never*), WORK (*majors*, *class*), ACHIEVEMENT (*earn*, *win*), LEISURE (*chat*, *movie*), HOME (*kitchen*, *family*), NONFLUENCIES (*umm*, *hm*), and FUTURE (*will*, *gonna*).

These categories are the most relevant in illustrating the emotional, topical, and psychological picture of conversation in tutoring when compared with the more on-task behavior of problem solving.

3 Discussion of Results

LIWC Category	T /S	Off Top *M*	Scaff *M*	Wil-coxon *p*-val	Paired t-test *t*-val	Co-hen's *d*
Social Process	T	11.15	7.75	<0.01	<0.01	1.37
	S	8.25	4.87	<0.01	<0.01	0.90
Positive Emotion	T	5.41	4.83	0.27	0.29	
	S	6.54	4.54	0.09	0.05	0.47
Tentative	T	3.10	1.91	<0.01	<0.01	1.08
	S	2.68	1.60	0.02	0.02	0.65
Work	T	2.90	1.10	<0.01	<0.01	0.86
	S	2.70	2.09	0.54	0.43	
Achieve	T	1.02	0.95	0.67	0.76	
	S	0.52	1.89	<0.01	<0.01	-0.92
Leisure	T	0.78	0.23	0.60	0.27	
	S	0.50	0.15	0.05	0.07	0.50
Home	T	0.30	0.04	0.02	0.05	0.53
	S	0.24	0.01	0.03	0.17	0.37
Nonfluen.	T	1.51	1.11	0.04	0.08	0.44
	S	3.89	4.14	0.17	0.82	
Future	T	1.13	1.23	0.80	0.66	
	S	0.74	1.35	0.01	0.04	-0.49

Table 1. LIWC Dimensions with Significant Results

Since a normal distribution of scores cannot be assumed in this analysis, comparisons between Off Topic conversation and Scaffolding dialogue were made by comparing the LIWC scores of the modes using both Wilcoxon's signed-rank test and a paired t-test, with similar outcomes. Effect sizes were also analyzed by calculating Cohen's *d*. Table 1 illustrates the significant results that emerged. In total, each category investigated occurs more in Off Topic than in Scaffolding, with the exception of a student's discussion of ACHIEVEMENT and FUTURE.

From this analysis, an interesting pattern of results emerges. The Off Topic mode had previously been characterized as a conversation that had nothing to do with the lesson at hand, which connoted that it is fairly irrelevant. However, Off Topic does not seem to be so wholly "off topic." Tutors and students in the Off Topic mode talk about work more often than they do in the Scaffolding mode, which is a mode where nothing but work is done. WORK words, according to the authors of LIWC, are mostly school-related. Off Topic may be a mode that allows the tutor to discuss test-taking skills, study strategies, and remind students what tasks need to be completed before the next tutoring session. For instance, one tutor divided up a study guide into manageable portions that needed to be completed every night so that the student would be prepared for an upcoming test. Previous to now, these conversations have only been qualitatively observed, but this supports a more in-depth analysis of what type of work tutors are talking about when they are supposedly discussing non-pedagogical topics.

This hypothesis is supported by the significant amount of conversation that takes place in Off Topic about the home; if FAMILY and FRIENDS (which may crop up in casual conversation about HOME-related topics) are not discussed significantly more in Off Topic, but HOME is, it may be that tutors are informing students of what sort of work needs to be done at home, and strategies to get work completed when on their own.

This may also explain why both students and tutors use more TENTATIVE words in Off Topic. Although it would seem that students should be more tentative and nonfluent when discussing difficult problem solving, they may be tentative in Off Topic when the tutor makes suggestions about studying and working. These suggestions of the tutor's may be framed using language like "maybe" and "perhaps" to make them more polite, and the student echoes this language in return. Thus, tentativeness may not come from uncertainty, but from suggestions couched in polite language.

It also appears that Off Topic conversation may not serve as a "pep talk" time; although it does contain more POSITIVE EMOTION words than Scaffolding, it does not expound upon the student's achievements. ACHIEVEMENT words are more common in Scaffolding, where students are receiving praise for their problem solving efforts. Off Topic conversation may seek to motivate the student in more subtle ways. By using more words that refer to SOCIAL PROCESSES (such as the third person plural and words like "talked"), the tutor and student may be building rapport with one another. This rapport may become important later on when the tutor gives the student blatantly negative feedback (Person et al., 2007), which can be motivationally damaging. Rapport may protect against flagging motivation in the student when the tutor uses "us" language and connects with the student in a more casual conversation.

4 Conclusions and Future Work

Our goal in this work was to use a simple linguistic analysis tool to uncover the hidden depths of an existing dialogue coding scheme. The use of such tools can paint a rich picture of the psychological, emotional, and topical content of a corpus, and can be used in two ways: first, it may help determine if a deeper inquiry into a hypothesis is warranted, and second, it can immediately orient future research towards key issues in a corpus without the less rigorous speculation and qualitative observations. The nature of broader coding schemes can come to be understood in a multifaceted manner using linguistic analysis, which may also inform future work.

Here, we have observed that off topic conversation in an expert tutoring dialogue corpus operates in a multidimensional way that is not irrelevant when studying the dynamics of an expert tutoring session. By using the LIWC tool developed by Pennebaker et al. (2001), themes concerning interpersonal rapport and global pedagogy emerge. The purpose of "off topic" conversation in tutoring may therefore be linked more to building a relationship between the tutor and the student, which is necessary for the trials of problem solving, and for the dispensation of "study strategies" that are more globally task-oriented, but are, nonetheless, important in understanding the pedagogical strategies of expert tutors. Off topic conversation was also hypothesized to function similarly in other tutorial work (Rosé, Kumar, Aleven, Robinson, and Wu, 2006).

One way of adding validity to these claims would be to investigate the topics broached in Off Topic through a topics model. In this way, recurring themes in off topic conversation can be revealed, and these themes can be aligned with the LIWC findings to see if a pattern emerges. From there, a new coding scheme may be devised to capture the multiple types of off topic conversation, which, for now, seem to be divided between interpersonal, rapport building and global pedagogy. This method of exploring a corpus has proven to be a useful approach when investigating possible avenues of improvement to coding schemes.

Acknowledgements

The research reported here was supported by the Institute of Education Sciences, U.S. Department of Education, through Grant R305A080594 to the University of Memphis. The opinions expressed are those of the authors and do not represent views of the Institute or the U.S. Department of Education.

References

Benjamin Bloom. 1984. The 2 sigma problem: The search for methods of group instruction as effective as one-to-one tutoring. *Educational Researcher*, 13:4-16.

Whitney Cade, Jessica Copeland, Natalie Person, and Sidney D'Mello. 2008. Dialogue modes in expert tutoring. *Proceedings of the 9th International Conference on Intelligent Tutoring Systems*, 470-479. Springer-Verlag, Berlin, Germany.

Michelene Chi, Marguerite Roy, and Robert Hausmann. 2008. Observing tutorial dialogues collaboratively: Insights about human tutoring effectiveness from vicarious learning. *Cognitive Science*, 32(2):301-341.

Art Graesser, Natalie Person, and Joseph Magliano. 1995. Collaborative dialogue patterns in naturalistic one-on-one tutoring. *Applied Cognitive Psychology*, 9:359-387.

François Mairesse and Marilyn Walker. 2006. Automatic Recognition of Personality in Conversation. In *Proceedings of the Human Language Technology Conference of the North American Chapter of the ACL*, 85–88. Association for Computational Linguistics, New York.

Rada Mihalcea and Carlo Strapparava. 2009. The Lie Detector: Explorations in the Automatic Recognition of Deceptive Language. In *Proceedings of the ACL-IJCNLP 2009 Conference Short Papers*, 309-312. Association for Computational Linguistics, Suntec, Singapore.

James Pennebaker, Martha Francis, and Roger Booth. 2001. *Linguistic Inquiry and Word Count (LIWC): LIWC2001*. Lawrence Erlbaum Associates, Mahwah, NJ.

Natalie Person, Blair Lehman, and Rachel Ozbun. 2007. Pedagogical and motivational dialogue moves used by expert tutors. Presented at the 17th Annual Meeting of the Society for Text and Discourse. Glasgow, Scotland.

Barbara Rogoff and William Gardner. 1984. Adult guidance of cognitive development. *Everyday cognition: Its development in social context*, 95-116. Harvard University Press, Cambridge, MA.

Carolyn Rosé, Rohit Kumar, Vincent Aleven, Allen Robinson, & Chih Wu. 2006. CycleTalk: Data driven design of support for simulation based learning. *International Journal of Artificial Intelligence in Education*, 16:195-223.

Making Conversational Structure Explicit: Identification of Initiation-response Pairs within Online Discussions

Yi-Chia Wang
Language Technologies Institute
Carnegie Mellon University
Pittsburgh, PA 15213, USA
yichiaw@cs.cmu.edu

Carolyn P. Rosé
Language Technologies Institute
Carnegie Mellon University
Pittsburgh, PA 15213, USA
cprose@cs.cmu.edu

Abstract

In this paper we investigate how to identify initiation-response pairs in asynchronous, multi-threaded, multi-party conversations. We formulate the task of identifying initiation-response pairs as a pairwise ranking problem. A novel variant of Latent Semantic Analysis (LSA) is proposed to overcome a limitation of standard LSA models, namely that uncommon words, which are critical for signaling initiation-response links, tend to be deemphasized as it is the more frequent terms that end up closer to the latent factors selected through singular value decomposition. We present experimental results demonstrating significantly better performance of the novel variant of LSA over standard LSA.

1 Introduction

In recent years, research in the analysis of social media (e.g., weblogs, discussion boards, and messengers) has grown in popularity. Unlike expository text, the data produced through use of social media is often conversational, multi-threaded, and more complex because of the involvement of numerous participants who are distributed both across time and across space. Recovering the multi-threaded structure is an active area of research.

In this paper, we form the foundation for a broader study of this type of data by investigating the basic unit of interaction, referred to as an **initiation-response pair** (Schegloff, 2007). Initiation-response pairs are pairs of utterances that are typically contributed by different participants, and where the first pair part sets up an expectation for the second pair part. Types of common initiation-response pairs include question-answer, assessment-agreement, blame-denial, etc. Note that although sometimes discussion forum interfaces make the thread structure of the interaction explicit, these affordances are not always present. And even in forums that have these affordances, the apparent structure of the discourse as represented through the interface may not capture all of the contingencies between contributions in the unfolding conversation. Thus, the goal of this investigation is to investigate approaches for automatically identifying initiation-response pairs in conversations.

One of the challenges in identifying initiation-response pairs is that the related messages are not necessarily adjacent to each other in the stream of contributed messages, especially within the asynchronous environment of social media. Furthermore, individual differences related to writing style or creative expression of self may also complicate the identification of the intended connections between contributions. Identification of initiation-response pairs is an important step towards automatic processing of conversational data. One potential application of this work is conversation summarization. A summary should include both the initiation and response as a coherent unit or it may fail to capture the intended meaning.

We formulate the task of identifying initiation-response pairs as a pairwise ranking problem. The goal is to distinguish message pairs that constitute an initiation-response pair from those that do not. We believe a ranking approach, where the degree of relatedness between a message pair can be considered in light of the relatedness between each of them and the surrounding messages within the same thread, is a more suitable paradigm for this task than a discrete classification-based paradigm.

Previous work on recovering conversational structure has relied on simple lexical cohesion

Human Language Technologies: The 2010 Annual Conference of the North American Chapter of the ACL, pages 673–676,
Los Angeles, California, June 2010. ©2010 Association for Computational Linguistics

measures (i.e., cosine similarity), temporal information (Lewis and Knowles, 1997; Wang et al., 2008), and meta-data (Minkov et al., 2006). However, relatively little work has investigated the importance of specifically **in-focus connections** between initiation-response pairs and utilized them as clues for the task. Consider, for example, the following excerpt discussing whether congress should pass a bill requiring the use of smaller cars to save the environment:

a) *Regressing to smaller **vehicles** would discourage business from producing more **pollution**.*
b) *If **CO2** emissions are lowered, wouldn't tax revenues be lowered as well? Are the democrats going to willingly give up Medicaid and social security?*

Although segment (b) is a reply to segment (a), the amount of word overlap is minimal. Nonetheless, we can determine that (b) is a response to (a) by recognizing the in-focus connections, such as "vehicles-CO2" and "pollution-CO2." To properly account for connections between initiations and responses, we introduce a novel variant of Latent Semantic Analysis (LSA) into our ranking model.

In section 2, we describe the Usenet data and how we extract a large corpus of initiation-response pairs from it. Section 3 explains our ranking model as well as the proposed novel LSA variation. The experimental results and discussion are detailed in Section 4 and Section 5, respectively.

2 Usenet and Generation of Data

The experiment for this paper was conducted using data crawled from the *alt.politics.usa Usenet* (User Network) discussion forum, including all posts from the period between June 2003 and June 2008. The resulting set contains 784,708 posts. The posts in this dataset also contain meta-data that makes parent-child relationships explicit (i.e., through the *References* field). Thus, we know 625,116 of the posts are explicit responses to others posts. The messages are organized into a total of 77,985 discussion threads, each of which has 2 or more posts.

In order to evaluate the quality of using the explicit reply structure as our gold standard for initiation-response links, we asked human judges to annotate the response structure of a random-selected medium-length discussion (19 posts) where we had removed the meta-data that indicated the initiation-reply structure. The result shows the accuracy of our gold standard is 0.89.

To set up the data as a pairwise ranking problem, we arranged the posts in the corpus into instances containing three messages each, one of which is a response message, one of which is the actual initiating message, and the other of which is a foil selected from the same thread. The idea is that the ranking model will be trained to prefer the actual initiating message in contrast to the foil.

The grain size of our examples is finer than whole messages. More specifically, positive examples are pairs of spans of text that have an initiation-reply relationship. We began the process with pairs of messages where the meta-data indicates that an initiation-reply relationship exits, but we didn't stop there. For our task it is important to narrow down to the specific spans of text that have the initiation-response relation. For this, we used the indication of quoted material within a message. We observed that when users explicitly quote a portion of a previously posted message, the portion of text immediately following the quoted material tends to have an explicit discourse connection with it. Consider the following example:

>> *Why is the quality of life of the child, mother,*
>> *and society at large, more important than the*
>> *sanctity of life?*
> *Because in the case of anencephaly at least,*
> *the life is ended before it begins.*
We disagree on this point. Why do you refuse to provide your very own positive definition of life? Do you believe life begins before birth? At birth? After birth? Never?

In this thread, the reply expresses an opinion against the first level quote, but not the second level quote. Thus, we used segments of text with single quotes as an initiation and the immediately following non-quoted text as the response. We extracted positive examples by scanning each post to locate the first level quote that is immediately followed by unquoted content. If such quoted material was found, the quoted material and the unquoted response were both extracted to form a positive example. Otherwise, the message was discarded.

For each post *P* where we extracted a positive example, we also extracted a negative example by picking a random post *R* from the same thread as *P*. We selected the negative example in such a way to make the task difficult in a realistic way. Choosing *R* from other threads would make the task too easy because the topics of *P* and *R* would most likely be different. We also stipulated that *R* cannot be the parent, grandparent, sibling, or child of *P*.

Together the non-quoted text of P and R forms a negative instance. Thus, the final dataset consists of pairs of message pairs $((p_i, p_j), (p_i, p_k))$, where they have the same reply message p_i, and p_j is the correct quote message of p_i, but p_k is not. In other words, (p_i, p_j) is considered as a positive example; (p_i, p_k) is a negative example. We constructed a total of 100,028 instances for our dataset, 10,000 (~10%) of which were used for testing, and 90,028 (~90%) of which were the learning set used to construct the LSA space described in the next section.

3 Ranking Models for Identification of Initiation-Response Pairs

Our pairwise ranking model[1] takes as input an ordered pair of message pairs $((p_i, p_j), (p_i, p_k))$ and computes their relatedness using a similarity function *sim*. Specifically,

$$(x_{ij}, x_{ik}) = (sim\ (p_i, p_j), sim\ (p_i, p_k))$$

where x_{ij} is the similarity value between post p_i and p_j; x_{ik} is the similarity value between post p_i and p_k. To determine which of the two message pairs ranks higher regarding initiation-response relatedness, we use the following scoring function to compare their corresponding similarity values:

$$score\ (x_{ij}, x_{ik}) = x_{ij} - x_{ik}$$

If the score is positive, the model ranks (p_i, p_j) higher than (p_i, p_k) and vice versa. A message pair ranked higher means it has more evidence of being an initiation-reply link, compared to the other pair.

3.1 Alternative Similarity Functions

We introduce and motivate 3 alternative similarity functions, where the first two are considered as baseline approaches and the third one is a novel variation of LSA. We argue that the proposed LSA variation is an appropriate semantic similarity measurement for identifying topic continuation and initiation-reply pairs in online discussions.

Cosine Similarity (*cossim*). We choose an approach that uses only lexical cohesion as our baseline. Previous work (Lewis and Knowles, 1997; Wang et al., 2008) has verified its usefulness for the thread identification task. In this case,

$$sim(p_i,p_j) = cossim(p_i,p_j)$$

where $cossim(p_i,p_j)$ computes the cosine of the angle between two posts p_i and p_j while they are represented as term vectors.

LSA Average Similarity (*lsaavg*). LSA is a well-known method for grouping semantically related words (Landauer et al., 1998). It represents word meanings in a concept space with dimensionality k. Before we describe how to compute average similarity given an LSA space, we explain how the LSA space was constructed in our work. First, we construct a term-by-document matrix, where we use the 90,028 message learning set mentioned at the end of Section 2. Next, LSA applies singular value decomposition to the matrix, and reduces the dimensionality of the feature space to a k dimensional concept space. This generated LSA space is used by both *lsaavg* and *lsacart* later.

For *lsaavg*, we follow Foltz et al. (1998):

$$sim(p_i, p_j) \quad lsaavg(p_i, p_j) \quad \cos\left(\frac{\sum_{t_a \in p_i} \vec{t_a}}{|p_i|}, \frac{\sum_{t_b \in p_j} \vec{t_b}}{|p_j|} \right)$$

The meaning of each post is represented as a vector in the LSA space by averaging across the LSA representations for each of its words. The similarity between the two posts is then determined by computing the cosine value of their LSA vectors.

This is the typical method for using LSA in text similarity comparisons. However, note that not all words carry equal weight within the vector that results from this averaging process. Words that are closer to the "semantic prototypes" represented by each of the k dimensions of the reduced vector space will have vectors with longer lengths than words that are less prototypical. Thus, those words that are closer to those prototypes will have a larger effect on the direction of the resulting vector and therefore on the comparison with other texts. An important consideration is whether this is a desirable effect. It would lead to deemphasizing those unusual types of information that might be being discussed as part of a post. However, one might expect that those things that are unusual types of information might actually be more likely to be the in-focus information within an initiation that responses may be likely to refer to. In that case, for our purposes, we would not expect this typical method for applying LSA to work well.

LSA Cartesian Similarity (*lsacart*). To properly account for connections between initiations and

[1] We cast the problem as a pairwise ranking problem in order to focus specifically on the issue of characterizing how initiation-response links are encoded in language through lexical choice. Note that once trained, pairwise ranking models can be used to rank multiple instances.

responses that include unusual words, we introduce the following similarity function:

$$sim(p_i, p_j) = lsacart(p_i, p_j) = \frac{\sum_{(t_a, t_b) \in p_i \times p_j} \cos(\vec{t_a}, \vec{t_b})}{|p_i||p_j|}$$

where we take the mean of the cosine values for all the word pairs in the Cartesian product of posts p_i and p_j. Note that in this formulation, all words have an equal chance to affect the overall similarity between vectors since it is the angle represented by each word in a pair that comes to play when cosine distance is applied to a word pair. Length is no longer a factor. Moreover, the averaging is across cosine similarity scores rather than LSA vectors.

4 Experimental Results

The results are found in Table 1. For comparison, we also report the random baseline (0.50).

	Random Baseline	Cos-Similarity	LSA-Average	LSA-Cart
Accuracy	0.50	0.66	0.60	**0.71**

Table 1. Overview of results

Besides the random baseline, LSA-Average performs the worst (0.60), with simple Cosine similarity (0.66) in the middle, and LSA-Cart (0.71) the best, with each of the pairwise contrasts being statistically significant. We believe the reason why LSA-Average performs so poorly on this task is precisely because, as discussed in last section, it deemphasizes those words that contribute the most unusual content. LSA-Cart addresses this issue.

To further understand this effect, we conducted an error analysis. We divided the instances into 4 sets based on the lexical cohesion between the response and the true initiation and between the response and the foil, by taking the median split on the distributions of these two cohesion scores. Our finding is that model performances vary by subset. In particular, we find that it is only in cases where the positive example has low lexical cohesion (e.g. our "vehicles-CO2" and "pollution-CO2" example from the earlier section), that we see the benefit of the LSA-Cart approach. In other cases, where the cohesion between the reply and the true initiation is high, Cos-Similarity performs best.

5 Discussion and Conclusion

We have argued why the task of detecting initiation-response pairs in multi-party discussions is important and challenging. We proposed a method for acquiring a large corpus for use to identify initiation-response pairs. In our experiments, we have shown that the ranking model using a variant of LSA performs best, which affirms our hypothesis that unusual information and uncommon words tends to be the focus of ongoing discussions and therefore to be the key in identifying initiation-response links.

In future work, we plan to further investigate the connection between an initiation-response pairs from multiple dimensions, such as topical coherence, semantic relatedness, conversation acts, etc. One important current direction is to develop a richer operationalization of the interaction that accounts for the way posts sometimes respond to a user, a collection of users, or a user's posting history, rather than specific posts per se.

Acknowledgments

We thank Mary McGlohon for sharing her data with us. This research was funded through NSF grant DRL-0835426.

References

David D. Lewis and Kimberly A. Knowles. 1997. Threading electronic mail: A preliminary study. *Information Processing and Management*, 33(2), 209–217.

Einat Minkov, William W. Cohen, Andrew Y. Ng. 2006. Contextual Search and Name Disambiguation in Email using Graphs. In *Proceedings of the International ACM Conference on Research and Development in Information Retrieval (SIGIR)*, pages 35–42. ACM Press, 2006.

Peter W. Foltz, Walter Kintsch, Thomas K. Landauer. 1998. Textual coherence using latent semantic analysis. *Discourse Processes*, 25, 285–307.

Thomas K. Landauer, Peter W. Foltz, and Darrell Laham. 1998. Introduction to latent semantic analysis. *Discourse Processes*, 25, 259-284.

Schegloff, E. 2007. *Sequence Organization in Interaction: A Primer in Conversation Analysis*, Cambridge University Press.

Yi-Chia Wang, Mahesh Joshi, William W. Cohen, Carolyn P. Rosé. 2008. Recovering Implicit Thread Structure in Newsgroup Style Conversations. In *Proceedings of the 2nd International Conference on Weblogs and Social Media (ICWSM II)*, Seattle, USA.

Engaging learning groups using Social Interaction Strategies

Rohit Kumar **Carolyn P. Rosé**
Language Technologies Institute
Carnegie Mellon University, Pittsburgh, PA, 15213
rohitk@cs.cmu.edu cprose@cs.cmu.edu

Abstract

Conversational Agents have been shown to be effective tutors in a wide range of educational domains. However, these agents are often ignored and abused in collaborative learning scenarios involving multiple students. In our work presented here, we design and evaluate interaction strategies motivated from prior research in small group communication. We will discuss how such strategies can be implemented in agents. As a first step towards evaluating agents that can interact socially, we report results showing that human tutors employing these strategies are able to cover more concepts with the students besides being rated as better integrated, likeable and friendlier.

1 Introduction

Conversational Agents (CAs) are autonomous interfaces that interact with users via spoken or written conversation. One of the applications of CAs is tutoring. Various research groups have developed tutoring agents in domains like reading, algebra, geometry, calculus, physics, computer literacy, programming, foreign languages, research methods and thermodynamics. Many of the evaluations show that CAs can be effective tutors (Arnott et. al., 2008; Kumar et. al., 2007; Graesser et. al., 2005).

Most systems that use CAs as tutors have been built for learning scenarios involving one student. Evaluation of learning technologies involving students working in groups with interactive agents has shown that learners are helped both by learning as a group and receiving tutorials from agents (Kumar et. al., 2007). However, some previous studies have reported that students learning in groups ignore the tutor's messages, unlike the case where students are individually tutored. Groups are more likely to abuse tutors than individual students.

We reason that the presence of other students in collaborative learning scenarios causes the agents to compete for the attention of the students. Since the agents are not adept at performing social interactive behavior, which makes up the bulk of formative communication in a group, they are quickly pushed to the periphery of the group.

Research on small group communication has identified twelve interaction categories that are commonly observed in small groups (Bales, 1950). These categories are broadly classified into task and social-emotional categories. Content presented by most current CAs mostly classifies under the task categories. In section 2, we will list the conversational strategies motivated from the three positive social-emotional interaction categories. Thereafter, the implementation and evaluation of a CA that interleaves these social interaction strategies while executing a task plan will be described.

2 Social Interaction Strategies

Balesian methodology (Bales, 1950) identifies three positive social-emotional interaction categories: showing solidarity, showing tension release and agreeing. Participants contribute turns of these categories to address the problems of re-integration, tension release and decision respectively. We have mapped these categories to practically implementable conversational strategies. This mapping is shown in table 1 ahead.

Each strategy is implemented as an instantiation of a conversational behavior. Most of the strategies listed in Table 1 are realized as prompts, triggered by rules based on agent plan, discourse and context features. For example, strategy 1e is triggered

Human Language Technologies: The 2010 Annual Conference of the North American Chapter of the ACL, pages 677–680,
Los Angeles, California, June 2010.

when one or more students in the group are found to be inactive for over 5 minutes. In this event, the tutor chooses to raise the status of the inactive students by eliciting contributions from them through a prompt like: *Do you have any suggestions Mike?* More implementation details of these strategies and triggers are discussed in the following section.

1. Showing Solidarity *Raises other's status, gives help, reward*
1a. Do Introductions *Introduce and ask names of all participants*
1b. Be Protective & Nurturing *Discourage teasing*
1c. Give Re-assurance *When student is discontent, asking for help*
1d. Complement / Praise *To acknowledge student contributions*
1e. Encourage *When group or members are inactive*
1f. Conclude Socially
2. Showing Tension Release *Jokes, laughs, shows satisfaction*
2a. Expression of feeling better *After periods of tension, work pressure*
2b. Be cheerful
2c. Express enthusiasm, elation, satisfaction *On completing significant steps of the task*
3. Agreeing *Shows passive acceptance, understands, concurs, complies*
3a. Show attention *To student ideas as encouragement*
3b. Show comprehension / approval *To student opinions and orientations*

Table 1. Social Interaction Strategies for three social-emotional interaction categories

3 WrenchTalker: Implementation

WrenchTalker is a CA we have built to employ the social interaction strategies listed in section 2. It helps teams of engineering students learn and apply basic concepts of mechanical stress while they participate in a freshmen lab project to design an aluminum wrench. Students can interact with this agent using a text-based chat environment.

The agent is built using the Basilica architecture (Kumar and Rosé, 2009). Under this architecture, CAs are modeled as a network of behavioral components. There are three types of components: actors (actuators / performers), filters (perceptors / annotators / cordinators) and memories. Figure 1 below shows a simplified depiction of the WrenchTalker component network.

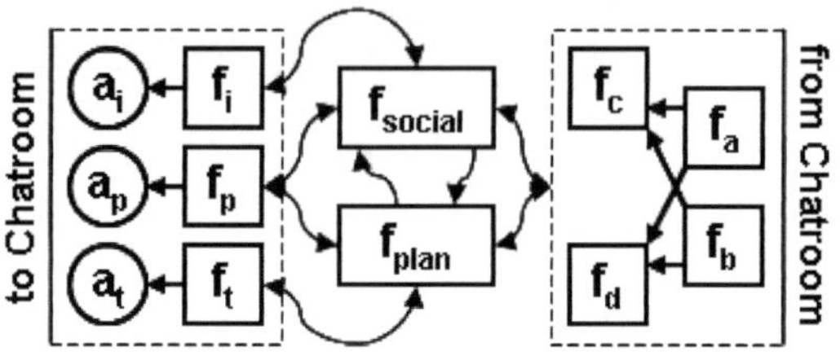

Figure 1. Component Network of WrenchTalker

Three of the actor and filter components correspond to three observable behaviors of the tutor, i.e., Introducing (a_i, f_i), Prompting (a_p, f_p) and Tutoring (a_t, f_t). Most of the other filter components form a sub-network that annotates turns with applicable semantic categories, accumulates them to identify inactive students and generates events that regulate the controllers.

The plan controller (f_{plan}) is responsible for executing the agent's interaction plan, which is comprised of 37 steps. The plan is executed largely sequentially; however the plan controller can choose to skip some steps in the interest of time. In the experiment described in section 5, the same plan controller is used in all three conditions. The social controller (f_{social}) implements the 12 strategies listed earlier. The strategies are triggered by rules based on combinations of three conditions: the last executed plan step, semantic categories associated with the most recent student turns and the ratio of tutor turns generated by f_{social} to f_{plan}. The first two conditions attempt to ensure that social behavior is suitable in the current conversational context and the third condition regulates the amount of social behavior by the CA.

The plan and social controllers are connected so that they regulate each other. For instance, when the plan controller is working, it blocks f_{social}. Upon completion of the blocking step, f_{social} is given control, which can then choose to perform a strategy by blocking f_{plan} before it progresses to the next step. Reflex strategies like 1b are not blocked.

Once the controllers determine a step or a strategy that is to be generated, the actors generate their turns. For example, strategy 1a is generated by actor a_i after it is triggered by the social controller.

We note that Basilica provides the flexibility to build complicated pipelines, as demonstrated in this case by the use of two controllers.

4 Related Work

To contextualize our research with other work on CAs, we classify agents with the social interaction strategies listed in Table 1 as *social interfaces* following the taxonomy proposed by Isbister (2002). Within this class of CAs, researchers have investigated the technical challenges and effects of conversational behavior that are similar in motivation to the ones we are exploring. Bickmore et. al. (2009) report that users found agents with autobiographies, i.e., back stories in first person more enjoyable and they completed more conversations with such agents. Dybala et. al. (2009) found that agents equipped with humor were evaluated as more human-like, funny and likeable. In a multiparty conversational scenario, Dohsaka et. al. (2009) found that an agent's use of emphatic expressions improved user satisfaction and user rating of the agent. We note that use of CAs as social interfaces has been found to have effects on both performance and perception metrics.

5 Experimental Design

In order to evaluate the effect of social interaction strategies listed in Table 1, we designed an experiment with three conditions. In the experimental condition (Social), students interacted with an agent that was equipped with our social interaction strategies, unlike the control condition (Task). In the third condition, a human tutor was allowed to intervene while the students interacted with a Task agent. In all three conditions, students go through the same task plan. However, the degree of social performance is varied from minimal (Task) to ideal (Human). We hypothesize that the human and social agents will be rated better than the Task agent.

We conducted a between subjects experiment during a freshmen computer aided engineering lab. 98 students participated in the experiment, which was held over six sessions spread evenly between two days. The two days of the experiment were separated by two weeks. Students were grouped into teams of three to four individuals. Students were grouped so that no two members of the same team sat next to each other during the lab, to ensure all communication was recorded. The teams were distributed between the three conditions.

Each session started with a follow-along tutorial of computer-aided analysis where the students analyzed a wrench they had designed earlier. The experimental manipulation happened during a collaborative design competition after the tutorial. Students were asked to work as a team to design a better wrench considering three aspects: ease of use, cost and safety. Students were instructed to make three new designs and calculate success measures of each of the three considerations. They were also told that a tutor will help them with two designs so that they are well-prepared to do the final design. No additional details about the tutor were given. The students communicated with each other and with the tutors using ConcertChat, an online environment that provides text-based instant messaging and workspace sharing facilities.

After spending 30-35 minutes on the design competition, each student filled out a questionnaire. It was comprised of eighteen questions on a seven point Likert-scale ranging from Strongly Disagree (1) to Strongly Agree (7). The questions were designed to elicit four types of ratings.

- Ratings about the tutor
- Ratings about the other team members
- Ratings about the design task
- Ratings about the team functioning

The questions in the first two classes elicited perceived liking and integration and checked whether the students noticed the tutor's display of the social interaction strategies. Task related questions asked about satisfaction, perceived legitimacy and discussion quality.

6 Results

Table 2 below shows the mean values for questionnaire categories apart from ratings about team members, since there were no significant effects related to those questions.

	D1	D2		T	S	H
Integration	3.85	3.94		3.03	*3.94*	**4.77**
Liking	3.68	3.63		2.78	3.53	**4.73**
Friendly	5.13	5.43		4.47	**5.56**	**5.83**
T.Releasing	4.49	4.63		3.84	4.61	**5.27**
Agreeing	4.30	4.45		3.97	4.44	4.73
Satisfaction	4.66	**5.77**		5.09	4.75	5.97

Table 2. Mean outcomes per condition ((T)ask,(S)ocial, (H)uman) and per day (Day1, and Day2)

The means are highlighted appropriately (**$p<0.001$**, **$p<0.05$**, *$p<0.08$*) to indicate significant differences from Day1 to Day2 and between the Task condition and each of the other two using a pairwise Tukey comparison.

First of all, we note that there is a significant difference in task satisfaction between the two days. We fine-tuned the timing parameters of the plan controller after day 1 so that the students had sufficient time to follow along with each of the steps. This was particularly useful for the task condition where the steps would be executed rapidly due to lack of regulation by the social controller.

On the right side of Table 2, we notice that the human tutors (H) were rated higher on being part of the team (Integration), being more liked, being friendlier and keeping the group more socially comfortable (T.Releasing). On the other hand, the social tutors (S) were rated to be friendlier and were only marginally better at being seen as part of the team.

	Strategy	**Social**	**Human**
Introducing	**1a**	2.67	3.80
Friendly	**1b-1e**	5.61	8.10
Concluding	**1f**	0.97	1.80
T.Releasing	**2a-2c**	5.81	1.77
Agreeing	**3a-3b**	1.78	4.90
Sum		16.83	22.17

Table 3. Mean counts of social turns by tutor

Note that human tutors were restricted to exhibit only social behaviors, which were displayed in addition to the same task related content given to students in the other two conditions. Clearly, the human tutors were better at employing the social interaction strategies. To further investigate this, we compare the number of turns corresponding to the broad categories of strategies in Table 3. Human tutors performed significantly more ($p<0.001$) social turns than the automated tutors in all strategies except showing tension release.

7 Conclusions

In order to make CAs that can participate in multi-party conversational scenarios, the agents must be able to employ Social Interaction Strategies. Here we have shown that the human tutors that use these strategies are better integrated into the group, and are considered more likeable and friendlier. These tutors also cover more steps and concepts and take less time to tutor the concepts, suggesting that the students are more engaged and responsive to them. On the other hand, automated tutors that employ these strategies in our current implementation do not show significant differences compared to task tutor.

We note a contrast between the performance of the human and the automated tutors with respect to the frequency with which they employ these strategies. Besides the frequent use of these strategies, we believe human tutors were better at identifying opportunities for employing these strategies, and they are able to customize the prompt to better suit the discourse context.

Acknowledgments

The research was supported by NSF grant number DUE 837661

References

Elizabeth Arnott, Peter Hastings and David Allbritton, 2008, Research Methods Tutor: Evaluation of a dialogue-based tutoring system in the classroom, *Behavior Research Methods*, 40 (3), 694-698

Robert F. Bales, 1950, *Interaction process analysis: A method for the study of small groups*, Addison-Wesley, Cambridge, MA

Timothy Bickmore, Daniel Schulman and Langxuan Yin, Engagement vs. Deceit: Virtual Humans with Human Autobiographies, 2009, *IVA*, Amsterdam

Kohji Dohsaka, Ryoto Asai, Ryichiro Higashinaka, Yasuhiro Minami and Eisaku Maeda, Effects of Conversational Agents on Human Communication in Though Evoking Multi-Party dialogues, 2009, *10th Annual SigDial*, London, UK

Pawel Dybala, Michal Ptaszynski, Rafal Rzepka and Kenji Araki, Humoroids: Conversational Agents that induce positive emotions with humor, 2009, *AAMAS*, Budapest, Hungary

Arthur C. Graesser, Patrick Chipman, Brian C. Haynes, and Andrew Olney, 2005, AutoTutor: An Intelligent Tutoring System with Mixed-initiative Dialogue, *IEEE Transactions in Education*, 48, 612-618

Katherine Isbister and Patrick Doyle, Design and Evaluation of Embodied Conversational Agents: A Proposed Taxonomy, 2002, *AAMAS Workshop: Embodied Conversational Agents*, Bologna, Italy

Rohit Kumar, Carolyn Rosé, Mahesh Joshi, Yi-Chia Wang, Yue Cui and Allen Robinson, Tutorial Dialogue as Adaptive Collaborative Learning Support, *13th AIED 2007*, Los Angeles, California

Rohit Kumar, Carolyn Rosé, Building Conversational Agents with Basilica, 2009, *NAACL*, Boulder, CO

Using Entity-Based Features to Model Coherence in Student Essays

Jill Burstein
Educational Testing Service
Princeton, NJ 08541
jburstein@ets.org

Joel Tetreault
Educational Testing Service
Princeton, NJ 08541
jtetreault@ets.org

Slava Andreyev
Educational Testing Service
Princeton, NJ 08541
sandreyev@ets.org

Abstract

We show how the Barzilay and Lapata entity-based coherence algorithm (2008) can be applied to a new, noisy data domain – *student essays*. We demonstrate that by combining Barzilay and Lapata's entity-based features with novel features related to grammar errors and word usage, one can greatly improve the performance of automated coherence prediction for student essays for different populations.

1 Introduction

There is a small body of work that has investigated using NLP for the problem of identifying coherence in student essays. For example, Foltz, Kintsch & Landauer (1998), and Higgins, Burstein, Marcu & Gentile (2004) have developed systems that examine coherence in student writing. Foltz, *et al.* (1998) systems measure lexical relatedness between text segments by using vector-based similarity between adjacent sentences; Higgins *et al*'s (2004) system computes similarity across text segments. Foltz *et al.*'s (1998) approach is in line with the earlier TextTiling method that identifies subtopic structure in text (Hearst, 1997). Miltsakaki and Kukich (2000) addressed essay coherence using Centering Theory (Grosz, Joshi & Weinstein, 1995). More recently, Barzilay and Lapata's (2008) approach (henceforth, BL08) used an entity-based representation to evaluate coherence. In BL08, *entities* (nouns and pronouns) are represented by their sentence roles in a text. The algorithm keeps track of the distribution of entity transitions between adjacent sentences, and computes a value for all transition types based on their proportion of occurrence in a text. BL08 apply their algorithm to three tasks, using well-formed newspaper corpora: text ordering, summary coherence evaluation, and readability assessment. For each task, their system outperforms a Latent Semantic Analysis baseline. In addition, best performance on each task is achieved using different system and feature configurations. Pitler & Nenkova (2008) applied BL08 to detect text coherence in well-formed texts.

Coherence quality is typically present in scoring criteria for evaluating a student's essay. This paper focuses on the development of models to predict *low*-and *high-coherence ratings* for essays. Student essay data, unlike newspaper text, is typically noisy, especially when students are non-native English speakers (NNES). Here, we evaluate how BL08 algorithm features can be used to model coherence in a new, noisy data domain -- *student essays*. We found that coherence can be best modeled by combining BL08 entity-based features with novel writing quality features. Further, our use of data sets from three different test-taker populations also shows that coherence models will differ across populations. Different populations might use language differently which could affect how coherence is presented. We expect to incorporate coherence ratings into e-rater®, ETS's automated essay scoring system (Attali & Burstein, 2006).

2 Corpus and Annotation

We collected approximately 800 essays (in total) across three data sets[1]: 1) adult, NNES test essays (TOEFL); 2) adult, native and NNES test essays; (GRE) 3) U.S. middle- and high-school native and NNES student essay submissions to *Criterion*®, ETS's instructional writing application.

Two annotators were trained to rate *coherence quality* based on how easily they could read an essay without stumbling on a *coherence barrier* (i.e., a confusing sentence(s)). Annotators rated

[1] TOEFL® is the Test of English as a Foreign Language, and GRE® is the Graduate Record Admissions Test.

Human Language Technologies: The 2010 Annual Conference of the North American Chapter of the ACL, pages 681–684,
Los Angeles, California, June 2010.

essays on a 3-point scale: 1) *low coherence*, 2) *somewhat coherent*, and 3) *high coherence*. They were instructed to ignore grammar and spelling errors, unless they affected essay comprehension.

During training, *Kappa* agreement statistics indicated that annotators had difficulty agreeing on the middle, *somewhat coherent* category. The annotation scale was therefore collapsed into a 2-point scale: *somewhat coherent* and *high coherence* categories were collapsed into the *high coherence* class (H), and *low-coherence* (L) remained unchanged. Two annotators labeled an overlapping set of about 100 essays to calculate inter-rater agreement; weighted Kappa was 0.677.

3 System

3.1 BL08 Algorithm

We implemented BL08's entity-based algorithm to build and evaluate coherence models for the essay data. In short, the algorithm generates a vector of *entity transition probabilities* for documents (essays, here). Vectors are used to build coherence models. The first step in the algorithm is to construct an entity grid in which all entities (*nouns and pronouns*) are represented by their roles (i.e., Subject **(S)**, Object **(O),** Other **(X)).** Entity roles are then used to generate *entity transitions* – the role transitions across adjacent sentences (e.g., Subject-to-Object, Object-to-Object). *Entity transition probabilities* are the proportions of different entity transition types within a text. The probability values are used then used as features to build a coherence model.

Entity roles can be represented in the following ways. In this study, consistent with BL08, different combinations are applied and reported (see Tables 2-4). Entities can be represented in grids with specified roles **(Syntax+)** **(S,O,X)**. Alternatively, roles can be reduced to show *only* the presence and absence of an entity **(Syntax-)** (i.e., Entity Present **(P)** or Not **(N).** Co-referential entities can be resolved **(Coreference+)** or not **(Coreference-).** Finally, the **Salience** option reflects the frequency with which an entity appears in the discourse: if the entity is mentioned two or more times, it is salient **(Salient+),** otherwise, not **(Salient-)**.

Consistent with BL08, we systematically completed runs using various configurations of entity representations (see Section 4).

Given the combination, the entity transition probabilities were computed for all labeled essays in each data set. We used *n-fold* cross-validation for evaluation. Feature vectors were input to C5.0, a decision-tree machine learning application.

3.2 Additional Features

In BL08, augmenting the core coherence features with additional features improved the power of the algorithm. We extended the feature set with writing quality features (Table 1). **GUMS** features describe the technical quality of the essay. The motivation for type/token features **(*_TT)** is to measure word variety. For example, a high probability for a "Subject-to-Subject" transition indicates that the writer is repeating an entity in Subject position across adjacent sentences. However, this does not take into account whether the same word is repeated or a variety of words are used. The **{S,O,X,SOX}_TT** (type/token) features *uncover* the actual words collapsed into the entity transition probabilities. **Shell nouns** (Atkas & Cortes, 2008), common in essay writing, might also affect coherence.

NNES essays can contain many spelling errors. We evaluated the impact of a context-sensitive spell checker **(SPCR+),** as spelling variation will affect the transition probabilities in the entity grid.

Finally, we experimented with a *majority vote method* that combined the best performing feature combinations.

4 Evaluation

For all experiments, we used a series of *n-fold cross-validation* runs with C5.0 to evaluate performance for numerous feature configurations. In Tables 2, 3 and 4, we report: baselines, results on our data with BL08's best system configuration from the summary coherence evaluation task (closest to our task), and our best systems. In the Tables, "best systems" combined feature sets and outperformed baselines. Rows in **bold** indicate final independent best systems that contribute to best performance in the *majority vote* method. Agreement is reported as Weighted Kappa (**WK**), Precision (**P**), Recall (**R**) and F-measure (**F**).

Baselines. We implemented three non-trivial baseline systems. **E-rater** indicates use of the full feature set from e-rater. The **GUMS** (GUMS+) feature baseline, uses the Grammar (G+), Usage

Feature Descriptor	Feature Description
GUMS	Grammar, usage, and mechanics errors, and style features from an AES system
S_TT **O_TT** **X_TT** **SOX_TT**[2] **P_TT**	Type/token ratios for actual words recovered from the entity grid, using the entity *roles.*
S_TT_Shellnouns **O_TT_Shellnouns** **X_TT_Shellnouns**	Type/token ratio of non-topic content, *shell nouns* (e.g., *approach, aspect, challenge*)

Table 1: New feature category description

(U+), Mechanics (M+), and Style (ST+) flags (subset of e-rater features) to evaluate a coherence model. The third baseline represents the best run using **type/token features** ({S,O,X,SOX}_TT), and **{S,O,X}_TT_Shellnouns** feature sets (Table 1). The baseline majority voting system includes e-rater, GUMS, and the best performing type/token baseline (see Tables 2-4).

Extended System. We combined our writing quality features with the core BL08 feature set. The combination improved performance over the three baselines, and over the best performing BL08 feature. Type/token features added to BL08 entity transitions probabilities improved performance of all single systems. This supports the need to *recover* actual word use. In Table 2, for TOEFL data, spell correction improved performance with the Mechanics error feature (where Spelling is evaluated). *This would suggest that annotators were trying to ignore spelling errors when labeling coherence.* In Table 3, for GRE data, spell correction improved performance with the Grammar error feature. *Spell correction did change grammar errors detected: annotators may have self-corrected for grammar.* Finally, the *majority vote* outperformed all systems. In Tables 3 and 4, Kappa was comparable to human agreement (K=0.677).

5 Conclusions and Future Work

We have evaluated how the BL08 algorithm features can be used to model coherence for student essays across three different populations. We found that the best coherence models for essays are built by combining BL08 entity-based features with writing quality features. BL08's outcomes showed that optimal performance was obtained by using different feature sets for different tasks. Our task was most similar to BL08's summary coherence task, but we used noisy essay data. The difference in the data types might also explain the need for our systems to include additional writing quality features.

Our *majority vote* method outperformed three baselines (and a baseline majority vote). For two of the populations, Weighted Kappa between system and human agreement was comparable. These results show promise toward development of an entity-based method that produces reliable coherence ratings for noisy essay data. We plan to evaluate this method on additional data sets, and in the context of automated essay scoring.

[2] Indicates an aggregate feature that computes the type/token ratio for entities that appear in any of S,O,X role.

References

Aktas, R. N., & Cortes, V. (2008). Shell nouns as cohesive devices in published and ESL student writing. *Journal of English for Academic Purposes*, 7(1), 3–14.

Attali, Y., & Burstein, J. (2006). Automated essay scoring with *e-rater* v.2.0 . *Journal of Technology, Learning, and Assessment, 4*(3).

Barzilay, R. and Lapata, M. (2008). Modeling local coherence: An entity-based approach. *Computational Linguistics,* 34(1), 1-34.

Foltz, P., Kintsch, W., and Landauer, T. K. (1998). The measurement of textual coherence with Latent Semantic Analysis. *Discourse Processes*, 25(2&3):285–307.

Higgins, D., Burstein, J., Marcu, D., & Gentile, C. (2004). Evaluating multiple aspects of coherence in student essays . *In Proceedings of HLT-NAACL 2004*, Boston, MA.

Grosz, B., Joshi, A., and Weinstein, S. 1995, Centering: A framework for modeling the local coherence of discourse. *Computational Linguistics*, 21(2): 203-226.

Hearst, M. A. (1997). TextTiling: Segmenting text into multi-paragraph subtopic passages. *Computational Linguistics*, 23(1):33–6

Miltsakaki, E. and Kukich, K. (2000). Automated evaluation of coherence in student essays. In *Proceedings of LREC 2000*, Athens, Greece

Pitler, E.,and Nenkova, A (2008). Revisiting Readability: A Unified Framework for Predicting

Text Quality. *In Proceedings of EMNLP 2008*, Honolulu, Hawaii.

		L (n=64)			H (n=196)			L+H (n=260)		
BASELINES: NO BL08 FEATURES	**WK**	**P**	**R**	**F**	**P**	**R**	**F**	**P**	**R**	**F**
(a) E-rater	0.472	56	69	62	89	82	86	79	79	79
(b) GUMS	0.455	55	66	60	88	83	85	79	79	79
(c) SOX_TT[3]	0.484	66	55	60	86	91	88	82	82	82
SYSTEMS: Includes BL08 FEATURES										
Coreference-Syntax+Salient+ (B&L08 summary task configuration)	0.253	49	34	40	81	88	84	75	75	75
(d) Coreference-Syntax-Salient-SPCR+M+	**0.472**	**76**	**45**	**57**	**84**	**95**	**90**	**83**	**83**	**83**
(e) Coreference+Syntax+Salient-GUMS+	**0.590**	**68**	**70**	**69**	**90**	**89**	**90**	**85**	**85**	**85**
(f) Coreference+Syntax+Salient-GUMS+O_TT_Shellnouns+	**0.595**	**68**	**72**	**70**	**91**	**89**	**90**	**85**	**85**	**85**
Baseline Majority vote: (a),(b), (c)	0.450	55	64	59	88	83	85	79	79	79
Majority vote: (d), (e), (f)	**0.598**	**69**	**70**	**70**	**90**	**90**	**90**	**85**	**85**	**85**

Table 2: Non-native English Speaker Test-taker Data (TOEFL): Annotator/System Agreement

		L (n=48)			H (n=210)			L+H (n=258)		
BASELINES: NO BL08 FEATURES	**WK**	**P**	**R**	**F**	**P**	**R**	**F**	**P**	**R**	**F**
(a) E-rater	0.383	79	31	45	86	98	92	86	86	86
(b) GUMS	0.316	68	27	39	85	97	91	84	84	84
(c) e-rater+SOX_TT[4]	0.359	78	29	42	86	98	92	85	85	85
SYSTEMS: INCLUDES BL08 FEATURES										
Coreference-Syntax+Salient+ (BL08 summary task configuration)	0.120	35	17	23	83	93	88	79	79	79
(d) Coreference+Syntax+Salient-SPCR+G+	**0.547**	**1.0**	**43**	**60**	**89**	**1.0**	**94**	**90**	**90**	**90**
(e) Coreference+Syntax-Salient-P_TT+	**0.462**	**70**	**44**	**54**	**88**	**96**	**92**	**86**	**86**	**86**
(f) Coreference+Syntax+Salient+GUMS+SOX_TT+	**0.580**	**71**	**60**	**65**	**91**	**94**	**93**	**88**	**88**	**88**
Baseline Majority vote: (a),(b), (c)	0.383	79	31	45	86	98	92	86	86	86
Majority vote: (d), (e), (f)	**0.610**	**1.0**	**49**	**66**	**90**	**1.0**	**95**	**91**	**91**	**91**

Table 3: Native and Non-Native English Speaker Test-taker Data (GRE): Annotator/System Agreement

		L (n=37)			H (n=226)			L+H (n=263)		
BASELINES: NO BL08 FEATURES	**WK**	**P**	**R**	**F**	**P**	**R**	**F**	**P**	**R**	**F**
(a) E-rater	0.315	39	46	42	91	88	89	82	82	82
(b) GUMS	0.350	47	41	43	90	92	91	85	85	85
(c) SOX_TT	0.263	78	19	30	88	99	93	88	88	88
SYSTEMS: INCLUDES BL08 FEATURES										
(d) Coreference-Syntax+Salient+ (BL08 summary task configuration)	**0.383**	**79**	**30**	**43**	**90**	**99**	**94**	**89**	**89**	**89**
(e) Coreference-Syntax-Salient-SPCR+	**0.424**	**67**	**38**	**48**	**90**	**97**	**94**	**89**	**89**	**89**
(f) Coreference+Syntax+Salient+S_TT+	**0.439**	**65**	**41**	**50**	**91**	**96**	**94**	**89**	**89**	**89**
Baseline Majority vote: (a),(b), (c)	0.324	43	41	42	90	91	91	84	84	84
Majority vote: (d), (e), (f)	**0.471**	**82**	**38**	**52**	**91**	**99**	**94**	**90**	**90**	**90**

Table 4: *Criterion* Essay Data*:* Annotator/System Agreement

[3] Type/token ratios from all roles using a Coreference+Syntax+Salient+ grid.
[4] Type/token ratios from all roles using Coreference+Syntax+Salient- grid.

Summarizing Microblogs Automatically

Beaux Sharifi, Mark-Anthony Hutton, and Jugal Kalita
University of Colorado at Colorado Springs
1420 Austin Bluffs Parkway
Colorado Springs, CO 80918, USA
{bsharifi, mhutton, jkalita}@uccs.edu

Abstract

In this paper, we focus on a recent Web trend called microblogging, and in particular a site called Twitter. The content of such a site is an extraordinarily large number of small textual messages, posted by millions of users, at random or in response to perceived events or situations. We have developed an algorithm that takes a trending phrase or any phrase specified by a user, collects a large number of posts containing the phrase, and provides an automatically created summary of the posts related to the term. We present examples of summaries we produce along with initial evaluation.

1 Introduction

Since Twitter's inception in 2006, it has grown at an unprecedented rate. In just four years, the service has grown to approximately 20 million unique visitors each month with users sending short 140-character messages (known as "tweets") approximately 40 million times a day. While the majority of these tweets are pointless babble or conversational, approximately 3.6% of these posts are topics of mainstream news (Pear Analytics, 2009). For example, Twitter has been cited as breaking many important events before traditional media, such as the attacks in Mumbai and the crash of the US Airways flight into the Hudson River.

In order to help users sort through the vast number of tweets that occur each day, Twitter.com has added a number of tools. For instance, Twitter's homepage displays important topics for three different ranges of time in order to see what topics are popular. For most topics, users are forced to read through related posts in order to try and understand why a topic is trending. In order to help users further, Twitter has partnered with the third-party website WhatTheTrend[1] in order to provide definitions of trending topics. WhatTheTrend allows users to manually enter descriptions of why a topic is trending. Unfortunately, WhatTheTrend suffers with spam and rants as well as lag time before a new trending topic is defined by a user.

While WhatTheTrend is a step in the right direction, a better approach is to automatically summarize important events as they occur in real time. We have developed such a method. Our method can automatically summarize a collection of microblogging posts that are all related to a topic into a short, one-line summary. Our results show that our automated summarizer produces summaries that are close to human-generated summaries for the same set of posts. For example, Table 1 below contains a sample of automatically produced summaries for some recently trending topics on Twitter.

2 Related Work

Some early work focused on summarizing results of database queries for presentation during natural language interactions (e.g., Kalita et al., 1986). Most summaries are generated for the purposes of providing a "gist" of a document or a set of documents to human readers (e.g., Luhn, 1958; Brandow et al., 1995). Summaries are sometimes also used as inputs to machine learning approaches, say for categorization. Kolcz et al. (2001) summarize textual documents in order to classify them, using the summaries as a feature to be input to a classifier. Most early studies used a news corpus like the Reuters dataset. As the Web started growing in size, the focus moved to Web pages.

[1] http://www.whatthetrend.com

Human Language Technologies: The 2010 Annual Conference of the North American Chapter of the ACL, pages 685–688,
Los Angeles, California, June 2010.

Topic	Automated Summary	Date
Ice Dancing	Canadians Tessa Virtue and Scott Moir clinch the gold in Olympic ice dancing; U.S. pair Davis and White win silver	2/22/2010
Dodgers	Phillies defeat Dodgers to take the National League Championship series.	10/21/2009
Limbaugh	Limbaugh dropped from group bidding for St. Louis Rams	10/14/2009
Dow Jones	The Dow Jones Industrial Average passes 10,000 for the first time since October 7th, 2008.	10/14/2009
Captain Lou	Wrestler, personality Captain Lou Albano dies at 76	10/14/2009
Bloomberg	Bloomberg Acquires Businessweek for Less Than $5 million	10/13/2009
G20	Trouble breaks out at G20 summit: Protesters and riot police have clashed ahead of the G20 summit in Pittsburgh	09/24/2009
AT&T	AT&T plans for iPhone MMS to arrive Friday	09/23/2009

Table 1. Example Summaries Produced by the Phrase Reinforcement Algorithm.

For example, Mahesh (1997) examines the effectiveness of Web document summarization by sentence extraction. Recently, there has been work on summarizing blogs (e.g. Zhou and Hovy, 2006; Hu et al., 2007). Most techniques focus on extraction: the selecting of salient pieces of documents in order to generate a summary. Applying extraction on microblogs at first appears irrelevant since a microblog post is already shorter than most summaries. However, extraction is possible when one considers extracting from multiple microblogs posts that are all related to a central theme.

3 Approach

3.1 Twitter API

Through an entirely HTTP-based API provided by Twitter, users can programmatically perform almost any task that can be performed via Twitter's web interface. For non-whitelisted users, Twitter restricts a user to 150 requests/hour. Furthermore, searches are limited to returning 1500 posts for a given request. Our summarizer has been shown to produce comparable automated summaries to human summaries with as few as 100 posts.

3.2 Phrase Reinforcement Algorithm

Given a trending topic, one can query Twitter.com for posts that contain the topic phrase. Presently, users would have to read these posts in order to comprehend and manually summarize their content. Instead, we automate this process using our Phrase Reinforcement Algorithm.

The central idea of the Phrase Reinforcement (PR) algorithm is to find the most commonly used phrase that encompasses the topic phrase. This phrase is then used as a summary. The algorithm was inspired from two simple observations: (1) users will often use the same word or sets of words adjacent to the topic phrase when describing a key idea and (2) users will often "re-tweet" (a Twitter form of quoting) the most relevant content for a trending topic. These two patterns create highly overlapping sequences of words when considering a large number of posts for a single topic. The PR algorithm capitalizes on these behaviors in order to generate a summary.

The Phrase Reinforcement algorithm begins with a starting phrase. This is typically a trending topic, but can be non-trending as well. Given the starting phrase, the PR algorithm submits a query to Twitter.com for a list of posts that each contains the phrase. Once the posts are retrieved, the algorithm filters the posts to remove any spam or other sources of irrelevant data (e.g. hyperlinks). Filtering is an important step in order to focus the algorithm on the most relevant content. We filter any spam by using a Naïve Bayes classifier which we trained using previously gathered spam content from Twitter.com. Next, non-English posts as well as duplicate posts are removed since we are concerned with English summaries only and want to prevent a single user from dominating a topic. Finally, given a set of relevant posts, we isolate the longest sentence from each post that contains the topic phrase. These sentences form the input into the PR algorithm.

Once we have the set of input sentences, the PR algorithm formally begins. The algorithm starts by building a graph representing the common sequences of words (i.e. phrases) that occur both before and after the topic phrase. The graph is generated such that it centers about a common root node representing the topic phrase. Adjacent to the root node are chains of common sequences of words found within the input sentences. In particular, each word is represented by a node and an associated count that indicates how many times the node's phrase occurs within the set of input sentences. The phrase of a node is simply the sequence of words generated by following the path from the node to the root node. To illustrate, consider the following set of input sentences for the topic "Ted Kennedy".

1. A tragedy: Ted Kennedy died today of cancer
2. Ted Kennedy died today
3. Ted Kennedy was a leader
4. Ted Kennedy died at age 77

Using these sentences, the PR algorithm would generate a graph similar to the one shown below in Figure 1.

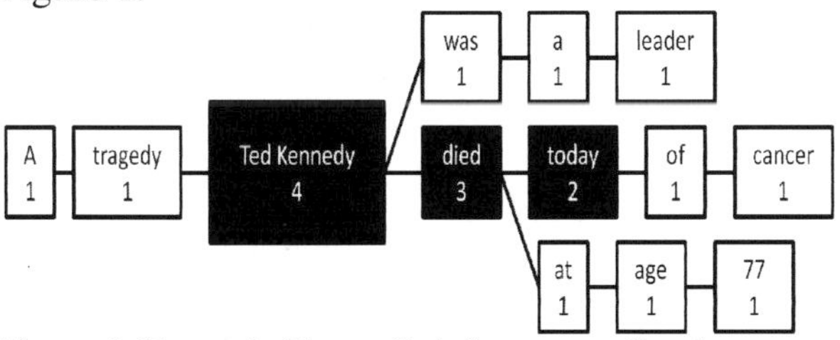

Figure 1. Example Phrase Reinforcement Graph.

In Figure 1, we see the node "today" has a count of two. This indicates that the phrase "Ted Kennedy died today" occurs exactly two times within the set of input sentences (in sentences 1 and 2). Likewise, the node "tradegy" has a count of one indicating the phrase "tragedy Ted Kennedy" only occurs one time (in sentence 1). In actuality, the PR algorithm would only add nodes to the graph with a count of at least two since it is looking for the most *common* phrase. These are shown as the black nodes in Figure 1. However, Figure 1 also includes unique nodes (shown in white) for helping illustrate the graph's structure.

After the graph is constructed, the PR algorithm assigns a weight to every node in order to prevent longer phrases from dominating the output. In particular, stop words are given a weight of zero while remaining words are given weights that are both proportional to their count and penalized the farther they are from the root node:

$$\begin{aligned} Weight(node) = Count(node) \\ - [RootDistance(node) \\ * \log_b Count(node)] \end{aligned}$$

In the above equation, the *RootDistance* of a node is simply the number of hops to get from the node to the root node and the logarithm base, b, is a parameter to the algorithm. Smaller values of b (e.g. 2) can be used for preferring shorter summaries over longer summaries.

Finally, once the graph is constructed and weighted, the PR algorithm is ready to generate a *partial summary*. To do so, the PR algorithm searches for the path with the most total weight by searching all paths that begin with the root node and end with a non-root node. This path is denoted as the best partial path since it only represents one half of the summary (i.e. the most common phrase occurring either before or after the topic phrase). In order to generate the remaining half of the summary, the PR algorithm is essentially repeated by initializing the root node with the partial summary and rebuilding the graph. The most heavily weighted path from this new graph is the final summary produced by the PR algorithm.

Using our example above and assuming that node weights are equal to their counts, the path with the most total weight is the path "Ted Kennedy died today of cancer" with a total weight of 11. This phrase would then be used as the root node of a new graph and the PR algorithm would be repeated. For this new graph, the only input sentence that contains this root phrase would be sentence 1. Therefore, the final summary for our example (assuming we allow unique phrases) would be sentence 1: "A tragedy: Ted Kennedy died today of cancer". However, if we only allow non-unique phrases in our graph (the black nodes), then our final summary would be "Ted Kennedy died today".

4 Results

In order to evaluate the PR algorithm, we gathered a set of testing data by collecting the top ten currently trending topics from Twitter's home page every day for five consecutive days. For each of the 50 trending topics, we retrieved the maximum number of posts from Twitter using its own API and then filtered the number of posts to 100 posts per topic. These posts were then given to two volunteers. The volunteers were instructed to simply generate the best summary possible using only the information contained within the posts and in 140 characters or less. Furthermore, automated summaries for each topic were also produced using the same 100 posts per topic. These summaries were then compared.

For comparing the manual and automated summaries, we adopted two of the metrics used by the Document Understanding Conference (DUC) of 2002 and 2004 (Lin and Hovy, 2003). First, we used their *Content* metric which asks a human judge to measure how completely an automated summary expresses the meaning of the manual summaries on a five point scale where 1 represents no meaning overlap and 5 represents complete meaning overlap. Next, we also used the automated evaluation metric ROUGE-1 developed by Lin (2004) which measures co-occurring unigram overlap between a set of manual and automated summaries. We restricted our automated evaluation to ROUGE-1 as opposed to the other ROUGE metrics since Lin indicates that this metric correlates highly with human judgments for very short summary tasks similar to the one we are performing (Lin, 2004).

For the 50 trending topics we used as our evaluation corpus, the PR algorithm produced an average Content score of 3.72 using $b = 100$ for our weighting measure. This result indicates our automated summaries express slightly less than most of the meaning of the manual summary content. To compare, we also used this same metric on our two sets of manual summaries which produced an average content score of 4.25. For the ROUGE-1 metric, the PR algorithm produced an average precision score of 0.31 and an average recall score of 0.30. Combining these scores using F_1-Measure, the PR algorithm produced a combined F_1 score of 0.30. Comparing the manual summaries against one another using ROUGE-1, they produced the same average precision, recall, and F_1 score of 0.34.

5 Future Work

Presently, we are working on extending our PR algorithm to providing real-time summaries within specific topics. We are experimenting with using a front-end classifier for producing trending topics within distinct categories and then summarizing around these topics in order to generate an automated real-time newspaper.

Acknowledgments

The work reported in this paper is partially supported by the NSF Grant ARRA: : CNS 0851783.

References

Brandow, R., Mitze K., and Rau, L.F. Automatic Condensation of Electronic Publications by Sentence Selection, Information Processing and Management, Vol 31, No 5, pp. 675-685, 1995.

Hu, M. and Sun, A. and Lim, E.P. Comments-oriented blog summarization by sentence extraction, ACM CIKM, pp. 901-904, 2007.

Kalita, J.K., Jones, M.L., and McCalla, G.I., Summarizing Natural Language Database Responses, Computational Linguistics, Volume 12, No. 2, pp. 107-124, 1986.

Kolcz, A., Prabhakarmurthi, V, and Kalita, J. Summarizing as Feature Selection for Text Categorization, CIKM '01, pp. 365-370, 2001.

Lin, C.Y. ROUGE: a Package for Automatic Evaluation of Summaries, Proceedings of Workshop on Text Summarization, 2004.

Lin, C.Y. and Hovy, E. Automatic evaluation of summaries using n-gram co-occurrence statistics, NAACL, pp. 71-78, 2003.

Luhn, P. The Automatic Creation of Literature Abstracts, in IRE National Convention, pp. 60-68, 1958.

Mahesh, K. Hypertext Summary Extraction for Fast Document Browsing, Working Notes of the AAAI Spring Symposium for the WWW, pp. 95-103, 1997.

Pear Analytics. Twitter Study, Retrieved 03 31, 2010, from http://www.scribd.com/doc/18548460/Pear-Analytics-Twitter-Study-August-2009, 2009.

Zhou, L. and Hovy, E. On the summarization of dynamically introduced information: Online discussions and blogs, AAAI-2006 Spring Symposium on Computational Approaches to Analyzing Weblogs, 2006.

Automatic Generation of Personalized Annotation Tags for Twitter Users

Wei Wu, Bin Zhang, Mari Ostendorf
Electrical Engineering
University of Washington, Seattle, WA
{weiwu, binz, ostendor}@uw.edu

Abstract

This paper introduces a system designed for automatically generating personalized annotation tags to label Twitter user's interests and concerns. We applied TFIDF ranking and TextRank to extract keywords from Twitter messages to tag the user. The user tagging precision we obtained is comparable to the precision of keyword extraction from web pages for content-targeted advertising.

1 Introduction

Twitter is a communication platform which combines SMS, instant messages and social networks. It enables users to share information with their friends or the public by updating their Twitter messages. A large majority of the Twitter users are individual subscribers, who use Twitter to share information on "what am I doing" or "what's happening right now". Most of them update their Twitter messages very frequently, in which case the Twitter messages compose a detailed log of the user's everyday life. These Twitter messages contain rich information about an individual user, including what s/he is interested in and concerned about. Identifying an individual user's interests and concerns can help potential commercial applications. For instance, this information can be employed to produce "following" suggestions, either a person who shares similar interests (for expanding their social network) or a company providing products or services the user is interested in (for personalized advertisement).

In this work, we focus on automatically generating personalized annotation tags to label Twitter user's interests and concerns. We formulate this problem as a keyword extraction task, by selecting words from each individual user's Twitter messages as his/her tags. Due to the lack of human generated annotations, we employ an unsupervised strategy. Specifically, we apply TFIDF ranking and TextRank (Mihalcea and Tarau, 2004) keyword extraction on Twitter messages after a series of text preprocessing steps. Experiments on randomly selected users showed good results with TextRank, but high variability among users.

2 Related Work

Research work related to Twitter message analysis includes a user sentiment study (Jansen et al., 2009) and information retrieval indexing. To our knowledge, no previously published research has yet addressed problems on tagging user's personal interests from Twitter messages via keyword extraction, though several studies have looked at keyword extraction using other genres.

For supervised keyword extraction, (Turney, 2000; Turney, 2003; Hulth, 2003; Yih et al., 2006; Liu et al., 2008) employed TFIDF or its variants with Part-of-Speech (POS), capitalization, phrase and sentence length, etc., as features to train keyword extraction models, and discriminative training is usually adopted. Yih et al. (2006) use logistic regression to extract keywords from web pages for content-targeted advertising, which has the most similar application to our work. However, due to the lack of human annotation on Twitter messages, we have to adopt an unsupervised strategy.

For unsupervised keyword extraction, TFIDF ranking is a popular method, and its effectiveness has been shown in (Hulth, 2003; Yih et al., 2006). TextRank and its variants (Mihalcea and Tarau, 2004; Wan et al., 2007; Liu et al., 2009) are graph-based text ranking models, which are derived from Google's PageRank algorithm (Brin and Page, 1998). It outperforms TFIDF ranking on traditional keyword extraction tasks. However, previous work on both TFIDF ranking and TextRank has been done mainly on academic papers, spoken documents or

Human Language Technologies: The 2010 Annual Conference of the North American Chapter of the ACL, pages 689–692,
Los Angeles, California, June 2010.

web pages, whose language style is more formal (or, less "conversational") than that of Twitter messages. Twitter messages contain large amounts of "noise" like emoticons, internet slang words, abbreviations, and misspelled words. In addition, Twitter messages are a casual log of a user's everyday life, which often lacks of a coherent topic sequence compared to academic papers and most spoken documents. Hence, it remains to see whether TFIDF ranking and TextRank are effective for identifying user's interests from Twitter messages.

3 System Architecture

Figure 1 shows the framework of our system for tagging Twitter user's interests. A preprocessing pipeline is designed to deal with various types of "noise" in Twitter messages and produce candidate words for user tags. Then the TFIDF ranking or TextRank algorithm is applied to select user tags from the candidate words.

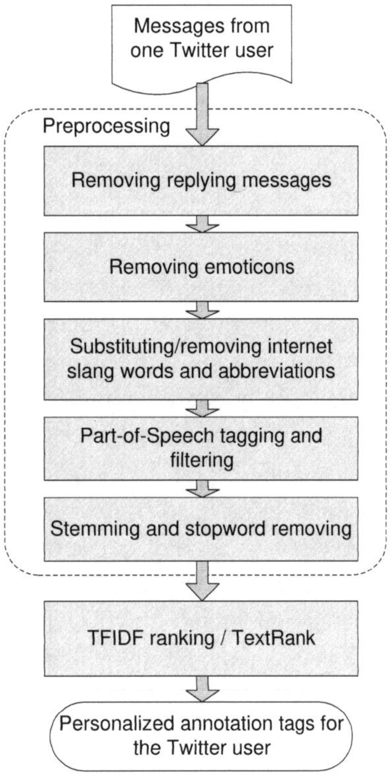

Figure 1: Framework of the personalized annotation tag generation system for Twitter users

3.1 Preprocessing

In addition to messages describing "What am I doing" or "what's happening right now", Twitter users also write replying messages to comment on other users' messages. This kind of message generally contains more information about the users they reply to than about themselves, and therefore they are removed in the preprocessing pipeline.

Emoticons frequently appear in Twitter messages. Although some of them help express user's sentiment on certain topics, they are not directly helpful for keyword analysis and may interfere with POS tagging in the preprocessing pipeline. Therefore, we designed a set of regular expressions to detect and remove them.

Internet slang words and abbreviations are widely used in Twitter messages. Most of them are out-of-vocabulary words in the POS tagging model used in the next step, and thus will deteriorate the POS tagging accuracy. Hence, we build a lookup table based on the list of abbreviations in the NoSlang online dictionary,[1] which we divide by hand into three sets for different processing. The first set includes 422 content words and phrases, such as "bff" (best friend forever) and "fone" (phone), with valid candidate words for user tags. The second set includes 67 abbreviations of function words that usually form grammatical parts in a sentence, such as "im" (i'm), "abt" (about). Simply removing them will affect the POS tagging. Thus, the abbreviations in both these sets are replaced with the corresponding complete words or phrases. The third set includes 4576 phrase abbreviations that are usually separable parts of a sentence that do not directly indicate discussion topics, such as "lol" (laugh out loud), "clm" (cool like me), which are removed in this step.

We apply the Stanford POS tagger (Toutanova and Manning, 2000) on Twitter messages, and only select nouns and adjectives as valid candidates for user tags. At the end of the preprocessing pipeline, the candidate words are processed with the rule-based Porter stemmer[2] and stopwords are filtered using a publicly available list.[3]

[1] www.noslang.com/dictionary

[2] tartarus.org/ martin/PorterStemmer/

[3] armandbrahaj.blog.al/2009/04/14/list-of-english-stop-words/

3.2 User Tag Extraction

3.2.1 TFIDF ranking

In the TFIDF ranking algorithm, messages from user u are put together as one document. The TFIDF value of word i from this user's messages is computed as

$$tfidf_{i,u} = \frac{n_{i,u}}{\sum_j n_{j,u}} \log(\frac{U}{U_i})$$

where $n_{i,u}$ is the count of word i in user u's messages, U_i is the number of users whose messages contain word i, and U is the total number of users in the Twitter corpus. For each user, words with top N TFIDF values are selected as his/her tags.

3.2.2 TextRank

According to the TextRank algorithm (Mihalcea and Tarau, 2004), each candidate word is represented by a vertex in the graph; edges are added between two candidate words according to their co-occurrence. In the context of user tag extraction, we build a TextRank graph with undirected edges for each Twitter user. One edge is added between two candidate words if they co-exist within at least one message; the edge weight is set to be the total count of within-message co-occurrence of the two words throughout all messages of this user.

Starting with an arbitrarily assigned value (e.g. 1.0), the rank value $R(V_i)$ of the candidate word at vertex V_i is updated iteratively according to the following equation,

$$R(V_i) = (1-d) + d \sum_{V_j \in E(V_i)} \frac{w_{ji}}{\sum_{V_k \in E(V_j)} w_{jk}} R(V_j)$$

where w_{ji} is the weight of the edge that links V_j and V_i, $E(V_i)$ is the set of vertices which V_i is connected to, and d is a damping factor that is usually set to 0.85 (Brin and Page, 1998). The rank update iteration continues until convergence. The candidate words are then sorted according to their rank values. Words with top-N rank values are selected as tags for this user.

4 Experiment

4.1 Experimental Setup

We employed the Twitter API to download Twitter messages. A unigram English language model was used to filter out non-English users. We obtained messages from 11,376 Twitter users, each of them had 180 to 200 messages. The word IDF for TFIDF ranking was computed over these users.

Precision (%)	TFIDF	TextRank
top-1	59.6	67.3
top-3	61.5	66.0
top-5	61.2	63.0
top-10	59.0	58.3

Table 1: Tagging precision on all users in the test set

We adopted an evaluation measure similar to the one proposed in (Yih et al., 2006) for identifying advertising keywords on web pages, which emphasizes precision. We randomly selected 156 Twitter users to evaluate the top-N precision of TFIDF ranking and TextRank. After we obtained the top-N outputs from the system, three human evaluators were asked to judge whether the output tags from the two systems (unidentified) reflected the corresponding Twitter user's interests or concerns according to the full set of his/her messages.[4] We adopted a conservative standard in the evaluation: when a person's name is extracted as a user tag, which is frequent among Twitter users, we judge it as a correct tag only when it is a name of a famous person (pop star, football player, etc). The percentage of the correct tags among the top-N selected tags corresponds to the top-N precision of the system.

4.2 Experimental Results

Table 1 gives the top-N precision for TFIDF and TextRank for different values of N, showing that TextRank leads to higher precision for small N. Although Twitter messages are much "noisier" than regular web pages, the top-N precision we obtained for Twitter user tagging is comparable to the web page advertising keyword extraction result reported in (Yih et al., 2006).

Figure 2 shows an example of the candidate word ranking result of a Twitter user by TextRank (the font size is set to be proportional to each word's TextRank value). By examining the Twitter messages, we found that this user is an information tech-

[4]The pairwise Kappa value for inter-evaluator agreement ranged from 0.77-0.83, showing good agreement.

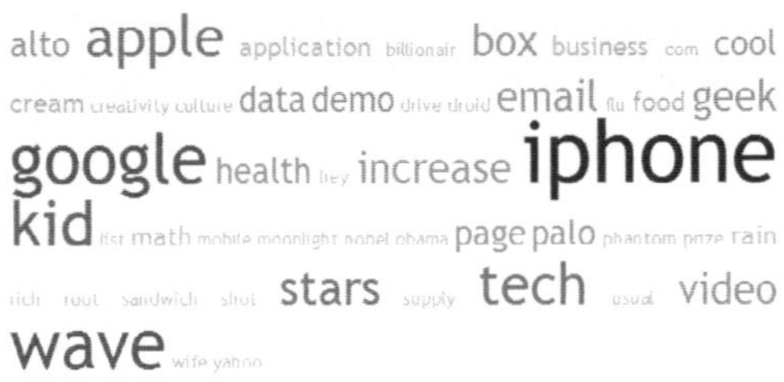

Figure 2: Example of a Twitter user's word ranks (the font size is proportional to each word's TextRank value)

Precision (%)				
top-N	σ >0.6	σ ≤0.6	H>5.4	H≤5.4
top-1	71.6	60.7	78.5	50.8
top-3	71.9	56.8	74.2	54.0
top-5	69.3	53.1	69.2	53.7
top-10	65.1	47.7	63.8	50.2

Table 2: TextRank tagging precision on users with different Top-10 TextRank value standard deviation (σ) and user message text entropy (H).

nology "geek", who is very interested in writing *Apple's iPhone applications*, and also a user of *Google Wave*. In this work, we use only isolated words as user tags, however, "google", "wave", and "palo", "alto" extracted in this example indicate that phrase level tagging can bring us more information about the user, which is typical of many users.

Although most Twitter users express their interests to some extent in their messages, there are some users whose message content is not rich enough to extract reliable information. We investigated two measures for identifying such users: standard deviation of the top-10 TextRank values and the user's message text entropy. Table 2 shows a comparison of tagging precision where the users are divided into two groups with a threshold on each of the two measures. It is shown that users with larger TextRank value standard deviation or message text entropy tend to have higher tagging precision, and the message text entropy has better correlation with the top-10 tagging precision than TextRank value standard deviation (0.33 v.s. 0.20 absolute).

5 Summary

In this paper, we designed a system to automatically extract keywords from Twitter messages to tag user interests and concerns. We evaluated two tagging algorithms, finding that TextRank outperformed TFIDF ranking, but both gave a tagging precision that was comparable to that reported for web page advertizing keyword extraction. We noticed substantial variation in performance across users, with low entropy indicative of users with fewer keywords, and a need for extracting key phrases (in addition to words). Other follow-on work might consider temporal characteristics of messages in terms of the amount of data needed for reliable tags vs. their time-varying nature, as well as sentiment associated with the identified tags.

References

S. Brin and L. Page. 1998. The anatomy of a large-scale hypertextual web search engine. *Computer Networks and ISDN Systems*, 30(1-7):107–117.

A. Hulth. 2003. Improved automatic keyword extraction given more linguistic knowledge. In *Proc. EMNLP*, pages 216–223.

B. J. Jansen, M. Zhang, K. Sobel, and A. Chowdury. 2009. Twitter power: Tweets as electronic word of mouth. *Journal of the American Society for Information Science and Technology*, 60(11):2169–2188.

F. Liu, F. Liu, and Y. Liu. 2008. Automatic keyword extraction for the meeting corpus using supervised approach and bigram expansion. In *Proc. IEEE SLT*, pages 181–184.

F. Liu, D. Pennell, F. Liu, and Y. Liu. 2009. Unsupervised approaches for automatic keyword extraction using meeting transcripts. In *Proc. HLT/NAACL*, pages 620–628.

R. Mihalcea and P. Tarau. 2004. Textrank: Bringing order into texts. In *Proc. EMNLP*.

K. Toutanova and C. D. Manning. 2000. Enriching the knowledge sources used in a maximum entropy part-of-speech tagger. In *Proc. EMNLP*, pages 63–77.

P. D. Turney. 2000. Learning algorithms for keyphrase. *Information Retrieval*, 2(4):303–336.

P. D. Turney. 2003. Coherent keyphrase extraction via web mining. In *Proc. IJCAI*, pages 434–439.

X. Wan, J. Yang, and J. Xiao. 2007. Towards an iterative reinforcement approach for simultaneous document summarization and keyword extraction. In *Proc. ACL*, pages 552–559.

W.-T. Yih, J. Goodman, and V. R. Carvalho. 2006. Finding advertising keywords on web pages. In *Proc. 15th International Conference on World Wide Web*, pages 213–222.

Language identification of names with SVMs

Aditya Bhargava and Grzegorz Kondrak
Department of Computing Science
University of Alberta
Edmonton, Alberta, Canada, T6G 2E8
{abhargava,kondrak}@cs.ualberta.ca

Abstract

The task of identifying the language of text or utterances has a number of applications in natural language processing. Language identification has traditionally been approached with character-level language models. However, the language model approach crucially depends on the length of the text in question. In this paper, we consider the problem of language identification of names. We show that an approach based on SVMs with n-gram counts as features performs much better than language models. We also experiment with applying the method to pre-process transliteration data for the training of separate models.

1 Introduction

The task of identifying the language of text or utterances has a number of applications in natural language processing. Font Llitjós and Black (2001) show that language identification can improve the accuracy of letter-to-phoneme conversion. Li et al. (2007) use language identification in a transliteration system to account for different semantic transliteration rules between languages when the target language is Chinese. Huang (2005) improves the accuracy of machine transliteration by clustering his training data according to the source language.

Language identification has traditionally been approached using character-level n-gram language models. In this paper, we propose the use of support vector machines (SVMs) for the language identification of very short texts such as proper nouns. We show that SVMs outperform language models on two different data sets consisting of personal names. Furthermore, we test the hypothesis that language identification can improve transliteration by pre-processing the source data and training separate models using a state-of-the-art transliteration system.

2 Previous work

N-gram approaches have proven very popular for language identification in general. Cavnar and Trenkle (1994) apply n-gram language models to general text categorization. They construct character-level language models using n-grams up to a certain maximum length from each class in their training corpora. To classify new text, they generate an n-gram frequency profile from the text and then assign it to the class having the most similar language model, which is determined by summing the differences in n-gram ranks. Given 14 languages, text of 300 characters or more, and retaining the 400 most common n-grams up to length 5, they achieve an overall accuracy of 99.8%. However, the accuracy of the n-gram approach strongly depends on the length of the texts. Kruengkrai et al. (2005) report that, on a language identification task of 17 languages with average text length 50 bytes, the accuracy drops to 90.2%. When SVMs were used for the same task, they achieved 99.7% accuracy.

Konstantopoulos (2007) looks particularly at the task of identifying the language of proper nouns. He focuses on a data set of soccer player names coming from 13 possible national languages. He finds that using general n-gram language models yields an average F_1 score of only 27%, but training the models specifically to these smaller data gives significantly better results: 50% average F_1 score for last names

Human Language Technologies: The 2010 Annual Conference of the North American Chapter of the ACL, pages 693–696,
Los Angeles, California, June 2010.

only, and 60% for full names.

On the other hand, Li et al. (2007) report some good results for single-name language identification using n-gram language models. For the task of separating single Chinese, English, and Japanese names, they achieve an overall accuracy of 94.8%. One reason that they do better is because of the smaller number of classes. We can further see that the languages in question are very dissimilar, making the problem easier; for example, the character "x" appears only in the list of Chinese names, and the bigram "kl" appears only in the list of English names.

3 Language identification with SVMs

Rather than using language models to determine the language of a name, we propose to count character n-gram occurrences in the given name, for n up to some maximum length, and use these counts as the features in an SVM. We choose SVMs because they can take a large number of features and learn to weigh them appropriately. When counting n-grams, we include space characters at the beginning and end of each word, so that prefixes and suffixes are counted appropriately. In addition to n-gram counts, we also include word length as a feature.

In our initial experiments, we tested several different kernels. The kernels that performed the best were the linear, sigmoid, and radial basis function (RBF) kernels. We tested various maximum n-gram lengths; Figure 1 shows the accuracy of the linear kernel as a function of maximum n-gram length. Polynomial kernels, a substring match–count string kernel, and a string kernel based on the edit distance all performed poorly in comparison. We also experimented with other modifications such as normalizing the feature vectors, and decreasing the weights of frequent n-gram counts to avoid larger counts dominating smaller counts. Since the effects were negligible, we exclude these results from this paper.

In our experiments, we used the LIBLINEAR (Fan et al., 2008) package for the linear kernel and the LIBSVM (Chang and Lin, 2001) package for the RBF and sigmoid kernels. We discarded any periods and parentheses, but kept apostrophes and hyphens, and we converted all letters to lower case. We removed very short names of length less than two. For all data sets, we held out 10% of the data

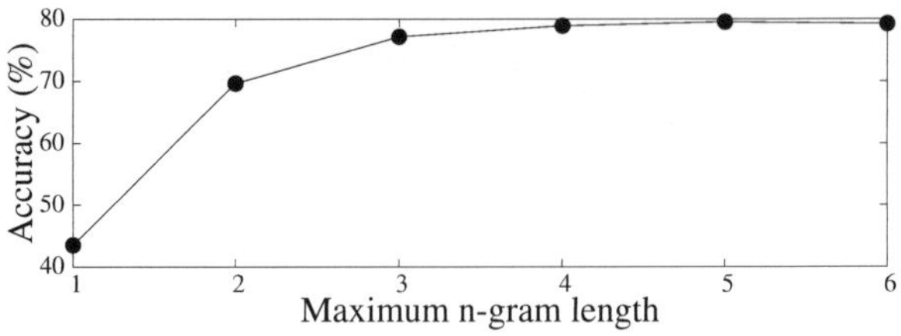

Figure 1: Cross-validation accuracy of the linear kernel on the Transfermarkt full names corpus.

as the test set. We then found optimal parameters for each kernel type using 10-fold cross-validation on the remaining training set. This yielded optimum maximum n-gram lengths of four for single names and five for full names. Using the optimal parameters, we constructed models from the entire training data and then tested the models on the held-out test set.

4 Intrinsic evaluation

We used two corpora to test our SVM-based approach: the Transfermarkt corpus of soccer player names, and the Chinese-English-Japanese (CEJ) corpus of first names and surnames. These corpora are described in further detail below.

4.1 Transfermarkt corpus

The Transfermarkt corpus (Konstantopoulos, 2007) consists of European soccer player names annotated with one of 13 possible national languages, with separate lists provided for last names and full names. Diacritics were removed in order to avoid trivializing the task. There are 14914 full names, with average length 14.8, and 12051 last names, with average length 7.8. It should be noted that these data are noisy; the fact that a player plays for a certain nation's team does not necessarily indicate that his or her name is of that nation's language. For example, *Dario Dakovic* was born in Bosnia but plays for the Austrian national team; his name is therefore annotated as German.

Table 1 shows our results on the Transfermarkt corpus. Because Konstantopoulos (2007) provides only F_1 scores, we used his scripts to generate new results using language models and calculate the accuracy instead, which allows us to be consistent with our tests on other data sets. Our results show that us-

Method	Last names	Full names
Language models	44.7	54.2
Linear SVM	**56.4**	**79.9**
RBF SVM	55.7	78.9
Sigmoid SVM	56.2	78.7

Table 1: Language identification accuracy on the Transfermarkt corpus. Language models have $n = 5$.

ing SVMs clearly outperforms using language models on the Transfermarkt corpus; in fact, SVMs yield better accuracy on last names than language models on full names. Differences between kernels are not statistically significant.

4.2 CEJ corpus

The CEJ corpus (Li et al., 2007) provides a combined list of first names and surnames, each classified as Chinese, English, or Japanese. There are a total of 97115 names with an average length of 7.6 characters. This corpus was used for the semantic transliteration of personal names into Chinese.

We found that the RBF and sigmoid kernels were very slow—presumably due to the large size of the corpus—so we tested only the linear kernel. Table 2 shows our results in comparison to those of language models reported in (Li et al., 2007); we reduce the error rate by over 50%.

5 Application to machine transliteration

Machine transliteration is one of the primary potential applications of language identification because the language of a word often determines its pronunciation. We therefore tested language identification to see if results could indeed be improved by using language identification as a pre-processing step.

5.1 Data

The English-Hindi corpus of names (Li et al., 2009; MSRI, 2009) contains a test set of 1000 names represented in both the Latin and Devanagari scripts. We manually classified these names as being of either Indian or non-Indian origin, occasionally resorting to web searches to help disambiguate them.[1] We discarded those names that fell into both categories

Method	Ch.	Eng.	Jap.	All
Lang. model	96.4	89.9	96.5	94.8
Linear SVM	**99.0**	**94.8**	**97.6**	**97.6**

Table 2: Language identification accuracy on the CEJ corpus. Language models have $n = 4$.

(e.g. "Maya") as well as those that we could not confidently classify. In total, we discarded 95 of these names, and randomly selected 95 names from the training set that we could confidently classify to complete our corpus of 1000 names. Of the 1000 names, 546 were classified as being of Indian origin and the remaining 454 were classified as being of non-Indian origin; the names have an average length of 7.0 characters.

We trained our language identification approach on 900 names, with the remaining 100 names serving as the test set. The resulting accuracy was **80%** with the linear kernel, **84%** with the RBF kernel, and **83%** with the sigmoid kernel. In this case, the performance of the RBF kernel was found to be significantly better than that of the linear kernel according to the McNemar test with $p < 0.05$.

5.2 Experimental setup

We tested a simple method of combining language identification with transliteration. We use a language identification model to split the training, development, and test sets into disjoint classes. We train a transliteration model on each separate class, and then combine the results.

Our transliteration system was DIRECTL (Jiampojamarn et al., 2009). We trained the language identification model over the entire set of 1000 tagged names using the parameters from above. Because these names comprised most of the test set and were now being used as the training set for the language identification model, we swapped various names between sets such that none of the words used for training the language identification model were in the final transliteration test set.

Using this language identification model, we split the data. After splitting, the "Indian" training, development, and testing sets had 5032, 575, and 483 words respectively while the "non-Indian" sets had 11081, 993, and 517 words respectively.

[1]Our tagged data are available online at `http://www.cs.ualberta.ca/~ab31/langid/`.

5.3 Results

Splitting the data and training two separate models yielded a combined top-1 accuracy of **46.0%**, as compared to **47.0%** achieved by a single transliteration model trained over the full data; this difference is not statistically significant. Somewhat counter-intuitively, using language identification as a pre-processing step for machine transliteration yields no improvement in performance for our particular data and transliteration system.

While it could be argued that our language identification accuracy of 84% is too low to be useful here, we believe that the principal reason for this performance decrease is the reduction in the amount of data available for the training of the separate models. We performed an experiment to confirm this hypothesis: we randomly split the full data into two sets, matching the sizes of the Indian and non-Indian sets. We then trained two separate models and combined the results; this yielded a top-1 accuracy of **41.5%**. The difference between this and the 46.0% result above is statistically significant with $p < 0.01$. From this we conclude that the reduction in data size was a significant factor in the previously described null result, and that language identification does provide useful information to the transliteration system. In addition, we believe that the transliteration system may implicitly leverage the language origin information. Whether a closer coupling of the two modules could produce an increase in accuracy remains an open question.

6 Conclusion

We have proposed a novel approach to the task of language identification of names. We have shown that applying SVMs with n-gram counts as features outperforms the predominant approach based on language models. We also tested language identification in one of its potential applications, machine transliteration, and found that a simple method of splitting the data by language yields no significant change in accuracy, although there is an improvement in comparison to a random split.

In the future, we plan to investigate other methods of incorporating language identification in machine transliteration. Options to explore include the use of language identification probabilities as features in the transliteration system (Li et al., 2007), as well as splitting the data into sets that are not necessarily disjoint, allowing separate transliteration models to learn from potentially useful common information.

Acknowledgements

We thank Sittichai Jiampojamarn for his assistance with the DIRECTL transliteration system, Shane Bergsma for his advice, and Stasinos Konstantopoulos for providing us with his scripts and data. This research was supported by the Natural Sciences and Engineering Research Council of Canada.

References

W. B. Cavnar and J. M. Trenkle. 1994. N-gram-based text categorization. In *Proc. of the Third Annual Symposium on Document Analysis and Information Retrieval*, pages 161–175.

C.-C. Chang and C.-J. Lin, 2001. *LIBSVM: a library for support vector machines*. Software available at `http://www.csie.ntu.edu.tw/~cjlin/libsvm`.

R.-E. Fan, K.-W. Chang, C.-J. Hsieh, X.-R. Wang, and C.-J. Lin. 2008. LIBLINEAR: A library for large linear classification. *Journal of Machine Learning Research*, 9:1871–1874.

A. Font Llitjós and A. W. Black. 2001. Knowledge of language origin improves pronunciation accuracy of proper names. In *Proc. of Eurospeech*, pages 1919–1922.

F. Huang. 2005. Cluster-specific named entity transliteration. In *Proc. of HLT-EMNLP*, pages 435–442.

S. Jiampojamarn, A. Bhargava, Q. Dou, K. Dwyer, and G. Kondrak. 2009. DirecTL: a language independent approach to transliteration. In *Proc. of ACL-IJCNLP Named Entities Workshop*, pages 28–31.

S. Konstantopoulos. 2007. What's in a name? In *Proc. of RANLP Computational Phonology Workshop*.

C. Kruengkrai, P. Srichaivattana, V. Sornlertlamvanich, and H. Isahara. 2005. Language identification based on string kernels. In *Proc. of International Symposium on Communications and Information Technologies*.

H. Li, K. C. Sim, J.-S. Kuo, and M. Dong. 2007. Semantic transliteration of personal names. In *Proc. of ACL*, pages 120–127.

H. Li, A. Kumaran, V. Pervouchine, and M. Zhang. 2009. Report of NEWS 2009 machine transliteration shared task. In *Proc. of Named Entities Workshop: Shared Task on Transliteration*, pages 1–18.

MSRI, 2009. Microsoft Research India. `http://research.microsoft.com/india`.

Integrating Joint n-gram Features into a Discriminative Training Framework

Sittichai Jiampojamarn[†] and **Colin Cherry**[‡] and **Grzegorz Kondrak**[†]

[†]Department of Computing Science
University of Alberta
Edmonton, AB, T6G 2E8, Canada
{sj,kondrak}@cs.ualberta.ca

[‡]National Research Council Canada
1200 Montreal Road
Ottawa, ON, K1A 0R6, Canada
Colin.Cherry@nrc-cnrc.gc.ca

Abstract

Phonetic string transduction problems, such as letter-to-phoneme conversion and name transliteration, have recently received much attention in the NLP community. In the past few years, two methods have come to dominate as solutions to supervised string transduction: generative joint n-gram models, and discriminative sequence models. Both approaches benefit from their ability to consider large, flexible spans of source context when making transduction decisions. However, they encode this context in different ways, providing their respective models with different information. To combine the strengths of these two systems, we include joint n-gram features inside a state-of-the-art discriminative sequence model. We evaluate our approach on several letter-to-phoneme and transliteration data sets. Our results indicate an improvement in overall performance with respect to both the joint n-gram approach and traditional feature sets for discriminative models.

1 Introduction

Phonetic string transduction transforms a source string into a target representation according to its pronunciation. Two important examples of this task are letter-to-phoneme conversion and name transliteration. In general, the problem is challenging because source orthography does not unambiguously specify the target representation. When considering letter-to-phoneme, ambiguities and exceptions in the pronunciation of orthography complicate conversion. Transliteration suffers from the same ambiguities, but the transformation is further complicated by restrictions in the target orthography that may not exist in the source.

Joint n-gram models (Bisani and Ney, 2002; Chen, 2003; Bisani and Ney, 2008) have been widely applied to string transduction problems (Li et al., 2004; Demberg et al., 2007; Jansche and Sproat, 2009). The power of the approach lies in building a language model over the operations used in the conversion from source to target. Crucially, this allows the inclusion of source context in the generative story. Smoothing techniques play an important role in joint n-gram models, greatly affecting their performance. Although joint n-gram models are capable of capturing context information in both source and target, they cannot selectively use only source or target information, nor can they consider arbitrary sequences within their context window, as they are limited by their back-off schedule.

Discriminative sequence models have also been shown to perform extremely well on string transduction problems. These begin with a Hidden Markov Model architecture, augmented with substring operations and discriminative training. The primary strength of these systems is their ability to include rich indicator features representing long sequences of source context. We will assume a specific instance of discriminative sequence modeling, DirecTL (Jiampojamarn et al., 2009), which achieved the best results on several language pairs in the NEWS Machine Transliteration Shared Task (Li et al., 2009). The same system matches or exceeds the performance of the joint n-gram approach on letter-to-phoneme conversion (Jiampojamarn et al., 2008). Its features are optimized by an online, margin-

Human Language Technologies: The 2010 Annual Conference of the North American Chapter of the ACL, pages 697–700,
Los Angeles, California, June 2010.

based learning algorithm, specifically, the Margin Infused Relaxed Algorithm, MIRA (Crammer and Singer, 2003).

In this paper, we propose an approach that combines these two different paradigms by formulating the joint n-gram model as a new set of features in the discriminative model. This leverages an advantage of discriminative training, in that it can easily and effectively incorporate arbitrary features. We evaluate our approach on several letter-to-phoneme and transliteration data sets. Our results demonstrate an improvement in overall performance with respect to both the generative joint n-gram approach and the original DIRECTL system.

2 Background

String transduction transforms an input string $\mathbf{x}$ into the desired output string $\mathbf{y}$. The input and output are different representations of the same entity; for example, the spelling and the pronunciation of a word, or the orthographic forms of a word in two different writing scripts.

One approach to string transduction is to view it as a tagging problem where the input characters are tagged with the output characters. However, since sounds are often represented by multi-character units, the relationship between the input and output characters is often complex. This prevents the straightforward application of standard tagging techniques, but can be addressed by substring decoders or semi-Markov models.

Because the relationship between $\mathbf{x}$ and $\mathbf{y}$ is hidden, alignments between the input and output characters (or substrings) are often provided in a pre-processing step. These are usually generated in an unsupervised fashion using a variant of the EM algorithm. Our system employs the many-to-many alignment described in (Jiampojamarn et al., 2007). We trained our system on these aligned examples by using the online discriminative training of (Jiampojamarn et al., 2009). At each step, the parameter update is provided by MIRA.

3 Features

Jiampojamarn et al. (2009) describe a set of indicator feature templates that include (1) context features (2) transition features and (3) linear-chain features.

context	$x_{i-c}\ y_i$ ... $x_{i+c}\ y_i$ $x_{i-c}x_{i-c+1}\ y_i$ ... $x_{i+c-1}x_{i+c}\ y_i$ ...... $x_{i-c}\dots x_{i+c}\ y_i$
transition	$y_{i-1}\ y_i$
linear-chain	$x_{i-c}\ y_{i-1}\ y_i$ ... $x_{i+c}\ y_{i-1}\ y_i$ $x_{i-c}x_{i-c+1}\ y_{i-1}\ y_i$ ... $x_{i+c-1}x_{i+c}\ y_{i-1}\ y_i$ ...... $x_{i-c}\dots x_{i+c},\ y_{i-1}\ y_i$
joint n-gram	$x_{i+1-n}y_{i+1-n}x_iy_i$ ... $x_{i-1}y_{i-1}x_iy_i$ $x_{i+1-n}y_{i+1-n}x_{i+2-n}y_{i+2-n}x_iy_i$ ... $x_{i-2}y_{i-2}x_{i-1}y_{i-1}x_iy_i$ ...... $x_{i+1-n}y_{i+1-n}\dots x_{i-1}y_{i-1}x_iy_i$

Table 1: Feature template

Table 1 summarizes these features and introduces the new set of *joint n-gram features*.

The context features represent the source side evidence that surrounds an input substring $\mathbf{x_i}$ as it generates the target output $\mathbf{y_i}$. These features include all possible n-grams that fit inside a source-side context windows of size $\mathbf{C}$, each conjoined with $\mathbf{y_i}$. The transition features enforce the cohesion of the generated output with target-side bigrams. The linear-chain features conjoin context and transition features.

The set of feature templates described above has been demonstrated to achieve excellent performance. The context features express rich information on the source side, but no feature template allows target context beyond $\mathbf{y_{i-1}}, \mathbf{y_i}$. Target and source context are considered jointly, but only in a very limited fashion, as provided by the linear chain features. Jiampojamarn et al. (2008) report that context features contribute the most to system performance. They also report that increasing the Markov order in the transition features from bigram to tri-

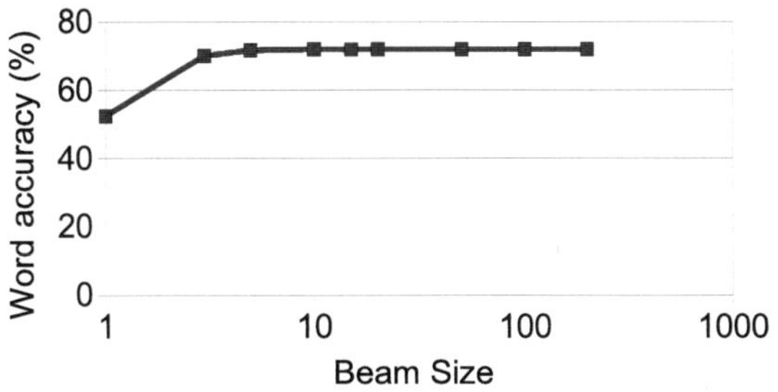

Figure 1: System accuracy as a function of the beam size

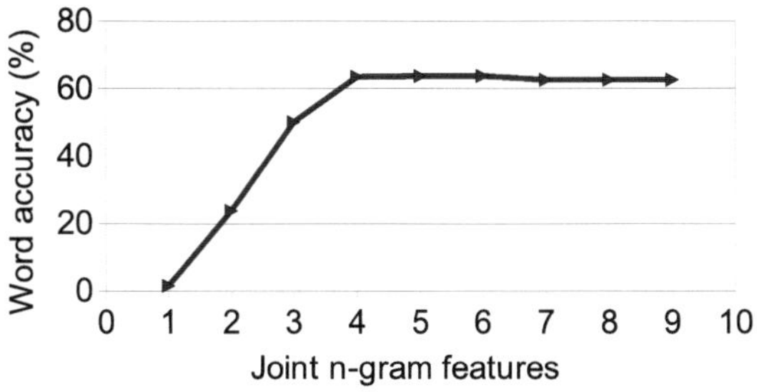

Figure 2: System accuracy as a function of n-gram size

gram results in no significant improvement. Intuitively, the joint information of both source and target sides is important in string transduction problems. By integrating the joint n-gram features into the online discriminative training framework, we enable the system to not only enjoy rich context features and long-range dependency linear-chain features, but we also take advantage of joint information between source and target substring pairs, as encoded by the joint n-gram template shown in the bottom of Table 1.

An alternative method to incorporate a joint n-gram feature would compute the generative joint n-gram scores, and supply them as a real-valued feature to the model. As all of the other features in the DIRECTL framework are indicators, the training algorithm may have trouble scaling an informative real-valued feature. Therefore, we represent these joint n-gram features as binary features that indicate whether the model has seen particular strings of joint evidence in the previous $\mathbf{n-1}$ operations when generating $\mathbf{y_i}$ from $\mathbf{x_i}$. In this case, the system learns a distinct weight for each substring of the joint n-gram.

In order to accommodate higher-order joint n-grams, we replace the exact search algorithm of Jiampojamarn et al. (2008) with a beam search. During our development experiments, we observed no significant decrease in accuracy after introducing this approximation. Figure 1 shows the system performance in terms of the word accuracy as a function of the beam size on a development set. The performance starts to converge quickly and shows no further improvement for values grater than 20. In the remaining experiments we set the beam size to 50.

We also performed development experiments with a version of the system that includes only joint n-gram indicators. Figure 2 shows the word accuracy with different values of n. The accuracy reaches its maximum for $n = 4$, and actually falls off for larger values of n. This anomaly is likely caused by the model using its expanded expressive power to memorize sequences of operations, overfitting to its training data. Such overfitting is less likely to happen in the generative joint n-gram model, which smooths high-order estimates very carefully.

4 Experiments and Results

We evaluate our new approach on two string transduction applications: (1) letter-to-phoneme conversion and (2) name transliteration. For the letter-to-phoneme conversion, we employ the English Celex, NETtalk, OALD, CMUdict, and the French Brulex data sets. In order to perform direct comparison with the joint n-gram approach, we follow exactly the same data splits as Bisani and Ney (2008). The training sizes range from 19K to 106K words. For the transliteration task, we use three data sets provided by the NEWS 2009 Machine Transliteration Shared Task (Li et al., 2009): English-Russian (EnRu), English-Chinese (EnCh), and English-Hindi (EnHi). The training sizes range from 10K to 30K words. We set $n = 6$ for the joint n-gram features; other parameters are set on the respective development sets.

Tables 2 and 3 show the performance of our new system in comparison with the joint n-gram approach and DIRECTL. The results in the rightmost column of Table 2 are taken directly from (Bisani and Ney, 2008), where they were evaluated on the same data splits. The results in the rightmost column of Table 3 are from (Jansche and Sproat, 2009), which was the best performing system based on joint

Data set	this work	DIRECTL	joint n-gram
Celex	**89.23**	88.54	88.58
CMUdict	**76.41**	75.41	75.47
OALD	**85.54**	82.43	82.51
NETtalk	**73.52**	70.18	69.00
Brulex	**95.21**	95.03	93.75

Table 2: Letter-to-phoneme conversion accuracy

Data set	this work	DIRECTL	joint n-gram
EnRu	**61.80**	61.30	59.70
EnCh	**74.17**	73.34	64.60
EnHi	**50.30**	49.80	41.50

Table 3: Name transliteration accuracy

n-grams at NEWS 2009. We report all results in terms of the word accuracy, which awards the system only for complete matches between system outputs and the references.

Our full system outperforms both DIRECTL and the joint n-gram approach in all data sets. This shows the utility of adding joint n-gram features to the DIRECTL system, and confirms an advantage of discriminative approaches: strong competitors can simply be folded into the model.

Comparing across tables, one can see that the gap between the generative joint n-gram and the DIRECTL methods is much larger for the transliteration tasks. This could be because joint n-grams are a poor fit for transliteration, or the gap could stem from differences between the joint n-gram implementations used for the two tasks. Looking at the improvements to DIRECTL from joint n-gram features, we see further evidence that joint n-grams are better suited to letter-to-phoneme than they are to transliteration: letter-to-phoneme improvements range from relative error reductions of 3.6 to 17.3, while in transliteration, the largest reduction is 3.1.

5 Conclusion

We have presented a new set of joint n-gram features for the DIRECTL discriminative sequence model. The resulting system combines two successful approaches for string transduction — DIRECTL and the joint n-gram model. Joint n-gram indicator features are efficiently trained using a large margin method. We have shown that the resulting system consistently outperforms both DIRECTL and strong joint n-gram implementations in letter-to-phoneme conversion and name transliteration, establishing a new state-of-the-art for these tasks.

Acknowledgements

This research was supported by the Alberta Ingenuity Fund and the Natural Sciences and Engineering Research Council of Canada.

References

Maximilian Bisani and Hermann Ney. 2002. Investigations on joint-multigram models for grapheme-to-phoneme conversion. In *Proc. ICSLP*, pages 105–108.

Maximilian Bisani and Hermann Ney. 2008. Joint-sequence models for grapheme-to-phoneme conversion. *Speech Communication*, 50(5):434–451.

Stanley F. Chen. 2003. Conditional and joint models for grapheme-to-phoneme conversion. In *Proc. Eurospeech-2003*.

Koby Crammer and Yoram Singer. 2003. Ultraconservative online algorithms for multiclass problems. *Journal of Machine Learning Research*, 3:951–991.

Vera Demberg, Helmut Schmid, and Gregor Möhler. 2007. Phonological constraints and morphological preprocessing for grapheme-to-phoneme conversion. In *Proc. ACL*, pages 96–103.

Martin Jansche and Richard Sproat. 2009. Named entity transcription with pair n-gram models. In *Proc. ACL-IJCNLP Named Entities Workshop*, pages 32–35.

Sittichai Jiampojamarn, Grzegorz Kondrak, and Tarek Sherif. 2007. Applying many-to-many alignments and Hidden Markov Models to letter-to-phoneme conversion. In *Proc. HLT-NAACL*, pages 372–379.

Sittichai Jiampojamarn, Colin Cherry, and Grzegorz Kondrak. 2008. Joint processing and discriminative training for letter-to-phoneme conversion. In *Proc. ACL*, pages 905–913.

Sittichai Jiampojamarn, Aditya Bhargava, Qing Dou, Kenneth Dwyer, and Grzegorz Kondrak. 2009. DirecTL: a language independent approach to transliteration. In *Proc. ACL-IJCNLP Named Entities Workshop*, pages 28–31.

Haizhou Li, Min Zhang, and Jian Su. 2004. A joint source channel model for machine transliteration. In *Proc. ACL*, pages 159–166.

Haizhou Li, A Kumaran, Vladimir Pervouchine, and Min Zhang. 2009. Report of NEWS 2009 machine transliteration shared task. In *Proc. ACL-IJCNLP Named Entities Workshop*, pages 1–18.

A Hybrid Morphologically Decomposed Factored Language Models for Arabic LVCSR

Amr El-Desoky, Ralf Schlüter, Hermann Ney
Lehrstuhl für Informatik 6 – Computer Science Department
RWTH Aachen University, D-52056 Aachen, Germany
{desoky,schluter,ney}@cs.rwth-aachen.de

Abstract

In this work, we try a hybrid methodology for language modeling where both morphological decomposition and factored language modeling (FLM) are exploited to deal with the complex morphology of Arabic language. At the end, we are able to obtain from 3.5% to 7.0% relative reduction in word error rate (WER) with respect to a traditional full-words system, and from 1.0% to 2.0% relative WER reduction with respect to a non-factored decomposed system.

1 Introduction

Arabic language is characterized by a complex morphological structure where different kinds of prefixes and suffixes are appended to the word stems producing a very large number of inflectional forms. This leads to poor language model (LM) probability estimates, and thus high LM perplexities (PPLs) causing problems in large vocabulary continuous speech recognition (LVCSR). One successful approach to deal with this problem is to consider LMs including morphologically decomposed words. Another approach is to use the factored language models (FLMs) which are powerful models that combine multiple sources of information and efficiently integrate them via a complex backoff mechanism (Bilmes and Kirchhoff, 2003).

Morphological decomposition is successfully used for Arabic LMs in several previous works. Some are based on linguistic knowledge, and others are based on unsupervised methods. Some of the linguistic methods are based on the Buckwalter Arabic Morphological Analyzer (BAMA) like in (Lamel et al., 2008). Alternatively, in our previous work (El-Desoky et al., 2009), we use the Morphological Analyzer and Disambiguator for Arabic (MADA) (Habash and Rambow, 2007). On the other side, most of the unsupervised methods are based on the minimum description length principle (MDL) like in (Creutz et al., 2007).

Another type of models is the FLM, in which words are viewed as vectors of K factors, so that $w_t := \{f_t^{1:K}\}$. A factor could be any feature of the word such as morphological class, stem, root or even a semantic feature. An FLM is a model over factors, i.e., $p(f_t^{1:K}|f_{t-1}^{1:K}, f_{t-2}^{1:K}, ..., f_{t-n+1}^{1:K})$, which could be reformed as a product of probabilities of the form $p(f|f_1, f_2, ..., f_N)$. The main idea of the model is to backoff to other factors when some word n-gram is not observed in the training data, thus improving the probability estimates.

In this work we try to combine the strengths of morphological decomposition and factored language modeling. Therefore, language models with factored morphemes are used. For this purpose, the LM training data are processed such that full-words are decomposed into prefix-stem-suffix format with different added features. We compare our approach with the standard full-word, decomposed word, and factored full-word n-gram approaches.

2 Factorization and Decomposition

We use MADA 2.0 in order to perform morphological analysis and attach a complete set of morphological tags to Arabic words in context. From those tags

Human Language Technologies: The 2010 Annual Conference of the North American Chapter of the ACL, pages 701–704,
Los Angeles, California, June 2010.

we derive three different features. Moreover, we derive a fourth feature based on the root of the word generated by "Sebawai" (Darwish, 2002). The list of features is:

- **"W"** (Word): word surface form.
- **"L"** (Lexeme): word lexeme.
- **"M"** (Morph): morphological description.
- **"P"** (Pattern): word after subtracting root.

The LM training corpora are processed so that words are replaced by the factored representation as required by SRILM-FLM extensions (Kirchhoff et al., 2008). Then, word decomposition is performed based on MADA as described in our previous publication (El-Desoky et al., 2009).

3 FLM topologies

In order to obtain a good performance via FLMs, we need to optimize the FLM parameters: the combination of the conditioning factors, backoff path, and smoothing options. For this purpose, we use a Genetic Algorithm based FLM optimization tool (GA-FLM) developed by Kirchhoff (2006) which seeks to minimize the PPL over some held-out text. Furthermore, we apply some manual optimization to fine tune the FLM parameters. For memory limitations, we only use factors up to 2 previous time slots (tri-gram like models). Finally, we come up with a set of competing FLMs with rather close PPLs. In Table 1, we record the PPLs measured for some held-out text. The first column gives the combination of the parent factors. So that, FLM_1 corresponds to the model $P(W_t|W_{t-1}, W_{t-2})$, which is the FLM equivalent of the standard tri-gram LM (our baseline model), while FLM_2 & FLM_3 correspond to the model $P(W_t|W_{t-1}, M_{t-1}, L_{t-1}, P_{t-1}, W_{t-2})$, however FLM_4 & FLM_5 correspond to the model $P(W_t|W_{t-1}, M_{t-1}, L_{t-1}, W_{t-2}, M_{t-2}, L_{t-2})$. The "gtmin" refers to the count threshold that is sufficient to have a language model hit at some node of the the backoff graph (for exact topologies, contact the first author). From Table 1, comparing PPLs (non-normalized) across factored and non-factored LMs, we see that using more factors other than the normal word could help decreasing the PPL. This is true for all the used types of vocabulary units.

	vocabulary		
FLM_x **parent factors**	**FW**	**PD**	**FD**
1: W1 W2 (baseline)	302.6	284.1	82.7
W1 M1 L1 P1 W2			
2: gtmin = 1	306.2	296.9	83.2
3: gtmin = 2-4	290.9	279.1	79.8
W1 M1 L1 W2 M2 L2			
4: gtmin = 1	300.2	291.1	83.6
5: gtmin = 2-4	294.5	283.7	81.1

Table 1: perplexities of the FLMs using vocabularies: (FW: 70k full-words; PD: partially decomposed with 20k ful-words + 50k morphemes; FD: 70k fully decomposed).

FLM_x **parent factors**	**WER [%]**
1: W1 W2 (baseline)	20.4
W1 M1 L1 P1 W2	
2: gtmin = 1	20.2
3: gtmin = 2-4	20.4
W1 M1 L1 W2 M2 L2	
4: gtmin = 1	**19.9**
5: gtmin = 2-4	20.3

Table 2: WERs using FLMs based on 70k full-words.

In order to select the best FLM topology, we run a simple one pass recognition for a small internal dev corpus derived from GALE data sets, consists of 40 minutes of audio data recorded during January to March 2007. The acoustic models are within-word tri-phone models trained using 1100h of audio material. The basic acoustic models are trained based on Maximum Likelihood (ML) method. Then, a discriminative training based on Minimum Phone Error (MPE) criterion is performed to enhance the models. A 70k full-words lexicon is used. The FLM training data consists of 206 Million running full-words. A standard bi-gram LM based on full-words is used to generate N-best lists, then N-best list rescoring is performed using the different FLM topologies shown in Table 1. We start by N = 1000-best down to 3-best sentences. Using N = 10 always gives the best results. The recognition WERs are recorded in Table 2. The least WER is obtained with FLM_4. We note that the best FLM does not correspond to the least PPL. This is because a higher "gtmin" value causes more backoff in cases of insufficient data leading to better estimates. Therefore, we select FLM_4 for the coming experiments.

4 Experimental Setup

Our recognition system is close to the one described in section 3. However, we use within and across-word models at different recognition passes. In addition, we use 70k or 256k lexicon of full-words or partially decomposed words. Alternatively, we evaluate the results on the GALE 2007 development and evaluation sets (dev07: 2.5h; eval07: 4h). Our recognizer works in 3 passes. In the first pass, within-word acoustic models are used with no adaptation, along with a standard bi-gram LM to generate lattices, followed by a standard tri-gram or 4-gram LM rescoring of lattices. The second pass does the same, but it uses across-word models with Constrained Maximum Likelihood Linear Regression (CMLLR) adaptation. Then, a third pass with additional Maximum Likelihood Linear Regression (MLLR) adaptation is performed, using a standard bi-gram LM to generate lattices or N-best lists. Then, one of the following is performed: **1)** lattice rescoring using standard tri-gram or 4-gram LM, **2)** N-best list rescoring using FLMs based on full-words, partially or fully decomposed words.

5 Experiments

In this section, we record our recognition results for: **1)** systems based on full-words, and **2)** systems based on decomposed words. Also, we introduce additional results for larger lexicon sizes.

5.1 Systems Based on Full-words

In this section, we present the WERs of our recognition systems based on full-words. Where, during the search, we use a lexicon of 70K full-words. In the first 2 passes, we use a standard bi-gram LM to generate lattices, followed by a standard tri-gram LM rescoring of lattices. However, in the third pass, we generate both lattices and N-best lists based on the same bi-gram LM. The final lattices and N-best lists are rescored using different LMs as shown in Table 3. In case we perform N-best list rescoring with a FLM, the N-best lists are processed to produce factored representation, followed by partial or full decomposition as previously described in section 2.

It is clear from Table 3 that the least WER is achieved when using N-best list rescoring using a full-words based FLM. This gives an absolute improvement of 0.8% (about 4.8% relative) compared to the standard tri-gram lattice rescoring. On the other hand, we have 0.6% absolute improvement (about 3.7% relative) compared to the standard 4-gram lattice rescoring. Decomposition does not help in this case. This is because the original N-best lists are generated in full-words format, whose decomposition might not lead to better LM scores. For this reason, we expect that it is better to start with a decomposed LM for lattice and N-best generation.

LM rescoring (3rd **pass)**	**Dev07 [%]**
tri-gram lattice resc. (baseline)	16.5
4-gram lattice resc.	16.3
N-best FLM resc.:	
+ FW (original N-best)	**15.7**
+ PD (decomposed N-best)	15.8
+ FD (decomposed N-best)	16.0

Table 3: WERs for 70k full-words systems.

LM rescoring (3rd **pass)**	**Dev07 [%]**
tri-gram lattice resc. (baseline)	14.7
4-gram lattice resc.	14.5
N-best FLM resc.:	
+ FW (re-joint N-best)	14.6
+ PD (original N-best)	**14.3**
+ FD (decomposed N-best)	14.4

Table 4: WERs for 70k partially decomposed systems (20k full-words + 50k morphemes).

5.2 Systems Based on Decomposed Words

This section introduces the WERs of our systems based on decomposed words. We use a similar setup as in section 5.1. However, we use a lexicon and a bi-gram LM based on a 70k partially decomposed words (20k full-words + 50k morphemes). Table 4 presents the results. As expected, we get the best WER when using N-best list rescoring with a FLM based on partially decomposed words. An absolute improvement of 0.4% (2.7% relative) is achieved compared to the new baseline. Compared to the old baseline of Table 3, we get an absolute improvement of 2.2% (13.3% relative).

5.3 Larger Lexicon Sizes

Now, we increase the size of our lexicon to 256k partially decomposed words (20k full-words + 236k

System	Dev07 [%]	Eval07 [%]
traditional full-words	14.9	16.5
partially decomposed		
+ 4-gram lat. resc. (baseline)	14.2	16.1
+ N-best FLM resc.:		
+ FW (re-joint N-best)	14.1	-
+ PD (original N-best)	**13.9**	**15.9**
+ FD (decomposed N-best)	14.0	-

Table 5: WERs for 256k full-words, and partially decomposed systems (20k full-words + 236k morphemes).

	70k vocabularies			256k vocabularies		
Corpus	**FW**	**PD**	**FD**	**FW**	**PD**	**FD**
Dev07	3.65	1.33	0.75	1.36	0.51	0.24
Eval07	4.82	1.94	1.13	1.85	0.64	0.41

Table 6: OOVs [%] of the used vocabularies.

morphemes). In addition, we use a standard 4-gram LM for rescoring the bi-gram lattices in the first 2 passes. To complete our comparisons, we record the WERs using traditional 256k full-words lexicon, standard bi-gram search, and standard 4-gram LM for lattice rescoring, with no decomposition or factorization. In Table 5, we see that the improvement persists for the larger lexicon. Compared to the new baseline, the 256k decomposed system achieves WER reductions of [dev07: 0.3% absolute (2.1% relative); eval07: 0.2% absolute (1.2% relative)] when using N-best list rescoring with a FLM based on partially decomposed words. Moreover, it improves over the traditional full-words by [dev07: 1.0% absolute (6.7% relative); eval07: 0.6% absolute (3.6% relative)]. The out-of-vocabulary rates (OOVs) are given in Table 6. It is worth noting that using fully decomposed lexicons as well as higher order LMs could not improve WERs, this we previously proved in (El-Desoky et al., 2009).

6 Conclusions

We have introduced a hybrid approach to Arabic language modeling. Our approach combines the strengths of both morphological decomposition and factored language modeling. Thus, we have used language models with factored morphemes. We have compared our approach to traditional approaches like: standard full-word n-grams, standard decomposed n-grams, and full-word based factored language models. Finally, we could achieve some improvements over all the traditional approaches. Nevertheless, we have only considered the use of factored language models in the rescoring phase.

Acknowledgments

This material is based upon work supported by the DARPA under Contract No. HR0011-06-C-0023. Any opinions, findings and conclusions expressed in this material are those of the authors and do not necessarily reflect the views of DARPA.

References

J. Bilmes and K. Kirchhoff. 2003. Factored language models and generalized parallel backoff. In *Proc. Human Language Technology Conf. of the North American Chapter of the ACL*, volume 2, pages 4 – 6, Edmonton, Canada, May.

M. Creutz, T. Hirsimki, M. Kurimo, A. Puurula, J. Pylkknen, V. Siivola, M. Varjokallio, E. Arisoy, M. Saraclar, and A. Stolcke. 2007. Morph-based speech recognition and modeling of out-of-vocabulary words across languages. *ACM Transactions on Speech and Language Processing*, 5(1), December.

K. Darwish. 2002. Building a shallow Arabic morphological analyzer in one day. In *ACL workshop on Computational approaches to semitic languages*, Philadelphia, PA, USA, July.

A. El-Desoky, C. Gollan, D. Rybach, R. Schlüter, and H. Ney. 2009. Investigating the use of morphological decomposition and diacritization for improving Arabic LVCSR. In *Interspeech*, pages 2679 – 2682, Brighton, UK, September.

N. Habash and O. Rambow. 2007. Arabic diacritization through full morphological tagging. In *Proc. Human Language Technology Conf. of the North American Chapter of the ACL*, volume Companion, pages 53 – 56, Rochester, NY, USA, April.

K. Kirchhoff, D. Vergyri, J. Bilmes, K. Duh, and A. Stolcke. 2006. Morphology-based language modeling for conversational Arabic speech recognition. *Computer Speech and Language*, 20(4):589 – 608, October.

K. Kirchhoff, J. Bilmes, and K. Duh. 2008. Factored language model tutorial. Technical report, Department of Electrical Engineering, University of Washington, Seattle, Washington, USA, February.

L. Lamel, A. Messaoudi, and J.L Gauvain. 2008. Investigating morphological decomposition for transcription of Arabic broadcast news and broadcast conversation data. In *Interspeech*, volume 1, pages 1429 – 1432, Brisbane, Australia, September.

Is Arabic Part of Speech Tagging Feasible Without Word Segmentation?

Emad Mohamed, Sandra Kübler
Indiana University
Department of Linguistics
Memorial Hall 322
Bloomington, IN 47405
USA
{emohamed,skuebler}@indiana.edu

Abstract

In this paper, we compare two novel methods for part of speech tagging of Arabic without the use of gold standard word segmentation but with the full POS tagset of the Penn Arabic Treebank. The first approach uses complex tags without any word segmentation, the second approach is segmention-based, using a machine learning segmenter. Surprisingly, word-based POS tagging yields the best results, with a word accuracy of 94.74%.

1 Introduction

Arabic is a morphologically rich language, in which a word carries not only inflections but also clitics, such as pronouns, conjunctions, and prepositions. This morphological complexity also has consequences for the part-of-speech (POS) annotation of Arabic: Since words can be complex, POS tags refer to segments rather than to whole words. Thus, the word `wsyrfEwnhA` (in Buckwalter transliteration; engl.: *and they will raise it*) is assigned the following POS tag: [CONJ+FUTURE_PARTICLE+IMPERFECT_VERB_PREFIX +IMPERFECT_VERB+IMPERFECT_VERB_SUFFIX_MASCULINE_PLURAL_3RD_PERSON+OBJECT_PRONOUN_FEMININE_SINGULAR] in the Penn Arabic Treebank (ATB) (Bies and Maamouri, 2003); the boundaries between segments are depicted by + signs. Automatic approaches to POS tagging either must assign such complex tags from a large tagset to complete words, or they must segment the word first and then assign POS tags to the segments. Previous approaches (Diab et al., 2004; Habash and Rambow, 2005; van den Bosch et al., 2007; AlGahtani et al., 2009) chose the segmentation approach but concentrated on POS tagging by using the segmentation provided by the ATB. Additionally, Diab et al. and Habash and Rambow used a reduced tagset. Diab et al. and Habash and Rambow used Support Vector Machines, the former with a standard windowing approach, the latter performing a full morphological analysis before POS tagging. Van den Bosch et al., whose approach is the most similar to ours, used memory-based learning with the full ATB tagset. They report a POS tagging accuracy of 91.5% (93.3% on known words, 66.4% on unknown words). However, they also evaluated on words as defined in the ATB, which differs from written Arabic in the treatment of affixes with syntactic functions (see section 2 for details). AlGahtani et al. used transformation-based learning combined with a morphological analysis for unknown words and words containing clitics. They reached a POS tagging accuracy of 96.9% on ATB1. Surprisingly, their results are lower for the experiment using the whole ATB (96.1%).

In this paper, we present two methods for Arabic POS tagging that do not require gold standard segmentation but can rather be used for naturally occurring Arabic. We investigate two different approaches: (1) Assigning complete POS tags to whole words, without any segmentation, and (2) a segmentation-based approach, for which we developed a machine learning based segmenter. In this approach, the words are first passed to the segmenter, then to the POS tagger. The first approach is surprisingly successful given the complex-

Human Language Technologies: The 2010 Annual Conference of the North American Chapter of the ACL, pages 705–708,
Los Angeles, California, June 2010.

ity of the task, reaching an accuracy on the word level of 94.74%, as compared to 93.47% for the segmentation-based approach. Thus, the result for the whole word approach is very close to the result obtained by using gold standard segmentation (94.91%). However, a more detailed analysis shows that this good performance of the word-based approach is due to its performance on known words while the few unknown words are more often misclassified: we reach an accuracy of 96.61% on known words but only 74.64% on unknown words.

2 Data, Methods, and Evaluation

Like the previous approaches, we base our experiments on the ATB, specifically on the after-treebank POS files, for extracting our training and test sets. More specifically, we use two sections of the ATB (P1V3 and P3V1) since those two sets do not contain duplicate sentences. This data set contains approximately 500,000 words. In order to be as representative of real-world Arabic, we use the non-vocalized version of the treebank. Since previous approaches, to our knowledge, used different data sets, our results are not directly comparable.

For both segmentation and POS tagging, we modified the ATB representation of words in order to obtain the text, as it would occur in newscasts. The ATB treats inflectional affixes, including the definite article `Al`, as part of a word but splits off those affixes that serve a syntactic function into separate words. In order to obtain text as it occurs in newscasts, we re-attached all conjunctions, prepositions, pronouns, and any elements that constitute parts of the word as an orthographic unit (with the exception of punctuation) to the word. The word `ltxbrh` (engl.: *in order to tell him*), for example, is represented as three words in the ATB, `l`, `txbr`, and `h`, but is treated as one single unit in our experiment. Our second modification concerns the null element in Arabic verbs. Since Arabic is pro-drop, the ATB annotation includes a null element in place of the omitted subject plus the POS tag it would receive. Since this information is not available in naturally occurring text, we delete the null element and its tag. For example, `{i$otaraY+(null)` and its tag PV+PVSUFF_SUBJ: 3MS would occur as `{i$otaraY` with the tag PV in our representation (we additionally remove the short vowels).

We perform 5-fold cross validation and use the same data split for all three types of experiments: (1) POS tagging using gold standard segmentation taken from the ATB, (2) POS tagging using a segmenter, and (3) POS tagging whole words with complex POS tags. The first experiment serves as the upper bound and as a comparison to previous approaches. The second experiment uses an automatic segmenter as a pre-processing component to the POS tagger. This means that the accuracy of the segmenter is also the upper limit of the POS tagger since errors in segmentation inevitably lead to errors in POS tagging. The last experiment uses full words and complex POS tags. The purpose of this experiment is to determine whether it is possible to tag complete words without segmentation.

The segmenter and the two POS taggers use memory-based learning. For segmentation, we use TiMBL (Daelemans and van den Bosch, 2005); for POS tagging MBT, a memory-based tagger (Daelemans et al., 1996). Memory-based learning is a lazy learning paradigm that does not abstract over the training data. During classification, the k nearest neighbors to a new example are retrieved from the training data, and the class that was assigned to the majority of the neighbors is assigned to the new example. MBT uses TiMBL as classifier; it offers the possibility to use words from both sides of the focus word as well as previous tagging decisions and ambitags as features. An ambitag is a combination of all POS tags of the ambiguity class of the word.

Word segmentation is defined as a per-letter classification task: If a character in the word constitutes the end of a segment, its class is '+', otherwise '-'. We use a sliding window approach with 5 characters before and 5 characters after the focus character, the previous decisions of the classifier, and the POS tag of the focus word assigned by the whole word tagger (cf. below) as features. The best results were obtained for all experiments with the IB1 algorithm with similarity computed as weighted overlap, relevance weights computed with gain ratio, and the number of k nearest neighbors equal to 1.

For POS tagging, we use the full tagset, with information about every segment in the word, rather than the reduced tagset (RTS) used by Diab et al. and Habash and Rambow, since the RTS assumes

Gold Standard Segmentation		Segmentation-Based Tagging		Whole Words
SAR	WAR	SAR	WAR	WAR
96.72%	94.91%	94.70%	93.47%	94.74%

Table 1: POS tagging results.

a segmentation of words in which syntactically relevant affixes are split from the stem. The word `w+y+bHv+wn+hA`, for example, in RTS is split into 3 separate tokens, `w`, `ybHvwn`, `hA`. Then, each of these tokens is assigned one POS tag, Conjunction for `w`, Imperfective Verb for `ybHvwn`, and Pronoun for `hA`. The split into tokens makes a preprocessing step necessary, and it also affects evaluation since a word-based evaluation is based on one word, the RTS evaluation on 3 tokens for the above example.

For all the POS tagging experiments, we use MBT. The best results were obtained with the Modified Value Difference Metric as a distance metric and with $k = 25$. For known words, we use the IGTree algorithm and 2 words to the left, their POS tags, the focus word and its ambitag, 1 right context word and its ambitag as features. For unknown words, we use IB1 as algorithm and the unknown word itself, its first 5 and last 3 characters, 1 left context word and its POS tag, and 1 right context word and its ambitag tag as features.

3 Experimental Results and Discussion

3.1 Word Segmentation

The memory-based word segmentation performs very reliably with a word accuracy of 98.23%. This also means that when the segmentation module is used as a pre-processing step for POS tagging, the accuracy of the tagger will have this accuracy as its upper bound. While there are cases where wrong segmentation results in the same number of segments, all of these words were assigned the wrong POS tags in our data. In an error analysis, we found that words of specific POS are more difficult to segment than others. Proper nouns constitute 33.87% of all segmentation errors, possibly due to the fact that many of these are either foreign names that resemble Arabic words (e.g. `Knt`, which is ambiguous between the English name *Kent*, and the Arabic verb *I was*), or they are ordinary nouns used as proper nouns but with a different segmentation (e.g. `AlHyAp`, engl.: *the life*). The POS tag with the second highest error rate was the noun class with 30.67%.

3.2 Part of Speech Tagging

Table 1 shows the results of the three POS tagging experiments described above. For the segmentation-based experiments, we report per-segment (SAR) and per-word (WAR) accuracy. As expected, POS tagging using gold standard segments gives the best results: 94.91% WAR. These results are approximately 3 percent points higher than those reported by van den Bosch et al. (2007). Although the results are not absolutely comparable because of the different data sets, this experiment shows that our approach is competitive. The next experiments investigate the two possibilities to perform POS tagging on naturally occurring Arabic, i.e. when gold segmentation is not available. The results of these experiments show that POS tagging based on whole words gives higher results (WAR: 94.74%) than tagging based on automatic segmentation (WAR: 93.47%). This result is surprising given that tagging whole words is more difficult than assigning tags to segments, as there are 993 complex tags (22.70% of which occur only once in the training set), versus 139 segment tags. A detailed error analysis of a previous but similar experiment can be found in Mohamed and Kübler (2010).

We assume that these results are an artifact of the ATB since it is based exclusively on newswire texts. This means that there is only a limited vocabulary, as shown by the very low rate of unknown words: across the five folds, we calculated an average of 8.55% unknown words. In order to test our hypothesis that unknown words are tagged more reliably with a segment-based approach, we performed an analysis on known and unknown words separately. The results of this analysis are shown in Table 2.

This analysis shows that for all experiments, the unknown words are tagged with a considerably

	Gold Standard Segmentation	Segmentation-Based Tagging	Whole Words
Known words	95.90%	95.57%	96.61%
Unknown words	84.25%	71.06%	74.64%

Table 2: POS results for known and unknown words.

lower accuracy. However, the loss of performance is more pronounced in the approaches without gold segmentation. It is also evident that tagging whole words reaches a higher accuracy than segment-based tagging for both known words and unknown words. From these results, we can conclude that while segmentation makes properties of the words available, it is not required for POS tagging. We also investigated the poor performance of the segmentation-based tagger. A closer look at the results for unknown words in segmentation-based tagging shows that 59.68% of the tagging errors are direct results from incorrect segmentation decisions. In comparison, for known words, only 6.24% of the incorrectly tagged words are also ill-segmented. This means that even though the quality of the segmenter is very high, the errors still harm the POS tagging step.

To make our results more comparable to those by Habash and Rambow (2005), we converted the test set with the POS tags from the whole word tagger to their tokenization and to a reduced tagset of 15 tags. In this setting, we reach a tokenization accuracy of 99.36% and a POS tagging accuracy of 96.41%. This is very close to the results by Habash and Rambow so that we conclude that high accuracy POS tagging for Arabic is possible without a full morphological analysis.

4 Conclusions and Future Work

We have presented a method for POS tagging for Arabic that does not assume gold segmentation, which would be unrealistic for naturally occurring Arabic. The approach we developed is competitive although it uses the full POS tagset, without any previous morphological analysis. The results of our experiments suggest that segmentation is not required for POS tagging. On the contrary, using whole words as basis for POS tagging yields higher accuracy, thus rendering a full morphological analysis or segmentation unnecessary. We reached the best results in tagging whole words both for known words and unknown words. These results were only marginally worse that the results obtained by the experiment based on gold segmentation.

The weakness of the segmentation-based approach is its low accuracy on unknown words. In the future, we will investigate knowledge-richer methods for segmentation. In particular, we will investigate whether an automatic vocalization step previous to segmentation will improve POS tagging accuracy for unknown words.

References

Shahib AlGahtani, William Black, and John McNaught. 2009. Arabic part-of-speech-tagging using transformation-based learning. In *Proceeedings of the 2nd International Conference on Arabic Language Resources and Tools*, Cairo, Egypt.

Ann Bies and Mohamed Maamouri. 2003. Penn Arabic Treebank guidelines. Technical report, LDC, University of Pennsylvania.

Walter Daelemans and Antal van den Bosch. 2005. *Memory Based Language Processing*. Cambridge University Press.

Walter Daelemans, Jakub Zavrel, Peter Berck, and Steven Gillis. 1996. MBT: A memory-based part of speech tagger-generator. In Eva Ejerhed and Ido Dagan, editors, *Proceedings of the 4th Workshop on Very Large Corpora*, pages 14–27, Copenhagen, Denmark.

Mona Diab, Kadri Hacioglu, and Daniel Jurafsky. 2004. Automatic tagging of Arabic text: From raw text to base phrase chunks. In *Proceedings of HLT-NAACL*, Boston, MA.

Nizar Habash and Owen Rambow. 2005. Arabic tokenization, part-of-speech tagging and morphological disambiguation in one fell swoop. In *Proceedings of ACL-2005*, pages 573—580, Ann Arbor, MI.

Emad Mohamed and Sandra Kübler. 2010. Arabic part of speech tagging. In *Proceedings of LREC*, Valetta, Malta.

Antal van den Bosch, Erwin Marsi, and Abdelhadi Soudi. 2007. Memory-based morphological analysis and part-of-speech tagging of Arabic. In Abdelhadi Soudi, Antal van den Bosch, and Günter Neumann, editors, *Arabic Computational Morphology*. Springer.

Arabic Mention Detection: Toward Better Unit of Analysis

Yassine Benajiba
Center for Computational Learning Systems
Columbia University
ybenajiba@ccls.columbia.edu

Imed Zitouni
IBM T. J. Watson Research Center
izitouni@us.ibm.com

Abstract

We investigate in this paper the adequate unit of analysis for Arabic Mention Detection. We experiment different segmentation schemes with various feature-sets. Results show that when limited resources are available, models built on morphologically segmented data outperform other models by up to 4F points. On the other hand, when more resources extracted from morphologically segmented data become available, models built with Arabic TreeBank style segmentation yield to better results. We also show additional improvement by combining different segmentation schemes.

1 Introduction

This paper addresses an important and basic task of information extraction: *Mention Detection* (MD)[1]: the identification and classification of textual references to objects/abstractions (i.e., *mentions*). These mentions can be either named (e.g. Mohammed, John), nominal (city, president) or pronominal (e.g. he, she). For instance, in the sentence "President *Obama* said *he* will visit ..." there are three mentions: *President, Obama* and *he*. This is similar to the Named Entity Recognition (NER) task with the additional twist of also identifying nominal and pronominal mentions. We formulate the mention detection problem as a classification problem, by assigning to each token in the text a label, indicating whether it starts a specific mention, is inside a specific mention, or is outside all mentions. The selection of the unit of analysis is an important step toward a better classification. When processing languages, such as English, using the word itself as the unit of analysis (after separating punctuations) leads to a good performance (Florian et al., 2004). For other languages, such as Chinese, character is considered as the adequate unit of analysis (Jing et al., 2003). In this paper, we investigate different segmentation schemes in order to define the best unit of analysis for Arabic MD. Arabic adopts a very complex morphology, i.e. each word is composed of zero or more *prefixes*, one *stem* and zero or more *suffixes*. Consequently, the Arabic data is sparser than other languages, such as English, and it is necessary to "segment" the words into several units of analysis in order to achieve a good performance.

(Zitouni et al., 2005) used Arabic morphologically segmented data and claimed to have very competitive results in ACE 2003 and ACE 2004 data. On the other hand, (Benajiba et al., 2008) report good results for Arabic NER on ACE 2003, 2004 and 2005 data using Arabic TreeBank (ATB) segmentation. In all published works, authors do not mention a specific motivation for the segmentation scheme they have adopted. Only for the Machine Translation task, (Habash and Sadat, 2006) report several results using different Arabic segmentation schemes. They report that the best results were obtained when the ATB-like segmentation was used. We explore here the four known and linguistically-motivated sorts of segmentation: punctuation separation, ATB, morphological and character-level segmentations. To our knowledge, this is the first paper which investigates different segmentation schemes to define the unit of analysis which best fits Arabic MD.

2 Arabic Segmentation Schemes

Character-level Segmentation: considers that each character is a separate token.

Morphological Segmentation : aims at segmenting

[1] We adopt here the ACE nomenclature: http://www.nist.gov/speech/tests/ace/index.html

Human Language Technologies: The 2010 Annual Conference of the North American Chapter of the ACL, pages 709–712,
Los Angeles, California, June 2010.

all affixes of a word. The morphological segmentation for the word والمكتب (wAlmktb — and the office)[2] could be: “و +ال +مكتب” (w +Al +mktb).

Arabic TreeBank (ATB) segmentation : This segmentation considers splitting the word into affixes only if it projects an independent phrasal constituent in the parse tree. As an example, in the word shown above والمكتب, the phrasal independent constituents are: the conjunction و (*w* — and) and the noun المكتب (*Almktb* — the office). The morphological segmentation of this word would lead to the following parse tree:

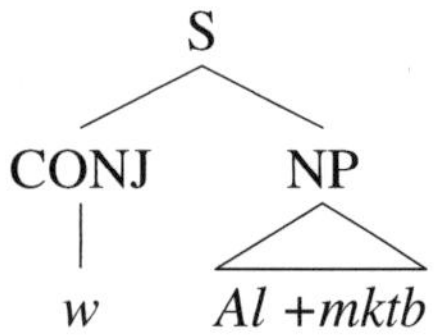

Since the ال (*Al*, the definite article) is not an independent constituent, it is not considered for ATB segmentation. Hence, for والمكتب, the ATB segmentation would be و +المكتب (w +Almktb).

Punctuation separation : it consists of separating the punctuation marks from the word.

Both ATB and morphological segmentation systems are based on *weighted finite state transducers* (WFST). The decoder implements a general Bellman dynamic programming search for the best path on a lattice of segmentation hypotheses that match the input characters (Benajiba and Zitouni, 2009). ATB and morphological segmentation systems have a performance of 99.4 and 98.1 F-measure respectively on ATB data.

The unit of analysis when doing classification depends on the used segmentation. When using the punctuation separation or character-based segmentations, the unit of analysis is the word itself (without the punctuation marks attached) or the character, respectively. The ATB and morphological segmentations are language specific and are based on different linguistic viewpoint. When using one of these two segmentation schemes, the unit of analysis is the morph (i.e. prefix, stem or suffix). Our goal in this paper is to find the unit of analysis that fits best Arabic MD.

[2]Throughout the paper, for each Arabic example we show between parenthesis its transliteration and English translation separated by “—”.

3 Mention Detection System

As explained earlier, we consider the MD task as a sequence classification problem where the class we predict for each unit of analysis (i.e., token) is the type of the entity which it refers to. We chose the maximum entropy (MaxEnt) classifier that can integrate arbitrary types of information and make a classification decision by aggregating all information available for a given classification. For more details about the system architecture, reader may refer to (Zitouni et al., 2009). The features used in our MD system can be divided into four categories:

Lexical Features: n-grams spanning the current token; both preceding and following it. A number of n equal to 3 turned out to be a good choice.

Stem n-gram Features: stem trigram spanning the current stem; both preceding and following it (Zitouni et al., 2005).

Syntactic Features: POS tags and shallow parsing information in a ± 2 window.

Features From Other Classifiers: outputs of MD and NER taggers trained on other data-sets different from the one we used here. They may identify types of mentions different from the mentions of interest in our task. For instance, such a tagger may identify dates or occupation references (not used in our task), among other types. Our hypothesis is that combining classifiers from diverse sources will boost performance by injecting complementary information into the mention detection models. We also use the two previously assigned classification tags as additional feature.

4 Data

Experiments are conducted on the Arabic ACE 2007 data. Since the evaluation tests set are not publicly available, we have split the publicly available *training* corpus into an 85%/15% data split. We use 323 documents (80,000 words, 17,634 mentions) for training and 56 documents (18,000 words, 3,566 mentions) as a test set. We are interested in 7 types of mentions: facility, Geo-Political Entity (GPE), location, organization, person, vehicle and weapon. We segmented the training and test set with four different styles building the following corpora:

Word$_s$: a corpus which is the result of running punctuation separation;

ATB$_s$: a corpus obtained by running punctuation separation and ATB segmentation;

Moph$_s$: a corpus where we conduct punctuation separation and morphological segmentation;

Char$_s$: a corpus where the original text is separated

into a sequence of characters.

When building MD systems on $Words_s$, ATB_s, $Morph_s$ and $Char_s$, the unit of analysis is the word, the ATB token, the morph and the character, respectively.

5 Experiments

We show in this section the experimental results when using Arabic MD system with different segmentation schemes and different feature sets. We explore in this paper four categories of features (c.f. Section 3):

Lex$_f$: lexical features;
Stem$_f$: Lex_f + morphological features;
Synt$_f$: $Stem_f$ + syntactic features;
Sem$_f$: $Synt_f$ + output of other MD classifiers.

Lex_f and $Stem_f$ features are directly extracted from the appropriate corpus based on the used segmentation style. This is different for Sem_f: we first run classifiers on the morphologically segmented data. Thereafter, we project those labels to other corpora. This is because, we use classifiers initially trained on morphologically segmented data such as ACE 2003, 2004 and 2005 data. In such data, two morphs belonging to the same word or ATB token may have 2 different mentions. During transfer, a token will have the label of the corresponding stem in the morphologically segmented data. One motivation to not re-train classifiers on each corpus separately is to be able to extract Sem_f features from classifiers with similar performance.

Table 1: Results in terms of F-measure per feature-set and segmentation scheme

	Lex_f	$Stem_f$	$Synt_f$	Sem_f
$Words_s$	66.4	66.6	69.0	77.1
ATB_s	70.1	69.8	72.1	**79.0**
$Morph_s$	**74.1**	**74.5**	**75.5**	78.3
$Char_s$	22.3	22.4	22.5	22.6

Results in Table 1 show that classifiers built on ATB_s and $Morph_s$ have shown to perform better than classifiers trained on data with other segmentation styles. When the system uses character as the unit of analysis, performance is poor. This is because the token itself becomes insignificant information to the classifier. On the other hand, when only punctuation separation is performed ($Words_s$), the data is significantly sparse and the obtained results achieves high F-measure (77.1) only when outputs of other classifiers are used. As mentioned earlier, classifiers used to extract those features are trained on $Morph_s$ (less sparse), which explains their remarkable positive impact since they resolve part of the data sparseness problem in $Words_s$. When using full morphological segmentation, the data is less sparse, which leads to less Out-Of-Vocabulary tokens (OOVs): the number of OOVs in the $Morph_s$ data is 1,518 whereas it is 2,464 in the ATB_s. As an example, the word الرهينة (Alrhynp — the hostage), which is person mention in the training data. This word is kept unchanged after ATB segmentation and is segmented to "ة+ رهين + ال" (Al+ rhyn +p) in $Morph_s$. In the development set the same word appears in its dual form without definite article, i.e. رهينتين. This word is unchanged in ATB_s and is segmented to "ين+ ت+ رهين" (rhyn +p +yn) in $Morph_s$. For the model built on ATB_s, this word is an OOV, whereas for the model built on $Morph_s$ the stem has been seen as part of a person mention and consequently has a better chance to tag it correctly. These phenomena are frequent, which make the classifier trained on $Morph_s$ more robust for such cases. Also, we observed that models trained on ATB_s perform better on long span mentions. We think this is because a model trained on ATB_s has access to larger context. One may argue that a similar behavior of the model built on the $Morph_s$ might be obtained if we use a wider context window than the one used for ATB_s in order to have similar contextual information. In order to confirm this statement, we have carried out a set of experiments using all features over $Morph_s$ data for a context window up to $-5/+5$, the obtained results show no improvement. Similar behavior is observed when looking to results on identified named (Nam.), nominal (Nom.) and pronominal (Pro.) mentions on ATB_s and $Morph_s$ (c.f. Table 2); we remind the reader that NER is about recognizing named mentions. When limited resources are available (e.g. Lex_f, $Stem_f$ or $Synt_f$), we believe that it is more effective to morphologically segment the text ($Morph_s$) as a pre-processing step. The use of morph as a unit of analysis reduces the data sparseness issue and at the same time allows better context handling when compared to character. On the other hand, when a larger set of resources are available (e.g., Sem_f), the use of the ATB token as a unit of analysis combined with morph-based features leads to better performance (79.0 vs. 78.3 on $Morph_s$). This is because (1) classifiers trained on ATB_s handle better the context and (2) the use of morph-based features (output of classifiers trained on morphologically segmented data) removes some of the data sparseness from which classifiers trained on ATB_s suffer. The obtained improvement in performance is statistically significant when using the stratified bootstrap re-sampling significance test (Noreen, 1989). We consider results as statistically significant when $p < 0.02$, which is the case in this paper. For an accurate MD system, we think it is appropriate to benefit from ATB_s tokens and $Morph_s$. We investigate in the following the combination of these two segmentation styles.

Table 2: Performance in terms of F-measure per level on ATB_s and $Morph_s$

	$Seg.$	Lex_f	$Stem_f$	$Synt_f$	Sem_f
Nam.	ATB_s	68.2	69.0	72.8	79.1
	$Morph_s$	73.4	73.8	75.3	78.7
Nom.	ATB_s	65.6	64.6	66.9	75.8
	$Morph_s$	71.7	72.2	72.9	75.4
Pro.	ATB_s	60.7	60.1	59.9	66.3
	$Morph_s$	63.0	67.2	65.7	65.1

5.1 Combination of ATB and Morph

We trained a model on ATB_s that uses output of the model trained on $Morph_s$ as additional information ($M2A_f$ feature). We proceed similarly by training a model on $Morph_s$ using output of the model trained on ATB_s ($A2M_f$ feature). We have obtained the features by a 15-way round-robin. Table 3 shows the obtained results.

Table 3: Results in terms of F-measure of the combination experiments

	Lex_f	$Stem_f$	$Synt_f$	Sem_f
ATB_s	70.1	69.8	72.1	79.0
ATB_s+$M2A_f$	70.7	70.8	73.1	**79.1**
$Morph_s$	74.1	74.5	75.5	78.3
$Morph_s$+$A2M_f$	**74.9**	**75.2**	**75.4**	78.6

Results show a significant improvement for models that are trained on ATB_s using information from $Morph_s$ in addition to Lex_f, $Stem_f$ and $Synt_f$ features. This again confirms our claim that the use of features from morphologically segmented text reduces the data sparseness and consequently leads to better performance. For Sem_f features, only a 0.1 F-measure points have been gained. This is because we are *already* using output of classifiers trained on morphologically segmented data, which resolve some of the data sparseness issue. The $Morph_s$ side shows that the obtained performance when the ATB_s output is employed together with the $Stem_f$ (75.2) is only 0.3 points below the performance of the system using $Synt_f$ (75.5).

6 Conclusions

We have shown a comparative study aiming at defining the adequate unit of analysis for Arabic MD. We conducted our study using four segmentation schemes with four different feature-sets. Results show that when only limited resources are available, using morphological segmentation leads to the best results. On the other hand, model trained on ATB segmented data become more powerful and effective when data sparseness is reduced by the use of other classifier outputs trained on morphologically segmented data. More improvement is obtained when both segmentation styles are combined.

References

Y. Benajiba and I. Zitouni. 2009. Morphology-based segmentation combination for arabic mention detection. *Special Issue on Arabic Natural Language Processing of ACM Transactions on Asian Language Information Processing (TALIP)*, 8(4).

Y. Benajiba, M. Diab, and P. Rosso. 2008. Arabic named entity recognition using optimized feature sets. In *Proc. of EMNLP'08*, pages 284–293.

R. Florian, H. Hassan, A. Ittycheriah, H. Jing, N. Kambhatla, X. Luo, N. Nicolov, and S. Roukos. 2004. A statistical model for multilingual entity detection and tracking. In *Proc.eedings of HLT-NAACL'04*, pages 1–8.

N. Habash and F. Sadat. 2006. Combination of arabic preprocessing schemes for statistical machine translation. In *Proceedings of ACL'06*, pages 1–8.

H. Jing, R. Florian, X. Luo, T. Zhang, and A. Ittycheriah. 2003. HowtogetaChineseName(Entity): Segmentation and combination issues. In *Proceedings of EMNLP'03*, pages 200–207.

E. W. Noreen. 1989. *Computer-Intensive Methods for Testing Hypotheses*. John Wiley Sons.

I. Zitouni, J. Sorensen, X. Luo, and R. Florian. 2005. The impact of morphological stemming on arabic mention detection and coreference resolution. In *Proc. of the ACL Workshop on Computational Approaches to Semitic Languages*, pages 63–70.

I. Zitouni, X. Luo, and R. Florian. 2009. A cascaded approach to mention detection and chaining in arabic. *IEEE Transactions on Audio, Speech and Language Processing*, 17:935–944.

An MDL-based approach to extracting subword units for grapheme-to-phoneme conversion

Sravana Reddy
Department of Computer Science
The University of Chicago
Chicago, IL 60637
sravana@cs.uchicago.edu

John Goldsmith
Departments of Linguistics
and Computer Science
The University of Chicago
Chicago, IL 60637
goldsmith@uchicago.edu

Abstract

We address a key problem in grapheme-to-phoneme conversion: the ambiguity in mapping grapheme units to phonemes. Rather than using *single* letters and phonemes as units, we propose learning chunks, or *subwords*, to reduce ambiguity. This can be interpreted as learning a lexicon of subwords that has minimum description length. We implement an algorithm to build such a lexicon, as well as a simple decoder that uses these subwords.

1 Introduction

A system for converting written words to their pronunciations is an important component of speech-related applications, especially in large vocabulary tasks. This problem, commonly termed "grapheme-to-phoneme conversion", or g2p, is non-trivial for several written languages, including English, since a given letter (grapheme) may represent one of several possible phonemes, depending on the context. Because the length of the context varies throughout the dictionary, fixed-length contexts may overfit some words, or inaccurately model others.

We approach this problem by treating g2p as a function from *contiguous sequences* of graphemes, which we call 'grapheme subwords', to sequences of phonemes ('phoneme subwords'), so that there is *minimal ambiguity* in finding the phoneme subword that corresponds to a given grapheme subword. That is, we seek to minimize both these quantities:

1. The conditional entropy of the phoneme subwords given a grapheme subword. This directly tackles the problem of ambiguity – a perfectly unambiguous phoneme subword conditional distribution would have entropy = 0.
2. The entropy of the grapheme subwords. This prevents the model from getting arbitrarily complex.

As a toy example, consider the following word-pronunciation[1] pairs:

time	T AY M
sting	S T IH NG
negation	N AH G EY SH AH N

There are at least 5 graphemes whose corresponding phoneme distribution is ambiguous ('i', 'e', 't', 'n', 'g'). In the segmentation below, every grapheme subword corresponds to only one phoneme subword:

t + ime	T + AY M
s + t + ing	S + T + IH NG
neg + a + tion	N AH G + EY + SH AH N

2 Related Work

Many grapheme-to-phoneme algorithms rely on something resembling subwords; these are mainly used to account for sequences of letters representing a single phoneme ('ph' for F), or vice versa ('x' for K S). Some of the early works that create one-to-one alignments between a word and its pronunciation address these cases by allowing a letter to map to one phoneme, a null phoneme, or 2-3 phonemes.

Jiampojamarn and Kondrak (2009) use expectation-maximization (EM) to learn many-to-many alignments between words and pronunciations, effectively obtaining subwords.

[1] All phonemes are denoted by their Arpabet representations.

Human Language Technologies: The 2010 Annual Conference of the North American Chapter of the ACL, pages 713–716,
Los Angeles, California, June 2010.

Joint-sequence models divide a word-pronunciation pair into a sequence of disjoint *graphones* or *graphonemes* – tuples containing grapheme and phoneme subwords. Such segmentations may include only trivial graphones containing subwords of length at most 1 (Chen, 2003). Other such models use EM to learn the maximum likelihood segmentation into graphones (Deligne and Bimbot, 1995; Bisani and Ney, 2008; Vozilla et al., 2003).

Subwords – or phrases – are used widely in machine translation. There is a large body of work on phrase extraction starting from word alignments; see Koehn et al. (2003) for a review. Marcu and Wong (2002) learn phrases directly from sentence pairs using a joint probability model.

3 Subword Extraction

3.1 Motivation for using MDL

Consider a lexicon of grapheme subwords $\mathcal{G}$ and phoneme subwords $\mathcal{P}$ that is extracted from a dictionary of word-pronunciation pairs, along with a joint probability distribution over $\mathcal{G}$ and $\mathcal{P}$. As stated earlier, our objective is to minimize the entropy of phoneme subwords conditioned on a given grapheme subword, as well as the entropy of the grapheme subwords. That is, we would like to minimize $H(\mathcal{P}|\mathcal{G}) + H(\mathcal{G})$, which is

$$H(\mathcal{G}, \mathcal{P}) = -\sum_{g \in \mathcal{G}} \sum_{p \in \mathcal{P}} pr(g,p) \log pr(g,p) \quad (1)$$

This objective can be restated as minimizing the *expected description length* of the lexicon, which is given by its entropy. This is reflected in the MDL principle (Rissanen, 1978), which seeks to find a lexicon such that the description length of the lexicon (and the compression of the data under the lexicon) is minimized.

3.2 Lexicon Induction

We begin with an initial alignment between a word's graphemes and the phonemes in its pronunciation for all word-pronunciation pairs in the training dictionary. These alignments are derived using the standard string edit distance dynamic programming algorithm (Wagner and Fischer, 1974), giving a list of tuples $t = [(w_1, r_1), (w_2, r_2), \ldots]$ for each word-pronunciation pair.[2] The set of all tuple lists t composes the training dictionary $\mathcal{T}$.

The initial lexicon is composed of all singleton graphemes and phonemes (including null). The probability $pr(g,p)$ is taken to be the number of times the tuple (g,p) occurs in $\mathcal{T}$ divided by the total number of tuples over all alignments in $\mathcal{T}$.

Following a procedure similar the word-discovery algorithm of de Marcken (1996), the lexicon is iteratively updated as sketched in Table 1. At no point do we delete singleton graphemes or phonemes.

The subwords in the final updated lexicon are then used to decode the pronunciations of unseen words.

4 G2P Decoding

4.1 Joint segmentation and decoding

Finding the pronunciation of a word based on the induced subword lexicon involves segmenting the word into a sequence of grapheme subwords, and mapping it to a sequence of phoneme subwords.

One possibility is carry these steps out sequentially: first parse the word into grapheme subwords, and then use a sequence labeling algorithm to find the best corresponding sequence of phoneme subwords. However, it is likely that the true pronunciation of a word is *not* derived from its best parse into grapheme units. For example, the best parse of the word 'gnat' is 'g nat', which yields the pronunciation `G N AE T`, while the parse 'gn at' would give the correct pronunciation `N AE T`.

Therefore, we search for the best pronunciation over *all segmentations* of the word, adapting the monotone search algorithm proposed by Zens and Ney (2004) for phrase-based machine translation.[3]

4.2 Smoothing

A bigram model is used over both the grapheme and phoneme subwords. These bigrams need to be smoothed before the decoding step. Adding an equal probability mass to unseen bigrams would fail to reflect simple phonotactics (patterns that govern sound

[2] Phoneme insertions and deletions are represented by the null grapheme and null phoneme respectively.

[3] The key adaptation is in using a bigram model over both graphemes and phonemes, rather than only phonemes as in the original algorithm.

Table 1: Concatenative algorithm for building a subword lexicon that minimizes description length. The input is $\mathcal{T}$, the set of alignments, and a threshold integer k, which is tuned using a held-out development set.

1	Update $pr(g,p)$ by computing the *posterior probabilities* of the tuple (g,p) in $\mathcal{T}$, using the forward-backward algorithm. Repeat once more to get an intermediate lexicon.
2	Compute the Viterbi parse of each $t \in \mathcal{T}$ under the lexicon derived in step 1.
3	Let A, the set of candidate tuples for addition to the lexicon, contain all tuples $(w_i w_{i+1}, r_i r_{i+1})$ such that (w_i, r_i) and (w_{i+1}, r_{i+1}) are adjacent more than k times in the computed Viterbi parses. For each $(g,p) \in A$, estimate the change in description length of the lexicon if (g,p) is added. If description length decreases, remove any null symbols within g and p, and add (g,p) to the lexicon.
4	Repeat steps 1 and 2.
5	Delete all tuples that do not occur in any of the Viterbi parses.
6	Compare the description length of the new lexicon with the lexicon at the start of the iteration. If the difference is sufficiently small, return the new lexicon; else, repeat from step 1.

sequences) in several cases. For example, the bigram `L UW K + S` is much more likely than `L UW K + Z`, since `S` is more likely than `Z` to follow `K`.

To introduce a bias towards phonotacticaly likely bigrams, we define the smoothed bigram probability of the subword a following a subword b. Given that b is made up of a sequence of l phonemes $b_1 b_2 \ldots b_l$, the probability is defined as the interpolation[4]:

$$pr_{new}(a|b) = \lambda_1 pr(a|b_1 b_2 \ldots b_l) + \lambda_2 pr(a|b_1 b_2 \ldots b_{l-1}) + \lambda_3 pr(a|b_1 b_2 \ldots b_{l-2})$$

Both the grapheme and phoneme subword bigrams are smoothed as described.

5 Results

We test our algorithm on the CMU Pronouncing Dictionary[5]. The dictionary is divided randomly into a training (90% of the data) and a test set. Performance is evaluated by measuring the *phoneme error rate* (PER) and the *word error rate* (WER).

The subword extraction algorithm converges in 3 iterations.We run the g2p decoder using the lexicon after 3 iterations, as well as after 0, 1 and 2 iterations. The results are shown in Table 2.

Table 2: Results after each iteration of subword extraction. While the maximum subword length after iteration 3 is 8, the vast majority of subwords have length 6 or less.

	# subwords	Max subword length	WER	PER
0	$\lvert\mathcal{G}\rvert : 27, \lvert\mathcal{P}\rvert : 40$	1	73.16	24.20
1	$\lvert\mathcal{G}\rvert : 819, \lvert\mathcal{P}\rvert : 1254$	2	48.39	12.43
2	$\lvert\mathcal{G}\rvert : 5430, \lvert\mathcal{P}\rvert : 4954$	4	28.32	7.16
3	$\lvert\mathcal{G}\rvert : 6417, \lvert\mathcal{P}\rvert : 5358$	6	26.31	6.29

Figure 1 compares the results of our method (denoted by **'MDL-Sub'**) to two baselines, at different values of *maximum subword length*. To evaluate the quality of our subwords, we substitute another extraction algorithm to create the lexicon – the grow-diag-final phrase extraction method (Koehn et al., 2005), denoted by 'GD' in the figure. We also run the implementation of Bisani and Ney (2008) – denoted by 'BN' – on the same data. BN is an example of a joint-sequence n-gram model, which uses a joint distribution $pr(\mathcal{G}, \mathcal{P})$ of graphemes and phonemes ('graphones'), conditioned on the preceding n-1 graphones for context information. Since this algorithm outperforms most of the existing g2p algorithms, it serves as a good point of comparison to the state of the art in g2p. The results of BN using an n-gram model are compared to MDL-Sub with an n-1 maximum subword length[6].

The MDL-Sub lexicon does significantly better than the phrases extracted by GD. While BN starts off doing better than MDL-Sub, the latter outperforms BN at longer subword lengths. Most of the additional errors in BN at that stage involve grapheme-to-phoneme ambiguity – phonemes like `AE`, `AA`, and `AH` being confused for one another when mapping

[4]In our experiments, we set $\lambda_1 = 0.5$, $\lambda_2 = 0.3$, $\lambda_3 = 0.2$.

[5]The CMU Pronouncing Dictionary. Available online at http://www.speech.cs.cmu.edu/cgi-bin/cmudict

[6]The contextual information of (n-1)-length subwords with bigrams is assumed to be roughly comparable to that of very short subwords over n-grams.

the grapheme 'a', and so on. Far fewer of these errors are produced by our algorithm. However, some of the longer subwords in MDL-Sub do introduce additional errors, mainly because the extraction algorithm merges smaller subwords from previous iterations. For example, one of the items in the extracted lexicon is 'icati' – a product of merging 'ic' and 'ati' – corresponding to `IH K EY SH`, thus generating incorrect pronunciations for words containing the string 'icating'.

Figure 1: Comparison of error rates.

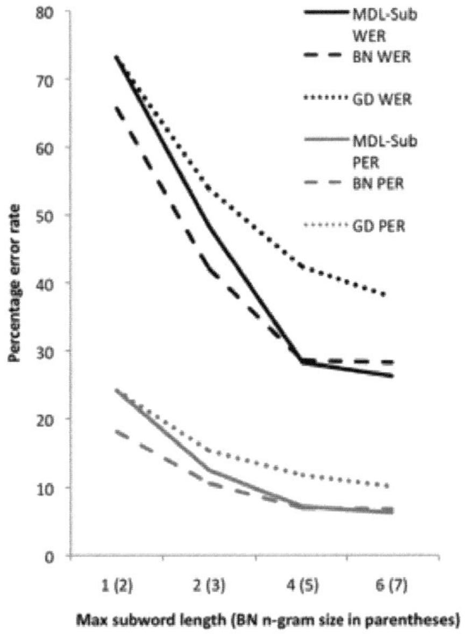

6 Conclusion

This paper deals with translational ambiguity, which is a major issue in grapheme-to-phoneme conversion. The core of our system consists of extracting subwords of graphemes and phonemes from the training data, so that the ambiguity of deriving a phoneme subword from a grapheme subword is minimized. This is achieved by formalizing ambiguity in terms of the minimum description length principle, and using an algorithm that reduces the description length of the subword lexicon at each iteration.

In addition, we also introduce a smoothing mechanism which retains some of the phonotactic dependencies that may be lost when using subwords rather than singleton letters and phonemes.

While retaining the basic approach to minimizing ambiguity, there are some avenues for improvement. The algorithm that builds the lexicon creates a more or less hierarchical structure – subwords tend to be composed from those extracted at the previous iteration. This appears to be the cause of many of the errors produced by our method. A subword extraction algorithm that does not use a strictly bottom-up process may create a more robust lexicon.

Our method of subword extraction could also be applied to phrase extraction for machine translation, or in finding subwords for related problems like transliteration. It may also be useful in deriving subword units for speech recognition.

References

Maximilian Bisani and Hermann Ney. 2008. Joint-sequence models for grapheme-to-phoneme conversion. *Speech Communication*, 50:434–451.

Stanley F Chen. 2003. Conditional and joint models for grapheme-to-phoneme conversion. In *Proceedings of Eurospeech*.

Carl G de Marcken. 1996. *Unsupervised Language Acquisistion*. Ph.D. thesis, MIT.

Sabine Deligne and Frederic Bimbot. 1995. Language modeling by variable length sequences: theoretical formulation and evaluation of multigrams. In *Proceedings of ICASSP*.

Sittichai Jiampojamarn and Grzegorz Kondrak. 2009. Online discriminative training for grapheme-to-phoneme conversion. In *Proceedings of Interspeech*.

Philipp Koehn, Franz Josef Och, and Daniel Marcu. 2003. Statistical phrase-based translation. In *Proceedings of HLT-NAACL*.

Philipp Koehn, Amittai Axelrod, Alexandra Birch Mayne, Chris Callison-Burch, Miles Osborne, and David Talbot. 2005. Edinburgh System Description for the 2005 IWSLT Speech Translation Evaluation. In *Proceedings of IWSLT*.

Daniel Marcu and William Wong. 2002. A phrase-based, joint probability model for statistical machine translation. In *Proceedings of EMNLP*.

Jorma Rissanen. 1978. Modeling by the shortest data description. *Automatica*.

Paul Vozilla, Jeff Adams, Yuliya Lobacheva, and Ryan Thomas. 2003. Grapheme to phoneme conversion and dictionary verification using graphonemes. In *Proceedings of Eurospeech*.

Robert Wagner and Michael Fischer. 1974. The string-to-string correction problem. *Journal of the ACM*.

Richard Zens and Hermann Ney. 2004. Improvements in phrase-based statistical machine translation. In *Proceedings of HLT-NAACL*.

Extracting Phrase Patterns with Minimum Redundancy for Unsupervised Speaker Role Classification

Bin Zhang, Brian Hutchinson, Wei Wu and Mari Ostendorf*
University of Washington, Seattle, WA 98125

Abstract

This paper addresses the problem of learning phrase patterns for unsupervised speaker role classification. Phrase patterns are automatically extracted from large corpora, and redundant patterns are removed via a graph pruning algorithm. In experiments on English and Mandarin talk shows, the use of phrase patterns results in an increase of role classification accuracy over n-gram lexical features, and more compact phrase pattern lists are obtained due to the redundancy removal.

1 Introduction

The identification of speaker roles is fundamental to the analysis of social content and information reliability in conversational speech. Previous work has primarily used supervised learning in automatic role classification. Barzilay et al. (2000) described a speaker role classification system for English broadcast news (BN), where the speakers were categorized into three types: anchor, journalist, and guest. The authors used supervised learning to discover n-gram signature phrases for speaker introduction and structural features such as duration, achieving an accuracy of 80% on ASR derived transcripts. Liu et al. (2006) studied speaker role classification on TDT-4 Mandarin BN data. Hidden Markov and maximum entropy models were used to label the sequence of speaker turns with the roles anchor, reporter, and other, based on n-gram features, which yielded 80% classification accuracy on human transcripts.

Hutchinson et al. (2010) extend previous work to the case of unsupervised learning, with the goal of portability across languages. That work explored speaker role classification using structural and n-gram features on talk show (or broadcast conversation (BC)) data. In this paper, we address a limitation of n-grams as features by proposing a method for learning phrases with gaps, which is particularly important for conversational speech, since there are more disfluencies that can cause failure of n-gram matching. In addition, we want to avoid topic words (e.g., proper nouns) in order to model speaker roles rather than topics. For example, for identifying the host, the phrase pattern "*We'll be back with * in a minute*" is more general than the n-grams "*We'll be back with John Smith in a minute*." To prevent these problems with n-grams, one must limit the length of learned n-grams, making them less discriminative.

Phrase patterns have been used in other NLP applications such as (Sun et al., 2007). To remove the redundancies in the automatically extracted phrase patterns, we propose a redundancy removal algorithm based on graph pruning that does not require role-labeled data. The resulting set of patterns is then used to extract lists of signature and conversational phrases, from which features are derived that are used to distinguish between the different roles. Using the phrase pattern-based lexical features in clustering, we obtain 82-89% speaker role classification accuracy on human transcripts of BC shows.

2 Method

Phrase patterns are generalizations of n-grams. A phrase pattern p of length n is an ordered list of words $(w_1, w_2, \ldots, w_n)$. It is matched by a word sequence of length $m \geq n$ if the sequence contains the words in the order defined by the pattern. Because the words in a phrase pattern need not appear contiguously in the sequence, phrase matching is less sensitive to disfluencies and topic words.

2.1 Phrase Pattern Extraction

Phrase patterns can be extracted by the sequential pattern mining algorithm PrefixSpan (Pei et al.,

* This research was funded by the Office of the Director of National Intelligence (ODNI), Intelligence Advanced Research Projects Activity (IARPA). All statements of fact, opinion or conclusions contained herein are those of the authors and should not be construed as representing the official views or policies of IARPA, the ODNI or the U.S. Government.

Human Language Technologies: The 2010 Annual Conference of the North American Chapter of the ACL, pages 717–720,
Los Angeles, California, June 2010.

2001). This algorithm efficiently extracts frequent phrase patterns in a corpus (i.e., relative frequency greater than a given threshold). Prior to the extraction, we perform text preprocessing including splitting the text into lines based on commas and periods to limit the pattern span, followed by case and punctuation removal. The extracted phrase patterns have variable length. As a result, longer patterns may contain shorter patterns. Phrase patterns with the same length may also be overlapped. These redundancies should be removed; otherwise, the same phrase may match several patterns, resulting in biased counts.

2.2 Phrase Pattern Redundancy Removal

Define a phrase pattern p as contained in another phrase pattern q if q contains all the words in p in the same order. p is called a parent pattern and q is the corresponding child pattern. Instead of constructing a tree as in (Siu et al., 2000) for variable length n-grams, we create a graph of phrase patterns based on containment, because a pattern can contain and be contained by multiple patterns. Our redundancy removal algorithm involves pruning this graph. With the nodes being the phrase patterns, the edges of the phrase pattern graph are constructed by connecting length-n phrase pattern p to length-$(n+1)$ phrase pattern q for all n, if p is contained in q. We connect only phrase patterns that differ by one word in length for computational efficiency, and this results in a multi-layer structure: the phrase patterns in each layer have the same length. For the convenience of pruning, a virtual node T is created as the "zeroth"-layer, and it is directly connected to all the nodes in the layer with the shortest pattern length.

Once a phrase pattern graph has been created, we prune the graph in order to remove the redundant nodes. First, we remove edges based on the ratio of counts $c(q)/c(p)$ between child node q and parent node p. A large ratio implies that the child appears in most of the cases where the parent appears. Hence, we keep the edge to indicate that the child can be used as a preferred substitute for the parent. On the other hand, the edge is removed if the ratio is small (less than a threshold t, see Fig. 1).

After this procedure is performed on all the edges in the graph, we determine whether a node is pruned based on its connectivity to parents and children. We

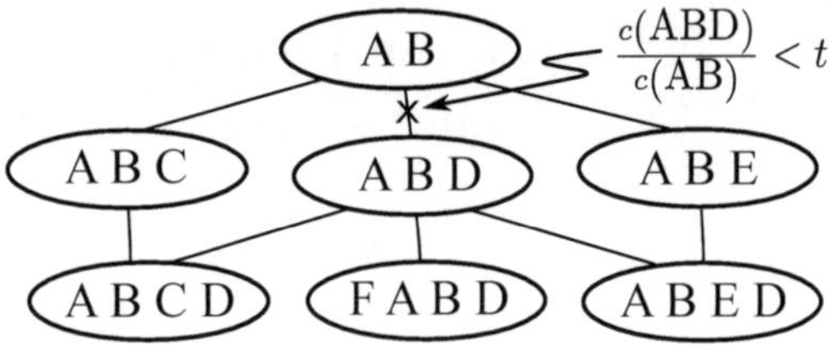

Figure 1: A fragment of an example phrase pattern graph. The letters represent words. The edge between "AB" and "ABD" is removed because the ratio of counts is less than the threshold.

define two levels of pruning, which differ in whether a node can be preserved even if its connections to parents are removed:

Conservative pruning A node is pruned if it has at least one child.

Aggressive pruning A node is pruned if it has at least one child or is not on a path connected to T.

Both methods were investigated, in case some useful phrase patterns ended up being pruned with the more aggressive approach.

2.3 Features Based on Phase Patterns

Although (Hutchinson et al., 2010) uses both lexical and structural features, here we use only lexical features to better assess impact. Once the graph pruning has provided a list of phrase patterns (eliminating phrases of length one because of low reliability), two subsets are extracted to represent signature phrases as might be used by a host and conversational phrases as might occur more frequently in live interviews. The signature statistic

$$\theta_1 = \frac{DF}{SF} + \alpha \log(f_{\mathrm{BC}}). \quad (1)$$

is based on the speaker frequency (SF, # speakers whose utterances match p), document frequency (DF, # shows that match p), and genre-dependent frequency f_{BC} (# occurrences of p in BC), all computed on the training data. The ratio $\frac{DF}{SF}$ favors phrases that occur in many documents but few speakers, e.g. one per show, as for a host. The log BC frequency term is a penalty to eliminate infrequent patterns. The conversation statistic

$$\theta_2 = \frac{f_{\mathrm{BC}}}{f_{\mathrm{BN}}+1} \mathbf{1}_{SF>\beta}. \quad (2)$$

uses frequency f_{BN} (# occurrences of p in BN), to look for phrases that are more frequent in BC data than BN, ideally live discussion phenomena. The indicator function $\mathbf{1}_{SF>\beta}$ eliminates phrases used by a small number of speakers to avoid topic-related phrases. Hyper-parameters α and β are tuned by inspecting the top phrase patterns after ranking. We use $\alpha = 10^{-3}, \beta = 500$ for English and $\alpha = 10^{-4}, \beta = 1000$ for Mandarin. Phrase patterns are ranked by the two statistics to generate lists of *signature* and *conversational* patterns, respectively.

During speaker-level feature extraction in role detection, each phrase pattern in the lists is matched against a speaker's utterances. The lexical features have two dimensions: the count of matches using the signature and conversational patterns, each normalized by the total number of patterns matched in the show to account for differences between shows.

3 Experiments

3.1 Task and Data

In the absence of speaker-role-labeled conversational speech training data, we perform unsupervised speaker role classification with three classes: host, expert guest, and soundbite. We evaluate on two human-labeled evaluation sets (English and Mandarin). The English eval set contains nine BC shows (150 speakers), while the Mandarin eval set contains 14 shows (140 speakers). There is an additional labeled Mandarin development set composed of ten shows (71 speakers). There are on average 7.6k words and 7.5k characters per show for English and Mandarin, respectively. The phrase patterns are learned from much larger corpora with speaker labels but without speaker role labels, including web transcripts for 310 English shows and quick rich transcripts for 4395 Mandarin shows. Because of the larger amount of Mandarin data, we use a lower threshold (5×10^{-5}) for phrase pattern extraction than for English (10^{-4}).

3.2 Classification

Spectral clustering (Shi and Malik, 2000) is used in this work, since we found it to outperform other clustering approaches such as k-means and Gaussian mixture models. Given a two-dimensional feature vector for each speaker in a show, we construct a speaker graph with edge weights defined by Gaussian similarity $\exp\left(-\frac{\|x_i - x_j\|^2}{2\sigma^2}\right)$. The spectral clustering is non-deterministic, because it uses k-means as its final step ($k = 3$), which is initialized by randomly choosing k samples as initial centroids. We vary σ as an integer from 1 to 100 in combination with different random initializations to generate multiple clustering alternatives, and then use a partition selection algorithm to pick the most common clustering among the candidates. We use domain knowledge to map speaker clusters into speaker roles: the cluster whose members have the largest average number of speaker turns is the host cluster, that with the smallest average number of turns is the soundbite cluster, and the remaining cluster contains the expert guests.

3.3 Results

The phase pattern pruning threshold t was tuned on the Mandarin dev set. We varied t from 0.1 to 0.9, and measured the classification accuracy. $t = 0.8$ was found to be optimal (Fig. 2).

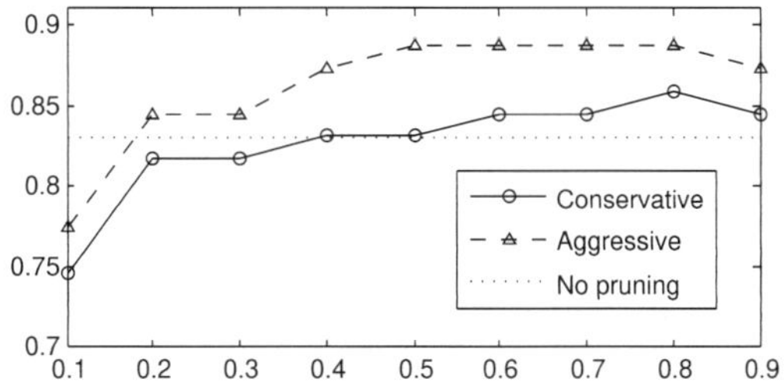

Figure 2: Accuracy on Man dev vs. pruning threshold t

The list of classification results on all the data sets is shown in Tab. 1. Aggressive pruning yields the best classification performance on all the data sets. It is also better than using n-gram matching for feature extraction (the last row of the table).

	Man dev	Man eval	Eng eval
No pruning	0.83	0.86	0.81
Cons. pruning	0.86	0.83	0.81
Aggr. pruning	**0.89**	**0.89**	**0.82**
N-gram	0.86	0.86	0.77

Table 1: Classification results

The size of phrase pattern lists is given in Tab. 2, and the number of redundant phrase patterns (the patterns that are contained in other patterns) is in Tab. 3 for different pruning levels. Using aggressive pruning, the list size and number of redundant phrase patterns are greatly reduced. However, the classification accuracy does not decrease. This demonstrates that the redundant phrase patterns are not helpful and can be harmful for this task.

Pruning level	Signature ptn.		Conv. ptn.	
	Eng	Man	Eng	Man
No pruning	2000	2000	1000	1000
Cons. pruning	1605	946	928	998
Aggr. pruning	244	370	465	835

Table 2: Phrase pattern list size

Pruning level	Signature ptn.		Conv. ptn.	
	Eng	Man	Eng	Man
No pruning	396	1331	337	142
Cons. pruning	35	307	334	142
Aggr. pruning	6	59	8	0

Table 3: Number of redundant phrase patterns in the list

The unsupervised speaker role classification system in (Hutchinson et al., 2010) uses both n-gram and structural features, giving classification accuracy on English and Mandarin eval sets of 0.86 and 0.84, respectively. Adding structural features to phrase-pattern-based lexical features improves the performance on English but not Mandarin, perhaps because soundbites in English tend to be much shorter than those in Mandarin.

3.4 Discussion

The experiments reflect differences between the two languages. We observe that the main gain in Mandarin comes from improved classification of hosts, due to the signature phrase patterns. In English, the improvement is attributed to improved classification of expert guests and soundbites, suggesting an improved conversational dimension of the lexical features. The performance difference of the two languages seems more related to the languages themselves, rather than the size of data sets on which phrase patterns are learned, because we were able to obtain similar performance on Mandarin even when the training set size is reduced.

Anecdotal inspection of the phrase patterns learned for the signature phrases suggests that the combination of redundancy pruning and the heuristic signature statistic is quite effective. For example, we observed English signature patterns such as "*back with after this*" and "*let's take a look at*." The former pattern can be matched by phrases with names or topics inserted, and the latter can be matched by "*let's just take a look at*" or "*let's take a brief look at*." In the Mandarin signature patterns, we also found patterns such as "今天 请到 演播室 的 嘉宾 是 * 的 * 教授" (*today the guest invited to the studio is Professor from*) and "谢谢 来自 * 的 报道" (*thanks to the report from*). These patterns can be considered to be templates for hosts, where the named-entities are skipped.

4 Conclusions

We have presented a method for extracting phrase patterns with minimum redundancy for speaker role classification. The proposed algorithm removes most of the redundancies in the phrase patterns, leading to more compact pattern lists and improved classification accuracy over n-gram lexical features. We can apply the algorithm to other applications such as text classification, where phrase patterns can be used in place of n-grams. One way to extend this work is to use the automatically extracted phrase patterns as initial features, and then employ supervised or semi-supervised learning techniques to learn a more discriminative feature set.

References

R. Barzilay et al. 2000. The Rules Behind Roles: Identifying Speaker Role in Radio Broadcasts *Proc. AAAI*, pp. 679–684.

Y. Liu. 2006. Initial Study on Automatic Identification of Speaker Role in Broadcast News Speech. *Proc. HLT*, pp. 81–84.

B. Hutchinson et al. 2010. Unsupervised Broadcast Conversation Speaker Role Labeling *Proc. ICASSP*, pp. 5322–5325.

G. Sun et al. 2007. Detecting Erroneous Sentences Using Automatically Mined Sequential Patterns. *Proc. ACL*, pp. 81–88.

J. Pei et al. 2001. PrefixSpan: Mining Sequential Patterns Efficiently by Prefix-projected Pattern Growth. *Proc. ICDE*, pp. 215–224.

M. Siu and M. Ostendorf. 2000. Variable N-grams and Extensions for Conversational Speech Language Modeling. *IEEE Transactions on Speech and Audio Processing*, 8(1):63–75.

J. Shi and J. Malik. 2000. Normalized Cuts and Image Segmentation. *IEEE Transactions on Pattern Analysis and Machine Intelligence*, 22(8):888–905.

Classification of Prosodic Events using Quantized Contour Modeling

Andrew Rosenberg
Department of Computer Science
Queens College CUNY, New York, USA
andrew@cs.qc.cuny.edu

Abstract

We present Quantized Contour Modeling (QCM), a Bayesian approach to the classification of acoustic contours. We evaluate the performance of this technique in the classification of prosodic events. We find that, on BURNC, this technique can successfully classify pitch accents with 63.99% accuracy (.4481 CER), and phrase ending tones with 72.91% accuracy.

1 Introduction

Intonation can significantly vary the intended meaning of a spoken utterance. In Standard American English, contrast is frequently indicated with an accent that has a steeper pitch rise – "I went to the **store** (not the library)" – than an accent that is used to indicate focus or introduce new information – "I went to the **store** (before going home)" . At phrase boundaries, rising pitch can indicate uncertainty or that the speaker is asking a question – "John likes Mary?" vs. "John likes Mary". Automatically detecting prosodic events and classifying their type allows natural language understanding systems access to intonational information that would unavailable if processing transcribed text alone.

The ToBI standard of intonation (Silverman et al., 1992) describes intonational contours as a sequence of High and Low tones associated with two types of prosodic events – pitch accents and phrase boundaries. The tones describe an inventory of *types* of prosodic events. In this work, we present Quantized Contour Modeling, a novel approach to the automatic classification of prosodic event types.

In Section 2, we describe related work on this task. We describe Quantized Contour Modeling in Section 3. Our materials are described in Section 4. Experimental results are presented and discussed in Section 5. We conclude and describe future directions for this work in Section 6.

2 Related Work

Five types of pitch accents – pitch movements that correspond to perceived prominence of an associated word – are defined in the ToBI standard(Silverman et al., 1992): H*, L*, L+H*, L*+H, H+!H*. In addition to these five, high tones (H) can be produced in a compressed pitch range indicated by (!H). For the purposes of the experiments described in this paper, we collapse high (H) and downstepped High (!H) tones into a single class leaving five accent types. The ToBI standard describes two levels of phrasing, intermediate phrases and intonational phrases which are comprised of one or more intermediate phrases. Each intermediate phrase has an associated phrase accent describing the pitch movement between the ultimate pitch accent and the phrase boundary. Phrase accents can have High (H-), downstepped High (!H-) or low (L-) tones. Intonational phrase boundaries have an additional boundary tone, to describe a final pitch movement. These can be high (H%) or low (L%). Intonational phrases have five possible phrase ending tone combinations, L-L%, L-H%, H-L%, !H-L% and H-H%. In section 5.3, we describe experiments classifying these phrase ending tones.

The *detection* of pitch accents and phrase boundaries has received significantly more research attention than the *classification* of accent types and phrase ending behavior. However, one technique that has been used in a number of research efforts is to simultaneously detect and classify pitch accent. This is done by representing pitch accent detection and classfication as a four-way classification task, where a token may be classified as UNACCENTED, HIGH, LOW, or DOWNSTEPPED. Both Ross and Ostendorf (1996) and Sun (2002) used this approach, reporting 72.4% and 77.0% accuracy respectively when evaluated on a single speakers. Levow also used this four-way classification for pitch accent detection and classification under supervised (2005), and unsupervised and semi-supervised learning approaches (2006). Using

Human Language Technologies: The 2010 Annual Conference of the North American Chapter of the ACL, pages 721–724,
Los Angeles, California, June 2010.

SVMs with only acoustic features, 81.3% accuracy at the syllable level is achieved. Using unsupervised spectral clustering, 78.4% accuracy is reported, while using the semi-supervised technique, Laplacian SVMs, 81.5% accuracy is achieved. Since these approaches simultaneously evaluate the detection *and* classification of pitch accents, direct comparison with this work is impossible.

Ananthakrishnan and Narayanan (2008) used RFC (Taylor, 1994) and Tilt (Taylor, 2000) parameters along with word and part of speech language modeling to classify pitch accents as H*, !H*, L+H* or L*. When evaluated on six BURNC speakers using leave-one-speaker-out cross-validation, accuracy of 56.4% was obtained. In the same work, the authors were able to classify L-L% from L-H% phrase-final tones in the BURNC with 67.7% accuracy. This performance was obtained using RFC F0 parameterization and a language model trained over categorical prosodic events.

3 Quantized Contour Modeling

In this section, we present a modeling technique, Quantized Contour Modeling. This technique quantizes the f0 contour of a word in the time and pitch domains, generating a low-dimensional representation of the contour. The pitch of the contour is linearly normalized to the range between the minimum and maximum pitch in the contour, and quantized into N equally sized bins. The time domain is normalized to the range [0,1] and quantized into M equally sized bins. An example of such a quantization is presented in Figure 1 where $N = 3$ and $M = 4$. Using this quantized representation of a pitch contour, we

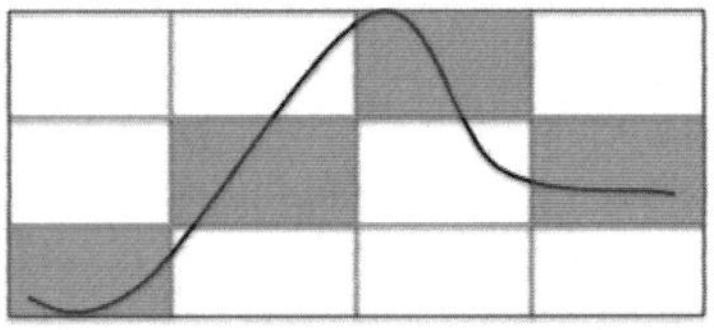

Figure 1: *Quantization with N=3 value and M=4 time bins.*

train a multinomial mixture model for each pitch accent type. Let the quantized contour be an M dimensional vector C where $C = (C_1, C_2, \ldots, C_M)$, where $C_i \in \{0 \ldots N-1\}$. We indicate pitch (f0) contours by C^{f0} and intensity contours by C^I. We train a multinomial model $p(type|C_i, i)$ for each time bin $i \in \{0 \ldots N-1\}$ with Laplace (add-one) smoothing. When using multinomial models, we quantize the mean of the pitch values assigned to a time bin. We use these pitch accent type models to classify a contour using the Bayesian classification function found in Equation 1. This formulation assumes that the values at each time are conditionally independent given the contour type. Also, we can modify the model incorporating a Markov hypothesis to include a sequential component by explicitly modeling the current and previous quantized values, as in Equation 2. We extend each of these models to model the energy contour shape simultaneously with the pitch contour. The classification technique allows for the number of pitch and energy value quantization bins to be distinct. However, in these experiments, we tie these, constraining them to be equal. The form of the classification functions using the energy contours are found in Figure 2.

Standard shape modeling

$$type^* = \operatorname*{argmax}_{type} p(type) \prod_i^M p(C_i|type, i) \quad (1)$$

Sequential f0 modeling

$$type^* = \operatorname*{argmax}_{type} p(type) \prod_i^M p(C_i|C_{i-1}, type, i) \quad (2)$$

Standard f0 + I modeling

$$type^* = \operatorname*{argmax}_{type} p(type) \prod_i^M p(C_i^{f0}, C_i^I|type, i) \quad (3)$$

Sequential f0 + I modeling

$$type^* = \operatorname*{argmax}_{type} p(type) \prod_i^M p(C_i^{f0}, C_i^I|C_{i-1}^{f0}, C_i^I, type, i) \quad (4)$$

Figure 2: *Quantized contour modeling classification formulae.*

4 Materials and Methods

We use two corpora that have been manually annotated with ToBI labels to evaluate the use of QCM in the classification of prosodic events. These two corpora are the Boston University Radio News Corpus (BURNC) (Ostendorf et al., 1995) and the Boston Directions Corpus (BDC) (Nakatani et al., 1995). The BURNC is a corpus of professionally read radio news data. A 2.35 hour, 29,578 word, subset from six speakers (three female and three male) has been prosodically annotated. The BDC is made up of elicited monologues spoken by four non-professional speakers, three male and one female. The BDC is divided into two subcorpora comprised of spontaneous and read speech. The 50 minutes of read speech contain 10,831 words. There are 60 minutes of annotated spontaneous material containing 11,627 words. Both are spoken by the same four speakers. In these experiments we evaluate these subcorpora separately, and refer to them as BDC-spon and BDC-read, respectively. The distribution of pitch accents and phrase-ending tones for these three corpora can be found in Figure 3.

Corpus	H*	L+H*	L*	L*+H	H+!H*
BDC-read	78.24%	13.72%	5.97%	1.36%	0.71%
BDC-spon	84.57%	6.32%	7.70%	0.68%	0.73%
BURNC	69.99%	21.64%	3.67%	0.34%	4.37%

Corpus	L-L%	L-H%	H-L%	!H-L%	H-H%
BDC-read	49.00%	35.62%	9.66%	4.29%	1.43%
BDC-spon	29.45%	32.57%	30.96%	4.40%	2.61%
BURNC	56.16%	38.38%	3.57%	0.68%	1.20%

Figure 3: *Distribution of prosodic event types in BURNC, BDC-read and BDC-spon corpora.*

In order to use QCM classification, we must first identify the region of an acoustic contour to quantify. Though there is evidence that acoustic evidence of prominence crosses the syllable boundary (Rosenberg and Hirschberg, 2009), it is largely held that the acoustic excursion corresponding to intonational prominence is centered around a syllable. To identify the region of analysis for QCM, we identify the accent-bearing syllable from the manual prosodic annotation, and quantize the contour extracted from the syllable boundaries. For the BURNC material, forced alignment syllable boundaries are available. However, no forced-alignment phone information is available for the BDC data. Therefore we apply Villing et al.'s (2004) envelope based pseudosyllabification routine to identify candidate syllabic regions. We use the pseudosyllable containing the accent annotation as the region of analysis for the BDC material. For classification of phrase ending intonation, we use the final syllable (or pseudosyllable) in the phrase as the region of analysis. To be clear, the accent and phrase boundary locations are derived from manual annotations; the intonational tones associated with these events are classified using QCM.

5 Prosodic Event Classification Results

In this section we present results applying QCM to the classification of pitch accents and phrase ending intonation. The work described in this section assumes the *presence* of prosodic events is known *a priori*. The approaches described can be seen as operating on output of an automatic prosodic event *detection* system.

5.1 Combined Error Rate

Automatic pitch accent classification poses an interesting problem. Pitrelli, et al. (Pitrelli et al., 1994) report human agreement of only 64.1% on accent classification in the ToBI framework. If downstepped variants of accents are collapsed with their non-downstapped forms this agreement improves to 76.1%. Second, pitch accents are overwhelmingly H* in most labeled corpus, including the BDC and BURNC material used in this paper. This skewed class distribution leads to a very high baseline, at or above the rate of human agreement. Because of this, we find accuracy an unreliable measure for evaluating the performance of this task. Multiple solutions can have similar accuracy, but radically different classification performance on minority classes. We therefore propose to use a different measure for the evaluation of pitch accent type classification. We define the Combined Error Rate (CER) as the mean of the weighted rates of Type I and Type II errors. The combination of these measures results in an increased penalty for errors of the majority class while being more sensitive to minority class performance than accuracy. Throughout this chapter, we will continue to report accuracy for comparison to other work, but consider CER to provide a more informative evaluation. To avoid confusion, accuracy will be reported as a percentage (%) while CER will be reported as a decimal.

$$CER = \frac{p(FP) + p(FN)}{2} \quad (5)$$

The Type I error rate measures the false positive rate for a given class (cf. Equation 6).

$$p(FP) = \sum_i p(C_i)p(FP_i) \quad (6)$$

We combine this measure with the Weighted Type II Error Rate (cf. Equation 7). The Type II error rate measures the false negative rate for a given class

$$p(FN) = \sum_i p(C_i)p(FN_i) \quad (7)$$

5.2 Pitch Accent Classification

The first step in applying Quantized Contour Modeling is to fix the desired quantization parameters. We do this by identifying a stratified 10% held out tuning set from the training data. We evaluate quantization sizes ranging between 2 and 7 for both the time and value parameters, leading to 36 candidates. Once we identify the best parameterization on this tuning data, we run ten-fold cross validation on the remaining data to evaluate the performance of each modeling technique (cf. Figure 2).

The classification accuracy and CER for each model is reported in Table 1 along with the number of time and value bins that were used. We first observe that modeling intensity information with f0 data does not improve classification performance. The alignment between pitch and intensity peaks have been shown to distinguish pitch accent types (Rosenberg, 2009); this relationship is not successfully captured by QCM. Moreover, we find that sequential modeling only leads to improvements in CER on BDC-read. On all corpora, the classification accuracy is improved, with statistically insignificant ($p > 0.05$) reductions in CER. This leads us to consider sequential modeling of pitch to be the best performing approach to the classification of pitch accent using QCM.

Method	BDC-read	BDC-spon	BURNC
f0	46.51/.3860(5,3)	**55.41/.4103(3,4)**	**47.56/.4444(4,4)**
Seq. f0	**73.17/.3667(6,7)**	81.20/.4156 (7,5)	63.99/.4481(7,7)
f0+I	37.53/.4094(3,3)	47.96/.4222(4,2)	48.36/.4472(2,2)
Seq. f0+I	74.08/.4032(7,3)	80.60/.4361(5,4)	66.97/.4530(6,5)
Baseline	78.22/.0000	84.57/.0000	70.23/.0000

Table 1: *Accuracy (%), CER, time and value bins from QCM pitch accent type classification experiments.*

5.3 Phrase-ending Tone Classification

As in Section 5.2, we identify the best performing quantization parameters on a stratified 10% tuning set, then run 10-fold cross validation on the remaining data. Results from QCM classification experiments classifying intonational phrase ending tone combinations – phrase accent and boundary tone – can be found in Table 2. We find

Method	BDC-read	BDC-spon	BURNC
f0	48.21(3,6)	40.26(2,2)	70.36 (5,2)
Seq. f0	53.86(2,2)	43.80(4,4)	71.77 (6,2)
f0+I	48.21(6,6)	38.28(6,6)	67.83(2,2)
Seq. f0+I	**57.94(6,6)**	**46.61(6,5)**	**72.91(7,7)**
Baseline	49%	32%	55%

Table 2: *Accuracy (%), time and value bins from QCM phrase ending tone classification experiments.*

that the simultaneous modeling of f0 and intensity consistently yields the best performance in the classification of phrase ending tones. These results all represent significant improvement over the majority class baseline. The interaction between pitch and intensity contours in the classification of phrase-ending intonation has not been thoroughly investigated and remains an open area for future research.

6 Conclusion and Future Work

In this paper we present a novel technique for the classification of two dimensional contour data, Quantized Contour Modeling (QCM). QCM operates by quantizing acoustic data into a pre-determined, fixed number of time and value bins. From this quantized data, a model of the value information is constructed for each time bin. The likelihood of new data fitting these models is then performed using a Bayesian inference.

We have applied QCM to the tasks of classifying pitch accent types, and phrase-ending intonation. The best performing parameterizations of QCM are able to classify pitch accent types on BURNC with 63.99% accuracy and .4481 Combined Error Rate (CER). QCM classifies phrase ending tones on this corpus with 72.91% accuracy.

These results do not represent the best performing approaches to these tasks. The best reported classification of pitch accent types on BURNC is 59.95% accuracy and .422 CER, for phrase ending intonation 75.09% (Rosenberg, 2009). However, the classification of phrase ending intonation is accomplished by including QCM posteriors in an SVM feature vector with other acoustic features.

This technique may be applicable to classifying other phenomena. Here we have used ToBI tone classifications as an intermediate representation of intonational phenomena. QCM could be used to directly classify turn-taking behavior, or dialog acts. Also, previous work has looked at using the same techniques to classify prosodic events and lexical tones in tonal languages such as Mandarin Chinese. QCM could be directly applied to lexical tone modeling; the only modification required would be a different segmentation routine.

References

S. Ananthakrishnan and S. Narayanan. 2008. Fine-grained pitch accent and boundary tone labeling with parametric f0 features. In *ICASSP*.

G.-A. Levow. 2005. Context in multi-lingual tone and pitch accent recognition. In *Interspeech*.

G.-A. Levow. 2006. Unsupervised and semi-supervised learning of tone and pitch accent. In *HLT-NAACL*.

C. Nakatani, J. Hirschberg, and B. Grosz. 1995. Discourse structure in spoken language: Studies on speech corpora. In *AAAI Spring Symposium on Empirical Methods in Discourse Interpretation and Generation*.

M. Ostendorf, P. Price, and S. Shattuck-Hufnagel. 1995. The boston university radio news corpus. Technical Report ECS-95-001, Boston University, March.

J. Pitrelli, M. Beckman, and J. Hirschberg. 1994. Evaluation of prosodic transcription labeling reliability in the tobi framework. In *ICSLP*.

A. Rosenberg and J. Hirschberg. 2009. Detecting pitch accents at the word, syllable and vowel level. In *HLT-NAACL*.

A. Rosenberg. 2009. *Automatic Detection and Classification of Prosodic Events*. Ph.D. thesis, Columbia University.

K. Ross and M. Ostendorf. 1996. Prediction of abstract prosodic labels for speech synthesis. *Computer Speech & Language*, 10(3):155–185.

K. Silverman, et al. 1992. Tobi: A standard for labeling english prosody. In *ICSLP*.

X. Sun. 2002. Pitch accent predicting using ensemble machine learning. In *ICSLP*.

P. Taylor. 1994. The rise/fall/connection model of intonation. *Speech Commun.*, 15(1-2):169–186.

P. Taylor. 2000. Analysis and synthesis of intonation using the tilt model. *Journal of the Acoustical Society of America*.

R. Villing, et al. 2004. Automatic blind syllable segmentation for continuous speech. In *ISSC*.

Investigations into the Crandem Approach to Word Recognition

Rohit Prabhavalkar, Preethi Jyothi, William Hartmann, Jeremy Morris, and Eric Fosler-Lussier
Department of Computer Science and Engineering
The Ohio State University, Columbus, OH
{prabhava, jyothi, hartmanw, morrijer, fosler}@cse.ohio-state.edu

Abstract

We suggest improvements to a previously proposed framework for integrating Conditional Random Fields and Hidden Markov Models, dubbed a Crandem system (2009). The previous authors' work suggested that local label posteriors derived from the CRF were too low-entropy for use in word-level automatic speech recognition. As an alternative to the log posterior representation used in their system, we explore frame-level representations derived from the CRF feature functions. We also describe a weight normalization transformation that leads to increased entropy of the CRF posteriors. We report significant gains over the previous Crandem system on the Wall Street Journal word recognition task.

1 Introduction

Conditional Random Fields (CRFs) (Lafferty et al., 2001) have recently emerged as a promising new paradigm in the domain of Automatic Speech Recognition (ASR). Unlike Hidden Markov Models (HMMs), CRFs are direct discriminative models: they predict the probability of a label sequence conditioned on the input. As a result, CRFs can capture long-range dependencies in the data and avoid the need for restrictive independence assumptions. Variants of CRFs have been successfully used in phone recognition tasks (Gunawardana et al., 2005; Morris and Fosler-Lussier, 2008; Hifny and Renals, 2009).

While the improvements in the phone recognition task are encouraging, recent efforts have been directed towards extending the CRF paradigm to the word recognition level (Zweig and Nguyen, 2009; Morris and Fosler-Lussier, 2009). The Crandem system (Morris and Fosler-Lussier, 2009) is one of the promising approaches in this regard. The Crandem system is directly inspired by the techniques of the Tandem system (Hermansky et al., 2000), where phone-label posterior estimates produced by a Multi-Layer Perceptron (MLP) are transformed into a suitable acoustic representation for a standard HMM. In both systems, the frame-based log posterior vector of $P(\text{phone}|\text{acoustics})$ over all phones is decorrelated using the Karhunen-Loeve (KL) transform; unlike MLPs, CRFs take into account the entire label sequence when computing local posteriors. However, posterior estimates from the CRF tend to be overconfident compared to MLP posteriors (Morris and Fosler-Lussier, 2009).

In this paper, we analyze the interplay between the various steps involved in the Crandem process. Is the local posterior representation from the CRF the best representation? Given that the CRF posterior estimates can be overconfident, what transformations to the posteriors are appropriate?

In Section 2 we briefly describe CRFs and the Crandem framework. We suggest techniques for improving Crandem word recognition performance in Section 3. Details of experiments and our results are discussed in Sections 4 and 5 respectively. We conclude with a discussion of future work in Section 6.

2 CRFs and the Crandem System

Conditional random fields (Lafferty et al., 2001) express the probability of a label sequence Q conditioned on the input data X as a log-linear sum of

Human Language Technologies: The 2010 Annual Conference of the North American Chapter of the ACL, pages 725–728,
Los Angeles, California, June 2010.

weighted feature functions,

$$p(Q|X) = \frac{\exp \sum_t \sum_j \lambda_j s_j(q_t, X) + \sum_j \mu_j f_j(q_{t-1}, q_t, X)}{Z(X)} \quad (1)$$

where $s_j(\cdot)$ and $f_j(\cdot)$ are known as state feature functions and transition feature functions respectively, and λ_j and μ_j are the associated weights. $Z(X)$ is a normalization term that ensures a valid probability distribution. Given a set of labeled examples, the CRF is trained to maximize the conditional log-likelihood of the training set. The log-likelihood is concave over the entire parameter space, and can be maximized using standard convex optimization techniques (Lafferty et al., 2001; Sha and Pereira, 2003). The local posterior probability of a particular label can be computed via a forward-backward style algorithm. Mathematically,

$$p(q_t = q|X) = \frac{\alpha_t(q|X)\beta_t(q|X)}{Z(X)} \quad (2)$$

where $\alpha_t(q|X)$ and $\beta_t(q|X)$ accumulate contributions associated with possible assignments of labels before and after the current time-step t. The Crandem system utilizes these local posterior values from the CRF analogously to the way in which MLP-posteriors are treated in the Tandem framework (Hermansky et al., 2000), by applying a log transformation to the posteriors. These transformed outputs are then decorrelated using a KL-transform and then dimensionality-reduced to be used as a replacement for MFCCs in a HMM system. While the MLP is usually reduced to 39 dimensions, the standard CRF benefits from a higher dimensionality reduction (to 19 dimensions). The decorrelated outputs are then used as an input representation for a conventional HMM system.

3 Improving Crandem Recognition Results

Morris and Fosler-Lussier (2009) indicate that the local posterior outputs from the CRF model produces features that are more heavily skewed to the dominant phone class than the MLP system, leading to an increase in word recognition errors. In order to correct for this, we perform a non-linear transformation on the local CRF posterior representation before applying a KL-transform and subsequent stages. Specifically, we normalize all of the weights λ_j and μ_j in Equation 1 by a fixed positive constant n to obtain normalized weights λ'_j and μ'_j. We note that the probability of a label sequence computed using the transformed weights, $p'(Q|X)$, is equivalent to taking the nth-root of the CRF probability computed using the unnormalized weights, with a new normalization term $Z'(X)$

$$p'(Q|X) = \frac{p(Q|X)^{1/n}}{Z'(X)} \quad (3)$$

where, $p(Q|X)$ is as defined in Equation 1. Also observe that the monotonicity of the nth-root function ensures that if $p(Q_1|X) > p(Q_2|X)$ then $p'(Q_1|X) > p'(Q_2|X)$. In other words, the rank order of the n-best phone recognition results are not impacted by this change. The transformation does, however, increase the entropy between the dominant class from the CRF and its competitors, since $p'(Q|X) < p(Q|X)$. As we shall discuss in Section 5, this transformation helps improve word recognition performance in the Crandem framework.

Our second set of experiments are based on the following observation regarding the CRF posteriors. As can be seen from Equation 2, the CRF posteriors involve a global normalization over the entire utterance as opposed to the local normalization of the MLP posteriors in the output softmax layer. This motivates the use of representations derived from the CRF that are 'local' in some sense. We therefore propose two alternative representations that are modeled along the lines of the linear outputs from an MLP. The first uses the sum of the state feature functions, to obtain a vector $f^{\text{state}}(X,t)$ for each time step t and input utterance X of length $|\mathcal{Q}|$ dimensions, where $\mathcal{Q}$ is the set of possible phone labels

$$f^{\text{state}}(X,t) = \left[\sum_j \lambda_j s_j(q, X) \right]^T \qquad \forall q \in \mathcal{Q} \quad (4)$$

where q is a particular phone label. Note that the lack of an exponential term in this representation ensures that the representation is less 'spiky' than the CRF posteriors. Additionally, the decoupling of the representation from the transition feature functions could potentially allow the system to represent relative ambiguity between multiple phones hypothesized for a given frame.

The second 'local' representation that we experimented with incorporates the CRF transition feature functions as follows. For each utterance X we perform a Viterbi decoding of the most likely state sequence $Q^{\text{best}} = \text{argmax}_Q\{p(Q|X)\}$ hypothesized for the utterance X. We then augmented the state feature representation with the sum of the transition features corresponding to the phone label hypothesized for the previous frame (q_{t-1}^{best}) to obtain a vector $f^{\text{trans}}(X,t)$ of length $|\mathcal{Q}|$,

$$f^{\text{trans}}(X,t) = \left[\sum_j \lambda_j s_j(q,X) + \sum_j \mu_j f_j(q_{t-1}^{\text{best}}, q, X)\right]^T \quad (5)$$

As a final note, following (Morris and Fosler-Lussier, 2009), our CRF systems are trained using the linear outputs of MLPs as its state feature functions and transition biases as the transition feature functions. Hence, f^{state} is a linear transformation of the MLP linear outputs down to $|\mathcal{Q}|$ dimensions.[1] Both f^{state} and f^{trans} can thus be viewed as an implicit mapping performed by the CRF of the input feature function dimensions down to $|\mathcal{Q}|$ dimensions. Note that the CRF implicitly uses information concerning the underlying phone labels unlike dimensionality reduction using KL-transform.

4 Experimental Setup

To evaluate our proposed techniques, we carried out word recognition experiments on the speaker-independent portion of the Wall Street Journal 5K closed vocabulary task (WSJ0). Since the corpus is not phonetically transcribed, we first trained a standard HMM recognition system using PLP features and produced phonetic transcriptions by force aligning the training data. These were used to train an MLP phone classifier with a softmax output layer, using a 9-frame window of PLPs with 4000 hidden layer units to predict one of the 41 phone labels (including silence and short pause). The linear outputs of the MLP were used to train a baseline Tandem system. We then trained a CRF using the MLP linear outputs as its state feature functions. We extract local posteriors as well as the two 'local' representations described in Section 3. These input representations were then normalized at the utterance level, before applying a KL-transformation to decorrelate them and reduce dimensionality to 39 dimensions. Finally, each of these representations was used to train a HMM system with intra-word triphones and 16 Gaussians per mixture using the Hidden Markov Model Toolkit (Young et al., 2002).

[1]We note that our system uses an additional state bias feature that has a fixed value of 1. However, since this is a constant term, it has no role to play in the derived representation.

System	Accuracy (%)
Crandem-baseline	89.4%
Tandem-baseline	91.8%
Crandem-NormMax	91.4%
Crandem-Norm5	92.1%
Crandem-state	91.7%
Crandem-trans	91.0%

Table 1: Word recognition results on the WSJ0 task

5 Results

Results for each of the experiments described in Section 4 are reported in Table 1 on the 330-sentence standard 5K non-verbalized test set. The Crandem-baseline represents the system of (Morris and Fosler-Lussier, 2009). Normalizing the CRF weights of the system by either the weight with largest absolute value (CRF-NormMax) or by 5 (tuned on the development set) leads to significant improvements ($p \leq 0.005$) over the Crandem baseline. Similarly, using either the state feature sum (Crandem-state) or the representation augmented with the transition features (Crandem-trans) leads to significant improvements ($p \leq 0.005$) over the Crandem baseline. Note that the performance of these systems is comparable to the Tandem baseline.

To further analyze the results obtained using the state feature sum representations and the Tandem baseline, we compute the mean distance for each phone HMM from every other phone HMM obtained at the end of the GMM-HMM training phase. The distance between two HMMs is computed as a uniformly weighted sum of the average distances between the GMMs of a one-to-one alignment of states corresponding to the two HMMs. GMM distances are computed using a 0.5-weighted sum of inter-dispersions normalized by self-dispersions (Wang et

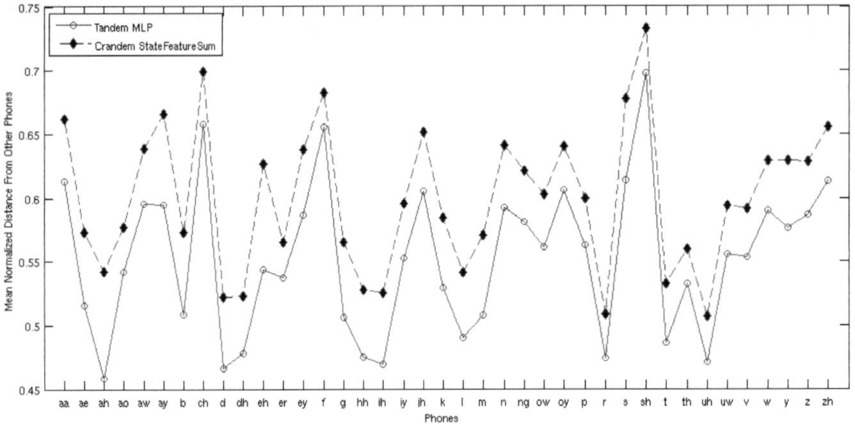

Figure 1: Normalized mean distances for each of the phone models from every other phone model trained using the Tandem MLP baseline and the state feature sum representation.

al., 2004). Distances between monomodal Gaussian distributions were computed using the Bhattacharyya distance measure. The phone HMM distances are normalized using the maximum phone distance for each system. As can be seen in Figure 1, the mean distances obtained from the state feature sum representation are consistently greater than the corresponding distances in the Tandem-MLP system, indicating larger separability of the phones in the feature space. Similar trends were seen with the transition feature sum representation.

6 Conclusions and Future Work

In this paper, we report significant improvements over the Crandem baseline. The weight normalization experiments confirmed the hypothesis that increasing the entropy of the CRF posteriors leads to better word-level recognition. Our experiments with directly extracting frame-level representations from the CRF reinforce this conclusion. Although our experiments with the systems using the state feature sum and transition feature augmented representation did not lead to improvements over the Tandem baseline, the increased separability of the phone models trained using these representations is encouraging. In the future, we intend to examine techniques by which these representations could be used to further improve word recognition results.

Acknowledgement: *The authors gratefully acknowledge support by NSF grants IIS-0643901 and IIS-0905420 for this work.*

References

A. Gunawardana, M. Mahajan, A. Acero, and J. Platt. 2005. Hidden conditional random fields for phone classification. Interspeech.

H. Hermansky, D. Ellis, and S. Sharma. 2000. Tandem connectionist feature stream extraction for conventional hmm systems. ICASSP.

Y. Hifny and S. Renals. 2009. Speech recognition using augmented conditional random fields. *IEEE Transactions on Audio, Speech, and Language Processing*, 17(2):354–365.

J. Lafferty, A. McCallum, and F. Pereira. 2001. Conditional random fields: Probabilistic models for segmenting and labeling sequence data. ICML.

J. Morris and E. Fosler-Lussier. 2008. Conditional random fields for integrating local discriminative classifiers. *IEEE Transactions on Acoustics, Speech, and Language Processing*, 16(3):617–628.

J. Morris and E. Fosler-Lussier. 2009. Crandem: Conditional random fields for word recognition. Interspeech.

F. Sha and F. Pereira. 2003. Shallow parsing with conditional random fields. NAACL.

Xu Wang, Peng Xuan, and Wang Bingxi. 2004. A gmm-based telephone channel classification for mandarin speech recognition. ICSP.

S. Young, G. Evermann, T. Hain, D. Kershaw, G. Moore, J. Odell, D. Ollason, D. Povey, V. Valtchev, and P. Woodland. 2002. *The HTK Book*. Cambridge University Press.

G. Zweig and P. Nguyen. 2009. A segmental crf approach to large vocabulary continuous speech recognition. ASRU.

Constraint-Driven Rank-Based Learning for Information Extraction

Sameer Singh **Limin Yao** **Sebastian Riedel** **Andrew McCallum**
Dept. of Computer Science
University of Massachusetts
Amherst MA 01003
{sameer,lmyao,riedel,mccallum}@cs.umass.edu

Abstract

Most learning algorithms for undirected graphical models require complete inference over at least one instance before parameter updates can be made. SampleRank is a rank-based learning framework that alleviates this problem by updating the parameters during inference. Most semi-supervised learning algorithms also perform full inference on at least one instance before each parameter update. We extend SampleRank to semi-supervised learning in order to circumvent this computational bottleneck. Different approaches to incorporate unlabeled data and prior knowledge into this framework are explored. When evaluated on a standard information extraction dataset, our method significantly outperforms the supervised method, and matches results of a competing state-of-the-art semi-supervised learning approach.

1 Introduction

Most supervised learning algorithms for undirected graphical models require full inference over the dataset (e.g., gradient descent), small subsets of the dataset (e.g., stochastic gradient descent), or at least a single instance (e.g., perceptron, Collins (2002)) before parameter updates are made. Often this is the main computational bottleneck during training.

SampleRank (Wick et al., 2009) is a rank-based learning framework that alleviates this problem by performing parameter updates *within* inference. Every pair of samples generated during inference is ranked according to the model and the ground truth, and the parameters are updated when the rankings disagree. SampleRank has enabled efficient learning for massive information extraction tasks (Culotta et al., 2007; Singh et al., 2009).

The problem of requiring a complete inference iteration before parameters are updated also exists in the semi-supervised learning scenario. Here the situation is often considerably worse since inference has to be applied to potentially very large unlabeled datasets. Most semi-supervised learning algorithms rely on marginals (GE, Mann and McCallum, 2008) or MAP assignments (CODL, Chang et al., 2007). Calculating these is computationally inexpensive for many simple tasks (such as classification and regression). However, marginal and MAP inference tends to be expensive for complex structured prediction models (such as the joint information extraction models of Singh et al. (2009)), making semi-supervised learning intractable.

In this work we employ a fast rank-based learning algorithm for semi-supervised learning to circumvent the inference bottleneck. The ranking function is extended to capture both the preference expressed by the labeled data, and the preference of the domain expert when the labels are not available. This allows us to perform SampleRank as is, without sacrificing its scalability, which is crucial for future large scale applications of semi-supervised learning.

We applied our method to a standard information extraction dataset used for semi-supervised learning. Empirically we demonstrate improvements over the supervised model, and closely match the results of a competing state-of-the-art semi-supervised learner.

2 Background

Conditional random fields (Lafferty et al., 2001) are undirected graphical models represented as factor

Human Language Technologies: The 2010 Annual Conference of the North American Chapter of the ACL, pages 729–732,
Los Angeles, California, June 2010.

graphs. A factor graph $G = \{\Psi_i\}$ defines a probability distribution over assignments $\mathbf{y}$ to a set of output variables, conditioned on an observation $\mathbf{x}$. A factor Ψ_i computes the inner product between the vector of sufficient statistics $\mathbf{f}(\mathbf{x}_i, \mathbf{y}_i)$ and parameters Θ. Let $Z(\mathbf{x})$ be the data-dependent partition function used for normalization. The probability distribution defined by the graph is:

$$p(\mathbf{y}|\mathbf{x}, \Theta) = \frac{1}{Z(\mathbf{x})} \prod_{\Psi_i \in G} e^{\Theta \cdot \mathbf{f}(\mathbf{x}_i, \mathbf{y}_i)}$$

2.1 Rank-Based Learning

SampleRank (Wick et al., 2009) is a rank-based learning framework for that performs parameter updates *within* MCMC inference. Every pair of consecutive samples in the MCMC chain is ranked according to the model and the ground truth, and the parameters are updated when the rankings disagree. This allows the learner to acquire more supervision per sample, and has led to efficient training of models for which inference is very expensive (Singh et al., 2009).

SampleRank considers two ranking functions: (1) the unnormalized conditional probability (model ranking), and (2) a *truth function* $\mathcal{F}(\mathbf{y})$ (objective ranking) which is defined as $-\mathcal{L}(\mathbf{y}, \mathbf{y}_L)$, the negative loss between the possible assignment $\mathbf{y}$ and the true assignment $\mathbf{y}_L$. The truth function can take different forms, such as tokenwise accuracy or F1-measure with respect to some labeled data.

In order to learn the parameters for which model rankings are consistent with objective rankings, SampleRank performs the following update for each consecutive pair of samples $\mathbf{y}^a$ and $\mathbf{y}^b$ of the MCMC chain. Let α be the learning rate, and $\Delta = \mathbf{f}(\mathbf{x}_i, \mathbf{y}_i^a) - \mathbf{f}(\mathbf{x}_i, \mathbf{y}_i^b)$, then Θ is updated as follows:

$$\Theta \xleftarrow{+} \begin{cases} \alpha\Delta & \text{if } \frac{p(\mathbf{y}^a|\mathbf{x})}{p(\mathbf{y}^b|\mathbf{x})} < 1 \wedge \mathcal{F}(\mathbf{y}^a) > \mathcal{F}(\mathbf{y}^b) \\ -\alpha\Delta & \text{if } \frac{p(\mathbf{y}^a|\mathbf{x})}{p(\mathbf{y}^b|\mathbf{x})} > 1 \wedge \mathcal{F}(\mathbf{y}^a) < \mathcal{F}(\mathbf{y}^b) \\ 0 & \text{otherwise.} \end{cases}$$

This update is usually fast: in order to calculate the required model ratio, only factors that touch changed variables have to be taken into account.

SampleRank has been incorporated into the FACTORIE toolkit for probabilistic programming with imperatively-defined factor graphs (McCallum et al., 2009).

3 Semi-Supervised Rank-Based Learning

To apply SampleRank to the semi-supervised setting, we need to specify the truth function $\mathcal{F}$ over both labeled and unlabeled data. For labeled data $\mathcal{Y}_L$, we can use the true labels. These are not available for unlabeled data $\mathcal{Y}_U$, and we present alternative ways of defining a truth function $\mathcal{F}_U : \mathcal{Y}_U \rightarrow \Re$ for this case.

3.1 Self-Training

Self-training, which uses predictions as truth, fits directly into our SampleRank framework. After performing SampleRank on training data (using $\mathcal{F}_L$), MAP inference is performed on the unlabeled data. The prediction $\hat{\mathbf{y}}_U$ is used as the ground truth for the unlabeled data. Thus the self-training objective function $\mathcal{F}_s$ over the unlabeled data can be defined as $\mathcal{F}_s(\mathbf{y}) = -\mathcal{L}(\mathbf{y}, \hat{\mathbf{y}}_U)$.

3.2 Encoding Constraints

Constraint-driven semi-supervised learning uses constraints to incorporate external domain knowledge when labels are missing (Chang et al., 2007; Mann and McCallum, 2008; Bellare et al., 2009). Constraints prefer certain label configurations over others. For example, one constraint may be that occurrences of the word "California" are preferred to have the label "location".

We can encode constraints directly into the objective function $\mathcal{F}_U$. Let a constraint i be specified as $\langle p_i, c_i \rangle$, where $c_i(\mathbf{y})$ denotes whether assignment $\mathbf{y}$ satisfies the constraint i $(+1)$, violates it (-1), or the constraint does not apply (0), and p_i is the constraint strength. Then the objective function is:

$$\mathcal{F}_c(\mathbf{y}) = \sum_i p_i c_i(\mathbf{y})$$

3.3 Incorporating Model Predictions

When the objective function $\mathcal{F}_c$ is used, every prediction on unlabeled data is ranked only according to the constraints, and thus the model is trained to satisfy all the constraints. This is a problem when the constraints prefer a wrong solution while the model favors the correct solution, resulting in SampleRank updating the model away from the true solution. To avoid this, the ranking function needs to balance preferences of the constraints and the current model.

One option is to incorporate the self-training objective function $\mathcal{F}_s$. A new objective function that combines self-training with constraints can be defined as:

$$\begin{aligned}\mathcal{F}_{sc}(\mathbf{y}) &= \mathcal{F}_s(\mathbf{y}) + \lambda_s \mathcal{F}_c(\mathbf{y}) \\ &= -\mathcal{L}(\mathbf{y}, \hat{\mathbf{y}}_U) + \lambda_s \sum_i p_i c_i(\mathbf{y})\end{aligned}$$

This objective function has at least two limitations. First, self-training involves a complete inference step to obtain $\hat{\mathbf{y}}_U$. Second, the model might have low confidence in its prediction (this is the case when the underlying marginals are almost uniform), but the self-training objective des not take this into account. Hence, we also propose an objective function that incorporates the model score directly, i.e.

$$\begin{aligned}\mathcal{F}_{mc}(\mathbf{y}) &= \log p(\mathbf{y}|\mathbf{x}, \Theta) + \log Z(x) + \lambda_m \mathcal{F}_c(\mathbf{y}) \\ &= \sum_{\Psi_i} \Theta \cdot \mathbf{f}(\mathbf{x}_i, \mathbf{y}_i) + \lambda_m \sum_i p_i c_i(\mathbf{y})\end{aligned}$$

This objective does not require inference, and also takes into account model confidence.

In both objective functions $\mathcal{F}_{sc}$ and $\mathcal{F}_{mc}$, λ controls the relative contribution of the constraint preferences to the objective function. With higher λ, SampleRank will make updates that never try to violate constraints, while with low λ, SampleRank trusts the model more. λ corresponds to constraint satisfaction weights ρ used in (Chang et al., 2007).

4 Related Work

Chang et al. propose constraint-driven learning (CODL, Chang et al., 2007) which can be interpreted as a variation of self-training: Instances are selected for supervision based not only on the model's prediction, but also on their consistency with a set of user-defined constraints. By directly incorporating the model score and the constraints (as in $\mathcal{F}_{mc}$ in Section 3.3) we follow the same approach, but avoid the expensive "Top-K" inference step.

Generalized expectation criterion (GE, Mann and McCallum, 2008) and Alternating Projections (AP, Bellare et al., 2009) encode preferences by specifying constraints on feature expectations, which require expensive inference. Although AP can use online training, it still involves full inference over each instance. Furthermore, these methods only support constraints that factorize according to the model.

Li (2009) incorporates prior knowledge into conditional random fields as variables. They require full inference during learning, restricting the application to simple models. Furthermore, higher-order constraints are specified using large cliques in the graph, which slow down inference. Our approach directly incorporates these constraints into the ranking function, with no impact on inference time.

5 Experiments

We carried out experiments on the Cora citation dataset. The task is to segment each citation into different fields, such as "author" and "title". We use 300 instances as training data, 100 instances as development data, and 100 instances as test data. Some instances from the training data are selected as labeled instances, and the remaining data (including development) as unlabeled. We use the same token-label constraints as Chang et al. (2007).

We use the objective functions defined in Section 3, specifically self-training (Self:$\mathcal{F}_s$), direct constraints (Cons:$\mathcal{F}_c$), the combination of the two (Self+Cons:$\mathcal{F}_{sc}$), and combination of the model score and the constraints (Model+Cons:$\mathcal{F}_{mc}$). We set $p_i = 1.0$, $\alpha = 1.0$, $\lambda_s = 10$, and $\lambda_m = 0.0001$.

Average token accuracy for 5 runs is reported and compared with CODL[1] in Table 1. We also report supervised results from (Chang et al., 2007) and SampleRank. All of our methods show vast improvement over the supervised method for smaller training sizes, but this difference decreases as the training size increases. When the complete training data is used, additional unlabeled data hurts our performance. This is not observed in CODL since they use more unlabeled data, which may also explain their slightly higher accuracy. Note that Self+Cons performs better than Self or Cons individually.

Model+Cons also performs competitively, and may potentially outperform other methods if a better λ_m is chosen. Note, however, that λ_m is much harder to tune than λ_s since λ_m weighs the contribution of the unnormalized model score, the range

[1]We report *inference without constraints* results from CODL. Their results that incorporated constraints were higher, but we do not implement this alternative due to the difficulty in balancing the model score and constraint weights.

Method	5	10	15	20	25	300
Sup. (CODL)	55.1	64.6	68.7	70.1	72.7	86.1
SampleRank	66.5	74.6	75.6	77.6	79.5	**90.7**
CODL	71	76.7	79.4	79.4	82	88.2
Self	67.6	75.1	75.8	78.6	80.4	88
Cons	67.2	75.3	**77.5**	78.6	79.4	88.3
Self+Cons	**71.3**	**77**	**77.5**	**79.5**	**81.1**	87.4
Model+Cons	69.8	75.4	75.7	79.3	79.3	90.6

Table 1: **Tokenwise Accuracy:** for different methods as we vary the size of the labeled data

of which depends on many different factors such as properties of the data, the learning rate, number of samples, proposal function, etc. For self+cons (λ_s), the ranges of the predictions and constraint penalties are fixed and known, making the task simpler.

Self training takes 90 minutes to run on average, while Self+Cons and Model+Cons need 100 minutes. Since the Cons method skips the inference step over unlabeled data, it takes only 30 minutes to run. As the size of the model and unlabeled data set grows, this saving will become more significant. Running time of CODL was not reported.

6 Conclusion

This work extends the rank-based learning framework to semi-supervised learning. By integrating the two paradigms, we retain the computational efficiency provided by parameter updates *within inference*, while utilizing unlabeled data and prior knowledge. We demonstrate accuracy improvements on a real-word information extraction dataset.

We believe that the method will be of greater benefit to learning in complex factor graphs such as joint models over multiple extraction tasks. In future work we will investigate our approach in such settings. Additionally, various sensitivity, convergence, and robustness properties of the method need to be analyzed.

Acknowledgments

This work was supported in part by the Center for Intelligent Information Retrieval, in part by SRI International subcontract #27-001338 and ARFL prime contract #FA8750-09-C-0181, and in part by The Central Intelligence Agency, the National Security Agency and National Science Foundation under NSF grant #IIS-0326249. Any opinions, findings and conclusions or recommendations expressed in this material are the authors' and do not necessarily reflect those of the sponsor.

References

Kedar Bellare, Gregory Druck, and Andrew McCallum. Alternating projections for learning with expectation constraints. In *UAI*, 2009.

Mingwei Chang, Lev Ratinov, and Dan Roth. Guiding semi-supervision with constraint-driven learning. In *ACL*, 2007.

Michael Collins. Discriminative training methods for hidden markov models: Theory and experiments with perceptron algorithm. In *ACL*, 2002.

Aron Culotta, Michael Wick, and Andrew McCallum. First-order probabilistic models for coreference resolution. In *NAACL/HLT*, 2007.

John Lafferty, Andrew McCallum, and Fernando Pereira. Conditional random fields: probabilistic models for segmenting and labeling sequence data. In *ICML*, 2001.

Xiao Li. On the use of virtual evidence in conditional random fields. In *EMNLP*, 2009.

Gideon S. Mann and Andrew McCallum. Generalized expectation criteria for semi-supervised learning of conditional random fields. In *ACL*, 2008.

Andrew McCallum, Karl Schultz, and Sameer Singh. FACTORIE: probabilistic programming via imperatively defined factor graphs. In *NIPS*, 2009.

Sameer Singh, Karl Schultz, and Andrew McCallum. Bi-directional joint inference for entity resolution and segmentation using imperatively-defined factor graphs. In *ECML/PKDD*, 2009.

Michael Wick, Khashayar Rohanimanesh, Aron Culotta, and Andrew McCallum. SampleRank: Learning preferences from atomic gradients. In *NIPS Workshop on Advances in Ranking*, 2009.

Softmax-Margin CRFs: Training Log-Linear Models with Cost Functions

Kevin Gimpel   Noah A. Smith
School of Computer Science
Carnegie Mellon University
Pittsburgh, PA 15213, USA
{kgimpel,nasmith}@cs.cmu.edu

Abstract

We describe a method of incorporating task-specific cost functions into standard conditional log-likelihood (CLL) training of linear structured prediction models. Recently introduced in the speech recognition community, we describe the method generally for structured models, highlight connections to CLL and max-margin learning for structured prediction (Taskar et al., 2003), and show that the method optimizes a bound on risk. The approach is simple, efficient, and easy to implement, requiring very little change to an existing CLL implementation. We present experimental results comparing with several commonly-used methods for training structured predictors for named-entity recognition.

1 Introduction

Conditional random fields (CRFs; Lafferty et al, 2001) and other conditional log-linear models (Berger et al., 1996) achieve strong performance for many NLP problems, but the conditional log-likelihood (CLL) criterion optimized when training these models cannot take a task-specific cost function into account.

In this paper, we describe a simple approach for training conditional log-linear models with cost functions. We show how the method relates to other methods and how it provides a bound on risk. We apply the method to train a discriminative model for named-entity recognition, showing a statistically significant improvement over CLL.

2 Structured Log-Linear Models

Let $\mathcal{X}$ denote a structured input space and, for a particular $x \in \mathcal{X}$, let $\mathcal{Y}(x)$ denote a structured output space for x. The size of $\mathcal{Y}(x)$ is often exponential in x, which differentiates structured prediction from multiclass classification. For named-entity recognition, for example, x might be a sentence and $\mathcal{Y}(x)$ the set of all possible named-entity labelings for the sentence. Given an $x \in \mathcal{X}$ and a $y \in \mathcal{Y}(x)$, we use a conditional log-linear model for $p_{\boldsymbol{\theta}}(y|x)$:

$$p_{\boldsymbol{\theta}}(y|x) = \frac{\exp\{\boldsymbol{\theta}^\top \boldsymbol{f}(x,y)\}}{\sum_{y' \in \mathcal{Y}(x)} \exp\{\boldsymbol{\theta}^\top \boldsymbol{f}(x,y')\}} \quad (1)$$

where $\boldsymbol{f}(x,y)$ is a feature vector representation of x and y and $\boldsymbol{\theta}$ is a parameter vector containing one component for each feature.

2.1 Training Criteria

Many criteria exist for training the weights $\boldsymbol{\theta}$. We next review three choices in detail. For the following, we assume a training set consisting of n examples $\{\langle x^{(i)}, y^{(i)} \rangle\}_{i=1}^{n}$. Some criteria will make use of a task-specific cost function that measures the extent to which a structure y differs from the true structure $y^{(i)}$, denoted by $\mathrm{cost}(y^{(i)}, y)$.

2.1.1 Conditional Log-Likelihood

The learning problem for maximizing conditional log-likelihood is shown in Eq. 3 in Fig. 1 (we transform it into a minimization problem for easier comparison). This criterion is commonly used when a probabilistic interpretation of the model is desired.

2.1.2 Max-Margin

An alternative approach to training structured linear classifiers is based on maximum-margin Markov networks (Taskar et al., 2003). The basic idea is to choose weights such that the linear score of each $\langle x^{(i)}, y^{(i)} \rangle$ is better than $\langle x^{(i)}, y \rangle$ for all alternatives $y \in \mathcal{Y}(x^{(i)}) \setminus \{y^{(i)}\}$, with a larger margin for those y with higher cost. The "margin rescaling" form of this training criterion is shown in Eq. 4. Note that the cost function is incorporated into the criterion.

2.1.3 Risk

Risk is defined as the expected value of the cost with respect to the conditional distribution $p_{\boldsymbol{\theta}}(y|x)$;

Human Language Technologies: The 2010 Annual Conference of the North American Chapter of the ACL, pages 733–736,
Los Angeles, California, June 2010.

on training data:

$$\sum_{i=1}^{n} \sum_{y \in \mathcal{Y}(x^{(i)})} p_{\boldsymbol{\theta}}(y|x^{(i)}) \text{cost}(y^{(i)}, y) \quad (2)$$

With a log-linear model, learning then requires solving the problem shown in Eq. 5. Unlike the previous two criteria, risk is typically non-convex.

Risk minimization first appeared in the speech recognition community (Kaiser et al., 2000; Povey and Woodland, 2002). In NLP, Smith and Eisner (2006) minimized risk using k-best lists to define the distribution over output structures. Li and Eisner (2009) introduced a novel semiring for minimizing risk using dynamic programming; Xiong et al. (2009) minimized risk in a CRF.

2.1.4 Other Criteria

Many other criteria have been proposed to attempt to tailor training conditions to match task-specific evaluation metrics. These include the average per-label marginal likelihood for sequence labeling (Kakade et al., 2002), minimum error-rate training for machine translation (Och, 2003), F_1 for logistic regression classifiers (Jansche, 2005), and a wide range of possible metrics for sequence labeling and segmentation tasks (Suzuki et al., 2006).

3 Softmax-Margin

The softmax-margin objective is shown as Eq. 6 and is a generalization of that used by Povey et al. (2008) and similar to that used by Sha and Saul (2006). The simple intuition is the same as the intuition in max-margin learning: high-cost outputs for $x^{(i)}$ should be penalized more heavily. Another view says that we replace the probabilistic score inside the $\exp$ function of CLL with the "cost-augmented" score from max-margin. A third view says that we replace the "hard" maximum of max-margin with the "softmax" ($\log \sum \exp$) from CLL; hence we use the name "softmax-margin." Like CLL and max-margin, the objective is convex; a proof is provided in Gimpel and Smith (2010).

3.1 Relation to Other Objectives

We next show how the softmax-margin criterion (Eq. 6) bounds the risk criterion (Eq. 5). We first define some additional notation:

$$\mathbb{E}_{(i)}[F] = \sum_{y \in \mathcal{Y}(x^{(i)})} p_{\boldsymbol{\theta}}(y \mid x^{(i)}) F(y)$$

for some function $F : \mathcal{Y}(x^{(i)}) \rightarrow \mathbb{R}$. First note that the softmax-margin objective (Eq. 6) is equal to:

$$\text{(Eq. 3)} + \sum_{i=1}^{n} \log \mathbb{E}_{(i)}[\exp \text{cost}(y^{(i)}, \cdot)] \quad (7)$$

The first term must be nonnegative. Taking each part of the second term, and using Jensen's inequality,

$$\begin{aligned} \log \mathbb{E}_{(i)}[e^{\text{cost}(y^{(i)},\cdot)}] &\geq \mathbb{E}_{(i)}[\log e^{\text{cost}(y^{(i)},\cdot)}] \\ &= \mathbb{E}_{(i)}[\text{cost}(y^{(i)}, \cdot)] \end{aligned}$$

which is exactly Eq. 5. Softmax-margin is also an upper bound on the CLL criterion because, assuming cost is nonnegative, $\log \mathbb{E}[\exp \text{cost}] \geq 0$. Furthermore, softmax-margin is a differentiable upper bound on max-margin, because the softmax function is a differentiable upper bound on the max function.

We note that it may also be interesting to consider minimizing the function $\sum_{i=1}^{n} \log \mathbb{E}_{(i)}[\exp \text{cost}(y^{(i)}, \cdot)]$, since it is an upper bound on risk but requires less computation for computing the gradient.[1] We call this objective the **Jensen risk bound** and include it in our experimental comparison below.

3.2 Implementation

Most methods for training structured models with cost functions require the cost function to decompose across the pieces of the structure in the same way as the features, such as the standard methods for maximizing margin and minimizing risk (Taskar et al., 2003; Li and Eisner, 2009). If the same conditions hold, softmax-margin training can be implemented atop standard CRF training simply by adding additional "features" to encode the local cost components, *only* when computing the partition function during training.[2] The weights of these "cost features" are not learned.

4 Experiments

We consider the problem of named-entity recognition (NER) and use the English data from the CoNLL 2003 shared task (Tjong Kim Sang and De Meulder, 2003). The data consist of news articles

[1] Space does not permit a full discussion; see Gimpel and Smith (2010) for details.

[2] Since $\text{cost}(y^{(i)}, y^{(i)}) = 0$ by definition, these "features" will never fire for the numerator and can be ignored.

$$\text{CLL:} \quad \min_{\boldsymbol{\theta}} \sum_{i=1}^{n} -\boldsymbol{\theta}^\top \boldsymbol{f}(x^{(i)}, y^{(i)}) + \log \sum_{y \in \mathcal{Y}(x^{(i)})} \exp\{\boldsymbol{\theta}^\top \boldsymbol{f}(x^{(i)}, y)\} \tag{3}$$

$$\text{Max-Margin:} \quad \min_{\boldsymbol{\theta}} \sum_{i=1}^{n} -\boldsymbol{\theta}^\top \boldsymbol{f}(x^{(i)}, y^{(i)}) + \max_{y \in \mathcal{Y}(x^{(i)})} \left(\boldsymbol{\theta}^\top \boldsymbol{f}(x^{(i)}, y) + \text{cost}(y^{(i)}, y)\right) \tag{4}$$

$$\text{Risk:} \quad \min_{\boldsymbol{\theta}} \sum_{i=1}^{n} \sum_{y \in \mathcal{Y}(x^{(i)})} \text{cost}(y^{(i)}, y) \frac{\exp\{\boldsymbol{\theta}^\top \boldsymbol{f}(x^{(i)}, y)\}}{\sum_{y' \in \mathcal{Y}(x^{(i)})} \exp\{\boldsymbol{\theta}^\top \boldsymbol{f}(x^{(i)}, y')\}} \tag{5}$$

$$\text{Softmax-Margin:} \quad \min_{\boldsymbol{\theta}} \sum_{i=1}^{n} -\boldsymbol{\theta}^\top \boldsymbol{f}(x^{(i)}, y^{(i)}) + \log \sum_{y \in \mathcal{Y}(x^{(i)})} \exp\{\boldsymbol{\theta}^\top \boldsymbol{f}(x^{(i)}, y) + \text{cost}(y^{(i)}, y)\} \tag{6}$$

Figure 1: Objective functions for training linear models. Regularization terms (e.g., $C \sum_{j=1}^{d} \theta_j^2$) are not shown here.

annotated with four entity types: person, location, organization, and miscellaneous. Our experiments focus on comparing training objectives for structured sequential models for this task. For all objectives, we use the same standard set of feature templates, following Kazama and Torisawa (2007) with additional token shape like those in Collins (2002b) and simple gazetteer features. A feature was included if it occurred at least once in training data (total 1,312,255 features).

The task is evaluated using the F_1 score, which is the harmonic mean of precision and recall (computed at the level of entire entities). Since this metric is computed from corpus-level precision and recall, it is not easily decomposable into features used in standard chain CRFs. For simplicity, we only consider Hamming cost in this paper; experiments with other cost functions more targeted to NER are presented in Gimpel and Smith (2010).

4.1 Baselines

We compared softmax-margin to several baselines: the structured perceptron (Collins, 2002a), 1-best MIRA with cost-augmented inference (Crammer et al., 2006), CLL, max-margin, risk, and our Jensen risk bound (JRB) introduced above.

We used L_2 regularization, experimenting with several coefficients for each method. For CLL, softmax-margin, max-margin, and MIRA, we used regularization coefficients $C \in \{0.01, 0.1, 1\}$. Risk has not always been used with regularization, as regularization does not have as clear a probabilistic interpretation with risk as it does with CLL; so, for risk and JRB we only used $C \in \{0.0, 0.01\}$. In addition, since these two objectives are non-convex, we initialized with the output of the best-performing CLL model on dev data (which was the CLL model with $C = 0.01$).[3] All methods except CLL and the perceptron make use of a cost function, for which we used Hamming cost. We experimented with different fixed multipliers m for the cost function, for $m \in \{1, 5, 10, 20\}$.

The hyperparameters C and m were tuned on the development data and the best-performing combination was used to label the test data. We also tuned the decision to average parameters across all training iterations; this has generally been found to help the perceptron and MIRA, but in our experiments had mixed results for the other methods.

We ran 100 iterations through the training data for each method. For CLL, softmax-margin, risk, and JRB, we used stochastic gradient ascent with a fixed step size of 0.01. For max-margin, we used stochastic subgradient ascent (Ratliff et al., 2006) also with a fixed step size of 0.01.[4] For the perceptron and MIRA, we used their built-in step size formulas.

4.2 Results

Table 1 shows our results. On test data, softmax-margin is statistically indistinguishable from MIRA, risk, and JRB, but performs significantly better than CLL, max-margin, and the perceptron ($p < 0.03$, paired bootstrap with 10,000 samples; Koehn,

[3] When using initialization of all ones for risk and JRB, results were several points below the results here, and with all zeroes, learning failed, resulting in 0.0 F-measure on dev data. Thus, risk and JRB appear sensitive to model initialization.

[4] In preliminary experiments, we tried other fixed and decreasing step sizes for (sub)gradient ascent and found that a fixed step of 0.01 consistently performed well across training objectives, so we used it for all settings for simplicity.

Method	Dev.	Test	(C, m, avg.?)
Perceptron	90.48	83.98	(Y)
MIRA	91.13	85.72	(0.01, 20, Y)
CLL	90.79	85.46	(0.01, N)
Max-Margin	91.17	85.28	(0.01, 1, Y)
Risk	91.14	85.59	(0.01, 10, N)
JRB	91.05	85.65	(0.01, 1, N)
Softmax-Margin	91.30	85.84	(0.01, 5, N)

Table 1: Results on development and test sets, along with hyperparameter values chosen using development set.

2004). It may be surprising that an improvement of 0.38 in F_1 could be significant, but this indicates that the improvements are not limited to certain categories of phenomena in a small number of sentences but rather appear throughout the majority of the test set. The Jensen risk bound performs comparably to risk, and takes roughly half as long to train.

5 Discussion

The softmax-margin approach offers (1) a convex objective, (2) the ability to incorporate task-specific cost functions, and (3) a probabilistic interpretation (which supports, e.g., hidden-variable learning and computation of posteriors). In contrast, max-margin training and MIRA do not provide (3); risk and JRB do not provide (1); and CLL does not support (2). Furthermore, softmax-margin training improves over standard CLL training of CRFs, is straightforward to implement, and requires the same amount of computation as CLL.

We have also presented the Jensen risk bound, which is easier to implement and faster to train than risk, yet gives comparable performance. The primary limitation of all these approaches, including softmax-margin, is that they only support cost functions that factor in the same way as the features of the model. Future work might exploit approximate inference for more expressive cost functions.

Acknowledgments

We thank the reviewers, John Lafferty, and André Martins for helpful comments and feedback on this work. This research was supported by NSF grant IIS-0844507.

References

A. Berger, V. J. Della Pietra, and S. A. Della Pietra. 1996. A maximum entropy approach to natural language processing. *Computational Linguistics*, 22(1):39–71.

M. Collins. 2002a. Discriminative training methods for hidden Markov models: Theory and experiments with perceptron algorithms. In *Proc. of EMNLP*.

M. Collins. 2002b. Ranking algorithms for named-entity extraction: Boosting and the voted perceptron. In *Proc. of ACL*.

K. Crammer, O. Dekel, J. Keshet, S. Shalev-Shwartz, and Y. Singer. 2006. Online passive-aggressive algorithms. *Journal of Machine Learning Research*, 7:551–585.

K. Gimpel and N. A. Smith. 2010. Softmax-margin training for structured log-linear models. Technical report, Carnegie Mellon University.

M. Jansche. 2005. Maximum expected F-measure training of logistic regression models. In *Proc. of HLT-EMNLP*.

J. Kaiser, B. Horvat, and Z. Kacic. 2000. A novel loss function for the overall risk criterion based discriminative training of HMM models. In *Proc. of ICSLP*.

S. Kakade, Y. W. Teh, and S. Roweis. 2002. An alternate objective function for Markovian fields. In *Proc. of ICML*.

J. Kazama and K. Torisawa. 2007. A new perceptron algorithm for sequence labeling with non-local features. In *Proc. of EMNLP-CoNLL*.

P. Koehn. 2004. Statistical significance tests for machine translation evaluation. In *Proc. of EMNLP*.

J. Lafferty, A. McCallum, and F. Pereira. 2001. Conditional random fields: Probabilistic models for segmenting and labeling sequence data. In *Proc. of ICML*.

Z. Li and J. Eisner. 2009. First- and second-order expectation semirings with applications to minimum-risk training on translation forests. In *Proc. of EMNLP*.

F. J. Och. 2003. Minimum error rate training for statistical machine translation. In *Proc. of ACL*.

D. Povey and P. C. Woodland. 2002. Minimum phone error and I-smoothing for improved discrimative training. In *Proc. of ICASSP*.

D. Povey, D. Kanevsky, B. Kingsbury, B. Ramabhadran, G. Saon, and K. Visweswariah. 2008. Boosted MMI for model and feature space discriminative training. In *Proc. of ICASSP*.

N. Ratliff, J. A. Bagnell, and M. Zinkevich. 2006. Subgradient methods for maximum margin structured learning. In *ICML Workshop on Learning in Structured Output Spaces*.

F. Sha and L. K. Saul. 2006. Large margin hidden Markov models for automatic speech recognition. In *Proc. of NIPS*.

D. A. Smith and J. Eisner. 2006. Minimum risk annealing for training log-linear models. In *Proc. of COLING-ACL*.

J. Suzuki, E. McDermott, and H. Isozaki. 2006. Training conditional random fields with multivariate evaluation measures. In *Proc. of COLING-ACL*.

B. Taskar, C. Guestrin, and D. Koller. 2003. Max-margin Markov networks. In *Advances in NIPS 16*.

E. F. Tjong Kim Sang and F. De Meulder. 2003. Introduction to the CoNLL-2003 shared task: Language-independent named entity recognition. In *Proc. of CoNLL*.

Y. Xiong, J. Zhu, H. Huang, and H. Xu. 2009. Minimum tag error for discriminative training of conditional random fields. *Information Sciences*, 179(1-2):169–179.

Bitext-Based Resolution of German Subject-Object Ambiguities

Florian Schwarck **Alexander Fraser** **Hinrich Schütze**
Institute for Natural Language Processing
University of Stuttgart
{koehlefn,fraser}@ims.uni-stuttgart.de

Abstract

We present a method for disambiguating syntactic subjects from syntactic objects (a frequent ambiguity) in German sentences taken from an English-German bitext. We exploit the fact that subject and object are usually easily determined in English. We show that a simple method disambiguates some subject-object ambiguities in German, while making few errors. We view this procedure as the first step in automatically acquiring (mostly) correct labeled data. We also evaluate using it to improve a state of the art statistical parser.

1 Introduction

Ambiguity of grammatical role is a problem when parsing a number of natural languages. In German, subject-object ambiguities are frequent. The sentence "Die Maus jagt die Katze" "the – mouse – chases – the – cat" exhibits such an ambiguity. Because word order is freer in German than in English, the sentence has two possible meanings: (i) The cat is chasing the mouse and (ii) the mouse is chasing the cat. We exploit the fact that such ambiguities are much less frequent in languages that possess a less flexible syntax than German. In English, the translation of the sentence "Die Maus jagt die Katze" is not ambiguous. If we have access to this translation, we can use this information to disambiguate the German sentence. The English translation is viewed as a surrogate for both contextual knowledge from the text and for world knowledge.

We present a method for disambiguating the subject and object roles in German sentences. We use an English-German *bitext* and exploit the fact that subject and object roles are rarely ambiguous in English. Using a new gold standard we created we show that our method disambiguates a significant proportion of subject-object ambiguities in German with high precision. We view this procedure as the first step in automatically acquiring (mostly) correct labeled data for training a statistical disambiguator that can be used on German text (even when no translation is available). In addition to measuring algorithm performance directly, we present experiments on improving the disambiguation of BitPar, a state of the art statistical parser.

2 Algorithm

Data and Word Alignment. We use the aligned English and German sentences in Europarl (Koehn, 2005) for our experiments. The corpus contains long and complex sentences. To establish translational correspondence between parallel sentences we use GIZA++ (Och and Ney, 2003). Its input is a tokenized parallel corpus. We lemmatized the text prior to aligning it.

Procedure. Figure 1 shows the architecture of our system. The boxes signify data sets, while the lines are processes applied to the data sets. The paper presents two applications. The first is the creation of a set of disambiguated German sentences (which involves word alignments in the upper right corner, and the use of parsers in the middle of the graphic). We also present a reranking of the N-best parses produced by BitPar (Schmid, 2004), a state of the art statistical parser (bottom of the graphic).

For processing of German we chose FSPar

Human Language Technologies: The 2010 Annual Conference of the North American Chapter of the ACL, pages 737–740,
Los Angeles, California, June 2010. ©2010 Association for Computational Linguistics

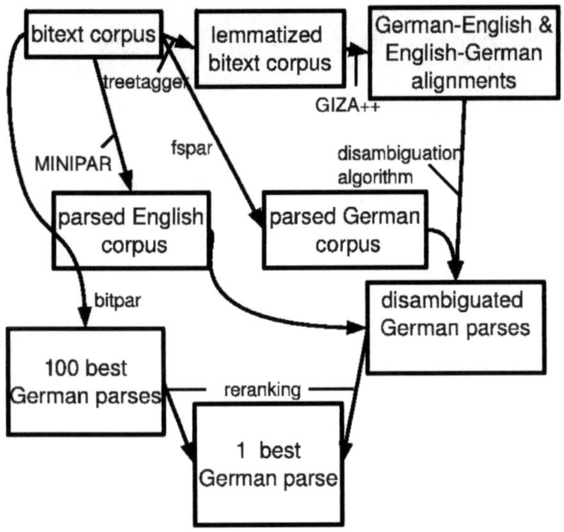

Figure 1: System Architecture

(Schiehlen, 2003), a fast shallow dependency parser. FSPar has extensive lexical knowledge which helps it to find subject-object ambiguities with high accuracy, but it does not try to resolve such ambiguities.

The key to our approach is to project syntactic roles from English text. For English parsing we used MINIPAR (Lin, 1998).

Based on FSPar's analysis, all German sentences with a subject-object ambiguity (about a third) were selected from EuroParl. The parallel English sentences were parsed with MINIPAR.

Words marked as ambiguous by FSPar were then processed using our algorithm. If an ambiguous German word was aligned to an English word that MINIPAR had (unambiguously) assigned the grammatical role of subject or object, then the syntactic role of the German word was defined by this information, see Figure 2.

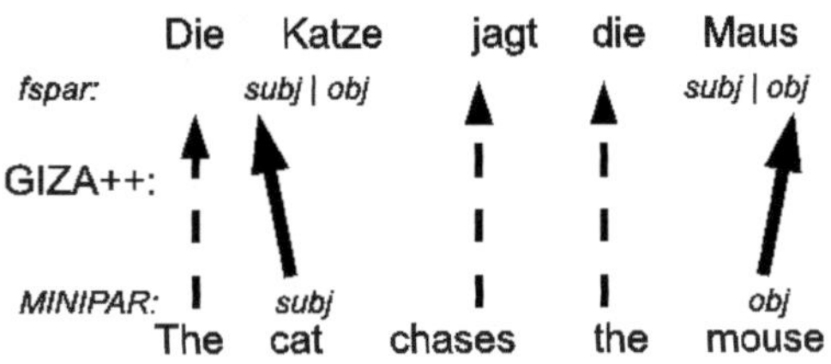

Figure 2: Disambiguation Algorithm

We used standard heuristics for improving word alignment (Och and Ney, 2003; Koehn et al., 2003), but there were many misalignments of ambiguous German words. In order for the procedure to work, we require that the German word to be disambiguated be aligned to the English subject or object. For this reason, we implemented *second guessing* based on a dictionary that lists for every German word the 10 most frequently aligned English words (found using the word alignment of all of Europarl). If an ambiguous German word was either unaligned or not aligned to the English subject or object, it was checked whether a dictionary translation was part of the parallel sentence and marked as subject or object by MINIPAR. If so, this dictionary word was used for disambiguation.

3 Evaluation

Gold Standard. We had access to a small set of gold standard parses (Padó and Lapata, 2009), but decided to create a larger corpus. We found that FSPar had acceptable performance for finding subject-object ambiguities[1]. The syntactic roles of words marked as ambiguous by FSPar were annotated. Four annotators annotated the syntactic roles in 4000 sentences using a graphical user interface (GUI). The GUI showed the ambiguous words in context and gave the annotator four different subject-object labels to choose from for each ambiguous word: *subject*, *object*, *expletive es* and *none*. Because the syntactic expletive "es" (English gloss: 'it') is frequent in German, as in "es scheint zu regnen" 'it appears to be raining,' we created a separate label for expletive "es", which is not treated as a subject.[2] The statistics are shown in table 1.

1000 sentences were annotated by all four annotators. Inter-annotator agreement was sufficient ($\kappa = 0.77$ on average (Carletta, 1996)).

Evaluation Measures. The output of our algorithm labels each word that FSPar classified as ambiguous with one of the three possible labels *subject*,

[1]FSPar has a very high precision in detecting subject-object ambiguities, as can be seen in Table 1 (approximately 0.955, the sum of two left columns divided by sum of all cells). We tried to get an idea of recall using the smaller gold standard. We made conservative assumptions about recall errors which we manually checked on a small sample, details are omitted. Using these assumptions led to an estimate for recall of 0.733, but true recall is likely higher.

[2]German "es" is also frequently used as a non-expletive, where it can take a syntactic role.

	subj	obj	expl_es	none
Annotator1	4152	3210	115	150
Annotator2	4472	3359	92	226
Annotator3	4444	3584	42	155
Annotator4	4027	3595	9	650

Table 1: Annotator decisions on the full gold standard

		DE2EN	Refined	GDFA	Intersection
	P	0.8412	0.8381	0.8353	0.8551
nosg	R	0.4436	0.3856	0.3932	0.3380
	F_1	0.5809	0.5282	0.5347	0.4845
	P	0.7404	0.7307	0.7310	0.7240
sg	R	0.5564	0.4873	0.4946	0.4528
	F_1	0.6353	0.5847	0.5900	0.5571
	P	0.9239	0.9203	0.9192	0.9277
filter-nosg	R	0.3940	0.3397	0.3461	0.2984
	F_1	0.5524	0.4962	0.5028	0.4515
	P	0.8458	0.8358	0.8369	0.8290
filter-sg	R	0.4839	0.4213	0.4279	0.3898
	F_1	0.6156	0.5602	0.5662	0.5302

Table 2: Precision, Recall and F_1 of the algorithm.

object and *no decision*[3]. We use the standard evaluation metrics **Precision** (P, the percentage of subject and object labelings in our hypothesis that are correct), **Recall** (R, the percentage of subject and object labelings in the gold standard that are correctly labeled in the hypothesis), and balanced **F** (F_1).

4 Experiments

Algorithm Performance. Table 2 shows the performance of our algorithm when evaluated against the manual annotation[4]. The lines *nosg*, *sg*, *filter-nosg* and *filter-sg* denote different configurations of the algorithm: Second guessing (section 2) was ("sg") or was not ("nosg") applied and filtering was ("filter") or was not applied. The filter increases precision by only keeping labels of subjects and objects that occur in the default order (e.g., the subject is to the left of the object in the main clause). As an aid to the user, FSPar presents such a determination of default order depending on its classification of clause type[5]. The columns indicate the heuristic postprocessing we applied to GIZA++'s alignment. *DE2EN* is the 1-to-N alignment calculated using German as the source language and English as the target language (i.e., each English word is linked to exactly zero or one German words).

As we see in table 2, with the most strict setup, *filter-nosg*, the algorithm resolves subject-object ambiguities with a precision of more than 92% but the best recall is only 39.4%, obtained using *DE2EN*. Second guessing increases recall but leads to losses in precision. The best precision result without the filter is 85.5%.

	configuration	P	R	F_1
1	top-1 (no change)	0.8088	0.8033	0.8060
2	relabeling *nosg*	0.7998	0.8176	0.8086
3	relabeling *filter-nosg*	0.8229	0.8344	0.8286
4	reranking *nosg*	0.8082	0.8123	0.8102
5	reranking *filter-nosg*	0.8145	0.8143	0.8144

Table 3: Precision, Recall and F_1 of changing BitPar decisions, DE2EN alignment

Improving BitPar's Subject-Object Decisions. For improving BitPar (which always tries to disambiguate subject-object), our baseline is the accuracy of the most probable parse shown in table 3, row 1.

Using the most probable parse from BitPar, we relabel a word "subject" or "object" if our system indicates to do so. With the algorithm alone we are able to improve recall (table 3, row 2). When we add the filter both precision and recall are improved (row 3). This experiment measures the improvement possible if our syntactic role information were directly integrated as a hard constraint into a parser (see section 5).

We now perform a simple reranking experiment, using BitPar's 100-best parses. For each sentence we choose the parse which agrees with as many of the subject/object decisions of the algorithm as possible (once again ignoring words where the algorithm chooses no decision). In case of ties in the number of agreements, we take the most probable parse. The results are in rows 4–5. Reranking increases F_1 by about 0.8%.

5 Related Work

Syntactic projection has been used to bootstrap treebanks in resource poor languages (Yarowsky and

[3]If *expletive es* or *none* was annotated, the system is correct if it does not make a decision.

[4]Because of problems with BitPar caused by preprocessing for FSPar, we use 11,279 sentences of the 13,000 annotated.

[5]Using this determination alone results in P 0.7728 R 0.8206 F 0.7960, very high recall but low precision.

Ngai, 2001; Hwa et al., 2005). In contrast with such work, we are addressing subject-object ambiguity in German. German parsers have no access to the contextual and world knowledge necessary to resolve this ambiguity.

Work on *projecting semantic roles* (Padó and Lapata, 2009; Fung et al., 2007) requires both syntactic parsing and semantic role labeling and is concerned with filling in the complete information in a semantic frame. Our approach is simpler and concerned only with syntactic disambiguation, not semantic projection. We focus only on difficult cases of subject-object ambiguity and although we do not always make a prediction, we obtain levels of precision that projection approaches making no use of knowledge of German syntax cannot achieve.

In *bitext parsing*, Burkett and Klein (2008) and Fraser et al. (2009) used feature functions defined on triples of (parse tree in language 1, parse tree in language 2, word alignment), combined in a log-linear model trained to maximize parse accuracy, requiring translated treebanks. We focus only on subject-object disambiguation in German, and annotated a new gold standard. We work on sentences that a partial parser has determined to be ambiguous. Fossum and Knight (2008) and Huang et al. (2009) improve English prepositional phrase attachment using features from an unparsed Chinese sentence. The latter work integrated the PP-attachment constraint (detected from the Chinese translation) directly into an English shift-reduce parser. As we have shown in the labeling experiment, integrating our subject-object disambiguation into BitPar could result in further increases beyond 100-best reranking.

6 Conclusion

We demonstrated the utility of bitext-based disambiguation of grammatical roles. We automatically created a large corpus of 164,874 disambiguated subject-object decisions with a precision of over 92%. This corpus will be of use in future research on syntactic role preferences and for the training of monolingual subject-object disambiguators. We presented a prototype application of subject-object disambiguation through a simple reranking of the 100-best list output by BitPar, and showed a possible further improvement if integrated in the parser. The new gold standard, which is publicly available, will hopefully be useful for work on both monolingual and bitext-based disambiguation.

Acknowledgments

This work was supported by Deutsche Forschungsgemeinschaft grants SFB 732 and MorphoSynt.

References

David Burkett and Dan Klein. 2008. Two languages are better than one (for syntactic parsing). In *EMNLP*.

Jean Carletta. 1996. Assessing agreement on classification tasks: The kappa statistic. *Computational Linguistics*, 22.

Victoria Fossum and Kevin Knight. 2008. Using bilingual Chinese-English word alignments to resolve PP-attachment ambiguity in English. In *AMTA*.

Alexander Fraser, Renjing Wang, and Hinrich Schütze. 2009. Rich bitext projection features for parse reranking. In *EACL*.

Pascale Fung, Zhaojun Wu, Yongsheng Yang, and Dekai Wu. 2007. Learning bilingual semantic frames: Shallow semantic parsing vs. semantic role projection. In *TMI*.

Liang Huang, Wenbin Jiang, and Qun Liu. 2009. Bilingually-constrained (monolingual) shift-reduce parsing. In *EMNLP*.

Rebecca Hwa, Philip Resnik, Amy Weinberg, Clara Cabezas, and Okan Kolak. 2005. Bootstrapping parsers via syntactic projection across parallel texts. *Nat. Lang. Eng.*, 11(3).

Philipp Koehn, Franz J. Och, and Daniel Marcu. 2003. Statistical phrase-based translation. In *HLT-NAACL*.

Philipp Koehn. 2005. Europarl: a parallel corpus for statistical machine translation. In *MT Summit X*.

Dekang Lin. 1998. Dependency-based evaluation of MINIPAR. In *Workshop on Eval of Parsing Systems*.

Franz J. Och and Hermann Ney. 2003. A systematic comparison of various statistical alignment models. *Computational Linguistics*, 29(1).

Sebastian Padó and Mirella Lapata. 2009. Cross-lingual annotation projection of semantic roles. *Journal of Artificial Intelligence Research*, 36:307–340.

Michael Schiehlen. 2003. A cascaded finite-state parser for German. In *Research Notes (EACL)*.

Helmut Schmid. 2004. Efficient parsing of highly ambiguous context-free grammars with bit vectors. In *COLING*.

David Yarowsky and Grace Ngai. 2001. Inducing multilingual POS taggers and NP bracketers via robust projection across aligned corpora. In *NAACL*.

Music, Language, and Computational Modeling: Lessons from the Key-Finding Problem

David Temperley
Eastman School of Music, University of Rochester
26 Gibbs St.
Rochester, NY 14604
dtemperley@esm.rochester.edu

Abstract

Recent research in computational music research, including my own, has been greatly influenced by methods in computational linguistics. But I believe the influence could also go the other way: Music may offer some interesting lessons for language research, particularly with regard to the modeling of cognition.

In this talk I will focus on an important problem in music cognition: the problem of key identification. I will argue that this problem is in some ways analogous to the problem of syntactic parsing in language. I will present a simple Bayesian model that performs well at the key-finding task. I will then consider some implications of the model for other issues. The model represents moment-to-moment changes in key over time and captures "reanalysis" effects in key perception. The model can be used to estimate the tonal ambiguity of a musical passage, and can also be used to estimate the probability of note patterns (just as a probabilistic grammar can be used to estimate the probability of word strings). An interesting question here concerns expectation: In forming expectations for the next surface element (note or word), do we consider all possible structures (syntactic structures or keys) or just the most probable one? Finally, the model sheds light on the concept of "information flow." It has been suggested that language reflects a tendency towards uniform density of information, in that less probable elements are spread out or elongated; I will suggest that the same may be true in music.

Slides for the talk will be available at my website, <www.theory.esm.rochester.edu/temperley>.

Human Language Technologies: The 2010 Annual Conference of the North American Chapter of the ACL, page 741,
Los Angeles, California, June 2010.

An Efficient Algorithm for Easy-First Non-Directional Dependency Parsing

Yoav Goldberg* and **Michael Elhadad**
Ben Gurion University of the Negev
Department of Computer Science
POB 653 Be'er Sheva, 84105, Israel
{yoavg|elhadad}@cs.bgu.ac.il

Abstract

We present a novel deterministic dependency parsing algorithm that attempts to create the easiest arcs in the dependency structure first in a non-directional manner. Traditional deterministic parsing algorithms are based on a shift-reduce framework: they traverse the sentence from left-to-right and, at each step, perform one of a possible set of actions, until a complete tree is built. A drawback of this approach is that it is extremely local: while decisions can be based on complex structures on the left, they can look only at a few words to the right. In contrast, our algorithm builds a dependency tree by iteratively selecting the best pair of neighbours to connect at each parsing step. This allows incorporation of features from already built structures both to the left and to the right of the attachment point. The parser learns both the attachment preferences and the order in which they should be performed. The result is a deterministic, best-first, $O(nlogn)$ parser, which is significantly more accurate than best-first transition based parsers, and nears the performance of globally optimized parsing models.

1 Introduction

Dependency parsing has been a topic of active research in natural language processing in the last several years. An important part of this research effort are the CoNLL 2006 and 2007 shared tasks (Buchholz and Marsi, 2006; Nivre et al., 2007), which allowed for a comparison of many algorithms and approaches for this task on many languages.

*Supported by the Lynn and William Frankel Center for Computer Sciences, Ben Gurion University

Current dependency parsers can be categorized into three families: local-and-greedy transition-based parsers (*e.g.*, MALTPARSER (Nivre et al., 2006)), globally optimized graph-based parsers (*e.g.*, MSTPARSER (McDonald et al., 2005)), and hybrid systems (*e.g.*, (Sagae and Lavie, 2006b; Nivre and McDonald, 2008)), which combine the output of various parsers into a new and improved parse, and which are orthogonal to our approach.

Transition-based parsers scan the input from left to right, are fast ($O(n)$), and can make use of rich feature sets, which are based on all the previously derived structures. However, all of their decisions are very local, and the strict left-to-right order implies that, while the feature set can use rich structural information from the left of the current attachment point, it is also very restricted in information to the right of the attachment point: traditionally, only the next two or three input tokens are available to the parser. This limited look-ahead window leads to error propagation and worse performance on root and long distant dependencies relative to graph-based parsers (McDonald and Nivre, 2007).

Graph-based parsers, on the other hand, are globally optimized. They perform an exhaustive search over all possible parse trees for a sentence, and find the highest scoring tree. In order to make the search tractable, the feature set needs to be restricted to features over single edges (first-order models) or edges pairs (higher-order models, e.g. (McDonald and Pereira, 2006; Carreras, 2007)). There are several attempts at incorporating arbitrary tree-based features but these involve either solving an ILP problem (Riedel and Clarke, 2006) or using computa-

Human Language Technologies: The 2010 Annual Conference of the North American Chapter of the ACL, pages 742–750,
Los Angeles, California, June 2010.

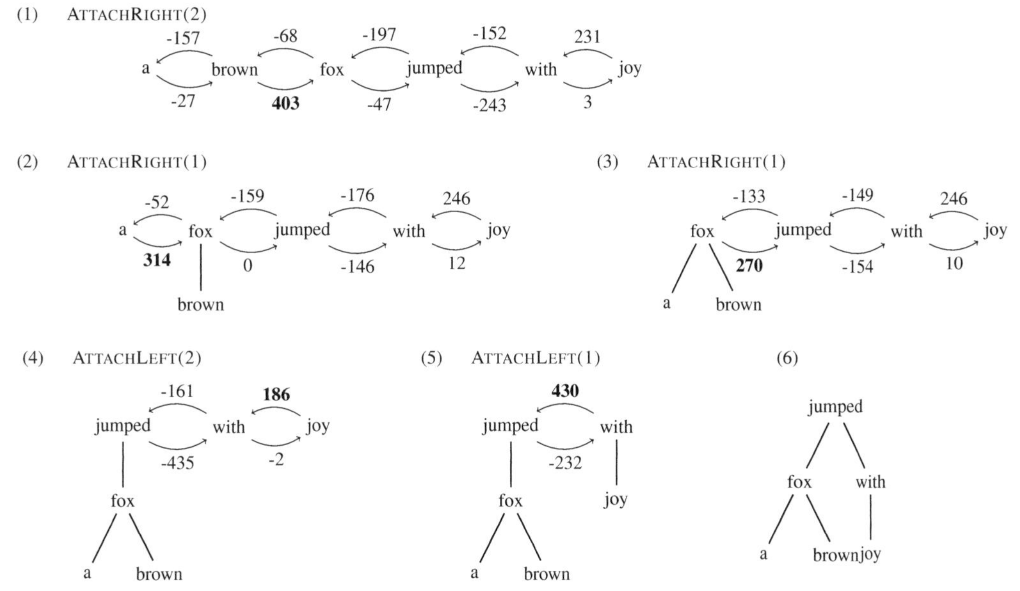

Figure 1: Parsing the sentence "a brown fox jumped with joy". Rounded arcs represent possible actions.

tionally intensive sampling-based methods (Nakagawa, 2007). As a result, these models, while accurate, are slow ($O(n^3)$ for projective, first-order models, higher polynomials for higher-order models, and worse for richer tree-feature models).

We propose a new category of dependency parsing algorithms, inspired by (Shen et al., 2007): nondirectional easy-first parsing. This is a greedy, deterministic parsing approach, which relaxes the left-to-right processing order of transition-based parsing algorithms. By doing so, we allow the explicit incorporation of rich structural features derived from both sides of the attachment point, and implicitly take into account the entire previously derived structure of the whole sentence. This extension allows the incorporation of much richer features than those available to transition- and especially to graph-based parsers, and greatly reduces the locality of transition-based algorithm decisions. On the other hand, it is still a greedy, best-first algorithm leading to an efficient implementation.

We present a concrete $O(nlogn)$ parsing algorithm, which significantly outperforms state-of-the-art transition-based parsers, while closing the gap to graph-based parsers.

2 Easy-first parsing

When humans comprehend a natural language sentence, they arguably do it in an incremental, left-to-right manner. However, when humans consciously annotate a sentence with syntactic structure, they hardly ever work in fixed left-to-right order. Rather, they start by building several isolated constituents by making easy and local attachment decisions and only then combine these constituents into bigger constituents, jumping back-and-forth over the sentence and proceeding from easy to harder phenomena to analyze. When getting to the harder decisions a lot of structure is already in place, and this structure can be used in deciding a correct attachment.

Our parser follows a similar kind of annotation process: starting from easy attachment decisions, and proceeding to harder and harder ones. When making later decisions, the parser has access to the entire structure built in earlier stages. During the training process, the parser learns its own notion of easy and hard, and learns to defer specific kinds of decisions until more structure is available.

3 Parsing algorithm

Our (projective) parsing algorithm builds the parse tree bottom up, using two kinds of actions: **AttachLeft(*i*)** and **AttachRight(*i*)** . These actions are applied to a list of partial structures $p_1, \ldots, p_k$, called $pending$, which is initialized with the n words of the sentence $w_1, \ldots, w_n$. Each action connects the heads of two neighbouring structures, making one of them the parent of the other, and removing the daughter from the list of partial structures. **ATTACHLEFT(*i*)** adds a dependency edge (p_i, p_{i+1}) and removes p_{i+1} from the list. **ATTACHRIGHT(*i*)** adds a dependency edge (p_{i+1}, p_i) and removes p_i from the list. Each action shortens the list of partial structures by 1, and after $n-1$ such actions, the list contains the root of a connected projective tree over the sentence.

Figure 1 shows an example of parsing the sentence "a brown fox jumped with joy". The pseudocode of the algorithm is given in Algorithm 1.

Algorithm 1: Non-directional Parsing

Input: a sentence= $w_1 \dots w_n$
Output: a set of dependency arcs over the sentence ($Arcs$)

1 $Acts = \{$ATTACHLEFT, ATTACHRIGHT$\}$
2 $Arcs \leftarrow \{\}$
3 $pending = p_1 \dots p_n \leftarrow w_1 \dots w_n$
4 **while** $length(pending) > 1$ **do**
5 $best \leftarrow \underset{\substack{act \in Acts \\ 1 \le i \le len(pending)}}{\arg\max} score(act(i))$
6 $(parent, child) \leftarrow$ edgeFor($best$)
7 $Arcs$.add($(parent, child)$)
8 $pending$.remove($child$)
9 **end**
10 **return** *Arcs*

$$\text{edgeFor(act(i))} = \begin{cases} (p_i, p_{i+1}) & \text{ATTACHLEFT}(i) \\ (p_{i+1}, p_i) & \text{ATTACHRIGHT}(i) \end{cases}$$

At each step the algorithm chooses a specific action/location pair using a function $score($**ACTION(*i*)**$)$, which assign scores to action/location pairs based on the partially built structures headed by p_i and p_{i+1}, as well as neighbouring structures. The $score()$ function is learned from data. This scoring function reflects not only the correctness of an attachment, but also *the order* in which attachments should be made. For example, consider the attachments (brown,fox) and (joy,with) in Figure (1.1). While both are correct, the scoring function prefers the (adjective,noun) attachment over the (prep,noun) attachment. Moreover, the attachment (jumped,with), while correct, receives a negative score for the bare preposition "with" (Fig. (1.1) - (1.4)), and a high score once the verb has its subject and the PP "with joy" is built (Fig. (1.5)). Ideally, we would like to score easy and reliable attachments *higher than* harder less likely attachments, thus performing attachments in order of confidence. This strategy allows us both to limit the extent of error propagation, and to make use of richer contextual information in the later, harder attachments. Unfortunately, this kind of ordering information is not directly encoded in the data. We must, therefore, learn how to order the decisions.

We first describe the learning algorithm (Section 4) and a feature representation (Section 5) which enables us to learn an effective scoring function.

4 Learning Algorithm

We use a linear model $score(x) = \vec{w} \cdot \phi(x)$, where $\phi(x)$ is a feature representation and $\vec{w}$ is a weight vector. We write $\phi_{act(i)}$ to denote the feature representation extracted for action act at location i. The model is trained using a variant of the structured perceptron (Collins, 2002), similar to the algorithm of (Shen et al., 2007; Shen and Joshi, 2008). As usual, we use parameter averaging to prevent the perceptron from overfitting.

The training algorithm is initialized with a zero parameter vector $\vec{w}$. The algorithm makes several passes over the data. At each pass, we apply the training procedure given in Algorithm 2 to every sentence in the training set.

At training time, each sentence is parsed using the parsing algorithm and the current $\vec{w}$. Whenever an invalid action is chosen by the parsing algorithm, it is not performed (line 6). Instead, we update the parameter vector $\vec{w}$ by decreasing the weights of the features associated with the *invalid* action, and increasing the weights for the currently highest scoring *valid* action.[1] We then proceed to parse the sentence with the updated values. The process repeats until a valid action is chosen.

Note that each single update does not guarantee that the next chosen action is valid, or even different than the previously selected action. Yet, this is still an aggressive update procedure: we do not leave a sentence until our parameters vector parses it cor-

[1]We considered 3 variants of this scheme: (1) using the highest scoring valid action, (2) using the leftmost valid action, and (3) using a random valid action. The 3 variants achieved nearly identical accuracy, while (1) converged somewhat faster than the other two.

rectly, and we do not proceed from one partial parse to the next until $\vec{w}$ predicts a correct location/action pair. However, as the best ordering, and hence the best attachment point is not known to us, we do not perform a single aggressive update step. Instead, our aggressive update is performed incrementally in a series of smaller steps, each pushing $\vec{w}$ away from invalid attachments and toward valid ones. This way we integrate the search of confident attachments into the learning process.

Algorithm 2: Structured perceptron training for direction-less parser, over one sentence.

Input: sentence,gold arcs,current $\vec{w}$,feature representation ϕ
Output: weight vector $\vec{w}$

1 $Arcs \leftarrow \{\}$
2 $pending \leftarrow sent$
3 **while** $length(pending) > 1$ **do**
4 $\quad allowed \leftarrow \{act(i) | isValid(act(i), Gold, Arcs)\}$
5 $\quad choice \leftarrow \underset{\substack{act \in Acts \\ 1 \leq i \leq len(pending)}}{\arg\max} \vec{w} \cdot \phi_{act(i)}$
6 $\quad$ **if** $choice \in allowed$ **then**
7 $\quad\quad (parent, child) \leftarrow$ edgeFor($choice$)
8 $\quad\quad Arcs$.add($(parent, child)$)
9 $\quad\quad pending$.remove($child$)
10 $\quad$ **else**
11 $\quad\quad good \leftarrow \underset{act(j) \in allowed}{\arg\max} \vec{w} \cdot \phi_{act(j)}$
12 $\quad\quad \vec{w} \leftarrow \vec{w} + \phi_{good} - \phi_{choice}$
13 **end**
14 **return** $\vec{w}$

Function `isValid` (*action,Gold,Arcs*)

1 $(p, c) \leftarrow$ edgeFor($action$)
2 **if** $(\exists c' : (c, c') \in Gold \wedge (c, c') \notin Arcs) \vee (p, c) \notin Gold$ **then**
3 $\quad$ **return** *false*
4 **return** *true*

The function $isValid(act(i), gold, arcs)$ (line 4) is used to decide if the chosen action/location pair is valid. It returns True if two conditions apply: (a) (p_i, p_j) is present in $gold$, (b) all edges $(\Box, p_j)$ in $gold$ are also in $arcs$. In words, the function verifies that the proposed edge is indeed present in the gold parse and that the suggested daughter already found all its own daughters.[2]

5 Feature Representation

The feature representation for an action can take into account the original sentence, as well as the entire parse history: $\phi_{act(i)}$ above is actually $\phi(act(i), sentence, Arcs, pending)$.

We use binary valued features, and each feature is conjoined with the type of action.

When designing the feature representation, we keep in mind that our features should not only direct the parser toward desired actions and away from undesired actions, but also provide the parser with means of choosing between several desired actions. We want the parser to be able to defer some desired actions until more structure is available and a more informed prediction can be made. This desire is reflected in our choice of features: some of our features are designed to signal to the parser the presence of possibly "incomplete" structures, such as an incomplete phrase, a coordinator without conjuncts, and so on.

When considering an action ACTION(i), we limit ourselves to features of partial structures around the attachment point: $p_{i-2}, p_{i-1}, p_i, p_{i+1}, p_{i+2}, p_{i+3}$, that is the two structures which are to be attached by the action (p_i and p_{i+1}), and the two neighbouring structures on each side[3].

While these features encode local context, it is local in terms of syntactic structure, and not purely in terms of sentence surface form. This let us capture some, though not all, long-distance relations.

For a partial structure p, we use w_p to refer to the head word form, t_p to the head word POS tag, and lc_p and rc_p to the POS tags of the left-most and right-most child of p respectively.

All our prepositions (IN) and coordinators (CC) are lexicalized: for them, t_p is in fact $w_p t_p$.

We define *structural*, *unigram*, *bigram* and *pp-attachment* features.

The *structural* features are: the length of the structures (len_p), whether the structure is a word (contains no children: nc_p), and the surface distance between structure heads ($\Delta_{p_i p_j}$). The *unigram* and *bigram* features are adapted from the feature set for left-to-right Arc-Standard dependency parsing de-

[2]This is in line with the Arc-Standard parsing strategy of shift-reduce dependency parsers (Nivre, 2004). We are currently experimenting also with an Arc-Eager variant of the non-directional algorithm.

[3]Our sentences are padded from each side with sentence delimiter tokens.

Structural	
for p in $p_{i-2}, p_{i-1}, p_i, p_{i+1}, p_{i+2}, p_{i+3}$	len_p , nc_p
for p,q in (p_{i-2}, p_{i-1}),(p_{i-1}, p_i),(p_i, p_{i+1}),$(p_{i+1}, pi + 2)$,(p_{i+2}, p_{i+3})	Δ_{qp} , $\Delta_{qp} t_p t_q$
Unigram	
for p in $p_{i-2}, p_{i-1}, p_i, p_{i+1}, p_{i+2}, p_{i+3}$	t_p , w_p , $t_p lc_p$, $t_p rc_p$, $t_p rc_p lc_p$
Bigram	
for p,q in (p_i, p_{i+1}),(p_i, p_{i+2}),(p_{i-1}, p_i),(p_{i-1}, p_{i+2}),(p_{i+1}, p_{i+2})	$t_p t_q$, $w_p w_q$, $t_p w_q$, $w_p t_q$ $t_p t_q lc_p lc_q$, $t_p t_q rc_p lc_q$ $t_p t_q lc_p rc_q$, $t_p t_q rc_p rc_q$
PP-Attachment	
if p_i is a preposition	$w_{p_{i-1}} w_{p_i} rc_{p_i}$, $t_{p_{i-1}} w_{p_i} rcw_{p_i}$
if p_{i+1} is a preposition	$w_{p_{i-1}} w_{p_{i+1}} rc_{p_{i+1}}$, $t_{p_{i-1}} w_{p_{i+1}} rcw_{p_{i+1}}$ $w_{p_i} w_{p_{i+1}} rc_{p_{i+1}}$, $t_{p_i} w_{p_{i+1}} rcw_{p_{i+1}}$
if p_{i+2} is a preposition	$w_{p_{i+1}} w_{p_{i+2}} rc_{p_{i+2}}$, $t_{p_{i+1}} w_{p_{i+2}} rcw_{p_{i+2}}$ $w_{p_i} w_{p_{i+2}} rc_{p_{i+2}}$, $t_{p_i} w_{p_{i+2}} rcw_{p_{i+2}}$

Figure 2: Feature Templates

scribed in (Huang et al., 2009). We extended that feature set to include the structure on both sides of the proposed attachment point.

In the case of unigram features, we added features that specify the POS of a word and its left-most and right-most children. These features provide the non-directional model with means to prefer some attachment points over others based on the types of structures already built. In English, the left- and right-most POS-tags are good indicators of constituency.

The *pp-attachment* features are similar to the bigram features, but fire only when one of the structures is headed by a preposition (IN). These features are more lexicalized than the regular bigram features, and include also the word-form of the right-most child of the PP (rcw_p). This should help the model learn lexicalized attachment preferences such as (hit, with-bat).

Figure 2 enumerate the feature templates we use.

6 Computational Complexity and Efficient Implementation

The parsing algorithm (Algorithm 1) begins with $n+1$ disjoint structures (the words of the sentence + ROOT symbol), and terminates with one connected structure. Each iteration of the main loop connects two structures and removes one of them, and so the loop repeats for exactly n times.

The argmax in line 5 selects the maximal scoring action/location pair. At iteration i, there are $n - i$ locations to choose from, and a naive computation of the argmax is $O(n)$, resulting in an $O(n^2)$ algorithm.

Each performed action changes the partial structures and with it the extracted features and the computed scores. However, these changes are limited to a fixed local context around the attachment point of the action. Thus, we observe that the feature extraction and score calculation can be performed once for each action/location pair in a given sentence, and reused throughout all the iterations. After each iteration we need to update the extracted features and calculated scores for only k locations, where k is a fixed number depending on the window size used in the feature extraction, and usually $k \ll n$.

Using this technique, we perform only $(k + 1)n$ feature extractions and score calculations for each sentence, that is $O(n)$ feature-extraction operations per sentence.

Given the scores for each location, the argmax can then be computed in $O(logn)$ time using a heap, resulting in an $O(nlogn)$ algorithm: n iterations, where the first iteration involves n feature extraction operations and n heap insertions, and each subsequent iteration involves k feature extractions and heap updates.

We note that the dominating factor in polynomial-time discriminative parsers, is by far the feature-extraction and score calculation. It makes sense to compare parser complexity in terms of these operations only.[4] Table 1 compares the complexity of our

[4]Indeed, in our implementation we do not use a heap, and opt instead to find the argmax using a simple $O(n)$ *max* operation. This $O(n^2)$ algorithm is faster in practice than the heap based one, as both are dominated by the $O(n)$ feature extraction, while the cost of the $O(n)$ *max* calculationis negligible compared to the constants involved in heap maintenance.

parser to other dependency parsing frameworks.

Parser	Runtime	Features / Scoring
MALT	$O(n)$	$O(n)$
MST	$O(n^3)$	$O(n^2)$
MST2	$O(n^3)$	$O(n^3)$
BEAM	$O(n * beam)$	$O(n * beam)$
NONDIR (This Work)	$O(nlogn)$	$O(n)$

Table 1: Complexity of different parsing frameworks. MST: first order MST parser, MST2: second order MST parser, MALT: shift-reduce left-to-right parsing. BEAM: beam search parser, as in (Zhang and Clark, 2008)

In terms of feature extraction and score calculation operations, our algorithm has the same cost as traditional shift-reduce (MALT) parsers, and is an order of magnitude more efficient than graph-based (MST) parsers. Beam-search decoding for left-to-right parsers (Zhang and Clark, 2008) is also linear, but has an additional linear dependence on the beam-size. The reported results in (Zhang and Clark, 2008) use a beam size of 64, compared to our constant of $k = 6$.

Our Python-based implementation[5] (the perceptron is implemented in a C extension module) parses about 40 tagged sentences per second on an Intel based MacBook laptop.

7 Experiments and Results

We evaluate the parser using the WSJ Treebank. The trees were converted to dependency structures with the Penn2Malt conversion program,[6] using the head-finding rules from (Yamada and Matsumoto, 2003).[7]

We use Sections 2-21 for training, Section 22 for development, and Section 23 as the final test set. The text is automatically POS tagged using a trigram HMM based POS tagger prior to training and parsing. Each section is tagged after training the tagger on all other sections. The tagging accuracy of the tagger is 96.5 for the training set and 96.8 for the test set. While better taggers exist, we believe that the simpler HMM tagger overfits less, and is more representative of the tagging performance on non-WSJ corpus texts.

Parsers We evaluate our parser against the transition-based MALT parser and the graph-based MST parser. We use version 1.2 of MALT parser[8], with the settings used for parsing English in the CoNLL 2007 shared task. For the MST parser[9], we use the default first-order, projective parser settings, which provide state-of-the-art results for English. All parsers are trained and tested on the same data. Our parser is trained for 20 iterations.

Evaluation Measures We evaluate the parsers using three common measures:

(unlabeled) Accuracy: percentage of tokens which got assigned their correct parent.

Root: The percentage of sentences in which the ROOT attachment is correct.

Complete: the percentage of sentences in which all tokens were assigned their correct parent.

Unlike most previous work on English dependency parsing, we *do not* exclude punctuation marks from the evaluation.

Results are presented in Table 2. Our non-directional easy-first parser significantly outperforms the left-to-right greedy MALT parser in terms of accuracy and root prediction, and significantly outperforms both parsers in terms of exact match. The globally optimized MST parser is better in root-prediction, and slightly better in terms of accuracy.

We evaluated the parsers also on the English dataset from the CoNLL 2007 shared task. While this dataset is also derived from the WSJ Treebank, it differs from the previous dataset in two important aspects: it is much smaller in size, and it is created using a different conversion procedure, which is more linguistically adequate. For these experiments, we use the dataset POS tags, and the same parameters as in the previous set of experiments: we train the non-directional parser for 20 iterations, with the same feature set. The CoNLL dataset contains some non-projective constructions. MALT and MST deal with non-projectivity. For the non-directional parser, we projectivize the training set prior to training using the procedure described in (Carreras, 2007).

Results are presented in Table 3.

[5] http://www.cs.bgu.ac.il/~yoavg/software/

[6] http://w3.msi.vxu.se/~nivre/research/Penn2Malt.html

[7] While other and better conversions exist (see, *e.g.*, (Johansson and Nugues, 2007; Sangati and Mazza, 2009)), this conversion heuristic is still the most widely used. Using the same conversion facilitates comparison with previous works.

[8] http://maltparser.org/dist/1.2/malt-1.2.tar.gz

[9] http://sourceforge.net/projects/mstparser/

Parser	Accuracy	Root	Complete
MALT	88.36	87.04	34.14
MST	90.05	93.95	34.64
NONDIR (this work)	89.70	91.50	37.50

Table 2: Unlabeled dependency accuracy on PTB Section 23, automatic POS-tags, including punctuation.

Parser	Accuracy	Root	Complete
MALT	85.82	87.85	24.76
MST	89.08	93.45	24.76
NONDIR (this work)	88.34	91.12	29.43

Table 3: Unlabeled dependency accuracy on CoNLL 2007 English test set, including punctuation.

While all models suffer from the move to the smaller dataset and the more challenging annotation scheme, the overall story remains the same: the non-directional parser is better than MALT but not as good as MST in terms of parent-accuracy and root prediction, and is better than both MALT and MST in terms of producing complete correct parses.

That the non-directional parser has lower accuracy but more exact matches than the MST parser can be explained by it being a deterministic parser, and hence still vulnerable to error propagation: once it erred once, it is likely to do so again, resulting in low accuracies for some sentences. However, due to the easy-first policy, it manages to parse many sentences without a single error, which lead to higher exact-match scores. The non-directional parser avoids error propagation by not making the initial error. On average, the non-directional parser manages to assign correct heads to over 60% of the tokens before making its first error.

The MST parser would have ranked 5th in the shared task, and NONDIR would have ranked 7th. The better ranking systems in the shared task are either higher-order global models, beam-search based systems, or ensemble-based systems, all of which are more complex and less efficient than the NONDIR parser.

Parse Diversity The parses produced by the non-directional parser are different than the parses produced by the graph-based and left-to-right parsers. To demonstrate this difference, we performed an Oracle experiment, in which we combine the output of several parsers by choosing, for each sentence, the parse with the highest score. Results are presented in Table 4.

Combination	Accuracy	Complete
Penn2Malt, Train 2-21, Test 23		
MALT+MST	92.29	44.03
NONDIR+MALT	92.19	45.48
NONDIR+MST	92.53	44.41
NONDIR+MST+MALT	93.54	49.79
CoNLL 2007		
MALT+MST	91.50	33.64
NONDIR+MALT	91.02	34.11
NONDIR+MST	91.90	34.11
NONDIR+MST+MALT	92.70	38.31

Table 4: Parser combination with Oracle, choosing the highest scoring parse for each sentence of the test-set.

A non-oracle blending of MALT+MST+NONDIR using Sagae and Lavie's (2006) simplest combination method assigning each component the same weight, yield an accuracy of 90.8 on the CoNLL 2007 English dataset, making it the highest scoring system among the participants.

7.1 Error Analysis / Limitations

When we investigate the POS category of mistaken instances, we see that for all parsers, nodes with structures of depth 2 and more which are assigned an incorrect head are predominantly PPs (headed by 'IN'), followed by NPs (headed by 'NN'). All parsers have a hard time dealing with PP attachment, but MST parser is better at it than NONDIR, and both are better than MALT.

Looking further at the mistaken instances, we notice a tendency of the PP mistakes of the NONDIR parser to involve, before the PP, an NP embedded in a relative clause. This reveals a limitation of our parser: recall that for an edge to be built, the child must first acquire all its own children. This means that in case of relative clauses such as "I saw the boy [who ate the pizza] with my eyes", the parser must decide if the PP "with my eyes" should be attached to "the pizza" or not *before* it is allowed to build parts of the outer NP ("the boy who..."). In this case, the verb "saw" and the noun "boy" are both outside of the sight of the parser when deciding on the PP attachment, and it is forced to make a decision in ignorance, which, in many cases, leads to mistakes. The globally optimized MST does not suffer as much from such cases. We plan to address this deficiency in future work.

8 Related Work

Deterministic shift-reduce parsers are restricted by a strict left-to-right processing order. Such parsers can rely on rich syntactic information on the left, but not on the right, of the decision point. They are forced to commit early, and suffer from error propagation. Our non-directional parser addresses these deficiencies by discarding the strict left-to-right processing order, and attempting to make easier decisions before harder ones. Other methods of dealing with these deficiencies were proposed over the years:

Several Passes Yamada and Matsumoto's (2003) pioneering work introduces a shift-reduce parser which makes several left-to-right passes over a sentence. Each pass adds structure, which can then be used in subsequent passes. Sagae and Lavie (2006b) extend this model to alternate between left-to-right and right-to-left passes. This model is similar to ours, in that it attempts to defer harder decisions to later passes over the sentence, and allows late decisions to make use of rich syntactic information (built in earlier passes) on both sides of the decision point. However, the model is not explicitly trained to optimize attachment ordering, has an $O(n^2)$ runtime complexity, and produces results which are inferior to current single-pass shift-reduce parsers.

Beam Search Several researchers dealt with the early-commitment and error propagation of deterministic parsers by extending the greedy decisions with various flavors of beam-search (Sagae and Lavie, 2006a; Zhang and Clark, 2008; Titov and Henderson, 2007). This approach works well and produces highly competitive results. Beam search can be incorporated into our parser as well. We leave this investigation to future work.

Strict left-to-right ordering is also prevalent in sequence tagging. Indeed, one major influence on our work is Shen *et.al.*'s bi-directional POS-tagging algorithm (Shen et al., 2007), which combines a perceptron learning procedure similar to our own with beam search to produce a state-of-the-art POS-tagger, which does not rely on left-to-right processing. Shen and Joshi (2008) extends the bidirectional tagging algorithm to LTAG parsing, with good results. We build on top of that work and present a concrete and efficient greedy non-directional dependency parsing algorithm.

Structure Restrictions Eisner and Smith (2005) propose to improve the efficiency of a globally optimized parser by posing hard constraints on the lengths of arcs it can produce. Such constraints pose an explicit upper bound on parser accuracy.[10] Our parsing model does not pose such restrictions. Shorter edges are arguably easier to predict, and our parses builds them early in time. However, it is also capable of producing long dependencies at later stages in the parsing process. Indeed, the distribution of arc lengths produced by our parser is similar to those produced by the MALT and MST parsers.

9 Discussion

We presented a *non-directional* deterministic dependency parsing algorithm, which is not restricted by the left-to-right parsing order of other deterministic parsers. Instead, it works in an *easy-first* order. This strategy allows using more context at each decision. The parser learns both *what* and *when* to connect. We show that this parsing algorithm significantly outperforms a left-to-right deterministic algorithm. While it still lags behind globally optimized parsing algorithms in terms of accuracy and root prediction, it is much better in terms of exact match, and much faster. As our parsing framework can easily and efficiently utilize more structural information than globally optimized parsers, we believe that with some enhancements and better features, it can outperform globally optimized algorithms, especially when more structural information is needed, such as for morphologically rich languages.

Moreover, we show that our parser produces different structures than those produced by both left-to-right and globally optimized parsers, making it a good candidate for inclusion in an ensemble system. Indeed, a simple combination scheme of graph-based, left-to-right and non-directional parsers yields state-of-the-art results on English dependency parsing on the CoNLL 2007 dataset.

We hope that further work on this non-directional parsing framework will pave the way to better understanding of an interesting cognitive question: which kinds of parsing decisions are hard to make, and which linguistic constructs are hard to analyze?

[10] In (Dreyer et al., 2006), constraints are chosen "to be the minimum value that will allow recovery of 90% of the left (right) dependencies in the training corpus".

References

Sabine Buchholz and Erwin Marsi. 2006. CoNLL-X shared task on multilingual dependency parsing. In *Proc. of CoNLL*.

Xavier Carreras. 2007. Experiments with a higher-order projective dependency parser. In *Proc. of CoNLL Shared Task, EMNLP-CoNLL*.

Michael Collins. 2002. Discriminative training methods for hidden markov models: Theory and experiments with perceptron algorithms. In *Proc of EMNLP*.

Markus Dreyer, David A. Smith, and Noah A. Smith. 2006. Vine parsing and minimum risk reranking for speed and precision. In *Proc. of CoNLL*, pages 201–205, Morristown, NJ, USA. Association for Computational Linguistics.

Jason Eisner and Noah A. Smith. 2005. arsing with soft and hard constraints on dependency length. In *Proc. of IWPT*.

Liang Huang, Wenbin Jiang, and Qun Liu. 2009. Bilingually-constrained (monolingual) shift-reduce parsing. In *Proc of EMNLP*.

Richard Johansson and Pierre Nugues. 2007. Extended constituent-to-dependency conversion for english. In *Proc of NODALIDA*.

Ryan McDonald and Joakim Nivre. 2007. Characterizing the errors of data-driven dependency parsing models. In *Proc. of EMNLP*.

Ryan McDonald and Fernando Pereira. 2006. Online learning of approximate dependency parsing algorithms. In *Proc of EACL*.

Ryan McDonald, Koby Crammer, and Fernando Pereira. 2005. Online large-margin training of dependency parsers. In *Proc of ACL*.

Tetsuji Nakagawa. 2007. Multilingual dependency parsing using global features. In *Proc. of EMNLP-CoNLL*.

Joakim Nivre and Ryan McDonald. 2008. Integrating graph-based and transition-based dependency parsers. In *Proc. of ACL*, pages 950–958, Columbus, Ohio, June. Association for Computational Linguistics.

Joakim Nivre, Johan Hall, and Jens Nillson. 2006. MaltParser: A data-driven parser-generator for dependency parsing. In *Proc. of LREC*.

Joakim Nivre, Johan Hall, Sandra Kübler, Ryan Mcdonald, Jens Nilsson, Sebastian Riedel, and Deniz Yuret. 2007. The CoNLL 2007 shared task on dependency parsing. In *Proc. of EMNLP-CoNLL*.

Joakim Nivre. 2004. Incrementality in deterministic dependency parsing. In *Incremental Parsing: Bringing Engineering and Cognition Together, ACL-Workshop*.

Sebastian Riedel and James Clarke. 2006. Incremental integer linear programming for non-projective dependency parsing. In *Proc. of EMNLP 2006*, July.

Kenji Sagae and Alon Lavie. 2006a. A best-first probabilistic shift-reduce parser. In *Proc of ACL*.

Kenji Sagae and Alon Lavie. 2006b. Parser combination by reparsing. In *Proc of NAACL*.

Federico Sangati and Chiara Mazza. 2009. An english dependency treebank à la tesnière. In *Proc of TLT8*.

Libin Shen and Aravind K. Joshi. 2008. Ltag dependency parsing with bidirectional incremental construction. In *Proc of EMNLP*.

Libin Shen, Giorgio Satta, and Aravind K. Joshi. 2007. Guided learning for bidirectional sequence classification. In *Proc of ACL*.

Ivan Titov and James Henderson. 2007. Fast and robust multilingual dependency parsing with a generative latent variable model. In *Proc. of EMNLP-CoNLL*.

Yamada and Matsumoto. 2003. Statistical dependency analysis with support vector machines. In *Proc. of IWPT*.

Yue Zhang and Stephen Clark. 2008. A tale of two parsers: investigating and combining graph-based and transition-based dependency parsing using beam-search. In *Proc of EMNLP*.

From Baby Steps to Leapfrog: How "Less is More" in Unsupervised Dependency Parsing*

Valentin I. Spitkovsky
Stanford University and Google Inc.
valentin@cs.stanford.edu

Hiyan Alshawi
Google Inc., Mountain View, CA, 94043
hiyan@google.com

Daniel Jurafsky
Stanford University, Stanford, CA, 94305
jurafsky@stanford.edu

Abstract

We present three approaches for unsupervised grammar induction that are sensitive to data complexity and apply them to Klein and Manning's Dependency Model with Valence. The first, *Baby Steps*, bootstraps itself via iterated learning of increasingly longer sentences and requires no initialization. This method substantially exceeds Klein and Manning's published scores and achieves 39.4% accuracy on Section 23 (all sentences) of the Wall Street Journal corpus. The second, *Less is More*, uses a low-complexity subset of the available data: sentences up to length 15. Focusing on fewer but simpler examples trades off quantity against ambiguity; it attains 44.1% accuracy, using the standard linguistically-informed prior and batch training, beating state-of-the-art. *Leapfrog*, our third heuristic, combines *Less is More* with *Baby Steps* by mixing their models of shorter sentences, then rapidly ramping up exposure to the full training set, driving up accuracy to 45.0%. These trends generalize to the Brown corpus; awareness of data complexity may improve other parsing models and unsupervised algorithms.

1 Introduction

Unsupervised learning of hierarchical syntactic structure from free-form natural language text is a hard problem whose eventual solution promises to benefit applications ranging from question answering to speech recognition and machine translation. A restricted version that targets dependencies and assumes partial annotation, e.g., sentence boundaries, tokenization and typically even part-of-speech (POS) tagging, has received much attention, eliciting a diverse array of techniques (Smith and Eisner, 2005; Seginer, 2007; Cohen et al., 2008). Klein and Manning's (2004) Dependency Model with Valence (DMV) was the first to beat a simple parsing heuristic — the right-branching baseline. Today's state-of-the-art systems (Headden et al., 2009; Cohen and Smith, 2009) are still rooted in the DMV.

Despite recent advances, unsupervised parsers lag far behind their supervised counterparts. Although large amounts of unlabeled data are known to improve semi-supervised parsing (Suzuki et al., 2009), the best unsupervised systems use less data than is available for supervised training, relying on complex models instead: Headden et al.'s (2009) Extended Valence Grammar (EVG) combats data sparsity with smoothing alone, training on the same small subset of the tree-bank as the classic implementation of the DMV; Cohen and Smith (2009) use more complicated algorithms (variational EM and MBR decoding) and stronger linguistic hints (tying related parts of speech and syntactically similar bilingual data).

We explore what can be achieved through judicious use of data and simple, scalable techniques. Our first approach iterates over a series of training sets that gradually increase in size and complexity, forming an initialization-independent scaffolding for learning a grammar. It works with Klein and Manning's simple model (the original DMV) and training algorithm (classic EM) but eliminates their crucial dependence on manually-tuned priors. The second technique is consistent with the intuition that learning is most successful within a band of the size-complexity spectrum. Both could be applied to more

*Partially funded by NSF award IIS-0811974; first author supported by the Fannie & John Hertz Foundation Fellowship.

Human Language Technologies: The 2010 Annual Conference of the North American Chapter of the ACL, pages 751–759,
Los Angeles, California, June 2010.

intricate models and advanced learning algorithms. We combine them in a third, efficient hybrid method.

2 Intuition

Focusing on simple examples helps guide unsupervised learning,[1] as blindly added confusing data can easily mislead training. We suggest that unless it is increased gradually, unbridled, complexity can overwhelm a system. How to grade an example's difficulty? The cardinality of its solution space presents a natural proxy. In the case of parsing, the number of possible syntactic trees grows exponentially with sentence length. For longer sentences, the unsupervised optimization problem becomes severely under-constrained, whereas for shorter sentences, learning is tightly reined in by data. In the extreme case of a single-word sentence, there is no choice but to parse it correctly. At two words, a raw 50% chance of telling the head from its dependent is still high, but as length increases, the accuracy of even educated guessing rapidly plummets. In model re-estimation, long sentences amplify ambiguity and pollute fractional counts with noise. At times, batch systems are better off using less data.

Baby Steps: Global non-convex optimization is hard. We propose a meta-heuristic that takes the guesswork out of initializing local search. Beginning with an easy (convex) case, it slowly extends it to the fully complex target task by taking tiny steps in the problem space, trying not to stray far from the relevant neighborhoods of the solution space. A series of nested subsets of increasingly longer sentences that culminates in the complete data set offers a natural progression. Its base case — sentences of length one — has a trivial solution that requires neither initialization nor search yet reveals something of sentence heads. The next step — sentences of length one and two — refines initial impressions of heads, introduces dependents, and exposes their identities and relative positions. Although not representative of the full grammar, short sentences capture enough information to paint most of the picture needed by slightly longer sentences. They set up an easier, incremental subsequent learning task. Step $k + 1$ augments training input to include lengths $1, 2, \ldots, k, k + 1$ of the full data set and executes local search starting from the (smoothed) model estimated by step k. This truly is grammar induction.

Less is More: For standard batch training, just using simple, short sentences is not enough. They are rare and do not reveal the full grammar. We find a "sweet spot" — sentence lengths that are neither too long (excluding the truly daunting examples) nor too few (supplying enough accessible information), using Baby Steps' learning curve as a guide. We train where it flattens out, since remaining sentences contribute little (incremental) educational value.[2]

Leapfrog: As an alternative to discarding data, a better use of resources is to combine the results of batch and iterative training up to the sweet spot data gradation, then iterate with a large step size.

3 Related Work

Two types of scaffolding for guiding language learning debuted in Elman's (1993) experiments with "starting small": data complexity (restricting input) and model complexity (restricting memory). In both cases, gradually increasing complexity allowed artificial neural networks to master a pseudo-natural grammar they otherwise failed to learn. Initially-limited capacity resembled maturational changes in working memory and attention span that occur over time in children (Kail, 1984), in line with the "less is more" proposal (Newport, 1988; 1990). Although Rohde and Plaut (1999) failed to replicate this[3] result with simple recurrent networks, other machine learning techniques reliably benefit from scaffolded model complexity on a variety of language tasks. In word-alignment, Brown et al. (1993) used IBM Models 1-4 as "stepping stones" to training Model 5. Other prominent examples include "coarse-to-fine"

[1]It mirrors the effect that boosting hard examples has for supervised training (Freund and Schapire, 1997).

[2]This is akin to McClosky et al.'s (2006) "Goldilocks effect."

[3]Worse, they found that limiting input *hindered* language acquisition. And making the grammar more English-like (by introducing and strengthening semantic constraints), *increased* the already significant advantage for "starting large!" With iterative training invoking the optimizer multiple times, creating extra opportunities to converge, Rohde and Plaut (1999) suspected that Elman's (1993) simulations simply did not allow networks exposed exclusively to complex inputs sufficient training time. Our extremely generous, low termination threshold for EM (see §5.1) addresses this concern. However, given the DMV's purely syntactic POS tag-based approach (see §5), it would be prudent to re-test Baby Steps with a lexicalized model.

approaches to parsing, translation and speech recognition (Charniak and Johnson, 2005; Charniak et al., 2006; Petrov et al., 2008; Petrov, 2009), and recently unsupervised POS tagging (Ravi and Knight, 2009). Initial models tend to be particularly simple,[4] and each refinement towards a full model introduces only limited complexity, supporting incrementality.

Filtering complex data, the focus of our work, is unconventional in natural language processing. Such scaffolding qualifies as *shaping* — a method of instruction (routinely exploited in animal training) in which the teacher decomposes a complete task into sub-components, providing an easier path to learning. When Skinner (1938) coined the term, he described it as a "method of successive approximations." Ideas that gradually make a task more difficult have been explored in robotics (typically, for navigation), with reinforcement learning (Singh, 1992; Sanger, 1994; Saksida et al., 1997; Dorigo and Colombetti, 1998; Savage, 1998; Savage, 2001). Recently, Krueger and Dayan (2009) showed that shaping speeds up language acquisition and leads to better generalization in abstract neural networks. Bengio et al. (2009) confirmed this for deep deterministic and stochastic networks, using simple multi-stage *curriculum* strategies. They conjectured that a well-chosen sequence of training criteria — different sets of weights on the examples — could act as a continuation method (Allgower and Georg, 1990), helping find better local optima for non-convex objectives. Elman's learners constrained the peaky solution space by focusing on just the right data (simple sentences that introduced basic representational categories) at just the right time (early on, when their plasticity was greatest). Self-shaping, they simplified tasks through deliberate omission (or misunderstanding). Analogously, Baby Steps induces an early structural locality bias (Smith and Eisner, 2006), then relaxes it, as if annealing (Smith and Eisner, 2004). Its curriculum of binary weights initially discards complex examples responsible for "high-frequency noise," with earlier, "smoothed" objectives revealing more of the global picture.

There are important differences between our results and prior work. In contrast to Elman, we use a large data set (WSJ) of real English. Unlike Bengio et al. and Krueger and Dayan, we shape a parser, not a language model. Baby Steps is similar, in spirit, to Smith and Eisner's methods. Deterministic annealing (DA) shares nice properties with Baby Steps, but performs worse than EM for (constituent) parsing; Baby Steps handedly defeats standard training. Structural annealing works well, but requires a hand-tuned annealing schedule and direct manipulation of the objective function; Baby Steps works "out of the box," its locality biases a natural consequence of a complexity/data-guided tour of optimization problems. Skewed DA incorporates a good initializer by interpolating between two probability distributions, whereas our hybrid, Leapfrog, admits multiple initializers by mixing structures instead. "Less is More" is novel and confirms the tacit consensus implicit in training on small data sets (e.g., WSJ10).

4 Data Sets and Metrics

Klein and Manning (2004) both trained and tested the DMV on the same customized subset (WSJ10) of Penn English Treebank's Wall Street Journal portion (Marcus et al., 1993). Its 49,208 annotated parse trees were pruned[5] down to 7,422 sentences of at most 10 terminals, spanning 35 unique POS tags. Following standard practice, automatic "head-percolation" rules (Collins, 1999) were used to convert the remaining trees into dependencies. Forced to produce a single "best" parse, their algorithm was judged on accuracy: its *directed score* was the fraction of correct dependencies; a more flattering[6] *undirected score* was also used. We employ the same metrics, emphasizing directed scores, and generalize WSJk to be the subset of pre-processed sentences with at most k terminals. Our experiments focus on $k \in \{1, \ldots, 45\}$, but we also test on WSJ100 and Section 23 of WSJ$^\infty$ (the entire WSJ), as well as the held-out Brown100 (similarly derived from the Brown corpus (Francis and Kucera, 1979)). See Figure 1 for these corpora's sentence and token counts.

[4] Brown et al.'s (1993) Model 1 (and, similarly, the first baby step) has a global optimum that can be computed exactly, so that no initial or subsequent parameters depend on initialization.

[5] Stripped of all empty sub-trees, punctuation, and terminals (tagged # and \$) not pronounced where they appear, those sentences still containing more than ten tokens were thrown out.

[6] Ignoring polarity of parent-child relations partially obscured effects of alternate analyses (systematic choices between modals and main verbs for heads of sentences, determiners for noun phrases, etc.) and facilitated comparison with prior work.

Corpus	*Sentences*	*POS Tokens*	*Corpus*	*Sentences*	*POS Tokens*
WSJ1	159	159	WSJ13	12,270	110,760
WSJ2	499	839	WSJ14	14,095	136,310
WSJ3	876	1,970	WSJ15	15,922	163,715
WSJ4	1,394	4,042	WSJ20	25,523	336,555
WSJ5	2,008	7,112	WSJ25	34,431	540,895
WSJ6	2,745	11,534	WSJ30	41,227	730,099
WSJ7	3,623	17,680	WSJ35	45,191	860,053
WSJ8	4,730	26,536	WSJ40	47,385	942,801
WSJ9	5,938	37,408	WSJ45	48,418	986,830
WSJ10	7,422	52,248	WSJ100	49,206	1,028,054
WSJ11	8,856	68,022	Section 23	2,353	48,201
WSJ12	10,500	87,750	Brown100	24,208	391,796

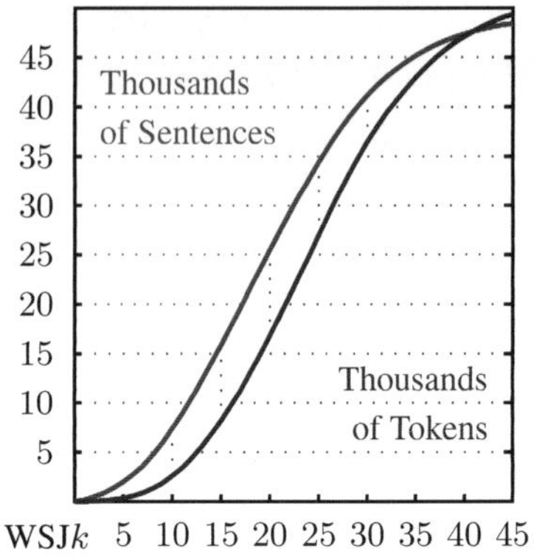

Figure 1: Sizes of WSJ$\{1, \ldots, 45, 100\}$, Section 23 of WSJ$^\infty$ and Brown100.

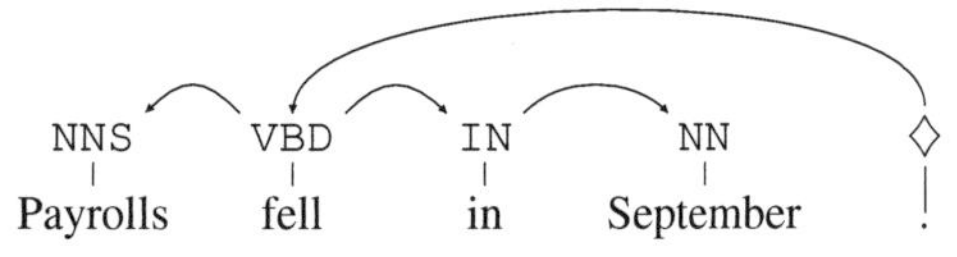

$$\begin{aligned}
\mathbb{P} = &\overbrace{(1-\mathbb{P}_{\text{STOP}}(\diamond, \texttt{L}, \texttt{T}))}^{0} &&\times \mathbb{P}_{\text{ATTACH}}(\diamond, \texttt{L}, \texttt{VBD})\\
\times\ &(1-\mathbb{P}_{\text{STOP}}(\texttt{VBD}, \texttt{L}, \texttt{T})) &&\times \mathbb{P}_{\text{ATTACH}}(\texttt{VBD}, \texttt{L}, \texttt{NNS})\\
\times\ &(1-\mathbb{P}_{\text{STOP}}(\texttt{VBD}, \texttt{R}, \texttt{T})) &&\times \mathbb{P}_{\text{ATTACH}}(\texttt{VBD}, \texttt{R}, \texttt{IN})\\
\times\ &(1-\mathbb{P}_{\text{STOP}}(\texttt{IN}, \texttt{R}, \texttt{T})) &&\times \mathbb{P}_{\text{ATTACH}}(\texttt{IN}, \texttt{R}, \texttt{NN})\\
\times\ &\mathbb{P}_{\text{STOP}}(\texttt{VBD}, \texttt{L}, \texttt{F}) &&\times \mathbb{P}_{\text{STOP}}(\texttt{VBD}, \texttt{R}, \texttt{F})\\
\times\ &\mathbb{P}_{\text{STOP}}(\texttt{NNS}, \texttt{L}, \texttt{T}) &&\times \mathbb{P}_{\text{STOP}}(\texttt{NNS}, \texttt{R}, \texttt{T})\\
\times\ &\mathbb{P}_{\text{STOP}}(\texttt{IN}, \texttt{L}, \texttt{T}) &&\times \mathbb{P}_{\text{STOP}}(\texttt{IN}, \texttt{R}, \texttt{F})\\
\times\ &\mathbb{P}_{\text{STOP}}(\texttt{NN}, \texttt{L}, \texttt{T}) &&\times \mathbb{P}_{\text{STOP}}(\texttt{NN}, \texttt{R}, \texttt{T})\\
\times\ &\underbrace{\mathbb{P}_{\text{STOP}}(\diamond, \texttt{L}, \texttt{F})}_{1} &&\times \underbrace{\mathbb{P}_{\text{STOP}}(\diamond, \texttt{R}, \texttt{T})}_{1}.
\end{aligned}$$

Figure 2: A simple dependency structure for a short sentence and its probability, as factored by the DMV.

5 New Algorithms for the Classic Model

The DMV (Klein and Manning, 2004) is a single-state head automata model (Alshawi, 1996) over lexical word classes $\{c_w\}$ — POS tags. Its generative story for a sub-tree rooted at a head (of class c_h) rests on three types of independent decisions: (i) initial direction $dir \in \{\texttt{L}, \texttt{R}\}$ in which to attach children, via probability $\mathbb{P}_{\text{ORDER}}(c_h)$; (ii) whether to seal dir, stopping with probability $\mathbb{P}_{\text{STOP}}(c_h, dir, adj)$, conditioned on $adj \in \{\texttt{T}, \texttt{F}\}$ (true iff considering dir's first, i.e., *adjacent*, child); and (iii) attachments (of class c_a), according to $\mathbb{P}_{\text{ATTACH}}(c_h, dir, c_a)$. This produces only projective trees.[7] A root token $\diamond$ generates the head of a sentence as its left (and only) child. Figure 2 displays an example that ignores (sums out) $\mathbb{P}_{\text{ORDER}}$.

The DMV lends itself to unsupervised learning via inside-outside re-estimation (Baker, 1979). Klein and Manning did not use smoothing and started with an "ad-hoc harmonic" completion: aiming for balanced trees, non-root heads attached dependents in inverse proportion to (a constant plus) their distance; $\diamond$ generated heads uniformly at random. This non-distributional heuristic created favorable initial conditions that nudged EM towards typical linguistic dependency structures.

5.1 Algorithm #0: Ad-Hoc* — A Variation on Original Ad-Hoc Initialization

Since some of the important implementation details are not available in the literature (Klein and Manning, 2004; Klein, 2005), we had to improvise initialization and terminating conditions. We suspect that our choices throughout this section do not match Klein and Manning's actual training of the DMV.

We use the following ad-hoc harmonic scores (for all tokens other than $\diamond$): $\tilde{\mathbb{P}}_{\text{ORDER}} \equiv 1/2$;

$$\tilde{\mathbb{P}}_{\text{STOP}} \equiv (d_s + \delta_s)^{-1} = (d_s + 3)^{-1},\ d_s \geq 0;$$
$$\tilde{\mathbb{P}}_{\text{ATTACH}} \equiv (d_a + \delta_a)^{-1} = (d_a + 2)^{-1},\ d_a \geq 1.$$

Integers $d_{\{s,a\}}$ are distances from heads to stopping boundaries and dependents.[8] We initialize training by producing best-scoring parses of all input sentences and converting them into proper probability distributions $\mathbb{P}_{\text{STOP}}$ and $\mathbb{P}_{\text{ATTACH}}$ via maximum-likelihood estimation (a single step of Viterbi training (Brown et al., 1993)). Since left and right children are independent, we drop $\mathbb{P}_{\text{ORDER}}$ altogether, mak-

[7]Unlike spanning tree algorithms (McDonald et al., 2005), DMV's chart-based method disallows crossing dependencies.

[8]Constants $\delta_{\{s,a\}}$ come from personal communication. Note that δ_s is one higher than is strictly necessary to avoid both division by zero and determinism; δ_a could have been safely zeroed out, since we never compute $1 - \mathbb{P}_{\text{ATTACH}}$ (see Figure 2).

ing "headedness" deterministic. Our parser carefully randomizes tie-breaking, so that all parse trees having the same score get an equal shot at being selected (both during initialization and evaluation). We terminate EM when a successive change in overall per-token cross-entropy drops below 2^{-20} bits.

5.2 Algorithm #1: Baby Steps — An Initialization-Independent Scaffolding

We eliminate the need for initialization by first training on a trivial subset of the data — WSJ1; this works, since there is only one (the correct) way to parse a single-token sentence. We plug the resulting model into training on WSJ2 (sentences of up to two tokens), and so forth, building up to WSJ45.[9] This algorithm is otherwise identical to Ad-Hoc*, with the exception that it re-estimates each model using Laplace smoothing, so that earlier solutions could be passed to next levels, which sometimes contain previously unseen dependent and head POS tags.

5.3 Algorithm #2: Less is More — Ad-Hoc* where Baby Steps Flatlines

We jettison long, complex sentences and deploy Ad-Hoc*'s initializer and batch training at WSJ$\hat{k}^*$ — an estimate of the sweet spot data gradation. To find it, we track Baby Steps' successive models' cross-entropies on the complete data set, WSJ45. An initial segment of rapid improvement is separated from the final region of convergence by a *knee* — points of maximum curvature (see Figure 3). We use an improved[10] L method (Salvador and Chan, 2004) to automatically locate this area of diminishing returns. Specifically, we determine its end-points $[k_0, k^*]$ by minimizing squared error, estimating $\hat{k}_0 = 7$ and $\hat{k}^* = 15$. Training at WSJ15 just misses the plateau.

5.4 Algorithm #3: Leapfrog — A Practical and Efficient Hybrid Mixture

Cherry-picking the best features of "Less is More" and Baby Steps, we begin by combining their models at WSJ$\hat{k}^*$. Using one best parse from each, for every sentence in WSJ$\hat{k}^*$, the base case re-estimates a new model from a *mixture* of twice the normal number of trees; inductive steps leap over $\hat{k}^*$ lengths, conveniently ending at WSJ45, and estimate their initial models by applying a previous solution to a new input set. Both follow up the single step of Viterbi training with at most five iterations of EM.

Our hybrid makes use of two good (conditionally) independent initialization strategies and executes many iterations of EM where that is cheap — at shorter sentences (WSJ15 and below). It then increases the step size, training just three more times (at WSJ$\{15, 30, 45\}$) and allowing only a few (more expensive) iterations of EM. Early termination improves efficiency and regularizes these final models.

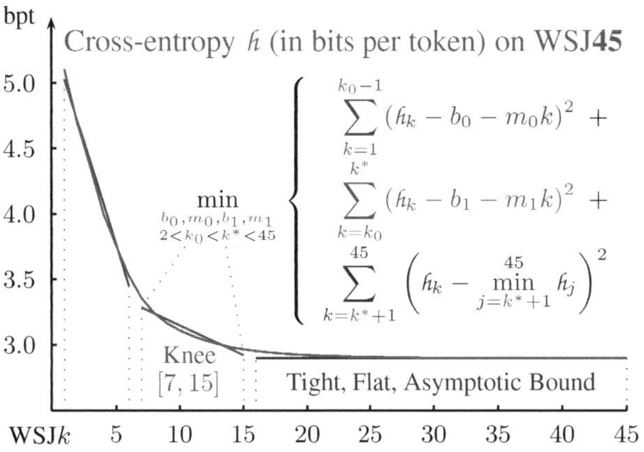

Figure 3: Cross-entropy on WSJ45 after each baby step, a piece-wise linear fit, and an estimated region for the knee.

5.5 Reference Algorithms — Baselines, a Skyline and Published Art

We carve out the problem space using two extreme initialization strategies: (i) the uninformed uniform prior, which serves as a fair "zero-knowledge" baseline for comparing uninitialized models; and (ii) the maximum-likelihood "oracle" prior, computed from reference parses, which yields a *skyline* (a reverse baseline) — how well any algorithm that stumbled on the true solution would fare at EM's convergence.

In addition to citing Klein and Manning's (2004) results, we compare our accuracies on Section 23 of WSJ$^\infty$ to two state-of-the-art systems and past baselines (see Table 2). Headden et al.'s (2009) lexicalized EVG is the best on short sentences, but

[9] Its 48,418 sentences (see Figure 1) cover 94.4% of all sentences in WSJ; the longest of the missing 790 has length 171.

[10] Instead of iteratively fitting a two-segment form and adaptively discarding its tail, we use *three* line segments, applying ordinary least squares to the first two, but requiring the third to be horizontal and tangent to a minimum. The result is a *batch* optimization routine that returns an *interval* for the knee, rather than a point estimate (see Figure 3 for details).

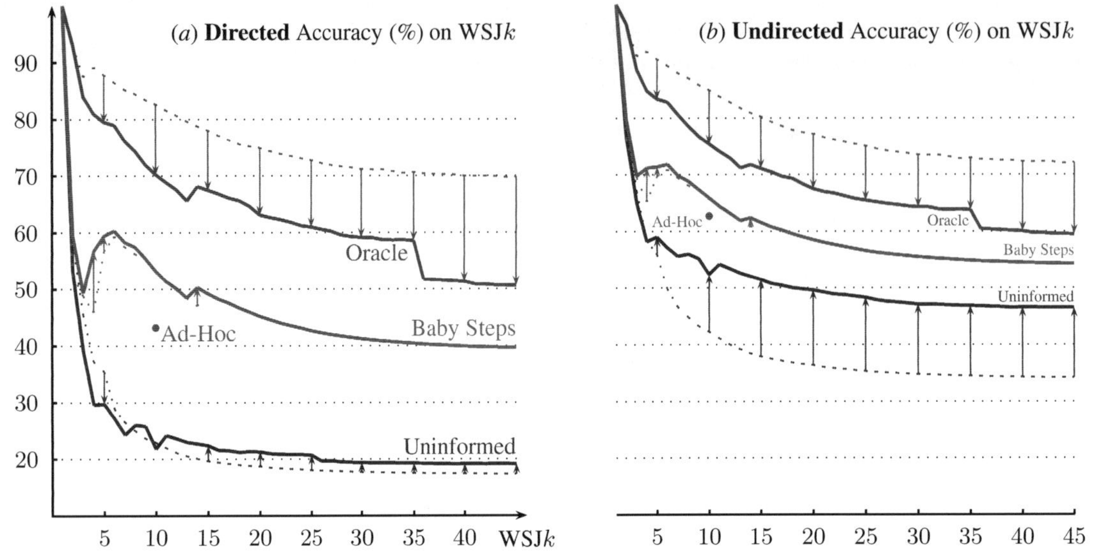

Figure 4: Directed and undirected accuracy scores attained by the DMV, when trained and tested on the same gradation of WSJ, for several different initialization strategies. Green circles mark Klein and Manning's (2004) published scores; red, violet and blue curves represent the supervised (maximum-likelihood oracle) initialization, Baby Steps, and the uninformed uniform prior. Dotted curves reflect starting performance, solid curves register performance at EM's convergence, and the arrows connecting them emphasize the impact of learning.

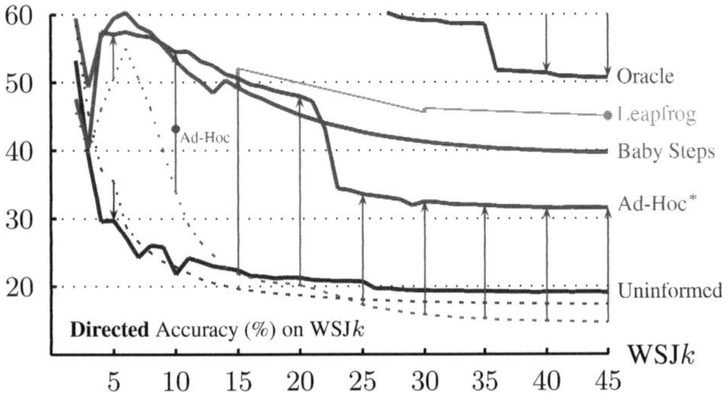

Figure 5: Directed accuracies for Ad-Hoc* (shown in green) and Leapfrog (in gold); all else as in Figure 4(*a*).

its performance is unreported for longer sentences, for which Cohen and Smith's (2009) seem to be the highest published scores; we include their intermediate results that preceded parameter-tying — Bayesian models with Dirichlet and log-normal priors, coupled with both Viterbi and minimum Bayes-risk (MBR) decoding (Cohen et al., 2008).

6 Experimental Results

We packed thousands of empirical outcomes into the space of several graphs (Figures 4, 5 and 6). The colors (also in Tables 1 and 2) correspond to different initialization strategies — to a first approximation, the learning algorithm was held constant (see §5).

Figures 4 and 5 tell one part of our story. As data sets increase in size, training algorithms gain access to more information; however, since in this unsupervised setting training and test sets are the same, additional longer sentences make for substantially more challenging evaluation. To control for these dynamics, we applied Laplace smoothing to all (otherwise unsmoothed) models and re-plotted their performance, holding several test sets fixed, in Figure 6.

We report undirected accuracies parenthetically.

6.1 Result #1: Baby Steps

Figure 4 traces out performance on the training set. Klein and Manning's (2004) published scores appear as dots (Ad-Hoc) at WSJ10: 43.2% (63.7%). Baby Steps achieves 53.0% (65.7%) by WSJ10; trained and tested on WSJ45, it gets 39.7% (54.3%). Uninformed, classic EM learns little about directed dependencies: it improves only slightly, e.g., from 17.3% (34.2%) to 19.1% (46.5%) on WSJ45 (learning some of the structure, as evidenced by its undirected scores), but degrades with shorter sentences, where its initial guessing rate is high. In the case of oracle training, we expected EM to walk away from supervised solutions (Elworthy, 1994; Meri-

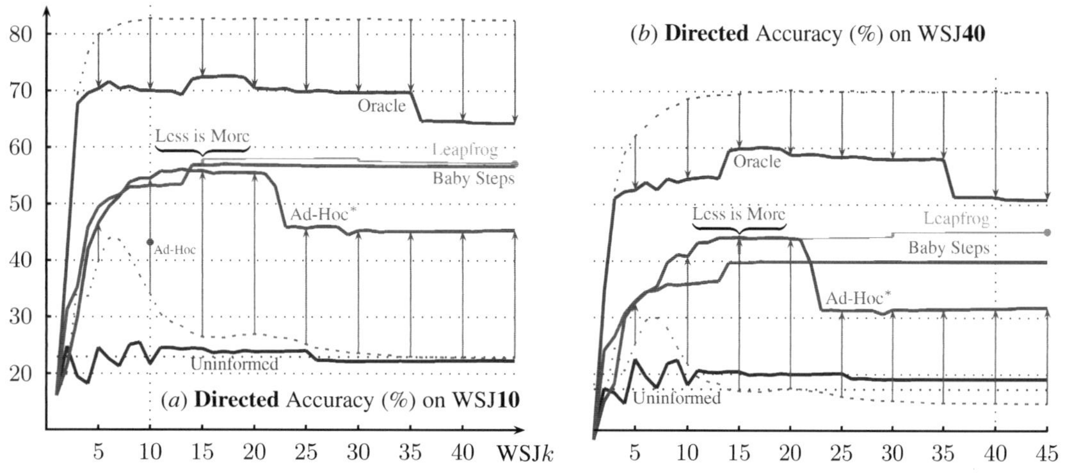

Figure 6: Directed accuracies attained by the DMV, when trained at various gradations of WSJ, smoothed, then tested against fixed evaluation sets — WSJ$\{10, 40\}$; graphs for WSJ$\{20, 30\}$, not shown, are qualitatively similar to WSJ40.

aldo, 1994; Liang and Klein, 2008), but the extent of its drops is alarming, e.g., from the supervised 69.8% (72.2%) to the skyline's 50.6% (59.5%) on WSJ45. In contrast, Baby Steps' scores usually do not change much from one step to the next, and where its impact of learning is big (at WSJ$\{4, 5, 14\}$), it is invariably positive.

6.2 Result #2: Less is More

Ad-Hoc*'s curve (see Figure 5) suggests how Klein and Manning's Ad-Hoc initializer may have scaled with different gradations of WSJ. Strangely, our implementation performs significantly above their reported numbers at WSJ10: 54.5% (68.3%) is even slightly higher than Baby Steps; nevertheless, given enough data (from WSJ22 onwards), Baby Steps overtakes Ad-Hoc*, whose ability to learn takes a serious dive once the inputs become sufficiently complex (at WSJ23), and never recovers. Note that Ad-Hoc*'s biased prior peaks early (at WSJ6), eventually falls below the guessing rate (by WSJ24), yet still remains well-positioned to climb, outperforming uninformed learning.

Figure 6 shows that Baby Steps scales better with more (complex) data — its curves do not trend downwards. However, a good initializer induces a sweet spot at WSJ15, where the DMV is learned best using Ad-Hoc*. This mode *is* "Less is More," scoring 44.1% (58.9%) on WSJ45. Curiously, even oracle training exhibits a bump at WSJ15: once sentences get long enough (at WSJ36), its performance degrades below that of oracle training with virtually no supervision (at the hardly representative WSJ3).

6.3 Result #3: Leapfrog

Mixing Ad-Hoc* with Baby Steps at WSJ15 yields a model whose performance initially falls between its two parents but surpasses both with a little training (see Figure 5). Leaping to WSJ45, via WSJ30, results in our strongest model: its 45.0% (58.4%) accuracy bridges half of the gap between Baby Steps and the skyline, and at a tiny fraction of the cost.

6.4 Result #4: Generalization

Our models carry over to the larger WSJ100, Section 23 of WSJ$^\infty$, and the independent Brown100 (see Table 1). Baby Steps improves out of domain, confirming that shaping generalizes well (Krueger and Dayan, 2009; Bengio et al., 2009). Leapfrog does best across the board but dips on Brown100, despite its safe-guards against over-fitting.

Section 23 (see Table 2) reveals, unexpectedly, that Baby Steps would have been state-of-the-art in 2008, whereas "Less is More" outperforms all prior work on longer sentences. Baby Steps is competitive with log-normal families (Cohen et al., 2008), scoring slightly better on longer sentences against Viterbi decoding, though worse against MBR. "Less is More" beats state-of-the-art on longer sentences by close to 2%; Leapfrog gains another 1%.

	*Ad-Hoc**	*Baby Steps*	*Leapfrog*		*Ad-Hoc**	*Baby Steps*	*Leapfrog*	
Section 23	44.1 (58.8)	39.2 (53.8)	43.3 (55.7)	@15	31.5 (51.6)	39.4 (54.0)	**45.0** (58.4)	@45
WSJ100	43.8 (58.6)	39.2 (53.8)	43.3 (55.6)		31.3 (51.5)	39.4 (54.1)	**44.7** (58.1)	
Brown100	43.3 (59.2)	42.3 (55.1)	42.8 (56.5)		32.0 (52.4)	42.5 (55.5)	**43.6** (59.1)	

Table 1: Directed and undirected accuracies on Section 23 of WSJ$^\infty$, WSJ100 and Brown100 for Ad-Hoc*, Baby Steps and Leapfrog, trained at WSJ15 and WSJ45.

			Decoding	WSJ10	WSJ20	WSJ$^\infty$
	Attach-Right	(Klein and Manning, 2004)	—	38.4	33.4	31.7
DMV	Ad-Hoc	(Klein and Manning, 2004)	Viterbi	45.8	39.1	34.2
	Dirichlet	(Cohen et al., 2008)	Viterbi	45.9	39.4	34.9
	Ad-Hoc	(Cohen et al., 2008)	MBR	46.1	39.9	35.9
	Dirichlet	(Cohen et al., 2008)	MBR	46.1	40.6	36.9
	Log-Normal Families	(Cohen et al., 2008)	Viterbi	59.3	45.1	39.0
	Baby Steps (@15)		*Viterbi*	*55.5*	*44.3*	*39.2*
	Baby Steps (@45)		*Viterbi*	*55.1*	*44.4*	*39.4*
	Log-Normal Families	(Cohen et al., 2008)	MBR	59.4	45.9	40.5
	Shared Log-Normals (tie-verb-noun)	(Cohen and Smith, 2009)	MBR	61.3	47.4	41.4
	Bilingual Log-Normals (tie-verb-noun)	(Cohen and Smith, 2009)	MBR	62.0	48.0	42.2
	Less is More (Ad-Hoc* @15)		*Viterbi*	*56.2*	*48.2*	*44.1*
	Leapfrog (Hybrid @45)		*Viterbi*	*57.1*	**48.7**	**45.0**
EVG	Smoothed (skip-val)	(Headden et al., 2009)	Viterbi	62.1		
	Smoothed (skip-head)	(Headden et al., 2009)	Viterbi	65.0		
	Smoothed (skip-head), Lexicalized	(Headden et al., 2009)	Viterbi	**68.8**		

Table 2: Directed accuracies on Section 23 of WSJ$\{10, 20, \infty\}$ for several baselines and recent state-of-the-art systems.

7 Conclusion

We explored three simple ideas for unsupervised dependency parsing. Pace Halevy et al. (2009), we find "Less is More" — the paradoxical result that better performance can be attained by training with less data, even when removing samples from the true (test) distribution. Our small tweaks to Klein and Manning's approach of 2004 break through the 2009 state-of-the-art on longer sentences, when trained at WSJ15 (the auto-detected sweet spot gradation).

The second, Baby Steps, is an elegant meta-heuristic for optimizing non-convex training criteria. It eliminates the need for linguistically-biased manually-tuned initializers, particularly if the location of the sweet spot is not known. This technique scales gracefully with more (complex) data and should easily carry over to more powerful parsing models and learning algorithms.

Finally, Leapfrog forgoes the elegance and meticulousness of Baby Steps in favor of pragmatism. Employing both good initialization strategies at its disposal, and spending CPU cycles wisely, it achieves better performance than both "Less is More" and Baby Steps.

Future work could explore unifying these techniques with other state-of-the-art approaches. It may be useful to scaffold on both data and model complexity, e.g., by increasing head automata's number of states (Alshawi and Douglas, 2000). We see many opportunities for improvement, considering the poor performance of oracle training relative to the supervised state-of-the-art, and in turn the poor performance of unsupervised state-of-the-art relative to the oracle models.[11] To this end, it would be instructive to understand both the linguistic and statistical nature of the sweet spot, and to test its universality.

Acknowledgments

We thank Angel X. Chang, Pi-Chuan Chang, David L.W. Hall, Christopher D. Manning, David McClosky, Daniel Ramage and the anonymous reviewers for many helpful comments on draft versions of this paper.

References

E. L. Allgower and K. Georg. 1990. *Numerical Continuation Methods: An Introduction*. Springer-Verlag.

[11]To facilitate future work, all of our models are publicly available at `http://cs.stanford.edu/~valentin/`.

H. Alshawi and S. Douglas. 2000. Learning dependency transduction models from unannotated examples. In *Royal Society of London Philosophical Transactions Series A*, volume 358.

H. Alshawi. 1996. Head automata for speech translation. In *Proc. of ICSLP*.

J. K. Baker. 1979. Trainable grammars for speech recognition. In *Speech Communication Papers for the 97th Meeting of the Acoustical Society of America*.

Y. Bengio, J. Louradour, R. Collobert, and J. Weston. 2009. Curriculum learning. In *ICML*.

P. F. Brown, V. J. Della Pietra, S. A. Della Pietra, and R. L. Mercer. 1993. The mathematics of statistical machine translation: Parameter estimation. *Computational Linguistics*, 19.

E. Charniak and M. Johnson. 2005. Coarse-to-fine n-best parsing and MaxEnt discriminative reranking. In *Proc. of ACL*.

E. Charniak, M. Johnson, M. Elsner, J. Austerweil, D. Ellis, I. Haxton, C. Hill, R. Shrivaths, J. Moore, M. Pozar, and T. Vu. 2006. Multilevel coarse-to-fine PCFG parsing. In *HLT-NAACL*.

S. B. Cohen and N. A. Smith. 2009. Shared logistic normal distributions for soft parameter tying in unsupervised grammar induction. In *Proc. of NAACL-HLT*.

S. B. Cohen, K. Gimpel, and N. A. Smith. 2008. Logistic normal priors for unsupervised probabilistic grammar induction. In *NIPS*.

M. Collins. 1999. *Head-Driven Statistical Models for Natural Language Parsing*. Ph.D. thesis, University of Pennsylvania.

M. Dorigo and M. Colombetti. 1998. *Robot Shaping: An Experiment in Behavior Engineering*. MIT Press/Bradford Books.

J. L. Elman. 1993. Learning and development in neural networks: The importance of starting small. *Cognition*, 48.

D. Elworthy. 1994. Does Baum-Welch re-estimation help taggers? In *Proc. of ANLP*.

W. N. Francis and H. Kucera, 1979. *Manual of Information to Accompany a Standard Corpus of Present-Day Edited American English, for use with Digital Computers*. Department of Linguistic, Brown University.

Y. Freund and R. E. Schapire. 1997. A decision-theoretic generalization of on-line learning and an application to boosting. *Journal of Computer and System Sciences*, 55(1).

A. Halevy, P. Norvig, and F. Pereira. 2009. The unreasonable effectiveness of data. *IEEE Intelligent Systems*, 24(2).

W. P. Headden, III, M. Johnson, and D. McClosky. 2009. Improving unsupervised dependency parsing with richer contexts and smoothing. In *Proc. of NAACL-HLT*.

R. Kail. 1984. *The development of memory in children*. W. H. Freeman and Company, 2nd edition.

D. Klein and C. D. Manning. 2004. Corpus-based induction of syntactic structure: Models of dependency and constituency. In *Proc. of ACL*.

D. Klein. 2005. *The Unsupervised Learning of Natural Language Structure*. Ph.D. thesis, Stanford University.

K. A. Krueger and P. Dayan. 2009. Flexible shaping: How learning in small steps helps. *Cognition*, 110.

P. Liang and D. Klein. 2008. Analyzing the errors of unsupervised learning. In *Proc. of HLT-ACL*.

M. P. Marcus, B. Santorini, and M. A. Marcinkiewicz. 1993. Building a large annotated corpus of English: The Penn Treebank. *Computational Linguistics*, 19(2).

D. McClosky, E. Charniak, and M. Johnson. 2006. Effective self-training for parsing. In *Proc. of NAACL-HLT*.

R. McDonald, F. Pereira, K. Ribarov, and J. Hajic. 2005. Non-projective dependency parsing using spanning tree algorithms. In *Proc. of HLT-EMNLP*.

B. Merialdo. 1994. Tagging English text with a probabilistic model. *Computational Linguistics*, 20(2):155–172.

E. L. Newport. 1988. Constraints on learning and their role in language acquisition: Studies of the acquisition of American Sign Language. *Language Sciences*, 10(1).

E. L. Newport. 1990. Maturational constraints on language learning. *Cognitive Science*, 14(1).

S. Petrov, A. Haghighi, and D. Klein. 2008. Coarse-to-fine syntactic machine translation using language projections. In *Proc. of EMNLP*.

S. O. Petrov. 2009. *Coarse-to-Fine Natural Language Processing*. Ph.D. thesis, University of California, Berkeley.

S. Ravi and K. Knight. 2009. Minimized models for unsupervised part-of-speech tagging. In *Proc. of ACL-IJCNLP*.

D. L. T. Rohde and D. C. Plaut. 1999. Language acquisition in the absence of explicit negative evidence: How important is starting small? *Cognition*, 72(1).

L. M. Saksida, S. M. Raymond, and D. S. Touretzky. 1997. Shaping robot behavior using principles from instrumental conditioning. *Robotics and Autonomous Systems*, 22(3).

S. Salvador and P. Chan. 2004. Determining the number of clusters/segments in hierarchical clustering/segmentation algorithms. In *Proc. of ICTAI*.

T. D. Sanger. 1994. Neural network learning control of robot manipulators using gradually increasing task difficulty. *IEEE Trans. on Robotics and Automation*, 10.

T. Savage. 1998. Shaping: The link between rats and robots. *Connection Science*, 10(3).

T. Savage. 2001. Shaping: A multiple contingencies analysis and its relevance to behaviour-based robotics. *Connection Science*, 13(3).

Y. Seginer. 2007. Fast unsupervised incremental parsing. In *Proc. of ACL*.

S. P. Singh. 1992. Transfer of learning by composing solutions of elemental squential tasks. *Machine Learning*, 8.

B. F. Skinner. 1938. *The behavior of organisms: An experimental analysis*. Appleton-Century-Crofts.

N. A. Smith and J. Eisner. 2004. Annealing techniques for unsupervised statistical language learning. In *Proc. of ACL*.

N. A. Smith and J. Eisner. 2005. Guiding unsupervised grammar induction using contrastive estimation. In *Proc. of the IJCAI Workshop on Grammatical Inference Applications*.

N. A. Smith and J. Eisner. 2006. Annealing structural bias in multilingual weighted grammar induction. In *Proc. of COLING-ACL*.

J. Suzuki, H. Isozaki, X. Carreras, and M. Collins. 2009. An empirical study of semi-supervised structured conditional models for dependency parsing. In *Proc. of EMNLP*.

Relaxed Marginal Inference and its Application to Dependency Parsing

Sebastian Riedel David A. Smith
Department of Computer Science
University of Massachusetts, Amherst
{riedel,dasmith}@cs.umass.edu

Abstract

Recently, relaxation approaches have been successfully used for MAP inference on NLP problems. In this work we show how to extend the relaxation approach to marginal inference used in conditional likelihood training, posterior decoding, confidence estimation, and other tasks. We evaluate our approach for the case of second-order dependency parsing and observe a tenfold increase in parsing speed, with no loss in accuracy, by performing inference over a small subset of the full factor graph. We also contribute a bound on the error of the marginal probabilities by a sub-graph with respect to the full graph. Finally, while only evaluated with BP in this paper, our approach is general enough to be applied with any marginal inference method in the inner loop.

1 Introduction

In statistical natural language processing (NLP) we are often concerned with finding the marginal probabilities of events in our models or the expectations of features. When training to optimize conditional likelihood, feature expectations are needed to calculate the gradient. Marginalization also allows a statistical NLP component to give confidence values for its predictions or to marginalize out latent variables. Finally, given the marginal probabilities of variables, we can pick the values that maximize these marginal probabilities (perhaps subject to hard constraints) in order to predict a good variable assignment.[1]

Traditionally, marginal inference in NLP has been performed via dynamic programming (DP); however, because this requires the model to factor in a way that lends itself to DP algorithms, we have to restrict the class of probabilistic models we consider. For example, since we cannot derive a dynamic program for marginal inference in second order non-projective dependency parsing (McDonald and Satta, 2007), we have non-projective languages such as Dutch using second order projective models if we want to apply DP. Some previous work has circumvented this problem for MAP inference by starting with a second-order projective solution and then greedily flipping edges to find a better non-projective solution (McDonald and Pereira, 2006).

In order to explore richer model structures, the NLP community has recently started to investigate the use of other, well-known machine learning techniques for marginal inference. One such technique is Markov chain Monte Carlo, and in particular Gibbs sampling (Finkel et al., 2005), another is (loopy) sum-product belief propagation (Smith and Eisner, 2008). In both cases we usually work in the framework of graphical models—in our case, with factor graphs that describe our distributions through variables, factors, and factor potentials. In theory, methods such as belief propagation can take any graph and perform marginal inference. This means that we gain a great amount of flexibility to represent more global and joint distributions for NLP tasks.

The graphical models of interest, however, are often too large and densely connected for efficient inference in them. For example, in second order

[1] With a loss function that decomposes on the variables, this amounts to Minimum Bayes Risk (MBR) decoding, which is often very effective.

Human Language Technologies: The 2010 Annual Conference of the North American Chapter of the ACL, pages 760–768,

dependency parsing models, we have $O(n^2)$ variables and $O(n^3)$ factors, each of which may have to be inspected several times. While belief propagation is still tractable here (assuming we follow the approach of Smith and Eisner (2008) to enforce tree constraints), it is still much slower than simpler greedy parsing methods, and the advantage second order models give in accuracy is often not significant enough to offset the lack of speed in practice. Moreover, if we extend such parsing models to, say, penalizing all pairs of crossing edges or scoring syntax-based alignments, we will need to inspect at least $O\left(n^4\right)$ factors, increasing our efficiency concerns.

When looking at the related task of finding the most likely assignment in large graphical models (i.e., MAP inference), we notice that several recent approaches have significantly sped up computation through *relaxation* methods (Tromble and Eisner, 2006; Riedel and Clarke, 2006). Here we start with a small subset of the full graph, and run inference for this simpler problem. Then we search for factors that are "violated" in the solution, and add them to the graph. This is repeated until no more new factors can be added. Empirically this approach has shown impressive success. It often dramatically reduces the effective network size, with no loss in accuracy.

How can we extend or generalize MAP relaxation algorithms to the case of marginal inference? Roughly speaking, we answer it by introducing a notion of *factor gain* that is defined as the KL divergence between the current distribution with and without the given factor. This quantity is then used in an algorithm that starts with a sub-model, runs marginal inference in it and then determines the gains of the not-yet-added factors. In turn, all factors for which the gain exceeds some threshold are added to the current model. This process is repeated until no more new factors can be found or a maximum number of iterations is reached.

We evaluate this form of *relaxed marginal inference* for the case of second-order dependency parsing. We follow Smith and Eisner's tree-aware belief propagation procedure for inference in the inner loop of our algorithm. This leads to a tenfold increase in parsing speed with no loss in accuracy.

We also contribute a bound on the error on marginal probabilities the sub-graph defines with respect to the full graph. This bound can be used both for terminating (although not done here) and understanding the dynamics of inference. Finally, while only evaluated with BP so far, it is general enough to be applied with any marginal inference method in the inner loop.

In the following, we first give a sketch of the graphical model we apply. Then we briefly discuss marginal inference. In turn we describe our relaxation algorithm for marginal inference and some of its theoretic guarantees. Then we present empirical support for the effectiveness of our approach, and conclude.

2 Graphical Models of Dependency Trees

We give a brief overview of the graphical model we apply in our experiments. We chose the grandparents and siblings model, together with language specific multiroot and projectivity options as taken from Smith and Eisner (2008). All our models are defined over a set of binary variables L_{ij} that indicate a dependency between token i and j of the input sentence W.

2.1 Markov Random Fields

Following Smith and Eisner (2008), we define a probability distribution over all dependency trees as a collection of edges $\mathbf{y}$ for a fixed input sentence W. This distribution is represented by an undirected graphical model, or Markov random field (MRF):

$$p_{\mathcal{F}}(\mathbf{y}) \stackrel{\text{def}}{=} \frac{1}{Z} \prod_{i \in \mathcal{F}} \Psi_i(\mathbf{y}) \qquad (1)$$

specified by an index set $\mathcal{F}$ and a corresponding family $(\Psi_i)_{\mathcal{F}}$ of **factors** $\Psi_i : \mathcal{Y} \mapsto \Re^+$. Here Z is the partition function $Z_{\mathcal{F}} = \sum_{\mathbf{y}} \prod_i \Psi_i(\mathbf{y})$.

We will restrict our attention to binary factors that can be represented as $\Psi_i(\mathbf{y}) = e^{\theta_i \phi_i(\mathbf{y})}$ with binary functions $\phi_i(\mathbf{y}) \in \{0,1\}$ and weights $\theta_i \in \Re$.[2] This

[2]These ϕ_i are also called *sufficient statistics* or *feature functions*, not to be confused with the features whose weighted sum forms the weight θ_i. The restriction to binary functions is without loss of generality since we can combine constraints on particular variable assignments into potential tables with several dimensions.

leads to

$$p_{\mathcal{F}}(\mathbf{y}) \stackrel{\text{def}}{=} \frac{1}{Z} \exp\left(\sum_{i \in \mathcal{F}} \theta_i \phi_i(\mathbf{y})\right)$$

as an alternative representation for $p_{\mathcal{F}}$. Note that when $\phi_i(\mathbf{y}) = 1$ we will say that Ψ_i **fires** for $\mathbf{y}$.

Note that a factor function $\Psi_i(\mathbf{y})$ can depend on any part of the observed input sentence W; however, for brevity we will suppress this extra argument to Ψ_i.

2.2 Hard and Soft Constraints on Trees

A particular model specifies its preference for set of dependency edges over another by a set of hard and soft constraints. We use hard constraints to rule out *a priori* illegal structures, such as trees where a word has two parents, and soft constraints to raise or lower the score of trees that contain particular good or bad substructures.

A **hard** factor (or constraint) Ψ_i evaluates an assignment $\mathbf{y}$ with respect to some specified condition and fires only if this condition is *violated*; in this case it evaluates to 0. It is therefore ruling out all configurations in which the condition does not hold. Note that a hard constraint Ψ_i corresponds to $\theta_i = -\infty$ in our loglinear representation.

For dependency parsing, we consider two particular hard constraints, each of which touches all edge variables in $\mathbf{y}$: the constraint **Tree** requires that all edges form a directed spanning tree rooted at the root node 0; the constraint **PTree** enforces the more stringent condition that all edges form a *projective* directed tree. As in (Smith and Eisner, 2008), we used algorithms from edge-factored parsing to compute BP messages for these factors. In our experiments, we enforced one or the other constraint depending on the projectivity of given treebank data.

A **soft** factor Ψ_i acts as a soft constraint that prefers some assignments to others. This is equivalent to saying that its weight θ_i is finite. Note that the weight of a soft factor is usually itself composed as a sum of (sub-)weights w_j for feature functions that have the same input-output behavior as $\phi_i(\mathbf{y})$ when conditioned on the current sentence. It is these w_j which are adjusted at training time.

We use three kinds of soft factors from Smith and Eisner (2008). In the full model, there are: $O(n^2)$ $\text{LINK}_{i,j}$ factors that judge dependency edges in isolation; $O(n^3)$ $\text{GRAND}_{i,j,k}$ factors that judge pairs of dependency edges in a grandparent-parent-child chain; and $O(n^3)$ $\text{SIB}_{i,j,k}$ factors that judge pairs of dependency edges that share the same parent.

3 Marginal Inference

Formally, given our set of factors $\mathcal{F}$ and an observed sentence W, marginal inference amounts to calculating the probability $\mu_i^{\mathcal{F}}$ that our binary features ϕ_i are active. That is, for each factor Ψ_i

$$\mu_i^{\mathcal{F}} \stackrel{\text{def}}{=} \sum_{\phi_i(\mathbf{y})=1} p_{\mathcal{F}}(\mathbf{y}) = E_{\mathcal{F}}[\phi_i] \quad (2)$$

For compactness, we follow the convention of Wainwright and Jordan (2008) and represent the belief for a variable using the marginal probability of its corresponding unary factor. Hence, if we want to calculate $p_{\mathcal{F}}(L_{ij})$ we use $\mu^{\mathcal{F}}_{\text{LINK}_{ij}}$ in place. Moreover we will use $\mu^{\mathcal{F}}_{\neg i} \stackrel{\text{def}}{=} 1 - \mu^{\mathcal{F}}_i$ when we need the probability of the event $\phi_i(\mathbf{y}) = 0$.

The two most prominent approaches to marginal inference in general graphical models are Markov Chain Monte Carlo (MCMC) and variational methods. In a nutshell, MCMC iteratively generates a Markov chain that yields $p_{\mathcal{F}}$ as its stationary distribution. Any expectation $\mu_i^{\mathcal{F}}$ can then be calculated simply by counting the corresponding statistics in the generated chain.

Generally speaking, variational methods frame marginal inference as an optimization problem. Either in the sense of minimizing the KL divergence of a much simpler distribution to the actual distribution $p_{\mathcal{F}}$, as in mean field methods. Or in the sense of maximizing a variational representation of the log-partition function over the set $\mathcal{M}$ of *valid* mean vectors (Wainwright and Jordan, 2008). Note that the variational representation of the log partition function involves an entropy term that is intractable to calculate in general and therefore usually approximated. Likewise, the set of constraints that guarantee vectors μ to be valid mean vectors is intractably large and is often simplified.

Because we use belief propagation (BP) as baseline to compare to, and as a subroutine in our proposed algorithm, a brief characterization of it is in order. BP can be seen as a variational method that uses the Bethe Free Energy as approximation to the entropy, and the set $\mathcal{M}_L$ of locally consistent mean vectors as an outer bound on $\mathcal{M}$. A mean vector is locally consistent if its beliefs on factors are consistent with the beliefs of the factor neighbors.

BP solves the variational problem by iteratively updating the beliefs of factors and variables based on the current beliefs of their neighbors. When applied to acyclic graphical models BP yields the exact marginals at convergence. For general graphs, BP is not guaranteed to converge, and the beliefs it calculates are generally not the true marginals; however, in practice BP often does converge and lead to accurate marginals.

4 Relaxed Incremental Marginal Inference

Generally the runtime and accuracy of a marginal inference method depends on size, density, tree-width and interaction strength (i.e. the magnitude of its weights) of the Graphical Model. For example, in Belief Propagation the number of messages we have to send in each iteration scales with the number of factors (and their degrees). This means that when we add a large number of extra factors to our model, such as the $O(n^3)$ grandparent and sibling factors for dependency parsing, we have to pay a price in terms of speed, sometimes even accuracy.

However, on close inspection often many of the additional factors we use to model some higher order interactions are somewhat unnecessary or *redundant*. To illustrate this, let us look at a second order parsing model with grandparent factors. Surely determiners are not heads of other determiners, and this should be easy to encourage using LINK features only. Hence, a grandparent factor that discourages a determiner-determiner-determiner chain seems unnecessary.

This raises two questions: (a) can we get away without most of these factors, and (b) can we efficiently tell which factors should be discarded. We will see in section 5 that question (a) can be answered affirmatively: with a only fraction of all second order factors we can calculate marginals that are very close to the BP marginals, and when used in MBR decoding, lead to the same trees.

Question (b) can be approached by looking at how a similar problem has been tackled in combinatorial optimization and MAP inference. Riedel and Clarke (2006) tackled the MAP problem for dependency parsing by an incremental approach that starts with a relaxation of the problem, solves it, and adds additional constraints only if they are violated. If constraints were added, the process is repeated, otherwise we terminate.

4.1 Evaluating Candidate Factors

To develop such an incremental relaxation approach to marginal inference, we generalize the notion of a violated constraint. What does it mean for a factor to be violated with respect to the solution of a marginal inference problem?

One answer is to interpret the violation of a constraint as "adding this constraint will impact our current belief". To assess the impact of adding factor Ψ_i to a sub-graph $\mathcal{F}' \subseteq \mathcal{F}$ we can then use the following intuition: if the distribution $\mathcal{F}' \cup \{i\}$ is very similar to the distribution corresponding to $\mathcal{F}'$, it is probably safe to say that the marginals we get from both are close, too. If we use the KL divergence between the (distributions of) $\mathcal{F}' \cup \{i\}$ and $\mathcal{F}'$ for our interpretation of the above mentioned closeness, we can define a potential *gain* for adding Ψ_i as follows:

$$g_{\mathcal{F}'}(\Psi_i) \stackrel{\text{def}}{=} D_{KL}\left(p_{\mathcal{F}'} \| p_{\mathcal{F}' \cup \{i\}}\right).$$

Together with a threshold ϵ on this gain we can now adapt the relaxation approach to marginal inference by simply replacing the question, "Is Ψ_i violated?" with the question, "Is $g_{\mathcal{F}'}(i) > \epsilon$?" We can see the latter question as a generalization of the former if we interpret MAP inference as the zero-temperature limit of marginal inference (Wainwright and Jordan, 2008).

The form of the gain function is chosen to be easily evaluated using the beliefs we have already available for the current sub-graph $\mathcal{F}'$. It is easy to show (see Appendix) that the following holds:

Proposition 1. *The gain of a factor Ψ_i with respect to the sub-graph $\mathcal{F}' \subseteq \mathcal{F}$ is*

$$g_{\mathcal{F}'}(\Psi_i) = \log\left(\mu_{\neg i}^{\mathcal{F}'} + \mu_i^{\mathcal{F}'} e^{\theta_i}\right) - \mu_i^{\mathcal{F}'} \theta_i \qquad (3)$$

That is, the gain of a factor Ψ_i depends on two properties of Ψ_i. First, the expectation $\mu_i^{\mathcal{F}'}$ that Ψ_i fires under the current model $\mathcal{F}'$, and second, its loglinear weight θ_i. To get an intuition for this gain, consider the limit $\lim_{\mu_i^{\mathcal{F}'} \to 1} g_{\mathcal{F}'}(\Psi_i)$ of a factor with positive weight that is expected to be active under $\mathcal{F}'$. In this case the gain becomes zero, meaning that the more likely Ψ_i fires under the current model, the less useful will it be to add according to our gain. For $\lim_{\mu_i^{\mathcal{F}'} \to 0} g_{\mathcal{F}'}(\Psi_i)$ the gain also disappears. Here the confidence of the current model in ϕ_i being inactive is so high that any single factor which indicates the opposite cannot make a difference.

Fortunately, the marginal probability $\mu_i^{\mathcal{F}'}$ is usually available after inference, or can be approximated. This allows us to maintain the same basic algorithm as in the MAP case: in each "inspection step" we can use the results of the last run of inference in order to evaluate whether a factor has to be added or not.

4.2 Algorithm

Algorithm 1 shows our proposed algorithm, *Relaxed Marginal Inference*. We are given an initial factor graph (for example, the first order dependency parsing model), a threshold ϵ on the minimal gain a factor needs to have in order to be added, and a solver S for marginal inference in the partial graphs we generate along the way.

We start by finding the marginals μ for the initial graph. These marginals are then used in step 4 to find the factors that would, when added in isolation, change the distribution substantially (i.e., by more than ϵ in terms of KL divergence). We will refer to this step as *separation*, in line with cutting plane terminology. The factors are added to the current graph, and we start from the top unless there were no new factors added. In this case we return the last marginals μ.

Clearly, this algorithm is guaranteed to converge: either we add at least one factor per iteration until we reach the full graph $\mathcal{F}$, or we converge before. However, it is difficult to make any general statements about the number of iterations it takes until convergence. Nevertheless, in our experiments we find that algorithm 1 converges to a much smaller graph after a small number of iterations, and hence we are always faster than inference on the full graph.

Finally, note that calculating the gain for all factors in $\mathcal{F} \setminus \mathcal{F}'$ in step 4 (separation) takes time proportional to $|\mathcal{F} \setminus \mathcal{F}'|$.

Algorithm 1 Relaxed Marginal Inference.

1: **require**:
   $\mathcal{F}'$*:init. graph,* ϵ*: threshold,* S*:solver,* R*: max. it*
2: **repeat**
   Find current marginals using solver S
3: $\mu \leftarrow$ marginals$(\mathcal{F}', S)$
   Find factors with high gain not yet added
4: $\Delta\mathcal{F} \leftarrow \{i \in \mathcal{F} \setminus \mathcal{F}' | g_{\mathcal{F}'}(\Psi_i) > \epsilon\}$
   Add factors to current graph
5: $\mathcal{F}' \leftarrow \mathcal{F}' \cup \Delta\mathcal{F}$
   Check: no more new factors were added or R reached
6: **until** $\Delta\mathcal{F} = \emptyset$ or iteration$>R$
   return the marginals for the last graph $\mathcal{F}'$
7: **return** μ

4.3 Accuracy

We have seen how to evaluate the potential gain when adding a single factor. However, this does not tell us how good the current sub-model is with respect to the complete graph. After all, while all remaining factors individually might not contribute much, in concert they may. We therefore present a (calculable) bound on the KL divergence of the partial graph from the full graph that can give us confidence in the solutions we return at convergence.

Note that for this bound we still only need feature expectations from the current model. Moreover, we assume all weights θ_i are positive—without loss of generality since we can always replace ϕ_i with its negation $1 - \phi_i$ and then change the sign of θ_i (Richardson and Domingos, 2006).

Proposition 2. *Assume non-negative weights, let* $\mathcal{F}' \subseteq \mathcal{F}$ *be a subset of factors,* $G \stackrel{def}{=} \mathcal{F} \setminus \mathcal{F}'$ *and* $\eta \stackrel{def}{=} \|\theta_G\|_1 - \langle \mu_G, \theta_G \rangle \geq 0$. *Then*

1. *for the KL divergence between* $\mathcal{F}'$ *and the full network* $\mathcal{F}$ *we have:*

$$D_{KL}\left(p_{\mathcal{F}'} \| p_{\mathcal{F}}\right) \leq \eta.$$

2. *for the error we make when estimating* ϕ_i*'s true expectation* $\mu_i^{\mathcal{F}}$ *by* $\mu_i^{\mathcal{F}'}$ *we have:*

$$-\left(e^{\eta} - 1\right) \mu_{\neg i}^{\mathcal{F}'} \leq \mu_i^{\mathcal{F}} - \mu_i^{\mathcal{F}'} \leq \left(e^{\eta} - 1\right) \mu_i^{\mathcal{F}'}.$$

This says that (1) we get closer to the full distribution and that (2) our marginals closer to the true marginals, if the remaining factors G either have a low total weight $\|\theta_G\|$, or the current belief μ_G already assigns high probability to the features ϕ_G being active (and hence $-\langle\mu_G, \theta_G\rangle$ is small). The latter condition is the probabilistic analog to constraints already being satisfied. Finally, since η can be easily calculated, we plan to investigate its utility as a convergence criterion in future work.

4.4 Related Work

Our approach is inspired by earlier work on relaxation algorithms for performing MAP inference by incrementally tightening relaxations of a graphical model (Anguelov et al., 2004; Riedel, 2008), weighted Finite State Machine (Tromble and Eisner, 2006), Integer Linear Program (Riedel and Clarke, 2006) or Marginal Polytope (Sontag et al., 2008). However, none of these methods apply to marginal inference.

Sontag and Jaakkola (2007) compute marginal probabilities by using a cutting plane approach that starts with the local polytope and then optimizes some approximation of the log partition function. Cycle consistency constraints are added if they are violated by the current marginals, and the process is repeated until no more violations appear. While this approach does tackle marginalization, it is focused on improving its accuracy. In particular, the optimization problems they solve in each iteration are in fact larger than the problem we want to relax.

Our approach is also related to edge deletion in Bayesian networks (Choi and Darwiche, 2006). Here edges are removed from a Bayesian network in order to find a close approximation to the full network useful for other inference-related tasks (such as combined marginal and MAP inference). The core difference to our approach is the fact that they ask which edges to *remove* from the full graph, instead of which to *add* to a partial graph. This requires inference in the full model—the very operation we want to avoid.

5 Experiments

In our experiments we seek to answer the following questions. First, how fast is our relaxation approach compared to full marginal inference at comparable dependency accuracy? This requires us to find the best tree in terms of marginal probabilities on the link variables (Smith and Eisner, 2008). Second, how good is the final relaxed graph as an approximation of the full graph? Finally, how does incremental relaxation scale with sentence length?

5.1 Data and Models

We trained and tested on a subset of languages from the CoNLL Dependency Parsing Shared Tasks (Nivre et al., 2007): Dutch, Danish, Italian, and English. We apply non-projective second order models for Dutch, Danish and Italian, and a projective second order model for English. To be able to compare inference on the same model, we trained using BP on the full set of LINK, GRAND, and SIB factors.

Note that our models would rank highly among the shared task submissions, but could surely be further improved. For example, we do not use any language specific features. Since our focus in this paper is speeding up marginal inference, we will search for better models in future work.

5.2 Runtime and Dependency Accuracy

In our first set of experiments we explore the speed and accuracy of relaxed BP in comparison to full BP. To this end we first tested BP configurations with at most 5, at most 10, and at most 50 iterations to find the best setup in terms of speed and accuracy. Smith and Eisner (2008) use 5 iterations but we found that by using 10 iterations accuracy could be slightly improved. Running at most 50 iterations led to the same accuracy but was significantly slower. Hence we only report BP results with 10 iterations here.

For relaxed BP we tested along three dimensions: the threshold ϵ on the gain of factors, the maximum number of BP iterations in the inner loop of relaxed BP, and the maximum number of relaxation iterations. A configuration with maximum relaxation iterations R, threshold ϵ, and maximum BP iterations B will be identified by $\text{Rel}_{R,\epsilon,B}$. In all settings we use the LINK factors and the hard factors as initial graph $\mathcal{F}'$.

Table 1 shows the results for several configurations and our four languages in terms of unlabeled dependency accuracy (percentage of correctly iden-

	Dutch		Danish		English		Italian	
Configuration	Acc.	Time	Acc.	Time	Acc.	Time	Acc.	Time
BP	84.9	0.665	88.1	1.44	88.3	2.43	87.4	1.68
$\text{Rel}_{\infty,0.0001,5}$	85.0	0.120	88.1	0.234	88.2	0.575	87.4	0.261
$\text{Rel}_{\infty,0.0001,50}$	84.9	0.121	88.2	0.236	88.3	0.728	87.4	0.266
$\text{Rel}_{1,0.0001,50}$	84.9	0.060	88.2	0.110	88.4	0.352	87.4	0.132

Table 1: Dependency accuracy (%) and average parsing time (sec.) using second order models.

tified heads) in comparison to the gold data, and average parsing time in seconds. Here parsing time includes both time spent for marginal inference and the MBR decoding step after the marginals are available.

We notice that by relaxing BP with no limit on the number of iterations we gain a 4-6 fold increase in parsing speed across all languages when using the threshold $\epsilon = 0.0001$, while accuracy remains as high as for full BP. This can be achieved with fewer BP iterations (at most 5) in each round of relaxation than full BP needs per sentence (at most 10). Intuitively this makes sense: since our factor graphs are smaller in each iteration there will be fewer cycles to slow down convergence. This only has a small impact on overall parsing time for languages other than English, since for most sentences even full BP converges after less than 10 iterations.

We also observe that running just one iteration of our relaxation algorithm ($\text{Rel}_{1,0.0001,50}$) is enough to achieve accurate solutions. This leads to a twofold speed-up in comparison to running relaxation until convergence (primarily because of fewer calls to the separation routine), and a 7-13 fold speed-up (tenfold on average) when compared to full BP.

5.3 Quality of Relaxed Subgraphs

How large is the fraction of the full graph needed for accurate marginal probabilities? And do we really need our relaxation algorithm with repeated inference or could we instead just prune the graph in advance? Here we try to answer these questions, and will focus on the Danish dataset. Note that our results for the other languages follow the same pattern.

In table 2, we present the average ratio of the sizes of the partial and the full graph in terms of the second order factors. We also show the total runtime needed to find the subgraph and run inference in it.

Configuration	Size	Time	Err.	Acc.
BP	100%	1.44	—	88.1
$\text{Rel}_{\infty,0.1,50}$	$\approx 0\%$	0.12	0.20	87.5
$\text{Rel}_{\infty,0.0001,50}$	0.8%	0.24	0.012	88.2
$\text{Rel}_{1,0.0001,50}$	0.8%	0.11	0.015	88.2
$\text{Pruned}_{0.1}$	42%	0.56	0.022	88.0
$\text{Pruned}_{0.5}$	22%	0.40	0.098	87.7

Table 2: Ratio of partial and full graph size (Size), runtime in seconds (Time), avg. error on marginals (Err.) and tree accuracy (Acc.) for Danish.

As a measure of accuracy for marginal probabilities we find the average error in marginal probability for the variables of a sentence. Note that this measure does not necessarily correspond to the true error of our marginals because BP itself is approximate and may not return the correct marginals.

The first row shows the full BP system, working on 100% of the factor graph. The next three rows look at relaxed marginal inference. We notice that with a low threshold $\epsilon = 0.1$ we pick almost no additional factors (0.003%), and this does affect accuracy. However, by lowering the threshold to 0.0001 and adding about 0.8% of the second order factors, we already match the dependency accuracy of full BP. On average we are also very close to the BP marginals.

Can we find such small graphs without running extra iterations of inference? One approach could be to simply cut off factors Ψ_i with absolute weights $|\theta_i|$ that fall under a certain threshold t. In the final rows of the table we test such an approach with $t = 0.1, 0.5$.

We notice that pruning can reduce the second order factors to 42% while yielding (almost) the same accuracy, and close marginals. However, it is 5 times slower than our fastest approach. When reducing

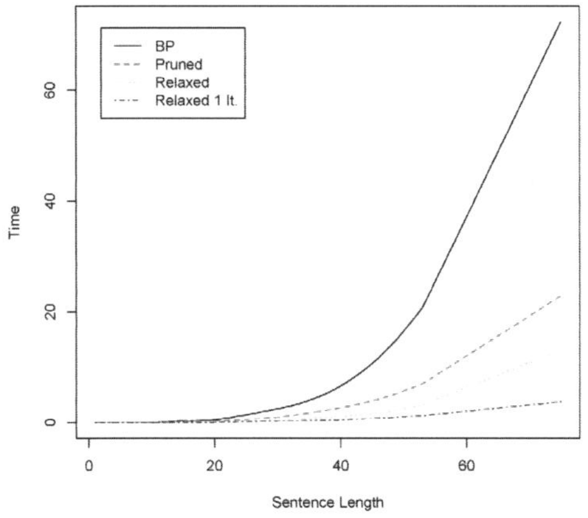

Figure 1: Total runtimes by sentence length.

size further to about 20%, accuracy drops below the values we achieved with our relaxation approach at 0.8% of the second order factors. Hence simple pruning removes factors that do have a low weight, but are still important to keep.

5.4 Runtime with Varying Sentence Length

We have seen how relaxed BP is faster than full BP on average. But how does its speed scale with sentence length? To answer this question figure 1 shows a plot of runtime by sentence length for full BP, pruned BP with threshold 0.1, $\text{Rel}_{\infty,0.0001,50}$ and $\text{Rel}_{1,0.0001,50}$.

The graph indicates that the advantage of relaxed BP over both full BP and Pruned BP becomes even more significant for longer sentences, in particular when running only one iteration. This shows that by using our technique, second order parsing becomes more practical, in particular for very long sentences.

6 Conclusion

We have presented a novel incremental relaxation algorithm that can be applied to marginal inference. Instead of adding violated constraints in each iteration, it adds factors that significantly change the distribution of the graph. This notion is formalized by the introduction of a gain function that calculates the KL divergence between the current network with and without the candidate factor. We show how this gain can be calculated and provide bounds on the error made by the marginals of the relaxed graph in place of the full one.

Our algorithm led to a tenfold reduction in runtime at comparable accuracy when applied to multilingual dependency parsing with Belief Propagation. It is five times faster than pruning factors by their absolute weight, and results in smaller graphs with better marginals.

In future work we plan to apply relaxed marginal inference to larger joint inference problems within NLP, and test its effectiveness with other marginal inference algorithms as solvers in the inner loop.

Acknowledgments

This work was supported in part by the Center for Intelligent Information Retrieval and in part by SRI International subcontract #27-001338 and ARFL prime contract #FA8750-09-C-0181. Any opinions, findings and conclusions or recommendations expressed in this material are the authors' and do not necessarily reflect those of the sponsor.

Appendix: Proof Sketches

For Proposition 1 we use the primal form of the KL divergence (Wainwright and Jordan, 2008)

$$D\left(p'_{\mathcal{F}} \| p_{\mathcal{F}}\right) = \log\left(Z_{\mathcal{F}} Z_{\mathcal{F}'}^{-1}\right) - \langle \mu_{F'}, \theta_{\mathcal{F}} - \theta_{\mathcal{F}'} \rangle$$

and represent the ratio $Z_{\mathcal{F}} Z_{\mathcal{F}'}^{-1}$ of partition functions as

$$\frac{Z_{\mathcal{F}}}{Z_{\mathcal{F}'}} = \sum_{\mathbf{y}} \frac{e^{\left\langle \theta_{\mathcal{F}'}, \phi_{\mathcal{F}'}(\mathbf{y}) \right\rangle}}{Z_{\mathcal{F}'}} e^{\langle \theta_G, \phi_G(\mathbf{y}) \rangle} = E_{\mathcal{F}'}\left[e^{\langle \theta_G, \phi_G \rangle}\right]$$

where $G \stackrel{\text{def}}{=} \mathcal{F} \setminus \mathcal{F}'$. With $G = \{i\}$ we get the desired gain.

For Proposition 2, part 1, we first pick a simple upper bound on $Z_{\mathcal{F}} Z_{\mathcal{F}'}^{-1}$ by replacing the expectation with $e^{\|\theta_G\|_1}$. Inserting this into the primal form KL divergence leads to the given bound. For part 2 we represent $p_{\mathcal{F}}$ using $p_{\mathcal{F}'}$

$$p_{\mathcal{F}}(\mathbf{y}) = Z_{\mathcal{F}'} Z_{\mathcal{F}}^{-1} e^{\langle \theta_G, \phi_G(\mathbf{y}) \rangle} p_{\mathcal{F}'}(\mathbf{y})$$

and reuse our above representation of $Z_{\mathcal{F}} Z_{\mathcal{F}'}^{-1}$. This gives

$$p_{\mathcal{F}}(\mathbf{y}) = E_{\mathcal{F}'}\left[e^{\langle \theta_G, \phi_G(\mathbf{y}) \rangle}\right]^{-1} p_{\mathcal{F}'}(\mathbf{y})\, e^{\langle \theta_G, \phi_G(\mathbf{y}) \rangle}$$

which can be upper bounded by lower bounding the expectation and upper bounding the log-linear term. For the latter we use $e^{\|\theta_G\|_1}$, for the first Jensen's inequality gives

$$E_{\mathcal{F}'}\left[e^{\langle \theta_G, \phi_G(\mathbf{y}) \rangle}\right]^{-1} \geq e^{E_{\mathcal{F}'}[\langle \theta_G, \phi_G(\mathbf{y}) \rangle]} = e^{\left\langle \theta_G, \mu_G^{\mathcal{F}'} \right\rangle}$$

where the equality follows from linearity of expectations. This yields $p_{\mathcal{F}}(\mathbf{y}) \leq p_{\mathcal{F}'}(\mathbf{y})\, e^{\eta}$ and therefore upper bounds on $\mu_i^{\mathcal{F}}$ and $\mu_{\neg i}^{\mathcal{F}}$. Basic algebra then gives the desired error interval for $\mu_i^{\mathcal{F}}$ in terms of $\mu_i^{\mathcal{F}'}$.

References

D. Anguelov, D. Koller, P. Srinivasan, S. Thrun, H.-C. Pang, and J. Davis. 2004. The correlated correspondence algorithm for unsupervised registration of nonrigid surfaces. In *Advances in Neural Information Processing Systems (NIPS '04)*, pages 33–40.

Arthur Choi and Adnan Darwiche. 2006. A variational approach for approximating bayesian networks by edge deletion. In *Proceedings of the Proceedings of the Twenty-Second Conference Annual Conference on Uncertainty in Artificial Intelligence (UAI-06)*, Arlington, Virginia. AUAI Press.

Jenny Rose Finkel, Trond Grenager, and Christopher Manning. 2005. Incorporating non-local information into information extraction systems by gibbs sampling. In *Proceedings of the 43rd Annual Meeting of the Association for Computational Linguistics (ACL' 05)*, pages 363–370, June.

R. McDonald and F. Pereira. 2006. Online learning of approximate dependency parsing algorithms. In *Proceedings of the 11th Conference of the European Chapter of the ACL (EACL '06)*, pages 81–88.

Ryan McDonald and Giorgio Satta. 2007. On the complexity of non-projective data-driven dependency parsing. In *IWPT '07: Proceedings of the 10th International Conference on Parsing Technologies*, pages 121–132, Morristown, NJ, USA. Association for Computational Linguistics.

J. Nivre, J. Hall, S. Kubler, R. McDonald, J. Nilsson, S. Riedel, and D. Yuret. 2007. The conll 2007 shared task on dependency parsing. In *Conference on Empirical Methods in Natural Language Processing and Natural Language Learning*, pages 915—932.

Matt Richardson and Pedro Domingos. 2006. Markov logic networks. *Machine Learning*, 62:107–136.

Sebastian Riedel and James Clarke. 2006. Incremental integer linear programming for non-projective dependency parsing. In *Proceedings of the Conference on Empirical methods in natural language processing (EMNLP '06)*, pages 129–137.

Sebastian Riedel. 2008. Improving the accuracy and efficiency of MAP inference for markov logic. In *Proceedings of the 24th Annual Conference on Uncertainty in AI (UAI '08)*, pages 468–475.

David A. Smith and Jason Eisner. 2008. Dependency parsing by belief propagation. In *Proceedings of the Conference on Empirical Methods in Natural Language Processing (EMNLP)*, pages 145–156, Honolulu, October.

D. Sontag and T. Jaakkola. 2007. New outer bounds on the marginal polytope. In *Advances in Neural Information Processing Systems (NIPS '07)*, pages 1393–1400.

David Sontag, T. Meltzer, A. Globerson, T. Jaakkola, and Y. Weiss. 2008. Tightening LP relaxations for MAP using message passing. In *Proceedings of the 24th Annual Conference on Uncertainty in AI (UAI '08)*.

Roy W. Tromble and Jason Eisner. 2006. A fast finite-state relaxation method for enforcing global constraints on sequence decoding. In *Joint Human Language Technology Conference/Annual Meeting of the North American Chapter of the Association for Computational Linguistics (HLT-NAACL '06)*, pages 423–430.

Martin Wainwright and Michael Jordan. 2008. *Graphical Models, Exponential Families, and Variational Inference.* Now Publishers.

Optimal Parsing Strategies for Linear Context-Free Rewriting Systems

Daniel Gildea
Computer Science Department
University of Rochester
Rochester, NY 14627

Abstract

Factorization is the operation of transforming a production in a Linear Context-Free Rewriting System (LCFRS) into two simpler productions by factoring out a subset of the nonterminals on the production's righthand side. Factorization lowers the rank of a production but may increase its fan-out. We show how to apply factorization in order to minimize the *parsing complexity* of the resulting grammar, and study the relationship between rank, fan-out, and parsing complexity. We show that it is always possible to obtain optimum parsing complexity with rank two. However, among transformed grammars of rank two, minimum parsing complexity is not always possible with minimum fan-out. Applying our factorization algorithm to LCFRS rules extracted from dependency treebanks allows us to find the most efficient parsing strategy for the syntactic phenomena found in non-projective trees.

1 Introduction

Gómez-Rodríguez et al. (2009a) recently examined the problem of transforming arbitrary grammars in the Linear Context-Free Rewriting System (LCFRS) formalism (Vijay-Shankar et al., 1987) in order to reduce the rank of a grammar to 2 while minimizing its fan-out. The work was motivated by the desire to develop efficient chart-parsing algorithms for non-projective dependency trees (Kuhlmann and Nivre, 2006) that do not rely on the independence assumptions of spanning tree algorithms (McDonald et al., 2005). Efficient parsing algorithms for general LCFRS are also relevant in the context of Synchronous Context-Free Grammars (SCFGs) as a formalism for machine translation, as well as the desire to handle even more general synchronous grammar formalisms which allow nonterminals to cover discontinuous spans in either language (Melamed et al., 2004; Wellington et al., 2006). LCFRS provides a very general formalism which subsumes SCFGs, the Multitext Grammars of Melamed et al. (2004), as well as mildly context-sensitive monolingual formalisms such as Tree Adjoining Grammar (Joshi and Schabes, 1997). Thus, work on transforming general LCFRS grammars promises to be widely applicable in both understanding how these formalisms interrelate, and, from a more practical viewpoint, deriving efficient parsing algorithms for them.

In this paper, we focus on the problem of transforming an LCFRS grammar into an equivalent grammar for which straightforward application of dynamic programming to each rule yields a tabular parsing algorithm with minimum complexity. This is closely related, but not equivalent, to the problem considered by Gómez-Rodríguez et al. (2009a), who minimize the fan-out, rather than the parsing complexity, of the resulting grammar. In Section 4, we show that restricting our attention to factorized grammars with rank no greater than 2 comes at no cost in parsing complexity. This result may be surprising, as Gómez-Rodríguez et al. (2009a) comment that "there may be cases in which one has to find an optimal trade-off between rank and fan-out" in order to minimize parsing complexity – in fact, no such trade-off is necessary, as rank 2 is always sufficient for optimal parsing complexity. Given this fact, we show how to adapt the factorization algorithm of Gómez-Rodríguez et al. (2009a) to return a transformed grammar with minimal parsing complexity and rank 2. In Section 5, we give a

Human Language Technologies: The 2010 Annual Conference of the North American Chapter of the ACL, pages 769–776,
Los Angeles, California, June 2010.

counterexample to the conjecture that minimal parsing complexity is possible among binarizations with minimal fan-out.

2 Background

A linear context-free rewriting system (LCFRS) is defined as a tuple $G = (V_N, V_T, P, S)$, where V_T is a set of terminal symbols, V_N is a set of nonterminal symbols, P is a set of productions, and $S \in V_N$ is a distinguished start symbol. Associated with each nonterminal B is a **fan-out** $\varphi(B)$, which tell how many discontinuous spans B covers. Productions $p \in P$ take the form:

$$p : A \to g(B_1, B_2, \ldots, B_r) \qquad (1)$$

where $A, B_1, \ldots B_r \in V_N$, and g is a function

$$g : (V_T^*)^{\varphi(B_1)} \times \ldots \times (V_T^*)^{\varphi(B_r)} \to (V_T^*)^{\varphi(A)}$$

which specifies how to assemble the $\sum_{i=1}^{r} \varphi(B_i)$ spans of the righthand side nonterminals into the $\varphi(A)$ spans of the lefthand side nonterminal. The function g must be **linear, non-erasing**, which means that if we write

$$g(\langle x_{1,1}, \ldots, x_{1,\varphi(B_1)} \rangle, \ldots, \langle x_{1,1}, \ldots, x_{1,\varphi(B_r)} \rangle) = \langle t_1, \ldots, t_{\varphi(A)} \rangle$$

the tuple of strings $\langle t_1, \ldots, t_{\varphi(A)} \rangle$ on the righthand side contains each variable $x_{i,j}$ from the lefthand side exactly once, and may also contain terminals from V_T.

We call r, the number of nonterminals on the righthand side of a production p, the **rank** of p, $\rho(p)$. The fan-out of a production, $\varphi(p)$ is the fan-out of its lefthand side, $\varphi(A)$. The rank of a grammar is the maximum rank of its rules,

$$\rho(G) = \max_{p \in P} \rho(p)$$

and similarly the fan-out of a grammar is the maximum fan-out of its rules, or equivalently, of its nonterminals:

$$\varphi(G) = \max_{B \in V_N} \varphi(B)$$

3 Parsing LCFRS

A bottom-up dynamic programming parser can be produced from an LCFRS grammar by generalizing the CYK algorithm for context-free grammars. We convert each production of the LCFRS into a deduction rule with variables for the left and right endpoints of each of the $\varphi(B_i)$ spans of each of the nonterminals $B_i, i \in [r]$ in the righthand side of the production.

The computational complexity of the resulting parser is polynomial in the length of the input string, with the degree of the polynomial being the number of distinct endpoints in the most complex production. Thus, for input of length n, the complexity is $O(n^c)$ for some constant c which depends on the grammar.

For a given rule, each of the r nonterminals has $\varphi(B_i)$ spans, and each span has a left and right endpoint, giving an upper bound of $c \leq 2 \sum_{i=1}^{r} \varphi(B_i)$. However, some of these endpoints may be shared between nonterminals on the righthand side. The exact number of distinct variables for the dynamic programming deduction rule can the written

$$c(p) = \varphi(A) + \sum_{i=1}^{r} \varphi(B_i) \qquad (2)$$

where $c(p)$ is the **parsing complexity** of a production p of the form of eq. 1 (Seki et al., 1991). To see this, consider counting the left endpoint of each span on the lefthand side of the production, and the right endpoint of each span on the righthand side of the production. Any variable corresponding to the left endpoint of a span of a righthand side nonterminal will either be shared with the right endpoint of another span if two spans are being joined by the production, or, alternatively, will form the left endpoint of a span of A. Thus, each distinct endpoint in the production is counted exactly once by eq. 2.

The parsing complexity of a grammar, $c(G)$, is the maximum parsing complexity of its rules. From eq. 2, we see that $c(G) \leq (\rho(G) + 1)\varphi(G)$. While we focus on the time complexity of parsing, it is interesting to note the space complexity of the DP algorithm is $O(n^{2\varphi(G)})$, since the DP table for each nonterminal is indexed by at most $2\varphi(G)$ positions in the input string.

4 Binarization Minimizes Parsing Complexity

An LCFRS production of rank r can be **factorized** into two productions of the form:

$$p_1 : A \rightarrow g_1(B_1, \ldots, B_{r-2}, X)$$
$$p_2 : X \rightarrow g_2(B_{r-1}, B_r)$$

This operation results in new productions that have lower rank, but possibly higher fan-out, than the original production.

If we examine the DP deduction rules corresponding to the original production p, and the first new production p_1 we find that

$$c(p_1) \leq c(p)$$

regardless of the function g of the original production, or the fan-out of the production's nonterminals. This is because

$$\varphi(X) \leq \varphi(B_{r-1}) + \varphi(B_r)$$

that is, our newly created nonterminal X may join spans from B_{r-1} and B_r, but can never introduce new spans. Thus,

$$\begin{aligned} c(p_1) &= \varphi(A) + \left(\sum_{i=1}^{r-2} \varphi(B_i) \right) + \varphi(X) \\ &\leq \varphi(A) + \sum_{i=1}^{r} \varphi(B_i) \\ &= c(p) \end{aligned}$$

As similar result holds for the second newly created production:

$$c(p_2) \leq c(p)$$

In this case, the fan-out of the newly created nonterminal, $\varphi(X)$ may be greater than $\varphi(A)$. Let us consider the left endpoints of the spans of X. Each left endpoint is either also the left endpoint of a span of A, or is the right endpoint of some nonterminal not included in X, that is, one of $B_1, \ldots B_{r-2}$. Thus,

$$\varphi(X) \leq \varphi(A) + \sum_{i=1}^{r-2} \varphi(B_i)$$

and applying this inequality to the definition of $c(p_2)$ we have:

$$\begin{aligned} c(p_2) &= \varphi(X) + \varphi(B_{r-1}) + \varphi(B_{r-2}) \\ &\leq \varphi(A) + \sum_{i=1}^{r} \varphi(B_i) \\ &= c(p) \end{aligned}$$

For notational convenience, we have defined the factorization operation as factoring out the last two nonterminals of a rule; however, the same operation can be applied to factor out any subset of the original nonterminals. The same argument that parsing complexity cannot increase still applies.

We may apply the factorization operation repeatedly until all rules have rank 2; we refer to the resulting grammar as a **binarization** of the original LCFRS. The factorization operation may increase the fan-out of a grammar, but never increases its parsing complexity. This guarantees that, if we wish to find the transformation of the original grammar having the lowest parsing complexity, it is sufficient to consider only binarizations. This is because any transformed grammar having more than two nonterminals on the righthand side can be binarized without increasing its parsing complexity.

5 The relationship between fan-out and parsing complexity

Gómez-Rodríguez et al. (2009a) provide an algorithm for finding the binarization of an LCFRS having minimal fan-out. The key idea is to search over ways of combining subsets of a rule's righthand side nonterminals such that subsets with low fan-out are considered first; this results in an algorithm with complexity polynomial in the rank of the input rule, with the exponent depending on the resulting minimum fan-out.

This algorithm can be adapted to find the binarization with minimum parsing complexity, rather than minimum fan-out. We simply use $c(p)$ rather than $\varphi(p)$ as the score for new productions, controlling both which binarizations we prefer and the order in which they are explored.

An interesting question then arises: does the binarization with minimal parsing complexity also have minimal fan-out? A binarization into a grammar of

$$A \to g(B_1, B_2, B_3, B_4)$$
$$g(\langle x_{1,1}, x_{1,2}\rangle, \langle x_{2,1}, x_{2,2}, x_{2,3}\rangle, \langle x_{3,1}, x_{3,2}, x_{3,3}, x_{3,4}, x_{3,5}\rangle, \langle x_{4,1}, x_{4,2}, x_{4,3}\rangle) =$$
$$\langle x_{4,1}x_{3,1}, x_{2,1}, x_{4,2}x_{1,1}x_{2,2}x_{4,3}x_{3,2}x_{2,3}x_{3,3}, x_{1,2}x_{3,4}, x_{3,5}\rangle$$

Figure 2: A production for which minimizing fan-out and minimizing parsing complexity are mutually exclusive.

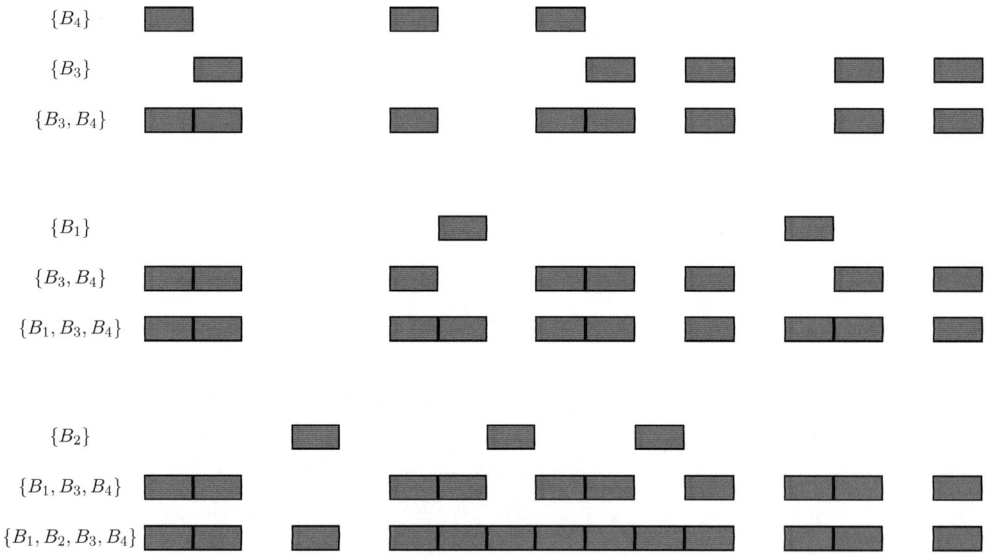

Figure 3: The binarization of the rule from Figure 2 that minimizes parsing complexity. In each of the three steps, we show the spans of each of the two subsets of the rule's righthand-side nonterms being combined, with the spans of their union (corresponding to a nonterminal created by the binarization) below.

function MINIMAL-BINARIZATION(p, $\prec$)
  workingSet $\leftarrow \emptyset$;
  agenda $\leftarrow$ priorityQueue($\prec$);
  for i from 1 to $\rho(p)$ **do**
    workingSet $\leftarrow$ workingSet $\cup\{B_i\}$;
    agenda $\leftarrow$ agenda $\cup\{B_i\}$;
  while agenda $\neq \emptyset$ **do**
    $p' \leftarrow$ pop minimum from agenda;
    if nonterms(p') $= \{B_1, \ldots B_{\rho(p)}\}$ **then**
      return p';
    for $p_1 \in$ workingSet **do**
      $p_2 \leftarrow$ newProd(p', p_1);
      find $p'_2 \in$ workingSet :
            nonterms(p'_2) = nonterms(p_2);
      if $p_2 \prec p'_2$ **then**
        workingSet $\leftarrow$ workingSet $\cup\{p_2\}\backslash\{p'_2\}$;
        push(agenda, p_2);

Figure 1: Algorithm to compute best binarization according to a user-specified ordering $\prec$ over productions.

fan-out f' cannot have parsing complexity higher than $3f'$, according to eq. 2. Thus, minimizing fan-out puts an upper bound on parsing complexity, but is not guaranteed to minimize it absolutely. Binarizations with the same fan-out may in fact vary in their parsing complexity; similarly binarizations with the same parsing complexity may vary in their fan-out. It is not immediately apparent whether, in order to find a binarization of minimal parsing complexity, it is sufficient to consider only binarizations of minimal fan-out.

To test this conjecture, we adapted the algorithm of Gómez-Rodríguez et al. (2009a) to use a priority queue as the agenda, as shown in Figure 1. The algorithm takes as an argument an arbitrary partial ordering relation on productions, and explores possible binarized rules in the order specified by this relation. In Figure 1, "workingSet" is a set of singleton nonterminals and binarized productions which are guaranteed to be optimal for the subset of nonterminals that they cover. The function "nonterms" returns, for a newly created production, the subset of the original nonterminals $B_1, \ldots B_r$ that it generates, and returns subsets of singleton nonterminals directly.

To find the binarization with the minimum fan-out f' and the lowest parsing complexity among binarizations with fan-out f', we use the following comparison operation in the binarization algorithm:

$$p_1 \prec_{\varphi c} p_2 \text{ iff } \varphi(p_1) < \varphi(p_2) \vee (\varphi(p_1) = \varphi(p_2) \wedge c(p_1) < c(p_2))$$

guaranteeing that we explore binarizations with lower fan-out first, and, among binarizations with equal fan-out, those with lower parsing complexity first. Similarly, we can search for the binarization with the lowest parsing complexity c' and the lowest fan-out among binarizations with complexity c', we use

$$p_1 \prec_{c\varphi} p_2 \text{ iff } c(p_1) < c(p_2) \vee (c(p_1) = c(p_2) \wedge \varphi(p_1) < \varphi(p_2))$$

We find that, in fact, it is sometimes necessary to sacrifice minimum fan-out in order to achieve minimum parsing complexity. An example of an LCFRS rule for which this is the case is shown in Figure 2. This production can be binarized to produce a set of productions with parsing complexity 14 (Figure 3); among binarizations with this complexity the minimum fan-out is 6. However, an alternative binarization with fan-out 5 is also possible; among binarizations with this fan-out, the minimum parsing complexity is 15. This binarization (not pictured) first joins B_1 and B_2, then adds B_4, and finally adds B_3.

Given the incompatibility of optimizing time complexity and fan-out, which corresponds to space complexity, which should we prefer? In some situations, it may be desirable to find some trade-off between the two. It is important to note, however, that if optimization of space complexity is the sole objective, factorization is unnecessary, as one can never improve on the fan-out required by the original grammar nonterminals.

6 A Note on Generative Capacity

Rambow and Satta (1999) categorize the generative capacity of LCFRS grammars according to their rank and fan-out. In particular, they show that grammars can be arranged in a two-dimensional grid, with languages of rank r and fan-out f having greater generative capacity than both grammars of rank r and fan-out $f-1$ and grammars of rank $r-1$

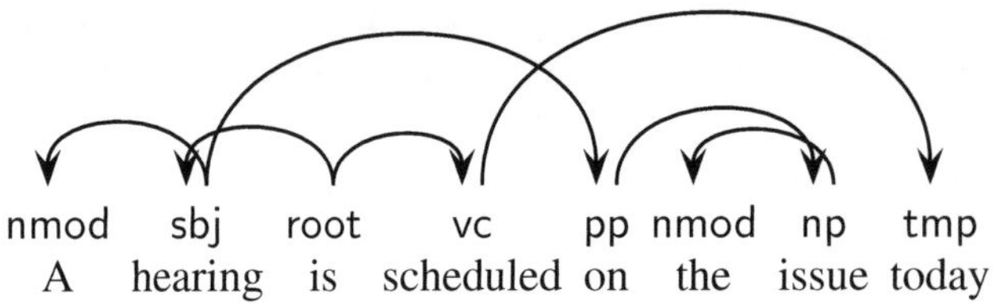

$$\begin{aligned}
\mathsf{nmod} &\rightarrow g_1 & g_1 &= \langle\, A \,\rangle \\
\mathsf{sbj} &\rightarrow g_2(\mathsf{nmod}, \mathsf{pp}) & g_2(\langle x_{1,1}\rangle, \langle x_{2,1}\rangle) &= \langle x_{1,1}\; \textit{hearing}\;, x_{2,1}\rangle \\
\mathsf{root} &\rightarrow g_3(\mathsf{sbj}, \mathsf{vc}) & g_3(\langle x_{1,1}, x_{1,2}\rangle, \langle x_{2,1}, x_{2,2}\rangle) &= \langle x_{1,1}\; \textit{is}\; x_{2,1} x_{1,2} x_{2,2}\rangle \\
\mathsf{vc} &\rightarrow g_4(\mathsf{tmp}) & g_4(\langle x_{1,1}\rangle) &= \langle\, \textit{scheduled}\;, x_{1,1}\rangle \\
\mathsf{pp} &\rightarrow g_5(\mathsf{tmp}) & g_5(\langle x_{1,1}\rangle) &= \langle\, \textit{on}\; x_{1,1}\rangle \\
\mathsf{nmod} &\rightarrow g_6 & g_6 &= \langle\, \textit{the}\,\rangle \\
\mathsf{np} &\rightarrow g_7(\mathsf{nmod}) & g_7(\langle x_{1,1}\rangle) &= \langle x_{1,1}\; \textit{issue}\,\rangle \\
\mathsf{tmp} &\rightarrow g_8 & g_8 &= \langle\, \textit{today}\,\rangle
\end{aligned}$$

Figure 4: A dependency tree with the LCFRS rules extracted for each word (Kuhlmann and Satta, 2009).

and fan-out f, with two exceptions: with fan-out 1, all ranks greater than one are equivalent (context-free languages), and with fan-out 2, rank 2 and rank 3 are equivalent.

This classification is somewhat unsatisfying because minor changes to a grammar can change both its rank and fan-out. In particular, through factorizing rules, it is always possible to decrease rank, potentially at the cost of increasing fan-out, until a binarized grammar of rank 2 is achieved.

Parsing complexity, as defined above, also provides a method to compare the generative capacity of LCFRS grammars. From Rambow and Satta's result that grammars of rank two and increasing fan-out provide an infinite hierarchy of increasing generative capacity, we see that parsing complexity also provides such an infinite hierarchy. Comparing grammars according to the parsing complexity amounts to specifying a normalized binarization for grammars of arbitrary rank and fan-out, and comparing the resulting binarized grammars. This allows us to arrange LCFRS grammars into total ordering over generative capacity, that is a one-dimensional hierarchy, rather than a two-dimensional grid. It also gives a way of categorizing generative capacity that is more closely tied to algorithmic complexity.

It is important to note, however, that parsing complexity as calculated by our algorithm remains a function of the grammar, rather than an intrinsic function of the language. One can produce arbitrarily complex grammars that generate the simple language a^*. Thus the parsing complexity of a grammar, like its rank and fan-out, can be said to categorize its *strong* generative capacity.

7 Experiments

A number of recent papers have examined dynamic programming algorithms for parsing non-projective dependency structures by exploring how well various categories of polynomially-parsable grammars cover the structures found in dependency treebanks for various languages (Kuhlmann and Nivre, 2006; Gómez-Rodríguez et al., 2009b).

Kuhlmann and Satta (2009) give an algorithm for extracting LCFRS rules from dependency structures. One rule is extracted for each word in the dependency tree. The rank of the rule is the number of children that the word has in the dependency tree, as shown by the example in Figure 4. The fan-out of the symbol corresponding to a word is the number of continuous intervals in the sentence formed by the word and its descendants in the tree. Projec-

complexity	arabic	czech	danish	dutch	german	port	swedish
20							1
18							1
16							1
15							1
13							1
12						2	3
11					1	1	1
10		2			6	16	3
9					7	4	1
8		4		7	129	65	10
7		3		12	89	30	18
6		178	11	362	1811	492	59
5	48	1132	93	411	1848	172	201
4	250	18269	1026	6678	18124	2643	1736
3	10942	265202	18306	39362	154948	41075	41245

Table 1: Number of productions with specified parsing complexity

tive trees yield LCFRS rules of fan-out one and parsing complexity three, while the fan-out and parsing complexity from non-projective trees are in principle unbounded.

Extracting LCFRS rules from treebanks allows us to study how many of the rules fall within certain constraints. Kuhlmann and Satta (2009) give an algorithm for binarizing LCRFS rules without increasing the rules' fan-out; however, this is not always possible, and the algorithm does not succeed even in some cases for which such a binarization is possible. Kuhlmann and Satta (2009) find that all but 0.02% of productions in the CoNLL 2006 training data, which includes various languages, can be binarized by their algorithm, but they do not give the fan-out or parsing complexity of the resulting rules. In related work, Gómez-Rodríguez et al. (2009b) define the class of *mildly ill-nested dependency structures* of varying gap degrees; gap degree is essentially fan-out minus one. For a given gap degree k, this class of grammars can be parsing in time $O(n^{3k+4})$ for lexicalized grammars. Gómez-Rodríguez et al. (2009b) study dependency treebanks for nine languages and find that all dependency structures meet the mildly ill-nested condition in the dependency treebanks for some gap degree. However, they do not report the maximum gap degree or parsing complexity.

We extracted LCFRS rules from dependency treebanks using the same procedure as Kuhlmann and Satta (2009), and applied the algorithm of Figure 1 directly to calculate their minimum parsing complexity. This allows us to characterize the parsing complexity of the rules found in the treebank without needing to define specific conditions on the rules, such as well-nestedness (Kuhlmann and Nivre, 2006) or mildly ill-nestedness, that may not be necessary for all efficiently parsable grammars. The numbers of rules of different complexities are shown in Table 1.

As found by previous studies, the vast majority of productions are context-free (projective trees, parsable in $O(n^3)$). Of non-projective rules, the vast majority can be parsed in $O(n^6)$, including the well-nested structures of gap degree one defined by Kuhlmann and Nivre (2006). The single most complex rule had parsing complexity of $O(n^{20})$, and was derived from a Swedish sentence which turns out to be so garbled as to be incomprehensible (taken from the high school essay portion of the Swedish treebank). It is interesting to note that, while the binarization algorithm is exponential in the worst case, it is practical for real data: analyzing all the rules extracted from the various treebanks takes only a few minutes. We did not find any cases in rules extracted from Treebank data of rules where minimizing parsing complexity is inconsistent with minimizing fan-out, as is the case for the rule of Figure 2.

8 Conclusion

We give an algorithm for finding the optimum parsing complexity for an LCFRS among grammars obtained by binarization. We find that minimum parsing complexity is always achievable with rank 2, but is not always achievable with minimum fan-out. By applying the binarization algorithm to productions found in dependency treebanks, we can completely characterize the parsing complexity of the extracted LCFRS grammar.

Acknowledgments This work was funded by NSF grants IIS-0546554 and IIS-0910611. We are grateful to Joakim Nivre for assistance with the Swedish treebank.

References

Carlos Gómez-Rodríguez, Marco Kuhlmann, Giorgio Satta, and David Weir. 2009a. Optimal reduction of rule length in linear conext-free rewriting systems. In *Proceedings of the 2009 Meeting of the North American chapter of the Association for Computational Linguistics (NAACL-09)*, pages 539–547.

Carlos Gómez-Rodríguez, David Weir, and John Carroll. 2009b. Parsing mildly non-projective dependency structures. In *Proceedings of the 12th Conference of the European Chapter of the ACL (EACL-09)*, pages 291–299.

A.K. Joshi and Y. Schabes. 1997. Tree-adjoining grammars. In G. Rozenberg and A. Salomaa, editors, *Handbook of Formal Languages*, volume 3, pages 69–124. Springer, Berlin.

Marco Kuhlmann and Joakim Nivre. 2006. Mildly non-projective dependency structures. In *Proceedings of the International Conference on Computational Linguistics/Association for Computational Linguistics (COLING/ACL-06)*, pages 507–514.

Marco Kuhlmann and Giorgio Satta. 2009. Treebank grammar techniques for non-projective dependency parsing. In *Proceedings of the 12th Conference of the European Chapter of the ACL (EACL-09)*, pages 478–486.

Ryan McDonald, Fernando Pereira, Kiril Ribarov, and Jan Hajič. 2005. Non-projective dependency parsing using spanning tree algorithms. In *Proceedings of Human Language Technology Conference and Conference on Empirical Methods in Natural Language Processing (HLT/EMNLP)*.

I. Dan Melamed, Giorgio Satta, and Ben Wellington. 2004. Generalized multitext grammars. In *Proceedings of the 42nd Annual Conference of the Association for Computational Linguistics (ACL-04)*, Barcelona, Spain.

Owen Rambow and Giorgio Satta. 1999. Independent parallelism in finite copying parallel rewriting systems. *Theor. Comput. Sci.*, 223(1-2):87–120.

H. Seki, T. Matsumura, M. Fujii, and T. Kasami. 1991. On multiple context-free grammars. *Theoretical Computer Science*, 88:191–229.

K. Vijay-Shankar, D. L. Weir, and A. K. Joshi. 1987. Characterizing structural descriptions produced by various grammatical formalisms. In *Proceedings of the 25th Annual Conference of the Association for Computational Linguistics (ACL-87)*.

Benjamin Wellington, Sonjia Waxmonsky, and I. Dan Melamed. 2006. Empirical lower bounds on the complexity of translational equivalence. In *Proceedings of the International Conference on Computational Linguistics/Association for Computational Linguistics (COLING/ACL-06)*, pages 977–984, Sydney, Australia.

The viability of web-derived polarity lexicons

Leonid Velikovich Sasha Blair-Goldensohn Kerry Hannan Ryan McDonald
Google Inc., New York, NY
{leonidv|sasha|khannan|ryanmcd}@google.com

Abstract

We examine the viability of building large polarity lexicons semi-automatically from the web. We begin by describing a graph propagation framework inspired by previous work on constructing polarity lexicons from lexical graphs (Kim and Hovy, 2004; Hu and Liu, 2004; Esuli and Sabastiani, 2009; Blair-Goldensohn et al., 2008; Rao and Ravichandran, 2009). We then apply this technique to build an English lexicon that is significantly larger than those previously studied. Crucially, this web-derived lexicon does not require WordNet, part-of-speech taggers, or other language-dependent resources typical of sentiment analysis systems. As a result, the lexicon is not limited to specific word classes – e.g., adjectives that occur in WordNet – and in fact contains slang, misspellings, multiword expressions, etc. We evaluate a lexicon derived from English documents, both qualitatively and quantitatively, and show that it provides superior performance to previously studied lexicons, including one derived from WordNet.

1 Introduction

Polarity lexicons are large lists of phrases that encode the polarity of each phrase within it – either positive or negative – often with some score representing the magnitude of the polarity (Hatzivassiloglou and McKeown, 1997; Wiebe, 2000; Turney, 2002). Though classifiers built with machine learning algorithms have become commonplace in the sentiment analysis literature, e.g., Pang et al. (2002), the core of many academic and commercial sentiment analysis systems remains the polarity lexicon, which can be constructed manually (Das and Chen, 2007), through heuristics (Kim and Hovy, 2004; Esuli and Sabastiani, 2009) or using machine learning (Turney, 2002; Rao and Ravichandran, 2009). Often lexicons are combined with machine learning for improved results (Wilson et al., 2005). The pervasiveness and sustained use of lexicons can be ascribed to a number of reasons, including their interpretability in large-scale systems as well as the granularity of their analysis.

In this work we investigate the viability of polarity lexicons that are derived solely from unlabeled web documents. We propose a method based on graph propagation algorithms inspired by previous work on constructing polarity lexicons from lexical graphs (Kim and Hovy, 2004; Hu and Liu, 2004; Esuli and Sabastiani, 2009; Blair-Goldensohn et al., 2008; Rao and Ravichandran, 2009). Whereas past efforts have used linguistic resources – e.g., WordNet – to construct the lexical graph over which propagation runs, our lexicons are constructed using a graph built from co-occurrence statistics from the entire web. Thus, the method we investigate can be seen as a combination of methods for propagating sentiment across lexical graphs and methods for building sentiment lexicons based on distributional characteristics of phrases in raw data (Turney, 2002). The advantage of breaking the dependence on WordNet (or related resources like thesauri (Mohammad et al., 2009)) is that it allows the lexicons to include non-standard entries, most notably spelling mistakes and variations, slang, and multiword expressions.

The primary goal of our study is to understand the characteristics and practical usefulness of such a lexicon. Towards this end, we provide both a qualitative and quantitative analysis for a web-derived English

Human Language Technologies: The 2010 Annual Conference of the North American Chapter of the ACL, pages 777–785,
Los Angeles, California, June 2010.

lexicon relative to two previously published lexicons – the lexicon used in Wilson et al. (2005) and the lexicon used in Blair-Goldensohn et al. (2008). Our experiments show that a web-derived lexicon is not only significantly larger, but has improved accuracy on a sentence polarity classification task, which is an important problem in many sentiment analysis applications, including sentiment aggregation and summarization (Hu and Liu, 2004; Carenini et al., 2006; Lerman et al., 2009). These results hold true both when the lexicons are used in conjunction with string matching to classify sentences, and when they are included within a contextual classifier framework (Wilson et al., 2005).

Extracting polarity lexicons from the web has been investigated previously by Kaji and Kitsuregawa (2007), who study the problem exclusively for Japanese. In that work a set of positive/negative sentences are first extracted from the web using cues from a syntactic parser as well as the document structure. Adjectives phrases are then extracted from these sentences based on different statistics of their occurrence in the positive or negative set. Our work, on the other hand, does not rely on syntactic parsers or restrict the set of candidate lexicon entries to specific syntactic classes, i.e., adjective phrases. As a result, the lexicon built in our study is on a different scale than that examined in Kaji and Kitsuregawa (2007). Though this hypothesis is not tested here, it also makes our techniques more amenable to adaptation for other languages.

2 Constructing the Lexicon

In this section we describe a method to construct polarity lexicons using graph propagation over a phrase similarity graph constructed from the web.

2.1 Graph Propagation Algorithm

We construct our lexicon using graph propagation techniques, which have previously been investigated in the construction of polarity lexicons (Kim and Hovy, 2004; Hu and Liu, 2004; Esuli and Sabastiani, 2009; Blair-Goldensohn et al., 2008; Rao and Ravichandran, 2009). We assume as input an undirected edge weighted graph $G = (V, E)$, where $w_{ij} \in [0, 1]$ is the weight of edge $(v_i, v_j) \in E$. The node set V is the set of candidate phrases for inclusion in a sentiment lexicon. In practice, G should encode semantic similarities between two nodes, e.g., for sentiment analysis one would hope that $w_{ij} > w_{ik}$ if v_i=*good*, v_j=*great* and v_k=*bad*. We also assume as input two sets of *seed phrases*, denoted P for the positive seed set and N for the negative seed set. The common property among all graph propagation algorithms is that they attempt to propagate information from the seed sets to the rest of the graph through its edges. This can be done using machine learning, graph algorithms or more heuristic means.

The specific algorithm used in this study is given in Figure 1, which is distinct from common graph propagation algorithms, e.g., label propagation (see Section 2.3). The output is a polarity vector $\mathbf{pol} \in \mathbb{R}^{|V|}$ such that $\mathbf{pol}_i$ is the polarity score for the ith candidate phrase (or the ith node in G). In particular, we desire $\mathbf{pol}$ to have the following semantics:

$$\mathbf{pol}_i = \begin{cases} > 0 & i^{th} \text{ phrase has positive polarity} \\ < 0 & i^{th} \text{ phrase has negative polarity} \\ = 0 & i^{th} \text{ phrase has no sentiment} \end{cases}$$

Intuitively, the algorithm works by computing both a positive and a negative polarity magnitude for each node in the graph, call them $\mathbf{pol}^+_i$ and $\mathbf{pol}^-_i$. These values are equal to the sum over the max weighted path from every seed word (either positive or negative) to node v_i. Phrases that are connected to multiple positive seed words through short yet highly weighted paths will receive high positive values. The final polarity of a phrase is then set to $\mathbf{pol}_i = \mathbf{pol}^+_i - \beta\mathbf{pol}^-_i$, where β a constant meant to account for the difference in overall mass of positive and negative flow in the graph. Thus, after the algorithm is run, if a phrase has a higher positive than negative polarity score, then its final polarity will be positive, and negative otherwise.

There are some implementation details worth pointing out. First, the algorithm in Figure 1 is written in an iterative framework, where on each iteration, paths of increasing lengths are considered. The input variable T controls the max path length considered by the algorithm. This can be set to be a small value in practice, since the multiplicative path weights result in long paths rarely contributing to polarity scores. Second, the parameter γ is a threshold that defines the minimum polarity magnitude a

Input: $G = (V, E)$, $w_{ij} \in [0, 1]$,
$P, N, \gamma \in \mathbb{R}$, $T \in \mathbb{N}$

Output: $\mathbf{pol} \in \mathbb{R}^{|V|}$

Initialize: $\mathbf{pol}_i, \mathbf{pol}^+_i, \mathbf{pol}^-_i = 0$, for all i
$\mathbf{pol}^+_i = 1.0$ for all $v_i \in P$ and
$\mathbf{pol}^-_i = 1.0$ for all $v_i \in N$

1. set $\alpha_{ij} = 0$ for all i, j
2. for $v_i \in P$
3. $F = \{v_i\}$
4.   for $t : 1 \ldots T$
5.   for $(v_k, v_j) \in E$ such that $v_k \in F$
6. $\alpha_{ij} = \max\{\alpha_{ij},\ \alpha_{ik} \cdot w_{kj}\}$
            $F = F \cup \{v_j\}$
7. for $v_j \in V$
8. $\mathbf{pol}^+_j = \sum_{v_i \in P} \alpha_{ij}$
9. Repeat steps 1-8 using N to compute $\mathbf{pol}^-$
10. $\beta = \sum_i \mathbf{pol}^+_i / \sum_i \mathbf{pol}^-_i$
11. $\mathbf{pol}_i = \mathbf{pol}^+_i - \beta \mathbf{pol}^-_i$, for all i
12. if $|\mathbf{pol}_i| < \gamma$ then $\mathbf{pol}_i = 0.0$, for all i

Figure 1: Graph Propagation Algorithm.

phrase must have to be included in the lexicon. Both T and γ were tuned on held-out data.

To construct the final lexicon, the remaining nodes – those with polarity scores above γ – are extracted and assigned their corresponding polarity.

2.2 Building a Phrase Graph from the Web

Graph propagation algorithms rely on the existence of graphs that encode meaningful relationships between candidate nodes. Past studies on building polarity lexicons have used linguistic resources like WordNet to define the graph through synonym and antonym relations (Kim and Hovy, 2004; Esuli and Sabastiani, 2009; Blair-Goldensohn et al., 2008; Rao and Ravichandran, 2009). The goal of this study is to examine the size and quality of polarity lexicons when the graph is induced automatically from documents on the web.

Constructing a graph from web-computed lexical co-occurrence statistics is a difficult challenge in and of itself and the research and implementation hurdles that arise are beyond the scope of this work (Alfonseca et al., 2009; Pantel et al., 2009). For this study, we used an English graph where the node set V was based on all n-grams up to length 10 extracted from 4 billion web pages. This list was filtered to 20 million candidate phrases using a number of heuristics including frequency and mutual information of word boundaries. A context vector for each candidate phrase was then constructed based on a window of size six aggregated over all mentions of the phrase in the 4 billion documents. The edge set E was constructed by first, for each potential edge (v_i, v_j), computing the cosine similarity value between context vectors. All edges (v_i, v_j) were then discarded if they were not one of the 25 highest weighted edges adjacent to either node v_i or v_j. This serves to both reduce the size of the graph and to eliminate many spurious edges for frequently occurring phrases, while still keeping the graph relatively connected. The weight of the remaining edges was set to the corresponding cosine similarity value.

Since this graph encodes co-occurrences over a large, but local context window, it can be noisy for our purposes. In particular, we might see a number of edges between positive and negative sentiment words as well as sentiment words and non-sentiment words, e.g., sentiment adjectives and all other adjectives that are distributionally similar. Larger windows theoretically alleviate this problem as they encode semantic as opposed to syntactic similarities. We note, however, that the graph propagation algorithm described above calculates the sentiment of each phrase as the aggregate of all the best paths to seed words. Thus, even if some local edges are erroneous in the graph, one hopes that, globally, positive phrases will be influenced more by paths from positive seed words as opposed to negative seed words. Section 3, and indeed this paper, aims to measure whether this is true or not.

2.3 Why Not Label Propagation?

Previous studies on constructing polarity lexicons from lexical graphs, e.g., Rao and Ravichandran (2009), have used the label propagation algorithm, which takes the form in Figure 2 (Zhu and Ghahramani, 2002). Label propagation is an iterative algorithm where each node takes on the weighted average of its neighbour's values from the previous iteration. The result is that nodes with many paths to seeds get high polarities due to the influence from their neighbours. The label propagation algorithm is known to have many desirable properties including convergence, a well defined objective function

Input: $G = (V, E)$, $w_{ij} \in [0, 1]$, P, N
Output: $\mathbf{pol} \in \mathbb{R}^{|V|}$
Initialize: $\mathbf{pol}_i = 1.0$ for all $v_i \in P$ and
$\mathbf{pol}_i = -1.0$ for all $v_i \in N$ and
$\mathbf{pol}_i = 0.0 \; \forall v_i \notin P \cup N$

1. for : t .. T
2. $\mathbf{pol}_i = \frac{\sum_{(v_i,v_j) \in E} w_{ij} \times \mathbf{pol}_j}{\sum_{(v_i,v_j)} w_{ij}}, \forall v_i \in V$
3. reset $\mathbf{pol}_i = 1.0 \; \forall v_i \in P$
   reset $\mathbf{pol}_i = -1.0 \; \forall v_i \in N$

Figure 2: The label propagation algorithm (Zhu and Ghahramani, 2002).

(minimize squared error between values of adjacent nodes), and an equivalence to computing random walks through graphs.

The primary difference between standard label propagation and the graph propagation algorithm given in Section 2.1, is that a node with multiple paths to a seed will be influenced by all these paths in the label propagation algorithm, whereas only the single path from a seed will influence the polarity of a node in our proposed propagation algorithm – namely the path with highest weight. The intuition behind label propagation seems justified. That is, if a node has multiple paths to a seed, it should be reflected in a higher score. This is certainly true when the graph is of high quality and all paths trustworthy. However, in a graph constructed from web cooccurrence statistics, this is rarely the case.

Our graph consisted of many dense subgraphs, each representing some semantic entity class, such as actors, authors, tech companies, etc. Problems arose when polarity flowed into these dense subgraphs with the label propagation algorithm. Ultimately, this flow would amplify since the dense subgraph provided exponentially many paths from each node to the source of the flow, which caused a reinforcement effect. As a result, the lexicon would consist of large groups of actor names, companies, etc. This also led to convergence issues since the polarity is divided proportional to the size of the dense subgraph. Additionally, negative phrases in the graph appeared to be in more densely connected regions, which resulted in the final lexicons being highly skewed towards negative entries due to the influence of multiple paths to seed words.

For best path propagation, these problems were less acute as each node in the dense subgraph would only get the polarity a single time from each seed, which is decayed by the fact that edge weights are smaller than 1. Furthermore, the fact that edge weights are less than 1 results in most long paths having weights near zero, which in turn results in fast convergence.

3 Lexicon Evaluation

We ran the best path graph propagation algorithm over a graph constructed from the web using manually constructed positive and negative seed sets of 187 and 192 words in size, respectively. These words were generated by a set of five humans and many are morphological variants of the same root, e.g., excel/excels/excelled. The algorithm produced a lexicon that contained 178,104 entries. Depending on the threshold γ (see Figure 1), this lexicon could be larger or smaller. As stated earlier, our selection of γ and all hyperparameters was based on manual inspection of the resulting lexicons and performance on held-out data.

In the rest of this section we investigate the properties of this lexicon to understand both its general characteristics as well as its possible utility in sentiment applications. To this end we compare three different lexicons:

1. **Wilson et al.**: Described in Wilson et al. (2005). Lexicon constructed by combining the lexicon built in Riloff and Wiebe (2003) with other sources[1]. Entries are are coarsely rated – strong/weak positive/negative – which we weighted as 1.0, 0.5, -0.5, and -1.0 for our experiments.

2. **WordNet LP**: Described in Blair-Goldensohn et al. (2008). Constructed using label propagation over a graph derived from WordNet synonym and antonym links. Note that label propagation is not prone to the kinds of errors discussed in Section 2.3 since the lexical graph is derived from a high quality source.

3. **Web GP**: The web-derived lexicon described in Section 2.1 and Section 2.2.

[1] See http://www.cs.pitt.edu/mpqa/

3.1 Qualitative Evaluation

Table 1 breaks down the lexicon by the number of positive and negative entries of each lexicon, which clearly shows that the lexicon derived from the web is more than an order of magnitude larger than previously constructed lexicons.[2] This in and of itself is not much of an achievement if the additional phrases are of poor quality. However, in Section 3.2 we present an empirical evaluation that suggests that these terms provide both additional *and* useful information. Table 1 also shows the recall of the each lexicon relative to the other. Whereas the Wilson et al. (2005) and WordNet lexicon have a recall of only 3% relative to the web lexicon, the web lexicon has a recall of 48% and 70% relative to the two other lexicons, indicating that it contains a significant amount of information from the other lexicons. However, this overlap is still small, suggesting that a combination of all the lexicons could provide the best performance. In Section 3.2 we investigate this empirically through a meta classification system.

Table 2 shows the distribution of phrases in the web-derived lexicon relative to the number of tokens in each phrase. Here a token is simply defined by whitespace and punctuation, with punctuation counting as a token, e.g., "half-baked" is counted as 3 tokens. For the most part, we see what one might expect, as the number of tokens increases, the number of corresponding phrases in the lexicon also decreases. Longer phrases are less frequent and thus will have both fewer and lower weighted edges to adjacent nodes in the graph. There is a single phrase of length 9, which is "motion to dismiss for failure to state a claim". In fact, the lexicon contains quite a number of legal and medical phrases. This should not be surprising, since in a graph induced from the web, a phrase like "cancer" (or any disease) should be distributionally similar to phrases like "illness", "sick", and "death", which themselves will be similar to standard sentiment phrases like "bad" and "terrible". These terms are predominantly negative in the lexicon representing the broad notion that legal and medical events are undesirable.

[2]This also includes the web-derived lexicon of (Kaji and Kitsuregawa, 2007), which has 10K entries. A recent study by Mohammad et al. (2009) generated lexicons from thesauri with 76K entries.

Phrase length	1	2	3
# of phrases	37,449	108,631	27,822

Phrase length	4	5	6	7	8	9
# of phrases	3,489	598	71	29	4	1

Table 2: Number of phrases by phrase length in lexicon built from the web.

Perhaps the most interesting characteristic of the lexicon is that the most frequent phrase length is 2 and not 1. The primary reason for this is an abundance of adjective phrases consisting of an adverb and an adjective, such as "more brittle" and "less brittle". Almost every adjective of length 1 is frequently combined in such a way on the web, so it not surprising that we see many of these phrases in the lexicon. Ideally we would see an order on such phrases, e.g., "more brittle" has a larger negative polarity than "brittle", which in turn has a larger negative polarity than "less brittle". However, this is rarely the case and usually the adjective has the highest polarity magnitude. Again, this is easily explained. These phrases are necessarily more common and will thus have more edges with larger weights in the graph and thus a greater chance of accumulating a high sentiment score. The prominence of such phrases suggests that a more principled treatment of them should be investigated in the future.

Finally, Table 3 presents a selection of phrases from both the positive and negative lexicons categorized into revealing verticals. For both positive and negative phrases we present typical examples of phrases – usually adjectives – that one would expect to be in a sentiment lexicon. These are phrases not included in the seed sets. We also present multiword phrases for both positive and negative cases, which displays concretely the advantage of building lexicons from the web as opposed to using restricted linguistic resources such as WordNet. Finally, we show two special cases. The first is spelling variations (and mistakes) for positive phrases, which were far more prominent than for negative phrases. Many of these correspond to social media text where one expresses an increased level of sentiment by repeating characters. The second is vulgarity in negative phrases, which was far more prominent than for positive phrases. Some of these are clearly appropri-

				Recall wrt other lexicons		
	All Phrases	Pos. Phrases	Neg. Phrases	Wilson et al.	WordNet LP	Web GP
Wilson et al.	7,628	2,718	4,910	100%	37%	2%
WordNet LP	12,310	5,705	6,605	21%	100%	3%
Web GP	178,104	90,337	87,767	70%	48%	100%

Table 1: Lexicon statistics. Wilson et al. is the lexicon used in Wilson et al. (2005), WordNet LP is the lexicon constructed by Blair-Goldensohn et al. (2008) that uses label propagation algorithms over a graph constructed through WordNet, and Web GP is the web-derived lexicon from this study.

POSITIVE PHRASES			**NEGATIVE PHRASES**		
Typical	**Multiword expressions**	**Spelling variations**	**Typical**	**Multiword expressions**	**Vulgarity**
cute	once in a life time	loveable	dirty	run of the mill	fucking stupid
fabulous	state - of - the - art	nicee	repulsive	out of touch	fucked up
cuddly	fail - safe operation	niice	crappy	over the hill	complete bullshit
plucky	just what the doctor ordered	cooool	sucky	flash in the pan	shitty
ravishing	out of this world	coooool	subpar	bumps in the road	half assed
spunky	top of the line	koool	horrendous	foaming at the mouth	jackass
enchanting	melt in your mouth	kewl	miserable	dime a dozen	piece of shit
precious	snug as a bug	cozy	lousy	pie - in - the - sky	son of a bitch
charming	out of the box	cosy	abysmal	sick to my stomach	sonofabitch
stupendous	more good than bad	sikk	wretched	pain in my ass	sonuvabitch

Table 3: Example positive and negative phrases from web lexicon.

ate, e.g., "shitty", but some are clearly insults and outbursts that are most likely included due to their co-occurrence with angry texts. There were also a number of derogatory terms and racial slurs in the lexicon, again most of which received negative sentiment due to their typical disparaging usage.

3.2 Quantitative Evaluation

To determine the practical usefulness of a polarity lexicon derived from the web, we measured the performance of the lexicon on a sentence classification/ranking task. The input is a set of sentences and the output is a classification of the sentences as being either positive, negative or neutral in sentiment. Additionally, the system outputs two rankings, the first a ranking of the sentence by positive polarity and the second a ranking of the sentence by negative polarity. Classifying sentences by their sentiment is a subtask of sentiment aggregation systems (Hu and Liu, 2004; Gamon et al., 2005). Ranking sentences by their polarity is a critical sub-task in extractive sentiment summarization (Carenini et al., 2006; Lerman et al., 2009).

To classify sentences as being positive, negative or neutral, we used an augmented vote-flip algorithm (Choi and Cardie, 2009), which is given in Figure 3. This intuition behind this algorithm is simple. The number of matched positive and negative phrases from the lexicon are counted and whichever has the most votes wins. The algorithm flips the decision if the number of negations is odd. Though this algorithm appears crude, it benefits from not relying on threshold values for neutral classification, which is difficult due to the fact that the polarity scores in the three lexicons are not on the same scale.

To rank sentences we defined the purity of a sentence X as the normalized sum of the sentiment scores for each phrase x in the sentence:

$$\mathsf{purity}(\mathsf{X}) = \frac{\sum_{\mathsf{x} \in \mathsf{X}} \mathbf{pol}_{\mathsf{x}}}{\delta + \sum_{\mathsf{x} \in \mathsf{X}} |\mathbf{pol}_{\mathsf{x}}|}$$

This is a normalized score in the range $[-1, 1]$. Intuitively, sentences with many terms of the same polarity will have purity scores at the extreme points of the range. Before calculating purity, a simple negation heuristic was implemented that reversed the sentiment scores of terms that were within the scope of negations. The term δ helps to favor sentences with multiple phrase matches. Purity is a common metric used for ranking sentences for inclusion in sentiment summaries (Lerman et al., 2009). Purity and negative purity were used to rank sentences as being positive and negative sentiment, respectively.

The data used in our initial English-only experi-

	Lexicon Classifier						Contextual Classifier					
	Positive			Negative			Positive			Negative		
	P	R	AP	P	R	AP	P	R	AP	P	R	AP
Wilson et al.	56.4	61.8	60.8	58.1	39.0	59.7	74.5	70.3	76.2	80.7	70.1	81.2
WordNet LP	50.9	61.7	62.0	54.9	36.4	59.7	72.0	72.5	75.7	78.0	69.8	79.3
Web GP	57.7	65.1†	69.6†	60.3	42.9	68.5†	74.1	75.0†	79.9†	80.5	72.6†	82.9†
Meta Classifier	-	-	-	-	-	-	76.6‡	74.7	81.2‡	81.8‡	72.2	84.1‡

Table 4: Positive and negative precision (P), recall (R), and average precision (AP) for three lexicons using either lexical matching or contextual classification strategies. † Web GP is statistically significantly better than Wilson et al. and WordNet LP ($p < 0.05$). ‡ Meta Classifier is statistically significantly better than all other systems ($p < 0.05$).

```
Input:   Scored lexicon pol, negation list NG,
         input sentence X
Output:  sentiment ∈ {POS, NEG, NEU}

set p, n, ng = 0
for x ∈ X
   if pol_x > 0 then p++
   else if pol_x < 0 then n++
   else if x ∈ NG then ng++
flip = (ng % 2 == 1)          //ng is odd
if (p > n & ¬flip) || (n > p & flip)
   return POS
else if (p > n & flip) || (n > p & ¬flip)
   return NEG
return NEU
```

Figure 3: Vote-flip algorithm (Choi and Cardie, 2009).

ments were a set of 554 consumer reviews described in (McDonald et al., 2007). Each review was sentence split and annotated by a human as being positive, negative or neutral in sentiment. This resulted in 3,916 sentences, with 1,525, 1,542 and 849 positive, negative and neutral sentences, respectively.

The first six columns of Table 4 shows: 1) the positive/negative precision-recall of each lexicon-based system where sentence classes were determined using the vote-flip algorithm, and 2) the average precision for each lexicon-based system where purity (or negative purity) was used to rank sentences. Both the Wilson et al. and WordNet LP lexicons perform at a similar level, with the former slightly better, especially in terms of precision. The web-derived lexicon, Web GP, outperforms the other two lexicons across the board, in particular when looking at average precision, where the gains are near 10% absolute. If we plot the precision-recall graphs using purity to classify sentences – as opposed to the vote-flip algorithm, which only provides an unweighted classification – we can see that at almost all recall levels the web-derived lexicon has superior precision to the other lexicons (Figure 4). Thus, even though the web-derived lexicon is constructed from a lexical graph that contains noise, the graph propagation algorithms appear to be fairly robust to this noise and are capable of producing large and accurate polarity lexicons.

The second six columns of Table 4 shows the performance of each lexicon as the core of a contextual classifier (Wilson et al., 2005). A contextual classifier is a machine learned classifier that predicts the polarity of a sentence using features of that sentence and its context. For our experiments, this was a maximum entropy classifier trained and evaluated using 10-fold cross-validation on the evaluation data. The features included in the classifier were the purity score, the number of positive and negative lexicon matches, and the number of negations in the sentence, as well as concatenations of these features within the sentence and with the same features derived from the sentences in a window of size 1.

For each sentence, the contextual classifier predicted either a positive, negative or neutral classification based on the label with highest probability. Additionally, all sentences were placed in the positive and negative sentence rankings by the probability the classifier assigned to the positive and negative classes, respectively. Mirroring the results of Wilson et al. (2005), we see that contextual classifiers improve results substantially over lexical matching. More interestingly, we see that the a contextual classifier over the web-derived lexicons maintains the performance edge over the other lexicons, though the gap is smaller. Figure 5 plots the precision-recall curves for the positive and negative sentence rank-

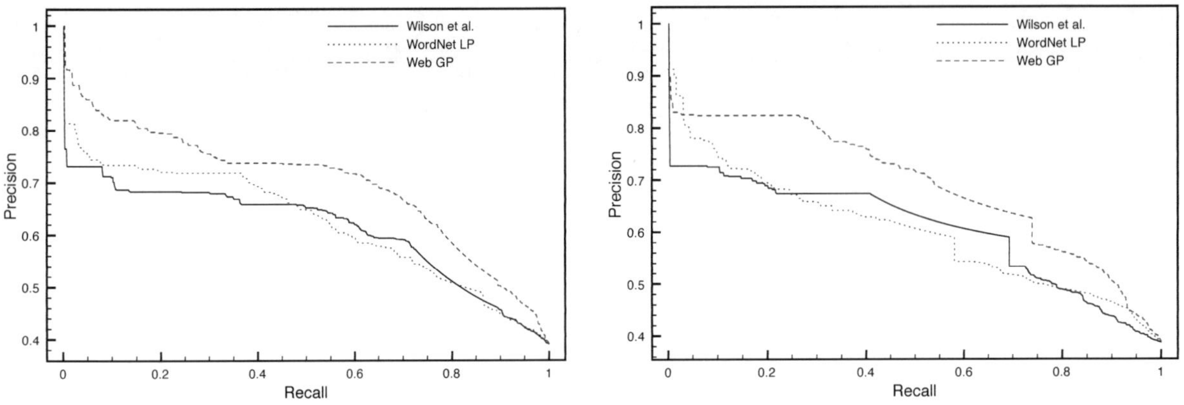

Figure 4: Lexicon classifier precision/recall curves for positive (left) and negative (right) classes.

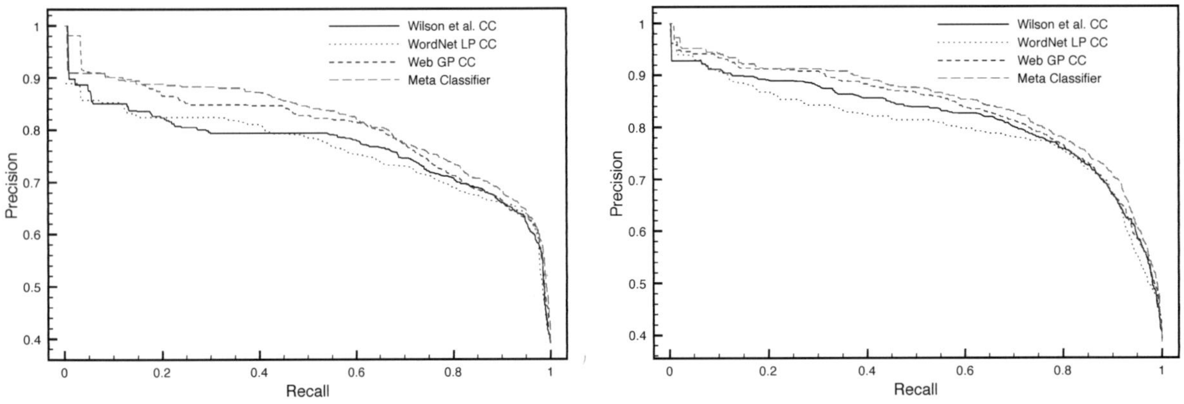

Figure 5: Contextual classifier precision/recall curves for positive (left) and negative (right) classes

ings, again showing that at almost every level of recall, the web-derived lexicon has higher precision.

For a final English experiment we built a meta-classification system that is identical to the contextual classifiers, except it is trained using features derived from all lexicons. Results are shown in the last row of Table 4 and precision-recall curves are shown in Figure 5. Not surprisingly, this system has the best performance in terms of average precision as it has access to the largest amount of information, though its performance is only slightly better than the contextual classifier for the web-derived lexicon.

4 Conclusions

In this paper we examined the viability of sentiment lexicons learned semi-automatically from the web, as opposed to those that rely on manual annotation and/or resources such as WordNet. Our qualitative experiments indicate that the web derived lexicon can include a wide range of phrases that have not been available to previous systems, most notably spelling variations, slang, vulgarity, and multiword expressions. Quantitatively, we observed that the web derived lexicon had superior performance to previously published lexicons for English classification. Ultimately, a meta classifier that incorporates features from all lexicons provides the best performance. In the future we plan to investigate the construction of web-derived lexicons for languages other than English, which is an active area of research (Mihalcea et al., 2007; Jijkoun and Hofmann, 2009; Rao and Ravichandran, 2009). The advantage of the web-derived lexicons studied here is that they do not rely on language specific resources besides unlabeled data and seed lists. A primary question is whether such lexicons improve performance over a translate-to-English strategy (Banea et al., 2008).

Acknowledgements: The authors thank Andrew Hogue, Raj Krishnan and Deepak Ravichandran for insightful discussions about this work.

References

E. Alfonseca, K. Hall, and S. Hartmann. 2009. Large-scale computation of distributional similarities for queries. In *Proceedings of the North American Chapter of the Association for Computational Linguistics (NAACL-HLT)*.

C. Banea, R. Mihalcea, J. Wiebe, and S. Hassan. 2008. Multilingual subjectivity analysis using machine translation. In *Proceedings of the Conference on Empirical Methods in Natural Language Processing (EMNLP)*.

S. Blair-Goldensohn, K. Hannan, R. McDonald, T. Neylon, G.A. Reis, and J. Reynar. 2008. Building a sentiment summarizer for local service reviews. In *NLP in the Information Explosion Era*.

G. Carenini, R. Ng, and A. Pauls. 2006. Multi-document summarization of evaluative text. In *Proceedings of the European Chapter of the Association for Computational Linguistics (EACL)*.

Y. Choi and C. Cardie. 2009. Adapting a polarity lexicon using integer linear programming for domain-specific sentiment classification. In *Proceedings of the Conference on Empirical Methods in Natural Language Processing (EMNLP)*.

S.R. Das and M.Y. Chen. 2007. Yahoo! for Amazon: Sentiment extraction from small talk on the web. *Management Science*, 53(9):1375–1388.

A Esuli and F. Sabastiani. 2009. SentiWordNet: A publicly available lexical resource for opinion mining. In *Proceedings of the Language Resource and Evaluation Conference (LREC)*.

M. Gamon, A. Aue, S. Corston-Oliver, and E. Ringger. 2005. Pulse: Mining customer opinions from free text. In *Proceedings of the 6th International Symposium on Intelligent Data Analysis (IDA)*.

V. Hatzivassiloglou and K.R. McKeown. 1997. Predicting the semantic orientation of adjectives. In *Proceedings of the European Chapter of the Association for Computational Linguistics (EACL)*.

M. Hu and B. Liu. 2004. Mining and summarizing customer reviews. In *Proceedings of the International Conference on Knowledge Discovery and Data Mining (KDD)*.

V.B. Jijkoun and K. Hofmann. 2009. Generating a non-english subjectivity lexicon: Relations that matter. In *Proceedings of the European Chapter of the Association for Computational Linguistics (EACL)*.

N. Kaji and M. Kitsuregawa. 2007. Building lexicon for sentiment analysis from massive collection of HTML documents. In *Proceedings of the Joint Conference on Empirical Methods in Natural Language Processing and Computational Natural Language Learning (EMNLP-CoNLL)*.

S.M. Kim and E. Hovy. 2004. Determining the sentiment of opinions. In *Proceedings of the International Conference on Computational Linguistics (COLING)*.

Kevin Lerman, Sasha Blair-Goldensohn, and Ryan McDonald. 2009. Sentiment summarization: Evaluating and learning user preferences. In *Proceedings of the European Chapter of the Association for Computational Linguistics (EACL)*.

R. McDonald, K. Hannan, T. Neylon, M. Wells, and J. Reynar. 2007. Structured models for fine-to-coarse sentiment analysis. In *Proceedings of the Annual Conference of the Association for Computational Linguistics (ACL)*.

R. Mihalcea, C. Banea, and J. Wiebe. 2007. Learning multilingual subjective language via cross-lingual projections. In *Proceedings of the Annual Conference of the Association for Computational Linguistics (ACL)*.

S. Mohammad, B. Dorr, and C. Dunne. 2009. Generating high-coverage semantic orientation lexicons from overtly marked words and a thesaurus. In *Proceedings of the Conference on Empirical Methods in Natural Language Processing (EMNLP)*.

B. Pang, L. Lee, and S. Vaithyanathan. 2002. Thumbs up? Sentiment classification using machine learning techniques. In *Proceedings of the Conference on Empirical Methods in Natural Language Processing (EMNLP)*.

P. Pantel, E. Crestan, A. Borkovsky, A. Popescu, and V. Vyas. 2009. Web-scale distributional similarity and entity set expansion. In *Proceedings of Conference on Empirical Methods in Natural Language Processing (EMNLP)*.

D. Rao and D. Ravichandran. 2009. Semi-Supervised Polarity Lexicon Induction. In *Proceedings of the European Chapter of the Association for Computational Linguistics (EACL)*.

E. Riloff and J. Wiebe. 2003. Learning extraction patterns for subjective expressions. In *Proceedings of the Conference on Empirical Methods in Natural Language Processing (EMNLP)*.

P. Turney. 2002. Thumbs up or thumbs down? Sentiment orientation applied to unsupervised classification of reviews. In *Proceedings of the Annual Conference of the Association for Computational Linguistics (ACL)*.

J. Wiebe. 2000. Learning subjective adjectives from corpora. In *Proceedings of the National Conference on Artificial Intelligence (AAAI)*.

T. Wilson, J. Wiebe, and P. Hoffmann. 2005. Recognizing contextual polarity in phrase-level sentiment analysis. In *Proceedings of the Conference on Empirical Methods in Natural Language Processing (EMNLP)*.

X. Zhu and Z. Ghahramani. 2002. Learning from labeled and unlabeled data with label propagation. Technical report, CMU CALD tech report CMU-CALD-02.

Dependency Tree-based Sentiment Classification using CRFs with Hidden Variables

Tetsuji Nakagawa*, **Kentaro Inui***[†] and **Sadao Kurohashi***[‡]
*National Institute of Information and Communications Technology
[†]Tohoku University
[‡]Kyoto University
tnaka@nict.go.jp, inui@ecei.tohoku.ac.jp, kuro@i.kyoto-u.ac.jp

Abstract

In this paper, we present a dependency tree-based method for sentiment classification of Japanese and English subjective sentences using conditional random fields with hidden variables. Subjective sentences often contain words which reverse the sentiment polarities of other words. Therefore, interactions between words need to be considered in sentiment classification, which is difficult to be handled with simple bag-of-words approaches, and the syntactic dependency structures of subjective sentences are exploited in our method. In the method, the sentiment polarity of each dependency subtree in a sentence, which is not observable in training data, is represented by a hidden variable. The polarity of the whole sentence is calculated in consideration of interactions between the hidden variables. Sum-product belief propagation is used for inference. Experimental results of sentiment classification for Japanese and English subjective sentences showed that the method performs better than other methods based on bag-of-features.

1 Introduction

Sentiment classification is a useful technique for analyzing subjective information in a large number of texts, and many studies have been conducted (Pang and Lee, 2008). A typical approach for sentiment classification is to use supervised machine learning algorithms with bag-of-words as features (Pang et al., 2002), which is widely used in topic-based text classification. In the approach, a subjective sentence is represented as a set of words in the sentence, ignoring word order and head-modifier relation between words. However, sentiment classification is different from traditional topic-based text classification. Topic-based text classification is generally a linearly separable problem ((Chakrabarti, 2002), p.168). For example, when a document contains some domain-specific words, the document will probably belong to the domain. However, in sentiment classification, sentiment polarities can be reversed. For example, let us consider the sentence "The medicine kills cancer cells." While the phrase *cancer cells* has negative polarity, the word *kills* reverses the polarity, and the whole sentence has positive polarity. Thus, in sentiment classification, a sentence which contains positive (or negative) polarity words does not necessarily have the same polarity as a whole, and we need to consider interactions between words instead of handling words independently.

Recently, several methods have been proposed to cope with the problem (Zaenen, 2004; Ikeda et al., 2008). However, these methods are based on flat bag-of-features representation, and do not consider syntactic structures which seem essential to infer the polarity of a whole sentence. Other methods have been proposed which utilize composition of sentences (Moilanen and Pulman, 2007; Choi and Cardie, 2008; Jia et al., 2009), but these methods use rules to handle polarity reversal, and whether polarity reversal occurs or not cannot be learned from labeled data. Statistical machine learning can learn useful information from training data and generally robust for noisy data, and using it instead of rigid rules seems useful. Wilson et al. (2005) proposed a method for sentiment classification which utilizes head-modifier relation and machine learning. However, the method is based on bag-of-features and polarity reversal occurred by content words is not handled. One issue of the approach to use sentence composition and machine learning is that only the whole sentence is labeled with its polarity in general corpora for sentiment classification, and each component of the sentence is not labeled, though such information is necessary for supervised ma-

Human Language Technologies: The 2010 Annual Conference of the North American Chapter of the ACL, pages 786–794,
Los Angeles, California, June 2010.

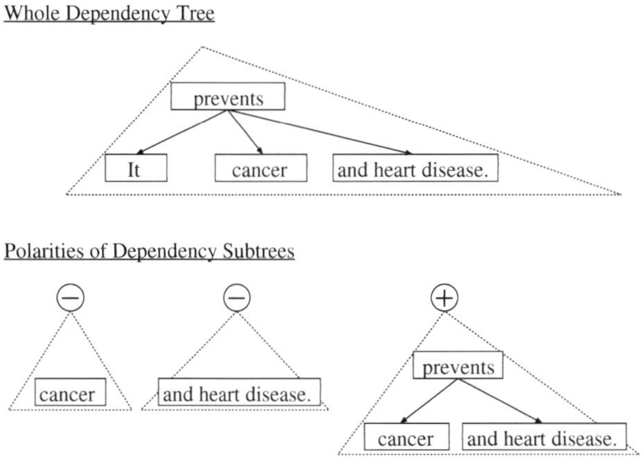

Figure 1: Polarities of Dependency Subtrees

Figure 2: Probabilistic Model based on Dependency Tree

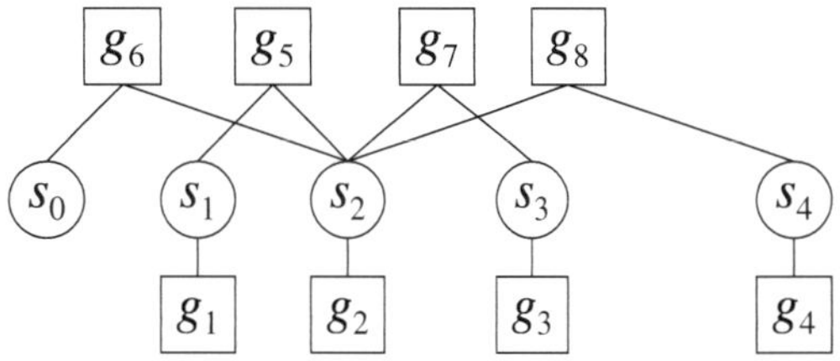

Figure 3: Factor Graph

chine learning to infer the sentence polarity from its components.

In this paper, we propose a dependency tree-based method for Japanese and English sentiment classification using conditional random fields (CRFs) with hidden variables. In the method, the sentiment polarity of each dependency subtree, which is not observable in training data, is represented by a hidden variable. The polarity of the whole sentence is calculated in consideration of interactions between the hidden variables.

The rest of this paper is organized as follows: Section 2 describes a dependency tree-based method for sentiment classification using CRFs with hidden variables, and Section 3 shows experimental results on Japanese and English corpora. Section 4 discusses related work, and Section 5 gives conclusions.

2 Dependency Tree-based Sentiment Classification using CRFs with Hidden Variables

In this study, we handle a task to classify the polarities (positive or negative) of given subjective sentences. In the rest of this section, we describe a probabilistic model for sentiment classification based on dependency trees, methods for inference and parameter estimation, and features we use.

2.1 A Probabilistic Model based on Dependency Trees

Let us consider the subjective sentence "It prevents cancer and heart disease." In the sentence, *cancer* and *heart disease* have themselves negative polarities. However, the polarities are reversed by modifying the word *prevents*, and the dependency subtree "prevents cancer and heart disease" has positive polarity. As a result, the whole dependency tree "It prevents cancer and heart disease." has positive polarity (Figure 1). In such a way, we can consider the sentiment polarity for each dependency subtree of a subjective sentence. Note that we use phrases as a basic unit instead of words in this study, because phrases are useful as a meaningful unit for sentiment classification[1]. In this paper, a *dependency subtree* means the subtree of a dependency tree whose root node is one of the phrases in the sentence.

We use a probabilistic model as shown in Figure 2. We consider that each phrase in the subjective sentence has a random variable (indicated by a circle in Figure 2). The random variable represents the polarity of the dependency subtree whose root node is the corresponding phrase. Two random variables are dependent (indicated by an edge in Figure 2) if their corresponding phrases have head-modifier relation in the dependency tree. The node denoted as *<root>* in Figure 2 indicates a virtual phrase which represents the root node of the sentence, and we regard that the random variable of the root node is the polarity of the whole sentence. In usual annotated corpora for sentiment classification, only each sentence is labeled with its polarity, and each phrase (dependency subtree) is not labeled, so all the random variables except the one for the root node are

[1]From an empirical view, in our preliminary experiments with the proposed method, phrase-based processing performed better than word-based processing in accuracy and in computational efficiency.

hidden variables that cannot be observed in labeled data (indicated by gray circles in Figure 2). With such a probabilistic model, it is possible to utilize properties such that phrases which contain positive (or negative) words tend to have positive (negative) polarities, and two phrases with head-modifier relation tend to have opposite polarities if the head contains a word which reverses sentiment polarity.

Next, we define the probabilistic model as shown in Figure 2 in detail. Let n denote the number of phrases in a subjective sentence, w_i the i-th phrase, and h_i the head index of the i-th phrase. Let s_i denote the random variable which represents the polarity of the dependency subtree whose root is the i-th phrase ($s_i \in \{+1, -1\}$), and let p denote the polarity of the whole sentence ($p \in \{+1, -1\}$). We regard the 0-th phrase as a virtual phrase which represents the root of the sentence. $\mathbf{w}, \mathbf{h}, \mathbf{s}$ respectively denote the sequence of w_i, h_i, s_i.

$$\mathbf{w} = w_1 \cdots w_n, \quad \mathbf{h} = h_1 \cdots h_n, \quad \mathbf{s} = s_0 \cdots s_n,$$
$$p = s_0.$$

For the example sentence in Figure 1, w_1 =*It*, w_2 =*prevents*, w_3 =*cancer*, w_4 =*and heart disease.*, $h_1 = 2$, $h_2 = 0$, $h_3 = 2$, $h_4 = 2$. We define the joint probability distribution of the sentiment polarities of dependency subtrees $\mathbf{s}$, given a subjective sentence $\mathbf{w}$ and its dependency tree $\mathbf{h}$, using log-linear models:

$$P_\Lambda(\mathbf{s}|\mathbf{w},\mathbf{h}) = \frac{1}{Z_\Lambda(\mathbf{w},\mathbf{h})} \exp\left\{\sum_{k=1}^{K} \lambda_k F_k(\mathbf{w},\mathbf{h},\mathbf{s})\right\}, \tag{1}$$

$$Z_\Lambda(\mathbf{w},\mathbf{h}) = \sum_{\mathbf{s}} \exp\left\{\sum_{k=1}^{K} \lambda_k F_k(\mathbf{w},\mathbf{h},\mathbf{s})\right\}, \tag{2}$$

$$F_k(\mathbf{w},\mathbf{h},\mathbf{s}) = \sum_{i=1}^{n} f_k(i,\mathbf{w},\mathbf{h},\mathbf{s}), \tag{3}$$

where $\Lambda = \{\lambda_1, \cdots, \lambda_K\}$ is the set of parameters of the model. $f_k(i,\mathbf{w},\mathbf{h},\mathbf{s})$ is the feature function of the i-th phrase, and is classified to *node feature* which considers only the corresponding node, or *edge feature* which considers both the corresponding node and its head, as follows:

$$f_k(i,\mathbf{w},\mathbf{h},\mathbf{s}) = \begin{cases} f_k^{\mathrm{n}}(w_i, s_i) & (k \in \mathbf{K}^{\mathrm{n}}), \\ f_k^{\mathrm{e}}(w_i, s_i, w_{h_i}, s_{h_i}) & (k \in \mathbf{K}^{\mathrm{e}}), \end{cases} \tag{4}$$

where $\mathbf{K}^{\mathrm{n}}$ and $\mathbf{K}^{\mathrm{e}}$ respectively represent the sets of indices of node features and edge features.

2.2 Classification of Sentiment Polarity

Let us consider how to infer the sentiment polarity $p \in \{+1, -1\}$, given a subjective sentence $\mathbf{w}$ and its dependency tree $\mathbf{h}$. The polarity of the root node (s_0) is regarded as the polarity of the whole sentence, and p can be calculated as follows:

$$p = \operatorname*{argmax}_{p'} P_\Lambda(p'|\mathbf{w},\mathbf{h}), \tag{5}$$

$$P_\Lambda(p|\mathbf{w},\mathbf{h}) = \sum_{\mathbf{s}:s_0=p} P_\Lambda(\mathbf{s}|\mathbf{w},\mathbf{h}). \tag{6}$$

That is, the polarity of the subjective sentence is obtained as the marginal probability of the root node polarity, by summing the probabilities for all the possible configurations of hidden variables. However, enumerating all the possible configurations of hidden variables is computationally hard, and we use sum-product belief propagation (MacKay, 2003) for the calculation.

Belief propagation enables us to efficiently calculate marginal probabilities. In this study, the graphical model to be solved has a tree structure (identical to the syntactic dependency tree) which has no loops, and an exact solution can be obtained using belief propagation. Dependencies among random variables in Figure 2 are represented by a factor graph in Figure 3. The factor graph consists of variable nodes s_i indicated by circles, and factor (feature) nodes g_i indicated by squares. In the example in Figure 3, $g_i (1 \leq i \leq 4)$ correspond to the node features in Equation (4), and $g_i (5 \leq i \leq 8)$ correspond to the edge features. In belief propagation, marginal distribution is calculated by passing messages (beliefs) among the variables and factors connected by edges in the factor graph (Refer to (MacKay, 2003) for detailed description of belief propagation).

2.3 Parameter Estimation

Let us consider how to estimate model parameters Λ, given L training examples $D = \{\langle \mathbf{w}^l, \mathbf{h}^l, p^l \rangle\}_{l=1}^{L}$. In this study, we use the maximum a posteriori estimation with Gaussian priors for parameter estimation. We define the following objective function $\mathcal{L}_\Lambda$, and calculate the parameters $\hat{\Lambda}$ which maximize the value:

$$\mathcal{L}_\Lambda=\sum_{l=1}^{L}\log P_\Lambda(p^l|\mathbf{w}^l,\mathbf{h}^l)-\frac{1}{2\sigma^2}\sum_{k=1}^{K}\lambda_k^2, \quad (7)$$

$$\hat{\Lambda}=\operatorname*{argmax}_{\Lambda}\mathcal{L}_\Lambda, \quad (8)$$

where σ is a parameter of Gaussian priors and is set to 1.0 in later experiments. The partial derivatives of $\mathcal{L}_\Lambda$ are as follows:

$$\frac{\partial\mathcal{L}_\Lambda}{\partial\lambda_k}=\sum_{l=1}^{L}\left[\sum_{\mathbf{s}}P_\Lambda(\mathbf{s}|\mathbf{w}^l,\mathbf{h}^l,p^l)F_k(\mathbf{w}^l,\mathbf{h}^l,\mathbf{s})-\sum_{\mathbf{s}}P_\Lambda(\mathbf{s}|\mathbf{w}^l,\mathbf{h}^l)F_k(\mathbf{w}^l,\mathbf{h}^l,\mathbf{s})\right]-\frac{1}{\sigma^2}\lambda_k. \quad (9)$$

The model parameters can be calculated with the L-BFGS quasi-Newton method (Liu and Nocedal, 1989) using the objective function and its partial derivatives. While the partial derivatives contain summation over all the possible configurations of hidden variables, it can be calculated efficiently using belief propagation as explained in Section 2.2. This parameter estimation method is same to one used for Latent-Dynamic Conditional Random Field (Morency et al., 2007). Note that the objective function $\mathcal{L}_\Lambda$ is not convex, and there is no guarantee for global optimality. The estimated model parameters depend on the initial values of the parameters, and the setting of the initial values of model parameters will be explained in Section 2.4.

2.4 Features

Table 1 shows the features used in this study. Features (a)–(h) in Table 1 are used as the node features (Equation (4)) for the i-th phrase, and features (A)–(E) are used as the edge features for the i-th and j-th phrases ($j=h_i$). In Table 1, s_i denotes the hidden variable which represents the polarity of the dependency subtree whose root node is the i-th phrase, q_i denotes the prior polarity of the i-th phrase (explained later), r_i denotes the polarity reversal of the i-th phrase (explained later), m_i denotes the number of words in the i-th phrase, $u_{i,k}$, $b_{i,k}$, $c_{i,k}$, $f_{i,k}$ respectively denote the surface form, base form, coarse-grained part-of-speech (POS) tag, fine-grained POS tag of the k-th word in the i-th phrase.

	Node Features
a	s_i
b	$s_i\&q_i$
c	$s_i\&q_i\&r_i$
d	$s_i\&u_{i,1},\cdots,s_i\&u_{i,m_i}$
e	$s_i\&c_{i,1},\cdots,s_i\&c_{i,m_i}$
f	$s_i\&f_{i,1},\cdots,s_i\&f_{i,m_i}$
g	$s_i\&u_{i,1}\&u_{i,2},\cdots,s_i\&u_{i,m_i-1}\&u_{i,m_i}$
h	$s_i\&b_{i,1}\&b_{i,2},\cdots,s_i\&b_{i,m_i-1}\&b_{i,m_i}$
	Edge Features
A	$s_i\&s_j$
B	$s_i\&s_j\&r_j$
C	$s_i\&s_j\&r_j\&q_j$
D	$s_i\&s_j\&b_{i,1},\cdots,s_i\&s_j\&b_{i,m_i}$
E	$s_i\&s_j\&b_{j,1},\cdots,s_i\&s_j\&b_{j,m_j}$

Table 1: Features Used in This Study

We used the morphological analysis system JUMAN and the dependency parser KNP[2] for processing Japanese data, and the POS tagger MXPOST (Ratnaparkhi, 1996) and the dependency parser MaltParser[3] for English data. KNP outputs phrase-based dependency trees, but MaltParser outputs word-based dependency trees, and we converted the word-based ones to phrase-based ones using simple heuristic rules explained in Appendix A.

The prior polarity of a phrase $q_i \in \{+1, 0, -1\}$ is the innate sentiment polarity of a word contained in the phrase, which can be obtained from sentiment polarity dictionaries. We used sentiment polarity dictionaries made by Kobayashi et al. (2007) and Higashiyama et al. (2008)[4] for Japanese experiments (The resulting dictionary contains 6,974 positive expressions and 8,428 negative expressions), and a dictionary made by Wilson et al. (2005)[5] for English experiments (The dictionary contains 2,289 positive expressions and 4,143 negative expressions). When a phrase contains the words registered in the dictionaries, its prior polarity is set to the registered polarity, otherwise the prior polarity is set to 0. When a phrase contains multiple words in the dictionaries, the registered polarity of the last (nearest to the end

[2] http://nlp.kuee.kyoto-u.ac.jp/nl-resource/

[3] http://maltparser.org/

[4] http://cl.naist.jp/~inui/research/EM/sentiment-lexicon.html

[5] http://www.cs.pitt.edu/mpqa/

of the sentence) word is used.

The polarity reversal of a phrase $r_i \in \{0, 1\}$ represents whether it reverses the polarities of other phrases (1) of not (0). We prepared polarity reversing word dictionaries, and the polarity reversal of a phrase is set to 1 if the phrase contains a word in the dictionaries, otherwise set to 0. We constructed polarity reversing word dictionaries which contain such words as *decrease* and *vanish* that reverse sentiment polarity. A Japanese polarity reversing word dictionary was constructed from an automatically constructed corpus, and the construction procedure is described in Appendix B (The dictionary contains 219 polarity reversing words). An English polarity reversing word dictionary was constructed from the General Inquirer dictionary[6] in the same way as Choi and Cardie (2008), by collecting words which belong to either NOTLW or DECREAS categories (The dictionary contains 121 polarity reversing words).

Choi and Cardie (2008) categorized polarity reversing words into two categories: function-word negators such as *not* and content-word negators such as *eliminate*. The polarity reversal of a phrase r_i explained above handles only the content-word negators, and function-word negators are handled in another way, since the scope of a function-word negator is generally limited to the phrase containing it in Japanese, and the number of function-word negators is small. The prior polarity q_i and the polarity reversal r_i of a phrase are changed to the following q'_i and r'_i, if the phrase contains a function-word negator (in Japanese) or if the phrase is modified by a function-word negator (in English):

$$q'_i = -q_i, \tag{10}$$

$$r'_i = 1 - r_i. \tag{11}$$

In this paper, unless otherwise noted, the word *polarity reversal* is used to indicate polarity reversing caused by content-word negators, and function-word negators are assumed to be applied to q_i and r_i in the above way beforehand.

As described in Section 2.3, there is no guarantee of global optimality for estimated parameters, since the objective function is not convex. In our preliminary experiments, L-BFGS often did not converge and classification accuracy was unstable when the initial values of parameters were randomly set. Therefore, in later experiments, we set the initial values in the following way. For the feature (A) in Table 1 in which s_i and s_j are equal, we set the initial parameter λ_i of the feature to a random number in $[0.9, 1.1]$, otherwise we set to a random number in $[-0.1, 0.1]$[7]. By setting such initial values, the initial model parameters have a property that two phrases with head-modifier relation tend to have the same polarity, which is intuitively reasonable.

3 Experiments

We conducted experiments of sentiment classification on four Japanese corpora and four English corpora.

3.1 Data

We used four corpora for experiments of Japanese sentiment classification: the Automatically Constructed Polarity-tagged corpus (ACP) (Kaji and Kitsuregawa, 2006), the Kyoto University and NTT Blog corpus (KNB) [8], the NTCIR Japanese opinion corpus (NTC-J) (Seki et al., 2007; Seki et al., 2008), the 50 Topics Evaluative Information corpus (50 Topics) (Nakagawa et al., 2008). The ACP corpus is an automatically constructed corpus from HTML documents on the Web using lexico-syntactic patterns and layout structures. The size of the corpus is large (it consists of 650,951 instances), and we used $1/100$ of the whole corpus. The KNB corpus consists of Japanese blogs, and is manually annotated. The NTC-J corpus consists of Japanese newspaper articles. There are two NTCIR Japanese opinion corpora available, the NTCIR-6 corpus and the NTCIR-7 corpus; and we combined the two corpora. The 50 Topics corpus is collected from various pages on the Web, and is manually annotated.

We used four corpora for experiments of English sentiment classification: the Customer Review data

[6] http://www.wjh.harvard.edu/ inquirer/

[7] The values of most learned parameters distributed between -1.0 and 1.0 in our preliminary experiments. Therefore, we decided to give values around the upper bound (1.0) and the mean (0.0) to the features in order to incorporate minimal prior knowledge into the model.

[8] http://nlp.kuee.kyoto-u.ac.jp/kuntt/

(CR)[9], the MPQA Opinion corpus (MPQA)[10], the Movie Review Data (MR) [11], and the NTCIR English opinion corpus (NTC-E) (Seki et al., 2007; Seki et al., 2008). The CR corpus consists of review articles about products such as digital cameras and cellular phones. There are two customer review datasets, the 5 products dataset and the 9 products dataset, and we combined the two datasets. In the MPQA corpus, sentiment polarities are attached not to sentences but expressions (sub-sentences), and we regarded the expressions as sentences and classified the polarities. There are two NTCIR English corpora available, the NTCIR-6 corpus and the NTCIR-7 corpus, and we combined the two corpora.

The statistical information of the corpora we used is shown in Table 2. We randomly split each corpus into 10 portions, and conducted 10-fold cross validation. Accuracy of sentiment classification was calculated as the number of correctly predicted labels (polarities) divided by the number of test examples.

3.2 Compared Methods

We compared our method to 6 baseline methods, and this section describes them. In the following, $p_0 \in \{+1, -1\}$ denotes the major polarity in training data, $\mathbf{H}_i$ denotes the set consisting of all the ancestor nodes of the i-th phrase in the dependency tree, and $\text{sgn}(x)$ is defined as below:

$$\text{sgn}(x) = \begin{cases} +1 & (x > 0), \\ 0 & (x = 0), \\ -1 & (x < 0). \end{cases}$$

Voting without Polarity Reversal The polarity of a subjective sentence is decided by voting of each phrase's prior polarity. In the case of a tie, the major polarity in the training data is adopted.

$$p = \text{sgn}\left(\sum_{i=1}^{n} q_i + 0.5 p_0 \right). \quad (12)$$

Voting with Polarity Reversal Same to *Voting without Polarity Reversal*, except that the polarities of phrases which have odd numbers of reversal phrases in their ancestors are reversed before voting.

$$p = \text{sgn}\left(\sum_{i=1}^{n} q_i \prod_{j \in \mathbf{H}_i} (-1)^{r_j} + 0.5 p_0 \right). \quad (13)$$

Rule The polarity of a subjective sentence is deterministically decided basing on rules, by considering the sentiment polarities of dependency subtrees. The polarity of the dependency subtree whose root is the i-th phrase is decided by voting the prior polarity of the i-th phrase and the polarities of the dependency subtrees whose root nodes are the modifiers of the i-th phrase. The polarities of the modifiers are reversed if their head phrase has a reversal word. The decision rule is applied from leaf nodes in the dependency tree, and the polarity of the root node is decided at the last.

$$s_i = \text{sgn}\left(q_i + \sum_{j:h_j = i} s_j (-1)^{r_i} \right), \quad (14)$$

$$p = \text{sgn}(s_0 + 0.5 p_0). \quad (15)$$

Bag-of-Features with No Dictionaries The polarity of a subjective sentence is classified using Support Vector Machines. Surface forms, base forms, coarse-grained POS tags and fine-grained POS tags of word unigrams and bigrams in the subjective sentence are used as features[12]. The second order polynomial kernel is used and the cost parameter C is set to 1.0. No prior polarity information (dictionary) is used.

Bag-of-Features without Polarity Reversal Same to *Bag-of-Features with No Dictionaries*, except that the voting result of prior polarities (one of positive, negative or tie) is also used as a feature.

Bag-of-Features with Polarity Reversal Same to *Bag-of-Features without Polarity Reversal*, except that the polarities of phrases which have

[9] http://www.cs.uic.edu/ liub/FBS/sentiment-analysis.html

[10] http://www.cs.pitt.edu/mpqa/

[11] http://www.cs.cornell.edu/People/pabo/movie-review-data/

[12] In experiments on English corpora, only the features of unigrams are used and those of bigrams are not used, since the bigram features decreased accuracies in our preliminary experiments as reported in previous work (Andreevskaia and Bergler, 2008).

Language	Corpus	Number of Instances	(Positive / Negative)
Japanese	ACP	6,510	(2,738 / 3,772)
	KNB	2,288	(1,423 / 865)
	NTC-J	3,485	(1,083 / 2,402)
	50 Topics	5,366	(3,175 / 2,191)
English	CR	3,772	(2,406 / 1,366)
	MPQA	10,624	(3,316 / 7,308)
	MR	10,662	(5,331 / 5,331)
	NTC-E	3,812	(1,226 / 2,586)

Table 2: Statistical Information of Corpora

Method	Japanese				English			
	ACP	KNB	NTC-J	50 Topics	CR	MPQA	MR	NTC-E
Voting-w/o Rev.	0.686	0.764	0.665	0.727	0.714	0.804	0.629	0.730
Voting-w/ Rev.	0.732	0.792	0.714	0.765	0.742	0.817	0.631	0.740
Rule	0.734	0.792	0.742	0.764	0.743	0.818	0.629	0.750
BoF-no Dic.	0.798	0.758	0.754	0.761	0.793	0.818	0.757	0.768
BoF-w/o Rev.	0.812	0.823	0.794	0.805	0.802	0.840	0.761	0.793
BoF-w/ Rev.	0.822	0.830	0.804	0.819	**0.814**	0.841	0.764	0.797
Tree-CRF	**0.846***	**0.847***	**0.826***	**0.841***	**0.814**	**0.861***	**0.773***	**0.804**

(* indicates statistical significance at $p < 0.05$)

Table 3: Accuracy of Sentiment Classification

odd numbers of reversal phrases in their ancestors are reversed before voting.

Tree-CRF The proposed method based on dependency trees using CRFs, described in Section 2.

3.3 Experimental Results

The experimental results are shown in Table 3. The proposed method Tree-CRF obtained the best accuracies for all the four Japanese corpora and the four English corpora, and the differences against the second best methods were statistically significant ($p < 0.05$) with the paired t-test for the six of the eight corpora. Tree-CRF performed better for the Japanese corpora than for the English corpora. For both the Voting methods and the Bag-of-Features methods, the methods with polarity reversal performed better than those without it[13].

Both BoF-w/ Rev. and Tree-CRF use supervised machine learning and the same dictionaries (the prior polarity dictionaries and the polarity reversing word dictionaries), but the latter performed better than the former. Our error analysis showed that BoF-w/ Rev. was not robust for erroneous words in the prior polarity dictionaries. BoF-w/ Rev. uses the voting result of the prior polarities as a feature, and the feature is sensitive to the errors in the dictionary, while Tree-CRF uses several information as well as the prior polarities to decide the polarities of dependency subtrees, and was robust to the dictionary errors. We investigated the trained model parameters of Tree-CRF, and found that the features (E) in Table 1, in which the head and the modifier have opposite polarities and the head word is such as *protect* and *withdraw*, have large positive weights. Although these words were not included in the polarity reversing word dictionary, the property that these words reverse polarities of other words seems to be learned with the model.

4 Related Work

Various studies on sentiment classification have been conducted, and there are several methods pro-

[13]The Japanese polarity reversing word dictionary was constructed from the ACP corpus as described in Appendix B, and it is not reasonable to compare the methods with and without polarity reversal on the ACP corpus. However, the tendency can be seen on the other 7 corpora.

posed for handling reversal of polarities. In this paper, our method was not directly compared with the other methods, since it is difficult to completely implement them or conduct experiments with exactly the same settings.

Choi and Cardie (2008) proposed a method to classify the sentiment polarity of a sentence basing on compositional semantics. In their method, the polarity of the whole sentence is determined from the prior polarities of the composing words by pre-defined rules, and the method differs from ours which uses the probabilistic model to handle interactions between hidden variables. Syntactic structures were used in the studies of Moilanen and Pulman (2007) and, Jia et al. (2009), but their methods are based on rules and supervised learning was not used to handle polarity reversal. As discussed in Section 1, Wilson et al. (2005) studied a bag-of-features based statistical sentiment classification method incorporating head-modifier relation.

Ikeda et al. (2008) proposed a machine learning approach to handle sentiment polarity reversal. For each word with prior polarity, whether the polarity is reversed or not is learned with a statistical learning algorithm using its surrounding words as features. The method can handle only words with prior polarities, and does not use syntactic dependency structures.

Conditional random fields with hidden variables have been studied so far for other tasks. Latent-Dynamic Conditional Random Fields (LDCRF) (Morency et al., 2007; Sun et al., 2008) are probabilistic models with hidden variables for sequential labeling, and belief propagation is used for inference. Out method is similar to the models, but there are several differences. In our method, only one variable which represents the polarity of the whole sentence is observable, and dependency relation among random variables is not a linear chain but a tree structure which is identical to the syntactic dependency.

5 Conclusion

In this paper, we presented a dependency tree-based method for sentiment classification using conditional random fields with hidden variables. In this method, the polarity of each dependency subtree of a subjective sentence is represented by a hidden variable. The values of the hidden variables are calculated in consideration of interactions between variables whose nodes have head-modifier relation in the dependency tree. The value of the hidden variable of the root node is identified with the polarity of the whole sentence. Experimental results showed that the proposed method performs better for Japanese and English data than the baseline methods which represents subjective sentences as bag-of-features.

Appendix

A Rules for Converting Word Sequence to Phrase Sequence

Let $v_1, \cdots, v_N$ denote an English word sequence, y_i the part-of-speech of the i-th word, and z_i the head index of the i-th word. The word sequence was converted to a phrase sequence as follows, by applying rules which combine two adjacent words:

```
LT ≡ {“,(,-LRB-,-LSB-,-LCB-,CC}
RT ≡ {”,),,,--,.,:,POS,-RRB-,-RSB-,-RCB-}
PP ≡ {IN,RP,TO,DT,PDT,PRP,WDT,WP,WP$,WRB}
NN ≡ {CD,FW,NN,NNP,NNPS,NNS,SYM,JJ}
do
 for i := 1 to N − 1
  if x_i and x_{i+1} are not yet combined ∧
   (x_i ∈ LT ∨
    x_{i+1} ∈ RT ∨
    ((y_i = y_{i+1} ∨ y_i = i + 1 ∨ y_{i+1} = i) ∧
     (x_i ∈ PP ∨
      (x_i ∈ NN ∧ x_{i+1} ∈ NN)))) then
   Combine the words v_i and v_{i+1}
until No rules are applied
```

B Construction of Japanese Polarity Reversing Word Dictionary

We constructed a Japanese polarity reversing word dictionary from the Automatically Constructed Polarity-tagged corpus (Kaji and Kitsuregawa, 2006). First, we collected sentences, each of which contains just one phrase having prior polarity, and the phrase modifies a phrase which modifies the root node. Among them, we selected sentences in which the prior polarity is not equal to the polarity of the whole sentence. We extracted all the words in the head phrase, and manually checked them whether they should be put into the dictionary or not. The rationale behind the procedure is that the prior polarity can be considered to be reversed by a certain word in the head phrase.

References

Alina Andreevskaia and Sabine Bergler. 2008. When Specialists and Generalists Work Together: Overcoming Domain Dependence in Sentiment Tagging. In *Proceedings of the 46th Annual Meeting of the Association for Computational Linguistics: Human Language Technologies*, pages 290–298.

Soumen Chakrabarti. 2002. *Mining the Web: Discovering Knowledge from Hypertext Data*. Morgan-Kauffman.

Yejin Choi and Claire Cardie. 2008. Learning with Compositional Semantics as Structural Inference for Subsentential Sentiment Analysis. In *Proceedings of the 2008 Conference on Empirical Methods in Natural Language Processing*, pages 793–801.

Masahiko Higashiyama, Kentaro Inui, and Yuji Matsumoto. 2008. Acquiring Noun Polarity Knowledge Using Selectional Preferences. In *Proceedings of the 14th Annual Meeting of the Association for Natural Language Processing*, pages 584–587. (in Japanese).

Daisuke Ikeda, Hiroya Takamura, Lev-Arie Ratinov, and Manabu Okumura. 2008. Learning to Shift the Polarity of Words for Sentiment Classification. In *Proceedings of the 3rd International Joint Conference on Natural Language Processing*, pages 296–303.

Lifeng Jia, Clement Yu, and Weiyi Meng. 2009. The Effect of Negation on Sentiment Analysis and Retrieval Effectiveness. In *Proceeding of the 18th ACM Conference on Information and Knowledge Management*, pages 1827–1830.

Nobuhiro Kaji and Masaru Kitsuregawa. 2006. Automatic Construction of Polarity-Tagged Corpus from HTML Documents. In *Proceedings of the COLING/ACL 2006 Main Conference Poster Sessions*, pages 452–459.

Nozomi Kobayashi, Kentaro Inui, and Yuji Matsumoto. 2007. Opinion Mining from Web Documents: Extraction and Structurization. *Journal of the Japanese Society for Artificial Intelligence*, 22(2):227–238.

Dong C. Liu and Jorge Nocedal. 1989. On the limited memory BFGS method for large scale optimization. *Mathematical Programming*, 45(3):503–528.

David J. C. MacKay. 2003. *Information Theory, Inference, and Learning Algorithms*. Cambridge University Press.

Karo Moilanen and Stephen Pulman. 2007. Sentiment Composition. In *Proceedings of the Recent Advances in Natural Language Processing International Conference*, pages 378–382.

Louis-Philippe Morency, Ariadna Quattoni, and Trevor Darrell. 2007. Latent-Dynamic Discriminative Models for Continuous Gesture Recognition. In *Proceedings of the 2007 IEEE Conference on Computer Vision and Pattern Recognition*, pages 1–8.

Tetsuji Nakagawa, Takuya Kawada, Kentaro Inui, and Sadao Kurohashi. 2008. Extracting Subjective and Objective Evaluative Expressions from the Web. In *Proceedings of the 2nd International Symposium on Universal Communication*.

Bo Pang and Lillian Lee. 2008. Opinion Mining and Sentiment Analysis. *Foundations and Trends in Information Retrieval*, 2(1-2):1–135.

Bo Pang, Lillian Lee, and Shivakumar Vaithyanathan. 2002. Thumbs up? Sentiment Classification using Machine Learning Techniques. In *Proceedings of the 2002 Conference on Empirical Methods in Natural Language Processing*, pages 79–86.

Adwait Ratnaparkhi. 1996. A Maximum Entropy Model for Part-of-Speech Tagging. In *Proceedings of the 1996 Conference on Empirical Methods in Natural Language Processing Conference*, pages 133–142.

Yohei Seki, David Kirk Evans, Lun-Wei Ku, Hsin-His Chen, Noriko Kando, and Chin-Yew Lin. 2007. Overview of Opinion Analysis Pilot Task at NTCIR-6. In *Proceedings of the 6th NTCIR Workshop*, pages 265–278.

Yohei Seki, David Kirk Evans, Lun-Wei Ku, Le Sun, Hsin-Hsi Chen, and Noriko Kando. 2008. Overview of Multilingual Opinion Analysis Task at NTCIR-7. In *Proceedings of the 7th NTCIR Workshop*.

Xu Sun, Louis-Philippe Morency, Daisuke Okanohara, and Jun'ichi Tsujii. 2008. Modeling Latent-Dynamic in Shallow Parsing: A Latent Conditional Model with Improved Inference. In *Proceedings of the 22nd International Conference on Computational Linguistics*, pages 841–848.

Theresa Wilson, Janyce Wiebe, and Paul Hoffmann. 2005. Recognizing Contextual Polarity in Phrase-Level Sentiment Analysis. In *Proceedings of the 2005 Joint Conference on Human Language Technology and Empirical Methods in Natural Language Processing*, pages 347–354.

Livia Polanyi Annie Zaenen. 2004. Contextual Lexical Valence Shifters. In *Proceedings of the AAAI Spring Symposium on Exploring Attitude and Affect in Text*.

Convolution Kernels for Opinion Holder Extraction

Michael Wiegand and **Dietrich Klakow**
Spoken Language Systems
Saarland University
D-66123 Saarbrücken, Germany
{Michael.Wiegand|Dietrich.Klakow}@lsv.uni-saarland.de

Abstract

Opinion holder extraction is one of the important subtasks in sentiment analysis. The effective detection of an opinion holder depends on the consideration of various cues on various levels of representation, though they are hard to formulate explicitly as features. In this work, we propose to use convolution kernels for that task which identify meaningful fragments of sequences or trees by themselves. We not only investigate how different levels of information can be effectively combined in different kernels but also examine how the scope of these kernels should be chosen. In general relation extraction, the two candidate entities thought to be involved in a relation are commonly chosen to be the boundaries of sequences and trees. The definition of boundaries in opinion holder extraction, however, is less straightforward since there might be several expressions beside the candidate opinion holder to be eligible for being a boundary.

1 Introduction

In recent years, there has been a growing interest in the automatic detection of opinionated content in natural language text. One of the more important tasks in sentiment analysis is the extraction of opinion holders. Opinion holder extraction is one of the critical components of an opinion question-answering system (i.e. systems which automatically answer opinion questions, such as "What does [X] like about [Y]?"). Such systems need to be able to distinguish which entities in a candidate answer sentence are the sources of opinions (= opinion holder) and which are the targets.

On other NLP tasks, in particular, on relation extraction, there has been much work on *convolution kernels*, i.e. kernel functions exploiting huge amounts of features without an explicit feature representation. Previous research on that task has shown that convolution kernels, such as sequence and tree kernels, are quite effective when compared to manual feature engineering (Moschitti, 2008; Bunescu and Mooney, 2005; Nguyen et al., 2009). In order to effectively use convolution kernels, it is often necessary to choose appropriate substructures of a sentence rather than represent the sentence as a whole structure (Bunescu and Mooney, 2005; Zhang et al., 2006; Moschitti, 2008). As for tree kernels, for example, one typically chooses the syntactic subtree immediately enclosing two entities potentially expressing a specific relation in a given sentence. The opinion holder detection task is different from this scenario. There can be *several* cues within a sentence to indicate the presence of a genuine opinion holder and these cues need not be member of a particular word group, e.g. they can be opinion words (see Sentences 1-3), communication words, such as *maintained* in Sentence 2, or other lexical cues, such as *according* in Sentence 3.

1. <u>The U.S. commanders</u> consider$_{opinion}$ the prisoners to be unlawful_combatants$_{opinion}$ as opposed to prisoners of war.

2. During the summit, <u>Koizumi</u> maintained$_{communication}$ a clear-cut_collaborative_stance$_{opinion}$ towards the U.S. and emphasized that the President was objective$_{opinion}$ and circumspect.

3. According$_{cue}$ to <u>Fernandez</u>, it was the worst_mistake$_{opinion}$ in the history of the Argentine economy.

Human Language Technologies: The 2010 Annual Conference of the North American Chapter of the ACL, pages 795–803,
Los Angeles, California, June 2010.

Thus, the definition of boundaries of the structures for the convolution kernels is less straightforward in opinion holder extraction.

The aim of this paper is to explore in how far convolution kernels can be beneficial for effective opinion holder detection. We are not only interested in how far different kernel types contribute to this extraction task but we also contrast the performance of these kernels with a manually designed feature set used as a standard vector kernel. Finally, we also examine the effectiveness of expanding word sequences or syntactic trees by additional prior knowledge.

2 Related Work

Choi et al. (2005) examine opinion holder extraction using CRFs with various manually defined linguistic features and patterns automatically learnt by the AutoSlog system (Riloff, 1996). The linguistic features focus on named-entity information and syntactic relations to opinion words. In this paper, we use very similar settings. The features presented in Kim and Hovy (2005) and Bloom et al. (2007) resemble very much Choi et al. (2005). Bloom et al. (2007) also consider communication words to be predictive cues for opinion holders.

Kim and Hovy (2006) and Bethard et al. (2005) explore the usefulness of semantic roles provided by FrameNet (Fillmore et al., 2003) for both opinion holder and opinion target extraction. Due to data sparseness, Kim and Hovy (2006) expand FrameNet data by using an unsupervised clustering algorithm.

Choi et al. (2006) is an extension of Choi et al. (2005) in that opinion holder extraction is learnt jointly with opinion detection. This requires that opinion expressions and their relations to opinion holders are annotated in the training data. Semantic roles are also taken as a potential source of information. In our work, we deliberately work with minimal annotation and, thus, do not consider any labeled opinion expressions and relations to opinion holders in the training data. We exclusively rely on entities marked as opinion holders. In many practical situations, the annotation beyond opinion holder labeling is too expensive.

Complex convolution kernels have been successfully applied to various NLP tasks, such as relation extraction (Bunescu and Mooney, 2005; Zhang et al., 2006; Nguyen et al., 2009), question answering (Zhang and Lee, 2003; Moschitti, 2008), and semantic role labeling (Moschitti et al., 2008). In all these tasks, they offer competitive performance to manually designed feature sets. Bunescu and Mooney (2005) combine different sequence kernels encoding different contexts of candidate entities in a sentence. They argue that several kernels encoding different contexts are more effective than just using one kernel with one specific context. We build on that idea and compare various scopes eligible for opinion holder extraction. Moschitti (2008) and Nguyen et al. (2009) suggest that different kinds of information, such as word sequences, part-of-speech tags, syntactic and semantic information should be contained in separate convolution kernels. We also adhere to this notion.

3 Data

As labeled data, we use the sentiment annotation of the *MPQA 2.0 corpus*[1]. Opinion holders are not explicitly labeled as such. However sources of *private states* and *subjective speech events* (Wiebe et al., 2003) are a fairly good approximation of the task. Previous work (Choi et al., 2005; Kim and Hovy, 2005; Choi et al., 2006) uses similar approximations.

4 Method

In this work, we consider all noun phrases (NPs) as possible candidate opinion holders. Therefore, the set of all data instances is the set of the NPs within the MPQA 2.0 corpus. Each NP is labeled as to whether it is a genuine opinion holder or not. Throughout this section, we will use Sentence 2 from Section 1 as an example.

4.1 The Different Levels of Representation

Several levels of representation are important for opinion holder extraction. Table 1 lists all the different levels that are used in this work. Generalized sequences employ *named-entity tags*, an OPINION tag for *opinion words* and a COMM tag for *communication words*[2]. Thus, in a generalized word se-

[1] `www.cs.pitt.edu/mpqa/databaserelease`

[2] Note that all candidate tokens are reduced to one generic CAND token. Thus, we hope to account for data sparseness in

quence (WRD_{GN}) a word is replaced by a generalized token whereas in a generalized part-of-speech sequence (POS_{GN}) a part-of-speech tag is replaced. For augmented constituent trees ($CONST_{AUG}$), the same sources of information are used. The difference to generalizing sequences is that instead of replacing words by generalized tokens, we add a node in the syntax tree with a generalized token so that it dominates the pertaining leaf node (see also nodes marked with $_{AUG}$ in Figure 2). All sources used for this type of generalization are known to be predictive for opinion holder classification (Choi et al., 2005; Kim and Hovy, 2005; Choi et al., 2006; Kim and Hovy, 2006; Bloom et al., 2007).

Note that the grammatical relation paths, i.e. $GRAM_{WRD}$ and $GRAM_{POS}$, can only be applied in case there is another expression in the focus in addition to the candidate of the data instance itself, e.g. the nearest opinion expression to the candidate. Section 4.4 explains in detail how this is done.

Predicate-argument structures (PAS) are represented by PropBank trees (Kingsbury and Palmer, 2002).

4.2 Support Vector Machines and Kernel Methods

Support Vector Machines (SVMs) are one of the most robust supervised machine learning techniques in which training data instances $\vec{x}$ are separated by a hyperplane $H(\vec{x}) = \vec{w} \cdot \vec{x} + b = 0$ where $w \in \mathbb{R}^n$ and $b \in \mathbb{R}$. One advantage of SVMs is that kernel methods can be applied which map the data to other feature spaces in which they can be separated more easily. Given a feature function $\phi : \mathbb{O} \rightarrow \mathbb{R}$, where $\mathbb{O}$ is the set of the objects, the kernel trick allows the decision hyperplane to be rewritten as:

$$H(\vec{x}) = \left(\sum_{i=1...l} y_i \alpha_i \vec{x}_i \right) \cdot \vec{x} + b =$$

$$\sum_{i=1...l} y_i \alpha_i \vec{x}_i \cdot \vec{x} + b = \sum_{i=1...l} y_i \alpha_i \phi(o_i) \cdot \phi(o) + b$$

where y_i is equal to 1 for positive and -1 for negative examples, $\alpha_i \in \mathbb{R}$ with $\alpha_i \geq 0, o_i \forall_i \in \{1, \ldots, l\}$ are the training instances and the product $K(o_i, o) = \langle \phi(o_i) \cdot \phi(o) \rangle$ is the kernel function associated with the mapping ϕ.

case there are several tokens making up the candidate.

4.3 Sequence and Tree Kernels

A sequence kernel (SK) measures the similarity of two sequences by counting the number of common subsequences. We use the kernel by Taylor and Christianini (2004) which has the advantage that it also considers subsequences of the original sequence with some elements missing. The extent of these *gaps* in a sequence is suitably reflected by a weighting function incorporated into the kernel.

Tree kernels (TKs) represent trees by their substructures. The feature space of these substructures, or fragments, is mapped onto a vector space. The kernel function computes the similarity of pairs of trees by counting the number of common fragments. In this work, we evaluate two tree kernels: Subset Tree Kernel (STK) (Collins and Duffy, 2002) and Partial Tree Kernel (PTK_{basic}) (Moschitti, 2006).

In STK, a tree fragment can be any set of nodes and edges of the original tree provided that every node has either all or none of its children. This constraint makes that kind of kernel well-suited for constituency trees which have been generated by context free grammars since the constraint corresponds to the restriction that no grammatical rule must be broken. For example, STK enforces that a subtree, such as *[VP [VBZ, NP]]*, cannot be matched with *[VP [VBZ]]* since the latter *VP* node only possesses one of the children of the former.

PTK_{basic} is more flexible since the constraint of STK on nodes is relaxed. This makes this type of tree kernel less suitable for constituency trees. We, therefore, apply it only to trees representing predicate-argument structures (PAS) (see Figure 1). Note that a data instance is represented by a set of those structures[3] rather than a single structure. Thus, the actual partial tree kernel function we use for this task, PTK, sums over all possible pairs PAS_l and PAS_m of two data instances x_i and x_j: $PTK(x_i, x_j) = \sum_{PAS_l \in x_i} \sum_{PAS_m \in x_j} PTK_{basic}(PAS_l, PAS_m)$.

To summarize, Table 2 lists the different kernel types we use coupled with the suitable levels of representation. This choice of pairing has already been motivated and empirically proven suitable on other

[3]i.e. all predicate-argument structures of a sentence in which the head of the candidate opinion holder occurs

Type	Description	Example
WRD	sequence of words	During the summit , Koizumi$_{CAND}$ maintained a clear-cut collaborative stance . . .
WRD_{GN}	sequence of generalized words	During the summit , CAND COMM OPINION . . .
POS	part-of-speech sequence	IN DET NN PUNC CAND VBD DET JJ JJ NN . . .
POS_{GN}	generalized part-of-speech sequence	IN DET NN PUNC CAND COMM OPINION . . .
$CONST$	constituency tree	*see Figure 2 without nodes marked* $_{AUG}$
$CONST_{AUG}$	augmented constituency tree	*see Figure 2*
$GRAM_{WRD}$	grammatical relation path labels with words	Koizumi$_{CAND}$ NSUBJ$\uparrow$ maintained DOBJ$\downarrow$ stance
$GRAM_{POS}$	grammatical relation path labels with part-of-speech tags	CAND NSUBJ$\uparrow$ VBD DOBJ$\downarrow$ NN
PAS	predicate argument structures	*see Figure 1(a)*
PAS_{AUG}	augmented predicate argument structures	*see Figure 1(b)*

Table 1: The different levels of representation.

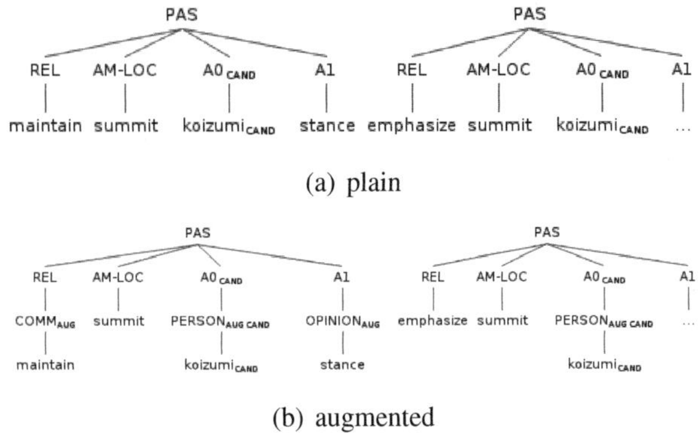

Figure 1: Predicate-argument structures (PAS).

tasks (Moschitti, 2008; Nguyen et al., 2009).

Type	Description	Levels of Representation
SK	Sequential Kernel	$WRD_{(GN)}$, $POS_{(GN)}$, $GRAM_{WRD}$, $GRAM_{POS}$
STK	Subset Tree Kernel	$CONST_{(AUG)}$
PTK	Partial Tree Kernel	PAS
VK	Vector Kernel	*not restricted*

Table 2: The different types of kernels.

4.4 The Different Scopes

We argue that using the entire word sequence or syntax tree of the sentence in which a candidate opinion holder is situated to represent a data instance produces too large structures for a convolution kernel. Since a classifier based on convolution kernels has to derive meaningful features by itself, the larger these structures are, the more likely noise is included in the model. Previous work in relation extraction has also shown that the usage of more focused substructures, e.g. the smallest subtree containing the two candidate entities of a relation, is more effective (Zhang et al., 2006). Unfortunately, in our task there is only one explicit entity we know of for each data instance which is the candidate opinion holder. However, there are several indicative cues within the context of the candidate which might be considered important. We identify three different cues being the nearest *predicate*, i.e. full verb or nominalization, *opinion word* and *communication word*[4]. For each of these expressions, we define a scope where the boundaries are the candidate opinion holder and the pertaining cue. Given these scopes, we can define resulting subsequences/subtrees and combine them. We further add two *background scopes*, one being the semantic scope of the candidate opinion holder and the entire sentence. As semantic scope we consider the subclause in which a candidate opinion holder is situated[5].

Figure 2 illustrates the different scopes. Abbreviations are explained in Table 3. As already mentioned in Section 4.1 for grammatical relation paths, a second expression in addition to the candidate opinion holder is required. These expressions can be derived from the different scopes, i.e. for $PRED$ it

[4] These three expressions may coincide but do not have to.

[5] Typically, the subtree representing a subclause has the closest S node dominating the candidate opinion holder as the root node and it contains only those nodes from the original sentence parse which are also dominated by that S node and whose path to that node does not contain another S node.

is the nearest predicate to the candidate, for OP it is the nearest opinion word and for $COMM$ it is the nearest communication word. For the background scopes SEM and $SENT$, however, there is no second expression in focus. Therefore, grammatical relation paths cannot be defined for these scopes.

Type	Description
$PRED$	scope with the boundaries being the candidate opinion holder and the nearest predicate
OP	scope with the boundaries being the candidate opinion holder and nearest opinion word
$COMM$	scope with the boundaries being the candidate opinion holder and the nearest communication word
SEM	semantic scope of the candidate opinion holder, i.e. subclause containing the candidate
$SENT$	entire sentence in which in the opinion holder occurs

Table 3: The different types of scope.

headword/governing category of CAND
is CAND capitalized/a person?
is CAND *subj|dobj|iobj|pobj* of OPINION/COMM?
is CAND preceded by *according to*? (Choi et al., 2005)
does CAND contain possessive and is followed by OPINION/COMM? (Choi et al., 2005)
is CAND preceded by *by* which is attached to OPINION/COMM? (Choi et al., 2005)
predicate-argument pairs in which CAND occurs
lemma/part-of-speech tag/subcategorization frame/voice of nearest predicate
is nearest predicate OPINION/COMM?
does CAND precede/follow nearest predicate?
words between nearest predicate and CAND (bag of words)
part-of-speech sequence between nearest predicate and CAND
constituency path/grammatical relation path from predicate to CAND

Table 4: Manually designed feature set.

4.5 Manually Designed Feature Set for a Standard Vector Kernel

In addition to the different types of convolution kernels, we also define an explicit feature set for a vector kernel (VK). Many of these features mainly describe properties of the relation between the candidate and the nearest predicate[6] since in our initial experiments the nearest predicate has always been the strongest cue. Adding these types of features for other cues, e.g. the nearest opinion or communication word, only resulted in a decrease in performance. Table 4 lists all the features we use. Note that this manual feature set employs all those sources of information which are also exploited by the convolution kernels. Some of the information contained in the convolution kernels can, however, only be represented in a more simplified fashion when using a manual feature set. For example, the first PAS in Figure 1(a) is converted to just the pair of predicate and argument representing the candidate (i.e. *REL:maintain_A0:Koizumi*). The entire PAS is not used since it would create too sparse features. Convolution kernels can cope with fairly complex structures as input since they internally match substructures. Manual features are less flexible since they do not account for partial matches.

[6]We select the nearest predicate by using the syntactic parse tree. Thus, we hope to select the predicate which syntactically relates to the candidate opinion holder.

5 Experiments

We used 400 documents of the MPQA corpus for five-fold crossvalidation and 133 documents as a development set. We report statistical significance on the basis of a paired t-test using 0.05 as the significance level. All experiments were done with the *SVM-Light-TK* toolkit[7]. We evaluated on the basis of exact phrase matching. We set the trade-off parameter $j = 5$ for all feature sets. For the manual feature set we used a polynomial kernel of third degree. These two critical parameters were tuned on the development set. As far as the sequence and tree kernels are concerned, we used the parameter settings from Moschitti (2008), i.e. $\lambda = 0.4$ and $\mu = 0.4$. Kernels were combined using plain summation. The documents were parsed using the Stanford Parser (Klein and Manning, 2003). Named-entity information was obtained by the Stanford tagger (Finkel et al., 2005). Semantic roles were obtained by using the parser by Zhang et al. (2008). Opinion expressions were identified using the Subjectivity Lexicon from the MPQA project (Wilson et al., 2005). Communication words were obtained by using the Appraisal Lexicon (Bloom et al., 2007). Nominalizations were recognized by looking

[7]available at `disi.unitn.it/moschitti`

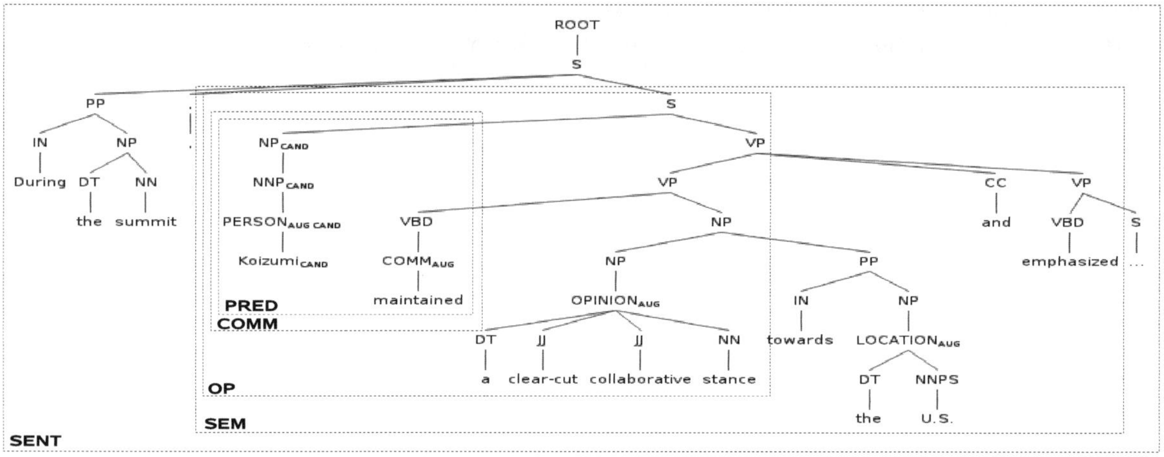

Figure 2: Illustration of the different scopes on a $CONST_{AUG}$; nodes belonging to the candidate opinion holder are marked with $_{CAND}$.

up nouns in NOMLEX (Macleod et al., 1998).

5.1 Notation

Each kernel is represented as a triple $\langle$*levelOfRepresentation* (Table 1), *Scope* (Table 3), *typeOfKernel* (Table 2)$\rangle$, e.g. $\langle CONST, SENT, STK\rangle$ is a Subset Tree Kernel of a constituency parse having the scope of the entire sentence. Note that not all combinations of these three parameters are meaningful. In the following, we will just focus on important and effective combinations. The kernel composed of manually designed features is denoted by just VK. The kernel composed of predicate-argument structures is denoted by $\langle PAS, SENT, PTK\rangle$.

5.2 Vector Kernel (VK)

The first line in Table 7 displays the result of the vector kernel using a manually designed feature set. It should be interpreted as a baseline. Due to the high class imbalance we will focus on the comparison of F(1)-Score throughout this paper rather than accuracy which is fairly biased on this data set. The F-Score of this classifier is at 56.16%.

5.3 Sequence Kernels (SKs)

For both sequence and tree kernels we need to find out what the best scope is, whether it is worthwhile to combine different scopes and what different layers of representation can be usefully combined.

The upper part of Table 5 lists the results of simple word kernels using the different scopes. The performance of the kernels using individual scopes varies greatly. The best scope is $PRED$ (1), the second best is SEM (2). The good performance of $PRED$ does not come as a surprise since the sequence is the smallest among the different scopes, so this scope is least affected by data sparseness. Moreover, this result is consistent with our initial experiments on the manual feature set (see Section 4.5).

Using different combinations of the word sequence kernels shows that $PRED$ and SEM (6) are a good combination, whereas OP, $COMM$, and $SENT$ (7;8;9) do not positively contribute to the overall performance which is consistent which the individual scope evaluation. Apparently, these scopes capture less linguistically relevant structure.

The next part of Table 5 shows the contribution of POS kernels when added to WRD kernels. Adding the corresponding POS kernel to the WRD kernel with $PRED$ scope (10) results in an improvement by more than 5% in F-Score. We get another improvement by approx. 3% when the corresponding SEM kernels (11) are added. This suggests that POS is an effective generalization and that the two scopes $PRED$ and SEM are complementary.

For the $GRAM_{WRD}$ kernel, the $PRED$ scope (12) is again most effective. We assume that this kernel most likely expresses meaningful syntactic relationships for our task. Adding the $GRAM_{POS}$ kernel (14) gives another boost by almost 4%.

Generalized sequence kernels are important.

Adding the corresponding WRD_{GN} kernels to the WRD kernel with $PRED$ and SEM scope results in an improvement from 47.77% (1) to 53.00% (15) which is a bit less than the combination of WRD and $POS_{(GN)}$ kernels (16). However, these types of kernels seem to be complementary since their combination provides an F-Score of 56.06% (17). This kernel combination already performs on a par with the manually designed vector kernel though less information is taken into consideration.

Finally, the best combination of sequence kernels (18) comprises WRD, WRD_{GN}, POS, and POS_{GN} kernels with $PRED$ and SEM scope combined with a $GRAM_{WRD}$ and a $GRAM_{POS}$ kernel with $PRED$ scope. The performance of 58.70% significantly outperforms the vector kernel.

5.4 Tree Kernels (TKs)

Table 6 shows the results of the different tree kernels. The table is divided into two halves. The left half (A) are plain tree kernels, whereas the right half (B) are the augmented tree kernels. As far as $CONST$ kernels are concerned, there is a systematic improvement by approximately 2% using tree augmentation. This proves that further non-syntactic knowledge added to the tree itself results in an improved F-Score. However, tree augmentation does not have any impact on the PAS kernels.

The overall performance of the tree kernels shows that they are much more expressive than sequence kernels. For instance, in order to obtain the same performance as of $\langle CONST_{AUG}, PRED, STK\rangle$ (19B), i.e. a single kernel with an F-Score 56.52, it requires several sequence kernels, hence much more effort. The performance of the different $CONST$ kernels relative to each other resembles the results of the WRD kernels. The best scope is $PRED$ (19). By far the worst performance is obtained by the $SENT$ scope (23). The combination of $PRED$ and SEM scope achieves an F-Score of 59.67% (25B) which is already slightly better than the best configuration of sequence kernels (18).

The performance of the PAS kernel (28A) with an F-Score of 53.51% is slightly worse than the best single plain $CONST$ kernel (19A). The PAS kernel and the $CONST$ kernels are complementary, since their best combination (29B) achieves an F-Score of 61.67% which is significantly better than the best combination of $CONST$ kernels (25B) or sequence kernels (18).

Combination	Acc.	Prec.	Rec.	F1
VK	93.63	53.28	59.37	56.16
best SKs	94.21	57.64	59.81	58.70
best TKs	94.16	56.18	**68.36**	61.67*
VK + best SKs	94.34	58.44	61.27	59.82*
VK + best TKs	94.33	57.41	68.03	62.27*
best SKs + best TKs	94.49	**59.22**	63.96	61.49*
VK + best SKs + best TKs	**94.53**	59.10	66.57	**62.61***†

Table 7: Results of kernel combinations (*: significantly better than best SKs; †: significantly better than best TKs; all convolution kernels are significantly better than VK).

5.5 Combinations

Table 7 lists the results of the different kernel type combinations. If VK is added to the best TKs, the best SKs, or both, a slight increase in F-Score is achieved. The best performance with an F-Score of 62.61% is obtained by combining all kernels.

6 Conclusion

In this paper, we compared convolution kernels for opinion holder extraction. We showed that, in general, a combination of two scopes, namely the scope immediately encompassing the candidate opinion holder and its nearest predicate and the subclause containing the candidate opinion holder provide best performance. Tree kernels containing constituency parse information and semantic roles achieve better performance than sequence kernels or vector kernels using a manually designed feature set. Best performance is achieved if all kernels are combined.

Acknowledgements

Michael Wiegand was funded by the German research council DFG through the International Research Training Group "IRTG" between Saarland University and University of Edinburgh.

The authors would like to thank Yi Zhang for processing the MPQA corpus with his semantic-role labeling system, the researchers from the MPQA project for helping to create an opinion holder corpus, and, in particular, Alessandro Moschitti for insightful comments and suggestions.

ID	Kernel	Acc.	Prec.	Rec.	F1
1	$\langle WRD, PRED, SK\rangle$	93.25	51.08	42.29	46.26
2	$\langle WRD, OP, SK\rangle$	92.77	46.38	32.52	38.21
3	$\langle WRD, COMM, SK\rangle$	92.42	43.70	35.99	39.46
4	$\langle WRD, SEM, SK\rangle$	93.16	50.32	34.65	41.04
5	$\langle WRD, SENT, SK\rangle$	90.60	29.90	27.29	28.53
6	$\langle WRD, PRED, SK\rangle + \langle WRD, SEM, SK\rangle$	93.78	56.55	41.36	47.77
7	$\sum_{j\in\{PRED,OP,COMM\}}\langle WRD, j, SK\rangle$	93.55	54.26	39.50	45.71
8	$\sum_{j\in Scopes\setminus SENT}\langle WRD, j, SK\rangle$	93.82	57.21	40.28	47.26
9	$\sum_{j\in Scopes}\langle WRD, j, SK\rangle$	93.63	55.15	39.52	46.03
10	$\langle WRD, PRED, SK\rangle + \langle POS, PRED, SK\rangle$	93.03	49.39	53.53	51.37
11	$\sum_{i\in\{PRED,SEM\}}(\langle WRD, i, SK\rangle + \langle POS, i, SK\rangle)$	93.86	55.60	53.22	54.38
12	$\sum_{i\in\{PRED,SEM\}}\langle WRD, i, SK\rangle + \langle GRAM_{WRD}, PRED, SK\rangle$	94.01	58.19	45.88	51.29
13	$\sum_{i\in\{PRED,SEM\}}\langle WRD, i, SK\rangle + \sum_{j\in\{PRED,OP,COMM\}}\langle GRAM_{WRD}, j, SK\rangle$	93.83	56.28	45.64	50.40
14	$\sum_{i\in\{PRED,SEM\}}\langle WRD, i, SK\rangle + \langle GRAM_{WRD}, PRED, SK\rangle + \langle GRAM_{POS}, PRED, SK\rangle$	93.98	56.59	53.92	55.21
15	$\sum_{i\in\{PRED,SEM\}}(\langle WRD, i, SK\rangle + \langle WRD_{GN}, i, SK\rangle)$	93.97	57.08	49.46	53.00
16	$\sum_{i\in\{PRED,SEM\}}(\langle WRD, i, SK\rangle + \langle POS_{GN}, i, SK\rangle)$	93.97	56.60	52.42	54.42
17	$\sum_{i\in\{PRED,SEM\}}(\langle WRD, i, SK\rangle + \langle WRD_{GN}, i, SK\rangle + \langle POS, i, SK\rangle + \langle POS_{GN}, i, SK\rangle)$	93.85	55.16	57.00	56.06
18	$\sum_{i\in\{PRED,SEM\}}(\langle WRD, i, SK\rangle + \langle WRD_{GN}, i, SK\rangle + \langle POS, i, SK\rangle + \langle POS_{GN}, i, SK\rangle)$ $+\langle GRAM_{WRD}, PRED, SK\rangle + \langle GRAM_{POS}, PRED, SK\rangle$	**94.21**	**57.64**	**59.81**	**58.70**

Table 5: Results of the different sequence kernels.

		A $i = CONST, j = PAS$				B $i = CONST_{AUG}, j = PAS_{AUG}$			
ID	Kernel	Acc.	Prec.	Rec.	F1	Acc.	Prec.	Rec.	F1
19	$\langle i, PRED, STK\rangle$	92.89	48.68	62.34	54.67	93.12	49.99	65.04	56.52
20	$\langle i, OP, STK\rangle$	93.04	49.49	54.71	51.96	93.27	50.93	59.06	54.68
21	$\langle i, COMM, STK\rangle$	92.76	47.79	55.89	51.50	92.96	49.03	58.85	53.47
22	$\langle i, SEM, STK\rangle$	93.70	54.40	52.13	53.23	93.90	55.47	56.59	56.03
23	$\langle i, SENT, STK\rangle$	92.42	44.34	39.92	41.99	92.50	45.20	42.40	43.74
24	$\sum_{k\in\{PRED,OP,COMM\}}\langle i, k, STK\rangle$	93.62	53.26	60.05	56.44	93.77	54.06	63.21	58.26
25	$\sum_{k\in\{PRED,SEM\}}\langle i, k, STK\rangle$	93.90	55.26	59.50	57.30	94.13	56.57	63.12	59.67
26	$\sum_{k\in Scopes\setminus SENT}\langle i, k, STK\rangle$	94.09	56.65	59.68	58.11	94.21	57.21	62.61	59.80
27	$\sum_{k\in Scopes}\langle i, k, STK\rangle$	94.14	57.41	57.88	57.63	94.29	**58.11**	61.10	59.56
28	$\langle j, SENT, PTK\rangle$	92.11	45.02	**69.96**	53.51	91.92	44.27	67.39	53.43
29	$\sum_{k\in\{PRED,SEM\}}\langle i, k, STK\rangle + \langle PAS, SENT, PTK\rangle$	94.05	55.68	66.01	**60.40**	94.16	56.18	**68.36**	**61.67**
30	$\sum_{k\in Scopes\setminus SENT}\langle i, k, STK\rangle + \langle PAS, SENT, PTK\rangle$	**94.30**	**57.95**	62.62	60.19	**94.36**	58.07	64.94	61.31

Table 6: Results of the different tree kernels.

References

Steven Bethard, Hong Yu, Ashley Thornton, Vasileios Hatzivassiloglou, and Dan Jurafsky. 2005. Extracting Opinion Propositions and Opinion Holders using Syntactic and Lexical Cues. In *Computing Attitude and Affect in Text: Theory and Applications*. Springer.

Kenneth Bloom, Sterling Stein, and Shlomo Argamon. 2007. Appraisal Extraction for News Opinion Analysis at NTCIR-6. In *Proceedings of NTCIR-6 Workshop Meeting*, Tokyo, Japan.

Razvan C. Bunescu and Raymond J. Mooney. 2005. Subsequence Kernels for Relation Extraction. In *Proceedings of the Conference on Neural Information Processing Systems (NIPS)*, Vancouver, Canada.

Yejin Choi, Claire Cardie, Ellen Riloff, and Siddharth Patwardhan. 2005. Identifying Sources of Opinions with Conditional Random Fields and Extraction Patterns. In *Proceedings of the Conference on Human Language Technology and Empirical Methods in Natural Language Processing (HLT/EMNLP)*, Vancouver, Canada.

Yejin Choi, Eric Breck, and Claire Cardie. 2006. Joint Extraction of Entities and Relations for Opinion Recognition. In *Proceedings of the Conference on Empirical Methods in Natural Language Processing (EMNLP)*, Sydney, Australia.

Michael Collins and Nigel Duffy. 2002. New Ranking Algorithms for Parsing and Tagging. In *Proceedings of the Annual Meeting of the Association for Computational Linguistics (ACL)*, Philadelphia, USA.

Charles. J. Fillmore, Christopher R. Johnson, and Miriam R. Petruck. 2003. Background to FrameNet. *International Journal of Lexicography*, 16:235 – 250.

Jenny Rose Finkel, Trond Grenager, and Christopher Manning. 2005. Incorporating Non-local Information into Information Extraction Systems by Gibbs Sampling. In *Proceedings of the Annual Meeting of the Association for Computational Linguistics (ACL)*, Ann Arbor, USA.

Soo-Min Kim and Eduard Hovy. 2005. Identifying Opinion Holders for Question Answering in Opinion Texts. In *Proceedings of AAAI-05 Workshop on Question Answering in Restricted Domains*, Pittsburgh, USA.

Soo-Min Kim and Eduard Hovy. 2006. Extracting Opinions, Opinion Holders, and Topics Expressed in Online News Media Text. In *Proceedings of the ACL Workshop on Sentiment and Subjectivity in Text*, Sydney, Australia.

Paul Kingsbury and Martha Palmer. 2002. From TreeBank to PropBank. In *Proceedings of the 3rd Conference on Language Resources and Evaluation (LREC)*, Las Palmas, Spain.

Dan Klein and Christopher D. Manning. 2003. Accurate Unlexicalized Parsing. In *Proceedings of the Annual Meeting of the Association for Computational Linguistics (ACL)*, Sapporo, Japan.

Catherine Macleod, Ralph Grishman, Adam Meyers, Leslie Barrett, and Ruth Reeves. 1998. NOMLEX: A Lexicon of Nominalizations. In *Proceedings of EURALEX*, Liège, Belgium.

Alessandro Moschitti, Daniele Pighin, and Roberto Basili. 2008. Tree Kernels for Semantic Role Labeling. *Computational Linguistics*, 34(2):193 – 224.

Alessandro Moschitti. 2006. Efficient Convolution Kernels for Dependency and Constituent Syntactic Trees. In *Proceedings of the 17th European Conference on Machine Learning (ECML)*, Berlin, Germany.

Alessandro Moschitti. 2008. Kernel Methods, Syntax and Semantics for Relational Text Categorization. In *Proceedings of the Conference on Information and Knowledge Management (CIKM)*, Napa Valley, USA.

Truc-Vien T. Nguyen, Alessandro Moschitti, and Giuseppe Riccardi. 2009. Convolution Kernels on Constituent, Dependency and Sequential Structures for Relation Extraction. In *Proceedings of the Conference on Empirical Methods in Natural Language Processing (EMNLP)*, Singapore.

Ellen Riloff. 1996. An Empirical Study of Automated Dictionary Construction for Information Extraction. *Artificial Intelligence*, 85.

John Taylor and Nello Christianini. 2004. *Kernel Methods for Pattern Analysis*. Cambridge University Press.

Janyce Wiebe, Theresa Wilson, and Claire Cardie. 2003. Annotating Expressions of Opinions and Emotions in Language. *Language Resources and Evaluation*, 1:2.

Theresa Wilson, Janyce Wiebe, and Paul Hoffmann. 2005. Recognizing Contextual Polarity in Phrase-level Sentiment Analysis. In *Proceedings of Human Language Technologies Conference/Conference on Empirical Methods in Natural Language Processing (HLT/EMNLP)*, Vancouver, Canada.

Dell Zhang and Wee Sun Lee. 2003. Question Classification using Support Vector Machines. In *Proceedings of the ACM Special Interest Group on Information Retrieval (SIGIR)*, Toronto, Canada.

Min Zhang, Jie Zhang, and Jian Su. 2006. Exploring Syntactic Features for Relation Extraction using a Convolution Tree Kernel. In *Proceedings of the Human Language Technology Conference of the North American Chapter of the ACL (HLT/NAACL)*, New York City, USA.

Yi Zhang, Rui Wang, and Hans Uszkoreit. 2008. Hybrid Learning of Dependency Structures from Heterogeneous Linguistic Resources. In *Proceedings of the Conference on Computational Natural Language Learning (CoNLL)*, Manchester, United Kingdom.

An Unsupervised Aspect-Sentiment Model for Online Reviews

Samuel Brody
Dept. of Biomedical Informatics
Columbia University
samuel.brody@dbmi.columbia.edu

Noemie Elhadad
Dept. of Biomedical Informatics
Columbia University
noemie@dbmi.columbia.edu

Abstract

With the increase in popularity of online review sites comes a corresponding need for tools capable of extracting the information most important to the user from the plain text data. Due to the diversity in products and services being reviewed, supervised methods are often not practical. We present an unsupervised system for extracting aspects and determining sentiment in review text. The method is simple and flexible with regard to domain and language, and takes into account the influence of aspect on sentiment polarity, an issue largely ignored in previous literature. We demonstrate its effectiveness on both component tasks, where it achieves similar results to more complex semi-supervised methods that are restricted by their reliance on manual annotation and extensive knowledge sources.

1 Introduction

Online review sites continue to grow in popularity as more people seek the advice of fellow users regarding services and products. Unfortunately, users are often forced to wade through large quantities of written data in order to find the information they want. This has led to an increase in research in the areas of opinion mining and sentiment analysis, with the aim of providing systems that can automatically analyze user reviews and extract the information most relevant to the user.

One example of such an application is generating a summary of the important factors mentioned in the reviews of a product (see Lerman et al. 2009). Another application is comparing two similar products. In this case, it is important to present to the user the aspects in which the products differ, rather than just provide a general star rating. A third example is systems for generating automatic recommendations, based on similarity between products, user reviews, and history of previous purchases. These types of application require an underlying framework to identify the important aspects of the product (also known as *features* or *attributes*), and the sentiment expressed by the review writer.

Unsupervised Methods are desirable for this task, for two reasons. First, due to the wide range and variety of products and services being reviewed, the framework must be robust and easily transferable between domains. The second reason is the nature of the data. Online reviews are often short and unstructured, and may contain many spelling and grammatical errors, as well as slang or specialized jargon. These factors often present a problem to methods relying exclusively on dictionaries, manually-constructed knowledge resources, and gazetteers, as they may miss out on an important aspect of the product or an indicator of sentiment. Unsupervised methods, on the other hand, are not influenced by the lexical form, and can handle unknown words or word-forms, provided they occur frequently enough. This insures that any emergent topic that is salient in the data will be addressed by the system.

In this paper, we present an unsupervised system which addresses the core tasks necessary to enable advanced applications to handle review data. We introduce a local topic model, which works at the sentence level and employs a small number of topics, to automatically infer the aspects. For sentiment detection, we present a method for automatically deriving an unsupervised seed set of positive and negative adjectives that replaces the manually constructed ones commonly used in the literature. Our approach is specifically designed to take into account the inter-

Human Language Technologies: The 2010 Annual Conference of the North American Chapter of the ACL, pages 804–812,
Los Angeles, California, June 2010.

action between the two tasks.

The rest of the paper is structured as follows. In Sec. 2 we provide relevant background, and place our method in the context of previous work in the field. We describe the data we used in Sec. 3, and our experiments on the aspect and sentiment-polarity components in Sec. 4 and 5, respectively. We conclude in Sec. 6 with a discussion of our results and findings and directions for future research.

2 Previous Approaches

In this paper, we focus on the detection of two principle elements in the review text: aspects and sentiment. In previous work these elements have been treated, for the most part, as two separate tasks.

Aspect The earliest attempts at aspect detection were based on the classic information extraction (IE) approach of using frequently occurring noun phrases (e.g., Hu and Liu 2004). Such approaches work well in detecting aspects that are strongly associated with a single noun, but are less useful when aspects encompass many low frequency terms (e.g., the *food* aspect of restaurants, which involves many different dishes), or are abstract (e.g. *ambiance* can be described without using any concrete nouns at all). Common solutions to this problem involve clustering with the help of knowledge-rich methods, involving manually-constructed rules, semantic hierarchies, or both (e.g., Popescu and Etzioni 2005, Fahrni and Klenner 2008). Titov and McDonald (2008b) underline the need for unsupervised methods for aspect detection. However, according to the authors, existing topic models, such as standard Latent Dirichlet Allocation (LDA) (Blei et al., 2003), are not suited to the task of aspect detection in reviews, because they tend to capture global topics in the data, rather than rateable aspects pertinent to the review. To address this problem, they construct a multi-grain topic model (MG-LDA), which attempts to capture two layers of topics - global and local, where the local topics correspond to rateable aspects. MG-LDA distinguishes tens of local topics, but the many-to-one mapping between these and rateable aspects is not explicit in the system. To resolve this issue, the authors extend their model in Titov and McDonald (2008a) and attempt to infer such a mapping with the help of aspect-specific ratings provided along with the review text.

Sentiment Sentiment analysis has been the focus of much previous research. In this discussion, we will only mention work directly related to our own. For a comprehensive survey of the subject, the reader is directed to Pang and Lee (2008).

Most previous approaches rely on a manually constructed lexicon of terms which are strongly positive or negative regardless of context. This information on its own is usually insufficient, due to lack of coverage and the fact that sentiment is often expressed through words whose polarity is highly domain and context specific. If a sentiment lexicon is available for one domain, domain adaptation can be used, provided the domains are sufficiently similar (Blitzer et al., 2007). Another common solution is through bootstrapping - using a seed group of terms with known polarity to infer the polarity of domain specific terms (e.g., Fahrni and Klenner 2008; Jijkoun and Hofmann 2009). The most minimalist example of this approach is Turney (2002), who used only a single pair of adjectives (*good* and *poor*) to determine the polarity of other terms through mutual information. For Chinese, Zagibalov and Carroll (2008) use a single seed word meaning *good*, and six common indicators of negation in their bootstrapping approach. Often, when using a context independent seed, large amounts of domain-specific data are required, in order to obtain sufficient co-occurrence statistics. Commonly, web queries are used to obtain such data.

Independently of any specific task, Hatzivassiloglou and McKeown (1997) present a completely unsupervised method for determining the polarity of adjectives in a large corpus. A graph is created, in which adjectives are nodes, and edges between them are weighted according to a (dis)similarity function based primarily on whether the two adjectives occurred in a conjunction or disjunction in the corpus. A heuristic approach is then used to split the graph in two. The group containing the adjectives with the higher average frequency is labeled as positive, and the other as negative.

Combined Approaches Aspects can influence sentiment polarity within a single domain. For example, in the restaurant domain, *cheap* is usually positive when discussing food, but negative when discussing the decor or ambiance. Many otherwise neutral terms (e.g., *warm, heavy, soft*) acquire a sentiment polarity in the context of a specific aspect.

Recent work has addressed this interaction in different ways. Mei et al. (2007) present a form of domain adaptation using an LDA model which treats positive and negative sentiment as two additional topics. Fahrni and Klenner (2008) directly address the specificity of sentiment to the word it is modifying. Aspects are defined by a manually specified subset of the Wikipedia category hierarchy. For sentiment, the authors use a seed set of positive and negative adjectives, and iteratively propagate sentiment polarity through conjunction relations (like those used by Hatzivassiloglou and McKeown 1997, above). Web queries are used to overcome the sparsity issue of these highly-specific patterns. In the IE setting, Popescu and Etzioni (2005) extract frequent terms, and cluster them into aspects. The sentiment detection task is formulated as a Relaxation Labeling problem of finding the most likely sentiment labels for opinion-bearing terms, while satisfying as many local constraints as possible. The authors use a variety of knowledge sources, web queries, and hand crafted rules to detect relations between terms (e.g., meronymy). These relations are used both for the clustering, and as a basis for the constraints.

Our approach is designed to be as unsupervised and knowledge-lean as possible, so as to make it transferable across different types of products and services, as well as across languages. Aspects are determined via a local version of LDA, which operates on sentences, rather than documents, and employs a small number of topics that correspond directly to aspects. This approach overcomes the problems of frequent-term methods, as well as the issues raised by Titov and McDonald (2008b). We use morphological negation indicators to automatically create a seed set of highly relevant positive and negative adjectives, which are guaranteed to be pertinent to the aspect at hand. These automatically-derived seed sets achieve comparable results to the use of manual ones, and the work of Zagibalov and Carroll (2008) suggests that the use of negation can be easily transfered to other languages.

3 Data

Our primary dataset is the publicly available corpus used in Ganu et al. (2009). It contains over 50,000 restaurant reviews from Citysearch New York[1]. Additionally, to demonstrate the domain independence of our system, we collected 1086 reviews for four leading netbook computers from Amazon.com.

For evaluation purposes, we used the annotated dataset from Ganu et al. (2009), which is a subset of 3,400 sentences from the Citysearch corpus. These sentences were manually labeled for aspect and sentiment. There were six manually defined aspect labels - *Food & Drink*, *Service*, *Price*, *Atmosphere*, *Anecdotes* and *Miscellaneous*. A sentence could contain multiple aspects, but, for our evaluation, we used only sentences with a single label. For sentiment, each sentence was given a single value - *Positive, Negative, Neutral* or *Conflict* (indicating a mixture of positive and negative sentiment).

We were also provided with a seed set of 128 positive and 88 negative adjectives used by Fahrni and Klenner (2008), which were specifically selected to be domain and target independent.

For the purpose of the experiments presented here, we focused on sentences containing noun-adjective pairs. Such pairs are one of the most common way of expressing sentiment about an aspect and allow us to capture the interaction between the two.

4 Aspect

4.1 Methodology

In order to infer the salient aspects in the data, we employed the following steps:

Local LDA We used a standard implementation[2] of LDA. In order to prevent the inference of global topics and direct the model towards rateable aspects (see Sec. 2), we treated each sentence as a separate document. The output of the model is a distribution over inferred aspects for each sentence in the data. The parameters we employed were standard, out-of-the-box settings ($\alpha = 0.1, \beta = 0.1$, 3000 iterations), with no specific tuning to our data. We ran the algorithm with the number of aspects ranging from 10 to 20, and employed a cluster validation scheme (see below) to determine the optimal number.

Model Order The issue of model order, i.e., determining the correct number of clusters, is an important element in unsupervised learning. A common

[1] `http://newyork.citysearch.com/`

[2] GibbsLDA++, by Xuan-Hieu Phan. Available at `http://gibbslda.sourceforge.net/`.

approach (Levine and Domany, 2001; Lange et al., 2004; Niu et al., 2007) is to use a cluster validation procedure. In such a procedure, different model orders are compared, and the one with the most consistent clustering is chosen. For the purpose of the validation procedure, we have a cluster corresponding to each aspect, and we label each sentence as belonging to the cluster of the most probable aspect.

Given the collection of sentences in our data, D, and two connectivity matrices C and $\hat{C}$, where a cell i,j contains 1 if sentences d_i and d_j belong to the same cluster, we define a consistency function F (following Niu et al. 2007):

$$F(C,\hat{C}) = \frac{\sum_{i,j} 1\{C_{i,j} = \hat{C}_{i,j} = 1, d_i, d_j \in \hat{D}\}}{\sum_{i,j} 1\{C_{i,j} = 1, d_i, d_j \in \hat{D}\}} \quad (1)$$

We then employ the following procedure:

1. Run the LDA model with k topics on D to obtain connectivity matrix C_k.
2. Create a comparison connectivity matrix R_k based on uniformly drawn random assignments of the instances.
3. Sample random subset D^i of size $\delta|D|$ from D.
4. Run the LDA model on D^i to obtain connectivity matrix C_k^i.
5. Create a comparison matrix R_k^i based on uniformly drawn random assignments of the instances in D^i.
6. Calculate $score_i(k) = F(\hat{C},C) - F(\hat{R},R)$ where F is given in Eq. 1.
7. Repeat steps 3 to 6 q times.
8. Return the average score over q iterations.

This procedure calculates the consistency of our clustering solution, using a similar sized random assignment for comparison. It does this on q subsets to reduce the effects of chance. The k with the highest score is chosen. In our experiments, we used $q = 5, \delta = 0.9$. For both our datasets (restaurants and netbooks), the highest-scoring k was 14.

Determining Representative Words For each aspect, we list all the nouns in the data according to a score based on their mutual information with regard to that aspect.

$$Score_a(w) = p(w,a) \cdot log \frac{p(w,a)}{p(w) \cdot p(a)} \quad (2)$$

Where $p(w), p(a), p(w,a)$ are the probabilities, according to the LDA model, of the word w, the aspect a, and the word w labeled with aspect a, respectively.

We then select, for each aspect, the top k_a ranking words, such that they cover 75% of the word-instances labeled by the LDA model with aspect label a. Due to the skewed frequency distribution of words, this is a relatively small portion of the words (typically 100-200). This set of representative words for each aspect is used in the sentiment component of our system (see Sec. 5.1).

4.2 Inferred Aspects

Table 1 presents the aspects inferred by our system for the restaurant domain. The inferred aspects cover all those defined in the manual annotation, but also distinguish between a finer granularity of aspects, based solely on the review text, e.g., between physical environment and ambiance, and between the attitude of the staff and the quality of the service.

In order to demonstrate that our method can be transfered between very different domains and categories of products, we also ran our algorithm on our set of netbook reviews. The inferred aspects are presented in Table 2. The system identifies important aspects relevant to our data. Some of these (e.g., software, hardware) might be suggested by human annotators, but some would probably be missed unless the annotators carefully read through all the reviews, e.g., the *Memory* aspect, which includes advice about upgrading specific models. This capability of our system is important, as it demonstrates that our method can be used to produce customized comparisons for the user and will take into account the important common factors, as well as the unique aspects of each item.

4.3 Evaluation

To determine the quality of our automatically inferred aspects, we compared the output of our system to the sentence-level manual annotation of Ganu et al. (2009). To each sentence in the data, the LDA model assigns a distribution $\{P(a)\}_{a \in A}$ over the set A of inferred aspects. By defining a threshold t_a for each aspect, we can label a sentence as belonging to aspect a if $P(a) > t_a$. By varying the threshold t_a we created precision-recall curves for the top three rateable aspects in the restaurant domain, shown in

Inferred Aspect	Representative Words	Manual Aspect
Main Dishes Bakery Food - General Wine & Drinks	chicken, sauce, rice, cheese, spicy, salad, hot, delicious, dessert, bagels, bread, chocolate menu, fresh, sushi, fish, chef, cuisine wine, list, glass, drinks, beer, bottle	Food & Drink
Ambiance / Mood Physical Atmosphere	great, atmosphere, wonderful, music, experience, relaxed bar, room, outside, seating, tables, cozy, loud	Atmosphere
Staff Service	service, staff, friendly, attentive, busy, slow table, order, wait, minutes, reservation, forgot	Staff
Value	portions, quality, worth, size, cheap	Price
Anecdotes Anecdotes	dinner, night, group, friends, date, family out, back, definitely, around, walk, block	Anecdotes
General Misc. - Location Misc.	best, top, favorite, city, NYC never, restaurant, found, Paris, (New) York, location place, eat, enjoy, big, often, stuff	Misc.

Table 1: List of automatically inferred aspects for the restaurant domain, with some representative words for each aspect (middle), and the corresponding aspect label from the manual annotation (right). Labels (left) were assigned by the authors.

Aspect	Representative Words	Aspect	Representative Words
Performance	power, performance, mode, fan, quiet	Mouse	mouse, right, touchpad, pad, buttons, left
Hardware	drive, wireless, bluetooth, usb, speakers, webcam	General	great, little, machine, price, netbook, happy
Memory	ram, 2GB, upgrade, extra, 1GB, speed	Purchase	amazon, purchased, bought, weeks, ordered
Software	using, office, software, installed, works, programs	Looks	looks, feel, white, finish, blue, solid, glossy
Usability	internet, video, web, movies, music, email, play	OS	windows, xp, system, boot, linux, vista, os
Portability	around, light, work, portable, weight, travel	Battery	battery, life, hours, time, cell, last
Comparison	netbooks, best, reviews, read, decided, research	Size	screen, keyboard, size, small, enough, big

Table 2: List of automatically inferred aspects for the netbook dataset, with representative words for each aspect .

Figure 1[3]. Although the data used in Titov and McDonald (2008a) was unavailable for direct comparison, our method exhibits similar behavior and performance (compare Fig. 4, there) on a domain with similar characteristics (abstract aspects which encompass many low frequency words). This demonstrates that our local version of LDA with few topics overcomes the issues which confronted the authors of that work (i.e., global topics and many-to-one mapping of topics to aspects), without requiring specially designed models or additional information in the form of user-provided aspect-specific ratings (see Sec. 2).

We believe the reason for this stems from the composition of online reviews. Since many reviews have similar mixtures of local topics (e.g., food, service), standard LDA prefers global topics, which distinguish more strongly between *reviews* (e.g., cuisine type, restaurant type). However, when employed at the sentence level, local topics (corresponding to rateable aspects) provide a stronger way to distinguish between individual *sentences*.

[3]We combined the probabilities of all the inferred aspects that match a single manually assigned aspect, according to the mapping in Table 1.

5 Sentiment

5.1 Methodology

For determining sentiment polarity, we developed the following procedure. For each aspect, we extracted the relevant adjectives, built a conjunction graph, automatically determined the seed set (or used a manual one, for comparison), and propagated the polarity scores to the rest of the adjectives. Details of each step are described below.

Extracting Adjectives As a pre-processing step, we parsed our data (using RASP, Briscoe and Carroll 2002). The parsed output was used to detect negation and conjunction. If an adjective *A* partic-

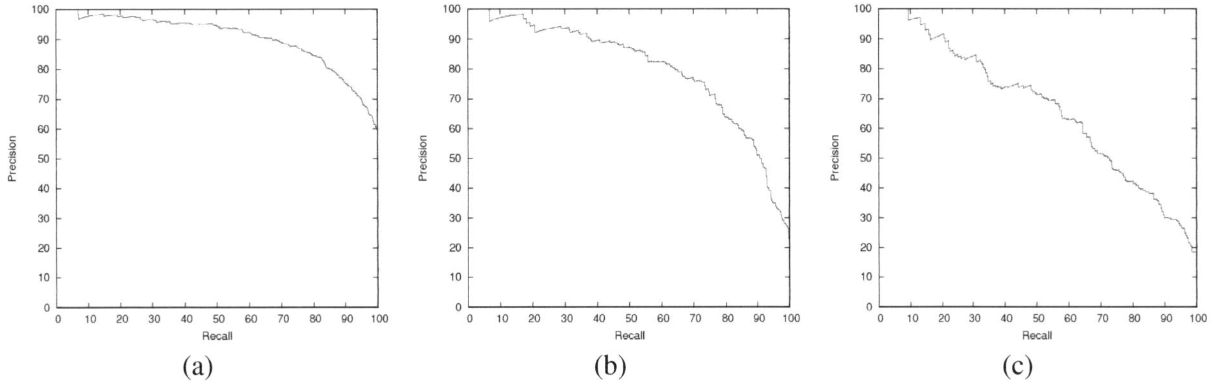

Figure 1: Precision / Recall curves for the top three rateable aspects: (a) *Food*, (b) *Service*, and (c) *Atmosphere*.

ipated in a negation in the sentence, it was replaced by a new adjective *not-A*. We then extract all cases where an adjective modified a noun. For example, from the sentence *"The food was tasty and hot, but our waiter was not friendly."* we can extract the pairs *(tasty, food), (hot, food), (not-friendly, waiter)*.

Building the Graph Our method for determining sentiment polarity is based on an adaptation of Hatzivassiloglou and McKeown (1997) (see Sec. 2).

Several issues confronted us when attempting to adapt their method to our task. In the original article, adjectives with no orientation were ignored. It is unclear how this can be easily done in an unsupervised fashion, and such sentiment-neutral adjectives are ubiquitous in real-world data. Furthermore, adjectives whose orientation depended on the context were also ignored. These are of particular interest in our task, and are likely to be missing or incorrectly labeled in standard sentiment dictionaries. For our purposes, since we need to handle adjectives expressing various shades of sentiment, not only strongly positive or negative ones, we are interested in a scoring method, rather than a binary labeling. Also, we do not want to use a general corpus, but rather the text from the reviews themselves. This usually means a much smaller corpus than the one used in the original paper, but has the advantage of being domain specific.

Our method of building the polarity graph differed in several ways from the original. First, we did not use disjunctions (e.g., 'but') as indicators of opposite polarity. The reason for this was that, in our domain of online reviews, disjunctions often did not convey contrast in polarity, but rather in perceived expectations, e.g., *"dainty but strong necklace"*, and *"cheap but delicious food"*.

Instead of using regular expressions to capture explicit conjunctions, we retrieved all cases where our parser indicated that two adjectives modified a single noun in the same sentence.

To ensure that aspect-specific adjectives are handled correctly, we built a separate graph for each aspect, by selecting the cases where the modified noun was one of the representative words for that aspect (see Sec. 4.1).

Constructing a Seed Set We used morphological information and explicit negation to find pairs of opposite polarity. Specifically, adjective pairs which were distinguished only by one of the prefixes *'un', 'in', 'dis', 'non',* or by the negation marker *'not-'* were selected for the seed set. Starting with the most frequent pair, we assigned a positive polarity to the more frequent member of the pair.

Then, in order of decreasing frequency, we assigned polarity to the other seed pairs, based on the shortest path either of the members had to a previously labeled adjective. That member received its neighbor's polarity, and the other member of the pair received the opposite polarity. When all pairs were labeled, we corrected for misclassifications by iterating through the pairs and reversing the polarity if that improved consistency, i.e., if it caused the members of the pair to match the polarities of more of their neighbors. Finally, we reverse the polarity of the seed groups if the negative group has a higher total frequency.

Propagating Polarity Our propagation method is based on the label propagation algorithm of Zhu and Ghahramani (2002). The adjectives in the positive and negative seed groups are assigned a polarity score of 1 and 0, respectively. All the rest start with a score of 0.5. Then, an update step is repeated. In update iteration t, for each adjective x that is *not in the seed*, the following update rule is applied:

$$p^t(x) = \frac{\Sigma_{y \in N(x)} w(y,x) \cdot p^{t-1}(y)}{\Sigma_{y \in N(x)} w(y,x)} \quad (3)$$

Where $p^t(x)$ is the polarity of adjective x at step t, $N(x)$ is the set of the neighbors of x, and $w(y,x)$ is the weight of the edge connecting x and y. We set this weight to be $1 + log(\#mod(y,x))$ where $\#mod(y,x)$ is the number of times y and x both modified a single noun. The update step is repeated to convergence.

5.2 Aspect-Specific Gold Standard

To evaluate the performance of the sentiment component of our system, we created an aspect-specific gold standard. For each of the top eight automatically inferred aspects (corresponding to the *Food, Service* and *Atmosphere* aspects in the annotation), we constructed a polarity graph, as described in Sec. 5.1. We retrieved a list of all adjectives that participated in five or more modifications of nouns from that specific aspect). Table 3 lists the number of such adjectives in each aspect. We split the data into ten portions and, for each portion, asked two volunteers to rate each adjective according to the polarity of the sentiment it expresses *in the context of the specified aspect*. The judges could select from the following ratings: *Strongly Negative*, *Weakly Negative*, *Neutral*, *Weakly Positive*, *Strongly Positive*, and *N/A*. As expected, exact inter-annotator agreement was low - only 54%, but when considering two adjacent ratings as equivalent (i.e, Strongly vs. Weakly Negative or Positive, and Neutral vs. Weakly Negative or Positive), agreement was 93.3%. This indicates there is some difficulty distinguishing between the fine-grained categories we specified, but high agreement at a coarser level, which advocates using a ranking approach for evaluation (see also Pang and Lee 2005). We therefore translated the annotator ratings to a numerical scale, from -2 (Strongly Negative) to $+2$ (Strongly Positive) at unit intervals. After discarding adjectives where one or more annotators gave a 'N/A' tag, we averaged the two annotator numerical scores, and used this data as the gold standard for our evaluation.

Aspect	# Adj.	# Rated	% Neu.
Mood	293	206	17%
Staff	155	122	3%
Main Dishes	287	185	25%
Physical Atmo.	161	103	21%
Bakery	180	129	23%
Food - General	192	144	28%
Wine & Drinks	111	75	18%
Service	89	57	5%
Total	1468	1021	–

Table 3: For each aspect, the number of frequently occurring adjectives for each aspect (# Adj.), number of adjectives remaining after removing those labeled 'N/A' (# Rated), and percent of rated adjectives labeled 'Neutral' by both annotators (% Neu.).

	Auto.		Manual	
Aspect	τ_k	D_k	τ_k	D_k
Mood	0.53	0.23	0.56	0.22
Staff	0.57	0.22	0.60	0.20
Main Dishes	0.19	0.40	0.38	0.31
Physical Atmo.	0.34	0.33	0.25	0.37
Bakery	0.33	0.33	0.35	0.33
Food - General	0.19	0.41	0.41	0.30
Wine & Drinks	0.32	0.34	0.52	0.24
Service	0.41	0.30	0.54	0.23
Average	0.36	0.32	0.45	0.27

Table 4: Kendall coefficient and distance scores for eight inferred aspects.

5.3 Evaluation Measures

Kendall's tau coefficient (τ_k) and Kendall's distance (D_k) are commonly used (e.g., Jijkoun and Hofmann 2009) to compare rankings. These measures look at the number of pairs of ranked items that agree or disagree with the ordering in the gold standard. The value of τ_k ranges from -1 (perfect disagreement) to 1 (perfect agreement), with 0 indicating an almost random ranking. The value of D_k ranges from 0 (perfect agreement) to 1 (perfect disagreement). It is important to note that only pairs that are ordered in the gold standard are used in the comparison.

5.4 Evaluation Results

Table 4 reports Kendall's coefficient (τ_k) and distance (D_k) values for our method when using our automatically derived seed set (Auto.). For comparison, we ran our procedure using the manually compiled seed set (Manual) of Fahrni and Klenner

Food - General: Mexican, *French*, Eastern, Turkish, European, Tuscan, Mediterranean, American, Cuban, Thai, Peruvian, Spanish, Korean, Vietnamese, Indian, African, Japanese, Italian, *Chinese*, Asian
Mood: Vietnamese, Brazilian, Turkish, Eastern, Caribbean, Cuban, Italian, Spanish, Japanese, European, Mediterranean, Colombian, Mexican, Asian, Indian, Thai, British, American, *French*, Korean, *Chinese*, Russian, Moroccan
Staff: British, European, *Chinese*, Indian, American, Spanish, Asian, Italian, *French*

Table 5: Polarity ranking of cuisine adjectives (from most positive) for three aspects.

(2008). Using the manual seed set obtains results that correspond better to our gold standard. Our automatic method also achieves good results, and can be used when a manual seed set is not available. More importantly, correlation with the gold standard may not indicate better suitability to the sentiment detection task in reviews. For instance, it is interesting to note that the worst correlation scores were on the *Main Dishes* and *Food - General* aspects. If we compare to Table 3, we can see these aspects have the highest percentage of adjectives rated as neutral by the annotators. However, in many cases, these adjectives actually carry some sentiment in their context. An example of this are adjectives describing the type of cuisine, which are objective, and therefore usually considered neutral by annotators. Table 5 shows the automatic ranking of cuisine type from positive to negative in three aspects. It is interesting to see that the rankings change according to the aspect, and certain cuisines are strongly associated with specific aspects and not with others. This is supported by Ganu et al. (2009), who observed during the annotation that, in the restaurant corpus, French and Italian restaurants were strongly associated with the service aspect. This trend can be identified automatically by our method, and at a much more detailed level than that noticed by a human analyzing the data.

6 Discussion & Future Work

Our experiments confirm the value of a fully unsupervised approach to the tasks of aspect detection and sentiment analysis. The aspects are inferred from the data, and are more representative than manually derived ones. For instance, in our restaurant domain, the manually constructed aspect list omitted or over-generalized some important aspects, while over-representing others. There was no separate *Drinks* category, even though it was strongly present in the data. The *Service* aspect, dealing with waiting time, reservations, and mistaken orders, was an important emergent aspect on its own, but was grouped under *Staff* in the manual annotation.

Adjectives can convey different sentiments depending on the aspect being discussed. For example, the adjective *'warm'* was ranked very positive in the *Staff* aspect, but slightly negative in the *General Food* aspect. A knowledge-rich approach might ignore such adjectives, thereby missing important elements of the review.

Finally, as online reviews belong to an informal genre, with inventive spelling and specialized jargon, it may be insufficient, for both aspect and sentiment, to rely only on lexicons. For example, our restaurant reviews included spelling errors such as *desert, decour/decore, anti-pasta, creme-brule, sandwhich, omlette, exelent, tastey,* as well as at least six different common misspellings of *restaurant*. There were also specialized terms, such as *Korma, Edamame, Dosa* and *Pho*, all of which do not appear in common dictionaries, and creative use of adjectives, such as *orgasmic* and *New-Yorky*.

This work has opened many avenues for future research and improvements. So far, we focused on adjectives as sentiment indicators, however, there have been studies showing that other parts of speech can be very helpful for this task (e.g., Pang et al. 2002; Benamara et al. 2007). Also, it would be interesting to take a closer look at the interactions between aspect and sentiment, especially at a multiple-sentence level (see Snyder and Barzilay 2007). Finally, we feel that the true test of the usability of our system should be through an application, and intend to proceed in that direction.

Acknowledgments

We'd like to thank Angela Fahrni and Manfred Klenner for kindly allowing us access to their data and annotation. We also wish to thank the volunteer annotators. This work was partially supported by a Google Research Award.

References

Benamara, Farah, Carmine Cesarano, Antonio Picariello, Diego Reforgiato, and V. S. Subrahmanian. 2007. Sentiment analysis: Adjectives and adverbs are better than adjectives alone. In *Proc. of the International Conference on Weblogs and Social Media (ICWSM)*.

Blei, David M., Andrew Y. Ng, and Michael I. Jordan. 2003. Latent dirichlet allocation. *Journal of Machine Learning Research* 3:993–1022.

Blitzer, John, Mark Dredze, and Fernando Pereira. 2007. Biographies, bollywood, boom-boxes and blenders: Domain adaptation for sentiment classification. In *Proc. of the 45th Annual Meeting of the Association of Computational Linguistics*. ACL, Prague, Czech Republic, pages 440–447.

Briscoe, Ted and John Carroll. 2002. Robust accurate statistical annotation of general text. In *Proc. of the 3rd LREC*. Las Palmas, Gran Canaria, pages 1499–1504.

Fahrni, Angela and Manfred Klenner. 2008. Old Wine or Warm Beer: Target-Specific Sentiment Analysis of Adjectives. In *Proc.of the Symposium on Affective Language in Human and Machine, AISB 2008 Convention*. pages 60 – 63.

Ganu, Gayatree, Noemie Elhadad, and Amelie Marian. 2009. Beyond the stars: Improving rating predictions using review text content. In *WebDB*.

Hatzivassiloglou, Vasileios and Kathleen R. McKeown. 1997. Predicting the semantic orientation of adjectives. In *Proc. of the 35th Annual Meeting of the Association for Computational Linguistics*. ACL, Madrid, Spain, pages 174–181.

Hu, Minqing and Bing Liu. 2004. Mining and summarizing customer reviews. In *KDD '04: Proc. of the tenth ACM SIGKDD international conference on Knowledge discovery and data mining*. ACM, New York, NY, USA, pages 168–177.

Jijkoun, Valentin and Katja Hofmann. 2009. Generating a non-english subjectivity lexicon: Relations that matter. In *Proc. of the 12th Conference of the European Chapter of the ACL (EACL 2009)*. ACL, Athens, Greece, pages 398–405.

Lange, Tilman, Volker Roth, Mikio L. Braun, and Joachim M. Buhmann. 2004. Stability-based validation of clustering solutions. *Neural Comput.* 16(6):1299–1323.

Lerman, Kevin, Sasha Blair-Goldensohn, and Ryan McDonald. 2009. Sentiment summarization: evaluating and learning user preferences. In *EACL '09: Proc. of the 12th Conference of the European Chapter of the Association for Computational Linguistics*. ACL, Morristown, NJ, USA, pages 514–522.

Levine, Erel and Eytan Domany. 2001. Resampling method for unsupervised estimation of cluster validity. *Neural Comput.* 13(11):2573–2593.

Mei, Qiaozhu, Xu Ling, Matthew Wondra, Hang Su, and ChengXiang Zhai. 2007. Topic sentiment mixture: modeling facets and opinions in weblogs. In *WWW '07: Proc. of the 16th international conference on World Wide Web*. ACM, New York, NY, USA, pages 171–180.

Niu, Zheng-Yu, Dong-Hong Ji, and Chew-Lim Tan. 2007. I2r: three systems for word sense discrimination, chinese word sense disambiguation, and english word sense disambiguation. In *SemEval '07: Proc. of the 4th International Workshop on Semantic Evaluations*. ACL, Morristown, NJ, USA, pages 177–182.

Pang, Bo and Lillian Lee. 2005. Seeing stars: Exploiting class relationships for sentiment categorization with respect to rating scales. In *Proc. of the ACL*. pages 115–124.

Pang, Bo and Lillian Lee. 2008. Opinion mining and sentiment analysis. *Foundations and Trends in Information Retrieval* 2(1-2):1–135.

Pang, Bo, Lillian Lee, and Shivakumar Vaithyanathan. 2002. Thumbs up?: sentiment classification using machine learning techniques. In *EMNLP '02: Proc. of the conference on Empirical methods in natural language processing*. ACL, Morristown, NJ, USA, pages 79–86.

Popescu, Ana-Maria and Oren Etzioni. 2005. Extracting product features and opinions from reviews. In *HLT '05: Proc. of the conference on Human Language Technology and Empirical Methods in Natural Language Processing*. ACL, Morristown, NJ, USA, pages 339–346.

Snyder, Benjamin and Regina Barzilay. 2007. Multiple aspect ranking using the good grief algorithm. In Candace L. Sidner, Tanja Schultz, Matthew Stone, and ChengXiang Zhai, editors, *HLT-NAACL*. The Association for Computational Linguistics, pages 300–307.

Titov, Ivan and Ryan McDonald. 2008a. A joint model of text and aspect ratings for sentiment summarization. In *Proc. of ACL-08: HLT*. ACL, Columbus, Ohio, pages 308–316.

Titov, Ivan and Ryan McDonald. 2008b. Modeling online reviews with multi-grain topic models. In *WWW '08: Proc. of the 17th international conference on World Wide Web*. ACM, New York, NY, pages 111–120.

Turney, Peter. 2002. Thumbs up or thumbs down? semantic orientation applied to unsupervised classification of reviews. In *Proc. of 40th Annual Meeting of the Association for Computational Linguistics*. ACL, Philadelphia, Pennsylvania, USA, pages 417–424.

Zagibalov, Taras and John Carroll. 2008. Automatic seed word selection for unsupervised sentiment classification of chinese text. In *COLING '08: Proc. of the 22nd International Conference on Computational Linguistics*. ACL, Morristown, NJ, USA, pages 1073–1080.

Zhu, X. and Z. Ghahramani. 2002. Learning from labeled and unlabeled data with label propagation. Technical report, CMU-CALD-02.

Joint Inference for Knowledge Extraction from Biomedical Literature

Hoifung Poon*
Dept. of Computer Sci. & Eng.
University of Washington
Seattle, WA 98195
hoifung@cs.washington.edu

Lucy Vanderwende
Microsoft Research
Redmond, WA 98052
Lucy.Vanderwende@microsoft.com

Abstract

Knowledge extraction from online repositories such as PubMed holds the promise of dramatically speeding up biomedical research and drug design. After initially focusing on recognizing proteins and binary interactions, the community has recently shifted their attention to the more ambitious task of recognizing complex, nested event structures. State-of-the-art systems use a pipeline architecture in which the candidate events are identified first, and subsequently the arguments. This fails to leverage joint inference among events and arguments for mutual disambiguation. Some joint approaches have been proposed, but they still lag much behind in accuracy. In this paper, we present the first joint approach for bio-event extraction that obtains state-of-the-art results. Our system is based on Markov logic and adopts a novel formulation by jointly predicting events and arguments, as well as individual dependency edges that compose the argument paths. On the BioNLP'09 Shared Task dataset, it reduced F1 errors by more than 10% compared to the previous best joint approach.

1 Introduction

Extracting knowledge from unstructured text has been a long-standing goal of NLP and AI. The advent of the World Wide Web further increases its importance and urgency by making available an astronomical number of online documents containing virtually unlimited amount of knowledge (Craven et al., 1999). A salient example domain is biomedical literature: the PubMed[1] online repository contains over 18 million abstracts on biomedical research, with more than two thousand new abstracts added each day; the abstracts are written in grammatical English, which enables the use of advanced NLP tools such as syntactic and semantic parsers.

Traditionally, research on knowledge extraction from text is primarily pursued in the field of information extraction with a rather confined goal of extracting instances for flat relational schemas with no nested structures (e.g, recognizing protein names and protein-protein interaction (PPI)). This restriction mainly stems from limitations in available resources and algorithms. The BioNLP'09 Shared Task (Kim et al., 2009) is one of the first that faced squarely information needs that are complex and highly structured. It aims to extract nested bio-molecular events from research abstracts, where an event may have variable number of arguments and may contain other events as arguments. Such nested events are ubiquitous in biomedical literature and can effectively represent complex biomedical knowledge and subsequently support reasoning and automated discovery. The task has generated much interest, with twenty-four teams having submitted their results. The top system by UTurku (Bjorne et al., 2009) attained the state-of-the-art F1 of 52.0%.

The nested event structures make this task particularly attractive for applying joint inference. By allowing information to propagate among events and arguments, joint inference can facilitate mutual disambiguation and potentially lead to substantial gain

* This research was conducted during the author's internship at Microsoft Research.

[1] http://www.ncbi.nlm.nih.gov/pubmed

Human Language Technologies: The 2010 Annual Conference of the North American Chapter of the ACL, pages 813–821,
Los Angeles, California, June 2010.

in predictive accuracy. However, joint inference is underexplored for this task. Most participants either reduced the task to classification (e.g., by using SVM), or used heuristics to combine manual rules and statistics. The previous best joint approach was Riedel et al. (2009). While competitive, it still lags UTurku by more than 7 points in F1.

In this paper, we present the first joint approach that achieves state-of-the-art results for bio-event extraction. Like Riedel et al. (2009), our system is based on Markov logic, but we adopted a novel formulation that models dependency edges in argument paths and jointly predicts them along with events and arguments. By expanding the scope of joint inference to include individual argument edges, our system can leverage fine-grained correlations to make learning more effective. On the development set, by merely adding a few joint inference formulas to a simple logistic regression model, our system raised F1 from 28% to 54%, already tying UTurku.

We also presented a heuristic method to fix errors in syntactic parsing by leveraging available semantic information from task input, and showed that this in turn led to substantial performance gain in the task. Overall, our final system reduced F1 error by more than 10% compared to Riedel et al. (2009).

We begin by describing the shared task and related work. We then introduce Markov logic and our Markov Logic Network (MLN) for joint bio-event extraction. Finally, we present our experimental results and conclude.

2 Bio-Event Extraction

We follow the BioNLP'09 Shared Task (Kim et al., 2009) on problem setup for bio-event extraction. A bio-molecular event (bio-event) refers to the change of state for bio-molecules such as DNAs and proteins. The goal is to extract these events from unstructured text such as biomedical abstracts. For each event, one needs to identify the trigger words that signifies the event and the theme arguments that undergo the change. In addition, for regulation events, the cause argument also needs to be identified if it is present. The task considers nine event types: `Expression`, `Transcription`, `Localization`, `Phosphorylation`, `Catabolism`, `Binding`, `Regulation`, `Positive_regulation`, and `Negative_regulation`. Only `Binding` can take multiple themes. Regulation events may take events as arguments. To facilitate evaluation, the task fixes the type of non-event arguments to protein and provides ground truth of protein mentions as input. [2]

Like any NLP task, ambiguity is a central problem. The same event can be expressed in many variations. For example, a `Negative_regulation` event may be signified by "inhibition", "down-regulation", "is abrogated by", to name a few. On the other hand, depending on the context, the same expression may represent different events. For example, "level" may signify any one of five event types in the training set, or signify none.

In addition, the nested event structures present new challenges to knowledge extraction systems. To recognize a complex event, besides from identifying the event type and trigger words, one also needs to identify its arguments and recursively identify their event structures. A mistake in any part will render a failure in this extraction.

The interdependencies among events and arguments naturally argue for joint predictions. For example, given the snippet "the level of VCAM-1 mRNA", knowing that "level" might signify an event helps to recognize the prepositional phrase (PP) as its theme. Conversely, the presence of the PP suggests that "level" is likely an event. Moreover, the word "mRNA" in the PP indicates that the event type is probably `Transcription`.

Most existing systems adopt a pipeline architecture and reduce the task to independent classifications of events and arguments. For example, the best system UTurku (Bjorne et al., 2009) first extracts a list of candidate triggers with types, and then determines for each pair of candidate triggers or proteins whether one is a theme or cause of the other. The triggers missed in the first stage can never be recovered in the second one. Moreover, since the second stage is trained with gold triggers as input, any trigger identified in the first stage tends to get at least

[2] The Shared Task also defines two other tasks (Tasks 2 and 3), which aim either to extract additional arguments (e.g., sites), or to determine if an event is a negation or speculation. In this paper, we focus on the core task (Task 1) as it is what most systems participate in, but our approach can be extended straightforwardly to handle the other tasks.

one argument, even though it may not be an event at all. As a result, the authors had to use an ad hoc procedure to trade off precision and recall for the final prediction task while training the first-stage extractor. In addition, each trigger or argument is classified independently using a multi-class SVM.

While joint inference can potentially improve accuracy, in practice, it is often very challenging to make it work (Poon and Domingos, 2007). The previous best joint approach for this task was proposed by Riedel et al. (2009) (labeled UT+DBLS in Kim et al. (2009)). Their system is also based on Markov logic (Domingos and Lowd, 2009). While competitive (ranked fourth in the evaluation), their system still lags UTurku by more than 7 points in F1.

Most systems, Riedel et al.'s included, classify each candidate argument path as a whole. A notable exception is the UTokyo system (Saetre et al., 2009), which incorporated sequential modeling by adapting a state-of-the-art PPI system based on MEMM. But they considered adjacent words in the sentence, which offered little help in this task, and their system trailed UTurku by 15 points in F1.

All top systems for event extraction relied heavily on syntactic features. We went one step further by formulating joint predictions directly on dependency edges. While this leverages sequential correlation along argument paths, it also makes our system more prone to the adverse effect of syntactic errors. Joint syntactic and semantic processing has received much attention lately (Hajic et al., 2009). In this paper, we explore using a heuristic method to correct syntactic errors based on semantic information, and show that it leads to significant performance gain for event extraction.

3 Markov Logic

In many NLP applications, there exist rich relation structures among objects, and recent work in statistical relational learning (Getoor and Taskar, 2007) and structured prediction (Bakir et al., 2007) has shown that leveraging these can greatly improve accuracy. One of the leading frameworks for joint inference is Markov logic, a probabilistic extension of first-order logic (Domingos and Lowd, 2009). A *Markov logic network (MLN)* is a set of weighted first-order clauses. Together with a set of constants, it defines a Markov network with one node per ground atom and one feature per ground clause. The weight of a feature is the weight of the first-order clause that generated it. The probability of a state x in such a network is given by $P(x) = (1/Z) \exp(\sum_i w_i f_i(x))$, where Z is a normalization constant, w_i is the weight of the ith clause, $f_i = 1$ if the ith clause is true, and $f_i = 0$ otherwise.

Markov logic makes it possible to compactly specify probability distributions over complex relational domains. Efficient inference can be performed using MC-SAT (Poon and Domingos, 2006). MC-SAT is a "slice sampling" Markov chain Monte Carlo algorithm that uses an efficient satisfiability solver to propose the next sample. It is orders of magnitude faster than previous MCMC algorithms like Gibbs sampling, making efficient sampling possible on a scale that was previously out of reach.

Supervised learning for Markov logic maximizes the conditional log-likelihood of query predicates given the evidence in the train data. This learning objective is convex and can be optimized using gradient descent, where the gradient is estimated using MC-SAT.

In practice, it is often difficult to tune the learning rate, especially when the number of groundings varies widely among clauses (known as *ill-conditioning* in numerical optimization). This problem is particularly severe in relational domains. One remedy is to apply preconditioning to the gradient. For example, Poon & Domingos (2007) divided the global learning rate by the number of true groundings of the corresponding clause in the training data, whereas Lowd & Domingos (2007) divided it by the variance of the clause (also estimated using MC-SAT). The latter can be viewed as approximating the Hessian with its diagonal, and is guaranteed optimal when the weights are not correlated (e.g., in logistic regression). Lowd & Domingos (2007) also used a scaled conjugate gradient algorithm to incorporate second-order information and further adapt the search direction.

The open-source Alchemy package (Kok et al., 2009) provides implementations of existing algorithms for Markov logic.

4 An MLN for Joint Bio-Event Extraction

In this section, we present our MLN for joint bio-event extraction. As standard for this task, we assume that Stanford dependency parses are available in the input. Our MLN jointly makes the following predictions: for each token, whether it is a trigger word (and if so, what is the event type), and for each dependency edge, whether it is in an argument path leading to a theme or cause.

To the best of our knowledge, the latter part makes this formulation a novel one. By breaking the prediction of an argument path into that on individual dependency edges, it can leverage the correlation among adjacent edges and make learning more effective. Indeed, compared to other top systems, our MLN uses a much simpler set of features, but is still capable of obtaining state-of-the-art results.[3] Computationally, this formulation is also attractive. The number of predictions is bounded by the number of tokens and edges, and is linear in sentence length, rather than quadratic.

Our MLN also handles the regulation events differently. We notice that events of the three regulation types often occur in similar contexts, and sometimes share trigger words (e.g., "involve"). Therefore, our MLN merges them into a single event type Regulation, and additionally predicts the regulation direction (Positive or Negative). This allows it to pool information shared by the three types.

Base MLN: The following are the main query predicates we used, along with descriptions:

Event(i): token i signifies an event;

EvtType(i, e): i is of event type e;

RegType(i, r): i is of regulation type r;

InArgPath(i, j, a): the dependency edge from i to j is in an argument path of type a, with a being either Theme or Cause.

If event i has type Positive_regulation, both EvtType(i, Regulation) and RegType(i, Positive) are true. Similarly for Negative_regulation. If the type is Regulation, only EvtType(i, Regulation) is true.

Table 1: Formulas in the base MLN.

Token(i, +t) ⇒ EvtType(i, +e)
Token(i, +t) ⇒ RegType(i, +r)
Token(j, +t) ∧ Dep(i, j, d) ⇒ EvtType(i, +e)
Dep(i, j, +d) ⇒ InArgPath(i, j, +a)
Dep(i, j, +d) ∧ Prot(i) ⇒ InArgPath(i, j, +a)
Dep(i, j, +d) ∧ Prot(j) ⇒ InArgPath(i, j, +a)
Token(i, +t) ∧ Dep(i, j, +d) ⇒ InArgPath(i, j, +a)
Token(j, +t) ∧ Dep(i, j, +d) ⇒ InArgPath(i, j, +a)

The main evidence predicates are:

Token(i, w): token i has word w;

Dep(i, j, d): there is a dependency edge from i to j with label d; [4]

Prot(i): i is a protein.

Our base MLN is a logistic regression model, and can be succintly captured by eight formulas in Table 1. All free variables are implicitly universally quantified. The "+" notation signifies that the MLN contains an instance of the formula, with a separate weight, for each value combination of the variables with a plus sign. The first three formulas predict the event type and regulation direction based on the token word or its neighbor in the dependency tree. The next five formulas predict whether a dependency edge is in an argument path, based on some combinations of token word, dependency label, and whether the nodes are proteins.

By default, we also added the unit formulas: Theme(x, y), Cause(x, y), EventType(x, +e), RegType(x, +r), which capture default regularities.

Joint Inference: Like any classification system, the formulas in the base MLN make independent predictions at inference time. This is suboptimal, because query atoms are interdependent due to either hard constraints (e.g., an event must have a type) or soft correlation (e.g., "increase" signifies an event and the dobj edge from it leads to a theme). We thus

[3]In future work, we plan to incorporate a much richer set of features; Markov logic makes such extensions straightforward.

[4]For convenience, we include the reverse dependency edges in the evidence. For example, if Dep(i, j, nn) is true, then so is Dep(j, i, −nn).

augment the base MLN with two groups of joint-inference formulas. First we incorporate the following hard constraints.

$$\texttt{Event(i)} \Rightarrow \exists \texttt{t}.\ \texttt{EvtType(i,t)}$$

$$\texttt{EvtType(i,t)} \Rightarrow \texttt{Event(i)}$$

$$\texttt{RegType(i,r)} \Rightarrow \texttt{EvtType(i,Regulation)}$$

$$\texttt{InArgPath(i,j,Theme)} \Rightarrow \texttt{Event(i)} \\ \vee\ \exists\, \texttt{k} \neq \texttt{j}.\ \texttt{InArgPath(k,i,Theme)}$$

$$\texttt{InArgPath(i,j,Cause)} \\ \Rightarrow \texttt{EvtType(i,Regulation)} \\ \vee\ \exists\, \texttt{k} \neq \texttt{j}.\ \texttt{InArgPath(k,i,Cause)}$$

$$\texttt{InArgPath(i,j,Theme)} \Rightarrow \texttt{Prot(j)} \\ \vee\ \exists\, \texttt{k} \neq \texttt{i}.\ \texttt{InArgPath(j,k,Theme)}$$

$$\texttt{InArgPath(i,j,Cause)} \Rightarrow \texttt{Event(j)} \vee \texttt{Prot(j)} \\ \vee\ \exists\, \texttt{k} \neq \texttt{i}.\ \texttt{InArgPath(j,k,Cause)}$$

The first three formulas enforce that events must have a type, that a token assigned an event (regulation) type must be an (regulation) event. The next four formulas enforce the consistency of argument path assignments: an argument path must start with an event, in particular, a cause path must start with a regulation event; a theme path must eventually trace to a protein, whereas a cause path may also stop at an event (which does not have a cause itself). To avoid looping, we forbid reverse edges in a path.[5]

Notice that with these constraints, adjacent edges in the dependency tree correlate with each other in their `InArgPath` assignments, much like in an HMM for linear sequences. Moreover, these assignments correlate with the event and event-type ones; knowing that `i` probably signifies an event makes it easier to detect an argument path, and vice versa. In addition, events that share partial argument paths can inform each other through the predictions on edges. In the experiments section, we will see that merely adding these hard constraints leads to 26-point gain in F1.

We also notice that different trigger words may use different dependencies to start an argument path of a particular type. For example, for many verbs, `nsubj` tends to start a cause path and `dobj` a theme path. However, for "bind" that signifies a `Binding` event, both lead to themes, as in "A binds B". Such soft regularities can be captured by a single joint formula: $\texttt{Token(i,+w)} \wedge \texttt{Dep(i,j,+d)} \Rightarrow \texttt{Event(i)} \wedge \texttt{InArgPath(i,j,+a)}$, which correlates event and argument type with token and dependency.

Linguistically-Motivated Formulas: Natural languages often possess systematic syntactic alternations. For example, for the word "increase", if both subject and object are present, as in "A increases the level of B", the subject is the cause whereas the object is the theme. However, if only subject is present, as in "The level of B increases", the subject is the theme. We thus augment the MLN with a number of context-specific formulas such as: $\texttt{Token(i,increase)} \wedge \texttt{Dep(i,j,nsubj)} \wedge \texttt{Dep(i,k,dobj)} \wedge \texttt{Event(i)} \wedge \texttt{Cause(i,j)}$.[6]

5 Learning And Inference

When training data comprises of many independent subsets (e.g., individual abstracts), stochastic gradient descent (SGD) is often a favorable method for parameter learning. By adopting small and frequent updates, it can dramatically speed up learning and sometimes even improve accuracy. Moreover, it easily scales to large datasets since each time it only needs to bring a few subsets into the memory.

In this paper, we used SGD to learn weights for our MLN. During this process, we discovered some general challenges for applying SGD to relational domains. For example, the ill-conditioning problem is particularly severe, and using a single learning rate either makes learning extremely slow or leads to divergence. Like Lowd & Domingos (2007), we combat this by dividing the learning rate by the variance. However, this still leads to divergence as learning progresses. The reason is that some weights are strongly correlated due to the joint formulas, especially the hard constraints. Therefore, the diagonal approximates the Hessian poorly. Inspired by Poon & Domingos (2007), for each formula, we count the numbers of true and false groundings in the train data, and add the smaller of the two plus one to the variance, before dividing the global rate by it.

[5]This is violated in some cases, and can be relaxed. We enforced it for simplicity in this paper.

[6]Available at `http://research.microsoft.com/-en-us/people/lucyv/naacl10`.

We found that this is effective for making learning stable in our experiments.

To compute the most probable state, we used MC-SAT to estimate the marginal probability of each query atom, and returned the ones with probability above a threshold. This allows us to easily trade off precision and recall by varying the threshold. To speed up burn-in, we followed Poon et al. (2009) and first ran MC-SAT with deterministic annealing for initialization.

6 Correcting Syntactic Errors With Semantic Information

Two typical types of syntactic errors are PP-attachment and coordination. For semantic tasks such as bio-event extraction, these errors also have the most adverse impact to performance. For example, for the snippet "involvement of p70 activation in IL-10 up-regulation by gp41", the Stanford parser makes two errors by attaching "up-regulation" to "activation" instead of "involvement", and attaching "gp41" to "involvement" instead of "up-regulation". This makes it very difficult to predict that "gp41" is the cause of "up-regulation", and that "up-regulation" is the theme of "involvement". For conjucts such as "IL-2 and IL-4 expressions", the parser will align "IL-2" with "expressions", which makes it difficult to recognize the expression event on "IL-2". For nested events like "gp41 regulates IL-2 and IL-4 expressions", this results in three extraction errors: IL-2 expression and the regulation event on it are missing, whereas an erroneous regulation event on IL-2 is predicted.

Syntactic errors are often incurred due to lack of semantic information during parsing (e.g., the knowledge that IL-2 and IL-4 are both proteins). In this paper, we used a heuristic method to fix such errors by incorporating two sources of semantic information: argument paths in training data and input protein labels. For conjuncts (signified by prefix `conj` in Stanford dependencies) between a protein and a non-protein, we check whether the non-protein has a protein child, if so, we remove the conjunct and reattach the first protein to the non-protein. For PP-attachments, we notice that often the errors can be fixed by reattaching the child to the closest node that fits a known attachment pattern (e.g., "up-regulation by PROTEIN"). We used the following heuristics to gather attachment patterns. For each argument path in the training data, if it consists of a single PP edge, then we add the combination of governor, dependency label, and dependent to the pattern. (Protein names are replaced with a special string.) If a path contains multiple edges, but a PP edge attaches to a word to the left of the event trigger (e.g., "gp41" attached to "involvement"), our system concludes that the dependent should instead be attached to the trigger and adds the corresponding pattern. In addition, we added a few default patterns like "involvement in" and "effect on". For each PP edge, the candidates for reattachment include the current governor, and the governor's parent and all rightmost descendants (i.e., its rightmost child, the rightmost child of that child, etc.) that are to the left of the dependent. We reattach the dependent to the closest candidate that fits an attachment pattern. If there is none, the attachment remains unchanged. In total, the fraction of reattachments is about 4%.

7 Experiments

We evaluated our system on the dataset for Task 1 in the BioNLP'09 Shared Task (Kim et al., 2009). It consists of 800 abstracts for training, 150 for development and 260 for test. We conducted feature development and tuned hyperparameters using the development set, and evaluated our final system on test using the online tool provided by the organizers. (The test annotations are not released to the public.) All results reported were obtained using the main evaluation criteria for the shared task.[7]

7.1 System

Our system first carries out lemmatization and breaks up hyphenated words.[8] It then uses the Stanford parser (de Marneffe et al., 2006) to generate dependencies. For simplicity, if an event contains multiple trigger words, only the head word is labeled.[9]

[7] Namely, "Approximate Span/Approximate Recursive Matching". See Kim et al. (2009) for details.

[8] E.g., "gp41-induced" becomes "gp41" and "induced", with a new dependency edge labeled `hyphen` from "induced" to "gp41". To avoid breaking up protein names with hyphens, we only dehyphenate words with suffix in a small hand-picked list.

[9] Most events have only one trigger, and the chosen words only need to lie within an approximate span in evaluation.

Table 2: Comparison of our full system with its variants and with UTurku on the development set.

	Rec.	Prc.	F1
BASE	17.4	67.2	27.7
BASE+HARD	49.4	58.5	53.6
FULL	51.5	60.0	**55.5**
−LING	50.5	59.6	54.7
−SYN-FIX	48.2	54.6	51.2
UTurku	51.5	55.6	53.5

We implemented our system as an extension to the Alchemy system (Kok et al., 2009). In particular, we developed an efficient parallelized implementation of our stochastic gradient descent algorithm using the message-passing interface (MPI). For learning, we used a mini-batch of 20 abstracts and iterated through the training files twice. For each mini-batch, we estimated the gradient by running MC-SAT for 300 samples; the initialization was done by running annealed MC-SAT for 200 samples, with temperature dropping from 10 to 0.1 at 0.05 decrements. For inference, we initialized MC-SAT with 1000 annealed samples, with temperature dropping from 10 to 0.1 at 0.01 decrements, we then ran MC-SAT for 5000 samples to compute the marginal probabilities. This implementation is very efficient: learning took about 20 minutes in a 32-core cluster with 800 training files; inference took a few minutes in average.

To obtain the final assignment, we set the query atoms with probability no less than 0.4 to true and the rest to false. The threshold is chosen to maximize F1 in the development set. To generate the events, we first found arguments for each trigger `i` by gathering all proteins and event triggers that were accessible from `i` along an argument path without first encountering another trigger. For triggers of base event types, we dropped other triggers from its argument list. For nested triggers, we generated events recursively by first processing argument triggers and generating their events, and then generating events for the parent trigger by including all combinations of argument events. For `Binding` triggers, we group its arguments by the first dependency labels in the argument paths, and generate events by a cross-product of the group members.

Table 3: Per-type recall/precision/F1 for our full system on the development set.

	Rec.	Prc.	F1
`Expression`	75.6	79.1	77.3
`Transcription`	69.5	73.1	71.3
`Phosphorylation`	87.2	87.2	87.2
`Catabolism`	85.7	100	92.3
`Localization`	66.0	85.4	74.5
`Binding`	39.1	61.8	47.9
`Positive_regulation`	41.8	51.0	46.0
`Negative_regulation`	39.3	56.2	46.3
`Regulation`	41.4	33.2	36.8

7.2 Results

We first conducted experiments on the development set to evaluate the contributions of individual components. Table 2 compares their performances along with that of UTurku. The base MLN (**BASE**) alone performed rather poorly. Surprisingly, by just adding the hard constraints to leverage joint inference (**BASE+HARD**), our system almost doubled the F1, and tied UTurku. In addition, adding the soft joint-inference formula results in further gain, and our full system (**FULL**) attained an F1 of 55.5. This is two points higher than UTurku and the best reported result on this dataset. The linguistically-motivated formulas are beneficial, as can seen by comparing with the system without them (**−LING**), although the difference is small. Fixing the syntactic errors with semantic information, on the other hand, leads to substantial performance gain. Without doing it (**−SYN-FIX**), our system suffers an F1 loss of more than four points. This verifies that the quality of syntactic analysis is important for event extraction. The differences between FULL and other variants (except -LING) are all statistically significant at 1% level using McNemar's test.

To understand the performance bottlenecks, we show the per-type results in Table 3 and the results at the predicate level in Table 4.[10] Both trigger and argument-edge detections leave much room for improvement. In particular, the system proposed many incorrect regulation triggers, partly because regulation triggers have the most variations

[10]Numbers in Table 3 refer to events, whereas in Table 4 to triggers. A trigger may signify multiple events, so numbers in Table 4 can be smaller than that in Table 3.

Table 4: Predicate recall/precision/F1 for our full system on the development set.

	Rec.	Prc.	F1
Expression	80.1	82.0	81.0
Transcription	68.8	71.0	69.8
Phosphorylation	87.5	92.1	89.7
Catabolism	84.2	100	91.4
Localization	62.5	86.2	72.5
Binding	62.4	82.4	71.1
Positive_regulation	65.8	70.7	68.2
Negative_regulation	58.3	71.7	64.3
Regulation	61.7	43.4	50.9
All triggers	68.1	71.7	69.9
Argument edge	69.0	71.8	70.4

Table 5: Comparison of our full system with top systems on the test set.

	Rec.	Prc.	F1
UTurku	46.7	58.5	52.0
JULIELab	45.8	47.5	46.7
ConcordU	35.0	61.6	44.6
Riedel et al.	36.9	55.6	44.4
FULL MLN	43.7	58.6	50.0

among all types. Our system did well in recognizing Binding triggers, but performed much poorer at the event level. This indicates that the bottleneck lies in correctly identifying all arguments for multi-theme events. Indeed, if we evaluate on individual event-theme pairs for Binding, the F1 jumps 15 points to 62.8%, with precision 82.7% and recall 50.6%.

Finally, Table 5 compares our system with the top systems on the test set. Our system trailed UTurku due to a somewhat lower recall, but substantially outperformed all other systems. In particular, it reduced F1 error by more than 10% compared to the previous best joint approach by Riedel et al. (2009).

7.3 Error Analysis

Through manual inspection, we found that many remaining errors were related to syntactic parses. The problem is particularly severe when there are nested or co-occuring PP-attachments and conjuncts (e.g., "increased levels of IL-2 and IL-4 mRNA and protein in the cell"). Our rule-based procedure in Section 6 has high precision in fixing some of these errors, but the coverage is limited. It also makes hard decisions in a preprocessing step, which cannot be reverted. A principled solution is to resolve syntactic and semantic ambiguities in a joint model that integrates reattachment decisions and extractions. This can potentially resolve more syntactic errors, as extraction makes more semantic information available, and is more robust to reattachment uncertainty.

In some challenging cases, we found further opportunities for joint inference. For example, in the sentence "These cells are deficient in FasL expression, although their cytokine IL-2 production is normal", "normal" signifies a Positive_regulation event over "IL-2 production" because of its contrast with "deficient". Such events can be detected by introducing additional joint inference rules that leverage syntactic structures such as subclauses.

We also found many cases where the annotations differ for the same expressions. For example, "cotransfection with PROTEIN" is sometimes labeled as both an Expression event and a Positive_regulation event, and sometimes not labeled at all. This occurs more often for regulation events, which partly explains the low precision for them.

8 Conclusion

This paper presents the first joint approach for bio-event extraction that achieves state-of-the-art results. This is made possible by adopting a novel formulation that jointly predicts events, arguments, as well as individual dependency edges in argument paths. Our system is based on Markov logic and can be easily extended to incorporate additional knowledge and linguistic features to further improve accuracy.

Directions for future work include: leveraging additional joint-inference opportunities, better integration of syntactic parsing and event extraction, and applying this approach to other extraction tasks and domains.

9 Acknowledgements

We give warm thanks to Sebastian Riedel and three anonymous reviewers for helpful comments and suggestions.

References

G. Bakir, T. Hofmann, B. B. Schölkopf, A. Smola, B. Taskar, S. Vishwanathan, and (eds.). 2007. *Predicting Structured Data*. MIT Press, Cambridge, MA.

Jari Bjorne, Juho Heimonen, Filip Ginter, Antti Airola, Tapio Pahikkala, and Tapio Salakoski. 2009. Extracting complex biological events with rich graph-based feature sets. In *Proceedings of the BioNLP Workshop 2009*.

Mark Craven, Dan DiPasquo, Dayne Freitag, Andrew McCallum, Tom Mitchell, Kamal Nigam, and Sean Slattery. 1999. Learning to construct knowledge bases from the world wide web. *Artificial Intelligence*.

Marie-Catherine de Marneffe, Bill MacCartney, and Christopher D. Manning. 2006. Generating typed dependency parses from phrase structure parses. In *Proceedings of the Fifth International Conference on Language Resources and Evaluation*, pages 449–454, Genoa, Italy. ELRA.

Pedro Domingos and Daniel Lowd. 2009. *Markov Logic: An Interface Layer for Artificial Intelligence*. Morgan & Claypool, San Rafael, CA.

Lise Getoor and Ben Taskar, editors. 2007. *Introduction to Statistical Relational Learning*. MIT Press, Cambridge, MA.

Jan Hajic, Massimiliano Ciaramita, Richard Johansson, Daisuke Kawahara, Maria Antonia Martii, Lluis Marquez, Adam Meyers, Joakim Nivre, Sebastian Pado, Jan Stepanek, Pavel Stranak, Mihai Surdeanu, Nianwen Xue, and Yi Zhang. 2009. The CoNLL-2009 Shared Task: syntactic and semantic dependencies in multiple languages. In *Proceedings of the Thirteenth Conference on Computational Natural Language Learning: Shared Task*.

Jin-Dong Kim, Tomoko Ohta, Sampo Pyysalo, Yoshinobu Kano, and Junichi Tsujii. 2009. Overview of BioNLP-09 Shared Task on event extraction. In *Proceedings of the BioNLP Workshop 2009*.

Stanley Kok, Parag Singla, Matt Richardson, Pedro Domingos, Marc Sumner, Hoifung Poon, and Daniel Lowd. 2009. The alchemy system for statistical relational ai. Technical report, Dept. of CSE, Univ. of Washington, http://alchemy.cs.washington.edu/.

Daniel Lowd and Pedro Domingos. 2007. Efficient weight learning for markov logic networks. In *Proceedings of the Eleventh European Conference on Principles and Practice of Knowledge Discovery in Databases*, pages 200–211, Warsaw. Springer.

Hoifung Poon and Pedro Domingos. 2006. Sound and efficient inference with probabilistic and deterministic dependencies. In *Proceedings of the Twenty First National Conference on Artificial Intelligence*, pages 458–463, Boston, MA. AAAI Press.

Hoifung Poon and Pedro Domingos. 2007. Joint inference in information extraction. In *Proceedings of the Twenty Second National Conference on Artificial Intelligence*, pages 913–918, Vancouver, Canada. AAAI Press.

Hoifung Poon, Colin Cherry, and Kristina Toutanova. 2009. Unsupervised morphological segmentation with log-linear models. In *Proceedings of NAACL-HLT*, Boulder, Colorado. ACL.

Sebastian Riedel, Hong-Woo Chun, Toshihisa Takagi, and Junichi Tsujii. 2009. A markov logic approach to bio-molecular event extraction. In *Proceedings of the BioNLP Workshop 2009*.

Rune Saetre, Makoto Miwa, Kazuhiro Yoshida, and Junichi Tsujii. 2009. From protein-protein interaction to molecular event extraction. In *Proceedings of the BioNLP Workshop 2009*.

Clinical Information Retrieval using Document and PICO Structure

Florian Boudin and Jian-Yun Nie
DIRO, Université de Montréal
CP. 6128, succursale Centre-ville
Montréal, H3C 3J7 Québec, Canada
{boudinfl,nie}@iro.umontreal.ca

Martin Dawes
Department of Family Medicine
McGill University, 515 Pine Ave W
Montréal, H2W 1S4 Québec, Canada
martin.dawes@mcgill.ca

Abstract

In evidence-based medicine, clinical questions involve four aspects: Patient/Problem (P), Intervention (I), Comparison (C) and Outcome (O), known as PICO elements. In this paper we present a method that extends the language modeling approach to incorporate both document structure and PICO query formulation. We present an analysis of the distribution of PICO elements in medical abstracts that motivates the use of a location-based weighting strategy. In experiments carried out on a collection of 1.5 million abstracts, the method was found to lead to an improvement of roughly 60% in MAP and 70% in P@10 as compared to state-of-the-art methods.

1 Introduction

As the volume of published medical literature continues to grow exponentially, there is more and more research for physicians to assess and evaluate and less time to do so. Evidence-based medicine (EBM) (Sackett et al., 1996) is a widely accepted paradigm in medical practice that relies on evidence from patient-centered clinical research to make decisions. Taking an evidence-based approach to searching means doing a systematic search of all the available literature, individually critically appraising each research study and then applying the findings in clinical practice. However, this is a time consuming activity. One way to facilitate searching for a precise answer is to formulate a well-focused and structured question (Schardt et al., 2007).

Physicians are educated to formulate their clinical questions according to several well defined aspects in EBM: Patient/Problem (P), Intervention (I), Comparison (C) and Outcome (O), which are called PICO elements. In many documents in medical literature (e.g. MEDLINE), one can find the elements of the PICO structure, but rarely explicitly annotated (Dawes et al., 2007). To identify documents corresponding to a patient's state, physicians also construct their queries according to the PICO structure. For example, in the question "*In children with pain and fever how does paracetamol compared with ibuprofen affect levels of pain and fever?*" one can identify the following PICO elements:

Patient/Problem: *children/pain and fever*
Intervention: *paracetamol*
Comparison: *ibuprofen*
Outcome: *levels of pain and fever*

Very little work, if any, has been carried out on the use of these elements in the Information Retrieval (IR) process. There are several reasons for that. It is not easy to identify PICO elements in documents, as well as in the question if these are not explicitly separated in it. Several studies have been performed on identifying PICO elements in abstracts (Demner-Fushman and Lin, 2007; Hansen et al., 2008; Chung, 2009). However, all of them are reporting coarse-grain (sentence-level) tagging methods that have not yet been shown to be sufficient for the purpose of IR. Moreover, there is currently no standard test collection of questions in PICO structure available for evaluation. On the other hand, the most critical aspect in IR is term weighting. One of the purpose of tagging PICO elements is to assign appropriate weights to these elements during the retrieval process. From this perspective, a semantic tagging of PICO elements may be a task that goes well beyond

Human Language Technologies: The 2010 Annual Conference of the North American Chapter of the ACL, pages 822–830,
Los Angeles, California, June 2010.

that is required for IR. It may be sufficient to have a method that assigns appropriate weights to elements rather than recognizing their semantic roles. In this paper, we will propose an approach to determine term weights according to document structure. This method will be compared to that using tagging of PICO elements.

In this paper, we first report an attempt to manually annotate the PICO elements in documents by physicians and use them as training data to build an automatic tagging tool. It turns out that there is a high disagreement rate between human annotators. The utilization of the automatic tagging tool in an IR experiment shows only a small gain in retrieval effectiveness. We therefore propose an alternative to PICO element detection that uses the structural information of documents. This solution turns out to be robust and effective. The alternative approach is motivated by a strong trend that we observe in the distribution of PICO elements in documents. We then make use of both PICO query and document structure to extend the classical language modeling approach to IR. Specifically, we investigate how each element of a PICO query should be weighted and how a location-based weighting strategy can be used to emphasize the most informative parts (i.e. containing the most PICO elements) of documents.

The paper is organized as follows. We first briefly review the previous work, followed by a description of the method we propose. Next, we present our experiments and results. Lastly, we conclude with a discussion and directions for future work.

2 Related work

There have been only a few studies trying to use PICO elements in the retrieval process. (Demner-Fushman and Lin, 2007) is one of the few such studies. The method they describe consists in re-ranking an initial list of retrieved citations. To this end, the relevance of a document is scored by the use of detected PICO elements, among other things. Several other studies aimed to build a Question-Answering system for clinical questions (Demner-Fushman and Lin, 2006; Andrenucci, 2008). But again, the focus has been set on the post-retrieval step, while the document retrieval step only uses a standard approach. In this paper, we argue that IR has much to gain by using PICO elements.

The task of identifying PICO elements has however gain more attention. In their paper, (Demner-Fushman and Lin, 2007) presented a method that uses either manually crafted pattern-matching rules or a combination of basic classifiers to detect PICO elements in medical abstracts. Prior to that, biomedical concepts are labelled by Metamap (Aronson, 2001) while relations between these concepts are extracted with SemRep (Rindflesch and Fiszman, 2003). Recently, supervised classification using Support Vector Machines (SVM) was proposed by (Hansen et al., 2008) to extract the number of trial participants. In a later study, (Chung, 2009) extended this work to other elements using Conditional Random Fields. Although these studies are reporting interesting results, they are limited in several aspects. First, many are restricted to some segments of the medical documents (e.g. Method section) (Chung, 2009), and in most cases, the test collection is very small (a few hundreds abstracts). Second, the precision and granularity of these methods have not yet been shown to be sufficient for the purpose of IR.

The structural information provided by markup languages (e.g. XML) has been successfully used to improve the IR effectiveness (INEX, 2002 2009). For such documents, the structure information can be used to emphasize some particular parts of the document. Thereby, a given word should not have the same importance depending on its position in the document structure.

Taking into account the structure can be done either at the step of querying or at the step of indexing. One way to integrate the structure at querying is to adapt query languages (Fuhr and Großjohann, 2001). These approaches follow the assumption that the user knows where the most relevant information is located. However, (Kamps et al., 2005) showed that it is preferable to use structure as a search hint, and not as a strict search requirement

The second approach consists in integrating the document structure at the indexing step by introducing a structure weighting scheme (Wilkinson, 1994). In such a scheme, the weight assigned to a word is not only based on its frequency but also on its position in the document. The structure of a document can be defined in terms of tags (e.g. title, section), each of those having a weight chosen either empirically or automatically by the use of optimizing techniques such as genetic algorithms (Trotman, 2005).

3 Using PICO elements in retrieval

In this section, we present an experiment on the manual annotation of PICO elements. We then describe an approach to detect these elements in documents and give some results on the use of these tagged elements in the retrieval process.

3.1 Manual annotation of PICO elements

We asked medical professionals to manually annotate the PICO elements in a small collection of abstracts from PubMed[1]. The instructions given to the annotators were fairly simple. They were asked to precisely annotate all PICO elements in abstracts with no restriction about the size of the elements (i.e. they could be words, phrases or sentences). More than 50 abstracts were manually annotated this way by at least two different annotators. Two annotations by two annotators are considered to agree if they share some words (i.e. they overlap). We computed the well known Cohen's kappa measure as well as an ad-hoc measure called `loose`. The latter uses PICO elements as units and estimates the proportion of elements that have been annotated by both raters.

Measure	P-element	I/C-element	O-element
kappa	0.687	0.539	0.523
loose	0.363	0.136	0.140

Table 1: Agreement measures computed for each element. Cohen's kappa and `loose` agreement are presented.

We can observe that there is a very low agreement rate between human annotators. The `loose` measure indicates that less than 15% of the I, C and O elements have been marked by both annotators. This fact shows that such human annotations can be hardly used to develop an automatic tagging tool for PICO elements, which requires consistent training data. We therefore try to develop a coarser-grained tagging method.

[1] `www.pubmed.gov`, PubMed is a service of the US National Library of Medicine that includes over 19 million citations from MEDLINE and other life science journals.

3.2 Automatic detection of PICO elements

Similarly to previous work, we propose a sentence-level detection method. The identification of PICO elements can be seen as a classification task. Even for a coarser-grain classification task, we are still lack of annotated data. One solution is to use the structural information embedded in some medical abstracts for which the authors have clearly stated distinctive sentence headings. Some recent abstracts in PubMed do contain explicit headings such as "PATIENTS", "SAMPLE" or "OUTCOMES", that can be used to locate sentences corresponding to PICO elements. Using that information, we extracted three sets of abstracts: Patient/Problem (14 279 abstracts), Intervention/Comparison (9 095) and Outcome (2 394).

Tagging each document goes through a three steps process. First, the document is segmented into plain sentences. Then each sentence is converted into a feature vector using statistical (e.g. position, length) and knowledge-based features (e.g. MeSH semantic type). Knowledge-based features were derived either from manually crafted cue-words/verbs lists or semantic types within the MeSH ontology[2]. Finally, each vector is submitted to multiple classifiers, one for each element, allowing to label the corresponding sentence. We use several algorithms implemented in the Weka toolkit[3]: decision trees, SVM, multi-layer perceptron and Naive Bayes. Combining multiple classifiers using a weighted linear combination of their prediction scores achieves the best results with a f-measure score of 86.3% for P, 67% for I/C and 56.6% for O in 10-fold cross-validation.

3.3 Use of detected elements in IR

We use language modeling approach to IR in this work. The idea is that a document is a good match to a query if its language model is likely to generate the query (Ponte and Croft, 1998). It is one of the state-of-the-art approaches in current IR research. Most language modeling work in IR use unigram language models –also called bags-of-words models– assuming that there is no structure in queries or documents. A typical way to score a document d as relevant to a query q is to use the *Kullback-Leibler*

[2] `www.nlm.nih.gov/mesh/`

[3] `www.cs.waikato.ac.nz/ml/index.html`

divergence between their respective LMs:

$$\text{score}(q, d) = \sum_{w \in q} P(w \mid M_q) \cdot \log P(w \mid M_d) \quad (1)$$
$$\propto -\text{KL}(M_q \parallel M_d)$$

where M_q is the LM of the query and M_d the LM of the document. $P(w \mid M_\rho)$ estimates the probability of the word w given the language model M_ρ. The most direct way to estimate these models is to use Maximum Likelihood estimation over the words:

$$P(w \mid M_\rho) = \frac{\text{count}(w, \rho)}{\mid \rho \mid}$$

where ρ is the observed document, $\text{count}(w, \rho)$ the number of times the word w occurs in ρ and $\mid \rho \mid$ the length of the document. Bayesian smoothing using *Dirichlet* priors is then applied to the maximum likelihood estimator to compensate for data sparseness.

We propose an approach that extend the basic LM approach to take into consideration the PICO element annotation. We assume that each element in the document has a different importance weight. Four more LMs are created, one for each elements. Given ω_e the weight of the PICO element e, $P(w \mid M_d)$ in equation 1 is re-defined as:

$$P_1(w \mid M_d) \propto P(w \mid M_d) + \sum_{e \in [P,I,C,O]} \omega_e \cdot P(w \mid M_e)$$

The right hand of the above equation is not a probability function. We could use a normalization to transform it. However, for the purpose of document ranking, this will not make any difference. Therefore, we will keep the un-normalized value.

We performed an extensive series of experiments using this model on the test collection described in Section 5. The results are shown in Table 2. It turns out that the best improvement we were able to obtain is very small (0.5% of MAP increase). There may be several reasons for that. First, the accuracy of the automatic document tagging may be insufficient. Second, even if elements are correctly identified in documents, if queries are treated as bags-of-words then any PICO element can match with any identical word in the query, whether it describe the same element or not. However, we also tested a naïve approach that matches the PICO elements in queries with the corresponding elements in documents. But this approach quickly turns out to be too restrictive and leads to bad results.

Measure	**Weighted elements**			
	P	I / C	O	Best†
MAP increase	0.0%	−0.2%	−0.1%	+0.5%

Table 2: Results using the PICO elements automatically detected in documents (†: $w_P = 0.5$, $w_I = 0.2$).

As we can see, this approach only brings limited improvement in retrieval effectiveness. This rises the question of the usability of such tagging method in its current performance state. We will see in the next section an alternative solution to this problem that relies on the distribution of PICO elements in documents.

4 Method

4.1 Distribution of PICO elements

PICO elements are not evenly distributed in medical documents, which often follow some implicit writing convention. An intuitive method is to weight higher a segment that is more probable to contain PICO elements. The distribution of PICO elements is likely to correlate to the position within the document. This intuition has been used in most of the supervised PICO detection methods which use location-based features. There has been several studies that cover the PICO extraction problem. However, as far as we know, none of them analyses and uses the positional ditribution of these elements within the documents for the purpose of IR. Biomedical abstracts can be typically represented by four ordered rhetorical categories which are Introduction, Methods, Results and Discussion (IMRAD) (Sollaci and Pereira, 2004). The reason is found in the need for speed when reviewing literature, as this format allows readers to pick those parts of particular interest. Besides, many scientific journals explicitly recommended this ordered structure.

The PICO dispersion is highly correlated to these rhetorical categories as some elements are more likely to occur in certain categories. For example, outcomes are more likely to appear in Results and/or Discussion parts. One could also expect to infer the role played by PICO elements in a clinical study. For example, the drug *pioglitazone* has not the same role in a clinical study if it appears as the main intervention (likely to occur in all parts) or as a comparative treatment (Methods and/or Results parts).

Instead of analysing the dispersion of PICO elements into the four IMRAD categories, we choose to the use automatically splitted parts. There are several reasons for that. First, the IMRAD categories are not explicitely marked in abstracts. An automatic tagging of these would surely result in some errors. Second, using a low granularity approach would provide more precise statistics. Furthermore, if one would use the dispersion of elements as a criterion to estimate how important each part is, an automatic partition would be a good choice because of its repeatability and ease to implement.

We divided each manually annotated abstract into 10 parts of equal length (P1 being the begining and P10 the ending) and computed statistics on the number of elements than occur in each of these parts. The Figure 1 shows the proportion of elements for each part. We can observe that PICO elements are not evenly distributed throughout the abstracts. Universally accepted rules that govern medical writing styles would be the first reason for that. It is clear that the beginning and ending parts of abstracts do contain most of the PICO elements. This gives us a clear indication on which parts should be enhanced when searching for these elements.

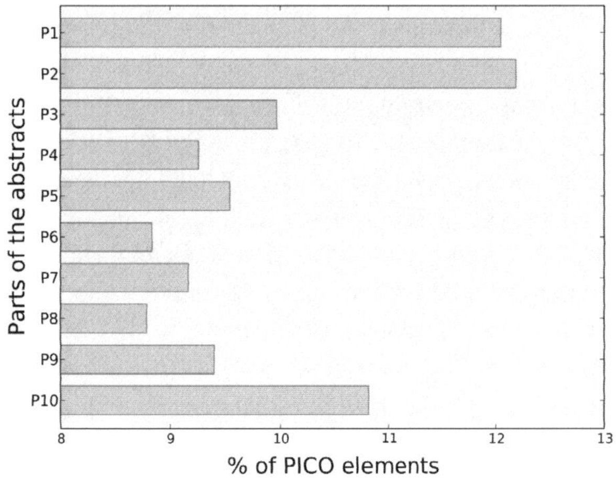

Figure 1: Proportion of PICO elements computed for each different part of abstracts.

Therefore, there may be several levels of granularity when using the PICO framework in IR. One can identify each PICO element in the document, whether it is described by a word, a phrase or a complete sentence. One can also use a coarser-grain approach, estimating from the distribution across documents the probability that each part contains a PICO element. As attempts to precisely locate PICO elements have shown that this task is particularly difficult, we propose to get rid this issue by using the second method.

4.2 Model definitions

We propose three different models that extend the classical language modeling approach. The first uses the structural information of documents, the second takes advantage of the PICO query structure while the third simply combine the first two models.

Model-1

Attempts to precisely locate PICO elements in documents have shown that this task is particularly difficult. We propose to get around this issue by introducing structural markers to convey document structure and use them as a means of providing location information. Accordingly, each document is represented as a series of successive parts. To integrate document structure into the ranking function, we estimate a series of probabilities that constraints the word counts to a specific part instead of the entire document. Each document d is then ranked by a weighted linear interpolation. Intuitively, the weight of a part should depend on how much information is conveyed by its words. Given γ_p the weight of the part $p \in [\text{TITLE}, \text{P1} \cdots \text{P10}]$, $P(w \mid M_d)$ in equation 1 is re-defined as:

$$P_2(w \mid M_d) \propto P(w \mid M_d) + \sum_{p \in d} \gamma_p \cdot P(w \in p \mid M_d)$$

Model-2

The PICO formulation of queries provides information about the role of each query word. One idea is to use this structural decomposition to thoroughly balance elements in the ranking function. For example, the weight given to the drug *fluoxetine* should be different depending on whether it refers to the intervention or comparison concept. The same goes for *obesity* which can be a problem or an outcome. To integrate this in the ranking function, we define a parameter δ_e that represents the weight given to query words belonging to the element $e \in [P, I, C, O]$. $f(w, e) = 1$ if $w \in e$, 0 otherwise. We re-defined $P(w \mid M_d)$ in equation 1 as:

$$P_3(w \mid M_q) \propto P(w \mid M_q) + \sum_{e \in [P,I,C,O]} \delta_e \cdot f(w, e) \cdot P(w \mid M_q)$$

Model-1+2

This is the combination of the two previously described models. We re-defined the scoring function as:

$$\text{score}(q, d) = \sum_{w \in q} P_3(w \mid M_q) \cdot \log P_2(w \mid M_d)$$

5 Experiments

In this section, we describe the details of our experimental protocol. We then present the results obtained with the three proposed models.

Experimental settings

We gathered a collection of nearly 1.5 million abstracts from PubMed with the following requirements: with abstract, humans subjects, in english and selecting the following publication types: RCT, reviews, clinical trials, letters, practice guidelines, editorials and meta-analysis. Prior to the index construction, each abstract is automatically divided into 10 parts of equal length, abstracts containing less than 10 words are discarded. The following fields are then marked: TITLE, P1, P2, ... P10 with P1 being the begining of the document and P10 the ending.

Unfortunately, there is no standard test collection appropriate for testing the use of PICO in IR and we had to manually create one. For queries, we use the Cochrane systematic reviews[4] on 10 clinical questions about different aspects of "*diabetes*". These reviews contain the best available information about an healthcare intervention and are designed to facilitate the choices that doctors face in health care. All the documents in the "Included studies" section are judged to be relevant for the question. These included studies are selected by the reviewers (authors of the review article) and judged to be highly related to the clinical question. In our experiments, we consider these documents as relevant ones. From the 10 selected questions, professors in family medicine have formulated a set of 52 queries, each of which was manually annotated according to the PICO structure. The resulting testing corpus is composed of 52 queries (average length of 14.7 words) and 378 relevant documents. Below are some of the alternative formulations of queries for the question "*Pioglitazone for type 2 diabetes mellitus*":

In patients with type 2 diabetes $^{(P)}$ | *does pioglitazone* $^{(I)}$ | *compared to placebo* $^{(C)}$ | *reduce stroke and myocardial infarction* $^{(O)}$

In patients with type 2 diabetes who have a high risk of macrovascular events $^{(P)}$ | *does pioglitazone* $^{(I)}$ | *compared to placebo* $^{(C)}$ | *reduce mortality* $^{(O)}$

We use cross-validation to determine reasonable weights and avoid over-fitting. We have divided the queries into two groups of 26 queries: Qa and Qb. The best parameters found for Qa are used to test on Qb, and vice versa. In our experiments, we use the KL divergence ranking (equation 1) as baseline. The following evaluation measures are considered relevant:

Precision at n ($P@n$). Precision computed on only the n topmost retrieved documents.

Mean Average Precision (MAP). Average of precisions computed at the point of each relevant document in the ranked list of retrieved documents.

MAP is a popular measure that gives a global quality score of the entire ranked list of retrieved documents. In the case of clinical searches, one could also imagine this scenario: a search performed by a physician who does not have the time to look into large sets of results, but for whom it is important to have relevant results in the top 10. In such case, $P@10$ is also an appropriate measure.

Student's t-test is performed to determine statistical significance. The Lemur Toolkit[5] was used for

[4] www.cochrane.org/reviews/

[5] www.lemurproject.org

all retrieval tasks. Experiments were performed with an "out-of-the-box" version of Lemur, using its tokenization algorithm and porter stemmer. The Dirichlet prior smoothing parameter was set to its default value $\mu = 2500$.

Experiments with model-1

We first investigated whether assigning a weight to each part of the document can improve the retrieval accuracy. It is however difficult to determine a set of reasonable values for all the parts together, as the value of one part will affect those of the others. In this study, we perform a two pass tuning. First, we consider the γ_p weights to be independent. By doing so, searching for the optimal weight distribution can be seen as tuning the weight of each part separately. When searching the optimal weight of a part, the weight for other parts is assigned 0. Second, these approximations of the optimum values are used as initial weights prior to the second pass. The final weight distribution is obtained by searching for the best weight combination around the initial values.

The Figure 2 shows the optimal weight distributions along with the best relative MAP increase for each part. A noticeable improvement is obtained by increasing the weights associated to the title/introduction and conclusion of documents. This is consistent with the results observed on the distribution of PICO elements in abstracts. Boosting middle parts of documents seems to have no impact at all. We can see that the two γ_p weight distributions (1-pass and 2-pass) are very close.

Performance measures obtained by model-1 are presented in Table 3. With 1-pass tuning, we observe a MAP score increase of 37.5% and a P@10 increase of 64.1%. After the second pass, scores are lower with 35% and 60.5% for MAP and P@10 respectively. This result indicates that there is possibly overfitting when we perform the two pass parameter tuning. It could also be caused by the limited number of query in our test collection. However, we can determine reasonable weights by tuning each part weight separately.

Experiments with model-2

We have seen that a large improvement could come from weighting each part accordingly. In a second series of experiments, we try to assign a different weight to each PICO element in queries. A grid search was used to find the optimal δ_e weights combination. The results are shown in Table 3.

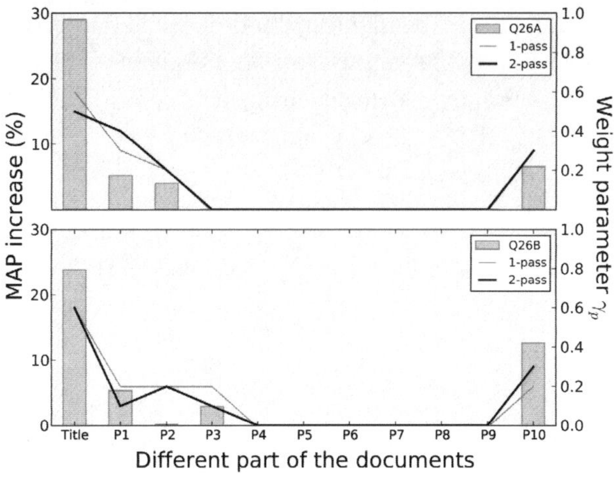

Figure 2: Best MAP increase for each part p (bar charts), corresponding 1 and 2-pass γ_p weights are also given.

We observe a MAP score increase of 22.5% and an increase of 11% in P@10. Though the use of a PICO weighting scheme increases the retrieval accuracy, there is clearly much to gain by using the document structure. The optimal $[\delta_p, \delta_i, \delta_c, \delta_o]$ weights distribution is $[0.3, 1.2, 0, 0.1]$ for Qa and $[0.2, 1, 0, 0.2]$ for Qb. That means that the most important words in queries belong to the Intervention element. This supports the manual search strategy proposed by (Weinfeld and Finkelstein, 2005), in which they suggested that I and P elements should be used first to construct queries, and only if too many results are obtained that other elements should be considered.

It is interesting to see that query words belonging to the Comparison element have to be considered as the least important part of a query. Even more so because they are in the same semantic group as the Intervention words. A reason for that could be the use of vague words such as "*no-intervention*" or "*placebo*". The methodology employed to construct the queries is also responsible. Indeed, physicians have focused on producing alternative formulations of 10 general clinical questions by predominantly modifying the one of the PICO elements. As a result, some of them do share the same vague Comparison words.

Experiments	MAP			P@10		
	Qb→Qa	Qa→Qb	% Avg.	Qb→Qa	Qa→Qb	% Avg.
Baseline	0.118	0.131		0.219	0.239	
Model-1 / 1pass	0.165	0.176	+37.5%‡	0.377	0.373	+64.1%‡
Model-1 / 2pass	0.165	0.170	+35.0%‡	0.354	0.381	+60.5%‡
Model-2	0.149	0.168	+22.5%‡	0.250	0.258	+11.0%
Model-1+2	0.198	0.202	+61.5%‡	0.385	0.392	+70.0%‡

Table 3: Cross-validation (train→test) scores for the baseline (Kullback-Leibler divergence), **model-1** with 1 and 2-pass tuning, **model-2** and their combination (**model-1+2**). Relative increase over the baseline is also given (averaged between Qa and Qb). (‡: t.test < 0.01)

Experiments with model-1+2

We have seen that both the use of a location-based weighting and a PICO-structure weighting scheme increase the retrieval accuracy. In this last series of experiments, we analyse the results of their combination. We can observe that fusing model-1 and model-2 allows us to obtain the best retrieval accuracy with a MAP score increase of 61.5% and a P@10 increase of 70.0%. It is a large improvement over the baseline as it means that instead of about two relevant documents in the top 10, our system can retrieve nearly four. These results confirm that both PICO framework and document structure can be very helpful for the IR process.

6 Conclusion

We presented a language modeling approach that integrates document and PICO structure for the purpose of clinical IR. A straightforward idea is to detect PICO elements in documents and use the elements in the retrieval process. However, this approach does not work well because of the difficulty to arrive at a consistent tagging of these elements. Instead, we propose a less demanding approach which assigns different weights to different parts of a document.

We first analysed the distribution of PICO elements in a manually annotated abstracts collection. The observed results led us to believe that a location-based weighting scheme can be used instead of a PICO detection approach. We then explored whether this strategy can be used as an indicator to refine document relevance. We also proposed a model to integrate the PICO information provided in queries and investigated how each element should be balanced in the ranking function. On a data set composed of 1.5 million abstracts extracted from PubMed, our method obtains an increase of 61.5% for MAP and 70% for P@10 over the classical language modeling approach.

This work can be much improved in the future. For example, the location-based weighting method can be improved in order to model a different weight distribution for each PICO element. As the distribution in abstracts is not the same among PICO elements, it is expected that differentiated weighting schemes could result in better retrieval effectiveness. In a similar perspective, we are continuing our efforts to construct a larger manually annotated collection of abstracts. It will be thereafter conceivable to use this data to infer the structural weighting schemes or to train a more precise PICO detection method. The focused evaluation described in this paper is a first step. Although the queries are limited to diabetes, this does not affect the general PICO structure in queries. We plan to extend the coverage of queries to other topics in the future.

Acknowledgements

The work described in this paper was funded by the Social Sciences and Humanities Research Council (SSHRC). The authors would like to thank Dr. Ann McKibbon, Dr. Dina Demner-Fushman, Lorie Kloda, Laura Shea, Lucas Baire and Lixin Shi for their contribution in the project.

References

A. Andrenucci. 2008. Automated Question-Answering Techniques and the Medical Domain. In *International Conference on Health Informatics*, volume 2, pages 207–212.

A.R. Aronson. 2001. Effective Mapping of Biomedical Text to the UMLS Metathesaurus: The MetaMap Program. In *AMIA Symposium*.

G. Chung. 2009. Sentence retrieval for abstracts of randomized controlled trials. *BMC Medical Informatics and Decision Making*, 9(1):10.

M. Dawes, P. Pluye, L. Shea, R. Grad, A. Greenberg, and J.Y. Nie. 2007. The identification of clinically important elements within medical journal abstracts: Patient-Population-Problem, Exposure-Intervention, Comparison, Outcome, Duration and Results (PECODR). *Informatics in Primary care*, 15(1):9–16.

D. Demner-Fushman and J. Lin. 2006. Answer extraction, semantic clustering, and extractive summarization for clinical question answering. In *ACL*.

D. Demner-Fushman and J. Lin. 2007. Answering clinical questions with knowledge-based and statistical techniques. *Computational Linguistics*, 33(1):63–103.

N. Fuhr and K. Großjohann. 2001. XIRQL: A query language for information retrieval in XML documents. In *SIGIR*, pages 172–180.

M.J. Hansen, N.O. Rasmussen, and G. Chung. 2008. A method of extracting the number of trial participants from abstracts describing randomized controlled trials. *Journal of Telemedicine and Telecare*, 14(7):354–358.

INEX. 2002-2009. Proceedings of the INitiative for the Evaluation of XML Retrieval (INEX) workshop.

J. Kamps, M. Marx, M. de Rijke, and B. Sigurbjörnsson. 2005. Structured queries in XML retrieval. In *CIKM*, pages 4–11.

J.M. Ponte and W.B. Croft. 1998. A language modeling approach to information retrieval. In *SIGIR*, pages 275–281.

T.C. Rindflesch and M. Fiszman. 2003. The interaction of domain knowledge and linguistic structure in natural language processing: interpreting hypernymic propositions in biomedical text. *Journal of Biomedical Informatics*, 36(6):462–477.

D.L. Sackett, W. Rosenberg, J.A. Gray, R.B. Haynes, and W.S. Richardson. 1996. Evidence based medicine: what it is and what it isn't. *British medical journal*, 312(7023):71.

C. Schardt, M. Adams, T. Owens, S. Keitz, and P. Fontelo. 2007. Utilization of the PICO framework to improve searching PubMed for clinical questions. *BMC Medical Informatics and Decision Making*, 7(1):16.

L.B. Sollaci and M.G. Pereira. 2004. The introduction, methods, results, and discussion (IMRAD) structure: a fifty-year survey. *Journal of the Medical Library Association*, 92(3):364.

A. Trotman. 2005. Choosing document structure weights. *Information Processing and Management*, 41(2):243–264.

J.M. Weinfeld and K. Finkelstein. 2005. How to answer your clinical questions more efficiently. *Family practice management*, 12(7):37.

R. Wilkinson. 1994. Effective retrieval of structured documents. In *SIGIR*, pages 311–317.

Topic Models for Image Annotation and Text Illustration

Yansong Feng and **Mirella Lapata**
School of Informatics, University of Edinburgh
10 Crichton Street, Edinburgh EH8 9AB, UK
Y.Feng-4@sms.ed.ac.uk, mlap@inf.ed.ac.uk

Abstract

Image annotation, the task of automatically generating description words for a picture, is a key component in various image search and retrieval applications. Creating image databases for model development is, however, costly and time consuming, since the keywords must be hand-coded and the process repeated for new collections. In this work we exploit the vast resource of images and documents available on the web for developing image annotation models without any human involvement. We describe a probabilistic model based on the assumption that images and their co-occurring textual data are generated by mixtures of latent topics. We show that this model outperforms previously proposed approaches when applied to image annotation and the related task of text illustration despite the noisy nature of our dataset.

1 Introduction

Recent years have witnessed the rapid growth of image collections available for searching and browsing over the Internet. Although image search engines are still in their infancy, initial research suggests that the deployed algorithms are not very accurate (Hawking et al., 1999). Given a query, search engines retrieve relevant pictures by analyzing the image caption (if it exists), textual descriptions found adjacent to the image, and other text-related factors such as the file name of the image. However, since they do not analyze the actual content of the images, search engines cannot be used to retrieve pictures from unannotated collections. The ability to perform the annotation task *automatically* would be of significant practical import for many image-based applications. Besides search and retrieval, other examples include browsing support (e.g., by clustering images into groups that are visually and semantically coherent) and story picturing (i.e., automatically suggesting images to illustrate text).

Automatic image annotation is a popular task in computer vision; a large number of approaches have been proposed in the literature under many distinct learning paradigms. These range from supervised classification (Smeulders et al., 2000; Vailaya et al., 2001) to instantiations of the noisy-channel model (Duygulu et al., 2002), to clustering (Barnard et al., 2002), and methods inspired by information retrieval (Feng et al., 2004; Lavrenko et al., 2003). Despite differences in application and formulation, all these methods essentially attempt to learn the correlation between image features and words from examples of annotated images. The Corel database has been extensively used as a testbed for the development and evaluation of image annotation models. It is a collection of stock photographs, divided into themes (e.g., *tigers*, *sunsets*) each of which are associated with keywords (e.g., *sun*, *sea*) that are considered appropriate descriptors for all images belonging to the same theme.

Unfortunately, the Corel database is not representative of the size or content of real-world image collections. It has a small number of themes with many closely related images which in turn share keyword descriptions. It is therefore relatively easy to learn the associations between images and keywords and do well on annotation and retrieval tasks (Tang and Lewis, 2007; Westerveld and de Vries, 2003). An appealing alternative is the use of resources where images and their annotations co-occur naturally. Examples include images found in news documents, consumer photo collections, Wikipedia articles, illustrated stories and so on. The key idea here is to treat the words in the surrounding text as annotations for the image. These annotations are undoubt-

Human Language Technologies: The 2010 Annual Conference of the North American Chapter of the ACL, pages 831–839,
Los Angeles, California, June 2010.

edly noisy, but plenty and cost-free. Moreover, the collateral text is often longer and more informative in comparison to the few keywords reserved for each image in Corel.

In this paper we propose a probabilistic image annotation model that learns to automatically label images under such noisy conditions. We use the database created in Feng and Lapata (2008) which consists of news articles, images, and their captions. Our model exploits the redundancy inherent in this multimodal dataset by assuming that images and their surrounding text are generated by a shared set of latent variables or topics. Specifically, we describe documents and images by a common multimodal vocabulary consisting of textual words and *visual terms* (visiterms). Due to polysemy and synonymy many words in this vocabulary will refer to the same underlying concept. Using Latent Dirichlet Allocation (LDA, Blei and Jordan 2003), a probabilistic model of text generation, we represent visual and textual meaning *jointly* as a probability distribution over a set of topics. Our annotation model takes these topic distributions into account while finding the most likely keywords for an image and its associated document. We also show how the model can be straightforwardly modified to perform automatic text illustration.[1] The task is routinely performed by news writers who often have to search large image collections in order to find suitable pictures for their text. Here, the model takes a document as input and suggests images that match its content. Experimental results on both tasks bring improvements over competitive models.

2 Related Work

A variety of learning methods have been applied to the image annotation task. These generally fall under two broad categories. Supervised methods define annotation as a classification task, e.g., by assuming a one-to-one correspondence between vocabulary words and classes or by grouping several words into a single class (see Chai and Hung 2008 for an overview). Unsupervised approaches attempt to discover the underlying connections between visual features and words, typically by introducing latent variables. Standard latent semantic analysis (LSA) and its probabilistic variant (PLSA) have been applied to this task (Hofmann, 2001; Monay and Gatica-Perez, 2007; Pan et al., 2004). More sophisticated models estimate the joint distribution of words and regional image features, whilst treating annotation as a problem of statistical inference in a graphical model (Barnard et al., 2002; Blei and Jordan, 2003; Wang et al., 2009).

Irrespectively of the underlying model or task at hand, much work has focused how to best represent the visual and textual modalities in order to exploit their synergy. Several approaches attempt to render images more word-like, by reducing the dimensionality of the image feature space (Bosch et al., 2008; Fei-Fei and Perona, 2005) or by learning a single representation for both visual and textual features (Monay and Gatica-Perez, 2007; Zhao and Grosky, 2003).

Our own work approaches the image annotation (and related story picturing) task from a slightly different angle. We train and test our model on images that contain implicit (and thus noisy) annotations that have not been specifically created for our task. On account of this, our model has access to knowledge sources other than the image and its keywords (i.e., the news article containing the image we wish to annotate). In Feng and Lapata (2008) we addressed this problem with a modified version of the continuous relevance annotation model (Lavrenko et al., 2003). Unlike other unsupervised approaches where a set of latent variables is introduced, each defining a joint distribution on the space of keywords and image features, the relevance model captures the joint probability of images and annotated words *directly*, without requiring an intermediate clustering stage (i.e., each annotated image in the training set is treated as a latent variable). We modified this model so as to exploit the information present in the document in two ways. First, in estimating the conditional probability of a keyword given an image, we also considered its likelihood in the collateral document. Secondly, we used an LDA model (trained on the document collection) to prune from the model's output words that are not representative of the document's topics.

The proposed approach differs from Feng and Lapata (2008) in three important respects: (a) document-based information is an integral part of our model as we predict caption words given the image *and* its accompanying document (b) LDA is no longer a post-processing step; our model relies on LDA to infer meaningful topics that capture the co-occurrence of visual features and words; (c) beyond image annotation, we show how the same framework can be applied to story picturing (Joshi et al., 2006), a task which has received less attention in the literature.

In terms of model structure, Blei and Jordan

[1]We use the terms "text illustration" and "story picturing" interchangeably throughout the paper.

(2003) and Monay and Gatica-Perez (2007) are closest to our work. The first model, known as correspondence LDA (CorrLDA), has been successfully employed for modeling annotated images in the Corel domain. CorrLDA also uses the notion of topic to model the generation of images and their captions. In this model, the visual modality drives the definition of the latent space to which the textual modality is linked. The second model is based on PLSA and learns a representation similar to ours consisting of textual and visual features. It is also trained using captioned images from the Corel database. We work with noisier and larger datasets. Our model exploits the captions accompanying the images as well as their surrounding documents. As a result, we obtain a similar number of textual and visual words; these are often imbalanced in the Corel database, where visual words are nearly 50 times more than textual words. The different nature of our data dictates the use of a model where the visual and textual modality are given equal importance in defining the latent space.

3 Problem Formulation

In this section we give a brief description of the image database we employ and also define the image annotation and story picturing tasks we are attempting here. As mentioned earlier, we use the dataset created in Feng and Lapata (2008).[2] It contains 3,361 articles that have been downloaded from the BBC News website[3]. Each article contains a news image which in turn is associated with a caption. The images are usually 203 pixels wide and 152 pixels high. The average caption length is 5.35 tokens, and the average document length 133.85 tokens. The captions vocabulary is 2,167 words and the document vocabulary is 6,253. The vocabulary shared between captions and documents is 2,056 words. In contrast to the Corel database, this dataset contains more complex images (with many objects) and has a larger vocabulary (Corel's vocabulary is approximately 300 words). An example of an abridged database entry is shown in Figure 1.

Due to the non-standard nature of the database we assume that the caption and news article describe the content of the image either directly or indirectly. It also follows that we may not be able to name all objects depicted in the image. Now, given these constraints our goal is twofold. Firstly, we will perform image annotation. Our model is trained on

A woman from East Sussex who bought an emu egg sold as a novelty food item on a farm on the Isle of Wight has managed to hatch it into a chick. Gillian Stone, from Bexhill, who breeds chickens, brought home three large green emu eggs from a holiday and put them in an incubator in her kitchen. Two turned out to be infertile, but after 52 days little Osborne hatched

Osborne the emu will grow to over 6ft tall

Table 1: Each entry in the BBC News database contains a document, an image, and its caption (shown in boldface).

document-image-caption tuples like the one shown in Table 1. During testing, we must infer the caption for an image. Secondly, we use the same dataset to perform automatic text illustration. During training, the model has access to the same collection of image-caption-document tuples. During testing, we are given a document and must find the images that best illustrate it.

4 Image and Document Representation

Words and images represent distinct modalities, images live in a continuous feature space, whereas words are discrete. Yet, both modalities on some level capture the same underlying concepts as they are used to describe the same objects. A common first step to all previous methods is the segmentation of the image into regions, using either a fixed-grid layout or an image segmentation algorithm. Regions are usually described by a standard set of features including color, texture, and shape which are treated as continuous vectors (e.g., Barnard et al. 2002; Blei and Jordan 2003) or in quantized form (e.g., Duygulu et al. 2002). Through this process, the low-level image features are made to resemble word-like units.

Here, we go one step further and represent each image by a bag of visual words, thereby converting visual features from a continuous onto a discrete space. In order to do this we use the Scale Invariant Feature Transform (SIFT) algorithm (Lowe, 1999). The general idea behind the algorithm is to first sample an image with the difference-of-Gaussians point detector at different scales and locations. Importantly, this detector is, to some extent, invariant to translation, scale, rotation and illumination changes. Each detected region is represented with a SIFT descriptor which is a histogram of edge directions at

[2] Available from http://homepages.inf.ed.ac.uk/s0677528/data.html.

[3] http://news.bbc.co.uk/

different locations. SIFT descriptors are quantized using the K-means clustering algorithm to obtain a discrete set of visual terms (visiterms) which form our visual vocabulary Voc_V. Each entry in this vocabulary stands for a group of image regions which are similar in content or appearance and assumed to originate from similar objects. More formally, each image I is expressed in a bag-of-words format vector, $[w_{v1}, w_{v2}, ..., w_{v_L}]$, where $w_{v_i} = n$ only if I has n regions labeled with v_i.

Since visual and textual modalities have now the same status—they are both represented as bags-of-words—we can also represent any image-caption-document tuple *jointly* as a mixed document d_{Mix}. The underlying assumption is that the two modalities express the same meaning which, as we explain below, can be operationalized as a probability distribution over a set of topics.

5 Modeling

Latent Dirichlet Allocation For ease of exposition, we first describe the basics of Latent Dirichlet Allocation (LDA; Blei et al. 2003), a probabilistic model of text generation and then move on to discuss our models which make use of probabilities estimated by LDA.

LDA can be represented as a three level hierarchical Bayesian model. Given a corpus consisting of M documents, Blei et al. (2003) define the generative process for a document d as follows:

1. Choose $\theta|\alpha \sim Dir(\alpha)$
2. For $n \in 1, 2, ..., N$:
   (a) Choose topic $z_n|\theta \sim Mult(\theta)$
   (b) Choose a word $w_n|z_n, \beta_{1:K} \sim Mult(\beta_{z_n})$

The mixing proportion over topics θ is drawn from a Dirichlet prior with parameters α whose role is to create a smoothed topic distribution. Once α and β are sampled, then each document is generated according to the topic proportions $z_{1:K}$ and word probabilities over topics β. The probability of a document d in a corpus is defined as:

$$P(d|\alpha,\beta) = \int_\theta P(\theta|\alpha)\left(\prod_{n=1}^{N}\sum_{z_k} P(z_k|\theta)P(w_n|z_k,\beta)\right)d\theta$$

Computing the posterior distribution $P(\theta, z|d, \alpha, \beta)$ of the hidden variables given a document is intractable in general. However, a variety of approximate inference algorithms have been proposed in the literature including variational inference which our model adopts (Blei et al., 2003). In this case, training an LDA model on a document collection will give two sets of parameters, the word probabilities given topics, $p(w|z_{1:K})$, and the topic proportions given documents, $P(z_{1:K}|d)$. The latter are document-specific, whereas the former represent the set of topics learned from the document collection.

Given a trained model, it is possible to do inference on an unseen document d_{new}:

$$p(w|d_{new}) \approx \sum_{k=1}^{K} P(w|z_k)\frac{\gamma_k}{\sum_{j=1}^{K}\gamma_j} \quad (1)$$

where $P(w|z_{1:K})$ are word probabilities over topics $z_{1:K}$ estimated during model training, and $\gamma_{1:K}$ are variational Dirichlet parameters obtained during inference on the new document (and can be considered as the posteriors of topic proportions over documents).

Image Annotation In the standard image annotation setting, a hypothetical model is given an image I and a set of keywords W, and must find the subset W_I ($W_I \subseteq W$) which appropriately describes image I:

$$W_I^* = \arg\max_W P(W|I) \quad (2)$$

The keywords are usually assumed to be conditionally independent on each other, so Equation (2) simplifies to:

$$W_I^* = \arg\max_W \prod_{w \in W} P(w|I) \quad (3)$$

Each entry in our database is an image-caption-document tuple (I, C, D). In this setting, we must find the subset of keywords W_I which appropriately describe image I with the help of the accompanying document D:

$$W_I^* = \arg\max_{W_t} P(W_t|I, D) \quad (4)$$

Here, W_t denotes a set of textual words (we use the subscript t to discriminate from the visual words which are not part of the model's output). We also assume that the keywords are conditionally independent of each other:

$$W_I^* = \arg\max_{W_t} P(W_t|I,D) = \arg\max_{W_t} \prod_{w_t \in W_t} P(w_t|I,D) \quad (5)$$

Since I and D are represented jointly as the concatenation of textual and visual terms, we may intuitively simplify the problem and use the mixed document representation d_{Mix} directly in estimating the conditional probabilities $P(w_t|I, D)$:

$$P(w_t|I,D) \approx P(w_t|d_{Mix}) \quad (6)$$

Substituting Equation (6) into (5) yields:

$$W_I^* \approx \arg\max_{W_t} \prod_{w_t \in W_t} P(w_t|d_{Mix}) \tag{7}$$

As mentioned earlier, we assume that the image and its associated text are generated by a mixture of latent topics which we infer using LDA. Specifically, we select the number of topics K and apply the LDA algorithm to a corpus consisting of documents $\{d_{Mix}\}$ in order to obtain the multimodal word distributions over topics $P(w|z_{1:K})$, and the estimated posterior of the topic proportions over documents $P(z_{1:K}|d_{Mix})$. We infer the topic proportions $P(z_{1:K}|d_{Mix_{new}})$ on a new document-image pair $d_{Mix_{new}}$ approximately using Equations (1) and (7):[4]

$$\begin{aligned} W_I^* &\approx \arg\max_{W_t} \prod_{w_t \in W_t} P(w_t|d_{Mix}) \qquad (8)\\ &= \arg\max_{W_t} \prod_{w_t \in W_t} \sum_{k=1}^{K} P(w_t|z_k)P(z_k|d_{Mix}) \\ &\approx \arg\max_{W_t} \prod_{w_t \in W_t} \sum_{k=1}^{K} P(w_t|z_k)\frac{\gamma_k}{\sum_{j=1}^{K}\gamma_j} \end{aligned}$$

where $P(w_t|z_k)$ are obtained during training, and $\gamma_{1:K}$ are inferred on the image-document test pair.

However, note that for an unseen image d_I and accompanying document d_D, the estimated topic proportions are solely based on variational inference which is an approximate algorithm. In order to render the model more robust, we smooth the topic proportions $P(z_{1:K}|d_{Mix})$ with probabilities based on a single modality:

$$P^*(z_{1:K}|d_{Mix}) \approx \tag{9}$$
$$q_1 P(z_{1:K}|d_{Mix}) + q_2 P(z_{1:K}|d_D) + q_3 P(z_{1:K}|d_I)$$

where $P(z_{1:K}|d_D)$ and $P(z_{1:K}|d_I)$ are inferred on d_D and d_I, respectively, and q_1, q_2, q_3 are smoothing parameters (which we tune experimentally on held-out data); q_3 is a shorthand for $(1-q_1-q_2)$.

In sum, calculating $P(W_t|I,D)$ boils down to estimating the probabilities $P(w_t|d_{Mix})$ according to Equations (8) and (9) which we obtain using the LDA model. We train LDA on the document collection $\{d_{Mix}\}$ and use inference to obtain the topic distributions of unseen image-document pairs. In the end, we obtain a ranked list of textual words w_t, the n-best of which are the annotations for image I.

[4]During training, the model has access to all three elements (I,C,D), so the mixed document d_{Mix} is the concatenation of the visual terms and words in the caption and document. During testing, the model is given an image and its accompanying document, so d_{Mix} contains words based on I and D, but not C.

Text Illustration Previous text illustration models are based on Corel-like databases with manual image descriptions (Barnard and Forsyth, 2001; Blei and Jordan, 2003) or instance-based learning using complex learning schemes (Joshi et al., 2006). Here, we present a relatively simple model, again under the topic mixture framework.

Given a test document D and a candidate image database $I_{1...N}$ with captions C, we must find the image or images which best describe the document. We can simply compute the probability of each visual term in the vocabulary given D by marginalizing over the document topics $z_{1:K}$:

$$P(w_v|D) = \sum_{z_{1:K}} P(w_v|z_k)P(z_k|d_D) \tag{10}$$

where w_v is a visual term and $P(w_v|z_k)$ the probability of w_v given topic z_k (as estimated on the training set).

Equation (10) delivers a ranked list of visual terms according to a given document. We could multiply these probabilities together mirroring Equation (7), however this is not reliable. In contrast to textual words, for which we may infer whether they are linguistically meaningful (e.g., by resorting to their part of speech), there is no easy way of knowing which visual words are important. Relying solely on frequency is not reliable either, as frequent visiterms may simply represent features common in all images (e.g., most images have some white color). To avoid a bias towards frequent but potentially irrelevant visual words, we output a fixed number of visual terms and select the image with the highest overlap as the correct illustration.

6 Experimental Setup

In this section we discuss our experimental design for assessing the performance of the models presented above. We give details on our training procedure and parameter estimation, describe our features, and present the baseline methods used for comparison with our models.

Data We evaluated the image annotation and text illustration tasks on the dataset described in Section 3. Documents and captions were part-of-speech tagged and lemmatized with Tree Tagger (Schmid, 1994). We excluded from the vocabulary low frequency words (appearing fewer than five times) and words other than nouns, verbs, and adjectives. For the image annotation task we follow the data split used in Feng and Lapata (2008). The training set contains 2,881 image-caption-document tuples; 240 tuples are reserved for development and 240 for testing. Our text illustration experiments, used 2,881 image-caption-document tuples for training. For the purposes of simulating a real story picturing engine environment, we created a large image pool of 450 image-caption pairs and tested on 300 of them.

Model Parameters For each image we extracted 150 (on average) SIFT features. These were quantized into a discrete set of visual terms using K-means. We varied K from 100 to 2,000. We trained the LDA topic model on the multimodal document collection $\{d_{Mix}\}$ and varied the number of topics from 15 to 1,000. The hyperparameter α was initialized to 0.1; the β probabilities were initialized randomly. The maximum number of iterations for variational inference was set to 1,000. We tuned the smoothing parameters q_1, q_2, and q_3 (see Equation (9)) on the development set. The best values were $q_1 = 0.84$, $q_2 = 0.12$, and $q_3 = 0.04$ (for both tasks). As the number of visual terms and topics are interrelated we exhaustively examined all possible combinations on the development set. We obtained best results on image annotation with 1,000 topics and 750 visual terms. On text illustration the best parameters were 1,000 topics and 2,000 visual terms.

Baselines For the image annotation experiments, we compared our model against the following baselines. Firstly, we trained a vanilla LDA model on the document collection without taking the images into account. This model estimates $P(w_t|D) = \sum_{k=1}^{K} P(w_t|z_k)P(z_k|D)$, the probability of textual word w_t given text document D. We assume that the most probable words are the captions for the accompanying image. Our second baseline is the extended relevance model (Feng and Lapata, 2008) that also takes the document into account but crucially assumes that the process of generating the images is independent from the process of generating its keywords.

We also compared our approach with two closely related latent variable models (developed for image-caption pairs), a PLSA-based model (Monay and Gatica-Perez, 2007) and CorrLDA (Blei and Jordan, 2003). The former model is an asymmetric version of PLSA; it estimates the topic structure solely from the textual modality and keeps it fixed for the visual modality. The technique is similar to *folding-in* (Hofmann, 2001), the standard PLSA procedure for inference in unseen documents and allows modeling an image as a mixture of latent topics that is defined only by one modality (in this case the caption words). CorrLDA first generates image regions from a Gaussian multinomial distribution parametrized with Dirichlet priors. Then, for each annotation word, it uniformly selects a region from the image and generates a word according to the topic used to generate that region. We optimized the parameters for both models on the development set. For CorrLDA, we followed the mean-field variational inference strategy proposed in Blei (2004). The optimal number of topics for PLSA, was 200 (with 2000 visual terms) and for CorrLDA 50.

For the text illustration experiments, the proposed model was compared with three baselines. The first one is essentially word overlap. We select the image whose caption has the largest number of words in common with the test document. The second one is a straightforward implementation of the vector space model (Salton and McGill, 1983) where documents and captions are represented by vectors whose components correspond to term-document co-occurrences. We followed common practice in weighting terms by their tf-idf values, and used the cosine similarity measure to find the image whose caption is most similar to the test document. Our third baseline uses a text-based LDA model to estimate document-caption similarity probabilistically, through topic sharing. The images most relevant to a document are found by maximizing the conditional probability of the candidate captions C given the document d_D: $P(C|d_D) = \prod_{w_c \in C} \sum_{k=1}^{K} P(w_c|z_k)P(z_k|d_D)$ (where w_c are the caption words, $P(w_c|z_k)$ the conditional distribution of each w_c given a topic z_k, and $P(z_k|d_D)$ the conditional distribution of z_k given d_D, the document we wish to illustrate.

Evaluation In the image annotation task we follow the evaluation methodology proposed in Duygulu et al. (2002). We are given an un-annotated image I and asked to automatically produce the n-best keywords. For all models discussed here, we report results with the top 10 annotation words using precision, recall and F1. In the text illustration task, we are given a test document d and a pool of candidate images $I_{1...N}$ with captions $C_{1...N}$. The model is expected to find an image from the candidate pool that matches the test document. We use equation (10) to output a ranked list of M_I visual terms. The image having the highest overlap with the top 30 visual terms is selected as the illustration for the test document. All illustration models were evaluated using top 1 accuracy, which is the percentage of successfully matched image-document pairs in the test set.

Model	Top 10		
	Precision	Recall	F1
CorrLDA	5.33	11.80	7.36
TxtLDA	7.30	16.90	10.20
PLSA	10.26	22.60	14.12
ExtRel	14.70	27.90	19.80
MixLDA	16.30	33.10	21.60

Table 2: Automatic image annotation results.

7 Results

Our results on the image annotation task are summarized in Table 2. Here, we compare our own model (MixLDA) which is trained on both visual and textual information against an LDA model based solely on textual information (TxtLDA), an extended version of the Continuous Relevance model that also exploits collateral document information (ExtRel; Feng and Lapata 2008), a PLSA model that prioritizes the textual over visual modality (Monay and Gatica-Perez, 2007), and CorrLDA (Blei and Jordan, 2003) which does the opposite. We performed significance testing on F1 using stratified shuffling (Noreen, 1989), an instance of assumption-free approximative randomization testing.

Let us first discuss the performance of TxtLDA and MixLDA. These two models are closely related — they both rely on the probabilities $P(w_t|d)$ to generate the image keywords — save one important difference. MixLDA uses a concatenated representation of words and visual features assuming that the two modalities have equal importance in defining the latent space, whereas TxtLDA considers only the textual modality. Our results show that MixLDA outperforms TxtLDA in terms of precision (by 9%), recall (by 16.2%). MixLDA improves F1 by 11.4%, and the difference is significant ($p < 0.01$).

PLSA significantly ($p < 0.01$) improves upon TxtLDA. The key difference is the visual information which makes up (to a certain extent) for the lack of richer textual data. Interestingly, CorrLDA performs significantly ($p < 0.01$) worse than both PLSA and TxtLDA. Recall that in CorrLDA word topic assignments are drawn from the image regions which are in turn drawn from a Gaussian distribution. Although this modeling choice delivers better results on the simpler Corel dataset, it does not seem able to capture the characteristics of our images which are noisier and more complex. Moreover, CorrLDA assumes that annotation keywords *must correspond* to image regions. This assumption is too restrictive in our setting where a single keyword may refer to many objects or persons in an image (e.g.,the word *badminton* is used to collectively describe an image depicting players, shuttlecocks, and rackets). As an aside, it is interesting to note, that neither PLSA nor CorrLDA achieve better results, when modified to take the captions *and* associated documents into account. PLSA scores are in the same ballpark (see Table 2), whereas CorrLDA performs worse, F1 decreases by 2%.

The extended relevance model improves considerably upon TxtLDA, CorrLDA, and PLSA but is significantly worse ($p < 0.01$) than MixLDA. On the surface, MixLDA seems similar to ExtRel, both models take advantage of visual and textual information. ExtRel smooths the conditional probability of a word given an image with the conditional probability of the same word given the document and uses an LDA model (trained on the document collection) to remove non-topical keywords from the model's output. MixLDA is conceptually simpler, LDA is the actual model rather than a post-processing step, and exploits the synergy between visual and textual information more directly. Topics are created based on both modalities which are treated on an equal footing. Compared to ExtRel, MixLDA improves precision by 1.6%, recall by 5.2% and the overall F1 by 1.8%.

Figure 1 illustrates examples of annotations gen-

TxtLDA	
Afghanistan, Taleban, soldier, British, zone, kill, force, Microsoft, **troop**, NATO	police, Burgess, time, letter, **crash**, case, death, operation, investigation, jail
MixLDA	
Afghanistan, **troop**, Blair, British, NATO, **helicopter**, soldier, support, **operation**, commander	**Diana**, police, case, **crash**, **Princess**, report, **death**, inquest, **Paris**, Burgess
Caption	
Troops need more Chinook helicopters to carry out operations	Princess Diana died in a car crash in Paris in 1997

Figure 1: Annotations generated by the TxtLDA and MixLDA models. Words in bold face indicate exact matches. The original captions are in the last row.

Model	Accuracy
TxtLDA	31.0
Overlap	31.3
VectorSpace	38.7
MixLDA	57.3

Table 3: Text Illustration results.

Europe's lunar satellite, the Smart 1 probe, is about to end its mission by crashing onto the Moon's surface. It will be a spectacular end for the robot which has spent the past 16 months testing innovative and miniaturized space technologies. Smart 1 has also produced detailed maps of the Moon's chemical make-up.

Figure 2: Top-3 illustrations for document in bottom row.

erated by TxtLDA and MixLDA for two images. For comparison, we also show the goldstandard image captions. Note that TxtLDA fails to generate any words relating to the objects shown in the image. It finds primarily words relating to the topics of the associated articles such as *troops* and *crash*. On the contrary, MixLDA is more successful at identifying the depicted objects, since it takes visual information into account.

Table 3 presents our results on the automatic text illustration task. Here, we compare our multimodal topic model (MixLDA) against three text-based baselines, namely word overlap (Overlap) a standard vector space model (VectorSpace), and TxtLDA. We examined whether differences in performance are statistically significant using a χ^2 test. As can be seen, MixLDA significantly ($p < 0.01$) outperforms these models by a wide margin (accuracy is 57.3% for MixLDA vs. 31.0% for TxtLDA, 38.7% for the vector space model, and 31.3% for word overlap). These results are encouraging given the simplicity of our model. They also indicate that substantial mileage can be gained by taking into account the visual modality.

Figure 2 shows the three best illustrations found by MixLDA and VectorSpace (incidentally, Overlap delivered the same ranking as VectorSpace). The images are presented in ranked order, i.e., the first image was given a higher score than the second one, etc. The document discusses Smart 1 Probe, a lunar satellite about to end its mission by crashing onto the moon's surface. MixLDA identifies an image depicting this satellite. The second best picture is also relevant, it resembles the moon's surface. The VectorSpace model does not find any related images, the first one is a DNA image, the second one depicts policemen at a crime scene and the third one Ben Nevis, the highest mountain in the British Isles.

8 Conclusions

In this paper we have presented a probabilistic approach for automatic image annotation and text illustration. Our model postulates that visual terms and words are generated by common (hidden) topics and is trained on a dataset consisting of images available on the Internet, their captions, and associated news articles. The annotations are implicit and the dataset is representative of the scale, diversity, and difficulty of real-world image collections. Overall, our results show that the model is robust to the noise inherent in such data. It improves upon competitive approaches that prioritize one modality over the other or exploit them indirectly. We also show that with minor modifications the model can be used to automatically illustrate a document with an appropriate image. Our method shows promise for multimodal search and image retrieval and other applications which have been traditionally text-based. An interesting future direction involves generating actual sentence descriptions rather than isolated keywords. Another relevant application is summarization. Our results suggest that taking visual information into account could potentially create more focused and accurate summaries.

The model presented here could be further improved in two ways. Firstly, we could allow an infinite number of topics and develop a nonparametric version that *learns* how many topics are optimal. Secondly, our model is based on word unigrams, and in this sense takes very little linguistic knowledge into account. Recent developments in topic modeling could potentially rectify this, e.g., by assuming that each word is generated by a distribution that combines document-specific topics and parse-tree-specific syntactic transitions (Boyd-Graber and Blei, 2009).

References

Barnard, K., P. Duygulu, D. Forsyth, N. de Freitas, D. Blei, and M. Jordan. 2002. Matching words and pictures. *Journal of Machine Learning Research* 3:1107–1135.

Barnard, K. and D. Forsyth. 2001. Learning the semantics of words and pictures. In *Proceedings of the 8th International Conference on Computer Vision*. Vancouver, BC, pages 408–415.

Blei, D. 2004. *Probabilistic Models of Text and Images*. Ph.D. thesis, U.C. Berkeley, Division of Computer Science.

Blei, D. and M. Jordan. 2003. Modeling annotated data. In *Proceedings of the 26th Annual International ACM SIGIR Conference*. Toronto, ON, pages 127–134.

Blei, D., A. Ng, and M. Jordan. 2003. Latent Dirichlet allocation. *Journal of Machine Learning Research* 3:993–1022.

Bosch, A., A. Zisserman, and X. Munoz. 2008. Scene classification using a hybrid generative/discriminative approach. *IEEE Transactions on Pattern Analysis and Machine Intelligence* 30(4):712–727.

Boyd-Graber, J. and D. Blei. 2009. Syntactic topic models. In *Proceedings of the 22nd Conference on Advances in Neural Information Processing Systems*. MIT, Press, Cambridge, MA, pages 185–192.

Chai, C. and C. Hung. 2008. Automatically annotating images with keywords: A review of image annotation systems. *Recent Patents on Computer Science* 1:55–68.

Duygulu, P., K. Barnard, J. de Freitas, and D. Forsyth. 2002. Object recognition as machine translation: Learning a lexicon for a fixed image vocabulary. In *Proceedings of the 7th European Conference on Computer Vision*. Copenhagen, Danemark, pages 97–112.

Fei-Fei, L. and P. Perona. 2005. A Bayesian hierarchical model for learning natural scene categories. In *Proceedings of the 2005 IEEE Computer Society Conference on Computer Vision and Pattern Recognition*. IEEE Computer Society Washington, DC, volume 2, pages 524–531.

Feng, S., V. Lavrenko, and R. Manmatha. 2004. Multiple Bernoulli relevance models for image and video annotation. In *Proceedings of the International Conference on Computer Vision and Pattern Recognition*. Washington, DC, pages 1002–1009.

Feng, Y. and M. Lapata. 2008. Automatic image annotation using auxiliary text information. In *Proceedings of ACL-08: HLT*. Columbus, OH, pages 272–280.

Hawking, D., N. Craswell, P. Thistlewaite, and D. Harman. 1999. Results and challenges in web search evaluation. *Computer Networks* 31(11):1321–1330.

Hofmann, T. 2001. Unsupervised learning by probabilistic latent semantic analysis. *Machine Learning* 41(2):177–196.

Joshi, D., J.Z. Wang, and J. Li. 2006. The story picturing engine—a system for automatic text illustration. *ACM Transactions on Multimedia Computing, Communications, and Applications* 2(1):68–89.

Lavrenko, V., R. Manmatha, and J. Jeon. 2003. A model for learning the semantics of pictures. In *Proceedings of the 17th Conference on Advances in Neural Information Processing Systems*. MIT, Press, Cambridge, MA.

Lowe, D. 1999. Object recognition from local scale-invariant features. In *Proceedings of International Conference on Computer Vision*. IEEE Computer Society, pages 1150–1157.

Monay, F. and D. Gatica-Perez. 2007. Modeling semantic aspects for cross-media image indexing. *IEEE Transactions on Pattern Analysis and Machine Intelligence* 29(10):1802–1817.

Pan, J., H. Yang, P. Duygulu, and C. Faloutsos. 2004. Automatic image captioning. In *Proceedings of the 2004 International Conference on Multimedia and Expo*. Taipei, pages 1987–1990.

Salton, G. and M.J. McGill. 1983. *Introduction to Modern Information Retrieval*. McGraw-Hill, New York.

Schmid, H. 1994. Probabilistic part-of-speech tagging using decision trees. In *Proceedings of the International Conference on New Methods in Language Processing*. Manchester, UK, pages 44–49.

Smeulders, A. W., M. Worring, S. Santini, A. Gupta, and R. Jain. 2000. Content-based image retrieval at the end of the early years. *IEEE Transactions on Pattern Analysis and Machine Intelligence* 22(12):1349–1380.

Tang, J. and P. H. Lewis. 2007. A study of quality issues for image auto-annotation with the Corel data-set. *IEEE Transactions on Circuits and Systems for Video Technology* 17(3):384–389.

Vailaya, A., M. Figueiredo, A. Jain, and H. Zhang. 2001. Image classification for content-based indexing. *IEEE Transactions on Image Processing* 10:117–130.

Wang, C., D. Blei, and L. Fei-Fei. 2009. Simultaneous image classification and annotation. In *Proceedings of CVPR*. Miami, FL, pages 1903–1910.

Westerveld, T. and A. P. de Vries. 2003. Experimental evaluation of a generative probabilistic image retrieval model on 'easy' data. In *Proceedings of the SIGIR Multimedia Information Retrieval Workshop*. Toronto, ON.

Zhao, R. and W. I. Grosky. 2003. Video shot detection using color anglogram and latent semantic indexing: From contents to semantics. In B. Furht and O. Marques, editors, *Handbook of Video Databases: Design and Applications*, CRC Press, pages 371–392.

Learning about Voice Search for Spoken Dialogue Systems

Rebecca J. Passonneau[1], Susan L. Epstein[2,3], Tiziana Ligorio[2], Joshua B. Gordon[4], Pravin Bhutada[4]

[1]Center for Computational Learning Systems, Columbia University
[2]Department of Computer Science, Hunter College of The City University of New York
[3]Department of Computer Science, The Graduate Center of The City University of New York
[4]Department of Computer Science, Columbia University
becky@cs.columbia.edu, susan.epstein@hunter.cuny.edu, tligorio@gc.cuny.edu, joshua@cs.columbia.edu, pravin.bhutada@gmail.com

Abstract

In a Wizard-of-Oz experiment with multiple wizard subjects, each wizard viewed automated speech recognition (*ASR*) results for utterances whose interpretation is critical to task success: requests for books by title from a library database. To avoid non-understandings, the wizard directly queried the application database with the ASR hypothesis (*voice search*). To learn how to avoid misunderstandings, we investigated how wizards dealt with uncertainty in voice search results. Wizards were quite successful at selecting the correct title from query results that included a match. The most successful wizard could also tell when the query results did not contain the requested title. Our learned models of the best wizard's behavior combine features available to wizards with some that are not, such as recognition confidence and acoustic model scores.

1 Introduction

Wizard-of-Oz (*WOz*) studies have long been used for spoken dialogue system design. In a relatively new variant, a subject (the *wizard*) is presented with real or simulated automated speech recognition (*ASR*) to observe how people deal with incorrect speech recognition output (Rieser, Kruijff-Korbayová, & Lemon, 2005; Skantze, 2003; Stuttle, Williams, & Young, 2004; Williams & Young, 2003, 2004; Zollo, 1999). In these experiments, when a wizard could not interpret the ASR output (*non-understanding*), she rarely asked users to repeat themselves. Instead, the wizard found other ways to continue the task.

This paper describes an experiment that presented wizards with ASR results for utterances whose interpretation is critical to task success: requests for books from a library database, identified by title. To avoid non-understandings, wizards used *voice search* (Wang et al., 2008): they directly queried the application database with ASR output. To investigate how to avoid errors in understanding (*misunderstandings)*, we examined how wizards dealt with uncertainty in voice search results. When the voice search results included the requested title, all seven of our wizards were likely to identify it. One wizard, however, recognized far better than the others when the voice search results did not contain the requested title. The experiment employed a novel design that made it possible to include system features in models of wizard behavior. The principal result is that our learned models of the best wizard's behavior combine features that are available to wizards with some that are not, such as recognition confidence and acoustic model scores.

The next section of the paper motivates our experiment. Subsequent sections describe related work, the dialogue system and embedded wizard infrastructure, experimental design, learning methods, and results. We then discuss how to generalize from the results of our study for spoken dialogue system design. We conclude with a summary of results and their implications.

2 Motivation

Rather than investigate full dialogues, we addressed a single type of turn exchange or adjacency pair (Sacks et al., 1974): a request for a book by its

Human Language Technologies: The 2010 Annual Conference of the North American Chapter of the ACL, pages 840–848, Los Angeles, California, June 2010.

title. This allowed us to collect data exclusively about an utterance type critical for task success in our application domain. We hypothesized that low-level features from speech recognition, such as acoustic model fit, could independently affect voice search confidence. We therefore applied a novel approach, *embedded WOz*, in which a wizard and the system together interpret noisy ASR.

To address how to avoid misunderstandings, we investigated how wizards dealt with uncertainty in voice search returns. To illustrate what we mean by uncertainty, if we query our book title database with the ASR hypothesis:

```
ROLL DWELL
```

our voice search procedure returns, in this order:

```
CROMWELL
ROBERT LOWELL
ROAD TO WEALTH
```

The correct title appears last because of the score it is assigned by the string similarity metric we use.

Three factors motivated our use of voice search to interpret book title requests: noisy ASR, unusually long query targets, and high overlap of the vocabulary across different query types (e.g., author and title) as well as with non-query words in caller utterances (e.g., "Could you look up . . .").

First, accurate speech recognition for a real-world telephone application can be difficult to achieve, given unpredictable background noise and transmission quality. For example, the 68% word error rate (*WER*) for the fielded version of Let's Go Public! (Raux et al., 2005) far exceeded its 17% WER under controlled conditions. Our application handles library requests by telephone, and would benefit from robustness to noisy ASR.

Second, the book title field in our database differs from the typical case for spoken dialogue systems that access a relational database. Such systems include travel booking (Levin et al., 2000), bus route information (Raux et al., 2006), restaurant guides (Johnston et al., 2002; Komatani et al., 2005), weather (Zue et al., 2000) and directory services (Georgila et al., 2003). In general for these systems, a few words are sufficient to retrieve the desired attribute value, such as a neighborhood, a street, or a surname. Mean utterance length in a sample of 40,000 Let's Go Public! utterances, for example, is 2.4 words. The average book title length in our database is 5.4 words.

Finally, our dialogue system, *CheckItOut*, allows users to choose whether to request books by title, author, or catalogue number. The database represents 5028 active patrons (with real borrowing histories and preferences but fictitious personal information), 71,166 book titles and 28,031 authors. Though much smaller than a database for a directory service application (Georgila et al., 2003), this is much larger than that of many current research systems. For example, Let's Go Public! accesses a database with 70 bus routes and 1300 place names. Titles and author names contribute 50,394 words to the vocabulary, of which 57.4% occur only in titles, 32.1% only in author names, and 10.5% in both. Many book titles (e.g., *You See I Haven't Forgotten, You Never Know*) have a high potential for confusability with non-title phrases in users' book requests. Given the longer database field and the confusability of the book title language, integrating voice search is likely to have a relatively larger impact in CheckItOut.

We seek to minimize non-understandings and misunderstandings for several reasons. First, user corrections in both situations have been shown to be more poorly recognized than non-correction utterances (Litman et al., 2006). Non-understandings typically result in re-prompting the user for the same information. This often leads to hyper-articulation and concomitant degradation in recognition performance. Second, users seem to prefer systems that minimize non-understandings and misunderstandings, even at the expense of dialogue efficiency. Users of the TOOT train information spoken dialogue system preferred system-initiative to mixed- or user-initiative, and preferred explicit confirmation to implicit or no confirmation (Litman & Pan, 1999). This was true despite the fact that a mixed-initiative, implicit confirmation strategy led to fewer turns for the same task. Most of the more recent work on spoken dialogue systems focuses on mixed-initiative systems in laboratory settings. Still, recent work suggests that while mixed- or user-initiative is rated highly in usability studies, under real usage it "fails to provide [a] robust enough interface" (Turunen et al., 2006). Incorporating accurate voice search into spoken dialogue systems could lead to fewer non-understandings and fewer misunderstandings.

3 Related Work

Our approach to noisy ASR contrasts with many other information-seeking and transaction-based dialogue systems. Those systems typically perform natural language understanding on ASR output before database query with techniques that try to improve or expand ASR output. None that we know of use voice search. For one directory service application, users spell the first three letters of surnames, and then ASR results are expanded using frequently confused phones (Georgila et al., 2003). A two-pass recognition architecture added to Let's Go Public! improved concept recognition in post-confirmation user utterances (Stoyanchev & Stent, 2009). In (Komatani et al., 2005), a shallow semantic interpretation phase was followed by decision trees to classify utterances as relevant either to query type or to specific query slots, to narrow the set of possible interpretations. CheckItOut is most similar in spirit to the latter approach, but relies on the database earlier, and only for semantic interpretation, not to also guide the dialogue strategy.

Our approach to noisy ASR is inspired by previous WOz studies with real (Skantze, 2003; Zollo, 1999) or simulated ASR (Kruijff-Korbayová et al., 2005; Rieser et al., 2005; Williams & Young, 2004). Simulation makes it possible to collect dialogues without building a speech recognizer, and to control for WER. In the studies that involved task-oriented dialogues, wizards typically focused more on the task and less on resolving ASR errors (Williams & Young, 2004; Skantze, 2003; Zollo, 1999). In studies more like the information-seeking dialogues addressed here, an entirely different pattern is observed (Kruijff-Korbayová et al., 2005; Rieser et al., 2005).

Zollo collected seven dialogues with different human-wizard pairs to develop an evacuation plan. The overall WER was 30%. Of the 227 cases of incorrect ASR, wizard utterances indicated a failure to understand for only 35% of them. Wizards ignored words not salient in the domain and hypothesized words based on phonetic similarity. In (Skantze, 2003), both users and wizards knew there was no dialogue system; 44 direction-finding dialogues were collected with 16 subjects. Despite a WER of 43%, the wizard operators signaled misunderstanding only 5% of the time, in part because they often ignored ASR errors and continued the dialogue. For the 20% of non-understandings, operators continued a route description, asked a task-related question, or requested a clarification.

Williams and Young collected 144 dialogues simulating tourist requests for directions and other negotiations. WER was constrained to be high, medium, or low. Under medium WER, a task-related question in response to a non-understanding or misunderstanding led to full understanding more often than explicit repairs. Under high WER, however, the reverse was true. Misunderstandings significantly increased when wizards followed non-understandings or misunderstandings with a task-related question instead of a repair.

In (Rieser et al., 2005), wizards simulated a multimodal MP3 player application with access to a database of 150K music albums. Responses could be presented verbally or graphically. In the noisy transcription condition, wizards made clarification requests about twice as often as that found in similar human-human dialogue.

In a system like CheckItOut, user utterances that request database information must be understood. We seek an approach that would reduce the rate of misunderstandings observed for high WER in (Williams & Young, 2004) and the rate of clarification requests observed in (Rieser et al., 2005).

4 CheckItOut and Embedded Wizards

CheckItOut is modeled on library transactions at the Andrew Heiskell Braille and Talking Book Library, a branch of the New York Public Library and part of the National Library of Congress. Borrowing requests are handled by telephone. Books, mainly in a proprietary audio format, travel by mail. In a dialogue with CheckItOut, a user identifies herself, requests books, and is told which are available for immediate shipment or will go on reserve. The user can request a book by catalogue number, title, or author.

CheckItOut builds on the Olympus/RavenClaw framework (Bohus & Rudnicky, 2009) that has been the basis for about a dozen dialogue systems in different domains, including Let's Go Public! (Raux et al., 2005). Speech recognition relies on PocketSphinx. Phoenix, a robust context-free grammar (*CFG*) semantic parser, handles natural language understanding (Ward & Issar, 1994). The Apollo interaction manager (Raux & Eskenazi, 2007) detects utterance boundaries using information from speech recognition, semantic parsing, and Helios, an utterance-level confidence annotator (Bohus & Rudnicky, 2002). The dialogue manager is implemented in RavenClaw.

To design CheckItOut's dialogue manager, we recorded 175 calls (4.5 hours) from patrons to librarians. We identified 82 book request calls, transcribed them, aligned the utterances with the speech signal, and annotated the transcripts for dialogue acts. Because active patrons receive monthly newsletters listing new titles in the desired formats, patrons request specific items with advance knowledge of the author, title, or catalogue number. Most book title requests accurately reproduce the exact title, the title less an initial determiner ("the," "a"), or a subtitle.

We exploited the Galaxy message passing architecture of Olympus/RavenClaw to insert a wizard server into CheckItOut. The hub passes messages between the system and a wizard's graphical user interface *(GUI)*, allowing us to collect runtime information that can be included in models of wizards' actions.

For speech recognition, CheckItOut relies on PocketSphinx 0.5, a Hidden Markov Model-based recognizer. Speech recognition for this experiment, relied on the freely available Wall Street Journal "read speech" acoustic models. We did not adapt the models to our population or to spontaneous speech, thus insuring that wizards would receive relatively noisy recognition output.

We built trigram language models from the book titles using the CMU Statistical Language Modeling Toolkit. Pilot tests with one male and one female native speaker indicated that a language model based on 7500 titles would yield WER in the desired range. (Average WER for the book title requests in our experiment was 71%.) To model one aspect of the real world useful for an actual system, titles with below average circulation were eliminated. An offline pilot study had demonstrated that one-word titles were easy for wizards, so we eliminated those as well. A random sample of 7,500 was chosen from the remaining 19,708 titles to build the trigram language model.

We used Ratcliff/Obersherhelp (*R/O*) to measure the similarity of an ASR string to book titles in the database (Ratcliff & Metzener, 1988). R/O calculates the ratio r of the number of matching characters to the total length of both strings, but requires $O(r^2)$ time on average and $O(r^3)$ time in the worst case. We therefore computed an upper bound on the similarity of a title/ASR pair prior to full R/O to speed processing.

5 Experimental Design

In this experiment, a user and a wizard sat in separate rooms where they could not overhear one another. Each had a headset with microphone and a GUI. Audio input on the wizard's headset was disabled. When the user requested a title, the ASR hypothesis for the title appeared on the wizard's GUI. The wizard then selected the ASR hypothesis to execute a voice search against the database.

Given the ASR and the query return, the wizard's task was to guess which candidate in the query return, if any, matched the ASR hypothesis. Voice search accessed the full backend of 71,166 titles. The custom query designed for the experiment produced four types of return, in real time, based on R/O scores:

- *Singleton*: a single best candidate (R/O $\geq$ 0.85)
- *AmbiguousList*: two to five moderately good candidates (0.85 > R/O $\geq$ 0.55)
- *NoisyList*: six to ten poor but non-random candidates (0.55 > R/O $\geq$ 0.40)
- *Empty*: No candidate titles (max R/O < 0.40)

In pilot tests, 5%-10% of returns were empty versus none in the experiment. The distribution of other returns was: 46.7% Singleton, 50.5% AmbiguousList, and 2.8% NoisyList.

Seven undergraduate computer science majors at Hunter College participated. Two were non-native speakers of English (one Spanish, one Romanian). Each of the possible 21 pairs of students met for five trials. During each trial, one student served as wizard and the other as user for a *session* of 20 title cycles. They immediately reversed roles for a second session, as discussed further below. The experiment yielded 4172 title cycles rather than the full 4200, because users were permitted to end sessions early. All titles were selected from the 7500 used to construct the language model.

Each user received a printed list of 20 titles and a brief synopsis of each book. The acoustic quality of titles read individually from a list is unlikely to approximate that of a patron asking for a specific title. Therefore, immediately before each session, the user was asked to read a synopsis of each book, and to reorder the titles to reflect some logical grouping, such as genre or topic. Users requested titles in this new order that they had created.

Participants were encouraged to maximize a session score, with a reward for the experiment winner. Scoring was designed to foster cooperative strategies. The wizard scored +1 for a correctly identified title, +0.5 for a thoughtful question, and -1 for an incorrect title. The user scored +0.5 for a successfully recognized title. User and wizard traded roles for the second session, to discourage participants from sabotaging the others' scores.

The wizard's GUI presented a real-time live feed of ASR hypotheses, weighted by grayscale to reflect acoustic confidence. Words in each candidate title that matched a word in the ASR appeared darker: dark black for Singleton or AmbiguousList, and medium black for NoisyList. All other words were in grayscale in proportion to the degree of character overlap. The wizard queried the database with a recognition hypothesis for one utterance at a time, but could concatenate successive utterances, possibly with some limited editing.

After a query, the wizard's GUI displayed candidate matches in descending order of R/O score. The wizard had four options: make a *firm choice* of a candidate, make a *tentative choice*, ask a *question*, or *give up* to end the title cycle. Questions were recorded. The wizard's GUI showed the success or failure of each title cycle before the next one began. The user's GUI posted the 20 titles to be read during the session. On the GUI, the user rated the wizard's title choices as correct or incorrect. Titles were highlighted green if the user judged a wizard's offered title correct, red if incorrect, yellow if in progress, and not highlighted if still pending. The user also rated the wizard's questions. Average elapsed time for each 20-title session was 15.5 minutes.

A questionnaire similar to the type used in PARADISE evaluations (Walker et al., 1998) was administered to wizards and users for each pair of sessions. On a 5-point Likert scale, the average response to the question "I found the system easy to use this time" was 4 (sd=0; 4=Agree), indicating that participants were comfortable with the task. All other questions received an average score of Neutral (3) or Disagree (2). For example, participants were neutral (3) regarding confidence in guessing the correct title, and disagreed (2) that they became more confident as time went on.

6 Learning Method and Goals

To model wizard actions, we assembled 60 features that would be available at run time. Part of our task was to detect their relative independence, meaningfulness, and predictive ability. Features described the wizard's GUI, the current title session, similarity between ASR and candidates, ASR relevance to the database, and recognition and confidence measures. Because the number of voice search returns varied from one title to the next, features pertaining to candidates were averaged.

We used three machine-learning techniques to predict wizards' actions: decision trees, linear regression, and logistic regression. All models were produced with the Weka data mining package, using 10-fold cross-validation (Witten & Frank, 2005). A decision tree is a predictive model that maps feature values to a target value. One applies a decision tree by tracing a path from the *root* (the top node) to a leaf, which provides the target value. Here the leaves are the wizard actions: firm choice, tentative choice, question, or give up. The algorithm used is a version of C4.5 (Quinlan, 1993), where gain ratio is the splitting criterion.

To confirm the learnability and quality of the decision tree models, we also trained logistic regression and linear regression models on the same data, normalized in [0, 1]. The logistic regression model predicts the probability of wizards' actions by fitting the data to a logistic curve. It generalizes the linear model to the prediction of categorical data; here, categories correspond to wizards' actions. The linear regression models represent wizards' actions numerically, in decreasing value: firm choice, tentative choice, question, give up.

Although analysis of individual wizards has not been systematic in other work, we consider the variation in human performance significant. Because we seek excellent, not average, teachers for CheckItOut, our focus is on understanding good wizardry. Therefore, we learned two kinds of models with each of the three methods: the *overall model* using data from all of our wizards, and individual *wizard models*.

Preliminary cross-correlation confirmed that many of the 60 features were heavily interdependent. Through an initial manual curation phase, we isolated groups of features with $R^2 > 0.5$. When these groups referenced semantically similar features, we selected a single representative from the group and retained only that one. For example, the features that described similarity between hypotheses and candidates were highly correlated, so we chose the most comprehensive one: the number of exact word matches. We also grouped together

Table 1. Raw session score, accuracy, proportion of offered titles that were listed first in the query return, and frequency of correct non-offers for seven participants.

Participant	Cycles	Session Score	Accuracy	Offered Return 1	Correct Non-Offers
W4	600	0.7585	0.8550	0.70	0.64
W5	600	0.7584	0.8133	0.76	0.43
W7	599	0.6971	0.7346	0.76	0.14
W1	593	0.6936	0.7319	0.79	0.16
W2	599	0.6703	0.7212	0.74	0.10
W3	581	0.6648	0.6954	0.81	0.20
W6	600	0.6103	0.6950	0.86	0.03

and represented by a single feature: three features that described the gaps between exact word matches, three that described the data presented to the wizard, nine that described various system confidence scores, and three that described the user's speaking rate. This left 28 features.

Next we ran CfsSubsetEval, a supervised attribute selection algorithm for each model (Witten & Frank, 2005). This greedy, hill-climbing algorithm with backtracking evaluates a subset of attributes by the predictive ability of each feature and the degree of redundancy among them. This process further reduced the 28 features to 8-12 features per model. Finally, to reduce overfitting for decision trees, we used pruning and subtree rising. For linear regression we used the M5 method, repeatedly removing the attribute with the smallest standardized coefficient until there was no further improvement in the error estimate given by the Akaike information criterion.

7 Results

Table 1 shows the number of title cycles per wizard, the raw session score according to the formula given to the wizards, and accuracy. *Accuracy* is the proportion of title cycles where the wizard found the correct title, or correctly guessed that the correct title was not present (asked a question or gave up). Note that score and accuracy are highly correlated (R=0.91, p=0.0041), indicating that the instructions to participants elicited behavior consistent with what we wanted to measure.

Wizards clearly differed in performance, largely due to their response when the candidate list did not include the correct title. Analysis of variance with wizard as predictor and accuracy as the dependent variable is highly significant (p=0.0006); significance is somewhat greater (p=0.0001) where session score is the dependent variable. Table 2 shows the distribution of correct actions: to offer a candidate at a given position in the query return (Returns 1 through 9), or to ask a question or give up. As reflected in Table 2, a baseline accuracy of about 65% could be achieved by offering the first return. The fifth column of Table 1 shows how often wizards did that (Offered Return 1), and clearly illustrates that those who did so most often (W3 and W6) had accuracy results closest to the baseline. The wizard who did so least often (W4) had the highest accuracy, primarily because she more often correctly offered no title, as shown in the last column of Table 1. We conclude that a spoken dialogue system would do well to emulate W4.

Overall, our results in modeling wizards' actions were uniform across the three learning methods, gauged by accuracy and F measure. For the combined wizard data, logistic regression had an accuracy of 75.2%, and F measures of 0.83 for firm choices and 0.72 for tentative choices; the decision tree accuracy was 82.2%, and the F measures for firm versus tentative choices were respectively 0.82 and 0.71. The decision tree had a root mean squared error of 0.306, linear regression 0.483. Table 3 shows the accuracy and F measures on firm choices for the decision trees by individual wizard, along with the numbers of attributes and nodes per

Table 2. Distribution of correct actions

Correct Action	N	%
Return 1	2722	65.2445
Return 2	126	3.0201
Return 3	56	1.3423
Return 4	46	1.1026
Return 5	26	0.6232
Return 7	7	0.1678
Return 8	1	0.0002
Return 9	2	0.0005
Question or Giveup	1186	28.4276
Total	4172	1.0000

Table 3. Learning results for wizards

Tree	Rank	Nodes	Attributes	Accuracy	F firm
W4	1	55	12	75.67	0.85
W5	2	21	10	76.17	0.85
W1	3	7	8	80.44	0.87
W7	4	45	11	73.62	0.83
W3	5	33	10	77.42	0.84
W2	6	35	10	78.49	0.85
W6	7	23	10	85.19	0.80

tree. Although relatively few attributes appeared in any one tree, most attributes appeared in multiple nodes. W1 was the exception, with a very small pruned tree of 7 nodes.

Accuracy of the decision trees does not correlate with wizard rank. In general, the decision trees could consistently predict a confident choice ($0.80 \leq F \leq 0.87$), but were less consistent on a tentative choice ($0.60 \leq F \leq 0.89$), and could predict a question only for W4, the wizard with the highest accuracy and greatest success at detecting when the correct title was not in the candidates.

What wizards saw on the GUI, their recent success, and recognizer confidence scores were key attributes in the decision trees. The five features that appeared most often in the root and top-level nodes of all tree models reported in Table 3 were:

- *DisplayType* of the return (Singleton, Ambiguous List, NoisyList)
- *RecentSuccess,* how often the wizard chose the correct title within the last three title cycles
- *ContiguousWordMatch,* the maximum number of contiguous exact word matches between a candidate and the ASR hypothesis (averaged across candidates)
- *NumberOfCandidates*, how many titles were returned by the voice search
- *Confidence,* the Helios confidence score

DisplayType, NumberOfCandidates and *ContiguousWordMatch* pertain to what the wizard could see on her GUI. (Recall that *DisplayType* is distinguished by font darkness, as well as by number of candidates.) The impact of *RecentSuccess* might result not just from the wizard's confidence in her current strategy, but also from consistency in the user's speech characteristics. The Helios confidence annotation uses a learned model based on features from the recognizer, the parser, and the dialogue state. Here confidence primarily reflects recognition confidence; due to the simplicity of our grammar, parse results only indicate whether there is a parse. In addition to these five features, every tree relied on at least one measure of similarity between the hypothesis and the candidates.

W4 achieved superior accuracy: she knew when to offer a title and when not to. In the learned tree for W4, if the *DisplayType* was *NoisyList*, W4 asked a question; if *DisplayType* was *AmbiguousList,* the features used to predict W4's action included the five listed above, along with the acoustic model score, word length of the ASR, number of times the wizard had asked the user to repeat, and the maximum size of the gap between words in the candidates that matched the ASR hypothesis.

To focus on W4's questioning behavior, we trained an additional decision tree to learn how W4 chose between two actions: offering a title versus asking a question. This 37-node, 8-attribute tree was based on 600 data points, with F=0.91 for making an offer and F=0.68 for asking a question. The tree is distinctive in that it splits at the root on the number of frames in the ASR. If the ASR is short (as measured both by the number of recognition frames and the words), W4 asks a question when *DisplayType* = *AmbiguousList* or *NoisyList,* either *RecentSuccess* ≤ 1 or *ContiguousWordMatch* = 0, and the acoustic model score is low. Note that shorter titles are more confusable. If the ASR is long, W4 asks a question when *ContiguousWordMatch* ≤ 1, *RecentSuccess* ≤ 2, and either *CandidateDisplay* = *NoisyList*, or *Confidence* is low, and there is a choice of titles.

8 Discussion

Our experiment addressed whether voice search can compensate for incorrect ASR hypotheses and permit identification of a user's desired book, given a request by title. The results show that with high WER, a baseline dialogue strategy that always offers the highest-ranked database return can nevertheless achieve moderate accuracy. This is true even with the relatively simplistic measure of similarity between the ASR hypothesis and candidate titles used here. As a result, we have integrated voice search into CheckItOut, along with a linguistically motivated grammar for book titles. Our current Phoenix grammar relies on CFG rules automatically generated from dependency parses of the book titles, using the MICA parser

(Bangalore et al., 2009). As described in (Gordon & Passonneau, 2010), a book title parse can contain multiple title slots that consume discontinuous sequences of words from the ASR hypothesis, thus accommodating noisy ASR. For the voice search phase, we now concatenate the words consumed by a sequence of title slots. We are also experimenting with a statistical machine learning approach that will replace or complement the semantic parsing.

Computers clearly do some tasks faster and more accurately than people, including database search. To benefit from such strengths, a dialogue system should also accommodate human preferences in dialogue strategy. Previous work has shown that user satisfaction depends in part on task success, but also on minimizing behaviors that can increase task success but require the user to correct the system (Litman et al., 2006).

The decision tree that models W4 has lower accuracy than other models' (see Table 3), in part because her decisions had finer granularity. A spoken dialogue system could potentially do as well as or better than the best human at detecting when the title is not present, given the proper training data. To support this, a dataset could be created that was biased toward a larger proportion of cases where not offering a candidate is the correct action.

9 Conclusion and Current Work

This paper presents a novel methodology that embeds wizards in a spoken dialogue system, and collects data for a single turn exchange. Our results illustrate the merits of ranking wizards, and learning from the best. Our wizards were uniformly good at choosing the correct title when it was present, but most were overly eager to identify a title when it was not among the candidates. In this respect, the best wizard (W4) achieved the highest accuracy because she demonstrated a much greater ability to know when *not* to offer a title. We have shown that it is feasible to replicate this ability in a model learned from features that include the presentation of the search results (length of the candidate list, amount of word overlap of candidates with the ASR hypothesis), recent success at selecting the correct candidate, and measures pertaining to recognition results (confidence, acoustic model score, speaker rate). If replicated in a spoken dialogue system, such a model could support integration of voice search in a way that avoids misunderstandings. We conclude that learning from embedded wizards can exploit a wider range of relevant features, that dialogue managers can profit from access to more fine-grained representations of user utterances, and that machine learners should be selective about which people to model.

That wizard actions can be modeled using system features bodes well for future work. Our next experiment will collect full dialogues with embedded wizards whose actions will again be restricted through an interface. This time, NLU will integrate voice search with the linguistically motivated CFG rules for book titles described earlier, and a larger language model and grammar for database entities. We will select wizards who perform well during pilot tests. Again, the goal will be to model the most successful wizards, based upon data from recognition results, NLU, and voice search results.

Acknowledgements

This research was supported by the National Science Foundation under IIS-0745369, IIS-084966, and IIS-0744904. We thank the anonymous reviewers, the Heiskell Library, our CMU collaborators, our statistical wizard Liana Epstein, and our enthusiastic undergraduate research assistants.

References

Bangalore, Srinivas; Bouillier, Pierre; Nasr, Alexis; Rambow, Owen; Sagot, Benoit (2009). *MICA: a probabilistic dependency parser based on tree insertion grammars. Application Note.* Human Language Technology and North American Chapter of the Association for Computational Linguistics, pp. 185-188.

Bohus, D.; Rudnicky, A.I. (2009). The RavenClaw dialog management framework: Architecture and systems. *Computer Speech and Language, 23*(3), 332-361.

Bohus, Daniel; Rudnicky, Alex (2002). *Integrating multiple knowledge sources for utterance-level confidence annotation in the CMU Communicator spoken dialog system* (Technical Report No. CS-190): Carnegie Mellon University.

Georgila, Kallirroi; Sgarbas, Kyrakos; Tsopanoglou, Anastasios; Fakotakis, Nikos; Kokkinakis, George (2003). A speech-based human-computer interaction system for automating directory assistance services. *International Journal of Speech Technology, Special Issue on Speech and Human-Computer Interaction, 6*(2), 145-59.

Gordon, Joshua, B.; Passonneau, Rebecca J. (2010). *An evaluation framework for natural language understanding in spoken dialogue systems.* Seventh International Conference on Language Resources and Evaluation (LREC).

Johnston, Michael; Bangalore, Srinivas; Vasireddy, Gunaranjan; Stent, Amanda; Ehlen, Patrick; Walker, Marilyn A., et al. (2002). *MATCH--An architecture for multimodal dialogue systems.* Proceedings of the 40th Annual Meeting of the Association for Computational Linguistics, pp. 376-83.

Komatani, Kazunori; Kanda, Naoyuki; Ogata, Tetsuya; Okuno, Hiroshi G. (2005). *Contextual constraints based on dialogue models in database search task for spoken dialogue systems.* The Ninth European Conference on Speech Communication and Technology (Eurospeech), pp. 877-880.

Kruijff-Korbayová, Ivana; Blaylock, Nate; Gerstenberger, Ciprian; Rieser, Verena; Becker, Tilman; Kaisser, Michael, et al. (2005). *An experiment setup for collecting data for adaptive output planning in a multimodal dialogue system.* 10th European Workshop on Natural Language Generation (ENLG), pp. 191-196.

Levin, Esther; Narayanan, Shrikanth; Pieraccini, Roberto; Biatov, Konstantin; Bocchieri, E.; De Fabbrizio, Giuseppe, et al. (2000). *The AT&T-DARPA Communicator Mixed-Initiative Spoken Dialog System.* Sixth International Conference on Spoken Dialogue Processing (ICLSP), pp. 122-125.

Litman, Diane; Hirschberg, Julia; Swerts, Marc (2006). Characterizing and predicting corrections in spoken dialogue systems. *Computational Linguistics, 32*(3), 417-438.

Litman, Diane; Pan, Shimei (1999). *Empirically evaluating an adaptable spoken dialogue system.* 7th International Conference on User Modeling (UM), pp. 55-46.

Quinlan, J. Ross (1993). *C4.5: Programs for Machine Learning.* San Mateo, CA: Morgan Kaufmann.

Ratcliff, John W.; Metzener, David (1988). Pattern Matching: The Gestalt Approach. *Dr. Dobb's Journal*, 46

Raux, Antoine; Bohus, Dan; Langner, Brian; Black, Alan W.; Eskenazi, Maxine (2006). *Doing research on a deployed spoken dialogue system: one year of Let's Go! experience.* Ninth International Conference on Spoken Language Processing (Interspeech/ICSLP).

Raux, Antoine; Eskenazi, Maxine (2007). *A Multi-layer architecture for semi-synchronous event-driven dialogue management.*IEEE Workshop on Automatic Speech Recognition and Understanding (ASRU 2007), Kyoto, Japan.

Raux, Antoine; Langner, Brian; Black, Alan W.; Eskenazi, Maxine (2005). *Let's Go Public! Taking a spoken dialog system to the real world.*Interspeech 2005 (Eurospeech), Lisbon, Portugal.

Rieser, Verena; Kruijff-Korbayová, Ivana; Lemon, Oliver (2005). *A corpus collection and annotation framework for learning multimodal clarification strategies.* Sixth SIGdial Workshop on Discourse and Dialogue, pp. 97-106.

Sacks, Harvey; Schegloff, Emanuel A.; Jefferson, Gail (1974). A simplest systematics for the organization of turn-taking for conversation. *Language, 50*(4), 696-735.

Skantze, Gabriel (2003). *Exploring human error handling strategies: Implications for Spoken Dialogue Systems.* Proceedings of ISCA Tutorial and Research Workshp on Error Handling in Spoken Dialogue Systems, pp. 71-76.

Stoyanchev, Svetlana; Stent, Amanda (2009). *Predicting concept types in user corrections in dialog.* Proceedings of the EACL Workshop SRSL 2009, the Second Workshop on Semantic Representation of Spoken Language, pp. 42-49.

Turunen, Markku; Hakulinen, Jaakko; Kainulainen, Anssi (2006). *Evaluation of a spoken dialogue system with usability tests and long-term pilot studies.* Ninth International Conference on Spoken Language Processing (Interspeech 2006 - ICSLP).

Walker, M A.; Litman, D, J.; Kamm, C. A.; Abella, A. (1998). Evaluating Spoken Dialogue Agents with PARADISE: Two Case Studies. *Computer Speech and Language, 12*, 317-348.

Wang, Ye-Yi; Yu, Dong; Ju, Yun-Cheng; Acero, Alex (2008). An introduction to voice search. *IEEE Signal Process. Magazine, 25*(3).

Ward, Wayne; Issar, Sunil (1994). *Recent improvements in the CMU spoken language understanding system.*ARPA Human Language Technology Workshop, Plainsboro, NJ.

Williams, Jason D.; Young, Steve (2004). *Characterising Task-oriented Dialog using a Simulated ASR Channel.* Eight International Conference on Spoken Language Processing (ICSLP/Interspeech), pp. 185-188.

Witten, Ian H.; Frank, Eibe (2005). *Data Mining: Practical Machine Learning Tools and Techniques* (2nd ed.). San Francisco: Morgan Kaufmann.

Zollo, Teresa (1999). *A study of human dialogue strategies in the presence of speech recognition errors.* Proceedings of AAAI Fall Symposium on Psychological Models of Communication in Collaborative Systems, pp. 132-139.

Zue, Victor; Seneff, Stephanie; Glass, James; Polifroni, Joseph; Pao, Christine; Hazen, Timothy J., et al. (2000). A Telephone-based conversational interface for weather information. *IEEE Transactions on Speech and Audio Processing, 8*, 85-96.

A Direct Syntax-Driven Reordering Model for Phrase-Based Machine Translation

Niyu Ge
IBM T.J.Watson Research
Yorktown Heights, NY 10598
niyuge@us.ibm.com

Abstract

This paper presents a direct word reordering model with novel syntax-based features for statistical machine translation. Reordering models address the problem of reordering source language into the word order of the target language. IBM Models 3 through 5 have reordering components that use surface word information but very little context information to determine the traversal order of the source sentence. Since the late 1990s, phrase-based machine translation solves much of the local reorderings by using phrasal translations. The problem of long-distance reordering has become a central research topic in modeling distortions. We present a syntax driven maximum entropy reordering model that directly predicts the source traversal order and is able to model arbitrarily long distance word movement. We show that this model significantly improves machine translation quality.

1 Introduction

Machine translation reordering models model the problem of the word order when translating a source language into a target language. For example in Spanish and Arabic, adjectives often come after the nouns they modify whereas in English modifying adjectives usually precede the nouns. When translating Spanish or Arabic into English, the position of the adjectives need to be properly reordered to be placed before the nouns to make fluent English.

In this paper, we present a word reordering model that models the word reordering process in translation. The paper is organized as follows. §2 outlines previous approaches to reordering. §3 details our model and its training and decoding process. §4 discusses experiments to evaluate the model and §5 presents machine translation results. §6 is discussion and conclusion.

2 Previous Work

The word reordering problem has been one of the major problems in statistical machine translation (SMT). Since exploring all possible reorderings of a source sentence is an NP-complete problem (Knight 1999), SMT systems limit words to be reordered within a window of length k. IBM Models 3 through 5 (Brown et.al. 1993) model reorderings based on surface word information. For example, Model 4 attempts to assign target-language positions to source-language words by modeling $d(j \mid i, l, m)$ where j is the target-language position, i is the source-language position, l and m are respectively source and target sentence lengths. These models are not effective in modeling reorderings because they don't have enough context and lack structural information.

Phrase-based SMT systems such as (Koehn et.al. 2003) move from using words as translation units to using phrases. One of the advantages of phrase-based SMT systems is that local reorderings are inherent in the phrase translations. However, phrase-based SMT systems capture reordering instances and not reordering phenomena. For example, if the Arabic phrase "*the car red*" and its English translation "the red car' is seen in the training data, phrase-based SMT is able to produce the correct English for the Arabic 'the car red'. However it will not be able to produce 'the blue car' for the Arabic '*the car blue*' if the training data does not contain this phrase pair. Phrases do not capture the phenomenon that Arabic adjectives and nouns need to be reordered. Another problem with phrase-based SMT is the problem of long-range reorderings. Recent work on reordering has been focusing on capturing general reordering

Human Language Technologies: The 2010 Annual Conference of the North American Chapter of the ACL, pages 849–857,
Los Angeles, California, June 2010.

phenomena (as opposed to instances) and on solving long-range reordering problems.

(Al-onaizan et.al. 2006) proposes 3 distortion models, the inbound, outbound, and pair models. They together model the likelihood of translating a source word at position i given that the source word at position j has just been translated. These models perform better than n-gram based language models but are limited in their use of only the surface strings.

Instead of directly modeling the distance of word movement, phrasal level reordering models model how to move phrases, also called *orientations*. Orientations typically apply to adjacent phrases. Two adjacent phrases can be either placed monotonically (sometimes called *straight*) or swapped (non-monotonically or *inverted*). Early orientation models do not use lexical contents such as (Zens et. al., 2004). More recently, (Xiong et.al. 2006; Zens 2006; Och et. al, 2004; Tillmann, 2004; Kumar et al., 2005, Ni et al., 2009) all presented models that use lexical features from the phrases to predict their orientations. These models are very powerful in predicting local phrase placements. More recently (Galley et.al. 2008) introduced a hierarchical orientation model that captures some non-local phrase reorderings by a shift reduce algorithm. Because of the heavy use of lexical features, these models tend to suffer from data sparseness problems. Another limitation is that these models are restricted to reorderings with no gaps and phrases that are adjacent.

We present a probabilistic reordering model that models directly the source translation sequence and explicitly assigns probabilities to the reorderings of the source input with no restrictions on gap, length or adjacency. This is different from the approaches of pre-order such as (Xia and McCord 2004; Collins et.al. 2005; Kanthak et. al. 2005; Li et. al., 2007). Although our model can be used to produce top N pre-ordered source, the experiments reported here do not use the model in the pre-order mode. Instead, the reordering model is used to generate a reorder lattice which encodes many reorderings and their costs (negative log probability). This reorder lattice is independent of the translation decoder. In principle, any decoder can use this lattice for its reordering needs. We have integrated the reorder lattice into a phrase-based. The experiments reported here are from the phrase-based decoder.

We present the reordering model based on maximum entropy models. We then describe the syntactic features in the context of Chinese to English translation.

3 Maximum Entropy Reordering Model

The model takes a source sequence of length n:

$$S = [s_1, s_2, \dots s_n]$$

and models its translation or *visit* order according to the target language:

$$V = [v_1, v_2, \dots v_n]$$

where v_j is the source position for target position j. For example, if the 2nd source word is to be translated first, then $v_1 = 2$. We find V such that

$$\arg\max_{V \in \{v\}} p(V \mid S) \qquad (1)$$

$$= \max \prod_{j=1}^{n} p(v_j \mid S, v_{1\dots} v_{j-1}) \qquad (2)$$

In equation (1) {υ} is the set of possible visit orders. We want to find a visit order V such that the probability p(V|S) is maximized. Equation (2) is a component-wise decomposition of (1).

Let

$$f = v_j \ \ and \ \ h = (S, v_1 \dots v_{j-1})$$

We use the maximum entropy model to estimate equation (2):

$$p(f \mid h) = \frac{1}{Z(h)} \exp(\sum_k \lambda_k \phi_k (f, h)) \quad (3)$$

where $Z(h)$ is the normalization constant

$$Z(h) = \sum_f \exp \sum_k \lambda_k \phi_k (f, h) \qquad (4)$$

In equation (3), $\phi_k(f, h)$ are binary-valued features. During training, instead of exploring all possible permutations, samples are drawn given the correct path only.

3.1 Feature Overview

Most of our features $\phi_k(f, h)$ are syntax-based. They examine how each parse node is reordered during translation. We also have a few non-syntax features that inspect the surface words and part-of-speech tags. They complement syntax features by capturing lexical dependencies and guarding against parsing errors. Instead of directly modeling the absolute source position v_j, we model the jump from the last source position v_{j-1}. All features share two common components: *j* (for *jump*), and *cov* (for *coverage*). *Jumps* are bucketed and capped at 4 to prevent data sparsity. *Coverage* is an integer indicating the visiting status of the words between the jump. Coverage is 0 if none of the words was visited prior to this step, 1 if all were visited, and 2 if some but not all were visited. (*j, cov*) are present in all features and are removed from the descriptions below. A couple of features use a variation of *Jump* and *Coverage*. These will be described in the feature description.

3.2 Parse-based Syntax Features

We use the sentence pair in Figure 1. as a working example when describing the features. Shown in the figure are a Chinese-English parallel sentence pair, the word alignments between them, and the Chinese parse tree. The parse tree is simplified. Some details such as part-of-speech tags are omitted and denoted by triangles. The first step is to determine the source visit sequence from the word alignment, also shown at the bottom of Figure 1. If a target is aligned to more than one source, we assume the visit order is left to right. In Figure 1, source words 2 and 8 are aligned to the English '*at*' and we define the visit sequence to be 8 following 2.

Chinese and English differ in the positioning of the modifiers. In English, non-adjectival modifiers follow the object they modify. This is most prominent in the use of relative clauses and prepositional phrases. Chinese in contrast is a pre-modification language where modifiers whether adjectival, clausal or prepositional typically precede the object they modify. In Figure 1., the Chinese prepositional phrase PP (in *lightly shaded* box in the parse tree) spanning range [2,8] precedes the verb phrase VP2 at positions [9,10]. These two phrases are swapped in English as shown by the two lightly shaded boxes in the alignment grid. The relative clause CP (in *dark shaded* box in the parse tree) in Chinese spanning range [3,6] precedes the noun phrase NP3 at position 7 whereas these two phrases are again swapped in English.

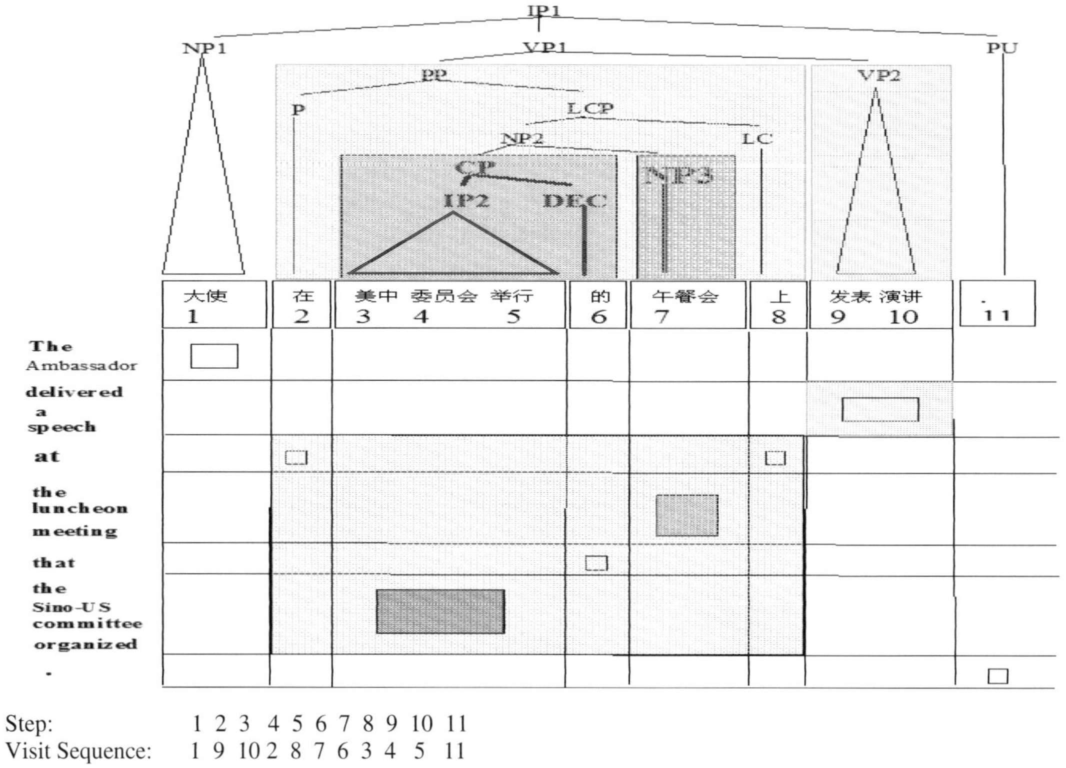

Figure 1. A Chinese-English Parallel Sentence with Chinese Parse

The phenomenon for the reordering model to capture is that node VP1's two children PP and VP2 (*lightly shaded*) need to be swapped regardless of how long the PP phrase is. This is also true for node NP2 whose two children CP and NP3 (*dark shaded*) need to be reversed.

Parse-based features model how to reorder the constituents in the parse by learning how to walk the parse nodes. For every non-unary node in the parse we learn such features as which of its child is visited first and for subsequent visits how to jump from one child to another. For the treelet VP1 → PP VP2 in Figure 1, we learn to visit the child VP2 first, then PP.

We now define the notion of '*node visit*'. When a source word s_i is visited at step *j*, we find its path to root from the leaf node denoted as $PathToRoot_i$. We say all the nodes contained in $PathToRoot_i$ are being visited at that step. Parse-based features are applied to every qualifying node in $PathToRoot_i$. Unary extensions do not qualify and are ignored. Since part-of-speech tags are unary branches, parse-based features apply from the lowest-level labels. Another condition depends on the jump and is discussed in section §3.4. All our features are encoded by a vector of integers and are denoted as ϕ (·) in this paper. We now describe the features.

3.2.1 First Child Features

The *first-child* feature applies when a node is visited for the first time. The feature learns which of the node's child to visit first. This feature learns such phenomena as translating the main verb first under a VP or translating the main NP first under an NP. The feature is defined as ϕ(*currentLabel, parentLabel, nthNode, j, cov)* where
currentLabel = label of the current parse node
parentLabel = label of the parent node
nthNode = an integer indicating the nth occurrence of the current node

In Figure 1, when source word 9 is visited at step 2, its *PathToRoot* is computed which is [VP2, VP1, IP1]. The *first-child* feature applied to VP2 is ϕ(VP2, VP1, 1, 4, 1) since
currentLabel = VP2; *parentLabel* = VP1;
nthChild = 1: VP2 is the 1st VP among its parent's children
j = 4: actual jump from 1 is 8 and is capped.
cov = 0: words in between the jump [1,9] are not yet visited at this step.
The semantics of this feature is that when a VP node is visited, the first VP child under it is visited first. This feature learns to visit the first VP first which is usually the head VP no matter where it is positioned or how many modifiers precede it.

3.2.2 Node Jump Features

This feature applies on all subsequent visits to the parse node. This feature models how to jump from one sibling to another sibling. This feature has these components: ϕ(*currentLabel, parentLabel, fromLable, nodeJump,cov)* where
fromLabel = the node label where the jump is from
nodeJump = node distance from that node
This feature effectively captures syntactic reorderings by looking at the node jump instead of surface distance jump. In our example, a *node-jump* feature for jumping from source 10 to 2 at step 4 at VP1 level is ϕ(PP, VP1, VP2, -1, 2) where
currentLabel = PP where source word 2 is under
parentLabel = VP1
fromLabel = VP2 where source word 10 is under
nodeJump = -1 since the jump is from VP2 to PP
cov = 2 because in between [2,10] word 9 has been visited and other words have not.

This feature captures the necessary information for the 'PP VP' reorderings regardless of how long the PP or VP phrase is.

3.2.3 Jump Over Sibling Features

To make a correct jump from one sibling to the other, siblings that are jumped over should also be considered. For example in Chinese, while jumping over a PP to cover a VP is a good jump, jumping over an ADVP to cover a VP may not be because adverbs in both Chinese and English often precede the verb they modify. The *jump-over-sibling* features help distinguish these cases. This feature's components are ϕ(*currentLabel, parentLabel, jumpOverSibling, siblingCov, j)* where *jumpOverSibling* is the label of the sibling that is jumped over and *siblingCov* is the coverage status of that sibling.

This feature applies to every sibling that is jumped over. At step 2 where the jump is from source 1 to 9, this feature at VP1 level is ϕ(VP2, VP1, PP, 0, 4) because PP is a sibling of VP2 and is jumped over, PP is not covered at this step, and the jump is capped to be 4.

3.2.4 Back Jump Sibling Features

For every forward jump of length greater than 1, there is a backward jump to cover those words that were skipped. In these situations we want to know how far we can move forward before we must jump backward. The *back-jump-sibling* feature applies when the jump is backward (distance is negative) and inspects the sibling to the right. It generates ϕ(*currentLabel, rightSiblingCov, j*). When jumping from 10 to 2 at step 4, this feature is ϕ(PP, 1, -4) where -4 is the *jump* and *currentLabel* = PP where source word 2 is under *rightSiblingCoverage* = 1 since VP2 has been completed visited at this time. This feature learns to go back to PP when its right sibling (VP2) is completed.

3.2.5 Broken Features

Translations do not always respect the constituent boundaries defined by the source parse tree. Consider the fragment in Figure 2.

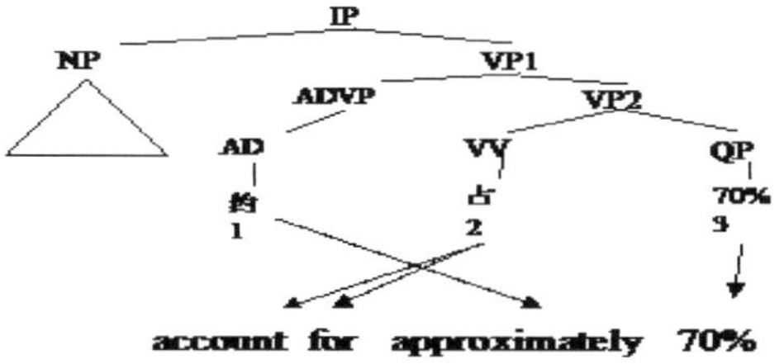

Figure 2. A '*Broken*' Tree

After the VV under VP2 is translated ("*account for*"), a transition is made to translate the ADVP ("*approximately*") leaving VP2 partially translated. We say that the node VP2 is *broken* at this step. This type of feature has been shown to be useful for machine translation (Marton & Resnik 2008). Here, *broken* features model the context under which a node is broken by observing the feature ϕ(*curTag, prevTag, parentLabel, j, cov*). For the transition of source word 2 to source word 1 in Figure 2, a broken feature applies at VP2: ϕ(AD, VV, VP2, -1 ,1). This feature learns that a VP can be broken when making a jump from a verb (VV) to an adverb (AD).

3.3 Non-Parse Features

Non-parse features do not use or use less fine-grained information from the parse tree.

3.3.1 Barrier Features

Barrier features model the intuition that certain words such as punctuation should not move freely. This phenomenon has been observed and shown to be helpful in (Xiong et. al., 2008). We call these words *barrier* words. Barrier features are ϕ(*barrierWord, cov, j*). All punctuations are barrier words.

3.3.2 Number of Zero Islands Features

Although word reorderings can involve words far apart, certain jump patterns are highly unlikely. For example, the coverage pattern '1010101010' where every other source word is translated would be very improbable. Let the right most covered source word be the *frontier*. For every jump, the *number-of-zero-islands* feature computes the number of uncovered source islands to the left of the frontier. Additionally it takes into account the number of parse nodes in between. This feature is defined as ϕ(*numZeroIslands, j, numParseNodesInBetween*). The number of parse nodes is the number of maximum spanning nodes in between the jump. The jump at step 2 from source 1 to 9 triggers this number-zero-island feature ϕ(1, 4, 1). The source coverage status at step 2 is 10000000100 because the first source word has been visited and the current visit is source 9. All words in between have not been visited. There is 1 contiguous sequence of 0's between the first '1' and the last '1', hence the *numZeroIslands* = 1. There is one parse node PP that spans all the source words from 2 to 8, therefore the last argument to the feature is 1. If instead, the transition was from source 1 to 8, then there would be 2 maximum spanning parse nodes for source [2,7] which are nodes P and NP2. The feature would be ϕ(1, 4, 2). This feature discourages scattered jumps that leave lots of zero islands and jump over lots of parse nodes.

3.4 Training

Training the maximum entropy reordering model needs word alignments and source-side parses. We use hand alignments from LDC. The training data statistics are shown in Table 1. We use the (Levy and Manning 2003) parser on Chinese.

Data	#Sentences	#Words
LDC2006E93	10,408	230,764
LDC2008E57	11,463	194,024

Table 1. Training Data

From the word alignments we first determine the source visit sequence. Table 2 details how the visit sequence is determined in various cases.

Alignment Type S-T	Visit Sequence
1-1	Left to right from target
m-1	Left to right from source
1-m	Left most target link
Ø	Attaches left

Table 2. Determining visit sequence

The first column shows alignment type from source (S) to target (T). 1-1 means one source word aligns to one target word. m-1 means many source words align to one target and vice versa. Ø means unaligned source words.

After the source visit sequence is decided, features are generated. Note that the height of the tree is not uniform for all the words. To preserve the structure and also alleviate the depth problem, we use the *lowest-level-common-ancestor* approach. For every jump, we generate features bottom up until we reach the node that is the common ancestor of the origin and the destination of the jump. In Figure 1 there is a jump from source 7 to 6 at step 7. The *lowest-level-common-ancestor* for source 6 and 7 is the node NP2 and features are generated up to the level of NP2. Features on this training data are shown in the second column in Table 5.

The MaxEnt model on this data is efficiently trained at 15 minutes per iteration (24 sentences/sec or 471 words/sec).

4 Experiments

4.1 Reorder Evaluation

To evaluate how accurate the reordering model is, we first compute its prediction accuracy. We choose the first 100 sentences from NIST MT03 as our test set for this evaluation. We manually word align them to the first set of reference using LDC annotation guidelines version 1.0 of April 2006. An average of 73% of the training sentences contain unaligned source words and over 87% of the test sentences contain unaligned source words. The unaligned source words are mostly function words. Because the visit sequence of unaligned source words are determined not by truth but by heuristics (Table 2), they pose a problem in evaluation.

We thus evaluate the model by measuring the accuracy of its decision conditioned on true history. We measure performance on the model's top-N choices for N = 1,2, and 3. Results are in Table 3. The table also shows the accuracy of no reordering in the *Monotone* column.

Top-N	Accuracy	Monotone
1	80.56%	65.39%
2	90.66%	-
3	93.05%	-

Table 3. Reordering model performance

Figure 3 plots accuracy vs. MaxEnt training iteration. Accuracy starts low at 74.7% and reaches is highest at iteration 8 and fluctuates around 80.5% thereafter.

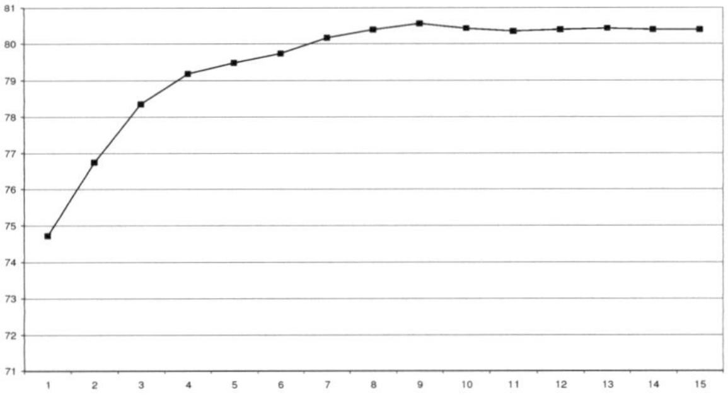

Figure 3. Accuracy vs. MaxEnt Training Iteration

We analyze 50 errors from the top-1 run. The errors are categorized and shown in Table 4.

Error Category	Percentage
Lexical	34%
Parse	30%
Model	20%
Reference	16%

Table 4. Error Analysis

'*Lexical*' errors are those that rise from lexical choice of source words. For example, an "ADVP VP" structure would normally be visited monotonically. However, in case of Chinese phrase '*so do*', they should be swapped. More than a third of the errors are of this nature. Errors in the *Refer-*

ence category are those that are marked wrong because of the particular English reference. The proposed reorderings are correct but they don't match the reference reorderings. Another 30% of the errors are due to parsing errors. The *Model* errors are due to two sources. One is the depth problem mentioned above. Local statistics for some very deep treelets overwhelm the global statistics and local jumps win over the long jumps in these cases. Another problem is the data sparseness. For example, the model has learned to reorder the 'PP VP' structure but there is not much data for 'PP ADVP VP'. The model fails to jump over PP into ADVP.

4.2 Feature Utility

We conduct ablation studies to see the utilities of each feature. We take the best feature set which gives the performance in Table 3 and takes away one feature type at a time. The results are in Table 5. The first row keeps all the features. The *Subtract* column shows performance after subtracting each feature while keeping all the other features. The *Add* column shows performance of adding the feature. Using just *first-child* features gets 75.97%. Adding *node-jump* features moves the accuracy to 78.40% and so on.

Features	#Features	Sub-tract	Add
-		80.56%	-
First Child	7,559	79.87%	75.97%
Node Jump	6,334	79.52%	78.40%
JumpOver Sib.	2,403	80.52%	79.00%
BackJump	602	80.48%	79.05%
Broken	15,183	80.30%	79.13%
Barrier	158	80.26%	79.22%
NumZ Islands	200	79.52%	80.56%

Table 5. Ablation study on features

5 Translation Experiments

5.1 Reorder Lattice Generation

The reordering model is used to generate reorder lattices which are used by machine translation decoders. Reorder lattices have been frequently used in decoding in works such as (Zhang et. al 2007, Kumar et.al. 2005, Hildebrand et.al. 2008), to name just a few. The main difference here is that our lattices encode probabilities from the reordering model and are not used to preorder the source. The lattice contains reorderings and their cost (negative log probability). Figure 4 shows a reorder lattice example. Nodes are lattice states. Arcs store source word positions to be visited (translated) and their cost and they are delimited by comma in the figure. Lower cost indicates better choice. Figure 4 is much simplified for readability. It shows only the best path (highlighted) and a few neighboring arcs. For example, it shows source words 1, 2, and 8 are the top 3 choices at step 1. Position 1 is the best choice with the lowest cost of 0.302 and so on.

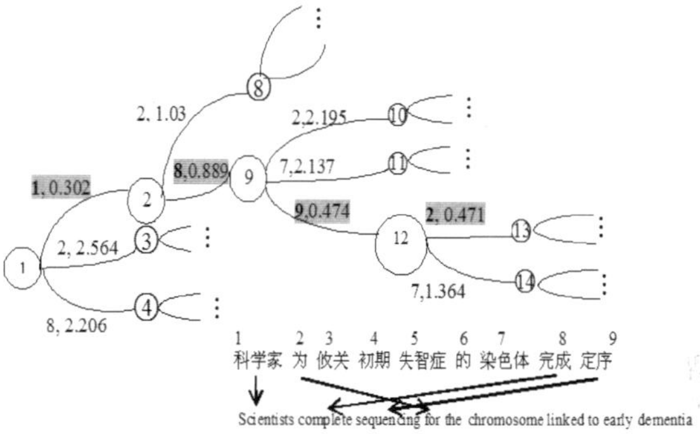

Figure 4. A lattice example

The sentence is shown at the bottom of the figure. The first part of the reference (true) path is indicated by the alignment which is source sequence 1, 8, 9, and 2. We see that this matches the lattice's top-1 choice.

Lattice generation takes source sentence and source parse as input. The lattice generation process makes use of a beam search algorithm. Every node in the lattice generates top-N next possible positions and the rest is pruned away. A coverage vector is maintained on each path to ensure each source word is visited exactly once. A wide beam width explores many source positions at any step and results in a bushy lattice. This is needed for machine translation because the parses are errorful. The structures that are hard for MT to reorder are also hard for parsers to parse. Labels critical to reordering such as CP are among the least accurate labels. Overall parsing accuracy is 83.63% but CP accuracy is 73.11%. We need a wide beam to include more long jumps to compensate the parsing errors.

5.2 Machine Translation

We run MT experiments on NIST Chinese-English test sets MT03-05. We compare the performance of using distance-based reordering and using maximum entropy reordering lattices. The decoder is a log-linear phrase based decoder. Translation models are trained from HMM alignments. A smoothed 5-gram English LM is built on the English Gigaword corpus and English side of the Chinese-English parallel corpora. In the experiments, lexicalized distance-based reordering allows up to 9 words to be jumped over. MT performance is measured by BLEUr4n4 (Papineni et.al. 2001).

The test set statistics and experiment results are show in Table 6. Decoding with MaxEnt reorder lattices shows significant improvement for all conditions.

Data	#Segs	Lex Skip-9	Reord Lattice	Gain
MT03	919	0.3005	0.3315	+3.1
MT04	1788	0.3250	0.3388	+1.38
MT05	1082	0.2957	0.3236	+2.79

Table 6. MT results

Figures 5 shows an example from MT output with word alignments to the Chinese input. The MaxEnt reordering model correctly reorders two source modifiers at source positions 8 and 22. The Skip9 output reorders locally whereas the MaxEnt lattice output shows much more complex reorderings.

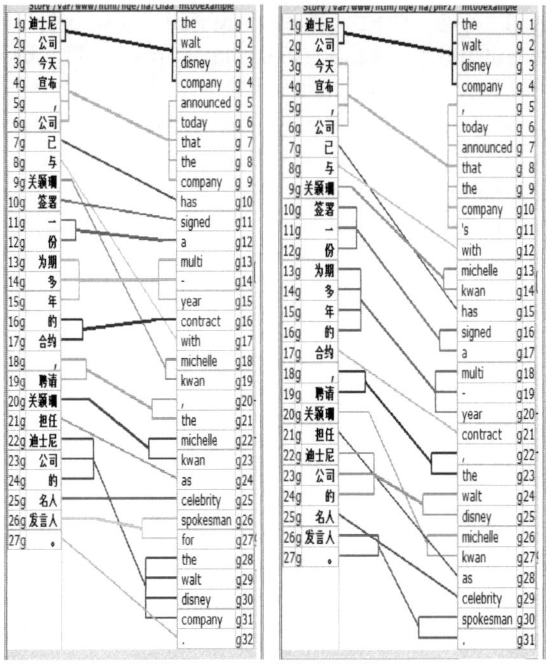

ME Lattice MT Skip9 MT

Figure 5. MT comparison

Our initial attempt at adding lexical pair jump features $\phi(fromWord, toWord, j)$ has not proved useful. It hurt accuracy by 3% (from 80% to 77%). We see from Table 4 that 34% of the errors are due to source lexical choices which indicates the weakness of the current lexical features. Regularization of the model might also make a difference with the lexical features.

Reordering and word choice in translation are not independent of each other. We have shown some initial success with a separate reordering model. In the future, we will build joint models on reordering and translation. This approach will also address some of the reordering problems due to source lexical idiosyncrasies.

6 Conclusions

We present a direct syntax-based reordering model that captures source structural information. The model is capable of handling reorderings of arbitrary length. Long-range reorderings are essential in translation between languages with great word order differences such as Chinese-English and Arabic-English. We have shown that phrase based SMT can benefit significantly from such a reordering model.

The current model is not regularized and feature selection by thresholding the feature counts is quite primitive. Regularizing the model will prevent overfitting, especially given the small training data set. Regularization will also make the ablation study more meaningful.

The reordering model presented here aims at capturing structural differences between source and target languages. It does not have enough lexical features to deal with lexical idiosyncrasies.

7 Acknowledgement

We would like to acknowledge the support of DARPA under Grant HR0011-08-C-0110 for funding part of this work. The views, opinions, and/or findings contained in this article are those of the author and should not be interpreted as representing the official views or policies, either expressed or implied, of the Defense Advanced Research Projects Agency or the Department of Defense.

References

A.S.Hildebrand, K.Rottmann, Mohamed Noamany, Qin Gao, S. Hewavitharana, N. Bach and Stephan Voga. 2008. *Recent Improvements in the CMU Large Scale Chinese-English SMT System.* In Proceedings of ACL 2008 (Short Papers)

C. Wang, M. Collins, and Philipp Koehn. 2007. *Chinese Syntactic Reordering for Statistical Machine Translation.* In Proceedings of EMNLP 2007

Chi-Ho Li, Dongdong Zhang, Mu Li, Ming Zhou, Minghui Li, and Yi Guan. 2007. *A Probabilistic Approach to syntax-based Reordering for Statistical Machine Translation.* In Proceedings of ACL 2007.

Christoph Tillmannn. 2004. *A Block Orientation Model for Statistical Machine Translation.* In Proceedings of HLT-NAACL 2004.

David Chiang. 2005. *A Hierarchical Phrase-based Model for Statistical Machine Translation.* In Proceedings of ACL 2005.

Dekai Wu. 1997. *Stochastic Inversion Transduction Grammars and Bilingual Parsing of Parallel Corpora.* Compuntational Linguistics, Vol. 23, pp 377-404

Deyi Xiong, Qun Liu, and Shouxun Lin. 2006. *Maximum Entropy Based Phrase Reordering Model for Statistical Machine Translation.* In Proceedings of ACL 2006.

Deyi Xiong, Min Zhang, Aiti Aw, Haitao Mi, Qun Liu and Shouxun Lin. 2008. *Refinements in FTG-based Statistical Machine Translation.* In Proceedings of ICJNLP 2008

Dongdong Zhang, Mu Li, Chi-Ho Li, and Ming Zhou. 2007. *Phrase Reordering Model Integrating Syntactic Knowledge for SMT.* In Proceedings of EMNLP 2007

Fei Xia and Michael McCord. 2004. *Improving a Statistical MT System with Automatically Learned Rewrite Patterns.* In Proceedings of COLING 2004.

Franz Josef Och and Hermann Ney. 2004. *The Alignment Template Approach to Statistical Machine Translation.* Computational Linguistics, Vol. 30(4). pp. 417-449

Kenji Yamada and Kevin Knight 2001. *A Syntax-based Statistical Translation Model.* In Proceedings of ACL 2001

Kevin Knight. 1999. *Decoding Complexity in Word Replacement Translation Models.* Computational Linguistics, 25(4):607-615

Kishore Papineni, Salim Roukos, Todd Ward, and Wei-jing Zhu. 2001. *A Method for Automatic Evaluation for MT.* In Proceedings of ACL 2001

Michael Collins, Philipp Koehn, and Ivona Kucerova. 2005. *Clause Restructuring for Statistical Machine Translation.* In Proceedings of ACL 2005.

Michell Galley, Christoph D. Manning. 2008. *A Simple and Effective Hierarchical Phrase Reordering Model.* Proceedings of the EMNLP 2008

Perter F. Brown, Stephen A. Della Pietra, Vincent J. Della Pietra, and Robert L. Mercer. 1993. *The Mathematics of Statistical Machine Translation.* Computation Linguistics, 19(2).

Philip Koehn, Franz Josef Och, and Daniel Marcu. 2003. *Statistical Phrase-based Translation.* In Proceedings of NLT/NAACL 2003.

Richard Zens, Hermann Ney, Taro Watanabe, and Eiichiro Sumita. 2004. *Reordering Constraints for Phrase-based Statistical Machine Translation.* In Proceedings of COLING 2004.

Richard Zens and Hermann Ney. 2006. *Discriminative Reordering Models for Statistical Machine Translation.* In Proceedings of the Workshop on Statistical Machine Translation, 2006.

Roger Levy and Christoph Manning. 2003. *Is it harder to parse Chinese, or the Chinese Treebank?* In Proceedings of ACL 2003

Shankar Kumar and William Byrne. 2005. *Local Phrase Roerdering Models for Statistical Machine Translation.* In Proceedings of HLT/EMNLP 2005

Stephan Kanthak, David Vilar, Evgeny Matusov, Richard Zens, and Hermann Ney. 2005. *Novel Reordering Approaches in Phrase-based Statistical Machine Translation.* In Proceedings of the Workshop on Building and Using Parallel Texts 2005.

Y. Al-Onaizan . K. 2006 *Distortion Models for Statistical Machine Translation.* In Proceedings of ACL 2006.

Yizhao Ni, C.J.Saunders, S. Szedmak and M.Niranjan 2009 *Handling phrase reorderings for machine translation.* In Proceedings of ACL2009

Yuqi Zhang, Richard Zens, and Hermann Ney. 2007. *Improved Chunk-level Reordering for Statistical Machine Translation.* In Proceedings of HLT/NAACL 2007.

Yuval Marton and Philip Resnik. 2008. *Soft Syntactic Constraints for Hierarchical Phrased-based Translation.* In Proceedings of ACL 2008.

Context-free reordering, finite-state translation

Chris Dyer and Philip Resnik
UMIACS Laboratory for Computational Linguistics and Information Processing
Department of Linguistics
University of Maryland, College Park, MD 20742, USA
redpony, resnik AT umd.edu

Abstract

We describe a class of translation model in which a set of input variants encoded as a context-free forest is translated using a finite-state translation model. The forest structure of the input is well-suited to representing word order alternatives, making it straightforward to model translation as a two step process: (1) tree-based source reordering and (2) phrase transduction. By treating the reordering process as a latent variable in a probabilistic translation model, we can learn a long-range source reordering model without example reordered sentences, which are problematic to construct. The resulting model has state-of-the-art translation performance, uses linguistically motivated features to effectively model long range reordering, and is significantly smaller than a comparable hierarchical phrase-based translation model.

1 Introduction

Translation models based on synchronous context-free grammars (SCFGs) have become widespread in recent years (Wu, 1997; Chiang, 2007). Compared to phrase-based models, which can be represented as finite-state transducers (FSTs, Kumar et al. (2006)), one important benefit that SCFG models have is the ability to process long range reordering patterns in space and time that is polynomial in the length of the displacement, whereas an FST must generally explore a number of states that is exponential in this length.[1] As one would expect, for language pairs with substantial structural differences (and thus requiring long-range reordering during translation), SCFG models have come to outperform the best FST models (Zollmann et al., 2008).

In this paper, we explore a new way to take advantage of the computational benefits of CFGs during translation. Rather than using a single SCFG to both reorder and translate a source sentence into the target language, we break the translation process into a two step pipeline where (1) the source language is reordered into a target-like order, with alternatives encoded in a context-free forest, and (2) the reordered source is transduced into the target language using an FST that represents phrasal correspondences.

While multi-step decompositions of the translation problem have been proposed before (Kumar et al., 2006), they are less practical with the rise of SCFG models, since the context-free languages are not closed under intersection (Hopcroft and Ullman, 1979). However, the CFLs are closed under intersection with regular languages. By restricting ourselves to a *finite-state* phrase transducer and representing reorderings of the source in a *context-free* forest, exact inference over the composition of the two models is possible.

The paper proceeds as follows. We first explore reordering forests and describe how to translate them with an FST (§2). Since we would like our reordering model to discriminate between good reorderings of the source and bad ones, we show how to train our reordering component as a latent variable in an end-to-end translation model (§3). We then presents experimental results on language pairs requiring small amounts and large amounts of reordering (§4). We conclude with a discussion of related

[1] Our interest here is the reordering made possible by varying the arrangement of the translation units, not the local word order differences captured inside memorized phrase pairs.

Human Language Technologies: The 2010 Annual Conference of the North American Chapter of the ACL, pages 858–866,
Los Angeles, California, June 2010.

work (§6) and possible extensions (§7).

2 Reordering forests and translation

In this section, we describe *source reordering forests*, a context-free representation of source language word order alternatives.[2] The basic idea is that for the source sentence, **f**, that is to be translated, we want to create a (monolingual) context-free grammar $\mathcal{F}$ that generates strings ($\mathbf{f'}$) of words in the source language that are permutations of the original sentence. Specifically, this forest should contain derivations that put the source words into an order that approximates how they will be ordered in the grammar of the target language.

For a concrete example, let us consider the task of English-Japanese translation.[3] Our input sentence is *John ate an apple*. Japanese is a *head-final language*, where the heads of phrases (such as the verb in a verb phrase) typically come last, and English is a *head-initial language*, where heads come first. As a result, the usual order for a declarative sentence in English is SVO (subject-verb-object), but in Japanese, it is SOV, and the desired translation is *John-ga ringo-o* [an apple] *tabeta* [ate]. In summary, when translating from English into Japanese, it is usually necessary to move verbs from their position between the subject and object to the end of the sentence.

This reordering can happen in two ways, which we depict in Figure 1. In the derivation on the left, a memorized phrase pair captures the movement of the verb (Koehn et al., 2003). In the other derivation, the source is first reordered into target word order and then translated, using smaller translation units. In addition, we have assumed that the phrase translations were learned from a parallel corpus that is in the original ordering, so the reordering forest $\mathcal{F}$ should include derivations of phrase-size units in the source order as well as the target order.

[2]Note that forests are isomorphic to context-free grammars. For example, what is referred to as the 'parse forest', and understood to encode all derivations of a sentence **s** under some grammar, can also be understood as being a context-free grammar itself that exactly generates **s**. We therefore refer to a forest as a grammar sometimes, or vice versa, depending on which characterization is clearer in context.

[3]We use English as the source language since we expect the parse structure of English sentences will be more familiar to many readers.

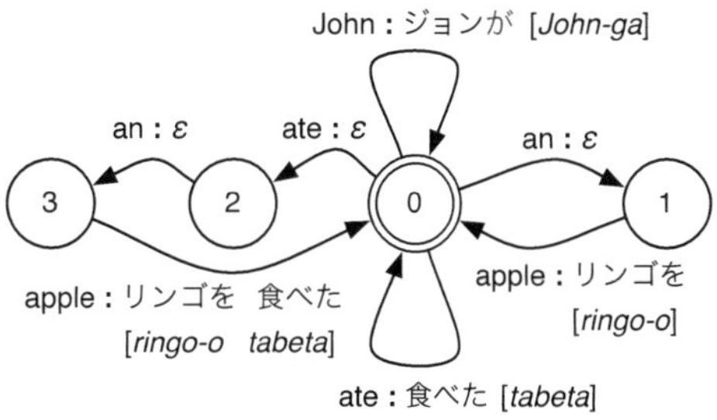

Figure 2: A fragment of a phrase-based English-Japanese translation model, represented as an FST. Japanese romanization is given in brackets.

A minimal reordering forest that supports the derivations depicted needs to include both an SOV and SVO version of the source. This could be accomplished trivially with the following grammar:

$$\begin{aligned} \mathrm{S} &\rightarrow \textit{John ate an apple} \\ \mathrm{S} &\rightarrow \textit{John an apple ate} \end{aligned}$$

However, this grammar misses the opportunity to take advantage of the regularities in the permuted structure. A better alternative might be:

$$\begin{aligned} \mathrm{S} &\rightarrow \textit{John}\ \mathrm{VP} \\ \mathrm{VP} &\rightarrow \textit{ate}\ \mathrm{NP} \\ \mathrm{VP} &\rightarrow \mathrm{NP}\ \textit{ate} \\ \mathrm{NP} &\rightarrow \textit{an apple} \end{aligned}$$

In this grammar, the phrases *John* and *an apple* are fixed and only the VP contains ordering ambiguity.

2.1 Reordering forests based on source parses

Many kinds of reordering forests are possible; in general, the best one for a particular language pair will be one that is easiest to create given the resources available in the source language. It will also be the one that most compactly expresses the source reorderings that are most likely to be useful for translation. In this paper, we consider a particular kind of reordering forest that is inspired by the reordering model of Yamada and Knight (2001).[4] These are generated by taking a source language parse tree and 'expanding' each node so that it

[4]One important difference is that our translation model is not restricted by the structure of the source parse tree; i.e., phrases used in transduction need not correspond to constituents in the source reordering forest. However, if a phrase does cross a constituent boundary between constituents A and B, then translations that use that phrase will have A and B adjacent.

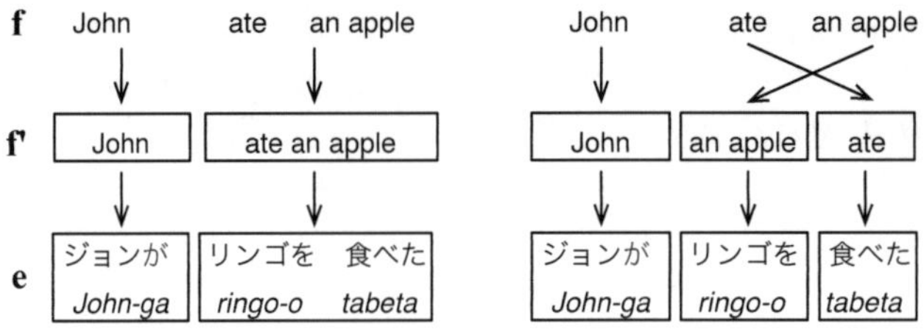

Figure 1: Two possible derivations of a Japanese translation of an English source sentence.

rewrites with different permutations of its children.[5]

For an illustration using our example sentence, refer to Figure 3 for the forest representation and Figure 4 for its isomorphic CFG representation. It is easy to see that this forest generates the two 'good' order variants from Figure 1; however, the forest includes many other derivations that will probably not lead to good translations. For this reason, it is helpful to associate the edges in the forest (that is, the rules in the CFG) with weights reflecting how likely that rule is to lead to a good translation. We discuss how these weights can be learned automatically in §3.

2.2 Translating reordering forests with FSTs

Having described how to construct a context-free reordering forest for the source sentence, we now turn to the problem of how to translate the source forest into the target language using a phrase-based translation model encoded as an FST, e.g. Figure 2. The process is quite similar to the one used when translating a source sentence with an SCFG, but with a twist: rather than representing the translation model as a grammar and parsing the source sentence, we represent the *source sentence* as a grammar (i.e. its reordering forest), and we use it to 'parse' the *translation model* (i.e. the FST representation of the phrase-based model). The end result (either way!) is a translation forest containing all possible target-language translations of the source.

Parsing can be understood as a means of computing the intersection of an FSA and a CFG (Grune and Jacobs, 2008). Since we are dealing with FSTs that define binary relations over strings, not FSAs defining strings, this operation is more properly *composition*. However, since CFG/FSA intersection is less cumbersome to describe, we present the algorithm in terms of intersection.

To compute the composition of a reordering forest, $\mathcal{G}$, with an FSA, F, we will make use of a variant of Earley's algorithm (Earley, 1970). Let weighted finite-state automaton $F = \langle \Sigma, Q, q_0, q_{\mathit{final}}, \delta, w \rangle$. Σ is a finite alphabet; Q is a set of states; q_0 and $q_{\mathit{final}} \in Q$ are start and accept states, respectively,[6] δ is the transition function $Q \times \Sigma \rightarrow 2^Q$, and w is the transition cost function $Q \times Q \rightarrow \mathbb{R}$. We use variables that refer to states in the FSA with the letters q, r, and s. We use x to represent a variable that is an element of Σ. Variables u and v represent costs. X and Y are non-terminals. Lowercase Greek letters are strings of terminals and non-terminals. The function $\delta(q, x)$ returns the state(s) that are reachable from state q by taking a transition labeled with x in the FSA.

Figure 5 provides the inference rules for a top-down intersection algorithm in the form of a weighted logic program; the three inference rules correspond to Earley's SCAN, PREDICT, and COMPLETE, respectively.

3 Reordering and translation model

As pointed out in §2.1, our reordering forests may contain many paths, some of which when translated will lead to good translations and others that will be bad. We would like a model to distinguish the two.

If we had a parallel corpus of source language sentences paired with 'reference reorderings', such a model could be learned directly as a supervised learning task. However, creating the optimal target-language reordering **f′** for some **f** is a nontrivial task.[7] Instead of trying to solve this problem, we opt to treat the reordered from of the source, **f′**, as a

[5]For computational tractability, we only consider all permutations only when the number of children is less than 5, otherwise we exclude permutations where a child moves more than 4 positions away from where it starts.

[6]Other FSA definitions permit sets of start and final states. We use the more restricted definition for simplicity and because in our FSTs $q_0 = q_{\mathit{final}}$.

[7]For a discussion of methods for generating reference re-

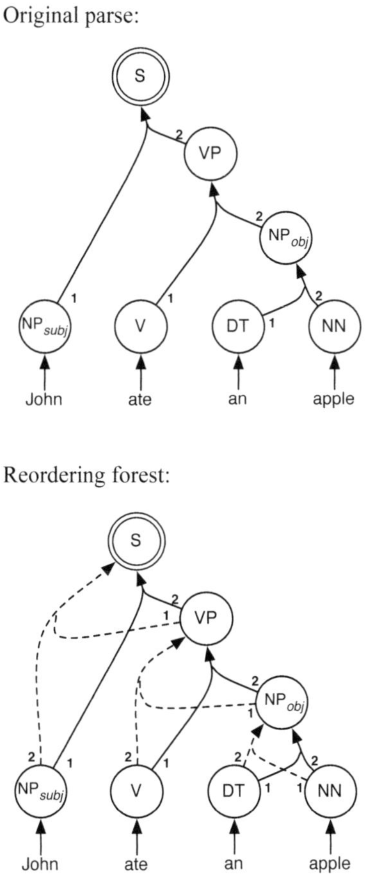

Figure 3: Example of a reordering forest. Linearization order of non-terminals is indicated by the index at the tail of each edge. The isomorphic CFG is shown in Figure 4; dashed edges correspond to reordering-specific rules.

Original parse grammar:	$\mathrm{S} \rightarrow \mathrm{NP_{subj}}\ \mathrm{VP}$
$\mathrm{VP} \rightarrow \mathrm{V}\ \mathrm{NP_{obj}}$	$\mathrm{NP_{obj}} \rightarrow \mathrm{DT}\ \mathrm{NN}$
$\mathrm{NP_{subj}} \rightarrow$ *John*	$\mathrm{V} \rightarrow$ *ate*
$\mathrm{DT} \rightarrow$ *an*	$\mathrm{NN} \rightarrow$ *apple*

Additional reordering grammar rules:

$\mathrm{S} \rightarrow \mathrm{VP}\ \mathrm{NP_{subj}}$

$\mathrm{VP} \rightarrow \mathrm{NP_{obj}}\ \mathrm{V}$

$\mathrm{NP_{obj}} \rightarrow \mathrm{NN}\ \mathrm{DT}$

Figure 4: Context-free grammar representation of the forest in Figure 3. The reordering grammar contains the parse grammar, plus the reordering-specific rules.

Initialization:

$$\frac{}{[S' \rightarrow \bullet S, q_0, q_0] : \overline{1}}$$

Inference rules:

$$\frac{[X \rightarrow \alpha \bullet x\beta, q, r] : u}{[X \rightarrow \alpha x \bullet \beta, q, \delta(r, x)] : u \otimes w(\delta(r, x))}$$

$$\frac{[X \rightarrow \alpha \bullet Y\beta, q, r]}{[Y \rightarrow \bullet\gamma, r, r] : u} \quad Y \xrightarrow{u} \gamma \in \mathcal{G}$$

$$\frac{[X \rightarrow \alpha \bullet Y\beta, q, s] : u \quad [Y \rightarrow \gamma\bullet, s, r] : v}{[X \rightarrow \alpha Y \bullet \beta, q, r] : u \otimes v}$$

Goal state:

$$[S' \rightarrow S\bullet, q_0, q_{\mathit{final}}]$$

Figure 5: Weighted logic program for computing the intersection of a weighted FSA and a weighted CFG.

latent variable in a probabilistic translation model. By doing this, we only require a parallel corpus of translations to learn the reordering model. Not only does this make our lives easier, since 'reference reorderings' are not necessary, but it is also intuitively satisfying because from a task perspective, we are not concerned with values of $\mathbf{f}'$, but only with producing a good translation $\mathbf{e}$.

3.1 A probabilistic translation model with a latent reordering variable

The translation model we use is a two phase process. First, source sentence $\mathbf{f}$ is reordered into a target-like word order $\mathbf{f}'$ according to a reordering model $r(\mathbf{f}'|\mathbf{f})$. The reordered source is then transduced into the target language according to a translation model $t(\mathbf{e}|\mathbf{f}')$. We require that $r(\mathbf{f}'|\mathbf{f})$ can be represented by a recursion-free probabilistic context-free grammar, i.e. a forest as in §2.1, and that $t(\mathbf{e}|\mathbf{f}')$ is represented by a (cyclic) finite-state transducer, as in Figure 2.

Since the reordering forest may define multiple derivations $\mathbf{a}$ from $\mathbf{f}$ to a particular $\mathbf{f}'$, and the transducer may define multiple derivations $\mathbf{d}$ from $\mathbf{f}'$ to a particular translation $\mathbf{e}$, we marginalize over these nuisance variables as follows to define the probability of a translation given the source:

$$p(\mathbf{e}|\mathbf{f}) = \sum_{\mathbf{d}} \sum_{\mathbf{f}'} t(\mathbf{e}, \mathbf{d}|\mathbf{f}') \sum_{\mathbf{a}} r(\mathbf{f}', \mathbf{a}|\mathbf{f}) \qquad (1)$$

Crucially, since we have restricted $r(\mathbf{f}'|\mathbf{f})$ to have the form of a weighted CFG and $t(\mathbf{e}|\mathbf{f}')$ to be an

orderings from word aligned parallel corpora, refer to Tromble and Eisner (2009).

FST, the quantity (1), which sums over all reorderings (and derivations), can be computed in polynomial time with dynamic programming composition, as described in §2.2.

3.2 Conditional training

While it is straightforward to use expectation maximization to optimize the joint likelihood of the parallel training data with a latent variable model, instead we use a log-linear parameterization and maximize conditional likelihood (Blunsom et al., 2008; Petrov and Klein, 2008). This enables us to employ a rich set of (possibly overlapping, non-independent) features to discriminate among translations. The probability of a derivation from source to reordered source to target is thus written in terms of model parameters $\Lambda = \{\lambda_i\}$ as:

$$p(\mathbf{e}, \mathbf{d}, \mathbf{f}', \mathbf{a}|\mathbf{f}; \Lambda) = \frac{\exp \sum_i \lambda_i \cdot H_i(\mathbf{e}, \mathbf{d}, \mathbf{f}', \mathbf{a}, \mathbf{f})}{Z(\mathbf{f}; \Lambda)}$$

$$\text{where } H_i(\mathbf{e}, \mathbf{d}, \mathbf{f}', \mathbf{a}, \mathbf{f}) = \sum_{r \in \mathbf{d}} h_i(\mathbf{f}', r) + \sum_{s \in \mathbf{a}} h_i(\mathbf{f}, s)$$

The derivation probability is globally normalized by the partition $Z(\mathbf{f}; \Lambda)$, which is just the sum of the numerator for all derivations of **f** (corresponding to any **e**). The H_i (written below without their arguments) are real-valued feature functions that may be overlapping and non-independent. For computational tractability, we assume that the feature functions H_i decompose with the derivations of $\mathbf{f}'$ and **e** in terms of *local* feature functions h_i. We also define $Z(\mathbf{e}, \mathbf{f}; \lambda)$ to be the sum of the numerator over all derivations that yield the sentence pair $\langle \mathbf{e}, \mathbf{f} \rangle$. Rather than training purely to optimize conditional likelihood, we also make use of a spherical Gaussian prior on the value of Λ with mean **0** and variance σ^2, which helps prevent overfitting of the model (Chen and Rosenfeld, 1998). Our objective is thus to select Λ minimizing:

$$\begin{aligned} \mathcal{L} &= -\log \prod_{\langle \mathbf{e}, \mathbf{f} \rangle} p(\mathbf{e}|\mathbf{f}; \Lambda) - \frac{||\Lambda||^2}{2\sigma^2} \\ &= -\sum_{\langle \mathbf{e}, \mathbf{f} \rangle} [\log Z(\mathbf{e}, \mathbf{f}; \Lambda) - \log Z(\mathbf{f}; \Lambda)] - \frac{||\Lambda||^2}{2\sigma^2} \end{aligned}$$

The gradient of $\mathcal{L}$ with respect to the feature weights has a parallel form; it is the difference in feature expectations under the reference distribution and the translation distribution with a penalty term due to the prior:

$$\frac{\partial \mathcal{L}}{\partial \lambda_i} = \sum_{\langle \mathbf{e}, \mathbf{f} \rangle} \mathbb{E}_{p(\mathbf{d}, \mathbf{a}|\mathbf{e}, \mathbf{f}; \Lambda)}[h_i] - \mathbb{E}_{p(\mathbf{e}, \mathbf{d}, \mathbf{a}|\mathbf{f}; \Lambda)}[h_i] - \frac{\lambda_i}{\sigma^2}$$

The form of the objective and gradient are quite similar to the traditional fully observed training scenario for CRFs (Sha and Pereira, 2003). However, rather than matching the feature expectations in the model to an observable feature value, we have to sum over the latent structure that remains after observing our target **e**, which makes the form of the first summand an expectation rather than just a feature function value.

3.2.1 Computing the objective and gradient

The objective and gradient that were just introduced can be computed in two steps. Given a training pair $\langle \mathbf{e}, \mathbf{f} \rangle$, we generate the forest of reorderings $\mathcal{F}$ from **f** as described in §2.1. We then compose this grammar with T, the FST representing the translation model, which yields $\mathcal{F} \circ T$, a translation forest that contains all possible translations of **f** into the target language, as described in §2.2. Running the inside algorithm on the translation forest computes $Z(\mathbf{f}; \Lambda)$, the first term in the objective, and the inside-outside algorithm can be used to compute $\mathbb{E}_{p(\mathbf{e}, \mathbf{d}, \mathbf{a}|\mathbf{f})}[h_i]$. Next, to compute $Z(\mathbf{e}, \mathbf{f}; \Lambda)$ and the first expectation in the gradient, we need to find the subset of the translation forest $\mathcal{F} \circ T$ that exactly derives the reference translation **e**. To do this, we again rely on the fact that $\mathcal{F} \circ T$ is a forest and therefore itself a context-free grammar. So, we use *this* grammar to parse the target reference string **e**. The resulting forest, $\mathcal{F} \circ T \circ \mathbf{e}$, contains all and only derivations that yield the pair $\langle \mathbf{e}, \mathbf{f} \rangle$. Here, the inside algorithm computes $Z(\mathbf{e}, \mathbf{f}; \Lambda)$ and the inside-outside algorithm can be used to compute $\mathbb{E}_{p(\mathbf{e}, \mathbf{d}, \mathbf{a}|\mathbf{f})}[h_i]$.

Once we have an objective and gradient, we can apply any first-order numerical optimization technique.[8] Although the conditional likelihood surface of this model is non-convex (on account of the latent variables), we did not find a significant initialization effect. For the experiments below, we initialized $\Lambda = \mathbf{0}$ and set $\sigma^2 = 1$. Training generally converged in fewer than 1500 function evaluations.

[8]For our experiments we used L-BFGS (Liu and Nocedal, 1989).

4 Experimental setup

We now turn to an experimental validation of the models we have introduced. We define three conditions: a small data scenario consisting of a translation task based on the BTEC Chinese-English corpus (Takezawa et al., 2002), a large data Chinese-English condition designed to be more comparable to conditions in a NIST MT evaluation, and a large data Arabic-English task.

For each condition, phrase tables were extracted as described in Koehn et al. (2003) with a maximum phrase size of 5. The parallel training data was aligned using the Giza++ implementation of IBM Model 4 (Och and Ney, 2003). The Chinese text was segmented using a CRF-based word segmenter (Tseng et al., 2005). The Arabic text was segmented using the technique described in Lee et al. (2003). The Stanford parser was used to generate source parses for all conditions, and these were then used to generate the reordering forests as described in §2.1.

Table 1 summarizes statistics about the corpora used. The reachability statistic indicates what percentage of sentence pairs in the training data could be regenerated using our reordering/translation model.[9] To train the reordering model, we used all of the reachable sentence pairs from BTEC, 20% of the reachable set in the Chinese-English condition, and all reachable sentence pairs under 40 words (source) in length in the Arabic-English condition.

Error analysis indicates that a substantial portion of unreachable sentence pairs are due to alignment (word or sentence) or parse errors; however, in some cases the reordering forests did not contain an adequate source reordering to produce the necessary target. For example, in Arabic, which is a VSO language, the treebank annotation is to place the subject NP as the 'middle child' between the V and the object constituent. This can be reordered into an English SVO order using our child-permutation rules; however, if the source VP is modified by a modal particle, the parser makes the particle the parent of the VP, and it is no longer possible to move the subject to the first position in the sentence. Richer reordering rules are needed to address this problem. Other solutions to the reachability problem include targeting reachable oracles instead of the reference translation (Li and Khudanpur, 2009) or making use of alternative training criteria, such as minimum risk training (Li and Eisner, 2009).

4.1 Features

We briefly describe the feature functions we used in our model. These include the typical dense features used in translation: relative phrase translation frequencies $p(\overline{e}|\overline{f})$ and $p(\overline{f}|\overline{e})$, 'lexically smoothed' translation probabilities $p_{lex}(\overline{e}|\overline{f})$ and $p_{lex}(\overline{f}|\overline{e})$, and a phrase count feature. For the reordering model, we used a binary feature for each kind of rule used, for example $\phi_{\mathrm{VP}\rightarrow\mathrm{V\ NP}}(\mathbf{a})$ would fire once for each time the rule VP $\rightarrow$ V NP was used in a derivation, **a**. For the Arabic-English condition, we observed that the parse trees tended to be quite flat, with many repeated non-terminal types in one rule, so we augmented the non-terminal types with an index indicating where they were located in the original parse tree. This resulted in a total of 6.7k features for IWSLT, 18k features for the large Chinese-English condition, and 516k features for Arabic-English.[10] A target language model was not used during the training of the source reordering model, but it was used during the translation experiments (see below).

4.2 Qualitative assessment of reordering model

Before looking at the translation results, we examine what the model learns during training. Figure 6 lists the 10 most highly weighted reordering features learned by the BTEC model (above) and shows an example reordering using this model (below), with the most English-like reordering indicated with a star.[11] Keep in mind, we expect these features to reflect what the best *English-like* order of the input should be. All are almost surprisingly intuitive, but this is not terribly surprising since Chinese and English have very similar large-scale structures (both are head initial, both have adjectives and quantifiers that precede nouns). However, we see two entries in the list (starred) that correspond to an En-

[9]Only sentences that can be generated by the model can be used in training.

[10]The large number of features in the Arabic system was due to the relative flatness of the Arabic parse trees.

[11]The italicized symbols in the English gloss are functional elements with no precise translation. Q is an interrogative particle, and DE marks a variety of attributive roles and is used here as the head of a relative clause.

Table 1: Corpus statistics

Condition	Sentences	Source words	Target words	Reachability
BTEC	44k	0.33M	0.36M	81%
Chinese-English	400k	9.4M	10.9M	25%
Arabic-English	120k	3.3M	3.6M	66%

glish word order that is ungrammatical in Chinese: PP modifiers in Chinese typically precede the VPs they modify, and CPs (relative clauses) also typically precede the nouns they modify. In English, the reverse is true, and we see that the model has indeed learned to prefer this ordering. It was not necessary that this be the case: since our model makes use of phrases memorized from a non-reordered training set, it could hav relied on those for all its reordering. Yet these results provide evidence that it is learning large-scale reordering successfully.

Feature	λ	note
VP $\rightarrow$ VE NP	0.995	
VP $\rightarrow$ VV VP	0.939	modal + VP
VP $\rightarrow$ VV NP	0.895	
VP $\rightarrow$ VP PP*	0.803	PP modifier of VP
VP $\rightarrow$ VV NP IP	0.763	
PP $\rightarrow$ P NP	0.753	
IP $\rightarrow$ NP VP PU	0.728	PU = punctuation
VP $\rightarrow$ VC NP	0.598	
NP $\rightarrow$ DP NP	0.538	
NP $\rightarrow$ NP CP*	0.537	rel. clauses follow

Input:

我 能 赶上 去 西尔顿 饭店 的 巴士 吗 ?

I CAN CATCH $[_{NP}[_{CP}$ GO HILTON HOTEL ***DE***] BUS] ***Q*** ?

(Can I catch a bus that goes to the Hilton Hotel ?)

5-best reordering:

I CAN CATCH $[_{NP}$ BUS $[_{CP}$ GO HILTON HOTEL ***DE***]] ***Q*** ?

★ I CAN CATCH $[_{NP}$ BUS $[_{CP}$ ***DE*** GO HILTON HOTEL]] ***Q*** ?

I CAN CATCH $[_{NP}$ BUS $[_{CP}$ GO HOTEL HILTON ***DE***]] ***Q*** ?

I CATCH $[_{NP}$ BUS $[_{CP}$ GO HILTON HOTEL ***DE***]] CAN ***Q*** ?

I CAN CATCH $[_{NP}$ BUS $[_{CP}$ ***DE*** GO HOTEL HILTON]] ***Q*** ?

Figure 6: (Above) The 10 most highly-weighted features in a Chinese-English reordering model. (Below) Example reordering of a Chinese sentence (with English gloss, translation, and partial syntactic information).

5 Translation experiments

We now consider how to apply this model to a translation task. The training we described in §3.2 is suboptimal for state-of-the-art translation systems, since (1) it optimizes likelihood rather than an MT metric and (2) it does not include a language model. We describe how we addressed these problems here, and then present our results in the three conditions defined above.

5.1 Training for Viterbi decoding

A language model was incorporated using cube pruning (Huang and Chiang, 2007), using a 200-best limit at each node during LM integration. To improve the ability of the phrase model to match reordered phrases, we extracted the 1-best reordering of the training data under the learned reordering model and generated the phrase translation model so that it contained phrases from both the original order and the 1-best reordering.

To be competitive with other state-of-the-art systems, we would like to use Och's minimum error training algorithm for training; however, we cannot tune the model as described with it, since it has far too many features. To address this, we converted the coefficients on the reordering features into a single reordering feature which then had a coefficient assigned to it. This technique is similar to what is done with logarithmic opinion pools, only the learned model is not a probability distribution (Smith et al., 2005). Once we collapsed the reordering weights into a single feature, we used the techniques described by Kumar et al. (2009) to optimize the feature weights to maximize corpus BLEU on a held-out development set.

5.2 Translation results

Scores on a held-out test set are reported in Table 2 using case-insensitive BLEU with 4 reference translations (16 for BTEC) using the original definition of the brevity penalty. We report the results of our model along with three baseline conditions, one with no-reordering at all (mono), the performance of a phrase-based translation model with distance-based distortion, the performance of our implementation of a hierarchical phrase-based translation model (Chiang, 2007), and then our model.

Table 2: Translation results (BLEU)

Condition	Mono	PB	Hiero	Forest
BTEC	47.4	51.8	52.4	**54.1**
Chinese-Eng.	29.0	30.9	32.1	**32.4**
Arabic-Eng.	41.2	45.8	**46.6**	44.9

6 Related work

A variety of translation processes can be formalized as the composition of a finite-state representation of input (typically just a sentence, but often a more complex structure, like a word lattice) with an SCFG (Wu, 1997; Chiang, 2007; Zollmann and Venugopal, 2006). Like these, our work uses parsing algorithms to perform the composition operation. But this is the first time that the *input* to a finite-state transducer has a context-free structure.[12] Although not described in terms of operations over formal languages, the model of Yamada and Knight (2001) can be understood as an instance of our class of models with a specific input forest and phrases restricted to match syntactic constituents.

In terms of formal similarity, Mi et al. (2008) use forests as input to a tree-to-string transducer process, but the forests are used to recover from 1-best parsing errors (as such, all derivations yield the same source string). Iglesias et al. (2009) use a SCFG-based translation model, but implement it using FSTs, although they use non-regular extensions that make FSTs equivalent to recursive transition networks. Galley and Manning (2008) use a context-free reordering model to score a phrase-based (exponential) search space.

Syntax-based preprocessing approaches that have relied on hand-written rules to restructure source trees for particular translation tasks have been quite widely used (Collins et al., 2005; Wang et al., 2007; Xu et al., 2009; Chang et al., 2009). Discriminatively trained reordering models have been extensively explored. A widely used approach has been to use a classifier to predict the orientation of phrases during decoding (Zens and Ney, 2006; Chang et al., 2009). These classifiers must be trained independently from the translation model using training examples extracted from the training data. A more ambitious approach is described by Tromble and Eisner (2009), who build a global reordering model that is learned automatically from reordered training data.

The latent variable discriminative training approach we describe is similar to the one originally proposed by Blunsom et al. (2008).

[12] Satta (submitted) discusses the theoretical possibility of this sort of model but provides no experimental results.

7 Discussion and conclusion

We have described a new model of translation that takes advantage of the strengths of context-free modeling, but splits reordering and phrase transduction into two separate models. This lets the context-free part handle what it does well, mid-to-long range reordering, and lets the finite-state part handle local phrasal correspondences. We have further shown that the reordering component can be trained effectively as a latent variable in a discriminative translation model using only conventional parallel training data.

This model holds considerable promise for future improvement. Not only does it already achieve quite reasonable performance (performing particularly well in Chinese-English, where mid-range reordering is often required), but we have only begun to scratch the surface in terms of the kinds of features that can be included to predict reordering, as well as the kinds of reordering forests used. Furthermore, by reintroducing the concept of a cascade of transducers into the context-free model space, it should be possible to develop new and more effective rescoring mechanisms. Finally, unlike SCFG and phrase-based models, our model does not impose any distortion limits.

Acknowledgements

The authors gratefully acknowledge partial support from the GALE program of the Defense Advanced Research Projects Agency, Contract No. HR0011-06-2-001. Any opinions, findings, conclusions or recommendations expressed in this paper are those of the authors and do not necessarily reflect the views of the sponsors. Thanks to Hendra Setiawan, Vlad Eidelman, Zhifei Li, Chris Callison-Burch, Brian Dillon and the anonymous reviewers for insightful comments.

References

P. Blunsom, T. Cohn, and M. Osborne. 2008. A discriminative latent variable model for statistical machine translation. In *Proceedings of ACL-HLT*.

P.-C. Chang, D. Jurafsky, and C. D. Manning. 2009. Disambiguating "DE" for Chinese-English machine translation,. In *Proc. WMT*.

S. F. Chen and R. Rosenfeld. 1998. A Gaussian prior for smoothing maximum entropy models. Technical Report TR-10-98, Computer Science Group, Harvard University.

D. Chiang. 2007. Hierarchical phrase-based translation. *Computational Linguistics*, 33(2):201–228.

M. Collins, P. Koehn, and I. Kucerova. 2005. Clause restructuring for statistical machine translation. In *Proceedings of ACL 2005*.

J. Earley. 1970. An efficient context-free parsing algorithm. *Communications of the Association for Computing Machinery*, 13(2):94–102.

M. Galley and C. D. Manning. 2008. A simple and effective hierarchical phrase reordering model. In *Proc. EMNLP*.

D. Grune and C. J. H. Jacobs. 2008. Parsing as intersection. In D. Gries and F. B. Schneider, editors, *Parsing Techniques*, pages 425–442. Springer, New York.

J. E. Hopcroft and J. D. Ullman. 1979. *Introduction to Automata Theory, Languages and Computation*. Addison-Wesley.

L. Huang and D. Chiang. 2007. Forest rescoring: Faster decoding with integrated language models. In *ACL*.

G. Iglesias, A. de Gispert, E. R. Banga, and W. Byrne. 2009. Hierarchical phrase-based translation with weighted finite state transducers. In *Proc. NAACL*.

P. Koehn, F. Och, and D. Marcu. 2003. Statistical phrase-based translation. In *Proc. of NAACL*, pages 48–54.

S. Kumar, Y. Deng, and W. Byrne. 2006. A weighted finite state transducer translation template model for statistical machine translation. *Journal of Natural Language Engineering*, 12(1):35–75.

S. Kumar, W. Macherey, C. Dyer, and F. Och. 2009. Efficient minimum error rate training and minimum Bayes-risk decoding for translation hypergraphs and lattices. In *Proc. ACL*.

Y.-S. Lee, K. Papineni, S. Roukos, O. Emam, and H. Hassan. 2003. Language model based Arabic word segmentation. In *Proc. ACL*.

Z. Li and J. Eisner. 2009. First- and second-order expectation semirings with applications to minimum-risk training on translation forests. In *Proc. EMNLP*.

Z. Li and S. Khudanpur. 2009. Efficient extraction of oracle-best translations from hypergraphs. In *Proc. NAACL*.

D. C. Liu and J. Nocedal. 1989. On the limited memory BFGS method for large scale optimization. *Mathematical Programming B*, 45(3):503–528.

H. Mi, L. Huang, and Q. Liu. 2008. Forest-based translation. In *Proceedings of ACL-08: HLT*, pages 192–199, Columbus, Ohio, June. Association for Computational Linguistics.

F. Och and H. Ney. 2003. A systematic comparison of various statistical alignment models. *Computational Linguistics*, 29(1):19–51.

S. Petrov and D. Klein. 2008. Discriminative log-linear grammars with latent variables. In *Advances in Neural Information Processing Systems 20 (NIPS)*, pages 1153–1160.

G. Satta. submitted. Translation algorithms by means of language intersection.

F. Sha and F. Pereira. 2003. Shallow parsing with conditional random fields. In *Proceedings of HLT-NAACL*, pages 213–220.

A. Smith, T. Cohn, and M. Osborne. 2005. Logarithmic opinion pools for conditional random fields. In *Proc. ACL*.

T. Takezawa, E. Sumita, F. Sugaya, H. Yamamoto, and S. Yamamoto. 2002. Toward a broad-coverage bilingual corpus for speech translation of travel conversations in the real world. In *Proceedings of LREC 2002*, pages 147–152, Las Palmas, Spain.

R. Tromble and J. Eisner. 2009. Learning linear order problems for better translation. In *Proceedings of EMNLP 2009*.

H. Tseng, P. Chang, G. Andrew, D. Jurafsky, and C. Manning. 2005. A conditional random field word segmenter. In *Fourth SIGHAN Workshop on Chinese Language Processing*.

C. Wang, M. Collins, and P. Koehn. 2007. Chinese syntactic reordering for statistical machine translation. In *Proc. EMNLP*.

D. Wu. 1997. Stochastic inversion transduction grammars and bilingual parsing of parallel corpora. *Computational Linguistics*, 23(3):377–404.

P. Xu, J. Kang, M. Ringgaard, and F. Och. 2009. Using a dependency parser to improve SMT for subject-object-verb languages. In *Proc. NAACL*, pages 245–253.

K. Yamada and K. Knight. 2001. A syntax-based statistical translation model. In *Proc. ACL*.

R. Zens and H. Ney. 2006. Discriminative reordering models for statistical machine translation. In *Proc. of the Workshop on SMT*.

A. Zollmann and A. Venugopal. 2006. Syntax augmented machine translation via chart parsing. In *Proc. of the Workshop on SMT*.

A. Zollmann, A. Venugopal, F. Och, and J. Ponte. 2008. A systematic comparison of phrase-based, hierarchical and syntax-augmented statistical MT. In *Proc. Coling*.

Improved Models of Distortion Cost for Statistical Machine Translation

Spence Green, Michel Galley, and **Christopher D. Manning**
Computer Science Department
Stanford University
Stanford, CA 94305
{spenceg,mgalley,manning}@stanford.edu

Abstract

The distortion cost function used in Moses-style machine translation systems has two flaws. First, it does not estimate the future cost of known required moves, thus increasing search errors. Second, all distortion is penalized linearly, even when appropriate re-orderings are performed. Because the cost function does not effectively constrain search, translation quality decreases at higher distortion limits, which are often needed when translating between languages of different typologies such as Arabic and English. To address these problems, we introduce a method for estimating future linear distortion cost, and a new discriminative distortion model that predicts word movement during translation. In combination, these extensions give a statistically significant improvement over a baseline distortion parameterization. When we triple the distortion limit, our model achieves a +2.32 BLEU average gain over Moses.

1 Introduction

It is well-known that translation performance in Moses-style (Koehn et al., 2007) machine translation (MT) systems deteriorates when high distortion is allowed. The *linear distortion cost model* used in these systems is partly at fault. It includes no estimate of future distortion cost, thereby increasing the risk of search errors. Linear distortion also penalizes all re-orderings equally, even when appropriate re-orderings are performed. Because linear distortion, which is a soft constraint, does not effectively constrain search, a *distortion limit* is imposed on the translation model. But hard constraints are ultimately undesirable since they prune the search space. For languages with very different word orders in which significant re-ordering is required, the distortion limit can eliminate the *oracle*, or "best," translation prior to search, placing an artificial limit on translation performance (Auli et al., 2009).

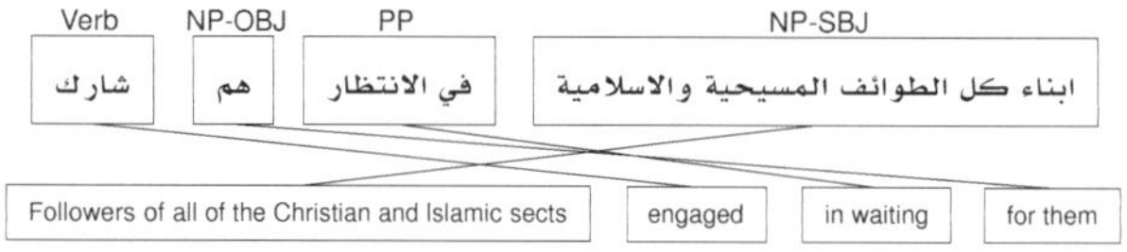

Figure 1: The oracle translation for this Arabic VOS sentence would be pruned during search using typical distortion parameters. The Arabic phrases read right-to-left, but we have ordered the sentence from left-to-right in order to clearly illustrate the re-ordering problem.

To illustrate this problem, consider the Arabic-English example in Figure 1. Assuming that the English translation is constructed left-to-right, the verb شارك *shaaraka* must be translated after the noun phrase (NP) subject. If P phrases are used to translate the Arabic source s to the English target t, then the (unsigned) linear distortion is given by

$$D(s,t) = p^1_{first} + \sum_{i=2}^{P} \left| p^{i-1}_{last} + 1 - p^i_{first} \right| \quad (1)$$

where p_{first} and p_{last} are the first and last source word indices, respectively, in phrase i. By this formula, the cost of the step to translate the NP subject before the verb is 9, which is high relative to the monotone translation path. Moreover, a conventional distortion limit (e.g., 5) would likely force translation of the verb prior to the full subject unless the exact subject phrase existed in the phrase table.[1] Therefore, the correct re-ordering is either improbable or impossible, depending on the choice of distortion parameters.

[1] Our constrained NIST MT09 Arabic-English system, which placed second, used a limit of 5 (Galley et al., 2009).

Human Language Technologies: The 2010 Annual Conference of the North American Chapter of the ACL, pages 867–875,
Los Angeles, California, June 2010.

The objective of this work is to develop a distortion cost model that allows the distortion limit to be raised significantly without a catastrophic decrease in performance. We first describe an admissible future cost heuristic for linear distortion that restores baseline performance at high distortion limits. Then we add a feature-rich discriminative distortion model that captures e.g. the tendency of Arabic verbs to move right during translation to English. Model parameters are learned from automatic bitext alignments. Together these two extensions allow us to triple the distortion limit in our NIST MT09 Arabic-English system while maintaining a statistically significant improvement over the low distortion baseline. At the high distortion limit, we also show a +2.32 BLEU average gain over Moses with an equivalent distortion parameterization.

2 Background

2.1 Search in Phrase-based MT

Given a J token source input string $\boldsymbol{f} = \{f_i^J\}$, we seek the most probable I token translation $\boldsymbol{e} = \{e_i^I\}$. The Moses phrase-based decoder models the posterior probability $p_\lambda\left(e_1^I | f_1^J\right)$ directly according to a log-linear model (Och and Ney, 2004), which gives the decision rule

$$\hat{e} = \arg\max_{I,e_1^I} \left\{ \sum_{m=1}^{M} \lambda_m h_m\left(e_1^I, f_1^J\right) \right\}$$

where $h_m\left(e_1^I, f_1^J\right)$ are M arbitrary feature functions over sentence pairs, and λ_m are feature weights set using a discriminative training method like MERT (Och, 2003). This search is made tractable by the use of beams (Koehn et al., 2003). Hypotheses are pruned from the beams according the sum of the current model score and a future cost estimate for the uncovered source words. Since the number of reordering possibilities for those words is very large—in theory it is exponential—an inadmissible heuristic is typically used to estimate future cost. The baseline distortion cost model is a weighted feature in this framework and affects beam pruning only through the current model score.

When we say *linear distortion*, we refer to the "simple distortion model" of Koehn et al. (2003) that is shown in Equation (1) and is converted to a cost by multiplying by -1. When extended to phrases, the key property of this model is that monotone decoding gives the least costly translation path. Reorderings internal to extracted phrases are not penalized. In practice, we commonly see n-best lists of hypotheses with linear distortion costs equal to zero. More sophisticated local phrase re-ordering models have been proposed (Tillmann, 2004; Zens and Ney, 2006; Koehn et al., 2007; Galley and Manning, 2008), but these are typically used in addition to linear distortion.

2.2 Arabic Linguistic Essentials

In this paper we use Arabic-English as a case study since we possess a strong experimental baseline. But we expect that the technique presented could be even more effective for high distortion language pairs such as Chinese-English and Hindi-English. Since the analysis that follows is framed in terms of Arabic, we point out several linguistic features that motivate our approach. From the perspective of the three criteria used to specify basic word order typology (Greenberg, 1966), Arabic is somewhat unusual in its combination of features: it has prepositions (not postpositions), adjectives post-modify nouns, and the basic word order is VSO, but SVO and VOS configurations also appear.

The implications for translation to English are: (1) prepositions remain in place, (2) NPs are inverted, and most importantly, (3) basic syntactic constituents must often be identified and precisely re-ordered. The VOS configuration is especially challenging for Arabic-English MT. It usually appears when the direct object is short—e.g., pronominal—and the subject is long. For example, translation of the VOS sentence in Figure 1 requires both a high distortion limit to accommodate the subject movement and tight restrictions on the movement of the PP. The particularity of these requirements in Arabic and other languages, and the difficulty of modeling them in phrase-based systems, has inspired significant work in source language preprocessing (Collins et al., 2005; Habash and Sadat, 2006; Habash, 2007).

Finally, we observe that target language models cannot always select appropriate translations when basic word order transformation is required. By not modeling source side features like agreement—which, in Arabic, appears between both verb and

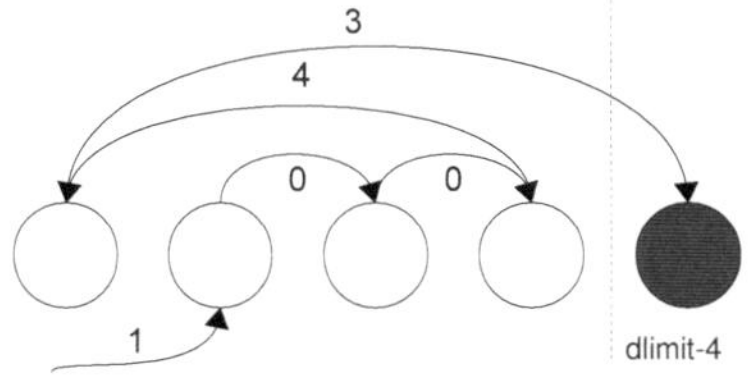

step k	F_k	Δ_{cost}	$D(s,t)$	$D(s,t) + \Delta_{cost}$
0	3	3	1	4
1	5	2	0	2
2	7	2	0	2
3	0	−7	4	−3
4	0	0	3	3
			8	**8**

Figure 2: Translation sequence in which the distortion limit is reached and the decoder is forced to cover the first skipped word. Future cost estimation penalizes the two monotone steps, yet total distortion cost remains unchanged.

subject, and adjective and noun—baseline phrase-based systems rely on the language model to specify an appropriate target word order (Avramidis and Koehn, 2008). Returning to Figure 1, we could have an alternate hypothesis *They waited for the followers of the Christian and Islamic sects*, which is acceptable English and has low distortion, but is semantically inconsistent with the Arabic.

	dlimit = 5	dlimit = 15
LINEAR	51.65	**49.35**
DEGREE 1.5	**51.69 (+0.04)**	48.73 (−0.62)
DEGREE 2	51.55 (−0.10)	48.40 (−0.95)

Table 1: BLEU-4 [%] dev set (MT04) scores (uncased) for several polynomial distortion models. Higher degree polynomial distortion models underperform at a high distortion limit (15).

3 The Cost Model

In this section we describe the new distortion cost model, which has four independent components.

3.1 Future Cost Estimation

Despite its lack of sophistication, linear distortion is a surprisingly effective baseline cost model for phrase-based MT systems. It can be computed in constant time, gives non-decreasing values that are good for search, and does not require an ancillary feature to adjust for the number of components in the calculation (e.g., language model scores are adjusted by the word penalty). Moreover, when a large training bitext is used, many local re-orderings are captured in the phrase table, so the decoder can often realize competitive performance by finding a best set of phrases with low distortion. But linear distortion is not the only unlexicalized alternative: we can use any function of the jump width. Table 1 shows development set (MT04) performance for polynomials of degree 1.5 and degree 2. The linear model is more effective than the higher order functions, especially at a higher distortion limit.

Nevertheless, Table 1 shows an unacceptable decrease in translation performance at the high distortion limit for all three polynomial models. In Moses, the reason is due in part to a dramatic underestimation of future re-ordering cost. Consider Figure 2 in which a distortion limit of 4 is used. The first word is skipped, and translation proceeds monotonically until the distortion limit forces the decoder to cover the first word. At low distortion limits, single phrases often saturate the distortion window, so underestimation is not problematic. But at high distortion limits, the decoder can skip many source positions at low cost before the search is constrained by the distortion limit. Words and phrases sprinkled carelessly throughout the hypotheses are evidence of errant search directions that have not been appropriately penalized by the distortion cost model.

To constrain search, we add an admissible future cost estimate to the linear model.[2] By definition, the model has a least cost translation path: monotone. Therefore, we can add to the baseline calculation $D(s,t)$ the cost of skipping back to the first uncovered source word and then translating the remaining positions monotonically. It can be verified by induction on $|\boldsymbol{C}|$ that this is an admissible heuristic.

Formally, let j represent the first uncovered index in the source coverage set $\boldsymbol{C}$. Let $\boldsymbol{C}_j$ represent the subset of $\boldsymbol{C}$ starting from position j. Finally, let j' represent the leftmost position in phrase p applied at translation step k. Then the future cost estimate F_k

[2]Moore and Quirk (2007) propose an alternate future cost formulation. However, their model seems prone to the same deterioration in performance shown in Table 1. They observed decreased translation quality above a distortion limit of 5.

is

$$F_k = \begin{cases} |C_j| + (j' + |p| + 1 - j) & \text{if } j' > j \\ 0 & \text{otherwise} \end{cases}$$

For $k > 0$, we add the difference between the current future cost estimate and the previous cost estimate $\Delta_{cost} = F_k - F_{k-1}$ to the linear penalty $D(s,t)$.[3] Table 2 shows that, as expected, the difference between the baseline and augmented models is statistically insignificant at a low distortion limit. However, at a very high distortion limit, the future cost estimate approximately restores baseline performance. While we still need a distortion limit for computational efficiency, it is no longer required to improve translation quality.

	dlimit = 5	dlimit = 15
BASELINE	51.65	49.35
FUTURECOST	51.73	51.65

Table 2: BLEU-4 [%] dev set scores (uncased) for the linear distortion with future cost estimation.

3.2 A Discriminative Distortion Model

So far, we have developed a search heuristic function that gives us a greater ability to control search at high distortion limits. Now we need a cost model that is sensitive to the behavior of certain words during translation. The model must accommodate a potentially large number of overlapping source-side features defined over the (possibly whole) translation sequence. Since we intend to train on automatic word alignments, data sparsity and noise are also risks. These requirements motivate two choices. First, we use a discriminative log-linear framework that predicts one of the nine discretized distortion classes in Figure 3. Let $d_{j,j'}$ indicate the class corresponding to a jump from source word j to j' computed as $(j+1-j')$. The discriminative distortion classifier is then

$$p_\lambda\left(d_{j,j'} | f_1^J, j, j'\right) = \frac{\exp\left[\sum_{m=1}^{M} \lambda_m h_m\left(f_1^J, j, j', d_{j,j'}\right)\right]}{\sum_{d^i_{j,j'}} \exp\left[\sum_{m=1}^{M} \lambda_m h_m\left(f_1^J, j, j', d^i_{j,j'}\right)\right]}$$

where λ_m are feature weights for the $h_m(f_1^J, j, j', d^i_{j,j'})$ arbitrary feature functions. This log conditional objective function is convex and can be optimized with e.g. a gradient-based procedure.

[3]One implementation choice is to estimate future cost to an artificial end-of-sentence token. Here the decoder incurs a penalty for covering the last word prior to completing a hypothesis. Although this implementation is inconsistent with Moses linear distortion, we find that it gives a small improvement.

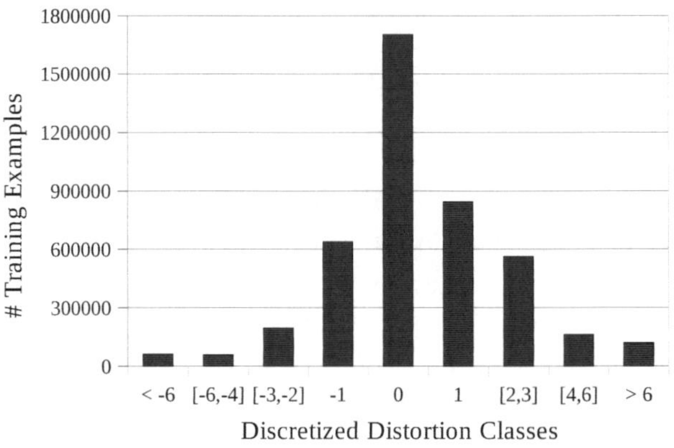

Figure 3: Distortion in Arabic-English translation is largely monotonic, but with noticeable right movement as verbs move around arguments and nouns around modifiers. The ability to predict movement decreases with the jump size, hence the increasing bin boundaries.

Second, we expect that many words will not be useful for predicting translation order.[4] In a large training bitext, it can be extremely tedious to identify informative words and word classes analytically. Our final decision is then to optimize the parameter weights λ_m using L_1 regularization (Andrew and Gao, 2007), a technique that can learn good models in the presence of many irrelevant features.[5] The L_1 regularizer saves us from filtering the training data (e.g., by discarding all words that appear less than an empirically-specified threshold), and provides sparse feature vectors that can be analyzed separately during feature engineering.

We train two independent distortion models. For a transition from source word j to j', we learn an *outbound* model in which features are defined with respect to word j. We have a corresponding *inbound*

[4]To train the models, we inverted and sorted the intersection alignments in the bitext. In our baseline system, we observed no decrease in performance between intersection and e.g. grow-diag. However we do expect that our method could be extended to multi-word alignments.

[5]We also add a Gaussian prior $p(\lambda) \backsim \mathcal{N}(0,1)$ to the objective (Chen and Rosenfeld, 1999). Using both L_1 and L_2 regularization is mathematically odd, but often helps in practice.

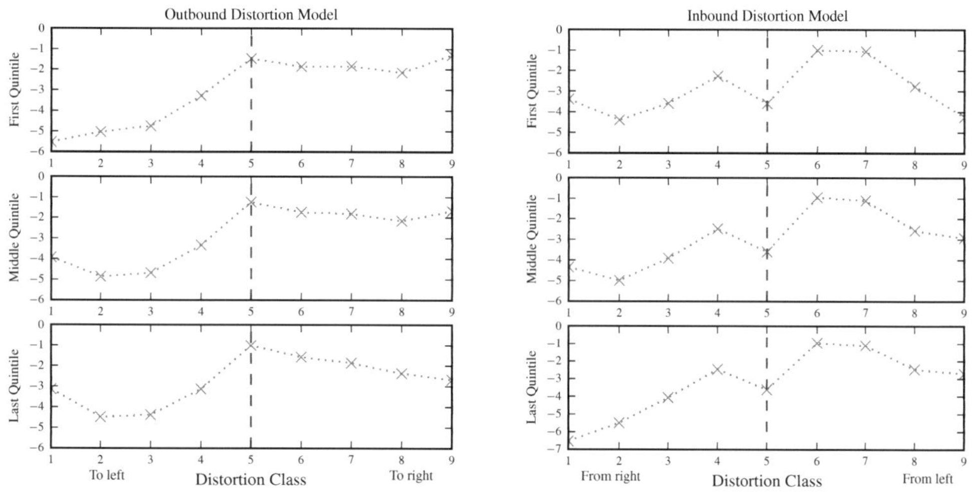

(a) شارك / VBD *shaaraka* ("he engaged") (b) الامريكي / JJ *al-aamriikii* ("American")

Figure 4: Selected discriminative cost curves (log scale) over three quintiles of the relative position feature. We condition on the word, POS, and length features. The classes correspond to those shown in Figure 3. (4a) The VSO basic word order is evident: early in the sentence, there is a strong tendency towards right movement around arguments after covering the verb. However, right movement is increasingly penalized at the end of the sentence. (4b) Adjectives post-modify nouns, so the model learns high inbound probabilities for jumps from positions earlier in the sentence. However, the curve is bi-modal reflecting right inbound moves from other adjectives in NPs with multiple modifiers.

model trained on features with respect to j'. At training time, we also add sentence beginning and ending delimiters such that inbound probabilities are learned for words that begin sentences (e.g., nouns) and outbound probabilities are available for tokens that end sentences (e.g., punctuation).

As a baseline, we use the following binary features: words, part-of-speech (POS) tags, relative source sentence position, and source sentence length. Relative source sentence position is discretized into five bins, one for each quintile of the sentence. Source sentence length is divided into four bins with bounds set empirically such that training examples are distributed evenly. To simplify the decoder integration for this evaluation, we have chosen context-free features, but the framework permits many other promising possibilities such as agreement morphology and POS tag chains.

Our models reveal principled cost curves for specific words (Figure 4). However, monotonic decoding no longer gives the least costly translation path, thus complicating future cost estimation. We would need to evaluate all possible re-orderings within the k-word distortion window. For an input sentence of length n, Zens (2008) shows that the number of re-ordering possibilities r_n is

$$r_n = \begin{cases} k^{n-k} \cdot k! & n > k \\ n! & n \leq k \end{cases}$$

which has an asymptotic complexity $\Theta(k^n)$. Instead of using an inadmissible heuristic as is done in beam pruning, we take a shortcut: we include the linear future cost model as a separate feature. Then we add the two discriminative distortion features, which calculate the inbound and outbound log probabilities of the word alignments in a hypothesis. Since hypotheses may have different numbers of alignments, we also include an alignment penalty that adjusts the discriminative distortion scores for unaligned source words. The implementation and behavior of the alignment penalty is analogous to that of the word penalty. In total, the new distortion cost model has four independent MT features.

4 MT Evaluation

4.1 Experimental Setup

Our MT system is Phrasal (Cer et al., 2010), which is a Java re-implementation of the Moses

dlimit = 5	MT03	MT05	MT06	MT08	Avg
MOSESLINEAR	52.31	52.67	42.97	41.29	
COUNTS	52.05	52.32	42.28	40.56	
FUTURE	52.26 (−0.05)	52.53 (−0.14)	43.04 (+0.07)	41.01 (−0.28)	−0.09
DISCRIM+FUTURE	**52.68* (+0.37)**	**53.13* (+0.46)**	**43.75** (+0.78)**	**41.82** (+0.53)**	+0.59

Table 3: BLEU-4 [%] scores (uncased) at the distortion limit (5) used in our baseline NIST MT09 Arabic-English system (Galley et al., 2009). **Avg** is a weighted average of the performance deltas. The stars for positive results indicate statistical significance compared to the MOSESLINEAR baseline (*: significance at $p \leq 0.05$; **: significance at $p \leq 0.01$)

dlimit = 15	MT03	MT05	MT06	MT08	Avg
MOSESLINEAR	51.04	51.35	41.01	38.83	
COUNTS	49.92	49.73	39.44	37.65	
LEX	50.96	51.21	41.87	39.38	
FUTURE	52.28** (+1.24)	52.45** (+1.10)	42.78** (+1.77)	41.01** (+2.18)	+1.66
DISCRIM+FUTURE	**52.36** (+1.32)**	**53.05** (+1.70)**	**43.65** (+2.64)**	**41.68** (+2.85)**	+2.32
num. sentences	*663*	*1056*	*1797*	*1360*	*4876*

Table 4: BLEU-4 [%] scores (uncased) at a very high distortion limit (15). DISCRIM+FUTURE also achieves a statistically significant gain over the MOSESLINEAR dlimit=5 baseline for MT05 ($p \leq 0.06$), MT06 ($p \leq 0.01$), and MT08 ($p \leq 0.01$).

decoder with the same standard features: four translation features (phrase-based translation probabilities and lexically-weighted probabilities), word penalty, phrase penalty, linear distortion, and language model score. We disable baseline linear distortion when evaluating the other distortion cost models. To tune parameters, we run MERT with the Downhill Simplex algorithm on the MT04 dataset. For all models, we use 20 random starting points and generate 300-best lists.

We use the NIST MT09 constrained track training data, but remove the UN and comparable data.[6] The reduced training bitext has 181k aligned sentences with 6.20M English and 5.73M Arabic tokens. We create word alignments using the Berkeley Aligner (Liang et al., 2006) and take the intersection of the alignments in both directions. Phrase pairs with a maximum target or source length of 7 tokens are extracted using the method of Och and Ney (2004).

We build a 5-gram language model from the Xinhua and AFP sections of the Gigaword corpus (LDC2007T40), in addition to all of the target side training data permissible in the NIST MT09 constrained competition. We manually remove Gigaword documents that were released during periods that overlapped with the development and test sets. The language model is smoothed with the modified Kneser-Ney algorithm, retaining only trigrams, 4-grams, and 5-grams that occurred two, three, and three times, respectively, in the training data.

We remove from the test sets source tokens not present in the phrase tables. For the discriminative distortion models, we tag the pre-processed input using the log-linear POS tagger of Toutanova et al. (2003). After decoding, we strip any punctuation that appears at the beginning of a translation.

4.2 Results

In Table 3 we report uncased BLEU-4 (Papineni et al., 2001) scores at the distortion limit (5) of our most competitive baseline Arabic-English system. MOSESLINEAR uses the linear distortion model present in Moses. COUNTS is a separate baseline with a discrete cost model that uses unlexicalized maximum likelihood estimates for the same classes present in the discriminative model. To show the effect of the components in our combined distortion model, we give separate results for linear distortion with future cost estimation (FUTURE) and for the combined discriminative distortion model (DISCRIM+FUTURE) with all four features: linear distortion with future cost, inbound and outbound proba-

[6]Removal of the UN data does not affect the baseline at a distortion limit of 5, and lowers the higher distortion baseline by −1.40 BLEU. The NIST MT09 data is available at http://www.itl.nist.gov/iad/mig/tests/mt/2009/.

Ar	NP-OBJ NP-TMP NP-SBJ Verb تولي الهولندي ياب دي هوب شيفر اليوم الاثنين مهامه
Reference	dutch national jaap de hoop scheffer today, monday, took up his responsibilities...
MosesLinear-d5	over dutchman jaap de hoop today , monday , in the post of...
MosesLinear-d15	dutch assumed his duties in the post of nato secretary general jaap de hoop today , monday...
Discrim+Future	the dutchman jaap de hoop today , monday , assumed his duties...

Figure 5: Verb movement around both the subject and temporal NPs is impossible at a distortion limit of 5 (MOSESLINEAR-d5). The baseline system at a high distortion limit mangles the translation (MOSESLINEAR-d15). DISCRIM+FUTURE (dlimit=15) correctly guides the search. The Arabic source is written right-to-left.

bilities, and the alignment penalty.

The main objective of this paper is to improve performance at very high distortion limits. Table 4 shows performance at a distortion limit of 15. To the set of baselines we add LEX, which is the lexicalized re-ordering model of Galley and Manning (2008). This model was shown to outperform other lexicalized re-ordering models in common use.

Statistical significance was computed with the approximate randomization test of Riezler and Maxwell (2005), which is less sensitive to Type I errors than bootstrap re-sampling (Koehn, 2004).

5 Discussion

The new distortion cost model allows us to triple the distortion limit while maintaining a statistically significant improvement over the MOSESLINEAR baseline at the lower distortion limit for three of the four test sets. More importantly, we can raise the distortion limit in the DISCRIM+FUTURE configuration at minimal cost: a statistically insignificant -0.2 BLEU performance decrease on average. We also see a considerable improvement over both the MOSESLINEAR and LEX baselines at the high distortion limit (Figure 5). As expected, future cost estimation alone does not increase performance at the lower distortion limit.

We also observe that the effect of conditioning on evidence is significant: the COUNTS model is categorically worse than all other models. To understand why, we randomly sampled 500 sentences from the excluded UN data and computed the log-likelihoods of the alignments according to the different models.[7] In this test, COUNTS is clearly better with a score of -23388 versus, for example, the inbound model at -38244. The explanation is due in part to optimization. The two discriminative models often give very low probabilities for the outermost classes. Noise in the alignments along with the few cases of long-distance movement are penalized heavily. For Arabic, this property works in our favor as we do not want extreme movement (as we might with Chinese or German). But COUNTS applies a uniform penalty for all movement that exceeds the outermost class boundaries, making it more prone to search errors than even linear distortion despite its favorable performance when tested in isolation.

Finally, we note that previous attempts to improve re-ordering during search (particularly long-distance re-ordering (Chiang, 2007)) have delivered remarkable gains for languages like Chinese, but improvements for Arabic have been less exceptional. By relaxing the distortion limit, we have left room for more sophisticated re-ordering models in conventional phrase-based decoders while maintaining a significant performance advantage over hierarchical systems (Marton and Resnik, 2008).

6 Prior Work

There is an expansive literature on re-ordering in statistical MT. We first review the development of re-ordering constraints, then describe previous cost models for those constraints in beam search decoders. Because we allow re-ordering during search, we omit discussion of the many different methods for preprocessing the source input prior to monotonic translation. Likewise, we do not recite prior work in re-ranking translations.

Re-ordering constraints were first introduced by Berger et al. (1996) in the context of the IBM translation models. The *IBM constraints* treat the source

[7] We approximated linear distortion using a Laplacian distribution with estimated parameters $\hat{\mu} = 0.51$ and $\hat{b} = 1.76$ (Goodman, 2004).

word sequence as a coverage set $\boldsymbol{C}$ that is processed sequentially. A source token is "covered" when it is aligned with a new target token. For a fixed value of k, we may leave up to $k - 1$ positions uncovered and return to them later. We can alter the constraint slightly such that for the first uncovered position $u \notin \boldsymbol{C}$ we can cover position j when

$$j - u < k \qquad j \notin \boldsymbol{C}$$

which is the definition of the distortion limit used in Moses. Variations of the IBM constraints also exist (Kanthak et al., 2005), as do entirely different regimes like the hierarchical *ITG constraints*, which represent the source as a sequence of blocks that can be iteratively merged and inverted (Wu, 1996). Zens and Ney (2003) exhaustively compare the IBM and ITG constraints, concluding that although the ITG constraints permit more flexible re-orderings, the IBM constraints result in higher BLEU scores.

Since our work falls under the IBM paradigm, we consider cost models for those constraints. We have said that linear distortion is the simplest cost model. The primary criticism of linear distortion is that it is unlexicalized, thus penalizing all re-orderings equally (Khalilov et al., 2009). When extended to phrases as in Equation (1), linear distortion is also agnostic to internal phrase alignments.

To remedy these deficiencies, Al-Onaizan and Papineni (2006) proposed a lexicalized, generative distortion model. Maximum likelihood estimates for inbound, outbound, and pairwise transitions are computed from automatic word alignments. But no estimate of future cost is included, and their model cannot easily accommodate features defined over the entire translation sequence. As for experimental results, they use a distortion limit that is half of what we report, and compare against a baseline that lacks a distortion model entirely. Neither their model nor ours requires generation of lattices prior to search (Zhang et al., 2007; Niehues and Kolss, 2009).

Lexicalized re-ordering models are the other significant approach to re-ordering. These models make local predictions about the next phrase to be translated during decoding, typically assigning costs to one of three categories: *monotone*, *swap*, or *discontinuous*. Both generative (Tillmann, 2004; Och and Ney, 2004; Koehn et al., 2007) and discriminative training (Tillmann and Zhang, 2005; Zens and Ney, 2006; Liang et al., 2006) algorithms have been proposed. Recently, Galley and Manning (2008) introduced a hierarchical model capable of analyzing alignments beyond adjacent phrases. Our discriminative distortion framework is not designed as a replacement for lexicalized re-ordering models, but as a substitute for linear distortion.

Finally, we comment on differences between our Arabic-English results and the well-known high distortion system of Zollmann et al. (2008), who find optimal baseline performance at a distortion limit of 9. First, they use approximately two orders of magnitude more training data, which allows them to extract much longer phrases (12 tokens v. our maximum of 7). In this setting, many Arabic-English re-orderings can be captured in the phrase table. Second, their "Full" system uses three language models each trained with significantly more data than our single model. Finally, although they use a lexicalized re-ordering model, no details are given about the baseline distortion cost model.

7 Conclusion

We have presented a discriminative cost framework that both estimates future distortion cost and learns principled cost curves. The model delivers a statistically significant +2.32 BLEU improvement over Moses at a high distortion limit. Unlike previous discriminative local orientation models (Zens and Ney, 2006), our framework permits the definition of global features. The evaluation in this paper used context-free features to simplify the decoder integration, but we expect that context-dependent features could result in gains for other language pairs with more complex re-ordering phenomena.

Acknowledgements

We thank the three anonymous reviewers and Daniel Cer for constructive comments, and Claude Reichard for editorial assistance. The first author is supported by a National Defense Science and Engineering Graduate (NDSEG) fellowship. This paper is based on work supported in part by the Defense Advanced Research Projects Agency through IBM. The content does not necessarily reflect the views of the U.S. Government, and no official endorsement should be inferred.

References

Y Al-Onaizan and K Papineni. 2006. Distortion models for statistical machine translation. In *ACL*.

G Andrew and J Gao. 2007. Scalable training of L1-regularized log-linear models. In *ICML*.

M Auli, A Lopez, H Hoang, and P Koehn. 2009. A systematic analysis of translation model search spaces. In *WMT*.

E Avramidis and P Koehn. 2008. Enriching morphologically poor languages for statistical machine translation. In *ACL*.

A Berger, P Brown, S Della Pietra, V Della Pietra, A Kehler, and R Mercer. 1996. Language translation apparatus and method using context-based translation models. *US Patent 5,510,981*.

D Cer, M Galley, D Jurafsky, and C D Manning. 2010. Phrasal: A statistical machine translation toolkit for exploring new model features. In *NAACL, Demonstration Session*.

S Chen and R Rosenfeld. 1999. A Gaussian prior for smoothing maximum entropy models. Technical Report CMU-CS-99-10S, Carnegie Mellon University.

D Chiang. 2007. Hierarchical phrase-based translation. *Computational Linguistics*, 33(2):201–228.

M Collins, P Koehn, and I Kucerova. 2005. Clause restructuring for statistical machine translation. In *ACL*.

M Galley and C D Manning. 2008. A simple and effective hierarchical phrase reordering model. In *EMNLP*.

M Galley, S Green, D Cer, P-C Chang, and C D Manning. 2009. Stanford University's Arabic-to-English statistical machine translation system for the 2009 NIST evaluation. Technical report, Stanford University.

J Goodman. 2004. Exponential priors for maximum entropy models. In *NAACL*.

JH Greenberg, 1966. *Some universals of grammar with particular reference to the order of meaningful elements*, pages 73–113. London: MIT Press.

N Habash and F Sadat. 2006. Arabic preprocessing schemes for statistical machine translation. In *NAACL*.

N Habash. 2007. Syntactic preprocessing for statistical machine translation. In *MT Summit XI*.

S Kanthak, D Vilar, E Matusov, R Zens, and H Ney. 2005. Novel reordering approaches in phrase-based statistical machine translation. In *ACL Workshop on Building and Using Parallel Texts*.

M Khalilov, J A R Fonollosa, and M Dras. 2009. Coupling hierarchical word reordering and decoding in phrase-based statistical machine translation. In *SSST*.

P Koehn, F J Och, and D Marcu. 2003. Statistical phrase-based translation. In *NAACL*.

P Koehn, H Hoang, A Birch, C Callison-Burch, M Federico, N Bertoldi, B Cowan, W Shen, C Moran, R Zens, C Dyer, O Bojar, A Constantin, and E Herbst. 2007. Moses: Open source toolkit for statistical machine translation. In *ACL, Demonstration Session*.

P Koehn. 2004. Statistical significance tests for machine translation evaluation. In *EMNLP*.

P Liang, B Taskar, and D Klein. 2006. Alignment by agreement. In *NAACL*.

Y Marton and P Resnik. 2008. Soft syntactic constraints for hierarchical phrased-based translation. In *ACL*.

R C Moore and C Quirk. 2007. Faster beam-search decoding for phrasal statistical machine translation. In *MT Summit XI*.

J Niehues and M Kolss. 2009. A POS-based model for long-range reorderings in SMT. In *WMT*.

F J Och and H Ney. 2004. The alignment template approach to statistical machine translation. *Computational Linguistics*, 30:417–449.

F J Och. 2003. Minimum error rate training for statistical machine translation. In *ACL*.

K Papineni, S Roukos, T Ward, and W-J Zhu. 2001. BLEU: a method for automatic evaluation of machine translation. In *ACL*.

S Riezler and J T Maxwell. 2005. On some pitfalls in automatic evaluation and significance testing in MT. In *ACL Workshop on Intrinsic and Extrinsic Evaluation Measures for Machine Translation and/or Summarization (MTSE'05)*.

C Tillmann and T Zhang. 2005. A localized prediction model for statistical machine translation. In *ACL*.

C Tillmann. 2004. A unigram orientation model for statistical machine translation. In *NAACL*.

K Toutanova, D Klein, C D Manning, and Y Singer. 2003. Feature-rich part-of-speech tagging with a cyclic dependency network. In *NAACL*.

D Wu. 1996. A polynomial-time algorithm for statistical machine translation. In *ACL*.

R Zens and H Ney. 2003. A comparative study on reordering constraints in statistical machine translation. In *ACL*.

R Zens and H Ney. 2006. Discriminative reordering models for statistical machine translation. In *WMT*.

R Zens. 2008. *Phrase-based Statistical Machine Translation: Models, Search, Training*. Ph.D. thesis, RWTH Aachen University.

Y Zhang, R Zens, and H Ney. 2007. Chunk-level reordering of source language sentences with automatically learned rules for statistical machine translation. In *SSST*.

A Zollmann, A Venugopal, F J Och, and J Ponte. 2008. A systematic comparison of phrase-based, hierarchical and syntax-augmented statistical MT. In *COLING*.

Why Synchronous Tree Substitution Grammars?

Andreas Maletti
Universitat Rovira i Virgili, Departament de Filologies Romàniques
Avinguda de Catalunya 35, 43002 Tarragona, Spain
andreas.maletti@urv.cat

Abstract

Synchronous tree substitution grammars are a translation model that is used in syntax-based machine translation. They are investigated in a formal setting and compared to a competitor that is at least as expressive. The competitor is the extended multi bottom-up tree transducer, which is the bottom-up analogue with one essential additional feature. This model has been investigated in theoretical computer science, but seems widely unknown in natural language processing. The two models are compared with respect to standard algorithms (binarization, regular restriction, composition, application). Particular attention is paid to the complexity of the algorithms.

1 Introduction

Every machine translation system uses a translation model, which is a formal model that describes the translation process. Either this system is hand-crafted (in rule-based translation systems) or it is trained with the help of statistical processes. Brown et al. (1990) discuss automatically trainable translation models in their seminal paper on the latter approach. The IBM models of Brown et al. (1993) are string-based in the sense that they base the translation decision on the words and the surrounding context. In the field of syntax-based machine translation, the translation models have access to the syntax (in the form of parse trees) of the sentences. Knight (2007) presents a good exposition to both fields.

In this paper, we focus on syntax-based translation models, and in particular, synchronous tree substitution grammars (STSGs), or the equally powerful (linear and nondeleting) extended (top-down) tree transducers of Graehl et al. (2008). Chiang and Knight (2006) gives a good introduction to STSGs, which originate from the syntax-directed translation schemes of Aho and Ullman (1972) [nowadays more commonly known as synchronous context-free grammars]. Roughly speaking, an STSG has rules in which a nonterminal is replaced by two trees containing terminal and nonterminal symbols. In addition, the nonterminals in the two trees are linked and a rule is only applied to linked nonterminals.

Several algorithms for STSGs have been discussed in the literature. For example, we can

- train them [see Graehl et al. (2008)],
- attempt to binarize them using the methods of (Zhang et al., 2006; Huang et al., 2009; DeNero et al., 2009b),
- parse them [see DeNero et al. (2009a)], or
- attempt to compose them.

However, some important algorithms are partial because it is known that the construction might not be possible in general. This is the case, for example, for binarization and composition.

In the theoretical computer science community, alternative models have been explored. Such a model is the multi bottom-up tree transducer (MBOT) of Arnold and Dauchet (1982) and Lilin (1981), which essentially is the bottom-up analogue of STSGs with the additional feature that nonterminals can have an arbitrary rank (the rank of a nonterminal of an STSG can be considered to be fixed to 1). This model is even more expressive than STSGs, but still offers good computational properties. In this contribution, we will compare STSGs and MBOTs with respect to some standard algorithms. Generally, MBOTs offer algorithmic benefits over STSG, which can be summarized as fol-

Human Language Technologies: The 2010 Annual Conference of the North American Chapter of the ACL, pages 876–884,
Los Angeles, California, June 2010.

lows:

- Every STSG can be transformed into an equivalent MBOT in linear time.
- MBOTs can be fully binarized in linear time whereas only partial binarizations (or asynchronous binarizations) are possible for STSGs.
- The input language of an MBOT M can be regularly restricted in $\mathcal{O}(|M| \cdot |S|^3)$, whereas the corresponding construction for an STSG M is in $\mathcal{O}(|M| \cdot |S|^{2\,\mathrm{rk}(M)+5})$ where $\mathrm{rk}(M)$ is the maximal number of nonterminals in a rule of the STSG M.
- MBOTs can be composed, whereas this cannot be achieved for STSGs.

Overall, we thus conclude that, from an algorithmic perspective, it would be beneficial to work with MBOTs instead of STSGs. However, the full power of MBOTs should not be tapped because, in general, MBOTs have the finite-copying property [see Engelfriet et al. (1980)], which complicates the algorithms for forward and backward application (see Section 7).

2 Preliminary definitions

An *alphabet* is a finite set of symbols. Our weighted devices use real-number weights, but the results translate easily to the more general setting of commutative semirings [see Golan (1999)]. A *weighted string automaton* as in Schützenberger (1961) and Eilenberg (1974) is a system (S, Γ, I, τ, F) where

- S and Γ are alphabets of states and input symbols, respectively,
- $I, F \colon S \to \mathbb{R}$ assign initial and final weights, respectively, and
- $\tau \colon S \times \Gamma \times S \to \mathbb{R}$ assigns a weight to each transition.

Let $w = \gamma_1 \cdots \gamma_k \in \Gamma^*$ be an input string of length k. A *run* on w is $r \colon \{0, \dots, k\} \to S$. The *weight* of the run r is $\mathrm{wt}(r) = \prod_{i=1}^{k} \tau(r_{i-1}, \gamma_i, r_i)$. The semantics of the automaton A then assigns to w the weight

$$A(w) = \sum_{r \text{ run on } w} I(r_0) \cdot \mathrm{wt}(r) \cdot F(r_k) \enspace .$$

A good introduction to weighted string automata can be found in Mohri (2009) and Sakarovitch (2009).

To simplify the theoretical discussion, we assume that each symbol that we use in trees has a fixed rank, which determines the number of children of each node with that label. A *ranked alphabet* $\Sigma = \bigcup_{k \geq 0} \Sigma_k$ is an alphabet whose symbols have assigned ranks. The set Σ_k contains all symbols of rank k. The set $T_\Sigma(V)$ of Σ-*trees* indexed by a set V is the smallest set such that $V \subseteq T_\Sigma(V)$ and $\sigma(t_1, \dots, t_k) \in T_\Sigma(V)$ for every $\sigma \in \Sigma_k$ and $t_1, \dots, t_k \in T_\Sigma(V)$. The size $|t|$ of the tree $t \in T_\Sigma$ is the number of occurrences of symbols from $\Sigma \cup V$ that appear in t. A context c is a tree of $T_{\Sigma \cup \{\Box\}}(V)$, in which the nullary symbol $\Box$ occurs exactly once. The set of all such contexts is $C_\Sigma(V)$. The tree $c[t]$ is obtained from c by replacing the symbol $\Box$ by t.

A *weighted synchronous tree substitution grammar* (STSG) is a system $(N, \Sigma, \Delta, I, P)$ where

- N is an alphabet of nonterminals,
- Σ and Δ are ranked alphabets of input and output symbols, respectively,
- $I \colon N \to \mathbb{R}$ assigns initial weights, and
- P is a finite set of productions $n \colon t \overset{a}{\leftrightarrow} u$ with $n \in N$, $t \in T_\Sigma(N)$, $a \in \mathbb{R}$, and $u \in T_\Delta(N)$ such that
  - every $n' \in N$ that occurs in t occurs exactly once in u and vice versa, and
  - $t \notin N$ or $u \notin N$.

Note that our distinction between nonterminals and terminals is rather uncommon for STSG [see Chiang (2005)], but improves the generative power. We chose the symbol "$\leftrightarrow$" because STSG productions are symmetric. The size $|n \colon t \overset{a}{\leftrightarrow} u|$ of a production is $|t| + |u|$, and the size $|M|$ of the STSG M is $\sum_{p \in P} |p|$. It is a *weighted tree substitution grammar* (TSG) if $t = u$ for all productions $n \colon t \overset{a}{\leftrightarrow} u \in P$. Further, it is in *normal form* if for every production $n \colon t \overset{a}{\leftrightarrow} u \in P$ there exist $\sigma \in \Sigma_k$, $\delta \in \Delta_k$, and nonterminals $n_1, \dots, n_k, n'_1, \dots, n'_k \in N$ such that $t = \sigma(n_1, \dots, n_k)$ and $u = \delta(n'_1, \dots, n'_k)$. A detailed exposition to STSGs and STSGs in normal form (also called synchronous context-free grammars) can be found in Chiang (2005). Further details on TSGs can be found in Berstel and Reutenauer (1982) and Fülöp and Vogler (2009).

Equal nonterminals in t and u of a production $n \colon t \overset{a}{\leftrightarrow} u \in P$ are *linked*. To keep the presentation simple, we assume that those links are re-

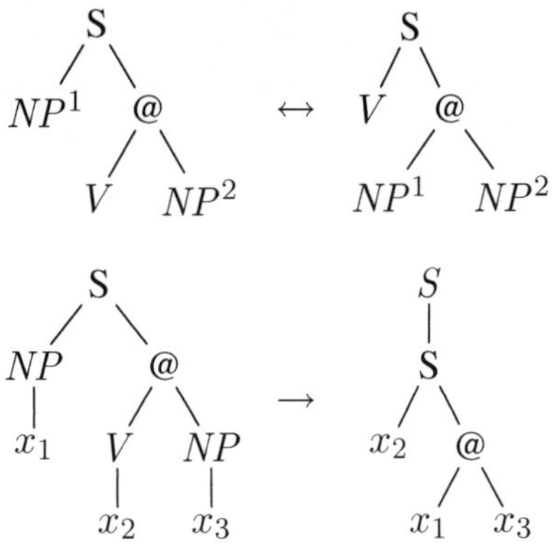

Figure 1: STSG production (top) and corresponding MBOT rule (bottom) where @ is an arbitrary symbol that is introduced during binarization.

membered also in sentential forms. In addition, we assume that $N \cap \Sigma = \emptyset$. For every $c, c' \in C_\Sigma(N)$ and $n \in N$, let $(c[n], c'[n]) \stackrel{a}{\Rightarrow} (c[t], c'[u])$ if

- there is a production $n \colon t \stackrel{a}{\leftrightarrow} u \in P$, and
- the explicit (the ones replacing $\Box$) occurrences of n in $c[n]$ and $c'[n]$ are linked.

Left-most derivations are defined as usual, and the weight of a derivation $D \colon \xi_0 \stackrel{a_1}{\Rightarrow} \cdots \stackrel{a_k}{\Rightarrow} \xi_k$ is $\mathrm{wt}(D) = \prod_{i=1}^{k} a_i$. The weight assigned by the grammar M to a pair $(t, u) \in T_\Sigma \times T_\Delta$ is

$$M(t, u) = \sum_{n \in N} I(n) \cdot \sum_{\substack{D \text{ left-most derivation} \\ \text{from } (n,n) \text{ to } (t,u)}} \mathrm{wt}(D) \enspace .$$

The second restriction on productions ensures that derivations are of finite length, and thus that the sums in the definition of $M(t, u)$ are finite.

In the following, we will use syntactic simplifications such as

- several occurrences of the same nonterminal in a tree (disambiguated by decoration).
- symbols that are terminals (of Σ and Δ) and nonterminals. We will print nonterminals in italics and terminal symbols upright.
- omission of the nonterminal n (or the weight a) of a rule $n \colon t \stackrel{a}{\leftrightarrow} u$ if the terminal n occurs at the root of t and u (or $a = 1$).
- $n \stackrel{a}{\rightarrow} t$ instead of $n \colon t \stackrel{a}{\leftrightarrow} t$ if it is a TSG.

A sample STSG production (using those simplifications) is displayed in Figure 1. Our STSGs are essentially equivalent to the (nondeleting and linear) extended tree transducers of Graehl et al. (2008) and Maletti et al. (2009).

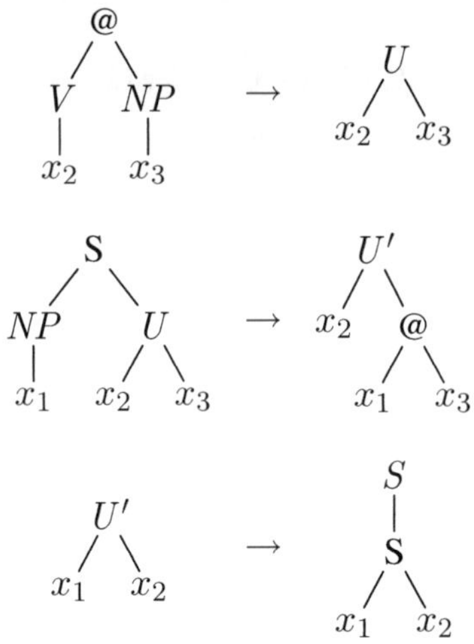

Figure 2: Sample MBOT rules in one-symbol normal form.

3 Multi bottom-up tree transducers

As indicated in the Introduction, we will compare STSGs to weighted multi bottom-up tree transducers, which have been introduced by Arnold and Dauchet (1982) and Lilin (1981). A more detailed (and English) presentation can be found in Engelfriet et al. (2009). Let us quickly recall the formal definition. We use a fixed set $X = \{x_1, x_2, \dots\}$ of (formal) variables. For a ranked alphabet S and $L \subseteq T_\Sigma(X)$ we let

$$S(L) = \{s(t_1, \dots, t_k) \mid s \in S_k, t_1, \dots, t_k \in L\}$$

and we treat elements of $S(L)$ like elements of $T_{\Sigma \cup S}(X)$.

Definition 1 *A weighted multi bottom-up tree transducer (MBOT) is a system $(S, \Sigma, \Delta, F, R)$ where*

- *S, Σ, and Δ are ranked alphabets of states, input symbols, and output symbols, respectively,*
- *$F \colon S_1 \to \mathbb{R}$ assigns final weights, and*
- *R is a finite set of rules $l \stackrel{a}{\rightarrow} r$ where $a \in \mathbb{R}$, $l \in T_\Sigma(S(X))$, and $r \in S(T_\Delta(X))$ such that*
  - *every $x \in X$ that occurs in l occurs exactly once in r and vice versa, and*
  - *$l \notin S(X)$ or $r \notin S(X)$.*

Roughly speaking, an MBOT is the bottom-up version of an extended top-down tree transducer, in which the states can have a rank different from 1. We chose the symbol "$\rightarrow$" because rules have a distinguished left- and right-hand side. The size $|l \stackrel{a}{\rightarrow} r|$ of

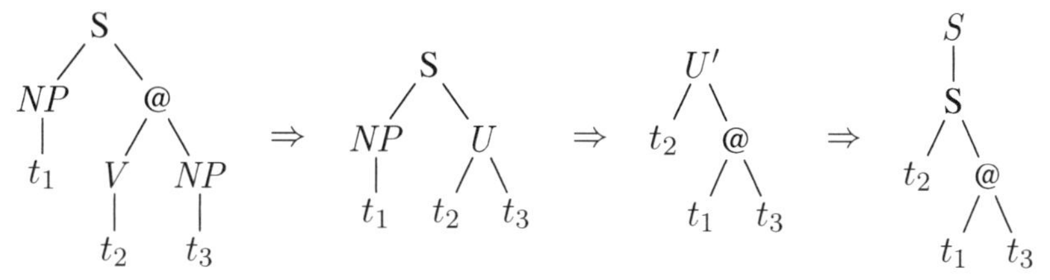

Figure 3: Derivation using the MBOT rules of Fig. 2.

a rule is $|l| + |r|$, and the size $|M|$ of an MBOT M is $\sum_{r \in R} |r|$. Again the second condition on the rules will ensure that derivations will be finite. Let us continue with the rewrite semantics for the MBOT $(S, \Sigma, \Delta, F, R)$. To simplify the presentation, we again assume that $S \cap (\Sigma \cup \Delta) = \emptyset$. We need the concept of substitution. Let $\theta\colon X \to T_\Delta$ and $t \in T_\Delta(X)$. Then $t\theta$ is the tree obtained by replacing every occurrence of $x \in X$ in t by $\theta(x)$.

Definition 2 *Let $c \in C_\Sigma(S(X))$ and $\theta\colon X \to T_\Delta$. Then $c[l\theta] \overset{a}{\Rightarrow} c[r\theta]$ if $l \overset{a}{\to} r \in R$. The weight of a derivation $D\colon \xi_0 \overset{a_1}{\Rightarrow} \cdots \overset{a_k}{\Rightarrow} \xi_k$ is $\mathrm{wt}(D) = \prod_{i=1}^{k} a_i$. The weight assigned by the MBOT M to a pair $(t, u) \in T_\Sigma \times T_\Delta$ is*

$$M(t,u) = \sum_{s \in S_1} F(s) \cdot \sum_{\substack{D \text{ left-most derivation} \\ \text{from } t \text{ to } s(u)}} \mathrm{wt}(D) \ .$$

We use the simplifications already mentioned in the previous section also for MBOTs. Figures 1 and 2 display example rules of an MBOT. The rules of Figure 2 are applied in a derivation in Figure 3. The first displayed derivation step uses the context $\mathrm{S}(NP(t_1), \square)$ and any substitution θ such that $\theta(x_2) = t_2$ and $\theta(x_3) = t_3$.

It is argued by Chiang (2005) and Graehl et al. (2008) that STSGs (and extended tree transducers) have sufficient power for syntax-based machine translation. Knight (2007) presents a detailed overview that also mentions short-comings. Since our newly proposed device, the MBOT, should be at least as powerful as STSGs, we quickly demonstrate how each STSG can be coded as an MBOT. An STSG production and the corresponding MBOT rule are displayed in Figure 1. Since the correspondence is rather trivial, we omit a formal definition.

Theorem 3 *For every STSG M, an equivalent MBOT can be constructed in time $\mathcal{O}(|M|)$.*

4 Binarization

Whenever nondeterminism enters the playfield, binarization becomes an important tool for efficiency reasons. This is based on the simple, yet powerful observation that instead of making 5 choices from a space of n in one instant (represented by n^5 rules), it is more efficient (Wang et al., 2007) to make them one-by-one (represented by $5n$ rules). Clearly, this cannot always be done but positive examples exist in abundance; e.g., binarization of context-free grammars [see CHOMSKY normal form in Hopcroft and Ullman (1979)].

Binarization of tree language devices typically consists of two steps: (i) binarization of the involved trees (using the auxiliary symbol @) and (ii) adjustment (binarization) of the processing device to work on (and fully utilize) the binarized trees. If successful, then this leads to binarized derivation trees for the processing device. In Figure 4 we show the binarization of the trees in an STSG production. Another binarization of the rule of Figure 4 is displayed in Figure 1. The binarization is evident enough, so we can assume that all trees considered in the following are binarized.

The binarization in Figure 1 is unfortunate because the obtained production cannot be factorized such that only two nonterminals occur in each rule. However, the binarization of Figure 4 allows the factorization into $\mathrm{S}(U, NP) \leftrightarrow \mathrm{S}(U, NP)$ and $U\colon @(NP, V) \leftrightarrow @(V, NP)$, which are fully binarized productions. However, in general, STSGs (or SCFGs or extended tree transducers) cannot be fully binarized as shown in Aho and Ullman (1972).

Zhang et al. (2006) and Wang et al. (2007) show the benefits of fully binarized STSGs and present a linear-time algorithm for the binarization of *binarizable* STSGs. We show that those benefits can be reaped for *all* STSGs by a simple change of model.

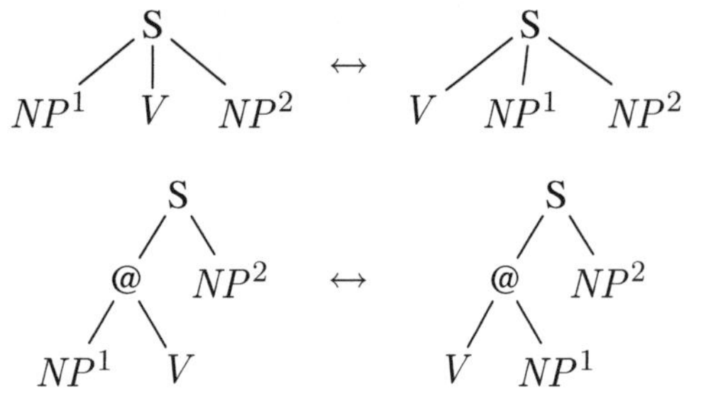

Figure 4: Binarization of trees in an STSG production. Top: Original — Bottom: Binarized trees.

We have already demonstrated that every STSG can be transformed into an equivalent MBOT in linear time. Next, we discuss binarization of MBOTs.

An MBOT is in *one-symbol normal form* if there is at most one input and at most one output symbol, but at least one symbol in each rule (see Figure 2). Raoult (1993) and Engelfriet et al. (2009) prove that every MBOT can be transformed into one-symbol normal form. The procedure presented there runs in linear time in the size of the input MBOT. Consequently, we can transform each STSG to an equivalent MBOT in one-symbol normal form in linear time. Finally, we note that a MBOT in one-symbol normal form has binarized derivation trees, which proves that we fully binarized the STSG.

Theorem 4 *For every STSG M an equivalent, fully binarized MBOT can be constructed in $\mathcal{O}(|M|)$.*

The construction of Engelfriet et al. (2009) is illustrated in Figure 2, which shows the rules of an MBOT in one-symbol normal form. Those rules are constructed from the unlucky binarization of Figure 1. In the next section, we show the benefit of the full binarization on the example of the BAR-HILLEL construction.

5 Input and output restriction

A standard construction for transformation devices (and recognition devices alike) is the regular restriction of the input or output language. This construction is used in parsing, integration of a language model, and the computation of certain metrics [see Nederhof and Satta (2003), Nederhof and Satta (2008), and Satta (2010) for a detailed account]. The construction is generally known as BAR-HILLEL construction [see Bar-Hillel et al. (1964) for the original construction on context-free grammars].

STSGs (and extended tree transducers) are symmetric, so that input and output can freely be swapped. Let M be an STSG and A a weighted string automaton with states S. In the BAR-HILLEL construction for M and A, the maximal rank $\mathrm{rk}(M)$ of a symbol in the derivation forest of M enters as an exponent into the complexity $\mathcal{O}(|M| \cdot |S|^{2\,\mathrm{rk}(M)+5})$. Since full binarization is not possible in general, the maximal rank cannot be limited to 2. In contrast, full binarization is possible for MBOTs (with only linear overhead), so let us investigate whether we can exploit this in a BAR-HILLEL construction for MBOTs.

Let $M = (S, \Sigma, \Delta, F, R)$ be an MBOT in one-symbol normal form. The symbols in $\Sigma \cup \Delta$ have rank at most 2. Moreover, let $G = (N, \Sigma, \Sigma, I, P)$ be a TSG in normal form. We want to construct an MBOT M' such that $M'(t, u) = M(t, u) \cdot G(t)$ for every $t \in T_\Sigma$ and $u \in T_\Delta$. In other words, each input tree should be rescored according to G; in the unweighted case this yields that the translation of M is filtered to the set of input trees accepted by G.

We occasionally write the pair (a, b) in angled parentheses ('$\langle$' and '$\rangle$'). In addition, we use the center line ellipsis '$\cdot\cdot$' (also with decoration) like a variable (especially for sequences).

Definition 5 *The input product $\mathrm{Prod}(M, G)$ is the MBOT $\mathrm{Prod}(M, G) = (S \times N, \Sigma, \Delta, F', R')$ where*

- *$F'(\langle s, n\rangle) = F(s) \cdot I(n)$ for every $s \in S$ and $n \in N$,*
- *for every rule $s(\cdot\cdot) \xrightarrow{a} s'(\cdot\cdot')\in R$ with $s, s' \in S$ and every $n \in N$, there exists a rule*

$$\langle s, n\rangle(\cdot\cdot) \xrightarrow{a} \langle s', n\rangle(\cdot\cdot') \in R' \ ,$$

- *for every rule $\sigma(s_1(\cdot\cdot_1), \dots, s_k(\cdot\cdot_k)) \xrightarrow{a} s(\cdot\cdot)$ in R with $\sigma \in \Sigma_k$ and $s, s_1, \dots, s_k \in S$, and every production $n \xrightarrow{b} \sigma(n_1, \dots, n_k) \in P$, the following rule is in R':*

$$\sigma(\langle s_1, n_1\rangle(\cdot\cdot_1), \dots, \langle s_k, n_k\rangle(\cdot\cdot_k)) \xrightarrow{ab} \langle s, n\rangle(\cdot\cdot) \ .$$

The first type of rule (second item) does not involve an input symbol, and thus the nonterminal of G is just forwarded to the new state. Since no step with respect to G is made, only the weight of the rule of M is charged. The second type of rule (third item) uses a rule of R with the input symbol σ

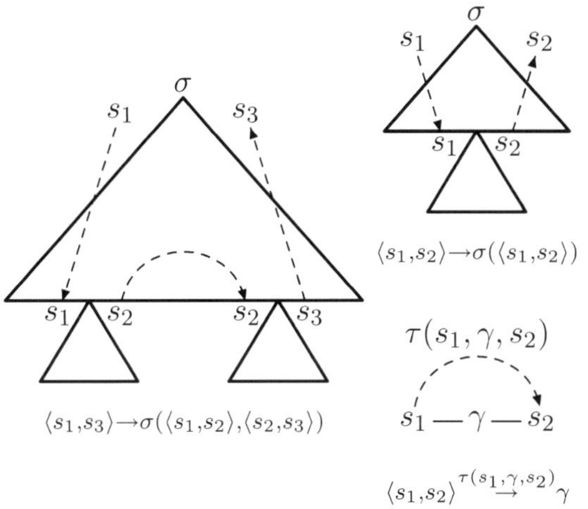

Figure 5: Constructing a TSG from a weighted string automaton.

and a production of P that also contains σ. The rule and the production are executed in parallel in the resulting rule and its weight is thus the product of the weights of the original rule and production. Overall, this is a classical product construction, which is similar to other product constructions such as Borchardt (2004). A straightforward proof shows that $M'(t, u) = M(t, u) \cdot G(t)$ for every $t \in T_\Sigma$ and $u \in T_\Delta$, which proves the correctness.

Next, let us look at the complexity. The MBOT $\mathrm{Prod}(M, G)$ can be obtained in time $\mathcal{O}(|M| \cdot |G|)$. Furthermore, it is known [see, for example, Maletti and Satta (2009)] that for every weighted string automaton A with states S, we can construct a TSG G in normal form, which has size $\mathcal{O}(|\Sigma| \cdot |S|^3)$ and recognizes each tree of T_Σ with the weight that the automaton A assigns to its yield. The idea of this construction is illustrated in Figure 5. Consequently, our BAR-HILLEL construction has the well-known complexity $\mathcal{O}(|M| \cdot |S|^3)$. This should be compared to the complexity of the corresponding construction for an STSG M, which is in $\mathcal{O}(|M| \cdot |S|^{2\,\mathrm{rk}(M)+5})$ where $\mathrm{rk}(M)$ is the maximal number of (different) nonterminals in a production of M. Thus, the STSG should be transformed into an equivalent MBOT in one-symbol normal form, which can be achieved in linear time, and the BAR-HILLEL construction should be performed on this MBOT.

Since STSGs are symmetric, our approach can also be applied to the output side of an STSG. However, it should be noted that we can apply it only to one side (the input side) of the MBOT. A construction for the output side of the MBOT can be defined, but it would suffer from a similarly high complexity as already presented for STSGs. More precisely, we expect a complexity of roughly $\mathcal{O}(|M| \cdot |S|^{2\,\mathrm{rk}(M)+2})$ for this construction. The small gain is due to the one-symbol normal form and binarization.

6 Composition

Another standard construction for transformations is (relational) composition. Composition constructs a translation from a language L to L'' given translations from L to L' and from L' to L''. Formally, given transformations $M' \colon T_\Sigma \times T_\Delta \to \mathbb{R}$ and $M'' \colon T_\Delta \times T_\Gamma \to \mathbb{R}$, the composition of M' and M'' is a tranformation $M' \,;\, M'' \colon T_\Sigma \times T_\Gamma \to \mathbb{R}$ with

$$(M' \,;\, M'')(t, v) = \sum_{u \in T_\Delta} M'(t, u) \cdot M''(u, v)$$

for every $t \in T_\Sigma$ and $v \in T_\Gamma$. Mind that the summation might be infinite, but we will only consider compositions, in which it is finite.

Unfortunately, Arnold and Dauchet (1982) show that the composition of two transformations computed by STSGs cannot necessarily be computed by an STSG. Consequently, there cannot be a general composition algorithm for STSGs.

Let us consider the problem of composition for MBOTs. Essentially, we will follow the unweighted approach of Engelfriet et al. (2009) to obtain a composition construction, which we present next. Let

$$M' = (S', \Sigma, \Delta, F', R') \quad \text{and}$$
$$M'' = (S'', \Delta, \Gamma, F'', R'')$$

be MBOTs in one-symbol normal form. We extend the rewrite semantics (see Definition 2) to trees that include symbols foreign to a MBOT. In other words, we (virtually) extend the input and output alphabets to contain all used symbols (in particular also the states of another MBOT). However, since we do not extend the set of rules, the MBOT cannot process foreign symbols. Nevertheless it can perform rewrite steps on known symbols (or apply rules that do not contain input symbols). We use $\Rightarrow_{R'}$ and $\Rightarrow_{R''}$ for derivation steps

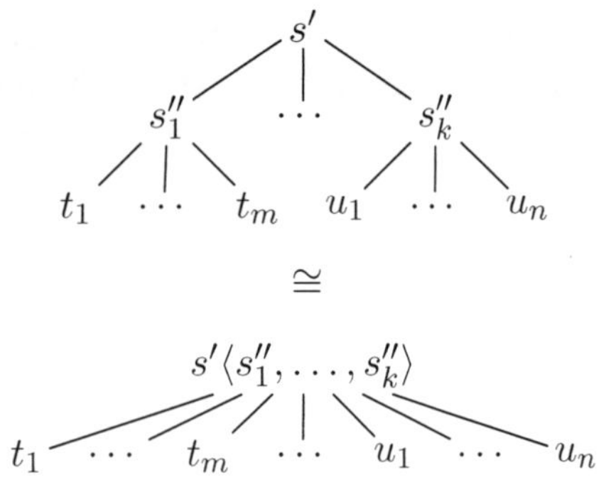

Figure 6: Identification in sentential forms.

that exclusively use rules of R' and R'', respectively. In addition, we identify $s'(s''_1(\cdot\cdot_1), \ldots, s''_k(\cdot\cdot_k))$ with $s'\langle s''_1, \ldots, s''_k \rangle(\cdot\cdot_1, \ldots, \cdot\cdot_k)$ for $s' \in S'$ and $s''_1, \ldots, s''_k \in S''$. This identification is illustrated in Figure 6.

Definition 6 *The MBOT $M' \,;M'' = (S, \Sigma, \Gamma, F, R)$ is such that*

- *for every $s' \in S'_k$ and $s''_1 \in S''_{\ell_1}, \ldots, s''_k \in S''_{\ell_k}$ we have $s'\langle s''_1, \ldots, s''_k \rangle \in S_{\ell_1 + \cdots + \ell_k}$,*
- *$F(s'\langle s' \rangle) = F'(s') \cdot F''(s'')$ for every $s' \in S'_1$ and $s'' \in S''_1$, and*
- *the rules $l \xrightarrow{a} r$ of R, all of which are such that the variables in l occur in order $(x_1, \ldots, x_k)$ from left-to-right, are constructed in 3 ways:*
  - *$l \overset{a}{\Rightarrow}_{R'} r$ by a single rule of R',*
  - *$l \overset{a}{\Rightarrow}_{R''} r$ by a single rule of R'', or*
  - *$l \overset{a_1}{\Rightarrow}_{R'} \xi \overset{a_2}{\Rightarrow}_{R''} r$ with $a = a_1 \cdot a_2$ and the applied rule of R' contains an output symbol.*

  If a rule $l \xrightarrow{a} r$ can be constructed in several ways (with exactly weight a), then the weights of all possibilities are added for the weight of the new rule.

Intuitively, a single rule of R' without output symbols is used in the first type (because otherwise r would have the wrong shape). In the second type, a single rule of R'' without input symbols is used. Finally, in the third type, first a rule of R' that produces an output symbol of Δ is used and then this symbol is processed by a single rule of R''. Note that every rule of R' can produce at most one output symbol and the rules of R'' either process none or one input symbol due to the assumption that M' and M'' are in one-symbol normal form. We illustrate a rule of the first in Figure 7.

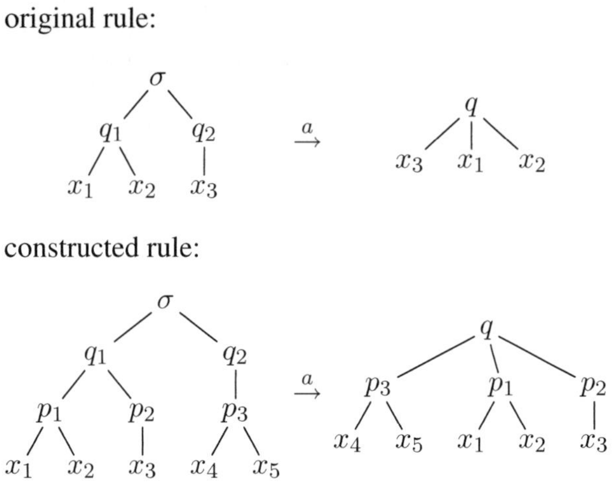

Figure 7: Example of a constructed rule of type 1.

The correctness proof of this construction can essentially (i.e., for the unweighted case) be found in Engelfriet et al. (2009). Before we can extend it to the weighted case, we need to make sure that the sum in the definition of composition is finite. We achieve this by requiring that

- for every $t \in T_\Sigma$ and $s \in S'_1$ there are finitely many $u \in T_\Delta$ such that $t \overset{a_1}{\Rightarrow} \cdots \overset{a_n}{\Rightarrow} s(u)$, or
- for every $v \in T_\Gamma$ and $s \in S''_1$ there are finitely many $u \in T_\Delta$ such that $u \overset{a_1}{\Rightarrow} \cdots \overset{a_n}{\Rightarrow} s(v)$.

In other words, M' may not have cyclic input ε-rules or M'' may not have cyclic output ε-rules. Now we can state the main theorem.

Theorem 7 *For all MBOTs M' and M'' with the above restriction the composition $M' \,;\, M''$ of their transformations can be computed by another MBOT.*

This again shows an advantage of MBOTs. The composition result relies essentially on the one-symbol normal form (or full binarization), which can always be achieved for MBOTs, but cannot for STSGs. Consequently, MBOTs can be composed, whereas STSGs cannot be composed in general. Indeed, STSGs in one-symbol normal form, which can be defined as for MBOTs, can be composed as well, which shows that the one-symbol normal form is the key for composition.

Finally, let us discuss the complexity of composition. Let $\mathrm{rk}(M')$ be the maximal rank of a state in S'. Then there are

- $\mathcal{O}(|M'| \cdot |S''|^{\mathrm{rk}(M')})$ rules of type 1,
- $\mathcal{O}(|M''| \cdot |S''|^{\mathrm{rk}(M')})$ rules of type 2, and

- $\mathcal{O}(|M'| \cdot |M''| \cdot |S''|^{\mathrm{rk}(M')})$ rules of type 3.

Each rule can be constructed in linear time in the size of the participating rules, so that we obtain a final complexity of $\mathcal{O}(|M'| \cdot |M''| \cdot |S''|^{\mathrm{rk}(M')})$. Note that if M' is obtained from an STSG M (via Theorem 4), then $\mathrm{rk}(M') \leq \mathrm{rk}(M)$. This shows that binarization does not avoid the exponent for composition, but at least enables composition in the general case. Moreover, the complexity could be slightly improved by the observation that our construction only relies on (i) M' having at most one output symbol per rule and (ii) M'' having at most one input symbol per rule.

7 Forward and backward application

We might want to apply a transformation not just to a single tree, but rather to a set of trees, which are, in some cases, already weighted. In general, the set of trees is given by a TSG G and we expect the result to be represented by a TSG as well. Forward and backward application amount to computing the image and pre-image of G under the transformation, respectively. Since STSG are symmetric, we need to solve only one of the problems if the transformation is given by an STSG. The other problem can then be solved by inverting the STSG (exchanging input and output) and using the method for the solved problem. We chose to address forward application here.

Forward application can be reduced to the problem of computing the co-domain (or range) with the help of a product construction for STSG, which is similar to the one presented in Definition 5. The co-domain cod_M of the tranformation computed by an STSG M assigns to each $t \in T_\Sigma$ the weight

$$\mathrm{cod}_M(t) = \sum_{u \in T_\Delta} M(t, u) \ .$$

This sum might not be well-defined. However, if $u \notin N$ for all productions $n \colon t \stackrel{a}{\leftrightarrow} u$ of the STSG, then the sum is well-defined and the output-side TSG (i.e., for every production $n \colon t \stackrel{a}{\leftrightarrow} u$ in the STSG there is a production $n \stackrel{a}{\to} u$ in the TSG) computes the co-domain. The restriction "$u \notin N$" guarantees that the output side is a TSG. Overall, domain, co-domain, and forward and backward applications (using the product construction) can be computed given such minor new requirements.

Also for transformations computed by MBOTs we can reduce the problem of forward application to the problem of computing the co-domain with the help of the product construction of Definition 5. However, the co-domain of an MBOT is not necessarily representable by a TSG, which is not due to well-definedness problems but rather the *finite-copying* property (Engelfriet et al., 1980) of MBOTs. This property yields that the co-domain might not be a regular tree language (or context-free string language). Consequently, we cannot compute forward or backward applications for arbitrary MBOT. However, if the MBOT is equivalent to an STSG (for example, because it was constructed by the method presented before Theorem 3), then forward and backward application can be computed essentially as for STSG. This can be understood as a warning. MBOT can efficiently be used (with computational benefits) as an alternative representation for transformations computed by STSG (or compositions of STSG). However, MBOT can also compute transformations, of which the domain or range cannot be represented by a TSG. Thus, if we train MBOT directly and utilize their full expressive power, then we might not be able to perform forward and backward application.

In the unweighted case, backward application can always be computed for MBOT. Moreover, it can be decided using (Ésik, 1984) whether all forward applications can be represented by TSGs. However, for a given specific TSG, it cannot be decided whether the forward application is representable by a TSG, which was proved by Fülöp (1994). A subclass of transformations computable by MBOT (that still contains all transformations computable by STSG), which allows all forward and backward applications, has been identified by Raoult (1993).

Conclusion and acknowledgement

We compared STSGs and MBOTs on several standard algorithms (binarization, regular restriction, composition, and application). We prove that MBOTs offer computational benefits on all mentioned algorithms as long as the original transformation is computable by an STSG.

The author was financially supported by the *Ministerio de Educación y Ciencia* (MEC) grants JDCI-2007-760 and MTM-2007-63422.

References

Alfred V. Aho and Jeffrey D. Ullman. 1972. *The Theory of Parsing, Translation, and Compiling*. Prentice Hall.

André Arnold and Max Dauchet. 1982. Morphismes et bimorphismes d'arbres. *Theoret. Comput. Sci.*, 20(1):33–93.

Y. Bar-Hillel, M. Perles, and E. Shamir. 1964. On formal properties of simple phrase structure grammars. In *Language and Information: Selected Essays on their Theory and Application*, pages 116–150. Addison Wesley.

Jean Berstel and Christophe Reutenauer. 1982. Recognizable formal power series on trees. *Theoret. Comput. Sci.*, 18(2):115–148.

Björn Borchardt. 2004. A pumping lemma and decidability problems for recognizable tree series. *Acta Cybernet.*, 16(4):509–544.

Peter F. Brown, John Cocke, Stephen A. Della Pietra, Vincent J. Della Pietra, Fredrick Jelinek, John D. Lafferty, Robert L. Mercer, and Paul S. Roossin. 1990. A statistical approach to machine translation. *Computational Linguistics*, 16(2):79–85.

Peter F. Brown, Stephen A. Della Pietra, Vincent J. Della Pietra, and Robert L. Mercer. 1993. Mathematics of statistical machine translation: Parameter estimation. *Computational Linguistics*, 19(2):263–311.

David Chiang and Kevin Knight. 2006. An introduction to synchronous grammars. In *Proc. ACL tutorial*.

David Chiang. 2005. A hierarchical phrase-based model for statistical machine translation. In *Proc. ACL*, pages 263–270.

John DeNero, Mohit Bansal, Adam Pauls, and Dan Klein. 2009a. Efficient parsing for transducer grammars. In *Proc. NAACL*, pages 227–235.

John DeNero, Adam Pauls, and Dan Klein. 2009b. Asynchronous binarization for synchronous grammars. In *Proc. ACL*, pages 141–144.

Samuel Eilenberg. 1974. *Automata, Languages, and Machines*. Academic Press.

Joost Engelfriet, Grzegorz Rozenberg, and Giora Slutzki. 1980. Tree transducers, L systems, and two-way machines. *J. Comput. System Sci.*, 20(2):150–202.

Joost Engelfriet, Eric Lilin, and Andreas Maletti. 2009. Extended multi bottom-up tree transducers: Composition and decomposition. *Acta Inform.*, 46(8):561–590.

Zoltán Ésik. 1984. Decidability results concerning tree transducers II. *Acta Cybernet.*, 6(3):303–314.

Zoltán Fülöp and Heiko Vogler. 2009. Weighted tree automata and tree transducers. In *Handbook of Weighted Automata*, chapter IX, pages 313–403. Springer.

Zoltán Fülöp. 1994. Undecidable properties of deterministic top-down tree transducers. *Theoret. Comput. Sci.*, 134(2):311–328.

Jonathan S. Golan. 1999. *Semirings and their Applications*. Kluwer Academic, Dordrecht.

Jonathan Graehl, Kevin Knight, and Jonathan May. 2008. Training tree transducers. *Computational Linguistics*, 34(3):391–427.

John E. Hopcroft and Jeffrey D. Ullman. 1979. *Introduction to Automata Theory, Languages and Computation*. Addison Wesley.

Liang Huang, Hao Zhang, Daniel Gildea, and Kevin Knight. 2009. Binarization of synchronous context-free grammars. *Computational Linguistics*, 35(4):559–595.

Kevin Knight. 2007. Capturing practical natural language transformations. *Machine Translation*, 21(2):121–133.

Eric Lilin. 1981. Propriétés de clôture d'une extension de transducteurs d'arbres déterministes. In *CAAP*, volume 112 of LNCS, pages 280–289. Springer.

Andreas Maletti and Giorgio Satta. 2009. Parsing algorithms based on tree automata. In *Proc. IWPT*, pages 1–12.

Andreas Maletti, Jonathan Graehl, Mark Hopkins, and Kevin Knight. 2009. The power of extended top-down tree transducers. *SIAM J. Comput.*, 39(2):410–430.

Mehryar Mohri. 2009. Weighted automata algorithms. In *Handbook of Weighted Automata*, pages 213–254. Springer.

Mark-Jan Nederhof and Giorgio Satta. 2003. Probabilistic parsing as intersection. In *Proc. IWPT*, pages 137–148.

Mark-Jan Nederhof and Giorgio Satta. 2008. Computation of distances for regular and context-free probabilistic languages. *Theoret. Comput. Sci.*, 395(2–3):235–254.

Jean-Claude Raoult. 1993. Recursively defined tree transductions. In *Proc. RTA*, volume 690 of LNCS, pages 343–357. Springer.

Jacques Sakarovitch. 2009. Rational and recognisable power series. In *Handbook of Weighted Automata*, chapter IV, pages 105–174. Springer.

Giorgio Satta. 2010. Translation algorithms by means of language intersection. Manuscript.

Marcel Paul Schützenberger. 1961. On the definition of a family of automata. *Information and Control*, 4(2–3):245–270.

Wei Wang, Kevin Knight, and Daniel Marcu. 2007. Binarizing syntax trees to improve syntax-based machine translation accuracy. In *Proc. EMNLP-CoNLL*, pages 746–754.

Hao Zhang, Liang Huang, Daniel Gildea, and Kevin Knight. 2006. Synchronous binarization for machine translation. In *Proc. NAACL-HLT*, pages 256–263.

An extractive supervised two-stage method for sentence compression

Dimitrios Galanis* and **Ion Androutsopoulos*+**
*Department of Informatics, Athens University of Economics and Business, Greece
+Digital Curation Unit – IMIS, Research Centre "Athena", Greece

Abstract

We present a new method that compresses sentences by removing words. In a first stage, it generates candidate compressions by removing branches from the source sentence's dependency tree using a Maximum Entropy classifier. In a second stage, it chooses the best among the candidate compressions using a Support Vector Machine Regression model. Experimental results show that our method achieves state-of-the-art performance without requiring any manually written rules.

1 Introduction

Sentence compression is the task of producing a shorter form of a single given sentence, so that the new form is grammatical and retains the most important information of the original one (Jing, 2000). Sentence compression is valuable in many applications, for example when displaying texts on small screens (Corston-Oliver, 2001), in subtitle generation (Vandeghinste and Pan, 2004), and in text summarization (Madnani et al., 2007).

People use various methods to shorten sentences, including word or phrase removal, using shorter paraphrases, and common sense knowledge. However, reasonable machine-generated sentence compressions can often be obtained by only removing words. We use the term *extractive* to refer to methods that compress sentences by only removing words, as opposed to *abstractive* methods, where more elaborate transformations are also allowed. Most of the existing compression methods are extractive (Jing, 2000; Knight and Marcu, 2002; McDonald, 2006; Clarke and Lapata, 2008; Cohn and Lapata, 2009). Although abstractive methods have also been proposed (Cohn and Lapata, 2008), and they may shed more light on how people compress sentences, they do not always manage to outperform extractive methods (Nomoto, 2009). Hence, from an engineering perspective, it is still important to investigate how extractive methods can be improved.

In this paper, we present a new extractive sentence compression method that relies on supervised machine learning.[1] In a first stage, the method generates candidate compressions by removing branches from the source sentence's dependency tree using a Maximum Entropy classifier (Berger et al., 2006). In a second stage, it chooses the best among the candidate compressions using a Support Vector Machine Regression (SVR) model (Chang and Lin, 2001). We show experimentally that our method compares favorably to a state-of-the-art extractive compression method (Cohn and Lapata, 2007; Cohn and Lapata, 2009), without requiring any manually written rules, unlike other recent work (Clarke and Lapata, 2008; Nomoto, 2009). In essence, our method is a two-tier over-generate and select (or rerank) approach to sentence compression; similar approaches have been adopted in natural language generation and parsing (Paiva and Evans, 2005; Collins and Koo, 2005).

2 Related work

Knight and Marcu (2002) presented a noisy channel sentence compression method that uses a language model $P(y)$ and a channel model $P(x|y)$, where x

[1] An implementation of our method will be freely available from http://nlp.cs.aueb.gr/software.html

Human Language Technologies: The 2010 Annual Conference of the North American Chapter of the ACL, pages 885–893,
Los Angeles, California, June 2010.

is the source sentence and y the compressed one. $P(x|y)$ is calculated as the product of the probabilities of the parse tree tranformations required to expand y to x. The best compression of x is the one that maximizes $P(x|y) \cdot P(y)$, and it is found using a noisy channel decoder. In a second, alternative method Knight and Marcu (2002) use a tree-to-tree transformation algorithm that tries to rewrite directly x to the best y. This second method uses C4.5 (Quinlan, 1993) to learn when to perform tree rewriting actions (e.g., dropping subtrees, combining subtrees) that transform larger trees to smaller trees. Both methods were trained and tested on data from the Ziff-Davis corpus (Knight and Marcu, 2002), and they achieved very similar grammaticality and meaning preservation scores, with no statistically significant difference. However, their compression rates (counted in words) were very different: 70.37% for the noisy-channel method and 57.19% for the C4.5-based one.

McDonald (2006) ranks each candidate compression using a function based on the dot product of a vector of weights with a vector of features extracted from the candidate's n-grams, POS tags, and dependency tree. The weights were learnt from the Ziff-Davis corpus. The best compression is found using a Viterbi-like algorithm that looks for the best sequence of source words that maximizes the scoring function. The method outperformed Knight and Marcu's (2002) tree-to-tree method in grammaticality and meaning preservation on data from the Ziff-Davis corpus, with a similar compression rate.

Clarke and Lapata (2008) presented an unsupervised method that finds the best compression using Integer Linear Programming (ILP). The ILP obejctive function takes into account a language model that indicates which n-grams are more likely to be deleted, and a significance model that shows which words of the input sentence are important. Manually defined constraints (in effect, rules) that operate on dependency trees indicate which syntactic constituents can be deleted. This method outperformed McDonald's (2006) in grammaticality and meaning preservation on test sentences from Edinburgh's "written" and "spoken" corpora.[2] However, the compression rates of the two systems were different (72.0% vs. 63.7% for McDonald's method, both on the written corpus).

We compare our method against Cohn and Lapata's T3 system (Cohn and Lapata, 2007; Cohn and Lapata, 2009), a state-of-the-art extractive sentence compression system that learns parse tree transduction operators from a parallel extractive corpus of source-compressed trees. T3 uses a chart-based decoding algorithm and a Structured Support Vector Machine (Tsochantaridis et al., 2005) to learn to select the best compression among those licensed by the operators learnt.[3] T3 outperformed McDonald's (2006) system in grammaticality and meaning preservation on Edinburgh's "written" and "spoken" corpora, achieving comparable compression rates (Cohn and Lapata, 2009). Cohn and Lapata (2008) have also developed an abstractive version of T3, which was reported to outperform the original, extractive T3 in meaning preservation; there was no statistically significant difference in grammaticality.

Finally, Nomoto (2009) presented a two-stage extractive method. In the first stage, candidate compressions are generated by chopping the source sentence's dependency tree. Many ungrammatical compressions are avoided using hand-crafted drop-me-not rules for dependency subtrees. The candidate compressions are then ranked using a function that takes into account the inverse document frequencies of the words, and their depths in the source dependency tree. Nomoto's extractive method was reported to outperform Cohn and Lapata's abstractive version of T3 on a corpus collected via RSS feeds. Our method is similar to Nomoto's, in that it uses two stages, one that chops the source dependency tree generating candidate compressions, and one that ranks the candidates. However, we experimented with more elaborate ranking models, and our method does not employ any manually crafted rules.

3 Our method

As already mentioned, our method first generates candidate compressions, which are then ranked. The candidate compressions generator operates by removing branches from the dependency tree of the

[2]See http://homepages.inf.ed.ac.uk/s0460084/data/.

[3]T3 appears to be the only previous sentence compression method whose implementation is publicly available; see http://www.dcs.shef.ac.uk/~tcohn/t3/.

input sentence (figure 1); this stage is discussed in section 3.1 below. We experimented with different ranking functions, discussed in section 3.2, which use features extracted from the source sentence s and the candidate compressions $c_1, \ldots, c_k$.

3.1 Generating candidate compressions

Our method requires a parallel training corpus consisting of sentence-compression pairs $\langle s, g \rangle$. The compressed sentences g must have been formed by only deleting words from the corresponding source sentences s. The $\langle s, g \rangle$ training pairs are used to estimate the propability that a dependency edge e of a dependency tree T_s of an input sentence s is retained or not in the dependency tree T_g of the compressed sentence g. More specifically, we want to estimate the probabilities $P(X_i|context(e_i))$ for every edge e_i of T_s, where X_i is a variable that can take one of the following three values: not_del, for not deleting e_i; del_u for deleting e_i along with its head; and del_l for deleting e along with its modifier. The head (respectively, modifier) of e_i is the node e_i originates from (points to) in the dependency tree. $context(e_i)$ is a set of features that represents e_i's local context in T_s, as well as the local context of the head and modifier of e_i in s.

The propabilities above can be estimated using the Maximum Entropy (ME) framework (Berger et al., 2006), a method for learning the distribution $P(X|V)$ from training data, where X is discrete-valued variable and $V = \langle V_1, \ldots, V_n \rangle$ is a real or discrete-valued vector. Here, $V = context(e_i)$ and $X = X_i$. We use the following features in V:

- The label of the dependency edge e_i, as well as the POS tag of the head and modifier of e_i.
- The entire head-label-modifier triple of e_i. This feature overlaps with the previous two features, but it is common in ME models to use feature combinations as additional features, since they may indicate a category more strongly than the individual initial features.[4]
- The POS tag of the father of e_i's head, and the label of the dependency that links the father to e_i's head.
- The POS tag of each one of the three previous and the three following words of e_i's head and modifier in s (12 features).
- The POS tag bi-grams of the previous two and the following two words of e_i's head and modifier in s (4 features).
- Binary features that show which of the possible labels occur (or not) among the labels of the edges that have the same head as e_i in T_s (one feature for each possible dependency label).
- Two binary features that show if the subtree rooted at the modifier of e_i or e_i's *uptree* (the rest of the tree, when e_i's subtree is removed) contain an important word. A word is considered important if it appears in the document s was drawn from significantly more often than in a background corpus. In summarization, such words are called signature terms and are thought to be descriptive of the input; they can be identified using the log-likelihood ratio λ of each word (Lin and Hovy, 2000; Gupta et al., 2007).

For each dependency edge e_i of a source training sentence s, we create a training vector V with the above features. If e_i is retained in the dependency tree of the corresponding compressed sentence g in the corpus, V is assigned the category not_del. If e_i is not retained, it is assigned the category del_l or del_u, depending on whether the head (as in the `ccomp` of "said" in Figure 1) or the modifier (as in the `dobj` of "attend") of e_i has also been removed. When the modifier of an edge is removed, the entire subtree rooted at the modifier is removed, and similarly for the uptree, when the head is removed. We do not create training vectors for the edges of the removed subtree of a modifier or the edges of the removed uptree of a head.

Given an input sentence s and its dependency tree T_s, the candidate compressions generator produces the candidate compressed sentences $c_1, \ldots, c_n$ by deleting branches of T_s and putting the remaining words of the dependency tree in the same order as in s. The candidates $c_1, \ldots, c_n$ correspond to possible assignments of values to the X_i variables (recall that $X_i = not\_del|del\_l|del\_u$) of the edges e_i of T_s.

[4]http://nlp.stanford.edu/pubs/maxent-tutorial-slides.pdf.

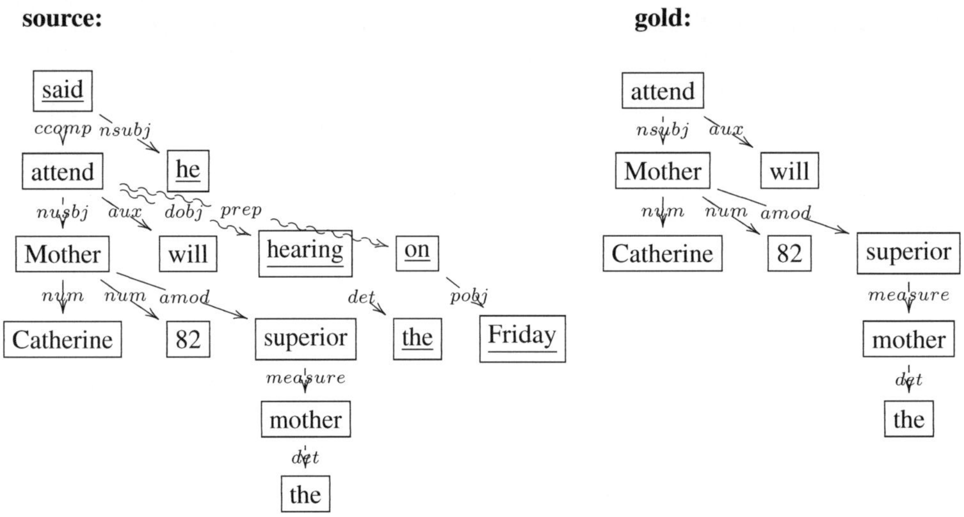

Figure 1: Dependency trees of a source sentence and its compression by a human (taken from Edinburgh's "written" corpus). The source sentence is: "Mother Catherine, 82, the mother superior, will attend the hearing on Friday, he said." The compressed one is: "Mother Catherine, 82, the mother superior, will attend." Deleted edges and words are shown curled and underlined, respectively.

Hence, there are at most 3^{m-1} candidate compressions, where m is the number of words in s. This is a large number of candidates, even for modestly long input sentences. In practice, the candidates are fewer, because del_l removes an entire subtree and del_u an entire uptree, and we do not need to make decisions X_i about the edges of the deleted subtrees and uptrees. To reduce the number of candidates further, we ignore possible assignments that contain decisions $X_i = x$ to which the ME model assigns probabilities below a threshold t; i.e., the ME model is used to prune the space of possible assignments.

When generating the possible assignments to the X_i variables, we examine the edges e_i of T_s in a top-down breadth-first manner. In the source tree of Figure 1, for example, we first consider the edges of "said"; the left-to-right order is random, but let us assume that we consider first the `ccomp` edge. There are three possible actions: retain the edge (not_del), remove it along with the head "said" (del_u), or remove it along with the modifier "attend" and its subtree (del_l). If the ME model assigns a low probability to one of the three actions, that action is ignored. For each one of the (remaining) actions, we obtain a new form of T_s, and we continue to consider its (other) edges. We process the edges in a top-down fashion, because the ME model allows del_l actions much more often than del_u actions, and when del_l actions are performed near the root of T_s, they prune large parts of the space of possible assignments to the X_i variables. Some of the candidate compressions that were generated for an input sentence by setting $t = 0.2$ are shown in Table 1, along with the gold (human-authored) compression.

3.2 Ranking candidate compressions

Given that we now have a method that generates candidate compressions $c_1, \ldots, c_k$ for a sentence s, we need a function $F(c_i|s)$ that will rank the candidate compressions. Many of them are ungrammatical and/or do not convey the most important information of s. $F(c_i|s)$ should help us select a short candidate that is grammatical and retains the most important information of s.

3.2.1 Grammaticality and importance rate

A simple way to rank the candidate compressions is to assign to each one a score intended to measure its *grammaticality* and *importance rate*. By grammaticality, $Gramm(c_i)$, we mean how grammatically well-formed candidate c_i is. A common way to obtain such a measure is to use an n-gram lan-

s: Then last week a second note, in the same handwriting, informed Mrs Allan that the search was on the wrong side of the bridge.
g: Last week a second note informed Mrs Allan the search was on the wrong side of the bridge.
c_1: Last week a second note informed Mrs Allan that the search was on the side. c_2: Last week a second note informed Mrs Allan that the search was. c_3: Last week a second note informed Mrs Allan the search was on the wrong side of the bridge. c_4: Last week in the same handwriting informed Mrs Allan the search was on the wrong side of the bridge.

Table 1: A source sentence s, its gold (human authored) compression g, and candidate compressions $c_1, \ldots, c_4$.

guage model trained on a large background corpus. However, language models tend to assign smaller probabilities to longer sentences; therefore they favor short sentences, but not necessarily the most appropriate compressions. To overcome this problem, we follow Cordeiro et al. (2009) and normalize the score of a trigram language model as shown below, where $w_1, \ldots, w_m$ are the words of candidate c_i.

$$Gramm(c_i) = \log P_{LM}(c_i)^{1/m} = (1/m) \cdot \log(\prod_{j=1}^{m} P(w_j|w_{j-1}, w_{j-2})) \quad (1)$$

The importance rate $ImpRate(c_i|s)$, defined below, estimates how much information of the original sentence s is retained in candidate c_i. $tf(w_i)$ is the term frequency of w_i in the document that contained ξ ($\xi = c_i, s$), and $idf(w_i)$ is the inverse document frequency of w_i in a background corpus. We actually compute $idf(w_i)$ only for nouns and verbs, and set $idf(w_i) = 0$ for other words.

$$ImpRate(c_i|s) = Imp(c_i)/Imp(s) \quad (2)$$

$$Imp(\xi) = \sum_{w_i \in \xi} tf(w_i) \cdot idf(w_i) \quad (3)$$

The ranking $F(c|s)$ is then defined as a linear combination of grammaticality and importance rate:

$$F(c_i|s) = \lambda \cdot Gramm(c_i) + (1-\lambda) \cdot \cdot ImpRate(c_i|s) - \alpha \cdot CR(c_i|s) \quad (4)$$

A compression rate penalty factor $CR(c_i|s) = |c|/|s|$ is included, to bias our method towards generating shorter or longer compressions; $|\cdot|$ denotes word length in words (punctuation is ignored). We explain how the weigths λ, α are tuned in following sections. We call LM-IMP the configuration of our method that uses the ranking function of equation 4.

3.2.2 Support Vector Regression

A more sophisticated way to select the best compression is to train a Support Vector Machines Regression (SVR) model to assign scores to feature vectors, with each vector representing a candidate compression. SVR models (Chang and Lin, 2001) are trained using l training vectors $(x_1, y_1), \ldots, (x_l, y_l)$, where $x_i \in \mathbb{R}^n$ and $y_i \in \mathbb{R}$, and learn a function $f : \mathbb{R}^n \rightarrow \mathbb{R}$ that generalizes the training data. In our case, x_i is a feature vector representing a candidate compression c_i, and y_i is a score indicating how good a compression c_i is. We use 98 features:

- $Gramm(c_i)$ and $ImpRate(c_i|s)$, as above.
- 2 features indicating the ratio of important and unimportant words of s, identified as in section 3.1, that were deleted.
- 2 features that indicate the average depth of the deleted and not deleted words in the dependency tree of s.
- 92 features that indicate which POS tags appear in s and how many of them were deleted in c_i. For every POS tag label, we use two features, one that shows how many POS tags of that label are contained in s and one that shows how many of these POS tags were deleted in c_i.

To assign a regression score y_i to each training vector x_i, we experimented with the following functions that measure how similar c_i is to the gold compression g, and how grammatical c_i is.

- Grammatical relations overlap: In this case, y_i is the F_1-score of the dependencies of c_i against those of the gold compression g. This measure has been shown to correlate well with human judgements (Clarke and Lapata, 2006). As in the ranking function of section 3.2.1, we add a compression rate penalty factor.

$$y_i = F_1(d(c_i)), d(g)) - \alpha \cdot CR(c_i|s) \quad (5)$$

$d(\cdot)$ denotes the set of dependencies. We call SVR-F1 the configuration of our system that uses equation 5 to rank the candidates.

- Tokens accuracy and grammaticality: Tokens accuracy, $TokAcc(c_i|s, g)$, is the percentage of tokens of s that were correctly retained or removed in c_i; a token was correctly retained or removed, if it was also retained (or removed) in the gold compression g. To calculate $TokAcc(c_i|s, g)$, we need the word-to-word alignment of s to g, and s to c_i. These alignments were obtained as a by-product of computing the corresponding (word) edit distances. We also want the regression model to favor grammatical compressions. Hence, we use a linear combination of tokens accuracy and grammaticality of c_i:

$$y_i = \lambda \cdot TokAcc(c_i|s, g) + (1 - \lambda) \cdot Gramm(c_i) - \alpha \cdot CR(c_i|s) \quad (6)$$

Again, we add a compression rate penalty, to be able to generate shorter or longer compressions. We call SVR-TOKACC-LM the configuration of our system that uses equation 6.

4 Baseline and T3

As a baseline, we use a simple algorithm based on the ME classifier of section 3.1. The baseline produces a single compression c for every source sentence s by considering sequentially the edges e_i of s's dependency tree in a random order, and performing at each e_i the single action (not_del, del_u, or del_l) that the ME model considers more probable; the words of the chopped dependency tree are then put in the same order as in s. We call this system Greedy-Baseline.

We compare our method against the extractive version of T3 (Cohn and Lapata, 2007; Cohn and Lapata, 2009), a state-of-the-art sentence compression system that applies sequences of transduction operators to the syntax trees of the source sentences. The available tranduction operators are learnt from the syntax trees of a set of source-gold pairs. Every operator transforms a subtree α to a subtree γ, rooted at symbols X and Y, respectively.

To find the best sequence of transduction operators that can be applied to a source syntax tree, a chart-based dynamic programming decoder is used, which finds the best scoring sequence q^*:

$$q^* = \arg\max_q score(q; w) \quad (7)$$

where $score(q; w)$ is the dot product $\langle \Psi(q), w \rangle$. $\Psi(q)$ is a vector-valued feature function, and w is a vector of weights learnt using a Structured Support Vector Machine (Tsochantaridis et al., 2005).

$\Psi(q)$ consists of: (i) the log-probability of the resulting candidate, as returned by a tri-gram language model; and (ii) features that describe how the operators of q are applied, for example the number of the terminals in each operator's α and γ subtrees, the POS tags of the X and Y roots of α and γ etc.

5 Experiments

We used Stanford's parser (de Marneffe et al., 2006) and ME classifier (Manning et al., 2003).[5] For the (trigram) language model, we used SRILM with modified Kneser-Ney smoothing (Stolcke, 2002).[6] The language model was trained on approximately 4.5 million sentences of the TIPSTER corpus. To obtain $idf(w_i)$ values, we used approximately 19.5 million verbs and nouns from the TIPSTER corpus.

T3 requires the syntax trees of the source-gold pairs in Penn Treebank format, as well as a trigram language model. We obtained T3's trees using Stanford's parser, as in our system, unlike Cohn and Lapata (2009) that use Bikel's (2002) parser. The language models in T3 and our system are trained on the same data and with the same options used by Cohn and Lapata (2009). T3 also needs a word-to-word alignment of the source-gold pairs, which was obtained by computing the edit distance, as in Cohn and Lapata (2009) and SVR-TOKACC-LM.

We used Edinburgh's "written" sentence compression corpus (section 2), which consists of source-gold pairs (one gold compression per source

[5]Both available from http://nlp.stanford.edu/.

[6]See http://www.speech.sri.com/projects/srilm/.

sentence). The gold compressions were created by deleting words. We split the corpus in 3 parts: 1024 training, 324 development, and 291 testing pairs.

5.1 Best configuration of our method

We first evaluated experimentally the three configurations of our method (LM-IMP, SVR-F1, SVR-TOKACC-LM), using the $F1$-measure of the dependencies of the machine-generated compressions against those of the gold compressions as an automatic evaluation measure. This measure has been shown to correlate well with human judgements (Clarke and Lapata, 2006).

In all three configurations, we trained the ME model of section 3.1 on the dependency trees of the source-gold pairs of the training part of the corpus. We then used the trained ME classifier to generate the candidate compressions of each source sentence of the training part. We set $t = 0.2$, which led to at most 10,000 candidates for almost every source sentence. We kept up to 1.000 candidates for each source sentence, and we selected randonly approximately 10% of them, obtaining 18,385 candidates, which were used to train the two SVR configurations; LM-IMP requires no training.

To tune the λ parameters of LM-IMP and SVR-TOKACC-LM in equations 4 and 6, we initially set $\alpha = 0$ and we experimented with different values of λ. For each one of the two configurations and for every different λ value, we computed the average compression rate of the machine-generated compressions on the development set. In the rest of the experiments, we set λ to the value that gave an average compression rate approximatelly equal to that of the gold compressions of the training part.

We then experimented with different values of α in all three configurations, in equations 4–6, to produce smaller or longer compression rates. The α parameter provides a uniform mechanism to fine-tune the compression rate in all three configurations, even in SVR-F1 that has no λ. The results on the development part are shown in Figure 2, along with the baseline's results. The baseline has no parameters to tune; hence, its results are shown as a single point. Both SVR models outperform LM-IMP, which in turn outperforms the baseline. Also, SVR-TOKACC-LM performs better or as well as SVR-F1 for all compression rates. Note, also, that the perfomance of the two SVR configurations might be improved further by using more training examples, whereas LM-IMP contains no learning component.

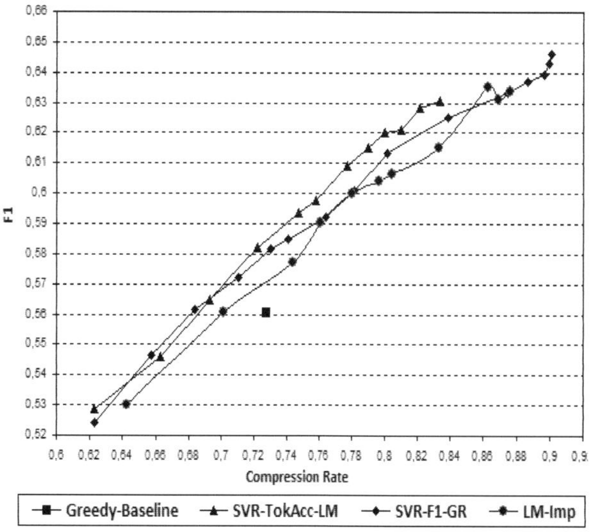

Figure 2: Evaluation results on the development set.

5.2 Our method against T3

We then evaluated the best configuration of our method (SVR-TOKACC-LM) against T3, both automatically ($F1$-measure) and with human judges. We trained both systems on the training set of the corpus. In our system, we used the same λ value that we had obtained from the experiments of the previous section. We then varied the values of our system's α parameter to obtain approximately the same compression rate as T3.

For the evaluation with the human judges, we selected randomly 80 sentences from the test part. For each source sentence s, we formed three pairs, containing s, the gold compression, the compression of SVR-TOKACC-LM, and the compression of T3, repsectively, 240 pairs in total. Four judges (graduate students) were used. Each judge was given 60 pairs in a random sequence; they did not know how the compressed sentenes were obtained and no judge saw more than one compression of the same source sentence. The judges were told to rate (in a scale from 1 to 5) the compressed sentences in terms of grammaticality, meaning preservation, and overall quality. Their average judgements are shown in Table 2, where the $F1$-scores are also included. Cohn and Lapata (2009) have reported very similar scores for T3 on a different split of the corpus (F1: 49.48%, CR: 61.09%).

system	G	M	Ov	F1 (%)	CR (%)
T3	3.83	3.28	3.23	47.34	59.16
SVR	4.20	3.43	3.57	52.09	59.85
gold	4.73	4.27	4.43	100.00	78.80

Table 2: Results on 80 test sentences. G: grammaticality, M: meaning preservation, Ov: overall score, CR: compression rate, SVR: SVR-TOKACC-LM.

Our system outperforms T3 in all evaluation measures. We used Analysis of Variance (ANOVA) followed by post-hoc Tukey tests to check whether the judge ratings differ significantly ($p < 0.1$); all judge ratings of gold compressions are significantly different from T3's and those of our system; also, our system differs significantly from T3 in grammaticality, but not in meaning preservation and overall score. We also performed Wilcoxon tests, which showed that the difference in the $F1$ scores of the two systems is statistically significant ($p < 0.1$) on the 80 test sentences. Table 3 shows the $F1$ scores and the average compression rates for all 291 test sentences. Both systems have comparable compression rates, but again our system outperforms T3 in $F1$, with a statistically significant difference ($p < 0.001$).

system	$F1$	CR
SVR-TOKACC-LM	53.75	63.72
T3	47.52	64.16

Table 3: $F1$ scores on the entire test set.

Finally, we computed the Pearson correlation r of the overall (Ov) scores that the judges assigned to the machine-generated compressions with the corresponding $F1$ scores. The two measures were found to corellate reliably ($r = 0.526$). Similar results have been reported (Clarke and Lapata, 2006) for Edinburgh's "spoken" corpus ($r = 0.532$) and the Ziff-Davis corpus ($r = 0.575$).

6 Conclusions and future work

We presented a new two-stage extractive method for sentence compression. The first stage generates candidate compressions by removing or not edges from the source sentence's dependency tree; an ME model is used to prune unlikely edge deletion or non-deletions. The second stage ranks the candidate compressions; we experimented with three ranking models, achieving the best results with an SVR model trained with an objective function that combines token accuracy and a language model. We showed experimentally, via automatic evaluation and with human judges, that our method compares favorably to a state-of-the-art extractive system. Unlike other recent approaches, our system uses no hand-crafted rules. In future work, we plan to support more complex tranformations, instead of only removing words and experiment with different sizes of training data.

The work reported in this paper was carried out in the context of project INDIGO, where an autonomous robotic guide for museum collections is being developed. The guide engages the museum's visitors in spoken dialogues, and it describes the exhibits that the visitors select by generating textual descriptions, which are passed on to a speech synthesizer. The texts are generated from logical facts stored in an ontology (Galanis et al., 2009) and from canned texts; the latter are used when the corresponding information is difficult to encode in symbolic form (e.g., to store short stories about the exhibits). The descriptions of the exhibits are tailored depending on the type of the visitor (e.g., child vs. adult), and an important tailoring aspect is the generation of shorter or longer descriptions. The parts of the descriptions that are generated from logical facts can be easily made shorter or longer, by conveying fewer or more facts. The methods of this paper are used to automatically shorten the parts of the descriptions that are canned texts, instead of requiring multiple (shorter and longer) hand-written versions of the canned texts.

Acknowledgements

This work was carried out in INDIGO, an FP6 IST project funded by the European Union, with additional funding provided by the Greek General Secretariat of Research and Technology.[7]

[7]Consult http://www.ics.forth.gr/indigo/.

References

A.L. Berger, S.A. Della Pietra, and V.J. Della Pietra. 2006. A maximum entropy approach to natural language processing. *Computational Linguistics*, 22(1):39–71.

D. Bikel. 2002. Design of a multi-lingual, parallel-processing statistical parsing engine. In *Proceedings of the 2nd International Conference on Human Language Technology Research*, pages 24–27.

C.C Chang and C.J Lin. 2001. LIBSVM: a library for Support Vector Machines. Technical report. Software available at http://www.csie.ntu.edu.tw/~cjlin/libsvm.

J. Clarke and M. Lapata. 2006. Models for sentence compression: A comparison across domains, training requirements and evaluation measures. In *Proceedings of COLING*, pages 377–384.

J. Clarke and M. Lapata. 2008. Global inference for sentence compression: An integer linear programming approach. *Artificial Intelligence Research*, 1(31):399–429.

T. Cohn and M. Lapata. 2007. Large margin synchronous generation and its application to sentence compression. In *Proceedings of EMNLP-CoNLL*, pages 73–82.

T. Cohn and M. Lapata. 2008. Sentence compression beyond word deletion. In *Proceedings of COLING*, pages 137–144.

T. Cohn and M. Lapata. 2009. Sentence compression as tree to tree tranduction. *Artificial Intelligence Research*, 34:637–674.

M. Collins and T. Koo. 2005. Discriminative reranking for natural language parsing. *Computational Linguistics*, 31(1):25–69.

J. Cordeiro, G. Dias, and P. Brazdil. 2009. Unsupervised induction of sentence compression rules. In *Proceedings of the ACL Workshop on Language Generation and Summarisation*, pages 391–399.

S. Corston-Oliver. 2001. Text compaction for display on very small screens. In *Proceedings of the NAACL Workshop on Automatic Summarization*, pages 89–98.

M.C. de Marneffe, B. MacCartney, and C. Manning. 2006. Generating typed dependency parses from phrase structure parses. In *Proceedings of LREC*, pages 449–454.

Dimitrios Galanis, George Karakatsiotis, Gerasimos Lampouras, and Ion Androutsopoulos. 2009. An open-source natural language generator for OWL ontologies and its use in protege and second life. In *Proceedings of the Demonstrations Session at EACL 2009*, pages 17–20, Athens, Greece, April. Association for Computational Linguistics.

S. Gupta, A. Nenkova, and D. Jurafsky. 2007. Measuring importance and query relevance in topic-focused multi-document summarization. In *Proceedings of ACL*, pages 193–196.

H. Jing. 2000. Sentence reduction for automatic text summarization. In *Proceedings of ANLP*, pages 310–315.

K. Knight and D. Marcu. 2002. Summarization beyond sentence extraction: A probalistic approach to sentence compression. *Artificial Intelligence*, 139(1):91–107.

C.W. Lin and E. Hovy. 2000. The automated acquisition of topic signatures for text summarization. In *Proceedings of ACL*, pages 495–501.

N. Madnani, D. Zajic, B. Dorr, N. F. Ayan, and J. Lin. 2007. Multiple alternative sentence compressions for automatic text summarization. In *Proceedings of DUC*.

C. D. Manning, D. Klein, and C. Manning. 2003. Optimization, maxent models, and conditional estimation without magic. In *tutorial notes of HLT-NAACL 2003 and ACL 2003*.

R. McDonald. 2006. Discriminative sentence compression with soft syntactic constraints. In *Proceedings of EACL*, pages 297–304.

T. Nomoto. 2009. A comparison of model free versus model intensive approaches to sentence compression. In *Proceedings of EMNLP*, pages 391–399.

D. Paiva and R. Evans. 2005. Empirically-based control of natural language generation. In *Proceedings of ACL*.

J. R. Quinlan. 1993. *C4.5: Programs for Machine Learning*. Morgan Kaufmann.

A. Stolcke. 2002. SRILM - an extensible language modeling toolkit. In *Proceedings of the International Conference on Spoken Language Processing*, pages 901–904.

I. Tsochantaridis, T. Hofmann, T. Joachims, and Y. Altun. 2005. Support vector machine learning for independent and structured output spaces. *Machine Learning Research*, 6:1453–1484.

V. Vandeghinste and Y. Pan. 2004. Sentence compression for automated subtitling: A hybrid approach. In *Proceedings of the ACL Workshop "Text Summarization Branches Out"*, pages 89–95.

Interpretation and Transformation for Abstracting Conversations

Gabriel Murray gabrielm@cs.ubc.ca **Giuseppe Carenini** carenini@cs.ubc.ca **Raymond Ng** rng@cs.ubc.ca
Department of Computer Science, University of British Columbia
Vancouver, Canada

Abstract

We address the challenge of automatically abstracting conversations such as face-to-face meetings and emails. We focus here on the stages of *interpretation*, where sentences are mapped to a conversation ontology, and *transformation*, where the summary content is selected. Our approach is fully developed and tested on meeting speech, and we subsequently explore its application to email conversations.

1 Introduction

The dominant approach to the challenge of automatic summarization has been *extraction*, where informative sentences in a document are identified and concatenated to form a condensed version of the original document. Extractive summarization has been popular at least in part because it is a binary classification task that lends itself well to machine learning techniques, and does not require a natural language generation (NLG) component. There is evidence that human abstractors at times use sentences from the source documents nearly verbatim in their own summaries, justifying this approach to some extent (Kupiec et al., 1995). Extrinsic evaluations have also shown that, while extractive summaries may be less coherent than human abstracts, users still find them to be valuable tools for browsing documents (He et al., 1999; McKeown et al., 2005; Murray et al., 2008).

However, these same evaluations also indicate that concise abstracts are generally preferred by users and lead to higher objective task scores. The limitation of a cut-and-paste summary is that the end-user does not know *why* the selected sentences are important; this can often only be discerned by exploring the context in which each sentence originally appeared. One possible improvement is to create *structured extracts* that represent an increased level of abstraction, where selected sentences are grouped according to phenomena such as *decisions*, *action items* and *problems*, thereby giving the user more information on why the sentences are being highlighted. For example, the sentence *Let's go with a simple chip* represents a decision. An even higher level of abstraction can be provided by generating new text that synthesizes or extrapolates on the information contained in the structured summary. For example, the sentence *Sandra and Sue expressed negative opinions about the remote control design* can be coupled with extracted sentences containing these negative opinions, forming a *hybrid summary*. Our summarization system ultimately performs both types of abstraction, grouping sentences according to various sentence-level phenomena, and generating novel text that describes this content at a higher level.

In this work we describe the first two components of our abstractive summarization system. In the *interpretation* stage, sentences are mapped to nodes in a conversation ontology by utilizing classifiers relating to a variety of sentence-level phenomena such as *decisions*, *action items* and *subjective sentences*. These classifiers achieve high accuracy by using a very large feature set integrating conversation structure, lexical patterns, part-of-speech (POS) tags and character n-grams. In the *transformation* stage, we select the most informative sentences by maximizing a function based on the derived ontology mapping and the coverage of weighted entities mentioned in the conversation. This transformation component utilizes integer linear programming (ILP) and we compare its performance with several greedy selection algorithms.

We do not discuss the generation component of our summarization system in this paper. The transformation component is still ex-

Human Language Technologies: The 2010 Annual Conference of the North American Chapter of the ACL, pages 894–902,
Los Angeles, California, June 2010.

tractive in nature, but the sentences that are selected in the transformation stage correspond to objects in the ontology and the properties linking them. Specifically, these are triples of the form $< participant, relation, entity >$ where a $participant$ is a person in the conversation, an $entity$ is an item under discussion, and a $relation$ such as *positive opinion* or *action item* links the two. This intermediate output enables us to create structured extracts as described above, with the triples also acting as input to the downstream NLG component.

We have tested our approach in summarization experiments on both meeting and email conversations, where the quality of a sentence is measured by how effectively it conveys information in a model abstract summary according to human annotators. On meetings the ILP approach consistently outperforms several greedy summarization methods. A key finding is that emails exhibit markedly varying conversation structures, and the email threads yielding the best summarization results are those that are structured similarly to meetings. Other email conversation structures are less amenable to the current treatment and require further investigation and possibly domain adaptation.

2 Related Research

The view that summarization consists of stages of *interpretation*, *transformation* and *generation* was laid out by Sparck-Jones (1999). Popular approaches to text extraction essentially collapse interpretation and transformation into one step, with generation either being ignored or consisting of post-processing techniques such as sentence compression (Knight and Marcu, 2000; Clarke and Lapata, 2006) or sentence merging (Barzilay and McKeown, 2005). In contrast, in this work we clearly separate interpretation from transformation.

The most relevant research to ours is by Kleinbauer et al. (2007), similarly focused on meeting abstraction. They create an ontology for the AMI scenario meeting corpus (Carletta et al., 2005), described in Section 5.1. The system uses topic segments and topic labels, and for each topic segment in the meeting a sentence is generated that describes the most frequently mentioned content items in that topic. Our systems differ in two major respects: their summarization process uses human gold-standard annotations of topic segments, topic labels and content items from the ontology, while our summarizer is fully automatic; and the ontology used by Kleinbauer et al. is specific not just to meetings but to the AMI scenario meetings, while our ontology applies to conversations in general.

While the work by Kleinbauer et al. is among the earliest research on abstracting multi-party dialogues, much attention in recent years has been paid to extractive summarization of such conversations, including meetings (Galley, 2006), emails (Rambow et al., 2004; Carenini et al., 2007), telephone conversations (Zhu and Penn, 2006) and internet relay chats (Zhou and Hovy, 2005).

Recent research has addressed the challenges of detecting decisions (Hsueh et al., 2007), action items (Purver et al., 2007; Murray and Renals, 2008) and subjective sentences (Raaijmakers et al., 2008). In our work we perform all of these tasks but rely on general conversational features without recourse to meeting-specific or email-specific features.

Our approach to transformation is an adaptation of an ILP sentence selection algorithm described by Xie et al. (2009). We describe both ILP approaches in Section 4.

3 Interpretation - Ontology Mapping

Source document interpretation in our system relies on a simple conversation ontology. The ontology is written in OWL/RDF and contains two core upper-level classes: Participant and Entity. When additional information is available about participant roles in a given domain, Participant subclasses such as ProjectManager can be utilized. The ontology also contains six properties that express relations between the participants and the entities. For example, the following snippet of the ontology indicates that *hasActionItem* is a relationship between a meeting participant (the property domain) and a discussed entity (the property range).

```
<owl:ObjectProperty rdf:ID="hasActionItem">
  <rdfs:domain rdf:resource="#Participant"/>
  <rdfs:range rdf:resource="#Entity"/>
</owl:ObjectProperty>
```

Similar properties exist for decisions, actions, problems, positive-subjective sentences, negative-subjective sentences and general extractive sentences (important sentences that may not match the other categories), all connecting conversation participants and entities. The goal is to populate the ontology with participant and entity instances from a given conversation and determine their relationships. This involves identifying the important entities and classifying the sentences in which they occur as being decision sentences, action item sentences, etc.

Our current definition of entity is simple. The entities in a conversation are noun phrases with mid-range document frequency. This is similar to the definition of concept as defined by Xie et al. (Xie et al., 2009), where n-grams are weighted by *tf.idf* scores, except that we use noun phrases rather than any n-grams because we want to refer to the entities in the generated text. We use mid-range document frequency instead of *idf* (Church and Gale, 1995), where the entities occur in between 10% and 90% of the documents in the collection. In Section 4 we describe how we use the entity's term frequency to detect the most informative entities. We do not currently attempt coreference resolution for entities; recent work has investigated coreference resolution for multi-party dialogues (Muller, 2007; Gupta et al., 2007), but the challenge of resolution on such noisy data is highlighted by low accuracy (e.g. F-measure of 21.21) compared with using well-formed text (e.g. monologues).

We map sentences to our ontology's object properties by building numerous supervised classifiers trained on labeled decision sentences, action sentences, etc. A general extractive classifier is also trained on sentences simply labeled as important. After predicting these sentence-level properties, we consider a participant to be linked to an entity if the participant mentioned the entity in a sentence in which one of these properties is predicted. We give a specific example of the ontology mapping using this excerpt from the AMI corpus:

1. A: And you two are going to work together on a *prototype* using *modelling clay*.
2. A: You'll get *specific instructions* from your *personal coach*.
3. C: Cool.
4. A: Um did we decide on a *chip*?
5. A: Let's go with a *simple chip*.

Example entities are italicized. Sentences 1 and 2 are classified as action items. Sentence 3 is classified as positive-subjective, but because it contains no entities, no $< participant, relation, entity >$ triple can be added to the ontology. Sentence 4 is classified as a decision sentence, and Sentence 5 is both a decision sentence and a positive-subjective sentence (because the participant is advocating a particular position). The ontology is populated by adding all of the sentence entities as instances of the Entity class, all of the participants as instances of the Participant class, and adding $< participant, relation, entity >$ triples for Sentences 1, 2, 4 and 5. For example, Sentence 5 results in the following two triples being added to the ontology:

```
<ProjectManager rdf:ID="participant-A">
<hasDecision rdf:resource="#simple-chip"/>
</ProjectManager>
```

```
<ProjectManager rdf:ID="participant-A">
<hasPos rdf:resource="#simple-chip"/>
</ProjectManager>
```

Elements in the ontology are associated with linguistic annotations used by the generation component of our system; since we do not discuss the generation task here, we presently skip the details of this aspect of the ontology. In the following section we describe the features used for the ontology mapping.

3.1 Feature Set

The interpretation component uses general features that are applicable to any conversation domain. The first set of features we use for ontology mapping are features relating to conversational structure. These are listed and briefly described in Table 1. The $Sprob$ and $Tprob$ features measure how terms cluster between conversation participants and conversation turns. There are simple features measuring sentence length (SLEN, SLEN2) and position (TLOC, CLOC). Pause-style features indicate how much time transpires between the previous turn, the current turn and the subsequent turn (PPAU, SPAU). For email conversations, pause features are based on the timestamps between consecutive emails. Lexical features capture cohesion (CWS) and cosine similarity between the sentence and the conversation (CENT1, CENT2). All structural features are normalized by document length.

Feature ID	Description
MXS	max *Sprob* score
MNS	mean *Sprob* score
SMS	sum of *Sprob* scores
MXT	max *Tprob* score
MNT	mean *Tprob* score
SMT	sum of *Tprob* scores
TLOC	position in turn
CLOC	position in conv.
SLEN	word count, globally normalized
SLEN2	word count, locally normalized
TPOS1	time from beg. of conv. to turn
TPOS2	time from turn to end of conv.
DOM	participant dominance in words
COS1	cos. of conv. splits, w/ *Sprob*
COS2	cos. of conv. splits, w/ *Tprob*
PENT	entro. of conv. up to sentence
SENT	entro. of conv. after the sentence
THISENT	entropy of current sentence
PPAU	time btwn. current and prior turn
SPAU	time btwn. current and next turn
BEGAUTH	is first participant (0/1)
CWS	rough ClueWordScore
CENT1	cos. of sentence & conv., w/ *Sprob*
CENT2	cos. of sentence & conv., w/ *Tprob*

Table 1: Features Key

While these features have been found to work well for generic extractive summarization, we use additional features for capturing the more specific sentence-level phenomena of this research.

- **Character trigrams** We derive all of the character trigrams in the collected corpora and include features indicating the presence or absence of each trigram in a given sentence.
- **Word bigrams** We similarly derive all of the word bigrams in the collected corpora.
- **POS bigrams** We similarly derive all of the POS-tag bigrams in the collected corpora.
- **Word pairs** We consider w_1, w_2 to be a word pair if they occur in the same sentence and w_1 precedes w_2. We derive all of the word pairs in the collected corpora and includes features indicating the presence or absence of each word pair in the given sentence. This is essentially a skip bigram where any amount of intervening material is allowed as long as the words occur in the same sentence.
- **POS pairs** We calculate POS pairs in the same manner as word pairs, above. These are essentially skip bigrams for POS tags.
- **Varying instantiation ngrams** We derive a simplified set of VIN features for these experiments. For each word bigram w_1, w_2, we further represent the bigram as p_1, w_2 and w_1, p_2 so that each pattern consists of a word and a POS tag. We include a feature indicating the presence or absence of each of these varying instantiation bigrams.

After removing features that occur fewer than five times, we end up with 218,957 total features.

4 Transformation - ILP Content Selection

In the previous section we described how we identify sentences that link participants and entities through a variety of sentence-level phenomena. Having populated our ontology with these triples to form a source representation, we now turn to the task of transforming the source representation to a summary representation, identifying the $< participant, relation, entity >$ triples for which we want to generate text. We adapt a method proposed by Xie et al. (2009) for extractive sentence selection. They propose an ILP approach that creates a summary by maximizing a global objective function:

$$maximize\ (1-\lambda) * \sum_i w_i c_i + \lambda * \sum_j u_j s_j \quad (1)$$

$$subject\ to\ \sum_j l_j s_j < L \quad (2)$$

where w_i is the *tf.idf* score for concept i, u_j is the weight for sentence j using the cosine similarity to the entire document, c_i is a binary variable indicating whether concept i is selected (with the concept represented by a unique weighted n-gram), s_j is a binary variable indicating whether sentence j is selected, l_j is the length of sentence j and L is the desired summary length. The λ term is used to balance concept and sentence weights. This method selects sentences that are weighted strongly and which cover as many important concepts as possible. As described by Gillick et al. (2009), concepts and sentences are tied together by two additional constraints:

$$\sum_j s_j o_{ij} \geq c_i \ \forall_i \quad (3)$$

$$s_j o_{ij} \leq c_i \ \forall_{i,j} \quad (4)$$

where o_{ij} is the occurence of concept i in sentence j. These constraints state that a concept can only be selected if it occurs in a sentence that is selected, and that a sentence can only be selected if all of its concepts have been selected.

We adapt their method in several ways. As mentioned in the previous section, we use weighted noun phrases as our entities instead of n-grams. In our version of Equation 1, w_i is the *tf* score of entity i (the *idf* was already used to identify entities as described previously). More importantly, our sentence weight u_j is the sum of all the posterior probabilities for sentence j derived from the various sentence-level classifiers. In other words, sentences are weighted highly if they correspond to multiple object properties in the ontology. To continue the example from Section 3, the sentence *Let's go with the simple chip* may be selected because it represents both a decision and a positive-subjective opinion, as well as containing the entity *simple chip* which is mentioned frequently in the conversation.

We include constraint 3 but not 4; it is possible for a sentence to be extracted even if not all of its entities are. We know that all the sentences under consideration will contain at least one entity because sentences with no entities would not have been mapped to the ontology in the form of $< participant, relation, entity >$ triples in the first place. To begin with, we set the λ term at 0.75 as we are mostly concerned with identifying important sentences containing multiple links to the ontology. In our case L is 20% of the total document word count.

5 Experimental Setup

In this section we describe our conversation corpora, the statistical classifiers used, and the evaluation metrics employed.

5.1 Corpora

These experiments are conducted on both meeting and email conversations, which we describe in turn.

5.1.1 The AMI Meetings Corpus

For our meeting summarization experiments, we use the *scenario* portion of the AMI corpus (Carletta et al., 2005), where groups of four participants take part in a series of four meetings and play roles within a fictitious company. There are 140 of these meetings in total, including a 20 meeting test set containing multiple human summary annotations per meeting (the others are annotated by a single individual). We report results on both manual and ASR transcripts. The word error rate for the ASR transcripts is 38.9%.

For the *summary annotation*, annotators wrote abstract summaries of each meeting and extracted sentences that best conveyed or supported the information in the abstracts. The human-authored abstracts each contain a general abstract summary and three subsections for "decisions," "actions" and "problems" from the meeting. A many-to-many mapping between transcript sentences and sentences from the human abstract was obtained for each annotator. Approximately 13% of the total transcript sentences are ultimately labeled as extracted sentences. A sentence is considered a decision item if it is linked to the decision portion of the abstract, and action and problem sentences are derived similarly.

For the *subjectivity annotation*, we use annotations of positive-subjective and negative-subjective utterances on a subset of 20 AMI meetings (Wilson, 2008). Such subjective utterances involve the expression of a private state, such as a positive/negative opinion, positive/negative argument, and agreement/disagreement. Of the roughly 20,000 total sentences in the 20 AMI meetings, nearly 4000 are labeled as *positive-subjective* and nearly 1300 as *negative-subjective*.

5.1.2 The BC3 Email Corpus

While our main experiments focus on the AMI meeting corpus, we follow these up with an investigation into applying our abstractive techniques to email data. The BC3 corpus (Ulrich et al., 2008) contains email threads from the World Wide Web Consortium (W3C) mailing list. The threads feature a variety of topics such as web accessibility and planning face-to-face meetings. The annotated portion of the mailing list consists of 40 threads. The threads are annotated in the same manner as the AMI corpus, with three human annotators per thread first authoring abstracts and then linking email thread sentences to the abstract sentences. The corpus also contains speech act annotations. Unlike the AMI corpus, however, there are no annotations for decisions, actions and problems, an issue addressed later.

5.2 Classifiers

For these experiments we use a maximum entropy classifier using the *liblinear* toolkit[1] (Fan et al., 2008). For each of the AMI and BC3 corpora, we perform 10-fold cross-validation on the data. In all experiments we apply a 20% compression rate in terms of the total document word count.

5.3 Evaluation

We evaluate the various classifiers described in Section 3 using the ROC curve and the area under the curve (AUROC), where a baseline AUROC is 0.5 and an ideal classifier approaches 1.

To evaluate the content selection in the transformation stage, we use weighted recall.This evaluation metric is based on the links between extracted sentences and the human gold-standard abstracts, with the underlying motivation being that sentences with more links to the human abstract are generally more informative, as they provide the content on which an effective abstract summary should be built. If M is the number of sentences selected in the transformation step, O is the total number of sentences in the document, and N is the number of annotators, then Weighted Recall is given by

$$recall = \frac{\sum_{i=1}^{M} \sum_{j=1}^{N} L(s_i, a_j)}{\sum_{i=1}^{O} \sum_{j=1}^{N} L(s_i, a_j)}$$

where $L(s_i, a_j)$ is the number of links for a sentence s_i according to annotator a_j. We can compare machine performance with human performance in the following way. For each annotator, we rank their sentences from most-linked to least-linked and select the best sentences until we reach the same word count as our selections. We then calculate their weighted recall score by using the other N-1 annotations, and then average over all N annotators to get an average human performance. We report all transformation scores normalized by human performance for that dataset.

6 Results

In this section we present results for our interpretation and transformation components.

[1]http://www.csie.ntu.edu.tw/ cjlin/liblinear/

6.1 Interpretation: Meetings

Figure 1 shows the ROC curves for the sentence-level classifiers applied to manual transcripts. On both manual and ASR transcripts, the classifiers with the largest AUROCs are the action item and general extractive classifiers. Action item sentences can be detected very well with this feature set, with the classifier having an AUROC of 0.92 on manual transcripts and 0.93 on ASR, a result comparable to previous findings of 0.91 and 0.93 (Murray and Renals, 2008) obtained using a speech-specific feature set. General extractive classification is also similar to other state-of-the-art extraction approaches on spoken data using speech features (Zhu and Penn, 2006)[2] with an AUROC of 0.87 on manual and 0.85 on ASR. Decision sentences can also be detected quite well, with AUROCs of 0.81 and 0.77. Positive-subjective, negative-subjective and problem sentences are the most difficult to detect, but the classifiers still give credible performance with AUROCs of approximately 0.76 for manual and 0.70-0.72 for ASR.

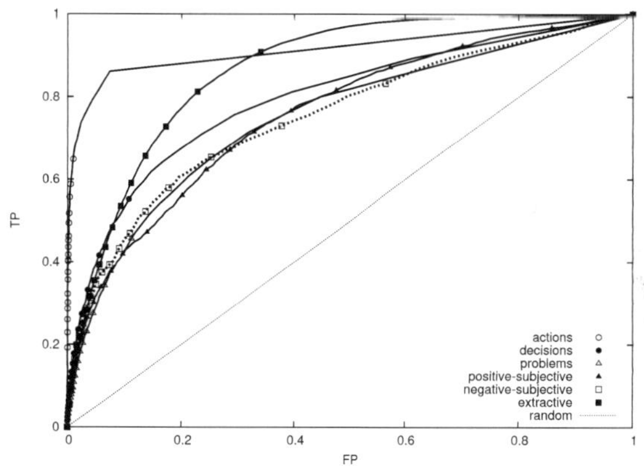

Figure 1: ROC Curves for Ontology Mapping Classifiers (Manual Transcripts)

6.2 Transformation: Meetings

In this section we present the weighted recall scores for the sentences selected using the ILP method described in Section 4. Remember, weighted recall measures how useful these sentences would be in generating sentences for an abstract summary. We also assess the performance of three baseline summarizers operating at the same compression level.

[2]Based on visual inspection of their reported best ROC curve

The simplest baseline (GREEDY) selects sentences by ranking the posterior probabilites output by the general extractive classifier. The second baseline (CLASS COMBO) averages the posterior probabilites output by *all* the classifiers and ranks sentences from best to worst. The third baseline (RETRAIN) uses the posterior probability outputs of all the classifiers (except for the extractive classifier) as new feature inputs for the general extractive classifier.

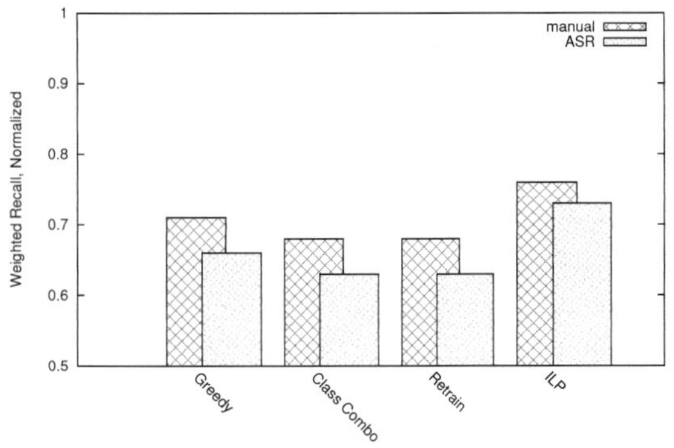

Figure 2: Weighted Recall Scores for AMI Meetings

Figure 2 shows the weighted recall scores, normalized by human performance, for all approaches on both manual and ASR transcripts. On manual transcripts, the ILP approach (0.76) is better than GREEDY (0.71) with a marginally significant difference (p=0.07) and is significantly better than CLASS COMBO and RETRAIN (both 0.68) according to t-test ($p < 0.05$) . For ASR transcripts, the ILP approach is significantly better than all other approaches ($p < 0.05$). Xie et al. (2009) reported ROUGE-1 F-measures on a different meeting corpus, and our ROUGE-1 scores are in the same range of 0.64-0.69 (they used 18% compression ratio).

6.3 Interpretation: Emails

We applied the same summarization method to the 40 BC3 email threads, with contrasting results. Because the BC3 corpus does not currently contain annotations for decisions, actions and problems, we simply ran the AMI-trained models over the data for those three phenomena. We can assess the performance of the extractive, positive-subjective and negative-subjective classifiers by examining the ROC curves displayed in Figure 3. Both the general extractive and negative-subjective classifiers have AUROCs of around 0.75. The positive-subjective classifier initially has the worst performance with an AUROC of 0.66, but we found that positive-subjective performance increased dramatically to an AUROC of 0.77 when we used only conversational features and not word bigrams, character trigrams or POS tags.

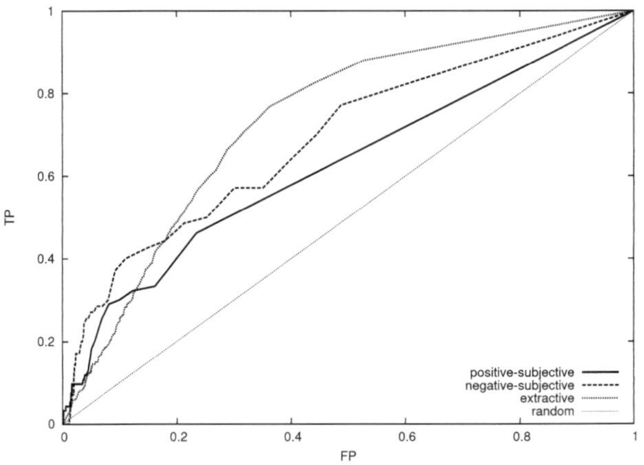

Figure 3: ROC Curves for Ontology Mapping Classifiers (BC3 Corpus)

6.4 Transformation: Emails

If we examine the weighted recall scores in Figure 4 we see that the ILP approach is worse than the greedy summarizers on the BC3 dataset. However, the differences are not significant between ILP and COMBO CLASS (p=0.15) and only marginally significant compared with RETRAIN and GREEDY (both p=0.08). The performance of the ILP approach varies greatly across email threads. The top 15 threads (out of 40) yield ILP weighted recall scores that are on par with human performance, while the worst 15 are half that.

6.4.1 Email Corpus Analysis

Due to the large discrepancy in performance on BC3 emails, we conducted additional experiments for error analysis. We first explored whether we could build a classifier that could discriminate the best 15 emails from the worst 15 emails in terms of weighted recall scores with the ILP approach, to determine whether there are certain features that correlate with good performance. Using the same fea-

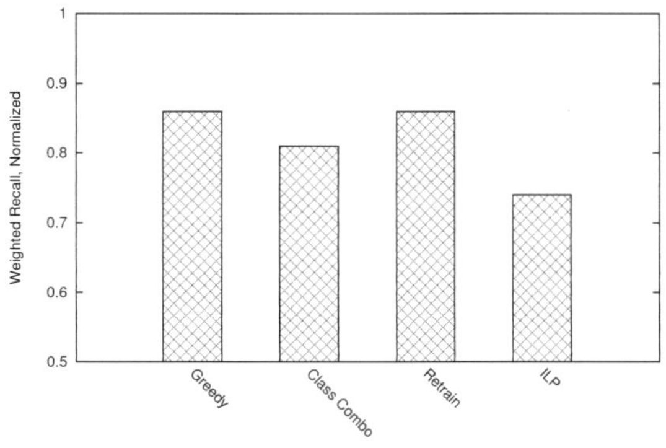

Figure 4: Weighted Recall Scores for BC3 Threads

Metric	Worst 15	Best 15
Weighted Recall	0.49	1.05
# Turns	6.27	6.73
# Participants	4.67	5.4
PPAU	0.18	0.12
BEGAUTH	0.31	0.18

Table 2: Selected Email Features, Averaged

tures described in Section 3.1, we built a logistic regression classifier on the two classes and found that they can be discriminated quite well (80% accuracy on an approximately balanced dataset) and that the conversation structure features are the most useful for discerning them. Table 2 shows the weighted recall scores and several conversation features that were weighted most highly by the logistic regression model. In particular, we found that the email threads that yielded good performance tended to feature more active participants (# Participants), were not dominated by a single individual (BEGAUTH), and featured a higher number of turns (# Turns) that followed each other in quick succession without long pauses (PPAU, pause as percentage of conversation length). In other words, these emails were structured more similarly to meetings. Note that since we normalize weighted recall by human performance, it is possible to have a weighted recall score higher than 1. On the 15 best threads, our system achieves human-level performance. Because we used AMI-trained models for detecting decisions, actions and problems in the BC3 data, it is not surprising that performance was better on those emails structured similarly to meetings. All of this indicates that there are many different types of emails and that we will have to focus on improving performance on emails that differ markedly in structure.

7 Conclusion

We have presented two components of an abstractive conversation summarization system. The *interpretation* component is used to populate a simple conversation ontology where conversation participants and entities are linked by object properties such as decisions, actions and subjective opinions. For this step we show that highly accurate classifiers can be built using a large set of features not specific to any conversation modality.

In the *transformation* step, a summary is created by maximizing a function relating sentence weights and entity weights, with the sentence weights determined by the sentence-ontology mapping. Our evaluation shows that the sentences we select are highly informative to generate abstract summaries, and that our content selection method outperforms several greedy selection approaches. The system described thus far may appear extractive in nature, as the transformation step is identifying informative sentences in the conversation. However, these selected sentences correspond to $< participant, relation, entity >$ triples in the ontology, for which we can subsequently generate novel text by creating linguistic annotations of the conversation ontology (Galanis and Androutsopolous, 2007). Even without the generation step, the approach described above allows us to create structured extracts by grouping sentences according to specific phenomena such as action items and decisions. The knowledge represented by the ontology enables us to significantly improve sentence selection according to intrinsic measures and to generate structured output that we hypothesize will be more useful to an end user compared with a generic unstructured extract.

Future work will focus on the generation component and on applying the summarization system to conversations in other modalities such as blogs and instant messages. Based on the email error analysis, we plan to pursue domain adaptation techniques to improve performance on different types of emails.

References

R. Barzilay and K. McKeown. 2005. Sentence fusion for multidocument news summarization. *Computational Linguistics*, 31(3):297–328.

G. Carenini, R. Ng, and X. Zhou. 2007. Summarizing email conversations with clue words. In *Proc. of ACM WWW 07, Banff, Canada.*

J. Carletta, S. Ashby, S. Bourban, M. Flynn, M. Guillemot, T. Hain, J. Kadlec, V. Karaiskos, W. Kraaij, M. Kronenthal, G. Lathoud, M. Lincoln, A. Lisowska, I. McCowan, W. Post, D. Reidsma, and P. Wellner. 2005. The AMI meeting corpus: A pre-announcement. In *Proc. of MLMI 2005, Edinburgh, UK*, pages 28–39.

K. Church and W. Gale. 1995. Inverse document frequency IDF: A measure of deviation from poisson. In *Proc. of the Third Workshop on Very Large Corpora*, pages 121–130.

J. Clarke and M. Lapata. 2006. Constraint-based sentence compression: An integer programming approach. In *Proc. of COLING/ACL 2006*, pages 144–151.

R.-E. Fan, K.-W. Chang, C.-J. Hsieh, X.-R. Wang, and C.-J. Lin. 2008. Liblinear: A library for large linear classification. *Journal of Machine Learning Research*, 9:1871–1874.

D. Galanis and I. Androutsopolous. 2007. Generating multilingual descriptions from linguistically annotated owl ontologies: the naturalowl system. In *Proc. of ENLG 2007, Schloss Dagstuhl, Germany.*

M. Galley. 2006. A skip-chain conditional random field for ranking meeting utterances by importance. In *Proc. of EMNLP 2006, Sydney, Australia*, pages 364–372.

D. Gillick, K. Riedhammer, B. Favre, and D. Hakkani-Tür. 2009. A global optimization framework for meeting summarization. In *Proc. of ICASSP 2009, Taipei, Taiwan.*

S. Gupta, J. Niekrasz, M. Purver, and D. Jurafsky. 2007. Resolving "*You*" in multi-party dialog. In *Proc. of SIGdial 2007, Antwerp, Belgium.*

L. He, E. Sanocki, A. Gupta, and J. Grudin. 1999. Auto-summarization of audio-video presentations. In *Proc. of ACM MULTIMEDIA '99, Orlando, FL, USA*, pages 489–498.

P-Y. Hsueh, J. Kilgour, J. Carletta, J. Moore, and S. Renals. 2007. Automatic decision detection in meeting speech. In *Proc. of MLMI 2007, Brno, Czech Republic.*

K. Spärck Jones. 1999. Automatic summarizing: Factors and directions. In I. Mani and M. Maybury, editors, *Advances in Automatic Text Summarization*, pages 1–12. MITP.

T. Kleinbauer, S. Becker, and T. Becker. 2007. Combining multiple information layers for the automatic generation of indicative meeting abstracts. In *Proc. of ENLG 2007, Dagstuhl, Germany.*

K. Knight and D. Marcu. 2000. Statistics-based summarization - step one: Sentence compression. In *Proc. of AAAI 2000, Austin, Texas, USA*, pages 703–710.

J. Kupiec, J. Pederson, and F. Chen. 1995. A trainable document summarizer. In *Proc. of the 18th Annual International ACM SIGIR Conference on Research and Development in Information Retrieval. Seattle, Washington, USA*, pages 68–73.

K. McKeown, J. Hirschberg, M. Galley, and S. Maskey. 2005. From text to speech summarization. In *Proc. of ICASSP 2005, Philadelphia, USA*, pages 997–1000.

C. Muller. 2007. Resolving *It*, *This* and *That* in unrestricted multi-party dialog. In *Proc. of ACL 2007, Prague, Czech Republic.*

G. Murray and S. Renals. 2008. Detecting action items in meetings. In *Proc. of MLMI 2008, Utrecht, the Netherlands.*

G. Murray, T. Kleinbauer, P. Poller, S. Renals, T. Becker, and J. Kilgour. 2008. Extrinsic summarization evaluation: A decision audit task. In *Proc. of MLMI 2008, Utrecht, the Netherlands.*

M. Purver, J. Dowding, J. Niekrasz, P. Ehlen, and S. Noorbaloochi. 2007. Detecting and summarizing action items in multi-party dialogue. In *Proc. of the 9th SIGdial Workshop on Discourse and Dialogue, Antwerp, Belgium.*

S. Raaijmakers, K. Truong, and T. Wilson. 2008. Multimodal subjectivity analysis of multiparty conversation. In *Proc. of EMNLP 2008, Honolulu, HI, USA.*

O. Rambow, L. Shrestha, J. Chen, and C. Lauridsen. 2004. Summarizing email threads. In *Proc. of HLT-NAACL 2004, Boston, USA.*

J. Ulrich, G. Murray, and G. Carenini. 2008. A publicly available annotated corpus for supervised email summarization. In *Proc. of AAAI EMAIL-2008 Workshop, Chicago, USA.*

T. Wilson. 2008. Annotating subjective content in meetings. In *Proc. of LREC 2008, Marrakech, Morocco.*

S. Xie, B. Favre, D. Hakkani-Tür, and Y. Liu. 2009. Leveraging sentence weights in a concept-based optimization framework for extractive meeting summarization. In *Proc. of Interspeech 2009, Brighton, England.*

L. Zhou and E. Hovy. 2005. Digesting virtual "geek" culture: The summarization of technical internet relay chats. In *Proc. of ACL 2005, Ann Arbor, MI, USA.*

X. Zhu and G. Penn. 2006. Summarization of spontaneous conversations. In *Proc. of Interspeech 2006, Pittsburgh, USA*, pages 1531–1534.

Quantifying the Limits and Success of Extractive Summarization Systems Across Domains

Hakan Ceylan and **Rada Mihalcea**
Department of Computer Science
University of North Texas
Denton, TX 76203
{hakan,rada}@unt.edu

Umut Özertem
Yahoo! Labs
701 First Avenue
Sunnyvale, CA 94089
umut@yahoo-inc.com

Elena Lloret and **Manuel Palomar**
Department of
Software and Computing Systems
University of Alicante
San Vicente del Raspeig
Alicante 03690, Spain
{elloret,mpalomar}@dlsi.ua.es

Abstract

This paper analyzes the topic identification stage of single-document automatic text summarization across four different domains, consisting of newswire, literary, scientific and legal documents. We present a study that explores the summary space of each domain via an exhaustive search strategy, and finds the probability density function (pdf) of the ROUGE score distributions for each domain. We then use this pdf to calculate the percentile rank of extractive summarization systems. Our results introduce a new way to judge the success of automatic summarization systems and bring quantified explanations to questions such as why it was so hard for the systems to date to have a statistically significant improvement over the lead baseline in the news domain.

1 Introduction

Topic identification is the first stage of the generally accepted three-phase model in automatic text summarization, in which the goal is to identify the most important units in a document, i.e., phrases, sentences, or paragraphs (Hovy and Lin, 1999; Lin, 1999; Sparck-Jones, 1999). This stage is followed by the topic interpretation and summary generation steps where the identified units are further processed to bring the summary into a coherent, human readable abstract form. The extractive summarization systems, however, only employ the topic identification stage, and simply output a ranked list of the units according to a compression ratio criterion. In general, for most systems sentences are the preferred units in this stage, as they are the smallest grammatical units that can express a statement.

Since the sentences in a document are reproduced verbatim in extractive summaries, it is theoretically possible to explore the search space of this problem through an enumeration of all possible extracts for a document. Such an exploration would not only allow us to see how far we can go with extractive summarization, but we would also be able to judge the difficulty of the problem by looking at the distribution of the evaluation scores for the generated extracts. Moreover, the high scoring extracts could also be used to train a machine learning algorithm.

However, such an enumeration strategy has an exponential complexity as it requires all possible sentence combinations of a document to be generated, constrained by a given word or sentence length. Thus the problem quickly becomes impractical as the number of sentences in a document increases and the compression ratio decreases. In this work, we try to overcome this bottleneck by using a large cluster of computers, and decomposing the task into smaller problems by using the given section boundaries or a linear text segmentation method. As a result of this exploration, we generate a probability density function (pdf) of the ROUGE score (Lin, 2004) distributions for four different domains, which shows the distribution of the evaluation scores for the generated extracts, and allows us to assess the difficulty of each domain for extractive summarization.

Furthermore, using these pdfs, we introduce a new success measure for extractive summarization systems. Namely, given a system's average score over a data set, we show how to calculate the per-

Human Language Technologies: The 2010 Annual Conference of the North American Chapter of the ACL, pages 903–911,
Los Angeles, California, June 2010.

centile rank of this system from the corresponding pdf of the data set. This allows us to see the true improvement a system achieves over another, such as a baseline, and provides a standardized scoring scheme for systems performing on the same data set.

2 Related Work

Despite the large amount of work in automatic text summarization, there are only a few studies in the literature that employ an exhaustive search strategy to create extracts, which is mainly due to the prohibitively large search space of the problem. Furthermore, the research regarding the alignment of abstracts to original documents has shown great variations across domains (Kupiec et al., 1995; Teufel and Moens, 1997; Marcu, 1999; Jing, 2002; Ceylan and Mihalcea, 2009), which indicates that the extractive summarization techniques are not applicable to all domains at the same level.

In order to automate the process of corpus construction for automatic summarization systems, (Marcu, 1999) used exhaustive search to generate the best *Extract* from a given *(Abstract, Text)* tuple, where the best *Extract* contains a set of clauses from *Text* that have the highest similarity to the given *Abstract*.

In addition, (Donaway et al., 2000) used exhaustive search to create all the sentence extracts of length three starting with 15 TREC Documents, in order to judge the performance of several summary evaluation measures suggested in their paper.

Finally, the study most similar to ours was done by (Lin and Hovy, 2003), who used the articles with less than 30 sentences from the DUC 2001 data set to find *oracle extracts* of 100 and 150 ($\pm$5) words. These extracts were compared against one summary source, selected as the one that gave the highest inter-human agreement. Although it was concluded that a 10% improvement was possible for extractive summarization systems, which typically score around the lead baseline, there was no report on how difficult it would be to achieve this improvement, which is the main objective of our paper.

3 Description of the Data Set

Our data set is composed of four different domains: newswire, literary, scientific and legal. For all the domains we used 50 documents and only one summary for each document, except for newswire where we used two summaries per document. For the newswire domain, we selected the articles and their summaries from the DUC 2002 data set,[1]. For the literary domain, we obtained 10 novels that are literature classics, and available online in text format. Further, we collected the corresponding summaries for these novels from various websites such as CliffsNotes (www.cliffsnotes.com) and SparkNotes (www.sparknotes.com), which make available human generated abstracts for literary works. These sources give a summary for each chapter of the novel, so each chapter can be treated as a separate document. Thus we evaluate 50 chapters in total. For the scientific domain, we selected the articles from the medical journal *Autoimmunity Reviews*[2] were selected, and their abstracts are used as summaries. Finally, for the legal domain, we gathered 50 law documents and their corresponding summaries from the European Legislation Website,[3] which comprises four types of laws - *Council Directives*, *Acts*, *Communications*, and *Decisions* over several topics, such as society, environment, education, economics and employment.

Although all the summaries are human generated abstracts for all the domains, it is worth mentioning that the documents and their corresponding summaries exhibit a specific writing style for each domain, in terms of the vocabulary used and the length of the sentences. We list some of the statistical properties of each domain in Table 1.

Domain	μ_{Dw}	μ_{Sw}	μ_R	μ_C	μ_{Cw}
Newswire	641	101	84%	1	641
Literary	4973	1148	77%	6	196
Scientific	1989	160	92%	9	221
Legal	3469	865	75%	18	192

Table 1: Statistical properties of the data set. μ_{Dw}, and μ_{Sw} represent the average number of words for each document and summary respectively; μ_R indicates the average compression ratio; and μ_C and μ_{Cw} represent the average number of sections for each document, and the average number of words for each section respectively.

[1] http://www-nlpir.nist.gov/projects/duc/data.html
[2] http://www.elsevier.com/wps/product/cws_home/622356
[3] http://eur-lex.europa.eu/en/legis/index.htm

4 Experimental Setup

As mentioned in Section 1, an exhaustive search algorithm requires generating all possible sentence combinations from a document, and evaluating each one individually. For example, using the values from Table 1, and assuming 20 words per sentence, we find that the search space for the news domain contains approximately $\binom{32}{5} \times 50 = 10,068,800$ summaries. The same calculation method for the scientific domain gives us $\binom{99}{8} \times 50 = 8.56 \times 10^{12}$ summaries. Obviously the search space gets much bigger for the legal and literary domains due to their larger text size.

In order to be able to cope with such a huge search space, the first thing we did was to modify the ROUGE 1.5.5[4] Perl script by fixing the parameters to those used in the DUC experiments,[5] and also by modifying the way it handles the input and output to make it suitable for streaming on the cluster.

The resulting script evaluates around 25-30 summaries per second on an Intel 2.33 GHz processor. Next, we streamed the resulting ROUGE script for each (document, summary) pair on a large cluster of computers running on an Hadoop Map-Reduce framework.[6] Based on the size of the search space for a (document, summary) pair, the number of computers allocated in the cluster ranged from just a few to more than one thousand.

Although the combination of a large cluster and a faster ROUGE is enough to handle most of the documents in the news domain in just a few hours, a simple calculation shows that the problem is still impractical for the other domains. Hence for the scientific, legal, and literary domains, rather than considering each document as a whole, we divide them into sections, and create extracts for each section such that the length of the extract is proportional to the length of the section in the original document. For the legal and scientific domains, we use the given section boundaries (without considering the subsections for scientific documents). For the novels, we treat each chapter as a single document (since each chapter has its own summary), which is further divided into sections using a publicly available linear text segmentation algorithm by (Utiyama and Isahara, 2001).[7] In all cases, we let the algorithm pick the number of segments automatically.

To evaluate the sections, we modified ROUGE further so that it applies the length constraint to the extracts only, not to the model summaries. This is due to the fact that we evaluate the extracts of each section individually against the whole model summary, which is larger than the extract. This way, we can get an overall ROUGE recall score for a document extract, simply by summing up the recall scores of each section extracts. The precision score for the entire document can also be found by adding the weighted precision scores for each section, where the weight is proportional to the length of the section in the original document. In our study, however, we only use recall scores.

Note that, since for the legal, scientific, and literary domains we consider each section of a document independently, we are not performing a true exhaustive search for these domains, but rather solving a suboptimal problem, as we divide the number of words in the model summary to each section proportional to the section's length. However, we believe that this is a fair assumption, as it has been shown repeatedly in the past that text segmentation helps improving the performance of text summarization systems (yen Kan et al., 1998; Nakao, 2000; Mihalcea and Ceylan, 2007).

5 Exhaustive Search Algorithm

Let $E_{i_k} = S_{i_1}, S_{i_2}, ..., S_{i_k}$ be the ith extract that has k sentences, and generated from a document D with n sentences $D = S_1, S_2, \ldots, S_n$. Further, let $len(S_j)$ give the number of words in sentence S_j. We enforce that E_{i_k} satisfies the following constraints:

$$\begin{aligned} len(E_{i_k}) &= len(S_{i_1}) + \ldots + len(S_{i_k}) \geq L \\ len(E_{i_{k-1}}) &= len(S_{i_1}) + \ldots + len(S_{i_{k-1}}) < L \end{aligned}$$

where L is the length constraint on all the extracts of document D. We note that for any E_{i_k}, the order of the sentences in $E_{i_{k-1}}$ does not affect the ROUGE scores, since only the last sentence may be

[4] http://berouge.com

[5] -n 2 -x -m -2 4 -u -c 95 -r 1000 -f A -p 0.5 -t 0

[6] http://hadoop.apache.org/

[7] http://mastarpj.nict.go.jp/ mutiyama/software/textseg/textseg-1.211.tar.gz

chopped off due to the length constraint.[8] Hence, we start generating sentence combinations $\binom{n}{r}$ in *lexicographic order*, for $r = 1...n$, and for each combination $E_{i_k} = S_{i_1}, S_{i_2}, ..., S_{i_k}$ where $k > 1$, we generate additional extracts E'_{i_k} by successfully swapping S_{i_j} with S_{i_k} for $j = 1, ..., k-1$ and checking to see if the above constraints are still satisfied. Therefore from a combination with k sentences that satisfies the constraints, we might generate up to $k-1$ additional extracts. Finally, we stop the process either when $r = n$ and the last combination is generated, or we cannot find any extract that satisfies the constraints for r.

6 Generating pdfs

Once the extracts for a document are generated and evaluated, we go through each result and assign its recall score to a range, which we refer to as a bin. We use $1,000$ equally spaced bins between 0 and 1. As an example, a recall score of 0.46873 would be assigned to the bin $[0.468, 0.469]$. By keeping a count for each bin, we are in fact building a histogram of scores for the document. Let this histogram be h, and $h[j]$ be the value in the jth bin of the histogram. We then define the normalized histogram $\widehat{h}$ as:

$$\widehat{h}[j] = \frac{N}{\sum_{i=1}^{N} h[j]} h[j] \qquad (1)$$

where $N = 1,000$ is the number of bins in the histogram. Note that since the *width* of each bin is $\frac{1}{N}$, the Riemann sum of the normalized histogram $\widehat{h}$ is equal to 1, so $\widehat{h}$ can be used as an approximation to the underlying pdf. As an example, we show the histogram $\widehat{h}$ for the newswire document AP890323-0218 in Figure 1.

We combine the normalized histograms of all the documents in a domain in order to find the pdf for that domain. This requires multiplying the value of each bin in a document's histogram, with all the other possible combinations of bin values taken from each of the remaining histograms, and assigning the result to the average bin for each combination. This can be done iteratively by keeping a moving average. We illustrate this procedure in Algorithm 1, where K represents the number of documents in a domain.

[8]Note that we do not take the coherence of extracts into account, i.e. the sentences in an extract do not need to be sorted in order of their appearance in the original document. We also do not change the position of the words in a sentence.

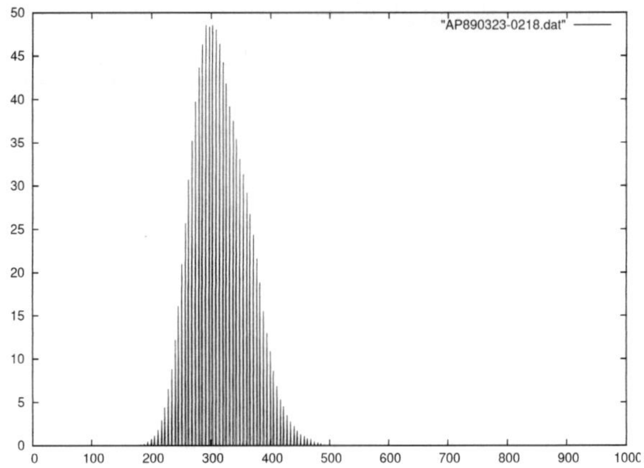

Figure 1: The normalized histogram $\widehat{h}$ of ROUGE-1 recall scores for the newswire document AP890323-0218.

Algorithm 1 Combine $\widehat{h}^i$'s for $i = 1, \ldots, K$ to create h_d, the histogram for domain d.

```
1:  h_d := {}
2:  for i = 1 to N do
3:      h_d[i] := ĥ^1[i]
4:  end for
5:  for i = 2 to K do
6:      h_t = {}
7:      for j = 1 to N do
8:          for k = 1 to N do
9:              a = round(((k * (i - 1)) + j)/i)
10:             h_t[a] = h_t[a] + (h_d[k] * ĥ^i[j])
11:         end for
12:     end for
13:     h_d := h_t
14: end for
```

The resulting histogram h_d, when normalized using Equation 1, is an approximation to the pdf for domain d. Furthermore, we used the $round()$ function in line 9, which rounds a number to the nearest integer, as the bins are indexed by integers. Note that this rounding introduces an error, which is distributed uniformly due to the nature of the $round()$ function. It is also possible to lower the affect of this error with higher resolutions (i.e. larger number of bins). In Figure 2, we show a sample h_d, obtained by combining 10 documents from the newswire do-

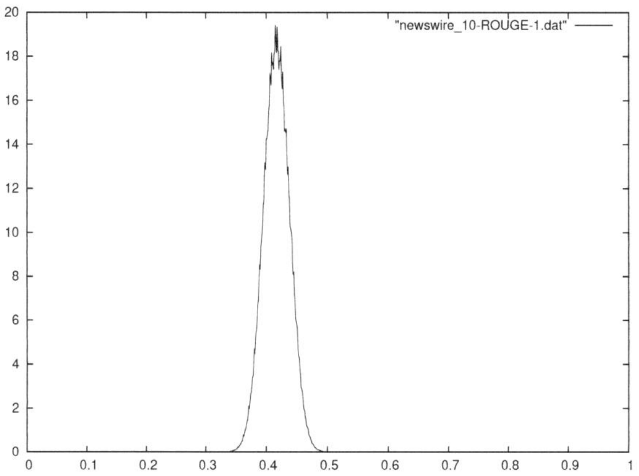

Figure 2: An example pdf obtained by combining 10 document histograms of ROUGE-1 recall scores from the newswire domain. The x-axis is normalized to [0,1].

main.

Recall from Section 4 that the documents in the literary, legal, and scientific domains are divided into sections either by using the given section boundaries or by applying a text segmentation algorithm, and the extracts of each section are then evaluated individually. Hence for these domains, we first calculate the histogram of each section individually, and then combine them to find the histogram of a document. The combination procedure for the section histograms is similar to Algorithm 1, except that in this case we do not keep a moving average, but rather sum up the bins of the sections. Note that when bin i and j are added, the resulting values should be expected to be half the times in bin $i+j$, and half the times in $i+j-1$.

7 Calculating Percentile Ranks

Given a pdf for a domain, the success of a system having a ROUGE recall score of S could be simply measured by finding the area bounded by S. This gives us the percentile rank of the system in the overall distribution. Assuming $0 \leq S \leq 1$, let $\widehat{S} = \lfloor N \times S \rfloor$, then the formula to calculate the percentile rank can be simply given as:

$$PR(S) = \frac{100}{N} \sum_{i=1}^{\widehat{S}} \widehat{h_d}[i] \tag{2}$$

	ROUGE-1			
Domain	μ	σ	max	min
Newswire	39.39	0.87	65.70	20.20
Literary	45.20	0.47	63.90	28.40
Scientific	45.99	0.68	71.90	24.20
Legal	72.82	0.28	82.40	62.80
	ROUGE-2			
Domain	μ	σ	max	min
Newswire	11.57	0.79	37.40	1.60
Literary	5.41	0.34	16.90	1.80
Scientific	10.98	0.60	33.30	1.30
Legal	28.74	0.29	40.90	19.60
	ROUGE-SU4			
Domain	μ	σ	max	min
Newswire	15.33	0.69	38.10	6.40
Literary	13.28	0.30	24.30	6.90
Scientific	16.13	0.50	35.80	6.20
Legal	35.63	0.25	45.70	28.70

Table 2: Statistical properties of the pdfs

8 Results

The ensemble distributions of ROUGE-1 recall scores per document are shown in Figure 3. The ensemble distributions tell us that the performance of the extracts, especially for the news and the scientific domains, are mostly uniform for each document. This is due to the fact that documents in these domains, and their corresponding summaries, are written with a certain conventional style. There is however a little scattering in the distributions of the literary and the legal domains. This is an expected result for the literary domain, as there is no specific summarization style for these documents, but somehow surprising for the legal domain, where the effect is probably due to the different types of legal documents in the data set.

The pdf plots resulting from the ROUGE-1 recall scores are shown in Figure 4.[9] In order to analyze the pdf plots, and better understand their differences, Table 2 lists the mean (μ) and the standard deviation (σ) measures of the pdfs, as well as the average minimum and maximum scores that an extractive summarization system can get for each domain.

By looking at the pdf plots and the minimum and maximum columns from Table 2, we notice that for

[9]Similar pdfs are obtained for ROUGE-2 and ROUGE-SU4, even if at a different scale.

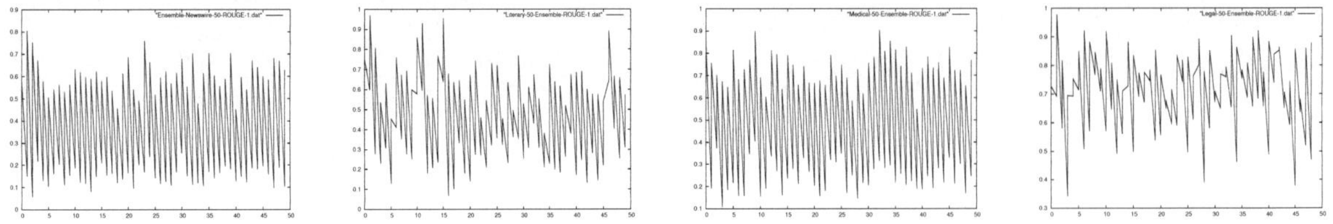

Figure 3: ROUGE-1 recall score distributions per document for Newswire, Literary, Scientific and Legal Domains, respectively from left to right.

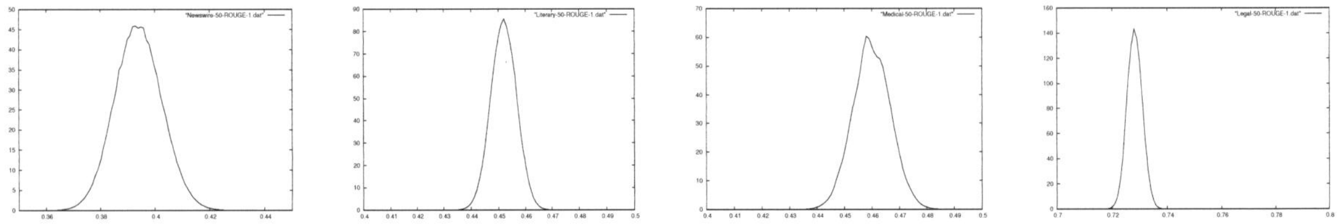

Figure 4: Probability Density Functions of ROUGE-1 recall scores for the Newswire, Literary, Scientific and Legal Domains, respectively from left to right. The resolution of the x-axis is increased to 0.1.

all the domains, the pdfs are long-tailed distributions. This immediately implies that most of the extracts in a summary space are clustered around the mean, which means that for automatic summarization systems, it is very easy to get scores around this range. Furthermore, we can judge the hardness of each domain by looking at the standard deviation values. A lower standard deviation indicates a steeper curve, which implies that improving a system would be harder. From the table, we can infer that the legal domain is the hardest while the newswire is the easiest.

Comparing Table 2 with the values in Table 1, we also notice that the compression ratio affects the performance differently for each domain. For example, although the scientific domain has the highest compression ratio, it has a higher mean than the literary and the newswire domains for ROUGE-1 and ROUGE-SU4 recall scores. This implies that although the abstracts of the medical journals are highly compressed, they have a high overlap with the document, probably caused by their writing style. This was in fact confirmed earlier by the experiments in (Kupiec et al., 1995), where it was found out that for a data set of 188 scientific articles, 79% of the sentences in the abstracts could be perfectly matched with the sentences in the corresponding documents.

Next, we confirm our experiments by testing three different extractive summarization systems on our data set. The first system that we implement is called *Random*, and gives a random score between 1 and 100 to each sentence in a document, and then selects the top scoring sentences. The second system, *Lead*, implements the lead baseline method which takes the first k sentences of a document until the length limit is reached. Finally, the last system that we implement is *TextRank*, which uses a variation of the PageRank graph centrality algorithm in order to identify the most important sentences in a document (Page et al., 1999; Erkan and Radev, 2004; Mihalcea and Tarau, 2004). We selected TextRank as it has a performance competitive with the top systems participating in DUC '02 (Mihalcea and Tarau, 2004). We would also like to mention that for the literary, scientific, and legal domains, the systems apply the algorithms for each section and each section is evaluated independently, and their resulting recall scores are summed up. This is needed in order to be consistent with our exhaustive search experiments.

The ROUGE recall scores of the three systems are shown in Table 3. As expected, for the literary and legal domains, the *Random*, and the *Lead* systems score around the mean. This is due to the fact that the leading sentences for these two domains do not indicate any significance, hence the *Lead* system just behaves like *Random*. However for the scientific and newswire domains, the leading sentences do have

	ROUGE-1		
Domain	Random	Lead	TextRank
Newswire	39.13	45.63	44.43
Literary	45.39	45.36	46.12
Scientific	45.75	47.18	49.26
Legal	73.04	72.42	74.82
	ROUGE-2		
Domain	Random	Lead	TextRank
Newswire	11.39	19.60	17.99
Literary	5.33	5.41	5.92
Scientific	10.73	12.07	12.76
Legal	28.56	28.92	31.06
	ROUGE-SU4		
Domain	Random	Lead	TextRank
Newswire	15.07	21.58	20.46
Literary	13.21	13.28	13.81
Scientific	15.92	17.12	17.85
Legal	35.41	35.55	37.64

Table 3: ROUGE recall scores of the Lead baseline, TextRank, and Random sentence selector across domains

	ROUGE-1		
Domain	Random	Lead	TextRank
Newswire	%39.18	%99.99	%99.99
Literary	%62.89	%62.89	%97.90
Scientific	%42.30	%95.56	%99.87
Legal	%79.47	%16.19	%99.99
	ROUGE-2		
Domain	Random	Lead	TextRank
Newswire	%39.57	%99.99	%99.99
Literary	%42.20	%54.32	%94.34
Scientific	%35.6	%96.03	%99.79
Legal	%36.68	%75.38	%99.99
	ROUGE-SU4		
Domain	Random	Lead	TextRank
Newswire	%40.68	%99.99	%99.99
Literary	%46.39	%46.39	%96.84
Scientific	%36.37	%97.69	%99.94
Legal	%23.53	%42.00	%99.99

Table 4: Percentile rankings of the Lead baseline, TextRank, and Random sentence selector across domains

importance so the *Lead* system consistently outperforms *Random*. Furthermore, although *TextRank* is the best system for the literary, scientific, and legal domains, it gets outperformed by the *Lead* system on the newswire domain. This is also an expected result as none of the single-document summarization systems were able to achieve a statistically significant improvement over the lead baseline in the previous Document Understanding Conferences (DUC).

The ROUGE scoring scheme does not tell us how much improvement a system achieved over another, or how far it is from the upper bound. Since we now have access to the pdf of each domain in our data set, we can find this information simply by calculating the percentile rank of each system using the formula given in Equation 2.

The percentile ranks of all three systems for each domain are shown in Table 4. Notice how different the gap is between the scores of each system this time, compared to the scores in Table 3. For example, we see in Table 3 that *TextRank* on scientific domain has only a 3.51 ROUGE-1 score improvement over a system that randomly selects sentences to include in the extract. However, Table 4 tells us that this improvement is in fact 57.57%.

From Table 4, we see that both *TextRank* and the *Lead* system are in the 99.99% percentile of the newswire domain although the systems have 1.20, 1.61, and 1.12 difference in their ROUGE-1, ROUGE-2, and ROUGE-SU4 scores respectively. The high percentile for the *Lead* system explains why it was so hard to improve over these baseline in previous evaluations on newswire data (e.g., see the evaluations from the Document Understanding Conferences). Furthermore, we see from Table 2 that the upper bounds corresponding to these scores are 65.7, 37.4, and 38.1 respectively, which are well above both the *TextRank* and the *Lead* systems. Therefore, the percentile rankings of the *Lead* and the *TextRank* systems for this domain do not seem to give us clues about how the two systems compare to each other, nor about their actual distance from the upper bounds. There are two reasons for this: First, as we mentioned earlier, most of the summary space consists of *easy* extracts, which make the distribution long-tailed.[10] Therefore even though we have quite a bit of systems achieving high scores, their number is negligible compared to the millions of extracts that are clustered around the mean. Secondly, we need a higher resolution (i.e. larger number of bins) in constructing the pdfs in order to be able to

[10]This also accounts for the fact that even though we might have two very close ROUGE scores that are not statistically significant, their percentile rankings might differ quite a bit.

see the difference more clearly between the two systems. Finally, when comparing two successful systems using percentile ranks, we believe the use of error reduction would be more beneficial.

As a final note, we also randomly sampled extracts from documents in the scientific and legal domains, but this time without considering the section boundaries and without performing any segmentation. We kept the number of samples for each document equal to the number of extracts we generated from the same document using a divide-and-conquer approach. We evaluated the samples using ROUGE-1 recall scores, and obtained pdfs for each domain using the same strategy discussed earlier in the paper. The resulting pdfs, although they exhibit similar characteristics, they have mean values (μ) around 10% lower than the ones we listed in Table 2, which supports the findings from earlier research that segmentation is useful for text summarization.

9 Conclusions and Future Work

In this paper, we described a study that explores the search space of extractive summaries across four different domains. For the news domain we generated all possible extracts of the given documents, and for the literary, scientific, and legal domains we followed a divide-and-conquer approach by chunking the documents into sections, handled each section independently, and combined the resulting scores at the end. We then used the distributions of the evaluations scores to generate the probability density functions (pdfs) for each domain. Various statistical properties of these pdfs helped us asses the difficulty of each domain. Finally, we introduced a new scoring scheme for automatic text summarization systems that can be derived from the pdfs. The new scheme calculates a percentile rank of the ROUGE-1 recall score of a system, which gives scores in the range [0-100]. This lets us see how far each system is from the upper bound, and thus make a better comparison among the systems. The new scoring system showed us that while there is a 20.1% gap between the upper bound and the lead baseline for the news domain, closing this gap is difficult, as the percentile rank of the lead baseline system, 99.99%, indicates that the system is already very close to the upper bound.

Furthermore, except for the literary domain, the percentile rank of the *TextRank* system is also very close to the upperbound. This result does not suggest that additional improvements cannot be made in these domains, but that making further improvements using only extractive summarization will be considerably difficult. Moreover, in order to see these future improvements, a higher resolution (i.e. larger number of bins) will be needed when constructing the pdfs.

In all our experiments we used the ROUGE (Lin, 2004) evaluation package and its ROUGE-1, ROUGE-2, and ROUGE-SU4 recall scores. We would like to note that since ROUGE performs its evaluations based on the n-gram overlap between the peer and the model summary, it does not take other summary quality metrics such as coherence and cohesion into account. However, our goal in this paper was to analyze the topic-identification stage only, which concentrates on selecting the right content from the document to include in the summary, and the ROUGE scores were found to correlate well with the human judgments on assessing the content overlap of summaries.

In the future, we would like to apply a similar exhaustive search strategy, but this time with different compression ratios, in order to see the impact of compression ratios on the pdf of each domain. Furthermore, we would also like to analyze the high scoring extracts found by the exhaustive search, in terms of coherence, position and other features. Such an analysis would allow us to see whether these extracts exhibit certain properties which could be used in training machine learning systems.

Acknowledgments

The authors would like to thank the anonymous reviewers of NAACL-HLT 2010 for their feedback.

The work of the first author has been partly supported by an award from Google, Inc. The work of the fourth and fifth authors has been supported by an FPI grant (BES-2007-16268) from the Spanish Ministry of Science and Innovation, under the project TEXT-MESS (TIN2006-15265-C06-01) funded by the Spanish Government, and the project PROMETEO Desarrollo de Tcnicas Inteligentes e Interactivas de Minera de Textos (2009/119) from the Valencian Government.

References

Hakan Ceylan and Rada Mihalcea. 2009. The decomposition of human-written book summaries. In *CICLing '09: Proceedings of the 10th International Conference on Computational Linguistics and Intelligent Text Processing*, pages 582–593, Berlin, Heidelberg. Springer-Verlag.

Robert L. Donaway, Kevin W. Drummey, and Laura A. Mather. 2000. A comparison of rankings produced by summarization evaluation measures. In *NAACL-ANLP 2000 Workshop on Automatic summarization*, pages 69–78, Morristown, NJ, USA. Association for Computational Linguistics.

G. Erkan and Dragomir R. Radev. 2004. Lexrank: Graph-based centrality as salience in text summarization. *Journal of Artificial Intelligence Research*, 22.

Eduard H. Hovy and Chin Yew Lin. 1999. Automated text summarization in summarist. In Inderjeet Mani and Mark T. Maybury, editors, *Advances in Automatic Text Summarization*, pages 81–97. MIT Press.

Hongyan Jing. 2002. Using hidden markov modeling to decompose human-written summaries. *Comput. Linguist.*, 28(4):527–543.

Julian Kupiec, Jan Pedersen, and Francine Chen. 1995. A trainable document summarizer. In *SIGIR '95: Proceedings of the 18th annual international ACM SIGIR conference on Research and development in information retrieval*, pages 68–73, New York, NY, USA. ACM.

Chin-Yew Lin and Eduard Hovy. 2003. The potential and limitations of automatic sentence extraction for summarization. In *Proceedings of the HLT-NAACL 03 on Text summarization workshop*, pages 73–80, Morristown, NJ, USA. Association for Computational Linguistics.

Chin-Yew Lin. 1999. Training a selection function for extraction. In *CIKM '99: Proceedings of the eighth international conference on Information and knowledge management*, pages 55–62, New York, NY, USA. ACM.

Chin-Yew Lin. 2004. Rouge: A package for automatic evaluation of summaries. In Stan Szpakowicz Marie-Francine Moens, editor, *Text Summarization Branches Out: Proceedings of the ACL-04 Workshop*, pages 74–81, Barcelona, Spain, July. Association for Computational Linguistics.

Daniel Marcu. 1999. The automatic construction of large-scale corpora for summarization research. In *SIGIR '99: Proceedings of the 22nd annual international ACM SIGIR conference on Research and development in information retrieval*, pages 137–144, New York, NY, USA. ACM.

Rada Mihalcea and Hakan Ceylan. 2007. Explorations in automatic book summarization. In *Proceedings of the 2007 Joint Conference on Empirical Methods in Natural Language Processing and Computational Natural Language Learning (EMNLP-CoNLL)*, pages 380–389, Prague, Czech Republic, June. Association for Computational Linguistics.

Rada Mihalcea and Paul Tarau. 2004. Textrank: Bringing order into texts. In *Conference on Empirical Methods in Natural Language Processing*, Barcelona, Spain.

Yoshio Nakao. 2000. An algorithm for one-page summarization of a long text based on thematic hierarchy detection. In *ACL '00: Proceedings of the 38th Annual Meeting on Association for Computational Linguistics*, pages 302–309, Morristown, NJ, USA. Association for Computational Linguistics.

Lawrence Page, Sergey Brin, Rajeev Motwani, and Terry Winograd. 1999. The pagerank citation ranking: Bringing order to the web. Technical report, Stanford InfoLab.

Karen Sparck-Jones. 1999. Automatic summarising: Factors and directions. In Inderjeet Mani and Mark T. Maybury, editors, *Advances in Automatic Text Summarization*, pages 1–13. MIT Press.

Simone Teufel and Marc Moens. 1997. Sentence extraction as a classification task. In *Proceedings of the ACL'97/EACL'97 Workshop on Intelligent Scallable Text Summarization*, Madrid, Spain, July.

Masao Utiyama and Hitoshi Isahara. 2001. A statistical model for domain-independent text segmentation. In *In Proceedings of the 9th Conference of the European Chapter of the Association for Computational Linguistics*, pages 491–498.

Min yen Kan, Judith L. Klavans, and Kathleen R. McKeown. 1998. Linear segmentation and segment significance. In *In Proceedings of the 6th International Workshop of Very Large Corpora*, pages 197–205.

Multi-document Summarization via Budgeted Maximization of Submodular Functions

Hui Lin
Dept. of Electrical Engineering
University of Washington
Seattle, WA 98195, USA
hlin@ee.washington.edu

Jeff Bilmes
Dept. of Electrical Engineering
University of Washington
Seattle, WA 98195, USA
bilmes@ee.washington.edu

Abstract

We treat the text summarization problem as maximizing a submodular function under a budget constraint. We show, both theoretically and empirically, a modified greedy algorithm can efficiently solve the budgeted submodular maximization problem near-optimally, and we derive new approximation bounds in doing so. Experiments on DUC'04 task show that our approach is superior to the best-performing method from the DUC'04 evaluation on ROUGE-1 scores.

1 Introduction

Automatically generating summaries from large text corpora has long been studied in both information retrieval and natural language processing. There are several types of text summarization tasks. For example, if an input query is given, the generated summary can be query-specific, and otherwise it is generic. Also, the number of documents to be summarized can vary from one to many. The constituent sentences of a summary, moreover, might be formed in a variety of different ways — summarization can be conducted using either *extraction* or *abstraction*, the former selects only sentences from the original document set, whereas the latter involves natural language generation. In this paper, we address the problem of generic extractive summaries from clusters of related documents, commonly known as *multi-document summarization*.

In extractive text summarization, textual units (e.g., sentences) from a document set are extracted to form a summary, where grammaticality is assured at the local level. Finding the optimal summary can be viewed as a combinatorial optimization problem which is NP-hard to solve (McDonald, 2007). One of the standard methods for this problem is called *Maximum Marginal Relevance* (MMR) (Dang, 2005)(Carbonell and Goldstein, 1998), where a greedy algorithm selects the most relevant sentences, and at the same time avoids redundancy by removing sentences that are too similar to already selected ones. One major problem of MMR is that it is non-optimal because the decision is made based on the scores at the current iteration. McDonald (2007) proposed to replace the greedy search of MMR with a globally optimal formulation, where the basic MMR framework can be expressed as a knapsack packing problem, and an integer linear program (ILP) solver can be used to maximize the resulting objective function. ILP Algorithms, however, can sometimes either be expensive for large scale problems or themselves might only be heuristic without associated theoretical approximation guarantees.

In this paper, we study graph-based approaches for multi-document summarization. Indeed, several graph-based methods have been proposed for extractive summarization in the past. Erkan and Radev (2004) introduced a stochastic graph-based method, *LexRank*, for computing the relative importance of textual units for multi-document summarization. In LexRank the importance of sentences is computed based on the concept of eigenvector centrality in the graph representation of sentences. Mihalcea and Tarau also proposed an eigenvector centrality algorithm on weighted graphs for document summarization (Mihalcea and Tarau, 2004). Mihalcea et al. later applied Google's *PageRank* (Brin and Page, 1998) to natural language processing tasks ranging

Human Language Technologies: The 2010 Annual Conference of the North American Chapter of the ACL, pages 912–920,
Los Angeles, California, June 2010.

from automatic keyphrase extraction and word sense disambiguation, to extractive summarization (Mihalcea et al., 2004; Mihalcea, 2004). Recent work in (Lin et al., 2009) presents a graph-based approach where an undirected weighted graph is built for the document to be summarized, and vertices represent the candidate sentences and edge weights represent the similarity between sentences. The summary extraction procedure is done by maximizing a submodular set function under a cardinality constraint.

Inspired by (Lin et al., 2009), we perform summarization by maximizing submodular functions under a *budget* constraint. A budget constraint is natural in summarization task as the length of the summary is often restricted. The length (byte budget) limitation represents the real world scenario where summaries are displayed using only limited computer screen real estate. In practice, the candidate textual/linguistic units might not have identical costs (e.g., sentence lengths vary). Since a cardinality constraint is a special case (a budget constraint with unity costs), our approach is more general than (Lin et al., 2009). Moreover, we propose a modified greedy algorithm (Section 4) and both theoretically (Section 4.1) and empirically (Section 5.1) show that the algorithm solves the problem near-optimally, thanks to submodularity. Regarding summarization performance, experiments on DUC'04 task show that our approach is superior to the best-performing method in DUC'04 evaluation on ROUGE-1 scores (Section 5).

2 Background on Submodularity

Consider a set function $f : 2^V \rightarrow \mathbb{R}$, which maps subsets $S \subseteq V$ of a finite ground set V to real numbers. $f(\cdot)$ is called normalized if $f(\emptyset) = 0$, and is *monotone* if $f(S) \leq f(T)$ whenever $S \subseteq T$. $f(\cdot)$ is called *submodular* (Lovasz, 1983) if for any $S, T \subseteq V$, we have

$$f(S \cup T) + f(S \cap T) \leq f(S) + f(T). \quad (1)$$

An equivalent definition of submodularity is the property of *diminishing returns*, well-known in the field of economics. That is, $f(\cdot)$ is submodular if for any $R \subseteq S \subseteq V$ and $s \in V \setminus S$,

$$f(S \cup \{s\}) - f(S) \leq f(R \cup \{s\}) - f(R). \quad (2)$$

Eqn. 2 states that the "value" of s never increases in the contexts of ever larger sets, exactly the property of diminishing returns. This phenomenon arises naturally in many other contexts as well. For example, the Shannon entropy function is submodular in the set of random variables. Submodularity, moreover, is a discrete analog of convexity (Lovasz, 1983). As convexity makes continuous functions more amenable to optimization, submodularity plays an essential role in combinatorial optimization.

Many combinatorial optimization problems can be solved optimally or near-optimally in polynomial time only when the underlying function is submodular. It has been shown that any submodular function can be *minimized* in polynomial time (Schrijver, 2000)(Iwata et al., 2001). Maximization of submodular functions, however, is an NP-complete optimization problem but fortunately, some submodular maximization problems can be solved near-optimally. A famous result is that the maximization of a monotone submodular function under a cardinality constraint can be solved using a greedy algorithm (Nemhauser et al., 1978) within a constant factor (0.63) of being optimal. A constant-factor approximation algorithm has also been obtained for maximizing monotone submodular function with a knapsack constraint (see Section 4.2). Feige et.al. (2007) studied unconstrained maximization of a arbitrary submodular functions (not necessarily monotone). Kawahara et.al. (2009) proposed a cutting-plane method for optimally maximizing a submodular set function under a cardinality constraint, and Lee et.al. (2009) studied non-monotone submodular maximization under matroid and knapsack constraints.

3 Problem Setup

In this paper, we study the problem of maximizing a submodular function under budget constraint, stated formally below:

$$\max_{S \subseteq V} \left\{ f(S) : \sum_{i \in S} c_i \leq \mathcal{B} \right\} \quad (3)$$

where V is the ground set of all linguistic units (e.g., sentences) in the document, S is the extracted summary (a subset of V), c_i is the non-negative cost of selecting unit i and $\mathcal{B}$ is our budget, and submodular function $f(\cdot)$ scores the summary quality.

The budgeted constraint arises naturally since often the summary must be length limited as mentioned above. In particular, the budget $\mathcal{B}$ could be the maximum number of words allowed in any summary, or alternatively the maximum number of bytes of any summary, where c_i would then be either number of words or the number of bytes in sentence i.

To benefit from submodular optimization, the objective function measuring the summary quality must be submodular. In general, there are two ways to apply submodular optimization to any application domain. One way is to force submodularity on an application, leading to an artificial and poorly performing objective function even if it can be optimized well. The alternative is to address applications where submodularity naturally applies. We are fortunate in that, like convexity in the continuous domain, submodularity seems to arise naturally in a variety of discrete domains, and as we will see below, extractive summarization is one of them. As mentioned in Section 1, our approach is graph-based, not only because a graph is a natural representation of the relationships and interactions between textual units, but also because many submodular functions are well defined on a graph and can naturally be used in measuring the summary quality.

Suppose certain pairs (i, j) with $i, j \in V$ are similar and the similarity of i and j is measured by a non-negative value $w_{i,j}$. We can represent the entire document with a weighted graph (V, E), with non-negative weights $w_{i,j}$ associated with each edge $e_{i,j}, e \in E$. One well-known graph-based submodular function that measures the similarity of S to the remainder $V \setminus S$ is the graph-cut function:

$$f_{\text{cut}}(S) = \sum_{i \in V \setminus S} \sum_{j \in S} w_{i,j}. \quad (4)$$

In multi-document summarization, redundancy is a particularly important issue since textual units from different documents might convey the same information. A high quality (small and meaningful) summary should not only be informative about the remainder but also be compact (non-redundant). Typically, this goal is expressed as a combination of maximizing the information coverage and minimizing the redundancy (as used in MMR (Carbonell and Goldstein, 1998)). Inspired by this, we use the following objective by combining a λ-weighted penalty term with the graph cut function:

$$f_{\text{MMR}}(S) = \sum_{i \in V \setminus S} \sum_{j \in S} w_{i,j} - \lambda \sum_{i,j \in S: i \neq j} w_{i,j}, \lambda \geq 0.$$

Luckily, this function is still submodular as both the graph cut function and the redundancy term are submodular. Neither objective, however, is monotone, something we address in Theorem 3. Although similar to the MMR objective function, our approach is different since 1) ours is graph-based and 2) we formalize the problem as submodular function maximization under the budget constraint where a simple greedy algorithm can solve the problem guaranteed near-optimally.

4 Algorithms

Algorithm 1 Modified greedy algorithm

```
G ← ∅
U ← V
while U ≠ ∅ do
    k ← arg max_{ℓ∈U} (f(G∪{ℓ}) − f(G)) / (c_ℓ)^r
    G ← G ∪ {k} if Σ_{i∈G} c_i + c_k ≤ B and
        f(G ∪ {k}) − f(G) ≥ 0
    U ← U \ {k}
end while
v* ← arg max_{v∈V, c_v≤B} f({v})
return G_f = arg max_{S∈{{v*},G}} f(S)
```

Inspired by (Khuller et al., 1999), we propose Algorithm 1 to solve Eqn. (3). The algorithm sequentially finds unit k with the largest ratio of objective function gain to scaled cost, i.e., $(f(G \cup \{\ell\}) - f(G))/c_\ell^r$, where $r > 0$ is the scaling factor. If adding k increases the objective function value while not violating the budget constraint, it is then selected and otherwise bypassed. After the sequential selection, set G is compared to the within-budget singleton with the largest objective value, and the larger of the two becomes the final output.

The essential aspect of a greedy algorithm is the design of the greedy heuristic. As discussed in (Khuller et al., 1999), a heuristic that greedily selects the k that maximizes $(f(G \cup \{k\}) - f(G))/c_k$ has an unbounded approximation factor. For example, let $V = \{a, b\}$, $f(\{a\}) = 1, f(\{b\}) = p$,

$c_a = 1, c_b = p + 1$, and $\mathcal{B} = p + 1$. The solution obtained by the greedy heuristic is $\{a\}$ with objective function value 1, while the true optimal objective function value is p. The approximation factor for this example is then p and therefore unbounded.

We address this issue by the following two modifications to the naive greedy algorithms. The first one is the final step (line 8 and 9) in Algorithm 1 where set G and singletons are compared. This step ensures that we could obtain a constant approximation factor for $r = 1$ (see the proof in the Appendix).

The second modification is that we introduce a scaling factor r to adjust the scale of the cost. Suppose, in the above example, we scale the cost as $c_a = 1^r, c_b = (p+1)^r$, then selecting a or b depends also on the scale r, and we might get the optimal solution using a appropriate r. Indeed, the objective function values and the costs might be uncalibrated since they might measure different units. E.g., it is hard to say if selecting a sentence of 15 words with an objective function gain of 2 is better than selecting sentence of 10 words with gain of 1. Scaling can potentially alleviate this mismatch (i.e., we can adjust r on development set). Interestingly, our theoretical analysis of the performance guarantee of the algorithm also gives us guidance about how to scale the cost for a particular problem (see Section 4.1).

4.1 Analysis of performance guarantee

Although Algorithm 1 is essentially a simple greedy strategy, we show that it solves Eqn. (3) globally and near-optimally, by exploiting the structure of submodularity. As far as we know, this is a new result for submodular optimization, not previously stated or published before.

Theorem 1. *For normalized monotone submodular function $f(\cdot)$, Algorithm 1 with $r = 1$ has a constant approximation factor as follows:*

$$f(G_f) \geq \left(1 - e^{-\frac{1}{2}}\right) f(S^*), \qquad (5)$$

where S^* is an optimal solution.

Proof. See Appendix. □

Note that an α-approximation algorithm for an optimization problem is a polynomial-time algorithm that for *all* instances of the problem produces a solution whose value is within a factor of α of the value of the an optimal solution. So Theorem 1 basically states that the solution found by Algorithm 1 can be at least as good as $(1 - 1/\sqrt{e})f(S^*) \approx 0.39 f(S^*)$ even in the worst case. A constant approximation bound is good since it is true for all instances of the problem, and we always know how good the algorithm is guaranteed to be without any extra computation. For $r \neq 1$, we resort to instance-dependent bound where the approximation can be easily computed per problem instance.

Theorem 2. *With normalized monotone submodular $f(\cdot)$, for $i = 1, \ldots, |G|$, let v_i be the ith unit added into G and G_i is the set after adding v_i. When $0 \leq r \leq 1$,*

$$f(G_i) \geq \left(1 - \prod_{k=1}^{i}\left(1 - \frac{c_{v_k}^r}{\mathcal{B}^r |S^*|^{1-r}}\right)\right) f(S^*) \qquad (6)$$

$$\geq \left(1 - \prod_{k=1}^{i}\left(1 - \frac{c_{v_k}^r}{\mathcal{B}^r |V|^{1-r}}\right)\right) f(S^*) \qquad (7)$$

and when $r \geq 1$,

$$f(G_i) \geq \left(1 - \prod_{k=1}^{i}\left(1 - \left(\frac{c_{v_k}}{\mathcal{B}}\right)^r\right)\right) f(S^*). \qquad (8)$$

Proof. See Appendix. □

Theorem 2 gives bounds for a specific instance of the problem. Eqn. (6) requires the size $|S^*|$, which is unknown, requiring us to estimate an upper bound of the cardinality of the optimal set S^*. Obviously, $|S^*| \leq |V|$, giving us Eqn. (7). A tighter upper bound is obtained, however, by sorting the costs. That is, let $c_{[1]}, c_{[2]}, \ldots, c_{[|V|]}$ be the sorted sequence of costs in nondecreasing order, giving $|S^*| < m$ where $\sum_{k=1}^{m-1} c_{[i]} \leq \mathcal{B}$ and $\sum_{k=1}^{m} c_{[i]} > \mathcal{B}$. In this case, the computation cost for the bound estimation is $O(|V| \log |V|)$, which is quite feasible.

Note that both Theorem 1 and 2 are for monotone submodular functions while our practical objective function, i.e. f_{MMR}, is not guaranteed everywhere monotone. However, our theoretical results still holds for f_{MMR} with high probability in practice. Intuitively, in summarization tasks, the summary is usually small compared to the ground set size ($|S| \ll |V|$). When $|S|$ is small, f_{MMR} is monotone and our theoretical results still hold. Precisely, assume that all edge weights are bounded: $w_{i,j} \in [0, 1]$ (which is the case for cosine similarity between non-negative vectors). Also assume that edges weights are independently identically distributed with mean μ, i.e. $\mathbb{E}(w_{i,j}) = \mu$. Given a budget $\mathcal{B}$, assume the maximum possible size of a solution is K. Let $\alpha = 2\lambda + 1$, and $\beta = 2K - 1$. Notice that $\beta \ll |V|$ for our summarization task. We have the following theorem:

Theorem 3. *Algorithm 1 solves the summarization problem near-optimally (i.e. Theorem 1 and Theorem 2 hold) with high probability of at least*

$$1 - \exp\left\{-\frac{2(|V| - (\alpha+1)\beta)^2\mu^2}{|V| + (\alpha^2 - 1)\beta} + \ln K\right\}$$

Proof. Omitted due to space limitation. □

4.2 Related work

Algorithms for maximizing submodular function under budget constraint (Eqn. (3)) have been studied before. Krause (2005) generalized the work by Khuller et al.(1999) on budgeted maximum cover problem to the submodular framework, and showed a $\frac{1}{2}(1 - 1/e)$-approximation algorithm. The algorithm in (Krause and Guestrin, 2005) and (Khuller et al., 1999) is actually a special case of Algorithm 1 when $r = 1$, and Theorem 1 gives a better bound (i.e., $(1 - 1/\sqrt{e}) > \frac{1}{2}(1 - 1/e)$) in this case. There is also a greedy algorithm with partial enumerations (Sviridenko, 2004; Krause and Guestrin, 2005) factor $(1 - 1/e)$. This algorithm, however, is too computationally expensive and thus not practical for real world applications (the computation cost is $O(|V|^5)$ in general). When each unit has identical cost, the budget constraint reduces to cardinality constraint where a greedy algorithm is known to be a $(1-1/e)$-approximation algorithm (Nemhauser et al., 1978) which is the best that can be achieved in polynomial time (Feige, 1998) if P $\neq$ NP. Recent work (Takamura and Okumura, 2009) applied the maximum coverage problem to text summarization (without apparently being aware that their objective is submodular) and studied a similar algorithm to ours when $r = 1$ and for the non-penalized graph-cut function. This problem, however, is a special case of constrained submodular function maximization.

5 Experiments

We evaluated our approach on the data set of DUC'04 (2004) with the setting of task 2, which is a multi-document summarization task on English news articles. In this task, 50 document clusters are given, each of which consists of 10 documents. For each document cluster, a short multi-document summary is to be generated. The summary should not be longer than 665 bytes including spaces and punctuation, as required in the DUC'04 evaluation. We used DUC'03 as our development set. All documents were segmented into sentences using a script distributed by DUC. ROUGE version 1.5.5 (Lin, 2004), which is widely used in the study of summarization, was used to evaluate summarization performance in our experiments [1]. We focus on ROUGE-1 (unigram) F-measure scores since it has demonstrated strong correlation with human annotation (Lin, 2004).

The basic textual/linguistic units we consider in our experiments are sentences. For each document cluster, sentences in all the documents of this cluster forms the ground set V. We built semantic graphs for each document cluster based on cosine similarity, where cosine similarity is computed based on the TF-IDF (term frequency, inverse document frequency) vectors for the words in the sentences. The cosine similarity measures the similarity between sentences, i.e., $w_{i,j}$.

Here the IDF values were calculated using all the document clusters. The weighted graph was built by connecting vertices (corresponding to sentences) with weight $w_{i,j} > 0$. Any unconnected vertex was removed from the graph, which is equivalent to pre-excluding certain sentences from the summary.

5.1 Comparison with exact solution

In this section, we empirically show that Algorithm 1 works near-optimally in practice. To determine how much accuracy is lost due to approximations, we compared our approximation algorithms with an exact solution. The exact solutions were obtained by Integer Linear Programming (ILP). Solving arbitrary ILP is an NP-hard problem. If the size of the problem is not too large, we can sometimes find the exact solution within a manageable time

[1] Options used: -a -c 95 -b 665 -m -n 4 -w 1.2

using a branch-and-bound method. In our experiments, MOSEK was used as our ILP solver.

We formalize Eqn. (3) as an ILP by introducing indicator (binary) variables $x_{i,j}, y_{i,j}, i \neq j$ and z_i for $i, j \in V$. In particular, $z_i = 1$ indicates that unit i is selected, i.e., $i \in S$, $x_{i,j} = 1$ indicates that $i \in S$ but $j \notin S$, and $y_{i,j} = 1$ indicates both i and j are selected. Adding constraints to ensure a valid solution, we have the following ILP formulation for Eqn. (3) with objective function $f_{\text{MMR}}(S)$:

$$\max \sum_{i \neq j, i,j \in V} w_{i,j} x_{i,j} - \lambda \sum_{i \neq j, i,j \in V} w_{i,j} y_{i,j}$$

$$\text{subject to: } \sum_{i \in V} c_i z_i \leq \mathcal{B},$$

$$x_{i,j} - z_i \leq 0, x_{i,j} + z_j \leq 1, z_i - z_j - x_{i,j} \leq 0,$$

$$y_{i,j} - z_i \leq 0, y_{i,j} - z_j \leq 0, z_i + z_j - y_{i,j} \leq 1,$$

$$x_{i,j}, y_{i,j}, z_i \in \{0, 1\}, \forall i \neq j, i, j \in V$$

Note that the number of variables in the ILP formulation is $O(|V|^2)$. For a document cluster with hundreds of candidate textual units, the scale of the problem easily grows involving tens of thousands of variables, making the problem very expensive to solve. For instance, solving the ILP exactly on a document cluster with 182 sentences (as used in Figure 1) took about 17 hours while our Algorithm 1 finished in less than 0.01 seconds.

We tested both approximate and exact algorithms on DUC'03 data where 60 document clusters were used (30 TDT document clusters and 30 TREC document clusters), each of which contains 10 documents on average. The true approximation factor was computed by dividing the objective function value found by Algorithm 1 over the optimal objective function value (found by ILP). The average approximation factors over the 58 document clusters (ILP on 2 of the 60 document clusters failed to finish) are shown in Table 1, along with other statistics. On average Algorithm 1 finds a solution that is over 90% as good as the optimal solution for many different r values, which backs up our claim that the modified greedy algorithm solves the problem near-optimally, even occasionally optimally (Figure 1 shows one such example).

The higher objective function value does not always indicate higher ROUGE-1 score. Indeed, rather than directly optimizing ROUGE, we optimize a surrogate submodular function that indicates the quality of a summary. Optimality in the submodular function does not necessary indicate optimality in ROUGE score. Nevertheless, we will show that our approach outperforms several other approaches in terms of ROUGE. We note that ROUGE is itself a surrogate for true human-judged summary quality, it might possibly be that f_{MMR} is a still better surrogate — we do not consider this possibility further in this work, however.

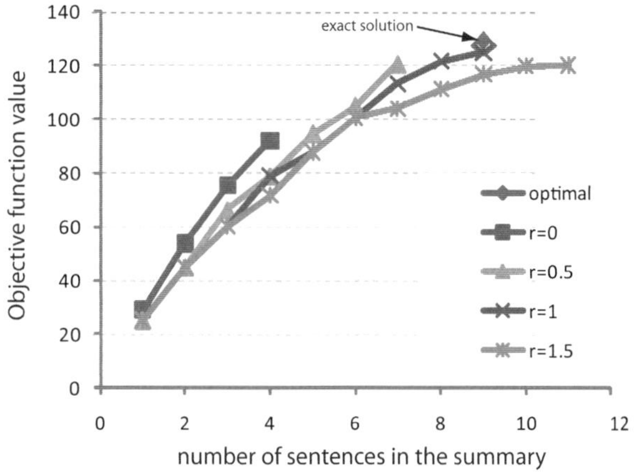

Figure 1: Application of Algorithm 1 when summarizing document cluster d30001t in the DUC'04 dataset with summary size limited to 665 bytes. The objective function was f_{MMR} with $\lambda = 2$. The plots show the achieved objective function as the number of selected sentences grows. The plots stop when in each case adding more sentences violates the budget. Algorithm 1 with $r = 1$ found the optimal solution exactly.

5.2 Summarization Results

We used DUC'03 (as above) for our development set to investigate how r and λ relate to the ROUGE-1 score. From Figure 2, the best performance is achieved with $r = 0.3, \lambda = 4$. Using these settings, we applied our approach to the DUC'04 task. The results, along with the results of other approaches, are shown in Table 2. All the results in Table 2 are presented as ROUGE-1 F-measure scores. [2]

We compared our approach to two other well-

[2] When the evaluation was done in 2004, ROUGE was still in revision 1.2.1, so we re-evaluated the DUC'04 submissions using ROUGE v1.5.5 and the numbers are slightly different from the those reported officially.

Table 1: Comparison of Algorithm 1 to exact algorithms on DUC'03 dataset. All the numbers shown in the table are the average statistics (mean/std). The "true" approximation factor is the ratio of objective function value found by Algorithm 1 over the ILP-derived true-optimal objective value, and the approximation bounds were estimated using Theorem 2.

	Approx. factor		ROUGE-1
	true	bound	(%)
exact	1.00	-	33.60/5.05
$r = 0.0$	0.65/0.15	≥0.19/0.08	33.50/5.94
$r = 0.1$	0.71/0.15	≥0.24/0.08	33.68/6.03
$r = 0.3$	0.88/0.11	≥0.37/0.06	34.77/5.49
$r = 0.5$	0.96/0.04	≥0.48/0.05	34.33/5.94
$r = 0.7$	0.98/0.02	≥0.56/0.05	34.08/5.41
$r = 1.0$	0.98/0.02	≥0.65/0.04	33.32/5.14
$r = 1.2$	0.97/0.02	≥0.48/0.05	32.54/4.69

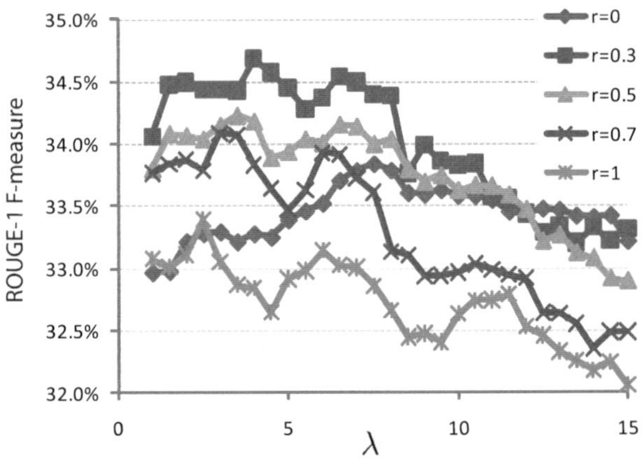

Figure 2: Different combinations of r and λ for f_{MMR} related to ROUGE-1 score on DUC'03 task 1.

known graph-based approaches, LexRank and PageRank. LexRank was one of the participating system in DUC'04, with peer code 104. For PageRank, we implemented the recursive graph-based ranking algorithm ourselves. The importance of sentences was estimated in an iterative way as in (Brin and Page, 1998)(Mihalcea et al., 2004). Sentences were then selected based on their importance rankings until the budget constraint was violated. The graphs used for PageRank were *exactly* the graphs in our submodular approaches (i.e., an undirected graph). In both cases, submodular summarization achieves better ROUGE-1 scores. The improvement is statistically significant by the Wilcoxon signed rank test at level $p < 0.05$. Our approach also outperforms the best system (Conroy et al., 2004), peer code 65 in the DUC'04 evaluation although not as significant ($p < 0.08$). The reason might be that DUC'03 is a poor representation of DUC'04 — indeed, by varying r and λ over the ranges $0 \leq r \leq 0.2$ and $5 \leq \lambda \leq 9$ respectively, the DUC'04 ROUGE-1 scores were all $> 38.8\%$ with the best DUC'04 score being 39.3%.

Table 2: ROUGE-1 F-measure results (%)

Method	ROUGE-1 score
peer65 (best system in DUC04)	37.94
peer104 (LexRank)	37.12
PageRank	35.37
Submodular ($r = 0.3, \lambda = 4$)	**38.39**

6 Appendix

We analyze the performance guarantee of Algorithm 1. We use the following notation: S^* is the optimal solution; G_f is the final solution obtained by Algorithm 1; G is the solution obtained by the greedy heuristic (line 1 to 7 in Algorithm 1); v_i is the ith unit added to G, $i = 1, \ldots, |G|$; G_i is the set obtained by greedy algorithm after adding v_i (i.e., $G_i = \cup_{k=1}^{i}\{v_k\}$, for $i = 1, \ldots, |G|$, with $G_0 = \emptyset$ and $G_{|G|} = G$); $f(\cdot) : 2^V \to \mathbb{R}$ is a monotone submodular function; and $\rho_k(S)$ is the gain of adding k to S, i.e., $f(S \cup \{k\}) - f(S)$.

Lemma 1. $\forall X, Y \subseteq V$,

$$f(X) \leq f(Y) + \sum_{k \in X \setminus Y} \rho_k(Y). \tag{9}$$

Proof. See (Nemhauser et al., 1978) □

Lemma 2. *For* $i = 1, \ldots, |G|$, *when* $0 \leq r \leq 1$,

$$f(S^*) - f(G_{i-1}) \leq \frac{\mathcal{B}^r |S^*|^{1-r}}{c_{v_i}^r}(f(G_i) - f(G_{i-1})), \tag{10}$$

and when $r \geq 1$,

$$f(S^*) - f(G_{i-1}) \leq \left(\frac{\mathcal{B}}{c_{v_i}}\right)^r (f(G_i) - f(G_{i-1})) \tag{11}$$

Proof. Based on line 4 of Algorithm 1, we have

$$\forall u \in S^* \setminus G_{i-1}, \frac{\rho_u(G_{i-1})}{c_u^r} \leq \frac{\rho_{v_i}(G_{i-1})}{c_{v_i}^r}.$$

Thus when $0 \leq r \leq 1$,

$$\sum_{u \in S^* \setminus G_{i-1}} \rho_u(G_{i-1}) \leq \frac{\rho_{v_i}(G_{i-1})}{c_{v_i}^r} \sum_{u \in S^* \setminus G_{i-1}} c_u^r$$
$$\leq \frac{\rho_{v_i}(G_{i-1})}{c_{v_i}^r} |S^* \setminus G_{i-1}| \left(\frac{\sum_{u \in S^* \setminus G_{i-1}} c_u}{|S^* \setminus G_{i-1}|} \right)^r$$
$$\leq \frac{\rho_{v_i}(G_{i-1})}{c_{v_i}^r} |S^*|^{1-r} \left(\sum_{u \in S^* \setminus G_{i-1}} c_u \right)^r$$
$$\leq \frac{\rho_{v_i}(G_{i-1})}{c_{v_i}^r} |S^*|^{1-r} \mathcal{B}^r,$$

where the second inequality is due to the concavity of $g(x) = x^r, x > 0, 0 \leq r \leq 1$. The last inequality uses the fact that $\sum_{u \in S^*} c_u \leq \mathcal{B}$. Similarly, when $r \geq 1$,

$$\sum_{u \in S^* \setminus G_{i-1}} \rho_u(G_{i-1}) \leq \frac{\rho_{v_i}(G_{i-1})}{c_{v_i}^r} \sum_{u \in S^* \setminus G_{i-1}} c_u^r$$
$$\leq \frac{\rho_{v_i}(G_{i-1})}{c_{v_i}^r} \left(\sum_{u \in S^* \setminus G_{i-1}} c_u \right)^r$$
$$\leq \frac{\rho_{v_i}(G_{i-1})}{c_{v_i}^r} \mathcal{B}^r.$$

Applying Lemma 1, i.e., let $X = S^*$ and $Y = G_{i-1}$, the lemma immediately follows. □

The following is a proof of Theorem 2.

Proof. Obviously, the theorem is true when $i = 1$ by applying Lemma 2.

Assume that the theorem is true for $i-1, 2 \leq i \leq |G|$, we show that it also holds for i. When $0 \leq r \leq 1$,

$$f(G_i) = f(G_{i-1}) + (f(G_i) - f(G_{i-1}))$$
$$\geq f(G_{i-1}) + \frac{c_{v_i}^r}{\mathcal{B}^r |S^*|^{1-r}} (f(S^*) - f(G_{i-1}))$$
$$= \left(1 - \frac{c_{v_i}^r}{\mathcal{B}^r |S^*|^{1-r}}\right) f(G_{i-1}) + \frac{c_{v_i}^r}{\mathcal{B}^r |S^*|^{1-r}} f(S^*)$$
$$\geq \left(1 - \frac{c_{v_i}^r}{\mathcal{B}^r |S^*|^{1-r}}\right) \left(1 - \prod_{k=1}^{i-1} \left(1 - \frac{c_{v_k}^r}{\mathcal{B}^r |S^*|^{1-r}}\right)\right)$$
$$f(S^*) + \frac{c_{v_i}^r}{\mathcal{B}^r |S^*|^{1-r}} f(S^*)$$
$$= \left(1 - \prod_{k=1}^{i} \left(1 - \frac{c_{v_k}^r}{\mathcal{B}^r |S^*|^{1-r}}\right)\right) f(S^*).$$

The case when $r \geq 1$ can be proven similarly. □

Now we are ready to prove Theorem 1.

Proof. Consider the following two cases:

Case 1: $\exists v \in V$ such that $f(\{v\}) > \frac{1}{2} f(S^*)$. Then it is guaranteed that $f(G_f) \geq f(\{v\})) > \frac{1}{2} f(S^*)$ due line 9 of Algorithm 1.

Case 2: $\forall v \in V$, we have $f(\{v\}) \leq \frac{1}{2} f(S^*)$. We consider the following two sub-cases, namely Case 2.1 and Case 2.2:

Case 2.1: If $\sum_{v \in G} c_v \leq \frac{1}{2}\mathcal{B}$, then we know that $\forall v \notin G, c_v > \frac{1}{2}\mathcal{B}$ since otherwise we can add a $v \notin G$ into G to increase the objective function value without violating the budget constraint. This implies that there is at most one unit in $S^* \setminus G$ since otherwise we will have $\sum_{v \in S^*} c_v > \mathcal{B}$. By assumption, we have $f(S^* \setminus G) \leq \frac{1}{2} f(S^*)$. Submodularity of $f(\cdot)$ gives us:

$$f(S^* \setminus G) + f(S^* \cap G) \geq f(S^*),$$

which implies $f(S^* \cap G) \geq \frac{1}{2} f(S^*)$. Thus we have

$$f(G_f) \geq f(G) \geq f(S^* \cap G) \geq \frac{1}{2} f(S^*),$$

where the second inequality follows from monotonicity.

Case 2.2: If $\sum_{v \in G} c_v > \frac{1}{2}\mathcal{B}$, for $0 \leq r \leq 1$, using Theorem 2, we have

$$f(G) \geq \left(1 - \prod_{k=1}^{|G|} \left(1 - \frac{c_{v_k}^r}{\mathcal{B}^r |S^*|^{1-r}}\right)\right) f(S^*)$$
$$\geq \left(1 - \prod_{k=1}^{|G|} \left(1 - \frac{c_{v_k}^r |S^*|^{r-1}}{2^r \left(\sum_{k=1}^{|G|} c_{v_k}\right)^r}\right)\right) f(S^*)$$
$$\geq \left(1 - \left(1 - \frac{|S^*|^{r-1}}{2^r |G|^r}\right)^{|G|}\right) f(S^*)$$
$$\geq \left(1 - e^{-\frac{1}{2}\left(\frac{|S^*|}{2|G|}\right)^{r-1}}\right) f(S^*)$$

where the third inequality uses the fact (provable using Lagrange multipliers) that for $a_1, \ldots, a_n \in \mathbb{R}^+$ such that $\sum_{i=1}^n a_i = \alpha$, function

$$1 - \prod_{i=1}^{n} \left(1 - \frac{\beta a_i^r}{\alpha^r}\right)$$

achieves its minimum of $1 - (1 - \beta/n^r)^n$ when $a_1 = \cdots = a_n = \alpha/n$ for $\alpha, \beta > 0$. The last inequality follows from $e^{-x} \geq 1 - x$.

In all cases, we have

$$f(G_f) \geq \min\left\{\frac{1}{2}, 1 - e^{-\frac{1}{2}\left(\frac{|S^*|}{2|G|}\right)^{r-1}}\right\} f(S^*)$$

In particular, when $r = 1$, we obtain the constant approximation factor, i.e.

$$f(G_f) \geq \left(1 - e^{-\frac{1}{2}}\right) f(S^*)$$

□

Acknowledgments

This work is supported by an ONR MURI grant (No. N000140510388), the Companions project (IST programme under EC grant IST-FP6-034434), and the National Science Foundation under grant IIS-0535100. We also wish to thank the anonymous reviewers for their comments.

References

S. Brin and L. Page. 1998. The anatomy of a large-scale hypertextual Web search engine. *Computer networks and ISDN systems*, 30(1-7):107–117.

Jaime Carbonell and Jade Goldstein. 1998. The use of MMR, diversity-based reranking for reordering documents and producing summaries. In *Proc. of SIGIR*.

J.M. Conroy, J.D. Schlesinger, J. Goldstein, and D.P. O'leary. 2004. Left-brain/right-brain multi-document summarization. In *Proceedings of the Document Understanding Conference (DUC 2004)*.

H.T. Dang. 2005. Overview of DUC 2005. In *Proceedings of the Document Understanding Conference*.

2004. Document understanding conferences (DUC). http://www-nlpir.nist.gov/projects/duc/index.html.

G. Erkan and D.R. Radev. 2004. LexRank: Graph-based Lexical Centrality as Salience in Text Summarization. *Journal of Artificial Intelligence Research*, 22:457–479.

U. Feige, V. Mirrokni, and J. Vondrak. 2007. Maximizing non-monotone submodular functions. In *Proceedings of 48th Annual IEEE Symposium on Foundations of Computer Science (FOCS)*.

U. Feige. 1998. A threshold of ln n for approximating set cover. *Journal of the ACM (JACM)*, 45(4):634–652.

G. Goel, , C. Karande, P. Tripathi, and L. Wang. 2009. Approximability of Combinatorial Problems with Multi-agent Submodular Cost Functions. FOCS.

S. Iwata, L. Fleischer, and S. Fujishige. 2001. A combinatorial strongly polynomial algorithm for minimizing submodular functions. *Journal of the ACM*, 48(4):761–777.

Yoshinobu Kawahara, Kiyohito Nagano, Koji Tsuda, and Jeff Bilmes. 2009. Submodularity cuts and applications. In *Neural Information Processing Society (NIPS)*, Vancouver, Canada, December.

S. Khuller, A. Moss, and J. Naor. 1999. The budgeted maximum coverage problem. *Information Processing Letters*, 70(1):39–45.

A. Krause and C. Guestrin. 2005. A note on the budgeted maximization of submodular functions. *Technical Rep. No. CMU-CALD-05*, 103.

J. Lee, V.S. Mirrokni, V. Nagarajan, and M. Sviridenko. 2009. Non-monotone submodular maximization under matroid and knapsack constraints. In *Proceedings of the 41st annual ACM symposium on Symposium on theory of computing*, pages 323–332. ACM New York, NY, USA.

Hui Lin, Jeff Bilmes, and Shasha Xie. 2009. Graph-based submodular selection for extractive summarization. In *Proc. IEEE Automatic Speech Recognition and Understanding (ASRU)*, Merano, Italy, December.

Chin-Yew Lin. 2004. ROUGE: A package for automatic evaluation of summaries. In *Text Summarization Branches Out: Proceedings of the ACL-04 Workshop*.

L. Lovasz. 1983. Submodular functions and convexity. *Mathematical programming-The state of the art,(eds. A. Bachem, M. Grotschel and B. Korte) Springer*, pages 235–257.

R. McDonald. 2007. A study of global inference algorithms in multi-document summarization. *Lecture Notes in Computer Science*, 4425:557.

R. Mihalcea and P. Tarau. 2004. TextRank: bringing order into texts. In *Proceedings of EMNLP*, Barcelona, Spain.

R. Mihalcea, P. Tarau, and E. Figa. 2004. PageRank on semantic networks, with application to word sense disambiguation. In *Proceedings of the 20th International Conference on Computational Linguistics (COLING-04)*.

R. Mihalcea. 2004. Graph-based ranking algorithms for sentence extraction, applied to text summarization. In *Proceedings of the ACL 2004 (companion volume)*.

2006. Mosek.

G.L. Nemhauser, L.A. Wolsey, and M.L. Fisher. 1978. An analysis of approximations for maximizing submodular set functions I. *Mathematical Programming*, 14(1):265–294.

A. Schrijver. 2000. A combinatorial algorithm minimizing submodular functions in strongly polynomial time. *Journal of Combinatorial Theory, Series B*, 80(2):346–355.

M. Sviridenko. 2004. A note on maximizing a submodular set function subject to a knapsack constraint. *Operations Research Letters*, 32(1):41–43.

H. Takamura and M. Okumura. 2009. Text summarization model based on maximum coverage problem and its variant. In *Proceedings of the 12th Conference of the European Chapter of the Association for Computational Linguistics*, pages 781–789. Association for Computational Linguistics.

Cross-lingual Induction of Selectional Preferences with Bilingual Vector Spaces

Yves Peirsman
QLVL, University of Leuven
Research Foundation – Flanders (FWO)
yves.peirsman@arts.kuleuven.be

Sebastian Padó
IMS, University of Stuttgart
pado@ims.uni-stuttgart.de

Abstract

We describe a cross-lingual method for the induction of selectional preferences for resource-poor languages, where no accurate monolingual models are available. The method uses bilingual vector spaces to "translate" foreign language predicate-argument structures into a resource-rich language like English. The only prerequisite for constructing the bilingual vector space is a large unparsed corpus in the resource-poor language, although the model can profit from (even noisy) syntactic knowledge. Our experiments show that the cross-lingual predictions correlate well with human ratings, clearly outperforming monolingual baseline models.

1 Introduction

Selectional preferences capture the empirical observation that not all words are equally good arguments to a given verb in a particular argument position (Wilks, 1975; Resnik, 1996). For instance, the subjects of the English verb *to shoot* are generally people, while the direct objects can be people or animals. This is reflected in speakers' intuitions. Table 1 shows that the combination *the hunter shot the deer* is judged more plausible than *the deer shot the hunter*. Selectional preferences do not only play an important role in human sentence processing (McRae et al., 1998), but are also helpful for NLP tasks like word sense disambiguation (McCarthy and Carroll, 2003) and semantic role labeling (Gildea and Jurafsky, 2002).

Computational models of selectional preferences predict such *plausibilities* for triples of a predicate p, an argument position a, and a head word h, such as

Predicate	Relation	Noun	Plausibility
shoot	subject	hunter	6.9
shoot	object	hunter	2.8
shoot	subject	deer	1.0
shoot	object	deer	6.4

Table 1: Predicate-relation-noun triples with human plausibility judgments on a 7-point scale (McRae et al., 1998)

(*shoot,object,hunter*). All recent models take a two-step approach: (1), they extract all triples (p, a, h) from a large corpus; (2), they apply some type of generalization to make predictions for unseen items. Clearly, the accuracy of these models relies crucially on the quality and coverage of the extracted triples, and thus on the syntactic analysis of the corpus. Unfortunately, corpora that are both large enough and have a very good syntactic analysis are only available for a handful of Western and Asian languages, which leaves all other languages without reliable selectional preference models.

In this paper, we propose a cross-lingual knowledge transfer approach to this problem: We automatically *translate* triples (p, a, h) from resource-poor languages into English, where large and high-quality parsed corpora are available and we can compute a reliable plausibility estimate. The translations are extracted from a *bilingual semantic space*, which can be constructed via bootstrapping from large unparsed corpora in the two languages, without the need for parallel corpora or bilingual lexical resources.

Structure of the paper. Section 2 reviews models for selectional preferences. In Section 3, we describe our approach. Section 4 introduces our experimental setup, and Sections 5 and 6 present and discuss our experiments. Section 7 wraps up.

Human Language Technologies: The 2010 Annual Conference of the North American Chapter of the ACL, pages 921–929,
Los Angeles, California, June 2010. ©2010 Association for Computational Linguistics

2 Selectional Preferences

The first broad-coverage model of selectional preferences was developed by Resnik (1996). To estimate the plausibility of a triple (p, a, h), Resnik first extracted all head words seen with predicate p in position a, $Seen_a(p)$, from a corpus. He then used the WordNet hierarchy to generalize over the head words and to create predictions for unseen ones. A number of studies has followed the same approach, exploring different ways of using the structure of WordNet (Abe and Li, 1996; Clark and Weir, 2002). While these approaches show good results, they can only make predictions for argument heads that are covered by WordNet. This is already a problem for English, and much more so in other languages, where comparable resources are often much smaller or entirely absent.

A promising alternative approach is to derive the generalizations from distributional information (Prescher et al., 2000; Padó et al., 2007; Bergsma et al., 2008). For example, the Padó et al. (2007) model computes vector space representations for all head words h and defines the plausibility of the triple (p, a, h) as a weighted mean of the vector space similarities between h and all h' in $Seen_a(p)$:

$$Pl(p, a, h) = \sum_{h' \in Seen_a(p)} \frac{w(h') \cdot sim(h, h')}{\sum_{h'} w(h')} \quad (1)$$

where $w(h')$ is a weight, typically frequency.

In this model, the generalization is provided by distributional similarity, which can be computed from a large corpus, without the need for additional lexical resources. Padó et al. found it to outperform Resnik's approach in an evaluation against human plausibility judgments. However, note that competitive results are only obtained by representing the head words in "syntactic" vector spaces whose dimensions consist of context words with their syntactic relation to the target rather than just context words. This is not surprising: Presumably, *hunter* and *deer* share a domain and are likely to have similar word-based context distributions, even though they differ with regard to their plausibility for particular predicate-argument positions. Only when the vector space can capture their different *syntactic* co-occurrence patterns can the model predict different plausibilities.

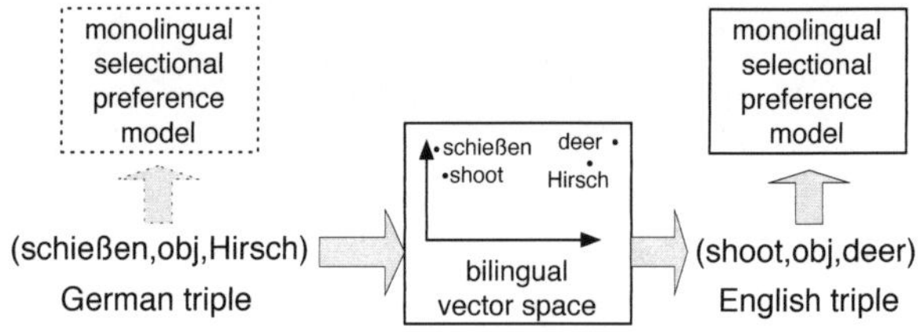

Figure 1: Predicting selectional preferences for a source language (e.g. German) by translating into a target language (e.g. English) with a bilingual vector space.

3 Cross-lingual selectional preferences

In order to compute reliable selectional preference representations, distributional models need to see at least some head words for each (p, a) combination. Manually annotated treebank corpora, which are becoming available for an increasing number of languages, are too small for this task. We therefore explore the idea of predicting the selectional preferences for such languages by taking advantage of large corpora with high-quality syntactic analyses in resource-rich languages like English. This idea falls into the general approach of *cross-lingual knowledge transfer* (see e.g. Hwa et al., 2005). The application to selectional preferences was suggested by Agirre et al. (2003), who demonstrated its feasibility by manual translation between Basque and English. We extend their experiments to an automatic model that predicts plausibility judgments in a resource-poor language (*source language*) by exploiting a model in a resource-rich language (*target language*).

Figure 1 sketches our method. We assume that there is not enough high-quality data to build a monolingual selectional preference model for the source language (shown by dotted lines). However, we can use a *bilingual vector space*, that is, a semantic space in which words of both the source and the target language are represented, to *translate* each source language word s into the target language by identifying its nearest (most similar) target word $tr(s)$:

$$tr(s) = \text{argmax}_t \, sim(s, t) \quad (2)$$

Now we can use a target language selectional preference model to obtain plausibilities for source triples:

$$Pl^s(p, a, h) = Pl^t(tr(p), a, tr(h)) \quad (3)$$

where the superscript indicates the language.

Eq. (3) gives rise to three questions: (1), How can we construct the bilingual space to model *tr*? (2), Is translating actually the appropriate way of transferring selectional preferences? (3), Is it reasonable to retain the source language argument positions like *subject* or *object*? The following subsections discuss (1) and (2); we will address (3) in Sections 5 and 6.

3.1 Bilingual Vector Spaces

Bilingual vector spaces are vector spaces in which words from two languages are represented (cf. Fig. 2). The dimensions of this space are labeled with bilingual context word pairs (like *secretly/heimlich* and *rifle/Gewehr* for German–English) that are mutual translations. By treating such context word pairs as single dimensions, the vector space can represent target words from both languages, counting the target words' co-occurrences with the context words from the respective language. In other words, a source-target word pair (s, t) will be assigned similar vectors in the semantic space if the context words of s are translations of the context words of t. Cross-lingual semantic similarity between words can be measured using standard vector space similarity (Lee, 1999).

Importantly, bilingual vector spaces can be built on the basis of co-occurrences drawn from two unrelated corpora for the source and target languages. Their construction does not require resources such as parallel corpora or bilingual translation lexicons, which might not be available for resource-poor source languages. Where parallel corpora exist, they often cover specific domains (e.g., politics), while many bilingual lexicons are prone to ambiguity problems.

The main challenge in constructing bilingual vector spaces is determining the set of dimensions, i.e., bilingual word pairs, using as little knowledge as possible. Most often, such pairs are extracted from small bilingual lexicons (Fung and McKeown, 1997; Rapp, 1999; Chiao and Zweigenbaum, 2002). As mentioned above, such resources might not be available. We thus follow an alternative approach by using frequent *cognates*, words that are shared between the two languages (Markó et al., 2005). Cognates can be extracted by simple string matching between the corpora, and mostly share their meaning (Koehn and Knight, 2002). However, they account for (at most) a small percentage of all interesting translation pairs.

To extend the set of dimensions available for the bilingual space, we use these cognates merely as a starting point for a *bootstrapping process*: We build a bilingual vector space with the initial word pairs as dimensions, and identify nearest neighbors between the two languages in the space. These are added as dimensions of the bilingual space, and the process is repeated. Since the focus is on identifying reliable source-target word pairs rather than complete coverage as in Eq. (2), we adopt a *symmetrical* definition of translation that pairs up only mutual nearest neighbors, and allows words to remain untranslated:[1]

$$tr_{sym}(s) = t \text{ iff } tr(s) = t \text{ and } tr(t) = s \qquad (4)$$

From the second iteration onward, this process introduces dimensions that are not identical graphemes, such as *Kind–child* and *Geschwindigkeit–speed*, and is iterated until convergence. Since each word of either language can only participate in at most one dimension, dimensions acquired in later steps can correct wrong pairs from previous steps, like the "false friend" German *Kind* 'child' – English *kind*, which is part of the initial set of cognates.

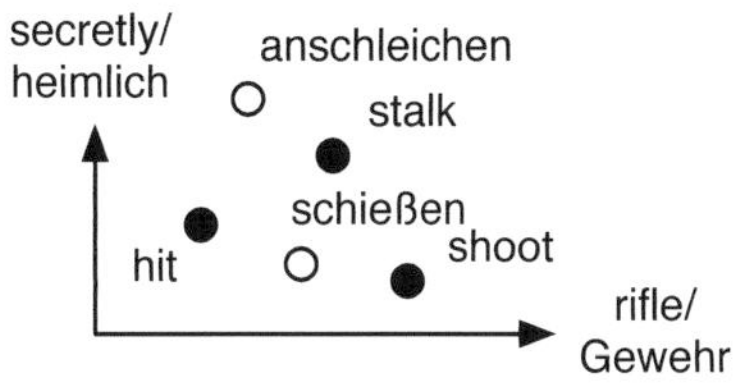

Figure 2: Sketch of a bilingual vector space for English (solid dots) and German (empty circles).

3.2 Translation and Selectional Preferences

As Figure 1 shows, the easiest way of exploiting a bilingual semantic space is to identify for each source word the target language word with the highest semantic similarity. For example, in Figure 2, the best translation of German *schießen* is its English nearest neighbor, *shoot*. However, it is risky to rely on the single nearest neighbor – it might simply be wrong. Even if it is correct, *data sparsity* is an issue: The translations may be infrequent in the target language, or the two translations of p and h may form unlikely collocates for target language-internal reasons (like

[1]To avoid unreliable vectors, we also adopt only the 50% most frequent of the tr_{sym} pairs. Frequency is defined as the geometric mean of the two words' monolingual frequencies.

difference in register) that do not reflect plausibility. A third issue are monolingual semantic phenomena like *polysemy* and *idioms*: The implausible German triple *(schießen,obj,Brise)* will be judged as very plausible due to the English idiom *to shoot the breeze*.

A look at the broader neighborhood of *schießen* suggests that its second and third-best English neighbors, *hit*, and *stalk*, can be used to *smooth* plausibility estimates for *schießen*. Instead of translating source language words by their single nearest neighbor, we will take its k nearest neighbors into account. This is defensible also from a more fundamental point of view, which suggests that the cross-lingual transfer of selectional preferences does *not* require literal translation in order to work. First, ontological models like Resnik's assume that *synonymous* words behave similarly with respect to selectional preferences. Second, recent work by Chambers and Jurafsky (2009) has induced "narrative chains", i.e., likely sequences of events, by their use of similar head words. Thus, we expect that all k nearest neighbors of a source predicate s are *informative* for the selectional preferences of s (like *schießen*) as long as they are either synonyms of its literal translation (*shoot/hit*) or come from the same narrative chain (*stalk/kill/...*).

It is also clear that smoothing does not always equate better predictions. Closeness in a word-based vector space can also just reflect semantic association. For example, Spanish *tenista* 'tennis player' is highly associated with English *tennis*, but is a bad translation in terms of selectional preferences. We assume that this problem is more acute for nouns than for verbs: The context of verbs is dominated by their arguments, which is not true for nouns. Consequently, close nouns in vector space can differ widely in ontological type, while close verbs generally have one or more similar argument slots. In our model, we will thus consider several verb translations, but just the best head word translation. For details, see Section 5.

4 Experimental Setup

Our evaluation uses English as the target language and two source languages: German (as a very close neighbor of English) and Spanish (as a more distant one). Neither of these languages are really resource-poor, but they allow us to compare our cross-lingual model against monolingual models, to emulate different levels of "resource poorness" and to examine the model's learning curve.

Plausibility Data. For German, we used the plausibility judgments collected by Brockmann (2002). The dataset contains human judgments for ninety triples sampled from the manually annotated 1 million word TiGer corpus (Brants et al., 2002): ten verbs with three argument positions (subject [SUBJ], direct object [DOBJ], and oblique (prepositional) object [POBJ]) combined with three head words. Models are evaluated against such datasets by correlating predicted plausibilities with the (not normally distributed) human judgments using Spearman's ρ, a non-parametric rank-order correlation coefficient.

We constructed a similar 90-triple data set for Spanish by sampling triples from two Spanish corpora (see below) using Brockmann's (2002) criteria. Human judgments for the triples were collected through the Amazon Mechanical Turk (AMT) crowdsourcing platform (Snow et al., 2008). We asked native speakers of Spanish to rate the plausibility of a simple sentence with the relevant verb-argument combination on a five-point Likert scale, obtaining between 12 and 17 judgments for each triple. For each datapoint, we removed the single lowest and highest judgments and computed the mean. We assessed the reliability of our data by replicating Brockmann's experiment for German with our AMT setup. With a Spearman ρ of almost .90, our own judgments correlate very well with Brockmann's original data.

Monolingual Prior Work and Baselines. For German, Brockmann and Lapata (2003) evaluated ontology-based models trained on TiGer triples and the GermaNet ontology. The results in Table 2 show that while both models are able to predict the data significantly, neither of the models can predict all of the data. We attribute this to the small size of TiGer.[2]

To gauge the limits of monolingual knowledge-lean approaches, we constructed two monolingual distributional models for German and Spanish according to the Padó et al. (2007) model (Eq. (1)). Recall that this model performs generalization in a syntax-based vector space model. We computed vector spaces from dependency-parsed corpora for the

[2]For each of the three argument positions and "all", Brockmann and Lapata report the results for the best parametrization of the models, which explains the apparently inconsistent results.

	Resnik	Clark & Weir
SUBJ	.408*	.268
DOBJ	.430*	.611***
POBJ	.330	.597***
all	.374***	.232*

Table 2: Monolingual baselines 1. Spearman correlations for ontology-based models in German as reported by Brockmann and Lapata (2003). *: $p < .05$; ***: $p < .001$

Lang.	German		Spanish			
Corpus	Schulte's HGC		AnCora		Encarta	
	ρ	Cov.	ρ	Cov.	ρ	Cov.
SUBJ	.34†	90%	.44*	80%	.14	100%
DOBJ	.51**	97%	.29	83%	-.05	100%
POBJ	.41*	93%	-.03	100%	—	—[3]
all	.33**	93%	.16	88%	.11	67%

Table 3: Monolingual baselines 2. Spearman correlation and coverage for distributional models. † : $p < .1$; *: $p < .05$; **: $p < .01$.

two languages, using the 2,000 most frequent lemma-dependency relation pairs as dimensions and adopting the popular pointwise mutual information metric as co-occurrence statistic. For German, we used Schulte im Walde's verb frame resource (Schulte im Walde et al., 2001), which contains the frequency of triples calculated from probabilistic parses of 30M words from the Huge German Corpus (HGC) of newswire. For Spanish, we consulted two syntactically analyzed corpora: the AnCora (Taulé et al., 2008) and the Encarta corpus (Calvo et al., 2005). At 0.5M words, the AnCora corpus is small, but manually annotated, whereas the larger, automatically parsed Encarta corpus amounts to over 18M tokens.

Table 3 shows the results for the distributional monolingual models. For German, we get significant correlations for DOBJ and POBJ, an almost significant correlation for SUBJs, and high significance for the complete dataset ($p < 0.01$). These figures rival the performance of the ontological models (cf. Table 2), without using ontological information. For Spanish, the only significant correlation with human judgments is obtained for subjects, the most frequent argument position, with the clean AnCora data. AnCora is presumably too sparse for the other argument positions. The large Encarta corpus, in turn, is very noisy, supporting our concerns from Section 2.

	n	noun	adj	verb	all
German	7340	.61	.57	.43	.56
Spanish	4143	.62	.67	.41	.58

Table 4: First-translation accuracy for German-English and Spanish-English translation (n: size of gold standard).

Cross-lingual Selectional Preferences. Our architecture for the cross-lingual prediction of selectional preferences shown in Figure 1 consists of two components, namely the bilingual vector space and a selectional preference model in the target language.

As our English selectional preference model, we again use the Padó et al. (2007) model, trained on a version of the BNC parsed with MINIPAR (Lin, 1993). The parameters of the syntactic vector space were the same as for the monolingual baseline models. The bilingual vector spaces were constructed from three large, unparsed, comparable monolingual corpora. For German, we used the HGC described above. For Spanish, we obtained a corpus with around 100M words, consisting of 2.5 years of crawled text from two major Spanish newspapers. For English, we used the BNC.

We first constructed initial sets of bilingual labels. For German–English, we identified 1064 graphemically identical word pairs that occurred more than 4 times per million words. Due to the larger lexical distance between Spanish and English, there are fewer graphemically identical tokens for this language pair. We therefore applied a Porter stemmer and found 2104 identical stems, at a higher risk of "false friends". We then applied the bootstrapping cycle from Section 3.1. The set of dimensions converged after around five iterations.

We evaluated the (asymmetric) nearest neighbor pairs from the final spaces, $(s, tr(s))$, against two online dictionaries.[4] Table 4 shows that 55% to 60% of the pairs are listed in the dictionaries, with parallel tendencies for both language pairs. The bilingual space performs fairly well for nouns and adjectives, but badly for verbs, which is a well-known weakness of distributional models (Peirsman et al., 2008).

Even taking into account the incompleteness of dictionaries, this looks like a negative result: more

[3]Since the Encarta data consists of individual dependency relations rather than trees, we could not model the POBJ data.

[4]DE-EN: www.dict.cc; ES-EN: www.freelang.net. Pairs $(s, tr(s))$ were only evaluated if the dictionary listed s.

than half of all verb translations are incorrect. However, following up on our intuitions from Section 3.2, we performed an analysis of the "incorrect" translations. It revealed that many of the errors in Table 4 are informative, semantically related words. Nearest neighbor target language verbs in particular tend to represent the same event type and take the same kinds of arguments as the source verb. Examples are German *gefährden* 'threaten' – English *affect*, and German *Neugier* 'curiosity' – English *enthusiasm*. We concluded that literal translation quality is a misleading figure of merit for our task.

Experimental rationale. Section 3 introduced one major design decision of our model: the question of how to treat the *argument position*, which cannot be translated by the bilingual vector space, in the cross-lingual transfer. We present two experiments that investigate the model's behavior in the absence and presence of knowledge about argument positions. Experiment 1 uses no syntactic knowledge about the source language whatsoever. In this situation, the best we can do is to assume that source language argument positions like SUBJ will correspond to the same argument position in the target language. Experiment 2 attempts to identify, for each source language argument position, the "best fit" position in the target language. This results in better plausibility estimates, but also means that we need at least some syntactic information about the source language. In both experiments, we vary the number of translations we consider for each verb.

5 Exp. 1: Induction without syntactic knowledge in the source language

This experiment assumes that argument positions simply carry over between languages. While this assumption clearly simplifies linguistic reality, it has the advantage of not needing any syntactic information about the source language. We thus model German and Spanish SUBJ relations by English SUBJ relations and DOBJs by DOBJs. In the case of (lexicalized) POBJs, where we cannot assume identity, we compute plausibility scores for *all* English POBJs that account for at least 10% of the predicate's argument tokens, and select the PP with the highest plausibility estimate. The k best "translations" of the predicate p, $tr_k(p)$, are turned into a single prediction using maximization, yielding the final model:

$$Pl^s_{\text{nosyn}}(p, a, h) = \max_{p_t \in tr_k(p)} Pl^t(p_t, a, tr(h)) \quad (5)$$

Note that this model does not use any source language information, except the bilingual vector space.

The results of Experiment 1 are given in Table 5 (coverage always 100%). For German, all predictions correlate significantly with human ratings, and most even at $p < 0.01$, despite our naive assumption about the cross-lingual argument position identity. The results exceed both monolingual model types (ontological, Tab. 2, and distributional, Tab. 3), notably without the use of syntactic data. In particular, the results for the POBJs, notoriously difficult to model monolingually, are higher than for SUBJs or DOBJs. We attribute this to the cross-lingual generalization which takes all prepositional arguments into account.

The Spanish dataset is harder to model overall. We obtain significantly high correlations for SUBJ, but non-significant results for DOBJ and POBJ. This corresponds well to the patterns for the monolingual AnCora corpus (Table 3). However, we outperform AnCora on the complete dataset, where it did not achieve significance, while the cross-lingual model does at $p < 0.01$ — again, even without the use of syntactic analyses. We attribute the overall lower results compared to German to systematic syntactic differences between English and Spanish. For example, animate direct objects in Spanish are realized as POBJs headed by the preposition *a*. Estimating the plausibility of such objects by looking at English POBJs is unlikely to yield good results. The use of a larger number of verb translations yields a clear increase in correlation for the German data, but inconclusive results for Spanish.

6 Exp. 2: Induction with syntactic knowledge in the source language

As discussed in Section 3.2, verbs that are semantically similar in the bilingual vector space may very well realize their (semantic) argument positions differently in the surface syntax. For example, German *teilnehmen* is correctly translated to English *attend*, but the crucial event argument is realized differently, namely as a POBJ headed by *an* in German and as a DOBJ in English. To address this problem, we

DE	1-best	2-best	3-best	4-best	5-best
SUBJ	.44*	.47**	.45*	.47**	**.54****
DOBJ	.39*	.39*	.52**	.54**	**.55****
POBJ	.58**	.61**	.61**	.61**	**.62****
all	.35**	.37**	.37**	.38**	**.40****

ES	1-best	2-best	3-best	4-best	5-best
SUBJ	.58**	**.64****	**.64****	.58**	.58**
DOBJ	.13	**.16**	.11	.07	.07
POBJ	**.13**	**.13**	.09	.14	.14
all	.34**	**.36****	.34**	.32**	.32**

Table 5: Exp.1: Spearman correlation between syntaxless cross-lingual model and human judgments for k best verb translations. Best k for each argument position marked in boldface. Coverage of all models: 100%.

learn a mapping function m that identifies the argument position a_t of a target language predicate p_t that corresponds best to an argument position a of a predicate p in the source language. Our simple model is in the same spirit as the cross-lingual plausibility model itself: It returns the argument position a_t of p_t for which the seen head words of (p, a) are most plausible when translated into the target language:[5]

$$m(p, a, p_t) = \operatorname*{argmax}_{a_t} \sum_{h \in Seen_a(p)} Pl^t(p_t, a_t, tr(h))$$

Parallel to Eq. (5), the cross-lingual model is now:

$$Pl^s_{\text{syn}}(p, a, h) = \max_{p_t \in tr_k(p)} Pl^t(p_t, m(p, a, p_t), tr(h)) \quad (6)$$

This model can recover English argument positions that correspond better to the original ones than the identity mapping. For example, on our data, it discovers the mapping for *teilnehmen an/attend* discussed above. A second example concerns the incorrect, but informative translation of *stagnieren* 'stagnate' as *boost*. Here the model recognizes that the SUBJ of *stagnieren* (the stagnating entity) corresponds to the DOBJ of *boost*.

Establishing m requires syntactic information in the source language, in order to obtain the set of seen head words $Seen_{a_s}(p_s)$. For this reason, Exp. 2 uses the parsed subset of the HGC (German), and the AnCora and Encarta corpora (Spanish). The results are shown in Table 6. We generally improve over

[5]To alleviate sparse data, we ignore argument positions of English verbs that represent less than 10% of its argument tokens.

DE	1-best	2-best	3-best	4-best	5-best
SUBJ	.55**	**.59****	.49**	.52**	.54**
DOBJ	.52**	.52**	.66**	.66**	**.68****
POBJ	.61**	.68**	**.70****	.69**	**.70****
all	.41**	.44**	.44*	.46**	**.48****

ES-A	1-best	2-best	3-best	4-best	5-best
SUBJ	**.52****	.47*	.42*	.41*	.42*
DOBJ	.52*^{c}	**.64****^{c}	.54*^{c}	.42*^{c}	.42*^{c}
POBJ	**.32**†	.18	.13	.13	.24
all	**.47****	.41**	.36**	.33**	.37**

ES-E	1-best	2-best	3-best	4-best	5-best
SUBJ	.40*	**.42***	.39*	.39*	.41*
DOBJ	**.21**	.02	.06	.13	.20

Table 6: Exp.2: Spearman correlation between syntax-aware cross-lingual model and human judgments for k best verb translations. ES-A: AnCora corpus, ES-E: Encarta corpus. Best k for each argument position in boldface. Coverage of all models: 100%, except ^{c}: 60%.

Exp. 1. For German, every single model now correlates highly significantly with human judgments ($p < 0.01$), and the correlation for the complete dataset increases from .40 to .48. For Spanish, we see very good results for the AnCora corpus. Compared to Exp. 1, we see a slight degradation for the SUBJs; however, the correlations remain significant for all values of k. Conversely, all predictions for DOBJs are now significant,[6] and the POBJs have improved at least numerically, which validates our analysis of the problems in Exp. 1. The best correlation for the complete dataset improves from .36 to .47. The results for the Encarta corpus disappoint, though. SUBJs are significant, but worse than for AnCora, and the DOBJs remain non-significant throughout. With regard to increasing the number of verb translations, Exp. 2 shows an almost universal benefit for German, but still mixed results for Spanish, which may indicate that verb translations for Spanish are still "looser" than the German ones.

In fact, most remaining poor judgments are the result of problematic translations, which stem from three main sources. The first one is sparse data. Infrequent German and Spanish words often receive unreliable vector representations. Some examples are the

[6]Note, however, that AnCora has an imperfect coverage for DOBJs (60%). This is because our Spanish dataset contains verbs sampled from Encarta that do not occur in AnCora.

German *Tau* ('dew', frequency of 180 in the HGC), translated as *alley*, and *Reifeprüfung* (German SAT, frequency 120), translated as *affiliation*. Both of these may also be due to the difference in genre between the HGC and the BNC. A second problem is formed by nearest neighbors that are ontologically dissimilar, as in the *tenista* 'tennis player'/*tennis* example from above. A final issue relates to limitations of the Padó et al. (2007) model, whose architecture is susceptible to polysemy-related problems. For instance, the Spanish combination (*excavar*, *obj*, *terreno*) was judged by speakers as very plausible, but its English equivalent (*excavate*, *obj*, *land*) is assigned a very low score by the model. This might be due to the fact that in the BNC, *land* occurs often in its political meaning, and forms an outlier among the head words for (*excavate*,*obj*).

How much syntactic information is necessary? The syntax-aware model requires syntactic information about the source language, which seems to run counter to our original motivation of developing methods for resource-poor languages. To address this point, we analyzed the behavior of the syntax-aware model for small syntactically analyzed corpora that contained only at most m occurrences for each predicate. We obtained the m occurrences by sampling from the syntactically analyzed part of the HGC; if fewer than m occurrences were present in the corpus, we simply used these. Figure 3 shows the training curve with 1 verb translation, averaged over n rounds ($n = 10$ for 5 arguments, $n = 5$ for 10 arguments, $n = 4$ for 20, 50 and 100 arguments). The general picture is clear: most of the benefit of the syntactic data is drawn form the first five occurrences for each argument position. This shows that a small amount of targeted syntactic annotation can improve the cross-lingual model substantially.

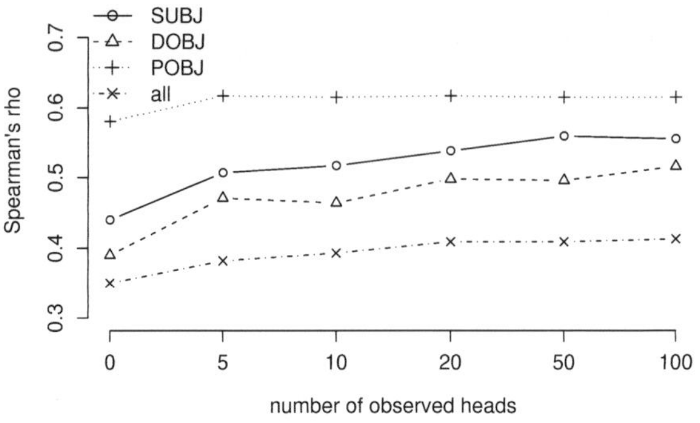

Figure 3: Training curve for the bilingual German–English model as a function of the number of observed head words per argument position in the source language.

7 Conclusions

In this article, we have presented a first unsupervised cross-lingual model of selectional preferences. Our model proceeds by automatically *translating* (predicate, argument position, head word) triples for resource-poor source languages into a resource-rich target language, where accurate selectional preference models are available. The translation is based on a bilingual vector space, which can be bootstrapped from large unparsed corpora in the two languages.

Our results indicate that bilingual methods can go a long way towards the modeling of selectional preferences in resource-poor languages, where bilingual lexicons, parallel corpora, or ontologies might not be available. Our experiments have looked at German and Spanish, where the cross-lingual models rival and even exceed monolingual methods that typically have to rely on small, clean "treebank"-style corpora or large, very noisy, automatically parsed corpora. We have also demonstrated that noisy syntactic data from the source language can be integrated in our model, where it helps improve the cross-lingual handling of argument positions. The linguistic distance between the languages can impact (1) the ability to find accurate translations and (2) the degree of syntactic overlap; nevertheless, as Agirre et al. (2003) show, the transfer is possible even for unrelated languages.

In this paper, we have instantiated the selectional preference model in the target language (English) with the distributional model by Padó et al. (2007). However, our approach is modular and can be combined with any other selectional preference model. We see two main avenues for future work: (1), The construction of properly bilingual models where source language information can also help to further improve the *target* language model (Diab and Resnik, 2002); (2), The extension of our cross-lingual mapping for the argument position to mappings that hold across multiple predicates as well as argument-dependent mappings like the Spanish direct objects, whose realization depends on their animacy.

References

Naoki Abe and Hang Li. 1996. Learning word association norms using tree cut pair models. In *Proc. ICML*, pages 3–11, Bari, Italy.

Eneko Agirre, Izaskun Aldezabal, and Eli Pociello. 2003. A pilot study of English selectional preferences and their cross-lingual compatibility with Basque. In *Proc. TSD*, pages 12–19, Brno, Czech Republic.

Shane Bergsma, Dekang Lin, and Randy Goebel. 2008. Discriminative learning of selectional preference from unlabeled text. In *Proc. EMNLP*, pages 59–68, Honolulu, HI.

Sabine Brants, Stefanie Dipper, Silvia Hansen, Wolfgang Lezius, and George Smith. 2002. The TIGER treebank. In *Proc. Workshop on Treebanks and Linguistic Theories*, Sozopol, Bulgaria.

Carsten Brockmann and Mirella Lapata. 2003. Evaluating and combining approaches to selectional preference acquisition. In *Proc. EACL*, pages 27–34, Budapest, Hungary.

Carsten Brockmann. 2002. Evaluating and combining approaches to selectional preference acquisition. Master's thesis, Universität des Saarlandes, Saarbrücken.

Hiram Calvo, Alexander Gelbukh, and Adam Kilgarriff. 2005. Distributional thesaurus vs. wordnet: A comparison of backoff techniques for unsupervised PP attachment. In *Proc. CICLing*, pages 177–188, Mexico City, Mexico.

Nathanael Chambers and Dan Jurafsky. 2009. Unsupervised learning of narrative schemas and their participants. In *Proc. ACL*, pages 602–610, Singapore.

Yun-Chuang Chiao and Pierre Zweigenbaum. 2002. Looking for candidate translational equivalents in specialized, comparable corpora. In *Proc. COLING*, pages 1–5, Taipei, Taiwan.

Stephen Clark and David Weir. 2002. Class-based probability estimation using a semantic hierarchy. *Computational Linguistics*, 28(2):187–206.

Mona Diab and Philip Resnik. 2002. An unsupervised method for word sense tagging using parallel corpora. In *Proc. ACL*, pages 255–262, Philadelphia, PA.

Pascale Fung and Kathleen McKeown. 1997. Finding terminology translations from non-parallel corpora. In *Proc. 3rd Annual Workshop on Very Large Corpora*, pages 192–202, Hong Kong.

Daniel Gildea and Daniel Jurafsky. 2002. Automatic labeling of semantic roles. *Computational Linguistics*, 28(3):245–288.

Rebecca Hwa, Philipp Resnik, Amy Weinberg, Clara Cabezas, and Okan Kolak. 2005. Bootstrapping parsers via syntactic projection across parallel texts. *Natural Language Engineering*, 11(3):311–325.

Philipp Koehn and Kevin Knight. 2002. Learning a translation lexicon from monolingual corpora. In *Proc. ACL-02 Workshop on Unsupervised Lexical Acquisition*, pages 9–16, Philadelphia, PA.

Lillian Lee. 1999. Measures of distributional similarity. In *Proc. ACL*, pages 25–32, College Park, MD.

Dekang Lin. 1993. Principle-based parsing without overgeneration. In *Proc. ACL*, pages 112–120.

Kornél Markó, Stefan Schulz, Olena Medelyan, and Udo Hahn. 2005. Bootstrapping dictionaries for cross-language information retrieval. In *Proc. SIGIR*, pages 528–535, Seattle, WA.

Diana McCarthy and John Carroll. 2003. Disambiguating nouns, verbs and adjectives using automatically acquired selectional preferences. *Computational Linguistics*, 29(4):639–654.

Ken McRae, Michael Spivey-Knowlton, and Michael Tanenhaus. 1998. Modeling the influence of thematic fit (and other constraints) in on-line sentence comprehension. *Journal of Memory and Language*, 38:283–312.

Sebastian Padó, Ulrike Padó, and Katrin Erk. 2007. Flexible, corpus-based modelling of human plausibility judgements. In *Proc. EMNLP-CoNLL*, pages 400–409, Prague, Czech Republic.

Yves Peirsman, Kris Heylen, and Dirk Geeraerts. 2008. Size matters. Tight and loose context definitions in English word space models. In *Proc. ESSLLI Workshop on Lexical Semantics*, pages 9–16, Hamburg, Germany.

Detlef Prescher, Stefan Riezler, and Mats Rooth. 2000. Using a probabilistic class-based lexicon for lexical ambiguity resolution. In *Proc. COLING*, pages 649–655, Saarbrücken, Germany.

Reinhard Rapp. 1999. Automatic identification of word translations from unrelated English and German corpora. In *Proc. ACL*, pages 519–526, College Park, MD.

Philip Resnik. 1996. Selectional constraints: An information-theoretic model and its computational realization. *Cognition*, 61:127–159.

Sabine Schulte im Walde, Helmut Schmid, Mats Rooth, Stefan Riezler, and Detlef Prescher. 2001. Statistical Grammar Models and Lexicon Acquisition. In *Linguistic Form and its Computation*, pages 389–440. CSLI Publications, Stanford, CA.

Rion Snow, Brendan O'Connor, Daniel Jurafsky, and Andrew Ng. 2008. Cheap and fast – but is it good? Evaluating non-expert annotations for natural language tasks. In *Proc. EMNLP*, pages 254–263, Honolulu, HI.

Mariona Taulé, M. Antònia Martí, and Marta Recasens. 2008. Ancora: Multilevel annotated corpora for Catalan and Spanish. In *Proc. LREC*, Marrakech, Morocco.

Yorick Wilks. 1975. Preference semantics. In E. Keenan, editor, *Formal Semantics of Natural Language*. Cambridge University Press.

Latent SVMs for Semantic Role Labeling using LTAG Derivation Trees*

Yudong Liu and **Gholamreza Haffari** and **Anoop Sarkar**
School of Computing Science
Simon Fraser University, British Columbia, Canada
{yudongl,ghaffar1,anoop}@cs.sfu.ca

Abstract

A phrase structure parse tree for a sentence can be generated by many different Lexicalized Tree-Adjoining Grammar (LTAG) derivation trees. In this paper, we use multiple LTAG derivations as latent features for semantic role labeling (SRL). We hypothesize that positive and negative examples of individual semantic roles can be reliably distinguished by possibly different latent LTAG-based features. We use latent support vector machines (LSVM) for the SRL task using these latent LTAG features. Our experiments on the PropBank-CoNLL'2005 dataset show that our method obtains 89.59% F1 score which is significantly better than the state of the art F1 score of 80.32% on this task.

1 Introduction

Semantic Role Labeling (SRL) aims to identify and label all the arguments for each predicate occurring in a sentence. It involves identifying constituents in the sentence that represent the predicate's arguments and assigning pre-specified semantic roles to them. The following example shows the semantic roles for the predicate *sell*, taken from the PropBank corpus (Palmer et al., 2005).

[$A0_{seller}$ *Ports of Call Inc.*] reached agreements to [V *sell*] [$A1_{\text{thing}}$ *its remaining seven aircraft*] [$A2_{\text{buyer}}$ *to buyers that weren't disclosed*] .

As in other natural language learning tasks, feature selection plays an important role in high performance SRL. SRL feature extraction has relied on various syntactic representations of input sentences, such as syntactic chunks (Hacioglu et al., 2004) and full syntactic parses (Gildea and Jurafsky, 2002), CCG derivations (Gildea and Hockenmaier, 2003) and dependency trees (Hacioglu, 2004) or integrated features from different parsers (Pradhan et al., 2005). Lexicalized Tree Adjoining Grammar (LTAG) derivation trees have been used for SRL (Chen and Rambow, 2003; Liu and Sarkar, 2007) who show that LTAG can localize predicate-argument dependencies to improve performance on the SRL task.

The LTAG derivations used in (Liu and Sarkar, 2007) were obtained by applying Magerman-Collins head percolation rules to Penn treebank (PTB) trees. However, more than one plausible LTAG derivation can be extracted from a single PTB tree. In this paper, we consider multiple LTAG derivations as a source of features for the SRL task. Since there are multiple LTAG derivations available for the single PTB tree, any single derivation tree extracted using one approach is not necessarily the best feature source for the SRL instance in question. By treating LTAG derivations as latent structures of a PTB tree, we use latent SVMs (LSVM) to learn which is the most suitable LTAG derivation for each SRL prediction instance.

2 Lexicalized Tree Adjoining Grammars

We assume some familiarity with Lexicalized Tree-Adjoining Grammar (LTAG); (Joshi and Schabes, 1997) is a good introduction to this formalism. A LTAG is defined to be a set of lexicalized *elementary trees* (*etree* for short), of which there are two types, *initial trees* and *auxiliary trees*. Etrees are composed through two operations, *substitution* and *adjunction*. The tree produced by composing the etrees is the *derived/parse tree* and the tree that records the history of composition is the *derivation tree* as shown in Fig. 1.

2.1 Generation of latent LTAG derivations

As in previous work on LTAG derivation tree extraction from the Penn TreeBank (Shen, 2004), we face two kinds of ambiguities in LTAG elementary tree extraction: *head choice* and *argument-adjunct*

* This research was partially supported by NSERC, Canada (RGPIN: 264905). Thanks to Mirella Lapata, Kristina Toutanova, Luke Zettlemoyer and the anonymous reviewers for their helpful comments.

Human Language Technologies: The 2010 Annual Conference of the North American Chapter of the ACL, pages 930–938,
Los Angeles, California, June 2010.

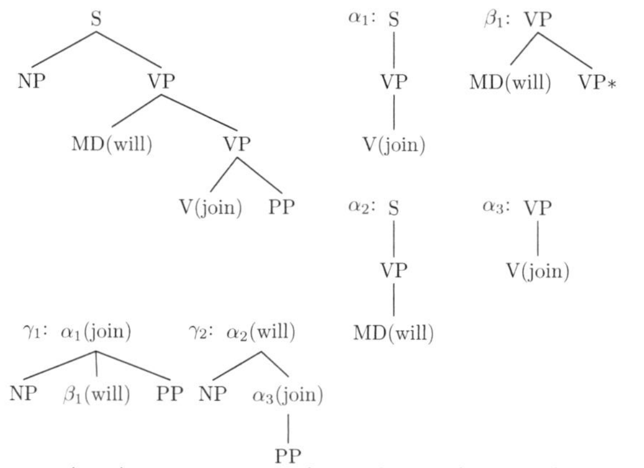

Figure 1: A parse tree schematic, and two plausible LTAG derivation trees for it: derivation tree γ_1 uses elementary trees α_1 and β_1 while γ_2 uses α_2 and α_3.

distinction. For each node in a parse tree, one of the daughter nodes is picked to be the head based on a heuristic rule that depends on the node labels, e.g. *V* is picked as the head daughter for node labeled *VP*. In LTAG-based statistical parsers, high accuracy is obtained by using the Magerman-Collins head-percolation rules in order to provide the etrees. (Chiang and Bikel, 2002) describes these heuristic rules in detail for the Collins parsing model (Collins, 1996) and (Chiang, 2000) describes the algorithm for converting a head-annotated parse tree into an LTAG derivation tree. In Fig. 1 the derivation tree γ_2 was created using this process. A *spine* of an etree is the path from lexical item to the root of the etree.

Argument-adjunct ambiguity is created if arguments are optionally localized using the substitution operation into the etree that is anchored with the predicate in conventional LTAG. Since this ambiguity is a core aspect of the SRL task, we do not use substitution in our grammar. In the resulting derivations, all etrees are in the spinal form (see α_1 in Fig. 1). These etrees are composed into LTAG derivations through *sister adjunction* which is commonly used in LTAG statistical parsers to deal with the relatively flat Penn Treebank trees (Chiang, 2000).

Given a predicate and parse tree, the latent LTAG derivations are created using the following method (illustrated by an example in Fig. 2). For each *predicate*, we apply 3 heuristic head-percolation rules to generate 3 head-annotated parse trees per predicate:

1. Magerman-Collins rules. (produces etree p_1 in Fig. 2)
2. Same as Rule 1, but label all consecutive VP nodes as head from the predicate until you see a non-VP node. (also produces etree p_1 in Fig. 2)
3. Same as Rule 1, but label all nodes as head from the predicate to the root of the PTB tree. (produces etree p_2 in Fig. 2)

For each head-annotated parse tree, different predicate etrees are extracted using the algorithm given in (Chiang, 2000) that converts head-annotated parse trees into LTAG derivations. For each predicate etree, we produce argument etrees which localize the constituent that may receive a semantic role (called the target, e.g. [NP] in Fig. 2). Each node from the target to the root of the parse tree is taken to be the root of an alternative argument etree. E.g. etrees a_1, a_3, a_5 in Fig. 2. Each target also produces additional latent derivations by choosing a different head child for the target. E.g. etrees a_1 and a_2 are identical except for different lexical anchors. When the number of intermediate etrees (defined as etrees between the predicate etree and argument etree in the LTAG derivation) is less than 3, we also consider all the possible variants for intermediate etrees based on the same strategy for generating argument etrees described above. E.g. etrees i_1 and i_2 in Fig. 2. Derivations rooted in i_1 do not generate the entire input tree T, and they don't have to because latent LTAG features only include information to link a predicate with its potential arguments. One LTAG derivation is different from another if the combination of predicate etree, argument etree, and intermediate etrees (if any) is different. Chapter 4 of (Liu, 2009) contains the pseudo-code for the algorithm that we use to generate the latent LTAG derivation trees. In our dataset on average we have ~130 derivation trees generated for each SRL instance.

3 Latent Support Vector Machines

We hypothesize that for each SRL classification task, positive and negative examples of individual semantic roles can be reliably distinguished by possibly different latent LTAG features, and thus the latent features can be used discriminatively using a max-margin SVM classifier that only picks the most predictive features. Inspired by (Cherry and Quirk, 2008), we apply Latent SVMs (LSVM) to the SRL task. LSVM is a relatively new methodology for

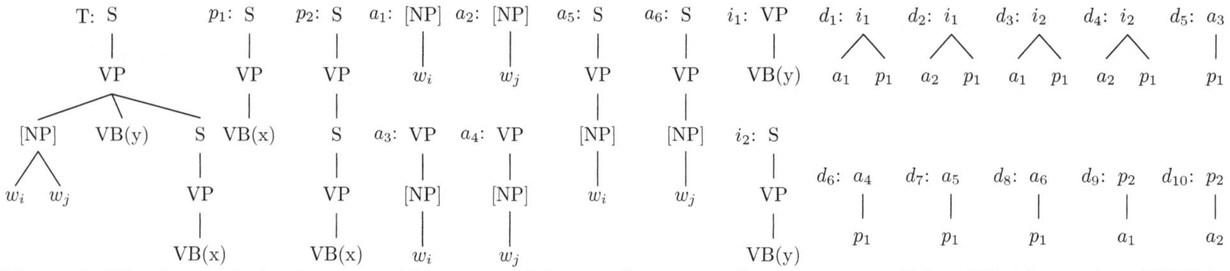

Figure 2: The latent derivation trees (d_i) extracted for predicate x and argument candidate NP (denoted as [NP]) in a parse tree fragment T. p_i: variants of predicate etree, a_i: variants of argument etrees, i_i: variants of intermediate etrees. In contrast to (Chen and Rambow, 2003) argument nodes do not have to be the root node of an etree.

discriminative training introduced by (Felzenszwalb et al., 2008) for object detection in computer vision. LSVMs are a generalization of classic SVMs to handle classification problems with latent structures with the properties we described above.

Let $D = \{\langle x_i, y_i \rangle\}_1^n$ be a set of labeled examples where x_i is an input and y_i is the output label, either $+1$ or -1. In classical SVMs, a weight vector $\mathbf{w}$ needs to be trained from D by optimizing the following objective function:

$$\arg\min_{\mathbf{w}} \frac{\lambda}{2}\|\mathbf{w}\|^2 + \sum_{i=1}^{n} \max(0, 1 - y_i f_{\mathbf{w}}(x_i)) \quad (1)$$

where $f_{\mathbf{w}}(x_i) = \mathbf{w} \cdot \Phi(x_i)$ and Φ is a feature vector for representing the input x_i. Each misclassification (when $y_i f_{\mathbf{w}}(x_i) < 1$) incurs a penalty proportional to the degree to which it violates the margin constraint.

In LSVMs, we introduce an extra dimensionality of latent structures, and classify input instances while simultaneously searching for a good latent structure. The score assigned to an input x is then defined as,

$$f_{\mathbf{w}}(x) = \max_{h \in H(x)} \mathbf{w} \cdot \Phi(x, h) \quad (2)$$

where H is a set of latent structures. As in classical SVMs, the weight vector is trained by solving Eqn. 1, where those latent annotations are preferred which induce low training error (the second term), and at the same time, lead to a low complexity classifier (the first term). In other words, the training instances are embedded into an appropriate extended feature space specific to the given classfication task. If there is only one possible latent structure for each input ($|H(x)| = 1$), then LSVM reduces to classical SVM.

To learn the model parameter $\mathbf{w}$, we use a coordinate descent algorithm to optimize Eqn. 1:

1. Find the best structure for each training example using the current weight vector:
$$\forall i : h_i \leftarrow \arg\max_{h \in H(x_i)} \mathbf{w} \cdot \Phi(x_i, h)$$
2. Using the current values for latent structures, learn the weight vector to minimize Eqn. 1 with $f_{\mathbf{w}}(x_i) = \mathbf{w} \cdot \Phi(x_i, h_i)$.

For SVM training in the second step, we use the freely available SvmSgd package[1] which implements *stochastic gradient descent* (SGD), an online learning algorithm for SVMs which is known to scale to millions of features and a large number of training examples (as is the case in the SRL task). The SGD algorithm selects a random training example at time t, and sets:

$$\mathbf{w}^{(t+1)} = \mathbf{w}^{(t)} - \eta \nabla F^{(t)}(\mathbf{w}^{(t)})$$

where $F^{(t)}(\mathbf{w})$ is the objective function specialized for the example chosen at time t, and η is the learning rate. The gradient $\nabla F^{(t)}(\mathbf{w})$ for our case is

$$\begin{cases} \lambda\mathbf{w} - y^{(t)}\Phi(x^{(t)}, h^{(t)}) & \text{if } y^{(t)}\mathbf{w} \cdot \Phi(x^{(t)}, h^{(t)}) < 1 \\ \lambda\mathbf{w} & \text{otherwise} \end{cases}$$

For our experiments, the space of latent features is structured, namely each latent LTAG derivation tree. However, the derivation tree is mapped into an unstructured set of latent features that are used in a linear kernel within the LSVM framework. More structured latent variables can also be used in LSVMs which need more sophisticated training algorithms (Yu and Joachims, 2009; Wang and Mori, 2009).

[1] *http://leon.bottou.org/projects/sgd*

Task	Positive Examples	Negative Examples
ID	219,556	349,629
A0	60,351	159,205
A1	80,486	139,070
A2	17,191	202,365
A3	3,005	218,551
A4	2,461	217,095

Table 1: The number of positive and negative training examples for the identification and classification tasks.

4 Semantic Role Labeling with LSVM

4.1 SRL Instance Generation

We use a commonly used architecture for building our SRL system. It consists of four stages: **pruning**, **argument identification**, **argument classification** and finally optionally we perform a **multi-class classification**. For SRL identification we train a binary LSVM classifier and for SRL classification we use the standard "one-vs-all" scheme. For each given training point $\langle x_i, y_i \rangle$, x_i is a constituent from the derived tree, and y_i is the output label. For identification, y indicates whether the current constituent that dominates a span is an argument or not. For each A_k classification, y indicates whether the current constituent, which has been already identified as an argument, has the A_k semantic role. In the pruning stage we only allow nodes that are sisters to nodes on the path from the predicate to the root *in the parse tree*. This is commonly used in the SRL community (c.f. (Xue and Palmer, 2004)). Pruning and parser errors provide an upper bound on the recall for any of our methods. We then generate the SRL training instances (positive and negative) from the pruned PTB trees. Table 1 shows the number of positive and negative instances that are generated from our training data for LSVM training. As in many SRL systems, this instance generation method makes an independence assumption among SRL instances extracted from the same sentence. However, we can obtain high performance without an explicit model of the frameset because with sufficiently discriminative features we never confuse a structural location in the parse during classification (A0, A1, etc.) and such a classifier will not predict two A0's in a row even though each prediction is independent.

Table 2: Features from the phrase-structure tree used in our system. Features with asterisk $*$ are not used for argument identification.

Basic features from (Gildea and Jurafsky, 2002)
• predicate lemma and voice
• phrase type and head word (phrase = candidate)
• path from phrase to predicate [1]
• position: phrase relative to predicate: before or after
• sub-cat records the immediate structure that expands from predicate's parent [2]
Additional features proposed by (Surdeanu et al. 2003; Pradhan et al., 2004, 2005)
• predicate POS
• head word POS
• first/last word/POS
• POS of word immediately before/after phrase
• path length [1]
• Lowest common ancestor path between phrase and predicate
• punctuation immediately before/after phrase$*$
• path trigrams$*$: up to 9 are considered
• head word named entity label such as "PER, ORG, LOC"$*$
• content word named entity label for PP parent node$*$
Additional features proposed by (Xue and Palmer, 2004)
• predicate_phrase type
• predicate_head word
• voice_position
• syntactic frame$*$

[1] In Fig. 1 $VP\uparrow VP\uparrow S\downarrow NP$ is the path from the predicate to a candidate phrase with path length 4.
[2] This feature is different from the **frame** feature which usually refers to all the semantic participants for the particular predicate.

4.2 Features

Table 2 lists the features that are extracted from PTB trees, and Table 3 listed the features we proposed that are extracted from the LTAG derivations mostly taken from (Liu and Sarkar, 2007) but we add n-gram features on etree spines. Our LTAG-based SRL systems use features from both Table 2 and Table 3.

5 Experiments

5.1 Experimental Setup

Training data (PropBank Sections 02-21), development set data (Section 24) and test data (Sec-

Table 3: Features from latent LTAG derivation trees used in our system. Head related features in Table 2 will be determined by the current LTAG derivation tree when they are used with the features in this table.

- pred etree (plus POS → voice)
- arg etree (plus POS → NE if any)
- reln of arg etree to pred etree: {child, parent, sibling, grandparent, uncle, other}
- distance between arg etree and pred etree: {0, 1, 2}
- label/index of attachment node between pred etree and parent (index of root = 0) [1]
- position1 of pred etree to its parent etree
- intermediate etree #1: predicate's parent etree, POS and lemma of anchor [2]
- label/index of attachment point of arg etree and its parent OR [3]
- label/index of attachment point of arg etree and its child [4]
- intermediate etree #2: arg's parent etree, POS and lemma of anchor OR [5]
- arg's child etree, POS and lemma of anchor [4]
- position2 of arg etree to its parent
- label of attachment between pred's parent etree and arg's parent etree [6]
- position3 of pred's parent etree to arg's parent etree
- position1 + position2 + position3 + relation
- position1 + position2 + position3 + distance
- relation + distance
- upto 9 trigrams of arg etree spine (from the head)
- upto 9 trigrams of pred etree spine (from the pred)

when relation is:

[1] parent or sibling or grandparent or uncle.
[2] sibling or grandparent or uncle.
[3] child or sibling or uncle.
[4] grandparent.
[5] sibling or uncle.
[6] uncle.

tion 23) are taken from CoNLL-2005 shared task data[2]. All the necessary annotation information such as predicates, parse trees from the Charniak parser (Charniak, 2000) as well as named entity labels are part of the data. The argument set we considered is the same as that of CoNLL-2005 shared task data, which includes {A0, A1, A2, A3, A4, A5} and 13 adjunct-like arguments such as AM-TMP and 11 referring arguments such as R-A0. The classification performance is evaluated using standard *Precision/Recall/F1* (p/r/f) scores.

We train 30 binary LSVM classifiers on the training data, one A_x or not-A_x binary classifier for each argument type that appears in the test set and development set.

We run LSVM training for a fixed number of iterations (39 in our experiments) and choose a stopping point based on performance on a heldout development set. There are 3 argument types (R-A3, R-A4 and R-AM-ADV) that never appear in the dev set, so we choose iteration 10 on the test set as the stopping point for them. In our experiment we use the default settings for SvmSgd. For more details, please refer to Chapter 4 of (Liu, 2009).

5.2 Results

Table 4 shows the results of LSVM-SRL using the CoNLL-2005 evaluation program on the CoNLL test data using the Charniak parse trees. We significantly outperform the previous best results on this dataset given in (Toutanova et al., 2008).

5.3 Analysis

To compare the relative utility of the LSVM for SRL, we have built two baseline systems:

- **Baseline1** is an SRL system that uses the features in Table 2 only. No LTAG derivation is introduced for each SRL instance.
- **Baseline2** is an SRL system that uses the features in Table 2 and Table 3. The LTAG derivation that is introduced for each SRL instance is generated using *Magerman-Collins* head percolation rules and *sister-adjunction* operation. This baseline replicates the SRL method in (Liu and Sarkar, 2007).

We use SvmSgd to train both baseline systems.

The weight initialization for LSVM-SRL is taken from Baseline2: the weights trained from Baseline2 are the initial weights for LSVM training. Some features may be shared between multiple latent LTAG derivations. We alternate between learning/updating the weights using SvmSgd and selecting the best latent derivation based on the updated weights. Table 5 shows the *Precision/Recall/Fscore* of LSVM-SRL and the baselines for each binary classification task. It shows that LSVM is producing very high precision with small gains in recall, which matches our intuition that the features are more predictive but do not address parser errors, and other issues that lead to low recall.

[2] http://www.lsi.upc.es/∼srlconll/.

	Our system						(Toutanova et al., 2008)					
label	corr.	excess	miss.	prec.	rec.	F1	corr.	excess	miss.	prec.	rec.	F1
Overall	11832	506	2245	95.90	84.05	**89.59**	11094	2452	2983	81.90	78.81	80.32
A0	3322	41	241	98.78	93.24	**95.93**	3168	417	395	88.32	88.30	88.31
A1	3907	342	1020	91.95	79.30	**85.16**	4004	909	923	81.50	81.27	81.38
A2	821	6	289	99.27	73.96	**84.77**	763	276	347	73.44	68.74	71.01
A3	129	13	44	90.85	74.57	**81.90**	96	32	77	75.00	55.49	63.79
A4	80	4	22	95.24	78.43	**86.02**	71	24	31	74.74	69.61	72.08
A5	4	6	1	40.00	80.00	53.33	4	0	1	100.00	80.00	**88.89**
AM-ADV	391	7	115	98.24	77.27	**86.50**	275	149	231	64.86	54.35	59.14
AM-CAU	48	4	25	92.31	65.75	**76.80**	36	17	37	67.92	49.32	57.14
AM-DIR	58	0	27	100.00	68.24	**81.12**	34	27	51	55.74	40.00	46.58
AM-DIS	290	7	30	97.64	90.62	**94.00**	241	54	79	81.69	75.31	78.37
AM-EXT	26	1	6	96.30	81.25	**88.14**	13	7	19	65.00	40.62	50.00
AM-LOC	271	0	92	100.00	74.66	**85.49**	206	104	157	66.45	56.75	61.22
AM-MNR	263	1	81	99.62	76.45	**86.51**	195	117	149	62.50	56.69	59.45
AM-MOD	547	2	4	99.64	99.27	**99.45**	540	11	11	98.00	98.00	98.00
AM-NEG	228	0	2	100.00	99.13	**99.56**	225	5	5	97.83	97.83	97.83
AM-PNC	81	0	34	100.00	70.43	**82.65**	45	38	70	54.22	39.13	45.45
AM-PRD	2	0	3	100.00	40.00	**57.14**	1	0	4	100.00	20.00	33.33
AM-REC	1	0	1	100.00	50.00	**66.67**	0	0	2	0.00	0.00	0.00
AM-TMP	895	54	192	94.31	82.34	**87.92**	786	195	301	80.12	72.31	76.92
R-A0	220	0	4	100.00	98.21	**99.10**	204	15	20	93.15	91.07	92.10
R-A1	149	3	7	98.03	95.51	**96.75**	128	31	28	80.50	82.05	81.27
R-A2	16	0	0	100.00	100.00	**100.00**	8	5	8	61.54	50.00	55.17
R-A3	0	0	1	0.00	0.00	0.00	0	0	1	0.00	0.00	0.00
R-A4	0	0	1	0.00	0.00	0.00	0	0	1	0.00	0.00	0.00
R-AM-ADV	2	1	0	66.67	100.00	**80.00**	0	0	2	0.00	0.00	0.00
R-AM-CAU	4	0	0	100.00	100.00	**100.00**	2	0	2	100.00	50.00	66.67
R-AM-EXT	1	1	0	50.00	100.00	**66.67**	0	0	1	0.00	0.00	0.00
R-AM-LOC	20	1	1	95.24	95.24	**95.24**	10	3	11	76.92	47.62	58.82
R-AM-MNR	5	12	1	29.41	83.33	**43.48**	2	2	4	50.00	33.33	40.00
R-AM-TMP	51	0	1	100.00	98.08	**99.03**	37	13	15	74.00	71.15	72.55
V	5126	141	141	97.32	97.32	97.32	5126	141	141	97.32	97.32	97.32

Table 4: Precision/Recall/Fscore% of the LSVM-SRL system compared to the state of the art on the PropBank/CoNLL-2005 shared task (Toutanova et al., 2008). Both systems use Charniak parser output.

Learning Curves Fig. 3 shows the learning curve evaluated on test data across the iterations of LSVM training. The largest improvement happens in the first iteration where the weights are updated for the first time; the performance levels off after a few iterations. A similar trend has been observed in the development set. To better understand the behavior of LSVMs, we analyse various aspects of the LSVM-SRL algorithm and experimental results.

Stability in LSVM Training In each training iteration LSVM picks the argmax latent LTAG derivation. Are the latent derivation trees stabilized during the LSVM learning iterations? Fig. 4 plots the percentage of the instances in the training data for which the latent derivation tree has changed compared to the immediately previous iteration. The model converges pretty quickly to its best latent annotation for the training data. Fig. 4 also shows the percentage of the instances for which the argmax derivation tree has not been observed in *all* previous iterations. For over 90% of the instances the derivation trees are changed in the first iteration, which is a drastic departure from the initial derivation trees (from Baseline2). The tendency to pick unseen derivation trees exists throughout the learning process, although it drops significantly after a few iterations.

Model Complexity Does LSVM training effectively minimize the complexity of the learned model by capturing feature sparsity? Each newly-selected previously unseen derivation tree (in Fig. 4) brings

class	Baseline1 (p/r/f)%			Baseline2 (p/r/f)%			LSVM-SRL (p/r/f)%			stop iter	recall bound
ID	87.71	84.86	86.26	89.00	85.21	87.01	98.96	86.38	**92.24**	12	86.90
A0	86.46	85.30	85.87	87.87	87.50	87.68	99.26	90.31	**94.57**	18	94.24
A1	78.70	83.72	81.13	84.56	82.16	83.34	99.69	82.00	**89.99**	22	84.37
A2	85.04	73.91	79.09	83.00	74.86	78.72	99.26	73.35	**84.36**	26	76.24
A3	77.04	65.82	71.00	83.46	67.09	74.39	98.48	76.47	**86.09**	18	78.24
A4	77.42	79.12	78.26	90.14	70.33	79.01	98.77	79.21	**87.91**	20	80.20
AM	80.85	81.39	81.11	82.10	81.87	81.99	97.73	85.31	**91.10**	22	85.75

Table 5: Results for individual binary classifiers, identification (ID) and A_x v.s. not-A_x classification. The stopping iteration was the one that gave highest accuracy on the dev set. The upper bound on recall is due to missing constituents in the Charniak parser output and due to pruning the tree.

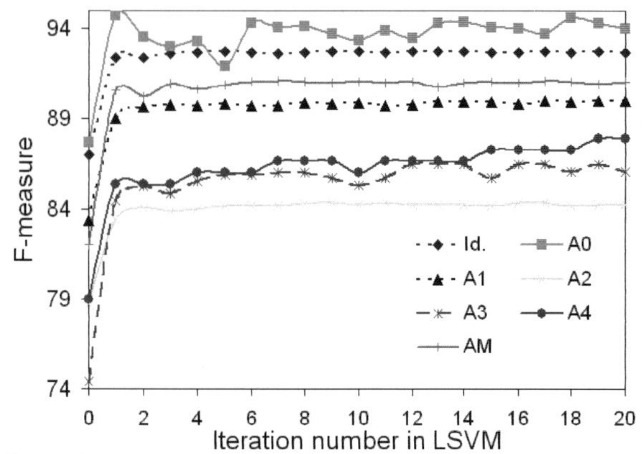

Figure 3: Fscore of identification and classification tasks on test data for each iteration of LSVM.

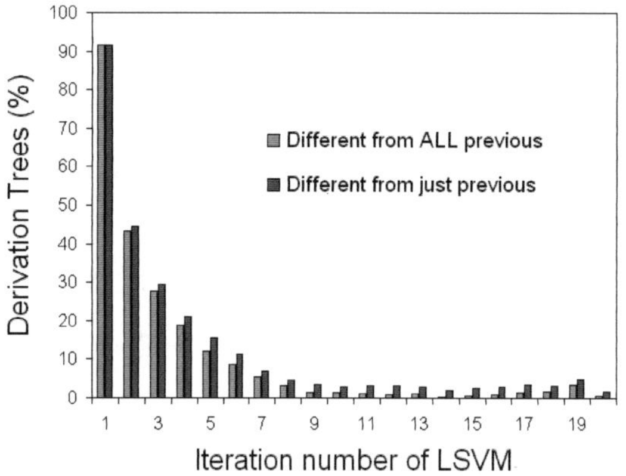

Figure 4: For each LSVM iteration in the identification task, the percentage of derivation trees which are different from the previous iteration versus those which are new and have not been observed in all previous iterations.

a set of new active features[3] into the model. Although new active features are added constantly to the model, Fig. 5 shows that the total number of active features decreases drastically during the first few learning iterations, and then stabilizes. In fact the model has picked a small set of features (8K features from the pool of 1,242,869 all possible features) having strong predictions for each individual task.

LSVM Initialization Does the initialization of the weight vector in LSVM matter? In our main experiments we initialize based on SVM training using linguistically plausible Magerman-Collins (MC) head rules. To compare against this initialization, for each training instance, we randomly select a derivation tree from its space of latent derivation trees, and we train a regular SVM with SvmSgd using this derivation tree (as we did in Baseline2). Over five random choices this approach gives an accuracy of $71.15{\pm}.79/86.11{\pm}.29/77.92{\pm}.36$. We then use these weights as the initial setting for LSVM training. E.g. in the A0 classification task, we have observed that p/r/f% is $84.54{\pm}8.00/86.44{\pm}2.12/85.33{\pm}4.49$ which is lower than initialization using MC head rules[4]. The results show that proper initialization matters a lot.

Why is LSVM so accurate? Fig. 6 is an example showing that LSVM finds ways to localize the predicate-argument relation in the LTAG derivation tree. In γ_1 tree, the predicate etree and the argument etree is far away from each other and their relation is not a *parent, child, sibling, grandparent* or *uncle* relationship. However in γ_2 tree these two etrees are localized as a *grandparent* relation. A more detailed analysis is shown in Table 6 where we show how the LSVM chosen derivation is different from the

[3] Active features are those which have non-zero values in the learned weight vector.

[4] The random initialization results are inflated since we chose the best results on the test set for the 5 runs rather than choosing a stopping point using the devset as in the results in Table 4.

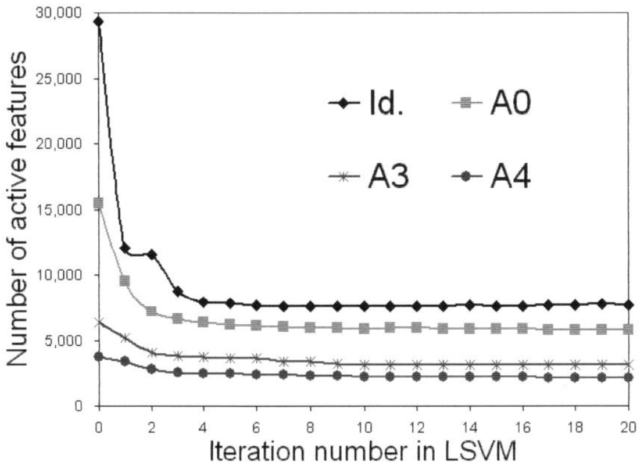

Figure 5: Number of active features during the iteration of LSVM for different tasks. These curves for the other classification tasks are similar to that of A0.

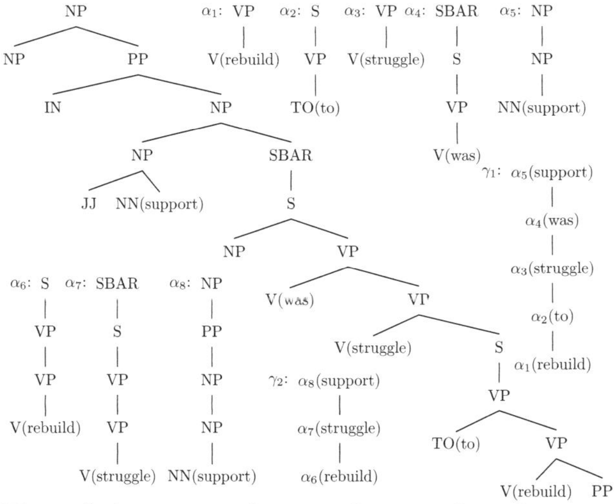

Figure 6: A parse tree fragment from test data where *rebuild* is the predicate and *support* is Arg1 of the predicate. γ_1 is the derivation tree from Baseline2, and γ_2 is the LSVM picked derivation tree. This is an example that is mis-predicted by Baseline2 but corrected by LSVM.

Magerman-Collins derivation (used by Baseline2), for each label (identification or ID, and A0...A4). From the examples that LSVM gets right but Baseline2 gets wrong, we count the percentage of differences between the LSVM argmax derivation and the Baseline2 derivation. We count the following differences: changed lexical head of argument etree (LexHd), a shorter distance between predicate etree and argument etree (SDist), a changed predicate etree (PredSP), a changed argument etree (ArgSP), and any changed intermediate etree (IntSP). LSVM does not change the lexical head frequently for the identification classifier. In contrast, LSVM creates a shorter distance between predicate etree and argument etree for identification (often by picking a different predicate etree), but not for classification. This is consistent with insights from (Pradhan et al., 2008) who say "...the more lexical/semantic features dominating the classification task where more general structural features are more dominant in the argument identification task."

	ID	A0	A1	A2	A3	A4
LexHd	26.1	44.5	47.7	74.4	28.6	18.8
SDist	79.9	18.4	15.9	5.3	3.9	6.3
PredSP	90.7	43.4	58.1	74.6	80.5	81.3
ArgSP	47.1	56.6	65.8	80.6	28.6	25.0
IntSP	5.7	17.1	14.7	2.3	14.3	6.2

Table 6: Percentage of LSVM corrected examples with changed substructures in LSVM chosen derivation tree.

To help understand the details of our implementation and to encourage replication of this result, the source code and the LSVM-SRL output on test data in CoNLL 2005 format can be downloaded from *http://natlang.cs.sfu.ca*.

6 Related and Future Work

(Cherry and Quirk, 2008) is the first application of LSVMs to NLP. They train a LSVM for language modeling which uses latent parse trees. We share the intuition that the latent features can be helpful in discrimination between positive and negative examples; in their case, latent CFG rules were used to judge (un)grammaticality of sentences.

The EM algorithm has been used in statistical parsing to explore the space of head-choice and head-percolation strategies (Chiang and Bikel, 2002; Shen, 2004). In both cases the heuristic Magerman-Collins rules always out-performed the learned rules in terms of parsing accuracy.

(Vickrey and Koller, 2008) is the only other work (that we know of) that uses latent features for SRL. They use hand-written sentence simplification rules and search for the most useful set of simplifications that can improve training error based on a log-linear model. Their model sums over the set of possible simplifications in contrast to our LSVM approach. We are currently exploring the use of log-linear models for SRL using latent LTAG features where we sum over the latent derivations.

References

Eugene Charniak. 2000. A maximum-entropy-inspired parser. In *NAACL-2000*.

John Chen and Owen Rambow. 2003. Use of deep linguistic features for the recognition and labeling of semantic arguments. In *EMNLP-2003*.

Colin Cherry and Chris Quirk. 2008. Discriminative, syntactic language modeling through latent SVMs. In *AMTA-2008*.

David Chiang and Daniel Bikel. 2002. Recovering latent information in treebanks. In *COLING-2002*.

David Chiang. 2000. Statistical parsing with an automatically extracted tree adjoining grammars. In *ACL-2000*.

Michael Collins. 1996. A new statistical parser based on bigram lexical dependencies. In *ACL-1996*.

Pedro Felzenszwalb, David McAllester, and Deva Ramanan. 2008. A discriminatively trained, multiscale, deformable part model. In *CVPR-2008*.

Daniel Gildea and Julia Hockenmaier. 2003. Identifying semantic roles using combinatory categorial grammar. In *EMNLP-2003*.

Daniel Gildea and Dan Jurafsky. 2002. Automatic labeling of semantic roles. *Computational Linguistics*, 58(3):245–288.

Kadri Hacioglu, Sameer Pradhan, Wayne Ward, James Martin, and Dan Jurafsky. 2004. Semantic role labeling by tagging syntactic chunks. In *CoNLL-2004 Shared Task*.

Kadri Hacioglu. 2004. Semantic role labeling using dependency trees. In *COLING-2004*.

Aravind Joshi and Yves Schabes. 1997. Tree-adjoining grammars. In G. Rosenberg and A. Salomaa, editors, *Handbook of Formal Languages*, pages 69–123. Springer, Berlin.

Yudong Liu and Anoop Sarkar. 2007. Experimental evaluation of LTAG-based features for semantic role labeling. In *EMNLP-2007*.

Yudong Liu. 2009. *Semantic role labeling using lexicalized tree adjoining grammars*. Ph.D. thesis, Simon Fraser University, Burnaby, BC, Canada.

Martha Palmer, Dan Gildea, and Paul Kingsbury. 2005. The proposition bank: An annotated corpus of semantic roles. *Computational Linguistics*, 31(1).

Sameer Pradhan, Wayne Ward, Kadri Hacioglu, James Martin, and Dan Jurafsky. 2005. Semantic role labeling using different syntactic views. In *ACL-2005*.

Sameer Pradhan, Wayne Ward, and James Martin. 2008. Towards robust semantic role labeling. *Computational Linguistics*, 34(2).

Libin Shen. 2004. Nondeterministic LTAG derivation tree extraction. In *Proc. TAG+7*.

Kristina Toutanova, Aria Haghighi, and Christopher Manning. 2008. A global joint model for semantic role labeling. *Computational Linguistics*, 34(2).

David Vickrey and Daphne Koller. 2008. Sentence simplification for semantic role labeling. In *Proceedings of ACL-08: HLT*.

Yang Wang and Greg Mori. 2009. Max-margin hidden conditional random fields for human action recognition. In *CVPR*.

Nianwen Xue and Martha Palmer. 2004. Calibrating features for semantic role labeling. In *EMNLP-2004*.

Chun-Nam Yu and Thorsten Joachims. 2009. Learning structural svms with latent variables. In *ICML '09*.

Unsupervised Induction of Semantic Roles

Joel Lang and **Mirella Lapata**
School of Informatics, University of Edinburgh
10 Crichton Street, Edinburgh EH8 9AB, UK
J.Lang-3@sms.ed.ac.uk, mlap@inf.ed.ac.uk

Abstract

Datasets annotated with semantic roles are an important prerequisite to developing high-performance role labeling systems. Unfortunately, the reliance on manual annotations, which are both difficult and highly expensive to produce, presents a major obstacle to the widespread application of these systems across different languages and text genres. In this paper we describe a method for inducing the semantic roles of verbal arguments directly from unannotated text. We formulate the role induction problem as one of detecting alternations and finding a canonical syntactic form for them. Both steps are implemented in a novel probabilistic model, a latent-variable variant of the logistic classifier. Our method increases the purity of the induced role clusters by a wide margin over a strong baseline.

1 Introduction

Semantic role labeling (SRL, Gildea and Jurafsky 2002) is the task of automatically classifying the arguments of a predicate with roles such as *Agent*, *Patient* or *Location*. These labels capture aspects of the semantics of the relationship between the predicate and the argument while abstracting over surface syntactic configurations. SRL has received much attention in recent years (Surdeanu et al., 2008; Màrquez et al., 2008), partly because of its potential to improve applications that require broad coverage semantic processing. Examples include information extraction (Surdeanu et al., 2003), question answering (Shen and Lapata, 2007), summarization (Melli et al., 2005), and machine translation (Wu and Fung, 2009).

Given sentences (1-a) and (1-b) as input, an SRL system would have to identify the verb predicate (shown in boldface), its arguments (*Michael* and *sandwich*) and label them with semantic roles (*Agent* and *Patient*).

(1) a. [Michael]$_{Agent}$ **eats** [a sandwich]$_{Patient}$.
 b. [A sandwich]$_{Patient}$ **is eaten** [by Michael]$_{Agent}$.

Here, sentence (1-b) is an alternation of (1-a). The verbal arguments bear the same semantic role, even though they appear in different syntactic positions: *sandwich* is the object of *eat* in sentence (1-a) and its subject in (1-b) but it is in both instances assigned the role *Patient*. The example illustrates the passive alternation. The latter is merely one type of alternation, many others exist (Levin, 1993), and their computational treatment is one of the main challenges faced by semantic role labelers.

Most SRL systems to date conceptualize semantic role labeling as a supervised learning problem and rely on role-annotated data for model training. PropBank (Palmer et al., 2005) has been widely used for the development of semantic role labelers as well as FrameNet (Fillmore et al., 2003). Under the PropBank annotation framework (which we will assume throughout this paper) each predicate is associated with a set of core roles (named *A0*, *A1*, *A2*, and so on) whose interpretations are specific to that predicate[1] and a set of adjunct roles (e.g., *Location* or *Time*) whose interpretation is common across predicates. In addition to large amounts of role-annotated data, SRL systems often make use of a parser to obtain syntactic analyses which subsequently serve as input to a pipeline of components concerned with

[1]More precisely, *A0* and *A1* have a common interpretation across predicates as *proto-agent* and *proto-patient* (Dowty, 1991).

Human Language Technologies: The 2010 Annual Conference of the North American Chapter of the ACL, pages 939–947,
Los Angeles, California, June 2010.

identifying predicates and their arguments (argument identification) and labeling them with semantic roles (argument classification).

Supervised SRL methods deliver reasonably good performance (a system will recall around 81% of the arguments correctly and 95% of those will be assigned a correct semantic role; see Màrquez et al. 2008 for details). Unfortunately, the reliance on labeled training data, which is both difficult and highly expensive to produce, presents a major obstacle to the widespread application of semantic role labeling across different languages and text genres. And although corpora with semantic role annotations exist nowadays in other languages (e.g., German, Spanish, Catalan, Chinese, Korean), they tend to be smaller than their English equivalents and of limited value for modeling purposes. Moreover, the performance of supervised systems degrades considerably (by 10%) on out-of-domain data even within English, a language for which two major annotated corpora are available. Interestingly, Pradhan et al. (2008) find that the main reason for this are errors in the assignment of semantic roles, rather than the identification of argument boundaries. Therefore, a mechanism for inducing the semantic roles observed in the data without additional manual effort would enhance the robustness of existing SRL systems and enable their portability to languages for which annotations are unavailable or sparse.

In this paper we describe an unsupervised approach to argument classification or *role induction*[2] that does not make use of role-annotated data. Role induction can be naturally formalized as a clustering problem where argument instances are assigned to clusters. Ideally, each cluster should contain arguments corresponding to a specific semantic role and each role should correspond to exactly one cluster. A key insight in our approach is that many predicates are associated with a standard linking. A linking is a deterministic mapping from semantic roles onto syntactic functions such as *subject*, or *object*. Most predicates will exhibit a standard linking, i.e., they will be predominantly used with a specific mapping. Alternations occur when a different linking is used. In sentence (1-a) the predicate *eat* is used with its standard linking (the *Agent* role is mapped onto the *subject* function and the *Patient* onto the *object*), whereas in sentence (1-b) *eat* is used with its passive-linking (the *Patient* is mapped onto *subject* and the *Agent* appears as a prepositional phrase). When faced with such alternations, we will attempt to determine for each argument the syntactic function it would have had, had the standard linking been used. We will refer to this function as the arguments' *canonical function*, and use the term *canonicalization* to describe the process of inferring these canonical functions in the case of alternations. So, in sentence (1-b) the canonical functions of the arguments *by Michael* and *sandwich* are *subject* and *object*, respectively.

Since linkings are injective, i.e., no two semantic roles are mapped onto the same syntactic function, the canonical function of an argument uniquely references a specific semantic role. We define a probabilistic model for detecting non-standard linkings and for canonicalization. The model specifies a distribution $p(F)$ over the possible canonical functions F of an argument. We present an extension of the logistic classifier with the addition of latent variables which crucially allow to learn generalizations over varying syntactic configurations. Rather than using manually labeled data, we train our model on observed syntactic functions which can be obtained automatically from a parser. These training instances are admittedly noisy but readily available and as we show experimentally a useful data source for inducing semantic roles. Application of the model to a benchmark dataset yields improvements over a strong baseline.

2 Related Work

Much previous work on SRL relies on supervised learning methods for both argument identification and argument classification (see Màrquez et al. 2008 for an overview). Most systems use manually annotated resources to train separate classifiers for different SRL subtasks (e.g., Surdeanu et al. 2008). A few approaches adopt semi-supervised learning methods. The idea here is to to alleviate the data requirements for semantic role labeling by extending existing resources through the use of unlabeled data. Swier and Stevenson (2004) induce role labels with a bootstrapping scheme in which the set of labeled instances is iteratively expanded using a classifier trained on previously labeled instances. Padó and Lapata (2009) project role-semantic annotations from an annotated corpus in one language onto an unannotated corpus in another language. And Fürstenau and Lapata (2009) propose a method

[2]We use the term *role induction* rather than *argument classification* for the unsupervised setting.

in which annotations are projected from a source corpus onto a target corpus, however within the same language.

Unsupervised approaches to SRL have been few and far between. Early work on lexicon acquisition focuses on identifying verbal alternations rather than their linkings. This is often done in conjunction with hand-crafted resources such as a taxonomy of possible alternations (McCarthy and Korhonen, 1998) or WordNet (McCarthy, 2002). Lapata (1999) proposes a corpus-based method that is less reliant on taxonomic resources, however focuses only on two specific verb alternations. Other work attempts to cluster verbs into semantic classes (e.g., Levin 1993) on the basis of their alternation behavior (Schulte im Walde and Brew, 2002).

More recently, Abend et al. (2009) propose an unsupervised algorithm for argument identification that relies only on part-of-speech annotations, whereas Grenager and Manning (2006) focus on role induction which they formalize as probabilistic inference in a Bayesian network. Their model defines a joint probability distribution over the particular linking used together with a verb instance and for each verbal argument, its lemma, syntactic function as well as semantic role. Parameters in this model are estimated using the EM algorithm as the training instances include latent variables, namely the semantic roles and linkings. To make inference tractable they limit the set of linkings to a small number and do not distinguish between different types of adjuncts. Our own work also focuses on inducing the semantic roles and the linkings used by each verb. Our approach is conceptually simpler and computationally more tractable. Our model is a straightforward extension of the logistic classifier with latent variables applied to all roles not just coarse ones.

3 Problem Formulation

We treat role induction as a clustering problem. The goal is to assign argument instances (i.e., specific arguments, occurring in an input sentence) into clusters such that each cluster contains instances with the same semantic role, and each semantic role is found in exactly one cluster. As we assume PropBank-style roles (Palmer et al., 2005), our model will allocate a separate set of clusters for each predicate and assign the arguments of a specific predicate to one of the clusters associated with it.

As mentioned earlier (Section 1) a linking is a deterministic mapping from semantic roles onto syntactic functions. Table 1 shows how frequently individual semantic roles map onto certain syntactic functions. The frequencies were obtained from the CoNLL 2008 dataset (see Surdeanu et al. 2008 for details) and constitute an aggregate across predicates. As can be seen, there is a clear tendency for a semantic role to be mapped onto a single syntactic function. This is true across predicates and even more so for individual predicates. For example, A0 is commonly mapped onto subject (SBJ), whereas A1 is often realized as object (OBJ). There are two reasons for this. Firstly, a predicate is often associated with a standard linking which is most frequently used. Secondly, the alternate linkings of a given predicate often differ from the standard linking only with respect to a few roles. Importantly, we do not assume that a single standard linking is valid

	A0	A1	TMP	MNR
SBJ	54514	19684	15	7
OBJ	3359	51730	93	54
ADV	162	3506	976	2308
TMP	5	60	15167	22
PMOD	2466	4860	142	62
OPRD	37	5554	1	36
LOC	17	145	43	157
DIR	0	178	15	6
MNR	5	48	13	3312
PRP	9	50	11	6
LGS	2168	36	2	2
PRD	413	830	31	38
NMOD	422	388	25	59
EXT	0	20	2	12
DEP	18	150	25	65
SUB	3	84	4	2
CONJ	198	331	22	8
ROOT	62	147	84	2
	64517	88616	16803	6404

Table 1: Contingency table between syntactic function and semantic role for two core roles *Agent* (A0) and *Patient* (A1) and two adjunct roles, *Time* (TMP) and *Manner* (MNR). Only syntactic functions occurring more than 1000 times are listed. Counts were obtained from the CoNLL 2008 training dataset using gold standard parses (the marginals in the bottom row also include counts of unlisted co-occurrences).

for all predicates. Rather, each predicate has its own standard linking. For example, in the standard linking for the predicate *fall*, A1 is mapped onto subject position, whereas in the standarad linking for *eat*, A1 is mapped onto object position.

When an argument is attested with a non-standard linking, we wish to determine the syntactic function it would have had if the standard linking had been used. This *canonical function* of the argument uniquely references a specific semantic role, i.e., the semantic role that is mapped onto the function under the standard linking. We can now specify an indirect method for partitioning argument instances into clusters:

1. Detect arguments that are linked in a non-standard way (detection).
2. Determine the canonical function of these arguments (canonicalization). For arguments with standard linkings, their syntactic function corresponds directly to the canonical function.
3. Assign arguments to a cluster according to their canonical function.

We distinguish between detecting non-standard linkings and canonicalization because in principle two separate models could be used. In our probabilistic formulation, both detection and canonicalization rely on an estimate of the probability distribution $p(F)$ over the canonical function F of an argument. When the most likely canonical function differs from the observed syntactic function this indicates that a non-standard linking has been used (detection). This most likely canonical function can be taken as the canonical function of the argument (canonicalization).

Arguments are assigned to clusters based on their inferred canonical function. Since we assume predicate-specific roles, we induce a separate cluster for each predicate. Given K clusters, we use the following scheme for determining the mapping from functions to clusters:

1. Order the functions by occurrence frequency.
2. For each of the $K-1$ most frequent functions allocate a separate cluster.
3. Assign all remaining functions to the K-th cluster.

4 Model

The detection of non-standard linkings and canonicalization both rely on a probabilistic model $p(F)$ which specifies the distribution over the canonical functions F of an argument. As is the case with most SRL approaches, we assume to be given a syntactic parse of the sentence from which we can extract labeled dependencies, corresponding to the syntactic functions of arguments. To train the model we exploit the fact that most observed syntactic functions will correspond to canonical functions. This enables us to use the parser's output for training even though it does not contain semantic role annotations.

Critically, the features used to determine the canonical function must be restricted so that they give no cues about possible alternations. If they would, the model could learn to predict alternations, and therefore produce output closer to the observed syntactic rather than canonical function of an argument. To avoid this pitfall we only use features at or below the node representing the argument head in the parse tree apart from the predicate lemma (see Section 5 for details).

Given these local argument features, a simple solution would be to use a standard classifier such as the logistic classifier (Berger et al., 1996) to learn the canonical function of arguments. However, this is problematic, because in our setting the training and application of the classifier happen on the same dataset. The model will over-adapt to the observed targets (i.e., the syntactic functions) and fail to learn appropriate canonical functions. Lexical sparsity is a contributing factor: the parameters associated with sparse lexical features will be unavoidably adjusted so that they are highly indicative of the syntactic function they occur with.

One way to improve generalization is to incorporate a layer of latent variables into the logistic classifier, which mediates between inputs (features defined over parse trees) and target (the canonical function). As a result, inputs and target are no longer directly connected and the information conveyed by the features about the target must be transferred via the latent layer. The model is shown in plate notation in Figure 1a. Here, X_i represents the observed input features, Y the observed target, and Z_j the latent variables. The number of latent variables influences the generalization properties of the model. With too few latent variables too little information will be transferred via the latent variables, whereas with too many latent variables generalization will degrade.

The model defines a probability distribution over the target variable Y and the latent variables Z, con-

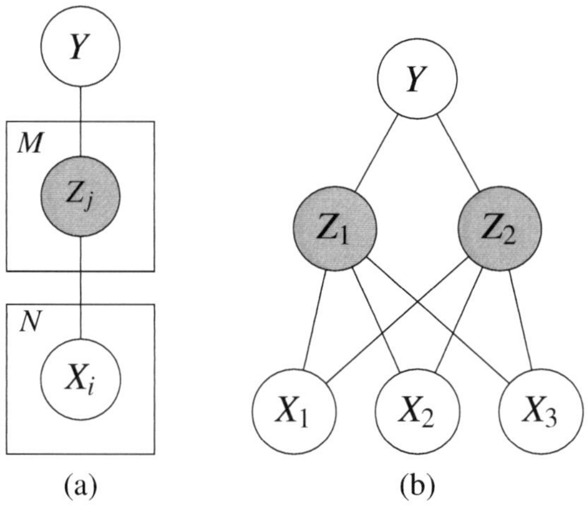

Figure 1: The logistic classifier with latent variables (shaded nodes) illustrated as a graphical model using (a) plate notation and (b) in unrolled form for $M=2$ and $N=3$.

ditional on the input variables X:

$$p(y,z|x,\theta) = \frac{1}{P(x,\theta)} \exp\left(\sum_k \theta_k \phi_k(x,y,z)\right) \quad (1)$$

We will assume that the latent variables Z_i are binary. Each of the feature functions ϕ_k is associated with a parameter θ_k. The partition function normalizes the distribution:

$$P(x,\theta) = \sum_y \sum_z \exp\left(\sum_k \theta_k \phi_k(x,y,z)\right) \quad (2)$$

Note that this model is a special case of a conditional random field with latent variables (Sutton and McCallum, 2007) and resembles a neural network with one hidden layer (Bishop, 2006).

Let (c,d) denote a training set of inputs and corresponding targets. The maximum-likelihood parameters can then be obtained by finding the θ maximizing:

$$\begin{aligned} l(\theta) &= \log p(d|c) \\ &= \sum_i \log \sum_z p(d_i,z|c_i) \\ &= \sum_i \log \frac{\sum_z \exp(\sum_k \theta_k \phi_k(c_i,d_i,z))}{P(c_i,\theta)} \end{aligned} \quad (3)$$

And the gradient is given by:

$$\begin{aligned} (\nabla l)_k &= \frac{\partial}{\partial \theta_k} l(\theta) \\ &= \sum_i \sum_z p(z|d_i,c_i)\phi_k(c_i,d_i,z) \\ &\quad - \sum_i \sum_{y,z} p(y,z|c_i)\phi_k(c_i,y,z) \end{aligned} \quad (4)$$

where the first term is the conditional expected feature count and the second term is the expected feature count.

Thus far, we have written the equations in a generic form for arbitrary conditional random fields with latent variables (Sutton and McCallum, 2007). In our model we have two types of pairwise sufficient statistics: $\beta(x,z) : \mathbb{R} \times \{0,1\} \to \mathbb{R}$, between a single input variable and a single latent variable, and $\gamma(y,z) : \mathcal{Y} \times \{0,1\} \to \mathbb{R}$, between the target and a latent variable. Then, we can more specifically write the gradient component of a parameter associated with a sufficient statistic $\beta(x_j,z_k)$ as:

$$\sum_i \sum_{z_k} p(z_k|d_i,c_i)\beta(c_{i,j},z_k) - \sum_i \sum_{z_k} p(z_k|c_i)\beta(c_{i,j},z_k) \quad (5)$$

And the gradient component of a parameter associated with a sufficient statistic $\gamma(y,z_k)$ is:

$$\sum_i \sum_{z_k} p(z_k|d_i,c_i)\gamma(d_i,z_k) - \sum_i \sum_{y,z_k} p(y,z_k|c_i)\gamma(y,z_k) \quad (6)$$

To obtain maximum-a-posteriori parameter estimates we regularize the equations. Like for the standard logistic classifier this results in an additional term of the target function and each component of the gradient (see Sutton and McCallum 2007). Computing the gradient requires computation of the marginals which can be performed efficiently using belief propagation (Yedidia et al., 2003). Note that due to the fact, that there are no edges between the latent variables, the inference graph is tree structured and therefore inference yields exact results. We use a stochastic gradient optimization method (Bottou, 2004) to optimize the target. Optimization is likely to result in a local maximum, as the likelihood function is not convex due to the latent variables.

5 Experimental Design

In this section we discuss the experimental design for assessing the performance of the model described above. We give details on the dataset, features and evaluation measures employed and present the baseline methods used for comparison with our model.

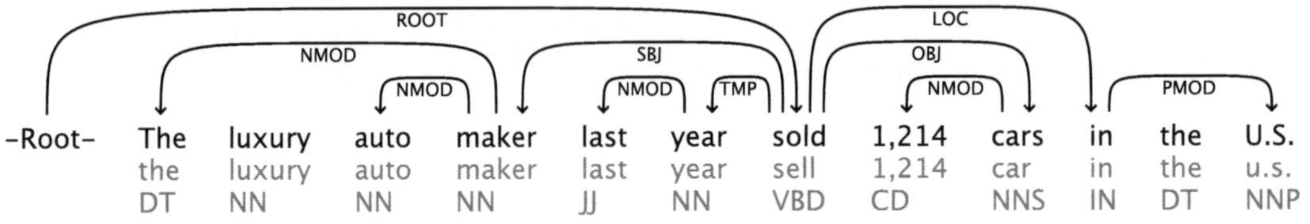

Figure 2: Dependency graph (simplified) of a sample sentence from the corpus.

Data Our experiments were carried out on the CoNLL 2008 (Surdeanu et al., 2008) training dataset which contains both verbal and nominal predicates. However, we focused solely on verbal predicates, following most previous work on semantic role labeling (Màrquez et al., 2008). The CoNLL dataset is taken form the Wall Street Journal portion of the Penn Treebank corpus (Marcus et al., 1993). Role semantic annotations are based on PropBank and have been converted from a constituent-based to a dependency-based representation (see Surdeanu et al. 2008). For each argument of a predicate only the head word is annotated with the corresponding semantic role, rather than the whole constituent. In this paper we are only concerned with role induction, not argument identification. Therefore, we identify the arguments of each predicate by consulting the gold standard.

The CoNLL dataset also supplies an automatic dependency parse of each input sentence obtained from the MaltParser (Nivre et al., 2007). The target and features used in our model are extracted from these parses. Syntactic functions occurring more than 1,000 times in the gold standard are shown in Table 1 (for more details we refer the interested reader to Surdeanu et al. 2008). Syntactic functions were further modified to include prepositions if specified, resulting in a set of functions with which arguments can be distinguished more precisely. This was often the case with functions such as ADV, TMP, LOC, etc. Also, instead of using the preposition itself as the argument head, we used the actual content word modifying the preposition. We made no attempt to treat split arguments, namely instances where the semantic argument of a predicate has several syntactic heads. These are infrequent in the dataset, they make up for less than 1% of all arguments.

Model Setup The specific instantiation of the model used in our experiments has 10 latent variables. With 10 binary latent variables we can encode 1024 different target values, which seems reasonable for our set of syntactic functions which comprises around 350 elements.

Features representing argument instances were extracted from dependency parses like the one shown in Figure 2. We used a relatively small feature set consisting of: the predicate lemma, the argument lemma, the argument part-of-speech, the preposition involved in dependency between predicate and argument (if there is one), the lemma of left-most/right-most child of the argument, the part-of-speech of left-most/right-most child of argument, and a key formed by concatenating all syntactic functions of the argument's children. The features for the argument *maker* in Figure 2 are [*sell, maker, NN, –, the, auto, DT, NN, NMOD+NMOD*]. The target for this instance (and observed syntactic function) is SBJ.

Evaluation Evaluating the output of our model is no different from other clustering problems. We can therefore use well-known measures from the clustering literature to assess the quality of our role induction method. We first created a set of gold-standard role labeled argument instances which were obtained from the training partition of the CoNLL 2008 dataset (corresponding to sections 02–21 of PropBank). We used 10 clusters for each predicate and restricted the set of predicates to those attested with more than 20 instances. This rules out simple cases with only few instances relative to the number of clusters, which trivially yield high scores.

We compared the output of our method against the gold-standard using the following common measures. Let K denote the number of clusters, c_i the set of instances in the i-th cluster and g_j the set of instances having the j-th gold standard semantic role label. Cluster purity (PU) is defined as:

$$PU = \frac{1}{K} \sum_i \max_j |c_i \cap g_j| \qquad (7)$$

We also used cluster accuracy (CA, Equation 8),

	PU		CA		CP		CR		CF1	
	Mic	Mac	Mic	Mac	Mic	Mac	Mic	Mac	Mic	Mac
SyntFunc	73.2	75.8	82.0	80.9	67.6	65.3	55.7	50.1	61.1	56.7
LogLV	72.5	74.0	81.1	79.4	64.3	60.6	59.7	56.3	61.9	58.4
UpperBndS	94.7	96.1	96.9	97.0	97.4	97.6	90.4	100	93.7	93.8
UpperBndG	98.8	99.4	99.9	99.9	99.7	99.9	100	100	99.8	100

Table 2: Clustering results using our model (LogLV) against the baseline (SyntFunc) and upper bounds (UpperBndS and UpperBndG).

cluster precision (CP, Equation 9), and cluster recall (CR, Equation 9). Cluster F1 (CF1) is the harmonic mean of precision and recall.

$$CA = \frac{TP+TN}{TP+FP+TN+FN} \quad (8)$$

$$CP = \frac{TP}{TP+FP} \qquad CR = \frac{TP}{TP+FN} \quad (9)$$

Here TP is the number of *pairs of instances* which have the same role and are in the same cluster, TN is the number of pairs of instances which have different roles and are in different clusters, FP is the number of pairs of instances with different roles in the same cluster and FN the number of pairs of instances with the same role in different clusters.

Baselines and Upper Bound We compared our model against a baseline that assigns arguments to clusters based on their syntactic function. Here, no attempt is made to correct the roles of arguments in non-standard linkings. We would also like to compare our model against a supervised system. Unfortunately, this is not possible, as we are using the designated CoNLL training set as our test set, and any supervised system trained on this data would achieve unfairly high scores. Therefore, we approximate the performance of a supervised system by clustering instances according to their gold standard role after introducing some noise. Specifically, we randomly selected 5% of the gold standard roles and mapped them to an erroneous role. This roughly corresponds to the clustering which would be induced by a state-of-the-art supervised system with 95% precision. Finally, we also report the results of the true upper bound obtained by clustering the arguments, based on their gold standard semantic role (again using 10 clusters per verb).

6 Results

Our results are summarized in Table 2. We report cluster purity, accuracy, precision, recall, and F1 for our latent variable logistic classifier (LogLV) and a baseline that assigns arguments to clusters according to their syntactic function (SyntFunc). The table also includes the gold standard upper bound (UpperBndG) and its supervised proxy (UpperBndS). We report micro- and macro-average scores.[3]

Model scores are quite similar to the baseline, which might suggest that the model is simply replicating the observed data. However, this is not the case: canonical functions differ from observed functions for approximately 27% of the argument instances. If the baseline treated these instances correctly, we would expect it to outperform our model. The fact that it does not, indicates that the baseline error rate is higher precisely on these instances. In other words, the model can help in detecting alternate linkings and thus baseline errors.

We further analyzed our model's ability to detect alternate linkings. Specifically, if we assume a standard linking where model and observation agree and an alternate linking where they disagree, we obtain the following. The number of true positives (correctly detected alternate linkings) is 27,606, the number of false positives (incorrectly marked alternations) is 32,031, the number of true negatives (cases where the model correctly did not detect an alternate linking) is 132,556, and the number of false negatives (alternate linkings that the model should have detected but did not) is 32,516.[4]. The analysis shows that 46% of alternations (baseline errors) are detected.

[3] Micro-averages are computed over instances while macro-averages are computed over verbs.

[4] Note that the true/false positives/negatives here refer to alternate linkings, not to be confused with the true/false positives in equations (8) and (9).

	PU		CA		CP		CR		CF1	
	Mic	Mac	Mic	Mac	Mic	Mac	Mic	Mac	Mic	Mac
SyntFunct	73.9	77.8	82.1	81.3	68.0	66.5	55.9	50.3	61.4	57.3
LogLV	82.6	83.7	87.4	85.5	79.1	74.5	73.3	68.5	76.1	71.4

Table 3: Clustering results using our model to detect alternate linkings (LogLV) against the baseline (SyntFunc).

We can therefore increase cluster purity by clustering only those instances where the model does not indicate an alternation. The results are shown in Table 3. Using less instances while keeping the number of clusters the same will by itself tend to increase performance. To compensate for this, we also report results for the baseline on a reduced dataset. The latter was obtained from the original dataset by randomly removing the same number of instances.[5] By using the model to detect alternations, scores improve over the baseline across the board. We observe performance gains for purity which increases by 8.7% (micro-average; compare Tables 2 and 3). F1 also improves considerably by 13% (micro-average). These results are encouraging indicating that detecting alternate linkings is an important first step towards more accurate role induction.

We also conducted a more detailed error analysis to gain more insight into the behavior of our model. In most cases, alternate linkings where $A1$ occurs in subject position and $A0$ in object position are canonicalized correctly (with 96% and 97% precision, respectively). Half of the detected non-standard linkings involve adjunct roles. Here, the model has much more difficulty with canonicalization and is successful approximately 25% of the time. For example, in the phrase *occur at dawn* the model canonicalizes LOC to ADV, whereas TMP would be the correct function. About 75% of all false negatives are due to core roles and only 25% due to adjunct roles. Many false negatives are due to parser errors, which are reproduced by the model. This indicates overfitting, and indeed many of the false negatives involve infrequent lexical items (e.g., *juxtapose* or *Odyssey*).

Finally, to put our evaluation results into context, we also wanted to compare against Grenager and Manning's (2006) related system. A direct comparison is somewhat problematic due to the use of different datasets and the fact that we induce labels for *all* roles whereas they collapse adjunct roles to a single role. Nevertheless, we made a good-faith effort to evaluate our system using their evaluation setting. Specifically, we ran our system on the same test set, Section 23 of the Penn Treebank (annotated with PropBank roles), using gold standard parses with six clusters for each verb type. Our model achieves a cluster purity score of 90.3% on this dataset compared to 89.7% reported in Grenager and Manning.

7 Conclusions

In this paper we have presented a novel framework for unsupervised role induction. We conceptualized the induction problem as one of detecting alternate linkings and finding their canonical syntactic form, and formulated a novel probabilistic model that performs these tasks. The model extends the logistic classifier with latent variables and is trained on parsed output which is used as a noisy target for learning. Experimental results show promise, alternations can be successfully detected and the quality of the induced role clusters can be substantially enhanced.

We argue that the present model could be usefully employed to enhance the performance of other models. For example, it could be used in an active learning context to identify argument instances that are difficult to classify for a supervised or semi-supervised system and would presumably benefit from additional (manual) annotation. Importantly, the framework can incorporate different probabilistic models for detection and canonicalization which we intend to explore in the future. We also aim to embed and test our role induction method within a full SRL system that is also concerned with argument identification. Eventually, we also intend to replace the treebank-trained parser with a chunker.

[5] This was repeated several times to ensure that the results are stable across runs.

References

Abend, O., R. Reichart, and A. Rappoport. 2009. Unsupervised Argument Identification for Semantic Role Labeling. In *Proceedings of ACL-IJCNLP*. Singapore, pages 28–36.

Berger, A., S. Della Pietra, and V. Della Pietra. 1996. A Maximum Entropy Approach to Natural Language Processing. *Computational Linguistics* 22(1):39–71.

Bishop, C. 2006. *Pattern Recognition and Machine Learning*. Springer.

Bottou, L. 2004. Stochastic Learning. In *Advanced Lectures on Machine Learning*, Springer Verlag, Lecture Notes in Artificial Intelligence, pages 146–168.

Dowty, D. 1991. Thematic Proto Roles and Argument Selection. *Language* 67(3):547–619.

Fillmore, C. J., C. R. Johnson, and M. R. L. Petruck. 2003. Background to FrameNet. *International Journal of Lexicography* 16:235–250.

Fürstenau, H. and M. Lapata. 2009. Graph Aligment for Semi-Supervised Semantic Role Labeling. In *Proceedings of EMNLP*. Singapore, pages 11–20.

Gildea, D. and D. Jurafsky. 2002. Automatic Labeling of Semantic Roles. *Computational Linguistics* 28(3):245–288.

Grenager, T. and C. Manning. 2006. Unsupervised Discovery of a Statistical Verb Lexicon. In *Proceedings of EMNLP*. Sydney, Australia, pages 1–8.

Lapata, M. 1999. Acquiring Lexical Generalizations from Corpora: A Case Study for Diathesis Alternations. In *Proceedings of the 37th ACL*. pages 397–404.

Levin, B. 1993. *English Verb Classes and Alternations: A Preliminary Investigation*. The University of Chicago Press.

Marcus, M., B. Santorini, and M. Marcinkiewicz. 1993. Building a Large Annotated Corpus of English: the Penn Treebank. *Computational Linguistics* 19(2):313–330.

Màrquez, L., X. Carreras, K. Litkowski, and S. Stevenson. 2008. Semantic Role Labeling: an Introduction to the Special Issue. *Computational Linguistics* 34(2):145–159.

McCarthy, D. 2002. Using Semantic Preferences to Identify Verbal Participation in Role Switching Alternations. In *Proceedings of the 1st NAACL*. Seattle, WA, pages 256–263.

McCarthy, D. and A. Korhonen. 1998. Detecting Verbal Participation in Diathesis Alternations. In *Proceedings of COLING/ACL*. Montréal, Canada, pages 1493–1495.

Melli, G., Y. Wang, Y. Liu, M. M. Kashani, Z. Shi, B. Gu, A. Sarkar, and F. Popowich. 2005. Description of SQUASH, the SFU Question Answering Summary Handler for the DUC-2005 Summarization Task. In *Proceedings of the HLT/EMNLP Document Understanding Workshop*. Vancouver, Canada.

Nivre, J., J. Hall, J. Nilsson, G. Eryigit A. Chanev, S. Kübler, S. Marinov, and E. Marsi. 2007. MaltParser: A Language-independent System for Data-driven Dependency Parsing. *Natural Language Engineering* 13(2):95–135.

Padó, S. and M. Lapata. 2009. Cross-lingual Annotation Projection of Semantic Roles. *Journal of Artificial Intelligence Research* 36:307–340.

Palmer, M., D. Gildea, and P. Kingsbury. 2005. The Proposition Bank: An Annotated Corpus of Semantic Roles. *Computational Linguistics* 31(1):71–106.

Pradhan, S. S., W. Ward, and J. H. Martin. 2008. Towards Robust Semantic Role Labeling. *Computational Linguistics* 34(2):289–310.

Schulte im Walde, S. and C. Brew. 2002. Inducing German Semantic Verb Classes from Purely Syntactic Subcategorisation Information. In *Proceedings of the 40th ACL*. Philadelphia, PA, pages 223–230.

Shen, D. and M. Lapata. 2007. Using Semantic Roles to Improve Question Answering. In *Proceedings of the EMNLP-CoNLL*. Prague, Czech Republic, pages 12–21.

Surdeanu, M., S. Harabagiu, J. Williams, and P. Aarseth. 2003. Using Predicate-Argument Structures for Information Extraction. In *Proceedings of the 41st ACL*. Sapporo, Japan, pages 8–15.

Surdeanu, M., R. Johansson, A. Meyers, and L. Màrquez. 2008. The CoNLL-2008 Shared Task on Joint Parsing of Syntactic and Semantic Dependencies. In *Proceedings of the 12th CoNLL*. Manchester, England, pages 159–177.

Sutton, C. and A. McCallum. 2007. An Introduction to Conditional Random Fields for Relational Learning. In L. Getoor and B. Taskar, editors, *Introduction to Statistical Relational Learning*, MIT Press, pages 93–127.

Swier, R. and S. Stevenson. 2004. Unsupervised Semantic Role Labelling. In *Proceedings of EMNLP*. Barcelona, Spain, pages 95–102.

Wu, D. and P. Fung. 2009. Semantic Roles for SMT: A Hybrid Two-Pass Model. In *Proceedings of NAACL HLT 2009: Short Papers*. Boulder, Colorado, pages 13–16.

Yedidia, J., W. Freeman, and Y. Weiss. 2003. Understanding Belief Propagation and its Generalizations. Morgan Kaufmann Publishers Inc., pages 239–269.

Probabilistic Frame-Semantic Parsing

Dipanjan Das   Nathan Schneider   Desai Chen   Noah A. Smith
School of Computer Science
Carnegie Mellon University
Pittsburgh, PA 15213, USA
{dipanjan@cs, nschneid@cs, desaic@andrew, nasmith@cs}.cmu.edu

Abstract

This paper contributes a formalization of frame-semantic parsing as a structure prediction problem and describes an implemented parser that transforms an English sentence into a frame-semantic representation. It finds words that evoke FrameNet frames, selects frames for them, and locates the arguments for each frame. The system uses two feature-based, discriminative probabilistic (log-linear) models, one with latent variables to permit disambiguation of new predicate words. The parser is demonstrated to significantly outperform previously published results.

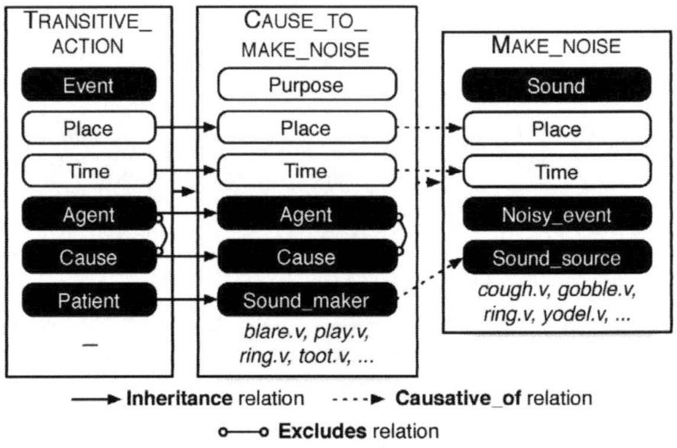

Figure 2. Partial illustration of frames, roles, and LUs related to the CAUSE_TO_MAKE_NOISE frame, from the FrameNet lexicon. "Core" roles are filled ovals. 8 additional roles of CAUSE_TO_MAKE_NOISE are not shown.

1 Introduction

FrameNet (Fillmore et al., 2003) is a rich linguistic resource containing considerable information about lexical and predicate-argument semantics in English. Grounded in the theory of frame semantics (Fillmore, 1982), it suggests—but does not formally define—a semantic representation that blends word-sense disambiguation and semantic role labeling.

In this paper, we present a computational and statistical model for frame-semantic parsing, the problem of extracting from text semantic predicate-argument structures such as those shown in Fig. 1. We aim to predict a frame-semantic representation as a *structure*, not as a pipeline of classifiers. We use a probabilistic framework that cleanly integrates the FrameNet lexicon and (currently very limited) available training data. Although our models often involve strong independence assumptions, the probabilistic framework we adopt is highly amenable to future extension through new features, relaxed independence assumptions, and semisupervised learning. Some novel aspects of our current approach include a latent-variable model that permits disambiguation of words not in the FrameNet lexicon, a unified model for finding and labeling arguments, and a precision-boosting constraint that forbids arguments of the same predicate to overlap. Our parser achieves the best published results to date on the SemEval'07 FrameNet task (Baker et al., 2007).

2 Resources and Task

We consider frame-semantic parsing resources.

2.1 FrameNet Lexicon

The FrameNet lexicon is a taxonomy of manually identified general-purpose **frames** for English.[1] Listed in the lexicon with each frame are several lemmas (with part of speech) that can denote the frame or some aspect of it—these are called **lexical units** (LUs). In a sentence, word or phrase tokens that evoke a frame are known as **targets**. The set of LUs listed for a frame in FrameNet may not be exhaustive; we may see a target in new data that does not correspond to an LU for the frame it evokes. Each frame definition also includes a set of frame elements, or **roles**, corresponding to different aspects of the concept represented by the frame, such as participants, props, and attributes. We use the term **ar-**

[1]Like the SemEval'07 participants, we used FrameNet v. 1.3 (http://framenet.icsi.berkeley.edu).

Human Language Technologies: The 2010 Annual Conference of the North American Chapter of the ACL, pages 948–956,
Los Angeles, California, June 2010.

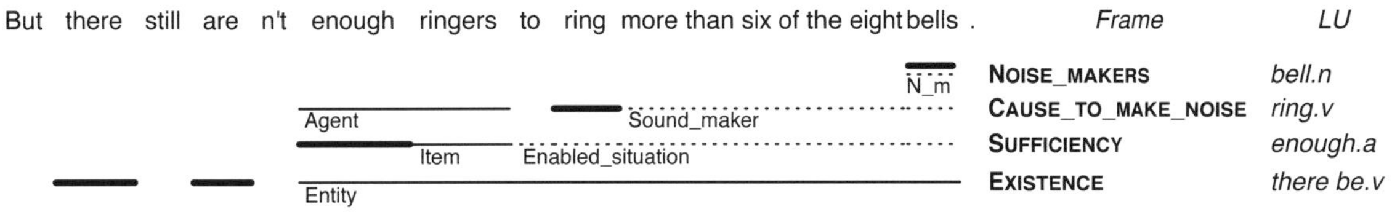

Figure 1. A sentence from PropBank and the SemEval'07 training data, and a partial depiction of gold FrameNet annotations. Each frame is a row below the sentence (ordered for readability). Thick lines indicate targets that evoke frames; thin solid/dotted lines with labels indicate arguments. "N_m" under *bells* is short for the Noise_maker role of the NOISE_MAKERS frame. The last row indicates that *there... are* is a discontinuous target. In PropBank, the verb *ring* is the only annotated predicate for this sentence, and it is not related to other predicates with similar meanings.

	FRAMENET LEXICON V. 1.3	
lexical	**exemplars**	
entries	*counts*	*coverage*
8379 LUs	139K sentences, 3.1M words	70% LUs
795 frames	1 frame annotation / sentence	63% frames
7124 roles	285K overt arguments	56% roles

Table 1. Snapshot of lexicon entries and exemplar sentences. Coverage indicates the fraction of types attested in at least one exemplar.

FULL-TEXT	*SemEval'07 data*								
ANNOTATIONS	**train**			**dev**			**test**		
Size							(*words*	*sentences*	*documents*)
all	43.3K	1.7K	22	6.3K	251	4	2.8K	120	3
ANC (travel)	3.9K	154	2	.8K	32	1	1.3K	67	1
NTI (bureaucratic)	32.2K	1.2K	15	5.5K	219	3	1.5K	53	2
PropBank (news)	7.3K	325	5	0	0	0	0	0	0
Annotations							(*frames/word*	*overt arguments/word*)	
all	0.23	0.39		0.22	0.37		0.37	0.65	
Coverage of lexicon							(*%_frames*	*%_roles*	*%_LUs*)
all	64.1	27.4	21.0	34.0	10.2	7.3	29.3	7.7	4.9
Out-of-lexicon types							(*frames*	*roles*	*LUs*)
all	14	69	71	2	4	2	39	99	189
Out-of-lexicon tokens							(*%_frames*	*%_roles*	*%_LUs*)
all	0.7	0.9	1.1	1.0	0.4	0.2	9.8	11.2	25.3

Table 2. Snapshot of the SemEval'07 annotated data.

gument to refer to a sequence of word tokens annotated as filling a frame role. Fig. 1 shows an example sentence from the training data with annotated targets, LUs, frames, and role-argument pairs. The FrameNet lexicon also provides information about relations between frames and between roles (e.g., INHERITANCE). Fig. 2 shows a subset of the relations between three frames and their roles.

Accompanying most frame definitions in the FrameNet lexicon is a set of lexicographic **exemplar sentences** (primarily from the British National Corpus) annotated for that frame. Typically chosen to illustrate variation in argument realization patterns for the frame in question, these sentences only contain annotations for a single frame. We found that using exemplar sentences directly to train our models hurt performance as evaluated on SemEval'07 data, even though the number of exemplar sentences is an order of magnitude larger than the number of sentences in our training set (§2.2). This is presumably because the exemplars are neither representative as a sample nor similar to the test data. Instead, we make use of these exemplars in features (§4.2).

2.2 Data

Our training, development, and test sets consist of documents annotated with frame-semantic structures for the SemEval'07 task, which we refer to collectively as the **SemEval'07 data**.[2] For the most part, the frames and roles used in annotating these documents were defined in the FrameNet lexicon, but there are some exceptions for which the annotators defined supplementary frames and roles; these are included in the possible output of our parser.

Table 2 provides a snapshot of the SemEval'07 data. We randomly selected three documents from the original SemEval training data to create a development set for tuning model hyperparameters. Notice that the test set contains more annotations per word, both in terms of frames and arguments. Moreover, there are many more out-of-lexicon frame, role, and LU types in the test set than in the training set. This inconsistency in the data results in poor recall scores for all models trained on the given data split, a problem we have not sought to address here.

[2] `http://framenet.icsi.berkeley.edu/semeval/FSSE.html`

Preprocessing. We preprocess sentences in our dataset with a standard set of annotations: POS tags from MXPOST (Ratnaparkhi, 1996) and dependency parses from the MST parser (McDonald et al., 2005) since manual syntactic parses are not available for most of the FrameNet-annotated documents. We used WordNet (Fellbaum, 1998) for lemmatization. We also labeled each verb in the data as having ACTIVE or PASSIVE voice, using code from the SRL system described by Johansson and Nugues (2008).

2.3 Task and Evaluation

Automatic annotations of frame-semantic structure can be broken into three parts: (1) *targets*, the words or phrases that evoke frames; (2) the *frame type*, defined in the lexicon, evoked by each target; and (3) the *arguments*, or spans of words that serve to fill roles defined by each evoked frame. These correspond to the three subtasks in our parser, each described and evaluated in turn: target identification (§3), frame identification (§4, not unlike word-sense disambiguation), and argument identification (§5, not unlike semantic role labeling).

The standard evaluation script from the SemEval'07 shared task calculates precision, recall, and F_1-measure for frames and arguments; it also provides a score that gives partial credit for hypothesizing a frame related to the correct one. We present precision, recall, and F_1-measure microaveraged across the test documents, report *labels-only* matching scores (spans must match exactly), and do not use named entity labels. More details can be found in Baker et al. (2007). For our experiments, statistical significance is measured using a reimplementation of Dan Bikel's randomized parsing evaluation comparator.[3]

2.4 Baseline

A strong baseline for frame-semantic parsing is the system presented by Johansson and Nugues (2007, hereafter J&N'07), the best system in the SemEval'07 shared task. For frame identification, they used an SVM classifier to disambiguate frames for known frame-evoking words. They used WordNet synsets to extend the vocabulary of frame-evoking words to cover unknown words, and then used a collection of separate SVM classifiers—one for each frame—to predict a single evoked frame for each occurrence of a word in the extended set.

J&N'07 modeled the argument identification problem by dividing it into two tasks: first, they classified candidate spans as to whether they were arguments or not; then they assigned roles to those that were identified as arguments. Both phases used SVMs. Thus, their formulation of the problem involves a multitude of classifiers—whereas ours uses two log-linear models, each with a single set of weights, to find a full frame-semantic parse.

TARGET IDENTIFICATION	P	R	F_1
Our technique (§3)	**89.92**	**70.79**	**79.21**
Baseline: J&N'07	*87.87*	*67.11*	*76.10*

Table 3. Target identification results for our system and the baseline. Scores in bold denote significant improvements over the baseline ($p < 0.05$).

3 Target Identification

Target identification is the problem of deciding which word tokens (or word token sequences) evoke frames in a given sentence. In other semantic role labeling schemes (e.g. PropBank), simple part-of-speech criteria typically distinguish predicates from non-predicates. But in frame semantics, verbs, nouns, adjectives, and even prepositions can evoke frames under certain conditions. One complication is that semantically-impoverished **support predicates** (such as *make* in *make a request*) do not evoke frames in the context of a frame-evoking, syntactially-dependent noun (*request*). Furthermore, only temporal, locative, and directional senses of prepositions evoke frames.

We found that, because the test set is more completely annotated—that is, it boasts far more frames per token than the training data (see Table 2)—learned models did not generalize well and achieved poor test recall. Instead, we followed J&N'07 in using a small set of rules to identify targets.

For a span to be a candidate target, it must appear (up to morphological variation) as a target in the training data or the lexicon. We consider multiword targets,[4] unlike J&N'07 (though we do not consider

[3]http://www.cis.upenn.edu/~dbikel/software.html#comparator

[4]There are 629 multiword LUs in the lexicon, and they correspond to 4.8% of the targets in the training set; among them are *screw up*.V, *shoot the breeze*.V, and *weapon of mass de-*

FRAME IDENTIFICATION (§4)	targets	exact frame matching P	R	F_1	partial frame matching P	R	F_1
Frame identification (oracle targets)	$*$	60.21	60.21	60.21	74.21	74.21	74.21
Frame identification (predicted targets)	auto §3	**69.75**	**54.91**	**61.44**	**77.51**	**61.03**	**68.29**
Baseline: J&N'07	*auto*	*66.22*	*50.57*	*57.34*	*73.86*	*56.41*	*63.97*

Table 4. Frame identification results. Precision, recall, and F_1 were evaluated under exact and partial frame matching; see §2.3. Bold indicates statistically significant results with respect to the baseline ($p < 0.05$).

discontinuous targets). Using rules from §3.1.1 of J&N'07, we further prune the list, with two modifications: we prune *all* prepositions, including locative, temporal, and directional ones, but do not prune support verbs. This is a conservative approach; our automatic target identifier will never propose a target that was not seen in the training data or FrameNet.

Results. Table 3 shows results on target identification; our system gains 3 F_1 points over the baseline.

4 Frame Identification

Given targets, the parser next identifies their frames.

4.1 Lexical units

FrameNet specifies a great deal of structural information both within and among frames. For frame identification we make use of frame-evoking **lexical units**, the (lemmatized and POS-tagged) words and phrases listed in the lexicon as referring to specific frames. For example, listed with the BRAGGING frame are 10 LUs, including *boast*.N, *boast*.V, *boastful*.A, *brag*.V, and *braggart*.N. Of course, due to polysemy and homonymy, the same LU may be associated with multiple frames; for example, *gobble*.V is listed under both the INGESTION and MAKE_NOISE frames. All targets in the exemplar sentences, and most in our training and test data, correspond to known LUs (see Table 2).

To incorporate frame-evoking expressions found in the training data but not the lexicon—and to avoid the possibility of lemmatization errors—our frame identification model will incorporate, via a latent variable, features based directly on exemplar and training **targets** rather than LUs. Let $\mathcal{L}$ be the set of (unlemmatized and automatically POS-tagged) targets found in the exemplar sentences of the lexicon and/or the sentences in our training set. Let $\mathcal{L}_f \subseteq \mathcal{L}$ be the subset of these targets annotated as evoking a particular frame f. Let $\mathcal{L}^l$ and $\mathcal{L}^l_f$ denote the lemmatized versions of $\mathcal{L}$ and $\mathcal{L}_f$ respectively. Then, we write *boasted*.VBD $\in \mathcal{L}_{\text{BRAGGING}}$ and *boast*.VBD $\in \mathcal{L}^l_{\text{BRAGGING}}$ to indicate that this inflected verb *boasted* and its lemma *boast* have been seen to evoke the BRAGGING frame. Significantly, however, another target, such as *toot your own horn*, might be used in other data to evoke this frame. We thus face the additional hurdle of predicting frames for unknown words.

The SemEval annotators created 47 new frames not present in the lexicon, out of which 14 belonged to our training set. We considered these with the 795 frames in the lexicon when parsing new data. Predicting new frames is a challenge not yet attempted to our knowledge (including here). Note that the scoring metric (§2.3) gives partial credit for *related* frames (e.g., a more general frame from the lexicon).

4.2 Model

For a given sentence $\mathbf{x}$ with frame-evoking targets $\mathbf{t}$, let t_i denote the ith target (a word sequence). Let t^l_i denote its lemma. We seek a list $\mathbf{f} = \langle f_1, \ldots, f_m \rangle$ of frames, one per target. In our model, the set of candidate frames for t_i is defined to include every frame f such that $t^l_i \in \mathcal{L}^l_f$—or if $t^l_i \notin \mathcal{L}^l$, then every known frame (the latter condition applies for 4.7% of the gold targets in the development set). In both cases, we let $\mathcal{F}_i$ be the set of candidate frames for the ith target in $\mathbf{x}$.

To allow frame identification for targets whose lemmas were seen in neither the exemplars nor the training data, our model includes an additional variable, ℓ_i. This variable ranges over the seen targets in $\mathcal{L}_{f_i}$, which can be thought of as **prototypes** for the expression of the frame. Importantly, frames are *predicted*, but prototypes are summed over via the latent variable. The prediction rule requires a probabilistic model over frames for a target:

$$f_i \leftarrow \text{argmax}_{f \in \mathcal{F}_i} \sum_{\ell \in \mathcal{L}_f} p(f, \ell \mid t_i, \mathbf{x}) \quad (1)$$

struction.N. In the SemEval'07 training data, there are just 99 discontinuous multiword targets (1% of all targets).

We adopt a conditional log-linear model: for $f \in \mathcal{F}_i$ and $\ell \in \mathcal{L}_f$, $p_{\boldsymbol{\theta}}(f, \ell \mid t_i, \mathbf{x}) =$

$$\frac{\exp \boldsymbol{\theta}^\top \mathbf{g}(f, \ell, t_i, \mathbf{x})}{\sum_{f' \in \mathcal{F}_i} \sum_{\ell' \in \mathcal{L}_{f'}} \exp \boldsymbol{\theta}^\top \mathbf{g}(f', \ell', t_i, \mathbf{x})} \quad (2)$$

where $\boldsymbol{\theta}$ are the model weights, and $\mathbf{g}$ is a vector-valued feature function. This discriminative formulation is very flexible, allowing for a variety of (possibly overlapping) features; e.g., a feature might relate a frame type to a prototype, represent a lexical-semantic relationship between a prototype and a target, or encode part of the syntax of the sentence.

Previous work has exploited WordNet for better coverage during frame identification (Johansson and Nugues, 2007; Burchardt et al., 2005, e.g., by expanding the set of targets using synsets), and others have sought to extend the lexicon itself (see §6). We differ in our use of a latent variable to incorporate lexical-semantic *features* in a discriminative model, relating known lexical units to unknown words that may evoke frames. Here we are able to take advantage of the large inventory of partially-annotated exemplar sentences.

Note that this model makes a strong independence assumption: each frame is predicted independently of all others in the document. In this way the model is similar to J&N'07. However, ours is a single conditional model that shares features and weights across all targets, frames, and prototypes, whereas the approach of J&N'07 consists of many separately trained models. Moreover, our model is unique in that it uses a latent variable to smooth over frames for unknown or ambiguous LUs.

Frame identification features depend on the preprocessed sentence $\mathbf{x}$, the prototype ℓ and its WordNet lexical-semantic relationship with the target t_i, and of course the frame f. Our model instantiates 662,020 binary features; see Das et al. (2010).

4.3 Training

Given the training subset of the SemEval'07 data, which is of the form $\left\langle \langle \mathbf{x}^{(j)}, \mathbf{t}^{(j)}, \mathbf{f}^{(j)}, \mathcal{A}^{(j)} \rangle \right\rangle_{j=1}^{N}$ ($N = 1663$ is the number of sentences), we discriminatively train the frame identification model by maximizing the following log-likelihood:[5]

$$\max_{\boldsymbol{\theta}} \sum_{j=1}^{N} \sum_{i=1}^{m_j} \log \sum_{\ell \in \mathcal{L}_{f_i^{(j)}}} p_{\boldsymbol{\theta}}(f_i^{(j)}, \ell \mid t_i^{(j)}, \mathbf{x}^{(j)}) \quad (3)$$

Note that the training problem is non-convex because of the summed-out prototype latent variable ℓ for each frame. To calculate the objective function, we need to cope with a sum over frames and prototypes for each target (see Eq. 2), often an expensive operation. We locally optimize the function using a distributed implementation of L-BFGS. This is the most expensive model that we train: with 100 CPUs, training takes several hours. (Decoding takes only a few minutes on one CPU for the test set.)

4.4 Results

We evaluate the performance of our frame identification model given gold-standard targets and automatically identified targets (§3); see Table 4.

Given gold-standard targets, our model is able to predict frames for lemmas not seen in training, of which there are 210. The partial-match evaluation gives our model some credit for 190 of these, 4 of which are exactly correct. The hidden variable model, then, is finding related (but rarely exact) frames for unknown target words. The net effect of our conservative target identifier on F_1 is actually positive: the frame identifier is far more precise for targets seen explicitly in training. Together, our target and frame identification outperform the baseline by 4 F_1 points. To compare the frame identification stage in isolation with that of J&N'07, we ran our frame identification model with the targets identified by their system as input. With partial matching, our model achieves a relative improvement of 0.6% F_1 over J&N'07 (though this is not significant).

While our frame identification model thus performs on par with the current state of the art for this task, it improves upon J&N's formulation of the problem because it requires only a single model, learns lexical-semantic features as part of that model rather than requiring a preprocessing step to expand the vocabulary of frame-evoking words, and is probabilistic, which can facilitate global reasoning.

5 Argument Identification

Given a sentence $\mathbf{x} = \langle x_1, \ldots, x_n \rangle$, the set of targets $\mathbf{t} = \langle t_1, \ldots, t_m \rangle$, and a list of evoked frames

[5] We found no benefit on development data from using an L_2 regularizer (zero-mean Gaussian prior).

$\mathbf{f} = \langle f_1, \ldots, f_m \rangle$ corresponding to each target, argument identification is the task of choosing which of each f_i's roles are filled, and by which parts of $\mathbf{x}$. This task is most similar to the problem of semantic role labeling, but uses frame-specific labels that are richer than the PropBank annotations.

5.1 Model

Let $\mathcal{R}_{f_i} = \{r_1, \ldots, r_{|\mathcal{R}_{f_i}|}\}$ denote frame f_i's **roles** (named frame element types) observed in an exemplar sentence and/or our training set. A subset of each frame's roles are marked as **core** roles; these roles are conceptually and/or syntactically necessary for any given use of the frame, though they need not be overt in every sentence involving the frame. These are roughly analogous to the core arguments A0–A5 and AA in PropBank. Non-core roles—analogous to the various AMs in PropBank—loosely correspond to syntactic adjuncts, and carry broadly-applicable information such as the time, place, or purpose of an event. The lexicon imposes some additional structure on roles, including relations to other roles in the same or related frames, and semantic types with respect to a small ontology (marking, for instance, that the entity filling the protagonist role must be sentient for frames of cognition). Fig. 2 illustrates some of the structural elements comprising the frame lexicon by considering the CAUSE_TO_MAKE_NOISE frame.

We identify a set $\mathcal{S}$ of spans that are candidates for filling any role $r \in \mathcal{R}_{f_i}$. In principle, $\mathcal{S}$ could contain any subsequence of $\mathbf{x}$, but in this work we only consider the set of contiguous spans that (a) contain a single word or (b) comprise a valid subtree of a word and all its descendants in the dependency parse produced by the MST parser. This covers 81% of arguments in the development data. The empty span is also included in $\mathcal{S}$, since some roles are not explicitly filled; in the development data, the average number of roles an evoked frame defines is 6.7, but the average number of overt arguments is only 1.7.[6] In training, if a labeled argument is not a valid subtree of the dependency parse, we add its span to $\mathcal{S}$.

Let $\mathcal{A}_i$ denote the mapping of roles in $\mathcal{R}_{f_i}$ to spans in $\mathcal{S}$. Our model makes a prediction for each $\mathcal{A}_i(r_k)$ (for all roles $r_k \in \mathcal{R}_{f_i}$) using:

$$\mathcal{A}_i(r_k) \leftarrow \operatorname{argmax}_{s \in \mathcal{S}} p(s \mid r_k, f_i, t_i, \mathbf{x}) \tag{4}$$

We use a conditional log-linear model over spans for each role of each evoked frame:

$$p_{\boldsymbol{\psi}}(\mathcal{A}_i(r_k) = s \mid f_i, t_i, \mathbf{x}) = \frac{\exp \boldsymbol{\psi}^\top \mathbf{h}(s, r_k, f_i, t_i, \mathbf{x})}{\sum_{s' \in \mathcal{S}} \exp \boldsymbol{\psi}^\top \mathbf{h}(s', r_k, f_i, t_i, \mathbf{x})} \tag{5}$$

Note that our model chooses the span for each role separately from the other roles and ignores all frames except the frame the role belongs to. Our model departs from the traditional SRL literature by modeling the argument identification problem in a single stage, rather than first classifying token spans as arguments and then labeling them. A constraint implicit in our formulation restricts each role to have at most one overt argument, which is consistent with 96.5% of the role instances in the training data.

Out of the overt argument spans in the training data, 12% are duplicates, having been used by some previous frame in the sentence (supposing some arbitrary ordering of frames). Our role-filling model, unlike a sentence-global argument detection-and-classification approach,[7] permits this sort of argument sharing among frames. The incidence of span *overlap* among frames is much higher; Fig. 1 illustrates a case with a high degree of overlap. Word tokens belong to an average of 1.6 argument spans each, including the quarter of words that do not belong to any argument.

Features for our log-linear model (Eq. 5) depend on the preprocessed sentence $\mathbf{x}$; the target t; a role r of frame f; and a candidate argument span $s \in \mathcal{S}$. Our model includes lexicalized and unlexicalized features considering aspects of the syntactic parse (most notably the dependency path in the parse from the target to the argument); voice; word ordering/overlap/distance of the argument with respect to the target; and POS tags within and around the argument. Many features have a version specific to the frame and role, plus a smoothed version incorporating the role name, but not the frame. These features

[6] In the annotated data, each core role is filled with one of three types of *null instantiations* indicating how the role is conveyed implicitly. E.g., the imperative construction implicitly designates a role as filled by the addressee, and the corresponding filler is thus CNI (constructional null instantiation). In this work we do not distinguish different types of null instantiations.

[7] J&N'07, like us, identify arguments for each target.

are fully enumerated in (Das et al., 2010); instantiating them for our data yields 1,297,857 parameters.

5.2 Training

We train the argument identification model by:

$$\max_{\psi} \sum_{j=1}^{N} \sum_{i=1}^{m_j} \sum_{k=1}^{|\mathcal{R}_{f_i^{(j)}}|} \log p_{\psi}(\mathcal{A}_i^{(j)}(r_k) \mid f_i^{(j)}, t_i^{(j)}, \mathbf{x}^{(j)}) \quad (6)$$

This objective function is concave, and we globally optimize it using stochastic gradient ascent (Bottou, 2004). We train this model until the argument identification F_1 score stops increasing on the development data. Best results on this dataset were obtained with a batch size of 2 and 23 passes through the data.

5.3 Approximate Joint Decoding

Naïve prediction of roles using Eq. 4 may result in overlap among arguments filling different roles of a frame, since the argument identification model fills each role independently of the others. We want to enforce the constraint that two roles of a single frame cannot be filled by overlapping spans. We disallow illegal overlap using a 10000-hypothesis beam search; the algorithm is given in (Das et al., 2010).

5.4 Results

Performance of the argument identification model is presented in Table 5. The table shows how performance varies given different types of perfect input: correct targets, correct frames, and the set of correct spans; correct targets and frames, with the heuristically-constructed set of candidate spans; correct targets only, with model frames; and ultimately, no oracle input (the full frame parsing scenario).

The first four rows of results isolate the argument identification task from the frame identification task. Given gold targets and frames and an oracle set of argument spans, our local model achieves about 87% precision and 75% recall. Beam search decoding to eliminate illegal argument assignments within a frame (§5.3) further improves precision by about 1.6%, with negligible harm to recall. Note that 96.5% recall is possible under the constraint that roles are not multiply-filled (§5.1); there is thus considerable room for improvement with this constraint in place. Joint prediction of each frame's arguments is worth exploring to capture correlations not encoded in our local models or joint decoding scheme.

The 15-point drop in recall when the heuristically-built candidate argument set replaces the set of true argument spans is unsurprising: an estimated 19% of correct arguments are excluded because they are neither single words nor complete subtrees (see §5.1). Qualitatively, the problem of candidate span recall seems to be largely due to syntactic parse errors.[8] Still, the 10-point decrease in precision when using the syntactic parse to determine candidate spans suggests that the model has trouble discriminating between good and bad arguments, and that additional feature engineering or jointly decoding arguments of a sentence's frames may be beneficial in this regard.

The fifth and sixth rows show the effect of automatic frame identification on overall frame parsing performance. There is a 22% decrease in F_1 (18% when partial credit is given for related frames), suggesting that improved frame identification or joint prediction of frames and arguments is likely to have a sizeable impact on overall performance.

The final two rows of the table compare our full model (target, frame, and argument identification) with the baseline, showing significant improvement of more than 4.4 F_1 points for both exact and partial frame matching. As with frame identification, we compared the argument identification stage with that of J&N'07 in isolation, using the automatically identified targets and frames from the latter as input to our model. With partial frame matching, this gave us an F_1 score of 48.1% on the test set—significantly better ($p < 0.05$) than 45.6%, the full parsing result from J&N'07. This indicates that our argument identification model—which uses a single discriminative model with a large number of features for role filling (rather than argument labeling)—is more powerful than the previous state of the art.

6 Related work

Since Gildea and Jurafsky (2002) pioneered statistical semantic role labeling, a great deal of com-

[8] Note that, because of our labels-only evaluation scheme (§2.3), arguments missing a word or containing an extra word receive no credit. In fact, of the frame roles correctly predicted as having an overt span, the correct span was predicted 66% of the time, while 10% of the time the predicted starting and ending boundaries of the span were off by a total of 1 or 2 words.

Argument Identification	targets	frames	spans	decoding	exact frame matching P	R	F_1	partial frame matching P	R	F_1
Argument identification (oracle spans)	*	*	*	naïve	86.61	75.11	80.45			
	*	*	*	beam §5.3	88.29	74.77	80.97			
Argument identification (full)	*	*	model §5	naïve	77.43	60.76	68.09			
	*	*	model §5	beam §5.3	78.71	60.57	68.46			
Parsing (oracle targets)	*	model §4	model §5	beam §5.3	49.68	42.82	46.00	57.85	49.86	53.56
Parsing (full)	auto §3	model §4	model §5	beam §5.3	**58.08**	**38.76**	**46.49**	**62.76**	**41.89**	**50.24**
Baseline: J&N'07	*auto*	*model*	*model*	*N/A*	*51.59*	*35.44*	*42.01*	*56.01*	*38.48*	*45.62*

Table 5. Argument identification results. $*$ indicates that gold-standard labels were used for a given pipeline stage. For full parsing, bolded scores indicate significant improvements relative to the baseline ($p < 0.05$).

putational work has investigated predicate-argument structures for semantics. Briefly, we highlight some relevant work, particularly research that has made use of FrameNet. (Note that much related research has focused on PropBank (Kingsbury and Palmer, 2002), a set of shallow predicate-argument annotations for *Wall Street Journal* articles from the Penn Treebank (Marcus et al., 1993); a recent issue of *CL* (Màrquez et al., 2008) was devoted to the subject.)

Most work on frame-semantic role labeling has made use of the exemplar sentences in the FrameNet corpus (see §2.1), each of which is annotated for a single frame and its arguments. On the probabilistic modeling front, Gildea and Jurafsky (2002) presented a discriminative model for arguments given the frame; Thompson et al. (2003) used a generative model for both the frame and its arguments; and Fleischman et al. (2003) first used maximum entropy models to find and label arguments given the frame. Shi and Mihalcea (2004) developed a rule-based system to predict frames and their arguments in text, and Erk and Padó (2006) introduced the Shalmaneser tool, which employs Naïve Bayes classifiers to do the same. Other FrameNet SRL systems (Giuglea and Moschitti, 2006, for instance) have used SVMs. Most of this work was done on an older, smaller version of FrameNet.

Recent work on frame-semantic *parsing*—in which sentences may contain multiple frames to be recognized along with their arguments—has used the SemEval'07 data (Baker et al., 2007). The LTH system of Johansson and Nugues (2007), our baseline (§2.4), performed the best in the SemEval'07 task. Matsubayashi et al. (2009) trained a log-linear model on the SemEval'07 data to evaluate argument identification features exploiting various types of taxonomic relations to generalize over roles. A line of work has sought to extend the coverage of FrameNet by exploiting VerbNet, WordNet, and Wikipedia (Shi and Mihalcea, 2005; Giuglea and Moschitti, 2006; Pennacchiotti et al., 2008; Tonelli and Giuliano, 2009), and projecting entries and annotations within and across languages (Boas, 2002; Fung and Chen, 2004; Padó and Lapata, 2005; Fürstenau and Lapata, 2009). Others have applied frame-semantic structures to question answering, paraphrase/entailment recognition, and information extraction (Narayanan and Harabagiu, 2004; Shen and Lapata, 2007; Padó and Erk, 2005; Burchardt, 2006; Moschitti et al., 2003; Surdeanu et al., 2003).

7 Conclusion

We have provided a supervised model for rich frame-semantic parsing, based on a combination of knowledge from FrameNet, two probabilistic models trained on SemEval'07 data, and expedient heuristics. Our system achieves improvements over the state of the art at each stage of processing and collectively, and is amenable to future extension. Our parser is available for download at `http://www.ark.cs.cmu.edu/SEMAFOR`.

Acknowledgments

We thank Collin Baker, Katrin Erk, Richard Johansson, and Nils Reiter for software, data, evaluation scripts, and methodological details. We thank the reviewers, Alan Black, Ric Crabbe, Michael Ellsworth, Rebecca Hwa, Dan Klein, Russell Lee-Goldman, Dan Roth, Josef Ruppenhofer, and members of the ARK group for helpful comments. This work was supported by DARPA grant NBCH-1080004, NSF grant IIS-0836431, and computational resources provided by Yahoo.

References

C. Baker, M. Ellsworth, and K. Erk. 2007. SemEval-2007 Task 19: frame semantic structure extraction. In *Proc. of SemEval.*

H. C. Boas. 2002. Bilingual FrameNet dictionaries for machine translation. In *Proc. of LREC.*

L. Bottou. 2004. Stochastic learning. In *Advanced Lectures on Machine Learning*. Springer-Verlag.

A. Burchardt, K. Erk, and A. Frank. 2005. A WordNet detour to FrameNet. In B. Fisseni, H.-C. Schmitz, B. Schröder, and P. Wagner, editors, *Sprachtechnologie, mobile Kommunikation und linguistische Resourcen*, volume 8. Peter Lang.

A. Burchardt. 2006. Approaching textual entailment with LFG and FrameNet frames. In *Proc. of the Second PASCAL RTE Challenge Workshop.*

D. Das, N. Schneider, D. Chen, and N. A. Smith. 2010. SEMAFOR 1.0: A probabilistic frame-semantic parser. Technical Report CMU-LTI-10-001, Carnegie Mellon University.

K. Erk and S. Padó. 2006. Shalmaneser - a toolchain for shallow semantic parsing. In *Proc. of LREC.*

C. Fellbaum, editor. 1998. *WordNet: an electronic lexical database.* MIT Press, Cambridge, MA.

C. J. Fillmore, C. R. Johnson, and M. R.L. Petruck. 2003. Background to FrameNet. *International Journal of Lexicography*, 16(3).

C. J. Fillmore. 1982. Frame semantics. In *Linguistics in the Morning Calm*, pages 111–137. Hanshin Publishing Co., Seoul, South Korea.

M. Fleischman, N. Kwon, and E. Hovy. 2003. Maximum entropy models for FrameNet classification. In *Proc. of EMNLP.*

P. Fung and B. Chen. 2004. BiFrameNet: bilingual frame semantics resource construction by cross-lingual induction. In *Proc. of COLING.*

H. Fürstenau and M. Lapata. 2009. Semi-supervised semantic role labeling. In *Proc. of EACL.*

D. Gildea and D. Jurafsky. 2002. Automatic labeling of semantic roles. *Computational Linguistics*, 28(3).

A.-M. Giuglea and A. Moschitti. 2006. Shallow semantic parsing based on FrameNet, VerbNet and PropBank. In *Proc. of ECAI 2006.*

R. Johansson and P. Nugues. 2007. LTH: semantic structure extraction using nonprojective dependency trees. In *Proc. of SemEval.*

R. Johansson and P. Nugues. 2008. Dependency-based semantic role labeling of PropBank. In *Proc. of EMNLP.*

P. Kingsbury and M. Palmer. 2002. From TreeBank to PropBank. In *Proc. of LREC.*

M. P. Marcus, M. A. Marcinkiewicz, and B. Santorini. 1993. Building a large annotated corpus of English: the Penn Treebank. *Computational Linguistics*, 19(2).

L. Màrquez, X. Carreras, K. C. Litkowski, and S. Stevenson. 2008. Semantic role labeling: an introduction to the special issue. *Computational Linguistics*, 34(2).

Y. Matsubayashi, N. Okazaki, and J. Tsujii. 2009. A comparative study on generalization of semantic roles in FrameNet. In *Proc. of ACL-IJCNLP.*

R. McDonald, K. Crammer, and F. Pereira. 2005. Online large-margin training of dependency parsers. In *Proc. of ACL.*

A. Moschitti, P. Morărescu, and S. M. Harabagiu. 2003. Open-domain information extraction via automatic semantic labeling. In *Proc. of FLAIRS.*

S. Narayanan and S. Harabagiu. 2004. Question answering based on semantic structures. In *Proc. of COLING.*

S. Padó and K. Erk. 2005. To cause or not to cause: cross-lingual semantic matching for paraphrase modelling. In *Proc. of the Cross-Language Knowledge Induction Workshop.*

S. Padó and M. Lapata. 2005. Cross-linguistic projection of role-semantic information. In *Proc. of HLT-EMNLP.*

M. Pennacchiotti, D. De Cao, R. Basili, D. Croce, and M. Roth. 2008. Automatic induction of FrameNet lexical units. In *Proc. of EMNLP.*

A. Ratnaparkhi. 1996. A maximum entropy model for part-of-speech tagging. In *Proc. of EMNLP.*

D. Shen and M. Lapata. 2007. Using semantic roles to improve question answering. In *Proc. of EMNLP-CoNLL.*

L. Shi and R. Mihalcea. 2004. An algorithm for open text semantic parsing. In *Proc. of Workshop on Robust Methods in Analysis of Natural Language Data.*

L. Shi and R. Mihalcea. 2005. Putting pieces together: combining FrameNet, VerbNet and WordNet for robust semantic parsing. In *Computational Linguistics and Intelligent Text Processing: Proc. of CICLing 2005*. Springer-Verlag.

M. Surdeanu, S. Harabagiu, J. Williams, and P. Aarseth. 2003. Using predicate-argument structures for information extraction. In *Proc. of ACL.*

C. A. Thompson, R. Levy, and C. D. Manning. 2003. A generative model for semantic role labeling. In *Proc. of ECML.*

S. Tonelli and C. Giuliano. 2009. Wikipedia as frame information repository. In *Proc. of EMNLP.*

Expected Sequence Similarity Maximization

Cyril Allauzen[1], **Shankar Kumar**[1], **Wolfgang Macherey**[1], **Mehryar Mohri**[2,1] **and Michael Riley**[1]
[1]Google Research, 76 Ninth Avenue, New York, NY 10011
[2]Courant Institute of Mathematical Sciences, 251 Mercer Street, New York, NY 10012

Abstract

This paper presents efficient algorithms for expected similarity maximization, which coincides with minimum Bayes decoding for a similarity-based loss function. Our algorithms are designed for similarity functions that are sequence kernels in a general class of positive definite symmetric kernels. We discuss both a general algorithm and a more efficient algorithm applicable in a common unambiguous scenario. We also describe the application of our algorithms to machine translation and report the results of experiments with several translation data sets which demonstrate a substantial speed-up. In particular, our results show a speed-up by two orders of magnitude with respect to the original method of Tromble et al. (2008) and by a factor of 3 or more even with respect to an approximate algorithm specifically designed for that task. These results open the path for the exploration of more appropriate or optimal kernels for the specific tasks considered.

1 Introduction

The output of many complex natural language processing systems such as information extraction, speech recognition, or machine translation systems is a probabilistic automaton. Exploiting the full information provided by this probabilistic automaton can lead to more accurate results than just using the one-best sequence.

Different techniques have been explored in the past to take advantage of the full lattice, some based on the use of a more complex model applied to the automaton as in rescoring, others using additional data or information for reranking the hypotheses represented by the automaton. One method for using these probabilistic automata that has been successful in large-vocabulary speech recognition (Goel and Byrne, 2000) and machine translation (Kumar and Byrne, 2004; Tromble et al., 2008) applications and that requires no additional data or other complex models is the minimum Bayes risk (MBR) decoding technique. This returns that sequence of the automaton having the minimum expected loss with respect to all sequences accepted by the automaton (Bickel and Doksum, 2001). Often, minimizing the loss function L can be equivalently viewed as maximizing a similarity function K between sequences, which corresponds to a kernel function when it is positive definite symmetric (Berg et al., 1984). The technique can then be thought of as an *expected sequence similarity maximization*.

This paper considers this expected similarity maximization view. Since different similarity functions can be used within this framework, one may wish to select the one that is the most appropriate or relevant to the task considered. However, a crucial requirement for this choice to be realistic is to ensure that for the family of similarity functions considered the expected similarity maximization is efficiently computable. Thus, we primarily focus on this algorithmic problem in this paper, leaving it to future work to study the question of determining how to select the similarity function and report on the benefits of this choice.

A general family of sequence kernels including the sequence kernels used in computational biology, text categorization, spoken-dialog classification, and many other tasks is that of *rational kernels* (Cortes et al., 2004). We show how the expected similarity maximization can be efficiently computed for these kernels. In section 3, we describe more specifically the framework of expected similarity maximization in the case of rational kernels and the corresponding algorithmic problem. In Section 4, we describe both a general method for the computation of the expected similarity maximization, and a more efficient method that can be used with a broad sub-family of rational kernels that verify a condition of non-ambiguity. This latter family includes the class of n-gram kernels which have been previously used to

Human Language Technologies: The 2010 Annual Conference of the North American Chapter of the ACL, pages 957–965,
Los Angeles, California, June 2010.

apply MBR to machine translation (Tromble et al., 2008). We examine in more detail the use and application of our algorithms to machine translation in Section 5. Section 6 reports the results of experiments applying our algorithms in several large data sets in machine translation. These experiments demonstrate the efficiency of our algorithm which is shown empirically to be two orders of magnitude faster than Tromble et al. (2008) and more than 3 times faster than even an approximation algorithm specifically designed for this problem (Kumar et al., 2009). We start with some preliminary definitions and algorithms related to weighted automata and transducers, following the definitions and terminology of Cortes et al. (2004).

2 Preliminaries

Weighted transducers are finite-state transducers in which each transition carries some weight in addition to the input and output labels. The weight set has the structure of a semiring.

A *semiring* $(\mathbb{K}, \oplus, \otimes, \overline{0}, \overline{1})$ verifies all the axioms of a ring except from the existence of a negative element $-x$ for each $x \in \mathbb{K}$, which it may verify or not. Thus, roughly speaking, a semiring is a ring that may lack negation. It is specified by a set of values $\mathbb{K}$, two binary operations $\oplus$ and $\otimes$, and two designated values $\overline{0}$ and $\overline{1}$. When $\otimes$ is commutative, the semiring is said to be *commutative*.

The *real semiring* $(\mathbb{R}_+, +, \times, 0, 1)$ is used when the weights represent probabilities. The *log semiring* $(\mathbb{R} \cup \{-\infty, +\infty\}, \oplus_{\log}, +, \infty, 0)$ is isomorphic to the real semiring via the negative-log mapping and is often used in practice for numerical stability. The *tropical semiring* $(\mathbb{R}\cup, \{-\infty, +\infty\}, \min, +, \infty, 0)$ is derived from the log semiring via the *Viterbi approximation* and is often used in shortest-path applications.

Figure 1(a) shows an example of a weighted finite-state transducer over the real semiring $(\mathbb{R}_+, +, \times, 0, 1)$. In this figure, the input and output labels of a transition are separated by a colon delimiter and the weight is indicated after the slash separator. A weighted transducer has a set of initial states represented in the figure by a bold circle and a set of final states, represented by double circles. A path from an initial state to a final state is an accepting path.

The weight of an accepting path is obtained by first $\otimes$-multiplying the weights of its constituent

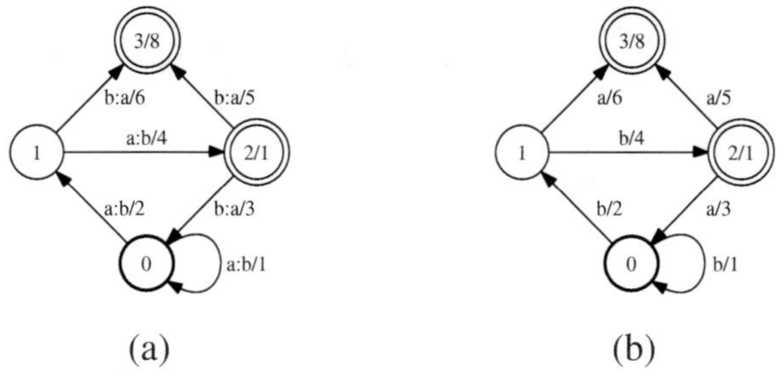

Figure 1: (a) Example of weighted transducer T over the real semiring $(\mathbb{R}_+, +, \times, 0, 1)$. (b) Example of weighted automaton A. A can be obtained from T by projection on the output and $T(aab, bba) = A(bba) = 1 \times 2 \times 6 \times 8 + 2 \times 4 \times 5 \times 8$.

transitions and $\otimes$-multiplying this product on the left by the weight of the initial state of the path (which equals $\overline{1}$ in our work) and on the right by the weight of the final state of the path (displayed after the slash in the figure). The weight associated by a weighted transducer T to a pair of strings $(x, y) \in \Sigma^* \times \Sigma^*$ is denoted by $T(x, y)$ and is obtained by $\oplus$-summing the weights of all accepting paths with input label x and output label y.

For any transducer T, T^{-1} denotes its *inverse*, that is the transducer obtained from T by swapping the input and output labels of each transition. For all $x, y \in \Sigma^*$, we have $T^{-1}(x, y) = T(y, x)$.

The *composition* of two weighted transducers T_1 and T_2 with matching input and output alphabets Σ, is a weighted transducer denoted by $T_1 \circ T_2$ when the semiring is commutative and the sum:

$$(T_1 \circ T_2)(x, y) = \sum_{z \in \Sigma^*} T_1(x, z) \otimes T_2(z, y) \quad (1)$$

is well-defined and in $\mathbb{K}$ for all x, y (Salomaa and Soittola, 1978).

Weighted automata can be defined as weighted transducers A with identical input and output labels, for any transition. Since only pairs of the form (x, x) can have a non-zero weight associated to them by A, we denote the weight associated by A to (x, x) by $A(x)$ and call it the *weight associated by A to x*. Similarly, in the graph representation of weighted automata, the output (or input) label is omitted. Figure 1(b) shows an example of a weighted automaton. When A and B are weighted automata, $A \circ B$ is called the *intersection* of A and B. Omitting the input labels of a weighted transducer T results in a weighted automaton which is said to be the *output projection of T*.

3 General Framework

Let X be a probabilistic automaton representing the output of a complex model for a specific query input. The model may be for example a speech recognition system, an information extraction system, or a machine translation system (which originally motivated our study). For machine translation, the sequences accepted by X are the potential translations of the input sentence, each with some probability given by X.

Let Σ be the alphabet for the task considered, e.g., words of the target language in machine translation, and let $L\colon \Sigma^* \times \Sigma^* \to \mathbb{R}$ denote a loss function defined over the sequences on that alphabet. Given a reference or hypothesis set $H \subseteq \Sigma^*$, minimum Bayes risk (MBR) decoding consists of selecting a hypothesis $x \in H$ with minimum expected loss with respect to the probability distribution X (Bickel and Doksum, 2001; Tromble et al., 2008):

$$\widehat{x} = \operatorname*{argmin}_{x \in H} \operatorname*{E}_{x' \sim X}[L(x, x')]. \quad (2)$$

Here, we shall consider the case, frequent in practice, where minimizing the loss L is equivalent to maximizing a similarity measure $K\colon \Sigma^* \times \Sigma^* \to \mathbb{R}$. When K is a sequence kernel that can be represented by weighted transducers, it is a *rational kernel* (Cortes et al., 2004). The problem is then equivalent to the following *expected similarity maximization*:

$$\widehat{x} = \operatorname*{argmax}_{x \in H} \operatorname*{E}_{x' \sim X}[K(x, x')]. \quad (3)$$

When K is a positive definite symmetric rational kernel, it can often be rewritten as $K(x, y) = (T \circ T^{-1})(x, y)$, where T is a weighted transducer over the semiring $(\mathbb{R}_+ \cup \{+\infty\}, +, \times, 0, 1)$. Equation (3) can then be rewritten as

$$\widehat{x} = \operatorname*{argmax}_{x \in H} \operatorname*{E}_{x' \sim X}[(T \circ T^{-1})(x, x')] \quad (4)$$

$$= \operatorname*{argmax}_{x \in H} \|A(x) \circ T \circ T^{-1} \circ X\|, \quad (5)$$

where we denote by $A(x)$ an automaton accepting (only) the string x and by $\|\cdot\|$ the sum of the weights of all accepted paths of a transducer.

4 Algorithms

4.1 General method

Equation (5) could suggest computing $A(x) \circ T \circ T^{-1} \circ X$ for each possible $x \in H$. Instead, we can compute a composition based on an automaton accepting all sequences in H, $A(H)$. This leads to a straightforward method for determining the sequence maximizing the expected similarity having the following steps:

1. compute the composition $X \circ T$, project on the output and optimize (epsilon-remove, determinize, minimize (Mohri, 2009)) and let Y_2 be the result;[1]
2. compute the composition $Y_1 = A(H) \circ T$;
3. compute $Y_1 \circ Y_2$ and project on the input, let Z be the result;[2]
4. determinize Z;
5. find the maximum weight path with the label of that path giving $\widehat{x}$.

While this method can be efficient in various scenarios, in some instances the weighted determinization yielding Z can be both space- and time-consuming, even though the input is acyclic. The next two sections describe more efficient algorithms.

Note that in practice, for numerical stability, all of these computations are done in the log semiring which is isomorphic to $(\mathbb{R}_+ \cup \{+\infty\}, +, \times, 0, 1)$. In particular, the maximum weight path in the last step is then obtained by using a standard single-source shortest-path algorithm.

4.2 Efficient method for n-gram kernels

A common family of rational kernels is the family of n-gram kernels. These kernels are widely use as a similarity measure in natural language processing and computational biology applications, see (Leslie et al., 2002; Lodhi et al., 2002) for instance.

The n-gram kernel K_n of order n is defined as

$$K_n(x, y) = \sum_{|z|=n} c_x(z) c_y(z), \quad (6)$$

where $c_x(z)$ is the number of occurrences of z in x. K_n is a positive definite symmetric rational kernel since it corresponds to the weighted transducer $T_n \circ T_n^{-1}$ where the transducer T_n is defined such that $T_n(x, z) = c_x(z)$ for all $x, z \in \Sigma^*$ with $|z| = n$.

[1] Equivalent to computing $T^{-1} \circ X$ and projecting on the input.

[2] Z is then the projection on the input of $A(H) \circ T \circ T^{-1} \circ X$.

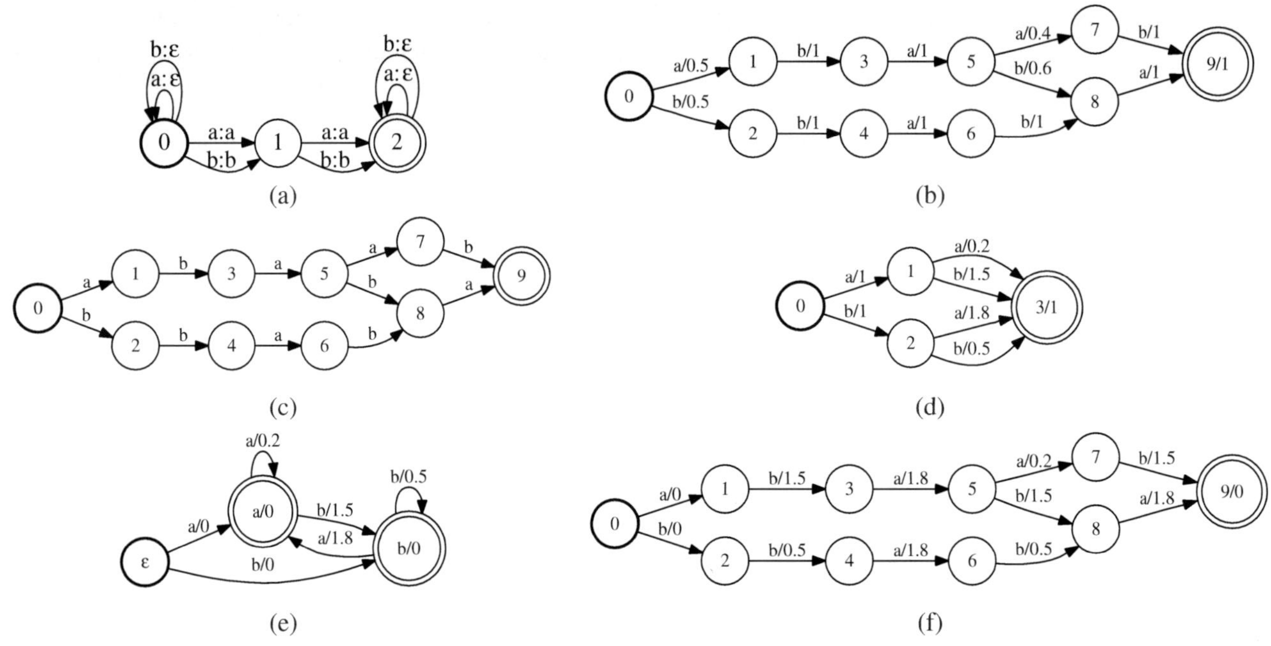

Figure 2: Efficient method for bigram kernel: (a) Counting transducer T_2 for $\Sigma = \{a, b\}$ (over the real semiring). (b) Probabilistic automaton X (over the real semiring). (c) The hypothesis automaton $A(H)$ (unweighted). (d) Automaton Y_2 representing the expected bigram counts in X (over the real semiring). (e) Automaton Y_1: the context dependency model derived from Y_2 (over the tropical semiring). (f) The composition $A(H) \circ Y_1$ (over the tropical semiring).

The transducer T_2 for $\Sigma = \{a, b\}$ is shown in Figure 2(a).

Taking advantage of the special structure of n-gram kernels and of the fact that $A(H)$ is an unweighted automaton, we can devise a new and significantly more efficient method for computing $\widehat{x}$ based on the following steps.

1. *Compute the expected n-gram counts in X:* We compute the composition $X \circ T$, project on output and optimize (epsilon-remove, determinize, minimize) and let Y_2 be the result. Observe that the weighted automaton Y_2 is a compact representation of the expected n-gram counts in X, i.e. for an n-gram w (i.e. $|w| = n$):

$$Y_2(w) = \sum_{x \in \Sigma^*} X(x) c_x(w) \\ = \mathop{\mathrm{E}}_{x \sim X} [c_x(w)] = c_X(w). \tag{7}$$

2. *Construct a context-dependency model:* We compute the weighted automaton Y_1 over the tropical semiring as follow: the set of states is $Q = \{w \in \Sigma^* \,|\, |w| \leq n \text{ and } w \text{ occurs in } X\}$, the initial state being ϵ and every state being final; the set of transitions E contains all 4-tuple (origin, label, weight, destination) of the form:

   - $(w, a, 0, wa)$ with $wa \in Q$ and $|w| \leq n - 2$ and
   - $(aw, b, Y_2(awb), wb)$ with $Y_2(awb) \neq 0$ and $|w| = n - 2$

   where $a, b \in \Sigma$ and $w \in \Sigma^*$. Observe that $w \in Q$ when $wa \in Q$ and that $aw, wb \in Q$ when $Y_2(awb) \neq 0$. Given a string x, we have

$$Y_1(x) = \sum_{|w|=n} c_X(w) c_x(w). \tag{8}$$

   Observe that Y_1 is a deterministic automaton, hence $Y_1(x)$ can be computed in $O(|x|)$ time.

3. *Compute $\widehat{x}$:* We compute the composition $A(H) \circ Y_1$. $\widehat{x}$ is then the label of the accepting path with the largest weight in this transducer and can be obtained by applying a shortest-path algorithm to $-A(H) \circ Y_1$ in the tropical semiring.

The main computational advantage of this method is that it avoids the determinization of Z in the

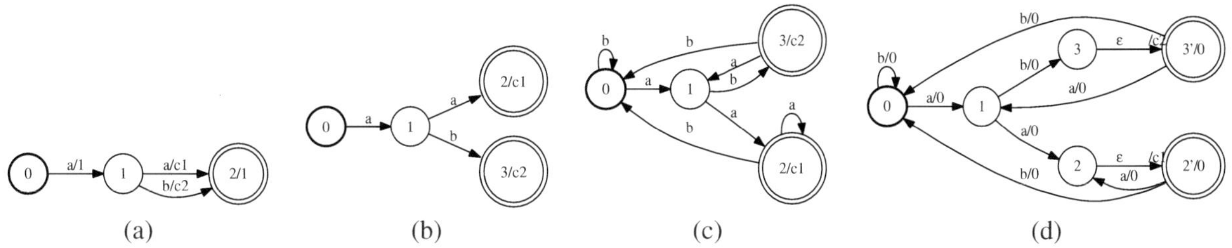

Figure 3: Illustration of the construction of Y_1 in the unambiguous case. (a) Weighted automaton Y_2 (over the real semiring). (b) Deterministic tree automaton Y_2' accepting $\{aa, ab\}$ (over the tropical semiring). (c) Result of determinization of $\Sigma^* Y_2'$ (over the tropical semiring). (d) Weighted automaton Y_1 (over the tropical semiring).

$(+, \times)$ semiring, which can sometimes be costly. The method has also been shown empirically to be significantly faster than the one described in the previous section.

The algorithm is illustrated in Figure 2. The alphabet is $\Sigma = \{a, b\}$ and the counting transducer corresponding to the bigram kernel is given in Figure 2(a). The evidence probabilistic automaton X is given in Figure 2(b) and we use as hypothesis set the set of strings that were assigned a non-zero probability by X; this set is represented by the deterministic finite automaton $A(H)$ given in Figure 2(c). The result of step 1 of the algorithm is the weighted automaton Y_2 over the real semiring given in Figure 2(d). The result of step 2 is the weighted automaton Y_1 over the tropical semiring is given in Figure 2(e). Finally, the result of the composition $A(H) \circ Y_1$ (step 3) is the weighted automaton over the tropical semiring given in Figure 2(f). The result of the expected similarity maximization is the string $\widehat{x} = ababa$, which is obtained by applying a shortest-path algorithm to $-A(H) \circ Y_1$. Observe that the string $\overline{x}$ with the largest probability in X is $\overline{x} = bbaba$ and is hence different from $\widehat{x} = ababa$ in this example.

4.3 Efficient method for the unambiguous case

The algorithm presented in the previous section for n-gram kernels can be generalized to handle a wide variety of rational kernels.

Let K be an arbitrary rational kernel defined by a weighted transducer T. Let X_T denote the regular language of the strings output by T. We shall assume that X_T is a finite language, though the results of this section generalize to the infinite case. Let $\overline{\Sigma}$ denote a new alphabet defined by $\overline{\Sigma} = \{\#_x : x \in X_T\}$ and consider the simple grammar G of context-dependent batch rules:

$$\epsilon \to \#_x / x\_\epsilon. \quad (9)$$

Each such rule inserts the symbol $\#_x$ immediately after an occurrence x in the input string. For batch context-dependent rules, the context of the application for all rules is determined at once before their application (Kaplan and Kay, 1994). Assume that this grammar is *unambiguous* for a parallel application of the rules. This condition means that there is a unique way of parsing an input string using the strings of X_T. The assumption holds for n-gram sequences, for example, since the rules applicable are uniquely determined by the n-grams (making the previous section a special case).

Given an acyclic weighted automaton Y_2 over the tropical semiring accepting a subset of X_T, we can construct a deterministic weighted automaton Y_1 for $\Sigma^* L(Y_2)$ when this grammar is unambiguous. The weight assigned by Y_1 to an input string is then the sum of the weights of the substrings accepted by Y_2. This can be achieved using weighted determinization.

This suggests a new method for generalizing Step 2 of the algorithm described in the previous section as follows (see illustration in Figure 3):

(i) use Y_2 to construct a deterministic weighted tree Y_2' defined on the tropical semiring accepting the same strings as Y_2 with the same weights, with the final weights equal to the total weight given by Y_2 to the string ending at that leaf;

(ii) let Y_1 be the weighted automaton obtained by first adding self-loops labeled with all elements of Σ at the initial state of Y_2' and then determinizing it, and then inserting new transitions leaving final states as described in (Mohri and Sproat, 1996).

Step (ii) consists of computing a deterministic weighted automaton for $\Sigma^* Y_2'$. This step corresponds to the Aho-Corasick construction (Aho and Corasick, 1975) and can be done in time linear in the size of Y_2'.

This approach assumes that the grammar G of batch context-dependent rules inferred by X_T is unambiguous. This can be tested by constructing the finite automaton corresponding to all rules in G. The grammar G is unambiguous iff the resulting automaton is unambiguous (which can be tested using a classical algorithm). An alternative and more efficient test consists of checking the presence of a *failure* or *default* transition to a final state during the Aho-Corasick construction, which occurs if and only if there is ambiguity.

5 Application to Machine Translation

In machine translation, the BLEU score (Papineni et al., 2001) is typically used as an evaluation metric. In (Tromble et al., 2008), a Minimum Bayes-Risk decoding approach for MT lattices was introduced.[3] The loss function used in that approach was an approximation of the log-BLEU score by a linear function of n-gram matches and candidate length. This loss function corresponds to the following similarity measure:

$$K_{LB}(x, x') = \theta_0 |x'| + \sum_{|w| \le n} \theta_{|w|} c_x(w) 1_{x'}(w). \tag{10}$$

where $1_x(w)$ is 1 if w occurs in x and 0 otherwise.

(Tromble et al., 2008) implements the MBR decoder using weighted automata operations. First, the set of n-grams is extracted from the lattice. Next, the posterior probability $p(w|X)$ of each n-gram is computed. Starting with the unweighted lattice $A(H)$, the contribution of each n-gram w to (10) is applied by iteratively composing with the weighted automaton corresponding to $\overline{w}(w/(\theta_{|w|} p(w|X))\overline{w})^*$ where $\overline{w} = \Sigma^* \setminus (\Sigma^* w \Sigma^*)$. Finally, the MBR hypothesis is extracted as the best path in the automaton. The above steps are carried out one n-gram at a time. For a moderately large lattice, there can be several thousands of n-grams and the procedure becomes expensive. This leads us to investigate methods that do not require processing the n-grams one at a time in order to achieve greater efficiency.

[3]Related approaches were presented in (DeNero et al., 2009; Kumar et al., 2009; Li et al., 2009).

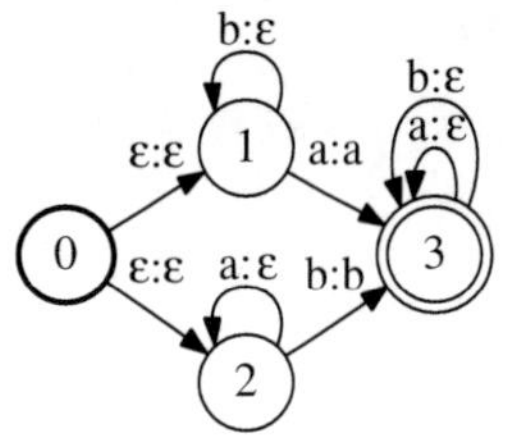

Figure 4: Transducer $\overline{T}_1$ over the real semiring for the alphabet $\{a, b\}$.

The first idea is to approximate the K_{LB} similarity measure using a weighted sum of n-gram kernels. This corresponds to approximating $1_{x'}(w)$ by $c_{x'}(w)$ in (10). This leads us to the following similarity measure:

$$\begin{aligned} K_{NG}(x, x') &= \theta_0 |x'| + \sum_{|w| \le n} \theta_{|w|} c_x(w) c_{x'}(w) \\ &= \theta_0 |x'| + \sum_{1 \le i \le n} \theta_i K_i(x, x') \end{aligned} \tag{11}$$

Intuitively, the larger the length of w the less likely it is that $c_x(w) \neq 1_x(w)$, which suggests computing the contribution to $K_{LB}(x, x')$ of lower-order n-grams ($|w| \le k$) exactly, but using the approximation by n-gram kernels for the higher-order n-grams ($|w| > k$). This gives the following similarity measure:

$$\begin{aligned} K_{NG}^k(x, x') = \theta_0 |x'| &+ \sum_{1 \le |w| \le k} \theta_{|w|} c_x(w) 1_{x'}(w) \\ &+ \sum_{k < |w| \le n} \theta_{|w|} c_x(w) c_{x'}(w) \end{aligned} \tag{12}$$

Observe that $K_{NG}^0 = K_{NG}$ and $K_{NG}^n = K_{LB}$.

All these similarity measures can still be computed using the framework described in Section 4. Indeed, there exists a transducer $\overline{T}_n$ over the real semiring such that $\overline{T}_n(x, z) = 1_x(z)$ for all $x \in \Sigma^*$ and $z \in \Sigma^n$. The transducer $\overline{T}_1$ for $\Sigma = \{a, b\}$ is given by Figure 4. Let us define the similarity measure $\overline{K}_n$ as:

$$\overline{K}_n(x, x') = (T_n \circ \overline{T}_n^{-1})(x, x') = \sum_{|w| = n} c_x(w) 1_{x'}(w). \tag{13}$$

Observe that the framework described in Section 4 can still be applied even though $\overline{K}_n$ is not symmetric. The similarity measures K_{LB}, K_{NG} and K_{NG}^k

	zhen					aren				
	nist02	nist04	nist05	nist06	nist08	nist02	nist04	nist05	nist06	nist08
no mbr	38.7	39.2	38.3	33.5	26.5	64.0	51.8	57.3	45.5	43.8
exact	37.0	39.2	38.6	34.3	27.5	65.2	51.4	58.1	45.2	45.0
approx	39.0	39.9	38.6	34.4	27.4	65.2	52.5	58.1	46.2	45.0
ngram	36.6	39.1	38.1	34.4	27.7	64.3	50.1	56.7	44.1	42.8
ngram1	37.1	39.2	38.5	34.4	27.5	65.2	51.4	58.0	45.2	44.8

Table 1: BLEU score (%)

	zhen					aren				
	nist02	nist04	nist05	nist06	nist08	nist02	nist04	nist05	nist06	nist08
exact	3560	7863	5553	6313	5738	12341	23266	11152	11417	11405
approx	168	422	279	335	328	504	1296	528	619	808
ngram	28	72	34	70	43	85	368	105	63	66
ngram1	58	175	96	99	89	368	943	308	167	191

Table 2: MBR Time (in seconds)

can then be expressed as the relevant linear combination of K_i and $\overline{K}_i$.

6 Experimental Results

Lattices were generated using a phrase-based MT system similar to the alignment template system described in (Och and Ney, 2004). Given a source sentence, the system produces a word lattice A that is a compact representation of a very large N-best list of translation hypotheses for that source sentence and their likelihoods. The lattice A is converted into a lattice X that represents a probability distribution (i.e. the posterior probability distribution given the source sentence) following:

$$X(x) = \frac{\exp(\alpha A(x))}{\sum_{y \in \Sigma^*} \exp(\alpha A(y))} \quad (14)$$

where the scaling factor $\alpha \in [0, \infty)$ flattens the distribution when $\alpha < 1$ and sharpens it when $\alpha > 1$. We then applied the methods described in Section 5 to the lattice X using as hypothesis set H the unweighted lattice obtained from X.

The following parameters for the n-gram factors were used:

$$\theta_0 = \frac{-1}{T} \text{ and } \theta_n = \frac{1}{4Tpr^{n-1}} \text{ for } n \geq 1. \quad (15)$$

Experiments were conducted on two language pairs Arabic-English (aren) and Chinese-English (zhen) and for a variety of datasets from the NIST Open Machine Translation (OpenMT) Evaluation.[4] The values of α, p and r used for each pair are given

	α	p	r
aren	0.2	0.85	0.72
zhen	0.1	0.80	0.62

Table 3: Parameters used for performing MBR.

in Table 3. We used the IBM implementation of the BLEU score (Papineni et al., 2001).

We implemented the following methods using the OpenFst library (Allauzen et al., 2007):

- *exact*: uses the similarity measure K_{LB} based on the linearized log-BLEU, implemented as described in (Tromble et al., 2008);
- *approx*: uses the approximation to K_{LB} from (Kumar et al., 2009) and described in the appendix;
- *ngram*: uses the similarity measure K_{NG} implemented using the algorithm of Section 4.2;
- *ngram1*: uses the similarity measure K^1_{NG} also implemented using the algorithm of Section 4.2.

The results from Tables 1-2 show that *ngram1* performs as well as *exact* on all datasets[5] while being two orders of magnitude faster than *exact* and overall more than 3 times faster than *approx*.

7 Conclusion

We showed that for broad families of transducers T and thus rational kernels, the expected similar-

[4]http://www.nist.gov/speech/tests/mt

[5]We consider BLEU score differences of less than 0.4% not significant (Koehn, 2004).

ity maximization problem can be solved efficiently. This opens up the option of seeking the most appropriate rational kernel or transducer T for the specific task considered. In particular, the kernel K used in our machine translation applications might not be optimal. One may well imagine for example that some n-grams should be further emphasized and others de-emphasized in the definition of the similarity. This can be easily accommodated in the framework of rational kernels by modifying the transition weights of T. But, ideally, one would wish to select those weights in an optimal fashion. As mentioned earlier, we leave this question to future work. However, we can offer a brief look at how one could tackle this question. One method for determining an optimal kernel for the expected similarity maximization problem consists of solving a problem similar to that of learning kernels in classification or regression. Let $X_1, \ldots, X_m$ be m lattices with $\text{Ref}(X_1), \ldots, \text{Ref}(X_m)$ the associated references and let $\widehat{x}(K, X_i)$ be the solution of the expected similarity maximization for lattice X_i when using kernel K. Then, the kernel learning optimization problem can be formulated as follows:

$$\min_{K \in \mathcal{K}} \frac{1}{m} \sum_{i=1}^{m} L(\widehat{x}(K, X_i), \text{Ref}(X_i))$$
$$\text{s. t. } K = T \circ T^{-1} \wedge \text{Tr}[K] \leq C,$$

where $\mathcal{K}$ is a convex family of rational kernels and $\text{Tr}[K]$ denotes the trace of the kernel matrix. In particular, we could choose $\mathcal{K}$ as a family of linear combinations of base rational kernels. Techniques and ideas similar to those discussed by Cortes et al. (2008) for learning sequence kernels could be directly relevant to this problem.

A Appendix

We describe here the approximation of the K_{LB} similarity measure from Kumar et al. (2009). We assume in this section that the lattice X is deterministic in order to simplify the notations. The posterior probability of n-gram w in the lattice X can be formulated as:

$$p(w|X) = \sum_{x \in \Sigma^*} 1_x(w) P(x|s) = \sum_{x \in \Sigma^*} 1_x(w) X(x) \quad (16)$$

where s denotes the source sentence. When using the similarity measure K_{LB} defined Equation (10), Equation (3) can then be reformulated as:

$$\widehat{x} = \operatorname*{argmax}_{x' \in H} \theta_0 |x'| + \sum_w \theta_{|w|} c_{x'}(w) p(w|X). \quad (17)$$

The key idea behind this new approximation algorithm is to rewrite the n-gram posterior probability (Equation 16) as follows:

$$p(w|X) = \sum_{x \in \Sigma^*} \sum_{e \in E_X} f(e, w, \pi_x) X(x) \quad (18)$$

where E_X is the set of transitions of X, π_x is the unique accepting path labeled by x in X and $f(e, w, \pi)$ is a score assigned to transition e on path π containing n-gram w:

$$f(e, w, \pi) = \begin{cases} 1 & \text{if } w \in e, p(e|X) > p(e'|X), \\ & \text{and } e' \text{ precedes } e \text{ on } \pi \\ 0 & \text{otherwise.} \end{cases} \quad (19)$$

In other words, for each path π, we count the transition that contributes n-gram w and has the highest transition posterior probability relative to its predecessors on the path π; there is exactly one such transition on each lattice path π.

We note that $f(e, w, \pi)$ relies on the full path π which means that it cannot be computed based on local statistics. We therefore approximate the quantity $f(e, w, \pi)$ with $f^*(e, w, X)$ that counts the transition e with n-gram w that has the highest arc posterior probability relative to predecessors in the entire lattice X. $f^*(e, w, X)$ can be computed locally, and the n-gram posterior probability based on f^* can be determined as follows:

$$\begin{aligned} p(w|\mathcal{G}) &= \sum_{x \in \Sigma^*} \sum_{e \in E_X} f^*(e, w, X) X(x) \\ &= \sum_{e \in E_x} 1_{w \in e} f^*(e, w, X) \sum_{x \in \Sigma^*} 1_{\pi_x}(e) X(x) \\ &= \sum_{e \in E_X} 1_{w \in e} f^*(e, w, X) P(e|X), \end{aligned} \quad (20)$$

where $P(e|X)$ is the posterior probability of a lattice transition $e \in E_X$. The algorithm to perform Lattice MBR is given in Algorithm 1. For each state t in the lattice, we maintain a quantity $\text{Score}(w, t)$ for each n-gram w that lies on a path from the initial state to t. $\text{Score}(w, t)$ is the highest posterior probability among all transitions on the paths that terminate on t and contain n-gram w. The forward pass requires computing the n-grams introduced by each transition; to do this, we propagate n-grams (up to maximum order -1) terminating on each state.

Algorithm 1 MBR Decoding on Lattices

Sort the lattice states topologically.
Compute backward probabilities of each state.
Compute posterior prob. of each n-gram:
for each transition e **do**
  Compute transition posterior probability $P(e|X)$.
  Compute n-gram posterior probs. $P(w|X)$:
  for each n-gram w introduced by e **do**
    Propagate $n-1$ gram suffix to h_e.
    if $p(e|X) > \text{Score}(w, T(e))$ **then**
      Update posterior probs. and scores:
      $p(w|X) \mathrel{+}= p(e|X) - \text{Score}(w, T(e))$.
      $\text{Score}(w, h_e) = p(e|X)$.
    else
      $\text{Score}(w, h_e) = \text{Score}(w, T(e))$.
    end if
  end for
end for
Assign scores to transitions (given by Equation 17).
Find best path in the lattice (Equation 17).

References

Alfred V. Aho and Margaret J. Corasick. 1975. Efficient String Matching: An Aid to Bibliographic Search. *Communications of the ACM*, 18(6):333–340.

Cyril Allauzen, Michael Riley, Johan Schalkwyk, Wojciech Skut, and Mehryar Mohri. 2007. OpenFst: a general and efficient weighted finite-state transducer library. In *CIAA 2007*, volume 4783 of *LNCS*, pages 11–23. Springer. http://www.openfst.org.

Christian Berg, Jens Peter Reus Christensen, and Paul Ressel. 1984. *Harmonic Analysis on Semigroups*. Springer-Verlag: Berlin-New York.

Peter J. Bickel and Kjell A. Doksum. 2001. *Mathematical Statistics, vol. I*. Prentice Hall.

Corinna Cortes, Patrick Haffner, and Mehryar Mohri. 2004. Rational Kernels: Theory and Algorithms. *Journal of Machine Learning Research*, 5:1035–1062.

Corinna Cortes, Mehryar Mohri, and Afshin Rostamizadeh. 2008. Learning sequence kernels. In *Proceedings of MLSP 2008*, October.

John DeNero, David Chiang, and Kevin Knight. 2009. Fast consensus decoding over translation forests. In *Proceedings of ACL and IJCNLP*, pages 567–575.

Vaibhava Goel and William J. Byrne. 2000. Minimum Bayes-risk automatic speech recognition. *Computer Speech and Language*, 14(2):115–135.

Ronald M. Kaplan and Martin Kay. 1994. Regular models of phonological rule systems. *Computational Linguistics*, 20(3).

Philipp Koehn. 2004. Statistical Significance Tests for Machine Translation Evaluation. In *EMNLP*, Barcelona, Spain.

Shankar Kumar and William J. Byrne. 2004. Minimum Bayes-risk decoding for statistical machine translation. In *HLT-NAACL*, Boston, MA, USA.

Shankar Kumar, Wolfgang Macherey, Chris Dyer, and Franz Och. 2009. Efficient minimum error rate training and minimum bayes-risk decoding for translation hypergraphs and lattices. In *Proceedings of the Association for Computational Linguistics and IJCNLP*.

Christina S. Leslie, Eleazar Eskin, and William Stafford Noble. 2002. The Spectrum Kernel: A String Kernel for SVM Protein Classification. In *Pacific Symposium on Biocomputing*, pages 566–575.

Zhifei Li, Jason Eisner, and Sanjeev Khudanpur. 2009. Variational decoding for statistical machine translation. In *Proceedings of ACL and IJCNLP*, pages 593–601.

Huma Lodhi, Craig Saunders, John Shawe-Taylor, Nello Cristianini, and Chris Watskins. 2002. Text classification using string kernels. *Journal of Machine Learning Research*, 2:419–44.

Mehryar Mohri and Richard Sproat. 1996. An Efficient Compiler for Weighted Rewrite Rules. In *Proceedings of ACL '96*, Santa Cruz, California.

Mehryar Mohri. 2009. Weighted automata algorithms. In Manfred Droste, Werner Kuich, and Heiko Vogler, editors, *Handbook of Weighted Automata*, chapter 6, pages 213–254. Springer.

Franz J. Och and Hermann Ney. 2004. The alignment template approach to statistical mchine translation. *Computational Linguistics*, 30(4):417–449.

Kishore Papineni, Salim Roukos, Todd Ward, and Wei-Jing Zhu. 2001. Bleu: a Method for Automatic Evaluation of Machine Translation. Technical Report RC22176 (W0109-022), IBM Research Division.

Arto Salomaa and Matti Soittola. 1978. *Automata-Theoretic Aspects of Formal Power Series*. Springer.

Roy W. Tromble, Shankar Kumar, Franz J. Och, and Wolfgang Macherey. 2008. Lattice minimum Bayes-risk decoding for statistical machine translation. In *Proceedings of the 2008 Conference on Empirical Methods in Natural Language Processing*, pages 620–629.

Accurate Non-Hierarchical Phrase-Based Translation

Michel Galley and **Christopher D. Manning**
Computer Science Department
Stanford University
Stanford, CA 94305
{mgalley,manning}@cs.stanford.edu

Abstract

A principal weakness of conventional (i.e., non-hierarchical) phrase-based statistical machine translation is that it can only exploit continuous phrases. In this paper, we extend phrase-based decoding to allow both source and target phrasal discontinuities, which provide better generalization on unseen data and yield significant improvements to a standard phrase-based system (Moses). More interestingly, our discontinuous phrase-based system also outperforms a state-of-the-art hierarchical system (Joshua) by a very significant margin (+1.03 BLEU on average on five Chinese-English NIST test sets), even though both Joshua and our system support discontinuous phrases. Since the key difference between these two systems is that ours is not hierarchical—i.e., our system uses a string-based decoder instead of CKY, and it imposes no hard hierarchical reordering constraints during training and decoding—this paper sets out to challenge the commonly held belief that the tree-based parameterization of systems such as Hiero and Joshua is crucial to their good performance against Moses.

1 Introduction

Phrase-based machine translation models (Och and Ney, 2004) advanced the state of the art by extending the basic translation unit from words to phrases. By conditioning translations on more than a single word, a statistical machine translation (SMT) system benefits from the larger context of a phrase pair to properly handle multi-word units and local reorderings. Experimentally, it was found that longer phrases yield better MT output (Koehn et al., 2003). However, while it is computationally feasible at training time to extract phrase pairs of nearly unbounded size (Zhang and Vogel, 2005; Callison-Burch et al., 2005), phrase pairs applicable at test time tend to be fairly short. Indeed, data sparsity often forces conventional phrase-based systems to segment test sentences into small phrases, and therefore to translate dependent words (e.g., the French *ne ... pas*) separately instead of jointly.

We present a solution to this sparsity problem by going beyond using only *continuous phrases*, and instead define our translation unit as any subset of words of a sentence, i.e., a *discontinuous phrase*. We generalize conventional multi-beam string-based decoding (Koehn, 2004) to allow variable-size discontinuities in both source and target phrases. Since each sentence pair can be more flexibly decomposed into translation units, it is possible to exploit the rich context of longer (possibly discontinuous) phrases to improve translation quality. Our decoder provides two extensions to Moses (Koehn et al., 2007): (a) to cope with source gaps, we follow (Lopez, 2007) to efficiently find all discontinuous phrases in the training data that also appear in the input sentence; (b) to enable target discontinuities, we augment translation hypotheses to not only record the current partial translation, but also a set of subphrases that may be appended to the partial translation at some later stages of decoding. With these enhancements, our best discontinuous system outperforms Moses with lexicalized reordering by 0.77 BLEU and 1.53 TER points on average.

We also show that our approach compares favorably to binary synchronous context-free grammar (2-SCFG) systems such as Hiero (Chiang, 2007), even though 2-SCFG systems also allow phrasal discontinuities. Part of this difference may be due to a difference of expressiveness, since 2-SCFG models impose hard hierarchical constraints that our models do not impose. Recent work (Wellington et al., 2006; Søgaard and Kuhn, 2009; Søgaard and

Human Language Technologies: The 2010 Annual Conference of the North American Chapter of the ACL, pages 966–974,
Los Angeles, California, June 2010. ©2010 Association for Computational Linguistics

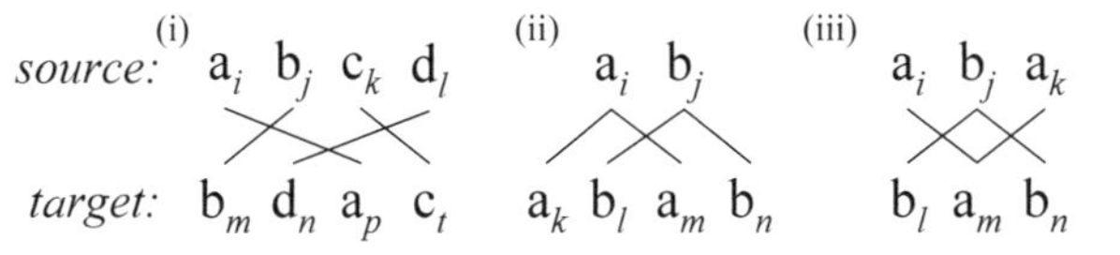

Figure 1: 2-SCFG systems such as Hiero are unable to independently generate translation units **a**, **b**, **c**, and **d** with the following types of alignments: (i) inside-out (Wu, 1997); (ii) cross-serial DTU (Søgaard and Kuhn, 2009); (iii) "bonbon" (Simard et al., 2005). Standard phrase-based decoders cope with (i), but not (ii) and (iii). Our phrase-based decoder handles all three cases.

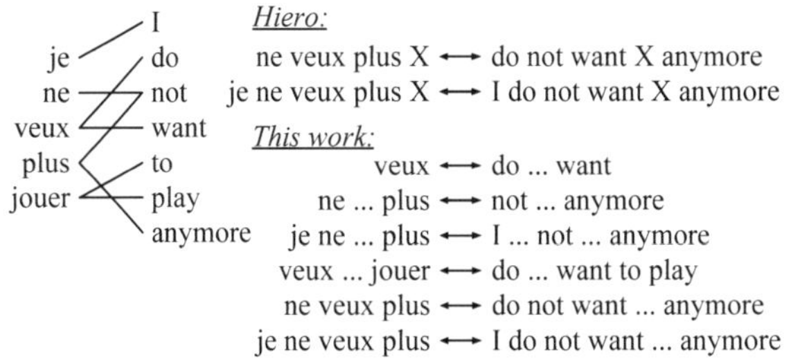

Figure 2: Due to hierarchical constraints, Hiero only extracts two discontinuous phrases from the alignment on the left, but our system extracts 11 (only 6 are shown).

Wu, 2009) has questioned the empirical adequacy of 2-SCFG systems, which are unable to perform any of the transformations shown in Fig. 1. For instance, using manually-aligned bitexts for 12 European languages pairs, Søgaard and Kuhn found that inside-out and cross-serial discontinuous translation units (DTU) account for 1.6% (Danish-English) to 18.6% (French-English) of all translation units. The empirical adequacy of 2-SCFG models would presumably be lower with automatically-aligned texts and if the study also included non-European languages. In contrast, phrase based systems can properly handle inside-out alignments when used with a reasonably large distortion limit, and all configurations in Fig. 1 are accounted for in our system. In our experiments, we show that our discontinuous phrase-based system outperforms Joshua (Li et al., 2009), a reimplementation of Hiero, by 1.03 BLEU points and 1.19 TER points on average. A final compelling advantage of our decoder is that it preserves the computational efficiency of Moses (i.e., time complexity is linear when a distortion limit is used), while SCFG decoders have a running time that is at least cubic (Huang et al., 2005).

2 Discontinuous Phrase Extraction

In this section, we introduce the extraction of discontinuous phrases for phrase-based MT. We will describe a decoder that can handle such phrases in the next section. Formally, we define the discontinuous phrase-based translation problem as follows. We are given a source sentence $\mathbf{f} = f_1^J = f_1, \ldots, f_j, \ldots, f_J$, which is to be translated into a target sentence $\mathbf{e} = e_1^I = e_1, \ldots, e_i, \ldots, f_I$. Unlike (Och and Ney, 2004), in this work, a sentence pair may be segmented into phrases that are not continuous, so each phrase is characterized by a coverage set, i.e., a set of word indices. Assuming that the sentence pair $(\mathbf{f}, \mathbf{e})$ is decomposed into K discontinuous phrases, we use $\mathbf{s} = (s_1, \ldots, s_K)$ and $\mathbf{t} = (t_1, \ldots, t_K)$ to respectively represent the decomposition of the source and target sentence into K word subsets that are complementary and non-overlapping. A pair of coverage sets (s_k, t_k) is said to be *consistent* with the word alignment A if the following condition holds:

$$\forall (i,j) \in A : i \in s_k \longleftrightarrow j \in t_k \quad (1)$$

For continuous phrases, finding all phrase pairs that satisfy this condition can be done in $O(nm^3)$ time (Och and Ney, 2004), where n is the length of the sentence and m is the maximum phrase length. The set of discontinuous phrases is exponential in the maximum span length, so phrase extraction must be tailored to a specific text (e.g., a given test sentence) for relatively large m values. Lopez (2007) presents an efficient solution using suffix arrays for finding all discontinuous phrases of the training data that are relevant to a given test sentence or test set. A complete overview of this technique is beyond the scope of this paper, though we will mention that it solves a phrase collocation problem by efficiently identifying collocated continuous phrases of the training data that also happen to be collocated in the test sentence. While this technique was primarily designed for extracting *hierarchical phrases* for Hiero (Chiang, 2007), it can readily be applied to the problem of finding all discontinuous phrases for our phrase-based system. Indeed, the suffix-array technique gives us for each input sentence a list of relevant source coverage sets. For each such s_k, we can easily enumerate each t_k satisfying Eq. 1. The

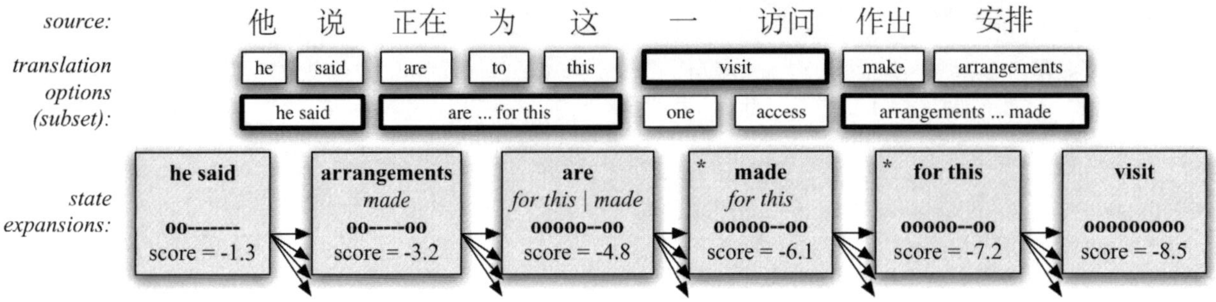

Figure 3: A particular decoder search path for the input shown at the top. Note that this example contains a cross-serial DTU (which interleaves *arrangements ... made* with *are ... for this*), a structure Hiero can't handle.

key difference between Hiero-style extraction and our work is that Eq. 1 is the *only* constraint.[1] Since our decoder doesn't impose hierarchical constraints, we exploit *all* discontinuous phrase pairs consistent with the word alignment, which often includes sound translations not captured by Hiero (e.g., *ne ... plus* translating to *not ... anymore* in Fig. 2).

3 Decoder

The core engine of our phrase-based system, Phrasal (Cer et al., 2010), is a multi-stack decoder similar to Moses (Koehn, 2004), which we extended to support variable-size gaps in the source and the target. In Moses, partial translation hypotheses are arranged into different stacks according to the total number of input words they cover. At every translation step, stacks are pruned using partial translation cost and a lower bound on the estimated future cost. Pruning is implemented using both threshold and histogram pruning, and Moses allows for hypothesis recombination between hypotheses that are indistinguishable according to the underlying models.

The key difference between Moses and our system is that, in order to account for target discontinuities, phrases that contains gaps in the target are appended to a partial translation hypothesis in multiple steps. Specifically, each translation hypothesis in our decoder is not only represented as a translation prefix and a coverage set as in Moses, but it also contains a set of isolated phrases (shown in italic in Fig. 3) that must be added to the translation at some later time. For instance, the figure shows how the phrase pair (作出安排, *arrangements ... made*) is being added to a partial translation. The prefix (*arrangements*) is immediately appended to form the hypothesis (*he said arrangements*), and the isolated phrase (*made*) is stored for later use.

Beam search algorithm.

1 create initial hypothesis $H_\emptyset$; add it to S^g_0
2 **for** $j = 0$ **to** J
3   **if** $j > 0$ **then**
4   **for** $n = 1$ **to** N
5   **for each** H_{new} **in** consolidate(H^c_{jn})
6   add H_{new} to S^g_j
7   **if** $j < J$ **then**
8   **for** $n = 1$ **to** N
9       $H_{old} := H^g_{jn}$
10       $u :=$ first uncovered source word of H_{old}
11   **for** $m = u$ **to** $u + distortionLimit$
12   **for each** (s_k, t_k) **in** translation_options(m)
13   **if** source s_k does not overlap H_{old} **then**
14             $H_{new} :=$combine(H_{old}, s_k, t_k)
15   add H_{new} to S^c_{j+l}, where $l = |s_k|$
16 **return** $\arg\max(S^g_J)$

Table 1: Discontinuous phrase-based MT.

A beam search algorithm for discontinuous phrase-based MT is shown in Table 1. Pruning is done implicitly in the table to avoid cluttering the pseudo-code. The algorithm handles $2J + 1$ stacks $S^g_0, S^g_1, \ldots, S^g_J$ and $S^c_1, \ldots, S^c_J$, where each stack may contain up to N hypotheses $H_{j1}, \ldots, H_{jN}$. The main loop of the algorithm alternates two stages: grow (lines 7–15) and consolidate (lines 3–6).[2] The grow stage is similar to standard phrase-

[1] In order to keep the number of phrases manageable, we additionally require that each (maximal) contiguous substring of s_k and t_k be connected with at least one word alignment.

[2] The distinction between S^g_i and S^c_i stacks ensures that the consolidate operation does not read and write hypotheses on the same stack. While it may seem effective to store hypotheses in

based MT: we take a hypothesis H^g_{jn} from S^g_j and combine it with a translation option (s_k, t_k), which yields a new hypothesis that is added to stack S^c_{j+l} (where $l = |s_k|$). The second stage, consolidate, lets the decoder select any number of isolated phrases (not necessarily all, and possibly zero) and append them in any order at the end of the current translation.[3] Consolidation operations are marked with stars in the figure (for simplicity, the figure does not display consolidations that keep hypotheses unchanged). We limit the number of isolated phrases to 4, which is generally enough to account for most transformations seen in the data. Any hypothesis in the last beam S^g_J is automatically discarded if it contains any isolated phrase.

One last difference with standard decoders is that we also handle source discontinuities. This problem is a known instance of MT by pattern matching (Lopez, 2007), which we already mentioned in the previous section. The function translation_options(m) of Table 1 returns the set of options applicable at position m using this pattern matching algorithm. Since this function is invoked a large number of times, it is important to precompute its return values for each m prior to decoding.

4 Features

Our system incorporates the same eight baseline features of Moses: two relative-frequency phrase translation probabilities $p(e|f)$ and $p(f|e)$, two lexically-weighted phrase translation probabilities (Koehn et al., 2003) $lex(e|f)$ and $lex(f|e)$, a language model probability, word penalty, phrase penalty, and linear distortion, and we optionally add 6 lexicalized reordering features as computed in Moses.

Our computation of linear distortion is different from the one in Moses, since we need to account for discontinuous phrases. We found that it is crucial to penalize discontinuous phrases that have relatively long gaps. Hence, in our computation of

different stacks depending on the number of isolated phrases, we have not found various implementations of this idea to work better than the algorithm described here.

[3]We let isolated phrases be reordered freely, with only three constraints: (1) the internal word order must be preserved, i.e., a phrase may not be split or reordered. (2) isolated phrases drawn from the same discontinuous phrase must appear in the specified order (i.e., the phrase *A* ... *B* ... *C* may not yield the translation *A* ... *C* ... *B*). (3) Empty gaps are forbidden.

5 Experimental Setup

Three systems are evaluated in this paper: Moses (Koehn et al., 2007), Joshua (Li et al., 2009) – a reimplementation of Hiero, and our phrase-based system. We made our best attempts to make our system comparable to Moses. That is, when no discontinuous phrases are provided to our system, it generates an output that is almost identical to Moses (only about 1% of translations differ on average). In both systems, we use the default settings of Moses, i.e., we set the beam size to 200, the distortion limit to 6, we limit to 20 the number of target phrases that are loaded for each source phrase, and we use the same default eight features of Moses. We use version 1.3 of Joshua with its default settings. Both Moses and our system are evaluated with and without lexicalized reordering (Tillmann, 2004).[4] We believe it to be fair to compare Joshua against phrase-based systems that exploit lexicalized reordering, since Hiero's hierarchical rules are also lexically sensitive.[5]

The language pair for our experiments is Chinese-to-English. The training data consists of about 28 million English words and 23.3 million Chinese words drawn from various news parallel corpora distributed by the Linguistic Data Consortium (LDC). In order to provide experiments comparable to previous work, we used the same corpora as (Wang et al., 2007). We performed word alignment using a cross-EM word aligner (Liang et al., 2006). For this, we ran two iterations of IBM Model 1 and two HMM iterations. Finally, we generated a symmetric word alignment from cross-EM Viterbi alignment using the Moses grow-diag heuristic in the case Moses and our system. In the case of Joshua, we used the grow-diag-final heuristic since this gave better results.

In order to train a competitive baseline given our computational resources, we built a large 5-gram language model using the Xinhua and AFP sections of the Gigaword corpus (LDC2007T40) in addition to the target side of the parallel data. This data represents a total of about 700 million words. We manually removed documents of Gigaword that were released during periods that overlap with those of our development and test sets. The language model was smoothed with the modified Kneser-Ney algorithm as implemented in SRILM (Stolcke, 2002), and we only kept 4-grams and 5-grams that occurred at least three times in the training data.

For tuning and testing, we use the official NIST MT evaluation data for Chinese from 2003 to 2008 (MT03 to MT08), which all have four English references for each input sentence. We used the 1664 sentences of MT06 for tuning and development and all other sets for testing. Parameter tuning was done with minimum error rate training (Och, 2003), which was used to maximize IBM BLEU-4 (Papineni et al., 2001). Since MERT is prone to search errors, especially with large numbers of parameters, we ran each tuning experiment four times with different initial conditions. We used n-best lists of size 200. In the final evaluations, we report results using both TER version 0.7.25 (Snover et al., 2006) and BLEU-4 (both uncased).

6 Results

We start by comparing some translations generated by the best configurations of Joshua, Moses, and our phrase-based decoder, systems we will empirically evaluate later in this section. Fig. 5 shows translations of our development set MT06, which were selected because our system makes a crucial use of discontinuous phrases. In the first example, the Chinese input contains 当 ... 时, which typically translates as *when*. Lacking an entry for the input phrase 当生命权被剥夺时 in its phrase table, Moses is unable to translate this segment appropriately, and must instead split this phrase to generate the translation *when the right was deprived of*, where 时 is translated into *of*. This is evidently a poor translation. Conversely, our system uses a discontinuous phrase to translate 当 ... 时, and translates the intervening words separately.

The remaining three translations all contain cross-serial DTUs (Søgaard and Kuhn, 2009) and thus would be difficult to generate using 2-SCFG systems. The second example motivates the idea

[4]We use Moses' default orientations: monotone, swap, and discontinuous. As far as this reordering model is concerned, we treat discontinuous phrases as continuous, i.e., we simply ignore what lies within gaps to determine phrase orientation.

[5](Tillmann, 2004) learns for each phrase a tendency to either remain monotone or to swap with other phrases. As noted in (Lopez, 2008), Hiero can represent the same information with hierarchical rules of the form uX, Xu, and XuX. Hiero actually models lexicalized reordering patterns that (Tillmann, 2004) does not account for, e.g., a transformation from X_1uX_2v to $X_2u'v'X_1$.

MT06 — segment 1589

Reference: Under such circumstances, when the right of existence was deprived, the only way remaining was to overthrow the existing dynasty by force and try to replace it.	*Joshua:* Under such circumstances, when life be deprived, can only resort to violence to overthrow the current dynasty, trying to replace,	*Moses:* Under such circumstances, when the right was deprived of, can only adopt the means of violence, in an attempt to overthrow the present dynasty replaced,	*This work:* Under such circumstances, when he was deprived of the right to life, it can only resort to violence in an attempt to overthrow the current dynasty replaced,

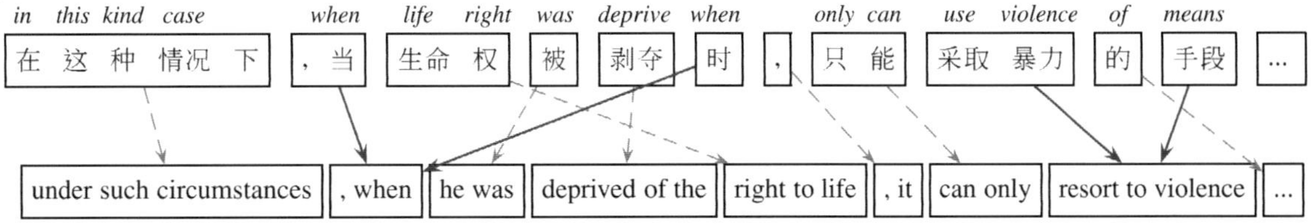

MT06 — segment 1044

Reference: CCP organization ministry demands to further enlarge strength of supervision of leading cadres and cadre selection and appointment	*Joshua:* Department demands further intensify supervision over the work of selecting and appointing leading cadres, and intensify	*Moses:* The central organization department, called on leading cadres, further increase the intensity of supervision over work of selecting and appointing cadres.	*This work:* The central organization department has called for further increase the intensity of supervision of leading cadres and the work of selecting and appointing cadres.

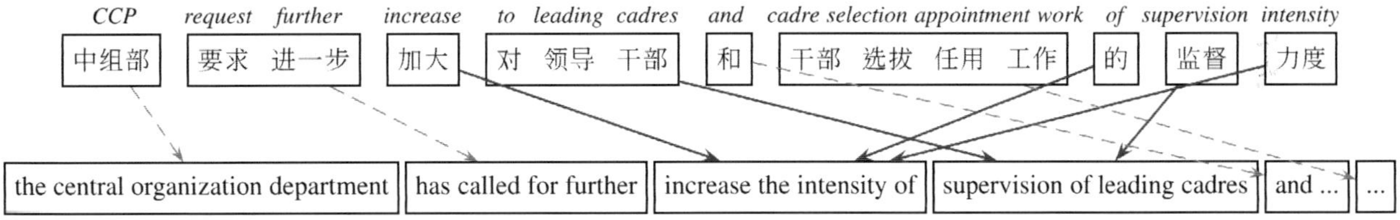

MT06 — segment 559

Reference: The government will take all possible measures to prevent similar incidents from happening in the future.	*Joshua:* Government will take all measures to prevent the re-occurrence of similar incidents in the future.	*Moses:* The government will take all measures to prevent the occurrence of similar incidents in the future.	*This work:* The government will take all measures to prevent similar incidents from happening again in the future.

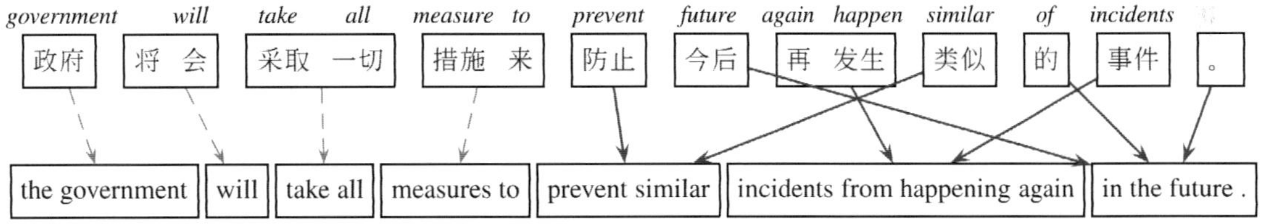

MT06 — segment 769

Reference: He also said that the arrangements are being made now for the visits.	*Joshua:* He also said that now is making arrangements for this visit.	*Moses:* He also said that the current visit is to make arrangements.	*This work:* He also said that the current arrangements are made for the visit.

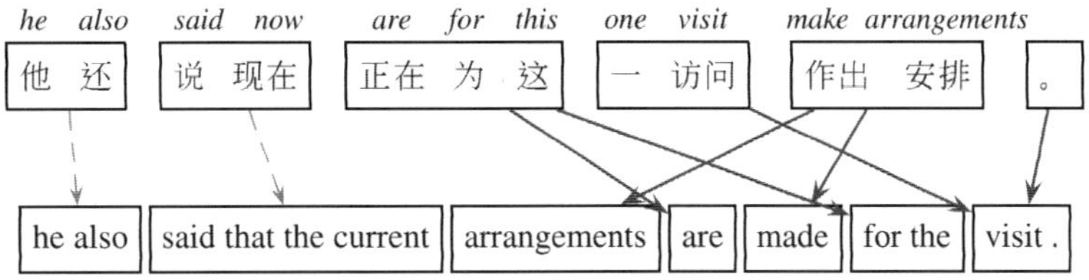

Figure 5: Actual translations produced by Joshua, Moses, and our system. For our system, we also display phrase alignments, including discontinuous phrase alignments. Results for these three systems here are displayed in rows 2, 4, and 8 of Table 2. The thick blue arrows represent alignments between discontinuous phrases, while red segmented arrows align continuous phrases.

	System	Gaps	LexR	MT06 (tune)		MT03		MT04		MT05		MT08		ALL	
				BLEU	TER	BLEU	TER	BLEU	TER	BLEU	TER	BLEU	TER	BLEU	TER
1	hierarchical	src	yes	33.55	58.04	33.25	59.73	36.03	58.92	32.03	61.11	26.30	61.30	31.70	58.21
2	(Joshua)	src+tgt	yes	33.84	58.11	33.47	59.85	36.10	58.82	32.17	61.20	26.61	61.21	31.90	58.22
3	phrase-based	no	no	33.17	59.24	32.60	60.80	35.38	59.55	31.15	62.43	25.56	61.98	31.08	59.14
4	(Moses)	no	yes	34.25	58.23	33.72	60.42	36.37	59.18	32.49	61.80	26.70	61.48	32.16	58.56
5	discontinuous phrase-based (this work)	src	no	33.77	58.56	33.20	60.42	36.17	59.13	31.75	61.62	25.99	61.47	31.68	58.60
6		tgt	no	33.27	58.98	32.95	60.42	35.41	59.35	31.08	62.45	25.69	61.71	31.17	58.93
7		src+tgt	no	33.86	58.26	33.32	60.02	36.36	58.56	31.87	61.35	26.13	61.29	31.81	58.25
8		src+tgt	yes	35.00	56.85	34.96	57.97	37.44	57.61	33.39	59.92	26.74	60.51	32.93	57.03
Improvement over hierarchical				**+1.16**	**−1.26**	**+1.49**	**−1.88**	**+1.34**	**−1.21**	**+1.22**	**−1.28**	+0.13	**−0.70**	**+1.03**	**−1.19**
Improvement over phrase-based				**+0.75**	**−1.38**	**+1.24**	**−2.45**	**+1.07**	**−1.57**	**+0.90**	**−1.88**	+0.04	**−0.97**	**+0.77**	**−1.53**
Number of sentences				*1664*		*919*		*1788*		*1082*		*1357*		*6810*	

Table 2: Our system compared again conventional and hierarchical phrase-based MT (Moses and Joshua). using uncased BLEUr4n4[%] and TER[%]. LexR indicates whether lexicalized reordering is enabled or not. We use randomization tests (Riezler and Maxwell, 2005) to determine significance of our best results (row 8) against Joshua (row 2) and Moses (row 4): differences marked in bold are significant at the $p \leq .01$ level.

that larger translation units, including discontinuous phrases, lead to better translations. The reference includes the translation *enlarge strength of supervision of leading cadres*, and our system is able to produce a translation that is almost identical (*increase the intensity of supervision of leading cadres*) using only two phrases, pulling together input words that are fairly far apart in the sentence. The third Chinese sentence has a word order quite different from English, but our decoder flexibly reorders it in a manner that can't be handled with SCFG decoders to give a word order (*prevent similar events from happening*) that matches the one in the reference. The last Chinese sentence includes the topicalization word 为 (*for*), which indicates the input sentence has no subject. One way to properly handle this translation is to turn the sentence into a passive in English (as in the reference), a transformation our system does, thanks to its support for complex reorderings.

Our main results are displayed in Table 2. First, Joshua systematically outperforms the Moses baseline (+0.82 BLEU point and −0.92 TER point on average), but performance of the two is about the same when Moses incorporates lexicalized reordering. This finding is consistent with previous work (Lopez, 2008). The results of our system displayed in rows 5–8 demonstrate that our system consistently outperforms Moses, whether they both use lexicalized reordering or not. The performance of our best system—i.e., with lexicalized reordering and both source and target gaps—is significantly better than the best Moses system (+0.77 BLEU and −1.53 TER). While the performance of our system without lexicalized reordering is close to that of Joshua, our system with lexicalized reordering significantly outperforms Joshua ($p \leq .01$) in 9 out of 10 evaluations. The single experiment where our improvement over Hiero is insignificant (i.e., BLEU on MT08) is mainly affected by a discrepancy of length (our brevity penalty on MT08 is 0.92).

It is interesting to notice that our system allowing phrasal discontinuities only on the source (row 5) performs almost as well as the system that allows them on both sides (row 7). For instance, while source discontinuities improve performance by 0.7 BLEU point on MT06, further enabling target discontinuities only raises performance by a mere 0.09 BLEU point. This naturally raises the question of whether our support for target gaps is ineffective, or whether target-discontinuous phrases are somewhat superfluous to the MT task. While it is certainly difficult to either confirm or deny the latter hypothesis, we can at least compare our handling of target-discontinuous phrases with hierarchical systems. In one additional set of experiments, we removed target-discontinuous phrases in Joshua prior to MERT and test time. Specifically, we removed all hierarchical phrases whose target side has the form uXv, $uXvX$, $XuXv$, and $uXvXw$, and only allowed rules whose target side has the form uX, Xu, XuX, XXu, or uXX. After this filtering, we found that target-discontinuous phrases in Joshua are also not crucial to its performance, since their removal only caused a drop of 0.2 BLEU point (row 1) and almost no change in terms of TER. We speculate that using target discontinuous phrases is more diffi-

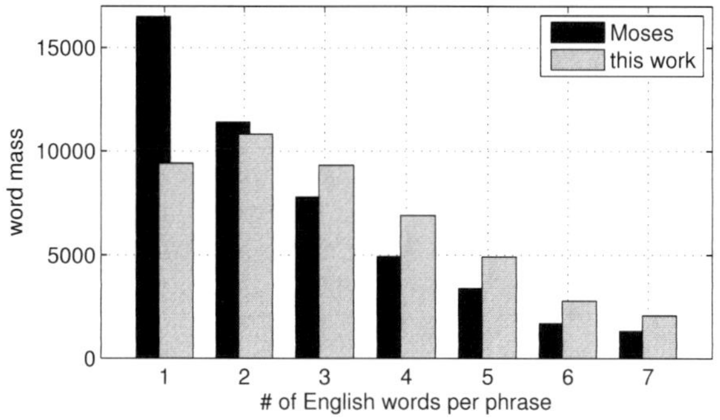

Figure 6: Phrase length histogram for MT06.

cult, since it represents a generation rather than just a matching problem.

In this paper, we have also argued that a main benefit of discontinuous phrases—and particularly source-discontinuous phrases—is that the decoder is allowed to use larger translation units than when restricted to continuous phrases. This claim is confirmed in Fig. 6. We find that our decoder makes effective use of the extended set of translation options at its disposal: While the Moses baseline translates MT06 with an average 1.73 words per phrase, adding support for discontinuities increases this average to 2.16, and reduces by 43% the use of single word phrases. On MT06, 53% of the translated sentences produced by our best system use at least one source-discontinuous phrase, and 9% of them exploit one or more target-discontinuous phrases.

7 Related Work

The main goal of this paper is to show that discontinuous phrases can greatly improve the performance of phrase-based systems. While some of the most recent phrase-based systems (Chiang, 2007; Watanabe et al., 2006) exploit context-free decoding algorithms (CKY, Earley, etc.) to cope with discontinuities, our system preserves the simplicity and speed of conventional phrase-based decoders, and in particular does not build any intermediate tree structure, does not impose any hard reordering constraints other than the distortion limit, and still achieves translation performance that is superior to that of a state-of-the-art hierarchical system.

A few previous non-hierarchical systems have also exploited phrasal discontinuities. The most notable previous attempt to incorporate gaps is described in (Simard et al., 2005). Simard et al. presents an extension to Moses that allows gaps in both source and target phrases, though each of their gap symbols must span exactly one word. This fact makes decoding simpler, since the position of all target words in a translation hypothesis is known as soon as the hypothesis is laid down, but fixed-size discontinuous phrases are less general and increase sparsity. By comparison, our gaps may span any number of words, so we have an increased ability to flexibly match the input sentence effectively. (Crego and Yvon, 2009) also handles gaps, though this work is applicable to an n-gram-based SMT framework (Mariòo et al., 2006), which is fairly different from the phrase-based framework.

8 Conclusions

In this paper, we presented a generalization of conventional phrase-based decoding to handle discontinuities in both source and target phrases. Our system significantly outperforms Moses and Joshua, two standard implementations of conventional and hierarchical phrase-based decoding. We found that allowing discontinuities in the source is more useful than target discontinuities in our system, though we found that this turns out to also be the case with the hierarchical phrases of Joshua. In future work, we plan to extend the parameterization of phrase-based lexicalized reordering models to be sensitive to these discontinuities, and we will also consider adding syntactic features to our models to penalize discontinuities that are not syntactically motivated (Marton and Resnik, 2008; Chiang et al., 2009). The discontinuous phrase-based MT system described in this work is part of Phrasal, an open-source phrase-based system available for download at http://nlp.stanford.edu/software/phrasal.

Acknowledgements

The authors thank three anonymous reviewers, Dan Jurafsky, Spence Green, Steven Bethard, Daniel Cer, Chris Callison-Burch, and Pi-Chuan Chang for their helpful comments. This paper is based on work funded by the Defense Advanced Research Projects Agency through IBM. The content does not necessarily reflect the views of the U.S. Government, and no official endorsement should be inferred.

References

Chris Callison-Burch, Colin Bannard, and Josh Schroeder. 2005. Scaling phrase-based statistical machine translation to larger corpora and longer phrases. In *Proc. of ACL*, pages 255–262.

Daniel Cer, Michel Galley, Dan Jurafsky, and Christopher Manning. 2010. Phrasal: A statistical machine translation toolkit for exploring new model features. In *Proc. of NAACL-HLT, Demonstration Session*.

David Chiang, Kevin Knight, and Wei Wang. 2009. 11,001 new features for statistical machine translation. In *Proc. of NAACL*, pages 218–226.

David Chiang. 2007. Hierarchical phrase-based translation. *Computational Linguistics*, 33(2):201–228.

Josep Crego and François Yvon. 2009. Gappy translation units under left-to-right SMT decoding. In *Proc. of EAMT*.

Liang Huang, Hao Zhang, and Daniel Gildea. 2005. Machine translation as lexicalized parsing with hooks. In *Proc. of the Ninth International Workshop on Parsing Technology*, pages 65–73.

Philipp Koehn, Franz Josef Och, and Daniel Marcu. 2003. Statistical phrase-based translation. In *Proc. of NAACL*, pages 48–54.

Philipp Koehn, Hieu Hoang, Alexandra Birch Mayne, Christopher Callison-Burch, Marcello Federico, Nicola Bertoldi, Brooke Cowan, Wade Shen, Christine Moran, Richard Zens, Chris Dyer, Ondrej Bojar, Alexandra Constantin, and Evan Herbst. 2007. Moses: Open source toolkit for statistical machine translation. In *Proc. of ACL, Demonstration Session*.

Philipp Koehn. 2004. Pharaoh: a beam search decoder for phrase-based statistical machine translation models. In *Proc. of AMTA*, pages 115–124.

Zhifei Li, Chris Callison-Burch, Chris Dyer, Juri Ganitkevitch, Sanjeev Khudanpur, Lane Schwartz, Wren N. G. Thornton, Jonathan Weese, and Omar F. Zaidan. 2009. Joshua: an open source toolkit for parsing-based MT. In *Proc. of WMT*.

Percy Liang, Ben Taskar, and Dan Klein. 2006. Alignment by agreement. In *Proc. of HLT-NAACL*, pages 104–111.

Adam Lopez. 2007. Hierarchical phrase-based translation with suffix arrays. In *Proc. of EMNLP-CoNLL*, pages 976–985.

Adam Lopez. 2008. Tera-scale translation models via pattern matching. In *Proc. of COLING*.

José B. Mariòo, Rafael E. Banchs, Josep M. Crego, Adrià de Gispert, Patrik Lambert, José A. R. Fonollosa, and Marta R. Costa-jussà. 2006. N-gram-based machine translation. *Computational Linguistics*, 32(4):527–549.

Yuval Marton and Philip Resnik. 2008. Soft syntactic constraints for hierarchical phrased-based translation. In *Proc. of ACL*, pages 1003–1011.

Franz Josef Och and Hermann Ney. 2004. The alignment template approach to statistical machine translation. *Computational Linguistics*, 30(4):417–449.

Franz Josef Och. 2003. Minimum error rate training for statistical machine translation. In *Proc. of ACL*.

Kishore Papineni, Salim Roukos, Todd Ward, and Wei-Jing Zhu. 2001. BLEU: a method for automatic evaluation of machine translation. In *Proc. of ACL*.

Stefan Riezler and John T. Maxwell. 2005. On some pitfalls in automatic evaluation and significance testing for MT. In *Proc. of Workshop on Evaluation Measures*, pages 57–64.

Michel Simard, Nicola Cancedda, Bruno Cavestro, Marc Dymetman, Eric Gaussier, Cyril Goutte, Kenji Yamada, Philippe Langlais, and Arne Mauser. 2005. Translating with non-contiguous phrases. In *Proc. of HLT-EMNLP*, pages 755–762.

Matthew Snover, Bonnie Dorr, Richard Schwartz, Linnea Micciulla, and John Makhoul. 2006. A study of translation edit rate with targeted human annotation. In *Proc. of AMTA*, pages 223–231.

Anders Søgaard and Jonas Kuhn. 2009. Empirical lower bounds on alignment error rates in syntax-based machine translation. In *Proc. of the Third Workshop on Syntax and Structure in Statistical Translation (SSST-3) at NAACL HLT 2009*, pages 19–27.

Anders Søgaard and Dekai Wu. 2009. Empirical lower bounds on translation unit error rate for the full class of inversion transduction grammars. In *Proc. of IWPT*, pages 33–36.

Andreas Stolcke. 2002. SRILM – an extensible language modeling toolkit. In *Proc. of ICSLP*, pages 901–904.

Christoph Tillmann. 2004. A unigram orientation model for statistical machine translation. In *Proc. of HLT-NAACL*, pages 101–104.

Chao Wang, Michael Collins, and Philipp Koehn. 2007. Chinese syntactic reordering for statistical machine translation. In *Proc. of EMNLP-CoNLL*.

Taro Watanabe, Hajime Tsukada, and Hideki Isozaki. 2006. Left-to-right target generation for hierarchical phrase-based translation. In *Proc. of ACL*.

Benjamin Wellington, Sonjia Waxmonsky, and I. Dan Melamed. 2006. Empirical lower bounds on the complexity of translational equivalence. In *Proc. of COLING-ACL*, pages 977–984.

Dekai Wu. 1997. Stochastic inversion transduction grammars and bilingual parsing of parallel corpora. *Computational Linguistics*, 23(3):377–404.

Ying Zhang and Stephan Vogel. 2005. An efficient phrase-to-phrase alignment model for arbitrarily long phrase and large corpora. In *Proc. of EAMT*.

Model Combination for Machine Translation

John DeNero,
UC Berkeley
denero@berkeley.edu

Shankar Kumar, Ciprian Chelba, and **Franz Och**
Google, Inc.
{shankarkumar,ciprianchelba,och}@google.com

Abstract

Machine translation benefits from two types of decoding techniques: consensus decoding over multiple hypotheses under a single model and system combination over hypotheses from different models. We present *model combination*, a method that integrates consensus decoding and system combination into a unified, forest-based technique. Our approach makes few assumptions about the underlying component models, enabling us to combine systems with heterogenous structure. Unlike most system combination techniques, we reuse the search space of component models, which entirely avoids the need to align translation hypotheses. Despite its relative simplicity, model combination improves translation quality over a pipelined approach of first applying consensus decoding to individual systems, and then applying system combination to their output. We demonstrate BLEU improvements across data sets and language pairs in large-scale experiments.

1 Introduction

Once statistical translation models are trained, a decoding approach determines what translations are finally selected. Two parallel lines of research have shown consistent improvements over the standard max-derivation decoding objective, which selects the highest probability derivation. *Consensus decoding* procedures select translations for a single system by optimizing for model predictions about n-grams, motivated either as minimizing Bayes risk (Kumar and Byrne, 2004), maximizing sentence similarity (DeNero et al., 2009), or approximating a max-translation objective (Li et al., 2009b). *System combination* procedures, on the other hand, generate translations from the output of multiple component systems (Frederking and Nirenburg, 1994). In this paper, we present *model combination*, a technique that unifies these two approaches by learning a consensus model over the n-gram features of multiple underlying component models.

Model combination operates over the component models' posterior distributions over translation derivations, encoded as a forest of derivations.[1] We combine these components by constructing a linear consensus model that includes features from each component. We then optimize this consensus model over the space of all translation derivations in the support of all component models' posterior distributions. By reusing the components' search spaces, we entirely avoid the hypothesis alignment problem that is central to standard system combination approaches (Rosti et al., 2007).

Forest-based consensus decoding techniques differ in whether they capture model predictions through n-gram posteriors (Tromble et al., 2008; Kumar et al., 2009) or expected n-gram counts (DeNero et al., 2009; Li et al., 2009b). We evaluate both in controlled experiments, demonstrating their empirical similarity. We also describe algorithms for expanding translation forests to ensure that n-grams are local to a forest's hyperedges, and for exactly computing n-gram posteriors efficiently.

Model combination assumes only that each translation model can produce expectations of n-gram features; the latent derivation structures of component systems can differ arbitrarily. This flexibility allows us to combine phrase-based, hierarchical, and syntax-augmented translation models. We evaluate by combining three large-scale systems on Chinese-English and Arabic-English NIST data sets, demonstrating improvements of up to 1.4 BLEU over the

[1] In this paper, we use the terms *translation forest* and *hypergraph* interchangeably.

Human Language Technologies: The 2010 Annual Conference of the North American Chapter of the ACL, pages 975–983,
Los Angeles, California, June 2010.

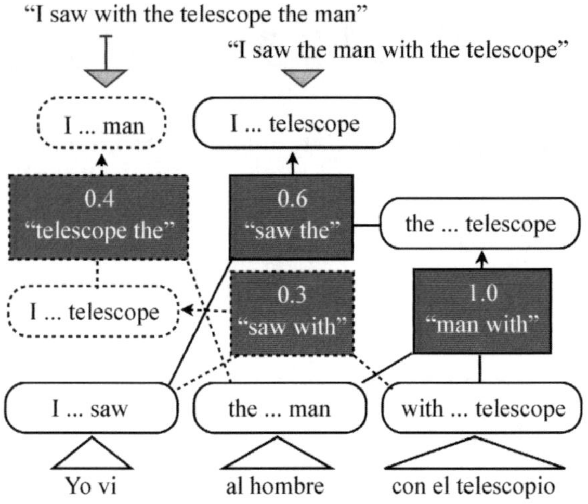

Figure 1: An example translation forest encoding two synchronous derivations for a Spanish sentence: one solid and one dotted. Nodes are annotated with their left and right unigram contexts, and hyperedges are annotated with scores $\theta \cdot \phi(r)$ and the bigrams they introduce.

best single system max-derivation baseline, and consistent improvements over a more complex multi-system pipeline that includes independent consensus decoding and system combination.

2 Model Combination

Model combination is a model-based approach to selecting translations using information from multiple component systems. Each system provides its posterior distributions over derivations $P_i(d|f)$, encoded as a weighted translation forest (i.e., translation hypergraph) in which hyperedges correspond to translation rule applications r.[2] The conditional distribution over derivations takes the form:

$$P_i(d|f) = \frac{\exp\left[\sum_{r\in d} \theta_i \cdot \phi_i(r)\right]}{\sum_{d'\in\mathcal{D}(f)} \exp\left[\sum_{r\in d'} \theta_i \cdot \phi_i(r)\right]}$$

where $\mathcal{D}(f)$ is the set of synchronous derivations encoded in the forest, r iterates over rule applications in d, and θ_i is the parameter vector for system i. The feature vector ϕ_i is system specific and includes both translation model and language model features. Figure 1 depicts an example forest.

Model combination includes four steps, described below. The entire sequence is illustrated in Figure 2.

[2]Phrase-based systems produce phrase lattices, which are instances of forests with arity 1.

2.1 Computing Combination Features

The first step in model combination is to compute n-gram expectations from component system posteriors—the same quantities found in MBR, consensus, and variational decoding techniques. For an n-gram g and system i, the expectation

$$v_i^n(g) = \mathbb{E}_{P_i(d|f)}\left[h(d,g)\right]$$

can be either an n-gram expected count, if $h(d,g)$ is the count of g in d, or the posterior probability that d contains g, if $h(d,g)$ is an indicator function. Section 3 describes how to compute these features efficiently.

2.2 Constructing a Search Space

The second step in model combination constructs a hypothesis space of translation derivations, which includes all derivations present in the forests contributed by each component system. This search space D is also a translation forest, and consists of the conjoined union of the component forests. Let R_i be the root node of component hypergraph D_i. For all i, we include all of D_i in D, along with an edge from R_i to R, the root of D. D may contain derivations from different types of translation systems. However, D only contains derivations (and therefore translations) that appeared in the hypothesis space of some component system. We do not intermingle the component search spaces in any way.

2.3 Features for the Combination Model

The third step defines a new combination model over all of the derivations in the search space D, and then annotates D with features that allow for efficient model inference. We use a linear model over four types of feature functions of a derivation:

1. Combination feature functions on n-grams $v_i^n(d) = \sum_{g\in\text{Ngrams}(d)} v_i^n(g)$ score a derivation according to the n-grams it contains.
2. Model score feature function b gives the model score $\theta_i \cdot \phi_i(d)$ of a derivation d under the system i that d is from.
3. A length feature ℓ computes the word length of the target-side yield of a derivation.
4. A system indicator feature α_i is 1 if the derivation came from system i, and 0 otherwise.

All of these features are local to rule applications (hyperedges) in D. The combination features provide information sharing across the derivations of different systems, but are functions of n-grams, and so can be scored on any translation forest. Model score features are already local to rule applications. The length feature is scored in the standard way. System indicator features are scored only on the hyperedges from R_i to R that link each component forest to the common root.

Scoring the joint search space D with these features involves annotating each rule application r (i.e. hyperedge) with the value of each feature.

2.4 Model Training and Inference

We have defined the following combination model $s_w(d)$ with weights w over derivations d from I different component models:

$$\sum_{i=1}^{I}\left[\sum_{n=1}^{4} w_i^n v_i^n(d) + w_i^{\alpha}\alpha_i(d)\right] + w^b\cdot b(d) + w^{\ell}\cdot \ell(d)$$

Because we have assessed all of these features on local rule applications, we can find the highest scoring derivation $d^* = \arg\max_{d\in D} s_w(d)$ using standard max-sum (Viterbi) inference over D.

We learn the weights of this consensus model using hypergraph-based minimum-error-rate training (Kumar et al., 2009). This procedure maximizes the translation quality of d^* on a held-out set, according to a corpus-level evaluation metric $B(\cdot;\mathbf{e})$ that compares to a reference set $\mathbf{e}$. We used BLEU, choosing w to maximize the BLEU score of the set of translations predicted by the combination model.

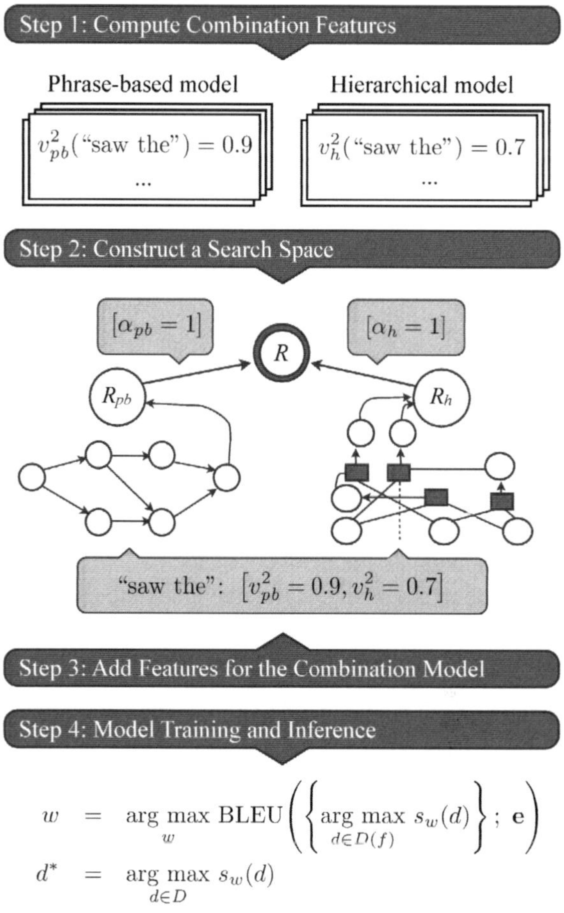

Figure 2: Model combination applied to a phrase-based (*pb*) and a hierarchical model (*h*) includes four steps. (1) shows an excerpt of the bigram feature function for each component, (2) depicts the result of conjoining a phrase lattice with a hierarchical forest, (3) shows example hyperedge features of the combination model, including bigram features v_i^n and system indicators α_i, and (4) gives training and decoding objectives.

3 Computing Combination Features

The combination features $v_i^n(d)$ score derivations from each model with the n-gram predictions of the others. These predictions sum over all derivations under a single component model to compute a posterior belief about each n-gram. In this paper, we compare two kinds of combination features, posterior probabilities and expected counts.[3]

Posterior probabilities represent a model's belief that the translation will contain a particular n-gram at least once. They can be expressed as $\mathbb{E}_{P(d|f)}[\delta(d,g)]$ for an indicator function $\delta(d,g)$ that is 1 if n-gram g appears in derivation d. These quantities arise in approximating BLEU for lattice-based and hypergraph-based minimum Bayes risk decoding (Tromble et al., 2008; Kumar et al., 2009). Expected n-gram counts $\mathbb{E}_{P(d|f)}[c(d,g)]$ represent the model's belief of how many times an n-gram g will appear in the translation. These quantities appear in forest-based consensus decoding (DeNero et al., 2009) and variational decoding (Li et al., 2009b).

[3]The model combination framework could incorporate arbitrary features on the common output space of the models, but we focus on features that have previously proven useful for consensus decoding.

Methods for computing both of these quantities appear in the literature. However, we address two outstanding issues below. In Section 5, we also compare the two quantities experimentally.

3.1 Computing N-gram Posteriors Exactly

Kumar et al. (2009) describes an efficient *approximate* algorithm for computing n-gram posterior probabilities. Algorithm 1 is an *exact* algorithm that computes all n-gram posteriors from a forest in a single inside pass. The algorithm tracks two quantities at each node n: regular inside scores $\beta(n)$ and n-gram inside scores $\hat{\beta}(n, g)$ that sum the scores of all derivations rooted at n that contain n-gram g.

For each hyperedge, we compute $\bar{b}(g)$, the sum of scores for derivations that *do not* contain g (Lines 8-11). We then use that quantity to compute the score of derivations that *do* contain g (Line 17).

Algorithm 1 Computing n-gram posteriors

1: **for** $n \in N$ in topological order **do**
2: $\quad \beta(n) \leftarrow 0$
3: $\quad \hat{\beta}(n, g) \leftarrow 0, \ \forall g \in \text{Ngrams}(n)$
4: $\quad$ **for** $r \in \text{Rules}(n)$ **do**
5: $\quad\quad w \leftarrow \exp\left[\theta \cdot \phi(r)\right]$
6: $\quad\quad b \leftarrow w$
7: $\quad\quad \bar{b}(g) \leftarrow w, \ \forall g \in \text{Ngrams}(n)$
8: $\quad\quad$ **for** $\ell \in \text{Leaves}(r)$ **do**
9: $\quad\quad\quad b \leftarrow b \times \beta(\ell)$
10: $\quad\quad\quad$ **for** $g \in \text{Ngrams}(n)$ **do**
11: $\quad\quad\quad\quad \bar{b}(g) \leftarrow \bar{b}(g) \times \Big(\beta(\ell) - \hat{\beta}(\ell, g)\Big)$
12: $\quad\quad \beta(n) \leftarrow \beta(n) + b$
13: $\quad\quad$ **for** $g \in \text{Ngrams}(n)$ **do**
14: $\quad\quad\quad$ **if** $g \in \text{Ngrams}(r)$ **then**
15: $\quad\quad\quad\quad \hat{\beta}(n, g) \leftarrow \hat{\beta}(n, g) + b$
16: $\quad\quad\quad$ **else**
17: $\quad\quad\quad\quad \hat{\beta}(n, g) \leftarrow \hat{\beta}(n, g) + b - \bar{b}(g)$
18: **for** $g \in \text{Ngrams}(\text{root})$ (all g in the HG) **do**
19: $\quad P(g|f) \leftarrow \frac{\hat{\beta}(\text{root}, g)}{\beta(\text{root})}$

This algorithm can in principle compute the posterior probability of any indicator function on local features of a derivation. More generally, this algorithm demonstrates how vector-backed inside passes can compute quantities beyond expectations of local features (Li and Eisner, 2009).[4] Chelba and Mahajan (2009) developed a similar algorithm for lattices.

3.2 Ensuring N-gram Locality

DeNero et al. (2009) describes an efficient algorithm for computing n-gram expected counts from a translation forest. This method assumes *n-gram locality* of the forest, the property that any n-gram introduced by a hyperedge appears in *all* derivations that include the hyperedge. However, decoders may recombine forest nodes whenever the language model does not distinguish between n-grams due to backoff (Li and Khudanpur, 2008). In this case, a forest encoding of a posterior distribution may not exhibit n-gram locality in all regions of the search space. Figure 3 shows a hypergraph which contains non-local trigrams, along with its local expansion.

Algorithm 2 expands a forest to ensure n-gram locality while preserving the encoded distribution over derivations. Let a forest (N, R) consist of nodes N and hyperedges R, which correspond to rule applications. Let $\text{Rules}(n)$ be the subset of R rooted by n, and $\text{Leaves}(r)$ be the leaf nodes of rule application r. The expanded forest (N_e, R_e) is constructed by a function $\text{Reapply}(r, L)$ that applies the rule of r to a new set of leaves $L \subset N_e$, forming a pair (r', n') consisting of a new rule application r' rooted by n'. P is a map from nodes in N to subsets of N_e which tracks how N projects to N_e. Two nodes in N_e are identical if they have the same $(n-1)$-gram left and right contexts and are projections of the same node in N. The symbol $\bigotimes$ denotes a set cross-product.

Algorithm 2 Expanding for n-gram locality

$N_e \leftarrow \{\}; R_e \leftarrow \{\}$
for $n \in N$ in topological order **do**
$\quad P(n) \leftarrow \{\}$
$\quad$ **for** $r \in \text{Rules}(n)$ **do**
$\quad\quad$ **for** $L \in \bigotimes_{\ell \in \text{Leaves}(r)} \left[P(\ell)\right]$ **do**
$\quad\quad\quad r', n' \leftarrow \text{Reapply}(r, L)$
$\quad\quad\quad P(n) \leftarrow P(n) \cup \{n'\}$
$\quad\quad\quad N_e \leftarrow N_e \cup \{n'\}$
$\quad\quad\quad R_e \leftarrow R_e \cup \{r'\}$

This transformation preserves the original distribution over derivations by splitting states, but maintaining continuations from those split states by duplicating rule applications. The process is analogous

[4] Indicator functions on derivations are not locally additive over the rules of a derivation, even if the features they indicate are local. Therefore, Algorithm 1 is not an instance of an expectation semiring computation.

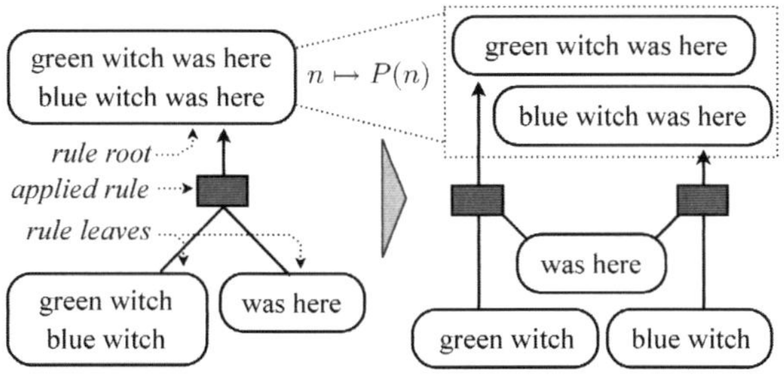

Figure 3: Hypergraph expansion ensures n-gram locality without affecting the distribution over derivations. In the left example, trigrams "green witch was" and "blue witch was" are non-local due to language model back-off. On the right, states are split to enforce trigram locality.

to expanding bigram lattices to encode a trigram history at each lattice node (Weng et al., 1998).

4 Relationship to Prior Work

Model combination is a multi-system generalization of consensus or minimum Bayes risk decoding. When only one component system is included, model combination is identical to minimum Bayes risk decoding over hypergraphs, as described in Kumar et al. (2009).[5]

4.1 System Combination

System combination techniques in machine translation take as input the outputs $\{e_1, \cdots, e_k\}$ of k translation systems, where e_i is a structured translation object (or k-best lists thereof), typically viewed as a sequence of words. The dominant approach in the field chooses a primary translation e_p as a *backbone*, then finds an alignment a_i to the backbone for each e_i. A new search space is constructed from these backbone-aligned outputs, and then a voting procedure or feature-based model predicts a final consensus translation (Rosti et al., 2007). Model combination entirely avoids this alignment problem by viewing hypotheses as n-gram occurrence vectors rather than word sequences.

Model combination also requires less total computation than applying system combination to consensus-decoded outputs. The best consensus decoding methods for individual systems already require the computation-intensive steps of model combination: producing lattices or forests, computing n-gram feature expectations, and re-decoding to maximize a secondary consensus objective. Hence, to maximize the performance of system combination, these steps must be performed for *each* system, whereas model combination requires only one forest rescoring pass over all systems.

Model combination also leverages aggregate statistics from the components' posteriors, whereas system combiners typically do not. Zhao and He (2009) showed that n-gram posterior features are useful in the context of a system combination model, even when computed from k-best lists.

Despite these advantages, system combination may be more appropriate in some settings. In particular, model combination is designed primarily for statistical systems that generate hypergraph outputs. Model combination can in principle integrate a non-statistical system that generates either a single hypothesis or an unweighted forest.[6] Likewise, the procedure could be applied to statistical systems that only generate k-best lists. However, we would not expect the same strong performance from model combination in these constrained settings.

4.2 Joint Decoding and Collaborative Decoding

Liu et al. (2009) describes two techniques for combining multiple synchronous grammars, which the authors characterize as joint decoding. Joint decoding does not involve a consensus or minimum-Bayes-risk decoding objective; indeed, their best results come from standard max-derivation decoding (with a multi-system grammar). More importantly, their computations rely on a correspondence between nodes in the hypergraph outputs of different systems, and so they can only joint decode over models with similar search strategies. We combine a phrase-based model that uses left-to-right decoding with two hierarchical systems that use bottom-up decoding — a scenario to which joint decoding is not applicable. Though Liu et al. (2009) rightly point out that most models can be decoded either left-to-

[5] We do not refer to model combination as a minimum Bayes risk decoding procedure despite this similarity because *risk* implies a belief distribution over outputs, and we now have multiple output distributions that are not necessarily calibrated. Moreover, our generalized, multi-model objective (Section 2.4) is motivated by BLEU, but not a direct approximation to it.

[6] A single hypothesis can be represented as a forest, while an unweighted forest could be assigned a uniform distribution.

right or bottom-up, such changes can have substantial implications for search efficiency and search error. We prefer to maintain the flexibility of using different search strategies in each component system.

Li et al. (2009a) is another related technique for combining translation systems by leveraging model predictions of n-gram features. K-best lists of partial translations are iteratively reranked using n-gram features from the predictions of other models (which are also iteratively updated). Our technique differs in that we use no k-best approximations, have fewer parameters to learn (one consensus weight vector rather than one for each collaborating decoder) and produce only one output, avoiding an additional system combination step at the end.

5 Experiments

We report results on the constrained data track of the NIST 2008 Arabic-to-English (ar-en) and Chinese-to-English (zh-en) translation tasks.[7] We train on all parallel and monolingual data allowed in the track. We use the NIST 2004 eval set (*dev*) for optimizing parameters in model combination and test on the NIST 2008 evaluation set. We report results using the IBM implementation of the BLEU score which computes the brevity penalty using the closest reference translation for each segment (Papineni et al., 2002). We measure statistical significance using 95% confidence intervals computed using paired bootstrap resampling. In all table cells (except for Table 3) systems without statistically significant differences are marked with the same superscript.

5.1 Base Systems

We combine outputs from three systems. Our phrase-based system is similar to the alignment template system described by Och and Ney (2004). Translation is performed using a standard left-to-right beam-search decoder. Our hierarchical systems consist of a syntax-augmented system (SAMT) that includes target-language syntactic categories (Zollmann and Venugopal, 2006) and a Hiero-style system with a single non-terminal (Chiang, 2007). Each base system yields state-of-the-art translation performance, summarized in Table 1.

[7]http://www.nist.gov/speech/tests/mt

		BLEU (%)			
		ar-en		**zh-en**	
Sys	**Base**	**dev**	**nist08**	**dev**	**nist08**
PB	MAX	51.6	43.9	37.7	25.4
PB	MBR	52.4*	44.6*	38.6*	27.3*
PB	CON	52.4*	44.6*	38.7*	27.2*
Hiero	MAX	50.9	43.3	40.0	27.2
Hiero	MBR	51.4*	43.8*	40.6*	27.8
Hiero	CON	51.5*	43.8*	40.5*	28.2
SAMT	MAX	51.7	43.8	40.8*	28.4
SAMT	MBR	52.7*	44.5*	41.1*	28.8*
SAMT	CON	52.6*	44.4*	41.1*	28.7*

Table 1: Performance of baseline systems.

	BLEU (%)			
	ar-en		**zh-en**	
Approach	**dev**	**nist08**	**dev**	**nist08**
Best MAX system	51.7	43.9	40.8	28.4
Best MBR system	52.7	44.5	41.1	28.8*
MC Conjoin/SI	**53.5**	**45.3**	**41.6**	**29.0***

Table 2: Performance from the best single system for each language pair without consensus decoding (*Best MAX system*), the best system with minimum Bayes risk decoding (*Best MBR system*), and model combination across three systems.

For each system, we report the performance of max-derivation decoding (MAX), hypergraph-based MBR (Kumar et al., 2009), and a linear version of forest-based consensus decoding (CON) (DeNero et al., 2009). MBR and CON differ only in that the first uses n-gram posteriors, while the second uses expected n-gram counts. The two consensus decoding approaches yield comparable performance. Hence, we report performance for hypergraph-based MBR in our comparison to model combination below.

5.2 Experimental Results

Table 2 compares model combination (MC) to the best MAX and MBR systems. Model combination uses a conjoined search space wherein each hyperedge is annotated with 21 features: 12 n-gram posterior features v_i^n computed from the PB/Hiero/SAMT forests for $n \leq 4$; 4 n-gram posterior features v^n computed from the conjoined forest; 1 length feature ℓ; 1 feature b for the score assigned by the base model; and 3 system indicator (SI) features α_i that select which base system a derivation came from. We refer to this model combination approach as MC

	BLEU (%)			
	ar-en		zh-en	
Strategy	**dev**	**nist08**	**dev**	**nist08**
Best MBR system	52.7	44.5	41.1	28.8
MBR Conjoin	52.3	44.5	40.5	28.3
MBR Conjoin/feats-best	52.7	44.9	41.2	28.8
MBR Conjoin/SI	53.1	44.9	41.2	28.9
MC 1-best HG	52.7	44.6	41.1	28.7
MC Conjoin	52.9	44.6	40.3	28.1
MC Conjoin/base/SI	53.5	45.1	41.2	28.9
MC Conjoin/SI	**53.5**	**45.3**	**41.6**	**29.0**

Table 3: Model Combination experiments.

Conjoin/SI. Model combination improves over the single best MAX system by 1.4 BLEU in ar-en and 0.6 BLEU in zh-en, and always improves over MBR.

This improvement could arise due to multiple reasons: a bigger search space, the consensus features from constituent systems, or the system indicator features. Table 3 teases apart these contributions.

We first perform MBR on the conjoined hypergraph (MBR-Conjoin). In this case, each edge is tagged with 4 conjoined n-gram features v^n, along with length and base model features. MBR Conjoin is worse than MBR on the hypergraph from the single best system. This could imply that either the larger search space introduces poor hypotheses or that the n-gram posteriors obtained are weaker. When we now restrict the n-gram features to those from the best system (MBR Conjoin/feats-best), BLEU scores increase relative to MBR-Conjoin. This implies that the n-gram features computed over the conjoined hypergraph are weaker than the corresponding features from the best system.

Adding system indicator features (MBR Conjoin+SI) helps the MBR-Conjoin system considerably; the resulting system is better than the best MBR system. This could mean that the SI features guide search towards stronger parts of the larger search space. In addition, these features provide a normalization of scores across systems.

We next do several model-combination experiments. We perform model combination using the search space of only the best MBR system (MC 1best HG). Here, the hypergraph is annotated with n-gram features from the 3 base systems, as well as length and base model features. A total of $3 \times 4 + 1 + 1 = 14$ features are added to each edge. Surprisingly, n-gram features from the additional systems did not help select a better hypothesis within the search space of a single system.

		BLEU (%)			
		ar-en		zh-en	
Approach	**Base**	**dev**	**nist08**	**dev**	**nist08**
Sent-level	MAX	51.8^*	44.4^*	40.8^*	28.2^*
Word-level	MAX	52.0^*	44.4^*	40.8^*	28.1^*
Sent-level	MBR	52.7^+	44.6^*	41.2	28.8^+
Word-level	MBR	52.5^+	44.7^*	40.9	28.8^+
MC-conjoin-SI		**53.5**	**45.3**	**41.6**	**29.0^+**

Table 4: BLEU performance for different system and model combination approaches. Sentence-level and word-level system combination operate over the sentence output of the base systems, which are either decoded to maximize derivation score (MAX) or to minimize Bayes risk (MBR).

When we expand the search space to the conjoined hypergraph (MC Conjoin), it performs worse relative to MC 1-best. Since these two systems are identical in their feature set, we hypothesize that the larger search space has introduced erroneous hypotheses. This is similar to the scenario where MBR Conjoin is worse than MBR 1-best. As in the MBR case, adding system indicator features helps (MC Conjoin/base/SI). The result is comparable to MBR on the conjoined hypergraph with SI features.

We finally add extra n-gram features which are computed from the conjoined hypergraph (MC Conjoin + SI). This gives the best performance although the gains over MC Conjoin/base/SI are quite small. Note that these added features are the same n-gram features used in MBR Conjoin. Although they are not strong by themselves, they provide additional discriminative power by providing a consensus score across all 3 base systems.

5.3 Comparison to System Combination

Table 4 compares model combination to two system combination algorithms. The first, which we call *sentence-level* combination, chooses among the base systems' three translations the sentence that has the highest consensus score. The second, *word-level* combination, builds a "word sausage" from the outputs of the three systems and chooses a path through the sausage with the highest score under a similar model (Macherey and Och, 2007). Nei-

	BLEU (%)			
	ar-en		**zh-en**	
Approach	**dev**	**nist08**	**dev**	**nist08**
HG-expand	52.7*	44.5*	41.1*	28.8*
HG-noexpand	52.7*	44.5*	41.1*	28.8*

Table 5: MBR decoding on the syntax augmented system, with and without hypergraph expansion.

	BLEU (%)			
	ar-en		**zh-en**	
Posteriors	**dev**	**nist08**	**dev**	**nist08**
Exact	52.4*	44.6*	38.6*	27.3*
Approximate	52.5*	44.6*	38.6*	27.2*

Table 6: MBR decoding on the phrase-based system with either exact or approximate posteriors.

ther system combination technique provides much benefit, presumably because the underlying systems all share the same data, pre-processing, language model, alignments, and code base.

Comparing system combination when no consensus (i.e., minimum Bayes risk) decoding is utilized at all, we find that model combination improves upon the result by up to 1.1 BLEU points. Model combination also performs slightly better relative to system combination over MBR-decoded systems. In the latter case, system combination actually requires more computation compared to model combination; consensus decoding is performed for *each* system rather than only once for model combination. This experiment validates our approach. Model combination outperforms system combination while avoiding the challenge of aligning translation hypotheses.

5.4 Algorithmic Improvements

Section 3 describes two improvements to computing n-gram posteriors: hypergraph expansion for n-gram locality and exact posterior computation. Table 5 shows MBR decoding with and without expansion (Algorithm 2) in a decoder that collapses nodes due to language model back-off. These results show that while expansion is necessary for correctness, it does not affect performance.

Table 6 compares exact n-gram posterior computation (Algorithm 1) to the approximation described by Kumar et al. (2009). Both methods yield identical results. Again, while the exact method guarantees correctness of the computation, the approximation suffices in practice.

6 Conclusion

Model combination is a consensus decoding strategy over a collection of forests produced by multiple machine translation systems. These systems can have varied decoding strategies; we only require that each system produce a forest (or a lattice) of translations. This flexibility allows the technique to be applied quite broadly. For instance, de Gispert et al. (2009) describe combining systems based on multiple source representations using minimum Bayes risk decoding—likewise, they could be combined via model combination.

Model combination has two significant advantages over current approaches to system combination. First, it does not rely on hypothesis alignment between outputs of individual systems. Aligning translation hypotheses accurately can be challenging, and has a substantial effect on combination performance (He et al., 2008). Instead of aligning hypotheses, we compute expectations of local features of n-grams. This is analogous to how BLEU score is computed, which also views sentences as vectors of n-gram counts (Papineni et al., 2002) . Second, we do not need to pick a backbone system for combination. Choosing a backbone system can also be challenging, and also affects system combination performance (He and Toutanova, 2009). Model combination sidesteps this issue by working with the conjoined forest produced by the union of the component forests, and allows the consensus model to express system preferences via weights on system indicator features.

Despite its simplicity, model combination provides strong performance by leveraging existing consensus, search, and training techniques. The technique outperforms MBR and consensus decoding on each of the component systems. In addition, it performs better than standard sentence-based or word-based system combination techniques applied to either max-derivation or MBR outputs of the individual systems. In sum, it is a natural and effective model-based approach to multi-system decoding.

References

Ciprian Chelba and M. Mahajan. 2009. A dynamic programming algorithm for computing the posterior probability of n-gram occurrences in automatic speech recognition lattices. Personal communication.

David Chiang. 2007. Hierarchical phrase-based translation. *Computational Linguistics*.

A. de Gispert, S. Virpioja, M. Kurimo, and W. Byrne. 2009. Minimum bayes risk combination of translation hypotheses from alternative morphological decompositions. In *Proceedings of the North American Chapter of the Association for Computational Linguistics*.

John DeNero, David Chiang, and Kevin Knight. 2009. Fast consensus decoding over translation forests. In *Proceedings of the Association for Computational Linguistics and IJCNLP*.

Robert Frederking and Sergei Nirenburg. 1994. Three heads are better than one. In *Proceedings of the Conference on Applied Natural Language Processing*.

Xiaodong He and Kristina Toutanova. 2009. Joint optimization for machine translation system combination. In *Proceedings of the Conference on Empirical Methods in Natural Language Processing*.

Xiaodong He, Mei Yang, Jianfeng Gao, Patrick Nguyen, and Robert Moore. 2008. Indirect-hmm-based hypothesis alignment for combining outputs from machine translation systems. In *Proceedings of the Conference on Empirical Methods in Natural Language Processing*.

Shankar Kumar and William Byrne. 2004. Minimum Bayes-risk decoding for statistical machine translation. In *Proceedings of the North American Chapter of the Association for Computational Linguistics*.

Shankar Kumar, Wolfgang Macherey, Chris Dyer, and Franz Och. 2009. Efficient minimum error rate training and minimum bayes-risk decoding for translation hypergraphs and lattices. In *Proceedings of the Association for Computational Linguistics and IJCNLP*.

Zhifei Li and Jason Eisner. 2009. First- and second-order expectation semirings with applications to minimum-risk training on translation forests. In *Proceedings of the Conference on Empirical Methods in Natural Language Processing*.

Zhifei Li and Sanjeev Khudanpur. 2008. A scalable decoder for parsing-based machine translation with equivalent language model state maintenance. In *ACL Workshop on Syntax and Structure in Statistical Translation*.

Mu Li, Nan Duan, Dongdong Zhang, Chi-Ho Li, and Ming Zhou. 2009a. Collaborative decoding: Partial hypothesis re-ranking using translation consensus between decoders. In *Proceedings of the Conference on Empirical Methods in Natural Language Processing*.

Zhifei Li, Jason Eisner, and Sanjeev Khudanpur. 2009b. Variational decoding for statistical machine translation. In *Proceedings of the Association for Computational Linguistics and IJCNLP*.

Yang Liu, Haitao Mi, Yang Feng, and Qun Liu. 2009. Joint decoding with multiple translation models. In *Proceedings of the Association for Computational Linguistics and IJCNLP*.

Wolfgang Macherey and Franz Och. 2007. An empirical study on computing consensus translations from multiple machine translation systems. In *EMNLP*, Prague, Czech Republic.

Franz J. Och and Hermann Ney. 2004. The Alignment Template Approach to Statistical Machine Translation. *Computational Linguistics*, 30(4):417 – 449.

Kishore Papineni, Salim Roukos, Todd Ward, and Wei-Jing Zhu. 2002. BLEU: A method for automatic evaluation of machine translation. In *Proceedings of the Association for Computational Linguistics*.

Antti-Veikko I. Rosti, Necip Fazil Ayan, Bing Xiang, Spyros Matsoukas, Richard Schwartz, and Bonnie J. Dorr. 2007. Combining outputs from multiple machine translation systems. In *Proceedings of the North American Chapter of the Association for Computational Linguistics*.

Roy Tromble, Shankar Kumar, Franz J. Och, and Wolfgang Macherey. 2008. Lattice minimum Bayes-risk decoding for statistical machine translation. In *Proceedings of the Conference on Empirical Methods in Natural Language Processing*.

Fuliang Weng, Andreas Stolcke, and Ananth Sankar. 1998. Efficient lattice representation and generation. In *Intl. Conf. on Spoken Language Processing*.

Yong Zhao and Xiaodong He. 2009. Using n-gram based features for machine translation system combination. In *Proceedings of the North American Chapter of the Association for Computational Linguistics*.

Andreas Zollmann and Ashish Venugopal. 2006. Syntax augmented machine translation via chart parsing. In *Proceedings of the NAACL 2006 Workshop on statistical machine translation*.

Detecting Emails Containing Requests for Action

Andrew Lampert †‡
†CSIRO ICT Centre
PO Box 76
Epping 1710
Australia
andrew.lampert@csiro.au

Robert Dale
‡Centre for Language Technology
Macquarie University 2109
Australia
rdale@science.mq.edu.au

Cecile Paris
CSIRO ICT Centre
PO Box 76
Epping 1710
Australia
cecile.paris@csiro.au

Abstract

Automatically finding email messages that contain requests for action can provide valuable assistance to users who otherwise struggle to give appropriate attention to the actionable tasks in their inbox. As a speech act classification task, however, automatically recognising requests in free text is particularly challenging. The problem is compounded by the fact that typical emails contain extraneous material that makes it difficult to isolate the content that is directed to the recipient of the email message. In this paper, we report on an email classification system which identifies messages containing requests; we then show how, by segmenting the content of email messages into different functional zones and then considering only content in a small number of message zones when detecting requests, we can improve the accuracy of message-level automated request classification to 83.76%, a relative increase of 15.9%. This represents an error reduction of 41% compared with the same request classifier deployed without email zoning.

1 Introduction

The variety of linguistic forms that can be used to express requests, and in particular the frequency with which indirect speech acts are used in email, is a major source of difficulty in determining whether an email message contains one or more requests. Another significant problem arises from the fact that whether or not a request is directed at the recipient of the email message depends on where in the message the request is found. Most obviously, if the request is part of a replied-to message that is contained within the current message, then it is perhaps more likely that this request was directed at the sender of the current message. However, separating out content intended for the recipient from other extraneous content is not as simple as it might appear. Segmenting email messages into their different functional parts is hampered by the lack of standard syntax used by different email clients to indicate different message parts, and by the *ad hoc* ways in which people vary the structure and layout of messages.

In this paper, we present our results in classifying messages according to whether or not they contain requests, and then show how a separate classifier that aims to determine the nature of the zones that make up an email message can improve upon these results. Section 2 contains some context and motivation for this work before we briefly review relevant related work in Section 3. Then, in Section 4, we describe a first experiment in request classification using data gathered from a manual annotation experiment. In analysing the errors made by this classifier, we found that a significant number of errors seemed to arise from the inclusion of content in parts of a message (e.g., quoted reply content) that were not authored by the current sender, and thus were not relevant other than as context for interpreting the current message content. Based on this analysis, we hypothesised that segmenting messages into their different functional parts, which we call **email zones**, and then using this information to consider only content from certain parts of a message for request classification, would improve request classifi-

Human Language Technologies: The 2010 Annual Conference of the North American Chapter of the ACL, pages 984–992,
Los Angeles, California, June 2010.

cation performance.

To test this hypothesis, we developed an SVM-based automated email zone classifier configured with graphic, orthographic and lexical features; this is described in more detail in (Lampert et al., 2009). Section 5 describes how we improve request classification performance using this email zone classifier. Section 6 summarises the performance of our request classifiers, with and without automated email zoning, along with an analysis of the contribution of lexical features to request classification, discussion of request classification learning curves, and a detailed error analysis that explores the sources of request classification errors. Finally, in Section 7, we offer pointers to future work and some concluding remarks.

2 Background and Motivation

Previous research has established that users routinely use email for managing requests in the workplace — e.g., (Mackay, 1988; Ducheneaut and Bellotti, 2001). Such studies have highlighted how managing multiple ongoing tasks through email leads to information overload (Whittaker and Sidner, 1996; Bellotti et al., 2003), especially in the face of an ever-increasing volume of email. The result is that many users have difficulty giving appropriate attention to requests hidden in their email which require action or response. A particularly lucid summary of the requirements placed on email users comes from work by Murray (1991), whose ethnographic research into the use of electronic messaging at IBM highlighted that:

> [Managers] would like to be able to track outstanding promises they have made, promises made to them, requests they've made that have not been met and requests made of them that they have not fulfilled.

This electronic exchange of requests and commitments has previously been identified as a fundamental basis of the way work is delegated and completed within organisations. Winograd and Flores were among the first to recognise and attempt to exploit this with their Coordinator system (Winograd and Flores, 1986). Their research into organisational communication concluded that "Organisations exist as networks of directives and commissives". It is on this basis that our research explores the use of requests (directive speech acts) and commitments (commissive speech acts) in email. In this paper, we focus on requests; feedback from users of the request and commitment classifier plug-in for Microsoft Outlook that we have under development suggests that, at least within the business context of our current users, requests are the more important of the two phenomena.

Our aim is to create tools that assist email users to identify and manage requests contained in incoming and outgoing email. We define a request as an utterance that places an obligation on an email recipient to schedule an action; perform (or not perform) an action; or to respond with some speech act. A simple example might be *Please call when you have a chance.* A more complicated request is *David will send you the latest version if there have been any updates.* If David (perhaps cc'ed) is a recipient of an email containing this second utterance, the utterance functions as a (conditional) request for him, even though it is addressed as a commitment to a third-party. In real-world email, requests are frequently expressed in such subtle ways, as we discuss in Section 4.

A distinction can be drawn between **message-level identification**—i.e., the task of determining *whether* an email message contains a request — and **utterance-level identification**—i.e., determining precisely where and how the request is expressed. In this paper, we focus on the task of message-level identification, since utterance-level identification is a significantly more problematic task: it is often the case that, while we might agree that a message contains a request or commitment, it is much harder to determine the precise extent of the text that conveys this request (see (Lampert et al., 2008b) for a detailed discussion of some of the issues here).

3 Related Work

Our request classification work builds on influential ideas proposed by Winograd and Flores (1986) in taking a language/action perspective and identifying speech acts in email. While this differs from the approach of most currently-used email systems, which routinely treat the content of email messages as homogeneous bags-of-words, there is a growing body of research applying ideas from Speech Act Theory (Austin, 1962; Searle, 1969) to analyse and enhance email communication.

Khosravi and Wilks (1999) were among the first to automate message-level request classification in email. They used cue-phrase based rules to classify three classes of requests: Request-Action, Request-Information and Request-Permission. Unfortunately, their approach was quite brittle, with the rules being very specific to the computer support domain from which their email data was drawn.

Cohen, Carvalho and Mitchell (2004) developed machine learning-based classifiers for a number of email speech acts. They performed manual email zoning, but didn't explore the contribution this made to the performance of their various speech act classifiers. For requests, they report peak F-measure of 0.69 against a majority class baseline accuracy of approximately 66%. Cohen, Carvalho and Mitchell found that unweighted bigrams were particularly useful features in their experiments, out-performing other features applied. They later applied a series of text normalisations and n-gram feature selection algorithms to improve performance (Carvalho and Cohen, 2006). We apply similar normalisations in our work. While difficult to compare due to the use of a different email corpus that may or may not exclude annotation disagreements, our request classifier performance exceeds that of the enhanced classifier reported in (Carvalho and Cohen, 2006).

Goldstein and Sabin (2006) have also worked on related email classification tasks. They use verb classes, along with a series of hand-crafted form- and phrase-based features, for classifying what they term **email genre**, a task which overlaps significantly with email speech act classification. Their results are difficult to compare since they include a mix of form-based classifications like **response** with more intent-based classes such as **request**. For requests, the results are rather poor, with precision of only 0.43 on a small set of personal mail.

The SmartMail system (Corston-Oliver et al., 2004) is probably the most mature previous work on utterance-level request classification. SmartMail attempted to automatically extract and reformulate action items from email messages for the purpose of adding them to a user's to-do list. The system employed a series of deep linguistic features, including phrase structure and semantic features, along with word and part-of-speech n-gram features. The authors found that word n-grams were highly predictive for their classification task, and that there was little difference in performance when the more expensive deep linguistic features were added. Based on this insight, our own system does not employ deeper linguistic features. Unfortunately, the results reported reveal only the aggregate performance across all classes, which involves a mix of both form-based classes (such as signature content address lines and URL lines), and intent-based classes (such as requests and promises). It is thus very difficult to directly compare the results with our system. Additionally, the experiments were performed over a large corpus of messages that are not available for use by other researchers. In contrast, we use messages from the widely-available Enron email corpus (Klimt and Yang, 2004) for our own experiments.

While several of the above systems involve manual processes for removing particular parts of message bodies, none employ a comprehensive, automated approach to email zoning.

We focus on the combination of email zoning and request classification tasks and provide details of how email zoning improves request classification — a task not previously explored. To do so, we require an automated email zone classifier. We experimented with using the Jangada system (Carvalho and Cohen, 2004), but found similar shortcomings to those noted by Estival et al. (2007). In particular, Jangada did not accurately identify forwarded or reply content in email messages from the email Enron corpus that we use. We achieved much better performance with our own Zebra zone classifier (Lampert et al., 2009); it is this system that we use for email zoning throughout this paper.

4 Email Request Classification

Identifying requests requires interpretation of the intent that lies behind the language used. Given this, it is natural to approach the problem as one of **speech act identification**. In Speech Act Theory, speech acts are categories like **assertion** and **request** that capture the intentions underlying surface utterances, providing abstractions across the wide variety of different ways in which instances of those categories might be realised in linguistic form. In this paper we focus on the speech acts that represent requests, where people are placing obligations upon others via actionable content within email messages.

The task of building automated classifiers is difficult since the function of conveying a request does not neatly map to a particular set of language forms; requests often involve what are referred to as **indirect speech acts**. While investigating particular surface forms of language is relatively unproblematic, it is widely recognised that "investigating a collection of forms that represent, for example, a particular speech act leads to the problem of establishing which forms constitute that collection" (Archer et al., 2008). Email offers particular challenges as it has been shown to exhibit a higher frequency of indirect speech acts than other media (Hassell and Christensen, 1996). We approach the problem by gathering judgments from human annotators and using this data to train supervised machine learning algorithms.

Our request classifier works at the message-level, marking emails as requests if they contain one or more request utterances. As noted earlier, we define a request as an utterance from the email sender that places an obligation on a recipient to schedule an action (e.g., add to a calendar or task list), perform an action, or respond. Requests may be conditional or unconditional in terms of the obligation they impose on the recipient. Conditional requests require action only if a stated condition is satisfied. Previous annotation experiments have shown that conditional requests are an important phenomena and occur frequently in email (Scerri et al., 2008; Lampert et al., 2008a). Requests may also be phrased as either a direct or indirect speech act.

Although some linguists distinguish between speech acts that require a physical response and those that require a verbal or information response, e.g., (Sinclair and Coulthard, 1975), we follow Searle's approach and make no such distinction. We thus consider questions requiring an informational response to be requests, since they place an obligation on the recipient to answer.[1]

Additionally, there are some classes of request which have been the source of systematic human disagreement in our previous annotation experiments. One such class consists of **requests for inaction**. Requests for inaction, sometimes called **prohibitives** (Sadock and Zwicky, 1985), prohibit action or request negated action. An example is: *Please don't let anyone else use the computer in the office*. As they impose an obligation on the sender, we consider requests for inaction to be requests. Similarly, we consider that meeting announcements (e.g., *Today's Prebid Meeting will take place in EB32c2 at 3pm*) and requests to read, open or otherwise act on documents attached to email messages (e.g., *See attached*) are also requests.

Several complex classes of requests are particularly sensitive to the context for their interpretation. Reported requests are one such class. Some reported requests, such as *Paul asked if you could put together a summary of your accomplishments in an email*, clearly function as a request. Others do not impose an obligation on the recipient, e.g., *Sorry for the delay; Paul requested your prize to be sent out late December*. The surrounding context must be used to determine the intent of utterances like reported requests. Such distinctions are often difficult to automate.

Other complex requests include instructions. Sometimes instructions are of the kind that one might 'file for later use'. These tend to not be marked as requests. Other instructions, such as *Your user id and password have been set up. Please follow the steps below to access the new environment*, are intended to be executed more promptly. Temporal distance between receipt of the instruction and expected action is an important factor to distinguish between requests and non-requests. Another influencing property is the likelihood of the trigger event that would lead to execution of the described action. While the example instructions above are likely to be executed, instructions for how to handle suspected anthrax-infected mail are (for most people) unlikely to be actioned.

Further detail and discussion of these and other

[1]Note, however, that not all questions are requests. Rhetorical questions are perhaps the most obvious class of non-request questions.

challenges in defining and interpreting requests in email can be found in (Lampert et al., 2008b). In particular, that paper includes analysis of a series of complex edge cases that make even human agreement in identifying requests difficult to achieve.

4.1 An Email Request Classifier

Our request classifier is based around an SVM classifier, implemented using Weka (Witten and Frank, 2005). Given an email message as input, complete with header information, our binary request classifier predicts the presence or absence of request utterances within the message.

For training our request classifier, we use email from the database dump of the Enron email corpus released by Andrew Fiore and Jeff Heer.[2] This version of the corpus has been processed to remove duplicate messages and to normalise sender and recipient names, resulting in just over 250,000 email messages. No attachments are included.

Our request classifier training data is drawn from a collection of 664 messages that were selected at random from the Enron corpus. Each message was annotated by three annotators, with overall kappa agreement of 0.681. From the full dataset of 664 messages, we remove all messages where annotators disagreed for training and evaluating our request classifier, in order to mitigate the effects of annotation noise, as discussed in (Beigman and Klebanov, 2009). The unanimously agreed data set used for training consists of 505 email messages.

4.2 Request Classification Features

The features we use in our request classifier are:

- message length in characters and words;
- number and percentage of capitalised words;
- number of non alpha-numeric characters;
- whether the subject line contains markers of email replies or forwards (e.g. `Re:`, `Fw:`);
- the presence of sender or recipient names;
- the presence of sentences that begin with a modal verb (e.g., *might*, *may*, *should*, *would*);
- the presence of sentences that begin with a question word (e.g, *who*, *what*, *where*, *when*, *why*, *which*, *how*);
- whether the message contains any sentences that end with a question mark; and
- binary word unigram and word bigram features for n-grams that occur at least three times across the training set.

Before generating n-gram features, we normalise the message text as shown in Table 1, in a manner similar to Carvalho and Cohen (2006). We also add tokens marking the start and end of sentences, detected using a modified version of Scott Piao's sentence splitter (Piao et al., 2002), and tokens marking the start and end of the message.

Symbol Used	Pattern
numbers	Any sequence of digits
day	Day names or abbreviations
pronoun-object	Objective pronouns: *me, her, him, us, them*
pronoun-subject	Subjective pronouns: *I, we, you, he, she, they*
filetype	.doc, .pdf, .ppt, .txt, .xls, .rtf
multi-dash	3 or more sequential '–' characters
multi-underscore	3 or more sequential '_' characters

Table 1: Normalisation applied to n-gram features

Our initial request classifier achieves an accuracy of 72.28%. Table 2 shows accuracy, precision, recall and F-measure results, calculated using stratified 10-fold cross-validation, compared against a majority class baseline. Given the well-balanced nature of our training data (52.08% of messages contain a request), this is a reasonable basis for comparison.

	Majority Baseline		No Zoning Classifier	
	Request	Non-Request	Request	Non-Request
Accuracy	52.08%		72.28%	
Precision	0.521	0.000	0.729	0.716
Recall	1.000	0.000	0.745	0.698
F-Measure	0.685	0.000	0.737	0.707

Table 2: Request classifier results without email zoning

An error analysis of the predictions from our initial request classifier uncovered a series of classification errors that appeared to be due to request-like signals being picked up from parts of messages such as email signatures and quoted reply content. It seemed likely that our request classifier would benefit from an email zone classifier that could identify and ignore such message parts.

[2] http://bailando.sims.berkeley.edu/enron/enron.sql.gz

5 Improving Request Classification with Email Zoning

Requests in email do not occur uniformly across the zones that make up the email message. There are specific zones of a message in which requests are likely to occur.

Unfortunately, accurate classification of email zones is difficult, hampered by the lack of standard syntax used by different email clients to indicate different message parts, and by the *ad hoc* ways in which people vary the structure and layout of their messages. For example, different email clients indicate quoted material in a variety of ways. Some prefix every line of the quoted message with a character such as '>' or '|', while others indent the quoted content or insert the quoted message unmodified, prefixed by a message header. Sometimes the new content is above the quoted content (a style known as **top-posting**); in other cases, the new content may appear after the quoted content (**bottom-posting**) or interleaved with the quoted content (**inline replying**). Confounding the issue further is that users are able to configure their email client to suit their individual tastes, and can change both the syntax of quoting and their quoting style (top, bottom or inline replying) on a per message basis.

Despite the likelihood of some noise being introduced through mis-classification of email zones, our hypothesis was that even imperfect information about the functional parts of a message should improve the performance of our request classifier.

Based on this hypothesis, we integrated Zebra (Lampert et al., 2009), our SVM-based email zone classifier, to identify the different functional parts of email messages. Using features that capture graphic, orthographic and lexical information, Zebra classifies and segments the body text into nine different email zones: author content (written by the current sender), greetings, signoffs, quoted reply content, forwarded content, email signatures, advertising, disclaimers, and automated attachment references. Zebra has two modes of operation, classifying either message fragments — whitespace separated sets of contiguous lines — or individual lines. We configure Zebra for line-based zone classification, and use it to extract only lines classified as author, greeting and signoff text. We remove the content of all other zones before we evaluate features for request classification.

6 Results and Discussion

Classifying the zones in email messages and applying our request classifier to only relevant message parts significantly increases the performance of the request classifier. As noted above, without zoning, our request classifier achieves accuracy of 72.28% and a weighted F-measure (weighted between the F-measure for requests and non-requests based on the relative frequency of each class) of 0.723. Adding the zone classifier, we increase the accuracy to 83.76% and the weighted F-measure to 0.838. This corresponds to a relative increase in both accuracy and weighted F-measure of 15.9%, which in turn corresponds to an error reduction of more than 41%. Table 3 shows a comparison of the results of the non-zoning and zoning request classifiers, generated using stratified 10-fold cross-validation. In a two-tailed paired t-test, run over ten iterations of stratified 10-fold cross-validation, the increase in accuracy, precision, recall and f-measure were all significant at p=0.01.

	No Zoning		With Zoning	
	Request	Non-Request	Request	Non-Request
Accuracy	72.28%		83.76%*	
Precision	0.729	0.716	0.849*	0.825*
Recall	0.745	0.698	0.837*	0.839*
F-Measure	0.737	0.707	0.843*	0.832*

Table 3: Request classifier results with and without email zoning (* indicates a statistically significant difference at p=0.01)

6.1 Lexical Feature Contribution

As expected, lexical information is crucial to request classification. When we experimented with removing all lexical (n-gram) features, the non-zoning request classifier accuracy dropped to 57.62% and the zoning request classifier accuracy dropped to 61.78%. In contrast, when we apply *only* n-gram features, we achieve accuracy of 71.49% for the non-zoning classifier and 83.36% for the zoning classifier. Clearly, lexical information is critical for accurate request classification, regardless of whether email messages are zoned.

Using Information Gain, we ranked the n-gram features in terms of their usefulness. Table 4 shows the top-10 unigrams and bigrams for our non-zoning request classifier. Using these top-10 n-grams (plus our non-n-gram features), we achieve only 66.34% accuracy. These top-10 n-grams do not seem to align well with linguistic intuitions, illustrating how the noise from irrelevant message parts hampers performance. In particular, there were several similar, apparently automated messages that were annotated (as non-requests) which appear to be the source of several of the top-10 n-grams. This strongly suggests that without zoning, the classifier is not learning features from the training set at a useful level of generality.

Word Unigrams	Word Bigrams	
	Word 1	Word 2
pronoun-object	let	*pronoun-object*
please	*pronoun-object*	know
iso	*start-sentence*	no
pronoun-subject	start	date
hourahead	hour	:
attached	;	hourahead
let	hourahead	hour
westdesk	*start-sentence*	start
parsing	westdesk	/
if	iso	final

Table 4: Top 10 useful n-grams for our request classifier without zoning, ranked by Information Gain

In contrast, once we add the zoning classifier, the top-10 unigrams and bigrams appear to correspond much better with linguistic intuitions about the language of requests. These are shown in Table 5. Using these top-10 n-grams (plus our non-n-gram features), we achieve 80% accuracy. This suggests that, even with our relatively small amount of training data, the zone classifier helps the request classifier to extract fairly general n-gram features.

Interestingly, although lexical features are very important, the top three features ranked by Information Gain are non-lexical: message length in words, the number of non-alpha-numeric characters in the message and the number of capitalised words in the message.

Word Unigrams	Word Bigrams	
	Word 1	Word 2
please	?	*end-sentence*
?	*pronoun-object*	know
pronoun-object	let	*pronoun-object*
if	*start-sentence*	please
pronoun-subject	if	*pronoun-subject*
let	*start-sentence*	thanks
to	please	let
know	*pronoun-subject*	have
thanks	thanks	*comma*
do	start	date

Table 5: Top 10 useful n-grams for our request classifier with zoning, ranked by Information Gain

6.2 Learning Curves

Figure 1 shows a plot of accuracy, precision and recall versus the number of training instances used to build the request classifier. These results are calculated over zoned email bodies, using the average across ten iterations of stratified 10-fold cross-validation for each different sized set of training instances, implemented via the `FilteredClassifier` with the `Resample` filter in Weka. Given our pool of 505 agreed message annotations, we plot the recall and precision for training instance sets of size 50 to 505 messages.

There is a clear trend of increasing performance as the training set size grows. It seems reasonable to assume that more data should continue to facilitate better request classifier performance. To this end, we are annotating more data as part of our current and future work.

6.3 Error Analysis

To explore the errors made by our request classifier, we examined the output of our zoning request classifier using our full feature set, including all word n-grams.

Approximately 20% of errors relate to requests that are implicit, and thus more difficult to detect from surface features. Another 10% of errors are due to attempts to classify requests in inappropriate genres of email messages. In particular, both marketing messages and spam frequently include request-like, directive utterances which our annotators all agreed would not be useful to mark as re-

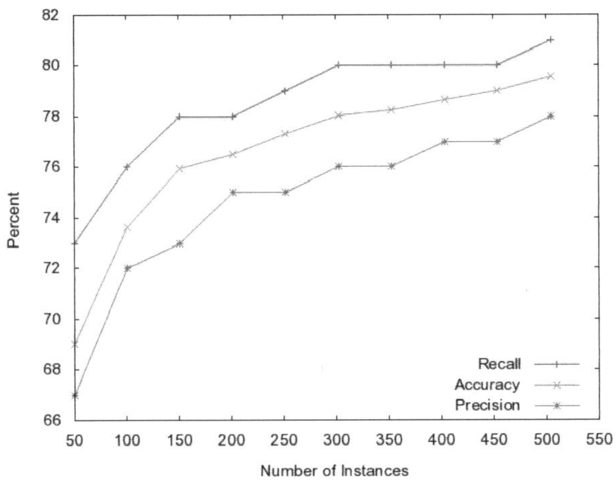

Figure 1: Learning curve showing recall, accuracy and precision versus the number of training instances

quests for an email user. Not unreasonably, our classifier is sometimes confused by the content of these messages, mistakenly marking requests where our annotators did not. We intend to resolve these classification errors by filtering out such messages before we apply the request classifier.

Another 5% of errors are due to request content occurring in zones that we ignore. The most common case is content in a forwarded zone. Sometimes email senders forward a message as a form of task delegation; because we ignore forwarded content, our request classifier misses such requests. We did experiment with including content from forwarded zones (in addition to the author, greeting and signoff zones), but found that this reduced the performance of our request classifier, presumably due to the additional noise from irrelevant content in other forwarded material. Forwarded messages are thus somewhat difficult to deal with. One possible approach would be to build sender-specific profiles that might allow us to deal with forwarded content (and potentially content from other zones) differently for different users, essentially learning to adapt to the different styles of different email users.

A further 5% of errors involve errors in the zone classifier, which leads to incorrect zone labels being applied to zone content that we would wish to include for our request classifier. Examples include author content being mistakenly identified as signature content. In such cases, we incorrectly remove relevant content from the body text that is passed to our request classifier. Improvements to the zone classifier would resolve these issues.

As part of our annotation task, we also asked coders to mark the presence of **pleasantries**. We define a pleasantry as an utterance that could be a request in some other context, but that does not function as a request in the context of use under consideration. Pleasantries are frequently formulaic, and do not place any significant obligation on the recipient to act or respond. Variations on the phrase *Let me know if you have any questions* are particularly common in email messages. The context of the entire email message needs to be considered to distinguish between when such an utterance functions as a request and when it should be marked as a pleasantry. Of the errors made by our request classifier, approximately 5% involve marking messages containing only pleasantries as containing a request.

The remaining errors are somewhat diverse. Close to 5% involve errors interpreting requests associated with attached files. The balance of almost 50% of errors involve a wide range of issues, from misspellings of key words such as *please* to a lack of punctuation cues such as question marks.

7 Conclusion

Request classification, like any form of automated speech act recognition, is a difficult task. Despite this inherent difficulty, the automatic request classifier we describe in this paper correctly labels requests at the message level in 83.76% of email messages from our annotated dataset. Unlike previous work that has attempted to automate the classification of requests in email, we zone the messages without manual intervention. This improves accuracy by 15.9% relative to the performance of the same request classifier without the assistance of an email zone classifier to focus on relevant message parts. Although some zone classification errors are made, error analysis reveals that only 5% of errors are due to zone misclassification of message parts. This suggests that, although zone classifier performance could be further improved, it is likely that focusing on improving the request classifier using the existing zone classifier performance will lead to greater performance gains.

References

Dawn Archer, Jonathan Culpeper, and Matthew Davies, 2008. *Corpus Linguistics: An International Handbook*, chapter Pragmatic Annotation, pages 613–642. Mouton de Gruyter.

John L Austin. 1962. *How to do things with words*. Harvard University Press.

Eyal Beigman and Beata Beigman Klebanov. 2009. Learning with annotation noise. In *Proceedings of the Joint Conference of the 47th Annual Meeting of the ACL and the 4th IJCNLP*, pages 280–287, Singapore.

Victoria Bellotti, Nicolas Ducheneaut, Mark Howard, and Ian Smith. 2003. Taking email to task: The design and evaluation of a task management centred email tool. In *Computer Human Interaction Conference*, CHI, pages 345–352, Ft Lauderdale, Florida.

Vitor R Carvalho and William W Cohen. 2004. Learning to extract signature reply lines from email. In *Proceedings of First Conference on Email and Anti-Spam (CEAS)*, Mountain View, CA, July 30-31.

Vitor R. Carvalho and William W. Cohen. 2006. Improving email speech act analysis via n-gram selection. In *Proceedings of HLT/NAACL 2006 - Workshop on Analyzing Conversations in Text and Speech*, pages 35–41, New York.

William W. Cohen, Vitor R. Carvalho, and Tom M. Mitchell. 2004. Learning to classify email into "speech acts". In *Conference on Empirical Methods in Natural Language Processing*, pages 309–316, Barcelona, Spain.

Simon H. Corston-Oliver, Eric Ringger, Michael Gamon, and Richard Campbell. 2004. Task-focused summarization of email. In *ACL-04 Workshop: Text Summarization Branches Out*, pages 43–50.

Nicolas Ducheneaut and Victoria Bellotti. 2001. E-mail as habitat: an exploration of embedded personal information management. *Interactions*, 8(5):30–38.

Dominique Estival, Tanja Gaustad, Son Bao Pham, Will Radford, and Ben Hutchinson. 2007. Author profiling for English emails. In *Proceedings of the 10th Conference of the Pacific Association for Computational Linguistics*, pages 263–272, Melbourne, Australia.

Jade Goldstein and Roberta Evans Sabin. 2006. Using speech acts to categorize email and identify email genres. In *Proceedings of the 39th Hawaii International Conference on System Sciences*, page 50b.

Lewis Hassell and Margaret Christensen. 1996. Indirect speech acts and their use in three channels of communication. In *Proceedings of the First International Workshop on Communication Modeling - The Language/Action Perspective*, Tilburg, The Netherlands.

Hamid Khosravi and Yorick Wilks. 1999. Routing email automatically by purpose not topic. *Journal of Natural Language Engineering*, 5:237–250.

Bryan Klimt and Yiming Yang. 2004. Introducing the Enron corpus. In *Proceedings of the Conference on Email and Anti-Spam (CEAS)*.

Andrew Lampert, Robert Dale, and Cécile Paris. 2008a. The nature of requests and commitments in email messages. In *Proceedings of EMAIL-08: the AAAI Workshop on Enhanced Messaging*, pages 42–47, Chicago.

Andrew Lampert, Robert Dal e, and Cécile Paris. 2008b. Requests and commitments in email are more complex than you think: Eight reasons to be cautious. In *Proceedings of Australasian Language Technology Workshop (ALTA2008)*, pages 55–63, Hobart, Australia.

Andrew Lampert, Robert Dale, and Cécile Paris. 2009. Segmenting email message text into zones. In *Proceedings of Empirical Methods in Natural Language Processing*, pages 919–928, Singapore.

Wendy E. Mackay. 1988. More than just a communication system: Diversity in the use of electronic mail. In *ACM conference on Computer-supported cooperative work*, pages 344–353, Portland, Oregon, USA.

Denise E. Murray. 1991. *Conversation for Action: The Computer Terminal As Medium of Communication*. John Benjamins Publishing Co.

Scott S L Piao, Andrew Wilson, and Tony McEnery. 2002. A multilingual corpus toolkit. In *Proceedings of 4th North American Symposium on Corpus Linguistics*, Indianapolis.

Jerry M. Sadock and Arnold Zwicky, 1985. *Language Typology and Syntactic Description. Vol.I Clause Structure*, chapter Speech act distinctions in syntax, pages 155–96. Cambridge University Press.

Simon Scerri, Myriam Mencke, Brian David, and Siegfried Handschuh. 2008. Evaluating the ontology powering smail — a conceptual framework for semantic email. In *Proceedings of the 6th LREC Conference*, Marrakech, Morocco.

John R. Searle. 1969. *Speech Acts: An Essay in the Philosophy of Language*. Cambridge University Press.

John Sinclair and Richard Malcolm Coulthard. 1975. *Towards and Analysis of Discourse - The English used by Teachers and Pupils*. Oxford University Press.

Steve Whittaker and Candace Sidner. 1996. Email overload: exploring personal information management of email. In *ACM Computer Human Interaction conference*, pages 276–283. ACM Press.

Terry Winograd and Fernando Flores. 1986. *Understanding Computers and Cognition*. Ablex Publishing Corporation, Norwood, New Jersey, USA, 1st edition. ISBN: 0-89391-050-3.

Ian Witten and Eiba Frank. 2005. *Data Mining: Practical machine learning tools and techniques*. Morgan Kaufmann, San Francisco, 2nd edition.

Evaluating Hierarchical Discourse Segmentation

Lucien Carroll
Linguistics Dept.
UC San Diego
San Diego, CA 92093
lucien@ling.ucsd.edu

Abstract

Hierarchical discourse segmentation is a useful technology, but it is difficult to evaluate. I propose an error measure based on the word error rate of Beeferman et al. (1999). I then show that this new measure not only reliably distinguishes baseline segmentations from lexically-informed hierarchical segmentations and more informed segmentations from less informed segmentations, but it also offers an improvement over previous linear error measures.

1 Introduction

Discourse segmentation is the task of identifying coherent clusters of sentences and the points of transition between those groupings. Discourse segmentation can be viewed as shallow parsing of discourse structure. The segments and the relations between them are left unlabeled, focusing instead on the boundaries between the segments (i.e., the bracketing).

Discourse segmentation is thought to facilitate automatic summarization (Angheluta et al., 2002; Boguraev and Neff, 2000), information retrieval (Kaszkiel and Zobel, 1997), anaphora resolution (Walker, 1997) and question answering (Chai and Jin, 2004). Automatic discourse segmentation, as shallow annotation of discourse structure, also provides a testing grounds for linguistic theories of discourse (Passonneau and Litman, 1997) and provides a natural unit of measure in linguistic corpora (Biber et al., 2004).

1.1 The structure of discourse

Research in discourse structure theory (Hobbs, 1985; Grosz and Sidner, 1986; Mann and Thompson, 1988; Kehler, 2002; Asher and Lascarides, 2003; Webber, 2004) and discourse parsing (Marcu, 2000; Forbes et al., 2003; Polanyi et al., 2004; Baldridge et al., 2007) has variously defined discourse structure in terms of communicative intention, attention, topic/subtopic structure, coherence relations, and cohesive devices. There is much disagreement about the units and elementary relations of discourse structure, but they agree that the structures are hierarchical, most commonly trees (Marcu, 2000), while others have argued for directed acyclic graphs (Danlos, 2004), or general graphs (Wolf and Gibson, 2004). In contrast, most of the segmentation research to date has focused on linear segmentation, in which segments are non-overlapping and sequential, and it has been argued that this sequence model is sufficient for many purposes (Hearst, 1994). I focus here on tree discourse segmentation, in which larger segments are composed of sequences of subsegments. This is potentially more informative and more faithful to linguistic theory than linear discourse segmentation is, but it poses a more challenging evaluation problem.

1.2 Hierarchical segmentation

Four studies have described hierarchical discourse segmentation algorithms, but none of them rigorously evaluated the segmentation in its hierarchical form. Yaari (1997) used a hierarchical clustering algorithm for hierarchical discourse segmentation, and to evaluate it, he linearized the tree (taking all boundaries equally) and compared the result-

Human Language Technologies: The 2010 Annual Conference of the North American Chapter of the ACL, pages 993–1001,
Los Angeles, California, June 2010.

ing precision and recall to contemporary linear segmentation algorithms. Slaney and Ponceleon (2001) used scale-space segmentation (an image segmentation algorithm) on the discourse's trajectory in a Latent Semantic Indexing (LSI) space (Landauer et al., 1998). They evaluated the algorithm by visual comparison with the heading-subheading structure of the text. Angheluta et al. (2002) applied a linear discourse segmentation algorithm recursively, segmenting each major segment into a sequence of subsegments. They used the result in a summarization system, and they evaluated the summarization system but not the segmentation itself. Eisenstein (2009) used a Bayesian latent topic model to find a hierarchical segmentation, and he comes the closest to quantitative evaluation of the whole segmentation. He evaluated it against three recursive segmentation algorithms on a corpus that had just two levels of segment depth and considers these two levels as separate and equally important. While each of these studies offers some insight into the validity of the hierarchical segmentation, none of these evaluation methods directly and quantitatively assesses the hierarchical segmentation as a whole.

Many state-of-the-art linear discourse segmentation algorithms also use hierarchical frameworks, making them applicable to hierarchical discourse segmentation with only trivial modification. For example, the C99 algorithm (Choi, 2000) applies contrast enhancement and divisive clustering to a matrix of lexical vector cosine similarities. The CWM algorithm (Choi et al., 2001) applies the same procedure to a similarity matrix of LSI vectors. Using these algorithms for hierarchical discourse segmentation simply requires keeping record of the boundary ranking, but until now they have only been used for linear segmentation.

1.3 The Beeferman error measure

Studies of linear discourse segmentation have revealed that discourse boundaries are inherently fuzzy. Human annotators demonstrate frequent disagreement about the number of segments and exactly where the transitions between segments occur, while still demonstrating statistically significant agreement (Passonneau and Litman, 1997). Because of this, conventional precision and recall measures penalize 'near misses' when they should be treated much the same as complete matches. The crossing-bracket measure (Carbone et al., 2004) is more forgiving, but still over-penalizes near misses and favors sparse bracketings. An error measure P_k proposed by Beeferman et al. (1999) compensates for the variation in boundary locations. It considers a moving window of width k equal to half the average segment length in the reference segmentation, where distances are measured in words or sentences, depending on whether word boundaries or sentence boundaries are considered possible discourse segment boundaries. The error is the average disagreement, between the reference segmentation and the evaluated segmentation, about whether the two ends of the window are in the same segment. Formally,

$$P_k = \frac{1}{N-k} \sum_{i=1}^{N-k} \delta(\delta(r_i, r_{i+k}), \delta(h_i, h_{i+k}))$$

where N is the total number of atoms (words or sentences) in the document, and k is the window width. The arguments r_i and h_i are the indices of the segments that contain atom i in the reference and hypothesized segmentations, respectively, and δ is the discrete delta function, evaluating to 1 if its arguments are equal and to 0 otherwise. Pevzner and Hearst (2001) proposed WindowDiff, a modification of P_k that indicates the average disagreement about how many boundaries lie within the window, replacing the inner δ functions with the count of segment boundaries between the two atoms. It is as sensitive to false positives as it is to false negatives, whereas P_k is more sensitive to false negatives.

There are still a few problems with these error measures. In penalizing false negatives and false positives equally, WindowDiff actually favors sparse segmentations. Whereas P_k scores the baseline strategies of no boundaries and all possible boundaries as within a few percent of 50% error, WindowDiff scores the all-boundaries baseline at 100% error for typical reference segmentations. Furthermore, in running the summation from $i = 1$ to $i = N - k$, both error measures count boundaries near the edges of the text less than boundaries near the middle of the text. A boundary that is $j < k$ atoms from the beginning or end of the text has weight $\frac{j}{k}$ relative to boundaries in the middle of the text. Finally, because of the hierarchical structure of many texts, it is quite possible that a reference segmentation might not include legitimate but fairly unimportant boundaries that a hypothesized segmentation does include. These unimportant boundaries should not count against the hypothesized segmentation, but in the linear segmentation paradigm, they necessarily do. The ideal error measure should distinguish more-informed algorithms from less-informed algorithms, treating equally uninformed baselines the same, and it should treat boundary placement errors according to the prominence of the boundaries, and not according to their positions within the text.

Building on work in evaluating linear segmentation, this study considers the evaluation of tree segmentations. I propose an error measure, derived from Beeferman et al.'s P_k (1999), for evaluating the alignment of a tree segmentation to a reference segmentation. I first show that this error measure is advantageous even for evaluating linear segmentations, and then I evaluate four hierarchical segmentation algorithms against a gold standard derived from encyclopedia articles.

2 A hierarchical measure

The proposed error measure is based on the intuition that prominent boundaries count more than less prominent boundaries. The hierarchical atom error rate E_{P_k} is the mean of Beeferman errors calculated over all linearizations of the segmentation tree (see Fig. 1). Assume a set R of reference boundaries and a set H of hypothesized boundaries each in rank order (prominent boundaries precede less prominent

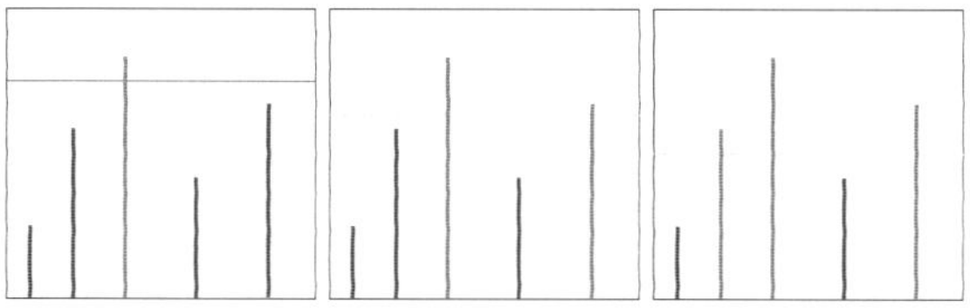

Figure 1: Sequential linearizations in computing hierarchical word error rate. The heights of the vertical lines represent the prominences of boundaries, and each horizontal line is one linearization. In the first step, only the highest boundary is used, producing just two segments. Each following step includes one more boundary.

ones). The error is calculated as

$$E_{P_k} = \frac{1}{|R|} \sum_i c_i P_k(R_i, H_i)$$

where

$$R_i = \{b_j : b_j \in R \wedge j \leq i\}$$

The elements of H_i are chosen such that $|H_i| = |R_i|$ and no $b_n \in H \setminus H_i$ is more prominent than any $b_j \in H_i$. If the reference boundaries are completely ordered, then $c_i = 1$ for all ranks i, but if some reference boundaries share ranks, one P_k term is calculated for each rank level in the reference segmentation, and weighted (c_i) by the number of boundaries that were at that level. In the degenerate case of linear segmentation, all segments have the same rank, and E_{P_k} reduces to the original P_k.

When hypothesized boundaries share ranks, each affected term in the summation is theoretically the average over all combinations (n boundaries at the next rank *Choose* r boundaries to complete H_i). But when the number of combinations is large, the computational complexity of the calculation can be reduced without sacrificing much accuracy by using a representative sampling of the combinations, as this closely approximates the average.

When the set of hypothesized boundaries is smaller than the set of reference boundaries, we could simply permit H_i to be smaller than R_i for large values of i, but that unnecessarily penalizes the hypothesized segmentation. The set of possible boundaries (word or sentence boundaries) which were not marked as segment boundaries can be understood to be segment boundaries of a baseline low ranking. Adding these unmarked boundaries to H, all at a single low rank, prevents incurring an undeserved penalty for false negatives.

In order to avoid undercounting boundaries near the beginning and end of the text, I consider the possibility of wrapping the window around from the beginning to the end of the text. In calculating P_k, the sum is understood to run from $i = 1$ to $i = N$, rather than stopping at $N - k$, and the atom index of the leading edge of the window $(i + k)$ generalizes to $((i + k) \bmod N)$.

3 Hierarchical replication of Choi et al.

As a preliminary test of the error measure, I evaluated two algorithms from Choi et al. (2001) on the standard segmentation data set that Choi (2000) compiled. Each file in that data is composed of 10 random portions of texts from the Brown Corpus (Francis and Kucera, 1979). The following results are based on the T_{3-11} subset, in which text segment lengths are uniformly distributed between 3 and 11 sentences. Since each file is composed of a sequence of text portions, the reference segmentation is linear, not hierarchical. Nevertheless, I evaluate hierarchical segmentation algorithms with the hierarchical measure, to show that treating linear segmentation as a special case of hierarchical segmentation solves the issue of unequal treatment of false positives and false negatives, and running the WindowDiff sum to N (wrapping the window around to the beginning) solves the problem of undercounting the boundaries near the text edges.

3.1 Segmentation algorithms

The C99 (Choi, 2000) and CWM (Choi et al., 2001) algorithms were evaluated. While these were designed and originally evaluated as linear segmentation algorithms, the hierarchical clustering they use makes hierarchical segmentation a trivial matter of retaining the order of the cluster splits. I refer to the hierarchical versions of these algorithms as HC99 and HCWM. The HC99 implementation used here is built directly from the C99 code which Choi released for educational use, and the HCWM implementation is based off that. The implementation uses a document-based LSI space built with Infomap-NLP[1] from the British National Corpus (Aston and Burnard, 1998), whereas the original CWM used sentence-based and paragraph-based LSI spaces derived from the Brown Corpus. Because of these differences, the implementation of HCWM reported here differs somewhat from the implementation of CWM reported by Choi et al. (2001).

The C99 and CWM algorithms include a criterion for optional automatic determination of the number of segments, but the hierarchical error measure does not penalize a segmentation for having more segments (defined by lower ranking boundaries) than the reference segmentation, so I used a constant number of segments, greater than in the reference segmentation, for the results reported here.

[1] Software available at http://infomap-nlp.sourceforge.net

One baseline (BIN) was constructed by a recursive bisection of segments, and another baseline (NONE) consisted of only the implicit boundaries at the beginning and end of the discourse, and all the possible intermediate boundaries (sentence breaks) are implicitly at one unmarked lower rank.

3.2 Results and Discussion

The calculated E_{P_k} error rates are displayed in Fig. 2.[2] The error for HC99 in Fig. 2a (12.5%) matches what Choi et al. (2001) reported (12%), while the error for HCWM (12.1%) is higher than that reported for the version with a paragraph-based 500-dimension LSI space (9%) but appears comparable to their sentence-based 400-dimension LSI space. (They do not report results for the sentence-based spaces on this T_{3-11} data set, but based on the results they report for a larger data set, it would appear to be about 12% for the T_{3-11} set.) The result for BIN (43.9%) is slightly lower than what Choi et al. (2001) reported for their equal-size segment baseline (45%). Since BIN would be an equal-segment baseline if there were only 8 segments per text, BIN should be similar to Choi et al's equal-size baseline. And the result for NONE (46.1%) agrees with Choi et al. (2001)'s results for their NONE (46%) baseline.

Comparison of graphs (a) and (b) in Fig. 2 shows that continuing the sum to wrap the window around to the beginning of the text generally lowers the measured error, to the greatest extent for BIN and least for HCWM. The average segment length in the reference segmentation is 7 sentences, so the window size k is usually 3 or 4 sentences, comparable to the minimum segment length (3). As a result, a boundary very rarely falls within k sentences of the text ends, and fully including these sentences in the sum leads to a lower error for segmentations like BIN that don't hypothesize boundaries near the text ends.

The E_{WD} hierarchical error rates (calculated according to WindowDiff) are consistently higher (Fig. 2c, d) than the corresponding E_{P_k}. WindowDiff

[2] The error rates in this section are calculated using the word-error rate for comparison with Choi's results, but since the candidate boundaries are actually the line breaks, the line-error rate would be more appropriate. Line error rates are 1% to 2% higher.

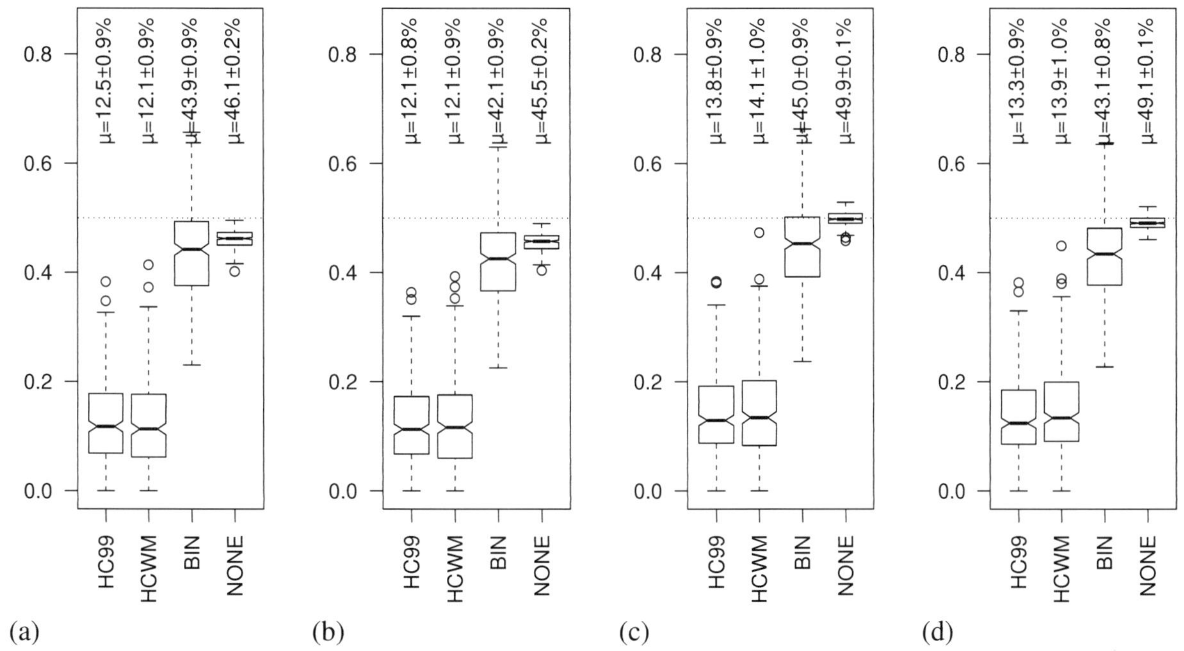

Figure 2: Distributions of E_{P_k} (a, b) and E_{WD} (c, d) for each of the hypothesized and baseline segmentation algorithms. The data in graphs (a) and (c) are calculated with sums that stop at $N-k$ (when the window reaches the end of the text), whereas (b) and (d) are calculated with sums that run to N (wrapping the window back to the beginning). The boxes indicate the quartiles, and the means with 95% confidence intervals are written above.

scores are never lower than P_k scores, because in order to count as in agreement, the two segmentations must agree about the number of boundaries within the window rather than just about whether there are boundaries within the window. But these scores are not much higher than EP_k either, even though the original linear WindowDiff measure sometimes assigns much higher scores. Under the original WindowDiff measure, with reference and hypothesized boundary sets of unequal size, the NONE baseline scores 43.8% (cf. P_k=43.5% for sum to N), while an ALL baseline scores 99.2% (cf. P_k=51.1% for sum to N). WindowDiff was designed to penalize false positives even when two boundaries are close together, a condition that P_k underpenalizes. When a hypothesized segmentation has more segments than the reference segmentation, the extra boundaries incur false positive penalties without corresponding false negative penalties, and WindowDiff assigns an error rate that is higher than the P_k error rate and sometimes even higher than the NONE baseline. But with the hierarchical E_{WD} error, extra boundaries are sampled or ignored, and so every false positive has a corresponding false negative, which limits the divergence between E_{WD} and E_{P_k} and keeps the E_{WD} error of informed segmentations below baseline errors. As with E_{P_k}, continuing the sum to N (Fig. 2d), has only a slight effect on the error, but the effect is most pronounced on BIN, reflecting the fact that BIN, like the reference segmentation systematically does not place boundaries near the text ends.

3.3 Conclusion

We have seen here that treating linear segmentations as a special case of hierarchical segmentations, having just one rank of marked boundaries but having implicit higher ranking boundaries at the text ends and implicit lower ranking boundaries at all 'non-boundaries', resolves the outstanding issues of unequal sensitivity that P_k and WindowDiff have. Furthermore, in sampling hypothesized boundaries to match the number of reference boundaries, the hierarchical conception of the error metric smoothly adapts to segmentations that overestimate or underestimate the number of segments. A segmentation can not do much worse than 50% (at chance) just by hypothesizing fewer or more segments than the reference segmentation 'knows' about. The major remaining strength of WindowDiff over the P_k metric is that P_k still undercounts errors when there are segments much smaller than the average size.

For these reasons, I adopt a version of E_{WD} that continues the sum to wrap the window around the end of the text. In addition, when I refer to the linear error measure in the following sections, I mean the special case of E_{WD} in which the information in the reference segmentation about the ranking of the marked boundaries is ignored, but boundary ranking information in the hypothesized segmentation (both marked and unmarked boundaries) is still used to select as many segment boundaries as are in the reference segmentation.

4 Wikipedia Evaluation

In this section, I compare the same two algorithms and baselines with two additional hierarchical segmentation algorithms, using a hierarchical reference segmentation. The reference segmentation corpus is derived from encyclopedia articles, and I use the hierarchical error measure developed in the previous sections. I also constrast the hierarchical error rates with measurements that ignore the boundary ranking information in the hypothesized or reference segmentations in order to highlight the difference between the performance on boundary position and the performance on boundary ranking.

4.1 Corpus and Algorithms

The evaluation corpus is derived from the *2006 Wikipedia CD* release.[3] The html pages were converted to flat text, removing boilerplate, navigation, info-boxes, and image captions. Heading text was replaced with a boundary marker, indicating the heading depth. The subcorpus used for this evaluation consists of articles with a heading depth of four (i.e. having html elements h2 through h5), a total of 66 articles. The texts were reformatted with an automatic sentence detector[4] to have one sentence per line, and then tokenized.[5]

In addition to the HC99 and HCWM algorithms used in the previous section, I use two algorithms described by Eisenstein (2009). The HIERBAYES algorithm (here, HBT) uses a multi-level latent topic model to perform joint inference over the locations and prominences of topic change boundaries. The GREEDY-BAYES algorithm (here, GBEM) uses a single-level latent topic model to find a linear segmentation, and recursively divides each of the segments.[6] Both algorithms internally decide the number of hypothesized boundaries, sometimes underestimating it and sometimes overestimating.[7]

4.2 Results and Discussion

The E_{WD} error rates for each of the hypothesized segmentations are presented in Fig. 3. As with the Choi data, the NONE baseline has an error rate at chance (50%), while the lexical algorithms perform better than that (highly statistically significantly ($p < .0001$) less than 50%, according to individual two-sided one-sample t-tests). However, they perform much worse than they did on the Choi data.

In spite of the relatively high error rates, the discriminating power of the evaluation measure is revealed by comparison of the fully hierarchical error rates (Fig. 3a) with the error rates that ignore the ranking information in the reference (Fig. 3b) or hypothesized (Fig. 3c) segmentations. For each of the lexical algorithms that were originally designed as linear segmentation algorithms (HC99, HCWM, and GBEM), the mean error is less in Fig. 3b against the linear standard (when reference segmentation boundary prominences are ignored) than in Fig. 3a under the fully hierarchical measure (two-tailed paired t-tests, each $p < .0001$). In contrast, HBT, designed as a hierarchical segmentation algorithm, obtains a lower error rate under the fully hierarchical E_{WD} measure (though the difference does

[3] Available from `http://schools-wikipedia.org/2006/`.

[4] From Ratnaparkhi's 'jmx' (`ftp://ftp.cis.upenn.edu/pub/adwait/jmx/jmx.tar.gz`).

[5] The evaluation code and corpus can be downloaded from `http://idiom.ucsd.edu/~lucien/segmentation`

[6] Both algorithms are part of the HBayesSeg package, available at `http://people.csail.mit.edu/jacobe/naacl09.html`

[7] Options for HBT were set to produce 3 levels of text-internal boundary prominence. Attempts to obtain more boundaries and more depth levels lead to deteriorated performance, because the search space grows geometrically with the number of levels (Eisenstein, p.c.)

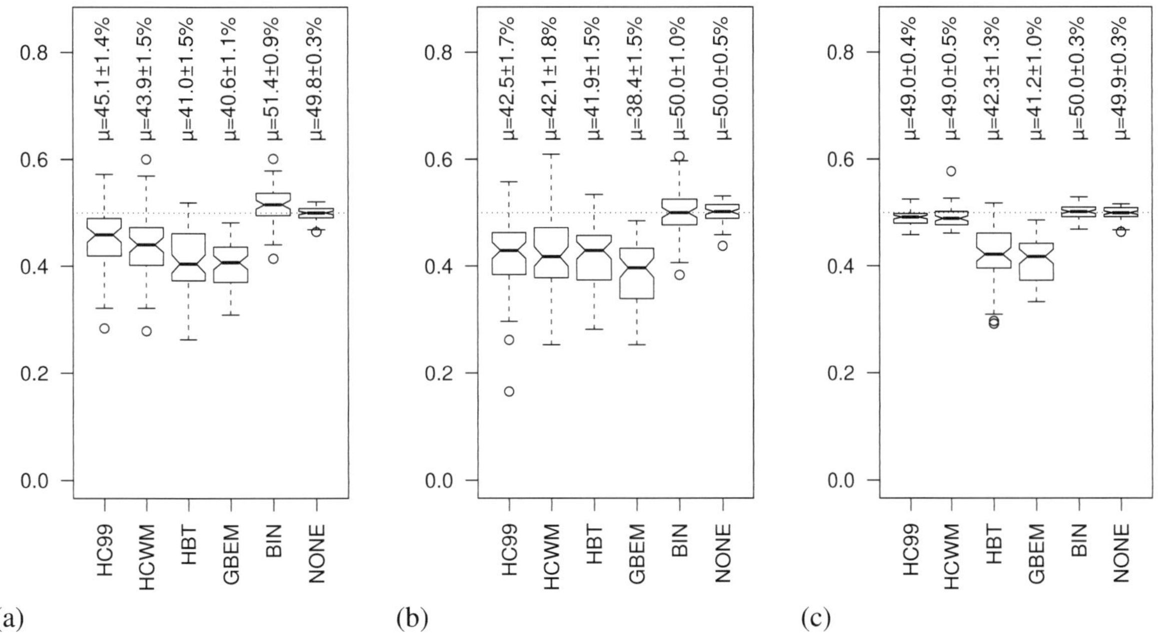

Figure 3: E_{WD} error rates for each of the segmentation algorithms. (a) Hierarchical error (b) Linear error (ignoring reference segmentation prominences) (c) Hierarchical error ignoring hypothesized segmentation prominences. Boxes show quantiles and means are written above, with 95% confidence intervals.

not reach significance: $p = 0.1$, two-tailed paired t-test). When instead the hypothesized boundary prominences are ignored (Fig. 3c), reducing them to linear segmentations but still evaluating against the hierarchical standard, the error rates of all the lexical algorithms are raised (in two-tailed paired t-tests, each $p < .0001$), but HBT and GBEM are only slightly affected, whereas HC99 and HCWM are almost raised to chance. While HBT and GBEM hypothesize about the same number of boundaries as the reference segmentation (13 and 22 text-internal boundaries on average, compared to 22 text-internal boundaries in the reference corpus), the HC99 and HCWM algorithms were made to hypothesize 54 boundaries for each text. The difference between their error rates in (Fig. 3a) and (Fig. 3c) shows that the HC99 and HCWM boundaries given the highest prominences corresponded much more closely to the reference boundaries than the hypothesized boundaries given the lowest prominences.

The mean scores for the BIN baseline are over 50% on the encyclopedia data. In contrast, the mean score for BIN on the Choi standard data (Fig. 2) was 45% for the linear measure and 43% for the hierarchical measure. Why did BIN do so poorly here when it performed well above chance on the Choi data? The difference is in the distributions of segment lengths. As seen in Fig. 4, the Choi data segment lengths are well-defined by their mean, because they were constructed with uniform distributions of segment length. On the other hand, the distribution of segment lengths in the encyclopedia data is more skewed, with many quite short segments and a few quite long segments.

The error rates for both HC99 and HCWM are much higher on the encyclopedia data than they are on the Choi data, and the error rates for HBT and GBEM are not much better. Choi's evaluation corpus was specifically designed to have obvious boundaries, whereas the boundaries in these discourse samples are much less obvious. As discussed by Kauchak and Chen (2005), even algorithms that obtain low error rates on newsfeed do not perform well on more fluid discourse, and while Ji and Zha (2003) reported quite low error on an expository text sample ($P_k = 12\%$), Kauchak and Chen (2005) report a best error rate of $P_k = 38.5\%$ on the encyclopedia corpus they used, and Malioutov and Barzi-

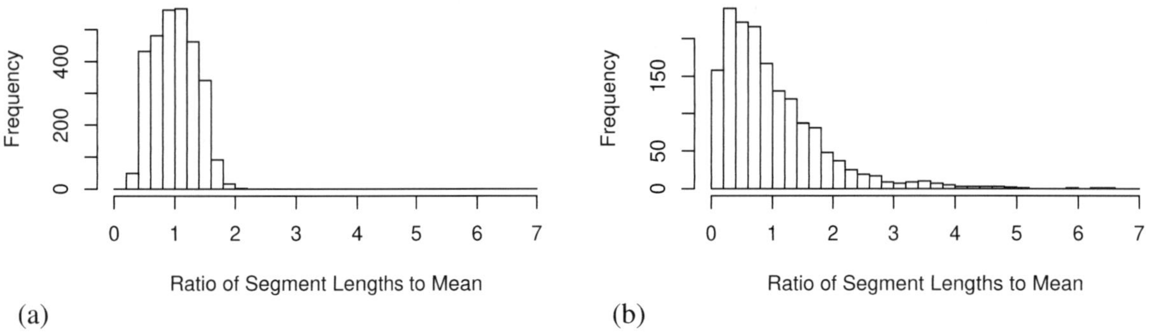

Figure 4: Distribution of sentences per segment for (a) Choi standard data (b) Wikipedia data

lay (2006) obtained P_k error rates between 30% and 40% on the lecture data they used, comparable to human annotator pairwise P_k ranging from 24% to 42%. C99 and CWM—like the other algorithms that make use of hierarchical representations of the text, such as Ji and Zha (2003) and Fragkou et al. (2004)—depend completely on lexical information. Another strand of research, including Galley et al. (2003) and Kauchak and Chen (2005), make use of a wide variety of linguistic and orthographic cues. And the discourse parsing systems take advantage of even more linguistic cues. The ideal segmentation algorithm needs to combine the advantages of each of these approaches, but the frameworks are not straightforwardly compatible. The Bayesian framework explored by Eisenstein and Barzilay (2008) is a potential route to a richer model, and they found their richer model beneficial for a meetings corpus but not for a textbook. The HBT and GBEM algorithms, which were based on that work, do not attempt to go beyond lexical cohesion, but it does provide a framework for hierarchical segmentation algorithms that take advantage of other cues.

5 Conclusions

In Section 2, I introduced a modification of the error measure developed by Beeferman et al. (1999) and Pevzner and Hearst (2001). I then showed that this modification, directed at evaluating hierarchical segmentations, also produces a more robust evaluation of linear segmentations as well. And applied to hierarchical segmentations, it successfully distinguishes lexically-informed segmentations from baseline segmentations, and it distinguishes hierarchical segmentations from segmentations composed of the same boundaries but without the boundary ranking information. As a more reliable evaluation of both linear and hierarchical segmentation algorithms, this error measure will facilitate the development of more richly informed segmentation algorithms.

Acknowledgments

In this research, I have benefited from resources at both San Diego State University and UC San Diego. This work has been enriched by the questions and advice of many people, including Eniko Csomay, Rob Malouf, Lara Taylor, Rebecca Colavin, Andy Kehler, and the NAACL anonymous reviewers. I am also grateful to Freddy Choi and Jacob Eisenstein for making their code and data available, and to Jacob for additional help running his code. All errors are my own.

References

Roxana Angheluta, Rik De Busser, and Marie-Francine Moens. 2002. The use of topic segmentation for automatic summarization. In *DUC 2002*.

Nicholas Asher and Alex Lascarides. 2003. *Logics of Conversation*. Cambridge University Press.

Guy Aston and Lou Burnard. 1998. *The BNC Handbook: Exploring the British National Corpus with SARA*. Edinburgh University Press.

Jason Baldridge, Nicholas Asher, and Julie Hunter. 2007. Annotation for and robust parsing of discourse structure of unrestricted texts. *Zeitschrift für Sprachwissenschaft*, 26(213):239.

Doug Beeferman, Adam Berger, and John D. Lafferty. 1999. Statistical models for text segmentation. *Machine Learning*, 34(1-3):177–210.

Douglas Biber, Eniko Csomay, James K. Jones, and Casey Keck. 2004. A corpus linguistic investigation of vocabulary-based discourse units in university registers. *Language and Computers*, 20:53–72.

Branimir Boguraev and Mary S. Neff. 2000. Discourse segmentation in aid of document summarization. In *33rd HICSS*.

Marco Carbone, Ya'akov Gal, Stuart Shieber, and Barbara Grosz. 2004. Unifying annotated discourse hierarchies to create a gold standard. In *Proceedings of 4th SIGDIAL Workshop on Discourse and Dialogue*.

Joyce Y. Chai and Rong Jin. 2004. Discourse structure for context question answering. In *HLT-NAACL 2004 Workshop on Pragmatics of Question Answering*, pages 23–30.

Freddy Choi, Peter Wiemer-Hastings, and Johanna Moore. 2001. Latent semantic analysis for text segmentation. In *Proceedings of 6th EMNLP*, pages 109–117.

Freddy Choi. 2000. Advances in domain independent linear text segmentation. In *Proceedings of NAACL-00*, pages 26–33.

Laurence Danlos. 2004. Discourse dependency structures as constrained DAGs. In *Proceedings of 5th SIGDIAL Workshop on Discourse and Dialogue*, pages 127–135.

Jacob Eisenstein and Regina Barzilay. 2008. Bayesian unsupervised topic segmentation. In *Proceedings of EMNLP 2008*.

Jacob Eisenstein. 2009. Hierarchical text segmentation from multi-scale lexical cohesion. In *Proceedings of NAACL09*.

Katherine Forbes, Eleni Miltsakaki, Rashmi Prasad, Anoop Sarkar, Aravind Joshi, and Bonnie Webber. 2003. D-LTAG system: Discourse parsing with a lexicalized tree-adjoining grammar. *Journal of Logic, Language and Information*, 12(3):261–279, June.

P. Fragkou, V. Petridis, and Ath. Kehagias. 2004. A dynamic programming algorithm for linear text segmentation. *Journal of Int Info Systems*, 23:179–197.

W. Nelson Francis and Henry Kucera. 1979. *BROWN Corpus Manual*. Brown University, third edition.

Michael Galley, Kathleen McKeown, Eric Fossler-Lussier, and Hongyan Jing. 2003. Discourse segmentation of multi-party conversation. In *41st ACL*.

Barbara J. Grosz and Candace L. Sidner. 1986. Attention, intentions, and the structure of discourse. *Computational Linguistics*, 12(3):175–204.

Marti Hearst. 1994. Multi-paragraph segmentation of expository text. In *32nd ACL*, pages 9 – 16, New Mexico State University, Las Cruces, New Mexico.

Jerry R Hobbs. 1985. On the coherence and structure of discourse. In *CSLI 85-37*.

Xiang Ji and Hongyuan Zha. 2003. Domain-independent text segmentation using anisotropic diffusion and dynamic programming. In *SIGIR'03*.

Marcin Kaszkiel and Justin Zobel. 1997. Passage retrieval revisited. In *Proceedings of 20th ACM SIGIR*, pages 178–185.

David Kauchak and Francine Chen. 2005. Feature-based segmentation of narrative documents. In *Proceedings of the ACL Workshop on Feature Engineering for Machine Learning in NLP*.

Andrew Kehler. 2002. *Coherence, reference and the theory of grammar*. CSLI Publications.

Thomas K. Landauer, Peter W. Foltz, and Darrell Laham. 1998. An introduction to latent semantic analysis. *Discourse Processes*, 25:259–284.

Igor Malioutov and Regina Barzilay. 2006. Minimum cut model for spoken lecture segmentation. In *Proceedings of the 21st International Conference on Computational Linguistics and 44th Annual Meeting of the ACL*, pages 25–32.

William Mann and Sandra Thompson. 1988. Rhetorical structure theory: Towards a functional theory of text organization. *Text*, 8(3):243–281.

Daniel Marcu. 2000. *The theory and practice of discourse parsing and summarization*. MIT Press.

Rebecca J. Passonneau and Diane J. Litman. 1997. Discourse segmentation by human and automated means. *Computational Linguistics*, 23(1):103–139.

Lev Pevzner and Marti Hearst. 2001. A critique and improvement of an evaluation metric for text segmentation. *Computational Linguistics*, 16(1).

Livia Polanyi, Chris Culy, Martin van den Berg, Gian Lorenzo Thione, and David Ahn. 2004. A rule based approach to discourse parsing. In *Proceedings of SIGDIAL*.

Malcolm Slaney and Dulce Ponceleon. 2001. Hierarchical segmentation: Finding changes in a text signal. *Proceedings of SIAM 2001 Text Mining Workshop*, pages 6–13.

Marilyn A. Walker. 1997. Centering, anaphora resolution, and discourse structure. In Aravind K. Joshi Marilyn A. Walker and Ellen F. Prince, editors, *Centering in Discourse*. Oxford University Press.

Bonnie Webber. 2004. D-LTAG: extending lexicalized TAG to discourse. *Cognitive Science*, 28:751–779.

Florian Wolf and Edward Gibson. 2004. Representing discourse coherence: A corpus-based analysis. In *20th COLING*.

Yaakov Yaari. 1997. Segmentation of expository texts by hierarchical agglomerative clustering. In *Proceedings of RANLP'97*.

Reformulating Discourse Connectives for Non-Expert Readers

Advaith Siddharthan
Department of Computing Science
University of Aberdeen
advaith@abdn.ac.uk

Napoleon Katsos
Research Centre for English and Applied Linguistics
University of Cambridge
nk248@cam.ac.uk

Abstract

In this paper we report a behavioural experiment documenting that different lexico-syntactic formulations of the discourse relation of *causation* are deemed more or less acceptable by different categories of readers. We further report promising results for automatically selecting the formulation that is most appropriate for a given category of reader using supervised learning. This investigation is embedded within a longer term research agenda aimed at summarising scientific writing for lay readers using appropriate paraphrasing.

1 Introduction

There are many reasons why a speaker/writer would want to choose one formulation of a discourse relation over another; for example, maintaining thread of discourse, avoiding shifts in focus and issues of salience and end weight. There are also reasons to use different formulations for different audiences; for example, to account for differences in reading skills and domain knowledge. In this paper, we present a psycholinguistic experiment designed to illuminate the factors that determine the appropriateness of particular realisations of discourse relations for different audiences. The second part of this paper focuses on training a natural language generation system to predict which realisation choices are more felicitous than others for a given audience. Our paraphrases include eight different constructions. Consider 1a.–d. below:

(1) a. Tom ate **because** he was hungry.
b. Tom ate **because of** his hunger.
c. Tom's hunger **caused** him to eat.
d. The **cause** of Tom's eating was his hunger.

These differ in terms of the lexico-syntactic properties of the discourse marker (shown in bold font). Indeed the discourse markers here are conjunctions, prepositions, verbs and nouns. As a consequence the propositional content is expressed either as a clause or a noun phrase ("*he was hungry*" vs "*his hunger*", etc.). Additionally, the order of presentation of propositional content can be varied to give four more lexico-syntactic paraphrases:

(1) e. **Because** Tom was hungry, he ate.
f. **Because of** his hunger, Tom ate.
g. Tom's eating **was caused by** his hunger.
h. Tom's hunger was the **cause** of his eating.

It is clear that some formulations of this propositional content are more felicitous than others; for example, 1a. seems preferable to 1d., but for a different propositional content, other formulations might be more felicitous (for instance, example 4, section 3.1, where the passive seems in fact preferable). While discourse level choices based on information ordering play a role in choosing a formulation, it is of particular interest to us that some decontextualised information orderings within a sentence are deemed unacceptable. Any summarisation task that considers discourse coherence should not introduce sentence-level unacceptability.

We now summarise our main research questions:

1. Are some formulations of a discourse relation more felicitous than others, given the same propositional content?
2. Does the reader's level of domain expertise affect their preferred formulation?
3. What linguistic features determine which formulations are acceptable?
4. How well can a natural language generator be trained to predict the most appropriate formulation for a given category of reader?

In this paper, we focus on causal relations because these are pervasive in science writing and are integral to how humans conceptualise the world. The 8 formulations selected are 2 information orderings

Human Language Technologies: The 2010 Annual Conference of the North American Chapter of the ACL, pages 1002–1010,
Los Angeles, California, June 2010.

of 4 different syntactic constructs; thus we explore a fairly broad range of constructions.

With regard to genre, we have a particular interest in scientific writing, specifically biomedical texts. Reformulating such texts for lay audiences is a highly relevant task today and many news agencies perform this service; e.g., Reuters Health summarises medical literature for lay audiences and BBC online has a Science/Nature section that reports on science. These services rely either on press releases by scientists and universities or on specialist scientific reporters, thus limiting coverage of a growing volume of scientific literature in a digital economy. Thus, reformulating technical writing for lay audiences is a research area of direct relevance to information retrieval, information access and summarisation systems.

At the same time, while there are numerous studies about the effect of text reformulation on people with different literacy levels or language deficits (see section 2), the issue of expert vs lay audiences has received less attention. Further, most studies focus on narrative texts such as news or history. However, as Linderholm et al. (2000) note, results from studies of causality in narrative texts might not carry over to scientific writing, because inferences are made more spontaneously during the reading of narrative than expository texts. Thus comparing expert vs lay readers on the comprehension of causal relations in scientific writing is a most timely investigation.

In section 2, we relate our research to the existing linguistic, psycholinguistic and computational literature. Then in section 3, we describe our psycholinguistic experiment that addresses our first two research questions and in section 4 we present a computational approach to learning felicitous paraphrases that addresses the final two questions.

2 Background and related work

2.1 Expressing causation

Linguists generally consider five different components of meaning (Wolff et al., 2005) in causal expressions: (a) occurrence of change in patient, (b) specification of endstate, (c) tendency and concordance, (d) directness and (e) mechanism. The expressions we consider in this paper, "because" (**conjunction**), "because of" (**preposition**) and "cause" as noun or verb (**periphrastic causatives**) express (a), (b) and in some instances, (c). This is in contrast to **affect verbs** that only express (a), **link verbs** that express (a–b), **lexical causatives** that express (a–d) and **resultatives** that express (a–e). These distinctions are illustrated by the sentences in example 2:

(2) a. Sara **kicked** the door. (affect verb – end state not specified)

b. The door's **breaking** was linked to Sara. (link verb – end state specified, but unclear that door has a tendency to break)

c. Sara **caused** the door to break. / The door broke **because of** Sara. (periphrastic / preposition – indirect; the door might have a tendency to break)

d. Sara **broke** the door. (lexical causative – directness of action is specified)

e. Sara **broke** the door **open**. (resultative – end state is "open")

There is much literature on how people prefer one type of causative over the other based on these five components of meaning (e.g. see Wolff et al. (2005)). What is less understood is how one selects between various expressions that carry similar semantic content. In this paper we consider four constructs "because of", "because", and "cause" as a verb and a noun. These express the components of meaning (a–c) using different syntactic structures. By considering only these four lexically similar constructs, we can focus on the role of the lexis and of syntax in determining the most felicitous expression of causation for a given propositional content.

2.2 Discourse connectives and comprehension

Previous work has shown that when texts have been manually rewritten to make discourse relations such as *causation* explicit, reading comprehension is significantly improved in middle/high school students (Beck et al., 1991). Further, connectives that permit pre-posed adverbial clauses have been found to be difficult for third to fifth grade readers, even when the order of mention coincides with the causal (and temporal) order; for instance, 3b. is more accessible than 3a. (e.g. from Anderson and Davison (1988)).

(3) a. **Because** Mexico allowed slavery, many Americans and their slaves moved to Mexico during that time.

b. Many Americans and their slaves moved to Mexico during that time, **because** Mexico allowed slavery.

Such studies show that comprehension can be improved by reformulating text; e.g., making causal relations explicit had a facilitatory effect for readers with low reading skills (Linderholm et al., 2000; Beck et al., 1991) and for readers with low levels of domain expertise (Noordman and Vonk, 1992). Further, specific information orderings were found to be facilitatory by Anderson and Davison (1988).

However, it has not been investigated whether readers with different levels of domain expertise are facilitated by any specific lexico-syntactic formulation among the many possible explicit realisations of a relation. This is a novel question in the linguistics literature, and we address it in section 3.

2.3 Connectives and automatic (re)generation

Much of the work regarding (re)generation of text based on discourse connectives aims to simplify text in certain ways, to make it more accessible to particular classes of readers. The PSET project (Carroll et al., 1998) considered simplifying news reports for aphasics. The PSET project focused mainly on lexical simplification (replacing difficult words with easier ones), but more recently, there has been work on syntactic simplification and, in particular, the way syntactic rewrites interact with discourse structure and text cohesion (Siddharthan, 2006). Elsewhere, there has been renewed interest in *paraphrasing*, including the replacement of words (especially verbs) with their dictionary definitions (Kaji et al., 2002) and the replacement of idiomatic or otherwise troublesome expressions with simpler ones. The current research emphasis is on automatically learning paraphrases from comparable or aligned corpora (Barzilay and Lee, 2003; Ibrahim et al., 2003). The text simplification and paraphrasing literature does not address paraphrasing that requires syntactic alterations such as those in example 1 or the question of appropriateness of different formulations of a discourse relation.

Some natural language generation systems incorporate results from psycholinguistic studies to make principled choices between alternative formulations. For example, SkillSum (Williams and Reiter, 2008) and ICONOCLAST (Power et al., 2003) are two contemporary generation systems that allow for specifying aspects of style such as choice of discourse marker, clause order, repetition and sentence and paragraph lengths in the form of constraints that can be optimised. However, to date, these systems do not consider syntactic reformulations of the type we are interested in. Our research is directly relevant to such generation systems as it can help such systems make decisions in a principled manner.

2.4 Corpus studies and treebanking

There are two major corpora that mark up discourse relations – the RST Discourse Treebank based on Rhetorical Structure Theory (Mann and Thompson, 1988), and the Penn Discourse Treebank (Webber et al., 2005). Neither is suitable for studies on the felicity of specific formulations of a discourse relation. As part of this research, we have created a corpus of 144 real text examples, reformulated in 8 ways, giving 1152 sentences in total.

There have been numerous corpus studies of discourse connectives, such as studies on the discourse-role disambiguation of individual cue-phrases in spoken and written corpora (e.g., Hirschberg and Litman (1993)), the substitutability of discourse connectives (e.g., Hutchinson (2005)), and indeed corpus studies as a means of informing the choice of discourse relations to consider in a theory (e.g., Knott and Dale (1994); Knott (1996)). A distinguishing feature of our approach relative to previous ones is an in-depth study of syntactic variations; in contrast, for example, Knott's taxonomy of discourse relations is based on the use of a substitution text that precludes variants of the same relation having different syntax.

3 Linguistic acceptability study

3.1 Dataset creation

We have constructed a dataset that can be used to gain insights into differences between different realisations of discourse relations. In the following, we will illustrate such rewriting situations using an example from a medical article. As mentioned previously, we are particularly interested in complex syntactic reformulations; in example 4 below, a. is from the original text and b.–h. are reformulations. There are two examples each of formulations using "*because*", "*because of*", the verb "*cause*" and the noun "*cause*" with different ordering of propositional content. This provides us with 8 formulations per example sentence; for example:

(4) a. Fructose-induced hypertension **is caused by** increased salt absorption by the intestine and kidney. **[cause_p]**

b. Increased salt absorption by the intestine and kidney **causes** fructose-induced hypertension. **[cause_a]**

c. Fructose-induced hypertension occurs **because of** increased salt absorption by the intestine and kidney. **[a_becof_b]**

d. **Because of** increased salt absorption by the intestine and kidney, fructose-induced hypertension occurs. **[becof_ba]**

e. Fructose-induced hypertension occurs **because** there is increased salt absorption by the intestine and kidney. **[a_bec_b]**

f. **Because** there is increased salt absorption by the intestine and kidney, fructose-induced hypertension occurs. **[bec_ba]**

g. Increased salt absorption by the intestine and kidney is the **cause of** fructose-induced hypertension. **[b_causeof_a]**

h. The **cause of** fructose-induced hypertension is increased salt absorption by the intestine and kidney. **[causeof_ab]**

Our corpus contains 144 such examples from three genres (see below), giving 1152 sentences in total. These 144 examples contain equal numbers of original sentences (18) of each of the 8 types. The manual reformulation is formulaic, and it is part of our broader research effort to automate the process using transfer rules and a bi-directional grammar. The example above is indicative of the process. To make a clause out of a noun phrase (examples 4c.–f.), we introduce either the copula or the verb "occur", based on a subjective judgement of whether this is an event or a continuous phenomenon. Conversely, to create a noun phrase from a clause, we use a possessive and a gerund; for example (simplified for illustration):

(5) a. Irwin had triumphed because he was so good a man.

b. The cause of Irwin's having triumphed was his being so good a man.

Clearly, there are many different possibilities for this reformulation; for example:

(5) b'. The cause of Irwin's *triumph* was his being so good a man.

b". The cause of Irwin's *triumph* was his *exceptional goodness as* a man.

As part of our wider research agenda, we are exploring automatic reformulation using transfer rules and a bi-directional grammar. In this context, given our immediate interest is in the discourse markers, we restrict our reformulation method to only generate sentences such as 5b. This not only makes automation easier, but also standardises data for our experiment by removing an aspect of subjectivity from the manual reformulation.

We used equal numbers of sentences from three different genres[1]:

- **PubMed Abstracts**: Technical writing from the Biomedical domain
- **BNC World**: Article from the British National Corpus tagged as World News
- **BNC Natural Science**: Article from the British National Corpus tagged as Natural Science. This covers popular science writing in the mainstream media

There were 48 example sentences chosen randomly from each genre, such that there were 6 examples of each of the 8 types of formulation)

3.2 Experimental setup

Human judgements for acceptability for each of the 1152 sentences in our corpus were obtained using the WebExp package (Keller et al., 2008 to appear).[2] We investigated acceptability because it is a measure which reflects both ease of comprehension and surface well-formedness.

The propositional content of 144 sentences was presented in 8 formulations. Eight participant groups (A–H) consisting of 6 people each were presented with exactly one of the eight formulations of each of 144 different sentences, as per a Latin square design. Thus, while each participant read an equal number of sentences in each formulation type, they never read more than one formulation of the same propositional content. Each group saw 18 original and 126 reformulated sentences in total, 48 from each genre. This experimental design allows all statistical comparisons between the eight types of causal formulations to be within-participants.

Acceptability judgements were elicited on the sentences without presenting the preceding context

[1]PubMed URL: http://www.ncbi.nlm.nih.gov/pubmed/
The British National Corpus, version 3 (BNC XML Edition). 2007. Distributed by Oxford University Computing Services on behalf of the BNC Consortium. http://www.natcorp.ox.ac.uk

[2]Note that the reformulations are, strictly speaking, grammatical according to the authors' judgement. We are testing violations of acceptability, rather than grammaticality per se.

from the original text. The participants were University of Cambridge students (all native English speakers with different academic backgrounds). Post experimentally we divided participants in two groups based on having a Science or a non-Science background[3]. Rather than giving participants a fixed scale (e.g. 1–7), we used the magnitude estimation paradigm, which is more suitable to capture robust or subtle differences between the relative strength of acceptability or grammaticality violations (see Bard et al. (1996); Cowart (1997); Keller (2000)).

3.3 Magnitude estimation

Participants were asked to score how acceptable a modulus sentence was, using any positive number. They were then asked to score other sentences relative to this modulus, using any positive number, even decimals, so that higher scores were assigned to more acceptable sentences. The advantage of Magnitude estimation is that the researcher does not make any assumptions about the number of linguistic distinctions allowed. Each subject makes as many distinctions as they feel comfortable. Scores were normalised to allow comparison across participants, following standard practice in the literature by using the z-score: For each participant, each sentence score was normalised so that the mean score is 0 and the standard deviation is 1:

$$z_{ih} = \frac{x_{ih} - \mu_h}{\sigma_h}$$

where z_{ih} is participant h's z-score for the sentence i when participant h gave a magnitude estimation score of x_{ih} to that sentence. μ_h is the mean and σ_h the standard deviation of the set of magnitude estimation scores for user h.

3.4 Results

42 out of 48 participants (19 science students and 23 non-science students) completed the experiment, giving us 3–6 ratings for each of the 1152 sentences. Figure 1 shows the average z-scores with standard error bars for Science and non-Science students for each of the three genres. The first six columns show the scores for only the 144 Original Sentences. Note that science students find PubMed sentences most acceptable (significantly more than BNC Natural Science; t-test, $p < .005$), while among non-science students there is a numerical tendency to find the world news sentences most acceptable. Both categories of participants disprefer sentences from the popular science genre. Columns 7–12 show the average z-scores for the 1008 reformulated sentences. Let us note that these are significantly lower than for the originals (t-test, $p < .001$).

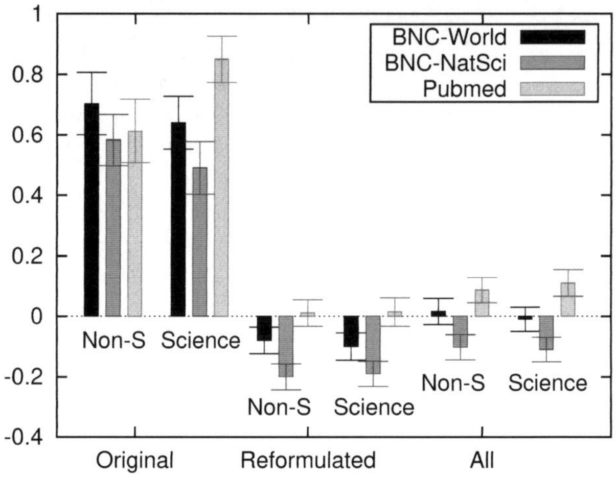

Figure 1: Preferences by Field of Study – **Science** or **Non-S**cience.

Some of these results are as expected. With regard to genre preferences, scientists might find the style of technical writing acceptable because of familiarity with that style of writing. Second, with regard to the average score for original and reformulated sentences, some reformulations just don't work for a given propositional content. This pulls the average for reformulated sentences down. However, on average 2 out of 7 reformulations score quite high.

It is interesting that the popular science genre is least preferred by both groups. This suggests that reformulating technical writing for lay readers is not a trivial endeavour, even for journalists.

Now consider Figure 2, which shows the average z-scores for only PubMed sentences for science and non-science students as a function of sentence type. For non-science students reading PubMed sentences, three formulations are strongly dispreferred – "a is caused by b", "because b, a" and "b is the

[3] Participants provided subject of study prior to participation in the experiment. Our classification of Science consists of Life Sciences(Genetics/Biology/etc), Chemistry, Environmental Science, Engineering, Geology, Physics, Medicine, Pharmacology, Veterinary Science and Zoology. Non-Science consists of Archaeology, Business, Classics, Education, Literature&Languages, International Relations, Linguistics, Maths, Music, Politics and Theology.

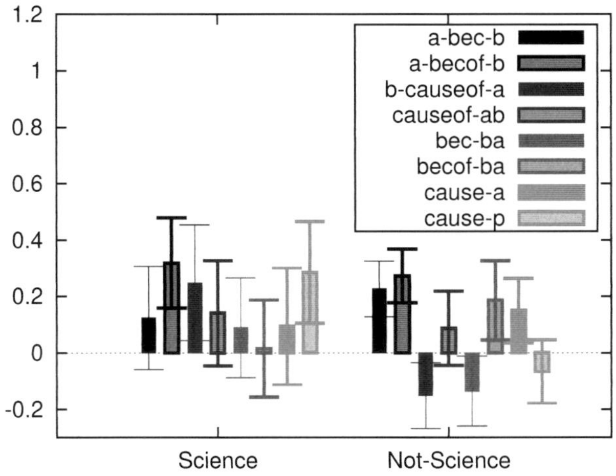

Figure 2: PubMed type preferences

cause of a". The last two are significantly lower than "a because b", "a because of b" and "because of b, a" (t-test, $.005 < p < .01$). On the contrary, there are no strong preferences among the science students and all the error bars overlap. Let us now look at some specific differences between science and non-science students:

1. Science students prefer sentences in the passive voice, while these are strongly dispreferred by non-science students. While active voice is the canonical form in English, much of science is written in the passive by convention. This difference can thus be explained by different levels of exposure.
2. Non-science students disprefer the use of "cause" as a noun while science students don't (columns 3–4 and 11–12).
3. Non-science students prefer "because of b, a" to "because b, a" while science students show the opposite preference.

The lack of strongly dispreferred formulations in the Science students is most likely due to two factors: (a) the group's familiarity with this genre and (b) their expert knowledge compensates for acceptability even for relatively odd formulations. In the absence of exposure and background knowledge, the non-Science students display clear preferences.[4]

Note that these preferences are not surprising. The preference for canonical constructs such as active voice and conjunction in infix position are well documented. Our claim however, is that blindly rewriting all instances of globally dispreferred constructs with globally preferred constructs is counterproductive because not all formulations are acceptable for any given propositional content. This claim is easily verified. Table 1 shows the average z-scores of non-science students when one formulation of each of the PubMed sentences is selected based only on the global preferences in Figure 2. Such rewriting invariably makes matters worse. In the next section we present a more intelligent approach.

Selection Method	Av. z
Always select original sentence	.61
Replace cause-p, b-causeof-a and causeof-ab with cause-a & bec-ba with a-bec-b	.48
Replace cause-p with cause-a, b-causeof-a with causeof-ab & bec-ba with a-bec-b	.47
Always select most preferred type (a-becof-b)	.27

Table 1: Selecting a formulation of PubMed sentences for non-science students using their global preferences.

4 Machine learning experiment

The first question we address is: for a given propositional content, which formulations are acceptable and which are not? This is a useful question for multiple reasons. In this paper, our interest stems from our desire to selectively rewrite causation based on the properties of the sentence as well as global preferences of categories of users. More generally, this information is important for summarisation tasks, where sentences might appear in different contexts and different information orderings might be desirable for reasons of coherence. Knowing which formulations are acceptable in isolation for a given propositional content is thus important.

Since Magnitude estimation scores are freescale, we first need to determine how high a score needs to be for that formulation to be considered acceptable. Our solution is to (a) treat the original formulation as acceptable and (b) treat any reformulations with a higher average z-score than the original as also acceptable. We find that roughly 3 formulations (the original and another two) out of 8 are acceptable on average. Our data is summarised below:

- 1152 Sentences in total (144 originals, 1008 reformulations)
    - 361 labelled as acceptable (31%; 144 originals, 217 reformulations)

[4]While we only show the averages for all sentences, the distributions for original and reformulated sentences look remarkably similar.

– 791 labelled as unacceptable (69%; 791 reformulations)

4.1 Features

We use shallow features derived from the sentence, as well as the textual genre. Sentences were parsed using the RASP parser (Briscoe and Carroll, 2002). The features we extract are as follows:

1. Type (8 values: cause_a, cause_p, a_bec_b, bec_ba, a_becof_b, becof_ba, a_causeof_b, causeof_ba)
2. Genre (3 values: pubmed, bnc-world, bnc-natsci)
3. Complexity: As an indication of the complexity of the propositional content, we use the following:
   (a) Length Features
     - length (in words) of the sentence and each clause
     - length (as proportion of total length) of each clause

   (b) Whether the causative is embedded in a relative clause or other construct
   (c) The presence or absence of copula in each clause (e.g., "because there is...")
   (d) Whether the causation is quantified (e.g., "a major cause of...")

The only feature that varies between the eight formulations of the same sentence is the "type" feature; the "genre" and "complexity" features are constant across reformulations. The reason for using 3(c–d) as features is that expressions such as "because there is" might be better formulated as "because of" and that it is hard to find an exact reformulation when quantifiers are present (e.g., "a major cause of" is not equivalent to "often because of").

Machine performance on this task is not very good (First Run, Table 2). The problem is that some propositional content is harder to formulate than others. Therefore good formulations of some propositional content might have much lower scores than even mediocre formulations of other propositional content. This makes it hard to learn a function that distinguishes good from bad formulations for any particular propositional content. To overcome this, we run the classifier twice. Given 8 formulations of 144 sentences $S_{i=1..144,j=1..8}$, the first run gives us 1152 probabilities $p_{weka1}(S_{ij})$ for the acceptability of each sentence, independent of propositional content (these are test-set probabilities using 10-fold cross-validation). We then run the machine learner again, with this new feature $relative$:

Classifier	Accuracy	Kappa
Baseline	.69	0
First Run	.72	.23
Second Run	.85	.65
Only PubMed	.89	.73

Table 2: Accuracy and Agreement of classifier relative to human judgement.

Genre	Class	P	R	F
All Genres	Good	.72	.78	.75
	Bad	.91	.89	.90
Only PubMed	Good	.89	.89	.89
	Bad	.89	.97	.92

Table 3: Precision, Recall and F-measure of classifier (second run) relative to human judgement.

- The ratio of the test-set probability (from the first run) to the highest of the 8 test-set probabilities for the different formulations of that sentence:

$$relative_{i=a,j=b} = \frac{p_{weka1}(S_{i=a,j=b})}{max_{i=a,j=1..8}(p_{weka1}(S_{i=a,j}))}$$

Thus probabilities for acceptability are normalised such that the best score for a given propositional content is 1 and the other 7 formulations score less than or equal to 1. The second classifier uses these relative probabilities as an extra feature.

4.2 Results

Our results are summarised in Table 2 (accuracy and agreement) and Table 3 (f-measure). We experimented with the Weka toolkit (Witten and Frank, 2000) and report results using "weka.classifiers.trees.J48 -C 0.3 -M 3" and 10-fold cross-validation for both runs.[5]

Table 2 shows that the first run performs at around baseline levels, but the second run performs significantly better (using z-test, p=0.01 on % Accuracy), with acceptable agreement of $\kappa = 0.65$[6]. This increases to 89% ($\kappa = .73$) when we only consider technical writing (PubMed genre). Table 3 shows that precision, recall and f-measure are also around .90 for PubMed sentences.

[5] J48 outperformed other Weka classifiers for this task.

[6] Following Carletta (1996), we measure agreement in κ, which follows the formula $K = \frac{P(A)-P(E)}{1-P(E)}$ where P(A) is observed, and P(E) expected agreement. κ ranges between -1 and 1. κ=0 means agreement is only as expected by chance. Generally, κ of 0.8 are considered stable, and κ of 0.69 as marginally stable, according to the strictest scheme applied in the field.

Left out feature	First Run		Second Run	
	Acc	κ	Acc	κ
Length	.71	-.01	.78	.33
Quantified	.71	.20	.75	.36
Embedded	.69	.15	.78	.37
Copula Present	.72	.20	.79	.44

Table 4: Accuracy and Kappa of classifier when complexity features are left out.

All our context features proved useful for the classification task, with the length features being the most useful. Table 4 shows the performance of the classifier when we leave out individual features.

It thus appears that we can determine the acceptable formulations of a sentence with high accuracy. The next question is how this information might be used to benefit a text regeneration system. To evaluate this, we combined our predictions with the user preferences visible in figure 2 as follows:

- We calculate a prior $prior_j$ for each formulation of type j using the z-score distribution for non-science students in Figure 2.
- We calculate $prior_{j=b}.p_{weka2}(S_{i=a,j=b})$ for each formulation $S_{i=a,j=b}$ of sentence a and type b, where $p_{weka2}(S_{i=a,j=b})$ is the probability returned by the classifier (second run) for formulation b of sentence a.
- **Selectively Reformulate:** We reformulate only the four dispreferred constructs (cause_p, bec_ba, causeof_ab, b_causeof_a) using the formulation for which the prior times the classifier probability is the maximum; i.e, for sentence a, we select $max_{i=a,j=1..8}(prior_j.p_{weka2}(S_{i=a,j}))$.

Table 5 shows the impact this reformulation has on the acceptability of the sentences. Our algorithm selects one formulation of each PubMed sentence based on our prior knowledge of the preferences of non-science students, and the Weka-probabilities for acceptability of each formulation of a sentence. Our selective reformulation increases the average z-score from .613 to .713. This is now comparable with the acceptability ratings of non-scientists for sentences from the world news genre. Note that reformulation only using priors resulted in worse results (Table 1).

However there remains scope for improvement. If we had an oracle that selected the best formulation of each sentence (as scored by non-scientists), this would result in an average score of 1.04.

Genre	Version	z-score
PubMed	Randomly Selected	−.17
PubMed	Original Sentences	.61
PubMed	Selectively Reformulate	.71
PubMed	Selected by Oracle	1.04
BNC World	Original Sentences	.70

Table 5: Average z-scores for non-science students. Selective reformulation increases the acceptability scores of sentences drawn from technical writing to levels comparable to acceptability scores of sentences drawn from news reports on world news (their most preferred genre).

5 Conclusions and future work

In this investigation we report that science and non-science university students have different global preferences regarding which formulations of causation are acceptable. Using surface features that reflect propositional complexity, a machine classifier can learn which of 8 formulations of a discourse relation are acceptable (with Accuracy $=$ .89 and Kappa $=$ .73 for sentences from the PubMed genre). Using the global preferences of non-science students as priors, and combining these with machine classifier predictions of acceptability, we have demonstrated that it is possible to selectively rewrite sentences from PubMed in a manner that is personalised for non-science students. This boosts the average z-score for acceptability from .613 to .713 on PubMed sentences, a level similar to scores of non-scientists for sentences from their most preferred World News genre. We have thus shown that there is potential for reformulating technical writing for a lay audience – differences in preferences for expressing a discourse relation do exist between lay and expert audiences, and these can be learnt.

While in this paper we focus on the discourse relation of causation, other discourse relations commonly used in scientific writing can also be realised using markers with different syntactic properties; for instance, *contrast* can be expressed using markers such as "while", "unlike", "but", "compared to", "in contrast to" or "the difference between". As part of our wider goals, we are in the process of extending the number of discourse relations considered. We are also in the process of developing a framework within which we can use transfer rules and a bi-directional grammar to automate such complex syntactic reformulation.

Acknowledgements

This work was supported by the Economic and Social Research Council (Grant Number RES-000-22-3272). We would also like to thank Donia Scott, Simone Teufel and Ann Copestake for many discussions that influenced the scope of this work, and John Williams and Theodora Alexopoulou for their suggestions on experimental design.

References

R.C. Anderson and A. Davison. 1988. Conceptual and empirical bases of readibility formulas. In Alice Davison and G. M. Green, editors, *Linguistic Complexity and Text Comprehension: Readability Issues Reconsidered.* Lawrence Erlbaum Associates, Hillsdale, NJ.

E.G. Bard, D. Robertson, and A. Sorace. 1996. Magnitude estimation for linguistic acceptability. *Language*, 72(1):32–68.

R. Barzilay and L. Lee. 2003. Learning to paraphrase: An unsupervised approach using multiple-sequence alignment. In *HLT-NAACL 2003*, pp 16–23.

I.L. Beck, M.G. McKeown, G.M. Sinatra, and J.A. Loxterman. 1991. Revising social studies text from a text-processing perspective: Evidence of improved comprehensibility. *Reading Research Quarterly*, pp 251–276.

E.J. Briscoe and J. Carroll. 2002. Robust accurate statistical annotation of general text. In *Proc. of the 3rd International Conference on Language Resources and Evaluation*, pp 1499–1504, Gran Canaria.

J. Carletta. 1996. Assessing agreement on classification tasks: The kappa statistic. *Computational Linguistics*, 22(2):249–254.

J. Carroll, G. Minnen, Y. Canning, S. Devlin, and J. Tait. 1998. Practical simplification of English newspaper text to assist aphasic readers. In *Proc. of AAAI98 Workshop on Integrating Artificial Intelligence and Assistive Technology*, pp 7–10, Madison, WI.

W. Cowart. 1997. *Experimental Syntax: applying objective methods to sentence judgement.* Thousand Oaks, CA: Sage Publications.

J. Hirschberg and D. Litman. 1993. Empirical studies on the disambiguation of cue phrases. *Computational Linguistics*, 19(3):501–530.

B. Hutchinson. 2005. Modelling the substitutability of discourse connectives. In *ACL '05: Proc. of the 43rd Annual Meeting on Association for Computational Linguistics*, pp 149–156, Morristown, NJ, USA. Association for Computational Linguistics.

A. Ibrahim, B. Katz, and J. Lin. 2003. Extracting paraphrases from aligned corpora. In *Proc. of The Second International Workshop on Paraphrasing*.

N. Kaji, D. Kawahara, S. Kurohash, and S. Sato. 2002. Verb paraphrase based on case frame alignment. In *Proc. of the 40th Annual Meeting of the Association for Computational Linguistics (ACL'02)*, pp 215–222, Philadelphia, USA.

F. Keller, S. Gunasekharan, N. Mayo, and M. Corley. 2008, to appear. Timing accuracy of web experiments: A case study using the webexp software package. *Behavior Research Methods.*

F. Keller. 2000. *Gradience in Grammar: Experimental and Computational Aspects of Degrees of Grammaticality.* Ph.D. thesis, University of Edinburgh.

A. Knott and R. Dale. 1994. Using linguistic phenomena to motivate a set of coherence relations. *Discourse Processes*, 18(1):35–62.

A. Knott. 1996. *A Data-Driven Methodology for Motivating a Set of Discourse Relations.* Ph.D. thesis, Ph. D. thesis, Centre for Cognitive Science, University of Edinburgh, Edinburgh, UK.

T. Linderholm, M.G. Everson, P. van den Broek, M. Mischinski, A. Crittenden, and J. Samuels. 2000. Effects of Causal Text Revisions on More-and Less-Skilled Readers' Comprehension of Easy and Difficult Texts. *Cognition and Instruction*, 18(4):525–556.

W. C. Mann and S. A. Thompson. 1988. Rhetorical Structure Theory: Towards a functional theory of text organization. *Text*, 8(3):243–281.

L. G. M. Noordman and W. Vonk. 1992. Reader's knowledge and the control of inferences in reading. *Language and Cognitive Processes*, 7:373–391.

R. Power, D. Scott, and N. Bouayad-Agha. 2003. Generating texts with style. *Proc. of the 4 thInternational Conference on Intelligent Texts Processing and Computational Linguistics.*

A. Siddharthan. 2006. Syntactic simplification and text cohesion. *Research on Language and Computation*, 4(1):77–109.

B. Webber, A. Joshi, E. Miltsakaki, R. Prasad, N. Dinesh, A. Lee, and K. Forbes. 2005. A Short Introduction to the Penn Discourse TreeBank. *Treebanking for discourse and speech: proceedings of the NODALIDA 2005 special session on Treebanks for spoken language and discourse.*

S. Williams and E. Reiter. 2008. Generating basic skills reports for low-skilled readers. *Natural Language Engineering*, 14(04):495–525.

I. Witten and E. Frank. 2000. *Data Mining: Practical Machine Learning Tools and Techniques with Java Implementations.* Morgan Kaufmann.

P. Wolff, B. Klettke, T. Ventura, and G. Song. 2005. Expressing causation in English and other languages. *Categorization inside and outside the laboratory: Essays in honor of Douglas L. Medin*, pp 29–48.

Tree Edit Models for Recognizing Textual Entailments, Paraphrases, and Answers to Questions

Michael Heilman Noah A. Smith
Language Technologies Institute
Carnegie Mellon University
Pittsburgh, PA 15213, USA
{mheilman,nasmith}@cs.cmu.edu

Abstract

We describe tree edit models for representing sequences of tree transformations involving complex reordering phenomena and demonstrate that they offer a simple, intuitive, and effective method for modeling pairs of semantically related sentences. To efficiently extract sequences of edits, we employ a tree kernel as a heuristic in a greedy search routine. We describe a logistic regression model that uses 33 syntactic features of edit sequences to classify the sentence pairs. The approach leads to competitive performance in recognizing textual entailment, paraphrase identification, and answer selection for question answering.

1 Introduction

Many NLP tasks involve modeling relations between pairs of sentences or short texts in the same language. Examples include recognizing textual entailment, paraphrase identification, and question answering. Generic approaches are, of course, desirable; we believe such approaches are also feasible because these tasks exhibit some similar semantic relationships between sentences.

A popular method for such tasks is Tree Edit Distance (TED), which models sentence pairs by finding a low or minimal cost sequence of editing operations to transform a tree representation of one sentence (e.g., a dependency or phrase structure parse tree) into a tree for the other. Unlike grammar-based models and shallow-feature discriminative approaches, TED provides an intuitive story for tree pairs where one tree is derived from the other by a sequence of simple transformations.

The available operations in standard TED are the following: insertion of a node, relabeling (i.e., renaming) of a node, and deletion (i.e., removal) of a node. While the restriction to these three operations permits efficient dynamic programming solutions for finding a minimum-cost edit sequence (Klein, 1989; Zhang and Shasha, 1989), certain interesting and prevalent phenomena involving reordering and movement cannot be elegantly captured. For example, consider the following sentence pair, which is a simplified version of a true entailment (i.e., the premise entails the hypothesis) in the development data for the RTE-3 task.

Premise: *Pierce built the home for his daughter off Rossville Blvd, as he lives nearby.*

Hypothesis: *Pierce lives near Rossville Blvd.*

In a plausible dependency tree representation of the premise, *live* and *Rossville Blvd* would be in separate subtrees under *built*. In the hypothesis tree, however, the corresponding nodes would be in a grandparent-child relationship as part of the same phrase, *lives near Rossville Blvd*. In general, one would expect that short transformation sequences to provide good evidence of true entailments. However, to account for the grandparent-child relationship in the hypothesis, TED would produce a fairly long sequence, relabeling *nearby* to be *near*, deleting the two nodes for *Rossville Blvd*, and then re-inserting those nodes under *near*.

We describe a tree edit approach that allows for more effective modeling of such complex reordering phenomena. Our approach can find a shorter and more intuitive edit sequence, relabeling *nearby* to be *near*, and then moving the whole subtree *Rossville Blvd* to be a child of *near*, as shown in Figure 1.

A model should also be able to consider characteristics of the tree edit sequence other than its overall length (e.g., how many proper nouns were deleted). Using a classifier with a small number of syntactic

Human Language Technologies: The 2010 Annual Conference of the North American Chapter of the ACL, pages 1011–1019,
Los Angeles, California, June 2010.

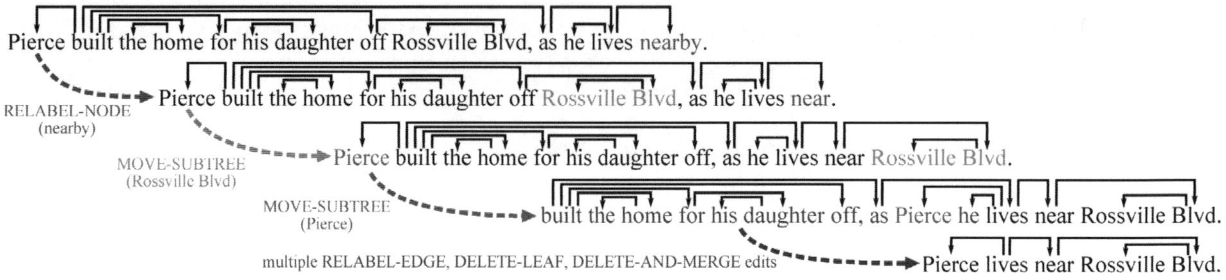

Figure 1: A tree edit sequence transforming a premise to an entailed hypothesis. Dependency types and parts of speech are omitted for clarity.

features, our approach allows us to learn—from labeled examples—how different types of edits should affect the model's decisions (e.g., about whether two sentences are paraphrases).

The structure of this paper is as follows. §2 introduces our model and describes the edit operations that were implemented for our experiments. §3 details the search-based procedure for extracting edit sequences for pairs of sentences. §4 describes the classifier for sentence pairs based on features of their corresponding edit sequences. §5 describes and presents the results of experiments involving recognizing textual entailment (Giampiccolo et al., 2007), paraphrase identification (Dolan et al., 2004), and an answer selection task for question answering (Wang et al., 2007). §6 addresses related work, and §7 provides concluding remarks.

2 Extended Tree Edit Sequences

This section defines a tree edit sequence and describes the operations used in our experiments.

We begin with some conventions. We use dependency trees as the structure upon which the tree edits will operate. The child nodes for a given parent are represented in a head-outward fashion such that the left and right children are separate lists, with the left- and right-most elements as the last members of their respective lists, as in most generative dependency models (Eisner, 1996). Each node consists of a lemmatized word token as its main label (hereafter, lemma), a part of speech tag (POS), and a syntactic relation label for the edge to its parent. We assume the root node has a special dummy edge label `ROOT`.

Let T_c be a "current tree" that is being transformed and let T_t be a "target tree" into which T_c will ultimately be transformed. Let $T(i)$ be a node with an index i into the tree T, where the indices are arbitrary (e.g., they could be word positions).

2.1 Definition

We define a tree edit sequence to be a series of edit operations that transform a source tree (the initial T_c) into a target tree T_t.[1] While TED permits only insert, relabel, and delete operations, edit sequences may contain more complex operations, such as moving entire subtrees and re-ordering child nodes.

2.2 Implemented Operations

For our experiments, we used the types of edit operations listed in Table 1.[2] The first six operations are straightforward extensions of the insert, relabel and delete operations allowed in TED. The final three operations, `MOVE-SUBTREE`, `NEW-ROOT`, and `MOVE-SIBLING`, enable succinct edit sequences for complex transformations. For a given current tree, there may be many instantiations of each operation (e.g., `DELETE-LEAF` could be invoked to delete any of a number of leaf nodes). Note that any tree can be transformed into any other simply by deleting all nodes from the one tree and inserting all the nodes in the other. However, our set of tree edit operations permits more concise and intuitive edit sequences.

3 Searching for Tree Edit Sequences

To model sentence pairs effectively, we seek a short sequence of tree edits that transforms one tree into another. The space of possible edit sequences, as with TED and many other methods involving trees,

[1] Such a sequence is sometimes called a "script" for TED.

[2] We leave for future work the exploration of other operations (e.g., swapping parent and child nodes).

Operation	Arguments	Description
INSERT-CHILD	node index j, new lemma l, POS p, edge label e, side $s \in \{left, right\}$	Insert a node with lemma l, POS p, and edge label e as the last child (i.e., farthest from parent) on side s of $T(j)$.
INSERT-PARENT	non-root node index j, new lemma l, new POS p, edge label e, side $s \in \{left, right\}$	Create a node with lemma l, POS p, and edge label e. Make $T(j)$ a child of the new node on side s. Insert the new node as a child of the former parent of $T(j)$ in the same position.
DELETE-LEAF	leaf node index j	Remove the leaf node $T(j)$.
DELETE-&-MERGE	node index j (s.t. $T(j)$ has exactly 1 child)	Remove $T(j)$. Insert its child as a child of $T(j)$'s former parent in the same position.
RELABEL-NODE	node index j, new lemma l, new POS p	Set the lemma of $T(j)$ to be l and its POS to be p.
RELABEL-EDGE	node index j, new edge label e	Set the edge label of $T(j)$ to be e.
MOVE-SUBTREE	node index j, node index k (s.t. $T(k)$ is not a descendant of $T(j)$), side $s \in \{left, right\}$	Move $T(j)$ to be the last child on the s side of $T(k)$.
NEW-ROOT	non-root node index j, side $s \in \{left, right\}$	Make $T(j)$ the new root node of the tree. Insert the former root as the last child on the s side of $T(j)$.
MOVE-SIBLING	non-root node index j, side $s \in \{left, right\}$, position $r \in \{first, last\}$	Move $T(j)$ to be the r child on the s side of its parent.

Table 1: Possible operations in our extended tree edit implementation. All are described as operations to tree T.

is exponentially large in the size of the trees. However, while dynamic programming solutions exist for TED (Klein, 1989; Zhang and Shasha, 1989), it is unlikely that such efficient algorithms are available for our problem because of the lack of locality restrictions on edit operations.[3]

3.1 Algorithm for Extracting Sequences

Rather than dynamic programming, we use greedy best-first search (Pearl, 1984) to efficiently find sensible (if not minimal) edit sequences. The distinguishing characteristic of greedy best-first search is that its function for evaluating search states is simply a heuristic function that estimates the remaining cost, rather than a heuristic function plus the cost so far (e.g., number of edits), as in other types of search.

Here, the initial search state is the source tree, the current state is T_c, and the goal state is T_t. The function for generating the successors for a given state returns returns trees for all possible specifications of operations on T_c (§2.2), subject to the minimal constraints to be described in §3.3. The enumeration order of the edits in the search procedure (i.e., the order in which states are explored) follows the order of their presentation in Table 1. In preliminary experiments, varying this order had no effect on the extracted transformations.

3.2 Tree Kernel Heuristic

In our greedy search approach, the evaluation function's value for a state depends only on the heuristic function's estimate of how different the current tree at that state is from the target tree. Using this function, at each step, the search routine chooses the next state (i.e., edit) so as to minimize the difference between the current and target trees.

We use a tree kernel to define the heuristic function. A kernel is a special kind of symmetric function from a pair of objects to a real number. It can be interpreted as the inner product of those objects represented in some real-valued feature space (Schölkopf and Smola, 2001). A tree kernel, as proposed by Collins and Duffy (2001), is a convolution kernel[4] whose input is a pair of trees and whose output is a positive number indicating the similarity of the sets of all their subtrees.

The dimensionality of the feature vector associated with a tree kernel is thus unbounded in general, and larger trees generally lead to larger kernel values. Direct use as a search heuristic would lead to the exploration of states for larger and larger trees, even ones larger than the target tree. Thus, as in

[3]Gildea (2003) proposes a dynamic programming algorithm for a related tree alignment problem, but it is still exponential in the maximum number of children for a node.

[4]Haussler (1999) provides a proof, which can be extended for our kernel, that tree kernels are valid kernel functions.

Equation 1, the search heuristic H "normalizes" the kernel K of the current tree T_c and target tree T_t to unit range by dividing by the geometric mean of the kernels comparing the individual trees to themselves.[5] Also, the normalized value is subtracted from 1 so as to make it a difference rather than a similarity. The search routine will thus reach the goal state when the heuristic reaches 0, indicating that the current and target trees are identical.

$$H(T_c) = 1 - \frac{K(T_c, T_t)}{\sqrt{K(T_c, T_c) \times K(T_t, T_t)}} \quad (1)$$

Kernels are most commonly used in the efficient construction of margin-based classifiers in the implied representation space (e.g., Zelenko et al., 2003). Here, however, the kernel helps to find a representation (i.e., an edit sequence) for subsequent modeling steps.

We are effectively mapping the source, current, and target trees to points on the surface of a high-dimensional unit sphere associated with the normalized kernel. In this geometric interpretation, the search heuristic in Equation 1 leads the search algorithm to explore reachable trees along the surface of this sphere, always choosing the one whose angle with the target tree is smallest, until the angle is 0. The path on the sphere corresponds to an edit sequence, from which we will derive edit features in §4 for classification.

Our kernel is based on the partial tree kernel (PTK) proposed by Moschitti (2006). It considers matches between ordered subsequences of children in addition to the full sequences of children as in Collins and Duffy (2001). This permits a very fine-grained measure of tree pair similarity. Importantly, if two nodes differ only by the presence or position of a single child, they will still lead to a large kernel function value. We also sum over the similarities between all pairs of nodes, similar to (Collins and Duffy, 2001).

Since the PTK considers non-contiguous subsequences, it is very computationally expensive. We therefore restrict our kernel to consider only contiguous subsequences, as in the contiguous tree kernel (CTK) (Zelenko et al., 2003).

[5]This normalized function is also guaranteed to be a kernel function (Schölkopf and Smola, 2001).

To define our kernel, we begin with a similarity function for pairs of nodes n_1 and n_2 that depends on their lemmas, POS tags, edge labels, and sides with respect to their parents:[6]

$$\begin{aligned} s(n_1, n_2) =& \delta(l(n_1), l(n_2)) \\ &\times \sum_{f \in \{l,e,p,s\}} \delta(f(n_1), f(n_2)) \end{aligned} \quad (2)$$

where δ returns 1 if its arguments are equivalent, 0 otherwise. l, e, p, and s are used here as functions to select the lemma, edge label, POS, and side of a node. Equation 2 encodes the linguistic intuition that the primary indicator of node similarity should be a lexical match between lemmas. If the lemmas match, then edge labels, POS, and the locations (sides) relative to their parents are also considered.

The kernel is defined recursively (starting from the roots), where n_i is a node in the set of nodes N_{T_i} in tree T_i:

$$K(T_1, T_2) = \sum_{n_1 \in \{N_{T_1}\}} \sum_{n_2 \in \{N_{T_2}\}} \Delta(n_1, n_2) \quad (3)$$

$$\Delta(n_1, n_2) = \mu \left(\lambda^2 s(n_1, n_2) + \sum_{J_1, J_2, |J_1| = |J_2|} \prod_{i=1}^{l(J_1)} \Delta(c_{n_1}[J_{1i}], c_{n_2}[J_{2i}]) \right) \quad (4)$$

$J_1 = \langle J_{11}, J_{12}, J_{13}, \ldots \rangle$ is an index sequence associated with any *contiguous* ordered sequence of children c_{n_1} of node n_1 (likewise for J_2). J_{1i} and J_{2i} point to the ith children in the two sequences. $|\cdot|$ returns the length of a sequence.

The kernel includes two decay factors: λ for the length of child subsequences, as in Zelenko et al. (2003) and Moschitti (2006); and μ for the height of the subtree, as in Collins and Duffy (2001) and Moschitti (2006). We set both to 0.25 in our experiments to encourage the search to consider edits leading to smaller matches (e.g., of individual parent-child dependencies) before larger ones.[7]

[6]The side of a node relative to its parent in a dependency tree is important: two parent nodes with the same children should not be considered exact matches if children are on different sides (e.g., *defeated the insurgents* and *the insurgents defeated*).

[7]From experiments with the paraphrase training set (§5.2), performance does not appear sensitive to the decay parameters. Settings of 0.1, 0.2, 0.3, and 0.4 led to 10-fold cross-validation

The main difference between our kernel and the CTK is that we sum over all pairs of subtrees (Equation 3). In contrast, the CTK only considers only one pair of subtrees. When the CTK is applied to relation extraction by Culotta and Sorensen (2004), each subtree is the smallest common subtree that includes the entities between which a relation may exist (e.g., the subtree for *Texas-based energy company Exxon Mobil* when extracting ORGANIZATION-LOCATION relations).

3.3 Constraints on the Search Space

For computational efficiency, we impose the following three constraints to simplify the search space. Note that the first two simply prune away obviously unhelpful search states.

1. For INSERT-CHILD, INSERT-PARENT, and RELABEL-NODE edits, the lemma and POS of the node to insert must occur in the target tree. Also, the pair consisting of the lemma for the node to insert and the lemma for its prospective parent must not appear more times in the resulting tree than in the target tree.
2. For MOVE-SUBTREE edits, the pair consisting of the lemma for the node to move and the lemma for its prospective parent must exist in the target tree.
3. For INSERT-CHILD and INSERT-PARENT edits, the edge labels attaching the newly inserted nodes to their parents are always the most frequent edge label for the given POS.[8] Further edits can modify these edge labels.

3.4 Search Error and Failure

The search does not always find optimal edit sequences, but most sequences seem reasonable upon inspection. However, for some cases, the search does not find a sequence in a reasonable number of iterations. We therefore set an upper limit of $maxIters = 200$ on the number of iterations.[9] In practice, this constraint is enforced a small fraction of the time (e.g., less than 0.1% of the time for the answer selection training data). If no goal state is found after $maxIters$ iterations, a special unknown sequence feature is recorded.

accuracy values that were not significantly different from each other. However, we did observe that increased search failure (§3.4) resulted from settings above 0.5.

[8]Edge label frequencies for each POS were computed from the training data for the MST parser (McDonald et al., 2005).

[9]$maxIters = 400$ for the textual entailment experiments to account for multi-sentence premises. For all tasks, extracting sequences took about 5 seconds on average per sentence pair with 1 GB of RAM on a 3.0 GHz machine.

4 Classification of Sequences

Given a training set of labeled sentence pairs, after extracting edit sequences, we train a logistic regression (LR) classification model (Hastie et al., 2001) on the labels and features of the extracted sequences.[10] We optimize with a variant of Newton's method (le Cessie and van Houwelingen, 1997).

The tree edit models use a set of 33 features of edit sequences to classify sentence pairs. We used the training data for the paraphrase task (§5.2) to develop this set. All features are integer-valued, and most are counts of different types of edits. Five are counts of the nodes in the source tree that were not edited directly by any operations (though their ancestors or descendants may have been). Table 2 describes the features in detail.

5 Experiments

Experiments were conducted to evaluate tree edit models for three tasks: recognizing textual entailment (Giampiccolo et al., 2007), paraphrase identification (Dolan et al., 2004), and an answer selection task (Wang et al., 2007) for question answering (Voorhees, 2004). The feature set and first tree edit model were developed for paraphrase, and then applied to the other tasks with very few modifications (all explained below) and no further tuning.[11]

5.1 Recognizing Textual Entailment

A tree edit model was trained for recognizing textual entailment (RTE). Here, an instance consists of

[10]In cross-validation experiments with the training data, we found that unregularized LR outperformed SVMs (Vapnik, 1995) and ℓ_2-regularized LR, perhaps due to the small number of features in our models.

[11]All datasets were POS-tagged using Ratnaparkhi's (1996) tagger and parsed for dependencies using the MST Parser (McDonald et al., 2005). Features were computed from POS and edge label information in the dependency parses. The WordNet API (Miller et al., 1990) was used for lemmatization only. An appendix with further experimental details is available at http://www.ark.cs.cmu.edu/mheilman/tree-edit-appendix/.

Feature	Description
totalEdits	# of edits in the sequence.
*X*Edits	#s of X edits (where X is one of the nine edit types in Table 1).
relabelSamePOS, relabelSameLemma, relablePronoun, relabelProper, relabelNum	#s of RELABEL-NODE edits that: preserve POS, preserve lemmas, convert between nouns and pronouns, change proper nouns, change numeric values by more than 5% (to allow rounding), respectively.
insertVorN, insertProper	#s of INSERT-CHILD or INSERT-PARENT edits that: insert nouns or verbs, insert proper nouns, respectively.
removeVorN, removeProper, removeSubj, removeObj, removeVC, removeRoot	#s of REMOVE-LEAF or REMOVE-&-MERGE edits that: remove nouns or verbs, remove proper nouns, remove nodes with subject edge labels, remove nodes with object edge labels, remove nodes with verb complement edge labels, remove nodes with root edge labels (which may occur after NEW-ROOT edits), respectively.
relabelEdgeSubj, relabeledgeObj, relabelEdgeVC, relabelEdgeRoot	#s of RELABEL-EDGE edits that: change to or from subject edge labels, change to or from object edge labels, change to or from verb complement edge labels, change to or from root edge labels, respectively.
uneditedNodes, uneditedNum, uneditedVerbs, uneditedNouns, uneditedProper	#s of unedited nodes: in total, that are numeric values, that are verbs, that are nouns, that are proper nouns, respectively.
unknownSeq	1 if no edit sequence was found and 0 otherwise (§3.4).

Table 2: Tree edit sequence classification features.

a "premise," which is a sentence or paragraph about a particular topic or event, and a "hypothesis," which is a single, usually short, sentence that may or may not follow from the premise. The task is to decide whether or not the hypothesis is entailed by the premise (Giampiccolo et al., 2007).

Tree edit sequences were extracted in one direction, from premise to hypothesis.[12] Since premises may consist of multiple sentences, we attach sentences as children of dummy root nodes, for both the premise and hypothesis. The model was trained on the development set (i.e., training data) for RTE-3 along with all the data from the RTE-1 and RTE-2 tasks. It was then evaluated on the RTE-3 test set. We report precision and recall for true entailments, and overall accuracy (i.e., percentage correct).

[12]It is counter-intuitive to model *adding* information through extensive insertions, for both entailment and answer selection.

System	Acc. %	Prec. %	Rec. %
Harmeling, 2007	59.5	-	-
de Marneffe et al., 2006	60.5	61.8	60.2
M&M, 2007 (NL)	59.4	**70.1**	36.1
M&M, 2007 (Hybrid)	**64.3**	65.5	63.9
Tree Edit Model	62.8	61.9	**71.2**

Table 3: Results for recognizing textual entailments. Precision and recall values are for the true entailment class. Results for de Marneffe et al. (2006) were reported by MacCartney and Manning (2008). Harmeling (2007) only reported accuracy.

We compare to four systems that use syntactic dependencies and lexical semantic information.[13] De Marneffe et al. (2006) described an RTE system that finds word alignments and then classifies sentence pairs based on those alignments. MacCartney and Manning (2008) used an inference procedure based on Natural Logic, leading to a relatively high-precision, low-recall system. MacCartney and Manning (2008) also tested a hybrid of the natural logic system and the complementary system of de Marneffe et al. (2006) to improve coverage. Harmeling (2007) took an approach similar to ours involving classification based on transformation sequences, but with less general operations and a more complex, heuristic procedure for finding sequences.

Table 3 presents RTE results, showing that the tree edit model performs competitively. While it does not outperform state-of-the-art RTE systems, the tree edit model is simpler and less tailored to this task than many other RTE systems based on similar linguistic information.

[13]The top-performing RTE systems often involve significant manual engineering for the RTE task. Also, many employ techniques that make them not very comparable to our approach (e.g., theorem proving). We also note that Kouylekov and Magnini (2005) report 55% accuracy for RTE-2 using TED. See Giampiccolo et al. (2007) for more RTE-3 results.

System	Acc. %	Prec. %	Rec. %
Wan et al., 2006	75.6	77	90
D&S, 2009 (QG)	73.9	74.9	**91.3**
D&S, 2009 (PoE)	**76.1**	**79.6**	86.0
Tree Edit Model	73.2	75.7	87.8

Table 4: Paraphrase identification results, with precision and recall measures for true (positive) paraphrases. Wan et al. (2006) report precision and recall values with only two significant digits.

System	MAP	MRR
Punyakanok et al., 2004	0.3814	0.4462
+WN	0.4189	0.4939
Cui et al., 2005	0.4350	0.5569
+WN	0.4271	0.5259
Wang et al., 2007	0.4828	0.5571
+WN	0.6029	0.6852
Tree Edit Model	**0.6091**	**0.6917**

Table 5: Results for the task of answer selection for question answering. +WN denotes use of WordNet features.

5.2 Paraphrase Identification

A tree edit model was trained and tested for paraphrase identification using the the Microsoft Research Paraphrase Corpus (Dolan et al., 2004). The task is to identify whether two sentences convey essentially the same meaning.

The standard training set was used to train the tree edit classification model to distinguish between true and false paraphrases. Since there is no predefined direction for paraphrase pairs, we extracted two sequences for each pair (one in each direction) and summed the feature values. The model was evaluated with the standard test set.

We report accuracy, positive class precision (i.e., percentage of predicted positive paraphrases that had positive gold-standard labels), and positive class recall (i.e., percentage of positive gold-standard labels that were predicted to be positive paraphrases).

We compare to two of the best performance approaches to paraphrase. One approach, by Wan et al. (2006), uses an SVM classifier with features based on syntactic dependencies, TED, unigram overlap, and BLEU scores (Papineni et al., 2002). The other system, by Das and Smith (2009), is based on a quasi-synchronous grammar (QG; Smith and Eisner, 2006), a probabilistic model that allows loose alignments between trees but prefers tree isomorphism. In addition to syntactic dependencies, the QG model utilizes entity labels from BBN Identifinder (Bikel et al., 1999) and lexical semantics knowledge from WordNet. Das and Smith (2009) also use a product of experts (PoE) (Hinton, 1999) to combine the QG model with lexical overlap features.

Table 4 shows the test set results for all of the systems. While the tree edit model did not outperform the other systems, it produced competitive results. Moreover, the tree edit model does not make use of BLEU scores (Wan et al., 2006), entity labeling components, lexical semantics knowledge sources such as WordNet (beyond lemmatization), or system combination techniques (Das and Smith, 2009).

5.3 Answer Selection for Question Answering

A tree edit model was trained for answer selection in question answering (QA). In this task, an instance consists of a short factual question (e.g., *Who wrote the 'Tale of Genji'?*) and a candidate answer sentence retrieved by the information retrieval component of a question answering system. For a positive instance, the text will correctly answer the question—though perhaps indirectly. It may also contain various extraneous information (e.g., *Kano script made possible the development of a secular Japanese literature, beginning with such Late Heian classics as Lady Murasaki's "Tales of Genji."*). For a given set of questions, the task here is to *rank* candidate answers (Wang et al., 2007).

The experimental setup is the same as in Wang et al. (2007). We trained the tree edit model on the manually judged positive and negative QA pairs from previous QA tracks at the Text REtrieval Conference (TREC-8 through TREC-12). The goal of the task is to rank answer candidates rather than classify them; therefore, after training a logistic regression classifier, we rank the answer candidates for a given question by their posterior probabilities of correctness according to the model.

We tested our model with QA pairs from TREC-13. We report Mean Average Precision (MAP) and Mean Reciprocal Rank (MRR), which are information retrieval measures for ranked lists.

Tree edit sequences were extracted only in one direction, from answer to question. We compare our tree edit model to three other systems as they are reported by Wang et al. (2007). Wang et al. use a QG model, incorporating information from dependency trees, entity labels from BBN Identifinder (Bikel et al., 1999), and lexical semantics knowledge from WordNet (Miller et al., 1990). Cui et al. (2005) developed an information theoretic measure based on dependency trees. Punyakanok et al. (2004) used a generalization of TED to model the QA pairs. For their experiments, Wang et al. also extended both of the latter models to utilize WordNet.

Table 5 displays answer selection results, including test set results for the baseline systems with and without lexical semantic information from WordNet. The tree edit model, which does not use lexical semantics knowledge, produced the best result reported to date. The results for the tree edit model are statistically significantly different (sign test, $p < 0.01$) from the results for all except the Wang et al. (2007) system with WordNet ($p > 0.05$).

5.4 Discussion

The parameter settings learned for the features in Table 2 were broadly similar for the three tasks. For example, operations involving changes to subjects and proper nouns tended to be associated with non-paraphrases, false entailments, and incorrect answers. We did not observe any interesting differences in the parameter values.

While the tree edit models perform competitively in multiple tasks by capturing relevant syntactic phenomena, it is clear that syntax alone cannot solve these semantic tasks. Fortunately, this approach is amenable to extensions, facilitated by the separation of the representation extraction and classification steps. Richer edits could be included; lexical semantics could be integrated into the classifier or the search heuristic; or edit sequences might be found for other types of trees, such as semantic parses.

6 Related Work

TED is a widely studied technique with many applications (Klein, 1989; Zhang and Shasha, 1989; Punyakanok et al., 2004; Schilder and McInnes, 2006). See Bille (2005) for a review. Chawathe and Garcia-Molina (1997) describe a tree edit algorithm for detecting changes in structured documents that incorporates edits for moving subtrees and reordering children. However, they make assumptions unsuitable for natural language, such as the absence of recursive syntactic rewrite rules. Bernard et al. (2008) use EM to learn the costs for simple insert, relabel, and delete edits, but they only discuss experiments for digit recognition and a task using artificial data.

Much research has focused on modeling word reordering phenomena and syntactic alignments (e.g., Gildea, 2003; Smith and Eisner, 2006; *inter alia*), and such methods have been applied successfully to semantic tasks (de Marneffe et al., 2006; Wang et al., 2007; Das and Smith, 2009). While we not describe connections to such approaches in detail due to space limitations, we note that theoretical connections are possible between transformations and alignments (Chawathe and Garcia-Molina, 1997).

Tree kernels have been applied to a variety of natural language tasks (Collins and Duffy, 2001; Zelenko et al., 2003; Culotta and Sorensen, 2004). Of particular interest, Zanzotto and Moschitti (2006) describe a kernel for RTE that takes tree pairs, rather than single trees, as input. To our knowledge, our use of a tree kernel as a search heuristic is novel.

7 Conclusion

We described tree edit models that generalize TED by allowing operations that better account for complex reordering phenomena and by learning from data how different edits should affect the models decisions about output variables of interest (e.g., the correctness of answers). They offer an intuitive and effective method for modeling sentence pairs. They led to competitive performance for three tasks: paraphrase identification, recognizing textual entailment, and answer selection for question answering.

Acknowledgments

We acknowledge partial support from the Institute of Education Sciences, U.S. Department of Education, through Grant R305B040063 to Carnegie Mellon University; and the National Science Foundation through a Graduate Research Fellowship for the first author and grant IIS-0915187 to the second author. We thank Mengqiu Wang and Dipanjan Das for their help with the data, André Martins for his geometric interpretation of our search procedure, and the anonymous reviewers for their comments.

References

M. Bernard, L. Boyer, A. Habrard, and M. Sebban. 2008. Learning probabilistic models of tree edit distance.

Pattern Recognition.

D. M. Bikel, R. Schwartz, and R. M. Weischedel. 1999. An algorithm that learns what's in a name. *Machine Learning*, 34.

P. Bille. 2005. A survey on tree edit distance and related problems. *Theoretical Computer Science*, 337.

S. Chawathe and H. Garcia-Molina. 1997. Meaningful change detection in structured data. In *Proc. of ACM SIGMOD*.

M. Collins and N. Duffy. 2001. Convolution kernels for natural language. In *Proc. of NIPS*.

H. Cui, R. Sun, K. Li, M. Kan, , and T. Chua. 2005. Question answering passage retrieval using dependency relations. In *Proc. of ACM-SIGIR*.

A. Culotta and J. Sorensen. 2004. Dependency tree kernels for relation extraction. In *Proc. of ACL*.

D. Das and N. A. Smith. 2009. Paraphrase identification as probabilistic quasi-synchronous recognition. In *Proc. of ACL-IJCNLP*.

M. de Marneffe, B. MacCartney, T. Grenager, D. Cer, A. Rafferty, and C. D. Manning. 2006. Learning to distinguish valid textual entailments. In *Proc. of the Second PASCAL Challenges Workshop*.

B. Dolan, C. Quirk, and C. Brockett. 2004. Unsupervised construction of large paraphrase corpora: Exploiting massively parallel news sources. In *Proc. of COLING*.

J. Eisner. 1996. Three new probabilistic models for dependency parsing: An exploration. In *Proc. of COLING*.

D. Giampiccolo, B. Magnini, I. Dagan, and B. Dolan, editors. 2007. *The third pascal recognizing textual entailment challenge*.

D. Gildea. 2003. Loosely tree-based alignment for machine translation. In *Proc. of ACL*.

S. Harmeling. 2007. An extensible probabilistic transformation-based approach to the third Recognizing Textual Entailment challenge. In *Proc. of ACL-PASCAL Workshop on Textual Entailment and Paraphrasing*.

T. Hastie, R. Tibshirani, and J. Friedman. 2001. *The Elements of Statistical Learning: Data Mining, Inference, and Prediction*. Springer.

D. Haussler. 1999. Convolution kernels on discrete structures. Technical Report ucs-crl-99-10, University of California Santa Cruz.

G. E. Hinton. 1999. Product of experts. In *Proc. of ICANN*.

P. N. Klein. 1989. Computing the edit-distance between unrooted ordered trees. In *Proc. of European Symposium on Algorithms*.

M. Kouylekov and B. Magnini. 2005. Recognizing textual entailment with tree edit distance algorithms. In *Proc. of the PASCAL RTE Challenge*.

S. le Cessie and J. C. van Houwelingen. 1997. Ridge estimators in logistic regression. *Applied Statistics*, 41.

B. MacCartney and C. D. Manning. 2008. Modeling semantic containment and exclusion in natural language inference. In *Proc. of COLING*.

R. McDonald, F. Pereira, K. Ribarov, and J. Hajič. 2005. Non-projective dependency parsing using spanning tree algorithms. In *Proc. of HLT-EMNLP*.

G. A. Miller, R. Beckwith, C. Fellbaum, D. Gross, and K. J. Miller. 1990. WordNet: An on-line lexical database. *International Journal of Lexicography*, 3(4).

A. Moschitti. 2006. Efficient convolution kernels for dependency and constituent syntactic trees. In *Proc. of ECML*.

K. Papineni, S. Roukos, T. Ward, and W.-J. Zhu. 2002. BLEU: a method for automatic evaluation of machine translation. In *Proc. of ACL*.

J. Pearl. 1984. *Heuristics: intelligent search strategies for computer problem solving*. Addison-Wesley.

V. Punyakanok, D. Roth, and W. Yih. 2004. Mapping dependencies trees: An application to question answering. In *Proc. of the 8th International Symposium on Artificial Intelligence and Mathematics*.

A. Ratnaparkhi. 1996. A maximum entropy part-of-speech tagger. In *Proc. of EMNLP*.

F. Schilder and B. T. McInnes. 2006. TLR at DUC 2006: approximate tree similarity and a new evaluation regime. In *Proc. of DUC*.

B. Schölkopf and A. J. Smola. 2001. *Learning with Kernels*. MIT Press.

D. A. Smith and J. Eisner. 2006. Quasi-synchronous grammars: Alignment by soft projection of syntactic dependencies. In *Proc. of HLT-NAACL Workshop on Statistical Machine Translation*.

V. N. Vapnik. 1995. *The Nature of Statistical Learning Theory*. Springer.

E. M. Voorhees. 2004. Overview of TREC 2004. In *Proc. of TREC*.

S. Wan, M. Dras, R. Dale, and C. Paris. 2006. Using dependency-based features to take the "para-farce" out of paraphrase. In *Proc. of the Australasian Language Technology Workshop*.

M. Wang, N. A. Smith, and T. Mitamura. 2007. What is the Jeopardy model? A quasi-synchronous grammar for QA. In *Proc. of EMNLP-CoNLL*.

F. M. Zanzotto and A. Moschitti. 2006. Automatic learning of textual entailments with cross-pair similarities. In *Proc. of COLING/ACL*.

D. Zelenko, C. Aone, and A. Richardella. 2003. Kernel methods for relation extraction. *J. of Machine Learning Research*, 3.

K. Zhang and D. Shasha. 1989. Simple fast algorithms for the editing distance between trees and related problems. *SIAM Journal of Computing*, 18.

Syntactic/Semantic Structures for Textual Entailment Recognition

Yashar Mehdad
FBK-IRST, DISI
University of Trento
Povo (TN) - Italy
mehdad@fbk.eu

Alessandro Moschitti
DISI
University of Trento
Povo (TN) - Italy
moschitti@disi.unitn.it

Fabio Massimo Zanzotto
DISP
University of Rome "Tor Vergata"
Roma - Italy
zanzotto@info.uniroma2.it

Abstract

In this paper, we describe an approach based on off-the-shelf parsers and semantic resources for the Recognizing Textual Entailment (RTE) challenge that can be generally applied to any domain. Syntax is exploited by means of tree kernels whereas lexical semantics is derived from heterogeneous resources, e.g. WordNet or distributional semantics through Wikipedia. The joint syntactic/semantic model is realized by means of tree kernels, which can exploit lexical relatedness to match syntactically similar structures, i.e. whose lexical compounds are related. The comparative experiments across different RTE challenges and traditional systems show that our approach consistently and meaningfully achieves high accuracy, without requiring any adaptation or tuning.

1 Introduction

Recognizing Textual Entailment (RTE) is rather challenging as effectively modeling syntactic and semantic for this task is difficult. Early deep semantic models (e.g., (Norvig, 1987)) as well as more recent ones (e.g., (Tatu and Moldovan, 2005; Bos and Markert, 2005; Roth and Sammons, 2007)) rely on specific world knowledge encoded in rules for drawing decisions. Shallower models exploit matching methods between syntactic/semantic graphs of texts and hypotheses (Haghighi et al., 2005). The matching step is carried out after the application of some lexical-syntactic rules that are used to transform the text T or the hypothesis H (Bar-Haim et al., 2009) at surface form level. For all these methods, the effective use of syntactic and semantic information depends on the coverage and the quality of the specific rules. Lexical-syntactic rules can be automatically extracted from plain corpora (e.g., (Lin and Pantel, 2001; Szpektor and Dagan, 2008)) but the quality (also in terms of little noise) and the coverage is low. In contrast, rules written at the semantic level are more accurate but their automatic design is difficult and so they are typically hand-coded for the specific phenomena.

In this paper, we propose models for effectively using syntactic and semantic information in RTE, without requiring either large automatic rule acquisition or hand-coding. These models exploit lexical similarities to generalize lexical-syntactic rules automatically derived by supervised learning methods. In more detail, syntax is encoded in the form of parse trees whereas similarities are defined by means of WordNet simlilarity measures or Latent Semantic Analysis (LSA) applied to Wikipedia or to the British National Corpus (BNC). The joint syntactic/semantic model is realized by means of novel tree kernels, which can match subtrees whose leaves are lexically similar (so not just identical).

To assess the benefit of our approach, we carried out comparative experiments with previous work: especially with the method described in (Zanzotto and Moschitti, 2006; Zanzotto et al., 2009). This constitutes our strong baseline as, although it can only exploit lexical-syntactic rules, it has achieved top accuracy in all RTE challenges. The results, across different RTE challenges, show that our approach constantly and significantly improves the

Human Language Technologies: The 2010 Annual Conference of the North American Chapter of the ACL, pages 1020–1028,
Los Angeles, California, June 2010.

baseline model. Moreover, our approach does not require any adaptation or tuning and uses a computation for the similarity function based on Wikipedia which is faster than the computation of tools based on WordNet or other resources (Basili et al., 2006).

The remainder of the paper is organized as follows: Section 2 critically reviews the previous work by highlighting the need of generalizing lexico-syntactic rules. Section 3 describes lexical similarity approaches, which can serve the generalization purpose. Section 4 describes how to integrate lexical similarity in syntactic structures using syntactic/semantic tree kernels (SSTK) whereas Section 5 shows how to use SSTK in a kernel-based RTE system. Section 6 describes the experiments and results. Section 7 discusses the efficiency and accuracy of our system compared with other RTE systems. Finally, we draw the conclusions in Section 8.

2 Related work

Lexical-syntactic rules are largely used in textual entailment recognition systems (e.g., (Bar-Haim et al., 2007; Dinu and Wang, 2009)) as they conveniently encode world knowledge into linguistic structures. For example, to decide whether the simple sentences are in the entailment relation:

$T_2 \Rightarrow ? H_2$

T_2	*"In 1980 Chapman killed Lennon."*
H_2	*"John Lennon died in 1980."*

we need a lexical-syntactic rule such as:

$$\rho_3 = \boxed{X}\,killed\,\boxed{Y} \rightarrow \boxed{Y}\,died$$

along with such rules, the temporal information should be taken into consideration.

Given the importance of lexical-syntactic rules in RTE, many methods have been proposed for their extraction from large corpora (e.g., (Lin and Pantel, 2001; Szpektor and Dagan, 2008)). Unfortunately, these unsupervised methods in general produce rules that can hardly be used: noise and coverage are the most critical issues.

Supervised approaches were experimented in (Zanzotto and Moschitti, 2006; Zanzotto et al., 2009), where lexical-syntactic rules were derived from examples in terms of complex relational features. This approach can easily miss some useful information and rules. For example, given the pair $\langle T_2, H_2 \rangle$, to derive the entailment value of the following case:

$T_4 \Rightarrow ? H_4$

T_4	*"In 1963 Lee Harvey Oswald murdered JFK"*
H_4	*"JFK died in 1963"*

we can only rely on this relatively interesting lexical-syntactic rule (i.e. which is in common between the two examples):

$$\rho_5 = (VP(VBZ)(NP\boxed{X})) \rightarrow (S(NP\boxed{X})(VP(VBZ\ \ died)))$$

Unfortunately, this can be extremely misleading since it also derives similar decisions for the following example:

$T_6 \Rightarrow ? H_6$

T_6	*"In 1956 JFK met Marilyn Monroe"*
H_6	*"Marilyn Monroe died in 1956"*

The problem is that the pairs $\langle T_2, H_2 \rangle$ and $\langle T_4, H_4 \rangle$ share more meaningful features than the rule ρ_5, which should make the difference with respect to the relation between the pairs $\langle T_2, H_2 \rangle$ and $\langle T_6, H_6 \rangle$. Indeed, the word *"kill"* is more semantically related to *"murdered"* than to *"meet"*. Using this information, it is possible to derive more effective rules from training examples.

There are several solutions for taking this information into account, e.g. by using FrameNet semantics (e.g., like in (Burchardt et al., 2007)), it is possible to encode a lexical-syntactic rule using the KILLING and the DEATH frames, i.e.:

$$\rho_7 = \begin{array}{l} KILLING(Killer:\boxed{X}, \\ Victim:\boxed{Y}) \end{array} \rightarrow \begin{array}{l} DEATH(\\ Protagonist:\boxed{Y}) \end{array}$$

However, to use this model, specific rules and a semantic role labeler on the specific corpora are needed.

3 Lexical similarities

Previous research in computational linguistics has produced many effective lexical similarity measures based on many different resources or corpora. For example, WordNet similarities (Pedersen et al., 2004) or Latent Semantic Analysis over a large corpus are widely used in many applications and for the definition of kernel functions, e.g. (Basili et al., 2006; Basili et al., 2005; Bloehdorn et al., 2006).

In this section we present the main component of our new kernel, i.e. a lexical similarity derived from different resources. This is used inside the syntactic/semantic tree kernel defined in (Bloehdorn and Moschitti, 2007a; Bloehdorn and Moschitti, 2007b) to enhance the basic tree kernel functions.

3.1 WordNet Similarities

WordNet similarities have been heavily used in previous NLP work (Chan and Ng, 2005; Agirre et al., 2009). All WordNet similarities apply to pairs of synonymy sets (synsets) and return a value indicating their semantic relatedness. For example, the following measures, that we use in this study, are based on path lengths between concepts in the Wordnet Hierarchy:

Path the measure is equal to the inverse of the shortest path length ($path\_length$) between two synsets c_1 and c_2 in WordNet

$$Sim_{Path} = \frac{1}{path\_length(c_1, c_2)} \tag{1}$$

WUP the Wu and Palmer (Wu and Palmer, 1994) similarity metric is based on the depth of two given synsets c_1 and c_2 in the WordNet taxonomy, and the depth of their least common subsumer (lcs). These are combined into a similarity score:

$$Sim_{WUP} = \frac{2 \times depth(lcs)}{depth(c_1) + depth(c_2)} \tag{2}$$

Wordnet similarity measures on synsets can be extended to similarity measures between words as follows:

$$\kappa_{\mathcal{S}}(w_1, w_2) = max_{(c_1,c_2) \in C_1 \times C_2} Sim_{\mathcal{S}}(c_1, c_2) \tag{3}$$

where $\mathcal{S}$ is Path or WUP and C_i is the set of the synsets related to the word w_i.

3.2 Distributional Semantic Similarity

Latent Semantic Analysis (LSA) is one of the corpus-based measure of distributional semantic similarity, proposed by (Landauer et al., 1998). Words $\vec{w_i}$ are represented in a document space. Each feauture is a document and its value is the frequency of the word in the document. The similarity is generally computed as a cosine similarity:

$$\kappa_{LSI}(w_1, w_2) = \frac{\vec{w_1}\vec{w_2}}{||\vec{w_1}|| \times ||\vec{w_2}||} \tag{4}$$

In our approach we define a proximity matrix P where $p_{i,j}$ represents $\kappa_{LSI}(w_i, w_j)$ The core of our approach lies on LSI (Latent Semantic Indexing) over a large corpus. We used singular value decomposition (SVD) to build the proximity matrix $P = DD^T$ from a large corpus, represented by its word-by-document matrix D.

SVD decomposes D (weighted matrix of term frequencies in a collection of text) into three matrices $U\Sigma V^T$, where U (matrix of term vectors) and V (matrix of document vectors) are orthogonal matrices whose columns are the eigenvectors of DD^T and $D^T D$ respectively, and Σ is the diagonal matrix containing the singular value of D.

Given such decomposition, P can be obtained as $U_k \Sigma_k^2 U_k^T$, where U_k is the matrix containing the first k columns of U and k is the dimensionality of the latent semantic space. This is efficiently used to reduce the memory requirements while retaining the information. Finally we computed the term similarity using the cosine measure in the vector space model (VSM).

Generally, LSA can be observed as a way to overcome some of the drawbacks of the standard vector space model, such as sparseness and dimensionality. In other words, the LSA similarity is computed in a lower dimensional space, in which second-order relations among words and documents are exploited (Mihalcea et al., 2006).

It is worth mentioning that the LSA similarity measure depends on the selected corpus but it benefits from a higher computation speed in comparison to the construction of the similarity matrix based on the WordNet Similarity package (Pedersen et al., 2004).

4 Lexical similarity in Syntactic Tree Kernels

Section 2 has shown that the role of the syntax is important in extracting generalized rules for RTE but it is not enough. Therefore, the lexical similarity described in the previous section should be taken into

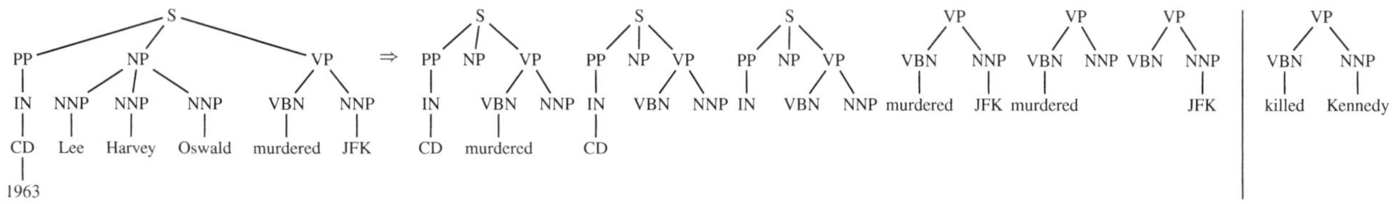

Figure 1: A syntactic parse tree (on the left) along with some of its fragments. After the bar there is an important fragment from a semantically similar sentence, which cannot be matched by STK but it is matched by SSTK.

account in the model definition. Since tree kernels have been shown to be very effective for exploiting syntactic information in natural language tasks, a promising idea is to merge together the two different approaches, i.e. tree kernels and semantic similarities.

4.1 Syntactic Tree Kernel (STK)

Tree kernels compute the number of common substructures between two trees T_1 and T_2 without explicitly considering the whole fragment space. The standard definition of the STK, given in (Collins and Duffy, 2002), allows for any set of nodes linked by one or more entire production rules to be valid substructures. The formal characterization is given in (Collins and Duffy, 2002) and is reported hereafter:

Let $\mathcal{F} = \{f_1, f_2, \ldots, f_{|\mathcal{F}|}\}$ be the set of tree fragments and $\chi_i(n)$ be an indicator function, equal to 1 if the target f_i is rooted at node n and equal to 0 otherwise. A tree kernel function over T_1 and T_2 is defined as $TK(T_1, T_2) = \sum_{n_1 \in N_{T_1}} \sum_{n_2 \in N_{T_2}} \Delta(n_1, n_2)$, where N_{T_1} and N_{T_2} are the sets of nodes in T_1 and T_2, respectively and $\Delta(n_1, n_2) = \sum_{i=1}^{|\mathcal{F}|} \chi_i(n_1)\chi_i(n_2)$.

Δ function counts the number of subtrees rooted in n_1 and n_2 and can be evaluated as follows:

1. if the productions at n_1 and n_2 are different then $\Delta(n_1, n_2) = 0$;

2. if the productions at n_1 and n_2 are the same, and n_1 and n_2 have only leaf children (i.e. they are pre-terminal symbols) then $\Delta(n_1, n_2) = \lambda$;

3. if the productions at n_1 and n_2 are the same, and n_1 and n_2 are not pre-terminals then $\Delta(n_1, n_2) = \lambda \prod_{j=1}^{l(n_1)} (1 + \Delta(c_{n_1}(j), c_{n_2}(j)))$, where $l(n_1)$ is the number of children of n_1, $c_n(j)$ is the j-th child of node n and λ is a decay factor penalizing larger structures.

Figure 1 shows some fragments (out of the overall 472) of the syntactic parse tree on the left, which is derived from the text T4. These fragments satisfy the constraint that grammatical rules cannot be broken. For example, *(VP (VBN (murdered) NNP (JFK)))* is a valid fragment whereas *(VP (VBN (murdered))* is not. One drawback of such kernel is that two sentences expressing similar semantics but with different lexicals produce structures which will not be matched. For example, after the vertical bar there is a fragment, extracted from the parse tree of a semantically identical sentences: `In 1963 Oswald killed Kennedy`. In this case, much less matches will be counted by the kernel function applied to such parse trees and the one of T4. In particular, the complete VP subtree will not be matched.

To tackle this problem the Syntactic Semantic Tree Kernel (SSTK) was defined in (Bloehdorn and Moschitti, 2007a); hereafter, we report its definition.

4.2 Syntactic Semantic Tree kernels (SSTK)

An SSTK produces all the matches of STK. Moreover, the fragments, which are identical but for their lexical nodes, produce a match proportional to the product of the similarity between their corresponding words. This is a sound definition. Indeed, since the structures are the same, each word in position i of the first fragment can be associated with a word located in the same position i of the second fragment. More formally, the fast evaluation of Δ for STK can be used for computing the semantic Δ for SSTK by simply adding the following step

0. if n_1 and n_2 are pre-terminals and $label(n_1) = label(n_2)$ then $\Delta(n_1, n_2) = \lambda \kappa_S(ch_{n_1}^1, ch_{n_2}^1)$,

where $label(n_i)$ is the label of node n_i and κ_S is a term similarity kernel, e.g. based on Wikipedia, Wordnet or BNC, defined in Section 3. Note that: (a) since n_1 and n_2 are pre-terminals of a parse tree they can have only one child (i.e. $ch^1_{n_1}$ and $ch^1_{n_2}$) and such children are words and (b) Step 2 of the original Δ evaluation is no longer necessary.

For example, the fragments: *(VP (VBN (murdered) NNP (JFK)))* has a match with *(VP (VBN (killed) NNP (Kennedy)))* equal to $\kappa_{\mathcal{S}}(murdered, kill) \times \kappa_{\mathcal{S}}(JFK, Kennedy)$.

Beside the novelty of taking into account tree fragments that are not identical it should be noted that the lexical semantic similarity is constrained in syntactic structures, which limit errors/noise due to incorrect (or, as in our case, not provided) word sense disambiguation.

Finally, it should be noted that when a valid kernel is used in place of $\kappa_{\mathcal{S}}$, SSTK is a valid kernel for definition of convolution kernels (Haussler, 1999). Since the matrix P derived by applying LSA produces a semi-definite matrix (see (Cristianini and Holloway, 2001)) we can always use the similarity matrix derived by LSA in SSTK. In case of Wordnet, the validity of the kernel will depend of the kind of similarity used. In our experiments, we have carried out single value decomposition and we have verified that our Wordenet matrices, Path and WUP, are indeed positive semi-definite.

5 Kernels for Textual Entailment Recognition

In this section, we describe how we use the syntactic tree kernel (STK) and the semantic/syntactic tree kernel (SSTK) for modeling lexical-syntactic kernels for textual entailment recognition. We build on the kernel described in (Zanzotto and Moschitti, 2006; Zanzotto et al., 2009) that can model lexical-syntactic rules with variables (i.e., first-order rules).

5.1 Anchoring and pruning

Kernels for modeling lexical-syntactic rules with variables presuppose that words in texts T are explicitly related to words in hypotheses H. This correlation is generally called anchoring and it is implemented with placeholders that co-index the syntactic trees derived from T and H. Words and intermediate nodes are co-indexed when they are equal or similar. For example, in the pair:

$T_8 \Rightarrow ? H_8$	
T_8	*"Lee Harvey Oswald was born in New Orleans, Louisiana, and was of English, German, French and Irish ancestry. In 1963* $\boxed{1}$ *Oswald murdered JFK* $\boxed{2}$*"*
H_8	*"JFK* $\boxed{2}$ *died in 1963* $\boxed{1}$*"*

Moreover, the set of anchors also allows us to prune fragments of the text T that are irrelevant for the final decision: we can discard sentences or phrases uncovered by placeholders. For example, in the pair $\langle T_8, H_8 \rangle$, we can infer that "*Lee H. . . ancestry*" is not a relevant fragment and remove it. This allows us to focus on the critical part for determining the entailment value.

5.2 Kernels for capturing lexical-syntactic rules

Once placeholders are available in the entailment pairs, we can apply the model proposed in (Zanzotto et al., 2009). This derives the maximal similarity between pairs of T and H based on the lexico-syntactic information encoded by the syntactic parse trees of T and H enriched with placeholders. More formally, the original kernel is based on the following equation:

$$maxSTK(\langle T, H \rangle, \langle T', H' \rangle) = max_{c \in C} \quad (5)$$
$$(STK(t(T,c), t(T',i)) + STK(t(H,c), t(H',i)),$$

where: (i) C is the set of all bijective mappings between the placeholders (i.e., the possible variables) from $\langle T, H \rangle$ into $\langle T', H' \rangle$; (ii) $c \in C$ is a substitution function, which implements such mapping; (iii) $t(\cdot, c)$ returns the syntactic tree enriched with placeholders replaced by means of the substitution c; and (iv) $STK(\tau_1, \tau_2)$ is a tree kernel function.

The new semantic-syntactic kernel for lexical-syntactic rules, maxSSTK, substitutes STK with SSTK in Eq. 5 thus enlarging the coverage of the matching between the pairs of texts and the pairs of hypotheses.

6 Experiments

The aim of the experiments is to investigate if our RTE system exploiting syntactic semantic kernels (SSTK) can effectively derive generalized lexico-syntactic rules. In more detail, first, we determine the best lexical similarity suitable for the task, i.e.

		No Semantic	Wiki	BNC	Path	WUP
RTE2	**j = 1**	63.12	63.5	62.75	62.88	**63.88**
	j = 0.9	63.38	**64.75**	62.26	63.88	64.25
RTE3	**j = 1**	66.88	**67.25**	**67.25**	66.88	66.5
	j = 0.9	67.25	**67.75**	67.5	67.12	67.38
RTE5	**j = 1**	65.5	**66.5**	65.83	66	66
	j = 0.9	65.5	**66.83**	65.67	66	66.33

Table 1: Accuracy of plain (WOK+STK+maxSTK) and Semantic Lexico-Syntactic (WOK+SSTK+maxSSTK) Kernels. The latter according to different similarities

distributional vs. Wordnet-based approaches. Second, we derive qualitative and quantitative properties, which justify the selection of one with respect to the other.

For this purpose, we tested four different version of SSTK, i.e. using Path, WUP, BNC and WIKI lexical similarities on three different RTE datasets. These correspond to the three different challenges in which the development set was provided.

6.1 Experimental Setup

We used the data from three recognizing textual entailment challenge: RTE2 (Bar-Haim ct al., 2006), RTE3 (Giampiccolo et al., 2007), and RTE5, along with the standard split between training and test sets. We did not use RTE1 as it was differently built from the others and RTE4 as it does not contain the development set.

We used the following publicly available tools: the Charniak Parser (Charniak, 2000) for parsing sentences and SVM-light-TK (Moschitti, 2006; Joachims, 1999), in which we coded our new kernels for RTE. Additionally, we used the Jiang&Conrath (J&C) distance (Jiang and Conrath, 1997) computed with `wn::similarity` package (Pedersen et al., 2004) to measure the similarity between T and H. This similarity is also used to define the text-hypothesis word overlap kernel (WOK).

The distributional semantics is captured by means of LSA: we used the java Latent Semantic Indexing (jLSI) tool (Giuliano, 2007). In particular, we precomputed the word-pair matrices for RTE2, RTE3, and RTE5. We built different LSA matrices from the British National Corpus (BNC) and Wikipedia (Wiki). The British National Corpus (BNC) is a balanced synchronic text corpus containing 100 million words with morpho-syntactic annotation. For Wikipedia, we created a model from the 200,000 most visited Wikipedia articles, after cleaning the unnecessary markup tags. Articles are our documents for creating the term-by-document matrix. Wikipedia provides the largest coverage knowledge resource developed by a community, besides the noticeable coverage of named entities. This further motivates the design of a similarity measure. We also consider two typical WordNet similarities (i.e., Path and WUP, respectively) as described in Sec. 3.1.

The main RTE model that we consider is constituted by three main kernels:

- WOK, i.e. the kernel based on only the text-hypothesis lexical overlapping words (this is an intra-pair similarity);
- STK, i.e. the sum of the standard tree kernel (see Section 4.1) applied to the two text parse-trees and the two hypothesis parse trees;
- SSTK, i.e. the same as STK with the use of lexical similarities as explained in Section 4.2;
- maxSTK and maxSSTK, i.e. the kernel for RTE, illustrated in Section 5.2, where the latter exploits similarity since it uses SSTK in Eq. 5.

Note that the model presented in (Zanzotto et al., 2009), our baseline, corresponds to the combination kernel: WOK+maxSTK. In this paper, in addition to the role of lexical similarities, we also study several combinations (we just need to sum the separated kernels), i.e. WOK+STK+maxSTK, SSTK+maxSSTK, WOK+SSTK+maxSSTK and WOK+maxSSTK.

Finally, we measure the performance of our system with the standard accuracy and then we determine the statistical significance by using the model

		STK	SSTK	maxSTK	maxSSTK	STK+maxSTK	SSTK+maxSSTK	∅
RTE2	+WOK	61.5	61.12	63.88	64.12	63.12	63.50	60.62
		52.62	52.75	61.25	59.38	61.25	58.75	-
RTE3	+WOK	66.38	66.5	66.5	67.0	66.88	67.25	66.75
		53.25	54.5	62.25	64.38	63.12	63.62	-
RTE5	+WOK	62.0	62.0	64.83	64.83	65.5	66.5	60.67
		54.33	57.33	63.33	62.67	61.83	62.67	-

Table 2: Comparing different lexico-syntactic kernels with Wiki-based semantic kernels

described in (Yeh, 2000) and implemented in (Padó, 2006).

6.2 Distributional vs. WordNet-based Semantics

The first experiment compares the basic kernel, i.e. WOK+STK+maxSTK, with the new semantic kernel, i.e. WOK+SSTK+maxSSTK, where SSTK and maxSSTK encode four different kinds of similarities, BNC, WIKI, WUP and Path. The aim is twofold: understanding if semantic similarities can be effectively used to derive generalized lexico-syntactic rules and to determine the best similarity model.

Table 1 shows the results according to No Semantics, Wiki, BNC, Path and WUP. The three pairs of rows represent the results over the three different datasets, i.e., RTE2, RTE3, and RTE5. For each pair, we have two rows representing a different j parameter of SVM. An increase of j augments the weight of positive with respect to negative examples and during learning it tunes-up the Recall/Precision rate. We use two values $j = 1$ (the default value) and $j = 0.9$ (selected during a preliminary experiment on a validation set on RTE2). $j = 0.9$ was used to minimally increase the Precision, considering that the semantic model tends to improve the Recall.

The results show that:

- WIKI semantics constantly improves the basic kernel (no Semantics) for any datasets or parameter.
- The distributional semantics is almost always better than the WordNet-based one.
- In one case WUP improves WIKI, i.e. 63.88 vs 63.5 and in another case BNC reaches WIKI, i.e. 67.25 but this happens for the default values of the j parameters, i.e. $j = 1$, which was not selected by our limited parameter validation.

Finally, the difference between the accuracy of the best WIKI kernels and the No Semantic kernels are statistically significant ($p << 0.05$).

6.3 Kernel Comparisons

The previous experiments (Sec. 6.2) show that Wikipedia-based distributional semantics provides an effective similarity to generalize lexico-syntactic rules (features). As our RTE kernel is a composition of other basic kernels, we experimented with different combinations to understand the role of each component. Moreover, to obtain results independent of parameterization we used the default parameter j.

Table 2 reports the accuracy of different kernels and their combinations on different RTE datasets. Each row describes the results for each dataset and it is split in two according to the use of WOK or not in the RTE model. In the each column, the different kernels are reported. For example, the entry in the 4th column and the 2nd row refers to the accuracy of SSTK in combination with WOK, i.e. WOK+SSTK for the RTE2.

We observe that: first WOK produces a very high accuracy in RTE challenges, i.e. 60.62, 66.75 and 60.67 and it is an essential component of RTE systems since its ablation always causes a large accuracy decrease. This is reasonable as the major source of information to establish entailment between sentences is their word overlap.

Second, STK and SSTK, when added to WOK, improve it on RTE2 and RTE5 but do not improve it on RTE3. This suggests a difficulty of exploiting syntactic information for RTE3.

Third, maxSTK+WOK relevantly improves WOK on RTE2 and RTE5 but fails in RTE3. Again, the syntactic rules (with variables) which this kernel

	BNC	WN	WIKI
RTE2	0.55	0.42	0.83
RTE3	0.54	0.41	0.83
RTE5	0.45	0.34	0.82

Table 3: Coverage of the different resources for the words of the three datasets

can provide are not enough general for RTE3. In contrast, maxSSTK+WOK improves WOK on all datasets thanks to its generalization ability.

Finally, STK and SSTK added to maxSTK+WOK or to maxSSTK+WOK tend to produce an accuracy increase, although not in every condition.

7 Discussion

7.1 Coverage and efficiency

As already mentioned, the practical use of Wikipedia to design lexical similarities is motivated by a large coverage. Deriving similarities from other resources such as WordNet is more time-consuming. To prove our claim, we performed an analysis on the coverage and efficiency in computing the pair term similarity.

Table 3 shows the coverage of the content words of the three datasets. The coverage of Wikipedia is about two times more than the other resources in all experimented datasets.

Speed	Milliseconds
LSA	0.54
WN with POS	5.3
WN without POS	15.2

Table 4: The comparison in terms of speed calculated over 10000 pairs after loading the model.

Moreover, Table 4 shows that the computation of the LSA matrix on Wikipedia is faster than using the WordNet similarity software (Pedersen et al., 2004). Even if the accuracy of some WordNet models can reach the one based on Wikipedia, the latter is preferable for the smaller computational cost.

7.2 Comparison with previous work

The results of our models show that lexical semantics for building more effective lexical-syntactic rules is promising. Here, we compare our approaches with other RTE systems to show that our results are indeed state-of-the-art. Unfortunately, deriving a reasonable accuracy value to represent the state-of-the-art is extremely difficult as many factors can determine the final score. For example, the best systems in RTE2 and RTE3 (Giampiccolo et al., 2007) have an accuracy 10% higher than the others but they generally use resources that are not publicly available.

	Average Acc.	Our rank	# participants
RTE2	59.8	3rd	23
RTE3	64.5	4th	26
RTE5	61.5	4th	20

Table 5: Comparison with other approaches to RTE

Table 5 shows the average accuracy of the participant systems, the rank of our system that we propose in this paper and the number of participants. Our model accuracy is absolutely above the average and it is ranked at the top positions. We can also carry out a finer comparison with respect to RTE2 (Bar-Haim et al., 2006). Our system results are the best when compared with systems using semantic models based on FrameNet, indeed the best ranked system in this class, i.e., (Burchardt et al., 2007), scores only 62.5. Among systems using logical inference, our model is instead the 3rd out of 8 systems using logical inference that perform worse than ours. Finally, it is the 2nd among systems using supervised machine learning models.

8 Conclusion

In this paper we presented a model to effectively include semantics in lexical-syntactic features for textual entailment recognition. We have experimentally shown that LSA-derived lexical semantics embedded in syntactic structures is a promising approach. The model that we have presented is one of the best system in the RTE challenges. Additionally, in contrast to many other methods it does not require large sets of handcrafted or corpus extracted lexical-syntactic rules.

Acknowledgements

The research of Alessandro Moschitti has been partially supported by Trustworthy Eternal Systems via Evolving Software, Data and Knowledge (EternalS, project number FP7 247758).

References

E. Agirre, E. Alfonseca, K. Hall, J. Kravalova, M. Paşca, and A. Soroa. 2009. A study on similarity and relatedness using distributional and wordnet-based approaches. In *NAACL '09: Proc. HLT/NAACL.*

R. Bar-Haim, I. Dagan, B. Dolan, L. Ferro, D. Giampiccolo, and I. Magnini, B. Szpektor. 2006. The ii PASCAL recognising textual entailment challenge. In *Proc. of the II PASCAL Challenges Workshop.*

R. Bar-Haim, I. Dagan, I. Greental, and E. Shnarch. 2007. Semantic inference at the lexical-syntactic level. In *AAAI'07: Proc. of the 22nd national conference on Artificial intelligence.*

R. Bar-Haim, J. Berant, and I. Dagan. 2009. A compact forest for scalable inference over entailment and paraphrase rules. In *Proc. of EMNLP.*

R. Basili, M. Cammisa, and A. Moschitti. 2005. Effective use of wordnet semantics via kernel-based learning. In *CoNLL.*

R. Basili, M. Cammisa, and A. Moschitti. 2006. A semantic kernel to classify texts with very few training examples. In *Informatica.*

S. Bloehdorn and A. Moschitti. 2007a. Combined syntactic and semantic kernels for text classification. In *ECIR.*

S. Bloehdorn and A. Moschitti. 2007b. Structure and semantics for expressive text kernels. In *Proc. of CIKM '07.*

S. Bloehdorn, R. Basili, M. Cammisa, and A. Moschitti. 2006. Semantic kernels for text classification based on topological measures of feature similarity. In *Proc. of ICDM 06, Hong Kong, 2006.*

J. Bos and K. Markert. 2005. Recognising textual entailment with logical inference. In *HLT '05: Proc. of the conference on HLT and EMNLP.*

A. Burchardt, N. Reiter, S. Thater, and A. Frank. 2007. Semantic Approach to Textual Entailment: System Evaluation and Task Analysis. In *Proc. of the 3rd-PASCAL Workshop on Textual Entailment*, Prague.

Y. S. Chan and H. T. Ng. 2005. Word sense disambiguation with distribution estimation. In *Proc. of IJCAI'05.*

Eugene Charniak. 2000. A maximum-entropy-inspired parser. In *Proc. of the 1st NAACL conference.*

M. Collins and N. Duffy. 2002. New ranking algorithms for parsing and tagging: kernels over discrete structures, and the voted perceptron. In *Proc. of ACL '02.*

N. Cristianini and R. Holloway. 2001. Latent semantic kernels.

G. Dinu and R. Wang. 2009. Inference rules and their application to recognizing textual entailment. In *Proc. of the EACL '09.*

D. Giampiccolo, B. Magnini, Ido Dagan, and B. Dolan. 2007. The third pascal recognizing textual entailment challenge. In *Proc. of the ACL-PASCAL Workshop on Textual Entailment and Paraphrasing.*

Claudio Giuliano. 2007. jLSI a for latent semantic indexing. *http://tcc.itc.it/research/textec/tools-resources/jLSI.html.*

A. D. Haghighi, A. Y. Ng, and C. D. Manning. 2005. Robust textual inference via graph matching. In *HLT '05: Proc. of the conference on HLT and EMNLP.*

David Haussler. 1999. Convolution kernels on discrete structures. Technical report.

J. J. Jiang and D. W. Conrath. 1997. Semantic similarity based on corpus statistics and lexical taxonomy. In *Proc. of the 10th ROCLING.*

Thorsten Joachims. 1999. Making large-scale support vector machine learning practical.

Landauer, Foltz, and Laham. 1998. Introduction to latent semantic analysis. In *Discourse Processes 25.*

D. Lin and P. Pantel. 2001. DIRT-discovery of inference rules from text. In *Proc. of the ACM KDD-01.*

R. Mihalcea, C. Corley, and C. Strapparava. 2006. Corpus-based and knowledge-based measures of text semantic similarity. In *Proc. of AAAI06.*

Alessandro Moschitti. 2006. Making tree kernels practical for natural language learning. In *Proc. of EACL.*

Peter Norvig. 1987. A unified theory of inference for text understanding. Technical report, USA.

Sebastian Padó, 2006. *User's guide to `sigf`: Significance testing by approximate randomisation.*

T. Pedersen, S. Patwardhan, and J. Michelizzi. 2004. Wordnet::similarity - measuring the relatedness of concepts. In *Proc. of 5th NAACL.*

D. Roth and M. Sammons. 2007. Semantic and logical inference model for textual entailment. In *Proc. of the ACL-PASCAL Workshop on Textual Entailment and Paraphrasing.*

I. Szpektor and I. Dagan. 2008. Learning entailment rules for unary templates. In *Proc. of COLING '08.*

M. Tatu and D. Moldovan. 2005. A semantic approach to recognizing textual entailment. In *HLT '05: Proc. of HLT/EMNLP.*

Z. Wu and M. Palmer. 1994. Verb semantics and lexical selection. In *Proc. of ACL.*

Alexander Yeh. 2000. More accurate tests for the statistical significance of result differences. In *Proc. of ACL 2000*, Morristown, NJ, USA.

F. M. Zanzotto and A. Moschitti. 2006. Automatic learning of textual entailments with cross-pair similarities. In *Proc. of ACL '06.*

F. M. Zanzotto, M. Pennacchiotti, and A. Moschitti. 2009. A machine learning approach to textual entailment recognition. *NATURAL LANGUAGE ENGINEERING.*

Automatic Metaphor Interpretation as a Paraphrasing Task

Ekaterina Shutova
Computer Laboratory
University of Cambridge
15 JJ Thomson Avenue
Cambridge CB3 0FD, UK
Ekaterina.Shutova@cl.cam.ac.uk

Abstract

We present a novel approach to metaphor interpretation and a system that produces literal paraphrases for metaphorical expressions. Such a representation is directly transferable to other applications that can benefit from a metaphor processing component. Our method is distinguished from the previous work in that it does not rely on any hand-crafted knowledge about metaphor, but in contrast employs automatically induced selectional preferences. Being the first of its kind, our system is capable of paraphrasing metaphorical expressions with a high accuracy (0.81).

1 Introduction

Metaphors arise when one concept is viewed in terms of the properties of the other. In other words it is based on *similarity* between the concepts. Similarity is a kind of association implying the presence of characteristics in common. Here are some examples of metaphor.

(1) News *travels* fast. (Lakoff and Johnson, 1980)

(2) How can I *kill* a process? (Martin, 1988)

(3) And then my heart with pleasure *fills*,
And *dances* with the daffodils.[1]

In metaphorical expressions seemingly unrelated features of one concept are associated with another concept. In the example (2) the *computational process* is viewed as something *alive* and, therefore, its forced termination is associated with the act of killing.

Metaphorical expressions represent a great variety, ranging from conventional metaphors, which we reproduce and comprehend every day, e.g. those in (1) and (2), to poetic and largely novel ones, such as (3). The use of metaphor is ubiquitous in natural language text and it is a serious bottleneck in automatic text understanding. In order to estimate the frequency of the phenomenon, we conducted a corpus study on a subset of the British National Corpus (BNC) (Burnard, 2007) representing various genres. We manually annotated metaphorical expressions in this data and found that 241 out of 761 sentences contained a metaphor or (rarely) an idiom. Due to such a high frequency of their use, a system capable of interpreting metaphorical expressions in unrestricted text would become an invaluable component of any semantics-oriented NLP application.

Automatic processing of metaphor can be clearly divided into two subtasks: *metaphor recognition* (distinguishing between literal and metaphorical language in text) and *metaphor interpretation* (identifying the intended literal meaning of a metaphorical expression). Both of them have been repeatedly addressed in NLP.

To date the most influential account of metaphor recognition has been that of Wilks (1978). According to Wilks, metaphors represent a violation of selectional restrictions in a given context. Consider the following example.

(4) My car *drinks* gasoline. (Wilks, 1978)

[1]taken from the verse "I wandered lonely as a cloud" written by William Wordsworth in 1804.

Human Language Technologies: The 2010 Annual Conference of the North American Chapter of the ACL, pages 1029–1037,
Los Angeles, California, June 2010.

The verb *drink* normally takes an *animate* subject and a *liquid* object. Therefore, *drink* taking a *car* as a subject is an anomaly, which may as well indicate metaphorical use of *drink*.

Most approaches to metaphor interpretation rely on task-specific hand-coded knowledge (Fass, 1991; Martin, 1990; Narayanan, 1997; Narayanan, 1999; Feldman and Narayanan, 2004; Barnden and Lee, 2002; Agerri et al., 2007) and produce interpretations in a non-textual format. However, the ultimate objective of automatic metaphor processing is a type of interpretation that can be directly embedded into other systems to enhance their performance. Thus, we define metaphor interpretation as a *paraphrasing task* and build a system that automatically derives literal paraphrases for metaphorical expressions in unrestricted text.

In summary, our system (1) produces a list of all possible paraphrases for a metaphorical expression (induced automatically from a large corpus); (2) ranks the paraphrases according to their likelihood derived from the corpus; (3) discriminates between literal and figurative paraphrases by detecting selectional preference violation and outputs the literal ones; and (4) disambiguates the sense of the paraphrases using WordNet (Fellbaum, 1998) inventory of senses.

We tested our system on a collection of metaphorical expressions representing verb-subject and verb-object constructions, where the verb is used metaphorically. To compile this dataset we manually annotated such phrases in a subset of the BNC using the metaphor identification procedure (MIP) (Pragglejaz Group, 2007). We then evaluated the quality of paraphrasing with the help of human annotators and created a gold standard for this task.

2 Experimental Data

Since we focus on single-word metaphors expressed by a verb, our annotation task can be viewed as verb classification according to whether the verbs are used metaphorically or literally. However, some verbs have weak or no potential of being a metaphor and, thus, our study is not concerned with them. We excluded the following verb classes: (1) auxiliary verbs; (2) modal verbs; (3) aspectual verbs (e.g. *begin, start, finish*); (4) light verbs (e.g. *take, give, put, get, make*).

2.1 The Corpus

Our corpus is a subset of the BNC. We sampled texts representing various genres: literature, newspaper/journal articles, essays on politics, international relations and history, radio broadcast (transcribed speech). The corpus contains 761 sentences and 13642 words.

2.2 Annotation Scheme

The annotation scheme we use is based on the principles of the metaphor identification procedure (MIP) developed by Pragglejaz Group (2007). We adopt their definition of *basic* sense of a word and their approach to distinguishing basic senses from the metaphorical ones. MIP involves metaphor annotation at the word level as opposed to identifying metaphorical relations (between words) or source–target domain mappings (between concepts or domains). Such annotation can be viewed as a form of word sense disambiguation with an emphasis on metaphoricity.

In order to discriminate between the verbs used metaphorically and literally we use the following procedure as part of our guidelines:

1. For each verb establish its meaning in context and try to imagine a more basic meaning of this verb on other contexts. As defined in the framework of MIP (Pragglejaz Group, 2007) basic meanings normally are: (1) more concrete; (2) related to bodily action; (3) more precise (as opposed to vague); (4) historically older.

2. If you can establish the basic meaning that is distinct from the meaning of the verb in this context, the verb is likely to be used metaphorically.

Consider the following example sentence:

(5) If he asked her to post a letter or buy some razor blades from the chemist, she was transported with pleasure.

In this sentence one needs to annotate four verbs that are underlined. The first 3 verbs are used in their basic sense, i.e. literally (*ask* in the context of "a person asking another person a question or a favour";

post in the context of "a person posting/sending a letter"; *buy* in the sense of "making a purchase"). Thus, they are tagged as literal. The verb *transport*, however, in its basic sense is used in the context of "goods being transported/carried by a vehicle". The context in this sentence involves "a person being transported by a feeling", which contrasts the basic sense in that the agent of *transporting* is an EMOTION as opposed to a VEHICLE. Thus, we can infer that the use of *transport* in this sentence is metaphorical.

2.3 Annotation Reliability

We tested reliability of this annotation scheme using multiple annotators on a subset of the corpus. The rest of the annotation was done by a single annotator.

Annotators We had three independent volunteer annotators, who were all native speakers of English and had some linguistics background.

Material and Task All of them received the same text taken from the BNC containing 142 verbs to annotate. They were asked to classify verbs as metaphorical or literal.

Guidelines and Training The annotators received written guidelines (2 pages) and were asked to do a small annotation exercise (2 sentences containing 8 verbs in total). The goal of the exercise was to ensure they were at ease with the annotation format.

Interannotator Agreement We evaluate reliability of our annotation scheme by assessing interannotator agreement in terms of κ (Siegel and Castellan, 1988). The classification was performed with the agreement of 0.64 (κ), which is considered reliable. The main source of disagreement was the high conventionality of some expressions, i.e. cases where the metaphorical etymology could be clearly traced, but the senses are highly lexicalized.

2.4 Phrase Selection

Only the phrases that were tagged as metaphorical by all of the annotators were included in the test set. Here are some examples of such phrases: *memories were slipping away; hold the truth back; stirred an unfathomable excitement; factors shape results; mending their marriage; brushed aside the accusations* etc. In order to avoid extra noise we placed some additional criteria to select the test phrases: (1) exclude phrases where subject or object referent is unknown, e.g. containing pronouns such as in *in which they [changes] operated*; (2) exclude phrases whose metaphorical meaning is realised solely in passive constructions (e.g. *sociologists have been inclined to [..]*); (3) exclude phrases where the subject or object of interest are represented by a named entity (e.g. *Then Hillary leapt into the conversation*); (4) exclude multiword metaphors (e.g. *go on pilgrimage with Raleigh or put out to sea with Tennyson*). The resulting test set contains 62 metaphorical expressions.

3 The Method

The system takes phrases containing annotated single-word metaphors (where a verb is used metaphorically, its context is used literally) as input. It generates a list of possible paraphrases that can occur in the same context and ranks them according to their likelihood derived from the corpus. Subsequently it identifies shared features of the paraphrases and the metaphorical verb using WordNet hierarchy of concepts and removes the unrelated concepts. Among the related paraphrases it then identifies the literal ones given the context relying on the automatically induced selectional preferences.

3.1 The Model for Paraphrase Ranking

We model the likelihood of a particular paraphrase as a joint probability of the following events: the interpretation (another term to replace the one used metaphorically) i co-occurring with the other lexical items from its context $w_1, ..., w_N$ in the relations $r_1, ..., r_N$ respectively.

$$L_i = P(i, (w_1, r_1), (w_2, r_2), ..., (w_N, r_N)), \quad (1)$$

where $w_1, ..., w_N$ and $r_1, ..., r_N$ represent the fixed context of the term used metaphorically in the sentence. This context will be kept as part of the paraphrase, and the term used metaphorically will be replaced.

We take each relation of the term in a phrase to be independent from the other relations of this term in this phrase. E.g. for a verb in the presence of both the subject and the object the `Verb-Subject` and `Verb-Object` relations would be considered to be independent events within the model. This yields the following approximation:

$$P(i,(w_1,r_1),(w_2,r_2),...,(w_N,r_N)) = P(i)\cdot P((w_1,r_1)|i)\cdot ...\cdot P((w_N,r_N)|i). \quad (2)$$

We can calculate the probabilities using maximum likelihood estimation

$$P(i) = \frac{f(i)}{\sum_k f(i_k)}, \quad (3)$$

$$P(w_n,r_n|i) = \frac{f(w_n,r_n,i)}{f(i)}, \quad (4)$$

where $f(i)$ is the frequency of the interpretation on its own, $\sum_k f(i_k)$ is the number of times this part of speech is attested in the corpus and $f(w_n,r_n,i)$ - the frequency of the co-occurrence of the interpretation with the context word w_n in the relation r_n. By performing appropriate substitutions into (2) we obtain

$$P(i,(w_1,r_1),(w_2,r_2),...,(w_N,r_N)) = \frac{f(i)}{\sum_k f(i_k)}\cdot\frac{f(w_1,r_1,i)}{f(i)}\cdot ...\cdot\frac{f(w_N,r_N,i)}{f(i)} = \frac{\prod_{n=1}^N f(w_n,r_n,i)}{(f(i))^{N-1}\cdot\sum_k f(i_k)} \quad (5)$$

This model is then used to rank the possible replacements of the term used metaphorically in the fixed context according to the data.

3.2 Parameter Estimation

The parameters of the model were estimated from the British National Corpus that was parsed using the RASP parser of Briscoe et al. (2006). We used the grammatical relations (GRs) output of RASP for BNC created by Andersen et al. (2008). The same output of RASP was used to identify the GRs in the metaphorical expressions themselves, as the metaphor corpus from which they were extracted is a subset of the BNC. To obtain the counts for $f(w_n,r_n,i)$ we extracted all the terms appearing in the corpus in the relation r_n with w_n for each lexical item - relation pair. The initial list of replacements for the metaphorical term was constructed by taking an overlap of the lists of terms for each lexical item - relation pair.

3.3 Identifying Shared Meanings in WordNet

It should be noted that the context-based model described in 3.1 overgenerates and hence there is a need to further narrow the search space. It is acknowledged in the linguistics community that metaphor is to a great extent based on similarity between the concepts involved. We exploit this fact to refine paraphrasing. After obtaining the initial list of possible substitutes for the metaphorical term, we filter out the terms whose meaning does not share any common features with that of the metaphorical term. Consider a Computer Science metaphor *kill a process*, which stands for *terminate a process*. The basic sense of *kill* implies an *end* or *termination* of life. Thus, *termination* is the shared element of the metaphorical verb and its literal interpretation.

Such overlap of features can be identified using the hyponymy relations in the WordNet taxonomy. Within the initial list of paraphrases we select the terms that are a hypernym of the metaphorical term or share a common hypernym with it[2]. To maximize the accuracy we restrict the hypernym search to three level distance in the taxomomy. The filtered lists of metaphorical verb replacements for some of the phrases from our dataset together with their log-likelihood are demonstrated in Table 1. Selecting the highest ranked paraphrase from this list as a literal interpretation will serve as a baseline.

3.4 Filtering Based on Selectional Preferences

The obtained lists contain some irrelevant paraphrases (e.g. *contain the truth* for *hold back the truth*) and some paraphrases where the substitute is used metaphorically again (e.g. *suppress the truth*). However, the task is to identify the literal interpretation, therefore, these need to be removed.

One way of dealing with both problems at once is to take into account selectional preferences of the verbs in our list. The verbs used metaphorically are likely to demonstrate strong semantic preference for the source domain, e.g. *suppress* would select for *movements (political)* rather than *ideas*, or *truth*, (the target domain), whereas the ones used literally (e.g.,

[2]We excluded the expressions containing a term whose metaphorical sense is included in WordNet from the test set, to ensure that the system does not rely on this extra hand-coded knowledge about metaphor.

Log-likelihood	Replacement
Verb-DirectObject	
hold back truth:	
-13.09	contain
-14.15	conceal
-14.62	suppress
-15.13	hold
-16.23	keep
-16.24	defend
stir excitement:	
-14.28	create
-14.84	provoke
-15.53	make
-15.53	elicit
-15.53	arouse
-16.23	stimulate
-16.23	raise
-16.23	excite
-16.23	conjure
Subject-Verb	
report leak:	
-11.78	reveal
-12.59	issue
-13.18	disclose
-13.28	emerge
-14.84	expose
-16.23	discover

Table 1: The list of paraphrases with the initial ranking

Association	Replacement
Verb-DirectObject	
hold back truth:	
0.1161	conceal
0.0214	keep
0.0070	suppress
0.0022	contain
0.0018	defend
0.0006	hold
stir excitement:	
0.0696	provoke
0.0245	elicit
0.0194	arouse
0.0061	conjure
0.0028	create
0.0001	stimulate
≈ 0	raise
≈ 0	make
≈ 0	excite
Subject-Verb	
report leak:	
0.1492	disclose
0.1463	discover
0.0674	reveal
0.0597	issue
≈ 0	emerge
≈ 0	expose

Table 2: The list of paraphrases reranked using selectional preferences

conceal) would select for *truth*. This would potentially allow us to filter out non-literalness, as well as unrelated verbs, by selecting the verbs that the noun in the metaphorical expression matches best.

We automatically acquired selectional preference distributions of the verbs in the paraphrase lists (for `Verb-Subject` and `Verb-Object` relations) from the BNC parsed by RASP. We first clustered 2000 most frequent nouns in the BNC into 200 clusters using the algorithm of Sun and Korhonen (2009). The obtained clusters formed our selectional preference classes. We adopted the association measure proposed by Resnik (1993) and successfully applied to a number of tasks in NLP including word sense disambiguation (Resnik, 1997). Resnik models selectional preference of a verb in probabilistic terms as the difference between the posterior distribution of noun classes in a particular relation with the verb and their prior distribution in that syntactic position regardless of the identity of the predicate. He quantifies this difference using the relative entropy (or Kullback-Leibler distance), defining the *selectional preference strength* as follows.

$$S_R(v) = D(P(c|v)||P(c)) = \sum_c P(c|v) \log \frac{P(c|v)}{P(c)}, \quad (6)$$

where $P(c)$ is the prior probability of the noun class, $P(c|v)$ is the posterior probability of the noun class given the verb and R is the grammatical relation in question. Selectional preference strength measures how strongly the predicate constrains its arguments. In order to quantify how well a particular argument class fits the verb, Resnik defines another measure called *selectional association*:

$$A_R(v,c) = \frac{1}{S_R(v)} P(c|v) \log \frac{P(c|v)}{P(c)}. \quad (7)$$

We use this measure to rerank the paraphrases and filter out those not well suited or used metaphorically. The new ranking is demonstrated in Table 2. The expectation is that the paraphrase in the first rank (i.e. the verb with which the noun in question has the highest association) represents the literal interpretation.

3.5 Sense Disambiguation

Another feature of our system is that having identified literal interpretations, it is capable to perform their word sense disambiguation (WSD). Disambiguated metaphorical interpretations are potentially a useful source of information for NLP applications dealing with word senses.

We adopt WordNet representation of a sense. Disambiguation is performed by selecting WordNet nodes containing those verbs that share a common hypernym with the metaphorical verb. The list of disambiguated interpretations for a random selection of phrases from our dataset is demonstrated in Table 3. However, we did not evaluate the WSD of the paraphrases at this stage.

4 Evaluation and Discussion

We evaluated the paraphrases with the help of human annotators in two different experimental settings.

Setting 1: the annotators were presented with a set of sentences containing metaphorical expressions and their rank 1 paraphrases produced by the system and by the baseline. They were asked to mark the ones that have the same meaning as the term used metaphorically and are used literally in the context of the paraphrase expression as correct.

We had 7 volunteer annotators who were all native speakers of English (one bilingual) and had no or sparse linguistic expertise. Their agreement on the task was 0.62 (κ), whereby the main source of disagreement was the presence of highly lexicalised metaphorical paraphrases. We then evaluated the system performance against their judgments in terms of *accuracy*. Accuracy measures the proportion of correct literal interpretations among the paraphrases in rank 1. The results are demonstrated in Table 4, the final systems identifies literal paraphrases with the accuracy of 0.81.

Setting 2: the annotators were presented with a set of sentences containing metaphorical expressions and asked to write down all suitable literal paraphrases for the highlighted metaphorical verbs. We had 5 volunteer subjects for this experiment (note that these were people not employed in the previous setting); they were all native speakers of English and had some linguistics background. We then compiled a gold standard by incorporating all of the annotations. E.g. the gold standard for the phrase *brushed aside the accusations* contains the verbs *rejected, ignored, disregarded, dismissed, overlooked, discarded*.

We compared the system output against the gold standard using *mean reciprocal rank* (MRR) as a measure. MRR is traditionally used to evaluate the performance of Question-Answering systems. We adapted this measure in order to be able to assess ranking quality beyond rank 1 and the recall of our system. An individual metaphorical expression receives a score equal to the reciprocal of the rank at which the first correct literal interpretation (according to the human gold standard) is found among the top five paraphrases, or 0 if none of the five paraphrases contains a correct interpretation. Once the individual reciprocal ranks of metaphorical expressions are estimated their mean is computed across the dataset. The MRR of our system equals 0.63 and that of the baseline is 0.55. However, it should be noted that given that our task is open-ended, it is hard to construct a comprehensive gold standard. For example, for the phrase *stir excitement* most annotators suggested only one paraphrase *create excitement*, which is found in rank 3. However, the top ranks of the system output are occupied by *provoke* and *stimulate*, which are more precise paraphrases, although they have not occurred to the annotators. Such examples result in the system's MRR being significantly lower than its accuracy at rank 1.

The obtained results are promising, the selectional preference-based reranking yields a considerable improvement in accuracy (26%) over the baseline. However, for one of the phrases in the dataset, *mend marriage*, the new ranking overruns the correct top suggestion of the baseline, *improve marriage*, and outputs *repair marriage* as the most likely literal interpretation. This is due to both the conventionality of some metaphorical senses (in this case *repair*) and to the fact that some verbs, e.g. *improve*, expose a moderate selectional preference strength, i.e. they are equally associated with a large number of classes. This demonstrates potential drawbacks of the selectional preference-based solutions. Another

Met. Expression	Top Int.	Its WordNet Sense
Verb-DirectObject		
stir excitement	provoke	**(arouse-1 elicit-1 enkindle-2 kindle-3 evoke-1 fire-7 raise-10 provoke-1)** - call forth (emotions, feelings, and responses): "arouse pity"; "raise a smile"; "evoke sympathy"
inherit state	acquire	**(get-1 acquire-1)** - come into the possession of something concrete or abstract: "She got a lot of paintings from her uncle"; "They acquired a new pet"
reflect concern	manifest	**(attest-1 certify-1 manifest-1 demonstrate-3 evidence-1)** - provide evidence for; stand as proof of; show by one's behavior, attitude, or external attributes: "The buildings in Rome manifest a high level of architectural sophistication"; "This decision demonstrates his sense of fairness"
brush aside accusation	reject	**(reject-1)** - refuse to accept or acknowledge: "we reject the idea of starting a war"; "The journal rejected the student's paper"
Verb-Subject		
campaign *surged*	improve	**(better-3 improve-2 ameliorate-2 meliorate-2)** - to make better: "The editor improved the manuscript with his changes"
report *leaked*	disclose	**(unwrap-2 disclose-1 let_on-1 bring_out-9 reveal-2 discover-6 expose-2 divulge-1 break-15 give_away-2 let_out-2)** - make known to the public information that was previously known only to a few people or that was meant to be kept a secret: "The auction house would not disclose the price at which the van Gogh had sold"; "The actress won't reveal how old she is"
tension *mounted*	lift	**(rise-1 lift-4 arise-5 move_up-2 go_up-1 come_up-6 uprise-6)** - move upward: "The fog lifted"; "The smoke arose from the forest fire"; "The mist uprose from the meadows"

Table 3: Disambiguated paraphrases produced by the system

Relation	Baseline	System
Verb-DirectObject	0.52	0.79
Verb-Subject	0.57	0.83
Average	0.55	0.81

Table 4: Accuracy with the evaluation setting 1

controvertial example was the metaphorical expression *tension mounted*, for which the system produced a paraphrase *tension lifted* with the opposite meaning. This error is likely to have been triggered by the feature similarity component, whereby one of the senses of *lift* would stem from the same node in WordNet as the metaphorical sense of *mount*.

5 Related Work

According to Conceptual Metaphor Theory (Lakoff and Johnson, 1980) metaphor can be viewed as an analogy between two distinct domains - the *target* and the *source*. Consider the following example:

(6) He *shot down* all of my arguments. (Lakoff and Johnson, 1980)

A mapping of a concept of *argument* (target) to that of *war* (source) is employed here. The idea of such interconceptual mappings has been exploited in some NLP systems.

One of the first attempts to identify and interpret metaphorical expressions in text automatically is the approach of Fass (1991). It originates in the work of Wilks (1978) and utilizes hand-coded knowledge. Fass (1991) developed a system called met*, capable of discriminating between literalness, metonymy, metaphor and anomaly. It does this in three stages. First, literalness is distinguished from non-literalness using selectional preference violation as an indicator. In the case that non-literalness is detected, the respective phrase is tested for being a metonymic relation using hand-coded patterns (such as CONTAINER-for-CONTENT). If the system fails to recognize metonymy, it proceeds to search the knowledge base for a *relevant analogy* in order to discriminate metaphorical relations from anomalous ones. E.g., the sentence in (4) would be represented in this framework as (*car,drink,gasoline*), which does not satisfy the preference (*animal,drink,liquid*), as *car* is not a hyponym of *animal*. met* then searches its knowledge base for a triple containing a hypernym of both the actual argument and the desired argument and finds (*thing,use,energy_source*), which represents the metaphorical interpretation.

Almost simultaneously with the work of Fass (1991), Martin (1990) presents a Metaphor Interpretation, Denotation and Acquisition System (MIDAS). The idea behind this work is that the more specific conventional metaphors descend from the general ones. Given an example of a metaphorical expression, MIDAS searches its database for a corresponding metaphor that would explain the anomaly. If it does not find any, it abstracts from the example to more general concepts and repeats the search. If it finds a suitable general metaphor, it creates a mapping for its descendant, a more specific metaphor, based on this example. This is also how novel metaphors are acquired. MIDAS has been integrated with the Unix Consultant (UC), the system that answers users questions about Unix.

Another cohort of approaches relies on performing inferences about entities and events in the source and target domains for metaphor interpretation. These include the KARMA system (Narayanan, 1997; Narayanan, 1999; Feldman and Narayanan, 2004) and the ATT-Meta project (Barnden and Lee, 2002; Agerri et al., 2007). Within both systems the authors developed a metaphor-based reasoning framework in accordance with the theory of conceptual metaphor. The reasoning process relies on manually coded knowledge about the world and operates mainly in the source domain. The results are then projected onto the target domain using the conceptual mapping representation. The ATT-Meta project concerns metaphorical and metonymic description of mental states and reasoning about mental states using first order logic. Their system, however, does not take natural language sentences as input, but logical expressions that are representations of small discourse fragments. KARMA in turn deals with a broad range of abstract actions and events and takes parsed text as input.

Veale and Hao (2008) derive a "fluid knowledge representation for metaphor interpretation and generation", called Talking Points. Talking Points are a set of characteristics of concepts belonging to source and target domains and related facts about the world which the authors acquire automatically from WordNet and from the web. Talking Points are then organized in *Slipnet*, a framework that allows for a number of insertions, deletions and substitutions in definitions of such characteristics in order to establish a connection between the target and the source concepts. This work builds on the idea of *slippage* in knowledge representation for understanding analogies in abstract domains (Hofstadter and Mitchell, 1994; Hofstadter, 1995). Consider the metaphor *Make-up is a Western burqa*:

Make-up =>
$\equiv$ typically worn by women
$\approx$ expected to be worn by women
$\approx$ must be worn by women
$\approx$ must be worn by Muslim women
Burqa <=

By doing insertions and substitutions the system arrives from the definition *typically worn by women* to that of *must be worn by Muslim women*, and thus establish a link between the concepts of *make-up* and *burqa*. Veale and Hao (2008), however, did not evaluate to which extent their method is useful to interpret metaphorical expressions occurring in text.

6 Conclusions

We presented a novel approach to metaphor interpretation and a system that produces literal paraphrases for metaphorical expressions. Such a representation is directly transferable to other applications that can benefit from a metaphor processing component. Our method is distinguished from the previous work in that it does not rely on any hand-crafted knowledge, other than WordNet, but in contrast employs automatically induced selectional preferences.

Our system is the first of its kind and it is capable of paraphrasing metaphorical expressions with a high accuracy (0.81). Although we reported results on a test set consisting of verb-subject and verb-object metaphors only, we are convinced that the described interpretation techniques can be similarly applied to other parts of speech and a wider range of syntactic constructions. Extending the system to deal with more types of phrases is part of our future work.

Acknowledgments

I am very grateful to Anna Korhonen, Simone Teufel, Ann Copestake and the reviewers for their helpful feedback on this work, Lin Sun for sharing his noun clustering data and the volunteer annotators. My studies and, thus, this research are funded by generosity of Cambridge Overseas Trust.

References

R. Agerri, J.A. Barnden, M.G. Lee, and A.M. Wallington. 2007. Metaphor, inference and domain-independent mappings. In *Proceedings of International Conference on Recent Advances in Natural Language Processing (RANLP-2007)*, pages 17–23, Borovets, Bulgaria.

O. E. Andersen, J. Nioche, E. Briscoe, and J. Carroll. 2008. The BNC parsed with RASP4UIMA. In *Proceedings of the Sixth International Language Resources and Evaluation Conference (LREC'08)*, Marrakech, Morocco.

J.A. Barnden and M.G. Lee. 2002. An artificial intelligence approach to metaphor understanding. *Theoria et Historia Scientiarum*, 6(1):399–412.

E. Briscoe, J. Carroll, and R. Watson. 2006. The second release of the rasp system. In *Proceedings of the COLING/ACL on Interactive presentation sessions*, pages 77–80.

L. Burnard. 2007. *Reference Guide for the British National Corpus (XML Edition)*. URL=http://www.natcorp.ox.ac.uk/XMLedition/URG/.

D. Fass. 1991. met*: A method for discriminating metonymy and metaphor by computer. *Computational Linguistics*, 17(1):49–90.

J. Feldman and S. Narayanan. 2004. Embodied meaning in a neural theory of language. *Brain and Language*, 89(2):385–392.

C. Fellbaum, editor. 1998. *WordNet: An Electronic Lexical Database (ISBN: 0-262-06197-X)*. MIT Press, first edition.

D. Hofstadter and M. Mitchell. 1994. The Copycat Project: A model of mental fluidity and analogy-making. In K.J. Holyoak and J. A. Barnden, editors, *Advances in Connectionist and Neural Computation Theory*, Ablex, New Jersey.

D. Hofstadter. 1995. *Fluid Concepts and Creative Analogies: Computer Models of the Fundamental Mechanisms of Thought*. HarperCollins Publishers.

G. Lakoff and M. Johnson. 1980. *Metaphors We Live By*. University of Chicago Press, Chicago.

J. H. Martin. 1988. Representing regularities in the metaphoric lexicon. In *Proceedings of the 12th conference on Computational linguistics*, pages 396–401.

J. H. Martin. 1990. *A Computational Model of Metaphor Interpretation*. Academic Press Professional, Inc., San Diego, CA, USA.

S. Narayanan. 1997. Knowledge-based action representations for metaphor and aspect (KARMA). Technical report, PhD thesis, University of California at Berkeley.

S. Narayanan. 1999. Moving right along: A computational model of metaphoric reasoning about events. In *In Proceedings of the National Conference on Artificial Intelligence (AAAI 99)*, pages 121–128, Orlando, Florida.

Pragglejaz Group (P. Crisp, R. Gibbs, A. Cienki, G. Low, G. Steen, L. Cameron, E. Semino, J. Grady, A. Deignan and Z. Kovecses). 2007. MIP: A method for identifying metaphorically used words in discourse. *Metaphor and Symbol*, 22:1–39.

P. Resnik. 1993. *Selection and Information: A Class-based Approach to Lexical Relationships*. Ph.D. thesis, Philadelphia, PA, USA.

P. Resnik. 1997. Selectional preference and sense disambiguation. In *ACL SIGLEX Workshop on Tagging Text with Lexical Semantics*, Washington, D.C.

S. Siegel and N. J. Castellan. 1988. *Nonparametric statistics for the behavioral sciences*. McGraw-Hill Book Company, New York, USA.

L. Sun and A. Korhonen. 2009. Improving verb clustering with automatically acquired selectional preferences. In *Proceedings of the 2009 Conference on Empirical Methods in Natural Language Processing*, pages 638–647, Singapore, August.

T. Veale and Y. Hao. 2008. A fluid knowledge representation for understanding and generating creative metaphors. In *Proceedings of the 22nd International Conference on Computational Linguistics (Coling 2008)*, pages 945–952, Manchester, UK.

Y. Wilks. 1978. Making preferences more active. *Artificial Intelligence*, 11(3):197–223.

Author Index